IN VOGUE

Six decades of fashion

GEORGINA HOWELL

ALLEN LANE

Copyright © The Condé Nast Publications Ltd, 1975

First published in 1975

Allen Lane
Penguin Books Ltd
17 Grosvenor Gardens London SW1

ISBN 0 7139 0739 8

_____

Research by Sheila Murphy
Design by Martin Bassett and Philip Clucas

_____

Printed in England by
Westerham Press Limited
Westerham, Kent

CONTENTS

THROUGH SIX DECADES

ON THE SOFA   1916   Maurice Beck & Macgregor   1926   1938

AT THE WHEEL   1919   1923   Helmut Newton   1965

IN THE AIR   Steichen   1926   Anton Bruehl   1937   William Klein   1961   Helmut Newton   1967

WITH ESCORTS   Pollard   1924   Eric   1936   Norman Parkinson   1960   David Bailey   1965

WITH THE CHILDREN   1936   Norman Parkinson

PREFACE

BEATRIX MILLER
Editor of *Vogue*

In October 1976, British *Vogue* celebrates its Diamond Jubilee,
60 years of reporting fashion, beauty, people, plays,
decoration, manners and attitudes.

According to James Laver's Time Spirit Theory,
that the forms of dress, apparently so haphazard,
so dependent on the whims of the designer,
have an extraordinary relevance to the spirit of the age, so,
browsing through old copies you catch the mood of the moment,
that moment. Mr I.S.V. Patcévitch, for 28 years President
and Chairman of Condé Nast said, 'each issue of *Vogue*,
this fragile and transitory product, performs a certain function.
It holds a mirror up to its times, a small mirror perhaps,
but a singularly clear, brilliant and revealing one.'

In a sense women and *Vogue* are synonymous and the role
women play is continuously reflected, albeit in a limited stratum
of society. The 60 years mirrored here embrace some of the most
crowded changes in social history and, in particular, the part
that women take in society and the world. So it is as natural
now to publish discoveries in science that affect people, men
and women, as it is to report on the latest Paris Collections.
Today, with a readership of over 2½ million, *Vogue*'s continuing
strength lies in its adherence to the original formula, maintaining
a constant viewpoint of style, quality and specialization while
continually evolving with the spirit of the time. Thus each issue
of the magazine is the tip of an iceberg of information,
creative intuition and research that has built up
over the years, just as this book is only one of
a potential hundred more.

1916-1923

The Great Escape

LUCILE

The Great War changed everything: way of life, attitudes, society, politics, people themselves mentally and physically. No war had ever involved so many civilians. Fashion in clothes and much else was turned upside down and no longer flowed in natural progressions and reactions. With hindsight, we know that World War 1 emancipated fashion, but while it was happening the breeches of 'farmerettes' and land girls, the trousers and overalls of the women munition workers and tram conductors, the uniforms of the nurses and postwomen were not considered part of fashion and scarcely surfaced to the pages of *Vogue*. Fashion dawdled in its tracks and simultaneously hopped a decade. Some people assumed that after the war there would be a rush of exaggerated impractical clothes as a reaction to serge suits and sensible proofed trenchcoats, others that women who had once known the freedom of trousers would never look back. Both were right. Fashion didn't catch up with itself until the mid-twenties. In the meantime sports clothes and jerseys took women forwards, crinolines, pagoda hips and tapered hems took them back. The cross currents brought to *Vogue* perhaps the oddest silhouette in the history of fashion. A woman might wear a hat of vulture quills two feet tall, a calf-length dress under a tunic dropping two points to touch the ground, the whole swathed with a tempest of monkey fur bands. In the evening she might wear a brocade tunic over a sagging nappy of chiffon, or a short crinoline in tiers of fur and lamé.

Coming out bang in the middle of the war, British *Vogue* was full of references to hard times and reduced incomes, but each issue was full of the fashion news from Paris. Under headlines such as 'Paris makes a brave show in spite of guns', or 'Paris lifts ever so little the ban on gaiety', *Vogue* managed to show the most extravagant of morale-boosting fashions. Once or twice a year there would be a page on 'A wardrobe for the woman war-worker . . . for the ten thousand women who are driving ambulances, working in canteens and nursing the wounded'. There were a few features on war topics: the Citroën munitions factory, an eyewitness's account of a night with a convoy, the new ambulances. *Vogue* recommended gifts for soldiers – horsehair gloves, air pillows and National War Bonds – and gave much space to the charity matinées that combined worthy war-work with society spectaculars. Lady Duff Gordon was photographed as 'the personification of the mystery and power of Russia' at the Ten Allies Costume Ball, Miss Fay Compton as a rose and Miss Viola Tree as a 'tall bramble' at the 'Our Day' matinée, Ethel Barrymore as Flanders at the Allied Nations pageant on Long Island. 'Dressing on a war income' was a regular feature, but not as helpful as it might have been, recommending that women should slim in order to use less fabric, and suggesting 'cleverly contrived neck arrangements' to change the look of a plain dress. In 1917 *Vogue* reported that the French government had banned jewels and evening dress at the Opéra,

Left: Miss Irene Hart, portrait by Hoppé, 1917

1. Oriental evening dress, shot silver tissue and orange tulle, 1919.

1. Lady Duff Gordon as Russia at the Ten Allies costume ball in New York. Sister of Elinor Glyn, Lady Duff Gordon ran the fashion house Lucile.
2. Lieut. Julian Cuthbert Orde, R.F.C.
3. Feminine adaptation of the British Warm, 1918.
4. The Duchess of Wellington knitting a sock.
5. The bold, flirtatious flapper, in this case musical comedy actress Molly Ramsden, brazenly smoking a cigarette.

the Odéon and the Comédie Française until the end of the war and had appealed to the public not to buy new dresses, and showed on the same page Doucet's irresistible evening wrap of rose panne velvet finished with skunk and tassels. There was a feature on 'Leave trousseaux' with adjuncts to 'make it [your] business to see that he carries away with him on his return to duty a refreshing vision of loveliness, and in particular to avoid the masculine', in other words the wartime innovations of 'service suits', waterproofs, wool underwear, thick stockings, tailored Viyella shirts, trench-coats and suits of uniform cloth copied from the soldiers' coats of black rubber or serge.

The first women to wear trousers and dungarees wore them be-cause they went with the job – dirty, hard jobs that women were taking over from the soldiers, train driving, plumbing, factory work, electrical engineering, window cleaning, farm labouring. Working clothes weren't considered part of fashion at all, just a temporary necessity like uniform, and *Vogue* reflected the attitude with one or two pages a year on equipment for ambulance drivers, compared with the main body of Paris fashion in every issue. Nevertheless short skirts and trousers became part of the vocabulary of fashion, and two coat designs arrived that stayed for good. The British Warm became the standard overcoat for men and women alike, with its deep revers, its epaulettes and buckled belt. From the mud of the front line came the trenchcoat, just as useful for landgirls or even commuters in taxiless cities. In rubberized cloth, it had double breasting, epaulettes and cuffstraps, an envelope flap across the shoulder fastening, and a button-on chin protector.

Society beauties had their portraits taken for *Vogue* by Hoppé, Hugh Cecil and Bertram Park. Ideally they were photographed in uniform, like Countess Bathurst in Red Cross outfit, or the Marchioness of Londonderry in the uniform of the Women's Service Legion. Failing that, they compensated in other ways. Mrs

Kermit Roosevelt's caption refers to her baby, and the career of her husband at the Front. The Duchess of Wellington is photo-graphed knitting a sock. Mrs Vincent Astor, photographed in a garden hat, has the intention of opening a convalescent home near Paris where wounded American soldiers may be nursed back to health. Lady Randolph Churchill 'has organized some very beautiful tableaux vivants for the matinée', and Miss Lucile Bald-win took 'active part, last autumn, in the Tuxedo Horticultural Society, which gave an exhibition for the Red Cross'. Musical comedy actresses and starlets did their bit, too. Lily Elsie appealed for cigarette papers for the Red Cross with a new photograph in *Vogue*, Doris Keane told *Vogue* she was going to put all her fan letters from soldiers into a book and sell it in aid of the Red Cross.

Vogue was packed with patriotic advertisements, all urging the public to spend money in the line of duty. 'In too many homes . . . these are the times of the darkest clouds. Yet assuredly it is true, and the old saying is justified of its belief, that every cloud has a silver lining. It is the writer's opinion the bright relief is the keeping up of the home . . . at Jelk's you can obtain the best furniture at the lowest prices.' There were appeals to women to think of their complexions: '. . . comes the remembrance of bitterly cold days when you were driving an Army Car, of hours spent in heated factories, and the wonder of what effect either has had on your complexion, hands and hair. Your mirror reassures you, Colleen Shampoos so soon restore lustre and life to the hair . . .' or, in a higher tone, 'It is lamentable that the far-famed beauty of the Englishwoman must suffer from the terrible strain her beloved country is undergoing. It is her duty to use every means in her power to prevent the effect on her beauty . . . You are urged to take one treatment at the elegant and most up-to-date "Cyclax" Salons.'

The soldiers came home from the trenches different men.

Hoppé

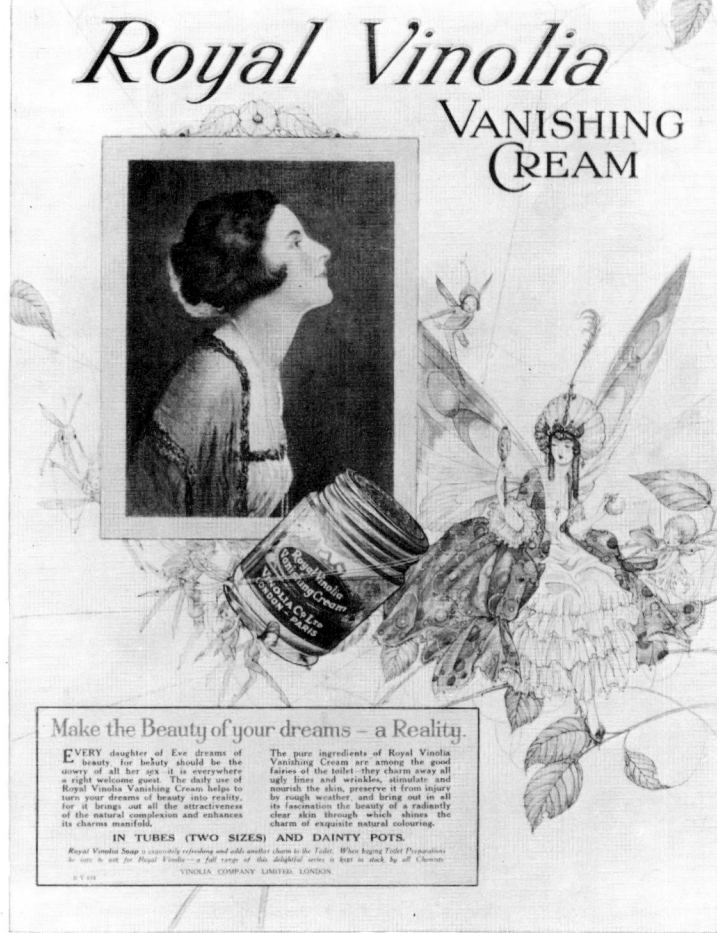

Royal Vinolia VANISHING CREAM

Make the Beauty of your dreams – a Reality.

EVERY daughter of Eve dreams of beauty for beauty should be the envy of all her sex—it is everywhere a right welcome guest. The daily use of Royal Vinolia Vanishing Cream helps to turn your dreams of beauty into reality, for it brings out all the attractiveness of the natural complexion and enhances its charms manifold.

The pure ingredients of Royal Vinolia Vanishing Cream are among the good fairies of the toilet—they charm away all ugly lines and wrinkles, stimulate and nourish the skin, preserve it from injury by rough weather, and bring out in all its fascination the beauty of a radiantly clear skin through which shines the charm of exquisite natural colouring.

IN TUBES (TWO SIZES) AND DAINTY POTS.

Royal Vinolia Soap is exquisitely refreshing and adds another charm to the Toilet. When buying Toilet Preparations be sure to ask for Royal Vinolia—a full range of this delightful series is kept in stock by all Chemists.

VINOLIA COMPANY LIMITED, LONDON.

Many were suffering from shell shock with nightmares and vivid daydreams, and if they recovered now they would probably go down with nervous breakdowns in 1921 or 1922. They were out of temper with Lloyd George and his Coalition government. They'd been promised a life fit for heroes at the end of the struggle, but they came home to an impoverished country in a state of confusion, and their jobs had been filled by women or men who had managed to avoid conscription. Officers, the husbands of *Vogue* readers, were given no unemployment benefits and high prices were followed by a slump. There was plenty to escape from.

Women had grown more confident, more independent, and had begun to earn their own living in factories and offices. They no longer wanted to be cooks, nurses, maids or dressmakers: as Dorothy Parker wrote in 1919, 'that sort of thing simply isn't being done, any more; it is considered positively unfeminine'. The war had killed one out of every seven eligible men, and seriously injured another, so marriage was not inevitable. Women were in better shape after years of rationed butter and sugar, and with the popularity of hockey and tennis. The hourglass figure of the old Gaiety girls now looked comic. Laced whalebone corsets had been superseded by camisole bras and rubber girdles. The flapper had arrived. The expression, which began as '*backfisch*' in Germany in the 1890s, had meant a very young tart before the war, but had come to mean the popular heroine of the munitions factory, a girl who rode on the flapper bracket of a motorbicycle, swore, smoked cigarettes publicly and sold flags with brazen flirtatiousness. This figure had little to do with the refined dignified dresses in *Vogue*, which regretted the fact in 1921: 'One cannot help wishing for a less independent, less hard, more feminine product than the average 20th. century girl.'

The new society had a new etiquette. At the end of 1918 class distinctions were temporarily relaxed. An aristocratic woman

Hoppé

might marry even into the labouring class as long as the man had a good war record. The 'new rich', the war profiteers, were hated by the new poor. Women were smoking in public, but the cigarettes had to be Egyptian and Turkish, not Virginian. It was considered all right to smoke in the restaurant car of a train, but vulgar on the top of a bus. Some women smoked in restaurants, and a waiter in one knocked a cigarette out of a lady's mouth. In 1919 new dance clubs and halls opened for tea dances, practice dances, subscription and victory dances. You could dance before lunch in private houses in London and the country. Before the war women danced the tango with hands on hips and pelvis thrust forward, faces white with rice powder, eyes blackened with kohl, called mascara. After the war they danced the kikikari or the shimmy with deadpan faces, a touch of lipstick, in a backless dress . . . 'I wish I could shimmy like my sister Kate, she shakes it like a bowl of jelly on a plate.' A clergyman in 1919 wrote, 'If these up-to-date

Fish

dances, described as the "latest craze", are within a hundred miles of all I hear about them, I should say that the morals of a pig-sty would be respectable in comparison.' *Vogue*, appealing to the mothers, found a tone of voice that combined tolerance with disapproval: 'a formal "coming out" seems to have gone the way of formal visits . . . Personally, one may feel that too much ease is being used too easily, particularly by people for whom formality might have served in place of those traditions which they lack . . . In any event, girls will grow up, bless them!' Debutantes in 1920 were sending out invitations in their own names to dances where there would be no chaperones. Girls were often invited to bring their own man.

Women's place was a debatable subject. As a reward for war services they were given the vote over thirty, but the government was counting on half the female population being too vain to give away their age, and the other half to put in 'safe' votes. 'From the princess to the humblest of munitions workers, the womanhood of Britain emerges from the ordeal with credentials which the future will acclaim', but many of the women who'd been praised for going out to work to help their country had their jobs snatched back in peacetime by Trades Unions: the soldiers wanted their work back again. Where women hung onto their jobs their pay was two-thirds that of a man. 'Votes for Women' gave way to 'Equal pay for Equal work'. The Sex Disqualification (Removal) Act of 1919 admitted women to many professions including the bar, and was followed up by acts to recognize women as morally responsible persons. In 1921 *Vogue* published 'Women and Education – a real Oxford for Women', to help appeal for funds for Oxford women's colleges. It was timed to accompany the announcement that the Queen would accept an honorary degree at Oxford. *Vogue* said, 'The women's part of the university will never possess the spirit which alone justifies Oxford's existence, until it has acquired the same freedom, intellectual as well as social, which characterizes the men's part.'

Oxford had admitted women to full membership in 1919, but Cambridge had refused with scenes of amazing ungallantry, hoisting high above the streets a female dummy in bloomers riding a bicycle, and was consequently in disgrace.

In 1919 a terrible epidemic of septic influenza swept through Europe and on round the world killing twenty-seven million people in all – twice as many as the war itself. In the United Kingdom there were 200,000 deaths, and people went about in public in antiseptic gauze masks. The dogs that accompanied them were muzzled, too: there had been an outbreak of rabies. There were high prices and strikes, peasouper fogs, and precious little coal. Even if your family were alive and together again, there was plenty to escape from and plenty to escape to. There was the light, bright note of the theatre – 'It will be a long time before the theatre can be serious again' – there was the cinema, there were cocktails and dancing, fancy dress balls, cabarets, weekend motoring and Fridays-to-Mondays. In summer families flooded to the seaside for their first holiday in five years: three hundred thousand visitors went to Blackpool, and women and children had to sleep in police cells while men slept out on the beaches and cliff tops. By the winter continental holidays were possible again for those who could afford them, and St Moritz was the place to go. *Vogue* ran a five-page feature on the right clothes to wear for skiing.

Of all escape valves, the films allowed you to live vicariously with the least effort. By 1919 half the population of Britain went

Ochsé Collection

Ira L. Hill

to the pictures twice a week. Charlie Chaplin who had been slated by the British press in 1915 as a young Englishman who was not doing his bit, was on everywhere, with Mary Pickford, whose baby ringlets and childish prettiness were much copied. *Vogue* published a pageful of the starlets who were trying to look like her. Her antithesis was wicked wicked Theda Bara, first of the vamps, an aggressive *femme fatale* launched on the first big publicity wave. She went to press interviews in a white limousine with Nubian footmen, primed with what she had to say: her name was an anagram of 'arab death', her nationality was to be revealed as French-Egyptian – she was really a Miss Goodman from Ohio. Her 'Kiss me, my fool' became a catch phrase. There was Clara Kimball Young, Tarzan's Jane, and sylph-like Lillian Gish, who starred in D. W. Griffith's *Birth of a Nation*, a four-hour film that consolidated the success of films as a new art form independent of the spoken word. She appeared in *Vogue* in 1918 in pictures from Griffith's war epic *Hearts of the World*, filmed in France in the recently recaptured village of Ham. Most often in *Vogue* was Geraldine Farrar, a beautiful opera singer who signed up with Samuel Goldwyn at $10,000 a week: in 1916 *Vogue* showed stills from Cecil B. De Mille's 'photo-drama' *Joan of Arc*, in which she took the starring part. Norma Talmadge was in almost every issue, a teenage leading lady at Vitagraph who went on to manage her own film company. For ultra-escapism there was Gloria Swanson, who appeared in a Sennett comedy as early as 1916. She was sensationally fashionable in all her films: De Mille insisted on it. In films like *For Better For Worse* (1919) and *The Affairs of Anatol* (1921) she staggered under the weight of jewels, furs and ostrich plumes. *Vogue* considered her a prime example of movie bad taste, but she made a tremendous hit with the British public.

The subtitles to films brought American slang to Britain, and it was much relished and disapproved of: 'Beatrix Esmond goes nix on the love-stuff' and 'You've dribbled a bibful, baby' were read

Rita Martin

1. Aquascutum's skiing suit, 1923: slate blue wool, double breasted, with strapped cuffs and military pockets.
2. Lillian Gish as she starred in David Griffith's *Hearts of the World*, 1918.
3. Sarah Bernhardt in her apartment in the Boulevard Péreire.
4. Florence Walton, famous dancer usually partnered by her husband Maurice. She wore gold and silver tissue dresses by Callot for her performances – when she was in New York they sent her one a week.
5. Gina Palerme, 1918. Delightful French musical comedy star who appeared in London at the Palace Theatre and the Duke of York's. Off stage, she might wear a chinchilla cape to the ground, with saluki dogs for accessories, or a velvet tam o'shanter and men's riding breeches.

out aloud by the audiences. *Vogue* wrote a piece on the murder of the English language. An American revue which came to London with Noël Coward in the cast had its name changed from *Oh Boy!* to *Oh Joy!* The feeling that Hollywood was hardly respectable meant that only a few screen stars were included in the magazine, although everyone who was anyone in the theatre could be seen in *Vogue* constantly.

Paris set the fashion, and the musical comedy and vaudeville actresses from London, Paris and Broadway wore the clothes to perfection. They were photographed as models if they were just beginning, as themselves when they'd arrived, and finally, when they were famous, in their own clothes from Callot and Poiret, Vionnet and Lanvin. Stars like Florence Walton and Gina Palerme were the staple diet of Paris designers. Yvonne Printemps took 80

de Givenchy

Lanvins to New York, and Florence Walton was sent a Callot dress a week. *Vogue* showed drawings of many of them.

Except for a brief falling-off in audiences in 1921 when a coal strike turned theatres into refrigerators, the stage had never done better or set more fashions. Costume design for important productions was always undertaken by couturiers, so that theatre design was naturally absorbed into fashion and new productions were scanned for fashion pointers. *Vogue* showed the best stage costumes from Hindu dancers' to Poiret's extravagant Oriental designs for *Agfar* at the Pavilion. There were sentimental comedies like *Paddy, the Next Best Thing* which ran for three years, and *Chu Chin Chow* which ran for five. There was Ibsen for problem plays, Galsworthy and Shaw revivals, Oscar Wilde, Gilbert & Sullivan and *Charley's Aunt*. Birmingham repertory theatre produced *Cymbeline* in modern dress, with warriors in khaki. In 1923 Cochran brought Eleanora Duse to England for the first time in seventeen years and began a migration of foreign plays and players to London. There was Sacha Guitry's *Grand Guignol* season and Carel Čapek's *R.U.R.* Somerset Maugham's *Our Betters* was too shocking, and *The Circle* was openly booed. Noël Coward's *The Young Idea* had only a short run in 1922. Public taste at this period was for something a little more sugary.

If the actresses showed *Vogue* readers how to look in the new clothes, it was the society queens who personified fashion for the designers themselves. Beauties whose portraits appeared and who really lived the life for which Paris fashion was designed were the Duchesse de Gramont (Madame Vionnet said that if she wanted to tell if a dress were right she had only to try it on the Duchesse); wealthy socialites Mrs Vanderbilt, Mrs Hatch and Countess Torby; Lady Lavery, a red-haired Irish-American from Chicago who married the painter Sir John Lavery in 1910 and became a well-known figure in London society. Her portrait was incorporated into her husband's design for Irish pound notes. There were the Duchess of Marlborough, the Queen of Spain, Lady Elizabeth Bowes-Lyon who was to become Queen, Princess Victoria, the Duchess of Sutherland, Mrs Dudley Ward who was seen everywhere with the Prince of Wales, and Mrs Ogden Mills, one of his hostesses in the U.S.A.

Bridging the gap between aristocrat and popular figure, Lady Diana Cooper was the daughter of the Duke of Rutland, a Red Cross nurse from the war, and the star of Max Reinhardt's *The Miracle*. A natural bohemian with a great appetite for life, she captured the public imagination, and her delicious blonde beauty together with the pastel colours she always wore were much copied. *Vogue* showed her portrait by Ambrose McEvoy, and her photograph taken by Bertram Park on the announcement of her marriage to Duff Cooper of the Grenadier Guards. Thousands of factory girls turned out to see her wedding.

Society life was much the same on both sides of the Channel, with lunches, art shows, theatre, concerts, cocktails, dancing, fancy dress balls, dinners. In London Dame Nellie Melba was singing at the Albert Hall, Madame Suggia playing the cello, John Goss singing, and Stravinsky performed at Wigmore Hall. According to *Vogue*'s critic the audience was full of 'poseurs and sycophants'. Under the headline 'Humours and Irrelevancies of the Nursery Music of Igor Stravinsky' he wrote, 'The first was a quasi-barbaric dance, only a few bars in length, but long enough, or short enough, to make people smile openly; at the second people laughed; at the third, a very solemn and ominous composition, people laughed still more.'

The first public appearance of *Façade* in 1923 brought the Sitwells into *Vogue* for the first time with a cautiously favourable review by Gerald Cumberland. Hidden behind a curtain painted by Frank Dobson, Edith Sitwell 'half sang, half shouted' her musical poetry through a Sengerphone. 'Her voice, beautiful in tone, full, resonant and clear, could, with effort, be heard above the decorative din of the music' by William Walton. This is Osbert Sitwell's own description of the reception: 'The front rows,

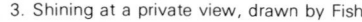

3. Shining at a private view, drawn by Fish.
4. Lady Lavery, 1916.
5. Tamara Karsavina in Caucasian costume, 1920

6. Lillah McCarthy in the dress and setting by the Omega Workshops for Israel Zangwill's farce *Too Much Money*, 1918.

3

4   Hoppé   5   Instead

6   Hugh Cecil

of art must be the breadth of its appeal.' He turned with relief to Sickert: 'One is glad and grateful to have been given this opportunity to study the work of one of the most honest, original and talented of English painters.' *Vogue* showed two wartime etchings of Nevinson, *The Road to Ypres* and *Flooded Trench on the Yser*; Nevinson remarked, 'the public is more interested in the war than it is in art.' All the leading painters and sculptors appeared in *Vogue*, and the more academic their approach the better reviewed they were. For the guidance of readers, *Vogue* produced a humourous guide illustrated by Fish, 'Shining at a Private View': suggested useful phrases were 'What rhythmic movement!' 'What green! What red! What yellow!' or failing anything else, 'How very brave.' Marie Laurençin, Laura Knight and Nina Hamnett were the women painters *Vogue* preferred, and Marie Laurençin was to draw covers for the magazine in the 1920s. In the field of applied arts, furniture from the Omega Workshop was shown, simple chairs and chests painted in confused colours described by a contemporary as being 'like a dragon's miscarriage'.

The greatest influence of all on fashion was the great and continuing inspiration of the Russian ballet. It was one consolation for the Russian Revolution that it had left half the Imperial Ballet permanently exiled abroad. Osbert Sitwell in *Great Morning* wrote, 'decoration was in the air . . . the currents that showed were mostly foreign, and reached life through the theatre . . . every chair-cover, every lamp-shade, every cushion reflected the Russian Ballet, the Grecian or Oriental visions of Bakst and Benois.' The barbaric beauty of the costumes and settings, the dancing of Karsavina, Lopokova, Pavlova, Nijinsky, Massine and the music of Rimsky-Korsakov, Balakirev, Debussy, Tchaikovsky combined in the most majestic and romantic of escapist fantasies. There was some doubt from *Vogue*'s theatre critic as to how one should react to them: 'There is really something a little incongruous in the Russian Ballet serving as a popular entertainment in a country which has begun to rage against wealth and leisure', and more doubts as to the audience's understanding of it: 'It is useless to pretend that the thousands who throng to see these ballets have the remotest idea as to what they really represent or signify.'

There was no fashion designer who had not been set off in a new direction by the Russian ballet, but perhaps those most influenced were Poiret, who took the whole thing in at a gulp, Callot, Dœuillet, Lucile, Redfern, Idare and Chanel in her embroideries.

especially, manifested their contempt and rage, and, albeit a good deal of applause countered the hissing . . . nevertheless the atmosphere was so greatly and so evidently hostile that at the end of the performance several members of the audience came behind the curtain to warn my sister not to leave the platform until the crowd had dispersed.' The first book reviews in the magazine discussed David Garnett's *Lady into Fox*, Michael Arlen's *These Charming People*, D. H. Lawrence's *Kangaroo*, Clive Bell's *On British Freedom* and Vita Sackville-West's *Grey Wethers*.

Vogue's reception of contemporary painting was far from adventurous. Modigliani, Matisse, Picasso and Vlaminck were found 'disappointing', but clearly worrying. 'Wanted,' wrote the critic, 'a revival of national art. The artists . . . foregathered in their little coteries, apart from the world, ply their esoteric mysteries more and more out of touch and sympathy with the great Heart of the People,' and he concluded, damningly, 'The ultimate standard

1. Slav influence: white crepe de chine dress with beaded waist, 1921.
2. Lucile's marguerite costume for the Ziegfeld Follies, 1919.
3. Tea gown of gold tissue, 1919.

LUCILE

Geometric prints, trellised and striped furs, silver and gold lace, brilliant linings, bead and silk embroidery, velvets and furs, boots, cockades and storms of feathers, glittering dragonfly lingerie and butterfly evening dresses with trains and wing sleeves, all that was most beautiful and extraordinary in Oriental fashion came straight off Diaghilev's stage. Until his death in 1929 there was nothing on the stage to rival the excitement his seasons aroused, although the original company had long since dispersed. The ballerinas naturally appeared very often in *Vogue*, and the next generation of dancers that had learnt from them: Mlle Rambert, who had learnt eurhythmics with Jacques Dalcroze and classical ballet with Nijinsky, and Madame Donnet, who founded the Ballet Philosophique. The passion for every kind of dancing was in the air. *Vogue* showed the schools of Marian Morgan and Margaret Morris, and photographed Isadora Duncan in America, with barefoot Woodland Dancers 'all born in Arcadia' responding freely to the open fields and sky.

In violent reaction to hard times and sensible clothes, the longing for escape and glamour brought a wave of fantastic fashion follies into *Vogue*. The theatrical came into the forefront of fashion. The modern woman in the gaiter suit turned into a beautiful barbarian in the evening, in a costume that might have been designed by Bakst. All Paris came out with evening dresses in tiers of shot tulle or silver lace and tea-rose brocade, with Turkish trousers of looped chiffon, lamé jackets, wings and trains of sparkling chiffon, turbans and fountains of ostrich feathers. Lucile's evening dresses, négligées and tea gowns are hardly different from her designs for the Ziegfeld Follies, and *Vogue* is filled with Egyptian gandouras, Caucasian waistcoats over dresses of metal bead embroidery, chains of gold and nets of pearls, butterfly sleeves of golden gauze, earrings dropping to the breast and head-dresses of shooting feathers. Oriental tea gowns, originally made to be worn between hunting and dressing for dinner, were worn now for informal dinners. Ida Rubinstein's dress by Worth looked like the saris of the Indian dancer Roshanara – who turned out to

be English. The Oriental influence came to an end in 1923 with a splendid 'Chinese Ball' in Paris, the French couturiers competing to dress the leading society figures.

If the greatest single influence on fashion was Oriental, the second was American. Both were enjoyed as a relief from wartime problems and restrictions, The prestige of America was never higher. The States had lost one-fiftieth of proportionate British losses in the war, yet had the glory of deciding the issue and bringing an end to the struggle. America came out of the war richer than before, whereas France and Britain were impoverished, Germany bankrupt, Austria destitute. Americans gave the lead in all social fashions, and brought jazz, films, coloured nail polish, rouge, cocktails, smoking and money into Europe. British *Vogue* was full of American social life, American cars, Venetian palaces erected

8

4

VIONNET

4. The Chinese Bal de l'Opéra in Paris, 1923: The
Duchess de Gramont costumed by Vionnet.

in Florida, American architect's houses, American resorts. Tourists from all over the States arrived in Britain from 1919 to buy up books, art, and sometimes houses wholesale. Agecroft Hall in Lancashire and Great Lodge in Essex were transported brick by brick and rebuilt in America. In return we got syncopated music, and what to do to it – the Baleta, the Maxina, the Twinkle, the Jog Trot, the Vampire, the Missouri Walk, the Elfreda. These new dances were practised in the restaurant-clubs that opened when the Licensing Act of 1921 allowed people to drink and dine at the same place. There was the Kit-Cat Club where you might see the Prince of Wales, the '43 where you might see Augustus John, Carpentier

Rehbinder

the boxer, or Chang the dope-gang king. To show how all the new dances should be done there were the Castles, Americans naturally, the first of a line of polished dancing couples that would include Maurice and Leonora Hughes, and Fred and Adèle Astaire. The Castles danced in hotels, cabarets and private soirées as well as on the stage. Mrs Vernon Castle, beautiful, vivacious and chic, appeared countless times in *Vogue*, lending her charm and elegance to fur coats, tennis dresses, riding habits, evening dresses, wedding dresses and every shape of hat.

Whatever was a source of inspiration and energy in any field was caught and turned into fashion in Paris – even when in 1923 Lord Carnarvon discovered the unrifled tomb of Tutankhamen at Luxor, and Ancient Egypt suddenly became fashionable. From 1916 to at least the mid-twenties the most important feature in any issue of *Vogue* was the 'Seen in Paris' fashion lead, and it was the great French designers whose clothes were drawn, photographed in the Bois, and seen on actresses, film stars and socialites the world over. Nine of the couture houses had kept open during the war, even presenting their collections while Big Bertha was showering the city with shells, or when the guns were audible not fifty miles away. Clothes were generally shown on mannikins, and in 1918 *Vogue* wrote, 'We were amused because the mannikins wore hats which were selected to suit their dresses, and consequently looked like real women of the world whom one might meet on a walk in the Bois'. Women ordered their clothes from sketches, or from examples shown on inanimate figures, and it was a great advance in 1919 when houses began to show their clothes on women who walked and turned around to demonstrate the look in action.

Best-established couture houses in Paris during the war were Worth, Doucet, Lanvin, Paquin and Poiret. Charles Frederick Worth had set the pattern for the *haute couture* by becoming dressmaker to the Empress Eugénie. He made for her the crinolines we see in Winterhalter portraits, the first ever tailor-made suit, introduced the train and then the bustle. His house carried on with splendid

and luxurious fashion. Jacques Doucet who trained Poiret, made restrained and elegant clothes, and was a connoisseur and patron of the arts. He was one of the first to buy paintings by the Impressionists, Picasso, and to collect Negro sculpture. Paul Poiret burst onto the scene in the first decade of the century, a megalomaniac, a dazzling designer of theatrical costume, and an inconsistent fashion dictator who urged women to abandon corsets on the one hand and on the other threw a lassoo round their ankles, in the form of hobble skirts. Trained by Doucet, he dressed Ida Rubinstein, Isadora Duncan, Eleanora Duse, Sarah Bernhardt, and in 1919 was making a comeback after a disastrous war (a law had to be passed specially for his benefit, forbidding soldiers to design their own uniforms). As the twenties approached his importance waned: he was never quite able to translate what was successful on the stage into clothes in which post-war women would be comfortable. He was the first couturier to launch perfumes and open a house for interior decoration; he initiated live models for fashion shows, the sunken bath, nail polish in Paris, and the private bar.

Jeanne Lanvin's reputation was made by the clothes she designed for her daughter, who became Comtesse de Polignac. Her love of Botticelli, stained glass windows and Impressionist paintings was reflected in her romantic clothes. She dressed the Princesse de Lucinge and Sasha Guitry's four wives.

Madame Paquin dressed the Queens of Belgium, Spain and Portugal and the queens of the *demi-monde*. A good businesswoman, she was elected chairman of the *haute couture* of Paris. Her contemporaries the Callot sisters introduced the fashion for lace blouses and silver and gold lamé evening dresses, and had to their credit trained Madeleine Vionnet, perhaps the greatest of all

Lachman

3   Delphi

the designers mentioned yet, who was a kind of architect of fashion. She designed a unique dress for each woman rather than a look, studying the client's proportions first on a wooden mannikin made to the exact dimensions. She chose the fabric and the line for the client's looks and character, and then cut with a mathematical precision. She invented cutting on the bias which changed the fit of clothes forever. Her clothes look nothing off, but come to life on the body. She only enjoyed dressing beautiful women, and didn't even care to dress herself particularly well: 'I was always short and I hate small women.' Her favourite client was the most elegant woman in Paris, the Duchesse de Gramont.

Gabrielle Chanel was the other great designer whose influence still affects fashion today. From a poor family, she cut up her aunt's curtains to dress a doll, and grew up into a designer with an instinct for what was just about to happen in fashion. A realist, she came up with just the thing people wanted to wear time and time again. 'Chanel' came to mean a whole look from sailor hat down to beige and black slingback shoes, even the scent in the air. She opened a millinery shop in the rue Cambon, nursed in a Deauville hospital during the war, and opened her own boutique afterwards. She made jersey chic in simple grey and navy dresses that were quite unlike anything women had worn before. She made blue pullovers and pleated skirts for the women who were replacing men in offices and factories, turned sports clothes into everyday clothes, made trousers elegant, and gave costume jewellery an intrinsic value of its own.

In London there were branches of Worth, Redfern and Paquin, there was Reville & Rossiter, and there was Lucile, the only famous house which made clothes specifically for smart London life. Lady

1. Chic interior, 1916: the rose and gray Paris dining room of the actress Eve Lavallière, decorated by Jils Garrine.
2. Ida Rubinstein, 1918. She came to Paris with Diaghilev and stayed. With her own company she staged gigantic spectacles incorporating ballet, opera and tragedy. For *Le Martyre de Saint Sébastien* she took the lead, D'Annunzio wrote the libretto, Bakst designed the costumes and sets, and Debussy composed the score. In the most fantastic trains and hats that Poiret could devise, she would walk down the middle of roads stopping the traffic all the way.
3. Society at L'Oasis, Poiret's nightclub in his garden, 1919.
4. Lina Cavalieri in pink and silver evening dress, 1916.

4
PAQUIN   Taponier   11

1

Lallie Charles

Duff Gordon ran her Lucile establishments in London, Paris, New York and Chicago. She closed the Paris branch during the war, returning from America to reopen in 1918. The sister of Elinor Glyn, she trained Molyneux. Lucile dresses were Oriental arabesques, dragonflies, pure enchantment: they were leisure clothes for escapists.

By 1920, the woman they dressed had a different shape. The hourglass figure from before the war had changed into a suppressed bosom and a slimmer, straighter torso. Pre-war underclothes had consisted of a bust-to-thigh whalebone corset with suspenders laced up over a drawstring shift and French drawers, and they were worn from the age of thirteen. After the war, with its shortages of butter and sugar, its work at the factory, its hockey and tennis, this was gradually simplified to a shapeless camisole bra and a girdle which reached from just above the waist to cover the hips. An American tourist in London was heard to say, 'Men won't dance with you if you're all laced up', and there were plenty of dances you couldn't do in corsets.

A curious anomaly in the simplified state of underclothes were the bathing suits worn right into the middle of the twenties – elaborate wrapover jersey dresses and baggy pants to the knee, or petal skirts and embroidered knickerbockers, worn over a brassière-cum-corset in rubber sheeting, with a turban on the head.

Sports clothes were the thin end of the wedge in making all kinds of fashion easier to move and work in. Comparing the elaborate fantasies of evening clothes with the pullover and pleated skirt of the golfer, or the cotton smock and trousers of the gardener, it's difficult to realize they were contemporary. Out of sports clothes came a garment which women could make at home, and which became the bread-and-butter fashion of the British – the jersey. It was new in 1919, and by the following year everyone had it: men soon followed with pullovers. These brisk and businesslike fashions, rather than the romantic extravagant ones, showed the direction of fashion for the following decade.

Women's looks had changed, too. '. . . and I heard, though I did not, myself, witness this,' reported *Vogue* in 1919, 'that during luncheon, at a well-known restaurant recently, a mutual friend of ours – it is not necessary to mention any name – was seen, not only to powder her nose in full view of everybody, but to redden her lips!' During the war, most women wore a touch of powder and a little eyelash dye, but nothing more until American tourists began flooding into Europe after the war, bringing with them lipstick, rouge, mascara and eyebrow pencil. Poiret was the first couturier to market his own scents and cosmetics: powder, lotion, cream, talcum, coloured nail polish, make-up base, rouge, eye shadow and stage make-up, but these were ahead of their time. Barbara Cartland describes herself in 1919: 'fair hair fluffed over the ears . . . red lips, subject of much criticism and many arguments, and a clear skin helped by chalk-white face powder. There were only three shades obtainable, dead white, yellow and almost brown!' The important beauty houses of Elizabeth Arden, Cyclax and Helena Rubinstein were among the first to advertise in British *Vogue*, but their products were complexion creams, not yet make-up.

Vogue's wartime issues show a marked difference between the looks of musical comedy actresses and society ladies: women on the stage, particularly Americans, knew how to use make up and weren't ashamed of wearing it. But everyone's hair, when photographed hatless, shows roughened, broken ends from too many permanents or too much marcel waving with hot tongs. Everyone wanted as much hair and as many curls as possible, and in 1917 *Vogue* showed a page of London actresses in the style of the young ideal, Mary Pickford. The higher and higher hats needed a good

2

3

Bertram Park

4

cushion of hair for anchorage, and there were advertisements in every issue for postiches and toupées 'absolutely impossible to detect'. Henna was still the only reliable way to brighten the colour of your hair, for although peroxide had been used for ten years, its effect on the hair was difficult to gauge and dangerous to repeat too often. In 1922 beauty suddenly became a fully fledged business, with the first ever articles on beauty farms and electrical massage. As the slim silhouette took over, the emphasis was on sport and beauty exercises.

After the curls and the Grecian chignons that were part and parcel of the fashion for all kinds of big hats, the small fitted cloche brought in the bob, which became the 'shingle' or the 'bingle' of the twenties, and finally the Eton crop. 'My dear, your hair is too beautiful,' says a bobbed girl to her long-haired friend in *Punch*. 'You really ought to have it cut off.' The first bob appears in *Vogue* in 1918, but this is two or three years before it became popular. By 1923 Benito is drawing a dozen variations of the same cut.

In 1923 *Vogue* showed the first sunlamp, as was to be found in the surgical wards of Princess Mary's Hospital – and a healthy tan began to be fashionable.

1. Society women are almost innocent of make up during the war years, and do not pluck their eyebrows. Hair is damaged from constant curling with hot tongs.
2. When Somerset Maugham first met Gladys Cooper in 1910 he said, 'She's the loveliest thing I've ever seen in my life.' Golden-haired, blue eyed, irresistibly the English rose, she was perfection in Reville's early costumes, and later in Molyneux: she almost always has an ostrich feather fan or boa at this time.
3. Here, Cherry Constant, from the chorus of *Theodore and Co.* at the Gaiety Theatre, 1916.
4. Black taffeta and embroidered tan silk bathing dresses belted over bloomers with bandanna handkerchiefs for turbans, 1920.

Bertram Park

1

2

CHANEL

Curtis Moffat and Olivia Wyndham

LADY DIANA COOPER

In *Vogue* Bakst said, 'Diana is the ideal woman, the belle of the hour', talking of the Goddess but intending a compliment to Lady Diana, described in another issue as 'untarnishable, the loveliest young Englishwoman of her generation'. Loved, admired and envied for three generations, she is a person of rare qualities, her captivating warmth and quick wit enforced by great energy and iron discipline. Always the centre of attention but quite unspoilt, she is naturally bohemian and adventurous and can take on any role — hostess, mechanic, farmer, author, ambassador, mother, actress, builder. Third and youngest daughter of the Duke of Rutland, she grew up at Belvoir Castle. The Duchess brought her up along highly unusual aesthetic lines. As a child she was always dressed in black velvet, as a debutante she wore grey and beige instead of the usual white and pink. At Ascot she was noticeable among the rosy straws in a black picture hat with sheaves of gold and silver wheat, and when she appeared in a group of debutantes dressed as swans for a pageant, she was the single black swan. Against parental opposition she married Mr Duff Cooper of the Grenadier Guards, and her role as the Madonna in Max Reinhardt's spectacle *The Miracle* made her a popular heroine in two continents. During the war she ran her own farm single-handed. An entry in her diary reads, 'The Pig Family Hutchinson is in splendid fatness and should make me a nice profit . . . I spend a lot of my time asphyxiated by the smell and bent double inside the stye shovelling their dung.' She appears in *Vogue* regularly, and her changes of appearance reflect the course of fashion since 1919.

1. 1919.
2. With her photograph as the Madonna, 1926.
3. 1930.
4. 1923.
5. 1937.
6. With her portrait by Ambrose McEvoy, at home in Little Venice, 1963.

5

6

4

15

1　　　　POIRET

2　　　　de Meyer

IRENE CASTLE

Irene Castle, and Vernon, her husband, were world-famous dancing partners, their most famous dances the tango, the one-step and the Castle Walk. Vernon Castle started his career as a vaudeville contortionist called The String Bean. They came from New York to Paris, and were nearly down and out when they were offered a job in cabaret at the Café de Paris. Dining at the restaurant as guests of the management the night before the job began, they were recognized by a Russian count and persuaded to perform an impromptu dance: it became part of their act for them to rise from the tables among the audience. A year or two later they were international celebrities, and returned to New York to open a combined restaurant and dancing school, Castle House. 'Castles in the Air' was the name of the nightclub over a theatre where they performed in the evening. By the time they were appearing in a revue called 'Watch your Step' they were earning $6,000 a week, and owned a country house in Manhasset, where Vernon Castle played polo and kept sporting dogs. When he was killed at Fort Worth in Texas in 1918, the result of a plane crash, Irene Castle continued her career alone, never dancing with another partner. She was the embodiment of 'modern', with her boyish, healthy looks, her hair which she bobbed early on, and her crisp, bold movements — the direct opposite of Mary Pickford's simpering ringleted baby looks.

1. In one of her dancing costumes for *Miss 1917*, a New York revue.
2. 1921.
3. 1918.

3

1. 1926.
2. Reboux hat, 1927.
3. 1920.

Scalioni

THE DUCHESSE DE GRAMONT

Madame Vionnet said of her, 'She was a real model, tall and beautiful. When I was making a dress, I had only to ask her to come and try it on and I knew exactly where it was wrong.' Formerly the Princess Maria Ruspoli of Italy, she became a famous Paris hostess who was said to have entertained 90,000 people in her lifetime.

VIONNET

Steichen

Génia Reinberg

LANVIN

The new chemise arrives, pioneered by Lanvin, Worth and Paquin, cut loose and full, belted under the bosom. Diet and exercise are recommended for the new silhouette, which is flat front and back, with gathered pleats under the arms. The chemise is voted 'practical, being perfectly adapted to the demands of modern life . . . comfortable, graceful and economical — for the number of these simple frocks that are made in the seclusion of the sewing-room to be worn later with the air of having issued from les Grandes Maisons is one of the secrets of the age. Moreover it is smart.' For the morning, it is made in serge or bure, for the afternoon velvet, for evening satin or in Worth's tinted tulles and muslins. There's a new 'georgette' satin, satin top, cotton base. Premet's chemise is shortened in front and worn over a petticoat trimmed in fur. Gabrielle Chanel,

'known the world over for her sports frocks, is this season making evening gowns — a straight chemise of black charmeuse, embroidered with gold irises from waist to hem'. At home, a more practical version of the chemise is advertised by Goochs.

The coats are the thickest and warmest in years. 'The three

dimensions of the top-coat are fixed,' says *Vogue*, 'they are the highest and longest and fullest possible.' Jackets of suits rise from the knee to finger length. *Vogue* features the wardrobes of two stars — Florence Walton with her new suits from Dœuillet and Callot, Lina Cavalieri with her taffeta and rose faille evening dresses from Paquin. Hemlines clear the ankles, fur trims everything. Some of the best suits are in jersey — the colours are 'robin's egg blue, nile green, orchid, lilac, pale rose and oyster white'. Sweaters are like suit jackets, trimmed in fur and belted over the full ankle-length skirt.

The hat is as necessary a part of the outdoor costume as shoes, and is only taken off in private houses. Babies wear knitted caps, children felt or straw cloches, grandmothers toques and turbans. To complement your hat, it's new to wear a necklace of ruffled tulle.

Left: LUCILE Black satin at home, 1917; photograph Thomas Fall.

1916

1

GOOCHS
VOGUE & VALUE

IN their bright, commodious salons Goochs are showing all the newest ideas for the season in Coats and Skirts, Afternoon and Evening Gowns, Coat Frocks, Millinery, Blouses, Furs, Travelling Coats, and Footwear.

Style, fit, and materials, all give a new meaning to Gooch Vogue, a yet higher standard to Gooch Value. Take a walk round the salons.

Gooch's Autumn Fashions Catalogue, just published, will be forwarded post free on request.

Goochs

BROMPTON RD · LONDON · S.W.

A TYPICAL EXAMPLE of Gooch Vogue and Value is seen in this very becoming Coat and Skirt at 13½ gs.

Tête de Nègre Poiret Hat, gold embroidery, exfact fee, 6½ gs

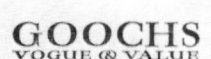

LUCILE

2

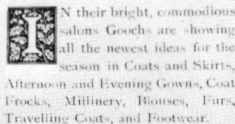

LUCILE

Rita Marti

3

20

ANDRÉ GROULT

THE *Arrol-Johnston* CAR

RILETTE

The Admiration of Everyone.

Arrol-Johnston Ltd., Makers of Cars, Dumfries.

Ira Hill

1. Gertie Millar in furs: photo Rita Martin.
2. Lucile suit.
3. Lucile's striped taffeta peg-top evening dress.
4. Fortuny dress.
5. André Groult 'sailor' in seal brown velvet.
6. Lanvin's tulle necklace.

1917

'Though Shops Have No Windows and Stocks are Underground, Paris Shows That Her Supreme Creative Qualities Remain Quite Unimpaired'

In spite of terrible pea-souper fogs, Paris produces a new spring silhouette out of the Russian ballet influence. The tonneau, or barrel skirt, often has peg top drapes and wings over the hips. At the same time couturiers are designing slim new day looks with a minimum of fabric: 'The war is responsible for so many things — for the new narrow skirts, for the colour of our frocks, for the shape of our hats, and for the texture (and price) of our gloves and shoes.'

It's a year of charity fetes and high hats, and everyone has an insatiable appetite for fur. You wrap furs round you however you can afford them, in coats or stoles, or you take a leaf out of Chanel's book and add bands of fur to jackets and hems. For evening, the Callot sisters introduce spun silver and gold tissues. Lucile's dresses and negligées show a new attention to sleeves. A gathered peplum makes the double-tiered evening dress the star of the year.

LUCILE

SPORTS

1. Snowproof Engadine skiing outfit.
2. Personal windscreen screwed onto a metal shoulder-frame, all packed away into a yellow leather case on arrival.
3. Green tweed gaiter suit.
4. Beige brocade and crepe evening dress with fur.
5. Jane Renouardt in Callot's tiered dress of cream tulle, silver and gold.

CALLOT

1917

1. Black-figured pale blue taffeta.
2. Black velvet dress and jacket,
black satin waistcoat.

DOEUILLET

1

The "JEANNETTE." Semi-evening or Afternoon Gown in best quality Chiffon Taffetas and Ninon de Soie, cut on most becoming lines and suitable for matron's wear. The bodice has sleeves of ninon and silk, vest of fine cream French lace, and finished at waist with handsome girdle and tassels in dull gold cord. Skirt has deep flounce of taffetas with top of ninon over dull gold insertion. In black, grey, nigger, and navy. **9** Gns.

The "GEORGETTE." Charming Afternoon Gown in good quality Georgette. Bodice embroidered in dull gold with large collar of flesh-pink Ninon de Soie, smart waistbelt of dull gold cord and metallic clasps. Skirt is finished with deep hem of Satin Meteor. In grey, saxe, navy, nigger, rose, and black. Large and medium sizes. **6½** Gns.

The "LOLETTE." Smart Afternoon or Semi-evening Gown in best quality Chiffon Taffetas. Bodice of Ninon de Soie veiled over dull gold metal lace. Skirt arranged with pleating of silk, trimmed Marabout. In nigger, brown, and black. **7½** Gns.

THESE three charming Gowns are indicative of the New Models for Spring.
They are smart and distinctive without being in any way extravagant.

WRITE FOR OUR SPRING CATALOGUE

It is a guide to economy, and may be had Post Free for the asking.

Peter Robinson's Oxford Street

Peter Robinson Ltd.

24

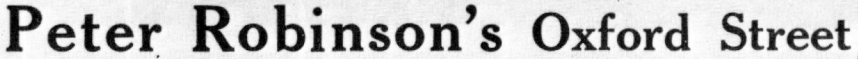

2

DOEUILLET

THE SLIM SILHOUETTE

LANVIN

JENNY

WORTH

LEWIS

1918

ARNOLD

'Not since the war began have the couturiers produced so many good models as have appeared this year, models that were conceived and stitched to the accompaniment of the boom of "Big Bertha".'

Chanel's fur-trimmed jersey costumes are making her a fortune. Fur trims everything — even black satin evening dresses. Belted tunics make double tiers of skirts, but the slim silhouette is taking over from last year's tonneau.

In a year of enforced economy blouses and waistcoats are becoming popular as additions that help you ring the changes. Washable frocks are acceptable, but 'there are times when one prefers to have economy inconspicuous . . . conceal the fact that your frock is washable with a detachable panel and girdle of grosgrain ribbon'. There's a new 'transformation' dress, for instance, 'a navy blue serge coat-dress with a front of light georgette crepe and what seems to be an underskirt of the same colour. One removes the dark serge frock and — presto — one is wearing a light blue frock with the same georgette crepe front. In this way the Parisienne is dressed for all day in one frock.'

The Comtesse de Talleyrand and the Comtesse de Fitz-James wear black tailored suits with handkerchief linen blouses through which you can see their strings of pearls. The Princesse de Broglie is noticed in a plain dress of a dark brown silk with a knotted sash, brown stockings and shoes, a brown hat with a grosgrain band.

Big-brimmed hats fly with chiffon veils, not only for motoring but for 'walking in a stiff breeze', to protect the complexion. More formal hats climb tall with quills, and with plumes of paradise and ostrich. As straw gets short, Paris milliners turn to silk and ribbon. The scope of sweaters has become wider over the last two years, and firms like Poirette are making beautiful and imaginative silk sweaters, with sailor collars, interesting textures, good use of colour.

As Paris becomes colder and bleaker, and the price of coal rises to 300 francs a ton, furs become more desirable and harder to get. The status symbol of the moment is to be completely wrapped in leopardskin, but for the many who can't afford it, 'There are nine and sixty ways of trimming suits these days, and every single furry one is right.' This is the first year of the craze for monkey fur, which appears as a ragged black fringe on hats, hems, muffs, and veils.

'Sometimes the pelts employed in these fashions are easily recognised; but it is best not to inquire too closely into the origin of some of the strange skins which have been cut into strips or folded into collars to trim many of the smartest frocks. They bear such concealing names as 'Jacquerette' or 'Péruvienne', and, while many women of curious disposition would like to know why, if they restrain their curiosity they may have more pleasure in wearing their furs.'

1. American Mrs Alexander Bache Pratt in furs, with a fashionable Alsatian.
2. Chanel's fur-trimmed jersey.
3. Paquin's monkey-fringed dress and coat.

1

2
CHANEL

3
PAQUIN

REVILLE

HATS

Lallie Charles

BRADLEY

MARIA GUY

1. Margaret Bannerman in a ribbon hat by Bradley.
2. Pewter tissue hat with jet beads and black paradise plumes. 'The effect is one of extreme elegance and unerring taste.'
3. Grey and fawn swathed crepe de chine, fawn quills.
4. Turban from Maria Guy in Russian sable and white ostrich feathers.
5. Tasselled mauve and white knitted sweater-suit.
6. Navy gabardine dress masquerading as a suit.

POIRETTE

5

6

de Meyer

DOEUILLET

1. Faith Celli in striped
ninon.
2. Dœuillet's is the
shortest new skirt.
3. Delysia looking
curious in a petalled
evening dress.
4 and 5. Both sides of
the picture — an
afternoon dress of
black charmeuse.

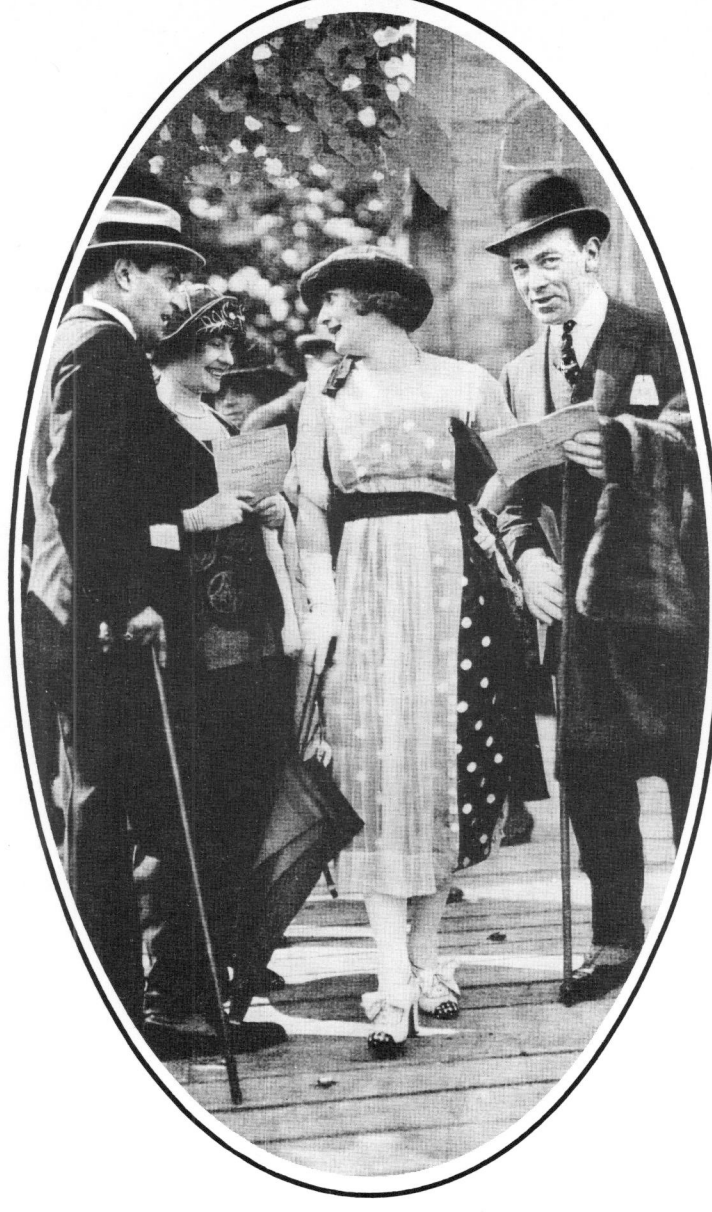

Gaby Deslys at Longchamp with Max Dearly, the actor: her foulard dress draped with chiffon. Famous for her glamour and her fantastic towering feather headdresses — she was called 'a human aviary' — she made no secret of her scandalous private life. Declaring 'Money is woman's only

bulwark against the world', she amassed a fabulous collection of jewels from her lovers, including a rope of pearls as long as herself from King Manuel of Portugal. When she died she left her money to the poor of Marseilles.

There's racing at Longchamp, and in Paris and London the season starts up again. At home there's professional cricket, yachting at Cowes, polo, and hunt balls in spite of a lack of male partners. At the Derby the favourite, Panther, comes in fourth. Dame Nellie Melba sings, the Russian ballet dances. At Wimbledon Mlle Suzanne Lenglen defeats Mrs Lambert Chambers. In Paris the city is packed, taxis are available again, and there are flowerstalls by the river. Poiret returns from the army to open up his salon, and with it a nightclub, L'Oasis, famous for not playing jazz. There is ragtime to dance to, or the new pasa doble and women dance in swaying fringes of beads or feathers.

Summer weekends include motoring, swimming and tennis. This is *Vogue's* list of equipment for a summer weekend: travelling dress, simple suit of wool jersey tweed or homespun with a smart tailored blouse. For walking, golf, motoring, a simple sports hat, low-heeled shoes. Face veil for walking in a breeze, sailing or motoring. Extra chiffon veil. Pleated skirt with a white blouse and coloured jumper for walking. Plain straw or felt hat, heavy white silk stockings, white buckskin shoes. Dark clocked stockings with grey or tan shoes for a change, a wool or silk scarf. Day frock, sports dress. Afternoon dress in organdie or silk. Suede or kid house shoes, stockings to match, hat. Two evening dresses for a Saturday to Monday, three for a

Friday to Monday. Dinner gown of satin or chiffon with a train, a less formal dance frock.

For the first time couturier collections are shown on living models. Women aren't content to choose from a sketch or a doll any more — they want to see how the clothes will move. In October a new house emerges, Molyneux. Captain Molyneux, who served his apprenticeship at Lucile in London, shows glamorous black evening dresses and ostrich feathers.

Formal afternoon dressing and sports suits are poles apart, but Chanel, Martial et Armand and Lanvin are beginning to find a large market between the two. The silhouette becomes slimmer; Lanvin's throwback crinolines are the exception. The summer uniform is a pale garden frock, the essential accessory a parasol, and a feather fan for evening. All evening dresses are fringed for dancing, with monkey fur, ostrich, steel beads, velvet ribbons or tassels of silk.

Hats have a new width at the sides, brims of pleated tulle, tricorne shapes, veiling . . . evening headdresses are made of ostrich feathers glycerined to make them heavy and drooping. 'At the theatre a handsome Englishwoman wore her dark hair wrapped round her small shapely head. She ornamented it with a novel diamond tiara, the centre a plume of black glycerine ostrich of which the rib was encrusted with diamonds'.

Henri Manuel

MOLYNEUX

1. Fringed black satin shawl.
2. Mistinguett in a black velvet
cape lined with stripes.
3 and 5. Day and evening of
the new house, Molyneux.
4. Sports clothes — navy
blazer, cream skirt, red
sailor hat; cream blouse
and skirt for tennis.

MOLYNEUX

LANVIN

LUCILE

7

6. A new bloused look
from Paris.
7. Black satin and crepe, net
ruffles, black straw
hat trimmed with
glycerine ostrich.
8. Gertrude Lawrence in a
tricorne by Edythe Brown.
9. Lanvin's new bouffant
crinolines are the exception
to the slim silhouette.

8

EDYTHE BROWN

9

LANVIN

REDFERN

REVILLE

The Comtesse d'Hautpoul by the polo field.   de Givenchy

Chanel's silhouette, staying close to the lines of the uncorseted figure, begins to make the bouffant skirts of Lanvin look old-fashioned, and the follies of Poiret too theatrical. Vionnet makes dresses that are works of art, but Chanel is more commercial. Everything she does makes news — the first quilted coat, the narrow crepe de chine dress inside a cage of tulle, and the suntan which she cultivates. *Vogue* publishes three pages of holiday beach clothes, still designed to protect you from too much sun, and three more on the backs of evening dresses, which begin at the waist. The one-year-old house of Molyneux proves itself with glamorous evening looks, and sets a fashion for hats weighted with feathers, ostrich feather fans from the Folies Bergères, bandeaux and yards of pearls. The most useful and easy way to dress is in knitted jackets or jumpers and pleated skirts, pioneered by Chanel and now generally accepted.

Hats spread out with ostrich feathers or tulle petals, and for evening there are diadems or bandeaux of silver leaves or gold tissue.

1920

CHANEL   1

De Givenchy

De Givenchy

ELSPETH PHELPS

3

4
VIONNET

5

6
CHANEL

1 and 2. The alternative
silhouettes.
3 and 6. Chanel's tulle bell
over a slim crepe de
chine dress.
4. Brown georgette crepe and
matching lace.
5. An English version of the
crinoline by Elspeth Phelps:
pink tulle with bands of skunk.
7. The sun is still something
from which to protect yourself
— in embroidered palest flesh
crepe.

7

MARGAINE LACROIX   de Meyer

9

10

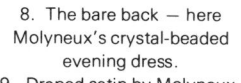

8. The bare back — here
Molyneux's crystal-beaded
evening dress.
9. Draped satin by Molyneux.
10. Cécile Sorel in Lucile's tea
gown of lavender and
silver lamé.

IRETTE

ELENID

1921

'The very smartest women seen during the morning promenade in the Bois, those who descend from a magnificent motor-car to walk for half an hour in the sunshine, wear strictly tailored Oxford grey suits absolutely plain, but with every accessory quite perfect'

Dresses are caught in naturally at the waist, and hems grow longer. Umbrellas or parasols are an essential part of the look. Lanvin produces a bright Riviera collection of Aztec embroideries, and Vionnet 'continues to make those "simple little things" — complex enough if one tries to copy them — and has her own distinctive way of utilizing fringe'. Fringes are everywhere: there are fringe sleeves, fringe hems, fringe cloaks.

'Owing to this craze for dancing, dining in restaurants where dancing takes place either during or after dinner has become very popular, and it is in such restaurants that one sees the newest clothes.' The newest are flat-chested and hemlines are any length, long and slender or bouffant and crinolined. Skirts drip handkerchief points to the floor, and *Vogue* shows a page of flame chiffon dresses by Ospovat, who dresses Lady Diana Cooper so beautifully.

The restaurant hat is a feather cartwheel, or a new favourite, the swagged hat, with a cascade of feathers or flowers falling over one shoulder. Reboux makes swags of cock feathers or flowers and fruit scattered on a chiffon streamer, Lewis adds tassels of chenille or jet, and Molyneux makes showers of glycerined ostrich feathers. The new motoring hat is a turban with long scarf ends to wear as a veil or a float.

'Most women at the present wear a very innocent sort of corset, which becomes more of a belt and less of a corset according to the suppleness of the figure for which it is designed. With some women, this is little more than a girdle to hold the stocking supporters; others like a bone back and front and even one over each hip. Hardly anyone goes further than this, and the corset is cut so that it gives support without restriction. Instead of tightening her bands, the woman who thinks that her figure is too generous now seeks some means of healthful reduction, and the change is one in which we should all rejoice. Very tight clothes never did anything to disguise avoirdupois, just misplaced it. But the absolutely uncorseted laissez-allez effect is no longer the proper one. One should have the appearance of being comfortably supported.'

REVILLE   Navy serge costume and pleated fawn crepe petticoat.

OSPOVAT

EAN PATOU   Rehbinder

MADELEINE ET MADELEINE   Rehbinder

1. Ospovat's flame chiffon with the year's uneven hemline.
2. White chiffon with crystal embroidery.

1. The Dolly sisters wearing fancy dress representing Ciro Pearls in which they won first prize at the Warriors' Day Ball, Covent Garden. They were Hungarian, originally Janzieska and Roszieska Deutch, known as Jenny and Rosie Dolly. They were almost identical, with black hair cut in fringes, and appeared in cabaret and on the stage. When Gordon Selfridge saw them at the Kit-Cat club he became infatuated with Jenny, on whom it is estimated he spent two million pounds between 1924 and 1931. He gave them the run of Selfridges and, more impressively, unlimited credit at his casinos in Le Touquet and Deauville. When Jenny won £40,000 and then lost £80,000 in a night, he sent her a diamond bracelet and Rosie a rope of pearls with a note, 'I hope this will make up for your losses last night, darling!' In the end, Jenny had to sell her jewellery and her château to pay her gambling debts. As Rosie married her third husband, she remarked, 'If this marriage doesn't take I will go into a nunnery', and her husband added, 'So will I!'

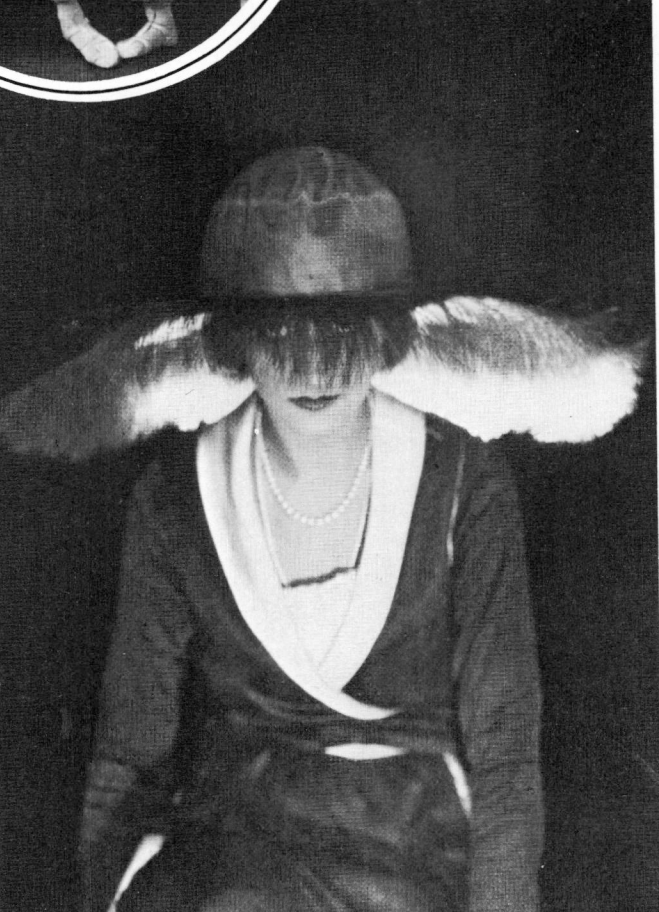

1

2 RENÉE   Brissaud

3

MERCIE McHARDY   Arjamand LEWIS   Génia Reinberg

BAKST

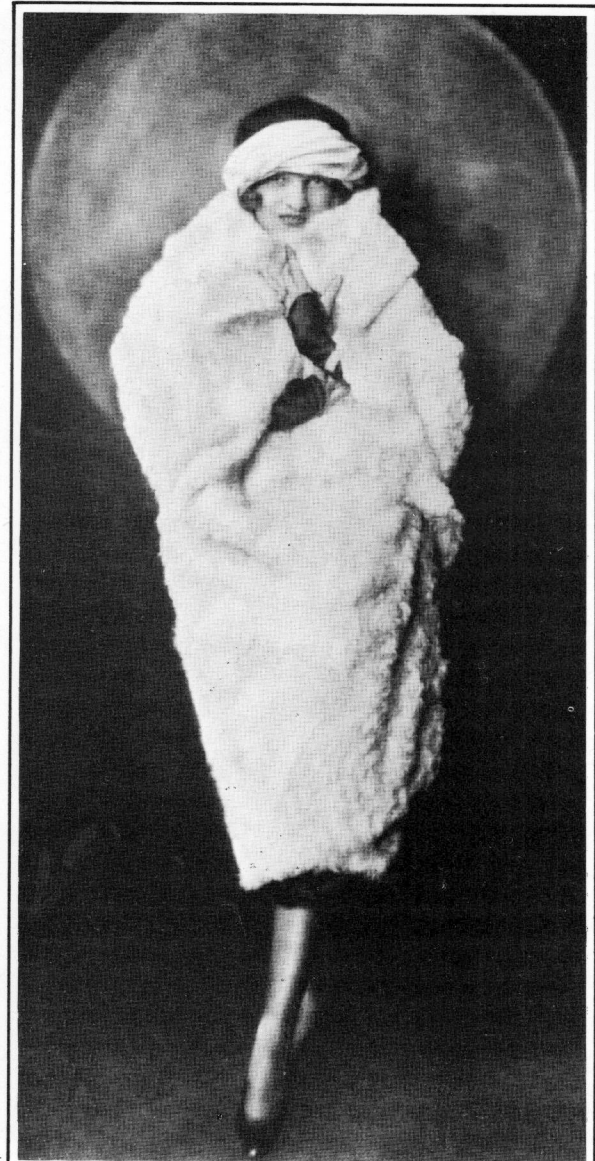

2. 'Mon mari — mon danseur':
sketch by Brissaud, dance frock
by Renée.
3. Duchess Sforza in Lewis's
silver lace hat with glycerined
ostrich feathers.
4. Ina Claire in a cloak of
green and gold brocade
designed by Bakst, with a
monkey collar.
5. Leonora Hughes in a rough
white caracul coat.
6. Bathing dress in crepe.
7. Summer frocks: lavender
and white gingham, green-
striped Japanese silk with a
white silk blouse.

THESE BATHING-SUITS PROVE THAT ONE MAY BE

IN THE WATER, AS OUT OF IT, JUST AS SMART

Meserole

41

1922

REBOUX   Flowerpot of picot straw with cock feathers and roses: sketch by Helen Dryden.

'In their street models for the spring of 1922, the couturiers have evolved a real "Paris fashion", such as we used to have when the women in all the capitals of the world wore the same puffed sleeves at the same time'

It is the year of the peasant in Paris and London. Lanvin makes the Breton suit, short braided jacket with lots of small buttons, big white organdie collar turning down over a red satin bow, sailor hat or round straw on the head. It's a look that Chanel will take up and make her own, but this year she's selling her own version of the peasant look — black crepe de chine dresses and overblouses covered with bright Balkan embroidery. The new suits by Jean Patou and others have hiplength jackets flared or waisted over long narrow skirts, hats, mufflers and the new buckled shoe, the accessory of the year. At Molyneux, metallic brocade and monkey fur fringes on pale dresses; and everywhere, fantastic sleeves.

The year of the royal wedding brings Princess Mary's trousseau into *Vogue* item by item: 'Individual Taste Combined with Beauty of Material and Design Result in a Charming Trousseau for the Nation's Bride.' Patriotically British, it consists of designs from Reville and Handley Seymour, with hats by Millicent.

LANVIN

LANVIN
1

DORVILLE

THE PEASANT
LOOK

2

1. Lanvin's Breton suit, manilla toillaine striped with chocolate braid, white organdie collar tied with red ribbon.

2. Chanel's Balkan embroideries, primary colours on black crepe de chine.
3. Travelling, 1922. One woman's luggage, by Vuitton, clothes by Molyneux.

3

1

LANVIN

A E Marty

2

A E Marty

3

LUCILE

1. New suit silhouettes—jackets flared or fitted.

2. The Riviera—Lanvin's sports clothes are perfection. For golfing, blue pullover with white collar and cuffs, full white flannel skirt. Centre, scarlet cheviot suit with the new short jacket. Right,

primrose wool jersey dress embroidered in checks of gold and silver thread.

3. Dolores models Lucile's shot green brocade with slashed sleeves.

4. Mme Stoisesco, poet (and the model for Proust's Mlle de Saint Loup), in evening dress.

Rehbinder

4

LANVIN   Black and white crepe.   Steichen

'Skirt lengths vary not only according to what designer creates them, and what lady wears them, but, also, according to the hour of the day when they are worn'

Chanel puts women into sweaters and pleated skirts 9-10 inches off the ground. 'The very short skirt at once suggests that the lady is dressed by Chanel who makes all her skirts short, whether for morning, afternoon or evening . . . the straight line is her medium of expression.' With cloche hats and bandeaux, a willowy flat silhouette and dropped waistlines, the look is universal: but hems are still undecided, wavering between ankle and calf. A slim figure is essential to the look, hence the emphasis on the outdoor life with sport, exercise, sunshine. Vionnet's crepe dresses are the most beautiful in Paris.

After the discovery of Tutankhamen's tomb Ancient Egypt suddenly becomes fashionable, with hieroglyphic embroideries, scarab and lotus jewellery, serpents, and stiff folds tied into the fronts of dresses. 'The concentration of fullness in front, which some call Indo-Chinese and others Egyptian, is very prominent in many collections, so that the plain flat — not to say, tight — back is everywhere in evidence.'

PARIS
AGREES TO DISAGREE
about
THE LENGTH
of
SKIRTS

IN Paris, at the present moment, there are many opinions about skirt lengths. Not only do the couturiers disagree among themselves, but, to make matters more confusing, the ladies whom they costume hold quite as conflicting views as the couturiers who dress them. Again, skirt lengths vary not only according to what designer creates them, and what lady wears them, but, also, according to the hour of the day when they are worn. The snapshots on this page illustrate some of the vagaries of Paris skirts. Take, for instance, the tailleurs shown at the lower left. The very short skirt at once suggests that the lady is probably dressed by Chanel who makes all her skirts short, whether for morning, afternoon, or evening. The more conservative skirt worn by her companion stops above the ankle. This is the length that Jenny makes. The lady at the lower right wears her skirt a little longer, while the Marquise de Saint-Sauveur, at the upper right, shows a hem-line fully ten inches off the ground.

The Parisienne treats the length of her afternoon frocks with the same diversity of opinion as her tailleur, but, generally speaking, she wears them two inches longer. In the centre is a snapshot of Madame Meyer wearing a smart frock which completely conceals her ankles, the length approved by Patou. In the afternoon frock at the left above, an effect of length is achieved by panels. This is the length approved by Vionnet

In London, skirts obey the same laws that obtain in Paris, the only difference being that, for the street, the English woman wears hers slightly longer than does the Parisienne. Also, the rules of length are more definite here; skirts are well above the ankle for the sports suit or severe tailleur; to the ankle for the elaborate tailleur; just below it for the afternoon frock; barely escaping the floor for the evening

1. The different lengths as they're being worn in London and Paris — two inches longer in London.

2. Gladys Cooper in Molyneux's silver turban and sheath with chiffon roses. The silver cloak is embroidered with pearls and lined with rose velvet.

3. Three-piece suit by Vladimir of soft green crepe de chine and hat worn low over the eyes.

4. Vionnet's summer crepes, appliquéd and printed. *Left*, black with crimson and scarlet poppies on green stems. *Centre*, black and white appliqué. *Right*, sky, tree and water colours in a reflection print.

MOLYNEUX

VLADIMIR

VIONNET

JENNY   DOUCET   DRECOLL

The Egyptian Look

DÉSIRÉE

Maurice Beck and Helen Macgregor

CHÉRUIT, PATOU   Meserole

5. Cathleen Nesbitt wears Désirée's Egyptian brocade with a Nile green georgette underskirt.

6. 'Dashing romance lurks' in the velvet-trimmed black taffeta modelled by Mrs Rudolph Valentino. Formerly Natasha Rambova — and born Winifred Shaugnessy De Wolf Hudnut, she had been a costume designer for Nazmova. Like her husband, to whom she had given a slave bracelet which he always wore in public, she believed in occultist powers. They lived in Beverly Hills in a house called 'Falcon's Lair'.

7. Cinema capes from Chéruit and Patou.

1924-1929

THE RECKLESS TWENTIES

By 1924 all the people had arrived, and the party was under full steam. It roared on until 1929, and expired with a Crash, leaving the guests bewildered and hung over. So much had happened in those six years, and ended so abruptly, that only a couple of years later the period seemed as distant as the days before the war. It is remembered as the Gay Twenties, the Roaring Twenties, but for the people who hadn't been asked to the party, nine-tenths of the population, it was a time of despair with hunger marches, dole queues and war heroes reduced to selling matches on the street. The undergraduates who rushed to man the buses and trains in the General Strike didn't know or care that the miners were striking for more work so that they could feed their families. There was a great distance between opposites which intensified the gaiety of the party-goers, the intolerance of the establishment and the misery of the working class.

Meanwhile the twenties in *Vogue* are a rich cocktail of society, the *avant-garde* and the popular jazz, Hollywood, reportage and criticism. The regular contributors included Aldous Huxley and Nancy Cunard, Clive Bell and Cecil Beaton, and called in features by Virginia Woolf, Noël Coward, Jean Cocteau, D. H. Lawrence, Evelyn Waugh, Vita Sackville-West, the Sitwells, and many more. *Vogue* extended its territory, and found an energetic style quite different from the tone of its first decade. The pages looked ten times more interesting with photographs by Steichen and Hoynin-

gen-Huene, Man Ray and Beaton, and came alive with subjects as different as Gertrude Stein – 'Certainly the union of oxygen with ostriches is not that of the taught tracer' – and the rhythms of the *Revue Nègre*:

> Skiddle up skat!
> Skiddle up skat!
> Oh, skiddle up, skiddle up,
> Skat! Skat! Skat!

Everything in the twenties was done after a cocktail, to jazz. How should a cocktail be drunk? 'Quickly, while it's still laughing at you,' replied Henry Craddock in the *Savoy Cocktail Book*. You bought the ice from the fishmonger for a shilling a lump, tied it up in a tea cloth and bashed it to bits on the floor. There was soon a cocktail shaker in every middle-class house, and *Vogue* showed designs for a private cocktail bar . . . 'Planning a Gay Corner Devoted to the Shaker, the Cherry and the Row of Happy Bottles'. Before the war you drank nothing until you sat down for dinner, but now there were dry Martinis, Side-cars, Bosom Caressers, Manhattans, Between the Sheets, or gin-and-ginger-beer. Marcel Boulestin, the famous restaurateur who wrote about food for *Vogue*, remarked, 'Cocktails are the most romantic expression of modern life . . . but the cocktail habit as practised in England now is a vice.'

Left: Josephine Baker at the Casino de Paris 1931, photograph Hoyningen Huene.
1. Covarrubias drawings.

Fish

1. The Sitwells, 1927
2. Florence Mills in *Dover Street to Dixie*
when it came to London in 1923.
3. John Howard Lawson's Broadway play
Processional, showing June Walker, the lead,
with part of the jazz band and the cubist
backcloth.
4. Design for a cocktail bar by Aubrey
Hammond.

In the morning, at tea time, and all night long people danced.
The Prince of Wales kept a band playing for an hour and a half
without a break while he one-stepped and Charlestoned with Mrs
Dudley Ward. Barbara Cartland describes how Friday-to-Monday
guests in the country would start dancing to the gramophone as
soon as they arrived, hurry upstairs to dress, drive fifteen or
twenty miles to a dance or a hunt ball and dance until five in the
morning. In London you went to a *thé dansant* at the Savoy for five
shillings, or twenty other places for less, and after the theatre you'd
take a taxi to the Berkeley, the Mayfair or the Embassy and dance
again to the music of the Savoy Orpheans, Le Roy Allwood or
Ambrose. When you tired of hotels there were nightclubs, but if
your favourite nightclub had just been raided and closed down,
there were still bottle parties, respectable at first, random later,
where there would be a Negro band and possibly a cabaret.

Jazz in the early twenties meant 'heavily punctuated, relentless
rhythm, with drums, rattles, bells, whistles, hooters and twanging
banjoes'. By the time Aldous Huxley wrote this description in *Antic
Hay*, the saxophone and trumpet had been added: 'Sweet, sweet
and piercing, the saxophone pierced into the very bowels of com-
passion and tenderness, pierced like a revelation from heaven . . .
More ripely and roundly, with a kindly and less agonizing volup-
tuousness, the 'cello meditated those Mohammedan ecstasies . . .
the violin admitted refreshing draughts of fresh air . . . and the
piano hammered and rattled away unmindful of the sensibilities
of the other instruments, banged away all the time, reminding
everyone concerned, in a thoroughly business-like way, that this
was a cabaret where people came to dance the fox trot.'

Round and round went the dancers all over Mayfair, usually in
fancy dress, women dressed as men, men as women, everybody
'terribly serious; not a single laugh, or the palest ghost of a smile.
Frantic noises and occasional cries of ecstasy come from half a
dozen negro players . . . Dim lights, drowsy odours and futurist
drawings on the walls and ceiling.'

The 'Original' Dixieland Jazz Band, white musicians, had
opened at the Hammersmith Palais as early as 1919, and there had

been a lot of diluted jazz since, but in 1925 the real thing was seen and heard in Paris. It had already happened in New York, where socialites went into the fringes of Harlem to dance and watch, and Negroes were invited up to Park Avenue apartments to teach the Charleston and the Black Bottom. The first all-coloured show written, produced and acted by Negroes was *Shuffle Along*, on Broadway in 1923. Since then there had been *Runnin' Wild*, *Chocolate Dandies*, *Honey*, and *Dover Street to Dixie*, and there was soon to be a King Vidor film *Hallelujah*, made in Hollywood with an all-black cast. The *Revue Nègre* was the first to come to Paris, and the audiences were almost knocked out by the waves of energy and noise which engulfed them from the footlights. Josephine Baker in her frill of bananas became an overnight sensation. Nancy Cunard was ecstatic about the 'perfect delight ... of Josephine Baker, most astounding of mulatto dancers, in her necklets, bracelets, and flouncing feathered loincloths. The fuzz has been taken out of her hair, which shines like a dark blue crystal, as she yodels (the nearest one can get to expressing it) and contorts her surprising form through a maze of complicated rhythms.' Another *Vogue* writer called her 'a woman possessed, a savage intoxicated with tom-toms, a shining machine à danser, an animal, all joint and no bones ... at one moment she is the fashion artist's model, at the next Picasso's.' A year or two later, when she'd opened her own nightclub in Paris, John McMullin went to interview her. 'She has come in without a wrap, and the length of her graceful body, which is light sealskin brown, is swathed in a full blue tulle frock with a bodice of blue snakeskin ... she wears an enormous diamond ring and a very impressive diamond bracelet. Her hair, which naturally grows in tight curls, is plastered close to her head with white of egg and looks as though it were painted on her head with black shellac. As she appears at the Folies Bergères, one is struck by her great decadence of line. When, for the finale, she wears only a diamanté maillot of tulle and red gloves with diamond balls hanging from the tips of her fingers, the effect is up to the wildest imagination of Beardsley.' She went everywhere in her Voisin car, painted brown and upholstered in brown snakeskin

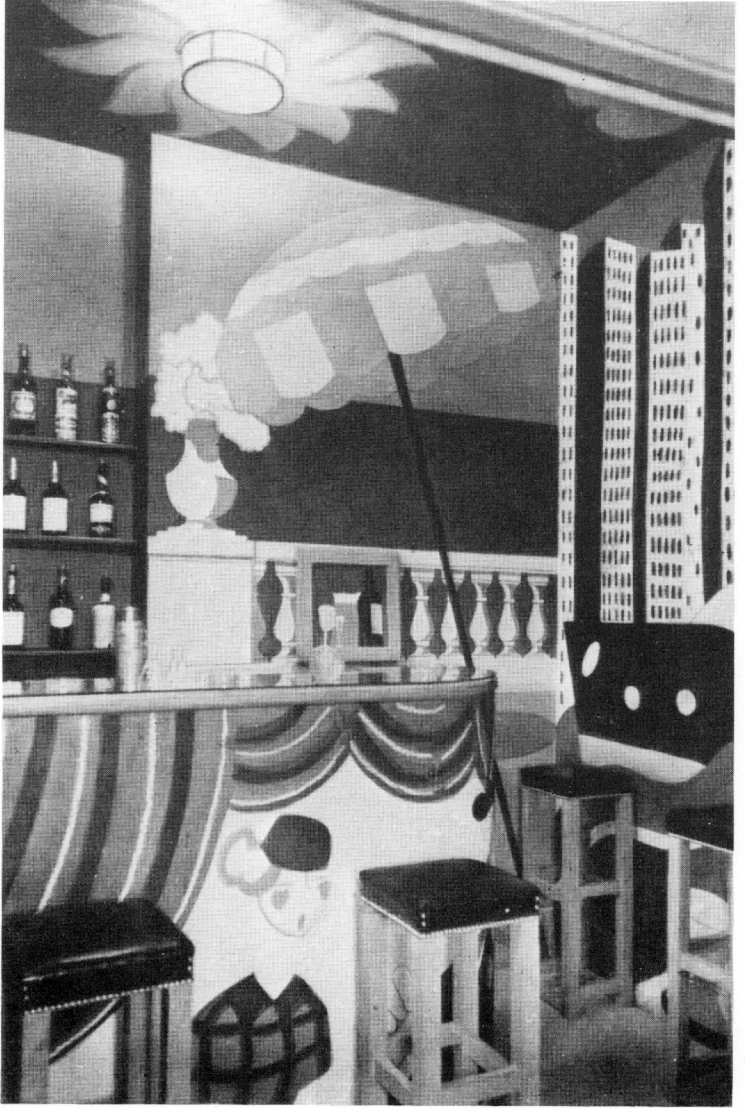

E.J. Mason

SCENE: "THE LAST JUMP," CABARET ON A SATURDAY NIGHT.

Here is Nick Fie Rastus with his "teasin' brown," getting in a word or two (I'll say he is) between dances and sips of that red ale which is the rage of Negro cabarets. Note the lady's neutral attitude, expressed by the chaste and exquisite clasping of her hands

THAT TEASIN' YALLA GAL

Seen in Paris in a cabaret or a "dancing" between the hours of 10 p.m. and 5 a.m. She gets right there each time, and don't you be making any mistake. A lady of mystery. Unescorted. Unescortable. Likely to have a greyhound at home. Impossible to tell the exact colour of her skin

KIND O' MELANCHOLY LIKE

He's jess natchely a quiet sort of fellow, dat boy is. Bin at dat table all night, sittin' down, waitin' for somebody, it seem. Don't nevah dance or sing or cut up. Nothin'. Jess sits over there, kind o' melancholy like. "You got to do bette'n dat, ole man. Ain't no time to git blue"

THE SHEIK OF DAHOMEY

Nothin'—Ah don't care whut it is—can get mah boy excited. Nothin'! And talk about havin' a way with wimmin, ain't nobody can tell him nothin' . . . He's a dressin' up fool, dat boy is, an' he sure's got luck with de high yalla ladies

Enter, The New Negro

Left, Negro types drawn by Miguel Covarrubias: captions by the negro poet Eric D. Walrond. 1. Nancy Cunard, journalist and poet. *Vogue's* Paris correspondent, 1927. She rimmed her eyes with kohl and wore African bangles to the elbows.

exactly matched to her own skin, accompanied by a maid, a chauffeur, and a white esquimau dog bearing on top of its head the red imprint of her kiss.

Josephine Baker was followed by Florence Mills and the Blackbirds. If Josephine Baker was a '*machine à danser*', Florence Mills was a poignant ragamuffin, all thin wrists and legs like toothpicks. All of a sudden everything black was the rage: black and white décor, Babangi masks, heads wrapped up in turbans, bracelets up the whole arm, jazz and all Negro dances, particularly the Charleston. 'In the 18th century we made money out of Negroes. In the 20th they make money out of us,' said *Vogue*. 'The Negro is at last coming into his own. The most distinguished art critics say his sculpture is better than that of Phidias; the musicians say he composes better than Beethoven; the dance-enthusiasts add that he dances better than Nijinsky; and the cabaret and music hall proprietors admit that he pays better than anyone.' The rhythms and characters of the Negro revue were beautifully given by the Mexican caricaturist Miguel Covarrubias with captions by a Negro poet, Eric D. Walrond . . . 'Nothin' – Ah don't care whut it is – can get mah boy excited. Nothin'! And talk about havin' a way with wimmin, ain't nobody can tell him nothin' . . . He's a dressin' up fool, dat boy is, an' he sure's got luck with de high yalla ladies.'

The new Negro had entered, created by the jazz spirit of their own invention, and people had suddenly to make their minds up about 'niggers'. *Books for the Morning Room Table* reviewed Carl Van Vechten's *Nigger Heaven* about life in Harlem, and David Garnett's *The Sailor's Return*. Writing about the latter, Edwin Muir wondered whether 'relations between a sailor and a negress are a fit subject for art; whether the theme is not too fantastic to have universal significance'. *Le Village Blanc* was a controversial book by Joe Alex about a party of French shipwrecked off Africa and captured by a tribe that had once been forced to exhibit itself in an exhibition native village in Paris. The chief turns them into an exhibition white village for the amusement of the tribe, with a bar, a café and a beauty parlour. Meanwhile Carl Einstein had written the definitive book on African sculpture *Negerplastik*, and the cubists had already absorbed Babangi masks and Dogon sculpture from the 1922 exhibition of French colonial art.

No sooner was jazz accepted as thrilling and artistic than there began to be a tendency among popular musicians to claim the credit for white culture. In 1926 *Vogue* was writing, 'How far syncopated music derives from the Negroes is doubtful, but certainly they are its best interpreters', and George Gershwin, well known for his 'Fascinatin' Rhythm' and 'Rhapsody in Blue', arrived in London to say, 'Well, sometimes I have got an inspiration from Negro spirituals. But it is doubtful if they are Negro at all. Paul Whiteman says they are mostly old English tunes.' Showing how to dance to the new tunes, old English or new American, were Maurice and Leonora Hughes, and Fred and Adèle Astaire. The Astaires drew enormous crowds in Gershwin's *Lady Be Good* in New York and London, 'Adèle squealing like a toy steam engine . . . Fred pat-a-flapping a proposal of marriage sans music', and Maurice Chevalier and Yvonne Vallée called their 1927 revue *Whitebirds* . . . 'a non-stop attaboy Charlestonized paean to the birds and the trees and the breeze – a lunatic dash past Nature at 60 miles an hour . . . if this man loves Nature, then all the nightingales will soon be drinking dry Martinis'.

Cars had a tremendous romantic appeal in the twenties, the appeal of speed, powerful machinery and status symbol rolled into one. Michael Arlen summed it up in this description of Iris Storm's car in *The Green Hat*, 'Like a huge yellow insect that had dropped to earth from a butterfly civilization, this car, gallant and suave, rested in the lowly silence of the Shepherd Market night. Open as a yacht, it wore a great shining bonnet, and flying over the crest of this great bonnet, as though in proud flight over the heads of scores of phantom horses, was that silver stork by which the gentle may be pleased to know that they have just escaped death beneath the wheels of a Hispano-Suiza car.'

In London gallery goers failed to see the point of much that was new in painting and sculpture. Clive Bell, writing in *Vogue* about Brancusi, complained, 'Within the last few months I have heard in London – in Paris, I think, that particular brand of imbecility is now known to be vulgar – the old familiar hee-haw, the fatuous comment, the time-worn joke, at the expense of one of the most serious of modern artists . . . the fools approach and read in their catalogues "L'oiseau" or "Tête d'une femme": peals of laughter. Is it possible these oafs suppose that the sculptor was trying to make a photographic likeness of a bird or a woman, and could get no nearer than this? No: people who could suppose that are not allowed out.' *Vogue* had come a long way from the 1919 review that said, 'Art cannot flourish without a wealthy and leisured class to savour it – a class which has sufficient time and energy to refine its taste and to sharpen its intellect in social encounters'. And in the popular press, 'Mr Ben Nicholson has three muddy nudes against wishy-washy backgrounds. It is obvious that the figures are not meant to be anatomically probable – one woman's ankles are three times the width of her neck; one wonders simply why he had to paint them.' Even in 1929, Epstein's Rima was daubed with tar and feathers. In *The Long Weekend* Robert Graves and Alan Hodge point out that the public were slowly being educated into seeing things in an impressionistic or post-impressionistic way by fashion sketches and advertisements. In the Underground, and in *Vogue*, you could see posters by McKnight Kauffer, and because they were not in an art gallery they were looked at without prejudice or suspicion.

Paris took the natural lead in all the arts except for films, and London followed. It was said the time lag in art fashions between France and educated England was about 12 years, and between educated England and the masses another two at least. Exhibitions held in the two cities in the mid-twenties summed up their relative positions. Wembley's Empire Exhibition was intended to enlarge the domestic market and encourage exports. Palaces of Art, Engineering and Industry jostled walled African towns, pagodas

Buffotot

Chevenon

1. Mirror-shelved library in Paris, 1928, with furniture of hardwood and snakeskin.
2. Lalique's glass dining room for the Paris Exhibition.
3. McKnight Kauffer poster, 1925.

and Indian tombs; the Great Dipper was the steepest in England. King George V's opening speech was relayed by radio and between six and seven million people heard his voice for the first time. Osbert Sitwell picked his way carefully through the sea of mud to pronounce the exhibition 'not ugly'.

In 1925 Paris opened the Decorative Arts Exhibition, the first on an international scale for over a century for which applied arts were the main reason. The exhibition gave its name to the style, which Osbert Lancaster calls 'Modernistic' and 'Functional', and Bevis Hillier defines as including Erté on one hand and the 'architectural nudism' of Le Corbusier on the other. Inspired by Cubism, the Bauhaus and Aztec art, it took its rich colours from the Russian ballet. Designs were intended for mass production in the new materials – plastics, ferro-concrete and vita-glass – and the aim was to combine art with industry. *Vogue* wrote, 'The Paris Exhibition is like a city in a dream, and the sort of dream that would give the psycho-analysts a good run for their money . . . Enormous fountains of glass play among life-size cubist dolls and cascades of music wash down from the dizzy summits of four gargantuan towers.' Instead of the simpering dummies that were usually used for fashion exhibitions, André Vigneau had made formalized wax or composition figures, Modiglianis with sculptured hair. They were silver, red, purple or natural wood colour, and showed the new clothes off beautifully, although they were found '*quelque peu troublant*'.

Poiret, who had been impressed by design education in Germany and Austria before the war, and had founded his textile and furnishing house Martine on revolutionary lines in 1922, was naturally involved in the exhibition. He made a merry-go-round of Paris figures including an apache dancer, a *modiste* and a fishwife. He designed three barges which he called 'Love', 'Organs' and 'Delights'; asked why, he answered, 'Women, always women.' 'Orgues' housed his new collection with wall hangings by Raoul Dufy, 'Délices' was a restaurant, and in 'Amours' Poiret sat playing a perfume piano, which fanned scented breezes at visitors when he pressed the notes for different scents.

The right clothes to wear for the functional pavilions and machine-turned constructions of the Art Deco exhibition were Sonia Delaunay's. A Russian who came from St Petersburg as an art student, she arrived in Paris in 1900 and married the painter Robert Delaunay. Her patchwork dresses are pure colour kaleido-scoped together into vivid geometric and abstract designs, jumbled alphabets and mosaics. They were made for golf and Bugattis, and she had cars painted to match the clothes. She shared with the vorticists and the expressionists a romantic feeling for speed, fragmentation and the influence of machines. She made coherent compositions like living paintings, and wasn't interested in the draping of cloth. Her husband said that she 'possessed colour in its atavistic state' and her clothes inspired poems – Blaise Cendrars's 'On her dress she has a body', and Tristan Tzara's

END OF BACKHAND DRIVE

4. Professor Lesieur and a pyramid of pupils, Comtesse Elie de Gaigneron, Princesse Guy de Faucigny-Lucinge and Mrs Harold Kingsland; photograph Lucien Eysserie.
5. Lady Mendl and instructor in her gardens at Antibes; photograph Lucien Eysserie.
6. Lelong tennis dress, 1928.
7. Benito's drawing of Chéruit's silver gauze dress, hand painted with lacquer-red, grey and black cubes, 1925.
8. One of Vigneau's grey wax mannequins for the Art Deco Exhibition, dressed by Lanvin and photographed by Man Ray.
9. Madame Agnès, the French milliner, in Futurist dress and earrings, 1925; photograph Steichen.

L'ange a glissé sa main
    dans la corbeille l'œil des fruits.
Il arrête les roues des autos,
    et le gyroscope vertigineux
    du cœur humain.

The woman who wore these clothes, or clothes by Vionnet, Chanel, Molyneux, Louiseboulanger or the new Schiaparelli is perfectly described in *Antic Hay*: 'fairly tall, but seemed taller than she actually was, by reason of her remarkable slenderness. Not that she looked disagreeably thin, far from it. It was a rounded slenderness. The Complete Man decided to consider her as tubular – flexible and tubular, like a section of boa constrictor . . . dressed in clothes that emphasized this serpentine slimness . . . on her head was a small, sleek black hat, that looked almost as though it were made of metal. It was trimmed on one side with a bunch of dull golden foliage.'

The serpentine slimness was an essential. If dancing and tennis weren't enough, then you took tablets and potions, slogged it out on electric camels and did physical jerks first thing in the morning. You bought rubber rollers with studs all over them, you went to Baden-Baden, or best of all you went down to the Riviera and took instruction from a dazzling 'professor' of physical fitness. *Vogue* was full of pictures of Princesses standing on their heads in pyramids, Duchesses turning cartwheels and Comtesses walking on their hands. Skirts and hair got shortest of all in 1926, and bosoms

55

were compressed with 'flatteners'. Bathing costumes were designed with swimming in mind, and the boiling summer of 1928 put the seal on the craze for sunbathing and getting a tan. Naturally there were many criticisms of the new woman. *Vogue* warned in 1924 that 'a siren with a "stinker" between her lips does not inspire an epigram or a lyric', but in 1928 Cecil Beaton was writing in the magazine, 'Our standards are so completely changed from the old that comparison or argument is impossible. We can only say, "But we *like* no chins! Du Maurier chins are as stodgy as porridge; we *prefer* high foreheads to low ones, we *prefer* flat noses and chests and schoolboy figures to bosoms and hips like water-melons in season. We like heavy eyelids; they are considered amusing and smart. We adore make-up and the gilded lily, and why not? Small dimpled hands make us feel quite sick; we like to see the forms of bones and gristle. We flatten out hair on purpose to make it sleek and silky and to show the shape of our skulls, and it is our supreme object to have a head looking like a wet football on a neck as thin as a governess's hatpin."' English girls who looked like this were handed a giant bouquet by a member of the suite of King Aman-aullah of Afghanistan who visited London in 1928. He told the *Daily News,* 'Look you, your English maidens are divinely beautiful, they are as fair as the pale moon which shines so gloriously in your western sky; their eyes are as bright as the eastern stars; and their complexion is just like the exquisite rose of Afghanistan.' That's what the reporter said he said, anyway.

The slim, brief look of twenties fashion was aided by the development of the artificial silk industry. Rayon printed well, it was light and cheap, and its production in the United States rose from eight million pounds weight in 1920 to fifty-three millions in 1925. By then everything a woman wore could be cut out of seven yards of fabric, and rayon stockings were cheap enough for almost everyone. Unlike the early art. silk stockings, these went right up the legs to the thighs, and came in sunburn colour, not just black and white.

The Art Deco exhibition had an immediate effect on design, bringing a grisly period of 'traditional' copying to an end. *Vogue* included a *House & Garden* supplement in the magazine from 1924, and showed the new decor in detail. There were flats like Mrs Viveash's 'tastefully in the movement. The furniture was upholstered in fabrics designed by Dufy – of enormous flowers, printed in grey and ochre on a white ground. There were a couple of lamp-shades by Balla. On the pale rose-stippled walls hung three portraits of herself by three different and entirely incongruous painters, a selection of the usual oranges and lemons, and a rather forbidding contemporary nude painted in two shades of green.' *Vogue* showed the later school of all-white décor, pioneered by Syrie Maugham, with white leather chairs, Kakemono pictures, white damask curtains fringed with monkey fur, and bleached Louis Quinze commodes. Mrs Maugham stripped the leaves off lilacs and peonies so that they looked like wax flowers, and hired very black Negroes to play for her parties. Rooms were thought of, not so much to be lived in, but as settings for parties. Chelsea studios were taken over by 'Bohemians', who scattered cushions on the floor, made Batik prints out of balloon silk left over from the war, and played Mahjong after dinner. Big houses were turned into flats, wood was faced in mirror glass, and everything was disguised as something else. 'Gramophones masquerade as cocktail cabinets,' said Osbert Lancaster, 'cocktail cabinets as book-cases; radios lurk in tea-caddies and bronze nudes burst asunder at the waist-line to reveal cigarette lighters.' Duncan Grant and Vanessa Bell worked together to paint furniture and panels: *Vogue* showed their work in Virginia Woolf's house in Tavistock Square and Maynard Keynes's rooms in Cambridge.

Mrs. Oliver Locker-Lampson is a very striking personage and looks like a Ruritanian Queen with her black hair threaded in long snake coils

Mrs. Herbert, whose marriage took place last month, was formerly Miss Marjorie du Pré; she is a very popular and well dressed young woman

Mrs. Kellett, who was formerly Miss Myrtle Atherley, is one of the most soignée and chic women who spend most of their time in the country

Lily Elsie has lovely bee-stung looking lips and corn-coloured hair. She is shortly, we hope, to act with Sir Gerald du Maurier in a "straight" play

Lady Louis Mountbatten is a chic matron with the highest heels, the most flashing bracelets and one of the most perfect complexions in London

PORTRAITS IN·PASSING

SKETCHES *by* CECIL BEATON

Mrs. McConnel (Elizabeth Pollock) wears a string of enormous bulbous pearls, a barbaric fringe dress and gold sandals

Mrs. Lionel Harris's white hair, flashing eyes and mouches are well known, and are to be seen at almost every charity ball and the dansant

The Hon. Mrs. Maurice Brett (Miss Zena Dare) was recently seen at a party looking lovelier than ever in white satin

1. Cecil Beaton drawings, 1927.
2. An all-white room in the style of Syrie Maugham, 1928, with cream leather chairs, cream damask curtains fringed with monkey fur, and glass-topped table.
3. A block of flats in a city of the future.
4. Amédée Ozenfant's studio house designed by Le Corbusier, 1926.
5. Mendelsohn's Einstein Tower at Potsdam, built in 1920, housing a laboratory and an observatory.
6. Maynard Keynes's rooms in King's College, Cambridge, with Duncan Grant's and Vanessa Bell's wall panels and curtains.

Fred Boissannas

E.J. Mason

Among the decoration, *Vogue* introduced the work of two architects who belonged fair and square in the machine age. Le Corbusier, who said, 'A house is a machine for living', designed rooms like operating theatres and buildings as severe as steamships. People who lived in his flats were allowed one picture, to be chosen from a picture-cupboard and changed as often as they liked. He believed that the construction should be clearly expressed in building, that kitchens and bathrooms should be given equal importance to drawing rooms and dining rooms. Eric Mendelsohn was a German architect, an expressionist whose organic buildings looked as if they were whizzing along at a hundred miles an hour, swooping round corners. He could have been the original for Otto Friedrich Silenus, the architect in Evelyn Waugh's *Decline and Fall*, who had 'first attracted Mrs Beste-Chetwynde's attention with the rejected design for a chewing-gum factory', and replaced her country house with one of ferro-concrete and aluminium.

There was to be a sad difference between these romantic Futurist ideas and the cheapened versions that would be built all over

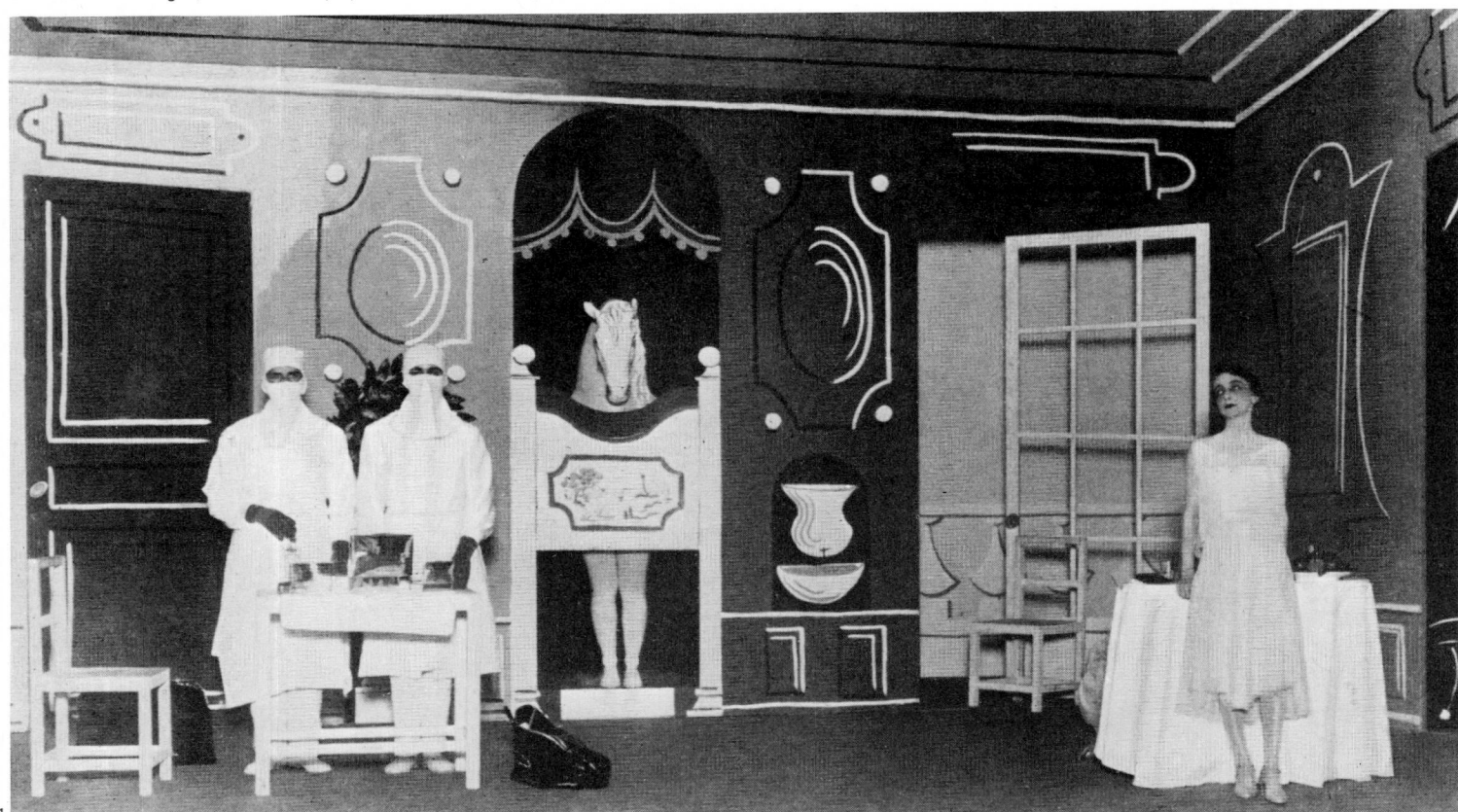

Waléry

Britain. Optimistic in 1925, *Vogue* was writing 'In the future those who work in great centres will either live in garden cities, which will encircle London and Paris, or else in tall buildings reasonably close to the business quarters. The dreary suburbs will disappear . . . it seems unlikely that most cities will increase in size. The Old World, at any rate, is greatly over-populated, and the size of urban populations depends eventually upon the size of fields upon which they depend for their food.'

The twenties gave women their freedom, sexually, through the work of Dr Marie Stopes and the setting up of birth control clinics, and politically. By the end of the decade the flapper vote had put five million more women on the electoral roll, which helped to bring in the second Labour government, fighting on unemployment. But it was not a political decade.

Ain't we got fun?
Not much money, oh! but honey!
Ain't we got fun?
There's nothing surer,
The rich get rich and the poor get – children.
In the meantime, in between time,
Ain't we got fun?

In Paris, the Cubists, Expressionists, Futurists, Dadaists and the new Surrealists were not shut off in separate boxes. They were writing and making films, putting on plays, decorating and philosophizing. Many were involved in the ballet. Picasso had painted the famous curtain for *Train bleu*, shown in 1924 with costumes by Chanel, sets by Laurens and choreography by Nijinska, Nijinsky's sister, and designed for *Parade, Pulcinella* and *The Three-*

Waléry

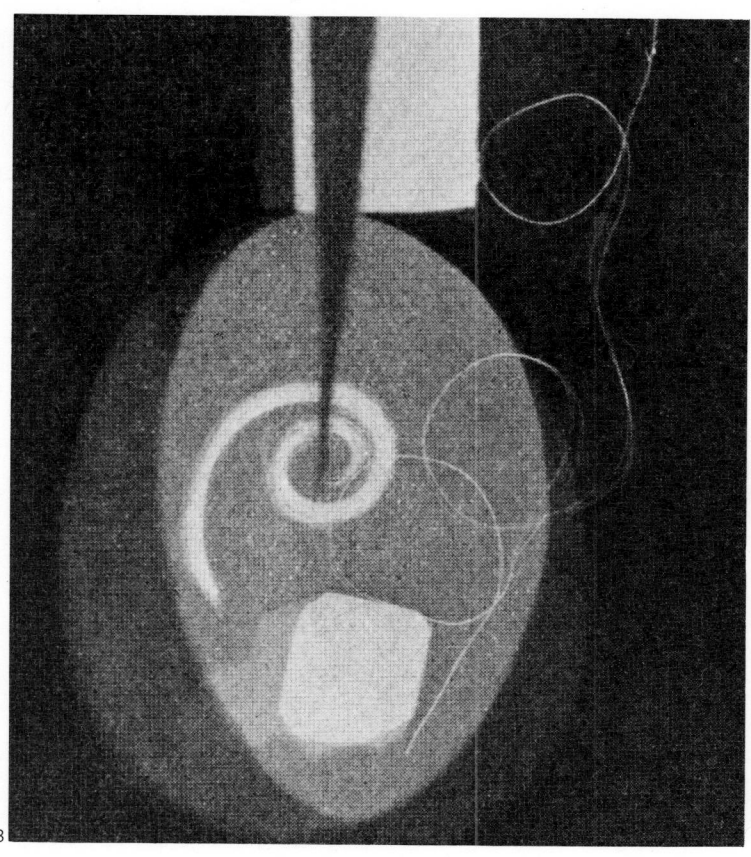

3

3. Two of Man Ray's 'rayographs'.
4. Cocteau drawing, 1925.
5. *Paysage animé* by Fernand Léger, 1925.

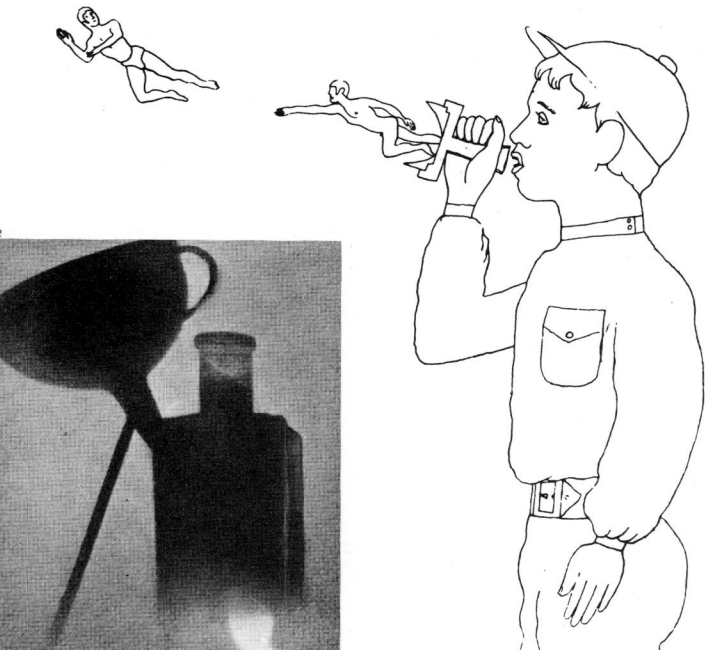

4

Cornered Hat. Matisse designed for Stravinsky's new one-act ballet *Le Chant du rossignol*, Braque for *Zéphyr et Flore*, Joan Miro and Max Ernst for *Romeo and Juliet*, and Marie Laurencin had designed some brief and modern costumes for Poulenc's *Les Biches*. In *Vogue* you could see Man Ray's mechanical experiments with film, composing photographs by exposing random objects directly to sensitive paper, and the latest work of Fernand Léger, key painter of the machine age whose pictures were composed like well-constructed aeroplanes or trains, in black and white with strong poster colours. The Surrealists' conference on sex in 1927 was ignored, with its relish for bad taste. The Surrealists savoured the *frissons* 'from the seduction of nuns and women who never washed, from outré sexual positions, from homosexual eccentricity'.

Jean Cocteau was a bridge between the arts, a gifted dilettante who helped initiate *Vogue* readers into the *avant-garde* by keeping three or four steps ahead. He had his first poems published at seventeen, and went on to write novels, ballets and plays, direct films, found a group of new musicians and publish his clever, tricky drawings. His one-act surreal tragedy *Orphée* was set in the technological present. Orpheus and Eurydice, in modern dress, confronted Death the operating surgeon with his two anaesthetists complete with rubber gloves, masks and surgical trolley. It caused some excitement, and *Vogue* called it at least the most interesting play of 1926. Another provocative play was Tristan Tzara's *Mouchoir de nuages*, with the actors sitting on stage, talking and making up, while the 'real' performance went on upon a small dais in the centre. This Roumanian Dadaist poet had staged the *Grand Spectacle du désastre* in 1920, which had succeeded only too well in rousing the audience to a pitch of fury.

The real centre of experimental theatre was Berlin. German Expressionism was an attempt to put a distance between the audience and the performance, to replace naturalism with stylization, to lose the individual in the mass. Characters were not given names, they were 'The Girl', 'The Boy', 'The Mother'. Bertolt Brecht said, 'I aim at an extremely classical, cold, highly intellectual style of performance. I am not writing for the scum who

5

want to have the cockles of their heart warmed.' The *Threepenny Opera* was performed in 1928. *Vogue* summed up the social criticism of Sternheim and Wedekind and Toller as 'dramatized Freud', and gave the parallel movement in German dancing, with Mary Wigmar leading her pupils in mass displays of gym and drill, the name 'tragic Tiller girls'. Berlin's favourite actress was Elizabeth Bergner, 'all nerves and delicacy', and Max Reinhardt, who turned crowd scenes into spectacular theatre all over Europe and America with Lady Diana Cooper's vehicle *The Miracle*, was the key figure in Expressionist theatre.

Expressionism was most successful in German films, which were acknowledged even in Hollywood as technically excellent at a fraction of the cost of American production. By 1924 they had a stronger grip on the British film market than British films themselves. The movement kicked off in 1919 with *The Cabinet of Doctor Caligari*, a nightmare fantasy set in a fairground, written by Carl Mayer and Hans Janowitz and directed by Robert Weine. Material objects took on an emotional significance by means of clever photography and disturbing prop design: angles were acute, chimneys set aslant on roofs, and shadows were painted on to jar with lighting effects. By 1926 the most successful film in Berlin was a Soviet propaganda film, *Battleship Potemkin*. The story of a mutiny and massacre in Odessa, it was called 'a marvel of mass acting and machinery in motion'. The same year *Vogue* published pictures of a new equally important film being made in Berlin, Fritz Lang's *Metropolis*, set in an underground city of the future with massed skyscrapers and terrifying machinery, and crowds surging through the maze in an attempt to escape from the flood.

That year Aldous Huxley in *Vogue* was criticizing Expressionist films for their pretentiousness and melodramatic ponderosity: 'A study of Felix the Cat would teach the German producers many valuable lessons.' He describes how Felix sings a few crotchets, seizes them and fits them together into a scooter, an easy thing to

de Meyer

At the turn of the decade there was a craze for dressing up in pageants and tableaux vivants as the Madonna, a saint or a nun, with attendant fashions for habits, drapes and wrapped heads – Paula Gellibrand's nun's-habit wedding dress, for instance. Its apogee was Lady Diana Cooper's prolonged appearance as the Madonna in *The Miracle*, for which she prepared herself by retreat into a convent.
1. Geraldine Farrar in Puccini's *Suor Angelica*, 1919.
2. Gladys Cooper in *The Betrothal*, 1921.
3. Lillah McCarthy in *Judith*, 1919.

Instead

Rita Martin

60

do on film, an impossible thing to do in words, and draws an analogy with the super-realist writers. 'The fact is that these "young" writers are rebelling, not against effete literary conventions, but against language itself. They are trying to make words do what they cannot do, in the nature of things. They are working in the wrong medium. The aim of the super realists is to free literature completely from logic and to give it the fantastic liberty of the dream. What they attempt to do – not very successfully – the camera achieves brilliantly.'

In England, there were three schools of writing, described by Ronald Blythe in *The Age of Illusion* as Bloomsbury, Mayfair, and the leafy Blankshire of Georgian Poetry, where few people went any more: Bloomsbury was the withdrawn and aristocratic drawing-room world of Lady Ottoline Morrell and the Woolfs, Clive and Vanessa Bell, Maynard Keynes and Lytton Strachey, with E. M. Forster on the perimeter. Mayfair, fabulously witty and irreverent, included Evelyn Waugh and Cyril Connolly. Still, for many readers, there was no writer like a dead writer and with this in mind Auden dedicated his *Poems* to Isherwood in 1930 with the words:

> Let us honour if we can
> The vertical man
> Though we value none
> But the horizontal one.

T. S. Eliot was one vertical man who was honoured and valued by contemporary writers. 'The Waste Land', written in 1922, acted as a catalyst. It had a note of gay disillusion and cynicism which they recognized as the mood of the decade:

> When lovely woman stoops to folly and
> Paces about her room again, alone,
> She smoothes her hair with automatic hand,
> And puts a record on the gramophone.

4. The children's escape from Fritz Lang's *Metropolis:* photograph of the film being made, in 1926.
5. Lady Ottoline Morrell, 1928.
6. Virginia Woolf in 1926 when she had written *Jacob's Room* and *Mrs Dalloway.* 'Try to imagine a mask that even without life, without intelligence would be beautiful. Then imagine this mask so impregnated with life and intelligence that it would seem to have been modelled by them. Imagine all this, and you will still have only a faint idea of the charm of Virginia Woolf's face, a charm that is the result of the most felicitous encounter of matter and soul in the face of a woman': Victoria Ocampo.

Cecil Beaton

Maurice Beck and Macgregor

Much of his work was a great deal more difficult. He said, 'genuine poetry can communicate before it is understood', and 'the poet is occupied with frontiers of consciousness beyond which words fail, though meanings still exist'. In Paris, Gertrude Stein was making connections between words as words, explained to *Vogue* readers by Edith Sitwell, who made poetry fun.

> With the flag.
> With the flag of sets.
> Sets of colour.
> Do you like flags.
> Blue flags smell sweetly.
> Blue flags in a whirl.
> The wind blows
> And the automobile goes.

'... Flags make her think of irises. Flags make her think of the wind. The wind makes her think of the speed of automobiles.'

James Joyce was more difficult than anyone. *Ulysses* had been published in 1922. Virginia Woolf wrote of 'a queasy undergraduate scratching his pimples', but T. S. Eliot said, 'How could anyone write again after achieving the immense prodigy of the last chapter?' Joyce said he had 'recorded, simultaneously, what a man says, sees, thinks and what such seeing, thinking, saying does to what you Freudians call the subconscious'.

Sexual deviation was becoming acceptable, at least by high society, due to the talent and gaiety of the homosexuals in the theatre and Mayfair, and due to the writers who put their predicament in readable form. 'And what is a "He-man?"' asked Gertrude Stein. 'Isn't it a large enough order to fill out to the dimensions of all that "a man" has meant in the past? A "He-man!"' This is how Scott Fitzgerald summed up the sexual education of the jazz age: 'We begin with the suggestion that Don Juan leads an interesting life (*Jurgen*, 1919); then we learn that there's a lot of sex around if we only knew it (*Winesburg, Ohio*, 1920), that adolescents lead very amorous lives (*This Side of Paradise*, 1920), that there are a lot of neglected Anglo-Saxon words (*Ulysses*, 1921), that older people don't always resist sudden temptations (*Cytherea*, 1922), that girls are sometimes seduced without being

1. Gertrude Lawrence, *left,* Beatrice Lillie, *right,* 1922.
2. Patrick Balfour and Cyril Connolly at home, 1927.
3. Noël Coward telephoning from his Ebury Street bedroom, 1927.

ruined (*Flaming Youth*, 1922), that even rape often turns out well (*The Sheik*, 1922), that glamorous English ladies are often promiscuous (*The Green Hat*, 1924), that in fact they devote most of their time to it (*The Vortex*, 1926), that it's a damn good thing too (*Lady Chatterley's Lover*, 1928), and finally that there are abnormal variations (*The Well of Loneliness*, 1928, and *Sodom and Gomorrah*, 1929).'

The London stage barely went further than Noël Coward's *The Vortex*, which shocked playgoers because drug-taking had never been a stage theme before. *Vogue* said, 'to excite emotions of pity or anxiety a play must contain people who rouse the sympathy of the audience by intelligence or character. The protagonists of "The Vortex" had neither, and as a result in the last act, instead of being stirred by their efforts to reform, one wished the son would continue to take drugs and the mother lovers, till they both died: a good riddance to bad rubbish.' Coward, at any rate, loved the publicity and was photographed in decadent satin pyjamas telephoning from the futurist bed of his Ebury Street flat. His *Fallen Angels* and *Sirocco* provoked 'cries of "rotter!" from the stalls, cat calls and shrieks from the gallery', but by 1927 his good lyrics and catchy tunes, light touch and perfect timing had won over audiences, and he had four shows running simultaneously. His leading lady, Gertrude Lawrence, perfectly matched the brittle, disillusioned mood of his plays. Languid and sunburnt, with a smoky voice, she gave fashion the overworked word casual, wearing a mink coat thrown over flannel trousers. She looked perfect in Molyneux's spotted pyjamas or his white satin evening dress as she leant against the balcony and sang 'Some day I'll find you'. 'She smoked cigarettes with a nuance that implied having just come out of bed and wanting to go back into it,' said Cecil Beaton. She had terrific style, and her arrival at the stage door was something worth waiting for, as she stepped out of her Hispano-Suiza with a corsage of orchids and a bevy of handsome young men with top hats and gardenias.

Bernard Shaw won the Nobel Prize for *Saint Joan* in 1924, with Sybil Thorndike in the lead. In the cast were Godfrey Winn, and Ernest Thesiger who left it for the new Cochran review. Cochran's Young Ladies were the best revue chorus of the day, and he was the leading showman and impresario of the twenties. He brought everything to London, from the Russian ballet to a cowboy rodeo, from prize fights to cabarets.

A great draw of the day was Tallulah Bankhead, who attracted in particular enormous crowds of female fans – more than any matinée idol – who choked the West End and crammed around the stage door. Her ambivalent appeal and tough wit made her an essential at smart parties, though her remarks could be killers. At a wedding she might remark, 'I've had both of them, and they were lousy', or at a first night, 'There's less in this than meets the eye.' She was a strange choice for Iris Storm in *The Green Hat*, Michael Arlen's successful novel made into a play. *Vogue* wrote, 'They take lovers as they take cocktails, and all the while use the words "clean" and "purity" as a chain-smoker uses cigarettes . . . you cannot make La Dame aux Camélias drive a Hispano-Suiza' – and you certainly would not have picked Tallulah Bankhead to play a Dame aux Camélias. A powerhouse of energy and a great show-off, she was described by Cecil Beaton as 'a wicked archangel . . . Medusa, very exotic, with a glorious skull, high pumice-stone cheekbones . . . Her cheeks are huge acid-pink peonies. Her eyelashes are built out with hot liquid paint to look like burnt matches, and her sullen, discontented rosebud of a mouth is painted the brightest scarlet, and is as shiny as Tiptree's strawberry jam.' She never stopped talking, and a friend who once took out a stopwatch and counted her words per minute calculated that she spoke

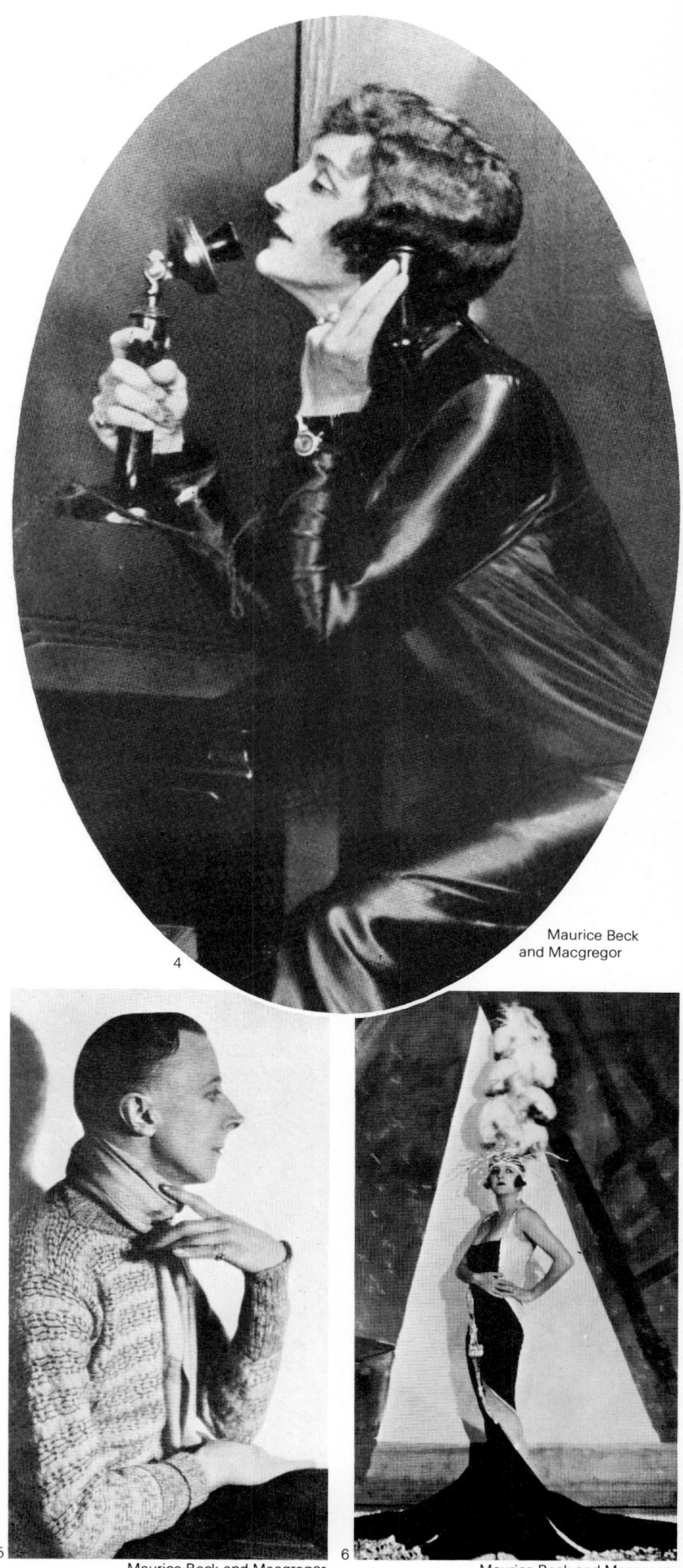

Maurice Beck and Macgregor

4

Maurice Beck and Macgregor

5

Maurice Beck and Macgregor

6

4. Lilian Braithwaite as Florence Lancaster in *The Vortex*, 1925.
5. Ernest Thesiger, 1925.
6. Delysia, Parisian actress and comedy star, who took the lead in Cochran revues of the early twenties, in 1925.

63

seventy thousand words a day – the wordage of *War and Peace* over a weekend. Emerging onto the street after lunch one day, she dropped a fifty dollar bill into the tambourine of a Salvation Army girl, and said, 'Don't bother to thank me, darling. I know what a perfectly *ghastly* season it's been for you Spanish dancers.'

Probably nothing gave so much pleasure to so many as the wireless. Everyone tuned in to the hour of dance band music in the evening, which left them whistling tunes like 'Bye Bye Blackbird', 'Valencia', or 'I Wonder Where My Baby is Tonight'. But popular music programmes were few and far between, sprinkled among chamber music and symphony concerts. John Reith, the General Manager of the British Broadcasting Company, saw that the radio was potentially as important as the printing press in terms of human enlightenment, and felt it as a religious duty to keep the B.B.C. free from commercialism and propaganda. The public re-

1

sented their diet of musical education, as the press, and *Vogue*'s music columnist Edwin Evans, were quick to point out. They called him 'the Judge of What We Ought To Want', and he bleakly replied, 'I do not pretend to give the public what it wants.' It was due to him that the announcers wore dinner jackets to read the nine o'clock news, and the public began to enjoy excellent radio plays and the best musical performances.

For sheer entertainment you went to the cinema. Everyone loved Felix the Cat, Bonzo Dog, Mickey Mouse and the slapstick comedies with Fatty Arbuckle, the nightmare acrobatics of prim, short-sighted Harold Lloyd who was always suspended by a sagging flag pole over a dizzy drop, and the surreal machine-infested world of poker-faced Buster Keaton. Every successful film was followed by its burlesque, and the melodrama of Rudolph Valentino's films were a rich inspiration to Laurel and Hardy. Charles Chaplin was still the most popular of all comedians, and *The Kid*, in which he adopts orphan Jackie Coogan, the most successful film of the twenties. Lon Chaney was Quasimodo in *The Hunchback of Notre Dame*, and it became a joke, when you saw a beetle scuttling over the floor, to shout, 'Don't kill it, it may be Lon Chaney in disguise.' Jim Tully told *Vogue* readers that Lon Chaney's father was a deaf and dumb Irish barber, that his mother was afflicted in the same way, and that he had learnt to mime by talking to them in sign language – a story that sounds as if it came from the press office. A quite different sort of film was a success in Britain when Robert Flaherty's documentary *Nanook of the North* was shown. About an Eskimo family, it showed how the camera could record domestic life without pretension or embarrassment.

Maurice Beck and
Macgregor

2

1. Picnic to music, 1925, with an Amplion portable loud speaker.
2. Rudolph Valentino doing a Nijinsky, 1924.

Opposite: Vogue's early drawn covers. *Top:* Early January 1919 by George Plank. Early March 1921 by George Plank. *Bottom:* Christmas 1916 by E.M.A. Steinmetz: Late September 1918 by George Plank. *Over page: Vogue* covers of the Jazz Age by Benito. Early May and late July 1926.

VOGUE

Early January 1919 — CONDÉ NAST & CO, LONDON — *One Shilling & Six Pence Net*

VOGUE

Early March 1921 — CONDÉ NAST & CO LTD — *One Shilling & Six Pence Net*

Steichen

The two big stars of the twenties were both Paramount properties, locked in a rivalry that made good gossip. Gloria Swanson arrived in Hollywood as a flat-figured extra from Chicago with brilliantined, spit-curled hair. Her camera-proof face, rather viciously beautiful, suited the most bizarre and exaggerated of fashions. She was a symbol of movie bad taste when she secured her social position by marrying the Marquis de la Falaise de Coudray, a 'docile nobleman with a reckless taste in spats'. She returned to her house in Hollywood and installed footmen in powdered wigs and satin knee-breeches.

Her rival Pola Negri, who was able to call herself Countess Dombski, was imported by Paramount because of her success in German films. She was overschooled by her studio, never caught on with the flapper fans as Gloria Swanson had, and was never very popular in Hollywood because she made no attempt to hide her contempt of American films and culture. She had some sort of affair with Rudolph Valentino, king of movie sheikhs and lounge lizards, and staged a dramatic fainting at his funeral that provoked more laughter than sympathy. She lost box office appeal towards the end of the decade and returned to Germany where, in 1936, she was once more starring in films and was rumoured to be a girl friend of Hitler.

Elinor Glyn's *Three Weeks* was a whale of a success, both the book and the film. A story about a Ruritanian Queen who enjoys three flaming weeks with Conrad Nagel on a bed of roses, it starred Eileen Pringle. Miss Pringle was reproved by the Deaf and Dumb Society who could see that when Conrad Nagel swept her into his arms her lips were saying 'If you drop me, you —, I'll break your neck.' Clara Bow was the It Girl who invented sex appeal – *Flaming*

Youth brought her 20,000 fan letters a week and made her everybody's sweetheart from 1925 to 1930. Sound came in in 1927, and by the end of 1928 the worst sound film could outdraw the best silent movie.

The greatest star of all arrived in the last years of the silent film. Greta Garbo was nineteen when she came to Hollywood in the entourage of Mauritz Stiller. Daughter of a poor labourer, she was the lather girl in a barber's shop when she had begun to play extras in a few Swedish films. She was different because she didn't give herself titles or airs, and her relationship with M.G.M. and reporters was one of icy formality. She hated publicity, and only asked to 'be alone'. On the screen her amazing beauty overwhelmed the audience. She didn't have to act, her slightest gesture conveyed more than other people's words. When her first talkie, Eugene O'Neill's *Anna Christie* arrived in 1930, her fans sat on the edges of their seats. They were dying to hear her voice, said to be guttural and thicky Swedish. They sighed with relief, then swooned with delight: her first words were 'Gif me a viskey, ginger ale on the side – and don't be stingy, baby.' When her shoulder length bob and slouch hat began to be universally copied, it signalled the end of the twenties.

By the end of the twenties fashionable restaurants could afford to spend £50,000 on redecorating, and cabarets brought in anything up to £1,000 a week. All the new restaurants and clubs were described in *Vogue*, and the people who went there. One of the smartest was the Kit-Cat where elegantly bored women looked over corsages of white orchids at cleanshaven young men with satin hair and wide shoulders: it was raided by the police the night after the Prince of Wales had dined there. Guests at Chez Victor, who

Curtis Moffat and Olivia Wyndham

crowded round the piano to hear Hutch sing 'The Man I Love', were appalled when Victor was convicted of breaking the Licensing Act and imprisoned. The Silver Slipper, with its glass floor and marvellous saxophonist, was the last big nightclub to be opened by Mrs Meyrick, who was imprisoned three times. Her clients over the years included a good cross section of twenties society, including Augustus John and Rudolph Valentino, J. B. Priestley and Sophie Tucker, Carpentier the boxer and Michael Arlen. You could find Tallulah Bankhead at Taglioni's, Epstein and his latest model at the Ham Bone in Soho, John at the Eiffel Tower, and end up at the Gargoyle eating scrambled eggs and drinking coffee by an open fire. In the dancing room was David Tennant's huge Matisse, for which Lady Latham made some Negro art curtains. As *Vogue* said, 'Everyone agrees that with Matisse you can't go wrong.'

This was the heyday of hostesses, with Elsa Maxwell for their queen. She would take over a whole nightclub or palace in any capital city and fill it with her set of international celebrities. At her parties there was a touch of the grotesque: you might have to blow a feather off a sheet or milk an artificial cow for your champagne. Mrs Corrigan was an avid party-giver who conquered London society by the extravagance of her hospitality. The most sought-after guests would find that they had won the gold cigarette cases in the tombola, and the all-star cabaret got more for their brief appearance at Mrs Corrigan's than for a week in the theatre. Finally, Mrs Corrigan would stand on her head to a drum-roll. They said, 'The only sound at night is Mrs Corrigan climbing', but they went. This was Cecil Beaton's description in *Vogue* of a typical party of the time, given by Mrs Guinness: 'people literally overflowing into the street . . . all the people one had ever known or even seen – up and down the big staircase, in the ballroom, along the corridors – "Hutch" singing in the ballroom while we all sat on the

floor – Edythe Baker playing to some of us in another room downstairs – Oliver Messel in the same room giving a ludicrously lifelike imitation of a lift-attendant describing the departments on each floor – Lady Ashley shining in a glittering short coat of silver sequins over her white dress – glimpses of the Ruthven twins – of Noël Coward looking happy and being amusing – Gladys Cooper in a Chanel rhinestone necklace that reached to the knees of her black velvet frock . . . impression after impression, before one sank and sank . . . to the supper room.'

Loelia Ponsonby, later the Duchess of Westminster, gave a different sort of party. She would ring up her friends at the last moment and ask them to come round with some food or champagne. Nine parties out of ten would be fancy dress. Evelyn Waugh in *Vile Bodies* wrote about 'Masked parties, savage parties, Victorian parties, Greek parties, Wild West parties, Russian parties, Circus parties, parties where one had to dress as someone else and almost naked parties in St John's Wood, parties in flats and studios and houses and ships and hotels and nightclubs, in windmills and swimming baths.' The swimming pool party given by Brian Howard and Elizabeth Ponsonby had a jazz band to which the guests danced in bathing suits. It caused a small scandal. The *Sunday Chronicle* wrote, 'Great astonishment and not a little indignation is being expressed in London over the revelation that in the early hours of yesterday morning a large number of society women were dancing in bathing dresses to the music of a Negro band at a "swim and dance" gathering organized by some of Mayfair's Bright Young People.' Brian Howard, down from Oxford, initiated 'Follow my Leader' through Selfridges, where a crowd of young people helpless with laughter tore about among the shoppers, jumping into lifts and climbing over the counters. Lord Bessborough and Prince Obolensky went to one of the Sutherlands'

Edmund Harrington

Cecil Beaton

parties as drunken waiters, taking over from house staff, finally keeling over with a crash of breaking china. Lady Diana Cooper wrote, 'there was a fancy ball at Ava Ribblesdale's last night, and all the women looked fifty per cent worse than usual – S. as Little Lord Fauntleroy quite awful, P. as a street Arab just dirty.' It was a good time for twins, and there was a pair at every party – the plain but jolly Ruthven sisters, the Ward twins and the Rowe twins, Joan and Kit Dunn, or Thelma Furness and Gloria Vanderbilt, twice the woman for being indistinguishable.

Society in the twenties was large enough to be heterogeneous and international, but small enough for the prime figures to be well known to readers of gossip columns. It was a clever, amusing, worldly set at best, greatly improved by overlapping with the theatre and the new rich. The Prince of Wales gave English society its lead, and his friends were actresses and self-made men. London's theatrical peerage included Zena Dare who had become the Hon. Mrs Maurice Brett, Gertie Millar (the Countess of Dudley), Rosie Boot of the Gaiety (the Marchioness of Headfort), Beatrice Lillie (Lady Peel), and Lady Inverclyde, who had been June on the stage. The well-known beauty Lady Ashley was rumoured to be the daughter of an ostler. As Sylvia Hawkes, her first job had been modelling at Reville, and she had been in the banned first London cabaret, 'Midnight Follies'. Her father-in-law, the Earl of Shaftesbury, was denying the engagement the day before the wedding, and none of the groom's family went to the marriage.

1. Iris and Viola Tree as London urchins at a 'children's party' party, 1926.
2. Mrs Gerard d'Erlanger, formerly Edythe Baker, 1929.
3. Lady Ashley, 1929.
4. Elsa Maxwell and friends at the Duc de Verdura's Palermo ball, 1929.

Interguglielmi

Cecil Beaton

Society women were the new fashion dictators. They wore couture clothes and lived by the season – Deauville in spring, the Riviera in summer, Scotland in autumn, London and Paris in the winter. Fashion had become a matter of personal style, and the embodiment of the new style was Mrs Dudley Ward, who practised the Charleston with the Prince of Wales at the Café de Paris early in the mornings. Neat as a pin, she wore natty check suits with a clove carnation and jingling bracelets, and dressed her daughters and herself to match in red gingham, with bows in the hair.

An exotic at the opposite end of the scale from Diana Cooper was Baba d'Erlanger, whose mother had brought her up to be highly unusual. As a child she had instead of a nanny a robed and turbaned mameluke, who followed her about like a page. The d'Erlangers lived in Byron's old house in Piccadilly, and gave marvellous children's parties to which Baba always wore gold. A *belle-laide* with a monkey face and scarlet lipstick, she became the Princesse Jean de Faucigny-Lucinge and set a fashion for wearing a tarbush cap and bunches of artificial fruit with a bathing suit.

The beauty of the moment was Paula Gellibrand, Baba

d'Erlanger's best friend, a heavy-lidded Modigliani with a look of fatigue and sophistication. A golden blonde with enormous blue eyes, she glossed them with Vaseline, wore hats dripping with wistaria and got married in a dress as plain as a nun's habit. A *Vogue* model, she married an unusual man, the Marquis de Casa Maury, Castilian by ancestry, Cuban by nationality, English by education. He was an ace driver of a Bugatti in the Grands Prix, and the owner of the first Bermuda-rigged schooner in Europe, doing the navigating himself. When Wall Street crashed he built the Curzon cinema. He spent seven months learning the trade under assumed names, sweeping up, working the projector, selling the tickets, until he knew enough to make a great success of the Curzon.

Finally there was Mrs Reginald Fellowes, who invented the almost insulting elegance that was to be the ambition of model girls up to the 1960s. She loved making other women look silly, usually managed it by looking much less 'dressed' than they did, arriving at greater elegance with far less apparent effort. She wore the same absolutely simple dress day after day, usually with a sequin

1. Mrs Dudley Ward, 1928.
2. Paula Gellibrand, 1929.
3. Mr and Mrs Michael Arlen at Cannes, 1928.
4. Cocktail time at Antibes, 1927.

Cecil Beaton

dinner jacket and a green carnation. Actually the dress was probably a different one every night, since she ordered plain linen dresses in dozens. Meeting a woman in the same dress at a nightclub once, she called for a pair of scissors and snipped off her ostrich trimming. Her jewellery was remarkable: she had handcuffs of emeralds, necklets of stones brought to her from India, and conch shells made of diamonds.

So much had happened in the twenties, and so many new influences felt, that the change in fashion was bound to be radical. The people who wore the clothes overtook the designers, who were obliged by the middle twenties to conform to the uniform of short skirts, dropped waists and simplicity demanded by the lives and tastes of their public. The most important designers to emerge from the twenties were the two most involved with new movements in other fields – Chanel, whose circle included Picasso, Cocteau and Stravinsky, and the new Schiaparelli, whose friends were the Surrealists.

THE CHANGING FACE

Florence Vandamm

2

GERTRUDE LAWRENCE

She arrived on the London scene in the early twenties at the same moment as Bea Lillie, who became Lady Peel: they were photographed in *Vogue* taking tea together in 1922, when Gertrude Lawrence looks timid, demure, an entirely different creature from the alluring worldly sophisticate she became in the mid-twenties. Her first starring role was in Ivor Novello's musical *A to Z*, which ran for 433 performances. She owes much of her success to her stage partnership with Noël Coward, whose flippant, cynical, casual plays like *Bitter Sweet* and *Private Lives* provided her with roles that perfectly suited her personality. 'Her manner and charm,' says Madge Garland, 'were such that by the time anyone found out she was not a beauty, it was too late, they were bewitched.' With her curdled voice, singing 'Some day I'll find you' in a bias white satin dress by Molyneux, she won all hearts. Her permanent contribution to fashion is the full-length mink coat worn over grey flannels, or perhaps the flame-coloured pyjama pants in which she fell off the sofa fighting with Laurence Olivier in *Bitter Sweet*.

1. Steichen's portrait of 1926.
2. 1922.
3. In Molyneux's satin and fox, for *Private Lives,* 1930.

1

Studio Sun

LADY ASHLEY

Formerly Sylvia Hawkes, a mannequin at Reville and a chorus girl at the Winter Garden, she took part in London's first cabaret show. Said to be the daughter of an ostler, she married Lord Ashley in the teeth of his family's opposition. Lord Ashley was the first of her five husbands — Douglas Fairbanks was the second. Tall, slender, with fair hair and a mild lisp, she was a perfect English rose. Both photographs, 1932.

Cecil Beaton

Hoyningen-Huene

1

Hugh Cecil

2

Hoyningen-Huene

1. 1923, on her
engagement to
Prince Jean-Louis
de Faucigny-Lucinge.
2. In Agnès's
Algerian hat, 1931.

BABA D'ERLANGER
Daughter of avant-garde decorator Baroness d'Erlanger she was always
dressed in gold as a child. When she grew up, a striking *belle-laide*, she
wore black paint under her eyes, brilliant red lipstick and long nails
enamelled maroon.

MARION MOREHOUSE
Steichen, who said 'Good fashion models have the qualities inherent in
a good actress', called her, 'The best fashion model I ever worked with.'
She was perfect for the clothes of the twenties, and perfect for
Steichen's formal, statuesque photographs. She later married the writer
e.e. Cummings and became a photographer herself.

3. 1925, in cloth
of gold veiled with
white chiffon by
Suzanne Talbot.
4. 1927, the
centre figure in
Chanel's white
satin crepe.

3 TALBOT

Steichen   4 CHANEL

Cecil Beaton

PAULA GELLIBRAND
Her look of exhausted sophistication was said to hide a perfectly simple, straightforward nature. She attracted attention at the Ritz, wearing a hat draped with wistaria, and became one of *Vogue's* first society models. Baroness d'Erlanger, mother of her friend Baba, encouraged her to gloss her eyelids with vaseline and wear simple, saintly clothes — nurses' coifs and nun's-habit dresses. She married the Marquis de Casa Maury.

'We have been passing through the awkward age, when instead of conversing we S.O.Sed in monosyllabic slang. It might be called the "Abbreviated Period – short skirts, short shrift, short credit and short names" . . . but you ain't seen nothin' yet'

LANVIN   Steichen

Black georgette crepe dress with high neck, steel discs for decoration, and sleeves slashed with white chiffon.

'The silhouette finds a straight line the smartest distance between two points'

There's a new Labour government and opinions are mixed — about Ramsay MacDonald's mode of dress, his ability to entertain, whether there will be a season or not. The hostess at 10 Downing Street is his daughter Ishbel MacDonald. Reporters interview her to find out if she is a modern girl. 'I've never been centred in a whirlpool of jazz and I do not intend to be,' she says. Lady Diana Cooper is in America playing in Max Reinhardt's *The Miracle*, her confidence boosted by her beautiful clothes by Ospovat. Every dashing lady has her own car, and *The Green Hat* by Michael Arlen is favourite reading. The hit of the year is Shaw's *Saint Joan;* asked why he wrote the play Shaw replies, 'To save Joan of Arc from John Drinkwater.' Jackie Coogan visits London and is treated like royalty. It's the year of *Le Train Bleu,* costumes by Chanel, curtains by Picasso. Moved from the Everyman to the West End, Coward's *The Vortex,* about a nogood mother and her drug-taking son, arouses a storm of protest. Everyone who can afford it is going abroad and hostess Mrs Laura Corrigan ('the only sound at night is Mrs Corrigan climbing') has gone to India, but makes arrangements for her Grand National house party by sending back reply-paid cables.

Vogue shows maternity clothes for the first time, and couturiers announce their London and Paris showings by advertisement. The smart places to go are Oddenino's and the Café de Paris.

Narrow, boneless and elastic girdles have taken over from the corset and the line is narrow and immaculately neat. The Prince of Wales visits Paris and inspires couturiers to collections of immaculate tailored suits in men's suitings and covert cloths. Navy and black are worn for town, white with coloured scarves or cloches for the country. Hems fall between the ankle and the calf of the leg, and the cloche sits so low on the head it hides the eyebrows. The accessories of the year are suede gloves worn a bit too large, a stubby fat umbrella, and Chanel's steel beads.

For evening add to the narrow silhouette gathered panels of tulle or bunches of feathers on the hips, or a train. The back is bared, the neckline modest. Chiffon evening dresses have feather boas or scarves, or butterfly wings floating from the shoulders. Satin is used for evening for the first time — Poiret's poppy and cornflower prints make evening pyjamas that look particularly good with the brief bobbed hair. Evening shoes are brocade slippers with embroidered toes or gemmed heels, and wraps are edged all round with fur.

For day you wear a suit with a hiplength jacket buttoned low and hanging dead straight over a straight skirt — Chanel's skirt is unbuttoned to show grey crepe pantalets. Seven-eighths coats hang open over their dresses — sometimes a light tunic with an underskirt of the coat fabric, or a low-waisted dress of printed crepe. Scarves tie in 'aeroplane bows' — stiffly, like propellers.

Left: The Grand Duchess Boris of Russia in a 'perfect sports dress', 1925: photograph Steichen.

75

RENÉE

CHANEL

MARTIAL ET ARMAND

1. Renée satin day suit.
2. Chanel skirt unbuttoned over crepe pantalets.
3. Martial et Armand cloche and propeller scarf.
4. The shortest evening hem is Chéruit's — here black satin.
5. Louiseboulanger grey covert-cloth suit, Reboux hat.
6. Chanel's chiffon evening dresses.
7. Lady Diana Cooper, back from New York, to help canvass for her husband, models a Henri Bendel brown velours hat for *Vogue*.
8. Nicole Groult's beige toile dress, for afternoon or 'informal restaurant wear.'
9. 'The pyjama is the smartest negligée' . . . and simpler versions are being worn for the beach and informal lunches at Deauville and the Venice Lido.

CHÉRUIT

LOUISEBOULANGER

6
CHANEL

7

HENRI BENDEL

8
NICOLE GROULT   Maurice Beck and Helen Macgregor

9

MOLYNEUX   MOLYNEUX   LANVIN

1925

DOVE

Nemtchinova of the Russian Ballet in Dove's black crepe de chine pyjamas appliquéd with vivid velvet flowers.

Maurice Beck and Macgregor

'You wanna be happy? Den watch dis kid! Ah tell de world dis sweetie sure kin make a funeral happy. Watch what she's fixin' fo' to do. Dance? She can't do nothin' else but! You show 'em sister'

Josephine Baker and the *Revue Nègre* arrive in Paris, and black jazz, black dancing, singing and talking bowl over young society. The exhibition of Arts Décoratifs gives its name to the new applied arts out of cubism, Egyptian art, Russian Ballet and the Bauhaus. Everyone's wearing Russian boots. Nancy Cunard has her scandalous affair with Henry Crowther, and Maynard Keynes staggers the intellectual world by marrying Lydia Lopokova. Tallulah Bankhead attracts a whole generation of female fans for her performance in *Fallen Angels* and *The Green Hat*. Everyone's humming 'Tea for Two', and Fred and Adèle Astaire are dancing Gershwin's *Lady Be Good* on Broadway. John Barrymore is Hamlet, Ida Rubinstein is in *La Dame aux Camélias* in Paris, Braque has done the decor for *Zéphyr et Flore* with Serge Lifar dancing, there's *No No Nanette,* and Mrs Mayrick is out of prison to open another nightclub, the Manhattan, where you can rub shoulders with Gordon Richards the jockey, Sophie Tucker, Rudolph Valentino and Paul Whiteman. 'Artists' in Chelsea studios give 'dos' nightly, the real painters are to be found in Cassis and Cagnes, and all over London the Bright Young People are chasing policemen's helmets and actresses' shoes.

Sonia Delaunay, the painter, works with Jacques Heim and produces patchwork colour coats that personify the jazz age. This year she puts the same design on a car — a 5CV Citroën. Geometric futurist fabrics are painted at Chéruit, Lanvin, Renée and Worth, and Vionnet cuts the shapes into the structure of the dress. Patou, Lanvin and Vionnet open sports shops, and *Vogue* runs features on exercise. The straight, slim silhouette begins to move with pleats and godets, bloused bodices, swaying fringes, flying scarves and streamers, but the fullness slips back into the slim form when still. Designers are learning from Vionnet's bias cut, and jabots, winged panels ripple. For evening there are butterfly backs and straight, slim fronts, and butterfly chiffons with wings drifting from the shoulders. There's a new sweater blouse, jewelled and embroidered over a matching skirt. Skirts get shorter and shorter, with evening handkerchief points or asymmetric hems. *Vogue* does its first feature on 'The Little Black Dress'. The fabrics are kasha, printed crepes, crepe de chine, alpaca, rep, poplin, silk serge, and any fabric with a ribbed texture. At home, tea gowns are replaced by satin pyjamas in cyclamen, fuchsia, violet and jade.

Maurice Beck and Macgregor

2

DOVE

1. Billie Burke in the new hat, a felt cloche with a crushed crown, and the new gloves, worn a size too big.
2. Dove's tea pyjamas in cyclamen brocade and green satin with an embroidered black satin jacket, modelled by 'the famous English beauty known as "Sumurun"'.
3. Ina Claire in a typical Chanel sports suit of 1925. She was the first actress to dress naturally for the films — Chanel's were the 'real clothes' she wore during the twenties in Hollywood and on Broadway. She might wear pale beige kasha dresses for drawing-room comedies or two-piece velveteen suits out of doors.
4. New freedom in the slim silhouette.

1

3

Steichen

CHANEL

Steichen

EARLY PARIS OPENINGS:

MOLYNEUX LELONG PATOU

4

1925

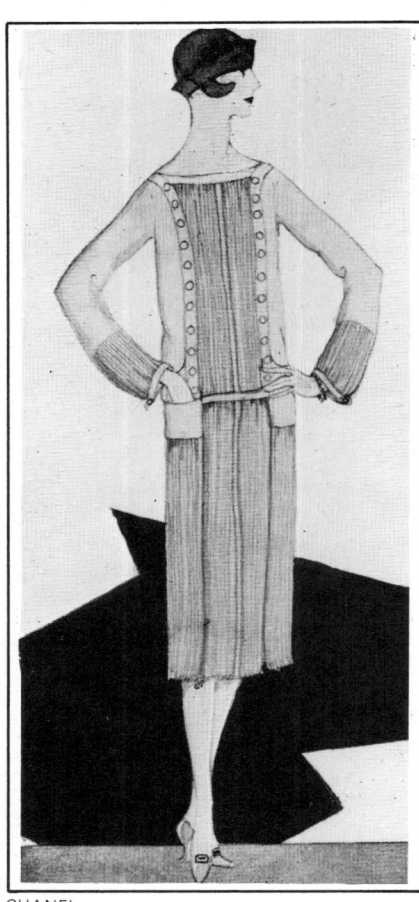

CHANEL

1. Chanel's grey crepella dress with pleated panels under the pockets, straight when still.
2. Vionnet's black velvet bias dress with crystal shoulder straps and crystal necklace embroidered on.
3. New backs for evening dresses.
4. Jean Patou's new sports department sells jersey and marocain bathing suits, which look as if you might be able to swim in them.
5. Flowered chiffon with the shortest, fullest evening skirt.
6. Lanvin's evening dress of gold brocade is embroidered with crystal and coral beads, with a bra top of peach tulle. Chéruit's cape is green and silver shot lamé with a skunk collar and green velvet lining.
7. English sports clothes — knitted suit, tweed topcoat, suede windcheater and kasha skirt
8. Isabel Jeans in Selfridge's straw hat and summer dress.

VIONNET

Douglas Pollard

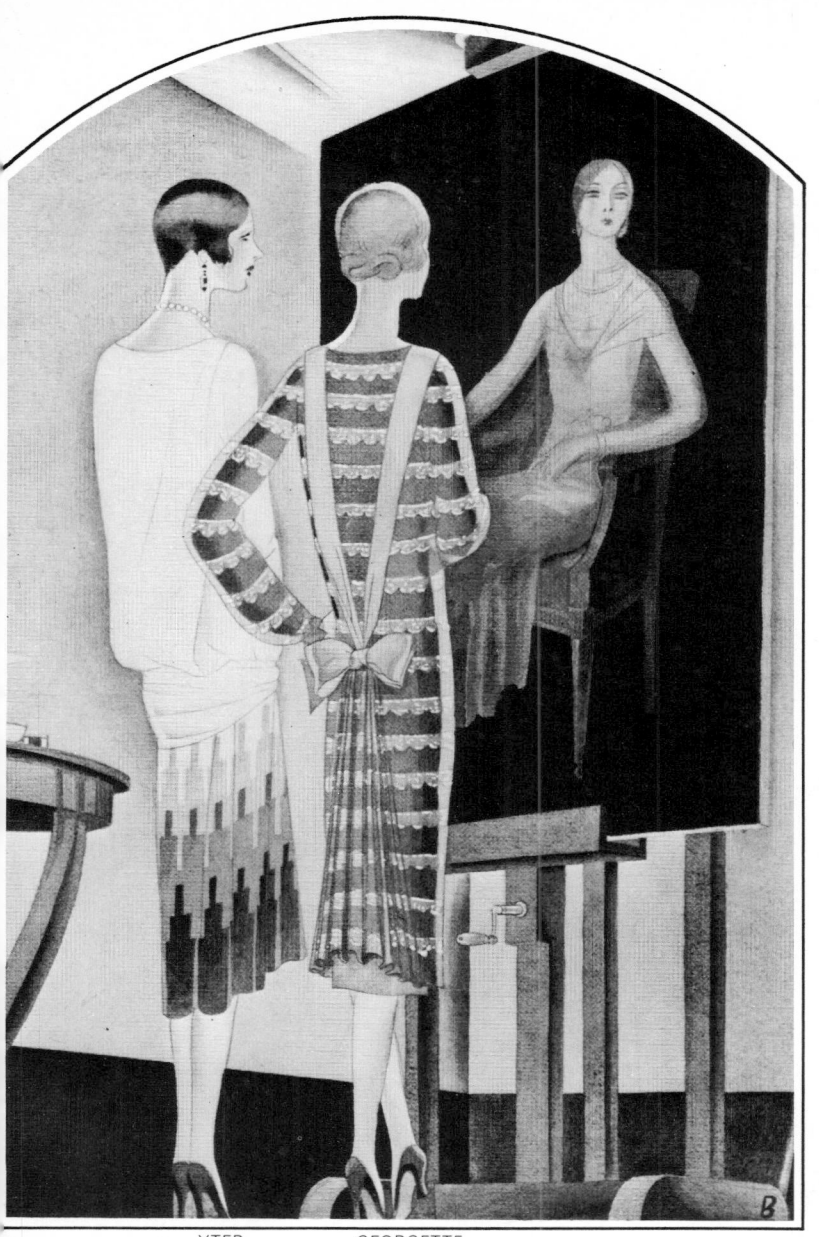

YTEB   GEORGETTE

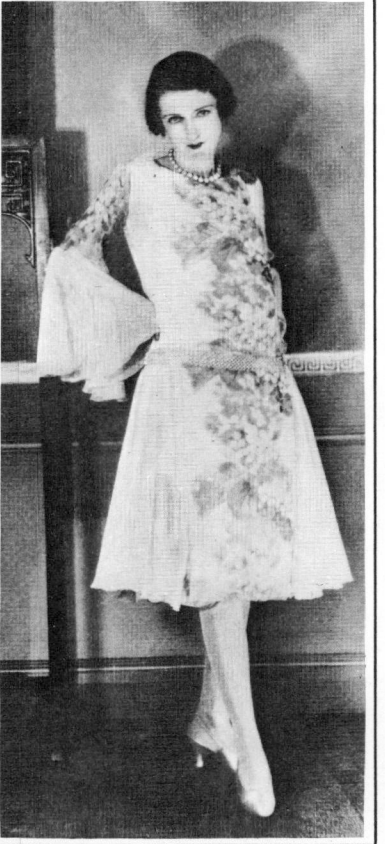

ARTELLE   Maurice Beck and Macgregor   LANVIN, CHÉRUIT   Steichen

4 PATOU   Fellows

7   Benito

8   Maurice Beck and Macgregor   81

1926

A man's shop, 1926

Shortsighted old lady to mannish young woman: 'Excuse me – did you say you were going up to Trinity or Girton next term?' *Punch cartoon*

The nine-day General Strike turns London upside down. Hyde Park is a milk depot, there are troops at Whitehall, and public transport comes to a stop. Commuters walk fifteen or twenty miles to work. It's the year of the Charleston, which sweeps the country and causes the vicar of St Aidan's in Bristol to declare, 'Any lover of the beautiful will die rather than be associated with the Charleston. It is neurotic! It is rotten! It stinks! Phew, open the windows!'

Skirts are at their shortest of the twenties, and sports clothes fill the foreground of fashion. *Vogue* writes on 'The Modern Rosalind' and the unfashionable can't tell the girls from the boys. Shoulders get broader, the fit is looser, and women go to men's shops to buy themselves plaid golfing socks, cardigans, ties and cravats, sleeveless V-neck sweaters, cuff links, cigarette holders and short dressing gowns. Chanel's tweed skirts with inverted pleats are much copied, and Chéruit brings out a new navy redingote, double-breasted with brass buttons.

On the other hand the dress silhouette softens. The cut is Vionnet's, a blouson dress tying around the hips into a front bow, lifting the skirt a little in front. Coats have fur collars, neat suits have frilly jabot blouses, and with them you wear two-tone leather shoes, suede purses and gloves. Daytime colours are navy, black and white, henna. Sports clothes are beige and brown or brilliant stripes and plaids. Evening dresses are pastel lace, white crepe, and all shades of mauve from palest lavender to ecclesiastic purple. Only the evening cloak is silver and gold, and any look borrowed from the Orient or the Russian ballet belongs in the tea-gown/pyjama category — even Poiret makes sports jumpers and pleated skirts.

1
PAM   Maurice Beck and Macgregor

2
CHANEL

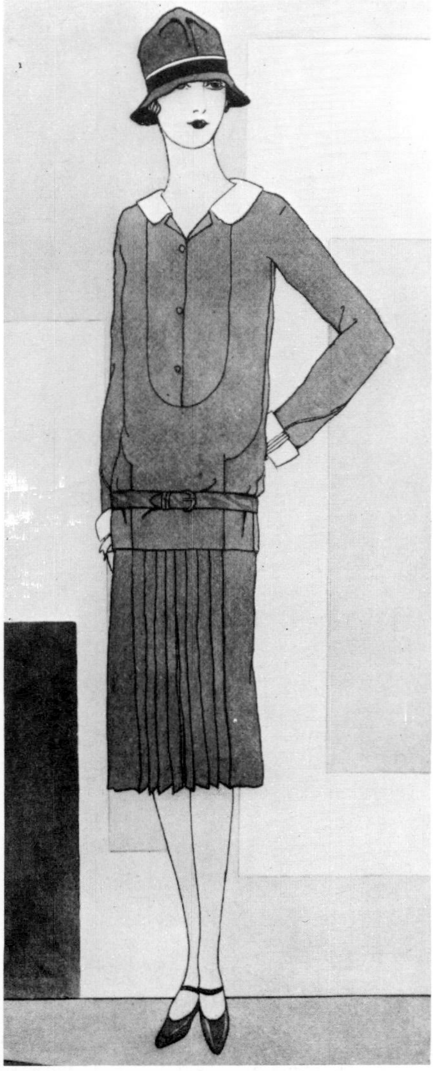

3
CHANEL

4
PATOU   Douglas Pollard

1. Three-piece travelling suit,
oatmeal angora with lynx collar and cuffs.
2. Chanel — black or purple crepella.
3. Chanel — grey-blue crepella with
collar and cuffs of white starched
linen, moiré belt.
4. Jean Patou — pleated skirt, black
jacket, white satin waistcoat.

1926

VIONNET 1 Francis

84 TALBOT

VIONNET   Sheeler

2

3

VIOLET NORTON   Maurice Beck and Macgregor

1. Vionnet's silver and gold dress shows her
marvellous cutting to perfection.
2. Vionnet's new sports shop sells dresses like this
one in natural kasha with monogram and navy
gored crepe de chine skirt.
3. Lime green and silver wrap from Violet Norton.
4. Travel by sea — with Chanel.
5. Winter sports at St Moritz.

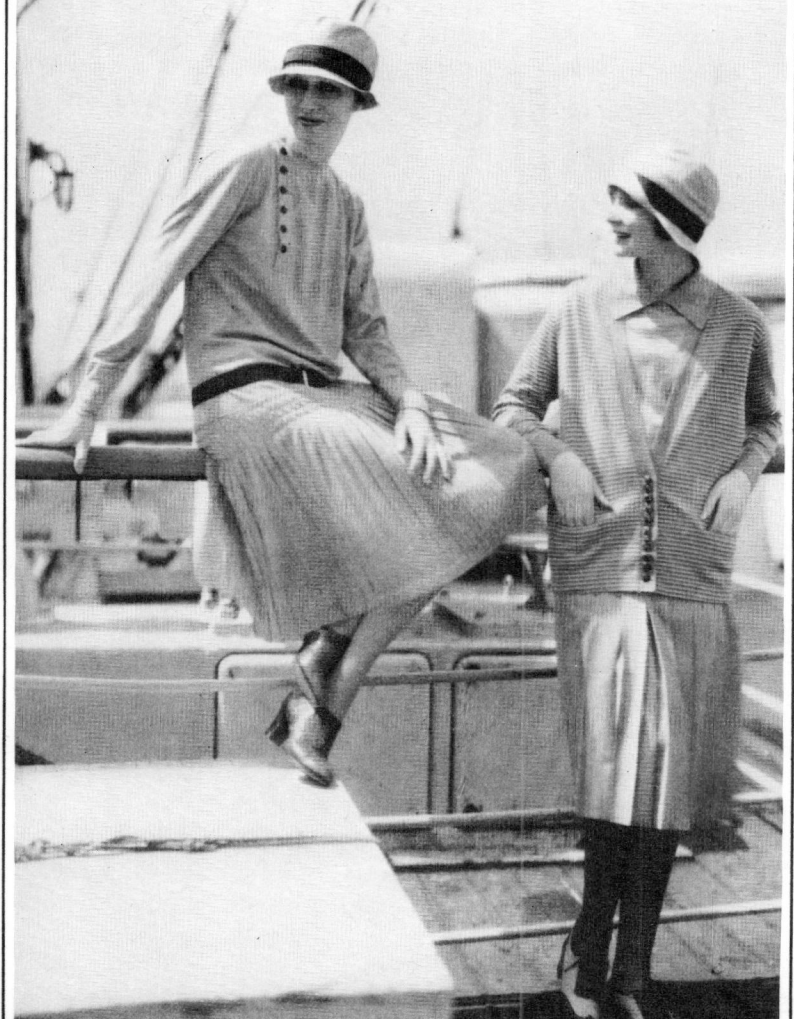

4

CHANEL   Steichen

5

Lepape

THE SUN

'We practically live in bathing suits and coconut oil'
Méraud Guinness, 1927

Year of the Surrealist conference on sex, Lindbergh's flight, and the new phrase 'sex appeal'. The sun is god, and society congregates at Cannes, Antibes, and the Venice Lido . . . there's Nancy Cunard in a gold dress with armfuls of barbaric bangles, her eyes made up with kohl 'which on first sight makes her unrecognisable'; Mrs Reginald Fellowes in a sequin dinner jacket with a green carnation, making news by wearing the same outfit night after night; the Duchess of Peneranda with her sunburned body and bare white dresses, flashing white teeth and brilliantined black hair; the Ruthven twins, the Dunne twins, the Morgan twins, Thelma Furness and Gloria Vanderbilt; Lady Louis Mountbatten, Mrs Cole Porter, Loelia Ponsonby . . . 'there are few French in Cannes'. The waterfront is lined with boutiques, Molyneux, Chanel, Poiret, Worth, Lanvin, offering special reductions and bargains for everyone who goes in. At home Noël Coward has 4 shows running simultaneously, and Cecil Beaton and Oliver Messel launch 1927 as the year of a million parties, most of them costume balls, with Beaton's costumes and Messel's masks. There's the Kit-Cat restaurant, the Café de Paris, and the cosy Gargoyle in Dean Street. There's a saxophonist you can't miss at the Silver Slipper, and Hutch singing 'The man I love' at Chez Victor, and Ciro's, where the Prince of Wales goes immediately on his return from his Canadian tour.

Sports clothes, in other words clothes for watching sports in, are the strongest influence in fashion. Looks designed for sports graduate to country day-dressing and then arrive in town. Chanel's country tweeds have just completed the course, particularly as she's opened a London shop this year: she pins a white piqué gardenia to the neck. Her 'lingerie touches' are copied everywhere — piping, bands of contrast, ruffles and jabots. She initiates fake jewellery, to be worn everywhere, even on the beach. Worth opens a sports shop here, and sells the new jumper suit — jersey overblouse and skirt in a combination of browns. Jackets get longer, and at the end of the year the skirt begins to drop. The new fur is a flared jacket of broadtail or shaved Persian lamb. The new indoor shoes are patent, called azuré, nacré or iridescent kid.

In reaction to the informal daytime tweeds, there's a silk afternoon dress to wear from three o'clock, and evening dresses look more formal, with draped, girdled or tucked hips. The newest are in printed chiffon, with flowers of the same fabric, or in a combination of white and flesh-coloured crepe. Shoppers come up from the country to buy their clothes from Harrods, Dickins & Jones, Debenham & Freebody, Marshall & Snelgrove and Harvey Nichols, and artificial silk is called 'rayon' from now on.

By the end of the year the shingle has become curly or waved, and *Vogue* asks, 'Shall we join the Long-Haired Ladies?' The black felt cloche of spring becomes the draped skullcap of winter — a helmet shape with one wing sweeping forward onto the cheek.

Three new houses make their first appearance in *Vogue* — Norman Hartnell, Elsa Schiaparelli and Galitzine.

1
NOWITZKY

2
HARVEY NICHOLS PATOU

4
PATOU   Hoyningen-Huene

1. Nowitzky bathing suits photographed on
the Venice Lido.
2. Two bathing suits: Harvey Nichols's in two
shades of orange jersey, Jean Patou's in
black and white crepe de chine with a
buttoned and monogrammed belt. The
printed silk beach shoes are from Patou.
3. Patou's bare-backed bathing costume,
tank top and shorts of red and white.
4. At the Bar Basque, Biarritz, in Patou
jumper suits.

3
PATOU   Lee Erickson   87

VIONNET

2

4
FORTUNY

3

Maurice Beck and Macgregor

1. Vionnet's rose and silver paillettes, matching pin and necklace.

2. Chanel's costume jewellery isn't meant to be mistaken for the real thing — most of it isn't even imitation. About now, she breaks her necklace of graduated pearls and strings them together as she finds them — setting a fashion for irregular beads. Here — a selection from London shops.

3. and 4. Mariano Fortuny's robes and velvets are famous, but almost impossible to get hold of from London. Here, making a unique appearance in British *Vogue*, his mushroom-pleat Greek robe in soft grey-blue satin on a drawstring-neck. The peplum hem is weighted with opalescent beads. Over it, a richer grey-blue velvet lined with ruby poplin, the velvet brushed with peacock and stamped with gold.

5. Mrs Cole Porter in cloche and fake beads.

6. New French hats, from Agnès and Marie Alphonsine.

7. Ilka Chase, daughter of American *Vogue's* editor-in-chief, models Chanel's eau de nil satin.

5

6

AGNÈS

AGNÈS

MARIE ALPHONSINE

CHANEL

7

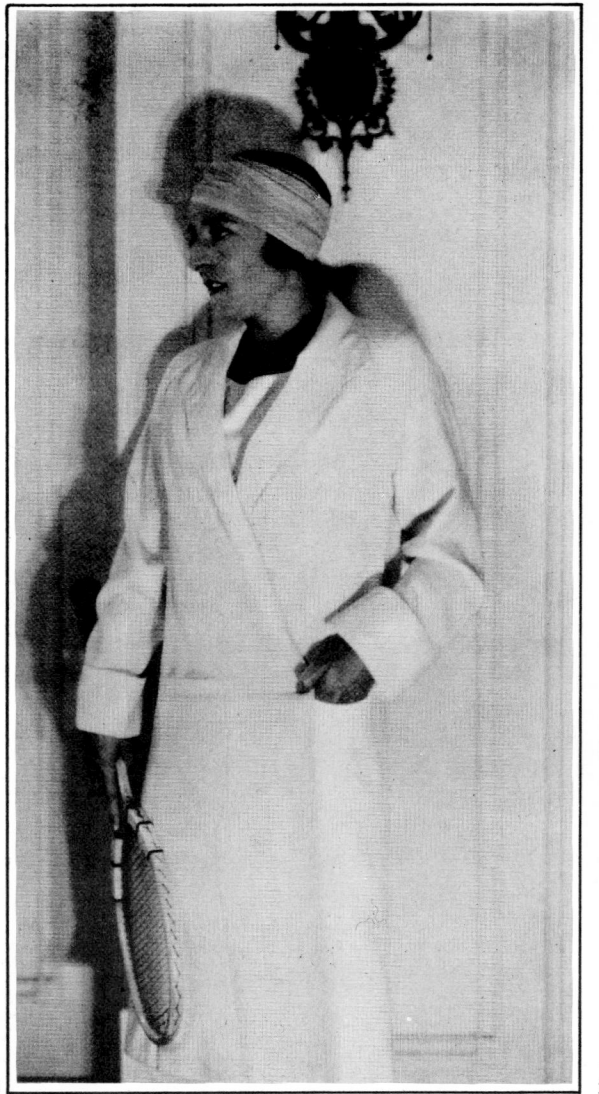

1

PATOU

2

CHANEL

Steicher

3

LOUISEBOULANGER   VIONNET   CHANEL

1. Suzanne Lenglen, 'hideously chic' in a white
bandeau, revolutionized tennis wear by
playing in a short, sleeveless, pleated dress
wrapped up here in a Patou coat.
2. Chanel—beige shaved lamb sports coat
and tweed dress.
3. Four country/town looks.
4. From Lady Paget's dress shop in Grafton
Street, a black and white silk dress matching
the lining of the coat, dots and stripes mixed.

4

Cecil Beaton

FIFINELLA   Steichen

5. Paquin's printed chiffon.
6. Garden party dress of white organdie
with an embroidered bolero.

AQUIN

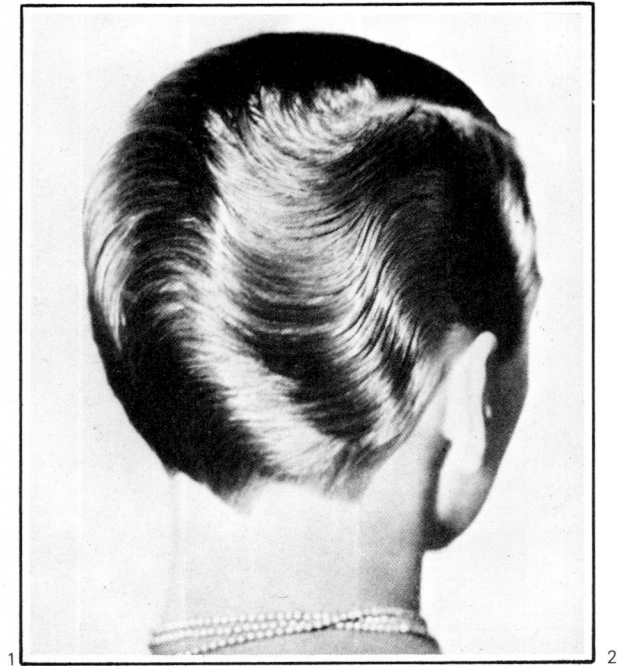

HARTNELL

Hugh Cecil

4

1. The waved shingle by Antoine.
2. First appearance of Norman Hartnell's name in *Vogue*, with this picture frock of pale blue taffeta with hand-painted flowers, pink chiffon bodice, orchid taffeta surplice.
3. The first Schiaparelli — and the first of her trompe l'oeil super-smart hand-knitted sweaters.
4. The hair-piece: by the end of the year women are adding to the shingle with a switch of false hair on a clasp.

'We shall be smart, but not hard; we shall gird our loins; there will be only one silhouette – the youthful one'

'To lose weight has become an obsession' and in its pursuit women go for treatments from Denglers to Brides, from Baden-Baden to Orsier, never forgetting to take their vitamins along with their cocktails – even dogs have a cocktail bar, dispensing water outside Vuitton in the Champs Elysées. As an accompaniment to drinks, the new potato crisps sell over a million packets this year. A very hot summer popularizes sunbathing at home as well as abroad – there are backless bathing suits so you can look evenly tanned in your backless evening dress. Rich smart women are flying all over the place: Lady Heath, Lady Bailey, Lady Anne Saville, Mrs Dulcibella Atkey and the redoubtable Duchess of Bedford, sixty years old before she set foot in a plane. The Dolly sisters are gambling away a fortune at Cannes, watched by a crowd six deep. *Vogue* tells you how to dress on £75 a year . . .'an evening dress from your little dressmaker, £4, three pairs of shoes, £6.10s, two hats, £3, lingerie and accessories, £2'.

Vogue gives women *carte blanche* to dress as they like – 'controlled by the permanent limitations of good taste and the current limitations of the mode'. The new 'runabout' dress is easy as any tennis dress. Waistlines begin to go up because of the fitted and moulded hipline, hems drop lower at the back, and the sweater of the year is Schiaparelli's, a *trompe l'oeil* scarf around the hips tying with a real tie on one side.

'As seen at Deauville or any other ville d'eau.'

1

CHANEL   VIONNET   PARIS TRADES   CHAMPCOMMUNAL

2 LANVIN   Hoyningen-Huene

3 SCHIAPARELLI, DRECOLL   Francis

WORTH

4   5 CHRISTABEL RUSSELL

1. Tweed ensembles.
2. Lanvin navy-blue and white bathing suit.
3. Another of Schiaparelli's trompe l'oeil sweaters, *left*;
right, Drecoll sports model in navy-blue and yellow.
4, 5 and 6. Three-piece suits: *left*, peach silk jumper with navy
bands, printed georgette skirt to match; *centre*, red crepe de chine
cardigan and skirt; *right*, clover-patterned sweater, deeply ribbed
over the hips.
7. The Marquise de Casa Maury — the beauty and model Paula
Gellibrand — with vaselined eyelids, wearing Worth's gold lamé with
pleated skirt and chiffon velvet cardigan.
8. Full tulle evening dress by Elspeth Fox-Pitt.
9. Schiaparelli's sweater (see No. 3) worn by Mrs Somerset
Maugham, *centre*, at Le Touquet.

94

7 WORTH

Cecil Beaton

6 FORTNUM & MASON

8 ELSPETH FOX-PITT

Bertram Park

9

SCHIAPARELLI

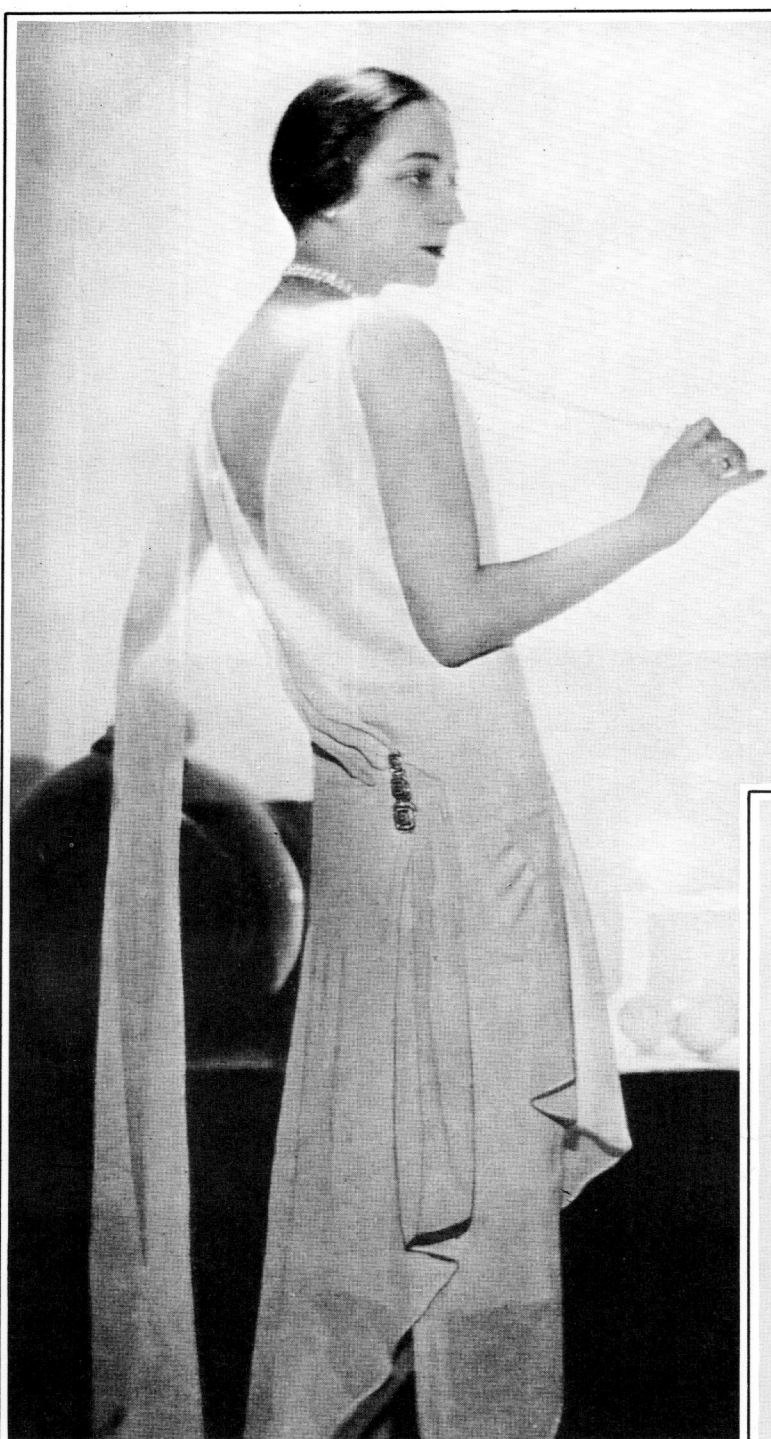

AIRY NOTHINGS
UNDERLIE
THE SUMMER MODE

PAUL CARET   Scaloni

1. Paul Caret evening dress in ivory Celanese
georgette.
2. Underwear — *left*, lace-trimmed washing satin
combinations with lowcut back, and *centre*, brassière
and corset of pink crepe de chine with écru lace.
3. Tiers by Chanel, in black crepe.

Cocktails at the 500, Bryan Howard in the centre   Howard and Joan Coster

'Automobiles, Movies and Bootlegging are the three biggest American industries.
After these . . . comes Beauty'   *Aldous Huxley, 1929*

There are machines to tone you, slim you and stretch you, skin nourishers, cleansers and lotions, and 'a face can cost as much in upkeep as a Rolls Royce'. This is what *Vogue's* fashion editor wears on her face: Arden's Ultra Amoretta foundation cream, powder, a little brilliantine over eyebrows and lashes — Coty's L'Origan — and Guerlain's pale lipstick. In town, Helena Rubinstein's sticky foundation called Creme Gypsy, sunburn colour, applied with a pad of cotton wool wrung out in cold water and drying to a light ochre. A little grease rouge, and two powders, first a light rachel then a deeper shade. Vaseline rubbed on the eyelid, with a blue or brown pencil line. Black mascara, brushed with a clean brush when still wet to take off excess, eyebrow pencil and a darker lipstick.

Dancing has slowed down. 'The most loved dance tunes of today are immersed in a delicious and quite artificial sentimentality, the kind of emotion that appeals only to the cynical or the sophisticated.' Two favourites of the year are 'Let's do it' and 'You're the cream in my coffee'. Rosita Forbes, the explorer, loves 'Glad Rag Doll', and Paula Gellibrand adores 'I can't give you anything but love, Baby'.

The bosom makes a gentle reappearance: most women are beginning to wear a 'combination corset', brassière and girdle in one, with a few light bones, cut to emphasize the waist. Or you can buy a bra-topped petticoat with divided legs to wear over a girdle. The day silhouette is simple, just a long jersey belted over pleats or a dress which, pure in line, has a complicated cut. Evening dresses are tiered, ruffled, bowed, butterfly-backed.

P. Mourgue

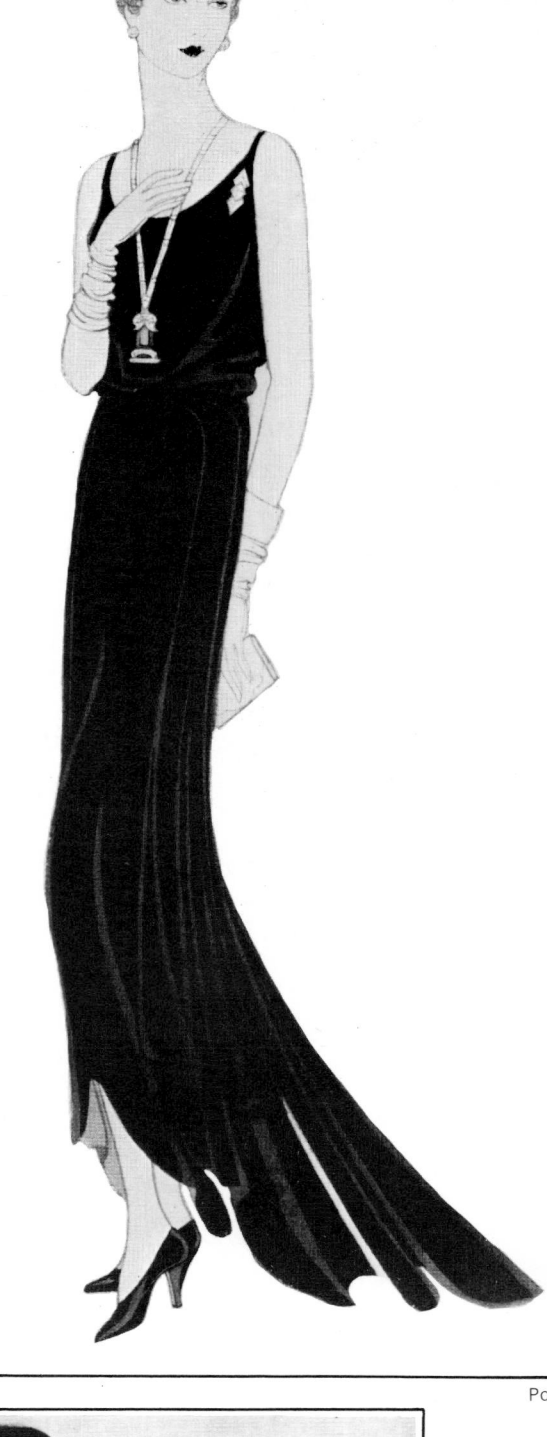

AUGUSTABERNARD

Pollard

1. *Vogue* cover for 1 May 1929.
2. Waisted black velvet evening dress by Augustabernard.
3. Corset from Roussel.
4. Bigger one-sided hats for winter from Maria Guy, *left*, and Reboux.

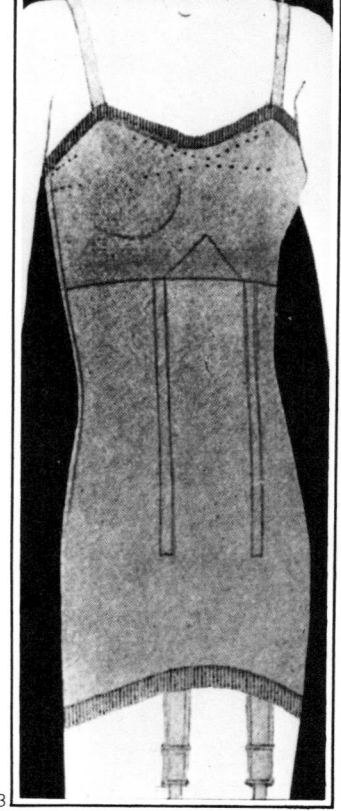

3 ROUSSEL

4 MARIA GUY

REBOUX

CHANEL

5. Chanel's new grège-brown jersey suit with hat, scarf, sweater and lining in red, blue and black stripes.
6. Beach trousers with big raffia hats.
7. Men's and women's jersey swimsuits.
8. Sleeveless Biarritz dress in white silk piqué with a sleeveless pale yellow jersey sweater belted in white and yellow grosgrain from Paris Trades. White folded felt hat, tan and white co-respondent shoes.

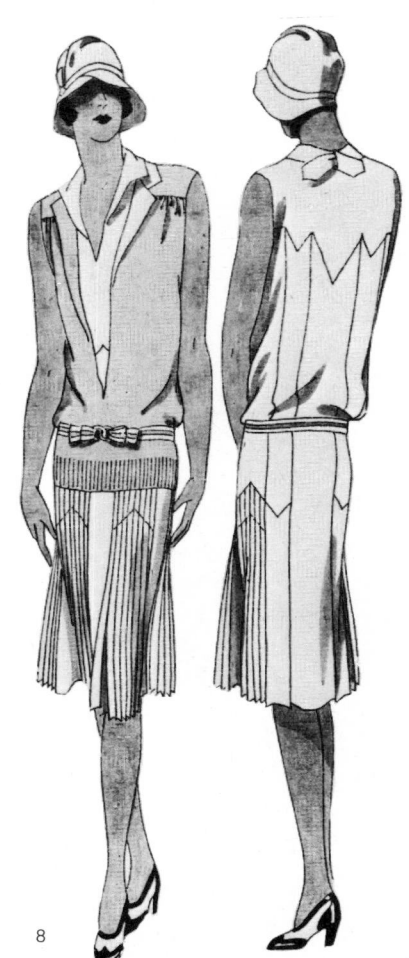

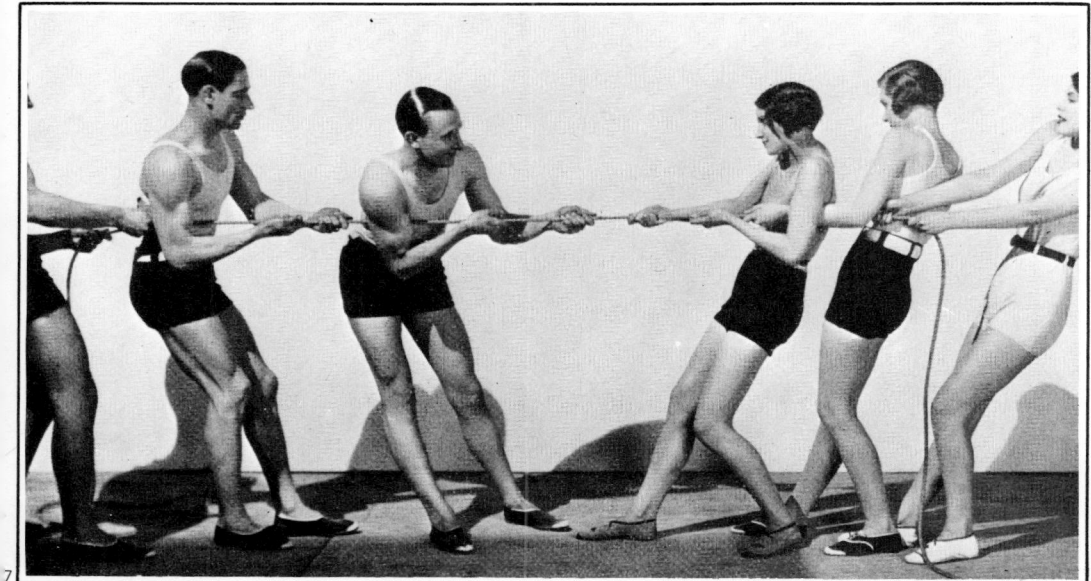

Hoyningen-Huene

1930–1939

The Threadbare Thirties

TO THE WOMEN OF BRITAIN

Your urgent duty calls you to-day, as never before, to ask in all your shopping for British goods.

Every time you buy British you are sure of getting the best quality in the world.

Every time you buy British you make work for your own fellow-countrymen.

Every time you buy British you help to improve your country's housekeeping account.

Scrutinize all advertisements.
Look at all labels.
Ask where the goods come from.

Insist, whenever you make a purchase, that you mean to

buy British
from the Empire at home and overseas
ISSUED BY THE EMPIRE MARKETING BOARD

December 1931.

The thick skin that protected the rich and secure in the twenties wore paper-thin in the thirties. Groucho Marx called the years of American Depression before the New Deal the Threadbare Thirties, but the slump was an international crisis and in Britain the unemployment figures reached three million, and feelings of anxiety and insecurity were at their highest since the middle of the war. Owing to the decline of world trade and the collapse of markets, Britain was pock-marked with Distressed Areas where almost the entire population was living on the meagre dole. A policy of national self-sufficiency was reuniting Germany and giving it identity and a sense of purpose, but Britain was divided and on the point of crisis when the National Government was formed in 1931, and politics began to invade the lives and conversation of people who had never thought politically before. Hunger marchers poured into London by the thousand instead of the hundred, and demonstrations were charged by police with batons – in Birkenhead the street fighting went on for three days. As an economy measure, the National Government had introduced reductions in unemployment pay subject to the Means Test. A man would come round, notice a new coat or find out if a boy did a paper round, and cut the allowance. Men whose families could not live on the dole as it was faced cuts and deductions of food tickets. Sympathy for them caused a rift in the Labour party, and the Left was joined by university undergraduates and dissatisfied or sensitive elements of the

middle and upper classes. University students who came out to see the hunger marchers spoke of the extraordinary sound of their feet, not marching like soldiers, but shuffling because of the flapping soles of their worn-out boots. In the twenties university students had rallied to the government in the General Strike. In the thirties they joined the marchers.

The situation was brought home to *Vogue*'s readership in other ways. Wal Hannington, organizer of the National Unemployed Workers' Movement, used the nuisance tactics exploited before the war by the Suffragettes and more recently by Gandhi's followers in India, to draw attention to the plight of the unemployed. One hundred unemployed moved right into *Vogue*'s territory when they invaded the Ritz one afternoon and asked for tea, provoking press features contrasting the lives of the unemployed with those of the Ritz tea-drinkers. Another stunt took place just before Christmas, when Oxford Street was crammed with shoppers. Unemployed men lay down head to toe, eight abreast across the road, and spread over themselves posters reading 'Work or Bread'. When the police arrived and dragged them onto the pavement, they immediately went back to their places in the road and had soon created a traffic jam that paralysed the West End.

Other facts you could not ignore were the scuffles of the Fascist party, led by Sir Oswald Mosley. Elected as Conservative member for Harrow at twenty, he had married Lord Curzon's daughter and

Left: Film star photograph, film star dress, 1932. Studio Sun's picture of an evening dress in Courtauld's Courgette, an artificial silk, in the quintessential thirties setting: a modern armchair, a bowl of white tulips.

101

1. Mrs Bryan Guinness, Sir Oswald Mosley's second wife, formerly Diana Mitford.
2. 'Vive le Front Plissé Populaire!' December 1936.
3. John Hoysradt, night-club satirist, as Mussolini. A former professor of history he was very popular in cabaret at the Dorchester in 1938 and 1939.

1   Cecil Beaton   2

3
102   Karger

subsequently quarrelled with both the Conservative and Labour parties. Unfortunately for him, his wife, who kept her Socialist convictions, was half Jewish. She died and left him free to marry in 1937, with Hitler as his best man, Mrs Bryan Guinness: otherwise Diana Mitford, sister of the 'Perfect Aryan Beauty' Unity Mitford. Both wives were well known to *Vogue* readers from the society pages.

For some time after Mussolini's takeover of Italy Fascism was vaguely respected, and Rothermere for the *Daily Mail* gave it his temporary support, but as the Blackshirts were seen to be using knuckledusters on hecklers and victimizing the 'Kikes' in the East End, and as Nazism grew year by year, the papers began to speak disparagingly of the 'rule of the rubber truncheon and the castor oil bottle'. In 1935 Margot Asquith was writing in *Vogue*, 'We do not believe in mock Mussolinis, silly shirts, self-advertising up-starts. We detest dictators . . . Men are tired of force and formula, they ardently desire to follow the things that make for peace.' *Vogue* had mentioned Mussolini in connection with fashion in 1933: 'À propos of an article in the Popolo d'Italia . . . Mussolini gives some good advice to the Nazis, including the warning, in view of a Prussian ordinance against lipstick and rouge – "Any power whatsoever is destined to fail before fashion. If fashion says skirts are to be short, you will not succeed in lengthening them, even with the guillotine." This statement by one dictator to another, acknow-ledging a power before which both are helpless, is of peculiar interest.'

Writers were now known for their politics, not their amusing novels. Evelyn Waugh was in favour of Fascism. Stephen Spender and Cecil Day Lewis represented the Left, and in spite of the Nazi hatred of modern art, Wyndham Lewis wrote a book in praise of Hitler. George Orwell, who was wounded in the Spanish Civil War, came back to write *Homage to Catalonia*; George Barker wrote his account. Aldous Huxley was now the intellectual leader of Constructive Pacifism and had published the *Encyclopedia of Pacifism*, before leaving for America with a handful of leading writers who could see the war coming and had no wish to take part in it.

In *Vogue*, the scope of the society and gossip pages was extended to include political topics. 'Our Lives from Day to Day' took on a political flavour from the beginning of the decade. 'At Mr Wells' we began with vodka and caviare to welcome Julian Huxley back from Moscow, who spoke of communal life to as perfect a small company of famous individualists as could be gathered together in a London flat.' In the same column, an irreverent mention of Gandhi on his visit to London – 'the famous little figure . . . looking very Mickey Mouse as he accepted tributes from the Ladies of India'. Asked whether he thought a dhoti sufficient garb for meeting the King, Gandhi had replied, 'The King wore enough for both of us'. On the advertising pages, readers were besought to 'Buy British', and on the fashion pages the models struck militaristic attitudes, the regimental suits that appeared in the mid-thirties giving copywriters a field day. 'Vive le Front Plisse Populaire!' . . . 'Newshirts for all parties' . . . 'Aux armes, Citoyennes! – the fashion cry of the moment'. Readers were told to 'March to the sound of drums by day', and shown suits with square epauletted shoulders, drummer boy frogging, gauntlet gloves and low heels, and hats with a 'forward putsch'.

One of *Vogue*'s most relevant pre-war features was a piece by Alan Stewart on finding out the real news. The silence that preceded the Abdication had brought it home to the public that the papers did not always print the whole news. Apart from what the press overlooked and chose to suppress, there were misrepresentations and actual censorship. The press continually referred to the unemployed as if they were too idle to look for work, and to the dole as though it were a comfortable wage. The facts were finally brought home by photographs of real life cases in *Picture Post*, founded on the lines of *Life* in 1938, which showed, for instance, the wife and four children of Alfred Smith waiting outside the Labour Exchange for his £2. 7s. 6d. weekly dole. Most people were in the dark about Germany's new rearmed power and the fresh European threats – just before the war angry letters to *The Times* denounced the B.B.C. for being alarmist because of its purely factual bulletins on the European situation. Alan Stewart's feature was called 'Every Woman her own Tabouis' – Geneviève Tabouis of the anti-Fascist *L'Œuvre* had a reputation for knowing what was going on behind the scenes. He said, 'If you lived in the United States, where the press is refreshingly bold and free, you wouldn't have to buy so many papers; but even in England you can discover almost all the news there is . . . those who skim five dailies know much more than those who read one only. If you take *The Times*, you should also take the *Daily Worker*. The *Daily Telegraph* and the *News Chronicle* also balance one another nicely . . . Unless you are Unity Mitford, it's unlikely that you will have much chance of a heart-to-heart talk with one of these Fuehrers, but it might be a good idea to have a look at the big shots of domestic politics. Go to a few political meetings, a Left Book Club Rally and persuade someone to get you into the House for a full dress Foreign Affairs debate.'

If politics were reflected only indirectly, the big scandal of the thirties happened well within *Vogue*'s scope. Mrs Simpson's name first appears in *Vogue* in 1935, obliquely mentioned in conjunction with groups including the Prince of Wales. We read that for cocktails 'hot sausages . . . are out of date, back numbers. You must think up something different. The Prince of Wales has hot buttered American soda biscuits, with cod's roe, served in hot silver breakfast dishes' and, a sentence or two further down the page, 'Mrs Simpson's food is of such a high standard that the intelligent guest fasts before going to have cocktails with her . . . Her hot dishes are famous.' At about this time Sir Samuel Hoare noticed Wallis Simpson for her 'sparkling jewels in very up-to-date Cartier settings'. *Vogue*'s references are so discreet that an inattentive reader might miss the point, but the two names are never far apart. 'The Prince of Wales went by boat to dine at St Tropez . . . and acquired a blue and white striped sailor's pullover . . . Tonight he dined at the restaurant on the quai, and when he got up to go on to another café for coffee, the entire company dining there got up and followed him, not even waiting to pay their bills . . .' and in the next column, 'All the smart clothes here come from Paris and London, not St Tropez. The best-dressed women, like Mrs Ernest Simpson, for example, have Schiaparelli's "pouch" dress in silk or printed cotton' – and she was photographed for *Vogue* in Schiaparelli's white linen trouser suit. When the King died, *Vogue* came out with a blank purple cover and wrote, 'The Reign Begins . . . Everything we know about the new occupant of the Throne suggests a keen, alert mind and forms the image of one who has mixed with a larger number of representative men and women than most other figures in history', and in the next issue, 'Mrs Ernest Simpson is now the best dressed woman in town.' Her immaculate, pin-neat elegance, like that of another hard-edged American contemporary, Mrs Diana Vreeland, who was to become editor of American *Vogue*, was much admired and copied in the thirties. It was a foil first for Schiaparelli's clothes, and later Mainbocher's.

Lady Furness, one of the Morgan twins who were often in *Vogue*, had introduced Mrs Simpson to the Prince of Wales and had lent her the train and feathers for the court appearance she made in spite of the rules about divorcees. In a conversation recorded by

4

5

James Laver in his anthology *Between the Wars*, when Lady Furness was leaving for a few weeks' holiday, Mrs Simpson said to her, 'Oh Thelma, the little man is going to be so lonely.' 'Well, dear,' replied Lady Furness, 'You look after him while I'm away. See that he does not get into any mischief.' On her return, she and the Simpsons were guests at Fort Belvedere: 'At dinner, I noticed that the Prince and Wallis seemed to have little private jokes. Once he picked up a piece of salad with his fingers. Wallis playfully slapped his hand. I . . . caught her eye and shook my head at her. She knew as well as everybody else that the Prince could be very friendly, but no matter how friendly, he never permitted familiarity . . . Wallis looked straight at me. That one cold, defiant stare told me the whole story. I left the Fort the following morning.' *Vogue* published honeymoon photographs of the Duke and Duchess at Schloss Wasserleonburg, one of 60 castles put at their disposal after the Abdication, and, tremendous scoop, published a portfolio of exclusive photographs by Cecil Beaton taken of them at the Chateau de Candé, the Duchess in the most elegant dresses from her Mainbocher trousseau.

Had fashion been the luxury many think it is, instead of a kind of barometer, the slump might have killed the couture – at least, for the years between the Crash and recovery. As it happened, the only Paris casualty was Augustabernard, who had just reopened in lavish new premises and who relied on a South American clientele who were all hit by the crisis at the same moment. Those houses which did not already have ready-to-wear sidelines now opened them, and even Chanel, who had one of the most expensive salons, cut her prices by half in 1932. In the first season after the Wall Street Crash, not a single American buyer came to Paris, and most of them did not return until 1933. The couture had always been prepared to wait a long time for payment, but at a time of fluctuating exchange rates this was a dangerous habit. Fortunately, all the couturiers had made so much money in the twenties that they had reserves. Their staff, who were underpaid anyway, were prepared to go on half-time, and, most important of all for the designers, the French fabric manufacturers were prepared to supply their materials on credit. A day dress took five yards of fabric in 1938, as opposed to the two yards it would have taken in the twenties. Not surprisingly, there was a vogue for economical and washable fabrics. Chanel was invited to England by Ferguson

to help promote their cottons as fashion fabrics, and in her 1931 collection she included thirty-five cotton evening dresses in piqué, lace, spotted muslin, organdie, lawn and net. These young and fresh looking dresses with their billowing skirts were the most popular evening dresses of the year with English debutantes, and with their fathers who paid the bills. Couture prices in the thirties however were not, even relatively, so very high: a plain Vionnet day dress in 1938 cost about £19, and now that it was in bad taste to look rich, there was a fashion for the 'poor' simple look. Ladies who were still fabulously rich went about in plain black dresses, furless wool coats and sweaters and slacks. *Vogue* wrote, 'It's no longer chic to be smart.' In the twenties Paris couturiers were showing four hundred outfits in a single collection. In the thirties these were whittled down to a hundred, and the showings were much better organized, with bureaux for the registration of models, a black book of cheap copyists to keep out, and press handouts to prevent misrepresentation.

It was an ill wind that made Paris less accessible to foreign clients. Now that fewer Londoners were going to Paris, London designers were given a boost and responded with new talent. Digby Morton set up his own couture business and was succeeded at Lachasse by Hardy Amies, Hartnell was prospering as the Queen's dressmaker, Molyneux and Charles Creed were to leave Paris for London at the outbreak of war. The designer Charles James, who made his reputation in America, was working in England during the early thirties and making a name for himself with the skill of his cutting and draping.

Fabrics were keeping pace with the ready-to-wear market. Artificial silk was now stronger and better made, and in 1939 the Americans began production of nylon, which they claimed to be more elastic than silk and one-and-a-half times stronger. *Vogue* drew a clothesline full of washable new clothes including a tailored linen suit, a beach dress with satinized stripes, an artificial silk jersey dress of awning stripes, and a frilled organdie and lace blouse. In shops people were asking for uncrushable fabrics like zingale, and for cottons, linens and spun rayons which were Sanforized – preshrunk. Schiaparelli matched Chanel's cottons with her own inevitably sensational experiments with Rhodophane, a glass fabric by Colcombet, and by using the nursery fabric Viyella for tailored blouses. She pioneered the use of Lightning

'If you are taking a lady out to lunch and find that she arrives with white eyelids and green eyelashes don't let off a piercing scream and telephone for an ambulance. Remember that it's her new way of making herself interesting—and comfort yourself with the thought that the colours might have been worse. If you ask her to dinner, she may arrive with a flight of blue birds doing vertically banked turns round the rim of her evening dress, or with her face obscured by a veil with real butterflies perched on top.'

Fasteners – zips – used first in sports skirts and finally in evening dresses, and loved to incorporate gadget clasps and motif buttons, made for her by craftsmen like Jean Clement.

The thirties in fashion was chiefly a neck and neck race between the rivals Schiaparelli and Chanel. Schiaparelli, although her influence was limited to this single decade, was the more sensational: she dressed Salvador Dali's wife free in return for inspiration, and her fashion follies were inspired jokes – the shoe hat, the 'chest of drawers' suit, the aspirin necklace and edible cinnamon buttons, the lacquered white hair. Her lasting innovation was perfectly sober – the combination of a dress with a matching jacket – but her colours were fantastic. She would put together fuchsia purple, shocking pink and black. It was typical of Schiaparelli that, when she decided she hated the modernistic mannikins given her to dress for the Exposition Internationale des Arts et Techniques in 1937, she buried them in flowers and slung up her new collection on a clothesline.

Chanel contemptuously referred to Schiaparelli as 'that Italian artist who makes clothes' (in much the same sense as Vionnet referred to Chanel as 'that modiste'), and her own clothes of the thirties were faultlessly elegant, modern, and matchlessly chic. With Chanel No. 5 and her incredible costume jewellery – 'It does not matter if they are real,' she said, 'so long as they look like junk!' – she revolutionized Hollywood glamour by dressing Ina Claire in the simplest of white satin pyjamas or tweed suits. Unlike Schiaparelli's musical comedy military suits, Chanel's were quite effortless, the collars small, the shoulders not noticeably padded, the waist left in its natural place and not drawn in tight. Over 40 herself, she knew what made a woman look younger, and invented cardigan jackets, dashing velveteen and ciré satin cinema suits, to be worn with flattering small hats. She made hornrimmed glasses a fashion accessory, and scotched forever Dorothy Parker's overquoted remark about girls who wear glasses. Her country clothes were a revelation to tweedy Englishwomen and she was her own best advertisement. 'Chanel,' said Lesley Blanch in 1938, 'demonstrated the fact that grey flannel trousers and a hairy wool sweater are nothing if not allied to swags of pearls, wrists clogged with barbaric bracelets and a netted coiffure top-knotted with masses of geraniums and chenille plumes.'

In the twenties only two or three couturiers stood out from the

1. Cinematographic photograph by Hoyningen-Huene, a master of lighting, 1933. The evening dress by Christabel Russell.
2. Cecil Beaton's photograph of Margot Asquith, 1935. Jean Harlow, when introduced to her, said, 'Pleased to meet you, Margot', sounding the T, and Margot Asquith replied, 'The T is silent, as in Harlow.'
3. Raoul Dufy's Ascot cover for *Vogue*, 29 May 1935.

4. Benito's Surrealist drawing of Chanel's black lace and Schiaparelli's wine crepe suit with leg of mutton sleeves.
5. Fashion photograph by Horst in Odeon style: Paquin's silver fox collared, white satin cape, 1935.
6. Salvador Dali, 1937, by Cecil Beaton.
7. Dali's sketch of his Dream House for the New York World Fair, 1939.

crowd because the look was universal. In the thirties each house had its own look, summed up by its most famous clients. Schiaparelli dressed Daisy Fellowes, the well-known fashion individualist. Molyneux was fortunate in dressing the beautiful and stylish Princess Marina, for whom he made the most flattering and well-behaved clothes that money could buy. Mainbocher, ex-editor of French *Vogue*, followed in the same tradition but his clothes acquired a harder image through his leading customer, the Duchess of Windsor. The two most sculptural of all fashion designers both began their Paris careers in the thirties: Alix, whose draped and folded silk jerseys already identify her by her later name, Madame Grès, and Balenciaga, who came to Paris at the beginning of the Spanish Civil War and had hardly time to be appreciated before the whole of Europe was at war again. Vionnet dressed Madame Martinez de Hoz, and Marcel Rochas, who is given the credit for the first padded shoulders, became famous overnight when eight ladies at a party in 1930 came face to face wearing the same Rochas dress. Charles Creed set a new standard in tailored suits for women.

By the thirties, *Vogue* had come into its fullest power over fashion. A word could make or break a collection. Couturiers would count the number of illustrations given to each house, and write off furious letters of complaint. Once the couture had recovered from the effects of the slump, it began to assume greater and greater importance. 'Now fashion is news, fashion is big business, fashion is the intimate concern of millions,' said *Vogue*, announcing in 1938 the first ever Collections Report to be broadcast from Paris to New York and relayed from there to London almost while the clothes were still being shown, A great deal of *Vogue*'s prestige was due to the metamorphosis of photography and the talents of *Vogue*'s excellent photographers. In the hands of Steichen, Hoyningen-Huene, Horst, Man Ray and Cecil Beaton, fashion photography was real art at last, technically perfect and beautifully lit, conveying the ideal realization of the dressmaker's skill and the spirit of the times. Some of the very best fashion drawings ever done were being executed at the same time by artists including Carl Ericsson (Eric), Count René Bouet Willaumez, René Bouché and Christian Bérard, a diabetic and opium addict, a gross, shabby and much-loved figure. Raoul Dufy, Giorgio de Chirico, Pavel Tchelitchew and Salvador Dali enlivened the covers and pages of *Vogue* with their drawings and paintings.

The first Surrealist Exhibition in England was shown in 1936, ten years after the Manifesto. It was greeted with derision. J. B. Priestley gave the reactionary view of the Surrealists when he wrote, 'They stand for violence and neurotic unreason. They are truly decadent. You catch a glimpse behind them of the deepening twilight of barbarism that may soon blot out the sky, until at last

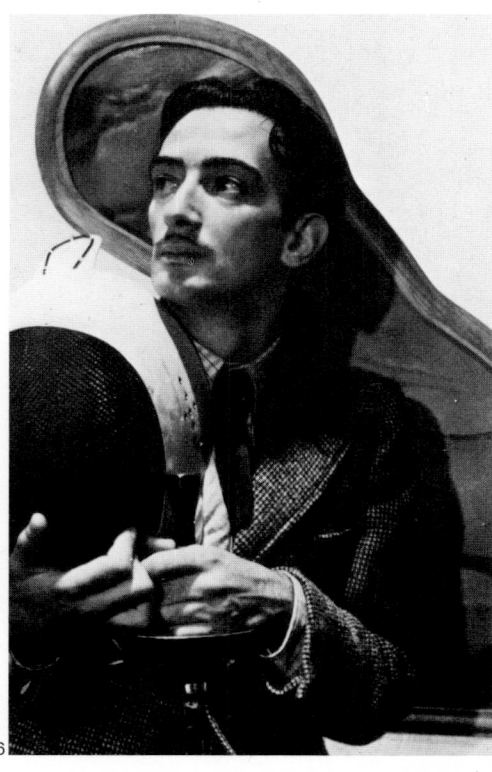

4

5

6

humanity finds itself in another long night . . . There are about too many effeminate or epicene young men, lisping and undulating. Too many young women without manners, balance, dignity . . . Too many people steadily lapsing into shaved and powdered barbarism.' Surrealism was already a familiar thing to most fashion photographers who travelled between London and Paris to work, but the exhibition made it topical and for a few years fashion illustration was dominated by Surrealism – ladies in evening dress carrying their own heads, models coiled in rope or poised by cracked mirrors, others sitting in evening dress with brooms and buckets, or on rubbish heaps. Dr M. F. Agha, Art Editor-in-Chief of *Vogue*, felt it necessary to write an explanatory dialogue: 'No one can tell me exactly what a Surrealist is. Can you?' 'A Surrealist is a man who likes to dress like a fencer, but does not fence; to wear a diving-suit, but does not dive . . . but descends to the lower depths of the subconscious . . . You know the old formula: "Man Bites Dog"? – only in this case the Dog has Paranoia, and the Man is really a couple of other guys.'

7

In a Surrealist film you could see, among other things, a cow sleeping in a Louis XIV salon; a man kicking a blind beggar; a burning tree, a giraffe, and a plough being thrown out of a window. At the end of the first performance of this, the producers were beaten up by the audience. Salvador Dali, who received reporters sitting on top of a desk on top of a bed with a loaf of bread on his head, drew for *Vogue* his Dream House designs for the New York World's Fair in 1939. *Vogue* wrote, 'three live mermaids . . . swim through flexible, rubberoid branches of trees, past long tendrils of typewriters. They swim past a writhing woman, chained to a piano, with the piano keys carved out of her rubberoid stomach . . . On a mammoth bed, a live woman is lying, asleep and dreaming three dreams . . . a double row of grisly, make-believe women, crowned with lobsters and girdled with eels, fades away into the distance.'

In the thirties *Vogue* began to cater for the mass fashion market. The technical improvements in fashion illustration showed the reader and the ready-to-wear manufacturers alike what to aim for, and sometimes how to cut: at first, designers had been anxious that too-accurate photography could give away their secrets. The models looked as glossy and perfect as film stars, and made women want to copy their hair and make-up. The magazine helped readers

directly by a concerted effort to show how to go about dressing fashionably with a limited amount of money, breaking down the given sum for essentials and accessories, leaving a margin for a beauty treatment, and adding it up neatly at the end. There was a 'Bargain of the Fortnight', and 'The Well Spent Pound', with an actual investigation into working girls' wardrobes at the end of the thirties: 'Some of the smartest girls we know turn themselves out on about £50 a year' . . . 'Business girls – they don't earn much – perhaps £5 a week. They perch on stools in snack bars for lunch. They save their pennies. That they can be well dressed is a miracle of England's ready-to-wear.' Suits for 6 gns., and dresses with coats for $8\frac{1}{2}$ gns., began to appear from Fenwick and Jaeger, classic coats with 'nothing to date them' from Aquascutum and Harrods, and Vogue Patterns were devised for everything from cotton evening dresses to knitting instructions for sweaters to go under wartime uniforms. When war was finally announced *Vogue* missed an issue and then got into wartime gear with monthly, instead of fortnightly issues, to comply with government regulations. *Vogue Beauty Book* and *Vogue House and Garden Book* were incorporated, and Pattern Double Numbers stepped up. 'Our policy is to maintain the standards of civilisation . . . We dedicate our pages to the support of important industries, to the encouragement of normal activities, to the pursuit of an intelligent and useful attitude

Steichen

to everyday affairs – and a determined effort to bring as much cheer and charm into our present life as is possible.' The first stern moral judgments – 'It's your job to spend gallantly, dress decoratively, be groomed immaculately – in short, to be a sight for sore eyes' – and condemnations of open-toed sandals in the city and women slopping about in slacks – 'Slack, we think, is the word' – gave way to talk about National Service work, blackouts, all-night canteens and cocktail-bar shelters, with an ever-increasing emphasis on practical inexpensive fashion. 'Brisk Action on the Mayfair Front' was a communiqué on the war activities of the designers – Stiebel was now a river policeman, Hardy Amies in the fire brigade, Dennis Glenny in the army, and most houses were opening up mail order departments or sending fitters out to tour the country.

In direct opposition to the effects of the slump on pre-war fashion, there was the irresistible, saturating glamour of American films. If the rich looked to Paris for their new fashions, working girls and the couturiers themselves kept an eye on the movies, 'the most perfect visual medium for the exploitation of fashion and beauty that ever existed'. Formerly the most vulgar dresses and hats of the early Gloria Swanson type, seen at fashion shows, provoked
108

whispers among *Vogue*'s editors of 'Phew! Pretty Hollywood!' but around the late twenties films caught up with fashion. One of the first attempts to reconcile film costume with real life fashion came in 1929, when Chanel was invited to Hollywood. It was a miserable failure. Elegant, contemporary and revolutionary though they were when Chanel designed them, the clothes dated overnight when hems dropped, and films still 'in the can' were suddenly obsolete. Nevertheless, the revolution went on. Stars of great personal chic refused to be dressed like Christmas trees in films, and 'bright young playwrights pointed out that duchesses do not eat breakfast in ballgowns', as Lesley Blanch wrote. Schiaparelli, Marcel Rochas, Molyneux, Alix, Jean Patou and Lanvin all made the trip to Hollywood, but this expensive and clumsy business gradually gave way to reliance on Hollywood's own indigenous and talented designers, the best-known of whom were Adrian and Howard Greer. By 1933 the question 'Who did that look first, Hollywood or Paris?' was inextricable, and *Vogue*, seriously attempting to work it out in a feature called 'Does Hollywood Create?' came to the conclusion that fashion ideas arrive 'by a sort of spontaneous combustion', giving credit for the fashion for page-

4 Steichen

5 Steichen

6

Garbo – hollowed eye sockets and plucked eyebrows
Dietrich – plucked eyebrows and sucked-in cheeks
Joan Crawford – the bow-tie mouth
Tallulah Bankhead – a sullen expression
Mae West – the hourglass figure and an attractive bawdiness
Constance Bennett – a glazed, bandbox smartness
Jean Harlow – platinum hair
Katherine Hepburn – red curls and freckles
Vivien Leigh – gypsy colouring, a glittering combination of white skin, green eyes and dark red hair

boy hair to Garbo, feather boas to Marlene Dietrich, and accolades for a sixth sense about the fashion future to Adrian and Howard Greer, who had to design their costumes months ahead of the release date, and make clothes that would not look outdated at the end of the run, perhaps two years later.

James Laver in *Vogue* called the camera the first 'engine for imposing types of beauty' and pointed out that 'one curious result of the power of the film has been the spread of type-consciousness to classes which have previously known nothing of such conceptions'. Every important film star appeared in *Vogue* and contributed some new look or fashion:

Vogue's models were often recognizable copies of these types of beauty, and in the thirties they were photographed in cinematographic style: in statuesque bias-cut white satin evening dresses draped on sofas beside glass bowls of white tulips, and lit from one side. It was a symptom of the new acceptability of films that *Vogue* took sittings on location out to Elstree studios, and photographed behind the scenes during filming, showing such oddities as a row of girls waiting to go on in Wanger's film *Vogues of 1938* resting their arms in arm stalls, 'necessary precaution against the least wrinkle, the slightest crease'.

109

1. Balenciaga's beautiful neo-Victorian dress in pale blue printed moiré, not in the least obscuring the figure.
2. Bandbox smart Constance Bennett, 1933, one of the most astute film stars where money was concerned. 'If she can't take it with her,' said her sister, Joan Bennett, she won't go'.
3. Carole Lombard in a rose and silver lamé dress by the Hollywood designer Travis Banton. She married Clark Gable and was killed in a plane crash on her way to meet him.
4. The Garbo effect on her contemporaries.

Single-handed, Hollywood evolved make-up from the crude materials of the twenties into the gigantic industry it is today. In 1931 the *Sunday Express* calculated that 1,500 lipsticks were being sold in London shops for every one sold ten years previously. Cosmetics and nail enamel were now sold from all hairdressers, large stores, chemists and Woolworths, and were applied with a skill learnt from the screen and from magazines. 'Glamour is all,' said *Vogue* in 1935, and tried to pin down what it meant: 'We decided it was the quality of illusion, not just personality. After all, Hitler has personality, but you couldn't call him glamorous.' When Adrian wrote about dressing Garbo for *Camille* he said, 'She brought to the sets, with her quality of aloofness, that mystery which is a part of her and a part of the theatre's integral glamour'. Unattainable glamour, embodied in the most famous stars of the thirties, Garbo and Dietrich, was the wistful other side of the threadbare thirties.

Make-up features in *Vogue* in the twenties had been rare and tentative, but in the thirties readers were taught the techniques of the stars point by point. In 'Seven Steps to Stardom', a beauty feature in January 1938, an ordinary looking girl is transformed into a 'Glamour Girl': first, a foundation of greasepaint over the face, with a streak of darker greasepaint narrowing the jaw, then blended eye shadows hollowing the eyes. Eyebrow pencil fines the browline, powder and rouge are brushed on and off again with a soft brush, lashes are blackened with mascara and thickened with artificial eyelashes. Finally, the mouth is defined with a pencil line and filled in with lipstick or lip rouge. In this way, glamour was thoroughly analysed and its effects calculated. When *Vogue* asked George Gershwin what he noticed first about a woman, he gave an answer typical of the new attitude:

> At 40 paces – her shape
> At 25 paces – her ankles and shoes
> At 10 paces – her face
> At 8 paces – her eyes
> At 5 paces – her mouth
> At no paces – her conversation.

Marlene Dietrich   Juliette Compton   Anna Sten   Tallulah Bankhead

Imported together with Hollywood innovations like false finger-nails and eyelashes – which had to be applied separately with glue – there was the new slang, assimilated just as readily. *Vogue* first used the adjective 'sexy' to describe an evening dress in 1936, the year of Lesley Blanch's first article as features editor of *Vogue*. Called 'On dit – and how!', it incorporated the new American expressions and described the new tone of voice. 'Mayfair is quite "sold" on American slang, and you have only to enter any one of these drawing rooms to be engulfed in a spate of transatlanticisms, which describe "swell guys" as being "the tops" or, its equivalent, "the Camembert"; "swell gals" as being "pretty smooth"; any variety of pleasures as "easy to take"; while the finer shades of pathos and bathos are now familiar to us as "sob-stuff" or "the jerkers". "Am I right, or am I *right*?" as they would phrase it.'

Hollywood films of the thirties followed the pattern of the De-pression and the New Deal. The first years of the Depression brought in Frankenstein and Dracula, followed by the realistic gangster film, Hollywood's attempt to attract an increasingly critical audience. Based on headline news stories, these ran straight into opposition from legions and clubs like the Daughters of the American Revolution, who objected that villains like Edward G. Robinson in *Little Caesar* had been turned into heroes, and who took offence at Spencer Tracy's words in *Quick Millions*: 'I'm too nervous to steal, too lazy to work . . . a man's a fool to go into legitimate business when you can clean up by applying business methods to organizing crime.' The 'confession' film, about girls who had traded on sex in the past and were trying to live it down, was almost as objectionable to moral America. In the purge that followed, film companies fell over backwards to comply with the Hays Office new Production Code. Jean Harlow's new film *Born to be Kissed* was changed in a moment of panic to *100 Per Cent Pure*, then more soberly renamed *The Girl from Missouri*. Hollywood then turned with relief to a sweeter and safer day. Films based on Dickens, Louisa May Alcott and Barrie brought to the screen Victorian life seen through a mist of nostalgia. The New Deal also brought in family films, musical spectaculars and screwball comedies.

Hoyningen-Huene

Neo-Victorianism was a major influence in the thirties. Victorian revivals like Dumas' *Lady of the Camellias* and Wilde's *The Importance of Being Earnest* were very popular on the stage, and so were modern plays on Victorian subjects like *The Barretts of Wimpole Street*: at one moment, three pseudo-historical plays about the Brontës were running at the same time.

The most successful of all musical, historical and costume shows was C. B. Cochran's 1932 production of Noël Coward's *Cavalcade*, a variety show that evoked the patriotism, security and sentiments of the Victorian age, and which appeared just when a great national effort was being made to overcome the Depression. A cast of 400 was brought up to the stage by six hydraulic lifts. *Vogue* wrote, 'Coming late into the darkened theatre, I was thrust into a world of 1900 . . . one of the actors stepped out in front of the curtain and announced the thrilling news that Mafeking had been relieved . . . the next scene revealed, not the stage, but the audience – a theatre of 1900 going mad over a Boer War victory; the people jumping from box to box, embracing one another; the women throwing fans into the air; the men their coats, ties and hats. The enthusiasm was infectious, and the whole theatre went mad, some people bursting into hysterical sobbing.' Coward said himself at the first night, 'In spite of the troublous times we are living in, it is still a pretty exciting thing to be English.' The British cinema also scored a major success with a historical subject, Alexander Korda's *The Private Life of Henry VIII* with Charles Laughton, followed by *Catherine the Great* with Flora Robson. There was a vogue for slashed and padded sleeves, velvet Tudor halos, shallow boaters with ribbon streamers as worn by Katherine Hepburn in *Little Women*, leg-of-mutton sleeves, and, from Norma Shearer in the film version of *Romeo and Juliet*, the Juliet bob, the Juliet cap, and the long, demure frock of full-skirted velvet with touches of white. The Victorian revival did not stop at clothes: in odd conjunction with functionalism, people were buying Victorian knick-knacks, sprigged curtains and heavy patterned wallpapers.

The movement was reinforced by Queen Elizabeth's own personal taste. With a good old-fashioned Scottish upbringing, she had conservative tastes and a love of daring finery. Dressed by Norman Hartnell, she wore velvet or furred suits, jewellery, flowers in the morning, a picture hat and a long full dress for receptions, and a crinoline for evening – 'full-skirted and décolleté in the Victorian, off-the-shoulder manner', and often in her favourite colour, powder blue. *Vogue* said, 'She is not a "fashionable" woman in the usual sense of the word. Yet her clothes superbly fulfil the two fundamental canons of good dressing. They fit her personality like a glove; and they are brilliantly suited to her way of life.' Her clothes on tour were tremendously admired and enjoyed by the public in France, America and Canada. In 1937 and 1938 every designer had fallen for the fairytale glamour of the sentimental crinoline – Patou, Molyneux, even Chanel, Vionnet and Alix.

The Duchess of Kent, Princess Marina, had lived with her father in Paris, and her sophisticated and innate elegance were Molyneux's best advertisement. *Vogue* drew a comparison between the Duchess and her great-aunt Queen Alexandra: 'There is the same classic purity of line, the same air of aloof elegance: the same charming, vague, rather wry smile: the same coiffure is topped by an identical hat . . . Women scan the papers for the Duchess' confirmation of fashion's newest trends.'

The health movement of the thirties made holiday camps popular, country resorts where campers lived in wooden huts and had their meals provided for them, spending their time walking, sunbathing, playing games and singing around the camp fire. *Vogue* went on location to take photographs round the floodlit Roe-

André Durst 2

Horst

3. 9 August 1939.
4. Princess Marina of Greece, beautiful and elegant in a dress by Molyneux, picture of 1934, the year of her marriage to the Duke of Kent. She set the seal of success on Molyneux's house by buying her trousseau there, and he continued to dress her beautifully in gentle, understated clothes — for instance, suits with fur collars and cuffs, evening dresses of bias satin with draped bateau necklines and ostrich feathers. She never adopted the padded shoulderline of the thirties, but originated many fashions of her own, such as the double pearl choker, the Edwardian hat tipped over the forehead: at George V's Jubilee she looked ravishing in a huge grey straw hat trimmed with grey ostrich feathers. It was criticized by the crowd for hiding half her face.
5. Amy Johnson, Mrs Mollison, in 1936. 'She dresses for record-breaking as if for a lunch date.' Here, on the wing of the B.A. Eagle she flew for the King's Cup.

hampton swimming club, showed playsuits and swimsuits in every summer issue, and advertised the new John Lewis country club, only 35 minutes from Paddington, where members could play tennis and croquet, go punting or swimming, and attend concerts and dances in the evening: 'The total bill for a weekend from Saturday afternoon to Sunday evening need not be more than ten shillings.' Sunbathing, nudism and hiking had all come from Germany at the time of the Weimar Republic, and all through the thirties Austria and Germany were the fashionable places for holidays abroad. Even in August 1939 *Vogue* included an advertisement for the German Railways Information Bureau: 'Germany, Land of Hospitality, offers everything you could wish for your holiday'. The result on fashion was a craze for Tyrolean peasant costume. The *Wandervogel* with his *lederhosen* was the romantic extension of the British hiker with his open-neck shirt, Borotra beret and shorts, and women took to dirndls of bright cheap cotton with a tight bodice, a bib or daisy braces, an apron and a feathered hat. 'The English have adopted the Tyrol as their own,' said *Vogue*, and described the same state of affairs in Paris, where the Princesse de Faucigny-Lucinge (Baba d'Erlanger that was) had just opened a shop selling only Tyrolean beachwear.

Open-air living had made women body-conscious and health-conscious. The slimming crazes of the twenties continued, but with the emphasis on keeping fit. Mrs Syrie Maugham, the decorator,

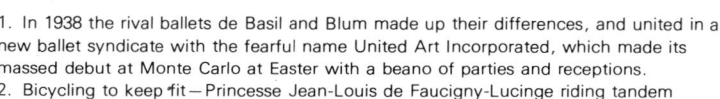

You need young stockings when Gerald tries to tango!

1. In 1938 the rival ballets de Basil and Blum made up their differences, and united in a new ballet syndicate with the fearful name United Art Incorporated, which made its massed debut at Monte Carlo at Easter with a beano of parties and receptions.
2. Bicycling to keep fit – Princesse Jean-Louis de Faucigny-Lucinge riding tandem behind Jacques Février.
3. 'Morley stockings keep the spring of youth', 1937.

was an obsessive dieter. 'Monday. Went to the first of Mrs Maugham's diet lunch parties . . . She decided to devote the first quiet spell to the interests of health and made it known to her friends that any who were feeling the effects of overeating and such a long siege of strenuous partying could come any day to lunch or dine with her on régime food.' Mrs Maugham finally went on the diet of diets. 'I starved for six weeks. Yes, literally, for six weeks I ate nothing at all . . . yet I never missed a day's work and feel better than I can ever remember.' *Vogue* profiled a New York model school in 1938, forerunner of those we know today, with 'Buddha' exercises, book-balancing for poise, lessons in dancing and make-up. People were so geared to keeping fit that the slightest excuse was enough to begin a craze for some particular exercise: when there was a French taxi strike in spring 1936, *Vogue* found 'Tout Paris on Wheels', men in dinner suits bicycling to the opera and women getting special cycling suits made up – Princesse de Faucigny-Lucinge rode tandem in a grey flannel shorts suit. The craze spread to the country, where country house stables were being filled up with secondhand bicycles for weekend guests. For those in London who would rather lose a few inches lying prone, Elizabeth Arden devised a warm paraffin Pack Treatment. The most popular way to get thin and healthy in the thirties was by dancing, and *Vogue* recommended tap lessons with Bunny Bradley, 'where Mr Cochran sends all his Young Ladies to be finished', and ballet with

Marie Rambert – together with a caution about taking it too seriously if you were already in your twenties. Zelda Fitzgerald's efforts to reach a professional standard when she was long past the ballet beginner age had contributed to her breakdown.

In 1936 Wilder Hobson wrote in *Vogue*, 'Swing is the musical fashion of the hour. Not to know the work of such swing artists as Thomas "Fats" Waller and Jack "Big Gate" Teagarden (gate meaning the ability to swing) is to confess such a dowdiness as would have been shown some years ago by someone who supposed the rumba to be one of the larger vertebrae. Judging by the heavy white-tie and Schiaparelli attendance at such New York swing saloons as the Onyx Club, swing music has penetrated the ritziest circles. It is even robust enough to appeal to Ernest Hemingway.' On liners, in the new Dorchester and the Savoy, down at the Locarno in Streatham, or even at home with the radiogram, people dressed up to the nines and danced all night to the smooth, glamorous sound of the big bands with their ranks of trumpets, clarinets and drums. The big bands, like some of the big cinemas, included crooners, tap dancers and showgirls in their performances, and teams of virtuosi would get to their feet and take the lead, playing extempore. Idols of the cinema audiences and best-loved of all the dancers in the dancing thirties – apart from the dazzling teenage Margot Fonteyn – were Fred Astaire and Ginger Rogers, one of whose most popular films was *The Castles*, about the earlier

Schenker

4. Fred Astaire in May 1939, when he was making
The Castles, a film about the earlier famous
dancers, with Ginger Rogers.
5. Summer fashion for staff, 1936, from Moss Bros.
6. The Big Apple, forerunner of jitterbug.

dancers Vernon and Irene Castle, *Vogue*'s heroine of the magazine's first decade. But whoever you were, you had to have rhythm. In the words of Irving Berlin's song, played by Jimmie Lunceford's band in 1937,

> He ain't got rhythm
> Every night he sits in the house alone.
> 'Cos he ain't got rhythm
> Every night he sits there and wears a frown.
> He attracted some attention
> When he found the fourth dimension,
> But he ain't got rhythm
> So no one's with him
> The loneliest man in town . . .

Louis Armstrong and Duke Ellington came on tour to show how swing should be played, and all the new dances came over from America. In February 1938 a forerunner of jitterbugging arrived in London, called 'The Big Apple' – a Negro euphemism for bottom. It involved lots of steps, including 'Kickin' the Mule', 'Truckin'' and 'Peelin' the Apple'. Lesley Blanch, writing about it in *Vogue*, came to the sad conclusion that the British did not have rhythm. 'Nostalgic university dons and their wives, in white tennis shoes and cross garters hung with little bells, bouncing dankly through the naiveties of Parson's Wedding and Jenny Pluck Pears, cannot be considered to represent the dancing public . . . [They]

go to the Hammersmith Palais de Dance, the Astoria in the Charing Cross Road, the new Paramount in Tottenham Court Road . . . to dance to first class bands of the Henry Hall and Roy Fox kidney, for 1*s.* 6*d.* in the afternoon and 2*s.* 6*d.* in the evening . . . the Big Apple demands a complete unselfconsciousness, which is not our national forte.'

The thirties changed the style of living and entertaining. People with town houses who had kept two or three servants now had only a cook. They closed up their basements, used the breakfast room as a kitchen, added a bath on the first floor and lived more or less as if they were in a flat. Cocktail parties turned into snack dinners. 'One has a sandwich, a whisky-and-soda, and goes in for a good supper after the play. I wonder if dinner is disappearing from our social scheme of life?' wondered *Vogue* in 1932. A few years later, even grand dinner parties turned out simpler food. 'Nobody has grand food any more . . . at Lady Colefax, we ate macaroni with cream and cheese, lamb with mint sauce, potato croquettes and spinach, and apple charlotte.' Reflecting the economical mood of the times, the thirties failed to produce any sensational new ideas for house decoration other than lighting, which was much improved by indirect lights and opaque bowls set directly into the ceiling or walls, and by the introduction of 'Anglepoise' reading lamps. The photographer Hoyningen-Huene mentioned the importance of good lighting when he was asked about the new Brick Top premises he

had been asked to decorate in Paris: 'I am going to light up the cabaret so that, after midnight, it will be becoming to middle-aged people who are slightly under the influence of liquor.' Schiaparelli's London flat was furnished entirely from John Lewis – 'It is so smart, so right and so practical' – with unpainted wood tables, rush-seat stools and armchair and divan covered in an unpatterned glazed chintz at 2s. 11d. a yard. Chanel's house in Menton was also the 'essence of simplicity, without superfluous furniture. But what there is is in the most perfect of its kind: old oak tables, chests, and cupboards, and in the airy bedrooms old Italian beds.'

Some of the best parties of the thirties are described by Cecil Beaton in his 'Social Scene' column. There were mystery parties like the one at which the footmen carried in a trunk, and everyone was asked to guess who was inside. The trunk was opened and a lady stepped out in a mask, scarf, heavy gloves and high boots. Mrs Michael Arlen guessed right: it was Gaby Morlay, the French actress. There were musical parties, like the one where Serge Lifar kicked off his shoes, leapt onto the piano and performed an impromptu dance. There was a craze for Victorian games like musical chairs, blindman's buff, and bobbing for apples – in 1932 'the latter game went out of favour very quickly as none of the women would risk losing their new eyelashes'. Most popular and exciting of all were the Scavenger parties started by Mrs Marshall Field in London and immediately copied by Elsa Maxwell. Dinner guests were given a list of things to obtain, and the one who collected most between ten and midnight won. Here is Elsa Maxwell's list:

E. J. Mason

One red bicycle lamp
One cooked sausage
One live animal other than a dog
One swan from the Bois de Boulogne
One slipper worn by Mistinguette that night
One handkerchief belonging to the Baron Maurice de Rothschild

O'Doyé

One hat from Mrs Reginald Fellowes
One live Duchess
One autographed photograph of royalty signed that night
One red stocking
One *Metro* ticket
One mauve comb
Three red hairs
One pompom from a sailor's hat
The cleverest man in Paris

That night, Mistinguette came offstage to find her dressing room ransacked and all her shoes gone. The next day, they were returned tied to flowering trees and bunches of white orchids.

Elsa Maxwell gave *Vogue* her seven rules for a good party. Ruthlessness – no lame ducks, no churchmen, no financiers or diplomats. Never let guests do what they want – guests never want to do what they want. Cram them into one room, which should be too small for the number invited. Light that room brilliantly. Never show any anxiety. Try to incur some opposition so that people take sides. Keep up plenty of noise. 'I once gave a party in a room too cold and cavernous ... so I hastily procured some beehives and, successfully concealing them in the room, the ears of the guests were assailed by a pleasant buzzing during lulls in the music.'

One of the wittiest parties was given by Miss Olga Lynn, at which guests were asked to come as a well-known book or play. Lady Eleanor Smith was *Vile Bodies*, Evelyn Waugh came as Wyndham Lewis's new book which was so expensive no one could afford it, Tallulah Bankhead was *The Open Book*, and Lord Knebworth, 'who sported a photograph of a Very August Pair', was *The Good Companions*.

In summer 1938 Lady Mendl gave a huge circus party, on Gatsby proportions. The hostess, in aquamarines, diamonds and a white organdie Mainbocher, was the ringmaster in the tan-bark ring,

Schall

with acrobats in satin and paillettes, ponies and clowns. Guests danced on a special composition dance floor under which there were millions of tiny springs, so that it gently heaved up and down with the rhythm. Constance Spry sent three aeroplanes of roses from London to Paris for the party, and in different parts of the garden three orchestras played jazz, Cuban rumbas and Hungarian waltzes. Concealed lighting turned the garden into a dream landscape with marble statues, fountains and urns of cut flowers ... For most of the people there, it was the last party.

1. Chanel's Riviera villa at Cap Martin, almost bare of furniture.
2. Schiaparelli's London flat, 1934, painted very pale blue and furnished from John Lewis. Here, her bare and simple dressing table with very good lighting.
3. 'Country costume at a ball in the Bois', 1931: the market gardeners' entry, Cole Porter in the cart with his wife and Princess Ilyinsky.
4. French chaperones, 1935. Three mothers appraise the débutantes.
5. Lady Mendl. As Elsie de Wolfe, the decorator, she is said to have been responsible for making America antique-conscious. She made a fortune in America, which she spent on her houses and her fantastic entertainments, bringing what Cecil Beaton calls 'the ruthlessness of a company director' to their planning and organization. She invented a cross-filing system so that her guests never had the same menu or sat next to the same people. 'When a new sandwich proved to be successful, she would dictate a memorandum that it must be photographed for *Vogue*.' She became better looking as she grew older, by dieting, facial surgery and by adopting pale blue hair, which later she allowed to grow white.

Nickolas
Murray

117

THE CHANGING FACE

THE DUCHESS OF WINDSOR

The Duchess, formerly Mrs Wallis Simpson, exemplified the crispest, neatest, hardest looks for the 30s. Even then, when every girl tried to look neat, she was described as looking strict and governessy. Never less than immaculate, she wore her hair parted in the centre, waved over the ears and pinned in a flat chignon at the back. Flattened to the head, it was brilliantined for shine, framing her clearcut features under a smart hat. She dressed first at Schiaparelli, wearing her white trouser suits in the South of France and her printed dresses in town, then turned to Mainbocher for her trousseau. He dressed her in slim crepes softened with a drape or a bow neck, in narrow bias evening dresses shined with sequins. In 1947 she was quick to adopt Christian Dior's New Look.

Man Ray

MAINBOCHER

1. 1935.
2. Honeymoon photograph at Wasserleonburg, 1937.
3. 1937.

PRINCESS NATALIE PALEY

Daughter of the Grand Duke Paul of Russia, she married Lucien Lelong whose clothes helped her become one of the best dressed beauties of the 30s. In 1935 she went to Hollywood to star in *Les Folies Bergères*, and later married again becoming Mrs Jack Wilson.

2 LELONG   Steichen

3 LELONG   Hoyningen-Huene

1. In Lelong's ermine-trimmed black crepe, 1930.
2. Dressed by Lelong, 1928: grey cloth coat, fox collar, grey-beige crepe dress, grey felt hat by Maria Guy.
3. In Lelong's stripes, Maria Guy's white hat, 1931.

Hoyningen-Huene

IYA, LADY ABDY
Wife of Sir Robert Abdy, a famous Russian
beauty with ash-blonde gently curling hair and
a prominent upper lip, over six feet tall.

1. Her new hairstyle, 1933, with a gold Alice band.
2. White feathers, 1932.

Dorothy Wilding

THE MORGAN TWINS
The much-publicized Morgan twins, identical except for a
small scar under Thelma's chin, from roller-
skating when she was a child. Thelma,
Viscountess Furness, left, was an escort of the
Prince of Wales, and introduced him to Mrs
Ernest Simpson; Gloria married Reginald
Vanderbilt. This year, 1932, marked the height
of the fashion for emphasized and
artificial eyelashes.

Hoyningen-Huene

1 SCHIAPARELLI   Cecil Beaton

MARLENE DIETRICH

Perfection of her type, Dietrich is the daughter of a Prussian policeman, born in December 1901 — 'Just say I'm 75 and let it go at that.' She originally wanted to be a concert violinist, but auditioned for Reinhardt and joined his drama school in 1921. Von Sternberg discovered her in Berlin for Lola in *The Blue Angel*, the film that made her famous. She dismissed her 17 previous films before Sternberg as 'nothing'. He said of her, 'To exhaust her is not possible'. When she first appeared in a man's suit and beret Paris booed her — and later, copied her. Her other contributions to women's looks: sucked-in cheeks and plucked eyebrows.

1. The epitome of glamour in Schiaparelli's Russian furs, 1936.
2. 1937.

TRAVIS BANTON   Steichen   121

1. Cock feather boa and dress by Schiaparelli, 1932.
2. In a tiered lace dress, possibly Fortuny's, 1917.
3. At the Duff Coopers' in Paquin's negligée, 1941.

SCHIAPARELLI   Hoyningen-Huene

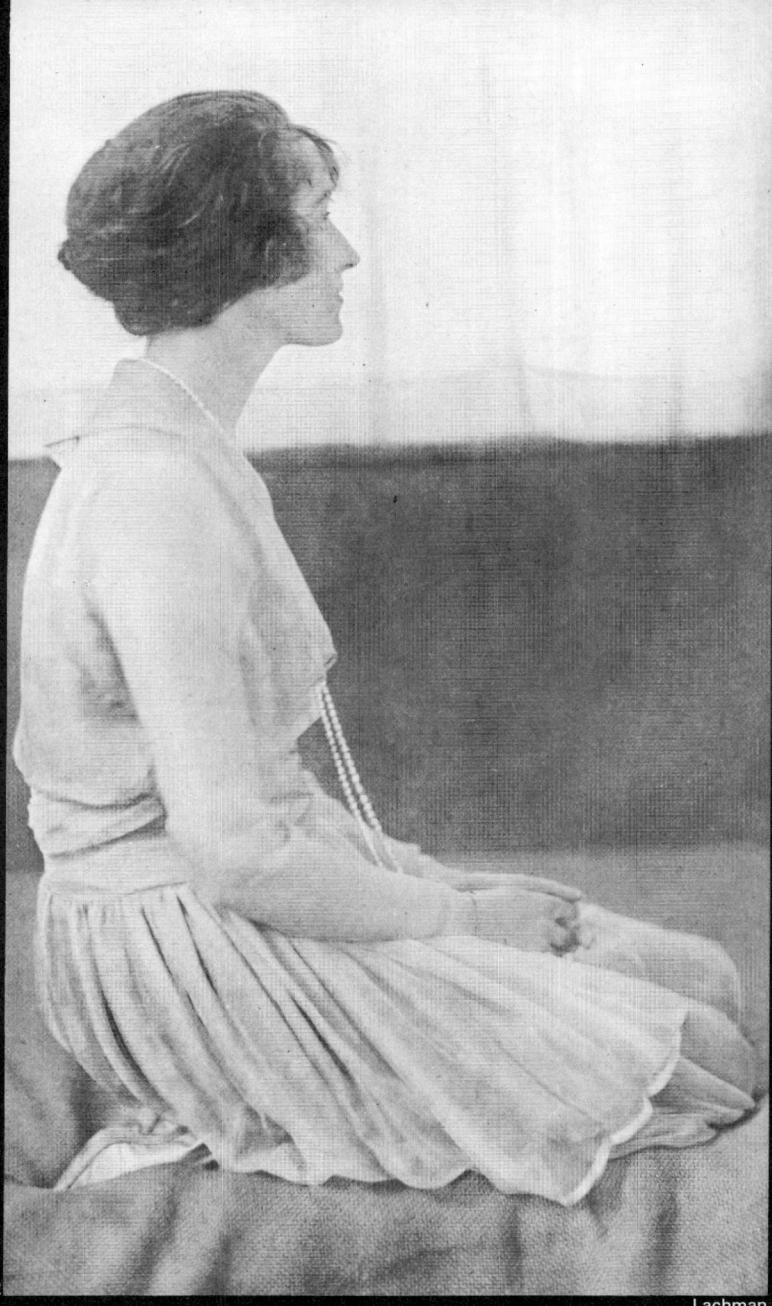

2   Lachman

3   PAQUIN   Cecil Beaton

THE HON. MRS REGINALD FELLOWES

Daisy Fellowes, formerly Princess Jean de Broglie, daughter of the Duc Decazes, was popularly known as the best-dressed woman in the world. Half American and half French, she was known for a brilliant studied simplicity, described by Cecil Beaton as a 'scrubbed classical look, an unparalleled air of slickness, trimness and cleanness . . . she had the air of having just come off a yacht, which she very likely had'. She enjoyed undercutting fashion, making other women look foolishly overdressed. She wore the same simple dress perpetually, cut in different colours of silk for evenings, linen for day. At Ascot, she appeared hatless; for an appearance at Court, where it was the custom to wear a long white dress, she drummed up a dead relative and wore a short black dress. Just before Paris was occupied, she escaped with her husband and daughter to London, where she settled down in the basement of the Duff Coopers' Westminster house, making a dining room out of the servants' hall and a bedroom out of the cellar. In 1941 she became the first President of the new Incorporated Society of London Fashion Designers, a job for which she was uniquely suited.

JOAN CRAWFORD

Hollywood star whose prolonged career began with
Our Modern Maidens in 1929. She gave the second
half of the thirties a fashion that was almost universal —
the crimson bow-tie mouth.

1. In Vionnet's white taffeta, 1938.
2. 1939.

Gertrude Lawrence's wardrobe by Molyneux for *Private Lives* sums up the day and evening looks of the year — fur-trimmed tweeds and a bias evening dress of panelled white satin. Everything she wears comes into general fashion, her beret, her tie and shirt, her open blazer, even her way of smoking a cigarette. Women use magnifying mirrors to make up their faces, with blue eyeshadow, blue or black mascara, pencilled and brilliantined plucked eyebrows. Hair is a little longer, but rolled up or curled at the back of the neck.

All skirts begin from a moulded or draped hip-yoke and flare to the calf of the leg. The best sellers are the light caped jersey dresses and the self-patterned jersey suits. Inside plain suits go the new lingerie blouses, printed chiffon with scarf necks, or silks with tucking and openwork. Dark dresses have white collars and cuffs, yokes and revers, in piqué, satin, or crepe. The new afternoon dress drops the hem nearly to the ankle, in draped wrapover crepe or chiffon, with a well-indicated waist and a full flared skirt.

For Ascot, you dress according to the weather. If it's bad, a frock of black satin with a white collar, a satin cardigan lined in white. If it's dull, a beige crepe with dipping skirt and fox-edged cape. If it's fine, a flowered chiffon to the ground with a big brimmed straw hat and gloves to the elbows.

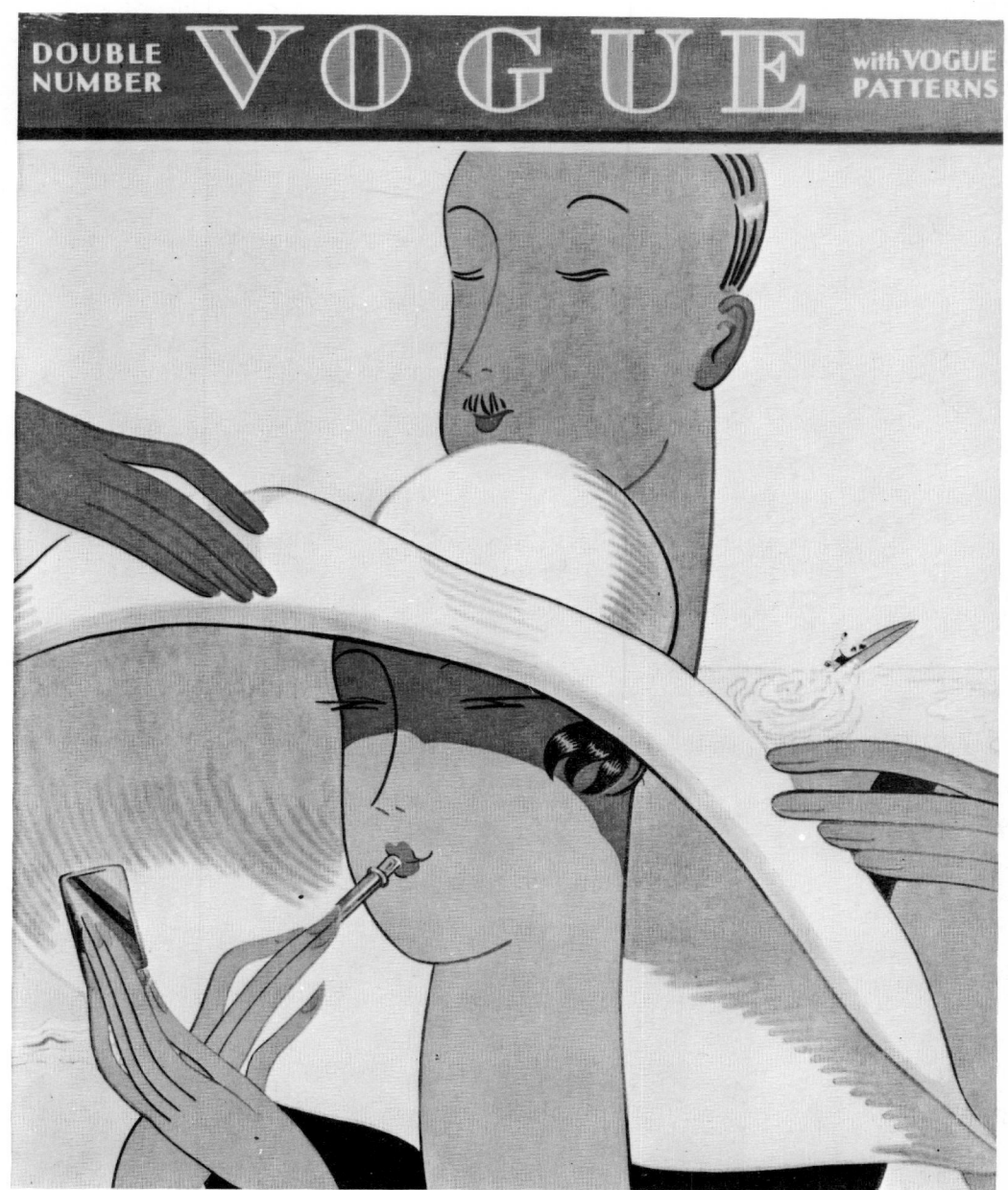

Cover, May 1930.

Left: White satin by Vionnet, 1939.

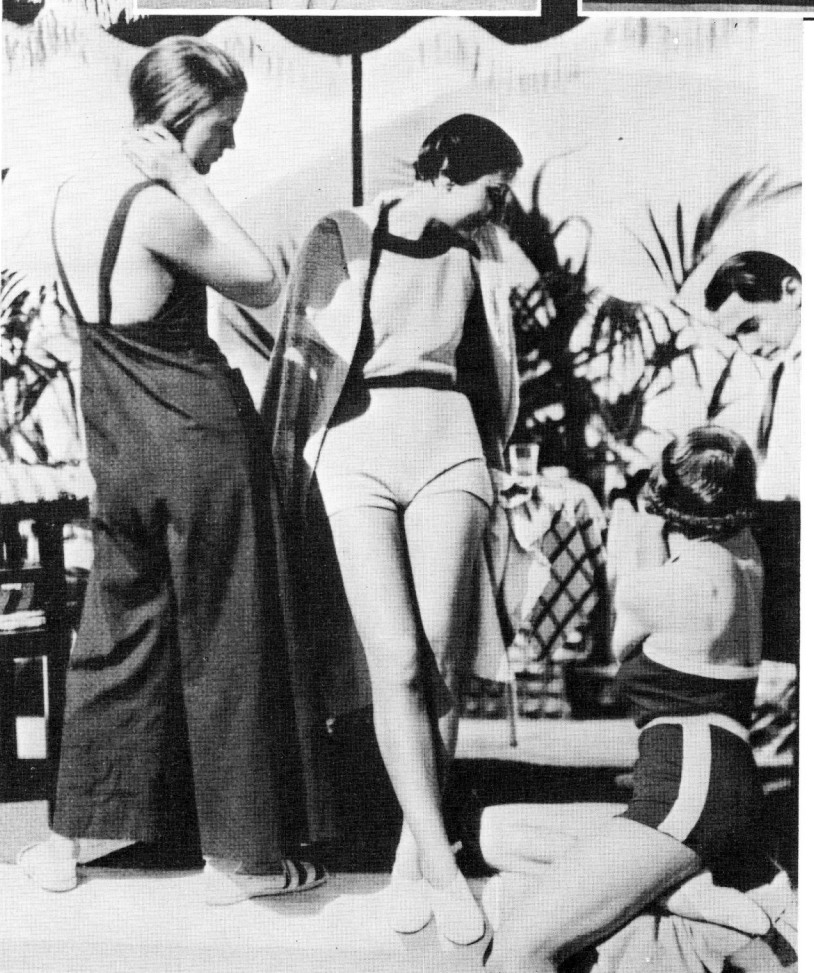

Hoyningen-Huene

1. The Maudie Littlehampton silhouette.
2. Vionnet's silk crepe afternoon dress, black and grège print, crossed and knotted at the waist.
3. Schiaparelli's black and white diagonal tweed, white shantung shirt buttoned onto the skirt.
4. Beach trousers and hand-knitted bathing suits.
5. Evening dresses by Vionnet in velvet cut to fall straight as columns when not in motion; photograph Steichen.
6. 'All smart hair is longer, but long hair is not smart.' Shoulder-length permed hair in a flat rolled chignon. Black lace dress by Chanel.
7. Motoring clothes: the biscuit tweed coat and skirt, with sleeveless woollen sweater and gaiters, cost 15½gn, together from Gamages.
8. Suit with pale top and dark skirt.

6

Steichen

8

VIONNET

Steichen

7

Howard and Joan Coster

1931

'Caught in the act of making up to beauty' with Pond's preparations.   Steichen

'There is more than an emphasis placed on natural feminine lines. There is exaggeration'

Clothes begin to broaden the shoulders and nip in the waist: skirts mould the hips and fall into flowing pleats. Shoes get higher heels, and late in the year the waist rises. Women are wearing their hair a little longer, but pressed close to the head to accommodate the essential new hat. The tilted mercury pierced with a quill introduces a wealth of original hats. Full length dresses or suits are worn for a formal tea, for the cinema and going out to dinner.

Fashion is swayed by two opposing influences. The financial situation is making itself felt, and *Vogue* writes about 'the new economy' and advertises *Vogue Patterns* on the cover: among the readers who send for them are Gloria Swanson and Moira Shearer. For the first time cheap washable fabrics are used for grand occasion clothes — Chanel shows a collection of 35 cotton evening dresses. Zips and the increasing sales of artificial silk make clothes cheaper. On the other hand, Hollywood sets a standard of sumptuous luxury. Women who can afford couture clothes take their lead from Paris, but the great cinema-going public copy the dresses and gowns of the screen stars. *Vogue* fills its pages with slinky cinema satins from Paris and the London shops, and takes location pictures in the Elstree studios.

A new designer opens in Paris. Mainbocher, formerly an American fashion artist and fashion editor of French *Vogue,* shows a new moulded sheath-dress and some intricately cut faille. Later, he will make his name by dressing Mrs Wallis Simpson. Lady Furness is spotted at Ciro's in a white dress, black pearls, and rings worn over her elbow-length matt black gloves. Daisy Fellowes in Paris sets a fashion for fresh flowers by wearing a daisy chain to a party, and her daughter Diana wears a Sam Browne belt of gardenias.

2 REVILLON

Cecil Beaton

1. White satin Court dress by Madame Hayward,
   who specializes in dresses for presentation.
2. Jeanne Stuart, 'one of the blonde hopes of the
   English stage', in Revillon's white satin pyjama suit.
3. Flannels and white wool shirt from Lillywhites.
4. Cinema satins. *Vogue* coins the phrase 'poured in'
   to describe the fit of a sheath dress.

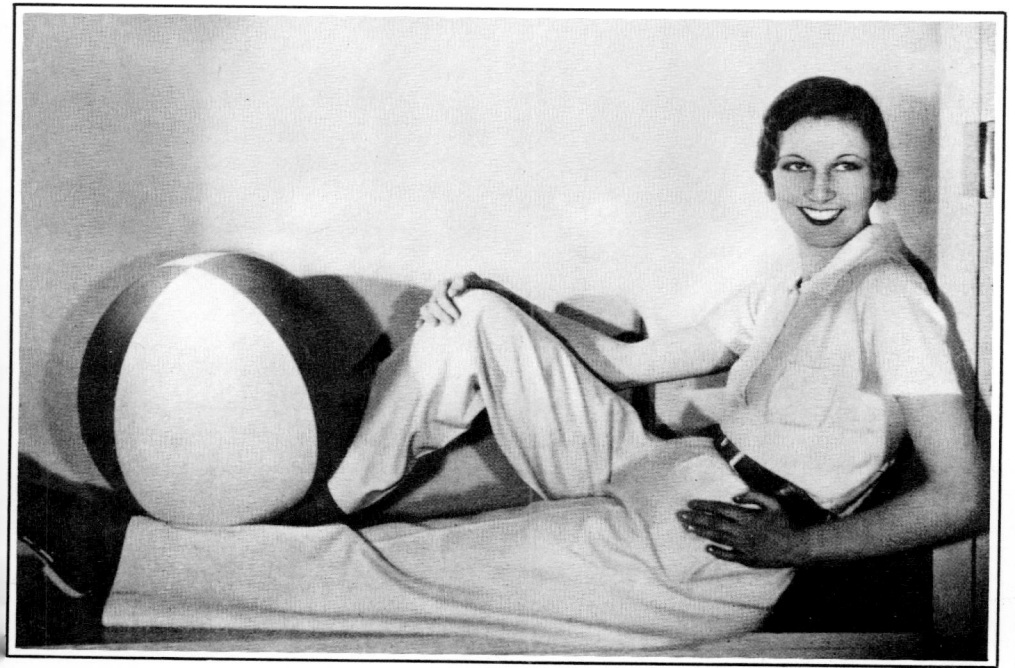

Lee Miller

4 HEIM

Hoyningen-Huene

1931

1
MAINBOCHER

2

Eric

3

Eric

1. *Left*, black and white coat cut like a jacket and
skirt, and, *right*, black rep dress.
2. The waistline rises in the autumn. Vionnet's
blouse and skirt.
3. English tweeds from the London ready to wear.
4. 'How to ruin a good dress' and wear it right,
demonstrated by Bea Lillie and photographed by Steichen.
5. Draped evening dresses in chiffon, point-de-
Venise and washable organdie.

HOW TO RUIN a GOOD DRESS

SHE critically surveys her new evening gown and then decides that the whole thing looks a little too plain. So she dresses it up a bit with a few long strands of imitation pearls. Her simple coiffure strikes her as unexciting, so she nips a ducky little clip in just where it shows to greatest advantage. At the last minute, her best young man sends her a massive shoulder spray, heavy with tin-foil, resplendent with changeable taffeta ribbons, and she pins that on too, pulling the décolletage regrettably askew.

Finally, someone tells her she is a *femme fatale*. She is enchanted and buys long glittering earrings, a diadem of brilliants for her hair, and giant court shoe-buckles, from under which peep coquettish wisps of tulle. To all this splendour, she adds a massive coral beaded bag, which swings from a long chain. One does not need to see to know that in due time she will produce from that bag a long chiffon handkerchief of the tie-and-die variety and a very long cigarette holder. Alone and unaided, she has ruined a good dress.

SUZANNE TALBOT   Hoyningen-Huene   5
                                                           CHANEL

131

1932-33

'A sock on your head and your chic on your sleeve'

Focus on the raised waist, emphasized by widened, heavier shoulders, means wearing a corset that pulls in the waist again — the new ones are two way stretch. The architectural V from shoulders to small fitted waist and, a mirror reflection, the flare of the skirt from the top of the hipbones, lends itself to a new fashion for stripes used on the bias. Now that zips can be set invisibly into seams, buttons are used for decoration, on revers and jabots, pockets and belts.

The big news story is Chanel's ciré satin cinema suit, but Schiaparelli's follies steal the limelight. She uses copper clamps for buttons, makes felt socks for hats that are copied everywhere, shellacs and lacquers sculptured hairdos, dusts evening hair with phosphorescent powder, and invents a short-lived, odd fashion for bustles added to backless evening dresses.

High necks and bows balance the tipped small hats or the basque berets, and the hat of hats to wear with ankle-length skirts after four o'clock is the big-brimmed sailor. Sweaters come up in the world and appear in town . . . 'the sweater has crashed even into late afternoon society'. They are brief and fitted, in everything from transparent silk to grocery string, with eyelets, rib textures and knots, puff sleeves and tied necklines. Chanel designs a ready-to-wear sweater collection for Harvey Nichols.

For evening, heavy crepes and dull satins give the flowing, folding, draping dresses their most statuesque quality yet. Boleros with puff sleeves take off to reveal bare backs, necklines in front going right up to the neck. This 'backward' movement shows up again in day clothes, with cowl-backed jackets rising behind the nape of the neck.

Hollywood's influence is at its strongest. Models wear bright lipstick like Joan Crawford's, and shadowed eyes. There is a fashion for artificial eyelashes, but it is confined to the

leisurely since they must be applied individually in a beauty salon, taking almost an hour an eye. *Vogue* reports on Garbo in man's evening dress and on the new designs by Adrian for films.

Three designers make their first appearance in *Vogue* — Teddy Tinling, Victor Stiebel and Charles James, whose influence on the ready-to-wear trade is immediately apparent.

Summer holiday fashions are set in

Saint Tropez, where clothes are beginning to be noticed for their theatricality. Madame Jeanne Duc, the modiste wife of the proprietor of l'Escale, does a line in little straw hats decorated with ribbons and fruit, Vachon (still in Saint Tropez) sells printed Provençal handkerchiefs for sunbathers to tie like boleros over their bathing suits, and Guy Baer sells original knitted sweaters.

2 AUGUSTABERNARD   Ben

3 SCHIAPARELLI

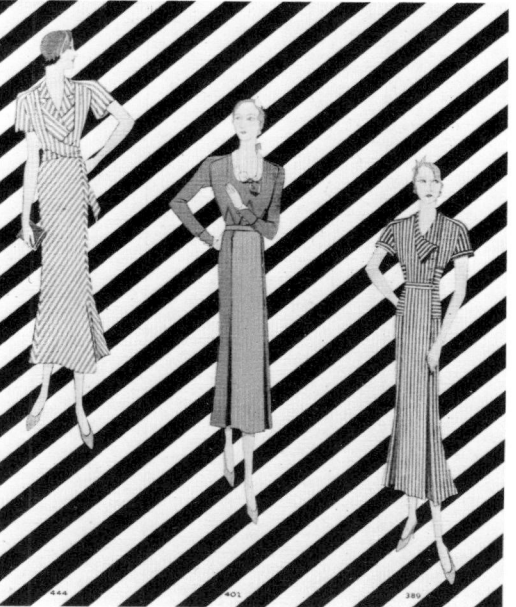

Hoyningen-Huene

1. For afternoon bridge, Rose Amado dress of green silk flecked with gold lamé and the new velvet bridge hat.
2. Augustabernard promoted the long narrow look for day and evening: here, pansy-purple crepe and blue fox boa.
3. Sports suit, grey and yellow tweed jacket, high necked blouse in silk jersey stiffened with yellow taffeta. First picture of the new Tyrolean hat.
4. Red and white spotted crepe de chine dress with a bodice cape by Mainbocher.
5. English spun silk 'washing frocks' in fashionable stripes.

1
LANVIN

Hoyningen-Huene

Dorothy Wilding

3
CHANEL

Cecil Beaton SCHIAPARELLI

5

1. Lanvin's beautiful new idea for evening: a shell-pink satin blouse wrapped and tied around a high-waisted black satin skirt.
2. The belted 1932 suit as worn by Miss Margaret Whigham, later Duchess of Argyll. She was the first debutante to organize her own publicity. She was charming to the press, gave press conferences, and naturally had flattering press coverage and was agreed to be the beauty of the year.
3. Blue and white plaid dress in British artificial silk.
4. Schiaparelli's bustle. . . . 'that new and much-talked of padding that juts out like a shelf just below a square-cut décolletage': maroon satin jersey.
5. New notions in summer bags, 1933.

7 VICTOR STIEBEL   Hoyningen-Huene

6. The 1933 look — Hollywood make up, sheer stockings
and high heels: advertisement for Kira silk stockings.
7. Victor Stiebel red, white and green striped chiffon for
Ascot Gold Cup Day.
8. The longer the skirt, the higher the heels: shoe
designs, 1933.
9. The cowl-backed silhouette, here in Lanvin's
astrakhan cape.

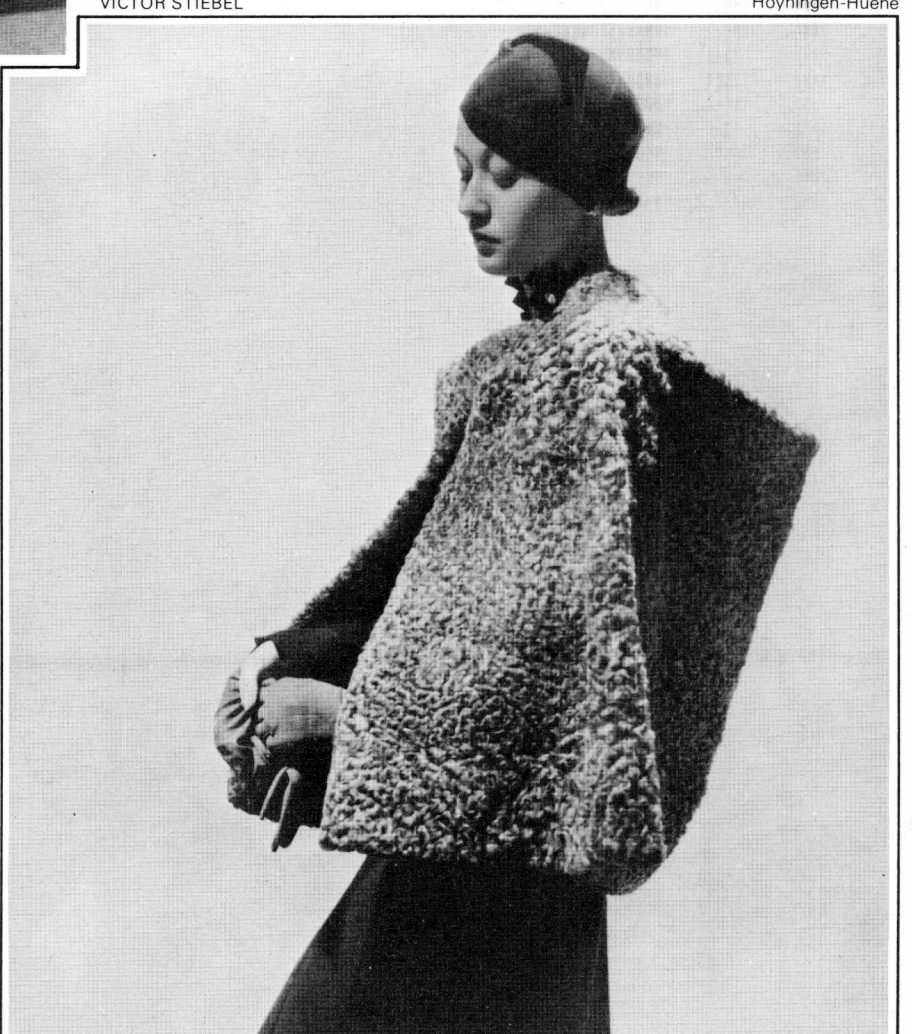

9 LANVIN   Hoyningen-Huene

Cecil Beaton

2 CHANEL   Cecil Beaton

1. The basque beret as worn by Dietrich: *left to right,* Agnès, Rose Descat, Agnès.
2. Mrs Marshall Field in a satin cinema suit.
3. Chanel designs ready to wear sweaters for Harvey Nichols.
4. Charles James's 12gn. spring suit in marine blue face-cloth. Raglan-sleeved top gathered onto a belt and the neck twisted with a spotted scarf.
5. The big-brimmed sailor, the hat sensation of 1932. Reboux hat, black crepe ankle-length dress by Lanvin.

4 CHARLES JAMES   Horst   5   Steichen

LOUISE BOURBON

The make-up, the hat, drawn by Eric

'Your very important profile will have the windswept, fleet lines of speedboat or aeroplane'

The look is hard and smart, best seen in profile. Hair blows back and up from an uncluttered hairline, a severe hat cuts across the head at a sharp angle, the lips are a vicious red, the waist is pinched, swagger coats make triangles over thin skirts. Fewer London customers and buyers go to Paris, and in *Vogue* the names Norman Hartnell, Digby Morton, Victor Stiebel and Charles Creed appear frequently. Schiaparelli invents the bird silhouette, with a jutting tail above the bottom. Designers are making the most of man-made fibres and effects — more lamé than ever, Cellophane and anthracite ribbon weaves, paillettes and sequins . . . 'the influence upon dress of this industrial age'. Hats are one-sided, 'giant flat phonograph discs' or pancake berets, and Schiaparelli's new poke bonnet.

Princess Marina's marriage to the Duke of Kent in November gives fashion an authoritative, stylish new heroine. *Vogue* draws her Molyneux trousseau item by item.

Symptom of the passion for rambling and hiking, for sunbathing and nudism, sports clothes become briefer than ever. Bathing suits are often slashed and backless, skirts divide or shrink into shorts. In the summer we see the Tyrolean look, with feathered fishing hats, daisy braces, bibs, aprons, dirndles and tight bodices. This year *Challenge to Death* is published, a book of essays written by leading pacifists.

1934

From Spain

Horst

1

2   SCHIAPARELLI   MAINBOCHER

Hoyningen-Huene

—to the Tyrol

1. Holiday clothes — Schiaparelli's mantilla sunhats, slacks and bathing suit tops.
2. Schiaparelli, *left,* and Mainbocher make the new box jacket part of their autumn collections.
3. Tyrolean outfit worn by Princess Jean de Faucigny-Lucinge (Baba d'Erlanger).
4. *Left,* navy jersey dress with touches of white piqué, *right,* tailored suit of checked tie silk.

ÈRE, JENNY

Hoyningen-Huene

1. Cellophane evening dress 'glistening like a magnificent black scarab', cape lined with black seal: by Alix, who later became Madame Grès.
2. Mainbocher's version of the sashed tunic evening dress in satin and wool.
3. One of the first two-piece bathing suits, Jacques Heim's black and white print sarong suit, with a big-brimmed hat.
4. Schiaparelli's bird silhouette in three spring suits; *left,* winged and tailed.
5. Schiaparelli's new poke bonnet: *Vogue* cover for 31 October 1934.

2 MAINBOCHER   Horst

3
JACQUES HEIM   Horst

4
SCHIAPARELLI

SCHIAPARELLI   Mourgue

VOGUE 1935·36

SCHIAPARELLI   White plaster mask with red feather eyelashes:
Vogue's Christmas cover for 1935.

'The Fashion battle cry of the moment "Aux Armes, Citoyennes!"'
... 'March to the sound of drums by day, dance to the music of lyres by night'

Daytime looks are severe and military, with square epauletted shoulders, frogging, plumed hats, low heels and gauntlet gloves. Schiaparelli leads the military camp with regiments of fitted suits, drummer boy jackets and a forward 'putsch' of hats. Women look 'tidy as tinkers', like Mrs Simpson in her Schiaparellis, with her meticulous grooming and attention to detail. In complete contrast to the soldierly daytime suits, evening dresses are statuesquely Greek or Indian, with Hindu jewellery — heavy carved and gemmed bracelets, rough diamonds fringed with pearls.

In 1936 King George V dies and the Prince of Wales becomes king. Mrs Simpson is still frequently mentioned, the *Queen Mary* is launched, and the *Hindenberg* crosses the Atlantic. On liners and in hotels people are dancing to swing played by the big bands. A new look is the tunic line, pulled tightly in at the waist with a stiff jutting peplum over a narrow skirt that is often of pinpleats tight as crinkled crepe. There are fabric prints of newspaper print, handwriting, radishes, buttons, pigs and matches.

Chanel's suits are gently fitted tweeds with open-neck white shirts, neither musical comedy, like Schiaparelli's, nor drab, like the London house Busvine, which has taken over Reville, with its heavy suits, box jackets, dark stockings and flat shoes.

Fresh air addiction has made women body-conscious and *Vogue's* beauty pages run separate spreads on feet, legs, hands and the figure. Cinema expertise with make-up filters through to the beauty pages, with face-shapers for accentuating the bone structure, red dots opening up the eyes, and red pencil defining the lips.

Schiaparelli's follies of the year: the white plaster mask with red feather eyelashes, black gloves with scarlet finger nails, pockets like bureau drawers, coarse hairnets anchoring pancake hats, tight blue satin trousers showing under the lifted hem of a black evening dress, and a bearskin coat from Iceland, with a wooden mask against snow glare.

'It's no longer smart to be chic,' says *Vogue*. Show the body as a superb piece of sculpture . . . the era of the dressmaker, all bits and pieces and complicated seaming, gives place to that of the mathematician and architect . . . the new London mode is neither streamlined nor sentimental. It is casual, bold, chunky and realistic. Textures rough rather than smooth: colours subtly coordinated.'

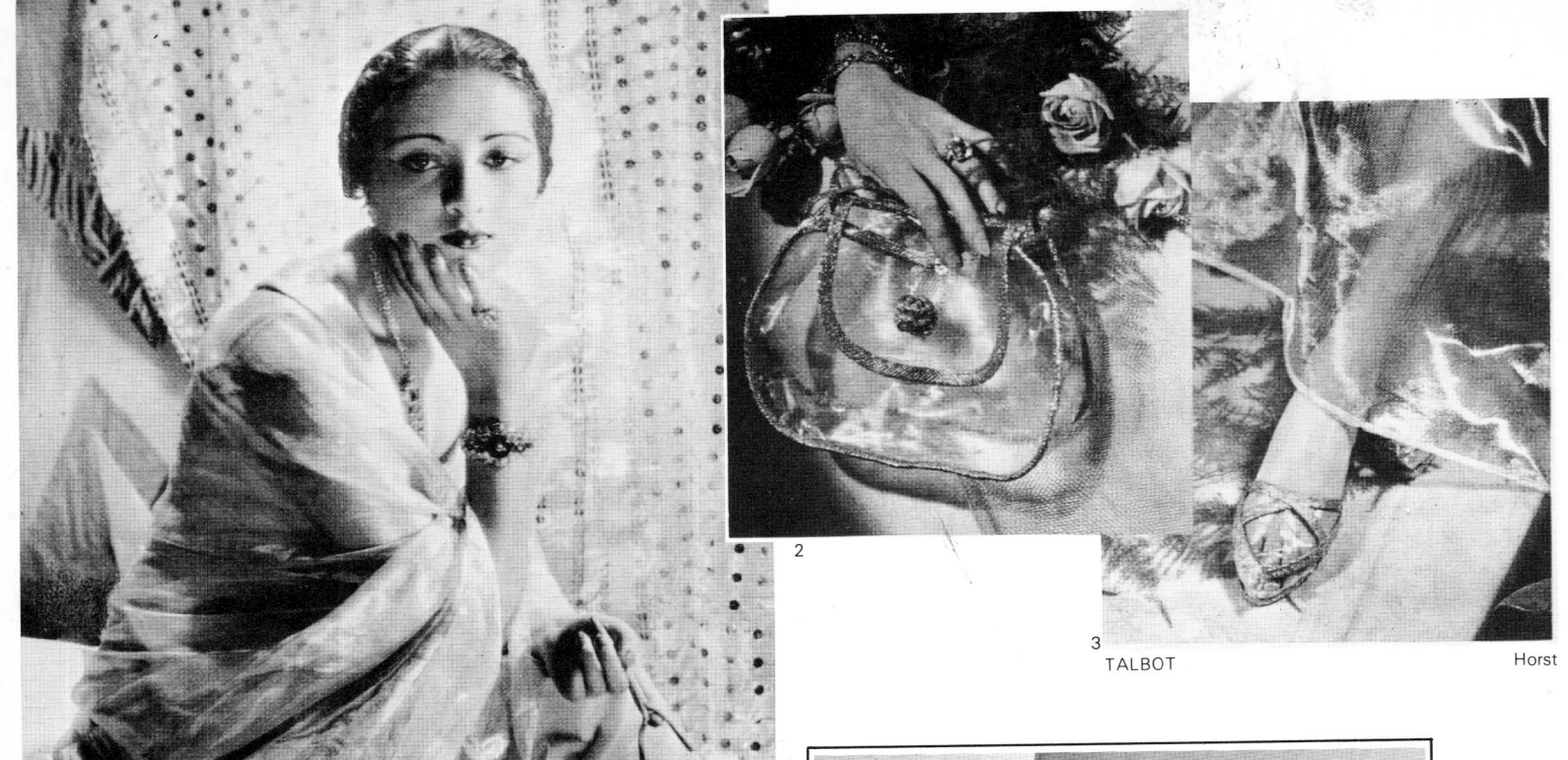

Cecil Beaton

2

TALBOT   Horst

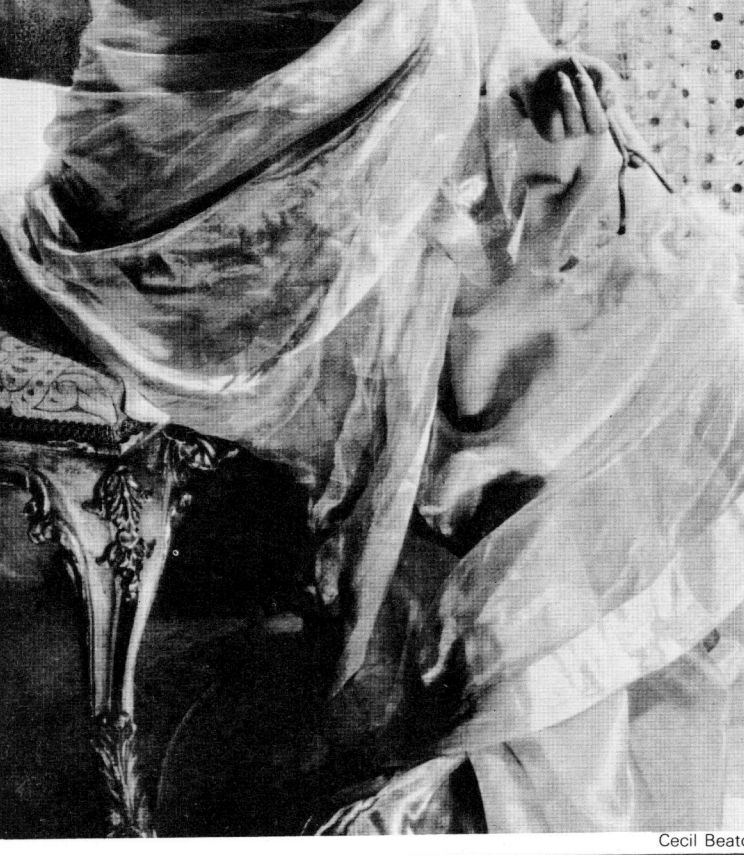

4   Horst

1. Princess Karam Kapurthala, a much admired Indian beauty who possibly inspired Schiaparelli's sari evening dresses.
2 and 3. Glass clothes, an invention of Schiaparelli's. A derivative of glass called Rhodophane, it is a brittle, fragile, transparent substance that has to be handled with care. Here, Talbot's bag and slipper.
4. Madame Max Ernst wearing Cartier's flexible, flat necklace and angular bangle of big yellow topazes.
5. Schiaparelli's sari dress in heavy white crepe.
6. Cellophane and accordion pleats: Vivien Leigh wears a Victor Stiebel dress, Cellophane over white taffeta.

5
SCHIAPARELLI

6
VICTOR STIEBEL   Horst

7. Long, red, brass-buttoned coat.
8. Cape and straight evening dress, lassoed by 'rope, hurtling out of oblivion, surrealist-fashion'.
9. A cavalcade of coats and capes.

8 SCHIAPARELLI   André Durst

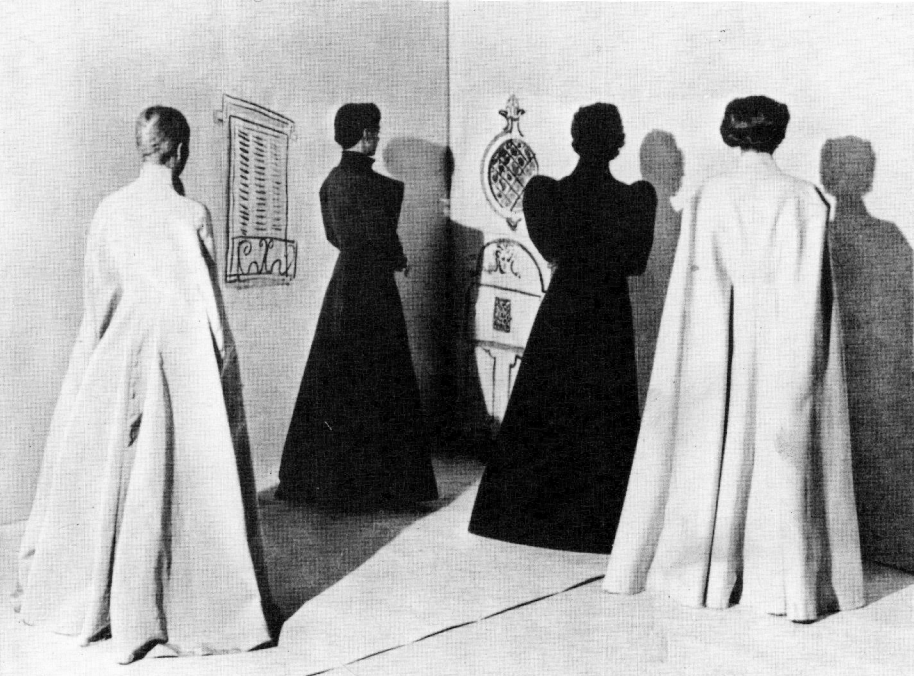

7
SCHIAPARELLI   Bérard   CHARLES JAMES   Cecil Beaton   143

TALBOT

1

2

4

VIONNET

Cecil Beaton

3. ALIX

Shaw Wildman

5

BATHING BREVITIES

Miles

1. 'The forward putsch in hats': Talbot's violet and green grosgrain turban and scarf.
2. Chanel's black velveteen cardigan suit, with a Florentine hat of beige and black velvet.
3. Alix's tunic-jacket in gold and blue brocade, with the lilt of a Bali dancer's coat.
4. Lady Brownlow in a white Vionnet afternoon dress with a bunch of white violets in her hat.
5. A shellful of Mr Cochran's Young Ladies in beach clothes.
6. Silver lamé trenchcoat, 8½gn., Fenwick.
7. Mainbocher beach outfits in white crash and checked gingham.

6

CHRISTIAN BÉRARD 7

1937-38

'Sex appeal is the prime motif of the Paris collections . . . and sex appeal is no longer a matter of subtle appeal'

'Sequins flash like a glance from a bright eye, and kill their man at ten yards'

'This year's recipe for chic is to strip to the waist, more or less, and then shelter under a cartwheel evening hat'

Colour floods through *Vogue* — cardinal red, coronation purple, emerald green, sulphur yellow, and Schiaparelli's brand new 'Shocking Pink' mixed with plummy maroons and metallic gold. Now you dress by colour, in a 'brief, boxy reefer in shrill blue, red and white plaid, worn with a deep red blouse and skirt'. You put two handkerchiefs in the pockets of a blue car coat, one fuchsia, one emerald. At night you dance to swing in a dress of pink and cerise, with gold accessories.

The new looks are all good useful factory looks, as if the designers already had war in mind. Hair is pinned up in the 'ready-for-bath' style, hidden under headscarves, suits are broad-shouldered and skimpy-skirted, and women clump around in wedge shoes on high cork soles. Schiaparelli makes an evening headscarf of gold embroidery. Evening dresses react by returning to Winterhalter crinolines, sentimentally tight waisted and frilled, although Schiaparelli and Molyneux retain a look of modern sophistication, and Alix tends to classical drapery as she will later under the name of Mme Grès.

Hats are quite ridiculous — 'leaning towers of grosgrain toppled into hats', huge haloes and cartwheels, huge brims draped with black veiling falling to the waist, and pure fantasies like Schiaparelli's wicker basket hat filled with Cellophane butterflies and flowers. Restaurants ban hats for the evening, and *Vogue* publishes a guide to what you can get away with where.

Two new looks that will resurface in the fifties: Schiaparelli's Mexican sombrero worn with cropped dungarees or slacks, and the American shirtwaister, with a bodice as full and

PIGUET   Tail-coated cape   Horst

pouchy as a Cuban bandleader's blouse.

Fundamental fashion news is Uplift, which has arrived from the cinema. Marian Jacks and Warners make the best uplift bras, and Schiaparelli makes an uplift sequin heart brassière built into the bodice of a narrow black dress . . . evenings are all afire with a Ziegfeld glitter of sequins.

Christian Bérard suggests new make

up: for a blonde, cyclamen rouge and deep blue lashes, for a brunette, brown suntan rouge, pomegranate lips.

The last word in chic is credited to Mrs Douglas Fairbanks for her short square box-jacket of sable, to Mrs Reginald Fellowes for her sapphire Mercury wing clipped to the lapel of her suit, and Vivien Leigh for her black velvet Flemish cap.

146

1
PAQUIN   Horst

2
MOLYNEUX

1. Merry Widow hat and
dress, audaciously cut,
filled in with not-so-modest
veiling.
2. Black velvet cartwheel
drooping an emerald
feather, narrow black
velvet dress split over
emerald satin.
3. Alix's Grecian
white jersey.
4. Velvet suit buttoned
with jewels.
5. Picture gown of
black tulle.

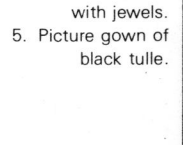

3

4
CHANEL   Horst

5 MOLYNEUX   Horst

1 CHANEL   Horst

2   Rawlings

SCHIAPARELLI

3

4   Eric

1. Gold lamé evening dress and chopped jacket of
                                    pressed pleats.
2. The 'ready for the bath' look, with a ribbon:
                              play suit by Rahvis.
3. Sequin jacket, lettuce green tweed over
                            corduroy trousers.
4. Boxy top coats in bright colours. *Left*, Maggy
         Rouff, wine, violet, green and brown;
              right, Alix, navy and rust.
5. Cockleshell bag of beige calf, and a basket-ball
    bag carried in a net — surely inspired by Dali.

5

CHIAPARELLI   Eric

7
VIONNET   Horst

6. Shocking pink dress, scooped below the breast one side and swathed with pink mousseline.

7. Suits look as though some clever person had taken a jacket from one suit, a skirt from another, and a blouse from a third. Here, a rare Vionnet day suit.

8. The shirt-waist silhouette from America.

9. Ferragamo, the Italian shoemaker, whose shoes are made entirely by hand, designs the first wedge evening shoes in gold kid and red satin.

9   149
FERRAGAMO

1. Weekend dressing — Strassner's white pullover, white wool slacks, striped blazer.

2. Schiaparelli's whole beach look — sombrero, chopped slacks, high cork sandals: *Vogue* cover, 22 June 1938.

3. 'If you haven't already started your tanning siege — try to get your first dose when you are entirely nude. It's more health-giving and it's infinitely better to get an even foundation to start with.'

4. 'Alison gets down to it — in her crinkled multi-striped cotton tub frock, 35s. 9d. Simpsons.'

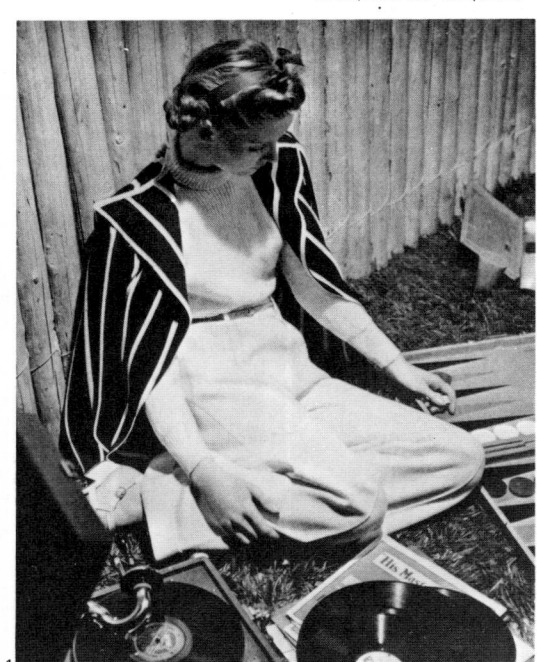

'The couturiers, every one, made the grand gesture. They caught the spirit of the moment with martial scarlet and black; they cast that nostalgic backward glance which people in troubled times bestow on a peaceful past'

'We deplore the crop of young women who take war as an excuse for letting their back hair down and parading about in slacks. Slack, we think, is the word . . . Determine, then – in this European jungle – to dress for dinner'

'Thousands of girls, trembling a bit, will go out looking for jobs this autumn. Thousands will get jobs. (Clothes will have something to do with this.) Thousands won't get jobs. (Clothes will have something to do with this, too.)'

BRAUN-SPIERER   Shoulderspan white felt Breton.

November *Vogue* is the first issue entirely produced under war conditions but from the start of the year clothes and copy are perfectly attuned to war, as though the designers knew it was coming. *Vogue* takes up its wartime attitude, 'It's your job to spend gallantly (to keep the national economy going), to dress decoratively, to be groomed immaculately — in short, to be a sight for sore eyes', and condemns slackness of appearance. There is a spread of candid camerawork showing the feet of women walking in Bond Street: 'We hope we shall be spared the sight of many little women in tailored suits running around London in open-toed sandals. Sister, watch your step.' Copy stresses economy, simplicity and practicability of the new uncrushable fabrics such as Zingal. Models are photographed on location in offices, on farms, in rainy London streets, even underwater. Leading looks are shirt dresses and simple suits with pleated skirts and 'nothing to date them', day dresses that can be worn to the office and go on, with a fur and muff, to a restaurant and dinner, and little-girl dresses — an extension of playsuits — with demure white collars and cuffs, tight waists, full short skirts, tucks, smocking and puff sleeves. Even Ascot skirts clear the turf by 17 inches.

Vogue patterns are for trousers for the volunteer owner-driver, a shirt for helping on the land, and knitting instructions for a sweater to go under uniform jackets.

The sweater has become the basis of most looks, even making the cover, worn with trousers and jewels. 'Sweaters appear, tough as you please, forever and a day, with our tweed skirts, with our golfing slacks. They appear, in highly sophisticated versions, with our town suits. Their social climb touches its peak when they appear, loaded with jewels, slashed with silk, over a grandly outsize evening skirt.'

Hair is Christy-waved and piled up on the head in curls and pompadours, or sausage-curled into a snood. Lips are painted into a bowtie shape, like Joan Crawford's, and coloured with Helena Rubinstein's 'Regimental Red' or Cyclax's 'Auxiliary Red'.

For evening, there are the Dorothy Lamour slinky crepes with plenty of uplift and a bare midriff, the draped chiffons used in contrasting panels, the simple cotton dance frocks. Fewer women now wear the crinolines that Norman Hartnell designs in powder blue and sequins for Queen Elizabeth. The London couturiers go to war and send out samples, fabric cuttings and saleswomen into the country towns. Hardy Amies joins the Fire Brigade, Victor Stiebel is a river policeman, Dennis Glenny is a soldier, and Digby Morton opens an off-the-peg department.

The clothes of 1939, the last that women invest in before the outbreak of war, will continue unchanged, like a fly in amber, throughout the war years.

1 LACHASSE

2

Siren into Suit

Digby Morton, famous tailleur, created this trouser suit in a bright tartan "Viyella." Beautifully warm to slip on over night-things in an emergency, with a hidey hood to cover your head. A lightning zip fastens it and military buttons trim the four patch pockets.

Viyella Thirty-six FASHION FABRICS

4 BARRI

1939

Vogue

1. Uncrushable heavy cotton suit in black and white plaid, showing lacy petticoats, photographed by André de Dienes who took some of the earliest pictures of an unsophisticated Marilyn Monroe.
2. Long-sleeved playsuits.
3. The first siren suit appears in *Vogue* as an advertisement for Viyella.
4. Day-length wine jersey restaurant dress, cleverly cut and draped with a fox hat and muff.
5. 1939 accessories — sunspectacles, blazing lipstick, plenty of glamour: *Vogue* cover, 9 August.
6. Helena Rubinstein's 'pick-up' masque. More and more often in the late 1930s, husbands would come home to find their wives looking like this.
7. Milada Mladora in a Kleinert periwinkle blue rubber bathing suit with rubber roses and rubber lace frills.
8. The foundation of the look — uplift and waspwaist.

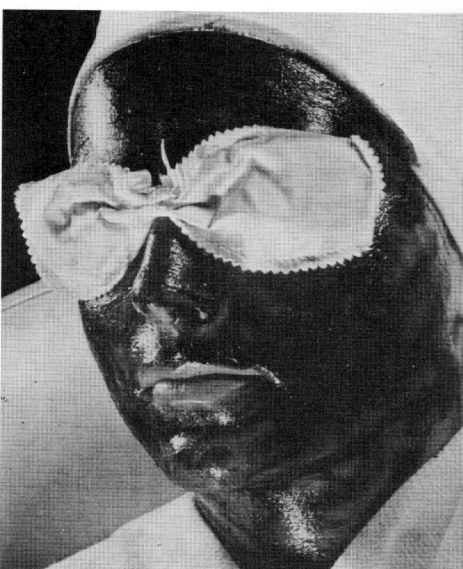

THE NIPPED-IN WAIST

DRESSES DEMAND IT —
— CORSETS CONTRIVE IT

Horst

1939

2 LELONG

1. For a secretary, little-girl dress in navy wool with white touches, Harrods.
2. Silk jersey dress in panels of white and navy wrapped with a white cummerbund.
3. Half and half fur coat, leopard-skin with a black wool back: jacket, Vionnet; hat, Talbot.
4. Dorothy Lamour evening dress of white crepe with uplift, bare midriff and bolero.
5. 'Mermaid or mummy,' call this silhouette what you will, the dress clings as closely, needs a twenty-inch waist, streamline hips and bee's knees to wear it. Patou's version is in his new, deep, winter green, with gold-fringe edging the jacket, sealing the skirt.
6. Worth's tangerine dress, with a pleated skirt, white bolero jacket, easily adaptable to the ready to wear.
7. Victorian straw, set on a butter-cup yellow snood.
8. Plum felt doll hat with a 'Skye terrier' fringe of ostrich, and Émile's sausage curls.

4
MOLYNEUX

5
PATOU

André Durst

7
RAHVIS

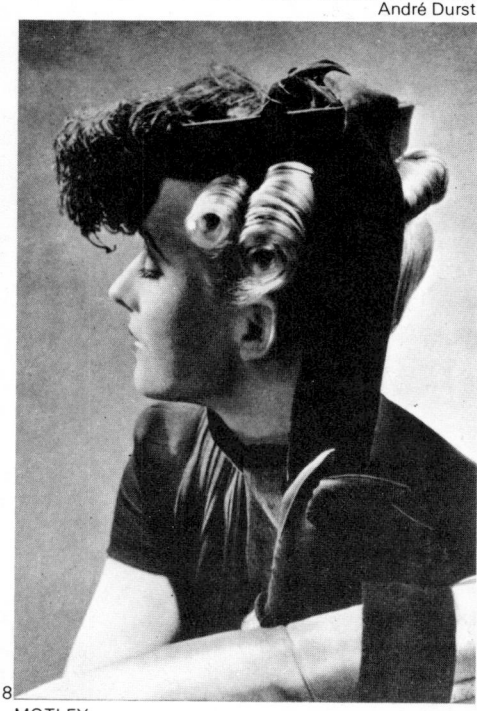

8
MOTLEY

155

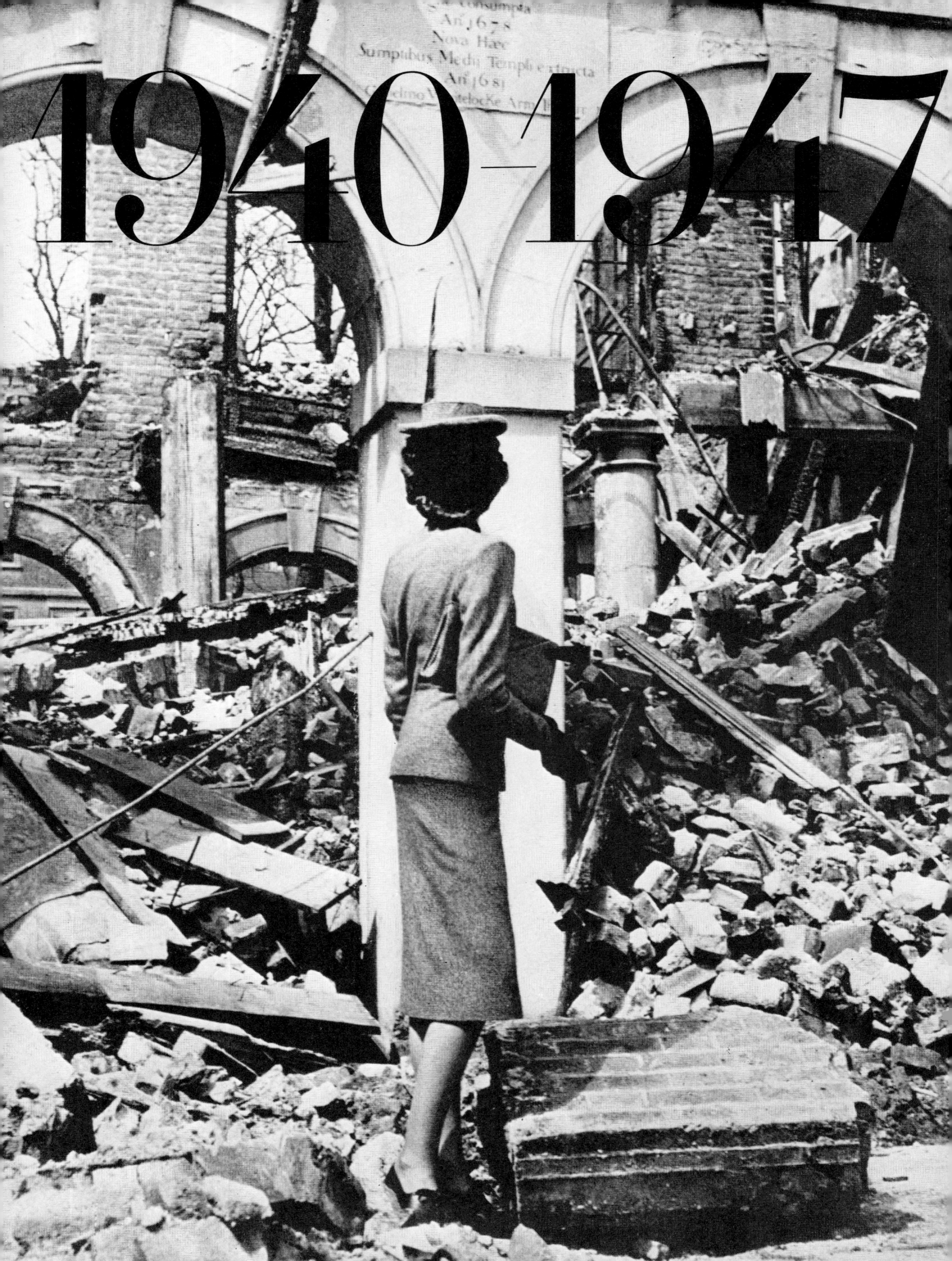

1940-1947

FASHION
BY GOVERNMENT ORDER

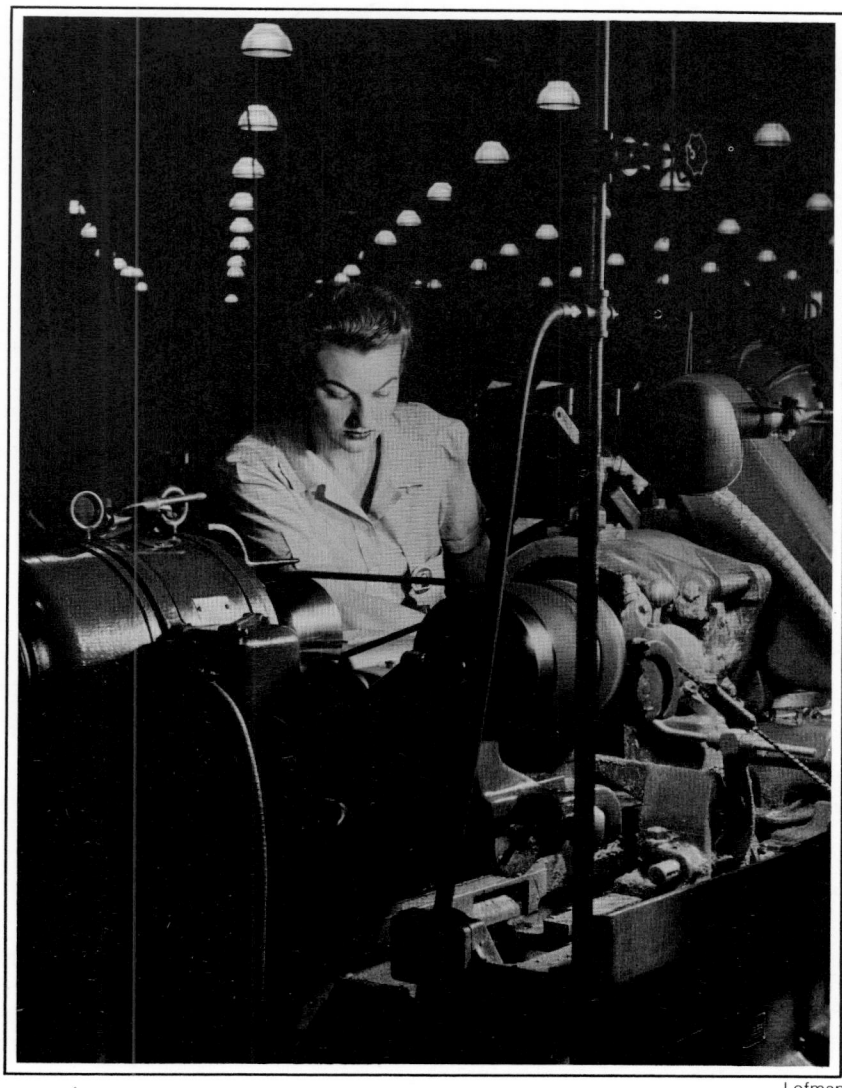

1

Lofman

By 1941 Londoners had settled down to a routine of chaos. Life was not only dangerous, but uncomfortable, dirty and odd. There were rabbits and chickens in backyards and on roofs, the park flower beds were full of cabbages and carrots, and habitual reserve gave way to smiles and offers of drinks. At the station, you were asked, 'Is your journey really necessary?' and a woman porter helped you with your cases. Places of entertainment were temporarily shut, and instead people went out to sleep; either in the dank and smelly municipal shelters or the muggy, convivial underground where, if you were lucky – or unlucky, some said – there might be an E.N.S.A. concert. People talked a different language, borrowed from the R.A.F., summed up by David Langdon in his cartoon of two civil servants, 'Give me a buzz on the intercom at eleven hundred hours and we'll bale out for coffee.'

Round every bombed house there spread a circle of debris, broken glass and pulverized coal which gradually settled on every surface, together with the Blitz smell of charred timber, gas and watersoaked dust. In the middle of the Blitz *Vogue* wrote, '"Come in and have a bath" rather than a drink, is the new social gesture – soap and water being a far more pleasing offer than any amount of gin.' The population was continually moving about, whether bombed out, evacuating, or snatching a weekend's leave at home.

The big hotels were crowded out. 'They are like luxury liners, their passengers signing on for an endlessly protracted, portless voyage.' They slept uneasily in the littered lounges, ate and danced in their crumpled clothes to the band – perhaps Lew Stone – while over their heads the roof spotters scanned the dark city. The problem of what to take with you, even for a night in the shelter, was a nightmare. 'All life is now lived in suitcases . . . the luggage-lugger has to decide between staggering under her all, or travelling light and free, but risking a return to nothing but demolition squads at work in the remnants of the area. "Safe as houses" now seems an obsolete phrase, and in rather poor taste, too.' It became common practice when you had dinner with friends to stay the night there. Guests camped in the basement or the bathroom, and dinner menus became a great deal simpler. 'You take what you can get, and make what you can of it, very often having to cook on an open fire, too. Onions being as scarce as peaches, even the most elegant cook can no longer baulk at hot-pots or stews as dinner-party fare.' *Vogue*'s social editor changed her milieu: 'a recent alarm found the Dorchester shelter filling up with celebrities – several ministers without portfolios or gas masks either, Lady Diana Cooper in full evening dress, Vic Oliver in serious mood, his wife Sarah Churchill sound asleep on the floor, and Leonora Corbett trying out a new

Left: 'Fashion is indestructible', perhaps Cecil Beaton's most famous fashion photograph, of a Digby Morton suit in the Temple's ruins, September 1941.
1. 'It must go on', 1942.

Here is VOGUE in spite of all!

OUTSIDE—on several nights, bombs have spattered within twenty yards. This street below our window now holds a new crater, and another length of the arcade has crashed. We were turned out temporarily for a time bomb

INSIDE—our offices have been strewn with broken glass. (See the freakishness of blast, that leaves a tumbler of water uncracked, unspilled.) Though five storeys up, our floors have been deep in soil and debris flung through the roof

BENEATH—we work on when our roof-watcher sends us down. Our editorial staff plan, lay-out, write. Our studio photograph in their wine-cellar-basement. Our fashion staff continue to comb the shops. Congestedly, unceremoniously but cheerfully, Vogue, like its fellow Londoners, is put to bed in a shelter

158   Lee Miller

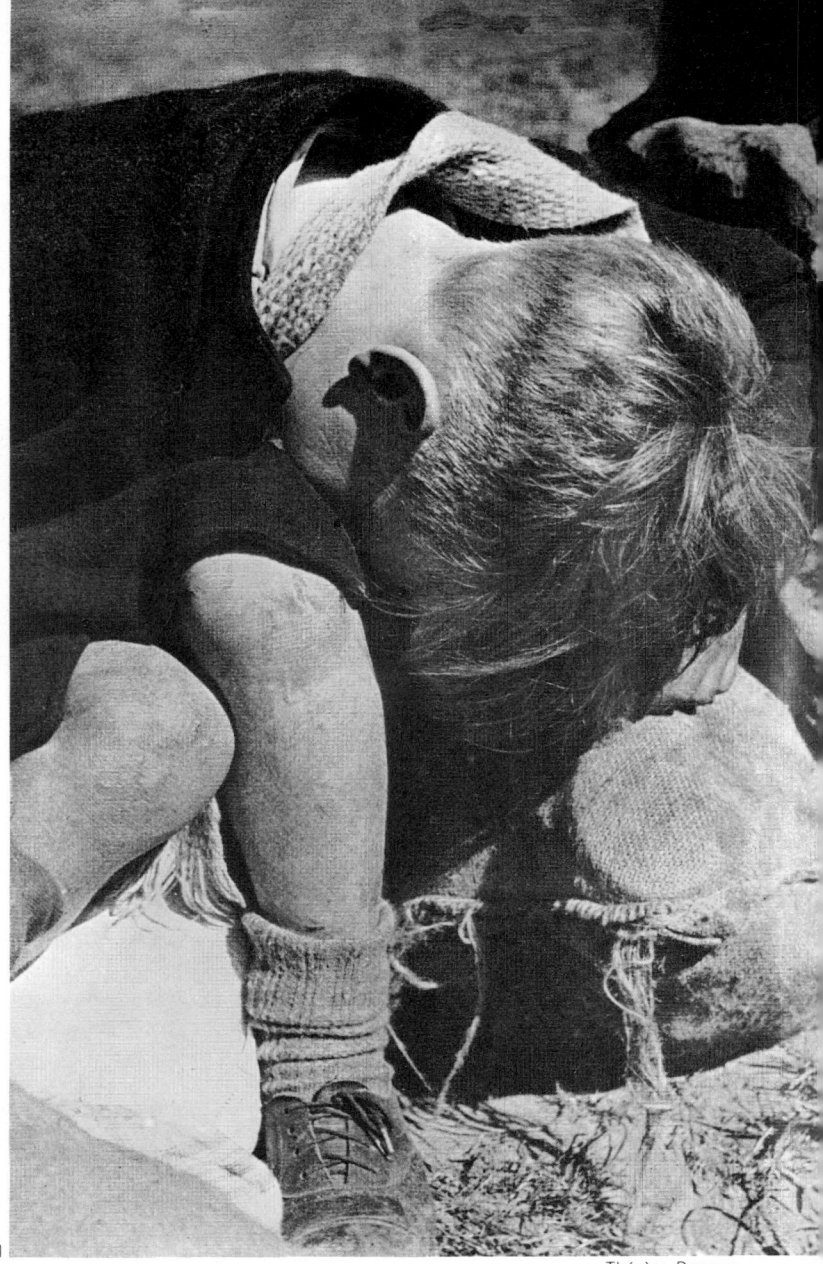

Thérèse Bonney

hairdo.' When the siren sounded in Mayfair, it often as not found the couturiers in the middle of complicated fittings. Captain Molyneux, his mouth full of pins, would ask his model, 'Do you want to go to the shelter?' and Sheila Wetton, today *Vogue*'s senior fashion editor, would obediently shake her head. At John Lewis the fittings were carried on in their shelters, while Dickens and Jones provided canteen refreshments for bomb-bound customers. 'At Grosvenor House, the new deep-shelter restaurant defies even sirens. It's left to the band to play All Clear, fitting the phrase to various tunes . . . Cinemas now flash All clear! All clear! across the screen regardless of the picture. It looked wonderful scrawled across Lillian Russell's 1880 bust, the other night.'

Vogue wrote complimentary features, 'I'm just back from town' and 'I'm just back from the country', giving the flavour of life in the summer of 1941. In town, 'Whole chunks of streets are up, choking dust turning people white . . . powdered glass tinkling about and everyone being too, too normal . . . errand *girls* instead of boys, bus conductorettes, waitresses at the Mirabelle . . . Piccadilly pretties now strut around in pseudo-sensible slacks . . . there are enormous determined cinema queues, and the Vic Wells ballet back again, and Flaganan and Allen, Oi-ing their way through the Black Vanities show, the theatrical success of the moment . . . You can hire hens by the week, they lay all over the back yard or balcony . . . in the evening nothing is fixed up ahead, and no one dreams of dressing up at night . . . Potato Bars have taken over from Milk Bars, and restaurants are full up all the time; an endless chain of meals emerging one into the next, all overlapping, women looking extra well groomed in uniform . . . Everyone's talking about

1. Homeless refugee child, 1942.
2. During the war farming had to be made to pay. The number of tractors increased from 60,000 to nearly a quarter of a million. Ploughing went on by night as well as by day, the blackout being waived for the purpose, and many of the drivers were women — during the war 90,000 enrolled in the Women's Land Army.
3. The much-needed bath, 1941 — to be clean during the Blitz was a luxury.
4. January 1940.

Lee Miller

Toni Frissel

Gerald Kelly's portrait of the Queen – we all know she has the most dazzling pink and white complexion, but why leave out the white? ... everywhere, the shrugging, shrilling Free French, the brightly coloured uniforms that fill the streets.' The progress of the war could be charted by the foreign uniforms in London – with the Allied troops, nearly 1½ million overseas troops were billeted in this country during the war.

In the country, 'all the big houses are commandeered ... ambulance classes, knitting bees for the Women's Institute, dressing for dinner with rigid formality, canteen stints and voluntary shifts of tractor driving and dairy work, everyone bicycling ... the difficulty of obtaining cosmetics – home-brewed lotions in the chemist's shop, car owners taking it in turns to drive into the nearest town with huge lists to do everyone's shopping for the week ... the farmer's wife sleeps under the dairy table with both her children, the vicar's wife makes for the crypt in her siren suit, the doctor's wife shares her fully equipped Anderson shelter'.

Weddings highlighted the many little austerities and restrictions of wartime life in Britain, from the rushed proposal to the ban on rice-throwing. Church bells were only to ring in case of parachute landings, there was no choir, no sugar icing for the cake, 'so enchanting tea-cosy covers have been invented to fit over plain cakes. For flowers and food, the bride takes what she can get ... the regimental flower, badge or squadron crest carried out in colour, the bouquet a mixed nosegay of any flowers in season, since the hothouses are occupied by fruit and vegetables.' The honeymoon might be a weekend in a borrowed cottage, petrol carefully saved for the purpose, or a few days in London, taking the opportunity

Vogue's-eye view of no margin for error
no margin for error no margin for error no margin for error no margin for error no margin for error no margin for error no margin for error no margin for error no margin for error no margin for error

Cecil Beaton

1. Sir Kingsley Wood, 1940.
2. 'The stuff of *Vogue*' — part of Cecil Beaton's waste paper hoard, 1942.
3. Lady Diana Cooper down on the farm, 1941.

Opposite: Schiaparelli dresses photographed by Horst, December 1947.
Over page, left: Vogue's break-the-rules issue, June 1971: 'It is in bad taste to dress extravagantly or showily when mingling with people who are all plainly dressed.' Satin shirt and shorts by Electric Fittings, shoes by Chelsea Cobbler, hair colour by Daniel and shape by Oliver of Leonard. Photograph by Peter Knapp.
Over page, right: Photograph by Art Kane, November 1963.

of collecting your friends together 'since no knowing, these days, when the next meeting may be'. The best presents were practical and portable, 'a portable wireless or gramophone, a portable Electrolux refrigerator that works on oil, electricity or gas ... treasures that money can't buy – a petrol coupon, honey in the comb, home-made jam'.

The 'Lend a hand on the land' posters brought townspeople into the country to help with the digging or haymaking. They were a mixed blessing to farmers, particularly the girls who turned up in high heels and their best dresses, but there were other more reliable sources of labour – soldiers, released from barracks for the day, and prisoners-of-war, working bands of 30 or 40 Germans or Italians dressed in blue dungarees patched with green. *Vogue* wrote many features about independent people who went 'back to the land' and produced their own food, some becoming successful farmers. There was Norman Parkinson, one of *Vogue*'s first-rank photographers then and now, who had volunteered for the Navy but had been told, 'You'd be more useful to us as a photographer', and worked on a propaganda magazine repudiating the statements of Lord Haw-Haw. At the same time he ran a farm. *Vogue* sent all the clothes for their country fashion shots down on the train, and Parkinson photographed them between mucking out the pigs and collecting swill. He wrote about the farm, 'Hotels, cafés and the cinema have bins with Park's Pig Food on the lid ... we collect the bins from the back door at four, and return for dinner by the front at eight. "Leave plenty on the side of your plate," we remind each other. "More for our pigs." ' Another Londoner running a farm was Lady Diana Cooper, who had set up a productive and profitable business with three acres, a cow and £50, and managed it single-handed until she accompanied her husband to Singapore. No Marie Antoinette, this amazingly versatile and adventurous society beauty, who had toured Europe and America as an actress, got up at 6.30 to milk the cow, feed the animals and make cheese. Another lynchpin of London society, Cecil Beaton, went down to photograph her, and was brainwashed. 'When you take into consideration the fact that their eggs replace "fixed" price fish, rare meat, or the canned foods which should be kept for emergency, fowls cannot fail to pay their way. By adding scrap to the rationed quota more fowls can be fed than have rations allotted to them.' Meanwhile Mrs John Betjeman in Berkshire was running a large vegetable and herb garden with the help of two evacuee schoolmasters, milking her goats twice a day,

driving herself about in a dogcart and riding the dawn parachute patrol on the downs.

In November 1942, *Vogue* pointed out to its readers another line of war work – welcoming the American servicemen to Britain. 'Remember, everything is twice as much fun to these American boys if there's a girl in it ... Frankness and informality are the keynotes to strike ... The American gullet is used to iced whisky, iced beer ... they'll like to hear the local history and superstitions.' In the pursuit of girls, the Americans had everything their own way. They were paid at least four times the basic British pay, they drove huge flashy cars, dispensed nylons, candy and packets of Lucky Strike, and gave their girlfriends a taste of glamour at the American base dances, with lavish food and drink, and the top dance bands like Glen Miller's, here on tour. As the British service-man bitterly remarked, 'The Americans are all right, except that they are overpaid, oversexed and over here.' When they finally de-parted things became a little greyer and quieter. Marghanita Laski remarked in 1946 *Vogue*, you couldn't count on finding a taxi outside the American Red Cross Clubs, and the young girls in the tube weren't chewing gum any more.

The immediate effects of the war on *Vogue* had been to put up the price from 1*s*. to 2*s*. in 1940, 2*s*. 6*d*. with *Vogue Pattern Book* included, and finally 3*s*. in 1942; and to contract the number of pages because of the paper shortage. Maxims such as 'Waste paper is vital to the war effort' and 'Use as little paper as possible for fires' were printed at the foot of the pages. The circulation, how-ever, increased, climbing from 52,000 in 1941 to 106,000 in 1949, and each issue was passed from hand to hand until up to twenty women had seen it. *Vogue*'s own advertisement in May 1941 said, 'Many more women are now buying *Vogue* than, on an average, used to take it in pre-war days. You've a copy in your hands – you're lucky. But every month there are countless people who miss their *Vogue* ... The trouble is, of course, that owing to official restrictions in the supply of paper, we just can't print as many copies as we'd like to. So it's a question of first come, first served. Please, if you're one of these fortunate first, don't be dog-in-a-manger about your *Vogue*. Share it with your friends. Invite them home and give them the run of your copy. And then, when you've read it all, studied it all and planned all your outfits – pass it on to someone else.'

The Second World War, unlike the First, brought no escapist

Opposite: Blouse by Albini, hat by Jean Charles Brosseau, face by Barbara Daly with Maybelline make up. Photograph by Sarah Moon, April 1972.
1. Jacqueline Cochran, ace airwoman, 1941.

follies, no fashion fantasies. They were impossible no less because of the wartime spirit than the government restrictions. In a speech to the Fashion Group of New York, Edna Woolman Chase, the American Editor-in-Chief, said, 'When people speak to me about this war they ask me "Isn't it going to be incredibly difficult to edit a luxury magazine like *Vogue* in times like these? Do you think that you can hope to survive?" My answer to that is – What kind of a magazine do they think this is? ... Fashions would not be fashions if they did not conform to the spirit and the needs and the restrictions of the current times.' Naturally, as fashion exactly reflects the mood of the times, the fashion was for clumpy shoes, clumsy suits, box coats and headscarves tied into turbans hiding 'a multitude of pins'. Just as even wealthy women in the Depression were dressing down in plain black dresses and furless coats, fashionable women before clothing restrictions were dressing in Utility-look suits or sweaters and slacks. 'It looks wrong to look wealthy,' said *Vogue*. 'The woman well-dressed in the meaning of today would not easily be rendered helpless or ridiculous.'

From the outset of war the magazine took what Pearson Phillips, the journalist, has called 'a positive and optimistic line'. *Vogue* needed to take that line as early as October 1940, when in 'No margin for error', it discussed Sir Kingsley Wood's budget that slapped a new Purchase Tax on clothes. 'His acts might suggest him no friend to fashion; but *Vogue* (hopefully) detects an ally. Because of him, designers will get together frankly, to pool their ideas and use their limited materials to present a united fashion front. Because of him, women will buy carefully and cleverly ... by the inescapable pressure of the Purchase Tax he will set them practising those sound dress maxims that *Vogue* has always preached. How often have we counselled against "the dress you buy and seldom wear" ... If women must buy less, they will buy better.'

Clothes rationing arrived in June 1941, by which time prices had nearly doubled in eighteen months. Coupons were distributed, and the rationing operated by a points system, a garment costing a number of coupon points irrespective of fabric and price. Utility clothes, however, fulfilled government requirements and sold at fixed prices. They were not subject to Purchase Tax. The Utility scheme involved at first 50 per cent and later 85 per cent of all cloth manufactured, controlling quality and price, and was reinforced by the Making of Clothes (Restrictions) Orders introduced in 1942, which covered nearly all clothing and restricted yardage

My coupons too?

and style. 'Dress restrictions simply pare away superfluities,' said *Vogue*, making the best of things. 'The progress of the war has made it necessary to prohibit all superfluous material and superfluous labour . . . Fashion is undergoing a compulsory course of slimming and simplification.' Readers were reminded, 'Subtraction, not addition, is the first of fashion rules – full liberty is liberty for excess as well as excellence.' On the other hand, 'The Board of Trade has now assessed our clothing requirements at 66 coupons – and margarine coupons at that – a horrid slight. It is now said that fashion's goose is properly cooked and done in, for want of the best butter. But fashion is indestructible and will survive even margarine coupons . . . you cannot ration a sense of style.' Noël Coward's new leading lady, Judy Campbell, pointed out enthusiastically, 'Rationing is marvellous in one respect. You can make lack of money look like lack of coupons.'

Most women found the disappearance of stockings and cosmetics even harder to accept than dress restrictions. The decline and fall of the stocking was the decline and fall of women's morale. The first blow was the ban on silk stockings in 1941, when, in January, *Vogue* recommended the substitutes – cotton, rayon and the hard-wearing heavy mesh – but by August even these were in such short supply that the advice became 'Discard stockings for casual wear at home and in the country substituting a plausible cream make up . . . wear sturdy stockings whenever suitable . . . wash and darn your precious rayon tenderly, taking them to the invisible menders at the first hint of a ladder.' Leg paint turned out to be thoroughly unsatisfactory, some kinds turning yellow in daylight, others rubbing off on skirts and leaving indelible marks. Worse was to come. By 1942 the Board of Trade warned that if women didn't go without stockings during the summer they would have to by winter. In a feature called 'Sock Shock', *Vogue* bravely published a picture of a woman in a smart summer afternoon dress, big hat – and ankle socks. 'Socks can contrive to look charming,' said *Vogue* brazenly. 'But we believe that it's easier to achieve a smart stockingless appearance with quite bare legs (smoothly tanned or made up) and footlets. We hope the Board will put these in production,' and meanwhile offered a knitting pattern for them. Lux advertisements, reminding the reader that Lux would one day come back on the market, ran this rhyme in 1945:

No wonder Julia shouts hurray!
Her sweetheart's home on leave today,
And frequent washing in the past
Has made his favourite stockings last.

Vogue's tone of voice had changed radically in the three years between 1939, when an editorial had rapped women over the knuckles for slopping about in town wearing open-toed sandals and slacks, and 1941: 'For the A.R.P. worker, the new, short coiffure. Long hair can be tied into a net turban which will hide under a tin hat. For the face, no make up, but a non-greasy, all-purpose cream, dusted with powder . . . Save your cosmetics for evenings out . . . That "too-good-to-be-true" look which only a personal maid can produce is absent – because the maid is absent, on munitions . . . Clothes look as if they had been taken care of, put on beautifully and then forgotten for more important things.' *Vogue*'s special issues were now devoted to Patterns and Renovations. At the beginning of the war, when there was still a pretence that fashion was changing and developing year by year, there were diagrams showing how you could alter last year's looks to this year's: later on, *Vogue* turned its attention to making the best of things. 'You can go hatless if you wear simple swept-back hair like this . . . you can go stockingless if you wear simple flat-heeled shoes like this.' Needs must, and the beauty pages, shrinking with the shrinking

supply of cosmetics, extolled the virtues of a healthy, brisk, scrubbed appearance. 'Polish yourself up: hair burnished and crisply cropped to the new length – it's a look that does not jar with uniform – with *women*'s uniform. Somehow, more and more, the eye unconsciously measures women up by this yardstick. Why does that shoulder-mane seem so out of date? Because it would look messy hanging on a uniform collar . . . What's wrong with those exquisite tapered nails? They couldn't do a hand's turn without breaking. The woman who could change instantly into uniform, or munitions overalls and look charming, soignée and right, is the smart woman of today' and exhorted women to keep 'nails rosy till the day when varnish vanishes: figure kept taut by exercise and good posture, with corsets a helping, but not a decisive factor . . . Wash-and-brush-up your face on occasion: because creams are rationed and soap is not.'

Prepared to make concessions over appearance in sacrificial wartime spirit, nevertheless *Vogue* was ready to take up cudgels when necessary. The line was firmly drawn in the August issue of 1942. The beauty column made the concessions. 'Today, you want to look as if you thought less about your face than about what you have to face; less about your figure than about how much you can do. You want to look as if you cared about your looks, yes, but cared more about being able to do a full day's work – whether it be in a factory, on the land, coping with a day nursery, or just managing your home single-handed as so many of us do today. You want to look beautiful, certainly – what woman in what age hasn't wanted to? . . . but you want it to be a beauty that doesn't jar with the times, a beauty that's heart-lifting not heart-breaking, a beauty that's beneficent but not beglamoured, and a beauty that's responsive – not a responsibility.'

But a special feature called 'It Must Go On' inveighed against the rumour that the supply of cosmetics, already curtailed to 25 per cent of peacetime output, might be cut further. 'Cosmetics are as essential to a woman as a reasonable supply of tobacco is to a man. A welfare officer at a munitions factory said, "£1,000 worth of cosmetics, distributed among my girls, would please them more than £1,000 in cash" . . . only when a woman looks her best can she feel and do her best. The supply should not be further reduced

by prejudice or puritanism – more frivolous than the cosmetics they censure.'

The war was a watershed for fashion, forcing the development of a stable ready-to-wear structure capable of prosperous large-scale production in the fifties. 'The geniuses who invented the Utility scheme had a great say in the development of the fashion industry,' said Frederick Starke, a leader in the better off-the-peg market. By controlling quantities and prices the Utility scheme forced manufacturers to choose their cloths wisely and cut economically. Standards of manufacture were improved by minimum-standard government regulations and by a public forced by coupon rationing to discriminate, and methods of manufacture were streamlined and better mechanized by the pressures of rushed uniform production. Sizing and costing were for the first time regularized and accurately worked out, and labour was reassessed. The fashion industry's workers came out of the war more secure: they were paid guaranteed wages and conditions of work were laid down. When in July 1942 the government took over extra factory space for the storage of munitions and other wartime equipment, many manufacturers had to get together to stay in business. By 1947 Frederick Starke had formed the London Model House Group, seven leading manufacturers who united to establish the prestige of British fashion abroad, and to present a united front to buyers and suppliers. In 1950 the Apparel and Fashion Industry's Association was to say, 'a revolution has taken place behind the smokescreen of wartime conditions'.

Meanwhile, London's couturiers had managed their own revolution. Early in the war *Vogue* said, 'Paris is in eclipse, making it London's opportunity to shine. Already in London are the Paris houses of Molyneux, Paquin, Worth; lending all the prestige of their Paris connection to the drive for dollars. Creed, too, is here . . . In England now, every branch of the fashion trade is stirring strongly. The challenge of the times has called forth, to admiration, qualities for which we have not always been conspicuous: initiative, speed, cooperation.'

In 1942 many of the couturiers were anxiously contemplating the possible next course of action of a government that had already introduced clothes rationing and the Utility scheme. There was

1

2

4 MOLYNEUX SCHIAPARELLI

1

just one way of proving London couture valuable to the national economy during the war, and that was export. The year before, nine couturiers had scored a success by cooperating in a special export drive, a collection for South America sent out under government auspices. *Vogue* had published a special South American edition to accompany the collection, and reproduced some of the photographs in British *Vogue*, where they looked conspicuously luxurious and glamorous among the regular diet of man-tailored tweeds and skimpy dresses. Norman Hartnell approached the managing director of Worth and other couturiers, urging a common front to the Board of Trade. Harry Yoxall, *Vogue*'s managing director, became the business head and entrepreneur of the new Incorporated Society of London Fashion Designers, aimed at developing the couture export market. The 'Inc Soc' was supported by fabric manufacturers and encouraged by the government. Early members were Norman Hartnell, Peter Russell, Worth, Angèle Delanghe, Digby Morton, Hardy Amies, Creed, Molyneux and Michael Sherard. The first president was the Hon. Mrs Reginald Fellowes, chief fashion personality of the early thirties, now camping in London in the basement of the Duff Coopers' house in Westminster.

In the spring of 1943, some well-designed, anonymous Utility clothes went into the market, the result of the Board of Trade's invitation to the couture to design basic garments subject to all the usual restrictions. Anne Scott-James had said, 'If Mayfair hasn't the skill to cut a good dress from three or four yards of material with five or six buttons it must learn – or go under'. It proved that it had, and it had turned the difficult situation to its own advantage.

For a magazine so closely concerned with Paris as *Vogue*, the blanket of silence that descended on the city during the Occupation was bound to change the character of the magazine, making it more insular but also more independent. Up to summer 1940 *Vogue* ran a regular 'Paris Sidelights' page, showing the character of the city essentially unchanged. Bettina Wilson wrote, 'Paris in the fifth month of the war is an attractive, comfortable, normal city with an intimate, almost country charm to life . . . you can enjoy such luxuries as smart hats and plentiful taxis, but nobody will look at you askance if you go hatless or ride your bicycle on fine days.

1. Fashion pages from *Album de la Mode,* 1942, the arts magazine published in Occupied Paris.
2. *Vogue* pin-up, 1943.
3. The Liberation of Paris — one of the glamorous girls in pretty clothes who provoked an envious pique in austerity Britain.

Hospitality in the home has practically become a cult – the war seems to have weakened, if not completely broken down, the impregnable barriers of French formality.' *Vogue* photographer, Arik Nepo, now a *poilu* in the French army, wrote from a barn, 'We're billeted in a barn. We tumbled in late one night, too tired to do anything but slump into the straw . . . Next morning some cut pictures out of magazines and stuck them on the walls. *Vogue*, naturally, had pride of place – being full of pretty girls, divinely dressed; what more could you want?' From the Paris Ritz *Vogue* reported, 'Mrs Reginald Fellowes and her family, Madame Schiaparelli and her daughter Gogo, Lady Mendl, the Comtesse de Montgomery and Mrs Corrigan all live on the first floor. Dropping in for a drink means visiting from one room to the next, perhaps meeting the Sacha Guitrys, Mlle Chanel, Jean Cocteau, who also have rooms there.' At Molyneux's mid-season collection there were Noël Coward, Madame la Générale Gamelin, and Mrs Fellowes – 'who knitted throughout the collection. There were four mannequins instead of 15, 30 models instead of 100, but those 30 struck clearly the informal note of the moment.' In poignant contrast to her circus ball of 1938, there were Lady Mendl's Sunday lunch parties at Versailles – 'small tables covered with oil cloth, corn beef hash to eat, and guests take away the dishes and sweep up crumbs'. The soup kitchen for out-of-work writers and musicians had a first night opening with all the familiar faces: the artistic poor paid 2 or 4 francs, according to circumstances, the wealthy visitors 20. Bettina Wilson wrote that the French were continually amazed by the fifteen-year-old look of the R.A.F. pilots on their first Paris leaves, sitting in every *boîte* and tapping their fingers and toes to the music 'to which no one is allowed to dance in Paris, except at special galas', and told the story of the Lopez-Willshaws' furniture, which had been willed to the Louvre after his death. During the first week of the war, a removals van drew into the courtyard with instructions from the curator of the Louvre to take the furniture away to a safe cellar for the duration, leaving the Lopez family sitting on the bamboo garden furniture in an empty salon.

There was grimmer news in July, when *Vogue* fashion artist Eric and his family left their home at Senlis, near Chantilly, to join a tide of refugees moving back from the German advance: as they left their house it was wrecked by a bomb. Seven months after the occupation of Paris *Vogue* received a batch of pictures relayed from New York, showing a deserted Champs Élysées, a tide of bicycles and a cycle taxi, a cross between a sidecar and push bike. 'Across the great gulf of silence – and of misunderstanding, which we still believe cannot be turned to enmity between our peoples – come pictures of a strangely subdued city.'

During the Occupation some twenty of the famous couture houses managed to stay open in Paris, with or without their chief designers. Schiaparelli and Mainbocher went to America, where Mainbocher stayed, and Molyneux, Creed, Angèle Delanghe went to London. 'One of the first things the Germans did,' said Lucien Lelong, President of the Couture Syndicate, 'was to break into the Syndicate offices and seize all documents pertaining to the French export trade.' M. Lelong successfully resisted all German efforts to remove the couture lock, stock and barrel to Berlin and Vienna. 'I told them that *la couture* was not a transportable industry, such as bricklaying.' Thanks to his negotiations, the couture houses managed to show two abbreviated collections a year. 'A few months later, in 1941 to be exact, due to the lack of materials, very severe restrictions were ordered and textile cards with the point system started. We soon realised that if this regulation was applied to our great fashion houses, it would mean closing them down immediately.' M. Lelong renewed his discussions with the Germans and succeeded in obtaining exemption from point restrictions for twelve houses. 'Unfortunately, the Germans noticed at the end of six months that ninety-two houses were operating, which led to more discussions. Finally we succeeded in keeping sixty. Over a period of four years, we had fourteen official conferences with the Germans . . . at four of them they announced that *la couture* was to be entirely suppressed, and each time we avoided the catastrophe. On another occasion, they demanded that 80 per cent of our workers go into war industries; this we managed to reduce to a 5 per cent quota, which in reality never exceeded 3 per cent.' He calculated that by the Liberation, 12,000 workers had been saved from unemployment and consequent labour in German war industries.

The export market was shut, and the couture had to depend on new clients, the recently moneyed class of black-marketeers, and many German wives, together with those of the Germans' French mistresses who dared to buy their clothes there. A great deal of subterfuge went on between the couturiers to get round German regulations. Bitter rivals in peacetime, they cooperated magnificently against the common enemy. When Madame Grès and

2

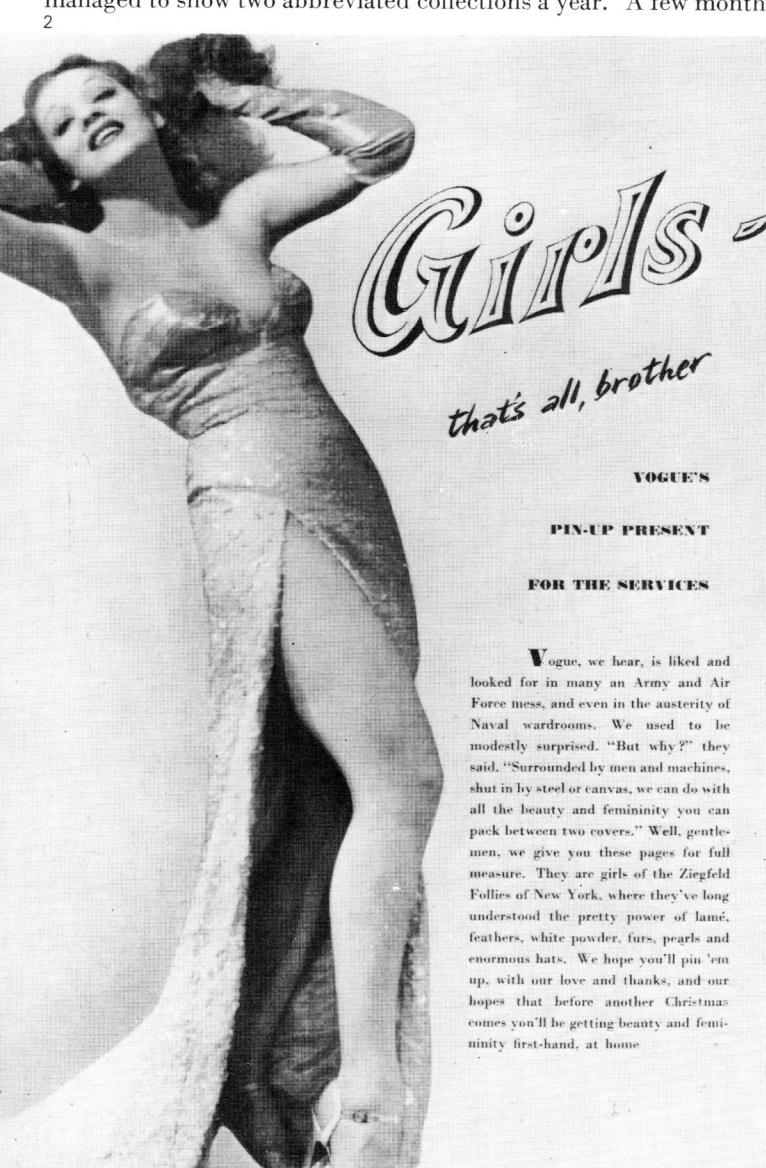

Lee Miller

Balenciaga were ordered to close their houses for two weeks because they had exceeded the authorized yardage for some of their models, the rest of the couture joined forces to finish their collections so that they could show on time.

Michel de Brunhoff, editor of French *Vogue*, was unable to publish it under the Germans. 'There was no honourable way; no way without compromise and collaboration. I stalled, and found slippery answers for the Germans when they suggested, and then ordered, that our magazines reopen with German backing.' Instead, M. de Brunhoff cooperated with *Le Figaro* to produce *Album de la Mode*, a magazine of the arts, theatre and fashion, from which *Vogue* reproduced some fashion pages after the Liberation.

The Liberation of Paris appears in *Vogue* as a personal triumph. With exceptional speed, *Vogue* showed photographs of the fighting in October 1944 – fire and smoke, a priest encouraging boys at a barricade, General de Gaulle as he passed the windows of *Vogue*'s former Paris office. Lee Miller, *Vogue*'s *femme soldat*, went to check up on Picasso, 'generous and voluble as ever', Boris Kochno (Diaghilev's discovery) and Bébé Bérard ('He has only one pair of trousers and has to wear an old trench coat as a skirt to work in'), Paul Eluard and Michel de Brunhoff. Elsa Schiaparelli went back to Paris, found that food cost five to twenty times as much as it had in 1939, and resolved to give women 'clothes that they can live in, not parade in'. Cecil Beaton found Colette muffled up in bed with hot-water bottles and nine fountain pens, writing her memoirs, Gertrude Stein writing about G.I.s and Democracy, and noticed a hopeful sign: 'two actors with salmon-painted faces emerging from a jeweller's shop while a moving picture camera grinds' – the film industry had started up again. Lee Miller reported, 'There is one hairdresser in all Paris who can dry hair: "Gervais" . . . He has rigged his dryers to stove pipes which pass through a furnace heated by rubble. The air is sent by fans turned by relay teams of boys riding a stationary tandem bicycle in the basement.'

In England, life was at its drabbest and most regimented. 'The penny plain of life is three farthings,' said *Vogue*, 'and the struggle to make up the difference takes so much of women's energy.' The public reaction to the Liberation fashion photographs – 'dazzling girls in full floating skirts, tiny waist-lines, top-heavy with built up pompadour front hair-dos and waving tresses; weighted to the ground with clumsy, fancy thick-soled wedge shoes' – was one of envious pique. *Vogue* sprang to the defence of Paris. 'If it surprises you to see pretty girls in pretty dresses, to see the beautiful clothes which the fashion houses never ceased to make, reflect that the life of France and her civilian technique of resistance must necessarily have been the reverse of England's. Here, it showed patriotism to obey regulations, to do the work required of us, to take no more than our rations. There, it showed patriotism to flout regulations, to avoid work except where it would not benefit the Germans (as in the luxury trades), to black-marketeer up to the hilt.'

The Liberation allowed readers to see their first Paris collections for four years. The designs had a mixed reception here and in America, where a ban was imposed on copying the full skirts and dressmaker details from photographs in fashion magazines. There was no question of being able to copy them here. In December *Vogue* published a manifesto by Lucien Lelong, which amounted to an apology. 'It was only after the Autumn Collections were shown that I received copies of English and American dress restrictions, and I now understand why certain journalists found the Paris Collections exaggerated. However, I must explain that my colleagues and I eliminated many models prepared before the liberation – replacing them by simple suits and coats which we felt better suited the circumstances arising from France's official re-entry into the War at the side of the Allies.'

With the end of the war clothes rationing tightened. There were shortages of everything from dried eggs to soap. Even bread was rationed, and the government spent £857,000 on a meat-substitute, an oily dull fish called snoek, which the press soon discovered was a large, ferocious cousin of the barracuda, which hissed and barked when annoyed. To give it a little much-needed glamour, the government published a series of snoek recipes, including 'Snoek Piquante'. However, nothing would make the public eat it, and at the time of the Festival of Britain a mysterious quantity of tinned fish came onto the market labelled 'Selected fish food for cats and kittens'.

The patient bearing with the minor horrors of war ended with the war. Now women were resentful of the shortages and restrictions: *Vogue*'s attitude changed from 'Dress restrictions simply pare away superfluities' to 'One has only to see a collection designed for export, and the same collection toned down to comply

1

Lee Miller

2

Lee Miller

It's easy . . . it's quick . . . it's delicious

Omelette: made with dried eggs — new laid eggs with nothing but the shell and water taken away. Appetising, digestible. So simple and easy, too. For the perfect omelette, try this way:

1 Quantities for two people. Mix 4 level tablespoons dried egg, with salt and pepper, and 4 tablespoons water till smooth. Beat well. Gradually add 4 more tablespoons water, keeping mixture very smooth. Again beat well.

2 Meanwhile, heat ½ oz. cooking fat in a frying pan (use the thickest one you have) until it starts to smoke. Pan and fat must be very hot. Pour egg in quickly.

3 As it cooks, lift edges with fork, allowing liquid egg to run under, until all is set. This takes from 1 to 1½ minutes. Don't overcook it. Now add, if you want to, grated cheese, chopped vegetables, meat, bacon etc. or herbs. Or jam. Fold over omelette away from handle of the pan so that it rolls over on to a hot plate.

ISSUED BY THE MINISTRY OF FOOD

3

with austerity at home, to realize how much fashion value has been lost in the process.' In February 1946 *Vogue* invited a Cambridge economist and broadcaster, Louis Stanley, to explain why, after nine years without new curtains, linen, upholstery or pretty clothes, we still could not get hold of new goods. Stanley called his feature 'The Second Battle of Britain' and said, 'It is bad enough when such goods do not exist, but to learn that they are being produced – the best this country can make – only not for domestic consumption is a bitter pill . . . Women are further exasperated by illustrations in periodicals and the national press showing exotic fashions in Paris, Brussels, New York, Stockholm, even Germany,' and went on to explain, 'We have to wipe out a deficit of £1,200,000,000 from Britain's balance of trade.' *Vogue* jettisoned the 'positive and optimistic line' on dress restrictions. 'It is unfair and economically unwise to leave our designers, one moment longer than is necessary, at such a disadvantage in relation to their competitors . . . we add our voice to those which ask the Board of Trade to abolish austerity as soon as practicable . . . and we hope that "as soon as practicable" will be construed with more urgency than it usually commands in Whitehall.' Marghanita Laski let fly: 'Patriotism is definitely NOT ENOUGH, and I, for one, am fed up. I'm fed up at home and I'm fed up when I go abroad. I don't like to see the foreigner pointing out a fellow-traveller (or could it be me?) and whispering, "You can see she's English – look at her clothes!"'

And yet no post-war look had evolved. James Laver, invited to make a prediction about the look to come, replied, 'Fashion has reached one of those turning points in history when everything may happen, just because anything may happen to the world. Neither in politics, nor in social life, nor in dress, nor in millinery are the lines yet laid down. We do not know yet *what* will get itself established.' One thing was certain, that the Board of Trade had created forbidden fruit and provided a violent psychological stimulus: women were eying clothes with passionate longing. When the New Look arrived, women were going to have it.

It arrived on 12 February 1947, at the freshly painted salon of a new young designer who had emerged from the ranks at Lucien Lelong. Christian Dior opened at 30 Avenue Montaigne, backed by Marcel Boussac, the textile millionaire, and at a stroke restored world confidence in Paris as fashion leader. The models swept in with fifteen, twenty-five, even eighty yards of fabric in their skirts, and spun up the aisle to the sounds of rustling petticoats and the crashing of ashtray stands. The New Look provoked extremes of delight in women, for whom each dress and suit was an orgy of all things most feminine and forbidden. Today no fashion innovation could equal the excitement of Dior's then, because it had been preceded by thirteen uninterrupted years of the square-shouldered Schiaparelli-initiated look.

Dior said, 'I designed clothes for flower-like women, with rounded shoulders, full, feminine busts, and hand-span waists above enormous, spreading skirts.' His models looked absolutely different from the women in the audience. Dior's newly-designed woman had soft neat shoulders, a wasp waist, a bosom padded for extra curve, and hips that swelled over shells of cambric or taffeta worked into the lining: the dressmaking techniques were immensely complicated, some Victorian, some newly evolved. She walked leaning backward to make the hips more prominent, and her skirt burst into pleats, sometimes stitched over the hips or blossoming out under the stiff curved peplum of her jacket. Her hem rustled around some twelve inches from the floor, from which it was divided by the sheerest of silk stockings and the highest of pointed shoes. She was delicious, and she made all other women green with envy.

Coffin

1 and 2. Gervais's human hair-dryers, Paris 1944.
3. Ministry of Food advertisement, 1944, for a dried egg omelette.
4. Christian Dior in 1947, the year of the New Look.

For *Vogue*, Dior's collection came at the end of a dull round of collections, too late to be justly dealt with in the March issue – there's a single line at the end of the Paris report, 'The season's sensation is the new house of Christian Dior – see next issue.' The April issue said, 'Christian Dior is the new name in Paris. With his first collection he not only shot into fame, but retrieved the general situation by . . . "the Battle of the Marne of the couture". His ideas were fresh and put over with great authority, his clothes were beautifully made, essentially Parisian, deeply feminine. Dior uses fabric lavishly in skirts – 15 yards in a woollen day dress, 25 yards in a short taffeta evening dress' and later, 'Fashion has moved decisively. Here are the inescapable changes. Always there is something prominent about the hips: in a shelf of peplum or a ledge of tucking; in bunched pleats or a bustle. The waist is breathtaking (except in the case of greatcoats). It is caught in with curved-to-the-form leather belts or wide, wide contrasting corselets or cummerbunds. Collars are clearly either/or: tiny or whoppers. Either way they are likely to stand up. Shoulders are gently natural. Sleeves are often pushed up; sometimes bulge at the wrists.' It was many years since the copy had been able to be so definite, so exact.

Women no sooner saw the New Look, but they had to have it. Dereta was one of the first off the mark in producing a grey flannel copy, and was taken aback to see 700 of them vanish from the rails of one West End shop within a fortnight. Naturally, because of the amount of fabric needed, the New Look could only appear in non-Utility clothes, of which production was limited. Yet manufacturers caught with large stocks of Utility 'man-tailored' suits lost money hand over fist: no one wanted them.

167

Sir Stafford Cripps summed up outraged official reaction: fury at the thwarting of fabric restrictions. He called a meeting of the British Guild of Creative Designers and suggested that they would be helping the national effort considerably if they would cooperate in keeping the short skirt popular – and the Guild obediently agreed to try. He then called in a committee of fashion journalists and, with the help of Harold Wilson, President of the Board of Trade, tried to persuade them to ignore Paris. They pointed out that their job was to report.

Several leading Labour party ladies including Mrs Bessie Braddock took up the struggle against what seemed to them to be a negation of all that women had won for themselves in two wars, making the classic mistake of thinking of female emancipation in male terms – that a woman has to be like a man to be free. To their attacks Christian Dior simply replied, 'I brought back the neglected art of pleasing'.

The New Look was such a success the new salon could hardly manage all their clients. I. Magnin took forty toiles, and Bergdorf Goodman, Bendel, Marshall Field, Eaton, Holt Renfrew took anything up to that number, ensuring that the whole of America would be wearing Dior or Dior copies. Buyers were still in the salon at two o'clock in the morning. The Dior staff worked eighteen hours a day. The two first famous customers were the Duchess of Windsor and Eva Peron, to be followed by Lady Marriott who ordered 40 models a season, Mrs Thomas Biddle, who had each dress repeated in four colours, Mrs David Bruce and 'all those beautiful English-women, victims of the currency restrictions in England' as the *première vendeuse* Suzanne Beguin put it – Lady Beatty, the Countess of Kenmare, Lady Peek ... and from Paris Baronne Alain de Rothschild, Madame Pierre Michelin and the Brazilian-born Madame Martinez de Hoz, formerly Vionnet's favourite client.

Unknown to Sir Stafford Cripps, the press and Norman Hartnell, there was a private showing of Dior's collection to the Queen, Princess Margaret and the Duchess of Kent at the French embassy in the autumn. Princess Margaret in due course gave her seal of approval to the New Look by wearing it everywhere. The Queen and the Duchess of Kent were soon wearing the new length and line as it influenced their own designers, Hartnell and Molyneux.

Another new designer, Pierre Balmain, had opened immediately after the war. He was a contemporary of Christian Dior at Lelong – in fact, they shared a desk and had once discussed the possibility of opening a salon together. A friend of Gertrude Stein, he had won her affection by making for her and for Alice B. Toklas 'nice warm suits', and she wrote a charming small piece about him for *Vogue*. At his first collection, Gertrude Stein whispered to Miss Toklas, 'We are the only people here wearing Balmain's clothes, but we must not let anyone know for we are not great advertisements for the world of fashion.'

A feature of the war and post-war years were the enormous queues to get into anything that was on. It took the Blitz or the appalling freak winter of 1946–7 to keep them away. From 1945 to 1950, 20 million people a week were going to the cinema: as one manager said, 'You can open a can of sardines and there's a line waiting to get in.' Shakespeare enjoyed a tremendous war-time revival, embodying for the audiences patriotism, historical romance and a secure sense of tradition in one. The Old Vic was bombed and became hydra-headed, with its companies covering the entire country. London lost its position as cultural head of Britain as companies scattered, museums and galleries closed down and musicians went on tour. London's loss was England's gain, and the provincial towns were able to see the best actors and productions available. Noël Coward took his players on the road in 1942 with *Blithe Spirit*, *Present Laughter* and *This Happy Breed*

– described by *Vogue* as '*Cavalcade* through the wrong end of opera glasses'. His first film was made at Denham with co-director David Lean. *In Which We Serve* was the story of a destroyer and the men who served on her, with Coward for the Captain, Celia Johnson as his wife, and Bernard Miles, Joyce Carey, John Mills and Kay Walsh in leading roles. It was notable for its realistic treatment of the subject, even down to a single swear word, and for its absence of condescension in dealing with the lower decks.

Whether it was Noël Coward and John Mills showing a stiff upper lip or Betty Grable and Rita Hayworth showing a bit of leg, films were a marvellous escape from reality. As *Vogue* said, 'Today's woman has less time to imagine, and a good deal of her imagining is done for her in the cinema.' Hollywood was earning about 70 million dollars a year in this country when in 1947 the Chancellor of the Exchequer, at this moment Dr Hugh Dalton, slapped a customs duty of 75 per cent on the value of all imported films, the sum to be prepaid. The day after, the Motion Picture Association

1. Noël Coward's first film, *In Which We Serve*, made at Denham in 1941-42.
2. Gertrude Stein with Alice B. Toklas, *left*, 1945.

1. Laurence Olivier and Vivien Leigh in 1940: 'The true-life love story of Scarlett O'Hara and *Rebecca's* Max de Winter was apotheosized in their Broadway *Romeo and Juliet* with Motley's décor and costumes.'
2. 'The uniform for the job', 1943: Cook, boat's crew, balloon operator, M.T. driver.

of America announced that all shipments of films were to be suspended immediately. Dr Dalton had blundered. True, he had presented the British film industry with the home market, but without the possibility of export to America, and much too soon – it was not yet ready to fill the gap. The improved standard of British wartime films – noted by *Vogue* in an optimistic feature called 'The coming heyday of British films' – was abandoned in the pressure to pour out cheap films to fill the cinemas. These were soon competing against the best American films that had been waiting for the embargo to be lifted, as it was a few months later by Harold Wilson as President of the Board of Trade. Rank lost over six million pounds in four years. By the spring of 1949, seventeen out of twenty-six British studios were idle, and on top of that there was the crushing entertainment tax. British films had ceased to be a paying production. Laurence Olivier said, 'It is wrong to say that British films don't pay – they pay very well, but they pay the wrong people.'

During the war the B.B.C.'s staff trebled in size, due to the boom in sound broadcasting, which eventually reached virtually every adult in the country. It was not just the news, preceded by the booming notes of Big Ben, that attracted listeners, it was the radio show I.T.M.A. with Tommy Handley, the Minister of Aggravation and Mysteries in the Office of Twerps, the Mayor of Foaming at the Mouth, Funf the German spy . . . *Much Binding in the Marsh* . . . *Bandwagon* . . . and in 1941 a different kind of programme, the *Brains Trust*, with philosopher Cyril Joad and his shrill opening, 'It depends what you mean by . . .', zoologist Julian Huxley, and retired naval officer A. B. Campbell, answering such questions as 'What is love?' and 'How do flies land on the ceiling?'

Elizabeth Bowen wrote about the function of the Third Programme for *Vogue*, stressing the need for drama writing on a high plane written specially for the air and commending Laurie Lee's *The Voyage of Magellan*, Louis MacNeice's *The Careerist* and Patric Dickinson's *The Wall of Troy*. 'To an extent, the programme is to create the listener: not less, the listener is to create the programme – by his response, mobility, curiosity, sensitiveness and willingness in approach to the not yet known. Third Programme is out to take long chances and risk wide shots.' She noticed with approval a new Europeanism of outlook, pointing out, 'We have an immense amount to catch up with. We need exactly the stimulus outside thought can supply.'

The museums reopened in 1945, and there were new foreign art books for sale in the book shops again. At the British Museum one of the first collections on show was the Sutton Hoo treasure, with an interesting tale behind it. Sutton Hoo's owner, Mrs Pretty, began in 1939 to have a persistent dream telling her, 'You must open the barrow by the river'. When, eventually, archaeologists broke into the mound they unearthed a huge Anglo-Saxon vessel bearing the richest series of funeral treasure ever unearthed in England – Byzantine silver dishes, enamelled flagons and jewels.

During and after the Second World War, as after the First, there was a preoccupation with the nature of the role of women, the theme appearing and reappearing in *Vogue*, sometimes in captions, sometimes in features or odd remarks. Discussing the work of Frances Hodgkins, who died in 1947, Myfanwy Evans said, 'Many women who are creative artists of any kind manage to achieve their work in spite of the fact that they also live normal (if

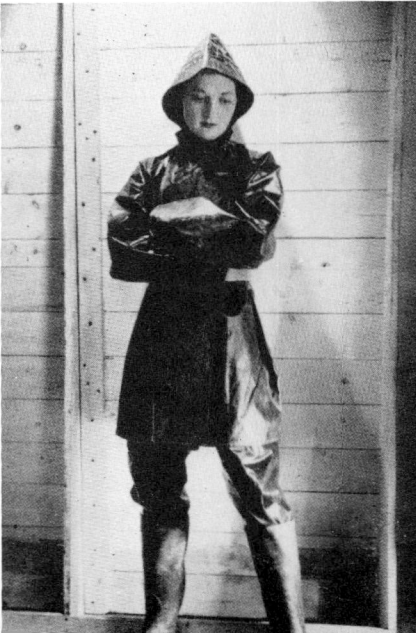

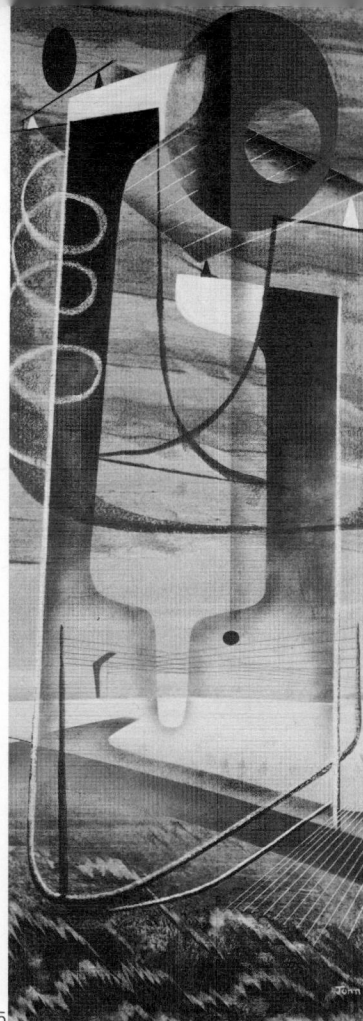

3. Frances Hodgkins painting, published in the year of her death, 1947, when she was 77.
4. Daphne du Maurier, 1946.
5. John Tunnard's illustration for Richard Busvine's feature on the future of television in 1945.

Felix Man   Coffin

nerve-wrecked) lives as women, with husband, home, children, clothes, servants and so on; it is the intensity with which they can withdraw from the world at the time that they are working that makes them into amateurs or professionals; the degree to which they can bear to be so much in the wrong as to be thoroughly selfish, at times, that makes them good or indifferent artists . . . a few take the most difficult way, and, remaining solitary, live or die by their work. Frances Hodgkins was one of these.' Anne Scott-James, reviewing *The Taming of the Shrew* at the rebuilt Old Vic, with Trevor Howard and Pat Burke, noticed, 'the Shrew was played like an honest child who grows into knowledge of guile and opportunism'. Again, Daphne du Maurier, writing in 1946 on doing nothing in the country: 'By this time I have had my bath, and am dressing, and am composing a letter to *The Times*, never published, on the subject of birth-control. The birthrate is falling, and I know why, and so do all the other women of my generation. It has nothing to do with insecurity or atom-bombs or the movies. It is because we don't *want* a lot of children, and had the women of past generations known how to limit their families they would have done so . . . Why are the churches empty? Because, with modern warfare, hellfire holds no terror for us. And was it only fear of the hereafter that made my lady in her crinoline go to church three times on a Sunday? No, it was boredom.' The feeling in the air was pinned, defined and concisely set out by Simone de Beauvoir in 'Femininity, the Trap', which appeared in *Vogue* in July 1947: the leading disciple of Jean-Paul Sartre's Existentialist philosophy, she had already published three novels and a play.

In 1947 Edith Piaf sang at the music halls and Existentialism was the new word in Paris. *Vogue* followed Sartre from the bar of the Pont Royal Hotel – 'no Bohemian café. It is like a shining Ritz bar on the left bank, and here Sartre drinks dry Martinis' – to a lecture at the Sorbonne. 'Sartre, short, broad, about thirty-eight, with thick glasses, sat at a small table and talked about the theatre. He spoke with extraordinary clearness and force, without confusion or metaphysics, or trailing ends of Existentialism, or roundhouse sentences . . . Speaking without notes and for one hour, he told these boys his theories about the theatre. His thesis is simply that

the drama now must be one of situation and not of character. That life is a series of choices and the way one chooses determines one's character, not the other way around.'

Mid-way through the forties, Richard Busvine had written in *Vogue*, 'Television, as a medium of entertainment, will eventually kill sound broadcasting stone dead, just as the talkies killed silent films. This development is recognised by the experts as the natural and inevitable outcome of television progress, and they therefore await with considerable impatience official resumption of the Television Service.' It was resumed in 1946, but not looked forward to by everyone with the same enthusiasm as Richard Busvine's experts. There were growing fears that the future industrial development of England, of which television and fashion were a part, would detract from the quality of life. Would the Britain of the future be the same Britain that had been fought for? Siegfried Sassoon voiced these fears. 'Up to about 30 years ago it was still quite reasonable to say that God made the country and man made the town . . . But the process of disfigurement has been insidious, because people accept it without realising the cumulative effect. These remarks are addressed (though only theoretically, I fear) to those who live in towns, but more especially to persons responsible for urban expansion, commercial exploitation of natural resources, and other energetic operations which can make a nice neighbourhood profitable and unpleasant . . . While I write these words, the hedges of England are white with hawthorn; meadows are bright with buttercups and the golden foot of May is on the flowers. Bees rejoice in the blossoming chestnut trees; the cuckoo shouts all day at nothing . . . One might almost believe that all's well with the world. But the urban and the rural district councillors think otherwise. For them a stretch of prime pasture land is an eligible building site; a leafy lane is a valuable road-frontage; and yonder copsy hillside has already been earmarked as the location for the latest thing in sewage farms. Next comes the county council road surveyor, companioned by an official from the Ministry of Transport who doesn't know an oak from an elm. Doomed are the delightful windings of the road Plumstead Episcopi to Crabtree Canonicorum.'

171

THE CHANGING FACE

DEBORAH KERR

At the beginning of her career after appearances in
films like *Major Barbara* and *Love on the Dole*, she followed up with a
triumphant stage appearance as Ellie Dunn in *Heartbreak House*. In
1943, when Cecil Beaton took this photograph, she was about to begin
work as Mary of Scotland for Gabriel Pascal. Her tranquil classic
beauty is at its best in this Molyneux black satin dress lined
with primrose crepe.

Cecil Beaton

MOLYNEUX

Cecil Beaton

1. Vivien Leigh in Molyneux star print dress
and black tweed jacket, 1941.
2. 1937, in Stiebel's magenta taffeta dress,
bordered with turquoise.
3. 1936.
4. 1941.

3

Rawlings

4

VIVIEN LEIGH

Vogue photographed Vivien Leigh as early as 1935, but her real fame came when she played Scarlett O'Hara in Selznick's 3¾ hour *Gone with the Wind*, which opened in Atlanta in December 1939, but appeared in Britain much later, delayed by wartime restrictions. Her marriage to Laurence Olivier put the seal on her success: her name was written in lights over three Broadway cinemas while she was playing Juliet to his Romeo on the New York stage, and later they appeared together in *Hamlet* at the very scene of the tragedy, Kronberg Castle, Elsinore. With her green eyes, her dark red hair, her beautiful pointed face, she looked marvellous in Victor Stiebel's evening dresses.

LORETTA YOUNG
Star in 1942 of
Bedtime Story and *The Men in Her Life*,
in a hat of spun glass and lace.

Horst

CONSTANCE BENNETT

A star of the thirties, Constance Bennett became the Hollywood evocation of the forties with her pompadour hairdo and her beautiful surprised-looking face. In 1926 she had married the wealthy Philip Plant. Four years afterwards, with a divorce and a million-dollar marriage settlement, she went back to Hollywood and stardom. As she eclipsed Gloria Swanson at the box office, she married Miss Swanson's former husband the Marquis de la Falaise. She always showed a good head for business, and her sister Joan Bennett was to say of her, 'If she can't take it with her, she won't go.'

1. 1941, Californian elegance from Irene: chalk-white crepe scarf and skirt, draped bodice the colour of tanned skin.
2. The exact wartime face — Constance Bennett's in 1940.

IRENE   Toni Frissell

LADY LOUIS MOUNTBATTEN

Lady Louis Mountbatten was known for the height of her heels, the brilliance of her smile and the blue of her eyes. She dressed beautifully, whether it was in a leather flying coat or in the faconné satins and patterned lamés that Worth made for her to take to Malta.

1. Painted by Salvador Dali, 1940: 'Last year she divided her time between her Brook Street penthouse and foreign travel. This year between Navy Comforts Committee work and country weekends.'
2. 1933.
3. 1943.

Horst

Clarence Bull

KATHERINE HEPBURN
Although Katherine Hepburn did much to spread the fashion for
neo-Victorian dress with Jo in *Little Women*, in private life she
has always liked trousers and no make up. She turned out to be
a superb comédienne in *Bringing up Baby*, 1938, six years after
her screen debut with John Barrymore. She was the first star
to have red curls and freckles.

Katherine Hepburn in the New York production of *The Lake*, 1934.
Opposite: Star of *The Philadelphia Story* opposite Cary Grant, 1940.

Steichen

1 MARCELLE

ADRIAN

INGRID BERGMAN

Toni Frissell

In 1941, 'the girl Hemingway would like for the star in the film version of *For Whom The Bell Tolls*'. Here in Adrian's white mousseline de soie dress with looped hems.

2 MOLYNEUX

ANN TODD

1. The forties face, in Marcelle's velvet pillbox, a cloud of spotted veiling tying under her chin: in 1944 she makes *Perfect Strangers*, a Korda production.
2. Star for a film about the Fleet Air Arm, *Ships with Wings*, from Ealing Studios, 1941. Dress by Molyneux.

MIGHTIER YET!
A FEW
CARELESS WORDS
MAY END IN THIS–
Many lives were lost in the last war through careless talk
Be on your guard ! Don't discuss movements of ships or troops
"CHEERIO, OLD LAD, GOOD LUC
CARELESS TALK CO
K UP THE
GHTING
ORCES

Lee Miller

'Last year women were running households. This year they are running canteens, voluntary organizations, service units – and taking orders as well as giving them. Last year time was no object: this week, next week, sometime . . . to dine, to dance, to meet, to marry '

'This year time is of the essence of the contract. Leave is reckoned in days, hours, minutes. Dates are timed to the split second and girls no longer keep boys waiting. "Are you free next Wednesday – 4.30–8? I've special leave." "Can you lunch today?" "Can you marry me tomorrow?" '

After the occupation of Paris at the end of May, attention is turned perforce to London design, ready-to-wear and the couture who bank on the export trade. Schiaparelli's wardrobe that she takes to America is the last Paris fashion in *Vogue* for four years. Suits range from the frankly military to the rather military, and in reaction there's a brief return to evening dress. For daytime relief there are duster hats with a scarf curtain falling over the hair, and built-up shoes, solid by day but as fanciful as you can find for evening. Purchase tax and shortage of fabric oblige women to buy less and more wisely. *Vogue* helps with diagrams showing how you can alter last year's looks and bring them up to date — although nothing has really changed.

Military Alliance between the air-force blue tweed and martial cut of this suit from Debenham and Freebody; $14\frac{1}{2}$ guineas

Molyneux's black mackintosh, lined in red tweed to match the dress and jacket, October 1940; photograph Cecil Beaton.

ON TOP at the Paris Mid-seasons

Dusters

They're sweeping Paris—
these handkerchief hats;
twisted into tight little pillboxes,
curtaining your curls.
Albouy, new milliner,
invented them

1   André Durst

2
SCHIAPARELLI   André Durst

3
BALENCIAGA

1. Fanciful duster hats by Albouy.
2. Schiaparelli's black and shocking pink — tight-waisted black suit with embroidered arrows, rosy pillbox.
3. Black wool jersey dress with violet yokes, silver fox shako and muff.
4. Mrs Max Aitken and a heap of aluminium for the aeroplane drive of her father-in-law Lord Beaverbrook, the Minister of Aircraft Production. This stunt turned into a fiasco when treasured saucepans were left unused because of their low aluminium content. Jaeger marron tweed coat.
5. *Vogue* cover of April 1940, showing the hard make up and Joan Crawford lips of the day.

JAEGER

1941

A deceptive jacket front gives a suit look for the coupon value of a dress, 11 coupons, 8½gns. at Bourne & Hollingsworth.

'Your wardrobe, instead of being a three-volume novel, will now be a short story in which every line will count'
'Il faut skimp, pour être chic'

Fashion now reaches its lowest ebb. Clothes rationing comes into force in June. *Vogue* tries to make the best of things but bewails the system. Utility clothes, two-thirds of all the clothes you can buy, fulfil government requirements and restrictions, and sell at fixed prices. The ban on silk stockings is another blow. In January *Vogue* is recommending the substitutes, but by August these too are in short supply. Cosmetics disappear from the counters, and Black Market make-up often contains a high proportion of lead, or at least brings you out in a guilty rash. 'Save your cosmetics for evenings out,' says *Vogue* in November, but most women have already been make-up-less for months.

The export drive is an essential source of income. Nine London-based couturiers combine in a collection for South America, sent out under government auspices. *Vogue's* copy accompanying the pictures has a wistful note: 'Though many of the models are necessarily remote from wartime life in England, yet still they hold much fashion interest for us.' In another export effort backed by government subsidy, the Cotton Board commissions artists, including Paul Nash, Graham Sutherland and Frank Dobson, to design new prints in co-operation with *Vogue,* couturiers and textile experts.

Vogue publishes a feature on looking your best in uniform with short hair, short nails and good posture, and praises the fashionable qualities of the British Warm — 'its pale beige colour is extremely becoming and its seven-eighths length has great chic. It looks wonderful (and even warmer) if lined with scarlet; but such splendour is reserved for those of field rank . . . its capacious pockets swallow up make-up and manicure kit without bulging.'

1
DERÉTA

London Fashions for South America

WORTH
PETER RUSSELL
WORTH

2

Cecil Beaton

1. Déreta advertisement, camel winter coat, fifteen coupons only.
2. Forbidden luxury — a spread from *Vogue's* special South American number supporting the co-operative London collection for export.
3. Mrs Christopher Sykes pulling off her overboots in the Ritz: bicycling to Government work she wears a mustard wool suit with wrapped and buttoned skirt made by her Polish dressmaker, Mme Przeworska.
4. The standby in the silk and flax shortage is rayon crepe, here in a Molyneux dress with a yoke of fuchsia sequins and a cyclamen sash.
5. Loretta Young in a net turban from Pissot and Pavy, knotted over a handful of tulips.

4

5

Cecil Beaton   PISSOT & PAVY

1941

RAHVIS, STRASSNER

Horst   4.

1. Rahvis's and Strassner's draped
evening dresses with
embroidered bands.
2. Tough coloured stockings, a
necessary substitute for short-lived
sheer ones: lilac, rose and
apple green.
3. Uniform hair made the best of —
three inches as worn in the services
and in factories. For A.R.P. workers
Vogue recommends tying long hair
into a net turban which will be
hidden under the tin hat, and for the
face 'no make-up but a non-greasy
all purpose cream dusted
with powder'.
4 and 5. New cotton prints:
above, John Armstrong's 'Fighting
Dream'; *below*, Paul Nash's
'Romney Marsh'.

Toni Frissell

'Fashion is undergoing a compulsory course of slimming and simplification ... the progress of the war has made it necessary to prohibit all superfluous material and superfluous labour'

'We are not saying that these clothes compete with the superb standard of pre-war days – but then neither does this life compare with that'

The Government gives Utility designs a much-needed boost by asking London couturiers to combine in a Utility collection for mass production. Molyneux, Hardy Amies, Digby Morton, Bianca Mosca, Peter Russell and Worth comply with Utility specifications to make topcoats, suits, afternoon dresses and cotton overalls that go anonymously into the shops in the spring of 1943. The stocking situation has become so bad that *Vogue* photographs a model in ankle socks.

Lack of every luxury forces emphasis on health, efficiency and practicality. 'Clothes look as if they had been taken care of, put on beautifully, and then forgotten for more important things. The woman well-dressed in the meaning of today would not easily be rendered helpless or ridiculous . . . that "too good to be true" look which only a personal maid can produce is absent — because the maid is absent, on munitions.' *Vogue* publishes a picture-strip showing you how to set your own hair, and trusts that the supply of cosmetics, already curtailed to 25 per cent of peacetime output, will not be further reduced. When the worse comes to the worst, 'there are four fundamental cosmetics you'll need, cosmetics which don't come out of jars and bottles . . . they are unrestricted, available to everybody: sleep, diet, exercise, rest for 20 minutes a day after lunch.'

The ideal wartime look: health and vigour, sleeves rolled back, socks pulled up.

185

1. Couturier-designed but anonymous Utility dresses commissioned by the Government: red and blue crepe.
2. Margaret Vyner shows how you can go hatless and stockingless in town, in a pale linen jumper suit from Fortnum & Mason and Pinet shoes.
3. The stocking situation has come to this: 'If we don't go without stockings this summer we shall go without stockings next winter.' The entire outfit from Fortnum & Mason, July 1942.

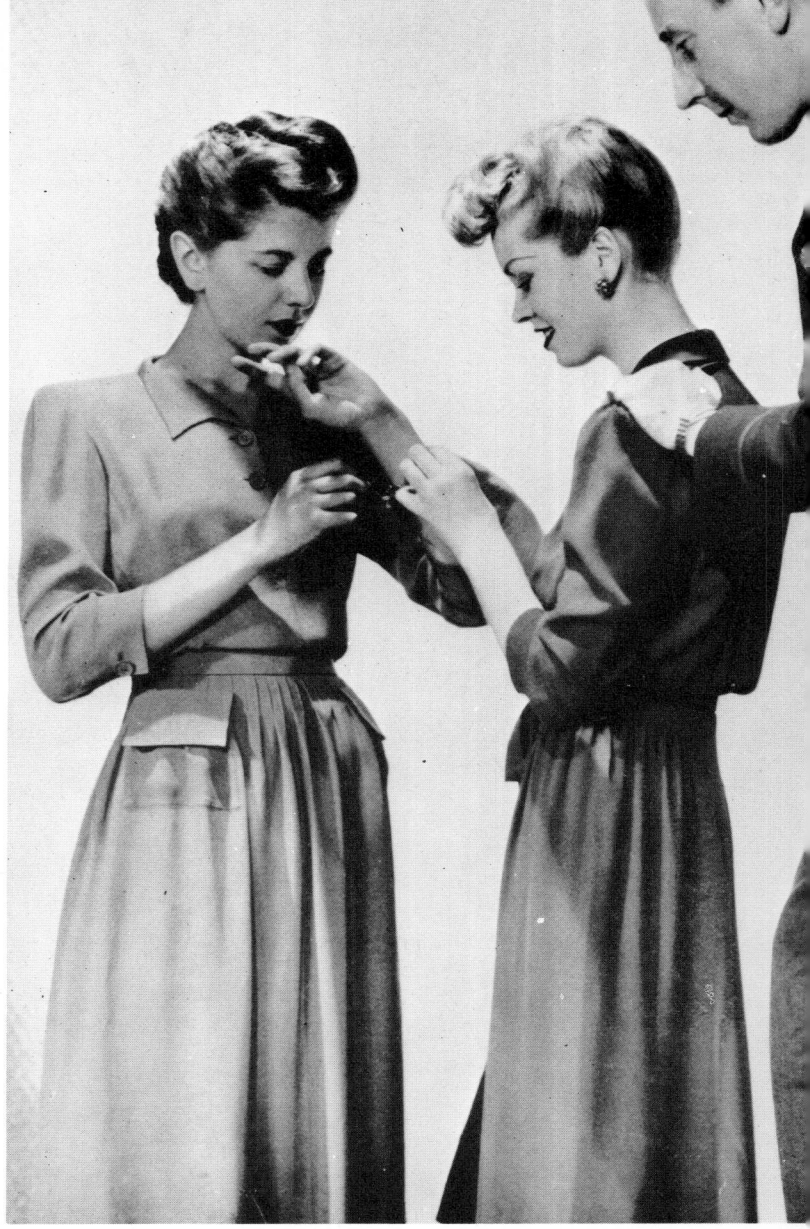

We can't have it both ways...

Even if we were not called to help, we could not leave men to fight this war alone. We asked for equal rights and we cannot have it both ways. It is only fair that we should face the music side by side with our men. Total war makes heavy demands on us. We must submit to routine and still keep the sparkle of unfettered days. We must take risks and show no sign of fear. We must work hard and let no weariness appear. We must remember that the slightest hint of a drooping spirit yields a point to the enemy. Never must careless grooming reflect a 'don't care' mood. Now that leisure and beauty-aids are limited, we can take pride in looking our best. Face value is more than ever high. Never should we forget that good looks and good morale are the closest of good companions.

PUT YOUR BEST FACE FORWARD.. *Yardley*

LE COQ D'OR RESTAURANT OPEN.

Lee Miller

It's a dream... it's HARELLA

Lee Miller

4. London couture suits in Utility tweeds, October 1942.
5. Entertaining the troops.
6. *Vogue* cover, May 1943: waistcoat, slacks and boxy jacket.   6

1942-43

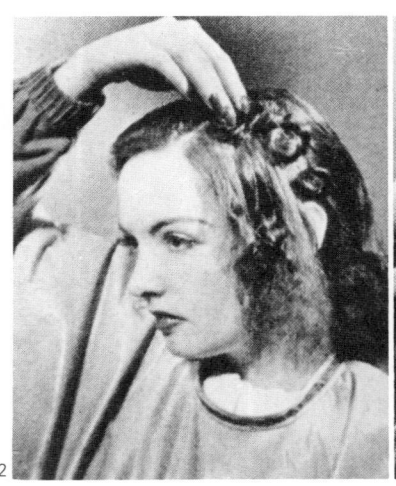

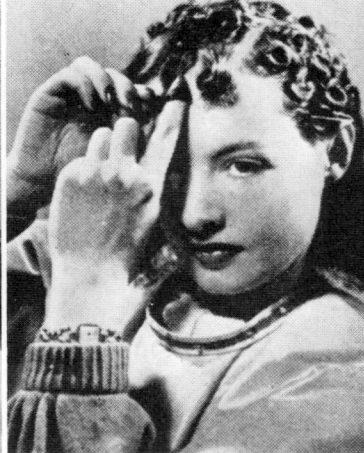

Baker

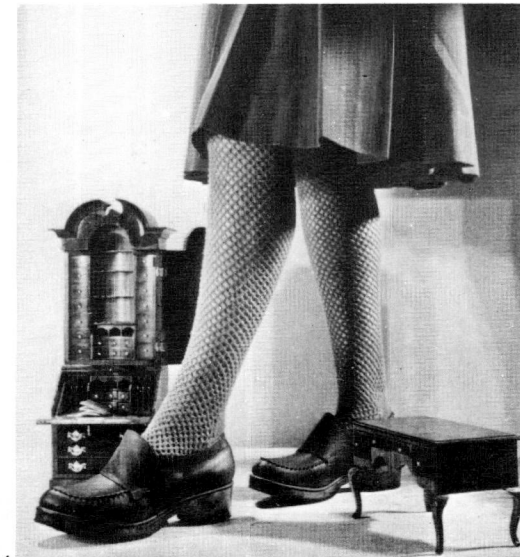

1. For limited incomes — *left*, twinset 26*s*. 9*d*., skirt 25*s*. 6*d*. *right*, twinset 26*s*. 5*d*. skirt 21*s*. 1*d*.
2. How to set your own hair: pompadour and curls, set with Kirbigrips.
3. 'Accessories, like other amenities, are getting scarcer, and are too costly to be lightly and lavishly bought.' Pancake and huge gloves in looped emerald green crochet.
4. Brevitt's wood-soled calf sabots 'to eke out the nation's shoe leather'. And to eke out the nation's stockings, heavy knits from a 6*d*. *Vogue* pattern.
5. A time for doing things by halves: 'As wardrobes wear out and coupons contract, a new fashion formula is needed . . . think in half terms for a change — a skirt and a shirt instead of a whole dress'. Black shirt and plaid skirt from Harrods.

Lee Miller   HARRODS   Horst

1944

Paris Liberation fashions
'The first free demonstration of the couture since 1940' *Lucien Lelong*

'... a flagrant violation of our imposed wartime silhouette' *The American War Production Board*

The Liberation of Paris in August allows *Vogue* readers to see the first Paris collection photographs since 1940. The autumn collections are given a mixed reception here and in America. The official reaction of both countries is an angry protest against such wastage of fabric and labour. In spite of the recently imposed L 85 restrictions in America, the manufacturers are quick to adopt the Liberation fashions, and a ban is imposed on copying from the photographs in fashion magazines. In Britain, there is no question of being able to copy the full skirts and dressmaker details.

Left: Molyneux's spare grey flannel suit with rounded revers and pockets; photograph Norman Parkinson.

MARGARET BARRY   JAYS

Norman Parkinson

2
AAGE THAARUP

SCHIAPARELLI

3

Lee Miller

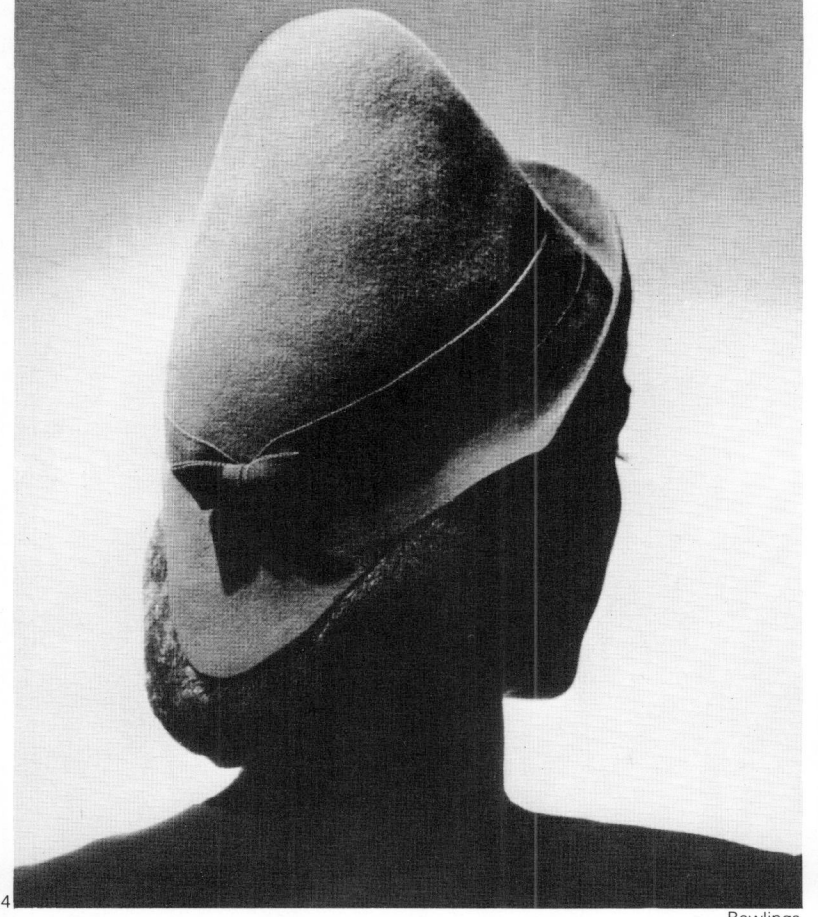

4

Rawlings

5

Joffé

6

Norman Parkinson

7

1. Norman Parkinson's photographs are a breath
of fresh air. Here, his 'change of weather' pictures,
showing the outside and inside of the 1944 wardrobe
(*left*, Margaret Barry, *right*, Jays).
2. Margot Fonteyn in the black felt Chinese hat designed
for her by Aage Thaarup.
3. Hourglass black wool coat lined in fur,
with a fur-trimmed turban.
4. Hat backward . . . hair down.
5. Hat forward . . . hair up.
6. Bicycling outfit: striped lisle shirt and divided
skirt in Moygashel spun rayon.
7. Rima advertisement.

1945-46

A 1945 silhouette: chinstrap hat, tight waist, stiff lampshade peplum, narrow longer skirt.

Joffé

'Neither in politics, nor in social life, nor in dress, nor in millinery are the lines yet laid down. We do not know yet *what* will get itself established'
James Laver, November 1946
The end of the war—and clothes rationing tightens. *Vogue*'s tone of voice, wearily patient in August 1945, 'when you read of beautiful fabrics and models being made "for export only", you would hardly be human if you did not feel a pang that they should be going out of your reach—and probably to women with fuller wardrobes than your own. But if your second thought can be "There go the means of bringing in food and raw material and the thousand things that England needs to live"—perhaps you won't feel so badly about it', acquires a sharper note by November—'these genius-thwarting austerity restrictions'. Life is to be drab for some time.

Vogue shows demobilization clothes for Servicewomen, 'You have a chance that seldom comes more than once in a lifetime—the chance of buying a completely new wardrobe', and in July 1945 publishes the first radioed

pictures and text from Moscow's Soviet State Fashion Show, in which judges pick 300 models for mass production from 1,100 shown.

In London, on 24 September 1946, the Council of Industrial Design opens the 'Britain Can Make It' exhibition at the Victoria and Albert Museum to prove that Britain can still produce the goods and to help raise the standard of design in everything from jugs and radios to dresses. The Fashion Hall is divided into three sections for inexpensive, medium-priced and couture clothes.

From Paris the news is hems lower, heels higher, waists nipped in with wired and boned corsets. Otherwise there is an air of indecision. In January *Vogue* reports 'Exaggeration of style has disappeared in Paris—austere elegance takes its place', in October 'Paris revels in femininity'. In fact, as James Laver says a month later, 'Fashion has reached one of those turning points in history when everything may happen . . . We do not know yet *what* will get itself established.'

There is a pregnant silence.

WOLSEY

Coffin

Penn

1. Yellow jersey dress with snakeskin belt.
2. 1946 straws in the wind — feathered cartwheel, deep neckline, draped longer skirt.
3. A new simplicity — white piqué dance dress from Ships, 1946.
4,5 and 6. 'Base your demobilization wardrobe on clothes like these.'

SHIPS

Blumenfeld

193

1945-46

BALENCIAGA

194

1 Eric

2

3 Eric

1 and 3. Eric draws evening silhouettes in 1946, showing the indecision of line and proportion.
2. Madame Rubio, the new Paris beauty, in a red faille dress with an embroidered bodice, 1946.
4. Hartnell's swathed purple sheath, 1946.
5. Indecision in length: the American handkerchief hem and swathed waist of 1946.
6. Dinner hat, 1945.
7. The 'Britain Can Make It' exhibition, September 1946: tucked and fitted grey dinner dress by Hardy Amies; beauty iron to stimulate circulation and spread face-cream evenly, by Countess Csaky.

5

Joffé

TURN ON FOR MORE

BRITAIN CAN MAKE IT

1. Corsets for the new nipped-in waists: 'veins of tiny wires and delicate bones make a wholly new way to let a woman look like a woman'. Here, blue grosgrain waspie used by Piguet and copied in England by Warners.
2. The first jeans in *Vogue*, July 1946 — royal blue and cropped to midcalf, from Simpsons.
3. Postwar beauty: pink-rouged cheeks, red lips, draped hair. Make up by Elizabeth Arden.
4. Forerunner of tights — pants and stockings in the same rib, 1946.
Right, Norman Parkinson's woman in white — 'wistful with the frustrations of youth, or the longing for a charm and an elegance abandoned without question during the wartime years, now hard to recover in a Utility world'? That was the longing that Dior's New Look answered.

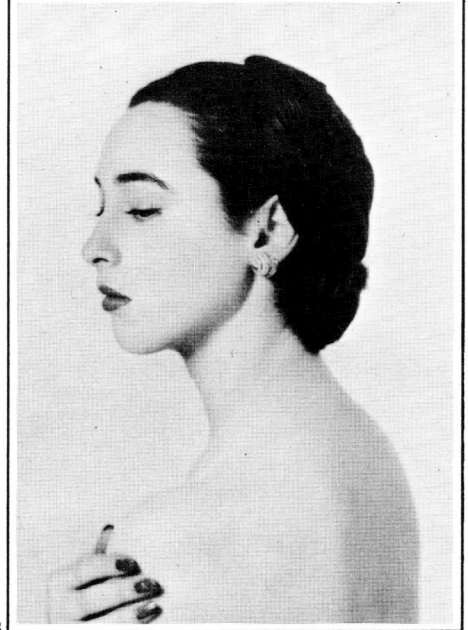

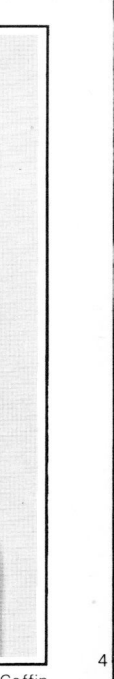

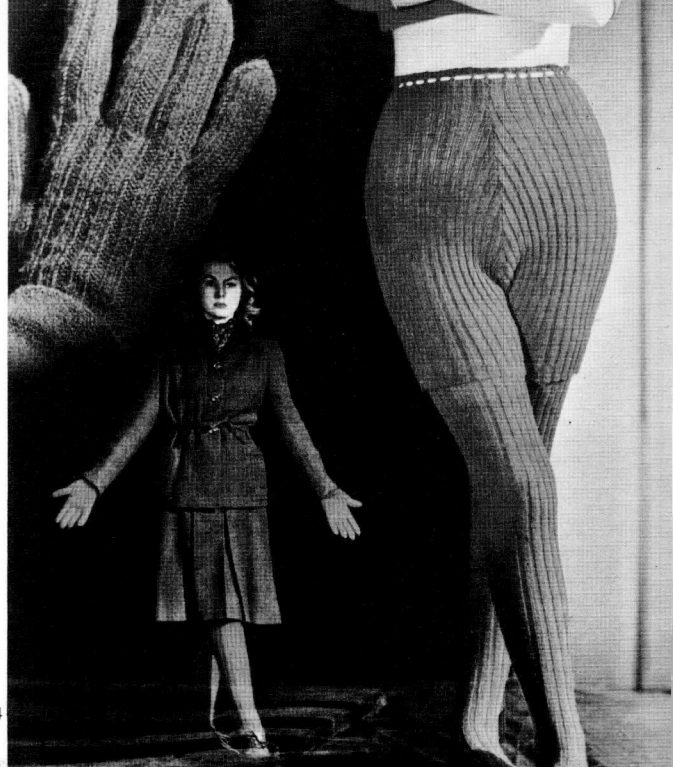

Coffin

1947

'The season's sensation is the new house of Christian Dior'

'The New Look wins – by a length!' *Commentator at Kempton Park's Easter meeting*

'Dior has saved the name of Paris' *Journalist at Dior's first collection*

'Bravo! Ravissant! Magnifique!' *Cries from the press at the collection*

'The longer skirt . . . the ridiculous whim of idle people . . . people who worry about longer skirts might do something more useful with their time' *Mrs Bessie Braddock*

'This New Look business is just completely silly' *Mrs Mabel Ridealgh, M.P.*

'There should be a law!' *Sir Stafford Cripps, President of the Board of Trade*

February 12, and to the women present at the first collection of Christian Dior, the war and its drab aftermath seems to be over at last. Dior, formerly a designer at Lucien Lelong, opens in pristine premises at 30 Avenue Montaigne, and with his New Look reinstates Paris as the authoritative leader of world fashion. At the end of the show, Englishwomen can be seen tugging their skimpy skirts down over their knees, feeling suddenly uncomfortable in their square-shouldered 'man-tailored' wartime suits.

Sir Stafford Cripps, President of the Board of Trade, sums up outraged official reaction. When the press seem reluctant to co-operate, Sir Stafford thumps the table and snorts, 'There should be a law.'

Meanwhile, in the autumn, unknown to the press, the public and Norman Hartnell, there is a special private showing of the Dior collection to the Queen, Princess Margaret and the Duchess of Kent at the French Embassy. Princess Margaret in due course gives the New Look her seal of approval by wearing it everywhere, and the Queen and the Duchess of Kent are soon wearing the new length and look as it influences their own designers, Hartnell and Molyneux. Coupons or no, the New Look has been adopted throughout the English ready-to-wear by December, and will continue as the dominant fashion look for the next ten years.

Dior's tight tussore jacket, 'padded to a teacup curve' over a long pleated black skirt.

DIOR

Bérard

1. Dior's New Look sketched at
Maxim's by Nobilé, April 1947.
2-6. Details from Dior's collection.
2. Shirtwaist collar and pleats.
3. Belted suit, box pleat skirt.
4. Safari hat, pleated dress.
5. Fan pleats.
6. Curved jacket, barrel skirt.

1 VICTOR STIEBEL

2 HARDY AMIES

3 RAHVIS

Coffin

GROUX   Coffin

1. Moira Shearer, latest addition to Covent Garden's
premières danseuses, in Victor Stiebel's ballet-length
black taffeta with an orchid pink organdie overskirt.
2. New Look influence in April: Hardy Amies's
crossover striped cotton dress with a ballet-
length skirt.
3. Rahvis's pink faille dress with a décolletage of
sequined black lace, photographed in the bomb-
shattered ruin of a beautiful house in
Grosvenor Square.
4. White straw and black felt hat.
5. The look and style of Penelope Dudley Ward is
'A figure with that thoroughbred look . . .
cameo profile . . . smooth and intelligent forehead . . .
gentian-blue eyes'.
6. October 1947: Dior drops the hem still lower. Fan-
pleated satin dress spinning out into a full skirt.
Velvet side-beret by Sygur. Photographed by Horst
at the Paris Exhibition of Housing and Urbanism.

6
DIOR   Horst

201

1948-1959

The new Avro Vulcan Bomber with Digby Morton suit, photographed by Norman Parkinson in 1954

The Fashion-conscious Fifties

Contemporary design in hats and chairs, summer 1950   Don Honeyman

Fashion was never the same after the fifties. Fundamental changes occurred thick and fast to revolutionize the industry and take it into new territories, involving bigger business than ever before. For the first time, looks and lines assumed a universal importance, making headline news in the papers all through the decade. Fashion became a new language capable of subtle interpretation, when boys and girls between 17 and 23 began to use clothes for group identification, provoking questions about fashion's role as signal, armour and decoration. For the first time in living memory, it was fashionable for men to be fashionable, a new preoccupation that cut right across society from the men about Mayfair to the Teddy Boys of the slum areas. New systems of mass production and the comparative prosperity of the late fifties made the average Englishwoman into one of the best-dressed women in the world, and the introduction of nylon made it possible for working girls in the cities to wear white and pale colours every day. Teenagers opened up a whole new category in the fashion market, and the teenage art-school designers who turned their attention to non-establishment fashion produced totally original looks, the first fashion to begin at source instead of being superimposed from abroad or adapted. These were the formative fashion years of the century – the fashion-conscious fifties.

The first ambition of the post-war years was to get back to normal. Britain was an almost bankrupt country faced with national shortages and a difficult balance of payments: austerity and rationing dragged on until 1954 in one form or another. The first sign of life had been women's appetite for the New Look, but on second sight its appeal was seen to be nostalgic, a reaction against the sexless clothes of wartime and the drudgery of home and work without a man around. Now in 1951 there was a gesture of hope and confidence in the future. The Festival of Britain was the last fling of the Labour government, a nationwide celebration of the country's contribution to civilization and a demonstration of its potential in many fields. In London the main exhibition was to be built on the blitzed South Bank site between Waterloo and Westminster bridges. The Festival Hall was the first building to be completed, a permanent fixture, and near it the Queen placed the stone for the future National Theatre. The bleak surrounding area began, under the organization of Gerald Barry and the designs of a team headed by Hugh Casson, to sprout pavilions and restaurants, constructions of cement and glass, striped awnings, flags and bunting, a Dome of Discovery with the largest unsupported roof in the world, and a towering Skylon which seems now to have been a premonition of the millions of television aerials which were to cover the country and shut down hundreds of cinemas in the course of the decade. The exhibition was bright and inviting by day, but at night it came into its own, turning into what Michael Frayn called 'a floodlit dream-world breathing music'. In *Vogue*'s eight-page Festival feature, leading off the Britannica issue, Marghanita Laski wrote, 'If all goes well ... what a country we shall live in, what a Britain we shall have! Through all our lifetimes, the man-made objects surrounding us have been devised, not to give visual pleasure, but unconsciously to assert that we are a people wealthy, provident, puritan, insular, keeping our feet firmly on the ground and not liking to make ourselves conspicuous. Suddenly on the South Bank, we discover that, no longer wealthy, we can be imaginative and experimental and ingenious, colourful, gaudy and gay.' Proving her point, *Vogue* declared, 'The most fastidious and fashion-conscious woman can dress immediately for any occasion in ready-to-wear clothes' and proved it with fashion from Jaeger, Susan Small, Dereta, and Marcus, Brenner, Rima and Mary Black.

In spite of this, *Vogue* gave the greatest emphasis all through the fifties to Paris, and for good reason. As the ready-to-wear market in America and Britain grew to giant proportions it depended more and more on Paris to act as authoritative pace-setter and to present new ideas that the public would recognize and look for in the shops. The fifties were a time of tyrannical dictatorship from Paris. Lines followed one another in quick succession: the envol line, the princess line, the tulip line, the I or H line, the A line, the trapeze line. It was a time when you couldn't be both fashionable and comfortable, unless you dressed at Chanel. You carried the weight of an enormous pyramid coat and you hobbled in pencil-slim skirts, always emphasized by photographing the model with one knee hidden behind the other. Collars turned up and bit into the chin, boned and strapless 'self-supporting' bodices made it difficult to bend, corsets pinched the waist and flattened the bust. 'Where has the waist gone?' asked *Vogue* in 1951, and answered, 'Anywhere but where you expect it.'

If you dressed in clothes from Paris or Paris copies, you wore stylized fashion with great but contrived glamour, geometric shapes, and exaggerated lines. Women obeyed Paris because of Christian Dior – no woman would forget during the fifties that a single collection had outdated everything in her wardrobe and made her self-conscious in a Utility suit. The consequence was that the fashion public were insecure, particularly about the length of their hems, and thought that every seasonal collection might bring a radical overnight change that would leave them with nothing to wear. The length of hems was headline news. Women M.P.s raged over 'short' skirts, and television news programmes quizzed women in the streets about what they thought of the new lengths.

The build up of public expectation exerted tremendous pressures on the Paris couturiers themselves. Although in fact no look could ever have the same effect as the New Look again – for first there would have to be no change for at least nine years – nevertheless the couturier trod a knife edge. Should the leading designers conflict too much in their lines, there was consternation and confusion among the buyers. Should they not change enough from the line of last season, buyers complained they were not being given a decisive lead. When Dior died of a heart attack in 1957, this public expectation was still intact. His '*Dauphin*', Yves Saint Laurent, was already signed up to a long and binding contract, and at the age of 21 found himself perched upon the multi-million franc edifice of the most influential fashion house in the world. He kept his balance with his first collection, when he launched the trapeze line – not too different from Dior's A line, but just different enough. In the salon people were trampled in the rush to embrace and congratulate him, and he had to appear like a king on the balcony

Anthony Denney

Henry Clarke

to wave to the cheering crowds below. 'Saint Laurent has saved France!' said the French headlines. 'The great Dior tradition will continue!' In the teeth of an unspoken agreement among the couture not to alter a hem length by more than two inches a season, Saint Laurent dropped the hem by three for his next collection. Twelve months later he bared the knees, and caused an uproar. A woman M.P. announced, 'I think it is ridiculous for a youth of 23 to try to dictate to sensible women. British women will not take any notice of this nonsense!' Radio programmes ran discussions on the likelihood of bare knees in Britain, and one newspaper headline said, 'Dior's man can do what he likes. We won't show our knees!' *Vogue* presented his collection in the kindest light, ignoring the shortest skirts and showing his new hobble hem first in its 'least exaggerated . . . utterly unalarming' form before leading up to the 'extreme trendsetter', and concluded, gallantly, 'When a new line is greeted with cries of indignation, it's a healthy sign . . . it means that the fashion world is alive and kicking.'

It was at this difficult moment in his career that the army draft, three times deferred, wrenched Saint Laurent from Dior. After two months he suffered a nervous and physical collapse, recuperated, and returned to Dior to find his assistant, the 35-year-old Marc Bohan, instated as chief designer. Saint Laurent sued and won £48,000 damages, which he used to open his own salon in 1962 with unqualified success and some of the staff from Dior.

If Dior had personified the old Paris, Chanel stood for the new. Dior's death left Chanel, who reopened in 1954, the despot of the couture. Her success was due to her overwhelming appeal directly to the wearers of her clothes. Her unalterable convictions about clothes and what they should do for women produced a phenomenon unique in the fifties – an unmistakable Paris look complete from head to toe that was flattering, easy to wear, and did not date. The envol, the princess, the tulip and all the other lines had the date stamped indelibly across them. After a year, they were finished. Chanel's was a classic line, refined again and again but never fundamentally changed. The fashionable woman's motto for the end of the decade could have been 'When in doubt, wear a Chanel'. They were as comfortable as a cardigan, you could run in them, they had real pockets where you could keep your cigarettes, and they gave a feeling of tremendous self-confidence.

In *Vogue*, the news of Chanel's return was the news of the year. In an exclusive interview before her first come-back Chanel gave Dior and the other couturiers a caustic going-over. 'A dress must function or on n'y tient pas. Elegance in clothes means being able to move freely . . . Look at today's dresses: strapless evening dresses cutting across a woman's front – nothing is uglier for a woman; boned horrors, that's what they are . . . these heavy dresses that won't pack into aeroplane luggage, ridiculous. All these boned and corseted bodices – out with them. What's the good of going back to the rigidity of the corset? No servants – no good having dresses that must be ironed by a maid each time you put them on,' and concluded the interview by saying, 'I am no longer interested in dressing a few hundred women, private clients; I shall dress thousands.' Opinion about her first collection was widely divided: she conceded nothing to the accepted stylization. *Vogue*'s cautious comment was 'At its best it has the easy livable look which is her great contribution to fashion history; at its worst it repeats the lines she made famous in the 'thirties: repeats rather than translates into contemporary terms.' By 1959 the contemporary terms had come into line with Chanel's convictions, and *Vogue*'s tone had changed completely. 'The heady idea that a woman should be more important than her clothes, which has been for almost 40 years Chanel's philosophy, has now permeated the fashion world.'

Perhaps the most unusual thing about Chanel was that she never

Norman Parkinson

1. Christian Dior, photographed by Anthony Denney at La Colle, Dior's isolated country house near Grasse, in 1957, within a year of his death.
2. Chanel told *Vogue*, 'Certain women wear a suit; certain suits wear women. In the first case the woman is bad; in the second, the suit is not good.' Here, Chanel's perfect combination: Comtesse Guy d'Arcangues, a private client, in her plaid tweed and checked silk suit.
3. The new Mayfair Edwardians, photographed in Savile Row in 1950.

minded being copied. Unlike other couturiers, who banned publication of photographs of their collections until the buyers had time to produce authentic copies from toiles, Chanel allowed pictures to be shown immediately and was happy for the streets to be full of Chanel copies even if they did not put a penny in her pocket. In this she was not unlike Mary Quant, who said, 'The whole point of fashion is to make fashionable clothes available to everyone', but she also showed a supreme confidence that quality would prevail – that the real Chanel suit would be instantly discernible from all fakes.

If Englishwomen of the fifties had never been better dressed, the men had never been so fashion-conscious either. In the prime P. G. Wodehouse years, a well-dressed man's appearance had to be remarkably inconspicuous – like Lord Emsworth, indistinguishable from his gardener – an inclination encouraged by rationing during the war when men had given up their clothing coupons to their wives and become shabbier than ever. After the war, attitudes began to change. The nostalgia which had provoked the New Look and made its success inevitable affected men's fashion too. Men-about-Mayfair began to dress in a way that owed something to Edwardian fashion, and by 1950 the look had evolved completely: curly bowlers and single-breasted coats with velvet collars and ticket pockets, trousers narrowed almost to drainpipes, and a rolled-up umbrella. The shirts they wore were striped, with the stripes running horizontally, and with stiff white collars. Suits had four-button jackets left undone over waistcoats with small lapels, some in rich velvet patterns. Recording the fashion, *Vogue* drew

1. 'She's 18, and she chooses trousers because somehow one always seems to end up sitting on the floor in her room . . .', Anthony Denney's teenager photograph. Yellow velvet pants, tapered and zipped with a cummerbund waist, flat pumps and a black jersey, blouse buttoned with jet.

2. 'The teenage thing', 1959. A 17-year-old apprentice hairdresser from Birmingham told Vogue, 'You can express yourself like, in clothes; you know, a nice dark red shirt with black verticals and a dark blue suit, a Perry Como and Italians; you're in there, sharp, playing it cool.'

1

Anthony Denney

2

attention to the fact that bowlers had become almost a uniform again since the recent order of the general commanding the London district that they should be worn by ex-Guards officers and Guards officers in civilian clothes. The four men *Vogue* photographed, Peter Coats, William Aykroyd, Mark Gilbey and Michael Chantry-Inchbald, were surprised to find within a year or two that they and their friends had been the inspiration for the Teddy Boys of South London, who adapted the single-breasting and velvet collars, the ticket pockets and loose fit into their own aggressively stylish look. The Teds wore plain white shirts with the collar turned up, or a bootlace tie, a silver chain round neck and wrist, a tattooed forearm and fingers, a thick draped suit and crêpe-soled brothel-creepers. Their hair was worn long and immaculately set in quiffs and side-boards, but greasy: Teddy Boys would go to a barber for 'styling', but drew the line at having it washed or dried under the dryer. For the first time the young had a fashion identity of their own.

The word 'teenager' itself was an import from America – a country where girls of six went regularly to the hairdresser and wore make-up at nine. Before the war there had been only 'girls' and 'youths'. Their independence was based on their earning capacity. A popular song was 'You gotta have something in the bank, Frank', and by 1958 the average wage was £8 a week for a boy, £6 for a girl: together just a living wage. There were jobs, shorter working hours, and somewhere to go afterwards. For the teenager in the mid-fifties there were jazz clubs, where students in 'wild-beast' sweaters jived with a girl in one hand and a bottle in the other, dance halls with a skiffle group or a rock 'n' roll band playing Bill Haley's 'Rock around the clock', clubs where juke boxes were fed by leather boys in black jeans and jackboots and studded jackets, and all day there were coffee bars, a refuge behind a bamboo grill overgrown with ivy and philodendron. Soon the West End was covered with Espressos, Wimpys, Bar-B-Ques, Moo-Cow Milk Bars and Chicken Inns.

Among the teenagers, it was the men's clothes rather than the girls' that identified their group, whether it was the Italian jacket, the fluorescent socks and the winkle-pickers of the East Enders or the shaggy sweaters, beards and sandals of the 'weekend beats'. It was a reversal of *Vogue*'s world in which women wore the conspicuous fashions and men were the decorous background. The girls from any of the groups might wear a buttoned cardigan with a string of beads and a narrow skirt, or a Sloppy Jo and tight jeans, or a tight sweater and a full skirt over layers of crackling petticoats. Towards the end of the fifties an art student look came into fashion with donkey jackets, falling-down hair, slim striped skirts, and a basket over the arm.

These were the first fashions that began in the street and worked upward into *Vogue*, and by 1959 the magazine was asking questions about the new trends. 'What does fashion represent? Decoration? Armour? A mood of society? For millions of working teenagers now, clothes like these are the biggest pastime in life: a symbol of independence, and the fraternity-mark of an age-group . . . The origins of the teenage look are urban and working class . . . and it has been taken up with alacrity by the King's Road. Contrariwise, it is itself influenced by the romantic concept of Chelsea.' By now, this look was growing out of English soil. America might have invented teenagers, but London was dressing them. As *Vogue* said, the look 'owes nothing to Paris or Savile Row; something to entertainment idols (the Tommy Steele haircut . . . the Bardot sex babe look); much to Italy, and surprisingly little to America (apart from a suggestion of the mechanized cowboy about motor cycling clothes): which may well be a symptom of a growing indifference to the American image'.

America was doing so well by the mid-fifties with her own line

in casual clothes from California – separates and co-ordinates, shirtwaisters and dirndls billowing out over drip-dry petticoats of crackle nylon, blue jeans derived from Levi Strauss's work pants for gold prospectors – that the French couture sent out a committee to study production methods, and returned surprised and impressed. More teenagers in Britain bought the 'sweater girl' bra, with its conical stiffened cups spiralled with stitching, than the copies of Dior's 'ban the bosom' corsets in 1954. In pursuit of a Jane Russell bosom girls bought a California bra – one was called the 'Hollywood Maxwell' – or shortened their shoulder straps and chanted the dormitory rhyme, 'I must, I must, achieve a bigger bust. I will, I will, make it bigger still. Hoorah, hoorah, I need a bigger bra.'

If America's influence was on the wane, it was because of a new generation of young British designers trained by the art schools into a practical knowledge of mass production, new methods of manufacture, sizing and grading, and production within limited price ranges. The Royal College of Art opened its School of Fashion Design in 1948, and its first professor of fashion was Madge Garland, a former fashion editor of *Vogue*. A long overdue acknowledgement of the kind of training needed, the school and similar departments throughout the country were quick to turn out uninhibited designs for non-establishment fashion. In 1953, the year *Vogue* started the regular 'Young Idea' feature for girls between 17 and 25, it published some ideas for skirts by the R.C.A. students: royal blue velveteen studded with silver buttons, turquoise felt slashed and slotted with velvet ribbon and tied with shoestrings, stovepipe trousers inside a double apron of glitter-scattered taffeta.

A product of art school, but not fashion school, was to give the young fashion movement its greatest impetus. Mary Quant, who failed to get her art teacher's diploma, was to be the 'major fashion force in the world outside Paris'. In 1955 she began her fashion

I dreamed I raced with the winds in my
maidenform bra

3. Tommy Steele, 'Buttons' in *Cinderella*, 1958. A home-grown rock idol and former seaman from Bermondsey.
4. Madge Garland, formerly *Vogue*'s fashion editor, by 1949 the first Professor of Fashion and principal of the new School of Fashion Design at the Royal College of Art. Photographed by Cecil Beaton in Bianca Mosca's blue-black brocade suit and Vernier's straw hat.

career in the workrooms of Erik, the milliner, and in November she opened Bazaar in the King's Road, a joint venture with her future husband, Alexander Plunket-Greene. She began by buying clothes in, but could not find the kind of fashion she wanted. Within a few months she was designing her own clothes, although totally ignorant of how to set about it: she began by buying fabrics across the counter at Harrods because she didn't know that they could be obtained wholesale. She found that Bazaar was becoming a meeting place, a kind of 'nonstop cocktail party', and that the clothes were bought off the rails almost as soon as they had been put there. Her bedsitter was full of sewing women working until late at night to put dresses in the shop the next morning. A year after the Quant revolution had begun, 19-year-old John Stephen came down from Glasgow and opened his first shop for teenagers, moving it soon afterwards to Carnaby Street.

Other revolutions had provided the fabrics without which the looks of the fifties could never have taken shape. From the basic silk, wool and cotton available at the beginning of the century, there were in the fifties dozens of alternatives, most of them crease-resistant or permanently pleated, glazed, shrink-proof, water-proof, moth-proof, and washable. Synthetics had begun to appear in fashion during the thirties, with Schiaparelli's 'Rhodophane' dress, and there was a cheap rayon or 'art. silk'. By 1938 there were Lastex tops and an improved, uncrushable rayon, but it was not

until the war, which had so many beneficial effects on the fashion industry, that textile manufacturers were forced back on their resources, and made the most of them. Nylon transformed the fifties wardrobe, making the petticoats that stood up by themselves and the almost invisible 12-denier stockings, the fake furs and the permanently pleated nightdresses, the laces and the knitting yarns. In 1954 *Vogue* published a glossary of man-made fibres including acetate, Dynel, Fibrolane, Orlon, rayon and Terylene. 'Putting on clean clothes daily,' as Madge Garland pointed out in her book *Fashion*, 'once thought to be an eccentricity of the Empress Josephine, is an habitual occurrence in the life of any girl.' Washable drip-dry clothes passed into the fashion repertoire of working city girls. Thick pullovers were made for the first time in powder blues and primrose yellows with Orlon and Courtelle; foundation garments were revolutionized, nylon fabrics in great variety making possible the two-way stretch doll-size girdle of 1952. Four years later one firm, English Rose, had 90 garments in their range, an increase of 60 since 1950, a number made possible by the different kinds of synthetic fibre.

The fifties were the time when women went out to work as a matter of course. In the 1920s when Van Dongen had painted 'The Lady Wants No Children' the question had been 'Job or children?': in the fifties women were prepared to take on two jobs in order to have the best of both worlds – and this at a time when children's

Herbert Matter

1. Nylon, which arrived from America after the war, revolutionizes fashion, 1951. Here, a nylon marquisette dress by Susan Small, photographed with the vast spinning room of the British Nylon Spinners' factory in Monmouthshire.
2. 'Stocking superlatives: the sheerest — 12-denier thinness, a new low (we are used to 15), just coming off the nylon machines.' This one by Charnos.
3. The pale thick-knit sweater, now easy to wash, quick to dry and able to hold its shape in Orlon or Courtelle. This one, lemon yellow Courtelle, by Playfair.

Vernier

nurses and maids were almost impossible to find. By the end of the decade, more than half the married women of Britain were going out to work. But T. W. Higginson could still have said, as he had nearly 100 years before, 'Like Charles Lamb, who atoned for coming late to the office in the morning by going away early in the afternoon, we have, first, half educated women, and then, to restore the balance, only half paid them.' A girl might earn about three-quarters of a man's wage, doing the same job in industry, and even when she was granted equal pay, did she get equal opportunities? Out of 150 top jobs in the B.B.C., only four were held by women. One of the two women governors, Mrs Thelma Cazalet-Keir, said, 'The B.B.C. conceded equal pay for women as long ago as 1926, but what's the good of that if no women get paid at the top level?' Jacqueline Wheldon, wife of B.B.C. producer Hew Wheldon, complained about the tone of voice in which television programmes addressed women, 'that jolly welfare-worker air, and that special sort of voice, as though every woman sitting at home was a moron . . . the term they used for us in the studio, I believe, was "Mums".' The publishing of Christabel Pankhurst's memoirs, *Unshackled*, provoked in *Vogue* a spirited debate between political commentator Henry Fairlie of the *Spectator* and *Daily Mail*, and working women. Mr Fairlie wrote that women were really reluctant victors in the battle for independence, and that they were the victims of a confidence trick by an industrial society to supply a cheap new source of labour. He declared that the typewriter had re-enslaved women, 'few of whom are happy until they have had a baby', and that cosmetics, fashion, and women's magazines were

all 'drugs to keep the slaves quiet'. In reply, Jean Mann, a J.P., invited Mr Fairlie to accompany her to the factories 'and look at the "exploited". They have wages and hours fixed by the Trade Unions. Ask these women if they would prefer their pre-emancipation jobs as servants, charwomen, cleaners, washerwomen!' Dame Sybil Thorndike said, 'If we are better persons as a result of freedom how can we have lost as women?' Margaret Casson, architect, drew attention to his 'curious assumption that because women are physically constructed to bear children they are therefore mentally and emotionally bound to enjoy domesticity above every other kind of life', and Shirley Conran, fabric designer, said, 'I chose to work because I found housekeeping easy and boring and because my husband is more interested in me as a fellow worker than as a super servant. What would Mr Fairlie rather we did when our children are past the baby stage? Embroider radiator screens?' Penelope Mortimer spoke for many working women when she said, summing up, 'Thoughtlessly, often effortlessly, one somehow manages to retain the affection and attention of one's family while voting, typing, earning. Even (and this is more remarkable) while cooking, cleaning the bottoms of saucepans, and administering Syrup of Figs. Could it be that, although a woman, one is a human being?'

In Anita Loos's 'Decline and Fall of Blondes', written for *Vogue* in 1951, she expressed her point with a difference. 'Any time we girls have to go to work the result, historically, is that we do things better than the opposite sex. I mean gentlemen will go to all the trouble of keeping office hours and holding Board Meetings and getting Mr Gallup to make a poll, and sending their Public Relations agents to Washington, in order to reach a decision which any blonde could reach while she was refurbishing her lipstick.'

The new word of the fifties was 'media'. Television had brought the meaning home to 26 million people by 1959, Aldous Huxley's 'television fodder', most of whom had been initiated by the televizing of the Coronation and had gone out to sign hire purchase agreements afterwards. The opening up of this enormous exploitable market came with Commercial Television in 1955, 'a national disaster', according to the Labour Party. So much was talked about 'subliminal' advertising that people began to doubt their own powers of resistance. In 1958 *Vogue* was writing, 'Having got ourselves thoroughly fussed about subliminal advertising and motivational research – the profitable quarrying of the depth-boys – we might return to ground level and look at the not so deep ideas employed upon our consciousness. The latest thought in cereal packages, expected here from America, is a celluloid gramophone record that can be cut out of the side of the package. Our sample performed, piercingly, "Goofy's Space-Trip to the Moon". "There's a big future for this little gimmick," say the instigators. "Birthday cards that sing Happy Birthday, aspirins with lullaby jingles!"'

In the new wave of commercialism, *Vogue*'s editorial policy moved closer to the fashion industry introducing an annual advertising award for good design, a colour range to help sell the new seasonal ranges in the shops, *Vogue* endorsements for featured fashions, and an attempt to catch the attention of specific markets and perform a reader's service in the introduction of Mrs Exeter in 1949 and Young Idea in 1953. After a pilot in 1945, *Vogue* initiated an annual talent contest from 1951, with a first prize of £50 and the offer of a job. This competition still operates today, and is the single way that a would-be journalist without contacts can walk straight into a job. Early winners included Cynthia Judah, Penelope Gilliatt, Anne Sharpley, Ann Scott-James, Isabel Quigly, Jill Butterfield and Edward Lucie-Smith. In 1952 the model competition began: 'Don't think, because no whistled tributes are forthcoming from corner boys, that you can't be a model.' In case of discouragement from family, *Vogue* added, 'You can reassure your father, your husband or your son, on one point: modelling is terribly respectable. Whatever you do, you will always be exemplarily clothed, and excessively chaperoned – by photographer, photographer's assistant, fashion editor (*stickler* for form), fashion editor's secretary, and studio girl.'

The technical age increased *Vogue*'s scope in several directions. On the features pages you might find a photograph of the new German Mopetta, a car no bigger than a big shopping basket, or a photograph of a pink daffodil or a blue-tinted mauve rose . . . 'no garden need now be without a yellow peony if you can spell Mlokosewitschii'. A picture of an experimental British Railways carriage, complete with reclining tweed seats, double glazed windows and thermostatic fan heating, might be paired with a new plastic greenhouse which allowed more ultra-violet light than did glass, or details of the new transatlantic telephone cable and what it might do for readers' calls to Australia.

There were new fashion photographs taken with telephoto lens, and unforgettable pictures by photographers of the calibre of Irving Penn and Norman Parkinson, whose perfected technique allowed them to realize inner fantasies. Penn's (usually 'lifts' from American *Vogue*) are of superb quality, to which end he will fly a planeload of electronic equipment across the ocean to the particular room he wants to work in, or smash to pieces an imperfect camera

Irving Penn

Norman Parkinson

rather than have it adjusted. Unlike Penn, Norman Parkinson prefers to work out of doors, and says, 'A studio is like an operating theatre. You go there to get part of yourself removed.' Taking a picture, he sets out like a water diviner – which he is – alive to every conjunction of ingredients that can produce magic. First day in a foreign country with a dress to photograph, he will tell the driver, 'Take the first right and the second left, the first right, the second left, until I tell you to stop', until 'the picture arrives'.

First of the 'send up' photographers, Antony Armstrong-Jones's pictures are outrageous moments caught by the camera when no one should have been looking – a girl teeters and falls into a river, fully dressed, a woman knocks over a couple of glasses as she rushes to embrace a man, the tide creeps up to cover the knees of a girl who has fallen asleep on a deckchair.

1. Vogue Pattern, photographed by Irving Penn, 1949.
2. The fashionable woman's image and how it changed between 1949 and 1957: Norman Parkinson's postwar heroine (*opposite*) was beautifully groomed and perfectly self-assured, Antony Armstrong-Jones's girl of the late fifties (*below*) was younger, less controlled, and supposedly unaware of the camera.
3. Twinset and pearls fashion, 1951. The caption read, 'The scene: a village pub. The theme: poise, dignity, the respect of person for person and class for class. The girl, quiet in dress and manners, waits while her husband gets drinks. The man, dropped in after work, takes his pint from a pewter mug, plays shove ha'penny on a well-made "slate" on an oak trestle table, has unselfconsciously pinned a rose in his coat.'
4. By 1957, *Vogue* was using cars as image-projectors. Here, a scampi belt Riley 2.6, with golf clubs, poodle and alpaca pile coat.

3

Norman Parkinson

4

Antony Armstrong-Jones

Norman Parkinson

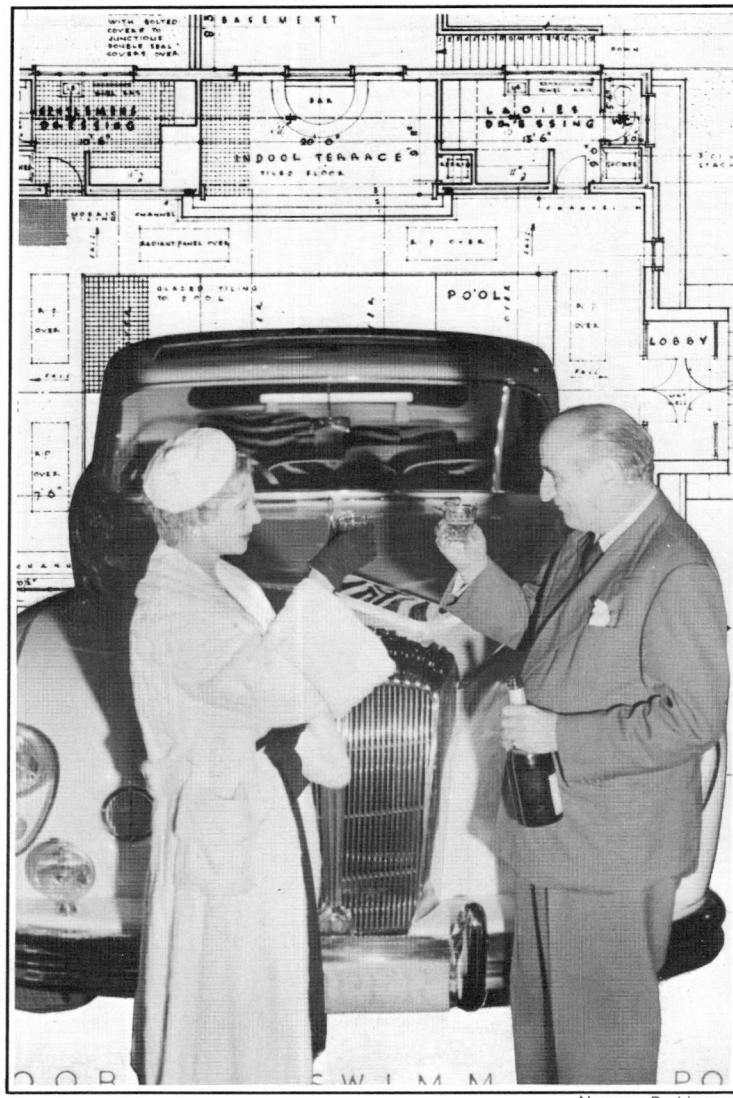

Norman Parkinson

Irving Penn

Common to the photographers who found their feet in the fifties was the independence and assurance of the model, who seemed to own the clothes and be carrying on her own life regardless of the camera, unless she faced it with a disconcerting awareness.

Vogue opened out into new territory with its features pages, edited by Siriol Hugh Jones then by Penelope Gilliatt, who was to marry John Osborne. Maria Callas faced James Dean across the pages; Gina Lollobrigida, 'the new Italian bombshell', jostled Joan Littlewood, 'a forthright genius with a band of idealists who toured the country in a lorry, clinging to the belief that the theatre is a popular art'; Satyajit Ray with his 'rapt fidelity, his realism and silence' lined up with Lady Docker and her new gold-plated, zebra-upholstered Daimler. *Vogue* was there to hear Liberace pronounce, 'It is good when fans get behind the life of a star who's a good clean citizen with a fine family life', and there to overhear Mike Todd telling a henchman, 'Now what about these cinemas? Save a lot of time if I had them both. Call 'em Liz's First House and Liz's Palace.' *Look Back in Anger* was described as 'the play that gave tongue to a generation scarcely speaking to its elders', the film *Gigi* as having produced the feeling that you were being sold something subliminally – 'M.G.M. good evenings start with Colette'. Penelope Gilliatt was quick to feel the tinge of 'Ealing-tight-little-island humour' in Alec Guinness's *The Horse's Mouth*. She asked Sidney Nolan what he thought of the performance. 'Very good,' he said. 'People usually play artists as though they were mad.' 'But, Sidney,' said his wife, 'this man was completely nutty.' 'Don't be silly,' said Sidney. 'He behaved just like I do.'

2

Norman Parkinson

John Deakin

The new writers' disillusionment with British politics and cant, system of privilege and genteel complacency, gave the old order a rough time from 1954, when Kingsley Amis published *Lucky Jim*. Osborne's *Look Back in Anger* at the Royal Court, with Alan Bates and Mary Ure, shocked people into self-awareness and marked a turning point in the decade, but it was in *The Entertainer* that he parodied most cruelly the decline of England through the deterioration of a seedy music hall performer. Reviewing John Braine's *Room at the Top* in its filmed version directed by Jack Clayton, the story of an anti-hero's climb through the British class system, Penelope Gilliatt wrote admiringly of what was dubbed 'kitchen-sink realism': 'Casually the camera-work states what a Northern town is like: cobbled streets, smudged views of chimneys, women cooking at ranges, wet slaps of washing to be dodged by children playing in the street. I know that remarking on this must sound like applauding a dress for being sufficiently in touch with reality to have a zip, but it is notable in our cinema.'

The anti-hero, who behaves disgracefully, but whose side we're on anyway, was not only a figure of British novels and plays but also of the new Hollywood films, which now produced the 'masculine brute rebellion'. Siriol Hugh Jones wrote, 'In the broad shoulders, the slouch, the regional accents and the beautiful broad peasant features of Richard Burton, the inescapable animal bulk of Marlon Brando, the neurotic-baker-boy puzzlement of Montgomery Clift, the sulking pout of Farley Granger – there lies glamour, there lies the heroic touch, the dream of 1952.' The heroine, whatever nationality, often had a new childishness – there was more than a

hint of the schoolgirl in Audrey Hepburn, of the baby in Marilyn Monroe and Brigitte Bardot.

The beginning of the men's hair cult was first noticed in Siriol Hugh Jones's feature 'Crew-cuts and Rough Diamonds', 1952, in which she said, 'I think the changing order of heroes is identified most easily along the hair-line . . . "pre-war hair" was well-cut and cared for, often even innocent of evil communications with brilliantine and other base messes. The post-war look is that of the crew-cut and its dire derivatives.'

It was not particularly surprising that the popular hero should have changed so much in a decade that had become insecure as quickly as it became self-aware. Bertrand Russell spoke of 'a fated and predetermined march towards disaster'. Sir Julian Huxley saw over-population as the gravest threat to man's future at a time when babies were being born 100 a minute to increase the world's population by nearly fifty millions a year. Meanwhile, hideous dormitory suburbs and bleak, boring new towns spread out to ruin the countryside in place of the glittering cities that had been visualized in the twenties. Not even the material prosperity of the late fifties could gloss over the disasters of Suez and Hungary, Korea, mistrust of politics and feelings of panic about the future that culminated in the Aldermaston marches and the demonstrations of civil disobedience. Television was at least the main factor in the new awareness, bringing the facts and the action of world affairs into the private lives of 26 million British viewers by 1959; no wonder the public was more involved and more anxious than it had ever been before.

THE CHANGING FACE

In the 1950s models became stars. Their names were well known, they could earn enormous salaries, and they were accorded film star status. Designers talked of models being their inspiration — there was Alla, the beautiful Eurasian girl at Dior, Bettina at Jacques Fath, Bronwen Pugh — later Lady Astor — at Balmain.

FIONA CAMPBELL-WALTER

Fiona Campbell-Walter, one of the great beauties of the time, was *Vogue*'s star British model, superbly photogenic, suitably haughty for the 1950s, and equally convincing in a mackintosh or tiara. She had the perfect proportions for a model, being 5 ft 8 ins tall with a 23 in waist, had long streamlined eyes and delicate features together with tawny hair which she lightened at the temples to widen her brow, and grew long enough to wear up or down. On her marriage to Baron Thyssen she gave up modelling.

1

Irving Penn

1. Irving Penn's 1952 photograph of America's top twelve international models, including mothers, magazine editors, a singer, a newspaper columnist, an actress and a designer.

2. Fiona Campbell-Walter, 'as finely bred as a champion greyhound', photographed in 1954 by Cecil Beaton. She returned to modelling in 1966.

2

AUDREY HEPBURN

Audrey Hepburn, real name Edda Hepburn van Heemstra, is a Belgian-born star actress of Irish-Dutch parentage. In 1952, when Norman Parkinson took this photograph, she was playing *Gigi* on Broadway, with 'fabulous personal success': her film *Secret People* was showing in England, and she had a Paramount contract waiting. In 1954, after *Roman Holiday* and *Sabrina Fair*, *Vogue* called her, Today's wonder-girl . . . She has so captured the public imagination and the mood of the time that she has established a new standard of beauty, and every other face now approximates to the 'Hepburn look'. Cecil Beaton said in *Vogue*, 'her appearance succeeds because it embodies the spirit of today . . . it took the rubble of Belgium, an English accent and an American success to launch the striking personality that best exemplifies our new Zeitgeist. Nobody ever looked like her before World War II . . . now thousands of imitations have appeared. The woods are full of emaciated young ladies with rat-nibbled hair and moon-pale faces.' She was 25, and she wore a 'monkey fur' fringe, highwayman coats, clergyman cassocks, and students pants, overalls and scarves, often with felt ballet pumps. She wore no powder, only a smudge of black greasepaint above and below her eyes. Cecil Beaton analysed her features, ' . . . character rather than prettiness; the bridge of the nose seems almost too narrow to carry its length, which flares into a globular tip with nostrils startlingly like a duck's bill. Her mouth is wide, with a cleft under the lower lip too deep for classical beauty, the delicate chin appears even smaller by contrast with the exaggerated width of her jaw bones . . . she owes a large debt to the ballet for her bearing and abandon in movement.' Through the years she has been a kind of barometer of fashion, looking each year as though she had been born for that minute in time.

Norman Parkinson

Cecil Beaton

BRIGITTE BARDOT

1. Brigitte Bardot, photographed by William Klein in 1959, three years after *And God Created Woman*. *Vogue* called her, 'the sensuous idol, a potent mixture of the sexy and the babyish, a seething milky bosom below a childish pout'. The phrase 'sex kitten' was coined to describe her. She reinforced her international success in 1965 with *Viva Maria*, and is still in demand today at forty years old.

LAUREN BACALL

2. Lauren Bacall told *Vogue* about her make up, 'For my peculiar face I look best when I look as though I'm not wearing any' and about clothes 'nothing itsy-bitsy—you shouldn't have to do too much to them, just wear them'.

BARBARA GOALEN

3. Barbara Goalen, Coffin's favourite model, appeared continually in *Vogue* from 1950, and could make the simplest cotton dress look expensive and smart. She personified the air of aloof sophistication that meant elegance throughout the decade, and looked perfect in stylized clothes that were extremely difficult to wear well. She is now Mrs Nigel Campbell.

Rutledge

137

Milton Greene

MARILYN MONROE

The first and last pictures to appear in *Vogue*. Olivier, Monroe, Rattigan, (*top*) were photographed in 1956 as they began work on the unhappy production *The Sleeping Prince:* Olivier told Monroe, 'Be sexy', which incapacitated her for weeks.

Bert Stern took the revealing last magazine pictures of her (*opposite*). News of her death came just as 15 September *Vogue* was going to press with this photograph, and *Vogue* said, 'The waste seems almost unbearable if out of her death comes nothing of insight into her special problems: no step towards a knowledge that might save, for the living, others as beautiful and tormented.'

GRACE KELLY

'Her composed, in-bred prettiness is rapidly revising Hollywood's idea of what's box-office. Public demand, since *Mogambo* and *Rear Window*, has landed her parts in *The Bridges at Toko-Ri, The Country Girl* and *Green Fire'*. 1955.

ANITA EKBERG

'In the colossal film version of *War and Peace*, just shown, she plays the Princess Elena Kouraguine, an invention of Tolstoy's that anticipated central heating. "Lissen", she said primly when we met her. "I am not an Iceberg. I am hot-blooded. I wear nothing under this." Our photographer, who takes snuff, has never taken it faster.' 1956.

Norman Parkinson

VOGUE

The Black and
White Idea

London Season

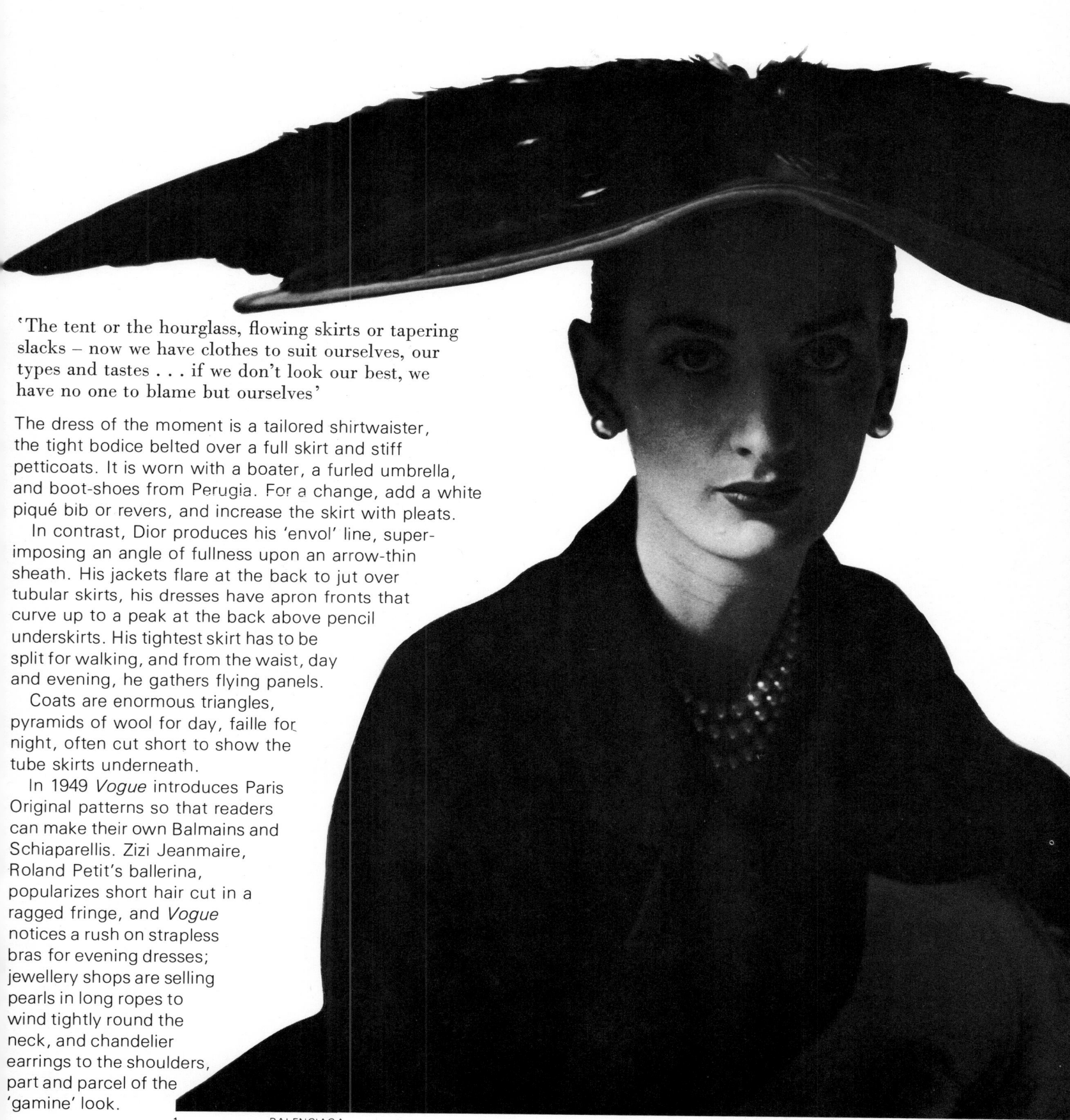

'The tent or the hourglass, flowing skirts or tapering slacks – now we have clothes to suit ourselves, our types and tastes . . . if we don't look our best, we have no one to blame but ourselves'

The dress of the moment is a tailored shirtwaister, the tight bodice belted over a full skirt and stiff petticoats. It is worn with a boater, a furled umbrella, and boot-shoes from Perugia. For a change, add a white piqué bib or revers, and increase the skirt with pleats.

In contrast, Dior produces his 'envol' line, super-imposing an angle of fullness upon an arrow-thin sheath. His jackets flare at the back to jut over tubular skirts, his dresses have apron fronts that curve up to a peak at the back above pencil underskirts. His tightest skirt has to be split for walking, and from the waist, day and evening, he gathers flying panels.

Coats are enormous triangles, pyramids of wool for day, faille for night, often cut short to show the tube skirts underneath.

In 1949 Vogue introduces Paris Original patterns so that readers can make their own Balmains and Schiaparellis. Zizi Jeanmaire, Roland Petit's ballerina, popularizes short hair cut in a ragged fringe, and Vogue notices a rush on strapless bras for evening dresses; jewellery shops are selling pearls in long ropes to wind tightly round the neck, and chandelier earrings to the shoulders, part and parcel of the 'gamine' look.

1   BALENCIAGA   Coffin

Left: Vogue's cover for June 1950, photographed by Irving Penn.
1. The shoulder-span hat: Balenciaga's grass-green faille with black wings.

1948-49

1
BRENNER   Lee Miller

2
CHRISTIAN DIOR   Coffin

1. Striped seersucker blouse, pale blue
pirate-length jeans.
2. 'Pencil slim' black wool dress with a check
envol jacket, Peter Pan collar tied with a
black taffeta bow, a black-velvet beret tipped
over the forehead. Perugia's check wool and
patent leather boots.
3. Victor Stiebel's debutante dress in layers
of tulle. The make up: sharp, pink and white
with pencilled eyebrows, streamlined eyes
and painted mouth. The hair, flattened to the
head as much as possible.
4. The gamine haircut, 1949, worn first by
Roland Petit's dazzling new ballerina Zizi
Jeanmaire.
5. Schiaparelli's slim silhouette with jutting
collar and peg-top skirt. Perugia's boots,
fitting like a stocking at the hemline.
6. Jacques Fath's lemon-yellow coat, a
tremendous triangle emphasized by the
buttoning; outsize collar.

NEW BEAUTIES continued

RENEE JEANMAIRE, newly risen star of Roland Petit's Ballets de Paris, electrified London and Paris by her dancing
in *Carmen*. She is small, dark, dazzling, with a nervous temperament in the finest sense of the word

3   4   Cecil Beaton
Hans Wild

The Tent
or the
Hourglass

5
Coffin

6   FATH

1950

Left: Irving Penn's portrait of Christian Dior's stylized, elegant mid-century woman demonstrated the acceptable *Vogue* way to smoke.
Right: Norman Parkinson's photograph of Enid Boulting in a Helena Geffers suit caused a sensation: American *Vogue*'s editor-in-chief cabled from New York SMOKING IN VOGUE SO TOUGH SO UNFEMININE!

1950

'Share the immense confidence of 1950, facing the unknown half of our century'

The most confident and high-spirited fashion since the mid-thirties, taking off from the New Look into exaggerated, geometric shapes, boldly asymmetric and stylized. The shirtwaister has competition in the new sheath dress, swathed and draped for evening. Balenciaga's sculptural formal designs for evening dresses steal the thunder—stiff paper taffetas blown up and rolled under into huge pumpkin skirts tipped up in the front, bows the size of umbrellas wrapping up the tightest sheaths, angles sharp as blades, buoyant curving widths in the skirts.

Hair is pressed to the head and seldom seen in the day without a hat, eyes become 'doe eyes', with painted flick-ups of eyeliner at the outer corners, complexions are made pink and white, lips sharp and vivid. Collars are sharp, high and turned up, waists are minimized by girdles that grip from rib cage to hips, peplums jut out above the narrowest skirts. To make skirts look even narrower at the knee, models are photographed with one leg behind the other, and the new trumpet skirt which flares out again below the narrowest point turns full length evening dresses into fishtail sheaths. The new shoe, day or evening, is the sling-back with a rounded toe.

1. Short evening dress, strapless lace corselet a[nd] swathed silk skirt sashe[d] the back. Sling-back la[ce] shoes.
2. Swinging redingote w[ith] huge jutting collar, whit[e] plush turban, black bam[boo] umbrella.
3. Pumpkin evening dre[ss] blown-out satin taffeta.

1 HARDY AMIES   Don Honeyman

2   DIOR   Irving Penn   3 BALENCIAGA   Irving Penn

'Where has the waist gone? Anywhere but where you expect it'

'She's eighteen, and she chooses trousers because somehow one always seems to end up sitting on the floor in her room, what with the gas ring and the gramophone being there already. There will be spaghetti and "coke"'

'The long supple torso, the little neat head, the longer skirt, this is the season at a glance from both capitals'

In 1951, year of the Festival of Britain, *Vogue* produces a special Britannica number devoted to British achievements with an 8-page feature on 'The Rise of the Ready-to-Wear': the most fastidious and fashion-conscious woman can dress immediately for any occasion in ready-to-wear clothes.'

Christian Dior's and Balenciaga's spring 1951 collections have several points in common, tipping the fashion balance in favour of a Chinese look — coolie hats, flick-up eyes, wide barrel-shaped jackets, black and white as the favourite colour combination. This is Dior's first collection without stiffened and padded interlinings, and he launches his immediately successful 'princess line' with dresses fitted through the midriff, waist unmarked. Balenciaga on the other hand puts plenty of stiffening into his jackets, cutting them to curve like shells over the body, and indicating the waist with a loose bow or an indented curve; his new middy line drops the waist to the hips.

Dior produces a new bloused jacket for his princess dress — a battlejacket when it's short, a middy jacket when it's gathered onto a wide belt at the hips. His new jumper suits with sailor collars fit at the hips over flat pleated skirts. Jacques Fath, who invented the 'guipure' girdle, 'has become a steadier star and made a glowingly brilliant show', offering as an alternative to the middy line a crisp, young suit with a cropped matador jacket showing a cummerbund waist and a full skirt bolstered with stiff petticoats. 'Instant Paris' additions for *Vogue* readers are a stole to wear day and evening, a bathing cap with a piece of black veiling, long evening gloves worn pushed down to the wrist for day, glittering diamanté or rhinestone earrings and bracelets, a string of graduated pearls.

Two new couturiers open in Paris in 1951: Castillo, designing for Lanvin, and Jacques Griffe, designing for Molyneux now that Captain Molyneux has had to resign because of his failing eyesight. In 1952, Givenchy opens in Paris and Cavanagh in London. Givenchy began by designing for the Schiaparelli boutique, and starts his independent career with a boutique collection. *Vogue* notes, 'He has a brilliant hand with separates — skirts with built up waistlines and "laundered" white blouses with large ruffled sleeves. He uses tri-colour schemes: garnet, sea green, black; sand, turquoise, white.'

A totally new influence begins to make itself apparent in fashion as the teenage market demands a look of its own. The earliest indications in *Vogue* are the tapered trousers and the stiff ballerina petticoats, the flat shoes, the 'chunky' sweaters. In March 1952 Norman Parkinson photographs a spread of square dancers in spinning skirts and pumps, with strapless tops or sweetheart necklines, and in November, Anthony Denney photographs a blueprint teenager complete with ponytail and Coca Cola.

Rawlings

BALENCIAGA

Right: Spring suit in charcoal shantung with a collarless yoke, a loose white gilet, and coolie hat.

227

2. Night and Day

Make up, night. . . 'The natural complexion is masked and paled with a creamy cake foundation and a clear-toned powder. Glowing colour is painted on the lips, every curve accentuated, the eyes are made mysterious with eyebrow pencil and a dusky shadow, and strip eyelashes of nylon.'

. . . *and day* 'The lipstick is the same, but this time the true line of the lips is followed, and mascara is the only eye flattery. The natural complexion is not masked but softly veiled with a light foundation and fluff of warm-tinted powder.'

2

4

DIOR

BALENCIAGA

Randall

5

Blumenfeld 3 DIOR

6

7
SUSAN SMALL
DAPHNE HUGHES

Anthony Denney

1. Agmar's suede bathing cap, hat of the moment, and the new emphasized eyebrows.

3. Accordion-pleated white crepe dress, Emba mutation mink coat, 1952.

4. Where is the waist? Under the arms, marked by a martingale in this Dior grey flannel dress and jacket. Beaver hat.

5. Where is the waist? Round the hips in this loose middy plaid suit by Balenciaga.

6. Trumpet skirt petticoat for evening.

7. Daphne Brooker, one of the winners of *Vogue's* first model contest in 1952 and now head of Kingston Fashion School, in a navy crepe jumper dress after Dior, with middy pleated skirt, sailor collar, Breton straw hat.

Irving Penn

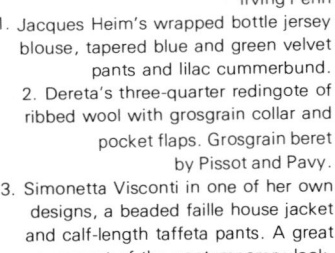

2 DERETA   Cecil Beaton

1. Jacques Heim's wrapped bottle jersey
blouse, tapered blue and green velvet
pants and lilac cummerbund.
2. Dereta's three-quarter redingote of
ribbed wool with grosgrain collar and
pocket flaps. Grosgrain beret
by Pissot and Pavy.
3. Simonetta Visconti in one of her own
designs, a beaded faille house jacket
and calf-length taffeta pants. A great
exponent of the contemporary look,
Simonetta, though still in her twenties in
1952, streaks her hair with grey.
4. Prints make a comeback — Dior's
shantung dustcoat with side slits,
box-pleat back.

3   Norman Parkinson

4 DIOR   Randall

SUSAN SMALL   Spotted chiffon dress with a green straw hat
by Simone Mirman; photograph Antony Armstrong-Jones

Coronation year – 'and Norman Hartnell celebrates with a collection of white and gold evening dresses'

'The sweater has grown in importance and size. Buy it two sizes larger than usual for a casual look. Add a sweater scarf, or fill in the V with rows and rows of pearls'

The dropped armhole dictates the shape that dominates both student and Paris-based fashion.

The teenage look for daytime is the 'mansize chunky sweater' with drainpipe pants and 'flatties': for evening, a full circle skirt in a bright felt—probably turquoise or kingfisher blue—with a tight poloneck sweater or a scoop-necked blouse tucked in.

From Paris, the same dropped, rounded, bulky shoulderline for suits and coats, the loose neck rolling off the body like an oversized sweater. Dior reintroduces padding over the bust with his 'tulip' line, and captures headlines by shortening his skirts to 16 inches from the ground—still two or three inches below the knee. Women are by now used to wearing skirts almost to their ankles, and are nervous of a change that might date their clothes as suddenly as the New Look did in 1947: *Vogue* soothes its readers, 'Dior always emphasizes that skirt length is a matter of individual proportions: he lived up to his own maxim by putting his ultra-short skirts only on petite model girls. In any case, a major fashion change must first be put over at full strength and then modified for general acceptance . . . the probability is that women will have their autumn skirts a couple of inches shorter than they might otherwise have done, and be ready for further shortening in the spring.'

London couture, 1953. The members of the
Incorporated Society of London Fashion
Designers with key models from their spring
collections, photographed by Norman
Parkinson.

1. Elspeth Champcommunal at Worth
2. Norman Hartnell
3. Hardy Amies
4. Victor Stiebel at Jacqmar
5. Michael Sherard
6. Digby Morton
7. Peter Russell
8. Mattli
9. Michael at Lachasse
10. Charles Creed
11. John Cavanagh

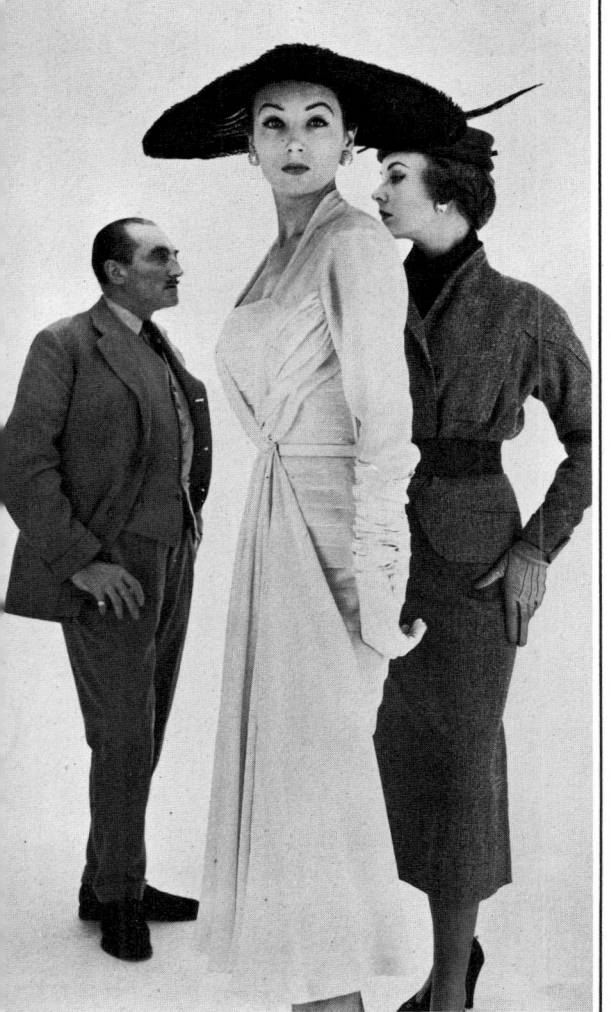

Norman Parkinson
2
Norman Parkinson

1. Travelling clothes: beige wool jersey separates, pleated skirt, short sleeved blouse top, cardigan and Kangol beret.

2. White ottoman dress and fitted jacket at Harrods, Simone Mirman headband of grape hyacinths and white straw, fine strip sandals by Delman.

3. Evening make up, summer 1953, with liquid rouge the new ingredient, used over the temples and under the brows. The rest of the make up goes on like this: a moisture cream under a tinted foundation, a heavy powder on top, a dark brown eyeshadow, pencilled eyebrows and eyeline, mascara, lipstick. Time, 18 min. 45 second.

4. Claire Bloom, between *Berlin Story* and *Ophelia* for the Old Vic, photographed for *Vogue* in Simone Mirman's hat of white currants mounted on net.

5. 'More Taste than Money' — cardigan coat of bird's eye jersey lined with denim, £13.6s. Black suede shower-cap hat.

6. Sleeveless balloon jacket, pinspot silk with a black rose; bloused over a V-neck black dress with black suede gloves.

7. The ideal shape for a Dior dress — Lefaucheur's foundation with nipped waist, flat back and carved-in midriff.

DIOR'S BOLD SKIRT LENGTH: BULK UNDER BULK ..

Bouché

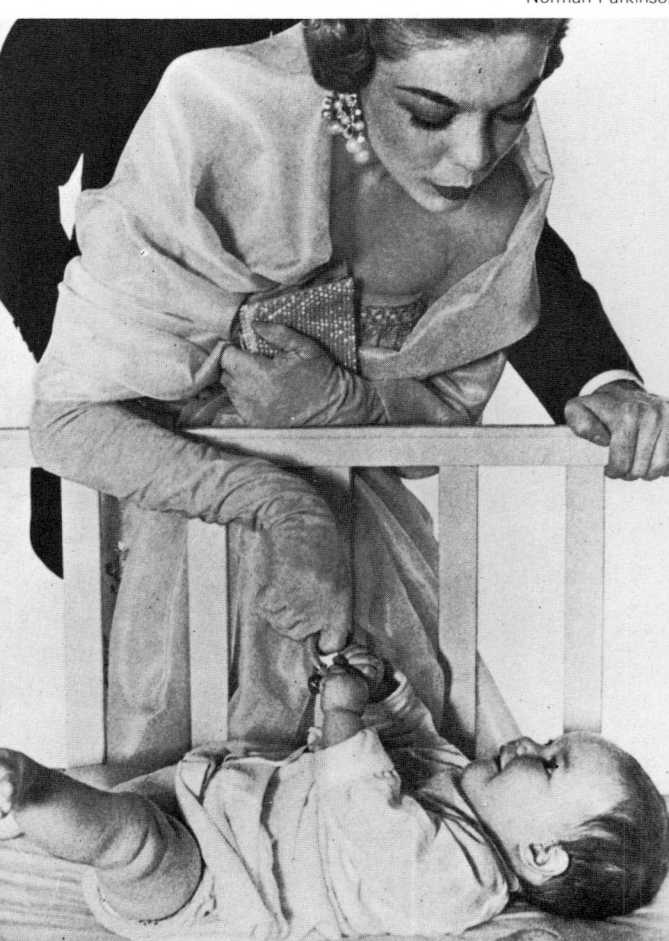

3

234

SIMONE MIRMAN

Anthony Denney

DOBETT

Norman Parkinson

BALENCIAGA

Henry Clarke

Frances
McLaughlin

1954

'The biggest news is personality news; Chanel's reopening. Her collection is the talk of Paris, with opinion violently divided. At its best it has the easy liveable look which is her great contribution to fashion history; at its worst it repeats the lines she made famous in the 'thirties: repeats rather than translates into contemporary terms'

Talking to *Vogue* before her comeback collection, Chanel promised there would be no 'fifties horrors'. She is as good as her word. She makes a young, easy-moving dashing collection that is truly more modern than the 'contemporary terms' of Dior's careful sophistication or Balenciaga's sculptural formality.

Vogue shows clothes from the Italian and Spanish collections — Pucci's brash jazzy Palio shirts, Simonetta's casual at-home pants, and Pertegaz's evening looks, immensely formal like those of another Spaniard, Balenciaga.

Now that she's made *Sabrina Fair*, Audrey Hepburn's is the best-known and most copied of all faces, and the classic Fiona Campbell-Walter is acknowledged as the most beautiful *Vogue* model.

'Trifling hats — the small, whole difference.' Anya Linden, soloist of the Sadler's Wells Ballet, in turquoise velvet by Vernier.

VERNIER   Cecil Beaton

1. Chanel's return — her beautiful navy jersey suit with squared shoulders, tucked white blouse with a bow tie, and sailor hat tipped to the back of the head.
2. Wenda Parkinson, photographed by her husband in Michael's elegant tussore suit widened at the shoulders over a striped black and white 'football sweater'.
3. Dior's sailor suit in soft navy jersey trimmed with satin ribbon.
4. Emilio Pucci's Palio-print silk shirt and bright corduroy pants: the shirts are already collector's pieces.

2 MICHAEL   Norman Parkinson

3 DIOR   Henry Clarke

CHANEL   Henry Clarke

4 PUCCI.   Rawlings   237

1 PERTEGAZ   Henry Clarke

2 CHANEL   Henry Clarke

1. Emerald paper taffeta
evening coat in tiers.
2. Chanel's shell pink jersey
cocktail dress — 'Dresses are
never gracious and
flattering enough'.
3. Dior's flat-bosomed evening
dress, skirt puffing from
the hips.
4. Balenciaga's ball dress of
spun-sugar net tied
with ribbon.

3 DIOR   Coffin

4

'A significant struggle is taking place in Paris. On the one side there are the designers whose achievement is to create clothes of so strong a shape that they look as if they could walk across the room alone . . . on the other side are the designers whose clothes are not superimposed on a body: they have no existence apart from it'

The first camp, designers of clothes with body and shape of their own, clothes popular with manufacturers and shops for their 'hanger appeal', are Dior, Givenchy, Balmain and Fath — now carried on by Jacques Fath's widow, Geneviève Fath.

Dior produces his new A line, a triangle widened from a small head and shoulders to a full pleated or stiffened hem. He uses stiff, strong fabrics such as tussore and faille. Variety comes from the placing of the crossbar waist — high for an empire line, below fingertip level at its lowest.

The second camp, whose clothes generally take their shape from the wearer in soft fabrics like jersey and silk tweed, include Chanel, Balenciaga's day clothes, Patou, Lanvin and Griffe.

An almost universal alternative to the A line is the slim tunic suit, sometimes called H and sometimes I, with the long jacket sometimes reaching to the knees over the even slimmer skirt. Chanel is the obvious exception to this hobble hem, with her easy jersey skirts widened with a deep inverted pleat.

Technological fashion assets now include one-size stretch stockings and lighter, softer stretch panti-girdles printed in vivid stripes or patterns.

Balenciaga's sinuous black I line tunic dress, great black fox collar giving weight at the top, and a flying panel from the shoulders.

BALENCIAGA

Henry Clarke

1955

1. Working girl's wool jersey suit in bright red with a shirty top, pleated skirt.
2. Stockbroker pinstripes — Michael's suit that is really a jacket and pinafore dress, Charles Creed's fitted black and white suit with a wing-collared white piqué blouse.
3. Dior's H line, with the narrowest of skirts, photograph Vernier.

Opposite: Scarlet velvet toque by Otto Lucas, flannel suit, by Bazaar. Photograph by Norman Parkinson, who called it 'Van Dongen' after the painting 'The Lady Wants No Children', November 1959.

Over page, left: Jersey wrap and trousers by Lovable, hat by Malyard. Photographed in the Seychelles by Norman Parkinson, December 1971.

Norman Parkinson

MICHAEL   CHARLES CREED

1. Dior's evening A line, black faille with a straw cartwheel hat.
2. Givenchy's oatmeal tweed dress with a semi-fitted, diagonally seamed waistline; photograph Henry Clarke.

Opposite: '1960s Deco.' Twenties peach chiffon embroidered with silver bugle beads, from the Purple Shop, Chelsea Antique Market. Photograph by Norman Parkinson, December 1969.

DIOR

1956-57

Christian Dior's death in 1957: 'He is sure of a high place in fashion history . . . His mantle has fallen upon young M. Yves Saint Laurent'

'. . . the big story of the shrinking skirt-length – from just-below-the-knee at Lanvin-Castillo to just-on-the-calf at Dior'

Waists are raised by almost all the Paris dictators bringing in a new suit with a cropped jacket showing a small cinched waist—best at Dior—sarong dresses wrapped high to one side, and the innovation of a stiff four-inch waspie belt that has the effect of raising the waist and exaggerating the hips at the same time: it will become the most copied accessory for years. Fashion catches up with Chanel and her comfortable jersey cardigan suits; she goes one better with contrasting braid, and invents a casual new skirt wrapped to one side with a trouser pocket in the seam. Coats are the thickest, softest and warmest ever, rounded like beehives,

funnel sleeves lost in the bulk, linings of fur. Colours are black, geranium red, fuchsia and shocking pink.

Christian Dior's last collection leaves a legacy, the waistless shift or chemise dress that narrows towards the hem, a refinement of Givenchy's 'sack', called the 'spindle' or 'chemmy dress', shortly to be known as the sac.

The hat is half the point of any new look now, usually a flowerpot toque pushed right down over the forehead, or a modified sou'wester with black veiling added or wrapping the face in a mesh cage, with a rose topknot. Eyes and lips are heavily outlined, visible at a hundred yards, and exaggerated still more to show through veils. Long cigarette holders come back to keep the sparks away.

Guy Laroche is an interesting new arrival in Paris, Audrey Hepburn has grown out her fringe, and in London Elizabeth Seal stars in *The Pyjama Game*; Henrietta Tiarks is deb of the year.

Elements of the mid-fifties – the 'sloppy Joe', here sleeveless and shocking pink; the waffle cotton shorts, the Chianti bottle and the spaghetti, the long cigarette holder.

     William Klein

1. The flowerpot hat, pushed down to the browline, in coffee cream satin slotted with a brown ribbon.
2. The glamour of a cocktail hat: mop of uncurled black ostrich, and a long cigarette holder to keep the sparks at a distance.
3. The veiled face with eyes and lips heavily outlined to show through.

OTTO LUCAS

Donald Silverstein

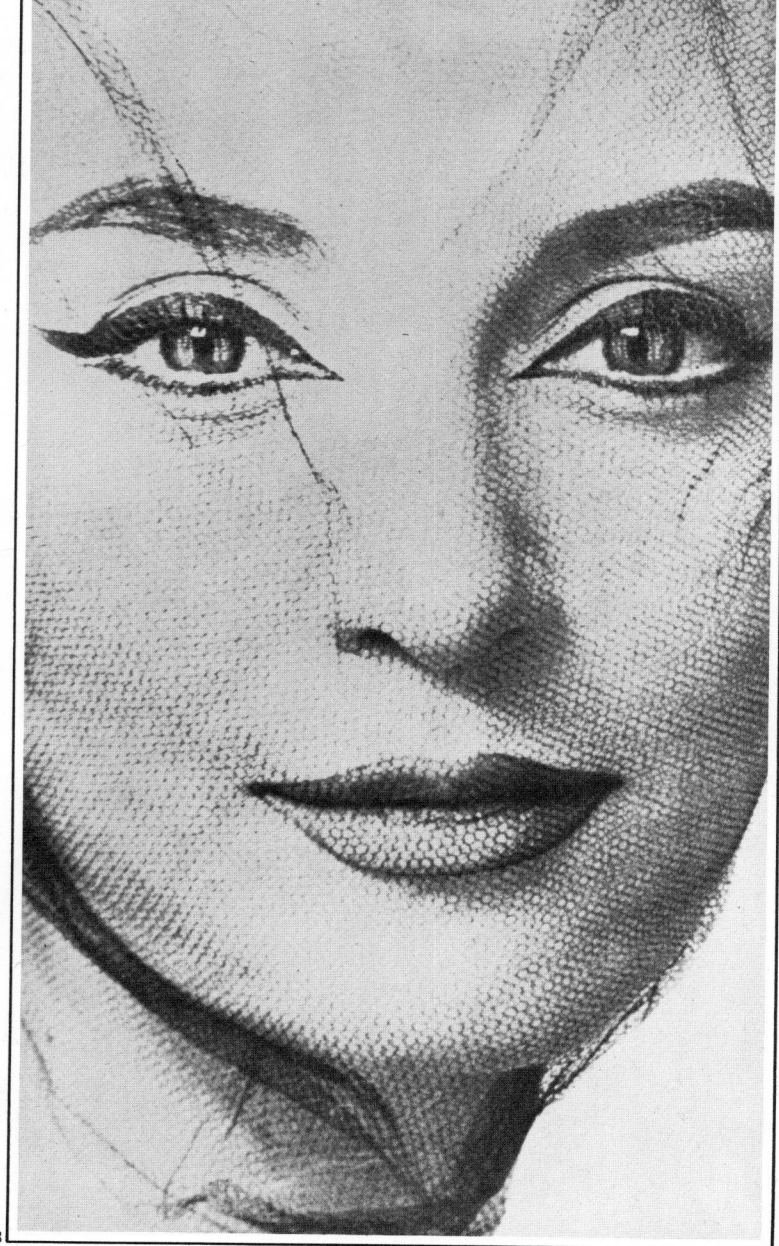

Henry Clarke

243

1
DIOR

William Klein

2
FATH

3
DIOR

Francis McLaughlin

4

William Klein

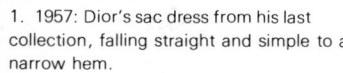

1. 1957: Dior's sac dress from his last collection, falling straight and simple to a narrow hem.
2. Fath's fragile lilac pleating, cape sleeves, boat neck tied at the back. Worn with a tulle turban in the nostalgic mood of 1957.
3. The big wrap from Paris, bulky, barrel-shape, cocooning. Christian Dior's coat, half a cape, in Prudhomme's thick grey wool, the armholes so deep that the huge sleeves are inset to the elbows. Worn with the new veiled flowerpot hat.
4. Shoes by Perugia. The ones marked with a white dot were made for Poiret in 1918; the rest are from Perugia's 1956 collection.
5. Domino cotton beach outfit; big shirt with sleeves to push up, brief shorts.
6. The universal twinset, worn by Elizabeth Seal, star of *The Pyjama Game*, with jangling bracelets and rolled-up jeans.
7. The glistening black PVC coat — vinyl-coated raincoat just about to become a classic.

5 HARVEY NICHOLLS

7

6 LENNOX   Norman Parkinson   DONALD BROOKS   245

1958

'Saint Laurent has saved France – the great Dior tradition will continue'

'Chanel, this perfect designer, whose first great period was in the twenties, seems more truly of today than many younger people'

'Chemise styles are in . . . trapezerie is gaining ground, and everywhere the high-rise influence prevails'

Yves Saint Laurent makes an enormous success of his first collection for Dior. *Vogue* reports, 'The newspaper sellers shouted "Saint Laurent has saved France" . . . the joy and relief were terrific — people cried, laughed, clapped and shook hands. For almost an hour no one could leave, and finally Saint Laurent had to appear in the street and wave to the cab drivers and passers by.' Backbone of his collection is the trapeze, 'the most important and fully formulated line in Paris', flaring gently from narrow shoulders to a shorter wider hemline just covering the knees.

By autumn the rest of Paris has adopted this length, only to find that Saint Laurent has dropped his hems to three inches below the knee — an unpopular move.

Only four years after her re-entry into the Paris couture, unrivalled now that Christian Dior is dead, Chanel's is the major fashion influence in the world. Her jersey suits and blazer jackets are copied all down the line to the local high street, and she is responsible for the popularity of men's shirts, jewelled cufflinks, gold chains and medallions, gilt and pearl earrings, Breton sailor hats, and sling-back shoes with contrasting toe caps. Because of her model-girls, women brush out their hair instead of flattening it to the head and have a fringe club-cut across the forehead.

Originating with Balenciaga and Givenchy there is the 'high-rise' waist, cinching the ribs above an almond-shaped skirt, gathered over the hips and narrowed at the hem. Bolero jackets are cropped to show the waist, and coats follow the same line when they are not flared into a trapeze.

Shaggy bright pink mohair jersey, sizes too big, with black needlecord drainpipes. Black Louis-heeled shoes piped in silver kid by Dolcis.

FENWICK

Norman Parkinson

1

1. Chinchilla, for the first time worked horizontally in this cardigan jacket worn with a grey flannel Garbo hat, gold bangles.
2. Bright navy jersey lined with the navy spotted silk of the blouse and Breton hat, with pearl earrings, heavy gold bangle.
3. Saint Laurent's trapeze line, backbone of his successful first collection for Dior. Simple black silk and wool dress, bow marking the high waist and hem raised to just cover the knee.
4. Grey and black striped wool trapeze dress in the London shops, 6 gns.

3

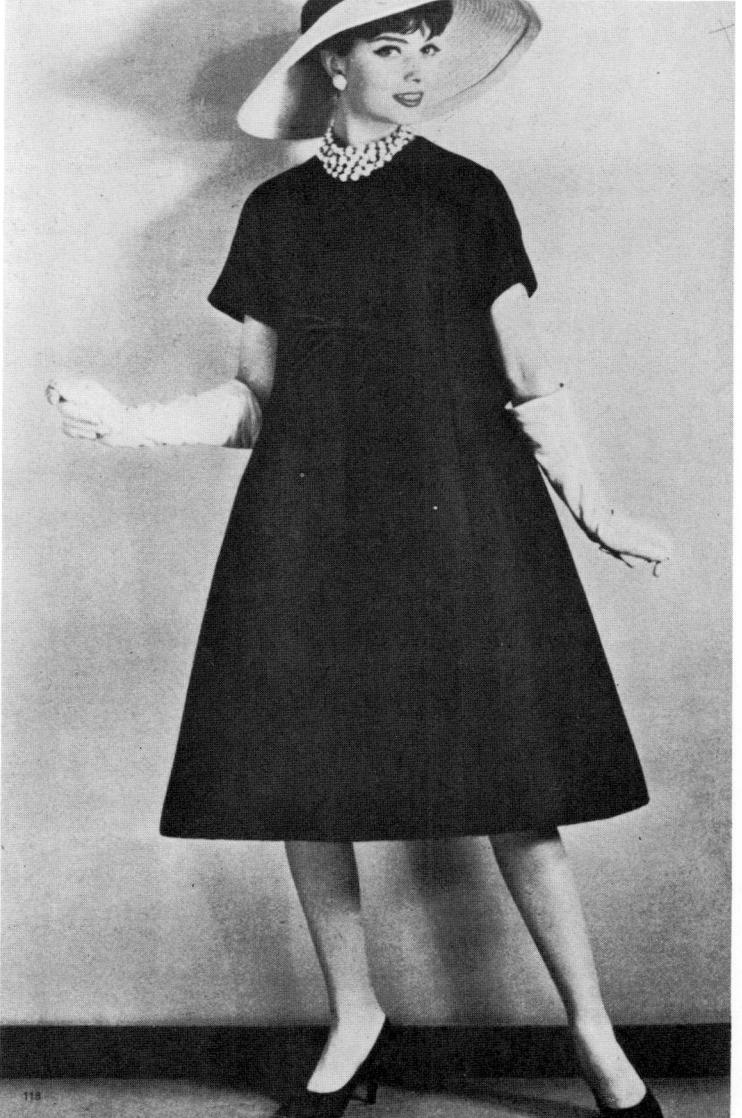

1. Antony Armstrong-Jones designed and photographed these ski clothes. Balloon anorak of orange and yellow proofed silk, with black leather knickerbockers.
2. The strapless evening-dress . . . Worth's in draped black chiffon.
3. Chanel's navy and white jersey suit hung with a mixture of gold chains.
4. The 1958 look, the Chanel look. Simple, unflattened hair, emphasis on the eyes, man's shirt with cuff links, heavy gold chains. Another 1958 development, the telescopic lens camera, taking in long-range details of Nelson's Column and Trafalgar Square.

KIKI BYRNE

2 WORTH

3
CHANEL
Henry Clarke

4 CHANEL
William Kleir

Striped cotton bikini, photograph Antony Armstrong-Jones

'The waist is back! The sack has had its day'

'Dior's man can do what he likes . . . We won't show our knees' – *Newspaper headline*

'"A woman should be more important than her clothes" – the 40-year-old philosophy of the fierce, wise, wonderful Coco Chanel'

In his badly-received autumn collection, Yves Saint Laurent at Dior raises the skirt to the knees, belts every waist and pulls the skirt in to a tight knee-band. The confidence invested in him last year is swept away by the outcry of the press, directed mainly at the skirt. *Vogue* presents his collection in the kindest light, ignoring the shortest skirts and showing the hobble first in its 'least exaggerated . . . utterly unalarming' form before leading up to the 'extreme trendsetter'. 'When a new line is greeted with cries of indignation, it's a healthy sign . . . it means that the fashion world is alive and kicking.'

The acceptable line from Paris is the 'body line', a wide, loose look universally cinched by a four-inch belt, with the hem two and a half inches below the knee.

Chanel at the end of the fifties is re-established as the most constant and popular of designers, offering a real alternative to this or that shortlived 'line'. In a time of great insecurity about fashion, she provides a glamorous, easy-to-wear, recognizable head-to-toe look that doesn't date. Her cardigan suits with chain-weighted jacket hems, beautiful linings and real pockets made to hold cigarettes and keys free the wearer from clothes-worries and give enormous self-confidence.

The long-hair cult begins with evening hair, real or false, swept up loosely round the head and marked like a turban with a big central jewel. High bead chokers built up the neck are the corollary to boat necklines and loose rolled-back collars.

Grey flannel makes the simple dresses and suits that dominate young fashion all winter, and becomes the first 'craze' of the sixties. *Vogue*'s new young photographers and copywriters combine in 'send up' fashion features that will be a feature of the sixties.

Irving Penn

SAINT LAURENT

SAINT LAURENT

CARDIN   Henry Clarke

The waist is back

4
SAINT LAURENT   Henry Clarke

1. Yves Saint Laurent's autumn 1959
collection for Dior raises the skirts to knee
level and introduces a provocative new line,
belted, with a knee level pull-in. It causes the
greatest fashion outcry since the New Look.
2. Yves Saint Laurent's black taffeta
ruffled with lace, worn with pink satin
winkle-pickers.
3. Pierre Cardin's navy worsted dress
with a cuffed boat neckline, belted waist,
and a barrel skirt with a deep front
pleat. The huge rolled-back straw hat
is almost Cardin's signature.
4. Pale blue shantung pleats, cape-
collared and belted by Yves Saint
Laurent for Dior's spring
collection.
5. A new evening look, long
hair—real or added—wrapped
round the head and jewelled, a
high Edwardian choker.
6. Princesse Odile de Croy in
Chanel's cardigan coat, nubbly
beige wool piped with navy
blue silk.

6
CHANEL

251

Henry Clarke

1960·1969

David Bailey

The Revolutionary Sixties

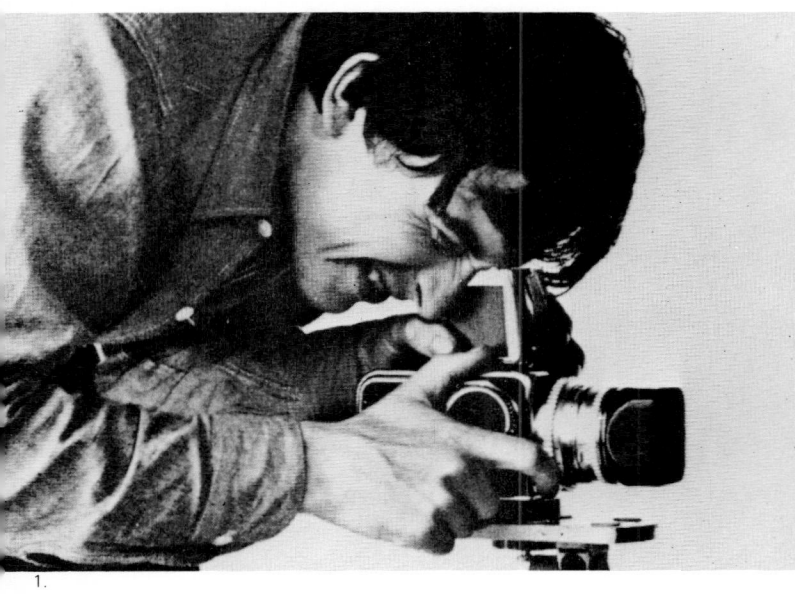

1.

Left: Jean Shrimpton in Mongolian lamb and over-the-knee boots, 1964.
1. David Bailey, 1965. 'They said that I wouldn't be a fashion photographer because I didn't have my head in a cloud of pink chiffon'.

'London is a city of and for the young,' wrote Peter Laurie in *Vogue* in 1964. 'Probably no other in the world offers us the opportunities that are here. Wherever enthusiasm, energy, iconoclasm or any kind of creative ability are needed, you'll find people in their mid-twenties or younger.' Britain had emerged from the turbulent last years of the fifties a changed country. 'In that period,' said American journalist John Crosby, writing for the *Daily Telegraph* colour supplement, 'youth captured this ancient island and took command in a country where youth had always before been kept properly in its place. Suddenly the young own the town.'

Everyone in the country who read the colour supplements or watched television could tell you who in particular owned the town, how they lived and the names of their friends. Yet the new social order was unrecognizable to members of the old establishment like Loelia, Duchess of Westminster, who told *Vogue*, 'London Society is a world which for better or worse no longer exists'. There was a new class system, and by the mid-sixties even *Private Eye* was referring – with disdain – to 'the new aristocracy'. They were all young, talented and concerned with the creation of 'image': pop singers, photographers, actors and model girls, pop artists, hairdressers, interior decorators, writers and designers. They came from all kinds of backgrounds. For instance, a cross-section of half a dozen, numbering David Bailey, Terence Donovan, Tony Armstrong-Jones, Alexander Plunket-Greene, Michael Caine and Terence Stamp, includes sons of an East Ham tailor, a Mile End lorry driver, an East End tugboat captain, a Billingsgate fishporter, a Q.C., and an organist. Because their prestige was founded on their talent, they shared a fierce respect for professionalism and treated any kind of amateurishness with contempt. They were aggressively self-confident, and – since nothing succeeds like success – became more so in the blaze of publicity. Any of them could have said in the words of Andrew Oldham, when joint manager of the Rolling Stones, 'I don't have to depend on other people's talents to get me on. I am good enough myself. I am good and I am going to get better.' There were no pretensions. When David Bailey published his *Box of Pin Ups*, designed by Mark Boxer and written by Francis Wyndham, he described the beginning of his career like this: 'I had a choice at this time, age 16, time Monday, 4.30 in the afternoon. I could either be a jazz musician, an actor, or a car thief ... They – from Mars or wherever they are – said I wouldn't be a fashion photographer because I didn't have my head in a cloud of pink chiffon. They forgot about one thing. I love to look at all women.' It was a feast for the press when he married French film star Catherine Deneuve in 1965, and the *Evening Standard* wrote, 'The bridegroom wore a light blue sweater ... and light green corduroy trousers', 'the bride

David Bailey

1

2

David Bailey

3

David Bailey

arrived smoking' and the best man, Mick Jagger, 'arrived with a blue denim suit and blue shirt with no tie'.

At every level, the sixties were a time of the young doing what they wanted better and more profitably than had been done before: a time of round pegs in round holes. Mary Quant had 'weathered the storm for the young designers' and in every field there were new opportunities to make revolutionary changes. Even in what had been the most reactionary circles, power was in the hands of the young. Roy Strong, talking to *Vogue* in 1967, when he was 'very young [at 32] to be the new Director of the National Portrait Gallery', was planning the first photographic exhibition in the museum's history. 'The great thing that all galleries have had to learn is that you have to go out to your public . . . Everybody's got it fixed in their mind that the National Portrait Gallery is terribly dull and dowdy, which, indeed, it was. Now the ordinary chap is coming in off the streets and saying, "Heavens, this is interesting, this is enjoyable." '

One thing Britain lacked, and felt the need of, was a young, dynamic political leader to fit the revolution, such as the U.S.A. had in President Kennedy. Between 1960 and 1963 the standing of Macmillan's government was falling sharply, and a note of envy

surfaced in *Vogue*, voiced by Mary Holland, who referred to America's 'new leader whose youth, vitality and firecracker energy make European statesmen seem like tired Victorians', and to 'the rest of us who still have old men at the top'. Part of *Vogue*'s interest in the President lay in his wife, Jacqueline Kennedy, who had won American *Vogue*'s talent contest in 1951 when, in answer to a question about People I Wish I Had Known, she had chosen Baudelaire, Oscar Wilde and Diaghilev. The good-looking and clothes-conscious Mrs Kennedy 'has resolutely eschewed the bun-fight and the honky-tonk of the American political scene and is inclined, instead, to the gentler practice of painting, conversation, literature and fashion'.

Quite soon the youth cult was blown up out of all proportion by thousands of features in the magazines and newspapers. Arthur Jones, writing about the mods and mids in *Vogue*, said as early as 1964, 'There *is* a teenage society, there are new standards in England that are not quite local nor Standard English; but the whole hopeful, dynamic thing is frozen by the gorgon stare of the old, the rich, the powerful.' There was also a new language invented by and for the teenagers: not the 'pad', 'Daddy-oh' and 'real gone' that issued from the American teenagers, but, using Arthur

Duffy

1. Mick Jagger, photographed by David Bailey in 1964 when Baby Jane Holzer, New York socialite, was quoted by Tom Wolfe as saying, 'Wait till you see the Stones! They're so sexy! They're pure sex! They're divine!' etc.
2. David Hemmings, starring as the fashion photographer in *Blow Up*, Antonioni's film about London in 1966.
3. Terence Stamp, restauranteur with his restaurant manager Rex Tilt: the 'Trencherman' was 'down the far end of the King's Road — I mean really the far end — past the plexiglass and plastic palazzi, where London becomes English again after hesitating between more Contemporary Living and freaked out West Coast manqué'.
4. Mary Quant and Alexander Plunket-Greene, 1962, when they were *Vogue*'s 'Ultra front-room people'.
5. The royal marriage, 1960. Special acknowledgement for Brian Duffy, who photographed the glass coach as it returned to the Palace.
6. Mrs Kennedy drawn by Bouché, 1961.
7. President Kennedy, 'more presidential, less golden boy than usual in this portrait by Irving Penn'.

Irving Penn

1. Peter Hall, effective head of the Royal Shakespeare Company, 'the contemporary theatre's greatest entrepreneur and Britain's most versatile director'. Terence Donovan photographed him in 1965, the year he produced Schoenberg's *Moses and Aaron* at Covent Garden.
2. 'A new Nijinsky has been born'. The 23-year-old Rudolf Nureyev photographed by Irving Penn in 1961.
3. Harold Pinter who made his name with *The Caretaker*, 'Clinical recorder of the queasy maladies of society' in 1963.

Terence Donovan

Irving Penn

Jones's examples, 'Tone, nip up the G's and con the drummer for some charge so we can have a circus before charp.'

In the middle sixties *Vogue* ran headlines like 'The World Suddenly Wants to Copy the Way We Look. In New York it's the London Look, in Paris it's Le Style Anglais . . . Where fashion influence came from Hollywood, the Left Bank and Italian films, English girls now not only have the nerve to be themselves but can enjoy watching others copy them.' Britain had a new image all round. America's attention had been caught by British theatrical talent since Osborne's *Look Back in Anger* had been voted the best foreign play of the season on Broadway in 1958. Since then there had been plays by Brendan Behan, Lionel Bart, Robert Bolt and Shelagh Delaney, the tremendous success of *Beyond the Fringe* and the Establishment team, and Anthony Newley's *Stop The World, I Want To Get Off*: New York critics were talking about a 'British domination of Broadway'. At the 1963 Paris Biennale it was British artists who had stolen the thunder, particularly David Hockney, Peter Blake, Peter Phillips and Allen Jones, all from the Royal College of Art. When David Hockney's exhibition opened in New York the next year, it was sold out on the first day. The same year, Dame Margot Fonteyn and Rudolf Nureyev of the Royal Ballet dancing in Vienna received an ovation that beat all records, with 89 curtain calls. Britain was no longer a respectable bowler-hatted gentleman with a stiff upper lip: the last remnants of that image had been dissolved for ever by the Profumo affair.

More than anything, it was the phenomenal success of the Beatles' American tour within a year of President Kennedy's assassination that put anything British on top. When they arrived at Kennedy Airport the whole country became Beatle-obsessed. Hardly anyone noticed when Sir Alec Douglas-Home arrived there five days later. In March, American advance sales for the sixth record, *Can't Buy Me Love*, were 2 million, and the next month they held not only the first five places in the American Top Hundred, but also the first two places in the LP charts. If what Andrew Oldham said was true, pop music was taking the place of religion and the Beatles were gods. America's supreme accolade was to give them Carnegie Hall for the first pop concert in its history; England's, perhaps, was the serious evaluation by *The Times*' music critic, who said, among other things, 'one gets the impression that they think simultaneously

of harmony and melody, so firmly are the major tonic sevenths and ninths built into their tunes, and the flat submediant key switches, so natural is the Aeolian cadence at the end of *Not a Second Time*' (the chord progression which ends Mahler's *Song of the Earth*) and admired 'the exhilarating and often quasi-instrumental vocal duetting, sometimes in scat or in falsetto, behind the melodic line; the melismas with altered vowels ("I saw her yesterday-ee-ay") which have not quite become mannered'.

Our other most popular export, the mini skirt, officially arrived in New York in 1965 with a British fashion show arranged by the Fashion House Group and held on board the *Queen Elizabeth*. The models in their thigh-high dresses stopped traffic on Broadway and in Times Square, and were seen on television all across the

4. The Beatles, 1963.
5. Marianne Faithfull, discovered by Andrew Oldham at a party. How did he know she had a voice? 'He didn't. I haven't.'
6. Sandie Shaw, whose first hit song 'There's Always Something There to Remind Me' sold over a quarter of a million records. Daughter of a Dagenham welder, she became equally popular in France.

David Bailey

David Bailey

U.S.A. Mary Quant made a fortune there the same year when she took 30 outfits on a whistle-stop tour of 12 cities in 14 days, the models showing the clothes to a non-stop dance routine and pop music. She soon had a business worth a million pounds, selling to the U.S.A., France, and nearly every other country in the Western world, designing 28 collections a year. She received her O.B.E. for services to the fashion industry in 1966, and went to Buckingham Palace in a mini skirt.

Both the designers and the wearers were enjoying a new form of expression. The outlets were the pop-playing boutiques, packed with clothes ideas by and for the young. In 1960 an American girl fresh from campus told *Vogue*, 'I had a sort of idea things might be a bit stodgy here, but I couldn't have been more wrong.

I have to put my hands in my pockets when I go around – especially all those small boutiques in Chelsea and Kensington.' You could try on as many clothes as you liked without being intimidated or reproached if you didn't buy: in fact it was sometimes difficult to find the assistant if you did want to buy. You never knew what you would find in a boutique. Seasonal cycles of stock were disrupted, and new looks arrived as soon as outworkers could get them finished, sometimes a few days after they had been designed. Girls who wanted to have first look at weekend stock learned to go along on a Friday evening when the boutiques took delivery and stayed open late. The fifteen- to nineteen-year-olds that had been a tiny fraction of the buying market in the mid-fifties grew in number until, in 1967, they were buying about half of all

1

the coats, dresses, knits and skirts being sold in the country. By then, to add to the deluge of ideas from home-grown designers, boutiques were selling every unusual thing in the world that you could wear, from rough Greek wool sweaters to saris; kimonos to harem pants; caftans to half-cured sheepskins from Turkey and Afghanistan. The fashion categories of the fifties, 'formal' and 'casual', had ceased to have any meaning. In 1960 *Vogue* photographed Mary Quant's dark striped pinafore with a black sweater for day, and on its own for going out to dinner. By 1965, the women at any smart party would be divided into two groups: half in the shortest skirts, half in full-length evening dresses, and neither feeling out of place.

One boutique that stands out from the rest because of its immediate and continuing popularity is Biba. Its originator and fashion designer, Barbara Hulanicki, began the original mail-order business in 1964, calling it after her sister. Her husband, Stephen Fitz-Simon directs all the business aspects and runs the Biba empire. As a

boutique, Biba started in undistinguished two-room premises off Kensington High Street. What made it different from the start was its dark, exotic, glittering interior, jumbled clothes, feathers, beads and Lurex spilling out over the counters like treasure in a cave. Its gimmick was the incredible cheapness of the clothes. There were no price tickets, but the poorest student could afford to say 'I'll have it' before asking 'How much?' In 1966, for £15, the price of a Mary Quant party dress, you could walk out of Biba in a new coat, dress, shoes, petticoat and hat. Stephen Fitz-Simon says, 'We could always spot a member of the trade turning a dress inside out to see how it was possible to sell it for so little.' Biba was often so crowded on a Saturday that there would be a queue waiting to be let in one by one as customers left, and Barbara Hulanicki remembers, 'We had to go out every day with a damp cloth to wipe the nose marks off the window.' By the end of the sixties the clothes were no longer so cheap and Biba was an all-in-one store, but it had more than a gimmick, it had an immediately recognizable image of its own. This is hard to define, being derived from Art Nouveau and Art Deco but, in the mood rather than the style, having more to do with the current idea of what they were like than the reality.

The sixties made Britain into a fashion leader and the most inventive country in the world. A million and one young designers were spilling out of the art schools, bursting with new ideas and practical expertise. As *Vogue* said in 1962, in a feature called Fresh Air in the Rag Trade: 'For the first time the young people who work in the rag trade are making and promoting the clothes they naturally like: clothes which are relevant to the way they live . . . ours is the first generation that can express itself on its own terms.' As David Bond put it, 'I tend to design clothes I'd like to see my girl friends in.' An unprecedented flow of talent was coming from the Royal College of Art under the aegis of Professor Janey Ironside – Zandra Rhodes, Marion Foale and Sally Tuffin, Bill Gibb, Ossie Clark, Graham Smith, Christopher McDonnell, Anthony Price. 'She taught by the tone of her voice,' said Graham Smith. 'She never told us that something was terrible. She didn't have to. She gave us the know-how and then left us the greatest freedom.' Not all the talent went into the boutiques. Jean Muir, for instance, our leading classic fashion designer, went to Jaeger for six years, and was backed by Courtaulds when she opened as Jane & Jane in 1962. She emerged independently with a unique standard in line and proportion – her clothes are meticulously controlled, demure, and reveal every line of the body. Zandra Rhodes finally found at Fortnum & Mason the freedom to extend her prints into clothes, making floating chiffons and crinoline nets coloured with a painter's palette. They are at the same time delicately executed and the last word in upstaging technique – you can't miss a girl in a Zandra Rhodes dress. Woollands 21 Shop, under the clever guidance of Vanessa Denza gave a boost to many of the best designers, including Ossie Clark, who made them a special collection while he was still at the Royal College of Art. Many, too, went to the best chain fashion shops such as Wallis: Jeffrey Wallis was a key figure in the recognition and promotion of British designing talent. He had already made the Chanel suit almost a uniform among well-off working women, and had kept the distinction and comfort of these suits by using the identical fabrics that Chanel had chosen. Equating good design with good profits, he told *Vogue*, 'The rise of positive thought that's strongly and independently creative is one of the most exciting things that's happened in England. Today a market exists of around 5,000,000 people in America, Europe and England all on the same fashion wavelength. Today the provinces are places like Texas, not Manchester. Young designers are springing up all the time; industry is creating the climate for them, top buyers the right type of background.'

Meanwhile in the face of this tremendous competition, the British couture members were growing fewer and fewer. In 1966 when they numbered seven, the hard facts were that a suit, with three fittings, came to between £90 and £200: a best-seller would not exceed an edition of 25. Even Michael, who dressed the most Parisian-minded of London's couture market, would have found it difficult had he not had an arrangement with Marks & Spencer, supervising their fashion design. Here and in Paris the couture began to turn to boutiques and ready-to-wear – Nina Ricci, Yves Saint Laurent, Cardin and Lanvin among others.

By 1967 fashion had finished with the 'space age' look, and designers began to see the future in terms of the present again. In the Courrèges heyday geometric haircuts, creaking welded plastics, silver and chalk white had become almost a uniform. 'Courrèges clothes are so beautiful,' said Andy Warhol. 'Everyone should look the same. Dressed in silver. Silver doesn't look like anything. It merges into everything. Costumes should be worn during the day

1. Biba's new boutique opens in the spring at 19-21 Kensington Church Street. Here, with her father, Teresa Topolski wears a striped cotton coat and dress in pale pinks. Coat, 57s. 6d., dress 47s. 6d., prices which make Biba into a frantic bargain hunt for school girls and students with very little money.

2. Barbara Hulanicki, beautiful originator of the Biba look, in 1964 a fashion illustrator. She has always worn polo-neck sweaters, boots, silver and gold: her hair is always perfect — she cuts it herself and never goes to a hairdresser — and she wears eye make-up, but no lipstick. Here, she wears a toffee and gold mesh sweater bought by her mother in the thirties.

Robert Freson

with lots of make-up.' Fashion had embraced brutalism and gone off at a wild tangent. In reaction there was a passion for the most romantic of dressing-up clothes. There were three schools of fashion – the flower power school, the ethnic peasant look, and *Viva Maria* ruffles and ringlets. By the end of the decade, nostalgia reigned; people turned back to the recent past for looks from the most heavily stylized and most easily identifiable decades. Girls were wearing slippery culottes, square-shouldered suits with scarlet lipstick, and beaded twenties dresses found in the antique markets. Bernard Nevill, whose Jazz Collection fabrics for Liberty had given the mood so much impetus, told *Vogue*, 'Initially Art Deco 69 was influenced by the flat florals and geometrics of Art Deco 25, which designers find fit so well the mood of Pop Culture. Now the trend is spreading in other directions as people collect the furniture, jewellery, ceramics and graphics of the period. And converging with this interest – a nostalgia for the 30s and 40s styles which are equally relevant now.' He emphasized the difference between Art Deco 69 and Art Deco 25. So much gets in the way of the reconstruction of a look from another time – the way you stand, your make up, how you want to appear, the underclothes you wear, the air you breathe – making the most careful copy only a parallel. The style that Aldous Huxley had described as 'A mixture of greenhouse and hospital ward furnished in the style of a dentist's operating chamber' was now the inspiration for the interiors of the smartest Chelsea houses and Regent's Park flats.

The scope of the fashion revolution can be seen at a glance in men's fashion. From the revival of Edwardian dandyism in the fifties via longer hair, printed shirts and no ties, polo-neck sweaters and skintight jeans, men were dressing in satin, chiffon, frills and lace by the end of the sixties. Mick Jagger wore a white organdie dress (with trousers) for an open air concert, and the mods appeared in high heels, with handbags and plucked eyebrows. Even the men who had changed their appearance least had changed a lot. Plain grey suits turned out close at hand to be made of rainbow weaves. 'Hooray Henrys' wore sheepskins, cavalry twills and paisley cravats: their trousers were cut in a slim backward curve, and their trouser hems were cut to lift over the instep. John Taylor of the *Tailor and Cutter* attributed it all to sex: 'It's simple; men want to look younger and more attractive now. England is not such a man's world as it was.' *Vogue* attributed it to women: 'The hand that rocks the cradle is at last having some influence on the droopy fawn cardigan and the grey socks round the ankle', and found that 'The Englishman's view that to be at all dandified is effete – or worse – is changing. After-shave lotions are established, deodorants a necessary commonplace, and colognes are catching on.' Fancy dress reached its height in 1968, when Christopher Gibbs urged *Vogue* readers to buy and wear the Diaghilev ballet costumes being auctioned at Sotheby's: 'There is nothing wrong in loving young men (though loving everyone is where it's at) . . . I'm sure Diaghilev would have been delighted to see his extravaganzas clothing the supple limbs of young Voguesters, bringing a pinch of the glory of All the Russias to dowdy gimcrack London . . . Come in colours, and the grey pox will never catch you. Heed only the poets and the painters and you'll never go wrong.'

Running away from the grey pox was a recurring theme of the decade. When Kenneth Tynan gave the name satire to the humour of *Beyond the Fringe*, a university review on the outskirts of the Edinburgh Festival in 1960, he remarked, 'England is complacent and the young are bored. There is the desire to hear breaking glass.' Humour had grown cruel and subtle since the early days of the rollicking moon-mad Goons, and it became the favourite weapon of the press. Peter Laurie was not entirely free of satirical intent himself when he wrote in *Vogue*, 'The intellectually aware will no doubt have noticed a new journalistic commodity in vogue among the cultured press: satire.' He pointed out that the Angry Young Men had quickly exhausted the value of sheer protest, but had uncovered a mine of social material which they had scarcely had time to work. Jonathan Miller said that the English seemed unable to be funny in their own voices, but in turning their attention to the target instead of the audience, the satirists found a new lightness of touch. 'There is an assumption that we are moderately well read and moderately familiar with what more serious artists and thinkers are doing,' said Peter Laurie, and Mary Holland wrote about *That Was The Week That Was* as 'this anarchic, unkind, uneven and often downright sick arrival to B.B.C. television . . . It is certainly not well-intentioned. It is sharp-tongued, cruel, sophisticated, and, praise be, firm in its belief that the audience is as clever as itself and capable of enjoying the same jokes.' Satire depended on a supply of targets ripe for sustained attack, and as these fell away towards the end of the sixties, this particular vein ran dry.

In the cinema, the decade began with long queues for foreign films. Londoners lost their interest in Cinerama, Todd A-O and Cinemascope, and went instead to the *nouvelle vague* films of Louis Malle, Claude Chabrol and Jean-Luc Godard, or the new Antonioni or Fellini from Italy. 'In the windy chill of London's Westbourne Grove,' said *Vogue* in 1960, 'people queue past the baker's shop and down the side street to see *Hiroshima Mon Amour*. There are four shows a day, all packed; no seats are bookable and

Peter Laurie

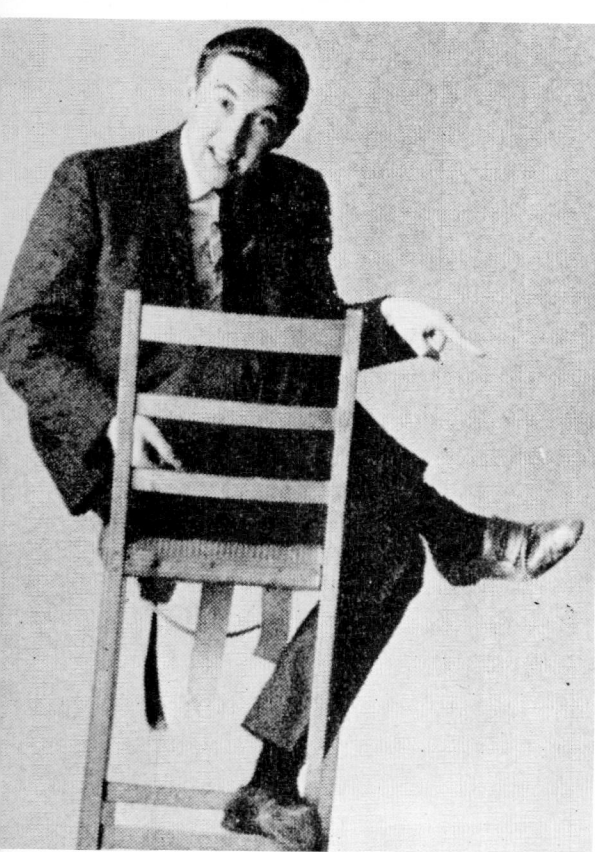

3   Peter Laurie

4   Peter Laurie

1. 'The attic dressers' drawn by Roger Law: dandies who dress in frilly shirts and frock coats from the Portobello Road, striped Edwardian suits from the attic and panamas, silver-topped canes and watch chains.

2. *Private Eye:* 'Its strength is that the editors write solely to please themselves'. Christopher Booker, William Rushton, Richard Ingrams.
3. David Frost of *'That Was The Week That Was'*.
4. Cabaret at The Establishment, Jeremy Geidt, John Fortune, John Bird and Eleanor Bron.

1

Avedon

2

Cecil Beaton

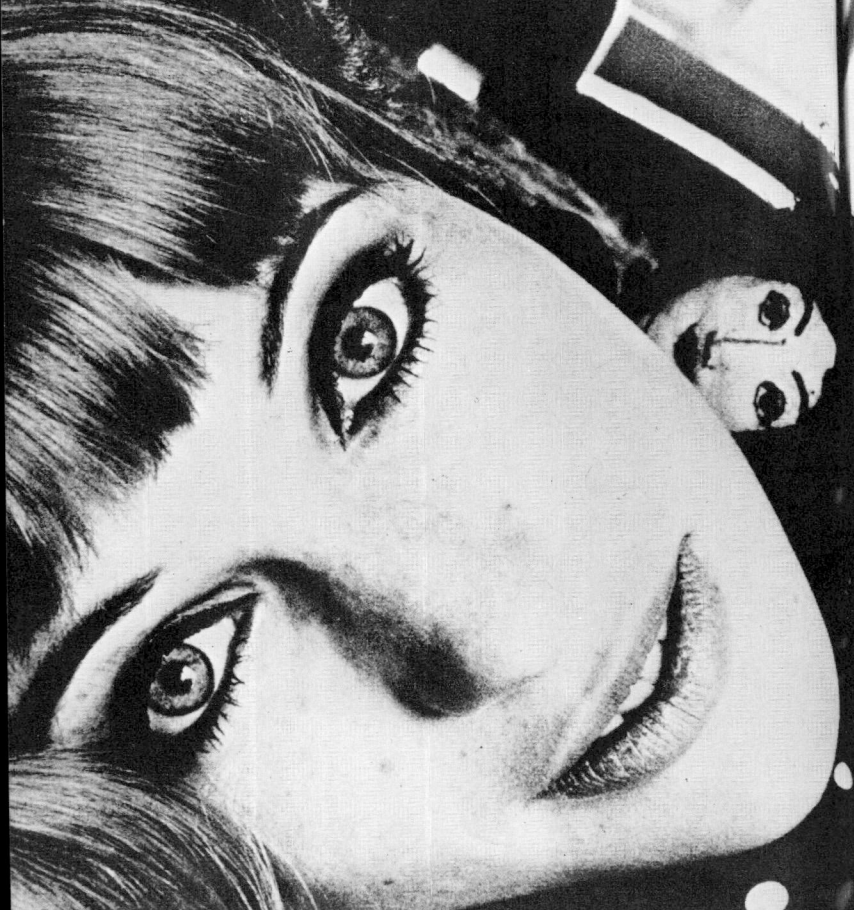

3

David Bailey

4

the telephone is permanently engaged. With this, his first feature film, director Alain Resnais joins the ranks of the new French film-makers who make us stand in line while many cinemas are half empty.' Resnais followed up with *Last Year in Marienbad*, developing the use of flashbacks to introduce the past into the present and give a feeling of *déjà vu*. Foreign films had a great influence on British directors, and the birth of neo-realist films like Karel Reisz's *Saturday Night and Sunday Morning*, produced by John Osborne's and Tony Richardson's Woodfall Films. 'With this film,' said Francis Wyndham, 'the British cinema has really grown up at last, indeed one might argue that this is the first British film ever made. It is about working class life today.' There followed a remarkable series of British films including *A Taste of Honey*, *The Loneliness of the Long Distance Runner*, *A Kind of Loving* and *Billy Liar*. Directors of all nationalities were aware of each other's work and films became much more cosmopolitan. To take three key films of the sixties, Richard Lester's Beatles vehicle *A Hard Day's Night*

and Joseph Losey's sinister *The Servant*, with brilliant performances by Dirk Bogarde and James Fox, were both made by Americans living and working in England, and Antonioni's *Blow-Up* by an Italian in London. A characteristic of the sixties was the fantasy fulfilment theme followed by a nightmarish ending – as in *Jules et Jim*, *Lolita* and *Bonnie and Clyde*.

'To those who say, "what was good enough for my father is good enough for me",' said the catalogue of the John Moores Liverpool exhibition, 'modern methods will not commend themselves in art as well as in transportation or heating.' After the 'British Painting of the Sixties' show at the Whitechapel, Edward Lucie-Smith introduced the work of a handful of dissimilar painters to *Vogue* readers and explained how wariness, toughness, worldliness and a scrupulous professionalism were now part of an artist's equipment. David Hockney, he said, 'has had the good fortune to find himself at the head of a well-defined new school of painting – the so-called "Pop Art" movement. What nobody seems to have

1. Avedon's portrait of *Funny Girl* Barbra Streisand in Grès navy linen poncho, and Roger Vivier's gold ball-heeled slippers. Barbra Streisand ('that second A, who needs it?') was made for success and fought for it. *Vogue* said, 'When she is being bothered — or thinks she is — she doesn't allow irritation to show; she simply darts out a beam of pure poison and lodges it in the annoyer.'
2. Audrey Hepburn in an Ascot dress designed by Cecil Beaton for *My Fair Lady*: all white and black. 'The costumes must step ahead of the past to have influence', said Cecil Beaton, 'but the ghost of my Aunt Jessie is present in all of them. I remember her as she returned from Paris with enormous five-foot-square boxes filled with hats and glittering finery', and Audrey Hepburn said, 'He makes you look the way you have always wanted to look' and asked for one of the costumes to keep.
3. Pauline Boty, 26, actress, painter, beauty, a distillation of the 1960s, who died tragically young.
4. Jane Asher, friend of Paul McCartney but also a considerable actress, with a dozen features and television films already behind her in 1964.
5. Frederico Fellini with a *Vogue* model, photographed by William Klein beside the 'gigantesco' poster for *La Dolce Vita*, the 'biggest and most controversial success in Italian movie history', 1960.

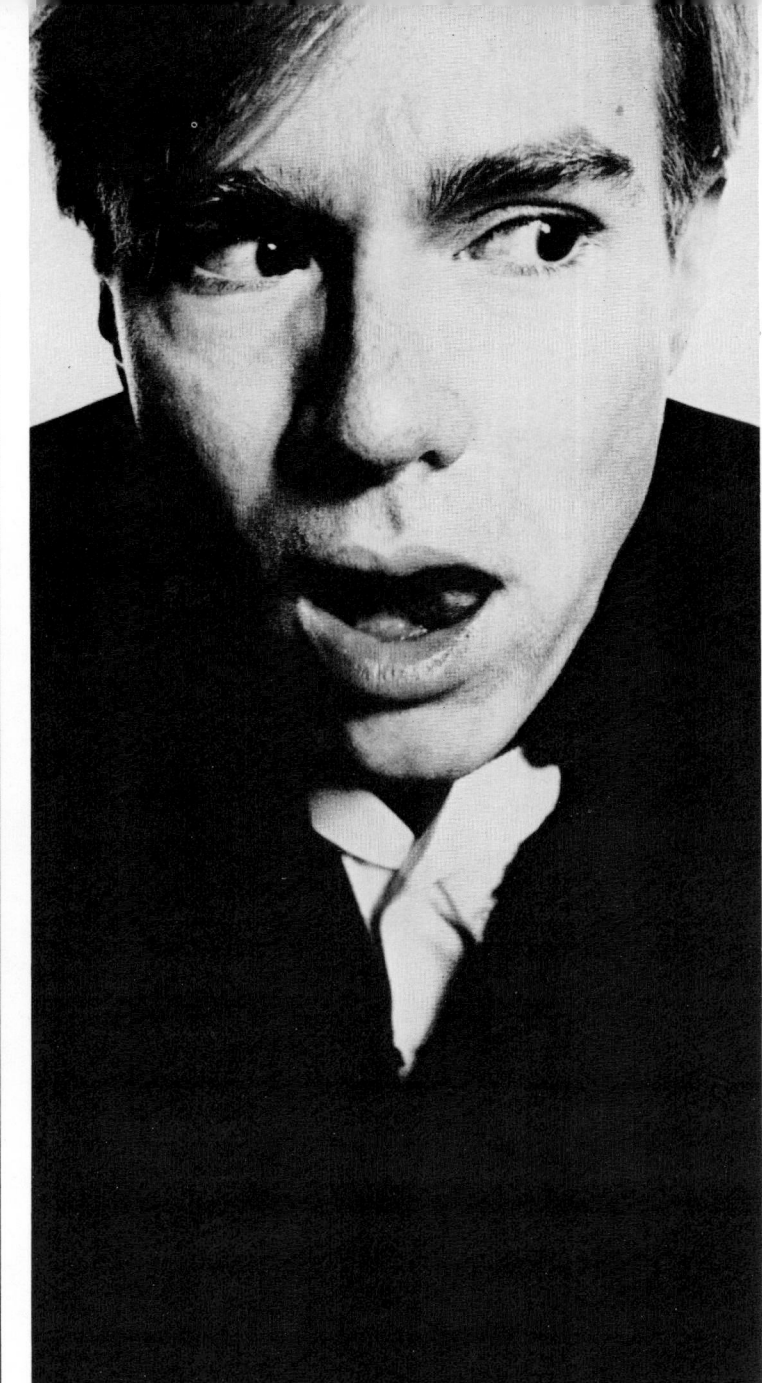

David Bailey

noticed is that Hockney is at his best just where he is least closely affiliated to Pop . . . he is a true narrative painter.' Howard Hodgkin was 'representative of a more sober kind of figurative painting . . . the nearest thing to a really classical artist'. Eschewing fashion in a fashion magazine, he told readers to look at a painting they would like to buy and see it as it would look in ten years' time – 1973 – 'just at the moment when it is most out of fashion, most *déjà vu*'. When *Vogue* interviewed Andy Warhol in 1965 he was more interested in Minimalism than Pop, and delivered to Polly Devlin a non-interview to go with his intentionally empty art-works. 'Edie is with us,' he informed her. 'The film with Edie for the festival is very beautiful. Half of it's out of focus and she does nothing . . . I flick on the switch and the film makes itself . . . Movies are so boring and you can sit and watch mine and think about yourself or whatever you want to think about. I don't know what I'm doing either. It keeps us busy.' He ventured that Tennessee Williams had written a script for him: 'Really only a title. It's "F and S". That's all. He wrote it. I'll make a film of it when I get back.' 'What does it mean?' 'What does it mean to you?' Does Warhol collect anything himself? 'All this art is finished . . . Squares on the wall. Shapes on the floor. Emptiness. Empty rooms . . . Redundant. That's what my art is all about.'

A year later, Elaine Dundy interviewed another celebrity of the sixties, Tom Wolfe, whose *Kandy-Kolored Tangerine-Flake Stream-line Baby* arrived in England via Jonathan Cape. His way of writing, his feud with the *New Yorker* and his extravagant form of dress had made him a V.I.P. in the U.S.A., and here he had a considerable impact on journalism, particularly on magazine and advertising copywriting. The new Wild Man of American literature, he had savagely attacked the *New Yorker* style, 'which requires that whenever you mention, say, an actor's name, you give the play he was in at the time, the cast, the theatre, and the length of time it ran and you get a fact-stuffed sentence that's quite beside the point . . . People only write in careful flowing sentences. They don't think that way and they don't talk that way.' Elaine Dundy described his clothes – a pale grey sharkskin suit and a tie twice as wide as usual with clowns dancing on it . . . 'It is necessary to refer to his clothes because he ascribes almost magical properties to them. "If that shirt and that shirt were running a race," he will say, pointing to what appear to be two identical shirts, "that shirt would win."' His style was hyperbolic, colloquial and immediate.

> I shall burst this placid pink shell
> I shall wake up slightly hungover,
> Favoured, adored, worshipped and clamoured for.
> I shall raise Hell and be a real
> Cut-up.

1. Edward Lucie-Smith's chosen painters, 1963. *Left*: David Hockney leaning on 'Two Friends'. *Centre above*: John Howlin below his 'I'll remember April'. *Centre below*: Ian Stephenson in front of 'Panchromatic'. *Right:* Howard Hodgkin and his 'Julia and Margaret'.
2. Andy Warhol, 1965.
3. Tom Wolfe, 'Wild Man' of American literature. Elaine Dundy said that he dressed to give offence to his viewers — to 'shake 'em up'. He himself said 'Everything's wrong with my coat . . .

too wide lapels, too much shoulder-padding and more buttons than a policeman's uniform', but he looked good in his clothes, as he was well aware.
4. *Hair*, America's Tribal Love-Rock Musical. Avedon photographed the writers James Rado and Gerome Ragni with Lynn Kellog who played Sheila.
5. Portraits in the style of new painters, photographed by David Montgomery. Looking like a Lichenstein, Charlotte Rampling.

3   Jack Robinson

4   Avedon

5   Montgomery

'The idea of what is news today is still a nineteenth-century concept,' he said. 'Perfect Journalism would deal constantly with one subject: Status.'

The dynamic turmoil of the late fifties and early sixties had become the nervous stimulation of the mid-sixties. In reaction to the orgy of commercialism that had characterized the decade, there was the alternative society of the idealists, the flower people using words like 'love' and 'freedom' in a woolly way. But it soon became evident that the alternative society was just as ripe for exploitation as any other. Underground magazines were paid for by record advertisements. *Hair* ('What do you want to be, besides dishevelled?') supposedly genuinely hippy, had an advance ticket sale of $250,000. In the U.S.A. flower-power was turning ugly in the heat of anti-Vietnam agitation: among the serious demonstrators were every kind of provocative revolutionary. In London the hippies found they could not live and buy pot by making candles and Batik prints alone. Rather than take National Assistance, a few dropped out and went to farm in the remotest parts of the country. For the most responsible and constructive thinkers – the Des Wilsons and the Naders – the conclusion seemed to be that we must do the best we can with what we have, working from inside the system to redress the balance and make good. With exploding populations and shrinking resources, the question already was, 'Is it too late?'

JEAN SHRIMPTON

Jean Shrimpton, top model and international figure of the 1960s, was the first high fashion model to be a favourite pin-up too. She was the most natural of models, and made the elegant and expensive clothes relate to the whole world of girls of her own age and type. She began modelling in 1960, and was only 19 when David Bailey's pictures of her began to dominate *Vogue* a couple of years later. *Vogue* called her 'just marvellously pretty' but it is a fact that it was almost impossible to take a bad picture of her — even in her passport picture she looks a great beauty. Barry Lategan says, 'She always looks as though being photographed is exactly what she wanted to do.' Jean Shrimpton told 'About Town' in a 1962 interview, 'I'm not a classical beauty. Nor beatnik really. But nearer beatnik than classical. I've been lucky, but I'm riding the crest of a wave. In a year everyone might be against my type of looks.' However she continues into the 1970s to have an uncontrived glamour that hasn't tarnished. She got out at the top, and lives in the country refusing modelling assignments and working at photography. She shows signs of real talent at the other side of the lens.

1. 1972.
2. Jean Shrimpton in New York: navy blazer suit by Slimma in a Chinatown telephone box, a pagoda in red, green and gold, 1962.
3. In a black dress by Fredrica, 1962.
4. Wallis cotton piqué suit, 1965.

2
SLIMMA   David Bailey

3
FREDRICA   David Bailey   David Bailey

4

John Encome

Avedon

Dave Budnick

Roberta Booth

VANESSA R[...]
1. Vanessa R[...]
1969. She is t[...]
the stage for [...]
1966. With h[...]
'the intellectu[...]
her first star v[...]
Lovely War. [...]
has never con[...]
heart has alw[...]

CATHERINE [...]
2. Perfectly b[...]
25 in 1969, sh[...]
Mississippi fo[...]
will have sing[...]
medium of th[...]
with the enig[...]
French star to[...]
'a cool combi[...]
school of acti[...]
non-acting.

VERUSCHKA [...]
3. Veruschka [...]
body painting[...]
or more often [...]

JEANNE MO[...]
4. Jeanne M[...]
well-known in[...]
Dangereuses,[...]
young fashion[...]
Dave Budnick[...]
girls in the Fre[...]
Maria in 1965[...]
in Britain.

JULIE CHRIS[...]
5. Julie Chri[...]
with a passin[...]
Vogue called[...]
film'. From d[...]
star in her o[...]
Darling, Dr Z[...]
eight well-kn[...]
in 1967.

SOPHIA LO[...]
6. Sophia Lo[...]
with one of [...]
seclusion in [...]
Rome. Soph[...]
has a cup of [...]
morning with[...]
lunch with h[...]
often skippin[...]
which I cons[...]
has no intere[...]
minutes.

Snowdon

ELIZABETH TAYLOR

Elizabeth Taylor is perhaps the last of the great world-famous movie stars, complete with diamonds, private planes and yachts, and a chain of husbands — Conrad Hilton, Michael Wilding, Michael Todd, Eddie Fisher and Richard Burton to date. British born, she evacuated with her family to Hollywood during the war and became a child star in such films as *Lassie Come Home* and *National Velvet.* She was posing for cheese-cake pictures when she was fifteen, and her amazing violet-eyed black-and-white beauty was already undeniable. Elizabeth Taylor and Richard Burton were thé world's most spectacular couple in the 1960s, and could guarantee an audience for any picture they played in. Even so, the blockbuster *Cleopatra* almost sank Twentieth Century Fox — to break even, it was said, the film had to bring in over 40 million dollars. By 1969 she had made 38 films, including her shattering performance with Burton in *Who's Afraid of Virginia Woolf.* In private life, she is extremely generous with her money where children's charities are concerned, donating around a million dollars a year, and has a large family of her own both by marriage and by adoption. 'Liz Taylor is 40,' ran *Life*'s cover in 1972,'. . . and all of us are suddenly middle-aged.'

1. 1953.
2. 1965.
3. In a wig designed to match her dog, 1972.
4. With Richard Burton at the 'Proust' ball given by Guy de Rothschild, 1972. She was dressed as Ida Rubinstein, in black taffeta and lace, emerald roses and a black egret cockade, all by Valentino; the Burton diamond on a black velvet ribbon around her neck.

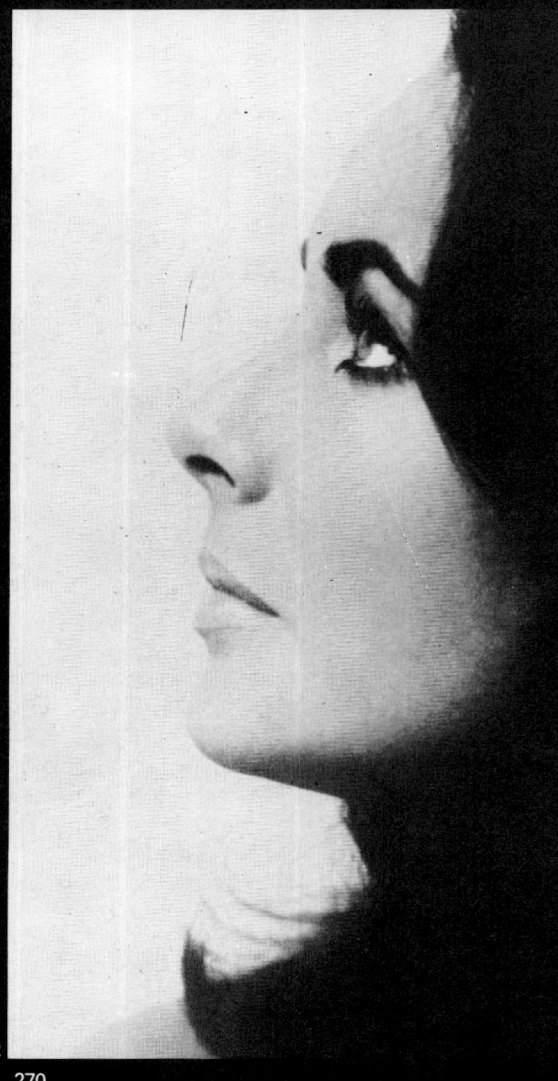

Cecil Beaton

Norman Parkinson

William Klein

270

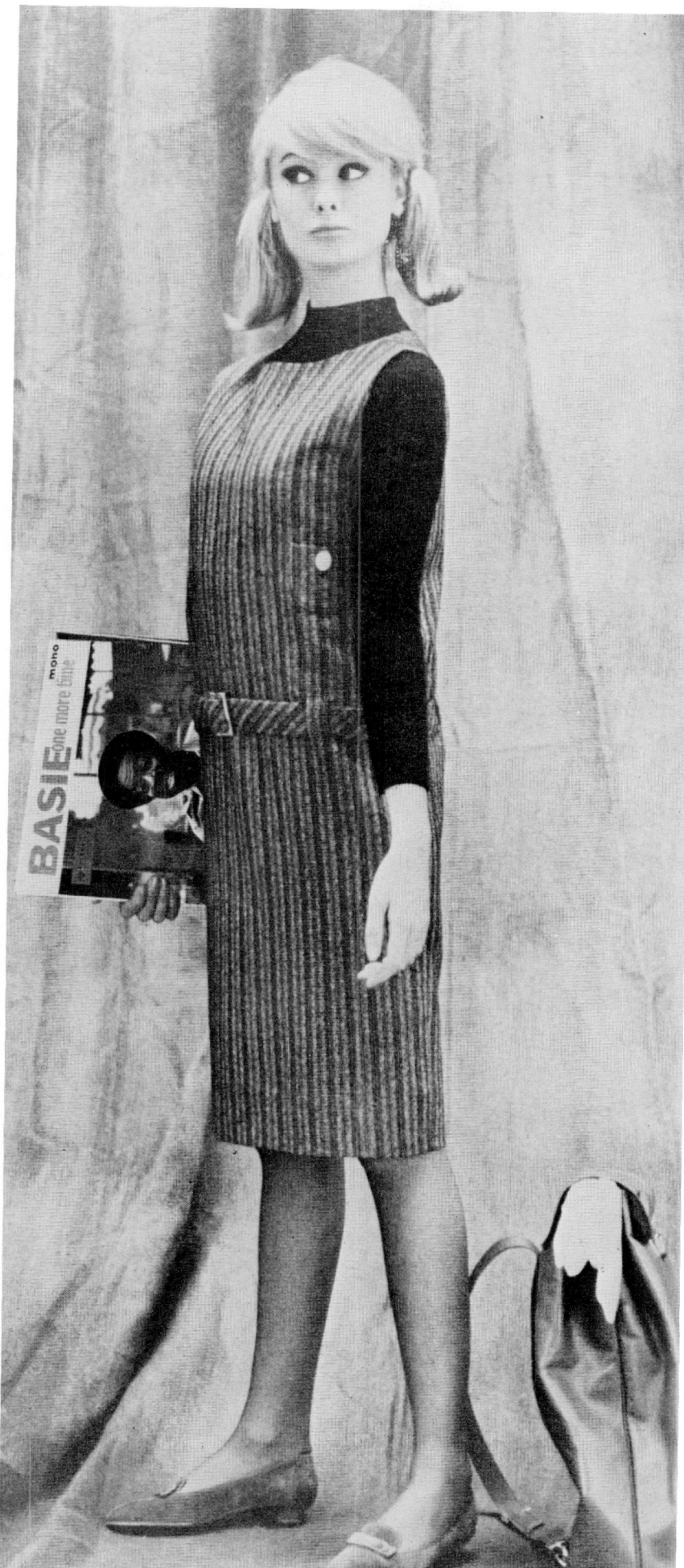

1
BAZAAR   Norman Parkinson

'Brevity is the soul of fashion'

'The beat look is the news at Dior . . . pale zombie faces; leather suits and coats; knitted caps and high turtleneck collars, black endlessly'

'St Tropez has burgeoned into one of the great playgrounds of the western world. It's Bardot and Sagan territory . . . an odd mixture of slightly scruffy insouciance and tremendous chic. Fashions started here one year are worn on beaches round the world the next'

'Young' begins to appear as the persuasive adjective for all fashions, hairstyles and ways of life: Bazaar's new clothes are prominent and after Bardot's pink gingham and *broderie anglaise* summer, even Paris begins to take St Tropez into account. Hair is backbrushed and waved, a long spiky fringe is brushed over the forehead, and eye make up begins to steal attention from lipstick. Best 'young' fashion investments are a pinafore, striped or flannel, to wear with or without a tight black sweater, and a leather suit, more tempting than a fur coat. Young Idea shows dark plaid knitted stockings, rainshirts, kneelength jeans worn inside a full unbuttoned skirt. The 'art student' look is everywhere, always qualified by *Vogue* 'not beat, not scruffy, but pretty'.

From Paris there are formal evening dresses, Chanel's rough white tweed cardigan suits edged with wide navy and scarlet braid — much copied, and a Wallis shops best seller — and Yves Saint Laurent's collection for Dior: a short skirt, gathered over the hips and tightened at the knee. At its most exaggerated, it's called the 'puffball' skirt. His 'beat' collection is the most unpopular look in Paris, and his last for Dior.

Page opposite: Patti Boyd wears Thocolette's topless Liberty lawn nightdress; photograph by David Bailey.
1. The art student pinafore from Bazaar, Young Idea's 1960 essential: grey and black stripes, worn with a tight black sweater and black stockings for day . . . and by itself for the evening, with a patent purse and stilettos.

1960

1   Duffy

2
McLaughlin-Gill

1. Blue and white striped kneelength jeans and matching skirt, wide-necked top and pointed pumps.
2. The bouffant hairdo, worn with pearls, white gloves, black broadtail jacket.
3. The 1960s leather suit. Sun spectacles are a new accessory.

KIKI
BYRNE

Claude
Virgin

4
SAINT LAURENT   Penn

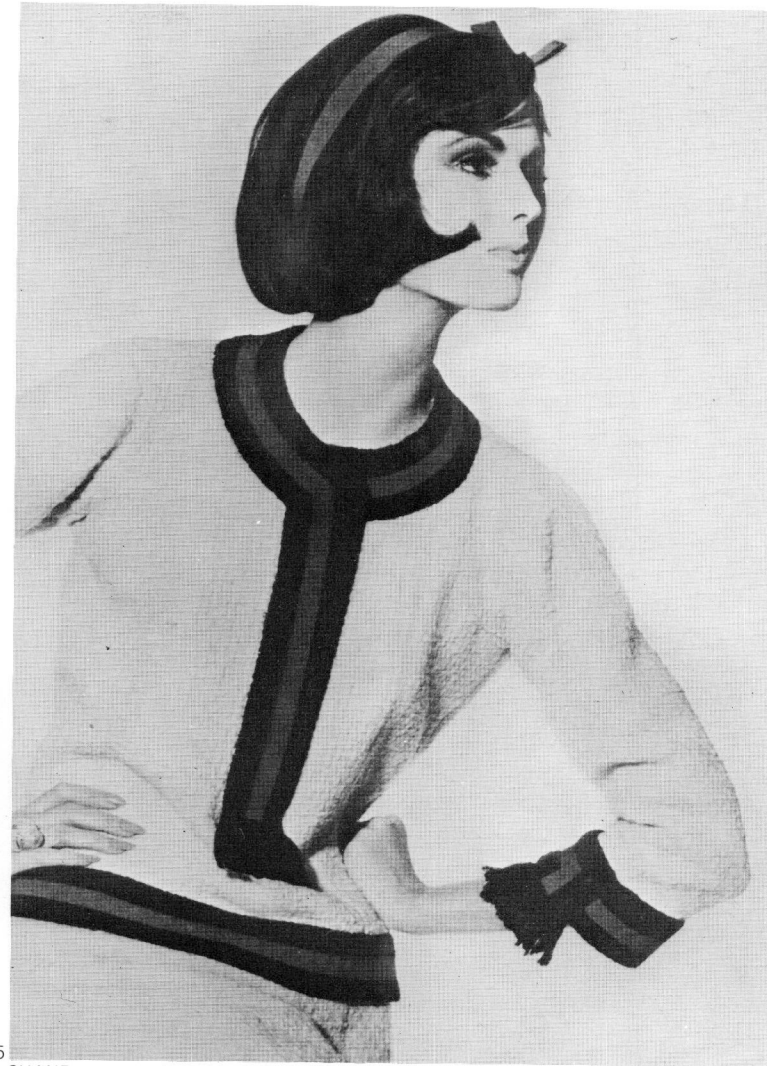

5 CHANEL   Penn

6
TRACY   Duffy

7 DIOR   Duffy

8 JEAN ALLEN   Duffy

4. Saint Laurent's unpopular last collection for Dior. 'The beat look, the Left Bank, is the news at Dior . . . pale zombie faces; leather suits and coats; knitted caps and high turtle-neck collars, black endlessly.'

5. Chanel's much copied 1960 suit: rough white tweed bound in navy braid.

6. Tom Courtenay, fresh from Konstantin in *The Seagull* at the Old Vic, said, 'I don't like that', to which the model, dressed in a gold lurex jersey cardigan suit replied, 'Well, try to like it.'

7. Kenneth More took time off from *The Greengage Summer* for the photograph. He liked the model's

Christian Dior dress: 'the bed jacket drape's wonderful'.

8. Lionel Bart working on *Blitz*, a follow-up to *Oliver* and *Fings*, said, 'It's amazing how I don't notice clothes . . . but she looks slightly off-beat, which I like.' The model is wearing a brown silk faille dress.

1961-62

'Young Idea is Gone on Moreau – clothes with the kind of tough gamin charm sparked off by Jeanne Moreau in the film *Jules et Jim*'

'What to wear with your new wig; chiffon culottes'

The 'Twist' arrives from France and is danced first at the Saddle Room. The Truffaut film *Jules et Jim* sets a fashion for grandmother spectacles with round wire frames, long mufflers, gaiters, boots, kilts, Gorblimey caps and knickerbockers. The culotte skirt is a new look, in suede, in tweed or chiffon. Bazaar and Kiki Byrne make sleeveless jumpersuits with pleated skirts, Mary Quant's in soft grey tweed bound with wide black braid. Girls are saving their money for the new coats — V-neck black leather cardigans, suede trenchcoats, or Gerald McCann's rabbit coat, the cheapest fur at 35 gn. Foreign buyers are becoming aware of the explosion of new British fashion talent: the London Fashion Week produces more than a million pounds worth of additional export business. In March 1962 *Vogue* applauds Edward Rayne's success in capturing the American press and buyers, bringing them over from Paris to see the shows of the Incorporated Society of London Fashion Designers, and getting them back in time for the Saint Laurent collection. Mary Quant makes a highly successful trip to America.

In Paris, 'The most heartfelt sounds during collections week were the bravos, ecstatic tears and kisses that greeted Marc Bohan after his first showing at Dior. It was the succès fou of Paris. Back again was the old Dior tradition of desirable, wearable clothes, each new design drawing choruses of oohs and aahs from the enraptured spectators.' Meanwhile Saint Laurent opens his independent couture house, and *Vogue* photographs a plain white dress with a cut out back and a circus pony turban, bought by Fortnum & Mason. His autumn collection brings the Left Bank look into the couture with total success. No one can deny the new elegance of his black ciré satins with ruffs of black mink, his rajah coats and tubular dresses worn with turbans and dark stockings, his long pulled-down tops and barrel skirts, all decorated with rich dark jewellery. Balenciaga makes a deep country suit in soft thick tweed with flat leather boots to the knee, and a slim city suit with belling peplum and hem. Bohan at Dior makes a dress that blouses over the waist, and bases a whole collection on matchbox seams, squaring off the silhouettes of suits and coats.

Wigs begin to edge into the fashion picture. Most hairdressers, *Vogue* reports, are telling their staff to cut down on back combing and advising clients to buy false pieces instead. Everyone wants more hair, adding thickness and height, whether the cut is short and curly or long, heavy and swinging. Lipsticks begin to pale down as eye make up gets heavier.

The new fluid all-in-one creams are the biggest make up revolution right now, giving an unpowdered matt complexion.

Jean Shrimpton and the *Jules et Jim* look: knickerbockers and Jackie Coogan cap, black leather jerkin and white cotton shirt.

Duff

SAINT LAURENT

Penn

1 GERALD McCANN

Peter Rand

1. The Left Bank look makes good now that Saint Laurent finds his independent fashion identity: black ciré satin cuffed in black mink.
2. Nine-tenths rabbit coat, 'affordable fur'.
3. Make up at full power in 1962, with the new all-in-one foundation creams.

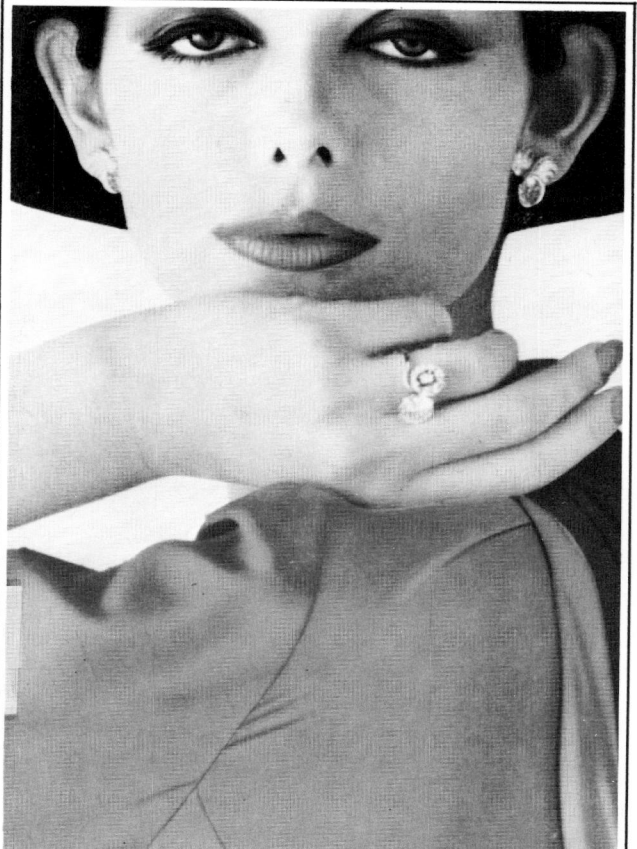

2

3

Claude Virgin

277

1961-62

1
POLLY PECK   Duffy

2   David Bailey

3 MOSBROOK   ANELLO & DAVIDE   Duffy

SUSAN SMALL   Peter Rand

MARC BOHAN   William Klein

1. *Jules et Jim*'s influence on Young Idea: here, grey cardigan suit with a V neck over a black leather sweater.

2. By 1962, the concensus among top hairdressers like Raphael and Leonard, André Bernard, Aldo of Aldobruno, Raymond and Steiner is that false pieces add height and bulk more satisfactorily than back-combing, which breaks the hair.

3. Yellow and black tartan kilt, with yellow shantung shirt and black high-heeled boots.

4. Instead of the little black dress, the schoolmarm blouse in tucked cotton with a black bow, long grey flannel skirt.

5. Marc Bohan's matchbox coat for Dior, in black and white check tweed with the bow of the dress showing at the neck.

6. From Yves Saint Laurent's first independent collection, a white silk crepe dress with a swimsuit back, a circus pony turban.

SAINT LAURENT   Helmut Newton

1963

'Boots, boots and more boots are marching up and down like seven leaguers, climbing to new leg lengths and taking with them stockings and kneesocks in thick depths of textures'

'The rule for dressing this winter: legs first'

'People are talking about . . . the secret rouging of knees above white socks'

Saint Laurent brings leather indoors, 'makes brass studs smarter than rubies' and shows women how to dress for their boots. He makes boots in alligator, covering the whole length of the legs to the thighs. Every woman who owns a tweed suit is buying a pair of boots, and there are dozens of heights and shapes to choose from. When legs show, they are covered in cables, paisleys, rugger socks, diamonds and tartans. 'There's a positive preoccupation with the fear of an arctic winter,' says *Vogue* in autumn, and it helps to sell Victorian vests and long underpants in stripes or diamonds edged with lace and made in stretchy Helanca, red flannel nightshirts and fur hats pulled down over the ears. In this year of the Profumo affair and Beatlemania, all the new looks are tied up with Vidal Sassoon's important new haircut — very hard, very architectural, a thick chopped bob that's shaped to bare the top of the neck, or falling a little longer in limp curves, straight as silk. Vidal Sassoon's talk of bone structure and head shape leads to rethinking in make up and a new interest in hats. *Vogue* talks of rouge being used not so much for colour as 'contouring the cheekbones', and James Wedge designs a collection of hats to go with the Sassoon cuts, sold from boutiques in the hair salons. Boo Field Reid makes more anti-establishment hats, including Bardot headscarves, Jules et Jim caps, and tweed baseball caps. The newest shape is the helmet fitting the head like a bathing cap, with a chin strap, in white fur by James Wedge, in black satin with a cartwheel brim by Dior. Herbert Johnson are selling as many bowlers to women as to men, in stitched dark velvets.

The Look for winter. Muffling brown check suit, with a skunk busby and boots of brown suede and patent leather, patterned tights and leather gloves.

David Bailey

MATITA

False eyelashes are an essential part of make up, but *Vogue* shows how to shape and trim them so that they only add a little thickness to the outer corners of the eyes. 'The beat look, left-bank pallor and the Cleopatra eye are off the beam: paint eye contours on with a thin line, using a tiny brush.'

1963 brings new young designers into *Vogue:* Foale and Tuffin from the R.C.A., with their cut-out shift dress; Roger Nelson, also from the College, with his designs for Woollands; Clive Evans who opens his couture house this year, and French designer Emmanuelle Khanh, working in Paris on her *'nouveau classique'* look. Her suits are meticulous and architectural, narrow and fitted tightly to the shoulder, every line curving. Onto this careful structure she adds exactly proportioned cuff and shoulder widths, revers and flaps curling away like petals. Her look is called 'the droop', and goes with the Vidal Sassoon haircut, and owl spectacles. Within a few months of *Vogue*'s first pictures, many ready-to-wear dresses and suits sprout long spaniel's ear collars.

Mary Quant launches her new Ginger Group — a collection of cheap clothes to be collected piece by piece and put together in endless variations. From Paris, bias shift dresses, Saint Laurent's peasant shirt and painter's smock, and Cardin's cut-out smocks baring the skin or the close-fitted dress beneath. Bohan makes a pinstripe suit for Dior, with leg o'mutton sleeves and kilt skirt, his signature a white gardenia worn with everything. Chanel goes from strength to strength: her newest suit is in rough rainbow tweed, thick as a thick-knit sweater. Saint Laurent's black and white geometric shifts are the easiest of all French looks to copy: in April, *Vogue* shows two spreads of them from the British ready-to-wear.

MARY QUANT   Terence Donovan

Peter Rand

1. Mary Quant's sailcloth sand-coloured dungarees with a black shirt.
2. The Vidal Sassoon haircut.
3. Emmanuelle Khanh, young French designer discovered by *Vogue*, wearing one of her own *'nouveau classique'* suits: cream checked Harris tweed, the silk shirt echoing the falling revers of the jacket.
4. New all-stretch corselette in Lycra net.

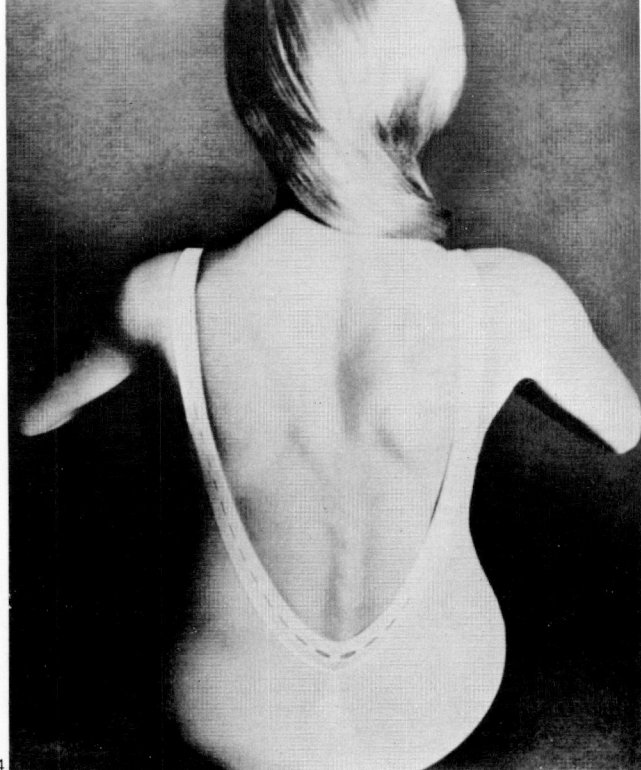

4

WARNER

Henry
Clarke

281

1 DIOR David Bailey

2 CHANEL Penn

MISS POLLY

282 3

4

TUFFIN & FOALE

Carapetian

SAINT LAURENT   Penn

SAINT LAURENT   Penn

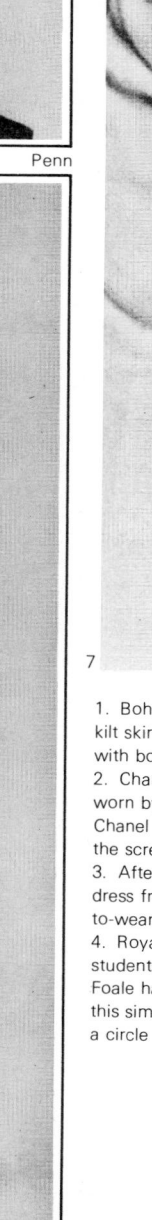

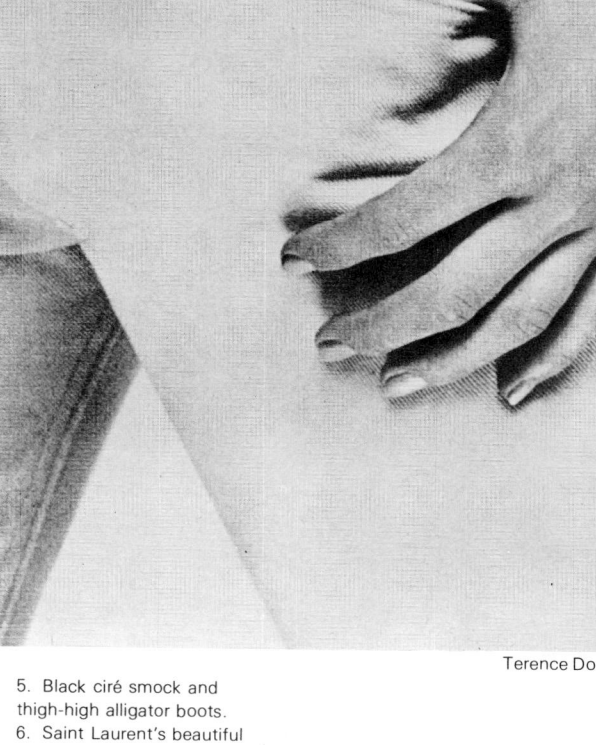

Terence Donovan

1. Bohan's leg o'mutton sleeves, kilt skirt in chalk stripe navy wool, with bowler and gardenia.
2. Chanel's navy jersey blazer suit worn by Anouk Aimée, who loves Chanel clothes on and off the screen.
3. After Saint Laurent — piebald dress from the London ready-to-wear.
4. Royal College of Art fashion students Sally Tuffin and Marion Foale have an early success with this simple shift dress cut out in a circle under each arm.

5. Black ciré smock and thigh-high alligator boots.
6. Saint Laurent's beautiful country tunic, bulky and loose with a narrow skirt, in Bernat Klein's mohair and wool tweed, worn with knitted wool stockings and flat walking shoes.
7. Jeans, the out-of-uniform uniform for the young.

1964

'Some of the occasions designers
apparently have in mind haven't
happened yet'
'Courrèges's skirts are the shortest in Paris'
'Courrèges invents the moon girl'
'White sets the pace at Courrèges'

The year of Courrèges. An expert tailor
trained at Balenciaga, he has been
producing his own collections since 1961,
but with his spring collection he suddenly
comes to the front of the Paris couture. To
the throbbing of tom-toms in his hot white
showroom on the avenue Kléber he parades
clothes that seem to be the projection of a
space age far ahead. *Vogue* says, 'White
sets the pace at Courrèges — tweeds,
gloves, kid boots, shoes, tunics, coats,
trousers are all white. Trouser suits are
lean, the trousers curved up at the ankle in
front, dipped over the heel at the back;
overblouses are straight and squarish,
jackets single breasted with a back half-
belt; skirts are the shortest in Paris —
above the knee. Coats are seven-eighths.'
From now on sixties fashion will revolve
round bare knees, the trouser suit, outsize
sunglasses, white leather boots, white and
silver.

This is also the first year of the ribbed
sweater and the small Liberty print, false
eyelashes with filaments added to give an
illusion of thickness and length. *Vogue*'s
pages are full of tawny tigresses like 'Baby
Jane' Holzer, wealthy jetsetter and
companion of Andy Warhol, and of the
Beatles' girl-friends Jane Asher and Patti
Boyd. In California, it's the year of Rudi
Gernreich's topless dress; in New York, of
Andy Warhol's camp culture and
underground movies.

1. Courrèges's 'moon girl': silver sequin pants tied with white satin
ribbon, white faille coat and suntanned midriff.
2. Courrèges makes his mark with his spring collection. Seven-eighths
coat in camel reversing to white gabardine over a white gabardine
dress, and trouser suit of white cotton matelasse with straight slit
trousers. Both worn with 'space helmets' and white kid boots.
3. Baby Jane Holzer demonstrates the craze for hair — the greatest
volume that can be contrived.
4. Jane Birkin wears a beautiful caramel wool coat by Dejac,
buttoned and half-belted, pleats at the back.
5. 1964 version of the Marlene Dietrich trouser suit in beige shantung,
trousers cut loose and straight, Canadian mink dropping off
the shoulders.

1
COURRÈGES   Penn

COURRÈGES

3

5

RICCI

1
ELMA   David Bailey

2 GERNREICH   David Bailey

1. White leather suit worn with white
lace stockings and white kid Courrèges
copy boots.
2. Rudi Gernreich's brave new world
— the Californian originator of the
topless bathing suit turns to camelhair
and checks, felt yashmaks and suede
balaclavas. His model wears scarlet
eye make-up.
3. Jane Asher, 'the envy of millions.
The Beatles are her fans,' in mustard
and black spotted cotton by Sally
Tuffin and Marion Foale.
4. Madame Grès's beautifully draped
evening dress of angora jersey, striped
in grey, blonde and white.
5. From Emmanuelle Khanh's
collection for Frank Usher, a white
rayon suit piped in bright red. Petalled
piqué bonnet, James Wedge.
6. The new cling sweater in sock
ribbing, pulled down hard in schoolboy
grey wool, tucked into a grey
flannel skirt.

3 TUFFIN & FOALE

1964

KHANH   Helmut Newton

JOHN LAING   David Bailey

GRÈS
Penn

1965

JOHN BATES   Duffy

Skimp cotton bikini dress in terracotta and navy, netted together in navy.

Opposite: Dresses, left to right, by Nettie Vogues, Diorling. Grace Coddington, fashion editor, in the water. Photograph by Helmut Newton, October 1973.
Over page, left: Make up by Christian Dior, felt cap by Charles Batten, heart necklace from Butler & Wilson. Photograph by Norman Parkinson, December 1973.
Over page, right: Face painted by Gil of Max Factor with a silk scarf by Karl Lagerfeld. Photograph by Clive Arrowsmith, November 1970.

'The world suddenly wants to copy the way we look. In New York it's the "London look", in Paris it's "*le style anglais*"'
'Every kind of English girl seems now to have the self-assurance praise and admiration give; every girl's an individualist – and a leader'
'Bras have been like something you wear on your head on New Year's Eve' – *Rudi Gernreich, American designer of the 'no bra' bra*

The Fashion House Group takes mini-skirts to America with a show on board the *Queen Elizabeth* berthed at New York. In Australia, Jean Shrimpton shocks race-goers with her mini-skirt four inches above the knees.

Skirts rise to mid-thigh, girls change over from stockings to tights and the London look becomes international. On the Continent and in America girls are approximating to 'the leggy, soft-skinned English blonde in country shoes, classic raincoat and grey flannel'. New examples of the type may come from anywhere: Françoise Dorléac, Françoise Hardy, Jane Birkin, Daliah Lavi, Jane Fonda. In March *Vogue* features 'The Attic Dressers', boys 'without the funds for Carnaby Street' who are dressing in dandy Victorian or Edwardian fashion from the street markets, Portobello, Brixton, or Church Street, Paddington, and out of dusty suitcases discovered in relations' attics. Ad men, with the money to pursue the look, are having made suits with waistcoats in pinstripes or grey flannel, which they wear with gold fob watches on chains, bow ties, and — if daring — a gangster hat. For evening, there are frilly shirts and velvet dinner jackets.

The dress of the moment is the see-through dress, with a netted midriff or made entirely of white crochet, necessitating another novelty, the invisible body stocking, flesh coloured and undecorated, pioneered in this country by Warners. Rudi Gernreich's soft 'no bra' bra firms the natural line without altering the shape or adding uplift; and this year, Mary Quant branches out into foundation-designing too.

Ossie Clark leaves Janey Ironside's fashion department at the R.C.A. this year and is quickly featured in *Vogue*. Ossie — 'After the war my father moved to a town called Oswaldtwistle and I've been called Ossie ever since' — began to make his name by designing a special collection for Woollands while still in his final term at College. Jean Muir, whose 'Jane & Jane' designs are constantly photographed in the magazine, begins to emerge with her own name on a small collection of beautifully simple maternity dresses.

In Paris, Edward Molyneux comes out of retirement, but only to sell to the trade. Yves Saint Laurent's Mondrian collection is based on a plain white jersey shift with lines and blocks in black and primary colours: the easiest thing in the world for the ready-to-wear market to copy. The first op art fabrics appear in the summer, versions of Bridget Riley's paintings.

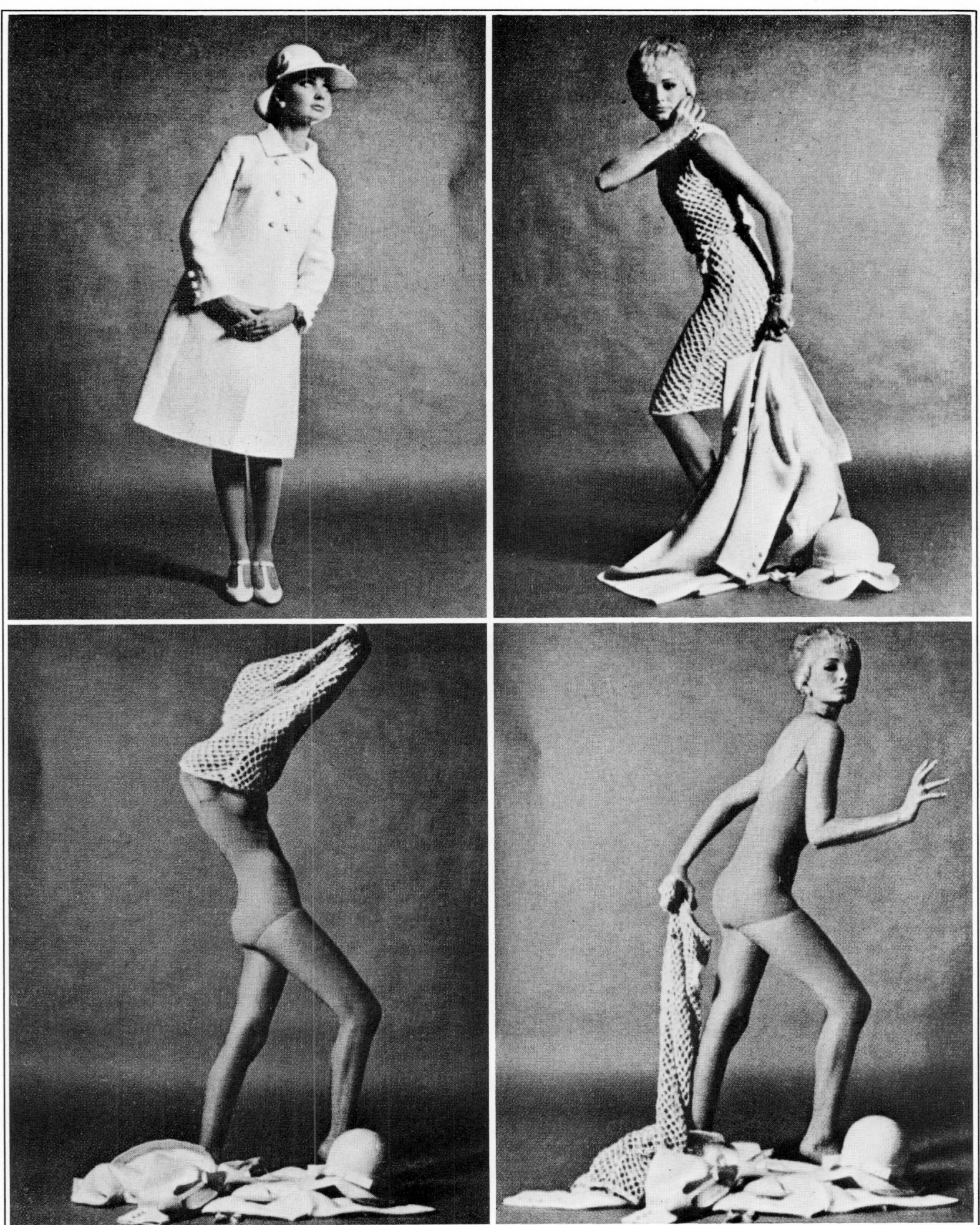

David Bailey

1965 layers: coat by Liza Spain, chenille dress by
Susan Small, Warners body stocking.

Opposite: Bianca Jagger in a box at the Théâtre de
France, with masked and white-powdered face by Serge
Lutens. Photographed by Eric Boman, March 1974.

1   W.H.I.

2   Penn

3   BONNIE CASHIN   Norman Parkinson

5

OSSIE CLARK

David Bailey

1. The crochet dress, made by Women's Home Industries to be worn over skin-coloured body stockings or camisole slips.
2. Diamanté mesh, Lord & Taylor, New York.
3. Blackberry leather tracksuit lined in silk, with a hooded jersey sweater.
4. 'Hypnotical Illusions': op art stripes designed by Getulio Alviani for Marucelli of Milan, photographed at the Temple of Rameses II on the west bank of the Nile.
5. New talent from the R.C.A., 23-year-old Ossie Clark, and his black and white quilted silk coat.

4

Henry
Clarke

1966

'Suddenly everyone's talking about Paco Rabanne, and his plastic fashion sculpture'
'Space projections . . . plastic, chrome, Dynel . . . everything silver, from visor to stockings and shoes'

The craziest fashion year of the sixties — a year in which make up becomes pure decoration, and you wear silver leather and plastic chain mail, skirts that show the whole length of your legs, mops of artificial hair coloured pink, green and purple, chrome jewellery, and visor sunglasses.

Paco Rabanne's plastics, small tiles linked together by chain, steal the show in Paris. Nearly all designers are infected with the mirage of 'space age fashion.' Cardin's dresses are half sculptures, little shifts suspended from ring collars, or cut out discs and squares. Saint Laurent makes his shifts in sheer organza, transparent except where they are striped or chevroned with silver sequins. Everywhere, from the couture to the ready-to-wear, the favourite dress is the briefest triangle, taking no account of the waist. It's worn with the shortest hair — Leonard cuts Twiggy's right back to the skull, shorter than a little boy's — huge plastic disc earrings, silver stockings, silver shoes laced up the leg, bangles of clear plastic and chrome. Silver leather or shirred silver nylon make the new jackets. Foale & Tuffin are just one of the shops selling suits with skirts and trousers matching the jackets, silver or contrasting corduroys. The craze for false hair reaches its peak with great mops and switches of Dynel, and eye make-up is designed to be seen from 100 yards, in streamlined eyeliners, black and white used alternately, and false eyelashes made still thicker with filament mascaras. Mary Quant's new make up is based on the face-decoration of 11 top models, and Verushka, America's surreal top model, is painting her body and face with flowers or colour abstractions.

These extreme looks need an extreme new kind of model girl, and *Vogue* photographs the Paris collections on the thinnest and most angular of them all — the spider-limbed black Donyale Luna, Ford plant manager's daughter from Detroit.

As alternatives to this new fashion brutalism, there are two new looks, Saint Laurent's gypsy print shifts or shirts-and-skirts with kerchiefs covering the hair, and the caftans that women are buying in Morocco or from the Indian boutiques in London. The caftan is undemanding, exotic, and a collector's piece and now becomes a classic. By the end of the sixties very few fashionable women won't have one.

Saint Laurent's autumn collection includes a few jokes, chiefly the pop dresses inspired by Andy Warhol, with vivid profiles of a face or a body scrawled over them in positive-negative contrast.

PACO RABANNE   David Bailey

1. 'The neon-lit kite coat', plastic diamonds on white crepe, by Paco Rabanne for Venet.
2. The Look: Dynel hair used in impossible thicknesses and colour combinations, and theatrical eye make up using alternate lines of black and white.
3. Front-zip silver Vinyl shift.
4. Scarlet kid coat and dress ruffed in racoon and lined in fleece.

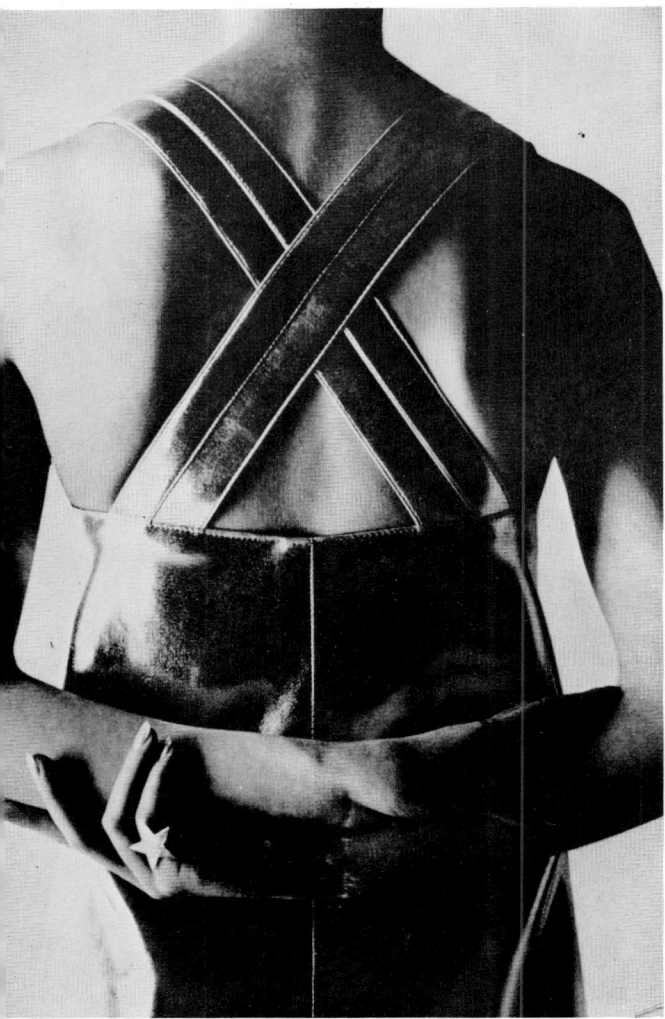

BONNIE CASHIN

Helmut Newton

JAN FINCH

David Bailey

293

1966

FOALE & TUFFIN   Traege

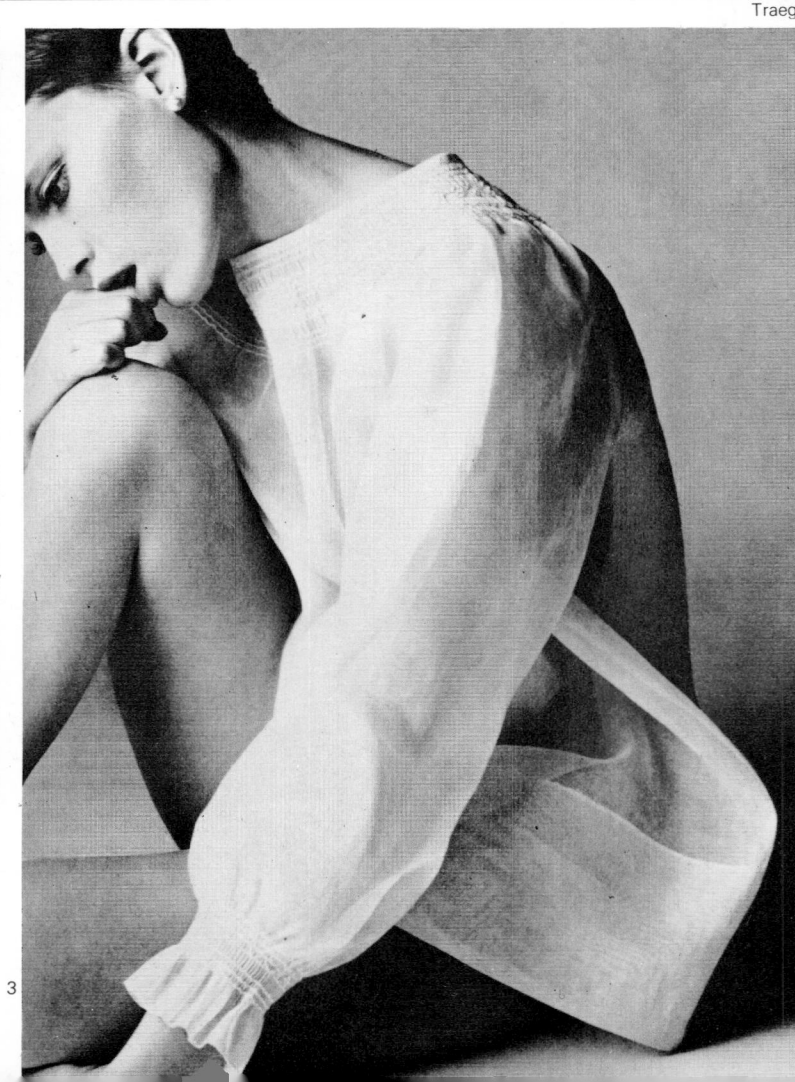

JULIAN ROBINSON   Bob Richardson

1. Grey and rust corduroy suit. Hat by James Wedge.
2. Dynel coat of powder-pink fluff.
3. Mia Farrow cuts her hair back to the skull, wears tiny pearl
studs in her ears, and sets a new style.

JOHN MARKS   RHONA ROY   David Bailey

4. Long white wool coat, worn by Susannah York, here with
Warren Beatty.

5. Lady Egremont wearing a sky blue caftan embroidered in white,
from northern Nigeria.

6. Patti Boyd (Mrs George Harrison) and her sister Jenny Boyd in
buckled red cotton dungaree dress by John Marks and navy spot shirt,
white crepe skirt by Rhona Roy.

1967-68

'On gusts of balalaika music from the Balkans, from hurdy-gurdy gypsy camps in Varna and the Ukraine, from straw-roofed Chechen villages, comes pure theatre for evening fashion. Give full rein to instincts for display and munificence with tinselled finery, brilliant skirts, silk embroidery, gold lace, tall boots, pattern used with pattern'

Hair arrives in London: 'Long, beautiful, gleaming, steaming, flaxen, waxen, curly, fuzzy, naggy, shaggy, ratty, matty, oily, greasy, fleecy, down-to-there hair like Jesus wore it halleluyah, I adore it hair!'

These two years mark the change in direction from futurist to romantic fashion. In reaction to the uniformity of geometric haircuts and 'functional' fashion, stiff carved tweed shifts and creaking plastic, women want to dress up and look wild and beautiful. The word 'romantic' now covers three kinds of dressing, all based on this wish to dress up again. The youngest is the flower power school, its prettiest exponent Patti Boyd, Mrs George Harrison, with her Red Indian leather fringes, headbands, and colour mixtures in layers of crepe and brocade — a kind of rag dressing mixed with bells, tassels and tinsel. Hair is loose, plaited or Afro fuzz, like Marsha Hunt's, star of *Hair*. The jetset version of this look is the wealthy ethnic gypsy, Ukrainian wedding dresses, Indian pantaloons, Afghan coats mixed with sheepskin and gold embroidery. In London you find it in the new Indian and middle-eastern boutiques that spring up all over the city and as special departments in the big stores. The last of the romantic looks is the ruffle-and-ringlet vogue, partly inspired by the Bardot/Moreau film *Viva Maria*, released last year, and it is available at shops like Annacat and Mexicana. By day it borrows kneebreeches and velvet suits from men, with ruffled shirts and long curly hair, by evening it becomes long demure dresses in fragile fabrics, frilled and tucked, with full milkmaid sleeves, bib fronts, and lace edgings. The hair is worn in ringlets or shoulder length curls, tied with bunches of ribbons.

The pop revolution burns out with a crackle of paper dresses. Expendable dresses come in poster prints or fabric patterns, in packs costing from 16*s.* to 22*s.* 6*d.* Biba sell a silver paper suit for £3, and there is a metal-sprayed Melinex dress that won't rip, tear, flare, crack or scratch, but makes such a noise that you can hear it in the next room. The micro skirt shrinks even more and becomes shorts, in grey flannel like a schoolboy's with shirt, tie and waistcoat for day, in organdie for one-piece shorts-dresses for the evening.

Ossie Clark's satin dresses with fabric prints by Celia Birtwell make the most revealing evening dresses in London, slashed or flowing against the body to show

1 DELISS   David Bailey

every line. Beside these hothouse dresses, which become a kind of status symbol, he turns to the recent past for fawn jersey tailored suits with square shoulders, a forties-through-sixties-eyes look.

Jean Muir, undiverted, develops her own tradition of simple, immaculate, intellectual fashion: dresses in Macclesfield silk, pyjama stripes or dressing gown paisleys, trouser suits made by an expert dressmaker.

1. Linen and lace peasant dress from Yugoslavia, pleated and embroidered in red silk, with a wide hem of flowered lace.
2. The Romantic evening look of the year, Viva Maria tucked and lacy cotton from Mexicana, blouse and bloomers.
3. Pale fringed doeskin, wrapped and tied.
4. Beginning of the hippy look: The Fool's painted walls at Apple, for the Beatles, and their clothes, clashing crepes, pieces of brocade, tassels and belts.

The Romantic Look

3 LESLEY   Traeger

MEXICANA
David Bailey

4 FOOL   Traeger

1
RICCI   David Bailey

2
CARDIN   Avedon   3 UNGARO   Pe

1. Navy braided suit with a monogrammed white silk shirt, navy scarf and hat.
2. Silver cast metal neck-sculpture supporting a sheath of black crepe. Sculpture by G. Mannoni.
3. Ungaro, trained at Balenciaga and Courrèges, opened independently in 1965, with 'another leap into space'. Here his yolk yellow canvas coat, blue pleat dress, and thigh-high Vinyl boots.
4. Watered purple velvet dress with white crepe tab and cuffs.
5. Saint Laurent's shock piece, sheer black chiffon with ostrich hips, a gold serpent wound round the waist.
6. Slimming by machine, a new form of faradism evolved by a Dr Hawkins in South Africa.

OHN BATES   David Bailey   SAINT LAURENT

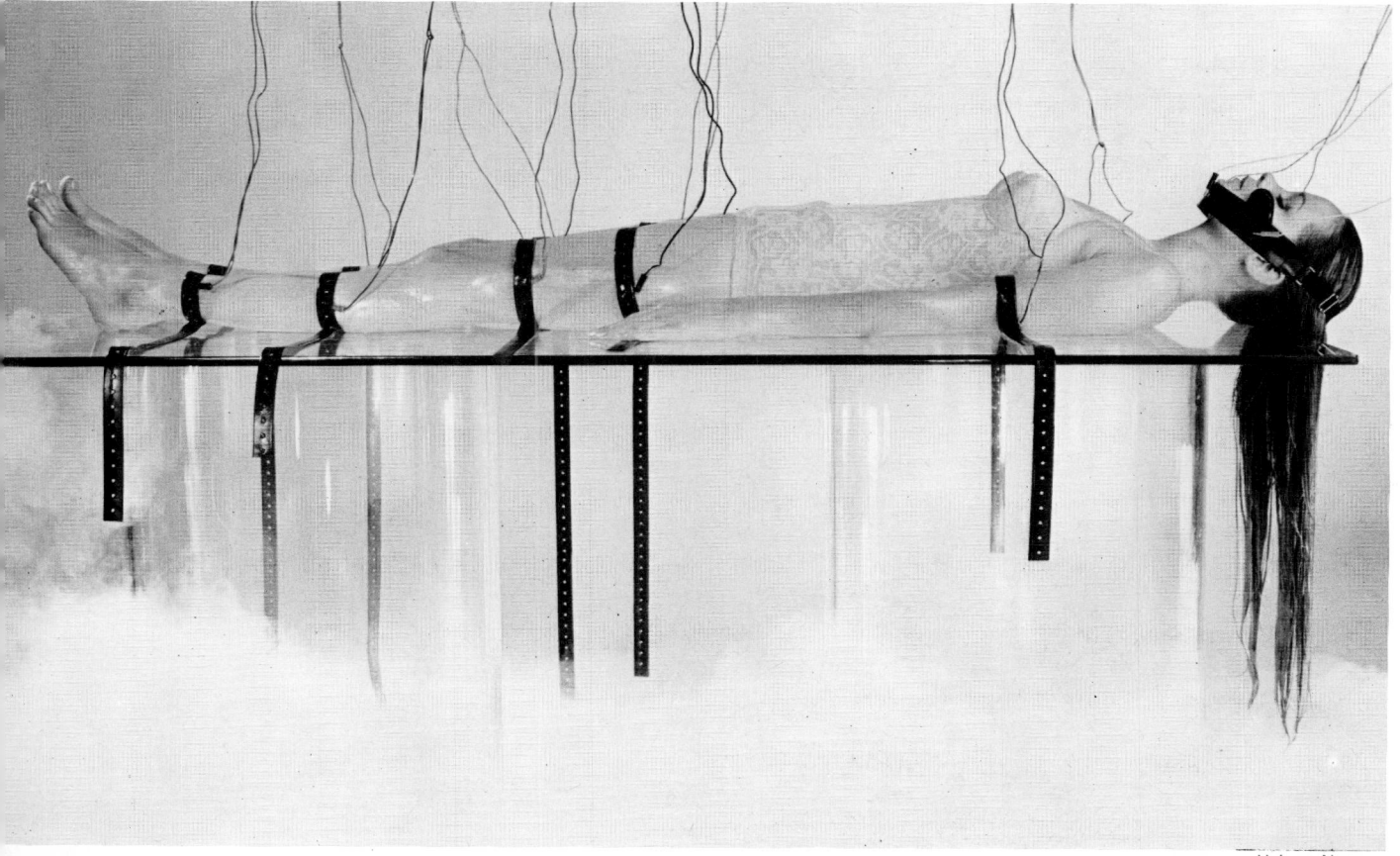

Helmut Newton

1969

'In fashion, the revolution is over. A new quiet reigns.' There has been an explosion of energy and excitement, linking together all the visual arts. A national upheaval, it has had international repercussions. It has brought us to the brink of space-age clothes, and stopped short at the notion of silver suits and transparent visors. Will it be like that? No, because what it will be like is growing now out of the life we lead'

'Brevity is the soul of fashion'

'The beat look is the news at Dior . . . pale zombie faces; leather suits and coats; knitted caps and high turtleneck collars, black endlessly'

Complete nudity is now permitted on the stage, and incomplete nudity in fashion: the most extreme looks from Paris, from Cardin, Ungaro, Courrèges, are now about the body instead of the space suit. By the autumn collections there is a freedom and wearability about all the important looks. Skirts are mini, knee-length, midi or maxi, 'Everything goes so long as it works for *you*.' There is Saint Laurent's frogged fitted hussar coat, or his caped highwayman coat to wear with trousers. Dior makes the easiest coat of all — just a wool dressing-gown wrapped and tied, with a big collar. All the tweeds are worn with crochet pudding-basin-hats pulled down to hide the hair, and long matching mufflers. Eyes are made up in technicolour, stockings are black, shoes are nanny's lace-ups.

Pop gives way to the pale pre-Raphaelite, hair in Ophelia ripples, eyes painted icing green or harebell blue, dresses are fantasies by Zandra Rhodes or Ossie Clark. The King's Road looks like a Russian ballet, and twenties beaded dresses with handkerchief points are treasured pieces. Art Deco is given impetus by Bernard Nevill's beautiful Jazz Collection prints for Liberty, and the antique clothes market opens up. You can dress as you please in any look, any length, and passers by don't turn a hair.

British fashion has never before had the world prestige it commands at the end of the sixties. In a fashion sense, it's as important, as sophisticated and more international than Paris. Buyers from all over the world look to the British ready-to-wear for the new tricks, and in London you can buy Saint Laurent ready-to-wear, Cerruti trouser suits, Missoni knits, Scandinavian cottons, the best couture and ready-to-wear from the Western world and every kind of exotica from far-away places. The indigenous talent discovered and trained in the art schools has produced Jean Muir, Ossie Clark, Mary Quant, Zandra Rhodes and Barbara Hulanicki of Biba, to name a few of the best British designers, and American painter Kaffe Fasset is living in London and inventing a new tapestry of patterns for knitting.

Avedon

1. Pale, ethereal beauty Ingrid Boulting, photographed with her hair wet-plaited and combed out when dry.
2. Pale chiffon dress with a shamrock print by Celia Birtwell.
3. Cobra print georgette, brown suede waistcoat appliquéd with the real thing.
4. Kaffe Fassett's tapestry pattern knit cardigan coat and stripe sweater, with suede trousers by Beged-Or.

2
OSSIE CLARK

Norman Parkinson

3
JEAN MUIR

4

KAFFE
FASSETT

David
Bailey

301

1 LESLIE POOLE

Barry Lategan

2 UNGARO

3 SAINT LAURENT

4 GIVENCHY

1. Tiered silk dress, ice cream pinks and blues, photographed with Bernard Nevill's Jazz Collection fabrics for Liberty, the Ideal Standard House door frame saved by Bernard Nevill, and part of his Deco collection.

2-4. Winter Collection: 'Everything goes (mini, midi, maxi) so long as it works for *you*.' Photographed by David Bailey.

5. Beautiful evening dress of mother-of-pearl printed panne velvet.

6. Cerruti's unisex look, well cut classics made for men and women. Here, scarlet and white paisley silk jackets and waistcoats with gabardine pants.

7. Clove wool dressing-gown coat.

5
SAINT LAURENT   David Bailey

6
CERRUTI   Patrick Lichfield   DIOR

7
                                                 David Bailey
                                                 303

1970·1975

Waste not, want not

The Uncertain Seventies

Eva Sereny

'The million dollar girl next door.' Lauren Hutton, the highest paid model in history —
two hundred thousand dollars a year in America for personifying Charles Revson's
Ultima beauty products. Not in spite of, but because of her gap teeth and her 'banana
nose', she is one of the beauties of our time.

Five years into the seventies, it seems that fashion has undergone a fundamental change. Even in the revolutionary sixties fashions were either 'in' or 'out': the differences were patently in the looks and lengths, the pace, and the fashionable age-group. Today the role of fashion has changed: the word 'fashion' itself conveys a multitude of different things to different people. Women now have lived through more fashions than at any other time. In 1970 and 1971 clothes became pure decoration – 'decoration, not labelling', *Vogue* emphasized – and the decorative revival spread outward from the houses of fashion designers to theatrical and movie circles, with hand-painted murals, ceilings sprayed with words and slogans, tigerskin-sprayed cars, cut-out tree silhouettes for the edges of rooms, pop-painted walls, toadstool chairs and flocked tea sets. Now, in London, you can find the whole range of fashion within a stone's throw – tweedy, ethnic, Hollywood, classic, glamorous, executive, nostalgic, pretty or international. Fashion has turned into repertoire. If clothes are modes of expression, fashion is a vocabulary. This is a point that has been emphasized again and again in *Vogue* during the 1970s: 'The real star of the fashion picture is the wearer, the real star of the issue is you ... Done right, fashion now is the expression of women who are free, happy, and doing what they want to be doing ... One woman lives dozens of different lives – one at home, another at work, another out in the evening, another in the country, another in the city, and at least two more for fun.' In 1971 *Vogue* made a point of breaking all the old fashion rules,

beautifully, finally asking, 'Is bad taste a bad thing?' This is a great milestone in the history of fashion. Enjoying this new freedom, women are no longer set pieces, arranged differently for each situation according to who will see them. In the Christmas 1974 issue, *Vogue* photographed Lauren Hutton, the highest paid model in history ($200,000 a year in America for personifying Charles Revson's Ultima beauty products), make-up-less, gap-toothed, tousle-haired, a 'million dollar girl next door'. In a previous issue, *Vogue* showed a kitchen gardener in beret, muffler, wrinkled wool tights, loose mohair knitted coat, and said, 'The clothes aren't smart, but they're very much in fashion. They obey the first rule of dress which is that clothes must be appropriate.' Replacing the worn-out dress roles of the past, women are pleasing themselves and giving pleasure to others by the originality and variety of their appearance, seldom conforming to anyone else's idea of what elegant means. In spite of the formidable talents of the best designers of our day – including Karl Lagerfeld, Yves Saint Laurent, Missoni – the people who really make today's look are the women who wear the clothes. It is safe to say that things will never be the same again.

Free as we seem to be, we are never without limits and boundaries. There are plenty of clothes we would *not* wear. The fashion of the too-recent past, for instance – which seems in the mid-seventies to begin in the mid-sixties; and no woman with her eyes open would walk about now in the skins of a rare animal and be the butt of raised eyebrows and uncomplimentary remarks. Fashion seems set

Left: 'The clothes aren't smart, but they're very much in fashion'. Printed wool skirt
by Daniel Hechter, with a mohair cardigan coat by Krizia and woollen stockings.

305

Henry Clarke

to evolve between the limits of the financial crisis and all its reper-cussions. In the 1960s clothes hinged on age. In the 1970s they will hinge on price. The fashion market is beginning to resolve itself between, on the one hand, the dead cheap – viz. the clothes in *Vogue*'s 'More Dash Than Cash' feature – and on the other hand, the expensive fashion investment. This category will not in the 1970s be confused with luxury – things you want but do not need. Luxury like fashion has changed its meaning, since the greatest luxury is always the thing in shortest supply. Luxuries today are, perhaps, time and peace. Fashion investments were redefined in *Vogue* in 1974 in a profile of an imaginary woman, the new fashion collector: 'She spends more money on her clothes than most women, but, when they're searching around for some-thing to wear, she's already perfectly dressed. When their clothes are beginning to look wrong, hers are right. So in the end, she probably spends no more than they.' Simplicity and quality do not become devalued – they are the only two fashion properties to hold their worth in *Vogue*'s fashion copy since 1916 – but in the 1970s they are not the whole story. Simple can also be plain and boring. An investment is really something that continues to give pleasure long after the novelty is over, and that means beautiful cloth, faultless cutting and making, and great discernment on the part of the designer and the buyer. One of *Vogue*'s chief functions today is to provide all that is necessary to give a reader this discerning eye. As one well dressed woman with very little money told a news-paper the other day, 'I always buy *Vogue*, that's my main extrava-gance'.

Alongside the noisy fashion revolution of the 1960s and early 1970s there has been a quiet revolution. The most fashionable clothes are for the first time being seen in context and on a par with the other arts, even to the point of holding their value long after their day is over. There have been increasing signs of this since the Victoria and Albert Museum's exhibition in 1960 of Heather Fir-bank's clothes, 'A Lady of Fashion', but as early as 1954 Richard Buckle's Diaghilev exhibition in Edinburgh and London displayed costumes as works of art, something over and above artefacts. A

pioneer private collector, Mrs Doris Langley Moore, who showed her fashion collection to the public whenever and wherever she could get accommodation for it, was offered a permanent site in 1959, and opened the Museum of Costume four years later in the beautiful Bath Assembly Rooms, where the clothes are charmingly arranged and displayed. The most recent important fashion ex-hibition has been Sir Cecil Beaton's 'Fashion', at the V & A in the winter of 1971–2. He showed a collection of 350 remark-able clothes dating from the 1880s, each one a milestone in fashion because of its origin or fabric, because of the design or the way it summed up the mood of its decade, or because of the woman who wore it and on what occasion. Dazzled by Balenciagas, Poirets, Vionnets, a Fortuny and a mass of Chanels, women gasped with horror at Cecil Beaton's story of how, six weeks before he had approached a Chicago millionaire whose deceased mother and wife had been famously fashionable, the widower had made a bonfire of all their clothes, many still unopened and unworn in their Paris boxes and tissue paper, dating back to the 1890s. A few decades ago this story would have been a joke: now, when that sort of perfection has almost disappeared (and with it many social injustices), it is a tragedy. Today dealers charge up to a hundred pounds for rare and beautiful clothes in perfect condition, and Sotheby's and Christie's regularly include costumes in their sales at which private collectors bid against museums.

A recent development in English middle-class life, a keen interest in food and good domestic design, has made Terence Conran a wealthy man. Say 'Habitat people' and everyone knows what you mean. Terence Conran himself admits that you could call the Habitat style 'Packaged Good Taste', but its success can be measured by the 22 Habitat stores in Britain, and the 18 scheduled to open up in France over the next five years, with the bourgeoisie panting for Le Style Britannique d'Habitat. 'His eye for design,'

1. Yves Saint Laurent and Madame Catroux in the white drawing room of his Paris apartment.
2. Engagement photograph by Norman Parkinson. Princess Anne in riding clothes and Captain Phillips in No. 1 dress uniform of his regiment, The Queen's Dragoon Guards.

David Bailey

David Bailey

said Antonia Williams in her interview with him, 'stems from his great love for the architecture of the Industrial Revolution, the factories and railways, locks and machinery, the work of Brunel and Morris and Mackintosh ... the basement life of Victorian and Edwardian England when things were beautiful because they were economical, because they were practical and because they were functional and because they weren't simply decorated to add grandeur to them.'

Whoever emerges in the second half of the seventies, it is sure that Germaine Greer will be remembered as a key figure of the decade. Her intelligent and beautifully written book, *The Female Eunuch*, gave rise to a great deal of journalistic debate and dinner-party bickering, but no one has yet added anything significant to what she had to say. Her argument is that women do not suffer from penis envy as Freud taught, but from the castration and distortion of the natural female personality. *The Female Eunuch* came out in the U.S.A. with a first printing of 75,000 copies, and serialization in three leading American magazines: it provoked swipes from Norman Mailer (whose *Prisoner of Sex* had recently been published). Kathleen Tynan interviewed Germaine Greer for *Vogue*, and found her 'boldly dressed and bra-less, with a long Pre-Raphaelite face, and a voice that can be coaxingly soft or stridently vulgar ... funny, outrageously coarse and direct about her pleasures ... a born teacher', who had once told her students, 'A teacher is yours to plunder'. Miss Greer, then lecturer in English at Warwick University, underground journalist, singer, dancer, actress, argues that it is not reform we need but a revolutionary change in our social structure. What we have to do is open up a bigger landscape, 'retrieve our power of invention', unleash our particular female energy on a world badly in need of it. 'To be *in* love is to be in dead trouble and to be deficient in the power of living and understanding the other person,' she says. 'The warning signal is when you're more anxious about losing the other person than seeing that they're happy, for then you lose your power of benevolence. What I'm supporting is a tenderness in sex which doesn't involve that edge of insecurity which makes you clutch, where you're only meant to take hold.' Her aim is to get the message of women's lib across, whether it means writing about the hazards of going to bed with Englishmen who are likely to suggest, 'Let's pretend you're dead', or 'not losing your temper when people ask you for the millionth time, "Do you hate men?"' Another liberationist, Midge Mackenzie, describes Germaine Greer as a 'phenomenon, a super-heroine ... who raises the possibilities for 5

Snowdon

Snowdon

other women. Although some of them feel that there is only room for one girl who both enjoys sex and has a Ph.D.'

With all this in the air, the Losey/Mercer film version of Henrik Ibsen's *A Doll's House*, made in 1973, acquired an extra edge of interest. Anthony Haden-Guest went to Roros in Norway, where the million-dollar production was being shot, and wrote that it was the scene of a few 'skirmishes in the sex-war'. The Ibsen conflicts came to life with Jane Fonda, 'fresh from anti-Vietnam peregrinations that have caused some of her fellow countrymen to demand her impeachment for treason'; her husband-to-be Tom Hayden, Vietnam activist and 'conspirator' with the Chicago Seven; Nancy Ellen Dowd, who had worked with Jane Fonda on a previous film *F.T.A. – Fuck the Army*; Delphine Seyrig, star of *Marienbad* and Buñuel's *The Discreet Charm of the Bourgeoisie*, active liberationist, accompanied by Michèle Richer who had fought alongside her on various abortion platforms; director Joe Losey who had left Hollywood during the Communist purge of the fifties; and playwright Joe Mercer, Marxist. Anthony Haden-Guest concluded that the director was not dealing with Jane Fonda alone, but with Nora Helmer herself. At the traditional end-of-the-film party, attended by the actors, the unit and several hundred citizens of Roros, all dressed up to the nines, Jane Fonda turned up in workforce jeans and industrial-strength boots.

Peter Brook's conception of *A Midsummer Night's Dream*, performed at Stratford in 1970, was one of the most astonishing theatrical productions of the early 1970s. Marina Warner, *Vogue*'s

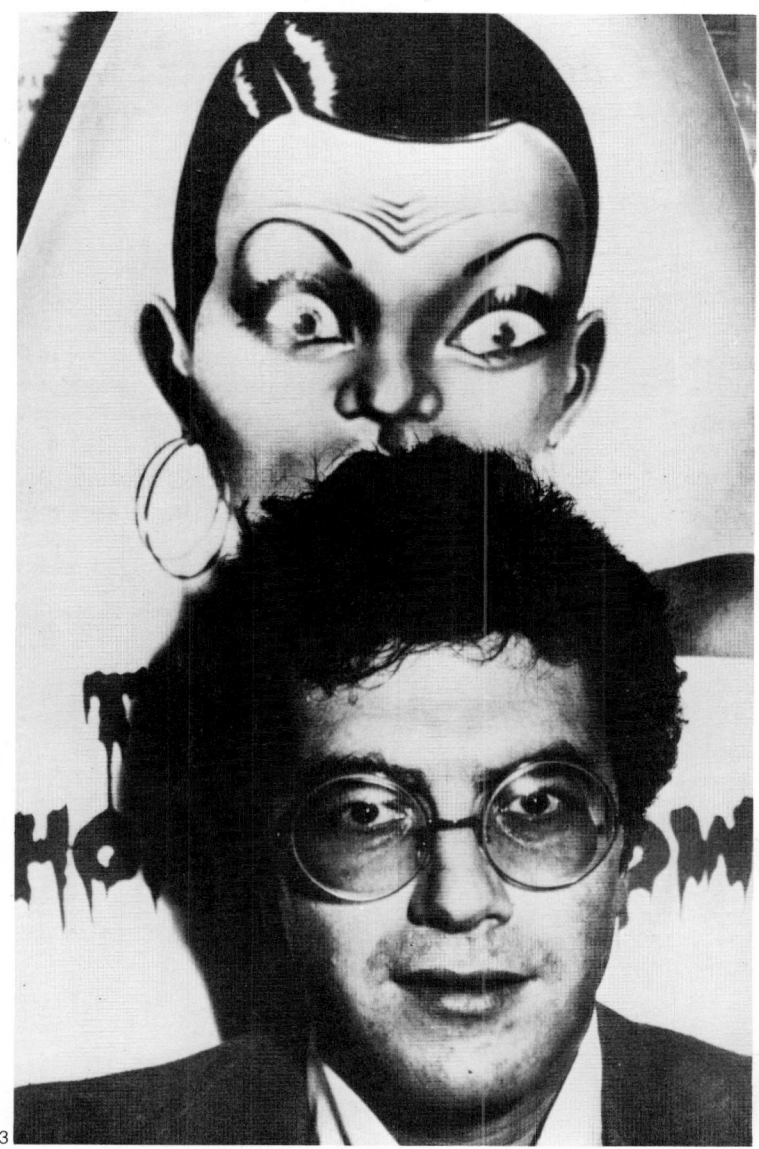

3

David Bailey

4

Dewe-Mathews

1. Liza Minnelli in *Cabaret* 'hitting her stride at last as the lusty Sally Bowles'.
2. George Melly, photographed by Snowdon, 1973. 'Some of his turns on stage are famous, 'notably Frankie and Johnnie, a one-man melodrama in which he sings, acts, changes sex, makes love, shoots himself, staggers about, collapses and dies into the audience, singing all the while.'
3. Michael White, impresario who has put on several successful 1970s shows, including *America Hurrah!*, *Oh Calcutta!*, and *The Rocky Horror Show*.
4. Ken Russell and his daughter Victoria. 11-year old Victoria played a groupie in her father's film of The Who's *Tommy*.

features editor, wrote, 'Peter Brook's production dives straight into the audience's imagination ... shakes the play to pieces, makes it astonishing and unrecognizable, yet loses none of Shakespeare's poetry.' Actors became acrobats in a set that was a stark white box, with ladders, firemen's poles, trapezes, swings and ropes. Titania's bed was a flying quilt of scarlet ostrich feathers, with coiled wire trees, fairies in sackcloth. The flower drug 'love-in-idleness' was a zinc plate spinning on a Perspex rod tossed back and forth between Puck and Oberon, and the play went on to wild percussion music from two bands seated high in the gallery, 'banging, whistling and shaking metal sheets, hissing and clicking'. As Marina Warner pointed out, it was a case of Theseus' own contention about theatre in the play scene that closes the *Dream*: 'The best in this kind are but shadows, and the worst are no worse, if imagination amend them.'

In films, the musical lived again in *Cabaret*, 'the film of the musical of the film of the play that was called *I am a Camera*, of the book that was called *Goodbye to Berlin* by Christopher Isherwood'; and lived again as self-parody in Ken Russell's *The Boy Friend*, launching Twiggy with Christopher Gable 'among lollipops and teddy bear kitsch and imitation Busby Berkeley routines'. It was an odd choice for Ken Russell after *The Devils*, set in the superstition-seized seventeenth century. His most recent venture is *Tommy*, The Who's rock opera: as Alexander Walker said in the *Evening Standard*, 'Ken Russell will try anything'. In the mid-seventies, directors of the *nouvelle vague*, François

Truffaut, Jean-Luc Godard, look like the living aristocracy of the cinema. In 1971 Truffaut talked to *Vogue* about his life in the cinema, and the split between Godard and himself since the days when they had grown up together as critics on the influential *Cahiers du Cinéma*. They made their first important films in the same year, 1959; Godard *Breathless*, and Truffaut *The 400 Blows*. Today Godard denounces Truffaut as conventional and frivolous, and Truffaut comments, in all kindness: 'Fundamentally, Godard's a dandy, struggling against his dandyism ... He finds it difficult to express himself, to find a language.' Truffaut himself, 'trim and small and solemn in a careful suit, smoking a Gitane and avoiding drinks or coffee because they disturb his sleep', lives a life dedicated to the cinema, has no home, and lives in a suite at the Georges V in Paris.

If *Death in Venice* has been the most beautiful film of the 1970s so far, it is not so easy to name the most exciting or the most vicious: there is plenty of competition. Small-budget films with unknown people for stars turn out to be better, often, than big-

David Bailey

budget ones: quicker and funnier and more surprising. Whatever the film, it is more than likely to have at least one scene put in for shock. 'Villains are heroes now,' said *Vogue* in 1971. 'Communication is brief, actions summary, titles terse. The beaten up and the beaters up, the mean and the sluttish are in the sun.'

Reflecting the focus of general concern, *Vogue* has in the early 1970s put emphasis on the pollution–conservation–preservation message. Since 1970 features have included the discovery of black holes in space, the origins of life, power and where it lies today, the reasons for advocating the Big Bang theory as the beginning of the universe, recycling, the possibility of life evolution on other planets, craftsmanship today and what happens to design students when they leave college, endangered buildings and what can be done to save them. In fashion captions for country clothes you read: 'Are they chopping down the trees? Ring your local C.P.R.E. branch. Is the river filthy? Ring Friends of the Earth. Plant your

1. Bjorn Andresen, the beautiful boy in Visconti's film of Thomas Mann's story *Death in Venice*.
2. Graham Palmer of the Waterway Recovery Group.
3. In 1972 when this picture was taken, David Essex was Jesus Christ in *Godspell*. Vogue said, 'He times his punch lines beautifully, dances disarmingly, and moves the audience to tears.' David Essex said, 'the only time I started to read the Bible was after I got the part'.
4. Marc Bolan, star singer of Tyrannosaurus Rex. When he went to Decca in 1965 they told him, 'With your face, boy, we'll make you a star.'
5. Francis Bacon photographed by Francis

Goodman, 1971, the year of his retrospective at the Grand Palais in Paris, an accolade only before accorded to one living painter, Picasso. John Gruen, in an interview with him for *Vogue*, said, 'The uniqueness of his style is based on a vision that concerns itself with precise yet never photographic observation.' Francis Bacon told him, 'I'm very interested in trying to do portraits, which now is almost an impossible thing to do, because you either make an illustration or a charged and meaningful appearance . . . how are you going to make a nose and not illustrate it?'
6. Allen Jones's drawing room, with his wife and two plastic dollies, 1970.

Richard Gloucester

Clive Arrowsmith

own trees for posterity, nurture the dandelion and the buttercup ... hang on to the butterflies and birds, the wild flowers and the free range animals.' The Friends of the Earth point out from *Vogue*'s pages that every year this country consumes a forest the size of Wales to make paper, most of which goes into dustbins, or that, although metals are amongst the simplest of materials to recycle, we throw away enough cans each year to make a pile 45,000 miles high. And James Cameron reminds us that 'There is no mystery, for example, about how to cure poverty, rationalize education, abolish road accidents, and eliminate the causes of war, and probably ninety-nine per cent of people want exactly these things. The only missing factor, as every sociologist has pointed out for donkey's years, is the ability to put the collective will and the available machinery to work.' If that factor cannot be reversed, 'toleration of the unacceptable will be replaced by acceptance of the intolerable'.

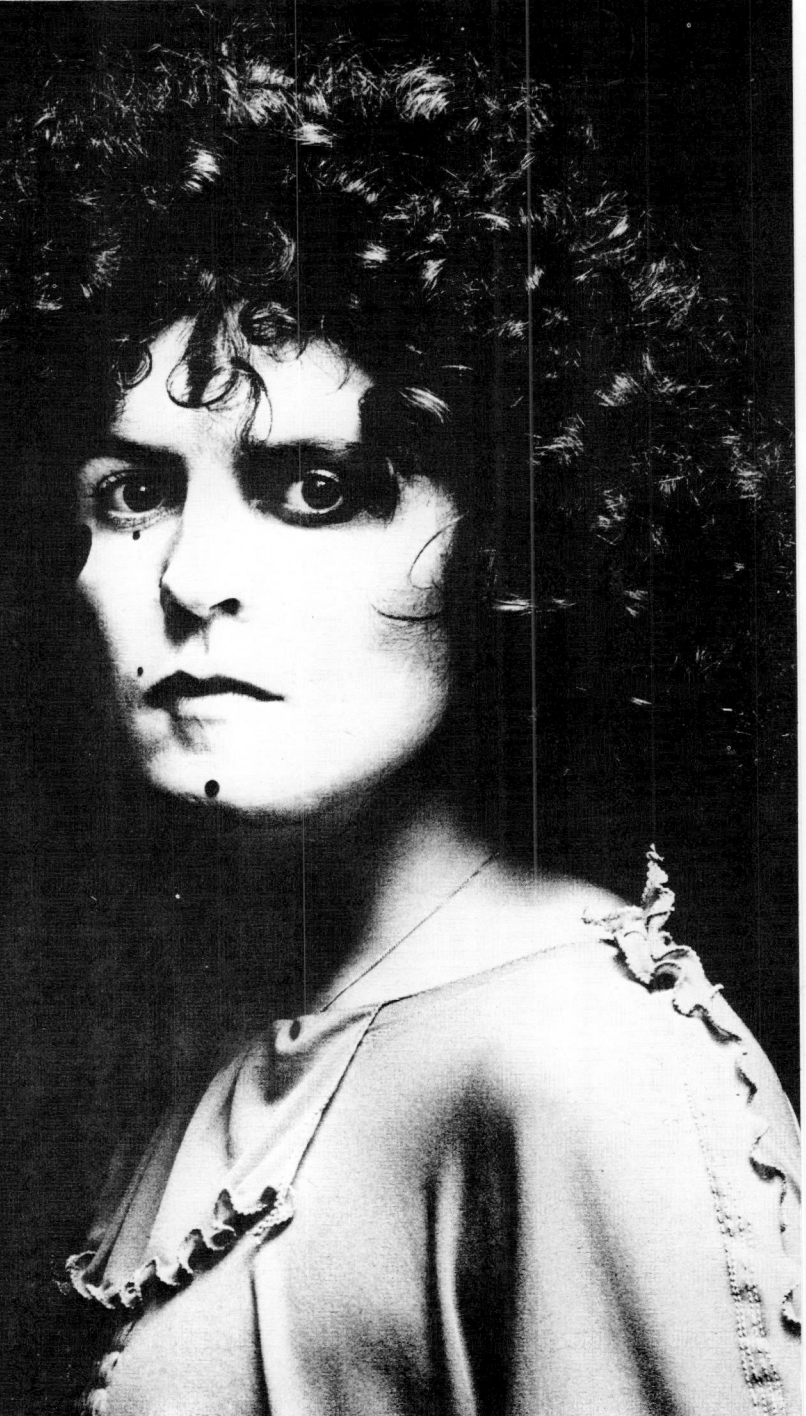

5

Francis Goodman

4   Richard Imrie

6   Norman Parkinson   311

THE CHANGING FACE

BIANCA JAGGER

Bianca Jagger, wife of Mick, mother of Jade, calls herself the only person who has become a star without having done a thing. She has a degree in political science, drinks tea in nightclubs, and is prepared to spend hours a day exercising and grooming herself for an evening appearance: she is known for making late and spectacular entrances, always looking beautiful.

1. 1973
2. 1974

OSSIE CLARK   David Hockney

Peter Sellers

LIZA MINNELLI

Liza Minnelli, who was 'bounced up and down on some of the finest knees in the motion picture business' is the daughter of Judy Garland and the hysterical star of *Cabaret*. A natural actress who can't stop, keyed up to a high pitch of energy, she is made to hold attention — a real star. Everyone is waiting for her to make another film: at the moment she's making a fortune in cabaret with a small c. Photographed here by Peter Sellers in 1973.

David Bailey

Pablo & Delia

AP

David Bailey

GRACE CODDINGTON

Grace Coddington, fashion editor and model, exerts considerable influence on the style of the 1970s through designers, who like her to wear their clothes, photographers, who like to photograph her, and models, who have copied her. She is able to change her style completely from time to time, through discipline and a make up technique only matched by Barbara Daly, and today wears her hair blazing red and frizzy with curls, her make up light, and her clothes by Saint Laurent, Sonia Rykiel, Jap, interspersed with one or two things from the antique markets. (See also the colour photograph opposite p.288).

. Pablo and Delia's drawing of themselves, *left*, and Grace Coddington, *right* (twice) in their own designs, 1972.
. Hair tucked away under a beret, in a biscuit crepe suit by Jap with a ow-neck blouse, photographed at Ajaccio harbour in 1974.
. As she looked in 1966.

3

David Bailey

Barry Lategan

Traeger

TWIGGY

Twiggy (Lesley Hornby), was still a child when *Vogue* began photographing her, a schoolgirl model with a naturally sophisticated and refined face: 'Lately,' said *Vogue* in 1972, 'she has grown up and into her face. Her eyebrows have changed into the finest of arches, her eyelashes have become silky, she wears a little shadow at the outer edges of her eyes and draws the cupid's bow of her mouth even sharper.' She is quick-witted and original, with a guffawing laugh and great charm. From model via dress- and sweater-design, she became a singer, tapdancer and film star with *The Boy Friend*. She says, '*The Boy Friend* changed things for me — after that, people began to take me a little more seriously. I loved modelling at the beginning, it was all I wanted, but I couldn't think of doing it now.' Already established in films, she had a television series of her own in 1974 and was Cinderella in the 1974-75 Christmas pantomime. As *Vogue*'s Cinderella, photographed by Barry Lategan, Twiggy was the cover of Christmas 1974 *Vogue*.

1. Twiggy in the seventies.
2. In black shorts and brown lizard waistcoat, 1967.
3. *Vogue* cover, Christmas 1974.

MARISA BERENSON

Marisa Berenson, jetsetter, heiress and model, is the grand-daughter of Schiaparelli. She took leading roles in *Cabaret*, *The Female Condition*, and looks like becoming a real star in Kubrick's *Barry Lyndon*, made on location in Ireland, playing opposite Ryan O'Neal.

1. 1972 by Avedon.
2. 1970.

David Bailey

Helmut Newton

DOMINIQUE SANDA

Dominique Sanda, international film star who began as a model, was discovered by Bresson for *Une Femme Douce*, and made her name with Bernardo Bertolucci's *The Conformist*, quickly followed by Vittorio De Sica's *The Garden of the Finzi-Continis*. Recent projects were *Steppenwolf, India Song*, and *Nove Cento* for Bertolucci. She told *Vogue*, 'Between the cinema and me it was, instantly, love.' She has a son, Ian. Here, in Saint Laurent's suit *à la Russe*.

ZANDRA RHODES   Clive Arrowsmith

'Clothes are a different thing from what they were. They are purely for decoration (not labelling) and they have more to do with you in particular than anything in general'

'What better time to paint your face, paint your clothes, paint your hair, your boots, your body?'

This year fashion becomes decoration, clothes become cosmetic. Hair is fuchsia pink or lime green, dresses are overlapping painted leaves or chiffon wisps trailing feathers, faces are painted in a rainbow of stripes or flowers (see pictures overleaf), necklaces are fringed leather bands painted with butterflies. This is the year of the embroidered Spanish shawl, the hand-painted boot, the layered haircut. Pablo & Delia, art students from Buenos Aires, arrive in London and tell *Vogue*, 'We are painters, and we have chosen fashion because it is a very, very lively manifestation, and we want to make free things, to create all the possibilities, in the language of fashion.' Leonard cuts the first important hairstyle of the 1970s, a cap of layered wisps following the shape of the head and blown dry instead of being set. By the end of the year it has become both longer and shorter — a short feathery cut with a thin veil of long hair covering the neck and shoulders, lightened or streaked in brilliant colours.

Everything is painted — necklaces, faces, hair, boots — and *Vogue* photographs models with picture faces: flowers, stripes, even parachutes. The fantasy continues to operate on the mass market level, designers aren't thinking 'This is for women in the AB income group'; they are thinking 'This is for a woman in a gypsy holiday mood'. Hats are right back in fashion for day and evening, and Liberty prints are collectors' items, to wear two or three at a time.

In the summer *Vogue* announces, 'The long skirt is here — and the first *Vogue* with not a short skirt in sight.' Jean Muir's collection provides an object lesson in the new lengths and how they depend on the balance of shape: the theme is tension at the top, freedom in the skirt. The proportion 'begins and ends with your body,' meaning a natural line, soft fluid fabrics and the bosom God gave you . . . 'Don't let them know you wear a bra,' says *Vogue*.

Far left: Pinafore and shirt by Pablo & Delia; photograph by Arthur Elgort in 1974.
Left: Pagoda dress of turquoise velvet with fur boots.

1

DIOR

320

Clive
Arrowsmith

GRAHAM PRICE

Clive Arrowsmith

2

BILL
GIBB

3

Clive Arrowsmith

JEAN MUIR   Clive Arrowsmith   JEAN MUIR   Barney Wan

Barry Lategan

LEONARD   Clive Arrowsmith

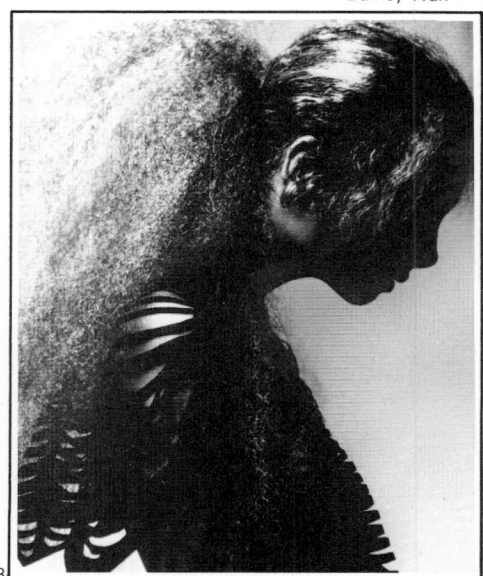

ARA GALLANT   Avedon

1. Dior's new coat proportion for trousers: tight bodice, bell skirt to mid-calf. In navy wool bound in braid.

2. Velvet knickerbockers and chiffon spot shirt loaded with decoration — bronze velvet shawl from The Purple Shop, cockade and hat, silk roses added to the shoes

3. Ziggurat pigskin jacket over knife pleats of jersey and tweed checks.

4 and 5. 'The long skirt is here': Jean Muir's collection says it all. *Left*, tucked and ribboned suede shirt. *Right*,

Barney Wan draws the new proportions from her summer show.

6. 18-year old *Vogue* beauty of the year, Lady Caroline Cholmondeley. Silver and enamel disc necklace by Dorothy Hogg of the R.C.A.

7. Leonard's haircut of the 1970s, layered and wispy, like a mob cap with a frill of fringes all round. Ends lightened by Daniel at Leonard.

8. Frizzed hair by Ara Gallant of New York.

1971

'Is bad taste a bad thing?'

'Fresh options, fantastic changes, breakthroughs . . .'

'There are no rules in the fashion game now. You're playing it and you make up the game as you go . . . you write your own etiquette, make up your face your own way, choose your own decorations, express yourself . . . faites vos jeux'

This year marks the height of fashion anarchy, when there is no leading right look, but every style adds to the vocabulary of the fashionable women — even 'bad' taste. Women are dressing to amuse themselves, not to improve their status or attract men, and *Vogue* runs a leading summer feature on the end of etiquette in fashion, asking 'Is bad taste a bad thing?'

There have never been so many different looks in fashion. The biggest category by far is the sensational: Zandra Rhodes's fantastic follies, Chloé's pastiche tap-dancers in silk gym-knickers, Thea Porter's oriental treasures, Pablo & Delia's baggy appliqué felts, Bill Gibb's elaborate patterns piled on together, and a new Japanese influence, tucked and quilted white cottons from Kenzo Takada of Jap, and Kansai Yamamoto's Kabuki theatre satins.

The forties and fifties craze, successor to the twenties and thirties, adds pedal-pushers, turban bows, red lipstick and box jackets to the repertoire, and flashy wedge-heeled platform shoes with peep toes and anklestraps appear with almost every look in the book.

A gentler nostalgia deepened by a sense of loss brings in a summer-in-the-country mood, with a flavour of early Colette, in shady straw hats with wreaths of poppies, flowered pinafores and aprons, faded cotton skirts, bonnets, collarless Liberty print blouses with full sleeves, bare feet in clogs. 'This is not a maternity feature,' writes *Vogue*, introducing calico and gingham smocks in spring, 'but what a great year to be pregnant.'

Shorts make a new appearance worn with puff-sleeves blouses, bows in the hair, lots of make up, fishnet tights and platform shoes — a joke tap-dancing look. 'Shorts are a sort of holiday from fashion,' warns *Vogue*. 'They look great on the right shape, in the right place,' but soon 'hotpants' are so popular that they are being worn by secretaries in city offices. Other alternatives to a skirt are dungarees in denim or quilted satin, worn with T shirts printed with the words 'Kiss me quick', 'Hallo sailor', 'Pow!' etc. The dandy trouser suit is by now a classic, three-button with a waistcoat or doublebreasted in tweedy checks.

Prints have never been better and there is a new way of wearing them. Saint Laurent puts spotted shirts with tile-pattern kilts and adds a patchwork-knit vest,

STIRLING COOPER — Arthur Elgort
Toggled tent coat and drainpipe trousers in green and brown plaid

Missoni puts a Spanish shawl print with brilliant stripes, and ready-to-wear designers everywhere are mixing up the Liberty cottons. In the same way, sweaters get more interesting. The new vest top that goes over the top of a long-sleeved sweater comes in colourways and patterns that relate, but do not match. Women begin to think in families of colours and pattern groups when they put their clothes together. In Italy Missoni takes this kind of dressing furthest, importing painters to experiment with effects in his modern Milan factory, and his many-coloured many-patterned layer dressing shows the way to a knitting revolution.

SAINT LAURENT   Barry Lategan

2 SYNDICA   Guy Bourdin

3 BUS STOP   BIBA   Jonvelle

1. Printed shirt, printed wool skirt, plaided patchwork vest:
a new kind of mixture from Saint Laurent Rive Gauche.
2. Layers of bubble-knit sweaters in mushroom pink, blue
and maroon.
3. Trouser suits for 'new tweedy people'.
4. 'Art can be a wearing business.'

PATRICK HUGHES   DAVID HOCKNEY   ELIZABETH FRINK   ALLEN JONES   323

1. White cottons designed by Kenzo Takada for Jap.
2. 'If all the world were summer.' Jonvelle's photograph of a Provençal country picnic, with Colette clothes.

1
JAP

Duc

2

Jonvelle

JAMES DREW

Clive Arrowsmith

The new look: fresh, sharp, crisp, with tidy short hair and a simple white shirt.

'Dress like a lady, in hat, gloves, ribbed cardigan and pleated skirt'

'Wear at least one thing you wouldn't be seen dead in – pearlised puce nail polish, little white embroidered gloves, a really hatty hat, a neat and tidy crisp summer dress'

'If you think you know all about sweaters, think again'
Sweaters, trousers and shoes dominate the fashion picture. Sweaters have become batwing or kimono-sleeved at Jap, wildly striped and patterned, bright as paint, and layered over other sweaters equally unconventional. Grainy speckled cardigans and knitted matching skirts give the effect of Donegal tweed, a winter favourite. Trousers are Oxford bags, pleated in to the waistband with side pockets and big turnups: by autumn, put with the new windcheater jackets, gathered onto striped elastic cuffs and waistband, they are a new kind of trouser suit. The summer look, blueprint Saint Laurent, is a combination of wide white gabardine trousers with cutaway red or navy vest, worn with cotton fishing hat and bright espadrilles. The jacket is loose and gathered from a yoke, a controlled smock shape. An alternative, easier to put together from the cheaper end of the ready-to-wear market, is the sailor suit, loose top with a sailor collar edged in navy or red stripes. 'All the nice girls love a sailor suit' says *Vogue*, and the shops are full of sailor sweaters, anchor-print shirts, spotted and striped trousers and T shirts with yachting motifs.

Shoes are preposterously high and vivid, the thick platform adding inches to already tall heels. Saint Laurent's rope-soled wedge espadrilles in primary colours lace up over bright contrasting tights, and for bare legs there are the new corksoled sandals. Best sellers at the Chelsea Cobbler are their high scalloped peeptoes with leather roses and anklestraps.

The wilder shores of fashion recede into evening fantasies, make up is lighter but just as bright, with less emphasis on the eyes, and Leonard's smooth short bobbed hair evens up the last of the layered ends. The condition of hair becomes a fetish and hairdressers lay in stocks of henna, which brightens the colour and adds shine and weight. In the summer there's a new fortyish hair style, brushed up into a curly topknot over the forehead, or a forehead roll with waved shoulderlength hair. Pillbox hats with veils go well with pinned-up hair and widened shoulders, and the period look is completed by the high anklestrap shoes. Newest equipment for model girls are the new coloured contact lenses, to give bright green or violet eyes.

'Try dressing like a lady' suggests *Vogue*: and Saint Laurent provides the greatest incentive with his long ribbed cardigans, bownecked silk shirts and striped or spotted shirtwaisters.

1   MIURA   JOHN CRAIG   DANIEL HECHTER   JEFF BANKS   Clive Arrowsmith

OSSIE CLARK   Clive Arrowsmith

1. New sporty sweaters.
2. Spots-and-stripes cakefrills, jacket and
baggy trousers.
3. Dusty blue velvet trouser suit,
peak-shouldered, wasp-waisted,
Oxford-bagged.

2   SALLY TUFFIN   Clive Arrowsmith

MISSONI

Barry Lategan

6

Peter Knapp

7

ZANDRA RHODES

Jonvelle

4. Missoni's new way to dress. Emerald checked knitted shirt worn over larger checked shirt, under square-necked jerkin with short checked sleeves.

5. Grainy wool cardigan and knitted skirt to match, with a bowneck shirt.

6. 'Change the colour and the shape of your hair.'

7. Zandra Rhodes's first sweater, pink, green, blue, with bat sleeves and duck tails, and her black silk jersey skirt with a lampshade frill.

Henry Clarke

327

1972

1
ALBINI
Guy Bourdin

2
SAINT LAURENT
Norman Parkinson

3
WALLIS
Zachariassen

1. Walter Albini's new classic with a new painted look: striped big-buttoned twinset, check shirt and button-through skirt.
2. The 1972 Saint Laurent look: knitted pudding basin hat, batwing suede windcheater with ribknit collar and cuffs, Donegal tweed skirt and crepe-soled lace ups.
3. Scarlet corduroy dolman jacket.
4. *Left*, loose white trousers, tight wrap bodice of green and white taffeta checks, cream straw hat. *Right*, long loose jacket and wide trousers in cotton.

4
SAINT LAURENT
Peter Knapp

'Do your clothes get along well together? Are they well related? Do they mix? They will now'

'The best looks now are simple and glamorous . . . classics with a difference'

'Clothes for the life you lead – and we're speaking to *you*'

'*Vogue* is a glossary of all the clothes for all the lives you lead concurrently,' says the magazine. 'We're speaking of dressing up and getting dressed in 5 minutes, driving the car and getting the shopping done, going away for the weekend and out for lunch.' As life gets more hectic, fashion gets simpler. Separates look new because they look uncontrived and easy: jackets, skirts and trousers in different colours and mixtures to put together with shirts and sweaters. 'Colourings make their effects by the combinations of colours in groups . . . Not just misty green for instance, but a greeny oatmeal cardigan over a lavender silk shirt and trousers checked with all three.' Even suits begin to look as though you'd picked each piece separately, with a jacket of one fabric put with a skirt or trousers of another. Jackets cue all the looks, simple and fitted or a bloused windcheater shape, in ciré, speckled velvet, checks with knitted edges, piqué for summer, sequins or fake fur for winter.

The sailor jersey gives way to the cricket sweater with shawl collar and striped edges, and tapestry jacquard knits join the mixture of patterns in the shops. From Paris and Italy come new ideas in knits, Saint Laurent's extra long cabled cardigan with V neck and cuffs ruffed with fur, and Missoni's soft knitted suits in bias plaid, fine sweater with a heavier cardigan and skirt.

There are hats for morning, noon and night: tam o' shanters and berets, thicknit pull-ons, skull caps of Lurex and pillboxes of sequins with a mist of black veiling.

There is an out-of-uniform uniform for students and school-leavers: floppy-brimmed hat, long straight hair, full-sleeved shirt or smock, and cotton skirt to the ground. Girls of this age flock to the new Biba, in the palatial premises of the former Derry & Toms in Kensington High Street, with acres of marble floor and glittering dark caves heaped like treasure with Lurex sweaters, satin cushions and slinky dresses — 'a Nickleodeon land of Art Deco with potted palms and mirrored halls'. Bibaland is a new centre where the young can go to read magazines and listen to records, try on clothes, do their food shopping, and eat or have a drink with friends.

1. Mink coat and jeans.

1

KATHERINE HAMNETT   BRENT SHERWOOD

David Bailey

1973

AVANT GARDE

1
LEONARD

Clive Arrowsmith

2

David Bailey

Bruce Laurence   COLETTE BREZAN   Norman Parkinson

4

6   RICHARD SMITH   Michael English

1. Leonard's shaded chalky beige-white ducktail hair, cropped, brushed up and forward. Colouring by Daniel at Leonard.
2. Long cabled cardigan furred in grey fox, pale grey to go with grey flannel pleats.
3. Dog's tooth checks on wool and acrylic, windcheater jacket bloused onto cream knit edges, with a shawl collar.
4. Beige and plum trellised twinset edged in stripes, Burgundy cord velvet skirt, and feathered velvet hat.
5. Twiggy in Biba sequins with matching mittens and skull cap, Deco necklace, photographed at the bar in Biba's Rainbow Room.
6. A highheeled speckled leather shoe on a perspex platform.

1973

1. Brown and black plaid knitted suit, rib-waist sweater belted over the skirt, and long loose cardigan with ribbed edges.
2. Jap's cream wool cricket sweater, shawl collar and cuffs striped in navy and wine.
3. Clean cut velvet jacket, spotted and dotted with grey, elastic bringing the waist in.
4. Navy jersey jacket, short sleeved white wool shirt, camel trousers, with a cream felt hat from James Drew.

1
MISSONI   David Bailey

2
JAP

Rose    3 JANICE WAINWRIGHT   David Montgomery   SAINT LAURENT   4

Barry
Lategan

JAP

Arthur Elgort

'Cleanliness is next to godliness. Keep the country country, hang on to the butterflies and birds, the wild flowers and the free range animals. Use your own energy and initiative unstintingly to protect the things you love. Are they chopping down the trees? Ring your local CPRE branch. Is the river filthy? Ring Friends of the Earth. Plant your own trees for posterity, nurture the dandelion and the buttercup.' Long loose striped wool polo-neck, brown and black, baggy brown wool V neck sweater round shoulders, beige wool skirt, all by Jap.

'The real star of the fashion picture now is the wearer'

'[Gardening clothes] The clothes aren't smart, but they're very much in fashion. They obey the first rule of dress which is that clothes must be appropriate'

'Meet the new fashion collector. She spends more money on her clothes than most women, but, when they're searching around for something to wear, she's already perfectly dressed. When their clothes are beginning to look wrong, hers are right. So in the end, she probably spends no more than they'

The utterly simple, the wrapped and layered, the nostalgic and the quite fantastic are all equally fashionable, and women use these categories as a kind of repertoire to pick from. No designer today can tell just how his look will be worn and changed by the wearer. Designers try to ensure their look by putting it together in great detail, with special hats, jewellery, shoes, make up — only to find that women take them apart again and make their own look from the pieces. In other words, any very fashionable woman now has to be a bit of a designer herself. Even the simplest Aquascutum coat looks quite different with frizzed red hair, kohl-rimmed eyes, two mufflers and a pixie hat. All the 'classics' are new looks, as can be seen by comparing a trench coat now with an original. Nostalgia in fashion takes many forms, from the junk market dress that looks 1975 with today's hair and make up to the new pastiche, but its most important contribution is an emphasis on quality, a quality that has almost disappeared from the affordable horizon. Pure fantasy is always with us in fashion as a way of bringing dreams to life, usually as evening looks, but lately also as country clothes for the city.

1
STEPHEN MARKS   David Bailey

2 SAINT LAURENT   Guy Bourdin

3
CHLOÉ   Helmut Newton

4
DIOR
Barry Lategan

5
Barry Lategan

1. The loose overdress to wear with or without a shirt, in denim blue cotton gathered from the yoke.
2. Black crepe with marguerites, print by Eric Boman with a white collar and white straw hat.
3. Pale rose-print dress with a cakefrill neck, cut on the bias, with shredded print flowers.
4. Crin hat with a veil for a brim.
5. 'More Dash Than Cash.' A whole winter's outfit for £34 27p.
6. Jap's glazed honey coloured cotton cape, cream silk shirt, cotton trousers and bowler.

Clive
Arrowsmith

335

1974-75

SAINT LAURENT

David Bailey

1. Perfectly simple and simply perfect white gabardine
jacket and fly button skirt, black and white striped
T shirt inside.
2. Blackberry bouclé shirt-tailed smock by Sheridan
Barnett, wool by Dormeuil. Cowled dickie, leg warmers,
skull cap and cotton satchel by Jap.
Photograph by Willie Christie.

BIBLIOGRAPHY

Battersby, Martin, *The Decorative 20s*, Studio Vista, 1969
Beaton, Cecil, *Fashion, an anthology*,
   (Catalogue to the V & A Exhibition, October 71 - January 1972)
Beaton, Cecil, *The Glass of Fashion*, Weidenfeld & Nicolson, 1954
Blythe, Ronald, *The Age of Illusion*, Penguin Books, 1963
Booker, Christopher, *The Neophiliacs,* Collins/Fontana, 1969
Cartland, Barbara, *We Danced All Night*, Arrow, 1970
Chamberlain, E.R. *Life in Wartime Britain*, Batsford, 1972
Contini, Mila, *Fashion*, Paul Hamlyn, 1965
Dormer, Jane, *Fashion in the 20s and 30s*, Ian Allan, 1973
Ewing, Elizabeth, *History of 20th Century Fashion*, Batsford, 1974
Flanner, Janet, *Paris was Yesterday*, ed. Irving Drutman, Viking, 1973
Garland, Madge, *Fashion*, Penguin Books, 1962
Garland, Madge, *The Indecisive Decade*, Macdonald, 1968
Graves, Robert, and Hodge, Alan, *The Long Weekend*,
   Faber & Faber, 1940; Penguin Books, 1971
Griffiths, Richard, and Mayer, Arthur, *The Movies*, Spring Books, 1957
Hadfield, John, ed., *Saturday Book 28*, Hutchinson, 1968
Hillier, Bevis, *Art Deco of the 20's & 30's*, Studio Vista, 1968
Hopkinson, Tom, ed., *Picture Post 1938-50*, Penguin Books, 1970
Laver, James, *Between the Wars*, Vista Books, 1961
Laver, James, *The Jazz Age*, Hamish Hamilton, 1964
Levin, Bernard, *The Pendulum Years (Britain in the 60s)*, Pan, 1970
Montgomery, John, *The Fifties*, George Allen & Unwin, 1965
Sissons, T.M.B. and French, P., eds., *Age of Austerity 1945-51*,
   Hodder & Stoughton, 1963
White, Palmer, *Poiret*, Studio Vista, 1973
Woolman Chase, Edna, *Always in Vogue*, Victor Gollancz, 1954

ACKNOWLEDGEMENTS

Many people have shared the burden of this book. I should like to thank Sheila Murphy, who had the enviable task of sifting through fifty-eight years of *Vogue* and choosing one-fiftieth of the material as a starting point, and Alex Kroll, Peter Carson and Eleo Gordon for the patience and care with which they gradually cut the book down to a manageable size.

I am grateful to Beatrix Miller and Georgina Boosey for their good advice and guidance, not to say forbearance when work on the book eclipsed my other work, and to Norman Parkinson and Sheila Wetton for their great help and long memories. Over the years a great number of gifted people have worked on *Vogue* and given the magazine its character and distinctive flavour in each decade. It has proved impossible to acknowledge them individually but to them belongs the credit for everything *In Vogue*.

I am grateful to Faber & Faber Ltd and Harcourt Brace Jovanovich Inc. for permission to quote from T.S. Eliot, *The Waste Land*; Faber & Faber Ltd and Random House Inc. for permission to quote from W.H. Auden, *Poems*.

I lastly want to thank my family who have lived with *In Vogue* for a year and a half: Michael, Thomas and particularly my mother, Gwen Howell, without whose unfailing help in times of crisis I should never have finished the book.

NOTE ON *VOGUE*

Vogue was founded in New York in 1892 as a society magazine and bought by Condé Nast in 1909. He turned it into America's leading fashion magazine and founded British *Vogue* in 1916. Edna Woolman Chase joined *Vogue* in 1895 and stayed for sixty years. She became editor of American *Vogue* in 1914 and later editor-in-chief. British *Vogue* was edited by Elspeth Champcommunal (1916-22), Dorothy Todd (1922-26), Alison Settle, O.B.E. (1926-35), Elizabeth Penrose (1935-40), Audrey Withers, O.B.E. (1940-60), Ailsa Garland (1961-64). The present editor is Beatrix Miller.

Many of the illustrations in this book had to be reproduced from the magazine as the original documents were no longer available. We hope that the interest of the subject matter will compensate for the occasional lack of quality.

INDEX

341

342

Clinical
Gastrointestinal
Endoscopy

Clinical Gastrointestinal Endoscopy

Gregory G. Ginsberg, M.D.
Associate Professor of Medicine
Gastroenterology Division
University of Pennsylvania School of Medicine;
Director of Endoscopic Services
Hospital of the University of Pennsylvania
Philadelphia, PA, USA

Michael L. Kochman, M.D., F.A.C.P.
Professor of Medicine
Co-Director, Gastrointestinal Oncology
Endoscopy Training Director
Gastroenterology Division
Hospital of the University of Pennsylvania
Philadelphia, PA, USA

Ian Norton, M.B.B.S., Ph.D., F.R.A.C.P.
Director of Endoscopy
Department of Gastroenterology and Hepatology
Concord Hospital
Sydney, Australia

Christopher J. Gostout, M.D.
Professor of Medicine
Mayo Clinic College of Medicine;
Consultant in Gastroenterology and Hepatology
Director of Endoscopic Research and Development
Mayo Clinic
Rochester, MN, USA

ELSEVIER
SAUNDERS

ELSEVIER
SAUNDERS

An imprint of Elsevier Inc

First published 2005

The right of Gregory G Ginsberg, Michael L Kochman, Ian Norton and Christopher J Gostout to be identified as author/s of this work has been asserted by them in accordance with the Copyright, Designs and Patents Act 1988

ISBN 0 7216 0282 7

British Library Cataloguing in Publication Data
A catalogue record for this book is available from the British Library

Library of Congress Cataloging-in-Publication Data

Clinical gastrointestinal endoscopy / editors, Gregory G. Ginsberg ... [et al.].
    p. ; cm.
  ISBN 0-7216-0282-7
  1. Enteroscopy. 2. Gastroscopy I. Ginsberg, Gregory G.
  [DNLM: 1. Endoscopy—methods. 2. Gastrointestinal Diseases—diagnosis. WI 141
C6427 2005]
RC804.E64C56 2005
616.3'407545—dc22

2004053670

Printed in China

Last digit is the print number: 9   8   7   6   5   4   3   2   1

Senior Editor: **Karen Bowler**
Developmental Editor: **Hilary Hewitt**
Project Manager: **Mary Stermel/Dan Fitzgerald**
Design Manager: **Andy Chapman**
Illustration Manager: **Mick Ruddy**
Illustrator: **Martin Woodward**
Marketing Manager(s) (UK/USA): **Jennie Finn/Laura Meiskey**

Contents

Contents

This symbol signifies that a chapter will be accompanied by a video clip on the attached DVD-ROM.

List of Contributors

Awni Taleb Abu-Sneineh, M.B.B.S.
Assistant Professor
University of Jordan;
Consultant Gastroenterologist
Jordan University Hospital
Amman, Jordan
8: *Patient Preparation and Pharmacotherapeutic Considerations*

James L. Achord, M.D.
Professor Emeritus
University of Mississippi Medical Center
Jackson, Mississippi
1: *The History of Gastrointestinal Endoscopy*

Mainor R. Antillon, M.D., M.B.A., M.P.H.
Associate Professor of Medicine
University of Colorado Health Science Center;
Director G-I Practice
University of Colorado Hospital
Denver, Colorado
35: *Endoscopic Therapy for Gastric Neoplasms*

Matthew R. Banks, B.Sc., M.R.C.P., Ph.D.
Registrar in Gastroenterology
Concord Hospital
Concord, Sydney, Australia
7: *Patient Assessment, Sedation, and Monitoring*

David E. Barlow, Ph.D.
Director of Technology Assessment
Olympus America, Inc.
Melville, New York
3: *How Endoscopes Work*

Todd H. Baron, M.D.
Professor of Medicine
Mayo Clinic College of Medicine;
Consultant
Mayo Clinic
Rochester, Minnesota
50: *Acute Pancreatitis and Peripancreatic Fluid Collections*

David J. Bjorkman, M.D., M.S.P.H., S.M.
Professor of Medicine
Interim Dean
University of Utah School of Medicine
Salt Lake City, Utah
12: *Assessment of Endoscopic Outcomes*

M. J. Bruno, M.D., Ph.D.
Assistant Professor
University of Amsterdam;
Gastroenterologist, Staff Member
Department of Gastroenterology and Hepatology
Academic Medical School
Amsterdam, The Netherlands
54: *Palliation of Malignant Pancreaticobiliary Obstruction*

David L. Carr-Locke, M.A., M.B., B.Chir., D.R.C.O.G., F.R.C.P.
Associate Professor of Medicine
Harvard Medical School;
Director of Endoscopy
Senior Physician
Brigham & Women's Hospital
Boston, Massachusetts
48: *Infections of the Biliary Tract*

Brooks D. Cash, M.D.
Assistant Professor of Medicine
Uniformed Services University of the Health Sciences;
Director of Clinical Research
Gastroenterology Division and Comprehensive Colorectal Cancer Center Initiative
National Naval Medical Center
Bethesda, Maryland
12: *Assessment of Endoscopic Outcomes*

Kenneth J. Chang, M.D.
Professor of Medicine
University of California
Irvine, California;
Executive Director
H.H. Chao Comprehensive Digestive Disease Center
University of California Medical Center
Orange, California
45: *Endoscopic Ultrasonography Guided Fine-Needle Aspiration of Pancreaticobiliary Lesions*

Wei-Kuo Chang, M.D.
Associate Professor
Division of Gastroenterology
Department of Medicine
National Defense Medical Center;
Attending Physician
Tri-Service General Hospital
Taipei, Taiwan
25: *Techniques in Enteral Access*

Yang Chen, M.D.
Professor of Medicine
University of Colorado Health Sciences Center
School of Medicine
Denver, Colorado;
Director of Endoscopy
University of Colorado Hospital
Aurora, Colorado
35: *Endoscopic Therapy for Gastric Neoplasms*

Kenneth D. Chi, M.D.
GI Fellow
Section of Endoscopy and Therapeutics
University of Chicago
Chicago, Illinois
34: *Evaluation of Gastric Polyps and Thickened Gastric Folds*

Nicholas I. Church, M.B.Ch.B., M.R.C.P.
Specialist Registrar in Gastroenterology
Western General Hospital
Edinburgh, United Kingdom
27: *Diagnosis and Staging of Esophageal Carcinoma*

Guido Costamagna, M.D., F.A.C.G.
Full Professor of Surgery
Catholic University;
Head, Digestive Endoscopy Unit
University Hospital
Roma, Italy
47: *Benign Biliary Strictures and Leaks*

Sanford M. Dawsey, M.D.
Senior Investigator
National Cancer Institute
Bethesda, Maryland
32: *Screening for Esophageal Squamous Cell Carcinoma and its Precursor Lesions*

James A. DiSario, M.D.
Professor of Medicine
Director of Therapeutic Endoscopy
University of Utah Health Sciences Center
Salt Lake City, Utah
46: *Choledocholithiasis*

Grace H. Elta, M.D.
Professor of Medicine
University of Michigan
Ann Arbor, Michigan
19: *Benign Strictures*

Gary W. Falk, M.D.
Staff Gastroenterologist
Cleveland Clinic Foundation
Cleveland, Ohio
28: *Diagnosis and Surveillance of Barrett's Esophagus*

Arnaldo Braga Feitoza, M.D.
Attending Surgeon
Digestive Endoscopy Unit
Department of Surgery
Hospital Aulino Feitosa
Telemaco Borba, Pabana, Brazil
11: *Postsurgical Endoscopic Anatomy*

David E. Fleischer, M.D.
Professor of Medicine
Mayo College of Medicine;
Chair Gastroenterology and Hepatology
Mayo Clinic Scottsdale
Scottsdale, Arizona
32: *Screening for Esophageal Squamous Cell Carcinoma and its Precursor Lesions*

Paul Fockens, M.D., Ph.D.
Director of Endoscopy
Academic Medical Center
University of Amsterdam
Amsterdam, The Netherlands
54: *Palliation of Malignant Pancreaticobiliary Obstruction*

Evan L. Fogel, M.D., M.Sc., F.R.C.P.
Associate Professor of Clinical Medicine
Indiana University Medical Center;
Rodebush VA Hospital
Indianapolis, Indiana;
Witham Hospital
Lebanon, Indiana
40: *Diagnostic Cholangiography*
49: *Sphincter of Oddi Dysfunction*

James T. Frakes, M.D., M.S.
Clinical Professor of Medicine
University of Illinois College of Medicine at Rockford;
Managing Partner
Rockford Gastroenterology Associates, Ltd.
Rockford, Illinois
2: *Setting Up an Endoscopy Facility*

Shai Friedland, M.D.
Assistant Professor of Medicine
Stanford University
Stanford, California;
Staff Gastroenterologist
VA Palo Alto
Palo Alto, California
38: *Colonoscopic Polypectomy and Endoscopic Mucosal Resection*
57: *New Techniques in Imaging*

Christopher J. Gostout, M.D.
Professor of Medicine
Mayo Clinic College of Medicine;
Consultant in Gastroenterology and Hepatology
Director of Endoscopic Research and Development
Mayo Clinic
Rochester, Minnesota
10: *Small-Caliber Endoscopy*

Takuji Gotoda, M.D.
Staff, Endoscopy Division
National Cancer Center Hospital
Tokyo, Japan
38: *Colonoscopic Polypectomy and Endoscopic Mucosal Resection*

Steven R. Granger, B.S., M.D.
General Surgery Resident
University of Utah School of Medicine
Salt Lake City, Utah
46: *Choledocholithiasis*

Frank G. Gress, M.D.
Associate Professor of Medicine
Division of Gastroenterology
Duke University School of Medicine
Duke University Medical Center
Durham, North Carolina
33: *Extraintestinal Endosonography (including celiac block)*

Naresh T. Gunaratnam, M.D.
Clinical Instructor
University of Michigan;
Director of Clinical Research
St. Joseph Mercy Hospital
Ann Arbor, Michigan
13: *Acute Nonvariceal Bleeding*

Kiyoshi Hashiba, M.D.
Director of Endoscopy
Hospital Sírio Libanês
Sao Paulo, Brazil
22: *Zenker's Diverticula*

Robert H. Hawes, M.D.
Professor of Medicine
Medical University of South Carolina
Charleston, South Carolina
52: *Chronic Pancreatitis, Stones, and Strictures*

Juergen Hochberger, M.D.
Assistant Professor of Medicine
Chief, Department of Gastroenterology
St. Bernward Academic Teaching Hospital
Hildesheim, Germany
42: *Difficult Cannulation and Sphincterotomy*

Marjolein Y.V. Homs, M.Sc.
Researcher
Department of Gastroenterology and Hepatology
Erasmus MC University Medical Center
Rotterdam, The Netherlands
30: *Endoscopic Palliation of Malignant Dysphagia and Esophageal Fistulas*

Douglas Howell, M.D.
Associate Clinical Professor of Medicine
University of Vermont Medical School;
Director, Pancreaticobiliary Center
Maine Medical Center
Portland, Maine
43: *Endoscopic Retrograde Cholangiopancreatography Tissue Sampling Techniques*

Maite Betés Ibáñez, Ph.D.
Associated Professor of Medicine
University of Navarra School of Medicine;
Staff Gastroenterologist
University Clinic of Navarra
Pamplona, Spain
17: *Chronic Gastrointestinal Bleeding*

Charles J. Kahi, M.D., M.Sc.
Assistant Professor of Medicine
Division of Gastroenterology and Hepatology
Indiana University School of Medicine
Indianapolis, Indiana
39: *Endoscopic Palliation of Colorectal Tumors*

David A. Katzka, M.D.
Associate Professor of Medicine
University of Pennsylvania School of Medicine;
Attending Physician
Hospital of the University of Pennsylvania
Philadelphia, Pennsylvania
20: *Achalasia*

Yakub I. Khan, M.B.B.S., M.D.
Consultant Gastroenterologist
Shaukat Khanum Hospital and Research Center
Lahore, Pakistan
13: *Acute Nonvariceal Bleeding*

Michael B. Kimmey, A.B., M.D.
Professor of Medicine
Division of Gastroenterology
Department of Medicine
University of Washington;
Director, Digestive Disease Center
University of Washington Medical Center
Seattle, Washington
26: *Acute Colonic Pseudo-Obstruction*

David James Koorey, M.B., B.S., Ph.D., F.R.A.C.P.
Senior Lecturer
University of Sydney;
Senior Staff Specialist
A W Morrow Gastroenterology and Liver Centre
Royal Prince Alfred Hospital
Sydney, Australia
36: *Management of Upper Gastrointestinal Familial Adenomatous Polyposis Syndrome and Ampullary Tumors*

Richard Kozarek, M.D.
Clinical Professor of Medicine
University of Washington;
Chief of Gastroenterology
Director, GI Institute
Virginia Mason Medical Center
Seattle, Washington
53: *Pancreatic Duct Leaks and Pseudocysts*

Karen L. Krok, M.D.
Gastroenterology Fellow
Johns Hopkins Hospital
Baltimore, Maryland
23: *Inflammatory Bowel Disease*

Glen A. Lehman, M.D.
Professor of Medicine and Radiology
Indiana University Medical Center
Indiana University School of Medicine
Indianapolis, Indiana
40: *Diagnostic Cholangiography*
49: *Sphincter of Oddi Dysfunction*

Blair S. Lewis, M.D.
Clinical Professor of Medicine
Mount Sinai School of Medicine
New York City, New York
16: *Obscure Gastrointestinal Bleeding*

Gary R. Lichtenstein, M.D.
Professor of Medicine
University of Pennsylvania School of Medicine;
Director, Center for Inflammatory Bowel Diseases
Hospital of the University of Pennsylvania
Gastroenterology Division
Department of Medicine
Philadelphia, Pennsylvania
23: *Inflammatory Bowel Disease*

David Lieberman, M.D.
Professor of Medicine
Chief, Division of Gastroenterology
Oregon Health and Science University
Portland, Oregon
37: *Colorectal Cancer Screening and Surveillance*

Takahisa Matsuda, M.D.
Staff, Endoscopy Division
National Cancer Center Hospital
Tokyo, Japan
38: *Colonoscopic Polypectomy and Endoscopic Mucosal Resection*

Stephen A. McClave, B.A., M.D.
Professor of Medicine
Division of Gastroenterology and Hepatology
Director of Clinical Nutrition
Chairman, Nutrition Support Teams
University of Louisville School of Medicine
Chairman, Nutrition Support Teams
Jewish Hospital
Louisville, Kentucky;
ASPEN, Director of Clinical Practice
Silver Spring, Maryland;
Chairman, ASGE Enteral Nutrition Special Interest Group
Deerfield, Illinois
25: *Techniques in Enteral Access*

Lee McHenry Jr., M.D.
Associate Professor of Medicine
Indiana University School of Medicine
Springmill Surgery Center
Indianapolis, Indiana
40: *Diagnostic Cholangiography*
49: *Sphincter of Oddi Dysfunction*

David C. Metz, M.D.
Professor of Medicine
Division of Gastroenterology
University of Pennsylvania School of Medicine;
Co-Director, GI Physiology Laboratory
Director, Acid Peptic Disease Program
Co-Director, Swallowing Disorders Program
Hospital of the University of Pennsylvania
Philadelphia, Pennsylvania
20: *Achalasia*

Marcia L. Morris, B.A., M.S.
President and CEO
Medical Service Associates, Inc.
Maplewood, Minnesota
6: *Electrosurgical Principles*

Miguel Muñoz-Navas, Ph.D.
Professor of Medicine
University of Navarra School of Medicine;
Director of the Department of Gastroenterology
and the Endoscopy Unit
University Hospital of Navarra
Pamplona, Spain
17: *Chronic Gastrointestinal Bleeding*

Douglas B. Nelson, M.D.
Staff Physician in Gastroenterology
Minneapolis VA Medical Center;
Associate Professor
University of Minnesota Medical School
Minneapolis, Minnesota
4: *Cleaning and Disinfecting Endoscopic Equipment*

Nam Q. Nguyen, M.B.B.S.
Gastroenterology Fellow
Royal Adelaide Hospital
Adelaide, South Australia
8: *Patient Preparation and Pharmacotherapeutic Considerations*

Nicholas Nickl, M.D.
Professor of Medicine
University of Kentucky Medical Center
Lexington, Kentucky
31: *Nonepithelial Tumors of the Esophagus and Stomach*

Ian Norton, M.B.B.S., Ph.D., F.R.A.C.P.
Director of Endoscopy
Department of Gastroenterology and Hepatology
Concord Hospital
Sydney, Australia
9: *Reporting, Documentation, and Risk Management*
36: *Management of Upper Gastrointestinal Familial Adenomatous Polyposis Syndrome and Ampullary Tumors*

Pankaj J. Pasricha, M.D.
Chief, Division of Gastroenterology and Hepatology
Bassel and Frances Blanton Distinguished Professor of Internal Medicine
Professor of Neuroscience & Cell Biology and Biomedical Engineering
The University of Texas Medical Branch
Galveston, Texas
55: *Endoluminal Surgery*

Ian D. Penman, M.D., F.R.C.P.
Senior Lecturer
Edinburgh University
Consultant Gastroenterologist
Western General Hospital
Edinburgh, United Kingdom
27: *Diagnosis and Staging of Esophageal Carcinoma*

Bret T. Petersen, M.D.
Consultant in Gastroenterology
Endoscopy Chair
Mayo Clinic and College of Medicine
Rochester, Minnesota
41: *Diagnostic Pancreatography*

Patrick Pfau, M.D.
Assistant Professor of Medicine
Director of Gastrointestinal Endoscopy
Section of Gastroenterology and Hepatology
University of Wisconsin Medical School
Madison, Wisconsin
21: *Ingested Foreign Objects and Food Bolus Impactions*

Bonnie J. Pollack, M.D.
Assistant Professor of Medicine
State University of New York at Stony Brook School of Medicine
Stony Brook, New York;
Associate Director of Gastrointestinal Endoscopy and Endoscopic Ultrasound
Winthrop University Hospital
Mineola, New York
33: *Extraintestinal Endosonography (including celiac block)*

Robert J. Ponec, M.D., F.A.C.P.
Clinical Assistant Professor of Medicine
Oregon Health and Science University
Portland, Oregon;
Salem Gastroenterology Consultant
Salem Hospital
Salem, Oregon
26: *Acute Colonic Pseudo-Obstruction*

Emad Rahmani, M.D., F.A.C.P.
Associate Professor of Clinical Medicine
Indiana University School of Medicine;
Director of Endoscopy
Wishard Memorial Hospital
Indianapolis, Indiana
39: *Endoscopic Palliation of Colorectal Tumors*

Elizabeth Rajan, M.D.
Assistant Professor of Medicine
Division of Gastroenterology and Hepatology
Mayo Clinic College of Medicine;
Consultant in Gastroenterology and Hepatology
Mayo Clinic
Rochester, Minnesota
56: *Bioabsorbable Stents*

Douglas K. Rex, M.D.
Professor of Medicine
Indiana University School of Medicine;
Director of Endoscopy
Indiana University Hospital
Indianapolis, Indiana
39: *Endoscopic Palliation of Colorectal Tumors*

Richard I. Rothstein, M.D.
Professor of Medicine
Dartmouth Medical School;
Chief, Section of Gastroenterology and Hepatology
Dartmouth-Hitchcock Medical Center
Lebanon, New Hampshire
18: *Gastroesophageal Reflux*

Ignacio Fernández-Urién Sáinz, M.D.
Clinical Associated Professor of Medicine
University of Navarra School of Medicine;
Staff Gastroenterologist
University Clinic of Navarra
Pamplona, Spain
17: *Chronic Gastrointestinal Bleeding*

Shiv Kumar Sarin, M.D., D.M.
Professor and Head
Department of Gastroenterology
G.B. Pant Hospital
New Delhi, India
14: *Portal Hypertensive Bleeding*

Thomas J. Savides, M.D.
Associate Professor of Clinical Medicine
University of California
San Diego, California
15: *Lower Gastrointestinal Bleeding*

Mark Schoeman, M.B.B.S., Ph.D., F.R.A.C.P.
Senior Lecturer in Medicine
University of Adelaide;
Head of Gastrointestinal Services
Royal Adelaide Hospital
Adelaide, South Australia
8: *Patient Preparation and Pharmacotherapeutic Considerations*

Kenneth W. Schroeder, M.D., Ph.D.
Consultant, Gastroenterology and Hepatology
Department of Medicine
Mayo Clinic College of Medicine
Rochester, Minnesota
9: *Reporting, Documentation, and Risk Management*

Barjest Chander Sharma, M.D., D.M.
Professor and Head
Department of Gastroenterology
G. B. Pant Hospital
New Delhi, India
14: *Portal Hypertensive Bleeding*

Stuart Sherman, M.D.
Professor of Medicine and Radiology
Director of ERCP
Indiana University School of Medicine
Indianapolis, Indiana
40: *Diagnostic Cholangiography*
49: *Sphincter of Oddi Dysfunction*

Peter D. Siersema, M.D., Ph.D.
Associate Professor of Medicine
Department of Gastroenterology and Hepatology
Erasmus MC University Medical Center
Rotterdam, The Netherlands
30: *Endoscopic Palliation of Malignant Dysphagia and Esophageal Fistulas*

Adam Slivka, M.D., Ph.D.
Associate Professor of Medicine
University of Pittsburgh;
Associate Chief, Division of Gastroenterology, Hepatology, and Nutrition
University of Pittsburgh Medical Center
Pittsburgh, Pennsylvania
51: *Acute Relapsing Pancreatitis*

Roy Soetikno, M.D., M.S.
Associate Professor
Stanford University School of Medicine
Stanford, California;
Chief of Endoscopy
Veterans Affairs Palo Alto Health Care System
Palo Alto, California
38: *Colonoscopic Polypectomy and Endoscopic Mucosal Resection*

Darius Sorbi, M.D.
Associate Professor
Mayo Medical School;
Senior Associate Consultant
Director, GI Endoscopy Unit
Mayo Clinic Scottsdale
Dix Hills, New York
10: *Small-Caliber Endoscopy*

Jennifer J. Telford, M.D., M.P.H.
Clinical Fellow
Harvard Medical School;
Fellow
Brigham and Women's Hospital
Boston, Massachusetts
48: *Infections of the Biliary Tract*

Mark D. Topazian, M.D.
Associate Professor of Medicine
Mayo Clinic College of Medicine;
Senior Associate Consultant
Mayo Clinic
Rochester, Minnesota
44: *Endoscopic Ultrasonography of Pancreatic and Biliary Diseases*

Anne-Marie van Berkel, M.D., Ph.D.
Gastroenterologist
Academic Medical Center
Amsterdam, The Netherlands
54: *Palliation of Malignant Pancreaticobiliary Obstruction*

Jacques Van Dam, M.D., Ph.D.
Professor of Medicine
Stanford University School of Medicine;
Clinical Chief and Director of Endoscopy
Stanford University Medical Center
Stanford, California
57: *New Techniques in Imaging*

Shyam Varadarajulu, M.D.
Assistant Professor of Medicine
Division of Gastroenterology-Hepatology
University of Alabama School of Medicine
Birmingham, Alabama
52: *Chronic Pancreatitis, Stones, and Strictures*

Kenneth K. Wang, M.D.
Associate Professor of Medicine
Mayo Clinic
Rochester, Minnesota
29: *Endoscopic Therapy for Superficial Esophageal Carcinoma*

James L. Watkins, M.D.
Associate Professor of Clinical Medicine
Indiana University Medical Center
Indianapolis, Indiana
40: *Diagnostic Cholangiography*
49: *Sphincter of Oddi Dysfunction*

Irving Waxman, M.D.
Professor of Medicine
Director of Endoscopy
University of Chicago
Chicago, Illinois
34: *Evaluation of Gastric Polyps and Thickened Gastric Folds*

George J.M. Webster, B.Sc., M.D., M.R.C.P.
Consultant Gastroenterologist
Department of Gastroenterology
The Middlesex Hospital
University College London Hospitals
London, United Kingdom
7: *Patient Assessment, Sedation, and Monitoring*

Wilfred Weinstein, M.D.
Professor of Medicine
Department of Medicine-Digestive Diseases
UCLA Center for The Health Sciences
Los Angeles, California
5: *Tissue Sampling, Specimen Handling, and Chromoendoscopy*

C. Mel Wilcox, M.D.
Professor of Medicine
University of Alabama;
Chief of Endoscopy
University Hospital
Birmingham, Alabama
24: *Infections of the Luminal Digestive Tract*

Preface

Welcome to the first edition of *Clinical Gastrointestinal Endoscopy*. This volume provides a comprehensive treatment of general and advanced gastrointestinal endoscopy and is prepared by leading authorities from around the globe. Authors were selected because of their personal contributions to the development of their assigned topics, acknowledged clinical prowess in the field, and proven track record as effective scientific writers. The result is a collection of the most authoritative and easily absorbed chapters available in endoscopy. The authors have taken the opportunity to design countless original diagrams, algorithms, and tables to precisely and easily display complex information. Each of the diagrams has been expertly redrawn to a consistent and attractive style. The authors have also lavished their exceptional collections of endoscopic photographs, EUS images, radiographs, and histomicrographs upon the book. Each of these stunning illustrations can be downloaded from the book's website (details and link are available on the enclosed DVD-ROM) so that you can use them in your presentations. Each of the world's leading contributors to this book has been asked to supply digital video demonstrating the diagnostic and therapeutic endoscopic procedures they cover. No other textbook offers real-time demonstrations of so many procedures from the world's experts—the reading experience has leapt from the page to the monitor. Each video clip, available on the enclosed DVD-ROM, has been meticulously edited to make the viewing experience efficiently educational.

These features make this volume essential reading for any fellow who is serious about endoscopy. This volume is also a vehicle for acquisition of new skills and an indispensable resource for practicing clinicians in both community and academic settings.

Clinical Gastrointestinal Endoscopy is divided into four main sections covering Equipment and General Principles of Endoscopy, Luminal Gastrointestinal Disorders, Pancreaticobiliary Disorders, and What's Next in Advanced Therapeutic Endoscopy? (a glimpse into the future). The first section elegantly describes the history of gastrointestinal endoscopy and then provides primers on how endoscopes, endoscopic devices, and endoscopy units function. There are many real practice-changing pearls of wisdom in these pages. Section II: Luminal Gastrointestinal Disorders is divided into benign and malignant disorders. The benign disorders subsection devotes five chapters to endoscopic diagnosis and treatment of gastrointestinal bleeding followed by detailed coverage of endoscopic approaches to strictures, enteral access, ingested foreign objects, and gastroesophageal reflux disease. The chapters on malignant disorders give complete coverage of endoscopic approaches to management of inflammatory, infectious, and functional disorders of the luminal digestive tract. The chapters on neoplastic disorders are divided into esophageal, gastroduodenal, and colorectal subsections. Within each subsection, endoscopic diagnosis, staging, palliation, and curative therapies are comprehensively covered. The pancreaticobiliary section details simple and advanced techniques in ERCP and EUS for the diagnosis and management of benign and malignant disorders of the pancreaticobiliary systems.

The editors draw on their collective decades of clinical endoscopic experience to clearly represent the core proven practice while energizing it with the cutting edge innovations. They are themselves the products of some of the powerhouses of gastrointestinal endoscopic training and practice: Georgetown University, Indiana University, Mayo Clinic, University of Michigan, and the University of Pennsylvania. They have worked painstakingly to develop a user-friendly and, at the same time, authoritative product. The publishers are to be congratulated on thumbing their noses at convention, developing a creative and richly illustrated volume, further improved by the DVD-ROM of the video demonstrations. The timelessness of most of the content will make this a "current" resource for many years.

Gregory G. Ginsberg, M.D.

Dedications

Developing a book of this scope and detail is a considerable undertaking for all involved. It is made possible and even pleasurable when supported by people who evidence excellence in the quality of their work and their passion for the subject matter. Such is the case with the coeditors, authors, and publishers involved herein.

I recruited my coeditors for their abilities to single out capable authors from diverse training and practice settings and to see that these authors delivered the goods in a reasonably timely manner. However, moreover, they are friends and professionals whom I admire. I thank them for their willing collaboration. A textbook is the sum of its parts, and I wish to express my sincerest appreciation to the individual authors for their personal investment in developing full, rich chapters. I am also appreciative of the organization, creativity, and professionalism on the part of the Elsevier publishing team, and, in particular, Rolla Couchman and Hilary Hewitt.

Influencing the development of this book, I gratefully acknowledge those who have shaped my career. I am indebted to my teachers during fellowship at Georgetown, Stanley Benjamin, David Fleischer, Firas Al-Kawas, Jim Lewis, Lou Korman, and Tim Lipman. I am appreciative of my division Chiefs at Penn, Peter Traber, Micheal Lucey, and Anil Rustgi, and to my divisional colleagues, many

outstanding fellows, nurses, and technical staff. There are many from the industry, too, with whom I have partnered in the development of new techniques and technologies and who have supported research and educational initiatives. Lastly, I acknowledge my father, David K. Ginsberg, M.D., who was among the early enthusiasts of gastrointestinal endoscopy and introduced me to the discipline subliminally by using our family movie camera to film his early endoscopic procedures. In the late 1960s and early 1970s, a typical home-movie viewing session would alternately feature birthdays, holidays, and endoscopic footage. Moreover, I acknowledge both mother and father for their example, encouragement, and guidance to this day.

I am fortunate enough to be able to thank my exceptional wife, Jane, who unselfishly supports my forays into projects like this in pursuit of professional development and satisfaction. Finally, I recognize my four (count 'em, four) lovely daughters, Jennifer, Kathleen, Elizabeth, and Meg, who are unending sources of warmth and humor.

I hope this book will enhance your knowledge and abilities, enrich your professionalism, and enable you to provide the best possible care for your patients.

Gregory G. Ginsberg

This book is dedicated to my family: my wife, Mary, and my children, Elyse and Sidney. Without their indulgences, this book would not have been possible.

Over the years a number of key individuals sparked and nurtured my interest in Gastroenterology and Therapeutic Endoscopy: Drs. Tom Layden and Jay Goldstein were critical early on in demonstrating to me the need for better diagnostics and additional effective therapies. Tachi Yamada, M.D. and Chung Owyang, M.D. had the foresight to allow me the specialized training, which I hope I have put to good use. Drs. Rick Boland, John DelValle, Grace Elta,

Robert Hawes, Michael Lucey, Jim Scheiman, Peter Traber, and Maurits Wiersema were instrumental in helping me acquire and define my skillset and in facilitating my clinical research and writing skills. My current colleagues at the University of Pennsylvania have been instrumental in providing critical insight and guidance.

Clifford G. Pilz, M.D. (1921–2005) deserves special mention. As my Chief of Medicine during my medical school, residency, and Chief Residency, he clearly defined the epitome of the all-knowing physician; no question too small to deserve an answer, no sign or symptom too subtle to be ignored.

Michael L. Kochman

It has truly been a pleasure working on this project, and for that I must first thank Greg Ginsberg for his faith in spite of the "tyranny of distance" involved in working with me, as well as my coeditors, contributing authors, and everyone at Elsevier.

It is no understatement that my career was reinvented at the Mayo Clinic and for that I will be eternally grateful for my many teachers and colleagues at Mayo, in particular Bret Petersen, Jonathan Clain, Gene DiMagno, Maurits Wiersema, and Todd Baron.

I must especially thank Chris Gostout for his remarkable enthusiasm and mentorship.

Lastly, I must thank my wonderful wife, Stephanie, for her unwavering support and my beautiful children, Sophie and Michael, for all the joy they give me as well as reminding me what's really important.

I hope that this book is helpful in your day-to-day practice and maybe helps spark some of the enthusiasm for endoscopy that I have been privileged to experience.

Ian Norton

As endoscopy continues to evolve into more exciting diagnostic and therapeutic capabilities, it is important to provide a strong base and resource upon which this evolution of endoscopy can grow. We accomplish this, in part, by the creation of textbooks crafted to be as comprehensive and as current as possible. On behalf of myself, my fellow coeditors, and, more importantly, the contributing authors of this text I have had the pleasure to work with, we are able to provide you with a valuable resource upon which to study the practice of endoscopy and better understand where endoscopy must go to enhance the care of our patients.

Christopher J. Gostout

Clinical
Gastrointestinal
Endoscopy

SECTION 1

Equipment and General Principles of Endoscopy

The History of Gastrointestinal Endoscopy

James L. Achord

Introduction

The role of the physician is to observe, detect anatomic abnormalities or disease, and conceive ways and means by which discovered deficiencies in function can be corrected or ameliorated. To extend the physical examination to areas that are hidden from external view such as within body orifices presents a problem of safe and effective access. In insatiable attempts to accomplish these goals, there is no human orifice and its recesses that has not been inspected, probed, prodded, and otherwise examined over the centuries. It was a compelling necessity to develop nonsurgical and safe methods to accomplish this purpose. Before the 20th century, numerous attempts to access these hidden cavities were plagued by instrumentation that was inadequate and dangerous.

The history of every science or technical development is invariably a series of small discoveries or innovations, often in fields remote from that under investigation. Small improvements, each resulting in incremental gains, lead toward the idealized goal. Oftentimes, changes that appear to be an advance are found to be an impediment by further discoveries, and one recognizes that a different way is better. Therefore, the task is never-ending.

The term *endoscopy* comes from the Greek prefix *endo-* (within) and the verb *skopein* (to view or observe). In this chapter, I summarize major developments in the field of gastrointestinal (GI) endoscopy. As in any summary, the contributions of some individuals are inevitably not cited and I apologize.

Early Efforts

The visual exploration and examination of body orifices date to Egyptian and later Greco-Roman times during which mechanical specula for viewing the vagina and anus were developed and used to a limited extent. Further progress was delayed by lack of sufficiently strong metals and the ability to form them into usable instruments and by the lack of adequate illumination. These initial efforts were directed at the genitourinary (GU) tract (i.e., cavities that are only a short and relatively straight distance from the exterior).

Phillip Bozzini, who published his work in 1805, is credited with the earliest known attempt to visualize the interior of a body cavity with a primitive endoscope (Fig. 1–1).[1-3] He devised a tin tube illuminated by a candle from which light was reflected by a mirror, a device he called a *lichtleiter* (light conductor). He used this device to examine the urethra, urinary bladder, and vagina, but it was an impractical instrument that never gained wide acceptance. Although

Figure 1–1. Bozzini's lichtleiter, 1805. (Reproduced from Edmonson JM: History of the instruments for gastrointestinal endoscopy. Gastrointest Endosc 37:S28, 1991.)

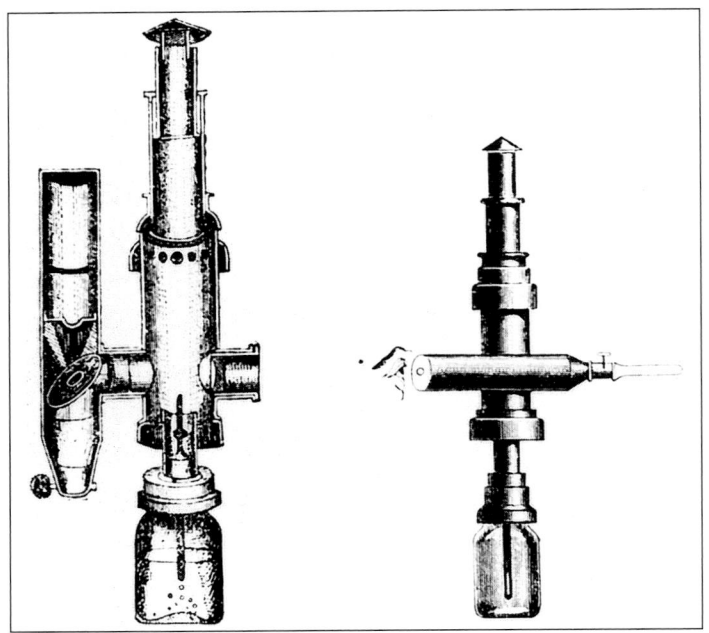

Figure 1-2. Desormeaux's endoscope, 1853. (Reproduced from Edmonson JM: History of the instruments for gastrointestinal endoscopy. Gastrointest Endosc 37:S29, 1991.)

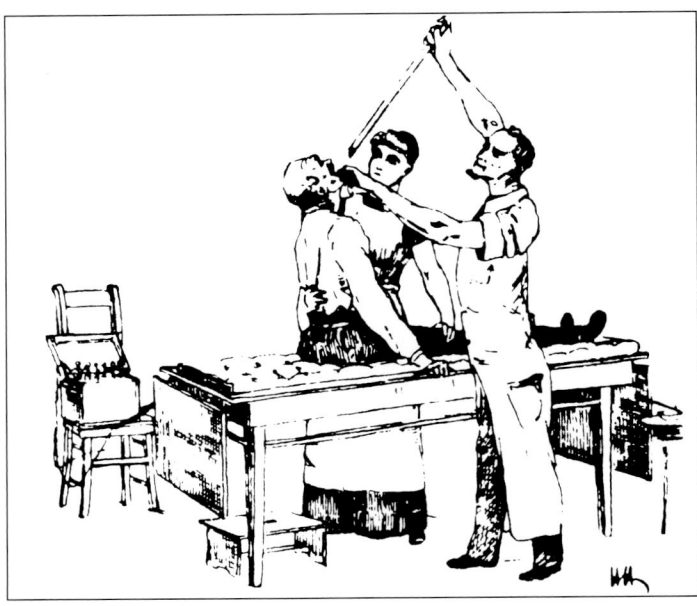

Figure 1-3. Kussmaul's gastroscope, 1868. (Reproduced from Edmonson JM: History of the instruments for gastrointestinal endoscopy. Gastrointest Endosc 37:S30, 1991.)

there were multiple attempts to develop more usable instruments, all were directed toward the GU tract and none were widely used. The most notable efforts were by Segalas in France in 1826 and Fisher in Boston in 1827[2]; both used straight metal tubes, but the lack of a satisfactory light source remained a major impediment. The next significant development was the instrument of Antonin J. Desormeaux in France.[3] Desormeaux's contribution in 1855 was a better, but still inadequate, light source using a lamp fueled with alcohol and turpentine ("gazogene") (Fig. 1–2). His instrument was based on that of Segalas. Others continued with efforts to improve the light source and the means to deliver it, but the devices were not satisfactory for the more inaccessible areas of the GI tract.

Rigid Gastrointestinal Endoscopes

Using a straight rigid metal tube passed over a flexible obturator and a cooperative sword swallower (Fig. 1–3), Adolf Kussmaul is credited as being the first to perform gastroscopy in 1868.[1-4] For a light source, he used a mirror reflecting light from the Desormeaux device, but he found it inadequate. He also quickly discovered that gastric secretions were a problem, despite using a flexible tube that he had developed earlier to empty the stomach before the procedure. The value of his efforts, however, was the demonstration that the curves and bends of the esophagus and esophagogastric junction could be traversed with careful manipulation and that the gastric pouch could be visualized. Kussmaul apparently demonstrated his "gastroscope" several times, but the illumination was too poor to allow a clinically useful image[3] and he abandoned his efforts.

Encouraged by the efforts of Kussmaul, others switched their attention to developing esophagoscopes because that organ is much easier to visualize and, therefore, required a less complex design than gastroscopes. The problems of perforation, at that time usually fatal, and of illumination remained major obstacles. Before the late 19th century, illumination of light reflected by a mirror into a straight metal tube continued to be used. As noted previously, several light sources were developed, but the intensity left much to be desired. Several innovations were developed to solve this problem, including a burning magnesium wire that produced a brilliant light but unacceptable heat and smoke. The most promising device seemed to be the brilliant light from a loop of platinum wire charged with direct current, introduced simultaneously by Bruck in Breslau and Milliot of Paris in 1882.[2] Although the illumination was good, there were major difficulties encountered with the considerable heat generated, necessitating a water cooling system, and the cumbersome batteries used for a power source. Nevertheless, it was an encouraging development and was used in several instruments that saw relatively wide use. These instruments were made obsolete just a few years later by Edison's incandescent electric light bulb introduced in 1879.

In 1886, the instrument maker Josef Leiter was the first to use the electric incandescent light bulb in a cystoscope just 7 years after Edison's introduction of the light bulb. With a few short-lived exceptions, all instruments after 1886 used Edison's invention. Working with Leiter, Johann von Mikulicz developed an unsuccessful gastroscope but a practical esophagoscope that he used extensively until distracted by his many other medical interests. At the turn of the 20th century, Chevalier Jackson, a talented otolaryngologist, also examined the esophagus and the stomach using a straight rigid tube and a distal electric light bulb, but few could match his talents in the GI tract. Under his influence, esophagoscopy was considered the exclusive province of ear, nose, and throat (ENT) departments in

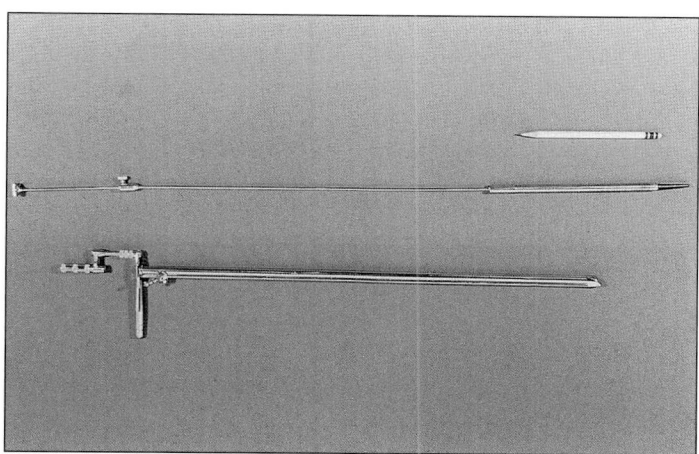

Figure 1–4. Eder-Hufford esophagoscope, the result of multiple attempts to develop a clinically useful instrument, 1949. (Personal photograph.)

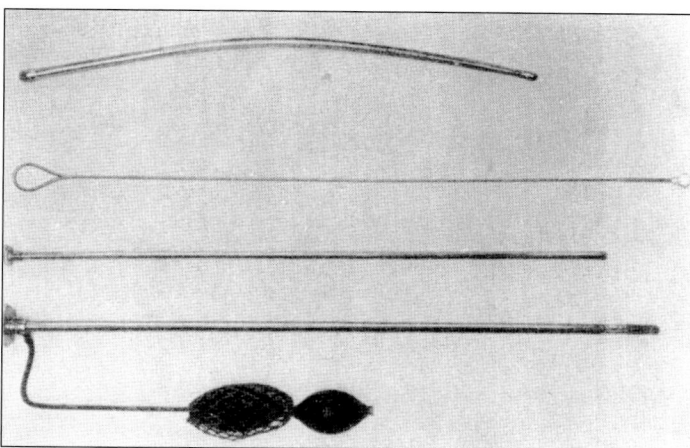

Figure 1–5. Elsner's gastroscope, 1911. (Reproduced from Edmonson JM: History of the instruments for gastrointestinal endoscopy. Gastrointest Endosc 37:S35, 1991.)

many community hospitals in the United States as late as the 1950s. The design of the esophagoscope remained that of a straight rigid tube, usually with a rubber finger-tipped obturator to make insertion safer. With the later addition of a 4× power lens on the proximal end and a distal incandescent bulb, various models were popular until the introduction of fiberoptics in 1961. The Eder-Hufford rigid esophagoscope (developed in 1949) (Fig. 1–4) was popular and still in use during my training from 1960 to 1962.

It was not until after 1900 that persistent effort to develop a usable gastroscope was successful. There were attempts to build a flexible instrument that used several lenses that were designed to be straightened after introduction; these instruments were fragile, easily damaged, and cumbersome. Straight tubes with simpler optics provided some usefulness, but perforations were still a problem.[1] In 1911, Elsner introduced a rigid gastroscope with an outer tube through which a separate inner optical tube with a flexible rubber tip and side-viewing portal could be passed (Fig. 1–5). The rubber tip, previously used in the esophagoscope obturator, was more crucial than it might appear, for it seemed to be, along with the later addition of a flexible metal coil proximal to it, the single feature that reduced the rate of perforation. Elsner's instrument actually worked as designed and was widely used, especially by Rudolph Schindler who called it the "mother of all instruments until 1932."[5] In 1922, Schindler introduced his own version of the Elsner gastroscope, the major innovation of which was the important addition of an air channel to clear the lens of secretions. With the Elsner gastroscope, Schindler examined the stomachs of several hundred patients and meticulously recorded his findings in each procedure. He published *Lehrbuch und Atlas der Gastreoskopie* in 1923, with descriptions and remarkably accurate drawings. He trained others in the technique and was responsible for wide acceptance of gastroscopy. The procedure was to first empty the stomach with a nasogastric tube followed by sedation. The patient was placed on the left side with an assistant who held the head rigidly extended to produce a straight path into the esophagus and thence into the stomach (the "sword swallower's technique"). The role of the assistant was critical. This effort is impressive and convinced many of the value of an expert examination of the stomach.

Semiflexible Gastroscopes

It became apparent that rigid straight tubes were not ideal for examination of the stomach. Fatal perforations continued to discourage the acceptance of the procedure. Visualization of the surface of the stomach was incomplete at best, with many consistently blind spots. These problems stimulated investigation of methods to manufacture flexible and safer instruments. The instruments were certainly not flexible by today's standards but were certainly more flexible than those straight, rigid instruments that came before. *Semiflexible*, with passive angulation of the distal portion of 34 degrees and sometimes more, was a more appropriate term.

In 1911, Michael Hoffman demonstrated that an image could be transmitted through a curved line by linking several short-focus prisms. Using this principle, several instruments were constructed, but these were neither satisfactory nor widely accepted. Rudolf Schindler, working with Wolf, the renowned instrument maker, constructed a semiflexible instrument with a rigid proximal portion and a distal portion (made elastic by coiled copper wire) that initially terminated with a rubber finger and, later, with a small rubber ball. Illumination was with a distal incandescent light bulb. Air insufflation was made possible with a rubber bulb, expanding the stomach wall to beyond the focal length of the Zeiss prisms. In 1932, the sixth and final version was patented. This instrument, known as the Wolf-Schindler gastroscope, greatly improved safety and efficacy of gastroscopy and was used throughout the world (Fig. 1–6). Thanks to the published meticulous work and enthusiasm of Schindler, whose designation as the "father of gastroscopy" is well deserved, the procedure was finally widely accepted as a valuable extension of the physical examination.

Schindler was born in Berlin in 1888. He gained considerable experience as an Army physician in World War I, when he became convinced that gastritis, then an often disparaged cause of symptoms, was a bona fide disease. His interest in gastritis was career long and undoubtedly stimulated his interest in gastroscopy. His Wolf-Schindler endoscope and his publications with drawings further enhanced what thereafter rapidly became a discipline. His

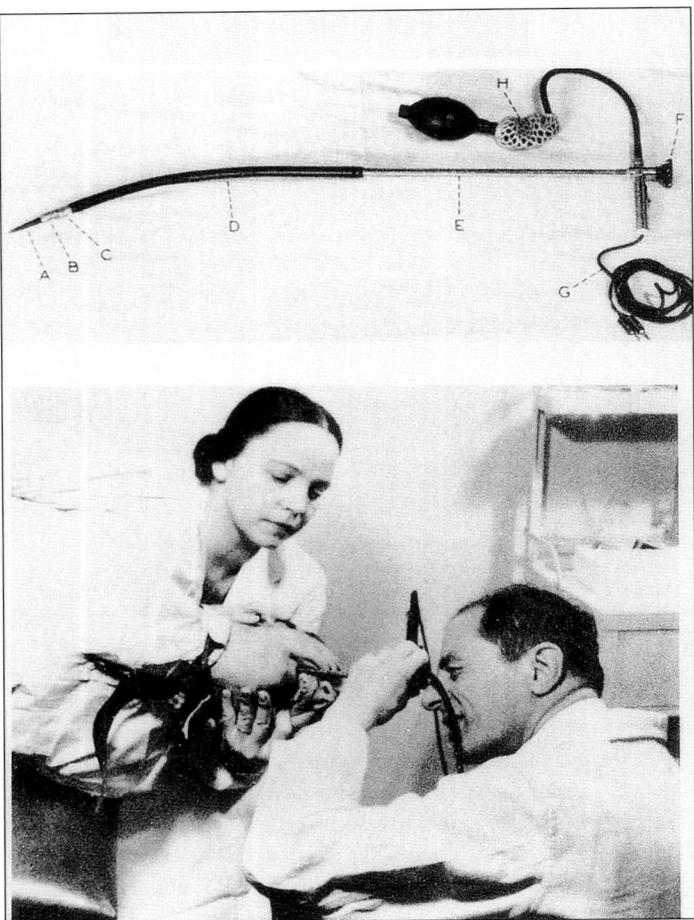

Figure 1-6. Wolf-Schindler "flexible" gastroscope *(top)* being used by Schindler *(bottom)* with his wife as the head holder. (Reproduced from Edmonson JM: History of the instruments for gastrointestinal endoscopy. Gastrointest Endosc 37:S37, 1991.)

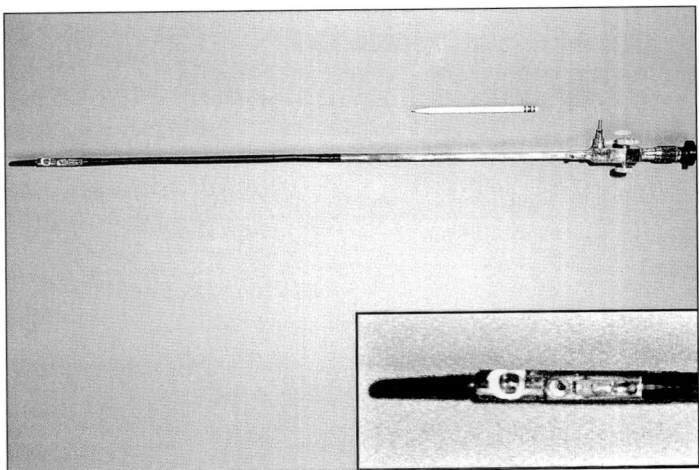

Figure 1-7. The Benedict operating gastroscope. (Personal photograph.)

enthusiasm for and talent in using the gastroscope led to what has been called his "gospel of gastroscopy"; he and others spread this gospel throughout academia and thence to the community of practicing physicians. Because of his Jewish background, he was put in "protective custody" by the Nazis, but with the help of Drs. Marie Ortmeyer and Walter Palmer and philanthropists in Chicago, he was able to immigrate to the United States in 1934.[1–4,7] Chicago became the hub of GI endoscopy, and it was here, in Schindler's home, that the first discussions were held about forming a new organization for GI endoscopy, now known after several name changes as the American Society of Gastrointestinal Endoscopy. In 1943, just 9 years after his emigration, Schindler left Chicago for Loma Linda University. Fifteen years later, in 1958, he accepted an appointment as Professor of Medicine at the University of Minas Gerais in Belo Horizone, Brazil. He returned to the United States in 1960 because of an eventually fatal illness of his wife and emigrated to his native Berlin in 1964 where he died in 1968 at the age of 80.[1] Despite his acclaim in endoscopy, he insisted that one must be a physician first and an endoscopist second. He was very knowledgeable in the field of general gastroenterology and published, without coauthors, a synopsis of the entire field in 1957.[6]

The Wolf-Schindler endoscope was introduced into the United States by Benedict, Borland, and many others. Schindler's emigration to Chicago saw a surge of interest in the United States; however, because of the war in Europe, the German source of instruments disappeared. Several U.S. companies, including the Cameron Company that produced its first instrument in 1940, worked with Schindler and others to produce a number of popular gastroscopes that were significant variations on the Wolf-Schindler.[8] This was followed by the Eder-Hufford semiflexible gastroscope in 1946[9] and by the gastroscope of the American Cystoscope Makers Inc. (ACMI) in 1950. The Eder-Palmer transesophagoscopic flexible gastroscope produced by the Eder Company in 1953 was a combination of the Eder-Hufford esophagoscope with a semiflexible gastroscope to be passed through it. Each, of course, had its proponents.

The era of the semiflexible gastroscope from 1932 to 1957 has been called "the Schindler era." He was chiefly responsible for transforming gastroscopy from a dangerous and seldom used procedure to one that was relatively safe and indispensable for evaluation of known or suspected disease of the stomach. He insisted that all those who planned to use the instrument be properly trained and that ". . . no manipulation inside of the body is without danger; therefore no endoscopic examination should be done without reasonable indication."[6] In today's vernacular, the risk approaches infinity if the benefit approaches zero.

Biopsy

Once instruments were available for visualization, it was apparent that tissue was needed to identify the nature of the observed abnormalities. Initially, instruments for blind biopsies were used, but a device that would allow the operator to directly biopsy abnormal tissue seen at endoscopy was needed. In 1948, the Benedict Operating Gastroscope, based on a 1940 model by Kenamore,[10] made direct biopsy possible (Fig. 1–7). The Benedict instrument, on which I was trained in 1960, was a popular instrument that was widely used. In the debates about the necessity for biopsy, Benedict,

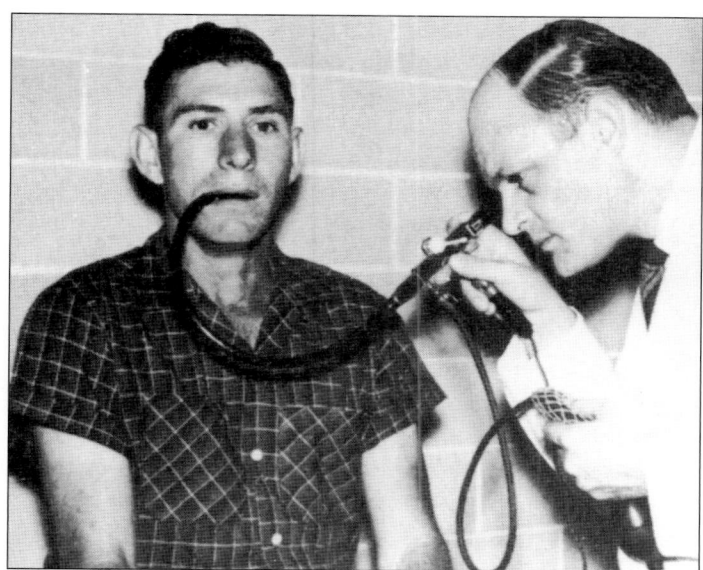

Figure 1–8. Dr. Hirschowitz examining the stomach of an outpatient. (Reproduced from Hirschowitz BI: Endoscopic examination of the stomach and duodenal cap with the fiberscope. Lancet 1:1074–1078, 1961.) (Reprinted with permission from Elsevier.)

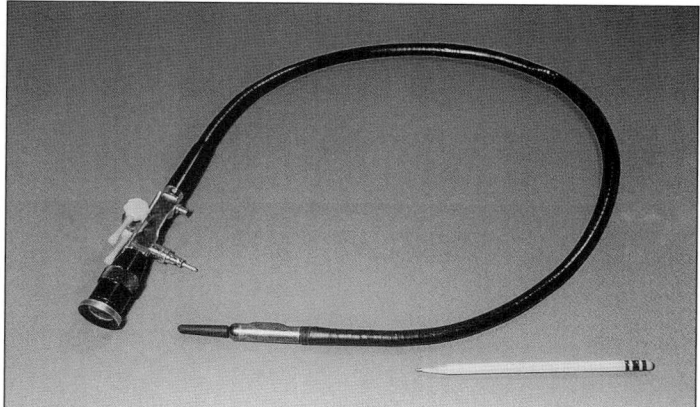

Figure 1–9. ACMI fiberscope, 1962. (Personal photograph.)

originally a surgeon who switched entirely to endoscopy, stated that gastroscopy was not a routine procedure and should be reserved for difficult problems in differential diagnosis but that "gastroscopic examination is not complete unless the gastroscopist has some means of biopsy readily available."[11] It soon became clear that the correlation between histology and a diagnosis based on visualization alone was oftentimes widely discrepant and that certain diagnoses could not be reliably made without tissue examination. Efforts such as wash and brush cytology continued and have persisted in various forms to the present.

Fiberoptics

By the 1950s, the ideal of a totally flexible GI endoscope with good visualization that could withstand the rigors of clinical use had not been realized, although the semiflexible instruments with their biopsy capabilities were satisfactory for most clinical purposes. These instruments were not rapidly abandoned by all with introduction of the remarkably flexible "fiberscope." The development of the science of fiberoptics and its application to endoscopes (scopes) truly revolutionized the diagnostic and, later, the therapeutic abilities of endoscopy. Its importance cannot be overstated in the development of this field. It was and is a marvelous and productive marriage of many areas of technology.

The principle of internal reflection of light along a conduction pathway was used by Heinrich Lamm in October 1930.[1] Unfortunately, the image was severely degraded by light escaping from the thin fibers of quartz that he used, although the potential for total flexibility was clearly present. He could not interest Schindler or others in his efforts, and the experiment was not continued. Almost 25 years later, in 1954, Basil Hirschowitz, in fellowship training at the University of Michigan, visited Hopkins and Kapany in London

to review their work[12] with glass fibers, which totally confirmed the work of Lamm and his predecessors. Dr. Hirschowitz became convinced that application of this principle could be used to develop a totally new and superior endoscope. He began work with a graduate student, Larry Curtiss, who developed a technique of coating glass fibers with glass of a different optical density, thereby preventing the escape of light and degradation of the image. This was the critical discovery that made the principle of internal reflection through glass fibers workable.

In 1957, Hirschowitz demonstrated his fiberscope, and he published his work in 1958[13] (Fig. 1–8). His audience was not very impressed, and it took another 3 years, working with ACMI, to produce a marketable scope, which he called the Hirschowitz Gastroduodenal Fiberscope. This was a very flexible side-viewing instrument with an electric light on its distal end, an air channel, and an adjustable focusing lens proximally. The tip did not have the obligatory rubber finger, and this omission was a source of criticism; one was added on a later model. Although some criticized the quality of the image, most believed its size and brightness was superior to that of the semiflexible scopes. This model, the ACMI 4990, was introduced to the market late in 1960 after being tested by Hirschowitz on himself and a number of patients.

In 1961, I was in gastroenterology fellowship at the Emory University Clinic with Spalding Schroder. I vividly recall his reaction when we first used our new fiberscope in about March 1962 (Fig. 1–9). When he finished our first examination, he turned to me and said, "Anybody want to buy a used Benedict operating scope?" I do not think we used it ever again. The Gastroduodenal Fiberscope was clearly superior in my young view and I finished my training with that instrument.

There were problems with the fiberscope noted by us and by others. The distal light source would become so heated that thermal injury to the gastric mucosa was possible unless the tip was continuously moved. In prolonged procedures protein in gastric secretions would coagulate on the bulb and the adjacent visualizing port, totally obscuring the lens. As the number of procedures with a single instrument increased, some glass fibers would break, producing small black dots in the visual field. This was a persistent problem with fiberscopes during their entire history and especially apparent in training programs where a single scope was used by

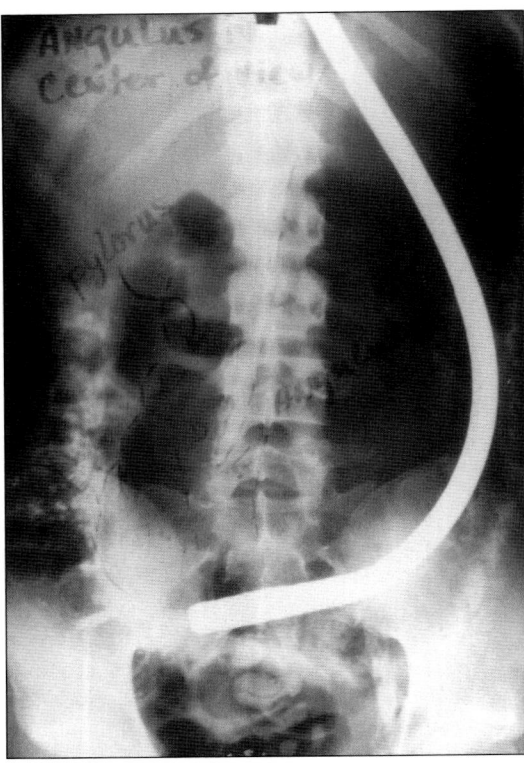

Figure 1-10. Visualization of the duodenum was sometimes obtained by overinflating the stomach. (Personal photograph.)

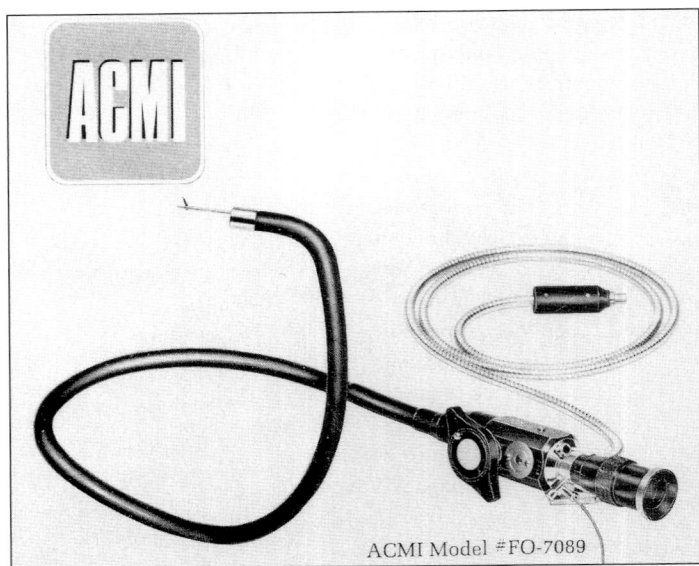

ACMI Model #FO-7089

Figure 1-11. The LoPresti forward-viewing esophago-gastroscope. (From advertisement in Gastrointest Endosc 16:79, 1970.)

several trainees on many patients. The side-viewing lens prevented visualization of the esophagus, and the scope had to be passed blindly through the pharyngeal orifice. This problem was also common with the previous semiflexible scopes in use and was not considered a defect at the time. The flexibility itself resulted in some difficulty in advancing, because attempts to push the instrument through the pylorus and into the gut simply resulted in more bowing in the gastric pouch (Fig. 1–10). Although one could sometimes visualize the duodenum, this was done by overinflating the stomach and thereby looking through the pylorus without actually entering it. If one managed to introduce the tip into the duodenum, as occasionally happened, the visual field was inside the focal length of the instrument and only a "red-out" was observed. Others had similar complaints.[4] Many did not believe that the additional expense of replacing the older, beloved instruments with which they had been successful for many years was warranted. Even ACMI officials did not see the fiberscope as totally replacing those instruments with lens systems.[2] Despite reservations, comparison and experiential studies demonstrated the advantages of the new fiberscopes.[14–17] Following the flagship ACMI model 4990, several models of the fiberscope were introduced by several companies, each with significant improvements including the controllable tip in the side-viewing ACMI model 5004. Visualization of the gastric pouch, including retroflexed views of the cardia, was complete.

The major objections to these instruments were the inability to pass the instrument under direct vision and to examine the esophagus; in addition, we could not consistently examine the area beyond the pylorus. Most of us were already fully trained in the use of the Eder-Hufford esophagoscope and, in the absence of a forward-

viewing fiberscope, we continued to use it. A forward-viewing scope was mandatory. Phillip A. LoPresti modified the tip to of the fiberscope to create the Foroblique fiberoptic esophagoscope in 1964.[18] It was possible to pass the instrument under direct vision, and we immediately discovered that we could not only examine the esophagus but also examine a large portion of the proximal stomach as well. At a length of 90 cm, however, we could not reach the duodenum. LoPresti, working with ACMI, produced the longer "Panview Mark '87' Gastro-Esophageal Endoscope" in 1970. By about 1971, the instrument had been lengthened to 105 cm with a four-way controllable tip capable of 180 degrees deflection (Fig. 1–11). The aptly labeled "panendoscope" was now a reality. Japanese and American manufacturers began to produce new models with such rapidity that endoscopists hardly had time to become thoroughly familiar with one before another, significantly improved (and more expensive), model was on the market. Patient comfort was greatly improved, and the relative safety of the fiberoptic endoscopes rapidly became apparent. By 1970, most gastroscopic examinations were done with fiberscopes. The development of a "teaching head" fiberoptic bundle with a light splitter and attached eyepiece, and attachment to the eyepiece of the scope, allowed two people to visualize the image. Dividing the light from the endoscope, however, considerably diminished the brightness of the image to both the operator and the observer. This device saw limited use and was used primarily in teaching institutions.

Endoscopic Retrograde Cholangiopancreatography

With access to the duodenum, the ampulla of Vater became visible. It followed that one should be able to inject contrast material into the bile and pancreatic ducts and increase diagnostic capabilities.

Initial attempts in 1968 by McCune and associates to modify an existing scope were only partially successful,[19] but these attempts did demonstrate that endoscopic visualization by injection of radiologic contrast agents into ducts was possible. In 1970, Machida and Olympus in Japan produced usable, side-viewing scopes with controllable tips and elevators to move the injection tube to the ampulla. Japanese endoscopists[20] developed the technique of endoscopic retrograde cholangiopancreatography (ERCP) with an 80% success rate. Vennes and Silvis[21] showed its utility in the United States and taught many physicians to use it.[4]

It was immediately apparent that if one could visualize the biliary and pancreatic ducts endoscopically (i.e., nonsurgically), one should by some means be able to apply long-established surgical techniques for treatment of choledocholithiasis and pancreatitis, such as sphincterotomy and stone removal. In 1974, just 4 years after the demonstration of the diagnostic utility of the new ERCP scopes, Kawai and colleagues[22] from Japan and Classen and Demling[23] in Germany independently developed methods of endoscopic electrosurgical sphincterotomy for extraction of biliary calculi in the common duct. Because this procedure requires great skill, Geenen[24] reported that in 1976, only 62 operative procedures had been done by 4 endoscopists and that 7 of these were failures. In 1983, Schuman[4] reported that several thousands of patients had undergone the procedure, and, by now, hundreds of thousands have been done. ERCP is now seldom used for purely diagnostic purposes; that need is being replaced by advanced radiologic techniques.

Photography

It is one thing to describe to others what one may see through any device and quite another to be able to show them. Certainly, the large impact of Schindler's early publications lay, in part, with the excellent color drawings he presented. Early on, however, neither cameras nor photographic films were so advanced as to allow good color reproduction or accurately sharp images in relatively poor lighting. Such documentation is essential for widespread appreciation of endoscopy by those who do not actually perform the procedure.

The first clinically useful photography came with improvements in film by Kodak and the construction of an external integrated camera by Segal and Watson in 1948.[25,26] Although the authors reported that some 61% of the images were of good quality, this was not the experience of all.[4] Although an intragastric camera was developed in 1848 by Lange and Meltzung, a clinically useful device was not available until 1950 when Uji, Sugiura, and Fukami, working with Olympus Corp.,[27] developed the Gastrocamera with synchronized flash that took good intragastric pictures and had a controllable distal portion. By following a prescribed pattern of rotation and flexion, a series of pictures were obtained that included the entire surface of the stomach. Its big disadvantage was that the operator could not see through the instrument and had to await development of the very narrow (5 mm) film before the results could be seen. Photographs for demonstration required additional time in the photo laboratory while enlargements were made. With the introduction of fiberoptic scopes in 1961 Olympus introduced a combination Gastrocamera fiberscope (GTF-A) in 1964, but, as reflected by Shuman,[4] "it was *just* a gastroscope" and never became

very popular. Simultaneously, rapid development and physician acceptance of fiberscopes with the ability to use technically advanced 35-mm cameras with an external adaptor made the Gastrocamera obsolete and it was abandoned.

Sigmoidoscopy and Colonoscopy

The problems presented by examination of the anus and rectum was relatively easy. Straight metal tubes were used and found in the ruins of Pompeii.[2] The basic design of the anoscope has not changed in the past century or more except that it is now made of disposable plastic. It still is a tapering short tube with an obturator that is removed after introduction through the anal sphincter.

Examination of the rectum and sigmoid required a longer tube, but no truly satisfactory device was available until 1894 when Howard A. Kelly of Johns Hopkins developed a 30-cm rigid tube with light reflected down the tube from a head lamp.[28] Tuttle incorporated a distal light source in his proctosigmoidoscope of 25 cm in 1903,[29] and these instruments have remained the basic design for the past 100 years. Within the past 15 years, disposable clear plastic tubes have been widely used. These are essentially a plastic version of the Kelly and Tuttle tubes with a distal electric light source, but they do allow visualization through the clear plastic. With the application of fiberoptics to sigmoidoscopy in the late 1960s, examination of the sigmoid colon became not only satisfactory but much more comfortable to the patient. In 1968, Bergin Overholt, who later went on to be the principal developer of colonoscopy using similar technology, presented his results of flexible sigmoidoscopy in 250 patients.[30] Although early flexible sigmoidoscopes were made in variable lengths, the current 60-cm length became the preferred one.

Examination of the colon above the sigmoid presents obvious additional problems of multiple curves and angulations amenable only to highly flexible instruments and trained operators. Certainly attempts using semiflexible instruments, all unsuccessful, were made and are reviewed by Edmondson.[2] It was not until the introduction of the flexible fiberscope that satisfactory examination of the length of the colon was possible. Attempts to use forward-viewing gastroscopes were not technically satisfactory, although several tried, including me. Turell presented his attempts in 1967 using a modified gastroscope, but he concluded that the instrument was not ready for routine clinical use.[31] By 1970, however, several manufacturers produced instruments specifically designed for colonoscopy, including ACMI, working with Gene Overholt in the United States, and Olympus Corp. in Japan. The primary problem with regularly accomplishing complete examinations to the cecum was not the instruments as much as the techniques necessary for passage of the scopes into the more proximal portions of the colon. Earlier pioneers in developing successful techniques still in use include Overholt, Wolf, Shinya, and Jerry Waye in the United States; Niwa and his colleagues in Japan; Salmon and Williams in England; Dehyle in Germany; and others.[4] Many of these early efforts were done with the guidance of fluoroscopy to negotiate the more difficult turns and to identify the actual area being observed, but, as experience was gained, fluoroscopy was no longer required. Learning under expert guidance and experience continues to be

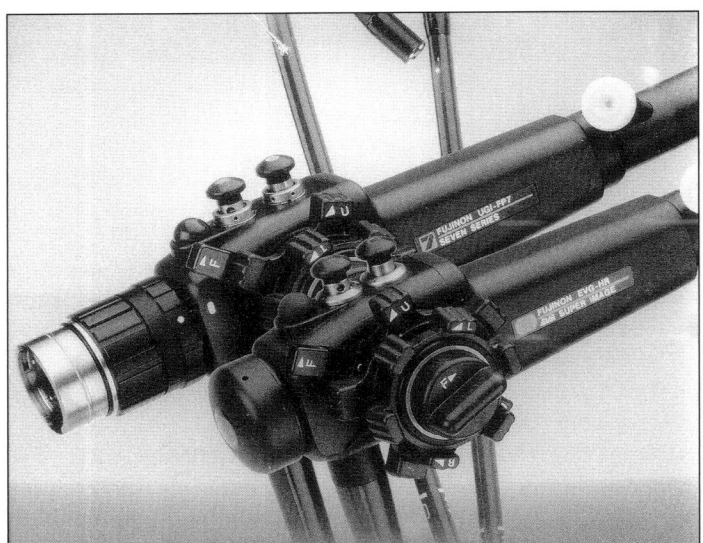

Figure 1–12. The Fujinon fiber optic panendoscope *(top)* and its successor, the Videopanendoscope *(bottom),* 1990, showing the two kinds of operating heads. (From advertisement in Gastrointest Endosc 36:240–241, 1990.)

more necessary in colonoscopy (and ERCP) than in upper endoscopy. By 1971, the diagnostic advantage of fiberoptic colonoscopy over single-contrast barium enema was firmly established,[32] and, by 1973, the efficacy and safety of polypectomy was established.[33]

Digital Endoscopy (Video Endoscopy)

In 1984, barely 20 years after introduction of the endoscopic fiberscope, Welch Allyn Inc. replaced the coherent fiberoptic image bundle in a colonoscope with a light-sensitive computer chip or charge-coupled device on which the image was focused by a small lens (see Chapter 3).[34] The digital signal was fed to a video processor that generated an image to a television monitor. The image did not occupy the entire screen, leaving space for information to be typed in by a keyboard. The resolution of the image was equal to that of the fiberscope. It was not necessary to change the basic mechanics of the fiberscope. The fiberoptic light bundle remained unchanged as did water, suction, and biopsy channels, and the deflection and locking mechanisms were not different. The basic elements of the videoendoscope have not changed, although a magnified image is now available. Since the original introduction by Welch Allyn, which no longer produces the VideoEndoscope, the market has been dominated by Olympus Corp., Fujinon, and Pentax. The technology was rapidly adapted to all endoscopes, both those used in gastroenterology and in other fields.

Advantages of the electronic instruments include an image that can be seen not only by the operator but also by anyone with access to a connected monitor in the same or another room. This feature greatly enhances the ability to teach others about the procedure and to inform other interested physicians about the findings in the individual patient. If desired, recording of procedures can be accomplished with videotape machines, and pictures of good quality of individual frames can be immediately made with externally integrated digital equipment. Individual endoscopists found that no adjustment of techniques was necessary when videoendoscopes were used, although they had to become accustomed to looking at the monitor screen rather than through an optical system with one eye (Fig. 1–12). This feature actually added to the useful length of the instrument because the whole scope could be held at the waist rather that brought to eye level. Recent innovations in colonoscopy instruments by Olympus include the ability to make a portion less flexible to facilitate navigation of difficult bends and turns. In addition, an enlarged image is now available that is an improvement in both vision and ease of manipulation.

A major disadvantage of videoendoscopes is one of cost. Whereas fiberoptic endoscopes, when they were still in use, could be purchased for less than $6000 and did not require processors or monitors, the latest videoendoscopes are priced over $20,000 and initial purchase of the entire package of endoscope, processing computer, monitors, and attachments may exceed $30,000. Initially, many questioned the wisdom of this added cost, which, of course, is passed on to the patient and the insurance companies.

Endoscopic Ultrasonography

Although the improvements in GI endoscopy are remarkable in the synthesis of diverse but complementary technologies, the information gained remains confined to what one can see from within the lumen of the gut. Simultaneous with these developments were those of computed tomography and external ultrasonographic tomograms. Conceptually, it was not only logical but compelling to look beneath the mucosa of the gut by incorporating into GI endoscopes miniaturized models of ultrasonographic transducers already in use. The ability to noninvasively explore tissue and organs in proximity to the gut obviously had exciting implications for diagnosis and therapy.

In 1976, in Germany, Lutz and Rosch,[35] working with Siemens Co., reported the use of a 1-cm ultrasonographic 4-MHz probe that could be passed through the biopsy channel of an Olympus TGF. They used it in two patients to successfully differentiate between pancreatic pseudocysts and tumors.[7] In 1980, two other groups developed endoscopic ultrasonography (EUS) devices that were incorporated onto the tip of conventional fiberscopes, one using a 5-MHz and the other a 10-MHz transducer.[36,37] These probes had good resolution at an acoustical focus depth of 3 cm. Others incorporated the transducer in the distal shaft of fiberoptic scopes and explored primarily the gut wall.[33,38] By 1985, ultrasonic transducers with variable frequencies incorporated into videoendoscopes were readily available, although expensive (over $100,000 for initial setup) (Fig. 1–13). It was immediately apparent that this procedure could accurately evaluate known or suspected intramural lesions of the gut,[39,40] and the procedure was rapidly expanded to include the esophagus; problems of diagnosis and recurrence of neoplasia, especially in the pancreas; portal hypertension; the colon and rectum; and bile ducts.[41] In 1991, Wiersema and his colleagues[42,43] demonstrated that EUS could be used to obtain fine needle aspiration cytology of mediastinal nodes and of nodes and lesions of the upper and lower GI tract. The addition of Doppler technology has now made possible the study of the flow through various channels, including the thoracic duct and blood vessel anastomosis.

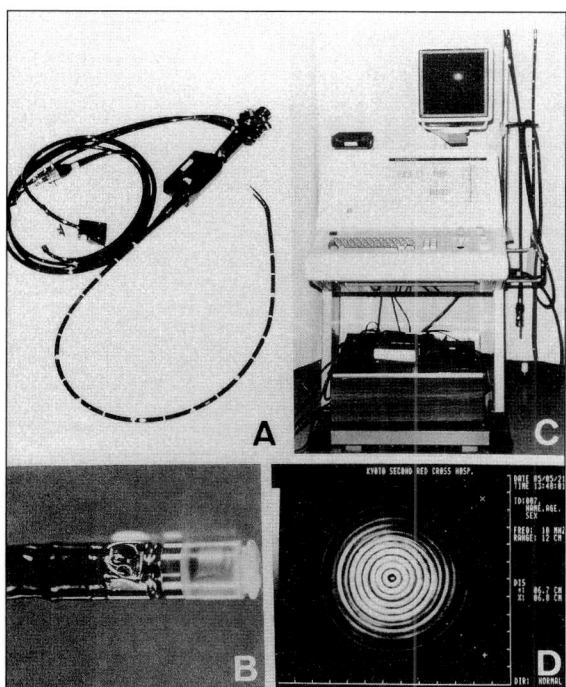

Figure 1-13. Ultrasonic endoscope system, model IV, made by Olympus Corp., 1986. (Reproduced from Yasuda K, Mukai H, Fujimoto S, et al: The diagnosis of pancreatic cancer by endoscopic ultrasonography. Gastrointest Endosc 34:1–8, 1988.)

The technique of using EUS instruments differs only slightly from using videoendoscopes, but prolonged training is necessary to accurately interpret the sonographic images obtained. EUS is not amenable to self-instruction. EUS training centers have been established in academic centers, but retraining of practicing physicians is a problem.[44]

Capsule Endoscopy (Wireless Endoscopy)

In 2000, Iddan and coworkers[45] reported the development of a capsule containing a tiny complementary metal oxide silicon (CMOS) camera that could be swallowed, take video (but slowed to 2 frames per second), and transmit them over 7 hours to a receiving digital storage unit worn by the patient as he or she goes about normal activities. These frames are then downloaded to a computer from which they are projected onto a monitor at a rate that can be controlled by the observer. Pictures of areas of interest can then be printed. Gastroenterologists in Israel conducted randomized trials comparing the efficacy of the wireless capsule with the efficacy of push enteroscopy and demonstrated superior results with the capsule.[46–48] Wireless capsule endoscopy has caught the imagination of gastroenterologists worldwide, and, in the past 2 years, a plethora of abstracts have been submitted to meetings. The findings are virtually unanimous in reporting better results in identifying lesions in the small bowel.[49] The capsule avoids the discomfort and need for sedation inherent in push enteroscopy. In addition to lack of biopsy

capability, a major disadvantage is the reported 1–2 hours of review time necessary, but this will certainly be overcome by training of nonphysician personnel to screen the multiple images produced. Although the major use of the capsule has been in elucidating the cause of occult bleeding from small bowel sources, where it appears superior to other methods, its future in other diseases, such as those in the colon, has already been indicated by studies largely reported by abstracts only. Its future is bright. It will be interesting to see how the principle of wireless endoscopy is married to videoendoscopes with direct wireless connection between the camera and the computer processor. For additional information, see also Chapter 3.

Summary

The development of endoscopy is a fascinating testimony to the ingenuity of humans. Instruments have evolved from dangerous straight tubes illuminated by light reflected from candles, through those somewhat flexible and safer instruments with an image transmitted through a series of prism lenses and illumination by an electric light bulb, to images transmitted through fiberoptic bundles with illumination transmitted by fiber bundles from an external source, to the present remarkably safe electronic instruments with digital images transmitted to a video screen through wires and processed by computers. Most recently, one can visualize the lumen of the gut without touching the patient. One can now not only visualize, biopsy tissue, and perform surgical procedures within the hidden cavities of the body but also indirectly see beneath the mucosa and into immediately adjacent organs. This is really a remarkable story and it ain't over yet!

To know and understand what has come before lends strength to efforts toward what is to be.

REFERENCES

1. Modlin IM: A Brief History of Endoscopy. Milano, Italy, MultiMed, 2000.
2. Edmonson JM: History of the instruments for gastrointestinal endoscopy. Gastrointest Endosc 37:S27–S56, 1991.
3. Haubrich WS: Gastrointestinal endoscopy. In Kirsner JB (ed): The Growth of Gastroenterologic Knowledge during the Twentieth Century. Philadelphia, Lea & Febiger, 1994, pp 474–490.
4. Schuman B: The development of the endoscope. In DiMarino Jr AJ, Benjamin SB (eds): Gastrointestinal Disease. An Endoscopic Approach, Volume I. Malden, MA, Blackwell Science, 1997, pp 9–24.
5. Schindler R: Gastroscopy. The Endoscopic Study of Gastric Pathology. Chicago, University of Chicago Press, 1950.
6. Schindler R: Synopsis of Gastroenterology. Philadelphia, Grune & Stratton, 1957.
7. Kirsner JB: American gastroscopy—Yesterday and today. Gastrointest Endosc 37:643–648, 1991.
8. Schindler R: An American built gastroscope. Am J Dig Dis 7:256–257, 1940.
9. Hufford AR: A new light weight, extra flexible gastroscope. Rev Gastroenterol 13:381–383, 1946.
10. Kenamore B: A biopsy forceps for the flexible gastroscope. Am J Dig Dis 7:539, 1940.
11. Benedict EB: Gastroscopic biopsy. Gastroenterology 37:447–448, 1959.

12. Hopkins HH, Kapany NS: A flexible fiberscope using static scanning. Nature 173:39–41, 1954.

13. Hirschowitz BI, Curtiss LE, Pollard HM: Demonstration of the new gastroscope, the "fiberscope." Gastroenterology 35:50–53, 1958.

14. Weisinger BB, Cramer AB, Zacharis LC: Comparative accuracy of the fiberscope and standard gastroscope in the diagnosis of gastric lesions: Preliminary report. Gastroenterology 44:858A, 1963.

15. Burnett W: An evaluation of the gastroduodenal fibrescope. Gut 3:361–365, 1962.

16. Cohen NN, Hughes RW, Manfredo HE: Experience with 1000 fibergastroscopic examinations of the stomach. Am J Dig Dis 11:943–950, 1966.

17. Paulson M, Gladsden ES: Esophagoscopy, gastroscopy, gastroenteroscopy, and proctosigmoidoscopy. In Moses Paulson M (ed): Gastroenterologic Medicine. Philadelphia, Lea & Febiger, 1969, pp 217–258.

18. LoPresti PA, Hilmi AM: Clinical experience with a new Foroblique fiber optic esophagoscope. Am J Dig Dis 9:690–697, 1964.

19. McCune WS, Shorb PE, Moscovitz H: Endoscopic cannulation of the ampulla of Vater: A preliminary report. Ann Surg 167:753–755, 1968.

20. Takagi K, Ikeda S, Nakagawa Y, Sakaguchi N, et al: Retrograde pancreatography and cholangiography by fiber duodenoscope. Gastroenterology 59:445–452, 1970.

21. Vennes JA, Silvis SE: Endoscopic visualization of bile and pancreatic ducts. Gastrointest Endosc 18:149–152, 1972.

22. Kawai K, Akasaka Y, Murakami K, et al: Endoscopic sphincterotomy of the ampulla of Vater. Gastrointest Endosc 20:148–151, 1974.

23. Classen M, Demling L: Endoskopische sphinckterotomie der papilla Vateri und steinextraktion aus dem ductus choledochus. Dtsch med Wochenschr 99:496–497, 1974.

24. Geenen JE: Endoscopic papillotomy. In Demling L, Classen M (eds): Endoscopic Sphincterotomy of the Papilla of Vater. Stuttgart, Germany, Georg Thieme, 1978.

25. Segal HL, Watson JS: Color photography through the flexible gastroscope. Gstroenterology 10:575–585, 1948.

26. Modlin IM: ibid, p 90.

27. Ashizawa S, Sakai Y: Gastrocamera; Its past and future. In Berry HL (ed): Gastrointestinal Panendoscopy. Springfield, IL, Charles C. Thomas, 1974, pp 223229.

28. Kelly HA: A new method of examination and treatment of diseases of the rectum and sigmoid flexure. Ann Surg 21:468–478, 1895.

29. Tuttle JP: A Treatise on Diseases of the Anus, Rectum, and Pelvic Colon. New York, Appleton and Co., 1903.

30. Overholt B: Flexible fiberoptic sigmoidoscopes. Cancer 19:80–84, 1969.

31. Turell R: Fiber optic sigmoidoscopes: Up to date developments. Am J Surg 113:305–307, 1967.

32. Wolff WI, Shinya H: Colonofiberoscopy. JAMA 217:1509–1512, 1971.

33. Wolff WI, Shinya H: Polypectomy via the fiberoptic colonoscope. Removal of neoplasms beyond the reach of the sigmoidoscope. N Engl J Med 288:329–332, 1973.

34. Sivak Jr MV, Fleischer DE: Colonoscopy with a VideoEndoscope: Preliminary experience. Gastrointest Endosc 30:1–5, 1984.

35. Lutz H, Rosch W: Transgastroscopic ultrasonography. Endoscopy 8:203–205, 1976.

36. Strohm WD, Phillip J, Hagenmuller F, Classen M: Ultrasonic tomography by means of an ultrasonic fiberendoscope. Endoscopy 12:241–244, 1980.

37. DiMagno EP, Buxton JL, Regan PT, et al: Ultrasonic endoscope. Lancet 1:629–631, 1980.

38. Gordon SJ, Rifkin B, Goldberg RB: Endoscopic evaluation of mural abnormalities of the upper gastrointestinal tract. Gastrointest Endosc 32:193–198, 1986.

39. Kawai K, Tanaka Y, Yasuda K: Clinical evaluation of endoscopic ultrasonography (EUS). Gastrointest Endosc 29:183A, 1983.

40. Sivak MV, George C: Endoscopic ultrasonography. Preliminary experience. Gastrointest Endosc 29:187A, 1983.

41. Symposium. Endoscopic ultrasonography. Gastrointest Endosc 36:S1–S46, 1990.

42. Wiersema MJ, Hawes RH, Wiersema LM, et al: Endoscopic ultrasonography as an adjunct to fine needle aspiration cytology of the upper and lower gastrointestinal tract. Gastrointest Endosc 38:35–39, 1992.

43. Rex RK, Tarver RD, Wiersema M, et al: Endoscopic transesophageal fine needle aspiration of mediastinal masses. Gastrointest Endosc 37:465–468, 1991.

44. Hoffman BJ, Hawes RH: Endoscopic ultrasound and clinical competence. Gastrointest Endosc Clin N Am 5:879–884, 1995.

45. Iddan G, Meron G, Glukhovsky A, et al: Wireless capsule endoscopy. Nature 405:417, 2000.

46. Appleyard M, Fireman Z, Glukhovsky A, et al: A randomized trial comparing wireless-capsule endoscopy with push enteroscopy for detection of small bowel lesions. Gastroenterology 119:1431–1438, 2000.

47. Appleyard M, Klukhovsky A, Swain P, Akasaka Y: Wireless-capsule diagnostic endoscopy for recurrent small-bowel bleeding. N Engl J Med 344:232–233, 2001.

48. Scapa E, Jacob H., Lewkowicz S, et al: Initial experience of wireless-capsule endoscopy for evaluating occult gastrointestinal bleeding and suspected small bowel pathology. Am J Gastroenterol 97:2776–2779, 2002.

49. Ell C, Remke S, May A, et al: The first prospective controlled trial comparing wireless capsule endoscopy with push enteroscopy in chronic gastrointestinal bleeding. Endoscopy 34:685–689, 2002.

Setting Up an Endoscopy Facility

James T. Frakes

Introduction

Safe and efficient performance of gastrointestinal endoscopy has the following requirements[1]:

- A properly trained endoscopist[2] with appropriate privileges to perform specific gastrointestinal endoscopic procedures[3]
- Properly trained nursing and ancillary personnel
- Operational, well-maintained equipment
- Adequately designed and equipped space for patient preparation, performance of procedures, and patient recovery
- Cleaning areas for reprocessing endoscopes and accessories
- Trained personnel and appropriate equipment to perform cardiopulmonary resuscitation
- A robust quality improvement assurance program[4,5]

Many of the aforementioned requirements for safe and efficient gastrointestinal endoscopy depend on the careful development of endoscopy areas, specifically the setting up or planning and design of an endoscopy facility. This chapter describes that process, beginning with laying the groundwork, including the development of a business plan and review of regulatory issues; site selection; facility planning and design, including patient flow and space needs; equipment requirements; staffing needs; and scheduling considerations.

Some additional issues such as endoscope cleaning and storage, tissue specimen processing and handling, recordkeeping and documentation, and quality assurance and improvement are discussed briefly but are covered in more detail in subsequent chapters of this book (see Chapters 4, 5, 7–9, 12).

Exploring Possibilities

TYPE OF FACILITY

There are numerous types of endoscopy facilities, including hospital endoscopy units, single- or multispecialty ambulatory surgery centers (ASCs), and office endoscopy suites. Each model has its unique set of advantages, disadvantages, and regulatory issues. The hospital and ASC environments are highly regulated by state and federal agencies and by third party accreditation bodies such as the Joint Commission on Accreditation of Healthcare Organizations (JCAHO), the Accreditation Association for Ambulatory Healthcare (AAAHC), and the American Association for Accreditation of Ambulatory Surgery Facilities (AAAASF). Private payers sometimes impose their own specific regulations. Office endoscopy suites, previously less regulated, have been subjected to more controls by state and federal agencies in recent years.

The decision regarding which type of facility to pursue is affected by the practice environment (solo practitioner, small or large group, single- or multispecialty group, independent or hospital-based) and local economics and politics. Regardless of the service location, high quality must be maintained. The American Society for Gastrointestinal Endoscopy (ASGE) has stated that the "standards for out-of-hospital endoscopic practice should be identical to those recognized guidelines followed in the hospital."

The hospital-based unit poses the fewest financial risks and demands for the endoscopist during the early phases of operation, and its use avoids alienating hospital administration by preserving hospital case volume. However, it affords the endoscopist little control over operations and offers him or her the lowest total financial return. Office endoscopy offers control and convenience with better financial return for the physician but poses some safety and liability concerns.[6] The single-specialty endoscopic ambulatory surgery center (EASC) provides the best of control, efficiency, convenience, and reimbursement for the physician owners and is extremely popular with patients, referring doctors, and payers.[7]

Irrespective of the type of facility to develop, formulating a business plan and understanding various regulatory issues are usually the first steps in the process.

BUSINESS PLAN

The decision to set up an endoscopy facility should occur only after detailed data gathering and the formulation of a business plan (market analysis, financial pro forma, implementation time line, etc.).[8,9] For a hospital-based unit or academic medical center, facility planners and accountants often perform these functions. For an office-based suite or an EASC, the tasks will fall to the physician owners, aided by numerous consultants, contractors, or corporate partners. Even with skilled help, however, development of an accurate and reliable business plan and pro forma are highly dependent on physician estimates, insights, and work habits. Physician input into the business plan makes the difference between a perfunctory exercise and an accurate predictor of future performance.

Endoscopy facilities represent small- to medium-sized investments requiring substantial financial resources and staff. Procedure volume must be sufficient to produce adequate revenue to cover the costs of building and running the facility and to generate a profit on investment. In general, three or four busy endoscopists performing 1200 to 1800 total procedures per year are required to offset the financial risk of the facility.[10]

Many factors influence the financial performance of an endoscopy facility. These include initial investment, expected volumes of service, revenue per unit of service, fixed operating costs, and variable costs per unit of service. The initial investment includes the cost of construction, equipment, and working capital for the first few months of operation. Strategic planning is important to anticipate group growth and demand for services in the coming 5 to 10 years.[9] The impact of managed care plans or other major health plans on the practice must also be anticipated. In addition, competition, new technology, population changes, and demographics might also affect case volume for the practice and the endoscopy facility.

A pro forma is a calculation examining the financial feasibility of a project based on anticipated investment and operating costs and revenues. The purpose of the pro forma is to reliably predict cash flows and profitability for the project. Initial investment costs have been defined previously. Also incorporated in the pro forma are estimated total costs per case based on estimated fixed and variable costs and expected case volume. Fixed costs are those that remain constant regardless of the number of procedures performed and include rent, interest, depreciation, taxes, insurance, amortization, and management fees. Variable costs, which account for the largest component of the average cost per case, include salaries and benefits, medical supplies, medications, equipment, maintenance and repair, administrative supplies, utilities, and accounting and legal fees. Break-even volumes can be determined by subtracting the variable expense per procedure from the average payment per procedure to indicate the contribution available to be used for overhead and profit. Dividing fixed costs by the contribution margin per procedure indicates the number of procedures needed to pay the fixed costs, also known as the break-even point. Additional service units above that level constitute profit. A simple example of a pro forma is provided by Fisk.[8]

The business plan and pro forma are mandatory in assessing the financial feasibility of the proposed endoscopy unit before construction. They further aid discussions in obtaining financing, and help the architect design the unit for anticipated volumes.

Regulatory and Certification Issues

Before planning and designing the facility, one must understand the relevant regulatory and certification issues. As with the business plan, units developed in a hospital or academic medical center usually benefit from administrators and planners familiar with these complex issues. However, physician owners of the office endoscopy suite or EASC must gain their own understanding.

A variety of agencies provide a myriad of rules and regulations concerning endoscopy facilities.[11-15] Legislation can come from federal, state, or local authorities. Regulations may come from federal agencies, state departments of health, and even third party accreditation organizations and private payers. Although these rules and regulations can seem excessive and needlessly costly, their intent is to ensure safe and successful outcomes for patients.

Regulations and certification issues for endoscopy facilities can be divided into six main categories including the following[11]:

- General federal regulatory laws and rules
- Facility state licensure
- Medicare certification
- Third party accreditation
- Physician credentialing
- Private payer requirements

GENERAL FEDERAL HEALTH-RELATED LAWS

Federal regulatory laws and rules include Fraud and Abuse Statutes (also known as anti-kickback laws), laws designed to prevent excessive or inappropriate payments. Endoscopy centers typically fall into a specific "safe harbor," a designation that protects EASC investors or shareholders from allegations of fraud or abuse. The safe harbor applies if the physician participants are surgeons or specialists engaged in the same surgical or medical practice specialty, including gastroenterology. These physicians can refer patients directly to their center and perform procedures on them as an extension of and significant part of their practices. Additional requirements of the safe harbor apply. Ownership of the facility, or remuneration from it, cannot be related to volume of referrals, services furnished, or the amount of business otherwise generated from that physician to the EASC. The amount of payment to physician owners from facility revenues must be directly proportional to the amount of each owner's capital investment. There must be no requirement that a passive investor make referrals to the EASC nor can the EASC or any investor make loans or guarantee a loan for a physician, if these funds are used to purchase ownership in the EASC. Furthermore, each physician must agree to treat Medicare and Medicaid patients. Finally, the physician owner must derive at least one third of his or her medical practice income from the performance of procedures that require an EASC or hospital endoscopy unit setting.

Other general federal health-related laws and rules relevant to endoscopy facilities include the False Claims Act and copayment waivers, Stark provisions, Health Insurance Portability and Accountability Act (HIPAA) provisions, and labor and employment issues.

The False Claims Act was designed to prevent false billings, claims that are medically unnecessary, and billings for inappropriately high payment. Copayment or deductible waivers may also be illegal if the government suspects such waivers are likely to induce referrals.

Stark provisions stem from the Ethics in Patients Referrals Act. They are closely related to fraud and abuse statutes but are civil rather than criminal laws. The regulatory body overseeing Medicare has ruled that a physician does not make an illegal referral for a procedure when he or she either personally performs the service or refers a patient to a partner to perform the service.

HIPAA provisions are rules and regulations covering patient health information disclosed by any covered health care entity, provider, or facility. Regarding labor and employment issues, numerous rules and regulations cover discrimination, harassment, protection of the disabled, and workplace safety. The Occupational Health and Safety Act (OSHA) of 1970 seeks to protect employees from recognized work hazards that might cause death or serious harm. For endoscopy centers, the OSHA requirements of major importance cover cleaning of endoscopic equipment, disinfection, and appropriate ventilation.

STATE LICENSURE

The state department of health licensing authority is interested in several features of a potential endoscopy facility. First and foremost, before any design and construction is undertaken, a careful review of the state's certificate of need (CON) requirements is needed. Some states will not allow construction of new facilities unless need is demonstrated. This process can be difficult, and prospective physician owners of endoscopy facilities may encounter opposition from hospitals, fearing competition and seeking to maximize use of their own facilities. Regarding specific construction guidelines, state regulators are most often interested in the flow of the facility, cleanliness, and control of infection within the procedure areas. Many states have adopted specific room sizes, acoustic regulations, door and hall size requirements, handicapped access provisions, requirements for exhaust systems, and specific fire codes. The state fire marshal will be concerned with emergency exits. Building codes from the National Fire Protection Association generally apply to endoscopy facilities built as new centers or as centers built in existing buildings. Many states also follow guidelines from the American Institute of Architects and the US Department of Health for design and construction of health care facilities.

MEDICARE CERTIFICATION

Medicare certification is usually sought after obtaining state licensure and is required for any facility seeking reimbursement for Medicare and Medicaid work. Medicare regulations and requirements are usually more extensive than those of the state and address governance of the facility, transfer agreements with a nearby hospital, continuous quality improvement activities, Medicare architectural requirements, and medical records. Additional standards concern organization and staffing, administration of drugs, and procurement of laboratory and radiology services. Two other requirements demand special attention as they relate to EASCs. First, the facility must be used exclusively for providing "surgical" services, a definition that includes most gastrointestinal endoscopies. This mandates a separation from other health care activities, separate staffing, and maintenance of special medical and financial records. Finally, the facility must comply with state licensure laws,[13] potentially difficult in some states because of restrictive CON requirements.

THIRD PARTY ACCREDITATION

After state licensure and Medicare certification have been obtained, some states or specific payers may require a third party accreditation before authorizing payments to an endoscopy facility. This can be provided by inspection from JCAHO, AAAHC, or AAAASF. Although these accreditations are typically achieved after state licensure, sometimes they can be pursued simultaneously with Medicare inspection. Under certain circumstances, Medicare will accept accreditation from one of the third party accreditors in lieu of its own survey. This is known as attaining "deemed status," and it obviates an additional inspection.

These third party accreditations focus on patient-related and organizational functions and, in the case of the EASC, concentrate on the "environment of care" or "facilities and environment." Third party inspection of a facility can be challenging and demands that the owners and operators fully understand each specific accrediting organization's standards. For example, a JCAHO survey scrutinizes five patient-focused functions and six organization-focused functions. Patient-related functions include patient rights and organization ethics, assessment of patients, care of patients, education of patients and family, and continuity of care. Organization functions include standards dealing with organization improvement; leadership; management of the environment of care; human resources; information; and surveillance, prevention, and control of infection. AAAHC and AAAASF inspections assess similar functions although these may be grouped under different organizational headings.

PHYSICIAN CREDENTIALING

Credentialing and privileging of physicians using the EASC may be mandated by federal, state, local, or third party organizations and include a formal application process, verification of licensure and drug enforcement administration status, malpractice history, admitting privileges, advanced cardiac life support (ACLS) status, and documentation of training.

PAYER REQUIREMENTS

Individual health plans or insurers may have their own regulatory requirements and these may vary significantly from payer to payer. Careful attention to local payer mix and any special regulations is necessary before designing and building an endoscopy facility to ensure qualification for payment.

As outlined previously, the regulatory and certification issues for endoscopy facilities are "complex, detailed, and broad."[11] Any physician wishing to develop an endoscopy facility must understand these rules of regulation and certification. Appropriate legal counsel should be considered mandatory.

Choosing a Site

For hospital-based endoscopy facilities, the facility's location is usually determined by the hospital's own planners and should include consideration of proximity to radiology, emergency department, and intensive care units. With office-based endoscopy or EASCs, physician owners choose the site. The site size and location require careful consideration because most office-based facilities or ASCs later expand to accommodate more physicians and patients. Preliminary land requirements are determined from space estimates (discussed later), parking requirements, appropriate landscaping or "green areas," and anticipated expansion.

For an office endoscopy suite or EASC, proximity to a hospital is desirable to minimize travel for patients requiring hospital transfer and for physician convenience. The site should be near but perhaps not on a major street to ease patient parking. Many patients coming to an ASC or office-based facility are elderly or may be anxious about their upcoming procedures. Access should be easy. Locating the physician offices adjacent to the ASC should be strongly considered, because it may be very efficient for staff and patients.

Facility Planning and Design

After forming a realistic business plan and acquiring an understanding of relevant regulatory and certification issues, attention then turns to the planning and design of the facility. Objectives must be articulated to the design professionals to ensure that the facility meets the needs of patients, endoscopists, and staff. Some points to keep in mind are as follows[16]:

- Allow adequate time for planning
- Set aside a regular block of time for discussion, review, and program development
- Choose experienced design professionals who communicate well
- Involve staff to ensure attention to their needs and wishes
- Prepare a statement of needs and goals to aid the architect in preparing a detailed program
- Prepare an inventory of equipment that will be used
- Visit other facilities to gather ideas worth incorporating
- Use flow studies to evaluate placement of functional elements
- Review preliminary drawings carefully
- If questions arise about the size or shape of a space, lay it out with tape on the floor and simulate work clearances

Planning and design of the facility will be a team project. The team will mainly involve a physician representing the endoscopists who will use the facility; two staff people, including the nurse responsible for patient care activities within the unit and the appropriate administrator; the architect; and the builder. The responsible physician must be given adequate time away from clinical duties to devote to planning, design, and oversight of the construction of the facility. Designated time must be set aside inasmuch as the process is ongoing and cannot be relegated to lunch hours and brief sessions whenever time can be stolen from clinical activities.

The architect is the primary professional involved in overseeing the entire project. It is wise to select an architect who specializes in medical buildings, particularly one who has experience in designing endoscopy facilities. Similarly, selection of a contractor who has experience in medical construction, particularly construction of endoscopy facilities, is important. Both architect and contractor must thoroughly understand the requirements of regulatory and

certifying bodies and local and state building codes. Sometimes the design and contracting can be provided by one company with both design and building capabilities. Although the physician representative, designated staff persons, architect, and contractor compose the major elements of the planning and design team, additional input may be needed from a mechanical engineer, electrical engineer, telephone contractor, information technology expert, and attorney.[17] Consideration might also be given to involving a lay person or "patient" to ensure sufficient attention to issues of patient comfort, dignity, and privacy.

PLANNING

The planning stage is concerned with deciding what activities will be conducted in the facility, what equipment will be needed, and how space will be allocated.

Scope of Activities

The first consideration is which endoscopic procedures will be performed in the facility.[18] The type of facility will, to a great extent, answer this question. The hospital-based facility will need to offer a wide range of endoscopic procedures, the only question being whether specialized procedures such as endoscopic retrograde cholangiopancreatography (ERCP), endoscopic ultrasound (EUS), laser endoscopy, or laparoscopy will be included.

For the office suite and EASC, services offered will be based on logistics and reimbursement ramifications. In these out-of-hospital facilities, procedures will usually be limited to "routine" high-volume procedures having predictable turnaround times and minimal recovery times and requiring standard equipment and less expensive accessories. In the EASC, it is critical that all procedures done be on the Medicare approved list to qualify for facility reimbursement. For both the office suite and the EASC, procedures will usually be limited to upper gastrointestinal endoscopy, esophageal dilation, and colonoscopy including polypectomy. Because of Medicare reimbursement guidelines, flexible sigmoidoscopy is now usually relegated to the office.

Predictably, rapid turnaround time is critical for the efficiently functioning EASC or office facility. Therefore, prolonged procedures or procedures that are unpredictable in duration such as ERCP are best done in the hospital. Procedures requiring prolonged recovery times such as liver biopsy are also best left for the hospital environment. Finally, procedures that require numerous and expensive accessories are best scheduled at the hospital because neither office suites nor EASCs can recover the costs of these accessories.

The question sometimes arises whether it is better to have a multispecialty or single specialty ASC. From the standpoint of services offered and equipment, the single-specialty EASC has the advantage of being the "focus factory."[19,20] In this environment, endoscopists, skilled gastrointestinal (GI) nurses, and administrative staff maximally use equipment of relatively low cost, performing predictably timed procedures with a rapid turnaround. The single-specialty EASC avoids the problem of the multispecialty facility where highly specialized equipment lies idle much of the time while physicians from differing specialties are performing their individual procedures.

Equipment

The greatest capital expense after the basic construction is that of equipment. Some tabulation of the equipment needed is necessary in the early planning stages and facility design. The basic equipment needed for an endoscopy unit is listed in Table 2–1.[1,18,21] A detailed discussion of individual items is not presented here, but a few points are useful in integrating the equipment needs into planning and design. In general, examining or procedure tables have been replaced by height-adjustable rolling procedural stretcher carts that allow patients, once properly gowned for endoscopy, to mount the moveable cart and not leave it until ready to leave the facility. These useful carts allow patients to be shuttled from preparation areas to procedure rooms and back to recovery areas and serve as procedure tables. This capability is very important to overall system efficiency and adds to patient safety by avoiding transfer to and from a procedure table.

Another major determinant of overall system speed and efficiency is the availability of endoscopes. This requires adequate numbers of endoscopes, high-level disinfection systems ("scope washers"), and adequate storage for extra endoscopes. Adequate numbers of endoscopes must be available to prevent inefficient down time in the unit. In most endoscopy suites, variable costs account for 80% or more of the total costs of providing endoscopic services, and 50% to 60% of this is attributable to staff salaries, wages, and benefits.[10] It is inefficient and fiscally unwise to have highly paid physicians and staff waiting for endoscopes. One of the most efficient scenarios is for one endoscopist to work out of two rooms so that he or she can move from room to room without major down time. This typically requires that each unit have three colonoscopes and three upper endoscopes for every two rooms in the facility. This allows two rooms to always be equipped for either upper endoscopy or colonoscopy with one endoscope always available to restock the next room during turnaround. The luxury of additional endoscopes per two rooms allows for the inevitable loss of an endoscope resulting from breakage and repair time. The high-volume, efficient endoscopy unit cannot afford to be penny wise and endoscope foolish when it comes to the number of endoscopes available.

Regarding esophageal dilators, the decision of whether to use a Savary or American dilator system versus balloons can have major economic consequences. This is less of an issue in the hospital where device costs can separately billed. However, in the office suite or the EASC, use of balloons may be problematic, particularly with Medicare or Medicaid patients, for whom the facility fee is set by regulation and extra costs for accessories cannot be passed on.

Physical Environment

Before beginning specific planning and design, it is worth considering some issues affecting space efficiency. It is the goal for physicians and staff to work as quickly and efficiently as possible while giving the patient the assurance that he or she is receiving appropriate care. System speed in the endoscopy facility usually comes from three delivery components:

1. Preparation and recovery of the patient
2. Reprocessing and return of endoscopes to the procedure room
3. Physician work habits

If the first two components operate properly, the number of procedure rooms available is not as important as the practice habits of the physician in performing procedures, talking to patients and their families, completing medical records, and returning to the procedure room.[22] In the efficient facility, physician discipline is needed, because room turnover and equipment reprocessing time can be rapid. Scheduled times for one physician operating out of two rooms with adequate staff and equipment can be easily allotted at 30 minutes for colonoscopies and 20 minutes for upper gastro-intestinal endoscopies (Rockford Gastroenterology Associates, Ltd., Rockford, Illinois, unpublished data).

Flow

Architects use flow diagrams to plan movement patterns in arranging space before actual design plans. Physician and nurse input is extremely important in arranging the flow relationships within the endoscopy facility to maximize efficiency, minimize travel distance, and achieve economy of movement. A basic flow diagram showing the components for a simple endoscopy unit is shown in Figure 2–1. The patterns of movement in a more complicated facility are conceptualized in Figure 2–2. Simple flow diagrams such as these

---

Table 2–1. Endoscopy Facility Equipment List

I. Major endoscopic and electrosurgical equipment
   A. Endoscopes, light sources, video processors, and monitors
   B. Electrocautery units and accessories
   C. Hemostasis unit (Heater Probe, Gold Probe, etc.)
   D. Physiologic monitoring devices including pulse oximetry, blood pressure and cardiac monitoring
II. Catheters, snares, forceps, and brushes
   A. Polypectomy snares
   B. Forceps
      1. Biopsy
         a. Regular or needle
         b. Hot biopsy
   C. Brushes
      1. Cleaning
      2. Cytology
   D. Graspers
   E. Retrieval baskets
III. Photo generator and image manager
IV. Esophageal dilators
   A. Wire-guided (Savary or American)
   B. Balloon
V. Rolling procedural stretcher carts with adjustable heights
VI. Suction equipment
VII. Pharmaceuticals
   A. Sedation and analgesia agents
      1. Benzodiazepines
      2. Narcotic analgesics
      3. Miscellaneous preference
   B. Benzodiazepine antagonists
   C. Narcotic antagonists
   D. Glucagon
   E. Atropine
   F. Topicals
VIII. Intravenous equipment, solutions, needles, and syringes
IX. Chemicals
   A. Formalin
   B. Disinfection solutions
X. Emergency cart, resuscitation equipment, supplies, and medications
XI. High-level disinfection equipment (cleaning trays, sinks, automatic endoscope washers, autoclave)
XII. Instrument storage cabinets
XIII. Blanket warmer
XIV. Radios and audio compact disc players
XV. Eyewash station

From references 1, 18, and 21.

can be elaborated into a functional relationship diagram as shown in Figure 2–3. Although this diagram suggests a floor plan, it is not a true floor plan. The sizes of the areas within the diagram are not proportional to the actual relative sizes of the rooms they represent. This type of functional relationship diagram shows the way that patients, staff, physicians, and equipment move through the facility. In the example of an ambulatory endoscopy center shown in Figure 2–3, both an endoscopy facility and an adjacent clinic facility are shown. The endoscopy facility on one side of the firewall can qualify as an ASC if the rules and regulations are followed and the endoscopy facility is separated from the clinic building by a required 1-hour fire rated wall-door construction system. This is usually achieved by using a wall with two layers of fire-rated gypsum board on either side of the structural wall supports and having the wall extend through the ceiling to the roof of the structure above.[22]

A functional relationship diagram can then be turned into an actual floor plan by assigning actual space requirements to the rooms that are represented. Figure 2–4 shows a sample architectural space program worksheet that can be used to turn a functional relationship diagram into a floor plan. Note that a 40% circulation allowance

must be added at the end of the tabulation to account for wall thicknesses, corridors, and so forth.[22]

DESIGNING THE ENDOSCOPY FACILITY

Marasco and Marasco[22] have suggested designing the endoscopy facility in modules. The modules to be designed include the following:

- Waiting module
- Business-reception module
- Preparation-recovery module
- Procedure room module
- Utility module
- Staff dressing module

Each of these modules are discussed separately because there are rules, regulations, and practical points to be kept in mind during design.

Waiting Module

There has been a marked shift toward outpatient-based endoscopy since the mid-1980s. This shift has major implications for the design and operation of the endoscopy facility. The patient's experience of the endoscopy facility oftentimes begins outside of the building in the parking lot. Patients arriving for endoscopy are often anxious and sometimes frightened. Maps with careful driving instructions and signs posted in the vicinity of the endoscopy facility can minimize confusion and offer reassurance. An all-weather canopy and automatic opening doors can be of major help to the elderly, ill, or disabled.

The reception and waiting room area provides an early impression of the endoscopy facility and should project efficiency and friendliness. Wheelchair storage should be available in this area, with wheelchairs stored out of sight. There must be adequate room for patients' escorts because one or two people usually accompany each patient scheduled for endoscopy. It is good to have a sub-waiting room for the endoscopy facility if there is an adjacent clinic area. A separate waiting area might be required under rules and regulations; even if not required, it might prove useful, because waiting times

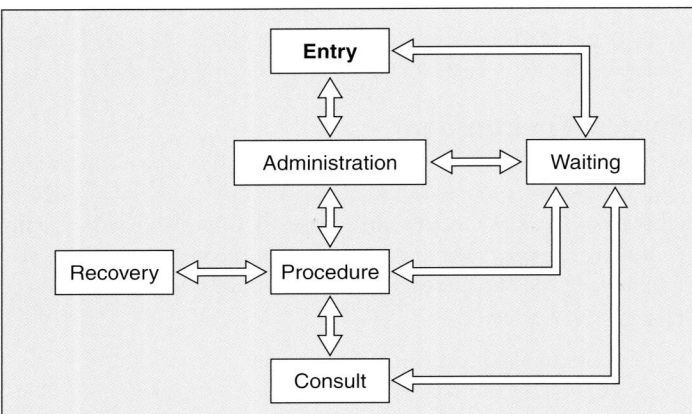

Figure 2–1. Flow diagram for a simple endoscopy unit. (Reproduced with permission from Rich ME: Office layout and design. In Overholt BF, Chobanian SJ (eds): Office Endoscopy. Baltimore, Williams & Wilkins, 1990.)

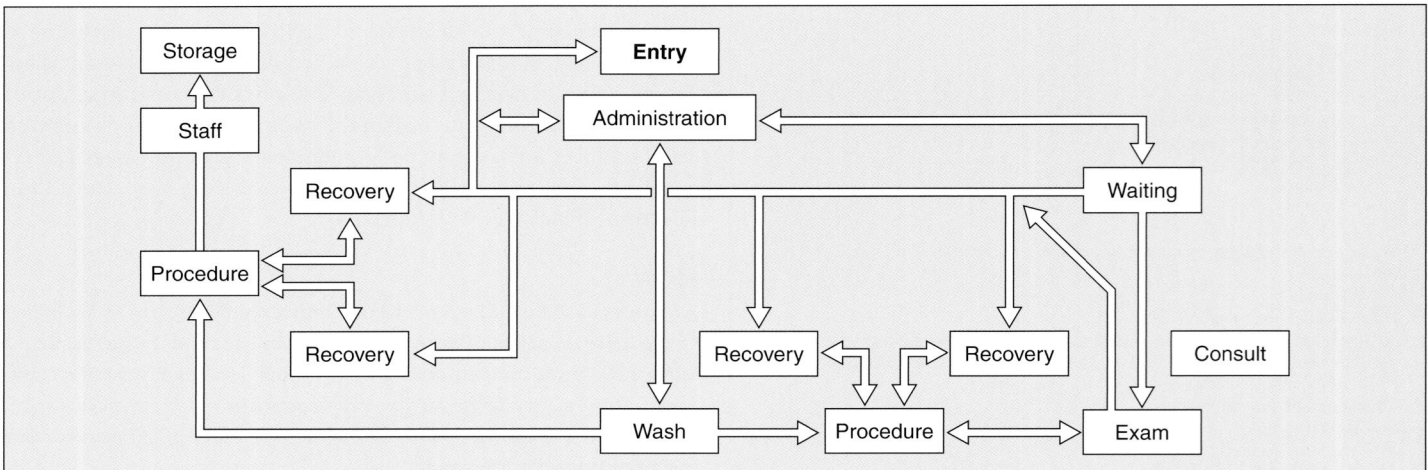

Figure 2–2. Flow diagram for a larger endoscopy unit. (Reproduced with permission from Rich ME: Office layout and design. In Overholt BF, Chobanian SJ (eds): Office Endoscopy. Baltimore, Williams & Wilkins, 1990.)

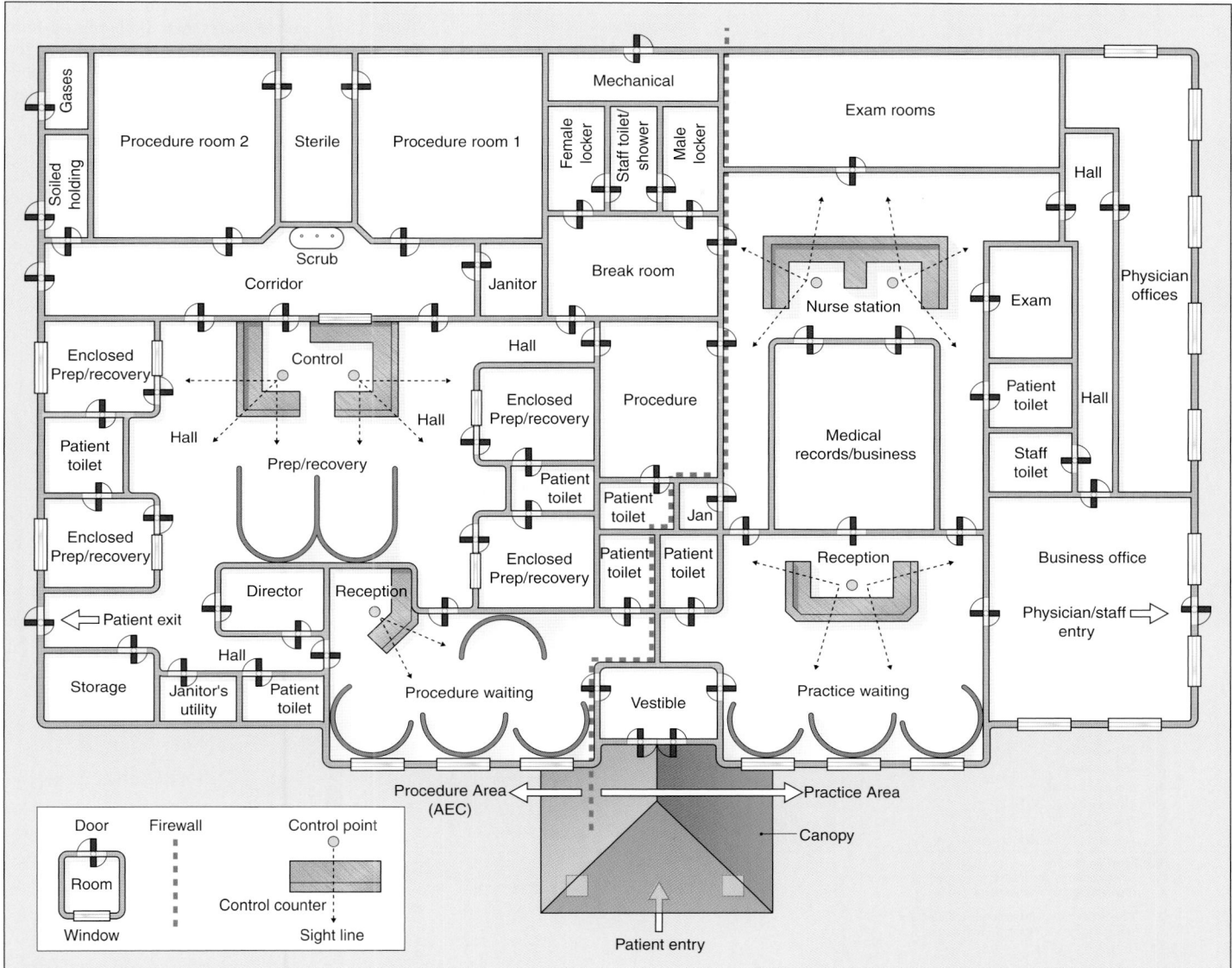

Figure 2–3. Functional relationship diagram of an ambulatory endoscopy center. (Reproduced from Marasco JA, Marasco RF: Designing the ambulatory endoscopy center. Ambulatory endoscopy centers. Gastrointest Endosc Clin N Am 12:193, 2002.)

for the clinic may be quite different from those for patients undergoing endoscopy. The waiting areas should be well appointed and equipped with a television set, videocassette player, and reading material. A toilet should be available near, but not directly off of, the waiting room. A small refreshment station near the reception area is also appreciated by escorts. The number of seats required is generally 2.5 times the number of patients in the building at any given time. An example of the general waiting area for Rockford Endoscopy Center, Rockford Gastroenterology Associates, Ltd., Rockford, Illinois is shown in Figure 2–5.

Business-Reception Module

The business-reception module includes reception area, billing stations, transcription, space for a director, files, and computer banks. Medicare requires that separate medical records be stored for the EASC portion of any facility that shares space with or adjoins

a clinic building. Careful attention to these storage requirements is important to ensure eligibility for Medicare certification. The records required by Medicare may be very limited and can be duplicated from the main records of the combined clinic/endoscopic facility. Often the practice and endoscopy areas can share a common business-reception module, but variances may be required from the state or the certifying body.

Preparation-Recovery Module

The preparation-recovery (prep-recovery) area of the endoscopy facility requires constant patient surveillance from the nursing staff. This area usually contains a nursing control station (Fig. 2–6), which allows unobstructed viewing of patients during the preparation and recovery stages of their visit.

The most efficient arrangement for preparation and recovery is to have them occur in the same place. Patient clothing can be stored in

ROOM	DESCRIPTION	AREA
A	Waiting Module		SF
1. Seats	☐ 2.0 to 2.5 x # of patients in building at once @ 18 SF/seat	_____ SF
2. Nourishment/TV	☐ 1 @ 10 SF =	_____ SF
3. Waiting room toilet	☐ 1 @ 55 SF =	_____ SF
4. Family room		_____ SF
B. Business Reception Module		SF
1. Reception area	☐ 50 SF/position	_____ SF
2. Billing		_____ SF
3. Transcription		_____ SF
4. Director		_____ SF
5. Files	☐ # of patients/year x 3 years divided by 100 patients/lineal feet = lineal feet @ 1.75 lineal feet per square feet	_____ SF
C. Control Module		SF
1. Control station	☐ 18 to 120 SF	_____ SF
2. Storage	☐ 20 to 30 SF	_____ SF
3. Dictation area	☐ 20 to 30 SF	_____ SF
D. Prep/Recovery Module		SF
1. Enclosed stations	☐ 2 per procedure room @ 100 SF =	_____ SF
	☐ Glassed enclosed procedure room side	_____
2. Recovery lounge	☐ 2 per procedure room @ 65 SF =	_____ SF
	☐ Recliner	_____
3. Toilet/dressing	☐ 1 per 2 prep/recovery stations @ 65 SF	
E. Operating Rooms (Procedure Room) Module		SF
1. See utilization chart for number		_____
2. Procedure rooms	☐ 270 SF	_____
	☐ Procedure room could be as little as 180 SF - discuss with state	
3. Scrub area	☐ See state regulations	
	☐ Could be inside room - if not then 10 SF	
F. Utility Module		SF
1. Sterilization	☐ 80 to 100 SF	_____ SF
	☐ Discuss with state	
2. Clean storage	☐ 10 to 40 SF	_____ SF
3. Dirty storage	☐ 20 to 50 SF	_____ SF
4. General storage	☐ 80 to 180 SF	_____ SF
5. Janitor's closet	☐ May need 2 - 15 to 20 SF	_____ SF
6. Gas storage	☐ 30 to 50 SF	_____ SF
7. Uninterruptible power source	☐ 20 to 40 SF	_____ SF
G. Staff Dressing Module		SF
1. Check state to see if separate male and female dressing rooms are needed	☐	_____ SF
2. Check state to see if separate toilet and/or shower is needed for male and female		
3. Dressing (male and/or female)	☐ 10 SF per locker - minimum 60 SF	_____ SF
	☐ 55 SF per toilet	_____ SF
	☐ 70 SF for shower and toilet	_____ SF
4. Break room	☐ Could be in practice area	_____ SF
	☐ 80 to 100 SF	
TOTAL NET AREA	**Sum of A through G**	_____ SF
40% CIRCULATION	**40% of Total Net**	_____ SF
TOTAL GROSS AREA	**Total Net + Circulation**	_____ SF

Figure 2–4. Architectural space program worksheet. (Reproduced from Marasco JA, Marasco RF: Designing the ambulatory endoscopy center. Ambulatory endoscopy centers. Gastrointest Endosc Clin N Am 12:194, 2002.)

a locked cabinet in the prep-recovery area, or can accompany the patient during transport to procedure room and back, stored underneath the rolling procedural stretcher cart. Patients can be rolled into procedure rooms on properly designed rolling carts that are also used as procedure tables. In this way, patients can move from preparation to procedure and back to recovery requiring no mounting or dismounting from wheelchairs or carts.

In general, at least two prep-recovery rooms or curtained bays are required per procedure room. Some patients who need additional recovery after they are able to dismount the procedure cart can be recovered in recliner chairs. A few curtained recliner chair areas can provide this extra recovery space. Corridors between procedure areas and prep-recovery spaces should be wide enough to provide easy patient cart movement. Toilets should be close to both prep-recovery and procedure areas.

Procedure Room Module

The number of procedure rooms is determined by the caseload of the endoscopy facility. This number is often overestimated. Much more important than the number of procedure rooms is the amount of recovery space available. In an efficient facility where turnaround time is quick, the number of procedure rooms can be minimized. It is most efficient for one endoscopist to have two rooms available so

Figure 2-5. General waiting area for Rockford Endoscopy Center, Rockford Gastroenterology Associates, Ltd., Rockford, Illinois. (Photograph by David Friedrich, Media Production, OSF Saint Anthony Medical Center, Rockford, Illinois.)

Figure 2-6. Nursing control station for preparation-recovery area. Rockford Endoscopy Center, Rockford Gastroenterology Associates, Ltd., Rockford, Illinois. (Photograph by David Friedrich, Media Production, OSF Saint Anthony Medical Center, Rockford, Illinois.)

that turnaround between cases can be very rapid. Using procedure rooms for recovery compromises efficiency by tying up a specialized procedure room. Block scheduling of a single endoscopist with two rooms offers maximum efficiency.

To determine the required number of procedure rooms, Marasco recommends using a utilization chart, an example of which is shown in Figure 2-7. By filling in the time of each of the time segments required in the endoscopy facility and adding the anticipated patient load, the number of procedure rooms needed can be estimated. Allowances should be made for growth in numbers of both physicians and patients over the subsequent 5 years. Generally, annual case loads increase 10% to 15% per year.[22] By using the patient load anticipated 5 years hence and dividing this load by the number of procedures per room per year, the number of required rooms can be calculated. Furthermore, by examining vertically on the utilization chart one can estimate the number of patients who will be in various stages within the endoscopy facility. This information can help predict the number of seats needed in the waiting room, the number of necessary procedure rooms, and the number of prep-recovery bays and recliner chairs needed.

The minimum size for an endoscopy room is probably 200 square feet,[1,16] but this is often inadequate to accommodate newer larger

videoendoscopy equipment and video monitors. Approximately 300 square feet are more appropriate for the modern endoscopy room.[1,22] Sometimes state licensing departments or Medicare will require a minimum size for an "operating room" that is inappropriately large for an endoscopy room. In that instance, a variance can be requested but is not automatically granted.

An example of an endoscopy procedure room layout is shown in Figure 2-8, which shows placement of the light source, videoprocessor, dual video monitors, electrocautery, and so forth. Many variations are possible to fit the preferences of the endoscopists and nursing staff. Rooms should be planned with equipment and supplies integrated into the layout and positioned strategically around the site of the patient on the procedural stretcher cart. The floor should be free of cables and wiring, these being arranged along the perimeter of the room or preferably above a dropped ceiling or in the walls. This allows physicians, staff, and equipment to move unfettered by cords and cables and avoids damaging these sensitive components. All endoscopic accessories, suction, oxygen, supplies, and all resuscitation equipment should be at hand. An emergency call button should be included in each procedure room and an emergency (crash) cart stored nearby. A typical endoscopy procedure room (Rockford Endoscopy Center) is shown in Figure 2-9.

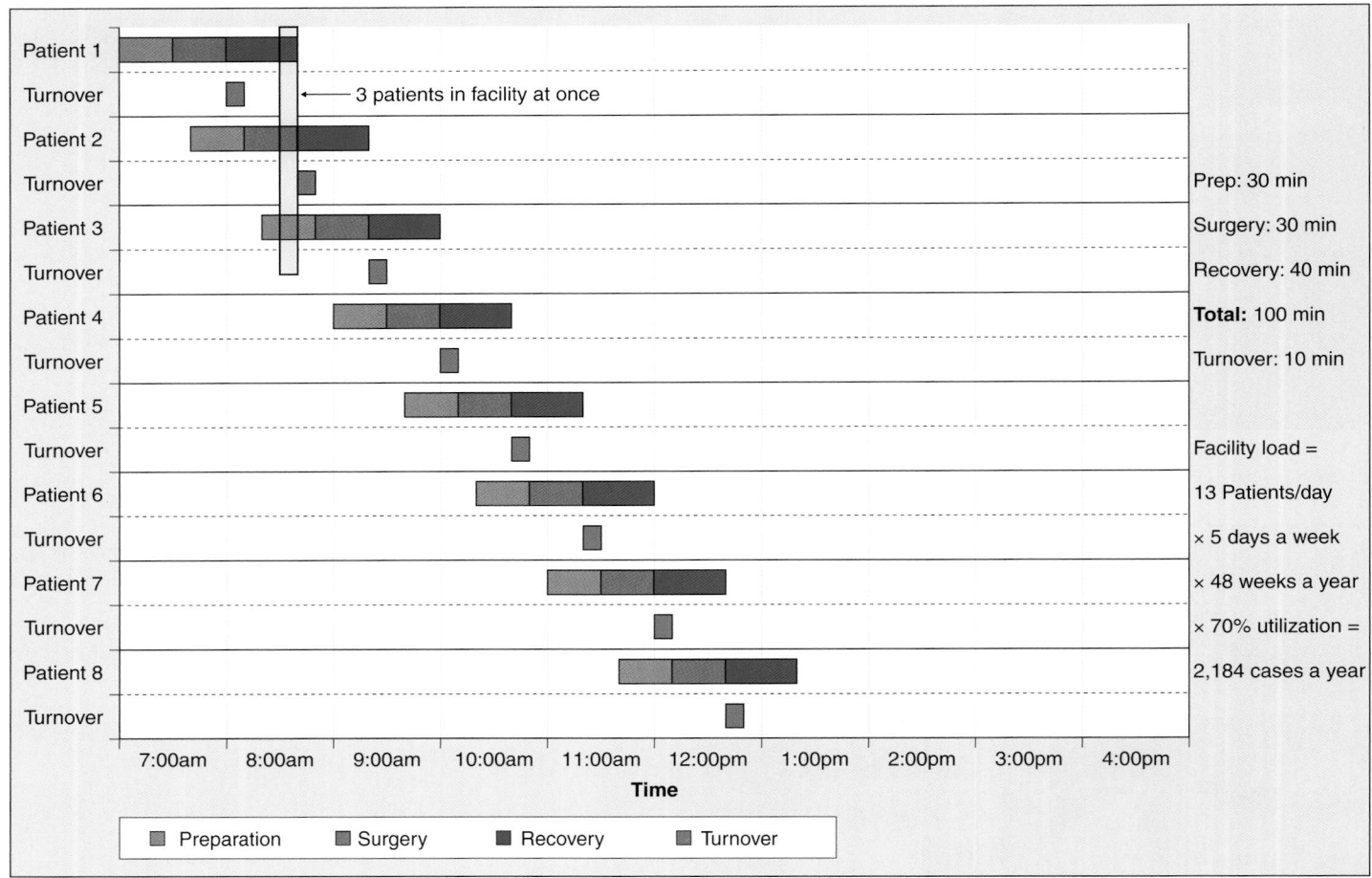

Figure 2–7. Sample procedure room utilization analysis. (Reproduced from Marasco JA, Marasco RF: Designing the ambulatory endoscopy center. Ambulatory endoscopy centers. Gastrointest Endosc Clin N Am 12:199, 2002.)

A more detailed discussion of basic clearances and human dimensional requirements are available in the book by Waye and Rich.[29]

Utility Module

Efficient equipment turnover time can be achieved by having appropriate equipment for rapid cleaning and high-level disinfection. In this scenario, the speed of the endoscopy facility is determined by the efficiency of the physician between procedures rather than by the number of procedure rooms.[22] Instrument cleaning and high-level disinfection can be accomplished by strategically placing the cleaning area between two procedure rooms or having an efficient large cleaning area within a short distance of several procedure rooms. Adequate numbers of endoscopes stored properly and reprocessed efficiently will ensure that the most expensive cost elements of the endoscopy facility—namely the physicians and nursing staff—are not kept waiting for equipment.

Cleaning rooms should be large and adequately ventilated with ample plumbing and power provisions for future changes. Oversized sinks are required, and there should be a place for soiled instruments to hang while waiting to be cleaned. Automated endoscope washers with multiple scope compartments, such as that shown in Figure 2–10, provide an efficient way of reprocessing endoscopes. A "pass through" window from soiled to clean utility areas should be available to maintain separation of "clean" and "dirty" areas. A closed cabinet for the storage of clean endoscopes is preferred to open storage, both to protect instruments and to prevent inadvertent sightings of instruments by anxious patients. Endoscope storage cabinets that circulate air through the endoscope channels provide added protection against moisture and bacterial growth within channels. Such a storage unit with channel air circulation is shown in Figure 2–11. Exhaust fans in the cleaning area are a must, as are provisions for disposal of toxic chemicals.

Also included in the utility module are storage areas. General storage for supplies must be readily accessible to the prep-recovery areas and the procedure rooms. There must be locked cabinets for storage of drugs. Biohazardous waste and gases such as oxygen must also be stored. An alternate power source, such as a battery back-up system or generator, is necessary to ensure uninterrupted power.

Staff Dressing Module

Requirements for dressing room spaces are different in the regulated and the unregulated endoscopy facility environments. Rules for the

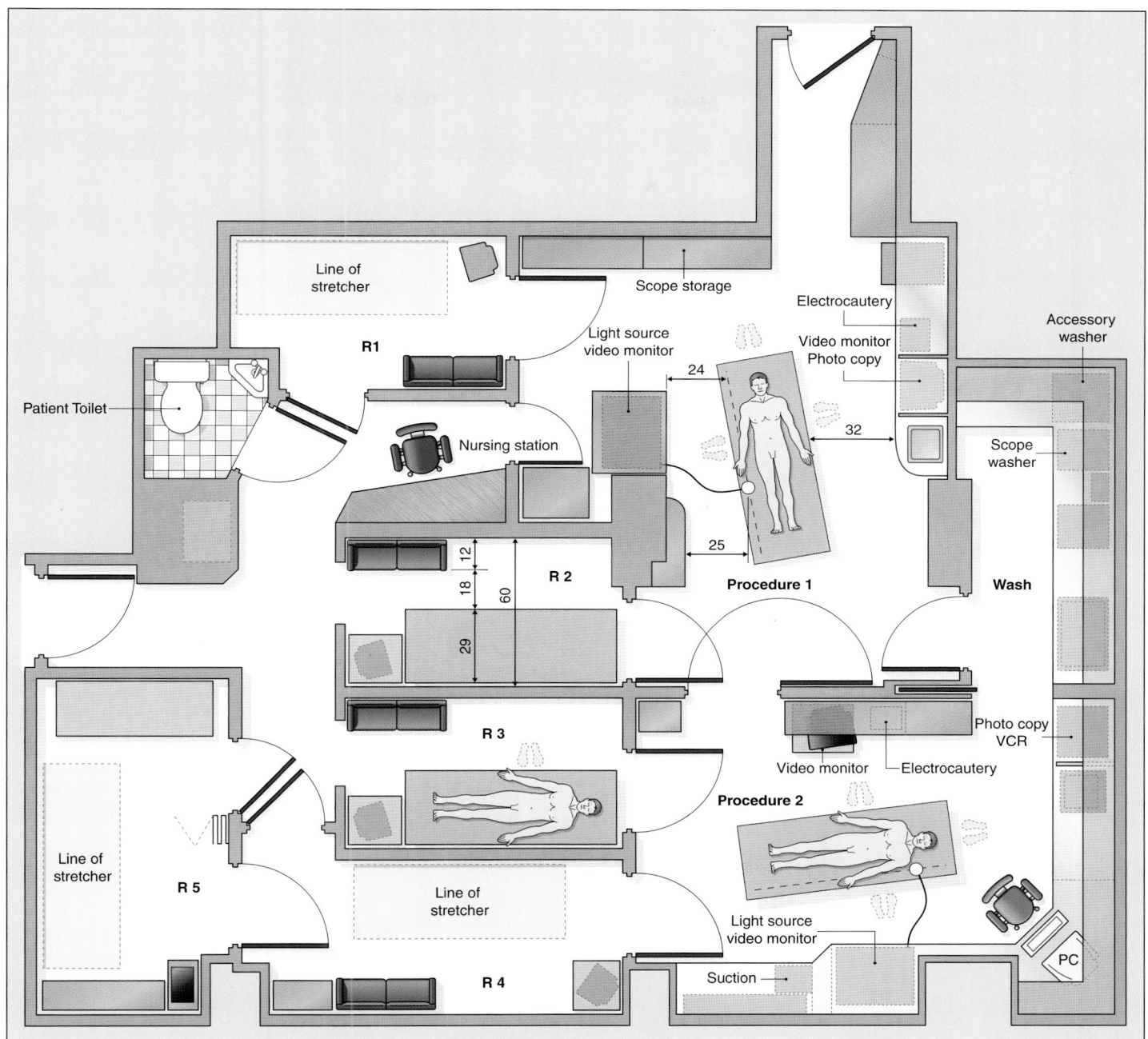

Figure 2-8. Example of endoscopy room layout. (Reproduced with permission from Rich ME: Office layout and design. In Overholt BF, Chobanian SJ (eds): Office Endoscopy. Baltimore, Williams & Wilkins, 1990.)

ASC or hospital may be quite different from the office. It is wise to know the regulations from the state department of health and from certification agencies. Male and female locker areas are generally required but variances can be requested to eliminate the need for unnecessary shower facilities. An additional part of the staff dressing module is the break room. Some state departments of health or certification bodies require a break room within the confines of the endoscopy facility. Careful attention to state and federal regulations is warranted to ensure that licensure and certification requirements are met.

SUMMARY OF PLANNING AND DESIGN

The design of the efficient endoscopy facility is facilitated by a functional relationship diagram showing the flow of patients through the facility. An architectural space program is then developed by tabulating the areas necessary and assigning space required. This architectural space program determines the size of the facility. A procedure room utilization calculation determines the number of procedure rooms and other areas necessary to handle the patient case load, and provisions should be made for case load growth. Careful attention to planning and design will result in the

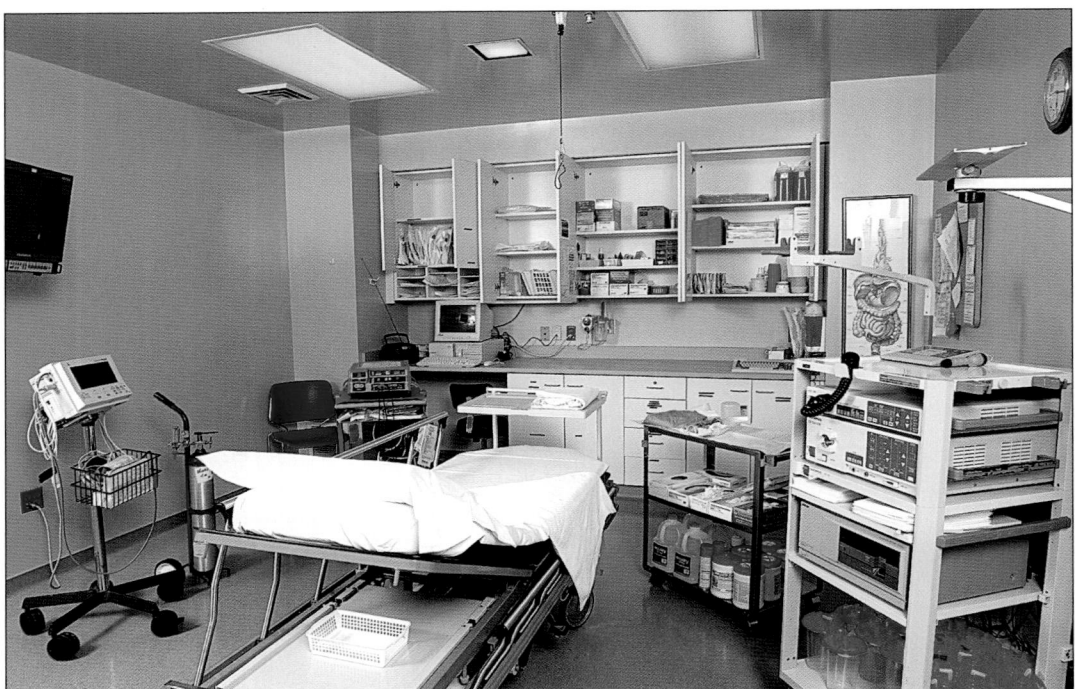

Figure 2–9. Typical endoscopy procedure room. Rockford Endoscopy Center, Rockford Gastroenterology Associates, Ltd., Rockford, Illinois. (Photograph by David Friedrich, Media Production, OSF Saint Anthony Medical Center, Rockford, Illinois.)

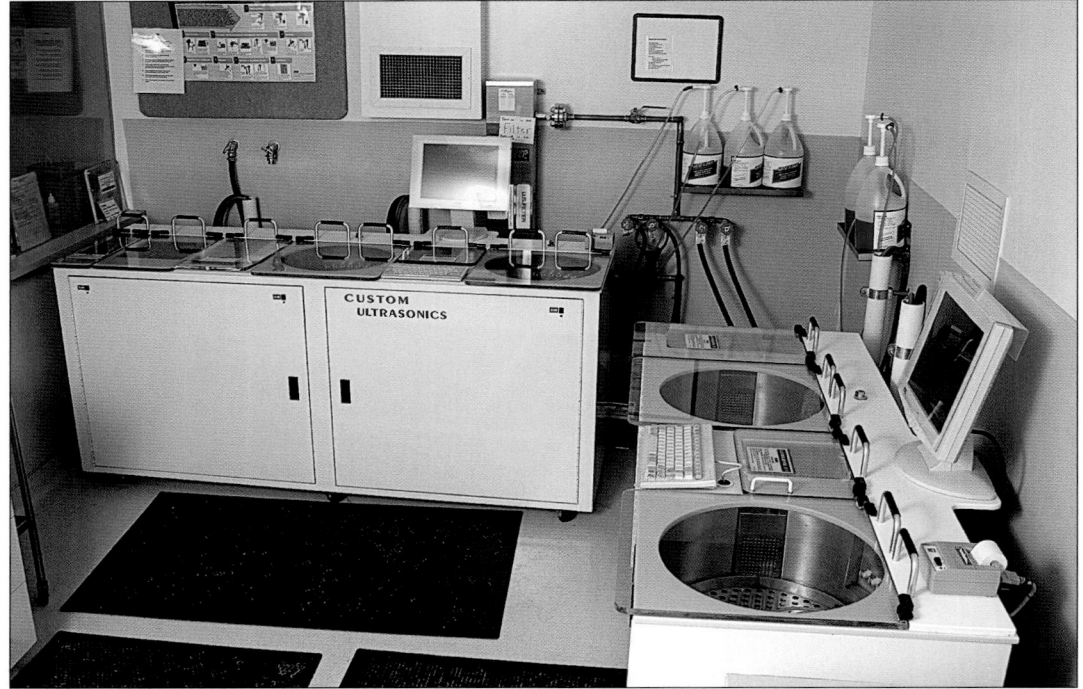

Figure 2–10. High-level disinfection unit for multiple endoscopes, Rockford Endoscopy Center, Rockford Gastroenterology Associates, Ltd., Rockford, Illinois. (Photograph by David Friedrich, Media Production, OSF Saint Anthony Medical Center, Rockford, Illinois.)

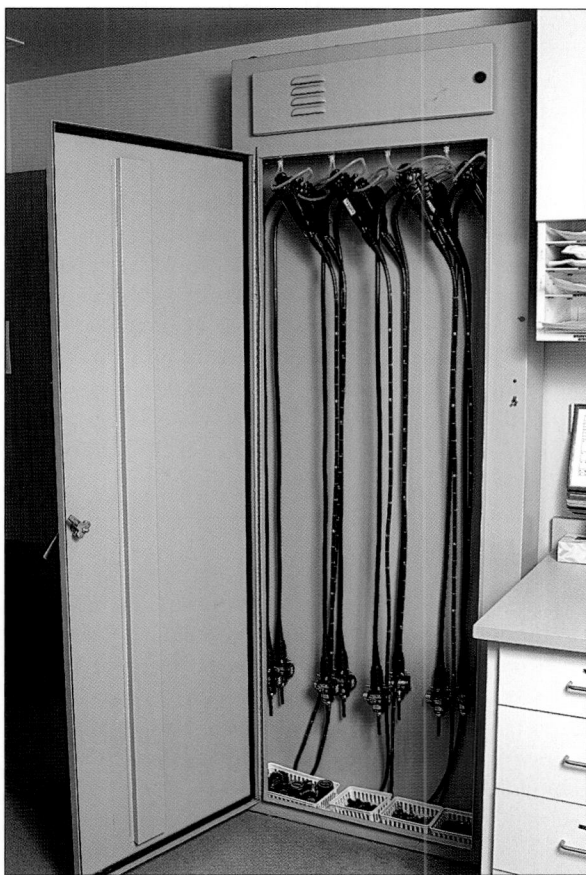

Figure 2-11. Endoscopy storage cabinet providing air circulation through endoscopy channels, Rockford Endoscopy Center, Rockford Gastroenterology Associates, Ltd., Rockford, Illinois. (Photograph by David Friedrich, Media Production, OSF Saint Anthony Medical Center, Rockford, Illinois.)

construction of a pleasant, efficient endoscopy facility that will meet the needs of patients, physicians, and staff.

Staffing and Scheduling

Decisions regarding staffing and scheduling are critical to the safe and efficient operation of the endoscopy facility, have a major impact on patient outcomes, and affect the financial viability of the endoscopy unit.

STAFFING

Decisions regarding staffing hinge on regulatory requirements, volumes of procedures, and case mix (disease acuity). Numerous federal and state regulations affect staffing decisions and a thorough knowledge of these requirements is necessary to ensure compliance with state licensing requirements, Medicare certification regulations, and third party accreditation standards.

Medicare guidelines stipulate that a registered nurse (RN) must be available on site during all hours of operation of a hospital or ASC endoscopy facility. The Nurse Practice Act of each individual state

also affects staffing decisions. This defines the scope of practice for RNs, Licensed Practical Nurses (LPNs), and other assistants or technicians. These Nurse Practice Acts may limit who can start intravenous (IV) lines, administer IV medications, or provide other clinical services.

To determine the number of full-time equivalents (FTEs) needed for staffing, one must quantify the time needed to care for a single patient, multiply this by the number of procedures scheduled daily, and divide by the work hours per day of a full-time employee. One current industry standard suggests an average time of 3 hours per procedure to admit, treat, and discharge a patient in an endoscopy facility (AMSURG Corporation, unpublished data).[30] Some factors that influence the decision to use RNs versus LPNs versus technicians include scope-of-practice regulations, salary costs, and availability. Regardless of the mix, care should always be directly supervised by an on-site RN.[31]

A typical two room endoscopy facility might be staffed as follows[30]:

- Procedure room number 1: one RN or LPN
- Procedure room number 2: one RN or LPN
- Cleaning room: one endoscope technician
- Preparation-recovery area: two RNs and one LPN, or one RN and two LPNs or technician (the LPN or technician should also be used to float between procedure rooms)

Each endoscopy facility would require at least one receptionist and perhaps a second clerical person. The use of dedicated endoscope technicians to perform cleaning and high-level disinfection and instrument setup promotes strict adherence to endoscope reprocessing guidelines and endoscope durability.

SCHEDULING

Most facilities use block scheduling to maximize efficiency and convenience. Block scheduling of one physician with two endoscopy rooms allows efficient movement of the endoscopist from one room to the next without delays caused by other endoscopists. It is possible for that individual to intermingle daily tasks such as telephone calls or chart review during any down time. Block scheduling also allows for time allotments based on the performance characteristics of individual endoscopists. Examples of block scheduling and tools for use in block scheduling have been published by McMillan.[30]

Equipment availability can affect scheduling. An ample number of endoscopes and rapid efficient cleaning and high-level disinfection will facilitate a more efficient schedule. The first patient of the day can be prepped in the procedure room if an additional procedural stretcher cart is available for each procedure room at the beginning of the day.

Time allotments for procedures vary from facility to facility. Reportedly, most facilities allow 45 minutes for colonoscopy and 30 minutes for upper gastrointestinal endoscopy.[30] Other facilities schedule more tightly, allowing 30 minutes for colonoscopy and 20 minutes for upper gastrointestinal endoscopy, including those with dilations (Rockford Gastroenterology Associates, Ltd., Rockford, Illinois, unpublished data). The tighter scheduling can be accommodated by efficient endoscopists, good staffing, adequate equipment, rapid turnaround time, and ample prep-recovery space (two to three prep-recovery bays per procedure room).

Careful staffing and scheduling is imperative to ensure high-quality care, good patient outcomes, and optimal fiscal performance of the endoscopy facility.

Documentation

An accurate and complete medical record must be kept for each patient and a log of the unit's overall activities (see Chapter 9).[1] The endoscopy report and nursing notes should include date, patient identification data, endoscopist, endoscopic procedure, indications, informed consent, extent of examination, duration of the procedure, findings, notation of tissue sampling, therapeutic interventions, complications, and limitations of the examination. Photographs, electronic images, and biopsy reports should also be part of the record. Quality indicators and patient outcomes should be tabulated and a method of regular peer review should develop.

Information management in an endoscopy facility affects all aspects of the operation including scheduling, billing and reimbursement, the patient medical record, procedure reports, clinical laboratory and anatomic pathology reports, imaging, pharmacy, patient education, performance improvement data, financial management, materials management and inventory, budgeting and forecasting, payroll and personnel, and staffing and scheduling.[32] Modern information technology may allow more efficient and effective operations within the facility.

Quality Improvement

Medicare regulations and third party accreditors require endoscopy facilities to engage in an ongoing comprehensive self-assessment of the quality of care provided. This process includes quality improvement efforts directed toward numerous facets of the operation of the facility. Reasons for quality improvement activities include ensuring that patients receive the highest quality of care possible; providing a competitive edge when seeking contracts; and addressing the recent emphasis of legislators and regulators on quality improvement activities as part of the licensure, certification, and accreditation process. A recent publication describes continuous quality improvement in the ambulatory endoscopy center.[33] The philosophies and tools presented in this article provide a framework for quality improvement activities in all endoscopy facilities. Attention to these activities will improve patient safety and patient care.

Summary

Gastrointestinal endoscopy has developed as a very important tool in the management of disorders of the gastrointestinal system since its introduction into clinical use in the early 1960s. It has transformed the discipline of gastroenterology. The growing use of increasingly complex endoscopic procedures and the evolution of endoscopy to the outpatient setting have fostered the careful development of endoscopy facilities that enable the delivery of endoscopic services in a safe efficient manner that is reassuring to the patient and produces good outcomes.

The process of setting up an endoscopy facility begins with exploring the types of facilities, developing a business plan, and researching relevant regulatory and certification issues. With those objectives accomplished, attention turns to planning the facility, including site selection, choosing equipment and planning the physical environment, and flow of patients and staff. Finally, the general plans for the facility are turned into specific architectural designs, which form the basis for construction of a pleasant efficient facility.

Once the facility is constructed careful attention to appropriate staffing, scheduling, documentation, and quality improvement activities promotes efficient and effective care, good patient outcomes, and responsible physical performance of the facility.

ACKNOWLEDGMENTS

The author acknowledges Nancy Garry, RN, Administrator, and Evon Dowd, RN, BS, CGRN, Supervisor of Rockford Endoscopy Center for their insights regarding the delivery of gastrointestinal endoscopic services, and Arnold M. Rosen, MD, and Brenda Paulson, Executive Secretary, for their help in preparing the manuscript. These colleagues at Rockford Gastroenterology Associates, Ltd. were very helpful in the creation of this chapter.

REFERENCES

1. American Society for Gastrointestinal Endoscopy: Establishment of gastrointestinal endoscopy areas. Gastrointest Endosc 50:910–912, 1999.
2. American Society for Gastrointestinal Endoscopy: Principles of training in gastrointestinal endoscopy. Gastrointest Endosc 49:845–853, 1999.
3. American Society for Gastrointestinal Endoscopy: Methods of granting hospital privileges to perform gastrointestinal endoscopy. Gastrointest Endosc 55:780–783, 2002.
4. American Society for Gastrointestinal Endoscopy: Quality improvement of gastrointestinal endoscopy. Gastrointest Endosc 49:842–844, 1999.
5. American Society for Gastrointestinal Endoscopy: Quality and outcomes assessment in gastrointestinal endoscopy. Gastrointest Endosc 52:827–830, 2000.
6. Pike IM: Outpatient endoscopy: Possibilities for the office. Ambulatory endoscopy centers. Gastrointest Endosc Clin N Am 12:247–261, 2002.
7. Frakes JT: Outpatient endoscopy: The case for the ambulatory surgery center. Ambulatory endoscopy centers. Gastrointest Endosc Clin N Am 12:215–227, 2002.
8. Fisk DA: Financial performance. In Baerg RD, Frakes JT, Mellow MH, Petrini JL (eds): The Development of an Ambulatory Endoscopy Center: A Primer. Manchester, MA, American Society for Gastrointestinal Endoscopy, 1998, pp 14–16.
9. Deas TM: Assessing the financial health of the endoscopy facility. Ambulatory endoscopy centers. Gastrointest Endosc Clin N Am 12:229–244, 2002.
10. Overholt BF: Office endoscopy or an endoscopic ambulatory surgery center? Gastroenterologist 1:99–106, 1993.
11. Ganz RA: Regulation and certification issues. Ambulatory endoscopy centers. Gastrointest Endosc Clin N Am 12:205–214, 2002.

12. Knox C, Mellow MH: Functional plan and architectural issues. In Baerg RD, Frakes JT, Mellow MH, Petrini JL (eds): The Development of an Ambulatory Endoscopy Center: A Primer. Manchester, MA, American Society for Gastrointestinal Endoscopy, 1998, pp 6–11.

13. Romansky M: Medicare certification of ambulatory surgical centers. In Baerg RD, Frakes JT, Mellow MH, Petrini JL (eds): The Development of an Ambulatory Endoscopy Center: A Primer. Manchester, MA, American Society for Gastrointestinal Endoscopy, 1998, pp 12–13.

14. Joint Commission on Accreditation of Healthcare Organizations: Ambulatory care accreditation. Available at http://www.jcaho.org (Accessed April 19, 2003).

15. Accreditation Association of Ambulatory Health Care: Products, resources. Available at http://www.aaahc.org (Accessed April 19, 2003).

16. Rich ME: Office layout and design. In Overholt BF, Chobanian SJ (eds): Office Endoscopy. Baltimore, Williams & Wilkins, 1990, pp 31–50.

17. Waye JD, Rich ME: Constructing the unit: Plans and problems. Planning an endoscopy suite for office and hospital. New York, Igaku-Shoin, 1990, pp 129–145.

18. Schapiro M: Office design and planning: The physician's viewpoint. In Overholt BF, Chobanian SJ (eds): Office Endoscopy. Baltimore, Williams & Wilkins, 1990, pp 9–29.

19. Herzlinger R: Market Driven Health Care: Who Wins, Who Loses in the Transformation of America's Largest Service Industry. Reading, MA, Addison-Wesley, 1997.

20. Deas TM Jr, Drerup DM: Endoscopic ambulatory surgery centers: Demise, service or thrive? J Clin Gastroenterol 29:253–256, 1999.

21. Waye JD, Rich ME: Program. Planning an Endoscopy Suite for Office and Hospital. New York, Igaku-Shoin, 1990, pp 33–45.

22. Marasco JA, Marasco RF: Designing the ambulatory endoscopy center. Ambulatory endoscopy centers. Gastrointest Endosc Clin N Am 12:185–204, 2002.

23. Rich ME: Office layout and design. In Overholt BF, Chobanian SJ (eds): Office Endoscopy. Baltimore, Williams & Wilkins, 1990, p 36.

24. Rich ME: Office layout and design. In Overholt BF, Chobanian SJ (eds): Office Endoscopy. Baltimore, Williams & Wilkins, 1990, p 38.

25. Marasco JA, Marasco RF: Designing the ambulatory endoscopy center. Ambulatory endoscopy centers. Gastrointest Endosc Clin N Am 12:193, 2002.

26. Marasco JA, Marasco RF: Designing the ambulatory endoscopy center. Ambulatory endoscopy centers. Gastrointest Endosc Clin N Am 12:194, 2002.

27. Marasco JA, Marasco RF: Designing the ambulatory endoscopy center. Ambulatory endoscopy centers. Gastrointest Endosc Clin N Am 12:199, 2002.

28. Rich ME: Office layout and design. In Overholt BF, Chobanian SJ (eds): Office Endoscopy. Baltimore, Williams & Wilkins, 1990, p 43.

29. Waye JD, Rich ME: The procedure zone. Planning an endoscopy suite for office and hospital. New York, Igaku-Shoin, 1990, pp 73–101.

30. McMillin DF: Staffing and scheduling in the endoscopy center. Ambulatory endoscopy centers. Gastrointest Endosc Clin N Am 12:285–296, 2002.

31. Society of Gastroenterology Nurses and Associates (SGNA): Role Delineation of Assistive Personnel. Position Statement, 2001. Chicago, SGNA, 2001.

32. Weinstein ML, Korman LY: Information management. Ambulatory endoscopy centers. Gastrointest Endosc Clin N Am 12:313–324, 2002.

33. Johanson JF: Continuous quality improvement in the ambulatory endoscopy center. Ambulatory endoscopy centers. Gastrointest Endosc Clin N Am 12:351–365, 2002.

FURTHER READING

American Society for Gastrointestinal Endoscopy: Policy and Procedure Manual for Gastrointestinal Endoscopy: Guidelines for Training and Practice. Chicago, American Society for Gastrointestinal Endoscopy, 1997.

Marasco RF, Marasco JA, Barkheimer J, et al: ASCs: Playing to win. Administrative Eyecare 6:12–51, 1997.

How Endoscopes Work

David E. Barlow

Overview

The flexible videoendoscope embodies more than 2 decades of refinements in solid-state imaging and mechanical design. Many different models are available, each having slightly different features, and each optimized for the portion of the gastrointestinal (GI) tract that it is designed to examine. Although alternative designs for the endoscope's control section have been proposed (e.g., "pistol-grip"), the basic shape and layout of the instrument are relatively unchanged since flexible endoscopes were first developed.

The basic components and controls of all flexible videoendoscopes are quite similar and are illustrated in Figure 3–1. The instrument is designed to be held and operated by the endoscopist's left hand. Some physicians use their left index finger to alternately control the suction and air/water valves, while the remaining fingers grip the instrument. Others use their left index finger for the suction valve, the middle finger for the air/water valve, and the final two to grip the instrument. The up and down angulation knob is manipulated by the physician's left thumb. The left and right angulation knob is controlled either by the thumb and first two fingers of the left hand or, alternatively, by the right hand. The endoscopist's right hand is primarily used to control the insertion tube—pushing, torquing, and withdrawing as necessary.

Insertion Tube

The endoscope's insertion tube is a major differentiating feature among endoscopes designed for gastroenterology. Although obvious differences exist dependent on the endoscope's application (e.g., the extra long length of the enteroscope, the thinness of a transnasal esophagoscope, and so forth), the subtler differences between endoscope models are just as important. This is especially true for colonoscopes. Although endoscopists may prefer using a particular colonoscope model for a variety of reasons, it is perhaps the instrument's insertion tube characteristics, which more than anything else, cause an endoscopist to pick a particular colonoscope as the instrument of choice. Indeed, if any single specification of the instrument can determine the speed and ease with which the endoscopist can insert the instrument, it is the mechanical characteristics of the insertion tube.

Endoscope manufacturers have put significant effort into refining the construction of the insertion tube and selecting ideal materials. Figure 3–2 shows the internal components of a typical colonoscope. The insertion tube usually contains (1) tubes for suction (biopsy), air, and water feeding; (2) often an additional tube for a forward water jet; (3) four angulation control wires; (4) fine electrical wires connecting the charge-coupled device (CCD) image sensor at the distal tip of the endoscope to the videoprocessor; and (5) delicate glass fibers for bringing light from the light source to the distal end of the endoscope. Colonoscopes with adjustable insertion tube flexibility have an additional component—a tensioning wire to control insertion tube stiffness. Duodenoscopes also have an additional wire/coil sheath running the length of the insertion tube for controlling the up and down position of the forceps elevator (see later discussion).

It is the task of the endoscope designer to pack all of these individual components into the smallest space possible but still to provide freedom for the components to move about without damaging the more fragile elements (CCD wires, fiberoptic strands) as the instrument is torqued and flexed during use. A dry powdered lubricant is applied to all internal components to reduce the stress that they place on each other during insertion tube manipulation.

INSERTION TUBE FLEXIBILITY

As previously mentioned, the handling characteristics of the insertion tube are extremely important, particularly for colonoscopes.

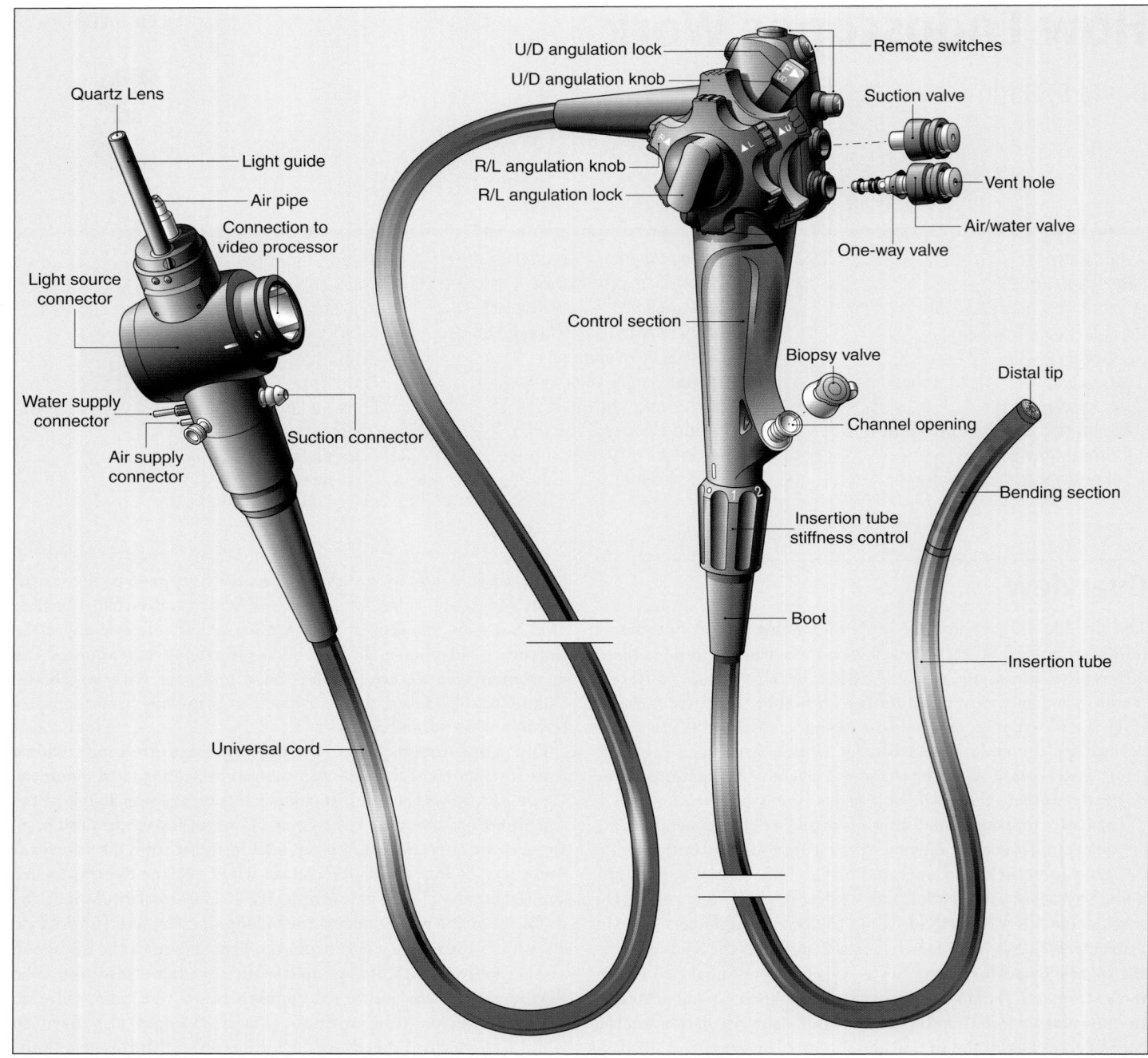

Quartz Lens

Light guide

Air pipe

Connection to
video processor

Light source
connector

Water supply
connector

Air supply
connector

Suction connector

Universal cord

U/D angulation lock

U/D angulation knob

Remote switches

Suction valve

R/L angulation knob

R/L angulation lock

Vent hole

Air/water valve

One-way valve

Control section

Biopsy valve

Distal tip

Channel opening

Bending section

Insertion tube
stiffness control

Boot

Insertion tube

Figure 3-1. Basic components of a standard flexible videoendoscope.

For easy insertion, the instrument must be capable of accurately transmitting all of the subtle movements and torque applied by the endoscopist. Any rotation that the endoscopist applies to the proximal portion of the shaft must be transferred to the distal tip of the instrument in a 1:1 ratio. The torqueability of the instrument is facilitated by flat, spiral metal bands that run just under the skin of the insertion tube (see Fig. 3–2). Because these bands are wound in opposite directions, they lock against one another as the tube is torqued, accurately transmitting rotation of one end of the tube to the other. At the same time, gaps between these spiral bands allow the shaft to flex freely. The bands also give the insertion tube its round shape. Their stiffness prevents the internal components of the insertion tube from being crushed by external forces.

These spiral bands are covered by fine strands of stainless steel wire, braided into a tubular mesh. A plastic polymer layer, typically black (or dark green on colonoscopes), is then extruded over this wire mesh to create the smooth outer surface of the insertion tube. The polymer layer provides an atraumatic, biocompatible, and watertight surface for the insertion tube. It is usually marked with numbers to gauge the depth of insertion.

Experience has shown that a more rigid insertion tube is optimal for examining the fixed anatomy of the upper GI tract. On the other

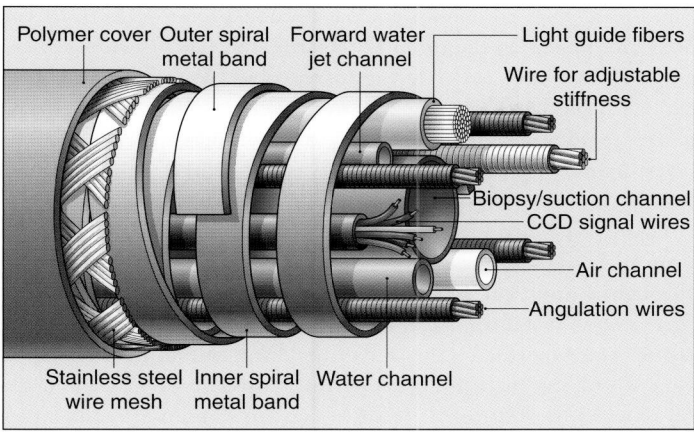

Figure 3–2. The internal components of a variable-stiffness colonoscope.

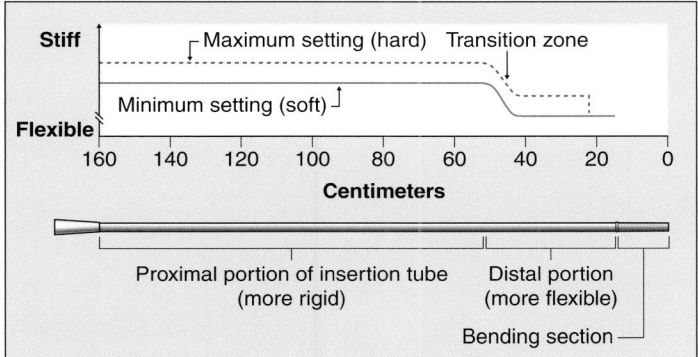

Figure 3–3. Graphical representation of insertion tube stiffness. Note variation; the distal 40 cm is more flexible. Furthermore, note the extra stiffness when the instrument is in the "stiff" setting *(dashed line)* versus in the soft setting *(solid line)*.

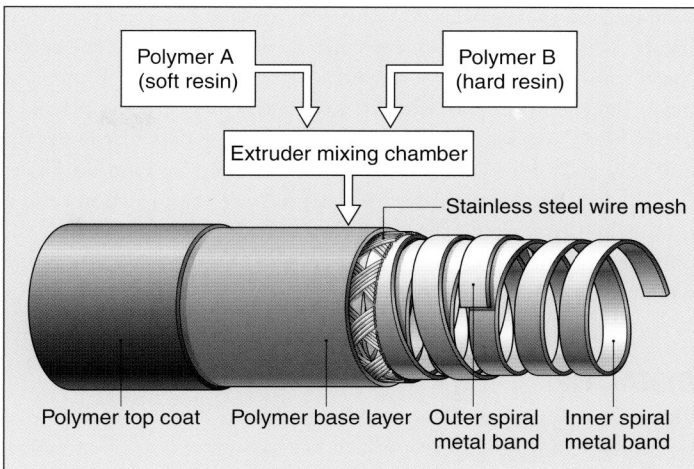

Figure 3–4. Instrument cover composition.

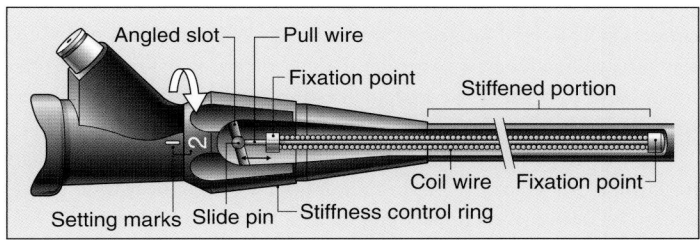

Figure 3–5. Mechanism for stiffening instrument (variable-stiffness colonoscope).

hand, the colon, with it's tortuosity and freely moving loops, is best examined by a more flexible instrument. Colonoscopists ideally want a tube that is flexible yet highly elastic. They want the instrument to be sufficiently floppy (nonrigid) to conform easily to the tortuous anatomy of the patient and to exert minimum force on the colon wall and attached mesentery. On the other hand, they want the instrument to have sufficient column strength to prevent buckling when the proximal end of the instrument is pushed. In addition to its flexibility, the colonoscope should have sufficient elasticity to pop back into a straightened condition when it is pulled back. This aids in removing loops. Obtaining the best combination of flexibility, elasticity, column strength, and torqueability is the art and science of insertion tube design. Often, improvements in one of these characteristics negatively affect one or more of the others. The final design is usually a compromise between these ideal characteristics, confirmed by months of clinical testing.

To further improve insertability, the flexibility of both gastroscope and colonoscope insertion tubes typically varies from end to end. As Figure 3–3 illustrates, the distal 40 cm of a colonoscope insertion tube is significantly more flexible than the proximal portion. This variation in flexibility is achieved by changing the formulation of the tube's outer polymer layer as it is extruded over the wire mesh

during manufacturing. As Figure 3–4 illustrates, the extruder contains two types of resins, one significantly harder than the other. Initially, as the distal end of the insertion tube passes through the machine, a layer of soft resin is applied to the distal 40 cm of the wire mesh. This soft resin is gradually replaced by the hard resin within a transition zone near the middle of the tube. The proximal portion of the insertion tube (50 to 160 cm) is then constructed totally from the hard resin.[4] The end result is an insertion tube that has a soft distal portion for atraumatically snaking through a tortuous colon, with a stiffer proximal portion that is effective at preventing loop reformation in those portions of the colon that have already been straightened by the colonoscope.

ADJUSTABLE FLEXIBILITY

Clinical experience has shown that endoscopists often disagree over what constitutes the ideal insertion tube. This may be due to differences in training, insertion technique, and/or past experience. In addition, some endoscopists have expressed a desire to change the characteristics of the insertion tube during the procedure, based either on insertion depth or the patient's anatomy. This has led to the development of an insertion tube with adjustable stiffness.[5] Colonoscopes with adjustable stiffness have a tensioning wire that runs the length of the insertion tube (see Fig. 3–2). The amount of tension in this wire is controlled by rotating a ring at the proximal end of the insertion tube, just below the control section (Fig. 3–5). When the pull wire in this stiffening system is in the "soft" position, the stiffening system provides no additional stiffness to the insertion tube beyond that provided by the wire mesh and polymer coat. As Figure 3–5 illustrates, when the control ring is rotated to one of the "hard" positions, an angled slot in the control ring pulls on the slide pin at the end of the pull wire, stretching the pull wire and placing it under heavy tension. This stiffens the coil wire that surrounds the pull wire and adds significant rigidity to the insertion tube. As Figure 3–3 illustrates, although the base stiffness of the insertion tube is established by varying the mixture of hard and soft resins in the polymer base layer, the insertion tube can be further stiffened at will during the procedure by rotating the stiffness control ring.

DISTAL TIP

Figure 3–6 illustrates the components found in the distal tip of a typical end-viewing endoscope such as a gastroscope or colonoscope. The larger of the circular glass lenses on the distal tip is the objective lens. This lens focuses a miniature image of the GI mucosa on the surface of a solid-state CCD image sensor. The image sensor sends a continuous stream of images back to the videoprocessor via a collection of very fine electrical wires. The objective lens and CCD unit are tightly sealed to prevent condensation from fogging the image, and to protect the imaging system from damage if fluid were to accidentally enter the instrument.

Light to illuminate the interior of the body travels through the instrument via fiberoptic illumination fibers. This light is then evenly dispersed across the endoscope's field of view via a light guide lens system. Some instruments have a single illumination system (as shown in Fig. 3–6). Other instruments have two fiberoptic bundles and two light guide lenses to improve illumination on both sides of the biopsy forceps (snare, etc.) and to facilitate the packing of components within the insertion tube.

The channel used for biopsy and suction exits close to the objective lens on the distal tip. The position of the biopsy channel relative to the objective lens determines how accessories appear in the image as they enter the visual field. For example, on some instruments, the snare or biopsy forceps appear to emanate from the lower right corner of the image. On other instruments, these accessories enter the visual field from the lower left corner and so forth.

The insertion tube also contains small tubes that carry air and water through the instrument (see Fig. 3–2). These tubes typically merge into a single tube a few inches from the distal tip (see

Fig. 3–9). This combined air/water tube then connects to the air/water nozzle on the tip of the instrument. Under control of the endoscopist, water can be fed across the objective lens to clean it, or air can be fed from the nozzle to insufflate the GI tract. Some gastroscopes and colonoscopes have an additional water tube and a water-jet nozzle on the distal tip for washing debris from the mucosa (see Fig. 3–6).

Figure 3–7 illustrates the components found in the distal end of a typical duodenoscope. Figure 3–7A is a schematic cross-section through the optical and illumination systems found in the duodenoscope's distal tip. Note that the objective lens for viewing the tissue is now located on the side of the distal end rather than on the very tip of the instrument. A prism is used to deflect the angle of view 90 to 105 degrees and to convert the instrument into a side-viewing endoscope. The illumination fibers are likewise steeply bent at the tip of the instrument, directing the light to emanate from the side. As in end-viewing instruments, an air/water nozzle positioned near the objective lens directs water across the lens to clean it, followed by air to blow away any remaining water droplets. Air from this nozzle is also used to insufflate the patient.

All duodenoscopes have a forceps elevator to actively deflect the tip of any accessory passed through the channel. The elevator

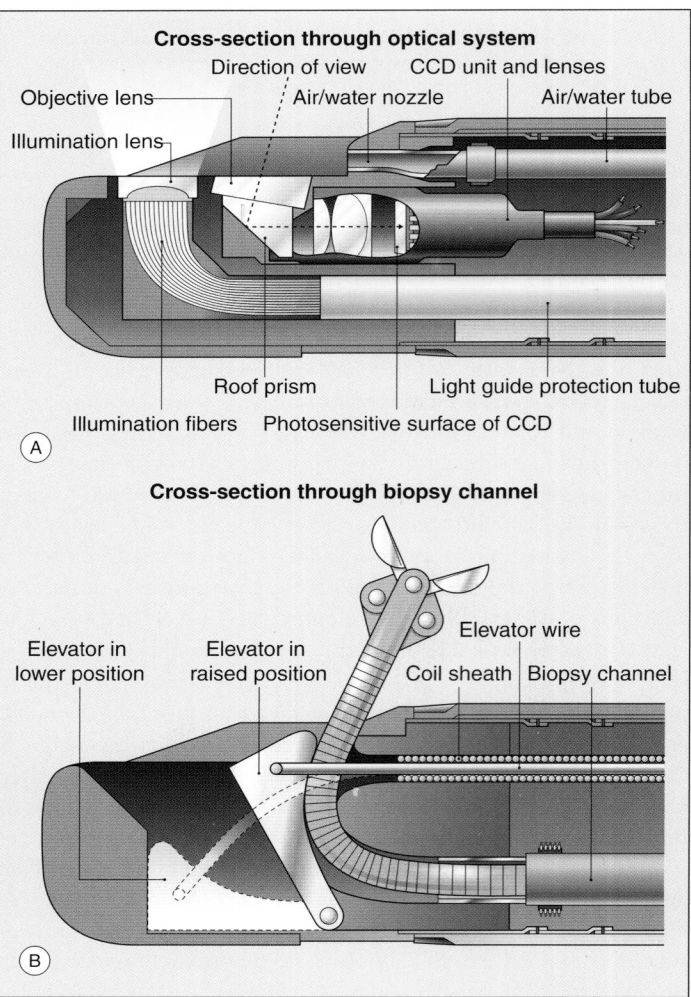

Figure 3–7. A and B, The duodenoscope distal tip assembly.

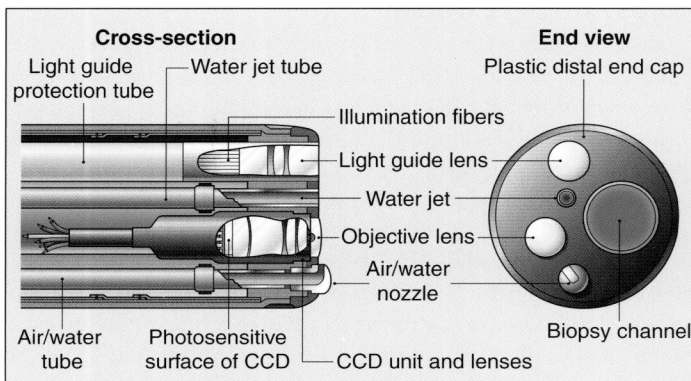

Figure 3–6. The colonoscope distal tip assembly.

mechanism is shown in Figure 3–7B. Normally this elevator lies in a recess within the tip of the endoscope (lowered position). However, when the endoscopist wishes to raise the accessory up into the field of view, he or she operates a thumb control on the control section of the instrument (not shown). This thumb control then pulls on the elevator wire, lifting the elevator out of its recess into a raised position, thereby deflecting the tip of the accessory in an antegrade direction up into the field of view.

BENDING SECTION AND ANGULATION SYSTEM

The distal tip of the endoscope's insertion tube can also be manipulated by the endoscopist. The deflectable portion, referred to as the bending section, is constructed quite differently from the rest of the insertion tube. As Figure 3–8 illustrates, the bending section is composed of a series of oddly shaped metal rings, each one connected to the ring on either side of it via a freely moving joint. These joints are constructed using a series of pivot pins, each one displaced from its neighbors by 90 degrees. One set of pivots allows the bending section to curl in the up and down direction. A second set allows the bending section to curl in the right and left direction. Together they enable the bending section to curl in any direction. The direction of the curl is controlled by four angulation wires that run the length of the insertion tube (see Fig. 3–2). These four wires are firmly attached to the tip of the bending section at the 3, 6, 9, and 12 o'clock positions, respectively. Pulling on the wire attached at the 12 o'clock position will cause the bending section to curl in the up direction, and achieves what endoscopists refer to as "UP tip deflection." Pulling on the wire attached at the 3 o'clock position

will cause RIGHT tip deflection. Pulling the other two wires will cause DOWN and LEFT deflection, respectively.

The endoscopist is able to pull on each of these wires in turn by rotating either the up and down or right and left angulation knobs. (For simplicity, Fig. 3–8 illustrates only the up and down angulation system.) Rotating the up and down and right and left knobs together produces a combined tip movement (e.g., upward and to the right) and allows the endoscopist to sweep the tip of the endoscope in any direction.

Air, Water, and Suction Systems

A schematic of a typical endoscopic air, water, and suction system is shown in Figure 3–9. An air pump in the light source provides air under mild pressure to a pipe protruding from the endoscope's light source connector. This air is carried by an air channel (tube) to the air/water valve on the control section. If this valve is not covered, the air simply exits from a hole in the top of the valve (see Fig. 3–1). This vent hole allows the air pump to pump freely when air is not needed, thus reducing wear and tear on the pump. If the endoscopist wants to insufflate the patient, he or she covers the vent hole with the tip of the finger. This closes off the vent and forces air down the air channel, exiting the instrument through the nozzle on the distal tip.

A one-way valve is incorporated into the shaft of the air/water valve (see Fig. 3–1) to hold air in the patient during examination. During endoscopy, the GI tract is typically insufflated to a pressure considerably above atmospheric pressure. If it were not for this

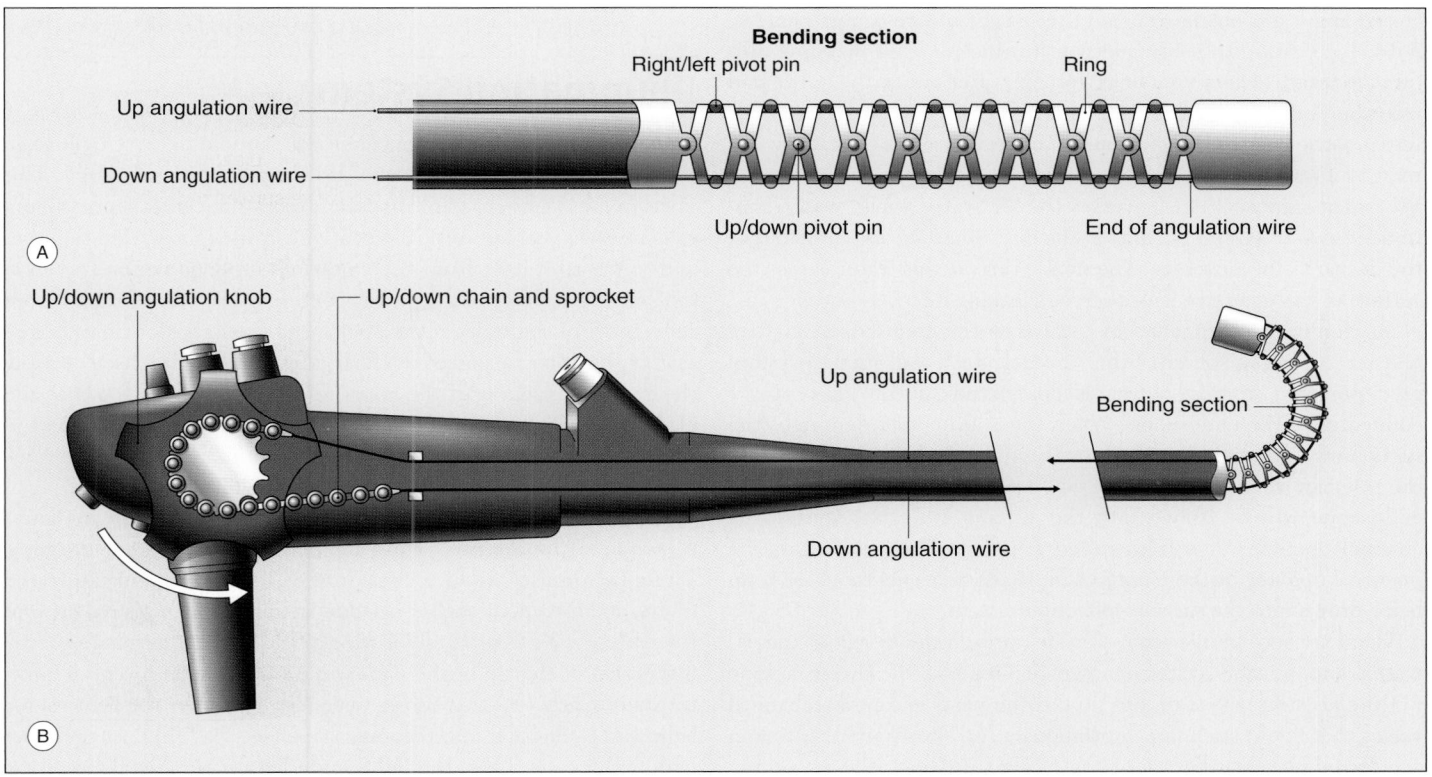

Figure 3–8. The angulation and bending system.

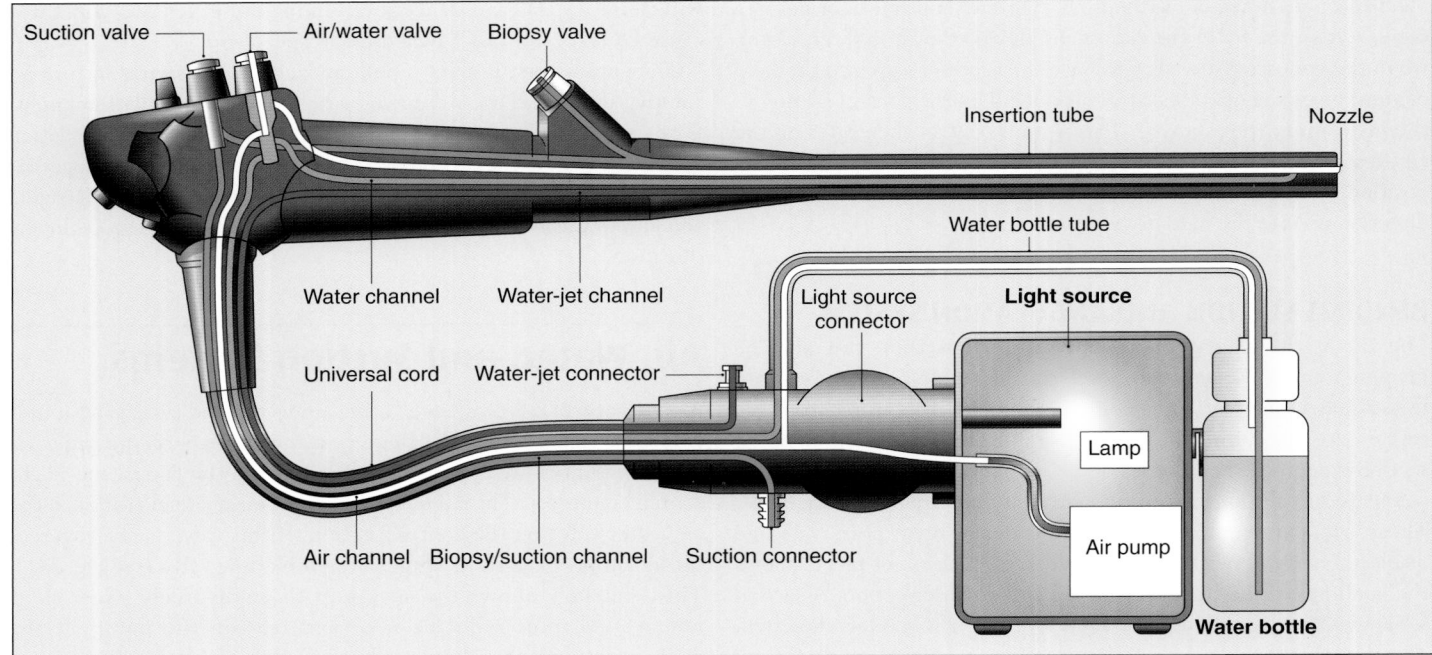

Figure 3–9. Configuration of the air, water, and suction systems.

one-way valve in the system, air from the organ under examination would flow back into the nozzle on the distal tip, up the air channel in the insertion tube, and out the hole in the air/water valve whenever the operator removed his or her finger from the valve. The antireflux valve is required to keep the patient insufflated.

Water, used to clean the objective lens during the procedure, is stored in a water bottle attached to the light source or cart (see Fig. 3–9). In addition to feeding air for insufflation, the air pump also pressurizes this water container, forcing water out of the bottle and into the endoscope. This water is then carried via a tube on the water bottle cap to the light source connector of the endoscope and then by a water channel up the universal cord to the air/water valve. When the endoscopist depresses the air/water valve, water continues down the water channel in the insertion tube and flows out of the nozzle at the distal tip. The nozzle directs this water across the surface of the objective lens, thereby cleaning it.

Suction is also controlled by a valve on the endoscope's control section. A suction source, either the hospital's wall suction system or a portable suction pump, is connected to the light source connector of the endoscope. When the endoscopist depresses the suction valve, suction is applied to the suction/biopsy channel within the insertion tube. Any fluid (or air) present at the distal tip of the endoscope will be drawn into the suction collection system. A channel-opening valve (also called a biopsy valve) closes off the proximal opening of the biopsy channel and prevents room air from being drawn into the suction collection system.

There are several inherent safety features in the design of the air, water, and suction system shown in Figure 3–9. These include (1) the air supply system has no moving parts and no mechanical valves that could stick in a continuously "on" position, resulting in accidental overinsufflation of the patient. Instead, the air simply exits the vent hole in the valve unless the physician has his finger

over this opening and (2) in the event that the suction system becomes obstructed and the endoscopist has difficulty with possible overinsufflation, he or she can simply quickly remove all valves from the endoscope. This stops all feeding of air and water and allows the patient's GI tract to depressurize through the open valve cylinders.

Illumination System

Endoscopes use an incoherent fiberoptic bundle to carry light from the external light source to the distal tip of the endoscope. This fiberbundle is composed of thousands of hairlike glass fibers (30 μm in diameter) that are optically coated to trap light within the fiber and to transmit light from end to end via a phenomenon known as *total internal reflection*. Light rays entering one end of such a fiber reflects off of the walls of the fiber many thousands of times before exiting the opposite end of the fiber. The types of glass used to make the core and cladding of the fiber and the thickness of the core and cladding are all carefully chosen to enable the fiberbundle to carry as much light as possible (see Kawahara[2] for a more complete discussion of fiberoptics).

Endoscopic light sources typically use 300-watt xenon arc lamps to produce the intense, white light needed for videoendoscopy. These lamps also produce considerable heat. Heat sinks, infrared filters, and forced-air cooling systems within the light source prevent the endoscope's fiberbundle from overheating and burning. A close inspection of the tip of the endoscope's light guide reveals a burn-resistant quartz lens that serves to collect light from the light source lamp and to direct it into the endoscope (see Fig. 3–1). At the other end of the endoscope, the light guide lens at the distal tip of the instrument spreads this light uniformly over the visual field (see

Fig. 3–6). An automatically controlled aperture (iris) in the light source controls the intensity of the light emitted from the endoscope tip (see Fig. 3–21). When the endoscope is in a large cavity such as the stomach and significant light is required, the aperture in the light source opens up, allowing the endoscope to transmit maximum light. On the other hand, when the endoscope tip is very close to the mucosa and illumination is bright, the aperture in the light source automatically closes down to reduce the amount of light exiting the light source. If the illumination is too low, the video image on the monitor will be dark and grainy. If the illumination is too strong, the image on the monitor will be washed out (i.e., "bloom"). The videoprocessor automatically keeps the brightness of the illumination within a range that is acceptable for the CCD image sensor by carefully controlling the amount of light produced by the light source.

Solid-State Image Capture

The image sensors used in videoendoscopes are typically referred to as CCDs. These sensors are solid-state imaging devices constructed of silicon semiconductor material. The silicon on the surface of the sensor is responsive to light. When a photon of light strikes the photosensitive surface of the CCD, it displaces an electron from a silicon atom at the surface. This produces a free, negatively charged electron in the silicon material along with a corresponding positively charged "hole" in the crystalline structure of the silicon where the electron was previously bound. This action is referred to as the *photoelectric effect* and is illustrated in Figure 3–10. As additional photons hit the surface of the sensor, additional free electrons and additional corresponding holes are created. The charges built up in the sensor are directly proportional to the amount of light falling on the CCD. Also, note that these charges are created regardless of the color of the light falling on the sensor.

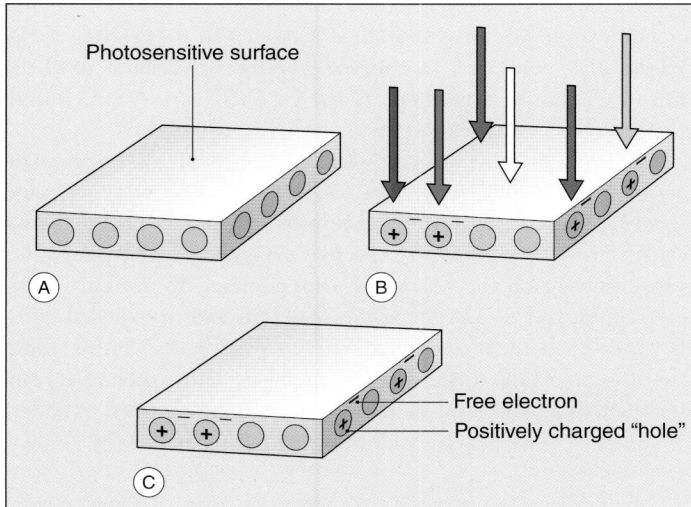

Figure 3–10. The photoelectric effect. Photons falling onto the surface of photosite liberate electrons, thus generating a charge proportional to the amount of light falling on that area.

Although a single photosensitive element is useful for measuring the brightness of light falling on a surface (as in a light meter), it cannot reproduce an image. To reproduce an image, the photosensitive surface must be divided up into a matrix of thousands of small, independent photosites. When an image is focused on the surface of such a sensor, the brightness of the image is automatically measured at each individual photosite within the matrix. Knowing the brightness of every point in the image will allow a vision system to accurately reproduce the image.

The CCD is a common component of such a solid-state vision system. The surface of a CCD image sensor is divided into a rectangular array of discrete photosites, individually referred to as picture elements, or *pixels*. Figure 3–11 illustrates a CCD sensor with such an array.

In a video image endoscope, the CCD is located in the distal tip of the instrument directly behind the objective lens (as shown in Fig. 3–6). The objective lens focuses a miniature image of the observed mucosa directly on the surface of this sensor. The pattern of light falling on the CCD (i.e., the image) is instantly converted into an array of stored electrical charges because of the photoelectric effect previously described. Because the charges stored in each of the individual pixels are isolated from neighboring pixels, the sensor faithfully transforms the optical image into an electrical replica of the image. This electrical representation is then processed and sent to a video monitor for reproduction.

As Figure 3–11 illustrates, pixels in dark areas of the image develop a low voltage, because of the generation of fewer charges. Pixels in brighter areas of the image develop a proportionately higher voltage, because of the creation of more electron/hole pairs. Each pixel is able to develop any level of charge, from some minimum to some maximum, depending on the brightness of the incident light. The conversion process from light to electrical charges is linear. Doubling the number of photons falling on a pixel doubles the number of charges generated at the pixel, until the storage capacity of the photosite is full.

READING THE IMAGE CREATED ON THE CHARGE-COUPLED DEVICE

After the CCD is exposed to the image, the charges developed in the CCD must be "read out" in an orderly manner and then processed to reproduce the original optical image. The manner in which the charges are moved about within the CCD as they are read out depends on the configuration of the CCD. The three most common types of CCDs are the line transfer CCD, the frame transfer CCD, and the interline transfer CCD.[1] Each of these CCD types has specific advantages in terms of the CCD's sensitivity to light (i.e., the brightness required of the endoscope's illumination system), the type of light source required (strobed vs. nonstrobed), the size of the CCD (which in turn affects the size of the endoscope's distal tip), and the speed at which the charges can be transferred out of the CCD.

The CCD schematically illustrated in Figure 3–11 is a line-transfer CCD. Figure 3–11A illustrates the projection of an optical image onto the photosensitive surface of the CCD. Electrical charges are developed at each photosite in the array after brief exposure to the image (Fig. 3–11B and C). For simplicity,

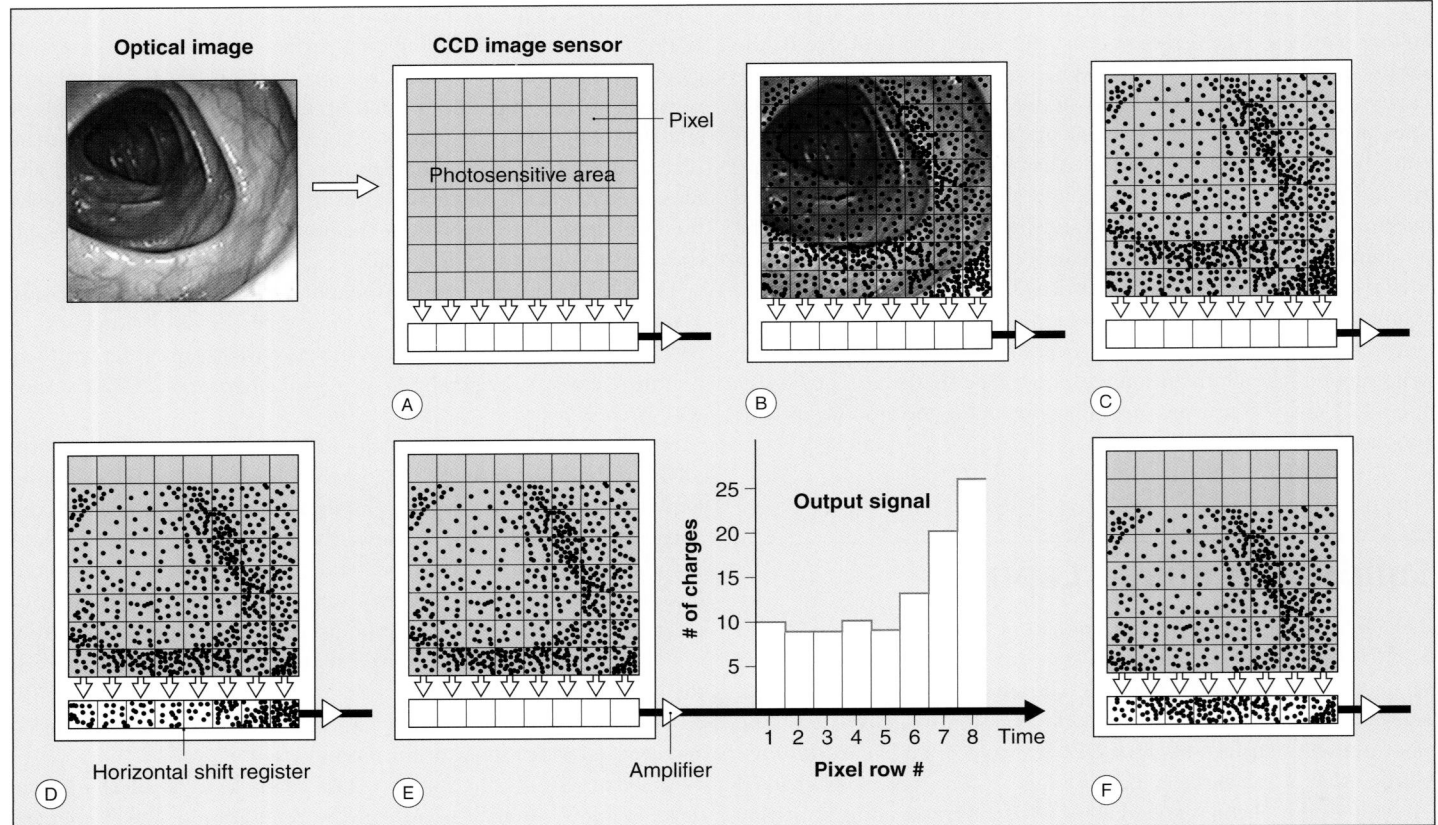

Figure 3–11. Image capture and read-out with a line-transfer charge-coupled device (CCD). Although an actual endoscopic CCD contains several hundred thousand pixels, for simplicity, the array illustrated contains only 64 pixels arranged in an 8-row by 8-column matrix. *A,* Image of mucosa is projected on the CCD's photosensitive surface. *B,* An electrical replica of the image is created because of the photoelectric effect. *C,* The electrical replica remains when shielded from light. *D,* The replica is shifted down one row pushing data from the bottom row into the horizontal shift register. *E,* The shift register is emptied, creating an output signal. *F,* The replica shifts down another row. The process repeats.

Figure 3–11 illustrates an array with only a very few pixels and only a very few resulting charges. These charges are represented by small dots within the photosites.

The charges within each pixel are then controlled and shifted over the surface of the CCD via electrodes adjacent to each photosite (these electrodes are not shown in Fig. 3–11). By varying the voltages applied to these electrodes, the electrons within individual pixels are transferred as charge packets from one pixel to another. Sequential voltage changes on these electrodes march the charges toward the bottom edge of the CCD and into a horizontal shift register (see Fig. 3–11D). The charges in the horizontal shift register are then passed through an output amplifier and are converted into an output signal. The output signal fluctuates in direct proportion to the number of charges stored in each pixel. At the point in the process illustrated in Figure 3–11E, the charges in bottom row of the original image has been read out and passed through the output amplifier and will be sent to the videoprocessor for reconstruction. The electrical representation of the entire image has shifted down one row on the CCD.

Once the horizontal shift register has been read out and cleared (emptied), the charges in each pixel of the array are then sequentially transferred down to the pixel below, resulting in a second shift of the image replica. This fills the horizontal shift register with the charges that were originally in the second-to-the-bottom row of the array, as shown in Figure 3–11F. The charges in the horizontal shift register are then again read out, resulting in an output signal that is representative of the brightness of the image falling on the second-to-the-bottom row of the original image. The processing of the image replica continues, in a similar step-by-step fashion, until the entire CCD has been read out. Once the CCD is read and cleared, it is ready for another exposure.

The charge-coupling process—the transfer of charges from pixel to pixel as packets—gives the CCD its name (charge-coupled device). The charges in the furthermost corners of the CCD are actually moved sequentially through several hundred photosites before they reach the horizontal shift register. In current video-endoscopes, the CCD is exposed, read out, and re-exposed 60 to 90 times each second. To maintain image fidelity during these repetitive transfers, it is essential that these charge packets remain intact with no loss or gain in charge quantity in the process of under-going hundreds of thousands of transfers per second as the CCD is being read out.

It should be noted that the photosensitive array of a line transfer CCD must be shielded from light during the entire time that the image is being moved and read out (the steps illustrated in Fig. 3–11C and following). This is necessary to prevent mixing

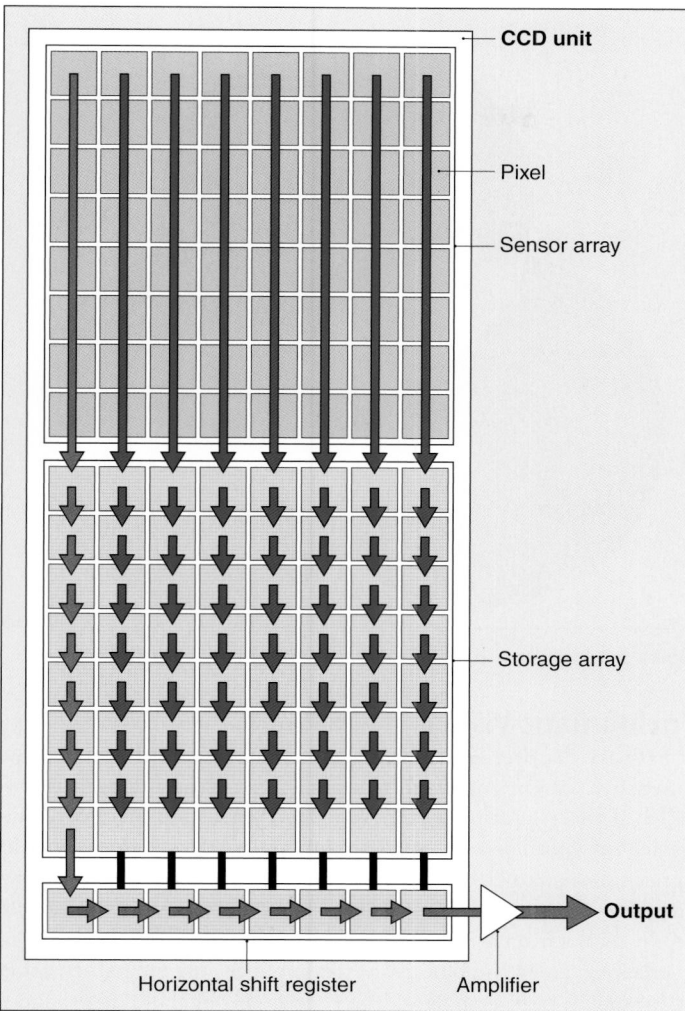

Figure 3–12. Schematic of a frame-transfer charge-coupled device (CCD).

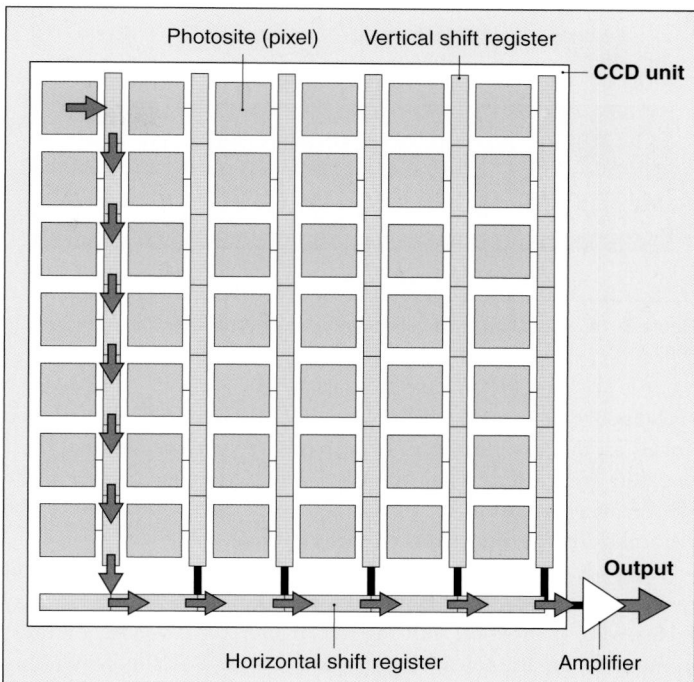

Figure 3–13. Schematic of an interline-transfer charge-coupled device (CCD).

information from the image under transfer with new charges being generated at the photosites by the light still falling on them. To preserve the original image, the photosites must be completely dark while the image replica is read out. One method of doing this in an endoscopic application is to strobe, or momentarily interrupt, the light emitted by the endoscope as the CCD is being read. This creates a momentary burst of light to expose the image sensor, followed by a brief period of darkness, as the CCD is read out and cleared. Endoscopists who have used a red, green, and blue (RGB) sequential endoscopy system (typically called a black and white CCD system) are quite familiar with the concept of strobed endoscopic light sources.

TYPES OF CHARGE-COUPLED DEVICES

One alternative to the line transfer CCD is a frame transfer CCD (illustrated in Fig. 3–12). The frame transfer CCD differs from the line transfer CCD in that the frame transfer CCD has a second array that is used only for charge storage. The first array is a photosite (sensor) array, that generates an electrical replica of the image, similar to that in a line transfer CCD. However, immediately

after creating the image replica, all of the charges created in the sensor array are transferred to the storage array in one quick transfer (illustrated by the long arrows in Fig. 3–12). Here they are held until they can be read out, line by line, in a process similar to a line transfer CCD (illustrated by the short arrows in Fig. 3–12). The red arrows in Figure 3–12 illustrate the path taken by the charges generated in the pixel in the upper left corner of the sensor array. Charges in other pixels take a similar path.

The advantage of the frame transfer CCD is that the device can collect light and generate charges in the sensor array at the same time that the storage array is being read out and processed. Because the frame transfer CCD has more time to gather light, it does not require as much illumination as a line transfer CCD. As a result, the number of lightguide fibers in the endoscope can be reduced. The disadvantage of frame transfer CCDs is that they are physically larger than line transfer CCDs because of the addition of the storage array. This additional size is a distinct drawback in endoscopic applications. In addition, frame transfer CCDs also require illumination strobing.

The interline transfer CCD is a hybrid of the previous two types. The interline CCD has vertical shift registers placed adjacent to each column of photosites (Fig. 3–13). Immediately after exposure, the charges developed at the photosites are transferred in one quick step to the adjacent vertical shift registers. Because of the rapid, one-step transfer of charges to the vertical shift registers, it is not necessary to interrupt illumination of the CCD during the read-out process. In the meantime, the charges in the vertical shift registers are transferred, step-by-step, down to the horizontal shift register, where they are then read out in a conventional manner. (The red arrows in Figure 3–13 illustrate the read-out path of charges generated in the upper left corner pixel.) The vertical shift registers are shielded from light, allowing them to be emptied as the CCD is

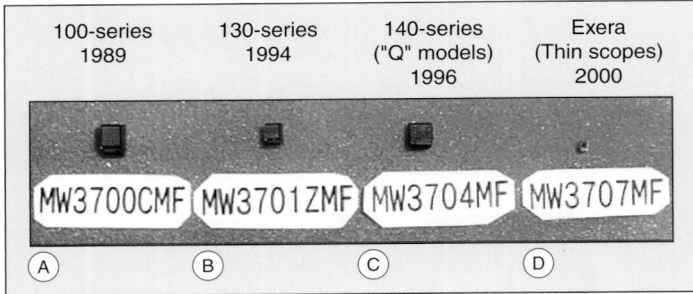

100-series 1989	130-series 1994	140-series ("Q" models) 1996	Exera (Thin scopes) 2000
MW3700CMF	MW3701ZMF	MW3704MF	MW3707MF
(A)	(B)	(C)	(D)

Figure 3–14. Reduction in size of charge-coupled devices (CCDs) from 1989 to 2000.

continuously exposed to light. The CCD thereby collects a second image as the first image is being read. When the vertical shift registers are finally empty, the newly created image replica in the sensor array is instantly transferred from the photosites to the vertical shift registers, and the process repeats.

A big advantage of the interline transfer CCD is that it does not require strobing of the illumination. Because the entire sensor array is cleared to the vertical shift registers in one step, the sensor array is immediately ready to capture the next image. So-called color chip endoscopes that use continuous, nonstrobed light sources are examples of interline transfer CCD systems.

All three types of CCDs described previously have been used in commercial videoendoscopes. Each type has its own advantages and disadvantages in terms of physical size, circuit complexity, light sensitivity and illumination requirements. Because of the predominance of color chip systems, the interline transfer CCD is currently the most commonly used CCD in endoscopy.

HISTORY OF ENDOSCOPE CHARGE-COUPLED DEVICE DEVELOPMENT

The first videoendoscopes were introduced in 1983 by Welch Allyn.[7] It was the miniaturization of CCDs used in handheld video cameras to a size that would fit within the distal tip of an endoscope that allowed the development of videoendoscopy. Since then, technology has continued to advance, allowing further reductions in the physical size of the CCD while increasing the number of pixels in the sensor array. This has allowed videoendoscopes to become progressively thinner, with larger channels and higher image resolution with each new generation. Figure 3–14 illustrates the progress made in reducing the size and increasing the resolution of the sensors used in Olympus endoscopes over the last 15 years.

REPRODUCTION OF COLOR

All solid-state image sensors are inherently monochromatic devices. They can reproduce only B&W images. The silicon photosites on the surface of the CCD develop charges in proportion only to the intensity (brightness) of the light falling on the array. They cannot distinguish the color of the incident light. (As shown in Fig. 3–10, a photon of red light produces the same charge as a photon of blue light and so forth.) For an endoscope to reproduce the necessary attribute of color, the system must have an additional means to analyze the color (wavelength) of the light falling on the sensor.

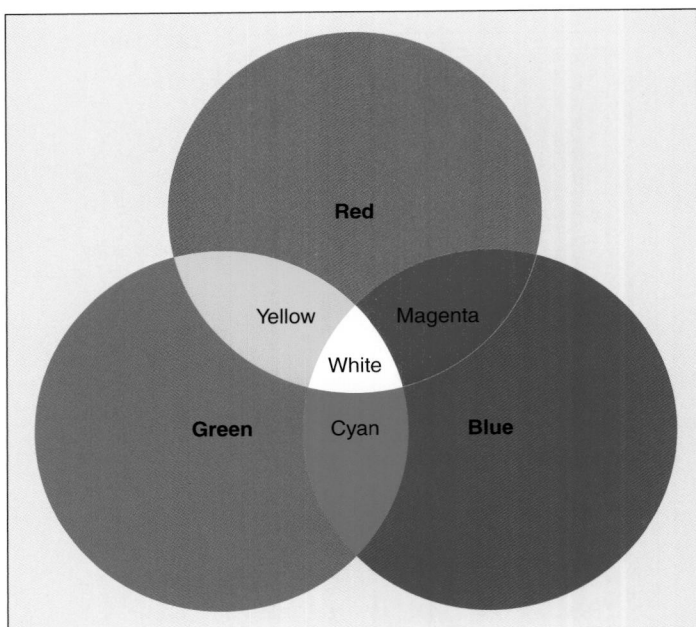

Figure 3–15. Illustration of the additive primary colors.

Trichromatic Vision

It has been discovered that nearly any color to which the human eye is sensitive can be matched by mixing light of only three colors—RGB. If three light projectors are fitted with RGB filters and the projected spotlights are overlapped, the resulting image would appear similar to that shown in Figure 3–15. The color resulting from the overlap of the red and green projectors is indistinguishable from monochromatic yellow light. Likewise, light from the overlapping green and blue projectors produces the mental sensation of looking at pure cyan light. The overlap of red and blue produces magenta. It is surprising that where all three of the projectors overlap in the center, the observer sees an area of pure white, with no hint of the three component colors. If the intensities of each of the three projectors are accurately controlled and varied, it is possible to reproduce virtually any spectral color in the central area of the overlap.

All video images are reconstructed using the three component colors of RGB. Because these three colors can be additively combined to mimic all other spectral colors they are commonly referred to as the three *additive primary colors*. It is these three colors, RGB, that are the colors of the phosphors used to create full color images on the face of a video monitor (Fig. 3–16).

Commercial videoendoscopes currently use two very different systems for recreating color. The first commercial video image endoscope, the VideoEndoscope introduced by Welch Allyn in 1983, was based on an RGB sequential imaging system. Many current instruments continue to use this system. The second system, the so-called color-chip endoscope, has now become the predominant system worldwide. Each color reproduction system has its own advantages and disadvantages, as explained later.

Red, Green, and Blue Sequential Imaging

The components of an RGB sequential videoscope system are schematically illustrated in Figure 3–16. The endoscope has a

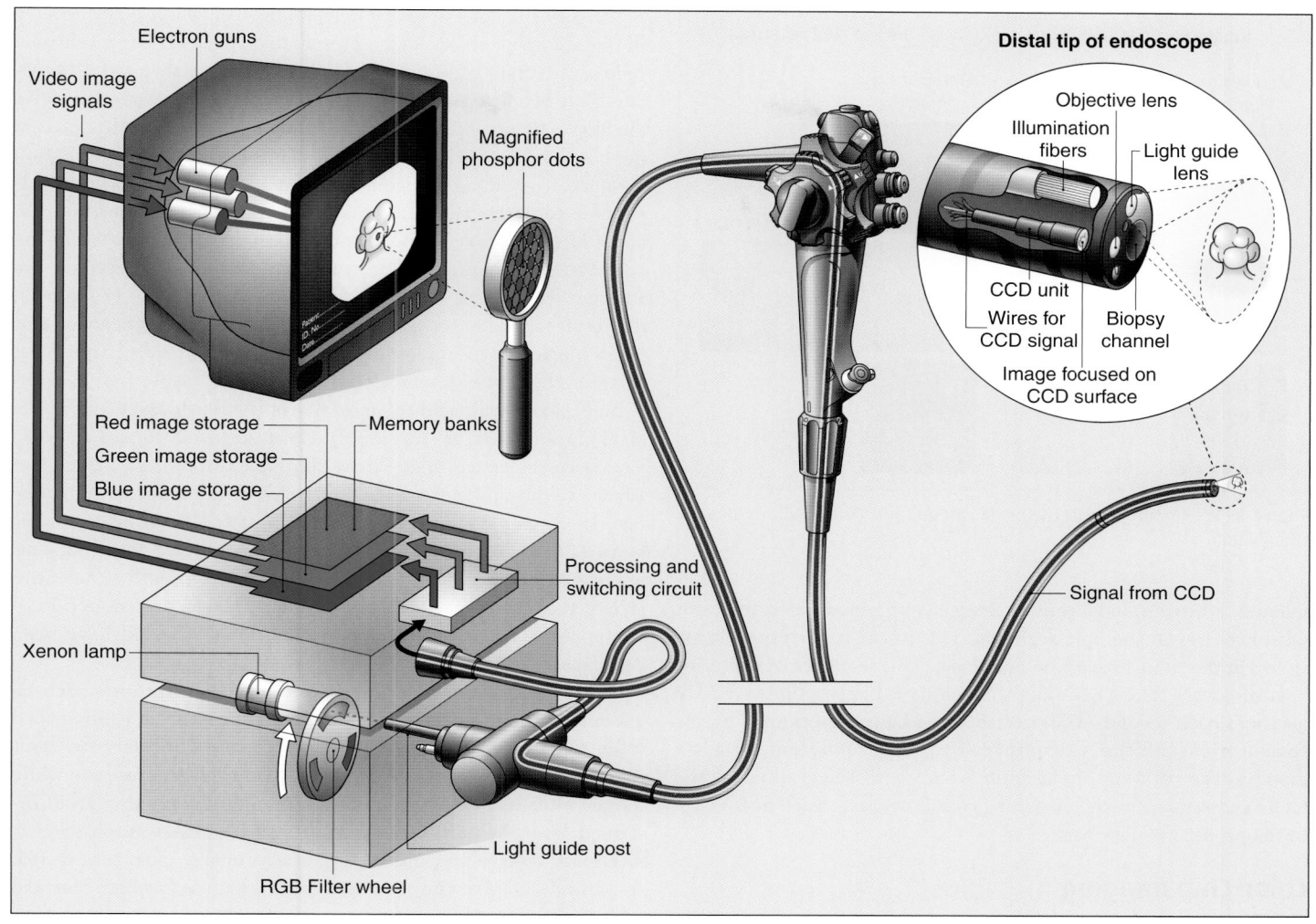

Figure 3–16. Schematic of a red, green, and blue (RGB) sequential endoscope imaging system.

monochromatic (B&W) CCD mounted in its distal tip. The objective lens at the tip of the endoscope focuses a miniature image of endoscope's field of view on the photosensitive surface of this CCD. This image is illuminated via a fiberoptic bundle running through the endoscope. This fiberoptic bundle carries light from a lamp within the light source to the distal tip of the endoscope. Unlike the light used for fiberoptic endoscopes, or the light used for color-chip endoscopes, this light is not continuous but is strobed or pulsed.

The high-intensity xenon lamp within the light source emits continuous white light with the approximate color temperature of sunlight. A rotating filter wheel with three colored segments (RGB) is placed between this lamp and the endoscope's light guide post. This filter wheel chops and colors the light falling on the endoscope's light guide bundle into alternating bursts of red, black (no light), green, black, blue, and black. When observed at the distal tip of the endoscope, this illumination appears to be a flickering white light, rather than the actual sequential bursts of RGB. Rotating at 20 to 30 revolutions/second, these three primary colors appear to merge, creating white illumination when observed with the unaided eye.

The purpose of this unique illumination system is to produce three separate monochromatic images, each obtained when the field of view is sequentially illuminated by the three primary colors in turn. During the fraction of a second when the red filter is in the light path, the GI mucosa is illuminated only by red light. The CCD image sensor captures a monochromatic (B&W) image of the mucosa as it appears under this red illumination (illustrated in Fig. 3–17). Tissue that is naturally reddish in color reflects heavily under red light and appears to be bright. Areas of the tissue with less red reflect red light weakly and appear dark under red illumination.

After a monochromatic image of the mucosa is obtained under red illumination, the filter wheel rotates to the adjacent opaque area of the wheel. At this point, the endoscopic illumination goes momentarily dark and the image on the CCD is read out, directed through a processing and switching circuit, and stored in the "red image" memory bank of the videoprocessor (see Fig. 3–16).

After the red image is stored, the filter wheel rotates to place the green filter in the light path. A monochromatic image of the mucosa as it appears under green illumination is then obtained by the CCD (see Fig. 3–17). This image is then read out and sent to the videoprocessor for storage in the "green image" memory bank. In a similar

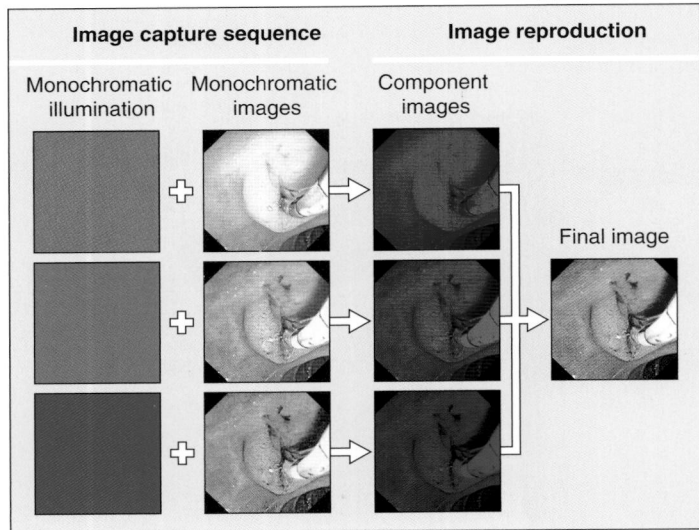

Figure 3–17. Image capture with red, green, and blue (RGB) sequential illumination.

manner, a third monochromatic image is obtained when the filter wheel rotates to the blue segment. This image is correspondingly stored in the "blue image" memory bank. This sequence of capturing a set of images for each of the three primary colors is repeated 20 to 30 times each second—the precise speed being determined by the specifications of the videoprocessor. Synchronization circuitry matches the rotation of the filter wheel with the readout of the CCD and sequences the switching circuit to direct each new image to the proper memory bank.

Color-Chip Imaging

As an alternative to the RGB sequential imaging system, some videoendoscopes use a color-chip imaging system. A color-chip CCD is essentially a B&W image sensor with a custom-fabricated, multicolored, microfilter bonded to its surface. This filter allows the CCD to directly and simultaneously resolve the component colors of the image. The term *instantaneous single-plate* CCD is sometimes used for this device to emphasize that all three color components are obtained concurrently by a single "plate," or CCD.

Endoscopes typically use a color-mosaic filter, like the type shown in Figure 3–18. It is possible to design a mosaic filter with any number of different color configurations; however, the color choices and the corresponding algorithm shown in Figure 3–18 are by far the most common. The colors used in this mosaic filter are yellow, cyan, and white (no filter). These segments are arranged in a 2 × 2 pixel box pattern that regularly repeats over the face of the CCD. Because the final output signals sent to the video monitor must be the standard RGB component images, the image produced behind this yellow, cyan, and white filter must be converted into its primary RGB components before display.

The processing algorithm for doing this is also illustrated in Figure 3–18 and works as follows. As Figure 3–19 will illustrate later, yellow filter elements absorb blue light but pass red and green light. This enables the pixels behind all yellow filter elements to receive both red and green information. Figure 3–19 shows that pixels behind cyan filter elements receive both the blue and the green

portions of the color spectrum. The filter-free white pixels receive all three primary colors. In a representative block of four pixels (one yellow, one cyan, and two white), three pixels receive red information, four pixels receive green information, and three pixels receive the blue component information (compare the colors of the pixels in the boxes in Fig. 3–18). By adding or subtracting the information obtained from adjacent pixels using an appropriate algorithm, it is possible to derive the individual RGB component values for each block of (four) pixels. For example, if the charges created in the cyan (green + blue) pixel are subtracted from the charges in the adjacent white (red + green + blue) pixel (see Fig. 3–18, step 1), the result is a value for the intensity of the red component for that pixel block. In a similar fashion, subtracting the charge level between the adjacent yellow (red + green) and white (red + green + blue) pixels will yield the intensity of the blue component in the pixel block (see Fig. 3–18, step 2). Once the values for red and blue have been calculated, they can be subtracted from the voltage of an adjacent white pixel, to calculate the green component value (see Fig. 3–18, step 3). At this point, each of the RGB intensities is known for the particular 2 × 2 block of pixels being analyzed. This process is then repeated for all 2 × 2 pixel blocks across the entire face of the CCD. When the process is completed, all required RGB component values for every pixel in the matrix will have been calculated.

One may question why it is desirable to go through such an extended process as the one just described if using an RGB-striped filter will yield the RGB component values directly, without calculation. The answer lies in the fact that a yellow, cyan, and white mosaic filter has a significant advantage in brightness over an RGB-striped filter. When RGB filter segments are used, each pixel is filtered to receive only one of the three primary colors (Fig. 3–19). A cyan-filtered pixel, on the other hand, is exposed to both blue and green light. Therefore, it is more heavily illuminated than a pure blue or pure green pixel. Likewise, pixels behind a yellow filter (red and green) or a white filter (no filtration = RGB) receive more photons (light) than pixels behind a pure RGB filter. Because of the increased light intensity passing through a yellow, cyan, and white mosaic filter, a CCD with this construction exhibits far greater light sensitivity than an RGB-striped CCD. The clear advantage of non-primary-colored filters is that because of the increased light sensitivity, color mosaic CCDs allow the videoscope designer to construct an endoscope with a smaller light guide fiber bundle, to maximize the endoscope's angle of view, and to increase the endoscope's depth of field. All of these characteristics improve optical performance but require additional light. For this reason all commercial color-chip endoscopes use color mosaic CCDs.

Reproduction of Motion

The color-chip videoscope has an inherent advantage over the RGB sequential videoscope in reproducing motion. The filter wheel in RGB videoprocessors typically rotates at 20 to 30 revolutions/second (rps). Because each of the color component images is captured individually, in sequence, it takes 1/30 second (with a 30-rps filter wheel) to capture the three component images that make up a single video image. If there is relative motion between the endoscope and the object being viewed, as often occurs during endoscopy, the three component images may differ slightly with

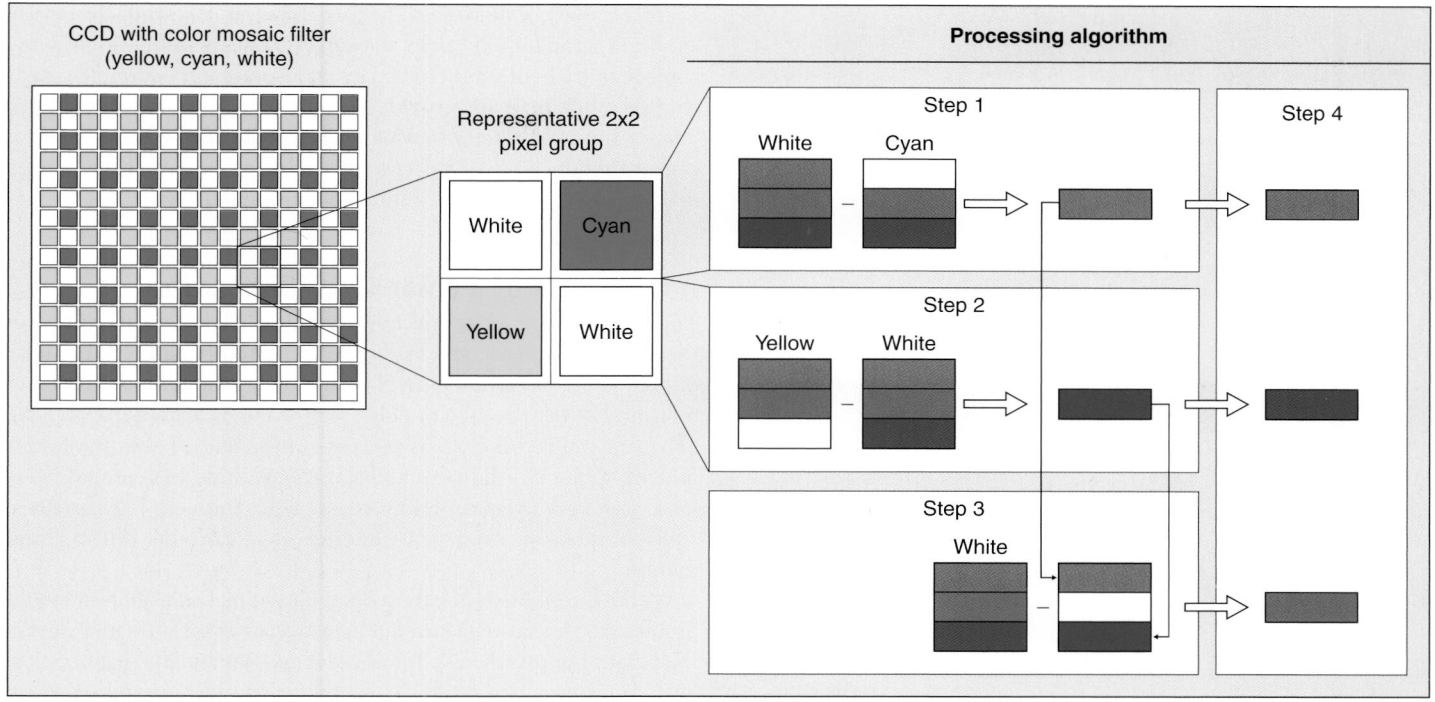

Figure 3–18. Color-chip charge-coupled device (CCD): Color-mosaic filter construction and processing algorithm.

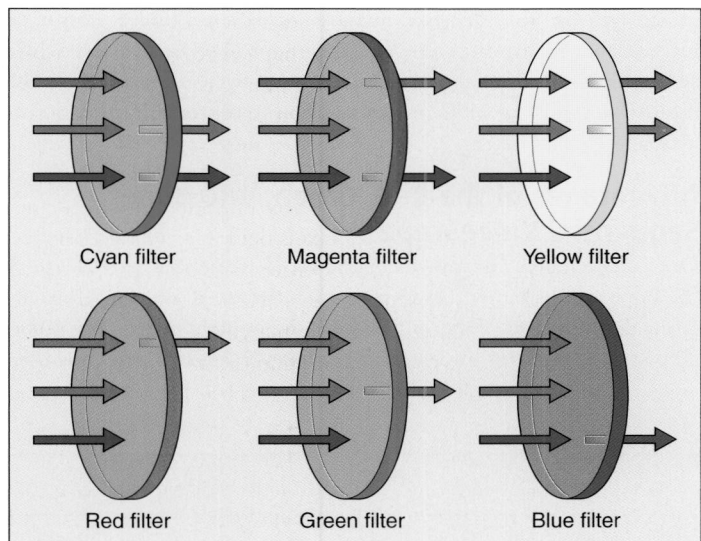

Figure 3–19. Effect of filter color on transmission of red, green, and blue light.

respect to object size and position. When these three RGB images are subsequently superimposed on the video monitor, it is likely that they will be misaligned. This misalignment will be clearly visible if the endoscopist happens to freeze the image while it is moving rapidly. Figure 3–20A illustrates the type of effect produced if the image (or part of the image) is moving while being captured. Note that the highlights, that appear as white spots on the nonmoving image (see Fig. 3–20B), now appear as separate RGB spots (Fig. 3–20A). In addition, the edges of the moving polyp in the figure have colored "ghost" fringes and all detail in the moving tissue is lost.

These problems are reduced in second generation RGB sequential videoprocessors. These processors incorporate an anti-color-slip circuit to analyze the video signal in real time and to freeze the image at the moment when color separation is at a minimum (see Fig. 3–20). In early RGB systems, the processor "froze" the image that was displayed on the monitor at the exact instant the image capture function was activated (i.e., the "freeze" button was depressed). Instead of capturing this initial image, activation of the freeze function on these newer RGB processors triggers a special capture circuit that analyzes the stream of incoming images for the next 0.25 second, that is, during the next five rotations of the filter wheel (see Fig. 3–20). From these five complete images (a total of 15 RGB component images), the circuit selects the set of RGB component images that exhibits the least amount of color separation. In the example shown in Figure 3–20, the capture circuit has found that there is considerable color slip in the image captured immediately after the freeze button was depressed. This results in colored fringes around the edges of objects that were moving, a color separation of normally white highlights, and an overall loss of image detail in the moving tissue (see Fig. 3–20A). On the other hand, the circuit has found that relative motion was minimal during RGB component images 7, 8, and 9; these were the third set of images captured after the freeze button was depressed (see Fig. 3–20B). The circuit therefore holds these three RGB component images in memory and displays them on the observation monitor as the best possible still image of the mucosa. However, this system does not reduce the strobing, color separation, and water-droplet flicker observed during real-time endoscopy.

Although the RGB sequential videoscope has difficulty reproducing motion, the color-chip videoscope is excellent at imaging moving tissue, because all three color components of the image are

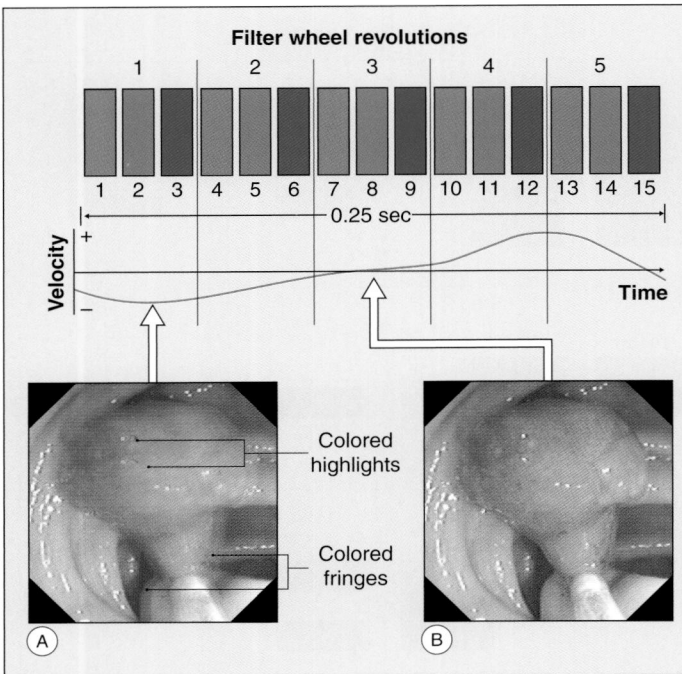

Figure 3-20. "Antislip" feature in a modern videoprocessor. *A,* Image captured during maximum motion. *B,* Sharp image when motion is at a minimum.

captured simultaneously. Because the illumination is continuous and unstrobed and the frame rate is consistent with contemporary TV standards, reproduction of moving images is smooth.

Another unique advantage of the color-chip videoscope is a feature that allows its effective shutter speed to be shortened to increase the sharpness of captured images. The color-chip system normally captures a new video image every 1/60 second. Although this time period is relatively short, quickly moving subjects that are frozen may appear to be slightly blurred (but with no color separation) because of movement during the capture period. To reduce this blur, it is advantageous to shorten the electronic capture period to a fraction of its normal time (e.g., from 1/60 second to

1/250 second). As in traditional film photography, the shorter the exposure period, the sharper the subject, but the more brightly the subject must be illuminated to prevent underexposure. The fast-shutter mode may not provide enough light for distant panoramic images, but in situations in which it is truly needed, the fast-shutter capture mode is very effective at producing bright, sharp, frozen images (i.e., close-up stills of quickly moving mucosa).

Advantages of a Color-Chip Videoscope

The color-chip videoscope has several inherent advantages over the RGB sequential system. These are listed in Table 3–1. Those discussed previously include (1) a smooth, natural reproduction of motion; (2) the absence of color separation on frozen images; and (3) a fast-shutter mode that prevents image blur of even the fastest moving subjects. Additional advantages include (4) compatibility with standard (non-strobing) xenon light sources, (5) increased transillumination, and (6) superior performance during laser therapy.

With RGB sequential endoscopes, abdominal transillumination is problematic because its strobed light output is substantially weaker than that of nonstrobed systems. Many RGB sequential light sources have a means for temporarily removing the spinning filter wheel from the light path when operating in the "transillumination" mode. This produces a steady, intense white light that is ideal for transillumination. However, once the filter wheel is removed, the image will be lost, because in most cases the illumination is so intense that it saturates the CCD, thus producing a totally white screen. Even if an image is visible, it will be in B&W because the filter wheel must be in its proper position to reproduce color.

Advantages of the Red, Green, and Blue Sequential Videoscope

One of the major advantages of the RGB sequential videoscope is the opportunity for increased resolution. Image resolution is heavily dependent on the number of pixels in the original image. The color-chip system requires information from several pixels, which is then

Table 3–1. Advantages and Disadvantages of a Color-Chip Videoscope

Advantages	Disadvantages
Color Chip System Smooth, natural reproduction of motion No color separation on captured images Fast shutter mode prevents image blur even when the subject is moving Uses standard (nonstrobing) xenon light source Transillumination is possible under normal viewing conditions Superior performance during laser therapy	Difficult to adapt for color analysis research
RGB Sequential System High-resolution image possible Each pixel images all three colors Advanced color analysis is possible by changing filters	Image slip between RGB component images "Rainbow effect" on rapidly moving objects Requires strobed light source Transillumination requires removing filter wheel and produces a B&W image Laser therapy is hindered by white aiming beam and image "bloom"

B&W, black and white; RGB, red, green, and blue.

processed via an algorithm, to obtain the RGB component values for a single point within the image.

However, in the RGB system, each pixel is illuminated by red, green, and blue light sequentially. Each pixel thus provides information on each of the three color components in turn. The fact that a single pixel can provide all three color components is an advantage for small imaging devices such as endoscopes. In practice, this advantage is not significant for most videoendoscopes, but it is a significant advantage when the thinnest possible endoscope is required (e.g., video choledochoscope).

Because the RGB sequential videoscope uses primary-colored filters and because the color components are isolated, captured, and processed separately within the videoprocessor, this type of videoscope provides very accurate color information. This potential advantage is not usually apparent with routine endoscopy; however, in image analysis research the RGB sequential system has the upper hand.

Laser Therapy with Videoendoscopes

No videoendoscope can be used effectively with any laser that operates within the visible spectrum. The intense laser light will totally saturate the CCD sensor, overpower the endoscopic image, and make observation of laser therapy impossible. However, it is possible to effectively adapt videoendoscopes for use with lasers that operate outside the visible spectrum. As an example, the neodymium:yttrium-aluminum-garnet (Nd:YAG) laser, which produces near-infrared light at 1060 nm, is compatible with appropriately modified videoscopes. Because the Nd:YAG laser operates outside the visible spectrum, endoscope manufacturers commonly protect the endoscope's CCD from the laser's light by covering it with a filter that transmits visible light (the image) but heavily absorbs the reflected laser light (near-infrared light). Whenever the laser is fired within the endoscopic field, this filter prevents the laser output from reaching the CCD, leaving the image undisturbed.

Even with such a filter, RGB sequential videoscopes have problems when used with nonvisible lasers. The first is a loss of the true color of the aiming beam. The helium-neon (He-Ne) aiming beam used in almost all Nd:YAG lasers appears as a red spot when observed with a fiberscope or a color-chip videoscope. When observed by an RGB sequential videoscope, however, the beam is always white. This is because the red aiming beam is on continuously and appears equally bright to the CCD during all portions of the RGB imaging cycle. As a result, the videoprocessor interprets the He-Ne beam as white. The bright, artificially white aiming beam displayed on the monitor obscures the tissue effect produced by the Nd:YAG laser and impairs observation of the laser's action. The loss of aiming beam color can be avoided by strobing the aiming beam in synchrony with the light source filter wheel. However, this modification is complex and costly.

Another problem of the RGB sequential endoscope is the relatively low brightness of its strobed illumination. This causes two problems: (1) the intensity of the laser aiming beam must be reduced because medical lasers have been traditionally designed to work with the intense illumination produced by fiberoptic endoscopes and (2) during periods of concentrated treatment, the tissue may glow at the point of laser impact. Because the burning tissue may be brighter than the videoscope's background illumination, the glowing tissue may cause the CCD to bloom and mask the local tissue effect of the laser.

In contrast, the color-chip videoscope uses intense, nonstrobed white light illumination, similar to that used with fiberscopes. The aiming beam retains its red color, and its intensity is usually not a problem. The result is a view similar to that seen through fiberoptic instruments. Because of these factors, the color-chip videoscope is the far better choice for endoscopic laser therapy.

Functions of a Typical Videoprocessor

Figure 3–21 schematically illustrates the functions of the various electrical circuits found within a typical RGB sequential videoprocessor. Many of these same functions are found in a color-chip videoprocessor. The CCD image sensor (located in the distal end of the endoscope) receives both power and timing signals from the videoprocessor. The timing signals control the readout of the CCD and the transfer of charges to and from the horizontal shift register (discussed earlier). From the shift register, the image signal is fed through an amplifier on the CCD and then into the preprocess circuitry of the videoprocessor.

The preprocess circuitry is responsible for electrically isolating the patient from the potentially dangerous high-voltage circuitry of the videoprocessor, for initiating automatic brightness control, and for adjusting the chroma (color) and white balance of the image. The preprocess circuitry further amplifies the signal and often performs additional image processing functions such as edge or structure enhancement.

The signal then passes through an analog-to-digital (A/D) converter, changing the signal from an analog to a digital format. The digitized image is then directed through a switching circuit for storage in one of the RGB image memory arrays. Images from the digital memories are next passed through a size-adjustment circuit that scales the relative size of the endoscopic image for presentation on the video monitor. A second circuit then adjusts the relative position of the endoscopic image (e.g., moves it to the right side of the monitor screen) and sizes and positions any subscreen image that may be added to the screen alongside the main image.

At this point, the developing image is still in a digital form, but it has been adjusted in size and position, with subscreen images (if any) added. The image then passes through a digital-to-analog (D/A) converter to change the image back to an analog format. Finally, the image passes through a postprocessing circuit that encodes the video signal to conform with a recognized video signal standard, allowing the image to be displayed on any standard video monitor.

Figure 3–21 also schematically illustrates some of the mechanical components of the videoprocessor and light source. Light from the light source lamp first passes through an infrared filter to remove nonvisible heat rays. The light then passes through a lens that focuses it on the tip of the fiberoptic light guide bundle within the universal cord of the endoscope. An iris in the light path controls the brightness of the light transmitted to the endoscope, and a filter

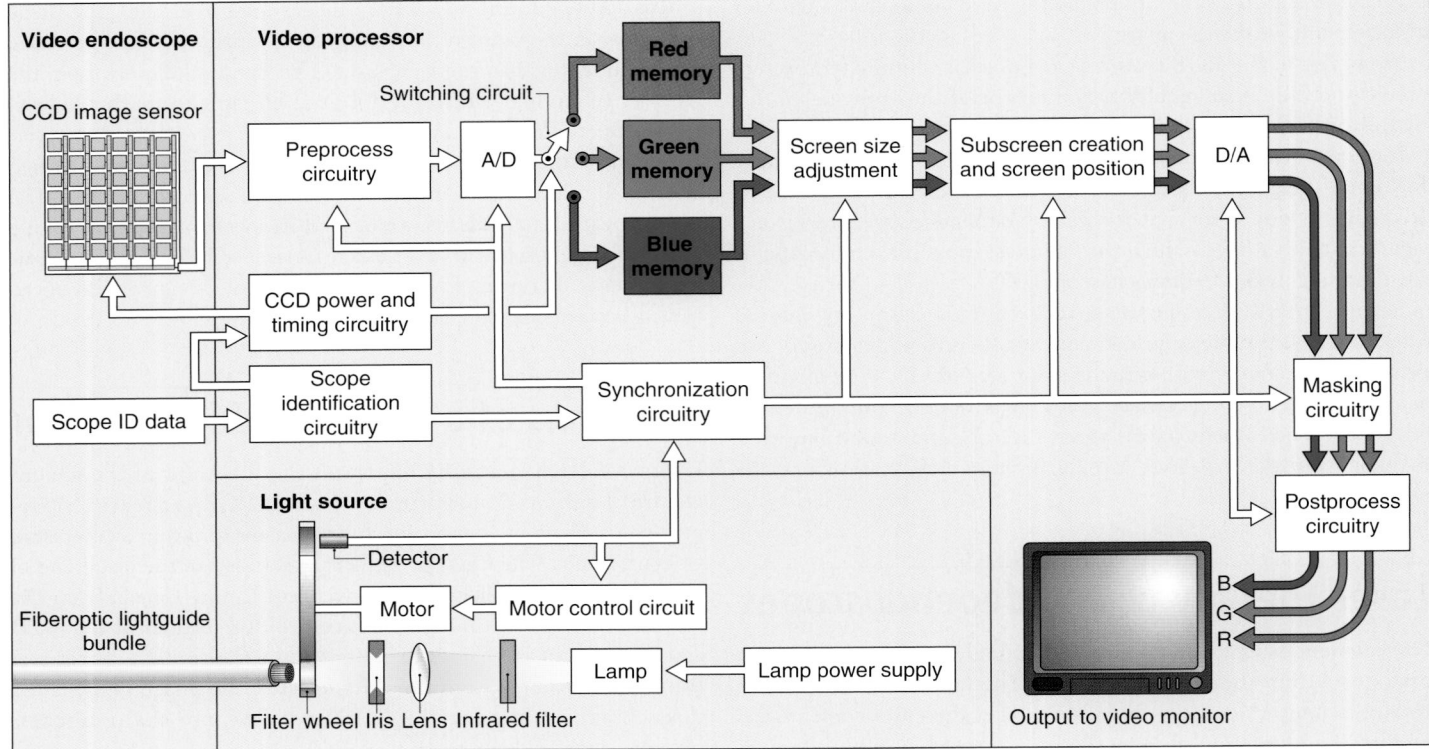

Figure 3–21. Schematic of videoprocessor and light source.

wheel modifies the color of the light (described previously). The motor rotating the filter wheel is regulated by a control circuit to ensure that the wheel spins at the precise speed required by the videoprocessor. Detectors placed adjacent to the filter wheel identify which filter segment (red, green, or blue) is currently in the light path.

Figure 3–21 also illustrates the synchronization circuitry that is within the videoprocessor to ensure that all functions of the videoprocessor and light source are coordinated with the video output signal. These functions include synchronization of filter wheel rotation, exposure and readout of the CCD, memory transfers within the videoprocessor, and image freeze control. Videoprocessors also generally require endoscope identification circuitry to identify the model (or type) of endoscope connected to the processor. Endoscope identification allows the system to compensate for differences in endoscope length and CCD type.

A major portion of the circuitry within a videoprocessor is designed around the specific CCD with which the processor is intended to operate. First-generation videoscopes used the same CCD for all endoscope models—from the largest colonoscope to the slimmest gastroscope. Current videoprocessors are designed to drive a family of CCDs, each of which differs in size and image resolution (see Fig. 3–14). An advantage of this strategy is that a family of compatible CCDs allows for a wide range of videoscopes—including large-diameter high-resolution instruments, specialty endoscopes, thin pediatric endoscopes, and large-channeled therapeutic instruments—to be compatible with the same videoprocessor. For a single videoprocessor to drive several different CCDs, the various CCDs must have similar electrical and

physical characteristics. In particular, the videoprocessor must specifically compensate for differences in pixel number, illumination requirements, data transfer rates, and drive circuitry. Despite the range of CCDs available for current videoprocessors, there are no videoprocessors that are compatible with both color-chip and RGB sequential endoscopes and it is not possible to interchange endoscopes or processors made by different manufacturers. Figure 3–21 summarizes many of the basic functions of a videoprocessor.

Video Standards

All cathode ray tube (CRT) monitors, whether used for computer or video applications, "paint" an image on the face of the monitor with a scanning electron beam. This beam typically starts in the monitor's upper left corner and scans the monitor horizontally, line by line, from top to bottom. The energy of this electron beam causes the RGB phosphor dots applied to the back of the screen to glow briefly, thus creating an image (see Fig. 3–16). Broadcast and closed-circuit TV systems use a system of interlace scan. The picture tube first scans all of the odd horizontal lines (1, 3, 5, and so on) and then goes back to complete the image by scanning the even lines (2, 4, 6, and so forth). The odd lines represent the first "field" of the image; the even lines represent the second field. Together, the two fields paint the entire screen once and create a single video "frame," or image. The process then starts over again, first one field, then the other, until a second complete picture or video frame is displayed.

In 1953, the National Television System Committee (NTSC) proposed a color encoding method that expanded on the RS-170A standard to create the first B&W-compatible, color TV standard for public broadcasting. The NTSC standard is still the universal color encoding method used in the United States, Canada, and Japan. (Most European countries conform to the incompatible PAL or SECAM color TV standards.) The NTSC video signal is a "composite" video signal, meaning the luminance (brightness) and chrominance (color) information are combined in one signal. Although a composite signal is convenient for broadcasting, image quality deteriorates as the color information is encoded into and decoded from the brightness signal. Because all common ancillary equipment (video monitors, videocassette recorders, etc.) accept NTSC composite video signals, all videoendoscope processors have NTSC composite output connectors on their rear panels.

In addition to an NTSC composite output, current video-processors also have a second set of connectors allowing for the output of the image in a luminance/chrominance (Y/C) video format (also called Super Video or S-Video). Y/C video connections maintain the brightness and chrominance information on two separate wires. Monitors, videocassette recorders, and other peripheral equipment communicating with Y/C signals provide better image quality than composite video equipment.

A third method of connecting video equipment, is to use four separate red, green, blue, sync (RGBS) cables. This video inter-connection method is the ideal means for preserving the original video image quality. Because the RGB image components and the synchronization signals are carried over four separate wires, this information is never mixed. Most videoscopes provide the option of using any or all of these three video connection methods (NTSC composite, Y/C, or RGBS). Most video monitors used for endoscopy also have inputs for all three types of signals and allow the user to select from these various configurations. For the best video reproduction, it is advisable to use RGBS or Y/C interconnections in place of the simpler NTSC wiring. (See Barlow[4] for a more complete discussion of the video standards used in endoscopy.)

Endoscopic Ultrasound Instrumentation

Although earlier endoscopic ultrasonography (EUS) instruments used fiberoptic imaging, video imaging now dominates this field as well. The current models of linear scanning instruments and the Olympus radial scanning instrument are oblique-viewing. The Pentax radial instrument is end-viewing. The previous discussion regarding overall instrument construction, insertion tube components, air, water, and suction systems, video imaging technology, and so forth generally apply to EUS instruments as well. However, to permit improved acoustic coupling, EUS instruments have a latex balloon at the tip that can be inflated or deflated with water. This requires additional infusion and suction controls compared with the standard endoscope.

EUS endoscopes obviously have additional components not found on standard endoscopes—the most important is a piezoelectric ultrasound transducer for obtaining the ultrasound image. Radial

instruments scan in a plane perpendicular to the long axis of the endoscope, generating a circular image with the endoscope at the center of the image. The Pentax radial instrument is electronic rather than mechanical. This permits Doppler function (current mechanical instruments do not have Doppler capability). However, the radial image is 270 degrees rather than 360 degrees generated by a mechanical rotating instrument. Linear instruments are all electronic curved array. They scan in an axis parallel to the long axis of the endoscope and the ultrasound in alignment with the instrument's biopsy channel. This permits a biopsy needle to be placed into adjacent tissues under real-time ultrasound guidance. To facilitate precise placement of the needle, an elevator is also present on these instruments, similar to that found in duodenoscopes.

Figure 3–22 schematically illustrates some of the additional components found in a mechanical radial scan EUS endoscope. The Olympus radial scanning instrument has an ultrasound transducer located in the tip of the endoscope, which rotates at a precisely con-trolled speed via a motor mounted at the top of the control section. An encoder informs the ultrasound system of the exact rotational position of the transducer at all times. Because the transducer requires electrical signals to generate and receive the ultrasound signals, a "slip ring" interface is required to couple these electrical signals to and from the rotating shaft that spins the transducer. All of these components are located at the top of the endoscope's

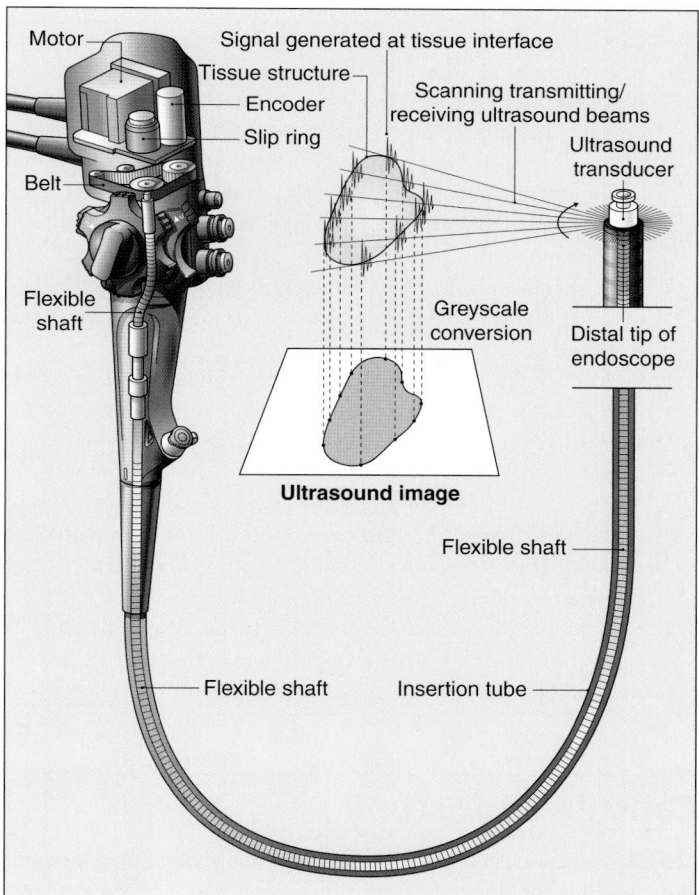

Figure 3–22. Schematic or a radial (mechanical) endoscopic ultrasound instrument.

control section. (Recently introduced EUS instruments have relocated these components to the light source connector to reduce the bulk and weight of the endoscope's control section.)

Factors to Consider When Evaluating a Video Image Endoscope

The video image endoscope is a technologically advanced and complex clinical tool. When these instruments first entered the market, published comparison reports of various commercially available models were common.[3,6,8] Now that the technology of video endoscopy has matured, such published comparisons are rare. It is difficult to identify any single design criterion as the deciding factor in selecting the best videoscope for a particular clinical application. When evaluating a videoendoscope the following criteria should be considered:

1. Image quality—Does the instrument have a sufficiently wide angle of view, with good depth of field, high image resolution, good image contrast, accurate color, clear frozen images, and a wide dynamic range (ability to see clearly in both light and dark areas of the image)?
2. Illumination characteristics—Does the instrument have adequate image brightness under all clinical conditions? Is illumination evenly distributed from image center to image edge? Does the system have responsive automatic brightness adjustment as viewing distances change?
3. Basic endoscope functions—Does the instrument have responsive handling and appropriate insertion tube characteristics? Does it have smooth tip angulation, a control section of appropriate shape and weight, conveniently positioned angulation knobs and valves, and good suction, insufflation, and lens washing performance?
4. Basic specifications—Does the manufacturer have a full range of instrument models, with a variety of insertion tube diameters and biopsy channel capacities?
5. Suitability for special therapeutic procedures—Is the videoendoscope well protected against image noise from electrosurgical generators? Is image quality acceptable when using lasers?
6. System features—Are the videoprocessor controls easy to understand? Are the endoscope switches for the control of remote devices easily accessible? Does the size and weight of the equipment allow for easy transportation?
7. System expansion and integration—Is the system capable of easily interfacing with hard copy devices, video tape recorders, and computerized image management systems?

Capsule Endoscopy

The past 5 years has witnessed the remarkably rapid development and clinical acceptance of capsule endoscopy. The first experiments in animals were published in the journal *Nature* in 2000,[9] and clinical trials for GI bleeding of obscure origin were first reported in

the literature in 2001.[10,11] Capsule endoscopy has been a major development in the trend toward minimally invasive examination of the GI tract. Currently, capsule endoscopy comprises three separate components:

1. Capsule
2. Receiving and storing system
3. Workstation for image integration (into a video) and analysis

CAPSULE

The current model of capsule (M2A, Given Imaging Inc., Israel) is 11 mm in diameter and 26 mm long. The capsule and its component parts are illustrated in Figure 3–23. One end of the capsule has a clear optical dome. The capsule is symmetrical in shape and small enough to tumble in the intestine; it therefore images the mucosa proximally or distally in a random fashion. Behind the clear dome is an aspherical lens with four light-emitting diodes (LEDs) arranged around it. The lens focuses the image onto a complementary metal-oxide semiconductor (CMOS) imager. Behind this are two silver oxide batteries, sufficient to power the LEDs and transmission for about 7 to 8 hours. A transmitter and antenna are located at the back of the capsule.

The capsule is packaged adjacent to a magnet. Removal of the capsule from the magnet trips a switch, activating the LEDs and transmission. Two images are regenerated and transmitted per second, synchronized with the LEDs' flashing illumination. This small amount of illumination is adequate because the bowel is collapsed (i.e., no air insufflation as is seen with standard endoscopy) and the image is very close to the optical dome.

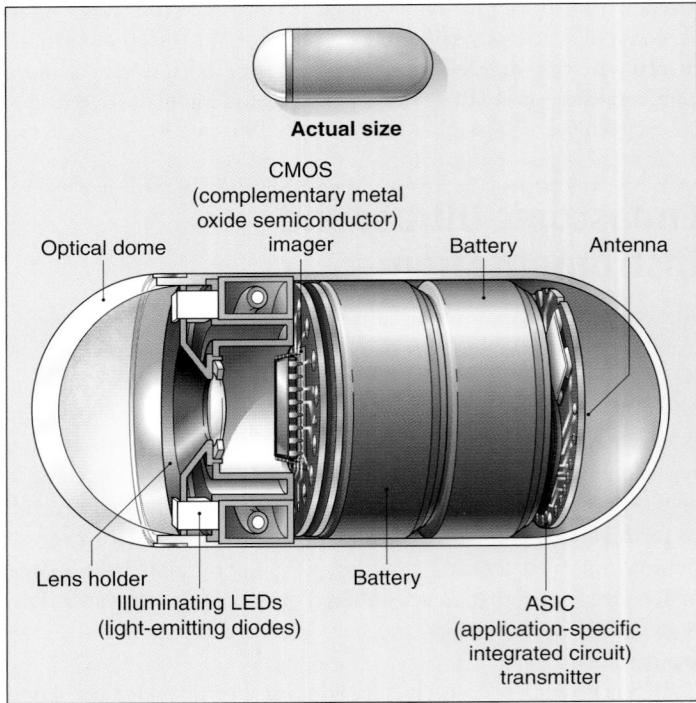

Figure 3–23. Schematic of the Given M2A capsule. (Property of Given Imaging [www.givenimaging.com].)

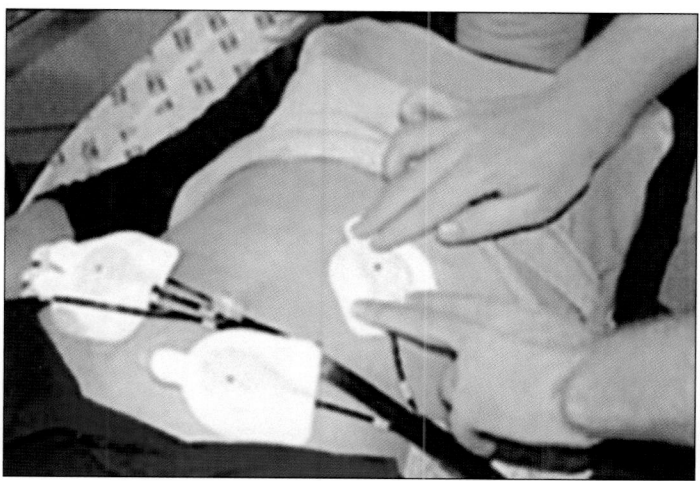

Figure 3–24. Lead placement for capsule endoscopy recording.

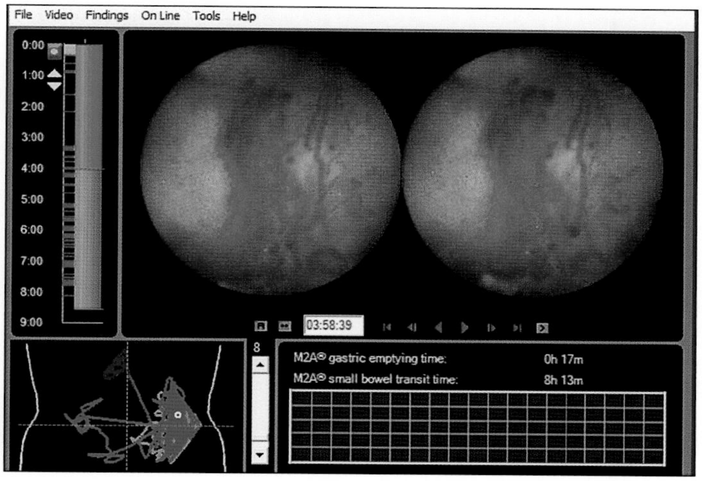

0:00	
1:00	
2:00	
3:00	
4:00	
5:00	
6:00	
7:00	
8:00	
9:00	

03:58:39

M2A® gastric emptying time: 0h 17m
M2A® small bowel transit time: 8h 13m

File   Video   Findings   On Line   Tools   Help

Figure 3–25. Typical Given capsule endoscopy workstation appearance.

RECEIVING AND STORING SYSTEM

The patient has a series of eight sensors taped to the anterior abdominal wall (Fig. 3–24). These detect the transmitted signal from the capsule. Furthermore, by measuring the relative strength of the signal from different sensors, the approximate location of the capsule within the abdomen can to determined. The latest generation of software for capsule endoscopy includes tracking of the capsule within the abdomen correlated with the image. The sensor leads connect to a small recording hard-drive worn on a belt. The belt also contains a rechargeable battery pack. The belt apparatus is relatively light and does not significantly impede normal nonexertional activities. The patient can ambulate and need not remain in the hospital during the recording phase.

WORKSTATION

After at least 7 hours, the sensors and belt are removed from the patient. The recording is downloaded to a computer workstation, which converts the approximately 50,000 images of the study into a video file of the patient's study on the computer's hard drive. The study is then viewed on the workstation screen as a video at speeds determined by the observer (Fig. 3–25).

REFERENCES

1. Barlow DE: Flexible endoscope technology: The video image endoscope. In Sivak MV Jr (ed): Gastroenterologic Endoscopy, 2nd ed, vol 1. Philadelphia, WB Saunders, 2000, pp 29—49.
2. Kawahara I, Ichikawa H: Flexible endoscope technology: The fiberoptic endoscope. In Sivak MV Jr (ed): Gastroenterologic Endoscopy, 2nd ed, vol 1. Philadelphia, WB Saunders, 2000, pp 16–28.
3. Knyrim K, Seidlitz H, Vakil N, et al: Optical performance of electronic imaging systems for the colon. Gastroenterology 96:776–782, 1989.
4. Moriyama H: Engineering characteristics and improvement of colonoscope for insertion. Early Colorectal Cancer 4:57–62, 2000.
5. Moriyama H: Variable stiffness colonoscope—structure and handling. Clin Gastroenterol 16:167–172, 2001.
6. Schapiro M: Electronic video endoscopy. A comprehensive review of the newest technology and techniques. Pract Gastroenterol 10:8–18, 1986.
7. Sivak MV Jr, Fleischer DE: Colonoscopy with a video endoscope. Preliminary experience. Gastrointest Endosc 30:1–5, 1984.
8. Video colonoscope systems. Health Devices 23:154–205, 1994.
9. Iddan G, Meron G, Glukhovsky A, Swain P: Wireless capsule endoscopy. Nature 405:417, 2000.
10. Appleyard M, Fireman Z, Glukhovsky A, et al: A randomized trial comparing wireless capsule endoscopy with push enteroscopy for the detection of small-bowel lesions. Gastroenterology 119:1431–1438, 2000.
11. Appleyard M, Glukhovsky A, Swain P: Wireless-capsule diagnostic endoscopy for recurrent small-bowel bleeding. N Engl J Med 344:232–233, 2001.

Cleaning and Disinfecting Endoscopic Equipment

Douglas B. Nelson

Introduction

Recent articles in the lay press suggesting that endoscopes are inadequately reprocessed have raised undue fear regarding the potential for transmission of infection during endoscopy. When current guidelines for endoscope cleaning and disinfection have been followed, this risk is virtually eliminated. However, this topic has largely been taken for granted by many endoscopists. Standardized cleaning and disinfection protocols have been available for some time, and, with few exceptions, changes have been gradual. This may have engendered some complacency on the part of endoscopists, to the point that many endoscopists were only vaguely aware of what went on "behind the curtain" of the endoscope reprocessing room; instruments were used on patients, taken away by gastrointestinal (GI) nurses or other health care personnel, reprocessed, and returned ready for patient use. As the amount of information available increases to patients via the Internet (often not based on scientific evidence), the endoscopist must be able to discuss this subject confidently with his or her patients.

Since the first report of fiberoptic GI endoscopy in 1961,[1] the endoscope has undergone almost continuous evolution in design. Although most of these developments have been aimed at improving the diagnostic and therapeutic capability of GI endoscopy, the introduction of fully immersible endoscopes in 1983 greatly facilitated cleaning and disinfection of the internal channels of the endoscope.[2,3] The development of video imaging technology, which provided a tremendous increase in the quality and resolution of the endoscopic image, had few implications for endoscope reprocessing. However, some changes have come at the cost of increasing complexity of design, presenting new challenges to cleaning and disinfection. The addition of an elevator lever to the duodenoscope allowed easier cannulation of the papilla during endoscopic retrograde cholangiopancreatography (ERCP), although the new exposed moveable part at the distal tip of the instrument and the associated control-wire channel also added new reprocessing steps. A similar type of elevator is also present on current endoscopic ultrasonography (EUS) endoscopes, or echoendoscopes. Echoendoscopes also possess an additional channel to inflate a balloon at the tip (needed to create the acoustic interface) that must be cleaned and disinfected. Another recent modification to some endoscope models is the inclusion of a dedicated water irrigation channel (other than the standard air and water channels), which also must be cleaned and disinfected (regardless of use). Current reprocessing guidelines are discussed in detail.

These guidelines, although applicable to nearly all GI endoscopes, do not apply to sheathed endoscopes systems. There is one Food and Drug Administration (FDA)-approved endoscopic sheath system that is commercially available.[4–8] Unlike the popular misconception of an "endoscope condom," the sheath is actually a part of the endoscope insertion tube and contains several channels. Because this is a complete endoscope system, the sheaths are not compatible with other endoscopes. Although the sheath is disposable and thus does not need conventional cleaning and disinfection (i.e., a new sheath is used for each procedure), the control dials on the handpiece are not protected and do require reprocessing. These dials are removable and require conventional cleaning and disinfection or sterilization. The two main disadvantages of the system are (1) sheath systems are not available for all types of endoscopes currently in use and (2) the imaging technology of the instrument uses fiberoptic rather than video-chip technology.[9] Readers should refer to the manufacturer's instructions for reprocessing this type of endoscope.

Principles of Disinfection

DEFINITIONS

Cleaning is a term that is simple to understand but difficult to precisely define in terms of a measurable endpoint. The official definition of cleaning used by the FDA is "the removal, usually with detergent and water, of adherent visible soil, blood, protein substances, and other debris from the surfaces, crevices, serrations, joints, and lumens of instruments, devices, and equipment by a manual or mechanical process that prepares the items for safe handling and/or further decontamination."[10] Although this seems to be straightforward, there is as yet no uniform consensus on how this

Table 4–1. Descending Order of Resistance of Microorganisms to Liquid Chemical Germicides

Prions (Transmissible Spongiform Encephalopathies Agents)
Creutzfeldt-Jakob (CJD)
Variant Creutzfeldt-Jakob (vCJD)

Bacterial Spores
Bacillus subtilis
Clostridium sporogenes

Mycobacteria
Mycobacterium tuberculosis

Nonlipid or Small Viruses
Poliovirus
Coxsackievirus
Rhinovirus

Fungi
Trichophyton spp.
Cryptococcus spp.
Candida spp.

Vegetative Bacteria
Pseudomonas aeruginosa
Salmonella choleraesuis
Enterococci

Lipid or Medium-Sized Viruses
Herpes simplex virus (HSV)
Cytomegalovirus (CMV)
Coronavirus
Hepatitis B virus (HBV)
Hepatitis C virus (HCV)
Human immunodeficiency virus (HIV)
Ebola virus

Modified from Bond WW, Ott BJ, Franke KA, McCracken JE: Effective use of liquid chemical germicides on medical devices: Instrument design problems. In Block SS (ed): Disinfection, Sterilization, and Preservation, 4th ed. Philadelphia, Lea & Fibiger, 1991, pp 1097–1106.

is operationally defined or what the endpoint of the process should be. How hot should the water be, and what concentration of detergent? How many times should the cleaning brush be passed down the endoscope channels? What does "visibly clean" mean, and how can this be applied to the internal channels of an endoscope that cannot be examined? There are a number of experimental methods that can be used to determine the efficacy of cleaning by the detection of residual protein, carbohydrate, blood, or viral/bacterial RNA/DNA,[11-16] although these are impractical for routine clinical use. However, despite the difficulty in precisely defining the process or the subsequent endpoint, there is ample evidence that endoscope cleaning (as currently performed) is an essential part of the disinfection process. Mechanical cleaning alone reduces microbial counts by approximately 10^3 to 10^6 (three to six logs), or a 99.9% to 99.9999% reduction.[17-24] It is equally clear that failure to adequately clean endoscopes or their accessories can defeat disinfection or sterilization processes,[25] and thus is an integral part of any endoscope reprocessing regimen.

Antiseptics are chemicals intended to reduce or destroy microorganisms on living tissue (e.g., skin), as opposed to disinfectants, which are used on inanimate objects (e.g., medical devices such as endoscopes).

Disinfection is defined broadly as the destruction of pathogenic and other types of microorganisms. There are three levels of disinfection: (1) *high-level disinfection*: the destruction of all mycobacteria, nonlipid or small viruses, fungi, vegetative bacteria, lipid or medium viruses, and most but not necessarily high numbers of spores; (2) *intermediate-level disinfection*: the destruction of all mycobacteria, vegetative bacteria, fungal spores, and some nonlipid viruses but not bacterial spores; and (3) *low-level disinfection*: the destruction of most bacteria (except mycobacteria), most viruses (except some nonlipid viruses), and some fungal spores (and not bacterial spores).[10] For liquid chemical germicides (LCGs), high-level disinfection is operationally defined as the ability to kill 10^6 mycobacteria (a six log reduction). The FDA defines a high-level disinfectant as a sterilant that is used for a shorter contact time.[26] This difference in the way that the same chemical is used to achieve different levels of disinfection/sterilization becomes important for endoscopy, because the contact times for sterilization with any given LCG are generally much longer (hours) than that for high-level disinfection (minutes) and may be detrimental to the endoscope. The relative resistance of various microorganisms to LCGs is shown in Table 4–1.

Sterilization is the destruction or inactivation of all microorganisms, or the absence of all microbial life. As an endpoint, it is an absolute (sterile or not sterile). However, the process is operationally defined as a 12-log reduction of bacterial endospores.[27] However, not all sterilization processes are alike. Steam and dry heat are the most extensively characterized; both are thermal methods that do not require the same physical contact as LCGs to achieve sterilization, and the processes are routinely monitored by the use of biologic indicators (e.g., spore test strips) to demonstrate that sterilization has been achieved. Although theoretically sterilization could be achieved with LCGs, the FDA and others have stated that these processes do not convey the same sterility assurance as other sterilization methods.[26,28,29]

The Spaulding classification system divides medical devices into categories based on the risk of infection involved with their use.[30,31] With some modifications, this classification scheme is widely accepted nationally and internationally, and has been used by the FDA, the Centers for Disease Control and Prevention (CDC), epidemiologists, microbiologists, and professional medical organizations to determine the degree of disinfection or sterilization needed for various medical instruments. Three categories of medical devices and their associated level of disinfection are recognized: (1) *critical:* these are defined as devices or instruments that are introduced into the human body and come into contact with normally sterile tissue or the vascular system; because of the potential for infection if the device is contaminated with microorganisms, these devices require sterilization; (2) *semicritical:* these are defined as devices that contact intact mucous membranes and do not ordinarily penetrate sterile tissue; they should receive at least high-level disinfection; and (3) *noncritical:* these devices do not ordinarily touch the patient or touch only intact epithelium (e.g., stethoscopes or patient carts); these items may be cleaned by low-level disinfection.

DISINFECTION AND GASTROINTESTINAL ENDOSCOPY

GI endoscopes are considered semicritical devices and thus should undergo at least high-level disinfection. This standard has been endorsed by the FDA[32]; the CDC[33]; and numerous professional

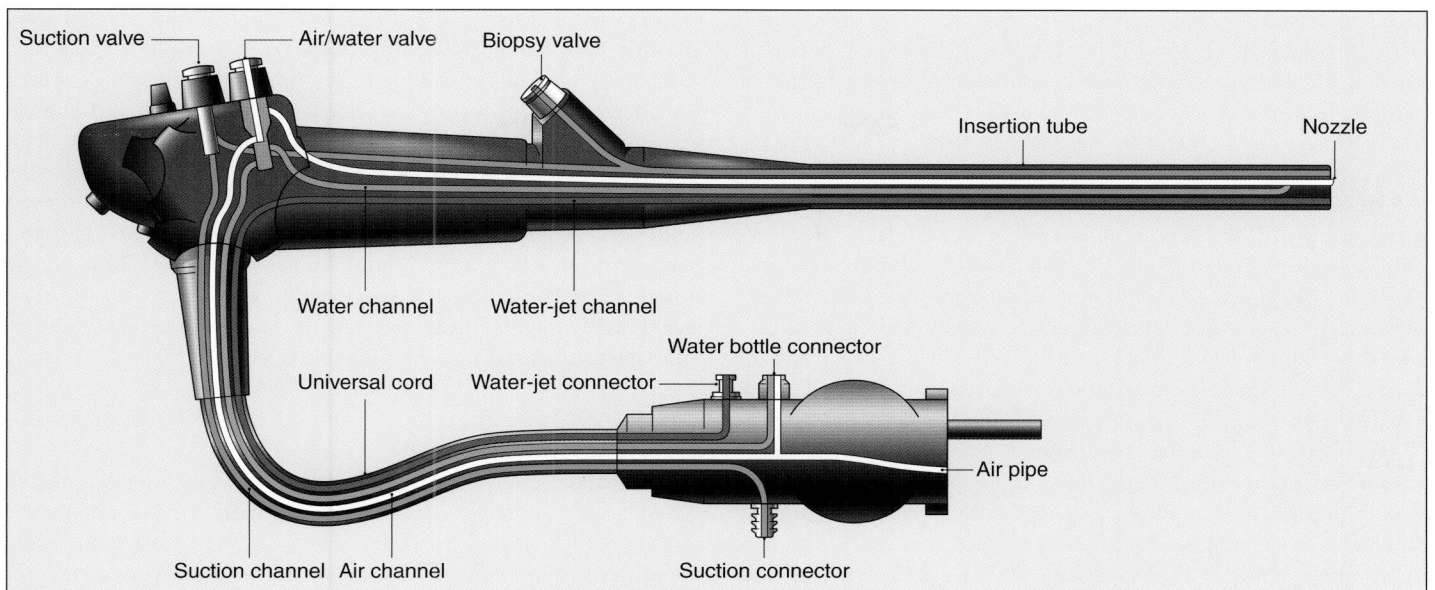

Figure 4–1. Schematic diagram of the internal channels of an endoscope. (Adapted from Olympus America. Copyright © Olympus America Inc. 2003.)

medical organizations including the American Society for Gastrointestinal Endoscopy (ASGE), the American College of Gastroenterology (ACG), the American Gastroenterology Association (AGA), the Society of Gastroenterology Nurses and Associates (SGNA), the Association of Perioperative Registered Nurses (AORN), the Association for Professionals in Infection Control and Epidemiology (APIC), and the American Society for Testing and Materials (ASTM).[34–37] Because of design considerations, GI endoscopes can be a challenge to clean and disinfect. Endoscopes are heat-labile instruments and thus cannot be steam autoclaved. They possess several long, narrow internal channels with bends (Fig. 4–1) that require exposure to the LCG to achieve high-level disinfection. In general, the air and water channels are too narrow to allow the passage of a cleaning brush (although the LCG is routinely circulated through this channel); however, one manufacturer has designed endoscope with an air and water channels that can be brushed.[38] Despite their complex internal design, high-level disinfection is not difficult to achieve with rigorous adherence to currently accepted guidelines.

Most accessory instruments used during endoscopy either contact the bloodstream (e.g., biopsy forceps, snares, and sphincterotomes) or enter sterile tissue spaces (e.g., the biliary tract) and are therefore classified as critical devices. As such, these devices require sterilization. Most accessories used during GI endoscopy are labeled by the FDA for single-use (i.e., disposable), and are intended to be discarded at the end of the procedure. Because these items are sterilized by the manufacturer, reprocessing is not an issue. However, some accessories are designed to be resterilized and reused and are designated as such by FDA. In this case, cleaning and sterilization is performed by the user according to the manufacturer's instructions.

The issue of sterilization of endoscopic accessories becomes considerably more complex when the reuse of single-use devices (SUDs) is considered. Although labeled as single-use (or dis-posable), many hospitals found that these devices could be safely cleaned, resterilized and reused, resulting in both decreased costs and reduced medical waste generation.[39–42] Despite the absence of evidence suggesting that this practice resulted in patient injury, the FDA issued a guidance document on August 14, 2000, that altered the agency's regulatory policy. The FDA considered the process of reprocessing (i.e., cleaning and sterilizing) a used SUD into a ready-for-patient-use device as "manufacturing," and as a result hospitals or third-party reprocessing companies that reprocessed SUDs were required to follow the same regulations as the original equipment manufacturers. These include premarket notification and approval requirements [510(k) and premarket approval application (PMA)], registration and listing, submission of adverse event reports, manufacturing and labeling requirements, tracking of devices, and correcting or removing from the market unsafe medical devices. Enforcement of these regulations was phased in over the subsequent 18 months (all aspects taking effect by February 14, 2002). The most onerous requirement was that a 510(k) or PMA was needed for each device that the institution intended to reprocess (which may be manufacturer and model-specific).[43] The regulatory burden imposed by these requirements essentially eliminated the practice of reprocessing of SUDs by most hospitals.

Risks of Inadequate Disinfection

Before discussing the specifics of current guidelines for endoscope cleaning and disinfection, it is helpful to understand how guidelines evolved over time in response to episodes of infection to minimize or eliminate vulnerabilities in the reprocessing procedure. Initially, endoscopes were simply washed with tap water and detergent, followed by exposure to alcohol.[44] In the 1970s, centers began using a variety of disinfectants to reprocess endoscopes.[45–52] In fact, the germicides used were generally antiseptic agents. Many of the agents that were considered to be effective at that time (e.g., alcohols, phenolics, iodophors, quaternary ammonium compounds, and chlorhexidine) have since been shown to be inadequate for high-level disinfection of GI endoscopes (Table 4–2).[53]

To standardize the cleaning and disinfection process, the ASGE, the AGA, and the ACG published joint guidelines on endoscope reprocessing in 1988. Key components of these guidelines were the emphasis on thorough manual cleaning of the instrument and all channels, high-level disinfection with an approved LCG (with a 10-minute exposure for glutaraldehyde specified at that time), a water rinse to remove residual sterilant, and a final drying step with forced air. The handles of nonimmersible endoscopes were to be cleaned with alcohol.[54] The British Society of Gastroenterology (BSG) published similar guidelines the same year, although notable differences included a recommended exposure time for glutaraldehyde of 4 minutes, the use of quaternary ammonium detergents as an acceptable second-line disinfectant, and only a brief mention of drying.[55] However, one of the authors of the BSG guidelines interpreted them as applying only to the insertion tube (which had direct patient contact) rather than the entire endoscope (particularly the control handpiece, which was not high-level disinfected) and recommended that if the handpiece was "extensively contaminated," or if the next patient was known to be immunocompromised, only then was high-level disinfection of the entire instrument necessary. If the instrument was not submersible, cleaning with alcohol and chlorhexidine was "practical."[56]

Recent guidelines in the United States from multiple organizations have been uniformly consistent (all endorsing a 20-minute exposure to glutaraldehyde at room temperature).[34–36,57] The importance of close adherence to reprocessing guidelines is apparent in the subsequent section. The major difference with formal guidelines originating outside the United States has been the endorsement of a shorter glutaraldehyde exposure time of 10 minutes.[58–60] Actual facility practices in other countries can vary substantially, highlighting the difficulty in generalizing reports of infection to the experience in the United States.[61–65]

SPECIFIC AGENTS

The most commonly reported infectious agent transmitted during GI endoscopy is *Pseudomonas aeruginosa*, with 227 cases described in the medical literature (see Table 4–2).[25] *P. aeruginosa* is an opportunistic pathogen that is widely found in the environment, and the organism thrives in a moist environment.[66] Endoscopes and their ancillary equipment are thus a potential reservoir and may serve a source of contamination. Early reports of *Pseudomonas* transmission during endoscopy (like those of other organisms at that time) were generally related to inadequate cleaning or the use of inadequate disinfectants; however, later reports have centered around these

Table 4–2. Pathogens Reportedly Transmitted During Gastrointestinal Endoscopy

Organism	Probable/Definite Cases	Failure(s) in Reprocessing Guideline
Pseudomonas aeruginosa	227	Failure to clean and disinfect between patients Inadequate cleaning Inadequate disinfectant Failure to disinfect all channels (particularly elevator channel) Failure to disinfect and sterilize water bottle Failure to dry with 70% alcohol Faulty or contaminated AER
Salmonella species	48	Inadequate cleaning Inadequate disinfectant Failure to sterilize forceps
Helicobacter pylori	10	Forceps not cleaned or sterilized between patients Inadequate cleaning Inadequate disinfectant
Klebsiella pneumoniae	5	Failure to dry with 70% alcohol Failure to disinfect elevator channel
Hepatitis C Virus	4	Inadequate disinfectant Inadequate exposure to LCG Failure to disinfect all channels with LCG Failure to sterilize forceps
Serratia marcescens	2	Inadequate disinfectant Failure to dry with 70% alcohol Failure to disinfect elevator channel
Enterobacter sp.	2	Inadequate cleaning Inadequate disinfectant
Hepatitis B Virus	1	Inadequate cleaning Inadequate disinfectant Failure to disinfect all channels with LCG
Trichosporon sp.	1	Failure to sterilize forceps

AER, automatic endoscope reprocessor; LCG, liquid chemical germicide.
From Nelson DB: Infectious disease complications of GI endoscopy: Part II, exogenous infections. Gastrointest Endosc 57:695–711, 2003.

major areas: (1) flawed automatic endoscope reprocessor (AER) units (responsible for well over half of the reported cases), (2) failure to regularly disinfect or sterilize the endoscope's irrigation bottle, (3) failure to recognize and disinfect the elevator channel of duodenoscopes, and (4) failure to completely dry the endoscope and all channels with a 70% alcohol solution followed by forced air.

There have been 48 cases of *Salmonella* sp. attributed to GI endoscopy.[25] In these reports, failure to mechanically clean the internal instrument channels was a uniform occurrence, and this was usually compounded by the use of an ineffective disinfectant. Because these were relatively early in the evolution of endoscope reprocessing (and preceded the guidelines standardizing these protocols), it is not surprising that there have been no reported cases of *Salmonella* transmission since 1987.

The 10 reported cases of endoscopic *Helicobacter pylori* transmission are almost as interesting as the initial confirmatory study by Marshall with self-inoculation. In one case, the author underwent endoscopy immediately after the instrument had been used in a patient known to harbor the organism. The endoscope was reprocessed by wiping the insertion tube with a paper towel soaked with benzethonium chloride and sucking the disinfectant through the instrument channels without cleaning. Perhaps predictably, the author then developed acute *H. pylori* infection.[67] Another case was associated with endoscopic research dealing with *H. pylori* and was attributed to failure to clean and sterilize (or even disinfect) the endoscopic biopsy forceps between subjects (although reprocessing of the endoscope or other ancillary study equipment is not mentioned).[68] The remaining cases were due to inadequate cleaning and the use of inadequate LCGs.

There is much less anxiety associated with the rare transmission of bacterial microorganisms than the disproportionate fear of viral infection. This is surprising in that the viruses of most concern (i.e., hepatitis B virus [HBV], hepatitis C virus [HCV], and human immunodeficiency virus [HIV]) are among the easiest microorganisms to destroy with standard reprocessing. Before the advent of the reprocessing guidelines in 1988, there were three cases of HBV attributed to endoscopy. Two early reports suggested a temporal relationship between the use of an endoscope in an HBV-positive individual preceding the case and subsequent development of HBV infection, although in both cases, no actual investigation was performed, and endoscope cleaning and disinfection were not acceptable by current standards.[69,70] In the third case, subtyping of the virus was used to confirm that transmission was likely. In this instance, the air and water channels were not exposed to glutaraldehyde.[71] Two recent cases of HBV infection attributed to endoscopy are unlikely.[25,72,73]

There have been four cases of HCV transmission during GI endoscopy, all originating outside the United States. In three cases, a breach in currently accepted endoscope-reprocessing guidelines was reported.[74,75] In the final case, the transmission was felt to be due to contamination of multidose vials used for sedation (and thus associated with the procedure but not the endoscope).[76] This was also the case with an outbreak of HCV at an endoscopy clinic in the United States. Although initially attributed to deficient endoscope reprocessing practices by the lay press, investigation by the New York State Department of Health determined that the cause was in fact the improper reuse of needles and contamination of multidose vials.[77,78] This highlights the importance of accepted infection control practices, which are discussed later.

There have been no reported cases of endoscopic transmission of HIV. Four studies have demonstrated that glutaraldehyde disinfection of endoscopes contaminated with HIV completely eliminates the virus.[79–81]

Although there have been 317 putative episodes of transmission of infection reported in the medical literature, in the absence of defective equipment (notably the automated endoscope reprocessor), there has been a failure to follow currently accepted guidelines for cleaning and disinfection in each case.[25] These deficient practices can be summarized as follows:

1. Mechanical cleaning of the endoscope and channels before disinfection has been inadequate or absent.
2. Use of an inadequate or ineffective disinfectant.
3. Failure to use an appropriate disinfectant for an adequate exposure period.
4. Failure to sterilize endoscopic accessory instruments.
5. Failure to dry the endoscope and all channels.

Liquid Chemical Germicides

The FDA defines a high-level disinfectant as a sterilant that is used under the same contact conditions except for a shorter contact time (Table 4–3). LCGs are ordinarily classified as sterilants by passing the Association of Official Analytical Chemists (AOAC) sporicidal test.[82] Older sterilants (e.g., ≥ 2% glutaraldehyde) were approved by the FDA for sterilization and high-level disinfection (although the prolonged exposure time required made this impractical). However, more recently approved sterilants, such as 0.55% *ortho*-phthalaldehyde (Cidex OPA) and hypochlorite 650 to 675 ppm (Sterilox) that are able to pass the AOAC sporicidal test have not been given an indication for device sterilization (i.e., high-level disinfection only).

The FDA has approved a number of LCGs for use as high-level disinfectants or sterilants in the reprocessing of endoscopes and other reusable medical devices. These include 2.4% or greater glutaraldehyde, 1.12% glutaraldehyde/1.93% phenol/phenate, 0.55% *ortho*-phthaldehyde, 0.2% peracetic acid, 7.5% hydrogen peroxide, 7.35% hydrogen peroxide/0.23% peracetic acid, 1.0% hydrogen peroxide/0.08% peroxyacetic acid, and hypochlorite 650 to 675 ppm active free chlorine.[82] Most of these sterilants are labeled for multiple reprocessing cycles for a specific time period. However, as these sterilants are reused, dilution occurs that can reduce their effectiveness. Product-specific test strips should regularly be used to monitor these solutions to ensure that they are above their minimum effective concentration (MEC). Solutions should be discarded whenever they fall below the MEC or when the use-life expires, whichever comes first. Users should consult with manufacturers of endoscopes and AERs (if used) for compatibility before selecting an LCG. This does not apply to 0.2% peracetic acid, which is not reusable (i.e., single use: each cycle requires new sterilant) or to the hypochlorite solution, which is generated from electrolysis of a saline solution for each cycle.[83–85]

Table 4-3. Disinfectants

FDA-Cleared Sterilants and High-Level Disinfectants for High-Level Disinfection of Endoscopes	Disinfectants Inadequate for High-Level Disinfection of Endoscopes (Examples)
≥2% glutaraldehyde	Phenolic solutions • Hexachlorophene
1.12% glutaraldehyde 1.93% phenol/phenate	Iodophor solutions • Povidone-iodine
0.55% *ortho*-phthalaldehyde	Quaternary ammonium solutions • Benzalkonium chloride • Benzethonium chloride • Cetrimide
7.5% hydrogen peroxide	Chlorhexidine
7.35% hydrogen peroxide 0.23% peracetic acid	Chlorhexidine/cetrimide
1.0% hydrogen peroxide 0.08% peracetic acid	Alkyldiaminoethylglycine HCL
0.2% peracetic acid	Ethyl or isopropyl alcohol*
Hypochlorite 650-675 ppm (active free chlorine)	

When used for high-level disinfection; appropriate for terminal drying.
FDA, Food and Drug Administration.
From Nelson DB: Infectious disease complications of GI endoscopy: Part II, exogenous infections. Gastrointest Endosc 57:695–711, 2003, with permission from the American Society for Gastrointestinal Endoscopy.

Automatic Endoscope Reprocessors

Historically, cleaning and high-level disinfection of endoscopes has been performed manually. The actual high-level disinfection step involved placing the mechanically cleaned endoscopes into a basin or container of the LCG (usually glutaraldehyde) that was also circulated through the internal channels of the instrument. However, exposure of endoscopy personnel to the LCG has been reported to cause respiratory, nasal, and skin problems.[86,87] AERs were designed to ensure that reprocessing is performed consistently and to replace some manual disinfection steps. An additional advantage is that AERs may minimize the exposure of endoscopy personnel to the LCG.[88] However, it is absolutely critical that users understand that endoscopes must be mechanically cleaned before reprocessing in an AER. Although these devices are occasionally referred to as "washer-disinfectors," there are currently no AERs that eliminate the need to mechanically clean the endoscope. It is also important to verify that the endoscope and the AER are compatible and use appropriate connectors.[89]

Cleaning and Disinfecting Endoscopes

A guideline for reprocessing GI endoscopes that has been endorsed by numerous gastroenterology, infection control, surgical, nursing, and hospital organizations contains detailed recommendations for this process.[90] A similar guideline by the Healthcare Infection Control Practices Advisory Committee (HICPAC) is currently in progress at the CDC.[91] The pertinent steps to achieve high-level disinfection of endoscopes from these guidelines are summarized in the following:

1. Perform pressure/leak testing after each use according to manufacturer guidelines.
2. Disconnect and disassemble endoscope components (e.g., air/water and suction valves) as far as possible and completely immerse the endoscope and components in the enzymatic detergent.
3. Meticulously clean the entire endoscope, including valves, channels, connectors, and all detachable parts with an enzymatic detergent compatible with the endoscope immediately after use, according to the manufacturer's instructions. Flush and brush all accessible channels to remove all organic (e.g., blood, tissue) and other residues. Repeatedly actuate the valves during cleaning to facilitate access to all surfaces. Clean the external surfaces and components of the endoscope using a soft cloth, sponge, or brushes.
4. Use brushes appropriate for the size of the endoscope channel, parts, connectors, and orifices (e.g., bristles should contact all surfaces) for cleaning. Cleaning items should be disposable or thoroughly cleaned and disinfected/sterilized between uses.
5. Discard enzymatic detergents after each use, because these products are not microbicidal and will not retard microbial growth.
6. Use a high-level disinfectant/sterilant cleared by the FDA for high-level disinfection (http://www.fda.gov/cdrh/ode/germlab.html).
7. The exposure time and temperature for disinfecting semicritical patient care equipment varies among the FDA-cleared high-level disinfectants. Follow the FDA-cleared label claim for high-level disinfection unless several well-designed experimental scientific studies, endorsed by professional societies,

demonstrate that an alternative exposure time is effective for disinfecting semicritical items. The FDA label claim for high-level disinfection with greater than 2% glutaraldehyde at 25°C ranges from 20 to 90 minutes depending on the product. However, multiple scientific studies and professional organizations support the efficacy of greater than 2% glutaraldehyde at 20 minutes at 20°C.

8. Select a disinfectant/sterilant that is compatible with the endoscope. The use of specific high-level disinfectants/sterilants on an endoscope should be avoided if the endoscope manufacturer warns against use because of functional damage (with or without cosmetic damage).

9. Completely immerse the endoscope and endoscope components in the high-level disinfectant/sterilant and ensure that all channels are perfused. Nonimmersible GI endoscopes should be phased out immediately.

10. If an AER is used, ensure that the endoscope and endoscope components can be effectively reprocessed in the AER (e.g., the elevator wire channel of duodenoscopes is not effectively disinfected by most AERs and this step must be performed manually). Users should obtain and review model-specific reprocessing protocols from both the endoscope and AER manufacturers and check for compatibility.

11. If an AER is used, place the endoscope and endoscope components in the reprocessor and attach all channel connectors according to the AER and endoscope manufacturers' instructions to ensure exposure of all internal surfaces with the high-level disinfectant/chemical sterilant.

12. If an AER cycle is interrupted, high-level disinfection or sterilization cannot be assured and should be repeated.

13. After high-level disinfection, rinse the endoscope and flush the channels with sterile, filtered, or tap water to remove the disinfectant/sterilant. Discard the rinse water after each use/cycle. Flush the channels with 70% to 90% ethyl or isopropyl alcohol and dry using forced air. The final drying steps greatly reduce the possibility of recontamination of the endoscope by waterborne microorganisms.

14. When storing the endoscope, hang it in a vertical position to facilitate drying (with caps, valves, and other detachable components removed as per manufacturer instructions).

15. Endoscopes should be stored in a manner that will protect the endoscope from contamination.

16. High-level disinfect or sterilize the water bottle (used for cleaning the lens and irrigation during the procedure) and its connecting tube at least daily. Sterile water should be used to fill the water bottle.

17. Perform routine testing of the liquid sterilant/high-level disinfectant to ensure MEC of the active ingredient. Check the solution at the beginning of each day of use (or more often) and document the results. If the chemical indicator shows that the concentration is less than the MEC, the solution should be discarded.

18. Discard the liquid sterilant/high-level disinfectant at the end of its reuse life (which may be single use) regardless of the MEC. If additional liquid sterilant/high-level disinfectant is added to an AER (or basin, if manually disinfected), the reuse life should be determined by the first use/activation of the original solution, that is, the practice of "topping off" of a liquid sterilant/high-level disinfectant pool does not extend the reuse life of the liquid sterilant/high-level disinfectant.

Although some have advocated that cleaned and disinfected endoscopes that have been stored should undergo an additional cleaning and disinfection process before the beginning of an endoscopy schedule, there are no data to support this as a routine practice. When GI endoscope cleaning and disinfection guidelines are strictly followed, and endoscopes are stored appropriately, this additional procedure is not necessary. However, in general if there is doubt about a cleaning and disinfection cycle, or the instrument is found to be wet after storage (or otherwise stored improperly), the endoscope should be reprocessed.

Disinfection Procedure Compliance

Adherence to established guidelines for the cleaning and disinfection of endoscopes is imperative. When these guidelines are followed, the risk of transmission of infection is virtually eliminated. However, this is not a reason for complacency, as compliance with existing reprocessing guidelines is not uniform. In 1991, Gorse and Messner[92] surveyed 2030 SGNA members and found that compliance with existing guidelines was as low as 67% in some areas. A collaborative study by the FDA and three state health departments published the following year investigated endoscope reprocessing at 26 health care facilities and found that 24% of patient-ready endoscopes were contaminated and that these were attributed to fundamental errors in the disinfection process.[93,94]

Although office endoscopy has recently been shown to be as safe as that practiced in more regulated settings (e.g., hospitals),[95] the absence of formal infection control programs and personnel may leave the office setting more vulnerable to compliance issues with regard to endoscope reprocessing. In one study of 19 family practice and internal medicine offices performing flexible sigmoidoscopy, all were found to deviate from accepted reprocessing guidelines in at least one area.[96]

Although two more recent studies suggest that compliance with reprocessing guidelines has improved,[97,98] there is room for improvement. The challenge facing the profession of GI endoscopy is to ensure that compliance with these guidelines is universal, regardless of the practitioner or setting.

Reprocessing Personnel

Only trained personnel who understand the importance of strict adherence to established protocols should perform endoscope reprocessing (as a corollary, untrained personnel should not reprocess endoscopes). This training should include device-specific reprocessing instructions (for both the endoscope and reprocessing equipment) and education regarding the biologic and chemical hazards associated with the cleaning and disinfection of endoscopes with LCGs. These individuals should meet annual competency standards for endoscope reprocessing. In addition, all health care personnel in the endoscopy suite should be trained in and adhere to standard infection control recommendations (e.g., standard precautions), including those to protect both patients and health care workers.[33]

Personal protective equipment, such as gloves, gowns, eyewear, and respiratory protection devices, should be readily available. This should be used, as appropriate, to protect reprocessing personnel from exposure to chemicals, blood, or other potentially infectious material.[99-101]

Novel Infectious Agents

Although rare, the impact of Creutzfeldt-Jakob disease (CJD) and variant Creutzfeldt-Jakob disease (vCJD) on endoscope reprocessing are addressed. These are degenerative neurologic disorders transmitted by proteinaceous infectious agents called prions (although this is a simplification). Prions are unusually resistant to disinfection by conventional chemical high-level disinfectants/sterilants.[102,103] Fortunately, the incidence rate of CJD in the United States is extremely low, with approximately 250 cases/year, or 0.97 cases per 1 million persons per year.[104] Furthermore, tissues and secretions that come into contact with the endoscope during procedures, such as saliva, gingival tissue, intestinal tissue, feces, and blood, are considered noninfectious by the World Health Organization.[102] A draft statement on CJD and medical device reprocessing from the CDC concluded that current guidelines for cleaning and disinfection of these instruments need not be changed.[35] Other infection control experts have concurred, citing the lack of exposure to high-risk tissue and the importance of mechanical cleaning in removing microbial contamination.[31,103] The clinical relevance of the recent finding of abnormal prion proteins in the olfactory (but not respiratory) epithelium of affected patients with regard to infection control or endoscope reprocessing is not clear.[105] It is reassuring to note that to date there have been no reported cases in the world literature of transmission of CJD (or any other transmissible spongiform encephalopathy, for that matter) by endoscopy.

More recently, vCJD, a rarer syndrome that is believed to be due to consumption of beef products containing the bovine spongiform encephalopathy (BSE) agent (possibly requiring a susceptible genotype by the individual) was recognized.[106] The only case of the disease reported in the United States was found in a 22-year-old patient who had moved from the United Kingdom. Despite active surveillance since 1990, BSE has not been detected in the United States.[107] Unlike CJD, the prions associated with vCJD can be detected in the lymphoid tissue of affected individuals (e.g., tonsil, appendix, and possibly ileum and rectum).[106,108-111] The prions in these tissues are present in lower concentrations and are approximately 50% less infective than central nervous system (CNS) tissue when homogenated and injected intracerebrally in mice.[112] The infectivity of intact tissue that might be encountered at endoscopy and the risk of subsequent transmission to another individual via gut inoculation is unknown but would undoubtedly be lower. Given the virtual absence of this disease in the United States, rigorous adherence to current guidelines for the cleaning and disinfection of endoscopes would seem to be adequate. There is no evidence that changes to current endoscopic practices or endoscope reprocessing guidelines are warranted, but these should be responsive to new information as it evolves.

REFERENCES

1. Hirschowitz BI: Endoscopic examination of the stomach and duodenal cap with the fiberscope. Lancet 1:1074–1078, 1961.
2. Ayliffe GA, Babb JR, Bradley CR: The immersible endoscope. Lancet 1:161, 1984.
3. Petersen BT: Gaining perspective on reprocessing of GI endoscopes. Gastrointest Endosc 50:287–291, 1999.
4. Rothstein RI, Littenberg B: Disposable, sheathed, flexible sigmoidoscopy: A prospective, multicenter, randomized trial. Gastrointest Endosc 41:566–572, 1995.
5. Schroy PC, Wilson S, Afdahl N: Feasibility of high-volume screening sigmoidoscopy using a flexible fiberoptic endoscope and a disposable sheath system. Am J Gastroenterol 91:1331–1337, 1996.
6. Sardinha TC, Wexner SD, Gilliland J, et al: Efficiency and productivity of a sheathed fiberoptic sigmoidoscope compared with a conventional sigmoidoscope. Dis Colon Rectum 40:1248–1253, 1997.
7. Mayinger B, Strenkert M, Hochberger J, et al: Disposable-sheath, flexible gastroscope system versus standard gastroscopes: A prospective, randomized trial. Gastrointest Endosc 50:461–467, 1999.
8. Bretthauer M, Hoff G, Thiis-Evensen E, et al: Use of a disposable sheath system for flexible sigmoidoscopy in decentralized colorectal cancer screening. Endoscopy 34:814–818, 2002.
9. ECRI: Endosheath endoscopic system. Health Devices 29:7–13, 2000.
10. Block SS: Definition of terms. In Block SS (ed): Disinfection, Sterilization, and Preservation, 5th ed. Philadelphia, Lippincott Williams & Wilkins, 2001, pp 19–28.
11. Knieler R: Manual cleaning and disinfection of flexible endoscopes—and approach to evaluating a combined procedure. J Hosp Infect 48(Suppl A):S84–87, 2001.
12. Alfa MJ, Olson N, DeGagne P, Jackson M: A survey of reprocessing methods, residual viable bioburden, and soil levels in patient-ready endoscopic retrograde cholangiopancreatography duodenoscopes used in Canadian centers. Infect Control Hosp Epidemiol 23:198–206, 2002.
13. Fantry GT, Zheng QX, James SP: Conventional cleaning and disinfection techniques eliminate the risk of endoscopic transmission of Helicobacter pylori. Am J Gastroenterol 90:227–232, 1995.
14. Deva AK, Vickery K, Zou J, et al: Detection of persistent vegetative bacteria and amplified viral nucleic acid from in-use testing of gastrointestinal endoscopes. J Hosp Infect 39:149–157, 1998.
15. Bécheur H, Harzic M, Colardelle P, et al: Contamination des endoscopes et des pinces à biopsies par le virus de l'hépatite C [French with English abstract]. Gastroenterol Clin Biol 24:906–910, 2000.
16. Deflandre J, Cajot O, Brixko C, et al: Risques de contamination par le virus de l'hépatite C des endoscopes utilisés dans un service hospitalier de gastroentérologie [French with English abstract]. Rev Med Liege 56:696–698, 2001.
17. Vesley D, Norlien KG, Nelson B, et al: Significant factors in the disinfection and sterilization of flexible endoscopes. Am J Infect Control 20:291–300, 1992.
18. Babb JR, Bradley CR: Endoscope reprocessing: Where do we go from here? J Hosp Infect 30:543–551, 1995.
19. Urayama S, Kozarek RA, Sumida S, et al: Mycobacteria and glutaraldehyde: Is high-level disinfection of endoscopes possible? Gastrointest Endosc 43:451–456, 1996.

20. Chu NS, McAlister D, Antonoplos PA: Natural bioburden levels detected on flexible gastrointestinal endoscopes after clinical use and manual cleaning. Gastrointest Endosc 48:137–142, 1998.

21. Cronmiller JR, Nelson DK, Salman G, et al: Antimicrobial efficacy of endoscopic disinfection procedures: A controlled, multifactorial investigation. Gastrointest Endosc 50:152–158, 1999.

22. Kovacs BJ, Chen YK, Kettering JD, et al: High-level disinfection of gastrointestinal endoscopes: Are current guidelines adequate? Am J Gastroenterol 94:1546–1550, 1999.

23. Vesley D, Melson J, Patricia S: Microbial bioburden in endoscope reprocessing and an in-use evaluation of the high-level disinfection capabilities of Cidex PA. Gastroenterol Nurs 22:63–68, 1999.

24. Foliente RL, Kovacs BJ, Aprecio RM, et al: Efficacy of high-level disinfectants for reprocessing GI endoscopes in simulated in-use testing. Gastrointest Endosc 53:456–462, 2001.

25. Nelson DB: Infectious disease complications of GI endoscopy: Part II, exogenous infections. Gastrointest Endosc 57:695–711, 2003.

26. Food and Drug Administration (FDA): Guidance for industry and FDA reviewers: Content and format of premarket notification [510(k) submissions for liquid chemical sterilants/high level disinfectants]. Rockville, MD, FDA, 2000.

27. Muscarella LF: What is disinfection, sterilization? Gastrointest Endosc 50:301–303, 1999.

28. Muscarella LF: Are all sterilization processes alike? AORN J 67:966–976, 1998.

29. Rutala WA, Weber DJ: Low-temperature sterilization technologies: Do we need to redefine sterilization? Infect Control Hosp Epidemiol 17:87–91, 1996.

30. Spaulding EH: Chemical disinfection and antisepsis in the hospital. J Hosp Res 9:5–31, 1972.

31. Favero MS, Bond WW: Disinfection of medical and surgical materials. In Block SS (ed): Disinfection, Sterilization, and Preservation, 5th ed. Philadelphia, Lippincott Williams & Wilkins, 2001, pp 881–917.

32. Draft guidance for the content of premarket notifications for endoscopes used in gastroenterology and urology. Rockville, MD, Food and Drug Administration, 1995.

33. Garner JS, Favero MS: CDC guideline for handwashing and hospital environmental control, 1985. Infect Control Hosp Epidemiol 7:231–243, 1986.

34. DiMarino AJ Jr, Leung J, Ravich W, et al: Reprocessing of flexible gastrointestinal endoscopes. Gastrointest Endosc 43:540–546, 1996.

35. Alvarado CJ, Reichelderfer M: APIC guidelines for infection prevention and control in flexible endoscopy. Am J Infect Control 28:138–155, 2000.

36. Standard practice for cleaning and disinfection of flexible fiberoptic and video endoscopes used in the examination of the hollow viscera. West Conshohocken, PA, American Society for Testing and Materials, 2000. F1518-00.

37. Recommended practices for use and care of endoscopes. 2002 Standards, Recommended Practices, and Guidelines. Denver, Association of periOperative Registered Nurses (AORN), 2002, pp 229–232.

38. Ishino Y, Ido K, Koiwai H, Sugano K: Pitfalls in endoscope reprocessing: Brushing of air and water channels is mandatory for high-level disinfection. Gastrointest Endosc 53:165–168, 2001.

39. Kozarek RA, Sumida SE, Raltz SL, et al: In vitro evaluation of wire integrity and ability to reprocess single-use sphincterotomes. Gastrointest Endosc 45:117–121, 1997.

40. Cohen J, Haber GB, Kortan P, et al: A prospective study of the repeated use of sterilized papillotomes and retrieval baskets for ERCP: Quality and cost analysis. Gastrointest Endosc 45:122–127, 1997.

41. Kozarek RA, Raltz SL, Ball TJ, et al: Reuse of disposable sphincterotomes for diagnostic and therapeutic ERCP: A one-year prospective study. Gastrointest Endosc 49:39–42, 1999.

42. Roach SK, Kozarek RA, Raltz SL, Sumida SE: In vitro evaluation of integrity and sterilization of single-use argon beam plasma coagulation probes. Gastrointest Endosc 94:139–143, 1999.

43. Food and Drug Administration (FDA): Enforcement priorities for single-use devices reprocessed by third parties and hospitals. Rockville, MD, FDA, 2000.

44. Axon AT, Phillips I, Cotton PB, Avery SA: Disinfection of gastrointestinal fibre endoscopes. Lancet 1:656–658, 1974.

45. Whalen GE: Risks of hepatitis: What can be done? [letter]. Gastrointest Endosc 22:48–49, 1975.

46. Tolon M, Thofern E, Miederer SE: Disinfection procedures of fiberscopes in endoscopy departments. Endoscopy 8:24–29, 1976.

47. Dunkerley RC, Cromer MD, Edmiston CE Jr, Dunn GD: Practical technique for adequate cleansing of endoscopes: A bacteriological study of pHisoHex and Betadine. Gastrointest Endosc 23:148-9, 1977.

48. Carr-Locke DL, Clayton P: Disinfection of upper gastrointestinal fiberoptic endoscopy equipment: An evaluation of a cetrimide chlorhexidine solution and glutaraldehyde. Gut 19:916–922, 1978.

49. Geenen JE, Pfeifer M, Simonsen L: Cleaning and disinfection of endoscopic equipment [letter]. Gastrointest Endosc 24:185–186, 1978.

50. Hedrick E: Cleaning and disinfection of flexible fiberoptic endoscopes used in gastrointestinal endoscopy. APIC 6:8–9, 1978.

51. Lindstaedt H, Krizek L, Miederer SE, Botzenhart K: Experience and problems in the disinfection of fibre endoscopes. Endoscopy 10:80–85, 1978.

52. Vennes JA, Geenen JE, Papp JP, Schapiro M: Endoscopically related infections and their prevention [letter]. Gastrointest Endosc 27:239–240, 1981.

53. Rutala WA: APIC guideline for selection and use of disinfectants. Am J Infect Control 24:313–342, 1996.

54. Infection control during gastrointestinal endoscopy: Guidelines for clinical application. Gastrointest Endosc 34:37S–40S, 1988.

55. Weller IV, Williams CB, Jeffries DJ, et al: Cleaning and disinfection of equipment for gastrointestinal flexible endoscopy: Interim recommendations of a Working Party of the British Society of Gastroenterology. Gut 29:1134–1151, 1988.

56. Sobala GM, Lincoln C, Axon AT: Does the endoscope control head need to be disinfected between examinations. Endoscopy 21:19–21, 1989.

57. Society of Gastroenterology Nurses and Associates: Standards of infection control in reprocessing of flexible gastrointestinal endoscopes. Gastroenterol Nurs 23:172–187, 2000.

58. British Society of Gastroenterology: Cleaning and disinfection of equipment for gastrointestinal endoscopy. Report of a Working Party of the British Society of Gastroenterology Endoscopy Committee. Gut 42:585–593, 1998.

59. European Society of Gastrointestinal Endoscopy: Guidelines on cleaning and disinfection in GI endoscopy. Endoscopy 32:77–83, 2000.

60. Leung JW: Working party report: Care of endoscopes. Reprocessing of flexible endoscopes. J Gastroenterol Hepatol 15:G73–77, 2000.

61. Arora A, Seth S, Tandon RK: Gastrointestinal endoscope disinfection practices in India: Results of a national survey. Indian J Gastroenterol 11:62–64, 1992.

62. Akamatsu T, Tabata K, Hironga M, et al: Transmission of Helicobacter pylori infection via flexible fiberoptic endoscopy. Am J Infect Control 24:396–401, 1996.

63. Orsi GB, Filocamo A, Di Stefano L, Tittobello A: Italian national survey of digestive endoscopy disinfection procedures. Endoscopy 29:732–740, 1997.

64. Alvarez SZ, Kothari K, Novis B, et al: Disinfection of endoscopic equipment. Gastrointest Endosc 49:668–670, 1999.

65. Brullet E, Ramirez-Armengol JA, Campo R, Board of the Spanish Association for Digestive Endoscopy: Cleaning and disinfection practices in digestive endoscopy in Spain: Results of a national survey. Endoscopy 33:864–868, 2001.

66. Pollack M: Pseudomonas aeruginosa. In Mandell GL, Bennett JE, Dolin R (eds): Principles and Practices of Infectious Diseases, 5th ed. Philadelphia, Churchill Livingstone, 2000, pp 2310–2335.

67. Miyaji H, Kohli Y, Azuma T, et al: Endoscopic cross-infection with *Helicobacter pylori* [letter]. Lancet 345:464, 1995.

68. Graham DY, Alpert LC, Smith JL, Yoshimura HH: Iatrogenic *Campylobacter pylori* infection is a cause of epidemic achlorhydria. Am J Gastroenterol 83:974–980, 1988.

69. Morris IM, Cattle DS, Smits BJ: Endoscopy and transmission of hepatitis B [letter]. Lancet 2:1152, 1975.

70. Seefeld U, Bansky G, Jaeger M, Schmid M: Prevention of hepatitis B virus transmission by gastrointestinal fibrescope: Successful disinfection with an aldehyde liquid. Endoscopy 13:238–239, 1981.

71. Birnie GG, Quigley EM, Clements GB, et al: Endoscopic transmission of hepatitis B virus. Gut 24:171–174, 1983.

72. Davis AR, Pink JM, Kowalik AM, et al: Multiple endoscopies in a Sydney blood donor found positive for hepatitis B and C antibodies. Med J Aust 164:571, 1996.

73. Federman DG, Kirsner RS: Leukocytoclastic vasculitis, hepatitis B, and the risk of endoscopy. Cutis 63:86–87, 1999.

74. Tennenbaum R, Colardelle P, Chochon M, et al: Hépatite C après cholangiographie rétrograde [French]. Gastroenterol Clin Biol 17:763–775, 1993.

75. Bronowicki J-P, Venard V, Botté C, et al: Patient-to-patient transmission of hepatitis C virus during colonoscopy. N Engl J Med 337:237–240, 1997.

76. Le Pogam S, Gondeau A, Bacq Y: Nosocomial transmission of hepatitis C virus [letter]. Ann Intern Med 131:794, 1999.

77. Frieden TR: Multi use vials letter (New York City Department of Health Web Site). Available at http://www.nyc.gov/html/doh/pdf/chi/ltr2-2002.pdf (accessed December 1, 2002).

78. Ramirez M: Cause of infection/Report: Anesthesiologist contaminated medicine vial. Newsday, July 3, 2002:A03.

79. Classen M, Dancygier H II, Gürtler L, Deinhardt F: Risk of transmitting HIV by endoscopes [letter]. Endoscopy 20:128, 1988.

80. Hanson PJ, Gor D, Clarke JR, et al: Contamination of endoscopes used in AIDS patients. Lancet 2:86–88, 1989.

81. Hanson PJ, Gor D, Jeffries DJ, Collins JV: Elimination of high titre HIV from fiberoptic endoscopes. Gut 31:657–659, 1990.

82. Food and Drug Administration: FDA-cleared sterilants and high level disinfectants with general claims for processing reusable medical and dental devices March 2003. Available at http://www.fda.gov/cdrh/ode/germlab.html (accessed April 28, 2003).

83. Selkon JB, Babb JR, Morris R: Evaluation of the antimicrobial activity of a new super-oxidized water, Sterilox, for the disinfection of endoscopes. J Hosp Infect 41:59–70, 1999.

84. Tsuji S, Kawano S, Oshita M, et al: Endoscope disinfection using acidic electrolytic water. Endoscopy 31:528–535, 1999.

85. Nelson D: Newer technologies for endoscope disinfection: Electrolyzed acid water and disposable-component endoscope systems. Gastrointest Endosc Clin N Am 10:319–328, 2000.

86. Norbäck D: Skin and respiratory symptoms from exposure to alkaline glutaraldehyde in medical services. Scand J Work Environ Health 14:366–371, 1988.

87. Gannon PFG, Bright P, Campbell M, et al: Occupational asthma due to glutaraldehyde and formaldehyde in endoscopy and x ray departments. Thorax 50:156–159, 1995.

88. Muscarella LF: Advantages and limitations of automatic flexible endoscope reprocessors. Am J Infect Control 24:304–309, 1996.

89. Sorin M, Segal-Maurer S, Urban C, et al: Nosocomial transmission of imipenem-resistant *Pseudomonas aeruginosa* following bronchoscopy associated with improper connection to the STERIS System 1 processor. Infect Control Hosp Epidemiol 20:514–516, 2001.

90. Nelson DB, Jarvis WR, Rutala WA, et al: Multi-society guidelines for reprocessing flexible gastrointestinal endoscopes. Gastrointest Endosc 58:1–8, 2003.

91. Rutala WA, Weber DJ, and the Healthcare Infection Control Practices Advisory Committee: Guideline for disinfection and sterilization in healthcare facilities. Am J Infect Control 2003 (in press).

92. Gorse GJ, Messner RL: Infection control practices in gastrointestinal endoscopy in the United States: A national survey. Infect Control Hosp Epidemiol 12:289–296, 1991.

93. Kaczmarek RG, Moore RM Jr, John M, et al: Multi-state investigation of the actual disinfection/sterilization of endoscopes in health care facilities. Am J Med 92:257–261, 1992.

94. Reynolds CD, Rhinehart E, Dreyer P, Goldman DA: Variability in reprocessing policies and procedures for flexible fiberoptic endoscopes in Massachusetts hospitals. Am J Infect Control 20:283–290, 1992.

95. United States General Accounting Office: Medicare physician payments: Medical settings and safety of endoscopic procedures (GAO-03-179). Washington, DC, United States General Accounting Office, 2002.

96. Jackson FW, Ball MD: Correction of deficiencies in flexible fiberoptic sigmoidoscope cleaning and disinfection technique in family practice and internal medicine offices. Arch Fam Med 6:578–582, 1997.

97. Cheung RJ, Ortiz D, DiMarino AJ Jr: GI endoscopic reprocessing practices in the United States. Gastrointest Endosc 50:362–368, 1999.

98. Muscarella LF: Current instrument reprocessing practices: Results of a national survey. Gastroenterol Nurs 24:253–260, 2001.

99. Occupational Safety and Health Administration (OHSA): Hazard Communication Standard. 29 CFR 1910.1200. Washington, DC, OSHA.

100. Occupational Safety and Health Administration: Occupational exposure to bloodborne pathogens: Final rule. Federal Register 56:64003-182, 1991.

101. Carr-Locke DL, Conn MI, Faigel DO, et al: Personal protective equipment. Gastrointest Endosc 49:854–857, 1999.

102. World Health Organization: WHO infection control guidelines for transmissible spongiform encephalopathies. WHO/CDS/CSR/APH/2000.3. Geneva, World Health Organization, 1999.

103. Rutala WA, Weber DJ: Creutzfeldt-Jakob disease: Recommendations for disinfection and sterilization. Clin Infect Dis 32:1348–1356, 2001.

104. Gibbons RV, Holman RC, Belay ED, Schonberger LB: Creutzfeldt-Jakob disease in the United States: 1979-1998 [letter]. JAMA 284:2322–2323, 2000.

105. Zanusso G, Ferrari S, Cardone F, et al: Detection of pathological prion protein in the olfactory epithelium in sporadic Creutzfeldt-Jakob disease. N Engl J Med 348:711–719, 2003.

106. Wadsworth JD, Joiner S, Hill AF, et al: Tissue distribution of protease resistant prion in variant Creutzfeldt-Jakob disease using a highly sensitive immunoblotting assay. Lancet 358:171–180, 2001.

107. Centers for Disease Control and Prevention: BSE and CJD information and resources. Available at http://www.cdc.gov/ncidod/diseases/cjd/cjd.htm (accessed December 11, 2002).

108. Hill AF, Zeidler M, Ironside JW, Collinge J: Diagnosis of new variant Creutzfeldt-Jakob disease by tonsil biopsy [letter]. Lancet 349:99–100, 1997.

109. Hilton DA, Fathers E, Edwards P, et al: Prion immunoreactivity in appendix before clinical onset of variant Creutzfeldt-Jakob disease. Lancet 352:703–704, 1998.

110. Hill AF, Butterworth RJ, Joiner S, et al: Investigation of variant Creutzfeldt-Jakob disease and other human prion diseases with tonsil biopsy samples. Lancet 353:183–189, 1999.

111. Ironside JW, Head MW, Bell JE, et al: Laboratory diagnosis of variant Creutzfeldt-Jakob disease. Histopathology 37:1–9, 2000.

112. Bruce ME, McConnell I, Will RG, Ironside JW: Detection of variant Creutzfeldt-Jakob disease infectivity in extraneural tissues [letter]. Lancet 358:208–209, 2001.

Tissue Sampling, Specimen Handling, and Chromoendoscopy

Wilfred Weinstein

CHAPTER

5

Techniques for Tissue Sampling

BIOPSY INSTRUMENTS

Pinch Biopsy Forceps

Reusable Versus Disposable Pinch Biopsy Forceps

Studies have assessed the durability of reusable forceps in regards to cost and safety.[1-4] With dedication and modest reprocessing costs, the reusable forceps have been shown to be safe and potentially cost effective. However, some hospital and ambulatory care centers do not want to invest in rigorous reprocessing standards and thus use disposable forceps.

Forceps Sizes

The most common pinch biopsy forceps used worldwide are ones that fit through a 2.8-mm biopsy channel. Infants and very young children often have biopsies taken with smaller forceps that fit through a 2.2-mm biopsy channel. Pediatric gastroenterologists use narrow-bore instruments generally for routine diagnostic biopsy if the child weighs less than 10 kg. In tiny infants, they may even use a bronchoscope.

The aim with pinch biopsy forceps is to obtain a biopsy that contains the full thickness of the mucosa in disorders that are not associated with a large increase in mucosal thickness such as hypertrophic gastropathies. The 2.8-mm channel biopsy forceps can generally obtain a full-thickness mucosal biopsy except for the gastric body, greater curve, where the folds are normally thickest. A biopsy that fails to contain the full thickness of the mucosa should be considered as partially inadequate except for biopsies taken to look at surface findings such as for *Helicobacter pylori* or *Giardia lamblia*.

The Large-Cup ("Jumbo") Forceps

The large-cup forceps require a large channel, a so-called therapeutic endoscope (biopsy channel 3.6 mm). The opened cups are 9 mm in the open span. Biopsies yield two to three times the surface area but are not generally much deeper (Fig. 5–1). Biopsies taken with these

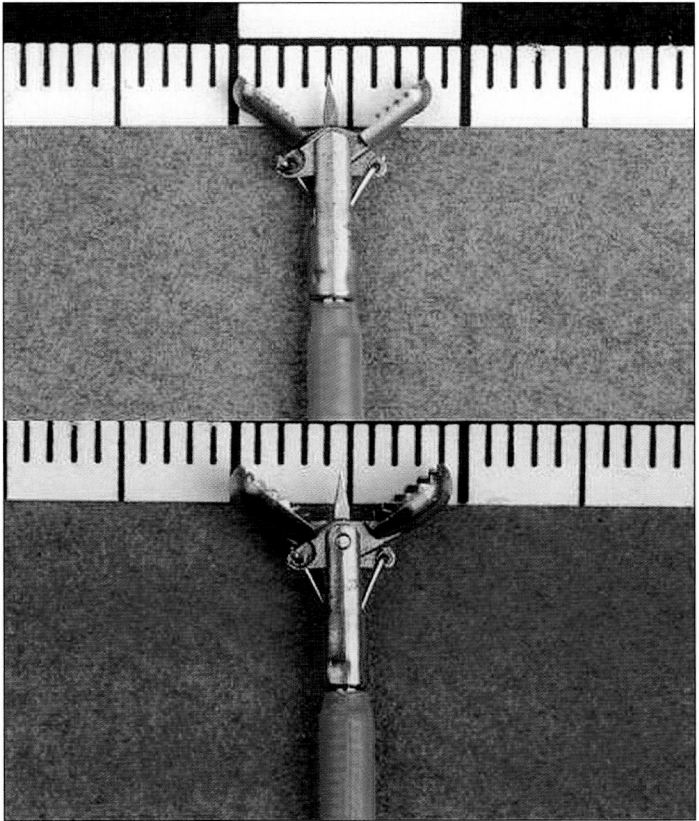

Figure 5–1. Biopsy forceps size comparisons. Comparison of regular (2.8-mm channel) forceps *(top)* and the large-cup forceps *(bottom)*. The open span of the smaller one is only 1 mm less than the 9-mm, open-span, large-cup (jumbo) forceps. The main difference between the two is the depth of the cups.

forceps usually contain very little submucosa or none at all. It is sometimes frustratingly difficult to get biopsies with sufficient submucosa when the objective is to diagnose amyloid, rule out Hirschsprung's disease, or hunt for vasculitis in submucosal blood vessels.

The large-cup forceps are clearly the one of choice for me whenever "tissue is the issue." They appear to be as safe as the more conventionally used smaller forceps.[5]

Part of the reason that only a minority of endoscopists use the large-cup forceps is because most endoscopes sold have a channel size (2.8 mm) that is too small to accommodate the larger forceps. However, there is also a puzzling antipathy toward the use of a larger forceps that obtain superior specimens, as if the larger forceps represented a serious threat.

One major advantage of the large-cup forceps is that the biopsies are much easier for the histotechnologist to orient in the laboratory. Orientation for embedding in paraffin is the key to maximizing the diagnostic yield from mucosal biopsies. Other advantages of large-cup forceps are that they contain proportionately less crush artifact, permit more precise evaluation of architecture, and are more likely to detect small, focal lesions.

Multiple Biopsy Specimen Forceps

Multiple biopsy specimen forceps are designed to obtain multiple specimens with a single pass. The disadvantage with prototypes to date is that each of the multiple-bite specimens are tiny, in the 2-mm range. In one study, the measurement of greater than 2 mm in one dimension was considered adequate, but the widths were not given; thus, it is impossible to tell if these were very slender. The problem with any biopsies that are individually small is that they are difficult for all but expert and specialized histotechnologists to orient properly for sectioning and producing high-quality sections. It is hoped that studies with new prototypes[6] will illustrate representative histology of what was considered average and interpretable and also provide the length-width dimensions of the biopsies.

Hot Biopsy Forceps

Hot biopsy forceps are insulated pinch biopsy forceps through which coagulation current is passed. The presumption has been that the hot biopsy leaves behind a burn that obliterates residual adenomatous tissue, but this idea has been challenged.[7] They have been used for diminutive colonic polyps, especially the tiny white ones in the rectum. If the hot biopsy forceps are to be used to quickly remove tiny polyps, a few should be taken first for histologic examination because the cautery artefact produced by the hot biopsy forceps commonly makes it impossible to differentiate hyperplastic from adenomatous polyps. It appears that these forceps are being used less often. They are safe in experienced hands,[8,9] but their use in the right colon is more likely to cause complications.[8,10]

Suction Biopsy

Suction biopsies are still sometimes used for biopsy in children.[11] The broadest application of suction biopsy in children has been in the diagnosis of Hirschsprung's disease. In this setting the measurement of biopsy distance from the anal verge is essential.[12]

Grasp Biopsies

Grasp biopsies are taken through a rigid sigmoidoscope using an alligator-jaw cutting forceps These are rarely used in clinical gastroenterology practice, but they may be useful for indurated distal rectal tumors that are difficult to grasp with the endoscopic biopsy forceps.

Cold Snare Biopsy

Looping small (<6 mm) polyps in the colon with a snare and cutting them off without electrocautery has been used in the colon[13,14] and appears to be safe. I have occasionally used a similar technique to remove multiple small (<6 mm) polyps in the stomach to distinguish hyperplastic from adenomatous polyps. Fundic gland polyps on the other hand have a characteristic appearance and location, and cold snare or any kind of snare is not generally required. The advantage to not applying electrocautery current to these smaller lesions is to avoid the electrocautery artefact that makes the histology uninterpretable. Cold snare biopsy should be used only by those who want to maintain an ongoing experience with the technique. One should always be prepared to apply a hemostasis probe if bleeding is excessive.

Furthermore, cold snare technique leaves a smaller mucosal defect than cautery-assisted polypectomy and, therefore, could potentially reduce the risk of secondary hemorrhage.

Laparoscopic Biopsies

Occasionally laparoscopic biopsies are used to obtain full-thickness biopsy specimens. This includes mapping of dysganglionosis[15] and full-thickness biopsies from various parts of the gastrointestinal (GI) tract for a variety of otherwise difficult-to-diagnose disorders[16] including some cases of intestinal pseudoobstruction.

Improving the Quality of Pinch Biopsies
How Close to the Biopsy Site Should One Position the Endoscope?

After biopsy targeting of focal lesions in disorders such as mucosa-associated lymphoid tissue (MALT), Barrett's esophagus, and ulcerative colitis, random biopsies are taken using landmarks or measurements. In these biopsy "mapping" circumstances, it is not necessary to be up close to biopsy sites or to clean each putative biopsy site of mucus or blood that has seeped over from adjacent biopsy sites. The biopsies can be taken blindly based on measurements or position, after the overall area has been cleared of any focal lesions that require biopsy first.

Pressure Against the Wall

Less tension on the wall helps get better quality biopsies. After the opened forceps are pressed against the wall, it is almost reflex to give a second push, thus indenting the wall even further before closing the forceps on the tissue. This unnecessary stretch may result in a shallower biopsy. A more attractive alternative is to have the lumen partially deflated beforehand or to gently touch the wall with the opened forceps and then apply several quick, staccato bursts of suction before clamping down on the tissue in the forceps cup.

Snapping the Forceps Back Quickly After It Is Closed on the Tissue

Some have thought that the biopsy forceps should be pulled away slowly to ensure that the submucosa falls away and thus to avoid overly deep biopsies. This is unnecessary because it provokes more crush artefact of the tissue. Excessive sampling of submucosa is certainly not a problem even with the large-cup forceps!

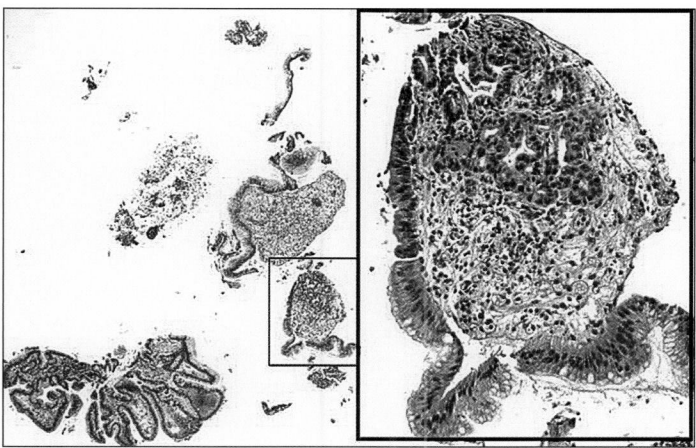

Figure 5–2. Double-bite inadequate biopsies of Barrett's esophagus taken for surveillance for dysplasia. All (except for one biopsy at the bottom) look like macrocytologies. One of these fragments *(inset)* shows high grade dysplasia.

Double Bites

Double bites refer to taking two biopsies with a single pass of the biopsy forceps. With the conventional-sized forceps, this double-bite technique often yields a tiny second biopsy, a *macrocytology* (Fig. 5–2). However, the double-bite technique may actually be done successfully in the colon and small bowel using the large-cup (jumbo) forceps. In the esophagus, the double-bite technique is difficult because of the need for angulation and risk of loss of the first biopsy obtained.[17] In the stomach, the size of the biopsies may be so generous with the first pass that there is scant room for a second biopsy.

To perform this technique, after the first biopsy is obtained, the closed forceps should be placed with slight pressure on the wall where the next biopsy is to be taken and the forceps are opened against a bit of wall pressure. This helps prevent the first biopsy from falling out into the lumen. After opening the forceps, a few staccato bursts of suction are applied, and the forceps are quickly closed to obtain the second biopsy. One does not always obtain two biopsies, but in the colon and small bowel this technique saves time when multiple biopsies are taken with the large-cup forceps.

In a prospective randomized study in 16 patients of esophageal and gastric biopsies, the samples from the first and second pass were deemed comparable but there was a significant risk of losing samples (18%). No measurements of biopsy size or photographs were provided.

The Turn-In Technique

In areas where one has to biopsy at an oblique angle or for gritty lesions, it helps enormously to use the turn-in technique especially in the esophagus.[18] The forceps are opened then drawn back flush with the endoscope tip. The tip of the endoscope is then deflected 90 degrees against the wall, thus allowing the forceps to be advanced *en face* from close up. They are advanced until resistance is met, then suction is applied briefly and the forceps are closed. It is not necessary to see what is being biopsied if random biopsies are being taken as in Barrett's surveillance. In the case of a focal lesion, the endoscope is positioned right over the lesion and then turned into it using the large up-down hand control knob on the endoscope. For those who want experience with the turn-in technique, the best is to try it in more spacious areas, such as the stomach, in the course of taking gastric biopsies.

The 6 O'clock Position and Biopsies of Gastroesophageal Junction (Cardia) Lesions

When areas are difficult to get at, rotation of the endoscope to the 6 o'clock position makes it infinitely easier to obtain biopsies and to target more accurately (Fig. 5–3). This is especially invaluable in biopsy surveillance of Barrett's esophagus in which the 12 o'clock aspect tends to be ignored for both visualization and biopsy targeting.

For lesions at the gastroesophageal (GE) junction, it is often invaluable to visualize the area on retroflexion in the stomach and

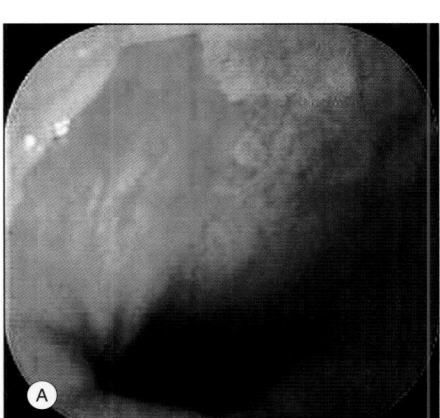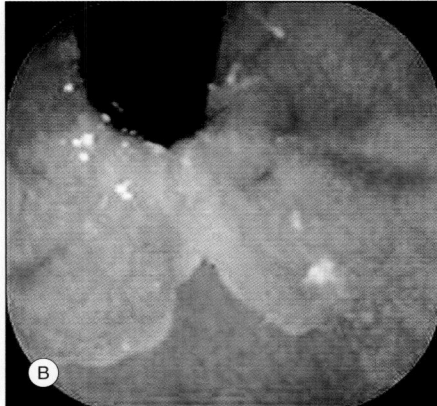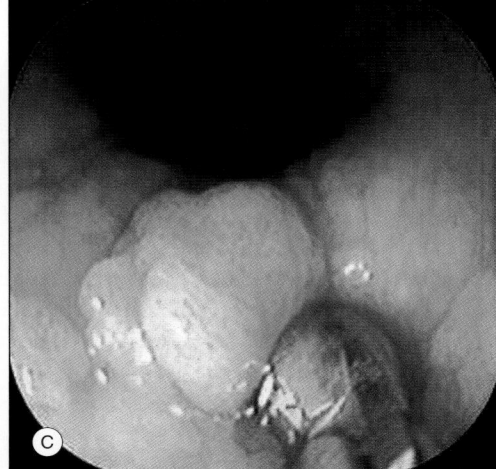

Figure 5–3. Value of viewing cardia lesions on retroflexion from the gastric side and positioning at 6 o'clock. *A,* End-on view of eccentric Z-line. *B,* Retroflexion view in the stomach. The eccentric part is positioned at 6 o'clock. Biopsy, if indicated, is easier from this aspect. *C,* Small gastroesophageal (GE) junction mass as viewed from the stomach on retroflexion and rotated to the 6 o'clock position for biopsy.

target biopsy or endoscopic mucosal resection (EMR) from this perspective (see Fig. 5–3C). This maneuver only works if the patient has a hiatal hernia. After the retroflexion is done in the stomach, air insufflation is put on the high mode and the endoscope is advanced by pulling backward until the endoscope tip advances right to the GE junction. In this way there is end-on visualization of a lesion. In addition, the endoscope can often be torqued slightly to place the lesion in or near the favored 6 o'clock position (see Fig. 5–3). If torque is required for biopsy positioning, the endoscopy assistant maintains it while the biopsy forceps are targeted to the lesion.

Reducing the Numbers of Uninterpretable Biopsies

Independent of which forceps or technique are used, one way to reduce the uninterpretability rate of biopsy is to have the endoscopy assistant indicate when a biopsy is nearly invisible or when there is only blood or mucus. Those should be discarded because they compromise the quality of sections overall when placed with adequate biopsies. In the process of taking biopsies a routine should be established whereby the endoscopy assistant calls out that a biopsy is adequate or otherwise.

Minimizing Biopsy Surveillance Antipathy

Part of the antipathy to surveillance biopsies is the drudgery of it all. When multiple biopsies are required, it helps enormously to have a second assistant in the room to run the forceps and handle the tissue while the other assistant monitors the patient. For upper endoscopic procedures such as Barrett's surveillance, it helps to have a well-sedated patient who does not keep bolting upright. The use of an anticholinergic such as glycopyrrolate 0.2 mg intravenous (IV) before the procedure reduces the secretions so that the endoscopy assistant may be freed from constantly suctioning the mouth.

TISSUE HANDLING
Transferring Biopsies from the Forceps to the Fixative

The best way to remove biopsies from the forceps is to use a blunt dental probe and push the biopsy out from the base of the opened forceps cups. If one pushes the biopsy out by pressing it from the top of the opened forceps, the biopsy may be squashed.

Shaking biopsies off the forceps into a fixative bottle may traumatize the biopsy tissue and cause denudation of the epithelium, especially from the gastric body. For those who want to continue the shake technique it might be useful to alert the pathologist to look for detached epithelium in biopsies from different parts of the GI tract. Some pathologists are so used to seeing a lot of detached epithelium that they believe that this is the best that endoscopists can achieve with endoscopic biopsies. When exudative lesions are biopsied for diagnosis, shaking biopsies into the fixative may peel off the exudate that contains the evidence for the presence of entities such as *Candida* or Herpes simplex, organisms that reside in the surface exudate.

Orientation of biopsies on support materials in the endoscopy units is not required in clinical practice and in inexperienced hands may lead to more tissue trauma. The key to having well-oriented biopsy specimens for histologic examination rests with the pathology

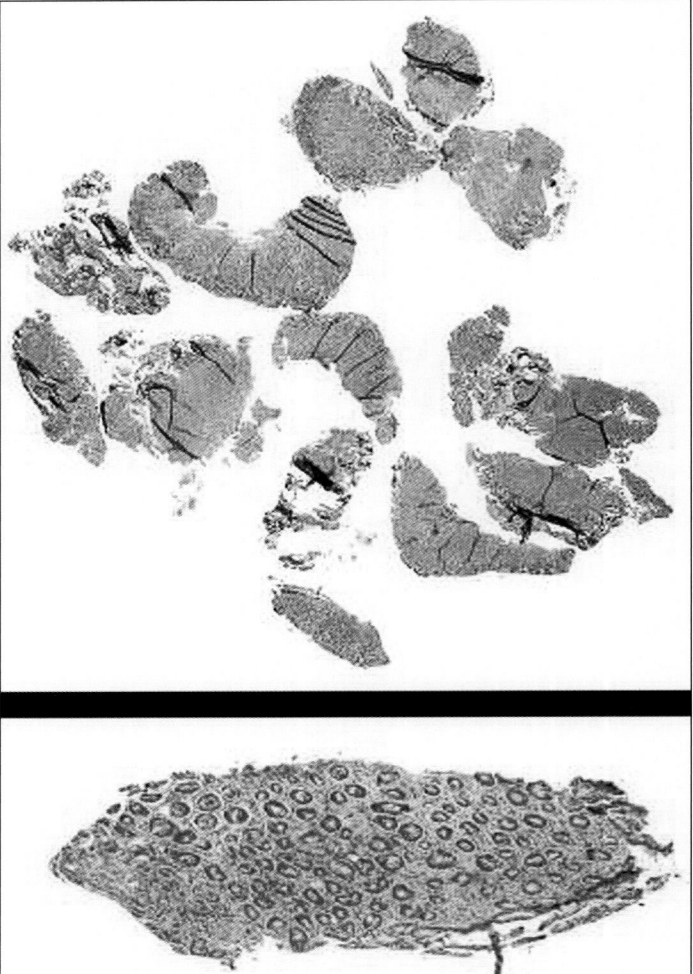

Figure 5–4. Too many biopsies placed into one fixative bottle and, hence, in one tissue block. Variable size fragments cannot be positioned en bloc; thus, each biopsy is not oriented. The dark lines represent tissue wrinkling in sectioning. The hallmark of grossly misoriented biopsies is shown below as cross-sectioned circles (doughnut effect) with no clue as to the real architecture.

histotechnologists' ability and motivation to embed the tissue *on its edge* in paraffin and obtain sections through the central core of the specimens.[19]

Number of Biopsies in a Fixative Bottle

One should never put more than four biopsies into a fixative bottle (Fig. 5–4). Most histotechnologists cannot line up more than four biopsies in a tissue block during embedding and section them so that all are represented in optimal orientation for interpretation. One argument that endoscopists use is that they put 10 or more in a single bottle to reduce the costs. They do not often get feedback that only half or fewer of those 10 specimens may be fully interpretable (see Fig. 5–4).

Polyps: Identifying the Stalk Region

When snare polypectomy is used for the removal of pedunculated or sessile polyps, the essential part of the specimen for cancer diagnosis is in the stalk region or the base, in the case of sessile polyps

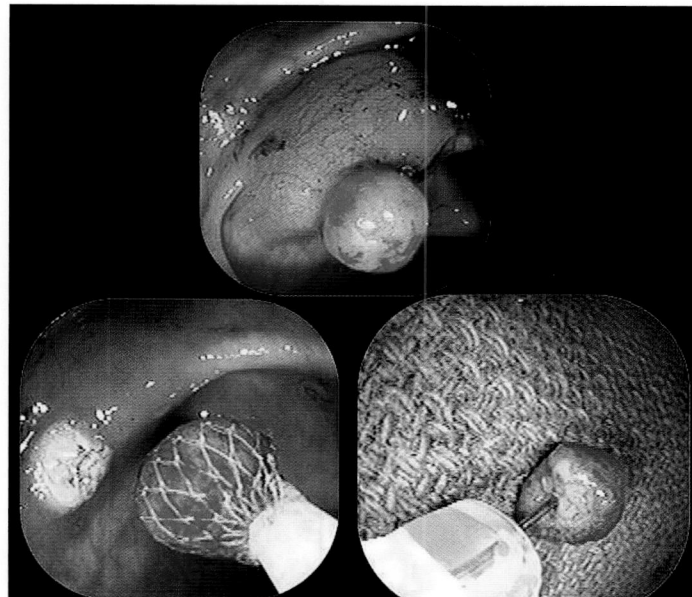

Figure 5–5. Polypectomy, first preinked. The base of the polyp has a needle inserted through to the tip of the polyp. In the laboratory, the polyp is bisected along the needle path and thus the central halves of the polyp will be embedded face down so that the base or stalk zone is represented in the first sections to be collected.

(Fig. 5–5). Stalks retract right after removal of the polyp and often shrink further and disappear after fixation. The best way to identify the stalk is to impale it with a short (1-inch) 25-gauge needle, right to the hub with the needle point emerging at the most convex part of the tip of the polyp (see Fig. 5–5). An alternative is to ink the polyp stalk or base after removal. After fixation for a few hours, the polyp is bisected with a scalpel or razor blade. The two bisected halves are embedded face down, and the first sections to come off are those that show the stalk region in its best orientation.[19]

Small Polyps

Small polyps are commonly retrieved into a suction trap. It appears that this does not damage the tissue. One key to doing it without getting it stuck in the suction channel is to have the polyp in a pool of liquid before suctioning. If there is none, some saline can be instilled first.

Shave Biopsy

When shave biopsy is used to remove larger sessile or pedunculated polyps in a piecemeal fashion, it is very important to submit the specimens marked at the cut sides or oriented mucosal side up. If the cut sides are marked and oriented, the pathologist can reconstruct the picture of a sessile adenoma. The diagnosis of cancer or its exclusion requires that the muscularis mucosae and upper submucosa be visualized. If multiple fragments are submitted with no orientation, the pathologist often cannot provide reassurance that invasion is not present.

Endoscopic Mucosal Resection

We, as endoscopists and the pathologists who handle these specimens, need to recognize that EMR specimens should be handled as are any resections for cancer or possible cancer. They are not merely larger biopsies.

It is preferable not to remove the lesions in pieces for the reasons discussed previously. Instead, the specimens should be oriented in such a way that there is no doubt in how to handle them. Handling EMR specimens requires a protocol worked out in advance for these lesions with the pathologists. The best scheme is to deliver the specimens fresh to pathology so that the pathologist examines it grossly and pins it out before placement in fixative. After fixation, the specimen should be cut into 2-mm strips and each embedded so that the whole specimen is represented in histologic slides.[20] In this way the patient and the endoscopist can be reassured that a focal or early lesion was analyzed optimally with respect to maximal invasion.

CYTOLOGY

Cytology in the Diagnosis of Infections

Of the three major potential infections of the esophagus, cytomegalovirus, *Candida albicans*, and Herpes virus, it is the latter two that are characterized by having the organisms in surface exudate. Cytomegalovirus is usually embedded deeper and is not commonly detected in smears of exudate for cytology.[21,22] Smears of exudates for cytologic examination may provide a rapid diagnosis, late in the day before a weekend. The brushings may also be used for culture, if desired. Exudate on the cytology brush is smeared onto slides just as for any other cytology. If a culture is desired, a second brushing is swirled around in a culture medium or the brush tip is cut off with wire cutters and left in the bottom of the culture medium container. With most esophageal infections, it is not necessary to obtain culture verification. Cytology for complementary diagnosis of other infections has been reported. These include tuberculosis,[23] zygomycosis,[24] and microfilaria.[25] Studies have reported the use of brush or imprint (of biopsies) cytology[26,27] for the diagnosis of *H. pylori* but are not commonly used. Aspirates of duodenal fluid have been used considerably in the past for the diagnosis of *G. lamblia*, but it appears that biopsies are at least as sensitive to make the diagnosis.[28] Aspirates of duodenal fluid in human immunodeficiency virus (HIV)-positive patients have been disappointing for diagnosis of infections in general, when compared with duodenal or jejunal biopsy.[29]

Cytology for Cancer or Dysplasia Diagnosis

Brush cytology is sometimes the only immediate diagnostic modality available in potentially malignant strictures with marked luminal compromise. One should exercise caution in passing the cytology brush into the lumen of a strictured area to do brushings.

Cytologic examinations outside of the endoscopic ultrasonography (EUS) setting are uncommonly performed.[30,31] Brush or other types of cytology at best are complementary to biopsy in the diagnosis of dysplasia and carcinoma. Cytology alone has not been shown to be accurate enough to bypass biopsy or to permit fewer biopsies to be taken.

Barrett's Esophagus

Barrett's esophagus is theoretically a good model in which to use cytology. When dysplasia and cancer occur, there is usually a field defect with multifocal dysplasia over a larger span than just a visible target lesion, if one is present. Even the cytology enthusiasts indicate that cytology and biopsy are complementary in Barrett's esophagus[22] and recognize that the cytologic diagnosis of low grade dysplasia is suboptimal.[21,31] Studies that examine cytology and biopsy have not included enough patients with dysplasia to know whether cytology would have an impact on surveillance practice efficiency and accuracy.[32] One could argue that any advantage of cytology over biopsy in small numbers of cases of carcinoma[32] must document that this is not due to relative inadequacy in sampling with the biopsy part of the protocol.

Techniques other than brush cytology have been used in Barrett's esophagus and other conditions. Imprint cytology is a technique in which the surface of the biopsy is touched to a glass slide for cytology and then the biopsy is also processed in the usual way.[33] It does not appear to offer any advantages.

With nonendoscopic cytology techniques, the idea is to be able to do surveillance with cytology alone, to then stratify subsets of patients for endoscopic biopsy for dysplasia, or to identify patients with Barrett's esophagus in screening patients with gastroesophageal reflux disease (GERD). The balloon approach[34] did not appear to be abrasive enough to obtain optimal cytologic sampling; thus, other techniques using mesh have been used in studies.[35]

Mass Screening for Squamous Cancer

In China, large-scale cytologic studies using nonendoscopic inflatable balloons have been used to try to identify those with dysplasia and carcinoma in areas with very high rates of squamous cancer of the esophagus.[36] In a study with balloon and sponge cytology samplers, compared with biopsy *at the same session*, sensitivities for squamous carcinoma were suboptimal with sensitivities less than 50% for dysplasia and carcinoma.[37]

Brush Cytology in Other Sites in the Gastrointestinal Tract

Studies have been reported in colorectal and gastric neoplasia.[38–40] As for esophageal strictures, if a lesion is difficult to biopsy then cytology may be valuable as a complementary technique.[41] The diagnosis of anal dysplasia especially in high-risk populations such as those with HIV can be difficult and anal cytology may, in future studies, be shown to play a role.[42,43] At present, its utility is unknown.

Molecular and Other Applications of Cytology

Not surprisingly studies are directed to using molecular pathology techniques in cytology just as in histology. These include colonic lavage cells for image cytometry,[44] obtaining cells for culture from the esophagus,[45] and biomarkers.[46]

DIALOGUE WITH THE PATHOLOGIST: THE SECOND ESSENTIAL PART OF OPTIMAL TISSUE HANDLING

A more detailed discussion of the pathologist-endoscopist interaction is available.[47]

Dialogue and communication with pathologists remains a weak link in the optimal use of biopsies in the management of patients.[48]

What Information Should the Pathologist Receive?

Tables 5–1 and 5–2 give the information that can be incorporated into a standardized biopsy requisition form. Table 5–1 gives examples of standardized biopsy locations. The endoscopy nurses can ensure that the scheme is kept as they write down the sites called out to

---

Table 5–1. Standardization of the Biopsy Locations for Endoscopy Reports and for the Pathology Requisition

Esophagus
LES, Z line and location of biopsy, all as centimeters from incisors. If no Barrett's esophagus, the LES region and Z line are assumed to be at the same location.

Stomach
Fundus
Body, Antrum (for each) greater or lesser curvature aspect; proximal, mid, or distal antrum or body

Duodenum and Jejunum
Bulb
2nd duodenum
Beyond 2nd duodenum is estimate only unless enteroscopy done under fluoroscopy

Ileum
As centimeters from ileocecal valve

Colon
Cecum
Ascending colon—cecum and ascending colon may normally have more inflammatory cells so separate them from biopsies from other sites
Hepatic flexure region
Transverse colon B if multiple sites here, then proximal, mid, distal
Splenic flexure region
Descending and sigmoid colon—if colon straight, as centimeters from anorectal margin; if not straight, then site descriptions as descending colon, sigmoid, rectum
Rectum B as such or if important focal rectal disease, as centimeters or relationship to the valves of Houston

LES, lower esophageal sphincter.
Modified from Weinstein WM: Mucosal biopsy techniques and interaction with the pathologist. Gastrointest Endosc Clin N Am 10:555–572, 2000.

Table 5–2. Information for the Pathologist: Lesion Descriptions, Relevant Medications, History, and Question for the Pathologist

Lesion Description
If abnormal, use simple language examples: thick folds instead of hypertrophic or edematous; thin instead of atrophic.
For description of a lesion, give what was seen rather than an interpretation (e.g., gastritis).

Biopsy Instrument
Detail type of instrument if different (e.g., hot biopsy forceps, electrocautery snare) than a pinch biopsy forceps.

For Polyps
Give size, whether sessile or pedunculated, and instrument used (e.g., biopsy forceps, hot biopsy forceps, or electrocautery snare).

Key Drugs
For all sites: any immunosuppressives, chemotherapy, or radiotherapy, current or recent nonsteroidal anti-inflammatory drugs (NSAIDs)
Stomach: proton pump inhibitors, dose and duration, recent or current antibiotics or bismuth compounds
Colon: type of prep, local or oral and type of oral, 5-ASA compounds or other IBD drugs

History
Brief, one or two lines usually suffices.

Question for the Pathologist
Be as specific as possible.

5-ASA, 5-amino salicylic acid; IBD, inflammatory bowel disease.
Modified from Weinstein WM: Mucosal biopsy techniques and interaction with the pathologist. Gastrointest Endosc Clin N Am 10:555–572, 2000.

them by the endoscopist. Table 5–2 details the other information to be provided to pathologists in order for them to be able to give more focused diagnoses and differential diagnoses.

The History

The history may be brief but relevant. For example, if a patient has diarrhea and has received chemotherapy, that should be stated if it has been recent. If radiotherapy has been given, the dates should be indicated so that the pathologist can look for the acute mucosal changes that occur soon after radiotherapy is begun versus the long-term effects that may occur months or years later.

The Questions for the Pathologist

Pathologists continue to put up with biopsies provided with no history and no question, for example, simply a label of "gastritis." This is equivalent to asking a clinician to do a physical examination and make a diagnosis without a history to help guide the examination.

Asking the right question or questions requires knowledge on the part of the endoscopist regarding what the biopsy can do in a given setting and what it cannot accomplish. Sometimes the question is simply, "What is this lesion?" Endoscopists need to have realistic expectations and not have the pathologists believe that they have to be apologists. The biopsy of polyps is a good example. Not infrequently, polyps are biopsied and the mucosa is normal. Instead of making a histologic diagnosis of "polypoid fold" or "mucosal tag" (apologist diagnoses), the pathologist should feel free to say "normal."

The questions for the pathologist can guide the final diagnosis. For example, if the endoscopist is evaluating a patient with a recent onset of diarrhea and believes it would be premature to label the patient with ulcerative colitis or Crohn's disease, the biopsy question might be: "rule out granulomas, focal versus diffuse inflammation and infectious pattern." If a small bowel biopsy is taken in a patient with malabsorption, the question might be "rule out flat mucosal lesion of celiac disease." If the question is to rule out celiac disease, the pathologist might give the celiac label with only minimal

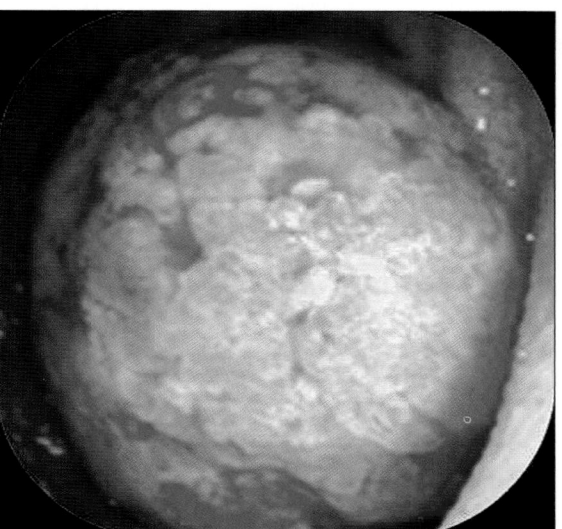

Figure 5–6. Large tumor of the transverse colon seen for the first time. The endoscopist's biopsies were accompanied by the question of "rule out cancer." The pathologist's diagnosis was "adenomatous change, cannot rule out cancer, and recommend rebiopsy." The endoscopist's question should have been "large mass, scheduled for resection, rule out adenomatous change."

abnormalities present (so-called Marsh 1 or 2 lesions), whereas it is not established that these abnormalities can cause overt malabsorption. The question for sessile polyps that are biopsied is simply rule out adenoma, not rule out complete excision. In a sessile polyp, to rule out total excision would require sectioning the whole dome-shaped biopsy from one end to the other.

When a cancer is found for the first time and the patient is slated for resection, the comment from the endoscopist should be "slated for surgery, rule out adenomatous change." If the question is to rule out cancer, then the diagnosis might come back as "adenoma present but cannot rule out cancer, recommend rebiopsy" (Fig. 5–6 illustrates this point).

Drugs

It is increasingly recognized that drugs may be responsible for a variety of pathologic conditions that were not imagined in the recent past. Table 5–2 outlines the information regarding drug or other therapy that can affect any part of the gut; some are site specific. Nonsteroidal anti-inflammatory drugs (NSAIDs) should be in the differential diagnosis of unusual lesions anywhere in the gut, although cause and effect in such instances are often difficult to prove. In lymphocytic or microscopic colitis, other drugs may be important (e.g., ranitidine).[49] It is not necessary to list all drugs that a patient takes. The importance of some drugs that a patient takes only becomes apparent after review of the biopsies. For example, in ischemic colitis in younger people without generalized athero-sclerotic disease, the possibility of a wider range of culpable drugs becomes important, including cocaine and oral contraceptives. These can be sought post hoc after the biopsies are interpreted.

What Can Pathologists Do To Improve Dialogue and Biopsy Diagnoses?

Modern GI biopsy diagnoses require that the pathologist knows the consequences of the diagnoses (e.g., lifelong gluten-free diet for celiac disease; difficulty with life insurance and worry about cancer with ulcerative colitis). The differential diagnoses should be focused and not just a litany of differential diagnoses that may be appropriate for a textbook but not for a diagnosis in clinical practice. This can all be achieved by regular dialogue including sharing publications between the endoscopist and the pathologist. Terminology for which there are action plans must be adhered to. For example, there are no published action plans for moderate dysplasia in either ulcerative colitis or Barrett's esophagus; thus, the pathologist should stick to indefinite, low grade, or high grade in the diagnosis of dysplasia.

Perhaps the two areas in GI pathology that need the most improvement are to avoid calling everything mild chronic inflammation and to improve biopsy-processing quality. The latter is still lacking in many pathology laboratories with regular production of cross-sectioned specimens and worse, tearing or chatter of tissue, and poor staining (see Fig. 5–4).

Chromoendoscopy

The focus on chromoendoscopy techniques in this section is on those that help target biopsies or removal of lesions. Chromoendoscopy involves the topical application of dyes to the mucosa, most often applied with a standard endoscopic retrograde cholangiopancreatography (ERCP) cannula or a special spray catheter.

Optical methods either alone or in combination with chromoendoscopy are likely to hold the key to better targeting, to increase biopsy yield in Barrett's esophagus and in some other disorders of the GI tract.[50]

Table 5–3 lists the staining agents and provides an overview of their staining characteristics and potential utility. There has been a renaissance of research interest in chromoendoscopy worldwide, occurring long after it was developed and first used primarily in Japan. However, chromoendoscopy is rarely to uncommonly used in clinical practice. Part of the reason is that the technique adds extra time to the procedure. In addition, except for simply highlighting focal lesions or diffuse mucosal abnormalities as in celiac disease, the other applications are more subjective in their interpretation. With a few exceptions, mainly related to highlighting lesions before their removal, there is as yet, no clear-cut evidence that chromoendoscopy should become part of routine clinical endoscopic practice.

PREPARATION OF THE PATIENT AND THE MUCOSA FOR CHROMOENDOSCOPY

If the use of Lugol's iodine is contemplated, it should be ascertained that the patient is not allergic to iodine. For methylene blue staining, the patient should be told that the urine and stool might adopt a blue color.

The enemy of good chromoendoscopy is surface mucus, blood, or retained food material.[51] The surface to be examined after application of dye should be washed. For the vital/absorptive dyes (e.g., Lugol's iodine, methylene blue), it is especially useful to wash with 20 mL or more of 10% N-acetylcysteine.[52] An alternative is to have the patient take a 20,000-unit pronase drink before the procedure.[53] This is then followed by another wash with water or saline after 1 to 2 minutes, using 100 mL or more of tap water to remove nonabsorbed stain. The washes can also contain a small amount of antifoam solution. Washes can be done using a 60-mL syringe with forceful pressure through the spray catheter or through a syringe without the spray catheter.

The use of anticholinergics such as glycopyrrolate 0.2 mg is effective in reducing secretions and the addition of glucagon (0.25 to 0.50 mg) just before or during the procedure helps to reduce peristalsis and spasm.

CONTRAST STAINS

Contrast stains help most in the delineation of superficial neoplastic lesions, such as in the stomach, and of all lesions before EMR.[20] In the latter instance, the often-irregular margins of the lesion to be excised are better defined. One disadvantage of contrast stains is that they require some experience to recognize what is normal mucosa and what is not. In the stomach, for example, pit openings and areae gastricae will look magnified and more irregular than the smooth unstained mucosa.

The most popular stain is the use of indigo carmine as a contrast stain (see Table 5–3). Although many experts indicate that it should not be washed off after application, some washing off after application leaves the innate color of the lesion in question still preserved (Fig. 5–7). Often all one needs are thin lines of stain in grooves or edges of lesions to define borders and provide a three-dimensional effect (see Fig. 5–7). Other stains can be used for contrast staining. Methylene blue (provided that there is no intestinal absorptive epithelium that binds the dye) can be used where simply contrast is desired, and even blood-stained mucosa, from an adjacent biopsy site, can be used to highlight lesions or mucosal detail.

Methylene blue can be used as a contrast stain in a different sense. When saline is being injected before mucosectomy, a few drops of methylene blue into a 30-mL syringe filled with saline will provide a sky blue color to the injected submucosa and provide a better contrast between the lesion to be removed and the uninvolved part of the submucosa below.[54]

Table 5–3. Stains for Chromoendoscopy

Stain Categories and Types	Concentration	Mechanism of Staining	Positive-Staining Color	Potential Utility	Staining Result
Contrast Stains*					
Indigo carmine	0.1%–0.4%	Pools in mucosal irregularities and grooves	Blue-violet (indigo)	For topographic accentuation of lesions	Creates a three-dimensional effect
Vital/Absorptive*					
Lugol's iodine	1%–4%	Absorbed by glycogen-containing epithelium	Dark green-brown to black	Squamous cancer	Negative
				Islands of residual Barrett's esophagus after ablation	Negative
				Esophagitis or any other process that depletes glycogen in squamous cells	Negative
Methylene blue	0.50%	Absorptive cells of small bowel and colon and metaplastic absorptive cells	Blue	Intestinal metaplasia of the stomach	Positive
				Adenomatous polyps of the duodenum	Negative
				Barrett's esophagus, intestinal epithelial component	Positive
				Gastric metaplasia of the duodenal bulb	Negative
Toluidine blue	1%	Nuclear DNA of malignant cells	Blue	Squamous cell carcinoma of the oropharynx and esophagus	Positive
Reactive Stains					
Congo red	0.3%–0.5%	pH < 3 yields blue-black color	Turns from red to blue-black	Map acid-secreting mucosa in survey studies	Color change confirms presence of oxyntic acid-secreting cells
Phenol red	0.10%	Alkaline pH color change	Turns from yellow to red	Map Helicobacter pylori infected epithelium for survey studies	Color change to red
Tattooing Agents†					
India ink	0.1% India ink or alternative commercial preparation	Permanent marking of lesion or site of former lesion	Black at injection site	Usual indication is for polyps removed and worrisome for cancer (superficial injection) or lesions to be removed at surgery (deep injection)	Permanent black color

*Cresyl violet and crystal violet have been used much less commonly as contrast and absorptive stains, respectively.
†Indocyanine green is used much less commonly as a tattooing agent.

THE ESOPHAGUS
Squamous Carcinoma and Dysplasia of the Esophagus

One of the most important potential applications of chromoendoscopy in the clinical arena is in the delineation of squamous carcinoma and dysplasia with Lugol's solution. The iodine in the solution stains the glycogen in normal squamous epithelium. Negative staining indicates a mucosal disorder.

Ten to 30 mL of the solution (see Table 5–3) is sprayed into the esophagus. This can be done efficiently by beginning at the GE junction and applying the spray as the endoscope is moved cephalad. The lumen can be partially collapsed, and when the upper extent of the sprayed area is reached it can be totally collapsed to permit apposition of the stained walls for more uniform staining. After 1 to 2 minutes, the lumen can be insufflated, and any pale-staining areas can be resprayed. The color ranges from dark green to brown to black in normal squamous epithelium. After 10 to 15 minutes the stain intensity starts to fade, sometimes dramatically.

Areas of dysplasia and carcinoma are glycogen depleted thus negative staining occurs.[55] The same holds for areas of eroded mucosa or mucosa markedly thinned by injury or regeneration,[56] for example after healing of erosive esophagitis or after restoration of neosquamous epithelium after ablation of Barrett's esophagus. In the latter instances, staining may be paler than usual and not completely negative.

Lugol's iodine highlights and makes visible areas of dysplasia or early carcinoma that can either be missed or poorly visualized in terms of margins. In a study in Linxian, China, which has one of the highest rates of esophageal cancer, the rate of dysplasia and cancer detection went from 62% to 96% with a specificity of 63% with the use of Lugol's stain.[57] The technique appears very useful to detect recurrent or metachronous lesions in centers that do EMR for early squamous esophageal carcinoma.[58,59] Lugol's iodine has also been

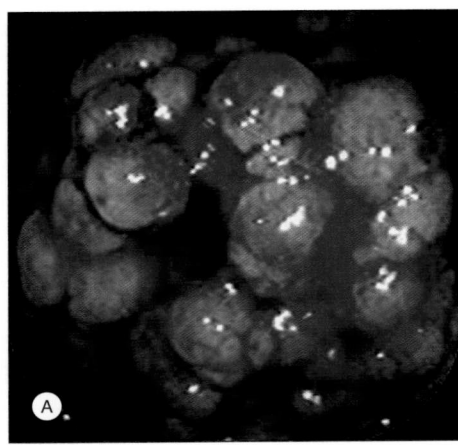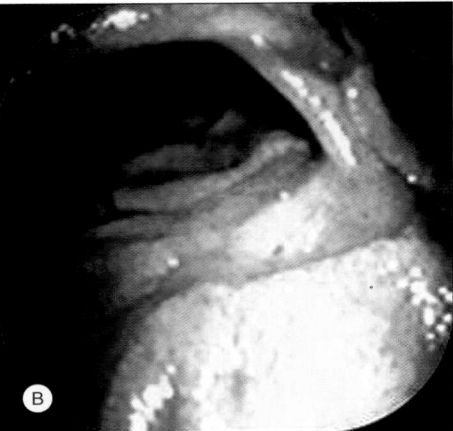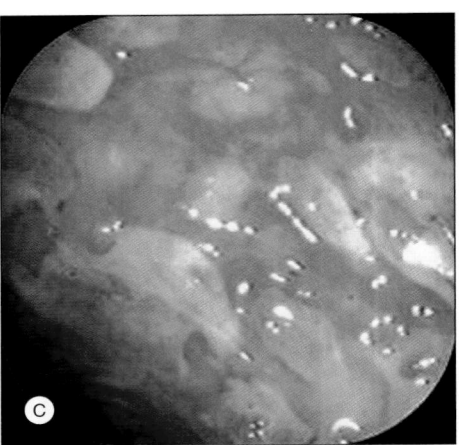

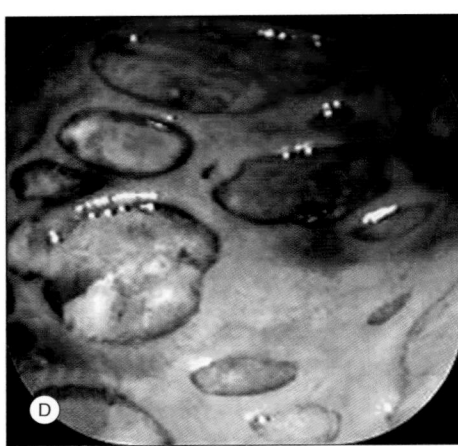

Figure 5-7. Contrast staining with indigo carmine. *A,* Clusters of gastric body fundic gland polyps in a patient with familial polyposis coli. *B,* Cookie-cutter erosions in the small bowel of a patient on nonsteroidal anti-inflammatory drugs (NSAIDs). Most of the dye has been washed off, and the residual dye in the grooves provides a three-dimensional effect. *C* and *D,* Rectosigmoid colon, unclassified inflammatory bowel disease. *C,* One initial impression was that of pseudomembranous colitis. *D,* After washing the lesions in *C,* the mucus and exudates filling the lesions vanished and the indigo carmine outlined saucer-shaped depressed ulcers or erosions.

tested in populations with an increased risk of squamous esophageal cancer such as head and neck cancers[60] and in those with abnormal exfoliative cytologies.[56]

Toluidine Blue

Toluidine blue has not been used to any extent since its early description.[61] It stains nuclear material of malignant cells, but esophageal ulcers and erosive esophagitis may give false-positive results.

Post Barrett's Ablation Search for Residual Barrett's Islands

After photodynamic therapy for dysplasia or after ablation studies in patients without dysplasia,[62,63] follow-up examinations are to search for areas of residual Barrett's esophagus for retreating. Application of Lugol's iodine to the previously ablated area makes it much easier to detect tiny islands of residual negative-staining Barrett's epithelium (Fig. 5-8).

Methylene Blue for the Detection of Barrett's Epithelium and Dysplasia

The most widely popularized staining method in research studies of Barrett's esophagus is with methylene blue (Fig. 5-9). Canto has done much of the seminal work with methylene blue.[65,66]

Methylene blue binds to intestinal absorptive epithelium, whether it is normal small intestine, the intestinal metaplasia that is characteristic of Barrett's esophagus, or intestinal metaplasia of the stomach. In Barrett's esophagus, there are two areas of interest in studies with methylene blue. One is to identify intestinal epithelium (positive staining) in apparent or possible short-segment Barrett's esophagus, and the second is to detect dysplasia by negative staining.

One sobering observation is that sprayed methylene blue induces oxidative damage of DNA when it is photosensitized by white light.[64] The concern in Barrett's epithelium is that the stain may further the promutagenic DNA damage that may already exist and raises the question about increased rate of carcinogenesis.[64] Clearly this requires more work and also might dictate the desirability of studying the other spray agents used in experimental studies of Barrett's esophagus.

The Methylene Blue Procedure

First, a mucolytic is given (N-acetylcysteine or pronase). Then 0.5% methylene blue is sprayed, and 2 minutes later the mucosa is washed off. More details are available in a recent comprehensive review including how to avoid staining clothing and admonitions to patients to not be dismayed by the passage of green urine and/or stool within the next day.[52] There is an acknowledged learning curve and the staining procedure adds 2 to 12 minutes to the procedure,[52] likely more on the order of 10 to 15 minutes, if one includes

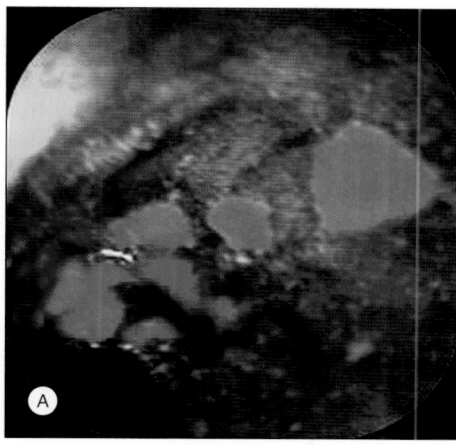

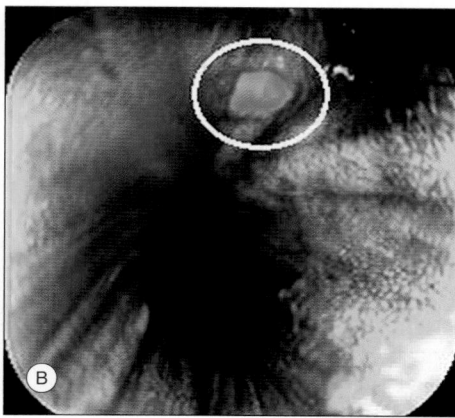

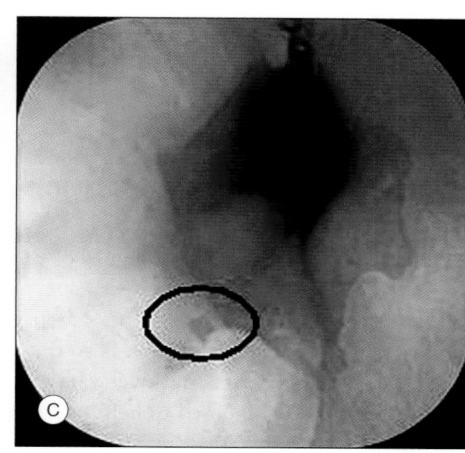

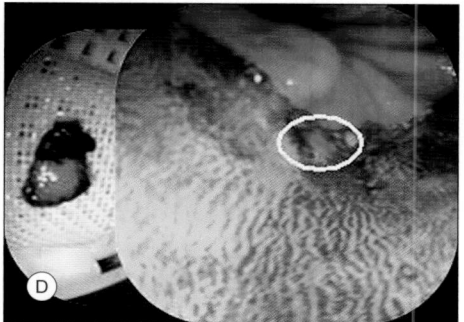

Figure 5-8. Lugol's iodine in the esophagus. *A,* Highlighted Barrett's islands before ablation in an experimental ablation study. Squamous cancer, dysplasia, and erosive esophagitis are also negative staining with Lugol's iodine. *B,* 6 weeks after initial ablation, tiny residual island of Barrett's epithelium remains. This island was not recognized before dye staining. *C* and *D,* Staining of a tiny island of columnar epithelium in a patient with gastroesophageal reflux disease (GERD). *C,* Before staining. *D,* Island rotated to 6 o'clock position after Lugol's iodine; the biopsy *(inset)* shows the excised negative-staining island surrounded by dark Lugol's-stained squamous mucosa.

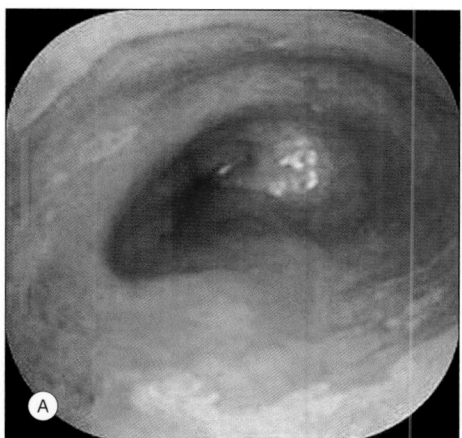

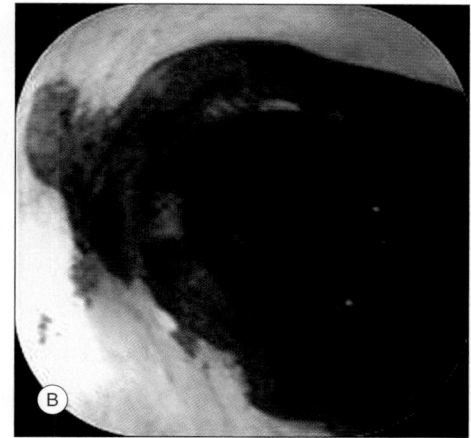

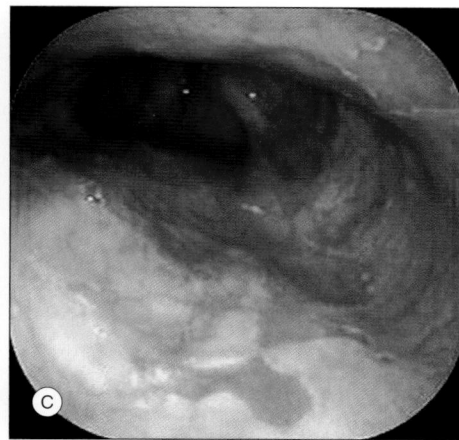

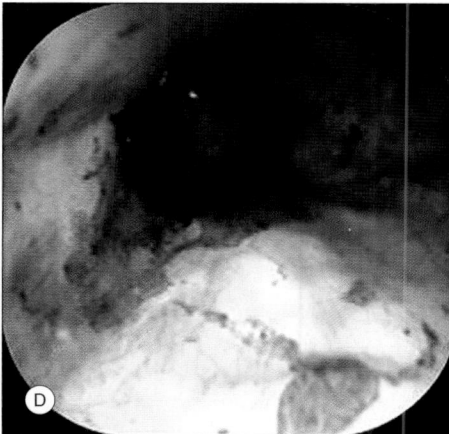

Figure 5-9. Methylene blue staining of long- and short-segment Barrett's esophagus. *A* and *B,* Long-segment Barrett's esophagus before and after staining. The staining intensity is dark and uniform. *C* and *D,* Short-segment Barrett's esophagus before and after staining. The staining intensity is lighter and more patchily distributed.

setup and postprocedure cleanup times. Canto advises that beginners in chromoendoscopy take multiple photographs and compare staining characteristics with pathologic diagnoses of biopsies of stained areas.[52]

Short-Segment Barrett's Esophagus and Intestinal Metaplasia of the Cardia

If biopsies of apparent 2-cm tongues of Barrett's at endoscopy are found to histologically have intestinal type goblet cells, then the diagnosis of short-segment Barrett's esophagus is made. If intestinal type goblet cells are absent, then Barrett's esophagus should not be diagnosed. Staining with methylene blue in suspect short-segment Barrett's esophagus is aimed to help increase the yield in biopsies of hitting areas with intestinal metaplasia (blue staining) to clinch the diagnosis.

When used for the detection of short-segment Barrett's esophagus ($\leq$ 3 cm in length), the staining pattern is less diffuse and patchier than in long segments of Barrett's esophagus (see Fig. 5–9). The reason is that in short-segment Barrett's esophagus there is a greater mix of intestinal and nonintestinal columnar cells present than in the more diffuse intestinal change of long-segment Barrett's esophagus.[65,66]

In short-segment Barrett's esophagus, proponents of the procedure report sensitivity for finding intestinal metaplasia as high as 98%[67]; more usual sensitivities are 80%[68] and may be as low as 60% to 70%,[69,70] but all usually report sensitivity that is higher than for random biopsies. The tenor of these studies is that fewer random biopsies are required with methylene blue staining. However, there is a body of conflicting data that shows no advantage over random biopsy, especially in short-segment Barrett's esophagus.[71–73] Each of the studies differs somewhat in study design and in how or whether the intensity or patchiness of staining is reported.

Methylene blue staining has also been used to identify intestinal metaplasia of the cardia right at the GE junction in those without endoscopically visible Barrett's esophagus.[74] In practice there is no clinical indication to biopsy a normal appearing Z-line. Intestinal metaplasia is not uncommon in asymptomatic individuals and certainly exists in patients with GERD without Barrett's esophagus.[75,76]

High Grade Dysplasia and Endoscopically Invisible Adenocarcinoma

Fewer studies have examined the potential role of methylene blue for early neoplastic change.[66,69,71,77] The objective here as with a host of other optical techniques is to target the areas most likely to contain neoplastic change and reduce the randomness of random biopsy.[50] These lesions should be negative staining with methylene blue because of transformation of the intestinal cells to neoplastic ones. In the ideal scenario, the blue staining nondysplastic Barrett's esophagus surrounds negative-staining dysplastic areas. The intensity of both the blueness and the paleness is variable.[52] The search for dysplasia in short-segment Barrett's esophagus is compounded by the fact that the nondysplastic short-segment Barrett's esophagus is often patchily distributed. It is more uniform in longer segment Barrett's esophagus (see Fig. 5–9). The sensitivity for high grade dysplasia[66,77] is much better than for low grade dysplasia.[69,71]

Other Staining Techniques in Barrett's Esophagus

Studies to detect intestinal metaplasia of the GE junction[78] and short-segment Barrett's esophagus have been reported using magnification endoscopy with indigo carmine or acetic acid. In a preliminary study, indigo carmine with magnification endoscopy has been used to attempt to characterize the different appearances of intestinal metaplasia of Barrett's esophagus and dysplasia.[79] Acetic acid (1.5%) changes the esophagus to a blanched white and leaves Barrett's esophagus and gastric mucosa looking red.[78,80]

Summary: Dye Staining in Barrett's Esophagus

Given the available data and the extra time involved, methylene blue or other dye techniques for detecting intestinal metaplasia and dysplasia are not likely to be incorporated into routine clinical practice. Targeted biopsy would be most desirable in short segment Barrett's esophagus (SSBE) to confirm Barrett's esophagus histologically and to target high grade dysplasia and endoscopically invisible adenocarcinoma. Further studies will likely clarify whether there is a role in clinical practice for dye staining in Barrett's esophagus.

THE STOMACH

Apart from the use of contrast stains to define subtle lesions (with[81] or without magnification endoscopy), there is no type of chromoendoscopy that has widespread applications in the stomach except for selected research indications. Congo red (see Table 5–3) has been used in studies to map out the extent of atrophic, non-acid-secreting mucosa in the gastric body and fundus.[82,83] Congo red and methylene blue were used in combination to help diagnose small gastric cancers[84] but are no longer used. Methylene blue stains intestinal metaplasia of the stomach a dark blue (Fig. 5–10), and it has been combined with magnification endoscopy to examine its utility in more precise characterization of intestinal metaplasia and gastric dysplasia.[85,86] Phenol red spray has been used in survey studies of the extent of *H. pylori* infection in the stomach (see Table 5–3), in both benign and malignant disease.[87,88]

THE SMALL INTESTINE
Celiac Disease

The endoscopic signs of celiac disease include loss of Kerckring's folds, scalloped folds, mosaic pattern (Fig. 5–11C), and visualization of underlying blood vessels. In one large study[89] using methylene blue after documenting the findings before spraying, endoscopists correctly identified 75 of 80 patients with the disease and 86 of 87 with normal mucosa. Although dye spraying made some of the changes more crisp, it did not add to the detection rate for these experienced endoscopists. In a study of patients with total and partial villous atrophy, magnification endoscopy plus chromoendoscopy with indigo carmine were statistically better for detection of small bowel lesions than standard endoscopy.[90] Finally, a smattering of different small bowel lesions were better seen with indigo carmine, but magnification endoscopy did not add to the yield.[91]

In suspect cases of celiac disease for an endoscopist not experienced in recognizing the endoscopic features, use of a stain

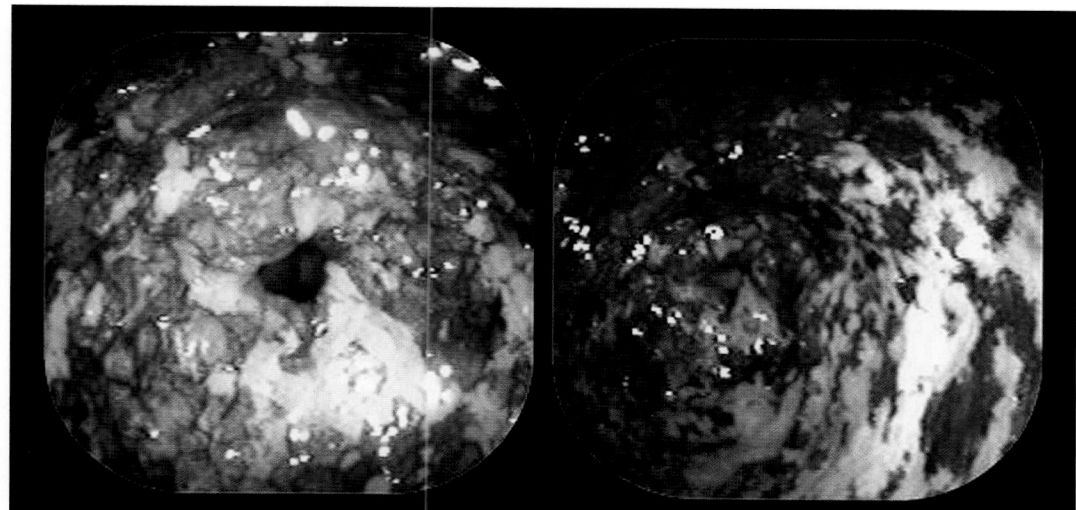

Figure 5-10. Methylene blue staining of the gastric antrum. There is major staining of much of the antrum indicating extensive intestinal metaplasia. Negative staining areas may represent nonintestinalized normal gastric surface epithelium or gastric dysplasia in a field of intestinal metaplasia.

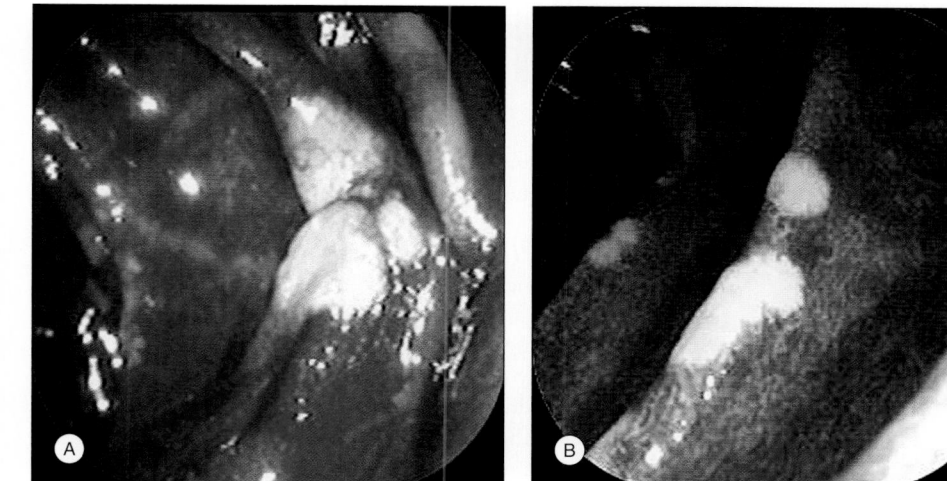
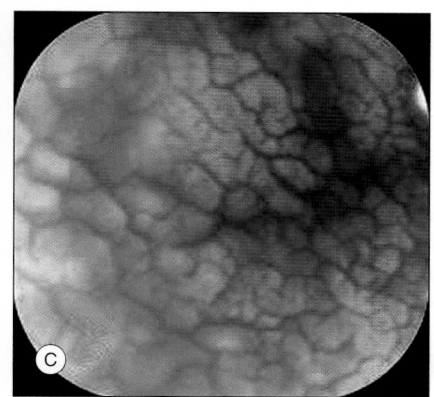

Figure 5-11. Small intestinal chromoendoscopy. *A* and *B,* Typical flat to minimally raised adenomas in the duodenum typical of those seen in familial polyposis coli. They are easily highlighted and more readily recognized with methylene blue staining. The methylene blue stains intestinal mucosa and leaves the adenomas negative staining. *C,* Indigo carmine contrast stain of the distal duodenum in a patient with celiac disease and a flat mucosa histologically. The typical mosaic, tilelike appearance of the flat mucosa is highlighted.

may make some of the features appear crisper. For endoscopists with a large experience with celiac disease, dye stains may not be helpful. However, any patient who has suspect celiac disease and is being endoscoped for this disease should have duodenal biopsies taken even if the typical endoscopic features are absent.

Other Small Bowel Lesions

In patients with multiple duodenal adenomas in familial adenomatous polyposis (FAP), methylene blue staining gives an excellent view of the overall terrain because it highlights negative-staining smaller lesions that may just appear as small plaquelike appearing flat lesions with normal endoscopy (see Fig. 5–11*A* and *B*). Furthermore, this stain or a contrast stain is very useful before EMR of one or more of these lesions.[20]

Small bumps in the duodenal bulb especially the proximal portion commonly represent oxyntic gland heterotopia with both gastric

surface epithelium and underlying oxyntic glands with parietal and chief cells. These are of no known clinical consequence, but if one wants to photograph their presumptive gastric nature a methylene blue spray will leave the bumps negative staining. The same principle applies to gastric surface metaplasia, a potential footprint of current or past inflammation.[92]

Methylene blue was used to identify the minor papilla or its orifice in patients with pancreas divisum,[93] but there are no tissue sampling indications here.

THE COLON

Polyps of the Colon

Chromoendoscopy has been directed to two aspects of polyps of the colon. One is to determine the difference between hyperplastic and adenomatous polyps on gross examination. The second is to increase

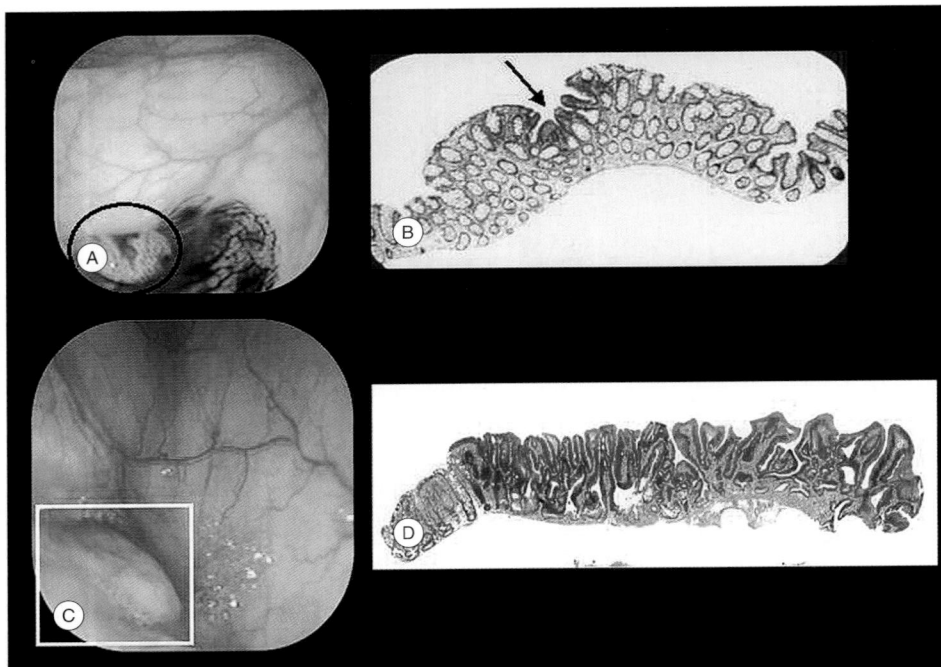

Figure 5–12. Types of flat adenomas with contrast. *A,* Indigo carmine shows the otherwise subtle depressed center of the tiny bump. *B,* The histology shows that the adenomatous part is depressed *(arrow)* and the bump effect is caused by the nonadenomatous elongated crypts. *C,* Flat nondepressed adenoma. The slightly yellowish mucus outlines the flat lesion. *D,* The histology illustrates the flat nature of the lesion. Contrast with the top picture *(B).*

the detection rate, especially of adenomas. The favorite stain has been indigo carmine spray, with or without magnifying endoscopy or high-resolution endoscopy. Other creative approaches to dye staining have put the dye into the electrolyte purging solution or into capsules.[94,95]

Hyperplastic Versus Adenomatous Polyps

A pit or pitted pattern denotes a hyperplastic polyp, and a grooved or sulcus appearance denotes adenoma. Most of the pioneering work on this was done in Japan.[96] Among a number of studies examining this potential is a U.S. prospective multicenter study. In this study, 92.3% of the polyps could be classified according to the dye staining pattern, and for adenomatous polyps the sensitivity, specificity, and negative predictive values were 82%, 82%, and 88%, respectively.[97]

Increased Detection Rate of Adenomas

Flat and depressed adenomas refer to adenomas that are pancake-like (with or without depressed centers) and not generally dome shaped (Fig. 5–12). One endoscopic definition that has been used is that they are either flat or depressed lesions with a height less than half of the diameter of the lesion.[98] To prove that they were not just a Japanese phenomenon, Saitoh, a Japanese endoscopist experienced in the detection of these lesions, was recruited to the United States. He performed left-sided colonic indigo carmine staining from splenic flexure to rectum for 211 patients' colonoscopies.[98] Flat and depressed lesions were found in 22.7%. These were more likely adenomas than hyperplastic polyps (87% vs. 67%), and the advanced lesions with high grade dysplasia or cancer were significantly smaller than comparable conventional polypoid lesions (10.75 vs. 20 mm). In a randomized controlled trial of 259 patients using total colonic dye spray, more diminutive adenomas were detected proximal to the sigmoid colon and more patients were identified with three or more adenomas.[99] Increased detection rates with indigo carmine

staining were also found in a Korean study; Korea has a lower incidence of colorectal neoplasia compared with Western countries.[100]

Application in Practice

The ability to distinguish between hyperplastic and adenomatous polyps holds some appeal, especially proximal to the rectum and distal sigmoid colon where hyperplastic polyps may be numerous and easy to identify as such because of their whitish appearance. Colon dye spray adds time to the colonoscopy procedure; these techniques require the desire and the gaining of a certain amount of experience. It remains to be seen whether their use in prospective studies will identify carcinomas at an earlier stage or whether optical techniques that can scan the mucosa will be the answer, at least to easier detection. The greatest theoretical potential for any optical aid is in finding flat adenomas in the 8- to 10-mm range that contain carcinoma. It is not known how many of these would be missed by experienced endoscopists with conventional colonoscopy nor what the temporal biologic behavior is of these lesions.

Chromoendoscopy and Inflammatory Bowel Disease

Chromoendoscopy was studied in a randomized controlled trial of at total of 174 patients with long-standing ulcerative colitis comparing conventional surveillance biopsy with total spray of the colon with methylene blue.[101] In the dye group, 32 lesions were detected with intraepithelial neoplasia (24 of 32 low grade; 24 of 32 in flat mucosa) compared with 10 lesions in the conventional endoscopy group (8 of 10 low grade; 4 of 10 in flat mucosa). The dye spray group also predicted the degree of histologic inflammation better than the conventional group but that is not the primary message.[102] As in most areas where chromoendoscopy is being studied, the question is whether the die is cast or whether optical techniques will one day prove simpler to perform, with equal or greater accuracy.[50]

REFERENCES

1. Kozarek RA, Attia FM, Sumida SE, et al: Reusable biopsy forceps: A prospective evaluation of cleaning, function, adequacy of tissue specimen, and durability. Gastrointest Endosc 53:747–750, 2001.
2. Hamilton MI, Sercombe J, Pounder RE: Control of intragastric acidity with over-the-counter doses of ranitidine or famotidine. Aliment Pharmacol Ther 15:1579–1583, 2001.
3. Jung M, Beilenhoff U, Pietsch M, et al: Standardized reprocessing of reusable colonoscopy biopsy forceps is effective: Results of a German multicenter study. Endoscopy 35:197–202, 2003.
4. Yang R, Ng S, Nichol M, Laine L: A cost and performance evaluation of disposable and reusable biopsy forceps in GI endoscopy. Gastrointest Endosc 51:266–270, 2000.
5. Levine DS, Blount PL, Rudolph RE, Reid BJ: Safety of a systematic endoscopic biopsy protocol in patients with Barrett's esophagus. Am J Gastroenterol 95:1152–1157, 2000.
6. Paternuosto M, Bottiglieri ME, Migliore G, et al: New biopsy forceps for gastrointestinal endoscopy. Endoscopy 34:933, 2002.
7. Peluso F, Goldner F: Follow-up of hot biopsy forceps treatment of diminutive colonic polyps. Gastrointest Endosc 37:604–606, 1991.
8. Gilbert DA, DiMarino AJ, Jensen DM, et al: Status evaluation: Hot biopsy forceps. American Society for Gastrointestinal Endoscopy. Technology Assessment Committee. Gastrointest Endosc 38:753–756, 1992.
9. Mann NS, Mann SK, Alam I: The safety of hot biopsy forceps in the removal of small colonic polyps. Digestion 60:74–76, 1999.
10. Williams CB: Small polyps: The virtues and the dangers of hot biopsy [editorial]. Gastrointest Endosc 37:394–395, 1991.
11. Thomson M, Kitching P, Jones A, et al: Are endoscopic biopsies of small bowel as good as suction biopsies for diagnosis of enteropathy? J Pediatr Gastroenterol Nutr 29:438–441, 1999.
12. Alizai NK, Batcup G, Dixon MF, Stringer MD: Rectal biopsy for Hirschsprung's disease: What is the optimum method? Pediatr Surg Int 13:121–124, 1998.
13. Tappero G, Gaia E, De Giuli P, et al: Cold snare excision of small colorectal polyps. Gastrointest Endosc 38:310–313, 1992.
14. Uno Y, Obara K, Zheng P, et al: Cold snare excision is a safe method for diminutive colorectal polyps. Tohoku J Exp Med 183:243–249, 1997.
15. Carvalho JL, Campos M, Soares-Oliveira M, Estevao-Costa J: Laparoscopic colonic mapping of dysganglionosis. Pediatr Surg Int 17:493–495, 2001.
16. Mazziotti MV, Langer JC: Laparoscopic full-thickness intestinal biopsies in children. J Pediatr Gastroenterol Nutr 33:54–57, 2001.
17. Padda S, Shah I, Ramirez FC: Adequacy of mucosal sampling with the "two-bite" forceps technique: A prospective, randomized, blinded study. Gastrointest Endosc 57:170–173, 2003.
18. Levine DS, Reid BJ: Endoscopic biopsy technique for acquiring larger mucosal samples. Gastrointest Endosc 37:332–337, 1991.
19. Lewin KJ, Riddell RH, Weinstein WM: Dialogue, handling of biopsies and resected specimens. In Lewin KJ, Riddell RH, Weinstein WM (eds): Gastrointestinal Pathology and Its Clinical Implications. New York, Tokyo, Igaku-Shoin, 1992, pp 15–18.
20. Soetikno RM, Gotoda T, Nakanishi Y, Soehendra N: Endoscopic mucosal resection. Gastrointest Endosc 57:567–579, 2003.
21. Saad RS, Mahood LK, Clary KM, et al: Role of cytology in the diagnosis of Barrett's esophagus and associated neoplasia. Diagn Cytopathol 29:130–135, 2003.
22. Geisinger KR: Endoscopic biopsies and cytologic brushings of the esophagus are diagnostically complementary. Am J Clin Pathol 103:295–299, 1995.
23. Jain S, Kumar N, Jain SK: Gastric tuberculosis. Endoscopic cytology as a diagnostic tool. Acta Cytol 44:987–992, 2000.
24. Pickeral JJ 3rd, Silverman JF, Sturgis CD: Gastric zygomycosis diagnosed by brushing cytology. Diagn Cytopathol 23:51–54, 2000.
25. Singh M, Mehrotra R, Shukla J, Nigam DK: Diagnosis of microfilaria in gastric brush cytology. A case report. Acta Cytol 43:853–855, 1999.
26. Cubukcu A, Gonullu NN, Ercin C, et al: Imprint cytology in the diagnosis of Helicobacter pylori. Does imprinting damage the biopsy specimen? Acta Cytol 44:124–127, 2000.
27. Ghoussoub RA, Lachman MF: A triple stain for the detection of Helicobacter pylori in gastric brushing cytology. Acta Cytol 41:1178–1182, 1997.
28. Gupta SK, Croffie JM, Pfefferkorn MD, Fitzgerald JF: Diagnostic yield of duodenal aspirate for G. lamblia and comparison to duodenal mucosal biopsies. Dig Dis Sci 48:605–607, 2003.
29. Bini EJ, Weinshel EH, Gamagaris Z: Comparison of duodenal with jejunal biopsy and aspirate in chronic human immunodeficiency virus-related diarrhea. Am J Gastroenterol 93:1837–1840, 1998.
30. Falk GW, Ours TM, Richter JE: Practice patterns for surveillance of Barrett's esophagus in the United States. Gastrointest Endosc 52:197–203, 2000.
31. Falk GW: Cytology in Barrett's esophagus. Gastrointest Endosc Clin N Am 13:335–348, 2003.
32. Geisinger KR, Teot LA, Richter JE: A comparative cytopathologic and histologic study of atypia, dysplasia, and adenocarcinoma in Barrett's esophagus. Cancer 69:8–16, 1992.
33. Yazgan Y, Demirturk L, Ozel AM, et al: Impact of imprint cytology in detecting short segment Barrett's esophagus. J Clin Gastroenterol 36:126–129, 2003.
34. Falk GW, Chittajallu R, Goldblum JR, et al: Surveillance of patients with Barrett's esophagus for dysplasia and cancer with balloon cytology. Gastroenterology 112:1787–1797, 1997.
35. Rader AE, Faigel DO, DiTomasso J, et al: Cytological screening for Barrett's esophagus using a prototype flexible mesh catheter. Dig Dis Sci 46:2681–2686, 2001.
36. Liu SF, Shen Q, Dawsey SM, et al: Esophageal balloon cytology and subsequent risk of esophageal and gastric-cardia cancer in a high-risk Chinese population. Int J Cancer 57:775–780, 1994.
37. Roth MJ, Liu SF, Dawsey SM, et al: Cytologic detection of esophageal squamous cell carcinoma and precursor lesions using balloon and sponge samplers in asymptomatic adults in Linxian, China. Cancer 80:2047–2059, 1997.
38. Geramizadeh B, Hooshmand F, Kumar PV: Brush cytology of colorectal malignancies. Acta Cytol 47:431–434, 2003.
39. Yu GH, Nayar R, Furth EE: Adenocarcinoma in colonic brushing cytology: High-grade dysplasia as a diagnostic pitfall. Diagn Cytopathol 24:364–368, 2001.
40. Geramizadeh B, Shafiee A, Saberfirruzi M, et al: Brush cytology of gastric malignancies. Acta Cytol 46:693–696, 2002.
41. Petrelli NJ, Letourneau R, Weber T, et al: Accuracy of biopsy and cytology for the preoperative diagnosis of colorectal adenocarcinoma. J Surg Oncol 71:46–49, 1999.
42. Moscicki AB, Hills NK, Shiboski S, et al: Risk factors for abnormal anal cytology in young heterosexual women. Cancer Epidemiol Biomarkers Prev 8:173–178, 1999.
43. Scholefield JH, Johnson J, Hitchcock A, et al: Guidelines for anal cytology—to make cytological diagnosis and follow up much more reliable. Cytopathology 9:15–22, 1998.
44. Keller R, Brandt B, Terpe HJ, et al: Cytology and image cytometry after colonic lavage: A complementary diagnostic tool in patients with ulcerative colitis. Dig Liver Dis 35:24–31, 2003.
45. Fitzgerald RC, Farthing MJ, Triadafilopoulos G: Novel adaptation of brush cytology technique for short-term primary culture of squamous and Barrett's esophageal cells. Gastrointest Endosc 54:186–189, 2001.
46. MacLennan AJ, Orringer MB, Beer DG: Identification of intestinal-type Barrett's metaplasia by using the intestine-specific protein villin and esophageal brush cytology. Mol Carcinog 24:137–143, 1999.
47. Lewin DN, Lewin KJ, Weinstein WM: Pathologist-gastroenterologist interaction. The changing role of the pathologist. Am J Clin Pathol 103(4 Suppl 1):S9–12, 1995.

48. Ofman JJ, Shaheen NJ, Desai AA, et al: The quality of care in Barrett's esophagus: Endoscopist and pathologist practices. Am J Gastroenterol 96:876–881, 2001.

49. Beaugerie L, Patey N, Brousse N: Ranitidine, diarrhoea, and lymphocytic colitis. Gut 37:708–711, 1995.

50. DaCosta R, Wilson BC, Marcon NE: Photodiagnostic techniques for the endoscopic detection of premalignant gastrointestinal lesions. Dig Endosc 15:153–173, 2003.

51. Acosta MM, Boyce HW Jr: Chromoendoscopy—where is it useful? J Clin Gastroenterol 27:13–20, 1998.

52. Canto MI, Yoshida T, Gossner L: Chromoscopy of intestinal metaplasia in Barrett's esophagus. Endoscopy 34:330–336, 2002.

53. Fujii T, Iishi H, Tatsuta M, et al: Effectiveness of premedication with pronase for improving visibility during gastroendoscopy: A randomized controlled trial. Gastrointest Endosc 47:382–387, 1998.

54. Munakata A, Uno Y: Colonoscopic polypectomy with local injection of methylene blue. Tohoku J Exp Med 173:377–382, 1994.

55. Nakanishi Y, Ochiai A, Yoshimura K, et al: The clinicopathologic significance of small areas unstained by Lugol's iodine in the mucosa surrounding resected esophageal carcinoma: An analysis of 147 cases. Cancer 82:1454–1459, 1998.

56. Freitag CP, Barros SG, Kruel CD, et al: Esophageal dysplasias are detected by endoscopy with Lugol in patients at risk for squamous cell carcinoma in southern Brazil. Dis Esophagus 12:191–195, 1999.

57. Dawsey SM, Fleischer DE, Wang GQ, et al: Mucosal iodine staining improves endoscopic visualization of squamous dysplasia and squamous cell carcinoma of the esophagus in Linxian, China. Cancer 83:220–231, 1998.

58. Shimizu Y, Tukagoshi H, Fujita M, et al: Metachronous squamous cell carcinoma of the esophagus arising after endoscopic mucosal resection. Gastrointest Endosc 54:190–194, 2001.

59. Nomura T, Boku N, Ohtsu A, et al: Recurrence after endoscopic mucosal resection for superficial esophageal cancer. Endoscopy 32:277–280, 2000.

60. Muto M, Hironaka S, Nakane M, et al: Association of multiple Lugol-voiding lesions with synchronous and metachronous esophageal squamous cell carcinoma in patients with head and neck cancer. Gastrointest Endosc 56:517–521, 2002.

61. Hix WR, Wilson WR: Toluidine blue staining of the esophagus. A useful adjunct in the panendoscopic evaluation of patients with squamous cell carcinoma of the head and neck. Arch Otolaryngol Head Neck Surg 113:864–865, 1987.

62. Weinstein WM: Is Barrett's esophagus dangerous? Endoscopy 34:1007–1009, 2002.

63. Weinstein WM: The prevention and treatment of dysplasia in gastroesophageal reflux disease: The results and the challenges ahead. J Gastroenterol Hepatol 17(Suppl):S113–S124, 2002.

64. Olliver JR, Wild CP, Sahay P, et al: Chromoendoscopy with methylene blue and associated DNA damage in Barrett's oesophagus. Lancet 362:373–374, 2003.

65. Canto MI, Setrakian S, Petras RE, et al: Methylene blue selectively stains intestinal metaplasia in Barrett's esophagus. Gastrointest Endosc 44:1–7, 1996.

66. Canto MI, Setrakian S, Willis J, et al: Methylene blue-directed biopsies improve detection of intestinal metaplasia and dysplasia in Barrett's esophagus. Gastrointest Endosc 51:560–568, 2000.

67. Kiesslich R, Hahn M, Herrmann G, Jung M: Screening for specialized columnar epithelium with methylene blue: Chromoendoscopy in patients with Barrett's esophagus and a normal control group. Gastrointest Endosc 53:47–52, 2001.

68. Kouklakis GS, Kountouras J, Dokas SM, et al: Methylene blue chromoendoscopy for the detection of Barrett's esophagus in a Greek cohort. Endoscopy 35:383–387, 2003.

69. Gangarosa LM, Halter S, Mertz H: Methylene blue staining and endoscopic ultrasound evaluation of Barrett's esophagus with low-grade dysplasia. Dig Dis Sci 45:225–229, 2000.

70. Sharma P, Topalovski M, Mayo MS, Weston AP: Methylene blue chromoendoscopy for detection of short-segment Barrett's esophagus. Gastrointest Endosc 54:289–293, 2001.

71. Wo JM, Ray MB, Mayfield-Stokes S, et al: Comparison of methylene blue-directed biopsies and conventional biopsies in the detection of intestinal metaplasia and dysplasia in Barrett's esophagus: A preliminary study. Gastrointest Endosc 54:294–301, 2001.

72. Breyer HP, Silva De Barros SG, Maguilnik I, Edelweiss MI: Does methylene blue detect intestinal metaplasia in Barrett's esophagus? Gastrointest Endosc 57:505–509, 2003.

73. Endo T, Awakawa T, Takahashi H, et al: Classification of Barrett's epithelium by magnifying endoscopy. Gastrointest Endosc 55:641–647, 2002.

74. Morales TG, Bhattacharyya A, Camargo E, et al: Methylene blue staining for intestinal metaplasia of the gastric cardia with follow-up for dysplasia. Gastrointest Endosc 48:26–31, 1998.

75. Hirota WK, Loughney TM, Lazas DJ, et al: Specialized intestinal metaplasia, dysplasia, and cancer of the esophagus and esophago-gastric junction: Prevalence and clinical data. Gastroenterology 116:277–285, 1999.

76. Lembo T, Ippoliti AF, Ramers C, Weinstein WM: Inflammation of the gastro-oesophageal junction (carditis) in patients with symptomatic gastro-oesophageal reflux disease: A prospective study. Gut 45:484–488, 1999.

77. Canto MI, Setrakian S, Willis JE, et al: Methylene blue staining of dysplastic and nondysplastic Barrett's esophagus: An in vivo and ex vivo study. Endoscopy 33:391–400, 2001.

78. Guelrud M, Herrera I, Essenfeld H, et al: Intestinal metaplasia of the gastric cardia: A prospective study with enhanced magnification endoscopy. Am J Gastroenterol 97:584–589, 2002.

79. Sharma P, Weston AP, Topalovski M, et al: Magnification chromoendoscopy for the detection of intestinal metaplasia and dysplasia in Barrett's oesophagus. Gut 52:24–27, 2003.

80. Lambert R, Rey JF, Sankaranarayanan R: Magnification and chromoscopy with the acetic acid test. Endoscopy 35:437–445, 2003.

81. Tajiri H, Doi T, Endo H, et al: Routine endoscopy using a magnifying endoscope for gastric cancer diagnosis. Endoscopy 34:772–777, 2002.

82. Tatsuta M, Okuda S: Location, healing, and recurrence of gastric ulcers in relation to fundal gastritis. Gastroenterology 69:897–902, 1975.

83. Asaka M, Sugiyama T, Nobuta A, et al: Atrophic gastritis and intestinal metaplasia in Japan: Results of a large multicenter study. Helicobacter 6:294–299, 2001.

84. Iishi H, Tatsuta M, Okuda S: Diagnosis of simultaneous multiple gastric cancers by the endoscopic Congo red–methylene blue test. Endoscopy 20:78–82, 1988.

85. Fennerty MB, Sampliner RE, McGee DL, et al: Intestinal metaplasia of the stomach: Identification by a selective mucosal staining technique [see comments]. Gastrointest Endosc 38:696–698, 1992.

86. Sanders DL, Pfeiffer RB, Hashimoto LA, et al: Pseudomembranous gastritis: A complication from aspergillus infection. Am Surg 69:536–538, 2003.

87. Iseki K, Tatsuta M, Iishi H, et al: Helicobacter pylori infection in patients with early gastric cancer by the endoscopic phenol red test. Gut 42:20–23, 1998.

88. Sakai N, Tatsuta M, Hirasawa R, et al: Low prevalence of Helicobacter pylori infection in patients with hamartomatous fundic polyps. Dig Dis Sci 43:766–772, 1998.

89. Niveloni S, Fiorini A, Dezi R, et al: Usefulness of videoduodeno-scopy and vital dye staining as indicators of mucosal atrophy of celiac disease: Assessment of interobserver agreement. Gastrointest Endosc 47:223–229, 1998.

90. Siegel LM, Stevens PD, Lightdale CJ, et al: Combined magnification endoscopy with chromoendoscopy in the evaluation of patients with suspected malabsorption. Gastrointest Endosc 46:226–230, 1997.

91. Kiesslich R, Mergener K, Naumann C, et al: Value of chromo-endoscopy and magnification endoscopy in the evaluation of duodenal abnormalities: A prospective, randomized comparison. Endoscopy 35:559–563, 2003.

92. Mertz H, Kovacs T, Thronson M, Weinstein W: Gastric metaplasia of the duodenum: Identification by an endoscopic selective mucosal staining technique. Gastrointest Endosc 48:32–38, 1998.

93. Park SH, de Bellis M, McHenry L, et al: Use of methylene blue to identify the minor papilla or its orifice in patients with pancreas divisum. Gastrointest Endosc 57:358–363, 2003.

94. Mitooka H, Fujimori T, Ohno S, et al: Chromoscopy of the colon using indigo carmine dye with electrolyte lavage solution. Gastrointest Endosc 38:373–374, 1992.

95. Mitooka H, Fujimori T, Maeda S, Nagasako K: Minute flat depressed neoplastic lesions of the colon detected by contrast chromoscopy using an indigo carmine capsule. Gastrointest Endosc 41:453–459, 1995.

96. Kudo S, Hirota S, Nakajima T, et al: Colorectal tumours and pit pattern. J Clin Pathol 47:880–885, 1994.

97. Eisen GM, Kim CY, Fleischer DE, et al: High-resolution chromoendoscopy for classifying colonic polyps: A multicenter study. Gastrointest Endosc 55:687–694, 2002.

98. Saitoh Y, Waxman I, West AB, et al: Prevalence and distinctive biologic features of flat colorectal adenomas in a North American population. Gastroenterology 120:1657–1665, 2001.

99. Brooker JC, Saunders BP, Shah SG, et al: Total colonic dye-spray increases the detection of diminutive adenomas during routine colonoscopy: A randomized controlled trial. Gastrointest Endosc 56:333–338, 2002.

100. Lee JH, Kim JW, Cho YK, et al: Detection of colorectal adenomas by routine chromoendoscopy with indigocarmine. Am J Gastroenterol 98:1284–1288, 2003.

101. Kiesslich R, Fritsch J, Holtmann M, et al: Methylene blue-aided chromoendoscopy for the detection of intraepithelial neoplasia and colon cancer in ulcerative colitis. Gastroenterology 124:880–888, 2003.

102. Bernstein CN: The color of dysplasia in ulcerative colitis. Gastroenterology 124:1135–1138, 2003.

103. Weinstein WM: Mucosal biopsy techniques and interaction with the pathologist. Gastrointest Endosc Clin N Am 10:555–572, 2000.

Electrosurgical Principles

Marcia L. Morris

Introduction

This chapter discusses electrosurgery as it is typically used in the gastrointestinal endoscopy setting.

Electrosurgery is surgery performed by electrical methods. Its development has been driven by the clinical need to control bleeding during surgical procedures. Although heat has been used medically to control bleeding for thousands of years, the use of electricity to produce heat in tissue has only been in general use since the mid-1920s and in flexible endoscopy since the 1970s.[1-3] Electrosurgery offers at least one unique advantage over mechanical cutting and thermal application: the ability to cut and coagulate tissue at the same time (Box 6–1). This advantage makes it the ideal surgical tool for the gastroenterologist.

Electricity

Four characteristics of electricity form a basis for the development of an understanding of the use of electrosurgery. They are current, voltage, circuit, and resistance *(impedance)*.

Electricity results from the phenomenon of negatively charged electrons moving from one atom to another. The term *current* is used to describe this electric charge in motion. The strength of the current is measured by the number of electrons passing a given point each second. *Voltage* is described as the force that drives the current

---

Box 6–1. Electrocautery vs. Electrosurgery

Electrocautery uses a simple direct current to heat an instrument that is then applied to tissue. The electric current never leaves the instrument and does not pass through the patient. An Olympus Heat Probe (Olympus America, Inc., Melville, NY) is an example of this technology. The term *electrocautery* is often incorrectly applied to all types of electrosurgical procedures. It is only correctly applied to this simple type of direct current device, which can produce only coagulation and no electrosurgical cutting.

---

around a complete *circuit* following the path of least resistance. In a simple, direct current, the electrons flow in only one direction. *Alternating currents* switch, or alternate, the direction of electron flow. The frequency of these alterations is measured in cycles per second or Hertz (Hz)—1 Hertz is equal to one cycle per second. *Impedance*, or resistance, is opposition to the flow of current and is measured in Ohms. Although often interchanged, the term *impedance* correctly refers to the opposition to the flow of an alternating current, whereas *resistance* is reserved for the case of a direct current.

MONOPOLAR AND BIPOLAR CIRCUITS

Because electricity requires a complete circuit in order for current to flow, electrosurgical accessories are designed to be either monopolar or bipolar. Bipolar instruments, such as Bicap probes (Circon/ACMI, Stamford, CT), have both the active and return electrodes built into the tip and are thus capable of completing the circuit through the probe without the use of a separate return electrode *(grounding pad)*.[4]

With a monopolar accessory, the circuit is completed via a grounding pad. To make the concept easy to visualize, we say that all of the electrons flow out of the accessory *(the active electrode)* through the patient and return to the generator through the grounding pad. In monopolar procedures, correct placement of the grounding pad is important to ensure the best dispersive effect of the energy as it exits the patient. Placement of a fresh disposable pad, crosswise, on the upper thigh is appropriate for most patients for most gastroenterology procedures.[5]

HIGH-FREQUENCY CURRENT IS USED FOR ELECTROSURGERY

Early pioneers in the development of electrosurgical devices discovered that applying an electric current to biologic tissue might produce different effects. The first was *electrolytic*. Charged molecules in the tissue flowed toward the poles of the electrodes if the current applied was direct or alternated very slowly.

Alternating the current more rapidly eliminated the electrolytic effect and produced the desired heating at the cellular level. However, a current alternating at less than 100,000 Hz (100 kHz) produced unwanted neuromuscular effects. (The response of the human body to the household frequency of 60 Hz is well known.)[6] When the electricity alternated at very high frequencies of about 300,000 Hz, most nerve and muscle activation was bypassed leaving predominantly the desired result of heating. The basis for the therapeutic use of all electrosurgery is this thermal effect.[6a]

CURRENT DENSITY

Current density is *the* defining variable in determining specific tissue effects in electrosurgery; however, it is the sum of the effects of all the other variables.

Current density is the measure of current concentration or, by definition, the current per unit area. The rate of heat generation and the resulting therapeutic effect is a function of the current density. It is a measure of intensity. Mathematically, the temperature rises as a square of the current density. Current that will boil water on a square millimeter area does not even feel warm on a square centimeter area.[7] The dramatic difference in surface area between the active electrode and the grounding pad is perhaps the best-understood example of this principle. Current density depends on the applied voltage, current, type of waveform, the tissue impedance, the size of the electrode, and the time that current is flowing. These *tissue effect variables* are addressed in detail. First, it is advantageous to look at the effect at the cellular level of the heating caused by sufficiently dense high-frequency current.

The application of high-frequency energy intensely to a precise area rapidly heats the tissue to 100° C and causes intracellular water to turn to steam.[8] The cell membrane explodes. This exploding path along an electrode, such as a wire, is what is referred to as *electrosurgical cutting*. In biologic tissue, voltage peaks must be greater than 200 Vp and sustained to create current intensity sufficient to create this effect.

With less total power applied, or for cells located farther from the electrode, the intracellular water is heated more slowly. At temperatures between 80° C and 100° C, the water vapor escapes from the cell without bursting the membrane, leaving the cell dry and shrunken with proteins denatured.[8,9] Electrosurgical coagulation has been the result. The ratio of the total number of cells "cut" to those "coagulated" determines the overall tissue effect (Box 6–2).

Waveform: The First Variable

Of the variables that determine tissue effect, the one that is the most influenced by electrosurgery generator design is that of the high-frequency waveform, or *output mode*.

The first electrosurgery generators assembled in the mid-1920s consisted of two separate units. A vacuum tube oscillator generating continuous high-frequency alternating current produced a cutting effect on tissue. In contrast, a spark gap oscillator producing a sharply damped, interrupted high-frequency alternating current

---

Box 6–2. A Current Density Analogy

As individual variables that account for changing tissue density are discussed, it is useful to have in mind the simple analogy of the microwave oven.

Microwaves use high-frequency electrical energy to heat the water in food without first heating a utensil or burner. This is similar to electrosurgery in heating tissue directly, unlike electrocautery that heats an implement and then the hot implement in turn is applied to tissue. Electrosurgery is to the microwave oven what electrocautery is to the standard stove.

One can imagine the change in a raw egg white in a microwave oven turned to the highest power setting. The resulting mess is a good example of electrosurgical cutting. Turning the microwave to its lowest setting can gently cook the egg white allowing it to turn white (coagulate and denature) with little popping (cutting). The intermediate settings on the microwave can produce some relative change in the percentage of egg white that explodes or coagulates—a blended effect. In electrosurgery, the waveform is analogous to the different microwave settings.

Continuing the analogy is helpful to intuitively make judgments about current density. Ten raw egg whites do not cook as quickly at the same power setting as one egg white does. The current density in the larger amount of tissue is lower, and, therefore, the heating is slower. This helps to visualize the difference that the size of a polyp makes when determining power settings. Less time or less power is needed to coagulate one egg white rather than ten. If one normally uses a powerful (high watt) microwave oven, one must choose higher settings to cook the same number of egg whites in a smaller oven. One can imagine how difficult it is to get an egg white that is already coagulated at a low setting to explode by then turning the power to high. The coagulated egg white is much more resistant to further energy penetration, and much of the water has already evaporated. How closely this resembles an overly desiccated polyp stalk stubbornly resisting excision!

The variables in the microwave equation—setting, watts, time, amount of food, and resulting temperature—behave very similarly to the variables that one considers in clinical electrosurgery: the waveform, power (current and voltage), time, current density, and the resulting tissue effect. The changing tissue effect is measured by its changing impedance.

---

caused coagulation. Early devices held these two entirely separate high-frequency oscillators in a single cabinet. A typical method of operating the device was for the practitioner to heartily throw a lever from one side to the other to change the desired tissue effect.

By 1968, semiconductor technology had developed to the point where the first *solid state* generator (ValleyLab) could be manufactured. It provided cut and coagulation currents in a single generator. In solid state generators (the only type now produced), continuous sinusoidal waveforms with fairly low voltage increasingly give way to a higher voltage waveform that is more and more interrupted (*modulated*) to take the tissue effect from one of mostly cutting to one of mostly coagulation (Fig. 6–1).

A continuous high-frequency waveform with a peak voltage of at least 200 (200 Vp) produces an intensity of current sufficient to create micro electric sparks between the active electrode and the target tissue. Such high current density along the leading edge of the electrode causes cells to literally explode, separating the tissue as if it were cut. As this cell vaporization continues, a micro steam layer is formed that helps to propagate the cutting effect.

Along the edges of the cut, there is always a margin of cells whose distance from the active electrode allows them to heat more slowly. These cells simply coagulate. The depth of this coagulated margin is directly related to the height of the peak voltage in the cutting waveform and the thickness of the electrode. Higher voltages leave a thicker margin of coagulation, and a thin wire leaves less coagulation than a flat blade.

Even with a continuous waveform, if the voltage never goes above 200 Vp, no cutting can occur. Such outputs lack the intensity to

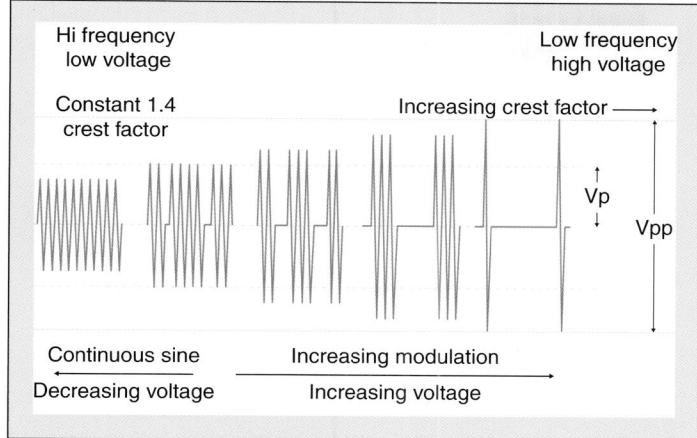

Figure 6–1. Electrosurgical waveform patterns.

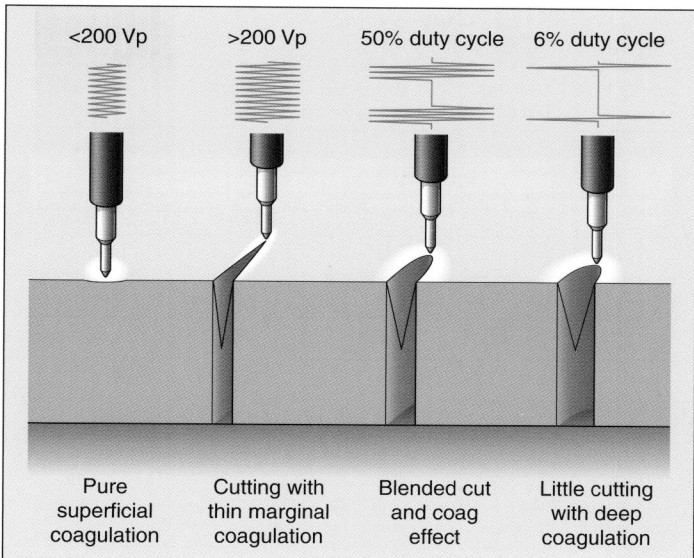

Figure 6–2. Tissue effect changes with changing waveform.

initiate the initial sparking necessary to produce the cutting effect. Instead, a superficial coagulation results.

To produce a deeper tissue effect with a lesser degree of electrosurgical cutting and an increasingly greater proportion of coagulated cells, the continuous waveform is interrupted or modulated. Interrupting the waveform delivers energy, even at the equivalent power settings, more slowly. To increase the depth of the coagulation the voltage spikes are increased. This is necessary because along the coagulating margins of the electrode path, the impedance is rising as the tissue is coagulated. The thin desiccated layer of coagulation produced by low-voltage continuous waveforms does not limit the penetration of these high-voltage spikes that force the current through the desiccated layer, increasing the depth of the coagulation (Fig. 6–2).[7]

Varying the degree of modulation and the voltage peaks allows the designers of electrosurgical generators to create output modes that hope to predict a predominate tissue effect. Unfortunately, the terminology used to communicate the design intent is by no means standardized.[6] Even between models from the same manufacturer, the same words may be used to describe different waveforms. It is the operator's responsibility to discern the type of output represented by the labeling on each generator used. The operator's manual provided with the unit is a good source for this and other, helpful information.[10]

Adding to the confusion of terminology is the fact that often the words used are not truly descriptive. Despite the fact that at least some margin of coagulation is always present, most electrosurgical generators have a continuous sine wave output with greater than 200 Vp labeled "pure cut." Increasingly common are generators that offer differing voltage levels in the cut mode, which offer differing depths of the coagulation along the margins. These are sometimes labeled "Cut Effect 1," "Cut Effect 2," and so forth.

Only a few generators have a waveform that is a continuous sine but never exceeds 200 Vp. Although continuous waveforms are usually associated with cutting, this extremely low voltage produces truly *pure* coagulation! This type of waveform may be named "soft coag" if used with a monopolar circuit, but it is also a good waveform choice in a bipolar circuit for endoscopic bipolar probes.

The modulated output that for a particular generator provides the deepest coagulation (hemostasis), with the least cutting, is often

misnamed "pure coag." Misnamed because as long as the voltage spikes—at least sometimes—over 200 Vp, some electrosurgical cutting is expected. It is this traditional but imprecise name that gives rise to such odd physician comments as "I always cut with pure coag."

Most generators are equipped with a varying number of modulated waveforms that fall between the extremes of nearly all cut or nearly all coagulation. These are typically named the "blended currents." This is perhaps the most descriptive name, because it correctly implies that some of the cells are vaporized, or cut, and some are coagulated. Increasingly modulated waveforms with increasingly high voltages produce tissue effects with increasing hemostasis and decreasing cutting.

The descriptions of these waveforms can be quantified by assigning them a *duty cycle*, which is the numerical percentage of the time the waveform is on (spiking) and the time it is off (interrupted). A waveform with a 6% duty cycle is on 6% of the time and off 94% of the total time. A continuous waveform has a 100% duty cycle. The peak voltage determines if a 100% duty cycle produces "pure" electrosurgical cutting or only "soft" coagulation. The terms *burst repetition rate* and *crest factor* are sometimes similarly used to quantify the degree to which a waveform is modulated (Table 6–1).

Power and Time

The next two variables that can be moderated to change tissue effect are the power setting and the time the current flows. They are intimately related because energy per unit of time is power measured in watts, and time multiplied by power equals total joules of heat produced. Time has the distinction of being the only electrosurgical variable that is completely controlled by the operator.

The final temperature (T) of the target tissue is defined by the equation: $\Delta T = J^2 p t / CD$, where t is time of current flow and CD is tissue density and its specific heat.[11] Given the same amount of

Table 6–1. Monopolar Output Names with Corresponding Duty Cycle

Duty Cycle (%)	Meditron UGI 3000B	Microvasive Endostat	ValleyLab SSE2	ValleyLab Force2	ValleyLab Force FX	ValleyLab ForceEZ	ERBE ICC 200E/A
100	Cut	Cut	Cut	Cut	Cut low (voltage limited) and cut pure	Cut pure and coag low 2 (330Vp) and coag low 3 (550Vp)	Autocut (Vp > 200) and soft coag (Vp < 200)
50	Blend 1	Blend	Blend	Blend 1	Cut blend	Cut blend	N/A
37	N/A	N/A	N/A	Blend 2	N/A	N/A	N/A
25	Blend 2	N/A	N/A	Blend 3	N/A	N/A	N/A
12	Blend 3	Coag	Coag	N/A	N/A	N/A	N/A
8	N/A	N/A	N/A	N/A	Desiccate	Coag low 1	N/A
4–6	Coag	N/A	N/A	Coag	N/A	N/A	Forced coag

Endostat is a trademark of Microvasive Corp. Operator's manual, 1992. SSE2, Force 2, Force EZ, Force FX are trademarks of Valleylab, Inc., a division of Tyco Healthcare. SSE 2 and Force 2 user's guides, 1994; Force FX user's guide, 1997, EZ-20 user's guide, 1999. ICC 200 E/A are trademarks of ERBE, USA, Inc. Operator's manual V 2.X, 2001. Meditron is a division of Cooper Surgical, Inc. UGI 3000 and UGI 3000B operator's manuals 1995–1999. Coag, coagulation; N/A, not applicable.

Table 6–2. Comparison of Bipolar Power Output Settings

Numerical Unit	Approximate Digital Setting (watts)
#1	6–10
#2	12–16
#3	12–20
#4 (most common setting)	20–26
#5	24–32
#6	28–38
#7	36–42
#8	38–46
#9	46–48
#10	50

Box 6–3. Examples of Suggested Waveforms for Typical Polypectomy

There is broad consensus among manufacturers and practitioners that a modulated, moderately high voltage output, with a duty cycle between 6% and 12%, a broad power curve, and power settings ranging between 15 and 40 watts is usually an excellent choice for conventional polypectomy. Notice that the generators shown all have an output selection of this type, although the name of the output is not consistent.

tissue, the same temperature can be achieved by selecting a high power and a short time or a lower power with a longer time. In either case, the same total amount of energy may be delivered but the electrosurgical effect can be radically different. One can imagine the difference in clinical effect between using a snare to deliver power set at 50 watts for 2 seconds or 20 watts for 5 seconds. The total joules of energy is equal (100 joules) but the tissue effect is not.[12] Another observation is that less tissue destruction occurs if the same total energy is delivered in short bursts rather than continuously. The pauses give the underlying tissue a chance to dissipate the heat.

The previous heat equation can be related to the change in tissue effect with a change in waveform by the following equation:

$$V \times C = P, \text{ where } V = \text{voltage}, C = \text{current}, \text{ and } P = \text{power in watts.}$$

If both the time and the power setting are kept constant, either a continuous (cut) or modulated (coag) waveform delivers the same total energy. The tissue effect, however, changes from one with little hemostasis and copious cutting to one with deep hemostasis and little electrosurgical cutting.

Because the ultimate target tissue effect is influenced by so many variables, electrosurgery generator manufacturers cannot provide simple "cook book" power setting directions. They do provide guidelines as to preferred waveform choices and power setting ranges for particular procedures. These guidelines are necessary due to the lack of standardization in both descriptive names and characteristics of outputs. The guidelines, however, do not substitute for a thorough understanding of the principles of electrosurgery and a complete familiarity with the particular generator in use.

A helpful design advance has been to replace the vague and nonlinear dial numbers of the past with digital watt displays.[13] With dial technology, it is rarely possible to duplicate the output from one generator with the same setting on another unit even if made by the same manufacturer.[14] Even with newer and more consistent digital settings, the power actually delivered compared with the setting displayed is accurate only within the tolerances set by the manufacturer. Many newer models achieve outputs within 1 or 2 watts of the selected display at usual power and impedances.

Power Curves, Microprocessor Control, and the Law of Ohm

Table 6–2 offers a general guide for translating numerical dial settings on older Bicap (Circon Corporation) generators to approximately equivalent bipolar digital outputs. Not all generators, however, produce the same type of bipolar outputs. The performance of endoscopic bipolar electrodes is enhanced if coupled with a generator that has a bipolar output with lower voltages (less sticking) and a *narrow power curve*, meaning that the power drops off sharply as impedance rises. Ideally, little power should be delivered by the time the impedance registers 500 Ohms.[15] This type of power curve enhances the probe's ability to deliver maximum power in low-impedance situations, such as frank blood, and then allows the power to decrease as the impedance increases with coagulation. This enhances the desirable self-limiting characteristic of this type of application.

The physical law that relates all of the electrosurgical variables has been elegantly summarized by Ohm in the equation $P = I^2R$. The $P = V \times C$ derivation of this equation has already been discussed in relating the type of waveform to total power. Ohm's law defines another principle crucial to a clinical understanding of electrosurgery: as impedance in tissue rises, power (either current and/or voltage) decreases. The narrow power curve discussed as ideal for bipolar probes is an excellent example of this fundamental principle.

A narrow power curve works well to produce superficial coagulation with either a monopolar or a bipolar contact electrode. It is not ideal for procedures such as snare polypectomy, in which maintaining adequate power to sustain at least some electrosurgical cutting along with deep coagulation is needed. To keep power constant in the face of rising impedance, either voltage or current must be increased.

To address this problem, research turned in the early 1980s to using microprocessors to measure and respond to changing impedance.[16] The result has been not only improved performance but also greatly increased safety in electrosurgical generator design.[17]

The first available performance control feature was designed to address the loss of power during rising impedance. Nearly every major brand of generator produced today has at least one output that has a broad power curve *(constant power)* feature. The microprocessor is designed to sense changing impedance and adjust either voltage or current to maintain the selected power. A *power curve* of a selected output is simply a graph provided by the generator manufacturer that attempts to represent how a given output typically behaves in the face of changing impedance. Although these graphs cannot completely characterize a generator's response, they can be useful.[18] They convey to the user the design intent of the microprocessor (Fig. 6–3).[19]

The initiation of cutting poses a hurdle for generators, especially if the electrode, such as a snare or papillotome wire, is pressed firmly against the tissue before the generator is activated.[20] This presents a large surface area with low current density and low impedance. The generator must provide especially high power to provide the intensity needed to create electrosurgical arcing and start the cutting effect. Often this initial power demand is greater than what is needed to continue the excision. A generator with a microprocessor designed to recognize these low-impedance loads and quickly provide high power helps ensure that adequate power is available when needed to start cutting without excessive stalling and unnecessary coagulation. The microprocessor can then automatically switch to the desired lower power levels to continue the procedure.

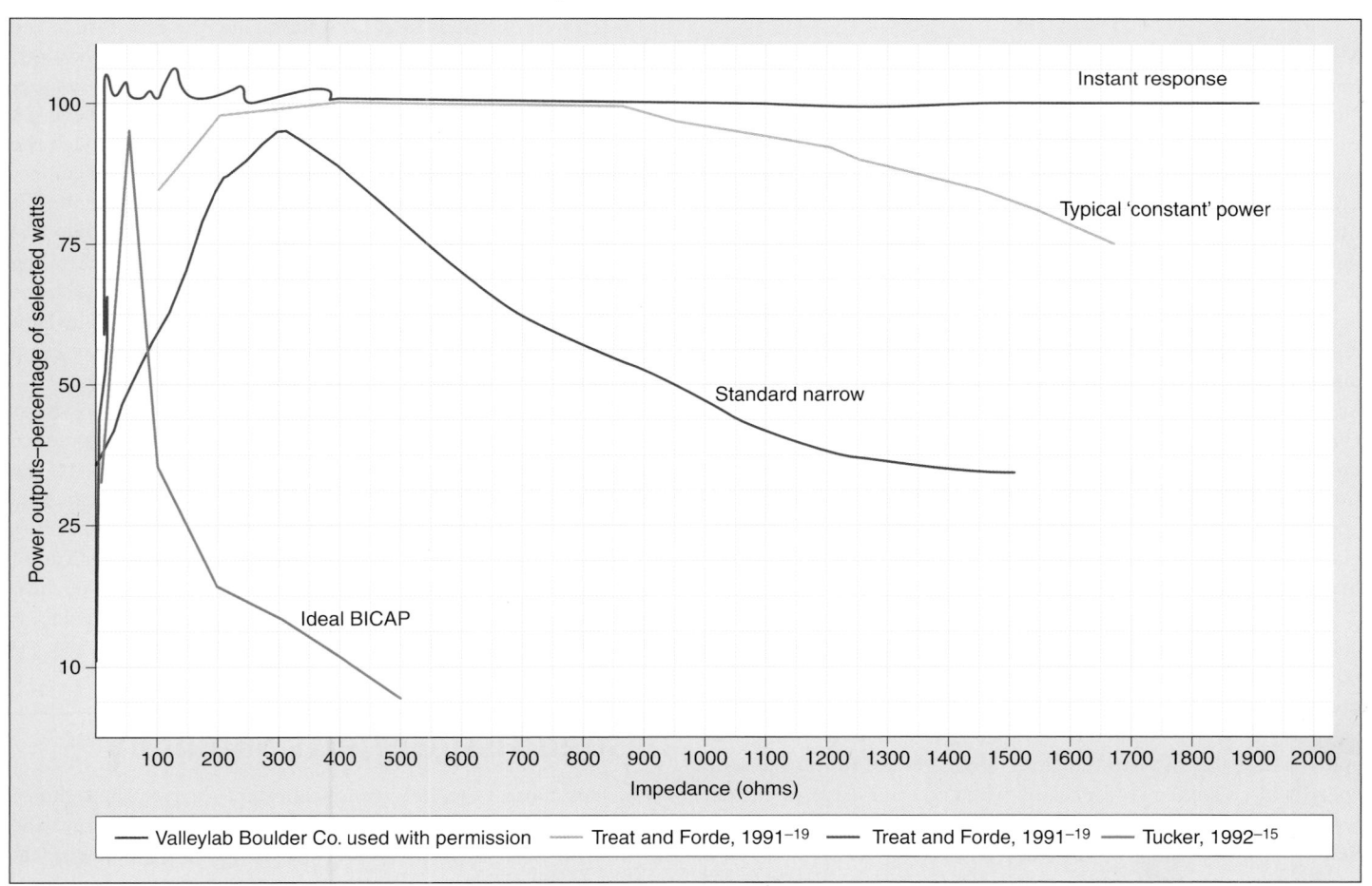

Figure 6–3. Typical power curves.

Another level of sophistication in microprocessor control is represented by generators that evaluate impedance changes millions of times per second. These adjust to keep the tissue *effect*, rather than the power, constant. Depending on the manufacturer and model, the current, the voltage, or both may rise and fall with changing impedance.

An example of layering of control designs is the EndoCut (Erbe USA, Inc., Marietta, GA) feature. It is a microprocessor control design that adjusts power constantly according to demand by allowing an initial instant start spike and then holding voltage constant while letting current float to adjust power. Superimposed over this is automatic alternating cutting and low-voltage coagulation, which eliminates the need to "tap" the pedal in sphincterotomy. Early studies indicate that the design has decreased the risk of zipper cutting and immediate bleeding in endoscopic sphincterotomy.[20-23]

At all levels, it is microprocessor enhancement that has made possible the increased safety of today's generators. Safety relevant parameters such as current leakage and grounding pad contact are continuously monitored by complex sensors with errors signaled by alarms. Automatic self-checks at power-up help electrosurgery generators enjoy an excellent record for reliability. Computerization offers the potential for innovation in generator design limited only by the challenge to engineers to produce controlled outputs that are safe, reliable, and clinically relevant.

Argon Plasma Coagulation

Most materials are insulators, in that the electrons are so tightly bound in the individual atoms that they do not permit a flow of electron charge. However, if an electric field acting on the material is high enough, the most loosely bound electrons are torn from their atoms allowing current flow. This process is called *ionization*. Different materials ionize more or less easily. Argon gas is one material that becomes conductive (ionized) quite easily. In its ionized state, it is called, like all ionized gases, a *plasma*.

In 1971 with the development of a plasma scalpel, technology to harness this phenomenon was introduced to medicine.[24] The first clinical applications were developed for use in open surgery procedures. Argon proved ideal not only because it is ionized at relatively low voltages but also because it forms a stable plasma phase, is chemically inert, and inexpensive. The units manufactured for use in open surgery, however, proved unsuitable for gastroendoscopic procedures because of high gas flow rates and a lack of flexible applicators. In 1991, the first systems designed for use in flexible endoscopy were produced and became available in the United States in late 1996 (Erbe USA, Inc.).[25]

The basic mechanism of argon plasma coagulation (APC) is the conduction of high-frequency thermal energy to target tissue via the now fluid electrons in the plasma arc. Indications for its use are producing coagulation for hemostasis or tissue devitalization. APC has many desirable characteristics that differentiate it from classic contact desiccation. These include a noncontact route that adds speed and convenience especially when treating large or diffuse lesions. The arc is not unidirectional but instead follows the electric field to tissue seeking to complete the monopolar circuit. APC produces a superficial eschar that is thinner, more flexible, and

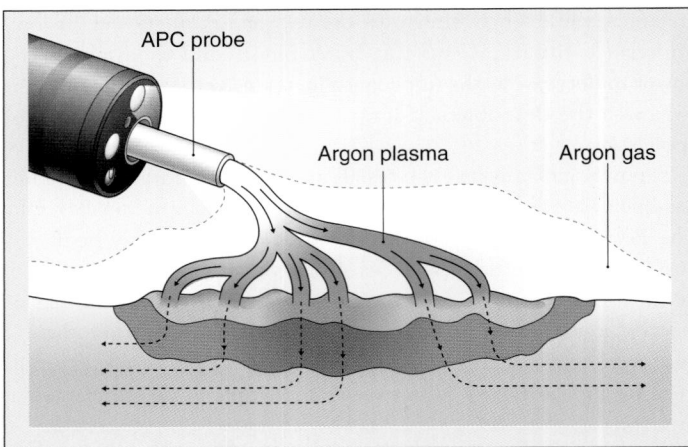

Figure 6-4. Argon plasma coagulation. (Redrawn from Grund KE, Farin G: New principles and applications of high-frequency surgery, including argon plasma coagulation. In The Annual of Gastrointestinal Endoscopy, 10th ed. London, Rapid Science Publishers, 1997.)

adherent than those produced with conventional means. Therefore the eschar may be less likely to rebleed.[26]

An APC system includes a gas source with control and a specialized electrosurgery generator to provide the voltage source. The actual ionization of the argon takes place when a slightly recessed electrode at the distal tip of the probe activates gas flowing through the flexible probe lumen. The physician has control of the distance the probe tip is held from the tissue, the flow rate of the gas, the power setting on the generator, and the time of application.

The length of the plasma arc between the probe tip and tissue is directly related to the power setting and the resistance of the target tissue and, to a lesser extent, the flow rate of argon. Although the design and advantages of APC systems are to provide a noncontact modality, the arc distance *in vivo* is usually only about 2 to 5 mm. It is clearly unsafe to embed the probe tip into the tissue while it is being activated.[24] Only the gas that has been ionized conveys the thermal effect to tissue. Excess argon outside the ionized arc zone has no thermal effect. Because higher flow rates of gas add little to the tissue effect, but more to patient discomfort because of extra distension, flow rates are commonly set at less than 2.0 L/m.

Overall, power settings between 40 and 90 watts are most commonly reported. In general, 40 to 60 watts are used to produce hemostasis of superficial vascular lesions, and 60 to 90 watts are used for tissue ablation.[24,27] One *in vivo* study found that muscle layer injury correlated closely with power, duration, and total joules of energy delivered.[28] As in all electrosurgery, time of application emerges as a critical physician-controlled variable. The use of short bursts of application, especially when working in the right colon, is desirable (Fig. 6-4).

Desired Tissue Effects Summary

Physicians control the electrosurgical effect through their choice of electrode, power setting, output mode, and application time. The tissue surrounding the active electrode is heated to a depth dependent on the current density and the time current is allowed to flow.

- Desiccation/broad hemostasis. Results from direct contact application of the active electrode with the target tissue. Accomplished with either monopolar or bipolar circuit. Most effectively achieved with broad electrodes—biopsy forceps, bipolar probes, and ball tip electrodes. Use of lowest possible power and voltage minimizes unwanted sticking and sparking. Time of application greatly affects depth of tissue injury. Rapid, broad noncontact hemostasis is achieved with APC.

- Fulguration. Noncontact application of high-voltage current without the assist of argon is *fulguration*. The distinction between a coagulation waveform that produces desiccation and one that produces fulguration is a matter of the height of the voltage peaks and whether or not the electrode is in direct contact with tissue. High voltages are required to induce current to arc through highly resistant, plain air. Because of unpredictable direction and depth of penetration caused by these intense, high-voltage sparks, true noncontact fulguration is rarely used in gastroenterology.

- Coaption. The concept of applying both pressure and current to seal a vessel. Most easily achieved with a bipolar probe and low-voltage bipolar output or a ball tip electrode with the lowest available voltage monopolar setting.

- Ablation. Used to destroy and eliminate surface tissue. This is most commonly achieved using a laser (e.g., neodymium: yttrium-aluminum-garnet [Nd:YAG]). Alternatives include APC on high power output or a contact electrode (such as a fistulatome) on a blended or coagulation setting of at least 6%.

- Cutting. For a cutting effect with minimal hemostasis, the thinnest wire electrodes are chosen with the lowest voltage cut waveform. Cut waveforms with increasing voltage increase the depth of the margin of hemostasis. Selecting a broader wire or moving the wire more slowly also increases hemostasis, as does choosing a waveform with some modulation. Modulated waveforms with duty cycles between 50% and 100% are common for cutting with hemostasis (coagulation). Coagulation increases as the duty cycle decreases.

Safety Considerations

As electrosurgery generator technology has advanced, safety has greatly improved. Overall, the safety record of electrosurgery is very good.[29] However, an understanding of the possible hazards is vital for operators to avoid errors or situations that increase the likelihood of complications.

IMPLANTED CARDIAC DEVICES

Patients with implanted cardiac devices can be at risk during the use of electrosurgery; however, its use with these devices is quite safe if properly monitored. The risk of malfunction of the pacemaker is greater with monopolar circuits; thus, one should use bipolar outputs if possible.[30] With the advice of a cardiologist and/or the device manufacturer, defibrillator units may need to be deactivated. Most newer pacemakers can withstand the use of monopolar electrosurgery, but it is still advisable to seek cardiac advice and

to place the patient return electrode so that current flows away from the patient's heart with as little distance as possible between electrodes. One should use short bursts of energy and continually monitor cardiac function during the procedure.[31] This important area is addressed in an excellent guideline available from the American Society for Gastrointestinal Endoscopy (ASGE) (www.asge.org).

GROUND REFERENCED VERSUS ISOLATED OUTPUT

Electric current always seeks ground and follows the path of least resistance. *Ground referenced* is a term used to describe largely outmoded types of electrosurgery generators in which the return electrode was attached to the metal chassis of the generator, which was in turn in contact with earth ground. These systems allowed the dangerous situation in which the current took any available path that was less resistant than the grounding pad route from the patient to earth. Sobering reports tell of *alternate site* burns either to the patient or to the physician when they unexpectedly became part of an unintended diversion for current seeking ground. Ground referenced units have been nearly universally replaced with generators that offer a safer solid state *isolated output* design. With an isolated output, the design favors *only* the pathway formed from the active electrode, through the patient, and back to the generator via the grounding pad. The international standard for isolated output generators requires that not more than 200 microamps of high-frequency current be allowed to return to the generator by any other path. These generators are designed to halt the delivery of power if these leakage current parameters are exceeded. With isolated generators, the risk of true alternate site burns has been virtually eliminated.[13] A point worth noting is that if a system were to allow excessive currents to leak to ground or back to the generator through an alternate path, an early sign would be diminished performance of the generator. It is for this reason that, if the operator notes sudden, unexplained loss of performance in a familiar procedure, the idea of increasing the power should not be the first thought but the last. It is prudent to first recheck the grounding pad, all cables, the active electrode, and the settings and alarm functions of the generator.

GROUNDING PAD SAFETY

Even with isolated output generators it is still possible to have a burn *at the site of the return pad* if it is incorrectly applied. Areas of decreased contact may allow the current density in remaining areas to become high enough to cause an exit burn on the patient. This hazard has been greatly reduced since the introduction in 1981 (ValleyLab) of contact quality monitoring, or split pad systems. Now widely available, these systems inactivate the generator and give an alarm if a condition arises at the pad site that might result in patient injury or if no grounding pad is attached to both the patient and the generator.[18]

DIRECT COUPLING

Other unintended site injuries can be explained by *direct coupling* in which a conductive element, such as a metal endoscope tip, comes into direct contact with an active electrode, such as a snare wire. In this case, the endoscope tip can allow a second pathway to the return electrode with unpredictable injury. This is avoided by keeping all active electrodes in view and advancing the accessory until the insulating sheath is past the endoscope tip. One should never proceed with an endoscope that has missing or damaged insulating distal tip hoods or other insulating features that are compromised.

UNANTICIPATED DIRECT BURNS

Unanticipated direct burns are usually the result of inadvertent activation of accessories when they are in contact with the grounded patient or burns to staff from damaged equipment. Any part of the grounded patient's body may be affected if an accessory were to be accidentally activated while lying on the bed, for example. It is a good rule to insist on fastidious control of accessories at all times, and, when an accessory is introduced through the scope, not to deliver power until the active tip is clearly in view. Monitoring the condition of all active cords and connecting cables should be routine.[10,32]

FLAMMABLE GASES

It is possible to ignite a fire in the colon in the presence of naturally occurring gases such as hydrogen and methane in the presence of oxygen. Thorough colon preparation using approved preparation techniques with solutions that do not contain mannitol or sorbitol is necessary even if the electrosurgery, including APC, is used only in the sigmoid colon or rectum.[33–35]

CAPACITIVE COUPLING AND INTERFERENCE

The heat produced by passing high-frequency current through resistive tissue is independent of the frequency; however, most electrosurgery generators operate within a range of 200 kHz to 3.3 megahertz (MHz). The lower range is set by the neuromuscular phenomenon, but the upper range is more loosely defined by a technical consideration. At very high frequencies, it becomes increasingly difficult to confine the current to the desired path because of capacitive coupling and radiated energy loss.

A capacitor exists whenever a nonconductor separates two conductors. A capacitor is created when an accessory, such as snare, is introduced through an endoscope. The wire and the metal interior components of the scope body are conductors. The insulating sheath of the snare and the covering components of the scope are insulators.

Capacitive coupling is an unpredictable event that can occur when high-frequency current passing through one of the conductors induces a current in the other conductor. A point of exposed metal in contact with tissue may be a vulnerable site as the induced current seeks a path to return to the generator. In addition to excessively high frequency, very high voltages also increase the likelihood of this event. Constant observance of the usual good practices of using the lowest voltages and lowest power possible for the procedure; wearing surgical gloves[36]; and always monitoring the condition of endoscopes, active cords, and accessories help to ensure that these sudden energy discharges are rare.[37]

It is more common for gastroenterologists to observe the case of radiated stray currents, because they may appear on video monitors as "snow" or interference on patient monitoring or videoprocessing equipment. This is especially true during the use of APC because of the higher than usual voltages and frequencies often used to ionize the gas and the noncontact method of application. The stray current in this situation is harmless unless the physician's view is dangerously obscured or patient-monitoring equipment is disrupted for more than a moment.

To reduce interference, the endoscopist may choose to attach a *scope feedback cord* (S cord: Olympus) from the endoscope to the generator or APC system. These cords provide a direct low-resistance path for leakage current back to the generator. Although the assumption is made that operators always check to see that the grounding pad is properly in place before the procedure is attempted, this becomes even more important if an S cord is used. If an S cord is used in the unlikely situation that the grounding pad return path is not available, the endoscope itself may become the return electrode.[9] The prevalence, however, of isolated output generators and relatively low power settings typical of gastroenterology procedures make the risk of injury from this situation minimal.

PATIENT RESPONSE DURING ELECTROSURGERY

Occasionally, a patient may "twitch" or complain of feeling something when electrosurgery is used. Nerve stimulation normally occurs with frequencies lower than 100,000 Hz, and electrosurgery generators usually operate at frequencies greater than 200,000 Hz. However, there are always nonlinear demodulation processes present at the electrosurgical site that produce very small amounts of low-frequency currents in the 1000 to 2000 Hz range. Although these small currents are quite harmless unless targeted directly to heart muscle, all electrosurgical generators incorporate blocking capacitors to minimize these unwanted low-frequency currents. However, they are present during all normal procedures and are more readily produced by the coagulation waveforms most commonly used in gastroenterology, and they increase with increasing generator power settings.[38] In addition to the waveform, demodulation current patterns are affected by tissue type, water content, and other uncontrollable factors so that patients vary greatly in their susceptibility. As long as patient movement is not a hazard, transient, minor, infrequent observations of this phenomenon are quite harmless. However, should the low-frequency capacitors in a generator ever fail, dangerous low-frequency currents of many milliamperes are possible but are immediately evident. In general, checking all active cords, grounding pad cables, and adapters regularly and maintaining scheduled equipment maintenance are the best safeguards.[39]

Conclusion

Electrosurgery is a safe and effective tool for tissue ablation and control of bleeding throughout the gut. In 1928, Dr. Harvey Cushing wrote, ". . . improvements and alterations in the apparatus and in our understanding of its possibilities are being so rapidly made that the developments of tomorrow can hardly be foreseen"—well said and still true.

ACKNOWLEDGMENTS

The mention of specific trademarked products are included only to increase the reader's understanding by providing concrete examples and should in no way be considered an endorsement of any specific product.

With thanks to the technical and educational departments and publications of the following corporations:

Erbe USA, Inc., 2225 Northwest Parkway, Marietta, GA 30067, 800-778-3723

Meditron, a division of Cooper Surgical, Inc., 95 Corporate Drive, Trumbull, CT 06611, 800-527-3530

Olympus America, Inc., 2 Corporate Center Drive, Melville, NY 11747, 800-848-9024

ValleyLab, a division of Tyco Healthcare, 5920 Longbow Drive, Boulder, CO, 80301, 800-255-8522

REFERENCES

1. Cushing H: Electrosurgery as an aid to the removal of intracranial tumors. Surg Gynecol Obstet 47:751–784, 1928.
2. Blackwood WD, Silvis E: Gastroscopic electrosurgery. Gastroenterology 61:305–314, 1971.
3. Shinya H, Wolff WI: Polypectomy via the fiber optic colonoscope. N Engl J Med 288:329–332, 1973.
4. Sanowski RA: Thermal application for gastrointestinal bleeding. J Clin Gastroenterol 8:239–244, 1986.
5. Anonymous: Part 4: Electrosurgery/coagulation. In Morris M (ed): SGNA Manual of GI Procedures, 4th ed. Chicago, Society of Gastroenterology Nurses and Associates, Inc, 2000, pp 131–135.
6. Sittner WR, Fitzgerald JK: High frequency electrosurgery. In Berci G (ed): Endoscopy. New York, Appleton-Century-Crofts, 1976, pp 214–221.
6a. Tucker RD: Principles of electrosurgery. In Sivak MV (ed): Gastroenterologic Endoscopy, Vol 1, 2nd ed. WB Saunders, 2000, pp 125–135.
7. Curtiss LE: High frequency currents in endoscopy: A review of principles and precautions. Gastrointest Endosc 20:9–12, 1973.
8. Tucker RD, Platz CF, Landas SK: Histologic characteristics of electrosurgical injuries. J Am Assoc Gynecol Laparoscopists 4:201–206, 1997.
9. Barlow DE: Endoscopic applications of electrosurgery: A review of basic principles. Gastrointest Endosc 28:73–76, 1982.
10. Veck S: An introduction to the principles of safety of electrosurgery. Br J Hosp Med 55(1–2):27–30, 1996.
11. Smith TL, Smith J: Radiofrequency electrosurgery. Oper Tech Otolaryngol Head Neck Surg 11:66–70, 2000.
12. Zinder JD: Common myths about electrosurgery. Otolaryngol Head Neck Surg 123:450–455, 2000.
13. Anonymous: Are Bovie CSV and other spark-gap electrosurgical units safe to use? Health Devices 24:293–294, 1995.
14. Waye J: Gastrointestinal polypectomy. In Waye J, Geenen J, Fleischer D, et al (eds): Techniques in therapeutic endoscopy. New York, Saunders/Gower Medical, 1987, pp 7.2–20.
15. Tucker RD, Sievert CE, Dramolowsky EV, et al: The interaction between electrosurgical generators, endoscopic electrodes and tissue. Gastrointest Endocs 38:118–122, 1992.
16. Tucker RD, Hurdlik TR, Silvis SE, et al: Automated impedance: A case study in microprocessor programming. Comput Biol Med 11:153–160, 1981.
17. Anonymous: Electrosurgical units. Health Devices 27:93–111, 1998.
18. Anonymous: Electrosurgical units. Health Devices 26:400–415, 1997.
19. Treat M, Forde K: A bipolar snare for endoscopic polypectomy. Endosc Rev 8(2):13–21, 1991.
20. Kohler A, Maier M, Benz C, et al: A new hf current generator with automatically controlled system (EndoCut mode) for endoscopic sphincterotomy-preliminary experience. Endoscopy 30:351–355, 1998.
21. Freeman M: Adverse events and success of ERCP. Gastrointest Endosc 56:S273–280, 2002.
22. Perini RF, Sadurski R, Hawes RH, et al: Post-sphincterotomy bleeding: Has the Erbe electrocautery helped? Gastrointest Endosc 53:AB88, 2001.
23. Norton ID, Bosco J, Meier PB, et al: A randomized trial of endoscopic sphincterotomy using 'pure-cut' versus 'EndoCut' electrical waveforms. Gastrointest Endosc 55:AB174, 2002.
24. Ginsberg G, Barkun AN, Bosco J, et al: Technology status evaluation report: The argon plasma coagulator. Gastrointest Endosc 55:807–810, 2002.
25. Farin G, Grund KE: Technology of argon plasma coagulation with particular regard to endoscopic applications. Endoscop Surg 2:71–77, 1994.
26. Platt RC, McGreevy T: Argon plasma electrosurgical coagulation. Technical monograph. Boulder, CO, Valleylab, 1996.
27. Anonymous: Clinical applications for argon plasma coagulation physician self study activity. Denver, Erbe USA, Inc, Education Design, 2002, pp 5–19.
28. Norton ID, Wang L, Levine A, et al: In vivo characterization of colonic thermal injury caused by argon plasma coagulation. Gastrointest Endosc 55:631–635, 2002.
29. Vilos G, Latendresse K, Gan BS: Electrophysical properties of electrosurgery and capacitive induced current. Am J Surg 182:222–225, 2001.
30. Veitch A: Endoscopic diathermy in patients with cardiac pacemakers. Endoscopy 30:544–547, 1998.
31. Madigan JD, Asim F, Choudhri BS, et al: Surgical management of the patient with an implanted cardiac device. Ann Surg 230:639–647, 1999.
32. Anonymous: Sparking from and ignition of damaged electrosurgical electrode cables. Health Devices 27:301–303, 1998.
33. Strocchi A, Bond JH, Ellis C, et al: Colonic concentrations of hydrogen and methane following colonoscopic preparation with an oral lavage solution. Gastrointest Endosc 36:580–582, 1990.
34. Avgerinos A, Kalantzis N, Rekoumis G, et al: Bowel preparation and the risk of explosion during colonoscopic polypectomy. Gut 25:361–364, 1984.
35. Taylor EW, Bentley S, Youngs D, et al: Bowel preparation and the safety of colonoscopic polypectomy. Gastroenterology 81:1–4, 1981.
36. Tucker RD, Ferguson S: Do surgical gloves protect staff during electrosurgical procedures? Surgery 110:892–895, 1991.
37. Tucker RD: Laparoscopic electrosurgical injuries: Survey results and their implications. Surg Laparosc Endosc 5:311–317, 1995.
38. Tucker RD, Sievert CE, Vennes JA, et al: Endoscopic radiofrequency electrosurgery. Gastrointest Endosc 36:412–413, 1990.
39. Tucker RD, Schmitt OH, Sievert CE, et al: Demodulated low frequency currents from electrosurgical procedures. Surg Gynecol Obstet 159:39–43, 1984.

Patient Assessment, Sedation, and Monitoring

Matthew R. Banks and George J.M. Webster

Introduction

Sedative and analgesic drugs are often used to facilitate endoscopic procedures. The principal aim of sedation is to maintain a cooperative patient, whereby the endoscopic procedure can be effectively and safely completed. The benefits of sedation thus relate to both patient satisfaction and the efficiency of the procedure. However, sedation is not without its problems. More than 50% of all reported endoscopic complications are related to sedation issues including aspiration, oversedation, hypoventilation, and airway obstruction.[1,2] Furthermore, sedation has time, cost, and staffing implications in terms of additional monitoring and recovery. With these issues in mind, there have been recent studies and expressed opinion in favor of unsedated endoscopy, with attempts at selecting tolerant patients (see Chapter 10).[3-6] The practice of unsedated endoscopy varies greatly both geographically and culturally, with particularly low rates in the United States.[7]

When using sedation, several factors may influence the class of sedative used, the depth of sedation, and the necessary level of anesthetic expertise present during the procedure. These include the length and complexity of the procedure, the degree of discomfort expected or experienced, and patient comorbidity. Moreover, patients vary in their sensitivity to sedation and their tolerance of endoscopy.

The level of sedation may be broadly considered within a spectrum from no sedation through general anesthesia (Table 7–1). The most often used level in endoscopic procedures is conscious sedation whereby the patient is able to make purposeful responses to verbal or tactile stimuli, with ventilatory and cardiovascular functions maintained. This level of sedation is normally achieved with a benzodiazepine alone or in combination with an opiate. However, there has been an increase in the use of deep sedation, most commonly with propofol.

This chapter discusses all aspects of sedation and patient safety. The importance of patient evaluation and risk assessment and presedation preparation and issues of consent are discussed. The attributes of sedative drugs are discussed in the context of level of sedation and monitoring required.

Table 7–1. Levels of Sedation	
Level 1: Minimal sedation	A drug-induced state, during which the patient responds normally to verbal commands. Cognitive function and coordination may be impaired. Ventilatory and cardiovascular function are unaffected.
Level 2: Conscious sedation	A drug-induced depression of consciousness, during which patients respond purposefully to verbal commands, either alone or accompanied by light tactile stimulation. A patent airway is maintained without help. Spontaneous ventilation is adequate, and cardiovascular function is usually maintained.
Level 3: Deep sedation	A drug-induced depression of consciousness, during which patients cannot be easily aroused but respond purposefully to repeated or painful stimulation. Patients may require assistance maintaining an airway. Spontaneous ventilation may be inadequate, and cardiovascular function is maintained.
Level 4: General anesthesia	Patients are not arousable, even by painful stimuli. Patients often require assistance in maintaining a patent airway. Positive pressure ventilation may be required because of respiratory depression or neuromuscular blockade. Cardiovascular function may be impaired.
From Bryson HM, Fulton BR, Faulds D: Propofol: An update of its use in anesthesia and conscious sedation. Drugs 50:513–559, 1995.	

Patient Evaluation and Preparation

Appropriate preprocedural evaluation of patients' history and physical findings reduces the risk of adverse outcomes and the potential for litigation (see Chapter 9).[8] Clinicians responsible for sedation should familiarize themselves with specific and relevant aspects of the medical history including abnormalities of major organ systems, previous adverse experience with sedation and analgesia, current medications and drug allergies, time of the last oral intake, and a history of alcohol or recreational drug use. A thorough physical examination is required particularly to assess the heart and lungs in addition to the airway. It may be useful to consider the patient in terms of the American Society of Anesthesiologists (ASA) status classification (Table 7–2). There is usually no indication to perform laboratory tests unless particular concern is raised by this assessment.

Although there are no data to support the provision of information about sedatives to patients, counseling may aid patient satisfaction. Patients undergoing sedation should be informed of the benefits, risks, and limitations associated with sedation and possible alternatives. This process should be part of the patient consent. Patients' expectations regarding the discomfort they are likely to experience while sedated during the procedure should be realistic and as accurate as possible.

Procedural Monitoring

Patients undergoing endoscopic procedures should have continuous monitoring before, during, and after the administration of sedatives.[9] Monitoring should only be discontinued when the patient is fully awake. Literature and medical opinion suggest that continuous recording of patient's level of consciousness, respiratory function, and hemodynamics reduces the risk of sedation-related adverse outcomes.[8] Early detection of adverse events induced by sedatives such as hypoxemia and cardiovascular compromise allows intervention to prevent life-threatening complications. Each of the parameters monitored are addressed.

LEVEL OF CONSCIOUSNESS

Decreasing levels of consciousness are associated with loss of reflexes that normally protect the airway and prevent hypoventilation. The response of patients to commands during sedation serves as a guide to their level of consciousness (see Table 7–1). During procedures in which verbal responses are not possible such as upper gastrointestinal (GI) endoscopy, other responses should be sought including hand movements or a nod of the head. Lack of response to verbal or tactile stimuli suggests a greater level of sedation and should be treated accordingly.

PULMONARY VENTILATION

Respiratory depression is probably the central event in sedation-related complications, and monitoring of ventilatory function reduces the risk of adverse outcomes. Ventilatory function can be monitored by observation of respiratory movement or by direct pulmonary auscultation. If ventilatory function cannot be observed, transcutaneous CO_2 and end-tidal CO_2 can be measured by capnography. Essentially, capnography measures CO_2 indirectly by light absorption in the infrared region of the electromagnetic spectrum. If the patient's ventilation is compromised, CO_2 retention occurs, which is identified as an early event on capnography often before oxygen desaturation.[10] Alternatively, respiratory activity can be continuously measured graphically using expired air CO_2 detectors.[11] This method can detect the early phases of respiratory depression. However, there have been no studies addressing whether capnography improves outcome in patients with conscious sedation.

PULSE OXIMETRY

Pulse oximetry is a noninvasive method of measuring oxygen saturation from a light signal transmitted through tissue, taking into account the pulsatile volume changes that occur. The probe differentiates the absorption of incidental light by the pulsatile arterial component from the static component, hence the term pulse oximeter. The pulse oximeter estimates the oxygen saturation by measuring the pulsatile signals across perfused tissue at two distinct wavelengths, which allows the differentiation of reduced hemoglobin and oxyhemoglobin. Oxyhemoglobin absorbs light in the infrared band, whereas reduced hemoglobin absorbs light in the red band. The functional oxygen saturation is defined as the ratio of oxyhemoglobin to all functional hemoglobins. The oxyhemoglobin dissociation curve is sigmoid, which limits the degree of desaturation that can be tolerated. Between 90% and 100% saturation, the partial pressure of arterial oxygen is maintained at a high level; however, below 90%, the curve becomes steeper and small drops in the oxygen saturation correspond to large drops in partial pressure. A variety of probes are available; however, the most commonly used probe is a reusable probe for use on fingers or toes.

Table 7–2. Definition of American Society of Anesthesiologists Comorbidity Status	
Class 1	Patient has no organic, physiologic, biochemical, or psychiatric disturbance. The pathologic process for which operation is to be performed is localized and does not entail systemic disturbance.
Class 2	Mild to moderate systemic disturbance caused either by the condition to be treated surgically or by other pathophysiologic processes
Class 3	Severe systemic disturbance or disease from whatever cause, even though it may not be possible to define the degree of disability with finality
Class 4	Severe systemic disorders that are already life threatening, not always correctable by operation
Class 5	The moribund patient who has little chance of survival but is submitted to operation in desperation

Pulse oximetry in sedated patients has been shown to improve assessment of respiratory status.[12] However, the routine use of pulse oximetry in unsedated endoscopy is not always indicated.[13] Although oximetry is not a substitute for monitoring ventilatory function, hypoxemia is more likely to be detected using oximetry in addition to clinical assessment. However, pulse oximeter probes occasionally detect peripheral oxygen saturation poorly, resulting in a falsely low or absent oxygen saturation reading. Failure rates have been demonstrated to be as high as 7%,[14] although the accepted error is 3% when compared with arterial blood gases.[15] Failure is more common in patients who are ASA status 3 and above; in patients with hypertension or hypotension, hypothermia, or pigmented skin; in the elderly; and in patients with renal failure. Pulse oximeters require adequate pulsations to distinguish arterial blood light absorption from venous blood and tissue light absorption. Therefore, the reading may be unreliable or absent if there is loss or diminution of the peripheral pulse. This may occur with blood pressure cuff inflation, improper positioning, hypothermia, hypotension, and peripheral vascular disease.

Although the response time of the pulse oximeter is fast, there may be a significant delay in the alveolar oxygen tension and change in oximeter reading.[16]

Some shades of nail polish may cause significantly lower saturation readings. This can be overcome by placing the probe across the finger rather than from nail to finger dorsum.

False alarms often occur during continuous monitoring and are usually due to motion artifact. Poor signal quality and sensor displacement are also common and can be avoided by changing position of the probe or warming a limb to improve circulation. Other maneuvers to reduce false alarms include delaying the time between detection of a low oxygen saturation and alarm activation, although this may lead to a delay in resuscitation in case of a true alarm.

HEMODYNAMIC MEASUREMENTS

Sedative agents and analgesics may have mild direct effects on hemodynamic control, such as hypotension, and hence on cardiovascular response to stressors. These changes can be detected by regular measurement of pulse and blood pressure. Moreover, changes in blood pressure and pulse may represent responses to hypoxemia, oversedation, or possibly patient distress to procedure-induced pain. Although there is no evidence demonstrating blood pressure monitoring during endoscopy influences morbidity and mortality, it has been suggested that both regular blood pressure measurements and pulse may be measured throughout procedures under sedation.[17] There is, however, wide variation in this practice. Continuous electrocardiogram (ECG) monitoring should be considered in high-risk patients such as those with disturbances in cardiac rhythm or ischemic heart disease. However, the necessity for ECG monitoring has not been demonstrated in clinical trials.

SUPPLEMENTAL OXYGEN

Oxygen given via nasal cannulae (for upper GI endoscopy) or via a mask has been demonstrated to reduce oxygen desaturation during sedated endoscopy[18,19] and should be given to all patients receiving sedation. However, because supplemental oxygen will delay the onset of hypoxemia in sedated patients who are hypoventilating, it is important not to rely solely on oximetry to monitor ventilation but also to use additional techniques including assessment of respiratory rate.

INTRAVENOUS ACCESS

In patients receiving intravenous sedatives, intravascular access should be maintained throughout the procedure until the patient is no longer at risk from cardiopulmonary depression. This provides immediate access for administration of reversal agents in case of oversedation or emergency drugs in case of arrhythmias. In patients who are receiving sedatives via nonintravascular routes (e.g., pediatric endoscopic procedures), intravenous access should also be attained if the patient is likely to have any cardiopulmonary depression.

Sedation and Consent

There are two issues surrounding consent and sedation. The first is that the patient should be fully informed of the indications, risks, and alternatives to sedation. The second is whether the patient is able to withdraw consent while under sedation. For example, if a sedated patient indicates during endoscopy that he or she wishes the procedure to be terminated, should the clinician complete the procedure or stop, given it may be in the patient's best interests to complete? In a recent study, 88% of colonoscopists stated that they would stop only after repeated requests by the sedated patient and only 45% thought patients were capable of making rational decisions while under sedation.[20] However, from the patient's perspective, opinion is equally divided into terminating the examination immediately or completing.

Staffing Levels and Training

The clinician performing a procedure will be unable to fully observe and assess the patient under sedation. Therefore, another individual should be available to monitor the patient's status in terms of conscious level, ventilatory function, and hemodynamic parameters. Furthermore, the presence of another individual is likely to improve patient comfort and satisfaction. There are several aspects of expertise required while managing sedated patients including knowledge of administered drugs and management of adverse events. All staff administering sedative drugs should be familiar with the pharmacology of all drugs used. In particular, staff should be aware of the time to onset of action, elimination half-life, interactions, adverse reactions, contraindications, and the pharmacology of appropriate antagonists. Specific areas of concern include the potentiation of sedative-induced respiratory depression by concomitantly administered opioids and benzodiazepines and inadequate time intervals between doses of sedatives. Furthermore, the individuals monitoring sedated patients should be able to recognize complications associated with the sedative drugs. Given that most complications associated with sedatives are cardiopulmonary, at least one individual should be familiar with advanced airway and ventilation management. Failing this, guidelines recommend an

Table 7–3. Appropriate Emergency Equipment Available When Using Sedative or Analgesic Drugs Capable of Causing Cardiorespiratory Depression

Intravenous equipment Gloves Tourniquets Alcohol wipes Sterile gauze Intravenous cannulas Intravenous tubing Intravenous fluids Needles and syringes
Basic airway management equipment Source of oxygen Suction Suction catheters (Yankauer catheters) Face masks Self-inflating breathing bag valve set Oral and nasal airways (Guerdel)
Advanced airway management equipment Laryngoscope handles and blades Endotracheal tubes Stylet
Pharmacologic antagonists Flumazenil Naloxone
Emergency medications Epinephrine Ephedrine Atropine Lidocaine Glucose (50%) Diphenhydramine Hydrocortisone and methylprednisolone Diazepam or midazolam

From Practice guidelines for sedation and analgesia by non-anesthesiologists: A report by the American Society of Anesthesiologists Task Force on sedation and analgesia by non-anesthesiologists. Anesthesiology 84:459–471, 1996.

advanced resuscitation provider be immediately available in the event of an emergency.[8] Resuscitation equipment must be readily available and should include a cardiac defibrillator, advanced airway and positive pressure ventilation equipment, and all the appropriate drugs including sedative antagonists (Table 7–3).[8]

Postprocedural Monitoring

After completion of the procedure, the patient is still at risk of sedative-related complications. Indeed, the risk of upper airway obstruction and hypoxemia after significant conscious sedation for endoscopic retrograde cholangiopancreatography (ERCP) appears to be greatest immediately after removal of the endoscope. Therefore, monitoring should continue until the patient has reached an acceptable level of consciousness, with normal ventilation, oxygenation, and hemodynamic parameters. Before discharge, although the patient's conscious level appears normal, it is recognized that there may be a prolonged period of amnesia with impairment of cognition and judgment. Patients may also be mildly dehydrated, especially after colonoscopy, and fluid replacement should be addressed.

Therefore, after an outpatient procedure, the patients should be advised of the following, which should apply for 24 hours after discharge:

- Not to drive
- Not to operate heavy or dangerous machinery
- Not to sign any legally binding documents
- To arrange escort home with an able companion
- Written instructions regarding the signs and symptoms of any adverse outcomes of the procedure and contact numbers for 24-hour advice

The benzodiazepine antagonist flumazenil has been demonstrated to enhance recovery from sedation and amnesia, without any risk of resedation in a placebo controlled study.[21] This clearly increases the expense of the procedure but may be preferable to patients. Because flumazenil will not preclude the need for postprocedural monitoring, the advantages of routine use may be negligible and are yet unproved. Furthermore, its routine use could lead to acute benzodiazepine withdrawal syndrome in patients who have not mentioned that they take regular benzodiazepines.

Drugs

Characteristics that would lend themselves to an ideal sedative agent include the following:

- Rapid onset of action
- Practical means of delivery
- Short half-life with rapid recovery
- Safe with predictable sedative response (pharmacodynamics)
- Effective, producing a calm, pain-free, cooperative patient

The most commonly used drugs are benzodiazepines used alone or in combination with an opiate. It is vital that clinicians become familiar with a small selection of specific sedatives (e.g., either meperidine or fentanyl). More recently, propofol has been used as an agent to induce deep sedation. The benzodiazepines midazolam and diazepam are often used and have been found to have similar efficacy.[22,23] However, midazolam is a more attractive agent because of its rapid onset of action, short half-life, and amnesic properties. Of the opiates, fentanyl and meperidine are most commonly used, with fentanyl being favored in light of its rapid action and absence of nausea. A combination of a benzodiazepine and an opiate is often used in endoscopy, although this may lead to a greater incidence of sedation-related complications.[24] In colonoscopy, opiates in combination with benzodiazepines are often used, but their combined use has not been shown to be more efficacious than benzodiazepines alone. Combination therapy in colonoscopy and upper GI endoscopy does not appear to improve pain and tolerance when compared with individual agents.[24–26] The literature generally suggests that administration of intravenous sedatives or analgesics is achieved safely by giving small incremental doses until the desired level of sedation is attained, rather than a single dose based on patient weight. Thus, the drug should be titrated with sufficient time elapsed between doses to allow for the full effect of each dose to be assessed before subsequent drug administration. Although not based on evidence, it has been suggested that opiate drugs are administered before benzodiazepines to titrate the latter carefully because of their greater sedative effects.

Droperidol has been used in the sedation of agitated patients. However, it is associated with hypotension and a prolonged recovery period. Moreover, the Food and Drug Administration has issued a warning after droperidol-induced cardiac arrhythmias.

Nitrous oxide has been used as a form of patient-controlled analgesia in several studies involving colonoscopy.[27,28] Potential benefits include an absence of sedation-related risks and a rapid recovery. In terms of patient tolerance, the studies were inconsistent, demonstrating no or reduced benefit when compared with traditional sedation.

Propofol and Deep Sedation

There are certain circumstances in which standard conscious sedation is inadequate, and patients may require deep sedation. These may include patients who are not tolerant of endoscopy under conscious sedation or in procedures that may be painful, prolonged, or complex, such as ERCP and endoscopic ultrasonography (EUS). Deep sedation can be achieved with benzodiazepine and narcotic combinations. Droperidol, diphenhydramine, and promethazine have all been combined with benzodiazepines and narcotics to potentiate the sedative effects to achieve deep sedation. Propofol is increasingly used for GI endoscopy because of its rapid onset, rapid recovery, and attainable depth of sedation. Propofol is an anesthetic agent with a rapid onset of action, amnesic properties, and a very short elimination half–life of 2 to 8 minutes, rendering it an attractive agent for endoscopic procedures. Furthermore, patients who regularly use sedatives and narcotics are often insensitive to standard benzodiazepine sedation and thus may benefit from propofol sedation. However, there are disadvantages associated with propofol use. Given the rapid elimination half-life, propofol must be continuously titrated to maintain sedation. Moreover, the narrow therapeutic window between conscious sedation, deep sedation, and anesthesia necessitates close monitoring. When compared with midazolam, the amnesic properties of propofol are inferior.[29] As a result of peripheral vasodilatation and impairment of cardiac contractility, propofol may cause profound hypotension.

PROPOFOL USE IN STANDARD ENDOSCOPIC PROCEDURES

Propofol has been compared with midazolam in several trials during standard endoscopic procedures.[30,31] Although the results are not consistent, propofol appears to improve patient cooperation and reduces recovery time. There does not appear to be any consistent difference in patient tolerance or safety. Due to the fact that propofol has no analgesic properties, its use in combination with fentanyl has been investigated and compared with standard benzodiazepine and narcotic combinations.[32,33] The results were inconsistent in terms of sedation, analgesia, recovery, and incidence of side effects, suggesting that propofol confers no additional benefit over standard sedation regimens.

PROPOFOL USE IN COMPLEX ENDOSCOPIC PROCEDURES

The use of propofol in complex and prolonged procedures has also been investigated. In a randomized trial, Wehrmann and coworkers[34] compared propofol with midazolam for ERCP and found patient cooperation to be superior and recovery times to be less in the propofol group; however, patient tolerance was the same. However, one patient in the propofol group required prolonged ventilatory support. The benefit of propofol over midazolam has been shown in two other studies for ERCP with EUS and ERCP with sphincter of Oddi manometry.[35,36]

NONANESTHETIST ADMINISTERED PROPOFOL

Given the narrow therapeutic window and potential for cardiopulmonary adverse events, many endoscopists favor the expertise of an anesthetist to administer and monitor propofol sedation. Using an anesthetist will incur additional costs that will offset any cost advantage gained by a more rapid sedation induction and recovery time. However, there is growing evidence to support the practice of nurse-administered propofol sedation (NAPS). In a study involving a series of more than 9000 patients given NAPS under the supervision of an endoscopist, NAPS was found to be safe and effective.[37] It is important to note that these nurses were trained and registered to administer and monitor propofol sedation, rather than nurse anesthetists. There were seven cases of respiratory compromise (three prolonged apnea, three laryngospasm, one aspiration) associated with upper endoscopy, which required mask ventilation only. The greater frequency of respiratory adverse events with upper endoscopy is probably related to the deeper level of sedation required to prevent reflex gagging. Thus, the ideal procedures for administration of NAPS are lower endoscopic procedures in which adverse complications are particularly low. The colonic perforation rate was less than 1:1000, and patients preferred NAPS over previous experiences with benzodiazepines.[37] Moreover, in a randomized study comparing NAPS and nurse administered midazolam for colonoscopy, time to sedation was more rapid with propofol, recovery was faster, and patients were more satisfied.[33] NAPS is also cost effective when compared with anesthetist-administered propofol.[35]

PROPOFOL PATIENT-CONTROLLED ANALGESIA

Patient-controlled analgesia and sedation (PCS) with propofol has been assessed in several studies. PCS using propofol and alfentanil were compared with diazepam and meperidine given as a bolus during colonoscopy in 66 randomized patients. PCS provided lighter sedation, less analgesia, and faster recovery with similar patient satisfaction.[38] In a more recent study, Kulling and colleagues[39] compared propofol and alfentanil PCS, continuous infusion, or NAPS and found PCS to exhibit a higher degree of patient satisfaction with faster recovery. Similar results were generated when comparing propofol PCS with midazolam.[40]

Table 7–4. American Society of Anesthesiologists (ASA) Taskforce Situations Associated with Difficult Airway Intubation

Patients with previous problems with anesthesia or sedation
Patients with a history of stridor, snoring, or sleep apnea
Patients with dysmorphic facial features, such as Pierre-Robin syndrome or trisomy 21
Patients with oral abnormalities, such as small opening (<3 cm in an adult); edentulous; protruding incisors; loose or capped teeth; high, arched palate; macroglossia; tonsillar hypertrophy; or a nonvisible uvula
Patients with neck abnormalities, such as obesity involving the neck and facial structures, short neck, limited neck extension, decreased hyoid-mental distance (<3 cm in an adult), neck mass, cervical spine disease or trauma, tracheal deviation, or advanced rheumatoid arthritis
Patients with jaw abnormalities such as micrognathia, retrognathia, trismus, or significant malocclusion

PROPOFOL AND PATIENT MONITORING

Patients undergoing procedures with propofol probably require more monitoring than those undergoing conscious sedation, although there is yet no evidence to support additional monitoring. Preprocedural assessment should include a full history of sedation-related risk factors and airway assessment. Risk factors would include conditions such as age extremes, cardiopulmonary disease, hepatic or renal impairment, narcotic and sedative use, and a potentially difficult airway for intubation (Table 7–4). Trials of NAPS have selected only patients with ASA status class 1 or 2 for propofol[37] (see Table 7–2). Furthermore, the ASA Taskforce states that if the patient has one or more sedation-related risk factors, coupled with the potential for deep sedation (with propofol), the incidence of adverse sedation-related events is likely to be high. In these circumstances, an anesthetist should be consulted before the procedure. Vargo and coworkers[11] have used capnography to guide propofol titration, thereby allowing respiratory depression to be identified early, although this was not shown to have an impact on outcome.

Pharyngeal Anesthesia in Sedation

Topical anesthetic agents are often used in addition to sedation to suppress the gag reflex and, thus, facilitate upper endoscopy. The most often used agent is lidocaine, administered as an aerosol spray to the pharynx. Other less commonly used agents include tetracaine, cetacaine, and benzocaine. All induce anesthesia for up to 1 hour with some evidence of impaired pharyngeal coordination.[41] Thus, patients should be advised not to eat or drink until sensation has returned to minimize the potential risk of bronchial aspiration. The data regarding the benefit of pharyngeal anesthesia given with sedation is conflicting.[42–44] Given that topical anesthetics have been associated with rare but potentially severe adverse reactions including methemoglobinemia,[45,46] their use should be limited to minimally sedated or unsedated patients.

Management of Oversedation

Sedatives have been implicated in more than 50% of all endoscopy-related complications, the most common adverse reactions being oversedation and respiratory depression. The expected mean desaturation during all sedated endoscopic procedures is about 3%

from baseline.[47] The availability of reversal agents for sedative drugs is associated with a deceased risk of sedation-related adverse events. Commonly used antagonists include flumazenil for benzodiazepines and naloxone for opioids. No antagonists exist for propofol, although the short elimination half-life lends to a rapid reversal of sedation. In patients who have received both a benzodiazepine and an opioid, flumazenil reverses sedation but not respiratory depression. Similarly, naloxone monotherapy has not been shown to reverse respiratory depression induced by opioid-benzodiazepine combinations. However, guidelines suggest that patients with combination therapy–induced respiratory depression should be given naloxone in addition to flumazenil.[17]

At the time of reversal or before reversal, the following steps should be observed:

- Basic airway management:
  - Clear airway including suction (if appropriate)
  - Jaw thrust maneuver
  - Guerdel airway if necessary
- Provide supplemental oxygen or increased oxygen
- Encourage or stimulate deep breaths
- Receive positive pressure ventilation if spontaneous ventilation is inadequate

Flumazenil and naloxone have previously been reserved for the treatment of oversedation and respiratory depression. However, the prolonged recovery times associated with the use of benzodiazepines has prompted research into the feasibility of using flumazenil routinely to reduce recovery times with potential cost savings.[21,48]

Unsedated Endoscopy

Given the risks and additional costs associated with the use of sedative drugs in endoscopy, unsedated endoscopy is increasingly being considered (see Chapter 10). In particular, the availability of ultrathin endoscopes (5 to 6 mm) has rendered unsedated endoscopy far more attractive. Several studies have demonstrated improved tolerance using the ultrathin compared with standard endoscopes.[49] The transnasal approach does not appear different from the per-oral route.[50,51] The benefits of unsedated endoscopy include a reduction in morbidity associated with sedative drugs, reduced patient monitoring, more rapid recovery, less time off work, and reduced cost. The potential disadvantages include poor patient satisfaction, with refusal to undergo repeat procedures, incomplete examination resulting from patient intolerance, and the reduced ability to perform therapeutic procedures. Furthermore, the refusal rate for unsedated upper GI endoscopy remains high.[52] Patient selection is of paramount importance before unsedated upper endoscopy. Several studies have suggested older age, low anxiety scores, tolerance of pharyngeal anesthesia, and a tolerance of prior endoscopy was associated with tolerance of unsedated upper endoscopy.[53,54] The data regarding the benefit of pharyngeal anesthesia in unsedated endoscopy are inconsistent, although the larger studies suggest improvement in patient tolerance and ease of performance.[55,56] There are several studies demonstrating colonoscopy can be completed successfully without sedation in up to 95% of patients in one series.[57,58] However, the refusal rate for unsedated colonoscopy remains high at up to 83%.[59]

Appendix: Pharmacology of Commonly Used Drugs

BENZODIAZEPINES

Benzodiazepines are central nervous system (CNS) depressants that induce sedation, hypnosis, amnesia, and anesthesia. The mechanism of action appears to intensify the physiologic inhibitory mechanisms mediated by gamma-aminobutyric acid (GABA).

Midazolam

Pharmacology

Midazolam is a short-acting benzodiazepine with an intravenous peak onset of action of between 2 and 5 minutes depending on the dose given and level of consciousness attained. If given with an opioid the action is more rapid (1.5 minutes) and sedation deeper, such that a dose reduction of approximately 30% is recommended. At doses sufficient to induce sedation, midazolam decreases the ventilatory response to raised CO_2 in normal patients and in particular patients with chronic airway limitation. The pharmacokinetic profile of midazolam is linear over the 0.05 to 0.4 mg/kg range, lending predictable dosage titration. The elimination half-life is 1 to 2.8 hours with a large volume of distribution. The drug is metabolized rapidly to 1-hydroxymethyl midazolam in the liver, conjugated and secreted in the urine.

Administration

Midazolam should be titrated in doses between 1 and 2 mg at intervals of 2 to 3 minutes to a total dose of 5 mg. Higher doses may be required but should be used with caution

Precautions and Adverse Reactions

When given with an opioid analgesic, there is an increased sedative effect necessitating the need for administration in small incremental steps. Sensitivity increases with age. Caution must be used when using midazolam in the elderly, in patients with hepatic or renal impairment, and in those with airflow limitation. Furthermore, because of a reduced rate of plasma clearance, patients with heart failure eliminate midazolam more slowly. Hypotension is a recognized association of midazolam particularly if given with an opioid.

Paradoxical reactions may occur with restlessness, agitation, and disinhibition, particularly in younger patients. It is important to recognize this phenomenon early because efforts to overcome this problem using escalating doses of benzodiazepine can lead to severe oversedation and apnea.

Contraindications

Midazolam should not be given to patients with myasthenia gravis, alcohol intoxication, or narrow angle glaucoma.

Interactions

The sedative effects of midazolam are enhanced by other CNS depressants including neuroleptics, alcohol, tranquilizers, antidepressants, analgesics, antiepileptics, and anxiolytics. The effects of midazolam are attenuated by drugs that induce cytochrome P-450 (rifampicin, carbamazepine, and phenytoin) and enhanced by inhibitors (erythromycin, diltiazem, antiviral agents, and fluconazole). In particular, midazolam should be given with care in patients on combination antiretroviral therapy.

Diazepam

Pharmacology

Diazepam is metabolized in the liver to the active metabolites temazepam, nordiazepam, and oxazepam, all of which are renally excreted. Plasma concentrations of diazepam and its active metabolites exhibit considerable interpatient variation. The intravenous plasma time curve is biphasic, with an initial rapid increase with a half-life of up to 3 hours and a second elimination phase with a half-life of 20 to 70 hours. The elimination half-life is increased in the elderly and in patients with renal and hepatic impairment.

Administration

The dose of diazepam should be titrated in doses of 2 to 4 mg to a total of up to 10 and 20 mg in some circumstances.

Precautions and Adverse Reactions

Care must be used in patients with renal, hepatic and cardiopulmonary impairment. Hypotension occurs rarely. Other precautions, contraindications, and drug interaction are similar to midazolam.

OPIOID ANALGESICS

Fentanyl

Pharmacology

Fentanyl is a synthetic opioid with an estimated 80-fold greater potency than morphine. Unlike other opioids, fentanyl does not induce histamine release. After intravenous injection, fentanyl reaches peak analgesic effects within 1 to 2 minutes, with a duration of 30 to 60 minutes. Serum concentrations decrease rapidly within 5 minutes to 20% of peak concentrations, followed by a slow decrease over 30 minutes. The drug is metabolized in the liver to active metabolites, all of which are excreted in the urine.

Administration

A dose of 50 to 100 µg should be given before benzodiazepine to enable accurate sedative dose titration.

Precautions and Adverse Reactions

Fentanyl causes respiratory depression for periods in excess of the analgesic effect. In light of the elimination, a reduced dose should be used in hepatic and renal impairment. In view of the potential for respiratory depression, care should be used in patients with pulmonary disease.

Contraindications

Fentanyl may cause severe bronchospasm and is thus contraindicated in asthma. Furthermore, fentanyl may cause severe muscle rigidity and is contraindicated in patients with myasthenia gravis.

Interactions

The sedative effect of fentanyl is enhanced by other CNS depressants such as other opioids, benzodiazepines, alcohol, neuroleptics, and tranquilizers. In particular, fentanyl has been associated with hypotensive adverse events with monoamine oxidase inhibitors and neuroleptics.

Meperidine/Pethidine
Pharmacology

Meperidine (known as pethidine in Europe and Australasia) is a synthetic opioid with both sedative and analgesic properties. As with other narcotics, meperidine causes respiratory depression and suppresses the cough reflex. The sedative and analgesic effects of meperidine after intravenous dosing occur within 2 to 4 minutes, and the analgesic effects can last up to 4 hours. The elimination half-life is 3.2 hours, in which metabolism is predominantly hepatic conjugation. Therefore, meperidine elimination is prolonged in patients with hepatic impairment.

Precautions and Adverse Reactions

Care should be taken when giving meperidine concurrently with other neurodepressants. The most common adverse reaction is respiratory depression. Meperidine may also result in profound hypotension. One active meperidine metabolite, normeperidine, has convulsant properties and elimination is prolonged in patients with renal impairment and old age. In these patients, high doses of meperidine may lead to convulsions, agitation, irritability, and tremors.

Administration

Meperidine should be given at an intravenous dose of 25 to 50 mg. Higher doses are more likely to result in adverse events.

Drug Interactions

The sedative effects of neurodepressants are all potentiated by meperidine. In addition, when given with phenothiazines, CNS toxicity and hypotension may occur. Interactions with monoamine oxidase inhibitors may be fatal and result in excitation, sweating, rigidity, hypertension or hypotension, and coma.

Propofol
Pharmacology

Propofol is distributed rapidly and induces sedation within 30 to 60 seconds. The half-life is only 2 to 8 minutes. Metabolism is by hepatic conjugation with renal excretion of inactive metabolites. Propofol is a centrally acting neural depressant without any analgesic properties and rapidly crosses the blood-brain barrier to potentiate GABA activity.

Contraindications

Known allergy to propofol.

Precautions and Adverse Reactions

The most important effect to be monitored with propofol is respiratory depression and apnea, occurring often with deep sedation. Hypotension is also common. Patients with ASA grade 3 or higher, the elderly, and patients using sedatives or opioid agents are at particular high risk for developing these cardiorespiratory complications. Apnea and hypotension occur in up to 75% of patients. In endoscopic trials using propofol, ventilatory support was necessary in up to 10% of patients, although incidence of respiratory depression necessitating support was far greater in complex procedures requiring a cooperative patient.[34] Excitatory phenomena such as tremors, twitches, hypertonus, and hiccups occur in up to 14%. Rarely, pulmonary edema, hypertension, cardiac arrhythmias, bronchospasm, and laryngospasm have occurred. Pain at the injection site is the most frequent local complication and occurs in 5% to 50% of patients.[60]

Administration

Propofol has been given in endoscopic studies by repeated bolus injections or as an infusion. Propofol is usually administered as an initial bolus dose of 20 to 40 mg followed by maintenance doses of 10 to 20 mg to attain the required level of sedation. Alternatively, propofol can be infused at a dose of 0.5 to 1.0 mg/kg over 1 to 5 minutes to induce deep sedation, followed by maintenance infusion at a dose of 1.5 to 3 mg/kg/hour.

Interactions

The sedative effect of propofol is enhanced by other sedative agents and analgesics when dose requirements are reduced.

Flumazenil
Pharmacology

Flumazenil is an imidazobenzodiazepine and antagonizes benzodiazepines through competitively inhibiting central receptors. Its effects are rapid, within 30 to 60 seconds, and it has an elimination half-life of 53 minutes. Clearance is entirely hepatic in which it is conjugated to form inactive metabolites.

Contraindications

Known sensitivity to flumazenil.

Precautions and Adverse Reactions

Care should therefore be taken when administering to patients with known benzodiazepine dependence, because this may precipitate withdrawal or even convulsions. Consideration should be given to the possibility of resedation and respiratory depression after the use of flumazenil. These patients should be monitored for an appropriate period based on the dose and duration of effect of the benzodiazepine used. Despite the use of reversal agents, patients should still be given postprocedural warnings as previously described. The use of flumazenil is not recommended in epileptic patients taking benzodiazepines, because this may give rise to convulsions. Seizures have been reported in patients with epilepsy and hepatic impairment.

Interactions

Flumazenil also blocks the effects of nonbenzodiazepines acting on benzodiazepine receptors such as zopiclone.

Administration

The recommended initial dose is 0.2 mg administered intravenously over 15 seconds. This can be repeated using 0.1-mg doses every 60 seconds to achieve reversal to a total dose of 2 mg.

Naloxone
Pharmacology

Naloxone is a competitive antagonist at opiate receptor sites and can reverse the sedative and respiratory effects of opiates. The effects of intravenous naloxone are apparent within 2 minutes with a 4-hour duration of action. Metabolism is via hepatic conjugation and renal excretion of the metabolites. Elimination half-life is 60 to 90 minutes.

Contraindications

Known hypersensitivity.

Precautions and Adverse Reactions

Care should be taken in patients who are dependent on opiates because naloxone can precipitate withdrawal syndrome. A rapid reversal of opioids can induce catecholamine release and cause excitation, ventricular arrhythmias, hypotension, pulmonary edema, convulsions, and death. Therefore, care should be used in patients with preexisting cardiac abnormalities.

Administration

Naloxone can be given intravenously or intramuscularly at an initial dose of 0.4 to 2 mg. Doses can be repeated at 2- to 3-minute intervals until a total dose of 10 mg is reached.

REFERENCES

 1. Freeman ML: Sedation and monitoring for gastrointestinal endoscopy. Gastrointest Endosc 4:475–475, 1994.
 2. Benjamin SB: Complications of conscious sedation. Gastrointest Endosc Clin N Am 6:277–286, 1996.
 3. Wang TH, Lin JT: Sedation for upper GI endoscopy in Taiwan. Gastrointest Endosc 50:888–889, 1999.
 4. Shaker R: A wake up call? Unsedated versus conventional esophagogastroduodenoscopy. Gastroenterology 117:1492–1495, 1999.
 5. Saeian K, Townsend WF, Rochling FA: Unsedated transnasal EGD: An alternative approach to conventional esophagogastroduodenoscopy for documenting Helicobacter pylori eradication. Gastrointest Endosc 49:297–301, 1999.
 6. Sorbi D, Gostout CJ, Henry J, Lindor KD: Unsedated small-caliber esophagogastroduodenoscopy (EGD) versus conventional EGD: A comparative study. Gastroenterology 17:1301–1307, 1999.
 7. Arrowsmith JB, Gerstman BB, Flescher DE, Benjamin SB: Results from the American Society for Gastrointestinal Endoscopy/US Food and Drug Administration collaborative study on complication rates and drug use during gastrointestinal endoscopy. Gastrointest Endosc 37:421–427, 1991.
 8. Practice guidelines for sedation and analgesia by non-anesthesiologists: A report by the American Society of Anesthesiologists Task Force on sedation and analgesia by non-anesthesiologists. Anesthesiology 84:459–471, 1996.
 9. Simon IB, Lewis RJ, Satava RM: A safe method for sedating and monitoring patients for upper and lower gastrointestinal endoscopy. Am Surg 57:219–221, 1991.
10. Nelson DB, Freeman NL, Silvis SE, et al: A randomized controlled trial of transcutaneous carbon dioxide monitoring during ERCP. Gastrointest Endosc 51:288–295, 2000.
11. Vargo JJ, Zuccaro G, Dumot JA, et al: Gastroenterologist-administered propofol for therapeutic upper endoscopy with graphic assessment of respiratory activity: A case series. Gastrointest Endosc 52:250–255, 2000.
12. Council on Scientific Affairs, American Medical Association: The use of pulse oximetry during conscious sedation. JAMA 270:1463–1468, 1993.
13. Banks MR, Kumar PJ, Mulcahy HE: Pulse oximetry saturation levels during routine unsedated diagnostic upper gastrointestinal endoscopy. Scand J Gastroenterol 36:105–109, 2001.
14. Moller JT, Pederson T, Rasmussen LS, et al: Randomized evaluation of pulse oximetry in 20,802 patients: I. Design, demography, pulse oximetry failure rate, and overall complication rate. Anesthesiology 78:436–444, 1993.
15. Alexander CM, Teller LE, Gross JB: Principles of pulse oximetry. Theoretical and practical considerations. Anesth Analg 68:368–376, 1989.
16. Verhoeff F, Sykes MK: Delayed detection of hypoxic events by pulse oximeters. Computer simulations. Anesthesia 45:103–109, 1990.
17. Waring JP, Baron TH, Hirota WK, et al: Guidelines for conscious sedation and monitoring during gastrointestinal endoscopy. Gastrointest Endosc 58:317–322, 2003.
18. Griffin SM, Chung SC, Leung JW: Effect of intranasal oxygen on hypoxia and tachycardia during endoscopic cholangiopancreatography. BMJ 300:83–84, 1990.
19. Bell GD, Bown S, Morden A: Prevention of hypoxaemia during upper gastrointestinal endoscopy by means of oxygen via nasal cannulae. Lancet 1:1022–1024, 1987.
20. Ward B, Shah S, Kirwan P, Mayberry JF: Issues of consent in colonoscopy: If a patient says 'stop' should we continue ? J R Soc Med 92:132–133, 1999.
21. Chang AC, Solinger MA, Yang DT, Chen YK: Impact of flumazenil on recovery after outpatient endoscopy: Placebo-controlled trial. Gastrointest Endosc 49:573–579, 1999.
22. Brouillette DE, Leventhal R, Kumar S, et al: Midazolam versus diazepam for combined esophagogastroduodenoscopy and colonoscopy. Dig Dis Sci 34:1265–1271, 1989.
23. Bell GD, Morden A, Coady T, et al: A comparison of diazepam and midazolam as endoscopy premedication assessing changes in ventilation and oxygen saturation. Br J Clin Pharmacol 26:595–600, 1988.
24. Rembacken BJ, Axon AT: The role of meperidine in sedation for colonoscopy. Endoscopy 27:244–247, 1995.
25. Froehlich F, Thorens J, Schwizer W: Sedation and analgesia for colonoscopy: Patient tolerance, pain and cardiorespiratory parameters. Gastrointest Endosc 45:1–4, 1997.
26. Laluna L, Allen ML, Dimarino AJ Jr: The comparison of midazolam and topical lidocaine spray versus the combination of midazolam, meperidine, and topical lidocaine spray to sedate patients for upper endoscopy. Gastrointest Endosc 53:289–291, 2001.
27. Forbes GM, Collins BJ: Nitrous oxide for colonoscopy: A randomized controlled study. Gastrointest Endosc 51:271–277, 2000.

28. Saunders BP, Fukumoto M, Halligan S, et al: Patient-administered nitrous oxide/oxygen inhalation provides effective sedation and analgesia for colonoscopy. Gastrointest Endosc 40:418–421, 1994.

29. Smith I, Monk TG, White PF, Ding Y: Propofol infusion during regional anesthesia: Sedative, amnestic and anxiolytic properties. Anesth Analg 79:313–319, 1994.

30. Carlsson U, Grattidge P: Sedation for upper gastrointestinal endoscopy: A comparative study of propofol and midazolam. Endoscopy 27:240–243, 1995.

31. Patterson KW, Casey PB, Murray JP, et al: Propofol sedation for outpatient upper gastrointestinal endoscopy: Comparison with midazolam. Br J Anaesth 68:108–111, 1992.

32. Koshy G, Nair S, Norkus EP, et al: Propofol versus midazolam and meperidine for conscious sedation in GI endoscopy. Am J Gastroenterol 95:1476–1479, 2000.

33. Sipe BW, Rex DK, Latinovich D, et al: Propofol versus midazolam/meperidine for outpatient colonoscopy: Administration by nurses supervised by endoscopists. Gastrointest Endosc 55:815–825, 2002.

34. Wehrmann T, Kokabpick S, Lembcke B, et al: Efficacy and safety of intravenous propofol sedation during routine ERCP: A prospective controlled study. Gastrointest Endosc 49:677–683, 1999.

35. Vargo JJ, Zuccaro G, Dumot JA, et al: Gastroenterologist-administered propofol versus meperidine and midazolam for ERCP and EUS: A randomized, controlled trial with cost effectiveness analysis. Gastroenterology 123:8–16, 2002.

36. Seifert H, Schmitt TH, Gultekin T, et al: Sedation with propofol plus midazolam versus propofol alone for interventional endoscopic procedures: A prospective randomized study. Aliment Pharmacol Ther 14:1207–1214, 2000.

37. Walker JA, McIntyre RD, Schleinitz PF, et al: Nurse-administered propofol sedation without anesthesia specialists in 9152 endoscopic cases in an ambulatory surgery center. Am J Gastroenterol 98:1744–1750, 2003.

38. Roseveare C, Seavell C, Patel P, et al: Patient-controlled sedation and analgesia, using propofol and alfentanil, during colonoscopy: A prospective, randomized controlled trial. Endoscopy 30:768–773, 1998.

39. Kulling D, Fantin AC, Biro P, et al: Safer colonoscopy with patient-controlled analgesia and sedation with propofol and alfentanil. Gastrointest Endosc 54:1–7, 2001.

40. Ng JM, Kong CF, Nyam D: Patient-controlled sedation with propofol for colonoscopy. Gastrointest Endosc 54:8–13, 2001.

41. Sulica L, Hembree A, Blitzer A: Swallowing and sensation: Evaluation of deglutation in the anesthetized larynx. Ann Otol Rhinol Laryngol 111:291–294, 2002.

42. Cantor DS, Baldridge ET: Premedication with meperidine and diazepam for upper gastrointestinal endoscopy precludes the need for topical anesthesia. Gastrointest Endosc 32:339–341, 1986.

43. Froehlich F, Schwizer W, Thorens J, et al: Conscious sedation for gastroscopy: Patient tolerance and cardiorespiratory parameters. Gastroenterology 108:697–704, 1995.

44. Davis DE, Jones MP, Kubik CM: Topical pharyngeal anesthesia does not improve upper gastrointestinal endoscopy in conscious sedated patients. Am J Gastroenterol 94:1853–1856, 1999.

45. Gunaratnam NT, Vazquez-Sequeiros E, Gostout CJ, Alexander GL: Methemoglobinemia related to topical benzocaine use: Is it time to reconsider the empiric use of topical anesthesia before sedated EGD? Gastrointest Endosc 52:692–693, 2000.

46. Patel D, Chopra S, Berman MD: Serious systemic toxicity resulting from use of tetracaine for pharyngeal anesthesia in upper endoscopic procedures. Dig Dis Sci 34:882–884, 1989.

47. Berg JC, Miller R, Burkhalter E: Clinical value of pulse oximetry during routine diagnostic and therapeutic endoscopic procedures. Endoscopy 23:328–330, 1991.

48. Bartelsman JF, Sars PR, Tytgat GN: Flumazenil used for reversal of midazolam-induced sedation in endoscopy outpatients. Gastrointest Endosc 36:S9–S12, 1990.

49. Dean R, Dua K, Massey B: A comparative study of unsedated transnasal esophagogastroduodenoscopy and conventional EGD. Gastrointest Endosc 44:422–426, 1996.

50. Elfant AB, Schneider DM, Bourke MJ: Prospective controlled trial of transnasal endoscopy (T-EGD) vs per-oral endoscopy (P-EGD) [abstract]. Gastrointest Endosc 43:311–317, 1996.

51. Craig A, Hanlon J, Dent J, Schoeman M: A comparison of transnasal and transoral endoscopy with small-diameter endoscopes in unsedated patients. Gastrointest Endosc 49:292–296, 1999.

52. Zaman A, Hahn M, Hapke R: A randomized trial of peroral versus transnasal unsedated endoscopy using a ultrathin videoendoscope. Gastrointest Endosc 49:279–284, 1999.

53. Mulcahy HE, Kelly P, Banks MR, et al: Factors associated with tolerance to, and discomfort with, unsedated diagnostic gastroscopy. Scand J Gastroenterol 36:1352–1357, 2001.

54. Campo R, Brullet E, Montserrat A, et al: Identification of factors that influence tolerance of upper gastrointestinal endoscopy. Eur J Gastroenterol Hepatol 11:201–204, 1999.

55. Campo R, Brullet E, Montserrat A, et al: Topical pharyngeal anesthesia improves tolerance of upper gastrointestinal endoscopy: A randomized double-blind study. Endoscopy 27:659–664, 1995.

56. Dhir V, Swaroop VS, Vazifdar KF, Wagle SD: Topical pharyngeal anesthesia without intravenous sedation during upper gastrointestinal endoscopy. Indian J Gastroenterol 16:10–11, 1997.

57. Rex DK, Imperiale TF, Portish V: Patients willing to try colonoscopy without sedation: Associated clinical factors and results of a randomized controlled trial. Gastrointest Endosc 49:554–559, 1999.

58. Cataldo PA: Colonoscopy without sedation. Dis Colon Rectum 39:257–261, 1996.

59. Early DS, Saiffudin T, Johnson JC: Patient attitudes towards undergoing colonoscopy without sedation. Am J Gastroenterol 94:1862–1865, 1999.

60. Valtaren M, Lisalo E, Kanto J, Rosenberg I: Propofol as an induction agent in children: Pain on injection and pharmacokinetics. Acta Anaesthesiol Scand 33:152–155, 1989.

61. Bryson HM, Fulton BR, Faulds D: Propofol: An update of its use in anesthesia and conscious sedation. Drugs 50:513–559, 1995.

Patient Preparation and Pharmacotherapeutic Considerations

CHAPTER

8

Mark Schoeman, Nam Q. Nguyen, and Awni Taleb Abu-Sneineh

Contents

Introduction

Correct patient preparation is essential for all endoscopic procedures because it contributes significantly to the safety and success of the procedure. This frequently translates into an improvement in outcome. There are a number of requirements that must be considered during the preparatory phase, and these are not limited to simple statements regarding fasting or how to complete a bowel preparation. The patient must have confidence that the clinician understands the clinical problem and has considered this information in making a decision about what endoscopic investigation is required. Once this has been established the clinician must consider issues such as timing and patient-specific factors that must be taken into account when preparing for an endoscopic procedure. If the patient has had this type of information explained, he or she is more likely to comply with preparation instructions in a safe manner. As part of this phase and as part of the explanation about what the procedure involves, it is also necessary to explain potential risks and complications. This all contributes to the process of obtaining informed consent, which is a crucial part of the preparation process.

Informed Consent

The process of informed consent will vary from country to country. In many parts of Europe, a formal consent is not required before endoscopic examinations. If the patient comes to have the procedure performed, these systems assume an implied consent. In other parts of the world such as in the United States and Australia, the consent process is a very detailed and potentially complex process that requires considerable attention by the endoscopist (see Chapter 9).

General Information about Patient Preparation

There are a number of aspects that must be considered when preparing patients for endoscopic examinations. These include the following:

- An understanding of the patient's particular clinical problem
- An awareness of the patient's clinical history
- A knowledge of the patient's recent (and past) medication history
- What procedure-specific preparation is required?
- What patient-specific preparation is required?
- Informed consent
- Postprocedure observation and discharge planning

The endoscopist must have knowledge of the indication for the procedure because this will not only determine what procedure is performed but also what interventions or treatment might be required during the procedure. Implicit also is an understanding of the patient's clinical history and the results of any recent investigations. The preprocedure assessment must extend to the patient's past medical and surgical history, previous endoscopy results, current medical therapy (including over-the-counter and intermittent medication), and drug allergies. Specific clinical history such as diabetes, a personal or family history of bleeding disorder, anesthetic reactions, or previous adverse reactions to other medical interventions (including reactions to radiologic contrast agents) should also be considered. Armed with this information the endoscopist is then able to determine not only the proper preparation but also any specific modifications that might be required for the individual patient (see Chapter 7).

Once the procedure preparation, risks, and potential complications have been discussed, the next phase of the explanatory process is to discuss discharge guidelines. Most endoscopic examinations are performed as day procedures, and frequently patient sedation is administered. Most institutions require that sedated patients are discharged in the care of a responsible person who can not only supervise transportation of the patient home but who is also able to respond to any delayed complications or difficulties. The level of postprocedure supervision depends on the type of intervention, specific patient factors such as mobility and age, or even such things as geographic isolation. These issues must be brought to the patient's attention before the procedure so that proper planning can take place before the examination. Difficulties with discharge arrangements should always be resolved before the endoscopic procedure and never left to be discussed after the procedure has been performed.

Although the previous process may seem cumbersome, there are significant advantages for both patient and endoscopist. These include the following:

- Ability to obtain informed consent
- Proper patient preparation
- Greater patient confidence with preparation
- Decreased failure to attend for endoscopic examinations
- Correct procedure being performed
- Improved diagnostic yield
- Decreased patient anxiety and potentially an improved patient tolerance of the procedure
- Improved discharge outcome

Preparation for Endoscopy and Enteroscopy[1]

Patients should not eat solid food for 6 hours or drink fluids for at least 4 hours before an elective endoscopy. These are minimum requirements. If a delay in gastric emptying is known or suspected, longer fasting or even a period of a fluid-only diet should be considered. If an adequate fasting time has not been completed, gastric lavage using a large-bore lavage tube may be necessary. In situations in which there is a delay in gastric emptying or in which there is an inadequate fasting time, there is a significant risk of pulmonary aspiration, and airway protection with airway intubation should be considered.

Normally it is acceptable for patients to take their usual medicines with a sip of water before endoscopy. Special consideration must be given to patients taking aspirin or anticoagulant medication or to those using hypoglycemic medication to treat diabetes (see separate section).

There are no data to support routine blood tests before diagnostic endoscopy, and screening tests are therefore not required. If a bleeding disorder is suspected or known, tests to evaluate this and direct therapy are indicated. Similarly if the patient's clinical condition is unstable or indicates that an abnormality in the blood tests is likely to be present, appropriate testing and correction of relevant abnormalities is indicated.

Preparation for Endoscopic Retrograde Cholangiopancreatography[1]

The preparation of patients for endoscopic retrograde cholangiopancreatography (ERCP) is similar to that for endoscopy. In general, patients undergoing ERCP almost always require sedation, and the duration of the procedure will be longer. This should be taken into account for the purposes of discharge planning.

Patients with suspected or proven biliary or pancreatic duct obstruction will generally be given prophylactic intravenous antibiotics (discussed in a later section). Antibiotics may also be given during or after the procedure if there is a clinical suspicion of inadequate duct drainage.

Before ERCP, it is important to determine if the patient has a known history of reaction to iodinated contrast agents. Although reaction to the contrast agent in allergic patients during ERCP is extremely uncommon, it is generally considered appropriate to administer prophylactic intravenous steroids, often in combination with an intravenous antihistamine agent. In severe cases, enlisting support of an anesthetist in case of a reaction is a prudent precaution. Appropriate resuscitation medication and facilities must be available.

Because the procedure is performed with radiologic imaging of the abdomen, patients who have had recent barium studies or other oral contrast agents should be checked to ensure that the field of view will be clear for the ERCP to be successfully completed. If there is residual contrast material in the gut, a formal bowel preparation may be required. Women of childbearing age must be asked if they are pregnant. If there is uncertainty, the ERCP may need to be deferred until the issue can be clarified. If ERCP is considered necessary in a pregnant woman, appropriate lead shielding of the lower abdomen is necessary to protect the fetus.

There are no data to support routine blood tests before diagnostic ERCP, and screening tests are generally not required. If a bleeding disorder is suspected or known, tests to evaluate this and direct therapy are indicated. Similarly if the patient's clinical condition is unstable or indicates that an abnormality in the blood tests is likely to be present, appropriate testing and correction of relevant abnormalities is indicated. For example, in patients presenting for ERCP with a history or signs of biliary obstruction, there exists the possibility of a disordered coagulation. Correction of this type of abnormality before the procedure is appropriate.

Preparation for Colonoscopy[1]

Of all endoscopic procedures, the quality of the preparation before colonoscopy has the greatest effect on the outcome of the procedure. The preparation is often regarded as the most unpleasant part of the procedure, and many patients are more concerned about this aspect than having the procedure performed. It is vital that the patient be given detailed verbal and written instructions in order for him or her to complete the preparation safely. If the correct preparation is not followed, the procedure will usually need to be deferred.

Good bowel preparation is essential to provide an optimal view for colonic examination and to minimize the risk of colonic trauma during the procedure resulting from poor view. To determine the correct preparation the clinician requires a careful patient assessment to determine which bowel cleansing agent should be used and what modifications to the patient's diet and regular medications are required.

Currently, the two widely accepted bowel preparations for colonoscopy are polyethylene glycol (PEG)–based solutions and sodium phosphate–based solutions. Stimulant and hyper-osmotic laxatives, such as castor oil, senna, mannitol, sorbitol, and lactulose, are no longer used as they are not very effective and carry risk of explosion during electrosurgical procedures.[2]

POLYETHYLENE GLYCOL–BASED PREPARATION

Golytely, developed in 1980, was the first osmotically balanced electrolyte purge solution. Since then, several modifications of the solution have been made to improve tolerability (Table 8–1). An oral purge using 4 L of a PEG-based solution, given the night before colonoscopy at the rate of approximately 1 L/hour, is associated with a good cleansing efficacy and reasonable patient tolerance.[3–5] Adding a flavor to the preparation is often preferred by patients. However, approximately 19% of patients are unable to complete the preparation because of its large volume and unpalatable taste.[6] Metoclopramide may be helpful in selected patients to decrease nausea and vomiting, although routine use of metoclopramide did not confer any significant benefit in a small, randomized trial.[7] PEG-based oral lavage (or indeed any form of bowel preparation) is contraindicated in patients with an ileus, significant gastric retention, suspected or established mechanical bowel obstruction, severe colitis, or neurologic impairment that prevents safe swallowing.[1] For patients with swallowing difficulties, a nasogastric tube can be used to administer the solution.

SODIUM PHOSPHATE–BASED PREPARATION

The sodium phosphate–based bowel preparation is a smaller volume and can be safely given to most healthy individuals. It is administered in split doses before the colonoscopy with the exact timing depending on the time that the colonoscopy is to be performed. It acts by exerting a hyperosmotic effect and by indirectly stimulating stretch receptors to increase peristalsis.[6] Available in both flavored and unflavored formulations, this bowel preparation has been shown to be superior in tolerance and at least as effective as PEG-based preparation.[6,9–12] However, because of its rapid osmotic effect and the possibility of significant hyperphosphatemia, it is recommended that this type of bowel preparation be avoided in patients sensitive to sudden volume shifts such as those with congestive heart failure and renal impairment. Caution is also required in patients with potential for disordered sodium or phosphate balance such as decompensated cirrhosis, small or large bowel dysmotility, and other preexisting electrolyte imbalances.[1,9,10,12] In addition, this preparation in not recommended in patients with proven or suspected inflammatory bowel disease because it can cause colonic inflammation and even aphthous ulceration in 25% of cases, compared with 2% to 3% in PEG-prepared patients.[13] Patients in whom this preparation is prescribed must be advised to drink as much clear fluids as can be tolerated to reduce the risk of dehydration and to facilitate the cleansing effect of the medication. For this reason it has been suggested that sodium phosphate–based preparations are not appropriate for elderly patients, but Thomson and coworkers[14] found that this preparation was safe, effective, and well tolerated in most elderly patients with a mean age of 72 years.

As part of the preparation, most patients will be advised to only have a clear liquid diet for 24 hours before examination.[1]

Routine blood testing before colonoscopy is not required but most clinicians recommend that antiplatelet and anticoagulation medications should be discontinued before the examination to minimize the risk of postprocedure bleeding (see later guidelines). In addition, any medication that might be associated with constipation should be temporarily stopped to facilitate the bowel cleansing process. In particular, oral iron can make the stool black and viscous, and this should be stopped at least 5 days before colonoscopic examination.[1] Lastly, specific instructions should be given to diabetic patients who are taking oral hypoglycemic medications and/or insulin to avoid periprocedural hypoglycemia.

Intravenous sedation is administered to most patients who undergo colonoscopy. It is, therefore, necessary for the patient to be fasted to reduce the potential for aspiration. The duration of fasting

Table 8–1. Different Formulations of PEG-Based Bowel Preparation						
Formulation	Na⁺ (meq/L)	K⁺ (meq/L)	Cl⁻ (meq/L)	HCO3⁻ (meq/L)	SO4⁻² (meq/L)	PEG3350 (gm/L)	Osmolality
Golytely	125	10	35	20	40	60	280
Nulytely	65	5	53	17	0	105	288
Colytely	125	10	35	20	80	60	280
Glycoprep	115	5	18	8	80	180	280
Colonlytely	125	10	35	20	40	59	280

PEG, polyethylene glycol.
Adapted from Keefe EB: Colonoscopy preps: What's best? Gastrointest Endosc 43:524–528, 1996.

can be comparatively brief because the patient will have only been on clear fluids for 24 hours before the procedure while undergoing bowel preparation. A fasting time of 2 to 4 hours is generally considered adequate.

There are a number of independent predictors of the potential for an inadequate bowel preparation such as a late colonoscopy start time; failure to follow preparation instructions; inpatient status; a procedural indication of constipation; use of tricyclic antidepressants; male gender; and a history of cirrhosis, stroke, dementia, or diabetes mellitus.[15–17] In these patients, a more prolonged bowel preparation may be required. For patients who continue to have a suboptimal preparation despite good compliance with the standard regimen, a 2-day clear fluid diet with preparation given on both days may be helpful. In addition, abstinence from fat within the diet for 1 week and a morning procedure time are recommended. In patients who develop nausea, vomiting, or excessive bloating, and who do not tolerate the preparation, one of the following measures can be used:

1. Stop the preparation early if a clear fecal fluid output is achieved.
2. Temporarily interrupt the preparation for 1 to 2 hours and then recommence.
3. Use a trial dose of metoclopramide.
4. Chill the bowel preparation solution.
5. Add clear, sugar-free flavor enhancers or lemon juice.
6. Slow the rate of consumption of the solution.

Preparation for Flexible Sigmoidoscopy[1]

Preparation before flexible sigmoidoscopy generally only requires cleansing of the left colon, and in some situations cleansing of the sigmoid and rectum is all that is needed. In most cases, this can be achieved by administering one or two enemas given 1 hour before the procedure. Currently, several types of enemas are available:

1. Microlax enema
2. Fleet enema (NaP)
3. Tap water enema
4. G&O enema (three parts glycerine, three parts olive oil, and three parts water)

A more extensive bowel preparation may be required in severely constipated patients or in those in whom a therapeutic procedure is required such as polypectomy or argon plasma coagulation therapy. In these cases, 2 L of PEG-based bowel preparation with 24 hours of clear fluid may be adequate. In contrast, bowel preparation may not be necessary in patients with active colitis or severe watery diarrhea. In general, patients undergoing flexible sigmoidoscopy do not receive intravenous sedation. If sedation is required, the patient should be advised to fast for 2 to 4 hours before the procedure.

Preparation for Endoscopic Ultrasound[1]

Patient preparation for this procedure is similar to upper gastrointestinal endoscopy. Patients must fast for 6 to 8 hours before the procedure. In patients in whom a biopsy or therapeutic intervention is considered necessary, a platelet count and coagulation studies may be appropriate before the procedure if a bleeding disorder is suspected. In addition, antiplatelet and anticoagulation therapies must be stopped 5 to 7 days before the procedure.

Preparation for Capsule Endoscopy or "Pill Cam"

Optimizing conditions for capsule endoscopy continues to be an area of interest. Most centers prefer a slightly longer fasting time than for routine endoscopy. In general, clear fluids are given after lunch on the day before the examination and the patient fasts for 12 hours before the examination is scheduled to begin. No medication should be taken within 2 hours of ingestion of the capsule. In some centers 2 L of a PEG-based bowel preparation regimen is given before the patient begins the 12-hour fast. This additional step might be particularly important if the patient has had a recent barium study or has had some other form of oral radiologic contrast agent. Some units ask the patient to ingest a small amount of antifoam preparation before the procedure, and some use a prokinetic such as metoclopramide. There are no data to indicate what is the optimal preparation regimen; therefore, the instructions can be individualized for the patient. It is prudent to review the patient's medication and consider holding any medication that might slow gastrointestinal motility. Iron supplements should be ceased at least 3 days prior to the examination.

Preparation for Endoscopic Procedures in Patients with Diabetes[1]

There are no controlled trials to guide preparation for endoscopic preparation in diabetic patients. The approach to these patients must be individualized, and factors such as usual glycemic control and the patient's ability to individually manage his or her diabetes are important considerations. There are no specific requirements in diabetic patients who are controlled on diet alone. In patients taking oral hypoglycemic agents, the medications are generally withheld during preparation for the procedure. During this time the patient must monitor their serum glucose and be able to get assistance if there is evidence of progressive hyperglycemia. Hypoglycemia is easily managed with sugar-containing clear fluids or candy. In patients taking insulin, dose reduction while undergoing the preparation is normal. Often the usual dose is given the evening before the procedure but only half the dose on the morning of the examination. The remaining dose can be given if appropriate after the procedure has been performed. Diabetic patients should preferentially be scheduled for a morning procedure and ideally be the first case for the day. During the preparation, the patient must monitor serum glucose and be given advice as to how to deal with either hypoglycemia or hyperglycemia.

Special Circumstances

PREPARATION FOR ENDOSCOPY IN CASE OF INGESTION OF A FOREIGN BODY OR FOR FOOD BOLUS OBSTRUCTION

Ingestion of foreign bodies occurs mainly in children and mentally disabled patients. Food bolus obstruction is relatively common in adults.[18,19] Endoscopic assessment and removal is the main modality of treatment for objects below the level of cricopharyngeal muscle. The nature of the patient symptoms will determine the urgency of the procedure. Emergency procedures should be performed for patients who are unable to swallow their saliva, those with sharp objects (fish bones, pins, dentures, and razor blades), and those with impacted disk batteries.[19,20] Plain x-ray films of the chest and neck may be advisable before the endoscopic procedure if the nature of the object or the site of obstruction is not clear from the history. The x-ray film may also show ectopic gas patterns to indicate a silent perforation. In general, oral radiologic contrast is best avoided because of the risk of aspiration and because it may obscure the endoscopic field.[21,22] With regard to food bolus impaction, glucagon can be given while the patient is waiting for the endoscopy, but this is usually unsuccessful and should not delay endoscopy.[23,24] Special attention should be given to airway protection to avoid the risk of airway obstruction during the procedure. Continuous oral suction and the availability of a laryngoscope are also important. General anesthesia with endotracheal intubation is indicated if airway protection is needed, but this is required in less than 25% of the cases.[25] In our experience, general anesthesia with muscle relaxation often facilitates removal of difficult or large items, particularly as they pass through the upper esophageal sphincter. This is particularly true for swallowed dentures (see Chapter 21).

PREPARATION FOR ENDOSCOPY IN PATIENTS WITH UPPER GASTROINTESTINAL BLEEDING

Preparation of an acutely bleeding patient for endoscopy requires additional precautions and care. The first step is to ensure that the patient is adequately resuscitated because any subsequent endoscopy is best performed when the patient is hemodynamically stable. If there is evidence of ongoing bleeding, urgent endoscopy with airway protection, even in an unstable patient, may be the best way of getting better clinical control of the situation. If time permits, a 6-hour fast is desirable, because this will improve the endoscopic view. Unfortunately, this is often not practical, particularly if there is evidence of active bleeding; therefore, gastric lavage may be required. Care must be taken not to suck too aggressively with the gastric lavage tube because significant mucosal trauma can occur and this can make interpretation of the subsequent endoscopic findings difficult. Some centers use antiemetic agents before urgent endoscopy in patients with suspected upper gastrointestinal bleeding to improve gastric emptying and thereby improve the endoscopic view. One randomized, placebo-controlled study has demonstrated improved endoscopic view with intravenous erythromycin administered 2 hours before endoscopy.[26]

Endoscopy in patients with upper gastrointestinal bleeding is usually performed after the patient has received intravenous sedation.[27] In many centers, emergency anesthetic assistance is frequently available, and there should be a low threshold to consider airway protection with endotracheal tube insertion. Significant pulmonary aspiration in an already unstable patient can have extremely serious consequences.

If the patient is suspected of having a bleeding peptic ulcer, consideration should be given to administering an intravenous proton pump inhibitor before the endoscopy. Studies have suggested that this can significantly improve outcome in these patients.[28–31] Similarly patients suspected of variceal bleeding may benefit from an octreotide infusion[32–34] (see Chapter 14).

PREPARATION FOR COLONOSCOPY IN PATIENTS WITH LOWER GASTROINTESTINAL BLEEDING

In patients with lower gastrointestinal bleeding, colonoscopy is the procedure of choice to identify the site of bleeding and in some circumstances allows therapeutic intervention[35] (see Chapter 15).

Before the procedure, patients should be resuscitated and have their general condition stabilized. Routine blood tests and coagulation profiles are generally performed in patients with gastrointestinal bleeding, and these should be corrected when appropriate. In general, most of the colonoscopies in patients with lower gastrointestinal bleeding are performed on a semiurgent basis to allow time for some sort of bowel preparation. The view at colonoscopy is often a problem in procedures performed urgently, although some studies suggest that urgent colonoscopy is not only technically possible and safe but also effective in controlling bleeding in some cases.[36,37] Blood itself is a cathartic; therefore, some clinicians are happy to perform the procedure in an unprepared bowel.[38] Most, however, prefer a bowel preparation and generally 4 L of PEG is given over 4 hours before the procedure.[36,39–41] This can be given orally or via a nasogastric tube. In elective procedures, the colon can be prepared in a standard fashion. Given that these patients are at higher risk of a disturbance of intravascular volume, it is generally advisable to avoid sodium phosphate–based preparations. A prokinetic agent may facilitate the bowel preparation.

In general, patients should not have barium studies before the colonoscopy because it will interfere with the view and may obscure flat mucosal lesions such as angiodysplasia. If an obstructive lesion is suspected, a clear water-soluble contrast agent such as Gastrografin should be used.

As for endoscopy in patients with upper gastrointestinal bleeding, it is important to ensure that the patient is appropriately sedated

Table 8–2. Risk Stratification of Bleeding for the Endoscopic Procedures and the Thromboembolic Conditions

	Low Risk	High Risk
Procedure classified according to risk of bleeding	Endoscopy, sigmoidoscopy and colonoscopy + biopsy ERCP without sphincterotomy Biliary/pancreatic stent without sphincterotomy EUS without FNA Enteroscopy	Polypectomy Biliary sphincterotomy Pneumatic or bougie dilation PEG insertion EUS with FNA Laser, argon ablation and coagulation Treatment of varices
Condition classified according to risk of thromboembolism if anticoagulation is discontinued	DVT Uncomplicated or paroxysmal nonvalvular atrial fibrillation Bioprosthetic valve Aortic prosthetic valve	Atrial fibrillation with valvular heart disease Mitral prosthetic valve Mechanical valve with prior thromboembolic event

DVT, deep venous thrombosis; ERCP, endoscopic retrograde cholangiopancreatography; EUS, endoscopic ultrasonography; FNA, fine needle aspiration; PEG, percutaneous endoscopic gastrostomy.
Reprinted from American Society for Gastrointestinal Endoscopy: Antibiotic prophylaxis for gastrointestinal endoscopy. Gastrointest Endosc 42:630–635, 1995, with permission from the American Society for Gastrointestinal Endoscopy.

and monitored during the procedure. In unstable patients, anesthetic assistance is advisable. In general these patients will already be fasted and a fasting time of 2 to 4 hours is appropriate. For stable patients, sedation as for routine colonoscopy is acceptable.

Antiplatelet and Anticoagulation Therapy

The decision to discontinue antiplatelet or anticoagulation therapy depends on two important factors: the risk of bleeding related to an endoscopic intervention and the risk of a thromboembolic event related to interruption of these medications. The risk stratification of these two factors is shown in Table 8–2. If anticoagulation therapy is only temporary, elective procedures should be delayed until the anticoagulation has been ceased.[42]

For anticoagulated patients who undergo a low-risk procedure, no adjustment to the anticoagulation therapy is needed, irrespective of the underlying condition. In contrast, anticoagulation therapy should be discontinued 3 to 5 days before the procedure in patients who undergo high-risk procedures, and anticoagulation therapy generally can be resumed the night of the procedure. The decision to obtain a preprocedure international normalized ratio (INR) should be individualized. For patients with high thromboembolic risk conditions, it is advisable to change the oral anticoagulants to intravenous heparin once the INR falls below the therapeutic level. Heparin should then be discontinued 4 to 6 hours before the procedure and can be resumed 2 to 6 hours after the procedure. In these patients, heparin and warfarin therapy should overlap until the INR has achieved the target therapeutic range.[43]

The exception is biliary sphincterotomy because the risk of major hemorrhage is between 10% and 15% if anticoagulation is resumed within 3 days of sphincterotomy.[44] The time to reinstitute anticoagulation therapy in patients following a sphincterotomy should be individualized and perhaps delayed if the risk of thromboembolism appears to be low.

In contrast, all endoscopic procedures can be performed in patients taking aspirin or other nonsteroidal anti-inflammatory drugs (NSAIDs) in standard doses provided that they do not have a preexisting bleeding disorder.[42] This recommendation is based on limited published studies suggesting that aspirin and NSAIDs in standard dose do not increase the risk of significant bleeding after gastroscopy or colonoscopy with biopsy, polypectomy, and even biliary sphincterotomy.[44,45] For newer antiplatelet agents, such as ticlopidine, clopidogrel, and dipyridamole, there are no data available to make a firm recommendation. However, it is advised to discontinue these agents 5 to 7 days before high-risk procedures, particularly in patients who are on concomitant aspirin or NSAID therapy.[42]

Management of Disorders of Hemostasis Before Endoscopic Examinations

The management of patients with hemostasis disorders should be individualized and when possible should be in close collaboration with an experienced hematologist in a specialized center with a special coagulation laboratory. The endoscopist must assess the risk of bleeding based on the procedural risk and the severity of the underlying disorder of hemostasis and plan the endoscopic procedure accordingly.[46]

von WILLEBRAND'S DISEASE
von Willebrand's disease (vWD) is the most common inherited disorder of hemostasis, and therapy before endoscopic procedures is dependent on the type of the vWD. For the less severe type I disease, treatment with desmopressin (DDAVP) starting 1 hour before the procedure and once daily thereafter for 2 to 3 days is adequate for patients undergoing diagnostic procedures and mucosal biopsies. However, for therapeutic procedures, infusion of factor VIII 1 hour before the procedure to achieve a factor VIII activity of 0.80 to 1.20 U/mL is required. After the procedure, factor VIII activity of at least 0.30 to 0.50 U/mL must be maintained for up to 2 weeks, to minimize the risk of rebleeding.[46] For the more severe

Table 8–3. Risk Stratification of Bacteremia and Infection for Endoscopic Procedures and Cardiac Conditions

Risk Level	Endoscopic Procedures with Risk of Bacteremia	Cardiac Conditions at Risk of Bacterial Endocarditis
Low risk	Gastroscopy, sigmoidoscopy and colonoscopy with or without mucosal biopsy, polypectomy and/or nonvariceal hemostasis interventions	Previous coronary bypass, cardiac pacemakers and implanted defibrillators, mitral valve prolapse (MVP) or previous rheumatic fever without valvular dysfunction or regurgitation
Intermediate risk		Most congenital cardiac malformation, rheumatic and other acquired valvular dysfunction (even after surgical correction), hypertrophic cardiomyopathy, MVP with valvular regurgitation
High risk	Esophageal stricture dilation, varix sclerosis, and ERCP with known or suspected bile duct obstruction	Prosthetic heart valves, previous history of endocarditis, surgically constructed systemic-pulmonary shunts or conduits

ERCP, endoscopic retrograde cholangiopancreatography.
Reprinted from American Society for Gastrointestinal Endoscopy: Antibiotic prophylaxis for gastrointestinal endoscopy. Gastrointest Endosc 42:630–635, 1995, with permission from the American Society for Gastrointestinal Endoscopy.

type II and III disease, the same factor VIII replacement regimen is required for both diagnostic (maintenance duration of 2 to 3 days) and therapeutic procedures (up to 2 weeks).[46]

HEMOPHILIA A AND B

Preprocedural assay of factor VIII or IX activity is essential to determine the dosage of replacement therapy in patients with hemophilia. Before the procedure, factor VIII infusion is required to achieve an activity of 0.80 to 1.20 U/mL. Postinfusion factor assay should be obtained to determine the patient's response to the infusion. For purely diagnostic procedures, no further infusion is required. If mucosal biopsies are performed, 75% of the initial dose should be given every 24 hours for an additional 2 to 3 days. If therapeutic procedures are performed, twice daily factor VIII infusion is required to achieve a maintenance activity of 0.30 to 0.50 U/mL for up to 2 weeks. Adequate factor VIII maintenance activity must be confirmed by at least daily factor VIII assay. Indications for factor IX replacement are identical to those for factor VIII infusion, except that the maintenance dose is administered at intervals of 24 hours because the half-life of factor IX is longer.[46]

LIVER DISEASE

The possible hemostatic defects in patients with liver disease are coagulopathy and thrombocytopenia. Correction is usually not required for diagnostic endoscopic procedures, but most centers would consider correction if the INR is greater than 2.5; correction is necessary if therapeutic maneuvers are needed. These recommendations are based on limited data. If high-risk procedures are carried out, correction of an INR of less than 1.4 to 1.7 is advisable.[46] This can be accomplished by a combination of fresh frozen plasma and vitamin K replacement. Correction of significant thrombocytopenia is discussed later.

RENAL FAILURE

The main hemostatic defect in patients with renal failure is an acquired qualitative platelet defect secondary to uremia. Fortunately, bleeding complications in these patients undergoing renal biopsy, abdominal surgery, liver and bone biopsies, or tooth extraction are rare.[47] In addition, preprocedural bleeding time measurement is not helpful because it does not predict outcome.[47] Platelet infusion is not routinely recommended, unless concurrent significant thrombocytopenia exists.[46] Because uremia is thought to be the cause of platelet dysfunction, dialysis with limited heparin shortly before high-risk procedures is recommended to lower serum urea nitrogen below 50 to 75 mg/dL.[46,48]

THROMBOCYTOPENIA

There are no prospective data on the need for prophylactic platelet transfusion, and the following guidelines have been based on decision analysis.[46,49,50] Platelet transfusion to raise the platelet count to higher than 20×10^9 platelets/litre is required for low-risk procedures and a count of greater than 50×10^9 platelets/litre is required for high-risk therapeutic procedures. For patients with immune thrombocytopenia, elective procedures should be postponed until an appropriate improvement in platelet count ($20–30\times10^9$ platelets/litre) is observed with standard therapy. If endoscopic procedures can not be postponed and immediate intervention is necessary, a platelet transfusion should be given just before the procedure.[46] If bleeding occurs after the procedure, further platelet transfusion should be given. Intravenous methylprednisolone and gamma globulin can be used if response to platelet transfusion is poor.[46]

Antibiotic Prophylaxis

Although the practice of antibiotic prophylaxis in gastrointestinal endoscopy is widely adopted, the evidence for its use is scanty and remains controversial. The risk of infectious complications from gastrointestinal endoscopic procedures appears to be low, and only very few published reports of infective endocarditis are directly attributable to an endoscopic procedure.[51]

So far, there are no prospective controlled trials to show that antibiotic prophylaxis before endoscopic procedures prevents infective endocarditis. Much of the data are inferred from surgical and dental studies.

Several procedural and patient factors must be considered for appropriate use of antibiotic prophylaxis before endoscopic procedure. These are outlined in Table 8–3.

Antibiotic prophylaxis against bacterial endocarditis is indicated for patients with high-risk lesions undergoing high-risk procedures. For low-risk bacteremic endoscopic procedures, antibiotic prophylaxis is not recommended for patients with low- to intermediate-risk valvular heart disease. It is advisable to consider prophylaxis on a case-by-case basis for patients undergoing low-risk procedures with high-risk valvular lesions, because there are insufficient data to support its routine use.[51]

Patients with low- or intermediate-risk valvular disease undergoing high-risk bacteremic endoscopic procedures should be assessed on a case-by-case basis. Current evidence does not support the use of prophylactic antibiotics for all patients with low-risk valvular disease.[51] The current recommended regimen is intravenous (IV) ampicillin 1 to 2 g and gentamicin 1.5 to 2.0 mg/kg, 30 minutes before the procedure, followed by amoxicillin 1.5 g orally 6 hours after the procedure. For penicillin-allergic patients, vancomycin 1 g IV can be substituted.

ANTIBIOTIC PROPHYLAXIS FOR PATIENTS WITH SYNTHETIC VASCULAR GRAFT

Animal studies suggest that there is an increased risk of synthetic graft infection before complete pseudointimal coverage.[52] A single IV dose of preprocedure antibiotic significantly reduces the risk of graft infection while waiting for complete pseudointimal formation.[53] For humans, complete pseudointimal coverage of aortic graft is achieved by 1 year. Therefore, it is reasonable to include patient with synthetic vascular grafts in the high-risk group mentioned previously for the first 12 months following graft placement. In these patients, the standard antibiotic regimen given previously has been recommended.[51]

ANTIBIOTIC PROPHYLAXIS FOR PATIENTS WITH PROSTHETIC JOINT

No routine antibiotic is recommended because there are no data to support the use in these cases.[51] Some institutions suggest that prosthetic joints should be covered with antibiotics for the first 3 months following insertion.

ANTIBIOTIC PROPHYLAXIS FOR PERCUTANEOUS ENDOSCOPIC GASTROSTOMY

Cefazolin 1 g (or equivalent) 30 minutes before percutaneous endoscopic gastrostomy insertion is routinely recommended for all patients who are not already on antibiotics, because the risk of peristomal wound infection is significantly reduced.[54] However, for patients who are already on appropriate antibiotic, no additional prophylaxis is required.[51]

ANTIBIOTIC PROPHYLAXIS FOR PATIENTS WITH CIRRHOSIS AND ASCITES OR IN THE IMMUNOCOMPROMISED PATIENT

There are few data for solid recommendation in these patients. Routine antibiotic prophylaxis is not recommended for patients who undergo low- to intermediate-risk procedures. However, for high-risk procedures, prophylaxis should be considered on a case-by-case basis, and the antibiotic regimen should be tailored to the specific perceived risk.[51]

REFERENCES

1. American Society for Gastrointestinal Endoscopy: Preparation of patients for GI endoscopy. Gastrointest Endosc 57:446–450, 2003.
2. Bigard MA, Gaucher P, Lassalles C: Fatal colonic explosion during colonoscopic polypectomy. Gastroenterology 77:1307–1308, 1979.
3. Thomas G, Brozinsky S, Isenberg J: Patient acceptance and effectiveness of a balanced lavage solution (Golytely) vs. the standard preparation for colonoscopy. Gastroenterology 82:435–437, 1982.
4. Matter SE, Rice PS, Campbell DR: Colonic lavage solutions: Plain versus flavored. Am J Gastroenterol 88:49–53, 1993.
5. Diab FH, Marshall JB: The palatability of five colonic lavage solutions. Alimentary Pharmacol Ther 10:815–818, 1996.
6. Hsu CW, Imperiale TF: Meta-analysis and cost comparison of polyethylene glycol lavage versus sodium phosphate for colonoscopy preparation. Gastrointest Endosc 48:276–231, 1998.
7. Brady CE, DiPalma JA, Pierson WP: Golytely lavage—Is metoclopramide necessary? Am J Gastroenterol 80:180–183, 1985.
8. Keefe EB: Colonoscopy preps: What's best? Gastrointest Endosc 43:524–528, 1996.
9. Vanner SJ, MacDonald PH, Paterson WG, et al: A randomized prospective trial comparing oral sodium phosphate with standard polyethylene glycol-based solution (Golytely) in the preparation of patients for colonoscopy. Am J Gastroenterol 85:422–427, 1990.
10. Kolts BE, Lyles WE, Achem SR, et al: A comparison of the effectiveness and patient tolerance of oral sodium phosphate, castor oil and standard electrolyte lavage for colonoscopy or sigmoidoscopy preparation. Am J Gastroenterol 88:1218–1221, 1993.
11. Cohen SM, Wexner SD, Binderow SR, et al: Prospective, randomized, endoscopic-blinded trial comparing pre-colonoscopy bowel cleansing methods. Dis Colon Rectum 37:689–692, 1994.
12. Frommer D: Cleansing ability and tolerance of three bowel preparations for colonoscopy. Dis Colon Rectum 40:100–104, 1997.
13. Zwas FR, Cirillo NW, El-Serag HB, Eisen RN: Colonic mucosal abnormalities associated with oral sodium phosphate solution. Gastrointest Endosc 43:463–466, 1996.
14. Thomson A, Naidoo P, Crotty B: Bowel preparation for colonoscopy: A randomized prospective trial comparing sodium phosphate and polyethylene glycol in a predominantly elderly population. J Gastroenterol Hepatol 11:101–107, 1996.
15. Church JM: Effectiveness of polyethylene glycol antegrade gut lavage bowel preparation for colonoscopy—Timing is the key! Dis Colon Rectum 41:1223–1225, 1998.
16. Ness RM, Manam R, Hoen H, Chalasani N: Predictors of inadequate bowel preparation for colonoscopy. Am J Gastroenterol 96:1797–1801, 2001.
17. Taylor C, Schubert ML: Decreased efficacy of polyethylene glycol lavage solution in the preparation of diabetic patients for outpatient colonoscopy: A prospective and blinded study. Am J Gastroenterol 96:710–715, 2001.
18. Vizcarrondo F, Brady PG, Nord HJ: Foreign bodies of the upper gastrointestinal tract. Gastrointest Endosc 29:208–210, 1983.
19. Mosca S, Manes G, Martino L, et al: Endoscopic management of foreign bodies in the upper gastrointestinal tract: Report on a series of 414 adult patients. Endoscopy 33:692–696, 2001.
20. Ginsberg GG: Management of ingested foreign objects and food bolus impactions. Gastrointest Endosc 41:33–38, 1995.
21. Cheng W, Tam PK: Foreign body ingestion in children: Experience with 1265 cases. J Pediatr Surg 34:1472–1476, 1999.

22. Eisen GM, Baron TH, Dominitz JA, et al: Guideline for the management of ingested foreign bodies. Gastrointest Endosc 55:802–806, 2002.
23. Ferrucci JT, Long JA: Radiological treatment of esophageal food impaction using intravenous glucagon. Radiology 125:25–28, 1977.
24. Trenkner SW, Maglinte DD, Lehman GA, et al: Esophageal food impaction: Treatment with glucagon. Radiology 149:401–403, 1983.
25. Webb WA: Management of foreign bodies of the upper gastrointestinal tract. Gastrointestinal Endoscopy 41:39–51, 1995.
26. Coffin B, Pocard M, Panis Y, et al: Erythromycin improves the quality of EGD in patients with acute upper GI bleeding: A randomized controlled study. Gastrointest Endosc 56:174–179, 2002.
27. Waye JD: Intubation and sedation in patients who have emergency upper GI endoscopy for GI bleeding. Gastrointest Endosc 51:768–771, 2000.
28. Javid G, Masoodi I, Zargar SA, et al: Omeprazole as adjuvant therapy to endoscopic combination injection sclerotherapy for treating bleeding peptic ulcer. Am J Gastroenterol 111:280–284, 2001.
29. Udd M, Miettinen P, Palmu A, et al: Regular-dose versus high-dose omeprazole in peptic ulcer bleeding: A prospective randomised double-blind study. Scand J Gastroenterol 36:1332–8, 2001.
30. Zed PJ, Loewen PS, Slavik RS, Marra CA: Meta-analysis of proton pump inhibitors in the treatment of bleeding peptic ulcers. Ann Pharmacother 35:1528–1534, 2001.
31. Higgins RM, Scates AC, Lantour JK: Intravenous proton pump inhibitors versus H2-antagonists for the treatment of GI bleeding. Ann Pharmacother 37:433–437, 2003.
32. Erstad BL: Octreotide for acute variceal bleeding. Ann Pharmacother 35:618–626, 2001.
33. Banares R, Albillos A, Rincon D, et al: Endoscopic treatment versus endoscopic plus pharmacologic treatment for acute variceal bleeding: A meta-analysis. Hepatology 35:609–615, 2002.
34. D'Amico G, Pietrosi G, Tarantino I, Pagliaro L: Emergency sclerotherapy versus vaso-active drugs for variceal bleeding in cirrhosis: A Cochrane meta-analysis. Gastroenterology 124:1277–1291, 2003.
35. Zuccarow G: Management of the adult patient with acute lower gastrointestinal bleeding. Am J Gastroenterol 93:1202–1208, 1998.
36. Jensen DM, Machicado GA, Jutabha R, Kovacs TO: Urgent colonoscopy for diagnosis and treatment of severe diverticular hemorrhage. N Engl J Med 342:78–82, 2000.
37. Jensen DM, Machicado GA: Diagnosis and treatment of severe hematochezia. The role of urgent colonoscopy after purge. Gastroenterology 95:1569–1567, 1988.
38. Rossini FP, Ferrari A, Spandre M, et al: Emergency colonoscopy. World J Surg 13:190–192, 1989.
39. Machicado GA, Jensen DM: Acute and chronic management of lower gastrointestinal bleeding: Cost-effective approaches. Gastroenterologist 3:189–201, 1997.
40. Faigel DA, Eisen GM, Baron TH, et al: Preparation of patients for GI endoscopy Gastrointest Endosc 57:446–450, 2003.
41. Thomas G, Brozinsky S, Isenberg JI: Patient acceptance and effectiveness of a balanced lavage solution (Golytely) versus the standard preparation for colonoscopy. Gastroenterology 82:435–437, 1982.
42. Eisen GM, Baron TH, Dominitz JA, et al: Guideline on the management of anticoagulation and antiplatelet therapy for endoscopic procedures. Gastrointest Endosc 55:775–779, 2002.
43. Geerts WH, Jay RM: Oral anticoagulants in the prevention and treatment of venous thromboembolism. In Poller I, Hirsch J (eds): Oral Anticoagulants. New York, Oxford University Press, 1996, pp 97–122.
44. Freeman M, Nelson D, Sherman S, et al: Complications of endoscopic biliary sphincterotomy. N Engl J Med 335:909–918, 1996.
45. Shiffman ML, Farrell MT, Yee YS: Risk of bleeding after endoscopic biopsy or polypectomy in patients taking aspirin or other NSAIDs. Gastrointest Endosc 40:458–462, 1994.
46. Van Os EC, Kamath PS, Goustout CJ, Heit JA: Gastroenterological procedures among patients with disorders of hemostasis: Evaluation and management recommendations. Gastrointest Endosc 50:536–543, 1999.
47. Diaz-Buxo JA, Donadio JV: Complications of percutaneous renal biopsy: An analysis of 1000 consecutive biopsies. Clin Nephrol 4:223–227, 1975.
48. Zachee P, Vermylen J, Boogaerts MA: Hematologic aspects of end-stage renal failure. Ann Hematol 69:33–40, 1994.
49. Schiffer CA: Prophylactic platelet transfusion. Transfusion 32:295–298, 1992.
50. Shulkin DJ, Fox KR, Stadtmauer EA: Guidelines for prophylactic platelet transfusions: Need for a concurrent outcomes management system. Qual Rev Bull 18:477–479, 1992.
51. American Society For Gastrointestinal Endoscopy: Antibiotic prophylaxis for gastrointestinal endoscopy. Gastrointest Endosc 42:630–635, 1995.
52. Malone J, Moore W, Campagna G, Bean B: Bacteremic infectability of vascular grafts: The influence of pseudointimal integrity and duration of graft function. Surgery 78:211–216, 1975.
53. Moore W, Rosson C, Hall A: Effect of prophylactic antibiotics in preventing bacteremic infection of vascular prostheses. Surgery 69:825–828, 1971.
54. Jain NK, Larson DE, Schroeder KW, et al: Antibiotic prophylaxis for percutaneous endoscopic gastrostomy. Ann Intern Med 107:824–828, 1987.

Reporting, Documentation, and Risk Management

Ian Norton and Kenneth W. Schroeder

Introduction

Endoscopic services have developed rapidly over the past 30 years such that the practice of gastroenterology is a procedural specialty for most practitioners. Procedural activities carry specific risks to the patient and expose the gastroenterologist to more potential for litigation than many other physicians. This is particularly the case with respect to gastroenterologists because most procedures are performed on "the walking well," patients without a defined major illness who, therefore, have little expectation of a poor outcome (compared, for example, to cardiologists performing infarct angioplasty). Despite this, a recent review of medical claims in the United States ranked gastroenterologists 23rd of 28 specialties in number of claims.[1]

It is an unfortunate reality of practice for gastroenterologists in many societies that malpractice litigation is a real possibility (or even probability) during their career. Nothing can eliminate this risk, but sound medical practice, good documentation, and appropriate informed consent processes will reduce the chance of both poor outcomes and litigation when adverse events occur. These are all elements of good practice; therefore, the principles outlined in this chapter are as relevant to those practicing in highly litigious environments (e.g., the United States and Australia) and in areas where litigation is almost nonexistent (e.g., New Zealand and parts of Western Europe). These regional differences are partly due to patient (consumer) expectation and to the local legal compensation framework.

Relationship of Medical Practice to Litigation

Several large studies have examined the impact of medical error on patient care.[2–5] Up to 36% of hospital admissions are associated with some form of error during the admission, usually trivial and of no clinical impact. However, a study of 20,000 surgical admissions noted an iatrogenic disability rate of 4.6%. Most of these were attributable to "acceptable risk," but the authors concluded that 17% of these injuries would have probably been successfully litigated. Thus, almost 1% of surgical admissions could result in a successful suit against the surgeon. However, in the Harvard Medical Practice Study[4] less than 2% of patients with an iatrogenic injury filed a claim. Clearly, other factors determine whether a claim is filed. Several studies have addressed this issue and have found that the major determinants of a patient's decision whether to sue are patient dissatisfaction and the physician's communicative and interpersonal skills.[6–9] The clear message here is that communication with the patient and family is of utmost importance, particularly when mishaps occur. Patients suffering a significant complication will often have their care transferred to the appropriate specialist for correction of the problem (e.g., intensivist or surgeon). It is an important risk management strategy to be available to the patient and family even if no longer participating in the direct care of the patient. This will demonstrate empathy and prevent anger arising from the perception of being "abandoned" by the physician.

CLAIMS AGAINST GASTROENTEROLOGISTS

Data in this area are difficult to assess because not all insurers are equally forthcoming with their data and some major U.S. institutions self-insure and do not release their data for review. However, the Physician Insurers Association of America pools information from 20 member insurers and periodically publishes their data.[1] These data have also been reviewed and published in the gastrointestinal (GI) literature.[10,11] The claims fall into the following groups:

1. Iatrogenic injury. Nearly 30% of claims related to improper endoscopic practice causing injury. Ninety-five percent of these cases were perforation or laceration of the gut and its sequelae. Other injuries such as pancreatitis, hemorrhage, dental injury, and falling from the bed while sedated also constituted claims.
2. Errors in diagnosis. About 25% of claims related to errors in diagnosis, two thirds of which were missed malignancies, particularly of the right colon and stomach. Missed colon cancer constituted more than 50% of colonoscopic claims and more than 75% of claims relating to sigmoidoscopy. Another

relatively frequent scenario was delay in diagnosis of malignancy through failure to perform endoscopic examinations. When claims against gastroenterologists were examined, another frequent scenario was delayed diagnosis of non-GI tract neoplasia, especially gynecologic and pulmonary. Clearly, gastroenterologists must be diligent in investigating the GI tract and in ensuring that their endoscopic examination is adequate (both in terms of bowel preparation and in ensuring that the cecum is reached, or if not, that further steps are taken to complete the evaluation). Furthermore, they must be clear where their duty of care to the patient ends. For example, a 60-year-old woman with new-onset abdominal bloating is referred to a gastroenterologist. It is not adequate to merely examine the bowel, find no abnormality, and reassure the patient. In this circumstance, the physician must either investigate further or make it clear to the referring physician and patient that, although the GI tract is normal, other possibilities (e.g., ovarian cancer) should be considered.

3. Medication error. This was relatively uncommon, accounting for less than 10% of gastroenterology claims. However, two notable areas are endoscopist-supervised sedation and prescription of corticosteroids and immunosuppressive agents.

Overall, approximately two thirds of claims against gastroenterologists could be considered "cognitive" and one third "procedural mishap." Problems with informed consent were factors in about half the cases.

Specific Endoscopic Procedures

In the Gerstenberger study of 610 endoscopic claims,[10,12] it is interesting to note that the relative risk of litigation arising from various procedures (relative to sigmoidoscopy) varied by less than a factor of two: sigmoidoscopy (1.0), gastroscopy (1.2), colonoscopy (1.7), and endoscopic retrograde cholangiopancreatography (ERCP) (1.6) despite the fact that ERCP and colonoscopy result in far more complications than sigmoidoscopy and gastroscopy. This seeming paradox is probably explained by the use of more intensive informed consent processes for ERCP and colonoscopy compared with the technically less challenging procedures. This illustrates the important principle of informed consent as a risk management strategy (discussed later).

Legal Principles in Medical Practice

PRINCIPLES OF TORT LAW

Claims for medical negligence fall under the principles of tort law. A knowledge of the principles of tort law is germane to the physician's understanding of his or her responsibilities. Torts are "civil wrongs" in which one private citizen has brought legal proceedings against another (in this case, the physician). It does not involve criminal behavior and is usually settled with financial compensation to the injured party (the award of "damages").

Tort law (with respect to medical negligence) involves four steps:

1. A duty. The physician's responsibility to the patient to comply with professional standards of practice.

2. A breach of duty. The physician did not fulfill that responsibility.
3. Causation. The physician's failure was a proximate cause of the patient's suffering.
4. Injury. The patient suffered a defined injury (physical, financial, or psychological).

Duty

The physician's duty to the patient comes from the doctor-patient relationship (i.e., a contract that the physician enters into with the patient to provide the patient with medical services to a reasonable standard). It is important to remember that this does not necessarily mean a consultation. An example of this might be a complication arising from a preparation suggested for a patient undergoing an open-access procedure. One way to reduce liability to the patient is to clearly demarcate where duty of care begins and ends. For example, if a physician diagnoses colon cancer, it is prudent to clearly document a management plan with subsequent specialists, to ensure that the patient understands the condition and how it is being managed, and to ensure that both the patient and his or her primary care physician are aware of this plan and how to take this management further. This will prevent complications from delay in definitive management and might help to reduce subsequent vicarious liability (e.g., the level of responsibility for subsequent malpractice by other health professionals).

A Breach of Duty

Once the patient-physician relationship is entered into, a breach of duty occurs when the physician fails to provide a reasonable standard of care. This reasonable standard is often difficult to define and will usually be established with the aid of expert witnesses. This does not mean to the level of an emeritus professor in that field but to a level acceptable to the physician's peers, that is, sound medical practice (published guidelines can be useful in this context but ironically are more often used for the plaintiff's case!). Many societies (e.g., the American Society for Gastrointestinal Endoscopy [ASGE], British Society of Gastroenterology [BSG], and Gastroenterological Society of Australia [GESA]) publish guidelines for endoscopic practice. The ASGE's set of guidelines, in particular, is an excellent resource that is available on the Internet. Of course, medical practice often varies depending on many variables such as comorbidities, patient wishes, physician expertise, and available resources. If one deviates substantially from common practice, it is essential to note the reasons for this in the medical record.

Causation

The plaintiff must prove that the physician's breach of duty caused the injury. The breach must be a "proximate cause" or a substantial (vs. remote) factor in bringing about the injury. For example, a patient with weight loss, back pain, and diabetes has an endoscopic ultrasound that fails to diagnose a pancreatic cancer. The patient is diagnosed with metastatic disease to the liver 2 months later. Although the endoscopist missed the lesion, it is unlikely that finding it would have altered the eventual outcome. This example also highlights the fact that no procedure is 100% sensitive, and the endoscopist's report and subsequent communication with the referring physician should reflect this fact, perhaps with suggestions for further assessment if the clinical suspicion is high.

Injury

The patient must be able to demonstrate some form of suffering. This will usually be physical, including the steps necessary to correct the initial injury (e.g., colonic perforation followed by surgery). In some circumstances, the injury could be psychological, although this is clearly harder to prove and quantify. Monetary losses because of the injury (e.g., medical costs, lost earnings, and future lost earnings) are also a relevant factor. Intangibles such as pain and suffering and emotional distress are also compensable in the United States.

Damages

As mentioned previously, the outcome of a successful malpractice suit is usually a monetary assessment of damages. The total payout may be composed of three types of damages:

1. General damages. This includes payment for pain and suffering.
2. Special damages. Compensation for medical expenses, lost earnings, future earning capacity, and so forth.
3. Punitive damages. This is a payment as a punishment for gross negligence. This usually means conscious indifference, fraud, or intentional harm and is rarely part of medical malpractice awards. Punitive damages may not be covered by malpractice insurance.

STANDARDS OF CARE

This is a legal concept that attempts to determine the duty that physicians must fulfill in their care of the patient. Failure to practice to this standard constitutes a breach of duty. The court usually determines this standard by hearing expert testimony and by reliance on published data such as peer-reviewed journal articles and practice guidelines.[13,14] Thus, the standard is tailored to the specific case under review and should reflect current practice at the time of the injury. Therefore, although society practice guidelines, publications, and so forth may be an important part of the evidence used to help determine this standard, they do not replace the court's or jury's determination in a particular case. Similarly, a case's judgment is not designed to dictate future clinical practice (although this often is the case).

The standard of care is best described as good patient care. It is not defined as best medical practice (e.g., the care provided by a world leader in a field) but rather on what would be expected from a peer under the same circumstances.

Majority and Minority Standards

There are often many ways to manage a clinical problem. In general, it is easier to defend the approach taken by most peers (the majority standard). Less common approaches or a minority standard may be valid but if used should ideally be accompanied by good documentation explaining why the usual clinical pathway was not followed and by clear documentation that alternative strategies and their relative risks and benefits were discussed with the patient. Many societies (e.g., the ASGE) publish excellent guidelines for endoscopic practice. Generally, adhering to guidelines such as these

is a good risk management strategy. Conversely, physicians who practice in ignorance of the majority standard do so at their peril.

DEFINING RESPONSIBILITY
Joint Liability and Comparative Fault

This concept recognizes that many health care workers may be involved in the circumstances leading to an adverse outcome. Therefore, the blame may be appropriately shared over many doctors, nurses, institutions, and so forth. For example, a colonic perforation is not, of itself, necessarily negligent. However, if it occurs with inadequate consent, liability may be shared by the endoscopist and by the referring physician and the nurse who obtained consent.

Respondeat Superior and Vicarious Liability

Respondeat superior is a legal term referring to the concept that a master is responsible for the mistakes of his servant. Vicarious liability means a corporation is responsible for the acts of its employees and agents. In this sense, a consultant supervising a fellow doing an ERCP may be liable for a proportion of the damages arising from a duodenal perforation. The degree of liability will vary depending on factors such as whether the patient had consented that the procedure would be performed by a trainee, the degree of seniority and supervision of the trainee, and whether the trainee was performing appropriately. Similarly, a physician may be held responsible for an adverse outcome resulting from incompetency by office staff, and hospitals may be held partly responsible for the mistakes of a physician in the employ of that institution.

INFORMED CONSENT

It is a basic legal principle that a competent individual has the right to determine what shall happen to his or her body. Thus, the physician must obtain the consent of the patient (or his or her legal guardian) before performing any procedure, with certain exceptions (discussed later). Historically, touching a patient without the patient's consent constituted a battery (a criminal offense). However, over time, negligence theory has tended to replace battery when cases of inadequate consent are tried. Hence, inadequate consent issues are likely to be heard in civil rather than criminal proceedings.

It is crucial to understand that informed consent is a *process*, not a signed piece of paper. Although most institutions use a signed consent form, it is usually a generic document and, therefore, may not reflect that the patient was aware of all the elements necessary for informed consent for that particular procedure in that particular patient. Nonetheless, a signed consent form is very useful in court as tangible evidence that a defendant did go through some process of consent and had the opportunity to ask questions.

Several elements constitute informed consent:

1. Risks. All procedures have some risk, and patients must be made aware of any risk that, in the view of a reasonable person, might have played a role in that specific patient's decision to proceed. This typically includes the most severe complications (e.g., death, hemorrhage, disability) and common side effects.

2. Benefits. The patient must understand why he or she is undergoing the procedure.
3. Alternatives. The patient must understand the relative risks and benefits of alternative investigations. The patient should also understand the alternative of not performing any procedure. Unfortunately, the courts have struggled with what constitutes reasonable disclosure of alternatives. Certainly, it should be a discussion of alternatives relevant to the patient concerned and not a recitation of medical casebook history.[15]
4. The opportunity to ask questions.

With regard to all these elements is the difficulty of standard of disclosure. Traditionally, the "professional standard of disclosure" has been used. This standard may be defined as "as much information as would have been provided by a physician's peers in the same situation" and was defined by a landmark case in 1960.[16] It assumes that the physician is acting in the best interest of the patient. However, it was noticed in the 1970s that this standard implies a somewhat paternalistic doctor-patient relationship that impinges on the patient's right to self-determination. Thus, the "lay" or "patient-oriented" standard has evolved. This was first enunciated in 1972 when a judge commented that:

> … a risk is thus material when a reasonable person, *in what the physician knows or should know to be the patient's position*, would be likely to attach significance to the risk or cluster of risks in deciding whether or not to forego the proposed therapy.[17]

In other words, the lay standard dictates that the physician must supply any information to which *that particular patient* would attach significance (e.g., a 1:10,000 risk of pharyngeal perforation might hold different significance to an opera singer compared with a layperson of the general public). This standard is potentially much more difficult for the physician to defend, because it requires a subjective assessment of what that *specific* patient would want to know.

It is important for the physician to avoid coercion of any sort. The physician should not be judgmental or emotive when explaining the procedure or the consequences of not following medical advice. Furthermore, it has been proposed by some that obtaining informed consent in the endoscopy room immediately before the procedure could be perceived as being coercive in that the patient, being prepared, gowned, having taken time off work, and possibly having an IV *in situ*, is unlikely to back out of the procedure. In addition, the endoscopy suite environment is unlikely to provide the patient with an adequate opportunity to ask questions. These issues are especially important in the open-access endoscopy setting.

Obviously, informed consent must be obtained in the language suitable to the patient's comprehension. If the patient only speaks a foreign language, consent should be obtained through a health professional or interpreter service. The patient's friends or relatives should not be used for interpreting; this may constitute a breach of confidentiality and the patient may be misled by the friend's or relative's own biases about what he or she wishes the patient to hear.

In one study, a videotape discussing the proposed procedure was shown to patients and was found to be as useful as discussion with the physician without the use of the tape. If information tapes are used, there must be the opportunity for the patient to ask questions that might arise from the viewing.[18]

Exceptions to Informed Consent

1. Emergency. To satisfy the requirements for emergency, the patient must be incapacitated such that he or she cannot provide consent and that delay in obtaining consent from other sources would put the patient at risk of permanent disability or death. It may occasionally be appropriate to perform additional procedures during the patient's consented procedure, which could not have been reasonably foreseen and for which allowing the patient to recover only to submit to another procedure would be unreasonable. For example, it would be reasonable to biopsy a suspected early esophageal malignancy during a gastroscopy performed to assess peptic ulcer disease. Another example is that a patient may require an intervention to correct a mishap that occurred during the procedure.
2. Waiver. A patient may occasionally assign his or her right to determination to the physician for the management of a specific condition. This must be well documented, ideally with a document signed by the patient.
3. Therapeutic privilege. This is an unusual situation in which the physician believes that fully informing the patient would be a detriment to the patient. This usually refers to emotional issues. Clearly, there is a danger here that mental health patients could be denied a basic right of self-determination. The physician must fully document why he or she has withheld information and should provide as much information to the patient as possible.
4. Legal mandate. In some circumstances, the court may order that a patient undergo a medical procedure without requiring the patient's consent. Obtaining concealed contraband and forensic pathology specimens are examples. A more difficult situation is performing a procedure on a minor against the wishes of the parent.
5. Incompetency. If the patient is incompetent to make decisions, the responsibility of providing informed consent defers to the patient's legal guardian.

Informed Refusal

The inverse of informed consent is informed refusal. If a patient refuses specific medical treatment, there is a duty of care for the physician to ensure that the refusal is informed. For example, it is negligent to allow a patient to leave hospital against medical advice without informing him or her of the risks of doing so.

Documentation

Sound documentation is an important risk management tool and a component of good medical practice. Nothing in a patient's management plan should be left to the memory of the physician. A case may come to trial years after the event. It is highly unlikely that the physician will be able to remember details of a consultation with the clarity of the plaintiff (on whom this brief patient-physician interaction has had a major impact). The plaintiff will thus appear to be a much more credible witness unless the physician has comprehensive notes. In general, a court will accept that something was discussed or did occur if it was documented in the notes at the time. Conversely, a court or jury may decide that a conversation did not occur if the plaintiff denies it and the physician only remembers the conversation or states that it is always his or her practice to discuss a certain aspect of care. Videotaping the consent process has been mentioned as a (somewhat extreme) method of documenting exactly what occurred.[19]

Medical record retention laws vary, and the physician should be acquainted with how long records of adults and minors need to be retained. The physician owns the record, but the patient has the right to control access to the information. The patient has a right to see the medical record and copy it for an appropriate fee.

Documents should be concise, logical, and legible. All entries must be dated. One should never make demeaning or insulting comments about the patient. If an error occurs, it should be struck through once (still legible) and a correction made, signed, and dated. *Notations must never be altered.* Forensic techniques are available to determine whether numbers and so forth have been changed subsequently. Notations can be corrected or supplemented if the changes are clearly identified and dated.

ELECTRONIC MEDIA

The gist of telephone conversations should be recorded in the notes. E-mail is increasingly used to communicate with other health professionals and patients. A physician using e-mail should consider using encryption software to protect confidentiality. All communications should be printed, and a hardcopy should be kept with the notes. Patients communicating with their physician via e-mail must understand that sending an e-mail does not mean that the physician has received and read it. (This can be done with an automatic reply message warning patients of a delay and urging them to call or go to the nearest hospital if their concern is urgent.) They should also be aware that in many circumstances e-mail is a poor substitute for a standard consultation. Care must be taken to ensure the security of data kept on computers and PDAs. These devices are of particular concern because they may easily be lost and may not have adequate password protection to prevent data retrieval; the data may contain sensitive patient information. For this reason, some institutions have banned the use of PDAs for resident staff for the purposes of any record keeping.

PROCEDURE DOCUMENTATION

Procedures may be documented by dictated or handwritten notes or by notes generated by databases. Irrespective of the method of documentation, all procedural reports should contain the following information:

- Date
- Patient identification (at least name and medical record number)
- Proceduralist
- Assistants present
- Instrument used
- Sedation
- Monitoring
- Use of topical anesthesia
- Indication
- Findings
- Interventions performed

- Impediments to the study (e.g., preparation)
- Complications
- Recommendations
- Follow-up

It is wise to include postprocedure documentation because many patients will have persistent amnesia attributable to the effects of sedation at the time of discussion before leaving the endoscopy unit (despite appearing to be alert). This documentation should include advice regarding driving, important decision making, or dangerous activities following sedation; follow-up arrangements; and a plan in case of emergency following the procedure. Depending on the findings of the procedure and the level of relationship between the endoscopist and the patient, it may or may not be appropriate to include a summary of the findings of the procedure. There are several software reporting systems that incorporate many of the necessary elements of the report. This may also include embedding of photographs that may be used both to document pathology and to document adequacy of the examination (e.g., documentation of visualization of the ileocecal valve).

Risk Management

Risk management is an evolving process that aims to identify potential sources of poor outcome and to undergo steps to correct these issues. Risk management has the following objectives:

1. To define instances that place the endoscopist at risk
2. To determine the frequency and significance of these instances
3. To apply risk management to individual cases
4. To develop preventative measures

Many of the issues already discussed compose important aspects of risk management.

1. Sound medical practice. The best defense against poor outcomes and possible litigation is good medical practice. An important aspect of this is efforts on the part of the individual and the institution to remain current with the medical literature and to practice in line with government statutes and societal guidelines. It is important to note that courts have been reluctant to accept financial constraint as a mitigating factor when assessing a poor outcome (although, of course, this may shift some blame from the individual to the institution).
2. Good documentation.
3. Informed consent.
4. Peer review. This is a vital mechanism to identify endemic problems and to recognize and discuss problems to prevent their recurrence. This must always be done in a nonthreatening manner so as to maintain a true reflection of the unit's complication profile. It should be a formal process, usually involving a meeting of all senior staff on a regular basis with recording of minutes.

   The physician should be aware of his or her own complication profile and where he or she stands relative to peers. Some very experienced proceduralists may have high complication rates because of the complexity of work that they perform and, in this circumstance, should have some way of illustrating their work mix. Patients have a right to know, in general terms, the physician's complication and outcome profile.

5. Adequate indemnity insurance. Some large institutions may self-insure their employees, but it is the responsibility of every physician to ensure that he or she has adequate indemnity coverage both for claims occurring now and for claims that may occur years into the future (although many states have a statute of limitation on medical malpractice claims).

Medico-Legal Consultation

A detailed discussion of this field is beyond the scope of this textbook. An expert medical witness provides an important service to the community, provided that the opinion is unbiased. The American College of Physicians has developed guidelines to assist physicians engaged in this activity. These guidelines state that appropriate expert witnesses should be appropriately licensed and board certified and should have been practicing in the area for at least 3 of the previous 5 years. Reasonable compensation should be provided, but contingency fees (i.e., fee structure based on the outcome of the case) are unethical. Some states cap the proportion of income that a physician can derive from this type of activity. This is an effort to prevent "hired guns" who will provide opinions clouded by a perception of what the client would like them to say.

The opinion should be unbiased, such that it should be irrelevant to the expert whether he or she is retained by the plaintiff or defendant. The opinion must be nonemotive. In most cases, being an expert witness will require a review of a medical record and summarizing an opinion regarding the patient's care. Because most cases are resolved long before trial, usually this is all that will be needed. If the case does proceed toward trial, the witness may merely be required to supply an affidavit, give a deposition, or, less commonly, be required to testify in court. When in court, witnesses should have detailed notes and not rely on their memory of the case. Answers should be succinct and directly respond to the question. It is crucial to only answer the question posed and fight the tendency to embellish an answer. If one does not know the answer to a question, one should say so. Again, one should be nonemotive and recognize that it may be the aim of one of the teams to discredit answers and determine whether indeed one is an expert.

REFERENCES

1. Physician Insurers Association of America: A risk management review of malpractice claims: Gastroenterology. Summary Report. Rockville, MD, Research Department, Physician Insurers Association of America, 2000.
2. Brennan TA, Leape L, Laird N, et al: Incidence of adverse events and negligence in hospitalized patients. N Engl J Med 324:370–376, 1991.
3. Leape L, Brennan TA, Laird N, et al: The nature of adverse events in hospitalized patients: Results of the Harvard Malpractice Study II. N Engl J Med 324:377–384 1991.
4. Localio RA, Lawthers AG, Brennan TA: Relationship between malpractice claims and adverse events due to negligence. N Engl J Med 325:245–251, 1991.
5. Brennan TA, Sox CM, Burstin HR: Relationship between negligent adverse events and the outcomes of medical malpractice. N Engl J Med 335:1963–1967, 1996.
6. Hickson GB, Clayton EW, Entman SS, et al: Obstetricians' prior malpractice experience and patients' satisfaction with care. JAMA 272:1583–1587, 1994.
7. Hickson GB, Federspiel CF, Pichert JW, et al: Patient complaints and malpractice risk. JAMA 287:2951–2957, 2002.
8. Levinson W, Roter DL, Mullooly JP, et al: Physician-patient communication: The relationship with malpractice claims among primary care physicians and surgeons. JAMA 277:553–559, 1997.
9. Hickson GB, Clayton EW, Githens PB, Sloan FA: Factors that prompted families to file medical malpractice claims following perinatal injuries. JAMA 267:1359–1363, 1992.
10. Gerstenberger PD, Plumeri PA: Malpractice claims in gastrointestinal endoscopy: Analysis of an insurance industry database. Gastrointest Endosc 39:132–138, 1993.
11. Medical Malpractice Claims and Risk Management in Gastroenterology and Gastrointestinal Endoscopy. American Society for Gastrointestinal Endoscopy Web site: Available at http://www.asge.org (Accessed October 31, 2003).
12. Gerstenberger PD: Malpractice in gastrointestinal endoscopy. Gastrointest Endosc Clin N Am 5:375–389, 1995.
13. Mello MM: Of swords and shields: The use of clinical practice guidelines in medical malpractice litigation. Univ Penn Law Rev 149:645–710, 2000.
14. Hyams AL, Shapiro DW, Brennan TA: Medical practice guidelines in malpractice litigation: An early retrospective. J Health Polit Policy Law 21:289–313, 1996.
15. Dunham v Wright, 423 F2d 940, 946 (3d Cir 1970).
16. Natanson v Klein, 186 Kan 393, 350 P2d 1093, reh'g denied, 187 Kan 186, 354 P2d 670 (1960).
17. 4 F2d 772 (1972) 45.
18. Agre P, Kurtz RC, Krause BJ: A randomized trial using videotape to present consent information for colonoscopy. Gastrointest Endosc 40:271–276, 1994.
19. Plumeri PA: Informed consent for gastrointestinal endoscopy in the '90s and beyond. Gastrointest Endosc 40:379, 1994.

Small-Caliber Endoscopy

 Darius Sorbi and Christopher J. Gostout

CHAPTER 10

Introduction

Intuitively, the practice of unsedated small-caliber endoscopy is appealing. Sedation may be responsible for a substantial proportion of the morbidity and mortality of endoscopic procedures. Furthermore, the administration of sedatives increases the preprocedure preparation, total procedure, and postprocedure recovery times. Finally, the patient and an accompanying person miss a full day of work, adding to the overall cost to the society. Thus, the ability to perform endoscopy without sedation could be advantageous.

Despite its potential safety and cost effectiveness, however, the practice of unsedated endoscopy has not gained wide acceptance in the United States. A number of factors may be responsible. These include inadequate evidence for efficacy, poor patient acceptance, lack of physician incentives, limited opportunities for training, cost of equipment, and medico-legal issues. The purpose of this chapter is to review the technique of unsedated small-caliber endoscopy with particular attention to the feasibility, tolerability, adequacy, safety, and cost effectiveness. The practice of unsedated esophagoscopy is also reviewed because the procedures are closely related.

A systematic review of the English-language literature was carried out. A Medline search was performed from January 1966 to March 2003 using the following key words: "sedationless," "small caliber," "ultrathin," and "unsedated." Publications pertaining to esophagogastroduodenoscopy (EGD) or esophagoscopy were reviewed. Each manuscript was assessed for evidence supporting the feasibility, tolerance, adequacy, safety, and cost effectiveness of unsedated small-caliber EGD (sc-EGD) or esophagoscopy.

Small-Caliber Endoscopy Insertion Techniques

Unsedated small-caliber upper endoscopy can be performed either transnasally or perorally. Transnasal endoscopy is feasible with endoscopes measuring 6 mm or less in outside diameter. Table 10–1

summarizes the specifications of the small-caliber endoscopes used in the reviewed studies and other endoscopes that are commercially available. Both video esophagogastroduodenoscopes and esophagoscopes are currently available. The former scopes have a working length of 1030 to 1330 mm and the latter a working length of only 600 mm. The outer diameter of the video esophagogastroduodenoscopes range between 5.1 and 6 mm. The esophagoscopes have an outside diameter of 3.1 or 4 mm. The relative outside diameters of the small-caliber pediatric and conventional esophagogastroduodenoscopes are shown in Fig. 10–1A. Some esophagogastroduodenoscopes allow right and left and up and down angulation, whereas others provide only one ratchet for up and down angulation (Fig. 10–1B).

Patient selection and preparation is of utmost importance. Uncooperative patients and young female patients with a high preprocedure anxiety level are not well suited for unsedated procedures. Because the tolerability of the procedure is related to the preprocedure anxiety, the procedure must be clearly explained before intubation. Topical anesthesia is commonly used before endoscope insertion. This can be in the form of a spray or jelly. The application of lidocaine jelly into the more patent nostril as determined by visual inspection is strongly advised with transnasal intubation. Pharyngeal anesthesia is recommended for both the transnasal and peroral approaches. Application of local vasoconstrictors may also be beneficial especially when a 6-mm-diameter instrument is inserted transnasally. If a 4-mm or smaller caliber endoscope is used, this may be of marginal value to aid insertion but may minimize epistaxis.

The procedure can be performed either in the standard left lateral decubitus position for conventional endoscopy or in the upright position (Fig. 10–2). Whether the upright position decreases the aspiration risk is not known. The procedure should be performed with minimal air insufflation. The endoscope should be inserted slowly and gently. Vigorous movements of the endoscope cause greater nasal discomfort with the transnasal route and more gagging with the peroral approach. During the procedure, continuing a conversation and demonstrating findings on the video monitor reassures patients and may improve tolerability and reduce discomfort.

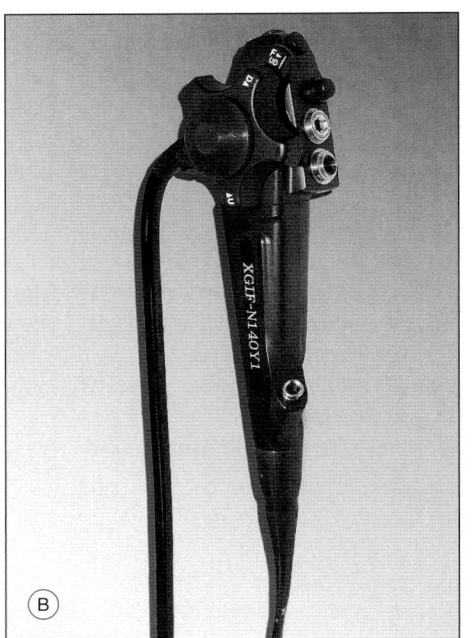

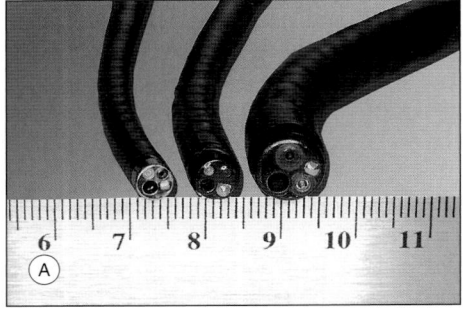

Figure 10–1. Small-caliber upper endoscopes. The distal ends of a small-caliber, a pediatric, and a conventional esophagogastroduodenoscope are shown *(A)* along with the handle of a small-caliber endoscope with only one ratchet for up and down control *(B)*.

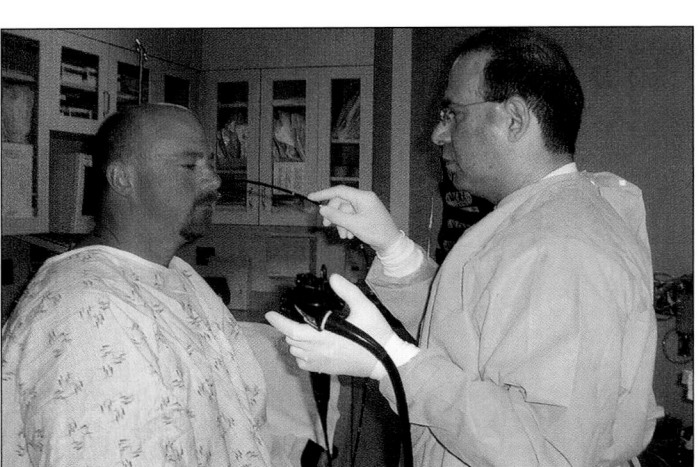

Figure 10–2. A patient is shown undergoing transnasal small-caliber esophagogastroduodenoscopy in the upright position.

Table 10–1. Fiberoptic and Video Small-Caliber Endoscopes Available for Unsedated Upper Endoscopy

Company/Model	Imaging	Outer Diameter* (mm)	Working Length (mm)	Instrument Channel (mm)	Angulation °Up/Down-°Right/Left
Pentax					
EG-1540	Video	5.1	1050	2.0	210/120-0/0
EG-1840	Video	6.0	1050	2.0	210/120-120/120
Olympus					
GIF-XP160	Video	5.9	1030	2.0	180/90-100/100
GIF-N230	Video	6.0	930	2.0	180/180-160/160
XGIF-N160Y1	Video	5.3	1330	2.0	180/180-0/0
GIF-N30	Fiberoptic	5.3	930	2.0	180/180-160/160
GIF-XP20	Fiberoptic	7.9	1030	2.0	210/90-100/100
XEF-DP[†]	Fiberoptic	3.1	600	—	90/90-0/0
LF-GP[†]	Fiberoptic	4	600	—	90/90-0/0
XEF 140I	Video	4	600	—	90/90-0/0
Fujinon					
EG-470 N/EG-270 N	Video	6.0	1100	2.0	210/90-100/100

The endoscopes with a working length of 600 mm are used for esophagoscopy only. Some esophagoscopes are battery operated.
Values correspond to the outside diameter of the insertion tube.
[†]*Denotes battery-operated esophagoscope.*

The technique for endoscope insertion is determined by several variables. Because it has not been established whether or not the peroral route is safer and better tolerated than the transnasal approach, the route of endoscope insertion should depend on the endoscopist's experience, patient preference, and endoscope diameter. Transnasal endoscopy is best performed with small-caliber endoscopes with a diameter of 6 mm or less. A biopsy can be obtained if a small-caliber endoscope with a 2-mm-diameter accessory channel is used. The pediatric biopsy forceps are required. The 4-mm or smaller esophagoscopes allow only a diagnostic examination. Because sedation is not used for the procedure, postprocedure recovery, aside from discharge instructions, is not necessary.

Unsedated Small-Caliber Upper Endoscopy

The impact of unsedated small-caliber endoscopy on the everyday practice of EGD is complex, and data from large randomized controlled trials are still lacking. Although lower procedure cost and complication rate would favor unsedated EGD, poor patient tolerance, inadequate visualization, and failure to complete the procedure could actually increase the cost of upper endoscopy secondary to repeated examination by sedated EGD.

Analyses of the few randomized controlled studies provide sufficient evidence that unsedated small-caliber upper endoscopy is feasible and tolerable in select patient groups. Most evidence, however, suggests that small-caliber endoscopy is slightly less sensitive. There are conflicting reports regarding the transnasal approach and whether or not it is preferred over the peroral route. Similarly, there are insufficient data regarding the safety of unsedated small-caliber endoscopy compared with sedated conventional endoscopy. Finally, the cost effectiveness of unsedated small-caliber endoscopy is yet to be determined. With that in mind, the following review summarizes the literature addressing the various aspects of unsedated small-caliber endoscopy.

TECHNICAL FEASIBILITY OF UNSEDATED SMALL-CALIBER ENDOSCOPY

Feasibility of unsedated small-caliber endoscopy is mainly a subjective measure defined by the endoscopist. It can be affected by a number of factors, including the diameter of the small-caliber endoscope, endoscope maneuverability, image quality, patient tolerability, and the skills of the endoscopist. Feasibility of unsedated endoscopy is particularly linked to tolerance, which is discussed in the next section. In the crudest sense, technical feasibility represents the successful completion of the intended procedure by intubating the duodenum if an EGD is being performed or intubating the stomach if esophagoscopy is being carried out. Several investigators have reported the feasibility of transoral or transnasal unsedated EGD.[1-13] The majority of these studies have not been prospective randomized controlled trials. Furthermore, the patient populations have been either small in size or not representative of the general U.S. population.

The following studies addressing the feasibility of EGD deserve attention. Wilkins and coworkers[1] randomized 72 patients to undergo either unsedated sc-EGD or sedated conventional EGD (c-EGD). Despite a highly selected and motivated U.S. Air Force community population, only 29 out of the 33 patients (88%) had a complete unsedated sc-EGD. In another controlled study, Mulcahy and coworkers[2] compared the feasibility of unsedated sc-EGD to unsedated c-EGD in 322 patients. EGD was completed in 160 of the 163 patients (98%) undergoing unsedated EGD with a 6-mm gastroscope compared with 145 out of the 159 patients (91%) undergoing unsedated EGD with a 9.8-mm gastroscope. They subsequently reported 39 (8%) failures in a prospective study of 508 patients undergoing routine unsedated gastroscopy.[3] Failure was associated with larger scope diameter (>9 mm), higher pre-procedure anxiety, and younger age. Ristikankare and colleagues[4] randomized 180 patients undergoing EGD to receive either intravenous (IV) midazolam, IV saline, or no IV access. Although the procedure was perceived "less difficult" in the IV midazolam group compared with the IV saline group, the difference was not statistically significant. The power to detect differences between the three groups was not determined in this study. Furthermore, the small patient population and the lack of validated criteria to assess the difficulty of an EGD limit the utility of the evidence. The feasibility of unsedated sc-EGD was also assessed as part of the multiphase Mayo Clinic Rochester study of a select group of highly motivated patients and volunteers.[5] The second portion of the duodenum was reached in 20 sedated and 20 unsedated volunteers in this prospective, nonrandomized study. Among the patients, 50 subjects successfully underwent sedated sc-EGD followed by sedated c-EGD, and 38 of the 40 patients underwent successful unsedated sc-EGD followed by sedated c-EGD. Overall, the technical feasibility was not significantly affected by sedation in this study. A type II error (failure to detect a significant difference when there is a difference), however, cannot be ruled out because the sample size to detect a significant difference was not calculated.

Investigators have also studied the feasibility of unsedated transnasal sc-EGD. Saeian and coworkers[6] demonstrated that unsedated transnasal esophagoscopy with a 5.3-mm gastroscope was feasible in 15 cirrhotic patients. The study was uncontrolled, and the population was very small. Zaman and colleagues[8] compared peroral and transnasal approaches for EGD with the same small-caliber instrument using a prospective randomized crossover study design. Of 105 patients, 60 (57%) agreed to undergo unsedated sc-EGD. Peroral unsedated EGD was feasible in 34 of 35 (97%) patients, including 4 who failed transnasal EGD and were crossed over. Unsedated transnasal EGD, on the other hand, was feasible in only 25 of 29 (86%) patients. The statistics were not reported and a sample size based on a study hypothesis was also not calculated before study initiation. Campo and coworkers[9] randomized 181 Spanish patients to undergo transnasal sc-EGD or peroral c-EGD. Insertion failed in six (3.3%) patients, four had been randomized to the transnasal and two to the peroral route. Craig and colleagues[12] performed a prospective randomized trial in Australia comparing the feasibility of unsedated transnasal to unsedated peroral sc-EGD. A complete examination was feasible in 74 of the 84 (88%) transnasal and 85 of the 86 (99%) transoral procedures, $p = .004$. Recently, Dumortier and coworkers[13] reported that unsedated transnasal

EGD was feasible in 1033 of 1100 (94%) patients studied prospectively at three French medical centers. Failures were mainly due to the inability to insert the small-caliber endoscope (62.7%). Other reasons included patient refusal and nasal pain. In their prior study published in 1999, they demonstrated that unsedated transnasal EGD was feasible in 82% of the study population and was associated with less nausea and choking.[14] The feasibility of transnasal sc-EGD was initially assessed in 100 patients in this two-phase study. One hundred fifty patients were then randomized to undergo peroral c-EGD with a 9.8-mm videoendoscope, peroral sc-EGD with a 6-mm videoendoscope, or transnasal sc-EGD with a 6-mm videoendoscope.

In summary, the evidence that supports the feasibility of unsedated upper endoscopy compared with sedated endoscopy is limited. One should remember that the randomized studies reviewed have failed to specify the study hypothesis and to calculate a sample size before study initiation. Thus, they may have failed to detect a difference because of a type II error. The studies have also used different caliber instruments, and there is some evidence suggesting that the feasibility of an unsedated examination may be better with smaller diameter instruments. Furthermore, none of the studies had sufficient power to examine whether unsedated endoscopy is feasible for all indications. Comparative studies comparing transnasal and peroral approaches have given variable results. However, the weight of the evidence suggests that transnasal intubation may not be feasible in all patients. Whether further technologic advances and decreased endoscope diameter will make the transnasal approach more feasible remains to be determined. Finally, although the reasons for refusal have not been addressed in most publications, several studies have revealed a large (about 40%) refusal rate in the United States, which will limit the adoption of an unsedated endoscopy approach in America.

TOLERABILITY OF UNSEDATED SMALL-CALIBER ENDOSCOPY

The tolerability of unsedated small-caliber esophagoscopy or EGD is of utmost importance. It directly affects patient or physician acceptance, examination adequacy, and technical feasibility. Many studies have measured the tolerability of unsedated upper endoscopy by evaluating specific symptoms such as gagging, choking, pain, and discomfort on a Likert scale. The tolerability of unsedated endoscopy varies considerably across countries and patient populations. Although unsedated upper endoscopy may be considered the norm in some countries, the idea may not be appealing to the American endoscopists and American patients. In fact, even regional differences may be noted within the United States. Tolerability is a complex variable, which is likely affected by numerous patient- and operator-related factors. These include patient education, prior endoscopic experience, preprocedure anxiety, patient age, patient gender, endoscopist skill, and technical performance of the endoscope. A prohibitively large and diverse patient population would be required to determine how all of these factors affect the tolerability and acceptance of unsedated endoscopy.

Catanzaro and coworkers[15] evaluated patient tolerability of unsedated endoscopy with a 4-mm esophagoscope. A total of 51 patients were enrolled in the study. Thirty patients underwent an unsedated procedure. Of these patients, 18 preferred the peroral and 12 the transnasal route. Patient tolerability and acceptability of unsedated esophagoscopy with the 4-mm esophagoscope compared favorably with a historical group of patients examined with a 3-mm esophagoscope. In an earlier study, Catanzaro and colleagues[16] assessed the use of a 3.1-mm battery-operated esophagoscope in an unsedated fashion. A total of 98 patients underwent examination with the battery-operated esophagoscope. Of the 56 patients undergoing an unsedated examination, 43 preferred the peroral approach. Although the endoscopist's perception of patient discomfort was not significantly different, the patients undergoing unsedated small-caliber esophagoscopy reported significantly more choking, pain, and overall discomfort with the 3.1-mm battery-operated esophagoscope. Faulx and coworkers[17] approached 98 patients to undergo unsedated 3.1-mm unsedated esophagoscopy before c-EGD. Only 46% of the 52 patients participating in the study preferred unsedated 3.1-mm esophagoscopy over c-EGD in the future. Sixteen patients chose the peroral approach and 36 patients the transnasal approach. Patients who chose the peroral route were more likely to prefer unsedated small-caliber endoscopy with the 3.1-mm esophagoscope compared with the transnasal approach (58% vs. 23%).

Saeian and colleagues[6] performed sedated c-EGD following unsedated sc-EGD and reported no significant difference in choking, discomfort, and sore throat in a population of 15 cirrhotic patients. In contrast, Wilkins and coworkers[1] reported increased gagging and choking in the 33 patients randomized to undergo unsedated sc-EGD compared with the 39 patients who underwent sedated c-EGD. However, most patients tolerated unsedated sc-EGD. A prospective American study found that only 52 of 98 patients (53%) approached agreed to undergo unsedated esophagoscopy with a 3.1-mm esophagoscope followed by sedated EGD.[17] Although one may argue that the willingness to undergo unsedated endoscopy may be hampered by undergoing tandem endoscopies, this is one of the few well-designed studies to address the impact of unsedated endoscopy on the practice of EGD. Of the 52 patients who underwent both procedures, only 46% preferred unsedated EGD. Patients who had transnasal esophagoscopy were less likely to prefer an unsedated procedure in the future compared with those who underwent peroral esophagoscopy (23% vs. 58%, respectively). Similarly, Zaman and colleagues[18] reported that 19 (31%) of 62 patients asked to undergo unsedated 6-mm transoral EGD followed by sedated transoral c-EGD refused. Of the 43 patients who agreed to undergo unsedated sc-EGD, 30 (70%) were willing to have unsedated sc-EGD in the future. However, a prospective randomized controlled trial from a center in the United Kingdom that routinely performs unsedated endoscopies concluded that endoscopists found unsedated examinations easier but patients reported significantly greater comfort with sedation.[19] Another United Kingdom trial that studied 62 elderly patients reported that an equal number of patients undergoing sedated or unsedated EGD described the procedure as "mildly unpleasant."[20] Of those who underwent unsedated EGD, 73% did not wish to be sedated for future EGD. Froehlich and colleagues[21] randomized 200 European patients to receive either IV midazolam with lidocaine spray, IV placebo with lidocaine spray, IV midazolam with placebo spray, or IV placebo with placebo spray and demonstrated that tolerability, assessed on a visual analog scale, was significantly improved in those who received IV sedation.

One major difficulty with the interpretation of the studies comparing the tolerability of unsedated endoscopy with sedated procedures is that benzodiazepines affect recall. Therefore, the timing of when the patient is questioned may affect the response to the questions. The only prospective controlled trial that compared two unsedated procedures found that patients reported less discomfort when peroral EGD was performed with a 6-mm endoscope compared with the 9.8-mm instrument.[2] Sedation during future examination was requested by 14% of those subjects who underwent examination with a 6-mm endoscope compared with 31% of patients examined with a 9.8-mm endoscope.

A few studies have compared the tolerability and acceptance of unsedated transnasal and peroral approaches. In a randomized U.S. trial of unsedated peroral versus transnasal sc-EGD, Zaman and coworkers[8] determined that 89% of the patients undergoing peroral and 69% of those undergoing transnasal EGD were willing to have unsedated sc-EGD in the future. On the other hand, a smaller U.S. study of 24 patients who had undergone transnasal unsedated EGD followed by c-EGD concluded that transnasal EGD was more acceptable.[10] However, a randomized Australian study of 170 patients found no significant difference in tolerability of unsedated sc-EGD with either route.[12] Recently, Dumortier and colleagues[13] reported that 95% of 1033 French patients who successfully underwent unsedated small-caliber transnasal EGD were willing to repeat it again. Furthermore, 91% of the 377 patients who had previously undergone unsedated transoral EGD preferred the transnasal route.

In summary, the majority of the literature suggests that unsedated endoscopy is not as tolerable as sedated endoscopies. There is also limited evidence supporting the use of smaller caliber instruments to make unsedated endoscopy more tolerable. The evidence in support of a transnasal approach to improve procedure tolerability is inconclusive because various studies have reported contradictory results. Acceptance of unsedated endoscopy appears moderate in patients who have successfully completed the procedure. For reasons not completely understood, American patients may be particularly unwilling to undergo unsedated endoscopy.

SAFETY OF UNSEDATED SMALL-CALIBER ENDOSCOPY

One of the arguments for advocating unsedated procedures is that the morbidity and mortality of endoscopic procedures is largely related to sedation. Although this may be true, the evidence is limited. The practice of sedated endoscopy is very safe, and complications are uncommon. The incidence of serious cardiorespiratory complications in an American Society for Gastrointestinal Endoscopy/U.S. Food and Drug Administration (ASGE/FDA) collaborative study of 21,011 procedures was 5.4 per 1000 cases and the incidence of death was 0.3 per 1000 cases.[22] A large retrospective German study found that the overall complication rate associated with sedated EGD was 0.009%.[23] Given the low complication rate of sedated EGD, any study to determine whether

unsedated EGD is safer would require an extremely large patient population.

The safety of unsedated EGD has been addressed in several small studies. Limited studies have reported no serious complications in 60 patients[5] and 170 patients[12] who underwent unsedated procedures. Epistaxis is unique to transnasal EGD and can occur in up to one out of five patients.[24] This is not surprising given that insertion of a soft small-bore nasogastric tube may result in epistaxis. The largest prospective study of unsedated transnasal EGD revealed epistaxis in 2.3%, nasal pain in 1.6%, and vasovagal reactions in 0.3% of the 1100 consecutive patients participating in the study at three French centers.

Much larger studies of unsedated EGD are needed to determine the true cardiorespiratory complication rate of the procedure. Unfortunately, cost prohibits the performance of such a large prospective randomized comparative study on the safety of unsedated and sedated EGD. Furthermore, although it appears that transnasal unsedated EGD is associated with an increased rate of minor complications (epistaxis) compared with peroral EGD, larger comparative studies with ultrathin endoscopes are required. In the absence of data from large prospective studies, the currently available safety data originate from small prospective or retrospective studies.

ADEQUACY OF UNSEDATED SMALL-CALIBER ENDOSCOPY AND BIOPSY

The data on the adequacy of examinations performed using small-caliber endoscopes are even more limited. Image quality, suctioning ability, adequacy of tissue sampling, and ability to perform therapeutic maneuvers are among the main determinants of "adequacy." The specifications of several small-caliber upper endoscopes are listed in Table 10–1. Most commercially available small-caliber endoscopes incorporate video charge-coupled devices (CCD) technology, although some studies have been performed with fiberoptic instruments. The outside diameter of these endoscopes ranges between 5 to 6 mm, approximately half the diameter of a conventional upper endoscope (Fig. 10–1A). The esophagoscopes have a working length of 600 mm to allow intubation of stomach. Some are battery operated and none allow biopsies. A thinner insertion tube may be too flexible, limiting passage through the pylorus and intubation of the second portion of the duodenum. Some manufacturers have marketed small-caliber endoscopes that have only unidirectional up-and-down tip deflection (Fig. 10–1B), whereas others have bidirectional up-and-down and right-and-left tip deflection similar to conventional instruments. The accessory channel of the small-caliber esophagogastroduodenoscopes is generally 2 mm. This limits the size of the biopsies that can be obtained and the ability to perform therapeutic interventions. The smaller diameter of the channels could also impair the ability to aspirate blood, secretions, and debris and the ability to wash the lens. A sample image of the gastroesophageal junction as viewed by a small-caliber endoscope is shown in Fig. 10–3, and a brief normal transnasal examination is presented as a video clip. Several publications addressing various aspects of adequacy are reviewed.

Wildi and coworkers[25] and Catanzaro and colleagues[15,16] have addressed the accuracy of the small-caliber esophagoscopes. Wildi

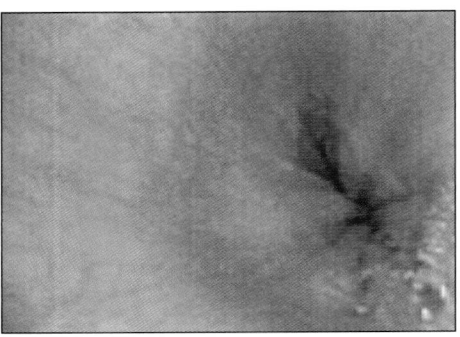

Figure 10–3. The endoscopic image of a normal squamocolumnar junction as viewed by a video esophagogastroduodenoscope is shown.

and coworkers assessed the diagnostic accuracy of sedated esophagoscopy performed by a nurse practitioner using a 4-mm esophagoscope compared with sedated c-EGD performed by an experienced gastroenterologist. Forty patients underwent tandem procedures in a blinded fashion. For all esophageal lesions, the sensitivity and specificity of the examination by the nurse practitioner were 75% and 98%, respectively. All four Schatski rings were missed.[25] Catanzaro and colleagues[15] reported a sensitivity, accuracy, and specificity of 91%, 98%, and 99% for detecting all esophageal lesions in their study of 51 patients undergoing esophagoscopy using the 4-mm esophagoscope. The first 24 patients underwent endoscopy using the battery-operated fiberoptic esophagoscope, and the following 27 patients were examined with the 4-mm video esophagoscope. In an earlier study, Catanzaro and coworkers[16] reported that the accuracy of esophageal examination with a 3.1-mm endoscope is substantially inferior to c-EGD. The sensitivity for detecting Barrett's esophagus, esophageal tumors, and esophageal varices was 54.5%, 66.7%, and 80%, respectively. Optical quality was reported as less than 4 on a scale of 1 to 5 in 42% of the cases.

In the study of Dumortier and colleagues,[13] endoscopic biopsies, obtained in 457 subjects undergoing a transnasal examination, were considered "sufficient." Four esophageal cancers and one gastric cancer were correctly diagnosed by biopsy. Although this is the largest study addressing the adequacy of samples obtained at the time of unsedated transnasal EGD, this outcome was not the primary or even secondary goal of the study. Furthermore, criteria for determining sample adequacy were not defined. Zaman and coworkers[18] reported that unsedated peroral sc-EGD with a video instrument missed 5 out of 59 lesions identified by c-EGD in 62 patients, yielding an accuracy of 92%. The optical quality of the images were rated as good in 84%, 65%, and 78% of the subjects when examining the esophagus, stomach, and duodenum, respectively. In a similar study of unsedated transnasal EGD, Dean and colleagues[10] found a sensitivity of 89% and a specificity of 97% using a fiberoptic instrument. In the only study examining the effect of sedation and endoscope caliber, Sorbi and coworkers[5] demonstrated that the accuracy for major endoscopic findings was 96% for the 50 patients who underwent sedated transoral sc-EGD and 97% for the 40 patients who underwent unsedated transoral sc-EGD. The view was particularly limited because of the inability to rapidly aspirate secretions and clear bubbles. These results suggest that caliber, and not sedation, may be the primary factor determining the accuracy

of unsedated small-caliber endoscopy. In fact, the 4-mm-diameter may be the lower limit for upper endoscopes to maintain adequate image quality.

Regardless of whether a video or a fiberoptic endoscope is used, studies comparing small-caliber upper endoscopy with conventional upper endoscopy have uniformly reported that the smaller caliber instruments have a slightly lower accuracy. Lesions missed by small-caliber instruments tend to be mild esophageal stenoses or located in the second portion of the duodenum. Although small-caliber endoscopes appear to be accurate for detecting common lesions, the studies have not addressed the accuracy of small-caliber endoscopy for detecting subtle rare mucosal abnormalities such as early malignancies. There is also insufficient evidence whether biopsies obtained by small-caliber endoscopes are adequate for detecting dysplasia in Barrett's esophagus.

COST EFFECTIVENESS OF UNSEDATED SMALL-CALIBER ENDOSCOPY

The major impetus behind the practice of unsedated endoscopy may well be cost. Elimination of sedation may significantly reduce the cost of endoscopy. The total expense of unsedated endoscopy, however, must be studied in view of its impact on the every day practice of EGD. Unsedated small-caliber endoscopy can result in savings only if the general population finds it acceptable and if most unsedated examinations are adequate and a repeat examination under sedation is not required.

The impact of unsedated endoscopy on the cost of EGD has been evaluated only in a few studies. In a case-control study, Gorelick and colleagues[26] assessed the potential cost savings associated with unsedated sc-EGD. Sixteen patients undergoing unsedated transoral sc-EGD were matched for age, gender, indication, and procedure day with a control group of 16 patients who underwent sedated c-EGD. The mean procedure room time was 16.3 minutes for unsedated sc-EGD and 34.9 minutes for sedated c-EGD ($p < .0005$). The mean recovery room time was 9.0 minutes for unsedated sc-EGD and 41.3 minutes for sedated c-EGD ($p < .00001$). The mean cost for unsedated sc-EGD was $462 and was considerably lower than the mean cost of sedated c-EGD that was reported as $587 ($p < .0006$). In a controlled study, Wilkins and coworkers[1] randomized 72 patients to undergo either unsedated sc-EGD or sedated c-EGD. The procedure time (mean ± SEM) for the 33 patients who underwent unsedated sc-EGD was 21.5 ± 2.3 minutes, whereas the procedure time for the 39 patients who underwent sedated c-EGD was 55.4 min ± 2.3 minutes. Without performing a formal cost analysis, they suggested that unsedated sc-EGD performed by primary care physicians could increase access while decreasing the cost of upper endoscopy. Bampton and colleagues[27] compared unsedated transnasal EGD with sedated transoral EGD. The mean procedure times of 15 minutes for the unsedated procedure and 20 minutes for the sedated EGD were not significantly different. However, the mean recovery time was 7 minutes for the unsedated transnasal examination compared with 37 minutes for the transoral sedated EGD, emphasizing the shorter recovery time when no sedation is administered. With the previous findings in mind, it should be noted that a formal cost effectiveness analysis of unsedated versus sedated endoscopy that accounts for variations in the patient population, patient acceptance, completion rates, and diagnostic accuracy is yet to be performed to determine the utility of this approach in the daily practice of upper endoscopy.

Conclusion

The practice of gastrointestinal endoscopy is constantly evolving. Unsedated small-caliber upper endoscopy is intuitively appealing and has become more popular with the availability of higher resolution small-caliber video endoscopes. Sufficient data exist supporting the feasibility of unsedated small-caliber endoscopy in selected patients. Furthermore, adequate data suggest that the sensitivity of the small-caliber endoscopes may be slightly less than c-EGD. Current literature, however, lacks sufficient evidence to provide guidelines on how to select the suitable patient population and whether or not unsedated endoscopy results in cost savings without significantly compromising comfort. Large, randomized, controlled studies and comprehensive cost effectiveness analyses are required to answer these questions.

REFERENCES

1. Wilkins T, Brewster A, Lammers J: Comparison of thin versus standard esophagogastroduodenoscopy. J Fam Pract 51:625–629, 2002.
2. Mulcahy HE, Riches A, Kiely M, et al: A prospective controlled trial of an ultrathin versus a conventional endoscope in unsedated upper gastrointestinal endoscopy. Endoscopy 33:311–316, 2001.
3. Mulcahy HE, Kelly P, Banks MR, et al: Factors associated with tolerance to, and discomfort with, unsedated diagnostic gastroscopy. Scand J Gastroenterol 36:1352–1357, 2001.
4. Ristikankare M, Hartikainen J, Heikkinen M, et al: Is routinely given conscious sedation of benefit during colonoscopy? Gastrointest Endosc 49:566–572, 1999.
5. Sorbi D, Gostout CJ, Henry J, Lindor KD: Unsedated small-caliber esophagogastroduodenoscopy (EGD) versus conventional EGD: A comparative study. [Comment]. Gastroenterology 117:1301–1307, 1999.
6. Saeian K, Staff D, Knox J, et al: Unsedated transnasal endoscopy: A new technique for accurately detecting and grading esophageal varices in cirrhotic patients. Am J Gastroenterol 97:2246–2249, 2002.
7. Shaker R, Saeian K: Unsedated transnasal laryngo-esophagogastroduodenoscopy: An alternative to conventional endoscopy. Am J Med 111(Suppl 8A):153S–156S, 2001.
8. Zaman A, Hahn M, Hapke R, et al: A randomized trial of peroral versus transnasal unsedated endoscopy using an ultrathin video-endoscope. [Comment]. Gastrointest Endosc 49(3 Pt 1):279–284, 1999.
9. Campo R, Montserrat A, Brullet E: Transnasal gastroscopy compared to conventional gastroscopy: A randomized study of feasibility, safety, and tolerance. Endoscopy 30:448–452, 1998.
10. Dean R, Dua K, Massey B, et al: A comparative study of unsedated transnasal esophagogastroduodenoscopy and conventional EGD. Gastrointest Endosc 44:422–424, 1996.
11. Belafsky PC, Postma GN, Daniel E, Koufman JA: Transnasal esophagoscopy. Otolaryngol Head Neck Surg 125:588–589, 2001.
12. Craig A, Hanlon J, Dent J, Schoeman M: A comparison of transnasal and transoral endoscopy with small-diameter endoscopes in unsedated patients. Gastrointest Endosc 49:292–296, 1999.
13. Dumortier J, Napoleon B, Hedelius F, et al: Unsedated transnasal EGD in daily practice: Results with 1100 consecutive patients. Gastrointest Endosc 57:198–204, 2003.
14. Dumortier J, Ponchon T, Scoazec JY, et al: Prospective evaluation of transnasal esophagogastroduodenoscopy: Feasibility and study on performance and tolerance. [Comment]. Gastrointest Endosc 49(3 Pt 1):285–291, 1999.
15. Catanzaro A, Faulx A, Isenberg GA, et al: Prospective evaluation of 4-mm diameter endoscopes for esophagoscopy in sedated and unsedated patients. Gastrointest Endosc 57:300–304, 2003.
16. Catanzaro A, Faulx A, Pfau PR, et al: Accuracy of a narrow-diameter battery-powered endoscope in sedated and unsedated patients. Gastrointest Endosc 55:484–487, 2002.
17. Faulx AL, Catanzaro A, Zyzanski S, et al: Patient tolerance and acceptance of unsedated ultrathin esophagoscopy. Gastrointest Endosc 55:620–623, 2002.
18. Zaman A, Hapke R, Sahagun G, Katon RM: Unsedated peroral endoscopy with a video ultrathin endoscope: Patient acceptance, tolerance, and diagnostic accuracy. Am J Gastroenterol 93:1260–1263, 1998.
19. Fisher NC, Bailey S, Gibson JA: A prospective, randomized controlled trial of sedation vs. no sedation in outpatient diagnostic upper gastrointestinal endoscopy. Endoscopy 30:21–24, 1998.
20. Solomon SA, Kajla VK, Banerjee AK: Can the elderly tolerate endoscopy without sedation? J R Coll Physicians Lond 28:407–410, 1994.
21. Froehlich F, Schwizer W, Thorens J, et al: Conscious sedation for gastroscopy: Patient tolerance and cardiorespiratory parameters. [Comment]. Gastroenterology 108:697–704, 1995.
22. Arrowsmith JB, Gerstman BB, Fleischer DE, Benjamin SB: Results from the American Society for Gastrointestinal Endoscopy/U.S. Food and Drug Administration collaborative study on complication rates and drug use during gastrointestinal endoscopy. Gastrointest Endosc 37:421–427, 1991.
23. Sieg A, Hachmoeller-Eisenbach U, Heisenbach T: [How safe is premedication in ambulatory endoscopy in Germany? A prospective study in gastroenterology specialty practices]. Deutsche Medizinische Wochenschrift 125:1288–1293, 2000.
24. Zuccaro G Jr: Sedation and sedationless endoscopy. Gastrointest Endosc Clin N Am 10:1–20, v, 2000.
25. Wildi SM, Wallace MB, Glenn TF, et al: Accuracy of esophagoscopy performed by a non-physician endoscopist with a 4-mm diameter battery-operated endoscope. Gastrointest Endosc 57:305–310, 2003.
26. Gorelick AB, Inadomi JM, Barnett JL: Unsedated small-caliber esophagogastroduodenoscopy (EGD): Less expensive and less time-consuming than conventional EGD. J Clin Gastroenterol 33:210–214, 2001.
27. Bampton PA, Reid DP, Johnson RD, et al: A comparison of transnasal and transoral oesophagogastroduodenoscopy. J Gastroenterol Hepatol 13:579–584, 1998.

Postsurgical Endoscopic Anatomy

Arnaldo Braga Feitoza

Introduction

Patients who have undergone surgical procedures that alter the anatomy of the upper gastrointestinal tract are often referred for endoscopic evaluation.[1] If meaningful and accurate diagnostic information is to be obtained in these patients, it is important that the endoscopist fully understand the anatomic changes resulting from the surgical procedures.[2] Knowledge of the new anatomy is essential to define the type of endoscope and accessories and to determine the need for supplementary studies during or before the endoscopic procedure.[3,4] In addition, accurate interpretation of endoscopic findings may permit the endoscopist to identify an unknown previous surgical procedure.

This chapter discusses the most common operations in the upper gastrointestinal tract that are relevant to the endoscopist. Technical details and common variations are described for each surgical procedure and correlated to the findings and to the anatomic alterations observed endoscopically. Surgical terms are also presented to assist the endoscopist in the interpretation of the surgical reports, which should always be reviewed before initiating the endoscopic examination.

Antireflux Procedures

NISSEN FUNDOPLICATION

Fundoplications to treat gastroesophageal reflux disease (GERD) are performed without gut resection to restore the competency of the cardia (Fig. 11–1). The plication has to be created over the distal esophagus just proximal to the cardioesophageal junction to be effective.[5] Modifications to the original fundoplication described by Nissen decreased the incidence of postoperative gas-bloat syndrome and dysphagia at the same time that the laparoscopic approach proved to be safe and reliable.[6–10] Shortening from 5 cm to 2 cm and loosening of the fundoplication resulted in the so-called floppy Nissen, which performed laparoscopically became the surgical gold

standard treatment for GERD.[11] The distal esophagus, the cardioesophageal junction, the gastric fundus, and the right and left crura are dissected in the same way for the open or laparoscopic procedure. Careful dissection is required to avoid transection of the nerve of Latarjet on the right side of the stomach. After reduction of the hernia, the left and right crura are approximated by sutures, gently snuggling the hiatus around the esophagus, which accommodates a previously inserted 60-Fr dilator (Fig. 11–1A). Division of the short gastric vessels may be required to mobilize the fundus.[12,13] The gastric fundus is passed behind the esophagus from left to right creating a 360-degree wrap by the placement of two or three sutures involving stomach-esophagus-stomach in the anterior portion of the wrap. The anterior and posterior vagus nervus are usually contained into the wrap, attached to the esophagus. At the end of the procedure, the wrap must lie below the diaphragm without tension (Fig. 11–1B).[14,15]

An intact Nissen fundoplication appears to the endoscopist as a narrow, easily transposable distal esophagus, with noninflamed mucosa, and reduced distension to air insufflation. An encircling redundant fold overlies the cardia on a retroflexed view and snuggles the endoscope. Edema accentuates the prominent cardia in the early postoperative setting and the area of the fundus becomes less capacious than normal. Late evaluation of the wrap may notice several rugal folds parallel to each other and to the markings on the insertion tube of the endoscope. Although this is a 360-degreee wrap, endoscopically the redundant fold appears as a 270-degree free cuff margin because the border continuous with the lesser curvature is not evident.[16] The crural closure should maintain the cardia below the diaphragm with the stomach completely insufflated with air. Occasionally, sutures in the distal esophagus may be observed, indicating migration through the wall or inappropriate penetration depth of the stitches during the procedure, associated or not with symptoms.[17]

Findings that could be associated with failure of the fundoplication include esophagitis, lack of the encircling fold on a retroflexed view, patulous gap between the endoscope tube and the wrap,

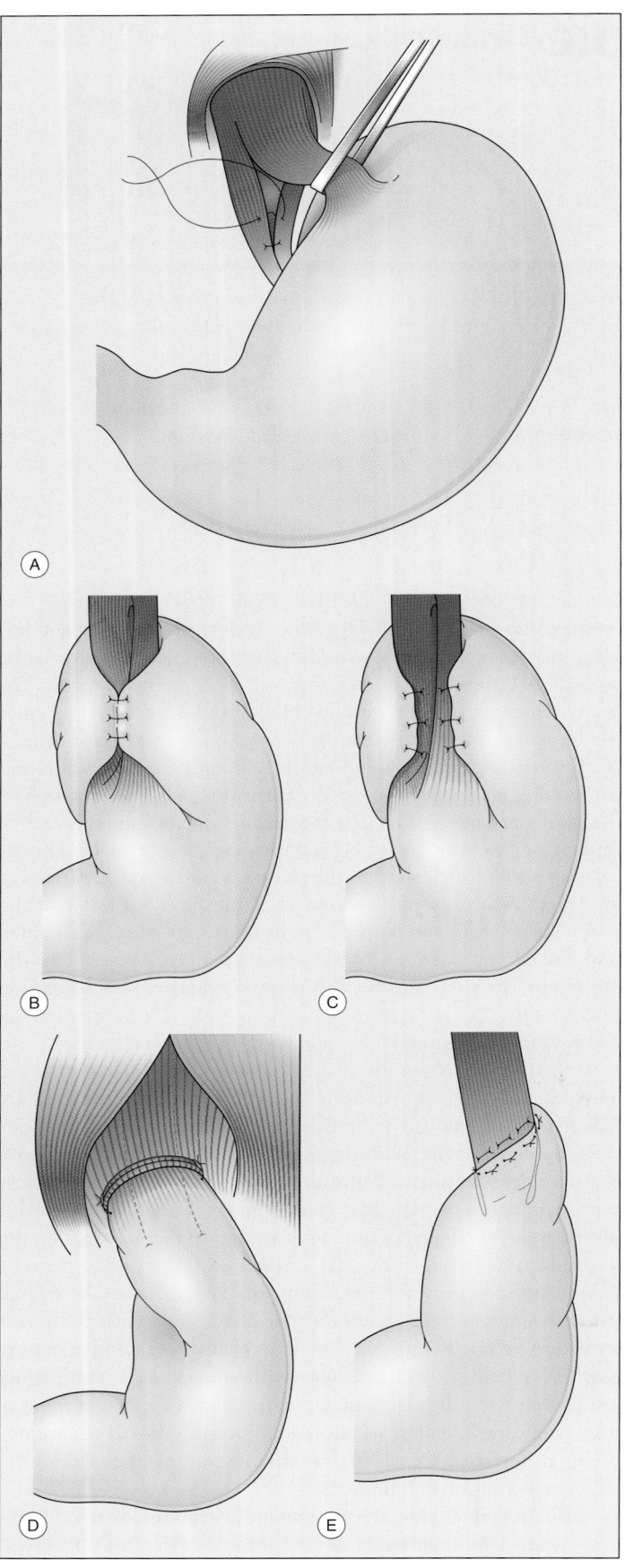

Figure 11–1. Drawings showing antireflux procedures. *A,* The esophageal hiatus is narrowed by sutures that approximate the crura of the diaphragm. *B,* Nissen fundoplication: a short and loose 360-degree wrap is created around the distal esophagus. *C,* Toupet fundoplication: a posterior partial wrap is created by suturing the edges of the stomach to the anterior esophagus, leaving a space in between. *D,* Dor procedure: a partial anterior fundoplication usually performed following a Heller myotomy. *E,* Belsey-Mark IV procedure: a partial wrap created through a thoracotomy by progressive invagination of the esophagus into the stomach.

migration of the wrap through an enlarged esophageal hiatus, hour-glass appearance of the proximal stomach indicating slippage through the valve, and irregularity in the dome shape of the fundus indicating parahiatal hernia. The squamocolumnar junction located more than 1 cm proximal to the margin of the wrap has been reported to be a major endoscopic clue in diagnosis of post-fundoplication problems.[18] Gastric retention may be related to damage to the vagus nerves during the procedure.[19] Some patients with persistent dysphagia present a tight wrap that causes resistance to the advance of the endoscope and may benefit from endoscopic dilation.[20]

PARTIAL FUNDOPLICATIONS (DOR/TOUPET)

Partial fundoplications are created with the fundus involving partially the distal esophagus. A Dor fundoplication is performed anteriorly, and the Toupet fundoplication is performed posteriorly (Fig. 11–1C and D). Both procedures can be performed to treat GERD; however, they are best indicated in patients who underwent a Heller myotomy (Dor) or with impaired esophageal body motility (Toupet).[21–23] Partial fundoplications also present a prominent fold overlying the cardia, which is not necessarily less evident than 360-degree wraps when observed endoscopically.[24]

BELSEY MARK IV

With the advent of laparoscopy, the Belsey Mark IV fundoplication is now only occasionally performed, because it requires a thoracotomy. A circumferential invagination of the distal esophagus into the proximal stomach is performed with two layers of stitches, including anchoring to the diaphragma in the last one. The crura are also sutured to narrow the esophageal hiatus. The final result is a 270-degree wrap around the distal esophagus, placed in the abdomen, and a hiatal repair (Fig. 11–1E).

Endoscopically, Belsey Mark IV and Nissen fundoplications are similar, with folds encircling the endoscope at the level of the cardia. However, coils of gastric rugae as seen after Nissen repair are not evident and there is an anterior compression that corresponds to the attachment of the esophagus to the diaphragm.[16]

COLLIS GASTROPLASTY

A short esophagus, usually due to chronic scarring resulting from GERD, can be repaired surgically through a Collis gastroplasty. The Collis gastroplasty creates a tubular segment of stomach in continuity to the esophagus, long enough to be encircled by a 360-degree fundoplication placed below the diaphragm. The fundoplication around this tubular segment within the positive pressure of the abdomen prevents the gastroesophageal reflux.[25] Short esophagus is declining possibly because patients with GERD are medically diagnosed and treated earlier.[26] Endoscopically, the squamocolumnar junction is observed above a short tubular segment of stomach, which may not distend properly because of the wrap. The Collis gastroplasty resembles the Nissen fundoplication on a retroflexed view with a less capacious fundus.

Operations Without Alteration of the Pancreaticobiliary Anatomy

BILLROTH I

Billroth I (BI) is the type of reconstruction after a partial gastrectomy in which the stomach is anastomosed to the duodenum (Fig. 11–2A).[27] The stomach resection is usually restricted to the antrum, and a truncal vagotomy is often associated. A considerable amount of remaining stomach with refluxed bile is observed endoscopically. The gastroduodenostomy is found toward the greater curvature. A prominent fold representing the closed part of the stomach is often observed along the lesser curvature ending at the gastroduodenostomy. A mucosal pattern change from gastric folds to flat duodenal surface indicates the anastomosis site. The duodenum is rectified, and the circular folds of the second portion are close to the anastomosis because of the partial resection of the bulb. Therefore, both major and minor papillae appear to be more proximal in the duodenum than in a patient with intact anatomy.

BILLROTH II

In a Billroth II (BII) reconstruction after a partial gastrectomy, the duodenal stump is closed and a gastrojejunostomy is created (Fig. 11–2B). This type of reconstruction is most commonly used in the treatment of gastric neoplasia, in which extensive resections are required. The remaining stomach is variable in length allowing the retroflexion maneuver if a long segment is present. The gastric remnant usually contains frothy bile and mucosal erythema from the alkaline reflux.[28] The gastrojejunostomy is located at the distal end of the stomach where two stomal openings corresponding to an end-to-side anastomosis can be identified. There are several surgical techniques to perform the gastrojejunostomy leading to distinct endoscopic presentations. The chosen technique depends on the surgeon preference, and there is no consensus for the ideal one. The gastrojejunostomy can vary in the size of the anastomosis, in the orientation of the jejunal loop to the stomach, and in the position of the anastomosis to the transverse colon. If the whole length of the transected stomach is anastomosed to the jejunum (oralis totalis or Polya), several rows of jejunal folds are observed between the two stomal openings (Fig. 11–3A). Conversely, if only a segment of the transected stomach is anastomosed to the jejunum (oralis partialis or Hoffmeister), few or no folds are evident. In this case, the stomach is partially closed, always from the lesser curvature, to reduce the diameter of the anastomosis, which is observed toward the greater curvature. Some surgeons attach the jejunal limb to the suture line that is closing the stomach to prevent dehiscence when performing an oralis partialis anastomosis (Fig. 11–3B).[29] In this case, a sharp angulation might be negotiated to enter the corresponding jejunal limb and a prominent fold may be seen emanating from the lesser curvature to the anastomosis. The small anastomosis diameter in association with the sharp angulation of this type of reconstruction may make the anatomy difficult to define endoscopically. Gastrojejunostomies performed with staplers are usually oralis partialis. In some cases, the stomach is completely closed at the

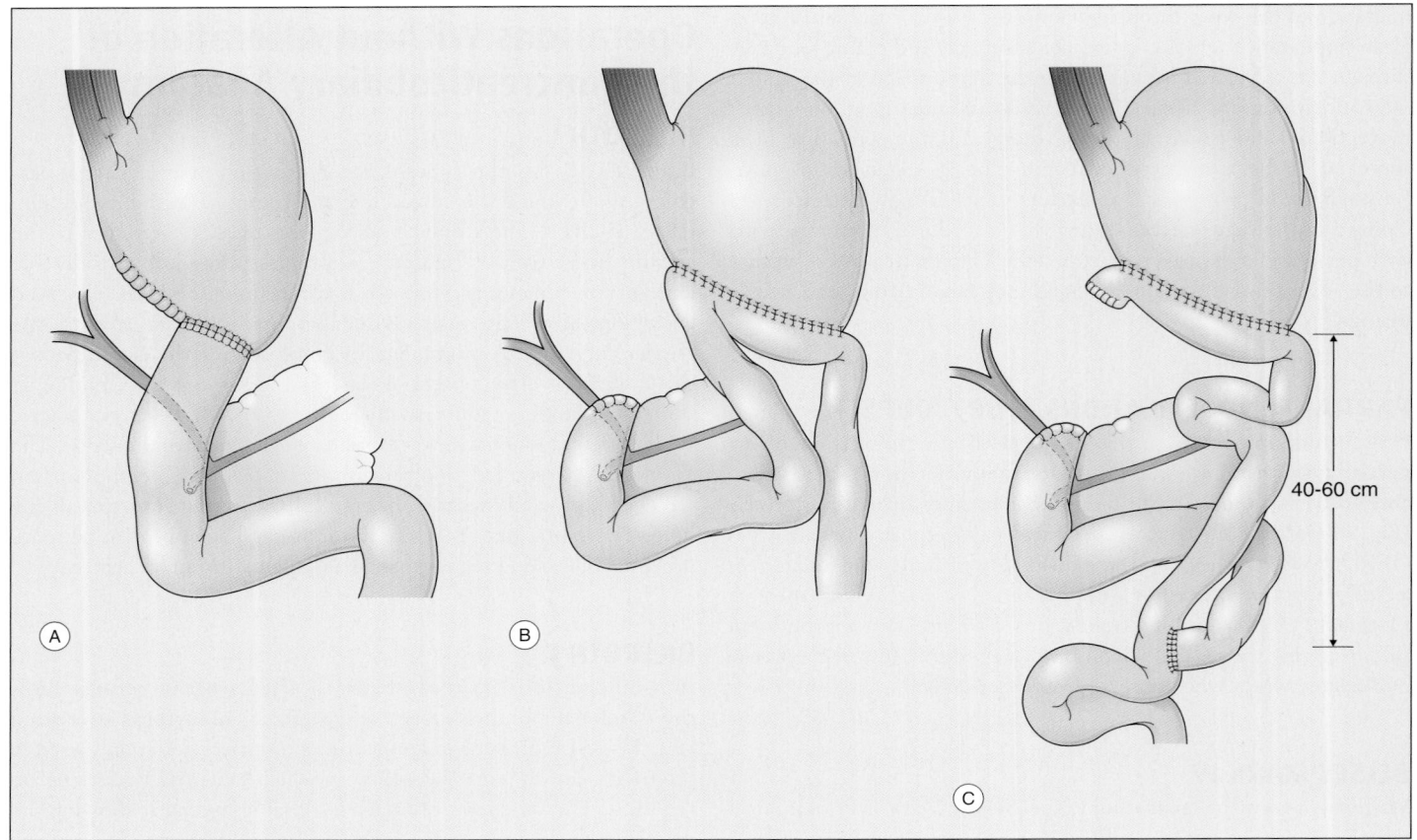

Figure 11-2. Drawings showing the three types of reconstruction after a partial gastrectomy. *A,* Billroth I: a gastroduodenostomy is performed toward the greater curvature. *B,* Billroth II: a gastrojejunostomy is created to reestablish the alimentary transit. Several variations may be observed in this type of reconstruction. *C,* Roux-en-Y: a gastrojejunostomy only with the efferent limb to prevent biliopancreatic reflux into the stomach. A 40- to 60-cm efferent limb leads to the jejunojejunostomy and afferent limb.

distal end and the gastrojejunal anastomosis is performed with a linear or a circular stapler in a side-to-side fashion at the posterior wall, 2 cm proximal to end of the stomach.[30] However, when observed endoscopically this side-to-side anastomosis is almost indistinguishable from a short end-to-side anastomosis.

The jejunum can be anastomosed to the stomach with the afferent limb attached to the greater curvature (isoperistaltic) or to the lesser curvature (antiperistaltic). The afferent limb refers to the jejunal limb that is in continuity with the duodenum while the efferent limb refers to the one that leaves the stomach toward the distal jejunum. Therefore, the two stomal openings observed endoscopically may represent the afferent or efferent limb depending on how the reconstruction was performed (Fig. 11–3C and *D*). If the reconstruction is isoperistaltic, the opening linked to the greater curvature will correspond to the afferent limb. If the reconstruction is antiperistaltic, the opening linked to the greater curvature will correspond to the efferent limb. Usually the stomal opening linked to the lesser curvature is more difficult to access with the endoscope because of the relative verticalization of the anastomosis.[31] Gastrectomies usually include the lesser more than the greater curvature in the resection. In addition, the information from surgical notes about the type of reconstruction, peristalsis and bile flow might help to define the limbs endoscopically. A careful observation of the anastomosis may demonstrate bile coming predominantly

from the afferent limb. Introducing the endoscope through this opening should reveal an increasing volume of bile as the endoscope advances toward the bulb, although bile may also be observed in the efferent limb. Visible peristaltic waves advancing away from the endoscope suggest that the instrument is in the efferent limb. Once the duodenal stump is reached, the flat mucosa of the residual bulb with a scarlike deformity in a cul-de-sac can be identified. A careful withdrawal of the endoscope will expose the major papilla, usually located at the right upper quadrant on the monitor screen. In patients with BII anatomy, the papilla is rotated 180 degrees in the endoscopic visual field. This "upside down" position requires distinct techniques to perform endoscopic retrograde cholangiopancreatography (ERCP), including dedicated sphincterotomes, needle-knife cut technique over the stent, or balloon dilation of the papilla[32–36] (see Chapter 42). If the duodenal stump cannot be identified, the endoscope should be withdrawn and the other limb intubated as far as possible. Fluoroscopic guidance may indicate that the efferent limb has been entered when the instrument is seen to pass deep into the pelvis. Conversely, passage of the endoscope into the right upper quadrant toward the liver or previous cholecystectomy clips suggests entry into the afferent limb.[37]

The length of the afferent limb also varies depending on the surgical technique. The afferent limb naturally fixed at the ligament of Treitz and surgically fixed to the stomach should be tensionless

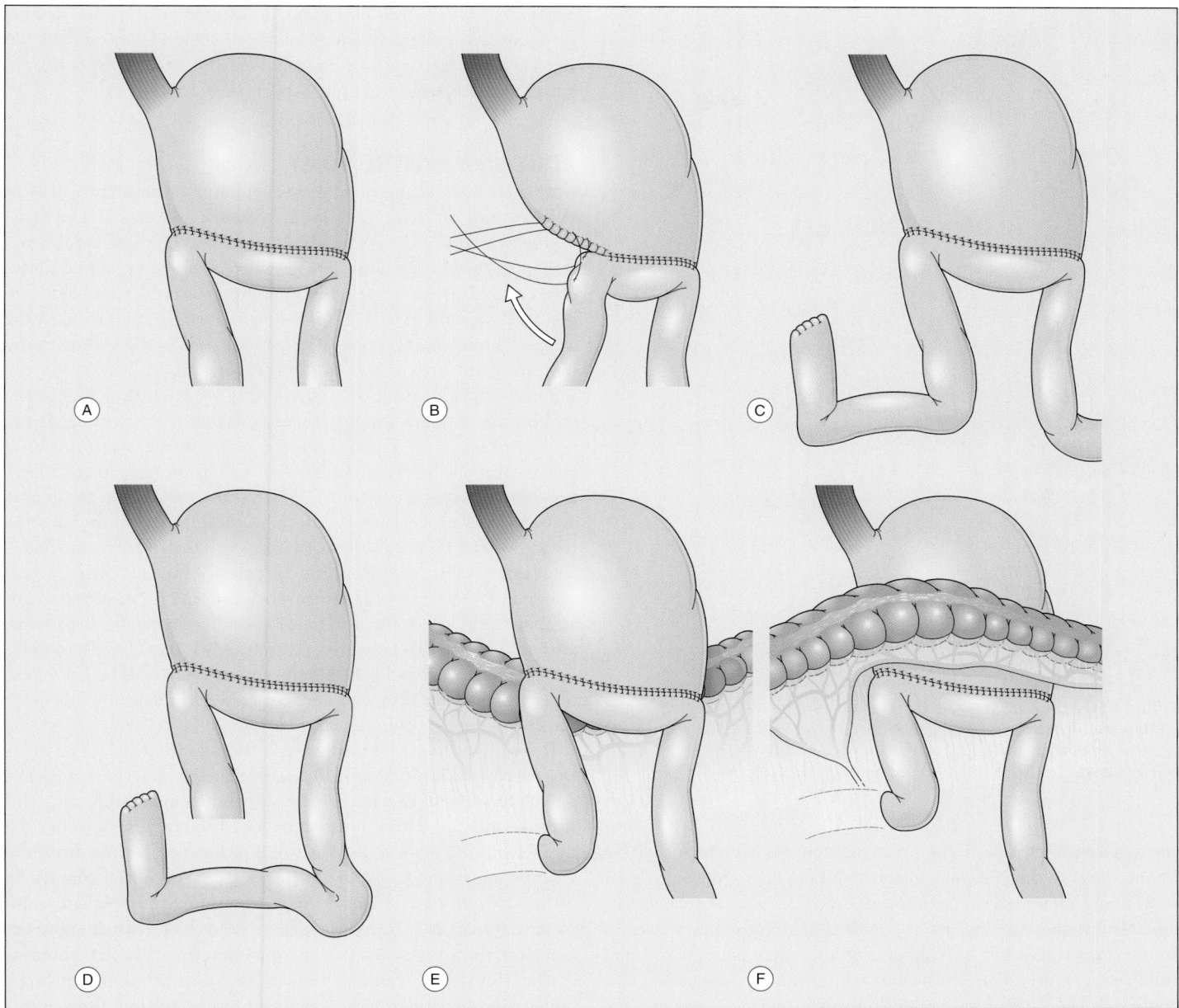

Figure 11–3. Drawings showing variations of the Billroth II reconstruction. *A,* Oralis totalis (Polya): the anastomosis occupies the entire length of the distal stomach. *B,* Oralis partialis (Hoffmeister): the anastomosis occupies only part of the distal stomach. In some cases, the jejunal limb is sutured to the lesser curvature to protect the suture line of the stomach from disruption. In this scenario, a sharp angulation must be negotiated to advance the endoscope through the stomal opening linked to the lesser curvature. *C,* Antiperistaltic anastomosis: the afferent limb is attached to the lesser curvature. *D,* Isoperistaltic anastomosis: the afferent limb is attached to greater curvature. *E,* Antecolic reconstruction: the anastomosis is anterior to the transverse colon leading to a longer afferent limb. *F,* Retrocolic reconstruction: the anastomosis passes through the mesocolon creating a shorter afferent limb.

but not redundant. There are two ways to position the afferent limb in relation to the transverse colon during a BII reconstruction. If an antecolic anastomosis is performed, the gastrojejunostomy is placed anterior to the transverse colon (Fig. 11–3E). Antecolic reconstructions frequently have long afferent limbs because of the distance between the ligament of Treitz and the remaining stomach, over the mesocolon, omentum, and transverse colon. Conversely, retrocolic reconstructions are performed through an opening in the transverse mesocolon, shortening the distance between the ligament of Treitz and the remaining stomach (Fig. 11–3F).[38,39] Antecolic and retrocolic

anastomoses are similar endoscopically, except for the unspecific observation obtained from the length of the limbs. Caution should be taken if a percutaneous endoscopic gastrostomy is indicated for a patient with a previous partial gastrectomy and retrocolic reconstruction.

The BII reconstruction can be associated with a side-to-side jejunojejunostomy, referred to as the Braun procedure (Fig. 11–4).[40] This procedure creates an anastomosis between the afferent and the efferent limb to divert bile from the gastric remnant and also to release the pressure of the afferent limb, supposedly preventing

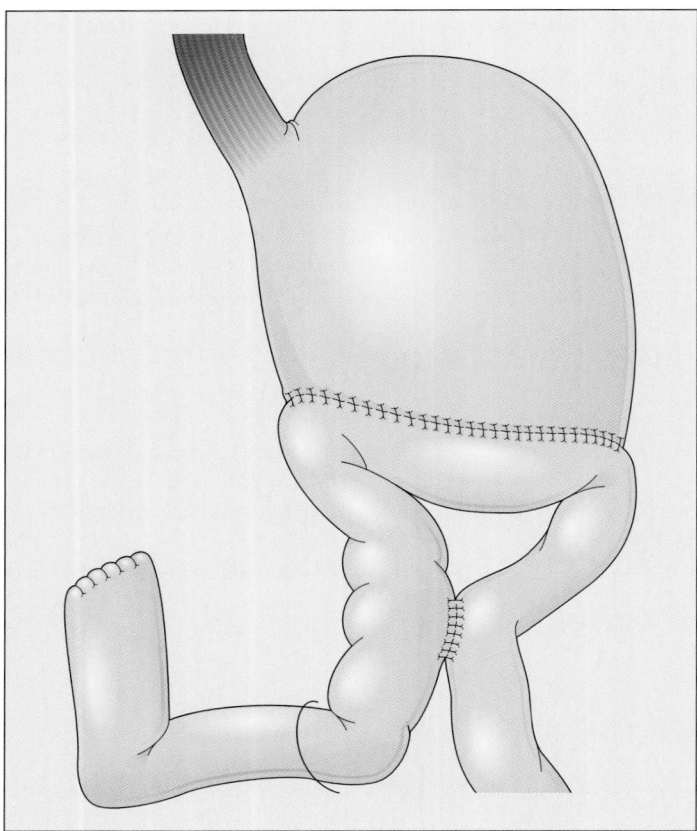

Figure 11–4. Drawing showing the Braun procedure after a Billroth II gastrectomy: an anastomosis between the afferent and efferent limb is created to prevent biliopancreatic reflux to the stomach or alleviate pressure in the afferent limb.

duodenal stump fistula.[41] The Braun anastomosis is performed 10 to 15 cm distal to the gastrojejunostomy and requires a longer afferent limb to accommodate the jejunojejunostomy.[42] Endoscopically, the gastrojejunostomy is similar to a standard BII. Frothy bile is present in the stomach because the Braun procedure only partially diverges biliopancreatic fluids from the gastrojejunostomy. After advancing the endoscope through either openings of the gastrojejunostomy, the side-to-side Braun anastomosis will be found in the afferent and efferent limb and three openings will be noted. One leads to the distal jejunum, another to the afferent limb, and the third one leads back to the stomach. A complete reverse intubation of the stomach may be carried out through the loop created with the Braun anastomosis. The same anatomic landmarks described for other BII procedures are of assistance in directing the endoscope through the limbs. However, a trial-and-error approach may be necessary to ultimately reach the duodenal stump. A higher rate of perforation has been reported during ERCP while traversing the afferent limb as compared with standard ERCP,[43,44] particularly when a stiff therapeutic duodenoscope is used. The Braun procedure has also been associated with perforations during ERCP. The use of a forward-viewing endoscope in these patients can reduce the risk of jejunal perforations,.[45] However, the ability to use a duodenoscope elevator may increase the success of the procedure, and a flexible diagnostic duodenoscope may be safer than a stiff therapeutic

instrument. If the papilla cannot be located with a side-viewing endoscope, a forward-viewing endoscope should be attempted and vice versa. Patients with excessively long afferent limb may require longer endoscopes to reach the papilla (see Chapter 42).

ROUX-EN-Y GASTRECTOMY

In this type of reconstruction, the jejunum is transected close to the ligament of Treitz, creating two distinct segments. The distal segment is sutured to the gastric remnant (gastrojejunostomy) becoming the efferent limb. The proximal segment is sutured to this efferent limb (jejunojejunostomy) approximately 40 cm below the gastrojejunostomy (Fig. 11–2C). The proximal segment is called the afferent limb, which connects the duodenum to the efferent limb instead of the stomach as in BII reconstructions. Therefore, the Roux-en-Y prevents biliopancreatic fluids from refluxing into the stomach in patients who have undergone gastric resection. It can be performed as the initial reconstruction after a gastrectomy or as the treatment for postgastrectomy syndrome resulting from a previous BII reconstruction.[46-48] Truncal vagotomy is commonly associated to prevent peptic ulcers in the efferent limb that is no longer washed by the alkaline contents of the biliopancreatic fluid.[49] The gastrojejunal anastomosis is end-to-side and two stomal openings are observed. The reconstruction can be isoperistaltic or antiperistaltic, antecolic or retrocolic, and oralis totalis or partialis, as described for BII. However, unlike the BII, one of the two limbs is extremely short and ends blindly almost immediately. Therefore, on entering a long limb with a patent lumen it is almost certain that the endoscope is within the efferent limb.

If the Roux-en-Y was performed after an initial BII reconstruction, the endoscopist should be aware that the blind limb might be patent for several centimeters before ending in a cul-de-sac. This short segment of patent limb occurs because conversion from a BII to a Roux-en-Y sometimes has to be performed farther from the gastrojejunostomy to avoid adhesions from the initial surgery. In effective Roux-en-Y reconstructions, the remnant stomach is completely clean of bile. However, because Roux-en-Y gastrojejunostomy increases the risk for delayed gastric emptying, residual contents in the stomach, including bezoars, and the afferent limb may impair visualization of these segments or progression of the endoscope. The absence of bile in an operated stomach should always alert the endoscopist for a Roux-en-Y reconstruction and the presence of residual food in this case should not lead to an erroneous conclusion of efferent limb obstruction. Total obstruction of the afferent limb in a BII reconstruction could also prevent bile to reflux to the stomach, mimicking a Roux-en-Y, but this is uncommon.[50] Conversely, presence of bile does not exclude a Roux-en-Y reconstruction. In this case, a short-length efferent limb may be responsible for the reflux. To be effective, the efferent limb has to measure at least 40 cm from the gastrojejunal anastomosis to the jejunojejunal anastomosis.[51] Longer limbs (up to 60 cm) may also be encountered.[52] Intubation through the efferent limb usually follows a straight route with variable looping. The enteroenteric anastomosis is usually end-to-side, but it may be side-to-side with a blind end (Fig. 11–5). In either case, the endoscope has to leave the efferent limb and enter the afferent limb to reach the major papilla in the duodenum (Fig. 11–5A).

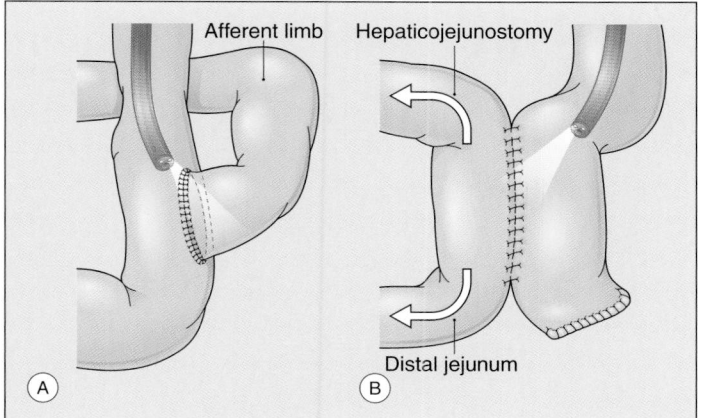

Figure 11–5. Drawings showing jejunojejunal anastomoses in Roux-en-Y reconstructions. *A,* Termino-lateral anastomosis in a Roux-en-Y gastrectomy. Two openings are observed at this level; one leads to the distal jejunum and the other to the ampulla via the afferent limb. *B,* Latero-lateral anastomosis in a hepaticojejunostomy: the endoscope has passed through the stomach, duodenum, and proximal jejunum reaching the jejunojejunal anastomosis. Three openings are noted, including a blind one. Note that in contrast to a Roux-en-Y gastrectomy (*A*), the loop in which the endoscope is located ends blindly.

If a side-to-side anastomosis is present, three openings will be observed. The one in continuity with the efferent limb leads to the distal jejunum, the other one to a blind distal end of the afferent limb, and the third one to the duodenum through the afferent limb. An end-to-side anastomosis will present two openings. One is a continuation of the efferent limb and leads to the distal jejunum; the other one leads to the afferent limb. Different degrees of angulation have to be negotiated to enter the afferent limb depending on the anastomosis configuration. Once the afferent limb is entered, progressively more bile should be seen until the duodenal stump is reached. A complete visualization of the Roux-en-Y gastrojejunostomy during a routine esophagogastroduodenoscopy (EGD) can be performed with a forward-viewing gastroscope, including the jejunojejunostomy. In contrast, when patients with Roux-en-Y gastrectomy require an ERCP, endoscopes with a longer insertion tube are usually needed (pediatric and adult colonoscopes, push-enteroscopes). In addition to the difficulties to reach the papilla, the small diameter of the working channel of these endoscopes and the short length of the endoscopic accessories contribute to the high rate of ERCP failures in these patients[53] (see Chapter 42).

GASTROJEJUNOSTOMY WITHOUT GASTRIC RESECTION

This procedure is performed to bypass the distal stomach or the duodenum mostly in cases of malignant obstruction that cannot be resected. In major duodenopancreatic trauma with a high risk for fistulas, a gastrojejunostomy may also be performed in association with a temporary closure of the pylorus as part of the duodenal exclusion.[54] Occasionally, the gastrojejunostomy is created prophylactically during the surgical exploration of a patient with unresectable adenocarcinoma of the head of the pancreas to prevent subsequent gastric outlet obstruction.[55] The gastrojejunostomy is

usually performed along the greater curvature of the distal body or the proximal antrum of the stomach (Fig. 11–6*A*). It may involve the anterior or the posterior wall at the surgeon discretion. In all cases, a side-to-side anastomosis is performed with the first jejunal loop that can be sutured without tension to the stomach. The anastomosis can be isoperistaltic or antiperistaltic, retrocolic, or antecolic as described for a BII gastroenteroanastomosis. The definition for the length of the anastomosis does not apply (oralis totalis/oralis partialis) because this is a side-to-side anastomosis. However, this anastomosis usually resembles an oralis partialis in length. The gastrojejunostomy presents endoscopically as a vertical anastomosis with two stomal openings that correspond to the afferent and efferent limb. Either one of the limbs may be in a superior (upper) or inferior (lower) position, depending on the technique used during the surgery. For example, if an isoperistaltic gastrojejunostomy has been created, the opening of the afferent limb should be expected in the upper position. The endoscopist should look carefully for a gastrojejunostomy in a patient with an upper tract obstruction who had undergone surgery. This anastomosis may become easily overlooked because it is typically not large, usually located among edematous gastric folds, and associated with gastric contents resulting from outlet obstruction. Ulcerations are also common and may impair intubation of the jejunal openings resulting from tissue retraction.[56] Access to the papilla can be achieved by passing the endoscope retrograde through the afferent limb when a gastric outlet obstruction has been established. The Braun procedure may be added to the gastrojejunostomy as previously described for BII reconstruction (Fig. 11–6*B*).

BARIATRIC SURGERY

The National Institutes of Health (NIH) Consensus Conference in 1985 recognized obesity as a health risk, acknowledged the importance of treating this condition and recommended the body mass index (BMI) to classify patients.[57,58] Indications for bariatric procedures are increasing because of the rise in prevalence of obesity, including childhood obesity, and the lack of effective nonsurgical treatments. Therefore, an increasing number of patients with altered anatomy and perhaps new diseases should be expected in endoscopy units, because gastrointestinal complaints are frequent after bariatric surgery. Indeed, the same complaints in uncomplicated postoperative courses can be present in patients with important surgical complications, which may require surgical revision.[59–61] In addition, some endoscopic findings may represent either a normal postsurgical appearance or a complication depending on the surgery that was performed.[62] An example is the endoscopic finding of a communication between a short proximal gastric pouch with a normal size remnant stomach. This communication is normally expected in a vertical banded gastroplasty (VBG), but it represents a failure (gastrogastric fistula) if the surgical procedure was a gastric bypass (GB). Therefore, the knowledge of the most common bariatric procedures is essential for optimal endoscopic assistance to bariatric patients and surgeons.

Surgical procedures to treat obesity have evolved during the last 5 decades. They can be simplified in two types, restrictive and malabsorptive.[63] Selection of one procedure over the other is based on the individual patient characteristics and surgeon preference.[64,65]

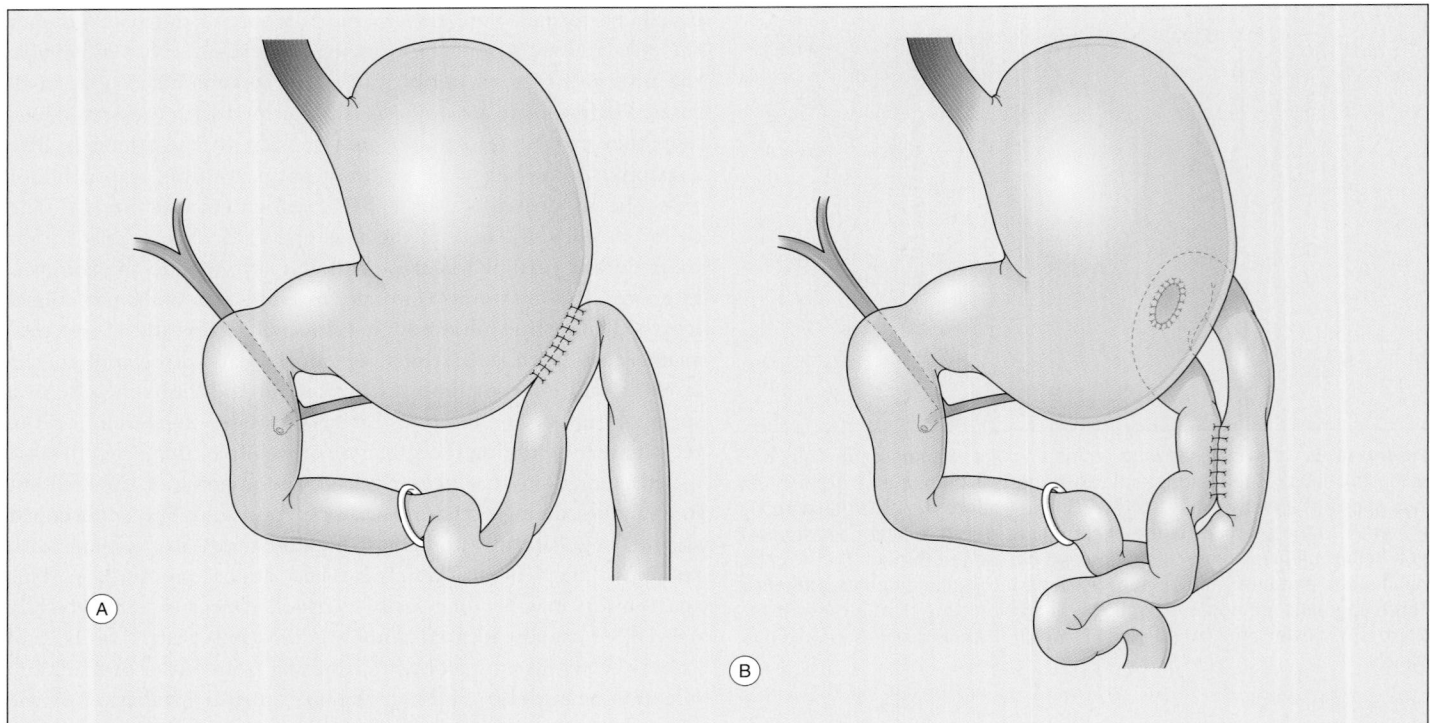

Figure 11–6. Drawings showing gastroenteroanastomoses. *A,* Antiperistaltic gastroenteroanastomosis created along the greater curvature. *B,* Isoperistaltic gastroenteroanastomosis created on the posterior wall of the stomach in association with the Braun procedure.

Jejunoileal Bypass

Jejunoileal bypass (JIB) was the first procedure proposed to induce malabsorption in 1954.[66] It is technically simple and safe because it involves only enteroanastomosis and the surgical steps are readily performed in the middle abdomen. In JIB, the proximal jejunum and the distal ileum are transected. The long jejunoileal segment in between these two transections is excluded from the intestinal transit by suturing the proximal margin in a close end and the distal margin to the sigmoid. An enteroanastomosis is performed between the proximal jejunum and the distal ileum, leaving a short segment of small bowel to absorption (Fig. 11–7). This procedure does not alter the endoscopic anatomy of the upper tract. JIB is no longer performed because of severe hepatic complications.[67] Patients with intact JIB should be considered to revert the operation.

Gastric Bypass

GB includes partition of the stomach creating a small-volume pouch (15 to 50 mL) in the proximal stomach.[68,69] With the distal stomach completely disconnected, the proximal gastric pouch is anastomosed with a Roux-en-Y limb that ranges from 50 to 200 cm to reestablish the alimentary transit (Fig. 11–8A).[70] For the endoscopist, GB may be compared with a Roux-en-Y gastrectomy. The differences are the size of the proximal gastric pouch, the length of the Roux limb, and the fact that the distal stomach is not resected. Surgical technical variations can be observed in GB regarding to the orientation of the pouch (horizontal vs. vertical), partition of the stomach (transection or not), use of a Silastic ring around the gastrojejunal stoma, length of the Roux limbs, and surgical access (laparoscopy vs. open surgery), among others.[71–73] The procedure proposed by Capella incorporates

a Silastic ring in the upper gastric pouch to prevent late stretching and also the suture of the Roux limb to the staple line of the pouch to prevent late gastrogastric fistulas (Fig. 11–8B).[74] GB is a restrictive and malabsorptive procedure.[75] Upper endoscopy in a patient with GB shows a small proximal pouch immediately after the esophagogastric junction with a narrow stoma leading to the small bowel and a long limb before reaching the jejunojejunal anastomosis, which may be inaccessible depending on the length of the limb. The gastric partition may include only the staple line, without division of the stomach (undivided bypass) or a complete transection of the stomach (divided bypass) (Fig. 11–8C). Undivided bypass presents a higher rate of fistulas between the pouch and the distal stomach compared with divided bypass. A gastrogastric fistula leads to a failure in weight loss and to a higher incidence of peptic ulcers beyond the gastrojejunal anastomosis. The gastrojejunostomy may be to the side or to the end of the jejunum or stomach. The small gastric pouch makes lateral and terminal gastric anastomoses indistinguishable. However, lateral and terminal anastomoses are different in the jejunal side. Lateral jejunal anastomosis presents two openings. One ends blindly shortly after the anastomosis; the other leads to the distal jejunum (efferent limb). Terminal anastomosis presents one opening that should be readily accessible endoscopically. The blind end of a lateral anastomosis should not be confused with stenosis of the efferent limb, particularly when scarring alters the anatomy. Abnormal endoscopic findings include esophagitis, pouch or esophagus dilation, stomal stenosis, stomal ulceration, prosthesis erosion at the stoma, and breakdown of the partition staple line. Stomal ulceration has been related to staple line dehiscence in which a gastrogastric fistula occurs, although other factors may be

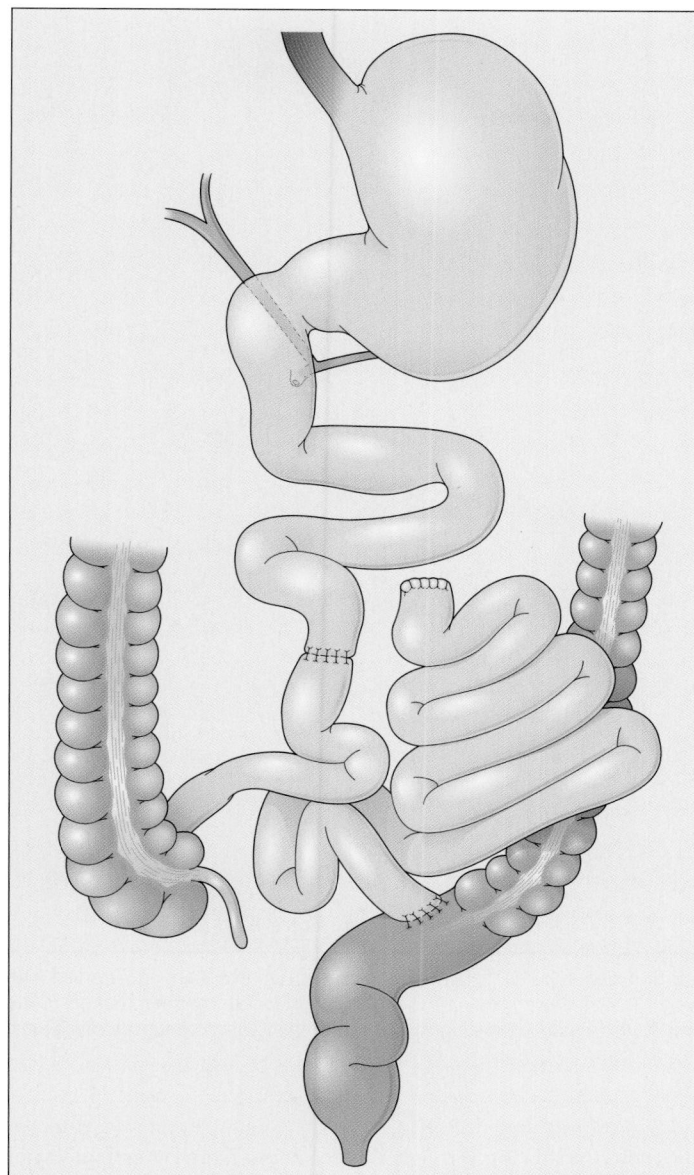

Figure 11–7. Drawing showing a jejunoileal bypass. This operation reduces the small bowel absorptive surface and leaves a long nonfunctional segment of small bowel. Endoscopically, there is no change in the anatomy for upper endoscopy and endoscopic retrograde cholangiopancreatography (ERCP).

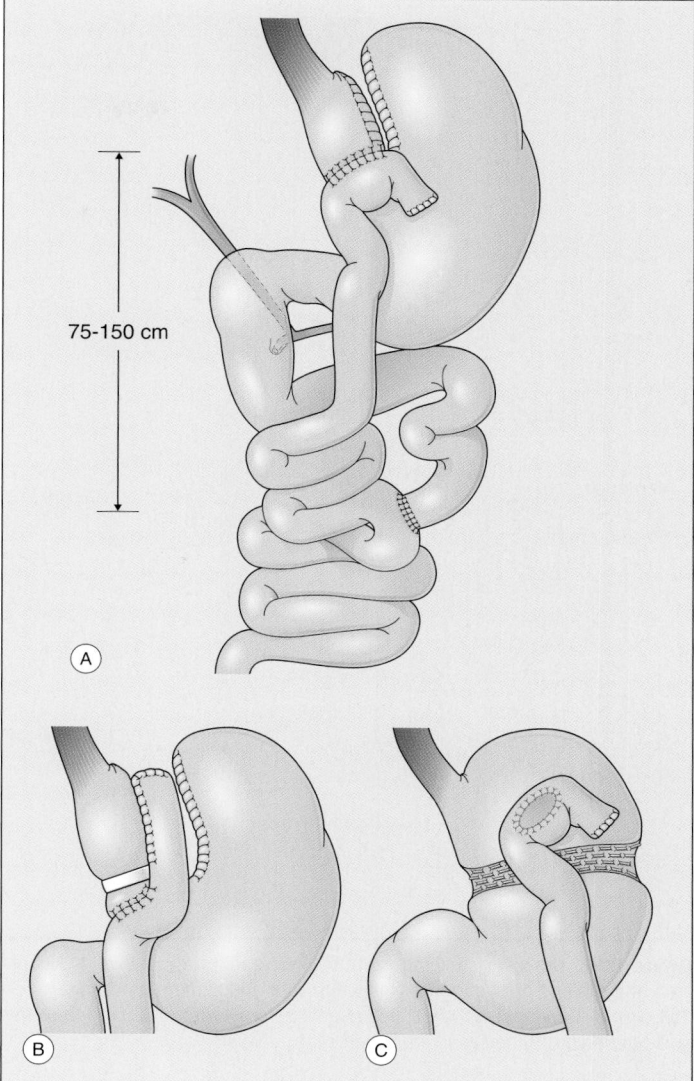

Figure 11–8. Drawings showing gastric bypass. *A,* A small volume pouch (15 to 50 mL) is created just beyond the gastroesophageal junction and anastomosed to a jejunal loop in a Roux-en-Y fashion. The efferent limb ranges from 75 to 150 cm. The distal stomach is not resected and may be used to create a gastrostomy through which the endoscope can be advanced to perform an endoscopic retrograde cholangiopancreatography (ERCP) or a gastroduodenoscopy. *B,* A technical variation that includes the attachment of the jejunal limb to the gastric partitioning to prevent gastrogastric fistulae and also the placement of a Silastic ring in the distal portion of the pouch to prevent dilation. *C,* Undivided gastric bypass: the staple line is not transected and the pouch is horizontal. This type of gastric bypass has been associated to failures in weight loss because of dilation of the pouch and disruption of the staple line.

involved.[76,77] Access to the major papilla and to the disconnected part of the stomach is often impossible per os in patients with GB.[78–80] A gastrostomy tract created in the distal stomach is used as an alternative to access these areas with the endoscope.[81,82]

Biliopancreatic Diversion

Biliopancreatic diversion (BPD) is a malabsorptive procedure to delay the involvement of bile and pancreatic juice in digestion.[83] BPD was first reported in 1979 by Nicola Scopinaro and colleagues and is also known as the Scopinaro procedure.[84] In BPD, the small bowel is divided creating two limbs. The distal limb is anastomosed to the stomach and the proximal limb to the ileum. After com-

pletion, the small bowel presents a new anatomic configuration with three distinct channels: common, alimentary, and biliopancreatic (Fig. 11–9*A*). BPD requires no small bowel resection and does not leave a nonfunctional small bowel segment. The results of the procedure depend on the length of the channels, which are variable because of the individual patient characteristics and surgeon preferences. Typically, a 50- to 100-cm common channel, and a 150- to 200-cm alimentary channel is created. The remaining small bowel

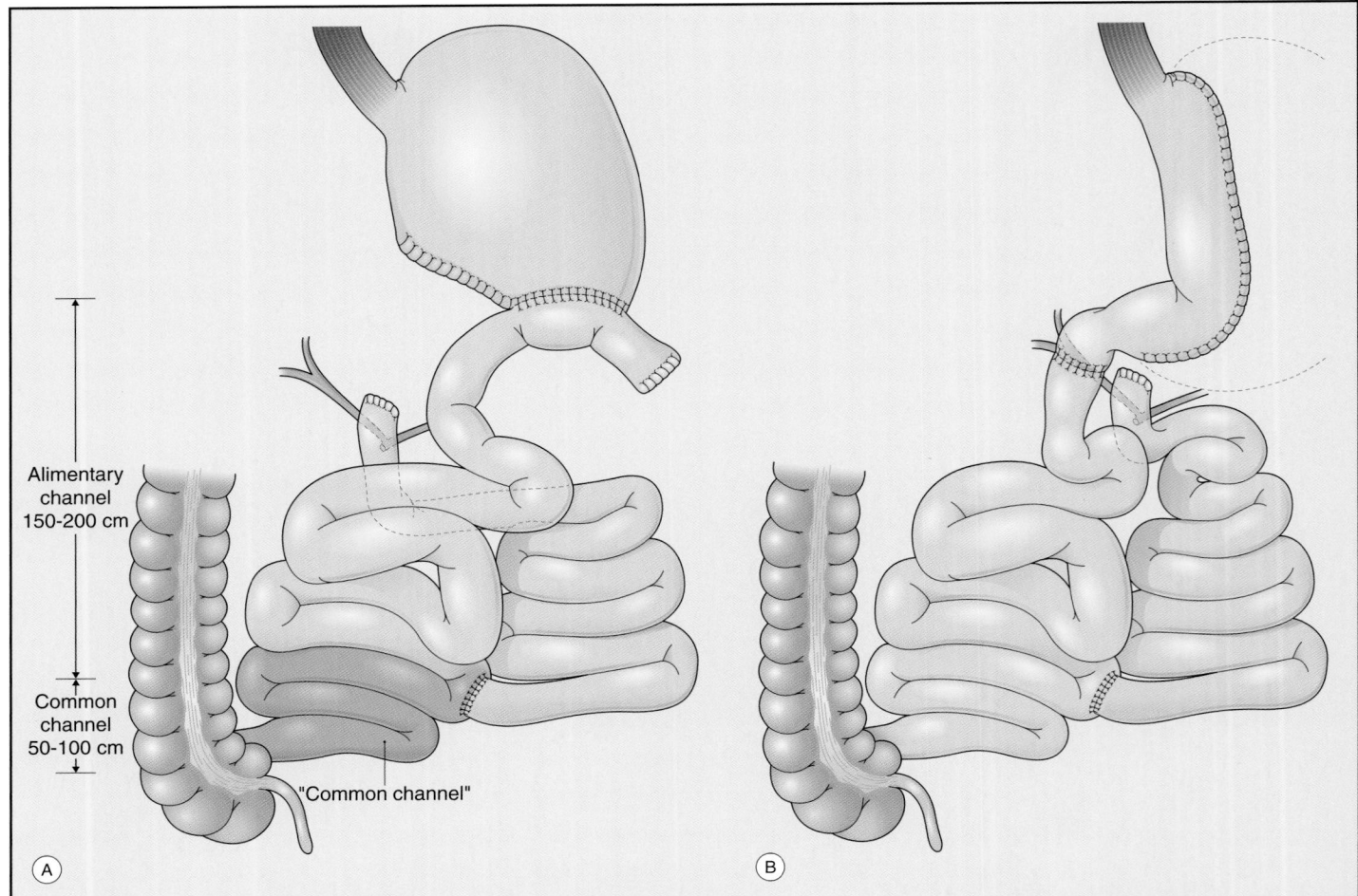

Figure 11–9. Drawings showing malabsorptive bariatric surgeries. *A,* Biliopancreatic diversion: a partial gastrectomy reconstructed in a Roux-en-Y fashion with long afferent and efferent limbs (biliopancreatic and alimentary channels, respectively). The shadowed area represents the short length common channel (50 to 100 cm). *B,* Duodenal switch: a sleeve gastrectomy with preservation of the pylorus leads to a duodenojejunostomy rather than a gastrojejunostomy. Jejunal limbs are reconstructed as in a biliopancreatic diversion.

constitutes the biliopancreatic channel. The common channel length is the determinant for long-term weight maintenance and steatorrhea, whereas the total common alimentary channel is for the temporary mild short-gut syndrome.[81] In addition, the stomach is altered by means of a partial resection or a GB to prevent peptic ulcer and to limit food intake. The gastric component of the BPD is easily accessible endoscopically and the findings vary according to the procedure that was performed. Nevertheless, bile should never be observed and peptic ulceration at the gastroenteroanastomosis and small bowel always carefully investigated. If a partial gastrectomy was chosen, the stomach resembles a Roux-en-Y gastrectomy with a short proximal gastric pouch. A GB may appear as a vertical small gastric pouch or a horizontal pouch that includes the fundus. In a horizontal pouch, the anastomosis with the jejunum should be observed toward the greater curvature. A GB does not include stomach resection, leaving a nonfunctional distal gastric segment, and it can be divided or undivided. Performing ERCP in a patient with BPD is nearly impossible per os because the endoscope has to be advanced all the way through the small bowel, except for the common channel, to reach the major papilla. Alternatives to access

the major papilla are through a gastrostomy (surgical or radiologic) or through a disrupted staple line between the pouch and the stomach. These alternatives apply only for patients who had a GB because gastric resection precludes both options.

Duodenal Switch

The duodenal switch (DS) procedure is a variation of the BPD. This procedure includes a sleeve gastrectomy preserving the pylorus and the anastomosis of the enteric limb end-to-end with the post-pyloric duodenum (Fig. 11–9B).[81] A lower prevalence of side effects has been reported for DS compared with BPD. The same principles described to BPD apply to DS during the endoscopic evaluation, except that a duodenojejunostomy rather than a gastrojejunostomy is present.

Vertical Banded Gastroplasty

Initial gastroplasty configurations proved inadequate in terms of weight loss and the procedure was refined by Mason into the VBG. VBG, a pure restrictive procedure, is the result of a search for a simpler operation compared with the GB.[85] VBG involves the

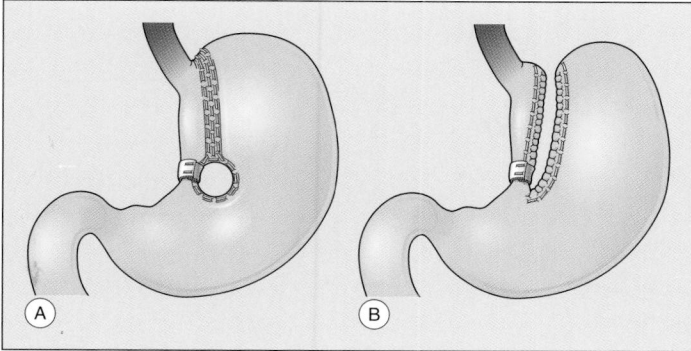

Figure 11–10. Drawings showing vertical banded gastroplasty. A 15-mL pouch is created at the angle of His and the outlet channel encircled by a circumferential band. *A,* A circular and a linear stapler are used to create this uncut gastroplasty. *B,* The staple line may be divided separating the two gastric parts to prevent gastrogastric fistula.

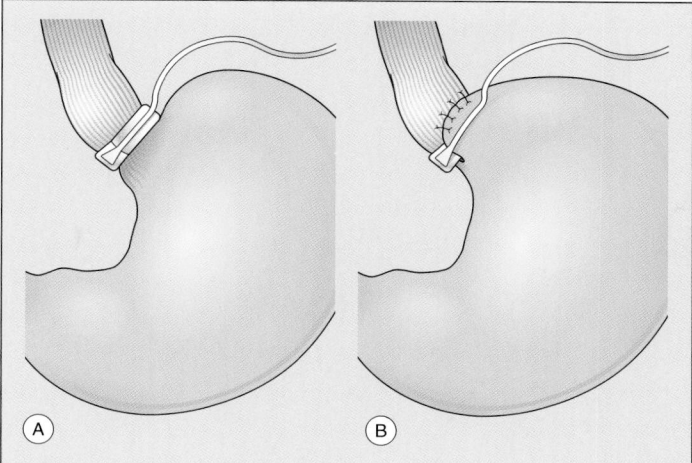

Figure 11–11. Drawings showing laparoscopic adjustable gastric banding. *A,* A 15-mL pouch is created in the proximal stomach with a banding device. The device can be adjusted to narrow the opening to the distal stomach by percutaneous injection of fluids. *B,* A gastrogastric suture is placed anteriorly over the band to prevent gastric herniation.

creation of a small pouch in the proximal stomach and the encirclement of the outlet channel to prevent dilation. The pouch is created along the lesser curvature with a stapled partition precisely at the angle of His to accommodate a volume of 15 mL or less. The outlet channel of the pouch is stabilized by the encirclement of a 5-cm circumference band or a Silastic ring (Fig. 11–10A). A technical variation includes dividing the stapled partition (Fig. 11–10B). Upper endoscopy in patients with intact VBG shows a small tubular pouch immediately after the esophagogastric junction with a narrow outlet channel that once transposed leads to the remaining distal stomach. Abnormal endoscopic findings include esophagitis, staple line dehiscence, food impaction, stenosis of the pouch outlet, and erosion of the gastric wall by the material used to encircle the outlet channel.[86,87] The remaining stomach, duodenal bulb, and biliopancreatic ducts are readily accessible for endoscopy if the outlet channel permits passage of the endoscope. The outlet channel is ideally 11 mm wide and 15 mm long, and it can be dilated endoscopically in cases of stenosis.

Laparoscopic Adjustable Gastric Banding

Laparoscopic adjustable gastric banding (LAGB) is a restrictive procedure largely used in some European countries.[88] LAGB involves placing a band around the proximal stomach to create a 15-mL pouch without the need of resecting or stapling the stomach (Fig. 11–11A). LAGB is now performed using a silicone material device that can be inflated with saline solution to adjust the gastric-pouch outflow. The inflatable part of the band device is connected by tubing to a reservoir implanted and secured to the abdominal fascia that can be accessed via a needle.[89] Adjustable silicone gastric bands reduce the risks of eroding the gastric wall and the incidence of uncontrolled vomiting compared with former types of gastric banding. Upper endoscopy in a patient with LAGB will show a small gastric pouch at the level of the cardia with a narrow outlet channel that leads to the distal normal stomach. Esophageal dilatation, esophagitis, gastric pouch dilatation, gastric slippage, outlet channel stenosis, and gastric wall erosion by the band device are the most common abnormal findings observed after LAGB.[90,91] Occasionally, a marked gastric fold surrounding the pouch outlet channel can be observed in a retroflexed view within the distal stomach. This fold

corresponds to the gastrogastric sutures placed anteriorly over the band device to decrease the risks of gastric herniation (Fig. 11–11B). Similar to the VBG, once the endoscope is advanced through the pouch-outlet channel, examination of the distal stomach, duodenum, and biliopancreatic ducts can be performed as in a regular endoscopy.

Operations with Alteration of the Pancreaticobiliary Anatomy

PANCREATICODUODENECTOMY (WHIPPLE PROCEDURE)

The Whipple procedure is performed to resect malignant or benign lesions in the head of the pancreas or in the second portion of the duodenum.[92] The extent of the resection classifies this procedure in classic or pylorus-preserving.

Classic Whipple Procedure

The gastric antrum, duodenum, head of the pancreas, and distal bile duct are resected in the classic Whipple procedure. This extensive resection lead to the proposal of at least 68 techniques for reconstruction of the alimentary and pancreaticobiliary tract during the evolution of this operation.[93] Currently, one well-accepted technique is to create all necessary anastomosis with a single limb of small bowel (Fig. 11–12A).[94,95] In this case, a side-to-side gastroenteroanastomosis will be encountered endoscopically, usually oralis partialis and with the resection limited to the antrum. Indeed, all the variations regarding orientation, position to the transverse colon, and stoma size described for the BII gastroenteroanastomosis apply here. On entering the afferent limb, which may vary from 40 to 60 cm and include a Braun procedure, the anastomosis with the biliary and pancreatic ducts can be identified. Sharp angulations resulting from fixation to adjacent organs may be encountered

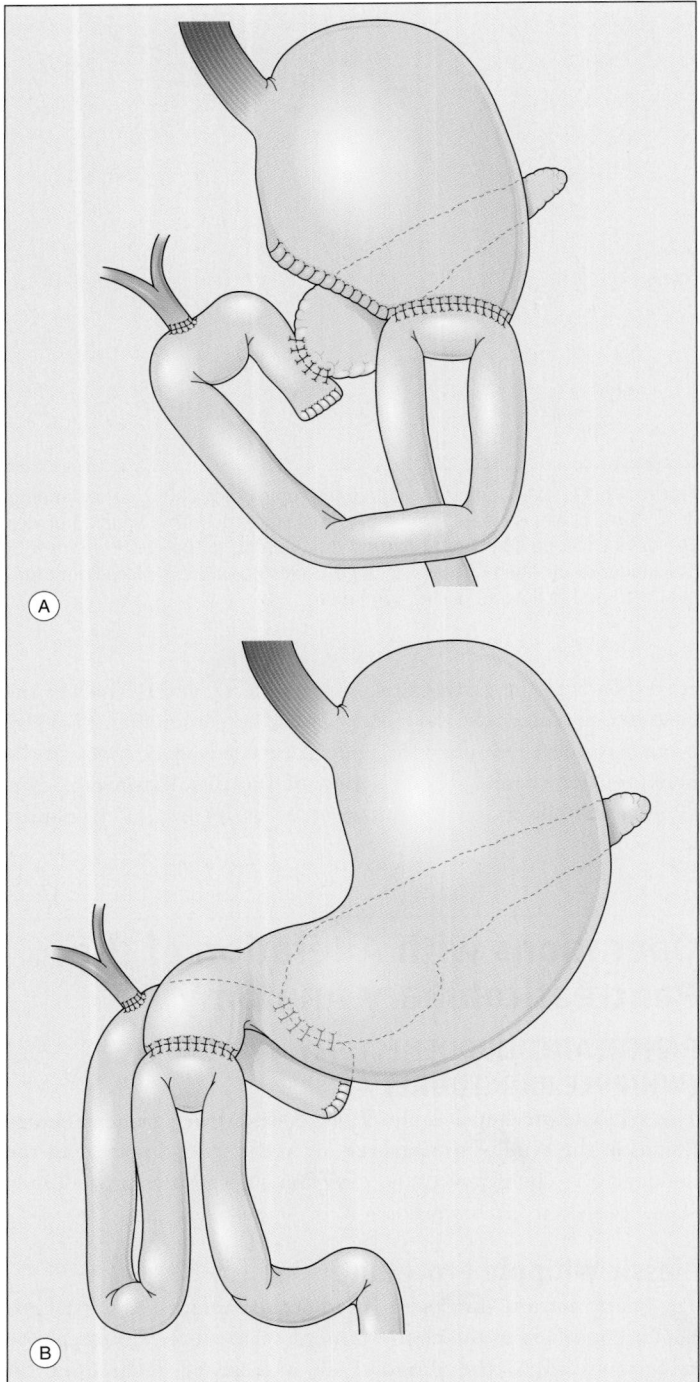

Figure 11–12. Drawings showing Whipple operations. *A,* Classic Whipple: resection of the distal stomach, head of the pancreas, distal biliary duct, and duodenum. A single loop of jejunum is used to the anastomoses with the stomach and biliary and pancreatic ducts. A partial isoperistaltic gastroenteroanastomosis is demonstrated. *B,* Pylorus-preserving Whipple: a duodenojejunostomy rather than a gastrojejunostomy is present in this procedure.

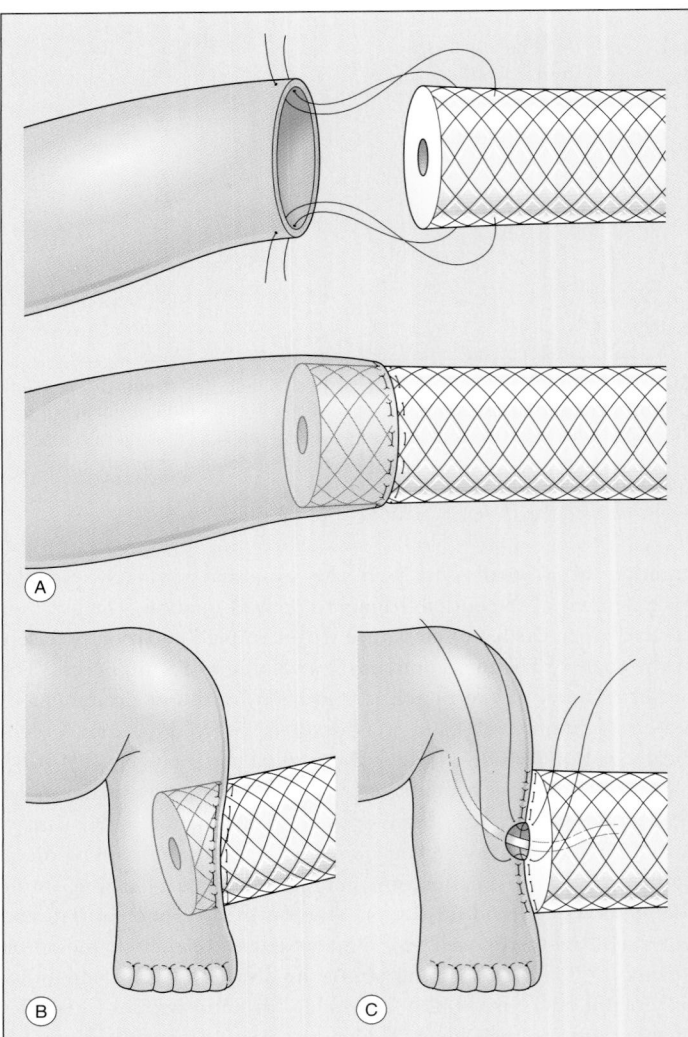

Figure 11–13. Drawings showing pancreaticojejunostomies. *A,* Terminoterminal "dunking" anastomosis where the pancreas is invaginated into the jejunum. *B,* Terminolateral dunking anastomosis. *C,* Mucosa-to-mucosa pancreaticojejunostomy.

mucosa anastomosis creates a small opening by suturing the pancreatic duct to the jejunal mucosa. The dunking anastomosis differs from the mucosa-to-mucosa anastomosis in that the pancreas is invaginated into the jejunum. Therefore, the opening of the pancreatic duct may varies from a flat, small-diameter anastomosis (mucosa-to-mucosa) to a protuberant sometimes downward-oriented anastomosis (lateral dunking), making the identification and cannulation of this duct technically challenging. The hepaticojejunostomy is located approximately 10 cm proximal (endoscopically) to the pancreaticojejunostomy. It is always an end-to-side anastomosis located in the antimesenteric border of the limb, occasionally subtle or hidden by a fold.

Pylorus-Preserving Whipple Procedure

The pylorus-preserving Whipple differs from the classic Whipple operation in that the stomach is not resected and a short segment of the proximal bulb remains to be anastomosed with the jejunum (Fig. 11–12B).[97] This modification has proved to decrease the morbidity

before reaching the blind end of the most proximal portion of the afferent limb, where the pancreaticojejunostomy will be found. The pancreaticojejunostomy may be end-to-end or end-to-side. In either case, the pancreaticojejunostomy may also be a mucosa-to-mucosa or a "dunking" anastomosis (Fig. 11–13A to C).[96] A mucosa-to-

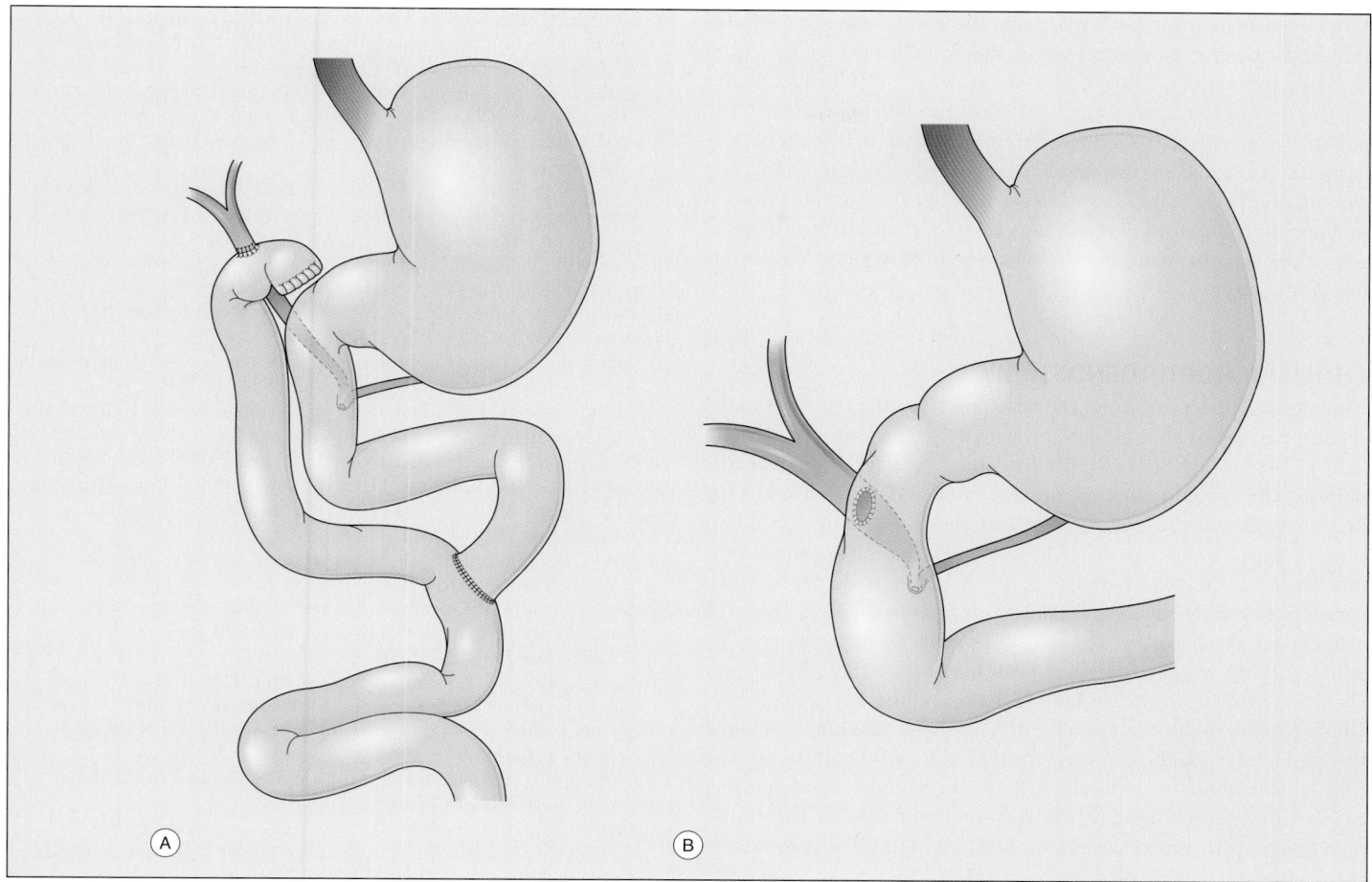

Figure 11–14. Drawings showing bilioenteric anastomoses. *A,* Roux-en-Y hepaticojejunostomy: the bile duct is anastomosed to a limb of jejunum in a lateral or terminal fashion. A side-to-side anastomosis preserves cannulation of the intrahepatic ducts through the papilla if no obstruction is present. The pancreatic duct remains accessible through the second portion of the duodenum. *B,* Choledochoduodenostomy: usually a side-to-side anastomosis readily accessible on the second portion of the duodenum. The distal bile duct may be filled with residual enteric contents leading to the sump syndrome.

of pancreaticoduodenectomies without compromising the oncologic principles of the resection. Therefore, a duodenojejunostomy rather than a gastrojejunostomy is observed in patients with a pylorus-preserving Whipple procedure. After traversing a normal stomach and the pylorus, a two-opening small-diameter anastomosis will be identified in a short segment of bulb. Depending on the orientation of the reconstruction, the afferent limb is to the right (antiperistaltic) or to the left (isoperistaltic). Antecolic or retrocolic anastomosis can also be observed, creating variations on the length of the jejunal limb. Usually, a trial-and-error approach is necessary to define the afferent limb, in which the pancreatic and biliary anastomosis are performed as described for the classic Whipple. In patients who have undergone a Whipple operation, the biliary and pancreatic anastomosis may be reached with a side-viewing or a forward-viewing endoscope.

ROUX-EN-Y HEPATICOJEJUNOSTOMY

Anastomosis of the hepatic duct to a loop of jejunum without disturbing the gastroduodenal anatomy is usually performed for biliary disease or during liver transplantation when the native bile duct cannot be used to create a duct-to-duct anastomosis.[98] The

hepaticojejunostomy is usually end-to-side, but side-to-side anastomosis can also be encountered (Fig. 11–14*A*). The anatomy of the stomach, duodenum, and pancreas are not altered and the endoscopic evaluation of these organs is similar to a nonoperated stomach. If the bile duct must be accessed, the endoscope has to be advanced through a normal stomach and duodenum before reaching the jejunojejunal anastomosis that will lead to a Roux limb with the hepaticojejunostomy. Therefore, long-length endoscopes are usually necessary, including the use of the overtube to prevent looping in the stomach, and failures to reach the biliary duct are common.[99,100] Opposed to the anatomy after a Roux-en-Y gastrectomy, the duodenojejunal limb merges into the small bowel rather than merge with a loop of small bowel. At the level of the jejunojejunostomy, three lumens (side-to-side) or two lumens (end-to-side) can be observed, depending on the reconstruction (Fig. 11–5*B*). One leads to the distal jejunum and other to the limb that contains the hepaticojejunostomy. The third lumen (only if side-to-side) observed along the initial limb occupied by the endoscope ends blindly just beyond the anastomosis. A trial-and-error approach to the first two limbs will reveal the one with the hepaticojejunostomy. The end-to-side hepaticojejunostomy is similar to the one described in the Whipple procedure, except that here the location is closer to the blind end of the limb. Different from the end-to-side, the side-to-side hepaticojejunostomy preserves the access to the biliary ducts through the major papilla if the distal common bile duct is not obstructed. In this case, a cholangiogram can be obtained with the aid of an occlusion balloon inflated proximal to the hepaticojejunostomy, avoiding the demanding insertion of the endoscope through the Roux limb. Air within the intrahepatic ducts is common in bilioenteric anastomosis and may be useful to evaluate patients in whom the hepaticojejunostomy is not reachable with the endoscope (air cholangiogram).[4,101]

CHOLEDOCHODUODENOSTOMY

Choledochoduodenostomy is the anastomosis of the bile duct to the second portion of the duodenum, usually performed in a side-to-side fashion (Fig. 11–14B). Endoscopically, after traversing the pylorus, the choledochoduodenostomy is found at the level of the major papilla on the opposite wall of the duodenum. The anastomosis may be sufficiently wide to allow visualization and partial intubation of the extrahepatic ducts. A side-to-side anastomosis presents two lumens. One leads to the proximal biliary tree; the other leads to the distal common bile duct. Because there is no alimentary diversion from the anastomosis, food impaction may occur in the distal common bile duct causing the sump syndrome, which may be the indication for ERCP in these patients.[102] Because the biliary duct can be accessed through the major papilla and also through the choledochoduodenostomy, a combination of accesses can be used to manipulate the different portions of the ducts, including anterograde cannulation of the papilla. The approach to the pancreatic duct is as for standard ERCP.

REFERENCES

1. Max MH, West B, Knutson CO: Evaluation of postoperative gastroduodenal symptoms: Endoscopy or upper gastrointestinal roentgenography? Surgery 86:578–582, 1979.
2. Donahue PE, Nyhus LM: Surgeon-endoscopists and the assessment of postoperative patients. South Med J 75:1570–1575, 1982.
3. Feitoza AB, Baron TH: Endoscopy and ERCP in the setting of previous upper GI tract surgery. Part I: Reconstruction without alteration of pancreaticobiliary anatomy. Gastrointest Endosc 54:743–749, 2001.
4. Feitoza AB, Baron TH: Endoscopy and ERCP in the setting of previous upper GI tract surgery. Part II: Postsurgical anatomy with alteration of the pancreaticobiliary tree. Gastrointest Endosc 55:75–79, 2002.
5. Little AG: Mechanisms of action of antireflux surgery: Theory and fact. World J Surg 16:320–325, 1992.
6. Nissen R: Eine einfache Operation zur Beeinflussung der Refluxoesophagitis. Schweiz Med Wochenschr 86:590–592, 1956.
7. Nissen R, Rosseti M: Surgery of hiatal hernia and other diaphragmatic hernias. J Int Coll Surg 43:663–674, 1965.
8. DeMeester TR, Bonavina L, Albertucci M: Nissen fundoplication for gastroesophageal reflux disease. Evaluation of primary repair in 100 consecutive patients. Ann Surg 204:9–20, 1986.
9. Peters JH, Heimbucher J, Kauer WK, et al: Clinical and physiologic comparison of laparoscopic and open Nissen fundoplication. J Am Coll Surg 180:385–393, 1995.
10. Hinder RA, Filipi CJ, Wetscher G, et al: Laparoscopic Nissen fundoplication is an effective treatment for gastroesophageal reflux disease. Ann Surg 220:472–481; discussion 481–483, 1994.
11. Donahue PE, Samelson S, Nyhus LM, et al: The floppy Nissen fundoplication. Effective long-term control of pathologic reflux. Arch Surg 120:663–668, 1985.
12. O'Boyle CJ, Watson DI, Jamieson GG, et al: Division of short gastric vessels at laparoscopic Nissen fundoplication: A prospective double-blind randomized trial with 5-year follow-up. Ann Surg 235:165–170, 2002.
13. Chrysos E, Tzortzinis A, Tsiaoussis J, et al: Prospective randomized trial comparing Nissen to Nissen-Rossetti technique for laparoscopic fundoplication. Am J Surg 182:215–221, 2001.
14. Horgan S, Pellegrini CA: Surgical treatment of gastroesophageal reflux disease. Surg Clin North Am 77:1063–1082, 1997.
15. Bowrey DJ, Peters JH: Laparoscopic esophageal surgery. Surg Clin North Am 80:1213–1242, 2000.
16. Johnson DA, Younes Z, Hogan WJ: Endoscopic assessment of hiatal hernia repair. Gastrointest Endosc 52:650–659, 2000.
17. Arendt T, Stuber E, Monig H, et al: Dysphagia due to transmural migration of surgical material into the esophagus nine years after Nissen fundoplication. Gastrointest Endosc 51:607–610, 2000.
18. Jailwala J, Massey B, Staff D, et al: Post-fundoplication symptoms: The role for endoscopic assessment of fundoplication integrity. Gastrointest Endosc 54:351–356, 2001.
19. Low DE: Management of the problem patient after antireflux surgery. Gastroenterol Clin North Am 23:371–389, 1994.
20. Malhi-Chowla N, Gorecki P, Bammer T, et al: Dilation after fundoplication: Timing, frequency, indications, and outcome. Gastrointest Endosc 55:219–223, 2002.
21. Gadenstatter M, Klingler A, Prommegger R, et al: Laparoscopic partial posterior fundoplication provides excellent intermediate results in GERD patients with impaired esophageal peristalsis. Surgery 126:548–552, 1999.
22. Hunter JG, Richardson WS: Surgical management of achalasia. Surg Clin North Am 77:993–1015, 1997.
23. Vogt D, Curet M, Pitcher D, et al: Successful treatment of esophageal achalasia with laparoscopic Heller myotomy and Toupet fundoplication. Am J Surg 174:709–714, 1997.
24. Mellinger JD, Ponsky JL: Endoscopic evaluation of the postoperative stomach. Gastrointest Endosc Clin N Am 6:621–639, 1996.
25. Trastek VF, Deschamps C, Allen MS, et al: Uncut Collis-Nissen fundoplication: Learning curve and long-term results. Ann Thorac Surg 66:1739–1744, 1998.
26. Horvath KD, Swanstrom LL, Jobe BA: The short esophagus: Pathophysiology, incidence, presentation, and treatment in the era of laparoscopic antireflux surgery. Ann Surg 232:630–640, 2000.
27. Sawye JL, Herrington JL: Vagotomy-antrectomy. In Wastell C, Nyhus LM, Donahue PE (eds): Surgery of the Esophagus, Stomach and Small Intestine. New York, Little, Brown, 1994, pp 520–530.
28. Ritchie WP Jr: Alkaline reflux gastritis. Gastroenterol Clin North Am 23:281–294, 1994.
29. Thon HJ, Loffler A, Buess G, et al: Is ERCP a reasonable diagnostic method for excluding pancreatic and hepatobiliary disease in patients with a Billroth II resection? Endoscopy 15:93–95, 1983.
30. Jameson LC: Stapling in esophageal and gastric surgery. In Wastell C, Nyhus LM, Donahue PE (eds): Surgery of the Esophagus, Stomach and Small Intestine. New York, Little, Brown, 1994, pp 572–587.
31. Aabakken L, Holthe B, Sandstad O, et al: Endoscopic pancreaticobiliary procedures in patients with a Billroth II resection: A 10-year follow-up study. Ital J Gastroenterol Hepatol 30:301–305, 1998.
32. Bedogni G, Bertoni G, Contini S, et al: Endoscopic sphincterotomy in patients with Billroth II partial gastrectomy: Comparison of three different techniques. Gastrointest Endosc 30:300–304, 1984.
33. Siegel JH, Cohen SA, Kasmin FE, et al: Stent-guided sphincterotomy. Gastrointest Endosc 40:567–572, 1994.
34. Prat F, Fritsch J, Choury AD, et al: Endoscopic sphincteroplasty: A useful therapeutic tool for biliary endoscopy in Billroth II gastrectomy patients. Endoscopy 29:79–81, 1997.

35. Bergman JJ, van Berkel AM, Bruno MJ, et al: A randomized trial of endoscopic balloon dilation and endoscopic sphincterotomy for removal of bile duct stones in patients with a prior Billroth II gastrectomy. Gastrointest Endosc 53:19–26, 2001.

36. van Buuren HR, Boender J, Nix GA, et al: Needle-knife sphincterotomy guided by a biliary endoprosthesis in Billroth II gastrectomy patients. Endoscopy 27:229–232, 1995.

37. Costamagna G, Mutignani M, Perri V, et al: Diagnostic and therapeutic ERCP in patients with Billroth II gastrectomy. Acta Gastroenterol Belg 57:155–162, 1994.

38. Mosca S: How can we reduce complication rates and enhance success rates in Billroth II patients during endoscopic retrograde cholangiopancreatography? Endoscopy 32:589–590, 2000.

39. Lin LF, Siauw CP, Ho KS, et al: ERCP in post-Billroth II gastrectomy patients: Emphasis on technique. Am J Gastroenterol 94:144–148, 1999.

40. Hintze RE, Adler A, Veltzke W, et al: Endoscopic access to the papilla of Vater for endoscopic retrograde cholangiopancreatography in patients with Billroth II or Roux-en-Y gastrojejunostomy. Endoscopy 29:69–73, 1997.

41. Olbe L, Becker HD: Partial gastrectomy with Billroth II resection and alternative methods. In Becker HD, Herfarth CH, Lierse W, Schreiber HW (eds): Surgery of the Stomach. Berlin, Springer-Verlag, 1987, pp 50–70.

42. Safrany L, Neuhaus B, Portocarrero G, et al: Endoscopic sphincterotomy in patients with Billroth II gastrectomy. Endoscopy 12:16–22, 1980.

43. Faylona JM, Qadir A, Chan AC, et al: Small-bowel perforations related to endoscopic retrograde cholangiopancreatography (ERCP) in patients with Billroth II gastrectomy. Endoscopy 31:546–549, 1999.

44. Costamagna G: ERCP and endoscopic sphincterotomy in Billroth II patients: A demanding technique for experts only? Ital J Gastroenterol Hepatol 30:306–309, 1998.

45. Kim MH, Lee SK, Lee MH, et al: Endoscopic retrograde cholangiopancreatography and needle-knife sphincterotomy in patients with Billroth II gastrectomy: A comparative study of the forward-viewing endoscope and the side-viewing duodenoscope. Endoscopy 29:82–85, 1997.

46. Delcore R, Cheung LY: Surgical options in postgastrectomy syndromes. Surg Clin North Am 71:57–75, 1991.

47. Haglund UH, Jansson RL, Lindhagen JG, et al: Primary Roux-Y gastrojejunostomy versus gastroduodenostomy after antrectomy and selective vagotomy. Am J Surg 159:546–549, 1990.

48. Donahue PE: Early postoperative and postgastrectomy syndromes. Diagnosis, management, and prevention. Gastroenterol Clin North Am 23:215–226, 1994.

49. Eagon JC, Miedema BW, Kelly KA: Postgastrectomy syndromes. Surg Clin North Am 72:445–465, 1992.

50. Burdick JS, Garza AA, Magee DJ, et al: Endoscopic management of afferent loop syndrome of malignant etiology. Gastrointest Endosc 55:602–605, 2002.

51. Steffes C, Fromm D: Postgastrectomy syndromes. In Zuidema GD (ed): Shackelford's Surgery of the Alimentary Tract, 4th ed. Philadelphia, WB Saunders, 1996, pp 166–184.

52. Schirmer BD: Gastric atony and the Roux syndrome. Gastroenterol Clin North Am 23:327–343, 1994.

53. Lehman GA: What are the determinants of success in utilization of ERCP in the setting of pancreatic and biliary diseases? Gastrointest Endosc 56(6 Suppl 2):S291–293, 2002.

54. Ivatury RR, Nassoura ZE, Simon R, et al: Complex duodenal injuries. Surg Clin North Am 76:797–812, 1996.

55. Lillemoe KD, Barnes SA: Surgical palliation of unresectable pancreatic carcinoma. Surg Clin North Am 75:953–968, 1995.

56. Nyhus LM, Sheaff CM: Recurrent ulcer. In Wastell C, Nyhus LM, Donahue PE (eds): Surgery of the Esophagus, Stomach and Small Intestine. New York, Little, Brown, 1994, pp 531–541.

57. Health implications of obesity. National Institutes of Health Consensus Development Conference Statement. Ann Intern Med 103:1073–1077, 1985.

58. Balsiger BM, Luque de Leon E, Sarr MG: Surgical treatment of obesity: Who is an appropriate candidate? Mayo Clin Proc 72:551–558, 1997.

59. Stellato TA, Crouse C, Hallowell PT: Bariatric surgery: Creating new challenges for the endoscopist. Gastrointest Endosc 57:86–94, 2003.

60. Byrne TK: Complications of surgery for obesity. Surg Clin North Am 81:1181–1193, 2001.

61. Knol JA: Management of the problem patient after bariatric surgery. Gastroenterol Clin North Am 23:345–369, 1994.

62. Papavramidis ST, Theocharidis AJ, Zaraboukas TG, et al: Upper gastrointestinal endoscopic and histologic findings before and after vertical banded gastroplasty. Surg Endosc 10:825–830, 1996.

63. Balsiger BM, Murr MM, Poggio JL, et al: Bariatric surgery. Surgery for weight control in patients with morbid obesity. Med Clin North Am 84:477–489, 2000.

64. Schirmer BD: Laparoscopic bariatric surgery. Surg Clin North Am 80:1253–1267, 2000.

65. Mason EE: Gastric surgery for morbid obesity. Surg Clin North Am 72:501–513, 1992.

66. Kremen AN, Linner JH, Nelson CH: Experimental evaluation of the nutritional importance of proximal and distal small intestine. Ann Surg 140:439–448, 1954.

67. Kaminski DL, Hermann VM, Martin S: Late effects of jejunoileal bypass operation on hepatic inflammation, fibrosis and lipid content. Hepatogastroenterology 32:159–162, 1985.

68. Fisher BL, Barber AE: Gastric bypass procedures. In Deitel M, Cowan GS Jr (eds): Update: Surgery for the Morbidly Obese Patient. Toronto, FD-Communications, 2000, pp 139–146.

69. Schauer PR, Ikramuddin S, Gourash W, et al: Outcomes after laparoscopic Roux-en-Y gastric bypass for morbid obesity. Ann Surg 232:515–529, 2000.

70. Murr MM, Balsiger BM, Kennedy FP, et al: Malabsorptive procedures for severe obesity: Comparison of pancreaticobiliary bypass and very long limb Roux-en-Y gastric bypass. J Gastrointest Surg 3:607–612, 1999.

71. Schauer PR, Ikramuddin S: Laparoscopic surgery for morbid obesity. Surg Clin North Am 81:1145–1179, 2001.

72. MacLean LD, Rhode BM, Nohr CW: Late outcome of isolated gastric bypass. Ann Surg 231:524–528, 2000.

73. Nguyen NT, Goldman C, Rosenquist CJ, et al: Laparoscopic versus open gastric bypass: A randomized study of outcomes, quality of life, and costs. Ann Surg 234:279–289; discussion 289–291, 2001.

74. Capella JF, Capella RF: An assessment of vertical banded gastroplasty-Roux-en-Y gastric bypass for the treatment of morbid obesity. Am J Surg 183:117–123, 2002.

75. Brolin RE: Gastric bypass. Surg Clin North Am 81:1077–1095, 2001.

76. Pope GD, Goodney PP, Burchard KW, et al: Peptic ulcer/stricture after gastric bypass: A comparison of technique and acid suppression variables. Obes Surg 12:30–33, 2002.

77. Schirmer B, Erenoglu C, Miller A: Flexible endoscopy in the management of patients undergoing Roux-en-Y gastric bypass. Obes Surg 12:634–638, 2002.

78. Peters M, Papasavas PK, Caushaj PF, et al: Laparoscopic transgastric endoscopic retrograde cholangiopancreatography for benign common bile duct stricture after Roux-en-Y gastric bypass. Surg Endosc 16:1106, 2002.

79. Silecchia G, Catalano C, Gentileschi P, et al: Virtual gastroduodenoscopy: A new look at the bypassed stomach and duodenum after laparoscopic Roux-en-Y gastric bypass for morbid obesity. Obes Surg 12:39–48, 2002.

80. Wright BE, Cass OW, Freeman ML: ERCP in patients with long-limb Roux-en-Y gastrojejunostomy and intact papilla. Gastrointest Endosc 56:225–232, 2002.

81. Baron TH. Vickers SM: Surgical gastrostomy placement as access for diagnostic and therapeutic ERCP. Gastrointest Endosc 48:640–641, 1998.

82. Sundbom M, Nyman R, Hedenstrom H, Gustavsson S: Investigation of the excluded stomach after Roux-en-Y gastric bypass. Obes Surg 11:25–27, 2001.

83. Marceau P, Hould FS, Lebel S, et al: Malabsorptive obesity surgery. Surg Clin North Am 81:1113–1127, 2001.

84. Scopinaro N, Gianetta E, Pandolfo N, et al: Bilio-pancreatic bypass. Proposal and preliminary experimental study of a new type of operation for the functional surgical treatment of obesity. Minerva Chir 31:560–566, 1976. (Italian)

85. Doherty C: Vertical banded gastroplasty. Surg Clin North Am 81:1097–1112, 2001.

86. Verset D, Houben JJ, Gay F, et al: The place of upper gastrointestinal tract endoscopy before and after vertical banded gastroplasty for morbid obesity. Dig Dis Sci 42:2333–2337, 1997.

87. Nguyen DQ, Buchwald H, Bolman RM 3rd, et al: Endoscopic laser treatment of obstructing polypropylene mesh after vertical banded gastroplasty. Gastrointest Endosc 51:616–617, 2000.

88. Pontiroli AE, Pizzocri P, Librenti MC, et al: Laparoscopic adjustable gastric banding for the treatment of morbid (grade 3) obesity and its metabolic complications: A three-year study. J Clin Endocrinol Metab 87:3555–3561, 2002.

89. DeMaria EJ: Laparoscopic adjustable silicone gastric banding. Surg Clin North Am 81:1129–1144, 2001.

90. Baldinger R, Mluench R, Steffen R, et al: Conservative management of intragastric migration of Swedish adjustable gastric band by endoscopic retrieval. Gastrointest Endosc 53:98–101, 2001.

91. Weiner R: A prospective randomized trial of different laparoscopic gastric banding techniques for morbid obesity. Surg Endosc 15:63–68, 2001.

92. Izbicki JR, Bloechle C, Knoefel WT, et al: Surgical treatment of chronic pancreatitis and quality of life after operation. Surg Clin North Am 79:913–944, 1999.

93. Trede M: Technique of Whipple pancreatoduodenectomy. In Trede M, Carter DC, Longmire WP (eds): Surgery of the Pancreas. New York, Churchill Livingstone, 1997, pp 487–498.

94. Farnell MB, Nagorney DM, Sarr MG: The Mayo Clinic approach to the surgical treatment of adenocarcinoma of the pancreas. Surg Clin North Am 81:611–623, 2001.

95. Pitt HA: Curative treatment for pancreatic neoplasms. Standard resection. Surg Clin N Am 75:891–904, 1995.

96. Toledo-Pereyra LH: The Pancreas—Principles of Medical and Surgical Practice. New York, Wiley, 1985.

97. Braasch JW, Gagner M: Pylorus-preserving pancreatoduodenectomy—technical aspects. Langenbecks Arch Chir 376:50–58, 1991.

98. Pfau PR, Kochman ML, Lewis JD, et al: Endoscopic management of post-operative biliary complications in orthotopic liver transplantation. Gastrointest Endosc 52:55–63, 2000.

99. Elton E, Hanson BL, Qaseem T, et al: Diagnostic and therapeutic ERCP using an enteroscope and a pediatric colonoscope in long-limb surgical bypass patients. Gastrointest Endosc 47:62–67, 1998.

100. Gostout CJ, Bender CE: Cholangiopancreatography, sphincterotomy, and common duct stone removal via Roux-en-Y limb enteroscopy. Gastroenterology 95:156–163, 1988.

101. Lim PL, Porter KG: Air as contrast for cholangiography in a patient with a history of allergy to radiopaque media. Endoscopy 31:S9, 1999.

102. Caroli-Bosc FX, Demarquay JF, Peten EP, et al: Endoscopic management of sump syndrome after choledochoduodenostomy: Retrospective analysis of 30 cases. Gastrointest Endosc 51:180–183, 2000.

Assessment of Endoscopic Outcomes

Brooks D. Cash and David J. Bjorkman*

Introduction

The development and refinement of flexible endoscopy has dramatically altered the diagnosis and management of many gastrointestinal (GI) diseases. The role of endoscopy has now extended beyond disorders of the luminal GI tract to include those involving the biliary tree, liver, and pancreas. Flexible endoscopy has become an integral part of the practice of gastroenterology. The important role of colonoscopy in the early detection and prevention of colorectal cancer has expanded the importance of this technology to the general population and other medical and surgical specialty areas.

As with any diagnostic or therapeutic intervention, it is vitally important that clinicians understand the indications, techniques, benefits, and risks associated with flexible endoscopy. Outcomes research provides insight into these important issues.

Definition of Outcomes Research

Outcomes research is defined as the study of "the outcomes of health care services and procedures used to prevent, diagnose, treat, and manage illness and disability."[1] Interpreted broadly, this definition encompasses research efforts that are designed to assess the delivery of health care resources and to determine the effects of such health care delivery on a variety of patient-centered outcomes such as quality of life, functional status, and survival. The definition of outcomes research may also be applied on a more practice-centered level when comparing different diagnostic or therapeutic techniques or when assessing the cost effectiveness of various health care delivery strategies. The overall goal of outcomes research is to identify optimal health care delivery strategies to maximize the benefit of these strategies to patients and society.

Over the last 2 decades, increasing demands have been placed on health care delivery by society in the setting of shrinking resources.

Patients are becoming active health care consumers who weigh the costs and benefits of the care that they receive or "purchase." Outcomes research provides a platform for the measurement of the effectiveness and benefit of medical care and allows comparisons of these outcomes based on cost and resource utilization to determine the quality of care.

The term *quality* is a vague term in the realm of health care delivery and is subject to wide ranges of interpretation. The Institute of Medicine defines quality as "the degree to which health services for individuals and populations increase the likelihood of desired health outcomes and are consistent with current professional knowledge."[2]

Importance of Outcomes Research

Outcomes research is a method of evaluating the value of current medical practices. Digestive diseases comprise a substantial portion of health care expenditures in the United States. These expenditures may be measured in terms of direct monetary costs, morbidity, mortality, the impact on quality of life, and decreased productivity. In 1985, the direct health care costs attributable to GI and digestive diseases were estimated to be more than $40 billion and constituted more than 10% of the health care costs in the United States.[3] GI disorders resulted in 22.8 million endoscopic procedures at a cost of more than $5 billion. Despite the widespread and frequent use of endoscopy, the appropriateness, quality, and value (outcomes) of endoscopic procedures remain largely unknown. In addition, there is wide variation in the use of GI endoscopy in different regions of the country. In one study that examined the appropriateness of upper GI endoscopy among different geographic regions with high, average, and low use, it was found that the indications for 28% of these procedures were equivocal or inappropriate.[4] Outcomes research is one approach to understanding the reasons for these variations in endoscopic practice and could provide data to determine the most effective and appropriate use of endoscopy.

Outcomes research is also important in providing a bridge for developing technology to move into clinical practice. Technology

---

*The opinions and assertions contained herein are the sole views of the authors and should not be construed as official or as representing the views of the U.S. Navy, the Department of Defense, or the Department of Veteran Affairs.

assessment typically occurs in three stages. The first phase, after the development of a new technology, is to determine the efficacy of a diagnostic or therapeutic technology. In other words, this phase determines whether or not the new technology will, under ideal and strictly controlled clinical circumstances, change the medical outcome of an individual patient. These types of studies typically are in the form of randomized controlled trials from tertiary medical centers and may not reflect the community practice experience. The second phase of technology assessment, the effectiveness phase, determines whether or not a new technology will change the medical outcome in routine clinical practice. Typically, these types of studies are performed at multiple centers with a varied patient population and cross-section of physician investigators. The third phase of technology assessment evaluates the efficiency of the technique. Efficiency studies address the economic impact of the technology by assessing the change in medical outcome resulting from the use of a new technology and its associated costs. Ultimately, this allows an estimate of the value, in terms of cost and benefit, that can be achieved as a result of technology integration. Consider computed tomography (CT) colonography (virtual colonoscopy) as an emerging technology. Multiple studies regarding the sensitivity and specificity of this technique for the identification of colorectal neoplasia have been performed. However, these trials represent only the efficacy phase of this technology assessment, measuring the ability of the methodology to identify lesions in highly specialized centers using optimal conditions and equipment. There have not been, to date, any published effectiveness trials examining the widespread application of this technology in a variety of clinical practices in a standardized screening population. As a result, it is difficult to extrapolate the results of the existing efficacy studies to large populations and recommend its widespread use in screening for colorectal cancer.[5]

Finally, outcomes research allows for quality assessment. This role is perhaps the most germane for the individual gastroenterologist. Because endoscopy has inherent risks, endoscopists have a responsibility to track and assess their outcomes and complications. This represents a very practical form of outcomes research. Identification of increased complication rates or decreased levels of patient satisfaction may identify areas for improvement in endoscopic practice. It is also likely that there will be increasing demand for data pertaining to individual physicians regarding their clinical outcomes, complication rates, and patterns of health care resource utilization from government agencies, third-party payers, and patients. Most importantly, the application of fundamental principles of outcomes research will allow individual endoscopists to collect and understand data regarding their own clinical practice, leading to improved patient care.

Use of Databases for Outcomes Research

Some of the most promising tools for accomplishing endoscopic outcomes research and quality assessment are large databases. These include administrative health care databases such as Medicare or regional health care claims databases and endoscopy-specific databases such as the Clinical Outcomes Research Initiative (CORI) and the Registry of Upper Gastrointestinal Bleeding and Endoscopy (RUGBE) datasets. The more general databases can provide important information such as mortality, hospitalization rates, length of stay, discharge diagnosis, charges, and resource utilization. These databases may be used to measure evaluated variation between different geographic and practice settings. The data are available quickly and at little cost and are less often complicated by confidentiality issues, because identifiable protected health information is not used. The data derived from these databases applies to a wide variety of patients and is in some ways less subject to the selection bias inherent in randomized controlled trials performed at tertiary care centers. In addition, administrative or claims data may be used to define epidemiologic patterns of various disease states. In contrast, the gastroenterology-specific databases are designed to track and provide outcomes specific to digestive disease states and the practice of endoscopy.

The limitations of the more generic databases stem from the fact that these databases often lack the detailed clinical data that investigators need and that data entry is often significantly flawed. Because the data in these collections are most often meant for claims and administrative purposes, data entry may be incomplete or misleading. There is often a relative lack of detailed information on individual patients such as comorbidities and demographic data.[6] Thus, although the use of generic claims and administrative databases is attractive from a societal point of view, such analyses are often very difficult to perform without the introduction of some bias. As a result, the conclusions derived from such analyses may be inherently limited.

Disease- or specialty-specific databases hold more promise for endoscopic outcomes and quality assessment than do the general databases. Two such databases that currently exist are the American Society of Gastrointestinal Endoscopy (ASGE) sponsored CORI project and the RUGBE database in Canada. In addition to these national databases, multiple proprietary endoscopic software packages have been developed and are used in endoscopic practice. Typically, these packages, such as Olympus Endoworks or Provalent and Pentax EndoPRO, are used day-to-day for endoscopy report generation. Multiple fields are accessible with preformatted, standardized endoscopic terms. There is typically an area for free text data entry as well. These types of databases are particularly useful for local quality assessment programs. For example, consider a large endoscopy center that has recently discovered a significant increase in endoscope repair costs. A simple query of the endoscopic database regarding the procedures involving the malfunctioning endoscopes might reveal a practice pattern that would lead to an intervention to correct the problem and reduce endoscope repair costs. More importantly, common outcomes such as complication rates, success rates, sedation patterns, and indications for and appropriateness of the procedure can, and should, be periodically measured.

Clearly, the most ambitious endoscopic outcomes research initiative at this time is the CORI project. The CORI database is a large endoscopic database that has its origins in the ASGE and its industry partners, who recognized that a formal assessment of endoscopic practice in varied settings was needed. The primary goal of the CORI database was to establish a computer-based practice consortium comprising multiple practice settings. The database, like the proprietary databases, may be used for day-to-day clinical care and for patient-centered outcomes and quality assessment research efforts. CORI, begun in 1995, is now operating at more than 70 sites with more than 500 participating physicians. Numerous publications and abstracts have been produced through careful analysis of the wealth of information in the database. These publications and research efforts have examined both general gastroenterology practice patterns and disease-specific outcomes. For instance, Lieberman and colleagues[7] have demonstrated that most upper endoscopic procedures at CORI sites were performed for dyspepsia and abdominal pain, dysphagia, gastroesophageal reflux disease, and suspected GI bleeding in descending order of frequency. Colonoscopy was most often performed for neoplasia surveillance, evaluation of hematochezia and positive fecal occult blood tests. They also demonstrated that there was a wide variation in the indications for endoscopy between academic and non-academic settings (Fig. 12–1). McCashland and colleagues[8] used the CORI database to show that right-sided colonic neoplasia is associated with increasing age and that women have a higher risk of isolated right-sided colonic neoplasia than men. These are but two examples of the power that is inherent in such a large, well-designed endoscopic database. Data from these databases could be potentially useful in developing guidelines for the standardization of endoscopic practice and for identifying important epidemiologic factors that would affect screening methods or recommendations for individual GI diseases.

Participation in the CORI database is free of charge and participants have access to the data from other centers. This allows participating physicians or practices to compare their practice patterns with national norms, analyze their own practice individually, participate in other research initiatives, or review ongoing database research. In addition, participation in the program may serve to demonstrate active and ongoing quality assurance initiatives to oversight authorities such as the Joint Commission for Accreditation of Healthcare Organizations (JCAHO) and the National Committee for Quality Assurance (NCQA).

Decision Analysis and Systematic Reviews

In an ideal world, the delivery of medical care would be completely based on clear clinical care evidence supporting the interventions implemented. Unfortunately, the available evidence demonstrates a clinical benefit in only 10% to 20% of the treatment that is delivered to patients for all of medicine.[9] Only relatively recently have endoscopic procedures and interventions been shown to benefit patients with upper GI bleeding or colorectal neoplasia.[10,11] One of the limitations to the development of clear-cut evidence to support benefit from endoscopic procedures is that clinical trials examining outcomes associated with many endoscopic procedures require a very large number of clinically similar patients to be adequately powered and must be necessarily prolonged to capture sufficient postendoscopy data. These features make endoscopic outcomes assessment inherently difficult to perform in prospective trials.

The use of decision analysis and systematic reviews offers several potential alternative methods of developing useful outcomes data without the limitations inherent in most endoscopic clinical care research. Decision analysis uses mathematical models to mimic clinical decisions and scenarios. Such analysis is based on estimates of disease prevalence and outcomes from various sources, including previous research and the consensus of experts in a particular field. Typically, a decision analysis contains a sensitivity analysis whereby certain variables are altered to quantify the subsequent changes in possible outcomes. This sensitivity analysis allows the key features in the clinical decision making algorithm to be identified and may serve to focus additional research efforts toward those areas. Decision analysis has been used in the past to assist in the development of clinical guidelines[12] and cost-effectiveness evaluations of colorectal cancer screening.[13]

Systematic reviews are compilations of multiple data points or studies in an effort to accept or reject a particular hypothesis. A systematic review may be qualitative or quantitative. Quantitative systematic reviews that mathematically combine data from multiple studies into a summary estimate of effect are called meta-analyses. In a meta-analysis, individual clinical trials are systematically appraised for similarity regarding the subject population, clinical problem, intervention, and outcome. If these features are similar

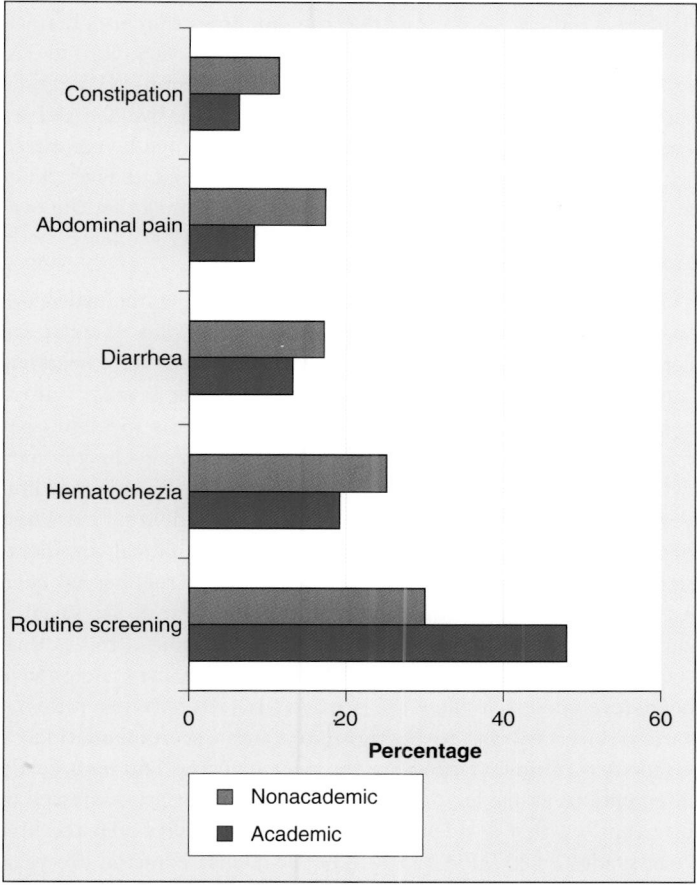

Figure 12–1. Variability in endoscopic indications in the United States: Nonacademic and academic settings. (Data from Lieberman DA, De Garmo PL, Fleischer DE, et al: Patterns of endoscopy in the United States. Gastroenterology 118:619–624, 2000.)

and the individual studies are of sufficient quality, data from individual clinical trials are pooled to increase the power of the primary analysis. This provides a summary estimate of the effect of the intervention that is more powerful than the estimate from the individual studies.

A qualitative systematic review does not allow pooling of data from individual studies, usually because the individual studies used different populations, interventions, or outcome measures. In this situation, investigators performing a qualitative systematic review independently critically appraise the existing research that is available regarding a particular treatment or intervention in an effort to develop a consensus opinion as to the outcomes associated with that particular intervention. Systematic reviews and meta-analyses have become increasingly important to clinicians who strive to practice evidence-based-medicine and, in the absence of adequately powered, lengthy, well-designed clinical trials, offer the best opportunity at this time to direct certain interventions that are still in question. Rigorous criteria detailing the design and methodology of systematic reviews and meta-analysis have been published elsewhere.[14]

Economic Analyses

Endoscopic procedures are relatively complex and expensive diagnostic and therapeutic interventions. As health care costs and third-party payer oversight continue to increase, endoscopists are under greater pressure to demonstrate that these procedures that they perform are both clinically effective and cost effective. The economic analyses inherent in outcomes research require some explanation. There are three different types of economic analyses: cost-minimization analysis, cost-utility analysis, and cost-benefit analysis.

COST-MINIMIZATION ANALYSES

Cost-minimization analyses are the simplest form of economic analysis. They assume that the same clinical outcome will be achieved by different approaches. The goal of a cost-minimization analysis is to identify the least expensive method to achieve that outcome or treat a particular condition. In a cost-minimization analysis, the costs associated with the detection and treatment of a particular condition are identified and expressed in terms of total cost to achieve the specified outcome or service.

COST-UTILITY ANALYSES

A cost-utility analysis extends these concepts further not only by identifying costs and outcomes associated with a particular condition or intervention but also by assigning a quality of life value (utility) to the various possible outcomes. Results of a cost-utility analysis are reported as a cost-utility ratio, the cost per quality-adjusted life-year gained. Expression of such a ratio, akin to cost-effectiveness ratios, permits comparison to other interventions that are generally accepted by society as reasonable and routine clinical practice.

COST-BENEFIT ANALYSES

Cost-benefit analyses are designed to guide policy decisions. They differ from cost-minimization and cost-utility analyses in that they quantify costs and benefits in the same units. Most often the units of measure of a cost-benefit analysis is the monetary value of the change in well-being resulting from an intervention or policy decision. It requires the extrapolation of benefit, such as cases of cancer prevented or life-years saved, to be reported as an actual dollar amount. Typically this amount is computed based on what a consumer would be "willing to pay" or give up, in terms of other consumption requiring monetary outlay. The results of a cost-benefit analysis are calculated by subtracting the costs (in monetary units) of a program or intervention from the benefits (in monetary units) that result from the program or intervention and are expressed as the net benefit. If the net benefit is positive, then the intervention passes the cost-benefit test. However, passing the cost-benefit test is not sufficient to endorse a particular intervention or program. It is also important to look at the "bottom-line" regarding the social acceptance and fiscal reasonableness of the costs relative to the benefits. Standards for what constitute reasonable "best practices" for many public policy interventions are put forth by the Office of Management and Budget (OMB) and are reported as cost-effectiveness ratios.

Cost-effectiveness analyses are a subset of cost-benefit analysis. A cost-effectiveness analysis measures the cost of the medical care delivered and also recognizes that the outcomes that are obtained through the delivery of that medical care may vary. Results are typically reported as the cost per specified health related outcome such as cost per life-year saved or adverse outcome avoided and are expressed in the form of a ratio. This ratio may then be compared with established cost-effectiveness ratios associated with other interventions. A cost-effectiveness analysis assumes that the outcome is a given and is thus performed to identify the least costly means of achieving the goal or outcome.

There is no benchmark for acceptability regarding minimal values that define a cost-effective intervention. Examples of what are considered to be cost-effective interventions include mammography screening ($21,400 per quality-adjusted life-year saved),[15] ultrasound screening for patients with carotid stenosis ($39,500 per quality-adjusted life-year saved),[16] and ultrasound screening in men with abdominal aortic aneurysms ($28,740 per quality-adjusted life-year saved).[17] Such decisions are not just dependent on costs and benefits but also on perception and ethical and political considerations. The cost effectiveness of cervical cancer screening has been estimated to be approximately $250,000 per year of life saved,[18] and although there is increasing debate as to the value of this testing, society continues to support its performance. Grading systems have been developed that allow the relative cost-effectiveness ratios of various interventions to be translated into recommendations.[19] Grade A recommendations are the most effective and least costly interventions available. Grade B recommendations are conferred to interventions that cost less than $20,000 per quality-adjusted life-year, grade C $20,000 to $100,000 per quality-adjusted life-year, and grade D greater than $100,000 per quality-adjusted life-year.

An example of the importance of economic analysis with respect to endoscopic practices may be found in the issues surrounding esophageal intestinal metaplasia (IM), or Barrett's esophagus, and esophageal cancer risk. It is widely recognized that IM is associated with an increased risk for the development of esophageal adeno-carcinoma. Clinical practice guidelines recommend periodic surveil-lance esophagoscopy with systematic esophageal biopsies for patients with the disorder.[20] However, the incidence of esophageal adenocarcinoma is relatively uncommon and a prospective ran-domized trial would require more than 5000 patients to be followed for more than 10 years to demonstrate a 50% reduction in mortality as a result of early detection through endoscopic surveillance.[21] In addition, there are potential complications that can result from upper endoscopy and it has been estimated that the cost for annual endoscopic screening for patients with IM would exceed $350 million.[22] Because of the obvious limitations in terms of obtaining outcomes in a prospective randomized controlled trial, Provenzale and colleagues[23] performed a cost-utility analysis to examine the appropriateness and optimal interval for endoscopic surveillance in patients with IM. These investigators used a decision analysis approach with varying intervention and outcome options and determined that screening with esophagoscopy annually with esophagectomy for high-grade dysplasia was the preferred method if only life expectancy were considered. When quality of life was included in the outcomes analysis, esophagoscopy every 2 to 3 years provided the greatest quality-adjusted life expectancy, and when costs were added to life expectancy and quality of life as part of the analysis, screening every 5 years had a similar incremental cost-effectiveness ratio to other widely accepted common medical interventions. One must realize, however, that this result is only one aspect of the conclusions that could be reached as a result of this analysis. One must also consider the ability and willingness of the potential payers to expend the resources for the intervention, the number of patients that must be screened, the potential benefit and harms associated with screening, and the societal acceptance of the intervention compared with historical benchmarks. Table 12–1 includes the features that should be present in a well-designed economic analysis and offers an appraisal method of such analyses for individual practitioners.

Endoscopic Quality Assessment

Since its introduction in the late 1950s, flexible fiberoptic endoscopy of the upper GI tract has assumed a primary role for the

Table 12–1. Steps in Evaluating an Economic Analysis

Determining the Validity the Design of an Economic Analysis
Were all relevant patient groups, interventions, and possible outcomes considered?
Are the outcomes linked to the best available evidence as determined by a systematic review of the literature?
Are the cost estimates accurate?
Was timing of costs and consequences considered?

Assessing the Results
What were the differences in costs and effects of different strategies?
Are there differences of costs and effects between subgroups?
Was a sensitivity analysis performed (correction for uncertainty)?

Applying the Results
Is the question and scenario encountered in routine clinical practice?
Are the assumptions for costs and benefit applicable to routine clinical practice?

diagnostic evaluation of symptoms such as gastroesophageal reflux disease (GERD), dyspepsia, dysphagia, and odynophagia.[24] Endoscopy has also proven itself to be the preferred therapeutic modality for bleeding GI lesions, the removal of esophageal and gastric foreign bodies, and the placement of enteral feeding devices.[25-28] Over the past 2 decades, new innovations such as photodynamic therapy and endoscopic approaches to GERD and Barrett's esophagus have continued to expand the potential role of esophagogastroduodenoscopy (EGD) as a therapeutic modality.

Similarly, the potential diagnostic and therapeutic roles of endoscopic retrograde cholangiopancreatography (ERCP) and colonoscopy have gained widespread acceptance over the preceding 2 decades and are now increasingly important aspects of the practice of gastroenterology. Unfortunately, merely being able to perform the procedure does not justify its performance. The procedural aspects of gastroenterology have come under a great deal of scrutiny during the same period because of the multitude of factors previously mentioned.[29] Thus, the need for outcomes research and outcomes assessment in the field of endoscopic gastroenterology has assumed a new prominence. The efficacy of the many of the aforementioned EGD-based procedures and the role of ERCP for multiple pancreati-cobiliary conditions and colonoscopy for colorectal cancer screening is not in question. What remains unproved for many of these accepted indications are the effects of these procedures on patient quality of life, mortality, and the relative cost per benefit achieved.

The field of GI endoscopy provides many opportunities for outcome assessment. More importantly, outcome assessment can improve the practice of endoscopy. Each endoscopic procedure has multiple potential outcomes that may be evaluated. Some of these include the technical success of the procedure, the diagnostic accuracy of the procedure, and the impact of the procedure on the patient's overall health and quality of life. These outcomes can be measured on multiple levels, from the individual endoscopist, to the general practice of endoscopy at a local, regional, or even national based setting (Table 12–2). The ASGE has developed guidelines for assessing outcomes in multiple endoscopic procedures.[30-32] These guidelines are meant to facilitate the widespread use of outcomes measures to monitor and improve the practice of endoscopy in any clinical setting. Each endoscopy unit and every endoscopist should be able to assess the quality of their endoscopic outcomes.

As new endoscopic techniques are developed, outcomes measure-ment should progress from evaluating efficacy (what we can do) to effectiveness (what we actually achieve). As the technology matures, the relevant outcomes should become more clinically oriented with a focus on mortality, quality of life, and costs of care. The ultimate result will be the optimal use of endoscopy to improve the lives of patients.

Conclusion

Endoscopic outcome assessments remain elusive. Because of the nature of many endoscopic procedures, short-term outcomes often do not provide meaningful data with regards to patient-centered issues such as quality of life and subsequent health care utilization. The potential impact of well-designed endoscopic outcomes research on the current practice of gastroenterology is tremendous

Table 12–2. Application of Endoscopic Outcomes Research

Local Practice Level
Quality assessment and improvement
Competence determination
Resource utilization
Guideline compliance
Oversight compliance
Procedural volume, success, complications, and trends
Individual variance tracking

Societal Level
Guideline formulation and adherence
Public health initiatives and screening recommendations

Cost Analysis
Practice variance analysis
Establishing standards of care
Macroeconomic resource utilization
Technology development and assessment

and such research is applicable at both local and societal levels. Outcomes research that addresses the benefit, both health related and economic, of endoscopy promises to shape future cancer screening initiatives and standardize the level of care that is currently delivered in the United States. Performing endoscopic outcomes research is often difficult because of the historical lack of large, inclusive database sets and the heretofore reliance on nonendoscopic and potentially inaccurate or incomplete claims datasets. The continued use and evaluation of both proprietary and nonproprietary endoscopic registries are expected to demonstrate the value of endoscopic procedures to the individual and to interested third parties. The use of these registries may also impact practice at a local level by facilitating examination of endoscopy unit practices and individual performance attributes that may then lead to quality improvement initiatives to further enhance the delivery of medical and endoscopic care. Although this area of research is still in its infancy, continued use and refinement of these technologies holds tremendous promise for the future and should be encouraged at all levels.

REFERENCES

1. Agency for Health Care Policy and Research: Medical treatment effectiveness research [Agency for Health Care Policy and Research Program note]. Rockville, MD, Department of Health and Human Services, Public Health Service, March 1990.
2. Lohr KN, Donaldson MS, Harris-Wehling J: Medicare: A strategy for quality assurance. V. Quality of care in a changing health care environment. QRB Qual Rev Bull 18:120–126, 1992.
3. Everhart JE: Summary. In Everhart JE (ed): Digestive Diseases in the United States: Epidemiology and Impact. U.S. Department of Health and Human Services, Public Health Service, National Institutes of Health, National Institute of Diabetes and Digestive and Kidney Diseases. Washington, DC, US Government Printing Office, 1994, NIH Publication 94-1447, ix–xii.
4. Chassin MR, Kosecoff J, Park RE, et al: Does inappropriate use explain geographic variations in the use of health care services? A study of three procedures. JAMA 258:2533–2537, 1987.
5. Cash BD, Schoenfeld P, Rex D: An evidence-based medicine approach to studies of diagnostic tests: Assessing the validity of virtual colonoscopy. Clin Gastroenterol Hepatol 1:136–144, 2003.
6. Eisen GM: Endoscopic databases and outcomes research. Gastrointest Endosc Clin N Am 9:587–594, 1999.
7. Lieberman DA, De Garmo PL, Fleischer DE, et al: Patterns of endoscopy in the United States. Gastroenterology 118:619–624, 2000.
8. McCashland TM, Brand R, Lyden E, et al: Gender differences in colorectal polyps and tumors. Am J Gastroenterol 96:882–886, 2001.
9. Donaldson MS, Capron AM: Patient outcome research teams: Managing conflict of interest. Washington, DC, National Academy, 1991.
10. Cook DJ, Guyatt GH, Salena BJ, Laine LA: Endoscopic therapy for acute nonvariceal upper gastrointestinal hemorrhage: A meta-analysis. Gastroenterology 102:139–148, 1992.
11. Winawer SJ, Zauber AG, Ho MN, et al: Prevention of colorectal cancer by colonoscopic polypectomy. N Engl J Med 339:1977–1981, 1993.
12. Ransohoff DF, Gracie WA, Schmittner JP: Guidelines of the American College of Physicians for the treatment of gallstones. Ann Intern Med 119:620–622, 1993.
13. Sonnenberg A, Delco F, Inadomi JM: Cost-effectiveness of colonoscopy in screening for colorectal cancer. Ann Intern Med 133:573–584, 2000.
14. Oxman AD, Cook DJ, Guyatt GH: Users' guides to the medical literature. VI. How to use an overview. Evidence-Based Medicine Working Group. JAMA 272:1367–1371, 1994.
15. Salzmann P, Kerlikowske K, Phillips K: Cost-effectiveness of extending screening mammography guidelines to include women 40 to 49 years of age. Ann Intern Med 127:955–965, 1997.
16. Yin D, Carpenter JP: Cost-effectiveness of screening for asymptomatic carotid stenosis. J Vasc Surg 27:245–255, 1998.
17. Frame PS, Fryback DG, Patterson C: Screening for abdominal aortic aneurysm in men ages 60 to 80 years: A cost-effectiveness analysis. Ann Intern Med 119:411–416, 1993.
18. Eddy DM: Screening for cervical cancer. Ann Intern Med 113:214–226, 1990.
19. Laupacis A, Feeny D, Detsky AS, et al: How attractive does a new technology have to be to warrant adoption and utilization? Tentative guidelines for using clinical and economic evaluations. CMAJ 146:473–481, 1992.
20. Sampliner RE: Updated guidelines for the diagnosis, surveillance, and therapy of Barrett's esophagus. Am J Gastroenterol 97:1888–1895, 2002.
21. Gallup Organization: A Gallup Organization National Survey: Heartburn Across America. Princeton, NJ, Gallup Organization, 1988.
22. Provenzale D: Economic analysis of endoscopic procedures. Gastrointest Endosc Clin N Am 9:573–586, 1999.
23. Provenzale D, Kemp JA, Arora S, et al: A guide for surveillance of patients with Barrett's esophagus. Am J Gastroenterol 89:670–680, 1994.
24. Morrissey JF, Reichelderfer: Gastrointestinal endoscopy. N Engl J Med 325:1214–1222, 1991.
25. Hay JA, Lyubashevsky E, Elashoff J, et al: Upper gastrointestinal hemorrhage clinical guideline determining the optimal hospital length of stay. Am J Med 100:313–322, 1996.

26. Consensus conference: Therapeutic endoscopy and bleeding ulcers. JAMA 262:1369–1372, 1989.
27. Webb WA: Management of foreign bodies in the upper gastrointestinal tract. Gastroenterology 94:204–216, 1988.
28. Ponsky JL, Gauderer MW: Percutaneous endoscopic gastrostomy: A non-operative technique for feeding gastrostomy. Gastrointest Endosc 27:9–11, 1981.
29. Schmitt CM: Procedure-specific outcomes assessment for esophagogastroduodenoscopy. Gastrointest Endosc Clin N Am 9:609–624, 1999.
30. Johanson JF, Schmitt C, Deas TM, et al: Quality and outcomes assessment in gastrointestinal endoscopy. Gastrointest Endosc 52:827–830, 2000.
31. Johanson JF, Cooper G, Eisen GM, et al: Quality assessment of ERCP. Gastrointest Endosc 56:165–169, 2002.
32. Johanson JF, Cooper G, Eisen GM, et al: Quality assessment of endoscopic ultrasound. Gastrointest Endosc 55:798–801, 2002.

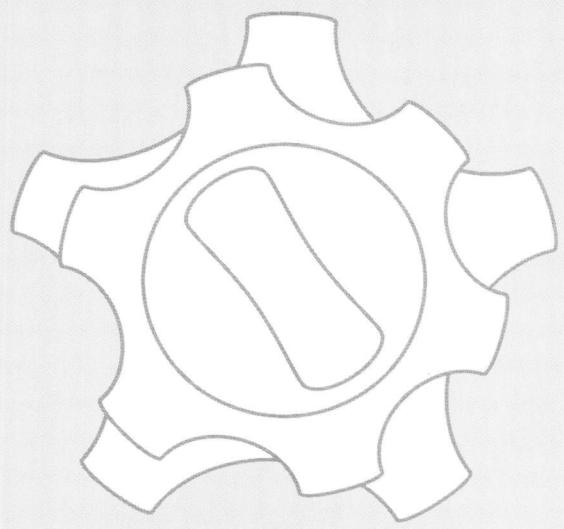

Luminal Gastrointestinal Disorders

Benign Disorders

Neoplastic Disorders
Esophagus
Gastroduodenum
Colorectum

Acute Nonvariceal Bleeding

Yakub I. Khan and Naresh T. Gunaratnam

Upper gastrointestinal (GI) bleeding is a common GI emergency and results in 300,000 to 350,000 hospital admissions annually in the United States. Bleeding from the upper GI tract is approximately five times more common than lower GI bleed and men are affected twice as commonly as women.[1] The mortality rate associated with upper GI bleeding is approximately 7% to 10%. However, patients developing GI hemorrhage while hospitalized for other reasons carry a much higher mortality rate of about 33%.[2] Endoscopic assessment and treatment of upper GI bleeding has evolved over the past 3 decades from a purely diagnostic role to one in which it is the standard for definitive therapy.

This chapter discusses the approach, assessment, and management strategies in a patient presenting with nonvariceal upper GI bleeding.

Table 13–1. Hemodynamics, Vital Signs, and Blood Loss		
Hemodynamics*	Blood Loss (%)†	Severity of Bleed
Shock (hypotension)	20–25	Massive
Postural hypotension	10–20	Moderate
Normal	<10	Minor

*Vital signs.
†Fraction of intravascular volume loss.
From Feldman M, Friedman LS, Sleisenger MH: Sleisenger and Fordtran's Gastrointestinal and Liver Disease. Philadelphia, WB Saunders, 2003, p 212.

Clinical Presentation

The presentation of GI bleeding depends on the volume and site of bleeding. Hematemesis is vomiting of blood. The source is usually proximal to the ligament of Treitz. This may be bright red indicating a recent or active bleed or "coffee ground" representing older blood reduced by acid in the stomach. Melena is black, tarry, and sticky stool with a specific foul odor by degradation of blood in the intestines and colon. A massive upper GI bleed can present as hematochezia (bright red blood per rectum) in 15% of the cases and carries a worse prognosis.[3]

Initial Evaluation

The initial assessment of the patient suspected of having an acute GI bleed must focus on hemodynamic stability so that resuscitative measures can be started without delay. A focused history and physical examination will provide vital information on the severity of bleeding and other confounding medical problems (coronary disease, chronic obstructive pulmonary disease [COPD], malignancy, etc.) that may affect medical management and therapeutic

intervention. Initial evaluation should focus on vital signs and orthostatic changes because postural hypotension represents a significant volume loss (>15%) and is a predictor of poor outcomes (Table 13–1).[4]

A peripheral intravenous (IV) access with two large-bore (at least 18 gauge) catheters or a central venous access must be achieved in patients with an acute bleed if hemodynamically unstable. Colloids (normal saline or lactated Ringer's) are the initial fluids of choice and are administered rapidly to restore intravascular volume. Continuous monitoring is required, especially for fragile patients with comorbid cardiopulmonary disease. Supplemental oxygen should be administered routinely.

Predisposing Factors

Complicating factors such as age (>65 years), comorbid conditions, coagulopathy, and medication must also be taken into account. Patients should be asked about nonsteroidal anti-inflammatory drug (NSAID) use. Acute upper and lower GI bleeding episodes are increased in patients taking aspirin and the effect appears to be dose related.[5] Patients taking low-dose (75 mg) aspirin are also at an increased risk for bleeding.[6] NSAIDs are probably the most important cause of peptic ulcer bleeding, which is a major cause of upper GI bleeding. GI bleeding is further complicated in patients receiving anticoagulation therapy.[7] Steroids and alendronate have been linked to increased risk when used concomitantly with NSAIDs.[8,9] Calcium channel antagonists have also been associated with an increased risk, but association is less clear.[10]

Nasogastric Aspirate

The diagnosis of the level of bleeding can be made by a careful history and physical examination. History of hematemesis from a reliable historian confirms the source to be proximal to the ligament of Treitz. Nasogastric (NG) tubes have been used extensively as part of the workup of acute GI bleeding. NG tubes can be very helpful in the localization of bleeding, because a bloody NG aspirate confirms the source to be from the upper tract. Use of saline or cold water lavage is no longer in practice because it was not shown to be effective in achieving hemostasis.[11,12] In the national survey of American Society of Gastrointestinal Endoscopy (ASGE), about 16% of patients were found to have active bleeding at the time of endoscopy with clear NG aspirates.[13] The bleeding sources in these patients also include esophagitis (10.7%) and varices (5.1%). The color of aspirate has been correlated with mortality: clear aspirate had 6% mortality, red blood had 18% mortality, and red blood with hematochezia had 30% mortality in the national ASGE survey.[14] Cuellar and coworkers[15] calculated sensitivity and specificity of physician assessment of active GI bleeding based on appearance of NG aspirate. It was found to be only 79% sensitive and 55% specific. It also held true for bilious aspirate (sensitivity 48%, specificity 74%). They did not recommend NG aspirates in the workup of acute GI bleeding, especially if endoscopy is planned in the next few hours.

Although NG lavage does not provide information about the etiology of bleeding, it can be useful to localize the source in a hemodynamically unstable patient because it is a quick easy test that is performed at bedside. A negative or bilious aspirate does not rule out upper GI bleeding. Testing of NG aspirate for occult blood is of no clinical value in acute GI hemorrhage and should be discouraged.

Laboratory Data

Laboratory tests appropriate at initial presentation include hemoglobin level, hematocrit, platelet count, prothrombin time, and partial thromboplastin time. Initial hemoglobin level may not depict the degree of bleeding. Thus, initial decision making must be on clinical grounds. It can take up to 72 hours for hemodilution to take place.[16] The blood urea nitrogen (BUN) level is elevated in GI bleed because blood proteins are degraded by the bacteria and released urea is reabsorbed. A raised BUN-to-creatinine ratio (>36) has been suggestive of an upper GI source of bleeding with a sensitivity of 90% and specificity of 27%.[17] This value can be helpful in the diagnosis; however, the clinical picture is often complicated by other medical illnesses (renal insufficiency, congestive heart failure [CHF], etc.) and polypharmacy. Other laboratory data of importance may include liver function tests, cardiac enzyme analysis, and a baseline electrocardiogram (ECG).

Risk Stratification

Most GI bleeds stop spontaneously without any recurrence. Approximately 20% of bleeds can continue or recur leading to patient morbidity and mortality.[18] Clinical factors have been identified that predict recurrent bleeding or poor outcome. Old age (>65 years), shock, comorbid illnesses, low hemoglobin on evaluation, melena, multiple transfusions (>4), hematochezia, fresh blood emesis or NG aspirate, and need for emergency surgery are clinical predictors resulting in an increased risk of rebleeding (Table 13–2).[19,20]

Based on these individual clinical criteria, a number of scoring systems have been formulated to try to stratify high-risk patients for appropriate intervention. The scoring criteria can be divided into those that include only clinical criteria to identify patients and those that include endoscopy criteria to predict patient outcome.

Blatchford and coworkers[21] devised a scoring system based on logistical regression data from 1748 consecutive patients of acute upper GI bleeding. The scoring system included admission hemoglobin, blood urea, pulse, systolic blood pressure presentation with syncope and melena, and evidence of hepatic disease and cardiac failure. They concluded that using their criteria could identify up to 20% of patients who have very low risk of needing treatment to control bleeding and thus can be offered outpatient treatment.

Cameron and colleagues[22] stratified 1349 (3-year period) consecutive patients to high, intermediate, or low risk based on initial clinical criteria that were developed using risk factors identified in earlier studies. Adverse outcomes (mortality, rebleed, need for intervention) were determined for each group. Two-week mortality in high-, intermediate-, and low-risk groups were 11.8%, 3.0%, and 0%, respectively. Rates of rebleeding were determined to be 44.1% in high risk, 2.3% in intermediate risk, and 0% in low risk, respectively. However, only 6% of the patients composed the low-risk group.

The development of clinical scoring systems are very encouraging because these can be used by emergency physicians, general practitioners, and junior house staff to effectively triage patients. However, they need validation in large cohorts in diverse populations before recommendations for general applications can be made.

Table 13–2. Statistically Significant Predictors of Persistent or Recurrent Bleeding

Risk Factor	Odds Ratio for Increased Risk
Age	
>65 yr	1.3
>70 yr	2.30
Shock (systolic BP <100 mm Hg)	1.2–3.65
Comorbid illness	1.6–7.63
Transfusion requirements	NA
Initial hemoglobin <10 g/dL	0.8–2.99
Coagulopathy (prolonged PT)	1.96 (1.46–2.64)
Melena	1.6
Blood in NG tube or stomach	1.1–11.5
Hematemesis	1.2–5.7
Continued bleeding	3.14 (2.4–4.12)

BP, blood pressure; NA, not available; NG, nasogastric; PT, prothrombin time. Modified from ref 19.

Table 13–3. Rockall Scoring System for Risk of Rebleeding and Death after Admission to Hospital for Acute Gastrointestinal Bleeding

Variable	Score			
	0	1	2	3
Age (yr)	<60	60–79	>80	
Shock	No shock (systolic BP >100 mm Hg, pulse <100 beats/min)	Tachycardia (pulse >100 beats/min, BP >100 mm Hg)	Hypotension (systolic <100 mm Hg, pulse >100 beats/min)	—
Comorbidity	Nil	—	Cardiac failure, ischemic heart disease, any major comorbidity	Renal failure, liver failure, disseminated malignancy
Diagnosis	Mallory-Weiss, no lesion or no SRH	All other diagnoses	Malignancy of upper GI tract	—
Major SRH	None or dark spot	—	Blood in upper GI tract, adherent clot, visible or spurting vessel	—

BP, blood pressure; GI, gastrointestinal; SRH, stigmata of recent hemorrhage.
Modified from ref 23.

Scoring Systems with Endoscopic Criteria

Multiple scoring systems have been developed using endoscopic findings in addition to clinical parameters to differentiate high-risk from low-risk patients for recurrent bleed. Rockall and colleagues[23] have developed a scoring system involving both clinical and endoscopic criteria (Table 13–3). The main aim is to predict risk of both rebleeding and mortality. The score consists of an initial calculation based on the patient's age, presence of comorbidity, and circulatory shock after endoscopy. Additional categorization of the bleeding lesion and the stigmata of hemorrhage enables the complete score to be calculated. A total score of less than three was associated with excellent prognosis, whereas a score greater than eight carried a high mortality. For cases with a score less than three, rebleeding occurred in less than 5% and mortality was 0%.

Multiple studies have been performed to validate the Rockall scoring system. Sanders and coworkers[24] prospectively studied 325 patients admitted to a specialized bleeding unit over a 3-year period. Rockall scores were calculated at presentation. All patients underwent endoscopy within 24 hours. For nonvariceal hemorrhage, increasing scores correlated with increased risk of rebleed ($p = .001$), but risk of death was not significantly linked to increasing score ($p > .05$). Rockall scores were significant for mortality ($p < .0005$; confidence interval [CI] 95%) and rebleeding ($p < .0005$) when variceal bleeds were also included in the analysis. The scoring system was shown by Vreeburg and colleagues[25] to be accurate for mortality but less so for rebleeding. It has been validated in other studies to be predictive and also cost effective.[26]

Hay and coworkers[27] derived a scoring system from the literature by using hemodynamics, time from bleeding, comorbidity and endoscopy findings. The patients were divided into low-, intermediate, and high risk based on the scoring system. Discriminatory ability and resource utilization were calculated by retrospective analysis. Use of the practice guidelines reduced hospital stay in low-risk patients from 4.6 to 2.9 days ($p < .001$). Other scoring system based on endoscopy findings have been proposed by Saeed and coworkers.[28]

The global clinical assessment of the patient before endoscopy and subsequent to endoscopy benefits from the categorization as to severity of bleeding and the use of criteria for rebleeding (Table 13–4).

Table 13–4. Severity of Bleeding: Clinical Criteria

Severity of Bleeding	Criteria
Mild	<1 g/dL drop in hemoglobin Minimal or no anemia Stable hemodynamics Infrequent melena Coffee-ground hematemesis
Moderate	1–2 g/dL drop in hemoglobin Anemia 10 g/dL Stable hemodynamics or tachycardia only Melena Hematemesis
Severe	>2 g/dL drop in hemoglobin Profound anemia (<10 g/dL) Hemodynamic instability (orthostatism; shock) Hematochezia or large-volume (>350 mL) frequent melena Repeated hematemesis
Rebleeding	>1.5 g/dL drop in hemoglobin Recurrent hematemesis Recurrent or increased frequency of melena/hematochezia

Prognostic Value of Endoscopic Findings

Previous endoscopic guidelines and studies have demonstrated endoscopic findings referred to as stigmata of recent hemorrhage (Fig. 13–1A to C). These endoscopic findings provide information on the risk of rebleeding and outcome and help to identify patients who would benefit from endoscopic therapy. Active bleeding and

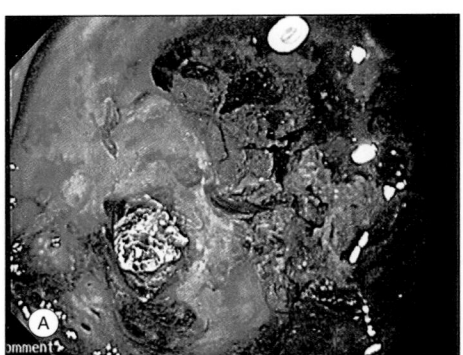
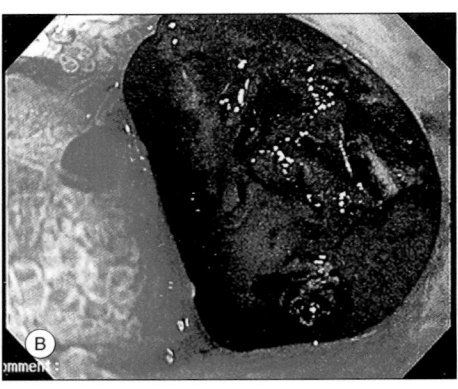
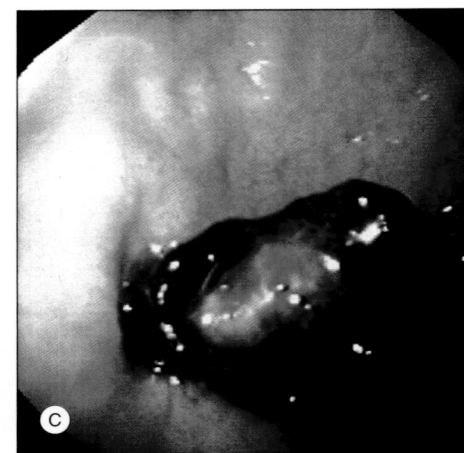

Figure 13-1. *A,* A visible vessel is seen as a dark protuberance near the central area of this duodenal bulb ulcer base. *B,* The involved ulcer is deeply penetrating and at least 2 cm in size. Both the penetration and ulcer size are worrisome, suggesting that the visible vessel seen in the previous photograph is a serosally based artery, which by location in the posterior duodenal bulb would implicate the gastroduodenal artery. *C,* An antral ulcer is seen with a densely adherent clot dangling from the ulcer base from a narrow point of attachment.

Table 13-5. Risk of Recurrent Bleeding by Endoscopic Criteria

Endoscopic Finding	Risk of Recurrent Bleeding (%)	Mortality (%)
Active bleeding	55	11
Visible vessel	43	11
Adherent clot	22	7
Flat spot	10	3
Clean base	5	2

Reproduced from Laine L, Peterson W: Bleeding peptic ulcer. N Engl J Med 331:717-727, 1994. Copyright © 1994 Massachusetts Medical Society. All rights reserved.

Table 13-6. Modified Forrest Criteria

Forrest Class	Type of Lesion
I A	Arterial spurting
I B	Active oozing
II A	Ulcer with nonbleeding visible vessel
II B	Ulcer with adherent clot on surface
II C	Ulcer with red or dark blue flat spot
III	Ulcer with clean base

a visible vessel in an ulcer base carry the highest risk of rebleed, whereas a clean base ulcer or flat spot have minimal risk (Table 13-5). In a prospective study over 6 years, Laine and colleagues[29] demonstrated that peptic ulcer with a clean base or a Mallory Weiss tear has a less than 2% risk of rebleeding. These patients could therefore be safely fed and discharged early from the hospital.

In 1974, Forrest and coworkers[30] first classified stigmata of recent hemorrhage based on endoscopic findings (Table 13-6). Visible vessel is the term used for an elevated area within the ulcer base. It is thought to be a coagulum overlying a pseudoaneurysm of an arterial vessel in the ulcer base.[31] The color of the lesion may be predictive of rebleeding; nonpigmented lesions (white-pale) have a higher risk (71%) than pigmented lesions (38%) in one experience.[32] The frequency with which a visible vessel can be found also depends on the timing of endoscopy and how aggressively an adherent clot is washed to expose the ulcer base. Chung and colleagues[33] reported disappearance of visible vessels in 62 patients who underwent endoscopy for 3 consecutive days.

The size and the depth of ulcer influence the bleeding rate. Increased ulcer size (>2 cm) is associated with an increased risk of rebleeding and mortality. The failure rate of therapeutic endoscopy is much higher in ulcers greater than 2 cm.[34]

Ulcers located high on the lesser curvature of the stomach and on the posteroinferior wall of the duodenal bulb also have a higher rate of rebleeding because of the proximity of the left gastric artery and gastroduodenal artery in these respective locations.[35]

Timing of Endoscopy

The timing of endoscopy has been a subject of debate, especially in patients who are clinically stable with no evidence of further bleeding. About 80% of patients with ulcers stop bleeding spontaneously, and it can be debated if endoscopy in these patients will alter patient outcome. However, a subset of these patients has clinical risk factors or endoscopic stigmata that make them high risk. Endoscopy findings provide vital additional information to effectively triage both high- and low-risk patients. It is now evident that early endoscopy provides essential data that affect patient triage. Kodali and coworkers[36] demonstrated that 21% of the patients with bleeding peptic ulcers had a clean base ulcer with a 3% risk of recurrent bleeding. They concluded that these patients can be discharged safely after endoscopy for outpatient management.

Longstreth and colleagues[37] developed practice guidelines for outpatient management based on retrospective data. The guidelines comprised early notification of a gastroenterologist; early endoscopy; and clinical, laboratory, and endoscopic criteria for outpatient care. Seventy-eight of 933 patients in this retrospective series and 34 of 141 patients in a prospective series received outpatient care. None in the retrospective series and one patient in prospective series were admitted for rebleeding, and no mortality was reported. Lai and coworkers[38] performed a similar study in which patients with low risk were managed as outpatients. No episodes of rebleeding or significant drop of hemoglobin were reported.

 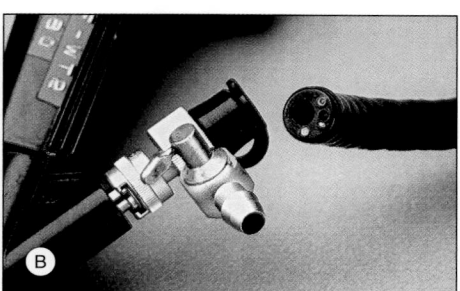

Figure 13-2. *A,* Comparison of the tips of the following endoscopes: diagnostic (tip diameter approximately 10 mm; channel size 2.8 mm); dual-channel therapeutic (tip diameter approximately 12 mm; channel sizes 3.4 mm and 2.8 mm); jumbo-channel therapeutic (tip diameter approximately 13 mm; channel size 6.0 mm). *B,* The jumbo-channel endoscope uses the biopsy channel port as the site for a separate suction line. A specialized toggle-type switch allows the suction to be controlled as desired and maintain use of the channel for devices. Use of the biopsy port with a second suction line is a practical method to deal with quick evacuation of blood and clot with any type of endoscope.

Lee and colleagues[39] showed that early endoscopy decreased the costs of care of patients with acute GI bleeding. Patients were prospectively randomized to receive endoscopy in the emergency room, and the control group underwent endoscopy in 1 to 2 days. Patients with low-risk findings were discharged from the emergency room. Endoscopy triage lead to early discharge of patients with low risk of rebleeding, without increasing morbidity and mortality. Median cost saving were $2068.

Cipolletta and coworkers[40] used endoscopic and clinical criteria to identify patients at low risk for recurrent bleeding. Patients were randomized to outpatient care versus hospital admission. No patient underwent surgery or died. Rates of recurrent bleeding were comparable (2.1% and 2.2%) in both groups. Median costs were $340 for outpatient and $3940 for inpatient group. They concluded that outpatient management of patients with low risk for recurrent bleeding is safe and cost effective.

Based on multiple studies confirming the beneficial effects of endoscopic therapy, urgent endoscopy and has been recommended by National Institute of Health[41] and ASGE[42] for patients who have active bleeding or who have clinical findings categorizing them at high risk for rebleeding. The definition of urgent endoscopy varies widely in various studies, from 2 to 24 hours after presentation to the hospital. It has been determined that 76% to 78% of the patients with acute GI bleeding undergo endoscopy within the first 24 hours.[43,44]

Preparation and Place for Endoscopy

Endoscopy is best undertaken in a fully equipped endoscopy suite where staff is trained in the use and maintenance of endoscopes and their related devices. Equipment must be available for cardiopulmonary monitoring during and after endoscopy. Stable hospitalized patients with mild to moderate bleeding can have endoscopy in an endoscopy unit. Patients with severe bleeding and hemodynamic compromise can be endoscoped at the bedside in the intensive care unit or emergency room. In certain settings, urgent endoscopy may be performed in the operating room to facilitate identification of a torrential bleeding site.

In patients with active or recent hemorrhage, residual blood in the stomach can limit the quality of examination. Poor visualization at the time of endoscopy has been associated with worse outcomes.[45] Multiple methods have been proposed to overcome this problem. Most commonly large-caliber NG tube lavage is used to clear the stomach. Instillation of 3% hydrogen peroxide[46] to dissolve small clots has been proposed. Use of an endoscope with a large accessory channel (up to 6 mm diameter) may be an effective method to remove clots and blood from the stomach.[47,48]

Two randomized controlled trials have looked into using erythromycin as a promotility agent to improve quality and yield of endoscopy.[49,50] Patients with acute GI bleeding were randomized to receive erythromycin (3 mg/kg IV) and were compared with the no treatment arm. The treatment group (erythromycin 3 mg/kg IV 20 to 60 minutes or 120 minutes before endoscopy) had an improved quality of endoscopic examination and resulted in reduced need for second-look endoscopy.

There are no data to suggest what the ideal endoscope is for both diagnosis and therapy (Fig. 13–2A and B). There is published experience with jumbo-channel instruments that can more efficiently evacuate blood and clot.[48,49] There are theoretic advantages for using therapeutic instruments with a large single channel or dual channels. The selection of these instruments are based on the intended use of a large coagulation probe and the availability of simultaneous suctioning. The large channels range from 3.4 to 4.2 mm diameter. Dual-channel instruments have a large or therapeutic channel and a small or diagnostic channel (2.8 mm diameter). These instruments have larger insertion tubes (>11 mm diameter) and generally have less retroflexion capability. Standard diagnostic endoscopes can be advantageous within the duodenum as can side-viewing duodenoscopes.

Causes of Nonvariceal Bleeding

GASTRIC AND DUODENAL ULCERS

Gastroduodenal ulcer disease is the most common cause of acute GI bleeding (Table 13–7). Ulcer disease is responsible for up to 50% of patients presenting with upper GI bleeding.[14,51] Hospitalization rate for ulcer-related GI bleeding has remained the same (40 to 60 cases per 100,000 patients) over the last 2 decades.[14,52]

Fifteen years ago, almost all peptic ulcers were considered idiopathic; in the 1980s and 1990s, most ulcer disease was attributed to

Table 13-7. American Society of Gastrointestinal Endoscopy Bleeding Survey: Endoscopic Diagnosis for Upper Gastrointestinal Bleeding in 2225 Patients

Diagnosis	Frequency (%)
Duodenal ulcer	24.3
Gastric erosions	23.4
Gastric ulcer	21.3
Varices	10.3
Mallory-Weiss tear	7.2
Esophagitis	6.3
Erosive duodenitis	5.8
Neoplasm	2.9
Stomal ulcer	1.8
Esophageal ulcer	1.7
Miscellaneous	6.8

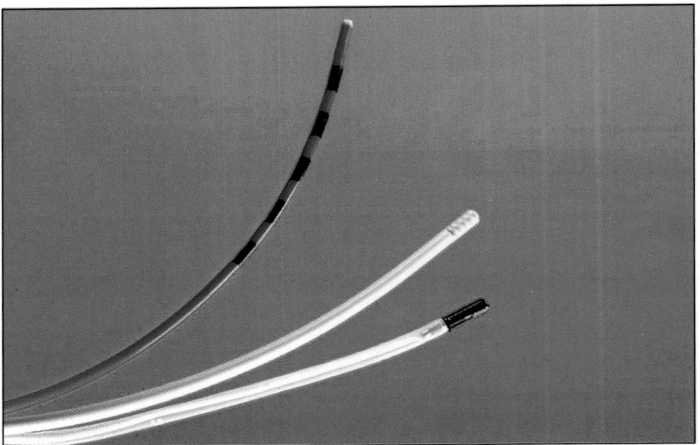

Figure 13-3. Coagulation probes: (from top down) Argon plasma coagulation end-firing probe, gold probe (Boston Scientific, Microvasive Endoscopy, Natick, MA), and heater probe (Olympus America, Melville, NY).

Helicobacter pylori and NSAIDs. *H. pylori* was found to be 90% of duodenal ulcers and 70% of gastric ulcers.[53] With awareness and aggressive therapy, there has been a decline in the prevalence of *H. pylori* in the Western world. The epidemiology of peptic ulcer has changed with a much higher percentage of *H. pylori*–negative ulcer disease now being reported.[54,55]

GI bleeding in patients with ulcers and high-risk features (active bleeding, nonbleeding visible vessel, densely adherent clot) commonly have continued or recurrent bleeding, and up to 35% require urgent surgery.[18] Over the last 15 to 20 years, endoscopic therapy has been demonstrated to benefit this population of patients.

Endoscopic therapy has been associated with reduction in the rates of rebleeding, blood transfusion, length of hospital stay, need for other therapeutic interventions, costs, and mortality.[56,57]

Indications for Endoscopic Therapy for Gastroduodenal Ulcers

Along with resuscitation, endoscopy is part of the initial care to triage patients in low- and high-risk categories. Endoscopic treatment for those with major stigmata for ulcer hemorrhage is indicated because it has demonstrated to improve outcome.

The National Institute of Health Consensus Conference in 1989 did not recommend any endoscopic treatment for patients with low-risk endoscopic stigmata. These include a clean-based ulcer or a dark nonprotuberent pigmented spot in the ulcer base. Endoscopic hemostasis is indicated to treat ulcers with major stigmata of recent hemorrhage. Patients who have active bleeding, spurting or oozing from the ulcer, a nonbleeding visible vessel in the ulcer base, and a densely adherent clot should receive endoscopic therapy.[19,58,59] In a recent meta-analysis by Bardou and coworkers,[60,61] endoscopic treatment was associated with statistically significant absolute decreases in rates of rebleeding, surgery, and mortality.

Nonbleeding Adherent Clot

The first randomized controlled study examining the management of major bleeding from ulcers with densely adherent clots was reported by Bleau and the Mayo Clinic GI Bleeding Team. Patients with adherent clots were randomized to receive medical therapy or endoscopic therapy. (Video 13–1). In the treatment arm, 1:10,000 epinephrine solution was injected in four quadrants around the ulcer before removing the overlying clot aggressively (cold snare, suction, manipulation with biopsy forceps and tip of the endoscope). Underlying stigmata were treated with heater probe (HP) coagulation. Rates of rebleeding were 34.3% in the medical treatment arm and 4.8% in the endoscopic treatment arm.[62] Jensen and coworkers[63] in a later, nearly identical study randomized 32 patients with severe bleeding and adherent clots to combination endoscopic therapy or medical management. In their study, after four-quadrant epinephrine injection, cold guillotining was used to shave off the clot to 3 to 4 mm above the ulcer base. The residual clot was treated with coaptive coagulation. Rebleeding rate in medical treatment group was 35.3% and 0% in the endoscopic therapy group.[63]

The underlying mechanism of rebleeding in case of an adherent clot is thought to be stigmata underlying the clot, which are the major determinants of rebleeding. Therefore, evaluation of the ulcer base is vital. Injection of 1:10,000 epinephrine appears to reduce the risk of bleeding and allows for the safe removal of the overlying clot.

Available Modalities for Endoscopic Therapy

Endoscopic therapy is undertaken routinely in patients with acute GI bleeding, with stigmata of recent hemorrhage. Endoscopic therapy can be broadly divided into four categories: injection therapy, thermal coaptive therapy, mechanical devices, and combination methods (Fig. 13–3). No single modality has been shown to be superior to others. Injection therapy and thermal modalities are believed to be equally effective. A meta-analysis of 12 randomized controlled trials 1813 patients randomized to injection or thermal therapy found no significant difference in continued or recurrent bleeding or need for surgery.[64] Combination therapies have gained more popularity because more data support use of combination therapy in specific situations.

Injection Therapy

Injection therapy is widely available and is one of the most common and established modalities used for ulcer hemostasis. Injection therapy is considered to be very safe, inexpensive, and easy to use with few clinically significant complications.

Epinephrine is the most established injection agent used for peptic ulcer injection therapy. Epinephrine diluted to 1:10,000 or 1:20,000 in normal saline is found to be the most effective and safest concentration.[65,66] The mechanism of action is thought to be vasoconstriction, platelet activation, and stimulation of the coagulation cascade.[67] In addition, a tamponade effect resulting from a volume of fluid into the ulcer base is also thought to be significant.[68] In a trial by Laine and Estrada,[69] comparison was made between normal saline injection (mean volume 30 mL) and bipolar electrocoagulation in patients with high-risk stigmata ulcer. Rates of rebleeding were 29% in injection group compared with 12% in thermocoagulation group. Mortality rates (6% vs. 2%) were not statistically significant.

Technique An injection needle with a retractable tip is used to inject 1:10,000 epinephrine solution in saline. Injection is undertaken in 0.5 to 1.0 mL increments in all four quadrants contiguous to the bleeding point. A total volume of 20 to 25 mL maybe injected until there is surrounding mucosal pallor and no bleeding or in the setting of spurting, a conversion from spurting to at least oozing. Alternatively, the injection can be made into a single site contiguous to the bleeding stigmata, and the epinephrine solution injected until there is resistance to injection and/or sufficient surrounding mucosal pallor. With chronic, fibrotic, and penetrating ulcers, there may not be any submucosa or musculeris to elevate with injected fluid. Injections should initially be made distal to the bleeding stigmata to raise the bleeding site toward the endoscope and view. Injections made proximal to the bleeding stigmata may impair access to the bleeding point because of elevation of the surrounding tissues and lifting the bleeding site away from the endoluminal view. Lin and coworkers[70] studied the effects of large-volume (mean 16.5 mL) versus small-volume (mean 8 mL) epinephrine injection as a single modality of treatment. The rebleeding rates were 15.4% in the large volume group and 30.8% in the small volume group. There were no differences in any other outcome measured between the two groups. They concluded that large volume greater than 13 mL of epinephrine can reduce rate of recurrent bleeding and is superior to smaller volumes. Alcohol injection is purposefully made in small amounts (0.5 mL per injection) and should not exceed 2 mL because of the desiccant properties and risk for eventual tissue necrosis with perforation.

Thermal Coaptive Therapy

Thermal methods include neodymium:yttrium-aluminum-garnet (Nd:YAG) laser, the HP, and electrocoagulation. Laser therapy and traditional monopolar coagulation are no longer popular because of lack of portability to bedside, high cost, and perforation risks. The multipolar electrocoagulation and HP are currently the most widely used thermal modalities. The advantages of these two devices are their efficacy; safety; portability; and the ability to combine irrigation, tamponade, and coagulation.

In coaptive coagulation, the probe is used to physically compress and tamponade the site of the bleeding vessel, followed by thermal energy sealing the walls of the vessel. In an animal model, arteries with a diameter of 2.5 mm can be coagulated with an HP using this technique.[71]

Technique

Bipolar probe: The technique has not been standardized and varies among the reported clinical trials. In canine models, the large (3.2 mm) probe produced better hemostasis than the smaller (2.3 mm) probe.[72,73] Laine[74] recommend forcefully applying the large (3.2 mm) bipolar coagulation probe (BICAP) on a low power setting for a prolonged duration, such as 14 seconds, or seven pulses of 2 seconds each. Jensen and coworkers[75] also used a low power setting with 10-second pulses on a BICAP II generator. The Gold probe has been shown to be effective at low power settings with longer pulse duration in clinical trials.

HP: The present technique for bleeding peptic ulcers involves using the larger HP, firm tamponade directly on the bleeding point or visible vessel, and coagulation with at least 120 J (four pulses of 30 J each) before moving the probe.[76]

Mechanical Devices

A number of mechanical devices, including clips, Endo-loop, and band ligators are now available for endoscopic treatment of GI bleeding. Although Endo-loop and band ligation have little role in treating peptic ulcer bleeding, use of clips have become very popular for emergency nonvariceal hemostasis (Fig. 13–4). The underlying mechanism of action is mechanical closure of the bleeding vessel. Randomized trials have compared use of clips alone or in combination with other therapies.

Among trials comparing clips with other endoscopic therapy, Cipolletta and colleagues[77] randomized 112 patients with major stigmata to HP or Hemoclip (HC) (Olympus Tokyo, Japan) therapy.

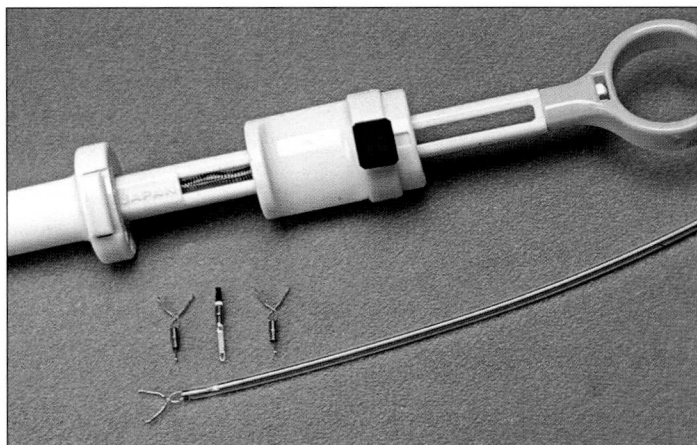

Figure 13–4. Original manually loaded Hemoclip (Olympus America, Melville, NY).

Table 13–8. Prospective Randomized Trials of Clipping and Other Therapies

Author	Treatments Compared	No. of Patients	Stigmata Treated	Initial Hemostasis (%)	Rebleeding (%)	Surgery (%)	Mortality (%)
Cipoletta, et al. (77)	HP	57	AB, NBVV	12 (60)	12 (21)	4 (7)	2 (3.5)
	Clip	56		13 (68)	1 (1.8)	2 (3.6)	2 (3.6)
Chou, et al. (78)	Dw Inj	40	AB, NBVV	39 (97.5)	11 (28.2)	5 (12.5)	2 (5)
	HP	39		40 (100)	4 (10.3)	2 (5.1)	1 (2.6)
Lin, et al. (79)	HP	40	AB, NBVV	40 (100)	2 (5)	1 (2.5)	1 (2.5)
	Clip	40		34 (85)	3 (8.8)	2 (5)	2 (5)

AB, active bleeding; Clip, hemoclip; Dw Inj, distilled water injection; HP, heater probe; NBVV, nonbleeding visible vessel.

Table 13–9. Prospective Randomized Trials of Clipping and Combination of Therapies

Author	Treatments Compared	No. of Patients	Stigmata Treated	Initial Hemostasis (%)	Rebleeding (%)	Surgery (%)	Mortality (%)
Chung, et al. (81)	Epi-HSE	41	AB, NBVV	39 (95.1)	6 (14.6)	6 (14.6)	1 (2.4)
	Clip	41		40 (97.6)	1 (2.4)	2 (4.9)	1 (2.4)
	Clip + HSE	42		41 (97.6)	4 (9.5)	1 (2.3)	1 (2.3)
Gevers, et al. (82)	Epi-polido	34	AB, NBVV	5 (85)	2 (15)		0 (0)
	Clip	35		13 (63)	12 (35)		0 (0)
	Clip + Epi-polido	32		8 (75)	8 (25)		3 (9)

AB, active bleeding; Clip, hemoclip; Epi-HSE, epinephrine hypertonic saline solution injection; Epi-polido, epinephrine-polidocanol solution injection; NBVV, nonbleeding visible vessel.

Rates of recurrent bleeding (21% vs. 1.8%) and need for surgery were significantly lower in the HC group. They concluded that HC therapy was safe and superior to HP. In a randomized study by Chou and coworkers,[78] HC therapy was found superior to distilled water injection therapy in patients with major stigmata (active bleeding vessel, nonbleeding visible vessel). In their study comparing HC (vs.) HP, Lin and colleagues[79] reported 85% initial hemostasis as compared with 100% in HP group. Rebleeding rate was 8.8% in HC and 5% in HP group (Table 13–8).

In trials comparing combination therapy, Villanueva and coworkers[80] randomized 250 patients to receive epinephrine injection alone and HC plus epinephrine injection for hemostasis of bleeding peptic ulcers. Initial hemostasis in both the groups were comparable (92% to 94%). In patients with active bleeding, rates of rebleeding was significantly higher in injection alone group (33%) compared with injection and HC (10%). Chung and coworkers[81] prospectively assigned 124 patients to HC, hypertonic saline-epinephrine (HSE), and combined treatment groups. Initial hemostasis was comparable in all groups. Rate of recurrent bleed in HC, HSE, and combination therapy groups were 2.4%, 14.6%, and 9.5%, respectively (Table 13–9). Gevers and colleagues[82] randomly assigned 101 patients with high-risk stigmata (active bleeding, nonbleeding visible vessel) to receive epinephrine, polidocanol injection, HC, or combined therapy. They reported more treatment failures in the HC group (34%) than injection therapy (6%). Failure of HC therapy was attributed to difficulty in clip placement and incomplete vessel compression. In a retrospective comparison, Buffoli and coworkers[83] did not find additional advantage of HC therapy when used in combination with epinephrine injection therapy. A favored trend toward reducing surgery was seen in the combination therapy group (0% vs. 7.4%).

Several randomized controlled trials investigating the use of endoscopic clips alone or in combination with other endoscopic modalities have reported variable success. The most important factor appears to be accurate positioning of a clip across the bleeding stigmata. This can be difficult for ulcers in sites such as high on the lesser curvature and posterior duodenal wall.[79] Endoscopic clipping devices have undergone improvements. The original individually loaded Olympus HC device has been transformed into a single preloaded device with rotation feature and a larger clip (wider). Another device (Triclip; Wilson Cook Medical, Winston-Salem, North Carolina) offers a three-pronged clip to enable placement and simultaneous irrigation capability. A third single-clip device (Boston Scientific Corporation, Natick, Massachusetts) offers the ability to open and close the clip, maximizing effective placement and minimizing the number of clips needed. A final device (Ethicon Endosurgery, Cincinnati, Ohio) offers the ability to selectively place the clip using a large-jaw forceps that can be opened and closed as desired over the bleeding site before deploying the clip, which is contained within the forceps jaws. This device offers the ability to place multiple clips. The tips of these clips, unlike others, overlap to lock the clip into the captured tissue.

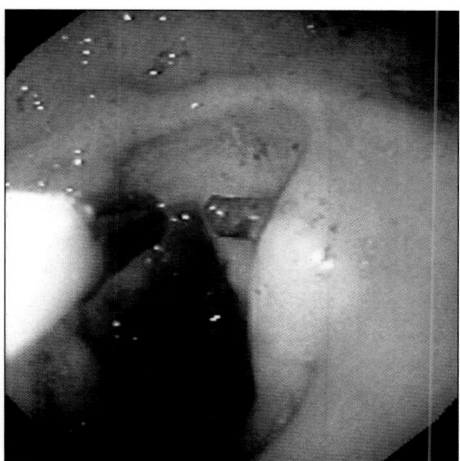

Figure 13–5. Large-sized heater probe and large-sized visible vessel protruding from an antral ulcer (not seen). Note the surrounding mucosal pallor from prior injection with 1:10,000 epinephrine.

Combination Therapy

There is a theoretical advantage of combining therapies to obtain lasting hemostasis using additive mechanisms. Injection therapy and thermal coagulation are the most popular combination therapies used (Fig. 13–5). Epinephrine causes vasoconstriction, reduced blood flow, and platelet activation, which potentiates the coaptive coagulation by thermal energy. Another advantage may be improved visualization of the target area for thermal coagulation after initial injection therapy in an actively bleeding ulcer. Combination therapy with both injection and coaptive therapy has been demonstrated to be superior to medical therapy alone.[62,63,84] There have been few randomized trials comparing combination therapy with endoscopic monotherapy (injection, thermal coagulation).

Chung and coworkers[85] in a randomized controlled trial compared epinephrine injection to epinephrine injection plus HP in actively bleeding ulcers. Outcomes as measured by clinical rebleeding, requirement for emergency surgery, blood transfusion, hospital stay, and mortality were not significantly different in the two groups. In a subgroup analysis, patients with major, active arterial bleeding had a better outcome regarding need for surgery (29.6% vs. 6.5%) and length of hospital stay (6 days vs. 4 days) after combination therapy. Combination therapy did not improve outcomes of patients with oozing of blood.

Lin and colleagues[86] compared epinephrine injection alone, bipolar electrocoagulation alone, and combined treatment using injection gold probe (Microvasive/Boston Scientific, Natick Massachusetts). Rebleeding rates of 6.7% in combination therapy (injection-gold probe), 30% in electrocoagulation ($p = .04$), and 35.5% in the injection therapy ($p = .01$) group were statistically significant. Combination therapy was also associated with reduced treatment failure rates and transfusion requirements.

Other Options

A variety of other agents have been used for injection therapy with variable results. These include agents causing tamponade (hypertonic saline, distilled water), sclerosing agents (ethanolamine, cyanoacrylate, polidocanol),[87–89] tissue desiccants (alcohol),[90] and agents stimulating clot formation (thrombin, fibrin glue).[91–94] There is little evidence that addition of other agents (sclerosants) significantly reduces the rate of rebleeding.[87–90] Sclerosants and especially desiccants have been associated with tissue necrosis of injected areas, clinical perforation, and death.

Thrombosis of the bleeding vessel is one aim of endoscopic therapy; injection of agents that stimulate clotting is an attractive proposition. Fibrin and thrombin have been used as agents to stimulate clot formation. Lin and coworkers[92] compared injection of fibrin glue with epinephrine for patients with high-risk stigmata (active bleeding, nonbleeding visible vessel). Rate of rebleeding was less in the fibrin group (15%) compared with the epinephrine group (56%). Pescatore and colleagues[93] compared epinephrine injection versus epinephrine plus fibrin glue injection in patients with high risk of rebleeding. There were no significant differences in rates of recurrent bleeding (24.3% and 21.5%, respectively, for epinephrine and epinephrine plus fibrin glue), surgery, or mortality between the two groups. Rutgeerts and colleagues[94] in a randomized trial of 850 patients with high-risk stigmata (active bleeding, nonbleeding visible vessel) compared single polidocanol injection, single fibrin glue injection, and daily fibrin glue injection until disappearance of visible vessel. All patients were pretreated with epinephrine injection. No significant difference in recurrent bleeding, transfusion, surgery, or mortality was reported between the single polidocanol and fibrin injection.

Kubba and coworkers[91] demonstrated reduced rates of rebleeding with combination of epinephrine and thrombin therapy (4.3%) when compared with epinephrine therapy (20%) alone. Balanzo and colleagues[95] did not find a significant difference when comparing epinephrine and epinephrine plus thrombin injection therapy. According to Church and coworkers,[96] combination of thrombin and HP did not confer any additional benefit over HP and placebo in patients with bleeding peptic ulcer. Fibrin glue and thrombin are expensive. Fibrin glue requires special preparation and dual-channel injection, one for fibrin and the other for thrombin. It does not allow for spontaneous availability and emergency use. Although promising, more convincing data are required to show superiority of these agents to currently available therapeutic options.

Role of Argon Plasma Coagulator

Argon plasma coagulation is a noncoaptive method that allows controlled noncontact electrocoagulation by means of monopolar energy delivered to the tissue through ionized gas (argon plasma). It has been used instead of standard electrocoagulation and preliminary data showed some promise. Cipolletta and coworkers,[97] in a prospective trial of 41 patients compared argon plasma coagulation (APC) with HP therapy. Rates of initial hemostasis, recurrent bleeding, emergency surgery, and 30-day mortality were comparable in both groups. Similar results have been reported by Chau and colleagues[98] in a large (185 cases) randomized trial comparing epinephrine plus HP with epinephrine plus APC. These data suggest that APC therapy seems to be safe and effective for treatment of ulcer bleeding; however, there is no obvious advantage of using or recommending APC over more established forms of endoscopic therapy.

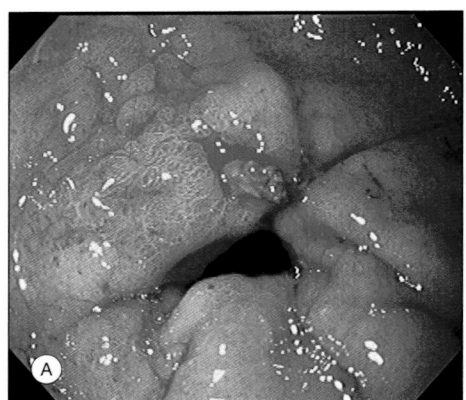
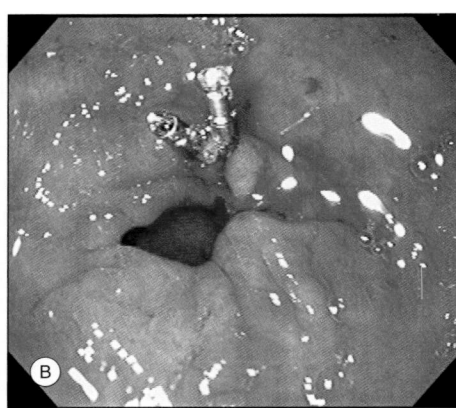

Figure 13-6. *A,* Antral ulcer with visible vessel (pigmented protuberance) at the lower left margin of the ulcer in a patient with thrombocytopenia. *B,* The ulcer has been completely closed with Hemoclips as primary therapy.

Recommendations for Endoscopic Stigmata

Arterial spurting: combination therapy, injection followed by coaptive coagulation

Nonbleeding visible vessel: monotherapy or combination therapy

Active oozing from focal spot in ulcer base: monotherapy, injection or coaptive coagulation

Adherent clot: combination therapy, injection followed by clot removal then coaptive coagulation

Pigmented flat spot or clean based ulcer: no therapy needed

Stigmata of recent hemorrhage and patient with coagulopathy: monotherapy or combination therapy followed by clipping or clipping alone (Fig. 13–6)

Role of Medical Therapy

In addition to endoscopic therapy, acid suppression therapy has been shown to benefit patients with bleeding peptic ulcers.[99,100] The role of gastric acid inhibition to stop bleeding or to prevent recurrent bleeding is related to stability of blood clot, which is favored by a higher gastric pH.[101,102] A pH of greater than 6 is required for platelet aggregation, whereas clot lysis occurs at pH below 6.

IV and oral histamine-2 (H₂) antagonists have been used for decades without any definite supporting evidence of their efficacy in decreasing rate of recurrent bleeding in these patients. Proton pump inhibitors (PPIs) have been found to be more effective than H₂-receptor antagonists in decreasing the rate of recurrent bleeding.[103] The findings of meta-analysis performed by Gisbert and coworkers[104] have found PPIs to be more effective than H₂-receptor antagonists in preventing persistent or recurrent bleeding. Their data suggested that beneficial effect of PPIs were mainly observed in those patients not having adjunct endoscopic therapy.

Lau and coworkers[105] reported results of a large double-blind randomized trial in which omeprazole was compared with placebo in patients receiving endoscopic therapy for bleeding ulcers. After receiving endoscopic therapy (active bleeding, nonbleeding visible vessel, stigmata under adherent clot), patients were randomized to IV omeprazole (8 mg/hr continuous infusion) versus placebo for 72 hours. Recurrent bleeding at 30 days, the primary end point of the study, occurred in 6.7% of the patients in the omeprazole group, as compared with 22.5% of the patients in the placebo group ($p < .001$). Most cases of rebleeding occurred within 72 hours of endoscopic therapy. Other randomized trials have also reported a decreased rate of rebleeding and in some cases surgery when comparing IV omeprazole to H₂-receptor antagonists or placebo after endoscopic therapy.[106] Among 156 patients with nonbleeding visible vessels and adherent clots, Sung and coworkers[107] demonstrated superiority of a combination of IV high-dose omeprazole infusion and endoscopic hemostasis over IV high-dose treatment alone.

Although no head-to-head studies are available at present, data are suggestive that proton pump inhibition is a class effect and that the improvement in rebleeding can be achieved by using omeprazole or pantoprazole (only IV PPI available in North America), 80-mg bolus followed by 8 mg/hour for 72 hours after endoscopic therapy (Table 13–10).

Table 13-10. Effectiveness of Omeprazole in Peptic Ulcer Bleeding

Study	Number	Edoscopic Therapy	Bleeding Rate		p Value
			Control	*Omeprazole*	
Khuroo, et al. (100)	220	No	40/110 (36%)	12/110 (11%)	<0.001
Lau, et al. (105)	240	Yes	24/120 (23%)	5/120 (7%)	<0.001
Sung, et al. (107)	156	Yes	7/78 (7%)	0/78 (0%)	0.01
Hasselgren, et al. (108)	322	Yes	26/163 (17%)	12/159 (8%)	N/S
Schaffalitzky de Muckadell, et al. (109)	229	Yes	37/118 (25%)	20/111 (18%)	N/S
Lin, et al. (110)	100	Yes	8/50 (16%)	0/50 (0%)	0.01

N/S, not specified.

Second-Look Endoscopy

Routine repeat (second-look) endoscopy is done at a variable time period after the index endoscopy, but most often 24 hours later with the intent of repeat endoscopic treatment of high-risk lesions, and has been advocated to be beneficial in some clinical situations. Few randomized trials have addressed the issue and show conflicting results. Messmann and coworkers[111] reported no improvements in outcomes when scheduled repeat endoscopy was compared with second endoscopy performed at recurrent bleeding. Villanueva and colleagues[112] noted a statistically nonsignificant trend toward better outcomes in the group that received routine second-look endoscopy within 24 hours. Saeed and colleagues[113] adopted an approach of scheduled retreatment to high-risk patients based on a composite clinical and endoscopic score and demonstrated significant benefit in the prevention of rebleeding. Pooled data on second-look endoscopy demonstrated that routine second-look endoscopy with retreatment significantly reduced the risk of recurrent bleeding compared with expectant management (absolute risk reduction 6.2%, $p < .01$, number needed to treat = 16).[114] The risk of surgery and death were not significantly influenced by second-look endoscopy. Cost effectiveness of repeat endoscopy has been verified in a hypothetical model[115] but no prospective studies are available to date.

Routine second-look endoscopy in all patients is not recommended. It may be justified in select high-risk patients. A second endoscopy may be useful in patients with a suboptimal index endoscopy because of poor visualization or other technical difficulties.

Dealing with Recurrent Bleeding

With research and advancements in endoscopic therapy, primary hemostasis has been achieved in more than 95% of patients with actively bleeding peptic ulcers and ulcers with stigmata of recent hemorrhage. Rebleeding can occur in up to 10% to 20% of these patients and there is a mortality rate of 4% to 10%. If rebleeding occurs, it occurs within 48 to 72 hours. Clinical judgment individualized to the patient must be used in the setting of rebleeding. A repeat endoscopy with repeated therapy in the absence of massive rebleeding has become accepted practice. Recurrent bleeding after a second endoscopic intervention should initiate plans for alternative interventions. These would become a consideration if the lesion has been technically challenging to access and deliver accurate therapy. If repeat endoscopy is to be considered a third time, then an alternative treatment should be considered (e.g., clipping, use of a larger coagulation probe). Repeated coagulation therapy increases the risk of perforation especially along the anterior duodenal wall. Angiography and surgery are the other options.

In a prospective randomized trial, Lau and coworkers[116] randomized 92 patients with recurrent bleeding after endoscopic hemostasis; 48 patients were assigned to repeat endoscopic therapy, and 44 patients were assigned to emergency ulcer surgery. Seventy-three percent (35 of 48) of patients had long-term control of bleeding by repeat endoscopic therapy. Twenty-seven percent required surgery, and there were 11 endoscopic failures with 2 perforations secondary to thermocoagulation. Overall fewer complications (14.6% vs. 36.4%) were noted in the repeat endoscopy group. This study suggests that a repeat endoscopy is effective in controlling rebleeding and in reducing the need for surgical intervention and its associated complications.

Failure of Endoscopic Therapy

Surgery for bleeding peptic ulcer has declined in the past 2 decades because of improvements in endoscopic hemostasis techniques and effective acid suppression therapy. However, active nonvariceal GI hemorrhage that overwhelms endoscopic intervention is referred to as torrential hemorrhage and requires urgent surgical operation. Therefore, it is imperative to obtain surgical consultation in all patients presenting with a major GI hemorrhage. Accurate prediction of patients who are likely to fail endoscopic management may allow for the scheduling of early semielective surgery. Wong and coworkers[117] analyzed risk factors associated with treatment failure with combined injection therapy and HP thermocoagulation. Hypotension, hemoglobin less than 10 g/dL, fresh blood in the stomach, ulcer with active bleeding, and large ulcers greater than 2 cm were independent risk factors predicting poor control of bleeding with endoscopy alone. In a prospective study by Chung and colleagues,[118] the presence of blood spurting and ulcers larger than 2 cm were significantly related to failure of endoscopic therapy. There are little data to support elective surgery in these patients although it sounds appealing in theory, because elective surgery carries a much lower mortality than emergent surgery. Maximal acid suppression therapy, close monitoring for signs of rebleeding, and surgical team on standby remains a sound treatment strategy.

Therapeutic Angiography

Therapeutic angiography is an alternative option for patients who have failed endoscopic therapy and are not candidates for surgery. Therapeutic options include selective intra-arterial vasopressin infusion or embolotherapy with microcoils, gelatin, or polyvinyl alcohol particles. Embolization has been shown to stop bleeding in massive gastroduodenal ulcers. Detection of bleeding site at the time of endoscopy provides vital information to the interventional radiologist to select the target area for catheterization. Technical success rates have been reported to be from 50% to 90%.[119–121] Known complications of embolization are bowel ischemia, necrosis with perforation, abscess formation, and hepatic infarction especially in patients with poor hepatic reserve.

Prevention of Recurrent Bleed

Prevention of recurrent ulcer disease and bleeding is very important in patients with ulcer hemorrhage. There are convincing data that treatment with PPIs prevents ulcer rebleeding.[102–109] Follow-up endoscopy is warranted to exclude malignancy in certain patients with gastric ulcer. The data linking persistent H. pylori with recurrent ulcer hemorrhage are compelling, making eradication of infection the best approach for these patients.[122–125] Most tests of active infection may exhibit increased false-negative rates in the setting of acute bleeding.[126–129] The optimal diagnostic approach may include testing for H. pylori by serology or antral biopsy at the time of

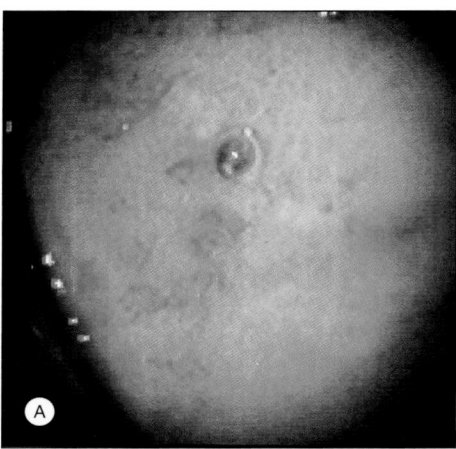 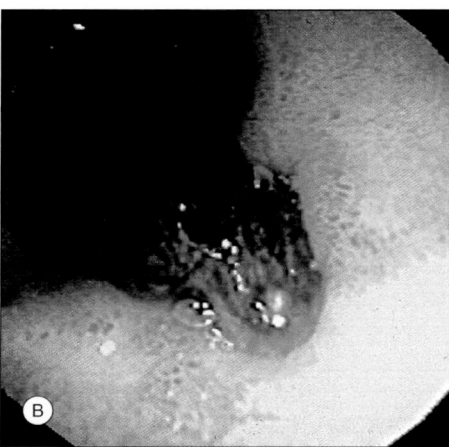 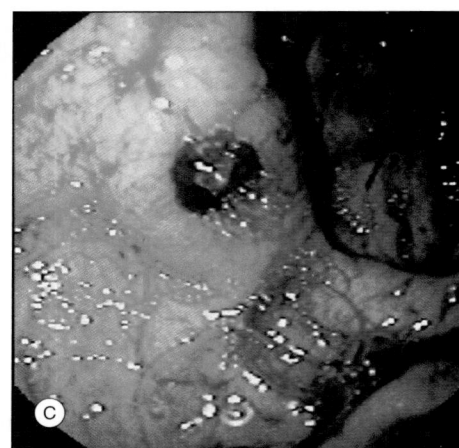

Figure 13-7. Dieulafoy's gastric lesions. *A,* A lesion with a thin rim of surrounding ulceration. *B,* Pale protruding artery with surrounding blood. *C,* Pale centrally protruding artery with surrounding mucosal defect.

endoscopy, with reconfirmation of negative results by repeat testing when the bleeding resolves. Oral therapy can be started immediately or during follow-up in patients found to have *H. pylori* infection.

Patients with peptic ulcer bleeding should be encouraged to discontinue NSAIDs use. If this is not possible, therapy with misoprostol (200 μg four times daily) or with omeprazole appears to be effective in prevention of gastroduodenal ulcers and erosions.[130,131] Switching to cyclooxygenase-2 (COX2) inhibitors is reasonable but would still require concurrent prophylaxis therapy.

DIEULAFOY'S LESION

The Dieulafoy's lesion (DL) is an uncommon cause of acute nonvariceal GI bleeding, but can be associated with sever recurrent hemorrhage. It was originally described by Gallard in 1884 and was designated "exulceratio simplex" by the French surgeon Georges Dieulafoy 14 years later. DL consists of an abnormal, submucosal "caliber-persistent artery" (1 to 3 mm diameter) that retains the serosal large caliber and typically protrudes through a small mucosal defect without any surrounding ulceration.[132] The underlying mechanism is poorly understood but is thought to be due to mechanical compression of the overlying mucosa by the large artery resulting in small erosion with rupture of vessel in to the lumen.[133]

DL accounts for 1.2% to 1.9% of cases of acute nonvariceal upper GI bleeding,[134,135] but incidence as high as 5.8% has been reported.[136] Although reported in all age groups, it predominantly presents in men of advanced age with multiple comorbid conditions.[135,137] Typically, a DL is located in the stomach usually within 6 cm of the gastroesophageal junction in 60% to 64% of cases and in the duodenum in another 14% to 18% of cases.[137,138]

Diagnosis

The endoscopic criteria for the diagnosis of DL are (1) active arterial spurting or micropulsatile streaming; (2) visualization of a protruding vessel with or without active bleeding or; (3) fresh, densely adherent clot with a narrow point of attachment, from a minute (less than 3 mm) mucosal defect or through normal surrounding mucosa (Fig. 13-7A to D).[139] Diagnosis at the time of endoscopy can be difficult because there is no identifying lesion (ulcer) to indicate the source. The diagnosis rates for initial endoscopy range from 49% to 63% and repeat endoscopy is often required. In view of the intermittent nature of bleeding from DL, the sensitivity of endoscopic diagnosis is likely to be increased through early endoscopy in patients with acute GI bleeding and especially recurrent bleeding while under observation.

Endoscopic Therapy

In the past, surgical resection has been the standard therapy to control bleeding in DL. With the advent of endoscopic techniques, management today is carried out by endoscopic methods in most patients. Hemostasis can be achieved by endoscopic treatment in more than 90% of the patients.[137,139] Endoscopic methods can be injection or thermal probe monotherapy, mechanical devices, or combination treatment. Most data are from cases series because randomized trials are difficult to perform because of the rarity of the condition.

Injection and Thermal Monotherapy

Multiple agents including epinephrine, a sclerosant, alcohol, hypertonic glucose, and cyanoacrylate glue have been reported for successful injection therapy. Although a there is a high initial success rate, there appears to be a high rate of rebleeding with injection monotherapy. Baettig and colleagues[136] treated 19 patients, using injection therapy with epinephrine or polidocanol and had a rebleeding rate of 21%, whereas Kasapidis and coworkers[140] in their retrospective analysis report a rebleeding rate of 55% in patients with DL treated with injection therapy using epinephrine, ethanolamine oleate (5%), or combination of the two.

Thermal probe monotherapy has been demonstrated to be effective but with variable success rates in small cohorts of patients. Lin and coworkers[141] had 100% success in their six patients, whereas Parra-Blanco and colleagues[142] had two of six patients with recurrent bleed after treatment with HP.

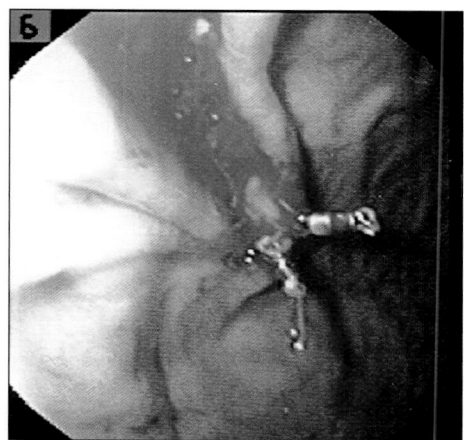

Figure 13–8. Fundal Dieulafoy's lesion treated by clipping.

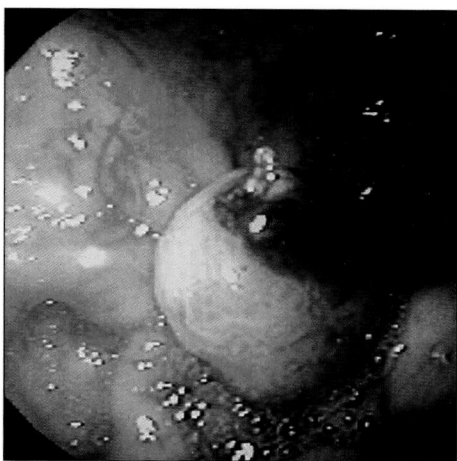

Figure 13–9. Gastric Dieulafoy's lesion (from Fig. 13.7C) treated by band ligation. Note the very prominent translucent protruding artery.

Combination Therapy

Combination therapy with injection followed by thermal probe coagulation does seem offer a more secure hemostasis by comparison with monotherapy (Video 13–2). The prior use of injection therapy with epinephrine may be a useful adjunct to slow or stop bleeding before targeted ablative therapy or before clot guillotine.

Stark and coworkers[143] presented their data of 10 years on management of DL. DL was found in 19 of 1124 consecutive patients with upper GI bleeding. Patients (18 of 19) treated with combination therapy with epinephrine injection and thermal therapy (17 HP; 1 BICAP) had a 100% success rate of initial hemostasis and only one patient rebled in the follow-up period. Kasapidis and colleagues[140] retrospectively compared injection therapy (epinephrine; ethanolamine) with thermal therapy alone or in combination with epinephrine injection. Initial hemostasis was achieved in all 18 patients. Five of nine patients had recurrent bleeding, whereas none of the patients in the other group (8/9 combined therapy; 1/9 HP only) rebled.

Mechanical Devices

Among mechanical devices, endo-clip application and endoscopic rubber band ligation have been successfully used to treat bleeding from DL. The rationale of using mechanical devices is the small size of the lesion with normal surrounding tissue, which can be compressed along with the caliber persistent artery.

Clipping   Like other lesions, clipping has also been used for DL (Fig. 13–8). Yamaguchi and coworkers[144] used HC application as first-choice hemostatic treatment for DL bleeding. Initial hemostasis was achieved in 94.1% of patients requiring 3.1 (mean; range 1 to 6) clips per patient. Rate of recurrent bleeding was 9.4%, which was successfully treated with repeat endoscopic therapy. None of the patients required surgery. Parra-Blanco[145] used HC application to control bleeding from DL in 69% of their patients. Initial success rate was 97% (17 of 18) with a mean of 2.7 clips per patient. Because clipping effects closure of the vessel and the associated acute mucosal defect, long-term prevention of recurrent bleeding after this form of therapy is unknown.

In a randomized prospective trial, Chung and colleagues[146] compared mechanical methods (HC and band ligation) to injection therapy with HSE. Of 24 patients, 12 were assigned to mechanical therapy (9 HC; 3 rubber band ligation) and 12 to injection therapy group. The mechanical therapy was more effective than injection therapy in terms of initial hemostasis (91.7% vs. 75%), recurrent bleeding (8.3% vs. 33.3%, $p < .05$) and need for surgery (0% vs. 17%).

Band Ligation   Matsui and coworkers[147] compared endoscopic band ligation (EBL) to bipolar electrocoagulation in patients with acute GI hemorrhage exclusive of chronic gastroduodenal disease (Fig. 13–9). Twenty-seven patients with DL had endoscopic therapy, with a success rate of 100% (13/13) for EBL versus 85.7% (12/14) for bipolar electrocoagulation. In a retrospective VA study, Mumtaz and colleagues[148] presented data of 23 patients with DL treated with EBL (14/23) and injection with or without thermal therapy. Initial hemostasis was achieved in all patients in both groups, and only one patient had early rebleeding (within 72 hours) in both groups. Nikolaidis and coworkers[149] retrospectively reviewed the results of EBL in 23 patients with DL. Initial hemostasis success rate was 96% (22 of 23). One patient with a jejunal DL required surgery for rebleeding. Unlike clipping, band ligation theoretically interrupts the vessel at its mucosal and submucosal levels. This may have better long-term outcome in the prevention of rebleeding.

Recurrent Bleeding

There is little evidence if acid suppression therapy is required or effective in preventing rebleeding from DLs. However, it is often administered either as empiric therapy for acute GI bleeding or to treat concurrent GI pathology. Short-term recurrent bleeding is common, occurring in 9% to 22% of cases. In case of rebleeding, repeat endoscopic therapy is recommended because it is successful in most patients. Long-term rates of recurrent bleeding is low once DL is completely treated. Studies have reported no recurrent bleeding with follow-up of up to 3 years after treatment[143,146]; however, repeat bleeding from the same site has been known to occur 6 years after the initial episode.[141]

In some patients with recurrent bleeding in whom a DL had been suspected within the proximal stomach, the caliber-persistent vessel had been identified and therapy directed by endoscopic ultrasound.[150,151]

Salvage Therapy

Despite a high success rate of endoscopic therapy, surgery may be required as salvage therapy in 3% to 16% of patients. The role of endoscopy for exact localization of the lesion is of extreme importance. Surgical oversewing of the vessel is associated with a higher risk of recurrent bleeding, and wedge resection of the area may be a better surgical procedure in these patients with refractory bleeding.[143] Angiography can be used not only to localize but also to selectively embolize the bleeding vessel. Varying success has been reported; it should be reserved for patients who have failed endoscopic therapy and are poor candidates for surgical intervention.

REFERENCES

1. Yavorski RT, Wong RK, Maydonovitch C, et al: Analysis of 3,294 cases of upper gastrointestinal bleeding in military medical facilities. Am J Gastroenterol 90:568–573, 1995.

2. Rockall TA, Logan RF, Devlin HB, et al: Incidence of and mortality from acute upper gastrointestinal haemorrhage in the United Kingdom. BMJ 311:222–226, 1995.

3. Wilcox CM, Alexander LN, Cotsonis G: A prospective characterization of upper gastrointestinal hemorrhage presenting with hematochezia. Am J Gastroenterol 92:231–235, 1997.

4. Silverstein FE, Gilbert DA, Tedesco FJ, et al: The national ASGE survey on upper gastrointestinal bleeding II. Clinical prognostic factors. Gastrointest Endosc 27:80–93, 1981.

5. Slattery J, Warlow CP, Shorrock CJ, et al: Risks of gastrointestinal bleeding during secondary prevention of vascular events with aspirin—analysis of gastrointestinal bleeding during the UK-TIA trial. Gut 37:509–511, 1995.

6. Swedish Aspirin Low-Dose Trial (SALT) of 75 mg aspirin as secondary prophylaxis after cerebrovascular ischaemic events. The SALT Collaborative Group. Lancet 338:1345–1349, 1991.

7. Wilcox CM, Truss CD: Gastrointestinal bleeding in patients receiving long term anticoagulation therapy. Am J Med 84:683–690, 1988.

8. Piper JM, Ray WA, Daugherty JR, et al: Corticosteroid use and peptic ulcer disease: Role of nonsteroidal anti-inflammatory drugs. Ann Intern Med 102:A84, 1991.

9. Graham DY, Malaty HM: Alendronate and naproxen are synergistic for development of gastric ulcers. Arch Intern Med 161:107–110, 2001.

10. Garcia Rodriguez LA, Cattaruzzi C, Troncon MG, Agostinis L: Risk of hospitalization for upper gastrointestinal tract bleeding associated with ketorolac, other nonsteroidal anti-inflammatory drugs, calcium antagonists and other antihypertensive drugs. Arch Intern Med 158:33–39, 1998.

11. Gilbert DA, Saunders DR: Iced saline lavage does not slow bleeding from experimental canine gastric ulcers. Dig Dis Sci 26:1065–1068, 1981.

12. Andrus C, Ponsky J: The effects of irrigant temperature in upper gastrointestinal hemorrhage: A requiem of iced saline lavage. Am J Gastroenterol 82:1062–1064, 1987.

13. Gilbert DA, Silverstein FE, Tedeaco FJ, et al: The national ASGE survey on upper gastrointestinal bleeding. III. Endoscopy in upper gastrointestinal bleeding. Gastrointest Endosc 27:94–102, 1981.

14. Silverstein FE, Gilbert DA, Tedeaco FJ, et al: The national ASGE survey on upper gastrointestinal bleeding. II. Clinical prognostic factors. Gastrointest Endosc 27:80–93, 1981.

15. Cuellar R, Gavaler J, Alexander J, et al: Gastrointestinal tract hemorrhage: The value of nasogastric aspirate. Arch Intern Med 150:1381–1384, 1990.

16. Ebert RA, Stead EA, Gibson JG: Response of normal subjects to acute blood loss. Arch Intern Med 68:578, 1940.

17. Ernst AA, Haynes ML, Weiss SJ: Usefulness of blood urea nitrogen/creatinine ratio in gastrointestinal bleeding. Am J Emerg Med 17:70–72, 1999.

18. Laine L, Peterson WL: Bleeding peptic ulcer. New Engl J Med 331:717–727, 1994.

19. Barkun A, Bardou M, Marshall JK: Consensus recommendations for managing Patients with nonvariceal upper gastrointestinal Bleeding. Ann Intern Med 139:843–857, 2003.

20. Huang C, Lichtenstein D: Nonvariceal upper gastrointestinal bleeding. Gastrointest Clin N Am 32:1053–1078, 2003.

21. Blatchford O, Murray WR, Blatchford M: A risk score to predict need for treatment for upper gastrointestinal hemorrhage. Lancet 356:1318–1321, 2000.

22. Cameron EA, Pratap JN, Inman S, et al: Three-year prospective validations of pre-endoscopic risk stratification in patients with acute upper-gastrointestinal haemorrhage. Eur J Gastroenterol Hepatol 14:497–501, 2002.

23. Rockall TA, Logan RF, Devlin HB, et al: Steering committee of National Audit of Acute Upper Gastrointestinal Haemorrhage. Risk assessment after acute gastrointestinal haemorrhage. Gut 38:316–321, 1996.

24. Sanders DS, Carter MJ, Goodchap RJ, et al: Prospective validation of Rockall risk scoring system for upper GI hemorrhage in subgroups of patients with varices and peptic ulcers. Am J Gastroenterol 97:630–635, 2002.

25. Vreeburg EM, Terwee CB, Snel P, et al: Validation of Rockall risk scoring system in upper gastrointestinal bleeding. Gut 44:331–335, 1999.

26. Dulai GS, Gralnek IM, Oei TT, et al: Utilization of health care resources for low-risk patients with acute, nonvariceal upper GI hemorrhage: An historical cohort study. Gastrointest Endosc 55:321–327, 2002.

27. Hay J, Lyubashevsky E, Elashoff J, et al: Upper gastrointestinal hemorrhage clinical guideline: Determining the optimal hospital length of stay. Am J Med 100:313–322, 1996.

28. Saeed Z, Ramirez F, Hepps K, et al: Prospective validation of the Baylor bleeding score for predicting the likelihood of rebleeding after endoscopic hemostasis of peptic ulcers. Gastrointest Endosc 41:561–565, 1995.

29. Laine L, Cohen H, Brodhead J, et al: Prospective evaluation of immediate versus delayed refeeding and prognostic value of endoscopy in patients with upper gastrointestinal hemorrhage. Gastroenterology 102:314–316, 1992.

30. Forrest JA, Finlayson ND, Sherman DJ: Endoscopy in gastrointestinal bleeding. Lancet 2:394–397, 1974.

31. Swain CP, Storey DW, Bown SG, et al: Nature of the bleeding vessel in recurrently bleeding gastric ulcers. Gastroenterology 90:595–608, 1986.

32. Freeman, ML, Cass OW, Peine CJ, Onstad GR: The non-bleeding visible vessel versus the sentinel clot: Natural history and risk of rebleeding. Gastrointest Endosc 39:359–366, 1993.

33. Chung SC, Leung JU, Lo KK, et al: Natural history of the sentinel clot: An endoscopic study [abstract]. Gastroenterology 98:31, 1990.

34. Branicki FJ, Coleman SY, Fok PJ, et al: Bleeding peptic ulcer: A prospective evaluation of risk factors for rebleeding and mortality. World J Surg 14:262–269, 1990.

35. Swain CP, Salmon PR, Northfield PC: Does ulcer position influence presentation and prognosis of acute gastrointestinal bleeding? Gut 27:A632, 1986.

36. Kodali VP, Peterson BT, Balm R, et al: Clean based peptic ulcer: Implications of cost effective management of acute gastrointestinal bleeding (AUGIB) [abstract] Am J Gastroenterol 90:1584, 1995.

37. Longstreth GF, Feitelberg SP: Outpatient care of selected patients with acute non-variceal upper gastrointestinal haemorrhage. Lancet 345:108–111, 1995.

38. Lai KC, Hui WM, Wong B, et al: A retrospective and prospective study on the safety of discharging selected patients with duodenal ulcer bleeding on the same day as endoscopy. Gastrointest Endosc 45:26–30, 1997.

39. Lee JG, Turnipseed S, Romano PS, et al: Endoscopy based triage significantly reduces hospitalization rates and costs of treating upper GI bleeding: A randomized controlled trial. Gastrointest Endosc 50:755–761, 1999.

40. Cipolletta L, Bianco MA, Rotondano G, et al: Outpatient management of low-risk nonvariceal upper GI bleeding. Gastrointest Endosc 55:1–5, 2002.

41. Consensus Development Panel: Therapeutic endoscopy and bleeding ulcers. JAMA 262:1369–1372, 1989.

42. A.S.G.E Standards of Practice Committee: The role of endoscopy in the management of non-variceal acute upper gastrointestinal bleeding. Guidelines for clinical application. Gastrointest Endosc 38:760–764, 1992.

43. Barkun AN, Chiba N, Enns R, et al: Use of national endoscopic database to determine the adoption of emerging pharmacological and endoscopic technologies in the everyday care of patients with upper GI bleeding: The RUGBE initiative [abstract]. Am J Gastroenterol 96:S261, 2001.

44. Vreeburg EM, Snel P, de Bruijne JW, et al: Acute upper gastrointestinal bleeding in the Amsterdam area: Incidence, diagnosis and clinical outcome. Am J Gastroenterol 92:236–243, 1997.

45. Stollman NH, Putcha RV, Neustater BR, et al: The ulcerated fundal pool in acute upper gastrointestinal bleeding: Implications and outcomes. Gastrointest Endosc 46:324–327, 1997.

46. Kalloo AN, Canto MI, Wadwa KS, et al: Clinical usefulness of 3% hydrogen peroxide in acute upper GI bleeding: A pilot study. Gastrointest Endosc 49:518–521, 1999.

47. Kodali VP, Petersen BT, Miller CA, Gostout CJ: A new jumbo-channel therapeutic gastroscope for acute upper gastrointestinal bleeding. Gastrointest Endosc 45:409–411, 1997.

48. Hintze RE, Binmoeller KF, Adler A, et al: Improved endoscopic management of severe gastrointestinal hemorrhage using a new wide-channel endoscope. Endoscopy 26:613–616, 1994.

49. Coffin B, Pocard M, Panis Y, et al: Erythromycin improves the quality of EGD in patients with acute upper GI bleeding: A randomized controlled study. Gastrointest Endosc 56:174–179, 2002.

50. Frossard JL, Spahr L, Queneau PE, et al: Erythromycin intravenous bolus infusion in acute upper gastrointestinal bleeding: A randomized, controlled, double-blind trial. Gastroenterology 123:17–23, 2002.

51. Skok P: The epidemiology of hemorrhage from the upper gastrointestinal tract in the mid-nineties—has anything changed? Hepatogastroenterology 45:2228–2233, 1998.

52. Czernichow P, Hochain P, Nousbaum JB, et al: Epidemiology and course of upper gastro-intestinal haemorrhage in four French geographical areas. Eur J Gastroenterol Hepatol 12:175–181, 2000.

53. Marshall BJ, McGechie DB, Rogers PA, et al: Pyloric Campylobacter infection and gastroduodenal disease. Med J Aust 142:439–444, 1985.

54. Ciociola AA, Mcsorely DJ, Turner K, et al: Helicobacter pylori rates in duodenal ulcer patients in the United States may be lower than previously estimated. Am J Gastroenterol 94:1834–1840, 1999.

55. Meucci G, Di Battista R, Abbiati C, et al: Prevalence and risk factors of Helicobacter pylori negative peptic ulcer. J Clin Gastroenterol 31:42–47, 2000.

56. Cook DJ, Salena B, Guyatt GH, Laine L: Endoscopic therapy for acute non-variceal upper gastrointestinal hemorrhage—a meta-analysis. Gastroenterology 102:130–148, 1992.

57. Sacks HS, Chalmers TC, Blum AL, et al: Endoscopic hemostasis: An effective therapy for bleeding peptic ulcers. JAMA 264:494–499, 1990.

58. Consensus statement on therapeutic endoscopy and bleeding ulcers. Consensus development panel. Gastrointest Endosc 36:S62–65, 1990.

59. British Society of Gastrointestinal Endoscopy Committee: Non-variceal upper gastrointestinal haemorrhage: Guidelines. Gut 51(Suppl IV):iv1–iv6, 2002.

60. Bardou M, Youssef M, Toubouti Y, et al: Newer endoscopic therapies decrease both re-bleeding and mortality in high risk patients with acute peptic ulcer bleeding: A series of meta-analyses [abstract]. Gastroenterology 123:A239, 2003.

61. Bardou M, Toubouti Y, Benhaberou-Brun D, et al: High dose proton pump inhibition decrease both re-bleeding and mortality in high risk patients with acute peptic ulcer bleeding. A series of meta-analyses [abstract]. Gastroenterology 123:A239, 2003.

62. Bleau BL, Gostout CJ, Sherman KE, et al: Recurrent bleeding from peptic ulcer associated with adherent clot: A randomized study comparing endoscopic treatment with medical therapy. Gastrointest Endosc 56:1–6, 2002.

63. Jensen DM, Kovacs TO, Jutabha R, et al: Randomized trial of medial or endoscopic therapy to prevent recurrent ulcer hemorrhage in patients with adherent clots. Gastroenterology 123:407–413, 2002.

64. Naveau S, Borotto E, Giruad J: Meta-analysis of endoscopic injection therapy versus thermal methods in peptic ulcer haemorrhage [abstract]. Gastroenterology 110:A207, 1996.

65. Chung SC, Leung JW, Steele RJ, et al: Endoscopic injection of adrenaline for actively bleeding ulcers: A randomized trial. BMJ 296:1631–1633, 1988.

66. Randall GA, Jensen DM, Hirabayashi K, et al: Controlled study of different sclerosing agents for coagulation of canine gut arteries. Gastroenterology 96:1271–1281, 1989.

67. O'Brien JR: Some effects of adrenaline and anti-adrenaline compounds on platelets in vitro and in vivo. Nature 200:763–764, 1963.

68. Lai KH, Peng SN, Guo WS, et al: Endoscopic injection for the treatment of bleeding ulcers: Local tamponade or drug effect? Endoscopy 26:338–241, 1994.

69. Laine L, Estrada R: Randomized trial of normal saline solution injection versus bipolar electrocoagulation for treatment of patients with high-risk bleeding ulcers: Is local tamponade enough? Gastrointest Endosc 55:6–10, 2002.

70. Lin HG, Hsieh YH, Tseng GY, et al: A prospective, randomized trial of large- versus small-volume endoscopic injection of epinephrine for peptic ulcer bleeding. Gastrointest Endosc 55:615–619, 2002.

71. Johnson JH, Jensen DM, Auth D: experimental comparison of endoscopic yttrium-aluminum-garnet laser, electrosurgery, and heater probe for canine arterial coagulation: Importance of compression and avoidance of erosion. Gastroenterology 92:1101–1108, 1987.

72. Jensen D, Hirabayashi, and CURE Hemostasis Research Group: A study of coagulation depths with BICAP and heater probe to improve endoscopic hemostasis of bleeding peptic ulcers [abstract]. Gastrointest Endosc 35:181, 1989.

73. Morris DL, Brearley, S, Thompson H, et al: A comparison of the efficacy and depth of gastric wall injury with 3.2 and 2.3 mm bipolar probes in canine arterial hemorrhage. Gastrointest Endosc 31:361–363, 1985.

74. Laine L: Determination of optimal technique for bipolar electrocoagulation treatment: An experimental evaluation of the BICAP and Gold probes. Gastroenterology 100:107–112, 1991.

75. Jensen DM, Kovacs TOG, Freeman M, et al: A multicenter randomized prospective study of Gold probe for hemostasis of very severe ulcer or Mallory-Weiss bleeding [abstract]. Gastroenterology 100(Suppl A):92, 1991.

76. Jensen DM: Heat probe for hemostasis of bleeding peptic ulcers: Techniques and results of randomized controlled trials. Gastrointest Endosc 36:S42–49, 1990.

77. Cipolletta L, Bianco MA, Marmo R, et al: Endoclips versus heater probe in preventing early recurrent bleeding from peptic ulcer: A prospective and randomized trial. Gastrointest Endosc 53:147–151, 2001.

78. Chou Y, Hsu P, Lai K, Lo C, et al: A prospective, randomized trial off endoscopic hemoclip placement and distilled water injection for treatment of high-risk bleeding ulcers. Gastrointest Endosc 57:324–328, 2003.

79. Lin HJ, Hsieh YH, Tseng GY, et al: A prospective, randomized trial of endoscopic hemoclip versus heater probe thermocoagulation for peptic ulcer bleeding. Am J Gastroenterol 97:2250–2254, 2002.

80. Villanueva C, Balanzo J, Sabat M, et al: Injection therapy alone or with combination with endoscopic hemoclip for bleeding peptic ulcer. Preliminary results of a randomized trial [abstract]. Gastrointest Endosc 43:281, 1996.

81. Chung IK, Ham JS, Kim HS, et al: Comparison of hemostatic efficacy of the endoscopic hemoclip method with hypertonic saline-epinephrine injection and a combination of the two for the management of bleeding peptic ulcers. Gastrointest Endosc 49:13–18, 1999.

82. Gevers AM, De Geode E, Simeons M, et al: A randomized trial comparing injection therapy with hemoclip and with injection combined with hemoclip for bleeding ulcers. Gastrointest Endosc 55:466–469, 2002.

83. Buffoli F, Graffeo M, Nicosia F, et al: Peptic ulcer bleeding: Comparison of two hemostatic procedures. Am J Gastroenterol 96:89–94, 2001.

84. Tekant Y, Goh P, Alexander DJ, et al: Combination therapy using adrenaline and heater probe to reduce rebleeding in patients with peptic ulcer haemorrhage: A prospective randomized trial. Br J Surg 82:223–226, 1995.

85. Chung SC, Lau JY, Sung JJ: Randomized comparison between adrenaline injection alone and adrenaline injection plus heat probe treatment for actively bleeding peptic ulcers. BMJ 314:1307–1311, 1997.

86. Lin HJ, Tseng GY, Perng CL, et al: Comparison of adrenaline injection and bipolar electrocoagulation for the arrest of peptic ulcer bleeding. Gut 44:715–719, 1999.

87. Choudari CP, Palmer KR: Endoscopic injection therapy for bleeding peptic ulcer: A comparison of adrenaline alone with adrenaline plus ethanolamine oleate. Gut 35:608–610, 1994.

88. Lee KJ, Kim JH, Hahm KB, et al: Randomized trial of N-butyl-2-cyanoacrylate compared with injection of hypertonic saline-epinephrine in the endoscopic treatment of bleeding peptic ulcers. Endoscopy 32:505–511, 2000.

89. Villanueva C, Balanzo J, Espinos JC, et al: Endoscopic injection therapy for bleeding ulcer: A prospective and randomized comparison of adrenaline alone or with polidocanol. J Clin Gastroenterol 17:195–200, 1993.

90. Chung SC, Leung JW, Leong HT, et al: Adding a sclerosant to endoscopic epinephrine injection in actively bleeding ulcers: A randomized trial. Gastrointest Endosc 39:611–615, 1993.

91. Kubba AK, Murphy W, Palmer KR: Endoscopic injection of bleeding peptic ulcer: A comparison of adrenaline alone with adrenaline plus human thrombin. Gastroenterology 111:623–628, 1996.

92. Lin H, Hsieh Y, Tseng G, et al: Endoscopic injection with fibrin sealant versus epinephrine for arrest of peptic ulcer bleeding: A randomized, comparative trial. J Clin Gastroenterol 35:218–221, 2002.

93. Pescatore P, Jornod P, Borovicka J, et al: Epinephrine versus epinephrine plus fibrin glue injection in peptic ulcer bleeding: A prospective randomized trial. Gastrointest Endosc 55:348–353, 2002.

94. Rutgeerts P, Rauws E, Wara P, et al: Randomized trial of single and repeated fibrin glue compared with injection of polidocanol in treatment of bleeding peptic ulcer. Lancet 350:692–696, 1997.

95. Balanzo J, Villanueva C, Sainz S, et al: Injection therapy for bleeding peptic ulcer. A prospective, randomized trial using epinephrine and thrombin. Endoscopy 22:157–159, 1990.

96. Church NI, Dallal HJ, Masson J, et al: A randomized trial comparing heater probe plus thrombin with heater probe plus placebo for bleeding peptic ulcer. Gastroenterology 125:396–403, 2003.

97. Cipolletta L, Bianco MA, Rotondano G, et al: Prospective comparison of argon plasma coagulator and heater probe in the endoscopic treatment of major peptic ulcer bleeding. Gastrointest Endosc 48:191–195, 1998.

98. Chau CH, Sui WT, Law BK, et al: Randomized controlled trial comparing epinephrine injection plus heater probe coagulation versus epinephrine injection plus argon plasma coagulation for bleeding peptic ulcers. Gastrointest Endosc 57:455–461, 2003.

99. Collins R, Langman M: Treatment with histamine H2 antagonists in acute upper gastrointestinal hemorrhage. Implications of randomized trials. N Engl J Med 313:660–666, 1985.

100. Khuroo MS, Yattoo GN, Javid G, et al: A comparison of omeprazole and placebo for bleeding peptic ulcer. N Engl J Med 336:1054–1058, 1997.

101. Peterson WL, Cook DJ: Antisecretory therapy for bleeding peptic ulcer. JAMA 280:877–878, 1998.

102. Saltzman JR, Zawacki JK: Therapy for bleeding peptic ulcers. N Engl J Med 336:1091–1093, 1997.

103. Brunner G, Chang J: Intravenous therapy with high doses of ranitidine and omeprazole in critically ill patients with bleeding peptic ulcerations of the upper gastrointestinal tract: An open, randomized controlled trial. Digestion 45:217–225, 1990.

104. Gisbert JP, Gonzalez L, Calvet X, et al: Proton pump inhibitors versus H2-antagonists: A metanalysis of their efficacy in treating bleeding peptic ulcer. Aliment Pharmacol Ther 15:917–926, 2001.

105. Lau JY, Sung JJ, Lee KK, et al: Effect of intravenous omeprazole on recurrent bleeding after endoscopic treatment of bleeding peptic ulcers. N Engl J Med 343:310–316, 2000.

106. Lanas A, Artal A, Blas JM, et al: Effect of parenteral omeprazole and ranitidine on gastric pH and the outcome of bleeding peptic ulcer. J Clin Gastroenterol 21:103–106, 1995.

107. Sung JJ, Chan FK, Lau JY, et al: The effect of endoscopic therapy in patients receiving omeprazole for bleeding ulcers with nonbleeding visible vessels or adherent clots. A randomized comparison. Ann Intern Med 139:237–243, 2003.

108. Hasselgren G, Lind T, Lundell L, et al: Continuous intravenous infusion of omeprazole in elderly patients with peptic ulcer bleeding. Results of a placebo-controlled multicenter study. Scand J Gastroenterol 32:328–333, 1997.

109. Schaffalitzky de Muckadell OB, Havelund T, Harling H, et al: Effect of omeprazole on the outcome of endoscopically treated bleeding peptic ulcers. Randomized double-blind placebo-controlled multicentre study. Scand J Gastroenterol 32:320–327, 1997.

110. Lin HJ, Lo WC, Lee FY, et al: A prospective randomized comparative trial showing that omeprazole prevents rebleeding in patients with bleeding peptic ulcers after successful endoscopic therapy. Arch Intern Med 158:54–58, 1998.

111. Messman H, Schaller P, Andus T, et al: Effect of programmed endoscopic follow-up examinations on the rebleeding rates of gastric and duodenal peptic ulcers treated by injection therapy: A prospective randomized controlled trial. Endoscopy 30:583–589, 1998.

112. Villanueva C, Balanzo J, Torras X, et al: Value of second-look endoscopy after injection therapy for bleeding peptic ulcer: A prospective and randomized trial. Gastrointest Endosc 40:34–39, 1994.

113. Saeed ZA, Cole RA, Ramirez FC, et al: Endoscopic retreatment after successful initial hemostasis prevents ulcer rebleeding: A prospective randomized trial. Endoscopy 28:288–294, 1996.

114. Marmo R, Rotondano G, Bianco MA, et al: Outcome for endoscopic treatment for peptic ulcer bleeding: Is second look necessary? A meta-analysis. Gastrointest Endosc 62–67, 2003.

115. Spiegel B, Ofman JJ, Woods K, Vakil N: Minimizing recurrent peptic ulcer hemorrhage after endoscopic hemostasis: The cost-effectiveness of competing strategies. Am J Gastroenterol 98:86–97, 2003.

116. Lau JY, Sung JJ, Lam YH, et al: Endoscopic retreatment compared with surgery in patients with recurrent bleeding after initial endoscopic control of bleeding ulcers. N Engl J Med 340:751–756, 1999.

117. Wong SK, Yu LM, Lau JY, et al: Prediction of therapeutic failure after adrenaline injection plus heater probe treatment in patients with bleeding peptic ulcer. Gut 50:322–325, 2002.

118. Chung IK, Kim EG, Lee MS, et al: Endoscopic factors predisposing to rebleeding following endoscopic hemostasis in bleeding peptic ulcers. Endoscopy 33:969–975, 2001.

119. Defreyne L, Vanlangenhove P, De Vos M, et al: Embolization as a first approach with endoscopically unmanageable acute nonvariceal gastrointestinal hemorrhage. Radiology 218:739–748, 2001.

120. Lang EK: Transcatheter embolization in management of hemorrhage from duodenal ulcer: Long-term results and complications. Radiology 182:703–707, 1992.

121. Aina R, Olivia VL, Therasse E, et al: Arterial embolotherapy for upper gastrointestinal hemorrhage: Outcome assessment. J Vasc Interv Radiol 12:195–200, 2001.

122. Graham DY, Hepps KS, Ramirez FC, et al: Treatment of Helicobacter pylori reduces the rate of rebleeding in peptic ulcer disease. Scand J Gastroenterol 28:939–942, 1993.

123. Labenz J, Borsch G: Role of Helicobacter pylori eradication in the prevention of peptic ulcer bleeding relapse. Digestion 41:1–4, 1994.

124. Rokkas T, Karameris A, Mavrogeorgis A, et al: Eradication of Helicobacter pylori reduces the possibility of rebleeding in peptic ulcer disease. Gastrointest Endosc 41:1–4, 1995.

125. Jaspersen D, Koerner T, Schorr W, et al: Helicobacter pylori eradication reduces the rate of rebleeding in ulcer hemorrhage. Gastrointest Endosc 41:5–9, 1995.

126. Grino P, Pascual S, Such J, et al: Comparison of diagnostic methods for Helicobacter pylori infection in patients with upper gastro-intestinal bleeding. Scand J Gastroenterol 36:1254–1258, 2001.

127. Lee JM, Breslin NP, Fallon C, O'Morain CA: Rapid urease tests lack sensitivity in Helicobacter pylori diagnosis when peptic ulcer disease presents with bleeding. Am J Gastroenterol 95:1166–1170, 2000.

128. Colin R, Czernichow P, Baty V, et al: Low sensitivity of invasive tests for detection of Helicobacter pylori infection in patients with bleeding ulcer. Gastroenterol Clin Biol 24:31–3, 2000.

129. Houghton J, Ramamoorthy R, Pandya H, et al: Human plasma is directly bactericidal against Helicobacter pylori in vitro, potentially explaining the decreased detection of Helicobacter pylori during acute upper GI bleeding. Gastrointest Endosc 55:11–16, 2002.

130. Graham DY, White RH, Moreland LW, et al: Duodenal and gastric ulcer prevention with misoprostol in arthritis patients taking NSAIDs. Misoprostol study group. Ann Intern Med 119:257–262, 1993.

131. Hawkey CJ, Karrasch JA, Szczpanski L, et al: Omeprazole compared with misoprostol for ulcers associated with nonsteroidal anti-inflammatory drugs. Omeprazole versus Misoprostol for NSAID-induced Ulcer Management (OMNIUM) Study Group. N Engl J Med 338:727–734, 1998.

132. Miko TL, Thomazy VA: The caliber persistent artery of the stomach: A unifying approach to gastric aneurysm, Dieulafoy's lesion, and submucosal arterial malformation. Hum Pathol 19:914–921, 1988.

133. Goldman R: Submucosal arterial malformation (aneurysm) of the stomach with fatal hemorrhage. Gastroenterology 46:589–594, 1964.

134. Norton ID, Peterson BT, Sorbi D, et al: Management and long-term prognosis of Dieulafoy lesion. Gastrointest Endosc 50:762–767, 1999.

135. Schmulewitz N, Baillie J: Dieulafoy lesions: A review of six years of experience at a tertiary referral center. Am J Gastroenterol 96:1688–1694, 2001.

136. Baettig B, Haecki W, Lammer F, Jost R: Dieulafoy's disease: Endoscopic treatment and follow up. Gut 34:1418–1421, 1993.

137. Reilly HF 3rd, al-Kawas FH: Dieulafoy's lesion. Diagnosis and management. Dig Dis Sci 36:1702–1707, 1991.

138. Veldhuyzen Van Zanten SJ, Bartelsman JF, Schipper ME, Tytgat GN. Recurrent massive haematemsis from Dieulafoy vascular malformations: A review of 101 cases. Gut 27:213–222, 1986.

139. Dy NM, Gostout CJ, Balm RK: Bleeding from endoscopically-identified Dieulafoy's lesion of the proximal small intestine and colon. Am J Gastroenterol 90:108–11, 1995.

140. Kasapidis P, Georgopoulos P, Delis V, et al: Endoscopic management and long-term follow-up of Dieulafoy's lesions in the upper GI tract. Gastrointest Endosc 55:527–531, 2002.

141. Lin HJ, Lee FY, Tsai YT, et al: Therapeutic endoscopy for Dieulafoy's disease. J Clin Gastroenterol 11:507–510, 1989.

142. Parra-Blanco A, Takahashi H, Mendez Jerez PV, et al: Endoscopic management of Dieulafoy lesions of the stomach: A case study of 26 patients. Endoscopy 29:834–839, 1997.

143. Stark M, Gostout CJ, Balm RK: Clinical features and endoscopic management of Dieulafoy's disease. Gastrointest Endosc 38:545–550, 1992.

144. Yamaguchi Y, Yamato T, Katsumi N, et al: Short-term and long-term benefits of endoscopic hemoclip application for Dieulafoy's lesion in the upper GI tract. Gastrointest Endosc 57:653–656, 2003.

145. Parra-Blanco A, Takahashi H, Mendez Jerez PV, et al: Endoscopic management of Dieulafoy lesions of the stomach: A case of 26 patients. Endoscopy 29:834–839, 1997.

146. Chung IK, Kim EJ, Lee MS, et al: Bleeding Dieulafoy's lesion and the choice of endoscopic method: Comparing the hemostatic efficacy of mechanical and injection methods. Gastrointest Endosc 52:721–724, 2000.

147. Matsui S, Kamisako T, Kudo M, Inou R: Endoscopic band ligation for control of nonvariceal upper GI Hemorrhage: Comparison with bipolar electrocoagulation. Gastrointest Endosc 55:214–218, 2002.

148. Mumtaz R, Shaukat M, Ramirez F: Outcomes of endoscopic treatment of gastroduodenal Dieulafoy's lesion with rubber band ligation and thermal/injection therapy. J Clin Gastroenterol 36:310–314, 2003.

149. Nikolaidis N, Zezos P, Giouleme O, et al: Endoscopic band ligation of Dieulafoy-like lesions in the upper gastrointestinal tract. Endoscopy 33:754–760, 2001.

150. Fockens P, Meenan J, Van Dullemen HM, et al: Dieulafoy's disease: Endosonographic detection and endosonography-guided treatment. Gastrointest Endosc 44:437–442, 1996.

151. Ribero A, Vazquez-Sequeiros E, Wiersema M: Doppler EUS-guided treatment of gastric Dieulafoy's lesion. Gastrointest Endosc 53:807–809, 2001.

Portal Hypertensive Bleeding

Shiv Kumar Sarin and Barjest Chander Sharma

Portal hypertension is defined as an increase in portal venous pressure greater than 5 mm Hg. It usually develops as a complication of cirrhosis (Table 14–1) and leads to development of variceal hemorrhage and ascites.

Varices are natural portosystemic collaterals or shunts, resulting from portal hypertension, and may occur at any site in the gut or even at ectopic sites. Collaterals occur where the portal venous system is in apposition to the systemic venous system, typically at the gastroesophageal (GE) junction; anorectum; and sometimes around the umbilicus, ovaries, and bare area of the liver.

Esophageal Varices

GRADING

Only about 50% of patients with cirrhosis develop varices, and in approximately 20% of patients, the varices are large.[1] The incidence of development and increase in the size of the varices is around 5% to 15% per year, depending on the Child's class[1] and the etiology.

Varices are easily diagnosed by upper gastrointestinal (GI) endoscopy and are categorized by their location into esophageal and gastric varices. Varices are most often seen in the distal esophagus and may extend beyond the Z line into the gastric cardia. The distal esophagus must be insufflated with air while assessing the variceal size. Esophageal varices can be graded using several classifications for documentation and research purposes.[2-5] According to Conn[2] the number of varices is graded as follows: 1+, a single varix; 2+, two or three varices; 3+, four to six varices; and 4+, more than six varices. The size of the varices is graded as follows: 1+, small varices only detectable on performing Valsalva maneuver; 2+, small varices (approximately 1 to 3 mm in diameter) visible without Valsalva maneuver; 3+, varices of moderate size (3 to 6 mm in diameter); and 4+, large varices (greater than 6 mm) (Fig. 14–1). Extent of esophageal involvement is graded as follows: 1+, terminal 3 cm; 2+, terminal 6 cm; 3+, terminal 9 cm; and 4+, involving more than the terminal 9 cm.

The Japanese Research Society for Portal Hypertension criteria[4] evaluate a number of endoscopic signs that include (1) *fundamental*

Table 14–1. Common Causes of Portal Hypertension		
Prehepatic	**Hepatic**	**Posthepatic**
Portal vein thrombosis	Presinusoidal • NCPF • IPH • Sarcoidosis • Schistosomiasis • Nodular regenerative hyperplasia • Myeloproliferative disorders	Inferior vena cava obstruction
Splenic vein thrombosis	Sinusoidal • Cirrhosis	Cardiac failure
Hepatoportal arteriovenous fistula	Postsinusoidal • Budd-Chiari syndrome • Veno-occlusive disease	Constrictive pericarditis
Splenomegaly		
IPH, idiopathic portal hypertension; NCPF, noncirrhotic portal fibrosis.		

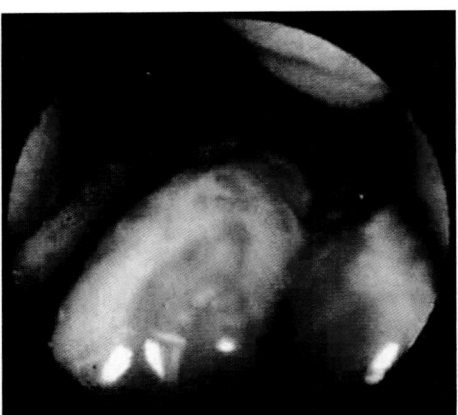

Figure 14–1. Endoscopic picture showing large esophageal varices with red color signs.

color of the varices: divided into white (Cw) and blue (Cb) color; (2) *red color signs*: dilated small vessels or microtelangiectasia on the variceal surface are subdivided into cherry red spot, red wale marking, and hematocystic spot. Depending on the number and the extent of distribution, each of these three red color signs are graded as absent (–), 1+, or 2+; (3) *form of varices*: small straight varices (F1), enlarged tortuous varices occupying less than one third of the esophageal lumen (F2), and largest sized coil-shaped varices occupying more than one third of the esophageal lumen (F3); (4) *location*: the longitudinal extent of the varices; located in the lower third of the esophagus, locus inferior (Li), varices extending up to the tracheal bifurcation, locus medialis (Lm), and varices that extended beyond the tracheal bifurcation, locus superior (Ls).

Although the commonest source of variceal bleeding is from the esophagus, in 10% to 30% of patients, bleeding could arise from other sites, especially after endoscopic obliteration of esophageal varices.

Certain types of varices are more likely to appear depending on the cause of portal hypertension. Gastric varices have been associated with portal or splenic vein thrombosis and hepatocellular carcinoma, and duodenal and biliary varices occur more with extrahepatic causes of portal hypertension.[6]

PATHOPHYSIOLOGY OF VARICEAL BLEEDING

The relationship between collateral blood flow and the transmural pressure gradient in varix is expressed as: $P1 - P2 = Q \times R$, where P1 and P2 is the pressure within and outside the varix, Q is the blood flow per unit of time, and R is the resistance to flow through the varix. Poiseulle's formula states that the resistance to flow may be expressed as follows: $R = 8 \, nl/\pi r^4$, where n is blood viscosity and l is length and r is radius of the vessel. The transmural pressure and radius of the varix along with the mural thickness of the varix (W) determines the wall tension of varix according to Laplace's law:

$$\text{Wall tension} = Q \times (8nl/\pi r^4) \times r/w$$

The propensity for a varix to bleed is directly linked to its wall tension. Theoretically, large long varices with a thin wall and high rates of flow are most prone to bleed. Decreasing collateral flow (by decreasing portal pressure or decreasing collateral resistance) or increasing wall thickness should decrease the risk of variceal rupture.

Because portal outflow resistance is relatively fixed, portal pressure is most commonly modulated by altering portal venous inflow.[1]

PREDICTORS OF FIRST VARICEAL BLEED

Graham and Smith[7] showed that after an initial variceal bleed, one third of patients died during initial hospitalization, another one third had a second bleed within 6 weeks, and only one third survived 1 year or more.

The severity of liver disease, large size of varices, and the presence of red color signs on endoscopy have been used by the North Italian Endoscopic Club (NIEC), as an index for the prediction of the first variceal bleeding. A patient with Child's C cirrhosis and large varices and red signs has a more than 76% risk of hemorrhage within 1 year, whereas a patient with Child's A cirrhosis and small varices and no red signs has a less than 10% likelihood of bleeding.[8] However, because only one third of patients that present with variceal hemorrhage have the previously mentioned risk factors, better definition of predictive factors is needed. We examined 12 clinical, endoscopic, and hemodynamic variables in 126 patients with portal hypertension, 72 bleeders and 54 nonbleeders. The variceal size and intravariceal pressure were the most important predictors of hemorrhage.[9] In another study, the risk of bleeding was 0%, 9%, 17%, 50%, and 72% when the variceal pressure was 13 or less mm Hg, greater than 13 but 14 or less mm Hg, greater than 14 but 15 or less mm Hg, greater than 15 but 16 or less mm Hg, and more than 16 mm Hg, respectively.[10]

Hepatic venous pressure gradient (HVPG) reflects in cirrhotics portal pressure and intravariceal pressure. Garcia-Tsao and coworkers[11] found that the HVPG was significantly higher in 49 patients who had bled from esophageal varices than in the 44 patients with cirrhosis who did not bleed (20.4 ± 5.1 vs. 16.0 ± 5.2). They also found that none of the patients who had bled had HVPG less than 12 mm Hg.

In one study, the portocaval pressure gradient (PPG) was found to decrease after transjugular intrahepatic portosystemic shunt (TIPS) procedure (from 19.7 ± 4.6 to 8.6 ± 2.7 mm Hg) and increased to more than 12 mm Hg (18.4 ± 7.46 mm Hg) in all patients who had rebleed.[12] Moitinho and coworkers[13] reported that patients admitted because of variceal bleeding who had an HVPG greater than 20 mm Hg measured within 48 hours had fivefold increased risk of (1) failure to control bleeding with the emergency treatment or (2) suffering early rebleeding. Dynamic measurements of HVPG are more valuable to assess the influence of therapeutic interventions or alcohol abstinence.[14]

Active bleeding at endoscopy was statistically shown to be an independent factor in predicting failure to control variceal bleeding.[15]

BACTERIAL INFECTION

Bacterial infections are common in variceal bleeding and occur in 35% to 66% of patients. Patients with bacterial infections and lack of antibiotic use have a higher risk of failure of control of bleeding and rebleeding.[16]

It is proposed that endotoxins released during bacterial infection result in an increase in portal pressure, through the introduction of endothelins (a potent substance for contraction of the stellate cells), vasoconstrictive cyclooxygenase products, and contraction of hepatic stellate cells. Furthermore, endotoxin-induced nitric oxide and prostacyclin induced by endothelin could inhibit platelet aggregation and reduced hemostasis at the level of the varix.

The hypothesis that antibiotic treatment in combination with oral nonselective β-blockers versus placebo may prevent variceal bleeding requires further evaluation.

NATURAL HISTORY OF ESOPHAGEAL VARICES

The prevalence and rate of growth of varices in cirrhotics is often related to the severity of liver disease. Child's class B or C cirrhotics should be screened at the time of diagnosis of cirrhosis, whereas patients with Child's A should be endoscoped only if there is evidence of portal hypertension. Patients who have no varices on screening endoscopy should be rescreened every two years if their liver function is stable or every 1 year if there are signs of hepatic decompensation. Because the development of large varices is greater in patients with small varices on initial endoscopy compared with patients with no varices, patients who have small varices on screening endoscopy should be rescreened every year.

It is unclear if any particular etiology of cirrhosis is associated with a higher risk of development or growth of varices.

About one third of patients with varices experience a variceal hemorrhage.[1] The 2-year bleeding risk in patients with cirrhosis and moderate to large varices is 25% to 30%. Lifelong risk of variceal bleeding is close to 50%.[17] In portal vein obstruction, the bleeding rate is even higher than in cirrhosis. The lifelong risk of bleeding is 80% with 50% of bleeds occurring before the age of 5 years.[17]

After varices start bleeding, the hemorrhage spontaneously stops in only 50% of cases. Those with Child's C cirrhosis and actively spurting varices are particularly prone to continue to bleed without active intervention. After cessation of active bleeding, the risk of rebleeding is higher for approximately 6 weeks. The risk of early rebleeding is greatest within the first 48 hours, and about half of all early rebleeding episodes occur during this time. The risk factors for early rebleeding include large varices, age older than 60 years, severity of initial bleed, renal failure, ascites, active bleeding on endoscopy, and red signs. Aggressive volume replacement may exacerbate the portal hypertension and precipitate early rebleeding.

The long-term course after an index bleed is punctuated by repeated episodes of variceal hemorrhage with its attendant risks of exsanguination, hepatic encephalopathy, and liver failure. The risk of recurrent bleeding is related to severity of liver failure, continued alcoholism, variceal size, renal failure, and presence of hepatoma. Approximately 70% of all untreated patients experience further bleeding or die within 1 year of their index bleeding.[7]

GASTRIC VARICES

Gastric varices are found in about one in five patients with portal hypertension. About 5% to 10% of patients with gastric varices may not have esophageal varices.

Gastric varices are more difficult to detect by endoscopy especially if they are small and isolated. Small varices in the fundus are often mistaken for a mucosal fold. Their identity as varices is based on their shape (grapelike clusters) and their bluish tinge. At endoscopic ultrasonography they could be seen as circular or linear anechoic channels within the gastric wall. The addition of color Doppler may confirm blood flow within varices and document obliteration of gastric varices after endoscopic treatment.

A simple classification of gastric varices depending on their anatomic location in the stomach can also help in understanding their natural history and approach to management.[18] Gastroesophageal varices (GOV) are located in esophagus and extend in continuity to lesser curve (GOV1) or greater curve (GOV2) of the stomach (Figs. 14–2, 14–3, and 14–4). Isolated gastric varices (IGV) are located usually on the fundus (IGV1) (Fig. 14–5), greater curve or other sites in the stomach or first part of duodenum (IGV2).

Gastric variceal bleeding has been reported to account for 3% to 30% of all acute variceal bleeding episodes. The risk of bleeding from gastric varices depends on their location. Although GOV1 constitute more than 70% of gastric varices, only 11% of GOV1 ever bleed. In contrast, although IGV1 constitute less than 8% of all gastric varices, 80% of IGV1 bleed.[19] IGV1 are often fed by spontaneous large collaterals that predispose to high incidence of hepatic encephalopathy. These spontaneous splenorenal collaterals partly decompress the portal vein and IGV1 are associated with lower portal pressures than esophageal varices. The IGV2 are rare (4.7% of all gastric varices); commonly seen in antrum (53%), duodenum (32%), or at both sites (11%); and rarely in body and fundus (4%). Overall, gastric varices bleed (Fig. 14–6) less often but more severely than esophageal varices.[20]

OTHER MANIFESTATIONS OF PORTAL HYPERTENSION

The common sequelae of portal hypertension include the development of varices in esophagus and stomach. Varices can also develop in other parts of the GI tract including the anorectal region, colon, and small intestine. Portal hypertensive gastropathy (PHG), colopathy, and enteropathy are other sequelae. Development of ascites, hepatopulmonary syndrome, portopulmonary syndrome, hepatorenal syndrome, hepatic encephalopathy, and cirrhotic cardiomyopathy are other manifestations of portal hypertension.

Management of Portal Hypertensive Bleeding

Major progress has taken place in the endoscopic, surgical, radiologic, and pharmacologic treatments for GI bleeding resulting from portal hypertension. Upper GI endoscopy, which should be carried out when the patient is in a stabilized hemodynamic condition, allows precise diagnosis and approach to specific treatment in 90% of cases.

Variceal hemorrhage is not the only cause of upper GI bleeding in patients with cirrhosis. The bleeding may be from gastric or duodenal varices, PHG, or peptic ulcer. Usually two clinically significant variceal bleeding episodes despite two adequate endoscopic treatments is defined as failure of endoscopic treatment at any time after index bleed.

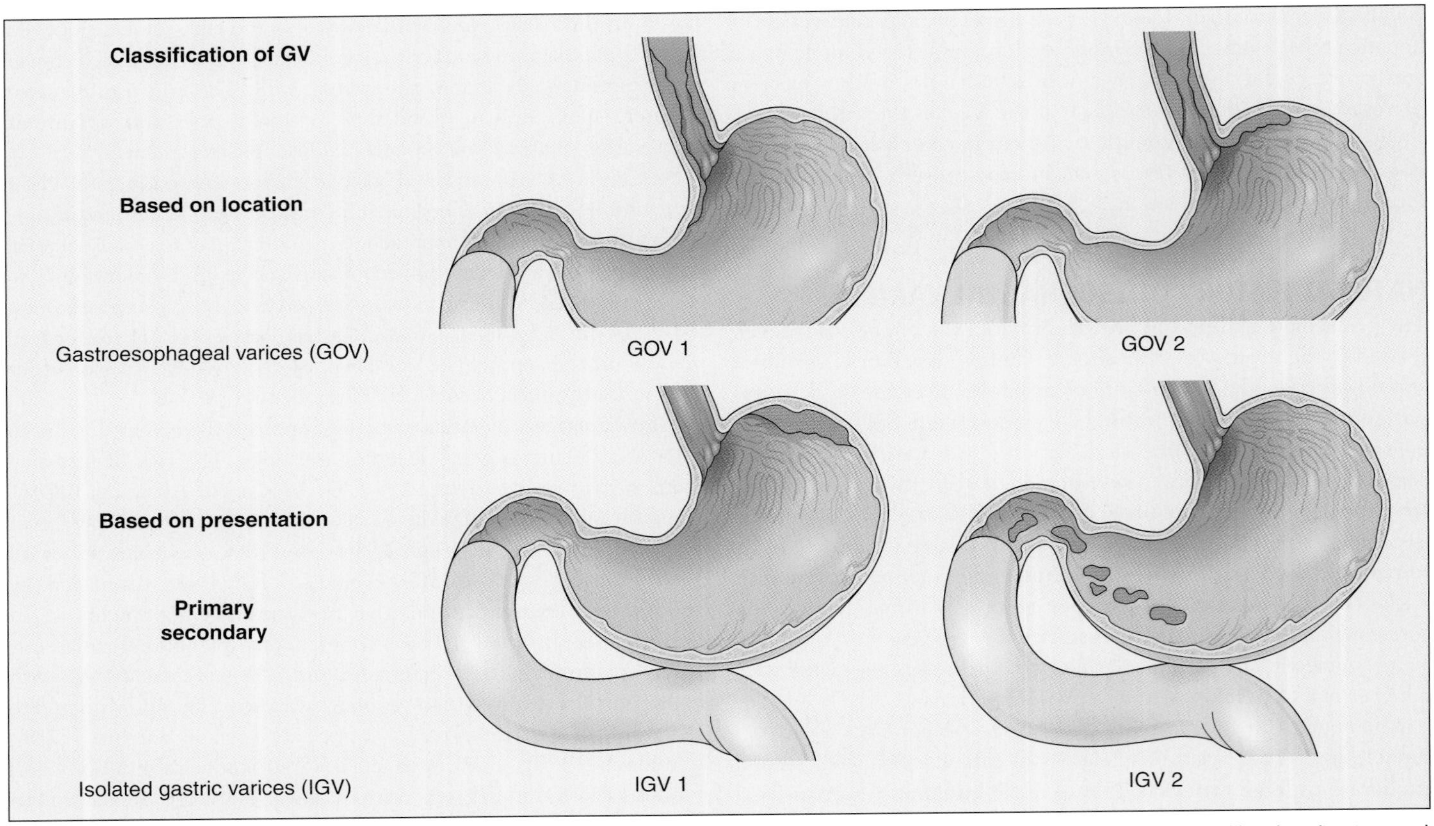

Classification of GV

Based on location

Gastroesophageal varices (GOV)

GOV 1

GOV 2

Based on presentation

Primary
secondary

Isolated gastric varices (IGV)

IGV 1

IGV 2

Figure 14–2. Sarin's classification of gastric varices based on the location. (Reproduced from Sarin SK, Kumar A: Gastric varices: Profile, classification, and management. Am J Gastroenterol 84:1244–1249, 1989, with permission from Blackwell Publishing Ltd.)

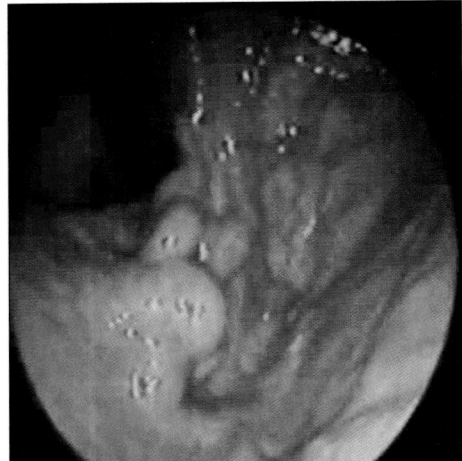

Figure 14–3. Endoscopic picture showing GOV1 type of gastric varices.

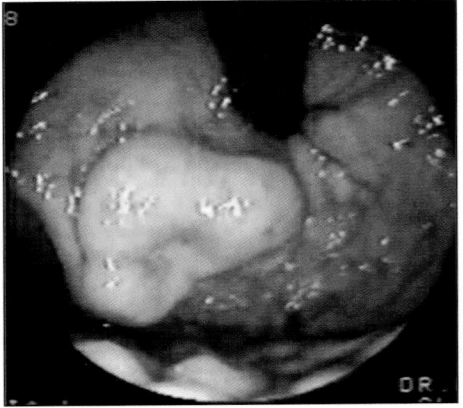

Figure 14–4. Endoscopic picture showing GOV2 type of gastric varices.

Although endoscopic therapy has no effect on the pathophysiologic mechanisms that lead to variceal bleeding, it is effective in the control of acute bleeding, prevention of rebleeding (secondary prophylaxis), and, to some extent, prevention of first episode of bleeding (primary prophylaxis) from esophageal varices.

MANAGEMENT OF ESOPHAGEAL VARICEAL BLEEDING

Active bleeding has been defined by the Baveno II Consensus Workshop as oozing or spurting at the time of endoscopy while clinically significant bleeding is defined as bleeding with a transfusion

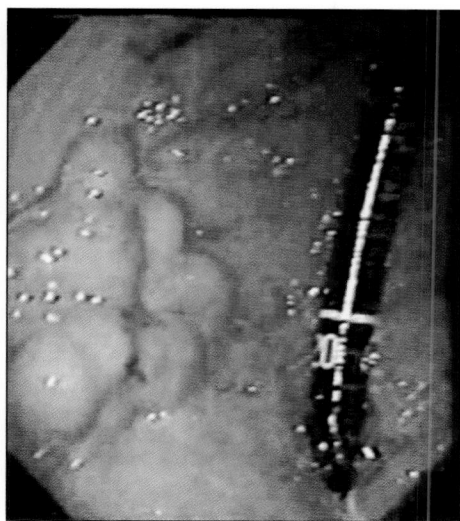

Figure 14–5. Endoscopic picture showing IGV1 type of gastric varices.

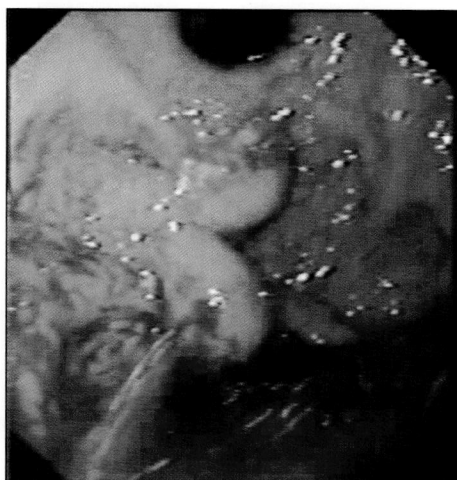

Figure 14–6. Endoscopic picture showing active bleeding from gastric varix.

requirement of 2 or more units of blood within 24 hours of time zero, together with a systolic blood pressure less than 100 mm Hg or a postural change of greater than 20 mm Hg and/or pulse rate greater than 100 beats/minute at time zero.[21]

Endoscopic Sclerotherapy for the Control of Acute Variceal Bleeding and Secondary Prophylaxis

Endoscopic sclerotherapy has been used for almost 60 years to treat bleeding esophageal varices and to eradicate varices. It consists of injection of a sclerosing agent into the lumen of varix (intravariceal) (Fig. 14–7) or immediately adjacent to the vessel to tamponade flow (paravariceal).[22]

The injected sclerosant achieves its immediate hemostatic effect by coagulation necrosis, and variceal thrombosis and subsequently the inflammation of the surrounding tissue and scarring leads to variceal obliteration. The most often used sclerosants are ethanolamine oleate, polidocanol, absolute alcohol, sodium tetradecyl sulfate, and sodium morrhuate with nearly comparable efficacy.[1,22–24] Absolute alcohol is a potent, aqueous, readily available low-cost agent and is comparable to 5% ethanolamine oleate and 3% sodium tetradecyl sulfate.[22,24] Endoscopic sclerotherapy is performed using free hand technique. Through the operating channel of the endoscope an injector with a retractile needle is passed, and the sclerosant is injected into the varix. During acute bleed, injections are directed at the bleeding site. If no stigmata of current or previous bleeding are found, all the varices are electively injected in a spiral form starting from a little above the GE junction and up to the lower 5 cm of the esophagus.

Normally, 1 to 3 mL of the sclerosant is injected at each site. An area of blanching of about 1 cm around the injection needle indicates adequate sclerosant injection. About 5 to 8 mL of sclerosant is generally sufficient during the first injection. Repeat sclerotherapy, which requires smaller quantities of the sclerosant, is performed at

1- to 3-week intervals until all varices are obliterated. An average of four to six sessions of sclerotherapy are needed. The variceal "kill time," that is, the time required for variceal obliteration, is shorter when EST sessions are performed once a week rather than once in 3 weeks. However, the survival is not improved, probably resulting from risk of bleeding from sclerotherapy ulcers.[25] In 5% to 20% of patients, bleeding recurs before obliteration of varices and in another 5% to 20% of patients, recurrent bleeding occurs after eradication of varices resulting from gastric varices or gastropathy. After obliteration, varices tend to recur over time in 50% to 70% of individuals.[1,26,27] Such varices are at risk of bleeding and surveillance endoscopy must be considered at periodic intervals.[1,26,27]

Endoscopic sclerotherapy can cause local or systemic complications (Table 14–2). Bacteremia is common during endoscopic sclerotherapy, and patients with active hemorrhage and those at risk for bacterial endocarditis or spontaneous bacterial peritonitis should receive antibiotics prophylactically. Superficial ulcers resulting from tissue necrosis are present in 90% of patients the day after endoscopic sclerotherapy and in 70% at 1 week.[28] Superficial ulcers are necessary accompaniments of sclerotherapy. Deep ulcers on the other hand often lead to rebleeding and stricture formation.

Serious complications are reported in 1% to 20% patients, with an overall mortality of 2% to 5%[29] (see Table 14–2). Minor complications such as pain, fever, and transient dysphagia are common.

Although esophageal dysmotility is frequent after intravariceal sclerotherapy, it does not lead to an increase in GE reflux.[30]

Efficacy of Endoscopic Sclerotherapy

Acute Bleed Endoscopic sclerotherapy can effectively arrest active esophageal variceal bleeding in about 95% of cases. It has been compared with balloon tamponade, vasopressin and its analogues, somatostatin, octreotide, and surgery and has been found to be equally or more effective.[1] Addition of tissue adhesive histoacryl (N-butyl-2-cyanoacrylate) to sclerotherapy has little benefit.

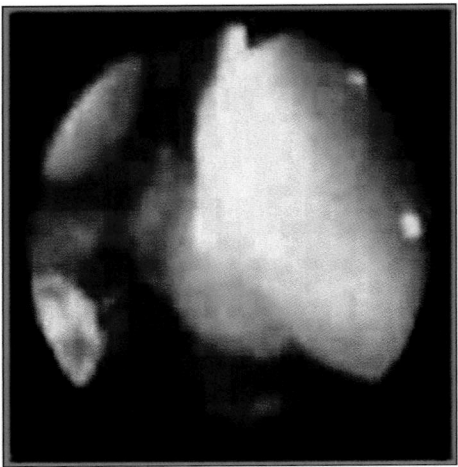
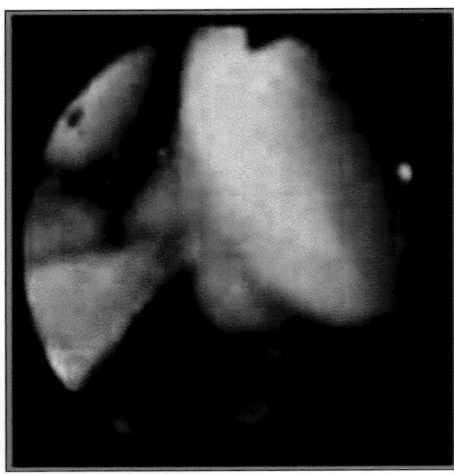
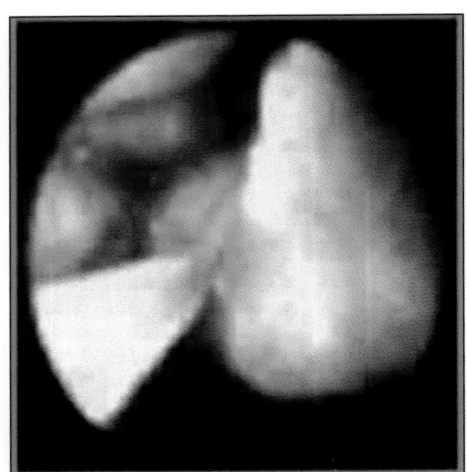

Figure 14–7. Endoscopic sclerotherapy of esophageal varices.

Table 14–2. Complications of Endoscopic Sclerotherapy

Esophageal	Local	Systemic
Ulcers	Mediastinitis	Sepsis
Bleeding	Pleural effusion	Hypoxia
Laceration		Aspiration pneumonia
Stricture		Spontaneous bacterial peritonitis
Dysmotility		Portal vein thrombosis
Perforation		

Data have been evaluated from many randomized clinical trials: sclerotherapy with concomitant drugs was found to be more effective in bleed control than either therapy given alone. However, there was no reduction in mortality.

Secondary Prophylaxis In eight trials involving more than 1100 patients, endoscopic sclerotherapy has been shown to decrease the risk of rebleeding (40% to 50% vs. 70%) and death (30% to 60% vs. 50% to 75%) compared with no treatment.[1] Complete obliteration of varices is more effective than incomplete eradication in preventing rebleeding and improving survival in patients with cirrhosis.[31,32] It has also been found to be helpful in cirrhotic patients with esophageal varices complicated by hepatocellular carcinoma. Sclerotherapy has been equally effective in patients with noncirrhotic portal hypertension.[33,34]

In twelve randomized controlled studies,[35,36] the combination of sclerotherapy and portal pressure reduction by β-blockers showed fewer bleeding recurrences compared with either treatment alone.

Endoscopic Sclerotherapy for Primary Prophylaxis

Primary prophylaxis of variceal bleeding or prevention of the first episode of variceal hemorrhage is the most logical approach to decrease the morbidity and mortality after a variceal bleed. Because only about 10% to 20% of patients bleed, it is important to carefully select patients who are at a high-risk of variceal hemorrhage. These include patients with large (>5 mm) varices, red-color signs, and moderate to severe liver disease.

The term *preprimary prophylaxis* is used to describe therapies to prevent the development of varices before they are apparent at endoscopy. *Early primary prophylaxis* is used to describe therapies that prevent increase in the size of small varices.

Endoscopic sclerotherapy has been compared with no treatment in 20 randomized trials that included 1756 patients, most of whom had medium- or large-sized varices. In the sclerotherapy group, there was a significant reduction in bleeding in 5 trials, increase in bleeding in 2 trials, and no difference in 13 trials.[37] Because of the significant heterogeneity in the results with regard to bleeding and mortality among the different trials,[38,39] prophylactic sclerotherapy is not recommended for primary prophylaxis.

Teran and colleagues[40] examined the cost effectiveness of variety of treatments in primary prophylaxis of variceal bleeding. They found that β-blockers were more cost effective than sclerotherapy or shunt surgery in patients with cirrhosis with a cost saving between $440 and $1460. The other treatments were not cost effective. Spiegel and coworkers[41] found empiric β-blocker therapy for the primary prophylaxis of variceal hemorrhage a cost-effective measure, because use of screening endoscopy to guide therapy adds significant cost with only marginal increase in effectiveness.

Endoscopic Variceal Ligation for Control of Acute Bleeding from Esophageal Varices and Secondary Prophylaxis

Endoscopic variceal ligation (EVL) is a technique in which a rubber band is placed with the help of an endoscope to strangulate a varix, resulting in its thrombosis and necrosis. The mucosa sloughs and a mural scar is formed. A banding device that consists of a cylinder preloaded with elastic rubber bands (Fig. 14–8) is attached to the tip of the endoscope, the varix is suctioned into the cylinder, and a trigger device allows the deployment of a band around the varix (Fig. 14–9). Single or multiple bands can be applied using different devices. Generally, five to eight bands are deployed circumferentially in one session.

Endoscopic band ligation is associated with fewer complications than endoscopic sclerotherapy. In contrast to chemical irritation from a sclerosant, the effect of band ligation is local and systemic complications are rare. Superficial mucosal ulcers are common, but stricture formation is rare.

Endoloops have been used as an alternative to rubber bands. They could be placed during the same endoscopy without taking the endoscope out (Figs. 14–10 and 14–11). Although they may exert more effective compressive force on tissue than bands, they may cause tear, if tightened excessively. Endoloops also need repeated loading.

Efficacy of Endoscopic Variceal Ligation

Acute Bleed The efficacy of EVL for the control of acute bleeding has been debated as technically, it may be difficult to visualize and band a bleeding varix. This could be overcome by placing four bands, one in each quadrant, just above the GE junction and

a second set 3 to 4 cm proximal. Steigmann and coworkers[42] randomized patients who bled from esophageal varices to sclerotherapy or ligation. The control of active bleeding was comparable, 77% in the sclerotherapy and 86% in the ligation group. Mortality was higher in the sclerotherapy (45%) compared with the ligation group (28%).

Avgerinos and colleagues[43] randomized 71 patients with cirrhosis having active variceal bleeding to ligation or sclerotherapy. The bleeding was controlled in 97% and 76% of patients in the ligation and sclerotherapy groups, respectively.

Secondary Prophylaxis EVL has been compared in 18 studies ($n = 1509$) to sclerotherapy for the prevention of recurrent bleeding. Meta-analyses have shown that the number of sessions, the time for obliteration, and the rebleeding rates are significantly lower with variceal ligation compared with sclerotherapy. However, variceal recurrence rates were higher with EVL (Table 14–3). A higher variceal recurrence with EVL is probably because ligation does not occlude the perforators as is done by injecting a sclerosant.

Many investigators have evaluated combining EVL with sclerotherapy during the same session (synchronous combination) for obliteration of esophageal varices. Laine and coworkers[44] and Saeed and colleagues[45] found that ligation alone was as effective with fewer complications (Table 14–4). On the other hand, to reduce high rate of variceal recurrence after band ligation, the concept of complementing ligation with sclerotherapy in metachronous fashion has found support.[46]

Other approaches to improve the rate of long-term eradication of esophageal varices after EVL by promoting fibrosis of the esophageal

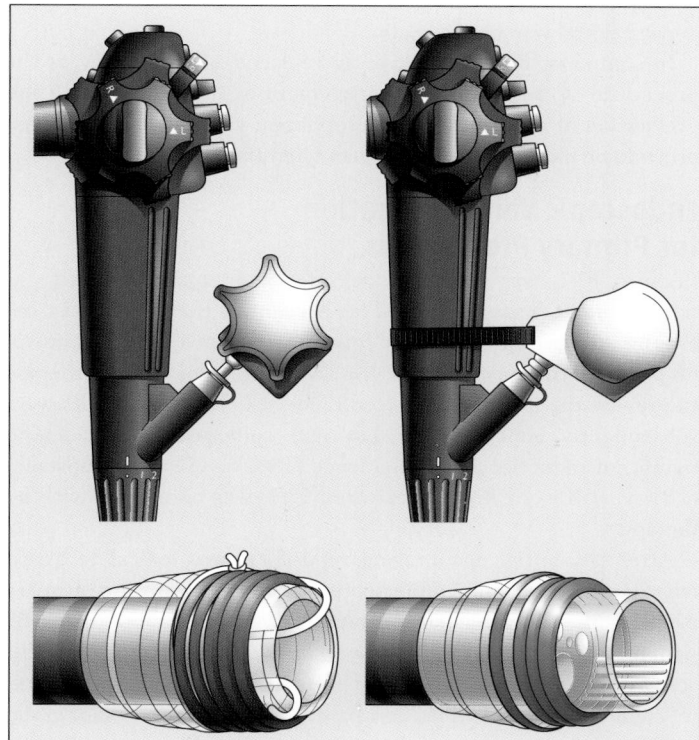

Figure 14–8. Band ligation set mounted on endoscope for band ligation of varices.

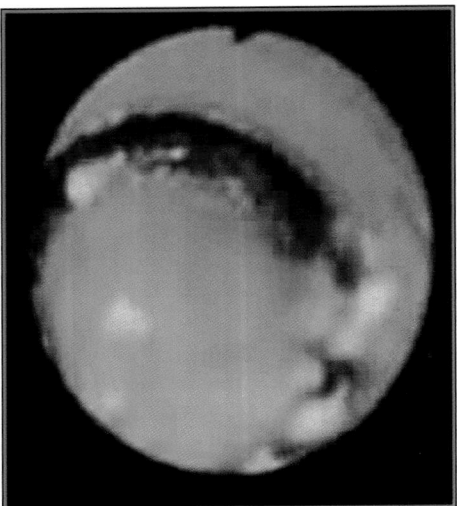

Figure 14-9. Endoscopic picture showing esophageal varix ligated with band.

wall, such as argon plasma coagulation,[47,48] low power diode laser treatment[47,49] and microwave,[50,51] are still experimental.

Our group observed a faster variceal eradication with ligation requiring fewer sessions but with a higher recurrence rate compared with sclerotherapy group over a follow-up period of 8.5 ± 4.4 months.[52] The incidence of PHG was higher after sclerotherapy than after band ligation (20.5% vs. 2.3%). The infrequent occurrence of PHG after band ligation may be due to the fact that band ligation does not occlude the esophageal perforators that allow blood to be drained away to paraesophageal collaterals resulting in lesser congestion of gastric microcirculation but higher rate of recurrence of esophageal varices. EVL has also been found effective in extra-hepatic portal venous obstruction.[53]

In summary, EVL has currently replaced sclerotherapy as the procedure of choice for the management of variceal bleeding and prevention of rebleeding from esophageal varices. This may even prove to be more cost effective than sclerotherapy.

Endoscopic Variceal Ligation for Primary Prophylaxis

Because EVL was found to be safer and equally effective as sclerotherapy, it was evaluated for preventing the first bleed from esophageal varices. Sarin and coworkers[54] showed, in a series of 68 patients, the superiority of the EVL compared with no therapy to prevent the first variceal bleed (Table 14–5). Their results were subsequently confirmed by Lay and colleagues,[55] who found significant reduction in the incidence (19% vs. 60%) and mortality (28% vs. 58%) of first bleed when EVL was compared with no therapy.

After the initial encouraging reports, it was logical to assess whether EVL is comparable to the current therapy for primary prophylaxis: the β-blocker therapy. Our group[56] randomized 89 patients with high-risk varices to receive EVL or propranolol. The actuarial probability of bleeding at 18 months was significantly lower in the EVL group (15.8%) compared with the propranolol group (43%). However, there was no survival benefit with EVL. Lui and colleagues[57] assigned 172 patients to endoscopic band ligation (n = 44), propranolol (n = 66), or isosorbide mononitrate (n = 62)

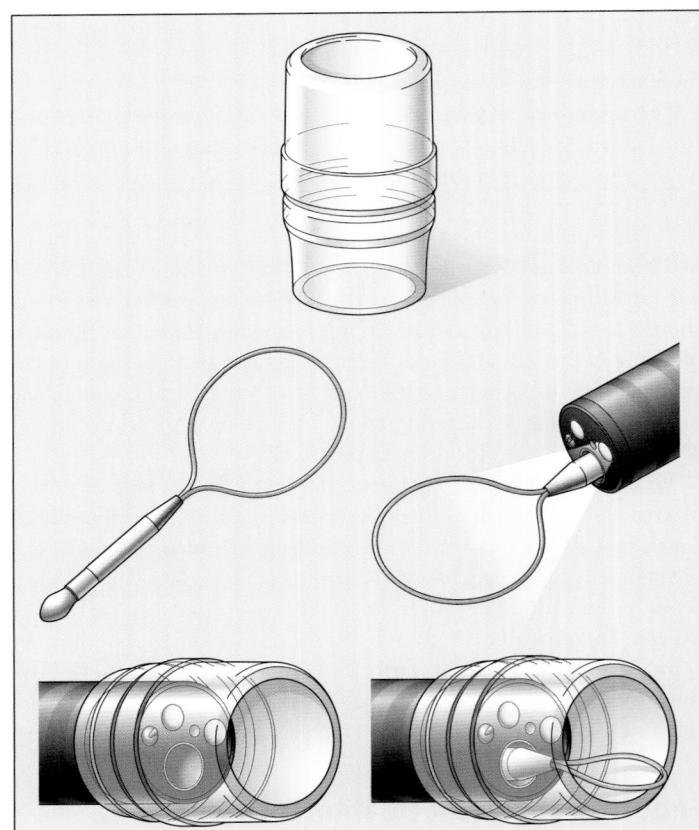

Figure 14-10. Endoloop parts and the Endoloop set mounted on endoscope.

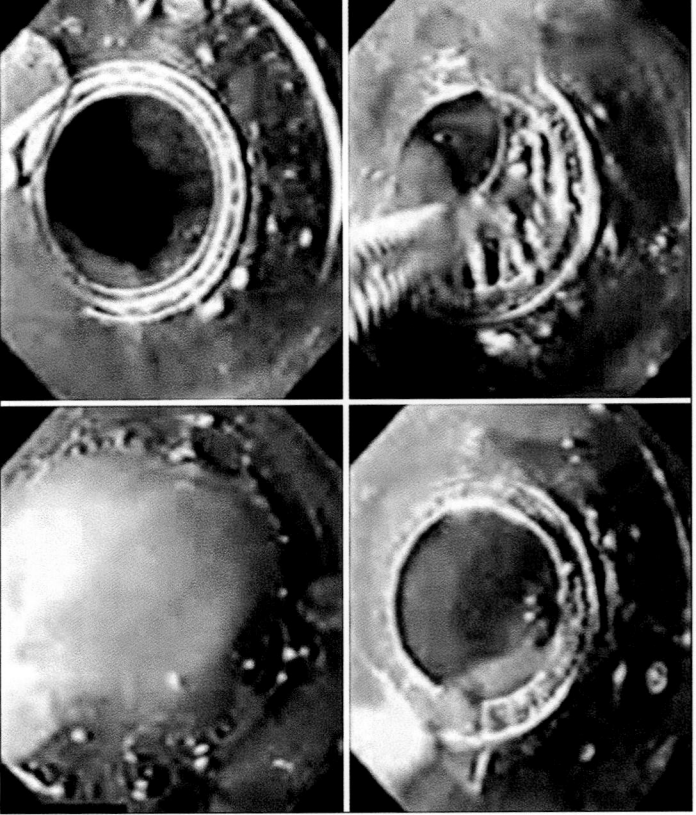

Figure 14-11. Endoscopic picture of ligation of esophageal varices with Endoloop.

Table 14–3. Results of Endoscopic Sclerotherapy Versus Endoscopic Variceal Ligation for Prevention of Rebleeding from Esophageal Varices

Reference	Therapy	N	Eradication (%)	Rebleeding (%)	Variceal Recurrence (%)	Follow-up
Hou, et al. (1995)[110]	EST	67	79	42	30	9.7 ± 6.4 mo
	EVL	67	86	19	48	10.5 ± 6.3 mo
Baroncini, et al. (1997)[111]	EST	54	92.5	19	13	53.4 ± 42 days
	EVL	57	93	16	30	496 ± 40 days
Sarin, et al. (1997)[52]	EST	48	93.8	21	7	8.3 ± 4.2 mo
	EVL	47	93.6	6	29	8.6 ± 4.6 mo
de la Pena, et al. (1999)[26]	EST	46	71	50	28	16 mo
	EVL	42	79	31	45	18 mo

EST, endoscopic sclerotherapy; EVL, endoscopic variceal ligation.

Table 14–4. Results of Endoscopic Variceal Ligation Versus Combined Endoscopic Variceal Ligation and Sclerotherapy for Esophageal Varices

References	Therapy	N	Eradication (%)	Rebleeding (%)	Variceal Recurrence (%)	Mortality (%)
Laine, et al. (1996)[44]	EVL	20	60	30	—	15
	EVL + EST	21	71	29	—	14
Saeed, et al. (1997)[45]	EVL	25	64	25	16	16
	EVL + EST	22	54.5	36	23	32
Lo, et al. (1998)[46]	EVL	35	—	31	43	29
	EVL + EST	37	—	8	14	19
Al Traif, et al. (1999)[115]	EVL	31	81	23	6	23
	EVL + EST	29	86	17	21	10
Djurdjevic, et al. (1999)[116]	EVL	51	92	10	26	12
	EVL + EST	52	88	14	24	14
Umehara, et al. (1999)[117]	EVL	26	80.8	—	72	15
	EVL + EST	25	84.0	—	22	12

EST, endoscopic sclerotherapy; EVL, endoscopic variceal ligation.

Table 14–5. Endoscopic Variceal Ligation Versus No Treatment for Prevention of First Bleeding from Esophageal Varices

Reference	Therapy	N	Eradication (%)	Variceal Bleeding (%)	Recurrence (%)	Mortality (%)
Sarin, et al. (1996)[54]	Control	33	—	39.4	—	24.2
	EVL	35	96	8.6	29	11.4
Lay, et al. (1997)[55]	Control	64	—	60	—	58
	EVL	62	60	19	42	28
Lo, et al. (1999)[112]	Control	63	—	21.8	—	36.5
	EVL	64	86	34.9	22	25
Omar, et al. (2000)[113]	Control	38	—	10.5	—	—
	EVL	36	—	2.8	—	—

EVL, endoscopic variceal ligation.

therapy (Table 14–6). On intention-to-treat analysis, variceal bleeding was observed in 7% of patients randomized to EVL, 14% of those randomized to propranolol, and 23% of those randomized to isosorbide mononitrate groups; the difference between EVL and nitrates was significant. A significant number of patients reported side effects with drug treatments (45% propranolol and 42% isosorbide mononitrate vs. 2% band ligation), resulting in withdrawal from treatment in 30% of propranolol and 21% of isosorbide mononitrate patients. There was no significant difference in mortality rates in the three groups.

There are several distinct advantages of EVL over β-blockers:

1. There are no contraindications (unless endoscopy is contra-indicated).
2. There is a required, short duration of therapy of 3 to 4 weeks; hence, there is improved compliance.
3. There is no need to measure hemodynamic parameters to assess 25% reduction in HVPG after drug therapy. In EVL, the achievable endpoint, the variceal eradication is visible endoscopically.

Table 14–6. Endoscopic Variceal Ligation Versus Propranolol or Isosorbide Mononitrate for Prevention of First Bleeding from Esophageal Varices

Reference	Therapy	N	Variceal Bleeding	Mortality (%)
Sarin, et al. (1999)[56]	Propranolol	44	43	11
	EVL	45	15	11.1
Lui, et al. (1999)[57]	Propranolol	66	9	21
	ISMN	62	19	19
	EVL	44	6.8	25
Song, et al. (2000)[114]	Propranolol	30	20	16.7
	EVL	31	9.7	9.7

EVL, endoscopic variceal ligation; ISMN, isosorbide mononitrate.

4. There is no need for indefinite therapy. It has been shown that patients who are on long-term propranolol therapy do not fare well on stopping the drug. The rebleeding rate becomes the same with higher morality as before having started the drug.

Two separate meta-analyses[58,59] of EVL for primary prophylaxis of variceal bleeding have been reported. The first meta-analysis included 283 patients included in four trials comparing EVL with β-blocker therapy. It showed that EVL reduced the risk of first hemorrhage from 16% in β-blocker–treated patients to 8% in EVL-treated patients (a relative risk reduction of 52%). However, no differences in bleeding-related or overall mortality were detected. The second meta-analysis comprised 601 patients included in five trials comparing EVL versus untreated controls. EVL reduced the overall risk of first hemorrhage from 18% to 4% with a relative risk reduction in overall mortality of 45% compared with no therapy.

At present, patients with high-risk varices should have an HVPG measurement and be given a nonselective β-blocker. If after 4 to 6 weeks, the HVPG is reduced by 25% or more or the gradient is less than 12 mm Hg with therapy, the drug should be continued. Band ligation should be reserved for patients who are nonresponders or have contraindications or intolerance to β-blockers.

Adjuvant and Alternate Treatments to Endoscopic Modalities in the Treatment of Acute Variceal Bleeding

Balloon tamponade using a triple-lumen Sengstaken–Blakemore tube or a four-lumen Minnesota tube stops acute variceal bleeding as efficiently as sclerotherapy. The Zimmon's tube allows endoscopy through the inflated rim of the balloon that abuts against the GE junction and compresses the bleeding varices. Routine use of balloon tamponade before therapeutic endoscopy may lead to more complications.[17,36,60,61]

Pharmacotherapy

Several vasoactive agents have been extensively evaluated with an aim to arrest active bleeding at the earliest, to prevent excessive blood loss, hepatic ischemia, and decompensation. Vasopressin or its analogue terlipressin and somatostatin or its analogues octreotide, lanreotide, and vapreotide have been studied.

The use of vasoactive drugs alone in acute variceal bleeding has not proved to be more effective than endoscopic treatment. Adding octreotide to EVL in patients with acute variceal bleeding has been of benefit in one study[62] but not in the other.[63] There is also some evidence to suggest that combined terlipressin and injection sclerotherapy decreases the incidence of rebleeding after sclerotherapy but with no effect in survival rate.[62] A trial comparing administration of somatostatin both before and after sclerotherapy for 5 days versus sclerotherapy alone suggested that somatostatin significantly reduced treatment failure and blood transfusion requirements but not mortality.[62] Similar results have also been reported by other workers.[64]

Reduction of portal pressure and HVPG is the rationale approach to prevent variceal bleeding. Eleven trials[39] involving 971 patients compared sclerotherapy with drugs (propranolol in 10 and nadolol plus isosorbide mononitrate in 1) for the prevention of recurrent bleeding (from any source; e.g., varices, portal hypertensive bleeding, or sclerotherapy ulcers). There was marked heterogeneity in the evaluation of rebleeding. In five studies, rebleeding was less frequent in patients randomized to drugs and in six studies in patients randomized to sclerotherapy. The pooled data showed that there was no significant difference between the two treatment modalities. There was no significant heterogeneity in the evaluation of survival. More patients randomized to sclerotherapy survived, but the result was not statistically significant. Moreover, the number of patients free of adverse events was significantly higher in the drug group compared with sclerotherapy group.

Pharmacologic therapy (β-blockers plus nitrates) has been found to be as effective as band ligation in preventing variceal rebleeding (Table 14–7).

Endoscopic band ligation (51 patients) was compared with propranolol or combination of propranolol plus isosorbide mononitrate (51 patients).[65] Nineteen patients had rebleeding in the pharmacotherapy group (median time 24 days) and 27 in the banding group (median time 24 days). At 1 year, 43.7% and 32% of the patients in the pharmacotherapy group compared with 53.8% and 22.5% in the banding group (p = ns) had rebled and died, respectively. In the prevention of variceal rebleeding, β-blockers with or without nitrates were found to be as effective as endoscopic band ligation.

Endoscopic band ligation was also compared with combination of band ligation, β-blockers, and sucralfate.[66] Sixty-two patients received band ligation alone, and 60 received combination therapy. After a median follow-up of 21 months, rebleeding and variceal recurrence occurred in 30% and 50% in the EVL group and in 11.6% and 26% patients in the combination group ($p < .05$).

Table 14–7. Randomized Controlled Trials Comparing Combination Pharmacotherapy with Endoscopic Therapy for Prevention of Variceal Rebleeding

Reference	Therapy	n	Rebleeding (%)	Deaths (%)	Follow-up (mo)
Villanueva, et al. (1996)[118]	Nadolol + ISMN	43	26	9	18
	Sclerotherapy	43	53	21	18
Villanueva, et al. (2001)[119]	Nadolol + ISMN	72	33	32	20
	Band ligation	72	49	42	22
Lo, et al. (2002)[120]	Nadolol +ISMN	61	57	13	24
	Band ligation	60	38	25	25
Patch, et al. (2002)[65]	Propranolol + ISMN	44	37	33	8
	Band ligation	47	53	33	12

ISMN, isosorbide mononitrate.

Acid Suppression

Many uncontrolled studies suggest a beneficial effect of acid suppression as an adjunct to sclerotherapy. In three controlled studies, the effect of sucralfate on healing of sclerotherapy-induced ulcers or preventing ulcer bleeding was found to be controversial. Ranitidine in one controlled study had a significant effect on ulcer healing, whereas omeprazole in another study had no effect.[67]

Antibiotics

Patients with acute GI bleeding are prone to systemic infections. Oral nonabsorbable and systemic antibiotics reduce the number of infections in early period after acute hemorrhage. A reduction in mortality in the antibiotic-treated patients has also been shown.[68,69]

Surgical Options

Trials comparing sclerotherapy to shunt surgery showed reduced rebleeding in the surgical group, but no consistent differences in mortality.[36,68] In a meta-analysis of four trials[36] comparing endoscopic sclerotherapy with esophageal transection and one with portacaval shunt in failures of medical therapy, there was no significant difference in failure to control bleeding or mortality, but rebleeding was significantly higher with endoscopic sclerotherapy. Orozco and coworkers[70] compared the elective treatment of variceal hemorrhage with β-blockers (propranolol), endoscopic sclerotherapy, and portal blood flow preserving surgical procedures (selective shunts and the Sugiura-Futagawa operation). They found that rebleeding rate was significantly lower in the surgical group as compared with other two groups. Survival was better for the low-risk patients (Child A) in the three groups, but when the three options were compared, no significant difference was found. Although advances in endoscopic therapy, liver transplantation, and advent of TIPS procedure have influenced the selection and outcome of patients with variceal bleeding, portosystemic shunt and esophagogastric devascularization remain important and effective options for selected patients.[71]

Transjugular Intrahepatic Portosystemic Shunt

TIPS has been compared with sclerotherapy in two meta-analysis, involving 811 and 750 patients, respectively.[72,73]

The median follow-up period ranged from 10 to 32 months in various trials. Both meta-analyses concluded that TIPS is more effective in preventing variceal rebleeding than endoscopic sclerotherapy (19% vs. 47%). However, because of the increased risk of post-treatment encephalopathy and the lack of improvement in survival, TIPS is not recommended as the first-line treatment for preventing variceal rebleeding. High rate of stent dysfunction requiring revision is another limitation of TIPS. Current recommendations by the National Digestive Diseases Advisory Board are to perform TIPS in patients with acute variceal bleeding that can not be controlled with endoscopic therapy or in patients with recurrent variceal bleeding refractory to or intolerant of conventional medical management including sclerotherapy and pharmacotherapy.

MANAGEMENT OF GASTRIC VARICES

The management of bleeding gastric varices depends on the natural history of different types of gastric varices. Although in nearly 60% of the patients GOV1 disappear with the obliteration of esophageal varices, the GOV2 and IGV1 require specific therapy.[74] The risk of bleeding from IGV1 was shown to correlate with variceal size (>10 mm), Child's class, and the presence of red color signs on varices.[1] IGV2, on the other hand, are uncommon varices, rarely bleed, and can be managed like IGV1. At present, endoscopic therapy of isolated gastric varices is indicated in the presence of active bleeding (spurting or oozing) and presence of a clot or other stigmata of recent bleed on the varix. Several issues related to gastric varices have not been well studied: the risk of bleeding from gastric varices after an episode of bleeding from esophageal varices, whether eradication of esophageal varices increases the risk of bleeding from gastric varices, and whether nonbleeding gastric varices that accompany bleeding esophageal varices should be prophylactically treated. At present empirically, the decision to treat gastric varices prophylactically could be made on the basis of location and size of gastric varices, presence of red color signs, Child's score, and the patient's access to cyanoacrylate treatment in the event of sudden hemorrhage.

Active bleeding from gastric varices can be controlled with injection sclerotherapy in 66% to 75% of cases (Tables 14–8 and 14–9). Rebleeding resulting from postsclerotherapy ulcers is common in isolated gastric varices. A combination of paravariceal and intravariceal sclerotherapy has been reported to achieve obliteration of gastric varices in about 40% of cases in a mean of four sessions, but the risk of bleeding with injection therapy is high.

Table 14-8. Endoscopic Sclerotherapy for Gastric Varices for Prevention of Rebleeding

Reference	Agent	N	Obliteration (%)	Rebleeding (%)	Recurrence (%)	Follow-up (mo)
Sarin, et al. (1988)[121]	AA (95%)	32	38	16	—	—
Gimson, et al. (1991)[122]	EO/glue	31	32.3	16	—	—
Chang, et al. (1996)[123]	STD (1.5%)	25	32	70	25	52 ± 37
Chang, et al. (1996)[123]	GW (50%)	26	81	30	4.8	57 ± 32
Sarin (1997)[124]	AA (95%)	60	72	23	0	24 ± 23

AA, absolute alcohol; EO, ethanolamine oleate; GW, glucose water; STD, sodium tetradecyl sulphate.

Table 14-9. Endoscopic Sclerotherapy for Gastric Varices in Active Gastric Variceal Bleeding

Reference	Agent	N	Success (%)	Rebleed (%)	Complications
Trudeau, et al. (1986)[125]	STD	9	100	90	Ulcer 89%
Gimson, et al. (1991)[122]	EO/glue	41	40	16	Ulcer 29% Perforation
Oho, et al. (1995)[80]	EO (5%)	24	67	25	—
Chang, et al. (1996)[123]	STD (1.5%)	25	80	70	Ulcer 30%
Chang, et al. (1996)[123]	GW (50%)	26	92	30	Ulcer 30%
Chiu, et al. (1997)[126]	STD (1.5%)	27	66.7	—	—
Sarin (1997)[124]	AA (95%)	18	67	34	Ulcer 100%
Ogawa, et al. (1999)[78]	EO (5%)	21	81	100	—
Sarin, et al. (2002)[77]	AA (95%)	8	62	25	—

AA, absolute alcohol; EO, ethanolamine oleate; GW, glucose water; STD, sodium tetradecyl sulphate.

Table 14-10. Gastric Variceal Ligation in the Management of Gastric Variceal Bleeding

Reference	Therapy	N	Active bleed (%)	Success (%)	Rebleeding (%)	Obliteration (%)
Yoshida, et al. (1994)[127]	GVL-S	10	10	100	10	100
Harada, et al. (1997)[128]	GVL-S	5	100	100	20	—
Cipolletta, et al. (1998)[129]	GVL-S	7	100	100	0	—
Yoshida, et al. (1999)[76]	GVL-S and EIS	35	23	100	3	97
Shiha and El-Sayed (1999)[75]	GVL	27	7	89	18.5	100

EIS, endoscopic injection sclerotherapy; GVL, gastric variceal ligation; GVL-S, gastric variceal snare ligation.

Endoscopic sclerotherapy does not achieve thrombosis of the entire varix, and the necrosis caused by it may induce massive bleeding[39] from the nonthrombosed high-flow gastric varix leading to high mortality.

Endoscopic ligation[75] and detachable snares[76] have also been used by some groups to control acute gastric variceal bleeding and reduce the risk of rebleeding (Table 14–10). However, there are limited efficacy data available.

Tissue Adhesive Agents

Tissue adhesive agents have been reported to be effective in treating bleeding gastric varices. Native cyanoacrylate (histoacryl [N-butyl-2-cyanoacrylate]) is a liquid with a consistency similar to water, lends itself to intravariceal injection. On contact with a physiologic medium such as blood, it rapidly polymerizes, forming a hard substance that plugs the bleeding varix and thus serves as a useful treatment option. However, the rapid polymerization can block the needle or damage the endoscope. Hence, histoacryl must be diluted with lipiodol (0.5:0.8 mL) to delay the polymerization reaction to complete the injection and remove the needle (Figs. 14–12 and 14–13). The individual dosage of cyanoacrylate per injection should be limited to 2 mL for fundal varices. Obliteration is tested by palpating the varix with the needle retracted. If soft, the varix is injected with additional aliquots of cyanoacrylate subsequently After 3 to 4 days of injection, necrosis occurs on the variceal walls and the cast is slowly extruded (Fig. 14–14). The extrusion process may last several weeks and sometimes even months.

With cyanoacrylate, control of active bleeding from gastric varices has been reported to range from 93% to 100% of patients, and rate of recurrent bleeding is generally less than 30%.[77–86] Huang and coworkers[84] reported 94% hemostasis in 90 patients with active or recent variceal bleeding from fundal varices. Tumorous gastric varices had a higher rebleeding rate than the tortuous and nodular type (34.4% vs. 17.2%).

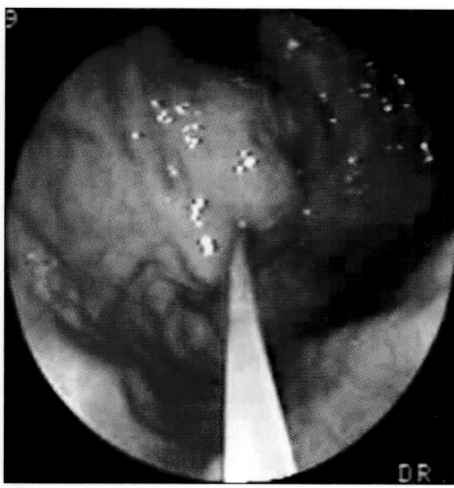

Figure 14–12. Endoscopic picture showing glue injection of gastric varix.

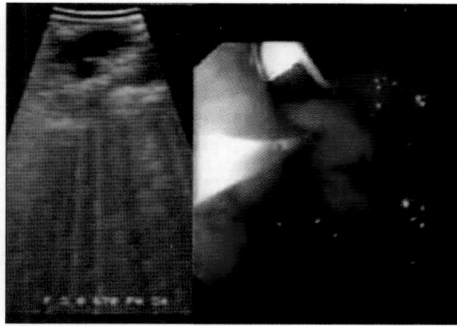

Figure 14–13. Endoscopic injection of gastric varices under endosonography monitoring.

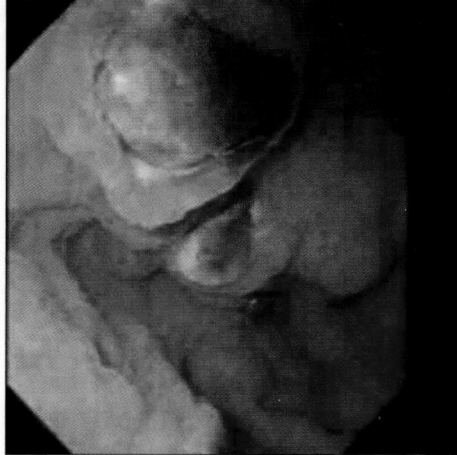

Figure 14–14. Endoscopic picture showing extrusion of glue cast from gastric varix.

Kind and coworkers[83] reported their 12-year experience with the use of histoacryl in 174 patients with bleeding gastric varices. The hemostasis rate was 97.1% with an early rebleeding rate of 15.5% and a hospital mortality rate of 19.5% (Table 14–11). Complications including chest pain and treatment-related, ulcer-induced bleeding occurred in 2.9% patients. However, they had high rebleeding rate in patients with prehepatic block with IGV1-type varices.

In our experience,[77] histoacryl was found to be more effective than absolute alcohol for controlling acute bleeding (89% vs. 62%) and obliteration of gastric varices (100% vs. 44%) (Table 14–12). Cyanoacrylate has also been shown to be superior to ethanolamine.[78] Combination of a sclerosing agent (ethanolamine oleate) and histoacryl has not been found to be of added advantage.[79,87] Glue injection has also been found superior to band ligation of gastric varices.[82] Repeat glue injection into the gastric varix to completely obliterate it may be better than injection on demand (on response to recurrent bleed).[85]

Adverse Effects of Cyanoacrylate Injection

Although uncommon, embolization of the adhesive into the lung, spleen, portal vein, renal vein, inferior vena cava, or brain (Fig. 14–15) poses a serious problem. Although the incidence varies from 2% to 5%, most often the embolization is small. Because of the fear of embolization, some workers prefer to inject undiluted cyanoacrylate. However, the disadvantage of using undiluted adhesive is that the accessory channel of the endoscope may get blocked or the injector needle may get stuck in the varix.[87,88] Cases of visceral fistula have also been described after glue injection.[89] Endoscopic ultrasonography with or without Doppler probe could be used to guide the injection of glue into gastric varices (see Fig. 14–13) and to assess adequate obliteration.[90] It could also help in assessing the paraesophageal collaterals and obliteration of perforators in esophageal variceal sclerotherapy or ligation.[91]

The hemostatic efficacy of glue injection coupled with the high mortality associated with nonendoscopic methods strongly favors glue injection as initial treatment in patients with active bleeding from GOV2 and IGV1. The treatment of GOV1 persisting after obliteration of esophageal varices must be separately planned. Modifications of the injection technique and new cyanoacrylate compounds such as acrylic glue (2-octyl-cyanoacrylate) may reduce or eliminate the risk of embolization.

Other Agents

Thrombin alone[92] or in combination with fibrinogen, "fibrin glue," is useful to stop excessive surface bleeding. Poly-N-acetyl glucosamine (P-GLc NAc) isolated from marine microalgae is a polysaccharide polymer, which was shown to quickly stop variceal hemorrhage in dogs. It is undergoing further evaluation.[93]

NONVARICEAL SOURCES OF PORTAL HYPERTENSIVE BLEEDING

Although mucosal changes can be seen from esophagus to rectum in portal hypertension, they are predominant in the stomach and are of two types: PHG and gastric antral vascular ectasia (GAVE). PHG, earlier called congestive gastropathy, relates to gastric mucosal changes seen endoscopically in patients with PHT. Mild PHG manifests as a mosaic-like pattern with or without discrete red spots and is unlikely to cause significant blood loss. In severe PHG, mucosal red spots become confluent and give rise to deeply erythematous areas that are susceptible to bleeding (Figs. 14–16 and 14–17). However, PHG could also be seen in nonportal hypertensive patients and healthy subjects.[94]

Table 14–11. Histoacryl Injection for Treatment of Gastric Varices

References	N	Hemostasis (%)	Rebleeding (%)	Mortality (%)	Follow-up (mo)
Lee, et al. (2000)[85]	47	95.7	12.8*/44.7†	17	24
Kind, et al. (2000)[83]	174	97.1	15.5	19.5	36
Battaglia, et al. (2000)[130]	32	96.8	34.4	18.7	45.4
Huang, et al. (2000)[84]	90	93.3	23.3	2.2	13
Sarin, et al. (2002)[77]	11	100	27	9	—

*≤ 48 hr; † >48 hr.

Table 14–12. Gastric Variceal Sclerotherapy Versus Glue Injection for Active Gastric Variceal Bleeding

Reference	Agent	N	Hemostasis (%)	Rebleeding (%)	Ulcer (%)	Mortality (%)
Oho, et al. (1995)[80]	EO	24	67	12.5	25	67
	HC	29	93	10	30	38
Sarin, et al. (1995)[131]	AA	8	62	25	82	25
	HC	9	89	22	65	25
Ogawa, et al. (1999)[78]	EO	21	81	35	—	23.8
	HC	17	100	0	—	0
Sarin, et al. (2002)[77]	AA	9	44	33	—	33
	HC	11	100	27	—	9

AA, absolute alcohol; EO, ethanolamine oleate; HC, histoacryl.

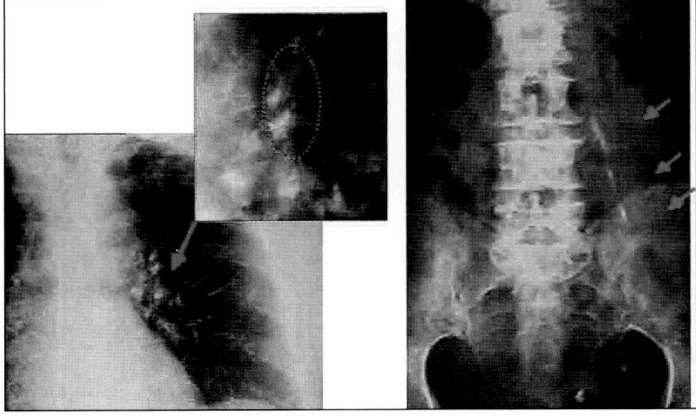

Figure 14–15. Microembolism *(arrow)* after glue injection on x-ray film of chest and abdomen.

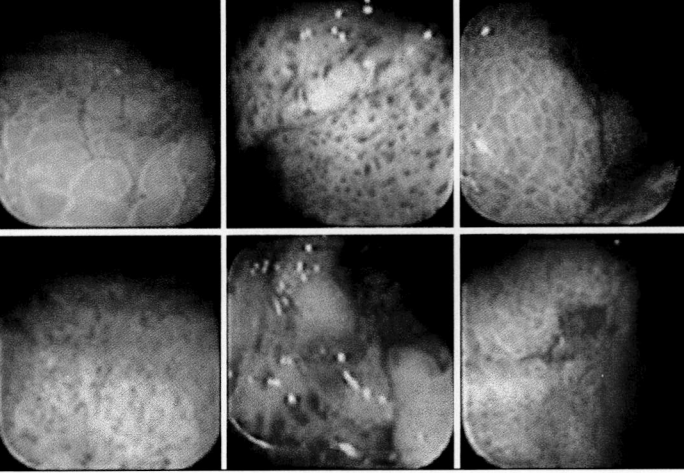

Figure 14–16. North Italian Endoscopy Club classification of portal hypertensive gastropathy.

PHG is a dynamic condition that can progress from mild to severe and vice versa or even disappear completely.

The clinical significance of PHG is still not clear because predictors of bleeding from PHG have not been clearly defined. It is generally agreed that severe lesions, previous sclerotherapy or ligation, diffuse distribution, presence of PHG before variceal obliteration, and advanced liver disease are associated with higher chances of PHG bleeding.

Acute bleeding from PHG is relatively rare, and bleeding from PHG is less severe than bleeding from GOV. After the first bleed from PHG, rebleed appears to be very common, with reported figures of 62% and 75%.

Effective treatment of PHG requires a reduction in the raised portal pressure, which can be accomplished pharmacologically by β-blockers with or without nitrates, radiologically by TIPS, by surgical shunts, or by liver transplantation. Argon plasma coagulation through endoscopy has been found to be effective in two of nine patients when performed every 2 to 3 weeks in one small series, but this is not an established therapy.[95]

Gastric Antral Vascular Ectasia

Two endoscopic manifestations of GAVE are currently recognized: (1) watermelon stomach and (2) diffuse antral vascular ectasia.

Endoscopic description of watermelon stomach is diagnostic and includes presence of longitudinal rugal folds traversing the antrum and converging on the pylorus; each contains a visible convoluted column of vessels, the aggregate resembling the stripes of watermelon. Some workers have described a more diffuse endoscopic form of GAVE (Fig. 14–18)[96,97] that at times is difficult to differentiate from PHG. However, it is histologically similar to watermelon stomach. It may sometimes help that PHG often involves the proximal stomach and occurs in association with a mosaic mucosal pattern.

Patients with GAVE present with significant occult or overt blood loss. Severe anemia is one of the commonest presentation and about 25 mL blood is estimated to be lost per day by these lesions.[97,98]

The etiology of GAVE remains uncertain. It is more prevalent among patients with chronic liver disease but not infrequently occurs in patients without hepatic pathology. When associated with cirrhosis, the evolution to portal hypertension does not seem a prerequisite. Portal pressure reduction does not improve the endoscopic appearance or bleeding propensity of GAVE. However, liver transplantation leads to rapid regression of the lesions. These features indicate that portal hypertension per se is not the sole pathogenetic mechanisms for GAVE.

At present, treatment of GAVE is unsatisfactory because reduction of portal pressure by β-blockers is of limited help. Drugs such as tranexamic acid, glucocorticoids, and estrogen-progesterone combination do help in reducing transfusion requirements, but their true efficacy remains equivocal.

Gostout and coworkers[98] reported endoscopic neodymium: yttrium-aluminium-garnet (Nd:YAG) laser coagulation to be effective in 12 of 13 patients after a median period of 6 months, eliminating the need for transfusion. Similar experience was reported by others[99] without complications. However, success in the diffuse form of GAVE is limited. Although surgical antrectomy can cure GAVE, liver transplantation is the best option.

Portal Hypertensive Enteropathy

Portal hypertension related mucosal abnormalities affecting the small intestine are less frequent[100] with low bleeding propensity. Diarrhea and protein-losing enteropathy, which improved after TIPS placement, could be other manifestations of PHE.

Portal Hypertensive Colopathy

Kozarek and coworkers[101] reported that 14 (70%) of their 20 cirrhotics had multiple vascular-appearing lesions (10 with cherry red spots, 6 with spider telangiectasias), 4 of whom also had endoscopic features suggesting a mild, chronic colitis, most commonly involving the right colon. We observed colopathy in 52% of patients with portal hypertension[102] more often in bleeders (52%) than in nonbleeders (12.5%).

PHC is rarely a cause of significant portal hypertensive bleeding.

Colopathy is usually diagnosed endoscopically and not histologically. Endoscopic lesions of PHC include colonic vascular ectasias or angiomata, mucosal abnormalities such as erythema, friability, and edema.[103,104]

MANAGEMENT OF OTHER GASTROINTESTINAL AND BILIARY VARICES

Anorectal Varices

In the lower GI tract, collaterals between the superior hemorrhoidal vein (portal) and the middle and inferior hemorrhoidal veins (systemic) result in anal and rectal varices. Hemorrhoids must be differentiated from anal varices; the former appear as purple, well-vascularized mucosa in the lower 4 cm of the anal canal. Varices in

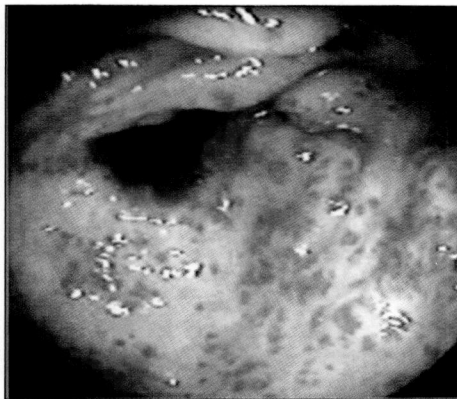

Figure 14–17. Endoscopic picture showing severe portal hypertensive gastropathy in antrum.

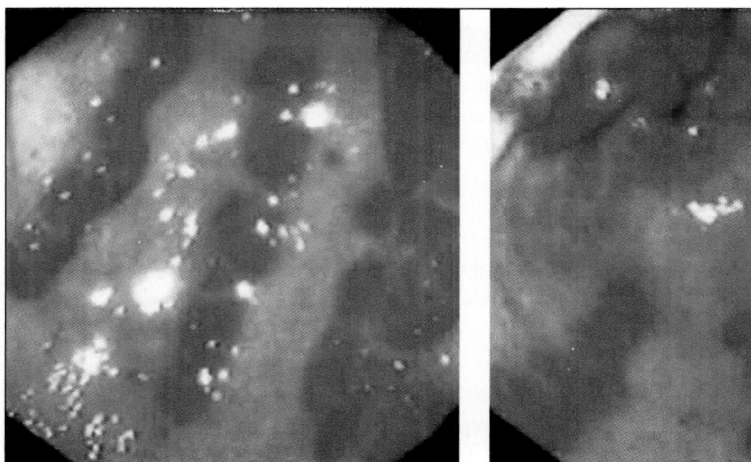

Figure 14–18. Endoscopic picture showing gastric antral vascular ectasia.

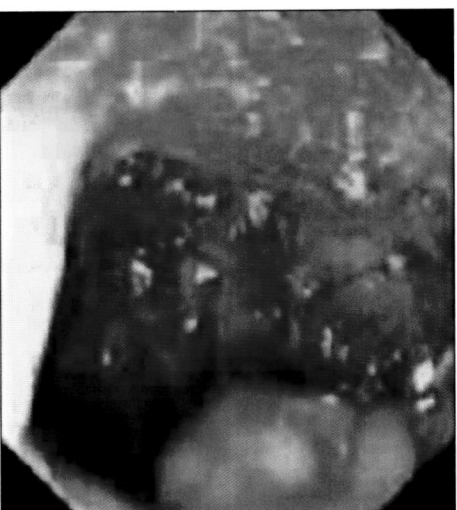

Figure 14–19. Endoscopic picture showing varix in second part of duodenum.

the anal canal appear as either discrete veins or saccular blue or slate grey swellings. Rectal varices start above the pectinate line and are easy to diagnose.

Anorectal varices are more common in patients with extrahepatic portal venous obstruction and noncirrhotic portal fibrosis (89%) as compared with cirrhosis (56%) and more so in bleeders than in nonbleeder patients.[105]

Unlike esophageal varices, anorectal varices rarely bleed, but if they bleed they often bleed massively. The incidence of bleeding from rectal varices was 1.4%, 6.7%, and 18% in the three studies, more so in patients with noncirrhotic portal hypertension.[102,105,106] For bleeding anorectal varices, endoscopic injection sclerotherapy, band ligation, embolization, cryosurgery and under-running of the varices with sutures have all been tried but often with limited success. Portosystemic shunt or TIPS are often needed to finally decompress and prevent rectal variceal bleeding.[6,22]

Duodenal Varices

Primary duodenal varices are rare and are usually found incidentally at the time of endoscopy, more often in patients with extrahepatic portal vein obstruction (EHPVO) or in cirrhotics with portal vein thrombosis (Fig. 14–19). Usually the afferent vessel of the duodenal varices is the superior or inferior pancreaticoduodenal vein originating in the portal vein trunk or superior mesenteric vein. The efferent vein drains into the inferior vena cava. In a review of 169 cases of bleeding ectopic varices, 17% occurred in the duodenum, 17% in the jejunum or ileum, 14% in the colon, 8% in the rectum, and 9% in the peritoneum.[107]

Duodenal varices more often are secondary, that is, appear after obliteration of esophageal varices. When a patient with portal hypertension has melena without hematemesis, the possibility of a bleeding duodenal varix should be considered. Sometimes these patients present with active upper GI bleed. Successful control of bleeding after injection of cyanoacrylate, sclerosant injection, or thrombin/sclerosant combination has been reported.[6,107] The data regarding band ligation of duodenal varices and other ectopic varices

are limited. Even in patients with reasonable liver functions, surgical mortality rates for treating actively bleeding duodenal varices range from 30% to 40%. Radiologic procedures such as selective embolization and TIPS may be effective but have not been extensively studied.

Jejunal and Ileal Varices

Varices involving the small intestine are rare. They are commonly found at the anastomotic sites and in adhesions. Patients who present with bleeding jejunal or ileal varices typically have a history of portal hypertension, prior abdominal surgery, and hematochezia without hematemesis. Small bowel varices can occur in the absence of cirrhosis when there is mesenteric or splenic vein thrombosis and even with concomitant nonbleeding esophageal varices. The common locations are ileum (47%) and jejunum (39%). Push enteroscopy and venous phase of angiography may reveal the bleeding source.

The small bowel varices can also be identified by wireless capsule endoscopy and retrograde ileoscopy. Successful sclerotherapy and glue injection to treat bleeding jejunal varices has been reported.[108]

Stomal Varices

The varicosities may form in and around the stoma in a patient who had colectomy for ulcerative colitis who develops PHT resulting from sclerosing cholangitis or in a cirrhotic with ileostomy. Bleeding is usually recurrent and problematic, with an estimated 3% to 4% risk of death at each episode. The time frame for development of these varices and hemorrhage from them is not clear but ranges from 1.5 to 348 months with an average of 28 months for colostomy and 48 months for ileostomy.

Local compression with gauze soaked in dilute epinephrine, sclerotherapy, and surgical variceal ligation are useful in temporarily controlling the bleed. Transcatheter embolization, disconnection of the stoma or portosystemic shunting, or TIPS placement have been used with variable success.

Biliary Varices

Varices have been reported in the gallbladder and the bile ducts, more often in patients with portal vein thrombosis. Usually varices of the biliary tree are found incidentally during ultrasound, Doppler, computed tomography (CT) scan, or endoscopic retrograde cholangiopancreatography (ERCP). At ERCP, bile duct varices may produce narrowing, irregularity and nodular extrinsic defects termed *portal biliopathy*.[109] Spontaneous bleeding from biliary varices is rare. Portal decompressive measures should relieve the venous dilation and consequent obstructive jaundice, if present.

Summary

Management of esophageal and gastric varices poses considerable challenge and requires a team approach and a dedicated intensive care unit (ICU). Combination of endoscopic band ligation with vasoactive drugs or with β-blockers to reduce portal pressure are effective in controlling active bleeding and preventing rebleeding. In patients nonresponsive to these measures, TIPS or rescue surgery must be offered. Although prevention of infection and hepatic encephalopathy can help improve survival, HVPG determines the outcome in such patients. Prevention of first variceal bleed from high-risk varices could be achieved by reduction in HVPG by β-blockers with or without adding nitrates. In subjects who do not achieve 20% or greater reduction in HVPG or have contraindications or side effects to β-blockers, EVL offers an equally effective and safe alternative. There is need to develop effective strategies to prevent development of varices or delay the increase in size of the small varices. Reduction in portal pressure does also help to reduce bleeding from PHG and ectopic varices but not from GAVE. Liver transplantation offers a lasting cure because it treats the cirrhotic liver and the portal hypertension syndrome.

REFERENCES

1. Luketic VA, Sanyal AJ: Esophageal varices. I. Clinical presentation, medical therapy, and endoscopic therapy. Gastroenterol Clin North Am 29:337–385, 2000.
2. Conn HO: Ammonia tolerance in the diagnosis of esophageal varices. A comparison of the endoscopic, radiologic and biochemical techniques. J Lab Clin Med 70:442–451, 1967.
3. Westaby D, Macdougall BR, Malia WM, et al: A prospective randomized study of two sclerotherapy techniques for esophageal varices. Hepatology 3:681–684, 1983.
4. Japanese Research Society for Portal Hypertension: The general rules for recording endoscopic findings on esophageal varices. Jpn J Surg 10:84–87, 1980.
5. Paquet KJ: Prophylactic endoscopic sclerosing treatment of the esophageal wall in varices: A prospective controlled randomized trial. Endoscopy 14:4–5, 1982.
6. Kotfila R, Trudeau W: Extraesophageal varices. Dig Dis 16:232–241, 1998.
7. Graham DY, Smith JL: The course of patients after variceal hemorrhage. Gastroenterology 80:800–809, 1981.
8. The North Italian Endoscopy Club for the Study and Treatment of Esophageal Varices: Predictors of the first variceal hemorrhage in patients with cirrhosis of the liver and esophageal varices. A prospective multicenter study. N Engl J Med 319:983–989, 1988.
9. Sarin SK, Sundaram KR, Ahuja RK: Predictors of variceal bleeding: An analysis of clinical, endoscopic and hemodynamic variables, with special reference to intravariceal pressure. Gut 30:1757–1764, 1989.
10. Nevens F, Bustami R, Scheys I, et al: Variceal pressure is a factor predicting the risk of a first variceal bleeding. A prospective cohort study in cirrhotic subjects. Hepatology 27:15–19, 1998.
11. Garcia-Tsao G, Groszmann R, Fisher RL, et al: Portal pressure, presence of gastroesophageal varices and variceal bleeding. Hepatology 5:419–24, 1985.
12. Casado M, Bosch J, Garcia-Pagan JC, et al: Clinical events after transjugular intrahepatic portosystemic shunt: Correlation with hemodynamic findings. Gastroenterology 114:1296–1303, 1998.
13. Moitinho E, Escorsell A, Bandi JC, et al: Prognostic value of early measurements of portal pressure in acute variceal bleeding. Hepatology 117:626–631, 1999.
14. Varobioff J, Groszmann RJ, Picabea E, et al: Prognostic value of hepatic venous pressure gradient measurements in alcoholic cirrhosis. A 10 year prospective study. Gastroenterology 111:701–709, 1996.
15. Ben-Ari Z, Cardin F, McCormick PA, et al: A predictive model for failure to control bleeding during acute variceal haemorrhage. J Hepatol 31:443–450, 1999.
16. Goulis J, Patch D, Burroughs AK: Bacterial infection in the pathogenesis of variceal bleeding. Lancet 353:139–142, 1999.
17. McKiernan PJ: Treatment of variceal bleeding. Gastrointest Endosc Clin N Am 11:789–812, 2001.
18. Sarin SK, Kumar A: Gastric varices: Profile, classification and management. Am J Gastroenterol 84:1244–1249, 1989.
19. Sarin SK, Lahoti D, Saxena SP, et al: Prevalence, classification and natural history of gastric varices: Long term follow up study in 568 portal hypertension patients. Hepatology 16:1343–1349, 1992.
20. Sarin SK, Lahoti D: Management of gastric varices. Bailliere Clin Gastroenterol 6:527–548, 1992.
21. de Franchis R (ed): Portal hypertension II. Proceedings of the Second Baveno International Consensus Workshop on Definitions, Methodology and Therapeutic Strategies. Oxford, England, Blackwell Science Ltd, 1996, pp 10–17.
22. Russo MW, Brown RS Jr: Endoscopic treatment of patients with portal hypertension. Gastrointest Endosc Clin N Am 11:1–14, 2001.
23. Sarin SK, Kumar A: Sclerosants for variceal sclerotherapy. A critical appraisal. Am J Gastroenterol 85:641–649, 1990.
24. Kochhar R, Goenka MK, Mehta S, Mehta SK: A comparative evaluation of sclerosants for esophageal varices. A prospective randomized controlled study. Gastrointest Endosc 36:127–130, 1990.
25. Sarin SK, Sachdev G, Nanda R, et al: Comparison of the two time schedules for endoscopic sclerotherapy: A prospective randomized controlled study. Gut 27:710–713, 1986.
26. de la Pena J, Rivero M, Sanchez E, et al: Variceal ligation compared with endoscopic sclerotherapy for variceal hemorrhage: Prospective randomized trial. Gastrointest Endosc 49:417–423, 1999.
27. Waked I, Korula J: Analysis of long term endoscopic surveillance during follow up after variceal sclerotherapy from a 13 years experience. Am J Med 102:192–199, 1997.
28. Sarin SK: Endoscopic sclerotherapy for esophago-gastric varices: A critical reappraisal. Aust NZ J Med 19:162–171, 1989.
29. deFranchis R: Prediction of first variceal hemorrhage in patients with cirrhosis of the liver and esophageal varices. N Engl J Med 319:983–989, 1988.
30. Sarin SK, Nanda R, Sachedev G, et al: Intravariceal versus paravariceal sclerotherapy: A prospective controlled randomized trial. Gut 28:657–662, 1987.
31. Seewald S, Seitz U, Yang AM, et al: Variceal bleeding and portal hypertension: Still a therapeutic challenge? Endoscopy 33:126–139, 2001.
32. Matsumoto H, Suzuki F, Souda K, et al: Improved long term survival following complete eradication of esophageal varices by sclerotherapy. Hepatogastroenterology 46:172–176, 1999.
33. Sarin S: Non-cirrhotic portal fibrosis. J Gastroenterol Hepatol 17(Suppl 3):S214–S223, 2002.
34. Sarin SK, Agarwal SR: Extrahepatic portal vein obstruction. Semin Liver Dis 22:43–58, 2002.
35. Kleber G, Steudel N, Fleig WE: Endoscopic treatment of portal hypertension. Digestion 59(Suppl 2):50–53, 1998.
36. D'Amico G, Pagliaro L, Bosch J: The treatment of portal hypertension. A metaanalytic review. Hepatology 22:332–353, 1995.
37. Pagliaro L, D'Amico G, Sorensen TI, et al: Prevention of first bleeding in cirrhosis: A meta-analysis of randomized trials of nonsurgical treatment. Ann Intern Med 117:59–70, 1992.
38. The Veteran Affairs Cooperative Variceal Sclerotherapy Group: Prophylactic sclerotherapy for esophageal varices in men with alcoholic liver disease. A randomized single blind, multicenter clinical trial. New Engl J Med 324:1779–1784, 1991.
39. Dagher L, Burroughs A: Variceal bleeding and portal hypertensive gastropathy. Eur J Gastroenterol Hepatol 13:81–88, 2001.
40. Teran JC, Imperiale TF, Mullen KD, et al: Primary prophylaxis of variceal bleeding in cirrhosis: A cost-effectiveness analysis. Gastroenterology 112:473–482, 1997.
41. Spiegel BM, Targownik L, Dulai GS, et al: Endoscopic screening for esophageal varices in cirrhosis: Is it ever cost effective? Hepatology 37:366–377, 2003.

42. Stiegmann GV, Goff JS, Michaletz-Onody PA, et al: Endoscopic sclerotherapy as compared with endoscopic ligation for bleeding esophageal varices. N Engl J Med 326:1527–1532, 1992.

43. Avgerinos A, Armonis A, Manolakopoulos S, et al: Endoscopic sclerotherapy versus variceal ligation in the long term management of patients with cirrhosis after variceal bleeding. A prospective randomized study. J Hepatol 26:1034–1041, 1997.

44. Laine L, Stein C, Sharma V: Randomized comparison of ligation versus ligation plus sclerotherapy in patients with bleeding esophageal varices. Gastroenterology 110:529–533, 1996.

45. Saeed ZA, Steigmann GV, Ramirez FC, et al: Endoscopic variceal ligation is superior to combined ligation and sclerotherapy for esophageal varices: A multicenter prospective randomized trial. Hepatology 25:71–74, 1997.

46. Lo GH, Lai KH, Cheng JS, et al: The additive effect of sclerotherapy to patients receiving repeated endoscopic variceal ligation: A prospective randomized trial. Hepatology 28:391–395, 1998.

47. Seewald S, Mendoza G, Seitz U, et al: Variceal bleeding and portal hypertension: Has there been any progress in the last 12 months. Endoscopy 35:136–144, 2003.

48. Nakamura S, Mitsunaga A, Murata Y, et al: Endoscopic induction of mucosal fibrosis by argon plasma coagulation (APC) for esophageal varices: A prospective randomized trial of ligation plus APC vs. ligation alone. Endoscopy 33:210–215, 2001.

49. Hino S, Kakutani H, Ikeda K, et al: Low power diode laser treatment using indocyanine green for eradication of esophageal varices. Endoscopy 33:873–875, 2001.

50. Hokari K, Kato M, Katagiri M, et al: A new combined therapeutic method for esophageal varices: Endoscopic variceal ligation followed by mucosal fibrosing with microwave. Dig Dis Week Abstract Book A458, 1998.

51. Kuga T, Higuchi K, Arakawa T, et al: Endoscopic treatment for esophageal varices with microwaves. Dig Dis Week Abstract Book A872, 1998.

52. Sarin SK, Govil A, Jain AK, et al: Prospective randomized trial of endoscopic sclerotherapy versus variceal band ligation for esophageal varices; influence on gastropathy, gastric varices and variceal recurrence. J Hepatol 26:826–832, 1997.

53. Zargar SA, Javid G, Khan BA, et al: Endoscopic ligation compared with sclerotherapy for bleeding esophageal varices in children with extrahepatic portal venous obstruction. Hepatology 36:666–672, 2002.

54. Sarin SK, Guptan RK, Jain AK, et al: A randomized controlled trial of endoscopic variceal band ligation for primary prophylaxis of variceal bleeding. Eur J Gastroenterol Hepatol 8:337–342, 1996.

55. Lay CS, Tsai YT, Teg CY, et al: Endoscopic variceal ligation in prophylaxis of first variceal bleeding in cirrhotic patients with high risk esophageal varices. Hepatology 25:1347–1350, 1997.

56. Sarin SK, Lamba GS, Kumar M, et al: Comparison of endoscopic ligation and propranolol for the primary prevention of variceal bleeding. N Engl J Med 340:988–993, 1999.

57. Lui HF, Stanley AJ, Forrest EH, et al: Primary prophylaxis of variceal haemorrhage: A randomized controlled trial comparing band ligation, propranolol and isosorbide mononitrate. Hepatology 30:318A, 1999.

58. D'Amico G, Pagiliaro L, Bosch J: Pharmacological treatment of portal hypertension: An evidence-based approach. Semin Liv Dis 19:475–505, 1999.

59. Imperiale TF, Chalasani N: A meta-analysis of endoscopic variceal ligation for primary prophylaxis of esophageal variceal bleeding. Hepatology 33:802–807, 2001.

60. Vargas HE, Gerber D, Abu-Elmagd K: Management of portal hypertension-related bleeding. Surg Clin North Am 79:1–22, 1999.

61. Jalan R, Hayes PC: UK guidelines on the management of variceal hemorrhage in cirrhotic patients. British Society of Gastroenterology. Gut 46(Suppl 3–4):1111–1115, 2000.

62. Vlavianos P, Westaby D: Management of acute variceal hemorrhage. Eur J Gastroenterol Hepatol 13:335–342, 2001.

63. Jenkins SA, Shields R, Davies M, et al: A multicentric randomized trial comparing octreotide and injection sclerotherapy in the management and outcome of acute variceal hemorrhage. Gut 41:526–533, 1997.

64. Villanueva C, Ortiz J, Sabat M, et al: Somatostatin alone or combined with emergency sclerotherapy in the treatment of acute esophageal variceal bleeding: A prospective randomized trial. Hepatology 30:384–389, 1999.

65. Patch D, Sabin CA, Goulis J, et al: A randomized, controlled trial of medical therapy versus endoscopic ligation for the prevention of variceal rebleeding in patients with cirrhosis. Gastroenterology 123:1013–1019, 2002.

66. Lo GH, Lai KH, Cheng JS, et al: Endoscopic variceal ligation plus nadolol and sucralfate compared with ligation alone for the prevention of variceal rebleeding: A prospective randomized trial. Hepatology 32:461–465, 2000.

67. McCormack G, McCormick PA: A practical guide to the management of esophageal varices. Drugs 57:327–335, 1999.

68. Garcia-Tsao G: Current management of the complications of cirrhosis and portal hypertension: Variceal hemorrhage, ascites, and spontaneous bacterial peritonitis. Gastroenterology 120:726–748, 2001.

69. Bernard B, Grange JD, Khac EN, et al: Antibiotic prophylaxis for the prevention of bacterial infections in cirrhotic patients with gastrointestinal bleeding: A meta-analysis. Hepatology 29:1655–1661, 1999.

70. Orozco H, Mercado MA, Chan C, et al: A comparative study of the elective treatment of variceal hemorrhage with beta-blockers, transendoscopic sclerotherapy, and surgery: A prospective, controlled, and randomized trial during 10 years. Ann Surg 232:216–219, 2000.

71. Rikkers LF: The changing spectrum of treatment for variceal bleeding. Ann Surg 228:536–546, 1998.

72. Papatheodoridis GV, Goulis J, Leandro G, et al: Transjugular intrahepatic portosystemic shunt compared with endoscopic treatment for prevention of variceal rebleeding; A meta-analysis. Hepatology 30:612–622, 1999.

73. Luca A, D'Amico G, La Galla R, et al: TIPS for prevention of recurrent bleeding in patients, with cirrhosis: Meta-analysis of randomized clinical trials. Radiology 212:411–421, 1999.

74. Sarin SK, Jain AK, Lamba GS, et al: Isolated gastric varices: Prevalence, clinical relevance and natural history. Dig Surg 20:42–47, 2003.

75. Shiha G, El-Sayed S: Gastric variceal ligation: A new technique. Gastrointest Endosc 49:437–441, 1999.

76. Yoshida T, Harada T, Shigemitsu T, et al: Endoscopic management of gastric varices using a detachable snare and simultaneous endoscopic sclerotherapy and O-ring ligation. J Gastroenterol Hepatol 14:730–735, 1999.

77. Sarin SK, Jain AK, Jain M, et al: A randomized controlled trial of cyanoacrylate versus alcohol injection in patients with isolated fundic varices. Am J Gastroenterol 97:1010–1015, 2002.

78. Ogawa K, Ishikawa S, Naritaka Y, et al: Clinical evaluation of endoscopic injection sclerotherapy using N-butyul-2-cyanoacrylate for gastric variceal bleeding. J Gastroenterol Hepatol 14:245–250, 1999.

79. Miyazaki S, Yoshida T, Barada T, et al: Injection sclerotherapy for gastric varices using N-butyl–2 cyanoacrylate and ethanolamine oleate. Hepatogastroenterology 45:1155–1158, 1998.

80. Oho K, Iwao T, Sumiao M, et al: Ethanolamine oleate versus butyl cyanoacrylate for bleeding gastric varices: A non randomized study. Endoscopy 27:349–354, 1995.

81. Akerman P, Raifman J, Siemens M, et al: Preliminary results of a prospective randomized trial of Histoacryl versus endoscopic band ligation (EBL) for acute esophagogastric variceal hemorrhage. Gastrointest Endosc 40:A247, 1994.

82. Lo GH, Lai KH, Cheng JS, et al: A prospective randomized trial of butyl cyanoacrylate injection versus band ligation in the management of bleeding gastric varices. Hepatology 33:1060–1064, 2001.

83. Kind R, Guglielmi A, Rodella L, et al: Bucrylate treatment of bleeding gastric varices: 12 years' experience. Endoscopy 32:512–519, 2000.

84. Huang YH, Yeh HZ, Chen GH, et al: Endoscopic treatment of bleeding gastric varices by N-butyl-2-cyanoacrylate (Histoacryl) injection: Long-term efficacy and safety. Gastrointest Endosc 52:298–301, 2000.

85. Lee YT, Chan FK, Ng EK, et al: EUS-guided injection of cyanoacrylate for bleeding gastric varices. Gastrointest Endosc 52:168–174, 2000.

86. Battaglia G, Morbin T, Paternello E, et al: Diagnostic et traitement endoscopique des varices gastriques. Acta Endosc 29:116–117, 1999.

87. Binmoeller KF: Glue for gastric varix: Some sticky issues. Gastrointest Endosc 52:298–301, 2000.

88. Bhasin DK, Sharma BC, Prasad H, Singh K: Endoscopic removal of sclerotherapy needle from gastric varix after N-butyl-2-cyanoacrylte injection Gastrointest Endosc 51:497–498, 2000.

89. Gostout CJ: What we need is a reliable plug. Am J Gastroenterol 97:1281–1283, 2002.

90. Obara K, Irisawa A, Saito A, et al: EUS monitoring of EIS. Endoscopy 30:A51, 1998.

91. Lo GH, Lai KH, Cheng JS, et al: Prevalence of paraesophageal varices and gastric varices in patients achieving variceal obliteration by banding ligation and injection sclerotherapy. Gastrointest Endosc 49:428–436, 1999.

92. Yang WL, Tripathi D, Therapondos G, et al: Endoscopic use of human thrombin in bleeding gastric varices. Am J Gastroenterol 97:1381–1385, 2002.

93. Kulling D, Vournakis JN, Woo S, et al: Endoscopic injection of bleeding esophageal varices with a poly-N-acetyl glucosamine gel formulation in the canine portal hypertension model. Gastrointest Endosc 49:764–777, 1999.

94. Sarin SK, Misra SP, Singal A, et al: Evaluation of incidence and significance of the mosaic pattern in patients with cirrhosis, noncirrhotic portal fibrosis and extrahepatic obstruction. Am J Gastroenterol 83:1235–1239, 1988.

95. Viggiano TR, Gostout CJ: Portal hypertensive intestinal vasculopathy. A review of the clinical, endoscopic and histopathologic features. Am J Gastroenterol 87:944–954, 1992.

96. Rider JA, Klotz AP, Kirsner JB: Gastritis with veno-capillary ectasia as a source of massive gastric hemorrhage. Gastroenterology 24:118–123, 1953.

97. Cales P, Payen JL, Berg P, et al: Antral vascular ectasia: New endoscopic and clinical spectrum. Gastroenterology 100:A38, 1991.

98. Gostout CJ, Ahlquist DA, Radford CM, et al: Endoscopic laser therapy for watermelon stomach. Gastroenterology 96:1462–1465, 1989.

99. Bourke MJ, Hope RL, Boyd P, et al: Endoscopic laser therapy for watermelon stomach. J Gastroenterol Hepatol 11:832–834, 1996.

100. Nagral AS, Joshi AS, Bhatia SJ, et al: Congestive jejunopathy in portal hypertension Gut 34:694–697, 1993.

101. Kozarek RA, Botoman VA, Bredfeldt JE, et al: Portal colopathy: Prospective study of colonoscopy in patients with portal hypertension. Gastroenterology 101:1192–1197, 1991.

102. Ganguly S, Sarin SK, Bhatia V, Lahoti D: The prevalence and spectrum of colonic lesions in patients with cirrhosis and non-cirrhotic portal hypertension. Hepatology 21:1226–1231, 1995.

103. Tam TN, Ng WW, Lee SD: Colonic mucosal changes in patients with liver cirrhosis. Gastrointest Endosc 42:408–412, 1995.

104. Chen LS, Lin HC, Lee FY, et al: Portal hypertensive colopathy in patients with cirrhosis. Scand J Gastroenterol 31:490–494, 1996.

105. Chawla Y, Dilawari JB: Anorectal varices: Their frequency in cirrhosis and non-cirrhotic portal hypertension. Gut 32:309–311, 1991.

106. Goenka MK, Kochhar R, Nagi B, Mehta SK: Rectosigmoid varices and other mucosal changes in patients with portal hypertension. Am J Gastroenterol 86:1185–1189, 1991.

107. Norton ID, Andrews JC, Kamath PS: Management of ectopic varices. Hepatology 28:1154–1158, 1998.

108. Getzlaff S, Benz CA, Schilling D, et al: Enteroscopic cyano-acrylate sclerotherapy of jejunal and gallbladder varices in a patient with portal hypertension. Endoscopy 33:462–464, 2001.

109. Chandra R, Kapoor D, Tharakan A, et al: Portal biliopathy. J Gastroenterol Hepatol 16:1144–1148, 2001.

110. Hou MC, Lin HC, Kuo BI, et al: Comparison of endoscopic variceal injection sclerotherapy and ligation for the treatment of esophageal variceal hemorrhage: A prospective randomized trial. Hepatology 21:1517–1522, 1995.

111. Baroncini D, Milandri GI, Boroni D, et al: A prospective randomized trial of sclerotherapy versus ligation in the elective treatment of bleeding esophageal varices. Endoscopy 29:235–240, 1997.

112. Lo GH, Lai KH, Cheng JS, et al: Prophylactic banding ligation of high risk esophageal varices in patients with cirrhosis: A prospective randomized trial. J Hepatol 31:451–456, 1999.

113. Omar MM, Attia M, Mostafa I: Prophylactic band ligation of large esophageal varices. J Hepatol 32(Suppl 2):73, 2000.

114. Song IH, Shin JW, Kim IH, et al: A prospective randomized trial between prophylactic endoscopic variceal ligation and propranolol administration for prevention of first bleeding in cirrhotic patients with high–risk esophageal varices. J Hepatol 32(Suppl 2):41, 2000.

115. Al Traif I, Fachartz FS, AI Jumah A, et al: Randomized trial of ligation versus combined ligation and sclerotherapy for bleeding esophageal varices. Gastrointest Endosc 50:1–6, 1999.

116. Djurdjevic D, Janosevic S, Dapcevic B, et al: Combined ligation and sclerotherapy versus ligation alone for eradication of bleeding esophageal varices: A randomized and prospective trial. Endoscopy 31:286–290, 1999.

117. Umehara M, Onda M, Tajiri T, et al: Sclerotherapy plus ligation versus ligation for the treatment of esophageal varices: A prospective randomized study. Gastrointest. Endosc 50:7–12, 1999.

118. Villanueva C, Balanzo J, Novella MT, et al: Nadolol plus isosorbide mononitrate compared with a sclerotherapy for the prevention of variceal rebleeding. N Engl J Med 334:1624–1629, 1996.

119. Villanueva C, Minana J, Ortiz J, et al: Endoscopic ligation compared with combined treatment with nadolol and isosorbide mononitrate to prevent recurrent variceal bleeding. N Engl J Med 345:647–655, 2001.

120. Lo GH, Chen WC, Chen MH, et al: Banding ligation versus nadolol and isosorbide mononitrate for the prevention of esophageal variceal rebleeding. Gastroenterology 123:728–734, 2002.

121. Sarin SK, Sachdev G, Nanda R, et al: Endoscopic sclerotherapy in the treatment of gastric varices. Br J Surg 75:747–750, 1988.

122. Gimson AE, Westaby D, Williams R: Endoscopic sclerotherapy in the management of gastric variceal haemorrhage. J Hepatol 13:274–278, 1991.

123. Chang KY, Wu CS, Chen PC: Prospective randomized trial of hypertonic glucose water and sodium tetradecyl sulfate for gastric variceal bleeding in patients with advanced liver cirrhosis. Endoscopy 28:481–486, 1996.

124. Sarin SK: Long term follow up of gastric variceal sclerotherapy: An eleven year experience. Gastrointest Endosc 46:8–14, 1997.

125. Trudeau W, Prindiville T: Endoscopic injection sclerosis in bleeding gastric varices. Gastrointest Endosc 32:264–268, 1986.

126. Chiu KW, Changchien CS, Chuah SK, et al: Endoscopic injection sclerotherapy with 1.5% Sotradecol for bleeding cardiac varices. J Clin Gastroenterol 24:161–164, 1997.

127. Yoshida T, Hayashi N, Suzumi S, et al: Endoscopic ligation of gastric varices using a detachable snare. Endoscopy 26:502–505, 1994.

128. Harada T, Yoshida T, Shigemitsu T, et al: Therapeutic results of endoscopic variceal ligation for acute bleeding of esophageal and gastric varices. J Gastroenterol Hepatol 12:331–335, 1997.

129. Cipolletta L, Bianco MA, Rotondano G, et al: Emergency endoscopic ligation of actively bleeding gastric varices with a detachable snare. Gastrointest Endosc 47:400–403, 1998.

130. Battaglia G, Morbin T, Paterello E, et al: Visceral fistulae as a complication of sclerotherapy for esophageal and gastric varices using isobutyl-2-cyanoacrylate. Gastrointest Endosc 52:267–270, 2000.

131. Sarin SK, Jain A, Guptan RC: A randomized trial of the efficacy of cyanoacrylate vs. alcohol in gastric variceal sclerotherapy; preliminary results [abstract]. Indian J Gastroenterol 14:A89, 1995.

Lower Gastrointestinal Bleeding

Thomas J. Savides

CHAPTER

15

Introduction

Acute severe lower gastrointestinal (GI) bleeding is a common problem for which colonoscopy can often result in diagnosis and possible treatment. It is often mild and self-limited. For purposes of this discussion, only moderately severe hematochezia, which results in decreased hematocrit greater than 8%, hospitalization, and possible blood transfusion, is considered. In addition, this chapter focuses only on colonic sources of lower GI bleeding, which is the most common site for severe hematochezia.

Epidemiology

Acute severe lower GI bleeding occurs with an annual hospitalization rate of 22 per 100,000 adult population, based on a retrospective study of middle-class Americans who were members of Kaiser Permanente Health Care system in San Diego.[1] Assuming that an average full-time clinical gastroenterologist is responsible for 50,000 adult lives, he or she would see more than 10 cases per year. Most cases occur in more elderly patients, given the increased frequency and risk for diverticulosis, vascular disease, and colonic malignancy.[1] The risk of lower GI bleeding is also associated with the use of aspirin and nonsteroidal anti-inflammatory drugs (NSAIDs).[2,3]

Initial Approach to the Patient with Severe Hematochezia

Initial patient assessment includes history, vital signs with orthostatic blood pressure determination, and physical and rectal examinations. Patients should be asked about whether they saw red blood or dark maroon blood, duration of symptoms, abdominal pain, prior history of lower GI, prior pelvic radiation, history of diverticulosis, and prior colon imaging studies. They should also be asked about use of medications associated with GI bleeding (aspirin, NSAIDs, anticoagulants, and *Ginkgo biloba*). Weight loss and/or a change in bowel habits suggest possible colon cancer. Abdominal pain suggests malignancy or an inflammatory process.

The most important parts of the physical examination are the vital signs and the stool examination. The presence of bright red blood on rectal examination strongly suggests the possibility of colonic bleeding. Bright red blood per rectum is always a colonic source unless it is accompanied by hypotension, which can occur during a severe upper gastrointestinal (UGI) or small bowel bleed with rapid transit of blood.[4] In the setting of hematochezia without hypotension, placement of a diagnostic nasogastric (NG) tube placement is usually unnecessary because it is unlikely that there is a severe UGI bleed without hypotension. If there is hypotension and hematochezia, a severe UGI bleed is possible, and an NG tube should be placed. A clear NG tube lavage does not always imply a lower GI source, because 16% of patients with duodenal ulcer bleeds have negative NG lavage.[5] If bile is seen in the NG tube lavage, it is unlikely to be an UGI bleed.

Physical examination should also focus on abdominal tenderness, surgical scars, and stigmata of liver disease. Most patients with severe hematochezia do not need placement of a NG tube for diagnostic lavage, unless there is a strong suspicion for an UGI source.

At least one large-bore (14- or 16-gauge) intravenous catheter should be placed, with two placed in the setting of ongoing bleeding. Blood should be sent for hematocrit, platelets, prothrombin time, partial thromboplastin time, chemistry panel, and type and cross-match for packed red blood cells. Resuscitation should be initiated simultaneously with assessment. Normal saline is infused as fast as needed to keep systolic blood pressure greater than 100 mm Hg and

Table 15–1. Early Predictors of Severity of Continued and/or Recurrent Lower Gastrointestinal Bleeding
Heart rate >100/min
Systolic blood pressure <115 mm Hg
Syncope
Nontender abdominal examination
Observed rectal bleeding during first 4 hours of hospital evaluation
Aspirin
More than two comorbid conditions
Strate LL, Orav EJ, Syngal S: Early predictors of severity in acute lower intestinal tract bleeding. Arch Intern Med 163:838–843, 2003, and Strate LL, Canale S, Ookubo R, et al: Risk stratification in acute lower intestinal bleeding: Prospective validation of a clinical prediction rule [abstract]. Gastroenterology 124:A-508, 2003.

pulse lower than 100 beats/minute. Patients are transfused with packed red blood cells, platelets, and fresh-frozen plasma as necessary to keep the hematocrit greater than 24%, platelet count greater than 50,000/mm^3, and prothrombin time less than 15 seconds. A GI endoscopist should be notified as soon as possible to expedite patient diagnosis and possible therapy. This is especially important in terms of coordinating timing of the bowel purge and procedure.

Most patients with lower GI bleeding can be admitted to internal medicine or gastroenterology services, rather than to the general surgery services, because these patients rarely require emergency surgical intervention and given their elderly age usually require management of their comorbid internal medicine type diseases. They should be admitted to an intensive care unit (ICU) or monitored intermediate care unit. Patients should have automatic blood pressure monitoring every 5 minutes if unstable and hourly if stable. Each patient should receive cardiac rhythm monitoring to observe for arrhythmias and to follow the heart rate as a sign of continued or recurrent bleeding. Laboratory-determined hematocrits (not finger-stick hematocrits, which are less reliable) should be obtained every 4 to 6 hours until the patient has a stable hematocrit. In cases of active bleeding, an indwelling bladder catheter should be placed to help monitor fluid status. Swan-Ganz catheter monitoring is unnecessary except for patients with a history of congestive heart failure or unstable cardiac disease. Patients older than the age of 60, or with risk factors for coronary artery disease, should also have serial electrocardiograms and cardiac enzyme evaluation to determine whether there is any cardiac ischemia.

Endoscopy of any sort should only be done when it can be performed safely and when the information may influence patient care. Patients should be medically resuscitated with fluids and transfusions before endoscopy. Ideally, they should be hemodynamically stable, with a heart rate of less than 100 beats/minute and systolic blood pressure greater than 100 mm Hg. The hematocrit, especially in elderly patients, should ideally be greater than 28%. Severe thrombocytopenia (platelet count less than 75,000/mm^3) should be corrected with transfusions before emergency endoscopy, and prolonged prothrombin time (>15 seconds) should be corrected with fresh-frozen plasma.

Middle-of-the-night endoscopy should be avoided if well-trained endoscopy nurses, appropriate endoscopy equipment, and surgical back-up are not available.

EARLY PREDICTORS OF SEVERITY IN ACUTE LOWER GASTROINTESTINAL BLEEDING

Early predictors (within 4 hours of admission) of severity for continued and/or recurrent bleeding after 24-hours of hospitalization include heart rate >100/min, systolic blood pressure <115 mmHg, syncope, nontender abdominal exam, observed rectal bleeding during the first four hours of hospital evaluation, aspirin, and more than two comorbid conditions (Table 15–1).[6] This prediction model has been prospectively validated, such that the low risk group had 0% rebleeding, the moderate risk group 45% rebleeding, and the high risk group 77% risk of rebleeding.[7] It is possible that factors such as these can be used to help triage patients to the appropriate level care, such as ICU, hospital ward, or outpatient evaluation, as well as urgent versus elective endoscopic evaluation.

MORTALITY OF HOSPITALIZED PATIENTS WITH SEVERE LOWER GASTROINTESTINAL BLEEDING

Patients who develop severe lower GI bleeding while hospitalized for other lesions have a much higher mortality rate than those admitted with lower GI bleeding. In a large Kaiser San Diego retrospective study, the in-hospital mortality rate for patients with lower GI bleeding that began as outpatients was 2.4%, compared with 23% for patients with in-hospital lower GI bleeding ($p < .001$).[1] Another study suggests that the mortality rate for patients in an ICU who begin having severe lower GI bleeding is 58%, with most of the bleeding coming from ischemic colitis.[8]

Diagnostic Options

Most patients will undergo initial evaluation with colonoscopy after bowel preparation, although in selected cases unprepped or enema-prepped flexible sigmoidoscopy may be performed. Other diagnostic tests may be used in selected cases or when colonoscopy is unsuccessful.

ANOSCOPY

Anoscopy can be useful if actively bleeding hemorrhoids are suspected. However, nearly every patient will require additional visualization of the more proximal colon using colonoscopy or possibly sigmoidoscopy.

FLEXIBLE SIGMOIDOSCOPY

Occasionally flexible sigmoidoscopy may be performed to quickly evaluate the left side of the colon for any bleeding site stigmata, rather than waiting for a full colonoscopy bowel preparation, and will result in a diagnosis in approximately 9% of cases.[9] This may be especially useful in patients with strongly suspected diverticular bleeding or ischemic colitis.

BARIUM ENEMA

There is no role for emergency barium enema in a patient with severe lower GI bleeding. This test is rarely diagnostic because it cannot demonstrate vascular lesions and may be misleading if only diverticula are present. It also fails to detect 50% of polyps greater than 10 mm in size.[10] Subsequent colonoscopy is needed for any suspicious lesions seen on barium enema, and no therapy can be performed.

NUCLEAR MEDICINE SCINTIGRAPHY

Nuclear medicine scintigraphy involves injecting a radiolabeled substance in the patient's bloodstream and then performing serial scintigraphy to detect focal collections of radiolabeled material. It has been reported to detect bleeding at a rate as low as 0.1 mL/minute.[11] The overall positive diagnostic rate is approximately 45%, with a 78% accuracy in the localization of the true bleeding site.[12] The most common false positive is when there is rapid transit of luminal blood such that labeled blood is detected in the colon although it originated in the UGI tract.

ANGIOGRAPHY

Angiography is positive when the arterial bleeding rate is at least 0.5 mL/minute.[13] The diagnostic yield depends on patient selection, timing of the procedure, and the skill of the angiographer, with positive yields in 12% to 69% of cases. An advantage of angiography is that embolization can be performed to control some bleeding lesions. However, there is also a 3% rate of major complications such as hematoma formation, femoral artery thrombosis, contrast dye reactions, renal failure, and transient ischemic attacks.[14]

COMPUTED TOMOGRAPHY COLONOGRAPHY

Computed tomography (CT) visualization of the colon is increasingly used to evaluate the colon for polyps and masses and may be of some benefit in lower GI bleeding. Faster scanners allow CT angiography, colonography, and evaluation of the small bowel to be performed. This potentially could allow diagnosis of both mass lesions and vascular lesions, which would be an advantage compared with the other radiologic imaging studies. One study from France reported that CT accurately diagnosed 17 of 19 lower GI bleeding sites, including diverticula, tumors, angiomas, and varices.[15]

COLONOSCOPY

Urgent colonoscopy using a rapid sulfate purge has been shown to be safe, to provide important diagnostic information, and sometimes to allow therapeutic intervention.[16] Patients usually ingest 4 to 6 L of polyethylene glycol (i.e., GoLYTELY) either orally or via NG tube over 3 to 5 hours until the rectal effluent is clear of stool, blood, and clots. Metoclopramide 10 mg may be given intravenously before the purge and repeated every 3 to 4 hours to facilitate gastric emptying and reduce nausea. It is probably best to avoid phosphosoda bowel preparations on suspected lower GI bleed patients because of potential risks of the high phosphate and sodium loads, although this has not been well studied.

Most "urgent" colonoscopy for lower GI bleeds is performed anywhere between 6 to 36 hours after the patient is admitted to the hospital. Because most bleeding stops spontaneously, cases are often performed more electively the day after initial hospitalization to allow the patient to receive blood transfusions and to have the bowel prep during the first day of hospitalization.

The overall diagnostic yield of a presumed or definite etiology using colonoscopy in lower GI bleeding ranges from 48% to 90%, with an average of 68%, based on a review of 13 studies.[12] The problem with interpreting these data is that it is often not possible to have a definite diagnosis of the cause of the bleeding unless bleeding stigmata are identified such as active bleeding, a visible vessel, an adherent clot, mucosal friability or ulceration, or the presence of fresh blood limited to a specific part of the colon. Many times a presumptive diagnosis will be made, especially in the case of diverticulosis, in which no blood is seen, but there is a potential bleeding site present.

The optimal time for performing urgent bowel preparation and colonoscopy is unknown. Theoretically, the sooner the endoscopy was performed, the higher the likelihood of finding a lesion that might be amenable to endoscopic hemostasis, such as a bleeding diverticulum or polyp stalk. However, a retrospective from Mayo Clinic suggested that there was no significant association between the time of endoscopy (0 to 12 hours, 12 to 24 hours, >24 hours) and the findings of active bleeding or other stigmata that would prompt colonoscopic hemostasis in patients with diverticular bleeding.[17] Early colonoscopy has been associated with shorter lengths of hospitalization days.[18]

Active bleeding or lesions at risk for rebleeding can be treated with colonoscopic hemostasis. This mostly applies to postpolypectomy bleeding and diverticula and is discussed later.

SURGERY

Surgical management is rarely needed for lower GI bleeding because most bleeding is either self-limited or easily managed with medical or endoscopic therapy. The main indications for surgery are malignant lesions and recurrent bleeding from diverticula. For this reason, it seems prudent that most stable patients be managed by internists and gastroenterologists, rather than surgical services.

Etiology and Pathogenesis of Severe Lower Gastrointestinal Bleeding

It is not always possible to visualize active bleeding during colonoscopy. The timing of endoscopy may influence this, in that earlier colonoscopy should increase the chances of detecting an actively bleeding lesion. A definite diagnosis of a bleeding lesion can usually be made if active bleeding is seen or there is an obvious stigma, such as clot or visible vessel. A presumptive diagnosis can be made if there is a suspicious lesion and no other possible sources. Table 15–2 shows the frequency of various presumed and/or definite sites of acute colonic bleeding. Potential colonic lesions amenable to endoscopic hemostasis include diverticula, postpolypectomy sites, angiomas, hemorrhoids, Dieulafoy's lesions, tumors, ulcers, and radiation proctitis.

Table 15–2. Etiology of Severe Lower Gastrointestinal Bleeding*	
Cause	Percent of Cases
Diverticulosis	33
Cancer/polyps	19
Colitis	18
Unknown	16
Angiodysplasia	8
Other	8
Postpolypectomy	6
Anorectal	4

*Summary of 1333 patients in seven published studies.
From Zuckerman GR, Prakash C: Acute lower intestinal bleeding. Part II: Etiology, therapy, and outcomes. Gastrointest Endosc 49:228–238, 1999.

DIVERTICULAR BLEEDING

Colonic diverticula are herniations of colonic mucosa and submucosa through the muscular layers of the colon. Diverticula in the colon are actually pathologic pseudodiverticula, because true diverticula contain all layers of the intestinal wall. Colonic diverticula seem to form when colonic tissue is pushed out by intraluminal pressure. Diverticula occur at the point of entry of the small arteries that supply the colon, the vasa recta, as they penetrate the circular muscle layer of the colonic wall. The entry points of the vasa recta are areas of relative weakness through which the mucosa and submucosa can herniate when under increased intraluminal pressure. They vary in diameter from a few milliliters to several centimeters. The most common location is the left colon. Most colonic diverticula are asymptomatic and remain uncomplicated.

Bleeding may occur from vessels at the neck or base of the diverticulum[19] (Fig 15–1).

Diverticula are common in Western countries, with a prevalence of 50% in older adults.[20] In contrast, fewer than 1% of continental African and Asian populations have diverticula.[21] This has lead to the hypothesis that regional differences in prevalence can be explained by the low amounts of dietary fiber in Western diets.

Presumably, the low-fiber diet results in less stool content, longer fecal transit time, increased colonic muscle contraction, and, ultimately, increased intraluminal pressure that results in the formation of propulsion diverticula. In addition, diverticula occur with increasing frequency with advanced age, which could be a result of weakening of the colonic wall and muscle tone. It has been estimated that 3% to 5% of patients with diverticulosis develop diverticular bleeding.[22] Although most diverticula are in the left colon, several series suggest that bleeding diverticula occur more often in the right colon.[19,22–24]

Patients with diverticular bleeding are typically elderly and present with *painless* hematochezia. They often have been taking aspirin or NSAIDS.[2] At least 75% of patients with diverticular bleeding stops spontaneously.[23] Those patients who stop bleeding usually require fewer than 4 units of blood. In one surgical series, surgical resection was needed in 60% of patients, most of whom had continued bleeding despite transfusion of 4 units of blood.[23] Patients with successful resection of a bleeding diverticulum had a rebleed rate of 4%.[23] Among patients who have stopped bleeding spontaneously, the rebleeding rate from colon diverticulosis is between 25% to 38% over the next 4 years.[1,23]

Urgent colonoscopy after rapid bowel preparation often reveals that patients have stopped bleeding by the time of colonoscopy, and only nonbleeding diverticula are detected. These patients are given the diagnosis of "presumptive diverticular bleed," because the diverticula are the only likely source of bleeding although no stigmata were identified.

Occasionally, urgent colonoscopy reveals stigmata of recent bleeding, such as active bleeding, a visible vessel, clot, or blood limited to one segment of the colon (Fig. 15–2). It seems possible that earlier colonoscopy in lower GI bleeding would result in a greater frequency of finding stigmata of recent diverticular bleeding, although a small case-series study from Mayo Clinic did not find any difference if colonoscopy was performed between 0 to 12 hours, 12 to 24 hours, or greater than 24 hours from the time of hospital admission.[17] There have been attempts to stratify diverticular bleeding at increased risk for rebleeding using the same endoscopic stigmata used in high-risk peptic ulcer bleeding (active bleeding, visible vessel, and clot), although the natural history for each

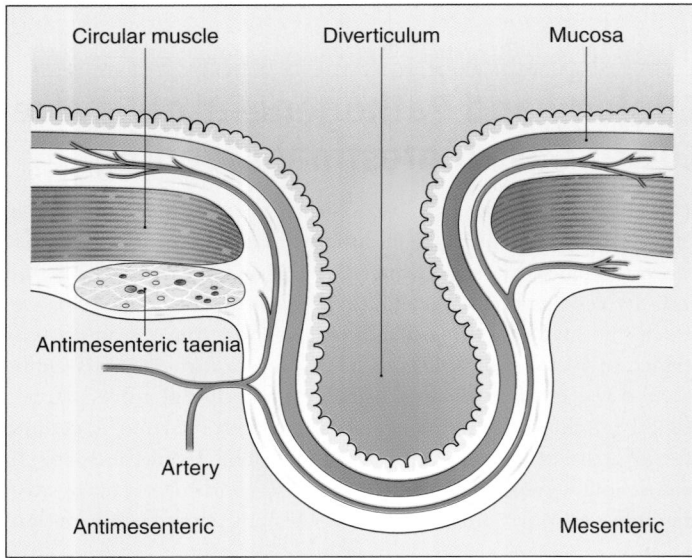

Figure 15–1. Vascular anatomy of colonic diverticulum.

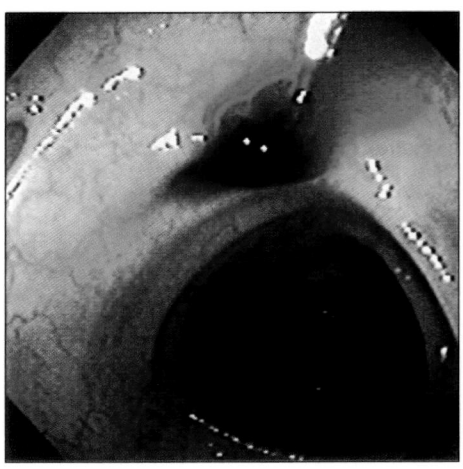

Figure 15–2. Active diverticular bleeding.

of these untreated stigmata is unknown. The "pigmented pro-tuberance" found on the edge of some diverticula at histopathology is usually clot at the edge of a ruptured blood vessel.[25] The UCLA/CURE group found that among 17 patients with stigmata of recent diverticular hemorrhage (6 active bleeding, 4 visible vessels, and 7 adherent clots) there was a very high rebleed rate of 53% and emergency surgery rate of 35%.[26]

Colonoscopic hemostasis of actively bleeding diverticula has been reported using bipolar probe coagulation, epinephrine injection, metallic clips, and fibrin glue.[25-32] If fresh red blood is seen in a focal segment of colon, then we try to carefully examine this segment of bowel to detect the exact bleeding site. If the bleeding is coming from the edge of the diverticulum or there is a pigmented protuberance on the edge, then we will initially inject 1:10,000 epinephrine in 1-mL aliquots using a sclerotherapy needle into four quadrants around the bleeding site. Then we use a bipolar probe at a low power setting (10 to 15 watts) and light pressure for a 1-second pulse duration to cauterize the diverticular edge and stop bleeding or flatten the visible vessel. If there is a nonbleeding adherent clot, we inject around the clot with 1:10,000 epinephrine in four quadrants with 1 mL per quadrant and then remove the clot in piecemeal fashion using a cold polyp snare. The clot is shaved down until it is 3 mm above the diverticulum, and then the underlying stigma is treated with bipolar probe coagulation as discussed previously.

After performing endoscopic hemostasis of a bleeding diverticulum, a permanent submucosal tattoo (India ink or SPOT) should always be placed in the adjacent mucosa to identify the site in case repeated colonoscopy or surgery is required for recurrent bleeding. For long-term management after colonoscopic hemostasis, patients are told to avoid aspirin and NSAIDs and to take a daily fiber supplement.

In 2000, Jensen and the UCLA/CURE group published their results on urgent colonoscopy for diagnosis and treatment of severe diverticular hemorrhage.[26] They found that 20% of patients with severe hematochezia had endoscopic stigmata suggesting a definite diverticular bleed. Compared with a historical control group with high-risk stigmata but no colonoscopic hemostasis, the group receiving colonoscopic hemostasis had a rebleed rate of 0% versus 53% and an emergency hemicolectomy rate of 0% compared with 35%. There were no rebleeding episodes in the patients who underwent colonoscopic hemostasis, after 3 years of follow-up.

In contrast to the UCLA experience, a smaller, retrospective review of the Duke University Medical Center Endoscopic Database revealed 13 patients with active bleeding or stigmata who received endoscopic treatment with epinephrine and/or bipolar coagulation.[33] Their 30-day rebleed rate was 38%, of whom four underwent surgery. Their long-term rebleed rate was 23% with a mean follow-up of 3 years.

Angiographic embolization can also be performed in selected cases of diverticular bleeding, but there is a risk of bowel infarction, contrast reactions, and renal failure. Angiography can be helpful before surgical resection.

Surgical resection for diverticular bleeding is usually reserved for recurrent bleeding episodes. It is best if guided by either colonoscopic, angiographic, or nuclear medicine studies showing the likely bleeding site. The need for surgery is often guided by certainty as to the bleeding site and medical comorbidity because diverticular

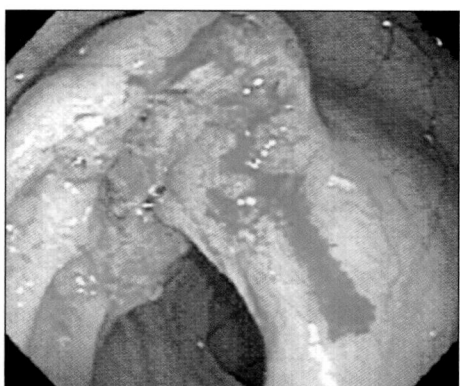

Figure 15–3. Colon cancer as a cause of severe hematochezia.

bleeding is often mild and the risks of surgical complications are increased in elderly patients.

COLON CANCER

Most patients with colon cancer present with occult GI blood loss rather than hematochezia. For adult patients with hematochezia, determining the presence or absence of a colon cancer is imperative, because early diagnosis improves survival. Because a cancer must ulcerate for overt bleeding to occur, most bleeding cancers present at a relatively advanced tumor stage (Fig. 15–3). Colon cancer can occur anywhere in the colon or rectum, but there is increased prevalence of right-sided tumors in elderly patients.

COLITIS

The term *colitis* refers to any form of inflammation of the colon. With regards to severe lower GI bleeding, this is usually ischemic colitis, inflammatory bowel disease, or possibly infectious colitis.

Ischemic colitis generally presents as hematochezia with mild left-sided abdominal discomfort. It results from mucosal hypoxia and is thought to be caused by hypoperfusion of the intramural vessels of the intestinal wall rather than by large vessel occlusion. Most cases do not have a recognizable cause, but associated conditions include recent aortic or cardiac surgery, vasculitis, and medications.[34,35] Because of collateral circulation, the ischemic involvement is usually segmental and primarily affects the mucosal aspect of the intestine. The colon is mostly affected in the watershed areas, such as the splenic flexure or rectosigmoid junction in which there is reduced collateral circulation, although ischemia can occur anywhere. The diagnosis is usually made by colonoscopy but can be suspected by "thumb-printing" on plain film radiographs or colonic wall thickening on CT scan. The colonoscopic appearance includes erythema, friability, and exudate (Fig. 15–4). Biopsies may be suggestive of ischemic changes but more importantly are used to exclude infectious changes or Crohn's disease. Ischemic colitis generally resolves in a few days and does not require colonoscopic hemostasis. In a large retrospective series from Kaiser, over a 4-year period there were no episodes of rebleeding from ischemic colitis.[1]

Inflammatory bowel disease affecting the colon can rarely cause severe acute lower GI bleeding. In a case series from the Mayo

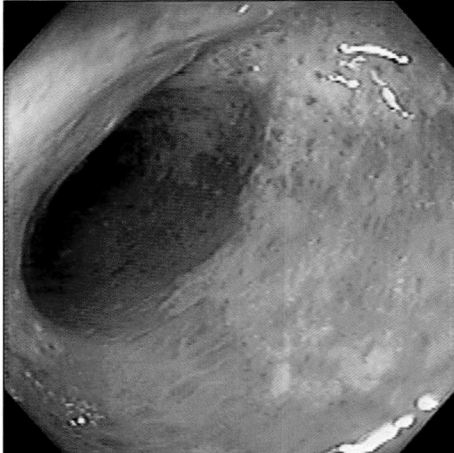

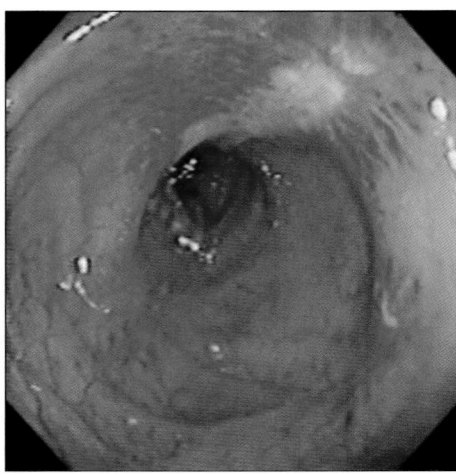

Figure 15-4. Ischemic colitis.

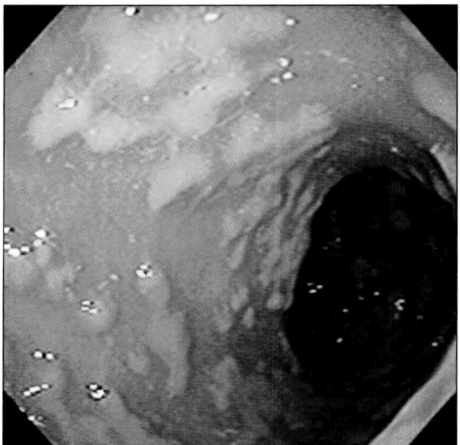

Figure 15-5. *Clostridium difficile* colitis.

Clinic, most patients had Crohn's disease.[36] Most patients were successfully treated medically. Three of the 31 patients in the series received endoscopic therapy with epinephrine injection alone or with bipolar coagulation, for adherent clots or oozing ulcers in Crohn's disease. These patients had no rebleeding. Twenty-three percent of patients had rebleeding a median of 3 days after the initial bleed (range 1 to 75 days). Thirty-nine percent of the Crohn's disease patients with severe bleeding required surgical management.

Infectious colitis should always be excluded in any patient with severe lower GI bleeding and colitis. Lower GI bleeding can occur with infection by *Campylobacter jejuni*, *Salmonella*, *Shigella*, invasive *Escherichia coli*, *E. coli* 0157, or *Clostridium difficile* (Fig. 15–5). Rarely is there significant blood loss. Diagnosis is made by stool cultures and flexible sigmoidoscopy.

ANGIODYSPLASIA

Colonic angiomas are also referred to as angiodysplasia, arteriovenous malformations, or vascular ectasias. They are generally uncommon, in that less than 1% of asymptomatic patients undergoing screening colonoscopy were found to have angiodysplasia.[37] The lesions seems to increase with age and may represent degeneration of previously normal blood vessels in the cecum and proximal ascending colon. Histopathology reveals a large, dilated, submucosal vein and, in advanced cases, dilated mucosal veins with small arteriovenous communications. Proposed explanations for angioma formation include the partial obstruction of submucosal veins passing through the colonic muscle layers, with eventual dilation of the submucosal and mucosal veins, and local mucosal ischemia.

Medical conditions associated with angiomas include chronic renal failure and hereditary hemorrhagic telangiectasia (Osler-Weber-Rendu syndrome). There have been reports suggesting that aortic stenosis is associated with lower GI bleeding, presumably from colonic angiomas.[38] The potential biologic explanation for this is that aortic stenosis causes defects in von Willebrand factor, which causes the patient to have decreased platelet adhesion and increased bleeding tendency, especially if there were preexisting mucosal GI lesions such as angiomas.[39,40] However, clinical studies do not support the association between aortic stenosis and the presence of angiomas.[41,42]

Bleeding from angiodysplasia is usually painless. The bleeding usually occurs from the right colon or cecum. In the past decade, it seems that the reported frequency of angiomas as the source of lower GI bleeding has decreased.[16,26] This may be because of better recognition of angiomas with improved endoscope technology and increased attribution to presumed diverticular bleeding as the cause of hematochezia. Endoscopic hemostasis has been successfully reported using thermal modalities (bipolar probe, heater probe, laser) and injection therapy.[43] Hormonal therapy has been reported as useful for decreasing bleeding from angiodysplasia, but a recent randomized controlled trial found no benefit.[44]

POSTPOLYPECTOMY BLEEDING

Postpolypectomy bleeding occurs after 1% to 6% of polypectomies, usually within the first 7 days.[45] It is generally mild and self-limited. Reported risk factors for postpolypectomy bleeding include large

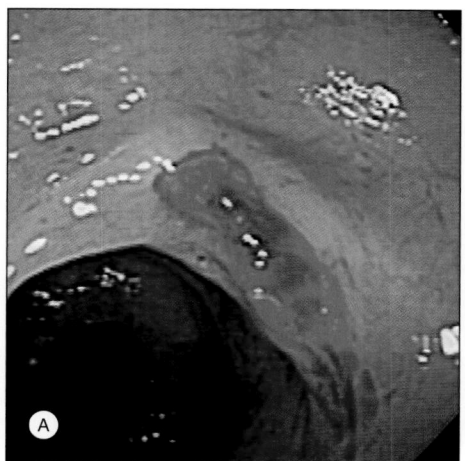 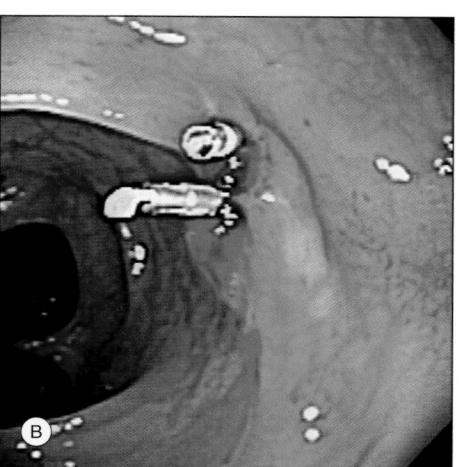

Figure 15–6. *A,* Postpolypectomy bleeding. *B,* Polypectomy site after placement of clips.

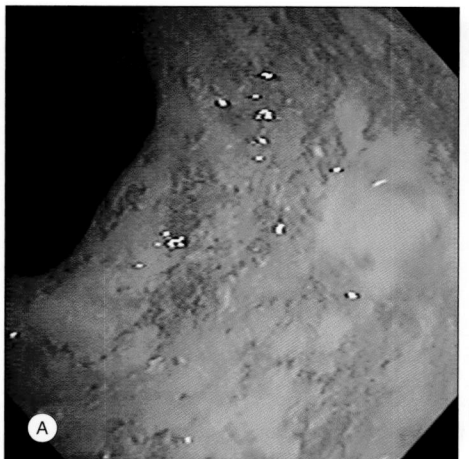 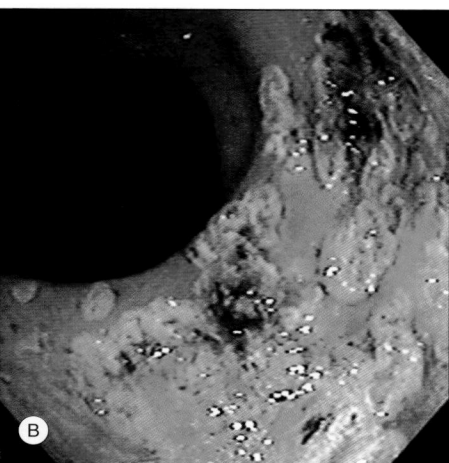

Figure 15–7. *A,* Radiation proctitis. *B,* Radiation proctitis after argon plasma coagulation.

polyps (>2 cm), thick stalks, sessile polyps, and right colon polyps.[45] Endoscopic management techniques include resnaring the stalk (without cautery), epinephrine injection, thermal coagulation, hemoclips, and endoloops (Fig. 15–6).[45–48]

A case series from the Mayo Clinic revealed the median time to bleeding after polypectomy was 5 days (range 0 to 17).[47] Sixty-five percent of patients received aspirin, NSAIDs, coumadin, heparin, or steroids after polypectomy; 76% of these patients required transfusions; and 96% were managed endoscopically with coagulation and/or epinephrine injection.

The *routine* use of placing hemoclips after colonic polypectomy or endoscopic mucosal resection does not decrease the subsequent postpolypectomy bleeding rate.[49] However, in selected patients who have had polypectomies and who were felt to be at increased risk for bleeding, prophylactic hemoclip placement or other endoscopic hemostasis may be considered.

RADIATION PROCTITIS

Radiation proctitis usually causes mild chronic hematochezia but occasionally can cause acute severe lower GI bleeding. Ionizing radiation can cause acute and chronic damage to the normal colon and rectum after radiation treatment for gynecologic, prostatic, bladder, or rectal tumors. Approximately 75% of patients who receive 4000 rads will develop acute, self-limited diarrhea, tenesmus, abdominal cramping, and rarely bleeding during the first few weeks. Chronic radiation effects occur 6 to 18 months after completion of treatment. Bowel injury resulting from chronic radiation is related to vascular damage, with subsequent mucosal ischemia, thickening, and ulceration. Much of this damage is felt to be due to chronic hypoxic ischemia and oxidative stress.

Flexible sigmoidoscopy reveals telangiectasia, friability, and ulceration in the rectum. Patients should be instructed to avoid all aspirin and NSAIDS and should be put on a high-fiber diet. Medical therapies with topic or oral 5-aminosalicylic acid, sucralfate, or steroids can be tried but are usually not successful.[50] Thermal therapy can be quite successful, including laser or argon plasma coagulation (Fig. 15–7).[51–53] Topical formalin applied directly to the rectal mucosa can reduce bleeding.[54] In refractory cases, hyperbaric oxygen can also provide successful management.[55,56] A few pilot studies suggest that antioxidant vitamins, such as vitamin A, C, and E, can also decrease bleeding from chronic radiation proctitis.[57]

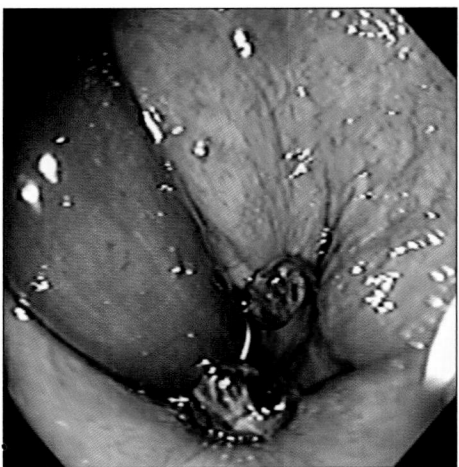

Figure 15–8. Hemorrhoid banding.

HEMORRHOIDS

Hemorrhoids are a plexus of veins just above the rectal squamocolumnar junction. Internal hemorrhoids are located above the dentate line, and external hemorrhoids are located below the dentate line. Symptomatic hemorrhoids are common in adults, mostly associated with prolonged straining during bowel movements, chronic constipation, pregnancy, obesity, and low-fiber diet. Bleeding is characterized by bright red blood per rectum that can coat the outside of the stool, may drip into the toilet bowel, and is present when wiping with tissue. Usually this is mild bleeding, but occasionally severe bleeding may occur from hemorrhoids.

The treatment of hemorrhoids usually starts with medical therapy consisting of fiber supplementation to soften stool, lubricant rectal suppositories (with or without steroids), and warm sitz baths. Anoscopic therapy can also be used including injection sclerotherapy, rubber band ligation, cryosurgery, infrared photocoagulation, and bipolar and direct current electrocoagulation. Recently, the use of a flexible endoscope and esophageal band ligation devices have also been described (Fig. 15–8).[58] Surgery is reserved for refractory bleeding not controlled with other mechanisms. Most patients respond to medical management.

RECTAL VARICES

In response to portal hypertension, varices can develop in the rectal mucosa between the superior hemorrhoidal veins (portal circulation) and the middle and inferior hemorrhoidal veins (systemic circulation). With anoscopy or sigmoidoscopy, rectal varices are seen as vascular structures located several centimeters above the dentate line. The incidence of rectal varices increases with the degree of portal hypertension. About 60% of patients with a history of bleeding esophageal varices have rectal varices. Rectal varices can be treated similarly to esophageal varices, with sclerotherapy, rubber band ligation, or portosystemic shunts.[59,60]

RECTAL DIEULAFOY'S LESION

Dieulafoy's lesions are large submucosal arteries without overlying mucosal ulceration, which can cause massive bleeding from any-

where in the GI tract, although bleeding is usually from the stomach. There have been reports of bleeding Dieulafoy's lesions in the rectum that were treated successfully with endoscopic hemostasis.[61,62]

Summary

The source of severe lower GI bleeding can usually be diagnosed by urgent colonoscopy. The differential diagnosis of lower GI bleeding includes diverticulosis, cancer, colitis, angiomas, postpolypectomy sites, radiation proctitis, internal hemorrhoids, and rectal varices. Patients should be stabilized with medical resuscitation and transfusion before urgent colonoscopy. Urgent colonic purge allows for earlier colonoscopy and the increased possibility for colonoscopic hemostasis. Bleeding diverticula and postpolypectomy bleeding can be treated with epinephrine injection, bipolar coagulation, and/or clipping. Radiation proctitis and angiomas can be treated with thermal coagulation. Most patients who have successful colonoscopic hemostasis will not have rebleeding. After endoscopic hemostasis, medical management can often help reduce the chances of rebleeding. Urgent colonoscopy should be performed in all patients with severe hematochezia suspected to have a lower GI bleed.

REFERENCES

1. Longstreth GF: Epidemiology and outcome of patients hospitalized with acute lower gastrointestinal hemorrhage: A population-based study. Am J Gastroenterol 92:419–424, 1997.
2. Foutch PG: Diverticular bleeding: Are nonsteroidal anti-inflammatory drugs risk factors for hemorrhage and can colonoscopy predict outcome for patients? Am J Gastroenterol 90:1779–1784, 1995.
3. Laine L, Connors LG, Reicin A, et al: Serious lower gastrointestinal clinical events with nonselective NSAID or coxib use. Gastroenterology 124:288–292, 2003.
4. Zuckerman GR, Trellis DR, Sherman TM, Clouse RE: An objective measure of stool color for differentiating upper from lower gastrointestinal bleeding. Dig Dis Sci 40:1614–1621, 1995.
5. Gilbert DA, Silverstein FE, Tedesco FJ, et al: The national ASGE survey on upper gastrointestinal bleeding. III. Endoscopy in upper gastrointestinal bleeding. Gastrointest Endosc 27:94–102, 1981.
6. Strate LL, Orav EJ, Syngal S: Early predictors of severity in acute lower intestinal tract bleeding. Arch Intern Med 163:838–843, 2003.
7. Strate LL, Canale S, Ookubo R, et al: Risk stratification in acute lower intestinal bleeding: Prospective validation of a clinical prediction rule [abstract]. Gastroenterology 124:A-508, 2003.
8. Probst A, Hunstiger M, Barnert J, et al: Characteristics of lower GI bleeding in critically ill patients—bleeding source and prognosis. Gastrointest Endosc 57:AB215, 2003.
9. Richter JM, Christensen MR, Kaplan LM, Nishioka NS: Effectiveness of current technology in the diagnosis and management of lower gastrointestinal hemorrhage. Gastrointest Endosc 41:93–98, 1995.
10. Winawer SJ, Stewart ET, Zauber AG, et al: A comparison of colonoscopy and double-contrast barium enema for surveillance after polypectomy. National Polyp Study Work Group. N Engl J Med 342:1766–1772, 2000.
11. Nicholson ML, Neoptolemos JP, Sharp JF, et al: Localization of lower gastrointestinal bleeding using in vivo technetium-99m-labelled red blood cell scintigraphy. Br J Surg 76:358–361, 1989.

12. Zuckerman GR, Prakash C: Acute lower intestinal bleeding: Part I: Clinical presentation and diagnosis. Gastrointest Endosc 48:606–617, 1998.

13. Baum S: Angiography and the gastrointestinal bleeder. Radiology 143:569–572, 1982.

14. Egglin TK, O'Moore PV, Feinstein AR, Waltman AC: Complications of peripheral arteriography: A new system to identify patients at increased risk. J Vasc Surg 22:787–794, 1995.

15. Ernst O, Bulois P, Saint-Drenant S, et al: Helical CT in acute lower gastrointestinal bleeding. Eur Radiol 13:114–117, 2003.

16. Jensen DM, Machicado GA: Diagnosis and treatment of severe hematochezia. The role of urgent colonoscopy after purge. Gastroenterology 95:1569–1574, 1988.

17. Smoot R, Gostout CJ, Rajan E, et al: Is early colonoscopy for acute diverticular bleeding needed? Gastrointest Endosc 55:AB123, 2002.

18. Strate LL, Syngal S: Timing of colonoscopy: Impact on length of hospital stay in patients with acute lower intestinal bleeding. Am J Gastroenterol 98:317–322, 2003.

19. Meyers MA, Alonso DR, Gray GF, Baer JW: Pathogenesis of bleeding colonic diverticulosis. Gastroenterology 71:577–583, 1976.

20. Stollman NH, Raskin JB: Diagnosis and management of diverticular disease of the colon in adults. Ad Hoc Practice Parameters Committee of the American College of Gastroenterology. Am J Gastroenterol 94:3110–3121, 1999.

21. Painter NS, Burkitt DP: Diverticular disease of the colon: A deficiency disease of Western civilization. Br Med J 2:450–454, 1971.

22. McGuire HH Jr, Haynes BW Jr: Massive hemorrhage for diverticulosis of the colon: Guidelines for therapy based on bleeding patterns observed in fifty cases. Ann Surg 175:847–855. 1972.

23. McGuire HH Jr: Bleeding colonic diverticula. A reappraisal of natural history and management. Ann Surg 220:653–656, 1994.

24. Wong SK, Ho YH, Leong AP, Seow-Choen F: Clinical behavior of complicated right-sided and left-sided diverticulosis. Dis Colon Rectum 40:344–348, 1997.

25. Foutch PG, Zimmerman K: Diverticular bleeding and the pigmented protuberance (sentinel clot): Clinical implications, histopathological correlation, and results of endoscopic intervention. Am J Gastroenterol 91:2589–2593, 1996.

26. Jensen DM, Machicado GA, Jutabha R, Kovacs TO: Urgent colonoscopy for the diagnosis and treatment of severe diverticular hemorrhage. N Engl J Med 342:78–82, 2000.

27. Yoshikane H, Sakakibara A, Ayakawa T, et al: Hemostasis by capping bleeding diverticulum of the colon with clips. Endoscopy 29:S33–S34, 1997.

28. Ramirez FC, Johnson DA, Zierer ST, et al: Successful endoscopic hemostasis of bleeding colonic diverticula with epinephrine injection. Gastrointest Endosc 43(2 Pt 1):167–170, 1996.

29. Savides TJ, Jensen DM: Colonoscopic hemostasis for recurrent diverticular hemorrhage associated with a visible vessel: A report of three cases. Gastrointest Endosc 40:70–73, 1994.

30. Lara LF, Bloomfeld RS: Endoscopic therapy for acute diverticular hemorrhage. Gastrointest Endosc 53:492, 2001.

31. Kim YI, Marcon NE: Injection therapy for colonic diverticular bleeding. A case study. J Clin Gastroenterol 17:46–48, 1993.

32. Andress HJ, Mewes A, Lange V: Endoscopic hemostasis of a bleeding diverticulum of the sigma with fibrin sealant. Endoscopy 25:193, 1993.

33. Bloomfeld RS, Rockey DC, Shetzline MA: Endoscopic therapy of acute diverticular hemorrhage. Am J Gastroenterol 96:2367–2372, 2001.

34. Brandt LJ, Boley SJ: AGA technical review on intestinal ischemia. American Gastrointestinal Association. Gastroenterology 118:954–968, 2000.

35. Brandt LJ, Boley SJ: Intestinal ischemia. In Feldman M, Friedman LS, Sleisenger MH (eds): Gastrointestinal and Liver Disease. Philadelphia, WB Saunders, 2002, pp 2321–2340.

36. Pardi DS, Loftus EV Jr, Tremaine WJ, et al: Acute major gastrointestinal hemorrhage in inflammatory bowel disease. Gastrointest Endosc 49:153–157, 1999.

37. Foutch PG, Rex DK, Lieberman DA: Prevalence and natural history of colonic angiodysplasia among healthy asymptomatic people. Am J Gastroenterol 90:564–567, 1995.

38. Heyde EC: Gastrointestinal bleeding in aortic stenosis. N Engl J Med 259:196, 1958.

39. Vincentelli A, Susen S, Le Tourneau T, et al: Acquired von Willebrand syndrome in aortic stenosis. N Engl J Med 349:343–349, 2003.

40. Sadler JE: Aortic stenosis, von Willebrand factor, and bleeding. N Engl J Med 349:323–325, 2003.

41. Imperiale TF, Ransohoff DF: Aortic stenosis, idiopathic gastrointestinal bleeding, and angiodysplasia: Is there an association? A methodologic critique of the literature. Gastroenterology 95:1670–1676, 1988.

42. Bhutani MS, Gupta SC, Markert RJ, et al: A prospective controlled evaluation of endoscopic detection of angiodysplasia and its association with aortic valve disease. Gastrointest Endosc 42:398–402, 1995.

43. Foutch PG: Angiodysplasia of the gastrointestinal tract. Am J Gastroenterol 88:807–818, 1993.

44. Junquera F, Feu F, Papo M, et al: A multicenter, randomized, clinical trial of hormonal therapy in the prevention of rebleeding from gastrointestinal angiodysplasia. Gastroenterology 121:1073–1079, 2001.

45. Waye JD, Kahn O, Auerbach ME: Complications of colonoscopy and flexible sigmoidoscopy. Gastrointest Endosc Clin N Am 6:343–377, 1996.

46. Uno Y, Satoh K, Tuji K, et al: Endoscopic ligation by means of clip and detachable snare for management of colonic postpolypectomy hemorrhage. Gastrointest Endosc 49:113–115, 1999.

47. Sorbi D, Norton I, Conio M, et al: Postpolypectomy lower GI bleeding: Descriptive analysis. Gastrointest Endosc 51:690–696, 2000.

48. Parra-Blanco A, Kaminaga N, Kojima T, et al: Hemoclipping for postpolypectomy and postbiopsy colonic bleeding. Gastrointest Endosc 51:37–41, 2000.

49. Shioji K, Suzuki Y, Kobayashi M, et al: Prophylactic clip application does not decrease delayed bleeding after colonoscopic polypectomy. Gastrointest Endosc 57:691–694, 2003.

50. Baum CA, Biddle WL, Miner PB Jr: Failure of 5-aminosalicylic acid enemas to improve chronic radiation proctitis. Dig Dis Sci 34:758–760, 1989.

51. Swaroop VS, Gostout CJ: Endoscopic treatment of chronic radiation proctopathy. J Clin Gastroenterol 27:36–40, 1998.

52. Taieb S, Rolachon A, Cenni JC, et al: Effective use of argon plasma coagulation in the treatment of severe radiation proctitis. Dis Colon Rectum 44:1766–1771, 2001.

53. Villavicencio RT, Rex DK, Rahmani E: Efficacy and complications of argon plasma coagulation for hematochezia related to radiation proctopathy. Gastrointest Endosc 55:70–74, 2002.

54. Parikh S, Hughes C, Salvati EP, et al: Treatment of hemorrhagic radiation proctitis with 4 percent formalin. Dis Colon Rectum 46:596–600, 2003.

55. Woo TC, Joseph D, Oxer H: Hyperbaric oxygen treatment for radiation proctitis. Int J Radiat Oncol Biol Phys 38:619–622, 1997.

56. Mayer R, Klemen H, Quehenberger F, et al: Hyperbaric oxygen—an effective tool to treat radiation morbidity in prostate cancer. Radiother Oncol 61:151–156, 2001.

57. Kennedy M, Bruninga K, Mutlu EA, et al: Successful and sustained treatment of chronic radiation proctitis with antioxidant vitamins E and C. Am J Gastroenterol 96:1080–1084, 2001.

58. Berkelhammer C, Moosvi SB: Retroflexed endoscopic band ligation of bleeding internal hemorrhoids. Gastrointest Endosc 55:532–537, 2002.

59. Hosking SW, Smart HL, Johnson AG, Triger DR: Anorectal varices, haemorrhoids, and portal hypertension. Lancet 1:349–352, 1989.

60. Firoozi B, Gamagaris Z, Weinshel EH, Bini EJ: Endoscopic band ligation of bleeding rectal varices. Dig Dis Sci 47:1502–1505, 2002.

61. Abdulian JD, Santoro MJ, Chen YK, Collen MJ: Dieulafoy-like lesion of the rectum presenting with exsanguinating hemorrhage: Successful endoscopic sclerotherapy. Am J Gastroenterol 88:1939–1941, 1993.

62. Meister TE, Varilek GW, Marsano LS, et al: Endoscopic management of rectal Dieulafoy-like lesions: A case series and review of literature. Gastrointest Endosc 48:302–305, 1998.

63. Zuckerman GR, Prakash C: Acute lower intestinal bleeding. Part II: Etiology, therapy, and outcomes. Gastrointest Endosc 49:228–238, 1999.

Obscure Gastrointestinal Bleeding

Blair S. Lewis

Introduction

Patients with obscure gastrointestinal (GI) bleeding are a minority of patients with bleeding but remain a unique and challenging set of patients to manage. These are patients who present with bleeding, either overtly with melena or maroon stools or occultly with iron deficiency anemia, and whose bleeding site is not detected despite evaluation with colonoscopy and upper endoscopy. Nearly one third of patients with isolated iron deficiency anemia rebleed and half of patients with overt bleeding rebleed. Often multiple transfusions are required to support these patients in whom repeated examinations by colonoscopy, upper intestinal endoscopy, barium enema, upper GI series, and bleeding scan are negative. In this group of patients, an early diagnosis of the bleeding site is rarely made.[1] The small intestine, beyond the duodenal bulb where inflammatory changes are common, is the most common location of the bleeding site in these patients despite it generally being an uncommon site of hemorrhage.[2] It is estimated that only 3% to 5% of all patients with GI bleeding have the site located between the second portion of the duodenum and the ileocecal valve.[3] Bleeding within the small bowel, unless massive, is often difficult to diagnose. Several factors are responsible for the inability to find the source of small bowel blood loss. In addition to being an unusual site of bleeding and thereby not routinely considered, the small bowel is relatively inaccessible as compared with the stomach and colon. The length of the small intestine, in addition to its free intraperitoneal location, vigorous contractility, and overlying loops confounds the usual diagnostic techniques. In addition to these technical problems, the bleeding rate may be slow or intermittent thereby not allowing identification by either angiography or bleeding scan. The yield of a small bowel series for diagnosing tumors of the small intestine is quite low and barium studies, even enteroclysis, cannot diagnose angioectasias, which are the most common cause of small intestinal bleeding. The distal small intestine has been relatively inaccessible to endoscopic intubation despite the development of various enteroscopes. Because of the inability to localize a bleeding site in the small bowel, these patients may present with prolonged occult blood loss or recurrent episodes of melena or maroon stool without a specific diagnosis.

It should be mentioned that although most physicians identify obscure bleeding with small intestinal bleeding, there are other sites of blood loss that can be overlooked. These causes include epistaxis, hemobilia, and even hemorrhoidal bleeding. Vascular lesions discussed in the sections ahead can also occur in the stomach or colon and can be missed because of incomplete examinations, poor patient preparation, or examination performance while the patient is anemic or hypotensive.

Patients with obscure bleeding by definition present with prolonged occult blood loss or recurrent episodes of melena or maroon stool without a specific diagnosis. In addition to the inability to diagnose patients with obscure GI bleeding, physicians who care for these patients are rightly concerned that the patient may have an occult malignancy. One of ten patients with obscure bleeding will have a small bowel tumor.[4] Unfortunately, cancer of the small bowel historically carries a poor prognosis. This is due in part to the low diagnostic ability of older testing, such as small bowel series. These patients typically present late in the course of their illness with symptoms of obstruction or metastatic disease. Studies have shown that if diagnosed early, prognosis of small bowel cancer is improved.[5]

An objective of physicians who care for patients with obscure bleeding is limiting an ongoing transfusion requirement. There is no effective medical therapy other than transfusion for bleeding intestinal angioectasias. Ablation therapy for angioectasias can be delivered either endoscopically or surgically and this choice is the crux of the decision analysis. Knowledge of the extent and severity of disease is necessary to make this decision. Thus, the key to improving the care and prognosis of these patients is improved diagnostic ability. From diagnosis comes proper and directed therapy.

In addition to these factors, there are the issues of the cost of caring for patients with obscure bleeding. The current medical literature lacks sufficient information on the costs associated with diagnosing obscure GI bleeding. The most comprehensive review of the economic literature for the period of 1985 to 1995 has limited information of value in understanding the costs and was not limited to obscure bleeding.[6]

There are various issues that contribute to the medical costs incurred in these patients. It may take considerable time to diagnose a patient with obscure bleeding. The median time to diagnose patients with obscure bleeding has been estimated as 2 years, with a range from 1 month to 8 years. In addition to this extended time to diagnosis, patients undergo numerous diagnostic tests and evaluations before a bleeding source is identified. Foutch and colleagues[7] reported that 39 patients undergoing push-enteroscopy for unidentified obscure bleeding had a total of 277 diagnostic tests performed before study entry. This was an average of 7.3 tests per patient. In this study, 49% of the patients continued to have an unknown bleeding source after push enteroscopy. The difficulties in locating the bleeding site with currently available diagnostic tools often result in the need for repeat testing, thus increasing the economic burden of obscure bleeding. In addition, patients with obscure bleeding may require blood transfusions and repeated hospitalizations. Flickinger and coworkers[8] reported 14 patients with obscure bleeding who had an average of five hospital admissions and an average of 46 units of blood transfused before undergoing intraoperative enteroscopy.

In an attempt to calculate the cost of obscure GI bleeding, Goldfarb and colleagues[9] reported costs incurred in 21 patients with obscure bleeding (Table 16–1). The mean length of time from first recognition of bleeding to study entry was 2.7 years. One patient who had gone 12 years since first bleed was excluded in this calculation. Because actual cost and charge data were not available, costs from a payer reimbursement perspective were based on average Medicare fees. Commercial reimbursements would be significantly higher. As demonstrated in Table 16–1, the costs associated with diagnosing obscure bleeding and treating the anemia are significant, averaging $33,630 per patient without a diagnosis made. Furthermore, data on other factors contributing to direct medical costs, such as physician visits, emergency department visits, and prescriptions, were not collected as part of the trial. Therefore, it would appear that these figures significantly underestimate the total cost of care and diagnosis of patients with obscure GI bleeding.

Finally, the nonmedical side of obscure bleeding should be considered. This includes the repeated testing that these patients are forced to undergo, the lifestyle changes that occur when faced with frequent hospitalizations and/or transfusions, and the personal medical costs of ongoing care. Patients with obscure bleeding often seek multiple medical opinions and "doctor-shop" searching for a resolution to their problem. They may think that they cannot travel because of the risk of bleeding. The psychosocial consequences of this problem are enormous. Again, rapid and correct diagnosis with definitive therapy would limit these issues.

Etiology

VASCULAR LESIONS OF THE SMALL BOWEL

There are a variety of causes of small bowel bleeding, each with its own bleeding pattern (Table 16–2). Vascular lesions are the most common cause of intestinal bleeding, accounting for 70% to 80%.[10] Vascular lesions of the bowel are not all the same. Although most vascular lesions appear endoscopically similar and can be a cause of bleeding, they consist of various pathologic identities (Table 16–3).[11]

Table 16–1. The Cost of Obscure Bleeding Based on 20 Patients

Procedure	Number of Events	Estimated Cost per Event ($)	Total Cost ($)	Cost per Patient ($)
Colonoscopy	73	660	48,180	2,409
Gastroscopy	83	590	48,970	2,449
Enteroscopy	22	590	12,980	649
Diagnostic radiology	38	220	8,360	418
Transfusion (units RBCs)	588	500	294,000	14,700
Inpatient hospitalizations	61	4,264	260,104	13,005
TOTAL COST			672,594	33,630

RBCs, red blood cells.
From Goldfarb N, Phillips A, Conn M, et al: Economic and health outcomes of capsule endoscopy. Dis Manage 5:123–135, 2002.

Table 16–2. Causes of Small Intestinal Bleeding by Bleeding Pattern

Brisk Bleeding: Melena, Hematochezia	Occult Bleeding
Angioectasia	Angioectasia
Leiomyoma	Adenocarcinoma
Leiomyosarcoma	Lymphoma
Jejunal diverticula	Carcinoid
Crohn's disease	Crohn's disease
Aortoenteric fistula	Zollinger-Ellison syndrome
Meckel's diverticulum	Vasculitis
Duplication cyst	Medications
Hemangioma	Infectious causes

Table 16–3. Classification of Vascular Anomalies

Angioectasia (vascular ectasia)
  Sporadic
  Associated with renal failure
  Associated with von Willebrand's disease
  Congestive gastropathy (see Fig. 16–5)
  Watermelon stomach (see Fig. 16–6)
Venous ectasia
Telangiectasia
Hemangiomas
Arteriovenous malformation
Caliber-persistent artery (Dieulafoy's lesion)

Angioectasias, or more aptly termed vascular ectasias, are dilated vessels, including capillaries, and contain no dysplastic tissue[12] (Figs. 16–1 to 16–4). These lesions can be found throughout the bowel and appear to recur and develop with aging. They are the most common vascular lesion; thus, the term angioectasia is typically applied to all small vascular lesions. Lewis and colleagues[13] reported the yield of standard pathologic examination when vascular lesions in the small intestine were identified endoscopically and then resected. All lesions appeared similarly endoscopically. The yield of routine pathologic examination was 57%. Pathologic examination of

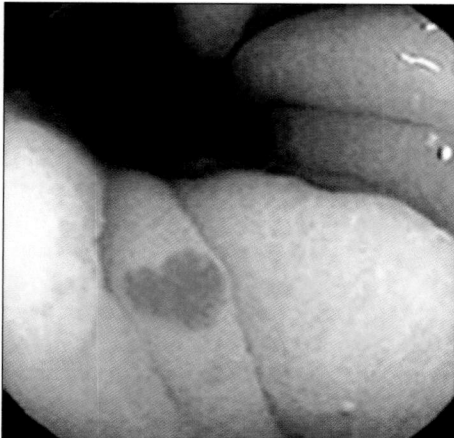

Figure 16–1. Gastric angioectasia.

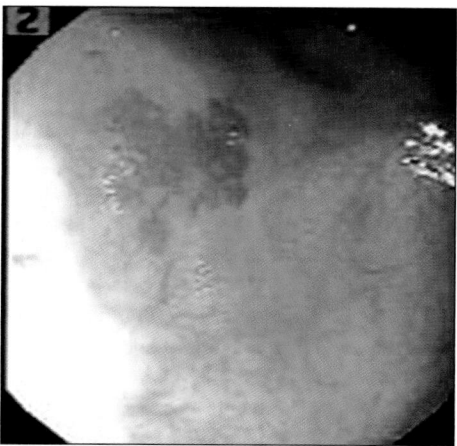

Figure 16–2. Colonic angioectasia.

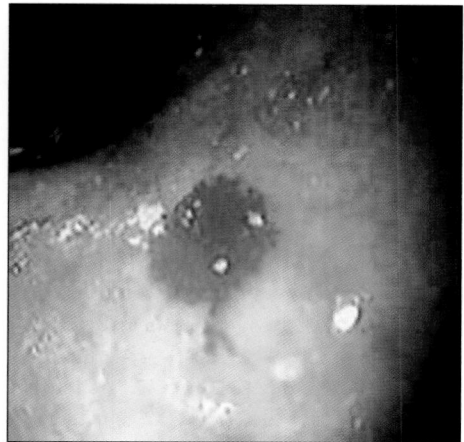

Figure 16–3. Rectal angioectasia.

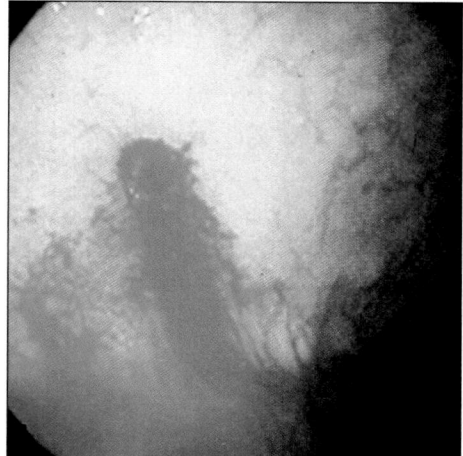

Figure 16–4. Dieulafoy's lesion in the gastric fundus.

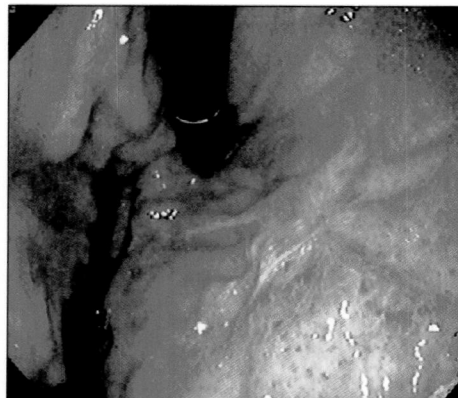

Figure 16–5. Retroflexed view of the gastric fundus demonstrating severe portal hypertensive gastropathy. Note erythema and "snakeskin" appearance of the mucosa.

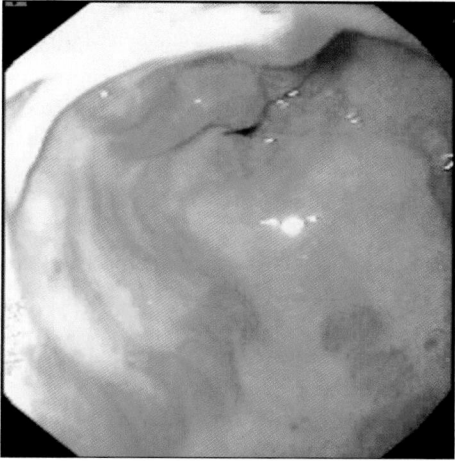

Figure 16–6. Watermelon stomach (gastric antral vascular ectasia).

14 patients' lesions revealed 8 identifiable vascular lesions including 5 angioectasias, 1 capillary hemangioma, 1 venous hemangioma, and 1 arteriovenous malformation (AVM). True angioectasias accounted for only 63% of identifiable lesions. Venous ectasias, also called plebectasias, differ from angioectasias and varices pathologically and clinically. These lesions consist of dilated submucosal veins usually with thin overlying mucosa. These venous varicosities have a normal endothelial lining and are non-neoplastic. They are not associated with liver disease. Endoscopically they appear as multiple bluish-red nodules and occur predominantly in the rectum and the esophagus. Small bowel lesions have also been described.[14] Clinically, they are an uncommon cause of bleeding and are usually asymptomatic. Telangiectasias differ from angioectasias by their diffuse nature, by their known tendency to recur, and by their associated skin or mucous membrane lesions. Pathologically, these hereditary lesions have dilated blood vessels throughout the bowel wall not just mucosally or submucosally as seen in angioectasias. Thinning of the arterial muscular layer is also considered specific for these lesions. Hereditary hemorrhagic telangiectasia (HHT) syndrome (Rendu-Osler-Weber syndrome) is the most common cause of intestinal telangiectasias. The inheritance pattern of this disease is autosomal dominant. Patients present with mucocutaneous lesions in the second and third decades, and epistaxis is the most common presenting symptom. GI bleeding (which occurs in approximately 15% of patients) develops later in life. Lesions tend to occur in the stomach and proximal small intestine. Turner's syndrome has also been associated with telangiectasias. The occurrence of bleeding in these patients is quite low, reported in 4 of 56 patients by Haddad and Wilkins[15] and none of 48 patients by Engel and Forbes.[16] Telangiectasias also occur in the calcinosis-Raynaud's-sclerodactyly-telangiectasia (CRST) syndrome. Although lesions usually occur on the hands, face, and mouth, gastric and small bowel telangiectasias may form and be a cause of bleeding.[17] Hemangiomas are neoplastic tumors made up of proliferating blood vessels, although rarely malignant. These lesions may be single or multiple, but once treated recurrence of bleeding is rare. Pathologically, these lesions are divided into capillary, cavernous, or mixed forms. Hemangiomas are also associated with skin lesions such as the cavernous hemangiomas of the skin in blue rubber bleb nevus syndrome or the cutaneous hemangiomas and soft tissue hypertrophy of Klippel-Trenaunay-Weber syndrome.[18] AVMs were once the term used to describe angioectasias. True AVMs are congenital lesions characterized by thick-walled arteries and veins without intervening capillaries forming a true arteriovenous fistula.[19] Muscular hypertrophy and eccentric intimal thickening is also seen. These lesions tend to occur in the younger patient and can be located anywhere in the GI tract, although they are most commonly found in the stomach and small intestine. These lesions, like hemangiomas, tend to be singular and do not recur.

Angioectasias are classically described as occurring in the right colon. Colonic angioectasias were initially described angiographically by Baum and coworkers[20] and by Boley and colleagues.[21] The colonic ectasias described by Boley were small and located predominantly in the cecum and ascending colon. Patients were older than the age of 60 and there was no gender predilection. All lesions in Boley's series were diagnosed by angiography, and 12 were further studied by stereomicroscopy after injection of the vasculature of the resected colon with a silicone-rubber compound. Angiographic and injection studies correlated well, showing the evolution from early to late lesions. Early lesions showed dilated tortuous submucosal veins on injection and late emptying veins on angiography. The so-called capillary tuft on angiography was shown by injection studies to be composed of clusters of dilated arterioles. Late lesions consisted of arteriovenous fistulas and were evidenced on angiographies by the presence of an early filling vein. Based on these findings, Boley suggested that angioectasias develop as a consequence of the normal, intermittent distention of the cecum and right colon causing recurrent obstruction to venous outflow where veins perforate the muscularis propria. The cecal location of these lesions was explained by its relatively large diameter producing relatively high wall pressures according to Laplace's law. With venous outflow obstruction, increased pressure would be transmitted to the capillary bed, dilating it. Over time, pressure would be transmitted to the precapillary sphincters, which in turn could become incompetent, creating an arteriovenous fistula. It is thus that Boley felt that angioectasias were a common degenerative disease of aging. His theory was supported when he examined 15 patients older than age 60 without bleeding or obstruction that had undergone right hemicolectomies for cancer. Eight of the 15 had submucosal ectasias and 4 had mucosal lesions. More recent studies suggest that angioectasia are an incidental finding at colonoscopy in 2% of nonbleeding individuals older than age 60.[22,23] Although these postulates are generally accepted, they remain only conjecture. Clinically it has not been shown that pressures generated in the cecum and right colon are enough to cause obstruction to venous outflow. Research that is more recent has revealed less mucosal vascular collagen type IV in colons with angioectasias than in normal colons.[24] This deficiency of collagen may place the colon at risk for the development of the vascular lesions. In other avenues of research, it has been shown that there are fibroblast and endothelial growth factors in the colons of patients with angioectasias, in marked contrast to that found in normal colons.[25] These new data suggest that colonic vascular ectasias are not formed by the degeneration of blood vessels but rather by angiogenesis. Research into the pathogenesis of HHT also points to angiogenesis as the cause.[26] HHT is a systemic hereditary illness associated with bleeding telangiectasias of every organ. This illness has recently been isolated to mutations on chromosome 9. It is postulated that the mutation alters endoglin, a transforming growth factor β (TGF-β) binding protein.[27] Endoglin is an integral membrane glycoprotein in endothelial cells of capillaries, arterioles, and venules. Endoglin binds transforming growth factor and this in turn leads to tissue growth, differentiation, motility, and remodeling. It is thought that the initiating event that leads to telangiectasia formation in patients with altered endoglin is tissue injury leading to abnormal tissue repair. Current research indicates that patients with HHT are a very heterogeneous group.[28] Presently, there are two HHT diseases, HHT1 and HHT2. HHT1 is the disease created by mutations on chromosome 9. At least 20 different mutations have been identified. Most simply, mutations in the q3 region are not associated with pulmonary vascular lesions, whereas mutations in the q34 region are associated with pulmonary disease. HHT2 is the disease created by mutations on chromosome 12 in the q13 region. This area codes for the activin receptor-like kinase gene. At least

14 different mutations have been described for this disease. With this knowledge, research into medical therapy aimed against angiogenesis is under way.

There have been no injection studies of small bowel angioectasias to help explain their pathophysiology. Since the time of early reports, vascular ectasias have been identified in the stomach and small intestine, although far less commonly than in the colon. Quintero[29] was the first to describe angioectasia of the stomach and duodenum that appeared similar to colonic lesions. Meyer and colleagues[30] reviewed 218 angioectasias found at postmortem examinations: 2.3% were located in the duodenum, 10.5% were located in the jejunum, and 8.5% were located in the ileum. Small bowel angioectasias are usually diagnosed endoscopically during either enteroscopy or intraoperative endoscopy. Angiography rarely diagnoses small intestinal vascular lesions. This is due to the multiple arterial arcades that feed the small bowel, limiting the identification of a late emptying or early filling vein or even a vascular tuft. Some pathophysiology other than the theory behind colonic vascular ectasias may be at play to explain the occurrence of angiodysplasias within the small bowel. Another difficulty in understanding angioectasias of the small intestine is that the various pathologies discussed previously present with similar clinical scenarios and similar endoscopic findings.

Vascular lesions of the small bowel can present with either brisk or occult bleeding. Patients may have only positive fecal occult blood testing or melena. Red or maroon blood per rectum is uncommon. Lewis and coworkers[31] reported that melena was the presenting sign in 64% of 102 patients with bleeding small bowel angioectasias, whereas 36% had occult blood in the stool. The reason why angioectasias bleed also remains unclear. Two theories are that bleeding results from high pressure bursting the thin walled capillary or that bleeding results from food abrading the mucosa. It has been noted pathologically that bleeding lesions are associated with thinning of overlying mucosa and ulceration in some cases. The fistula may cause localized ischemia of the mucosa leading to thinning and ulceration of the mucosa, the final pathway to bleeding.[10] This theory also correlates with the endoscopic finding of "anemic halos" associated with angioectasias. A ring of pale mucosa is seen endoscopically around some angioectasias similar to the anemic halos dermatologists describe with telangiectasias of the skin. These pale rings are felt to be secondary to the shunting of blood.[32] Their presence endoscopically confirms the vascular nature of the lesion seen.

Angioectasias have been associated with several other clinical disorders including aortic stenosis, chronic renal failure, and von Willebrand's disease (vWD). Aortic stenosis has long been implicated as a cause of bleeding from the right colon and, by inference, the formation of angioectasias.[33] Although the cardiac lesion was not etiologic in the formation of angioectasias, it may be causative in their bleeding because of the change in pulse pressure.[8] Although some studies report a cessation of bleeding after aortic valve replacement, long-term follow-up has not substantiated that claim.[34,35] Imperiale and Ransohoff[36] reviewed the literature and found only four controlled studies that addressed the association of idiopathic GI bleeding and aortic stenosis. None addressed the presence of angioectasias directly. Imperiale and Ransohoff also found major methodologic deficiencies in these studies that included non-blinded data collection, noncomparable diagnostic workup between groups, nonblinded ascertainment of exposure, and noncomparable demographic susceptibility. Mehta and colleagues[37] performed echocardiography in 29 patients with colonic angioectasia. Although 76% of the patients had a systolic murmur that was felt to be related to flow, none had evidence of true aortic stenosis. Thus, there is little evidence that aortic stenosis is an independent risk factor for the development of or bleeding from angioectasias.

The natural history of angioectasias is also still not known. It is estimated that less than 10% of all patients with colonic angioectasia will eventually bleed. Foutch and coworkers[38] followed eight patients with incidentally found colonic angioectasia for a mean of 3 years and none developed bleeding. Richter and colleagues[39] reported 15 patients with incidental ectasias diagnosed at colonoscopy, who were followed for a mean of 23 months, and none developed bleeding. Once lesions have bled, their tendency to rebleed is also not fully known. Although physicians are eager to treat these lesions, it may be that up to 50% will not rebleed. Hutcheon and coworkers[40] reported six patients who were treated with only blood transfusions after having a transfusion-dependent bleed from colonic vascular lesions. There was a 91% decrease in transfusions during the follow-up period. Richter[39] reported 36 patients treated conservatively after having documented bleeding from colonic angioectasia: 26% rebled at 1 year and 46% rebled at 3 years. In a cohort study of medical therapy of bleeding angioectasia, Lewis and coworkers[41] reported a spontaneous cessation of bleeding in 44% of patients with small bowel angioectasia during a 13.1-month mean follow-up. In all of these studies, the propensity for rebleeding was not dependent on the type of bleeding that the patient experienced.

TUMORS OF THE SMALL BOWEL

Tumors are the second most common cause of small bowel bleeding.[42,43] Small bowel tumors account for only 5% of all GI tract tumors. They account for 5% to 10% of all cases of small intestinal hemorrhage.[44,45] Most are benign. These patients are generally younger than patients with angioectasia of the small bowel, with an average age of 51 compared with 69. Bleeding is the presenting complaint in 25% to 53% of patients with small bowel tumors. Frank bleeding is most common with either melena or maroon blood per rectum. Lewis and coworkers[31] reported this presentation in 62% of 13 patients with small bowel tumors, whereas 38% presented with occult blood in the stool. According to Lewis and coworkers, the type of bleeding, whether frank blood loss or occult blood in the stool, is not an effective means of differentiating bleeding secondary to an angioectasia versus a small bowel tumor. Because bleeding is often the sole symptom, the diagnosis is often delayed, contributing to the poor prognosis in patients with malignant tumors. In 1995, 4600 new cases of small intestinal cancer were reported along with 1120 deaths.[43] Tumors are typically missed by most radiographic tests; thus, before the advent of small intestinal endoscopy, tumors of the small bowel generally carried a dismal prognosis. In 1980, Herbsman and colleagues[46] reported that survival of more than 6 months for adenocarcinoma of the small bowel was rare. Even in the days of endoscopy, the endoscopic appearance of a small bowel mass can be deceiving. The endoscopist may only able to say that a tumor is present and not know the true pathology. Many small bowel tumors are submucosal also adding to the difficulty of visual diagnosis and even diagnosis by endoscopic biopsy. Submucosal tumors include gastrointestinal stromal tumors (GISTs), carcinoids, lipomas, and metastatic disease. With the small space of the small bowel and a large tumor, the typical changes suggestive of a submucosal process may be missed. Typically, the endoscopist looks for visible mucosa and a vascular pattern across the tumor to confirm its submucosal nature. Bridging folds may also help in this regard. In the small bowel, the mucosa may be pulled so tightly over the mass that it becomes transparent, masking the standard changes. GISTs can vary in size and the endoscopic appearance does not judge the size of the extramucosal component. Occasionally, central ulceration or umbilication may be seen. Lymphomas can have several different appearances. A classification of these appearances has been created and includes a nodular pattern, an infiltrative pattern, and an ulcerating pattern.[47] Halphen and coworkers,[48] in a review of 120 patients with primary small bowel lymphoma, found the infiltrative pattern, in which the mucosa is firm and motionless, to be most indicative of lymphoma. The other patterns may be mimicked by celiac disease and radiation enteritis among others. Adenocarcinoma is circumferential and often quite exophytic, appearing like the endoscopic appearance of colon cancer. Metastatic melanoma can often be suspected by its pigmented nature. Carcinoid can be suggested when multiple submucosal nodules or masses are seen. It should also be mentioned that certain illnesses increase the risk of developing small bowel malignancy. Celiac disease increases the risk of both adenocarcinoma and lymphoma. Crohn's disease increases the risk of developing adenocarcinoma as does familial polyposis and Peutz-Jeghers syndrome. Human immunodeficiency virus (HIV) infection increases the risk of small bowel lymphoma and Kaposi's sarcoma.

GISTs are mesenchymal neoplasms that previously were classified as smooth muscle tumors. Twenty-five percent of GISTs are found in the small bowel, and they can be located at any level.[49] Prognosis is not dependent on location but rather on the state of the tumor at the time of diagnosis. Histologically, GISTs vary from spindle cell tumors to epithelioid and pleomorphic lesions. Malignancy is determined pathologically by a mitotic rate over 5 per 50 high-power field (HPF) or size greater than 5 cm. They are the most common small bowel tumors that bleed. Bleeding may be brisk and occurs when there is central tumor necrosis and subsequent ulceration of the overlying mucosa. Because of their vascularity, 99m technetium (Tc) pertechnetate scanning may be positive in GISTs, and angiography has been reported to show a tumor blush in 86% of lesions.[43] There is no sex predilection, and these lesions are most often seen in the fifth to seventh decade. Gradual but more chronic blood loss is usually associated with other small bowel tumors including carcinoid, adenocarcinoma, and lymphomas. GISTs may grow more serosally than intraluminally, and this dumb-bell configuration with a small mucosal component can make both radiographic and endoscopic diagnosis difficult.

Adenomatous polyps and adenocarcinomas are most often found within the proximal bowel with 90% of lesions located within the duodenum and the first 20 cm of the jejunum (see also Chapter 36). Lymphomas on the other hand tend to involve the distal jejunum or ileum. Carcinoid can be found throughout the small bowel although multicentric lesions in the mid small bowel are most common.

Metastatic disease can also migrate to the small bowel; melanoma and breast cancer are most common, although colonic cancer can also metastasize to the small intestine. Pancreatic cancer can directly invade the duodenum and present with bleeding.

ULCERATION OF THE SMALL BOWEL

Ulcerative diseases within the small intestine are another group of entities that cause small bowel bleeding. In this category, Crohn's disease is the most common. Gross bleeding is unusual in Crohn's disease, occurring in 4% to 10% of patients with ileitis.[50] Transmural inflammation, the pathologic hallmark of the disease can erode into large submucosal vessels causing massive bleeding. These episodes are usually self-limited and not recurring. Bleeding is not usually the sole symptom in these patients, because most also have the more common symptoms of Crohn's disease such as diarrhea and abdominal pain.

Meckel's diverticulum is a remnant of the vitelline duct and is usually located approximately 100 cm from the ileocecal valve. This anomaly occurs in 2% of the population and is more common in men than women. It is the cause of bleeding in two thirds of men younger than the age of 30 presenting with small bowel bleeding.[51] Bleeding is almost always brisk resulting from ulceration within the diverticulum or the adjoining ileum secondary to acid production from ectopic gastric mucosa lining the diverticulum wall. Preoperative diagnosis is uncommon, although radionuclide scanning using 99mTc pertechnetate is available to label parietal cells within the gastric mucosa. Intestinal duplication cysts can also be lined with ectopic gastric mucosa, leading to ulceration and bleeding. Unlike a Meckel's diverticulum, these congenital cysts may be located anywhere in the bowel.

Zollinger-Ellison syndrome, certain infections, medications, and various vasculitides can also cause small bowel ulcerations. Postbulbar ulcerations occur in gastrinomas with ulcers not only described in the second portion of the duodenum but also in the third and forth portions and in the jejunum. It has been reported that postbulbar ulcerations in the duodenum occur in 14% and that jejunal ulcers occur in 11% of patients with Zollinger-Ellison syndrome.[52] Small bowel infections with tuberculosis, syphilis, typhoid, and histoplasmosis can also be causes of bleeding. Medications such as potassium, nonsteroidal anti-inflammatory drugs (NSAIDs), and 6-mercaptopurine can also cause small bowel ulcerations and bleeding. The mechanism of injury by potassium appears to be secondary to its affect on mesenteric circulation. In high doses, potassium decreases mesenteric blood flow and stenosing ulcers of the small intestine have been found to have the pathologic features of ischemic injury.[53] NSAIDs commonly affect the small bowel. Postmortem studies report that 8.4% of patients on long-term NSAIDs have small bowel ulcerations.[54] Patients typically present with iron deficiency anemia, and acute bleeding is unusual.

Vasculitis can affect the bowel in several different ways.[55] A patient's presentation depends on the size of the vessels involved. Although large artery vasculitis, as with aortitis, can lead to arterial occlusion and subsequent bowel gangrene and perforation, venulitis and obstruction of venous return leads to mucosal edema and malabsorption. Vasculitis of medium and small arteries generally cause GI bleeding. Medium-sized arteries develop aneurysms, which can rupture and massively bleed as seen in polyarteritis nodosa. Other necrotizing vasculitides of the bowel are seen in rheumatoid arthritis (although usually affecting the colon) and systemic lupus erythematosus. Vasculitis of small arteries, the vasa recta, or the intramural arterioles presents with pain, fever, and occult bleeding. Infectious and inflammatory processes usually affect these vessels such as with tuberculosis, amyloidosis, sarcoidosis, and multiple myeloma.[56] Hypersensitivity vasculitis, a vasculitis usually affecting the smaller vessels in response to a specific antigen, is seen in Henoch-Schönlein purpura. Radiation injury to the bowel can also cause a vasculitis and subsequent bleeding. Irradiation of the bowel initially affects the intestinal mucosa directly causing ulceration and bleeding. Late injury usually occurs 6 to 24 months after radiation treatment as a consequence of a progressive occlusive vasculitis.[57] Injury rarely occurs with total doses of less than 4000 rads, and greater amounts of radiation increase the risk of late enteritis as does preexisting abnormalities of mesenteric blood flow such as in congestive heart failure.

DIVERTICULA OF THE SMALL BOWEL

Jejunal diverticula can cause small bowel bleeding. These are acquired pseudodiverticula that develop on the mesenteric border of the intestine at the site of perforating blood vessels. Jejunal diverticula, found in 1% to 2% of individuals in autopsy studies, are usually asymptomatic. It is estimated that less than 5% of all people with jejunal diverticula actually bleed from them.[58] Therefore, when discovered on a small bowel series, small bowel diverticula should be considered incidental findings because angiographic or radionuclide scanning evidence of active bleeding is necessary to conclude that the diverticula are the site of blood loss. When bleeding does occur from jejunal diverticula, it is usually massive and can be associated with mortality as high as 20%.

VASCULAR ANOMALIES OF THE SMALL BOWEL

There are several other vascular anomalies that may cause bleeding within the small bowel. Small bowel varices can be a cause of massive bleeding. These lesions are usually located within the duodenum and proximal jejunum.[59] They are extraserosal and thus are rarely a cause of bleeding. Small bowel varices are most commonly associated with prehepatic causes of portal hypertension such as malignancy.

Bleeding from an aortoenteric fistula is massive and life threatening. Fistulas are typically secondary, occurring in patients after abdominal aorta aneurysm surgery. However, primary aortoenteric fistulas can also occur.[60] Typically fistulas form at the anastomosis of the Dacron graft or are paraprosthetic in the proximal portion of the graft. The duodenum is the typical site of intestinal involvement, but fistulas to the ileum and other regions of bowel have been described. Patients who are particularly prone to fistula formation are those with complicated graft surgery. This includes those who have graft infection postoperatively or those who required reoperation. Fistula formation typically occurs early in the postoperative period. The classic history is that of a herald bleed with massive bleeding that stops suddenly. Endoscopy, angiography and even computed tomography (CT) scanning cannot completely exclude this diagnosis and often exploratory surgery is necessary to make sure that the duodenum is free from the aorta.

Caliber-persistent arteries, those arteries that fail to narrow and decrease in size as they penetrate the submucosa, may occur throughout the gut.[61,62] The most common location for this anomaly is the gastric fundus within 6 cm of the esophagogastric junction, the so-called Dieulafoy's lesion[63] (see Fig. 16–4). Pathologically, the caliber-persistent artery has no associated aneurysm, although it has also been called a cirsoid aneurysm, and there is no mucosal ulceration associated with the lesion. This arterial lesion, named after a surgeon who described it, usually occurs in males between ages 30 to 50. Although the stomach is the most common location of this lesion, both duodenal and jejunal Dieulafoy's lesions have been reported.[64,65] Bleeding is painless and massive. Diagnosis is often difficult. Patients present with bleeding but may have no lesions visible endoscopically. Once treated, bleeding will not recur because these lesions are considered congenital and the occurrence of more than one has not been reported.

Diagnosis
RADIOLOGY

Small bowel series has long been considered the main stay in the evaluation of the small intestine.[66] However, data show a relatively low yield of positive findings for patients with occult bleeding or iron deficiency. Although most Crohn's disease and large ulcerations of the small intestine can readily be diagnosed using this standard examination,[67] it is estimated that only approximately 5% of small bowel follow-through examinations will detect an intestinal bleeding site. Rabe and coworkers[68] reported a yield of 5.6% in a series of 215 small bowel series performed for obscure bleeding. Fried and colleagues[69] made no diagnoses in 28 examinations. Gordon and coworkers[70] made diagnoses in 3 of 46 patients (6.5%) with iron deficiency anemia who underwent small bowel follow-through examinations. These included one with a jejunal ulcer and two with an abnormal terminal ileum. Rockey and Cello[71] evaluated 29 patients with iron deficiency anemia and negative upper endoscopies and colonoscopies using enteroclysis in 26 and small bowel series in 3. No lesions were identified.

Enteroclysis has been shown to have an increased sensitivity over the standard small bowel follow-through examination. Gurian and colleagues[72] retrospectively compared 88 consecutive enteroclysis studies and 52 routine small bowel series in the same patients. Enteroclysis made a correct diagnosis in 96% of these patients, whereas small bowel series only made diagnoses in 72% of 18 examinations. The false-negative rate for enteroclysis was 7.6%, whereas the false-negative rate for small bowel series was 41.6%. Missed diagnoses on small bowel series included missed Crohn's disease, small bowel obstruction, and a small bowel malignancy. This improved diagnostic yield of enteroclysis over small bowel series has been confirmed by other studies as well.[73–75] The failure of small bowel series may be technical or it may be secondary to errors during the reading of the films. Maglinte and coworkers[76] reported 42 small bowel lesions diagnosed by enteroclysis but missed by small bowel series. Thirty lesions (71%) were not seen on the small bowel series in retrospect, but 12 (29%) were seen retrospectively and thus were initially missed secondary to interpretive errors. Despite the advantages of enteroclysis over small bowel series, Ott and coworkers[77] reported that enteroclysis requires more time, has more side effects (gagging and retching), and involves more radiation exposure than routine small bowel series. They concluded that small bowel series was still a preferable screening examination. Long-term follow-up studies have confirmed that a normal enteroclysis study does exclude the presence of small bowel disease. Barloon and colleagues[78] obtained follow-up on 75 patients who had normal enteroclysis examinations for a minimum follow-up period of 3 years. Sixty-nine patients were still free of disease, and the specificity of enteroclysis was calculated to be 92%.

Enteroclysis appears to be an effective tool in the evaluation of patients with small bowel bleeding. Rex and colleagues[79] reported that enteroclysis has a yield of 10% in 125 patients with obscure GI bleeding. Diagnoses included Meckel's diverticulum, Crohn's disease, adenocarcinoma, metastatic melanoma, leiomyoma, and leiomyosarcoma. Antes and coworkers[80] retrospectively reported a similar yield of 11% in a group of 124 patients with obscure GI bleeding. Moch and colleagues[81] reported a yield of 25% for enteroclysis performed in patients with obscure bleeding. Findings at enteroclysis in 32 of 128 patients included 10 cancers, 3 angioectasias, 2 mural hematomas, radiation enteritis, sprue, Meckel's diverticulum, and an ulcer. Enteroclysis was positive in 14 patients, was falsely negative in 2 in whom a structural lesion was ultimately found, and was falsely positive in 1. It is unclear how angioectasias were diagnosed by enteroclysis in this report, because barium radiographic modalities are incapable of diagnosing these mucosal lesions.

Several investigators have combined push enteroscopy with enteroclysis.[82,83] Push enteroscopy evaluates the proximal small bowel and then facilitates the placement of a catheter for the performance of enteroclysis. This improves patient tolerance of the enteroclysis because conscious sedation is used for the endoscopic portion.[84] Willis and coworkers[85] reported a yield of 8% in patients with bleeding for enteroclysis performed after push enteroscopy. They discovered two cancers in a group of 24 patients with obscure bleeding.

The application of magnetic resonance imaging (MRI) technology to the performance of enteroclysis is being developed.[86] Oral magnetic particles provide a negative or black luminal contrast agent, and this improves not only the visualization of the intestinal lumen but also the intestinal wall. Similarly, combining CT scanning with enteroclysis may improve the visualization within the small bowel.[87] CT enterography has been used only in Crohn's disease to this point and has not been applied to patients with obscure bleeding.[88]

RADIOISOTOPE SCANNING

Radioisotope bleeding scans are often used when there is suspected lower GI bleeding.[89] Its ready availability, low cost, and absence of complications have lead to its universal acceptance. It is often a prerequisite for emergency angiography. Red blood cells are labeled either *in vitro* or *in vivo* with a radionuclide tag, and during an acquisition time of 1 to 2 hours, as little as 5 mL of intraluminal blood will give a "positive" scan. Small bowel bleeding can be identified on nuclear scans as the tracer-labeled blood takes a serpiginous route through the gut in subsequent pictures, unlike the course of blood in colonic bleeding that follows a more specific movement pattern. The effectiveness of the scan is somewhat dependent on the affinity between the radioactive technetium and the red cell. *In vitro* labeling results in a tighter bond between the tag and the red cell, whereas multiple transfusions can adversely alter the binding mechanism limiting the effectiveness of the scan.[90] Unfortunately, although this test may confirm the small intestine as the site of bleeding, close approximation to the actual location within the bowel is not possible. Positive scans require other modalities to truly identify or specifically localize or tag the site of blood loss. A so-called advantage to red blood cell scans is the intravascular half-life of 24 hours permitting a longer scanning time whereby sequential scans increase the probability of identifying the bleeding site. However, delayed scans obtained 12 to 24 hours after injection may yield misleading information, by identifying areas of blood pooling but not the site of active bleeding. Emslie and coworkers[91] reported the outcome in 21 patients with positive technetium scanning. Fourteen patients had the site confirmed by either angiography or surgery. All of the false-positive studies were positive at greater than 15 hours. The authors concluded that technetium scanning is effective in localizing bleeding when positive within the continuous phase of imaging.

Other literature fails to confirm the effectiveness of radioisotope scanning. The literature is retrospective and generally poorly identifies the group being studied. Most studies address patients with active lower GI bleeding or those referred for scanning. Suzman and colleagues[92] reported retrospectively on 224 patients with active lower GI bleeding: 115 patients (51%) had positive scans of which 96 could be localized to an isolated site and 88 (92%) of these sites were in the colon. Of the 224 patients, 50 patients underwent surgery for bleeding, 37 patients had a localizing scan before surgery, and this was correct in 36 patients. Patients with a positive scan were five more times likely to require surgery. It is unclear if this association attests to the effectiveness of the scan or to the severity of the individual patient's bleeding. Rantis and coworkers[93] reported results in 72 patients who had 80 scans. This was a retrospective report of patients with acute GI bleeding. Scans were positive in 47.5%, and a site of bleeding was confirmed in 22 of the 38 positive scans. The sensitivity of scanning was 84.6%, and the specificity was 70.4%. The accuracy of localization was 72.7%. Other studies report similar data.[94] Voeller and colleagues[95] reported the clinical application of bleeding scans in 103 patients and showed that the scans fail to localize bleeding in 85% of patients. The authors concluded that the scan is not an adequate screen for angiography and it cannot be used to guide subsequent surgery.

Meckel's scans using 99mTc pertechnetate that binds to parietal cells is another nuclear scan used in the evaluation of small bowel bleeding. The sensitivity for this test is reported to be 75% to 100% with false-positive scans reported in 15% of instances and false-negatives reported in 25%.[96] Pentagastrin and cimetidine have been shown to increase the uptake of pertechnetate by parietal cells and a so-called enhanced Meckel's scan using either of these pharmacologic agents has been used to increase the sensitivity of this test.[97]

ANGIOGRAPHY

Angiography can detect bleeding at a rate of 0.5 mL/minute. This radiographic technique can localize a site of bleeding in 50% to 72% of patients with massive hemorrhage, but this yield decreases to 25% to 50% when active bleeding has slowed or stopped.[98] In addition to the demonstration of active bleeding, angiography can diagnose nonbleeding lesions such as angioectasias and small bowel tumors. Diagnosis of angioectasias within the small intestine can be difficult because such small lesions may vasoconstrict with reductions in blood pressure and intravascular volume associated with bleeding. Initially, it was felt that angiography was the only way to diagnose colonic angioectasias. Boley and coworkers[99] described different features characteristic of these lesions. Their report of 45 angiograms in 25 patients with bleeding showed right colonic angioectasias confirmed pathologically in 18.[94] Three separate signs were seen in these patients and were considered diagnostic. A slowly filling vein was the most common finding in 92%. This vein, densely opacified and dilated, is located intramurally and persists after other mesenteric veins have emptied. Its presence supports the proposed pathophysiologic mechanism, namely obstruction to venous outflow. The next most frequent radiographic finding was a vascular tuft found in 68%. These tufts correlating with the dilated honeycomb complexes were often noted in the arterial phase at the end of an ileocolic branch artery. The third radiographic finding was an early filling vein occurring in 56%. The vein, either the ileocolic vein or some other localized vein is seen in the arterial phase before visualizing other mesenteric veins. It represents a true arteriovenous fistula. Patients can have one or more of these findings. Forty-four percent of these patients had all three. Although these signs are characteristic, they are not commonly found in practice. Angiography for small intestinal angioectasias has an especially low yield, because angiographic interpretation is more difficult within the small bowel mesenteric arteriolar arcades. An examination of 60 patients with bleeding revealed that, of 14 patients with chronic occult bleeding, only 2 had true-positive studies and 2 had false-negative studies.[100] Of 28 patients with recurrent acute bleeding, 2 had true-positive examinations and 4 had false-negative examinations. Of 16 patients with acute bleeding, 3 true positives and 1 false negative were found. In total, 7 true positives and 7 false negative occurred in 14 patients with known angioectasias of the colon and/or the small bowel. These results do not include extravasation that was found in 2 patients.

Stress angiography has been advocated by several centers. This technique administers vasodilator, anticoagulants, and/or thrombolytic agents in patients with obscure bleeding. Angiography is performed after this to determine a site of blood loss. All authors suggest placing the patient in an intensive care unit setting, having cross-matched blood, and having a surgeon available should bleeding be massive. Mernagh and coworkers[101] reported the yield of angiography in 18 patients with chronic GI blood loss. Initial angiography provided a diagnosis in six patients including three with small bowel angioectasias, one colonic angioectasia, and two with small bowel tumors. Twelve patients were then heparinized for 24 hours and the angiogram was repeated. This provided an additional diagnosis in six patients including three with small bowel angioectasias and two with colonic angioectasias. The yield of angiography was doubled using heparin. Bloomfeld and colleagues[102] retrospectively reported seven patients with obscure bleeding who received urokinase plus heparin plus tolazidine before angiography. Extravasation was produced in two patients (29%). Both were patients with colonic diverticular bleeding.

Another innovation in the field of radiology is helical CT angiography. Ettorre and coworkers[103] reported the use of helical CT in 18 patients with obscure bleeding. This procedure involves injection of a contrast agent intra-arterially, either mesenteric arteriography or abdominal aortography, just before CT scanning. Ettorre and coworkers found a bleeding site in 13 of the 18 patients for a yield of 72%. Of the ultimately diagnosed small bowel causes of bleeding, CT diagnosed seven of the nine patients. Diagnoses included two angioectasias of the small bowel and two small bowel tumors.

ENTEROSCOPY

Endoscopic evaluation of the distal duodenum and large areas of the jejunum and ileum has been termed enteroscopy.[104] At present, there are two nonsurgical methods available: push enteroscopy and capsule endoscopy. Both Sonde and Rope-way enteroscopy techniques, although historically important in the evaluation of obscure bleeding, have largely been abandoned.[105] Intraoperative enteroscopy is considered the ultimate endoscopic evaluation of the small bowel.

During push enteroscopy, an endoscope is advanced beyond the ligament of Treitz into the proximal jejunum.[106] Although designated instruments have been made for this examination, most experience has been based using an orally passed adult or pediatric colonoscope.[107] With these routinely available instruments, it is possible to intubate the jejunum for approximately 40 to 60 cm beyond the ligament of Treitz. Longer instruments have been developed, and coupled with the development of an overtube that limits looping of the endoscope shaft, deeper intubation of the jejunum is possible.[108,109] Designated push enteroscopes measure 200 to 250 cm. These instruments can use an overtube, which is initially backloaded onto the shaft of this orally passed endoscope. Once the endoscope tip is within the jejunum, the overtube is advanced down the esophagus until its distal tip rests within the prepyloric antrum or even into the jejunum. The stiffening tube acts to limit intragastric and intraduodenal bulb looping of the push enteroscope, a hindrance to deep small bowel intubation. The push enteroscope is then advanced deep into the small bowel, effectively bringing endoscopic evaluation and therapeutic intervention to the entire jejunum and possibly the proximal ileum. Studies have shown that overtubes do increase depth of insertion although there appears to be limit to the insertion depth not based on endoscope working length.[110]

Push enteroscopy is useful when looking for a cause of small intestinal bleeding. Reported yields have varied from 13% to 38%. Messer and coworkers[111] using a pediatric colonoscope reported finding the bleeding site in 20 of 52 patients (38%) with obscure bleeding. Findings included angioectasias in 9 and small bowel tumors in 11. Fouch and colleagues[7] used an orally passed adult colonoscope and reported a yield of 38% in their report of examinations of 39 patients. Angioectasias were the most common finding accounting for 80% of the diagnoses. Chong and coworkers[112a] reported finding a possible cause of bleeding in 64% of 55 patients using a 2-m long push enteroscope in combination with an overtube. It is important to note that up to 25% to 65% of culprit lesions seen at push enteroscopy are within reach of standard gastroscopy (proximal to ampulla of Vater).[112b,112c,112d]

Push enteroscopy is therapeutic and diagnostic. Using bipolar cautery, Foutch and coworkers[7] were able to fulgurate angioectasias in 11 of 12 patients. Control of bleeding was obtained in 8 of the 11 treated patients. Askin and Lewis[113] followed 55 patients after cauterization of jejunal angioectasias for an average period of 30 months. These patients required significantly fewer total transfusions and had a significantly reduced transfusion requirement when compared with their precauterization history and when compared with a cohort of patients with intestinal angioectasias who were not cauterized. Landi and coworkers[114a] reported the long-term follow-up of patients with obscure bleeding evaluated by push enteroscopy. They studied 105 patients followed for an average of 2 years. Overall, 31% of patient continued to bleed. This risk of rebleeding was stratified by the diagnosis at push enteroscopy. If the examination was negative, 27% rebled; if angioectasias were treated, 56% bled; if some other diagnosis was made, 24% rebled. The risk of continued bleeding was also increased if the patient had multiple episodes of bleeding before the push examination and if the patient required blood transfusion.

More recently, a enteroscope traction system has been developed using an overtube and enteroscope, both with a balloon at their distal end.[114b,114c] By sequentially inflating the balloons and gaining traction on the small bowel, the intestine can be pleated onto the overtube. This technique can to performed either antegrade or retrograde via colonoscopy and terminal ileoscopy. Preliminary data suggest that total enteroscopy is possible in most patients, with the possibility of therapeutic interventions as well. Further data are needed to evaluate this new technique.

CAPSULE ENDOSCOPY

An endoscopic capsule (Given Imaging Limited, Yoqneam, Israel) was developed to obtain images from the entire small bowel. The capsule, measuring 11 × 26 mm, contains 6 light-emitting diodes (LEDs), a lens, a color camera chip, two silver oxide batteries, a radio frequency transmitter, and an antenna. The camera is a complementary metal oxide semiconductor (CMOS) chip. This chip requires less power than present charged-coupled device (CCD) chips found on videoendoscopes and digital cameras, and it can operate at very low levels of illumination. The capsule obtains two images per second and transmits the data via radiofrequency to a recording device worn about the patient's waist. This recording device is a minicomputer with 5 gigabytes of memory, allowing storage of the 57,600 images obtained during a typical 8-hour examination. Once the study is completed, the recording device is downloaded to a computer workstation whose software provides the images to the computer screen. The capsule is disposable and does not need to be retrieved by the patient. It is passed naturally. Presently, there are three contraindications to capsule endoscopy. These include patients with swallowing disorders (although the capsule can be placed endoscopically), patients with implanted pacemakers and defibrillators, and patients with small bowel obstruction.

The typical procedure entails having a patient present in the morning of the examination after a 12-hour fast. Oral iron supplementation is discontinued 3 days before the examination. The recording device is initialized with the patient's personal data to avoid confusion should multiple recorders be used simultaneously. A sensor array is applied to the patient's abdomen that will capture the signals from the capsule and carry them to the recording device. The recorder is then placed in a belt around the patient's waist. There is also a battery pack to power the recording device. The patient then swallows the activated capsule with a glass of water. Typically, a patient drinks 250 to 500 mL of water. The patient can then be discharged from the facility, although he or she cannot eat for an additional 4 hours. During the day, the patient can be fully active. The patient then returns to the facility after 8 hours, and the sensor array and recording device are removed. The patient is discharged, and the images in the recording device are downloaded to the workstation.

In addition to the video images, the system is designed to grossly identify the capsule's location within the small bowel. There is an algorithm in the workstation software that determines the capsule's location in two dimensions based on the signal strength to the individual sensors of the sensor array. The computer algorithm was tested by comparing the computer's localization with fluoroscopic images obtained during a capsule examination in 17 volunteers.[115] The distance of the capsule location from the umbilicus was compared in 92 different measurements. The mean distant between computer estimation of location and fluoroscopic localization was 3.8 cm with a standard deviation of 2.2 cm. A drawing of the small bowel passage is produced that provides a location for each of the approximately 57,600 images obtained during the 8 hours. This localization is an estimate only, because not only does the capsule move within the intestine but also the small bowel moves within the abdominal cavity. Thus, the proximal jejunum can be located in the right lower quadrant or the left upper quadrant. In addition, the bowel's location is related to the position of the patient. For example, the small bowel can sag to the pelvis while a patient is standing. However, when the diagram produced is combined with the knowledge of the length of time the capsule has been in the small bowel, along with the time between pyloric passage and the identified lesion and the amount of visible bowel traversed to the lesion and from the lesion to the ileocecal valve, an approximation of the location of the lesion can be made.

In addition to localization software, the system also contains an image recognition algorithm that identifies red pixels in the data. This identifies possible areas of bleeding or the possible presence of vascular lesions. Liangpunsakul and colleagues[116] examined this technology in 24 patients. They reported a sensitivity of 72% and a positive predictive value of 81%.

Capsule technology was initially developed to report temperature, pressure, and pH levels inside the body. This technology dates from 1954. The present endoscopic capsule was developed by Dr. Gavriel Idan in 1981.[117] The initial report of the capsule's use was published detailing the quality of the capsule's images in 10 healthy volunteers.[118] The capsule was subsequently studied in nine canines.[119] Colored beads ranging in size from 3 to 6 mm were sewn into the canine small intestine. A total of 9 to 13 beads were placed in each dog. Capsule endoscopy was able to significantly identify more beads than push enteroscopy. After this study, a short report of capsule endoscopy use on a compassionate basis was published. Four patients with obscure GI bleeding were reported in whom bleeding sites were identified with capsule endoscopy.[120] In the first clinical trial, push enteroscopy was compared with capsule endoscopy in 21 patients with obscure GI bleeding.[121] Capsule endoscopy was superior to push enteroscopy in the evaluation of obscure bleeding. Capsule endoscopy made a diagnosis in 11/20 (55%) and findings included angioectasias, fresh blood, a tumor, and an ileal ulcer. Push enteroscopy made a diagnosis in 6/20 (30%); all findings were angioectasias. No additional diagnoses were made by push enteroscopy, and the capsule identified lesions found distally in the small bowel were not reachable by push enteroscopy. A trial from Germany has also been reported.[122] In 32 patients with obscure GI bleeding, capsule endoscopy was superior in providing a diagnosis. These results were statistically significant. The yield of capsule endoscopy in this series was 66%, whereas push enteroscopy's yield was 28%. The French study by Saurin and coworkers[123] reported a capsule endoscopy yield of 67% in 60 patients with obscure bleeding. These yields are clearly higher when compared with other literature concerning the yields of enteroscopy, both push and sonde, and radiographic studies in patients with obscure GI bleeding.

Capsule endoscopy has also been compared with x-ray studies of the small bowel. Costamagna and colleagues[124] reported superiority of capsule endoscopy to small bowel series in 20 patients. Eliakim and coworkers[125] reported a comparison of capsule endoscopy to small bowel series and CT scanning in 20 patients with suspected Crohn's disease. Capsule endoscopy detected all the lesions seen on small bowel series and CT scanning and detected additional lesions in 47% of cases. Capsule endoscopy was shown to be statistically superior to small bowel series. The literature continues to demonstrate the superiority of capsule endoscopy to other imaging modalities of the small bowel.[126] Although there have only been a few published series, there have been many abstracts confirming the efficacy of capsule endoscopy. There has been no difference in yield when the technology is applied to patients with overt bleeding compared with those who present with iron deficiency anemia.

Despite the apparent superiority of capsule visualization of the small bowel, there remain several concerns with this new technology. One concern is the possibility of capsule retention. Experience reveals that this occurs in approximately 1% of examinations. Barkin and Friedman[127] reported experience in 937 capsule studies. A total of seven cases of capsule retention occurred, 0.75%. All seven had obstructing ulcers of the small bowel that led to retention. None of the patients became symptomatic of obstruction despite having the capsule retained proximal to a stricture. Six of the seven had undergone pre-examination small bowel series and this was normal in all six. Thus, it is apparent that a normal small bowel series does not protect a patient from having a capsule becoming caught internally. It has been concluded that retention identifies a site of pathology that led to the study. This pathology is typically NSAID strictures, Crohn's disease, or partially obstructing tumors.

A second concern of physicians is the intensity of reading a capsule study. Typical examinations obtain images over 8 hours. Because images are obtained at a rate of two images per second, a total of 57,600 images are produced during 8 hours of acquisition.

The computer workstation allows images to be viewed singly or as a video stream. Although obtained at 2 images/second, images may be reviewed at up to 40 images/second. Because an abnormality may be present on only one image, most physicians familiar with the system believe that lesions could easily be missed at the faster rates. A single image is only on the monitor for less than 0.02 second when viewing at 40 images/second. A consensus conference of users in 2003 agreed that 15 frames/second is the fastest acceptable rate of review. At this rate, 57,600 images can be seen in 64 minutes. This takes only into account running the images as a video without stopping to examine individual images. Lewis and Swain[121] reported the viewing times of 20 examinations performed using the Given system. They averaged 56 minutes to review only the small bowel images with a range of 34 to 94 minutes. Ell and coworkers[122] also reported taking an average of 50 minutes in examining the small bowel data of 32 patients. The range was from 30 to 120 minutes. Costamagna[124] reported taking 2 hours to review each study. It was unclear in this study if the images reviewed included the gastric and colonic portions. Average small bowel passage is 4 hours and thus without viewing the gastric and colonic portions of the examination, a physician must review a minimum of 28,800 images. The time it takes to review the capsule study is extremely important, because it is a limiting factor to capsule endoscopy's acceptance by gastroenterologists. In an editorial, Fleischer[128] stated that "the time required to read the studies (60 to 90 minutes) does not make economic or practice sense." In an effort to shorten the review time, software has been developed to allow the reader to view two images simultaneously.[129] Dual-image reading places two images, one full second of image collection, on one screen, side-by-side. This could theoretically shorten the reading time by as much as 50%. In addition, to the length of time that the review takes, physicians are also concerned about reading the studies properly and not missing lesions. Suspected blood indicator software can also aid in reading a study. Fleischer also expressed concern that "without concentration on the part of the physician, a lesion could be missed."

Surgery

Exploratory surgery is often considered in the patient with recurrent obscure GI bleeding. Unfortunately, there is a low success rate for simple exploration when unaccompanied by other simultaneous evaluations such as intraoperative endoscopy. Although surgery appears to be the most straightforward modality, exact localization of the bleeding site is required when resecting the small intestine. Unlike the colon, large areas of the small bowel cannot be resected. The patient is at risk of becoming a nutritional cripple with chronic diarrhea. Because vascular lesions are the most common cause of bleeding in the small bowel and because such lesions are not grossly palpable or visible, the site of bleeding must be identified and tagged, either preoperatively or intraoperatively, to limit the resected area. Intraoperatively, a number of methods have been used with limited success.[130] Simple palpation and transillumination of the intestine can occasionally identify large vascular abnormalities and submucosal tumors, but more often areas felt to represent bleeding sites are not. Clots within the small intestine have been palpated and been mistaken for polyps. In the patient with active bleeding, reflux of blood proximally obviates the assumption that the most proximal extent of the intraluminal blood column marks its source. Transillumination may identify areas of pooling intraluminal blood but may miss the sources of slow or intermittent bleeding and often does not reveal vascular abnormalities. It is so uncommon to approach the obscurely bleeding patient with exploration alone that yields quoted come from reports in the 1960s. Retzlaff and coworkers[131] reported the results of simple exploration in 100 patients with obscure bleeding. This experience came before the advent of preoperative endoscopy; thus, the yield reported of 31% must be discounted, because it included diagnoses that today would have been made preoperatively. If one excludes diagnoses readily made today by endoscopy, such as peptic ulcer disease, colon cancer, and esophageal varices, the yield of exploration reported by Retzlaff and coworkers falls to 10%.

INTRAOPERATIVE ENTEROSCOPY

Intraoperative enteroscopy remains the most common form of total small bowel endoscopic examination.[132] Techniques to perform this examination involve either intubating the proximal jejunum with an orally passed colonoscope or using push enteroscope before performance of the laparotomy or placement of the endoscope through a mid small bowel enterotomy. The endoscopic examination is performed by having the surgeon grasp the endoscope tip and hold a short segment of bowel straight to allow endoscopic inspection. The view is best seen by dimming the overhead lights, which also allows the surgeon to look at the transilluminated bowel. Once examined both internally and externally, the small bowel is pleated onto the shaft of the endoscope and the next section of bowel is examined. Generally, examination is performed only during intubation because mucosal trauma occurs with the pleating causing artifact that may be confused with the appearance of angioectasia.[133] Identified lesions are marked serosally with a suture. At the end of the examination, the endoscope is withdrawn and sites of resection are identified by the sutures. Lewis and coworkers[134] reported the results of intraoperative enteroscopy in 23 patients using oral placement of a colonoscope. The ileocecal valve was reached in 60% of cases and the distal ileum within 2 feet of the valve was reached in 15%. The pleating of the small bowel proved traumatic. Mucosal lacerations occurred in 50% and perforations occurred in 5%. Lewis and coworkers did not encounter prolonged ileus because of the trauma to the bowel, but it has been described after intraoperative enteroscopy with a cessation of bowel function up to 11 days postoperatively.[135] Intraoperative enteroscopy can be ineffective in the actively bleeding patient, because intraluminal blood can obscure the view.[136] Intra-abdominal adhesions from previous laparotomy can also make intraoperative enteroscopy difficult.

Laparoscopic-assisted enteroscopy is being explored in several centers around the world. Only animal studies and case reports are presently in the literature.[137] Technique issues involve the placement of laparoscopic trocars before the oral passage of an enteroscope and advancement of the enteroscope during the examination. Presently, most success has been encountered with laparoscopically exteriorizing a loop of mid small bowel and placing the enteroscope through this portal.[138]

Yields of intraoperative enteroscopy in identifying the site of blood loss have been reported in the ranges of 70% to 100%.[139–144] Angioectasias are the most common nonpalpable cause of bleeding, but radiation enteritis, ulcerations, and even strictures may require endoscopic identification. Although intraoperative enteroscopy offers endoscopic cauterization with either intraoperative laser or coagulation probe application, resection is considered definitive. Kendrick and coworkers[145] reported the experience in 70 patients with obscure bleeding who came to intraoperative enteroscopy. A diagnosis was made in 74% with angioectasias accounting for 54% of the findings, ulcers accounted for 31%, tumors for 11%, and diverticula for 4%. Unfortunately, 32-month follow-up revealed only 52% without bleeding. Douard and colleagues[146] reported experience in 20 patients in whom a diagnosis was made in 16 and 6 rebled in the 19-month follow-up period.

Several other intraoperative methods have been used with less success than intraoperative endoscopy to identify small bowel bleeding sites. Multiple enterotomies are often inaccurate in locating the source of bleeding and place the patient at increased jeopardy from postoperative leak or infection. Some surgeons create the enterotomy and then inspect the bowel with a rigid sigmoidoscope. Wide resection of the small intestine may leave the patient with chronic diarrhea or malabsorption or worse with the relevant site of bleeding unexcised. Placement of an enterostomy may help localize the source of bleeding to a proximal or distal location, but localization that is more specific is impractical and requires repeated laparotomies.

Intraoperative angiography is another tool that has been successful in identifying bleeding sites within the small intestine.[147] An initial diagnostic angiography must be obtained in a patient. Greater success has been obtained when the catheter can be advanced into a subsegmental artery that feeds the identified lesion. At laparotomy, the small intestine along the mesenteric border is marked with metal clips. Repeat intraoperative angiography is performed and identification of the relevant segment of the intestine is made by its close proximity to the various clips. Because this requires sophisticated radiographic equipment, some surgeons elect to perform the laparotomy in the radiology suite. To simplify this method, preoperative angiographic marking of a bleeding site can also be accomplished. This requires superselective catheters placed as close to the bleeding point as possible. Leaving the catheter in place or embolizing the vessel with a metal coil allows the surgeon to palpate the bleeding site. Injection of vital dyes such as indigo carmine will stain the bowel for 5 days and is another way to minimize the length of resection. Successful localization with injection of methylene blue has also been reported.[148] Because these techniques have missed their mark on occasions, some authors advocate injecting the artery of the specimen with barium and x-raying the specimen to confirm excision of the lesion before closing the abdomen.

Doppler ultrasonography has been used intraoperatively to identify angioectasias initially suspected during transillumination.[149] The handheld probe detects the increased blood flow through these shunts. Some authors have also advocated measuring venous pressure and oxygen saturation.[104] The lack of appropriate desaturation or "step-down" in the mesenteric vein suggests that it is being fed preferentially by an arteriovenous fistula.

In the actively bleeding patient who has a positive bleeding scan before surgery, intraoperative scintigraphy has been successful in localizing the bleeding site to a specific loop of bowel.[104] The gamma camera is brought to the operating room as the laparotomy is performed. The bowel is clamped every 30 cm to prevent run off of blood. Each segment is then scanned and the appropriate segment can be resected. The use of a gamma camera as opposed to the use of an uncollimated, handheld Geiger counter permits more accurate and direct imaging of larger areas of the intestine in a shorter period. The use of atraumatic clamps minimizes the effect of backwash of intraluminal blood, improving the accuracy of localization and helping to reduce the length of intestine resected.

Diagnostic and Therapeutic Approaches

The American Gastroenterological Association (AGA) medical position statement concerning the evaluation and management of obscure bleeding was published in January of 2000, before the initial studies using capsule endoscopy.[150] The position statement proposes progressive testing with bleeding scans and angiography for those patients with active bleeding and repeat endoscopy, enteroscopy, enteroclysis, or small bowel series for those not actively bleeding. With continued blood loss, intraoperative enteroscopy is suggested.

The extent of the evaluation of the patient with obscure bleeding is dependent on two major factors: the extent of the bleeding and the age of the patient. Patients with occult blood in their stool but no associated anemia most likely do not require evaluation beyond colonoscopy unless upper tract symptoms are present. Certainly, advanced testing beyond colonoscopy and upper endoscopy is not warranted in this group. Patients with an ongoing transfusion requirement need a full evaluation. The most common cause of obscure bleeding in this group is angioectasia, accounting for up to 80% of causes. These patients are typically older than 60 years. Small bowel tumors are the most common cause of obscure bleeding in patients younger than the age of 50. Young patients should be handled differently than older patients. Management decisions in the older group are often quite difficult because the natural history of angioectasias is still not known. It is estimated that less than 10% of all patients with angioectasia will eventually bleed. Once lesions have bled, their tendency to rebleed is also not known. Although physicians are anxious to treat these lesions, it may be that as many as 50% will not rebleed.

In the patient presenting obscure GI bleeding with either positive fecal occult blood testing and associated anemia or overt bleeding with melena or maroon blood per rectum, colonoscopy and upper endoscopy should be performed. Barium studies can be considered but should not replace endoscopic examinations. In the face of continued bleeding and initially negative colonoscopy and upper endoscopy, repeated endoscopic examinations can be worthwhile. Repeated barium studies are not indicated. Once all the standard examinations are negative, the small bowel may be assumed to be the source of blood loss.

Capsule endoscopy may be the answer to the longstanding desire for the complete endoscopic examination of the entire small bowel.

Capsule endoscopy has only been evaluated by three small trials thus far and outcomes studies need to be performed. However, early worldwide experience suggests that this examination may prove to be the preferred method of small bowel evaluation, because of the length of the small bowel examined, the quality of the examination, and the noninvasive nature of the test. Using capsule endoscopy, the evaluation of patients with GI bleeding in the future may be very different from current practice. Capsule endoscopy may become the third test in the evaluation of patients with GI bleeding, once upper endoscopy and colonoscopy are negative. In the patient with active bleeding, capsule endoscopy can confirm the small bowel as the site of bleeding, providing a location. Even if the study is negative for the small bowel in the actively bleeding patient, the study may indicate that the bleeding is actually colonic or even gastric in origin. In the patient with active bleeding within the small intestine, the capsule will guide further evaluation and therapy. A patient with a small bowel tumor detected by capsule endoscopy will proceed directly to laparoscopic surgery. If the site of bleeding is identified in the proximal small bowel and there is no mass, push enteroscopy will be used to reidentify the site and cauterize the lesion. In cases in which a distal small bowel site is identified, surgical intervention coupled with intraoperative enteroscopy will be necessary. Because the entire small bowel has been examined with the capsule examination, surgery can be targeted and a laparoscopic-assisted approach coupled with intraoperative enteroscopy to examine only the suspected area will be performed. This will simplify the surgical option. In patients with isolated iron deficiency or a more occult or intermittent type of bleeding, capsule endoscopy will be used similarly to identify an intestinal bleeding lesion and thereby direct subsequent testing or treatment. The early diagnosis of tumors of the small bowel will be obtained and those with negative examinations will be reassured. Although outcomes studies are needed, it would appear that the early use of capsule endoscopy would not only allow more rapid diagnosis and thus improved patient care but also could lessen the costs associated with obscure bleeding. Repeated colonoscopy and upper endoscopy would be avoided and with a diagnosis, repeat hospitalizations and transfusions could be averted. There is little doubt in my mind that practice guidelines will change with increased experience with using capsule endoscopy.

In the patient presenting with positive fecal occult blood testing, colonoscopy and upper endoscopy should be performed. Barium studies can be considered but should not replace endoscopic examinations. In the face of continued bleeding and initially negative colonoscopy and upper endoscopy, repeated endoscopic examinations can be worthwhile. Repeated barium studies are not indicated. Once all the standard examinations are negative, the small bowel may be assumed to be the source of blood loss. Push enteroscopy should be considered early because of its relative ease of performance and ability to provide therapy. Further evaluations are not usually warranted, however, unless the patient requires transfusion. The exception to this rule is in younger patients who tolerate anemia well and thus avoid transfusion despite ongoing bleeding. In these cases, despite its low yield, a small bowel series or, preferably, an enteroclysis, is recommended to ensure that no gross, obvious bleeding site exists. Exploratory laparoscopy is an effective method of diagnosing and treating small bowel tumors in young patients.

With massive hemorrhage from the small bowel, bleeding scan and or angiography usually rapidly identifies the site of bleeding. Exploratory surgery is usually successful. If at surgery, there is no palpable cause of bleeding, one cannot trust that the proximal most end of the blood in the bowel is the site of hemorrhage. At these times, intraoperative scintigraphy or endoscopy can be useful to identify the exact site and thereby limit the amount of bowel resected. The actual cause of bleeding may not be diagnosed by endoscopy, but the site can be identified as the area with the freshest blood. If preoperative angiography is positive, vital staining or embolization with a metal coil, which can then be palpated at surgery, can aid subsequent surgery.

Difficulty in diagnosis commonly is encountered in the patient presenting with slower bleeding. Once all the standard examinations are negative, the small bowel is assumed to be the source of blood loss. Further evaluation is clearly indicated in those patients that have an ongoing transfusion requirement. Despite the low yield, a small bowel series or enteroclysis is recommended to ensure that no gross, obvious bleeding site exists such as a large tumor or Crohn's disease. Push enteroscopy should be considered before repeating any of the previous examinations such as upper endoscopy or colonoscopy when searching for an obscure cause of bleeding. The finding of a tumor will lead to surgery, and discovered angioectasias can be cauterized. Bleeding scans and angiography are withheld unless the patient is actively bleeding. Although acutely obtained bleeding scans may be positive, they do not aid in directing therapy but merely confirm that bleeding is intestinal. Delayed views from a bleeding scan are not worthwhile. Some authors have also advocated stress angiography or pharmacoangiography, although the true yields are not known. Heparinization does not increase bleeding but merely continues bleeding at the same rate. Vasodilator and antithrombolytic agents can be dangerous and I do not advocate their use. Exploratory surgery can then be carried out coupled with intraoperative endoscopy in a select group of patients. When diffuse angioectasias of the small intestine are discovered by enteroscopy, surgery is not indicated. There have been reports of successful treatment of bleeding angioectasias using medical therapy.

Medical therapy of vascular lesions is contrary to current practice. Endoscopic or surgical therapy is considered best at present because of its ease; relatively good long-term results; and the lack of a clearly effective, well-tolerated medical therapy. Medical therapy is usually reserved for diffuse vascular diseases of the bowel, when vascular lesions are located in relatively inaccessible locations, in patients with continued bleeding despite endoscopic or surgical management, or in patients who are not candidates for either endoscopic or surgical therapy. Fortunately, such patients are quite uncommon. Diffuse lesions generally do not include multiple lesions in a single segment of bowel. Gastric antral vascular ectasia (GAVE) syndrome, which involves a myriad of vascular lesions within the gastric antrum, is treated endoscopically. Similarly, multiple cecal vascular lesions without evidence of other vascular lesions would be treated endoscopically or surgically. Diffuse lesions most often involve more than one location in the bowel (e.g., stomach and small bowel). This is an uncommon occurrence. Berner and coworkers[4] reported the results of enteroscopy in 450 patients with obscure bleeding. Only four patients had vascular lesions within the stomach, duodenum, jejunum, and ileum. Diffuse illness of the bowel may suggest the presence of a systemic illness such as HHT or cirrhosis. Such systemic illness is another reason to pursue a medical alternative. Medical therapy is also indicated in patients with lesions located in inaccessible portions of the bowel. Generally, this suggests lesions within the distal jejunum and ileum. These situations presently require surgery and if the patient cannot tolerate surgery, medical therapy may be tried. The last group of patients in whom medical therapy is indicated is those patients with continued bleeding after endoscopic or surgical therapy. These are the most frustrating group—those who continue to bleed despite appropriate management. Lewis and coworkers[134] reported the follow-up results of exploratory laparotomy and intraoperative enteroscopy in 20 patients with bleeding from vascular lesions of the small bowel. Of these, nine developed rebleeding postoperatively, including two patients with diffuse vascular lesions of the small bowel. These rebleeding patients would be best managed medically postoperatively.

Medical therapy has been pursued along several lines:

1. Supportive care. The most common form of medical therapy has been simple supportive care. This may include iron therapy and avoidance of aspirin and other anticoagulants. Transfusions may be necessary, occasionally on a regular basis.

2. Estrogens. The second form of medical therapy has been the use of estrogens. Hormonal therapy for bleeding from vascular malformations has been used since the 1950s. It was initially noted that a woman with HHT had epistaxis that varied with her menstrual cycle.[151] Estrogen-progesterone therapy for epistaxis in HHT patients has been used in uncontrolled fashion since. A controlled trial has failed to show any benefit from this therapy.[152] Estrogen has been used in GI bleeding in several case reports, two uncontrolled trials,[153,154] and four controlled trials.[155,156] Junquera and coworkers[157] reported the results of a multicenter, randomized trial of hormonal therapy in 68 patients with bleeding angioectasias. Patients were randomized to receive placebo or ethynylestradiol 0.01 mg plus norethisterone 2 mg daily for a minimum of 1 year. There was no difference between these two groups either in number of transfusions or number of bleeding episodes. Thirty-nine percent in the treatment group continued to bleed, and 46% in the placebo group continued to bleed. In addition, many patients cannot tolerate hormonal treatment. Lewis and colleagues[41] reported that 57% of the treated patients complained of side effects of hormonal therapy including vaginal bleeding, fluid retention, congestive heart failure, and gynecomastia among others. Therapy was stopped in 40%. There was no evidence of significant side effects. Thus, it does not appear that hormonal therapy is effective in stopping or reducing bleeding from angioectasia.

3. Miscellaneous. There have been other medical attempts to control bleeding from intestinal vascular lesions. Somatostatin has been used with some reported success, although it was used in an uncontrolled fashion.[158-160] Use of octreotide in a dose of 0.1 mg subcutaneously twice daily has been used and resulted reduced blood loss. It is postulated that the medication works by reducing splanchnic blood flow and by enhancing platelet aggregation. In addition, there has been a

report using aminocaproic acid (Amicar) in two patients with HHT and GI bleeding.[161] Patients were treated with 1 and 1.5 g twice daily and bleeding decreased. It is postulated that aminocaproic acid, which is an inhibitor of the fibrinolytic system, allows fibrin to close bleeding sites. Thalidomide use in obscure bleeding has also been reported in case report.[162] It was felt to work because of its antiangiogenic property. Clearly, additional studies of these medical therapies are needed.

Summary

I advocate several basic tenants before instituting any therapy for vascular lesions of the bowel. First, therapy should only be considered for bleeding vascular lesions. Nonbleeding lesions do not require intervention either medical or surgical. Long-term studies show a low bleeding rate when these lesions are followed. Thus, it is recommended that no prophylactic therapy should be given to incidentally found ectasias. Second, a bleeding dyscrasia should also always be considered in patients with recurrent bleeding and a bleeding time, prothrombin time, and partial thromboplastin time should be obtained. GI angioectasia has been associated with vWD.[163,164] Fressinaud and Meyer[165] reported an international survey of 297 centers dealing with patients with vWD. The incidence of angioectasia in patients with acquired vWD was 11.7%. These patients had a median age of 69 years. Patients with congenital vWD had a 2% incidence of angioectasias in type II disease and a 4.5% incidence in type III disease. These patients had a median age of 55 years. The authors concluded that the association between angioectasia and vWD is not a coincidence and that angioectasias formation was associated with the absence of high-molecular-weight multimers of von Willebrand's factor, which is only seen in type II and III disease and acquired vWD. Third, the treating physician must define the treatment goals. In a patient with profuse bleeding or bleeding for an extended period, one might not expect complete cure. Thus, a realistic treatment goal may be to limit transfusions and be able to manage the anemia of bleeding with iron therapy, oral or parenteral. At the same time, the initial presentation should not dissuade the physician from one therapy versus another. Treatment outcomes are not determined by the type of bleeding a patient experiences. Active bleeding is not a prerequisite for endoscopic therapy, and occult bleeding or iron deficiency is not a prerequisite for medical therapy. Fourth, that which is treatable should be treated. Often patients with diffuse vascular lesions of the small bowel can have their bleeding controlled with simple cauterization of the most proximal lesions. Complete and total ablation of all vascular lesions is often unnecessary to eliminate a transfusion requirement. Fifth, there is no uniform therapy. Therapy is individually decided on in this set of diseases. There is no role for empiric right hemicolectomy nor any empiric therapy for presumed but unconfirmed vascular diseases of the bowel. Each treatment is individually decided. Sixth, if surgery is contemplated, the entire bowel must be evaluated preoperatively or intraoperatively because of the high incidence of concomitant disease elsewhere in the bowel.

REFERENCES

1. Peterson W: Obscure gastrointestinal bleeding. Med Clin North Am 72:1169–1176, 1988.
2. Lewis B, Waye J: Bleeding from the small intestine. In Sugawa C, Schuman B, Lucas C (eds): Gastrointestinal Bleeding. New York, Igaku-Shoin, 1992, pp 178–188.
3. Netterville R, Hardy J, Martin R: Small bowel hemorrhage. Ann Surg 167:949–957, 1968.
4. Berner J, Mauer K, Lewis B: Push and sonde enteroscopy for obscure GI bleeding. Am J Gastroenterol 89:2139–2142, 1994.
5. Szold A, Katz L, Lewis B: Surgical approach to occult GI bleeding. Am J Surg 163:90–92, 1992.
6. Sahai AV, Pineault R: An assessment of the use of costs and quality of life as outcomes in endoscopic research. Gastrointest Endosc 46:113–118, 1997.
7. Foutch PG, Sawyer R, Sanowski R: Push-enteroscopy for diagnosis of patients with gastrointestinal bleeding of obscure origin. Gastrointest Endosc 36:337–341, 1990.
8. Flickinger EG, Stanforth AC, Sinar DR: Intraoperative video panendoscopy for diagnosing sites of chronic intestinal bleeding. Am J Surg 157:137–142, 1989.
9. Goldfarb N, Phillips A, Conn M, et al: Economic and health outcomes of capsule endoscopy. Dis Manage 5:123–135, 2002.
10. Lewis B: Vascular diseases of the small intestine. In DiMarino A, Benjamin S (eds): Gastrointestinal Disease: An Endoscopic Approach. Malden, MA, Blackwell Science, 1997, pp 541–550.
11. Lewis B: Vascular anomalies. In Schlesinger M, Fordtran J, Petersen W, Fleischer D (eds): Advances in Gastrointestinal Diseases. Philadelphia, WB Saunders, 1992, pp 3:105–112.
12. Harford W: Gastrointestinal angiodysplasia: Clinical features. Endoscopy 20:144–148, 1988.
13. Lewis B, Mauer K, Harpaz N, et al: The correlation of endoscopically identified vascular lesions to their pathologic diagnosis [abstract]. Gastrointest Endosc 39:344, 1993.
14. Peoples J, Kartha R, Sharif S: Multiple phlebectasia of the small intestine. Am Surg 47:373–376, 1981.
15. Haddad H, Wilkins L: Congenital anomalies associated with gonadal aplasia, review of 53 cases. Pediatrics 23:885–902, 1959.
16. Engel E, Forbes A: Cytogenetic and clinical findings in 48 patients with congenitally defective or absent ovaries. Medicine 44:135–164, 1965.
17. Rosenkrans P, de Rooy D, Bosman F, et al: Gastrointestinal telangiectasia as a cause of severe blood loss in systemic sclerosis. Endoscopy 12:200–204, 1980.
18. Golitz L: Heritable cutaneous disorders that affect the gastrointestinal tract. Med Clin North Am 64:829–846, 1980.
19. Ottinger L, Vickery A: A 30 year history of recurrent gastrointestinal bleeding. N Engl J Med 305:211–218, 1981.
20. Baum S, Athanasoulis C, Waltman A, et al: Angiodysplasia of the right colon: A cause of gastrointestinal bleeding. AJR Am J Roentgenol 129:789–794, 1977.
21. Boley S, Sammartano R, Adams A, et al: On the nature and etiology of vascular ectasias of the colon. Gastroenterology 72:650–660, 1977.
22. Hochter W, Weingart W, Kuhner E, et al: Angiodysplasia in the colon and rectum—endoscopic morphology, localization, and frequency. Endoscopy 17:182–185, 1985.
23. Heer M, Sulser H, Hany A: Angiodysplasia of the colon: An expression of occlusive vascular disease. Hepatogastroenterology 34:127–131, 1987.
24. Roskell D, Biddolph S, Warren B: Apparent deficiency of mucosal vascular collagen type IV associated with angiodysplasia of the colon. J Clin Pathol 51:18–20, 1998.
25. Junquera F, Saperas E, de-Torres I, et al: Increased expression of angiogenic factors in human colonic angiodysplasia. Am J Gastroenterol 94:1070–1076, 1999.

26. Sabba C, Cirulli A, Rizzi R, et al: Angiogenesis and hereditary telangiectasia. Rendu-Osler-Weber disease. Acta Haematol 106:214-219, 2001.
27. McAllister KA, Grogg KM, Johnson DW, et al: Endoglin, a TGF-β binding protein of endothelial cells, is the gene for hereditary haemorrhagic teleangiectasia type 1. Nat Genet 8:345–351, 1994.
28. Marchuk D, Guttmacher A, Penner J, Ganguly P: Report on the workshop on hereditary hemorrhagic telangiectasia, July 10-11, 1997. Am J Med Genet 76:269–273, 1998.
29. Quintero E: Upper gastrointestinal bleeding caused by gastroduodenal vascular malformations. Dig Dis Sci 31:897–905, 1986.
30. Meyer C, Troncale F, Galloway S, Sheahan D: Arteriovenous malformations of the bowel: An analysis of 22 cases and a review of the literature. Medicine 60:36–48, 1981.
31. Lewis B, Kornbluth A, Waye J: Small bowel tumors: The yield of enteroscopy. Gut 32:763–765, 1991.
32. Brandt L: Anemic halos around telangiectasias. Gastroenterology 92:1282, 1987.
33. Weaver G, Alpern H, Davis J, et al: Gastrointestinal angiodysplasia associated with aortic valve disease: Part of a spectrum of angiodysplasia of the gut. Gastroenterology 77:1–11, 1979.
34. Scheffer S, Leatherman L: Resolution of Heyde's syndrome of aortic stenosis and gastrointestinal bleeding after aortic valve replacement. Ann Thorac Surg 42:477–480, 1986.
35. Cappell M, Lebwohl O: Cessation of recurrent bleeding from gastrointestinal angiodysplasias after aortic valve replacement. Ann Intern Med 105:54–57, 1986.
36. Imperiale T, Ransohoff D: Aortic stenosis, idiopathic gastrointestinal bleeding and angiodysplasia: Is there an association. Gastroenterology 95:1670–1676, 1988.
37. Mehta P, Heinsimer J, Bryg R, et al: Reassessment of the association between gastrointestinal arteriovenous malformations and aortic stenosis. Am J Med 86:275–277, 1989.
38. Foutch P, Rex D, Lieberman D: Prevalence and natural history of colonic angiodysplasia among healthy asymptomatic people. Am J Gastroenterol 90:564–567, 1995.
39. Richter J, Christensen M, Colditz G: Angiodysplasia: Natural history and efficacy of therapeutic interventions. Dig Dis Sci 34:1542–1546, 1989.
40. Hutcheon D, Kabelin J, Bulkley G, Smith G: Effect of therapy on bleeding rates in gastrointestinal angiodysplasia. Am Surg 53:6–9, 1987.
41. Lewis B, Salomon P, Rivera-MacMurray S, et al: Does hormonal therapy have any benefit for bleeding angiodysplasia? J Clin Gastroenterol 15:99–103, 1992.
42. Rossini F, Risio M, Pennazio M: Small bowel tumors and polyposis syndromes. Gastrointest Endosc Clin N Am 9:93–114, 1999.
43. Conn M. Tumors of the small intestine. In DiMarino A, Benjamin S (eds): Gastrointestinal Disease: An Endoscopic Approach. Malden, MA, Blackwell Science, 1997, pp 551–566.
44. Martin L, Max M, Richardson J, Peterson G: Small bowel tumors: Continuing challenge. South Med J 73:981–985, 1980.
45. Ashley S, Wells S: Tumors of the small intestine. Semin Oncol 15:116–28, 1988.
46. Herbsman H, Wetstein L, Rosen Y, et al: Tumors of the small intestine. Curr Probl Surg 17:121–182, 1980.
47. Barakat M: Endoscopic features of primary small bowel lymphoma: A proposed endoscopic classification. Gut 23:36–41, 1982.
48. Halphen M, Najjar T, Jaafoura H, et al: Diagnostic value of upper intestinal fiber endoscopy in primary small intestinal lymphoma. Cancer 58:2140–2145, 1986.
49. Miettinen M, Lasota J: Gastrointestinal stromal tumors (GISTs): Definition, occurrence, pathology, differential diagnosis and molecular genetics. Pol J Pathol 54:3–24, 2003.
50. Farmer R, Hawk W, Turnbull R: Clinical patterns in Crohn's disease: A statistical study of 615 cases. Gastroenterology 68:627–635, 1975.
51. Brown C, Olshaker J: Meckel's diverticulum. Am J Emerg Med 6:157–164, 1988.
52. Ellison E, Wilson S: The Zollinger-Ellison syndrome: Reappraisal and evaluation of 260 registered cases. Ann Surg 160:512–515, 1964.
53. Allen A, Boley S, Schultz L, et al: Potassium-induced lesions of the small bowel. JAMA 193:997–1006, 1965.
54. Morris A: Nonsteroidal anti-inflammatory drug enteropathy. Gastrointest Endosc Clin N Am 9:125–133, 1999.
55. Harris M, Lewis B: Systemic diseases affecting the mesenteric circulation. Surg Clin North Am 72:245–259, 1992.
56. Sorbi D, Conio M, Gostout C: Vascular disorders of the small bowel. Gastrointest Endosc Clin N Am 9:71–92, 1999.
57. Sher M, Bauer J: Radiation-induced enteropathy. Am J Gastroenterol 85:121–128, 1990.
58. Akhrass R, Yaffe M, Fischer C, et al: Small-bowel diverticulosis: Perceptions and reality. J Am Coll Surg 184:383–388, 1997.
59. Lewis B, Waye J: Duodenal varices. IM Intern Med Specialist 10:19, 1989.
60. Grande J, Ackermann D, Edwards W: Aortoenteric fistulas. A study of 28 autopsied cases spanning 25 years. Arch Pathol Lab Med 113:1271–1275, 1989.
61. Case 24-1991, case records of the Massachusetts General Hospital. N Engl J Med 324:1726–1732, 1991.
62. Fockens P, Tytgat G: Dieulafoy's disease. Gastrointest Endosc Clin N Am 6:739–752, 1996.
63. Eidus L, Rasuli P, Manion D, Heringer R: Caliber-persistent artery of the stomach (Dieulafoy's vascular malformation). Gastroenterology 99:1507–1510, 1990.
64. Deutsch G, Hanly M, Yeh K: Jejunal cirsoid aneurysm: A rare cause of massive lower gastrointestinal hemorrhage. Am Surg 64:1179–1182, 1998.
65. Blecker D, Bansal M, Zimmerman R, et al: Dieulafoy's lesions of the small bowel causing massive gastrointestinal bleeding: Two case reports and literature review. Am J Gastroenterol 96:902–905, 2001.
66. Lewis B: Radiology versus endoscopy of the small bowel. Gastrointest Clin N Am 9:13–27, 1999.
67. Bowden T: Endoscopy of the small intestine. Surg Clin North Am 69:1237–1247, 1989.
68. Rabe F, Becker G, Begozzi M, et al: Efficacy study of the small-bowel examination. Radiology 140:47–50, 1981.
69. Fried A, Poulos A, Hatfield D: The effectiveness of the incidental small-bowel series. Radiology 140:45–46, 1981.
70. Gordon SR, Smith RE, Power GC: The role of endoscopy in the evaluation of iron deficiency anemia in patients over the age of 50. Am J Gastroenterol 89:1963–1967, 1994.
71. Rockey DC, Cello, JP: Evaluation of the gastrointestinal tract in patients with iron-deficiency anemia. N Engl J Med 329:1691–1695, 1993.
72. Gurian L, Jendrzejewski J, Katon R, et al: Small-bowel enema: An underutilized method of small-bowel examination. Dig Dis Sci 27:1101–1108, 1982.
73. Bessette J, Maglinte D, Kelvin F, Chernish S: Primary malignant tumors in the small bowel: A comparison of the small-bowel enema and conventional follow-through examination. AJR Am J Roentgenol 153:741–744, 1989.
74. Vallance R: An evaluation of the small bowel enema based on an analysis of 350 consecutive examinations. Clin Radiol 31:227–232, 1980.
75. Dixon P, Roulston M, Nolan D: The small bowel enema: A ten year review. Clin Radiol 47:46–48, 1993.
76. Maglinte D, Burney B, Miller R: Lesions missed on small-bowel follow-through: Analysis and recommendations. Radiology 144:737–739, 1982.
77. Ott D, Chen Y, Gelfand D, et al: Detailed per-oral small bowel examination vs. enteroclysis. Radiology 155:29–34, 1985.
78. Barloon T, Lu C, Honda H, Berbaum K: Does a normal small-bowel enteroclysis exclude small-bowel disease? Abdom Imaging 19:113–115, 1994.

79. Rex D, Lappas J, Maglinte D: Enteroclysis in the evaluation of suspected small intestinal bleeding. Gastroenterology 97:58–60, 1989.

80. Antes G, Neher M, Hiemeyer V, Burger A: Gastrointestinal bleeding of obscure origin: Role of enteroclysis. Eur Radiol 6:851–854, 1996.

81. Moch A, Herlinger H, Kochman M, et al: Enteroclysis in the evaluation of obscure gastrointestinal bleeding. AJR Am J Roentgenol 163:1381–1384, 1994.

82. McGovern R, Barkin J: Enteroscopy and enteroclysis: An improved method for combined procedure. Gastrointest Radiol 15:327–328, 1990.

83. Cohen M, Barkin J: Enteroscopy and enteroclysis: The combined procedure. Am J Gastroenterol 84:1413–1415, 1989.

84. Aliperti G, Zuckerman G, Willis J, Brink J: Enteroscopy with enteroclysis. Gastrointest Endosc Clin N Am 6:803–810, 1996.

85. Willis J, Chokshi H, Zuckerman G, Aliperti G: Enteroscopy-enteroclysis: Experience with a combined endoscopic-radiographic technique. Gastrointest Endosc 45:163–167, 1997.

86. Faber S, Stehling M, Holzknecht N, et al: Pathologic conditions in the small bowel: Findings at fat-suppressed gadolinium-enhanced MR imaging with an optimized suspension of oral magnetic particles. Radiology 205:278–282, 1997.

87. Raptopoulos V, Schwartz R, McNicholas M, et al: Multiplanar helical CT enterography in patient's with Crohn's disease. Am J Roentgenol 169:1545–1550, 1997.

88. Doerfler O, Ruppert-Kohlmayr A, Reittner P, et al: Helical CT of the small bowel with an alternative oral contrast material in patients with Crohn disease. Abdom Imaging 28:313–318, 2003.

89. Markisz J, Front D, Royal H: An evaluation of 99M-Tc labeled red blood cell scintigraphy for the detection and localization of gastrointestinal bleeding sites. Gastroenterology 83:394–398, 1982.

90. Bunker S, Brown J, McAuley R: Detection of gastrointestinal bleeding sites: Use of in vitro Tc 99m-labelled RBC's. JAMA 247:789–792, 1982.

91. Emslie J, Zarnegar K, Siegel M, Beart R: Technetium-99m-labeled red blood cell scans in the investigation of gastrointestinal bleeding. Dis Colon Rectum 39:750–754, 1996.

92. Suzman M, Talmor M, Jennis R, et al: Accurate localization and surgical management of active lower gastrointestinal hemorrhage with technetium-labeled erythrocyte scintigraphy. Ann Surg 224:29–36, 1996.

93. Rantis P, Harford F, Wagner R, Henkin R: Technetium-labeled red blood cell scintigraphy: Is it useful in acute lower gastrointestinal bleeding? Int J Colorect Dis 10:210–215, 1995.

94. Garofalo T, Abdu R: Accuracy and efficacy of nuclear scintigraphy for the detection of gastrointestinal bleeding. Arch Surg 132:196–199, 1997.

95. Voeller G, Bunch G, Britt L: Use of technetium-labeled red blood cell scintigraphy in the detection and management of gastrointestinal hemorrhage. Surgery 110:799–804, 1991.

96. Brown C, Olshaker J: Meckel's diverticulum. Am J Emerg Med 6:157–164, 1988.

97. Yeker D, Buyukunal C, Benli M, et al: Radionuclide imaging of Meckel's diverticulum: Cimetidine versus pentagastrin plus glucagon. Eur J Nucl Med 9:316–319, 1984.

98. Browder W, Cerise E, Litwin M: Impact of emergency angiography in massive lower gastrointestinal bleeding. Ann Surg 204:530–536, 1986.

99. Boley S, Sprayregen S, Sammartano R, et al: The pathophysiologic basis for the angiographic signs of vascular ectasias of the colon. Radiology 125:615–621, 1977.

100. Fiorito J, Brandt L, Kozicky O, et al: The diagnostic yield of superior mesenteric angiography: Correlation with the pattern of gastrointestinal bleeding. Am J Gastroenterol 84:878–881, 1989.

101. Mernagh J, O'Donovan N, Somers S, et al: Use of heparin in the investigation of obscure gastrointestinal bleeding. Can Assoc Radiol J 52:232–235, 2001.

102. Bloomfeld R, Smith T, Schneider A, Rockey D: Provocative angiography in patients with gastrointestinal hemorrhage of obscure origin. Am J Gastroenterol 95:2807–2812, 2000.

103. Ettorre G, Francioso G, Garribba A, et al: Helical CT angiography in gastrointestinal bleeding of obscure origin. AJR Am J Roentgenol 168:727–730, 1997.

104. Gilbert D, Buelow R, Chung R, et al: Status evaluation: Enteroscopy. Gastrointest Endosc 37:673–677, 1991.

105. Lewis B: Enteroscopy. Gastrointest Endosc Clin N Am 10:101–116, 2000.

106. MacKenzie J: Push enteroscopy. Gastrointest Endosc Clin N Am 9:29–36, 1999.

107. Lewis B, Waye J: Small bowel enteroscopy: A comparison of findings with push and sonde enteroscopy in 81 patients with GI bleeding of obscure origin. Gastrointest Endosc 34:207, 1988.

108. Barkin J, Lewis B, Reiner D, et al: Diagnostic and therapeutic jejunoscopy with a new, longer enteroscope. Gastrointest Endosc 38:55–58, 1992.

109. Shimizu S, Tada M, Kawai K: Development of a new insertion technique in push-type enteroscopy. Am J Gastroenterol 82:844–847, 1987.

110. Waye J: Small-bowel endoscopy. Endoscopy 35:15–21, 2003.

111. Messer J, Romeu J, Waye J, Dave P: The value of proximal jejunoscopy in unexplained gastrointestinal bleeding. Gastrointest Endosc 30:151, 1984.

112a. Chong J, Tagle M, Barkin J, Reiner D: Small bowel push-type fiberoptic enteroscopy for patients with occult gastrointestinal bleeding or suspected small bowel pathology. Am J Gastroenterol 89:2143–2146, 1994.

112b. Descamps C, Schmit A, Van Gossum A: "Missed" upper gastrointestinal tract lesions may explain "occult" bleeding. Endoscopy 31:452–455, 1999.

112c. Pennazio M, Rossini FP: Main issues in push enteroscopy. Ital J Gastroenterol Hepatol 30:96–101, 1998.

112d. Zaman A, Katon RM: Push enteroscopy for obscure gastrointestinal bleeding yields a high incidence of proximal lesions within reach of a standard endoscope. Gastrointest Endosc 47:372–376, 1998.

113. Askin M, Lewis B: Push enteroscopic cauterization: Long-term follow-up of 83 patients with bleeding small intestinal angiodysplasia. Gastrointest Endosc 43:580–583, 1996.

114a. Landi B, Cellier C, Gaudric M, et al: Long-term outcome of patients with gastrointestinal bleeding of obscure origin explored by push enteroscopy. Endoscopy 34:355–559, 2002.

114b. Yamamoto H, Sugano K: A new method of enteroscopy—the double-balloon method. Can J Gastroenterol 17:273–274, 2003.

114c. Yamamoto H, Sekine Y, Sato Y, et al: Total enteroscopy with a nonsurgical steerable double-balloon method. Gastrointest Endosc 53:216–220, 2001.

115. Fischer D, Shreiber R, Meron G, et al: Localization of a wireless capsule endoscope in the GI tract. Gastrointest Endosc 53:AB126, 2001.

116. Liangpunsakul S, Mays L, Rex D: Performance of Given Suspected Blood Indicator. Gastrointest Endosc 57:AB164, 2003.

117. Meron G: The development of the swallowable video capsule (M2A). Gastrointest Endosc 6:817–819, 2000.

118. Iddan G, Meron G, Glukhovsky A, Swain P: Wireless capsule endoscopy. Nature 405:417, 2000.

119. Appleyard M, Fireman Z, Glukhovsky A, et al: A randomized trial comparing wireless capsule endoscopy with push enteroscopy for the detection of small-bowel lesions. Gastroenterology 119:1431–1438, 2000.

120. Appleyard M, Glukhovsky A, Swain P: Wireless-capsule diagnostic endoscopy for recurrent small-bowel bleeding. N Engl J Med 344:232–233, 2001.

121. Lewis B, Swain P: Capsule endoscopy in the evaluation of patients with suspected small intestinal bleeding: Results of a pilot study. Gastrointest Endosc 56:39–53, 2002.

122. Ell C, Remke S, May A, et al: The first prospective controlled trial comparing wireless capsule endoscopy with push enteroscopy in chronic gastrointestinal bleeding. Endoscopy 34:685–689, 2002.

123. Saurin J, Delvaux M, Gaudin H, et al: Diagnostic value of endoscopic capsule in patients with obscure digestive bleeding: Blinded comparison with video push-enteroscopy. Endoscopy 35:576–584, 2003.

124. Costamagna G, Shah S, Riccioni M, et al: A prospective trial comparing small bowel radiographs and video capsule endoscopy for suspected small bowel disease. Gastroenterology 123:999–1005, 2002.

125. Eliakim R, Fischer D, Suissa A, et al: Wireless capsule video endoscopy is a superior diagnostic tool in comparison to barium follow-through and computerized tomography in patients with suspected Crohn's disease. Eur J Gastroenterol Hepatol 15:363–367, 2003.

126. Scapa E, Jacob H, Lewkowicz S, et al: Initial experience of wireless-capsule endoscopy for evaluating occult gastrointestinal bleeding and suspected small bowel pathology. Am J Gastroenterol 97:2776–2779, 2002.

127. Barkin J, Friedman S: Wireless capsule endoscopy requiring surgical intervention: The world's experience. Am J Gastroenterol 97:S–298, 2002.

128. Fleischer D: Capsule endoscopy: The voyage is fantastic—will it change what we do. Gastrointest Endosc 56:452–456, 2002.

129. Davidson T, Shreiber R, Jacob H: Multi-viewing of video streams: A new concept for efficient review of capsule endoscopy studies. Gastrointest Endosc 57:AB164, 2003.

130. Biener A, Palestro C, Lewis B, Katz L: Intraoperative scintigraphy for active small intestinal bleeding. Surg Gynecol Obstet 171:388–392, 1990.

131. Retzlaff J, Hagedorn A, Bartholomen L: Abdominal exploration for gastrointestinal bleeding of obscure origin. JAMA 177:104–107, 1961.

132. Delmotte J, Gay G, Houcke P, et al: Intraoperative endoscopy. Gastrointest Endosc Clin N Am 1:61–69, 1999.

133. Frank M, Brandt L, Boley S: Iatric submucosal hemorrhage: A pitfall of intraoperative endoscopy. Am J Gastroenterol 75:209–210, 1981.

134. Lewis B, Wenger J, Waye J: Intraoperative enteroscopy versus small bowel enteroscopy in patients with obscure GI bleeding. Am J Gastroenterol 86:171–174, 1991.

135. Whelan R, Buls J, Goldberg S, et al: Intraoperative endoscopy: University of Minnesota experience. Am Surg 55:281–286, 1989.

136. Bowden T, Hooks V, Mansberger A: Intraoperative gastrointestinal endoscopy. Ann Surg 191:680–687, 1980.

137. Chung R: Laparoscopy-assisted jejunal resection for bleeding leiomyoma. Surg Endosc 12:162–163, 1998.

138. Matsushita M, Hajiro K, Takakuwa H, Fujikawa T: Laparoscopically assisted panenteroscopy for gastrointestinal bleeding of obscure origin. Gastrointest Endosc 46:474–475, 1997.

139. Bowden T, Hooks V, Teeslink C, et al: Occult gastrointestinal bleeding, locating the cause. Am Surgeon 46:80–87, 1980.

140. Strodel W, Eckhauser F, Knol J, et al: Intraoperative fiberoptic endoscopy. Am Surg 50:340–344, 1984.

141. Mathus-Vliegen E, Tytgat G: Intraoperative endoscopy: Technique, indications and results. Gastrointest Endosc 32:381–384, 1986.

142. Apelgren K, Vargish T, Al-Kawas F: Principles for use of intraoperative enteroscopy for hemorrhage from the small bowel. Am Surg 54:85–87, 1988.

143. Desa L, Ohri S, Hutton K, et al: Role of intraoperative enteroscopy in obscure gastrointestinal bleeding of small bowel origin. Br J Surg 78:192–195, 1991.

144. Lau W, Wong S, Yuen W, et al: Intraoperative enteroscopy for bleeding angiodysplasias of the small intestine. Surg Gynecol Obstet 168:341-344, 1989.

145. Kendrick M, Buttar N, Anderson M, et al: Contribution of intraoperative enteroscopy in the management of obscure gastrointestinal bleeding. J Gastrointest Surg 5:162–167, 2001.

146. Douard R, Wind P, Panis Y, et al: Intraoperative enteroscopy for diagnosis and management of unexplained gastrointestinal bleeding. Am J Surg 180:181–184, 2000.

147. Fazio V, Zelas P, Weakley F: Intraoperative angiography and localization of bleeding from the small intestine. Surg Gynecol Obstet 151:637–640, 1980.

148. Anthanasoulis C, Moncure A, Greenfield A, et al: Intraoperative localization of small bowel bleeding sites with combined angiographic methods and methylene blue injection. Surgery 87:77–84, 1980.

149. Cooperman M, Martin E, Evans W, Carey L: Use of Doppler ultrasound in intraoperative localization of intestinal arteriovenous malformations. Ann Surg 190:24–26, 1979.

150. American Gastroenterological Association Medical Position Statement: Evaluation and management of occult and obscure gastrointestinal bleeding. Gastroenterology 118:197–200, 2000.

151. Koch H, Escher G, Lewis J: Hormonal management of hereditary hemorrhagic telangiectasia. JAMA 149:1376–1380, 1952.

152. Vase P: Estrogen treatment of hereditary hemorrhagic telangiectasia. Acta Med Scand 209:393–396, 1981.

153. Bronner M, Pate M, Cunningham J, et al: Estrogen-progesterone therapy for bleeding gastrointestinal telangiectasias in chronic renal failure. Ann Intern Med 105:371–374, 1986.

154. Junquera F, Santos J, Saperas E, et al: Estrogen and progesterone treatment in digestive hemorrhage caused by vascular malformations. Gastroenterol Hepatol 18:61–65, 1995.

155. van Cutsem E, Rutgeerts P, Vantrappen G: Treatment of bleeding gastrointestinal vascular malformations with oestrogen-progesterone. Lancet 335:953–955, 1990.

156. Van Cutsem E: Georges Brohee Prize. Oestrogen-progesterone, a new therapy of bleeding gastrointestinal vascular malformations. Acta Gastroenterol Belg 56:2–10, 1993.

157. Junquera F, Feu F, Papo M, et al: A multicenter, randomized clinical trial of hormonal therapy in the prevention of rebleeding from gastrointestinal angiodysplasia. Gastroenterology 121:1073–1079, 2001.

158. Rossini F, Arrigoni A, Pennazio M: Octreotide in the treatment of bleeding due to angiodysplasia of the small intestine. Am J Gastroenterol 88:1424–1427, 1993.

159. Nordquist L, Wallach P: Octreotide for gastrointestinal bleeding of obscure origin in an anticoagulated patient. Dig Dis Sci 47:1514–1515, 2002.

160. Nardone G, Rocco A, Balzano T, Budillon G: The efficacy of octreotide therapy in chronic bleeding due to vascular abnormalities of the gastrointestinal tract. Aliment Pharmacol Ther 13:1429–1436, 1999.

161. Saba H, Morelli G, Logrono L: Brief report: Treatment of bleeding in hereditary hemorrhagic telangiectasia with aminocaproic acid. N Engl J Med 330:1789–1790, 1994.

162. Shurafa M, Kamboj G: Thalidomide for the treatment of bleeding angiodysplasias. Am J Gastroenterol 98:221–222, 2003.

163. Duray P, Marcal J, Livolsi V, Fisher R, et al: Gastrointestinal angiodysplasia: A possible component of von Willebrand's disease. Hum Pathol 15:539–544, 1984.

164. Ahr D, Rickles F, Hoyer L, et al: von Willebrand's disease and hemorrhagic telangiectasia. Am J Med 62:452–458, 1977.

165. Fressinaud E, Meyer D: International survey of patients with von Willebrand disease and angiodysplasia. Thromb Haemost 70:546, 1993.

Chronic Gastrointestinal Bleeding

Miguel Muñoz-Navas, Maite Betés Ibáñez, and Ignacio Fernández-Urién Sáinz

Introduction

Chronic gastrointestinal (GI) hemorrhage may be overt or occult. Overt bleeding is defined as chronic if it is persistent but not severe enough to cause circulatory compromise. It may be seen in the form of melena or red rectal bleeding. If occult, the clinical presentation is typically with anemia, with evidence of occult bleeding on testing of the stools. In some patients, chronic hemorrhage may be clinically interleaved with acute episodes.[1] Acute GI bleeding is discussed in detail in other chapters.

Chronic GI bleeding includes common clinical scenarios; however, the meaning and diagnostic criteria for the different terms are not well delineated.[2] Chronic bleeding from the gut is always significant, and in particular it must be remembered that malignant tumors of the gut may be present and curable.

There is no universal agreement as to the nomenclature of GI lesions that can cause chronic bleeding, but a simple classification is presented in Table 17–1. In this chapter, we focus on the most frequent causes of chronic GI bleeding.

Vascular lesions are an important cause of chronic GI bleeding. They may be solitary, multiple, or diffuse and may exist as isolated abnormalities or be part of a syndrome or a systemic disorder. The taxonomy of vascular abnormalities in the GI tract has been inconsistent and a source of confusion.[3,4] It may be based on histologic characteristics, gross appearance, or association with systemic diseases. These considerations permit categorization into three broad groups:

- Vascular tumors, which may be benign (e.g., hemangiomas) or malignant (e.g., Kaposi's sarcoma or angiosarcoma).

- Vascular anomalies associated with congenital or systemic diseases, such as blue rubber bleb nevus syndrome (BRBNS), Klippel-Trénaunay-Weber syndrome (KTWS), Ehlers-Danlos syndrome, pseudoxanthoma elasticum, the CREST variant of scleroderma (calcinosis, Raynaud's phenomenon, esophageal dysmotility, scleroderma, and telangiectases), and hereditary hemorrhagic telangiectasia (HHT).

- Acquired or sporadic lesions, such us angiodysplasias, gastric antral vascular ectasia (VE), radiation-induced VEs, and Dieulafoy's lesions.

Angiodysplasia of the Gastrointestinal Tract

VE of the GI tract, also referred to as angiodysplasia or less accurately as arteriovenous malformation (AVM), is a distinct clinical and pathologic entity.[5–7] It is the most common vascular abnormality of the GI tract and probably the most frequent cause of lower intestinal bleeding after age 60 years. Although the terms *angiodysplasias* and *arteriovenous malformations* have been used synonymously, the term *angiodysplasia* (Greek *angeion*, "vessel"; *dys*, "bad" or "difficult"; *plasis*, "a molding") means a poorly formed vessel but with a lesser connotation of congenital origin than with the word *malformation*. Angiodysplasias are usually distinguished from telangiectasias, which, although anatomically similar, are usually referred to in the context of systemic or hereditary diseases.

Because most vascular abnormalities are detected during endoscopy, a taxonomy based on endoscopic appearance has been

Table 17–1. Causes of Chronic Gastrointestinal Bleeding

Gastrointestinal Lesions	
Within Reach of an Upper Endoscope	**May Be Beyond Reach of an Upper Endoscope**
Esophagitis	Celiac sprue
Cameron's erosions	Crohn's disease
Peptic ulcer disease	Intestinal lymphoma
Gastritis/erosions	Small bowel angiodysplasia
Duodenitis/erosions	Small bowel tumors
Angiodysplasia	Small bowel ulcers and erosions, including NSAID/other drug-induced lesions
Portal-hypertensive gastropathy	Small bowel diverticulosis
Gastric/esophageal cancer	Small bowel varices
Gastric/duodenal polyps	Lymphangioma
Gastric/duodenal lymphoma	Radiation enteritis
Partial gastrectomy	Blue rubber bleb nevus syndrome
GAVE	Osler-Weber-Rendu syndrome
Dieulafoy's lesion	Small bowel polyposis syndromes
	Gardner's syndrome
	Amyloidosis
	Meckel's diverticulum
	Hemosuccus pancreaticus, hemobilia
	Klipple-Trénaunay-Weber syndrome

Colonic Lesions	
Colon polyps	Colitis/IBD
Colon cancer	Parasitic infestation
Angiodysplasia	Hemorrhoids
Colonic ulcers	Diverticular bleeding

GAVE, gastric antral vascular ectasia; IBD, inflammatory bowel disease; NSAID, nonsteroidal anti-inflammatory drug.

proposed.[8] The classification system recognizes the location, size, and number of angiodysplasias.

PATHOGENESIS

Angiodysplasias are composed of ectatic, dilated, thin-walled vessels that are lined by endothelium alone or by only small amounts of smooth muscle. Their anatomy has been best demonstrated by studies in which casts of the vessels were made by injecting a silicone material.[9] These studies demonstrated that the most prominent feature in angiodysplasias are dilated tortuous submucosal veins. Small arteriovenous communications are present due to incompetence of the precapillary sphincter. Enlarged arteries are also present in larger angiodysplasias and may be associated with arteriovenous fistulas, which explains why bleeding can occur in some patients.

Histologic examination demonstrates dilated vessels in the mucosa and submucosa, sometimes covered by a single layer of surface epithelium. These features are shared by angiodysplasias in the colon and stomach.[10]

The pathogenesis of angiodysplasias is not well understood. Four theories have been proposed:

1. Angiodysplasias may develop in response to chronic partial, intermittent, low-grade obstruction of the submucosal veins at the point where they penetrate the muscle layers of the colon.[9] Following this logic, the prevalence of VEs in the right colon can be attributed to a greater tension in the cecal wall compared with that other parts of the colon, according to Laplace's principle. Over many years, repeated contraction and distention of the cecum results in dilation and tortuosity of the submucosal vein and, later, the venules and capillaries draining into it. Finally, the capillary rings dilate, the precapillary sphincters become incompetent, and a tiny arteriovenous fistula develops.

2. Angiodysplasias may be a complication of chronic mucosal ischemia, which can occur during episodes of bowel obstruction or straining stools.[11]

3. Angiodysplasias may be a complication of local ischemia associated with cardiac, vascular, or pulmonary disease.[12]

4. Angiodysplasias may be congenital, which is probably more likely in young patients or those who have angiodysplasias associated with congenital diseases.

Increased expression of angiogenic factors have been found in human colonic angiodysplasias.[13]

EPIDEMIOLOGY AND NATURAL HISTORY

The prevalence of GI angiodysplasias in the overall population is not well known because asymptomatic individuals usually do not undergo endoscopic evaluation. VEs have been seen in 0.2% to 2.9% of "nonbleeding persons"[14,15] and in 2.6% to 6.2% of patients evaluated specifically for occult blood in the stool, anemia, or hemorrhage.[14–16]

Angiodysplasias occur most often in the colon, where they are an important cause of lower GI bleeding, particularly in patients older than 60,[17–19] although presentation in patients in their 30s has been described.[20] There is no gender predilection.

CLINICAL MANIFESTATIONS

Angiodysplasias can remain clinically silent or cause bleeding. Patients who bleed typically present with occult blood loss and are more likely than other patients with GI bleeding to have had prior admissions for GI bleedings.[21]

Bleeding from vascular lesions typically is recurrent and low grade, although approximately 15% of patients present with massive hemorrhage. The nature and degree of bleeding frequently vary in the same patient with different episodes, and patients may have bright red blood, maroon-colored stools, and melena on separate occasions. In 20% to 25% of episodes, only tarry stools are passed, and in 10% to 15% of patients, bleeding is evidenced only by iron deficiency anemia, with stools that are intermittently positive for occult blood.[22] The spectrum reflects the varied rate of bleeding from the ectatic capillaries and venules. In more than 90% of instances, bleeding stops spontaneously. In the past, as many as 30% of patients with vascular lesions had had "blind" surgery for presumed diverticular or idiopathic bleeding. With the advent of endoscopy, the percentage of patients who have had operations has decreased, because most lesions are identified and treated at the time of the first episode.[23]

Stomach and Duodenum

Angiodysplasias of the stomach have been incriminated as the cause of blood loss in 4% to 7% of patients with GI bleeding.[17,24] However, angiodysplasias in the stomach or duodenum are found incidentally in approximately 50% of cases[25] with these lesions.

The risk that an incidentally found gastric or duodenal angiodysplasia will subsequently bleed is uncertain. On the other hand, patients who have bled from gastric or duodenal angiodysplasias are at increased risk of subsequent bleeding. This was illustrated in a series of 30 patients with gastric or duodenal angiodysplasias; 77% had experienced at least one episode of overt bleeding before diagnosis.[17]

Small Intestine

Angiodysplasias can be found throughout the small intestine. Most series that have evaluated small intestine angiodysplasias have included patients with GI bleeding of unclear etiology despite upper endoscopy and colonoscopy. In one series using push enteroscopy, small intestinal angiodysplasias were considered to be responsible for bleeding in 33 of 83 patients with iron deficiency anemia that was unexplained after upper endoscopy and colonoscopy.[26]

Colon

The colon is the most common site of angiodysplasias in the GI tract; colonic lesions are most often found in cecum and ascending colon.

Angiodysplasias of the colon account for approximately 20% to 30% of cases of acute lower GI bleeding, which is comparable in frequency to colonic diverticular bleeding.[27]

An angiodysplasia can be confidently considered a source of GI bleeding only if it is seen to be active bleeding. The risk of subsequent bleeding in patients who are found to have nonbleeding colonic angiodysplasia is not well established. The number of lesions and the presence of coexisting coagulopathy or platelet dysfunction may be important determinants. Patients who have bled from colonic angiodysplasias are at increased risk for subsequent bleeding.[9]

CONDITIONS WITH INCREASED PREVALENCE

End-Stage Renal Disease

Angiodysplasia is the second most common cause of GI bleeding in patients with end-stage renal disease.[28] These lesions account for about 20% and 30% of upper and lower GI bleeds, respectively,[28] and approximately half of recurrent upper GI bleeds.[29] In a prospective study of upper GI hemorrhage over a 50-month period, VE was the etiology of upper GI hemorrhage in 13% of patients with renal insufficiency and was the etiology of bleeding more often in patients with renal insufficiency than in those with normal renal function.[30] The prevalence of VE as a cause of upper GI bleeding was related to the duration of renal failure and the requirement of hemodialysis. The lesions can occur anywhere along the GI tract and are usually multiple.[29]

The reason for the increased prevalence among patients with end-stage renal disease is unknown. One possible explanation is that the lesions are detected more frequently because of the increased risk of bleeding associated with uremia-induced platelet dysfunction.

von Willebrand's Disease

An association between angiodysplasias and congenital or acquired von Willebrand's disease has been reported.[31,32] This association may reflect an increased tendency for angiodysplasias to become clinically evident because of the underlying coagulopathy.

Aortic Stenosis

Approximately 50% of patients with bleeding VEs have evidence of cardiac disease, and as many as 25% have been reported to have aortic stenosis. Bleeding from angiodysplasias in patients with aortic stenosis (Heyde's syndrome) has been repeatedly reported but remains controversial.[33] In support of this relationship is the observation that bleeding may be improved after aortic valve replacement.[34–36] Two possible explanations have been proposed to explain this observation. Patients with aortic stenosis may develop an acquired form of von Willebrand's disease, which may be reversed after aortic valve replacement.[37–39] The mechanism is thought to involve mechanical disruption of von Willebrand multimers during turbulent passage through the narrowed valve.[40] Thus, patients with aortic stenosis may be more likely to bleed from existing angiodysplasias. The observation that angiodysplasias persist following aortic valve replacement despite cessation of bleeding supports this hypothesis.[10,41]

Another explanation is that existing angiodysplasias may bleed as a result of ischemic necrosis in patients who have a low cardiac output.[11] However, this suggestion is inconsistent with the observations that bleeding angiodysplasias have not been associated with other forms of heart disease associated with a low cardiac output, and a low cardiac output is a late complication of aortic stenosis.

Several retrospective, uncontrolled studies[42,43] and a prospective, controlled investigation[44] do not substantiate a causative role or association of aortic valve diseases with colon VE. Replacement of the aortic valve for control of bleeding secondary to these vascular lesions is not universally accepted.[23] A logical approach to the patients with both lesions is to first treat the colonic lesion endoscopically, regardless of whether the patient's cardiac status warrants surgery. If valve replacement is necessary and endoscopic therapy is unsuccessful, further endoscopic or surgical treatment of the colonic angiodysplasia may be delayed until after cardiac surgery. Further attempts at endoscopic treatment or surgical resection are then indicated if bleeding recurs.[45]

Progressive Systemic Sclerosis

Vascular lesions are a prominent feature of progressive systemic sclerosis, especially in the CREST variant.[46] Angiodysplasias are usually distinguished from telangiectasias, which, although anatomically similar, are usually referred to in the context of systemic or hereditary diseases. In patients with progressive systemic sclerosis, sites most frequently involved by telangiectases are the hands, lips, tongue, and face, but gastric, intestinal, and colorectal lesions have been reported. These tiny lesions may be the source of occult or clinically significant bleeding and are the best treated, if possible, by endoscopic electrocoagulation or photocoagulation.[47]

DIAGNOSIS

Angiodysplasias are usually diagnosed during endoscopy. They have a characteristic appearance of a 5- to 10-mm, cherry-red, fernlike pattern of arborizing, ectatic blood vessels radiating from a central vessel (Fig. 17–1). This pattern should be specifically looked for because angiodysplasias may be confused with other erythematous mucosal lesions or with normal vessels (Table 17–2).[23,48]

Because traumatic and endoscopic suction artifacts may resemble vascular lesions, all lesions must be evaluated immediately on insertion of the colonoscope rather than during withdrawal. "Anemic halos" are often seen surrounding vascular lesions of the bowel. Although these do not differentiate the various types of vascular lesions, they distinguish true vascular lesions from artifacts.[45] Pinch biopsy samples of vascular lesions obtained during endoscopy are usually nonspecific; therefore, the risk of performing biopsies of these abnormalities is not justified.

The sensitivity of colonoscopy for the detection of angiodysplasias in unknown because angiography would be required as a gold standard, but sensitivity probably exceeds 80%.[18] Angiodysplasias may be difficult to visualize during colonoscopy in patients who do not have an optimal bowel cleaning. Because the appearance of vascular lesions is influenced by blood pressure, blood volume, and state of hydration, such lesions may be not evident in patients with severely reduced blood volumes or who are in shock, until red cell and volume deficits are corrected. Cold water lavage of the colon, as is sometimes done to clean the luminal surface from debris during colonoscopy, may mask underlying VEs.[49] Meperidine also may diminish the prominence of some vascular abnormalities because of a transient decrease in mucosal blood flow; its use could be minimized and its effects reversed by naloxone to detect colonic vascular lesions more accurately. Use of naloxone can enhance the appearance of normal colonic vasculature in about 10% of patients and can cause ectasias to appear (2.7%) or increase in size (5.4%).[50] However, it is unclear if the use of naloxone could lead to any significant clinical benefit given the uncertainty that a nonbleeding angiodysplasia is the cause of bleeding during standard colonoscopy, much less one that has been augmented by giving naloxone. Furthermore, reversal of narcotic analgesia may cause an uncomfortable subsequent examination, particularly if therapeutics are performed.

Because angiodysplasias are often multiple and may be located throughout the GI tract, it may be necessary to examine the entire bowel to detect all potential bleeding lesions. Endoscopic examination of the small bowel is limited by its significant length and distance from accessible orifices. Wireless capsule endoscopy is a new technology that allows visualization of the small bowel, which has been developed to facilitate examination of this inaccessible

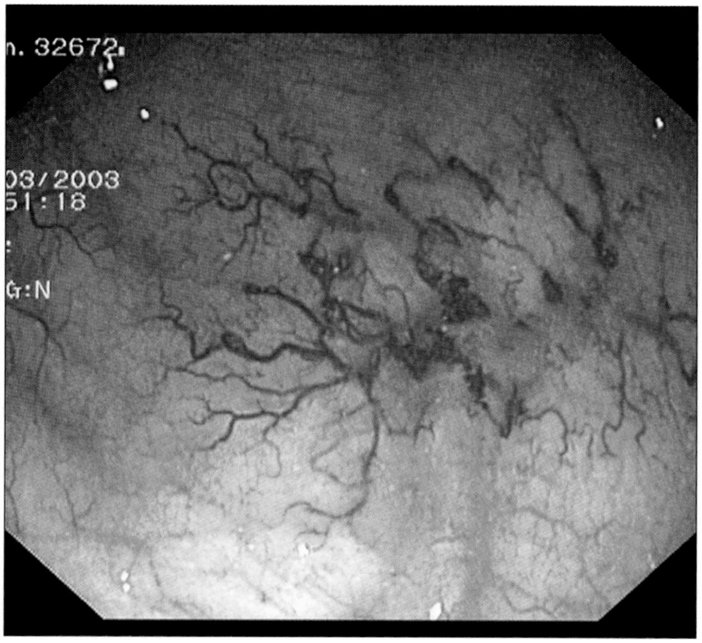

Figure 17–1. Typical angiodysplasia in the right colon. Angiodysplastic lesions are seen as slightly dilated tortuous vessels.

Table 17-2. Lesions Confused with Vascular Ectasias on Endoscopy		
	Vascular	Arteriovenous malformations
		Angiomas
		Phlebectasias
		Spiders
		Telangiectases
		Varices
		Venous stars
	Nonvascular	Trauma
		Polyps
		Adenomatous
		Hyperplastic
		Lymphoid
	Colitis	Ischemic
		Infectious
		Radiation
		Inflammatory bowel disease

portion of the GI tract.[51,52] It was approved for clinical use late in 2001. The capsule endoscope contains a miniature video camera, a light source, batteries, and a receiver attached to the body that allow images to be captured. The strength of the signal is used to calculate the position of the capsule in the body. Imaging of the esophagus, stomach, and colon is typically brief and incomplete or hampered by anatomy and preparation, respectively. The most common indication for capsule endoscopy is the evaluation of obscure GI bleeding after negative upper endoscopy, push enteroscopy, colonoscopy, and small bowel radiography.[53] In general, capsule endoscopy provides successfully imaged small-bowel pathologic features (Fig. 17–2). Although this technology cannot be used for biopsy or therapy, it may be valuable in the assessment of bleeding in patients with negative results on gastroscopy and colonoscopy. A canine model compared wireless capsule endoscopy to push enteroscopy for the detection of colored beads placed surgically throughout the small intestine.[54] Capsule endoscopy had a sensitivity of 64% and specificity of 92% compared with 37% and 97% for push enteroscopy. The first clinical report on capsule endoscopy detailed its use in 20 patients with obscure GI bleeding.[55] To date, many series pertaining to the use of capsule endoscopy in the evaluation of obscure bleeding have been published in abstract form. Capsule endoscopy identified likely sources of blood loss in 21% to 31% of patients. The most common findings were angiodysplasias, varices, ulcers, and tumors. The first prospective controlled trial comparing wireless capsule endoscopy with push enteroscopy[56] has been recently published. In this study, capsule endoscopy had the highest diagnostic yield in chronic GI bleeding and was significantly superior to push enteroscopy. The authors suggested that capsule endoscopy can help reduce the number of diagnostic procedures in these patients. Correlation between the proposed capsule localization of small bowel pathology and localization at surgery has not been validated. Future capsule designs may emerge with expanded capabilities that include fluid sampling, mucosal biopsy, targeted labeling, and controlled movement. With future innovation and study, the indications for capsule endoscopy will likely expand and become more focused.

Angiography is used to determine the site and nature of lesions during bleeding. It may permit therapy in patients who are bleeding and can identify some vascular lesions even when bleeding has ceased. The three reliable angiographic signs that diagnose VEs are a densely opacified, slowly emptying, dilated, tortuous vein; a vascular tuft; and an early-filling vein.[57] A fourth sign, extravasation of contrast material, identifies the site of bleeding when bleeding volume is at least 0.5 mL/minute but does not contribute to the diagnosis of ectasia.

Nuclear scan is another diagnostic technique that can be used in selected patients.[58,59]

Helical computed tomographic (CT) angiography may provide another method to diagnose angiodysplasias. Its accuracy may be high,[60] although studies are needed to better understand the role of this technique in the management of patients with GI bleeding.

MANAGEMENT

Management of bleeding VEs consists of three phases[23]: (1) diagnosis; (2) conversion of the emergency situation to an elective one by control of the acute hemorrhage; and (3) definitive treatment of the lesions by colonoscopic ablation, angiography, or surgical removal.

The natural history of colonic VE is benign in healthy, asymptomatic people, and the risk of bleeding is small.[61] It is estimated that only about 50% of those lesions ever bleed. Moreover, there is a risk of bleeding and perforation following attempts at endoscopic obliteration. For incidentally found lesions, endoscopic therapy is not warranted.[62]

Pharmacologic Treatment

The goals of pharmacologic therapy are to control bleeding and to prevent rebleeding.

Iron Formulations

In patients with occult bleeding, bleeding from angiodysplasia is more likely in those who have continued occult bleeding, multiple lesions, and a bleeding diathesis. Therefore, a graduated approach is reasonable in these patients beginning with iron replacement therapy if needed and pursuing more aggressive therapeutic options if required by clinical circumstances.[62,63]

In patients with overt bleeding, actively bleeding angiodysplasia should be treated.

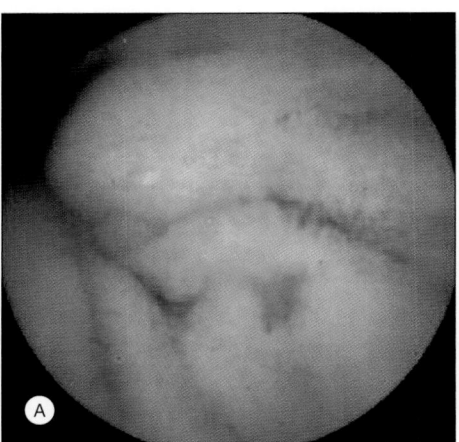
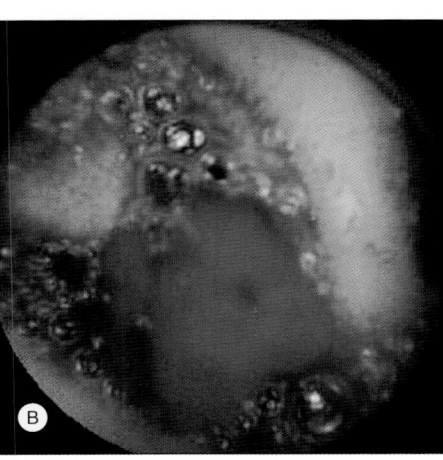

Figure 17–2. Small bowel angiodysplasias in patients with obscure gastrointestinal bleeding diagnosed by wireless capsule endoscopy. *A,* Nonbleeding angiodysplasia. *B,* Active bleeding angiodysplasia.

Hormonal Therapy

Hormonal therapy, usually with conjugated estrogens, has been used to treat patients with VEs of the GI tract in an attempt to reduce or terminate bleeding.[64] The mechanisms by which such agents might work are not known, although procoagulant effects and endothelial injury are popular theories. The results of several prospective, controlled trials examining hormonal therapy have been divergent.[65–67] In a long-term observational study, combination hormonal therapy was shown to stop bleeding in patients with occult GI bleeding of obscure origin, likely to have resulted from small bowel angiodysplasias.[67]

The literature regarding hormonal therapy for bleeding GI mucosal vascular abnormalities has been reviewed recently.[68] Although uncontrolled studies suggest that combination estrogen-progesterone therapy prevents bleeding episodes resulting from angiodysplasia, the evidence from a recent placebo-controlled trial suggests that this therapy is ineffective.[69] These authors considered that efficacy of hormonal therapy in these patients remains to be proven by a large, randomized, placebo-controlled trial with long follow-up.[70]

This pharmacologic therapy is not free from complications. Main side effects include fluid retention, uterine bleeding, increased plasma triglycerides, pancreatitis, hypercoagulability, breast tenderness or enlargement, headache, and an increased incidence of gallbladder disease. Contraindications for hormonal therapy include thromboembolic disease, cholestatic jaundice, endometrial hyperplasia, known or suspected breast cancer or estrogen-dependent neoplasia, vaginal bleeding in women, and gynecomastia in men. In clinical practice, estrogen-progesterone therapy should be used for patients with symptomatic recurrent episodic bleeding in which other therapies have failed.

Octreotide

The efficacy of octreotide in the treatment of angiodysplasias has been limited to case reports and small series in which a response has been reported in some patients.[71–73] The dosage can be tapered to the lowest quantity that prevents rebleeding. A 6-month course of therapy has been used to treat most patients. Mild GI side effects have been reported. Inflammation at the injection site has been noted. Mild steatorrhea and mild hyperglycemia may result from the inhibition of pancreatic exocrine and endocrine secretion. Octreotide therapy alters gallbladder contractility, inducing biliary sludge. A small number of patients develop acute cholecystitis. Cost effectiveness of this treatment has not been demonstrated.

Endoscopic Treatment

The goal of endoscopic therapy is thrombosis of the bleeding vessel. Studies directly comparing the effectiveness of the different approaches have not been performed. The approach depends on the location of the lesion, the experience of the endoscopist, and the availability of equipment.

- **Bipolar or heater probe coagulation** is said to be effective for treatment of GI angiodysplasias,[74,75] and they have replaced monopolar coagulation,[12] which may be less effective and more risky.[76]

- **Injection of a sclerosant**, such as ethanolamine, has been used to obliterate lesions.[77] However, sclerosants should probably be avoided until additional data on safety and efficacy are available.[45]
- **Elastic band ligation** has been used and seems to be safe to treat angiodysplasias of the stomach.[78,79] However, the walls of the small and large intestine are thinner (especially the right colon), and a high suction pressure could result in band entrapment of all layers of the intestinal wall, with the subsequent risk of complications, mainly delayed perforation.[80]
- **Lasers,** including argon and Nd-YAG lasers, have been used.[81–83] These techniques require expensive equipment and specific training, and serious complications have been reported.
- **Argon plasma coagulation (APC)** uses high frequency energy transmitted to tissue by ionized gas. This technique has been used for a variety of bleeding lesions, including angiodysplasias.[84,85] Its great advantage over laser or photodynamic therapy is the limited depth of tissue injury and its lower cost. This property is because the argon stream always seeks electrically conductive areas of tissue, thus avoiding the coagulated zones, which have lost their electric conductivity because of desiccation. This detail empowers APC with the capacity to limit its effect to approximately 3 mm. However, perforation of the cecum has been reported.[84] Preliminary results of a controlled trial comparing APC to bipolar electrocoagulation for bleeding angiodysplasias suggested that both techniques were safe but that APC was slower and less convenient.[86]
- **Cryotherapy** has been recently shown as a safe and effective treatment from diffuse mucosal lesions of the GI tract.[87]

The effectiveness of endoscopic treatment of angiodysplasias is difficult to assess given the lack of prospective controlled trials. Recurrent bleeding from cecal VEs appears to be reduced after laser therapy or ablation via the heater probe or bipolar (Bicap) coagulators, but patients usually need more than one session of endoscopic hemostasis.[88] Each endoscopic technique appears to be effective and relatively safe. Perforation of the GI tract, however, is a risk, particularly with electrocoagulation or laser therapy. The main risks of thermal therapy for colonic VEs are severe bleeding in 5% of patients and postcoagulation syndrome in 1.7% of cases.[75] Endoscopic treatment of vascular lesions in patients known to have coagulation disorders carries an increased risk of procedure-induced hemorrhage. When treating large lesions, experienced endoscopists recommend[45] to first ablate the periphery of the lesion to create a collar of edema that, in theory, reduces the vascular supply to the lesion and thereby diminishes the potential for immediate or delayed hemorrhage. In the cecum, care must be taken to avoid full distention because this decreases the thickness of its wall and increases the risk of perforation.

Although acute bleeding can appear to be successfully treated, rebleeding is common and is often from other lesions. Recurrent bleeding can be expected in approximately 20% of patients with colonic VEs and in a grater percentage of those with associated coagulopathies, renal failure, portal hypertension, or additional upper GI vascular lesions.[45]

Considering these results together, it is reasonable to attempt endoscopic therapy in patients with accessible lesions in whom the clinical settings favors an intervention that may have only short-term success. Patients who have multiple lesions or have an underlying bleeding diathesis may be less likely to benefit from endoscopic therapy and are at increased risk of complications. Such patients may benefit from attempts to improve their bleeding tendency.

In preparation for endoscopic ablation of vascular lesions, aspirin, nonsteroidal anti-inflammatory agents, anticoagulants, and anti-platelet agents should be withdrawn at least 1 week to 10 days before the procedure. Care should be taken not to distend the cecum fully, because the wall would be further thinned and the risk of perforation increased.[23] After therapy, patients must be cautioned not to resume full doses of anticoagulants or antiplatelet agents for 2 weeks. Tissue damage and sloughing in the treated area are maximum at about 10 days, and the onset of hemorrhage may be delayed until that time.

Angiography

Angiography may localize the site of active bleeding and permit embolization or infusion of vasopressin to stop the bleeding. Because angiography occasionally causes serious complications such as arterial thrombosis, contrast reactions, and acute renal failure, its use before definitive surgical therapy has been questioned.[89] Angiography should be reserved for patients with life-threatening bleeding who are not surgical candidates or for those in whom localization of lesions is desired before surgical resection.

Vasopressin infusions, either intravenously or intra-arterially through the angiographic catheter, successfully arrest hemorrhage from VEs in more than 80% of the patients in whom extravasation is demonstrated.[15] The intravenous route appears to be as effective as the intra-arterial route when the bleeding is in the left colon, but intra-arterial administration is more successful when the bleeding is from the right colon or small bowel. Infarction of the sigmoid colon and severe arterial spasm and ischemia of a leg have been seen following vasopressin infusions into the inferior mesenteric artery (IMA) given at the same rate as that used in the superior mesenteric artery (SMA). These complications may be avoided by infusing less than 0.4 unit/minute (the dose of SMA infusions), recognizing the lesser blood flow of the IMA.

Surgery

Surgical resection is definitive for lesions that have been clearly identified as the source of bleeding. However, recurrent bleeding may occur from lesions elsewhere in the GI tract. Preoperative or intraoperative enteroscopy and wireless capsule endoscopy may be helpful for localizing lesions.

Right hemicolectomy remains the treatment of choice for a patient who has bled and whose right colonic VEs have been identified by either colonoscopy or angiography if (1) the bleeding continues, (2) endoscopic ablation is not available, and (3) endoscopic ablation has been unsuccessful or is not feasible for technical reasons.[23] In the latter two situations, right hemicolectomy is done as an elective procedure once active bleeding is controlled. It is important that the entire right half of the colon be removed to ensure that no VEs are left behind. Because 50% to 80% of bleeding diverticula are located in the right side of the colon, the risks of leaving the left colon containing diverticula, which might the source of the bleeding, are far outweighed by the increased morbidity and mortality of the more extensive subtotal colectomy. Recurrent bleeding can be expected in up to 20% of patients so treated. Subtotal colectomy should be performed only as a last resort.[23]

Richter and coworkers[15] studied the course of 101 patients with angiodysplasias to determine the natural history and compare the efficacy of medical therapy, endoscopic electrocoagulation, and surgery (right hemicolectomy). Similar rates of recurrent bleeding were observed for medically and endoscopically treated groups during a mean follow-up of 22 months. Surgically treated patients had a frequency of recurrent bleeding less than half that of the other groups.

Hereditary Hemorrhagic Telangiectasia

HHT or Osler-Weber-Rendu disease is an uncommon, autosomal dominant disorder characterized by telangiectases and AVMs that affect many organs including the skin, lips, oral and nasopharyngeal membranes, tongue (Fig. 17–3A), lungs, GI tract, liver and brain[90,91] and can result in bleeding.

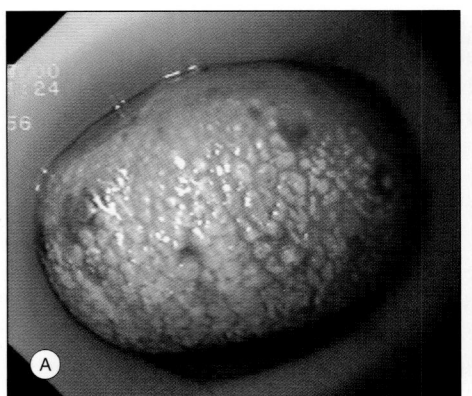
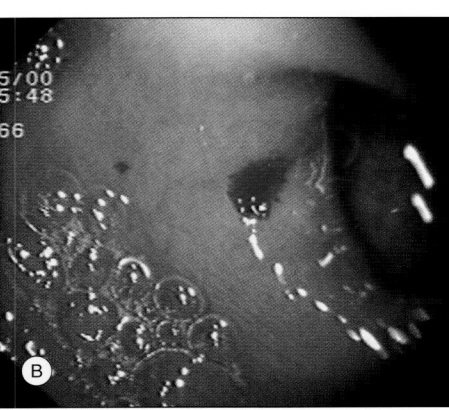

Figure 17–3. Hereditary hemorrhagic telangiectasia or Osler-Weber-Rendu syndrome. Patient with multiple telangiectases involving (A) the tongue and (B) the stomach.

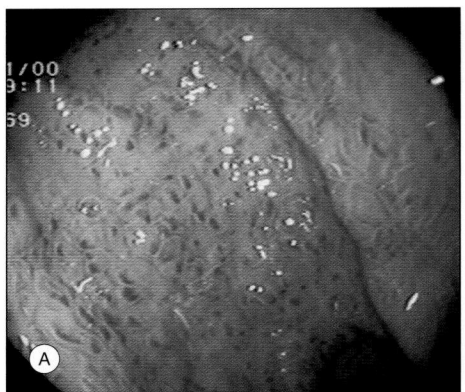

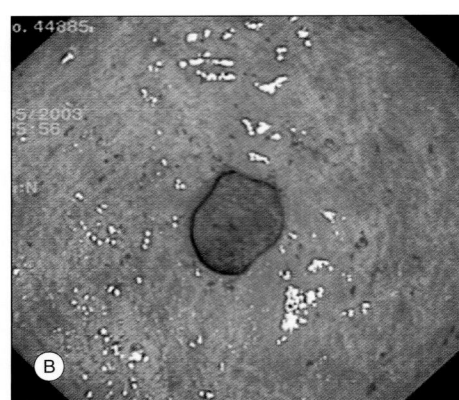

Figure 17-4. Portal hypertensive gastropathy *(A)* with a mosaic pattern and cherry-red spots in the body of the stomach and *(B)* localized in the antrum of a cirrhotic patient.

CLINICAL MANIFESTATIONS

Manifestations of HHT are not generally present at birth but develop with increasing age. Epistaxis is usually the earliest sign of disease, often occurring in childhood; pulmonary AVMs become apparent from puberty, whereas mucocutaneous and GI telangiectasia develop progressively with age.[92]

A family history has been reported in approximately 80% of patients with this disease[93] but is less common in those who manifest bleeding after the age of 50 years.[45]

GI bleeding does not usually start until the fifth or sixth decade,[94] occurs in 25% to 33% of patients with HHT, is challenging to treat, and can cause significant morbidity, resulting in severe anemia and high blood transfusion requirements.[95,96]

Endoscopy may reveal telangiectases in the stomach (Fig. 17–3*B*), duodenum, small bowel or colon that are punctiform, well-defined, red-blue spots, with a fernlike border, usually flat, although they may be 1 to 3 mm nodules, similar in size and appearance to those of the nasal and oral mucosa.[94] The lesions are more common in the stomach, duodenum, or jejunum than in the colon.[92] Capsule endoscopy may contribute to the diagnosis of small intestinal telangiectases.[91,97]

Selective mesenteric arteriography may be necessary to localize the precise bleeding site.[1]

MANAGEMENT

Therapies for GI bleeding range from a variety of pharmacologic agents to endoscopic or surgical treatment.

Drug therapies include ethynylestradiol and norethisterone,[65,98] danazol,[99] and aminocaproic acid.[100]

Endoscopic therapy is the most effective form of treatment in stopping hemorrhage from actively bleeding lesions. Unfortunately, because of the multiplicity of lesions, bleeding often recurs.[93] There are several reports of endoscopic therapy, including sclerotherapy with sodium morrhuate,[101] with ethanol, and with polidocanol[102]; monopolar and bipolar coagulation and heater probe[103,104]; APC[102]; yttrium aluminum garnet laser[105]; and clip application.[106]

Surgical therapy has limited success because of recurrent disease,[92] but it may be useful for emergency control of hemorrhage from discrete lesions identified as the source of the bleeding that do not respond to medical or endoscopic therapy.[93]

Gastric Vascular Lesions in Patients with Cirrhosis

After variceal bleeding, hemorrhagic gastritis has been accepted as the most frequent cause of upper GI bleeding in cirrhotic patients with portal hypertension.[107] The term *hemorrhagic gastritis* has included bleeding from various nonvariceal mucosal lesions, such as multiple ulcerations, portal hypertensive gastropathy (PHG), and gastric antral vascular ectasia (GAVE).[107–109]

PHG and GAVE can cause acute and chronic upper GI blood loss. These conditions frequently, but not invariably, are diagnosed by upper endoscopy. Although they are fairly prevalent, only 15% to 20% of subjects experience symptomatic GI blood loss.

PORTAL HYPERTENSIVE GASTROPATHY

PHG is the term used to describe the endoscopic appearance of gastric mucosa, with a characteristic mosaic-like pattern with or without red spots, seen in patients with cirrhotic or noncirrhotic portal hypertension. The mosaic pattern appears as white reticular network separating areas of raised red or pink mucosa resembling the skin of a snake (snakeskin appearance). PHG is seen mainly in the body and the fundus of the stomach, but it is also seen rarely in the gastric antrum (Fig. 17–4). These changes are not unique to gastric mucosa. Similar changes are also rarely seen in the small intestine and colon especially in the presence of extrahepatic portal hypertension. When PHG is severe, it can include discrete cherry-red spots, fine pink speckling, or scarlatina-type rash, collectively called red marks.[110] The characteristic histologic finding of PHG is dilated capillaries and venules in the mucosa and submucosa without erosion, inflammation, or fibrinous thrombi.[111]

Classification

There is no general consensus on the endoscopic classification of PHG. The most widely used classification is the one recommended by McCormack and coworkers[111] who classified PHG into mild and severe (Table 17–3). Mild PHG is defined by the presence of only a mosaic-like pattern, whereas severe PHG is diagnosed when red point lesions, cherry-red spots, or black-brown spots are present.

Table 17–3. Classification of Portal Hypertensive Gastropathy

McCormack and coworkers[111]	Tanoue and coworkers[112]	NIEC[113]
Mild Fine pink speckling (scarlatina-type rash) Superficial reddening Mosaic pattern	**Grade I** Mild reddening Congestive mucosa	**Mosaic pattern** Mild: diffuse pink areola Moderate: flat red spot Severe: diffuse red areola
Severe Discrete red spots Diffuse hemorrhagic lesion	**Grade II** Severe redness and a fine reticular pattern separating the areas of raised edematous mucosa	**Red mark lesion** Discrete Confluent (diffuse)
	Grade III Point bleeding + grade II	**Black-brown spot**
NIEC, New Italian Endoscopic Club.		

Its popularity relates in part to its simplicity and also its ability to predict the risk of bleeding, with an increased risk of gastric hemorrhage in severe (38% to 62%) compared with mild cases (3.5% to 31%).[108,109] However, often the observed endoscopic findings are of an intermediate severity and are not well represented as being either mild or severe. Tanoue and colleagues and the New Italian Endoscopic Club have since described a more detailed scoring system.[110,112,113] Tanoue and coworkers[112] classified PHG into four grades (grade 0 = none, grade 1 = mild, grade 2 = moderate, grade 3 = severe). This grading permits more informative description of the observed endoscopic findings.

A simpler classification system as recommended by McCormack and colleagues has a better intraobserver and interobserver agreement and reproducibility.[114] Further work must be done to improve the currently available grading system.

Prevalence

Prospective studies have reported that PHG is present in more than 50% of patients with cirrhosis.[115,116] The reported prevalence varies widely due to patient selection, absence of uniform criteria and classification, and more importantly, the differences in interobserver and intraobserver variation.[117]

Although PHG is usually seen in association with either esophageal or gastric varices, there is no direct linear correlation between portal pressure and the presence or severity of PHG.[118] The cause of portal hypertension is unlikely to be a significant factor.[119–121] The prevalence of PHG does not seem to have a linear relationship with the severity of liver disease as reported by a recent study, which showed the lowest prevalence of severe PHG in Child C patients.[113] This may suggest that other hitherto unidentified factors may play a role in the pathogenesis of PHG. However, there is a general agreement that the prevalence of PHG does increase with variceal obliteration.[120]

Pathogenesis

Portal hypertension and not liver disease seems to be the key factor for the development of PHG because PHG is equally common in portal hypertensive patients with or without liver disease.[122,123] Moreover, the improvement or disappearance of PHG in many patients after transjugular intrahepatic portosystemic shunt (TIPS) and shunt surgery suggests that there is a significant association between PHG and portal hypertension. However, the severity and the presence of PHG do not have a linear correlation with the severity of portal hypertension.[118] Chronic elevation in portal pressure and increased splenic circulation may increase gastric mucosal blood flow, and this may be one explanation for the development of PHG. The actual measurement of gastric blood flow using Doppler has shown variable results, suggesting that there may be other explanations for the pathogenesis of PHG.[124,125] The severity of PHG may increase with more advanced liver disease as shown in some studies, but the results are not consistent.[113,118,119] There have been many other explanations for the pathogenesis of PHG. There is experimental evidence to suggest that gastric mucosal defense mechanisms are impaired in the presence of portal hypertension.[126–128]

Aggravation of PHG after variceal banding or sclerotherapy might be caused by alterations in local hemodynamics after obliteration of the esophageal varices.[129,130] Hepatofugal flow velocity is increased in the left gastric vein in direct relationship with the enlarging size of esophageal varices. Gastric mucosal blood flow is higher in cirrhotic patients whose extrahepatic collaterals are predominantly via esophageal varices. Therefore, obliteration of the esophageal collateral venous network may cause higher flow velocity in the gastric vascular bed. It has been speculated that the extravasation of sclerosant into the mediastinum during sclerotherapy may result in chemical vagotomy, and this may cause esophageal dysmotility and delayed gastric emptying, leading to the development of PHG.[131] However, there is no direct evidence to suggest that delayed gastric emptying causes PHG.

Natural History and Complications

The overall incidence of acute bleeding from PHG is low and is seen mostly in those with more severe PHG. Bleeding is often mild, and a transfusion requirement is usually limited to one to two units of blood. Prevalence of chronic bleeding cannot be reliably estimated because of the uncertainty of making a firm diagnosis. Major determinants of bleeding from PHG are length of time the patients had PHG and the extent and severity of lesions. The mortality associated with bleeding from PHG is very low because most bleeds are minor compared with variceal bleeding. Death caused by PHG is unusual and is not an independent risk factor for survival.

The presence and severity of PHG seem to change with time. Although some workers believe that PHG is a progressive lesion,[116,132] others have observed that it may regress in a fair proportion of patients.[133] This variability in results could be due to differences in the patient population, the time when the lesions appear, or the influence of endoscopic intervention for varices. An important factor that is known to influence the development of PHG is endoscopic sclerotherapy.[119] In one study, during a follow-up of 2 years, the severity of PHG fluctuated with time in 25%, improved in 23%, remained stable in 29%, and deteriorated in 23%.[113] Endoscopic sclerotherapy and banding seems to worsen the severity of PHG and increases the risk of bleeding.[111,112,129,130] In one study, 44% of patients developed PHG after variceal eradication by sclerotherapy compared with only 9% before sclerotherapy.[120] The results in this prospective study suggested that if gastropathy persists for more than 3 months, it is likely to persist for longer periods. In a minority, PHG lesions may still regress within a period of 6 months but are unlikely to regress beyond this period; when PHG was present before endoscopic therapy for varices, the lesions often persisted or progressed after obliteration of esophageal varices. The frequency of bleeding from PHG in these circumstances was high. It is for these reasons that they recommend that such patients be followed-up with serial endoscopies and that the benefits of beta-blockers therapy be evaluated as prophylaxis against PHG bleeding.[120] However, the efficacy of serial endoscopies simply for monitoring of the progression of PHG remains to be proven.[134]

Management

Clinically significant bleeding is seen only in association with severe PHG. Effective treatment requires a reduction in the portal pressure.

Pharmacologic Treatment

The aim of pharmacologic treatment is (1) to control hemorrhage in patients with actively bleeding PHG and (2) to prevent rebleeding in patients with known PHG.

- **Nonselective beta-blockers**, such as **propranolol** and **nadolol**, have been shown to reduce portal pressure and gastric mucosal blood flow. In small studies, propranolol has been shown to reduce bleeding related to PHG.[135,136] In a randomized, controlled trial of 56 patients with PHG, multivariate analysis showed that absence of propranolol treatment was the only predictive variable for rebleeding.[115] In conclusion, the use of propranolol in PHG leads to endoscopic improvement, a cessation of bleeding in acutely hemorrhaging patients, and a decreased incidence of rebleeding from severe PHG. Pharmacologic therapy is typically long-term due to evidence the discontinuation of therapy can lead to rebleeding from PHG. Other medications such as prednisone, estrogen, and progesterone are ineffective for bleeding-related PHG.
- Given the proven beneficial effects of **vasoactive agents** such as **somatostatin, octreotide,** and **terlipressin** in variceal bleeding, their role in the management of PHG has also been evaluated. Somatostatin has been shown to reduce gastric mucosal blood

flow by decreasing splanchnic blood flow.[137] Similar effects are also seen with vasopressin and Glypressin. In patients with acute bleeding, an uncontrolled study has shown an efficacy with both somatostatin and octreotide.[138] However, a recent study showed that the decrease in portal pressure is only transient; therefore, use of somatostatin or octreotide is unlikely to benefit patients with chronic PHG bleeding.[139] The use of these agents should be limited to patients with acute bleeding.

There are no clinical trials directly comparing the efficacy of propranolol versus octreotide for active hemorrhage related to PHG. Some authors use octreotide first in patients with acute bleeding because it is better tolerated than propranolol in this setting.[140]

Endoscopic Treatment

Endoscopic treatment does not have a significant role in the management of PHG bleeding because the bleeding is often mild and diffuse. If an active bleeding site is identified, it could be managed by injection of sclerosant or cauterization using the heater or bipolar probe. Although laser therapy has been shown to be safe and effective in reducing GAVE-associated bleeding, it is not known whether laser therapy is effective or safe in patients with severe PHG when the predominant lesion is in the gastric antrum.[141]

Noninvasive and Invasive Surgery

Both TIPS and shunt surgery have shown to be effective for PHG bleeding in anecdotal reports. In a study by Orloff and coworkers,[142] portocaval shunting successfully controlled bleeding, and the gastric mucosa had reverted to normal on follow-up gastroscopies in all 12 patients with repeated bleeding unresponsive to propranolol. TIPS was shown to improve PHG in 9 of 10 patients.[143] Furthermore, it successfully stopped recurrent bleeding refractory to medical therapy in one of these patients. Thus, TIPS offers another therapeutic option for patients who have bleeding refractory to medical therapy especially if they are poor candidates for surgical shunts (i.e., Child's class C cirrhosis).[144]

Despite these encouraging anecdotal reports, most authors[140] think that TIPS or shunt surgery should be used only as the last resort in these patients because the risks outweigh the benefits. Currently, the only treatment that could be recommended for prophylaxis of PHG bleeding is nonselective beta-blockers such as propranolol or nadolol. Pharmacologic therapy is typically long-term due to evidence the discontinuation of therapy can lead to rebleeding from PHG.[144] Efficacy of therapy can be followed clinically and endoscopically as evidenced by improved mucosal appearance and evidence of diminished portal hypertension.

GASTRIC ANTRAL VASCULAR ECTASIA

GAVE was first described in 1984 by Jabbari and coworkers.[145] These authors coined the term "watermelon stomach" from its resemblance to the skin of the namesake fruit. The acronym GAVE describes a vascular lesion of the antrum that consists of tortuous, dilated vessels radiating outward from the pylorus, like spokes from a wheel, and resembling the dark stripes on the surface of a watermelon (Fig. 17–5A). The typical histologic appearance of GAVE includes marked dilation of capillaries and collecting venules in the

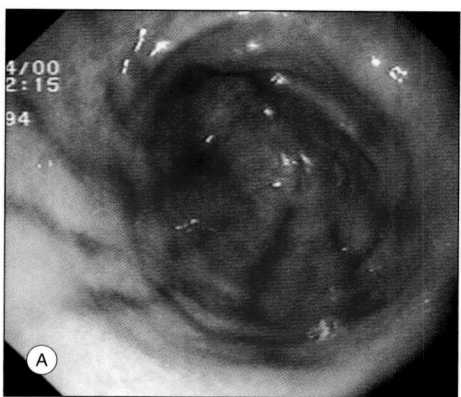 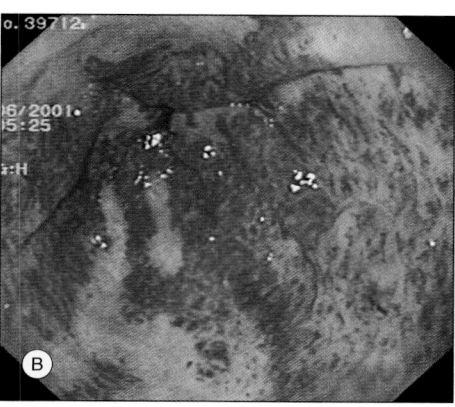

Figure 17–5. Two different forms of gastric antral vascular ectasia. *A,* Watermelon stomach. *B,* Diffuse antral vascular ectasia.

gastric mucosa and submucosa with areas of intimal thickening characterized by fibromuscular hyperplasia, fibrohyalinosis, and thrombi.[108,109,145,146]

An increasing number of reports of GAVE, however, have included some cases in which the endoscopic appearance showed spotty erythemas diffusely scattered in the antral area and coalesced (diffuse antral VE or "honeycomb stomach").[3,24] Diffuse antral VE is now recognized as the same entity as watermelon stomach, and both are regarded as GAVE[25] (Fig. 17–5B).

The diffuse form is the predominant pattern in patients with cirrhosis. Noncirrhotic patients with GAVE are typically middle-aged or older women, and GAVE is found in association with achlorhydria, atrophic gastritis, the CREST syndrome, and after bone marrow transplantation.[25,46,147]

Pathogenesis

The pathogenesis of GAVE is poorly understood, and there is no single unifying hypothesis. Possible mechanisms include humoral factors and mechanical causes.[108,109,148,149]

Spahr and colleagues[150] observed that GAVE was not improved by successful portal decompression following TIPS (one patient) or by endoscopic laser therapy (one patient), whereas the antral mucosal lesions disappeared completely after liver transplantation. This may suggest that GAVE could be related to increased secretion of yet unidentified vasoactive substances in the presence of liver disease. For example, glucagon and nitric oxide were found to be increased in cirrhotic patients. Local disturbances in vascular tone must be involved to explain that VEs develop specifically in the antrum.

The proponents of the mechanical theory have suggested that chronic intermittent venous obstruction associated with powerful muscular contractions of the antrum and pylorus or repeated trauma associated with a loosely attached antral mucosa and prolapse of the antral mucosa through the pylorus may cause GAVE.[145,146,151] The fibromuscular hyperplasia seen at histology in GAVE supports the hypothesis of repeated mechanical stress induced by gastric peristalsis.

Relationship Between Portal Hypertensive Gastropathy and Gastric Antral Vascular Ectasia

Some researchers believe that GAVE and PHG are different manifestations of the same pathogenetic process, whereas others view them as separate entities.[109] These lesions can be differentiated by endoscopic and histologic findings. PHG is always associated with portal hypertension and is observed mostly in the fundus and corpus of the stomach; mucosal red spots and the so-called mosaic pattern are present and the histologic examination only shows VE in the mucosa without signs of inflammation. By contrast, GAVE can occur in both cirrhotic and noncirrhotic patients. Lesions are found almost exclusively in the antrum and red spots are either aggregated in linear stripes (as in the watermelon stomach) or diffusely spread. Histologically, VE are present in the mucosa and are associated with inflammation, fibrin thrombi, fibrohyalinosis, and spindle cell proliferation.

In severe PHG, the red marks may have a striped appearance and may have a close resemblance to GAVE. It is not uncommon to see GAVE-like appearance in patients with portal hypertension, and GAVE-like appearance is seen more commonly in patients with portal hypertension compared with those without portal hypertension.[114] The dilemma is whether one should call this appearance GAVE or severe PHG. The histologic appearance of GAVE is different from PHG, but mucosal biopsies are rarely deep enough to make a firm diagnosis and it may not be completely safe to do repeated biopsies in patients with portal hypertension and severe PHG. Bleeding from GAVE, unlike PHG, is not known to respond to nonselective beta-blockers.[109,152] However, a therapeutic challenge is not clinically useful to differentiate these two entities because the response to beta-blockers is variable in patients with PHG. In a recent study, Kamath and coworkers[153] showed that patients with GAVE, in the absence of background mosaic appearance, did not respond to TIPS compared with those with PHG.

It has been suggested that the same gastric vascular alteration related to portal hypertension may appear different, grossly and histologically, depending on the anatomic location of the stomach.[116] The hemodynamics of venous drainage of the antrum are different from body or fundus of the stomach. It can be argued that the typical histologic changes, fibrosis and thrombosis, seen in GAVE may also be seen with more chronic and severe PHG. The variable response to beta-blockers and TIPS may be a reflection of the advanced histologic changes.[109] Some authors believe that the term GAVE should be reserved for the presence of typical, linear, red lesions in the gastric antrum without the mosaic-like appearance of mucosal background in the rest of the stomach. When there is evidence of mosaic-like pattern or evidence of more severe PHG in the body and fundus, they favor classifying it as a spectrum of PHG.[114]

Management

Bleeding from gastric mucosal lesions in patients with portal hypertension is a serious complication although bleeding is usually slow and insidious and rarely massive and life threatening. However, multiple transfusions may be required during the follow-up.

Endoscopic therapy generally is preferred because of its efficacy, but pharmacologic treatment may be used as adjunct therapy or in patients with persistent bleeding from mucosal areas not amenable to endoscopic therapy.

Pharmacologic Treatment

- Although **combination hormonal therapy** has been shown to be effective in controlling bleeding from GAVE in some case reports or small trials,[154–157] it does not improve the endoscopic appearance of this lesion. As with other pharmacologic therapies, hormonal therapy provides an alternative to endoscopic therapy when extensive vascular abnormalities are present. Furthermore, it eliminates the risk of circumferential scarring and stenosis that can occur with the endoscopic modalities discussed.
- The use of **tranexamic acid** for GAVE has only been reported in one case report.[158] Given the limited experience with anti-fibrinolytics for GI bleeding, the use of this agent should be reserved for refractory patients who have failed other measures.[140]
- **Octreotide** was used in one trial, with successful results.[71] However, at least one case report failed to show a response of GAVE to octreotide.[159]
- **Treatment with beta-blockers** has been reported to be successful in controlling bleeding from gastric mucosal lesions in cirrhotic patients. However, in these reports, it is unclear whether patients bled from PHG or from GAVE.[115,136] It is worth noting that, in the study from Spahr and colleagues,[150] treatment with the nonselective beta-blocker nadolol did not control chronic bleeding from GAVE. In addition, the results of this study clearly showed that the decrease in portal hypertension following TIPS or shunt surgery was not effective in controlling chronic blood loss related to GAVE.[150]

Endoscopic Treatment

The current first-line therapy for GAVE consists of endoscopic ablation. The aim of endoscopic therapy to eliminate or reduce significantly the blood transfusion requirements of a patient with bleeding.

- In a trial by Bourke and coworkers,[160] **Nd:YAG laser coagulation** was used in 11 consecutive patients with GAVE. Transfusion dependence was eliminated in two thirds of the patients and was lessened in the remaining patients. In this trial, an average of three sessions per patient was required; sucralfate was used to prevent iatrogenic ulceration. Endoscopic laser therapy is repeated every 2 to 4 weeks until most of the lesions disappear and the hemoglobin remains stable. One study has indicated that the mean number of treatments needed to obliterate the vascular lesions and eliminate the need for transfusions was less for Nd:YAG laser when compared with APC (2.33 ± 0.27 vs. 5.75 ± 0.89).[161]

- **APC.** As with the Nd:YAG laser, large surface areas of involved mucosa can be adequately treated during a single endoscopic session. Several case reports have described the successful use of APC for the management of GAVE.[162,163] Compared with Nd:YAG laser, APC is easier to use. Avoidance of the need to approach the target in a near perpendicular manner makes this an attractive tool for use. The equipment is less expensive than a laser unit. In addition, the fibers used are less expensive and the time to set up the equipment for use is less, allowing more efficient use of time in the endoscopy suite.
- **The heater probe** uses a thermal element that heats the device tip that results in tissue coagulation. Petrini and colleagues[164] described the successful use of a heater probe for management of GAVE. An average of four sessions was required to eliminate the transfusion requirements and improve endoscopic appearance in 8 of 10 patients.

The major problem with GAVE is continued blood loss requiring repeated blood transfusions. Ikeda and coworkers[165] recently presented a 10-year endoscopic follow-up study from discrete initial lesions to the full picture of GAVE. They reported that latent hemorrhage occurred at a quite early stage as the coalesced lesions formed and that the vascular lesions of GAVE should be eradicated at this stage.

Although generally the Nd:YAG laser and APC are preferred over heater probe for the treatment of GAVE because of their ability to cover a greater surface area, the endoscopic therapeutic modality chosen also depends on the individual experience of the endoscopist and local availability.[140]

Surgery

In the study from Spahr and colleagues,[150] in one patient who underwent a surgical shunt, chronic bleeding was never controlled despite a complete normalization of portal pressure. Similarly, it has been reported that portocaval shunt surgery proved ineffective in treating chronic GI blood loss related to GAVE in a patient with portal hypertension as a result of nodular regenerative hyperplasia.[166]

Antrectomy provides the most definitive therapy for GAVE as illustrated by low rates of rebleeding and anemia recurrence.[167–169] However, surgery carries a significant risk of mortality in cirrhotic patients with portal hypertension. TIPS placement may make antrectomy easier and faster by avoiding operative blood losses related to the presence of collaterals secondary to portal hypertension. However, TIPS should be restricted to cirrhotic patients with good liver function, because of the risk of TIPS induced progressive liver failure.[150] Given the comorbid illnesses typically associated with GAVE as well as the advanced age of most patients, surgery is considered salvage therapy for patients that have not responded to a reasonable trial of endoscopic or pharmacologic therapies.[140]

Portal Colopathy

Over the past 2 decades, awareness of the association between portal hypertension and changes in the intestinal circulation has

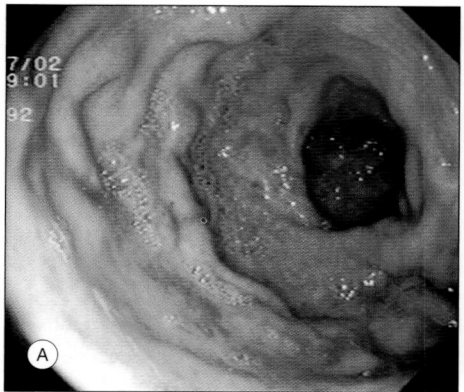 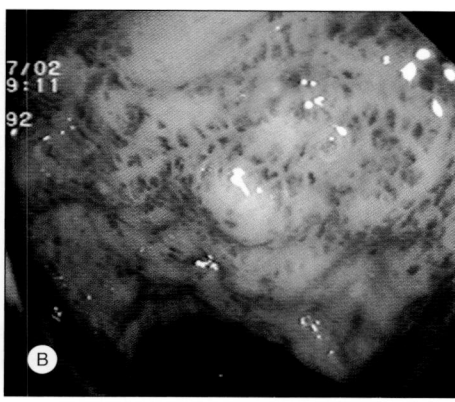

Figure 17–6. Portal colopathy. *A,* Portal hypertension causing collateral circulation in the rectum. *B,* Colitis with granularity, erythema, friability, and cherry-red spots.

Table 17–4. Summary of Published Studies on the Prevalence of Colonic Abnormalities in Patients with Cirrhosis

Study	Number of patients	Colitis-like lesions (%)	Vascular lesions (%)	Rectal varices (%)	Hemorrhoids (%)
Kozarek et al.[170]	20	20	70	25	Ns
Naveau et al.[171]	64	Ns	25	20	Ns
Chen at al.[172]	35	Ns	49	46	Ns
Tam et al.[173]	75	11	84	13	Ns
Rabinovitz et al.[174]	412	32	Ns	4	25
Scandalis et al.[175]	38	58	0	8	39
Goenka et al.[176]	75	Ns	12	89	41
Ganguly et al.[177]	50	6	52	44	Ns
Misra et al.[178]	70	27	49	40	36
Bresci et al.[179]	50	10	16	34	70
Bini et al.[181]	437	38	13	9	46

Ns, not stated.

increased. The fundamental pathologic change is a vasculopathy. Portal hypertensive vasculopathy most often involves the stomach (PHG) and can be a source of bleeding. The significance of small bowel involvement (enteropathy) is unknown. Colon involvement (colopathy) has been associated with bleeding. Several studies have described the colonic findings associated with cirrhosis and portal hypertension.[170–179] Colorectal lesions associated with portal hypertension and cirrhosis include hemorrhoids, varices (portosystemic collaterals that develop because of portal hypertension, Fig. 17–6A) focal and diffuse telangiectasias, and spiders. The term *portal colopathy* has been used to describe colonic lesions resembling the vascular lesions of portal gastropathy and the diffuse colitis-like appearance seen in patients with portal hypertension[170,171] (Fig. 17–6B). There is confusion regarding the diagnostic criteria and clinical significance of this condition. This might be attributable to imprecise terminology, lack of uniform endoscopic descriptions, interobserver variability, and the absence of distinctive histopathologic features.[180] Therefore, in previously published studies, the prevalence of colonic abnormalities in patients with cirrhosis varied widely (Table 17–4), and the true prevalence of portal colopathy is unknown. Because all patients in some studies were referred for colonoscopy based on clinical indications,[181] these reviews may have overestimated the true prevalence of portal colopathy.

Conflicting data have been published regarding the relationship between the prevalence of portal colopathy and Child-Pugh classification in cirrhotic patients.[82,170,172,177,179,181] In a recent study,[181] portal gastropathy, 2+ or larger esophageal varices, Child-Pugh class C cirrhosis, and the use of beta-blockers were independent predictors of portal colopathy; the use of beta-blockers was protective. Portal hypertensive colopathy and gastropathy might not be distinct entities but regional manifestations of portal hypertension. Furthermore, they might share similar mechanisms with regard to pathogenesis.

The histology of the colitis-like mucosal abnormalities from most patients with portal hypertension is that of nonspecific, mild inflammation. Several studies have shown that the endoscopic appearance of colonic mucosal edema and erythema is not associated with significant inflammatory infiltrates but rather with mucosal vessel changes.[171,181–183] Based on these findings, some authors suggest the use of the term *colopathy* when referring to the mucosal abnormalities of the colon in patients with cirrhosis.[181] This avoids the suggestion of the involvement of inflammatory cells in the pathogenesis of a disease that lacks a definitive etiologic mechanism.

Several endoscopic classification systems exist to grade the severity of mucosal changes in patients with portal gastropathy.[111,113] To date, there are no classification systems for grading the severity of mucosal abnormalities in cirrhotic patients with portal colopathy, making comparisons between studies difficult. Bini and coworkers,[181] based on their findings, proposed that portal colopathy could be classified into three grades: grade 1, erythema of the colonic mucosa; grade 2, erythema along with a mosaic-like appearance of the mucosa; and grade 3, vascular lesions of the colon, including cherry-red spots, telangiectasias, or angiodysplasia-like lesions.

The same authors[181] observed for the first time an increase in the prevalence of portal colopathy in cirrhotic patients who had undergone band ligation and/or sclerotherapy of esophageal varices. They suggested that, similarly with PHG, it may be that portal colopathy is related to the levels of portal pressure and that obliteration of esophageal varices may cause a redistribution of blood flow in similar ways in the stomach and colon. Prospective studies are necessary to validate this observation.

MANAGEMENT

Beta-adrenergic blockers are usually the first-line therapy in patients with portal colopathy. The lesions of portal colopathy are considered amenable to the same thermal therapies as for GAVE and PHG, although no controlled trials have been published at this time.[23,70]

TIPS may be useful as a second-line treatment in patients with recurrent portal hypertensive bleeding from colonic angiodysplasia-like lesions who do not tolerate or are unresponsive to treatment with beta-adrenergic blockers.[184]

Hemangiomas

CLINICAL MANIFESTATIONS

Hemangiomas are the second most common vascular lesion of the colon. Considered by some to be true neoplasms, they are generally thought to be hamartomas because most are present at birth. They may be solitary or multiple lesions limited to one segment of the GI tract, or they may be part of diffuse GI or multisystem angiomatoses. Individual hemangiomas may be classified as cavernous, capillary, or mixed types. Most are small (Fig. 17–7), ranging from few millimeters to 2 cm, but larger lesions do occur, especially in the rectum (see cavernous hemangioma of the rectum). In the presence of GI bleeding, hemangiomas of the skin should suggest the possibility of associated bowel lesions.[45]

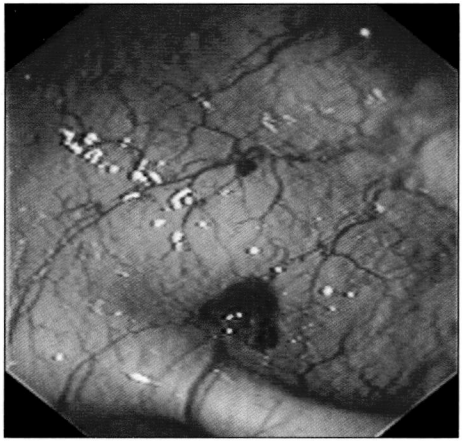

Figure 17–7. Solitary hemangioma of the colon.

Hemangiomas causing upper GI hemorrhage are most commonly identified in the upper small intestine. These benign vascular tumors, almost all of which are cavernous hemangiomas, appears as single or multiple red, purple or blue nodular lesions. These lesions generally should not be treated endoscopically. Angiographic therapy may stop bleeding; however, the most effective treatment is surgical.

Bleeding from colonic hemangiomas usually is low, producing occult blood loss with anemia or melena. Hematochezia is less common, except in large, cavernous hemangiomas of the rectum, which may cause massive hemorrhage. Diagnosis is best established by endoscopy, including enteroscopy, because roentgenologic studies, including angiography, frequently are normal although the presence of calcifications representing phleboliths within hemangiomas has been described.

MANAGEMENT

Hemangiomas that are small, solitary, or few in number can be treated by colonoscopic coagulation using a laser or some other thermal mode. Colonoscopic excision of small lesions has been described,[185] including removal of small lesions for the purpose of diagnosis in patients with multiple hemangiomas.[186] Amano and colleagues[187] reported electrosurgical snare polypectomy of a large, pedunculated, polypoid cavernous hemangioma that arose in the sigmoid colon in a 28-year-old man who presented with prolapse of the lesion through the anus. Although complications of colonoscopic excision of hemangiomas appear to be rare, the number of reports is small and it is therefore difficult to determine the safety of colonoscopic treatment. This may depend on size and gross morphology of the lesion (e.g., sessile vs. pedunculated) and the technical feasibility of endoscopic treatment. Large or multiple lesions usually require surgical resection of either the hemangioma alone or the involved segment of colon.

CAVERNOUS HEMANGIOMA OF THE RECTUM

A distinct form of colonic hemangioma is the cavernous hemangioma of the rectum.[45] These lesions are usually not associated with another GI hemangiomas and are extensive, involving the entire rectum or portions of the rectosigmoid colon. The massive bleeding resulting from these rectal hemangiomas often necessitates excision of the rectum by either abdominal-perineal or low-anterior resection; ligation and embolization of major feeding vessels have been used successfully. Attempts at local control have been of value in some instances, but mostly these have been only temporarily effective.

Blue Rubber Bleb Nevus Syndrome

CLINICAL MANIFESTATIONS

BRBNS, also known as Bean's syndrome, is a rare, probably inherited disorder, characterized by cutaneous hemangiomas and vascular tumors of the GI tract, that can also involve other organs as the brain, kidneys, lungs, eyes, oronasopharynx, parotids, liver, spleen, heart, pleura, peritoneum, pericardium, skeletal muscles, bladder, penis, and vulva.[188–190]

The lesions usually appear in early childhood and tend to increase in size and number with age. They are usually blue, raised, and easily compressible with light palpation. The contained blood can be emptied by direct pressure, leaving a wrinkled blue sac that slowly refills over several seconds or minutes.[23]

Skin lesions may be present throughout the body, particularly predominating on the upper limbs (Fig. 17–8A) and trunk.[191]

The GI lesions are usually multiple and may involve any portion of the GI tract but are most common in the small bowel and in the distal part of the colon.[23] The characteristic GI lesion is a discrete mucosal nodule with an overlying central bluish red cap resembling a nipple but may be a flat macular dark bluish red spot or a raised polypoid nodule with a central vascular cap[189,192] (Fig. 17–8B and C).

Most patients are asymptomatic. Loss of blood from the GI tract is the major problem and commonly causes chronic anemia.[192,193] The onset of GI bleeding may be at any time from early childhood to middle age.[1]

The lesions can also cause intestinal intussusception[194] and numerous extraintestinal problems, such as orthopedic deformities associated with bone involvement,[188] neurologic defects resulting from central nervous system involvement[195] and spinal cord compression,[196] pulmonary hypertension resulting from vascular obliteration, hemothorax and hemopericardium,[197] exophthalmos and loss of vision secondary to eye involvement,[190] or disseminated intravascular coagulation and thrombocytopenia.[198]

DIAGNOSIS

When BRBNS is suspected, and depending on the clinic, a search should be conducted, including some of the following techniques: gastroscopy, colonoscopy, enteroscopy,[189] capsule endoscopy, endoscopic ultrasound (US),[199] enteroclysis, US, computed tomography (CT),[193] magnetic resonance imaging,[191,195] radionuclide-tagged red blood cell scan,[197] and angiography.[200]

TREATMENT

Most patients respond to supportive therapy, such as iron supplementation and blood transfusion when required.[192] For recurrent bleeding, medical, endoscopic and surgical therapy have been used.

Medical therapy includes the use of corticosteroids,[198,201] antifibrinolytic agents,[202] gamma globulin,[198] interferon,[201] and octeotride.[202]

Endoscopic management appears to be safe and useful, although the lesions can be transmural, which implies a theoretical increase in risk for bowel perforation as a complication. There are several reports of endoscopic therapy, including sclerotherapy with absolute alcohol,[203] sodium morrhuate,[204] epinephrine and polidocanol,[205] band ligation,[193,205] polypectomy,[191,193,206] bipolar coagulation,[207] and laser therapy.[207,208]

Angiographic embolization can be useful for treating acute bleeding and preventing further bleeding.[209]

Successful surgical excision of the bleeding lesions or segmental resection of the involved gut has been performed[210] and can be aided by intraoperative endoscopy.[211]

Klippel-Trénaunay-Weber Syndrome

CLINICAL MANIFESTATIONS

KTWS, also known as nevus vasculosus hypertrophicus, is a rare nonhereditary congenital vascular malformation, secondary to a generalized mesodermal development abnormality.[212] Originally described by Klippel and Trénaunay in 1900, it is characterized by bony or soft tissue hypertrophy, usually affecting one extremity (Fig. 17–9A); hemangiomas and/or lymphangiomas; and varicosities or venous malformations, appearing at birth or in childhood.

Visceral hemangiomas have been described involving organs such as the GI tract (Fig. 17–9B), liver, spleen, bladder, kidney, lung, and heart.[213]

GI hemorrhage is a potential serious complication secondary to diffuse vascular malformations involving the GI tract. GI bleeding usually begins in the first decade of life and may be recurrent and mild or severe.[213] Its severity may be enhanced by a consumption coagulopathy because of intravascular clotting within the venous sinusoids of the hemangiomas.[45] The most common reported cause of GI bleeding is attributed to diffuse cavernous hemangiomas of the distal colon and rectum[214] found in 1% to 12.5% of cases.[213,215] Less frequent causes of GI bleeding are rectal or rectovaginal varices caused by obstruction of the internal iliac system, esophageal varices secondary to prehepatic portal hypertension because of cavernous transformation or hypoplasia of the portal vein,[216] and jejunal hemangiomas.[217]

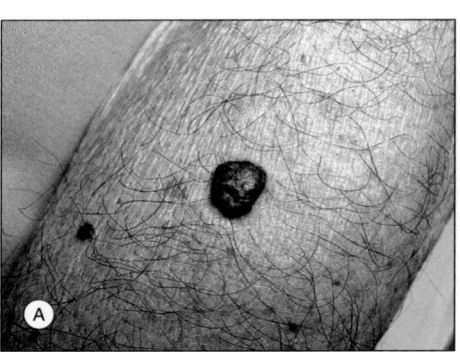
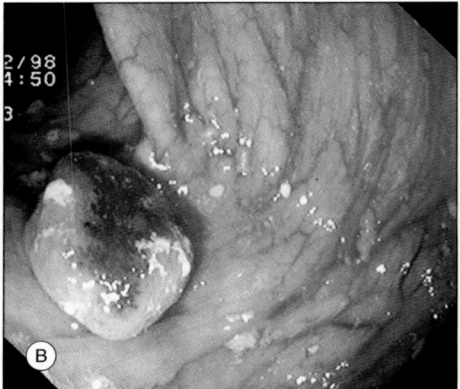
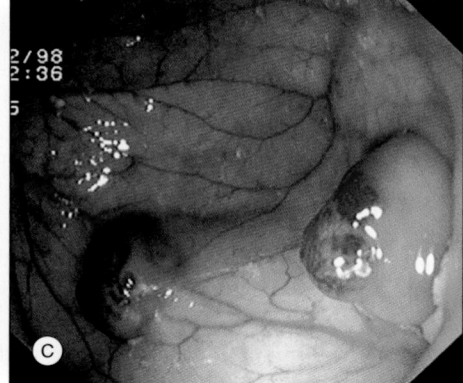

Figure 17–8. Multiple hemangiomatosis or blue rubber bleb nevus syndrome. A, Typical dark blue nodular lesions of the skin. B and C, Lesions involving the colon.

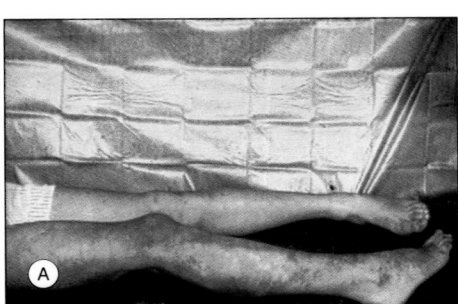
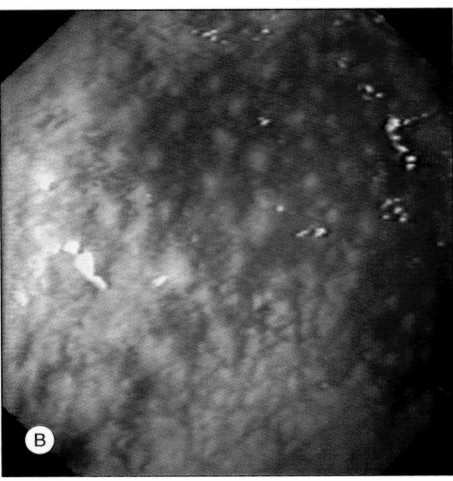

Figure 17–9. Klippel-Trénaunay-Weber syndrome involving the gastrointestinal tract. *A,* Hypertrophic leg resulting from venous hypertension and stasis. *B,* Rectal hemangioma in the same patient.

Colonic obstruction and ascites secondary to massive hemangiomatous-lymphangiomatous retroperitoneal masses may occur.[218]

DIAGNOSIS

Radiologic investigations play an important role in assessing colorectal involvement and occasionally finding the specific bleeding site. The presence of phleboliths on a plain abdominal radiograph in these very young patients suggest that they have angiomatosis.[213] Barium studies can demonstrate luminal distensible narrowing, with a scalloped mucosal outline because of the presence of varicosities or submucosal hemangiomas.[45,219] CT and magnetic resonance imaging of the abdomen and pelvis provide a simple, noninvasive means of assessing visceral hemangiomatous masses and identifying upward extension in the pelvis and abdomen.[219] An abdominal angiography is required preoperatively for defining the anatomy and extent of the intestinal involvement to guide surgical intervention.[217]

At colonoscopy, the rectum and the lower part of the colon may show visible mucosal vessels or compressible nodules and extensive bluish angiomatous submucosal lesions. Biopsy of the lesions should be avoided, because it may precipitate severe hemorrhage.[213] Lesions in deeper layers of the wall can be assessed by endoscopic ultrasonography.[220]

TREATMENT

The treatment varies from conservative to surgical measures, depending on the clinical symptoms and risk of complications. Transfusion dependency, life-threatening bleeding episodes, and poor quality of life require definitive therapy.[213] When the entire rectum is severely involved, surgery is sometimes necessary, by means of an abdominoperineal resection of the involved rectum and colon, with a permanent colostomy,[215] or with a colon pouch anal anastomosis.[221]

Angiographic embolization may be useful if a specific active bleeding site is found[213] or preoperatively.[221]

Endoscopic therapy has a limited role because of the commonly diffuse nature of the intestinal hemangiomas[222] and is reserved for management of localized lesions or ablation of postoperative residual disease. The use of argon[223] and neodymium laser[222] or sclerosis with formaldehyde and absolute alcohol[224] have been reported with success. APC and the photodynamic therapy[213] may be very efficient but their use in this disease has not yet been reported.

Radiation Injury of the Gastrointestinal Tract

RADIATION PROCTITIS

Clinical Manifestations

Radiotherapy is a common treatment modality used for several pelvic malignancies. Despite progress in radiation techniques, adjacent organs remain exposed to chronic radiation injury, which occurs in 2% to 25% of patients.[225]

The rectum, a fixed organ in the pelvis, has a glandular-type epithelium in which the cells undergo a rapid turnover. This organ is, therefore, particularly vulnerable to ionizing radiation and to radiation-induced complications. The incidence of such complications is proportional to the dose and its degree of spreading and to the volume and method of irradiation (external or by brachytherapy).[225] Intracavitary radiation delivery has been shown to increase the risk of developing chronic radiation proctitis.[226]

Risk factors for radiation-induced damage include history of abdominal surgery, arteriosclerosis, obesity, diabetes, and concomitant chemotherapy.[225,227]

Radiation injury to the intestine has acute and chronic phases. Acute radiation injury occurs during or immediately after treatment and results from direct cellular damage. This injury inhibits division of the intestinal crypt stem cells, and the lamina propria becomes infiltrated with inflammatory cells resulting in loss of cellular function and mucosal inflammation. Clinical symptoms of acute radiation proctitis—diarrhea and tenesmus—are usually self-resolving,

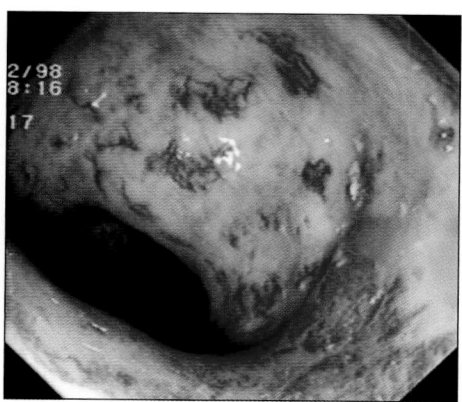

Figure 17–10. Radiation-induced proctitis with pale mucosa, edema, and neovascularization.

requiring only symptomatic treatment and typically are not therapeutic challenges.[228]

Chronic radiation proctitis is histologically characterized by submucosal collagen proliferation, endarteritis of arterioles, and thrombi in vessel lumens, leading to submucosal fibrosis, chronic mucosal ischemia, and progressive epithelial atrophy.[229]

Clinical symptoms of chronic radiation usually begin months to years after the initial radiation exposure with a median of 8 to 16 months[229,230] but with latencies as long as 30 years.[231]

Symptoms include rectal bleeding, diarrhea, rectal pain, fecal urgency, tenesmus, obstructed defecation (in patients who have developed stenosis), and less commonly fecal incontinence and fistulas. Many patients have multiple symptoms with a significantly negative impact on their daily activities.[228] Bleeding may be severe enough to require frequent hospital admissions and blood transfusions; up to 55% of cases may require support with blood transfusions before undergoing definitive therapy.[232]

Diagnosis

Flexible sigmoidoscopy or colonoscopy and biopsy are helpful to assess the extent and severity of radiation injury. Endoscopic examination shows prominent telangiectasia, erythema, and friability (Fig. 17–10); spontaneous or contact bleeding; and, less frequently, ulceration, stenosis, and fistulas. There is often a distinct margin between normal and abnormal tissue that relates to the edge of the radiation field.[232]

Barium enema may be helpful in investigating patients suspected of having fistulas or strictures. It may show distortion and narrowing of the colon and rectum, although it tends to underestimate the severity of radiation injury.[233]

Anorectal physiology **manometry studies** reveal reduced rectal compliance, rectal volumes, anal resting pressures, and internal anal sphincter length.[234,235]

Treatment
Medical Therapies
The traditional approach to treatment of chronic radiation proctitis has been directed toward decreasing the inflammation observed in irradiated rectal tissue with the use of anti-inflammatory agents such as aminosalicylic acid derivatives and corticosteroids.[228] Not surprisingly, the response to such agents has been disappointing. Other approaches such as promoting healing in damaged tissue with short-chain fatty acid enemas,[236] oral and rectal sucralfate,[230,237] antioxidant vitamins,[228] or hormonal therapy with an estrogen-progesterone combination[238] have been tried with partial success.

Recently the use of hyperbaric oxygen has demonstrated moderate success; unfortunately this therapy is expensive and inconvenient, requiring between 20 and 40 treatment sessions.[239,240]

Endoscopic Therapies
Different endoscopic therapies have been described for rectal bleeding in this condition:

- **Topical formalin** application for radiation injury was first reported in radiation-induced cystitis.[241] Its mechanism of action is likely to be due to a local chemical cauterization of the inflamed or fragile telangiectatic rectal mucosa.[232] The treatment is inexpensive and easy to perform. The technique involves the direct application of 4% formalin to the affected area in the rectum, either with formalin-soaked gauze[242] or by direct instillation.[243] Direct application under visualization is better than blind irrigation, because it avoids unnecessary complications and contact of formalin with normal mucosa. The application continues until mucosal blanching occurs, usually within 2 to 3 minutes.[244] The perianal area should be protected with careful draping to avoid formalin injury.[232] The short-term success of the technique with complete cessation of bleeding ranges between 59% and 100%.[232] Recurrent symptomatic relapses have been treated successfully with repeated applications. Complications have been described such as painful fissures of the anal margins, perianal ulcerations,[245] stool incontinence, and rectal ulcerations and strictures.[243]
- **Bipolar electrocoagulation** and **heater probe** are more effective than medical therapy at improving the quality of life.[246]
- **Argon,**[247] **Nd:YAG,**[248] and **KTP laser**[249] have been reported to be effective in the short-term treatment of this disease with a marked decrease in bleeding in 87% of treated patients.[232] Repeated treatment is needed because symptoms tend to recur.[247] Laser therapy has the advantage of being a precise technique that does not involve tissue contact, is well tolerated, and improves activities of daily life. Disadvantages include its high cost; the need for protective precautions; and the risk of rectal ulcer,[249] bowel perforation, and rectovaginal fistulas.[232]
- **APC.** Many authors consider APC to be first-line therapy for radiation proctitis. When the lesions are circumferential, at least two sessions are provided to electrocoagulate each hemicircumference separately. A month later an endoscopy is performed, and a further electrocoagulation is applied if lesions persist.[225] A median of 3-3.7 treatment sessions is necessary for control of bleeding.[232,250] APC is relatively ineffective in patients with excessive bleeding, because of the absorption of current by blood on the surface. Care must be taken not to overdistend the bowel with argon gas insufflation.[232] Because of its limited depth of penetration, morbidity is usually minor and consists of gas bloating, tenesmus, transient abdominal

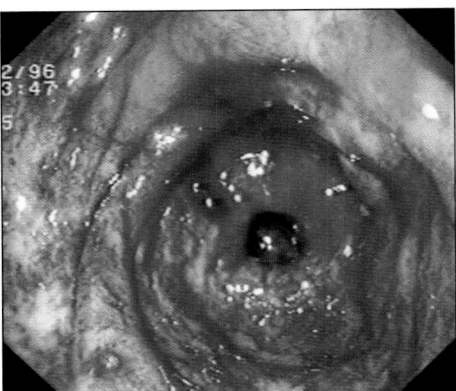

Figure 17–11. Radiation-induced gastritis with erythema, friability, and ulcerated mucosa.

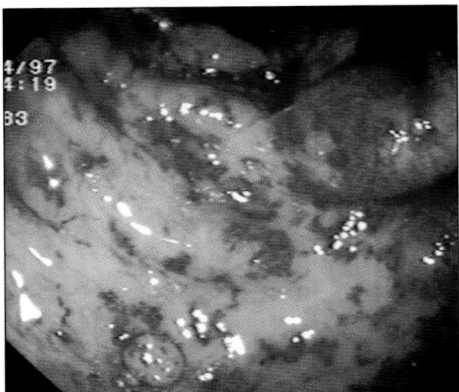

Figure 17–12. Radiation-induced duodenitis with edema, friability, and diffuse telangiectases.

or anal pain, and diarrhea in about 20% of cases.[251] Major complications are exceptional but include rectovaginal fistula,[252] chronic rectal ulceration, anal or rectal stricture,[225] and perforation.[253]

- **Endoscopic cryotherapy** using nitrous oxide has recently been described in a small group of patients with radiation proctitis with complete control of bleeding in all patients.[87] It was also highly effective in patients with multiple AVMs (86%) and watermelon stomach (71%) but less effective in patients with radiation gastritis and duodenitis (40%). Cryotherapy was applied every 2 to 3 days until all lesions were fully treated. The average number of therapeutic sessions needed to stop the bleeding was 3.6. Cryotherapy resulted in superficial tissue necrosis that was usually completely healed within 3 months after the final treatment sessions. Cryotherapy was remarkably safe with only benign self-limited adverse events.

Surgery

Surgical treatment is now considered a last resort and should be reserved only for patients who have intractable symptoms that have failed to respond to medical therapy and for patients with fistulas, because surgery is associated with frequent morbidity and mortality.[254] Proctectomy and a Hartmann's procedure, abdominoperineal resection, and coloanal anastomosis are the surgical options. Resection of the affected rectum needs dissection in an irradiated field with potential complications that range from bleeding to anastomotic leaks and sepsis.[230]

RADIATION GASTRITIS

Gastric complications resulting from radiotherapy are uncommon, but injury can occur when the stomach lies within the radiation field of an adjacent extragastric tumor.[255] A high total dose, usually greater than 5000 rads and high daily fraction appear to be the main risk factors.[256]

Acute vasculopathy may progress to a prolonged and progressive obliterate endarteritis, vasculitis, and endothelial proliferation, leading to mucosal ischemia, ulceration, mucosal telangiectasias, and fibrosis.[257]

Unlike radiation proctitis, GI bleeding from chronic radiation gastritis is rare with very few cases reported.[257,258] When it is present, it shows a diffuse process with multiple bleeding sites leading to significant blood loss, requiring multiple blood transfusions, prolonged hospitalizations, and repeated endoscopies. Endoscopically the mucosa of the stomach appears friable and granular with multiple telangiectasias (Fig. 17–11).

Other possible severe complications are perforation and gastric outlet obstruction.[229]

There is very little information in the literature on the management of radiation-induced complications in the stomach.[229] Prolonged blood loss must be treated with iron and folic acid supplements and with transfusions. Aminocaproic acid has been reported to be effective in control of bleeding in one patient.[257]

Bleeding can be controlled by different endoscopic techniques, such as APC[258] and cryotherapy.[87]

Surgery may be necessary if other treatment fails,[256,259] but it is associated with high morbidity.[257]

RADIATION INJURY OF THE SMALL BOWEL

The small intestine is particularly susceptible to radiation injury[255] (Fig. 17–12).

Radiation injury to the small intestine most often occurs in the clinical setting of radiotherapy for rectal, urologic, gynecologic, or retroperitoneal malignancies. The degree of injury appears proportional to radiation dosage delivered to the segment of small bowel that lies within the radiation field. The relative fixed position of the duodenum and distal ileum within the abdominal cavity make these portions particularly vulnerable to radiation-induced injury. Predisposing factors in the progression of radiation injury include excessive radiation, previous abdominal surgery that fixes loops of bowel in place, underlying cardiovascular disease, and an asthenic habitus.[260]

The mechanism of injury is vascular damage with progressive localized ischemia. This leads to telangiectatic lesions and ulceration of the mucosa, fibrosis with stricturing, and less frequently fistula formation or even perforation.

The clinical manifestations of chronic radiation typically occur 1 to 2 years after exposure and range from malabsorption, hemorrhage, bowel obstruction, fistulas, and abscess formation secondary to perforation.[261]

Bleeding can be managed with the same endoscopic techniques that are used in radiation proctitis.

The treatment is difficult and sometimes surgery is necessary.[260] Resection of the involved small bowel segment is preferable to bypass.[89]

Cameron Ulcers and Erosions

Patients with sliding hiatal hernias, mainly large hernias, may develop Cameron ulcers or erosions. These mucosal lesions are usually localized on the crest of the mucosal folds, on the lesser curve of the stomach, at the level of the diaphragmatic hiatus.[262]

Cameron lesions can be found in 5% of all patients with hiatal hernias.[263]

The cause of Cameron lesions is still unclear, but it is thought that mechanical trauma and perhaps ischemia and acid mucosal injury play a primary role in their pathogenesis.

Cameron lesions present clinically with chronic GI bleeding and associated iron deficiency anemia. These lesions can also present as acute upper GI bleeding in up to one third of cases.[263]

Treatment includes antisecretory therapy and supplemental iron. In about one third of patients, Cameron lesions may persist or recur despite antisecretory medication, in which case surgical repair of the associated hernia may be required.[263]

REFERENCES

1. Spencer J, Camillieri M: Chronic gastrointestinal haemorrhage. In Bouchier IAD, Allan RN, Hodgson HJF, Keighley MRB (eds): Gastroenterology: Clinical Science and Practice. London, WB Saunders, 1993, pp 988–1003.
2. Zuckerman GR, Prakash C, Askin MP, et al: AGA technical review on the evaluation and management of occult and obscure gastrointestinal bleeding. Gastroenterology 118:201–221, 2000.
3. Moore JD, Thompson NW, Appleman HD, et al: Arteriovenous malformation of the gastrointestinal tract. Arch Surg 111:381–389, 1976.
4. Duray PH, Marcal JM Jr, Livolsi VA, et al: Small intestinal angiodysplasia in the elderly. J Clin Gastroenterol 6:311–319, 1984.
5. Boley SJ, Sammartano RJ, Adams A, et al: On the nature and etiology of vascular ectasias of the colon: Degenerative lesions of aging. Gastroenterology 72:650–660, 1977.
6. Naveau S, Leger-Ravet MB, Houdayer C, et al: Nonhereditary colonic angiodysplasias: Histomorphometric approach to their pathogenesis. Dig Dis Sci 40:839–842, 1995.
7. Foutch PG: Angiodysplasia of the gastrointestinal tract. Am J Gastroenterol 88:807–818, 1993.
8. Schmit A, Van Gossum A: A proposal for an endoscopic classification of digestive angiodysplasias for therapeutic trials. Gastrointest Endosc 48:659, 1998.
9. Boley SJ, DiBiase A, Brandt LJ, et al: Lower intestinal bleeding in the elderly. Am J Surg 137:57–64, 1979.
10. Weaver GA, Alpern HD, Davis JS, et al: Gastrointestinal angiodysplasia associated with aortic valve disease: Part of a spectrum of angiodysplasia of the gut. Gastroenterology 77:1–11, 1979.
11. Baum S, Athanasoulis CA, Waltman AC, et al: Angiodysplasia of the right colon: A cause of gastrointestinal bleeding. Am J Roentgenol 129:789–794, 1977.
12. Rogers BH: Endoscopic diagnosis and therapy of mucosal vascular abnormalities of the gastrointestinal tract occurring in elderly patients and associated with cardiac, vascular and pulmonary disease. Gastrointest Endosc 16:134–138, 1980.
13. Junquera F, Saperas E, De Torres I, et al: Increased expression of angiogenic factors in human colonic angiodysplasia. Am J Gastroenterol 94:1070–1076, 1999.
14. Danesh BJ, Spiliadis C, Williams CB, et al: Angiodysplasia, an uncommon cause of colonic bleeding: Colonic evaluation of 1,050 patients with rectal bleeding and anemia. Int J Colon Dis 2:218–222, 1987.
15. Richter JM, Christensen MR, Colditz GA, et al: Angiodysplasia: Natural history and efficacy of therapeutic interventions. Dig Dis Sci 34:1542–1546, 1989.
16. Rockey DC: Gastrointestinal tract evaluation in patients with iron deficiency anemia. Semin Gastrointest Dis 10:53–64, 1999.
17. Clouse RE, Costigan DJ, Mills BA, et al: Angiodysplasia as a cause of upper gastrointestinal bleeding. Arch Intern Med 145:458–461, 1985.
18. Richter JM, Hedberg SE, Athanasoulis CA, et al: Angiodysplasia: Clinical presentation and colonoscopic diagnosis. Dig Dis Sci 29:481–485, 1984.
19. Boley SJ, Sammartano R, Brandt LJ, et al: Vascular ectasias of the colon. Surg Gynecol Obstet 149:353–559, 1979.
20. Jesudason SR, Devasia A, Mathen VI, et al: The pattern of angiodysplasia of the gastrointestinal tract in a tropical country. Surg Gynecol Obstet 161:525–531, 1985.
21. Cappell MS, Gupta A: Changing epidemiology of gastrointestinal angiodysplasia with increasing recognition of clinically milder cases: Angiodysplasia tend to produce mild chronic gastrointestinal bleeding in a study of 47 consecutive patients admitted from 1980 to 1989. J Gastroenterol 87:201–206, 1992.
22. Boley SJ, Brandt LJ: Vascular ectasia of the colon. Dig Dis Sci 31:26S–42S, 1986.
23. Greenwald DA, Brandt LJ: Vascular lesions of the gastrointestinal tract. In Feldman M, Friedman LS, Sleisenger MH (eds): Gastrointestinal and Liver Disease. Pathophysiology, Diagnosis, Management. Philadelphia, WB Saunders, 2002, pp 2341–2351.
24. Moreto M, Figa M, Ojembarrena E, et al: Vascular malformations of the stomach and duodenum: An endoscopic classification. Endoscopy 18:227–229, 1986.
25. Marwick T, Kerlin P: Angiodysplasia of the upper gastrointestinal tract. Clinical spectrum in 41 cases. J Clin Gastroenterol 8:404–407, 1986.
26. Schmit A, Gay F, Adler M, et al: Diagnostic efficacy of push-enteroscopy and long term follow-up of patients with small bowel angiodysplasias. Dig Dis Sci 41:2348–2352, 1996.
27. Browder W, Cerise EJ, Litwin MS: Impact of emergency angiography in massive lower gastrointestinal bleeding. Ann Surg 204:530–536, 1986.
28. Porush JG, Faubert PF: Chronic renal failure. In Porush JG, Faubert PF (eds): Renal Disease in the Aged. Boston, Little, Brown, 1991, p 285.
29. Zuckerman GR, Cornette GL, Clouse RE, et al: Upper gastrointestinal bleeding in patients with chronic renal failure. Ann Intern Med 102:588–592, 1985.
30. Chalasani N, Cotsonis G, Wilcox CM: Upper gastrointestinal bleeding in patients with chronic renal failure: Role of vascular ectasia. Am J Gastroenterol 91:2329–2332, 1996.
31. Duray PH, Marcal JM Jr, LiVolsi VA, et al: Gastrointestinal angiodysplasia: A possible component of von Willebrand's disease. Hum Pathol 15:539–544, 1984.
32. Alhumood SA, Devine DV, Lawson L, et al: Idiopathic immune-mediated acquired von Willebrand's disease in a patient with angiodysplasia: Demonstration of an unusual inhibitor causing a functional defect and rapid clearance of von Willebrand factor. Am J Hematol 60:151–157, 1999.

33. Imperiale TF, Ransohoff DF: Aortic stenosis, idiopathic gastrointestinal bleeding, and angiodysplasia: Is there an association? A methodologic critique of the literature. Gastroenterology 95:1670–1676, 1988.

34. King RM, Pluth JR, Giuliani ER: The association of unexplained gastrointestinal bleeding with calcific aortic stenosis. Ann Thorac Surg 44:514–516, 1987.

35. Cappell MS, Lebwohl O: Cessation of recurrent bleeding from gastrointestinal angiodysplasias after aortic valve replacement. Ann Intern Med 105:54–57, 1986.

36. Scheffer SM, Leatherman LL: Resolution of Heyde's syndrome of aortic stenosis and gastrointestinal bleeding after aortic valve replacement. Ann Thorac Surg 42:477–480, 1986.

37. Warkentin TE, Moore JC, Morgan DG: Aortic stenosis and bleeding gastrointestinal angiodysplasia: Is acquired von Willebrand's disease the link? Lancet 340:35–37, 1992.

38. Veyradier A, Balian A, Wolf M, et al: Abnormal von Willebrand factor in bleeding angiodysplasias of the digestive tract. Gastroenterology 120:346–353, 2001.

39. Warkentin TF, Moore JC, Morgan DG: Gastrointestinal angio-dysplasia and aortic stenosis. N Engl J Med 347:858–859, 2002.

40. O'Brien JR, Etherington MD, Brant J, Watkins J: Decreased platelet function in aortic valve stenosis: High shear platelet activation then inactivation. Br Heart J 74:641–644, 1995.

41. Bourdette D, Greenberg B: Twelve-year history of gastrointestinal bleeding in a patient with calcific aortic stenosis and hemorrhagic telangiectasia. Dig Dis Sci 24:77–79, 1979.

42. Mehta PM, Heinsimer JA, Bryg RJ, et al: Reassessment of the association between gastrointestinal arteriovenous malformations and aortic stenosis. Am J Med 86:275–277, 1989.

43. Oneglia C, Sabatini T, Rusconi C, et al: Prevalence of aortic valve stenosis in patients affected by gastrointestinal angiodysplasia. Eur J Med 2:75–78, 1993.

44. Bhutani MS, Gupta SC, Markert RJ, et al: A prospective controlled evaluation of endoscopic detection of angiodysplasia and its association with aortic valve disease. Gastrointest Endosc 42:398–402, 1995.

45. Brandt LJ, Boley SJ: Vascular disorders of the colon. In Sivak MV Jr (ed): Gastroenterologic Endoscopy, 2nd ed. Philadelphia, WB Saunders, 2000, pp 1324–1350.

46. Sjogren R: Gastrointestinal features of scleroderma. Curr Opin Rheumatol 8:569–575, 1996.

47. Duchini A, Sessoms SL: Gastrointestinal hemorrhage in patients with systemic sclerosis and CREST syndrome. Am J Gastroenterol 93:1453–1456, 1998.

48. Stamm B, Heer M, Buhler H, et al: Mucosal biopsy of vascular ectasia (angiodysplasia) of the large bowel detected during routine colonoscopic examination. Histopathology 9:639–646, 1985.

49. Brandt LJ, Mukhopadhyay D: Masking of colon vascular ectasias by cold water lavage. Gastrointest Endosc 49:141–142, 1999.

50. Brandt LJ, Spinnell MK: Ability of naloxone to enhance the colonoscopic appearance of normal colon vasculature and colon vascular ectasias. Gastrointest Endosc 49:79–83, 1999.

51. Iddan G, Meron G, Glukhovsky A, et al: Wireless capsule endoscopy. Nature 405:725–729, 2000.

52. Gong F, Swain P, Mills T: Wireless endoscopy. Gastrointest Endosc 51:725–729, 2000.

53. Ginsberg GG, Barkun AN, Bosco JJ, et al: Wireless capsule endoscopy. Gastrointest Endosc 56:621–624, 2002.

54. Appleyard M, Fireman Z, Glukhovsky A, et al: A randomized trial comparing wireless capsule endoscopy with push enteroscopy for the detection of small-bowel lesions. Gastroenterology 119:1431–1438, 2000.

55. Lewis B, Swain P: Capsule endoscopy in the evaluation of patients with suspected small intestinal bleeding: The results of the first clinical trial [abstract]. Gastrointest Endosc 53:AB70, 2001.

56. Ell C, Remke S, May A, et al: The first prospective controlled trial comparing wireless capsule endoscopy with push enteroscopy in chronic gastrointestinal bleeding. Endoscopy 34:685–689, 2002.

57. Boley SJ, Sprayregen S, Sammartano RJ, et al: The pathophysio-logic basis for the angiographic signs of vascular ectasias of the colon. Radiology 125:615–621, 1977.

58. Dusold R, Burke K, Carpentier W, et al: The accuracy of technetium-99m-labeled red cell scintigraphy in localizing gastrointestinal bleeding. Am J Gastroenterol 89:345–348, 1994.

59. Levy R, Barto W, Gani J: Retrospective study of the utility of nuclear scintigraphic-labelled red cell scanning for lower gastrointestinal bleeding. ANZ J Surg 73:205–209, 2003.

60. Junquera F, Quiroga S, Saperas E, et al: Accuracy of helical computed tomographic angiography for the diagnosis of colonic angiodysplasia. Gastroenterology 119:293–299, 2000.

61. Foutch PG, Rex DK, Lieberman DA: Prevalence and natural history of colonic angiodysplasia among healthy asymptomatic people. Am J Gastroenterol 90:564–567, 1995.

62. Brandt LJ: A cecal angiodysplastic lesion is discovered during diagnostic colonoscopy performed for iron-deficiency anemia associated with stool positive for occult blood. What therapy would you recommend? Am J Gastroenterol 83:710–711, 1988.

63. Wilcox CM, Alexander LN, Clark WS: Prospective evaluation of the gastrointestinal tract in patients with iron deficiency anemia and no systemic or gastrointestinal signs or symptoms. Am J Med 103:405–409, 1997.

64. Granieri R, Mazzulla JP, Yarborough GW: Estrogen-progesterone therapy for recurrent gastrointestinal bleeding secondary to gastrointestinal angiodysplasia. Am J Gastroenterol 83:556–558, 1988.

65. Van Cutsem E, Rutgeerts P, Vantrappen G: Treatment of bleeding gastrointestinal vascular malformations with oestrogen-progesterone. Lancet 335:953–955, 1990.

66. Lewis B, Salomon P, Rivera-MacMurray S, et al: Does hormonal therapy have any benefit for bleeding angiodysplasia? J Clin Gastroenterol 15:99–103, 1992.

67. Barkin JS, Ross BS: Medical therapy for chronic gastrointestinal bleeding of obscure origin. Am J Gastroenterol 93:1250–1254, 1998.

68. Marshall JK, Hunt RH: Hormonal therapy for bleeding gastrointestinal mucosal vascular abnormalities: A promising alternative. Eur J Gastroenterol Hepatol 9:521–525, 1997.

69. Junquera F, Feu F, Papo M, et al: A multicenter, randomized, clinical trial of hormonal therapy in the prevention of rebleeding from gastrointestinal angiodysplasia. Gastroenterology 121:1073–1079, 2001.

70. Junquera F, Saperas E, Piqué JM: Hormonal therapy in angiodysplasia: Should we completely abandon its use?(reply). Gastroenterology 123:2156–2157, 2002.

71. Nardone G, Rocco A, Balzano T, et al: The efficacy of octreotide therapy in chronic bleeding due to vascular abnormalities of the gastrointestinal tract. Aliment Pharmacol Ther 13:1429–1436, 1999.

72. Orsi P, Guatti-Zuliani C, Okolicsanyi L: Long-acting octreotide is effective in controlling rebleeding angiodysplasia of the gastrointestinal tract. Dig Liver Dis 33:330–334, 2001.

73. Bowers M, McNulty O, Mayne E: Octreotide in the treatment of gastrointestinal bleeding caused by angiodysplasia in two patients with von Willebrand's disease. Br J Hematol 108:524–527, 2000.

74. Askin MP, Lewis BS: Push-enteroscopic cauterization: Long-term follow-up of 83 patients with bleeding small intestinal angiodysplasia. Gastrointest Endosc 43:580–583, 1996.

75. Jensen DM, Machicado GA: Colonoscopy for diagnosis and treatment of severe lower gastrointestinal bleeding: Routine outcomes and cost analysis. Gastrointest Endosc Clin N Am 7:477–498, 1997.

76. Trudel JL, Fazio VW, Sivak MV: Colonoscopic diagnosis and treatment of arteriovenous malformations in chronic lower gastrointestinal bleeding: Clinical accuracy and efficacy. Dis Colon Rectum 31:107—110, 1988.

77. Bemvenuti GA, Julich MM: Ethanolamine injection for sclerotherapy of angiodysplasia of the colon. Endoscopy 30:564–569, 1998.

78. Weilert F, Smith AC: Endoscopic band ligation of gastric angiodysplasia. N Z Med J 111:320, 1998.

79. Campo R, Brullet E: Endoscopic treatment of gastric angiodysplasia with elastic band ligation. Gastrointest Endosc 43:502–504, 1996.

80. Campo R, Brullet E, Montané JM, et al: Elastic band ligation in the bowel: Is it really safe? Gastrointest Endosc 47:105–106, 1998.

81. Gostout CJ, Bowyer BA, Ahlquist DA, et al: Mucosal vascular malformations of the gastrointestinal tract: Clinical observations and results of endoscopic Neodymium: Yttrium-Aluminum-Garnet laser therapy. Mayo Clin Proc 63:993–1003, 1988.

82. Naveau S, Aubert A, Poynard AT, et al: Long-term results of treatment of vascular malformations of the gastrointestinal tract by Neodymium YAG laser photocoagulation. Dig Dis Sci 35:821–826, 1990.

83. Cello JP, Grendell JH: Endoscopic laser treatment for gastrointestinal vascular ectasias. Ann Intern Med 104:352–354, 1986.

84. Wahab PJ, Mulder CJ, den Hartog G, et al: Argon plasma coagulation in flexible gastrointestinal endoscopy: Pilot experiences. Endoscopy 29:176–181, 1997.

85. Johanns W, Luis W, Janssen J, et al: Argon plasma coagulation (APC) in gastroenterology: Experimental and clinical experiences. Eur J Gastroenterol Hepatol 9:581–587, 1997.

86. Jensen SM, Jutabha R, Kovaks TO: A randomized prospective study of endoscopic hemostasis with argon plasma coagulator (APC) compared to gold probe (GP) for bleeding angiomas [abstract]. Gastrointest Endosc 49:A442, 1999.

87. Kantsevoy SV, Cruz-Correa MR, Vaughn CA, et al: Endoscopic cryotherapy for the treatment of bleeding mucosal vascular lesions of the GI tract: A pilot study. Gastrointest Endosc 57:403–406, 2003.

88. Hutcheon DF, Kabelin J, Bulkley GB, et al: Effect of therapy on bleeding rates in gastrointestinal angiodysplasia. Am Surg 53:6–9, 1987.

89. Cohn SM, Moller BA, Zieg PM, et al: Angiography for preoperative evaluation in patients with lower gastrointestinal bleeding: Are the benefits worth the risks? Arch Surg 133:50–55, 1998.

90. Garcia-Tsao G, Korzenik JR, Young L, et al: Liver disease in patients with hereditary hemorrhagic telangiectasia. N Engl J Med 343:931–936, 2000.

91. Longacre AV, Gross CP, Gallitelli M, et al: Diagnosis and management of gastrointestinal bleeding in patients with hereditary hemorrhagic telangiectasia. Am J Gastroenterol 98:59–65, 2003.

92. Begbie ME, Wallace GM, Shovlin CL: Hereditary hemorrhagic telangiectasia (Osler-Weber-Rendu syndrome): A view from the 21st century. Postgrad Med 79:18–24, 2003.

93. Rockey DC: Gastrointestinal bleeding. In Feldman M, Friedman LS, Sleisenger MH (eds): Gastrointestinal and Liver Disease. Philadelphia, WB Saunders, 2002, pp 211–248.

94. Guttmacher AE, Marchuk DA, White RI: Hereditary hemorrhagic telangiectasia. N Engl J Med 333:918–924, 1995.

95. Kjeldsen AD, Kjeldsen J: Gastrointestinal bleeding in patients with hereditary hemorrhagic telangiectasia. Am J Gastroenterol 95:415–418, 2000.

96. Sharma VK, Howden CW: Gastrointestinal and hepatic manifestations of hereditary hemorrhagic telangiectasia. Dig Dis 16:169–174, 1998.

97. Yousfi M, Sharma V, Leighton J, et al: Video capsule endoscopy for obscure gastrointestinal bleeding and iron deficiency anemia [abstract]. Gastroenterology 122:A18, 2002.

98. Hisada T, Kuwabara H, Tsunoda T, et al: Hereditary hemorrhagic telangiectasia showing severe anemia which was successfully treated with estrogen. Intern Med 34:589–592, 1995.

99. Haq AU, Glass J, Netchvolodoff CV, et al: Hereditary hemorrhagic telangiectasia and danazol. Ann Intern Med 109:171, 1988.

100. Annichino-Bizzacchi JM, Facchini RM, Torresan MZ, et al: Hereditary hemorrhagic telangiectasia response to aminocaproic acid treatment. Thromb Res 96:73–76, 1999.

101. Young W, Gilbert V, Feinsat T, et al: The recurrent upper gastrointestinal bleeding in hereditary hemorrhagic telangiectasia (Osler's disease) successfully treated by endoscopic sclerotherapy. Gastrointest Endosc 28:148–152, 1982.

102. Kitamura T, Tanabe S, Koizumi W, et al: Rendu-Osler-Weber disease successfully treated by argon plasma coagulation. Gastrointest Endosc 54:525–527, 2001.

103. Machicado GA, Jensen DM: Upper gastrointestinal angiomata: Diagnosis and treatment. Gastrointest Endosc Clin N Am 1:241–262, 1991.

104. Takazawa J, Motoya M, Okamura S, et al: A case of Rendu-Osler-Weber disease treated with electrocautery. Prog Dig Endosc 19:148–150, 1981.

105. Harada K, Mizushima K, Ono M, et al: A case of Osler's disease treated with laser coagulation. Gastroenterological Endosc 22:400–407, 1980.

106. Iwanuma Y, Haba T, Maekawa T: A case of Rendu-Osler-Weber disease with bleeding from mucosal telangiectasia of the stomach treated by endoscopic hemostasis using clip. Prog Dig Endosc 45:180–181, 1994.

107. Rector WG, Reynolds TB: Risk factors for hemorrhage from esophageal varices and acute gastric erosions. Clin Gastroenterol 14:139–153, 1985.

108. Quintero E, Pique JM, Bombi JA, et al: Gastric antral vascular ectasias causing bleeding in cirrhosis. A distinct entity associated with hypergastrinemia and low serum levels of pepsinogen I. Gastroenterology 93:1054–1061, 1987.

109. Payen JL, Cales P, Voigt JJ: Severe portal hypertensive gastropathy and antral vascular ectasia are distinct entities in patients with cirrhosis. Gastroenterology 108:138–144, 1995.

110. Spina GP, Arcidiacono R, Bosch J, et al: Gastric endoscopic features in portal hypertension: Final report of a consensus conference, Milan, Italy, September 19, 1992. J Hepatol 21:461–467, 1994.

111. McCormack TT, Sims J, Eyre-Brook I, et al: Gastric lesions in portal hypertension: Inflammatory gastritis or congestive gastropathy? Gut 26:1226–1232, 1985.

112. Tanoue K, Hashizume M, Wada H, et al: Effects of endoscopic injection sclerotherapy on portal hypertensive gastropathy: A prospective study. Gastrointest Endosc 38:582–585, 992.

113. Primignani M, Carpinelli L, Preatoni P, et al: Natural history of portal hypertensive gastropathy in patients with liver cirrhosis. The New Italian Endoscopic Club for the study and treatment of esophageal varices (NIEC). Gastroenterology 119:181–187, 2000.

114. Thuluvath PJ. Portal hypertensive gastropathy. Am J Gastroenterol 97:2973–2978, 2002.

115. Pérez-Ayuso RM, Piqué JM, Bosch J, et al: Propranolol in prevention of recurrent bleeding from severe portal hypertensive gastropathy in cirrhosis. Lancet 337:1431–1434, 1991.

116. Pique JM: Portal hypertensive gastropathy. Baillieres Clin Gastroenterol 11:257–270, 1997.

117. Calès P, Zabotto B, Meskens C, et al: Gastroesophageal endoscopic features in cirrhosis. Observer variability, interassociations, and relationship to hepatic dysfunction. Gastroenterology 98:156–162, 1990.

118. Iwao T, Toyonaga A, Oho K, et al: Portal-hypertensive gastropathy develops less in patients with cirrhosis and fundal varices. J Hepatol 26:1235–1241, 1997.

119. Sarin SK, Sreenivas DV, Lahoti D, et al: Factors influencing development of portal hypertensive gastropathy in patients with portal hypertension. Gastroenterology 102:994–999, 1992.

120. Sarin SK, Shahi HM, Jain M, et al: The natural history of portal hypertensive gastropathy: Influence of variceal eradication. Am J Gastroenterol 95:2888–2893, 2000.

121. Gupta R, Saraswat VA, Kumar M, et al: Frequency and factors influencing portal hypertensive gastropathy and duodenopathy in cirrhotic portal hypertension. J Gastroenterol Hepatol 11:728–733, 1996.

122. Bayraktar Y, Balkanci F, Uzunalimoglu B, et al: Is portal hypertension due to liver cirrhosis a major factor in the development of portal hypertensive gastropathy? Am J Gastroenterol 91:554–558, 1996.

123. Masuko E, Homma H, Ohta H, et al: Rheologic analysis of gastric mucosal hemodynamics in patients with cirrhosis. Gastrointest Endosc 49:371–379, 1999.

124. Panes J, Bordas JM, Pique JM, et al: Increased gastric mucosal perfusion in cirrhotic patients with portal hypertensive gastropathy. Gastroenterology 103:1875–1882, 1992.

125. Ohta M, Hashizume M, Higashi H, et al: Portal and gastric mucosal hemodynamics in cirrhotic patients with portal-hypertensive gastropathy. Hepatology 20:1432–1436, 1994.

126. Nishizaki Y, Kaunitz JD, Oda M, et al: Impairment of gastric mucosal defenses measured in vivo in cirrhotic rats. Hepatology 20:445–452, 1994.

127. Ohta M, Yamaguchi S, Gotoh N, et al: Pathogenesis of portal hypertensive gastropathy: A clinical and experimental review. Surgery 131:S165–S170, 2002.

128. Kawanaka H, Tomikawa M, Jones MK, et al: Defective mitogen-activated protein kinase (ERK2) signaling in gastric mucosa of portal hypertensive rats: Potential therapeutic implications. Hepatology 34:990–999, 2001.

129. Sarin SK, Misra SP, Singal A, et al: Evaluation of the incidence and significance of the "mosaic pattern" in patients with cirrhosis, noncirrhotic portal fibrosis, and extrahepatic obstruction. Am J Gastroenterol 83:1235–1239, 1988.

130. Lo GH, Lai KH, Cheng JS, et al: The effects of endoscopic variceal ligation and propranolol on portal hypertensive gastropathy: A prospective, controlled trial. Gastrointest Endosc 53:579–584, 2001.

131. Balan KK, Grime JS, Sutton R, et al: Do alterations in the rate of gastric emptying after injection sclerotherapy for oesophageal varices play any role in the development of portal hypertensive gastropathy? HPB Surg 11:141–150, 1999.

132. D'Amico G, Montalbano L, Traina M, et al: Natural history of congestive gastropathy in cirrhosis. The Liver Study Group of V. Cervello Hospital. Gastroenterology 99:1558–1564, 1990.

133. Hou MC, Lin HC, Chen CH, et al: Change of portal hypertensive gastropathy following EVL or sclerotherapy. Hepatology 20:104A, 1994.

134. Gostout CJ: Portal hypertensive gastropathy: Much ado about nothing? Am J Gastroenterol 95:2682–2684, 2000.

135. Lebrec D, Poynard T, Hillon P, et al: Propranolol for prevention of recurrent gastrointestinal bleeding in patients with cirrhosis: A controlled study. N Engl J Med 305:1371–1374, 1981.

136. Hosking SW, Kennedy HJ, Seddon I, et al: The role of propranolol in congestive gastropathy of portal hypertension. Hepatology 7:437–441, 1987.

137. Li MK, Sung JJ, Woo KS, et al: Somatostatin reduces gastric mucosal blood flow in patients with portal hypertensive gastropathy: A randomized, double-blind crossover study. Dig Dis Sci 41:2440–2446, 1996.

138. Kouroumalis EA, Koutroubakis IE, Manousos ON: Somatostatin for acute severe bleeding from portal hypertensive gastropathy. Eur J Gastroenterol Hepatol 10:509–512, 1998.

139. Escorsell A, Bandi JC, Andreu V, et al: Desensitization to the effects of intravenous octreotide in cirrhotic patients with portal hypertension. Gastroenterology 120:161–169, 2001.

140. Garcia N, Sanyal AJ: Portal hypertensive gastropathy and gastric antral vascular ectasia. Curr Treat Options Gastroenterol 4:163–171, 2001.

141. Gostout CJ, Ahlquist DA, Radford CM, et al: Endoscopic laser therapy for watermelon stomach. Gastroenterology 96:1462–1465, 1989.

142. Orloff MJ, Orloff MS, Orloff SL, et al: Treatment of bleeding from portal hypertensive gastropathy by portacaval shunt. Hepatology 21:1011–1017, 1995.

143. Urata J, Yamashita Y, Tsuchigame T, et al: The effects of trans-jugular intrahepatic portosystemic shunt on portal hypertensive gastropathy. J Gastroenterol Hepatol 13:1061–1067, 1998.

144. Panes J, Pique JM. Therapeutic options for bleeding portal hypertensive gastropathy [editorial]. J Gastroenterol Hepatol 13:977—979, 1998.

145. Jabbari M, Cherry R, Lough JO, et al: Gastric antral vascular ectasia: The watermelon stomach. Gastroenterology 87:1165–1170, 1984.

146. Lee FI, Costello F, Flanagan N, et al: Diffuse antral vascular ectasia. Gastrointest Endosc 30:87–90, 1984.

147. Toyota M, Hinoda Y, Nakagawa N, et al: Gastric antral vascular ectasia causing severe anemia. J Gastroenterol 31:710–713, 1996.

148. Pérez-Ayuso RM, Piqué JM, Saperas E et al: Gastric vascular ectasias in cirrhosis: association with hypoacidity not related to gastric atrophy. Scand J Gastroenterol 24:1073–1078, 1989.

149. Lowes R, Rode J: Neuroendocrine cell proliferation in gastric antral vascular ectasia. Gastroenterology 97:207–212, 1989.

150. Spahr L, Villeneuve JP, Dufresne MP, et al: Gastric antral vascular ectasia in cirrhotic patients: Absence of relation with portal hypertension. Gut 44:739–742, 1999.

151. Suit PF, Petras RE, Bauer TW, et al: Gastric antral vascular ectasia: A histologic and morphometric study of the "watermelon stomach". Am J Surg Pathol 11:750–757, 1987.

152. Gilliam JH, Geisinger KR, Wu WC, et al: Endoscopic biopsy is diagnostic in gastric antral vascular ectasia. The "watermelon stomach." Dig Dis Sci 34:885–888, 1989.

153. Kamath PS, Lacerda M, Ahlquist DA, et al: Gastric mucosal responses to intrahepatic portosystemic shunting in patients with cirrhosis. Gastroenterology 118:905–911, 2000.

154. Tran A, Villeneuve JP, Bilodeau M, et al: Treatment of chronic bleeding from gastric antral vascular ectasia (GAVE) with estrogen-progesterone in cirrhotic patients: An open pilot study. Am J Gastroenterol 94:2909–2911, 1999.

155. Moss SF, Ghosh P, Thomas DM, et al: Gastric antral vascular ectasia: Maintenance treatment with oestrogen-progesterone. Gut 33:715–717, 1992.

156. Schoonbroodt D, Horsmans Y, Hoang P, et al: Vascular gastric lesions, Crest syndrome, and primary biliary cirrhosis: Efficacy of estrogen-progesterone treatment. Gastroenterol Clin Biol 18:649–651, 1994.

157. Mannning R: Estrogen/progesterone treatment of diffuse antral vascular ectasia. Am J Gastroenterol 90:154–156, 1995.

158. McCormick PA, Ooi H, Crosbie O: Tranexamic acid for severe bleeding gastric antral vascular ectasia in cirrhosis. Gut 42:750–752, 1998.

159. Barbara G, De Giorgio R, Salvioli B, et al: Unsuccessful octreotide treatment of the watermelon stomach. J Clin Gastroenterol 26:345–346, 1998.

160. Bourke MJ, Hope RL, Boyd P, et al: Endoscopic laser therapy for watermelon stomach. J Gastroenterol Hepatol 11:832–834, 1996.

161. Bjorkman DJ, Buchi KN: Endoscopic laser therapy of the watermelon stomach. Lasers Surg Med 12:478–481, 1992.

162. Eloubeidi MA, Branch MS: Clinical images. Watermelon stomach. Dig Dis 17:123, 1999.

163. Focke G, Seidl C, Grouls V: Treatment of watermelon stomach (GAVE syndrome) with endoscopic argon plasma coagulation (APC). A new therapy approach. Leber Magen Darm 26:254–259, 1996.

164. Petrini JJ, Johnston J: Heat probe treatment for antral vascular ectasia. Gastrointestinal Endosc 35:324–328, 1989.

165. Ikeda M, Ishida H, Nakamura E, et al: An endoscopic follow-up study of the development of diffuse antral vascular ectasia. Endoscopy 28:390–393, 1996.

166. Cales P, Voigt JJ, Payen JL, et al: Diffuse vascular ectasia of the antrum, duodenum and jejunum in a patient with nodular regenerative hyperplasia. Lack of response to portosystemic shunt or gastrectomy. Gut 34:558–561, 1993.

167. Borsch G: Diffuse gastric antral vascular ectasia: The "watermelon stomach" revisited [letter]. Am J Gastroenterol 82:1333–1334, 1987.

168. Gostout CJ, Viggiano TR, Ahlquist DA, et al: The clinical and endoscopic spectrum of the watermelon stomach. J Clin Gastroenterol 15:256–263, 1992.

169. Kurger R, Ryan M, Dickson K, et al: Diffuse vascular ectasia in the gastric antrum. Am J Gastroenterol 82:421–426, 1987.

170. Kozarek RA, Botoman VA, Bredfeldt JE, et al: Portal colopathy: Prospective study of colonoscopy in patients with portal hypertension. Gastroenterology 101:1192–1197, 1991.

171. Naveau S, Bedossa P, Poynard T, et al: Portal hypertensive colopathy: A new entity. Dig Dis Sci 36:1774–1781, 1991.

172. Chen LS, Lin HC, Lee FY, et al: Portal hypertensive colopathy in patients with cirrhosis. Scand J Gastroenterol 31:490–494, 1996.

173. Tam TN, Ng WW, Lee SD: Colonic mucosal changes in patients with liver cirrhosis. Gastrointest Endosc 42:408–412, 1995.

174. Rabinovitz M, Schade RR, Dindzans VJ, et al: Colonic disease in cirrhosis: An endoscopic evaluation in 412 patients. Gastroenterology 99:195–199, 1990.

175. Scandalis N, Archimandritis A, Kastanas K, et al: Colonic findings in cirrhotics with portal hypertension: A prospective colonoscopic and histological study. J Clin Gastroenterol 18:325–329, 1994.

176. Goenka MK, Kochhar R, Nagi B, et al: Rectosigmoid varices and other mucosal changes in patients with portal hypertension. Am J Gastroenterol 86:1185–1189, 1991.

177. Ganguly S, Sarin SK, Bhatia V, et al: The prevalence and spectrum of colonic lesions in patients with cirrhotic and noncirrhotic portal hypertension. Hepatology 21:1226–1231, 1995.

178. Misra SP, Dwiverdi M, Misra V: Prevalence and factors influencing hemorrhoids, anorectal varices, and colopathy in patients with portal hypertension. Endoscopy 28:340–345, 1996.

179. Bresci G, Gambardella L, Parisi G, et al: Colonic disease in cirrhotic patients with portal hypertension: An endoscopic and clinical evaluation. J Clin Gastroenterol 26:222–227, 1998.

180. Viggiano TR, Gostout CJ: Portal hypertensive intestinal vasculopathy: A review of the clinical, endoscopic, and histopathologic features. Am J Gastroenterol 87:944–954, 1992.

181. Bini EJ, Lascarides CE, Micale PL, et al: Mucosal abnormalities of the colon in patients with portal hypertension: An endoscopic study. Gastrointest Endosc 52:511–516, 2000.

182. Lamps LW, Hunt CM, Green A, et al: Alterations in colonic mucosal vessels in patients with cirrhosis and noncirrhotic portal hypertension. Hum Pathol 28:527–535, 1998.

183. Munakata A, Nakajima H, Sasaki Y, et al: Does portal hypertension modify colonic mucosal vasculature? Quantification of alteration by image processing and topology. Am J Gastroenterol 90:1997–2001, 1995.

184. Balzer C, Lotterer E, Kleber G, et al: Transjugular intrahepatic portosystemic shunt for bleeding angiodysplasia-like lesions in portal-hypertensive colopathy. Gastroenterology 115:167–172, 1998.

185. Fraiberg EN, Ahmed S: Colonoscopic excision of a polypoidal cavernous hemangioma of the cecum. Gastrointest Endosc 31:109, 1985.

186. Pontecorvo C, Lombardi S, Mottola L, et al: Hemangiomas of the large bowel. Report of a case. Dis Colon Rectum 26:818–820, 1983.

187. Amano K, Seko A, Nagura K, et al: A case of polypoid cavernous hemangioma of the sigmoid colon excised by colonoscopic polypectomy. Gastroenterol Jpn 28:712–718, 1993.

188. Beck PL, Aspinall AI, Kilvert VM, et al: Blue rubber bleb nevus syndrome. Gastrointest Endosc 56:598–600, 2002.

189. Oksuzoglu BC, Oksuzoglu G, Cakir U, et al: Blue rubber bleb nevus syndrome. Am J Gastroenterol 91:780–782, 1996.

190. Rodrigues D, Bourroul ML, Ferrer AP, et al: Blue rubber bleb nevus syndrome. Rev Hosp Clin Fac Med Sao Paulo 55:29–34, 2000.

191. Ertem D, Acar Y, Kotiloglu E, et al: Blue rubber bleb nevus syndrome. Pediatrics 107:418–421, 2001.

192. Muñoz-Navas M, Fernández-Urién I, Espinet E, et al: Blue rubber bleb nevus syndrome, three cases. Rev Esp Enf Digest 96:344–345, 2004.

193. Bak YT, Oh CH, Kim JH, et al: Blue rubber bleb nevus syndrome: Endoscopic removal of the gastrointestinal hemangiomas. Gastrointest Endosc 45:90–92, 1997.

194. Tyrrel RT, Baumgartner BR, Montemayor KA: Blue rubber bleb nevus syndrome: CT diagnosis of intussusception. Am J Roentgenol 154:105–106, 1990.

195. Kim SJ: Blue rubber bleb nevus syndrome with central nervous system involvement. Pediatr Neurol 22:410–412, 2000.

196. Garen PD, Sahn EE: Spinal cord compression in blue rubber bleb nevus syndrome. Arch Dermatol 130:934–935, 1994.

197. Fernandes C, Silva A, Coelho A, et al: Blue rubber bleb naevus: Case report and literature review. Eur J Gastroenterol Hepatol 11:455–457, 1999.

198. Aihara M, Konuma Y, Okawa K, et al: Blue rubber bleb nevus syndrome with disseminated intravascular coagulation and thrombocytopenia: Successful treatment with high-dose intravenous gammaglobulin. Tohoku J Exp Med 163:111–117, 1991.

199. Romao Z, Pontes J, Lopes H, et al: Endosonography in the diagnosis of "blue rubber bleb nevus syndrome": An uncommon cause of gastrointestinal tract bleeding. J Clin Gastroenterol 28:262–265, 1999.

200. Jennings M, Ward P, Maddocks JL: Blue rubber bleb naevus disease: An uncommon cause of gastrointestinal tract bleeding. Gut 29:1408–1412, 1988.

201. Boente MD, Cordisco MR, Frontini MD, et al: Blue rubber bleb nevus (Bean syndrome): Evolution of four cases and clinical response to pharmacologic agents. Pediatr Dermatol 16:222–227, 1999.

202. Gonzalez D, Elizondo BJ, Haslag S, et al: Chronic subcutaneous octreotide decreases gastrointestinal blood loss in blue rubber-bleb nevus syndrome. J Pediatr Gastroenterol Nutr 33:183–188, 2001.

203. Dwivedi M, Misra SP: Blue rubber bleb nevus syndrome causing upper GI hemorrhage: A novel management approach and review. Gastrointest Endosc 55:943–946, 2002.

204. Arguedas MR, Wilcos CM: Blue rubber bleb nevus syndrome. Gastrointest Endosc 50:544, 1999.

205. Sala T, Urquijo JJ, Lopez-Viedma B, et al: Blue nevus syndrome: Endoscopic treatment by sclerosis and banding ligation. Gastroenterol Hepatol 22:136–138, 1999.

206. Shimada S, Namikawa K, Maeda K, et al: Endoscopic polypectomy under laparotomy throughout the alimentary tract for a patient with blue rubber bleb nevus syndrome. Gastrointest Endosc 45:423–427, 1997.

207. Maunoury V, Turck D, Brunetaud JM, et al: Blue rubber bleb nevus syndrome: 3 cases treated with a Nd:YAG laser and bipolar electrocoagulation. Gastroenterol Clin Biol 14:593–595, 1990.

208. Dieckmann K, Maurage C, Faure N, et al: Combined laser-steroid therapy in blue rubber bleb nevus syndrome: Case report and review of the literature. Eur J Pediatr Surg 4:372–374, 1994.

209. Yacoub M, Gnaoui A, Abroug S, et al: The "blue rubber bleb nevus" (Bean's syndrome): Uncommon cause of gastrointestinal bleeding. Ann Pediatr 40:157–161, 1993.

210. Wong SH, Lau WY: Blue rubber-bleb nevus syndrome. Dis Colon Rectum 25:371–374, 1982.

211. Watanabe Y, Sato M, Tokui K, et al: Multiendoscope-assisted treatment for blue rubber bleb nevus syndrome. Surg Endosc 14:595, 2000.

212. Baskerville PA, Ackroyd JS, Browse NL: The etiology of Klippel-Trénaunay syndrome. Ann Surg 202:624–627, 1985.

213. Wilson CL, Wong LM, Chua H, et al: Bleeding from cavernous angiomatosis of the rectum in Klippel-Trénaunay syndrome. Report of three cases and literature review. Am J Gastroenterol 96:2783—2788, 2001.

214. Duque JM, Muñoz-Navas M, Betes MT, et al: Colonic involvement in the Klippel-Trénaunay-Weber syndrome. Rev Esp Enferm Dig 92:44–45, 2000.

215. Gandolfi L, Rossi A, Stasi G, et al: The Klippel-Trénaunay syndrome with colonic hemangioma. Gastrointest Endosc 33:442–445, 1987.

216. Bataller R, Sans M, Escorsell A, et al: Esophageal variceal bleeding caused by hypoplasia of the portal vein in a patient with the Klippel-Trénaunay syndrome. Am J Gastroenterol 93:275–276, 1998.

217. Brown R, Ohri SK, Ghosh P, et al: Case report. Jejunal vascular malformation in Klippel-Trénaunay syndrome. Clin Radiol 44:134–136, 1991.

218. Telander RL, Kaufman BH, Gloviczki P, et al: Prognosis and management of lesions of the trunk in children with Klippel-Trénaunay syndrome. J Pediatr Surg 19:417–422, 1984.

219. Yeoman LJ, Shaw D: Computerized tomography appearances of pelvic haemangioma involving the large bowel in childhood. Pediatr Radiol 19:414–416, 1989.

220. Vazquez-Sequeiros E, Sorbi D, Kamath PS, et al: Klippel-Trénaunay syndrome: Role of EUS. Gastrointest Endosc 54:660–661, 2001.

221. Lehmann TG, Dux M, von Herbay A, et al: Klippel-Trénaunay syndrome with involvement of the rectum. Surgical therapy after interventional radiologic preparation. Chirurg 71:228–233, 2000.

222. Myers BM: Treatment of colonic bleeding in Klippel-Trénaunay syndrome with combined partial colectomy and endoscopic laser. Dig Dis Sci 38:1351–1353, 1993.

223. Azizkhan RG: Life-threatening hematochezia from a rectosigmoid vascular malformation in Klippel-Trénaunay syndrome: Long-term palliation using an argon laser. J Pediatr Surg 26:1125–1128, 1991.

224. Garteiz D, Robledo F, de la Fuente M, et al: Klippel-Trénaunay syndrome. Rev Gastroenterol Mex 64:181–185, 1999.

225. Taïeb S, Rolachon A, Cenni JC, et al: Effective use of argon plasma coagulation in the treatment of severe radiation proctitis. Dis Colon Rectum 44:1766–1771, 2001.

226. Deitel M, Vasic V: Major intestinal complications of radiotherapy. Am J Gastroenterol 72:65–70, 1979.

227. Cho KH, Lee CK, Levitt SH: Proctitis after conventional external radiation therapy for prostate cancer: Importance of minimizing posterior rectal dose. Radiology 195:699–703, 1995.

228. Kennedy M, Bruninga K, Mutlu EA, et al: Successful and sustained treatment of chronic radiation proctitis with antioxidant vitamins E and C. Am J Gastroenterol 96:1080–1084, 2001.

229. Coia LR, Myerson RJ, Tepper JE: Late effects of radiation therapy on the gastrointestinal tract. Int J Radiation Oncology Biol Phys 31:1213–1226, 1995.

230. Gul YA, Prasannan S, Jabar FM, et al: Pharmacotherapy for chronic hemorrhagic radiation proctitis. World J Surg 26:1499–1502, 2002.

231. Lucarotti ME, Mountford RA, Bartolo DC: Surgical management of intestinal radiation injury. Dis Colon Rectum 34:865–869, 1991.

232. Tagkalidis PP, Tjandra JJ: Chronic radiation proctitis. ANZ J Surg 71:230–237, 2001.

233. Johnson RJ, Carrington BM: Pelvic radiation disease. Clin Radiol 45:4–12, 1993.

234. Varma JS, Smith AN, Busuttil A: Correlation of clinical and manometric abnormalities of rectal function following chronic radiation injury. Br J Surg 72:875–878, 1985.

235. Varma JS, Smith AN, Busuttil A: Function of the anal sphincters after chronic radiation injury. Gut 27:528–533, 1986.

236. Talley NA, Chen F, King D, et al: Short-chain fatty acids in the treatment of radiation proctitis: A randomized, double-blind, placebo-controlled, cross-over pilot trail. Dis Colon Rectum 40:1046–1050, 1997.

237. Sasai T, Hiraishi H, Suzuki Y, et al: Treatment of chronic post-radiation proctitis with oral administration of sucralfate. Am J Gastroenterol 93:1593—1595, 1998.

238. Wurzer H, Schafhalter-Zoppoth I, Brandstätter G, et al: Hormonal therapy in chronic radiation colitis. Am J Gastroenterol 93:2536–2538, 1998.

239. Warren DC, Feehan P, Slade JB, et al: Chronic radiation proctitis treated with hyperbaric oxygen. Undersea Hyperb Med 24:181–184, 1997.

240. Woo TC, Joseph D, Oxer H: Hyperbaric oxygen treatment for radiation proctitis. Int J Radiat Oncol Biol Phys 38:619–622, 1997.

241. Brown RB: A method of management of inoperable carcinoma of the bladder. Med J Aust 1:23–24, 1969.

242. Roche B, Chautems R, Marti MC: Application of formaldehyde for treatment of hemorrhagic radiation-induced proctitis. World J Surg 20:1092–1095, 1996.

243. Counter SF, Froese DP, Hart MJ: Prospective evaluation of formalin therapy for radiation proctitis. Am J Surg 177:396–398, 1999.

244. Seow-Choen F, Goh HS, Eu KW, et al: A simple and effective treatment for hemorrhagic radiation proctitis using formalin. Dis Colon Rectum 36:135–138, 1993.

245. Saclarides TJ, King DG, Franklin JL, et al: Formalin installation for refractory radiation-induced hemorrhagic proctitis. Dis Colon Rectum 39:196–199, 1996.

246. Jensen DM, Machicado GA, Cheng S, et al: A randomized prospective study of endoscopic bipolar electrocoagulation and heater probe treatment of chronic rectal bleeding from radiation telangiectasia. Gastrointest Endosc 45:20–25, 1997.

247. Taylor JG, DiSario JA, Buchi KN: Argon laser therapy for hemorrhagic radiation proctitis: Long-term results. Gastrointest Endosc 39:641–644, 1993.

248. Carbatzas C, Spencer GM, Thorpe SM, et al: Nd:YAG laser treatment for bleeding from radiation proctitis. Endoscopy 28:497–500, 1996.

249. Taylor JG, DiSario JA, Bjorkman DJ: KTP laser therapy for bleeding from chronic radiation proctopathy. Gastrointest Endosc 52:353–357, 2000.

250. Kaassis M, Oberti F, Burtin P, et al: Argon plasma coagulation for the treatment of hemorrhagic radiation proctitis. Endoscopy 32:673–676, 2000.

251. Villavicencio RT, Rex DK, Rahmani E: Efficacy and complications of argon plasma coagulation for hematochezia related to radiation proctopathy. Gastrointest Endosc 55:70–74, 2002.

252. Silva RA, Correia AJ, Dias LM, et al: Argon plasma coagulation therapy for hemorrhagic radiation proctosigmoiditis. Gastrointest Endosc 50:221–224, 1999.

253. Sousan EM, Mathieu N, Roque I, et al: Bowel explosion with colonic perforation during argon plasma coagulation for hemorrhagic radiation-induced proctitis. Gastrointest Endosc 57:412–413, 2003.

254. Swaroop VS, Goustout GJ: Endoscopic treatment of chronic radiation proctopathy. J Clin Gastroenterol 27:36–40, 1998.

255. Cohn SM, Bickston S: Radiation injury in the gastrointestinal tract. In Yamada T (ed): Textbook of Gastroenterology. Philadelphia, Lippincott Williams & Wilkins, 2003, pp 2760–2771.

256. Flobert C, Cellier C, Landi B, et al: Gastrite hémorragique sévère d'origine radique. Gastroenterol Clin Biol 22:232–234, 1998.

257. Grover N, Johnson A: Aminocaproic acid used to control upper gastrointestinal bleeding in radiation gastritis. Dig Dis Sci 42:982–984, 1997.

258. Morrow JB, Dumot JA, Vargo JJ: Radiation-induced hemorrhagic carditis treated with argon plasma coagulator. Gastrointest Endosc 51:498–499, 2000.

259. Yeung YP, Ho CM, Wong KH, et al: Surgical treatment of recalcitrant radiation-induced gastric erosions. Head Neck 22:303–306, 2000.

260. Sher ME, Bauer J: Radiation-induced enteropathy. Am J Gastroenterol 85:121–128, 1990.

261. Nguyen N, Antoine JE, Dutta S, et al: Current concepts in radiation enteritis and implications for future clinical trials. Cancer 95:1151–1163, 2002.

262. Cameron AJ, Higgins JA: Linear gastric erosion. A lesion associated with large diaphragmatic hernia and chronic blood loss anemia. Gastroenterology 91:338–342, 1986.

263. Weston AP: Hiatal hernia with Cameron ulcers and erosions. Gastrointest Endosc Clin N Am 6:671–679, 1996.

Gastroesophageal Reflux

Richard I. Rothstein

Introduction

Gastroesophageal reflux disease (GERD) is one of the most common gastrointestinal (GI) disorders, and the burden of disease brought on by gastroesophageal reflux is the costliest among GI disorders in the United States.[1] Although most individuals experience symptoms of GERD infrequently, approximately 14% of Americans report GERD episodes at least once per week, and up to 7% describe daily symptoms of heartburn or regurgitation.[2] In addition, the extraesophageal manifestations of GERD, including laryngeal inflammation, chronic cough, and asthma, are being recognized with increasing frequency. Individuals bothered by GERD symptoms score themselves as having their quality of life affected more than individuals with angina pectoris or mild heart failure.[3] The impact of GERD on quality of life worsens in parallel with the severity of symptoms and is the same for GERD sufferers with erosive esophagitis or nonerosive reflux disease (NERD).[4] The consequences of chronic GERD are significant and include the development of peptic esophageal strictures, esophageal intestinal metaplasia, and adenocarcinoma.[5]

Although some degree of gastroesophageal reflux and distal esophageal acid contact is considered normal and physiologic, it should be asymptomatic. Symptomatic and complicated GERD evolves from an imbalance in the mechanisms that prevent excessive entrance of the refluxate into the distal esophagus. Competence of the esophagogastric junction (EGJ) is the primary defense factor, and esophageal acid clearance, epithelial and tissue resistance, and refluxate causticity are also important elements in the pathophysiology of GERD.[6] Among the contributing pathophysiologic factors, low resting lower esophageal sphincter pressure (LESP) is associated with more severe reflux disease and erosive esophagitis, and the severity of reflux disease in patients with hiatal hernia has been positively correlated with the size of the hernia sac.[7,8]

The contribution of transient lower esophageal sphincter relaxations (tLESRs) to excessive exposure of the esophagus to acid and pepsin is becoming increasingly better understood. Patients with GERD have a larger fraction of tLESRs associated with reflux than normal controls and longer duration of esophageal acid exposure as a result.[9] The contribution of tLESRs to GERD is more important for patients with nonerosive or mild erosive disease, whereas individuals with more severe grades of esophagitis often have other factors (hiatal hernia, hypotensive lower esophageal sphincter [LES]) permitting prolonged acid exposure.[10]

Successful treatment for GERD should provide adequate symptom relief, heal reflux-induced esophagitis, maintain long-term symptom remission, and prevent complications associated with GERD. In addition, an ideal therapy would have a minimal risk of morbidity and mortality and would be cost effective for both patients and the health care system. Treatment options for GERD focus on minimizing the exposure of the esophageal epithelium to gastric secretions and fortifying the antireflux barrier at the EGJ. Medical therapies have focused mainly on acid suppression, most recently with proton pump inhibitors (PPIs), whereas surgical therapies have targeted the EGJ most commonly with fundoplication. Both medical and surgical strategies have had varying success in achieving treatment objectives, although they are roughly comparable in clinical outcomes[11,12] and have been, in general, safe.

Pharmacologic treatments have been shown to be safe and effective for relieving symptoms, healing esophagitis, maintaining remission, and preventing the recurrence of strictures.[13,14] However, they usually require daily dosing, which may be a barrier for some patients, and may require increased dosing over time. In addition, although acid inhibitors may provide 85% to 95% relief of pyrosis, they often fail to improve the common GERD symptom of regurgitation for many individuals, reducing overall satisfaction with medical management of GERD.[15]

Surgery is an option for patients who do not achieve satisfactory results from management with medications or who do not wish to continue their dependency on frequent use of these agents. In 1956, Rudolf Nissen published his initial experience with the open fundoplication, termed *gastroplication*, and it became the most popular standard surgical treatment option until 1991, when laparoscopic antireflux surgery was introduced.[16] With the obvious benefits of a minimally invasive approach, laparoscopic fundoplication has supplanted the original open thoracic and transabdominal approaches.[17] Performed by experienced surgeons, laparoscopic fundoplication has been shown to be about 90% effective controlling reflux symptoms, but up to half of surgically treated patients may eventually require medications to control their recurrent symptoms 10 years postoperatively.[11,12,18]

Similar to pharmacologic treatment, laparoscopic fundoplication provides symptom relief, facilitates the healing of the esophagus, and maintains symptom remission. This minimally invasive surgical approach can decrease postoperative recovery and complications for patients. However, a lack of randomized controlled trials comparing laparoscopic fundoplication to other therapies makes it difficult to adequately assess its relative efficacy. Nonetheless, it is clear that the initial impact of laparoscopic fundoplication on patients' quality of life is not insignificant, with usually 1 day of hospitalization and 3 weeks of postoperative recovery that includes dietary modifications and restriction of certain exercises and activities. The operative therapy appears to be generally safe, but 5% to 8% of patients exhibit new postoperative symptoms such as dysphagia, bloating, increased flatus, diarrhea, and an inability to eructate or vomit.[18–20] There is also an extremely rare possibility of mortality related to general anesthesia or other perioperative factors. In addition, the laparoscopic surgical approach has a high upfront cost, which is comparable to the cost for many years of medical treatment. Published cost-efficacy models of surgical versus medical GERD treatment do not always factor in the costs of postoperative complications and repeat surgical interventions, resulting in assumptions that may underestimate the true cost of surgical intervention.[21–24] Surgical procedures to treat GERD that are performed in the community hospital setting have fewer optimal outcomes compared with those performed in more experienced centers of excellence, and this must be considered when making individualized recommendations for treatment.[25]

In this background of medical versus surgical management, innovative endoscopic therapies have emerged as a treatment option for individuals with GERD. Designed for the outpatient arena, these procedures are less invasive than laparoscopic fundoplication, usually require only conscious sedation and promise rapid recovery. These interventions can provide long-term benefit for GERD sufferers. They also may be considered a "bridge" therapy because patients who undergo the endoscopic treatments can still elect to be treated with chronic medications or surgical intervention if the endoscopic therapy does not provide full symptom relief or if symptoms later recur. These endoscopic antireflux treatments are in evolution, and most initial reports address symptom relief in short-term follow-up studies of mild GERD patients. There are only a few peer-reviewed original reports available for each of these new techniques, and only one published sham-controlled trial. Although other data have been presented in abstract form, few studies have incorporated large enough numbers of subjects and intention-to-treat analysis, issues required to provide valid demonstration of effect.

The endoscopic techniques may be categorized into three groups:

1. Sewing and plication at the cardia and gastroesophageal junction,
2. Radiofrequency (RF) thermal therapy to the LES
3. Injection and implantation of biopolymers at the gastroesophageal junction (Table 18–1)

Table 18-1. Endoscopic Treatments for Gastroesophageal Reflux Disease

Plication and Sewing
Submucosal
Bard EndoCinch
Wilson-Cook Endoscopic Suturing Device
Full-thickness
NDO Plicator
Syntheon Anti-Reflux Device

Radiofrequency Thermal Treatment
Curon Stretta

Injection and Implantable
Plexiglas (PMMA) microspheres
Boston Scientific expansile polymer Enteryx
Medtronic hydrogel Gatekeeper

Some of these endoscopic treatments are reversible, and most are repeatable. Still in development, these endoscopic approaches have shown promise in providing short-term symptom relief for patients with mild GERD. Long-term outcome and sham-controlled studies are underway for many of these devices and techniques and will further provide much needed peer-reviewed evidence for expanded application of these techniques.

Endoscopic Techniques

ENDOLUMINAL PLICATION AND SEWING TECHNIQUE

Endoluminal plication and sewing techniques enable clinicians to place sutures or "staples" at the cardia during flexible upper endoscopy. These techniques may treat the symptoms of GERD, addressing its pathophysiology, by producing an alteration of the angle of His, lengthening or augmenting the LES mechanism, or refashioning the valve at the cardioesophageal junction.[6] The plication and sewing techniques are repeatable and reversible.

Bard EndoCinch

Device

More than 15 years ago the first endoscopic sewing and plication instrument was designed and techniques to apply this instrument were developed over several subsequent years.[26–31] This early work evolved into the currently Food and Drug Administration (FDA)-approved Bard EndoCinch system (Bard Endoscopic Technologies, Billerica, MA), and more than 5000 clinical procedures have now been performed worldwide with this device. Approved for the treatment of GERD, the EndoCinch instrument permits sewing techniques that may also be used to treat perforations, oversew bleeding sites, attach devices to the luminal surface, and create changes in anatomy for antiobesity surgery.

The Bard EndoCinch device consists of several components (Fig. 18–1) and is placed via an overtube into the patient. The sewing capsule is attached to the distal tip of a standard videogastroscope. This capsule has a hollow cavity into which surface tissue is suctioned. A handle, which is mounted to the biopsy port on the control arm of the gastroscope, drives the needle that runs through the biopsy channel to create a stitch. The handle

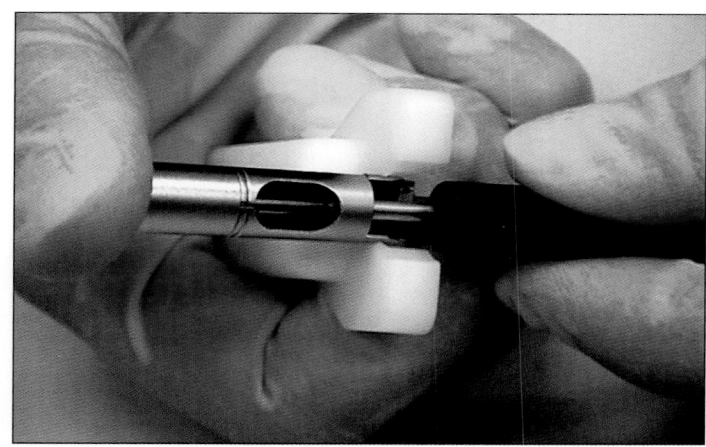

Figure 18-1. Bard EndoCinch sewing capsule being attached to distal end of videogastroscope.

controls the advance of the hollow-core needle, into which 3-0 monofilament suture is back-loaded. A metal t-tag attached to the suture is captured into the tip of the mounted capsule after being driven forward by a stiff wire pushed through the hollow needle by the handle. Because the endoscope used for suturing has the sewing capsule mounted on its tip, a second videogastroscope is required for the EndoCinch procedure and is used to fasten the ends of the suture material together after two stitches have been created with the sewing endoscope as discussed later.

The original device and technique required the use of a knot-pusher and a guillotine catheter to perform extracorporeal knot tying and intragastric knot cutting and were used by the investigators in the initial published pivotal trial. Revised versions included a catheter with a small ring and peg to cinch the two ends of the suture while cutting the suture material. This technical advance eliminated the need for hand-tying knots and substantially reduced the time needed to perform each plication (set of two stitches cinched together).

Technique[32,33]

The procedure is similar to a routine upper endoscopy that is longer in duration and requires higher doses of sedation. The pharynx is sprayed with a topical anesthetic, and conscious sedation is administered. Using one of the two videogastroscopes required to create an endoscopic gastric plication, a routine upper endoscopy is performed. One scope has the mounted suturing capsule; the other is used for the initial viewing, passing the guidewire, and cinching and cutting the suture material. After reviewing the landmarks, a guidewire is advanced through the gastroscope into the distal stomach, and the gastroscope is removed while keeping the guidewire in position.

An overtube is loaded onto a 15-mm Savary-type esophageal dilator and advanced into position over the guidewire. The dilator and wire are subsequently removed from the patient, and the overtube remains as a conduit for subsequent instrument passage and exchanges. The overtube extends down through the proximal third of the esophagus. The gastroscope with mounted sewing capsule is then placed into the overtube and advanced down the esophagus to the level of the squamocolumnar junction.

Stitches to form plications can be placed in several patterns: linear, circumferential, or helical (vertically staggered), and typically one anticipates placing two to three plications at a session. The usual target for placement of plications is 1 cm below the z-line at 3, 6, and 9 o'clock for circumferential pattern and at 3, 2, and 1 cm below the z-line for the linear configuration. The helical configuration can be applied to small hiatal hernias and involves the placement of four to six plications in an ascending staggered order from about 3 cm below the gastroesophageal junction to the z-line.

For any of these stitch configurations, when the target area is identified for apposition of the sewing capsule to the gastric surface, suction is applied to the capsule via an accessory tubing, thereby drawing the adjacent tissue into the capsule cavity. After waiting 10 seconds, the handle is depressed, forcing the t-tag and needle through the suctioned tissue; withdrawing the handle leaves the tag captured into the tip of the sewing capsule. Release of suction and forward advancement of the endoscope releases the stitched tissue and the endoscope is then withdrawn through the overtube. The same t-tag is reloaded into the hollow-core needle to place a second stitch at a location within 1 to 1.5 cm of the initial stitch. The second stitch is placed as for the first one, and the endoscope is removed. The suture ends are now extracorporeal and can be adjusted gently to remove any redundant loop.

The other gastroscope is now needed to finish the plication. In the original technique, half-hitches were hand tied and pushed to the surface of the stomach with the knot-pusher. Each subsequent half-hitch (five to six total) was performed with entry and removal of the endoscope via the overtube, and the final step involved removal of the pushing catheter and insertion of the guillotine catheter into the biopsy channel of the gastroscope. After back-threading the suture ends through this cutting catheter and using the suture as a guide to the gastric surface, a quick back-tug on the catheter would cut the ends of the knot at the stomach surface. The total time to create one plication with this original method was about 15 minutes. The new cinching and cutting catheter reduces the time to create a plication to about 5 minutes. The repetitive hand-tying steps and exchange of pushing and cutting catheters is replaced by the passage of one cinching catheter back-loaded onto the suture material and guided to the gastric surface where the cinching tag is placed and sutures are cut in one action (Fig. 18–2). Other refinements in the technique continue to be described and include the use of mucosal cautery in the area to be stitched, which may provide for mucosal apposition that results in more durable plications and reduced chance of suture pull-through.

Preclinical Data

A study of the endoscopic sewing machine to form a gastroplasty in dogs demonstrated the capabilities of the early plication device. Manometry performed before and after the procedures showed a significant increase in LESP (13.3 vs. 4.6 mm Hg) and gastric yield pressure (19 vs. 10 mm Hg).[29] A later study in a porcine model showed similar augmentation of the LESP postgastroplasty, with a median sphincter pressure increase from 3 to 6 mm Hg and an increase in sphincter length from 3 to 3.75 cm.[34] The median time pH was less than 4 decreased significantly from 9.3% to 0.2% postprocedure in these pigs. Animal studies have demonstrated that most endoscopically placed stitches are located at a mean depth of

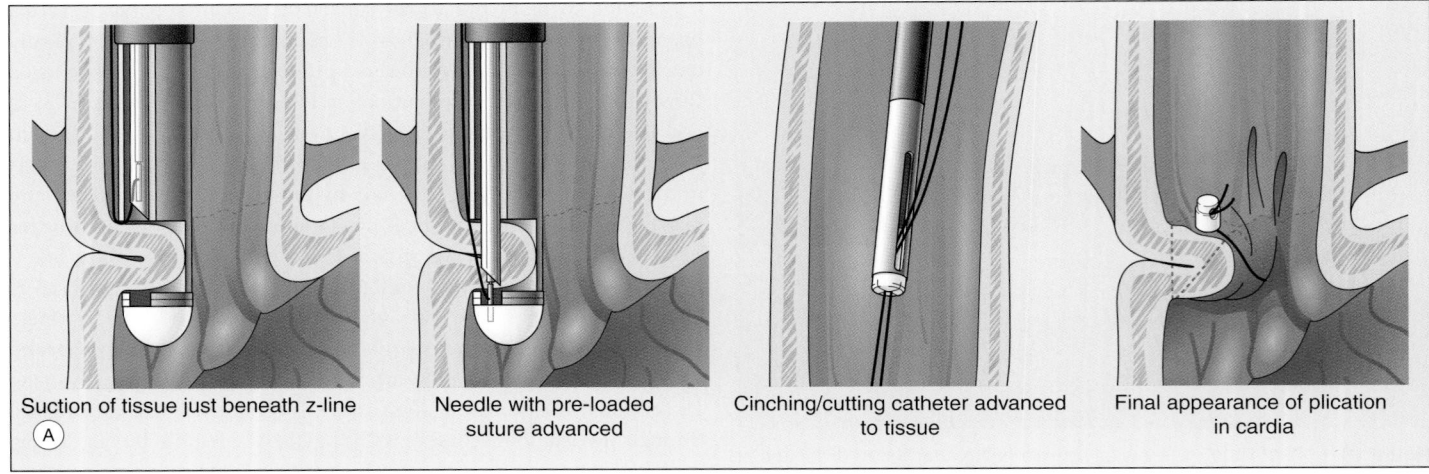

Suction of tissue just beneath z-line   Needle with pre-loaded suture advanced   Cinching/cutting catheter advanced to tissue   Final appearance of plication in cardia

(A)

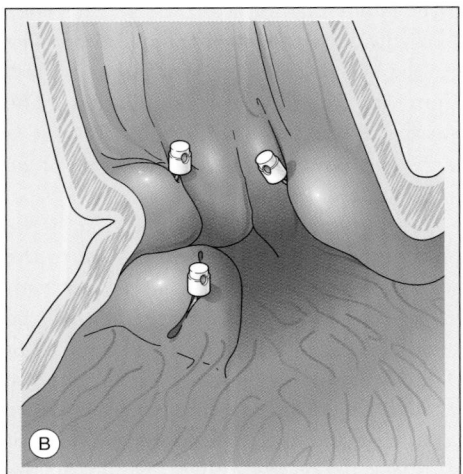

(B)

Figure 18-2. *A,* EndoCinch technique for creation of gastric plication. *B,* Three EndoCinch plications completed.

2.8 mm (i.e., in the submucosa) and that no difference in depth occurred after shorter versus longer tissue suction times (10 vs. 30 seconds).[35] The depth of suture placement correlated to overall thickness of the stomach, with occasional transmural stitches seen.

An interesting study of the histopathologic response to intraluminal plications in a New Zealand rabbit model showed that fusion between pleated mucosal folds did not occur irrespective of suture-penetration depth.[36] Fusion did occur easily when serosal surfaces were fastened together. This has implications because the deeper full-thickness plicators are evaluated in regards to durability of the plication and clinical outcomes in treated GERD patients.

Clinical Experience

The initial American multicenter trial that provided data to the FDA for approval of the device involved 64 patients from eight sites.[37] It suggested that endoluminal gastric plication is a safe outpatient treatment for GERD, with the expectation that about two thirds of patients will be successfully treated at 6 months' follow-up. Inclusion criteria were three or more episodes per week of heartburn when off antisecretory medications (with or without erosive esophagitis), benefit from and dependency on continued use of antisecretory drugs for symptom control, and documented acid

reflux by pH monitoring. Exclusion criteria included dysphagia, more than mild erosive esophagitis while on medications, body mass index (BMI) greater than 40 kg/m^2, GERD refractory to antisecretory therapy, and a hiatal hernia greater than 2 cm in length. Treatment success was defined as a decrease in the heartburn severity score of 50% in addition to a reduction in the use of antireflux medications to less than four doses per month. Subjects underwent endoscopy, esophageal manometry, ambulatory pH monitoring, symptom severity scoring, and quality of life assessments before and after endoscopic therapy. Patients were randomized to either linear or circumferential plication configurations. The initial mean heartburn symptom score was 62.7, falling significantly to a mean of 16.7 and 17 at 3 and 6 months postprocedure, respectively. Initial regurgitation scores significantly improved in the short-term follow-up. No difference was found in LES resting pressure or length. Twenty-five percent of patients had grade 2 esophagitis at baseline, whereas 19% had it at 6-month follow-up. The percent total time that pH was ≤4, the total number of reflux episodes, and the percent upright time that pH was ≤4 were all significantly improved at 6 months' follow-up. However, improvement in symptoms did not always correlate to improvement of esophagitis or pH profiles. Quality of life scores at 6 months postprocedure were significantly improved for social functioning and bodily pain. There was no difference in any outcomes related to linear versus circumferential placement of the stitches. Most importantly, at 6 months' follow-up, 62% of patients were taking less than four doses of medications per month and were considered treatment successes.

Adverse events included pharyngitis (31%), vomiting (14%), abdominal and/or chest pain (14% to 16%), and two episodes of minor mucosal tear thought to have been related to the use of the large overtube. One subject experienced a suture microperforation that was treated conservatively with brief hospitalization.

Two recent reviews[32,33] summarized the clinical outcomes data from the published pivotal trial and from numerous small studies whose data are so far only available in abstract form. The results from these other investigators have shown similar benefits during short-term follow-up.

In a series from the United Kingdom and Sweden, 102 patients who were treated with linear plications and followed a median of 12 weeks had significant improvement in heartburn symptoms and percent total time that the pH was <4. In contrast to the U.S. study, the European investigators demonstrated a significant augmentation of LES length and resting tone.[38] A small American multicenter experience from tertiary and community settings reported the outcomes for 88 GERD patients who underwent circumferential endoluminal gastroplication. At short-term follow-up (duration not specified) heartburn resolved completely in 85% and to less than three episodes per week in 6%, whereas 9% had no improvement. Regurgitation resolved in 90%. Seventy-four percent of patients discontinued medications for reflux symptoms, and 17% took "occasional" doses.[39] A report from the Mayo Clinic showed a less satisfactory outcome from a study of 23 subjects with a mean 6.7-month follow-up. Interestingly, 24% of patients had undergone a repeat session of plication treatment, suggesting that the initial treatment failed to adequately control symptoms. Although about two thirds of patients had partial or complete relief of their heartburn symptoms, only 20% were able to be off antireflux medications.[40]

Further experience in humans was described by the group from Adelaide, South Australia.[41] They treated 15 subjects who had symptomatic GERD, with two circumferential plications about 1 cm below the squamocolumnar junction. The endoscopic suturing significantly reduced 24-hour esophageal acid exposure from 9.6% to 7.4% at 6 months, and this effect was durable at the 1-year follow-up. Seven patients (47%) remained off acid suppressing medications at 6 and 12 months after their procedures. This study also demonstrated that the treated individuals had a significant 37% decrease in transient LES relaxations and an augmentation of LESP from 4.2 to 6.2 mm Hg.

Other investigators have reported similar significant clinical outcomes in short-term follow-up.[42-44]

Two-Year Follow-up

An understanding of the cost effectiveness of this procedure will come from an analysis of longer term outcomes. A preliminary report of 33 patients from the initial U.S. multicenter investigator group followed for up to 2 years demonstrated persistent improvement in heartburn severity and frequency.[45] However, regurgitation was no longer significantly improved. Twenty-five percent of the patients were completely off antisecretory medications, whereas 28% were on minimal medications to control symptoms. The remaining patients were on their original doses of antisecretory medications (41%) or had undergone surgical fundoplication (two patients). In another similar report of 23 patients, only 22% continued to be off antisecretory medicines at 2-year follow-up.[46] An additional 30% required less than 50% of the original dose. The remaining 11 patients had either a need for antisecretory medications greater than 50% of the time or had undergone antireflux surgery. It is important to highlight that these outcomes were from cohorts of patients whose procedure was performed during the investigators' learning curve and that additional experience with the plication procedure (including optimizing the correct number and location of plications) may improve the long-term outcomes. Longer term follow-up data were recently presented from a cohort of 85 patients from a U.S. multicenter clinical site collaboration followed prospectively for 2 years after receiving one to three plications.[47] Fifty-one percent of the patients had no GERD symptoms or only occasional symptoms; 41% of patients were off all PPIs and another 15% took less than one PPI dose per week. Acid exposure testing in 68 patients (80% of the original group) at 3 to 6 months' follow-up showed a significant change from mean pH 9.4 to 5.8 with normalization of pH seen in 39%.

Improvement to Technique

To potentially improve the durability of plications, suture retention, and clinical outcome after the EndoCinch gastric plication procedure, investigators in Indianapolis randomized subjects to receive preliminary cautery to the mucosa before plicating.[48] One half of the study patients received a 2-cm wide 25-watt bipolar electrocautery applied to the lesser curve before the standard procedure, whereas the others were plicated in the usual fashion. The preliminary results showed a clinical benefit to the supplemental cautery group over controls and better stitch retention. Further study must be undertaken to determine the optimal technique.

Helical placement of the sutures is a modification of the initial linear or circumferential patterns and is useful to cover more surface of the upper stomach, especially when a moderate-sized hiatal hernia is present. The pattern of stitch placement begins distal to the squamocolumnar junction and works around the proximal stomach in an ascending spiral. Although some have described a benefit of the helical pattern over traditional stitch placements,[49] a recent prospective study did not show an outcome difference of one pattern of suturing over any other.[50]

Sham-Controlled Trial

A sham-controlled, randomized, blinded single institution EndoCinch study has recently been completed.[51] Subjects were included if they were older than 18 years and if they had symptomatic GERD at least 3 days a week and were dependent on taking daily PPIs or histamine-2 blockers (H2B) for symptom control. Documented acid reflux disease by 24-hour pH monitoring off PPI or H2B with a pH ≤4 more than 4% of the time was required for enrollment. Subjects with abnormal esophageal peristalsis on manometry, esophagitis worse then grade B (LA classification), a hiatal hernia greater than 3 cm, an esophageal stricture, presence of dysphagia, previous gastroesophageal or cardiothoracic surgery, or the presence of comorbidities classified ≥3 by the American Society of Anesthesiologists (ASA) grading criteria were excluded. Women who were pregnant or intended to become pregnant were also excluded.

For the sham procedure, patients were prepared as for the real intervention, with comparable use of intravenous conscious sedation, passage and placement of the oroesophageal tube, and exchange of endoscopes in a pattern to mimic the true EndoCinch procedure. A similar dialogue was followed during the sham procedure that tried to mimic that of the true intervention. To maintain blinding, the patients and the study coordinator who interacted with the patients before and after the procedures were not aware of the assignment and interaction, with only the endoscopist and in-room assistants knowing this information.

At 3 months' follow-up, heartburn frequency was improved in a larger proportion of patients after EndoCinch treatment when compared with the sham group (69% vs. 31%, $p = .03$). There was no significant difference in heartburn severity (81% vs. 50%), regurgitation (53% vs. 56%), or bothersome score (75% vs. 50%). More subjects in the gastric plication group discontinued their daily acid suppressing medications when compared with the sham group (75% vs. 25.0%, $p = .01$); however, no difference was found when comparing the discontinuation of all acid suppressive medications (56% vs. 25%). Acid exposure significantly improved in the EndoCinch vs. sham groups (pH difference: -4.0 vs. $+1.0$, $p = .03$), but normalized only in two (12.5%) of the treated patients. We did not detect a difference between the treatment effect on LESP or quality of life measures.

This study highlighted the significant sham-response rate and the need for randomized controlled trials of sufficient size to understand the true effectiveness of novel endoscopic therapies for GERD.

Wilson-Cook Sewing System
Device
Another submucosal stitching instrument, the Wilson-Cook Endoscopic Suturing Device (Wilson-Cook Medical, Winston-Salem, NC), was recently approved by the FDA. The flexible sewing (Sew-Right) and knot-tying (Ti Knot) devices (Fig. 18–3) are passed via an accessory channel mounted to a flexible videoendoscope and no oroesophageal overtube is required. The Sew-Right device has a diameter of 5.2 mm and uses a dual-needle system with a continuous loop of suture. The left and right needle selection is performed by moving a toggle switch in the handle. Tissue suctioned into the distal end of the instrument can be stitched with one of the needles. Suctioning occurs via a vacuum port on the handle of the instrument. Releasing suction and rotating the instrument permits adjacent gastric tissue to be suctioned and stitched by the second needle. These needles pick up ferrules attached to the ends of the braided polyester suture and the ends are withdrawn through the accessory channel as the instrument is removed. Similar to the technique for EndoCinch, the Ti Knot device can cut and crimp together the suture ends in a fastener. As for the EndoCinch

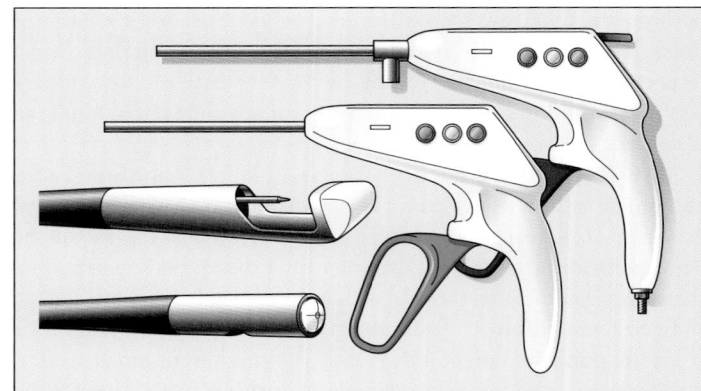

Figure 18–3. Wilson-Cook Endoscopic Suturing Device: Sew-Right and Ti-Knot instruments.

technique, each plication takes 10 to 15 minutes to perform. There is very limited preclinical and clinical experience with this device, which has been used successfully for placement of stitches and plications.

Procedure and Technique
The procedure is performed in similar fashion to that for the Bard EndoCinch. The patient is medicated with conscious sedation. A routine endoscopy is performed and anatomic features are reviewed. The external accessory channel is attached to the shaft of the endoscope and together gently passed to the stomach. Through the channel, the flexible Sew-Right device is passed and with the toggle switch selecting the right-sided needle, the instrument is advanced to the cardia. Under direct vision, the tissue to be stitched, usually within a centimeter of the gastroesophageal junction, is suctioned into the distal port on the instrument. With the tissue captured, the handle is squeezed to advance the right needle through the tissue, where it captures the ferrule with attached suture end and pulls it back through the tissue as the needle returns to its resting position. Suction is released, and the toggle switch is moved to engage the left needle. Choosing an area that is about 1.5 cm from the initial stitch, the tissue from this second location is suctioned into the tip of the Sew-Right instrument and the handle operated to deploy the left needle through and back to create the second stitch.

With both suture ends captured into the Sew-Right instrument, it is slowly withdrawn out of the accessory channel. The continuous suture material now has stitched two areas of the proximal stomach, and cutting and fastening the suture ends together will create a plication or pleat. This is accomplished with the Ti-Knot instrument. The suture exiting the accessory channel is cut from the Sew-Right device and back-loaded into the Ti-Knot instrument. The Ti-Knot instrument is advanced down the external accessory channel, and, similar to the EndoCinch procedure, the cutting and crimping device is positioned at the mucosal surface. Actuating the handle of the Ti-Knot instrument crimps the titanium cylinder knot to hold the suture ends in place and simultaneously cuts the suture ends, releasing the instrument, which is then withdrawn through the channel (Fig. 18–4). A series of linear or circumferential plications can be formed by repeating the Sew-Right and Ti-Knot

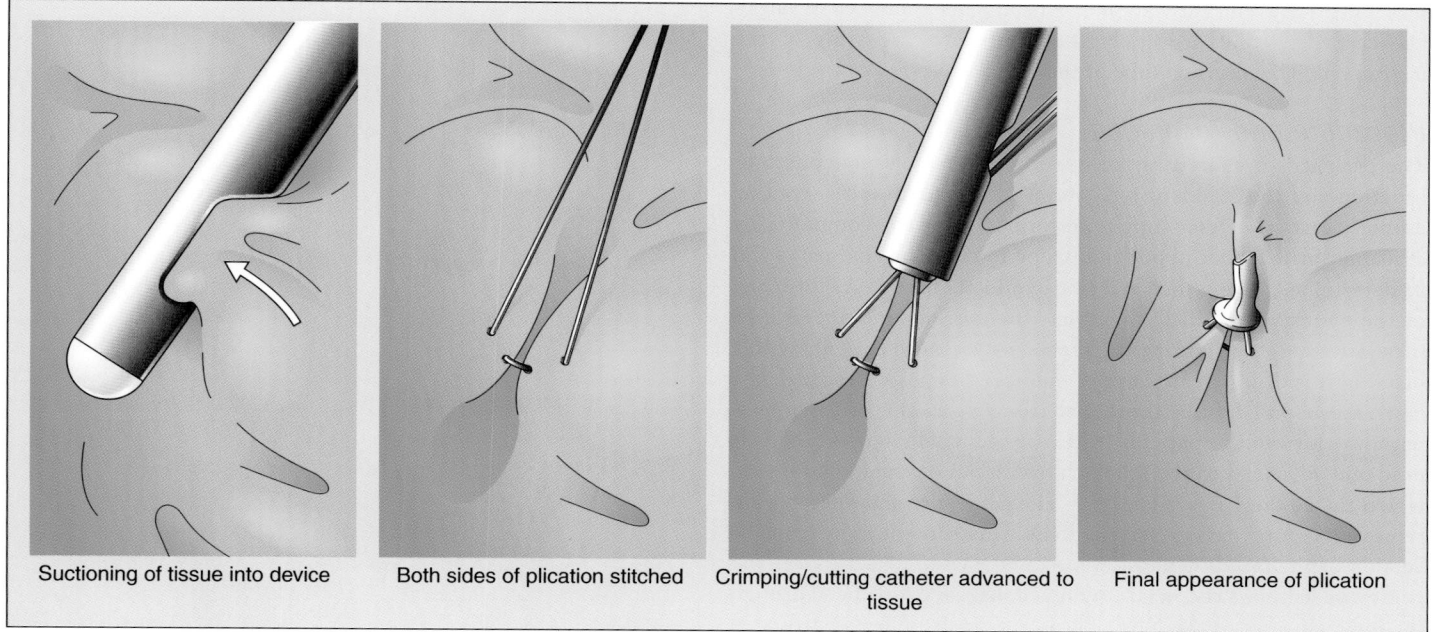

| Suctioning of tissue into device | Both sides of plication stitched | Crimping/cutting catheter advanced to tissue | Final appearance of plication |

Figure 18–4. Wilson-Cook Endoscopic Suturing Device technique for creating gastric plication.

sequences. Each plication takes about 15 minutes to complete. There is no consensus on number and location of these pleats for optimal effect.

Preclinical Data

In early animal studies, the device was shown to place stitches in the submucosal layer of the stomach. In a study with a swine model, endoscopic ultrasound and upper endoscopy were carried out at baseline and after the placement of two gastroplications in the proximal cardia at 3 weeks' follow-up.[52] The investigators found a focal increase in the thickness of the muscularis propria layer at the gastroesophageal junction near the mucosal suture site. Hypertrophy of the circular smooth muscle layer was seen *in vivo*, and these findings were confirmed histologically from the *ex vivo* stomach.

Clinical Data

No published, peer-reviewed GERD treatment outcome data are yet available for the Wilson-Cook device, although a small number of patients have been treated for this indication.

NDO Plicator
Device

The NDO Plicator (NDO Surgical, Mansfield, MA) is an instrument designed to create a full-thickness serosa-to-serosa apposition of the proximal cardia (Fig. 18–5). It has recently undergone clinical study in a U.S. multicenter trial[53] and received FDA approval for marketing as an antireflux therapy. In the pivotal open-label trial, the earliest version of the NDO device was placed via an esophageal overtube, and a 5.9-mm videogastroscope was inserted through the core of the instrument to provide direct visualization of the cardia

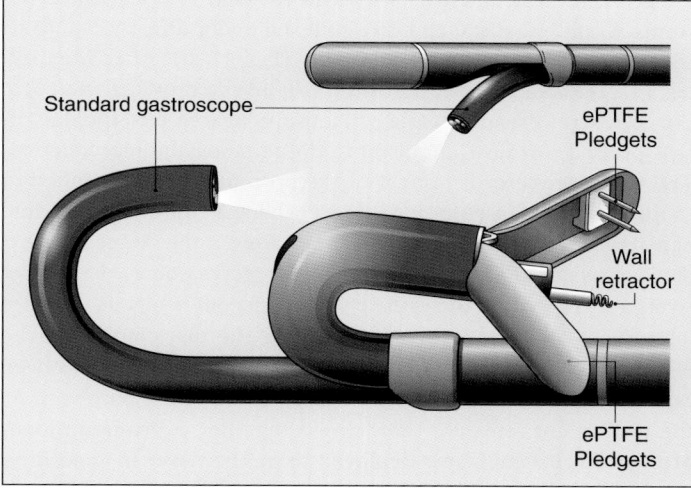

Figure 18–5. NDO Plicator device.

while the plication was being created. The most recent version of the instrument can be passed without an overtube and still accepts a small pediatric videogastroscope for viewing the operative field. The NDO instrument is reusable after reprocessing, and deploys single-use, preformed suture-based implants.

The NDO instrument has controls on the instrument handle that actuate the opening and closing of its arms at the distal end of the instrument shaft and for deployment of the preformed implant. Through the center of the instrument, a stainless steel cork-screw–shaped tissue retractor is passed to engage tissue from that area to be plicated. The implant, pre-tied 2-0 polypropylene with polytetrafluoroethylene bolsters, is loaded onto the arms of the instrument. The current system has the implant contained in single-use cartridges that are easily mounted onto the arms of the instrument. The insertion tube of the device is 45-Fr.

Procedure and Technique

The patient is prepared for an upper endoscopy, using conscious sedation and the standard left lateral position. An initial routine esophagogastroduodenoscopy is performed using any commercially available small-caliber upper endoscope to view the landmarks and to determine the presence and size of a hiatal hernia. As for many of the endoscopic GERD therapies, the current practice recommendations are for limiting the procedure to those patients with a hiatal hernia of less than 2 cm. A guidewire is passed through the gastroscope and left in the distal stomach as the endoscope is withdrawn from the patient. In the pivotal trial, an overtube was used and advanced to the stomach over a Savary-type dilator into which the guidewire was inserted. The guidewire and dilator were removed before passage of the NDO instrument. The current version of the instrument allows it to be passed directly over the guidewire without the need for an esophageal overtube. Through the hollow center of the NDO Plicator, a small-caliber gastroscope is passed, and, on reaching the stomach, it is advanced further and retroflexed to allow complete viewing of the targeted region to be plicated in the proximal cardia.

The NDO instrument is advanced forward into an insufflated stomach, and the distal end is retroflexed under direct vision using the control on the instrument handle (Fig. 18–6). After identifying a target area for plication anteriorly in the proximal stomach, the cork-screw–shaped tissue retractor is engaged into the muscularis propria, within 1 cm distal to the squamocolumnar junction. The tissue retractor is critical to the procedure. It is intended to capture the muscularis propria thus enabling a "full-thickness" fold of gastric wall to be drawn into the open arms of the device. There is obvious twisting of the mucosa of the target tissue as the deeper layers are engaged by the catheter tip and its outer sheath. The two instrument arms are opened by turning the dial control on the instrument handle, and the proximal stomach tissue that has been captured with the cork-screw catheter is pulled between them. As the instrument arms are then closed together, a pre-tied mono-filament suture implant is deployed to fix the tissue in apposition just beneath the gastroesophageal junction. The tissue retraction catheter is disengaged and withdrawn back into its channel. The instrument arms are subsequently opened to release the plicated tissue, occasionally requiring some manipulation of the endoscope position to gain freedom from the manipulated tissue, and then closed again to allow removal of the NDO instrument in the straightened position.

Preclinical Data

Several preclinical trials were performed to determine the safety and efficacy of this novel therapy.[54,55] Procedures were performed in survived live miniswine, including observation of the procedure by concurrent laparoscopy to document the full-thickness characteristic of this treatment. These animals were followed for 12 weeks with no complications noted. To gain an understanding of the effectiveness of the full-thickness plication and to determine an

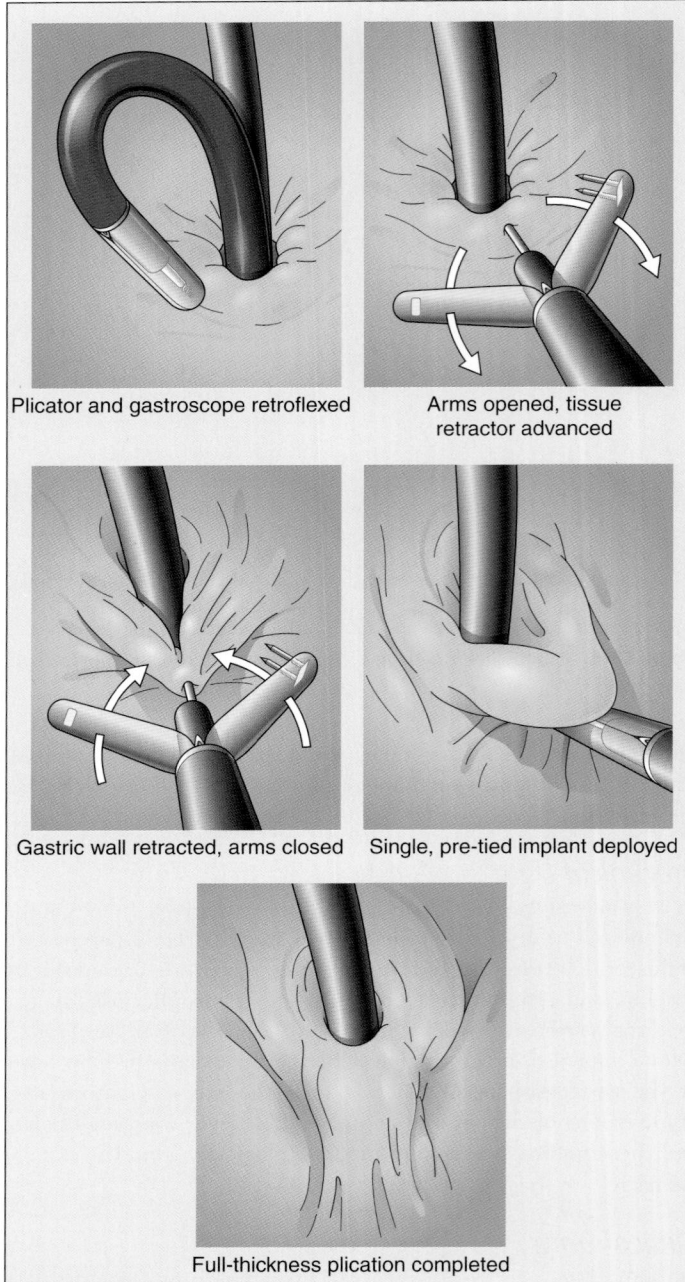

Plicator and gastroscope retroflexed

Arms opened, tissue retractor advanced

Gastric wall retracted, arms closed

Single, pre-tied implant deployed

Full-thickness plication completed

Figure 18–6. NDO Plicator technique.

optimal placement of the implant in the stomach, an *ex vivo* porcine stomach model was created to monitor intragastric and yield pressures. While preserving baseline esophageal diameters, the full-thickness plications raised the average gastric yield pressures by about eightfold.

Clinical Data

A pilot human study was conducted on six GERD patients in India.[56] These individuals had symptomatic reflux and good response to acid suppression and had abnormal acid exposure time

 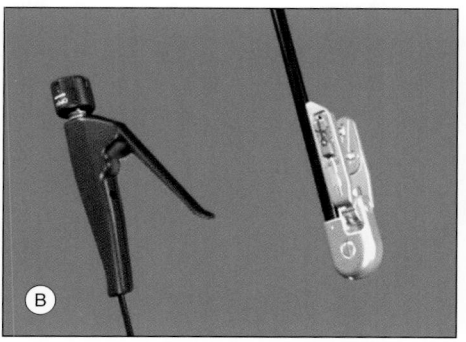 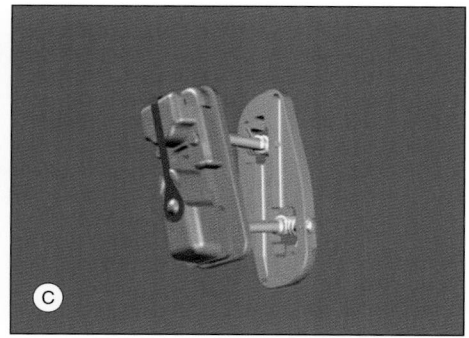

Figure 18–7. *A,* Syntheon AntiReflux Device. *B,* Proximal and distal ends of device and *(C)* titanium implant.

in the distal esophagus. The mean procedure time was 21 minutes. At 6 months after the treatment, five of the six patients no longer required their acid suppressive medications to control the GERD symptoms. Twelve months post-treatment, the GERD symptom scores and quality of life assessments remained significantly improved from baseline.

A pivotal multicenter open-label study was conducted at seven participating centers, enrolling 64 GERD subjects.[53] These individuals had chronic heartburn, were dependent on acid inhibitory agents, and had relief of symptoms from these medications. Excluded from enrollment were individuals with a hiatal hernia greater than 2 cm, individuals with high-grade esophagitis (>3 Savary-Miller), and those with esophageal intestinal metaplasia (Barrett's). All subjects had one plication placed (mean procedure time 17.2 minutes). The 6-month follow-up showed a 67% symptom score improvement, and 74% of patients were off their previously required PPI medications. Normalization of pH occurred for only 30% of the participants at the short-term follow-up, similar to that seen for the other endoscopic therapies. No change in esophageal manometric parameters was seen post-treatment. Seventy percent of patients have continued off their PPI medications in a recent follow-up assessment at 12 months. Adverse procedure-related events included pharyngitis (41%), abdominal pain (20%), chest pain (17%), GI disorder (17%), eructation (14%), dysphagia (11%), and nausea (6%). Serious adverse events included dyspnea during the procedure in two subjects. One of these required endotracheal intubation to avoid the airway compromise caused by the esophageal overtube. One patient had a pneumothorax, which was treated conservatively. Two patients developed a pneumoperitoneum; one underwent a laparoscopic exploration, which did not show a perforation, and the other had an obvious gastric tear repaired endoscopically with endoclips and managed conservatively with antibiotics. It was thought that the first patient had air enter the peritoneum under insufflation pressure, which exited out the holes created by the needles as they delivered the implant, and the second patient had trauma from the exposed first-generation instrument arms. The arms in the current version are now covered by a flexible membrane, and no other trauma has been noted subsequently.

No sham-controlled study has yet been conducted, although one is anticipated. In the pilot NDO trial, only one plication was placed, and further study with single versus multiple plications would

be valuable. Procedure time for one NDO plication (mean of 17 minutes) is shorter than that to complete the typical Bard EndoCinch or Wilson-Cook Endoscopic Suturing Device procedure (assuming at least two plications placed per session with those instruments). There were some significant safety issues with the initial NDO device, which should be obviated by the design modifications of the most recent instrument version.

Syntheon Plication Device
Device
The Syntheon Anti-Reflux Device (ARD) (Syntheon/ID, Miami, FL) is another full-thickness plicator, and it is now undergoing study in an open-label multicenter clinical trial. The instrument is passed over a guidewire, and a standard gastroscope is passed alongside the device rather than through it (as described previously for the NDO). The plicator places a titanium metal implant to appose the serosal surfaces (Fig. 18–7).

Technique
Following routine upper endoscopy to assess the landmarks, a guidewire is left in the distal stomach as the endoscope is withdrawn. The semiflexible instrument is loaded onto the guidewire, and, taking care to keep the orientation correct (long arm against tongue), the proximal part of the plicating device is advanced to the stomach. The gastroscope is then reintroduced alongside of the instrument and advanced to the stomach. The gastroscope is retroflexed to view the closed device and to allow positioning within the cardia. The device is then withdrawn toward the cardia and the arms are opened, allowing proximal stomach tissue to be pulled between them with a special tissue retractor deployed through the biopsy channel of the observing endoscope. The instrument shaft is easily manipulated separately and independently from the endoscope. The goal is to target an area of the anterior cardia between the fundus and lesser curve. The targeted area is easily secured by the unique curved hooks of the tissue retractor. The arms of the ARD instrument are subsequently closed to apply the metal fastener and then reopened to release it. Closed again, the instrument is then removed from the stomach behind the gastroscope as it is withdrawn (made easier by the use of a snare placed between the closed instrument arms, securing it up against the distal tip of the endoscope) (Fig. 18–8).

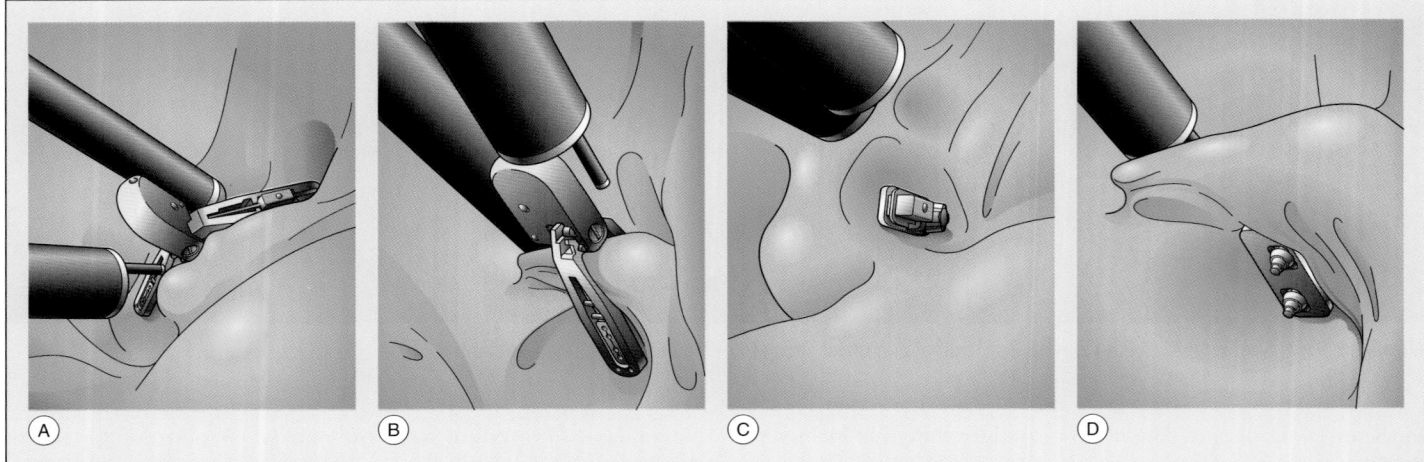

Figure 18–8. *A,* Device arms opened and tissue retractor engaged to pull cardia into open arms. *B,* Arms closed to form full-thickness plication. *C,* Female side of implant observed. *D,* Male side of implant observed.

Clinical Data

The time to perform the technique is comparable to that for the NDO plicator, and, similarly, only one plication is being performed in the pivotal trial. This initial trial is nearing completion, and outcome results and safety details are awaited. A sham-controlled trial is under design and will follow the initial safety and efficacy evaluation.

Other Sewing and Plicating Devices

Intraluminal transgastric valvuloplasty was described by a group of investigators who incorporated the use of two percutaneous endoscopic gastrostomy ports that permit minimally invasive access to the operative field in the stomach cardia.[57,58] In the original animal work, a standard gastroscope passed transorally allowed inspection of the stomach and identification of its landmarks and assisted in the positioning of the gastrostomy ports. The gastroscope was removed, and a 60-Fr intraluminal invaginator was passed into position under direct vision using a laparoscope passed via one of the gastrostomy ports. This instrument secures the tissue at the squamocolumnar junction and pulls it intraluminally, creating a circumferential intragastric "nipple" valve (Fig. 18–9).

This intussuscepted full-thickness valve is secured with eight biodegradable staples, two placed into each of the four quadrants circumferentially. In the baboon study, over the follow-up period of 6 months, no dysphagia, weight loss, or other significant adverse events were noted. During the endoscopic follow-up in 12 baboons at 6 months, most staples were observed to be embedded in tissue with the nipple-type valve observed in all of the animals, albeit less than fully intact in half. Postprocedure augmentation in total LES length and intra-abdominal length were seen, but the intervention did not alter resting LESP. The authors concluded that this intraluminal valvuloplasty approach may improve competency of the LES and appeared well tolerated in the animal model. Future evolution of the technique to allow a fully transoral approach (and avoid the need of gastrostomy ports) is currently under study. This would further reduce the "invasion" and make this technique even more attractive as a treatment option for GERD.

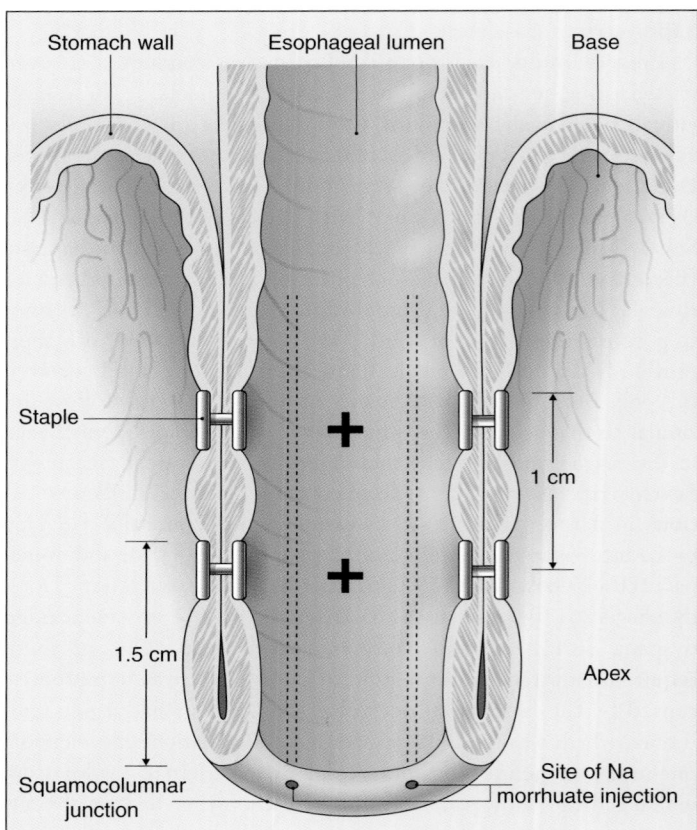

Figure 18–9. Intraluminal valvuloplasty demonstrating intussuscepted gastroesophageal junction with staples. (Reprinted from Mason RJ, Filipi CJ, DeMeester TR, et al: A new intraluminal antigastroesophageal reflux procedure in baboons. Gastrointest Endosc 45:283–290, 1997, with permission from the American Society for Gastrointestinal Endoscopy.)

Other device manufacturers are seeking creative solutions for the endoscopic treatment of GERD. Some of these have been described and used in animal models, such as the Olympus Eagle Claw sewing system and a novel linear stapling device,[59,60] whereas others are still in the early design phase.

RADIOFREQUENCY THERMAL THERAPY
Curon Stretta

Device
The Stretta System (Curon Medical, Inc., Sunnyvale, CA) uses an endoluminal delivery of low-power, temperature-controlled RF energy into the muscularis propria of the gastroesophageal junction for the treatment of GERD.[61] Approved for use by the FDA in 2000, more than 5000 patients have now been treated. The system uses a special 20-Fr diameter balloon-basket single-use catheter that contains four radially distributed curved 25-gauge, 5.5-mm length nickel-titanium needles (Fig. 18–10). Each needle has dual-thermocouple temperature sensors to maintain consistent energy delivery to the LES muscular layer. Ports in the catheter provide intraprocedural cold water irrigation to reduce mucosal heating and prevent surface tissue injury. The bougie-like catheter is advanced into the esophagus over a guidewire that enters the distal tip and exits proximal to the balloon. The catheter handle has a thumb control to deploy and retract the needles. The handle connects to wall suction, water irrigation, and the RF generator.

The RF monopolar generator is a computerized control module unit that controls and delivers the RF energy to the needle electrodes (Fig. 18–11). It provides pure sine-wave energy at 465 kHz and 2 to 5 watts to four individually controlled channels. The system has temperature feedback control and can discontinue power to an individual needle electrode if tissue temperature exceeds 100° C, if the mucosal surface temperature exceeds 50° C, or if recorded impedance exceeds 1000 Ohms. The target temperature for tissue thermal treatment is 85° C.

Procedure and Technique
The Stretta procedure is typically performed in the outpatient setting using conscious sedation. After attaching the catheter to the control module and placing a grounding dispersive electrode to the patient's back, a standard upper endoscopy is performed to view the landmarks and determine whether a hiatal hernia greater than 3 cm in length or Barrett's esophagus is present (which would preclude the procedure). After recording the distance from the incisors to the squamocolumnar junction, the gastroscope is removed as a 0.035- to 0.039-inch outer diameter soft-tipped guidewire is advanced through the endoscope and left in the distal stomach. The treatment catheter is then advanced over the guidewire and advanced to the stomach. The guidewire is then withdrawn out of the patient, and the catheter handle is attached to suction. The first set or "ring" of thermal lesions is created 1 cm above the squamocolumnar junction. This is accomplished by inflating the balloon to 2.5 psi and deploying the needles into the deep tissues of the distal esophagus. The impedance value will fall significantly when the needle electrode passes from air into the solid muscular tissue. Currently, the RF energy is delivered to each electrode for 60 seconds. In case of rapid mucosal tissue heating, the balloon basket can be reduced in size or the flow rate of the irrigating water increased, and a brisk reduction in tissue temperature is observed. After the delivery of energy, the needles are retracted and the catheter repositioned for the next deployment and activation. The full Stretta procedure involves placing the deep intramuscular coagulation points in four antegrade rings that straddle the gastroesophageal junction from 1 cm above to just beneath the squamocolumnar junction in ½-cm increments and two retrograde "pull-back" rings in the cardia (Fig. 18–12). Each antegrade ring deploys the needles twice at about

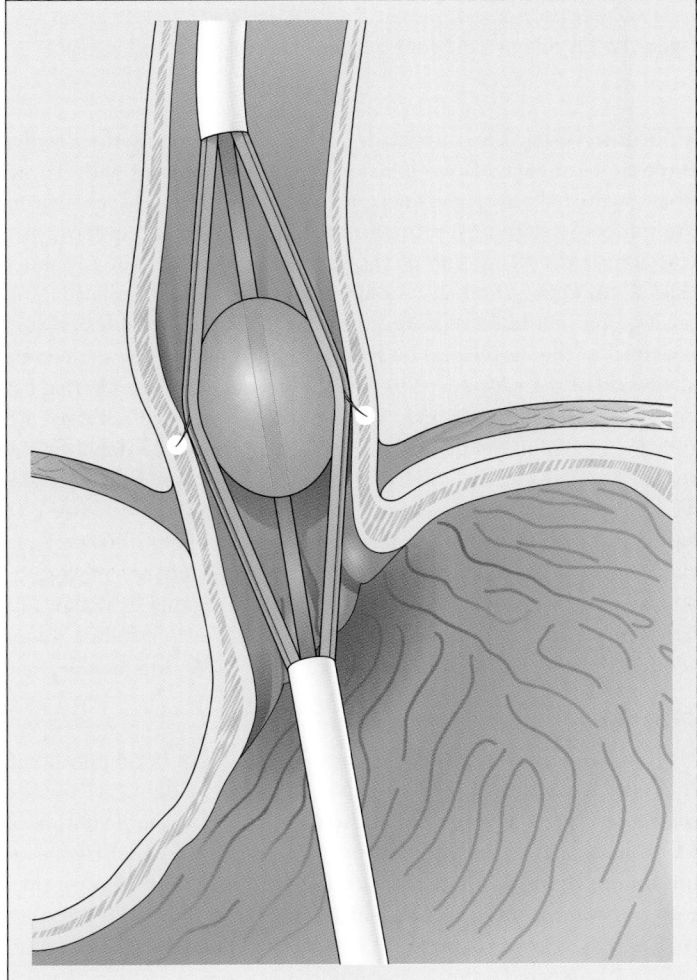

Figure 18–11. Stretta technique—placement of the catheter.

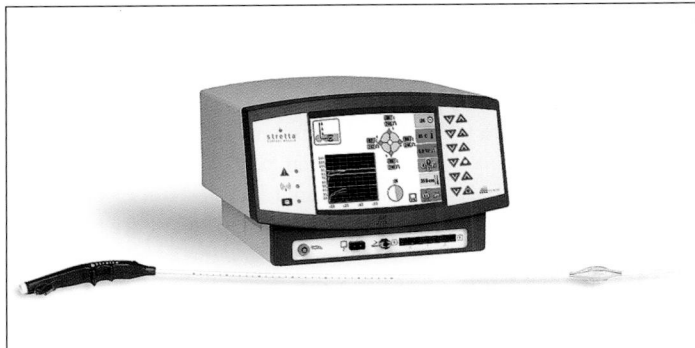

Figure 18–10. Curon Stretta catheter and radiofrequency (RF) generator control module.

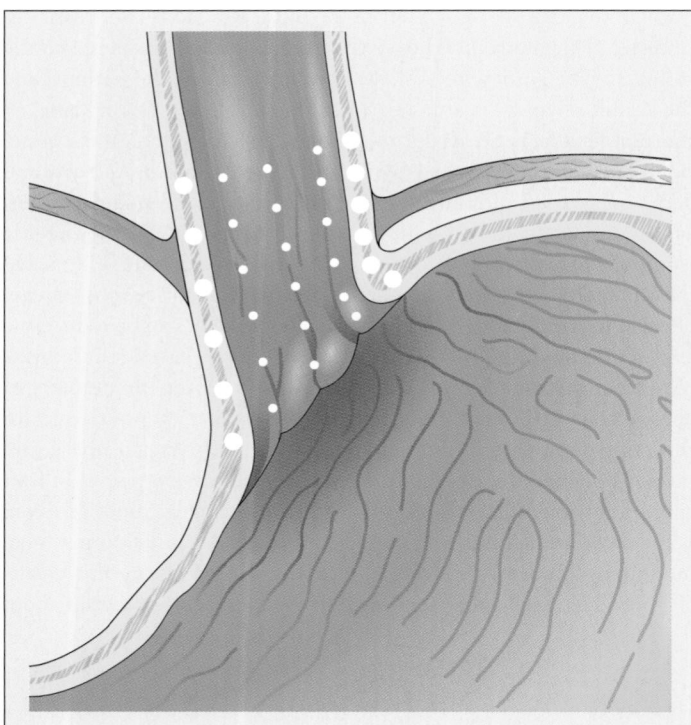

Figure 18–12. Stretta technique—creation of full set of thermal lesions.

45-degrees apart. The retrograde pullback rings deploy the needles three times at each of two positions in the cardia: once with 25 mL of air in the balloon at pullback and once with 22 mL of air. During the pullback phase of treatment, the catheter is held under gentle traction. If the distal end of the catheter moves proximally more than 2 cm above the known z-line distance, balloon inflation and positioning should be repeated to avoid placing thermal lesions too proximal in the esophageal body. It is helpful to pass the endoscope along side of the catheter after the first or second antegrade ring has been completed, to check the position and level of the RF treatments. Adjustment upward or downward can be done for the remaining rings so that the target area is appropriately covered. There is a tendency for the catheter to move distally when the balloon is inflated, and the interval endoscopy is helpful to perform the procedure more accurately, adjusting the delivery pattern as appropriate to cover the targeted area. The endoscope is withdrawn before the energy delivery recommences. The procedure takes about 45 minutes to complete and is, by its nature, irreversible.

Preclinical Data

Using a porcine model and incorporating the use of botulinum toxin to relax the LES pretreatment, RF energy delivery to the gastroesophageal junction demonstrated significant augmentation of LESP and gastric yield pressure.[62] One week after 100 units of botulinum toxin was injected into the LES region of 20 pigs, they were randomized to no treatment (control $n = 7$) or RF treatment ($n = 13$). The control group LESP fell 27% at 9 weeks. In contrast, the Stretta-treated group had a similar decrease of LESP at 1 week after the BOTOX injection, with a mean increase of 21% in LESP at 8 weeks post-treatment. Both groups underwent gastric yield

pressure testing (defined as when there was a manometric common channel effect and gross esophageal reflux event), with the treated animals showing a 75% augmentation of gastric yield pressure post-treatment. Three Yucatan minipigs were further evaluated at 6 months post-RF treatment and showed a 68% increase in LESP and a 114% increase in gastric yield pressure at that time. After RF treatment, there was demonstrable thickening of the muscular wall seen in a dog model by histopathology[63] and a porcine model with endosonography.[64]

Two human trials have reinforced the findings from an earlier animal trial and showed significant reductions in tLESRs after the RF treatment.[63,65,66]

Clinical Data

In the uncontrolled initial Stretta multicenter trials, which studied symptomatic GERD patients who had at least some benefit from their antisecretory medications, the 6-month and 1-year results showed significant improvement in all GERD-specific parameters including heartburn scores (median 4 decreased to 1), GERD health-related quality of life scales (median 27 decreased to 9), and distal acid exposure time post-treatment (median 10.6% reduced to 6.4%).[67,68] At the longer term follow-up, PPI medication requirement fell from 88.1% to 30%, whereas 40% were off all antireflux medications at 12 months. LESP did not increase, and the percent of patients with esophagitis before or after treatment was not significantly different. No major complications were seen in these initial reports, and subsequent study has shown no adverse effects on vagal nerve function or gastric emptying. There were 8.6% minor complications seen from the initial trial: superficial mucosal injury (2.5%), fever (1.7%), chest discomfort (1.7%), transient dysphagia (0.8%), sedation-related hypotension (0.8%), and topical anesthesia allergy (0.8%). Patients had been excluded from the initial studies if they had a hiatal hernia greater than 3 cm in length, active severe esophagitis, significant dysphagia, previous esophagogastric surgery, long-segment esophageal intestinal meta-plasia, collagen vascular disease, or pregnancy.

A recent subgroup analysis was performed between the "responder" and "nonresponder" groups from the U.S. open Stretta trial, to better understand the correlation of successful outcome to reduction in acid exposure as opposed to a possible alteration in sensitivity of the esophageal body.[69] Responder subgroups showed significant improvement in esophageal acid exposure, whereas non-responders did not. Changes in the GERD-HRQL and heartburn severity scores did correlate with changes in acid exposure. One effect of the Stretta procedure may be to decrease esophageal acid exposure, and optimizing this effect may translate to better clinical outcomes.

The Stretta device was released commercially in 2000, and more than 5000 procedures have now been performed in the United States. Although there was no systematic collection of outcomes data from most of these cases, a registry of 558 patients who were treated with Stretta at 33 institutions with a mean follow-up of 8 months showed significant GERD symptom control, with 51% no longer using their antisecretory medication, and high patient satisfaction.[70]

This degree of success in uncomplicated GERD patients has been seen by other investigators, and the improvement in GERD symptoms was achieved safely.[71,72–74] A modification of the Stretta technique for patients with large hiatal hernias and for those patients who are postlaparoscopic Nissen fundoplication has been proposed.[75]

Unfortunately, there have been several perforations and three deaths now associated with the Stretta procedure, although these occurred early after the marketing release. No additional serious complications have been reported, and the provision of adequate training to address the learning curve of this and any new treatment will help avoid further device-related problems. Similar to the other endoscopic antireflux treatments, Stretta has been mainly performed in patients with hiatal hernias that are less than 2 cm and with mild GERD in general.

Sham-Controlled Study

A recent sham-controlled study of 64 GERD patients showed the Stretta treatment (performed in 35 patients) to be superior to sham (in 29 patients) for control of heartburn symptoms and improvement in quality of life at 6 months after the intervention.[76] Patients who received the sham treatment were prepared for the procedure in the same fashion as those undergoing the RF treatment. After conscious sedation, routine upper endoscopy was carried out. A sham catheter with identical feel and characteristics to the real treatment catheter was passed into position. This sham catheter had no needles to deploy, but a dialogue similar to that for the real treatment was used by the investigators and assistants to mimic the real treatment as closely as possible. After 6 months, sham-treated patients were offered the real procedure if they were still symptomatic.

Interestingly, although there were more Stretta-treated versus sham subjects who responded to the intervention (defined as >50% improvement in GERD quality of life score) at 6 months (61% vs. 30%) and more treated versus sham who were without daily heartburn symptoms at this follow-up interval (61% vs. 33%), no differences in reduction of daily medication use was evident between the groups. There was no difference in esophageal acid exposure times comparing the two groups at 6 months. This finding emphasizes that the main utility of endoscopic GERD treatment may be for the nonerosive patient (most individuals with GERD), with no demonstrated consistent ability of these minimally invasive procedures to effectively heal erosive esophagitis.

INJECTION AND IMPLANTATION THERAPY

History

Animal Studies

Beginning in the early 1980s, implantation of an inert biocompatible material was considered for the treatment of GERD, and an initial animal study showed the potential utility of bovine dermal collagen and Teflon paste injected into the distal esophagus in a dog model.[77] Most surgically manipulated dogs showed improvement in some reflux parameters after injection and implantation. The utility of hylan gel implantation was also studied in dogs; however, the association of abnormal pulmonary findings subsequent to the implantation of the hylan gel with dimethyl sulfoxide (DMSO) limited any further study.[78]

Clinical Studies

An initial human trial of injected bovine collagen was undertaken in 1988 in 10 GERD patients who were not fully responding to their antireflux medications (histamine receptor antagonists, prokinetics, antacids).[79] These subjects had esophagitis on endoscopy or excessive distal esophageal acid exposure by pH monitoring. They underwent injection of bovine collagen generally into four quadrants at the squamocolumnar junction, with implants extending above and below this area and a mean implant volume of 85 mL implanted over several sessions. There was a 50% to 75% reduction in reflux symptoms and medication requirements reported after the treatment and significant improvement in esophageal acid exposures. The short-term results were encouraging, but the effect was not long-lasting. At the 12-month follow-up, most of the reflux parameters had returned to near baseline levels and most patients were back on medications. At endoscopy, there was resorption of the implant material. The early success and lack of durable effect led the investigators to propose the characteristics of an ideal implantable material, the "Lehman" criteria (Table 18–2).

Additional study was pursued among other agents with a potential for persistence of the implanted material. A small study from Greece showed the short-term efficacy of polymethylmethacrylate (PMMA, Plexiglas) beads in bovine collagen,[80,81] and, in another small study, polytetrafluoroethylene (Polytef) showed similar short-term improvements.[82] More recently, ethylene vinyl alcohol injection (Enteryx, Boston Scientific Corp, Natick, MA) and hydrogel biopolymer implantation (Gatekeeper) are undergoing evaluation for efficacy and safety in the treatment of patients with GERD. Enteryx is a biocompatible polymer that is implanted into the muscle layer of the LES, and Gatekeeper is a biocompatible hydrogel implant that is placed into a submucosal pocket just at or above the gastroesophageal junction.

Plexiglas

A pilot clinical trial using submucosal injection of PMMA microspheres in 3.5% bovine gelatin solution has been reported.[80,81] Ten patients who were on PPIs to control reflux-related symptoms and who had abnormal esophageal acid exposure times were recruited to the study. Treatment sessions took between 10 and 30 minutes, with a mean volume of about 32 mL implanted.

Table 18–2. Lehman Criteria for Ideal Injectable Implant Material

Low viscosity (injectable through 5-Fr catheter, 25-gauge needle)
Biologically inert at implantation site, and if metastatic:
   Noncarcinogenic
   Nonallergenic
   Nonimmunogenic
Low side effect profile
Nonbiodegradable
High persistence at implantation site
Low cost
Capable of resisting mechanical strain
Sterile
Favorable elasticity and plasticity
No adverse effect on adjacent musculature
No refrigeration required for storage

From Lehman GA: The history and future of implantation therapy for gastroesophageal reflux disease. Gastrointest Endosc Clin N Am 13:157–165, 2003.

Patients were followed-up at 6 and 14.5 months after therapy. Results showed significant improvement in GERD symptom scores and distal acid exposure times after the intervention compared with baseline values, although no patients normalized their 24-hour total time of pH <4. Seven of 10 of the subjects were completely off antireflux medications at the short-term follow-up. Two patients experienced transient chest pain at the time of the implantation, and no serious complications developed post-treatment. Clusters of PMMA microspheres were identified by endoscopic ultrasonography 6 months postimplantation and were seen to be scattered circumferentially in the submucosa and occasionally in the muscular layer. No further clinical study has been described with this agent since this pilot project.

Enteryx

Device

This biocompatible expansile polymer consists of 8% ethylene vinyl alcohol mixed with radiopaque tantalum powder, in a solution of DMSO. Liquid when initially injected, this solution becomes an inert spongy mass as it interacts with fluid in the tissue. The implantable material is purchased together with DMSO-compatible injector needle and syringes. The Enteryx mixture must be constantly agitated (shaken) for at least 10 minutes before drawing the solution into the syringe for the initial injection. This allows the tantalum powder to be dispersed evenly and suspended in the ethylene vinyl alcohol/DMSO solution. The Enteryx remaining in the vial and syringes containing Enteryx should continue to be shaken by an assistant in the room so that subsequent injections will be performed with a fully suspended solution. The injector needle is primed and flushed with the DMSO. The Enteryx solution is drawn into the provided syringes, and the injector needle is loaded with the material to nearly the full length of the catheter. The flexible injector needle catheter is now ready to be passed through the biopsy port of a standard gastroscope to create the appropriate implants.

Procedure and Technique[83,84]

The patient undergoes a standard upper endoscopy, including usual monitoring and preparation, after standard and specific informed consent. Some patients may be given a prophylactic antibiotic. The Enteryx procedure requires the use of fluoroscopy. Following the administration of conscious sedation, a routine upper endoscopy is carried out, carefully recording the anatomic landmarks and especially noting the squamocolumnar (z-line) demarcation. The DMSO compatible 4-mm, 23-gauge injector needle is advanced through the endoscope to the mucosal surface at the squamocolumnar junction. Advancement of the needle and endoscope permits the needle to enter the tissues at an acute angle at or just proximal to the squamocolumnar line. The Enteryx solution is injected very slowly by the assistant, at a rate of about 1 mL/minute. Heat is generated during the polymerization and the rate of injection must therefore be extremely slow and methodical.

Fluoroscopy shows the pattern of injection as the material is injected into the surrounding tissues. The endoscopist must watch both the fluoroscopic image to look at the pattern of injected material and the intraluminal image to watch for submucosal implantation or extravasation. Injection is stopped if the injection is observed to be too superficial (submucosal) or transluminal with dissipation or streaming in. However, if a localized radiodense collection of the polymer is observed after injection of the first several tenths of a milliliter, the injection is continued for about 1 or 2 mL at the same site. The injection may continue around the gastroesophageal junction in an arc. In this case, the injection may continue for several more milliliters as an arc is observed to form (Figs. 18–13 and 18–14) In general, most treatment sessions involve the placement of multiple collections of 1 mL or more placed circumferentially around the gastroesophageal junction, for a goal of between 6 and 8 mL of intramuscularly implanted Enteryx. Following each injection of material, the needle is left in place in the puncture site for at least 20 seconds to allow the Enteryx to begin to solidify and to reduce leakage out of the injection site on withdrawal of the needle.

Patients tolerate an outpatient procedure. Postprocedure pain is to be expected. This is usually handled with oral analgesics and is typically transient. The DMSO vehicle causes patients to exhale an intense garlic odor for several hours after the procedure. Patients may complain of dysphagia, which is transient. Patients are generally instructed to eat a soft diet for a few days postprocedure and wean themselves off their antisecretory agents over the next week or two. The Enteryx procedure is repeatable if symptoms are not fully controlled after the first implantation, and the same technique that was used for the initial treatment is followed. About 25% of subjects in the initial pivotal trial of Enteryx were retreated.[85] Enteryx implantation, in contrast to some other GERD endotherapies, is not a reversible technique.

Preclinical Data

Increased gastric yield pressure was demonstrated postimplantation of Enteryx in a porcine model using water infusion.[86] Interestingly, this augmentation took at least 6 weeks to develop, suggesting the need for chronic remodeling and fibrosis for this effect. This study showed no increase in lower esophageal length or tone after implantation of Enteryx. The investigators proposed that a change in sphincter compliance might explain the enhanced barrier effect at the gastroesophageal junction.

During this same animal study, to learn more about the safety of Enteryx, injections of the biopolymer were performed into tissues of the mediastinum and peritoneum. No significant sequelae followed implantation into these structures, and no migration of the implantations was noted following whole-body radiography to identify the location of the tantalum.

The accuracy of implantation was assessed in a group of volunteers who were going to have an esophagectomy and underwent three or four implants of 1 to 2 mL of Enteryx preoperatively.[87] Eighty-eight percent of the attempted implants were accurately placed into the esophageal wall using the standard technique. Four of the injections were found subserosally or attached to the exterior of the esophagus.

Clinical Outcomes

A pilot study was reported on 15 subjects with GERD, who demonstrated augmentation of LESP and improvement in heartburn score and antireflux medication use post-treatment.[88] Assessed by radiography 6 months postimplant, 9 of 15 patients had more than

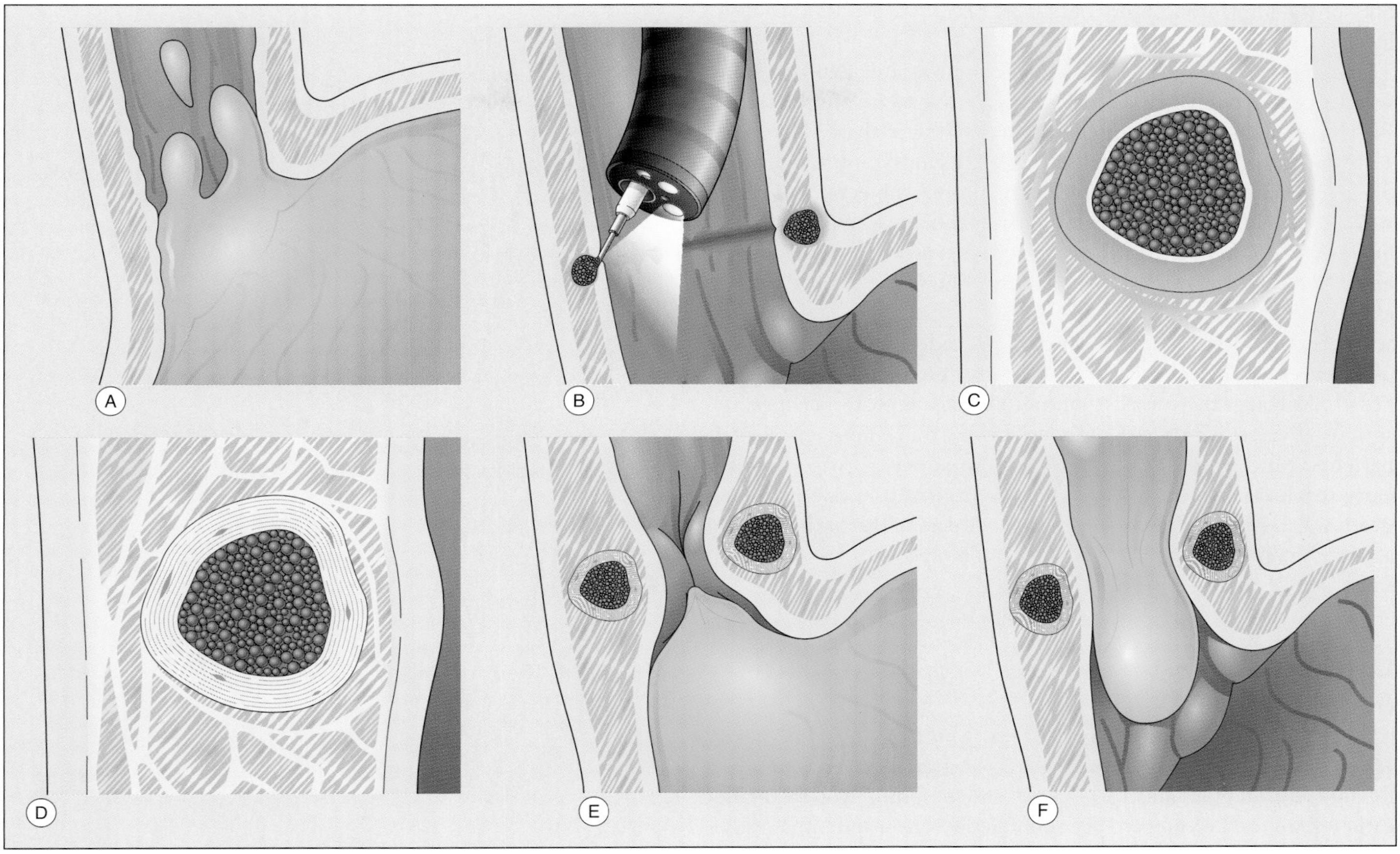

Figure 18–13. Boston Scientific Enteryx—technique of injection.

Figure 18–14. Enteryx—fluoroscopic demonstration of arc-type injection.

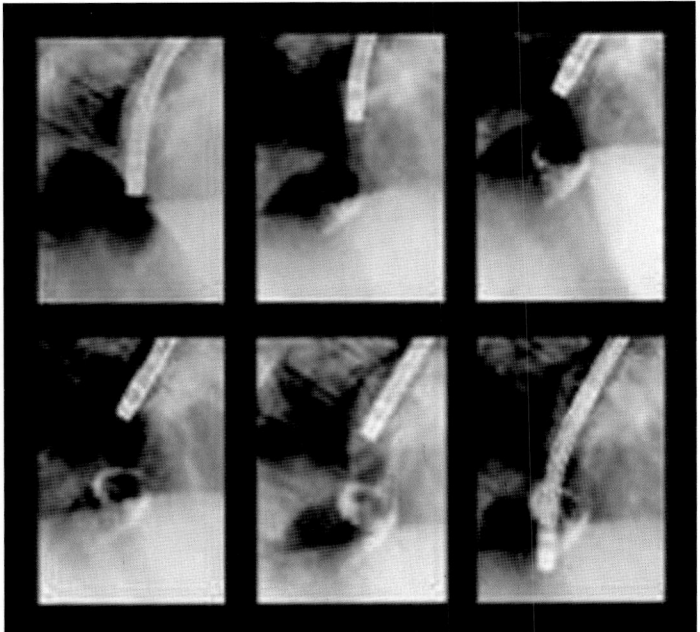

50% of the implanted Enteryx in place. LESP was reported to have increased from 12.2 to 16.7 mm Hg.

The results of the pivotal international multicenter Enteryx study were recently published and showed PPI use to be eliminated in 74% of treated subjects at 6 months and in 70% of these subjects at 12 months' follow-up.[85,89] pH scores significantly improved, with 38.8% normalization at 12 months in studied subjects, and there was a 1-cm LES length augmentation after therapy (2 cm at baseline increased to 3 cm post-treatment). There was no effect on incidence or severity of esophagitis after treatment. The GERD-HRQL scores after Enteryx therapy were comparable to those obtained on anti-secretory medications. The average procedure time was about 34 minutes. At 2-year follow-up, 64% of these patients remain off PPIs.[90] Although there was significant chest pain postprocedure, no serious adverse events were reported from this cohort of treated patients. Mild dysphagia was seen in a minority of subjects with early resolution. In the postmarketing phase of use, one patient's death was related to the use of Enteryx. A postmarketing long-term assessment study and a multicenter, randomized, sham-controlled Enteryx trial are under way.

Gatekeeper

Device

The Gatekeeper Reflux Repair System (Medtronic, Minneapolis, MN) consists of a transoral wire-guided overtube. A 1-mm diameter flexible endoscopic injector needle and a 1-mm trocar needle catheter are used to prepare the submucosal region and implant the polyacrylonitrile-based hydrogel (HYPAN) prosthesis.

Technique

The Gatekeeper device uses a 16-mm diameter overtube instrument through which is passed a standard or pediatric-sized video-gastroscope that is used to monitor the treatment field and to provide suction within the overtube. Suction draws the mucosa and submucosa into multiple shallow holes in the distal part of the Gatekeeper overtube to stabilize it in place as the hydrogel prostheses are introduced submucosally. With the subject given conscious sedation, a typical upper endoscopic examination is carried out, noting the landmarks and the distance to the squamo-columnar junction. After placing a guidewire into the distal stomach, the endoscope is removed and the Gatekeeper overtube is advanced over the wire to straddle the squamocolumnar junction. The flexible gastroscope is then introduced through the appropriate channel of the Gatekeeper instrument and advanced to its distal end. Suction is applied within the endoscope to draw the adjacent mucosa and submucosa into the device. Using the flexible sclerotherapy-type needle, saline is injected submucosally to create a pocket into which the hydrogel implant will be placed after the pocket is pierced by a sharp trocar. The implant is directed into submu-cosal position by a push-rod. The polyacrylonitrile-based hydrogel implants are 20 × 2 mm small and resemble pieces of "pencil lead" when introduced but swell to their full size (approximately 15 mm diameter) within a day when hydrated (Figs. 18–15 and 18–16). Usually, four to six implants are placed in a radial fashion into the submucosa at a treatment session, each implantation taking about 5 minutes to perform after about 10 minutes to prepare and place

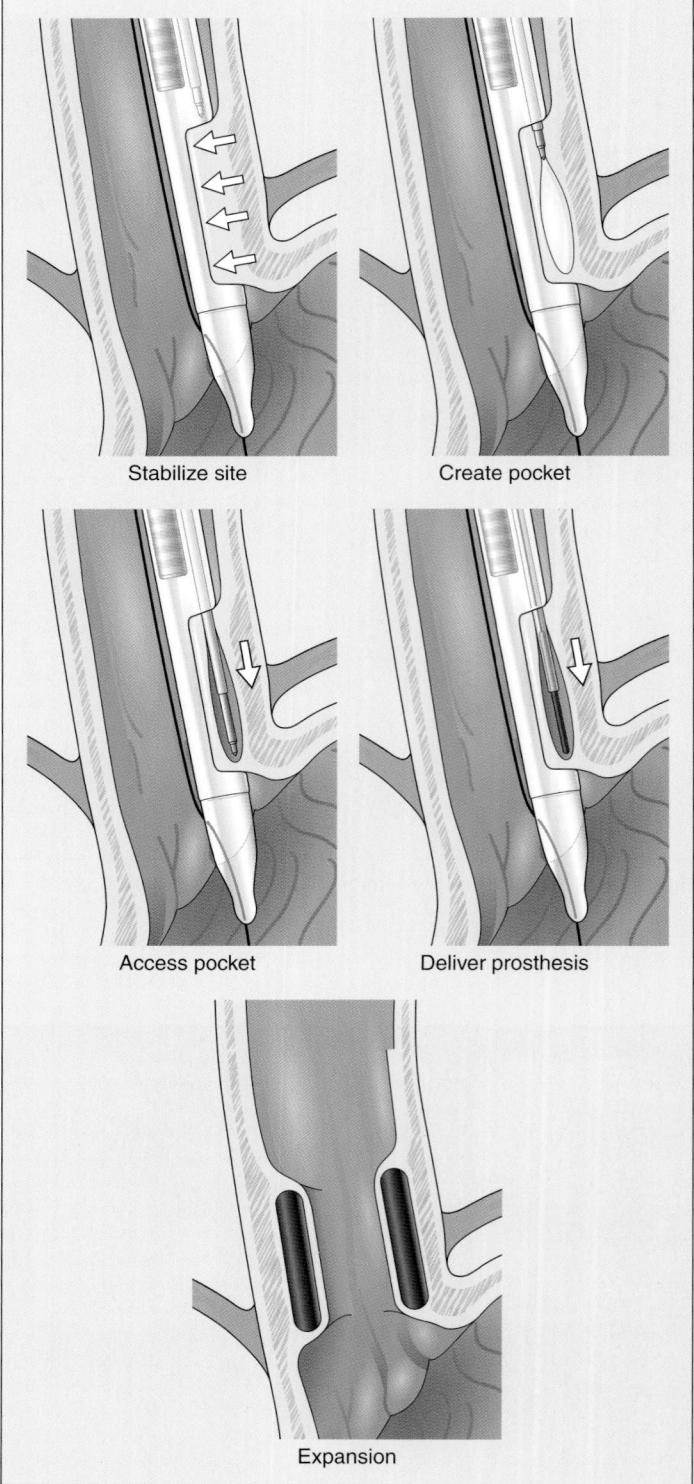

Stabilize site   Create pocket

Access pocket   Deliver prosthesis

Expansion

Figure 18–15. Medtronic Gatekeeper technique—implantation steps.

the Gatekeeper instrument. The instrument is rotated into the next position after releasing suction from the gastroscope, and then the whole process is repeated as for the placement of the initial prosthesis. One advantage of this implantation technique is its easy reversibility if needed, accomplished by using a needle knife to

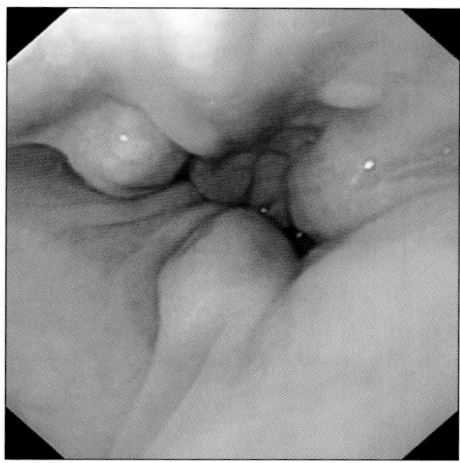

Figure 18–16. Gatekeeper—view of submucosal implants in distal esophagus.

Table 18–3. Common Inclusion and Exclusion Criteria for Gastrointestinal Reflux Disease Endotherapy Pivotal Trials
Inclusion Criteria Chronic symptoms of heartburn and regurgitation Response of GERD symptoms to acid suppression Abnormal ambulatory pH study with excessive distal esophageal acid contact time Normal esophageal manometry Ability to consent to the procedure
Exclusion Criteria Hiatal hernia greater than 2 cm, or in some studies 3 cm Severe erosive esophagitis Esophageal strictures or varices Intestinal metaplasia and Barrett's esophagus (for some studies, short-segment IM allowed) Previous esophagogastric surgery Pregnancy Obesity with BMI >35 High anesthesia risk (ASA class III or greater)
ASA, American Society of Anesthesiologists; BMI, body mass index; GERD, gastroesophageal reflux disease; IM, intestinal metaplasia.

incise the mucosa over the upper edge of an implant, which can then be gently suctioned out from its submucosal pocket by using a variceal banding "cap" attached to the distal endoscope.

Preclinical Data

Although the Gatekeeper technique requires specific training to place the hydrogel implants in the correct manner, it is easily learned, and data from an animal trial using farm pigs and miniswine showed that 98% of delivery attempts were successful.[91] Eighty-eight percent of the hydrogel implants were present for periods up to 6 months. Eighteen of 19 prostheses were retained at 3 years in long-term follow-up. The implants were easily removable in less than 5 minutes.

Clinical Data

A pilot study initiated at the Academic Medical Center of the University of Amsterdam in the Netherlands in which 10 GERD patients underwent the Gatekeeper procedure showed that the implants were successfully placed in 97% of attempts.[92] The procedures, which were accomplished in 22 minutes or less, improved the median reflux symptom scores at 1 and 6 months' follow-up. Four of 9 patients were off their acid-suppressing medicines, and 3 reduced their PPI dosage by at least 50% at the short-term follow-up. In a follow-up European multicenter trial, 30 additional patients underwent the Gatekeeper procedure. The introduction of the implant submucosally was successful in 94% of attempts, with a mean procedural time of 23 minutes. At 1 month postimplantation, 110 of 128 prostheses were still in position, and at 6 months, 47 of 62 were in correct position. Two serious adverse events occurred in this cohort: one patient suffered a pharyngeal perforation, which resolved after conservative management and was thought related to the older design of the now-modified overtube instrument, and one patient had severe postprandial nausea that resolved after endoscopic removal of the prostheses.

An international, multicenter, randomized, sham-controlled Gatekeeper trial has recently commenced and will be a pivotal trial for efficacy and safety outcomes with this technique.

Indications and Contraindications for Gastroesophageal Reflux Disease Endoscopic Therapy

The clinical experience with the endoscopic GERD treatments has mainly been for patients meeting the inclusion and exclusion criteria outlined in Table 18–3. Because none of these therapies have been shown to effectively heal esophagitis and only one third of treated patients from the pivotal trials achieve normalization of the distal acid contact time, their use as monotherapy for patients with erosive GERD is difficult to support. It is possible that GERD endotherapy may be useful as an adjunct to continued pharmacologic therapy to control symptoms or heal esophagitis, although we have no evidence-based medicine to support this indication. Whether these treatments should be used to provide relief of symptoms in patients with Barrett's esophagus, in light of the low rate of pH normalization, is as unclear as the lack of consensus as to the value of normalizing esophageal acid exposure pharmacologically in these same patients.[93] Future study for other groups, such as those with extraesophageal symptoms, longer segment Barrett's, pregnancy, failed laparoscopic Nissen, and prebariatric or postbariatric surgery, should be considered and undertaken.

Preoperative History and Considerations

Comprehensive evaluation must be performed before considering a patient for endoscopic treatments and much time should be spent in reviewing the expectations of the individual considering these management options. Patients should be questioned about prior surgical history and chronic medical conditions. The standard preprocedural evaluations generally include esophagogastroduodenoscopy (EGD), esophageal manometry, and ambulatory pH monitoring. The EGD permits a preprocedural assessment of the anatomy and a search for conditions that might preclude the use of the endoscopic approach (large hiatal hernia, long-segment Barrett's, severe erosive disease, stricture, concomitant upper GI disease). Manometry is useful to identify significant esophageal dysmotility including achalasia. The endoscopic procedures can be performed in patients with minor esophageal motor disturbances. Patients with very low LES tone (<6 mm Hg) may not respond as well to endotherapy as those with more normal tone because most of the studies have not shown major improvement in LES tone or length, but this has not been studied systematically because these patients were excluded from most of the initial studies.

Obviously, consideration should be taken for those patients on anticoagulation when manipulation of the tissues by endotherapy is entertained. Patients with portal hypertension should be excluded, in the presence of gastric or esophageal varices.

Variations and Unusual Situations

A preliminary report suggested that the EndoCinch device may be effective in patients with hiatal hernias larger than 2 cm; only patients with hiatal hernias smaller than 2 cm were included in the initial pivotal trial.[49] However, patients with larger hiatal hernias required more plications than those with smaller hiatal hernias. The use of a helical or staggered placement, rather than a circumferential or linear pattern, may benefit in patients with these larger hernias.[50,94] A modification of the Stretta technique for patients with larger hiatal hernias was described, and further experience is awaited to confirm this modified technique.[7] In that same report, the author reflected on modification of the usual Stretta technique for patients who are post Nissen fundoplication.

There are very limited data on the use of endoscopic antireflux procedures in patients with extraesophageal manifestations of GERD. An initial report on 32 GERD patients with pulmonary symptoms (wheezing 47%, cough 81%) and daily heartburn (75%) and/or daily regurgitation (50%) demonstrated significant clinical improvement at a mean follow-up of 6 months. In this patient cohort, wheezing was reduced to 6.3% and cough reduced to 19%, with significant improvements in heartburn symptom score and in regurgitation.[95] Data from another experienced group suggest a similar outcome and should direct further investigation in this problematic population of GERD patients.[96]

Postoperative Care

Standard postprocedural orders for the endoscopic GERD treatments have included use of antiemetics to avoid vomiting, which may potentially disrupt some of the suture-based interventions.

Following the procedure, a discussion is held with the patient to review any dietary restriction, medication use, activities, and the follow-up that will occur. The patient is examined to determine any evidence for adverse procedural outcome and may be given a prescription for analgesic medication to use. Most patients are observed for about 2 hours after the intervention.

Patients may be scheduled for a return office visit at 1 month after the endoscopic treatment. Patients are instructed to adhere to a liquid diet with progression to a soft diet for several days after the procedure. They are advanced to a regular diet by 96 hours, as long as no significant dysphagia is present. Activities are limited on the day of the procedure, but most treated patients are back to their usual schedules by the next day. Some clinicians request that their plication-treated patients not lift more than 15 pounds during the first postprocedure week.

Following full-thickness plicator therapies, some clinicians prescribe a week of antibiotics for the treated patients, whereas others just give the recommended standard preprocedural antibiotic prophylaxis.

Complications

Adverse events occurring in the group of 64 subjects during the pivotal Bard EndoCinch trial[37] included pharyngitis (31%), vomiting (14%), abdominal pain (14%), chest pain (16%), mucosal tear (3%), hypoxia (6%), gastric bleeding (3%), and suture perforation (2%). In the postmarketing experience, there have been a few patients requiring transfusions for GI bleeding. No deaths have been associated with the use of this device.

Adverse events occurred in 8.6% (10 patients) in the group of 118 subjects from the pivotal Curon Stretta trial[68] and included low-grade fever (1.7%), superficial mucosal injury (2.5%), chest pain (1.7%), transient dysphagia (0.8%), sedation-related hypotension (0.8%), and submental swelling resulting from topical anesthetic allergy (0.8%). In the postmarketing experience, there have been perforations and two deaths reported. These were in the early postrelease period. Since that time, increased efforts to improve clinician education and device improvements including the modification to guidewire-directed catheters has reduced the overall adverse event rate. In a comparison study against laparoscopic Nissen fundoplication, the complication rate was 1.7% (minor transient gastroparesis) compared with 11% major complications (enterotomies, pneumothorax, slipped Nissen, paraesophageal and incisional hernias) in the surgically treated group.[71]

In the pivotal NDO trial in which 64 patients underwent a full-thickness placation,[53] transient, mild adverse events included pharyngitis (41%), abdominal pain (20%), chest pain (17%), GI disorder (17%), eructation (14%), dysphagia (11%), and nausea (6%). Serious adverse events included two subjects with hypoxia after placement of the overtube, one subject with pneumothorax with hospital admission and conservative management, one subject with pneumoperitoneum with subsequent negative exploratory laparoscopic examination, and one subject with gastric perforation that was observed intraprocedurally, closed endoscopically with clips, and watched conservatively on postprocedural antibiotics.

In the initial pivotal Enteryx trial in which 85 subjects underwent injection of ethylene vinyl alcohol into the LES,[89] complications included chest pain (92%), which resolved within 14 days in 83% of affected individuals, and dysphagia (20%), which resolved within 2 to 12 weeks. During the initial postmarketing interval there has been a death, in which a direct injection into the aortic wall resulted in a fistula and in subsequent fatal GI hemorrhage.

Chest pain and referred pain to the left supraclavicular area is usual and expected after treatment with Enteryx, Gatekeeper, NDO, and ARD. This is generally managed well with mild oral analgesics.

Comparison to Laparoscopic Surgery

The efficacy of the EndoCinch device compared with laparoscopic fundoplication was evaluated in a preliminary report that included 18 patients treated endoscopically and 16 age-matched patients who underwent laparoscopic Nissen fundoplication.[97] The mean duration of the procedure (52 vs. 116 minutes) and hospital stay (0.05 vs. 3.3 days) were shorter in those undergoing the endoscopic procedure. Symptoms scores, need for PPIs, and quality of life were significantly improved in both groups. However, patients undergoing laparoscopic Nissen fundoplication showed greater control of esophageal acid exposure. Study of a cohort of 27 patients treated with EndoCinch compared with laparoscopic Nissen[98] showed similar short-term symptomatic improvement between the two groups, but follow-up satisfaction with the laparoscopic Nissen intervention was higher (96%) compared with the endoscopic gastric plication group (78%). More recently, the early outcomes (at a mean of about 8 months) in 47 subjects with "refractory GERD" who underwent the EndoCinch procedure were compared with the early outcomes in a cohort of 40 subjects referred for laparoscopic Nissen fundoplication.[99] Overall, 66% of the endoscopic gastric plication treated group were satisfied with their treatment in comparison with 93% of the group treated by laparoscopic surgical intervention. Postprocedural antireflux PPI and prokinetic medication use was 32% in the endoscopically treated group and 13% in the surgically managed cohort ($p = .03$).

One study was recently published that compared the short-term results of the RF Stretta procedure in 65 patients to the short-term results in 75 patients undergoing laparoscopic Nissen fundoplication in one institution.[71] The groups were different in that patients with Barrett's esophagus, hiatal hernias larger than 2 cm, and LESP less than 8 mm Hg were assigned to surgical intervention and excluded from endoscopic management. At 6 months, quality of life scores were similarly improved for both groups. At this follow-up, 58% of Stretta-treated patients were off all PPI medications and an additional 31% had reduced their doses significantly, whereas 97% of the surgically treated group were off all PPIs. Both groups appeared to be satisfied with their chosen intervention.

Future Trends

We have seen the initial data for clinical outcomes and safety for the first group of endoscopic treatments for GERD. As has been already stated, these results, largely, were from the learning curve experiences of the initial investigators performing these procedures in carefully defined symptomatic patients. Although successful for most patients in controlling reflux symptoms and allowing significant or total discontinuation of acid suppressive medications, the follow-up intervals have been mainly short term, and during longer term follow-up there appears to be a diminution of beneficial effect.

To improve the efficacy, techniques using currently available devices may need to be modified. Optimizing techniques will require study of varying the number and location of plications; the number, volume, and location of injectable or implantable agents; and the number and location of RF thermal lesions. On the other hand, currently available devices for GERD treatment have many limitations. The ability to effectively place the instruments and devices is occasionally limited, and not all areas of the upper stomach are easily accessed with some of the current instrument designs. To improve intraluminal tissue manipulation, new and better technology is needed.

Robotics technology, which has been most applied and studied in the surgical specialties, has the potential to revolutionize endoscopic practice in the future.[100] Robots as endoscopic therapeutic assistants would play a role much like that of surgical robots. These assistants could be for passive positioning, for assisting in moving instruments or accessories, or for actual driving of the endoscopic tools as directed by the endoscopist.

Telemanipulators could provide the endoscopist with the advantages seen for those used in the laparoscopic surgical arena. Using joystick or other manual controls, while positioned at a control console, the endoscopist could direct small and interchangeable instruments introduced into the stomach via the oral cavity. The endoscopist would have access to intraluminal and transluminal sites and structures with an ability to perform complex and predictable diagnostic and therapeutic maneuvers. The endoscopist would have hands, arms, and eyes inside the patient, and an armamentarium of flexible instruments would provide a tool kit for new procedures and techniques. Intraluminal procedures for GERD would be possible with precision and enhanced visualization, removal of hand tremor, and augmented articulation and positioning among the obvious benefits.

The technology of computer-assisted telerobotic endoscopic surgery has been developed by endoVia (Norwood, MA), and early work with this device is laying the foundation for more complex procedures.[101] This system consists of three components: the endoscopist's interface, a control system, and a drive unit. The endoscopist's interface is a pair of control handles (like joysticks) that allow the operator to direct the position and orientation of the instruments and to actuate their "open-close" or other functions. The system operator can be seated comfortably at a console while controlling the handles and has a video display screen for viewing the operative field (Fig. 18–17). The control system consists of the motors, position sensors, motion control electronics, and system computer that translate movements of the interface handles into precise instrument motions. The drive unit is made up of a package of motors mounted on a sliding platform that move in response to signals from the control system to drive the disposable instruments, which are mounted on sliding platforms. The exchangeable instruments are placed through guide tubes, which are mounted externally to the flexible endoscope. The disposable instruments are capable of motion with up to 6 degrees of freedom and may have electrocautery capability. Tissue graspers, scissors, needle drivers, and a "hot" needle-knife have been made and tested. An array of endoscopic procedures using these novel articulating accessories, such as treatment of GERD, is on the horizon.

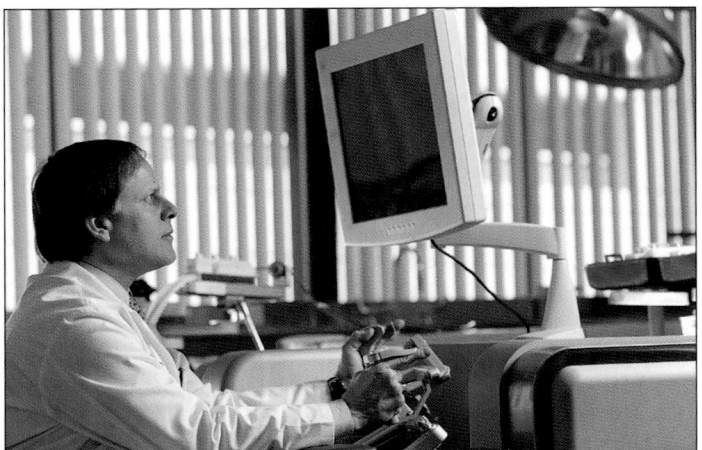

Figure 18–17. Computer-assisted robot for endoscopic surgery.

Table 18–4. Order of Studies and Outcome Measures for New Endoscopic Gastrointestinal Reflux Disease Therapies

Proof of principal studies
Pilot human studies
Multicenter prospective open-label trials
Prospective, randomized, sham-controlled studies demonstrating that the new therapy is superior to placebo
Prospective, randomized, controlled studies comparing the new therapy to an established therapy for GERD

GERD, gastroesophageal reflux disease.
Reprinted from Edmundowicz SA: Injection therapy of the lower esophageal sphincter for the treatment of GERD. Gastrointest Endosc 59:545–552, 2004, with permission from the American Society for Gastrointestinal Endoscopy.

Summary

GERD affects a large segment of the population. Its presentation can be classical, with heartburn and regurgitation, or, less commonly, it can present with extraesophageal symptoms of chest pain and laryngeal and/or pulmonary symptoms. Patients with GERD are significantly bothered in their quality of life and seek effective treatments. Medical therapy has been successful and is safe for long-term use. The only alternative until recently had been surgical intervention, mainly with the laparoscopic Nissen fundoplication. Outcomes for surgical and pharmacologic treatments, when medication dosing was not fixed, appear equivalent in prospective studies. However, many patients are not satisfied with their daily dependency on antisecretory medications and their GERD symptoms rapidly return when these agents are not taken. Many individuals are concerned about the invasiveness of standard surgical intervention, even laparoscopic, and the potential side effects that, although typically short-lived, may persist and affect the quality of their lives.

Endoscopic treatment of GERD offers an alternative to these two "pillars" of therapy. Although not efficacious for all treated patients, the initial success rate for control of symptoms and ability to stop antisecretory medication is in the 65% to 85% range for these novel techniques in up to 1-year follow-up. For most, but not all of these treatments, the durability falls, and, by the second postprocedural year, less than half of treated patients are able to remain off medications because their GERD symptoms have returned.

These data are mainly from the initial trials and early experiences of the investigators, much of which was during their learning curve intervals. It is anticipated that further experience with the devices, coupled with optimized techniques, would yield more substantial and durable outcomes.

Although new therapies need to be reviewed for clinical efficacy, their safety profiles require close monitoring. GERD is a benign condition for the most part, and substantial procedure-related morbidity and mortality (even if rare) will not support the ongoing use of these new devices and techniques. Attention to adequate training and credentialing will be important for these new procedures, just as it has been for the introduction of many of our expanding endoscopic therapeutic procedures.

Additional science, including well-designed randomized prospective trials, sham-controlled trials, and multicenter trials that are adequately powered are needed to provide the data to effectively assess the clinical utility. Comparative trials between endotherapy, surgical, and/or medical therapy are necessary.

The ideal patients for these treatments have yet to be identified. The persistence of erosive esophagitis and the low rate of normalization of distal esophageal acid exposure after treatment should direct our use of these treatments in those patients with NERD. The use of an endoscopic antireflux procedure adjunctively in patients partially responsive to medications needs further assessment. Consideration for use in patients who fall outside the usual inclusion criteria used in the initial clinical trials will provide us with much needed additional information concerning the broader application of these interventions. Attention to optimizing the instruments and techniques will likely yield improved clinical outcomes. It is an interesting time in the evolution of this exciting new therapy (Table 18–4).

Much remains to be understood. Are these techniques ready for prime time or should they continue to be studied in so-called centers of excellence? Should one become an early adopter or await further experience? Which of these devices and techniques will be in clinical use 5 years from now, and which will no longer be offered? The answers to these and so many more questions will come from additional clinical experience and from the rigorous scholarship of ongoing research. Nonetheless, the initial experience with endoscopic therapy for GERD has been impressive, with reasonable symptom control, improvement in quality of life, and reduction in medication use. The future will bring additional devices and techniques, and the lessons learned from GERD endotherapy will serve us well as we expand the arena of intraluminal and transluminal endoscopic surgery.

REFERENCES

1. Sandler RS, Everhart JE, Donowitz M, et al: The burden of selected digestive diseases in the United States. Gastroenterology 122:1500–1511, 2002.

2. Locke GR, Talley NJ, Fett SL, et al: Prevalence and clinical spectrum of gastroesophageal reflux: A population based study in Olmstead County, Minnesota. Gastroenterology 112:1448–1456, 1997.

3. Dimenas E, Glise H, Hallerback B, et al: Quality of life in patients with upper gastrointestinal symptoms. An improved evaluation of treatment regimens? Scand J Gastroenterol 28:681–687, 1993.

4. Revicki DA, Wood M, Maton PN, Sorensen S: The impact of gastroesophageal reflux disease on health-related quality of life. Am J Med 104:252–258, 1998.

5. Lagergren J, Bergstrom R, Lindgren A, Nyren O: Symptomatic gastroesophageal reflux as a risk factor for esophageal adenocarcinoma. N Engl J Med 340:825–831, 1999.

6. Kahrilas PJ, Pandolfino JE: The target of therapies: Pathophysiology of gastroesophageal reflux disease. Gastrointest Endosc Clin N Am 13:1–17, 2003.

7. Kahrilas PJ: GERD pathogenesis, pathophysiology, and clinical manifestations. Cleve Clin J Med 70(Suppl 5):S4–19, 2003.

8. Jones MP, Sloan SS, Rabine JC, et al: Hiatal hernia size is the dominant determinant of esophagitis presence and severity in gastroesophageal reflux disease. Am J Gastroenterol 96:1711–1717, 2001.

9. Mittal RK, McCallum RW: Characteristics and frequency of transient relaxations of the lower esophageal sphincter in patients with reflux esophagitis. Gastroenterology 95:593–599, 1988.

10. van Herwaarden MA, Samsom M, Smout AJ: Excess gastroesophageal reflux in patients with hiatus hernia is caused by mechanisms other than transient LES relaxations. Gastroenterology 119:1439–1446, 2000.

11. Lundell L, Miettinen P, Myrvold HE, et al: Continued (5-year) follow-up of a randomized clinical study comparing antireflux surgery and omeprazole in gastroesophageal reflux disease. J Am Coll Surg 192:172–179, 2001.

12. Spechler SJ, Lee E, Ahnen D, et al: Long-term outcome of medical and surgical therapies for gastro-esophageal reflux disease: Follow-up of a randomized controlled trial. JAMA 285:2331–2338, 2001.

13. Klinkenberg-Knol EC, Nelis F, Dent J, et al: Long-term omeprazole treatment in resistant gastro-esophageal reflux disease: Efficacy, safety and influence on gastric mucosa. Gastroenterology 118:661–669, 2000.

14. Chiba N, DeGara CJ, Wilkinson JM, et al: Speed of healing and symptom relief in grade II-IV gastro-esophageal reflux disease: A meta-analysis. Gastroenterology 112:1798–1810, 1997.

15. Crawley JA, Schmitt CM: How satisfied are chronic heartburn sufferers with their prescription medications? Results of the patient unmet needs survey. JCOM 7:29–34, 2000.

16. Modlin IM, Kidd M, Lye KD: Historical perspectives on the treatment of gastroesophageal reflux disease. Gastrointest Endosc Clin N Am 13:19–55, 2003.

17. Rattner D, Brooks D: Patient satisfaction following laparoscopic and open antireflux surgery. Arch Surg 130:289–294, 1995.

18. Liu JY, Woloshin S, Laycock WS, Schwartz LM: Late outcomes after laparoscopic surgery for gastroesophageal reflux. Arch Surg 137:397–401, 2001.

19. Eubanks T, Omelanczuk P, Richards DC, et al: Outcomes of laparoscopic anti-reflux procedures. Am J Surg 179:391–395, 2000.

20. Anvari M, Allen C: Five-year comprehensive outcomes evaluation in 181 patients after laparoscopic Nissen fundoplication. J Am Coll Surg 196:51–59, 2003.

21. van den Boom G, Go P, Hameeteman W, et al: Cost-effectiveness of medical versus surgical treatment in patients with severe or refractory gastroesophageal reflux disease in the Netherlands. Scand J Gastroenterol 31:1–9, 1996.

22. Huedebert G, Marks L, Wilcox C, et al: Choice of long-term strategy for the management of patients with severe esophagitis. A cost-utility analysis. Gastroenterology 112:1078–1086, 1997.

23. Viljakka M, Nevalainen J, Isolauri J: Lifetime costs of surgical versus medical treatment of severe gastroesophageal reflux disease in Finland. Scand J Gastroenterol 32:766–772, 1997.

24. Lafullarde T, Watson D, Jamieson G, et al: Laparoscopic Nissen fundoplication. Five-year results and beyond. Arch Surg 136:180–184, 2001.

25. Vakil N, Shaw M, Kirby R: Clinical effectiveness of laparoscopic fundoplication in a U.S. community. Am J Med 114:1–5, 2003.

26. Swain CP, Mills TN: An endoscopic sewing machine. Gastrointest Endosc 32:36–37, 1986.

27. Swain CP: Endoscopic sewing and stapling machines. Endoscopy 29:205–210, 1997.

28. Swain CP, Brown G, Mills TN: An endoscopic stapling device: Development of a new flexible endoscopically controlled device for placing multiple transmural staples in gastrointestinal tissue. Gastrointest Endosc 35:338–339, 1989.

29. Gong F, Swain CP, Kadirkamanathan SS, et al: Cutting thread at flexible endoscopy. Gastrointest Endosc 44:667–674, 1996.

30. Kadirkamanathan SS, Evans DF, Gong F, et al: Antireflux operations at flexible endoscopy using endoluminal stitching techniques: An experimental study. Gastrointest Endosc 44:133–143, 1996.

31. Swain P, Park P, Mills T: Bard EndoCinch: The device, the technique, and pre-clinical studies. Gastrointest Endosc Clin N Am 13:75–88, 2003.

32. Rothstein RI: Endoscopic therapy for gastroesophageal reflux disease: Sewing/plication techniques. Up-to-Date Version 12.2. February 19, 2004 [Online textbook].

33. Rothstein RI, Filipi CJ: Endoscopic suturing for gastroesophageal reflux disease: Clinical outcomes with the Bard EndoCinch. Gastrointest Endosc Clin N Am 13:89–101, 2003.

34. Kadirkamanathan SS, Yazaki E, Evans DF, et al: An ambulant porcine model of acid reflux used to evaluate endoscopic gastroplasty. Gut 44:782–788, 1999.

35. Rothstein RI, Moodie K: Depth of endoscopically placed sutures [abstract]. Gastrointest Endosc 51:AB144, 2000.

36. Feitoza AB, Gostout CJ, Rajan E, et al: Endoluminal gastroplications: A histopathologic analysis of intraluminal suture plications. Gastrointest Endosc 57:868–876, 2003.

37. Filipi C, Lehman G, Rothstein RI, et al: Transoral endoscopic suturing for gastroesophageal reflux disease: A multicenter trial. Gastrointest Endosc 53:416–422, 2001.

38. Swain CP, Park PO, Kjellin T, et al: Endoscopic gastroplasty for the treatment of gastro-esophageal reflux disease [abstract]. Gastrointest Endosc 51:144, 2001.

39. Raijman I, Ben-Menachem T, Reddy G, et al: Symptomatic response to endoluminal gastroplication (ELGP) in patients with gastroesophageal reflux disease (GERD): A multi-center experience [abstract]. Gastrointest Endosc 53:AB74, 2001.

40. Maple JT, Alexander JA, Gostout CJ, et al: Endoscopic gastroplasty for GERD: Not as good as billed? A single-center, 6-month report [abstract]. Am J Gastroenterol 96:S22, 2001.

41. Tam WC, Holloway RH, Dent J, et al: Impact of endoscopic suturing of the gastroesophageal junction on lower esophageal sphincter function and gastroesophageal reflux in patients with reflux disease. Am J Gastroenterol 99:195–202, 2004.

42. Mahmood Z, McMahon B, Khosa F, et al: EndoCinch therapy for gastro-esophageal reflux disease: A one year prospective follow up. Gut 52:34–39, 2003.

43. Liu JJ, Knapp R, Carr-Lock DL: Treatment of medication refractory gastroesophageal reflux disease with endoluminal plication [abstract]. Gastrointest Endosc 55:AB257, 2002.

44. Arts J, Slootmaekers S, Sifrim D, et al: Endoluminal gastroplication (EndoCinch) in GERD patients refractory to PPI therapy [abstract]. Gastroenterology 122:AB39117, 2002.

45. Rothstein RI, Pohl H, Grove M, et al: Endoscopic gastric plication for the treatment of GERD: Two year follow-up results [abstract]. Am J Gastroenterol 96S:107, 2001.

46. Haber GB, Marcon NE, Kortan P, et al: A 2-year follow-up of 25 patients undergoing endoluminal gastric plication (ELGP) for gastroesophageal reflux disease (GERD) [abstract]. Gastrointest Endosc 53:116, 2000.

47. Chen YK, Raijman I, Ben-Menachem T, et al: Long-term experience with endoluminal gastroplication (ELGP): Clinical and economic outcomes of the US multicenter trial [abstract]. Gastrointest Endosc 57:AB100, 2003.

48. Lehman GA, Dunne DP, Hieston K, et al: Suturing plication of the cardia with EndoCinch device: Effect of supplemental cautery. A human prospective randomized trial [abstract]. Gastrointest Endosc 55:AB260, 2002.

49. Raijman I, Ben-Menachem T, Starpoli AA, et al: Endoluminal gastroplication (ELGP) improves GERD symptoms in patients with large hiatal hernias [abstract]. Gastrointest Endosc 55:AB255, 2002.

50. Filipi CJ, Gerhardt JD: Comparison of endoluminal gastroplication configuration techniques [abstract]. Am J Gastroenterol 97:AB89, 2002.

51. Rothstein RI, Hynes M, Grove M, Pohl H: Endoscopic gastric plication (EndoCinch) for GERD: A randomized, sham-controlled, blinded, single-center study [abstract]. Gastrointest Endosc 59:AB111, 2004.

52. Liu JJ, Glickman JN, Saltzman J: Effect of mucosal sutures on the muscularis propria layer at the gastroesophageal junction [abstract]. Gastrointest Endosc 59:AB240, 2004.

53. Pleskow D, Rothstein RI, Kozarek R, et al: Endoscopic full-thickness plication for GERD: A multicenter study. Gastrointest Endosc 59:163–171, 2004.

54. Chuttani R, Kozarek R, Critchlow J, et al: A novel endoscopic full-thickness plicator for treatment of GERD: An animal model study. Gastrointest Endosc 56:116–122, 2002.

55. Chuttani R: Endoscopic full-thickness plication: The device, technique, pre-clinical and early clinical experience. Gastrointest Endosc Clin N Am 13:109–116, 2003.

56. Chuttani R, Sud R, Sachdev G, et al: A novel endoscopic full-thickness plicator for the treatment of GERD: A pilot study. Gastrointest Endosc 58:770–776, 2003.

57. Mason RJ, Filipi CJ, DeMeester TR, et al: A new intraluminal antigastroesophageal reflux procedure in baboons. Gastrointest Endosc 45:283–290, 1997.

58. DeMeester TR: Microvasive gastric stapler: The device, technique, and preclinical results. Gastrointest Endosc Clin N Am 13:117–133, 2003.

59. Hu B, Sun L, Lau YW, et al: Endoscopic suturing without extra-corporeal knots: The Eagle Claw V [abstract]. Gastrointest Endosc 59:AB114, 2004.

60. Edmundowicz SA, Perrone JM, Siegel LC, et al: Randomized controlled evaluation of a novel endoscopic stapling system in an animal model for GERD [abstract]. Gastrointest Endosc 59:AB148, 2004.

61. Utley DS: The Stretta procedure: Device, technique, and pre-clinical study data. Gastrointest Endosc Clin N Am 13:135–145, 2003.

62. Utley DS, Kim MS, Vierra MA, Triadafilopoulos G: Augmentation of lower esophageal sphincter pressure and gastric yield pressure after radiofrequency energy delivery to the gastroesophageal junction: A porcine model. Gastrointest Endosc 52:81–86, 2000.

63. Kim MS, Holloway R, Dent J, Utley DS: Radiofrequency energy (RFe) delivery to the gastric cardia inhibits triggering of transient lower esophageal sphincter relaxations in dogs. Gastrointest Endosc 57:17–22, 2003.

64. Chang KJ, Utley DS: Endoscopic ultrasound (EUS) in-vivo assessment of radiofrequency (RF) energy delivery to the gastroesophageal (GE) junction in a porcine model [abstract]. Gastrointest Endosc 53:AB165, 2001.

65. DiBaise JK, Brand RE, Quigley EM: Endoluminal delivery of radio-frequency energy to the gastroesophageal junction uncomplicated GERD: Efficacy and potential mechanism of action. Am J Gastroenterol 97:833–842, 2002.

66. Tam WC, Schoeman MN, Zhang Q, et al: Delivery of radio-frequency energy (RFe) to the lower esophageal sphincter (LES) and gastric cardia inhibits transient LES relaxations and gastro-esophageal reflux in patients with reflux disease. Gut 52:479–485, 2003.

67. Triadafilopoulos G, DiBiase JK, Nostrant TT, et al: Radiofrequency energy delivery to the gastro-esophageal junction for the treatment of GERD. Gastrointest Endosc 53:407–415, 2001.

68. Triadafilopoulos G, DiBaise JK, Nostrant TT, et al: The Stretta procedure for the treatment of GERD: 6 and 12 month follow-up of the U.S. open label trial. Gastrointest Endosc 55:149–156, 2002.

69. Triadafilopouos G: Changes in GERD symptom scores correlate with improvement in esophageal acid exposure after the Stretta procedure. Surg Endosc 18:1038–1044, 2004.

70. Wolfsen HC, Richards WO: The Stretta procedure for the treatment of GERD: A registry of 558 patients. J Laparoendosc Adv Surg Tech 12:395–402, 2002.

71. Richards WO, Houston HL, Torquati A, et al: Paradigm shift in the management of gastroesophageal reflux disease. Ann Surg 237:638–649, 2003.

72. Houston H, Khaitan L, Holzman M, Richards WO: First year experience of patients undergoing the Stretta procedure. Surg Endosc 17:401–404, 2003.

73. Reymunde A, Santiago N: The Stretta procedure is an effective alternative to long-term PPI therapy for patients with GERD: Clinical experience after 82 consecutive procedures [abstract]. Am J Gastroenterol 96:S34, 2001.

74. Mansell DE: Extended follow-up in patients treated with the Stretta procedure: A report on 29 patients [abstract]. Gastrointest Endosc 55:AB194, 2002.

75. Noar MD, Igari Y, Mulock D, et al: The large hiatal hernia and failed Nissen fundoplication: Initial report of successful treatment using modified radiofrequency ablation (Stretta) technique [abstract]. Am J Gastroenterol 96:S27, 2001.

76. Corley DA, Katz P, Wo J, et al: Radiofrequency energy to the gastroesophageal junction for treatment of GERD (the Stretta procedure): A randomized, sham-controlled, multicenter clinical trial. Gastroenterology 125:668–676, 2003.

77. O'Connor KW, Madison ST, Smith DJ, et al: An experimental endoscopic technique for reversing gastroesophageal reflux in dogs by injecting inert material in the distal esophagus. Gastrointest Endosc 30:275–280, 1984.

78. Lehman GA: The history and future of implantation therapy for gastroesophageal reflux disease. Gastrointest Endosc Clin N Am 13:157–165, 2003.

79. O'Connor MD, Lehman GA: Endoscopic placement of collagen at the lower esophageal sphincter to inhibit gastroesophageal reflux—a pilot study of 10 medically intractable patients. Gastrointest Endosc 34:106–112, 1988.

80. Feretis C, Benakis P, Dimopoulos C, et al: Endoscopic implantation of Plexiglas (PMMA) microspheres for the treatment of GERD. Gastrointest Endosc 53:423–426, 2001.

81. Feretis C, Benakis P, Dimopoulos C, et al: Plexiglas (polymethyl-methacrylate) implantation: Technique, pre-clinical and clinical experience. Gastrointest Endosc Clin N Am 13:167–178, 2003.

82. Shafik A: Intraesophageal Polytef injection for the treatment of reflux esophagitis. Surg Endosc 10:329–331, 1996.

83. Loius H, Deviere J: Endoscopic implantation of Enteryx for the treatment of gastroesophageal reflux disease: Technique, pre-clinical and clinical experience. Gastrointest Endosc Clin N Am 13:191–200, 2003.

84. Edmundowicz SA: Injection therapy of the lower esophageal sphincter for the treatment of GERD. Gastrointest Endosc 59:545–552, 2004.

85. Johnson DA, Ganz R, Aisenberg J, et al: Endoscopic, deep mural implantation of Enteryx for the treatment of GERD: 6-month follow-up of a multicenter trial. Am J Gastroenterol 98:250–258, 2003.

86. Mason R, Hughes M, Lehman G, et al: Endoscopic augmentation of the cardia with a biocompatible injectable polymer (Enteryx) in a porcine model. Surg Endosc 16:386–391, 2002.

87. Peters JH, Silverman DE, Stein A: Lower esophageal sphincter injection of a biocompatible polymer. Accuracy of implantation assessed by esophagectomy. Surg Endosc 17:547–550, 2003.

88. Deviere J, Pastorelli A, Hubert L, et al: Endoscopic implantation of a biopolymer in the lower esophageal sphincter for gastroesophageal reflux: A pilot study. Gastrointest Endosc 55:335–341, 2002.

89. Johnson DA, Ganz R, Aisenberg J, et al: Endoscopic implantation of Enteryx for the treatment of GERD: 12-month results of a prospective multicenter trial. Am J Gastroenterol 98:1921–1930, 2003.

90. Cohen L, Johnson DA, Ganz R, et al: Enteryx solution, a minimally invasive injectable treatment for GERD: Analysis of extended follow-up through 24 months [abstract]. Am J Gastroenterol 98:A71, 2003.

91. Easter DW, Yurek M, Johnson G: Long-term retention of endoscopically placed hydrogel prostheses at the lower esophageal sphincter in pigs. Surg Endosc 18:448–451, 2004.

92. Fockens P: Gatekeeper reflux repair system: Technique, pre-clinical and clinical experience. Gastrointest Endosc Clin N Am 13:179–189, 2003.

93. Triadafilopoulos G: Proton pump inhibitors for Barrett's esophagus. Gut 46:144–146, 2000.

94. Raijman I, Walters R, Garza C, et al: Helical endoluminal gastroplication (ELGP) compared with standard ELGP in patients with gastroesophageal reflux disease (GERD) [abstract]. Gastrointest Endosc 55:AB260, 2002.

95. Shahrier M, Raijman I, Starpoli A, et al: Endoluminal gastroplication (ELGP) improves acid-related symptoms in GERD patients [abstract]. Gastroenterol 122:263, 2002.

96. Liu JJ, Knapp R, Carr-Lock DL: Treatment of medication refractory gastroesophageal reflux disease with endoluminal gastroplication [abstract]. Gastrointest Endosc 55:AB257, 2002.

97. Mahmood Z, Byrne PJ, McCullough J, et al: A comparison of Bard EndoCinch transoesophageal endoscopic placation (BETEP) with laparoscopic fundoplication (LNF) for the treatment of gastro-esophageal reflux disease (GORD) [abstract]. Gastrointest Endosc 55:AB90, 2002.

98. Velanovitch V, Ben-Menachem T, Goel S: Case-control comparison of endoscopic fundoplication with laparoscopic fundoplication in the treatment of gastroesophageal reflux disease [abstract]. Gastroenterol 120:A115, 2001.

99. Chadalavada R, Lin E, Swafford V, et al: Comparative results of endoluminal gastroplasty and laparoscopic antireflux surgery for the treatment of GERD. Surg Endosc 18:261–265, 2004.

100. Rothstein RI, Rosen J, Young JS: Improving efficiency in endoscopy with robotic technology. Gastrointest Endosc Clin N Am 14:679–696, 2004.

101. Rothstein RI, Ailinger RA, Peine W: Computer-assisted endoscopic robot system for advanced therapeutic procedures [abstract]. Gastrointest Endosc 59:AB112, 2004.

Benign Strictures

Grace H. Elta

Benign strictures occur throughout the gastrointestinal (GI) tract, although they are most common in the esophagus. This chapter focuses on the endoscopic diagnosis and therapy of these strictures including a review of the long-term outcome data available.

Esophageal Strictures

The most common presenting symptom is solid food dysphagia. Although there continues to be some debate about whether a barium esophagram or an upper endoscopy is the best initial test in patients with dysphagia,[1] many gastroenterologists favor endoscopy because the diagnoses that benefit from a barium x-ray, such as achalasia and Zenker's diverticulum, are uncommon and endoscopy offers both diagnosis and treatment in most patients. Dysphagia can be a symptom of gastrointestinal reflux disease (GERD) without the presence of a stricture.[2] Narrowing of the esophagus to 13 mm or less (39 French) is the diameter at which dysphagia typically occurs. Mild degrees of stenosis can be missed endoscopically; thus, patients with persistent dysphagia after a normal endoscopy and a therapeutic trial of a proton pump inhibitor should have a barium esophagram subsequently performed.

The most common etiology of benign esophageal stricture is GERD (Fig. 19–1). Because of the widespread use of proton pump inhibitors, peptic strictures are becoming less common[3] and are recurring less frequently.[4] They are usually at their worst at the initial presentation.[5] Another etiology of esophageal strictures is corrosive strictures, resulting from either alkali or strong acid ingestion. Compared with peptic strictures, corrosive strictures require more dilation sessions and the chance of recurrence is higher.[6] Other less common causes of esophageal stricture include radiation-, infection-,[7] pill-,[8] and sclerotherapy-induced esophageal strictures[9] (Table 19–1). Extrinsic compression of the esophagus can also cause symptomatic esophageal stenosis. The most common

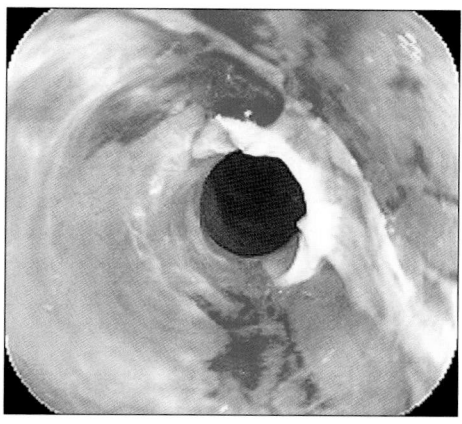

Figure 19–1. Recurrent peptic esophageal stricture in a patient allergic to proton pump inhibitors who has had two failed fundoplications.

causes of extrinsic esophageal compression are mediastinal tumors such as breast and lung cancer and lymphoma, although compression by lymph nodes in tuberculosis and histoplasmosis and by vascular structures such as an aberrant right subclavian artery (arteria lusoria)[10,11] also occur. Recently, small-caliber esophagus has been described in patients with eosinophilic esophagitis.[12,13] This syndrome may overlap with "corrugated ring esophagus"[14] and may describe patients who are at higher risk for complications from dilation.

DILATION OF ESOPHAGEAL STRICTURES

Most reported series on the treatment of benign esophageal strictures are composed predominately or exclusively of patients with peptic strictures. Consequently, published guidelines on the management of strictures are based primarily on the results of

Table 19–1. Benign Diseases that Cause Dysphagia	
Mucosal disease	Gastrointestinal reflux disease (GERD) (peptic stricture)
	Caustic injury (corrosive ingestion, sclerotherapy)
	Radiation injury
	Pill-induced esophagitis
	Rings and webs
	Infectious esophagitis
Motility disorders	Achalasia
	Scleroderma or CREST syndrome
	Hypothyroidism
	Other motility disorders
Mediastinal compression	Mediastinal infections (tuberculosis, histoplasmosis)
	Arteria lusoria

Table 19–2. Esophageal Dilators	
Mercury- or tungsten-filled bougies	Maloney (tapered tip)
	Hurst (blunt tip)
Wire-guided polyvinyl bougies	Savary
	American Endoscopy
	Celestin (step wise diameter increase)
Balloon dilators	Through the scope (TTS)
	Controlled radial expansion (CRE) through the scope
	Over-a-wire fluoroscopic control

studies of patients with peptic lesions.[1,15] There are three primary types of dilator choices (Table 19–2). The first, and historically most widely used, is the mercury- or tungsten-filled rubber bougies, either blunt tipped (Hurst) or tapered tip (Maloney). Except for home dilation performed by patients, the weighted bougies have been replaced by wire-guided tapered polyvinyl bougies or by balloons in many endoscopy units. The major advantage to the wire-guided bougie is the security of knowing that the tip is directed through the stricture rather than into a side wall. This security is heightened by the use of fluoroscopy for the wire-guided bougie dilation, although it is not necessary unless the stricture is extremely narrow or tortuous. There are several manufacturers of wire-guided bougies. The Celestin dilator has a series of short steps, which increase the diameter in a stepwise manner, rather than a smooth taper. In the United States, the Savary (Wilson-Cook) and American Endoscopy (Bard) bougies are the most popular. They differ in the length of the taper and the method for making them radiopaque. Available diameters range from 5 to 20 mm (15 to 60 French).

Fluoroscopic guidance is purported to improve the safety of esophageal dilation, although the data published to support this contention is unconvincing.[16] In a study of 145 patients treated with Maloney dilators, fluoroscopy was found to alter the dilation technique in 24%.[17] It was found particularly useful for ensuring proper dilator passage in patients with large hiatal hernias. It has been argued that a wire guide of the bougie alleviates the need for fluoroscopic control. Only in very tight, long, or tortuous strictures where the wire does not freely pass through the stricture is fluoroscopy needed. In a study of more than 300 patients using wire-guided bougienage, only 8% of the patients required fluoroscopic-guided dilation.[18]

Balloon dilators can also be used over a wire under fluoroscopic control. At some institutions, this is performed by interventional radiology. However, the most popular balloons are through the scope (TTS). They are passed through the biopsy channel of an endoscope and have a soft tip that is passed under direct vision through the stricture. The efficacy of the balloon is improved if water (or contrast medium), rather than air, is used for inflation because fluids are less compressible in tight strictures. TTS balloons vary in length from 3 to 8 cm although the longer ones (5 to 8 cm) are usually used for the esophagus. Available inflation diameters range from 6 to 20 mm (18 to 54 French). The most recent development in balloon dilation is the controlled radial expansion (CRE) balloons. They each have three different inflation steps that achieve gradated dilation. An in vitro study has shown that the CRE balloons deliver a consistently reproducible and progressively greater dilating force.[19] The three dilation steps are 1 to 1.5 mm apart for all of the CRE balloon sizes. For example, the 6-mm or 18 French balloon achieves 12 French at the first inflation step, 15 French at the second, and 18 French at the final dilation step. The 18-mm balloon has three steps at 16, 17, and 18 mm (48, 51, and 54 French). Advantages for TTS balloons are that dilation can be performed immediately during the endoscopy and that the endoscope can be passed through the stricture following dilation. This facilitates complete endoscopic examination with biopsy and cytology. The major disadvantage of balloons is that they are more expensive and some are relatively fragile.

In bougienage, dilation is accomplished by the radial vector of an axially directed force. In contrast, balloon dilators deliver the entire dilating force radially and simultaneously over the entire length of the stenosis rather than progressively from the proximal to the distal extent. There is less longitudinal shear stress with balloons.[20] For balloons, the radial vector force is that exerted by the circumference of the balloon, and the magnitude of this force is related to the length and curvature of the balloon waist at the onset of dilation. Therefore, the dilating force is greater if the stricture is tighter and longer.[21]

There are relatively few patients studied in randomized trials comparing the efficacy and safety of the different dilator types[22–29] (Table 19–3). Of six randomized controlled studies comparing wire-guided bouginage with balloon dilation, four concluded that wire-guided bougie was modestly better than balloon for reduction of dysphagia; one found that balloon dilation was modestly better than bougie for prevention of recurrence, required fewer sessions, and had less procedural discomfort; and one found no difference with regard to relief of dysphagia or the need for repeat dilation. There appears to be no clear superiority in these various outcome measurements for one technique over another. One study comparing the risk of perforation of Maloneys, wire-guided bouginage, and balloons concluded that Maloney dilation had a greater risk of perforation than the other two techniques.[24] Most endoscopy units have both balloon and wire-guided bougie devices available.

ESOPHAGEAL DILATION TECHNIQUE

Patient preparation should include holding warfarin or correcting coagulation defects before the procedure. Transient bacteremia is common with dilation; thus, high-risk patients should receive antibiotics.[30]

Table 19–3.Comparison of Balloon versus Wire-guided Bougie Dilation

Study	Ref	Number of Patients	Dilators Compared	Outcome
Scolapio et al. (1999)	23	251	Savary vs. 2 balloon types	No difference in immediate or 1 year relief of dysphagia
Cox et al. (1988)	25	65	Savary vs. balloon	Better relief of dysphagia with bougie
Shemesh and Czerniak (1990)	27	60	Savary vs. balloon	Savary slightly more effective
Saeed et al. (1995)	22	34	Savary vs. balloon	Balloon slightly better for prevention of recurrence, less procedure discomfort, and required fewer treatment sessions
Tytgat (1989)	26	60	Savary vs. balloon	Bougie modestly better than balloon for relief of dysphagia
Tulman (1981)	29	93	Balloon vs. Celestin and Eder-Puestow	Bougie modestly better for relief of dysphagia and maintenance of patency

There is no clear consensus on the optimal size to which a peptic stricture should be dilated. Dysphagia appears to occur when the esophagus is narrowed below 13 mm (39 French). Most series report dilation to gauge diameters between 40 and 60 French with good relief of symptoms and very low complication rates.[31,32] Although no study has documented a higher perforation risk with larger dilator sizes, it is generally assumed that little therapeutic benefit exists with dilation greater than 50 to 54 French, and the possibility of increased risk exists.

When dilating a stricture with bougies, the initial dilator size chosen should approximately equal the estimated stricture diameter. It has been recommended that the stepwise increase in bougie size should be not more than three sizes above that at which significant resistance is felt, the "rule of threes." There are no studies to validate that adherence to this rule increases safety of the procedure. Clearly reported series of patients treated by balloon dilation often use balloons diameters that are larger than the rule of threes. Also, in a large series of more than 400 patients in which multiple dilators or a single large dilator (≥45 French) was passed in a single session with only one perforation observed.[33] However, given the risks of perforation and hemorrhage, it seems prudent to not try to accomplish too much dilation in a single setting. Patients can be brought back in 1 to 2 weeks for repeat sessions to achieve an adequate dilation.

COMPLICATIONS OF ESOPHAGEAL DILATION

The major complications of esophageal dilation are perforation and bleeding. Although there is considerable variation in the studies available, the overall serious complication rate appears to be 0.5% with perforation and bleeding approximately equal in frequency.[34,35] It has been suggested that "blind" Maloney dilation has a higher perforation rate than wire-guided bougie.[24] However, if wire-guided techniques are reserved for the tighter, longer, more difficult strictures, they may actually show more complications. Perforation usually is obvious with the patient exhibiting distress and in pain. Subcutaneous emphysema may not develop quickly. A chest x-ray and water-soluble x-ray contrast swallow examination should be performed if perforation is suspected. Surgical consultation is mandatory although many confined perforations have been managed conservatively with no oral intake and intravenous antibiotics. Bleeding severe enough to require transfusions often leads to a

repeat endoscopy to determine if endoscopic therapy is required, although most bleeding from esophageal tears stops spontaneously.

Transient bacteremia frequently complicates esophageal dilation. Studies of blood cultures periprocedure suggest that bacteremia occurs in 20% to 45% of cases.[36,37] Despite this high frequency of bacteremia, infectious complications have rarely been reported.[38,39] Antibiotic prophylaxis is currently recommended for stricture dilation in patients with high-risk conditions, such as prosthetic valves, a history of endocarditis, systemic-pulmonary shunt, or a synthetic vascular graft (<1 year old). There are insufficient data to make a firm recommendation for patients with intermediate-risk conditions such mitral valve prolapse with insufficiency, rheumatic valvular dysfunction, hypertropic cardiomyopathy, or congenital cardiac malformations or for patients with low-risk conditions such as cirrhosis and ascites.[40] However, many clinicians use antibiotic prophylaxis for dilation therapy for any level of patient risk.

STRICTURE RECURRENCE

Before proton pump inhibitors were available, approximately 60% of patients required repeat dilations for recurrent dysphagia.[41,42] With proton pump inhibitor therapy, as few as 30% of patients with peptic strictures require repeat dilations within 1 year.[43] Neither the severity of the initial stricture nor the size of the dilator used appears to have an influence on the likelihood of stricture recurrence.[44]

The technique of self-bougienage can be taught to patients who require very frequent esophageal dilation despite intensive medical therapy and for whom surgery is either contraindicated or unacceptable. There are very limited published data on self-bougienage, but it appears to be both safe and effective.[45] Given the efficacy of proton pump inhibitors, self-bougienage may be primarily of historical interest.

RECALCITRANT ESOPHAGEAL STRICTURES

Refractory strictures are more commonly due to corrosive injury or surgical anastomoses than peptic etiology.[46-48] Steroid injection has been recommended for refractory benign esophageal strictures.[49,50] Using a 23-gauge sclerotherapy needle, four to six aliquots of 0.25 mL of triamcinolone acetonide (10 mg/mL) are injected into the proximal edge of the stricture and into the strictured segment immediately prior to dilation. A study of 14 patients with corrosive strictures showed a marked decrease in the dilation requirement compared with their own historical control.[51] Similar success has been reported in a series of 31 patients with strictures resulting from a variety of causes including 12 patients with peptic etiology and 8 postsurgical anastomotic strictures, radiation therapy induced, pill-induced, and sclerotherapy-induced strictures. Intralesional steroid injection led to a significant reduction in the number of dilation sessions in all subjects.[50] Although there are no controlled or randomized studies available, given the safety of steroid injection, it is reasonable to try this therapy in the uncommon patient refractory to standard dilation and medical therapy.

Another endoscopic treatment that has recently been reported in the treatment of benign anastomotic esophageal stenosis is the use of electrocautery.[52] Six radial incisions, each about 2 to 3 mm long, are made using a needle knife sphincterotome. None of these patients had undergone previous dilation with bougies or balloons.

Surgical treatment of refractory strictures is another alternative. There are two major approaches: (1) antireflux surgery with intraoperative stricture dilation and (2) esophageal reconstruction such as a gastric pull through or colonic interposition. For peptic strictures that are associated with esophageal shortening, a lengthening procedure such as a Collis gastroplasty may be needed in addition to the antireflux surgery. Comparison of surgical treatment for peptic strictures by antireflux surgery and intraoperative dilation versus nonsurgical therapy show similar success rates.[53,54] The major advantage to surgery is the decreased need for long-term medical therapy. However, with long-term follow-up, most patients have reinstituted antireflux medications regularly.[55] One difficult subset of esophageal peptic stricture patients is those with esophageal motility disorders such as scleroderma. The abnormal esophageal motor function and mechanical obstruction caused by fundoplication can result in significant postoperative dysphagia, although there are reports of scleroderma patients with excellent surgical outcomes.[56] For severe strictures, often not resulting from peptic etiology, surgical resection and reconstruction is required with the substantially higher morbidity and mortality.

The use of self-expanding metallic stents (SEMS) for the treatment of refractory benign esophageal strictures has been reported.[57] Early success is high, although late complications, primarily stricture above the stents, have been reported.[58,59] In general, SEMS are contraindicated for the treatment of benign strictures because of difficult long-term complications. The recent introduction of silicone-covered plastic expandable endoprosthetics is promising for the remediation of selected strictures.

Esophageal Rings and Webs

Episodic and nonprogressive dysphagia without weight loss is characteristic of an esophageal web or a distal esophageal ring (Schatzki ring). The first episode often occurs during a hurried meal or with alcohol. The patient notes that the food is stuck in the distal esophagus and can often be passed by drinking large quantities of liquids. The offending food is frequently a piece of bread or steak and hence the description "steakhouse syndrome."[60]

ESOPHAGEAL RINGS

The distal esophagus contains two rings, the A and B (Schatzki) rings. The A or muscular ring is the proximal border of the lower esophageal sphincter. It is covered by squamous epithelium and can only very rarely be demonstrated on esophagram. If it is symptomatic, it can be treated by passage of a 50 French bougie or by injection of botulinum toxin.[61]

In contrast, the B ring, otherwise known as the mucosal or Schatzki ring, is very common and is found in 6% to 14% of subjects undergoing barium GI series.[62] It is a thin membrane that has squamous epithelium on its upper surface and columnar epithelium on its lower surface; thus, it demarcates the squamocolumnar junction. It is composed of mucosa and submucosa, and there is no muscularis propria. It is felt that most Schatzki rings are congenital in origin, although a relationship to GERD has been proposed.[63] It remains unclear how many are truly scar tissue caused by acid reflux. Most rings demonstrated at upper endoscopy or on barium esophagrams are asymptomatic. When the esophageal lumen is narrowed to less than or equal to 13 mm, rings can cause solid food dysphagia and food impactions. Rings causing dysphagia are effectively treated by passage of a single large (50 or 54 French) bougie or by a series of dilators of progressively larger diameter. Although passage of a single large dilator is the most popular means of therapy, there are no studies to confirm the superiority of this technique over the gradual dilation typically used for peptic strictures. Repeat dilations are required in most patients with Schatzki rings because 90% have recurrent dysphagia within 3 years. This again raises a question of the relation to acid reflux and the possible benefit of proton pump inhibitors.[64] An alternative treatment for rings is four-quadrant biopsy causing disruption of the ring. In a randomized study comparing this technique with passage of a single 52-French Maloney dilator, there was no difference in efficacy or in durability of response with 12-month follow-up.[65] Electrocautery incision of Schatzki's rings has also been reported.[66,67] A recent study of 11 patients with recurrent dysphagia despite previous large caliber dilation found that the addition of endoscopic incision to the dilation provided a longer dysphagia-free interval compared with repeated bougienage.[68]

ESOPHAGEAL WEBS AND THE "CORRUGATED" ESOPHAGUS

Esophageal webs are one or more thin horizontal membranes of squamous epithelium within the upper and mid esophagus. Unlike rings, they rarely encircle the lumen but protrude from the anterior wall extending laterally but not posteriorly. Webs may be asymptomatic but do cause solid food dysphagia and can present at any age. They are usually fragile membranes responding well to dilation with bougienage after initial rupture by the endoscope[69] (Fig. 19–2). An association between cervical webs and iron deficiency anemia in adults (especially women) has been described as the Plummer-Vinson or Paterson-Kelly syndrome. This has also been associated with celiac sprue. The pathogenesis of this syndrome is unclear.

A syndrome of multiple webs also called "corrugated ringed esophagus" has been described in men who have long-standing dysphagia since childhood. Dilation relieves the dysphagia, although these patients are prone to significant mucosal tears; thus, cautious

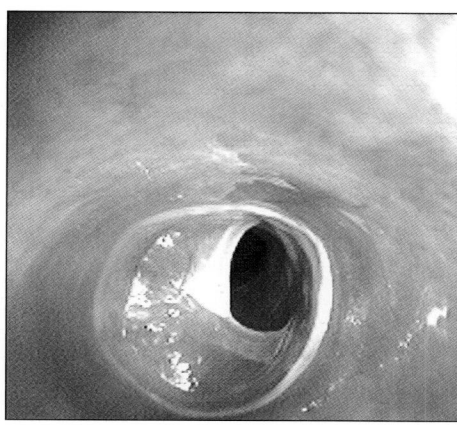

Figure 19–2. Upper esophageal web in a patient with iron deficiency anemia.

dilation has been recommended. Some authorities consider this a form of congenital esophageal stenosis.[70] This condition may be associated with eosinophilic esophagitis in children and adults. It has also been reported that some patients with ringed esophagus have underlying gastroesophageal reflux and may benefit from proton pump therapy.[71]

Gastric, Pyloric, and Small Bowel Strictures

The major question for patients with nonesophageal strictures is the appropriateness of balloon dilation versus surgical therapy. This decision depends on the etiology of the stenosis and the long-term outcome for dilation therapy. When dilation therapy is chosen, most nonesophageal stenoses are best treated with balloon dilation. These can be placed over an endoscopically or radiographically placed wire or passed through the endoscope. Balloons passed through the endoscope (TTS or CRE) have the advantage of allowing completion of the endoscopic examination after dilation and are the most popular. Similar to esophageal balloons, the CRE balloons allow three-step dilation with a single balloon, although the steps are only 1 mm apart and the balloons are significantly more expensive than single-sized TTS balloons. Pyloric (and colonic) balloons are shorter in length than esophageal balloons with usual lengths of 3 to 4 cm. Some experts recommend the use of fluoroscopy and 10% to 25% contrast solution with endoscopic balloons to better assess the bulb apex or C loop wall during inflation.[72] Technical variables such as the duration of balloon insufflation, the frequency and adequacy of dilation, and the size of balloons used have not been standardized. The successful use of Savary Gilliard dilators for obstruction of the distal stomach and duodenal bulb has also been reported in case reports.[73]

CAUSES OF NONESOPHAGEAL UPPER GASTROINTESTINAL TRACT STRICTURES

The most common site for nonesophageal upper gastrointestinal (UGI) tract strictures is at the pylorus, although gastric, anastomotic, and duodenal strictures also occur. Peptic ulcer disease is the most

Table 19–4. Benign Causes of Stomach or Pyloric Stenoses

Peptic ulcer disease (nonsteroidal anti-inflammatory drug (NSAID) > *Helicobacter pylori*)
Postoperative
Corrosive ingestion
Crohn's disease
Radiation therapy

common cause of gastric outlet obstruction, although *Helicobacter pylori* infection is infrequent[74]; a history of nonsteroidal anti-inflammatory drug (NSAID) use is very common. The initial technical failure rate of pyloric dilation, or an "intention to treat" analysis, is not reported in most case series. One report of 46 consecutive patients with benign gastric outlet obstruction had initial technical failure in 5 patients (11%).[75] A second series reported technical failure in 5 out of 54 patients (9.3%).[72] In the patients in whom dilation therapy is technically possible, sustained relief was reported in as few as 16% to 50% of patients[72,76] although most series[77,78] have long-term successful outcomes in 70% of patients. No prospective or controlled studies are available.

Postoperative strictures may occur at any site, including efferent and afferent limb anastomoses in patients with prior Billroth II surgery and at gastric bypass sites for bariatric surgery. A recent report of fluoroscopic balloon dilation of gastric outlet obstruction following surgery for morbid obesity reports 50% of 28 patients experiencing relief of symptoms.[79] A combined use of electro-surgical incision and balloon dilatation has been reported successful in five patients with refractory postoperative pyloric stenosis.[80]

Other causes of stomach or pyloric stenoses include a history of corrosive ingestion, prior radiation therapy, and Crohn's disease (Table 19–4). Three patients with gastric outlet obstruction resulting from prior corrosive ingestion were treated successfully with intralesional steroid injections combined with TTS balloon dilation.[81] There are several reports of balloon dilation for obstructive gastroduodenal Crohn's disease[82–84] (Video 19–1). Initial symptomatic relief occurs although a high rate of recurrence is reported. Repeat dilations may be required if there is a strong interest in avoiding surgery. Long fibrous strictures resulting from Crohn's disease appear less likely to respond to endoscopic treatment.

CONTRAINDICATIONS AND COMPLICATIONS

Contraindications to balloon dilation include deep ulceration at the stenosis or uncorrectable coagulopathy. Although reported series are too small to really assess the risk of active ulceration in the stricture, it is presumed that this does increase the risk of perforation. Perforation rates of 4% to 7.4% have been reported in small case series.[77,72] In one study of 54 patients, two of the four perforations occurred in patients with active ulceration and all four occurred with large balloon diameters (16 and 20 mm).[72]

One frequent adverse outcome reported is ulcer and stricture recurrence. One retrospective review of 19 patients who had undergone balloon dilation for nonmalignant pyloric stenoses with a median follow-up of 45 months found that all patients had immediate symptomatic relief but that only 16% experienced sustained relief.[76] Eighty-four percent of patients had recurrence of symptoms of gastric outlet obstruction with the median time to recurrence being 9 months. NSAID intake was not studied in this relapsed group of patients, although it was noted that recurrence was more likely in women. In another series of 41 patients treated successfully with TTS dilation, only 14 patients (30%) remained disease free at 3 years follow-up.[75] Twenty-one patients required subsequent surgery, 18 for recurrent obstructions, 2 for interval perforations, and 1 for bleeding. These outcomes have led some experts to recommend initial surgical treatment for patients who are good operative candidates. In contrast, prolonged symptom relief is reported successful in up to ⅔ of treated patients, especially if they continue acid suppressive therapy.[77] It seems reasonable to discuss these outcomes and potential complications with patients and to include them in the decision of trying endoscopic dilation treatment before surgery.

Another potential adverse outcome of endoscopic dilation of gastric or duodenal stenoses is the potential for misdiagnosis of malignant obstruction resulting in delay in treatment.[72]

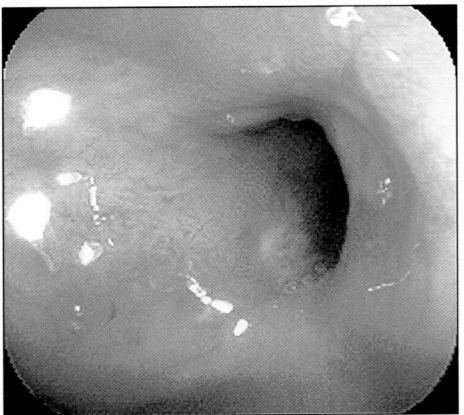

Figure 19–3. Anastomotic ileocolonic stricture in a patient with clinically quiescent Crohn's disease. Two shallow ulcers are present at the stricture.

Benign Colonic and Ileocolonic Strictures

Similar to gastroduodenal strictures, the most important initial treatment decision for colonic and ileocolonic strictures is whether one should attempt balloon dilation or proceed directly to surgical treatment. This decision depends on the etiology of the stricture and the patient's wishes. An important caveat to remember is that only symptomatic strictures require treatment. Many colonic strictures noted at colonoscopy are not causing obstructive symptoms and are best left untreated. TTS balloon dilators are available for use during colonoscopy. They are the same length (3 to 4 cm) as pyloric dilation balloons and indeed are often marketed for both locations being sufficiently long for the colonoscope. Both CRE and TTS balloons are available in the standard 18 to 54 French sizes, although larger "anastomotic" balloons at 20 mm (60 French) and 25 mm (75 French) are also available. There are some data to support a higher clinical success for colonic dilation when balloons of greater diameter than 51 French are used.[85] Radiologically guided balloon dilation has also been reported successful in LGI tract strictures as have polyvinyl over-the-guide wire dilators.[86,87] Case reports using SEMS are available in benign colonic strictures,[88] although this is not routinely recommended because of the long-term patency problems associated with permanent metal stents in the GI tract.[89]

CAUSES OF BENIGN LOWER GASTROINTESTINAL TRACT STRICTURES

The most common site for LGI tract strictures is at surgical anastomoses. Etiologies of benign LGI stenoses include postoperative, Crohn's disease (most of which occur at previous surgical anastomotic sites), diverticular, ischemic, NSAID-related colopathy, and radiation-induced (Table 19–5).

More than 150 patients with Crohn's LGI strictures treated with endoscopic balloon dilation have been reported in case series.[90–94] No controlled studies are available. Most of the strictures occur at previous surgical anastomoses although de novo Crohn's strictures have also been treated (Fig. 19–3). In the one prospective study of

Table 19–5. Benign Causes of Lower Gastrointestinal Stenoses

Surgical anastomoses
Crohn's disease (most often also at anastomoses)
Diverticular disease
Ischemia
Nonsteroidal anti-inflammatory (NSAID) colopathy
Radiation-induced

55 patients submitted to 78 dilation procedures, the procedure was technically successful in 70 (90%).[91] Successful passage of the 13.6-mm diameter colonoscope through the stricture immediately after the dilation occurred in 73% of the dilations. Another large retrospective case series reported that the median number of dilations per patient was one, although many patients did undergo two or three sessions.[92] There are two reports of combined local steroid injection and balloon dilation for a total of 27 patients.[95,96] The response rate from this combined therapy appears similar to other series of balloon dilation alone for Crohn's disease; thus, it is difficult to know if adding local steroid injection improves clinical outcome. Long-term clinical benefit is reported in 41% to 62% of the larger series[91,92] and up to 72% to 80% in some smaller ones.[93,94] Although general anesthesia has been used for some treatments, most patients have conscious sedation. Complications appear to occur infrequently with balloon dilation of Crohn's strictures. Perforation has been the major concern and was reported in 1.6% to 8% of procedures. Colonic perforation usually requires surgical repair; however, this is not a dreaded outcome because surgery in a prepped bowel is the alternative treatment required for failure of treatment. However, the potential for perforation and surgical repair does emphasize the importance of not performing endoscopic dilation unless the LGI stricture is symptomatic.

Balloon dilation treatment of postoperative colorectal anastomotic strictures is reported in more than 120 patients.[85,97–99] None of these are prospective or controlled trials but are case series. Success rates appear to be slightly better than stricture dilation in Crohn's disease, although this may simply be reporting bias. Complications of perforation and bleeding occur in up to 7.8% of patients.[85] Refractory strictures have been treated with a combination of

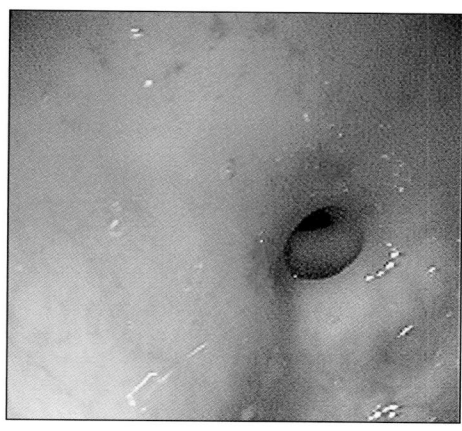

Figure 19–4. Ascending colon stricture resulting from prior nonsteroidal anti-inflammatory drug (NSAID) use.

balloon dilation and endoscopic incision with an electrocautery needle knife (6 patients) or with balloon dilation and endoscopic laser treatment (10 patients).[100,101] The success rate in both of these small series was 80% to 90%.

NSAID colopathy can also lead to colonic strictures, often with a "diaphragm type" appearance.[102–104] These strictures are usually in the right colon and often are not narrow enough to cause obstructive symptoms. However, multiple case reports of successful balloon dilation for tight NSAID strictures are reported as a viable option to surgical resection (Fig. 19–4). Discontinuation of NSAIDs is an important part of therapy.

Radiation-induced colorectal strictures are some of the most challenging stenoses to treat. Surgical management carries a high mortality unless simple bypass with colostomy or ileostomy is performed. For this reason, endoscopic dilation has been attempted with Savary-Gilliard dilators,[105] balloon dilators,[106] and permanent metal stent placement.[107] The decision for the type of treatment for radiation strictures should be made after surgical consultation and careful consideration of patient wishes.

CONTRAINDICATIONS AND COMPLICATIONS: DILATION OF BENIGN COLONIC STRICTURES

Contraindications to an attempt at LGI dilation are coagulopathy, deeply ulcerated strictures, and long strictures. The major complications are bleeding and perforation. An additional adverse outcome is failure to respond to dilation therapy either initially or with frequent relapses.

REFERENCES

1. Spechler SJ: AGA technical review on treatment of patients with dysphagia caused by benign disorders of the distal esophagus. Gastroenterology 117:223–254, 1999.
2. Dakkak M, Hoare RC, Maslin SC, et al: Oesophagitis is as important as oesophageal stricture diameter in determining dysphagia. Gut 34:152–155, 1993.
3. Marks RD, Richter JE, Rizzo H, et al: Omeprazole versus H2-receptor antagonists in treating patients with peptic stricture and esophagitis. Gastroenterology 106:907–915, 1994.
4. Barbezat GO, Schlup M, Lubcke R: Omeprazole therapy decreases the need for dilatation of peptic oesophageal strictures. Aliment Pharmacol Ther 13:1041–1045, 1999.
5. Agnew SR, Pandya SP, Reynolds RP, et al: Predictors for frequent esophageal dilations of benign peptic strictures. Dig Dis Sci 41:931–936, 1996.
6. Broor SL, Kumar A, Chari ST, et al: Corrosive esophageal strictures following acid ingestion: Clinical profile and results of endoscopic dilatation. J Gastroenterol Hepatol 4:56–61, 1989.
7. Wilcox CM: Esophageal strictures complicating ulcerative esophagitis in patients with AIDS. Am J Gastroenterol 94:339–343, 1999.
8. Colina RE, Smith M, Kikendall JW, et al: A new probable increasing cause of esophageal ulceration: Alendronate. Am J Gastroenterol 92:704–706, 1997.
9. Maddern JG, Horowitz M, Jamieson GG, et al: Abnormalities of esophageal and gastric emptying in progressive systemic sclerosis. Gastroenterology 97:922–926, 1984.
10. Stork T, Gareis R, Krumholz K, et al: Aberrant right subclavian artery (arteria lusoria) as a rare cause of dysphagia and dyspnea in a 79 year-old woman with right mediastinal and retrotracheal mass, and co-existing coronary artery disease. Vasa 30:225–228, 2001.
11. Woods RK, Sharp RJ, Holcomb GW 3rd, et al: Vascular anomalies and tracheoesophageal compression: A single institution's 25-year experience. Ann Thorac Surg 72:434–438, 2001.
12. Teitelbaum JE, Fox VL, Twarog FJ, et al: Eosinophilic esophagitis in children: Immunopathological analysis and response to fluticasone propionate. Gastroenterology 122:1216–1225, 2002.
13. Vasilopoulos S, Murphy P, Auerbach A, et al: The small-caliber esophagus: An unappreciated cause of dysphagia for solids in patients with eosinophilic esophagitis. Gastrointest Endosc 55:99–106, 2002.
14. Morrow JB, Vargo JJ, Goldblum JR, et al: The ringed esophagus: Histologic features of GERD. Am J Gastroenterol 96:984–989, 2001.
15. The ASGE Standards of Practice Committee: Balloon dilation of gastrointestinal tract strictures. Gastrointest Endosc 48:702–704, 1998.
16. McClave SA, Brady PG, Wright RA, et al: Does fluoroscopic guidance for Maloney esophageal dilation impact on the clinical endpoint of therapy: Relief of dysphagia and achievement of luminal patency. Gastrointest Endosc 43:93–97, 1996.
17. Tucker LE: The importance of fluoroscopic guidance for Maloney dilation. Am J Gastroenterol 87:1709–1711, 1992.
18. Kozarek RA, Patterson DJ, Ball TJ, et al: Esophageal dilation can be done safely using selective fluoroscopy and single dilation sessions. J Clin Gastroenterol 20:184–188, 1995.
19. Goldstein JA, Barkin JS: Comparison of the diameter consistency and dilating force of the controlled radial expansion balloon catheter to the conventional balloon dilators. Am J Gastroenterol 95:3423–3427, 2000.
20. McLean GK, LeVeen RF: Shear stress in the performance of esophageal dilation: Comparison of balloon dilation and bougienage. Radiology 172:983–986, 1989.
21. Abele JE: The physics of esophageal dilatation. Hepatogastroenterology 39:486–489, 1992.
22. Saeed ZA, Winchester CB, Ferro PS, et al: Prospective randomized comparison of polyvinyl bougies and through-the-scope balloons for dilation of peptic strictures of the esophagus. Gastrointest Endosc 41:189–195, 1995.
23. Scolapio JS, Pasha TM, Gostout CJ, et al: A randomized prospective study comparing rigid to balloon dilators for benign esophageal strictures and rings. Gastrointest Endosc 50:13–17, 1999.
24. Hernandez LJ, Jacobson JW, Harris MS: Comparison among the perforation rates of Maloney, balloon, and Savary dilation of esophageal strictures. Gastrointest Endosc 51:460–462, 2000.
25. Cox JG, Winter RK, Maslin SC, et al: Balloon or bougie for dilatation of benign oesophageal stricture? An interim report of a randomised controlled trial. Gut 29:1741–1747, 1988.

26. Tytgat GN: Dilation therapy of benign esophageal stenoses. World J Surg 13:142–148, 1989.

27. Shemesh E, Czerniak A: Comparison between Savary-Gilliard and balloon dilatation of benign esophageal strictures. World J Surg 14:518–521, 1990.

28. Yamamoto H, Hughes RW Jr, Schroeder KW, et al: Treatment of benign esophageal stricture by Eder-Puestow or balloon dilators: A comparison between randomized and prospective nonrandomized trials. Mayo Clin Proc 67:228–236, 1992.

29. Tulman AB, Boyce HW Jr: Complications of esophageal dilation and guidelines for their prevention. Gastrointest Endosc 27:229–234, 1981.

30. Bautista-Casanovas A, Varela-Cives R, Estevez Martinez E, et al: What is the infection risk of oesophageal dilatations? Eur J Pediatr 157:901–903, 1998.

31. Pereira-Lima JC, Ramires RP, Zamin I Jr, et al: Endoscopic dilation of benign esophageal strictures: Report on 1043 procedures. Am J Gastroenterol 94:1497–1501, 1999.

32. Dumon JF, Meric B, Sivak MV Jr, et al: A new method of esophageal dilation using Savary-Gilliard bougies. Gastrointest Endosc 31:379–382, 1985.

33. Kozarek RA, Patterson DJ, Ball TJ, et al: Esophageal dilation can be done safely using selective fluoroscopy and single dilating sessions. J Clin Gastroenterol 20:184–188, 1995.

34. Silvis SE, Nebel O, Rogers G, et al: Endoscopic complications. Results of the 1974 American Society for Gastrointestinal Endoscopy surgery. JAMA 235:928–930, 1976.

35. Kozarek RA: Hydrostatic balloon dilation of gastrointestinal stenoses: A national survey. Gastrointest Endosc 32:15–19, 1986.

36. Botoman VA, Surawicz CM: Bacteremia with gastrointestinal endoscopic procedures. Gastrointest Endosc 32:342–346, 1986.

37. Nelson DB, Sanderson SJ, Azar MM: Bacteremia with esophageal dilation. Gastrointest Endosc 48:563–567, 1948.

38. Yin TP, Dellipiani AW: Bacterial endocarditis after Hurst bougienage in a patient with a benign oesophageal stricture. Endoscopy 15:27–28, 1983.

39. Schlitt M, Mitchem L, Zorn G, et al: Brain abscess after esophageal dilation for caustic stricture: Report of three cases. Neurosurgery 17:947–951, 1985.

40. ASGE Standard of Practice Committee: Antibiotic prophylaxis for gastrointestinal endoscopy. Gastrointest Endosc 42:630–635, 1995.

41. Ogilvie AL, Ferguson R, Atkinson M: Outlook with conservative treatment of peptic oesophageal stricture. Gut 21:23–25, 1980.

42. Hands LJ, Papavramidis S, Bishop H, et al: The natural history of peptic oesophageal stricture treated by dilation and anti-reflux therapy alone. Ann R Coll Surg Engl 71:306–309, 1989.

43. Smith PM, Kerr GD, Cockel R, et al: A comparison of omeprazole and ranitidine in the prevention of recurrence of benign esophageal stricture. Gastroenterology 107:1312–1318, 1994.

44. Agnew SR, Pandya SP, Reynolds RP, et al: Predictors for frequent esophageal dilations of benign peptic strictures. Dig Dis Sci 41:931–936, 1996.

45. Grobe JL, Kozarek RA, Sanowski RA: Self-bougienage in the treatment of benign esophageal strictures. J Clin Gastroenterol 6:109–112, 1984.

46. Duseja A, Chawla YK, Singh RP, et al: Dilatation of benign esophageal strictures: 10 year's experience with Celestin dilators. J Gastroenterol Hepatol 15:26–29, 2000.

47. Lahoti D, Broor SL, Basu PP, et al: Corrosive esophageal strictures: Predictors of response to endoscopic dilation. Gastrointest Endosc 41:196–200, 1995.

48. Ikeya T, Ohwada S, Ogawa T, et al: Endoscopic balloon dilation for benign esophageal anastomotic stricture: Factors influencing its effectiveness. Hepato Gastroenterol 46:959–966, 1999.

49. Zein NN, Greseth JM, Perrault J: Endoscopic intralesional steroid injections in the management of refractory esophageal strictures. Gastrointest Endosc 41:596–598, 1995.

50. Lee M, Kubik CM, Polhamus CD, et al: Preliminary experience with endoscopic intralesional steroid injection therapy for refractory upper gastrointestinal strictures. Gastrointest Endosc 41:598–601, 1995.

51. Kochhar R, Ray JD, Sriram PV, et al: Intralesional steroids augment the effects of endoscopic dilation in corrosive esophageal strictures. Gastrointest Endosc 49:509–513, 1999.

52. Brandimarte G, Tursi A: Endoscopic treatment of benign anastomotic esophageal stenosis with electrocautery. Endoscopy 34:399–401, 2002.

53. Little AG, Naunheim KS, Ferguson MK, et al: Surgical management of esophageal strictures. Ann Thorac Surg 45:144–147, 1988.

54. Spechler SL: Comparison of medical and surgical therapy for complicated gastroesophageal reflux disease in veterans. N Engl J Med 326:786–792, 1992.

55. Spechler SJ, Lee E, Ahnen D, et al: Long-term outcome of medical and surgical therapies for gastroesophageal reflux disease: Follow-up of a randomized controlled trial. JAMA 285:2331–2338, 2001.

56. Poirier NC, Taillerfer R, Topart R, et al: Antireflux operations in patients with scleroderma. Ann Thorac Surg 58:66–72, 1994.

57. Fiorini A, Fleischer D, Valero J, et al: Self-expanding metal coil stents in the treatment of benign esophageal strictures refractory to conventional therapy: A case series. Gastrointest Endosc 52:259–262, 2000.

58. Ackroyd R, Watson DI, Devitt PG, et al: Expandable metallic stents should not be used in the treatment of benign esophageal strictures. J Gastroenterol Hepatol 16:484–487, 2001.

59. Lee JG, Hsu R, Leung JW: Are self-expanding metal mesh stents useful in the treatment of benign esophageal stenoses and fistulas? An experience of four cases. Am J Gastroenterol 95:1857–1859, 2000.

60. DeVault KR: Lower esophageal (Schatzki's) ring: Pathogenesis, diagnosis, and therapy. Dig Dis 14:323–329, 1996.

61. Hirano I, Gilliam J, Goyal RK: Clinical and manometric features of the lower esophageal muscular ring. Am J Gastroenterol 95:43–49, 2000.

62. Johnson AC, Lester DD, Johnson S, et al: Esophagogastric ring: Why and when we see it, and what it implies: A radiologic-pathologic correlation. South Med J 85:946–952, 1992.

63. Marshall JB, Kretschmar JM, Diaz-Arias AA: Gastroesophageal reflux as a pathogenic factor in the development of symptomatic lower esophageal rings. Arch Intern Med 150:1669–1672, 1990.

64. Jamieson H, Hinder RA, DeMeester TR, et al: Analysis of thirty-two patients with Schatzki's ring. Am J Surg 158:563–566, 1989.

65. Chotiprasidhi P, Minocha A: Effectiveness of single dilation with Maloney dilator versus endoscopic rupture of Schatzki ring using biopsy forceps. Dig Dis Sci 45:281–284, 2000.

66. Guelrud M, Villasmil L, Mendez R: Late results in patients with Schatzki ring treated by endoscopic electrosurgical incision of the ring. Gastrointest Endosc 33:96–98, 1987.

67. Burdick JS, Venu RP, Hogan WJ: Cutting the defiant lower esophageal ring. Gastrointest Endosc 39:616–619, 1993.

68. DiSario JA, Pedersen PJ, Bichis-Canoutas C, et al: Incision of recurrent distal esophageal (Schatzki) ring after dilation. Gastrointest Endosc 56:244–248, 2002.

69. Sreenivas DV, Kumar A, Mannar KV, et al: Results of Savary-Gilliard dilatation in the management of cervical web of esophagus. Hepatogastroenterology 49:188–190, 2002.

70. Oh CH, Levine MS, Katzka DA, et al: Congenital esophageal stenosis in adults: Clinical and radiographic findings in seven patients. Am J Roentgenol 176:1179–1182, 2001.

71. Morrow JB, Vargo JJ, Goldblum JR, et al: The ringed esophagus: Histological features of GERD. Am J Gastroenterol 96:984–989, 2001.

72. Lau JY, Chung SC, Sung JJ, et al: Through-the-scope balloon dilation for pyloric stenosis: Long-term results. Gastrointest Endosc 43:98–101, 1996.

73. Pai CG: Use of Savary-Gilliard dilators for strictures of the distal stomach and duodenal bulb. Gastrointest Endosc 50:866–867, 1999.

74. Gibson JB, Behrman SW, Fabian TC, et al: Gastric outlet obstruction resulting from peptic ulcer disease requiring surgical intervention is infrequently associated with Helicobacter pylori infection. J Am Coll Surg 191:32–37, 2000.

75. Hewitt PM, Krige JE, Funnell IC, et al: Endoscopic balloon dilatation of peptic pyloroduodenal strictures. J Clin Gastroenterol 28:33–35, 1999.

76. Kuwada SK, Alexander GL: Long-term outcome of endoscopic dilation of nonmalignant pyloric stenosis. Gastrointest Endosc 41:15–17, 1995.

77. Kozarek RA, Botoman VA, Patterson DJ: Long-term follow-up in patients who have undergone balloon dilation for gastric outlet obstruction. Gastrointest Endosc 36:558–561, 1990.

78. Boylan JJ, Gradzka MI: Long-term results of endoscopic balloon dilatation for gastric outlet obstruction. Dig Dis Sci 44:1883–1886, 1999.

79. Vance PL, deLange EE, Shaffer HA Jr, et al: Gastric outlet obstruction following surgery for morbid obesity: Efficacy of fluoroscopically guided balloon dilation. Radiology 222:70–72, 2002.

80. Hagiwara A, Sonoyama Y, Togawa T, et al: Combined use of electrosurgical incisions and balloon dilatation for the treatment of refractory postoperative pyloric stenosis. Gastrointest Endosc 54:504–508, 2001.

81. Kochhar R, Sriram PV, Ray JD, et al: Intralesional steroid injections for corrosive induced pyloric stenosis. Endoscopy 30:734–736, 1998.

82. Kelly SM, Hunter JO: Endoscopic balloon dilatation of duodenal strictures in Crohn's disease. Postgrad Med J 71:623–624, 1995.

83. Matsui T, Hatakeyama S, Ikeda K, et al: Long-term outcome of endoscopic balloon dilation in obstructive gastroduodenal Crohn's disease. Endoscopy 29:640–645, 1997.

84. Kimura H, Sugita A, Nishiyama K, et al: Treatment of duodenal Crohn's disease with stenosis: Case report of 6 cases. Jpn J Gastroenterol 97:697–702, 2000.

85. Kozarek RA: Hydrostatic balloon dilation of gastrointestinal stenoses: A national survey. Gastrointest Endosc 32:15–19, 1986.

86. McNicholas MM, Gibney RG, MacErlaine DP: Radiologically guided balloon dilatation of obstructing gastrointestinal strictures. Abdom Imaging 19:102–107, 1994.

87. Morini S, Hassan C, Cerro P, et al: Management of an ileocolonic anastomotic stricture using polyvinyl over-the-guidewire dilators in Crohn's disease. Gastrointest Endosc 53:384–387, 2001.

88. Cascales-Sanchez P, Garcia-Olmo D, Julia-Molla E: Long-term expandable stent as a definitive treatment for benign rectal stenosis. Br J Surg 84:840–841, 1997.

89. Kozarek RA, Ball TJ, Patterson DJ: Metallic self-expanding stent application in the upper gastroesophageal tract: Caveats and concerns. Gastrointest Endosc 38:1–6, 1992.

90. Breysem Y, Coremans G, Hendrickx G: Endoscopic balloon dilation of colonic and ileo-colonic Crohn's strictures: Long-term results. Gastrointest Endosc 38:142–147, 1992.

91. Couckuyt H, Gevers AM, Coremans G, et al: Efficacy and safety of hydrostatic balloon dilatation of ileocolonic Crohn's strictures: A prospective longterm analysis. Gut 36:577–580, 1995.

92. Thomas-Gibson S, Brooker JC, Hayward CM, et al: Colonoscopic balloon dilation of Crohn's strictures: A review of long-term outcomes. Eur J Gastroenterol Hepatol 15:485–488, 2003.

93. Dear KL, Hunter JO: Colonoscopic hydrostatic balloon dilatation of Crohn's strictures. J Clin Gastroenterol 33:315–318, 2001.

94. Williams AJ, Palmer KR: Endoscopic balloon dilatation as a therapeutic option in the management of intestinal stricture resulting from Crohn's disease. Br J Surg 78:453–454, 1991.

95. Brooker JC, Beckett CG, Saunders BP, et al: Long-acting steroid injection after endoscopic dilation of anastomotic Crohn's strictures may improve the outcome: A retrospective case series. Endoscopy 35:333–337, 2003.

96. Ramboer C, Verhamme M, Dhondt E, et al: Endoscopic treatment of stenosis in recurrent Crohn's disease with balloon dilation combined with local corticosteroid injection. Gastrointest Endosc 42:252–255, 1995.

97. Venkatesh KS, Ramanujam PS, McGee S: Hydrostatic balloon dilatation of benign colonic anastomotic strictures. Dis Colon Rectum 35:789–791, 1992.

98. Skreden K, Wiig JN, Myrvold HE: Balloon dilation of rectal strictures. Acta Chir Scand 153:615–617, 1987.

99. Aston NO, Owen WJ, Irving JD: Endoscopic balloon dilatation of colonic anastomotic strictures. Br J Surg 76:780–782, 1989.

100. Hagiwara A, Togawa T, Yamasaki J, et al: Endoscopic incision and balloon dilatation for cicatricial anastomotic strictures. Hepatogastroenterology 46:997–999, 1999.

101. Luck A, Chapius P, Sinclair G, et al: Endoscopic laser stricturotomy and balloon dilatation for benign colorectal strictures. ANZ J Surg 71:594–597, 2001.

102. Gopal DV, Katon RM: Endoscopic balloon dilation of multiple NSAID-induced colonic strictures: Case report and review of the literature on NSAID-related colopathy. Gastrointest Endosc 50:120–123, 1999.

103. Weinstock LB, Hammoud Z, Brandwin L: Nonsteroidal anti-inflammatory drug-induced colonic stricture and ulceration treated with balloon dilatation and prednisone. Gastrointest Endosc 50:564–566, 1999.

104. Smith JA, Pineau BC: Endoscopic therapy of NSAID-induced colonic diaphragm disease: Two cases and a review of published reports. Gastrointest Endosc 52:120–125, 2000.

105. Triadafilopoulos G, Sarkisian M: Dilatation of radiation-induced sigmoid stricture using sequential Savary-Gilliard dilators. A combined radiologic-endoscopic approach. Dis Colon Rectum 33:1065–1067, 1990.

106. Johansson C: Endoscopic dilation of rectal strictures: A prospective study of 18 cases. Dis Colon Rectum 39:423–428, 1996.

107. Yates MR, Baron TH: Treatment of a radiation–induced sigmoid stricture with an expandable metal stent. Gastrointest Endosc 50:422–426, 1999.

Achalasia

David A. Katzka and David C. Metz

Introduction

Achalasia is a relatively rare disease affecting both sexes and involving all races. It was described centuries ago; however, perhaps because of its relative rarity, little is known about its cause. Similarly, there are still questions concerning the etiology, diagnosis, and management of achalasia. These include such basic questions as (1) what is the gold standard for the diagnosis of achalasia, (2) what is the best treatment algorithm for the condition, and (3) by what criteria should we follow patients to determine whether treatment has been successful? This chapter attempts to provide an in-depth review of achalasia and to provide a practical approach to these questions or at least to determine why they may still not be answerable at this time!

Etiology

The etiology of achalasia is unknown, but a good theoretical construct that might explain the sequence of events is as follows. An external source of injury (infectious or otherwise) occurs in a genetically susceptible individual. This injury triggers an auto-immune response, which in turn causes chronic damage to intra-mural esophageal and lower esophageal sphincter (LES) neurons possibly including central vagus nerve connections. The chronic neural damage results in depletion of all nerve elements, but there is a relatively greater loss of inhibitory nerve control of the LES, specifically, nitric oxide synthase, thereby leaving a net increased stimulatory effect on LES function. This overall stimulatory effect causes incomplete LES relaxation and hypertonicity (i.e., spasm) of the sphincter. The neural dysfunction also causes a relative and often complete hypotonia of the esophageal body, but whether this is primarily from nerve injury or secondary to chronic functional obstruction of the LES is unknown. With ongoing injury, secondary inflammation supervenes leading to neural destruction and fibrotic replacement with worsening LES dysfunction and esophageal hypotonia (i.e., loss of peristalsis). The result is progressive esophageal dilatation worsening dysmotility and esophageal failure. Figure 20–1 illustrates the putative events in the development of achalasia.

Extensive experimental data support this hypothesis. First, the neurotropic virus, varicella zoster (but not herpes simplex 1 or cytomegalovirus), has been detected by *in situ* hybridization in cardiomyotomy specimens from achalasia patients.[1] In addition, Chagas' disease, a disease caused by *Trypanosoma cruzi*, a protozoan that is endemic in Central and South America, causes esophageal disease that may be indistinguishable from achalasia on manometric and radiographic grounds as a consequence of denervation of Auerbach's plexus.[2] Second, certain investigators have demonstrated an association between white subjects with achalasia and the class II human leukocyte antigen (HLA) DQ1.[3] In fact, this genetic relationship has been characterized more specifically as an association with the DQB1*0602 and DRB1*15 HLA alleles.[4] Third, antimyenteric[5] and antimuscarinic cholinergic receptor autoantibodies[6] have been detected in patients with achalasia. Fourth, studies of surgical specimens from patients with achalasia have demonstrated a chronic inflammatory infiltrate leading to ganglionic destruction and fibrosis.[7-11] Fifth, vagal dysfunction has been demonstrated both in natural and experimental animal models of achalasia.[12,13] Sixth, a selective deficiency of nitric oxide synthase, the predominant inhibitory neurotransmitter of the LES, has been demonstrated in both animal models and patients with achalasia.[14,15] Seventh, patients with less advanced forms of achalasia (from both a clinical and radiographic point of view) have more inflammation and less fibrosis in the ganglia of the LES than do patients with more advanced forms of the disease,[10,16] suggesting that LES basal and residual tone may increase and esophageal body function deteriorates as the disease progresses.[17] Clearly, much more data are needed to prove this hypothesis. The data referred to were generated from a relatively small number of patients, given the rarity of the disease. Furthermore, the abnormalities described are rarely identified in all patients with achalasia. For example, only three of nine patients had detectable varicella zoster in the myenteric plexus[1] and only 7 of 18 had antimyenteric neuronal

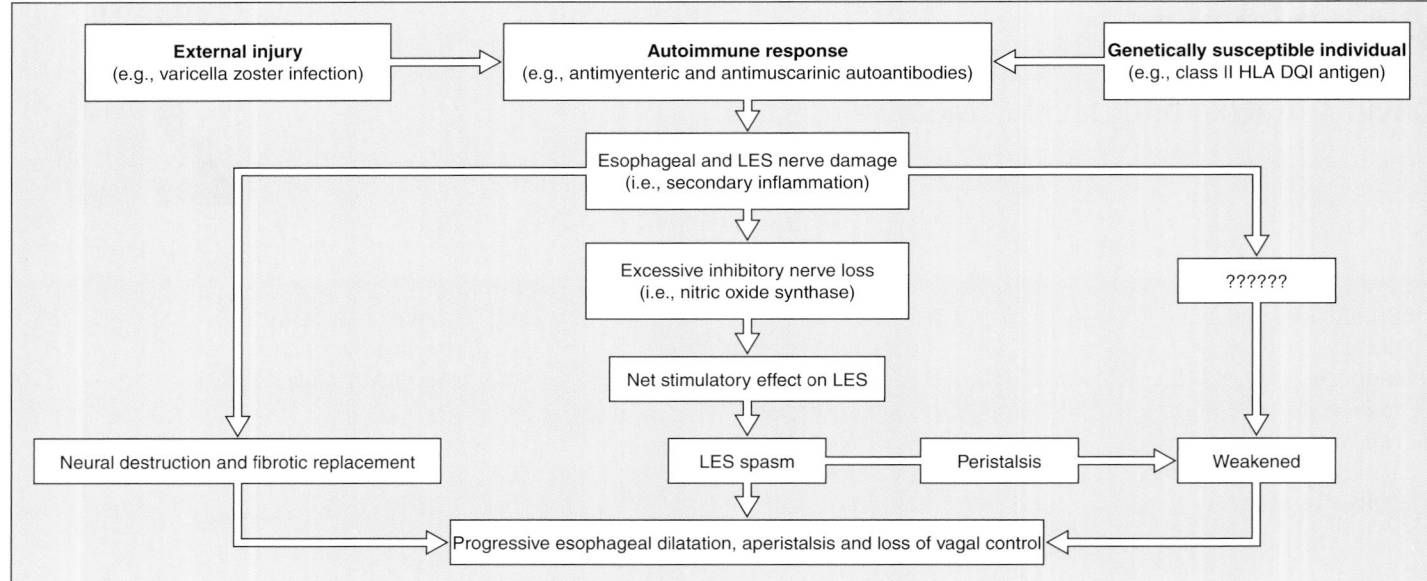

Figure 20–1. Putative etiology of achalasia.

antibodies.[4] Still, these preliminary findings are encouraging, particularly because the general theory proposed here may apply to other gastrointestinal disease states in addition to achalasia (e.g., chronic idiopathic pseudoobstruction).

Diagnosis

The diagnosis of achalasia is based on clinical, radiologic, and manometric criteria because the pathologic equivalent is still being studied. In addition, pathologic specimens are not routinely accessible except after cardiomyotomy in which case, hopefully, the diagnosis has already been made! Occasionally, the radiologic appearance (usually with barium swallow but occasionally with computed tomography [CT] scanning or routine chest x-ray film) or manometric tracing alone may be diagnostic of achalasia (in patients presenting with a compatible clinical syndrome). However, in most patients, the diagnosis is based on a constellation of findings using all three criteria.

SYMPTOMS

The hallmark symptoms of achalasia are dysphagia, chest pain, and regurgitation (Table 20–1). Indeed, various series of patients with achalasia have reported dysphagia in 82% to 100% of cases, chest pain in 17% to 95%, and regurgitation in 59% to 81%.[18–23] Dysphagia occurs typically for both solids and liquids, but, often, solid food dysphagia precedes liquid dysphagia. Some patients with early disease describe the need to "wash down their food with water," which possibly affords relief by raising a sufficient head of pressure above to overcome the LES spasm below. In others, there may be superimposed acute episodes of solid food dysphagia in which patients present with symptoms suggestive of food impaction that resolve spontaneously or are severe enough to warrant endoscopic removal. Chest pain often occurs during ingestion and may signify

Table 20–1. Symptoms of Achalasia

Major Symptoms	Frequency (%)*
Dysphagia	82–100
Chest pain	17–95
Regurgitation	59–81
Weight loss	32

Minor Symptoms
Slow eating
Stereotypical maneuvers during eating
Halitosis
Heartburn
Accumulation of oral debris at night
Staining of the pillow during sleep
Nocturnal coughing or choking
Acute airway obstruction
Inability to belch
Postprandial syncope
Dental caries
Asthma
Pneumonia

See text for references.

food impaction. However, a spasm-like chest pain that may mimic gastroesophageal reflux disease (i.e., heartburn) or cardiac pain (i.e., angina) may also occur spontaneously. The origin of the chest pain is generally unclear and it may be somewhat independent of the mechanisms that cause dysphagia and regurgitation. This is suggested by data demonstrating that chest pain commonly persists after achalasia treatment that is effective for the other two major symptoms.[23] Regurgitation may occur from minutes to hours after ingestion of a meal. Indeed, patients may even identify food in the regurgitant that they ingested many days before. Patients with severe disease may not even be able to drink a glass of water without regurgitating. The nature of the regurgitant may be useful to differentiate achalasia from gastroesophageal reflux disease. In achalasia, the regurgitant is typically described as non-sour or non-bitter and patients may mention that it "tastes just like it did when it was initially swallowed." Because of the difficulty with eating, weight loss is also a common feature of achalasia; seen in 32% of patients in one recent study.[24] In our experience, a careful history emphasizing and dissecting the major symptoms of dysphagia, chest pain, regurgitation, and weight loss can be quite specific for the diagnosis of achalasia, although we are constantly surprised by the varied patterns of presentation of this unusual disease.

As with many chronic disease states in which life-threatening consequences are rare and take months to years to develop, achalasia is a disease that lends itself to self-accommodation on the part of the patient. Behavioral adaptation may lead to the emergence of a whole host of subtle compensatory symptoms accompanied by denial or de-emphasis of the more classic symptoms described previously (see Table 20–1). For example, one recent study[24] elicited numerous compensatory symptoms including slow eating and other stereotypical maneuvers to aid swallowing such as walking, standing, sitting straight up, or arching of the neck during swallowing. Potential patients should also be interviewed about other subtle symptoms including halitosis, heartburn, accumulation of oral debris or staining of the pillow during sleep, nocturnal coughing or choking, acute airway obstruction,[25,26] an inability to belch because of upper esophageal sphincter dysfunction,[27,28] and even postprandial syncope.[29] Heartburn, the cardinal symptom of gastroesophageal reflux, is particularly important because its presence is often erroneously felt to be a strong negative indicator of achalasia. Although unproved, the sensation may be a consequence of bacterial fermentation of retained ingested foodstuff leading to lowering of the esophageal luminal pH. Other important symptoms often erroneously ascribed to gastroesophageal reflux disease include the presence of dental caries (from food bathing the teeth at night), asthma, and a history of pneumonia (presumably from micro-aspiration). In fact, accurately differentiating between gastroesophageal reflux disease and achalasia by history alone may be surprisingly difficult, given that the two diseases represent completely opposite ends of the pathophysiologic spectrum.

RADIOGRAPHY

Achalasia may be suspected on routine chest x-ray film (particularly a lateral view) by the presence of an air-fluid level and/or a dilated esophagus. However, barium swallow is the most reliable radiographic method for making the diagnosis (Fig. 20–2). The pathognomonic findings include a smooth tapered narrowing of the gastroesophageal junction (the so-called bird's beak appearance) with a proximally dilated esophagus that may be filled with fluid or food debris. Features of candidal infection, a consequence of long-standing esophageal stasis, may also be present. However, on this basic template, there is remarkable heterogeneity. The degree of esophageal dilatation may vary from minimal to massive and end-stage disease may reveal sigmoidization of the esophagus. Similarly, the diameter of the gastroesophageal junction may range from less than 1 mm to greater than 8 mm. Radiographs may also demonstrate single or multiple distal esophageal diverticula of varying size or a corkscrew or "spastic" appearance with several simultaneous lumen-obliterating contractions (some term this vigorous achalasia). To

assess and characterize these esophageal radiographic findings, various scoring systems have been devised.[18,24] However, although these scoring systems help to standardize interpretation of radiographic appearance, which may be useful from a research point of view, it is important to note that there is generally very poor correlation between symptom severity and radiographic score.[24] This limitation is further discussed in the treatment section.

Finally, there has been an old tenet in esophagology that a hiatal hernia is unusual in achalasia.[30] More recent data have questioned this dictum demonstrating the presence of a hiatal hernia in 10 of 71 radiographs reviewed from patients with achalasia (14.5%) as compared with 9 of 35 patients (25.7%) aged 51 years or older, a frequency that is similar to the normal population.[31] This makes intuitive sense because achalasia may develop at any age, sometimes in the presence of long-standing gastroesophageal reflux disease with a hiatal hernia that preceded the development of the achalasia. Perhaps, older studies may have suffered from either underdiagnosis of hiatal hernia or overenrollment of younger patients.

ESOPHAGEAL MANOMETRY

In the absence of a true gold standard, manometry is the single best test for the diagnosis of achalasia (Fig. 20–3). However, the manometric diagnosis of achalasia has undergone great revision in recent years. Whereas classic teaching requires the presence of a hypertensive LES with incomplete relaxation (i.e., an increased residual pressure) and esophageal body aperistalsis, it is now clear that these classic criteria do not occur in all patients. Part of the reason for this reevaluation has come from prolonged combined ambulatory pH and manometric recordings in which peristaltic contractions, complete LES relaxation, and even acid reflux may be demonstrated intermittently in patients who otherwise fulfill the classic criteria on stationary manometry.[32] As a result, it now seems conceivable that "normal" manometric findings might occur on stationary manometry as well in achalasia patients, depending on the timing of the study. Toward this end, Hirano and coworkers[33] in their study of 58 patients with achalasia recently proposed a manometric heterogeneity in patients with achalasia including features such as a normal basal LES pressure, normal residual pressures, high-amplitude contractions, varying lengths of aperistalsis, and even the presence of transient LES relaxations (the hallmark of gastroesophageal reflux disease). Of course, in interpreting this important study, one might wonder what the gold standard for the diagnosis of achalasia was in these "atypical" patients. This study again demonstrates the importance of making the diagnosis of achalasia based on a combination of compatible clinical, radiographic, and manometric findings in a specific patient rather than routinely relying on classic criteria. Similarly, Vantrappen and coworkers,[34] in their landmark paper proposed that diffuse esophageal spasm is in itself one end of the spectrum of achalasia. After this lead, several case reports have now demonstrated spasm-type manometric (and perhaps radiographic) findings either as a component of established achalasia or as an early manifestation of dysmotility that may evolve into achalasia in due course.[35,36] Currently, many esophagologists consider diffuse esophageal spasm a true variant of achalasia. Furthermore, attention

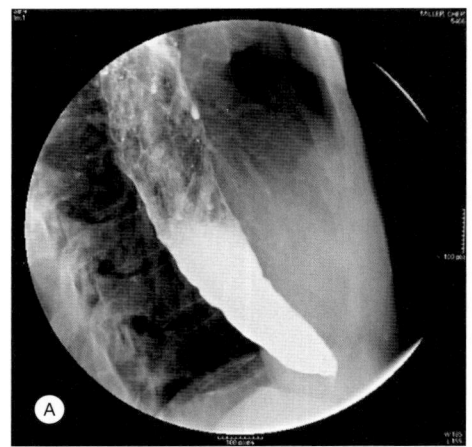

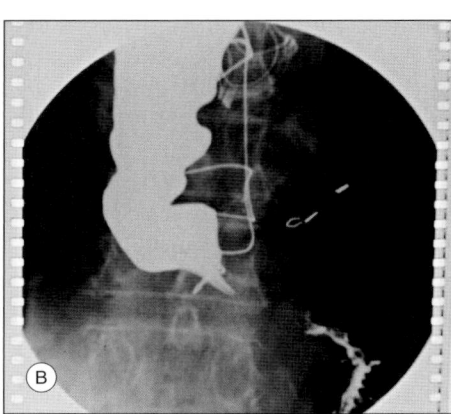

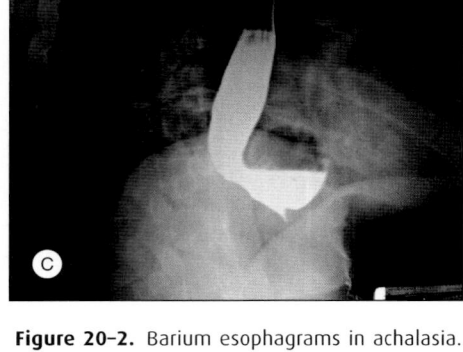

Figure 20–2. Barium esophagrams in achalasia. *A*, Classic. *B*, Vigorous achalasia. *C*, Epiphrenic diverticulum. *D*, Multiple diverticula. *E*, Food retention and sigmoidization.

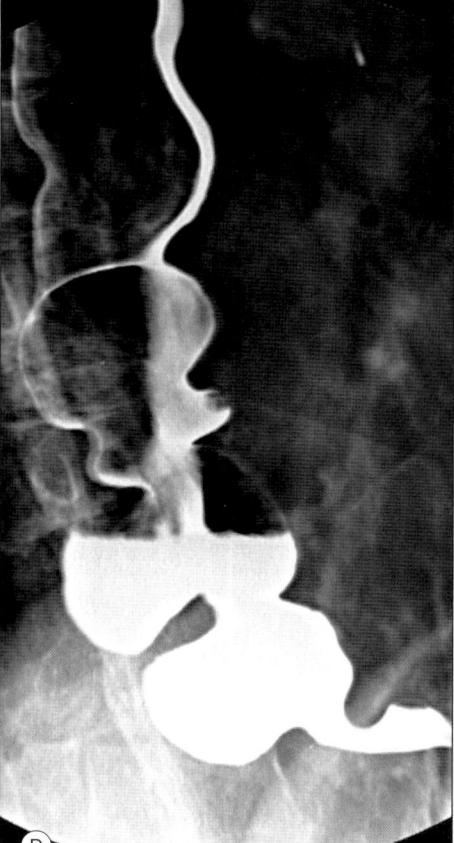

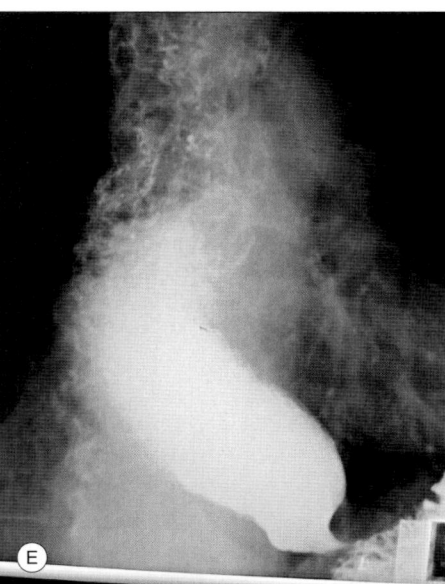

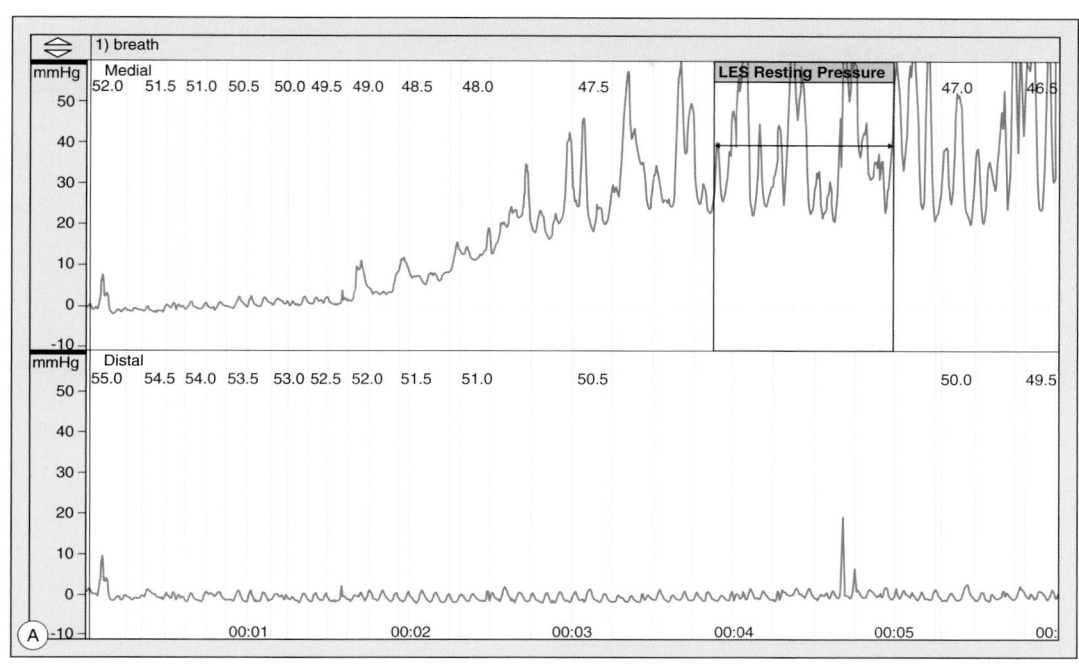

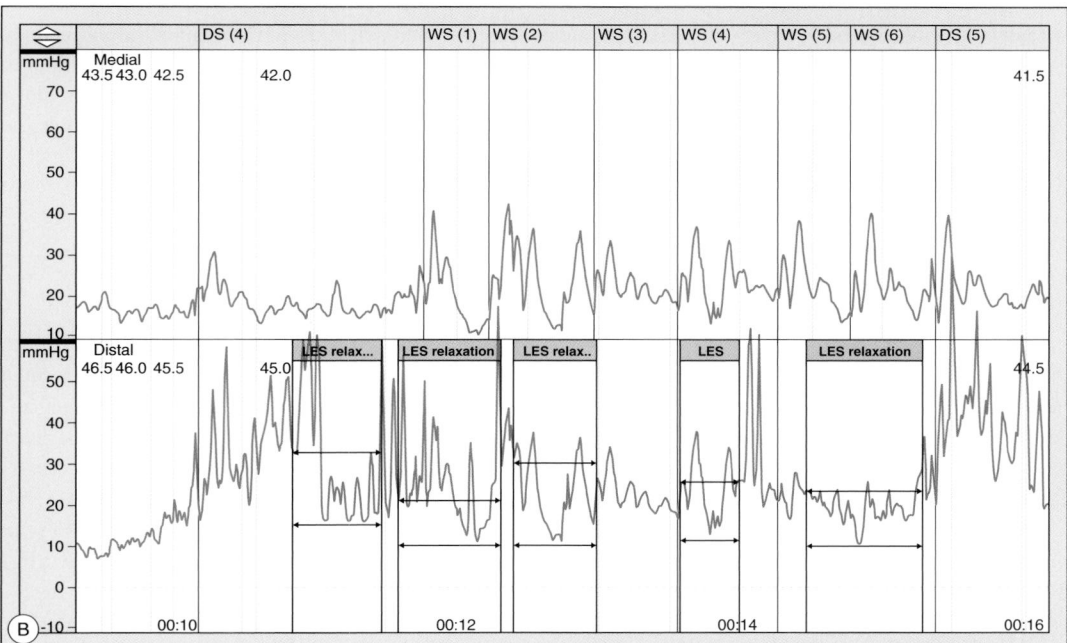

Figure 20–3. Manometric tracings of achalasia. *A,* Hypertensive lower esophageal sphincter. *B,* Incomplete lower esophageal sphincter (LES) relaxation.

Continued

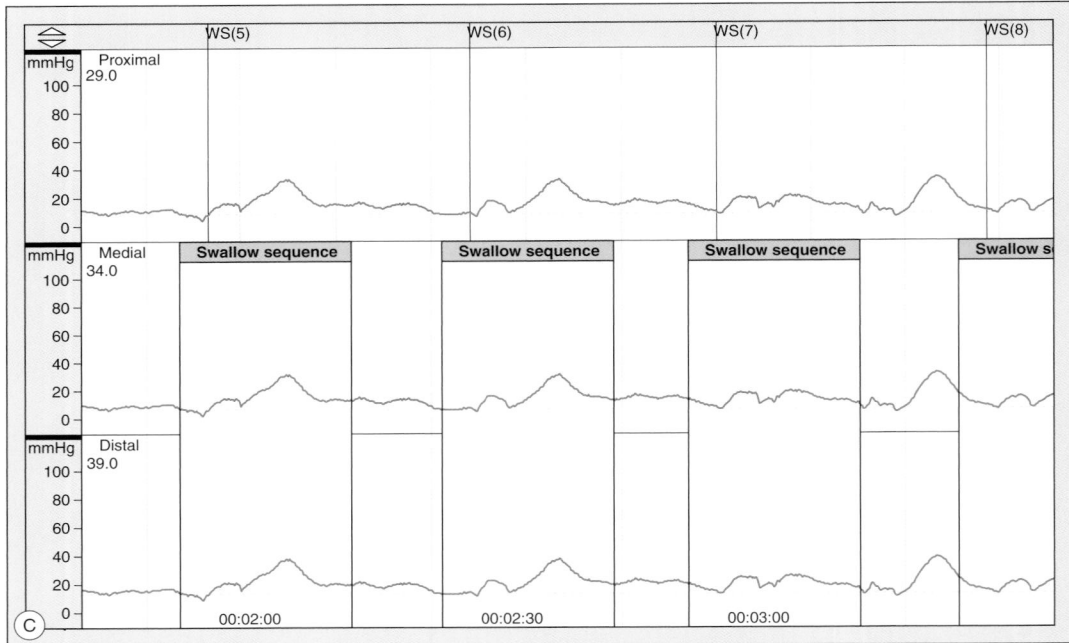

Figure 20-3, cont'd. Manometric tracings of achalasia. *C,* Aperistalsis with mirror images.

has also focused on the concept of vigorous achalasia, which is distinguished from classical achalasia by the presence of high-amplitude nonperistaltic esophageal body contractions. Vigorous achalasia may also represent an early manometric manifestation of the disease, before the development of complete aperistalsis. Although pathologic studies have demonstrated progression of histologic injury within the myenteric plexus during the transition from vigorous to classic achalasia,[9] clinical studies comparing radiographic appearance and response to therapy in vigorous and classic achalasia have not borne out these differences.[37]

ENDOSCOPY

Obvious achalasia, may occasionally be diagnosed during upper gastrointestinal endoscopy. As with barium radiography, endoscopic findings may include the presence of retained food in the esophagus (or, more commonly, pooled saliva), frank esophageal dilatation, and a tight LES/gastroesophageal junction region that characteristically "pops" open with mild to moderate pressure. However, for more subtle cases, endoscopy may appear completely normal, thus discouraging its use for diagnosis. Furthermore, because endoscopy is now used more and more as a therapeutic modality for patients with achalasia, a firm diagnosis should preferably be made before endoscopic intervention (i.e., making a decision to perform botulinum toxin injection or pneumatic dilatation requires advanced planning, which is best done before endoscopy). However, upper endoscopy is of particular importance in the diagnosis of secondary achalasia because of a gastroesophageal junction tumor, which may mimic primary achalasia in all of its manifestations. Secondary achalasia is discussed in more detail at the end of this chapter.

Several studies have also examined the role of endoscopic ultra-sonography in diagnosing achalasia.[38,39] Although some studies suggest that patients with achalasia may have increased LES and esophageal body wall thickness, these findings are not present in all patients. Currently, endoscopic ultrasonography should be considered a research tool for patients with primary achalasia. Its role in secondary achalasia is discussed later.

Treatment

Before prescribing treatment options for patients with achalasia, a number of important therapeutic principles must be kept in mind (Table 20–2). The first is the need to individualize the definition of a treatment threshold because no defined criteria exist. To date, investigators have been unable to define specific criteria for therapy or to evaluate treatment response. This controversy arises from data demonstrating extremely poor correlation between symptoms and radiographic appearance both before and after treatment. For example, one recent study[24] comparing both the number and severity of achalasia symptoms with radiographic scores (based on predefined radiographic parameters such as the degree of esophageal dilatation, the LES diameter, and the presence or absence of sigmoidization or retained food debris) found no correlation at all between symptoms and x-ray appearance either before or after treatment. Other studies have had similar results.[40,41] Thus, one has to decide whether treatment should be based on symptoms or x-ray appearance. For patients who are particularly symptomatic, treatment is usually indicated regardless of radiologic studies.

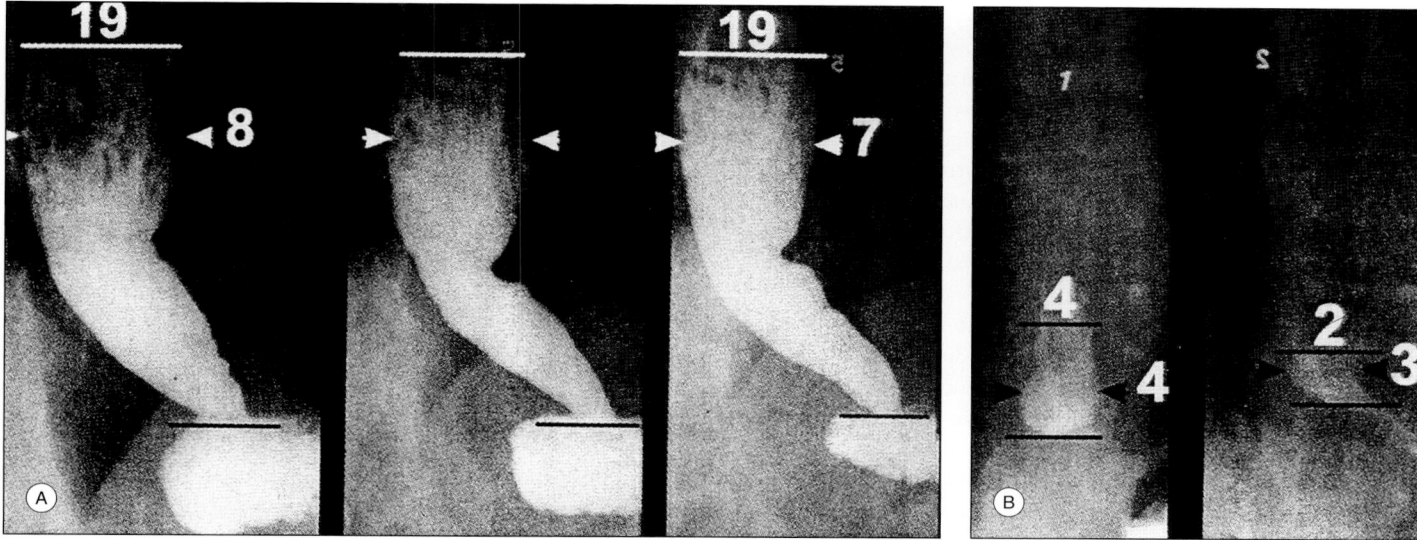

Figure 20–4. Esophagrogram after ingestion of 250 mL of barium. Height of barium column is indicated by the transverse line and numeric values. Width of the barium column is indicated by arrows and numeric values. *A,* Premyotomy barium columns at 1, 2, and 5 minutes. *B,* Postmyotomy barium columns at 1 and 2 minutes. (From Kostic SV, Rice TW, Baker ME, et al: Timed barium esophagogram: A simple physiologic assessment for achalasia. J Thorac Cardiovasc Surg 120:935–946, 2000.)

Table 20–2. Therapeutic Principles in Achalasia

1. In the absence of predefined criteria, the definition of a treatment threshold should be individualized.
    a. There is extremely poor correlation between symptoms and radiographic appearance both before and after treatment.
    b. Older patients respond better to therapy with botulinum toxin injection or balloon dilatation than do younger patients.
    c. It is unknown whether early therapeutic intervention alters the natural history of achalasia or not.
2. There is controversy surrounding the use of standardized symptom or radiographic assessment for patient management.
    a. Symptom scoring methods have not been found to be very useful clinically.
    b. The "timed" barium swallow should be considered standard for all research studies in achalasia, but it may have limited utility in general clinical practice.
3. The risks and benefits (including duration of response) must be factored into treatment decisions.
4. There is marked heterogeneity amongst therapeutic studies so that an individual patient may not be representative of the population studied.
5. The methodology used to report results of therapeutic intervention vary from study to study.

However, does one treat a 30-year-old man with marked sigmoidization of the esophagus and retained debris who has stable weight and minimal symptoms? Similarly, does a patient without weight loss and minimal esophageal dilatation on esophagram who complains only of regurgitation thrice weekly merit surgical myotomy? These are some of the potential clinical decisions that will be made purely based on best clinical judgment with little data for guidance. In addition, one must keep in mind age when evaluating symptoms and treatment response. Studies have demonstrated that older patients with achalasia (greater than 45 to 60 years depending on the study) tend to have better symptomatic responses to treatment. This has been shown both with botulinum toxin injection[42] and with pneumatic dilatation.[43] Whether this represents an objective or subjective improvement is unclear because older patients tend to have esophagi that are less sensitive to stimulation[44]; therefore, this population may be less reliable in conveying objective improvement. Furthermore, there have as yet been no outcome trials designed to demonstrate whether early therapeutic intervention leads to an improved clinical outcome or not.

The second issue is whether one should standardize the criteria used for symptom assessment or radiographic evaluation. There is a wide variation in the way individual physicians take histories from patients with achalasia. Specific symptom scoring methods have been proposed to address this problem to allow standardized evaluation of treatment responses, but they have not been found to be very useful clinically.[24,45,46] Similarly, there is also great variability in the way a barium swallow is performed among different radiology departments. Difference exists in terms of the amount and consistency of oral contrast given, the performance of video techniques versus static images, the use of double- versus single-contrast imaging, and the number and rate of swallows administered. As a result, some investigators have studied the use of a standardized "timed" barium swallow.[40,47,48] The proposed technique requires ingestion of low-density barium sulfate suspension within 30 to 45 seconds (the maximum amount tolerated is measured) with spot films taken at 1, 2, and 5 minutes. The height and width of the barium column is measured at each time point and the rate of esophageal emptying from 1 to 5 minutes is recorded (Fig. 20–4).[46] In one of the studies using this technique,[47] 32 patients with near complete symptom relief after therapy were followed. Initially, there was a significant association between patient symptoms and barium height improvement although esophageal barium emptying was less predictive of the symptomatic response during longer term follow-up. Despite this limitation, however, patients whose symptom response correlated best with emptying were far less likely to have symptomatic relapse during follow-up. Whether these standardized approaches, either symptomatic (i.e., subjective) or radiographic (i.e., objective), help improve patient outcome is unclear. In addition, in the face of an abnormal timed barium swallow but little symptomatic residual post-treatment, we may still be left with the question of whether to treat the x-ray film or the patient. However, we do believe strongly that standardization of symptoms and radiographic findings should be done for any type of achalasia research trial.

The third treatment principle is the need to weigh the risks of any planned procedure against the expected duration of treatment response for the individual patient. When choosing among the three standard treatment options (botulinum toxin injection, pneumatic dilatation, and surgical myotomy), procedure risk seems to correlate with efficacy. Thus, a healthy young patient may be viewed quite differently from an older or poor operative risk patient in terms of initial treatment options. The former would be a better candidate for pneumatic dilatation or surgical myotomy with the expectation of a durable response, whereas the latter may be a better candidate for repeated botulinum toxin injection at intervals.

Fourth, when evaluating the results of therapeutic studies, one must bear in mind that most studies deal with a heterogeneous population of patients with varying degrees of disease severity. Moreover, because of significant variability among patients in terms of specific symptoms,[24] extrapolating symptom response rates from clinical studies to individual patients may not always be valid. Furthermore, because of the rarity of this disease, most achalasia studies group patients with all stages of severity together for analysis. Therefore, these data include therapeutic responses from patients with minimal esophageal dilatation and some LES opening to those with frank sigmoidization, complete aperistalsis, and severe LES spasm. Although the proportion of patients with end-stage disease may be similar among some studies, they are often excluded in others. In one study evaluating the efficacy of Heller myotomy for achalasia, symptomatic success was clearly related to preoperative disease stage.[49] The relatively small numbers of achalasia patients in general also predisposes to type II errors in study design. Finally, the precise and specific details of how therapeutic procedures (botulinum toxin injection, pneumatic dilatation, and surgical myotomy) are performed often vary greatly among operators.

Fifth, many surgical series measure symptom response rates on a four-point scale consisting of excellent, good, fair, and poor categories. However, when overall outcome is presented, these subgroups may be combined into two groups only to reflect satisfactory or successful outcomes (excellent plus good) as opposed to unsatisfactory on unsuccessful outcomes (fair plus poor). Thus, a study suggesting that two therapeutic modalities are equally effective for achalasia because a similar proportion of patients had successful outcomes may in fact contain disparate numbers of patients with excellent versus good symptomatic responses because the two categories were combined to reflect equal success.

BOTULINUM TOXIN INJECTION

From the innovative work of Pashricha and coworkers,[50] botulinum toxin injection into the LES has become a cornerstone of treatment for achalasia. There are three reasons why gastroenterologists have embraced this approach to treatment: it is easy to administer, it is safe, and it works. Because of its extremely favorable risk-to-benefit ratio, we commonly use botulinum toxin injection as a temporizing measure in patients presenting with severe disease who are concerned about undergoing more invasive procedures or in those at poor risk for more invasive procedures. The precise injection technique is amazingly unspecified. In Pashricha's original work "the lower esophageal sphincter was visualized endoscopically by identification of the sphincteric rosette typically seen at the squamocolumnar junction. Botulinum toxin was injected through a 5-mm sclerotherapy needle into the region of the lower esophageal sphincter." In a more recent report by Kolbasnik and colleagues,[51] botulinum toxin was administered "approximately 5 mm above the Z line." In a study by Annese and coworkers,[52] the toxin was injected into "the LES region identified at endoscopy." The fact that all these studies show similar efficacy for botulinum toxin injection suggests that the precise site(s) of injection may not be critical to the technique's success. It is worth noting that the LES is generally longer in patients with achalasia (approximately 5 cm) as compared with control subjects and gastroesophageal reflux disease patients. It is unknown whether clinical results vary with botulinum toxin injection into the proximal, mid, or distal LES region. In addition, there are no clear data to support an advantage to administering the injection using endoscopic ultrasonography guidance or from a retroflexed position in the gastric cardia. Our personal techniques for administering botulinum toxin for achalasia emphasize the following points. Good localization of the LES region is essential. This is best achieved by straddling back and forth between the stomach and distal esophagus to check position before injection because the increased LES tone may "grab" the endoscope making the proximal border of the LES appear higher at times. The endoscope is kept approximately 5 mm above the squamocolumnar junction and then swung in the direction of the anticipated injection site to permit an en face angle of injection. The sclerotherapy injection catheter is then used to push the wall of the LES region away from the endoscope thereby maintaining a perpendicular relationship to the esophageal wall (to avoid a tangential injection). With the tip of the catheter firmly opposed to the mucosa, the needle is deployed and a submucosal injection is administered. We generally use 20 units of toxin injected sequentially into each quadrant with the final injection being administered from a retroflexed position below (i.e., 100 units in total). Additional important aspects of botulinum toxin administration include not preparing the solution until just before its use (because it is extremely expensive), using nonbacteriostatic saline without preservatives (preservatives may destroy the toxin), admixing the toxin with the saline solution by slowly injecting the saline into the vial followed by gently rolling the vial back and forth (to prevent denaturing of the toxin), and making sure that the sclerotherapy catheter is fully flushed before injection (to prevent submucosal injection of air). Figure 20–5 illustrates performance of an injection using this technique.

That botulinum toxin works well for patients with achalasia has been clear from the first published trial.[53] Numerous subsequent trials[54–56] have confirmed this fact. The symptom response after one injection ranges from 64% to 100%.[52–56] Manometric and radiologic

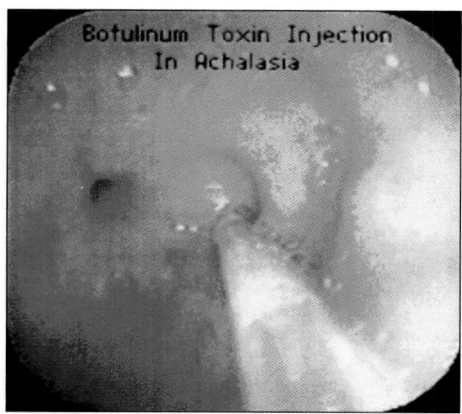

Figure 20–5. Botulinum toxin injection photograph.

parameters in these studies also improve significantly. There is a 33% to 49% reduction in basal LES pressure and a 35% to 47% reduction in esophageal retention. The duration of response ranges from 7.1 to 11 months. Prolonged responses (>2 years) have been documented in several patients. In addition, patients who respond well to their initial injection appear to also respond well to a second injection. However, studies vary on the symptomatic response to a second injection in initial nonresponders (from 0% to 33%). We believe a second injection is worthwhile in patients who initially fail to respond, particularly if the patient is elderly or a poor operative risk. Data on the efficacy of a third or fourth injection are scant, but anecdotal and published data suggest it may still work. As discussed, age may be an important predictor of response to botulinum toxin injection. For example, in Pashricha's initial study,[53] patients older and younger than 50 years had an 82% and 43% chance of responding symptomatically, respectively. Other, but not all, studies show similar trends.[54] Another predictor of success is the presence of vigorous achalasia, although the number of patients available for analysis is very small.[53] This is not unexpected because vigorous achalasia may represent an earlier form of the disease process in which esophageal peristalsis is less impaired. The single most important predictor of symptomatic response, both initially and long term is a documented reduction in LES pressure (this holds true in general for all achalasia treatment modalities). For example, one study[54] demonstrated that a fall in basal LES pressure to less than 20 mm Hg predicted a 100% symptomatic response. Interestingly, one study only[55] suggested that a low basal LES pressure pre-treatment was also predictive of a better outcome (see Pachrisha figures). Side effects of botulinum toxin injection are infrequent. Studies have reported transient chest pain, heartburn-type symptoms, and rash. In one case report,[57] a 10-year-old girl with achalasia developed a sinus tract between the esophagus and fundus, but this occurred after six botulinum toxin injections.

PNEUMATIC DILATATION

In evaluating studies of pneumatic dilatation for achalasia, evaluation of the precise method used and the age of the study are paramount for two reasons. First, as discussed previously, there is marked variation in the precise details of the technique used. For

example, methods vary from brief 3- to 5-second dilatations at 12 to 15 pounds per square inch (PSI),[58] to maintaining an average dilatation pressure of 7 PSI for less than 30 seconds, to maintaining a pressure of 6 to 12 PSI for up to 2 minutes. Whether such variations in technique influence outcome has not been well studied. Studies specifically examining the effect of the dilator size or the duration or number of inflations have not shown any clear differences,[59,60] although one early study did show an increased benefit if a larger balloon size was used (35 mm vs. 30 mm)[60] and another demonstrated a benefit to inflating the balloon to a pressure of greater than 7 PSI.[58] Second, it is also important to recognize that there has been a progressive change in the types of dilators used over time. Earlier studies described the use of the rather bulky, cumbersome Brown-McCarty or Mosher bags. However, these have been replaced over the past decade by Rigiflex dilators. Although the Rigiflex dilator is considered easier to use, there are only little data suggesting that it actually yields superior results.[61]

It must be stressed that there is no agreed-on method for balloon dilatation and many methodologic variations exist based mainly on anecdotal, personal experience. We emphasize the following points regarding performance of balloon dilatation for achalasia. We always start with a 30-mm balloon Rigiflex dilator. Although the data suggest that there may be an incremental benefit to using a larger diameter balloon,[59] we prefer to start off with the smaller 30-mm balloon in the hopes of limiting the likelihood of perforation. We are willing to repeat the procedure with a 35-mm balloon at a later setting if the initial dilatation is unsuccessful but we are very averse to using the 40-mm balloon given its high rate of perforation and the fact that alternate therapies (especially laparoscopic myotomy) are so successful. Balloon dilatations are always performed under fluoroscopic guidance. Before the actual procedure, it is essential to test the balloon for leaks by inflating it fully with saline or water. It is also important to check the location of the radiopaque markers on the balloon surface for later reference during the procedure, because they are commonly not located in the center of the balloon. The actual dilatation is always preceded by an upper endoscopy to ensure that the esophagus is clear of luminal contents, to exclude an obvious carcinoma, to gauge the extent of esophageal tortuosity, and to identify the presence or absence of a hiatal hernia to permit appropriate LES location fluoroscopically. The balloon is then passed under fluoroscopic guidance over a rigid guidewire with a soft flexible tip. It is important to confirm that the guidewire traverses the diaphragm before deployment of the balloon dilator. The balloon is maneuvered until it traverses the LES region and the position is verified fluoroscopically. We first inflate the balloon to about 2 to 3 PSI to confirm appropriate positioning of the balloon looking for a "waist" in its center. This commonly is just below, not at, the diaphragm. The catheter is then fixed in place by grasping it firmly against the bite block. If there is too much give on the catheter it will be squeezed inferiorly by the hypertensive LES during inflation. The balloon is then inflated slowly up to a limit of 10 PSI. During the process, we attempt to first identify the waist and then notice its obliteration to confirm that the balloon reached its full diameter. We prefer to deflate the balloon as soon as the waist is obliterated rather than maintaining full inflation for any set period of time. We do not exceed a balloon pressure of 10 PSI based on data suggesting an increased chance of perforation above this

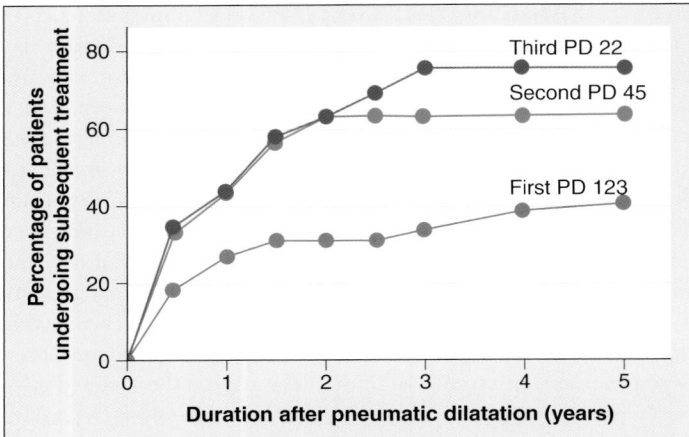

Figure 20-6. Efficacy of repeated balloon dilatations in patients with achalasia. (From Parkman HP, Reynolds JC, Ouyang A, et al: Pneumatic dilatation or esophagomyotomy treatment for idiopathic achalasia: Clinical outcomes and cost analysis. Dig Dis Sci 38:75-85, 1993.)

Table 20-3. Predictors of Response to Balloon Dilatation

Durable first response
Absence of early relapse (within 2 months)
Older patients do better
Absence of advanced disease
LES pressure
? Complete balloon distension

LES, lower esophageal sphincter.

limit.[63] The dilator and guidewire are then removed and examined for blood to confirm that the LES region has been torn. We generally do not reintubate the esophagus endoscopically, but we always follow therapeutic dilatation with a gastrograffin swallow immediately after the patient has awakened from the intervention. This is primarily to exclude a procedural perforation rather than an attempt to document efficacy, although it must be stressed that postdilatation spasm may hide a perforation that presents later as the spasm resolves.

There is general consensus amongst most authorities that a single, successful balloon dilatation has a duration of efficacy in the order of a few years. Specifically, 5-year follow-up data show that the effect of a single dilatation remains effective in 30% to 50% of patients.[60,62-64] Typically, patients require two to three dilatations over a 5-year period to stay in remission. In Parkman's classic study,[65] three dilatations maintained remission in 90% of patients after 5 years follow-up (Fig. 20-6). Only 15% of patients required myotomy during this period (although two of these were a consequence of procedurally induced perforation). There have also been longer term follow-up studies reported.[66] In one of these,[66] pneumatic dilatation was effective in 61 of 72 patients followed for a mean length of 6.5 years and a second dilatation was required in only 4 patients. One patient responded for 25 years with a single procedure! Another series[60] followed patients for more than 15 years at which time the therapeutic response to balloon dilatation was classified as excellent in 12%, good in 28%, moderate in 20%, and poor in 40% with a median dilatation requirement of four. However, two caveats must be kept in mind when evaluating these long-term follow-up studies. First, a significant number of patients were lost to follow-up, which hampers the quality of the report.[67] Second, one of the reports[68] describes the personal experience of one of the most experienced esophagologists in the world and it is unclear whether physicians with less experience can expect similar outcomes or not.

As with botulinum toxin injection, it is clear that pneumatic dilatation works well for patients with achalasia. An effective symptom response occurs in most patients, and, unlike botulinum toxin injection, the effect may be quite durable. There are also objective data demonstrating that the technique is effective in terms of producing a reduction in LES pressure and esophageal diameter and improved esophageal emptying by scintigraphy.[59,60] On the other hand, patients commonly require repeated procedures and some patients have little, if any, response. For example, one study[60] demonstrated little or no improvement in 12 of 54 patients (23%), 4 weeks postdilatation. Thus, there is a wide range of potential outcomes from no response at all to long-term resolution of symptoms.

Several factors have been proposed as useful predictors of a response to balloon dilatation (Table 20-3). First (and intuitively), the more frequent the dilatations are needed to induce remission, the less likely they are to provide long-term responses. This has been shown in 5-year studies when multiple dilatations are required for symptom control.[60] Second, early relapse (i.e., within 2 months) predicts a poor long-term outcome.[58,60] Third, age is also an important predictor of success. In various studies, older age may be defined as older than 40 years,[58,60] older than 45 years,[63] or older than 60 years.[64] In one of these studies,[58,60] four of five patients younger than 18 years had symptomatic relapse within 2 months. Moreover, in another study of 132 patients,[64] patients younger than 60 years were much more likely to need myotomy (14 patients) than patients older than 60 years (only one patient). Fourth, advanced stage achalasia is also less likely to respond to dilatation. Many studies evaluating balloon dilatation specifically exclude patients with sigmoidization of the esophagus because such patients are felt to have end-stage disease that is unlikely to respond to any therapeutic modality other than esophagectomy. From an objective point of view, neither radiographic findings nor the degree of esophageal emptying postdilatation are able to predict long-term clinical course.[62] However, absolute LES pressure does appear to correlate with long-term clinical benefit (Fig. 20-7), and, in some cases, a reassessment of LES pressure postprocedure may be helpful.[62] As discussed previously, newer balloons and greater diameter balloons have not clearly been shown to influence outcome, although one study suggested that higher balloon inflation pressures and radiographic visualization of a fully expanded balloon diameter predicted greater success.[62]

Pneumatic balloon dilatation of the LES for achalasia is by no means a risk-free procedure. The most concerning complication is esophageal perforation. Most studies quote a perforation rate of between 0% and 6%.[59,64,69-72] This is particularly important because esophageal perforation may have a poor outcome even with rapid careful management. The quoted mortality rate from

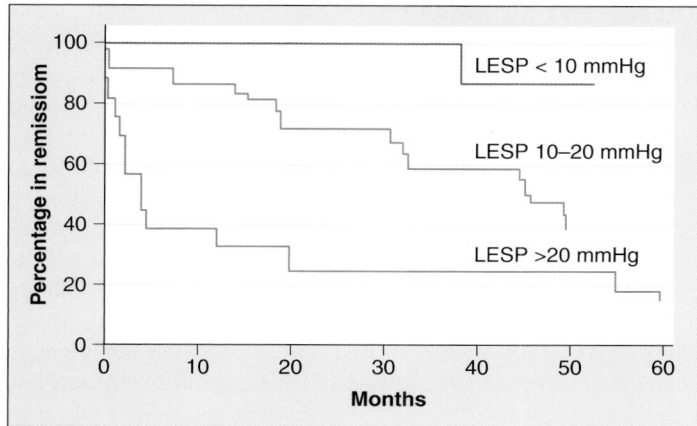

Figure 20-7. Correlation between postdilation lower esophageal sphincter pressure (LESP) and clinical outcome. (From Eckardt VF, Aignherr C, Bernhard G: Predictors of outcome in patients with achalasia treated by pneumatic dilation. Gastroenterology 103:1732–1738, 1992.)

traumatic esophageal perforation is 10%.[73,74] Factors associated with an increased likelihood of esophageal perforation after balloon dilatation include (1) a first dilatation, (2) high-amplitude esophageal contractions, and (3) malnutrition.[58,75,76] Perforation rates may be lower in the Rigiflex era[75] possibly contributed to by the use of lower inflation pressures and shorter inflation times as compared with prior reports. Still, patients must be cautioned very carefully before dilatation. They especially need to be made aware that the operative management of a traumatic esophageal perforation generally requires an open approach through either the chest or the abdomen), whereas a primary Heller myotomy is easily accomplished laparoscopically in most cases.

Other worrisome complications of balloon dilatation include hematomata (which rarely may cause esophageal obstruction[61]) and chest pain. As expected, chest pain is quite common and at times it may be severe enough to warrant hospitalization even if contrast studies fail to show a perforation. Interestingly, achalasia patients who present initially with chest pain are more likely to develop severe chest pain after balloon dilatation.[58]

Long-term complications may also develop postdilatation. Gastroesophageal reflux is common when measured by ambulatory pH monitoring,[77] but it usually is not severe and it responds readily to proton pump inhibitor therapy. Nevertheless, severe reflux complications such as esophageal stricture formation and even Barrett's esophagus have been reported.[58] The development of a diverticulum in the distal esophagus after balloon dilatation has also been described,[58] but whether this represents true diverticular formation or an esophageal ballooning from an effective dilatation-induced myotomy[78] is unclear.

SURGICAL MYOTOMY

Surgical cardiomyotomy (the Heller procedure) is an important and effective therapy achalasia. It has stood the test of time (many long-term series have been published), it is relatively safe, and it has been successfully adapted to a minimally invasive laparoscopic approach (e.g., references 79–105). Five to 10 years after surgery, patient

satisfaction remains high with good to excellent results persisting in 85% to 90% of patients. Laparoscopic myotomy, a newer technique for which the available duration of follow-up is shorter by necessity, seems to be associated with similar outcomes to traditional open myotomy. When compared with pneumatic dilatation, myotomy (whether performed in an open or laparoscopic fashion) outperforms dilatation.[69,79–82] However, there are two important limiting factors that keep pneumatic dilatation a viable option. First, is the ever-present, albeit small, risk of perioperative complications. Second, is the steep learning curve involved in learning to perform laparoscopic myotomy reliably (at least 20, but probably more, cases). Several series note that most, if not all, serious complications occur within the first 20 to 30 patients.[94,106] Like many other foregut surgical procedures, the results of laparoscopic myotomy are best if the procedure is performed by an expert, experienced surgeon.

The mortality from Heller myotomy is low, rarely exceeding 1% in expert hands. Major early complications that not uncommonly result include inadvertent mucosal perforation (up to 25%), pneumothorax, inadvertent splenectomy (<4%), and vagotomy. Most of these complications are managed easily without significant long-term sequela. However, it is important to recognize that the morbidity and mortality of pneumatic dilatation is far lower. Longer term technical complications include an incomplete myotomy, which fails to cure the problem (in approximately 5% to 10% of cases), or conversely, gastroesophageal reflux disease (which may, in a small percentage of cases, lead to Barrett's esophagus and/or stricture formation). One of the interesting surgical controversies regarding the performance of a Heller myotomy is the ongoing debate about how precisely to perform the operation. For example, debates continue over whether the thoracoscopic or laparoscopic approach is better and whether an antireflux procedure should be performed at the same time and, if so, what type of antireflux surgery is best. Those who argue against the need for an antireflux procedure point out that a carefully performed thoracoscopic or laparoscopic myotomy permits excellent visualization of the gastroesophageal junction allowing preservation of the vagus nerve and oblique sling fibers of the cardia resulting in only minor traumatic mobilization of the lower esophagus through the diaphragmatic crural sphincter. As a consequence, reflux is unlikely to occur[106] as is borne out by some studies, which show no differences in the development of reflux symptoms whether an antireflux operation is performed or not.[87] On the other hand, numerous other series have identified a high incidence postoperatively of reflux symptoms, abnormal ambulatory pHmetry scores, and the subsequent development of peptic strictures and Barrett's esophagus (e.g., reference 101). Furthermore, there is a fine line between not extending the myotomy too far down the cardia (leading to reflux) and paying the price with an incomplete myotomy (leading to failure and requiring a repeat operation). Consequently, we believe that most patients, if not all, should undergo an antireflux procedure with a laparoscopic myotomy, specifically. If the thoracoscopic approach is used, we do not believe an antireflux operation is essential. However, this approach is less attractive given the ease, lower complication rate, shorter hospital stay, and less postoperative pain associated with the laparoscopic approach. The final debate regarding antireflux surgery is the precise type of antireflux procedure to perform. Surgeons continue to debate over whether to perform a loose, but complete, fundoplication (i.e., a Nissen operation) as opposed to one of the partial fundoplication (e.g., the Dorr or Toupet procedures). To date no clear recommendations have emerged.

Occasionally, patients with end-stage achalasia require esophagectomy. Numerous studies have shown that a favorable surgical outcome is closely related to the preoperative stage of disease.[49] It is not at all surprising that patients with marked sigmoidization and dilatation of the esophagus will not respond well to sphincter-directed therapy alone. What little data are available regarding these end-stage patients suggest that esophagectomy (either with a gastric pull-up or with a colonic or jejeunual interposition) enables most of these patients to regain their weight and eat within the expected limitations of any patient undergoing a total esophagectomy.[107,108]

Finally, successful robot-assisted laparoscopic Heller myotomy has been described.[109] This technique provides further potential advances over a standard laparoscopic approach by providing a three-dimensional view of the gastroesophageal junction thereby restoring depth perception to the operator and by improving precision by scaling down the surgeon's movements so that large movements of the robotic console are translated into smaller movements in the patient. Robotic surgery also eliminates hand tremor.

MISCELLANEOUS TREATMENTS

Pharmacologic therapy for achalasia has been used in the past and is presently undergoing further investigation. Sublingual nifedipine has been reported to improve symptoms, esophageal retention, and LES pressures.[110,111] This approach may be useful in isolated, rare instances, but potential side effects and lack of published long-term efficacy limit its use. Similarly, sildenafil, by augmenting nitric oxide effects, lowers the LES pressure and improves some manometric measurements in patients with achalasia.[112] However, symptoms are not improved significantly so that there are no indications for its use at this time. Finally, expandable metal stents have been attempted in six poor surgical candidates with achalasia.[113] Unfortunately, there was no sustained symptom relief and the 1-month mortality was extremely high, suggesting no role for this approach at the present time.

TREATMENT SUMMARY

Trying to reach consensus on the appropriate initial treatment strategy for achalasia is one of the great debates in esophagology. Even decision models cannot agree, with one recent study siding with pneumatic dilatation[114] and another with laparoscopic cardiomyotomy.[115] Furthermore, the latter publication even indicated a preference for botulinum toxin injection over balloon dilatation.[115] Each of the three major approaches has its own advantages and disadvantages (Table 20–4). Botulinum toxin injection is easy to perform, generally works well, has only a small chance of significant complications, and can be given multiple times. One recent placebo controlled trial even demonstrated similar outcomes for symptom control and objective measurements of changes in LES pressure and esophageal retention in patients randomized to pneumatic dilatation or botulinum toxin injection,[52] although the number of patients studied was small (16 in toto) and the trend was in favor of dilatation. On the other hand, the duration of effect with botulinum toxin is much shorter than that with either balloon dilatation or surgical myotomy requiring either repeated injections or ultimately a more definitive intervention such as balloon dilatation or surgical myotomy. In comparing balloon dilatation to surgical myotomy, the available data favor a surgical approach especially when one factors in the advantages afforded by using the laparoscopic approach and, in the future, robot-assisted techniques. Although, anecdotal evidence[115] has suggested that dilatation induced esophageal perforation may be repaired laparoscopically with little lost as compared with an elective procedure, this is by no means generally accepted. Thus, the disadvantages of balloon dilatation over surgical myotomy includes both a poorer efficacy and a potentially missed opportunity to undergo a minimally invasive procedure. Indeed, some medical centers have all but abandoned pneumatic dilatation in favor of laparoscopic myotomy. We have not yet embraced this approach completely, but the number of dilatations we are performing currently has decreased markedly.

Our general approach for the management of patients with achalasia is as follows. Botulinum toxin injection is our preferred initial management strategy for patients who are elderly, poor operative risks or who have an unclear or incomplete form of achalasia (i.e., as a diagnostic trial in Katzka and coworkers[117]). We

Table 20–4. Advantages and Disadvantages of Various Initial Approaches for the Treatment of Achalasia

Therapy	Advantages	Disadvantages	Comments
Botulinum toxin injection	Easy to perform Generally effective Safe Repeatable ? Diagnostic utility	Short effect duration	Useful for poor surgical risks, the elderly, acute management of malnourished patients
Balloon dilatation	Avoids anesthesia Generally effective Outpatient procedure More effective in elderly	? Surgery better Perforation risk Perforation requires open repair	Requires an expert operator with surgical backup. Reserve for poor operative risks or patients reluctant for surgery
Surgical myotomy	Effective Safe Can be combined with antireflux surgery	In-patient stay Not 100% effective Anesthesia risk	Ideal approach in healthy young individuals

also favor this approach initially for patients who present in extremis to permit stabilization of their condition before definitive therapy is undertaken later or for those who are reluctant to undergo definitive therapy until we can demonstrate the likely benefit of lowering LES pressure by another means later on. For young, healthy patients (arbitrarily, one might say, younger than 25 years), laparoscopic myotomy is indicated initially. We favor combining their cardio-myotomy with a loose fundoplication at the same time. For older patients (arbitrarily say older than 60 years) but otherwise in good health, pneumatic dilatation may be indicated initially. We believe that the initial management of choice in healthy patients between 25 and 60 years old (actually most patients seen in clinical practice) is not clearly defined. We believe it is important to offer all the available options in as unbiased a manner as possible, which requires consultation with both a gastroenterologist and a laparoscopic surgeon, although we also believe it important to stress the lack of durability with botulinum toxin injection that otherwise seems a quick, easy fix. For patients who respond poorly initially or in whom there is a rapid return of symptoms after a less risky procedure, the next step up should be offered early in the treatment process rather than performing the previously ineffective approach repeatedly. Finally, we also believe it worthwhile to offer patients presenting with apparently end-stage disease an initial attempt at sphincter-directed therapy before resorting to an esophagectomy because of the poor relationship between radiologic findings and outcome. Under these conditions, we favor botulinum toxin injection as a safe, initial diagnostic approach in determining the likely efficacy of future sphincter-directed therapy.

Achalasia and Cancer

The relationship of achalasia with cancer deserves special mention (Table 20–5). The disease has two important associations with malignancy. First is the development of an achalasia-like syndrome as consequence of malignancy (i.e., secondary achalasia) and second is the development of malignancy in patients with long-standing achalasia (i.e., secondary malignancy).

SECONDARY ACHALASIA

Secondary achalasia accounts for approximately 2.4% to 4% of all cases of achalasia.[118,119] Malignancy may cause an achalasia-like syndrome through two unrelated mechanisms. The first is through direct anatomic compression or infiltration of the LES[120] mandating the performance of a careful upper endoscopy with careful retroflexion in all patients. The second is through an antibody-

mediated paraneoplastic effect on esophageal function. In a recent study of 13 patients with tumor-induced achalasia,[121] 11 cases had direct involvement of the LES with penetration into the muscularis propria. Three of these cases demonstrated extensive neoplastic involvement of the myenteric plexus of the LES. Interestingly, ganglion cells appeared normal suggesting that the effect is purely due to an obstruction to esophageal outflow. That some of these malignancies induced achalasia through extrinsic compression alone is supported by case reports of benign processes such as mediastinal fibrosis, surgical procedures, or large pancreatic pseudocysts also causing achalasia-like syndromes.[122,123] In one of the patients in the aforementioned series, anti-Hu antibodies (antineuronal nuclear antibody type 1) were detected. Histologic analysis of the LES in this patient revealed marked lymphocytic myenteric plexus inflammation and marked depletion of ganglion cells identical to that seen in primary achalasia. Several types of malignancy cause secondary achalasia. Their distribution depends partly on the mechanism involved. For malignancies that cause achalasia by direct involvement of the distal esophagus, adenocarcinoma of the cardia or gastroesophageal junction (with or without Barrett's esophagus) predominates,[119] but many other types of cancer have also been described including cancer of the breast, liver, prostate, lung, pleura, pancreas, cervix, and uterus.[121,124–128] For paraneoplastic achalasia, small cell carcinoma of the lung predominates, but other cancer types including lymphoma have also been described.[121,129]

The diagnosis of secondary achalasia requires a high index of suspicion. Although these patients tend to be older, have a shorter duration of symptoms, and commonly exhibit weight loss, studies have shown that even with these "red flags" primary achalasia is still statistically much more common.[130] Furthermore, the onset of achalasia symptoms may precede signs of cancer by months or even years[131] in patients with paraneoplastic achalasia. One clue may be the presence of other neurologic symptoms or the presence of a more global gastrointestinal motility syndrome (e.g., colonic pseudo-obstruction) together with the presence of achalasia symptoms. In addition, whereas patients with paraneoplastic achalasia may appear radiologically and endoscopically identical to primary disease, patients with secondary achalasia from direct tumor involvement tend to have longer areas of distal esophageal narrowing and less esophageal dilatation than patients with primary achalasia.[132] Endoscopically, as opposed to the characteristic "pop" that one feels on traversing the LES with primary achalasia, there is moderate to severe resistance during endoscopic passage. Despite the absence of firm data, we favor careful anatomic evaluation of the LES region with endoscopic ultrasonography or CT scanning in elderly patients with significant weight loss who present with the new onset of rapidly progressive symptoms. Another option is to perform endoscopic ultrasound at the time of endoscopy, which is what we favor. In addition, CT scanning should also be considered in patients with a long history of cigarette smoking or associated pulmonary symptoms.

Treatment for secondary achalasia is usually directed at the tumor. The one exception might be patients with paraneoplastic disease, especially those with antibody-confirmed disease but no obvious primary tumor in whom a botulinum toxin injection may be effective (reference 131 and anecdotal personal observation).

Table 20–5. Achalasia and Malignancy

Secondary Achalasia
Gastroesophageal junction tumor
Paraneoplastic achalasia
Secondary Malignancy

SECONDARY MALIGNANCY

The second association of achalasia with malignancy is the increased risk of squamous cell carcinoma and perhaps adenocarcinoma of the esophagus in patients with longstanding primary disease. The estimated relative risk of developing squamous cell carcinoma of the esophagus in achalasia is 8- to 140-fold higher than in the normal population.[133-135] In a recent long-term follow-up study of 249 patients with achalasia (a mean of 12 years), 6 (2.4%) developed esophageal cancer. Esophageal cancer generally develops at a younger age in patients with achalasia. Symptoms of achalasia generally precede the development of squamous cell carcinoma of the esophagus by 17 to 20 years.[133-135] Consequently, there has been a long debate regarding the role, if any, of endoscopic surveillance in patients with achalasia, which remains unresolved. One recent report described the potential role of flow cytometric analysis of esophageal biopsy specimens as a means of surveying these patients, but this recommendation was based on a single case report.[137] Furthermore, there are no data available to demonstrate whether effective treatment of achalasia reduces the development of esophageal cancer.

REFERENCES

1. Robertson CS, Martin BA, Atkinson M: Varicella-zoster virus DNA in the esophageal myenteric plexus in achalasia. Gut 34:299–302, 1993.
2. Wong RK, Maydonovitch CL, Metz SJ, et al: Significant DQw association with achalasia. Dig Dis Sci 34:349–352, 1989.
3. Verne GN, Hahn AB, Pineau BC, et al: Association of LSA-DR and -DQ alleles with idiopathic achalasia. Gastroenterology 117:26–31, 1999.
4. Ruiz-de-Leon A, Mendoza J, Sevilla-Mantilla C, et al: Myenteric antiplexus antibodies and class II HLA in achalasia. Dig Dis Sci 47:15–19, 2002.
5. Verne GN, Sallusto JE, Baker EY: Anti-myenteric neuronal antibodies in patients with achalasia. A prospective study. Dig Dis Sci 42:307–313, 1997.
6. Goin JC, Sterin-Borda L, Bilder CR, et al: Functional implications of circulating muscarinic cholinergic receptor autoantibodies in chagasic patients with achalasia. Gastroenterology 117:798–805, 1999.
7. Cassella RR, Brown AL, Sayre GP, Ellis FH Jr: Achalasia of the esophagus: Pathologic and etiologic considerations. Ann Surg 160:474–479, 1964.
8. Goldblum JR, Whyte RI, Orringer MB, Appelman HD: Achalasia. A morphologic study of 42 resected specimens. Am J Surg Pathol 18:327–337, 1994.
9. Goldblum JR, Rice TW, Richter JE: Histopathologic features in esophagomyotomy specimens from patients with achalasia. Gastroenterology 111:648–654, 1996.
10. Clark SB, Rice TW, Tubbs RR, et al: The nature of the myenteric infiltrate in achalasia. An immunohistochemical analysis. Am J Surg Pathol 24:1153–1158, 2000.
11. Tottrup A, Fredens K, Funch-Jensen P, et al: Eosinophil infiltration in primary esophageal achalasia. A possible pathogenic role. Dig Dis Sci 34:297–303.
12. Higgs B, Kerr FW, Ellis FH Jr: The experimental production of esophageal achalasia by electrolytic lesions in the medulla. J Thorac Cardiovasc Surg 50:613–625, 1965.
13. Holland CT, Satchell PM, Farrow BR: Selective vagal afferent dysfunction in dogs with congenital idiopathic megaesophagus. Auton Neurosci 99:18–23, 2002.
14. Mearin F, Mourelle M, Guarner F, et al: Patients with achalasia lack nitric oxide synthase in the gastro-esophageal junction. Eur J Clin Invest 23:724–728, 1993.
15. Sivarao DV, Mashimo HL, Thatte HS, Goyal RK: Lower esophageal sphincter is achalasic in nNOS(–/–) and hypotensive in W/W(v) mutant mice. Gastroenterology 121:34–42, 2001.
16. Whyte RI, Orringer MB, Appelman HD: Achalasia. A morphologic study of 42 resected specimens. Am J Surg Pathol 18:327–337, 1994.
17. Mearin F, Vasconez C, Zarate N, Malagelada JR: Esophageal tone in patients with total aperistalsis: Gastroesophageal reflux disease versus achalasia. Am J Physiol 279:G374–379, 2000.
18. Vantrappen G, Hellemans J, Deloof W, et al: Treatment of achalasia with pneumatic dilatations. Gut 12:268–275, 1971.
19. Okike N, Payne WS, Neufeld DM, et al: Esophagomyotomy versus forceful dilatation for achalasia of the esophagus: Results in 899 patients. Ann Thorac Surg 28:119–123, 1979.
20. Wong RK, Johnson LF: Achalasia. In Castell DO, Johnson LF (eds): Esophageal Function in Health and Disease. New York, Elsevier Biomedical, 1983, pp 99–123.
21. Howard PJ, Maher L, Pryde A, et al: Five year prospective study of the incidence, clinical features, and diagnosis of achalasia in Edinburgh. Gut 33:1011–1015, 1992.
22. Eckardt VF, Kohne U, Westermeier T: Risk factors for diagnostic delay in achalasia. Dig Dis Sci 42:580–585, 1997.
23. Eckardt VF, Stauf B, Bernhard G: Chest pain in achalasia: Patient characteristics and clinical course. Gastroenterology 116:1300–1304, 1999.
24. Blam ME, Delfyett W, Levine MS, et al: Achalasia: A disease of varied and subtle symptoms that do not correlate with radiographic findings. Am J Gastroenterol 97:1916–1923, 2002.
25. Becker DJ, Castell DO: Acute airway obstruction in achalasia. Possible role of defective belch reflex. Gastroenterology 97:1323–1326, 1989.
26. Arcos E, Medine C, Mearin F, et al: Achalasia presenting as acute airway obstruction. Dig Dis Sci 45:2079–2083, 2000.
27. Dudnick RS, Castell JA, Castell DO: Abnormal upper esophageal sphincter function in achalasia. Am J Gastroenterol 87:1712–1715, 1992.
28. Massey B, Hogan WJ, Dodds WJ, Dantas RO: Alteration of the upper esophageal sphincter belch reflex in patients with achalasia. Gastroenterology 103:1574–1579, 1992.
29. Schima W, Sterz F, Pokieser P: Syncope after eating. N Engl J Med 328:1572, 1993.
30. Binder HJ, Clemett AR, Thayer WR, et al: Rarity of hiatus hernia in achalasia. N Eng J Med 272:680–682, 1965.
31. Goldenberg SP, Vos C, Burrell M, Traube M: Achalasia and hiatal hernia. Dig Dis Sci 37:528–531, 1992.
32. Van Herwaarden MA, Sansom M, Smout AJ: Prolonged manometric recordings of esophagus and lower esophageal sphincter in achalasia patients. Gut 49:813–821, 2001.
33. Hirano I, Tatum RP, Shi G, et al: Manometric heterogeneity in patients with idiopathic achalasia. Gastroenterology 120:789–798, 2001.
34. Vantrappen G, Janssens J, Hellemans J, et al: Achalasia, diffuse esophageal spasm, and related motility disorders. Gastroenterology 76:450–457, 1979.
35. Anggiansah A, Bright NF, McCullagh M, Owen WJ: Transition from nutcracker esophagus to achalasia. Dig Dis Sci 35:1162–1166, 1990.
36. Golioto M, McGrath K, Smith J, Brazer S: Achalasia with high-amplitude esophageal body contractions. Dig Dis Sci 46:1960–1962, 2001.
37. Goldenberg SP, Burrell M, Fette GG, et al: Classic and vigorous achalasia: A comparison of manometric, radiographic, and clinical findings. Gastroenterology 101:743–748, 1991.
38. Miller LS, Liu JB, Barbarevich CA, et al: High-resolution endoluminal sonography in achalasia. Gastrointest Endosc 42:545–549, 1995.

39. Van Dam J, Falk GW, Sivak MV, et al: Endosonographic evaluation of the patient with achalasia: Appearance of the esophagus using the echoendoscope. Endoscopy 27:185–190, 1995.

40. Kostic SV, Rice TW, Baker ME, et al: Timed barium esophagogram: A simple physiologic assessment for achalasia. J Thorac Cardiovasc Surg 120:935–946, 2000.

41. Eckardt VF, Aignherr C, Bernhard G: Predictors of outcome in patients with achalasia treated by pneumatic dilation. Gastroenterology 103:1732–1738, 1992.

42. Neubrand M, Scheurlen C, Schepki M, Sauerbruch T: Long-term results and prognostic factors in the treatment of achalasia with botulinum toxin. Endoscopy 34:519–523, 2002.

43. Robertson CS, Fellows IW, Mayberry JF, Atkinson M: Choice of therapy for achalasia in relation to age. Digestion 40:244–250, 1988.

44. Lasch H. Castell DO. Castell JA: Evidence for diminished visceral pain with aging: Studies using graded intraesophageal balloon distension. Am J Physiol 272(1 Pt 1):G1–3, 1997.

45. Ellis FH, Olsen AM: Achalasia of the esophagus. In Ellis FH, Olsen AM (eds): Major Problems in Clinical Surgery, vol 9. Philadelphia, WB Saunders, 1969, p 205.

46. Vantrappen G, Hellemans J: Treatment of achalasia and related motor disorders. Gastroenterology 79:144–154, 1980.

47. Vaezi MF, Baker ME, Achkar E, Richter JE: Timed barium esophagram: Better predictor of long term success after pneumatic dilation in achalasia than symptom assessment. Gut 50:765–770, 2002.

48. De Oliveira JM, Birgisson S, Doinoff C, et al: Timed barium swallow: A simple technique for evaluating esophageal emptying in patients with achalasia. AJR Am J Roentgenol 169:473–479, 1997.

49. Pechlivanides G, Chrysos E, Athanasakis E, et al: Laparoscopic Heller cardiomyotomy and Dor fundoplication for esophageal achalasia. Arch Surg 16:1240–1243, 2001.

50. Pashricha PJ, Rai R, Ravich WJ, et al: Botulinum toxin for achalasia: Long-term outcome and predictors of response. Gastroenterology 110:1410–1415, 1996.

51. Kolbasnik J, Waterfall WE, Fachnie B, et al: Long-term efficacy of Botulinum toxin in classical achalasia: A prospective study. Am J Gastroenterol 94:3434–3439, 1999.

52. Annese V, Basciani M, Perri F, et al: Controlled trial of botulinum toxin injection versus placebo and pneumatic dilation in achalasia. Gastroenterology 111:1418–1424, 1996.

53. Pasricha PJ, Ravich WJ, Hendrix TR, et al: Intrasphincteric botulinum toxin for the treatment of achalasia. N Engl J Med 332:774–778, 1995.

54. Cuilliere C, Ducrotte P, Zerbib R, et al: Achalasia: Outcome of patients treated with intrasphincteric injection of botulinum toxin. Gut 41:87–92, 1997.

55. Neubrand M, Scheurlen C, Schepki M, Sauerbruch T: Long-term results and prognostic factors in the treatment of achalasia with botulinum toxin. Endoscopy 34:519–523, 2002.

56. Kolbasnik J, Waterfall WE, Fachnie B, et al: Long-term efficacy of Botulinum toxin in classical achalasia: A prospective study. Am J Gastroenterol 94:3434–3439, 1999.

57. Sukerek H, Tolia V: Clinical quiz. J Pediatr Gastroenterol Nutr 35:38–39, 2002.

58. Csendes A, Velasco N, Braghetto I, Henriquez A: A prospective randomized study comparing forceful dilatation and esophagomyotomy in patients with achalasia of the esophagus. Gastroenterology 80:789–795, 1981.

59. Gelfand MD, Kozarek RA: An experience with polyethylene balloons for pneumatic dilation in achalasia. Am J Gastroenterol 84:924–927, 1989.

60. Eckardt VF, Kanzler G, Westermeier T: Complications and their impact after pneumatic dilation for achalasia: Prospective long-term follow-up study. Gastrointest Endosc 45:349–353, 1997.

61. Kim CH, Cameron AJ, Hsu JJ, et al: Achalasia: Prospective evaluation of relationship between lower esophageal sphincter pressure, esophageal transit, and esophageal diameter and symptoms in response to pneumatic dilation. Mayo Clin Proc 68:1067–1073, 1993.

62. Eckardt VF, Aignherr C, Bernhard G: Predictors of outcome in patients with achalasia treated by pneumatic dilation. Gastroenterology 103:1732–1738, 1992.

63. West RL, Hirsch DP, Bartelsman JF, et al: Long term results of pneumatic dilation in achalasia followed for more than 5 years. Am J Gastroenterol 97:1346–1351, 2002.

64. Nair LA, Reynolds JC, Parkman HP, et al: Complications during pneumatic dilation for achalasia or diffuse esophageal spasm. Analysis of risk factors, early clinical characteristics, and outcome. Dig Dis Sci 38:1893–1904, 1993.

65. Parkman HP, Reynolds JC, Ouyang A, et al: Pneumatic dilatation or esophagomyotomy treatment for idiopathic achalasia: Clinical outcomes and cost analysis. Dig Dis Sci 38:75–85, 1993.

66. Robertson CS, Fellows IW, Mayberry JF, Atkinson M: Choice of therapy for achalasia in relation to age. Digestion 40:244–250, 1988.

67. Penagini R, Cantu P, Mangano M, et al: Long-term effects of pneumatic dilatation on symptoms and lower esophageal sphincter pressure in achalasia. Scand J Gastroenterol 37:380–384, 2002.

68. Katz PO, Gilbert J, Castell DO: Pneumatic dilatation is effective long-term treatment for achalasia. Dig Dis Sci 43:1973–1977, 1998.

69. Arvanitakis C: Achalasia of the esophagus. A reappraisal of esophagomyotomy vs. forceful pneumatic dilation. Dig Dis Sci 20:841–846, 1975.

70. Sanderseon DR, Ellis FH, Olsen AM: Achalasia of the esophagus: Results of therapy by dilation. Chest 48:116–121, 1970.

71. Vantrappen G, Hellemans J, Deloof W, et al: Treatment of achalasia with pneumatic dialtions. Gut 12:268–275, 1971.

72. Fellows IW, Oglivie AL, Atkinson M: Pneumatic dilatation in achalasia. Gut 12:268–275, 1983.

73. Bladergroen MR, Lowe JE, Postlethwait RW: Diagnosis and recommended management of esophageal perforation and rupture. Ann Thorac Surg 42:235–239, 1986.

74. Wesdorp IC, Bartelsman JF, Huibregtse K, et al: Treatment of instrumental esophageal perforation. Gut 25:398–404, 1984.

75. Borotto E, Gaudric M, Danel B, et al: Risk factors of esophageal perforation during pneumatic dilatation for achalasia. Gut 39:9–12, 1996.

76. Fennerty B: Esophageal perforation during pneumatic dilatation for achalasia: A possible association with malnutrition. Dysphagia 5:227–228, 1990.

77. Shoenut JP, Duerksen D, Yaffe CS: A prospective assessment of gastroesophageal reflux before and after treatment of achalasia patients: Pneumatic dilation versus transthoracic limited myotomy Am J Gastroenterol 92:1109–1112, 1997.

78. Rubesin SE, Kennedy M, Levine MS, et al: Distal esophageal ballooning following Heller myotomy. Radiology 167:345–347, 1988.

79. Okike N, Payne WS, Meufeld DM, et al: Esophagomyotomy versus forceful dilation for achalasia of the esophagus: Results in 899 patients. Ann Thorac Surg 28:119–125, 1979.

80. Csendes A, Braghetto I, Henriquez A, Cortes C: Late results of a prospective randomised study comparing forceful dilatation and esophagomyotomy in patients with achalasia. Gut 30:299–304, 1989.

81. Suarez J, Mearin F, Boque R, et al: Laparoscopic myotomy vs. endoscopic dilation in the treatment of achalasia. Surg Endosc 16:75–77, 2002.

82. Yon J, Christensen J: An uncontrolled comparison of treatments for achalasia. Ann Surg 182:672–676, 1975.

83. Paricio PP, Martinez de Haro L, Ortiz A, Aguayo JL: Achalasia of the cardia: Long-term results of esophagomyotomy and posterior partial fundoplication. Br J Surg 77:1371–1374, 1990.

84. Sariyannis C, Mullard KS: Esophagomyotomy for achalasia of the cardia. Thorax 30:539–542, 1975.

85. Hirashima T, Sato H, Hara T, et al: Results of esophagocardioplasty with gastric patch treatment of esophageal achalasia. Ann Surg 188:38–42, 1978.

86. Ellis FH, Crozier RE, Watkins E: Operation for esophageal achalasia. Results of esophagomyotomy without an antireflux operation. J Thorac Cardiovasc Surg 88:344–351, 1984.

87. Jordan PH Jr: Longterm results of esophageal myotomy for achalasia. J Am Coll Surg 193:137–145, 2001.

88. Pai G, Ellison R, Rubin JW, Moore HV: Two decades of experience with modified Heller's myotomy for achalasia. Ann Thorac Surg 38:201–206, 1984; objective evaluation of the results of esophago-myotomy in 100 patients with achalasia of the esophagus. Surgery 104:469–475, 1988.

89. Black J, Vorbach AN, Leigh Collis J: Results of Heller's operation for achalasia of the esophagus. The importance of hiatal hernia repair. Br J Surg 63:949–953, 1976.

90. Wingfield HV, Karwowski A: The treatment of achalasia by cardiomyotomy. Br J Surg 59:281–284, 1972.

91. Ben-Meir A, Urbach DR, Khajanchee YS, et al: Quality of life before and after laparoscopic Heller myotomy for achalasia. Am J Surg 181:471–474, 2001.

92. Patti MG, Molena D, Fisichella PM, et al: Laparoscopic Heller myotomy and Dor fundoplication for achalasia: Analysis of successes and failures. Arch Surg 136:870–877, 2001.

93. Reference deleted in page proofs.

94. Finley RJ, Clifton JC, Stewart KC, et al: Laparoscopic Heller myotomy improves esophageal emptying and the symptoms of achalasia. Arch Surg 136:892–896, 2001.

95. Maher JW, Conklin J, Heitshusen DS: Thoracoscopic esophagomyotomy for achalasia. Surgery 130:570–577, 2001.

96. Yamamura MS, Gilstger JC, Myers BS, et al: Laparoscopic Heller myotomy and anterior fundoplication for achalasia results in a high degree of patient satisfaction. Arch Surg 135:902–906, 2000.

97. Luketich JD, Fernando HC, Christie NA, et al: Outcomes after minimally invasive esophagomyotomy. Ann Thorac Surg 72:1909–1913, 2001.

98. Ackroyd R, Watson EI, Devitt PG, Jamieson GG: Laparoscopic cardiomyotomy and anterior partial fundoplication for achalasia. Surg Endosc 15:683–686, 2001.

99. Diener U, Patti MG, Molena D, et al: Laparoscopic Heller myotomy relieves dysphagia in patients with achalasia and low LES pressure following pneumatic dilatation. Surg Endosc 15:687–690, 2001.

100. Finley RJ, Clifton JC, Stewart KC, et al: Laparoscopic Heller myotomy improves esophageal emptying and the symptoms of achalasia. Arch Surg 136:892–896, 2001.

101. DiSimone MP, Felice V, D'Errico A, et al: Onset timing of delayed complications and criteria of follow-up after operation for esophageal achalasia. Ann Thorac Surg 61:1106–1111, 1996.

102. Holzman MD, Sharp KW, Lapido JK et al: Laparoscopic surgical treatment of achalasia. Am J Surg 173:308–311, 1997.

103. Ancona E, Anselmino M, Zanitto G, et al: Esophageal achalasia: Laparoscopic versus conventional open Heller-Dor operation. Am J Surg 170:265–270, 1995.

104. Raiser F, Perdikis G, Hinder RA, et al: Heller myotomy via minimal-access surgery. An evaluation of antireflux procedures. Arch Surg 131:593–598, 1996.

105. Watson EI, Devitt PG, Jamieson GG: Laparoscopic cardiomyotomy and anterior partial fundoplication for achalasia. Surg Endosc 15:683–686, 2001.

106. Robertson GS, Lloyd DM, Wicks ACB, et al: Laparoscopic Heller's cardiomyotomy without an antireflux procedure. Br J Surg 82:957–959, 1995.

107. Peters JH, Kauer WK, Crookes PF, et al: Esophageal resection with colon interposition for end-stage achalasia. Arch Surg 130:632–637, 1995.

108. Gupta NM, Goenka MK, Behera A, Bhasin DK: Transhiatal esophagectomy for benign obstructive conditions of the esophagus. Br J Surg 84:262–264, 1997.

109. Shah J, Rockall R, Carzi A: Robot-assisted laparoscopic Heller's cardiomyotomy. Surg Laparosc Endosc Percutan Tech 12:30–32, 2002.

110. Berger K, McCallum RW: Nifedipine in the treatment of achalasia. Ann Intern Med 96:61–62, 1982.

111. Coccia G, Bortolotti M, Michetti P, Dodero M: Return of esophageal peristalsis after nifedipine therapy in patients with idiopathic achalasia. Am J Gastroenterol 87:1705–1708, 1992.

112. Bortolotti M, Mari C, Lopilato C, et al: Effects of sildenafil on esophageal motility of patients with idiopathic achalasia. Gastroenterology 118:253–257, 2000.

113. Mukherjee S, Kaplan DS, Parasher G, Sipple MS: Expandable metal stents in achalasia—is there a role? Am J Gastroenterol 95:2185–2188, 2000.

114. O'Connor JB, Singer ME, Imperiale TF, et al: The cost-effectiveness of treatment strategies for achalasia. Dig Dis Sci 47:1516–1525, 2002.

115. Urbach DR, Hansen PD, Khajanchee YS, Swanstrom LL: A decision analysis of the optimal initial approach to achalasia: Laparoscopic Heller myotomy with partial fundoplication, thoracoscopic Heller myotomy, pneumatic dilation, or botulinum toxin injection. J Gastrointest Surg 5:192–205, 2001.

116. Bell N: Laparoscopic repair of perforation from pneumatic dilatation.

117. Katzka DA, Castell DO: Use of botulinum toxin as a diagnostic/therapeutic trial to help clarify an indication for definitive therapy in patients with achalasia. Am J Gastroenterol 94:637–642

118. Sandler RS, Bozymksi EM, Orlando RC: Failure of clinical criteria to distinguish between primary achalasia and achalasia secondary to tumor. Dig Dis Sci 27:209–213, 1982.

119. Moonka R, Patti MG, Feo CV, et al: Clinical presentation and evaluation of malignant pseudoachalasia. J Gastrointest Surg 3:456–461, 1999.

120. Raymond L, Lach B, Shamji FM: Inflammatory etiology of primary esophageal achalasia: An immunohistochemical and ultrastructural study of Auerbach's plexus. Histopathology 35:445–453, 1999.

121. Liu W, Fackler W, Rice TW, et al: The pathogenesis of pseudoachalasia. A clinicopathologic study of 13 cases of a rare entity. Am J Surg Pathol 26:784–788, 2002.

122. Awad ZT. Selima MA. Filipi CJ: Pseudoachalasia as a late complication of gastric wrap performed for morbid obesity: Report of a case. Surg Today 32:906–909, 2002.

123. Colarian JH, Sekkarie M, Rao R: Pancreatic pseudocyst mimicking idiopathic achalasia. Am J Gastroenterol 93:103–105, 1998

124. Tanigawa H, Kida Y, Kuwao S, et al: Hepatoid adenocarcinoma in Barrett's esophagus associated with achalasia: First case report. Pathol Int 52:141–146, 2002.

125. Bholat OS, Haluck RS: Pseudoachalasia as a result of metastatic cervical cancer. J Soc Laparoendosc Surg 5:57–62, 2001.

126. Song CW, Chun HJ, Kim CD, et al: Association of pseudo-achalasia with advancing cancer of the gastric cardia. Gastrointest Endosc 50:486–491, 1999.

127. Lopez-Liuchi JV, Kraytem A, Uldry PY: Oesophageal achalasia secondary to pleural mesothelioma. J R Soc Med 92:24–25, 1999.

128. Moonka R, Patti MG, Feo CV, et al: Clinical presentation and evaluation of malignant pseudoachalasia. J Gastrointest Surg 3:456–461, 1999.

129. Lucchinetti CF, Kimmel DW, Lennon VA: Paraneoplastic and oncologic profiles of patients seropositive for type 1 antineuronal nuclear autoantibodies. Neurology 50:652–657, 1998.

130. Sandler RS, Bozymksi EM, Orlando RC: Failure of clinical criteria to distinguish between primary achalasia and achalasia secondary to tumor. Dig Dis Sci 27:209–213, 1982.
131. Valera RA, Brazer SR: Botulinum toxin for suspected pseudo-achalasia. Am J Gastroenterol 90:1319–1321, 1995.
132. Woodfield CA, Levine MS, Rubesin SE, et al: I. Diagnosis of primary versus secondary achalasia: Reassessment of clinical and radiographic criteria. AJR Am J Roentgenol 175:727–731, 2000.
133. Brossard E, Ollyo JB, Fontolliet C, et al: Achalasia and squamous cell carcinoma of the esophagus: Is an endoscopic surveillance justified? [abstract]. Gastroenterology 102:A4, 1992.
134. Meijssen MA, Tilanus HW, van Blankenstein M, et al: Achalasia complicated by esophageal squamous cell carcinoma: A prospective study of 195 patients. Gut 33:155–158, 1992.
135. Just-Viera JO, Haight C: Achalasia and carcinoma of the esophagus. Surg Gynecol Obstet 128:1081–1095, 1969.
136. Brucher BL, Stein HJ, Bartels H, et al: Achalasia and esophageal cancer: Incidence, prevalence, and prognosis. World J Surg 25:745–749, 2001.
137. Porschen R, Molsberger G, Kuhn A, et al: Achalasia-associated squamous cell carcinoma of the esophagus: Flow-cytometric and histologic evaluation. Gastroenterology 108:545–549, 1995.

Ingested Foreign Objects and Food Bolus Impactions

CHAPTER
21

Patrick Pfau

Introduction

Ingested gastrointestinal (GI) foreign bodies and food bolus impactions occur often and are the second most common endoscopic emergency after GI bleeding. The actual incidence of foreign bodies and food impaction is unknown and little controlled data exist on the management of foreign body ingestions.

Although most GI bodies do not result in serious clinical sequelae or mortality,[1] it has been estimated that up to 1500 deaths annually in the United States are attributed to ingested foreign bodies and food impactions.[2–4] As a result of the frequency and the potential for negative consequences, it is important for the gastroenterologist and endoscopist to understand the patients at risk for ingestion of foreign bodies, the best method for a prompt diagnosis, and the best management with avoidance of unwanted complications. Few prospective trials exist in the field of foreign body ingestion, and our understanding is based on large case series, reviews, and reports describing specific new techniques of management.

Epidemiology

Most foreign body ingestions occur in the pediatric population. Eighty percent of foreign body ingestions occur in children with most ingestions occurring between the ages of 6 months and 3 years.[5] Pediatric ingestions are almost always accidental, resulting from the child's natural oral curiosity.[6] The most common items ingested by children are coins but also often include small toys, crayons, buttons, pins, jewels, and disc batteries.[7,8,9]

Accidental ingestion in adults occurs in a variety of groups of patients. Dentures or dental work are the most common risk factors for accidental foreign body ingestion resulting from impaired tactile sensation during swallowing.[10,11] Certain careers such as roofing, tailor, or seamstress have increased rates of foreign body ingestion because of accidental occupational swallowing of nails or needles. The other large patient group who accidentally ingest foreign bodies are those with compromised judgment or senses such as found in the very elderly, demented, or intoxicated. Accidental coin ingestion

has been encountered in young college students secondary to an increasingly popular tavern game ("Quarters") in which a quarter may inadvertently be swallowed.[12]

Intentional ingestion of foreign bodies is frequent in psychiatric patients or prisoners[13,14] (Fig. 21–1). These patients ingest foreign bodies for a secondary gain and often ingest multiple objects and have a previous history of foreign body ingestion. An often cited patient has a recorded 2533 foreign bodies documented during his ingestion career.[15]

Esophageal food impaction is a much more common problem than true foreign body ingestion with an estimated annual incidence of 13 episodes per 100,000 people.[16] Most (75% to 100%) patients who present with a food impaction have some type of predisposing esophageal pathology.[16–19] The most commonly observed abnormalities associated with food impaction are Schatzki's rings and peptic strictures. Less commonly found as the predisposing cause are webs, extrinsic compression, surgical anastomoses, fundoplication wraps, and bariatric gastroplasties.[20] Esophageal cancer

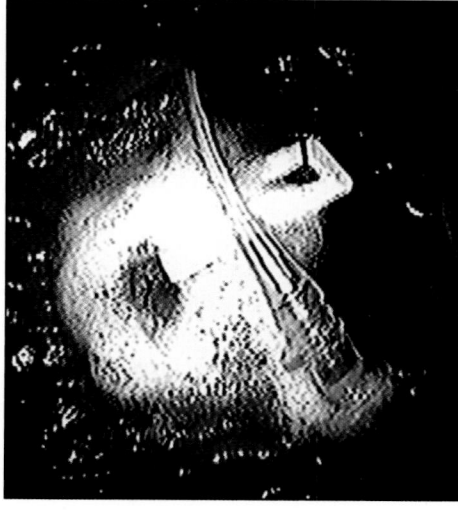

Figure 21–1. Endoscopic image of an intravenous Heplock ingested in the hospital by a prisoner with a psychiatric history.

very rarely presents with acute food bolus impaction.[21] Motility disorders such as achalasia, diffuse esophageal spasm, and nutcracker esophagus are infrequent causes of food impactions.[22] Food impaction rarely occurs in children and happens more often in patients older than the fourth or fifth decade of life.

The type of food impaction correlates with the local cuisine and dietary habits of a specific region. In the United States, meat is the most common food impaction, particularly beef, chicken, or hot dogs. In Asia and coastal countries, fish and fish bones are the most common food to result in impaction and mucosal trauma in either the esophagus or oropharynx.[23,24]

Pathophysiology and Pathogenesis

Most ingested foreign bodies (80% to 90%) and food bolus impactions pass spontaneously without clinical sequelae.[1] However, 10% to 20% require nonoperative, usually endoscopic, intervention and 1% may eventually require surgery.[19,21,25] Therefore, it is important to understand how ingested foreign bodies can result in significant disease and in which parts of the GI tract foreign bodies are most likely to cause damage (Fig. 21–2). This will ensure appropriate use of endoscopic and surgical intervention.

The most common complications related to foreign bodies are obstruction and perforation. Once through the esophagus, most objects, including sharp objects pass through the intestinal tract without consequence.[1,26] However, among patients presenting with symptoms related to a foreign body, the perforation rate has been estimated to be as high as 5% overall and up to 35% for sharp and pointed objects.[21,27] Esophageal perforation is the most frequent cause of significant morbidity and mortality and can result in mediastinitis, lung abscess, pneumothorax, peritonitis, and cardiac tamponade.[28] The risk of perforation of the esophagus increases dramatically when foreign bodies or food boluses are left impacted in the esophagus for greater than 24 hours. Other reported complications, including those that have been reported to lead to fatalities, include GI bleeding, aortoenteric fistulae, aspiration, abscess formation, and true rarities such as perforation of the heart and lead and zinc toxicity.[29–35]

Food boluses by definition result in obstruction and possible complication only in the esophagus. True ingested foreign bodies can occur anywhere along the digestive tract but are most likely to occur in locations where there is an anatomic sphincter, acute angulation, physical narrowing, or a congenital malformation[26] (see Fig. 21–2).

The posterior hypopharynx is the first area of the GI tract in which a foreign body may become lodged, particularly small sharp objects such as chicken or fish bones.[36,37] In the esophagus, there are four areas of physical narrowing where a food bolus or foreign body is likely to impact. These include the upper esophageal sphincter, the level of the aortic arch, the crossing of the main stem bronchus, and the lower esophageal sphincter and gastroesophageal junction. All of these areas have been shown to be areas of true luminal narrowing with diameters of 23 mm or less in the adult patient.[38] Independent of the physiologic areas of narrowing, most food boluses are associated with esophageal pathology including rings, webs, diverticula, and peptic strictures.[2] Finally, although more

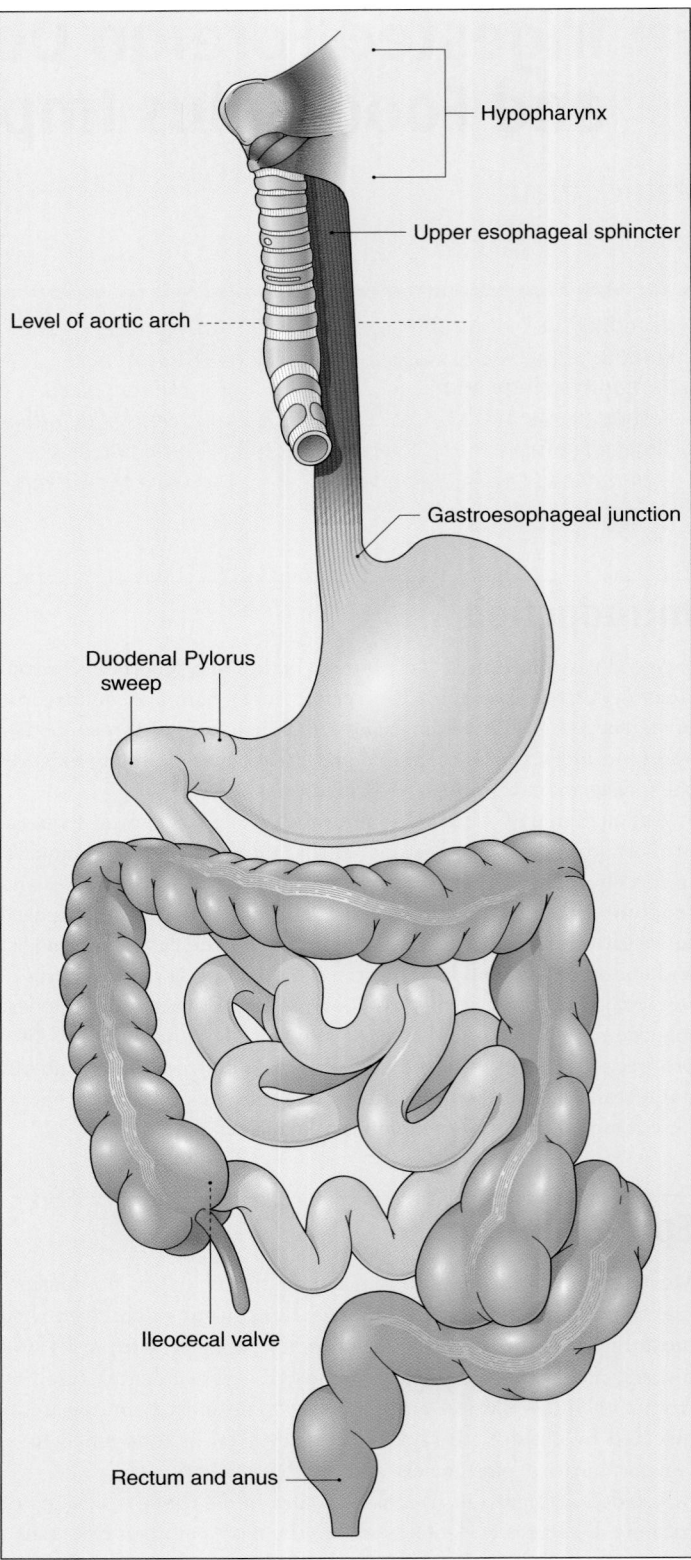

Figure 21–2. Gastrointestinal areas of luminal narrowing and angulation that predispose to foreign body impaction and obstruction. (Adapted with permission from Feldman M, Friedman LS, Sleisenger MH (eds): Sleisenger & Fordtrans Gastrointestinal and Liver Disease, Vol 1, 7th ed. London, Saunders, 2002, p 387.)

disputed, esophageal motor disturbances such as achalasia, diffuse esophageal spasm, or segmental variations in peristalsis may contribute to food and foreign body impactions.[39–42]

Once in the stomach, most foreign bodies pass through the GI tract without complications in 1 to 2 weeks. Exceptions are certain objects that are unable to pass through the pylorus. Objects with a diameter of greater than 2 cm and objects longer than 5 cm have difficulty passing through the pylorus or the duodenal bulb and sweep.[26,36,43]

In the small intestine, three points of impedance exist where a foreign body may become lodged and result in obstruction. These include the duodenal C-loop where long objects may get "hung-up" and result in perforation. The narrowing and angulation of the ligament of Treitz can result in foreign body obstruction and even smaller objects that were able to pass through the pylorus and ligament of Treitz may cause a distal small bowel obstruction by becoming impacted at the ileocecal valve. Patients with small bowel disease, history of adhesions, or partial small bowel obstructions may have greater difficulty passing foreign bodies through the small intestine.

Most objects, once in small intestine and colon, do not cause damage. The bowel tends to naturally protect itself against foreign bodies. A foreign body stimulates peristalsis and axial flow in the small intestine, which results in the foreign body traveling with the blunt end leading and the sharp end trailing.[44] As the foreign body travels further into the large intestine, it usually becomes centered in the lumen surrounded by stool making a complication even less likely.[2]

Rectal foreign bodies are often inserted into the rectum via the anorectal route. However, occasionally an ingested foreign body may traverse the entire GI tract to the rectum before further passage is impaired by the internal and external sphincters.

Clinical Features

HISTORY AND PHYSICAL EXAMINATION

History of ingestion including timing of ingestion, type of foreign body ingested, and onset of symptoms is usually reliable in communicative adults. History is particularly reliable for food impactions because patients are usually symptomatic and can detail the exact onset of symptoms. Small sharp objects or fish bones often present with a foreign body sensation or odynophagia in the posterior pharynx or cervical esophagus. This occurs even if the foreign body has passed to the stomach because of a small mucosal laceration. Esophageal obstruction, partial or complete, usually results in symptoms. Esophageal obstruction may cause substernal chest pain, dysphagia, gagging, vomiting, or a sensation of choking.[45] More complete obstruction can lead to drooling and the inability to handle oral secretions.

The type of symptoms may aid in determining whether an esophageal foreign body is still present and where in the esophagus it may be located. If the patient presents with dysphagia, dysphonia, or odynophagia, there is almost an 80% chance that a foreign body or food impaction will be present. If the symptom is only retrosternal pain or a pharyngeal discomfort, less than 50% of

patients will have an identifiable foreign object.[46] The patient may be able to successfully localize the object in the posterior pharynx or at the level of the cricopharyngeal muscle. However, for objects located more distally in the esophagus and into the stomach, patient localization becomes poor with an accuracy of 30% to 40% in the esophagus and almost 0% in the stomach.[47,48] Once in the stomach, small intestine, or colon, the only symptoms described are secondary to a complication resulting from the foreign body such as obstruction, perforation, or bleeding.

The history and symptoms for true foreign bodies is less reliable than food impaction because true foreign bodies are often ingested by children, mentally impaired adults, or adults who have ingested the foreign body for secondary gain. Even in esophageal foreign bodies, 20% to 38% of children are asymptomatic.[47,49] Furthermore, in children and noncommunicative adults, there may be no history of a foreign body ingestion from the patient or the caregiver in up to 40% of cases,[50] necessitating a high degree of suspicion. Symptoms are more subtle and include drooling, poor feeding, blood-stained saliva, or a failure to thrive.[50,51] Respiratory compromise may occur with aspiration or a proximally located esophageal foreign body that compresses the trachea causing wheezing and stridor.[50,52]

Past medical history is important in regard to previous episodes of either food impaction or foreign body ingestion. Previous food impaction or a previous need of esophageal dilation makes recurrent episodes more likely. Patients with previous true foreign body ingestion are often patients who are multiple ingestors who are more likely to ingest multiple objects and complex objects.

Physical examination aids little in determining the presence or location of a foreign body but is important to detect potential ingestion related complications. Determination of airway and level of consciousness is crucial before any endoscopic or nonendoscopic intervention. Lung examination should be performed to detect the presence of wheezing or aspiration. Esophageal or oropharyngeal perforation may result in swelling, erythema, or crepitus of the neck or chest region. Abdominal examination aids in determining the signs of an obstruction or perforation.

Diagnosis

Diagnostic evaluation should begin with plain film radiographs. Patients with suspected foreign body ingestion should undergo anteroposterior and lateral radiographs of the chest and abdomen to help determine the presence, type, and location of a foreign body[27] (Fig 21–3). Anteroposterior and lateral neck and chest films are suggested if there is a suspicion of a foreign body in the esophagus versus the trachea or if there is a foreign object that may be obscured by overlying spine[50,53] (Fig. 21–4). Plain x-ray films also aid in detecting complications such as aspiration, abdominal free air, or subcutaneous emphysema.[45,54]

Radiographic studies are more controversial in children. Because history is often poor from children, mouth-to-anus screening films have been advocated in suspected foreign body ingestions.[27] Others have suggested a more directed approach or nonradiographic methods in determining the presence and location of foreign bodies in children.[55]

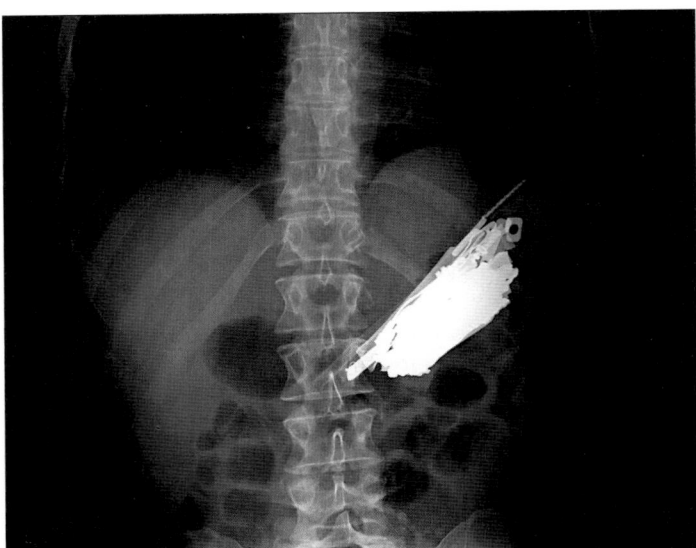

Figure 21-3. Radiograph of patient who had ingested all of the letter keys of a standard typewriter. Because of the size and complexity of this ingested foreign object, laparotomy was required for successful removal.

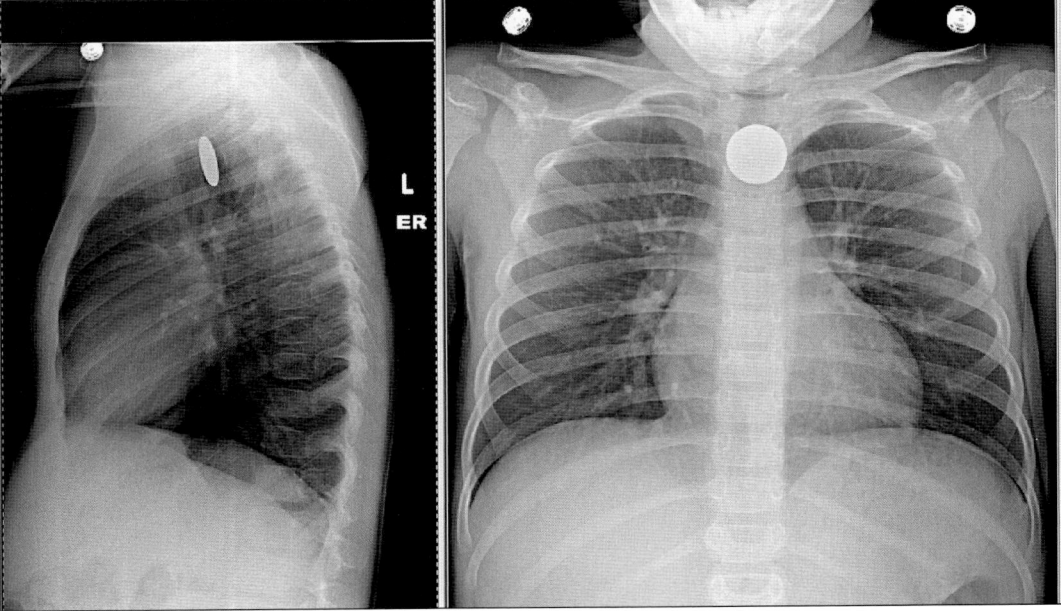

Figure 21-4. Anteroposterior and lateral chest x-ray film of child with suspected coin ingestion showing the coin clearly in the proximal esophagus. (Image courtesy of Dr. Ken L. Schreibman, Department of Radiology, University of Wisconsin Medical School.)

Plain x-ray films are satisfactory in some true foreign bodies and occasionally in food ingestions with larger bones. However, many objects including plastic, wood, and glass are not radiopaque, and small fish or chicken bones and thin metal objects are not readily seen.[9] False-negative rates with plain x-ray films are as high as 47% and false-positive rates are close to 20% in the investigation of foreign bodies.[46,56] Furthermore, 35% of films read by a nonradiologist for the presence of foreign bodies have been found to be misread.[57]

Generally, it is accepted that barium studies should not be performed in the evaluation of GI foreign bodies. If aspiration occurs, the hypertonic contrast agents used can cause acute pulmonary edema.[58] Barium evaluation can delay a necessary therapeutic endoscopic procedure by interfering with endoscopic visualization and complicating removal of a foreign body.[59]

Advanced imaging may be used in unusual or difficult to diagnose cases and may aid in detecting soft tissue inflammation or the presence of an abscess. Three-dimensional computed tomography (CT) has been used to diagnose foreign bodies not seen with other imaging, and magnetic resonance imaging (MRI) may have a role in demonstrating soft tissue periesophageal pathology.[50,60]

Because of the concern of radiation in the pediatric population, handheld metal detectors have become increasingly popular as a noninvasive method to determine the presence and location of ingested metal objects, particularly coins, in children. Metal detectors have been shown repeatedly to have sensitivities and specificities greater than 90% in detecting metallic esophageal foreign bodies in both experienced and inexperienced hands.[55,61,62] Thus, metal detectors can be used as a screening tool before intervention in children who are poor historians with minimal symptoms.

Diagnostic endoscopy provides the most accurate diagnostic modality in suspected ingested foreign bodies and food impactions. Any patient with persistent symptoms and a continued clinical suspicion of a GI foreign body should undergo an upper endoscopy even after negative or unrevealing radiographic evaluation.[63] This approach ensures the correct diagnosis of food impactions, nonradiopaque objects, and radiopaque objects that are obscured by overlying bony structures.[26]

Endoscopy is the best method to detect underlying pathology such as esophageal strictures that contribute to a food impaction or foreign body that would not pass readily through the GI tract. Endoscopy also can closely examine the GI mucosa to assess for laceration or damage that may contribute to continuing symptoms after a foreign body has spontaneously passed. Foremost, diagnostic endoscopy is directly linked to when endoscopy will be used for therapy—treatment or extraction of a known or suspected foreign body.

Diagnostic endoscopy is not indicated when small, blunt objects are known to have passed into the stomach and the patient is asymptomatic. These objects traverse the pylorus and the rest of the GI tract without complications. If a foreign body is known to have passed the ligament of Treitz, diagnostic and therapeutic endoscopy will be of little added benefit. Rare exceptions are sharp objects that can be safely extracted with an enteroscope. Finally, diagnostic endoscopy is contraindicated when there is physical examination or radiographic evidence of a bowel perforation anywhere in the GI tract or a small bowel obstruction beyond the ligament of Treitz secondary to the foreign body.

Treatment

In providing any treatment of GI foreign bodies, it must always be remembered that 75% to 90% of GI foreign bodies pass through the GI tract spontaneously without complication.[19,64] Two recent studies have emphasized conservative management, with 86% to 97% of foreign bodies passing spontaneously with minimal complications.[65,66] Importantly, esophageal foreign bodies were excluded from the these studies. Although conservative management is successful in most nonesophageal foreign bodies, a more appropriate treatment plan if immediate endoscopy is not performed is to have a policy of expectant management and then selective endoscopy based on type, size, and location of the ingested object.[67]

A number of medical therapies for esophageal foreign bodies or food impactions have been studied as primary treatment or in conjunction with endoscopic therapy. The most often used medication is glucagon, a smooth muscle relaxant that significantly reduces lower esophageal sphincter pressure with doses as low as 0.25 mg.[68] Glucagon has reported successes of 12% to 58% in treating esophageal food impactions.[69,70] However, a randomized trial found

glucagon no better than placebo in treating children with coins lodged in the esophagus.[71] Glucagon is generally safe but may result in nausea, abdominal distension, and rarely vomiting. Glucagon does not work with a fixed obstruction present, which is often found with esophageal foreign bodies and food impactions. Furthermore, glucagon does not provide definitive examination and treatment of coexisting esophageal pathology as will flexible endoscopy. Finally, glucagon may help when used with endoscopy by lowering lower esophageal sphincter pressure and facilitating the endoscope pushing a food impaction into the stomach.[72]

Nitroglycerin and nifedipine are other smooth muscle relaxants that have been anecdotally described as promoting passage of esophageal impactions into the stomach.[27] Medical methods that have been described but should be avoided are gas-forming agents, emetics, and papain meat tenderizer. Gas-forming agents combined with a smooth muscle relaxant have been reported to have success rates of almost 70% in clearing esophageal foreign bodies into the stomach.[73] However, esophageal rupture and perforation have occurred with these agents, particularly if there is a fixed obstruction or if the foreign body has been present greater than 6 hours.[74,75] Papain, a meat tenderizer used for the treatment of food impaction, and emetics are two methods that should never be used because of the risk of esophageal necrosis, perforation, and aspiration.[2,76,77]

The radiologic literature has multiple descriptions of methods to remove esophageal foreign bodies under fluoroscopic guidance. Reported methods include extraction with Foley balloon catheters, suction catheters, wire baskets, or a magnetic catheter to extract ferromagnetic metal objects.[54,78] The largest experience has been with Foley catheters in which the catheter is passed either nasally or orally into the esophagus and past the foreign body. The balloon is then inflated and withdrawn to deliver the foreign body to the oropharynx where it can be retrieved. Although high success rates have been reported, the major drawback is loss of control of the foreign body, particularly at the level of the upper esophageal sphincter and laryngopharynx. Complications reported include nosebleeds, dislodgment of the foreign body in the nose, laryngospasm, vomiting, and, of greatest concern, aspiration with resultant airway obstruction and even death.[79,80] Because radiologic methods do not match the efficacy or safety of endoscopy, few indications exist for their use. Radiologic methods to remove foreign bodies or food impactions should be limited to when endoscopy is not available or cannot be available within 12 to 24 hours.

Flexible endoscopy has clearly become the diagnostic and therapeutic method of choice in both true GI foreign bodies and food boluses in the pediatric and adult population. This is based on multiple large series using endoscopy for the treatment of GI foreign bodies with success rates greater than 95% and associated morbidity and mortality reported at 0% in most studies but always less than 5%.[7,16,17,19,59,81-83] Although treatment failures are rare, predictors of endoscopic failure and complications include intentional ingestion, ingestion of multiple complex foreign bodies, and lack of patient cooperation.[27]

Because most GI foreign bodies pass through the GI tract uneventfully, the indication and timing for intervention with endoscopy is important. Generally, if a patient is symptomatic, intervention is required. For esophageal foreign bodies, this includes patients with odynophagia, dysphagia, vomiting, inability to handle secretions, drooling, chest pain, or the sensation of a present foreign body. Once past the esophagus, symptoms of obstruction or perforation may necessitate surgical rather than endoscopic intervention.

If the patient is not overtly symptomatic or cannot accurately give a history concerning their symptoms, the location and characteristics of the foreign body define the need for intervention.

Generally, all esophageal foreign bodies and food impactions require intervention in an urgent or emergent fashion. No foreign body should be allowed to remain lodged in the esophagus greater than 24 hours. The time a foreign body is present in the esophagus is directly related to an increase in complications.[84,85]

For most objects that reach the stomach, observation is acceptable because the risk of complications once the object is out of the esophagus is greatly diminished. Sharp objects are the primary exception and should be removed from the stomach and duodenum if they are within reach of the endoscope because the risk of perforation can be as high as 15% to 35%.[86] Long objects greater than 5 cm and large objects greater than 2 cm are unlikely to pass the duodenal sweep or pylorus, respectively, and thus attempts to remove them should be made.

Observation is recommended for small blunt objects in the stomach, which usually pass without complication. Even sharp or complex foreign bodies that fail endoscopic retrieval can initially be observed because the minority of even these objects result in significant complications.[65,66] In the more complex foreign bodies that are not extracted with the endoscope, periodical radiographs should be obtained to document progression through the GI tract (Fig. 21–5). Close attention should be paid to symptoms such as fever, distension, vomiting, or abdominal pain that could suggest obstruction or perforation. For objects that are not extracted the amount and timing of observation and radiographs should be individualized as transit time varies greatly based on patient and type of object ingested.[87]

Before initiating endoscopic therapy for foreign bodies and food boluses, proper procedure, equipment, and patient preparation will increase the success rate while maintaining a low complication rate. The endoscopist should be aware of the type of foreign bodies that may be encountered in that particular patient and the safest method to remove these objects. Before endoscopy, it is beneficial to perform a "dry run" on a similar object *ex vivo*.[19] This allows proper retrieval device selection and makes the extraction safer and easier.

Endoscopes, endoscopic retrieval devices, and accessory equipment available to assist in removal of foreign bodies and food impactions are listed in Table 21–1. Before an attempt at removing

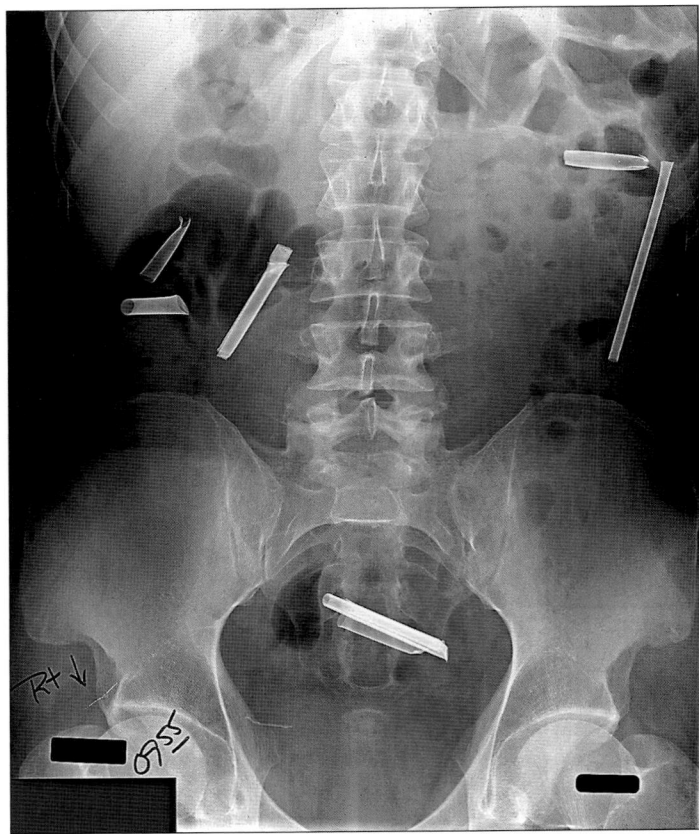

Figure 21–5. Radiograph demonstrating passage of broken television antenna throughout the intestine. Patient eventually passed all the pieces of the antenna without complication.

complex foreign bodies an endoscopy suite should be equipped with a minimum of a rat-tooth forceps, polypectomy snares, Dormia baskets, and retrieval nets.[1,88]

Standard-sized overtubes that extend past the upper esophageal sphincter and overtubes of length 45 to 60 cm that extend past the lower esophageal sphincter should be available. An overtube provides airway protection, allows frequent passes of the endoscope, and protects the mucosa from superficial and deep lacerations.[89] The longer overtube can aid in removing sharp objects and objects that cannot be pulled retrogradely through the lower esophageal sphincter. A latex protector hood that can be simply attached to the end of the endoscope also helps prevent mucosal trauma in retrieval of sharp objects when overtubes are not available or when objects cannot easily be pulled through an overtube.[90,91]

Table 21–1. Equipment for Treatment and Removal of Gastrointestinal Foreign Bodies and Food Impactions

Endoscopes	Overtubes	Accessory Equipment
Flexible endoscope Rigid endoscope Laryngoscope	Standard esophageal overtube 45–60 cm foreign body overtube	Retrieval net Grasping forceps Dormia basket Polypectomy snare Magnetic extractor Steigmann-Goff variceal ligator cap Latex protector hood

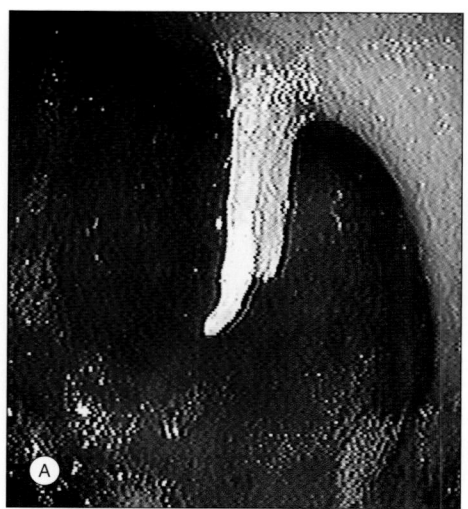 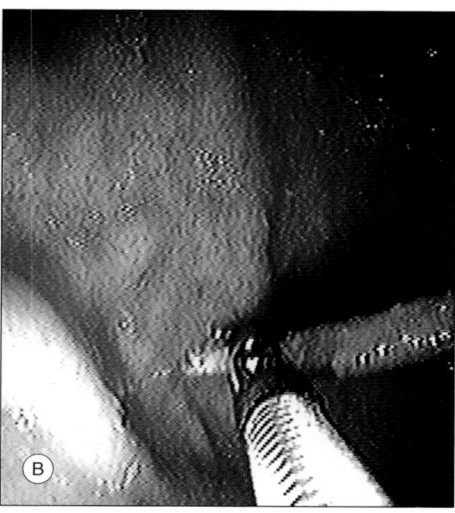

Figure 21-6. Endoscopic photograph of a patient who presented with abdominal pain 3 days after ingesting a toothpick *(A)*. The toothpick was imbedded deep into the stomach wall but was successfully extracted with a rat-tooth forceps through an overtube without difficulty *(B)*. (See attached video clip).

The flexible endoscope is the preferred endoscopic method for treating GI foreign bodies and food impactions because of the high success rate, low complication rate, availability, and affordability.[26] Rigid esophagoscopy has equal efficacy to flexible endoscopy in the treatment of esophageal foreign bodies, but it always requires general anesthesia and few endoscopists have experience with the rigid endoscope. Flexible nasoendoscopes have been suggested as an alternative to standard flexible endoscopes but have been shown to have no additional benefit and may fail more often for foreign bodies below the cricopharyngeus.[92] Laryngoscopes with the aid of a Kelly or McGill forceps should be available and may help in the removal of small, sharp objects at the hypopharynx.

Intravenous conscious sedation provides enough needed sedation in most adult patients with foreign bodies or food impactions. General anesthesia with endotracheal intubation in certain patients is preferred because it provides complete control over the airway and the patient. General anesthesia should be used in most pediatric patients and should be considered in uncooperative patients and patients with multiple or complex foreign bodies in whom removal will take an extended period of time.

Finally, an *ex vivo* study has shown that success and speed of foreign body retrieval is directly related to endoscopist experience.[89] For complex foreign bodies, the most experienced endoscopist at an institution should attempt endoscopic retrieval. If concern exists about experience with foreign body retrieval or a lack of necessary endoscopic equipment and accessories, the patient should be transferred to a tertiary care center for successful treatment and extraction of the foreign body.

SHARP OBJECTS

Sharp and pointed objects account for one third of all perforations caused by GI foreign bodies and if untreated up to 15% to 35% of sharp/pointed foreign bodies may lead to a GI complication.[93] Bones, toothpicks, and dental bridgework are the most common inadvertently swallowed sharp foreign bodies (Fig. 21–6 and Video 21–1). More complex and varied pointed objects are seen in patients with psychiatric illnesses or incarcerated patients. Among these populations, common objects ingested are razor blades, pins, needles, nails, writing instruments, and metal wires.

Sharp objects in the esophagus should be addressed in an emergent fashion with an attempt to remove the object within at least 24 hours. Because of the risk of perforation, attempts should be made to retrieve any sharp object within the reach of the endoscope. When removing sharp ingested foreign bodies, Chevalier Jackson's axiom should be remembered: "advancing points puncture, trailing points do not."[94] When removing sharp objects, the foreign body should be grasped in a position so that the sharp or pointed end trails distally to the endoscope, thus lowering the chance of a significant procedure-related perforation or mucosal trauma during extraction.

Polypectomy snares and foreign body retrieval forceps such as a rat-tooth or alligator forceps are the most commonly used devices for removing sharp foreign bodies with the most endoscopic control. If the size and shape of the foreign body prohibits easy withdrawal of the object an overtube, either standard or foreign body overtube (45 to 60 cm) should be used to protect the esophagus, airway, and oropharynx.[91] An alternative is a soft latex protector hood that provides mucosal protection. The hood is simply placed and sometimes tied to the end of the endoscope with suture and folded back on itself to obtain endoscopic visualization. After the foreign body is grasped, as it is pulled through the lower or upper esophageal sphincter the hood flips over the end of the endoscope and the tightly grasped foreign body, which is protected within the hood (Fig. 21–7). Commercially available hoods exist or alternatively a modified latex glove has been described to be used with similar methodology for the removal of sharp gastric foreign bodies.[95]

Sharp objects that are beyond the reach of the endoscope or cannot be safely removed with the endoscope can still be observed with a relatively low chance of complication. Sharp objects should be followed more closely, and surgery should be considered if the object does not progress on serial radiographs or if there is any evidence of abdominal pain; fever; or overt signs of obstruction, perforation, or bleeding.

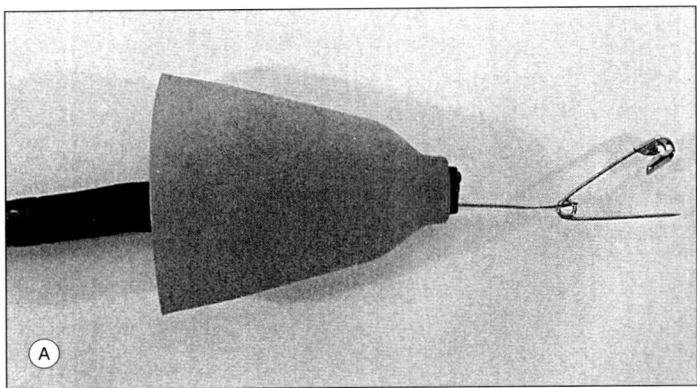
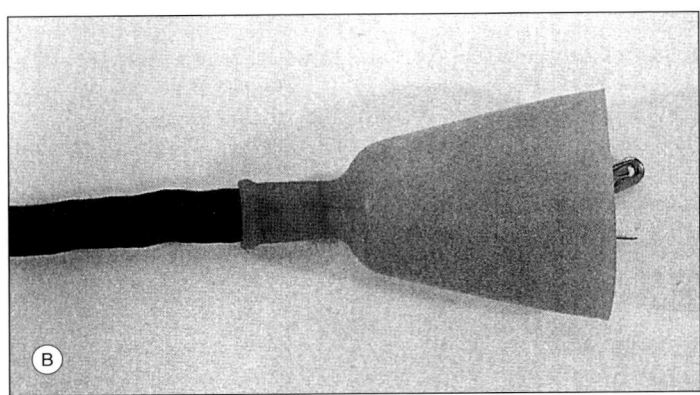

Figure 21-7. A latex protector hood with the hood pulled back providing full visualization and allowing the endoscopist to easily grasp a sharp object *(A)*. As the protector hood is pulled back through the lower esophageal sphincter, the hood flips forward protecting the gastrointestinal mucosa from the sharp object *(B)*. (With permission from Feldman M, Friedman LS, Sleisenger MH (eds): Sleisenger & Fordtrans Gastrointestinal and Liver Disease, Vol 1, 7th ed. London, Saunders, 2002, p 393.)

COINS AND BUTTON BATTERIES

Coins and button batteries are the most common and one of the most dangerous foreign bodies in children, respectively. Coins in the esophagus that are not promptly removed can result in pressure necrosis of the esophageal wall with possible perforation or fistulization. In children, before attempted endoscopic removal, airway protection should be provided via general anesthesia with endotracheal intubation. In adults, dimes and pennies, measuring 17 and 18 mm, respectively, will pass through the esophagus, but larger coins may become lodged. For an adult, an overtube can be used for airway protection if the coin can be pulled through it. Pinch biopsy forceps should be avoided because greater control is provided with a rat-tooth forceps or a basket. The preferred retrieval device for coins is a retrieval net that allows easy snaring of the coin and also protects the airway as the coin is pulled past the larynx.[89] Retrieval with a net can be performed by directly snaring the coin in the esophagus and then pulling out the endoscope, net, and coin in toto. Alternatively, if there is no resistance, the coin can be gently pushed into the stomach and then more easily snared and retrieved by the net and subsequently removed via the mouth.

Objects of 2.5 cm or less can pass through the pylorus. This includes all coins except half dollars (30 mm) or silver dollars (38 mm). Thus, once a coin enters the stomach, observation with conservative management is sufficient in most patients.[96,97] Patients may maintain a regular diet, but if the coin does not pass in approximately 4 weeks it should be removed endoscopically.[93]

Button batteries are of special concern because they may contain an alkaline solution that can rapidly cause a liquefaction necrosis of esophageal tissue resulting in perforation or fistula formation. Ten percent of ingested button batteries become symptomatic; children younger than 5 years are the most common victims.[97] The mechanism of injury can be caused by direct corrosive action, low-voltage burns, and pressure necrosis.[19] Thus, any clinical suspicion or radiographic evidence of a disc battery localized in the esophagus should prompt emergent endoscopy.

In the retrieval of button disc batteries, it is crucial to protect the airway with endotracheal tube intubation in children or an overtube

in adults or older children. Traditionally, the button battery had a high endoscopic failure rate of up to 60% of cases because its shape and contour made it difficult to grasp.[98] The use of the Roth retrieval net has solved this problem, making retrieval of button batteries successful in almost all cases. The battery can be retrieved from the esophagus or pushed into the stomach and retrieved. A stone retrieval basket also works with a high success rate but slightly less control than a retrieval net.

Once in the stomach or beyond, button batteries rarely cause problems and are generally treated with observation only.[99] If the battery reaches the duodenal sweep, 85% will pass through the GI tract within 72 hours.[100] Batteries located beyond the esophagus require endoscopy if the patient develops symptoms or the battery remains in the stomach for 48 hours on repeat radiograph.[77]

LONG OBJECTS

Objects longer than approximately 5 to 10 cm may have difficulty passing the duodenal sweep, resulting in perforation or obstruction. Objects of concern are toothbrushes, spoons and forks, and pens and pencils. The objects can easily be grasped with a snare or basket. The object must be grabbed at the end of the object to allow retrograde removal through the lower esophageal sphincter, esophagus, and upper esophageal sphincter. Grasping the object near the center orients the object in a horizontal plane, prohibiting pulling the long object through the lower esophageal sphincter or the esophagus. A long overtube that passes the gastroesophageal junction is beneficial because the object can be pulled into the overtube, and the foreign body, overtube, and endoscope all can be removed as a single entity.

NARCOTIC PACKETS

Ingested narcotic packets are found in two types of patients, the "body stuffer" and the "body packer." The body stuffer is a user or dealer who, to avoid arrest, "stuffs" varying amount of drugs into often poorly made packets before ingesting them. The body packer, in the process of smuggling drugs, "packs" much larger amounts of drugs into carefully prepared, usually latex or plastic, packages that are designed to withstand GI tract transit.[101,102]

Diagnosis is usually made because of an arrest and confession by the patient. Of more concern, patients may present with intestinal obstruction or experience toxic effects of the drugs that they have ingested. Up to 26% of patients who have ingested narcotic packets may have symptoms related to the narcotic ingested with serious symptoms and even death in almost 5%.[103] Toxicology screens may identify the drug, detect leakage, and allow the correct reversal agent to be administered. Abdominal radiographs and CT scans of patients with ingested narcotic packets show multiple round or sausage-shaped radiopacities, but false-negative imaging is well described.[102–104]

Endoscopy for removal of narcotic packets is contraindicated because of the danger of rupture of the package resulting in a toxicology emergency.[1] Observation with a clear liquid diet is recommended with lavage and purgatives best avoided because of the risk of the rupture. Surgery is used for failure of the packets to progress, intestinal obstruction, and occasionally for acute rupture.[26]

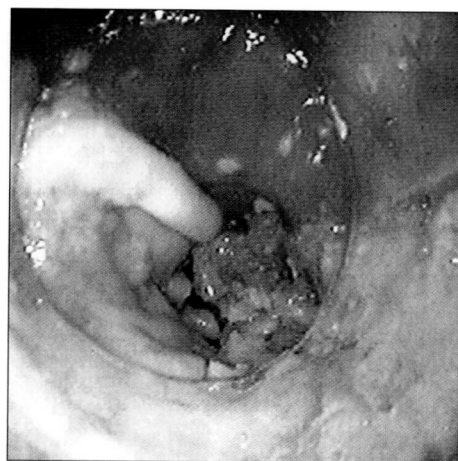

Figure 21–8. Endoscopic photograph in a patient with esophageal cancer who developed dysphagia after eating chicken noodle soup. An overtube was placed allowing multiple passes of the endoscope to successfully extract the food.

FOOD BOLUS IMPACTION

Esophageal food bolus impaction is the most common "foreign body" in adults that can cause symptoms and require endoscopic intervention. In the United States, the most common impacted foods are meat products including beef, chicken, pork, and hot dogs.[20,21] Food impaction may occur in association with alcohol ingestion during which the patient may not chew food as carefully, leading to the terms "steakhouse syndrome" and "backyard barbecue syndrome." In Asia and coastal areas, the most common food foreign body is fish bones. Fish bones rarely cause food impaction but cause symptoms because of the sharp and pointed ends of bones.

Food boluses may pass spontaneously; thus, endoscopic intervention must be based on symptoms. If there is evidence of near or complete obstruction with the patient unable to handle their secretions, salivating, or drooling, endoscopy should be performed on an urgent basis. If the patient has the sensation of the food bolus passing either spontaneously or after preendoscopy glucagon, a gentle trial of fluids then solids may be sufficient and endoscopy can be avoided. However, if there is any concern that the food bolus remains, endoscopy should be performed because all esophageal food impactions should be removed in 12 to 24 hours. Furthermore, endoscopy is indicated because of the high esophageal-related pathology associated with food impactions.

The accepted first endoscopic method used for the treatment of esophageal food impactions is the "push technique." This technique entails gently pushing of the esophageal food bolus into the stomach with the endoscope. Before pushing the food bolus into the stomach, an attempt should be made to steer the endoscope around the impaction and into the stomach. This allows assessment of the nature and degree of any obstructive esophageal pathology beyond the food bolus. Generally, if an endoscope can be advanced around a food bolus and past any obstruction, the push technique should be successful. After steering around the food bolus, the endoscope is pulled back proximal to the food impaction and the impaction is

gently pushed forward. This is aided by esophageal muscle relaxation induced by sedation, expansion of the esophageal lumen with endoscopic air insufflation, and intravenous glucagon if it has been given.[27]

Even if the endoscope cannot be initially maneuvered around the impaction, a trial of gently pushing the food bolus can be safely attempted. However, forcefully pushing the endoscope or blindly advancing dilators or retrieval devices past the food bolus is not recommended because of the high percentage of patients with esophageal pathology.[1,27] For larger food impactions, particularly meats such as chicken or beef that can be broken apart, the push technique can be performed after breaking the meat into smaller pieces with a forceps or snare. The push technique has been found to have success rates greater than 95% and complications approaching 0% in the treatment of food impactions.

Certain cases of food impactions cannot be safely pushed into the stomach and must be retrieved with the endoscope via the mouth. An overtube is useful to protect the airway and allow multiple passes of the endoscope (Fig. 21–8). This is particularly useful in meat impactions in which the food shreds and breaks into multiple pieces before it can be completely removed. Standard endoscopic grasping forceps, snares, and baskets used under direct visualization can be used alone or together. The Roth retrieval net can be particularly useful in managing food impactions because the food bolus can be contained completely within the net avoiding the use of an overtube and minimizing the risk of aspiration.[105] For well-impacted food boluses, the use of a Steigmann-Goff endoscopic ligator can be used to suction up large pieces of food that can be removed via the mouth with an overtube in place.[106,107]

Up to 75% to 100% of patients with food impactions are found to have esophageal pathology at the time of the index or follow-up endoscopy.[16,17,19] Furthermore, more than half of patients with food bolus impactions have abnormal 24-hour pH studies and almost half have abnormal esophageal manometry tests.[18] In most patients if a benign stricture or Schatzki's ring is visualized after clearance of the food bolus, the narrowing can be effectively and safely dilated at the

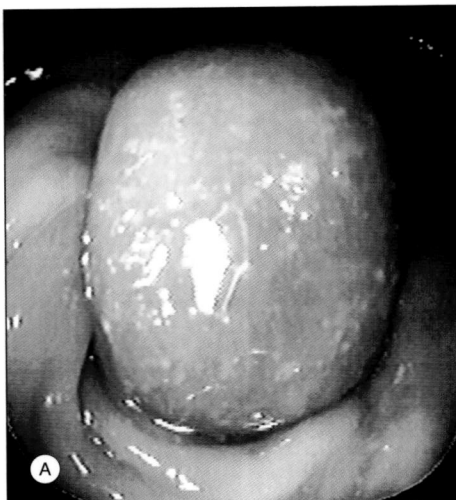

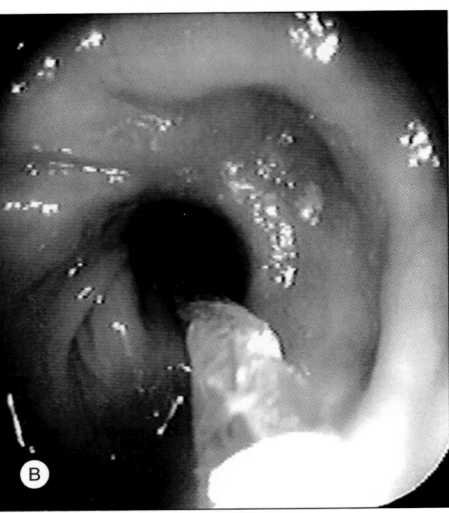

Figure 21–9. Endoscopic image of a jelly bean that had caused acute impaction in the distal esophagus (A). This was treated with the push technique. A peptic stricture was then successfully dilated with a balloon at the time of the same endoscopy (B).

time of the same endoscopy (Fig. 21–9). Occasionally, esophageal mucosal erythema, edema, and abrasions from the food bolus or the endoscope may interfere with accurate endoscopic diagnosis and safe dilation treatment. These patients can be placed on acid suppression and have an elective endoscopy with possible dilation in approximately 4 to 6 weeks.

Postoperative Care

For uncomplicated removal of true foreign bodies or food bolus impactions, postoperative care should be no different from standard endoscopy. Each institution should follow its routine postprocedure recovery guidelines according to whether the procedure was performed under conscious sedation or general anesthesia. Thus, most patients with foreign bodies and food impactions can be treated as outpatients. If the patient recovers without sequelae, the patient, family, or parents should observe the patient for any sign of complications in the next 24 hours. Food bolus patients should be educated in methods of reducing further impactions including eating more slowly, chewing foods thoroughly, and avoiding troublesome foods.[27]

Consideration should be made for admitting certain patients for 24-hour observation postprocedure. These include young children, patients with multiple or complex foreign bodies, and patients in whom extraction and treatment of the foreign body was technically difficult.

If the extraction was difficult, if there was any evidence on endoscopy of a complication secondary to the foreign body or the endoscope, or if the patient shows signs of a complication postprocedure, the patient requires observation and further investigation. The largest concern is esophageal perforation and the best outcomes and survival occur when this is recognized early.[19] Any evidence of postprocedure fever, tachycardia, shortness of breath, chest or abdominal pain, or crepitus should lead to prompt plain x-ray films followed by contrast radiographic studies and surgical consultation.

Complications

The complication rate of endoscopic treatment of GI foreign bodies or food impactions ranges from no complications found in most studies to 1.8%.[7,16,17,19,21,59,108] The most common complication associated with endoscopic removal of foreign bodies is esophageal perforation. Although no prospective data exist, risk factors thought to increase the complication rate are the uncooperative patient, the multiple ingestor, the deliberate ingestor such as a prisoner or psychiatric patient, and the removal of sharp and pointed objects. Other complications reported with endoscopic removal of foreign bodies are GI bleeding, aspiration, and cardiopulmonary complications secondary to sedation. These complications do not occur at a rate significantly different from the complication rate found in standard upper endoscopy.

Future Trends

Paralleling the development and availability of flexible endoscopes, endoscopy has become the diagnostic modality of choice and the standard of care for the treatment of ingested foreign bodies and impacted food boluses. No rival technology or method used in the treatment of foreign bodies is available and none is likely to match the efficacy or safety of endoscopic methods in the future.

However, despite the frequency of foreign bodies treated with upper endoscopy, information is lacking on the actual incidence of foreign bodies, and treatment recommendations are still based primarily on retrospective collections of data. The main future challenge is the thorough collection of prospective data concerning patients with foreign bodies and food boluses and how these patients may best be treated with GI endoscopy both in the community and at tertiary endoscopy centers. With this data, the individual endoscopist will be able to offer the optimal treatment to the often encountered patient with an ingested foreign body or food impaction.

REFERENCES

1. Eisen GM, Baron TH, Dominitz JA, et al: Guideline for the management of ingested foreign bodies. Gastrointest Endosc 55:802–806, 2002.
2. Lyons MF, Tsuchida AM: Foreign bodies of the gastrointestinal tract. Med Clin North Am 77:1101–1114, 1993
3. Clerf LH: Historical aspects of foreign bodies in the food and air passages. South Med J 68:1449–1454, 1975.
4. Devanesan J, Pisani A, Sharman P, et al: Metallic foreign bodies in the stomach. Arch Surg 112:664–665, 1977.
5. Webb WA: Management of foreign bodies in the upper gastrointestinal tract. Gastroenterology 94:204–216, 1988.
6. O'Brien GC, Winter DC, Kirwan WO, et al: Ingested foreign bodies in the paediatric patient. Ir J Med Sci 170:100–102, 2001.
7. Kim JK, Kim SS, Kim JI, et al: Management of foreign bodies in the gastrointestinal tract: An analysis of 104 cases in children. Endoscopy 31:301–304, 1999.
8. Arana A, Hauser B, Hachimi-Idrissi S, et al: Management of ingested foreign bodies in childhood and review of the literature. Eur J Pediatr 160:468–472, 2001.
9. Cheng W, Tam PK: Foreign-body ingestion in children: Experience with 1265 cases. J Pediatr Surg 34:1472–1476, 1999.
10. Gunn A: Intestinal perforation due to swallowed fish or meat bone. Lancet 1:125–128, 1966.
11. Bunker PG: The role of dentistry in problems of foreign body in the air and food passage. J Am Dent Assoc 64:782–787, 1962.
12. Gluck M: Coin ingestion complicating a tavern game. West J Med 150:343–344, 1989.
13. O'Sullivan ST, Reardon CM, McGreal GT, et al: Deliberate ingestion of foreign bodies by institutionalized psychiatric hospital patients and prison inmates. Ir J Med Sci 165:294–296, 1997.
14. Losanoff JE, Kjossev KT: Gastrointestinal crosses: An indication for surgery. J Clin Gastroenterol 33:310–314, 2001.
15. Chalk SG, Faucer H: Foreign bodies in the stomach. Arch Surg 16:494–500, 1928.
16. Longstreth GF, Longstreth KJ, Yao JF: Esophageal food impaction: Epidemiology and therapy. A retrospective, observational study. Gastrointest Endosc 53:193–198, 2001.
17. Vicari JJ, Johanson JF, Frakes JT: Outcomes of acute esophageal food impaction: Success of the push technique. Gastrointest Endosc 53:178–181, 2001.
18. Lacy PD, Donnelly MJ, McGrath JP, et al: Acute food bolus impaction: Aetiology and management. J Laryngol Otol 111:1158–1161, 1997.
19. Webb WA: Management of foreign bodies of the upper gastrointestinal tract: Update. Gastrointest Endosc 41:39–51, 1995.
20. Weinstock LB, Shatz BA, Thyssen EP: Esophageal food bolus obstruction: Evaluation of extraction and modified push technique in 75 cases. Endoscopy 31:421–425, 1999.
21. Vizcarrondo FJ, Brady PG, Nord HJ: Foreign bodies of the upper gastrointestinal tract. Gastrointest Endosc 29:208–210, 1983.
22. Breumelhof R, Van Wijk HJ, Van Es CD, et al: Food impaction in nutcracker esophagus. Dig Dis Sci 35:1167–1171, 1990.
23. Lim CT, Quah RF, Loh LE: A prospective study of ingested foreign bodies in Singapore. Arch Otolaryngol Head Neck Surg 120:96–101, 1994.
24. Ngan JH, Fok PJ, Lai EC, et al: A prospective study on fish bone ingestion. Experience of 358 patients. Ann Surg 211:459–462, 1990.
25. Nandi P, Ong GB: Foreign body of the esophagus: Review of 2394 cases. Br J Surg 65:5–9, 1978.
26. Ginsberg GG: Management of ingested foreign objects and food bolus impactions. Gastrointest Endosc 41:33–38, 1995.
27. Pfau PR, Ginsberg GG: Foreign bodies and bezoars. In Fordtran JS, Schleiseinger MH (eds): Gastrointestinal and Liver Disease. Pathophysiology/Diagnosis/Management. Philadelphia, WB Saunders, 2002, pp 386–398.
28. Brady P: Esophageal foreign bodies. Gastroenterol Clin North Am 20:691–701, 1991.
29. Jiraki K: Aortoesophageal conduit due to a foreign body. Am J Forensic Med Pathol 17:347–348, 1996.
30. Simic MA, Budakov BM: Fatal upper esophageal hemorrhage caused by a previously ingested chicken bone: Case report. Am J Forensic Med Pathol 19:166–168, 1998.
31. Spitz L, Kimber C, Nguyen K, et al: Perforation of the heart by a swallowed open safety-pin in an infant. J R Coll Surg Edinb 43:114–116, 1998.
32. Drnovsek V, Fontanez-Garcia D, Wakabayashi MN, et al: Gastrointestinal case of the day. Pyogenic liver abscess caused by perforation by a swallowed wooden toothpick. Radiographics 19:820–822, 1999.
33. Sevastos N, Rafailidis P, Kolokotronis K, et al: Primary aortojejunal fistula due to a foreign body: A rare cause of gastrointestinal bleeding. Eur J Gastroenterol Hepatol 14:797–800, 2002.
34. McNutt TK, Chambers-Emerson J, Dethlefsen M, et al: Bite the bullet: Lead poisoning after ingestion of 206 lead bullets. Vet Hun Toxicol 43:288–289, 2001.
35. Bennett DR, Baird CJ, Chan KM, et al: Zinc toxicity following massive coin ingestion. Am J Forensic Med Pathol 18:148–153, 1997.
36. Stack LB, Munter DW: Foreign bodies in the gastrointestinal tract. Emerg Med Clin North Am 14:493–521, 1996.
37. O'Flynn P, Simp R: Fish bones and other foreign bodies. Clin Otolaryngol 18:231–233, 1993.
38. Bloom RR, Nakano PH, Gray SW, et al: Foreign bodies of the gastrointestinal tract. Am Surg 10:618–621, 1986.
39. Rohl L, Aksglaede K, Funch-Jensen P, Thommesen P: Esophageal rings and strictures: Manometric characteristics in patients with food impaction. Acta Radiol 41:275–279, 2000.
40. McCord GS, Staiano A, Clouse RE: Achalasia, diffuse spasm, and non-specific motor disorders. Baillerres Clin Gastroenterol 5:307–335, 1991.
41. Tibbling L, Bjorkhoel A, Jansson E, et al: Effect of spasmolytic drugs on esophageal foreign bodies. Dysphagia 10:126–127, 1995.
42. Stein HJ, Schwizer W, DeMeester TR, et al: Foreign body entrapment in the esophagus of healthy subjects—a manometric and scintigraphic study. Dysphagia 7:220–225, 1992.
43. Koch H: Operative endoscopy. Gastrointest Endosc 24:65–68, 1977.
44. Davidhoff E, Towne JB: Ingested foreign bodies. N Y State Med J 75:1003–1007, 1975.
45. Taylor RB: Esophageal foreign bodies. Emerg Clin North Am 5:301–311, 1987.
46. Herranz-Gonzalez J, Martinez-Vidal J, Garcia-Sarandeses A, et al: Esophageal foreign bodies in adults. Otolaryngol Head Neck Surg 105:649–654, 1991.
47. Connolly AA, Birchall M, Walsh-Waring GP, et al: Ingested foreign bodies: Patient guided localization is a useful clinical tool. Clin Otolaryngol 17:520–524, 1992.
48. Lee J: Bezoars and foreign bodies of the stomach. Gastrointest Endosc Clin North Am 6:605–619, 1996.
49. Binder L, Anderson WA: Pediatric gastrointestinal foreign body ingestions. Ann Emerg Med 13:112–117, 1984
50. Muniz AE, Joffe MD: Foreign bodies, ingested and inhaled. JAAPA 12:22–24, 1999.
51. Choudhury CR, Bricknell MC, MacIver D: Oesophageal foreign body, an unusual cause of respiratory symptoms in a three week old baby. J Laryngol Otol 106:556–557, 1992.
52. Yoshida C, Peura D: Foreign bodies in the esophagus. In Castell D (ed): The Esophagus. Boston, Little, Brown, 1995, pp 379–394.
53. Webb WA, Taylor MB: Foreign bodies of the upper gastrointestinal tract. In Taylor MB (ed): Gastrointestinal Emergencies, 2nd ed. Philadelphia, Lippincott Williams & Wilkins, 1996, pp 204–216.
54. Shaffer HA, de Lange EE: Gastrointestinal foreign bodies and strictures: Radiologic interventions. Curr Prob Diagn Radiol 23:205–249, 1994.

55. Bassett KE, Schunk JE, Logan L: Localizing ingested coins with a metal detector. Am J Emerg Med 17:338–341, 1999.

56. Hodge D, Tecklenburg F, Fleischer G: Coin ingestion: Does every child need a radiograph? Ann Emerg Med 14:443–446, 1985.

57. Jones NS, Lannigan FJ, Salama NY: Foreign bodies in the throat: A prospective study of 388 cases. J Laryngol Otol 105:104–108, 1991.

58. Mosca S: Management and endoscopic techniques in cases of ingestion of foreign bodies. Endoscopy 32:232–233, 2000.

59. Mosca S, Manes G, Martino L, et al: Endoscopic management of foreign bodies in the upper gastrointestinal tract: Report on a series of 414 adult patients. Endoscopy 33:692–696, 2001.

60. Takada M, Kashiwagi R, Sakane M, et al: 3D-CT Diagnosis for ingested foreign bodies. Am J Emerg Med 18:192–193, 2000.

61. Seikel K, Primm PA, Elizondo BJ, et al: Handheld metal detector localization of ingested metallic foreign bodies, Arch Pediatr Adolesc Med 153:853–857, 1999.

62. Gooden EA, Forte V, Papsin B: Use of a commercially available metal detector for the localization of metallic foreign body ingestion in children. J Otolaryngol 29:218–220, 2000.

63. Ciriza C, Garcia L, Suarez P, et al: What predictive parameters best indicate the need for emergent gastrointestinal endoscopy after foreign body ingestion? J Clin Gastroenterol 31:23–28, 2000.

64. Velitchkov NG, Grigorov GI, Losanoff JE, et al: Ingested foreign bodies of the gastrointestinal tract. Retrospective analysis of 542 cases. World J Surg 20:1001–1005, 1996.

65. Kurkciyan I, Frossard M, Kettenbach J, et al: Conservative management of foreign bodies in the gastrointestinal tract. Z Gastroenterol 34:173–177, 1996.

66. Weiland ST, Schurr MJ: Conservative management of ingested foreign bodies. J Gastrointest Surg 6:496—500, 2002.

67. O'Sullivan ST, McGreal GT, Reardon CM, et al: Selective endoscopy in management of ingested foreign bodies of the upper gastrointestinal tract: Is it safe? Int J Clin Pract 51:289–292, 1997.

68. Colon V, Grade A, Pullman G, et al: Effect of doses of glucagon used to treat food impaction on esophageal motor function of normal subjects. Dysphagia 14:27–30, 1999.

69. Ferrucci JT, Long LA: Radiologic treatment of esophageal food impaction using intravenous glucagon. Radiology 125:25–28, 1977.

70. Trenker SW, Maglinte DT, Lehman G, et al: Esophageal food impaction: Treatment with glucagon. Radiology 149:401–403, 1983.

71. Mehta D, Attia M, Quintana E, et al: Glucagon use for esophageal coin dislodgment in children: A prospective double-blind, placebo-controlled trial. Acad Emerg Med 8:200–203, 2001.

72. Alaradi O, Bartholomew M, Barkin JS: Upper endoscopy and glucagon: A new technique in the management of acute esophageal food impaction. Am J Gastroenterol 96:912–913, 2001.

73. Robbins MI, Shortsleeve MJ: Treatment of acute esophageal food impaction with glucagon, an effervescent agent, and water. AJR Am J Roentgenol 162:325—328, 1994.

74. Kaszar-Seibert DJ, Korn WT, Bindman DJ, et al: Treatment of acute esophageal food impaction with a combination of glucagon, effervescent agent, and water. AJR Am J Roentgenol 154:533–534, 1990.

75. Smith JC, Janower ML, Geiger AH: Use of glucagon and gas-forming agents in acute esophageal food impaction. Radiology 159:567–568, 1986.

76. Maini S, Rudralingam M, Zeitoun H, et al: Aspiration pneumonitis following papain enzyme treatment for oesophageal meat impaction. J Laryngol Otol 115:585–586, 2001.

77. Litovitz T, Scmitz BF: Ingestion of cylindrical and button batteries: An analysis of 2382 cases. Pediatrics 89:747–757, 1992.

78. Paulson EK, Jaffe RB: Metallic foreign bodies in the stomach: Fluoroscopic removal with a magnetic orogastric tube. Radiology 174:191–194, 1990.

79. Hawkins DB: Removal of blunt foreign bodies from the esophagus. Ann Otol Rhinol Laryngol 99:935–940, 1990.

80. Schunk JE, Harrison AM, Corneli HM, et al: Fluoroscopic Foley catheter removal of esophageal foreign bodies in children: Experience with 415 cases. Pediatrics 94:709–714, 1994.

81. Blair SR, Graeber GM, Cruzzavala JL, et al: Current management of esophageal impactions. Chest 104:1205–1209, 1993.

82. Thapa BR, Singh K, Dilawari JB: Endoscopic removal of foreign bodies from the gastrointestinal tract. Indian Pediatr 30:1105–1110, 1993.

83. Khurana AK, Saraya A, Jain N, et al: Management of foreign bodies of the upper gastrointestinal tract. Trop Gastroenterol 19:32–33, 1998.

84. Bonadio WA, Emslander H, Milner D, et al: Esophageal mucosal changes in children with an acutely ingested coin lodged in the esophagus. Pediatr Emer Care 10:333–334, 1994.

85. Chaikhouni A, Kratz JM, Crawford MA: Foreign bodies of the esophagus. Am Surg 51:173–179, 1985.

86. Henderson CT, Engel J, Schlesinger P: Foreign body ingestion: Review and suggested guidelines for management. Endoscopy 19:68–71, 1987.

87. Macgregor D, Ferguson J: Foreign body ingestion in children: An audit of transit time. J Accid Emerg Med 15:371–373, 1998.

88. Nelson DB, Bosco JJ, Curtis WD, et al: ASGE technology status evaluation report. Endoscopic retrieval devices. February 1999. American Society for Gastrointestinal Endoscopy. Gastrointest Endosc 50:932–934, 1999.

89. Faigel DO, Stotland BR, Kochman ML, et al: Device choice and experience level in endoscopic foreign object retrieval: An in vivo study. Gastrointest Endosc 45:490–492, 1997.

90. Bertoni G, Pacchione Sassatelli R, et al: A new protector device for safe endoscopic removal of sharp gastroesophageal foreign bodies in infants. J Pediatr Gastroenterol Nutr 16:393–396, 1993.

91. Bertoni G, Sassatelli R, Conigliaro R, et al: A simple latex protector hood for safe endoscopic removal of sharp-pointed gastroesophageal foreign bodies. Gastrointest Endosc 44:458–461, 1996.

92. Chu KM, Choi HK, Tuen HH, et al: A prospective randomized trial comparing the use of the flexible gastroscope versus the bronchoscope in the management of foreign body ingestion Gastrointest Endosc 47:23–27, 1998.

93. Byrne WJ: Foreign bodies, bezoars, and caustic ingestion. Gastrointest Endosc Clin N Am 4:99–119, 1994.

94. Jackson C, Jackson CL: Diseases of the Air and Food Passages of Foreign Body Origin. Philadelphia, WB Saunders, 1937.

95. Kao LS, Nguyen T, Dominitz J, et al: Modification of a latex glove for the safe endoscopic removal of a sharp gastric foreign body. Gastrointest Endosc 52:127–129, 2000.

96. Stringer MD, Capps SN: Rationalizing the management of swallowed coins in children. BMJ 302:1321–1322, 1991.

97. Temple AR, Veltri JC: One year's experience in a regional poison control center. The Intermountain Regional Poison Control Center. Clin Toxicol 12:27–89, 1978

98. Litovitz TL: Button battery ingestions. JAMA 249:2495–2500, 1983.

99. Chan YL, Chang SS, Kao KL, et al: Button battery ingestion: An analysis of 25 cases. Chan Gung Med J 25:169–174, 2002.

100. Litovitz TL: Battery ingestions: Product accessibility and clinical course. Pediatrics 75:469–476, 1985.

101. McCarron NM, Wood JD: The cocaine "body packer" syndrome: Diagnosis and treatment. JAMA 250:1417–1420, 1983.

102. Caruna DS, Weinbach B, Goerg D, et al: Cocaine packer ingestion. Ann Intern Med 100:73–74, 1984.

103. June R, Aks SE, Keys N, et al: Medical outcome of cocaine bodystuffers. J Emerg Med 18:221–224, 2000.

104. Eng JG, Aks SE, Marcus C, et al: False-negative abdominal CT scan in a cocaine body stuffer. Am J Emerg Med 18:192–193, 2000.

105. Neustater B, Barkin JS: Extraction of an esophageal food impaction with a Roth retrieval net. Gastrointest Endosc 43:66–67, 1996.

106. Mamel JJ, Weiss D, Pouagare M, et al: Endoscopic suction removal of food boluses from the upper gastrointestinal tract using Steigmann-Goff friction fit adapter. An improved method for removal of food impactions. Gastrointest Endosc 41:593–596, 1995.

107. Pezzi JS, Shiau YF: A method for removing meat impactions from the esophagus. Gastrointest Endosc 40:634–636, 1994.

108. Classen M, Farthmann EF, Seifert E, et al: Operative and therapeutic techniques in endoscopy. Clin Gastroenterol 7:741–763, 1978.

Zenker's Diverticula

Kiyoshi Hashiba

CHAPTER

22

Introduction

The Zenker's type of diverticulum is the most important diverticulum of the esophagus. It usually causes symptoms that typically require surgical treatment. It can also be treated endoscopically. Endoscopic therapy is appealing because most of the severely symptomatic patients are elderly people.

Epidemiology

Zenker's diverticulum (ZD) is a false diverticulum first described by Ludlow in 1769.[1] X-ray studies have shown its incidence to be around 0.1% of upper gastrointestinal (GI) barium studies.[2] Eighty percent of patients are older than 60 years,[3] and it is more frequent in males.[3] The occurrence in children is rare,[4] and no differences have been mentioned concerning race or geographic areas.

Pathogenesis

ZDs appear at weak points in the posterior wall of the hypopharynx when there is a lack of coordination between the pharyngeal constrictor and the cricopharyngeus muscles.[5] Fibrosis of the cricopharyngeus muscle and the striated muscle of the upper esophagus has been recently cited as the cause of such incoordination.[6,7] Contraction of the pharyngeal constrictor muscle combined with the absence of relaxation of the cricopharyngeus muscle results in impaired passage of a fecal bolus with a consequent marked increase in pressure, allowing the mucosa and submucosa to bulge through inherent weak sites between the descending fibers of inferior constrictor and the transverse cricopharyngeus muscles, which, in fact, constitute the most distal part of the inferior constrictor (Fig. 22–1). Some authors postulate that incomplete upper sphincter opening is likely to cause dysphagia not the incoordination.[6] A bulging mucous membrane sac could also pass through or immediately beneath the cricopharyngeus muscle.

Clinical Features

There is a well-established relationship of anatomic changes to clinical symptoms.[8] When the ZD is small, the patient has the sensation of having a foreign body in the throat. A common complaint is throat irritation with excessive mucus. As the ZD increases in size, regurgitation of food and mucus begins to occur after meals and also when the patient lies down. If the diverticula sac is very large and the opening is transverse, the preferential route of food will be into the ZD (Fig. 22–2). Symptoms of dysphagia during early deglutition will appear and patients may lose a significant amount of weight. With clinical aggravation, pulmonary aspiration complications become common.

Pathology

The ZD arises in the hypopharynx. The wall of the sac is formed only by the mucosa and submucosa. Thus, it is not a true diverticulum. As a diverticulum, it forms a pouch and usually descends along the left side of the neck. However, it may be present on either side. In advanced phases of the disease, the mucosa may become inflamed. An increased incidence in cancer has been associated with a ZD. The ZD is commonly found in association with other esophageal disease, such as hiatal hernia, gastroesophageal reflux, esophageal membranes (in 50% of the cases), achalasia, and polyps.[9,10]

Differential Diagnosis

A contrast study is useful to investigate dysphagia during early deglutition, especially for medication (e.g., pills), and to assess a suspected large ZD. If the diverticulum is not small, the diagnosis is also easily established in the anteroposterior projection (Fig. 22–3). The diverticulum lies in the midline and extends to the left. However, in the case of a small ZD, the x-ray study of the lateral

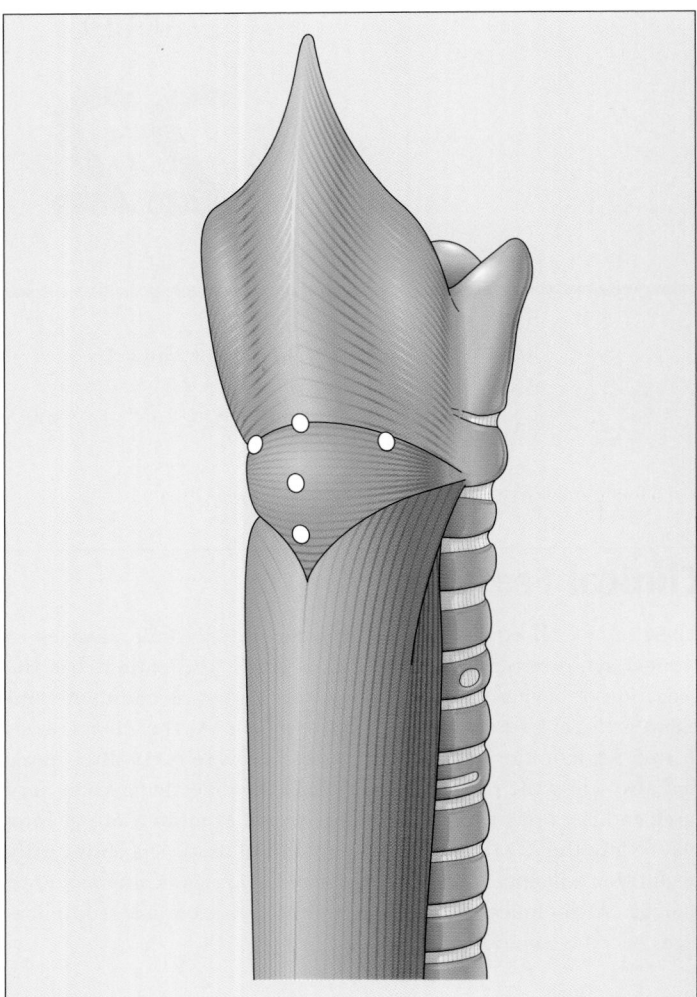

Figure 22–1. A schematic view of hypopharynx. The white dots show sites of weakness from which a Zenker's diverticulum can develop.

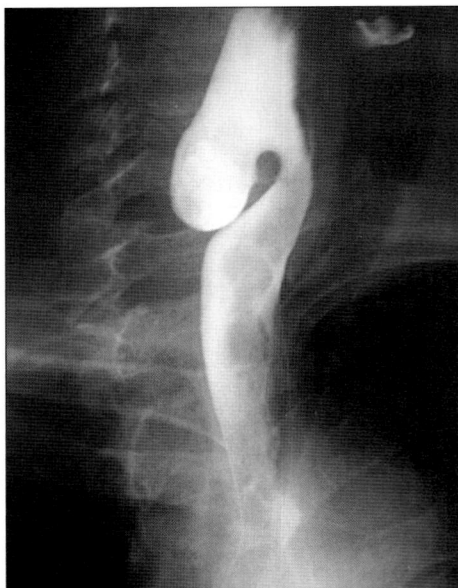

Figure 22–2. Lateral x-ray study of esophagus showing a Zenker's diverticulum.

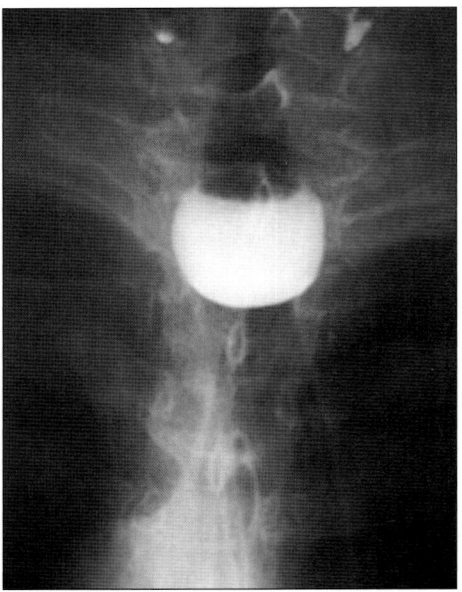

Figure 22–3. Frontal upper gastrointestinal (GI) barium study of esophagus showing a Zenker's diverticulum (ZD). The preferential flow for the contrast bolus is into the ZD.

projection is important (see Fig. 22–2). When aspiration is suspected, an x-ray study without barium meal is needed. In such a case, iodine contrast should be used to avoid complications resulting from aspiration of the barium meal into the lung. Sometimes it is necessary to clear the diverticula from retained foods to avoid filling defects that mimic mucosal lesions. Alternatively, an endoscopic examination may serve as the primary diagnostic study. For many years, this was not recommended. In early phases of the disease, when ZD cannot yet be detected, the difficulty found in inserting the endoscope into the esophagus is the most common basis for the suspicion of ZD. When a patient presents with symptoms apparently related to early deglutition, the possibility of a ZD must be considered in case of such difficulty. After the diagnosis of ZD has been established, endoscopy should be performed to evaluate the diverticulum. Mucosal abnormalities can occur that warrant biopsy (Fig. 22–4). The incidence of cancer is higher in the ZD mucosa than in the normal esophageal mucosa. Endoscopy is not dangerous in experienced hands, and insertion into the esophagus lumen is usually achieved, often with the help of a flexible accessory used as a guide (Fig. 22–5). As the diverticulum increases progressively from a small protruding area to a sac, it usually descends down

the left side of the neck. However, it may present on either side of the region where an alteration is detected. A long period of fast should always be recommended before the endoscopic procedure. During the diagnostic procedure, in cases of superficial trauma or biopsy, antibiotics should be prescribed. If a perforation is suspected, an upper GI barium study must be avoided. The preferential flow of contrast will be near the perforation opening because of the alteration and dysfunction of cricopharyngeus muscle (Fig. 22–6). A careful endoscopic examination can be helpful, but it will increase the pneumomediastinum (Fig. 22–7).

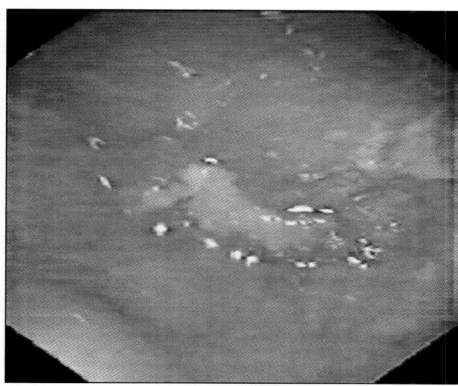

Figure 22–4. An ulcerated lesion in a Zenker's diverticulum.

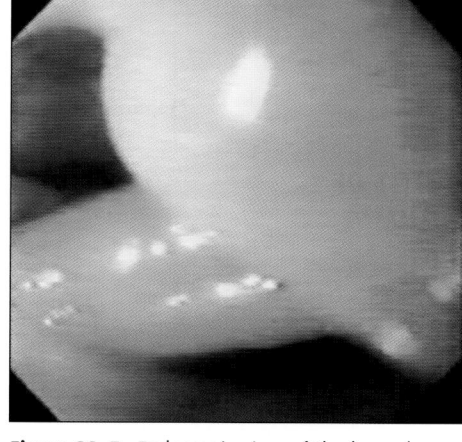

Figure 22–5. Endoscopic view of the hypopharynx in a Zenker's diverticulum (ZD) patient. A guidewire is inserted in the esophageal lumen.

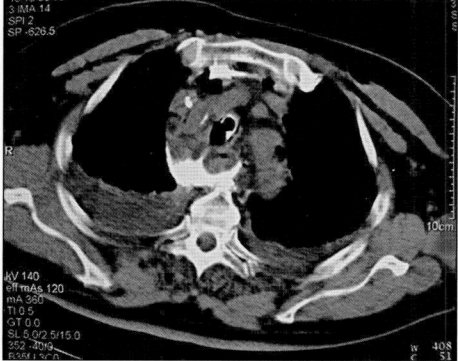

Figure 22–6. Computed tomography in a patient with perforation in the hypopharynx after an upper gastrointestinal (GI) barium study.

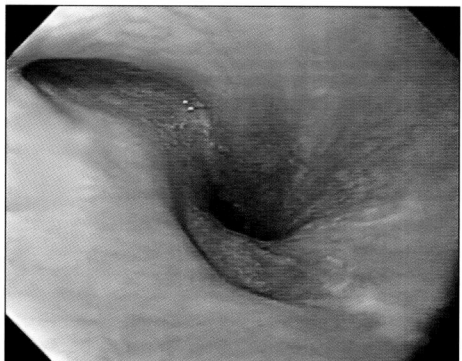

Figure 22–7. Endoscopic view in a patient with a small Zenker's diverticulum (ZD) suspected to have a perforation in an upper gastrointestinal endoscopy. The perforation appears at the left side of hypopharynx.

Treatment

When the patient's initial complaint is dysphagia and ZD can only be suspected from the x-ray study, clinical improvement can result from dilatation with a large flexible tube. In advanced cases, the standard treatment has been open surgery with resection of the ZD and a cricopharyngeal myotomy. Inversion of the sac has been performed by some surgeons. Cricopharyngeal myotomy is the key component of the surgery. The absence of a cricopharyngeal myotomy is probably the reason for the failure of treatment with resection of the diverticulum only.[11,12] For many years, the surgical treatment was performed in two stages to avoid mediastinitis and pulmonary complications. Many surgeons currently perform a one-stage operation with the esophagus intubated or an endoscope placed inside the diverticulum to determine the ZD position and to prevent excessive resection of tissue with subsequent stricture. For a small ZD, some recommend cricopharyngeal myotomy only. The most frequent complication of surgical treatment is the development of a pharyngocutaneous fistula in the early postoperative course. When spontaneous healing does not occur, endoscopic

dilatation of the esophagus and fibrin injection around the internal orifice with or without placement of clips at the same site has been successful. A recent randomized study by Bowdler and Stell[13] compared inversion with resection, in association with cricopharyngeal myotomy. Improved outcome with lower incidence of fistulae were obtained with inversion. Recognized complications of the conventional approach are mediastinitis, laryngeal paralysis, stricture, and recurrence.

Endoscopic treatment is not new. In 1917, Mosher[14] described an endoscopic transoral diverticulotomy, but this method was soon abandoned because of complications. In 1960, Dohlman and Mattson[15] presented their endoscopic technique using electrocoagulation to divide the septum between the esophagus and the diverticulum. Another transoral technique was proposed by Collard and coworkers[16] in 1993 using an Endo GIA 30 2.5-cm stapler to cut the muscular septum. In this case, the cut edges were stapled with metallic clips, which avoided contamination of the mediastinum and ensured hemostasis of the wound edges. This procedure requires general anesthesia, and the postoperative course is uncomfortable. Moreover, it is not certain that a sufficient myotomy can be performed by the device, resulting in a small remaining pouch. Recently a simple, low-cost endoscopic technique was described, which is performed without general anesthesia and can be used in most cases with good results and a low morbidity rate.

ENDOSCOPIC TREATMENT OF ZENKER'S DIVERTICULUM[17]

Technique

Preparation

The procedure should be performed in fasted patients. Those with a deep ZD must have only liquid foods on the day preceding the endoscopic treatment; just before the operation, gargling with a liquid antiseptic mouthwash is necessary. An antibiotic (2-g cephalosporin) that covers oral flora is given intravenously before the procedure. The diverticulotomy takes place under monitored sedation with intravenously administered benzodiazepine and meperidine and topical anesthesia with lidocaine.

Diverticulotomy

The procedure of dividing the muscular septum between the diverticulum and esophagus is performed with an end-viewing endoscope. If the patient has not had an upper GI endoscopy recently, the first step is an endoscopic examination of the diverticulum—an important measure not only to plan the treatment but also to detect potential neoplasia.[18] Pathology in the remaining esophagus, stomach, and duodenum also must be excluded. A 0.035-inch wire is inserted into the esophagus as a guide to introduce a 12-Fr semiflexible tube or small (6–7 mm) Savary-type dilator. This optimizes exposure of the septum between the ZD and the esophagus lumen and also protects the opposite esophageal wall from thermal injury. The division of the septum is performed with a needle-knife and a blended monopolar current similar to sphincterotomy. Bleeding can be minimized by blending more coagulation than cut. Because the visual field is limited, even a small amount of blood impairs visualization of the incision. The incision begins at the top of the septum (Fig. 22–8) and continues toward the bottom (Fig. 22–9), at the midline of the septum. However, when the ZD is shallow, the incision can begin at the bottom of the diverticula and extend upward to the septal margin. In either case, it is convenient to create a coagulation mark at the most distal point of the intended incision, because, given the edema and other local alterations at the end of the cut, it can be difficult to know exactly where the bottom of the ZD is. The transverse fibers of the cricopharyngeus muscle are usually clearly seen across the bottom of the divided septum (see Fig. 22–9). Analgesics are prescribed at discharge. This procedure can be performed in an outpatient setting. Patients are allowed to resume oral intake of liquid 8 hours after the procedure and are advanced to a regular diet as tolerated. Some patients may not be able to fast completely over this extended time period and will therefore require hospitalization. Some authors suggest that a dilatation procedure before the septal incision facilitates the procedure. Recently, Sakai and coworkers[19] showed a technique using a transparent cap attached to the distal end of the forward-viewing endoscope that may enhance the view of the septum during the cut.

Results

Endoscopic diverticulotomy (ED) has been performed in one session with complete incision of the cricopharyngeal muscular septum. Dysphagia disappears promptly after the procedure, even when total incision of the septum has not been achieved. Other symptoms including regurgitation, halitosis, nocturnal coughing, and respiratory distress disappear after the procedure. In our first series, 17 of 47 patients (36%) underwent ED in one session and 30 (64%) needed more than one session (mean value 2.2). Forty-five of the patients (96%) showed a noticeable improvement in symptoms after the first session, and all experienced minimal to no dysphagia. Cough and halitosis also disappeared. Division of the septum was not complete in 17 patients after the first session, but the improvement of dysphagia was marked. Bleeding usually occurred during the procedure but was universally self-limited. During the postprocedure clinical course, bleeding is rare and has been controlled endoscopically. Cervical emphysema is not uncommon and can be manually detected after there has been complete section

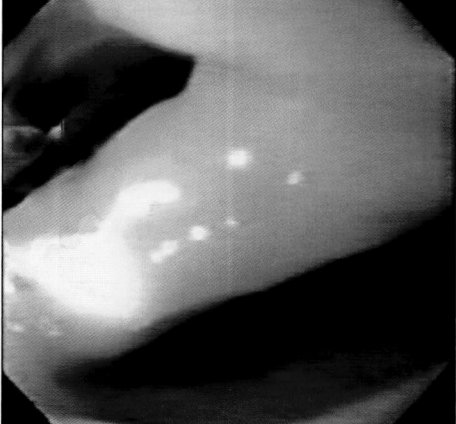

Figure 22–8. Endoscopic view of the typical muscular septum separating the diverticulum *(right)* from the esophageal lumen *(left)*. The endoscopic diverticulotomy starts from the top of the septum at the midline of the septum.

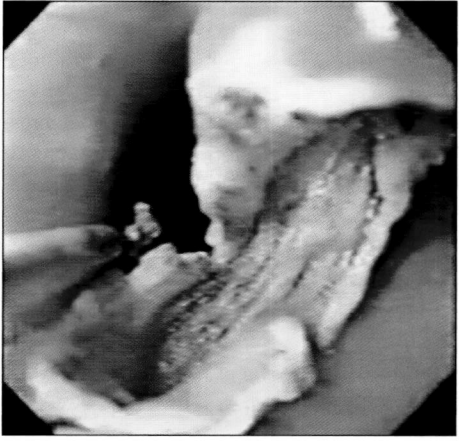

Figure 22–9. The final appearance after incising the septum.

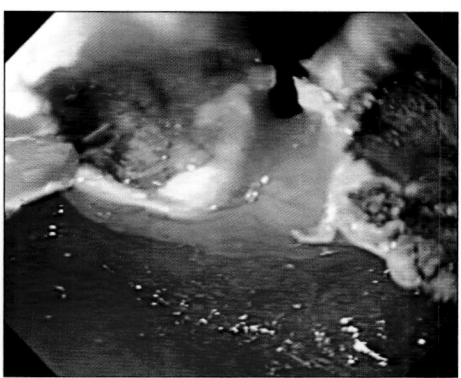

Figure 22–10. A symptomatic patient after endoscopic diverticulotomy. Two incisions are made, lateral to the midline, to release the remaining symptomatic septum.

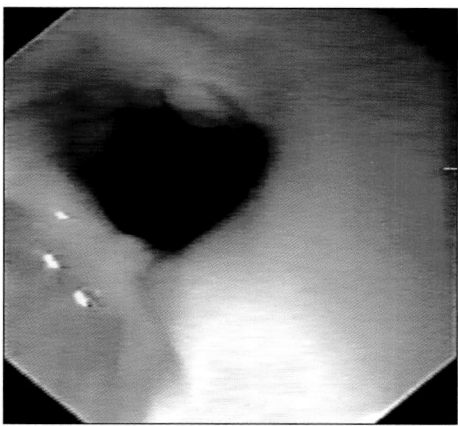

Figure 22–11. A small pouch remains *(lower left),* limited by a residual septum, during follow-up after a complete diverticulotomy.

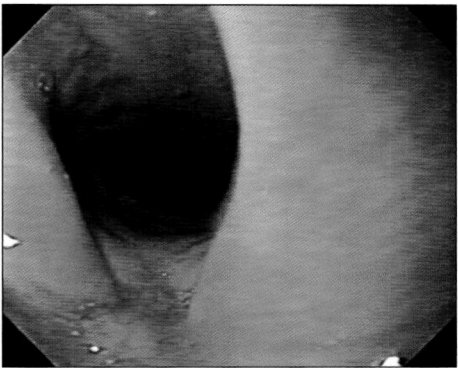

Figure 22–12. Follow-up endoscopy. The septum has been eliminated within the midportion.

of the septum. It may increase with coughing immediately after the incision. Eighty-three percent of the patients in our first series began oral intake of liquids and ice cream on the first day after the ED and began solid food in the subsequent days. In two patients, endoscopic control 1 month later revealed stenosis of the esophageal entrance and a new diverticulotomy incision was performed for resolution of the dysphagia. In case of septal recurrence, the preferred method is to perform two incisions, lateral to the midline of the septum (Fig. 22–10). However, it is important that the incisions be close to the midline to avoid laryngeal injury. Serious complications such as mediastinitis and fistula can occur but are rare. Follow-up periods for our earliest patient series ranged from 1 day to 1 year. In many cases, follow-up endoscopy revealed a small remaining pouch at the bottom of the ZD, despite a complete section (Fig. 22–11). Rarely, a residual septum is not seen (Fig. 22–12).

Similarly, even in patients without symptoms, radiologic study has shown that the diverticulum did not disappear completely. Long-term follow-up experience suggests that contrast study is not an ideal evaluation of the results of diverticulotomy because, in most cases, especially in patients without symptoms, the study reveals a small residual pouch. This is why some authors distinguish between clinical and radiologic recurrence.[2] In successful cases, manometry has revealed a reduction of the upper esophageal sphincter pressure.[11]

Future Trends

For an endoscopist experienced with ED, ED has become the first line of therapy. In this setting conventional surgery is reserved for endoscopic failures.

Suture of the cut edges is desirable to avoid bleeding, as is the experience with endoscopic staple-assisted esophagodiverticulostomy proposed by Collard and colleagues[16] and Scher and Richtsmeier.[20] Because suturing methods are being intensively developed in endoscopy, this modification of the procedure will be desirable in the endoscopic treatment of ZD. The placement of metallic clips could become an option. However, clip size may be suboptimal and there is a potential for mechanical discomfort for the patient.

REFERENCES

1. Ludlow A: A case of obstructed deglutition from a preternatural dilatation of a bag formed in pharynx. Med Observations Inquiries 3:85–101, 1767.
2. Bertelsen S, Aasted A: Results of operative treatment of hypopharingeal diverticulum. Thorax 31:544–547, 1976.
3. Holinger PH, Schild JA: The Zenker's (hypopharyngeal) diverticulum. Ann Otol 78:679–688, 1969.
4. Meadows JA Jr: Esophageal diverticula in infants and children. South Med J 63:691–694, 1970.
5. Bell C: Surgical Observations. London, Longmans, Greene, 1816.
6. Cook IJ, Jamieson GG, Blumberg P, et al: Pathogenesis and treatment of Zenker's diverticulum. Chirurgia 116:673–678, 1990.
7. Lerut T, van Raemdonck D, Guelinckx P, et al: Zenker's diverticulum: Is a myotomy of the cricopharyngeus useful? How long should it be? Hepatogastroenterology 39:127–131, 1992.
8. Lahey FH, Warren KW: Esophageal diverticula. Surg Gynecol Obstet 98:1–4, 1954.
9. Gage-White L: Incidence of Zenker's diverticulum with hiatus hernia. Laryngoscope 98:527–530, 1988.
10. Gullane PJ, Willet JM, Heeneman H, et al: Zenker's diverticulum. J Otolaryngol 12:53–57, 1983.
11. Broll R, Kramer T, Kalb K, et al: Manometric follow-up after resection of Zenker's diverticulum. Z Gastroenterol 30:142–146, 1992.
12. Wheeler D: Diverticula of the Foregut. Radiology 49:476–482, 1947.

13. Bowdler DA, Stell PM: Surgical management of posterior pharyngeal pulsion diverticula: Inversion versus one-stage excision. Br J Surg 74:988–990, 1987.
14. Mosher HP: Webs and pouches of the esophagus, their diagnosis and treatment. Surg Gynecol Obstet 25:175–187, 1917.
15. Dohlman G, Mattson D: The endoscopic operation for hypopharyngeal diverticula. Ann Otol Rhinol Laryngol 71:744–752, 1960.
16. Collard JM, Otte J, Kestens PJ: Endoscopic stapling technique of esophagodiverticulostomy for Zenker's diverticulum. Ann Thorac Surg 56:573–576, 1993.
17. Hashiba K, Paula AL, Silva JGN, et al: Endoscopic treatment of Zenker's diverticulum. Gastrointest Endosc 49:93–97, 1999.
18. Pierce WS, Johnson J: Squamous cell carcinoma arising in a pharyngoesophageal diverticulum. Cancer 24:1068–1070, 1969.
19. Sakai P, Ishioka S, Maluf-Filho F, et al: Endoscopic treatment of Zenker's diverticulum with an oblique-end hood attached to the endoscope. Gastrointest Endosc 54:760–763, 2001.
20. Scher RL, Richtsmeier WJ: Endoscopic staple-assisted esophagodiverticulostomy for Zenker's diverticulum. Laryngoscope 106:951–956, 1996.

Inflammatory Bowel Disease

Karen L. Krok and Gary R. Lichtenstein

Introduction

Inflammatory bowel disease (IBD) is an idiopathic, chronic intestinal condition that is characterized by episodes of relapse and remission. The diagnosis of Crohn's disease or ulcerative colitis is dependent on the clinical presentation and the findings on imaging studies.

Endoscopy is the most sensitive method to evaluate mucosal changes and is the only method available for providing histologic information. It is indicated to evaluate unexplained diarrhea and to aid in the differential diagnosis of IBD. Endoscopy is used to investigate radiographic abnormalities, such as mass lesions and strictures. In patients with IBD, it is crucial to determine the extent of disease, the disease activity, and to have a good working knowledge of the efficacy of various medical therapies used to treat patients with IBD such that the appropriate medication can be applied in the correct clinical scenario. Endoscopy also is indicated in the screening and surveillance for dysplasia and cancer. Colonoscopy, flexible sigmoidoscopy, and esophagogastroduodenoscopy (EGD) offer therapeutic benefits as well, including stricture dilatation, stent placement, and bleeding control. Endoscopic retrograde cholangiopancreatography (ERCP) is used often to evaluate for the potential of primary sclerosing cholangitis and recently the role of video capsule endoscopy in patients with known or suspected IBD has begun to evolve.

Normal Appearance of the Bowel

Endoscopically, the normal colon appears to glisten and is salmon-pink in color. There is a visible network of branching vessels identified throughout the colon. The smoothness of the mucosal surface and the absence of nodules or irregular polyps are the hallmarks of a healthy colon. There is a classic triangulated or semicircular configuration of the interhaustral markings. Contact bleeding or friability is not seen in a normal, healthy colon.

The rectum has a more vascular appearance. Its vessels increase in caliber the further distal they are, producing more prominent vasculature.

Early Lesions of Inflammatory Bowel Disease

CROHN'S DISEASE

The earliest endoscopic lesions in Crohn's disease are considered to be tiny punched-out ulcers in an otherwise normal-appearing mucosa. These then enlarge and aggregate to form larger surface ulcerations. Normal mucosa surrounds the ulcerations until late in the disease. Scanning electron microscopy has identified surface erosions only 100 to 200 µm in size surrounded by M cells, which may be the entry point for whatever the etiologic agent is found to be in Crohn's disease.[1]

ULCERATIVE COLITIS

Ulcerative colitis triggers an increase in the surface blood flow, which causes the earliest lesions endoscopically to be diffuse erythema and vascular congestion. The mucosa looks like "wet sandpaper"; the edema produces a fine granular appearance and dulls the mucosal vascular architecture. The engorged mucosa bleeds readily when touched by the endoscope and as inflammation progresses, spontaneous bleeding occurs secondary to minute surface ulcerations that have been formed.

Importance of Assessing Extent of Disease

Establishing the extent of intestinal inflammation is essential in attempting to differentiate Crohn's disease from ulcerative colitis. This effort may be helpful to help guide medical therapy, to establish the risk of colorectal carcinoma, and to decide when to consider surgery. Colonoscopy with multiple biopsies is the standard for defining extent of disease and excluding other forms of inflammation. Biopsies are more sensitive than macroscopic evaluation in determining the degree of inflammation and hence increase the diagnostic yield of an endoscopy considerably; biopsies from macroscopically normal mucosa can reveal microscopic areas of inflammation. Skip lesions are suggestive of Crohn's disease, whereas ulcerative colitis tends to be a more circumferential and contiguous disease.

Biopsies of the terminal ileum are often critical in the differentiation of Crohn's disease from ulcerative colitis. Involvement of the ileum is highly suggestive of Crohn's disease. Proximal biopsies often are revealing in a patient with resistant proctitis and a normal-appearing barium study. Up to 50% of these patients will have proximal inflammation present on biopsy. In addition to this, proximal biopsies that are negative for inflammation identify patients with primarily rectal or left-sided colonic involvement; these patients usually respond to medicated suppositories or enemas and evidence shows that the addition of topical therapy offers significant benefit for these patients.[2]

Assessing Disease Severity

Over the past 30 years, many disease activity indexes have been formulated. These indices are useful mostly in clinical trials, in which the necessity to characterize severity and response to treatment in a reproducible fashion from institution to institution and from study to study is imperative. They also allow for enrollment of homogeneous groups of patients. An ideal index of activity would be simple to use, encompass the variability of disease manifestations, and be easily reproducible. No index thus far has been widely adopted by gastroenterologists in their clinical practice and no index can replace a good clinical history and clinical judgment.

CROHN'S DISEASE

The Crohn's Disease Activity Index (CDAI) was developed in 1976 by Best and coworkers[3] as part of the National Cooperative Crohn's Disease Study. It is the gold standard index for any Crohn's disease clinical trial. A multivariant regression analysis was performed and eight variables were identified as predictors of disease activity. These are number of stools, abdominal pain, general well-being, extra-intestinal complications, antidiarrheal agents used in the previous 7 days, abdominal mass felt on palpation, hematocrit, and body weight (Table 23–1). CDAI scores range from 0 to 600. A score of less than 150 corresponds to relative disease quiescence (remission), 150 to 219 is mildly active disease, 220 to 450 is moderately active disease, and a score of greater than 450 is indicative of severe disease. A decrease in greater than 100 points indicates a clinically significant improvement in disease activity (termed clinical response). Older literature suggests that a clinical response is defined by a decrease in CDAI by greater than 70 points. The limitations of the CDAI include the complexity of the calculation needed by the physician, the weight placed on subjective complaints such as general well-being and abdominal pain, and the requirement of the patient to keep a diary for 7 days.

The Harvey-Bradshaw index,[4] or the Simple index, is less complicated than the CDAI and uses five variables recorded on one occasion (Table 23–2). No diary is needed and no laboratory values are required. The five variables are general well-being, abdominal pain, abdominal mass, number of liquid stools, and systemic complications. Each variable is weighted the same. Studies have found that the Harvey-Bradshaw Index correlates well with the CDAI.[5]

The Crohn's Disease Endoscopic Index of Severity (CDEIS)[6] is a third index and the first to use endoscopic data in assessing disease severity. This prospectively developed index was established in 1989 by the French group of Groupe d'Etudes Therapeutique des Affections Inflammatoires du Tube Digestif (GETAID) and, after being validated in a large multicenter trial,[6] is now the gold standard for evaluation of endoscopic, rather than clinical, activity. The bowel is divided into five segments (the rectum, the sigmoid and left colon, the transverse colon, the right colon, and the ileum) and a numerical score is assigned based on objective endoscopic criteria: the presence or absence of deep or superficial ulcerations and the extent of surface involved by the disease (Table 23–3). Scores range from 0 to 44 with higher scores indicating more severe disease. The CDEIS is reproducible, but it is rather time consuming for the physician to calculate a score, which hinders its use outside of clinical trials. It also has failed to correlate with patient's symptoms or other indicators of clinical activity.[7] The main goal of therapy in Crohn's disease has been to achieve remission from disease symptoms rather than to achieve endoscopic remission. Endoscopic severity previously had not been shown to correlate reliably with prognosis nor to predict a clinical response to therapy.[8] However, there are recent studies with infliximab treatment that imply that there is a longer remission and fewer disease events in patients achieving endoscopic remission.[9,10] This may alter the role that endoscopy has in the evaluation of the clinical course of Crohn's disease.

In 2002, a second severity index based on endoscopic findings was proposed, the Simple Endoscopic Score for Crohn's Disease (SES-CD).[11] Because endoscopic remission has become one of the goals

Table 23–1. Crohn's Disease Activity Index

Variable	Description	Scoring	Multiplier
Number of liquid stools	Sum of 7 days		×2
Abdominal pain	Sum of 7 days ratings	0 = none 1 = mild 2 = moderate 3 = severe	×5
General well-being	Sum of 7 days ratings	0 = generally well 1 = slightly under par 2 = poor 3 = very poor 4 = terrible	×7
Extraintestinal complications	Number of listed complications	Arthritis/arthralgia, iritis/uveitis, erythema nodosum, pyoderma gangrenosum, aphthous stomatitis, anal fissure/fistula/abscess, fever >37.8°C	×20
Antidiarrheal drugs	Use in previous 7 days	0 = no 1 = yes	×30
Abdominal mass		0 = no 2 = questionable 5 = definite	×10
Hematocrit	Expected − observed Hct	Males: 47 − observed Females: 42 − observed	×6
Body weight	Ideal/observed ratio	[1− (ideal/observed)] × 100	×1 (not <−10)

From Best WR, Becktel JM, Singleton JW, et al: Development of a Crohn's disease activity index. National Cooperative Crohn's Disease Study. Gastroenterology 70:439–444, 1976.

Table 23–2. Harvey Bradshaw Index (Simple Index)

Variable	Scoring	Total
General well-being	0 = very well 1 = slightly below par 2 = poor 3 = very poor 4 = terrible	
Abdominal pain	0 = none 1 = mild 2 = moderate 3 = severe	
Number of liquid stools daily	—	
Abdominal mass	0 = no 1 = dubious 2 = definite 3 = definite and tender	
Extraintestinal complications	Arthritis/arthralgia, iritis/uveitis, erythema nodosum, pyoderma gangrenosum, aphthous stomatitis, anal fissure/fistula/abscess	

From Harvey RF, Bradshaw JM: A simple index of Crohn's disease activity. Lancet 1:514, 1980.

for monitoring treatment in clinical trials, there is a need for a simpler endoscopic activity assessment than the CDEIS. The bowel is divided into the same five segments as in the CDEIS, and a score of 0 to 3 is assigned based on endoscopic criteria—presence of ulcers, degree of ulcerated surface, degree of affected surface, presence of narrowings, and the number of affected segments (Table 23–4). This is easier and faster to calculate than the CDEIS. The reproducibility of the SES-CD was as good as was found with the CDEIS, and it reliably correlated with the CDEIS, the present gold standard. However, like the CDEIS, the correlation of SES-CD results with clinically active disease was weak. The role of endoscopic assessment of severity of disease in clinical practice is still being developed.

ULCERATIVE COLITIS

The first qualitative grading system for ulcerative colitis was developed by Truelove and Witts[12] in 1955. This classification

Table 23–3. Scoring System for Crohn's Disease Endoscopic Index of Severity

Scoring	Rectum	Sigmoid and Left Colon	Transverse Colon	Right Colon	Ileum	Total
Deep ulcerations (12 if present)						Total 1
Superficial ulcerations (12 if present)						Total 2
Surface involved by disease (cm)						Total 3
Surface involved by ulcerations (cm)						Total 4
Total 1 + Total 2 + Total 3 + Total 4 =						Total A
Number of segments totally or partially explored =						n
Total A/n =						Total B
If an ulcerated stenosis is present anywhere add 3 =						C
If a nonulcerated stenosis is present anywhere add 3 =						D
Total B + C + D =						CDEIS

From Mary JY, Modigliani R: Development and validation of an endoscopic index of the severity for Crohn's disease: A prospective multicentre study. Groupe d'Studes Therapeutiques des Affections Inflammatoires du Tube Digestif (GETAID). Gut 30:983–989, 1989.

Table 23–4. Definitions of the Simple Endoscopic Score for Crohn's Disease Variables

Variable	0	1	2	3
Presence of ulcers	None	Aphthous ulcers (0.1–0.5 cm)	Large ulcers (0.5–2.0 cm)	Very large ulcers (>2.0 cm)
Ulcerated surface	None	<10%	10%–30%	>30%
Affected surface	Unaffected segment	<50%	50%–75%	>75%
Presence of narrowings	None	Single, can be passed	Multiple, can be passed	Cannot be passed
Number of affected segments	All variables = 0	At least one variable ≥1	—	—

To determine the simple endoscopic score for Crohn's disease (SES-CD), the equation is SES-CD = sum of all variables − 1.4 × (number of affected segments).
Daperno M, Van Assche G, Bulois P, et al: Development of Crohn's disease endoscopic score (CDES): A simple index to assess endoscopic severity of Crohn's disease [abstract]. Gastroenterology 122:A216, 2002.

Table 23–5. Truelove and Witts' Classification of Severity in Ulcerative Colitis

Mild	Diarrhea: fewer than 4 bowel movements daily, with only small amounts of blood No fever No tachycardia Erythrocyte sedimentation rate (ESR) <30 mm/hr
Moderate	Activity between mild and severe
Severe	Diarrhea: ≥6 bowel movements daily, with blood Fever: mean evening temperature >37.5°C or a temperature of >37.5°C on at least 2 of 4 days at any time of the day Tachycardia: mean pulse >90 beats/min Anemia: Hemoglobin <7.5 g/dL compared to normal, allowing for recent transfusions ESR >30 mm/hr

From Truelove SC, Witts LJ: Cortisone in ulcerative colitis. Final report on a therapeutic trial. Br Med J 2:1041–1048, 1955.

system divides patients into mild, moderate, or severe disease based on five criteria: temperature, heart rate, hemoglobin, erythrocyte sedimentation rate, and diarrheal symptoms (Table 23–5). Initially when this index was described, only definitions for patients with mild and severe disease were described. This index is simple, quick, and easily applied and can rapidly identify the sickest patients with ulcerative colitis.

Powell-Tuck and coworkers[13] developed a scoring system to be used in their clinical trial that incorporated clinical data and endoscopic criteria. This scoring system includes a wider range of symptoms than the Truelove and Witts scoring system and includes examination for abdominal tenderness and a sigmoidoscopic scoring system. Assessment of the macroscopic sigmoidoscopic appearance is subjective, and studies have found poor correlation between the colonoscopic findings and the Powell-Tuck Activity Score.[14] This suggests that sigmoidoscopy is not the most accurate method of assessing disease activity once the diagnosis of ulcerative colitis has been established.

Table 23–6. The Simple Colitis Activity Index	
Symptoms	**Score**
Bowel frequency (day)	
1–3	0
4–6	1
7–9	2
>9	3
Bowel frequency (night)	
1–3	1
4–6	2
Urgency of defecation	
Hurry	1
Immediately	2
Incontinence	3
Blood in stool	
Trace	1
Occasionally frank	2
Usually frank	3
General well-being	
Very well	0
Slightly below par	1
Poor	2
Very poor	3
Terrible	4
Extracolonic features	1 per manifestation

From Walmsley RS, Ayres RC, Pounder RE, et al: A simple clinical colitis activity index. Gut 43:29–32, 1998.

The Simple Colitis Activity Index[15] was developed to aid in the initial evaluation of exacerbations of ulcerative colitis by outpatient physicians. It was compared with the established Powell-Tuck Activity Score and the authors found good correlation between the two indices ($p < .0001$). This simpler index includes six clinical criteria: bowel frequency (day), bowel frequency (night), urgency of defecation, blood in stool, general well-being, and extracolonic manifestations (Table 23–6). Because this index does not use endoscopic or laboratory data, it may be used as an initial assessment in the outpatient setting and possibly by patients themselves as a guide to modifying treatment and the need to seek further medical advice.

The Ulcerative Colitis Disease Activity Index (UCDAI) was designed in 1987 by Dr. Lloyd Sutherland and coworkers[16] to provide an objective basis for assessing drug efficacy. Four variables are measured, with each receiving a numerical value of 0 (normal) to 3 (most severe); a total value of 12 indicates the most severe disease. These variables are stool frequency, amount of blood in stool, endoscopic appearance of colonic mucosa, and a physician's assessment of disease severity. One of the potential strengths of this index is its incorporation of endoscopic appearance. A clinical response to therapy is defined as a reduction in the UCDAI score by 2 or more points. This index is very similar to another well-accepted index, often called the "Mayo Score," developed by investigators at the Mayo Clinic.[17]

It should be stressed that none of the aforementioned indices that have been described for patients with ulcerative colitis has been validated. They have been accepted as being appropriate without proper formal validation.

Preparation of Patients for Gastrointestinal Endoscopy

LOWER FLEXIBLE GASTROINTESTINAL ENDOSCOPY (COLONOSCOPY AND FLEXIBLE SIGMOIDOSCOPY)

The quality of the colonoscopy or flexible sigmoidoscopy depends on the effectiveness of the bowel preparation. Bowel cleansing should leave no residual fecal material and only very little fluid. An inadequate bowel preparation has many repercussions: it impairs visualization and colonoscopic diagnosis, it may require the procedure to be rescheduled, and it prolongs insertion time that not only adds to patient discomfort[18] but also increases the cost of the procedure.[19]

In a study comparing GoLytely, NuLytely, and Fleet Phospho-Soda, Ell and colleagues[20] demonstrated a statistically significant benefit to using GoLytely over the other two preparations in achieving effective cleansing of the entire colon before colonoscopy. There was no difference in patient satisfaction between the three preparations. In this study, the patients ate a regular breakfast on the day before the examination and thereafter only had clear fluids; they were not to eat anything on the day of the colonoscopy. The bowel cleansing regimen occurred in two stages, with divided doses the day prior and the on the morning of the procedure. A short interval between bowel preparation and the colonoscopy has yielded better cleansing results.[21] The GoLytely preparation in the past had been considered to be the gold standard for bowel cleansing before colonoscopy. It should be noted that none of these studies were performed in patients with IBD, and Fleet Phospho-Soda enemas have been implicated in the development of an acute colitis.

For a flexible sigmoidoscopy, patient studies have not shown a clearly superior method for bowel preparation. The addition of magnesium citrate to the regimen does appear to improve the quality of the study over enemas alone.[22,23] Patients may consider a completely oral regimen more easily tolerated than one that includes enemas,[24] but the best preparation probably would be one that includes both oral magnesium citrate and one to two Fleet enemas.[25] These have yet to be adequately assessed in blinded controlled trials for patients with IBD.

UPPER ENDOSCOPY

There is no preparation required for a patient to undergo an upper gastrointestinal (GI) endoscopy. Patients should ingest no solids for at least 6 hours before the procedure and no liquids for at least 4 hours. If a patient has a gastric emptying disorder, a longer period of fasting may be required.

Indications for Gastrointestinal Endoscopy in Inflammatory Bowel Disease

LOWER FLEXIBLE GASTROINTESTINAL ENDOSCOPY

Endoscopy plays a key role in not only the diagnosis of Crohn's disease but also in its management. Although other radiologic modalities often are complementary to the diagnosis and treatment

Table 23-7. Indications for Lower Endoscopy in Inflammatory Bowel Disease

Cancer screening
Determination of disease activity
Determination of disease extent
Early diagnosis
Evaluation of unexplained diarrhea
Monitor therapy
Perioperative evaluation
Stricture management

Table 23-8. Endoscopic Appearance of Crohn's Disease and Ulcerative Colitis

Endoscopic Appearance	Crohn's Disease	Ulcerative Colitis
Rectum	Spared	Involved
Vascular pattern	Normal	Early loss of vascular markings
Mucosal involvement	Skip lesions	Continuous
Ulcers	Within inflamed mucosa	Within normal mucosa
Mucosal granularity	Present	Present ("wet sandpaper")
Mucosal friability	Present	Present
Cobblestoning	Present	Absent
Thick interhaustral septum	Present	Present
Pseudopolyps	Present	Present
Narrowing of lumen	Present	Present
Strictures	Present	Present
Fistula	Present	Absent
Ulcerations in terminal ileum	Present	Absent
Mucosal bridge	Present	Present

of Crohn's disease, endoscopy is the only method that allows for biopsies to be taken. Table 23–7 lists indications for colonoscopy in IBD. Colonoscopy is usually performed during the initial evaluation of ulcerative colitis and Crohn's disease to confirm the diagnosis, assess disease severity, and determine the extent of the disease. It also plays an important role in assessing the disease response to therapy and is important in performing endoscopic surveillance for dysplasia and/or cancer.

Colonoscopy and flexible sigmoidoscopy are contraindicated in patients with known or suspected peritonitis, bowel perforation, or colonic necrosis.[26] Severe coagulopathy, thrombocytopenia, or neutropenia also are contraindications for the procedure. In addition, toxic megacolon and fulminant colitis generally are relative contraindications for the procedure secondary to their increased risk of colonic perforation.

UPPER GASTROINTESTINAL ENDOSCOPY

Upper GI endoscopy is used to evaluate upper GI symptoms in patients with IBD. Biopsies of normal gastric mucosa in patients with indeterminant colitis may aid in the diagnosis of Crohn's colitis. In patients with known Crohn's disease, it allows for the diagnosis of Crohn's disease of the esophagus, stomach, and duodenum. It also can be therapeutic in the treatment of strictures or upper GI bleeding.

Crohn's Disease

LOWER GASTROINTESTINAL ENDOSCOPY

Colonoscopy is performed in the initial diagnosis of Crohn's disease to confirm the diagnosis and assess the extent of the disease. Intubation of the terminal ileum should be attempted in all patients; there is an 80% to 97% success rate of insertion of the colonoscope into the distal ileum.[27,28] Biopsies of the terminal ileum should be taken because Crohn's ileitis can appear macroscopically normal. Endoscopic involvement of the ileum is usually associated with Crohn's disease, but patients with pancolonic involvement who have ulcerative colitis can have backwash ileitis, a patchy inflammation without ulceration that extends a few centimeters into the terminal ileum. Biopsies are required to differentiate the two diagnoses.

A flexible sigmoidoscopy may be appropriate to perform when a colonoscopy was recently performed or when the inflammation is known to be limited to the left side of the colon.[29] In patients with severe disease activity, a colonoscopy may be contraindicated secondary to the severe degree of inflammation; whereas a flexible sigmoidoscopy can be useful to confirm that a patient's symptoms are related to their Crohn's disease and not an infectious or other form of colitis. A flexible sigmoidoscopy can also be used to confirm a diagnosis of irritable bowel syndrome (IBS) by excluding other inflammatory or neoplastic disorders. In IBS, there is normal colonic anatomy, but there may be nonspecific findings of increased colonic mucus, mural spasm, and an increased sensitivity to painful stimuli during flexible sigmoidoscopy.[30]

Colonic perforation is the most common major complication of a diagnostic colonoscopy, with a risk of approximately 0.25%.[31,32] In patients with severe colitis, a suspected abscess, toxic megacolon, or signs or symptoms of a bowel obstruction, colonoscopy is generally not recommended because the risk of perforation is greatly increased. A very small scope (6-mm outer diameter) can be used for assessment of the rectum and sigmoid; this technique practically eliminates the risk of colonic perforation. The proximal extent of disease can then be evaluated by computed tomography (CT) scan. The most common reason to abort a colonoscopy in patients with Crohn's disease is related to the presence of severe inflammation with large, deep ulcerations, which carry an increased risk of perforation.

The endoscopic appearance of IBD usually is not specific enough to make the definitive diagnosis of ulcerative colitis versus Crohn's disease; the accuracy of colonoscopy in differentiating between the two forms of inflammatory colitis is 85% to 90%.[33] There are some features that can favor one diagnosis over the other (Table 23–8). Endoscopically, Crohn's disease tends to vary with disease duration and severity. The rectum is typically spared, with the most severe involvement occurring in the cecum and right colon; the most common patterns of disease distribution are ileocolitis (40% to 50%), ileitis (30% to 40%), and colitis (15% to 25%). Classically, the disease is discontinuous, forming skip areas; these are areas of disease that are separated by normal mucosa.

In early Crohn's disease, small punched out aphthous ulcers are typically seen on the background of normal mucosa (Fig. 23–1A and B). Aphthous ulcers are a result of submucosal lymphoid follicle expansion and penetration through the mucosa. As the disease

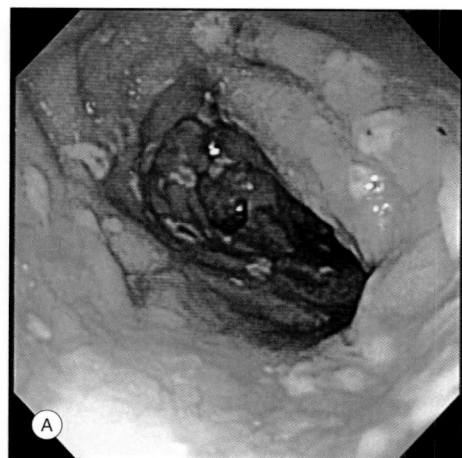
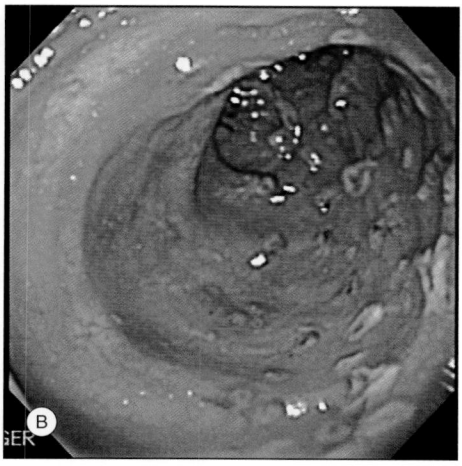

Figure 23-1. *A* and *B,* Multiple aphthous ulcers seen in recurrent Crohn's disease in the neoterminal ileum of the ileocolic anastomosis 3 months after resection.

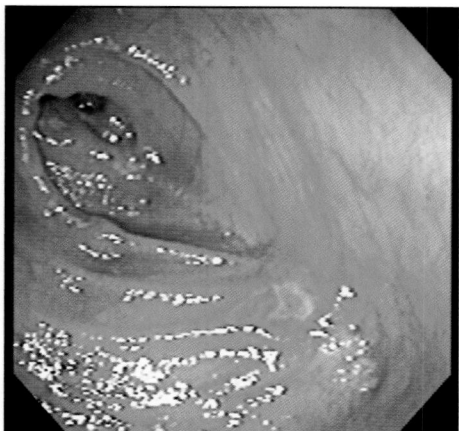

Figure 23-2. Stellate colonic ulcers in a patient with Crohn's disease.

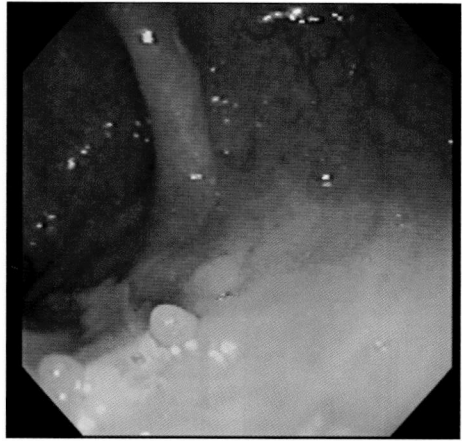

Figure 23-3. Irregularly shaped ulcerations in a patient with Crohn's disease.

progresses, these superficial ulcerations enlarge and coalesce to become long and linear and may take on the appearance of a star ("stellate ulcers") (Fig. 23–2). These ulcerations then can deepen throughout the bowel wall to lead to abscess and fistula formation. With increasing chronicity, submucosal edema and injury results in a cobblestoning appearance, which practically is pathognomonic for Crohn's disease; cobblestoning consists of uniform nodulations that are low in height with a broad base. Patients with severe disease can have large linear ulcers ("bear claw" ulcers) and deep serpiginous ulcers (Figs. 23–3 and 23–4). Strictures can form in areas with transmural circumferential inflammation. Patients with moderate to severe disease activity may be endoscopically indistinguishable from patients with ulcerative colitis and many other diseases (Fig. 23–5).

Histologically, there is transmural inflammation with predominantly lymphocytic infiltration. Granulomas are the hallmark of Crohn's disease, although they are present in only 10% to 25% of biopsy specimens. They are more common in the early stages of the disease.[34] Granulomas can be found throughout the GI tract and in macroscopically normal areas. For this reason, it is advocated that upper GI endoscopy with biopsy be performed when the differentiation between ulcerative colitis and Crohn's disease is not clear.

UPPER GASTROINTESTINAL ENDOSCOPY

One of the hallmarks of Crohn's disease is that it can affect the entire GI tract, from the mouth to the anus. Involvement of the upper GI tract was previously felt to be an uncommon site of disease, with a prevalence of less than 4%.[35,36] Routine use of endoscopy has found a prevalence closer to 50% to 60%.[37] Dysphagia, odynophagia, epigastric pain, and stomatitis are the most common symptoms, although most patients are asymptomatic.[38-40]

Endoscopic features of Crohn's disease in the esophagus tend to be nonspecific, including aphthous ulcers, cobblestoning, stricture formation, friability, and granularity. Huchzermeyer and coworkers[41] described two different stages of esophageal involvement. The first stage is a milder and earlier form of the disease. There is erythema and edema that progresses to aphthous ulcerations with intervening normal mucosa, resembling a cobblestoning appearance. In the second stage, there is esophageal stricturing and stenosis. Histologically, it is rare to see a granuloma on a biopsy of the esophagus; 75% of biopsies show active chronic inflammation and 30% show ulcerations.[38]

The antrum and duodenum are the most common sites of involvement of the upper GI tract (Fig. 23–6*A* and *B*). Gastroduodenal

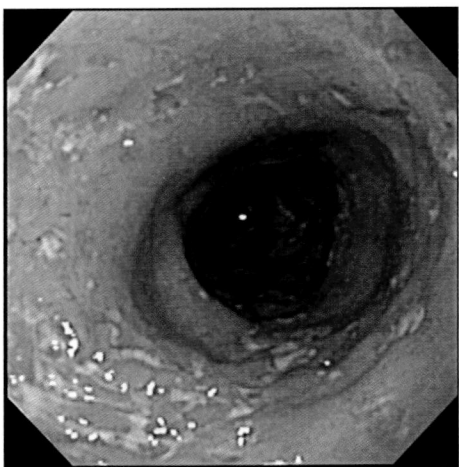

Figure 23–4. Multiple serpiginous ulcerations of the rectum in a patient with Crohn's disease.

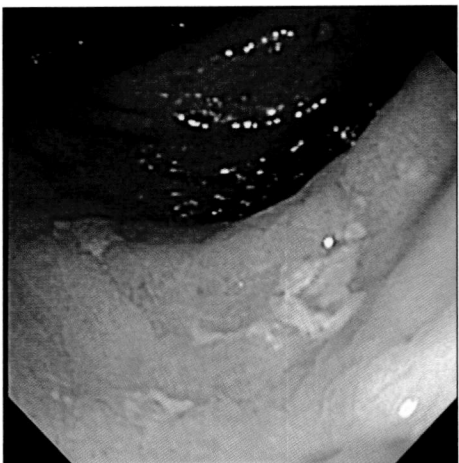

Figure 23–5. Ulcers in the colon in patients with Behçet's disease cannot be differentiated endoscopically from patients with Crohn's disease.

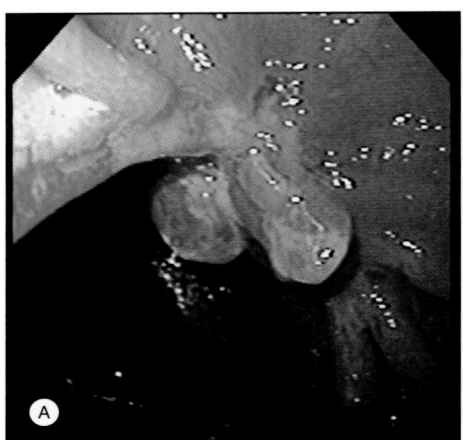

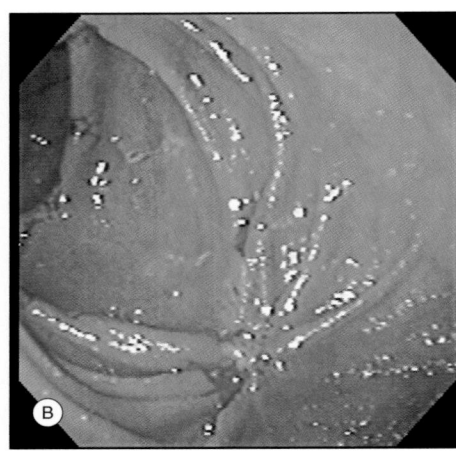

Figure 23–6. *A,* Duodenal active ulceration in a patient with Crohn's disease. *B,* Duodenal bleeding in an active ulcer in the same patient with Crohn's disease.

disease is contiguous in approximately 60% of patients, with only 40% having duodenal disease solely.[42] Unlike the round and oval ulcers seen in peptic ulcer disease, the ulcerations in gastroduodenal Crohn's disease tend to be more serpiginous and longitudinal.[35] Mucosal erythema and nodularity, cobblestoning, and strictures have also been described.[36,42] The descending duodenum is often the most severely affected. The pathognomonic granulomas are found in approximately 40% of biopsies taken from the duodenum.[42]

Ulcerative Colitis

LOWER GASTROINTESTINAL ENDOSCOPY

In ulcerative colitis, the inflammatory response is directed solely at the colon and is limited to the mucosa and submucosa. The disease starts in the rectum in 95% of cases, which causes one to reconsider the diagnosis of ulcerative colitis in any patient with rectal sparing. The inflammation usually occurs in a circumferential, contiguous pattern.

Early in the disease, there is loss of the vascular pattern and congestion. The smooth and glistening appearance of normal colonic mucosa is replaced by a more granular appearing mucosa caused by disruption of the normal light reflection. There is blunting of the normal finely branched mucosal vascular pattern, blunting of the intrahaustral folds caused by mucosal edema, and diffuse mucosal erythema.

At later stages, the edematous mucosa acquires a sandpaper-like appearance and becomes very friable. This leads to easy mucosal bleeding, even in response to being brushed lightly by the endoscope or a cotton swab. With severe disease, mucopus, a yellow-white exudate, may be present. Disruption of the colonic mucosa develops and small shallow ulcers can develop and progress to large deep ulcerations. These large ulcerations can coalesce to form areas of completely destroyed mucosa; pseudopolyps or mucosal bridges can form from the congested mucosal remnants present in the denuded areas (Fig. 23–7A and B and Fig. 23–8A and B).[43] Usually pseudopolyps are not clinically significant, but in patients with long-standing ulcerative colitis, they require a biopsy because they resemble adenomatous and malignant polyps (Fig. 23–9).

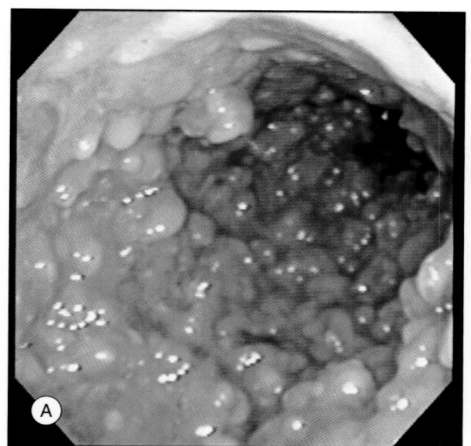 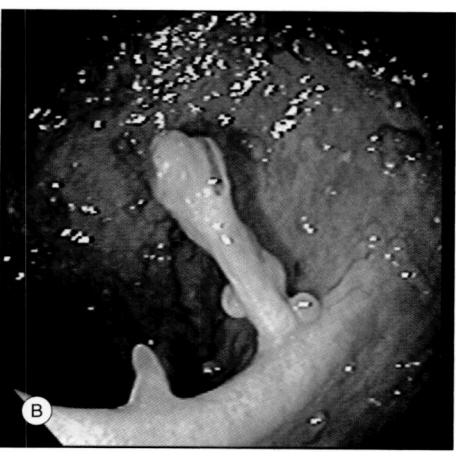

Figure 23–7. *A* and *B,* Pseudopolyps in a patient with ulcerative colitis.

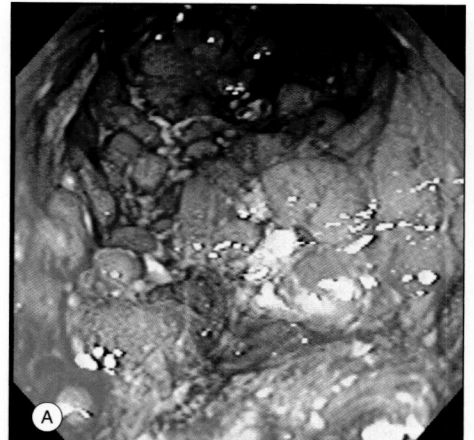 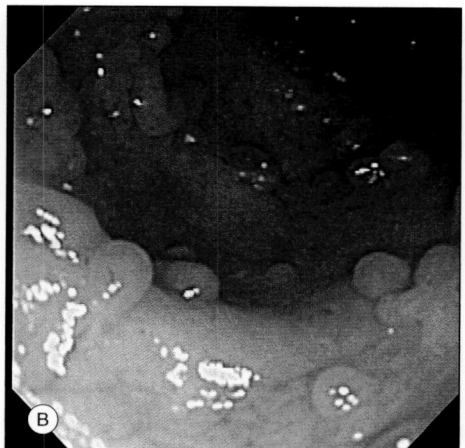 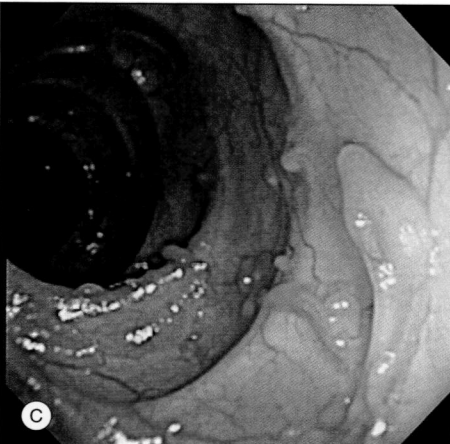

Figure 23–8. *A,* Pseudopolyps in a patient with severe ulcerative colitis. *B* and *C,* Pseudopolyps in the same patient after treatment.

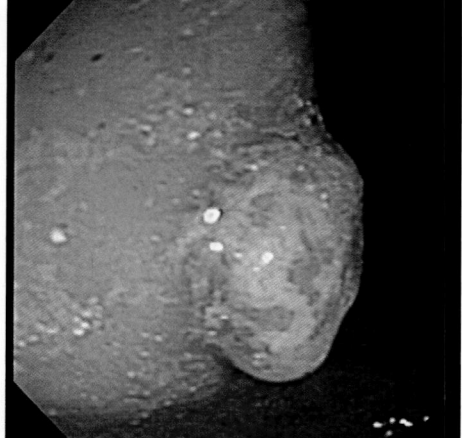

Figure 23–9. Large pseudopolyp in the rectum of a patient with longstanding ulcerative colitis.

Toxic megacolon is one of the dreaded complications of colitis; although more often seen in patients with ulcerative colitis, it is found in Crohn's disease as well. In severe colitis, there is damage to the neural plexus and muscularis propria that can lead to neuromuscular dysfunction. This can result in progressive colonic dilatation leading to a toxic megacolon.

In chronic ulcerative colitis, the colon appears smooth, shortened and noncompliant (rigid) on colonoscopy. There is loss of the haustral folds caused by thickening of the muscularis mucosa and submucosal fibrosis. The colon has a characteristic pipelike appearance.

The terminal ileum can also be involved in 10% to 20% of patients with panulcerative colitis. There is erythema, an abnormal vascular pattern, and superficial erosions in the distal 5 cm of the terminal ileum secondary to this backwash ileitis. This is almost always found in the setting of a dilated and incompetent ileocecal valve. Although this ileitis does not cause any clinical symptoms, there are retrospective data that suggest that backwash ileitis is associated with an increased risk of colorectal cancer (CRC).[44]

UPPER GASTROINTESTINAL ENDOSCOPY

Because ulcerative colitis, by definition, does not affect the upper GI tract, an upper endoscopy would not be performed routinely. One of the few reasons to perform an upper endoscopy is if the diagnosis of ulcerative colitis is in question; this test can look for evidence of inflammatory disease elsewhere in the GI tract to establish the diagnosis of Crohn's disease.

Strictures and Mass Lesions

DIFFERENTIATING MALIGNANT FROM BENIGN STRICTURES

The healing response to the chronic inflammation found in IBD is thought to result in intestinal strictures. It is believed that, in healing, there is recruitment of fibroblasts and other structural components, which promote fibrosis and luminal narrowing leading to strictures (Fig. 23–10).[45] The sheer number and diversity of cell types in the intestine makes it difficult to identify a solitary cell responsible for the fibrosis seen in IBD. Stricture formation is found more often in patients with Crohn's disease than with ulcerative colitis because of the transmural nature of inflammation seen in Crohn's disease (Figs. 23–11 and 23–12). The prevalence of colonic strictures in Crohn's disease ranges from 4% to 5% in surgical data[46] to 8% to 9% using endoscopic data.[47]

With all strictures, it is imperative to assess for any evidence of malignancy. Although strictures are more often found in patients with Crohn's disease, those associated with ulcerative colitis have a higher frequency of malignancy. The rate of malignancy in patients who have strictures is 7% to 11% in Crohn's disease,[48] compared with approximately 25% in ulcerative colitis.[49] Efforts should be made to exclude malignancy when performing a colonoscopy (Fig. 23–13). This includes visualizing the entire length of the stricture and beyond and using a narrower pediatric colonoscope,

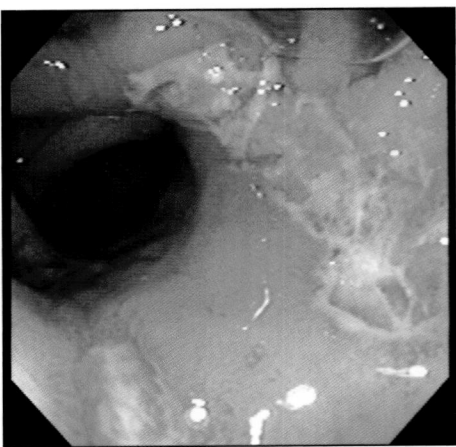

Figure 23–10. Multiple active ulcers in a patient with fibrostenotic Crohn's disease.

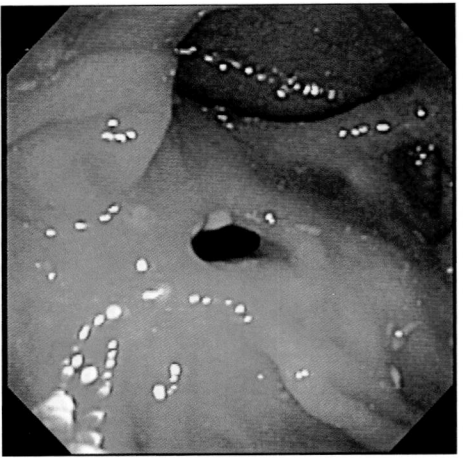

Figure 23–11. Crohn's stricture at the anastomosis.

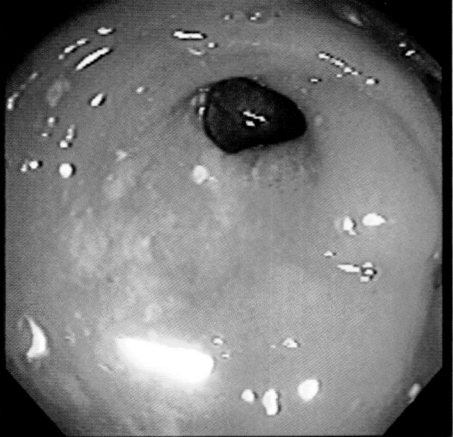

Figure 23–12. Stricture at the ileocolic anastomosis.

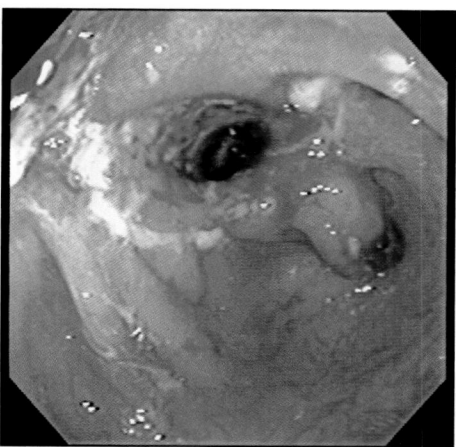

Figure 23–13. Ulceration and nonmalignant stricture in a patient with active Crohn's disease in the descending colon.

push enteroscope, or gastroscope if necessary. Biopsy specimens should be obtained from the edge and the core of the stricture. Endoscopic features suggesting malignancy within a stricture are rigidity of the edge, an eccentric lumen, nodularity within the stricture, and an abrupt shelflike margin. Even if the biopsy is negative for malignancy, these highly suspicious lesions should be treated as if they were malignant, because carcinoma complicating IBD can extend submucosally. Surgery should be considered in all patients with biopsy-proven malignant strictures, those with highly suspicious lesions based on gross endoscopic assessment, and those in which a colonoscope is unable to pass to survey the remainder of the colon.

ROLE OF BALLOON DILATATION OF STRICTURES

Strictures that are deemed to be benign may be treated without surgical resection by using through-the-scope (TTS) balloon dilatation. Strictures most amenable for endoscopic therapy are short (typically less than 8 cm), isolated, and located in areas of only mild inflammation. The overall success rate of TTS balloon dilatation ranges from 50% to 85%.[50–56] Dilatation can be repeated in cases of symptomatic recurrence; both Couckuyt and colleagues[50] and Sabate and coworkers[57] found a 40% success rate of TTS dilatation, but they also found a 40% probability of patients requiring surgery at 5-year follow-up. The complication rate of TTS balloon dilatation ranges from 2.9% to 8%, with colonic perforation being the most common complication.[50,54,57] No prospective randomized controlled studies have been performed to compare endoscopic treatment of strictures directly with surgical stricturoplasty.

Steroid injections at the time of dilatation have been proposed to improve the results of balloon dilatation. Ramboer and coworkers[52] treated 13 patients with symptomatic strictures that precluded the passage of a standard 13-mm colonoscope. Although there was no control group, this study offered promising results because all 13 patients experienced immediate relief and none required surgery at 47 months of follow-up. The success of the combined therapy

may be secondary to a local anti-inflammatory effect of the corticosteroids and/or a decrease in the tendency toward fibrosis after dilatation. Prospective randomized studies need to be done to further evaluate the use of steroids during balloon dilatation.

Differential Diagnosis

DIFFERENTIATING CROHN'S DISEASE FROM ULCERATIVE COLITIS

The accuracy of colonoscopy in differentiating Crohn's disease from ulcerative colitis is approximately 85% to 90%.[33] Establishing an accurate diagnosis is important because the treatment, surgical options, and prognosis often are significantly distinct between the two forms of colitis. It is also important to reevaluate the original diagnosis and to continue to evaluate patients with an "indeterminant colitis," because these diseases often evolve over time. Two studies looked at this phenomenon. Moum and coworkers[58] studied 527 patients with ulcerative colitis and 88% had their diagnosis confirmed at 2 years' follow-up; 91% of the 228 patients with Crohn's disease had their diagnosis confirmed. In 36 patients that were originally listed as indeterminant colitis, at 2 years, 33% and 17% were reclassified as having either ulcerative colitis or Crohn's disease, respectively. Langevin and colleagues[59] studied 96 patients with ulcerative proctitis, and, over a 29-month period, 14% developed features more consistent with Crohn's disease.

The expression of perinuclear antineutrophil cytoplasmic antibodies (pANCA) is present in most patients with ulcerative colitis, but 10% to 30% of patients with Crohn's disease also have this antibody; these appear to be a subset of patients with Crohn's disease who have a more ulcerative colitis-like pattern of disease: left-sided colitis, rectal bleeding, and mucus discharge.[60] The anti-*Saccharomyces cerevisiae* antibody (ASCA) also is helpful in IBD. This is present in 50% to 70% of patients with Crohn's disease and in only 7% to 14% of patients with ulcerative colitis.[61] These serologic tests have not proven to play a significant role in establishing a diagnosis for an indeterminant colitis. In the rare case in which an individual has IgG and IgA ASCA positivity (the so-called double ASCA positive), there has been an excellent correlation with the presence of Crohn's disease.

Lesions such as inflammatory polyps (pseudopolyps) and mucosal bridges can occur in both forms of IBD. Mucosal bridges develop when two adjacent ulcers meet by burrowing beneath an area of inflamed mucosa, and, as the area heals, re-epithelialization of the ulcers and the undersurface of the mucosal strip produces a mucosal covered tube connected at both ends. There is a loss of haustral folds and linear scar formation in the healing process of both forms of colitis. The endoscopic evidence of inflammatory polyps, mucosal bridges, loss of haustral folds, or linear scarring does not offer any mechanism to differentiate ulcerative colitis from Crohn's disease.

It is most difficult to distinguish between ulcerative colitis and Crohn's disease when there is severe and active disease present. In the later stages of both diseases, the two forms of colitis can resemble each other so closely endoscopically that the diagnosis may not be possible until more time has passed and the patient is re-examined. The most helpful distinguishing features in Crohn's disease are the presence of aphthous ulcers, the cobblestoning appearance, and the focal and asymmetric distribution of the colitis. In ulcerative colitis, the more important differentiating endoscopic features are the small ulcers in a diffusely inflamed mucosa and the granularity and friability of the mucosa.[33]

Multiple biopsies are needed for making an accurate diagnosis. Each biopsy is labeled according to its location in the colon, because the pattern of inflammation is often very important in establishing a diagnosis. Focal inflammation is more consistent with Crohn's disease, whereas progressively increasing inflammation of the distal colon is more suggestive of ulcerative colitis.

Intubation of the terminal ileum and a biopsy of the small bowel are imperative in establishing a diagnosis. Although there may be backwash ileitis in patients with pancolonic involvement who have ulcerative colitis, there are no actual ulcerations seen and most often the ileum is free of disease in patients with ulcerative colitis; up to two thirds of patients with Crohn's disease have ileal involvement. The ileocecal valve is often patent in ulcerative colitis, whereas in Crohn's disease it is contracted and difficult to intubate.

DIFFERENTIATING CROHN'S DISEASE AND ULCERATIVE COLITIS FROM INFECTIOUS COLITIS

The initial diagnosis of IBD can be challenging, because there are many conditions that share the same clinical presentation (Table 23–9). In a patient with a diarrheal illness that lasts for more than 2 weeks, IBD and infectious colitis are important considerations. A careful history including travel information, diet, and antibiotic usage and stool studies and an endoscopy with biopsies often are required to make the diagnosis. It may initially be difficult to distinguish idiopathic IBD from infectious colitis because many of the clinical symptoms are similar. The endoscopic appearance of the mucosa and the histologic changes in inflammatory and infectious colitis may also be practically identical. Determining the accurate diagnosis depends on an experienced endoscopist, a reliable pathologist, and subsequent visits with the patient to observe the disease progression.

A flexible sigmoidoscopy and rectal biopsy are often adequate enough to distinguish between inflammatory and infectious colitis; a complete colonoscopy usually is not required.[62] However, if a diagnosis is unable to be made based on a flexible sigmoidoscopy alone, both proximal and distal biopsies of the right colon can be useful. In a patient with unexplained diarrhea of at least 4 to 6 weeks' duration, who has severe symptoms, nocturnal or frequent

---

Table 23–9. Differential Diagnosis of Inflammatory Bowel Disease

Behçet's syndrome
Diversion colitis
Diverticulitis
Graft-versus-host disease
Infectious colitis
Ischemic colitis
Malignancy
Microscopic colitis
Pseudomembranous and drug-induced colitis
Radiation colopathy

---

watery stools, weight loss, an elevated erythrocyte sedimentation rate or who is immunocompromised, it is reasonable to perform a colonoscopy with biopsies.[63] Approximately 30% of patients with mucoid bloody diarrhea and suspected IBD actually have an infectious etiology for their diarrhea.[64] In addition, many patients who present with IBD also are superinfected.[65] In one study, 36% of patients with refractory ulcerative colitis had cytomegalovirus (CMV) found on rectal biopsy.[66]

Endoscopic features seen more commonly in infectious colitis include free pus, an intense reddening of the surface mucosa, and yellowish exudates that partially or completely cover the mucosal surface. Patchy inflammation within the same colonic segment that consists of multiple small areas of inflammation with intervening normal appearing mucosa is one of the more characteristic endoscopic features of infectious colitis.[64] In the ensuing paragraphs, a brief description of some of the most common causes of infectious colitis and their distinctive endoscopic findings is presented.

Actinomycosis

Actinomyces israelii is an anaerobic gram-positive bacterium that is found in the mouth, lungs, and GI tract. The most common site of GI tract involvement is the ileocecal region, and it can produce a suppurative, granulomatous infection with a propensity for fistula formation and a release of "sulfur granules."[67] Symptoms include weight loss, night sweats, draining fistulas, and abdominal masses.[68] The diagnosis is confirmed by culture and histopathologic evaluation.

Amebiasis

Amebic colitis *(Entamoeba histolytica)* is a protozoan infection that primarily affects the large bowel.[69] It is most often seen in patients who recently immigrated from developing countries and who recently traveled to developing countries. Symptoms can vary from none to explosive diarrhea, tenesmus, fever, and abdominal cramps. Colonoscopic appearance during the acute phase resembles ulcerative colitis, but in the chronic phase it appears more like Crohn's disease. The most common segments involved are the cecum and right colon, with the rectum and sigmoid less often involved.[70] Toxic megacolon may develop in severe cases of amebiasis. Colonoscopy reveals granular, friable, and erythematous mucosa with discrete large ulcers covered by yellowish, mucopurulent exudates.[71] Biopsies of the margins of the ulcers provide a 60% to 90% yield of trophozoites to make the diagnosis.[72]

Balantidium coli

Balantidium coli is a protozoan transmitted by pigs that only rarely affects the colon. This infection causes varying degrees of inflammation in the rectosigmoid that initially may resemble Crohn's disease or amebiasis. The ulcers vary from scattered and superficial to multiple and deep. To make the diagnosis, the characteristic trophozoites can be found in scrapings from the rectal ulcers or in tissue samples.

Campylobacter jejuni

Campylobacter jejuni is a bacterial pathogen that typically causes a self-limited infectious diarrhea. It is the most commonly identified bacterial pathogen in cases of diarrhea in the United States.[73] It can resemble both ulcerative colitis and Crohn's disease.[74,75] Typically, the organism produces mucosal erythema and friability in the early stages and diffuse exudates over the mucosa that makes it indistinguishable from ulcerative colitis. The rectum is usually involved and the right colon is rarely affected; up to 50% of patients may present with rectal bleeding and tenesmus similar to ulcerative colitis. Less commonly, the colonoscopic appearance resembles Crohn's disease with hyperemia, friability, edema, and scattered small ulcers. Extraintestinal manifestations, such as erythema nodosum and peripheral arthritis, may be present.[76] Hepatosplenomegaly may occur from *Campylobacter* infections.[77] Twenty percent of patients may relapse or have a prolonged illness that may mimic IBD. Dark-field or phase-contrast examination of fresh stool may be diagnostic.[76]

Chlamydia trachomatis

Chlamydia trachomatis is the etiologic agent for lymphogranuloma venereum (LGV), a sexually transmitted infection that may cause proctitis and rectal stricturing. Discrete ulcers and friable mucosa often are seen in the rectum and may extend to the descending colon. The presence of stenosis and fistula formation may make this difficult to distinguish from Crohn's disease. Cultures and/or serologic tests are needed to establish the diagnosis.

Clostridium difficile or Pseudomembranous Colitis

Clostridium difficile is a bacterial infection that typically presents with watery diarrhea and crampy abdominal pain after a course of antibiotic therapy.[78] The characteristic colonoscopic finding is a pseudomembrane consisting of raised, yellow-white adherent plaques that range from 2 mm to 8 mm in diameter[79]; these pseudomembranes stud the surface of a moderately inflamed mucosa. The plaques typically occur in the rectum but occasionally can occur exclusively in the proximal colon.[80] The diagnosis is confirmed by fecal assay for C. *difficile* toxin A or B.[81]

Cytomegalovirus

CMV is an opportunistic infection that affects immunocompromised patients, most commonly in patients with acquired immunodeficiency syndrome (AIDS) whose CD_4 count is less than 100. Patients can be asymptomatic or may complain of abdominal pain and bloody diarrhea. The presence of discrete, punched-out shallow ulcerations is a hallmark for this disease (Fig. 23–14A and B). This can be difficult to distinguish from Crohn's disease, because there may be normal appearing mucosa adjacent to these ulcerations; unlike Crohn's disease, CMV ulcers are usually single and vary in size from 2 mm to 6 mm. Isolated right-sided disease is not uncommon. The diagnosis is made with a biopsy of the ulcer edges and finding CMV inclusion bodies on hematoxylin and eosin staining.[82] Multiple biopsies may be required because of the low density of infected cells.[83]

Escherichia coli 0157:H7

Escherichia coli 0157:H7 is a bacterial infection that produces a hemorrhagic colitis and also can lead to a hemolytic uremic syndrome and thrombotic thrombocytopenic purpura. It is associated with contaminated undercooked beef products. Endoscopically, the mucosa appears edematous, hyperemic, and friable, mimicking Crohn's disease.[84]

Herpes Simplex

Herpes simplex proctitis, another sexually transmitted infection, produces anal pain, tenesmus, rectal discharge, and constipation. It rarely affects any part of the colon more proximal than the rectum. The combination of external perianal vesicles and rectal lesions with mucosa that is erythematous, friable, and ulcerated in the distal 10 cm of the rectum is highly suggestive of herpes simplex infection. These perianal vesicles can progress to deep ulcerations. Lymphadenopathy, impotence, urinary retention, and lumbosacral dysesthesia can develop.[85] To diagnose this infection, one would perform viral cultures of rectal swabs or biopsies.[86]

Histoplasma capsulatum

Histoplasmosis is a mycotic infection that rarely infects the colon. When it is present, there is usually mucosal hyperemia, friability, ulcerations, lymph node hypertrophy, and pseudopolyps in the ileocecal region.[87] This mimics Crohn's disease in its predominantly right-sided distribution and its noncontiguous nature.[88] The diagnosis should be considered in immunocompromised hosts and travelers from endemic areas. The organism is identified by serology, culture or by DNA probe.

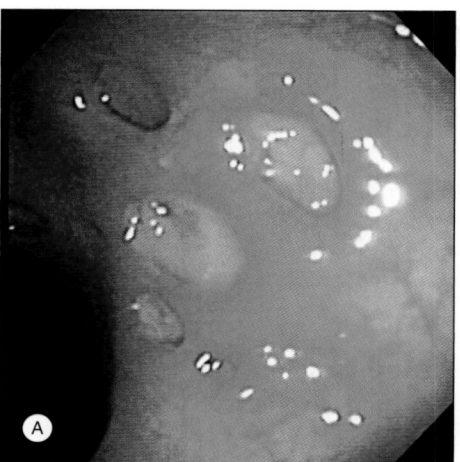
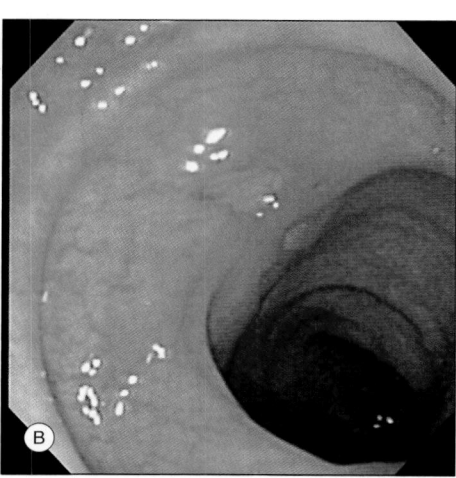

Figure 23–14. *A* and *B*, Cytomegalovirus (CMV) ulceration in immunocompromised host after a renal transplant.

Mycobacterium tuberculosis

Mycobacterium tuberculosis can affect any part of the large bowel and terminal ileum.[89] The rectum is often spared. Usually, there is a deformity of the ileocecal valve and luminal narrowing present in the ileocecal area. On colonoscopy, it often can be difficult to distinguish colonic tuberculosis from Crohn's disease. Both produce ulcerations bordered by edema and erythema and the ulcers are often located in areas of otherwise normal-appearing mucosa. There may be cobblestoning as a result of submucosal involvement, thickening of the bowel wall, and inflammatory pseudopolyps. Two distinctions between Crohn's disease and *M. tuberculosis* endoscopically are that in the later stages the ulcers often have a rolled edge and lack the sharp definition that is seen in Crohn's disease and that the areas of normal mucosa are shorter in colon affected by *M. tuberculosis*. Mass lesions or tuberculomas can develop and fistulization may be present between loops of bowel. Caseating granulomas can be found in biopsies to diagnose *M. tuberculosis*.[90]

Neisseria gonorrhoeae

Neisseria gonorrhoeae, like other sexually transmitted diseases such as herpes simplex virus (HSV) and LGV, produces a proctitis. A creamy rectal discharge or rectal bleeding, rectal friability, and erythema are usually present.[91] Anal intercourse is the largest risk factor for developing this proctitis. Cultures are required to distinguish this from ulcerative colitis.[92]

Salmonella

Salmonellosis is a bacterial diarrheal illness that usually lasts less than 2 months. It primarily involves the small bowel, spares the rectum, and only affects the colon sporadically. Early in the disease, there is edema, hyperemia, and granularity of the mucosa that then progresses to petechial hemorrhages and mucosal friability. Typhoid fever, a distinctive acute systemic febrile infection caused by *Salmonella*, is a result of a heat-labile enterotoxin that on invasion of the mucosa causes an influx of water and electrolytes into the lumen of the bowel.[93,94] As invasion occurs, localized infections develop and the bacteremia may produce a fever, headache, delirium, maculopapular rash ("rose spots"), leukopenia, and splenomegaly.[95] On endoscopy, one sees volcano-like ulcerations with a surrounding border of erythema.[96]

Schistosoma mansoni

Schistosoma mansoni is a parasite that is found mostly in tropical climates and may be difficult to diagnose because it is not found on routine ova and parasite examination; the encysted schistosomes are found in the resected polyps or biopsies.[97] Schistosomiasis produces a severely inflamed colon with multiple proximal polyps that have a whitish surface exudate. The polyps are produced by the inflammatory response to the degenerating ova. Often the rectum and sigmoid colon are completely normal, but when they are involved, this disease mimics ulcerative colitis; in these cases, there are shallow ulcerations with hyperemia, friability, and edema of the mucosa.

Shigella dysenteriae

Shigella dysenteriae is a gram-negative bacterium that causes bacillary dysentery or shigellosis. The disease can be divided into two phases.[98] The first phase, occurring in the first 1 to 2 days, consists of watery diarrhea and cramping; this phase is mediated by an enterotoxin. The second phase is caused by invasion of the organism into the large intestine and produces fever, cramps, bloody diarrhea, and tenesmus. Although patchy in appearance, the endoscopic appearance often resembles ulcerative colitis because there are multiple ulcers with considerable exudate. The mucosa often appears magenta colored because of the intense erythema. This is diagnosed with stool culture, which is only positive in 50% of cases.

Strongyloides stercoralis

Strongyloides stercoralis is a helminth infection that has ongoing cycles of autoinfection resulting from the internal production of infective larvae. It is found mostly in tropical climates. It produces nausea, diarrhea, GI bleeding, and weight loss. Endoscopically, it may produce a brown pigmentation in a speckled distribution. The diagnosis is made by detecting the rhabditiform larvae in the stool or by detecting the organism in biopsies.

Treponema pallidum

Treponema pallidum causes syphilis and is another sexually transmitted infection that leads to a proctitis. There are often lesions in the anal or anorectal region that can resemble both Crohn's disease and ulcerative colitis.

Yersinia enterocolitica

Yersinia enterocolitica is an enteroinvasive bacterium that produces abdominal pain, fever, and diarrhea; symptoms can last for months. Its diffuse erythema, friability, and edema throughout the entire colon produces a similar appearance to ulcerative colitis.[99] Less often, there is involvement of the ileum with aphthous ulcers adjacent to normal mucosa, which resembles Crohn's disease.[99] Extraintestinal symptoms such as arthritis, erythema nodosum, and aphthous stomatitis can also occur. The diagnosis can be challenging because the laboratory must inoculate the proper medium for this bacteria to grow and it can often take several weeks to demonstrate growth of the organism.

OTHER INFLAMMATORY DISORDERS OF THE COLON

Disinfectant Colitis

Colonic mucosal damage can occur from the inadequate rinsing of the cleaning solutions that are used to disinfect colonoscopes.[100] Colonoscopic instillation of fluid containing residual hydrogen peroxide instantaneously causes compromise to the mucosal stroma, resulting in mucosal blanching and effervescence; these white plaquelike lesions form a "pseudolipomatosis" colitis and produce the "snow white" sign.[101] Glutaraldehyde solution is also used in disinfecting the colonoscope; this causes direct injury to the crypt epithelium. Disinfectant colitis is a rare complication of colonoscopy.

Diverticular-Associated Colitis

Colonoscopy is not usually warranted in acute diverticulitis and often is contraindicated because there can be resistance to the passage of the colonoscope secondary to the pronounced tortuosity, fixation, and redundancy of the colon. When performed, exuding pus and inflammation around the orifice of a single diverticulum may be present. There is often severe spasm of the diseased segment without the typical redness, granularity, or friability found in most forms of inflammatory colitis.

In diverticular disease, the mucosa found on the tips of several adjacent hypertrophied folds may be patchy, mottled, and reddened. The redness is actually many tiny petechial dots; there is pressure generated by the muscular activity of the narrowed and hypertrophied colon that leads to capillary rupture. Unlike IBD, this mucosa is not friable and does not bleed easily when touched by the tip of the colonoscope. When a large enough segment is involved, the mucosa may become friable and spontaneous bleeding can occur.

On biopsy, there is a lack of inflammatory cell response. Instead, there is a characteristic hemorrhagic infiltration that is diagnostic of diverticular colitis.

Ischemic Colitis

Acute ischemic colitis presents with symptoms of severe abdominal pain, rectal bleeding, and abdominal distention. Atherosclerosis is the most common risk factor, but atrial fibrillation, congestive cardiomyopathy, recent aortic surgery, and hypercoagulability have also been associated with it.[102] The most common sites of ischemia are the descending colon distal to the splenic flexure, the sigmoid colon, and the rectum.[103] There are varying degrees of ischemic injury. There can be complete full-thickness necrosis, transient mucosal necrosis with partial resolution and residual scarring and stricture formation, or simply transient mucosal necrosis with complete resolution of the ischemia.

On endoscopy, mild ischemia produces only slightly edematous mucosa. Severe ischemia causes hemorrhagic, friable, and ulcerated mucosa and often has a characteristic plum red to blue black coloration. These ulcerations resemble aphthous ulcers, but the clinical history and acuity usually excludes Crohn's disease from the differential. A biopsy can also differentiate ischemic from inflammatory colitis; ghost cells are pathognomonic for ischemia but are rarely seen.[104] Usually, there are nonspecific findings of submucosal hemorrhage, vascular congestion, and interstitial edema.

Nonsteroidal Anti-Inflammatory Drug Colopathy

Nonsteroidal anti-inflammatory drugs (NSAIDs) have been associated with reactivation of quiescent ulcerative colitis and Crohn's disease.[105] In addition to this form of colitis, NSAIDs are also associated with their own de novo nonspecific colitis. The mechanism for this is unclear, but it is thought to relate to prostaglandin inhibition and increased intestinal permeability. Symptoms include hematochezia, diarrhea, ulcerations, perforations, abdominal pain, and iron deficiency anemia.[106] The diagnosis is based on history in conjunction with endoscopic evidence of submucosal fibrosis and focal inflammatory lesions.

Preparation-Related Colitis

Toxic or caustic materials introduced into the rectum by enema or suppository can cause a colitis. Phospho-Soda enemas cause a loss of normal vascular pattern, granularity, and friability in the distal colon.[107] Oral sodium phosphate has also been shown to cause

mucosal abnormalities.[108] Small aphthous-like ulcerations are formed, which macroscopically can resemble Crohn's disease but pathologically are easily differentiated.

Radiation Colitis

Colonic mucosa can be damaged by radiation to the pelvis and abdomen. This most commonly occurs in the treatment of cervical and prostate cancers. Most commonly, the distal sigmoid and proximal rectum are involved. Acutely, a patient often experiences a self-limited illness that consists of diarrhea, tenesmus, and occasional rectal bleeding. Chronic radiation colitis produces rectal bleeding that can present up to 20 years after the initial radiation. On colonoscopy, the mucosa is granular and friable with evidence of spontaneous bleeding and telangiectasias in the rectum and sigmoid (Fig. 23–15). Radiation colitis can resemble ulcerative colitis and idiopathic proctitis.

Solitary Rectal Ulcer Syndrome

Solitary rectal ulcer syndrome (SRUS) is a rare disorder of unknown etiology whose cardinal feature is isolated erythema or ulceration of a part of the rectal wall. Rectal bleeding, mucous production, constipation, rectal discomfort, and urgency also are usually present. Up to 26% of patients with SRUS are initially misdiagnosed.[109] Ulcerated SRUS may be mistaken for IBD, and some patients have even been treated with high-dose steroids. Polypoid lesions (colitis cystica profunda, seen in association with the SRUS), usually found on the anterior rectal wall, have been mistaken for neoplasms. Histologically, SRUS is unique; there is evidence of fibrous obliteration of the lamina propria with disorientation of the muscularis mucosa and extension of smooth muscle fibers into the lamina propria.

This syndrome affects men and women equally and the mean age of onset is 49 years.[110] The mean reported duration of symptoms before diagnosis ranges from 3 to 5 years.[110–112] The diagnosis can often be made on sigmoidoscopy. Ulceration is not universally present, with polypoid, nonulcerated lesions, and erythematous areas also seen; in one series, the prevalence of ulceration was 57%, the prevalence of polypoid lesions were 25%, and the prevalence of patches of hyperemic mucosa was 18%.[111]

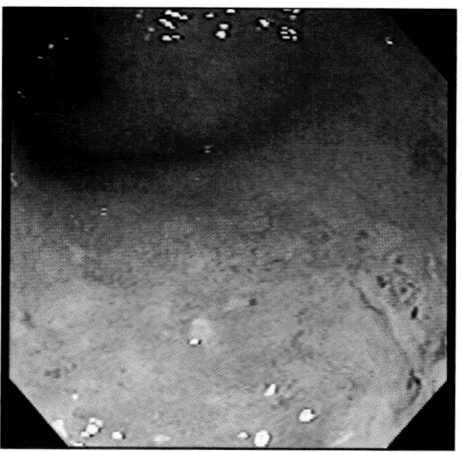

Figure 23–15. Moderately severe radiation proctitis.

There is no specific cure for SRUS. Topical steroids and sulfasalazine enemas are not effective.[111,113] Sucralfate enemas have been used, which lead to symptomatic and macroscopic improvement, but the histologic changes persisted.[114] Biofeedback techniques such as correction of pelvic floor defecatory behavior; regulation of toilet habits; and encouragement to stop laxatives, suppositories, and enemas have been shown to be useful[115,116] and should now be the first-line therapy for patients with SRUS. Surgery plays only a minor role in the treatment of SRUS and should be reserved for patients with intractable symptoms and those with evidence of rectal prolapse; there is symptomatic improvement in approximately 56% of patients, but 33% are often unchanged or worse.[117]

Cancer in Inflammatory Bowel Disease

Both ulcerative colitis and Crohn's disease are associated with an increased risk for developing CRC and precancerous dysplastic epithelial changes. In the general population, CRC is the third leading cause of death in the United States in both men and women and the second leading cause of cancer death overall. This may be one of the most preventable forms of cancer, because routine colonoscopies allow detection and removal of precancerous polyps. Knowledge of CRC risk in patients with IBD is inadequate, despite the obvious conclusion that this is one of the most frightening aspects of the diagnosis of IBD. Physicians need to educate their patients and stress the importance of screening.

There is no debate that ulcerative colitis bears a high risk for the development of CRC. A recent meta-analysis of 116 studies by Eaden and coworkers[118] showed that the prevalence of CRC in patients with ulcerative colitis is approximately 3.7%. The risk for CRC increased with duration of disease; there was a 2% incidence of cancer after 10 years, a 9% incidence after 20 years, and a 19% incidence after 30 years of disease. The development of cancer accounts for one third of deaths related to ulcerative colitis.

In contrast, data exist that both support and refute the hypothesis that Crohn's disease is associated with an increased risk of CRC. However, increasing data demonstrate a similar risk for CRC in Crohn's disease as in ulcerative colitis. Gillen and coworkers[119] studied patients with extensive Crohn's disease of the colon and equally extensive ulcerative colitis and found that the relative and the absolute 20-year cumulative incidence of CRC were virtually identical in both groups. Earlier studies did not adjust for the absence of colonic disease, a history of colonic resection, or the duration or extent of disease,[120–122] and this probably resulted in the apparently lower risk of CRC in Crohn's disease. Ekbom and colleagues[123] found that the relative risk of CRC in patients with Crohn's disease irrespective of disease localization was approximately 2.5, but in Crohn's colitis the relative risk was 5.6, which is similar to the relative risk seen in ulcerative colitis.

Several factors have been suggested to be associated with a higher risk for CRC in patients with IBD (Table 23–10). Most studies have examined risk factors for patients with ulcerative colitis, but it is generally extrapolated that these are probably risk factors in patients

Table 23–10. Risk Factors for Colorectal Carcinoma in Ulcerative Colitis
Age at onset of disease
Anatomic extent of disease
Disease activity
Duration of disease
Family history of colorectal cancer
Primary sclerosing cholangitis

with Crohn's disease also. Increasing duration of disease is a risk factor, with CRC rarely being diagnosed when ulcerative colitis has been present for less than 8 years; hence, typically surveillance with colonoscopy does not begin until after 8 years of pancolonic disease. The age of onset has been suggested to be related to the risk of developing CRC.[124,125] A family history of CRC is also a risk factor; patients with IBD who have a first-degree relative with CRC have a relative risk of 2.5 and 3.7, respectively, for developing CRC, and if the first-degree relative was diagnosed before the age of 50 with CRC the relative risk is 9.2.[126]

The extent of the disease is also a risk factor for developing CRC in most studies. It has been reported that the incidence ratios for the risk of CRC in patients with proctitis is 1.7, for patients with disease extending beyond the rectum but no further than the hepatic flexure is 2.8, and for patients with disease beyond the hepatic flexure in 14.8.[125]

Patients with ulcerative colitis and primary sclerosing cholangitis (PSC), a progressive, fibrotic, cholestatic hepatobiliary inflammatory disease, appear to be at increased risk for CRC. Soetikno and coworkers[127] performed a meta-analysis of 11 studies to further study this. They found an approximate fourfold increased risk for CRC in patients with ulcerative colitis and PSC, when compared with those with ulcerative colitis alone. The explanation for this association is unknown.

The detection of colitis-associated CRC during colonoscopy is difficult because the dysplasia may be present in macroscopically normal mucosa; it has been suggested that only 20% to 50% of intraepithelial neoplasias can be detected by routine colonoscopy.[128] Cancers in ulcerative colitis grow in a diffusely infiltrating pattern, also hindering the macroscopic diagnosis of dysplasia.[129]

Dysplasia is broadly classified as flat or raised based on its appearance endoscopically. Flat dysplasias occur most often in macroscopically normal mucosa and represent 95% of the dysplasia found.[130] When macroscopically detectable, there is thickened mucosa with mild discoloration and a velvety appearance with evidence of nodularity. If flat dysplasia is found on biopsy, then the patient should undergo a colectomy. Raised dysplasia, or dysplasia-associated lesion or mass (DALM), is found in less than 5% of the patients with dysplasia. These can be further subdivided into adenoma-like and non–adenoma-like dysplasia. The latter are composed of plaques, masses, or strictured lesions and are prone to progress to colon cancer[131]; these patients, like patients with flat dysplasia, should undergo total colectomy. The adenoma-like DALMs appear as discrete sessile or pedunculated polyps. If these are noted on colonoscopy, the patient should undergo polypectomy and biopsy; if the biopsy is negative for adenocarcinoma, then the patient does not require a colectomy but rather only increased surveillance. Further studies with long-term follow-up are required to determine the natural history of these lesions.

Surveillance programs that focus on colonoscopy with biopsies have been the main method used to detect dysplasia and early cancers in patients with IBD. There are no randomized controlled trials, prospective cohort studies, or case-control studies that definitively prove a benefit for surveillance colonoscopy, but anecdotal and circumstantial evidence appear to suggest one. Moreover, no randomized controlled trials will probably ever be done, because most physicians would consider it unethical to withhold surveillance colonoscopy from a patient with IBD.

Because it can be challenging to determine macroscopically if dysplasia is present, the standard of care is to obtain four-quadrant jumbo biopsies every 10 cm between the rectum and the cecum, for a total of 40 to 50 random biopsies per colonoscopy in patients with ulcerative colitis. It has been estimated that 33 biopsies are required to give 90% confidence in the detection of dysplasia if it is indeed present.[132]

Chromoendoscopy (CE) may prove to be a more efficient way to biopsy the colon. In CE, various dyes are sprayed onto the colonic mucosa to allow for more detailed evaluation of the mucosal surface. Recent studies have shown that not only does the CE allow for better differentiation between the neoplastic and non-neoplastic changes in the colon based on the staining pattern[133] but also it improves early diagnosis of adenomas and CRCs.[134] Kiesslich and colleagues[135] showed in a randomized, controlled trial that methylene blue-aided CE permits more accurate diagnosis of the extent and severity of the inflammatory activity in ulcerative colitis compared with conventional colonoscopy. More targeted biopsies were possible and a statistically significant higher number of intraepithelial neoplasias were detected in the CE group, 32 versus 10 in the conventional colonoscopy group. This tool may prove to be extremely beneficial in the diagnosis of early CRCs in patients with IBD. The colonoscopies do take longer to perform, but with more experience and the increasing sensitivity of the biopsies, it still would appear to be a superior surveillance method to standard colonoscopy.

Pouchitis

Pouchitis is an acute inflammatory condition of a pouch or reservoir occurring after a restorative proctocolectomy or continent ileostomy. Ten years after surgery, pouchitis occurs in 30% to 46% of patients.[136,137] Symptoms of pouchitis include diarrhea, urgency, abdominal pain, tenesmus, bleeding, and incontinence. If a patient previously had experienced extraintestinal symptoms of their ulcerative colitis, these may often recur during an episode of pouchitis.

The cause of pouchitis is unknown. It has been related to stasis of intestinal contents and bacterial proliferation within the ileal reservoir. This hypothesis is strengthened by data that treatment with metronidazole or ciprofloxacin decreases patient's symptoms; recurrence may arise after cessation of the antibiotics.[138] Impaired utilization of short-chain fatty acids[139] and recurrent colitis in an ileal mucosa that has undergone colonic metaplasia[140] have also been suggested in the etiology of pouchitis. Women may experience

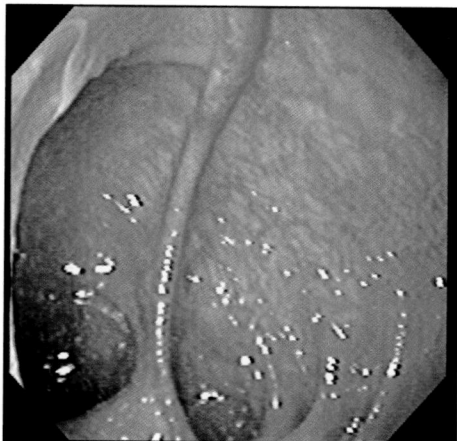

Figure 23–16. Mild pouchitis in a patient with ulcerative colitis.

pouchitis more often than men, 74% versus 47%, respectively.[141] Smoking, for unclear reasons, may actually be protective against pouchitis.[142]

Pouchitis is diagnosed by endoscopy and biopsy (Fig. 23–16). Endoscopically, the mucosa appears erythematous, friable, and nodular. There is a loss of the normal vascular pattern and contact bleeding. Aphthous ulcers may also be found within the pouch; for this reason, Crohn's disease must be excluded. The differential diagnosis in a patient with pouchitis is either pouchitis with Crohn's-disease-like features or actual Crohn's disease in a patient that had been misdiagnosed as having ulcerative colitis before surgery; the latter occurs in up to 10% of patients.[143] The endoscopist should always advance the scope proximal to the pouch to the ileum above the pouch and biopsies should be taken from there. Pouchitis should never spill over into the ileum above the pouch, and if inflammation is found in the ileum above the pouch, the diagnosis of Crohn's disease should be seriously considered.

Dysplasia can occur in the rectal mucosa adjacent to the ileorectal anastomosis because a small amount of rectum remains in patients who have had ileal pouches. For this reason, patients should undergo periodic surveillance sigmoidoscopy with rectal mucosa biopsy for the evaluation of dysplasia. Risk factors that have been suggested for the development of dysplasia include a history of primary sclerosing cholangitis or pouchitis.[144]

Intraoperative Endoscopy

Intraoperative endoscopy has been performed to locate areas of inflammation in the small bowel that are not well defined by radiography before surgery. This is accomplished by inserting the endoscope in a retrograde fashion from the distal opening of the small intestine up to the ligament of Treitz. The benefit of this procedure is questionable, because, although more lesions are found intraoperatively than in radiography preoperatively, the findings do not relate to postoperative recurrence of Crohn's disease.[145] In one study, more than half of the lesions found on intraoperative endoscopy were not found radiographically before surgery; however, this endoscopic data only modified surgery in 2 of 20 patients.[146]

The endoscopic findings usually do not affect the decision of the surgeon.[147] The anastomosis can be made in an area of relatively inflamed bowel or at areas of microscopic involvement, because this does not seem to be a factor in the postoperative recurrence rate of Crohn's disease.[148-150] Patients treated with radical resections and those treated with nonradical resections have the same recurrence rate; hence, a nonradical resection is the preferred surgery for patients with Crohn's disease.[151]

Endoscopy and Ileostomy

When the entire colon is removed for a patient with IBD, the patient can be left with a standard Brooke ileostomy, an ileoanal anastomosis with a pouch, or a continent ileostomy. An upper endoscope is often used for examination of the stoma because of its thin diameter and small radium of tip deflection. The endoscope usually can visualize the distal 10 or 20 cm of the ileostomy stoma (Fig. 23–17).

Ileoscopy can be beneficial in evaluating a patient with indeterminant colitis who has undergone colectomy and is scheduled for an ileoanal anastomosis. If there is evidence of Crohn's disease, this would argue against proceeding with the ileoanal procedure.

This examination is best performed when the patient is in the supine position and can often be done without sedation.

Capsule Endoscopy

Imaging the small bowel is always a challenge for the gastroenterologist, and, until recently, the methods used to visualize the small intestine were unsatisfactory. CT scan of the abdomen can show transmural thickening and extramural complications, including peri-intestinal fat stranding and mesenteric lymphadenopathy, but it is not sensitive enough to detect mucosal inflammation. Push endoscopy has been used more often, but it is extremely uncomfortable, can take between 15 and 45 minutes, and requires sedation and analgesia and there is a danger of perforation.[152] Conventional endoscopic techniques are limited by the length of the small bowel;

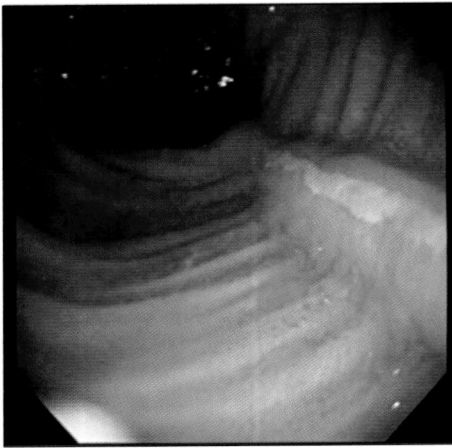

Figure 23–17. Granulation and ulceration along the suture line in a patient with ileoanal pouch.

the endoscope can only examine 10 to 20 cm beyond the ligament of Treitz. Another approach is examination of the entire small intestine by intraoperative endoscopy. This is obviously a more invasive method that carries the standard complication risks of general anesthesia and surgery.[153]

The development of the wireless capsule endoscopy has offered a new modality for visualizing the small bowel. The capsule enteroscope contains a miniature video camera, a light source, batteries, and a radio transmitter. Video images are transmitted by radio waves to the sensor array that is attached to the person. This allows for images of the entire GI tract (for a period of up to 8 hours) to be captured and stored in a portable recorder.

Capsule endoscopy has been shown to be superior to the standard small bowel examination with barium for suspected small bowel disease.[154] For obscure GI bleeding, barium follow-through was much worse when compared with capsule endoscopy in making a diagnosis, 5% versus 31%, respectively.[154] In 20 patients with suspected small bowel disease, barium follow-through was diagnostic in 20% of patients, whereas capsule endoscopy was diagnostic in 45% of patients, suspicious in 40%, and nondiagnostic in 15% of patients.[154]

In Crohn's disease, capsule endoscopy to be a superior diagnostic tool when compared with barium follow-through and CT. Eliakim and coworkers[155] found that capsule endoscopy established new diagnoses, confirmed existing diagnoses, enlarged the extent of the disease, and ruled out suspicious Crohn's disease in 70% of patients. Barium follow-through only accomplished this in 37% of patients. In addition to this, capsule endoscopy detected all of the lesions detected by barium follow-through and CT and found additional lesions in 47% of cases. It was also able to rule out lesions found in other modalities in 16% of cases, making capsule endoscopy both more sensitive and specific than barium follow-through and CT. Fireman and colleagues[156] evaluated the effectiveness of wireless capsule endoscopy in patients with suspected Crohn's disease of the small bowel that had previously been undetected by barium follow-though and CT and found a diagnostic yield of 71%. The capsule was able to detect mucosal erosions, ulcers, and strictures and the degree of severity ranged from mild to severe.

Capsule endoscopy is well tolerated by patients. One of the limitations of the procedure is the time that is required for the physician to review all of the images; a review of the images should obviously be performed by individuals who are experienced in viewing and interpreting endoscopic images. This is proving to be a novel technique of great potential in the evaluation of Crohn's disease with nonobstructive small bowel involvement. It should also be noted that at present there is no validated endoscopic scoring system that has been validated for patients with Crohn's disease. This endeavor is now ongoing.

Endoscopic Retrograde Cholangiopancreatography

PSC is one of the most devastating complications of IBD, occurring in up to 5% of patients with ulcerative colitis and less commonly in Crohn's disease. PSC is a cholestatic disease in which a nonsuppurative, chronic inflammation involves the biliary tree leading to progressive strictures. ERCP is the gold standard for diagnosis of PSC. Findings on ERCP include diffuse multifocal annular strictures of the intrahepatic and extrahepatic bile ducts and a characteristic "beads on a string" appearance on cholangiogram. ERCP offers the ability to biopsy and brush these strictures to exclude the diagnosis of cholangiocarcinoma.[157] It also plays a key role in the nonoperative management of cholangitis associated with stricture formation, by allowing for dilatation and stenting of dominant strictures.[158,159]

PSC can develop before any evidence of colitis is found. Up to 80% of cases of PSC are associated with IBD, most with ulcerative colitis, hence the recommendation that patients undergo colonoscopy with surveillance biopsy specimens to assess for the presence of subclinical colitis.

Conclusions

Although other radiographic imaging modalities are complementary in the diagnosis of IBD, endoscopy plays the key role in diagnosing and managing IBD. Colonoscopy with biopsy is the most sensitive method to detect, diagnose, and differentiate Crohn's disease and ulcerative colitis from all other forms of colitis. Endoscopy is integral in treating many of the complications of IBD, including stricture formation and bleeding. As the diseases progress, both ulcerative colitis and Crohn's colitis patients must be routinely evaluated by colonoscopy to assess for any evidence of dysplasia.

The gastroenterologist must be well trained to recognize the multitude of endoscopic appearances of IBD. These images and a solid clinical history are crucial in the diagnosis and management of patients with IBD.

REFERENCES

1. Fujimura Y, Kamoi R, Iida M: Pathogenesis of aphthoid ulcers in Crohn's disease: Correlative findings by magnifying colonoscopy, electron microscopy, and immunohistochemistry. Gut 38:724–732, 1996.
2. Hinojosa J, Abad A, Panes J, et al: Multicenter, randomized trial comparing oral, topical and oral plus topical mesalamine in the prevention of relapse in distal ulcerative colitis (DUC). Gastroenterology 120:58, 2001.
3. Best WR, Becktel JM, Singleton JW, et al: Development of a Crohn's disease activity index. National Cooperative Crohn's Disease Study. Gastroenterology 70:439–444, 1976.
4. Harvey RF, Bradshaw JM: A simple index of Crohn's-disease activity. Lancet 1:514, 1980.
5. de Dombal FT, Softley A: IOIBD report no 1: Observer variation in calculating indices of severity and activity in Crohn's disease. International Organisation for the Study of Inflammatory Bowel Disease. Gut 93:727–733, 1987.
6. Mary JY, Modigliani R: Development and validation of an endoscopic index of the severity for Crohn's disease: A prospective multicentre study. Groupe d'Studes Therapeutiques des Affections Inflammatoires du Tube Digestif (GETAID). Gut 30:983–989, 1989.
7. Cellier C, Sahmoud T, Froguel E, et al: Correlations between clinical activity, endoscopic severity, and biological parameters in colonic or ileocolonic Crohn's disease. A prospective multicentre study of 121 cases. Groupe d'Etudes Therapeutiques des Affections Inflammatoires du Tube Digestif (GETAID). Gut 35:231–235, 1994.
8. Landi B, Anh TN, Cortot A, et al: Endoscopic monitoring of Crohn's disease treatment: A prospective, randomized clinical trial. The Groupe d'Etudes Therapeutiques des Affections Inflammatoires Digestives. Gastroenterology 102:1647–1653, 1992.
9. Colombel JF, Rutgeerts P, Yan S, et al: Infliximab maintenance treatment results in lower hospitalization rate in Crohn's disease patients [abstract]. Gastroenterology 122:A613, 2002.
10. D'Haens G, Norman M, Baert F, et al: Endoscopic healing after infliximab treatment for Crohn's disease provides a longer time to relapse [abstract]. Gastroenterology 122:A100, 2002.
11. Daperno M, Van Assche G, Bulois P, et al: Development of Crohn's disease endoscopic score (CDES): A simple index to assess endoscopic severity of Crohn's disease [abstract]. Gastroenterology 122:A216, 2002.
12. Truelove SC, Witts LJ: Cortisone in ulcerative colitis. Final report on a therapeutic trial. Br Med J 2:1041–1048, 1955.
13. Powell-Tuck, J, Brown RL, Lennard-Jones JE: A comparison of oral prednisolone given as a single or multiple daily doses for active proctocolitis. Scand J Gastroenterol 13:833–837, 1978.
14. Gomes P, du Boulay C, Smith CL, et al: Relationship between disease activity indices and colonoscopic findings in patients with colonic inflammatory bowel disease. Gut 27:92–95, 1986.
15. Walmsley RS, Ayres RC, Pounder RE, et al: A simple clinical colitis activity index. Gut 43:29–32, 1998.
16. Sutherland LR, Martin F, Greer S, et al: 5-aminosalicylic acid enema in the treatment of distal ulcerative colitis, proctosigmoiditis, and proctitis. Gastroenterology 92:1894–1898, 1987.
17. Schroeder KW, Tremaine WJ, Ilstrup DM: Coated oral 5-aminosalicylic acid therapy for mildly to moderately active ulcerative colitis. A randomized study. N Engl J Med 317:1625–1629, 1987.
18. Kim WH, Cho YJ, Park JY, et al: Factors affecting insertion time and patient discomfort during colonoscopy. Gastrointest Endosc 52:600–605, 2000.
19. Rex DK, Imperiale TF, Latinovich DR, et al: Impact of bowel preparation on efficiency and cost of colonoscopy. Am J Gastroenterol 97:1696–1700, 2002.
20. Ell C, Fischbach W, Keller R, et al: A randomized, blinded, prospective trial to compare the safety and efficacy of three bowel-cleansing solutions for colonoscopy. Endoscopy 35:300–304, 2003.
21. Church JM: Effectiveness of polyethylene glycol antegrade gut lavage bowel preparation for colonoscopy: Timing is the key. Dis Colon Rectum 41:1223–1225, 1998.
22. Sharma VK, Chockalingham S, Clark V, et al: Randomized, controlled comparison of two forms of preparation for screening flexible sigmoidoscopy. Am J Gastroenterol 92:198–200, 1997.
23. Osgard EM, Jackson JL, Strong JS: A randomized trial comparing three methods of bowel preparation for flexible sigmoidoscopy. Am J Gastroenterol 93:1126–1130, 1998.
24. Fincher RK, Osgard EM, Jackson JL, et al: A comparison of bowel preparations for flexible sigmoidoscopy: Oral magnesium citrate combined with oral bisacodyl, one hypertonic phosphate enema, or two hypertonic phosphate enemas. Am J Gastroenterol 94:2122–2127, 1999.
25. Herman M, Shaw M, Loewen B: Comparison of three forms of bowel preparations for screening flexible sigmoidoscopy. Gastroenterol Nurs 24:178–181, 2001.
26. Cappell MS: Gastrointestinal endoscopy in the high risk patient. Dig Dis 14:228–244, 1996.
27. Gaisford W: Fiberendoscopy of the cecum and terminal ileum. Gastrointest Endosc 21:13–18, 1974.
28. Nagasako K, Yazawa C, Takemoto T: Biopsy of the terminal ileum. Gastroinest Endosc 19:7–10, 1972.

29. Bitton A: Medical management of ulcerative proctitis, proctosigmoiditis, and left-sided colitis. Semin Gastrointest Dis 12:263–274, 2001.

30. Cullingford GL, Coffey JF, Carr-Locke DL: Irritable bowel syndrome: Can the patient's response to colonoscopy help with diagnosis? Digestion 52:209–213, 1992.

31. Baillie J: Complications of endoscopy. Endoscopy 26:185–203, 1994.

32. Anderson ML, Pasha TM, Leighton JA: Endoscopic perforation of the colon: Lessons from a 10-year study. Am J Gastroenterol 95:3418–3422, 2000.

33. Pera A, Bellando P, Caldera V, et al: Colonoscopy in inflammatory bowel disease. Diagnostic accuracy and proposal of an endoscopic score. Gastroenterology 92:181–5, 1987.

34. Potzi R, Walgram M, Lochs H, et al: Diagnostic significance of endoscopic biopsy in Crohn's disease. Endoscopy 21:60–62, 1989.

35. Rutgeerts P, Onette E, Vantrapen G, et al: Crohn's disease of the stomach and duodenum: A clinical study with emphasis on the value of endoscopy and endoscopic biopsies. Endoscopy 12:288–294, 1980.

36. Danzi JT, Farmer RG, Sullivan BH Jr, et al: Endoscopic features of gastroduodenal Crohn's disease. Gastroenterology 70:9–13, 1976.

37. Alcantara M, Rodriguez R, Potenciano JL, et al: Endoscopic and bioptic findings in the upper gastrointestinal tract in patients with Crohn's disease. Endoscopy 25:282–286, 1993.

38. Decker GA, Loftus EV, Pasha TM, et al: Crohn's disease of the esophagus: Clinical features and outcomes. Inflamm Bowel Dis 7:113–119, 2001.

39. D'Haens G, Rutgeerts P, Geboes K, et al: The natural history of esophageal Crohn's disease: Three patterns of evolution. Gastroinest Endosc 40:296–300, 1994.

40. Weinstein T, Valderrama E, Pettei M, et al: Esophageal Crohn's disease: Medical management and correlation between clinical, endoscopic and histologic features. Inflamm Bowel Dis 3:79–83, 1997.

41. Huchzermeyer H, Paul F, Seifert K, et al: Endoscopic results in five patients with Crohn's disease of the esophagus. Endoscopy 8:75–81, 1976.

42. Nugent F, Roy M: Duodenal Crohn's disease: An analysis of 89 cases. Am J Gastroenterol 84:249–254, 1989.

43. Scotiniotis I, Rubesin SE, Ginsberg GG: Imaging modalities in inflammatory bowel disease. Gastroenterol Clin North Am 78:1331–1352, 1994.

44. Heuschen UA, Hinz U, Allemeyer EH, et al: Backwash ileitis is strongly associated with colorectal carcinoma in ulcerative colitis. Gastroenterology 120:841–847, 2001.

45. Lawrance IC, Maxwell L, Doe W: The response of intestinal mucosal fibroblasts to profibrogenic cytokines in inflammatory bowel disease. Inflamm Bowel Dis 7:226–36, 2001.

46. Farmer RG, Hawk WA, Turnball RB Jr: Indications for surgery in Crohn's disease: Analysis of 500 cases. Gastroenterology 71:245–250, 1976.

47. Waye JD: Endoscopy in inflammatory bowel disease. Clin Gastroenterol 279–296, 1980.

48. Yamazaki Y, Ribeiro M, Sachar DB, et al: Malignant colorectal strictures in Crohn's disease. Am J Gastroenterol 86:882–885, 1991.

49. Gumaste V, Sachar DB, Greenstein AJ: Benign and malignant colorectal strictures in ulcerative colitis. Gut 33:938–941, 1992.

50. Couckuyt H, Gevers AM, Coremans G, et al: Efficacy and safety of hydrostatic balloon dilation of ileocolonic Crohn's strictures: A prospective long term analysis. Gut 36:577–580, 1995.

51. Linares L, Moreira LF, Andrews H, et al: Natural history and treatment of anorectal strictures complicating Crohn's disease. Br J Surg 75:653–655, 1998.

52. Ramboer C, Verhamme M, Dhondt E, et al: Endoscopic treatment of stenosis in recurrent Crohn's disease with balloon dilation combined with local corticosteroid injection. Gastrointest Endosc 42:252–255, 1995.

53. Thomas-Gibson S, Brooker JC, Ayward CM, et al: Colonoscopic balloon dilation of Crohn's strictures: A review of long-term outcomes. Eur J Gastroenterol Hepatol 15:465–468, 2003.

54. Blomberg B, Rolny P, Jarnerot G: Endoscopic treatment of anastomotic strictures in Crohn's disease. Endoscopy 23:195–198, 1991.

55. Breysem Y, Janssens JF, Coremans G, et al: Endoscopic balloon dilation of colonic and ileocolonic Crohn's strictures: Long-term results. Gastrointest Endosc 38:142–147, 1992.

56. Dear KL, Hunter JO: Colonoscopic hydrostatic balloon dilatation of Crohn's strictures. J Clin Gastroenterol 33:315–318, 2001.

57. Sabate JM, Villarejo J, Bouhnik Y, et al: Hydrostatic balloon dilatation of Crohn's strictures. Aliment Pharmacol Ther 18:409–413, 2003.

58. Moum B, Ekbom A, Vatn M, et al: Inflammatory bowel disease: Re-evaluation of the diagnosis in a prospective population based study in southeastern Norway. Gut 40:328–332, 1997.

59. Langevin S, Menard DB, Haddad H, et al: Idiopathic ulcerative proctitis may be the initial manifestation of Crohn's disease. J Clin Gastroenterol 15:199–204, 1992.

60. Vasiliauskas E, Plevy S, Landers C, et al: Perinuclear antineutrophil cytoplasmic antibodies in patients with Crohn's disease define a clinical subgroup. Gastroenterology 110:1810–1819, 1996.

61. Abreu M, Vasiliauskas EA, Kam LY, et al: Use of serologic tests in Crohn's disease. Clin Perspect Gastroenterol 4:155–164, 2001.

62. Dundas SA, Dutton J, Skipworth P: Reliability of rectal biopsy in distinguishing between chronic inflammatory bowel disease and acute self-limiting colitis. Histopathology 31:60–66, 1997.

63. Marshall J, Singh R, Diaz-Arias A: Chronic unexplained diarrhea: Are biopsies necessary if colonoscopy is normal? Am J Gastroenterol 90:372–376, 1995.

64. Tedesco F, Hardin R, Hardin R, Harper R, et al: Infectious colitis endoscopically simulating inflammatory bowel disease: A prospective evaluation. Gastrointest Endosc 29:195–197, 1983.

65. Bayerdorffer E, Hochter W, Schwarzkopf-Steinhauser G, et al: Bioptic microbiology in the differential diagnosis of enterocolitis. Endoscopy 18:177–181, 1986.

66. Cottone M, Pietrosi G, Martorana G, et al: Prevalence of cytomegalovirus infection in severe refractory ulcerative and Crohn's colitis. Am J Gastroenterol 96:773–775, 2001.

67. Ratliff DA, Carr N, Cochrane JP: Rectal stricture due to actinomycosis. Br J Surg 73:589–590, 1986.

68. Thompson JR, Watts R Jr, Thompson WC: Actinomycetoma masquerading as an abdominal neoplasm. Dis Colon rectum 25:368–370, 1982.

69. Crowson T, Hines C: Amebiasis diagnosed by colonoscopy. Gastrointest Endosc 24:254–255, 1978.

70. Nevin RW: The surgical aspects of intestinal amoebiasis. Ann R Coll Surg Engl 29:69–84, 1947.

71. Radhakrishnan S, Al Nakib B, Shaikn H, et al: The value of colonoscopy in schistosomal, tuberculous, and amebic colitis: Two-year experience. Dis Colon Rectum 29:891–895, 1986.

72. Li E, Stanley SL Jr: Protozoa: Amebiasis. Gastroenterol Clin North Am 25:471–492, 1996.

73. Preliminary FoodNet data on the incidence of foodborne illnesses—selected sites, United States, 2000. Morb Mortal Wkly Rep 50:241–246, 2001.

74. Blaser M, Parson R, Lou-Wang W: Acute colitis caused by Campylobacter fetus ss jejuni. Gastroenterology 78:448–453, 1980.

75. Loss R, Mangla J, Pereira M: Campylobacter colitis presenting as inflammatory bowel disease with segmental colonic ulcerations. Gastroenterology 79:138–140, 1980.

76. Blaser MJ, Reller LB: Campylobacter enteritis. N Engl J Med 305:1444—1452, 1981.

77. Guerrant RL, Lahita RG, Winn WC, et al: Campylobacteriosis in man: Pathogenic mechanisms and review of 91 bloodstream infections. Am J Med 65:584–592, 1978.

78. Kelly CP, Pothoulakis C, LaMont JT: Clostridium difficile colitis. N Engl J Med 330:257–262, 1993.

79. Jacobs NF Jr: Antibiotic-induced diarrhea and pseudomembranous colitis. Postgrad Med 95:111–120, 1994.

80. Tedesco FJ, Corless JK, Brownstein RE: Rectal sparing in antibiotic-associated pseudomembranous colitis: A prospective study. Gastroenterology 83:1259–1260, 1982.

81. Fekety R, Shah AB: Diagnosis and treatment of *Clostridium difficile* colitis. JAMA 269:71–75, 1993.

82. Patra S, Samal SC, Chacko A, et al: Cytomegalovirus infection of the human gastrointestinal tract. J Gastroenterol Hepatol 14:973–976, 1999.

83. Wilcox CM, Straub RF, Schwartz DA: Prospective evaluation of biopsy number for the diagnosis of viral esophagitis in patients with HIV infection and esophageal ulcer. Gastrointest Endosc 44:587–593, 1996.

84. Ilnyckyj A, Greenberg H, Bernstein C: *Escherichia coli* 0157:H7 infection mimicking Crohn's disease. Gastroenterology 112:995–999, 1992.

85. Anderson MD, Cerda JJ: AIDS-related infections of the GI tract and hepatobiliary tract. Pract Gastroenterol 13:37–46, 1989.

86. Nahass GT, Goldstein BA, Zhu LY, et al: Comparison of Tzanck smear, viral culture, and DNA diagnostic methods in detection of *Herpes simplex* and varicella-zoster infection. JAMA 268:2541–2544, 1992.

87. Haws C, Long R, Caplan G: Histoplasma capsulatum as a cause of ileocolitis. Am J Roentgenol 128:692–694, 1977.

88. Clarkston W, Bonacini M, Peterson I: Colitis due to *Histoplasma capsulatum* in the acquired immune deficiency syndrome. Am J Gastroenterol 86:913–916, 1991.

89. Bhargava DK, Tandon HD, Chawla TC, et al: Diagnosis of ileocecal and colonic tuberculosis by colonoscopy. Gastrointest Endosc 31:68–70, 1985.

90. Havath KD, Whelan RL: Intestinal tuberculosis: Return of an old disease. Am J Gastroenterol 93:692–696, 1998.

91. McMillan A, Lee FD: Sigmoidoscopic and microscopic appearance of rectal mucosa in homosexual men. Gut 22:1035–1041, 1981.

92. Kilpatrick ZM: Gonorrheal proctitis. N Engl J Med 287:967–969, 1972.

93. D'Aoust JY: Pathogenicity of food borne Salmonella. Int J Food Microbiol 12:17–40, 1991.

94. Hornick RB, Greisman S: On the pathogenesis of typhoid fever. Ann Intern Med 138:357–359, 1978.

95. Montefusco PP, Geiss AC, Randall S: Typhoid fever and massive intestinal hemorrhage. Contemp Surg 24:61–65, 1984.

96. Hepps K, Sutton F, Goodgame R: Multiple left-sided colon ulcers due to typhoid fever. Gastrointest Endosc 37:479–480, 1991.

97. Mohamed A, Al Karawi M, Yasawy M: Schistosomal colonic disease. Gut 31:439–442, 1990.

98. Khuroo MS, Mahajan R, Zargar SA, et al: The colon in shigellosis: Serial colonoscopic appearances in *Shigella dysenteriae* I. Endoscopy 22:35–38, 1990.

99. Matsumoto T, Iida M, Matsui T, et al: Endoscopic findings in *Yersinia enterocolitica* enterocolitis. Gastrointest Endosc 36:583–587, 1990.

100. Ryan C, Potter G: Disinfectant colitis. Rinse as well as you wash [editorial]. J Clin Gastroenterol 21:6–9, 1995.

101. Bilotta JJ, Wayne JD: Hydrogen peroxide enteritis: The "snow white" sign. Gastrointest Endosc 35:428–430, 1989.

102. Reinus JF, Brandt LJ, Boley SJ: Ischemic disease of the bowel. Gastroenterol Clin North Am 19:319–343, 1990.

103. Scowcroft C, Sanowski R, Kozarek R: Colonoscopy in ischemic colitis. Gastrointest Endosc 27:156–161, 1981.

104. Dignan CR, Greenson JK: Can ischemic colitis be differentiated from C. *difficile* colitis in biopsy specimens? Am J Surg Pathol 21:706–710, 1997.

105. Walt R, Hawkey C, Langman M: Colitis associated with non-steroidal anti-inflammatory drugs [letter]. BMJ 288:238, 1984.

106. Davies N: Toxicity of nonsteroidal anti-inflammatory drugs in the large intestine. Dis Colon Rectum 38:1311–1321, 1995.

107. Meisel J, Bergman D, Graney D, et al: Human rectal mucosa: Proctoscopic and morphological changes caused by laxatives. Gastroenterology 72:1274–1279, 1977.

108. Zwas F, Cirillo N, El-Serag H: Colonic mucosal abnormalities associated with oral sodium phosphate solution. Gastrointest Endosc 43:463–466, 1996.

109. Kuipers HC, Schreve RH, Hoedmakers H: Diagnosis of functional disorders of defecation causing the solitary rectal ulcer syndrome. Dis Colon Rectum 29:126–129, 1986.

110. Tjandra JJ, Fazio VW, Church JM, et al: Clinical conundrum of solitary rectal ulcer. Dis Colon Rectum 35:227–234, 1992.

111. Martin CJ, Parks TG, Biggart JD: Solitary rectal ulcer syndrome in Northern Ireland. 1971-1980. Br J Surg 68:744–747, 1981.

112. Ford MJ, Anderson JR, Gilmour HM, et al: Clinical spectrum of "solitary ulcer" of the rectum. Gastroenterology 84:1533–1540, 1983.

113. White CM, Findlay JM, Price JJ: The occult rectal prolapse syndrome. Br J Surg 67:528–530, 1980.

114. Zagar SA, Khuroo MS, Mahajan R: Sucralfate retention enemas in solitary rectal ulcer. Dis Colon Rectum 34:455–457, 1991.

115. Vaizey CJ, Roy AJ, Kamm MA: Prospective evaluation of the treatment of solitary rectal ulcer syndrome with biofeedback. Gut 41:817–820, 1997.

116. Binnie NR, Papachrysostomou M, Clare N, et al: Solitary rectal ulcer: The place of biofeedback and surgery in the treatment of the syndrome. World J Surg 16:836–840, 1992.

117. Sitzler PA, Kamm MA, Nicholls RJ, et al: Long-term clinical outcome of surgery for solitary rectal ulcer syndrome. Br J Surg 85:1246–1250, 1998.

118. Eaden JA, Abrams KR, Mayberry JF: The true risk of colorectal cancer in ulcerative colitis: A meta-analysis. Gastroenterology 48:526–535, 2001.

119. Gillen CD, Walmsley RS, Prior P, et al: Ulcerative colitis and Crohn's disease: A comparison of the colorectal cancer risk in extensive colitis. Gut 35:1590–1592, 1994.

120. Gyde SN, Prior P, Macartney JC, et al: Malignancy in Crohn's disease. Gut 21:1024–1029, 1980.

121. Persson PG, Karlen P, Bernell O, et al: Crohn's disease and cancer: A population-based cohort study. Gastroenterology 107:1675–1679, 1994.

122. Weedon DD, Shorter RG, Ilstrup DM, et al: Crohn's disease and cancer. N Engl J Med 289:1099–1103, 1973.

123. Ekbom A, Helmick C, Zack M, et al: Increased risk of large-bowel cancer in Crohn's disease with colonic involvement. Lancet 336:357–359, 1990.

124. Karlen P, Lofberg R, Brostrom O, et al: Increased risk of cancer in ulcerative colitis: A population-based cohort study. Am J Gastroenterol 94:1047–1052, 1999.

125. Ekbom A, Helmick C, Zack M, et al: Ulcerative colitis and colorectal cancer: A population-based study. N Engl J Med 323:1228–1233, 1990.

126. Askling J, Dickman PW, Karlen P, et al: Family history as a risk factor for colorectal cancer in inflammatory bowel disease. Gastroenterology 120:1356–1362, 2001.

127. Soetikno RM, Lin OS, Heidenreich PA, et al: Increased risk of colorectal neoplasia in patients with primary sclerosing cholangitis and ulcerative colitis: A meta-analysis. Gastrointest Endosc 56:48–54, 2002.

128. Ransohoff DF, Ridell RH, Levin B: Ulcerative colitis and colonic cancer problems in assessing diagnostic usefulness of mucosal dysplasias. Dis Colon Rectum 28:383–388, 1985.

129. Vieth M, Stolte M, Mueller E, et al: Bioptical differential diagnosis of adenomas, dysplasias and carcinomas in patients with ulcerative colitis. Leber Magen Darm 3:125–132, 2000.

130. Tytgat GNJ, Dhir V, Gopinath N: Endoscopic appearance of dysplasia and cancer in inflammatory bowel disease. Eur J Cancer 31:1174–1177, 1995.

131. Odze RD: Adenomas and adenoma-like DALMs in chronic ulcerative colitis: A clinical, pathological and molecular review. Am J Gastroenterol 94:1746–1750, 1999.

132. Levine D, Reid B: Endoscopic biopsy technique for acquiring larger mucosal samples. Gastrointest Endosc 37:332–337, 1991.

133. Kudo S, Tamura S, Nakajima T, et al: Diagnosis of colorectal tumorous lesions by magnifying endoscopy. Gastrointest Endosc 44:8–14, 1996.

134. Rembacken BJ, Fujii T, Cairns A, et al: Flat and depressed colonic neoplasms: A prospective study of 1000 colonoscopies in the UK. Lancet 355:1211–1214, 2000.

135. Kiesslich R, Fritsch J, Holtmann M, et al: Methylene blue-aided chromoendoscopy for the detection of intraepithelial neoplasia and colon cancer in ulcerative colitis. Gastroenterology 124:880–888, 2003.

136. Lohmuller JL, Emberton JH, Dozois RR, et al: Pouchitis and extra-intestinal manifestations of inflammatory bowel disease after ileal-pouch-anal anastomosis. Ann Surg 211:622–627, 1990.

137. Penna C, Dozois R, Tremaine W, et al: Pouchitis after ileal pouch-anal anastomosis for ulcerative colitis occurs with increased frequency in patients with associated primary sclerosing cholangitis. Gut 38:234–239, 1996.

138. Gionchetti P, Rizzello F, Venturi A, et al: Oral bacteriotherapy as maintenance treatment in patients with chronic pouchitis: A double-blind, placebo-controlled trial. Gastroenterology 119:305–309, 2000.

139. Sagar P, Taylor B, Goodwin P, et al: Acute pouchitis and deficiencies of fuel. Dis Colon Rectum 38:488–493, 1995.

140. deSilva H, Millard P, Kettlewell M, et al: Mucosal characteristics of pelvic ileal pouches. Gut 32:61–65, 1991.

141. Simchuk EJ, Thirlby RC: Risk factors and true incidence of pouchitis in patients after ileal pouch-anal anastomoses. World J Surg 24:851–856, 2000.

142. Merrett MN, Mortensen N, Kettlewell M, et al: Smoking may prevent pouchitis in patients with restorative proctocolectomy for ulcerative colitis. Gut 38:362–364, 1996.

143. Keighley M: Review article: The management of pouchitis. Aliment Pharmacol Ther 10:449–457, 1996.

144. Gullberg K, Stahlberg D, Liljeqvist L, et al: Neoplastic transformation of the pelvic pouch mucosa in patients with ulcerative colitis. Gastroenterology 112:1487–1492, 1997.

145. Esaki M, Matsumoto T, Hizawa K, et al: Intraoperative enteroscopy detects more lesions but is not predictive of postoperative recurrence in Crohn's disease. Surg Endosc 15:455–459, 2001.

146. Lescut D, Vanco D, Bonniere P, et al: Perioperative endoscopy of the whole small bowel in Crohn's disease. Gut 34:647–649, 1993.

147. Klein O, Colombel J, Lescut D, et al: Remaining small bowel endoscopic lesions at surgery have no influence on early anastomotic recurrences in Crohn's disease. Am J Gastroenterol 90:1949–1952, 1995.

148. Whelan G, Farmer R, Fazio V, et al: Recurrence after surgery in Crohn's disease. Gastroenterology 88:1826–1833, 1985.

149. Hamilton SR, Reese J, Pennington L, et al: The role of resection margin frozen section in the surgical management of Crohn's disease. Surg Gynecol Obstet 160:57–62, 1985.

150. Chardavoyne R, Flint GW, Pollack S, et al: Factors affecting recurrence following resection for Crohn's disease. Dis Colon Rectum 29:495–502, 1985.

151. Pennington L, Hamilton SR, Bayless TM, et al: Surgical management of Crohn's disease: Influence of disease at margin of resection. Ann Surg 163:94–98, 1992.

152. Swain CP: The role of endoscopy in clinical practice. Gastrointest Endosc Clin N Am 9:135–144, 1999.

153. Ress AM, Benaccin JC, Sarr MG: Efficacy of intraoperative enteroscopy in diagnosis and prevention of recurrent, occult gastrointestinal bleeding. Am J Gastroenterol 89:2143–2146, 1994.

154. Costamagna G, Shah SK, Riccioni ME, et al: A prospective trial comparing small bowel radiographs and video capsule endoscopy for suspected small bowel disease. Gastroenterology 123:999–1005, 2002.

155. Eliakim R, Fischer D, Suissa A, et al: Wireless capsule video endoscopy is a superior diagnostic tool in comparison to barium follow-through and computerized tomography in patients with suspected Crohn's disease. Eur J Gastroenterol Hepatol 15:363–367, 2003.

156. Fireman Z, Mahajna E, Broide E, et al: Diagnosing small bowel Crohn's disease with wireless capsule endoscopy. Gut 52:390–392, 2003.

157. Ponsioen CY, Vrouenraets SM, van Milligen de Wit AW, et al: Value of brush cytology for dominant strictures in primary sclerosing cholangitis. Endoscopy 31:305–309, 1999.

158. Lee JG, Schutz SM, England RE, et al: Endoscopic therapy of sclerosing cholangitis. Hepatology 21:661–667, 1995.

159. van Milligen de Wit AW, van Bracht J, Rauws EA, et al: Endoscopic stent therapy for dominant extrahepatic bile duct strictures in primary sclerosing cholangitis. Gastrointest Endosc 44:293–299, 1996.

Infections of the Luminal Digestive Tract

C. Mel Wilcox

Introduction

The management of luminal gastrointestinal (GI) tract infections has been an essential component of the practice of gastroenterology since the birth of our subspecialty. Over the last 3 decades, however, the emergence of endoscopy with mucosal biopsy as a safe and accurate diagnostic tool for patients with suspected infection has elevated the GI endoscopist to a key partner in the management team. The importance of the endoscopist is best appreciated for patients who develop GI complications after organ transplantation and for those with acquired immunodeficiency syndrome (AIDS). In these settings, infections are the most frequent complications, and the differential diagnosis and diagnostic approach to GI symptoms often differ from the normal host. This chapter provides an overview of GI infections from the endoscopist's perspective based on organ system because the clinical presentation generally points to the site of gut involvement and thus dictates the diagnostic strategy.

Several common themes emerge that are applicable to all GI infections. These include the following:

1. The clinical presentation is dictated by the infecting pathogen.
2. The severity and chronicity of infection for the immunosuppressed patient is dictated by the cause, duration, and type of immunodeficiency.
3. The endoscopic features of any GI infection are variable and overlapping making definitive diagnosis by biopsy essential.

immunosuppressed patients, the incidence and severity of infection is linked to the cause and degree of the immunodeficiency state. For example, patients undergoing solid organ transplantation are at the highest risk of infection early on after transplantation because of profound medication-induced immunodeficiency. It is during this period that latent infections become manifest and susceptibility to infections is greatest. Over time, however, as drug-induced immunosuppression is tapered, the incidence of infections falls. For human immunodeficiency virus (HIV)-infected patients, the incidence of GI infections rises markedly as immune function deteriorates and the infection risk can be accurately stratified by the absolute CD4 lymphocyte count.[1,2] Two additional factors that commonly play a role in the genesis of infection in both the immunosuppressed and normal hosts include medication exposure, such as to antibiotics or corticosteroids, and hospitalization; both of these factors may predispose to the development of infection.

The array of luminal GI infections is broad and parallels the unique epidemiologic factor(s) of each patient. A number of infectious pathogens are termed opportunistic because they generally complicate only immunodeficiency states. The specific immunodeficiency state, its pathophysiology, and severity dictate the spectrum of complicating pathogen(s). Furthermore, within a specific risk group (e.g., solid organ transplantation), the causes and frequency of infections differ because of the variable levels of immune suppression. For example, infections are more commonly observed after heart than liver transplantation because more potent

Epidemiology

The prevalence, incidence, and etiology of luminal GI tract infections are influenced by many factors (Table 24–1). In the normal host, luminal GI infections generally occur at random after exposure to a pathogen and are self-limited. Exposure may take many forms such as occupational (day care centers), dietary, environmental (contaminated water), and even medications. Coexisting host factors may promote the clinical expression of infection and either attenuate or exacerbate the disease. For

Table 24–1. Factors Involved in the Prevalence and Type of GI Infections

Exposure
Presence/cause of immunodeficiency
  Transplant and type
  AIDS
  Cancer
Geographic location
Hospital setting
Medication exposure(s)

AIDS, acquired immunodeficiency syndrome; GI, gastrointestinal.

and prolonged drug-induced immunosuppression is required to prevent cardiac rejection. Rarely, opportunistic infections have been observed in the apparently normal host, but in contrast to the immunodeficient patient, these infections are typically self-limited.[3,4] In general, the more severe the immunodeficiency state required for development of an opportunistic infection, the less likely the pathogen will be observed in the normal host. For example, although herpes simplex virus (HSV) is a well-recognized pathogen in otherwise healthy people,[3] HSV esophagitis occurs most often in patients with some predisposing factor(s). In contrast, until the advent of transplantation, cytomegalovirus (CMV) was a rare pathogen, and its identification in any patient suggests some type of immune dysfunction.[4,5] CMV is now regarded as one of the most common opportunistic infections. This frequency of infection relates to the high prevalence of prior exposure to CMV, as reflected by seropositivity rates of more than 90% in developed countries[6] and to the fact that CMV disease generally occurs from recrudescence of latent infection during periods of profound immunosuppression.

The frequency of GI infections has been changing (primarily decreasing) in the immunosuppressed patient. Extensive research has defined the time course and spectrum of infections that complicate immune deficiency states.[7] Based on these observations, targeted preemptive antimicrobial prophylaxis has become the standard of care against many of these infections during periods of greatest vulnerability. Different classes of agents are used at varying time points depending on the infection risk and pathogen(s) associated with the level of immune impairment. However, antimicrobial prophylaxis is associated with an increased risk for other infections and to the development of drug resistance. For example, the use of prophylaxis for *Pneumocystis carinii* in AIDS is associated with a rise in the prevalence of other opportunistic infections, such as viral disease, because patients are now living longer.[8] The implementation of *Candida* prophylaxis in selected patients undergoing transplantation and the widespread use of oral antifungal therapies in AIDS has reduced the incidence of fungal infections but has been linked with drug resistance to *Candida* species.[9] The use of highly active antiretroviral therapy for HIV-infected patients has drastically reduced the frequency of GI complications, both infections and neoplasms.[10–12] More selective immunosuppressive therapy, such as with cyclosporine, has been beneficial in reducing the incidence of infections post transplant.[13] Methods for prophylaxis other than use of antimicrobials have also played a beneficial role in the reduction of opportunistic infections. In high-risk transplant patients, the use of CMV-seronegative organs and blood products for seronegative recipients, use of leukocyte-depleted platelets for patients after bone marrow transplantation, and the administration of preemptive antiviral therapy have all reduced the incidence of CMV disease.[14–16]

With the rise in international travel for both business and pleasure, geography plays an increasingly important role in the prevalence of some GI infections. Pathogens are endemic in certain portions of the world and in specific regions within countries. In the United States, histoplasmosis is endemic in the Midwestern states and Mississippi Valley, and coccidioidomycosis is endemic in the American southwest. *Mycobacterium tuberculosis* (TB) is endemic in third world countries and involvement of the GI tract is well recognized. *Penicillium marneffei* has recently been described as a pathogen and appears limited geographically to Southeast Asia.[17] Traveler's diarrhea, usually caused by enteropathogenic *Escherichia coli*, is characteristically seen with travel to Mexico and other developing countries.[18]

In summary, the frequency of luminal GI infections, the spectrum of pathogens, severity of infection, and organ involvement are dictated by the combination of exposure, predilection (host factors), and organ-specific tropism of the infecting pathogen. A careful history regarding potential exposure(s); cause; stage of immunodeficiency, if present; and specific epidemiologic factors germane to the clinical presentation will determine the potential causes of infection.

Pathogenesis

The pathogenic mechanisms of luminal GI infections are (1) exposure to a pathogen, (2) reactivation of prior infection (recrudescence), (3) overgrowth of a commensal organism, and (4) local spread or dissemination. The specific organ(s) involved with any infectious process, other than local spread, is dictated by the organ-specific tropism of the infecting pathogen. For example, *Candida* and HSV almost exclusively infect squamous epithelium, whereas *Campylobacter jejuni* and *Shigella* species are colonic pathogens.

Inherent to any discussion of pathogenesis is the issue of host-related factors. A number of nonspecific and immune-based defense mechanisms both prevent and attenuate GI infections.[19] These defenses may be altered by disease, by medications, or as a part of the aging process. Saliva provides an effective physical barrier because of its physical properties, and immunoglobulins that are present in saliva and in intestinal secretions provide an important early line of defense. Gastric acid is a barrier to enteropathogens, and hypochlorhydria has been shown to be a risk factor for the development of cholera and other GI infections.[20] GI motility moves ingested pathogens through the gut and prevents stasis, which can lead to bacterial overgrowth. Inherent antibacterial proteins secreted by Paneth cells, termed defensins, appear to play a key role in the host response to bacterial infections of the gut.[21]

The mucosal immune system is composed of inflammatory cells, most notably T cells.[19] After exposure to a foreign antigen, these cells differentiate into helper or cytotoxic cells depending on whether the cells express the CD4 or CD8 receptor. The release of cytokines by these cells plays a key role in limiting infection but can also result in tissue damage. The critical role of the mucosal immune system in preventing and controlling infections is best demonstrated by the array and severity of luminal GI infections witnessed in AIDS, in which a progressive loss of CD4 lymphocytes from both the systemic circulation and the mucosal-based immune system occurs.[22,23] Loss of these cells predisposes to small intestinal infections by opportunistic infections such as cryptosporidiosis and microsporidiosis. Likewise, lymphocyte dysfunction, either medication-induced or as part of an immune deficiency state, predisposes to symptomatic primary infection or recrudescence (e.g., CMV).

Most of the viral GI infections considered here result from recrudescence of infection rather than recent exposure (primary infection). Normally, exposure to these infections occurs during childhood, and the systemic and mucosal-based immune systems keep these infections controlled. However, with immunodeficiency, disease may then become overt.

Candida is a commensal organism of the oropharynx and esophagus. Although *Candida* is usually present in small numbers, overt disease can be observed even in the normal host under select conditions such as antibiotic use; inhaled or ingested corticosteroids; antiacid therapy or hypochlorhydria states; diabetes mellitus; alcoholism; malnutrition; old age; radiation therapy to the head, neck, and chest; and esophageal motility disturbances. Alterations in cellular immunity lead to candidal colonization and superficial infection, and humoral immunity (granulocytes) prevents invasive disease and dissemination. Bacterial esophagitis is a polymicrobial infection consisting of oral flora, particularly gram-positive organisms, including *Streptococcus viridans*, staphylococci, and other bacilli. This rare cause of esophagitis occurs under conditions of absolute granulocytopenia or severely impaired granulocyte function in which these commensal bacteria invade mucosa that has been damaged from reflux disease, from radiation therapy, or chemotherapy, leading to an active local infection and potential dissemination.[24]

GI infections may result secondarily from active disease in adjacent organs. Esophageal disease may be caused by contiguously infected mediastinal lymph nodes or pulmonary parenchymal infection[25] and by spread of infection via a draining fistula or obstructed lymphatics, resulting in tracheoesophageal fistula.[26] Widespread lymphohematogenous dissemination of opportunistic infections causes either diffuse or focal disease anywhere in the gut, and this process is generally limited to only the most severely immunocompromised patients.[27,28]

Most intestinal infections result in tissue inflammation although of varying degrees. Local upregulation of cytokines plays a central role in the local immune response to the pathogen but may also cause tissue injury. For example, CMV esophagitis is associated with high mucosal concentrations of the proinflammatory cytokine tumor necrosis factor-α.[29] Toxin production and virulence factors play a key role in the clinical expression and tissue damage caused by many GI infections, especially bacterial infections.[30]

In summary, luminal digestive tract infections occur under specific epidemiologic conditions and in the appropriate host. The tissue-based immune system is critical for preventing opportunistic infections, and, when absent, infection with such pathogens may be chronic and potentially life-threatening. Exposure to the pathogen is important; however, concurrent predisposing factors that were elucidated previously, such as antibiotic and/or chemotherapy exposure, can play a pathogenic role in both the normal and immunosuppressed host.

Clinical and Endoscopic Features

A number of factors guide the approach to the patient with suspected GI infection. Given the breadth of potential etiologic pathogens, the diagnostic strategy should be based on the character and chronicity of the symptoms, the organ system(s) involved, and findings on physical examination. As noted previously, for the immunosuppressed patient, the cause and severity of the immunodeficiency syndrome play an important role in the diagnostic approach.

ESOPHAGUS
Clinical Features

The most prevalent cause of esophageal infection in both the normal host and immunosuppressed patient is *Candida* followed by the herpes viruses.[5,31–34] CMV occurs more commonly in the AIDS patient, whereas HSV is more often observed in the normal host and non–HIV-infected immunosuppressed patients. Odynophagia is the characteristic symptom of esophageal infection, and infections resulting in esophageal ulceration almost uniformly cause odynophagia.[5,35] Although less common, dysphagia may be observed with esophageal infections, especially *Candida* esophagitis, or may represent esophageal obstruction or dysmotility from the infection or its sequelae. Bleeding is generally observed only when there is ulceration, and although generally mild, it can be severe if there is an associated coagulopathy.[36] Pulmonary symptoms may predominate when there is fistula formation to the tracheobronchial tree or coexistent pulmonary involvement. Patients with AIDS often have multiple coexisting esophageal disorders, which further complicate management.[5,37]

Physical examination, particularly of the oropharynx, may be helpful in suggesting the diagnosis of esophageal infection. Approximately two thirds of patients with AIDS and esophageal candidiasis have oral candidiasis (thrush).[38] In other immunocompromised patients, oropharyngeal candidiasis is also commonly associated with esophageal candidiasis.[5] It should be recognized, however, that thrush may be absent if antifungal therapy, such as nystatin, is currently administered. Furthermore, the presence of oropharyngeal candidiasis does not prove that *Candida* is the only cause of symptoms nor does the absence of oropharyngeal candidiasis exclude *Candida* esophagitis. Patients with chronic mucocutaneous candidiasis may have fungal involvement of various mucous membranes, hair, nails, and skin and have a history of adrenal or parathyroid dysfunction. Coexistent oropharyngeal ulceration is common in patients with HSV esophagitis but is infrequent in patients with CMV esophagitis or other systemic infections.[39,40]

After *Candida* species, herpes viruses are the most frequent infectious agents that cause esophagitis. Post transplant, HSV and CMV occur with equal frequency as causes of esophagitis,[5] whereas in patients with AIDS, HSV esophagitis is relatively uncommon and far less frequent than CMV. In a study of 100 HIV-infected patients with esophageal ulcer, HSV was only found in 9 (in 4, it was a copathogen with CMV).[34] HSV esophageal infection commonly presents with the sudden onset of severe odynophagia, heartburn, or chest pain.[39] Autopsy studies suggest that esophageal symptoms may be absent. Herpes labialis (i.e., cold sores) and oropharyngeal ulcers may coexist, antedate, or develop during the esophageal infection, whereas skin infection is rare.[5] A number of systemic manifestations including low-grade fever or upper respiratory symptoms may precede the onset of esophageal symptoms. In untreated immunocompetent persons, spontaneous resolution of HSV esophageal infection occurs within 2 weeks of the onset of symptoms. Rarely,

Table 24–2. Differential Diagnosis of Endoscopic Findings Based on Organ System and Pathogen

Finding	Esophagus	Stomach	Small Bowel	Colon
Plaque	Candida HSV	Cryptococcus MAC	MAC Cryptococcus	*Clostridium difficile* CMV
Inflammation*	HSV CMV	CMV Cryptococcus Cryptosporidia	Cryptosporidia	Bacteria CMV
Erosion/ulcer	Any infection	CMV TB Syphilis	CMV Cryptosporidia and Cryptococcus	Bacteria CMV Histo Ameba Strongyloides
Stricture	CMV TB Histo Blasto	Cryptosporidia TB	CMV TB	CMV TB
Mass	CMV TB	CMV	CMV	CMV Histo

*Edema, subepithelial hemorrhage.
Blasto, Blastomyces; CMV, cytomegalovirus; Histo, Histoplasma; HSV, herpes simplex virus; MAC, Mycobacterium avium complex; TB, Mycobacterium tuberculosis.

bleeding is the initial presentation and may be observed in the absence of esophageal complaints.

Odynophagia is almost uniformly present and is characteristically severe with CMV esophagitis. Chest pain, weight loss, and fever may be reported. The onset of symptoms is often more subacute than the acute presentation of HSV. A prior or coexistent diagnosis of CMV infection in other organs (e.g., retinitis or colitis) is not infrequent. Although rare in transplant patients, retinitis may be observed in approximately 15% of AIDS patients at the time of diagnosis of GI disease.[40]

The frequency of esophageal involvement with other pathogens is rare. Bacterial esophagitis has been observed in patients with severe neutropenia, usually those with hematologic malignancies, but occasionally it is observed after bone marrow transplantation,[33] diabetic ketoacidosis,[41] or steroid therapy. The presentation is similar to the presentation with other infection agents. Bacteria reported to involve the esophagus include *Brucella*,[42] *Actinomyces*,[43] *Nocardia*,[44] and *Bartonella henselae*.[45] The symptoms of esophageal TB depend on the degree and type of involvement.[26,46,47] Systemic symptoms of fever and weight loss are common. Pulmonary complaints often predominate because of a fistula to the trachea, bronchus, or pleural space. Dysphagia may be prominent with the formation of long strictures or traction diverticula resulting from the fibrotic response. Upper GI hemorrhage caused by esophageal ulcers or tuberculous arterioesophageal fistulas may be the primary manifestation. Bleeding caused by extensive mucosal disease has been described in an AIDS patient with esophageal *Mycobacterium avium* complex (MAC).[48,49] Fungi other than *Candida* species and parasitic diseases have rarely been reported to involve the esophagus.[50–55]

Barium radiography plays a minor role in the diagnosis of esophageal infection. In any patient, the presence of severe odynophagia limits the ability to drink barium, thereby hampering the adequacy of the examination. Although specific barium esophagram findings may be more typical for certain disorders,[56] given the potential overlap,

many of the findings are nonspecific and endoscopy with biopsy is generally indicated. Furthermore, the wide spectrum of causes coupled with the specific antimicrobial regimen that are required necessitates a definitive diagnosis rather than empirical antimicrobial therapy. Nevertheless, a sinus tract or fistulous connection to the bronchial tree or mediastinum at the level of the hilum is highly suggestive of TB but may also be the result of malignancy. An esophageal neoplasm may be mimicked by an ulcerated tuberculous granulomatous mass or CMV ulcer.[57–59] Chest radiography or computed tomography (CT) scan of the chest may support the diagnosis of TB.

Endoscopic Features

The characteristics of the esophageal lesion(s) provide very important diagnostic clues. The location, size, and appearance of all endoscopic abnormalities should be documented, because these features form the basis of the differential diagnosis and are useful for comparison on follow-up endoscopic examinations. Importantly, the differential diagnosis of the lesion will dictate how the lesion(s) should be sampled and what recommendations for diagnostic testing should be made on the biopsy and/or cytologic specimens (discussed later). Serologic testing plays no significant role in the diagnosis of acute infectious esophagitis.

Endoscopic examination of the esophagus is the most sensitive and specific method for diagnosing esophageal candidiasis (Table 24–2). The gross endoscopic appearance of *Candida* esophagitis is pathognomonic (Fig. 24–1) and may be graded according to published criteria.[60] A large, well-circumscribed ulceration should not be attributed to *Candida*. The endoscopic characteristics of HSV esophagitis reflect the pathologic changes; it appears as discrete, usually small (less than 1 cm), well-circumscribed shallow ulcers; a diffuse erosive esophagitis; or rarely vesicles[5,61] (Fig. 24–2). Small, scattered lesions covered with exudate mimic esophageal candidiasis. Deep ulcers, as seen with CMV, are very rare. CMV esophagitis is characteristically associated with one or more ulcerations that can be quite striking in patients with AIDS. Nevertheless, as with other infections, variability has been reported with an appearance ranging from multiple shallow ulcers, to solitary giant ulcers, to a diffuse superficial esophagitis[62] (Fig. 24–3). Although serologic testing is not helpful because of the high rate of prior exposure to CMV, the absence of CMV DNA or antigenemia in the blood would suggest an alternative diagnosis. Esophageal TB can present with a fistula to the tracheobronchial tree easily visualized endoscopically and rarely as an ulcer or mass lesion resembling a neoplasm. In normal hosts from endemic areas in South America, *Trypanosoma cruzi* may involve the myenteric plexus of the esophagus resulting in Chagas' disease and an appearance that is indistinguishable clinically, radiographically, manometrically, and endoscopically from idiopathic achalasia.[63] This diagnosis may be established by antibody testing. The endoscopic appearances of other rare infections have been described in case reports and resemble other infections.

STOMACH

Clinical Features

Symptomatic gastric infections are much less prevalent than those of the esophagus. The primary gastric pathogens are *Helicobacter pylori* and CMV; parasites and mycobacteria are also reported but are uncommon. Because of the relative infrequency of gastric infections, our understanding of the presentation and endoscopic findings of most of these infections are based on case reports or small series. With the exception of *H. pylori*, most infections of the stomach occur in the setting of an immunodeficiency. Gastric infections are typically manifested by upper abdominal pain that is generally steady and may radiate to the back. Associated symptoms are common and include nausea with or without vomiting; vomiting may be prominent when mucosal infection is severe. Infrequently, nausea alone in the absence of abdominal pain may be observed. Fever and weight loss are variable. Diarrhea may be the prominent symptom if the infecting pathogen also involves the small bowel. Bleeding, both occult and overt, is usually a marker of mucosal ulceration. However, because most gastric infections are superficial, severe bleeding is unusual unless there is an associated coagulopathy. As in the esophagus, the primary symptom is dictated by the infecting pathogen. For example, CMV gastric infection typically produces ulceration; thus, abdominal pain with or without bleeding is the most frequent presentation. Mucosal infections that result in gastritis without ulceration such as cryptosporidiosis are more commonly manifested by nausea without pain or may be asymptomatic. *H. pylori* infection of the stomach is considered an asymptomatic infection in most people regardless of immune status.[64]

Physical examination is generally unrevealing. Mild abdominal pain may be elicited on palpation of the epigastrium. A Hemoccult-positive stool is nonspecific.

Radiologic studies may suggest the presence of gastric infection. Although abnormalities can often be identified, the findings are typically nonspecific and further investigation with endoscopy is often required. Barium findings of gastric infection may include fold thickening or ulceration, whereas the most common CT finding is wall thickening, usually diffuse, and focal lesions mimicking a mass lesion (Fig. 24–4).

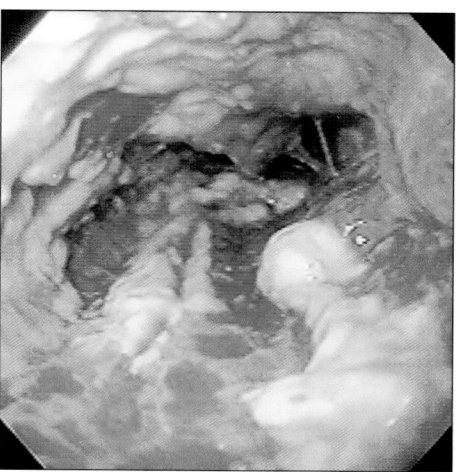

Figure 24-1. *Candida* esophagitis—multiple yellow plaques coating the esophageal lumen. In several areas the plaque has been removed, showing a normal-appearing underlying mucosa.

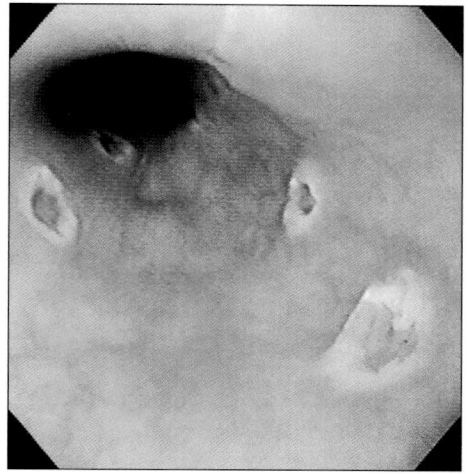

Figure 24-2. Herpes simplex virus esophagitis—multiple small ulcers, some of which have a "volcano" appearance typical for herpes simplex virus. Note that the intervening mucosa is normal.

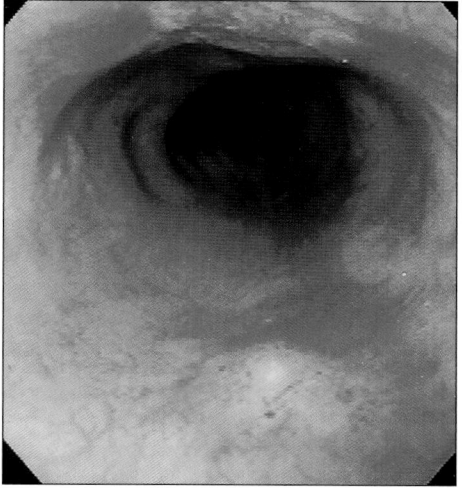

Figure 24-3. Cytomegalovirus esophagitis—two ulcers in the midesophagus with normal surrounding mucosa.

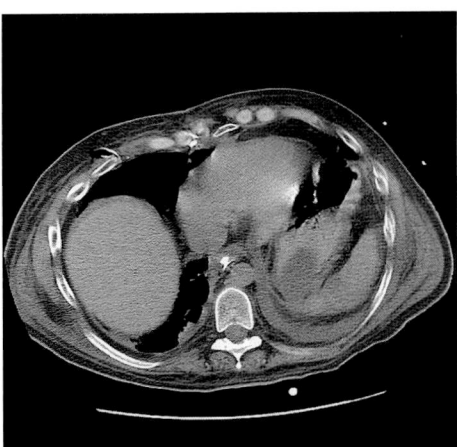

Figure 24–4. Gastric mucormycosis. Large hypodense area in the gastric wall on computed tomography (CT) scan.

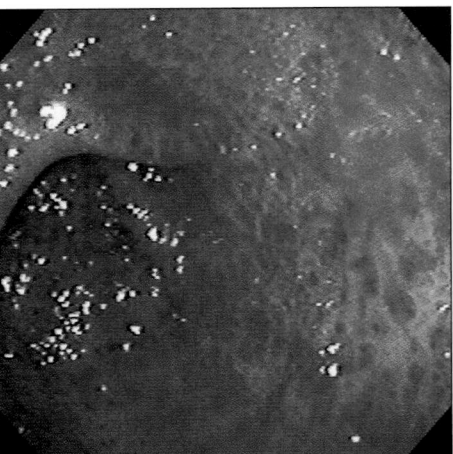

Figure 24–5. Cytomegalovirus gastritis—diffuse subepithelial hemorrhage, some of which is confluent in the gastric antrum. Several small erosions were also present in this patient.

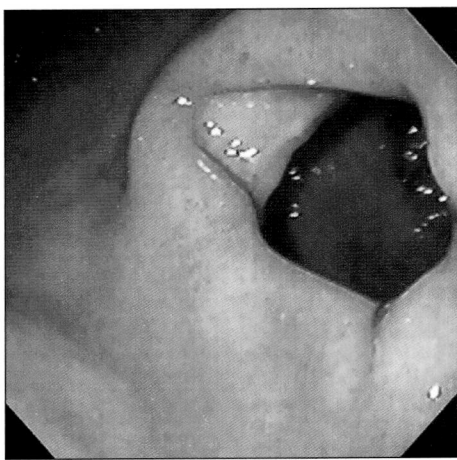

Figure 24–6. Pyloric channel ulcer resulting from cytomegalovirus—hemicircumferential ulceration with a clean base in the pyloric channel. This lesion resembles a peptic ulcer.

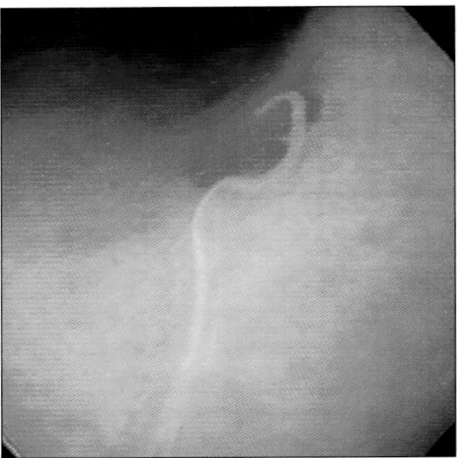

Figure 24–7. Anisakiasis—well-circumscribed area of subepithelial hemorrhage with a small worm emanating from the center of the hemorrhage. The worm was removed with biopsy forceps.

Endoscopic Features

Like all GI infections, the primary endoscopic abnormality is dictated by the infecting pathogen, and the severity of disease both clinically and endoscopically is dependent on the presence and degree of immunodeficiency. CMV, the most common opportunistic gastric pathogen, generally presents with a diffuse gastritis characteristically with a hemorrhagic component[65] (Fig. 24–5). Mucosal breaks are typical with focal or diffuse erosions or frank ulceration(s) (Fig. 24–6) that may be large, are usually well circumscribed, and may mimic a malignancy.[57] Large ulcerations have also been described with fungi and secondary syphilis.[66,67] The endoscopic features of gastric cryptosporidiosis and mycobacterial infection may appear as inflammation, polyps, or even antral narrowing.[68–72] In the normal host, gastric anisakiasis has been associated with ingestion of raw fish and the *Anisakis* larvae may be visualized land removed at the time of endoscopy[73,74] (Fig. 24–7).

SMALL INTESTINE

Clinical Features

The etiology of small bowel infection is dominated by parasitic disorders. In the normal host, *Giardia* infection predominates. With the exception of CMV, opportunistic small bowel infections are uncommon in the transplant patient but are a hallmark of AIDS when *Cryptosporidium* and Microsporidia are frequent pathogens. Although typically a pathogen complicating immunodeficiency syndromes, self-limited cryptosporidiosis has been observed in the normal host usually during single-source outbreaks and may be a more common cause of acute diarrhea than once thought.[75] MAC, a pathogen principally restricted to patients with AIDS, is a common small bowel pathogen that is widely disseminated at the time of diagnosis (Fig. 24–8). A localized proximal small bowel infection can occur with CMV, and distal ileitis has been reported with CMV, bacteria, mycobacteria, fungi, and parasites.[76–85]

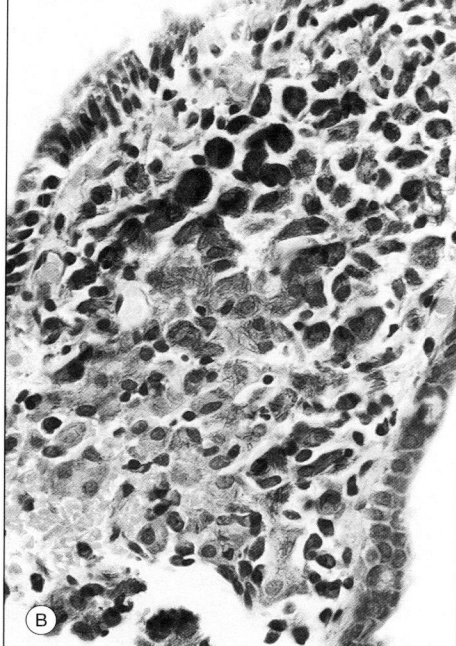

Figure 24-8. Duodenal *Mycobacterium avium* complex (MAC). *A,* Multiple well-circumscribed papular lesions typical for intestinal MAC. *B,* Acid-fast staining of mucosal biopsies shows numerous mycobacteria filling the lamina propria.

Diarrhea is the hallmark of small bowel infections with the severity and chronicity dependent on the etiology and the host. Severe watery diarrhea causing dehydration is characteristic of intestinal cryptosporidiosis, whereas less severe disease is observed with most other pathogens. Although crampy abdominal pain may be seen with any diarrheal disorder, more constant discomfort would be most typical for CMV enteritis and MAC.[48] Symptoms of malabsorption may be prominent when the infection is diffuse and severe, although overt steatorrhea suggests pancreatic rather than small intestinal disease. Significant borborygmi may occur when the diarrhea is more voluminous. Because CMV generally causes focal mucosal ulceration sparing the intervening mucosa, abdominal pain and overt bleeding can be observed in the absence of diarrhea. Weight loss may be profound with some infections. As noted, a distal ileitis, as reported from CMV, bacteria, TB, MAC, and parasites including *Isospora*, may result in a right lower quadrant pain syndrome. An acute abdomen can result from intestinal perforation and is most commonly due to CMV.[84]

The physical examination is variable from normal to cachexia and dehydration. Dehydration and electrolytes abnormalities would suggest a more severe process such as cryptosporidiosis. Abdominal tenderness may be elicited and would suggest CMV or perhaps MAC. Occult blood in the stool is nonspecific. Extraintestinal signs and symptoms may be associated with *Yersinia* species infection.[85]

Radiologic studies are of limited use in the setting of suspected small bowel infection. Small bowel barium studies may obscure stool studies if needed. CT can be helpful if thickened small bowel segments are visualized, although the differential diagnosis is broad.[81,83,86]

Endoscopic Features
The endoscopic findings of small bowel infections vary from normal to widespread hemorrhage and ulceration. Focal erosions and ulcerations are typical for a viral infection with CMV, whereas minimal

mucosal changes, if any, are common with parasitic diseases. Ulcers have also been reported from *Toxoplasma.*[80] Small bowel atrophy is associated with some of these infections and endoscopically mimics celiac sprue.[87,88] MAC infection has a characteristic appearance of small to confluent nodular lesions often with a yellow color resembling Whipple's disease (see Fig. 24–8). Disseminated fungal infections can also present with small nodular lesions.[89] Rarely, obstructive symptoms may predominate if there is an obstructive process. Stricture and ulceration of the ileum is typical for TB and rare for CMV (Fig. 24–9); these are best characterized by radiographic rather than endoscopic examination.[86,90,91] Ileitis can also be observed with some bacterial infections including *Yersinia* species and *Salmonella* species.[81,82,92] It should be recognized that

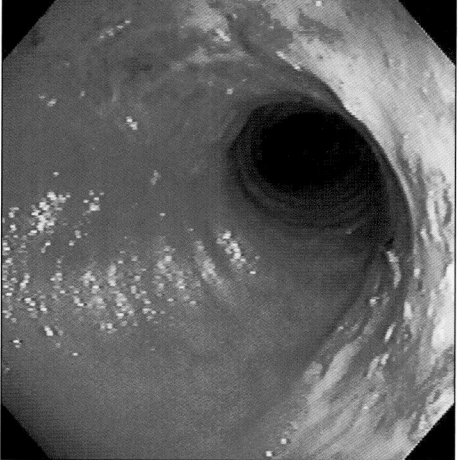

Figure 24-9. Cytomegalovirus ileitis—well-circumscribed hemicircumferential ulceration at the ileocolonic anastomosis after heart transplant and right hemicolectomy.

the endoscopic and radiographic features of any severe ileitis may mimic Crohn's disease. The diffuse nature of most small bowel infections highlights the importance of ileal examination with mucosal biopsy if colonoscopy is performed.

COLON
Clinical Features

In contrast to the upper GI tract, bacteria are the most common colonic pathogens. *Campylobacter* is the most prevalent isolate in most series of acute infectious diarrhea and colitis.[30] Depending on the clinical setting, CMV is the most frequent opportunistic pathogen, whereas *Clostridium difficile* remains an important pathogen in all patients regardless of immune status.

Diarrhea and abdominal pain are the cardinal manifestations of colonic infection. Acute diarrhea with urgency, tenesmus, and small volume bleeding are typical for bacterial colitis in any patient regardless of immune status. Although colonic infection is typically acute, especially in the normal host, a chronic or recurrent diarrhea may be observed in the immunodeficient patient. If the proximal colon is preferentially involved, right-sided abdominal pain may predominate. Bleeding is uniform with *E. coli* 0157H7 enteritis, and this infection should not be considered in its absence.[93] Parasitic diseases can involve the colon and either present acutely (amebic disease) or present with a chronic watery disease (cryptosporidiosis); concomitant small bowel disease is seen with cryptosporidiosis. Microsporidia do not infect the colon.[87] Colonic CMV infection characteristically manifests as a chronic watery diarrhea; pain is often a prominent feature, and both occult and overt bleeding may occur. Fever is common in bacterial infection, less so with CMV, and absent in most parasitic disorders. MAC can involve the colon, and although rare in developed countries, TB involvement of the colon is well recognized.[90] Toxic megacolon and perforation may complicate severe infection with either bacteria or viruses.[94]

The physical examination is generally dictated by the infecting pathogen. With acute bacterial colitis, the patient may appear toxic and have significant abdominal tenderness suggesting an acute abdomen and the pain may predominate over the diarrhea. Fever and abdominal pain may also be the main features of severe C. *difficile* colitis. Laboratory studies may demonstrate a leukocytosis with left shift but are otherwise nonspecific.

The most common radiographic study used in colonic infection is CT scanning. These studies are often performed because of the marked pain that is observed. Colonic wall thickening, which may be dramatic, is the typical finding for any colitis and may be found on routine abdominal radiographs (Fig. 24–10). Additional findings on CT may include small bowel thickening or lymphadenopathy.[94-96] Depending on the infectious cause, the radiographic abnormalities may be either focal or diffuse. Barium enema examination, if indicated, should not be performed in patients with suspected colonic infection until all stool studies are collected.

Endoscopic Features

The endoscopic findings in colonic infection range from normal to severe pancolonic edema and ulceration typical for a fulminant ulcerative colitis. *Campylobacter, Shigella,* and *Salmonella* infections may appear similar endoscopically with mucosal edema, subepithelial hemorrhage, erosions, and ulcers of varying size (Fig. 24–11). Distal disease is typical for *Campylobacter* and *Shigella* infections, whereas infections with *Salmonella* and *Yersinia* preferentially involve the right colon and ileum.[97-100] *Salmonella typhi* result in lymphoid hyperplasia leading to ulceration at the site of Peyer's patches; this may explain the geographic location in the bowel.[101]

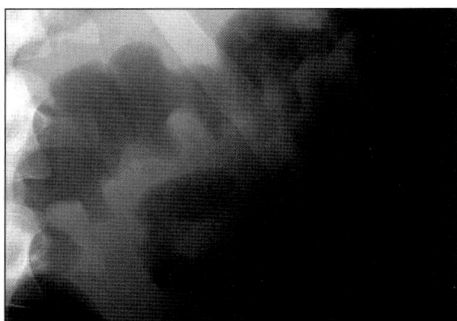

Figure 24–10. Thumbprinting of the colon. Characteristic thumbprinting seen on this plain abdominal radiograph of a patient with bacterial colitis.

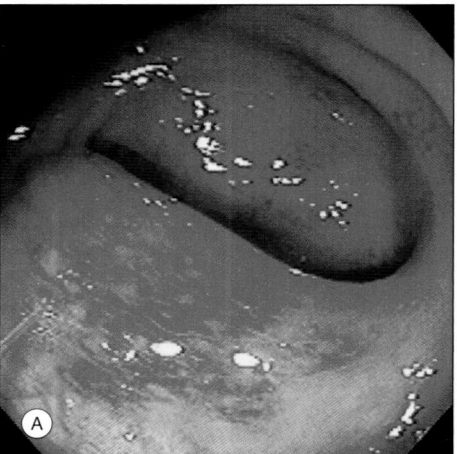

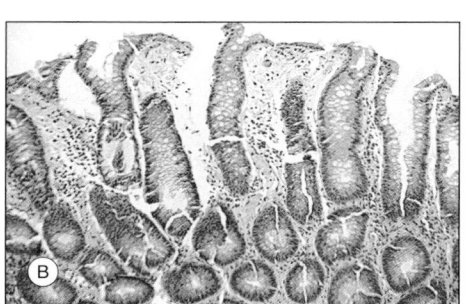

Figure 24–11. Campylobacter colitis. *A,* Focal area of subepithelial hemorrhage and erosion in the cecum. *B,* Hematoxylin and eosin staining from cecal biopsies show preserved architecture, mucosal edema, subepithelial hemorrhage, and acute inflammatory cells. These findings are typical for acute self-limited colitis resulting from a bacterial infection.

However, with any bacterial colitis, the colitis may be patchy, segmental, or diffuse. C. *difficile* colitis has a well-recognized appearance of plaque-like lesions that are typically confluent and are generally present in the distal colorectum (Fig. 24–12). When the disease is severe, mucosal edema is prominent. Subepithelial hemorrhage is characteristic of CMV infection as is ulceration of variable distribution (Fig. 24–13). An appearance of inflammatory bowel disease, either ulcerative colitis or Crohn's disease, has been described with bacteria and CMV.[102,103] HSV can rarely involve the colon, but generally only the distal rectum and anus are involved given the tropism of HSV for squamous mucosa. Amebic colitis may resemble a fulminant colitis or more commonly cause multiple ulcers that can be mistaken for idiopathic inflammatory bowel disease[104,105] (Fig. 24–14). The colonoscopic findings of cryptosporidiosis may be minimal edema or normal-appearing colon. TB may present with a mass lesion or serpiginous ulceration and nodularity.[90] Fungi have rarely been reported to involve the colon with histoplasmosis noted to cause ulceration or mass lesions resembling carcinoma.[106] Helminthic and other pathogens of the colon have also been described.[107,108] As noted, abdominal CT may be helpful when evaluating for complications such as toxic megacolon.[109–111]

Pathology

The pathologic features of GI infections are dependent on the infecting pathogen, and tissue tropism dictates the organ(s) of involvement. The gross pathologic appearance of esophageal candidiasis ranges from a few white or yellow plaques on the mucosal surface to a dense, thick plaque coating the mucosa and encroaching on the esophageal lumen. Although potentially misinterpreted as "ulcer," this plaque material is composed of desquamated squamous epithelial cells, admixed with fungal organisms, inflammatory cells, and bacteria.[60] True ulceration (granulation tissue) is rarely caused by *Candida* alone and has been documented most commonly in patients with profound granulocytopenia or when *Candida* is a coinfection with another cause of ulceration.[37] More deep-seated submucosal infections can occur with some fungi, and disseminated fungal infections can lead to ulceration.

Viral infection characteristically results in mucosal erosion and ulceration regardless of the site of infection. HSV infection is generally limited to squamous mucosa, where the earliest manifestation is a vesicle. As these vesicles enlarge and ulcerate, they coalesce to form larger superficial lesions, which are typically focal leaving the intervening mucosa normal. Microscopic examination of the squamous epithelial cells at the ulcer edge reveals multinucleation, ground-glass nuclei, and eosinophilic Cowdry's type A inclusion bodies that may take up half of the nuclear volume. With progression, these inclusion bodies may be surrounded by haloes and may become more basophilic, filling, enlarging, and deforming the nucleus. The histologic hallmark of CMV esophagitis is mucosal ulceration. Although variable, deep ulcers are very characteristic for disease in AIDS, whereas in other immunocompromised patients, lesions tend to remain more superficial. Despite the depth of the lesions, perforation is rare. In contrast to HSV, the viral cytopathic effect of CMV is located in endothelial and mesenchymal cells in the granulation tissue of the ulcer base rather than in squamous cells. Inclusions are large (cytomegalo) and often have an eosinophilic appearance that may be located either in the nucleus or in the cytoplasm.[112] The inclusions can assume an atypical appearance especially in patients with AIDS[113]; immunohistochemical stains play a valuable role in selected patients to confirm the

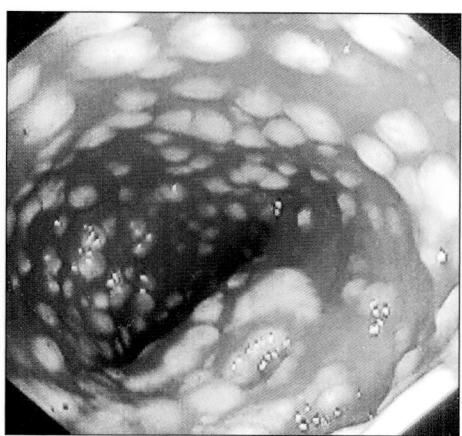

Figure 24–12. *Clostridium difficile* colitis. Typical yellow plaques in the distal colon.

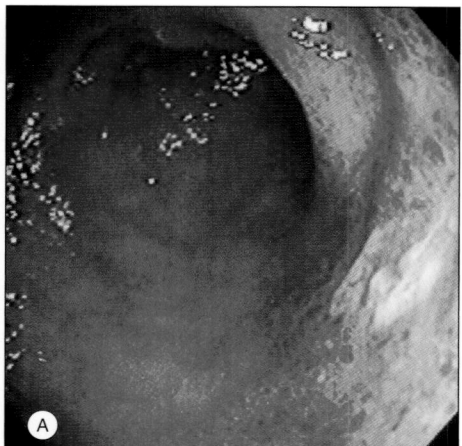

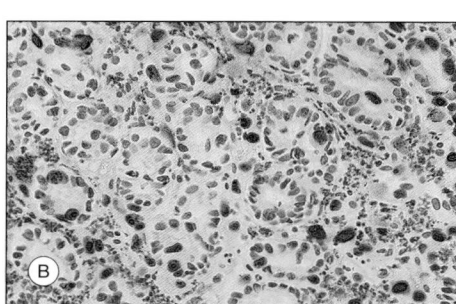

Figure 24–13. Cytomegalovirus (CMV) colitis. *A,* Diffuse subepithelial hemorrhage typical for CMV infection. *B,* Immunohistochemical stain for CMV antigens highlights the numerous infected cells.

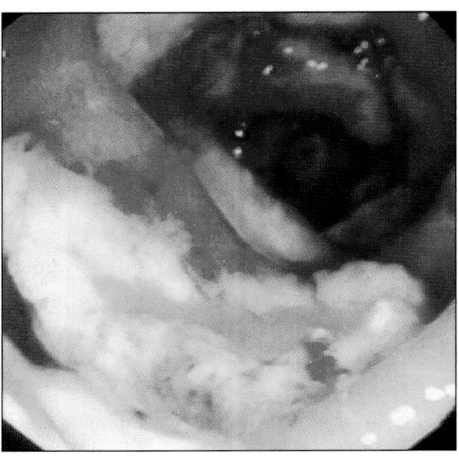

Figure 24–14. Amebic colitis—patchy erosions and ulcer suggestive of inflammatory bowel disease. (Courtesy of John L. Meisel, MD.)

presence of CMV, and they often highlight more infected cells than are appreciated by routine hematoxylin and eosin staining[114] (see Fig. 24–13B). As noted, CMV may coexist with HSV or *Candida* or other pathogens in patients with AIDS.

The gross pathologic appearance of bacterial esophagitis depends on the etiologic pathogen and ranges from diffuse, shallow ulcerations to ulcers associated with erythema, plaques, pseudomembranes, nodules, or hemorrhage. Microscopic examination reveals pseudomembranes and bacterial invasion that may be superficial and limited to squamous epithelium or may be invasive and transmural with infiltration of blood vessels (i.e., phlegmonous esophagitis). Esophageal actinomycosis is characterized by ulceration and sinuses leading from abscess cavities with sulfur granules and filamentous gram-positive branching bacteria seen on tissue biopsies.[43] In the one reported case, *B. henselae* esophagitis resulted in multiple nodules resulting from a lobulated proliferation of capillary vessels lined by plump endothelial cells.[45] Bacterial infection of the stomach is generally limited to *H. pylori* infection, which has the characteristic active chronic gastritis often with lymphoid aggregates.[115] Phlegmonous gastritis, whose pathogenesis is not well understood, may involve both gram-positive and gram-negative bacilli.[116] Acute bacterial colitis is pathologically demonstrated by crypt abscess with a preponderance of polymorphonuclear leukocytes and preservation of the mucosal architecture. These features help distinguish these processes from idiopathic inflammatory bowel disease.[117]

TB generally results in disease secondarily from paraesophageal infected nodes in the midesophagus at the level of the carina. In other parts of the gut, primary mucosal infection can occur. Esophageal disease can also be manifested by tracheoesophageal fistula. Histologically, granulomas are often present in ulcer tissue, with mycobacteria identifiable by mycobacterial staining. MAC, in contrast to TB, may not result in well-formed granulomas. Staining for MAC often yields an abundance of organisms (see Fig. 24–8B), whereas tuberculous bacilli may be few in number even in patients with AIDS.

Although generally an excellent stain, hematoxylin and eosin staining may not identify all pathogens. A variety of pathogen-specific stains are available to aid in the identification of nearly all common GI infections (with the exception of nonherpes viruses).

These stains highlight infecting pathogens and make identification easier. Immunohistochemical stains for viral antigens are very helpful when examining for herpes viruses.[118] Because a battery of stains is not routinely performed on all biopsy specimens, communication with the pathologist is essential to ensure appropriate pathologic evaluation.[119]

Differential Diagnosis

The diagnostic considerations are determined by the clinical presentation, risk group and severity of immunodeficiency, and the specific endoscopic findings. Although overlap is broad, some endoscopic abnormalities are typical for a specific pathogen and may be organ specific (see Table 24–2).

In the esophagus, CMV esophagitis and the idiopathic esophageal ulcer of AIDS are difficult to differentiate.[120,121] These two processes generally result in one or more large ulcers. Pill-induced esophagitis must be excluded by history because the pathologic findings of esophageal biopsies are similar. Likewise, distal esophageal ulcer may suggest gastroesophageal reflux disease, and the histopathologic features cannot distinguish the idiopathic esophageal ulcer from gastroesophageal reflux disease. However, the clinical history is different, and the endoscopic appearance helps suggest gastroesophageal reflux. Small esophageal ulcers can be observed in the acute phase of HIV infection, which can mimic viral or pill-induced esophagitis.[122] Esophageal strictures can result from opportunistic infections.[123] The history coupled with mucosal biopsy helps differentiate infection from gastroesophageal reflux disease.

The appearance of the small bowel is similar in many infections and can be normal. The cause of bacterial colitis, with the exception of C. *difficile*, can rarely be differentiated by presentation or endoscopic appearance alone, although some infections may favor a proximal or distal location. In this setting, stool culture and blood culture may be diagnostic. In an immunosuppressed patient with chronic diarrhea, one or more colonic ulcers associated with subepithelial hemorrhage are highly suggestive for CMV, but this appearance can result from other disorders as well.

Treatment

Fortunately, effective antimicrobial therapies are available for most GI infections (Table 24–3). The pathogen rather than the organ of involvement dictates the treatment regimen. Systemic therapy should be provided for patients with severe disease and associated immunodeficiency. In the normal host, many infections are acute and self-limited and therefore require no specific therapy. In fact, antimicrobial therapy may be contraindicated and potentially harmful with some infections such as E. *coli* 0157H7 in which antibiotic therapy may be associated with hemolytic uremic syndrome in children.[124] For HIV-infected patients, treatment of the underlying immunodeficiency with highly active antiretroviral drugs is quite effective and is fundamental to the treatment of any opportunistic infection in this setting. Indeed, antiretroviral therapy alone can result in remission of some opportunistic infections and AIDS-associated neoplasms, which underscores the importance of

Table 24–3. Suggested Regimens for the Treatment of Luminal GI Infections

Pathogen	Drug	Dosage	Route	Duration	Efficacy (%)
Candida	Ketoconazole	200–400 mg/day	PO	7–14 day	<80
	Fluconazole	100 mg/day	PO/IV	7–14 day	~80
	Itraconazole	200 mg/day	PO	7–14 day	~80
	Amphotericin B	0.5 mg/kg/day	PO/IV	7 day	>95
Histoplasma	Amphotericin B	—	IV	—	>90
	Ketoconazole	—	—	—	—
Other fungi	Amphotericin B	—	—	—	—
CMV	Ganciclovir	5 mg/kg	IV	2–4 wk	~75
	Foscarnet	bid	IV	2–4 wk	~75
	Valganciclovir	90 mg/kg bid	PO	14 day	>90
		900mg bid			
HSV	Acyclovir	400 mg five times/day	PO/IV	14 day	>90
	Valacyclovir	1 g tid	PO	14 day	>90
	Famciclovir	500 mg tid	PO	14 day	>90
	Foscarnet	90 mg/kg bid	IV	14 day	>95
	Ganciclovir	5 mg/kg bid	IV	14 day	>95
Mycobacteria	Same as for pulmonary disease				
Bacteria	Based on infecting species				
Idiopathic ulcer	Prednisone	40 mg/day, taper	PO	4 wk	>90
	Thalidomide	200–300 mg/day	PO	4 wk	>90

bid, twice a day; CMV, cytomegalovirus; GI, gastrointestinal; IV, intravenous; HSV, herpes simplex virus; PO, per os; tid, three times a day.

immune reconstitution in any setting.[125,126] Likewise, in the transplant patient, reducing the dosage of immunosuppressive drugs, when possible, plays an important adjunctive role in the management of any opportunistic infection.

INDICATIONS AND CONTRAINDICATIONS

Luminal GI infections are generally suspected clinically, and the diagnosis can often be established by noninvasive studies. For example, small bowel and colonic infections, which are manifested by diarrhea, can be diagnosed by routine stool studies. Blood cultures in the febrile patient may be diagnostic and bone marrow examination may also be helpful in selected situations in which a disseminated infection is suspected. In the appropriate setting, endoscopic evaluation may not be indicated initially; instead, empiric therapy directed at suspected pathogens may be the best initial strategy. For the HIV-infected patient at risk for esophageal candidiasis, in whom oropharyngeal candidiasis is found, an empiric trial of fluconazole therapy should be performed first and endoscopic evaluation should be reserved for the nonresponder (discussed later). Although stool studies may identify a pathogen in a patient who is not severely ill and in whom diarrhea is chronic, when the infection is acute and severe, early endoscopy may be helpful in suggesting the etiology and directing therapy until the biopsy results return.

The contraindications for endoscopic evaluation are generally similar to any other patient. Severe coagulopathy must be recognized and treated appropriately if mucosal biopsies are anticipated. However, the endoscopic appearance alone, as noted previously, may be diagnostic in some cases, obviating a need for routine biopsy.

PREOPERATIVE HISTORY AND CONSIDERATIONS

The clinical history and epidemiologic features dictate the potential cause of intestinal infection. Patients at risk for pulmonary TB must be recognized before upper endoscopy is performed so that the appropriate respiratory precautions are exercised. Specialized media for endoscopic biopsies may be required in some settings. Culture media for mycobacteria should be available when TB is considered. As noted, coagulopathy must be recognized before endoscopy.

In patients with AIDS and thrush, the presence of dysphagia and/or odynophagia usually indicates *Candida* esophagitis. Therefore, in the symptomatic patient with associated thrush, an empirical trial of antifungal therapy should be instituted, reserving endoscopy for those patients who fail to respond. Further evaluation should be delayed no longer than 1 week for patients with severe persistent symptoms because the response to antifungal therapy is rapid, with clinical improvement occurring in most patients within days.[127,128] If patients fail to improve with empirical antifungal therapy, endoscopy should be performed because disorders other than *Candida* are identified in most patients.[129] This empirical strategy has not been critically studied in the transplant setting; however, clinical experience suggests it is effective. Empiric therapy for acute diarrhea in other immunosuppressed patients is commonly practiced but little studied.

DESCRIPTION OF TECHNIQUES

No specific techniques are generally required for the endoscopic evaluation of GI infection. Based on the suspected cause clinically, endoscopically, and pathologically, additional stains may be required, thereby necessitating close collaboration with the pathologist to accurately diagnose these infections. Because most infections can be

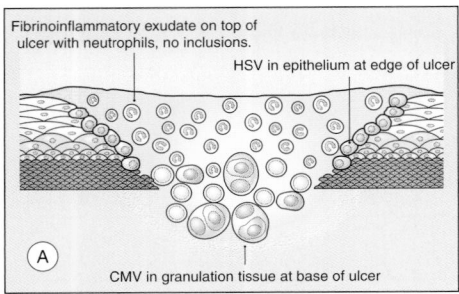
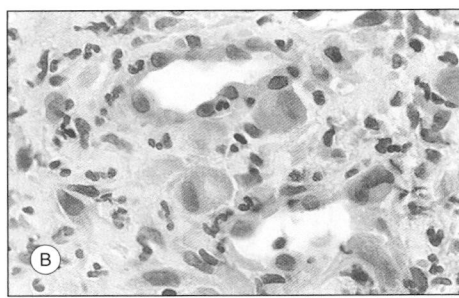
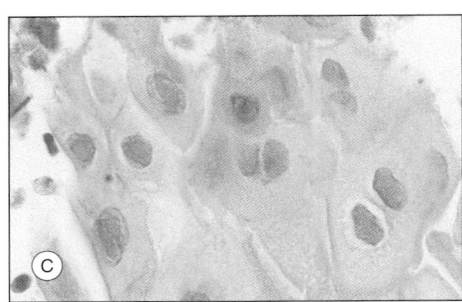

Figure 24–15. *A,* Location of viral cytopathic effect in mucosal ulceration. Herpes simplex virus can be found at the ulcer edge, whereas cytomegalovirus (CMV) is located in granulation tissue deep in the ulcer bed. *B,* Large cells with intranuclear inclusions typical for CMV. *C,* Multinucleated cells in squamous tissue typical for HSV. (From Lazenby AJ: Gastroenterologist/pathologist partnership. Tech Gastrointest Endosc 4:95–100, 2002.)

diagnosed on tissue biopsy alone, multiple biopsies of endoscopic abnormalities should be performed to increase diagnostic yield. Even when the mucosa appears normal, multiple biopsies should be taken when infection is suspected. During endoscopy, mucosal lesions can be brushed and submitted for cytologic evaluation or biopsied for histologic diagnosis.[130] Esophageal brushings with cytologic evaluation may be diagnostically helpful in certain diseases such as those resulting from *Candida* and HSV but are not helpful for diagnosis of CMV disease. Viral culture of biopsy specimens may increase the diagnostic yield, although both false positives and false negatives occur, and they are less sensitive than multiple biopsies.[131] Use of shell vial techniques improves the turnaround time for CMV culture to 48 hours. Bacterial culture of colonic biopsies has been found in some series to enhance the diagnostic yield. Cytologic brushings[132] and endoscopic mucosal biopsies should be taken from the ulcer edge when HSV disease is suspected, because the viral cytopathic effect is best identified in epithelial cells rather than in granulation tissue in the ulcer bed. In contrast, the ulcer base must be biopsied when viral infection is suspected with CMV (Fig. 24–15). Multiple biopsies (up to 10) may be required to establish the diagnosis in patients with AIDS and should be taken from the base of the ulcer.[133] Culture of an aliquot of stool obtained at colonoscopy and bacterial culture of mucosal biopsies may increase the diagnostic yield.[134,135]

As mentioned previously, a number of histologic stains are available to identify pathogens. Immunohistochemical staining on biopsy samples using specific monoclonal antibodies to viruses such as HSV and CMV will help confirm the diagnosis when the viral cytopathic effect is difficult to appreciate. We generally rely on histology for the diagnosis of viral GI infections and use brushings and viral culture selectively. A technique first described for gastric biopsies, whereby the forceps are tilted into the lesion and the tissue is avulsed, is especially useful for taking samples from esophageal lesions (Fig. 24–16). Lastly, as noted previously, communication with the pathologist is essential so that appropriate attention can be drawn to specific pathogens and so that special stains can be performed.

VARIATIONS AND UNUSUAL SITUATIONS

Although the endoscopic findings are well recognized for some pathogens, a number of peculiar endoscopic abnormalities have

been previously reported. In general, if an infection is suspected, a systematic endoscopic approach as noted previously should be taken.

POSTOPERATIVE CARE

Management after the endoscopic examination should parallel any other patient. Close follow-up with the pathologist may yield a preliminary diagnosis within 24 hours.

COMPLICATIONS

Complications from endoscopy in the immunocompromised patients are similar to the normal host. There have been rare reports of bacteremia after endoscopic examination in patients with neutropenia. In this setting, antibiotic therapy before endoscopy is appropriate. Bleeding is generally self-limited but may occur in the anticoagulated patient. Although multiple biopsies may be felt to be unsafe, they should be performed for any ulcer, and the risk of perforation is extraordinarily low. Vigorous biopsy of esophageal ulceration appears safe with no reported cases of biopsy-induced perforation.[123]

Future Trends

The GI endoscopist will continue to play an important role in the management of GI infections, because of the ability to directly visualize the GI tract and to perform mucosal biopsies. Future advancements will likely be most notable for molecular techniques to identify infections. These techniques could involve specific use of markers in the blood or, more likely, use assays on mucosal tissue to search for microbial DNA fingerprints. These technologies should expedite the diagnosis and improve both sensitivity and specificity. Further refinements in immunosuppressive regimens coupled with tailored antimicrobial prophylaxis will further reduce the incidence of infections in the transplant setting. Just like the birth of HIV-1 decades ago, it is likely that further unforeseen infections will arise in the future, necessitating a collective approach involving a variety of disciplines, including the GI endoscopist.

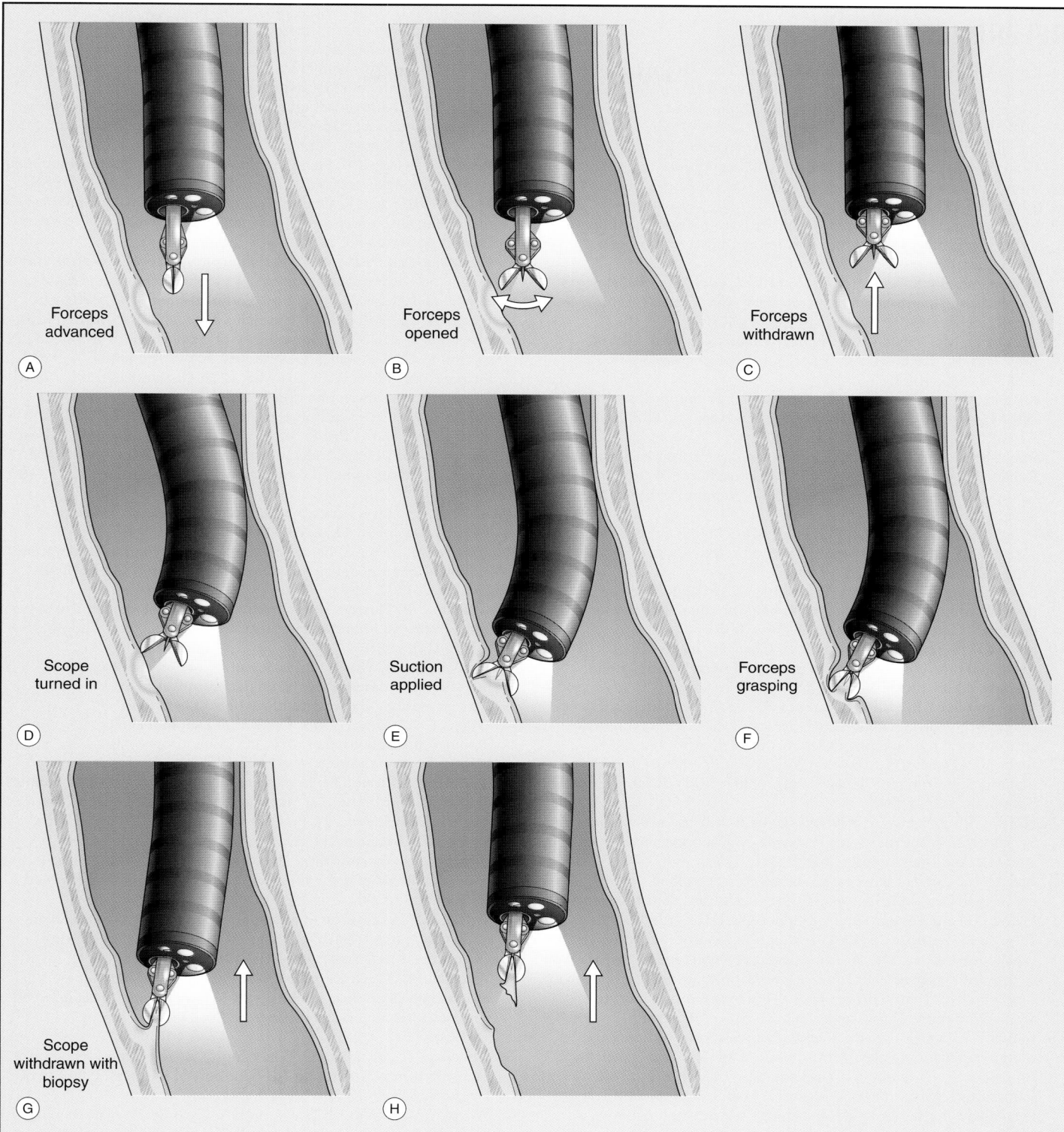

Figure 24–16. Biopsy technique for esophageal ulceration. The scope is turned into the lesion to sample the ulcer. Larger mucosal samples can be acquired in this fashion. (Redrawn from Wilcox CM: Approach to esophageal disease in AIDS: A primer for the endoscopist. Tech Gastrointest Endosc 4:59–65, 2002.)

REFERENCES

1. Seage GR 3rd, Losina E, Goldie SJ, et al: The relationship of preventable opportunistic infections, HIV-1 RNA, and CD4 cell counts to chronic mortality. J Acquir Immune Defic Syndr 30:421–428, 2002.

2. Bacellar H, Munoz A, Hoover DR, et al., for the Multicenter AIDS Cohort Study: Incidence of clinical AIDS conditions in a cohort of homosexual men with CD4+ cell counts <100/mm^3. J Infect Dis 170:1284–1287, 1994.

3. Ramanathan J, Rammouni M, Baran J Jr, et al: Herpes simplex virus esophagitis in the immunocompetent host: An overview. Am J Gastroenterol 95:2171–2176, 2000.

4. Venkataramani A, Schlueter AJ, Spech TJ, et al: Cytomegalovirus esophagitis in an immunocompetent host. Gastrointest Endosc 40:392–393, 1994.

5. Baehr PH, McDonald GB: Esophageal infections: Risk factors, presentation, diagnosis, and treatment. Gastroenterology 106:509–532, 1994.

6. Kothari A, Ramachandran VG, Gupta P, et al: Seroprevalence of cytomegalovirus among voluntary blood donors in Delhi, India. J Health Popul Nutr 20:348–351, 2002.

7. Rubin RR: Infections in the liver and renal transplant patient. In Rubin RH, Young LS (eds): Clinical Approach to Infection in the Compromised Host, 2nd ed. New York, Plenum Publishing, 1988, p 561.

8. Porter K, Fairley CK, Wall PG, et al: AIDS defining diseases in the UK: The impact of PCP prophylaxis and twelve years of change. Int J STD AIDS 7:252–257, 1996.

9. Fichtenbaum CJ, Koletar S, Yiannoutsos C, et al: Refractory mucosal candidiasis in advanced human immunodeficiency virus infection. Clin Infect Dis 30:749–756, 2000.

10. Brodt HR, Kamps BS, Gute P, et al: Changing incidence of AIDS-defining illness in the era of antiretroviral combination therapy. AIDS 11:1731–1738, 1997.

11. Monkemuller KE, Call SA, Lazenby AJ, et al: Declining prevalence of opportunistic gastrointestinal disease in the era of combination antiretroviral therapy. Am J Gastroenterol 95:457–462, 2000.

12. Jones JL, Hanson DL, Dworkin MS, et al: Surveillance for AIDS-defining opportunistic illnesses, 1992-1997. MMWR CDC Surveill Summ 48:1–22, 1999.

13. Hofflin JM, Potasman I, Baldwin JC, et al: Infectious complications in heart transplant recipients receiving cyclosporine and corticosteroids. Ann Intern Med 106:209–216, 1987.

14. Boeckh M: Current antiviral strategies for controlling cytomegalovirus in hematopoietic stem cell transplant recipients: Prevention and therapy. Transpl Infect Dis 1:165–178, 1999.

15. Turgeon N, Fishman JA, Basgoz N, et al: Effect of oral acyclovir or ganciclovir therapy after preemptive intravenous ganciclovir therapy to prevent cytomegalovirus disease in cytomegalovirus seropositive renal and liver transplant recipients receiving antilymphocyte antibody therapy. Transplantation 66:1780–1786, 1998.

16. Kanda Y, Mineishi S, Saito T, et al: Response-oriented preemptive therapy against cytomegalovirus disease with low-dose ganciclovir: A prospective evaluation. Transplantation 73:568–572, 2002.

17. Ranjana KH, Priyokumar K, Singh TJ, et al: Disseminated Penicillium marneffei infection among HIV-infected patients in Manipur state, Indian J Infect 45:268–271, 2002.

18. De Las Casas C, Adachi J, Dupont H: Review article: Travellers' diarrhoea. Aliment Pharmacol Ther 13:1373–1378, 1999.

19. James SP: Cellular immune mechanisms of defense in the gastrointestinal tract. In Blaser MJ, Smith PD, Ravdin JI, et al (eds): Infections of the Gastrointestinal Tract. New York, Raven Press, 1995, pp 213–236.

20. Evans CA, Gilman RH, Rabbani GH, et al: Gastric acid secretion and enteric infection in Bangladesh. Trans R Soc Trop Med Hyg 91:681–685, 1997.

21. Salzman NH, Ghosh D, Huttners KM, et al: Protection against enteric salmonellosis in transgenic mice expressing a human intestinal defensin. Nature 422:522–526, 2003.

22. Zeitz M, Ullrich R, Schneider T, et al: Mucosal immunodeficiency in HIV/SIV infection. Pathobiology 66:151–157, 1998.

23. Kotler DP: Characterization of intestinal disease associated with human immunodeficiency virus infection and response to antiretroviral therapy. J Infect Dis 179:S454–456, 1999.

24. Walsh TJ, Belitsos NJ, Hamilton SR: Bacterial esophagitis in immuno-compromised patients. Arch Intern Med 146:1345–1348, 1986.

25. Marshall JB, Singh R, Demmy TL, et al: Mediastinal histoplasmosis presenting with esophageal involvement and dysphagia: Case study. Dysphagia 10:53–58, 1995.

26. Devarbhavi HC, Alvares JF, Radhikidevi M: Esophageal tuberculosis associated with esophagotracheal or esophagomediastinal fistula: Report of 10 cases. Gastrointest Endosc 57:588–592, 2003.

27. Forsmark CE, Wilcox CM, Darragh TM, et al: Disseminated histo-plasmosis in AIDS: An unusual case of esophageal involvement and gastrointestinal bleeding. Gastrointest Endosc 36:604–605, 1990.

28. Grimes MM, LaPook JD, Bar MH, et al: Disseminated Pneumocystis carinii infection in a patient with acquired immunodeficiency syndrome. Hum Pathol 18:307–308, 1987.

29. Wilcox CM, Harris PR, Redman TK, et al: High mucosal levels of tumor necrosis factor alpha messenger RNA in AIDS-associated cytomegalovirus-induced esophagitis. Gastroenterology 114:77–82, 1998.

30. Ina K, Kusugami K, Ohta M: Bacterial hemorrhagic enterocolitis. J Gastroenterol 38:111–120, 2003.

31. Bonacini M, Young T, Laine L: The causes of esophageal symptoms in human immunodeficiency virus infection. Arch Intern Med 151:1567–1572, 1991.

32. Graham SM, Flowers JL, Schweitzer E, et al: Opportunistic upper gastrointestinal infection in transplant recipients Surg Endosc 9:146–150, 1995.

33. McDonald GB, Sharma P, Hackman RC, et al: Esophageal infections in immunosuppressed patients after marrow transplantation. Gastroenterology 88:1111–1117, 1985.

34. Wilcox CM, Schwartz DA, Clark WS: Esophageal ulceration in human immunodeficiency virus infection: Causes, diagnosis, and management. Ann Intern Med 123:143–149, 1995.

35. Bashir RM, Wilcox CM: Symptom-specific use of upper gastrointestinal endoscopy in human immunodeficiency virus-infected patients yields high dividends. J Clin Gastroenterol 23:292–298, 1996.

36. Vanegas F, Montalvo RD, Alvarex OA, et al: Massive upper gastrointestinal hemorrhage due to cytomegalovirus infection in two patients with acquired immunodeficiency syndrome. South Med J 93:235–238, 2000.

37. Wilcox CM: Evaluation of a technique to evaluate the underlying mucosa in patients with AIDS and severe Candida esophagitis. Gastrointest Endosc 42:360–363, 1995.

38. Wilcox CM, Straub RF, Clark WS: Prospective evaluation of oropharyngeal findings in human immunodeficiency virus-infected patients with esophageal ulceration. Am J Gastroenterol 90:1938–1941, 1995.

39. Genereau T, Lortholary O, Bouchaud O, et al: Herpes simplex esophagitis in patients with AIDS: report of 34 cases. Clin Infect Dis 22:926–931, 1996.

40. Wilcox CM, Straub RF, Schwartz DA: Cytomegalovirus esophagitis in AIDS: A prospective study of clinical response to ganciclovir therapy, relapse rate, and long-term outcome. Am J Med 98:169–176, 1995.

41. Ezzell JH Jr, Bremer J, Adamec TA: Bacterial esophagitis: An often forgotten cause of odynophagia. Am J Gastroenterol 85:296–298, 1990.

42. Laso FJ, Cordero M, Giarcia-Sanchez: Esophageal brucellosis: A new location of Brucella infection. Clin Invest 72:393–395, 1994.

43. Arora AK, Nord JK, Olofinlade JO, et al: Esophageal actinomycosis: A case report and review of the literature. Dysphagia 18:27–31, 2003.

44. Kim J, Minamoto GY, Grieco MH: Nocardial infection as a complication of AIDS: Report of six cases and review. Rev Infect Dis 13:624–629, 1991.
45. Chang AD, Drachenberg CI, James SP: Bacillary angiomatosis associated with extensive esophageal polyposis: A new mucocutaneous manifestation of acquired immunodeficiency disease (AIDS). Am J Gastroenterol 91:2220–2223, 1996.
46. Seivewright N, Feehally J, Wicks AC: Primary tuberculosis of the esophagus. Am J Gastroenterol 79:842–843, 1984.
47. Griga T, Duchna HW, Orth M, et al: Tuberculous involvement of the esophagus with oesophagobronchial fistula. Dig Liv Dis 34:528–531, 2002.
48. Gray JR, Rabeneck L: Atypical mycobacterial infection of the gastrointestinal tract in AIDS patients. Am J Gastroenterol 89:1521–1524, 1989.
49. Cappell MS, Gupta A: Gastrointestinal hemorrhage due to gastrointestinal Mycobacterium avium intracellulare of esophageal candidiasis in patients with the acquired immunodeficiency syndrome. Am J Gastroenterol 87:224–229, 1992.
50. Margolis PS, Epstein A: Mucormycosis esophagitis in a patient with the acquired immunodeficiency syndrome. Am J Gastroenterol 89:1900–1902, 1994.
51. Choi JH, Yoo JH, Chung IJ, et al: Esophageal aspergillosis after bone marrow transplant. Bone Marrow Transplant 19:293–294, 1997.
52. Ng FH, Wong SY, Chang CM, et al: Esophageal actinomycosis: A case report. Endoscopy 29:133, 1997.
53. Khandekar A, Moser D, Fidler WJ: Blastomycosis of the esophagus. Ann Thorac Surg 30:76–79, 1980.
54. Kazlow PG, Shah K, Benkov KJ, et al: Esophageal cryptosporidiosis in a child with acquired immune deficiency syndrome. Gastroenterology 91:1301–1303, 1986.
55. Laguna F, Garcia-Samaniegh J, Soriano V, et al: Gastrointestinal leishmaniasis in human immunodeficiency virus-infected patients: Report of five cases and review. Clin Infect Dis 19:48–53, 1994.
56. Levine MS: Radiology of esophagitis: A pattern approach. Radiology 179:1–7, 1991.
57. Laguna F, Garcia-Samaniego J, Alonso MJ, et al: Pseudotumoral appearance of cytomegalovirus esophagitis and gastritis in AIDS patients. Am J Gastroenterol 88:1108–1111, 1993.
58. Rich JD, Crawford JM, Kazanjian SN, et al: Discrete gastrointestinal mass lesions caused by cytomegalovirus in patients with AIDS: Report of three cases and review Clin Infect Dis 15:609–614, 1992.
59. Laajam MA: Primary tuberculosis of the esophagus: Pseudotumoral presentation. Am J Gastroenterol 79:839–841, 1984.
60. Wilcox CM, Schwartz DA: Endoscopic-pathologic correlates of Candida esophagitis in acquired immunodeficiency syndrome. Dig Dis Sci 41:1337–1345, 1996.
61. McBane RD, Gross JR Jr: Herpes esophagitis: Clinical syndrome, endoscopic appearance, and diagnosis in 23 patients. Gastrointest Endosc 37:600–603, 1991.
62. Wilcox CM, Straub RA, Schwartz DA: Prospective endoscopic characterization of cytomegalovirus esophagitis in patients with AIDS. Gastrointest Endosc 40:481–484, 1994.
63. Lages-Silva E, Crema E, Ramirez LE, et al: Relationship between trypanosome cruzi and human chagasic megaesophagus: Blood and tissue parasitism. Am J Trop Med Hyg 65:435–441, 2001.
64. McQuaid KR: Eradication of H. pylori in nonulcer dyspepsia. How much analysis do we need? J Clin Gastroenterol 36:291–296, 2003.
65. Ruiz AR Jr, Borum ML: Cytomegalovirus hemorrhagic gastritis. AIDS Patient Care STDS 15:1–5, 2001.
66. Sheu BS, Lee PC, Yang HB: A giant gastric ulcer causes by mucormycosis infection in a patient with renal transplantation. Endoscopy 30:S60–61, 1998.
67. Greenstein DB, Wilcox CM, Schwartz DA: Gastric syphilis. Report of seven cases and review of the literature. J Clin Gastroenterol 18:4–9, 1994.
68. Coppola F, Recchia S, Ferrari A, et al: Visceral leishmaniasis in AIDS with gastric involvement. Gastrointest Endosc 38:76–78, 1992.

69. Rossi P, Rivasi F, Codeluppi M, et al: Gastric involvement in AIDS associated cryptosporidiosis. Gut 43:476–477, 1998.
70. Tromba JL, Inglese R, Rieders B, et al: Primary gastric tuberculosis presenting as pyloric outlet obstruction. Am J Gastroenterol 86:1820–1822, 1991.
71. Cersosimo E, Wilkowske CJ, Rosenblatt JE, et al: Isolated antral narrowing associated with gastrointestinal cryptosporidiosis in acquired immunodeficiency syndrome. Mayo Clin Proc 67:553–556, 1992.
72. Chalasani N, Lazenby AJ, Wilcox CM: Unusual endoscopic features of gastric and duodenal cryptosporidiosis in AIDS. Gastrointest Endosc 45:525–527, 1997.
73. Ikeda K, Kumashiro R, Kifune T: Nine cases of acute gastric anisakiasis. Gastrointest Endosc 35:304–308, 1989.
74. Lopez-Serrano MC, Gomez AA, Daschner A, et al: Gastroallergic anisakiasis: Findings in 22 patients. J Gastroenterol Hepatol 15:503–506, 2000.
75. Leav BA, Mackay M, Ward HD: Cryptosporidium species: New insights and old challenges. Clin Infect Dis 36:903–908, 2003.
76. Kotler DP, Baer JW, Scholes JV: Isolated ileitis due to cytomegalovirus in a patient with AIDS. Gastrointest Endosc 37:571–574, 1991.
77. Schneebaum CW, Nivick DM, Chabon AB, et al: Terminal ileitis associated with Mycobacterium avium-intracellulare infection in a homosexual man with acquired immune deficiency syndrome. Gastroenterology 92:1127–1132, 1987.
78. Gumbs MA, Girishkumar H, Yousuf A, et al: Histoplasmosis of the small bowel in patients with AIDS. Postgrad Med J 76:367–369, 2000.
79. Gompels MM, Todd J, Peters BS, et al: Disseminated strongyloidiasis in AIDS: Uncommon but important. AIDS 5:329–332, 1991.
80. Bertoli F, Espino M, Arosemena JR 5th, et al: A spectrum in the pathology of toxoplasmosis in patients with acquired immunodeficiency syndrome. Arch Pathol Lab Med 119:214–224, 1995.
81. Balthazar EJ, Charles HW, Megibow AJ: Salmonella- and Shigella-induced ileitis: CT findings in four patients. J Comput Assist Tomogr 20:375–378, 1996.
82. Puylaert JB, Van der Zant FM, Mutsaers JA: Infectious ileocecitis caused by Yersinia, Campylobacter and Salmonella: Clinical, radiological and US findings. Eur Radiol 7:3–9, 1997.
83. Gorschluter M, Marklein G, Hofling K, et al: Abdominal infections in patients with acute leukaemia: A prospective study applying ultrasonography and microbiology. Br J Haematol 117:351–358, 2002.
84. Meza AD, Bin-Sagheer S, Zuckerman MJ, et al: Ileal perforation due to cytomegalovirus infection. J Natl Med Assoc 86:145–148, 1994.
85. Saebo A, Lessen J: Acute and chronic gastrointestinal manifestations associated with yersinia enterocolitica infection. A Norwegian 10-year follow-up study on 458 hospitalized patients. Ann Surg 215:250–255, 1992.
86. Wisser J, Zingerman B, Wasik M, et al: Cytomegalovirus pseudotumor presenting as bowel obstruction in a patient with acquired immunodeficiency syndrome. Am J Gastroenterol 87:771–774, 1992.
87. Kotler DP, Orenstein JM: Clinical syndromes associated with microsporidiosis. Adv Parasitol 40:321–349, 1998.
88. Shah VH, Rotterdam H, Kotler DP, et al: All that scallops is not celiac disease. Gastrointest Endosc 51:717–720, 2000.
89. Chalasani N, Lazenby AJ, Wilcox CM: Unusual endoscopic features of gastric and duodenal cryptosporidiosis in AIDS. Gastrointest Endosc 45:525–527, 1997.
90. Muneef MA, Memish Z, Mahmoud SA, et al: Tuberculosis in the belly: A review of forty-six cases involving the gastrointestinal tract and peritoneum. Scand J Gastroenterol 36:528–532, 2001.
91. Knollmann FD, Grumewald T, Adler A, et al: Intestinal disease in acquired immunodeficiency syndrome: Evaluation by CT. Eur Radiol 7:1419–1429, 1997.

92. Stolk-Engelaar VM, Hoogkamp-Korstanje JA: Clinical presentation and diagnosis of gastrointestinal infections by Yersinia enterocolitica in 261 Dutch patients. Scand J Infect Dis 28:571–575, 1996.

93. Griffin PM, Ostroff SM, Tauxe RV, et al: Illnesses associated with Escherichia coli O157:H7 infections. A broad clinical spectrum. Ann Intern Med 109:705–712, 1988.

94. Kirkpatrick ID, Greenberg HM: Gastrointestinal complications in the neutropenic patient: Characterization and differentiation with abdominal CT. Radiology 226:668–674, 2003.

95. Macari M, Balthazar EJ, Megibow AJ. The accordion sign at CT: A nonspecific finding in patients with colonic edema. Radiology 221:743–746, 1999.

96. Suri S, Gupta S, Suri R: Computed tomography in abdominal tuberculosis. Br J Radiol 72:92–98, 1999.

97. Shigeno T, Akamatsu T, Fujimori K, et al: The clinical significance of colonoscopy in hemorrhagic colitis due to enterohemorrhagic Escherichia coli O157:H7 infection. Endoscopy 34:311–314, 2002.

98. Rutggerts P, Geboes K, Ponette E, et al: Acute infective colitis causes by endemic pathogens in western Europe: Endoscopic features. Endoscopy 14:212–219, 1982.

99. Khuroo MS, Mahajan R, Zargar SA, et al: The colon in shigellosis: Serial colonoscopic appearance in Shigella dysenteriae I. Endoscopy 22:35–38, 1990.

100. Wong SY, Ng FH, Kwok KH, et al: Skip colonic ulceration in typhoid ileo-colitis. J Gastroenterol 34:700–701, 1999.

101. Hepps K, Sutton FM, Goodgame RW: Multiple left-sided colon ulcers due to typhoid fever. Gastrointest Endosc 37:479–480, 1991.

102. Tedesco FJ, Hardin RD, Harper RN, et al: Infectious colitis endoscopically simulating inflammatory bowel disease: A prospective evaluation. Gastrointest Endosc 29:195–197, 1983.

103. Wilcox CM, Chalasani N, Lazenby A, et al: Cytomegalovirus colitis in acquired immunodeficiency syndrome: A clinical and endoscopic study. Gastrointest Endosc 48:39–43, 1998.

104. Takahashi T, Gamboa-Dominguez A, Gomez-Mendez TJ, et al: Fulminant amebic colitis: Analysis of 55 cases. Dis Colon Rectum 40:1362–1367, 1997.

105. Ebecken R: Amebic colitis simulating ulcerative colitis. Gastrointest Endosc 51:641–642, 2000.

106. Garcia RA, Jagirdar J: Colonic histoplasmosis in acquired immunodeficiency syndrome mimicking carcinoma. Ann Diagn Pathol 7:14–19, 2003.

107. Linder JD, Monkemuller KE, Lazenby AJ, et al: Streptococcus bovis bacteremia associated with strongyloides stercoralis colitis. Gastrointest Endosc 52:796–798, 2000.

108. Bellomo AR, Perlman DC, Kaminsky DL, et al: Pneumocystis colitis in a patient with the acquired immunodeficiency syndrome. Am J Gastroenterol 87:759–761, 1992.

109. Beaugerie L, Ngo Y, Goujard F, et al: Etiology and management of toxic megacolon in patients with human immunodeficiency virus infection. Gastroenterology 107:858–863, 1994.

110. Chaudhuri A, Bekdash BA: Toxic megacolon due to Salmonella: A case report and review of the literature. Int J Colorectal Dis 17:275–279, 2002.

111. Dallal RM, Harbrecht BG, Boujoukas AJ, et al: Fulminant Clostridium difficile: An underappreciated and increasing cause of death and complications. Ann Surg 235:363–372, 2002.

112. Beaugerie L, Cywiner-Golenzer C, Monfort L, et al: Definition and diagnosis of cytomegalovirus colitis in patients infected by human immunodeficiency virus. J Acquir Immune Defic Syndr Hum Retrovirol 14:423–429, 1997.

113. Schwartz DA, Wilcox CM: Atypical cytomegalovirus inclusions in gastrointestinal biopsy specimens from patients with the acquired immunodeficiency syndrome: Diagnostic role of in situ nucleic acid hybridization. Hum Pathol 23:1019–1026, 1992.

114. Orenstein JM, Dieterich DT: The histopathology of 103 consecutive colonoscopy biopsies from 82 symptomatic patients with acquired immunodeficiency syndrome. Arch Pathol Lab Med 125:1042–1046, 2001.

115. El-Zimaity HM, Segura AM, Genta RM, et al: Histologic assessment of Helicobacter pylori status after therapy: Comparison of Giemsa, Diff-Quik, and Genta stains. Mod Pathol 11:288–291, 1998.

116. Schultz MJ, van der Hulst RW, Tytgat GN: Acute phlegmonous gastritis. Gastrointest Endosc 44:80–83, 1996.

117. Anand BS, Malhotra V, Bhattacharya SK, et al: Rectal histology in acute bacillary dysentery. Gastroenterology 90:654–660, 1986.

118. Monkemuller KE, Bussian AH, Lazenby AJ, et al: Special histologic stains are rarely beneficial for the evaluation of HIV-related gastrointestinal infections. Am J Clin Pathol 114:387–394, 2000.

119. Lazenby AJ: Gastroenterologist/pathologist partnership. Tech Gastrointest Endosc 4:95–100, 2002.

120. Wilcox CM, Schwartz DA: Endoscopic characterization of idiopathic esophageal ulceration associated with human immuno-deficiency virus infection. J Clin Gastroenterol 16:251–256, 1993.

121. Frager D, Kotler DP, Baer J: Idiopathic esophageal ulceration in the acquired immunodeficiency syndrome: Radiologic reappraisal in 10 patients. Abdom Imaging 19:2–5, 1994.

122. Schacker T, Collier AC, Hughes J, et al: Clinical and epidemiologic features of primary HIV infection. Ann Intern Med 125:257–264, 1996.

123. Wilcox CM: Esophageal strictures complicating ulcerative esophagitis in patients with AIDS. Am J Gastroenterol 94:339–343, 1999.

124. Safdar N, Said A, Gangnon RE, et al: Risk of hemolytic uremic syndrome after antibiotic treatment of Escherichia coli O157:H7 enteritis: A meta-analysis. JAMA 288:996–1001, 2002.

125. Carr A, Marriott D, Field A, et al: Treatment of HIV-1 associated microsporidiosis and cryptosporidiosis with combination antiretroviral therapy. Lancet 351:256–261, 1998.

126. Murdaca G, Campelli A, Setti M, et al: Complete remission of AIDS/Kaposi's sarcoma after treatment with a combination of two nucleoside reverse transcriptase inhibitors and one non-nucleoside reverse transcriptase inhibitor. AIDS 16:304–305, 2002.

127. Wilcox CM, Alexander LN, Clark WS, et al: Fluconazole compared with endoscopy for human immunodeficiency virus-infected patients with esophageal symptoms. Gastroenterology 110:1803–1809, 1996.

128. Lai YP, Wu MS, Chen MY, et al: Timing and necessity of endoscopy in AIDS patients with dysphagia or odynophagia. Hepatogastroenterology 45:186–189, 1998.

129. Wilcox CM, Straub RF, Alexander LN, et al: Etiology of esophageal disease in human immunodeficiency virus-infected patients who fail antifungal therapy. Am J Med 101:599–604, 1996.

130. Geisinger KR: Endoscopic biopsies and cytologic brushings of the esophagus are diagnostically complementary. Am J Clin Pathol 103:295–299, 1995.

131. Goodgame RW, Genta RM, Estrada R, et al: Frequency of positive tests for cytomegalovirus in AIDS patients: Endoscopic lesions compared with normal mucosa. Am J Gastroenterol 88:338–343, 1993.

132. Wilcox CM: Approach to esophageal disease in AIDS: A primer for the endoscopist. Tech Gastrointest Endosc 4:59–65, 2002.

133. Wilcox CM, Straub RF, Schwartz DA: A prospective evaluation of biopsy number for the diagnosis of viral esophagitis in patients with HIV infection and esophageal ulcer. Gastrointest Endosc 44:587–593, 1996.

134. Matsumoto T, Iida M, Kimura Y, et al: Culture of colonoscopically obtained biopsy specimens in acute infectious colitis. Gastrointest Endosc 40:184—187, 1994.

135. Barbut F, Beaugerie L, Delas N, et al: Comparative value of colonic biopsy and intraluminal fluid culture for diagnosis of bacterial acute colitis in immunocompetent patients. Infectious Colitis Study Group. Clin Infect Dis 29:356–360, 1999.

Techniques in Enteral Access

CHAPTER

25

Stephen A. McClave and Wei-Kuo Chang

Introduction

Using the gut and providing nutritional support by the enteral route play a pivotal role in patient outcome in the critical care setting. When there is failure to obtain enteral access and gut disuse ensues, the gut becomes a proinflammatory organ, increasing oxidative stress and the risk of complications.[1] Early enteral access and use of the gut, in contrast, promote or support the mass of gut-associated lymphoid tissue (GALT) and mucosal-associated lymphoid tissue (MALT) at distant sites such as the liver, lungs, and kidney.[2] This process contributes to orderly immune function and a reduction in the rate of long-term complications. The sicker the patient, the greater the need to maintain gut integrity, and enteral nutrition support becomes a therapeutic tool or pharmacologic agent capable of changing outcome by reducing nosocomial infection, multiple organ failure, and hospital length of stay.[3,4] Recent literature confirms that aggressive enteral tube feeding decreases the rate of complications when compared with standard therapy (patients are on their own to advance to oral diet as tolerated) or total parenteral nutrition (TPN).[5,6]

However, obtaining enteral access early in the course of a critically ill patient may be difficult. Patients in this setting are at the height of the hypermetabolic response, often requiring high doses of narcotic analgesia and sedation; thus, they are prone to ileus, gastroparesis, and high gastric residual volumes. Transporting these patients to the radiology suite for placement of feeding tubes is difficult, because they are unstable. Such transport leads to delays in getting enteral tubes placed and has been shown to increase the risk of complications (e.g., aspiration, hemodynamic instability, and new cardiac dysrhythmias).[7,8] Bedside techniques to place feeding tubes are essentially blinded, which carries some additive risk. Although bedside techniques may be sufficient in a large number of patients in

the critical care setting, the success rate for bedside placement decreases as disease severity increases, and there is greater need to place the tube lower in the gastrointestinal (GI) tract.

In long-term acute care and in the chronic management of patients recovering from stroke and neurologic injury, percutaneous endoscopic techniques provide a more reliable semipermanent enteral access, affording a number of options in a variety of patients. Getting a tube down below the stomach into the small bowel has been shown to reduce the incidence of regurgitation and aspiration.[9,10] In a recent meta-analysis, small bowel feeding was shown to significantly reduce the incidence of aspiration pneumonia when compared with gastric feeding.[11] In patients with severe gastroparesis, percutaneous endoscopic techniques may provide a gastrostomy tube for decompression and a direct jejunostomy tube for continued enteral feeding. In patients with recurrent flares of chronic pancreatitis, placement of an endoscopic jejunostomy tube may provide therapeutic options that preserve nutritional status, decrease dependance on narcotic analgesia, and reduce the number of hospitalizations per year. In patients with dysphagia resulting from neurologic injury, these percutaneous endoscopic feeding tubes are easily removable should the patient recover function and resume adequate volitional oral intake.

The role of the endoscopist in these settings is critical. The endoscopist has the skills to place the tube at the appropriate level in the GI tract, and most of the techniques can be performed at the bedside in the intensive care unit (ICU) without transport to the radiology suite. The endoscopist has the expertise in gut physiology, enabling adequate monitoring of enteral feeding. Endoscopists have the capabilities to provide simple techniques by which to manage complications. In the absence of such expertise for enteral access, the use of TPN increases significantly, a change in management strategy that may negatively affect patient outcome.

How to Establish an Endoscopy Service for Enteral Access

Several important steps should be taken to set up an effective endoscopic enteral tube service. The strength of the nutrition literature is so strong regarding the beneficial effects of enteral feeding in the critical care setting that nutrition support teams are under significant pressure to get enteral tubes in early and get enteral feeds started quickly. The endoscopist should establish rapport with the nutrition support team and provide a timely response to consults for request for enteral access. This can be facilitated by flexibility with potential time slots in the endoscopy schedule to make room for add-on cases. It is important to provide same-day service when a request for access is placed to deliver the best patient care. In general, it helps to treat a request for enteral access for a patient in the ICU as one would respond to a request to evaluate a GI bleeder.

The two most important endoscopes needed to outfit an endoscopy enteral tube service are a pediatric colonoscope and a small-caliber gastroscope with an insertion tube outer diameter less than 6 mm. A pediatric colonoscope is an excellent choice for endoscopic nasoenteric tube (ENET), percutaneous endoscopic gastrojejunostomy (PEGJ), and direct percutaneous endoscopic jejunostomy (DPEJ) because of its length and relative stiffness. Although a push enteroscope can be a substitute for the pediatric colonoscope, the greater flexibility of the small bowel enteroscope insertion tube promotes looping in the stomach. The small-caliber gastroscope has the advantage that it can be passed via the transnasal route at the bedside without sedation, making it an ideal choice in cases requiring ENET placement. When a 28-Fr percutaneous endoscopic gastrostomy (PEG) is in place, this same endoscope may be passed directly through the PEG for purposes of conversion to a PEGJ.

The endoscopist should be encouraged to learn one technique well for each of the four procedures (ENET, PEG, PEGJ, and DPEJ), and later try other techniques to find his or her personal favorite. Fluoroscopy is valuable early in the learning curve, but all of these techniques may be performed easily at the bedside or in the endoscopy suite without fluoroscopy. The ability to come to the ICU and place these tubes endoscopically without fluoroscopy avoids the need to transport the patient out of the ICU, increases flexibility in scheduling, and avoids the cost and potential exposure to radiation involved with fluoroscopy. Having appropriate colonoscopic length ancillary devices, such as wires, biopsy forceps, and snares and other accessories such as clipping devices (to secure the distal tube tip to the intestinal mucosa) or bandage clips (to secure the proximal end of the tube to the skin), improves the efficiency and success rate for these procedures. It is important to maximize lubrication when working with feeding tubes, by activating the hydrophilic lubricant on the inner surface of the tube by water infusion and by applying a vegetable spray or surgical lubricant to the outer surface.

Endoscopic Nasoenteric Tubes

ENET placement is most commonly required in the critical care setting. Severity of critical illness, complications of sepsis and multiple organ failure, and therapeutic strategies such as placement on mechanical ventilation are all factors indicating the need for early enteral access. Establishing enteral access and initiating enteral feeds is considered part of the basic resuscitation of these patients. ENET placement is specifically reserved for those critically ill patients who demonstrate intolerance to initial nasogastric feeding (because of poor gastric emptying, ileus, regurgitation, or aspiration) and those who require jejunal feeding because of acute pancreatitis. Several techniques have been described for ENET placement.

OVER-THE-GUIDEWIRE TECHNIQUE

The over-the-guidewire technique may be more difficult technically than other ENET procedures because of the oronasal transfer and wire exchanges (removing the endoscope from the wire and placing the feeding tube over the wire). However, this technique is the one ENET procedure that most reliably places the feeding tube at or below the ligament of Treitz. Before performing endoscopy, the oronasal transfer tube is placed through one nostril, brought out the mouth, and then clamped to the side using a hemostat. The pediatric colonoscope is passed through the mouth down the esophagus and stomach into the small bowel. As the endoscopist traverses the duodenum, it is important to pay attention to landmarks of the duodenal bulb, the C-loop, and then the distal duodenum leading to the ligament of Treitz. Paying attention to these landmarks helps assure the endoscopist as to the location of the tip of the endoscope within the GI tract. Passing the scope one to two loops below the ligament of Treitz helps to anchor the tip of the wire ultimately during subsequent wire exchanges (Fig. 25–1A). Once the scope has been passed as deep as possible, the wire is extended out from the end of the scope until it meets gentle resistance.

The first wire exchange involves removing the endoscope off the wire without displacing the tip. The key point to this aspect of the procedure is that the endoscopist places one hand on the scope as he or she removes it from the mouth and the other hand on the wire as it is passing into the operating channel of the scope at the other end (Fig. 25–1B). An assistant may support the weight of the scope, keeping it from bowing in the middle during the wire exchange. The tip of the wire protrudes from the patient's mouth at the point at which the colonoscope has been withdrawn off the wire. The oronasal transfer of the wire, if done incorrectly, will cause a loop to form in the mouth and/or displacement of the tip of the wire from the small bowel back into the stomach. The tip of the wire is placed through the oronasal transfer tube, passing the excess wire out of the end of the transfer tube protruding from the nose (Fig. 25–1C). Before the final loop protruding from the mouth is withdrawn or eliminated, the index finger is passed through the mouth, pinning the wire against the posterior wall of the oropharynx (Fig. 25–1D). While firmly holding the wire against the posterior pharyngeal wall, traction is placed on the end of the wire protruding from the nose, completely eliminating the loop protruding through the mouth (Fig. 25–1D). With the wire now protruding from the nose, the final wire exchange is made, carefully passing the feeding tube over the wire (Fig. 25–1E). Again, the endoscopist is careful to place one hand at the nose as he or she inserts the tube, with the other hand at the opposite end of the feeding tube where the wire is being withdrawn. The rate of the tube passing down into the nose

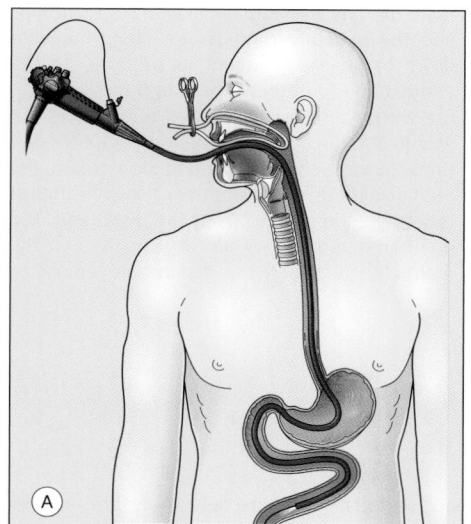
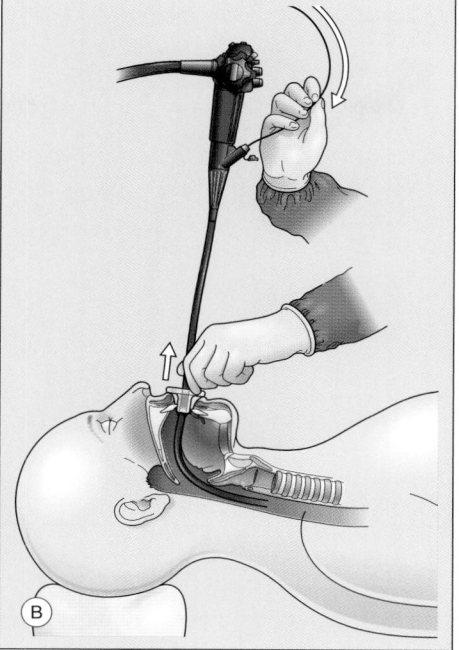
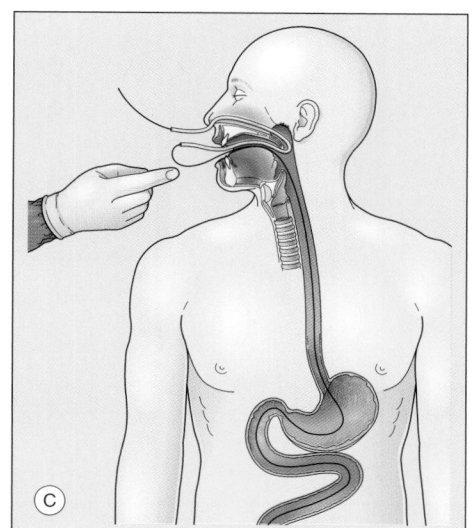
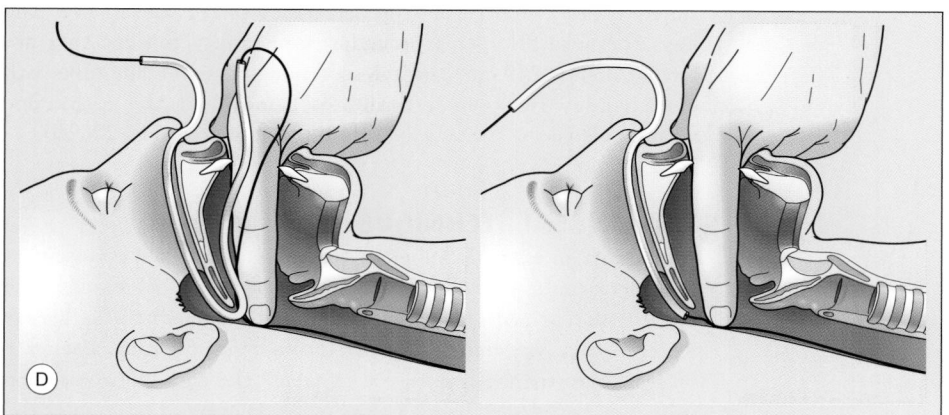
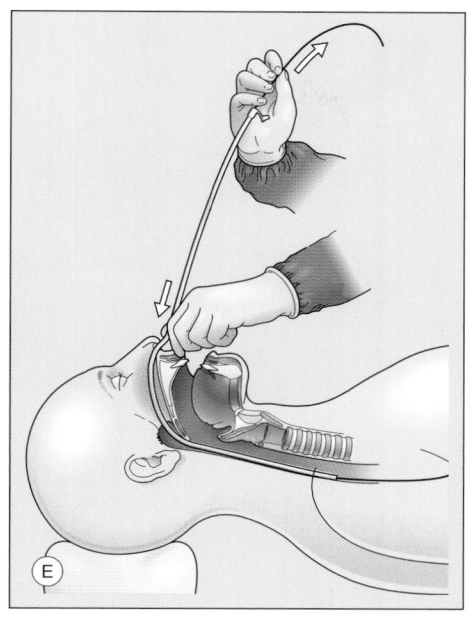

Figure 25–1. Over-the-guidewire endoscopic nasoenteric tube (ENET) technique. *A,* The pediatric colonoscope is passed down below the ligament of Treitz and the wire extended out beyond the end of the scope. *B,* In the initial wire transfer, the scope is withdrawn out from the mouth at the same rate the guidewire is passed down through the operating channel, to prevent displacement of the wire tip from its position in the small bowel. *C,* With the wire protruding out through the mouth, the tip of the wire is then passed through the oronasal transfer tube. *D,* The index finger is then used to pin the wire against the posterior pharyngeal wall while traction is placed on the wire protruding out through the nose, pulling on the wire until the wire is straight and tension is felt against the finger in the posterior pharynx. *E,* In the final wire transfer, the feeding tube is passed over the wire down through the nares at the exact same rate that the wire is withdrawn out from the distal end of the feeding tube, again to avoid displacing the wire tip.

should match exactly centimeter for centimeter the rate of the wire being withdrawn at the other end to avoid deflecting the tip of the wire (Fig. 25–1*E*).

DRAG AND PULL TECHNIQUE

The drag and pull technique is facilitated by placing one or two extra guidewires (for a total of two or three) through the nasoenteric tube before placement. Two to 3 cm of the soft tip of one wire should protrude out through the distal end of the tube. This assembly is then passed down through the nose into the stomach,

followed by passage of the endoscope down through the mouth into the stomach. Once in the stomach, long biopsy forceps are used to grab the soft tip of the wire protruding from feeding tube. The scope holding the wire is then passed into the small bowel, hopefully down to or beyond the ligament of Treitz (Fig. 25–2*A*).

From the point of deepest insertion, the endoscope is then slowly withdrawn back toward the stomach as the biopsy forceps holding the wire are advanced holding the tip of the wire in place in the small bowel. Once the scope is positioned back into the stomach, the feeding tube is advanced over the wire down to its tip, which is still being held by the biopsy forceps (Fig. 25–2*B*). Only at this point

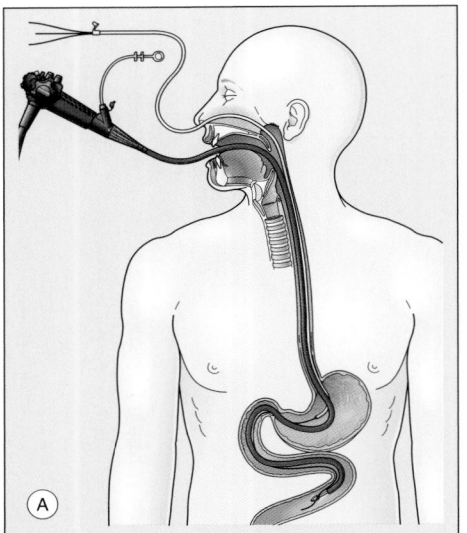

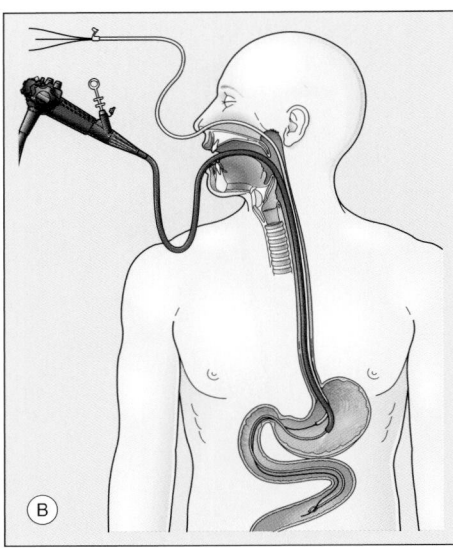

Figure 25–2. Drag and pull endoscopic nasoenteric tube (ENET) technique. *A,* The feeding tube is stiffened with three guidewires and then passed into the stomach, where one of the three guidewires is passed out beyond the end of the feeding tube. This one wire is grabbed with biopsy forceps and the pediatric colonoscope drags the wire down below the ligament of Treitz. *B,* As the endoscope is withdrawn back into the stomach, the biopsy forceps are pushed out to hold the wire in position below the ligament of Treitz. With the endoscope still positioned in the stomach, the feeding tube is advanced over the wire until it meets the biopsy forceps at the distal end. The endoscope is then withdrawn out through the mouth before all of the guidewires are removed.

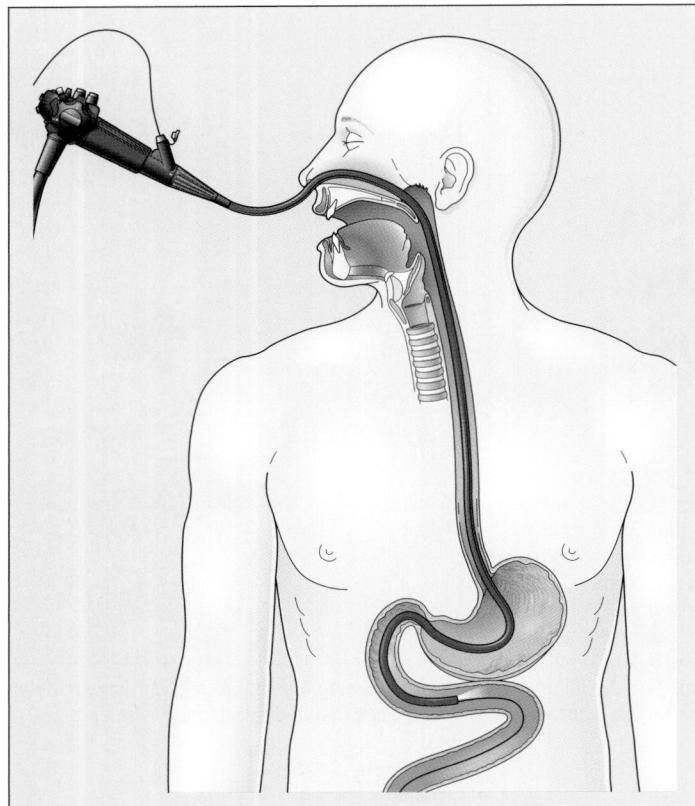

Figure 25–3. Transnasal endoscopic nasoenteric tube (ENET) technique. After first placing biopsy forceps down through the operating channel to stiffen the endoscope, a small-caliber (<6-mm diameter) gastroscope is passed through the nares down into the stomach and beyond the pylorus. A guidewire is passed through the operating channel out beyond the end of the endoscope, and then the endoscope is subsequently withdrawn. The final feeding tube is passed over the wire.

are the biopsy forceps opened and the wire released. The biopsy forceps are then withdrawn back into the scope, and the scope is slowly withdrawn back out through the esophagus and mouth. The keys to success for this procedure are biopsy forceps that are long enough (≥240 cm) and the stiffening of the feeding tube with extra guidewires (which facilitates removal of the endoscope without displacing the tube back into the stomach) (Fig. 25–2B).

TRANSNASAL TECHNIQUE

Availability of a small-caliber gastroscope affords the endoscopist the opportunity for a simple technique for ENET placement. The key to success with this instrument are placement of a biopsy forceps or a savory guidewire down through the operating channel to increase the stiffness and ease with which the endoscope insertion tube may be passed through the bowel. Transnasal passage of the scope is tolerated well by the patient and sedation may not be necessary. After intubating the esophagus and stomach, the scope is passed as far as possible, usually to the third or fourth portion of the duodenum. At this point, the stiffening device in the biopsy channel is withdrawn and a guidewire is placed down through the operating channel out as far as possible until meeting gentle resistance (Fig. 25–3). Using the wire exchange system described in the over-the-guidewire technique, the gastroscope is then withdrawn off the wire. Obviously, no oropharyngeal transfer of the wire is required, and the feeding tube may be passed immediately and directly over the wire. Wire exchanges are somewhat more tenuous and difficult with this procedure, because the wire is usually not passed as deep into the small bowel as in the over-the-guidewire technique described earlier, and the tip may be displaced more easily back into the stomach.

ALTERNATIVE OPTIONS

In a simpler version of the previously mentioned drag and pull technique, knotted suture line is attached to the distal end of the

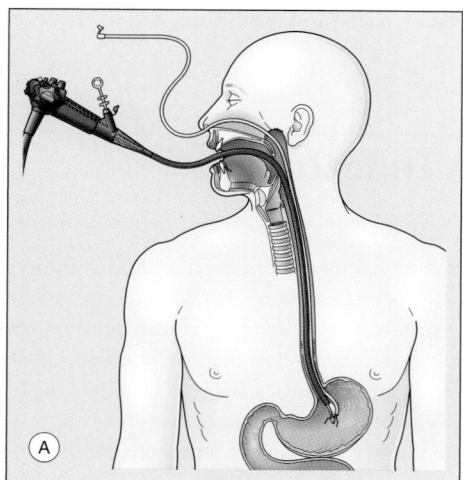

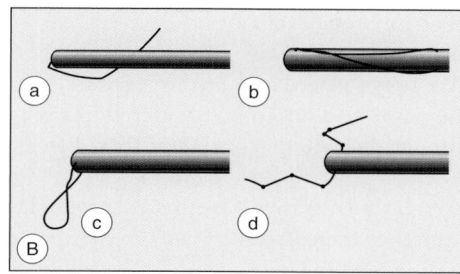

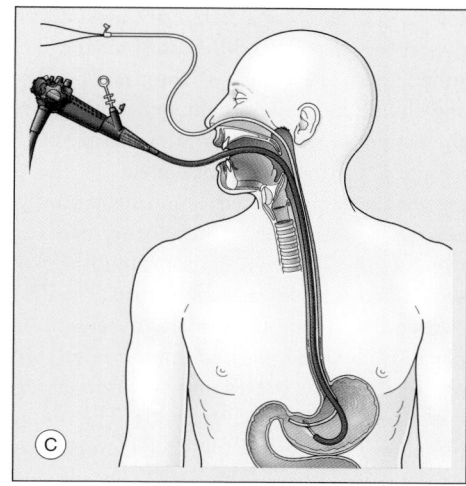

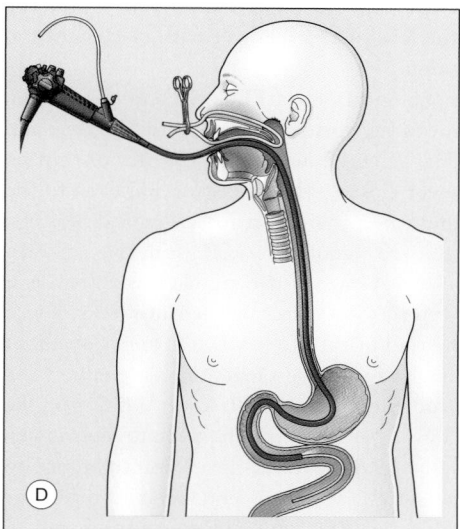

Figure 25–4. Additional endoscopic nasoenteric tube (ENET) options. *A,* One option involves two knotted sutures, attached to the distal end of the feeding tube, which is then passed through the nares down into the stomach. Biopsy forceps passed through the gastroscope grab the knotted suture and drag the tube down below the pylorus into the distal duodenum. *B,* This figure shows how the knotted suture is superior to a single or double suture line (which may adhere with gastric juices and mucous to the feeding tube) and a loop of suture (which may become tangled and twisted). *C,* A second option involves two or three guidewires passed through the feeding tube, which is subsequently passed through the nares down in to the stomach. The endoscope is passed through the mouth down into the stomach where biopsy forceps are used to push or shove the stiffened feeding tube through the pylorus. The tube can then be advanced further down into the distal duodenum by pushing from the outside. *D,* Another option involves the passage of an 8-Fr feeding tube through the operating channel of a therapeutic gastroscope, which has been passed to the distal duodenum or proximal jejunum. After advancing the feeding tube out beyond the end of the endoscope, the endoscope is withdrawn out from the mouth and the tube is transferred via a larger oronasal transfer tube out through the nose.

feeding tube and then the tube is passed through the nares down into the stomach. The endoscopist simply passes the scope through the mouth down into the stomach grabbing the knotted suture with biopsy forceps (Fig. 25–4A). It can be surprisingly difficult and frustrating to drag the tip of the feeding tube through the pylorus and down into the duodenum. The success of this sometimes awkward procedure is improved by using knotted suture line instead of a loop or single strand on the tip of the tube (Fig. 25–4B), by adding a second guidewire to stiffen the enteral tube to prevent displacement on withdrawing the endoscope, and by keeping the biopsy forceps 1 to 2 cm out away from the tip of the scope to enhance visualization (Fig. 25–4A).

In another alternative technique, one or two extra guidewires (for a total of two or three) are added to the feeding tube to increase stiffness, and then the tube is passed through the nares down into the esophagus and stomach. The endoscope is passed through the mouth down into the stomach, and the tip of the stiffened tube is simply pushed or nudged using open biopsy forceps through the pylorus into the duodenal bulb (Fig. 25–4C). Continuing to watch endoscopically from the stomach, the endoscopist pushes the stiffened feeding tube from the outside proximal end in an effort to pass the distal tip around the C-loop and into the third and fourth portion of the duodenum (Fig. 25–4C).

A reliable alternative method uses an 8-Fr nasoenteric tube, which is passed through the biopsy or device channel of the endoscope after it has been passed through the esophagus and stomach into the small bowel. This procedure's success is enhanced by using a large-channel therapeutic endoscope and a small-bore (8 Fr) nasoenteric tube whose proximal feeding cap can be removed. Because the scope is passed through the mouth, it does require placement of an oronasal transfer tube and the subsequent transfer of the tube from the mouth out through the nose (Fig. 25–4D) using the technique described in the over-the-guidewire technique.

SECURING TUBE WITH NASAL BRIDLE

For any case in which the time and expense of endoscopic placement of a nasoenteric tube is required, consideration should be given to securing the tube with a nasal bridle. Although this technique may seem barbaric and overly punitive to the patient, selection of the proper tube for the nasal bridle results in a degree of discomfort that is no different from the presence of the nasoenteric tube alone. The timing of the nasal bridle placement is important and should be done initially before endoscopy is performed (before the patient is agitated from the passage of the endoscope). Two 5-Fr neonatal feeding tubes are ideal for the bridle. The first tube is passed through one nares and brought out the mouth, while the second is passed through the other nares and likewise brought out the mouth. The two ends protruding from the mouth are then secured together by a single suture (Fig. 25–5). Traction is placed on one end protruding from the nares, pulling the nasal bridle into place (pulling the knotted juncture out through the nares such that one of the tubes passes into the nares around the nasal septum and out the other nares) (Fig. 25–5). The oronasal transfer tube is then placed and the rest of the ENET procedure commences thereafter. At the completion of the ENET placement, the tube is simply taped to the nasal bridle beginning 1 cm below the nose, wrapping the tape

downward over the feeding tube and bridle until the bridle is completely covered.

Percutaneous Endoscopic Gastrostomy

Placement of a PEG tube provides a more reliable and semipermanent enteral access compared with the ENET and should be considered in any patient requiring artificial nutrition support for greater than 4 weeks' duration. Because an incision is made, those patients who are not already on antibiotics require a single dose of antibiotic prophylaxis (a third-generation cephalosporin is appropriate) at the time of the initial procedure. Identifying landmarks with an indelible marker such as the midline and the left costal margin provides good orientation during procedure and avoids the possibility of lacerating the left lobe of the liver with placement too close to the left costal margin.

In the past, the traditional location for PEG placement has been in the left upper quadrant in the vortex formed by the midline and the left costal margin (Fig. 25–6A). Relocating the site of routine PEG placement down lower close to the umbilicus and even to the right of the midline should be considered for two good reasons. First, as shown on computerized tomography (CT) scan (Fig. 25–6B), the area of greatest interface between the stomach with anterior wall that provides the shortest, most direct passage into the stomach is located at this site. The traditional site in the left upper quadrant creates a tract that is longer and more tangential as it enters the stomach. However, even more importantly, this lower position on the abdomen places the PEG in the antrum, which facilitates conversion of the PEG to a PEGJ should the patient develop intolerance to feeding later on. Site selection is further enhanced by instilling 500 mL of air through the nasogastric tube into the stomach and by obtaining an abdominal film in the hour before PEG placement.

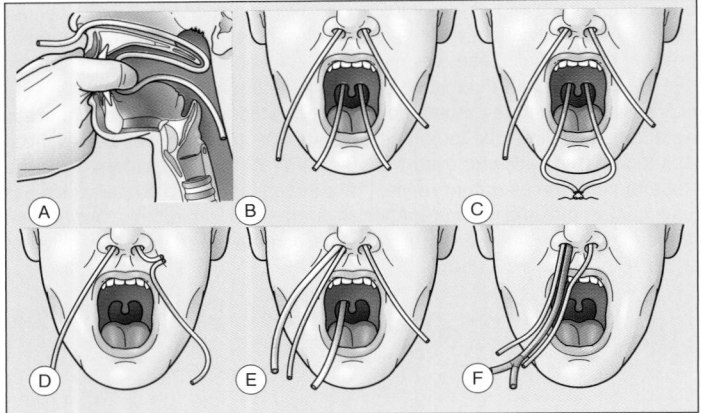

Figure 25–5. Bridle technique for securing endoscopic nasoenteric tube (ENET).

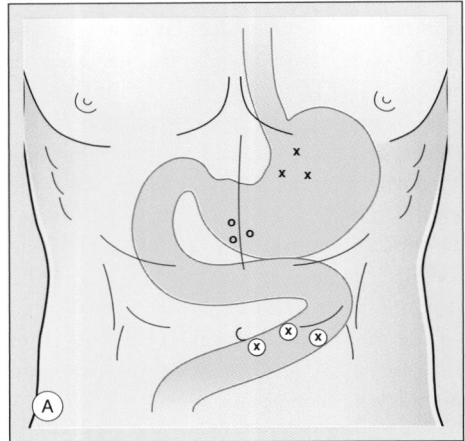
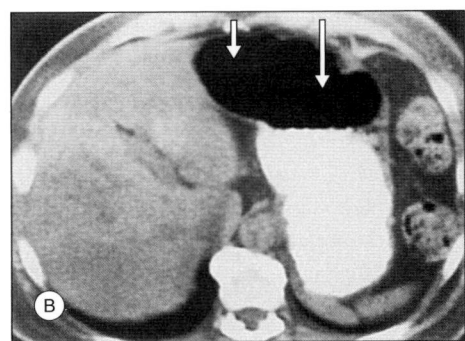
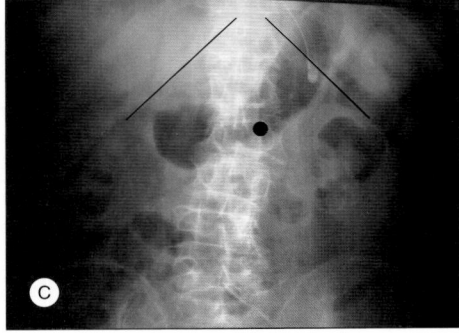

Figure 25–6. Steps to localize percutaneous endoscopic gastrostomy (PEG), percutaneous endoscopic gastrojejunostomy (PEGJ), and direct percutaneous endoscopic jejunostomy (DPEJ) sites. *A,* The traditional PEG site is marked by the "x"s in the left upper quadrant. Better placement is above the umbilicus, close to the midline, or slightly to the patient's right of midline position. The PEG is in the gastric antrum, which is ideal should the patient require conversion later to a PEGJ. X with circles show the tremendous variability in the site for DPEJ placement, which can occur anywhere from the left costal margin down to the left iliac crest. *B,* Computerized tomography (CT) scan shows that the PEG site slightly above or to the patient's right of the umbilicus coincides with the area with the most direct, perpendicular, and shortest tract into the gastric antrum. Traditional sites in the left upper quadrant have a longer, more tangential tract into the midbody or even lower fundus. *C,* Placing a coin in the umbilicus and injecting 500 mL of air through a nasogastric tube before PEG placement helps identify the gastric antrum, easing selection of the PEG site.

Putting a coin in the umbilicus serves as an obvious landmark on the abdominal film, the position of which can be compared with the costal margin. The position of the air bubble with respect to the coin and the costal margins help select the specific PEG site (Fig. 25–6C).

Palpating the stomach and obtaining translumination through the abdominal wall is necessary for proper PEG site selection. If there is any question (especially in cases of obesity), a safe tract technique may be used to ensure that no intervening loop of bowel exists between the stomach and the anterior abdominal wall (Fig. 25–7). Using a 21- to 23-gauge spinal needle and a syringe with 1 to 2 mL of saline, the needle is passed through the abdominal wall at the proposed PEG site. If bubbles appear in the saline just as the needle passes into the lumen of the stomach (as seen by endoscopy), there is some reassurance that the tract is appropriate. If bubbles appear before the needle passes into the stomach, there may be an intervening loop of bowel present (Fig. 25–7). PEG tubes should be selected that can be easily converted to a PEGJ should intolerance develop, and at least 20- to 24-Fr diameter may be selected to minimize chance of clogging. The length of the skin incision should be adequate just to accommodate the diameter of the feeding tube.

PONSKY PULL AND SACHS-VINE PUSH TECHNIQUE

The Ponsky pull and Sachs-Vine push techniques are virtually indistinguishable, provide no real advantage over the other, and may be selected based on personal preference of the operator. Once the PEG site is selected, the skin is anesthetized, a small incision is made, and the initial trocar is passed into the stomach. In the Sachs-Vine push technique, a single-stranded wire is passed through the trocar into the stomach and secured by a snare passed through the endoscope. With the Ponsky pull technique, a blue double-stranded wire loop is passed through the trocar and grabbed by the snare (Fig. 25–8A).

The wire passed by either technique is then brought out the mouth. In the Sacks-Vine push technique, a long 1½- to 2-foot plastic pointed leader is fused to the proximal end of the feeding tube, facilitating passage over a guidewire. This assembly is pushed down the wire through the esophagus and out through the gastric and abdominal wall (Fig. 25–8B). In contrast, the Ponsky pull technique involves a loop on the end of the feeding tube that is affixed to the double-stranded blue loop of wire protruding from the patient's mouth. Attaching the two wire loops is made easier by remembering the phrase "blue through," which describes the blue double-stranded wire being passed first through the loop on the end of the feeding tube (Fig. 25–8B). Once the knot between the wire loops is secured, the feeding tube is then pulled down through the esophagus into the stomach and out through the abdominal wall into the final position (Fig. 25–8C).

As a general rule when setting the external bumper, a slightly loose fit with approximately 1 cm of play causes fewer subsequent complications than a tight fit that can later lead to pressure necrosis and buried bumper syndrome. A quick and easy procedure to facilitate setting adequate tension between the bumpers involves following the PEG tube down through the esophagus by snaring the endoscope to the internal bolster (Fig. 25–9A). As shown in the top of Figure 25–9A, snaring one third of the internal bolster makes it easy to release the bolster once the scope is led down into the stomach. As the tube is pushed or pulled down through the esophagus and stomach, the endoscope is brought down easily with it into position into the stomach. Once the snare is released, the external bolster may be set with the internal bolster under direct endoscopic visualization (Fig. 25–9B). Drawing a figure and marking the exact number on the tube for the position of the external bolster is a valuable aid for nursing care and may be placed on the chart for reference at any time (Fig. 25–9B).

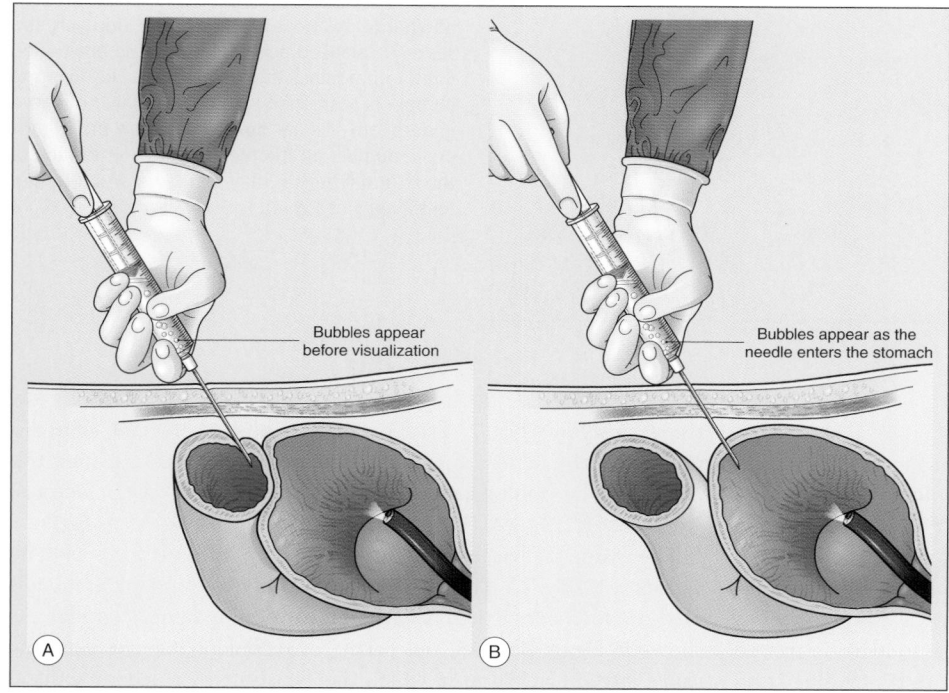

Figure 25–7. The safe tract technique for percutaneous endoscopic gastrostomy (PEG) placement helps avoid inadvertent tracking through an adjacent loop of bowel before passage into the stomach.

Bubbles appear before visualization

Bubbles appear as the needle enters the stomach

A

B

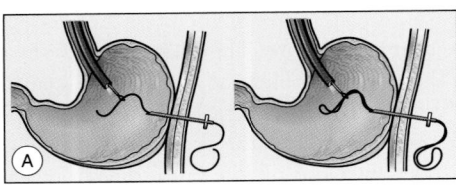

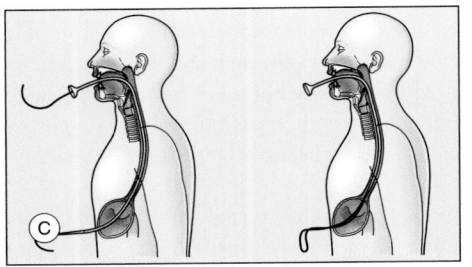

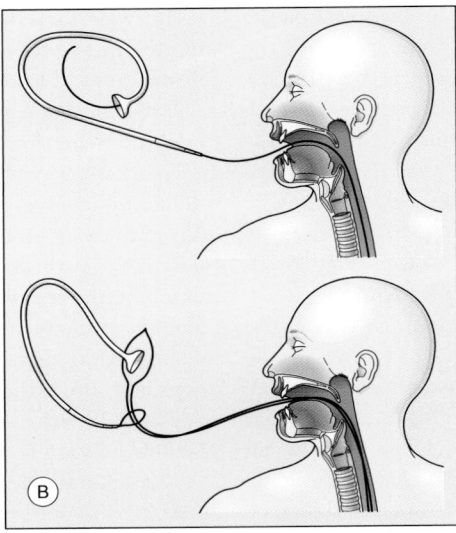

Figure 25–8. Comparison of the Sachs-Vine push versus the Ponsky pull technique for percutaneous endoscopic gastrostomy (PEG) placement. *A,* In the Sachs-Vine technique, a single wire is passed through the trocar and grabbed with the snare, whereas a wire loop is passed through the trocar in the Ponsky pull technique. *B,* A long, 2-foot plastic leader attached directly to the feeding tube allows the entire ensemble to passed or pushed over the wire in the Sachs-Vine push technique, whereas the blue wire loop can be attached to a wire loop on the end of the feeding tube in the Ponsky pull technique allowing the tube to be pulled into position. *C,* In the Sachs-Vine technique, the tube attached to the plastic leader is pushed through the esophagus and out through the gastric wall, whereas in the Ponsky pull technique, the wire loop pulls the feeding tube down through the esophagus and out through the gastric wall.

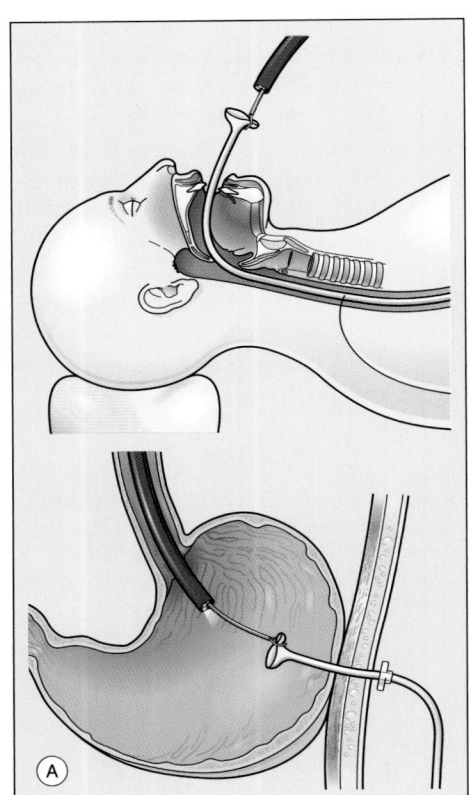

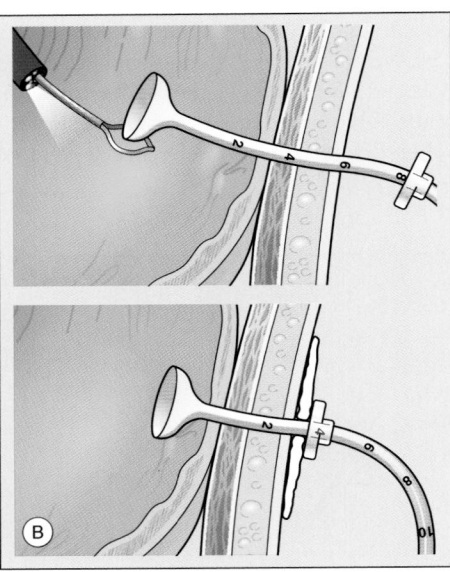

Figure 25–9. Following the percutaneous endoscopic gastrostomy (PEG) tube down into place and positioning the external bolster for appropriate tension. *A,* Just before the feeding tube is pushed or pulled down through the oropharynx and esophagus, a snare passed through the endoscope is snared to the internal bolster of the feeding tube securing the endoscope to the tube. The endoscope is then pulled down through the oropharynx and esophagus as the PEG is brought down into position. *B,* Once in the stomach, the snare is released and the bumper is positioned gently up against the gastric wall. The external bumper is positioned with a single layer of gauze underneath. A final figure indicating the appropriate number on the feeding tube for position of the external bolster may be drawn and recorded on the patient's chart.

RUSSEL INTRODUCER TECHNIQUE

In patients with a large exophytic oropharyngeal or esophageal carcinoma, the Russel introducer technique should be considered to avoid tumor implantation of the PEG site. This is a technique commonly used by radiologists but is easily performed by the endoscopist. Localization of the PEG site, position of the endoscope, and passage of the initial trocar are identical to the previous two techniques. With the trocar in place, a guidewire is passed into the stomach and then held firmly by a snare protruding from the endoscope (Fig. 25–10A). Gentle external traction is maintained on the wire from outside the abdomen throughout the procedure by pulling against the end held by the snare inside the stomach.

The stomach has to first be secured to the anterior wall by T-fasteners (Fig. 25–10A). Although a variety of commercial models of these fasteners exists, the design for deployment is similar. As shown in Figure 25–10A, this particular technique involves a narrow gauge introducer trocar in which the T-fastener is placed in a distal

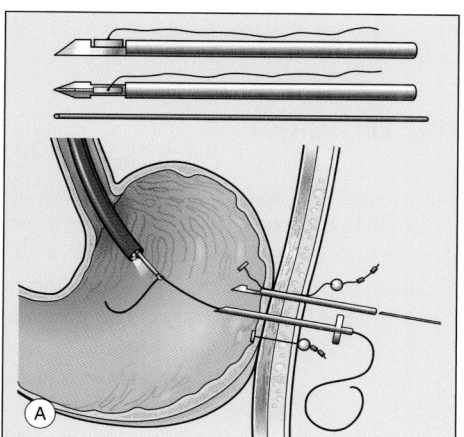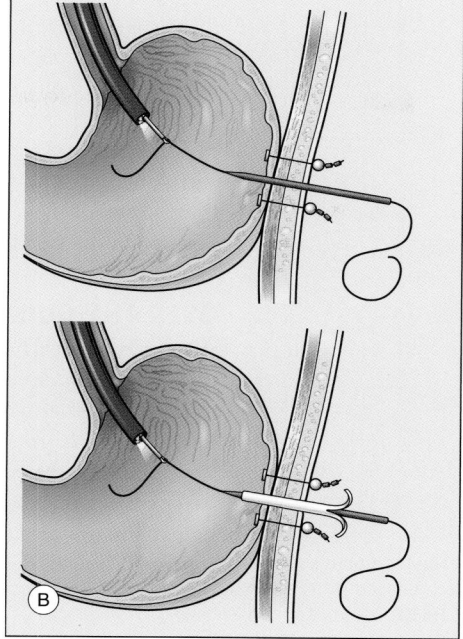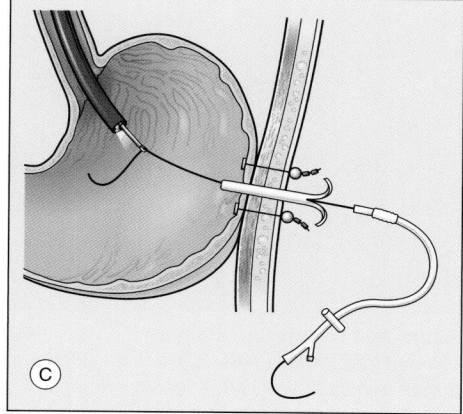

Figure 25–10. The Russell introducer percutaneous endoscopic gastrostomy (PEG) technique. *A,* After initial placement of the trocar and passage of a single stranded wire, the wire is held with some tension against external traction by a snare passed through the endoscope within the stomach. T-fasteners are then passed to secure the stomach up against the anterior abdominal wall. The top of this figure shows how the T-fasteners with attached suture are released by the canula device. *B,* Once the stomach is secured to the anterior abdominal wall, the tract is dilated over the guidewire by three Seldinger dilators of increasing size. After the last dilation, a peel-away sheath over the final dilator is passed into position and the dilator is removed. *C,* After first preloading an external bumper on the feeding tube, the feeding tube is passed over the wire through the peel-away sheath into the stomach where the internal bolster is inflated, the peel-away sheath is removed, and the external bolster is positioned down against the skin.

slot. After making a nick in the skin with a scalpel blade, the device is passed through the abdominal wall. The T-fastener is deployed in the stomach by a central canula. After removing the small trocar and canula for the T-fastener, a cotton roller ball and two metal fastening devices are cinched down until there is mild tension on the outer abdominal wall against the T-fastener on the inside of the stomach. Crimping the two metal fasteners holds the T-fastener in place. Anywhere from two to four T-fasteners should be placed circumferentially around the trocar before proceeding further (Fig. 25–10*A*).

With the stomach affixed to the anterior wall by the T-fasteners, the tract over the wire is dilated by Seldinger-type dilators of increasing size. Two to three dilators are passed over the wire as external traction is again placed against the snare holding the wire on the inside of the stomach (Fig. 25–10*B*). Once the tract has been fully dilated, a peel-away sheath overlying a larger bore canula is passed over the wire and into the stomach (Fig. 25–10*B*, bottom).

Most of the Russel introducer kits do not come with an external bolster and are designed or anticipated instead to be sutured to the skin. A simple homemade external bolster may be created by a short segment from any small Salem sump, Foley catheter, or other larger gauge feeding tube, and placed over the feeding tube before passage into the stomach (Fig. 25–10*C*). Once the external bolster is in place, the feeding tube may be placed over the wire through the peel-away sheath into the stomach. The internal balloon is then inflated, the peel-away sheath is removed, and the external bolster is then placed into position (Fig. 25–10*C*).

Percutaneous Endoscopic Gastrojejunostomy

For patients with documented intolerance to gastric feeding with nausea, vomiting, high gastric residual volumes, or evidence of gastroparesis, the PEGJ provides an easy although less reliable access to the small bowel. The success of this procedure is related to a number of factors. Localization of the PEG in the antrum is most important. The PEG should be cut down to approximately 10 cm in length to afford a maximum length of the jejunal tube for passage into the small bowel. If the PEGJ is performed at the time of initial PEG placement, then antibiotic prophylaxis should be used. A site just to the right and above the umbilicus is the best site for placement into the antrum. A pediatric colonoscope is important to try to get one to two loops below the ligament of Treitz. Biopsy forceps of at least 240 cm in length are important to have a sufficient working length beyond the tip of the colonoscope. The endoscopist should not use a snare to place wires in this procedure, because it can be difficult to extract the snare from the tip of the wire once it is positioned in the small bowel.

One of the most important elements in the success of this procedure is the function of an air retention valve (Fig. 25–11). Although a number of commercial models are available (top of Fig. 25–11), a homemade air valve can be made from the cap of the feeding tube (creating a hole with a pair of scissors) (bottom of Fig. 25–11). The air valve allows passage of a wire or a snare through the

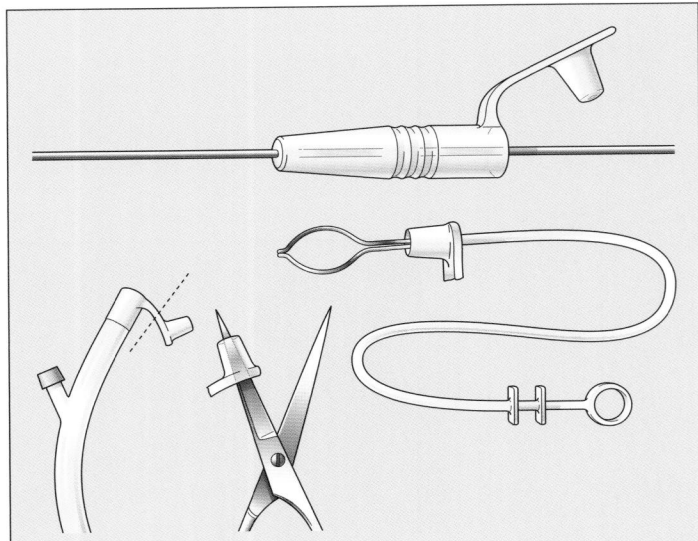

Figure 25–11. Commercial and homemade air valves. The top figure shows a commercial air valve passed over the guidewire, which is used most often during percutaneous endoscopic gastrojejunostomy (PEGJ) conversions. A homemade air valve may be created by cutting off the valve plug on a feeding tube, coring the valve out with a pair of scissors, and then passing a snare or wire through the valve.

PEG into the stomach without losing air insufflation. Failure to use or create an air valve significantly prolongs the procedure and can make visualization very difficult when passing the endoscope from the stomach into the small bowel.

THROUGH-THE-SNARE TECHNIQUE

This technique is the most reliable way to successfully position a PEGJ tube into the proximal jejunum at or below the ligament of Treitz. After cutting the PEG down to 10 cm, an air retention valve is fashioned and the snare is passed through the hole in the valve positioned in the PEG and on into the stomach. The snare is opened allowing the pediatric colonoscope to be passed down through the esophagus and stomach, through the snare, and on into the small bowel. Once the endoscope has been passed into the small bowel, the snare is closed once to make sure the scope has passed through the snare. The air plug may be backed out of the PEG at this point to decompress the stomach and prevent curling of the scope. The scope is passed hopefully one to two loops beyond the ligament of Treitz. At its deepest penetration, a guidewire is passed out further into the jejunum until gentle resistance is met. The key to success of this technique is the selection of a very long 480-cm standard guidewire. The usual wire that comes with PEG and PEGJ kits is usually substantially shorter than this (Fig. 25–12A). Using proper wire exchange techniques, the endoscope is withdrawn back to the proximal stomach above the level of the snare, keeping the tip of the wire in position in the small bowel (Fig. 25–12B). Once the scope has been brought back to approximately 45 cm (from the incisors), the air valve is placed back into the PEG to insufflate the stomach and confirm position of the scope above the snare (Fig. 25–12B). The snare is then closed on the wire and a loop of the wire is pulled out through the PEG to the outside (Fig. 25–12C). The endoscopist

separates the loop with his or her fingers and has an assistant pull on the proximal wire extending out from the proximal operating channel of the endoscope. The movement of one side of the loop helps identify that end of the wire coming from the endoscope (Fig. 25–12C). This end of the wire is then pulled out through the PEG, resulting in a straightened guidewire passing through the PEG and down into the small bowel (Fig. 25–12D). The jejunal tube is then passed over the wire (using good wire exchange technique) into position in the small bowel.

OVER-THE-GUIDEWIRE TECHNIQUE

Although this technique appears to be more simplified than the through-the-snare technique, it may be slightly more frustrating for proper placement of the jejunal tube well down into the small bowel. For this technique, an air retention valve is placed over a wire, and then the wire is passed through the PEG into the stomach. After passing the endoscope through the esophagus into the stomach, biopsy forceps are used to grasp the wire and walk it on down into the small bowel. The key to the success of this procedure is again using biopsy forceps that are at least 240 cm in length, to afford a sufficient working length out beyond the end of the colonoscope. The colonoscope is passed hopefully down to a level at or below the ligament of Treitz (Fig. 25–13A). With the biopsy forceps still holding the wire, they are slowly advanced as the scope is withdrawn back into the proximal stomach. The jejunal tube is then passed over the wire all the way down until it strikes the biopsy forceps still holding the tip of the wire in the small bowel (Fig. 25–13B). Only at this point are the biopsy forceps opened, releasing the wire. The biopsy forceps are withdrawn back into the endoscope. It is important for the endoscopist to realize that if shorter biopsy forceps are used, the jejunal tube may strike the forceps holding the end of the wire while there is still a significant length of jejunal tube remaining outside the PEG. Although it is appropriate to open the biopsy forceps and release the wire at this point, the added length of the jejunal tube outside the PEG as the jejunal tube is pushed down and seated into position in the PEG often forms a loop in the stomach and the procedure has to be repeated.

TRANS-PERCUTANEOUS ENDOSCOPIC GASTROSTOMY GASTROSCOPY TECHNIQUE

This technique may be performed with a small caliber gastroscope, as long as the patient's original PEG is 28-Fr in diameter. The technique can be performed through a PEG tube of smaller diameter, but a bronchoscope or ureteroscope may need to be substituted. The key to success with any of these small endoscopes is to stiffen the instrument by placing a biopsy forceps or a stiff guidewire down through the operating channel. Failure to do so will cause excessive looping in the stomach and possible inability to transcend the pylorus. In this simple technique, the endoscope is passed through the PEG, down through the pylorus and through the third and fourth portion of the duodenum. It is difficult to get beyond the ligament of Treitz with this scope alone, but passing the wire out through the end of the scope once it is positioned in the distal duodenum may allow passage of the wire into the proximal jejunum below the ligament of Treitz. The scope is then withdrawn and the jejunal tube is placed over the guidewire (Fig. 25–14).

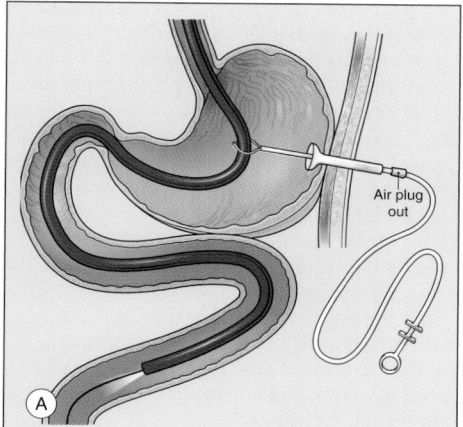

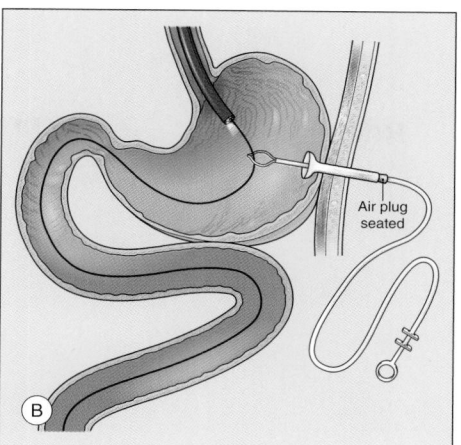

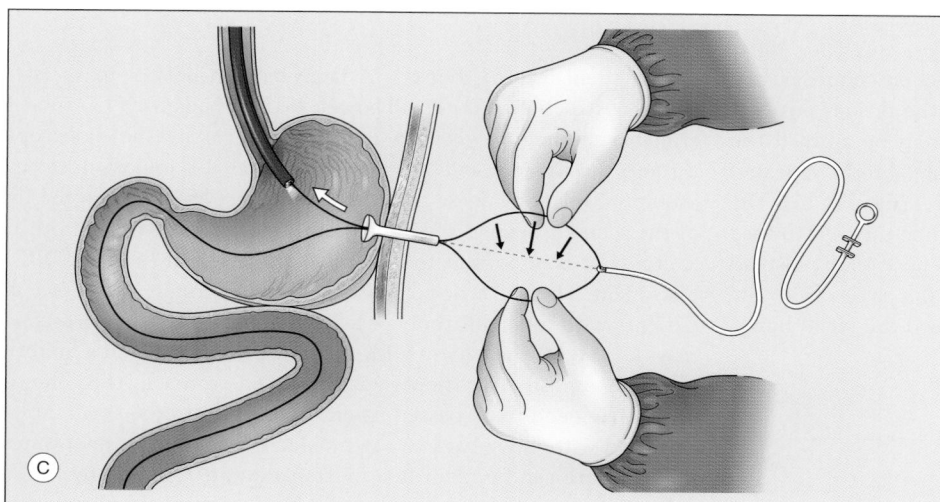

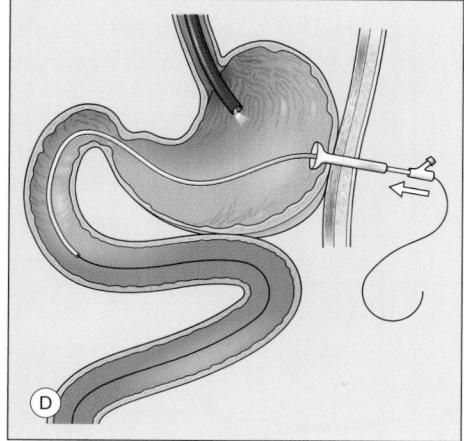

Figure 25–12. Through-the-snare percutaneous endoscopic gastrojejunostomy (PEGJ) technique. *A,* After initial placement of the percutaneous endoscopic gastrostomy (PEG), the PEG tube is cut down short to approximately 10 cm, and then a snare placed through a homemade or commercial air valve is passed into the stomach. A pediatric colonoscope is passed into the stomach, through the snare, and then down into the small bowel below the ligament of Treitz (after which the wire is extended beyond the end of the scope). *B,* Using careful wire transfer technique, the endoscope is withdrawn back to the proximal stomach, keeping the tip of the wire in place below the ligament of Treitz. The air plug may be seated to allow visualization of the snare within the stomach. The snare is then closed on the wire, which is pulled out through the PEG. *C,* While the assistant holds the wire loop coming out from the PEG, the operator pulls on the wire extruding from the operating channel of the scope, to indicate which side of the wire loop represents the proximal end of the wire. That loop is then pulled out through the PEG. *D,* The final jejunal extension tube is passed over the single stranded wire, which should be still positioned well below the ligament of Treitz.

SECURING THE PERCUTANEOUS ENDOSCOPIC GASTROJEJUNOSTOMY

The most frustrating aspect of the PEGJ procedure is that the jejunal tube commonly migrates back into the stomach. Two techniques may help prevent this. One is to use a rotatable hemoclip (Olympus America, Melville, NY) device to clip a suture affixed to the distal end of the feeding tube to the intestinal mucosa. Although this is easy to perform, the hemoclip only holds the suture reliably in place for 7 to 10 days. A second technique is shown in Figure 25–15, in which an anchor is created with a 1-cm segment from some other piece of tubing. A Salem sump, Foley catheter, or some other feeding tube may be used to create the 1-cm anchor. A 20-cm length of suture is affixed to the distal end of the feeding tube and then secured to the anchor. The anchor is simply placed over the guidewire ahead of the jejunal feeding tube in the final step of the PEGJ procedure, as the jejunal tube is passed over the wire into position in the small bowel (Fig. 25–15).

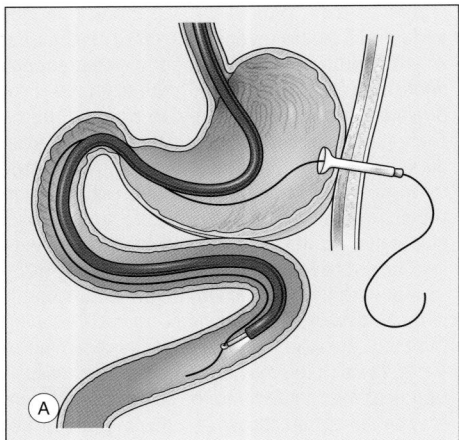
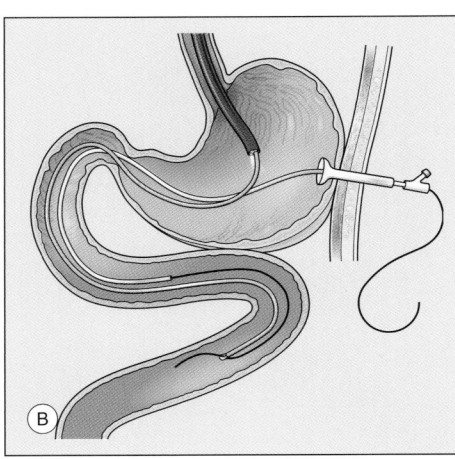

Figure 25–13. Over-the-guidewire percutaneous endoscopic gastrojejunostomy (PEGJ) technique. *A,* A single stranded guidewire passed through a valve (which is seated in the percutaneous endoscopic gastrostomy [PEG]) is grasped by biopsy forceps (passed down through a pediatric colonoscope). The endoscope holding the wire (via biopsy forceps) is passed down into the small bowel below the ligament of Treitz. *B,* The endoscope is then withdrawn back into the stomach as the biopsy forceps are pushed outward through the end of the scope, holding the wire in place below the ligament of Treitz. Once the scope has been withdrawn back into the proximal stomach, the jejunal extension tube is passed over the wire until the distal end strikes the biopsy forceps at the end of the wire.

It is important at the completion of the PEGJ procedure by any of these methods that the operator confirms the proper position endoscopically. If the jejunal tube forms a loop up toward the gastroesophageal junction, the procedure may need to be repeated to achieve deeper positioning into the small bowel (Fig. 25–16). The natural action of this loop is to displace the tube upward toward the fundus, out from the small bowel. Proper positioning instead should have the appearance that the jejunal tube passes from the PEG directly toward the pylorus and down into the small bowel (Fig. 25–16).

Direct Percutaneous Endoscopic Jejunostomy

Although DPEJ may be the most technically demanding procedure for enteral access, it provides probably the most reliable semi-permanent access for the patient who has had difficulty with gastroparesis, nausea, vomiting, and previous intolerance to gastric feeding. Similar to an initial PEG placement, antibiotic prophylaxis is required for the DPEJ technique. Although the DPEJ technique is very similar to the Ponsky pull or Sachs-Vine push technique for PEG, a number of important differences exist. First, a much larger area of the abdomen from the costal margins bilaterally down to the iliac crests on both sides may need to be prepped, because transillumination may occur anywhere over the abdomen. If the patient has had previous partial gastrectomy and rerouting of the GI tract, the DPEJ may end up being placed significantly to the right of the midline. The DPEJ is a two-person procedure, requiring someone at the level of the skin and a skilled endoscopist with the scope. The endoscopist should anticipate taking much longer time to transilluminate (anywhere from 5 to 30 minutes) and finger palpate a site. It is most appropriate to use a 21- to 23-gauge spinal needle as a sounding needle in attempts to intubate the small bowel. Again, the endoscopist should anticipate many more needlesticks with the small gauge spinal needle compared with the PEG technique. The Ponsky pull technique is better suited for DPEG. The plastic leader on the Sachs-Vine push technique may not be long enough to reach the small bowel site. Most importantly, a tube should be selected

with a small internal bolster. A large balloon bolster may cause partial obstruction of the small bowel. A 15-Fr pediatric PEG tube is available commercially with a flat bolster. In passing the endoscope through the stomach and into the small bowel, it is important to pay attention to landmarks so that the endoscopist knows when the tip of the scope is beyond the duodenum. In a patient with Billroth II anatomy, it is important to document the efferent limb for DPEJ placement. The pediatric colonoscope is the instrument of choice in patients with intact anatomy or a "virgin abdomen." A gastroscope may be used for the patient with a partial gastrectomy and a Billroth II reanastomosis. In patients with an intact stomach, the colonoscope may need to be passed its entire length into the small intestines and withdrawn back to the proximal duodenum several times before a site can be identified by transillumination and by finger palpation.

At the beginning of the procedure, the physician at the skin should have the anesthetic needle and syringe in one hand and the sounding needle in the other hand. As he or she gets transillumination, a quick brief injection of the local anesthetic is followed by a quick abrupt puncture with the sounding needle. Care should be taken not to pass the sounding needle more proximally into the shaft of the endoscope. The endoscopist should place a snare through the instrument and out into the lumen, anticipating passage of the

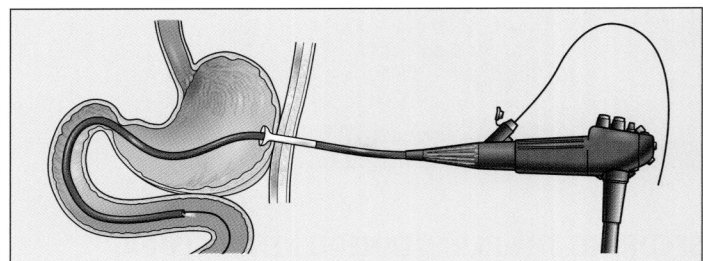

Figure 25–14. Trans-percutaneous endoscopic gastrostomy (PEG) gastroscope percutaneous endoscopic gastrojejunostomy (PEGJ) technique. After first stiffening the small-caliber 5.5-mm gastroscope with a biopsy forceps, the endoscope is passed through the PEG down to the distal duodenum and proximal jejunum. After removing the biopsy forceps, a single-stranded guidewire is passed out through the end of the endoscope hopefully beyond the ligament of Treitz. After the scope is withdrawn, the jejunal extension tube is passed over the wire.

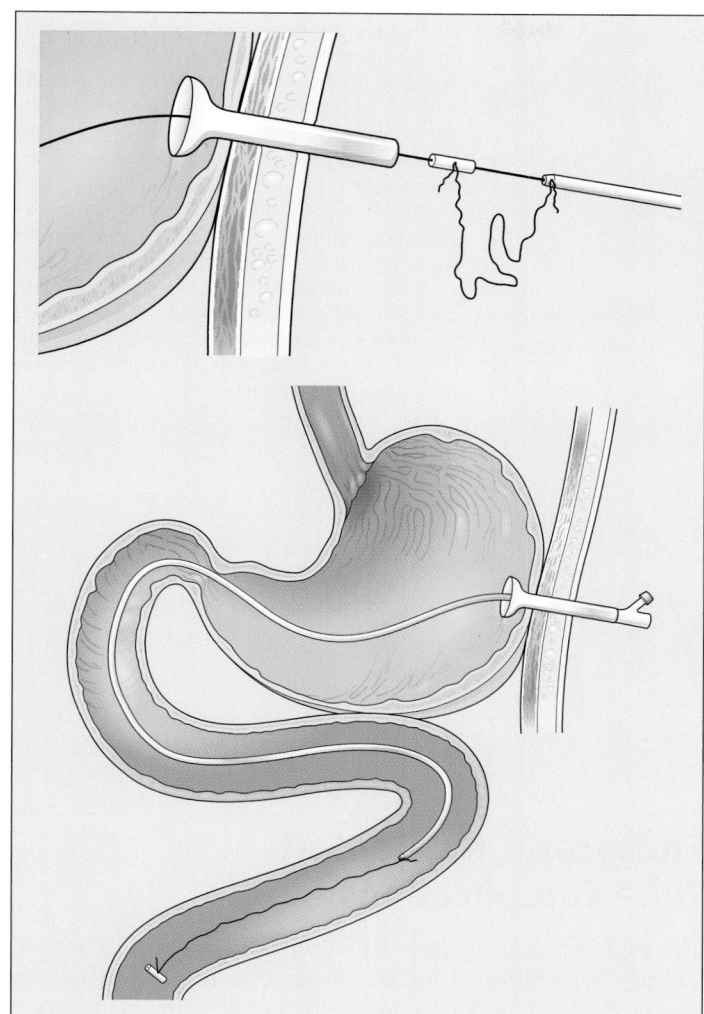

Figure 25–15. Creation of a percutaneous endoscopic gastrojejunostomy (PEGJ) anchor. A single 1-cm section of tubing is created from any tube that is roughly the same diameter as the feeding tube, which is then attached to the distal end of the feeding tube via a 20-cm silk suture. The anchor segment is preloaded on the guidewire ahead of the feeding tube and then passed down into position in the distal duodenum and proximal jejunum. After removal of the wire, the anchor hopefully will pass distally and help hold the distal tip of the jejunal extension tube in place.

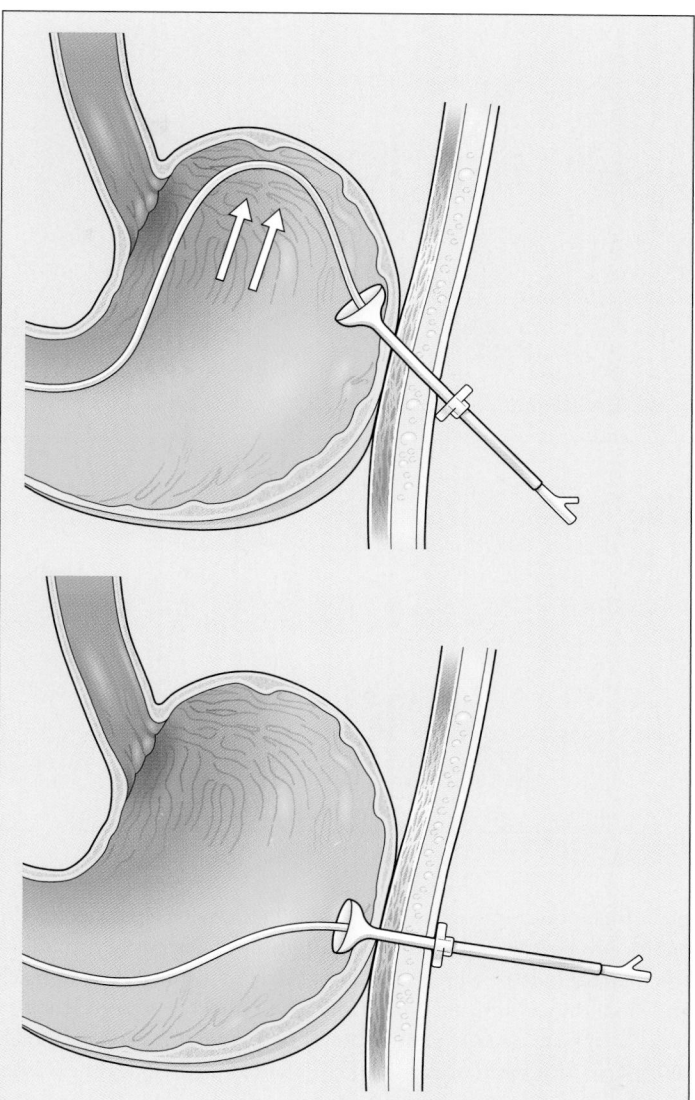

Figure 25–16. Appropriate position of the jejunal extension tube after percutaneous endoscopic gastrojejunostomy (PEGJ) conversion. Poor placement is demonstrated by the upper figure, which shows that the jejunal tube passes toward the gastroesophageal junction before looping and then passing down to the pylorus. If the tube is left in this position after placement, this loop will serve to displace the tip of the jejunal tube back into the stomach. The figure below shows proper positioning of the jejunal extension tube, in which the tube passes from the percutaneous endoscopic gastrostomy (PEG) directly toward the pylorus and on into the small bowel.

sounding needle into the lumen of the small bowel (Fig. 25–17A). Once the small bowel is intubated, the sounding needle is grasped firmly with the snare and held in place by the endoscopist. The skin physician then takes the trocar and passes alongside the sounding needle in the same axis to achieve intubation in the small bowel (Fig. 25–17B). Glucagon may be given intravenously at this point to maintain a hypotonic bowel. A recent commercial model of a DPEJ device has combined the sounding needle and trocar together as one piece, making this section of the DPEJ technique a one-step procedure. Once the trocar is passed into the lumen of the small bowel, the snare is released from the sounding needle and repo-

sitioned on the trocar. The sounding needle is withdrawn and removed. Still holding the bowel in place with the snare affixed to the trocar, a wire is passed through the trocar into the small bowel, and the snare is slipped off the trocar, grabbing the wire within the lumen of the small bowel (Fig. 25–17C). The wire is then fed through the trocar as the endoscopist removes the wire out through the stomach, esophagus, and the patient's mouth. Only at this point (Fig. 25–17D) is further local anesthesia applied in the area of the wire, and an incision is made with the scalpel.

With the wire protruding out from the patient's mouth, the DPEJ tube is placed using either the Ponsky pull or the Sachs-Vine

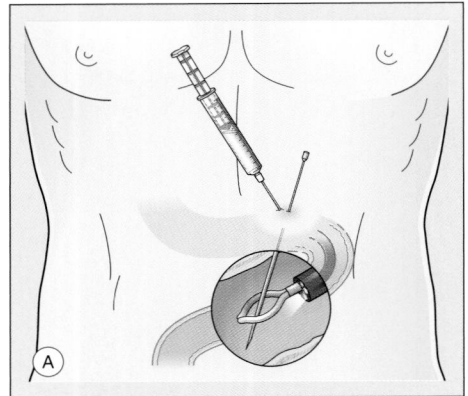
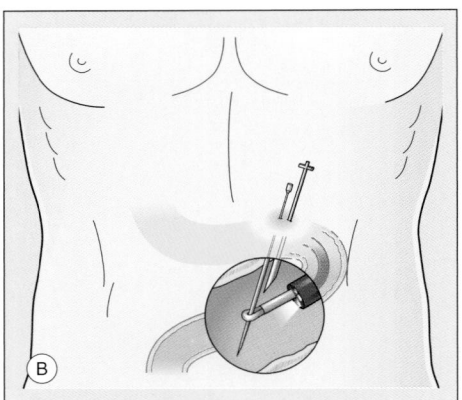
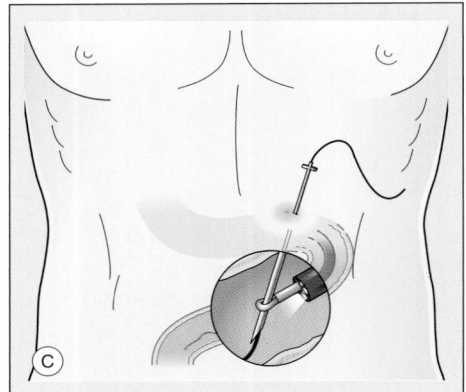
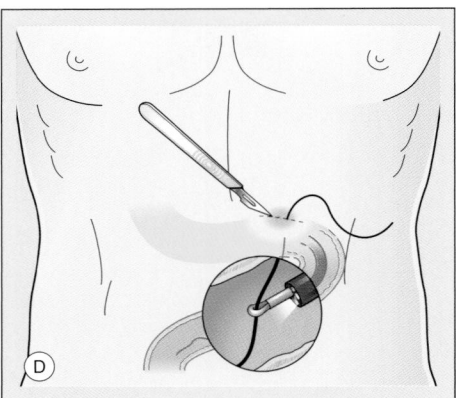

Figure 25-17. Direct percutaneous endoscopic jejunostomy (DPEJ) technique. *A,* After quick initial skin anesthesia, a 23-gauge sounding needle is passed into the small bowel and grasped with a snare passed through the operating channel of the endoscope positioned in the small bowel. *B,* While holding the sounding needle in place with the snare, the trocar is passed at the same angle into the small bowel. The snare is opened, the sounding needle is withdrawn, and the snare is transferred to the trocar. *C,* A guidewire is then passed through the trocar, the snare is opened enough to fall back onto the wire, and then the trocar is removed. *D,* Only after the wire has been grabbed firmly by the snare should the skin incision be made over the guidewire. Once the wire has been withdrawn out through the mouth, the final placement is made using the Ponsky Pull or Sachs-Vine Push technique.

push technique. In comparison to the PEG (where passage of the endoscope postplacement is optional), it may be necessary to follow the internal bolster with the endoscope down through the stomach and small bowel into final position. The bolster has a tendency to pop down from one segment of bowel to the next. It can be difficult to confirm final position of the DPEJ "blinded feel" alone, by measuring the distances (using the calibrated markings on the tube) between the skin and the internal bolster, or by palpating the internal bolster transabdominally with tension on the tubes. Securing the end of the endoscope to the internal bolster with a snare (such as described earlier for the PEG procedure) will help facilitate this process.

Postprocedure Care

Patient management and care of the enteral access site postplacement is essentially the same for all of the percutaneous techniques. Patients are generally held nil per os (NPO) for 3 to 4 hours after initial placement, after which feeds may be initiated. Starting at a lower infusion rate of 25 mL/hour, feeds may be advanced as tolerated quickly every 6 to 12 hours such that goal infusion rate is obtained within 24 to 48 hours. For the first 7 to 10 days, hydrogen peroxide should be used once per day to clean the access site, after which soap and water washes should be sufficient (continued peroxide washes may be corrosive). Bandage dressings should be changed daily over this initial period. There should be ½ to 1 cm of play between the skin and external bolster. After 7 to 10 days, the frequency of dressing changes may be decreased.

Endoscopic Nasoenteric Tube Complications

The most common complication of the ENET procedure is postinsertion displacement. Tubes placed intentionally in the small bowel may be displaced back into the stomach in 3.7% to 7% of cases.[12] Inadvertent removal of the nasoenteric tube completely occurs in 21% to 41% of patients.[13,14] Surprisingly, inadvertent removal does not always occur in a setting with the typical profile of the patient with altered mental status. Most cases of inadvertent removal involve patients with normal mental status, occurring as a result of routine nursing duties (arising from bed, transport out of the unit, physical therapy) when there has been failure to secure the tube by proper methods.[13] Securing the distal end of the nasoenteric feeding tube by using a hemoclip (securing a suture on the tip of the tube to the intestinal mucosa) will not prevent displacement of the tube manually by the patient. Securing the proximal end with a nasal bridle or some kind of bandage clipping device (securing the proximal end to the skin) is needed. Displacement of nasoenteric tubes on initial placement occurs in 0.3% to 15% of cases (mean 3% to 4%), but this is related more to blinded, bedside techniques using aspirate pH and auscultatory methods.[12,14,15] In these cases, pneumothorax, bronchopleural fistula, and even empyema (resulting from infusion of formula into the lung) may occur.[12] These latter complications do not usually occur as a result of endoscopic placement.

Additional minor complications include epistaxis, persistent gagging, knotting, breaking and kinking of the tube, or occlusion of the tube from clogging of the formula. Clogged feeding tubes are best treated with a pancreatin (Viokase) tablet crushed in warm water with bicarbonate, placed in a 10-mL syringe, and used as an irrigating solution. This has been shown in formal testing to be superior to a variety of soft drinks and papain (or meat tenderizer).[16] If the clot fails to clear with this irrigating solution alone, an endoscopic retrograde cholangiopancreatography (ERCP) catheter should be placed down through the tube to the level of the clot and infusion of the irrigating solution should be delivered directly at the site of the clot. If the clogged tube persists, further efforts to clear the clot may be accomplished by a mechanical declogging device such as an endoscopy brush or spiral-shaped mechanical declogger that can actually be rotated or screwed through the obstruction.

Sinusitis is a complication of prolonged nasoenteric tube placement and should be a consideration in patients with such tubes who develop an unexplained fever. The incidence of sinusitis based on opacification of sinuses on radiograph or CT scan tends to be over-reported at approximately 25%, whereas needle puncture and culture of effluent from the sinuses more accurately places the incidence at approximately 11.4%.[17] Esophageal stricture is a theoretical complication of long standing nasoenteric tubes, but the incidence is not clear and is probably under-reported. A longstanding nasal bridle, in place for greater than 1 to 2 months' duration, may erode through the nasal septum.

Percutaneous Endoscopic Gastrostomy Complications

Reports from the literature of overall complications related to PEG placement indicate that this minimally invasive procedure has low morbidity and negligible mortality.[18,19] Two large series published 10 to 15 years ago showed that the incidence of minor complications ranged from 4.9% to 13%, with major complications ranging from 1.3% to 3%.[18,19] Mortality in these two large series was only 0.2% to 1%.[18,19] Two large more recent series published within the past 3 years duplicated these results, showing that the rate of minor complications ranged from 10.3% to 10.7% and the rate of major complications ranged from 1% to 2.4%.[20,21] There was no mortality in these more recent series. Minor complications described in these reports include peristomal wound infections, tube disintegration, clogging, leakage, prolonged ileus, late inadvertent extubation, subcostal neuralgia, laceration of the left lobe of the liver, and delayed closure after removal. Major complications reported include aspiration, peritonitis, early premature removal, tumor implantation at the PEG site, buried bumper syndrome, gastrocolocutaneous fistula, necrotizing fasciitis, and hemorrhage.[18–21]

A benign pneumoperitoneum occurs in up to 40% of cases after routine PEG placement.[22] In the absence of peritoneal signs (e.g., rebound tenderness), this finding is innocuous and does not preclude feeding within 4 hours of tube placement. Pneumoperitoneum may or may not be accompanied by a large air-filled distended stomach, which can easily be decompressed by uncapping the newly placed PEG tube.[23] Prolonged ileus after PEG placement was described in 1% of patients in one large series.[21]

The incidence of aspiration after PEG placement is difficult to determine because of varying definitions (witnessed aspiration event versus new infiltrate on chest radiograph vs. aspiration of gastric contents labeled with a radioisotope or fluoroscopic colorimetric microsphere). The risk of aspiration immediately related to the procedure of PEG placement has been reported to be less than 1% of cases[18,24] and is thought to be related to oversedation, over-inflation of the stomach, and performance of the procedure in the supine position. Aspiration as a long-term complication of PEG placement has been reported in up to 18% of cases.[25] In one small prospective study, patients randomized to PEG placement had lower gastroesophageal reflux (as measured by 24-hour pH monitoring) compared with patients randomized to nasogastric feeding.[26] Risk for aspiration long-term is related to patient age (older than 70), reduced level of consciousness, history of neuromuscular disease, delayed gastric emptying, endotracheal intubation, trauma to the abdomen or pelvis, bolus versus continuous feeds, and nursing care.[27,28] Risk for aspiration increases fourfold when patients are moved from the ICU (low patient-to-nurse ratio) out to the medical or surgical floor (high ratio).[27] These studies reporting aspiration post-PEG placement do not usually differentiate aspiration of contaminated oropharyngeal secretions from regurgitation and aspiration of contaminated gastric contents. At lease three studies would suggest that the aspiration of contaminated oropharyngeal secretions is at least an equivalent if not greater factor in colonizing the trachea and upper respiratory tree than aspiration of bacteria-laden gastric contents.[29–31] Poor oral health has been well defined as an additional risk factor for aspiration in patients on tube feeding.[32]

Buried bumper is an under-reported syndrome ranging from ulceration underneath the internal bolster to total erosion of the PEG tube out through the gastric and abdominal wall. It most often occurs as a result of excessive tension between the external and internal bolster, but additional predisposing factors include smaller, stiffer internal bolsters (made from silicone compared with polyurethane), presence of malnutrition or poor wound healing, or a significant weight gain in response to feeding.[24] Buried bumper syndrome may present simply as increased leakage around the PEG, infection at the PEG site, immobility of the catheter, resistance to infusion, or abdominal pain occurring with infusion of formula.[23,24,33,34] A wide variety of techniques are described in the literature to manage this complication. Usually the PEG tube has to be removed either by pulling it back into the stomach and out through the mouth or by pulling it out through the abdominal wall. In patients in whom the PEG tube has not been used from several weeks to months, the internal bolster may be completely buried within the gastric or abdominal wall. In this situation, a needle-knife thermocoagulation catheter may be required to cut down to the bolster to facilitate removal.[33]

Gastrocolocutaneous fistulas may occur because of inadvertent puncture of an overlying loop of bowel at the time of initial placement or as a delayed complication occurring because of migration or erosion of the tube over time into the colon.[24,35] Insufficient transillumination, inadequate gastric insufflation at the time of initial placement, or previous abdominal surgery in which a loop of bowel may be tacked down by scar tissue are all risk factors increasing the likelihood for this complication.[23,24] Gastrocolocutaneous fistula may present acutely with peritonitis, infection, fasciitis, or obstruction to flow of infusion of the formula. More often, it occurs chronically, presenting after several months with either stool appearing around the PEG tube or as insidious diarrhea in which the stool has the appearance of formula identical to that infused into the PEG. Frequently, this complication is not identified until the tube is removed and stool appears at the ostomy site. This complication is managed by first documenting the complication with radiographic contrast studies. Surprisingly, it is managed easily by simply removing the PEG, placing a bandage over the defect, and allowing the site to heal. Operative takedown is only required if the fistula fails to close.[23,24]

PEG site infection is one the most common complications of PEG placement. Risk for developing PEG site infection is related to patient factors (e.g., diabetes, obesity, malnutrition, or chronic use of steroids), factors involving technique (pull or push type PEGs vs. introducer PEGs, small incisions, and lack of antibiotic prophylaxis), and nursing care (excessive traction on the bolsters). The incidence of wound infection around the PEG site ranges from 5.4% to 17%,[25,36,37] but the majority (more than 70%) are minor in degree.[38] Antibiotic prophylaxis at the time of initial placement is an important measure to reduce the incidence of this complication. In an older study, a single dose of antibiotic prophylaxis at the time of placement reduced the incidence of PEG site infection from 32% to 7% ($p < .05$).[39] In a more recent study, a single dose of one or two antibiotics at the time of placement reduced the incidence of PEG site infection significantly from 13.2% to 0.5% compared with controls receiving no antibiotic prophylaxis ($p < .01$).[38] Patients already on concurrent antibiotics do not need additional prophylaxis at the time of PEG placement.[40] If infection develops around the PEG site, usually intravenous antibiotics and local wound care are sufficient to correct the complication. Surgical incision and drainage are rarely required. Actual peritonitis occurs less often in 0.4% to 1.5% of cases[18,24,35,41] and is differentiated from simple PEG site infection by the development of peritoneal signs and rebound tenderness. Again, prompt broad-spectrum intravenous antibiotics are usually sufficient. However, in the presence of peritonitis, contrast studies should be performed to rule out the presence of a leak. If there is leakage into the peritoneum, then surgical intervention is required.[24]

Hemorrhage is a rare complication involving less than 2.5% of cases.[24,35] A variety of etiologic factors may contribute to this complication, including direct puncture of a blood vessel or traumatic tearing of the esophagus or stomach on initial placement, concomitant peptic ulcer disease, development of gastric ulcer underneath the internal bolster, or erosion of the posterior gastric wall opposite from the internal bolster of the PEG tube.[24,35] Management involves urgent endoscopy to document the source and appropriate steps to achieve hemostasis.

Leakage around the PEG site is reported in only 1% to 2% of cases,[21,41] but this probably represents under-reporting of the incidence of this complication. Etiologic factors include corrosive agents (vitamin C ascorbic acid infused with formula, increased gastric acid arising from stop orders for prescribed acid-reducing agents, and continued peroxide washes of the site after initial placement), cutaneous fungal infection around the site, development of granulation tissue, side-torsion on the tube creating ulceration on one wall of the tract, absence of an external bolster (allowing to-and-fro motion of the PEG tube through the tract), buried bumper syndrome, and PEG site infection. Management again depends on defining the exacerbating factors, which can usually be ascertained by careful examination of the PEG site. Initial physical examination should rule out PEG site infection, make sure there is no fixation of the tube (suggesting buried bumper syndrome), and make sure there is no ulceration of the tract indicating side-torsion. The patient's list of medications should be reviewed, a proton pump inhibitor should be added if this agent has not been ordered, ascorbic acid should be stopped, and consideration should be given to providing an antifungal cream or zinc oxide to the site. Side-torsion creating ulceration in the tract may require stabilization of the PEG tube with a vertical clamp (which prevents side-to-side motion). Granulation tissue around the PEG site may be treated with silver nitrate sticks. Options of an external bolster may be easily corrected by replacing the PEG tube with a replacement PEG set that contains an external bolster or by creating a homemade external bolster from the funneled end of a Foley catheter. PEG site infection should be treated, as should existence of the buried bumper syndrome according to previously described methods. In some cases, the tract may be damaged to the point that diverting the stream of infused formula down into the small bowel (by converting the PEG to a PEGJ) or completely removing the PEG tube and placing a nasoenteric aspirate/feed tube to allow the site to heal may be required in more severe cases.

Accidental extubation of the PEG tube occurs in anywhere from 1.6% to 4.4% of cases, half of which occur prematurely before complete maturation of the PEG site.[20,25,35,37,42] Normally the PEG site should mature over 7 to 10 days with the gastric wall fused to the anterior abdominal wall. Maturation of the PEG tract may be delayed up to 3 to 4 weeks in the presence of chronic steroid use, malnutrition, or ascites. Management is surprisingly simple a long as no peritonitis is present.[35] A nasogastric (NG) tube can be placed for decompression, a broad-spectrum antibiotic should be started, and the PEG may be replaced within 7 to 10 days. Only if peritonitis develops is surgical intervention required.[35] Once the PEG tract is mature, simple bedside replacement with a PEG tube may be sufficient or endoscopic placement if the site closes down.

Less common complications of PEG placement include tumor implantation at the PEG site, development of a bronchoesophageal fistula, migration of the internal balloon bolster causing gastric outlet obstruction at the level of the pylorus, reversible apnea, subcostal neuralgia, and development of a gastroileocutaneous fistula.[20,43–47]

Percutaneous Endoscopic Gastrojejunostomy and Direct Percutaneous Endoscopic Jejunostomy Complications

For obvious reasons, patients requiring placement of a PEGJ are at risk for all of the complications previously described for placement of a routine PEG tube. The most common additional problem encountered with PEGJ tubes is inadvertent migration of the jejunal tube from the small bowel back into the stomach, which occurs in

27% to 42% of cases.[48-50] A number of factors contribute to this complication including a large dilated atonic stomach, failure to cut the PEG tube down to a shortened length, shorter length of the jejunal tube, placement of the initial PEG high in the stomach, surgical PEG placement (in which the PEG tube is tunneled pointing toward the gastroesophageal junction), and recurrent nausea and vomiting. Steps that can be taken at the time of initial placement to reduce this complication include positioning the PEG tube immediately above and to the right of the umbilicus so that the entrance is in the gastric antrum, cutting the PEG tube down to approximately 10 cm in length, selecting a jejunal tube with the greatest length, and making sure that there is no loop in the stomach as the jejunal tube passes from the PEG to the pylorus. As mentioned earlier in the section on technique of PEGJ placement, securing the distal end to the intestinal mucosa with a hemoclip or placement of an anchor device may help hold the jejunal tube in place for a brief time.

Complications arising from DPEJ placement again differ very little from routine PEG placement. Of note is the fact that a jejunocolocutaneous fistula may occur. Intermittent small bowel obstruction may occur with a larger balloon-type internal bolster is selected for the procedure. Volvulus leading to necrotic bowel has been described with DPEG.[51]

Conclusion

Nutrition support teams across the country are pressured to obtain early enteral access, because the weight of the literature shows that early use of the gut and maintenance of gut integrity significantly affects patient outcome. These teams rely on a skilled endoscopist to obtain enteral access, monitor enteral tube feeding, and help troubleshoot problems when the issue of intolerance arises. When a short-term nasoenteric feeding is required, or more long-term percutaneous access is needed, a variety of techniques exist for almost any patient situation. Under each category of access, the endoscopist should learn one main technique well and then experiment enough with all of the techniques to know which one suits him or her best. Proper choice of instrument, correct accessory devices, and selection of the appropriate technique for the individual patient needs should optimize the chances for success and minimize the risk of complications when performing endoscopic procedures to obtain enteral access.

REFERENCES

1. McClave SA, Mallampalli A: Nutrition in the ICU, Part I: Enteral feeding—When and why? J Crit Illness 16:197–204, 2001.
2. Kudsk KA: Importance of enteral feeding in maintaining gut integrity. JPEN J Parenter Enteral Nutr 25:S2–S8, 2001.
3. Kudsk KA, Croce MA, Fabian TC: Enteral versus parenteral feeding. Effects on septic morbidity after blunt and penetrating abdominal trauma. Ann Surg 215:503–513, 1992.
4. McClave SA, Snider HL: The gut in nutritional management of acute pancreatitis. Clin Perspect Gastroenterol 2:86–92, 1999.
5. Braunschweig CL, Levy P, Sheean PM, Wang X: Enteral compared with parenteral nutrition: A meta-analysis. Am J Clin Nutr 74:534–542, 2001.
6. Lewis SJ, Egger M, Sylvester PA, Thomas S: Early enteral feeding versus "nil by mouth" after gastrointestinal surgery: Systematic review and meta-analysis of controlled studies. BMJ 323:1–5, 2001.
7. Smith I, Fleming S, Cernaianu A: Mishaps during transport from the intensive care unit. Crit Care Med 18:278–281, 1990.
8. Evans A, Winslow EH: Oxygen saturation and hemodynamic response in critically ill, mechanically ventilated adults during intrahospital transport. Am J Crit Care 4:106–111, 1995.
9. Heyland DK, Drover JW, Macdonald S, et al: Effect of postpyloric feeding on gastroesophageal regurgitation and pulmonary microaspiration: Results of a randomized controlled trial. Crit Care Med 29:1495–1501, 2001.
10. Lien HC, Chang CS, Chen GH: Can percutaneous endoscopic jejunostomy prevent gastroesophageal reflux in patients with preexisting esophagitis? Am J Gastroenterol 95:3439–3443, 2000.
11. Heyland DK, Drover JW, Dhaliwal R, Greenwood J: Optimizing the benefits and minimizing the risks of enteral nutrition in the critically ill: Role of small bowel feeding. JPEN J Parenter Enteral Nutr 26(6 Suppl):S51–55; discussion S56–57, 2002.
12. Levy H: Nasogastric and nasoenteric feeding tubes. Gastroenterol Endosc Clin North Am 8:529–550, 1998.
13. McClave SA, Sexton LK, Spain DA, et al: Enteral tube feeding in the intensive care unit: Factors impeding adequate delivery. Crit Care Med 27:1252–1256, 1999.
14. Metheny N, Dettenmeier P, Hampton K, et al: Detection of inadvertent respiratory placement of small-bore feeding tubes: A report of 10 cases. Heart Lung 19:631–638, 1990.
15. Roubenoff R, Ravich WJ: Pneumothorax due to nasogastric tubes. Report of four cases, review of the literature, and recommendations for prevention. Arch Intern Med 149:184–188, 1989.
16. Marcuard SP, Stegall KL, Trogdon S: Clearing obstructed feeding tubes. JPEN J Parenter Enteral Nutr 13:81–83, 1989.
17. George DL, Falk PS, Umberto Meduri G, et al: Nosocomial sinusitis in patients in the medical intensive care unit: A prospective epidemiological study. Clin Infect Dis 27:463–470, 1998.
18. Larson DE, Burton DD, Schroeder KW, et al: Percutaneous endoscopic gastrostomy: Indications, success, complications, and mortality in 314 consecutive patients. Gastroenterology 93:48–52, 1987.
19. Grant JP: Percutaneous endoscopic gastrostomy. Ann Surg 217:168–174, 1993.
20. Rimon E: The safety and feasibility of percutaneous endoscopic gastrostomy placement by a single physician. Endoscopy 33:241–244, 2001.
21. Lin HS, Ibrahim HZ, Kheng JW, et al: Percutaneous endoscopic gastrostomy: Strategies for prevention and management of complications. Laryngoscope 111:1847–1852, 2001.
22. Gottfried EB, Plumser AB, Clair MR: Pneumoperitoneum following percutaneous endoscopic gastrostomy. Gastroenterol Endosc 32:397–399, 1986.
23. Baskin WN: Enteral access techniques. Gastroenterologist 4:S40–S56, 1996.
24. Safidi BY, Marks JM, Ponsky JL: Percutaneous endoscopy gastrostomy. Gastroenterol Endosc Clin North Am 8:551–558, 1998.
25. James A, Kapur K, Hawthorne AB: Long-term outcome of percutaneous endoscopic gastrostomy feeding in patients with dysphagic stroke. Age Ageing 27:671–676, 1998.
26. Johnson DA, Hacker JF, Benjamin SB, et al: Percutaneous endoscopic gastrostomy effects on gastroesophageal reflux and the lower esophageal sphincter. Am J Gastroenterol 82:622–624, 1987.
27. Mullan H, Roubenoff RA, Roubenoff R: Risk of pulmonary aspiration among patients receiving enteral nutrition support. JPEN J Parenter Enteral Nutr 16:160–164, 1992.
28. McClave SA, DeMeo MT, DeLegge MH, et al: North American Summit on Aspiration in the Critically Ill Patient: Consensus statement. JPEN J Parenter Enteral Nutr 26(6 Suppl):S80–85, 2002.

29. Pingleton SK, Hinthorn DR, Liu C: Enteral nutrition in patients receiving mechanical ventilation. Multiple sources of tracheal colonization include the stomach. Am J Med 80:827–832, 1986.

30. Torres A, el-Ebiary M, Gonzalez J, et al: Gastric and pharyngeal flora in nosocomial pneumonia acquired during mechanical ventilation. Am Rev Respir Dis 148:352–357, 1993.

31. Bonten MJ, Gaillard CA, van Tiel FH, et al: The stomach is not a source for colonization of the upper respiratory tract and pneumonia in ICU patients. Chest 105:878–884, 1994.

32. DeRiso AJ 2nd, Ladowski JS, Dillon TA, et al: Chlorhexidine gluconate 0.12% oral rinse reduces the incidence of total nosocomial respiratory infection and nonprophylactic systemic antibiotic use in patients undergoing heart surgery. Chest 109:1556–1561, 1996.

33. Ma MM, Semlacher EA, Fedorak RN, et al: The buried gastrostomy bumper syndrome: Prevention and endoscopic approaches to removal. Gastroenterol Endosc 4:505–508, 1995.

34. Boyd JW, DeLegge MH, Schamburek RD, et al: The buried bumper syndrome: A new technique for safe, endoscopic PEG removal. Gastroenterol Endosc 41:508–511, 1995.

35. Schapiro GD, Edmundowicz SA: Complications of percutaneous endoscopic gastrostomy. Gastroenterol Endosc Clin North Am 6:409–422, 1996.

36. Lockett MA, Templeton ML, Byrne TK, Norcross ED: Percutaneous endoscopic gastrostomy complications in a tertiary-care center. Am Surg 68:117–120, 2002.

37. Dwyer KM, Watts DD, Thurber JS, et al: Percutaneous endoscopic gastrostomy: The preferred method of elective feeding tube placement in trauma patients. J Trauma 52:26–32, 2002.

38. Gossner L, Keymling J, Hahn EG, Ell C: Antibiotic prophylaxis in percutaneous endoscopic gastrostomy (PEG): A prospective randomized clinical trial. Endoscopy 31:119–124, 1999.

39. Jain NK, Larson DE, Schroeder KW, et al: Antibiotic prophylaxis for percutaneous endoscopic gastrostomy. Ann Intern Med 107:824–828, 1987.

40. Sturgis TM, Yancy W, Cole JC, et al: Antibiotic prophylaxis in percutaneous endoscopic gastrostomy. Am J Gastroenterol 91:2301–2304, 1996.

41. Abuksis G, Mor M, Segal N, et al: Percutaneous endoscopic gastrostomy: High mortality rates in hospitalized patients. Am J Gastroenterol 95:128–132, 2000.

42. Galat SA, Gerig KD, Porter JA, et al: Management of premature removal of the percutaneous endoscopic gastrostomy. Am Surg 56:733–736, 1990.

43. De Vogelaere K, De Backer A, Vandenplas Y, Deconinck P: Gastroileocutaneous fistula: An unusual complication of percutaneous endoscopic gastrostomy. Endoscopy 32:S3–4, 2000.

44. Clancy MJ, Hunter DC: Tube migration causing gastric outlet obstruction: An unusual complication of percutaneous endoscopic gastrostomy. Endoscopy 32:S58, 2000.

45. Bilijam C, Hulsbergen M, Bosman D, Taminiau J: Bronchoesophageal fistula as a complication of percutaneous endoscopic gastrostomy. Endoscopy 32:S26–27, 2000.

46. Segal D, Michaud L, Guimber D, et al: Late-onset complications of percutaneous endoscopic gastrostomy in children. J Pediatr Gastroenterol Nutr 33:495–500, 2001.

47. Schiano TD, Pfister D, Harrison L, et al: Neoplastic seeding as a complication of percutaneous endoscopic gastrostomy. Am J Gastroenterol 89:131–133, 1994.

48. Fan AC, Baron TH, Rumalla A, Harewood GC: Comparison of direct percutaneous endoscopic jejunostomy and PEG with jejunal extension. Gastrointest Endosc 56:890–894, 2002.

49. Doede T, Faiss S, Schier F: Jejunal feeding tubes via gastrostomy in children. Endoscopy 34:539–542, 2002.

50. DiSario JA, Foutch PG, Sanowski RA: Poor results with percutaneous endoscopic jejunostomy. Gastroenterol Endosc 36:257–260, 1990.

51. Rumalla A, Baron TH: Results of direct percutaneous endoscopic jejunostomy, an alternative method for providing jejunal feeding. Mayo Clin Proc 75:807–810, 2000.

Acute Colonic Pseudo-Obstruction

CHAPTER

26

Robert J. Ponec and Michael B. Kimmey

Introduction

Acute colonic pseudo-obstruction (ACPO) is a disorder characterized by massive dilatation of the colon in the absence of mechanical obstruction. This severe motility disturbance, also known as Ogilvie's syndrome,[1] usually develops in hospitalized patients and is associated with a variety of medical and surgical conditions. The tension on the colon wall resulting from the extreme dilatation can lead to ischemic necrosis and perforation, especially in the cecum. The rate of spontaneous perforation has been quoted to be from 3% to 15% with an attendant 40% to 50% mortality rate.[2–5]

Despite the potential risk of perforation, approximately 75% of patients with ACPO recover over an average of 3 to 5 days when treated with a variety of conservative measures.[3,4] During the sometimes prolonged recovery phase, however, ACPO contributes greatly to the patients' discomfort and immobilization and may delay institution of enteral nutrition.

Both the risk of perforation and the morbidity of the long recovery have lead to a search for effective and safe therapies, not only to prevent perforation but also to speed resolution. Very few controlled trials have evaluated the standard therapies used for ACPO. Nonetheless, conservative management strategies such as nasogastric suction and measures to correct precipitating factors have been the mainstay of treatment.

For the minority (about 25%) of patients who fail to respond to conservative therapy or for those who have severe, prolonged colonic dilatation risking perforation, more active interventions are instituted. In the past, surgical cecostomy or hemicolectomy were the main options in severe or refractory cases. Then, colonoscopy and various radiologic procedures were reported to help decompress the colon.[5–10] More recently, medications such as neostigmine have been shown to be effective.[11] The timing and combination of conservative and more active interventions must be individualized according to the severity of the ACPO and the patient's comorbidities.

Epidemiology

ACPO is relatively uncommon. It can be triggered by a variety of acute medical and surgical illnesses. Typically, rapid onset abdominal distension begins within a few days of the onset of the underlying illness.[2]

Because ACPO is uncommon, one must look at reviews that examine several years of reported cases to be able to draw conclusions about the epidemiology of the condition. A number of case reports and reviews describe specific triggers. However, each proposed underlying condition only seems to be associated with the development of ACPO in only a very small percentage of cases. ACPO has been reported after a variety of surgeries including orthopedic, urologic, gynecologic, neurologic, and organ transplants.[3,4,12–21] It is seen in obstetrics after both vaginal deliveries and cesarean sections.[3,22,23] Trauma and burn patients sometimes develop ACPO.[3,4,12,24] A variety of medical illnesses are known to cause ACPO including sepsis, respiratory failure, mechanical ventilation, renal failure, myocardial infarction, vascular emergencies, and cancer.[3,4,12,25–35] A number of medications can precipitate ACPO, especially narcotic analgesics and any medication that decreases peristalsis, such as tricyclic antidepressants or anticholinergic drugs.[5,7,36–38] See Table 26–1 for a review of these associated conditions. Although the connection between any of these causes and ACPO is most likely through a disturbance in the autonomic innervation of the bowel, other variables such as patient age, comorbidities, and factors such as immobility, medications, and electrolyte imbalances are thought to help precipitate the onset in an individual patient.[2]

In one review of 351 ACPO cases from 1948 to 1980, 88% followed surgery, trauma, or acute medical illnesses.[3] The remaining 12% were classified as idiopathic. This review reported a 15% perforation rate, with a 45% mortality in those with colonic perforation. This high mortality was attributed in part to the fact that these patients already had serious underlying medical and/or surgical problems.

In another review of 400 patients from 1970 to 1985, 95% of the cases had identifiable underlying medical, surgical, or obstetric conditions.[4] This left only 5% to be categorized as idiopathic. ACPO usually developed within 5 days of onset of the underlying condition. The median patient age was about 60 years and the male to female ratio was 1.5:1. Perforation rate was 20% and mortality in those who perforated was about 40%. Overall, mortality in the group was 15%. Mortality rate was affected by age, cecal diameter, length of dilatation of colon, presence of ischemia in bowel wall,

Table 26–1. Conditions Associated with Acute Colonic Pseudo-Obstruction

Surgical	Obstetrical	Trauma	Medical Illnesses	Medications
Orthopedic	Normal delivery	Fractures	Sepsis	Narcotic analgesics
Urologic	Cesarean section	Burns	Neurologic disorders	Tricyclic antidepressants
Gynecologic			Cancer	Anesthetic agents
Abdominal			Chemotherapy	Antiparkinsonian drugs
Transplant			Radiation therapy	Anticholinergics
			Hypothyroidism	
			Myocardial infarction	
			Stroke	
			Respiratory failure, mechanical ventilation	
			Renal failure	
			Electrolyte imbalance (potassium, magnesium, calcium, phosphorous)	
			Viral infections (herpes, varicella zoster)	

and patient comorbidities. One important observation in this review was that patients with cecal diameter ranging from 8 cm to 25 cm usually had viable colon without significant ischemia. Thus, cecal size alone is not the only factor in the risk of perforation. Other variables such as the acuity of the onset and the duration of distension were also potentially important factors.

Pathogenesis

In 1948, Ogilvie[1] first described massive colonic distension in two patients who had the onset of abdominal distension over a few weeks, rather than the more acute presentation that we currently refer to as "Ogilvie's." Both patients were ultimately found to have widespread intra-abdominal malignancy with retroperitoneal involvement of nerve plexuses, leading Ogilvie to speculate that disruption of the autonomic innervation of the colon was the underlying cause of the disorder.[1]

Despite the variety of possible triggers of ACPO, the presentation is remarkable consistent. Generally, patients develop severe abdominal distension within 5 days of the onset of the medical or surgical insult. The intestinal dilatation is usually most pronounced in the colon, especially proximal to the splenic flexure. On x-ray examination, the appearance is very similar to that of a patient who actually has an obstruction near the upper left colon, leading to the title of "pseudo-obstruction." These facts have led to the hypothesis that the final common pathway of the development of the disease is an acute cessation of effective colonic motility resulting from a disruption of the autonomic supply of the left side of the colon. One hypothesis was that excess sympathetic stimulation of the colon was inhibiting contraction. This seemed supported by the observation that this occurred in any sort of severe physical stress. In addition, epidural anesthesia to decrease sympathetic output has been reported to be beneficial treatment for ACPO.[39] On the other hand, when guanethidine was used to block sympathetic tone, there was very little effect on colonic function in ACPO patients.[40]

The leading current theory about the pathogenesis of ACPO is that a decrease in parasympathetic stimulus to the colon is more important than an excess of sympathetic input.[41] In the study of guanethidine mentioned previously, patients were first given guanethidine and then treated with neostigmine to block acetyl-cholinesterase. Patients had a prompt return of colonic contraction only after the neostigmine, leading to the idea that a loss of parasympathetic tone is important in the development of ACPO. Some speculate that the parasympathetic deficiency is most pronounced in the left colon because of disruption of supply from the sacral plexus. This may explain why the left colon is contracted and aperistaltic in ACPO. Since these pioneering studies, the one medical treatment that has had the most consistent success in treatment of ACPO has been the use of neostigmine to cause a sudden increase in acetylcholine concentration at parasympathetic nerve synapses and thus an increase in colon peristalsis.

Other factors that undoubtedly contribute to the pathogenesis of ACPO are chronic underlying bowel motility disorders and constipation, patient immobility, electrolyte imbalance, medications such as narcotics, and mechanical ventilation. These other factors may contribute to the autonomic imbalance, directly suppress muscular function of the colon, or simply increase the amount of gas that is entering the digestive tract.

The most feared complication of ACPO is colon perforation. When it happens, it usually occurs in the right colon, especially the cecum. The pathophysiology of this relates to high wall tension in the cecum leading to ischemic necrosis and then wall disruption. The right colon, which naturally has a thinner wall and larger diameter than the left side, will have the highest wall tension when the colon is distended. This is described well by Laplace's law: $T = P \times R/2d$, where T is wall tension, P is pressure in colon lumen, R is the radius of the colon, and d represents the thickness of the colonic wall. This equation helps to explain how, in the setting of severe distension of the thin-walled cecum, small changes colonic radius can lead to relatively large changes in wall tension and thus increase the risk of perforation. Usually the perforation risk is not very high in patients with cecal diameter below 12 cm. Paradoxically, studies have shown that patients with ACPO and cecal diameter in excess of 25 cm can recover without incident. Thus, other variables such as elasticity of the muscle wall, adequacy of blood supply, and time course of distension must be important as well in determining whether the colon will remain viable. For instance, some studies indicate an association between the duration of ACPO and perforation risk and indicate that those with persistence of distension for more than 5 days have higher perforation rates.[42]

Clinical Features

ACPO is seen mainly in patients who are hospitalized for an acute medical, surgical, obstetrical, or traumatic event. The condition progresses at a variable rate, usually over 2 to 7 days. The nearly universal symptom is progressive abdominal distension. The reported frequency of other symptoms is quite varied. Abdominal pain (10% to 80%), nausea (10% to 60%), vomiting (10% to 60%), diarrhea (30% to 40%), constipation (40% to 50%), and respiratory compromise resulting from distension have all been reported.[3–5,7] Patients with ischemia and perforation are much more likely to have abdominal pain and fever.

Physical examination findings include a markedly distended abdomen that is usually tympanitic to percussion. Bowel sounds are often present. Although some tenderness has been noted in up to 60% of patients in some reports, significant tenderness or guarding should raise suspicion for perforation.

Laboratory abnormalities can include an elevated white blood count in up to 25% in those without perforation and in close to 100% in those with perforation.[4] Abnormalities in electrolytes such as potassium, calcium, magnesium, and phosphorus and abnormalities in thyroid function are not necessarily caused by ACPO but are thought to contribute to colonic dysfunction. Thus, these laboratory results should be checked and corrected, if abnormal.

Abdominal x-ray films show colonic distension, usually most pronounced in the cecum, ascending, and transverse colon. In contrast with patients with severe obstipation, the colon is distended primarily with gas not stool. There is often an apparent "cutoff" near the splenic flexure with a collapsed left colon. The location of the cutoff varies. In one review, the cutoff was at the splenic flexure in 56% of patients, at the hepatic flexure in 18%, and at the descending or sigmoid colon in 27%. Although the small bowel is said to usually have less dilatation in ACPO, one report indicated up to 80% of patients had some small bowel dilatation. Air-fluid levels have been reported in up to 40%. Of course, x-ray evidence of gas in the bowel wall or free intraperitoneal air is indicative of colonic perforation. Radiographic water-soluble contrast enemas are often needed to rule out a true mechanical obstruction. As discussed in the treatment section, the use of water-soluble contrast has been reported to have a therapeutic effect in some patients.[43]

Differential Diagnosis

Two major considerations in the differential diagnosis of ACPO are mechanical bowel obstruction and toxic megacolon resulting from an enteric infection or inflammatory bowel disease (IBD). In addition, patients with chronic colonic pseudo-obstruction are sometimes first diagnosed when they are hospitalized for other reasons, making it important to first establish that the condition is truly acute and not chronic.

Mechanical colon obstruction from causes such as colon cancer, sigmoid volvulus, and diverticulitis must be confidently ruled out before considering specific therapies for ACPO. Often the fact that

patients with ACPO continue to have watery bowel movements is helpful to indicate that a complete obstruction is unlikely. In some cases, the presence of some gas in the rectum or throughout the entire colon also helps to rule out obstruction. Nonetheless, neither of these parameters is totally reliable. Thus, either a water-soluble contrast enema or a colonoscopy may be required to rule out mechanical obstruction.

Toxic megacolon resulting from infections such as *Clostridium difficile* should be considered in patients who have been exposed to antibiotics or prolonged care in a hospital or nursing facility, where they may have contracted the infection. Generally, such patients had severe diarrhea before the onset of the abdominal distension. Other colonic infections leading to toxic megacolon have been reported, particularly in immunosuppressed patients. In some cases, these patients seem to have a presentation indistinguishable from classical ACPO. However, when the colonic distension is due to infection, patients usually have an elevated white blood cell count; thickening of bowel wall on x-ray films; and endoscopic evidence of severe colonic erythema, edema, ulceration, or pseudomembranes on flexible sigmoidoscopy. Stool studies for enteric pathogens and C. *difficile* toxin are important in this setting.[44]

Similarly, toxic megacolon resulting from IBD can usually be differentiated from ACPO by a review of clinical history, laboratory results, x-ray films, and findings on sigmoidoscopy.[45] Patients with IBD should have had a history of diarrhea (often bloody) and abdominal cramps before the development of the colonic distension. Blood test results usually show leukocytosis. Abdominal x-ray films often show bowel wall edema. Sigmoidoscopy should show changes consistent with IBD.

Lastly, the presence of chronic pseudo-obstruction can often be excluded by a careful review of the patient's history, old records, and prior abdominal radiographs, when available.

Treatment

Because ACPO is relatively uncommon, there have been few controlled trials of the treatments that are currently considered the standard of care. Most of the information is from reviews, observational studies, and case presentations. Therapy is generally divided into conservative measures and active interventions. Because at least 75% of patients with ACPO resolve with a combination of conservative measures, these are generally tried first for at least 24 to 48 hours in most patients before more active interventions are considered.[46] The reported success from these measures ranges from 33% to 100%.[24–26]

The following sections describe conservative therapy, medication therapy, colonoscopy, and surgical approaches for ACPO. These treatments are often combined. For example, conservative measures are typically continued when more active interventions are added. The order and combination of these measures must be individualized to a patient's clinical presentation and course. Figure 26–1 outlines a proposed treatment algorithm for most patients with ACPO, modified from the recent American Society for Gastrointestinal Endoscopy (ASGE) practice guideline on treatment of this condition.[46]

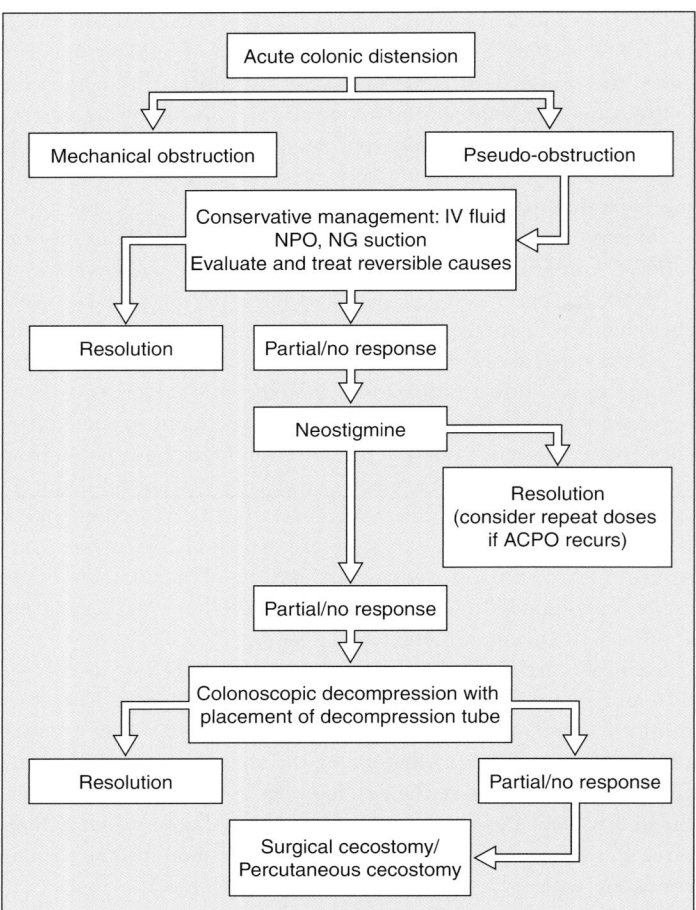

Figure 26–1. A suggested algorithm for the management of acute colonic pseudo-obstruction (ACPO) is shown. This algorithm has been adopted from the Practice Guideline published by the American Society for Gastrointestinal Endoscopy. (From Eisen GM, Baron TH, Dominitz JA, et al: Acute colonic pseudo-obstruction. Gastrointest Endosc 56:789–792, 2002.)

CONSERVATIVE THERAPY

Conservative measures for treatment of ACPO include most, if not all, of the following, depending on individual circumstances.[36] The patient is made nil per os (NPO) and nasogastric suction is used to prevent even more gas from entering the gastrointestinal (GI) tract. Patients are mobilized as much as possible. If the patient is bed-bound, then the patient's position should be changed often from side to side and, when possible, into the prone and knee-to-chest position. A search for contributing factors should be done with correction of as many as possible. For example, one should withdraw medications that interfere with colonic motility such as narcotic analgesics, anticholinergics, and calcium channel blockers. Electrolyte imbalance (especially potassium, calcium, magnesium, and phosphorous) should be corrected. Regular rectal examinations, as often as every 6 hours, have been advocated as a way to encourage passage of colonic gas. Alternatively, placement of a rectal tube can be considered for this purpose. Gentle tap water enemas are controversial but are advocated by some as a way to liquefy remaining stool. A water-soluble contrast enema can also liquefy stool and is useful for excluding mechanical obstruction. Some

authors have reported a stimulant effect on motility that sometimes speeds recovery.[43] However, the use of any enema runs a small but real risk of perforation in these circumstances. Prophylactic antibiotics have not been studied. If a patient has a fever and/or elevated white blood cell count, then broad-spectrum antibiotics can be considered while a careful evaluation is under way for signs of colonic ischemia, perforation, or for other infections.

Generally, conservative measures are continued for 24 to 48 hours before one moves to more active interventions. This is not based on controlled data but rather on the observation that patients whose severe colon dilatation (over 12 cm) persists for 4 to 5 days run a higher risk of ischemia and perforation.[4]

Although conservative therapy is generally successful, return of colon function in responders takes an average of 5 days. During this time, patients are contending with the consequences of ACPO including distension, pain, delay in institution of enteral nutrition, compromised respiratory status, and delay in ambulation that can lead to other morbidities such as thromboembolism, atelectasis, and pneumonia. In addition, patients are at risk of colonic perforation during this time. These facts have led to a search for a safe and effective treatment not only for those who are refractory to conservative measures but also for a treatment to provide a more prompt resolution early in the course of the illness.

A number of active interventions have been reported to be useful for ACPO. They include medications such as neostigmine,[11] colonoscopy with or without placement of a decompression tube,[47–53] Gastrografin enema,[43] radiologic procedures such as placement of a transanal decompression tube,[10] cecostomy, and surgical resection of part of the colon.

MEDICAL THERAPY

In the past, patients who either failed to respond to conservative measures or were felt to have impending perforation were treated with surgery, such as cecostomy. When colonoscopic decompression was shown to be effective, it became the mainstay of treatment of such patients. Most recently, medications that stimulate colon motility have been of interest.

The most promising medication thus far for treatment of ACPO is neostigmine, an inhibitor of acetylcholinesterase. Neostigmine causes a transient but significant increase in acetylcholine concentration, resulting in a pronounced increase in cholinergic stimulus throughout the body, including in the colon. The leading theory about the pathogenesis of ACPO is that there is an autonomic imbalance, with an increase in sympathetic tone and a decrease in the parasympathetic stimulus to the colon. Both of these changes are thought to have a negative impact on colon motility. This theory has led to studies of drugs that either decrease sympathetic tone or increase parasympathetic tone as means to restore colon function. In the 1960s, Neely and Catchpole[54] studied the effects of guanethidine (a sympathetic antagonist) and neostigmine (Prostigmine) (a cholinergic drug) on small bowel motility and found that these medications seemed to restore peristalsis. In 1992, Hutchinson and Griffiths[40] treated 11 ACPO patients first with guanethidine and then with neostigmine. They found that 8 of 11 patients had prompt return of bowel motility but only after the neostigmine infusion. In 1995, Stephenson and coworkers[16]

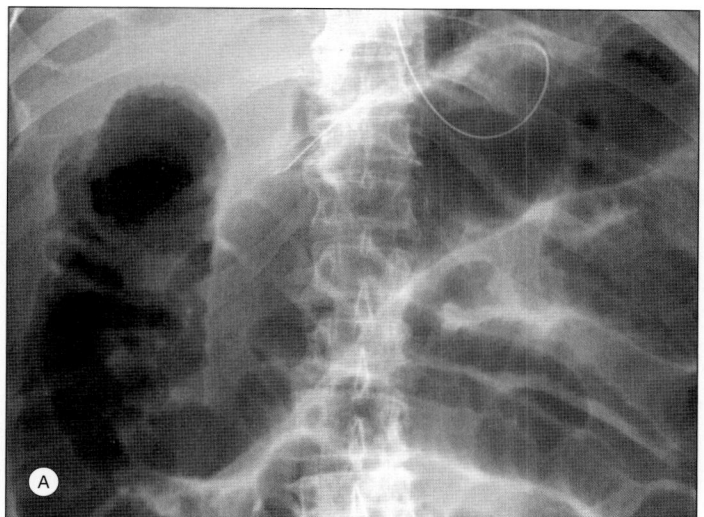 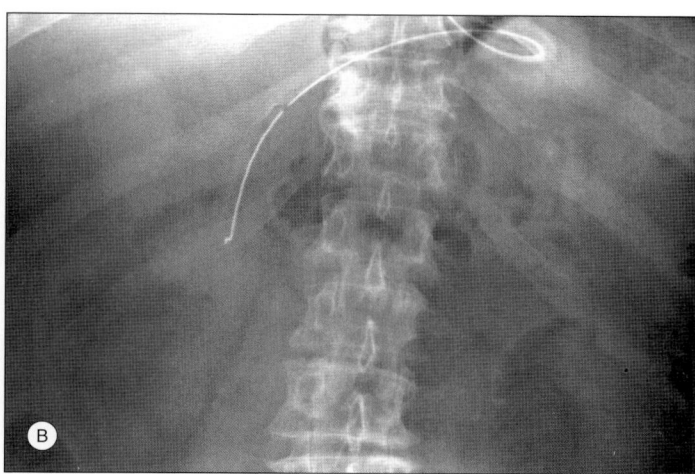

Figure 26–2. *A,* A dilated transverse colon and hepatic flexure are shown in a patient with acute colonic pseudo-obstruction. Note that a nasogastric tube is present in the stomach. *B,* Three hours following administration of neostigmine, colonic gas is no longer present. The nasogastric tube remains in place. (Reproduced from Ponec RJ, Saunders MD, Kimmey MB: Neostigmine for the treatment of acute colonic pseudo-obstruction. N Engl J Med 341:137–141, 1999. Copyright © 1999 Massachusets Medical Society. All rights reserved.)

presented results of a study showing that 11 of 12 ACPO patients treated with 2.5 mg of intravenous neostigmine had prompt resolution of their condition. These observations have been confirmed by subsequent studies including prompt clinical resolution in 75% of ACPO cases as presented by Turefano-Fuentes and coworkers[55] in 1997 and in 26 of 28 cases treated by Trevisani and colleagues,[56] whose results were published in 2000. Recent physiologic studies on neostigmine indicate that its indirect effect on muscarinic receptors in the bowel wall, presumably through increased local acetylcholine concentrations, results in increased colonic tone and increased coordinated colonic propulsion.[57]

Because ACPO often resolves with conservative therapy alone, controlled trials of neostigmine and other therapies are important. The only controlled trial published to date was performed at the University of Washington[11] and was published in 1999. Twenty-one patients with ACPO (refractory to at least 24 hours of conservative measures and with a cecal diameter greater than 10 cm) were randomized to receive either 2.0 mg of neostigmine or saline by a 3-minute intravenous infusion administered by a physician, blinded to the treatment allocation. The responses recorded included immediate passage of flatus and stool; the amount of decrease in the measured abdominal girth; and the change in the diameters of the cecum, ascending, and transverse colon on abdominal x-ray films obtained 3 hours later (Fig. 26–2). Ten of the 11 patients randomized to neostigmine had prompt resolution with substantial responses in all of the measured endpoints. The one nonresponder subsequently had a response when an open-label neostigmine dose was given 3 hours later. The median time to passage of flatus was 4 minutes (range 3 to 30 minutes). None of the patients given placebo responded, despite the continuation of conservative measures in all patients. Seven patients from the placebo group were treated with open-label neostigmine 3 hours later and all had a prompt response. Since this publication, several uncontrolled studies have also reported similar results with usually about 80% to 90% of patients showing a prompt response to the drug.[58–61]

Some studies have shown success with repeated doses of the drug for patients with partial responses and recurrences.[16]

Neostigmine side effects include abdominal pain, nausea, vomiting, sweating, excess salivation, bronchospasm, and symptomatic bradycardia. Patients at risk for bradycardia such as those with preexisting bradyarrhythmias or those on beta-blockers are at potentially higher risk of complications from neostigmine, as are those with severe bronchospasm. Thus, some caution in patient selection is needed. Nonetheless, neostigmine can be used in most patients with ACPO when the proper monitoring and precautions are in place. Patients should be kept supine on a pad or bed pan for the first 30 minutes after neostigmine and should be monitored by continuous electrocardiogram (ECG) and frequent, intermittent blood pressure determinations. Transient bradycardia can occur but usually resolves quickly without treatment because of the short half-life of neostigmine. Atropine should be immediately available but should be given only if the bradycardia is severe, prolonged, or associated with significant hypotension or persistent symptoms. Although neostigmine is partly cleared by plasma cholinesterase, about one half of the clearance takes place in the kidneys; thus, patients with renal failure have a prolonged half-life of neostigmine. In anephric patients, the elimination half-life is about 180 minutes compared with the 80 minutes seen in patients with normal renal function.[62]

Because it appears to be rapidly effective in most patients with ACPO and has a low side effect profile compared with other active therapies such as colonoscopy or surgery, neostigmine appears early in the suggested treatment algorithm.[46,63,64] Most studies indicate that, as long as conservative measures are continued, the recurrence rate of ACPO after neostigmine is low.[11] Nonetheless, repeat doses can be tried in case of recurrence before one resorts to more invasive techniques. Because the elimination half-life is 80 minutes, retreatment is not advisable at intervals less than every 3 hours.

Other medical therapies have been reported, including prokinetics such as metoclopramide,[65] erythromycin,[66,67] and cisapride.[68] Most reports on these other agents have been anecdotes of one or two patients. The published reports on use of metoclopramide have been disappointing. Some have questioned the wisdom of applying a prokinetic such as metoclopramide out of concern that its main stimulus is on emptying the upper gut. This theoretically may deliver even more gas to the colon without adequate stimulus of the colon itself and worsen the distension there.

COLONOSCOPY

Colonoscopy can be useful in treating ACPO in a number of ways. First, it can be used to suction the extra gas and decompress the colon directly. Colonoscopy can also be used to rule out mechanical obstruction and to check for signs of colonic mucosal ischemia and necrosis. Lastly, it can be used to place a guidewire into the proximal colon, over which a decompression tube can be placed. The reported rate of intubation proximal to the hepatic flexure in the setting of ACPO is up to 70%.[5]

Although there are no controlled trials proving its efficacy, colonoscopic decompression has been central in the therapy of ACPO patients who fail conservative measures. Its successful use was first reported in 1977 by Kukora and Dent.[6] Since then, a number of uncontrolled studies have reported initial clinical success with colonoscopy in about 70 % of cases.[7,8,17,25] Nonetheless, a high recurrence rate of up to 40% may lead to repeated colonoscopy.[5,47,69] Several authors have reported a lower recurrence rate if a decompression tube is left in place, especially if it is proximal to the hepatic flexure.[48–50] One institution compared the recurrence rate of colonoscopy with decompression tube placement with historical controls of colonoscopy alone and found recurrence rates of 0% versus 45%, respectively.[51] Some have criticized uncontrolled studies on colonoscopic decompression because they have not had control groups of conservative therapy alone (which may have differed over time) and have a referral bias of only studying patients specifically referred for the purpose of colonoscopic decompression.[5,52]

A summary of expert consensus on several aspects of therapeutic colonoscopy for ACPO follows.[53] Colonoscopy in ACPO patients is technically difficult (performed in the unprepared colon of seriously ill patients) and carries an increased perforation risk of 1% to 3%.[7,52] It should only be performed by expert endoscopists. Preparatory enemas are not needed because the stool remaining in the colon is usually already liquefied. In addition, enemas may increase the risk of perforation in patients with ACPO. Air insufflation must be kept to a minimum. As each new dilated segment is entered with the colonoscope, it should be decompressed as much as possible without causing loss of visualization. Cecal intubation is desired. One should try to advance the colonoscope beyond the hepatic flexure.

Traditionally, it has been said that, if mucosal ischemia is found, the colonoscope should be withdrawn and the patient should be sent for urgent surgical resection, usually of the right colon, which is most often involved. More recently, successful treatment with conservative measures and tube decompression has been reported even in patients with endoscopic evidence of ischemia.[70]

A tube for decompression should be placed at the initial colonoscopy. Various techniques have been described. The most popular and most effective to date is the placement of a guidewire through the colonoscope when the colonoscope tip is in the cecum or at least proximal to the hepatic flexure. The colonoscope is then withdrawn over the wire and then the wire is used to guide a decompression tube into position. This is best done with the help of fluoroscopy to avoid the common problems of coiling of the tube and distal migration of the tip all the way back to the left colon during placement. There are commercially available decompression kits that use a 0.035-inch wire and catheters that range from 7 to 14 Fr in diameter. Other authors suggest using stiffer wires and the use of larger tubes, such as a modified 18-Fr Levin or nasogastric tube. The tube is then taped securely to the buttock and is flushed with water at least every 6 hours to decrease clogging.

Daily abdominal x-ray films should be performed after colonoscopy and tube placement. The diameter of the colon in the cecum, ascending colon, and transverse colon should be tracked and one should be vigilant for signs of free intraperitoneal air. Although there is sometimes a dramatic decrease in colonic dilatation immediately after decompression, more commonly the colonic dilatation decreases gradually (Fig. 26–3). One study showed that the mean change in cecal diameter both 4 hours and 1 day after colonoscopic decompression was only about 2 cm.[71]

One report describes an alternative method for advancing a transanal decompression tube into the proximal colon using a steerable tricomponent coaxial catheter under fluoroscopic guidance.[10] Successful placement proximal to the hepatic flexure and decompression was seen in four consecutive patients.

SURGERY

Surgery is now reserved for ACPO patients who fail medical and colonoscopic therapy or for those with signs of colonic perforation. Retrospective studies have shown that surgery is associated with higher morbidity and mortality than the other therapies. This probably reflects the fact that the patients selected for surgery had more severe ACPO and more serious underlying conditions, although the extra morbidity of general anesthesia and an abdominal operation in such patients undoubtedly also has a significant impact.

For patients without peritoneal signs, tube cecostomy is advocated. For those with peritoneal signs, a more extensive exploration is recommended with the surgical findings guiding the type of intervention.[2] For instance, in those patients with a viable cecum, a tube cecostomy can still be done. However, if there is significant ischemia or perforation, then colonic resection is advised with the decision whether to do a primary anastomosis versus an ileostomy and mucous fistula depending on the patient's condition and the degree of peritoneal contamination. Cecostomy has a high success rate in terms of decompression of the right colon.

In addition to the more traditional open surgical approach and placement of a Foley catheter or similar drain into the cecum, there are other variations of the technique. One is to perform laparoscopy first to check cecal viability and then to use the laparoscope to help place a cecostomy tube. T-fasteners are used to hold the cecal wall up against the abdominal wall.[72] Some argue that, with the availability and effectiveness of neostigmine and colonoscopy, surgery should now be reserved for those patients who have signs of perforation or peritonitis. Its use for decompression in refractory cases should be infrequent.[73]

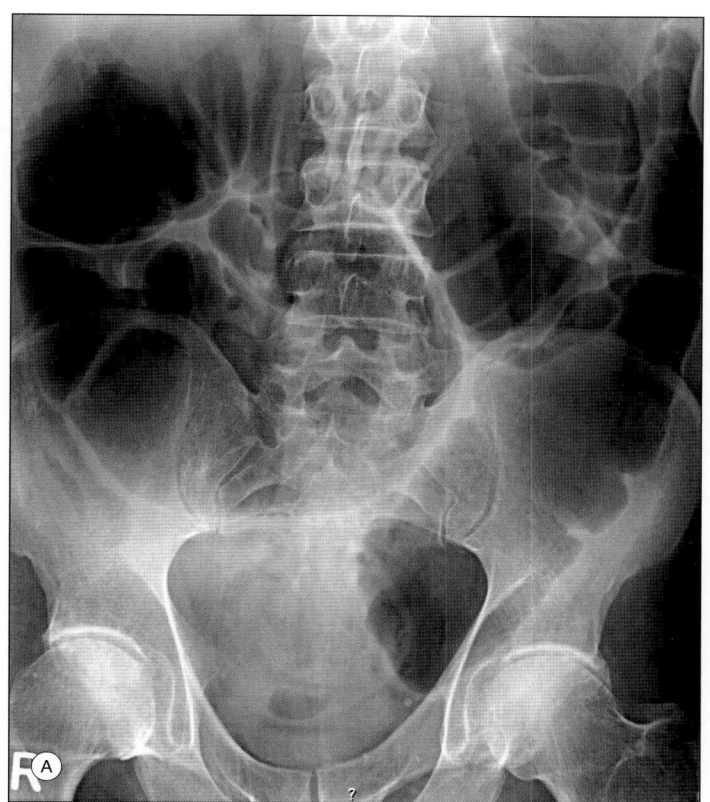
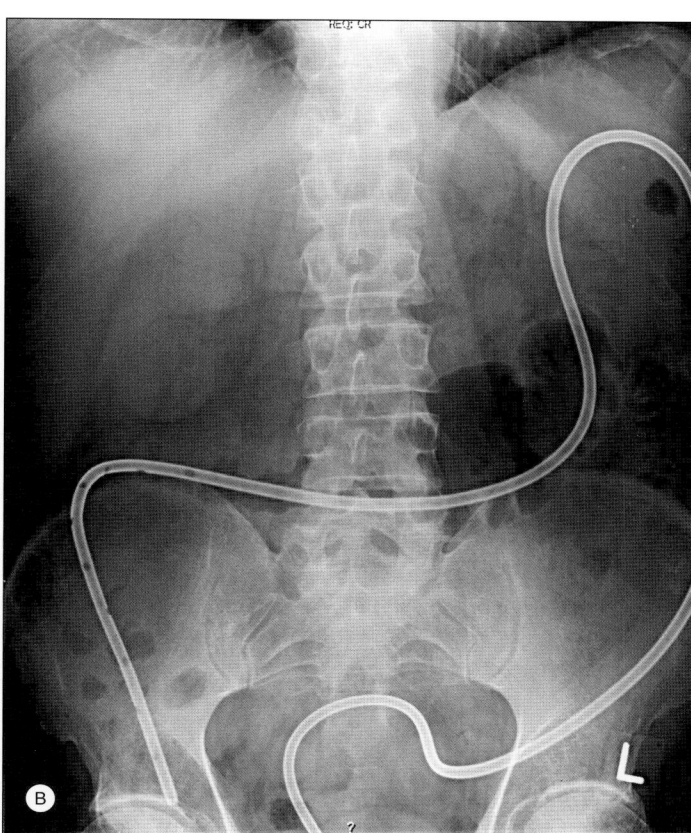

Figure 26–3. *A,* A Plain abdominal radiograph from a patient with acute colonic pseudo-obstruction is shown. *B,* An additional radiograph following colonoscopy and placement of a 14-Fr colonic decompression tube reveals a significant reduction in colonic gas. (Reprinted from Nietsch H, Kimmey MB: Acute colonic pseudo-obstruction. In Waye J, Rex DK, Williams CB [eds]: Colonoscopy: Principles and Practice. London, Blackwell Science, 2004, pp 596–602.)

Other methods of placing cecal tubes have been reported. One involves using a colonoscope in the cecum to guide placement of a transcutaneous trocar and guidewire[74] (a percutaneous endoscopic cecostomy). The wire is then used to place a latex mushroom catheter of the type used as percutaneous endoscopic gastrostomy tubes. Radiologic methods have used fluoroscopy or computed tomography (CT) scan to guide placement of T-fasteners and drainage tubes into the cecum.[9,75,76]

Of course, all of the techniques that involve placing a hole in the cecum run the significant risk of wound infections, leakage, and peritonitis. Local operative complications and the morbidity of anesthesia and open abdominal surgery in patients who are generally already very ill make surgery a last resort for treatment of ACPO. This is especially true given the fact that conservative measures, medical therapies, and colonoscopy can successfully treat nearly all of the cases.

Future Trends

The major challenges in studying therapy for ACPO are that it is an uncommon condition that most often occurs in seriously ill hospitalized patients. It causes perforation in about 3%. Thus, prospective, controlled studies designed to prove a difference in hard endpoints such as perforation and death are not likely to be forthcoming. However, controlled trials that track intermediate endpoints such as colon diameter and resolution of the distension are possible.

Most cases of ACPO resolve with conservative therapy, but the time to resolution can be a number of days, making spontaneous resolution still a significantly morbid event. In addition, these sick patients do not tolerate invasive procedures well. Thus, emphasis should be placed on finding therapies that simply speed resolution safely and with minimal dependence on invasive procedures. Future studies of ACPO fall into three categories: prevention, medication therapies, and interventional therapies.

Because ACPO can occur as the result of nearly any severe medical or surgical insult, it is hard to imagine how to prevent it completely. Nonetheless, there are certain situations that are especially associated with ACPO, such as severe trauma, major orthopedic procedures, and pelvic surgeries. Although this has not been systematically studied, it is logical to hypothesize that early, prophylactic application of some of the measures described previously in the section of conservative therapy might actually prevent some of the cases.

Medication therapies will probably be the biggest area of future research in ACPO. For instance, safer prokinetic agents could be applied earlier and more liberally. Many have speculated that neostigmine might be rendered easier and safer to use if patients were concomitantly treated with another agent to block some of the unwanted systemic cholinergic side effects, without lessening the therapeutic benefit of the neostigmine. Glycopyrrolate, an acetylcholine receptor antagonist, has been proposed for this purpose. Some physiologic measurements have shown that patients who were pretreated with glycopyrrolate do still have a significant increase in colonic motility after neostigmine administration.[77] Whether this combination would enjoy the apparent success of neostigmine alone remains to be proven. The use of intravenous or oral medications to prevent recurrence is another potential area for future study. One hypothesis is that bowel-selective prokinetic agents (e.g., tegaserod) might be used to decrease the high recurrence rate that is often seen in patients who have had successful initial decompressive therapy. If successful, such medicines could also be used in prophylaxis as well in high-risk situations, such as trauma patients.

Lastly, although colonoscopy already has a high success rate of about 70% for initial therapy, improvements in minimally invasive endoscopic and radiologic techniques for placement of decompression tubes will be of further benefit.

REFERENCES

1. Ogilvie H: Large-intestine colic due to sympathetic deprivation: A new clinical syndrome. BMJ 2:671–673, 1948.
2. Dorudi S, Berry AR, Kettlewell MG: Acute colonic pseudo-obstruction. Br J Surg 79:99–103, 1992.
3. Nanni G, Garbini A, Luchetti P, et al: Ogilvie's syndrome (acute colonic pseudo-obstruction): Review of literature (October 1948 to March 1980) and report of four additional cases. Dis Colon Rectum 25:157–166, 1982.
4. Vanek VW, Al-Salti M: Acute colonic pseudo-obstruction (Ogilvie's syndrome) an analysis of 400 cases. Dis Colon Rectum 29:203–210, 1986.
5. Jetmore AB, Timmcke AE, Gathright B, et al: Ogilvie's syndrome: Colonoscopic decompression and analysis of predisposing factors. Dis Colon Rectum 35:1135–1142, 1992.
6. Kukor JS, Dent TL: Colonoscopic decompression of massive nonobstructive cecal dilation. Arch Surg 112:512–517, 1997.
7. Geller A, Petersen BT, Gostout CJ: Endoscopic decompression for acute colonic pseudo-obstruction. Gastrointest Endosc 44:144–150, 1996.
8. Bode WE, Beart RW, Spencer RJ, et al: Colonoscopic decompression for acute pseudoobstruction of the colon (Ogilvie's syndrome): Report of 22 cases and review of the literature. Am J Surg 147:243–245, 1984.
9. Crass JR, Simmons RL, Frick MP, et al: Percutaneous decompression of the colon using CT guidance in Ogilvie syndrome. AJR 144:475–476, 1985.
10. Bender GN, Do-Dai DD, Briggs LM: Colonic pseudo-obstruction: Decompression with a tricomponent coaxial system under fluoroscopic guidance. Radiology 188:395–398, 1993.
11. Ponec RJ, Saunders MD, Kimmey MB: Neostigmine for the treatment of acute colonic pseudo-obstruction. N Engl J Med 341:137–141, 1999.
12. Spira IA, Rodrigues R, Wolff WI: Pseudo-obstruction of the colon. Am J Gastroenterol 65:397–408, 1976.
13. Elmaraghy AW, Schemitsch EH, Burnstein MJ, et al: Ogilvie's syndrome after lower extremity arthroplasty. Can J Surg 42:133–137, 1999.
14. Clarke HD, Berry DJ, Larson DR, et al: Acute pseudo-obstruction of the colon as a postoperative complication of hip arthroplasty. J Bone Joint Surg Am 79A:1642–1647, 1997.
15. Terhune D, Petrochko N, Jordan G, et al: Ogilvie's syndrome developing after ethanol ablation of renal cell carcinoma. J Urol 133:838–839, 1985.
16. Stephenson BM, Morgan AR, Salaman JR, et al: Ogilvie's syndrome: A new approach to an old problem. Dis Colon Rectum 38:424–427, 1995.
17. Love R, Starling JR, Sollinger HW, et al: Colonoscopic decompression for acute colonic pseudo-obstruction (Ogilvie's syndrome) in transplant recipients. Gastrointest Endosc 34:426–429, 1988.
18. O'Malley KJ, Flechner SM, Kapoor A, et al: Acute colonic pseudo-obstruction (Ogilvie's syndrome) after renal transplantation. Am J Surg 177:492–496, 1999.
19. Koneru B, Selby R, O'Hair DP, et al: Nonobstructing colonic dilation and colonic perforations following renal transplantation. Arch Surg 125:610–613, 1990.
20. Cakir E, Baykal S, Haydar U, et al: Ogilvie's syndrome after cervical discectomy. Clin Neurol Neurosurg 103:232–233, 2001.
21. Caner H, Bavbek M, Albayrak A, et al: Ogilvie's syndrome as a rare complication of lumbar disc surgery Can J Neurol Sci 27:77–78, 2000.
22. Imai A, Mikamo H, Kawabata I, et al: Acute colonic pseudo-obstruction of the colon (Ogilvie's syndrome) during pregnancy. J Med 21:331–336, 1990.
23. Shaxted EJ, Jukes R: Pseudo-obstruction of the bowel in pregnancy. Br J Obstet Gynaecol 86:411–413, 1979.
24. Estela CM, Burd DA: Conservative management of acute pseudo-obstruction in a major burn. Burns 25:523–525, 1999.
25. Fausel CS, Goff JS: Nonoperative management of acute idiopathic colonic pseudo-obstruction (Ogilvie's syndrome). West J Med 143:50–54, 1985.
26. Sloyer AF, Panella VS, Demas BE, et al: Ogilvie's syndrome: Successful management without colonoscopy. Dig Dis Sci 33:1391–1396, 1988.
27. Breccia M, Girmenia C, Mecarocci S, et al: Ogilvie's syndrome in acute myeloid leukemia: Pharmacological approach with neostigmine. Ann Hematol 80:614–616, 2001.
28. Schuffler MD, Baird HW, Fleming R, et al: Intestinal pseudo-obstruction as the presenting manifestation of small-cell carcinoma of the lung. Ann Intern Med 98:129–134, 1983.
29. Ikehara O: Vincristine-induced paralytic ileus: Role of fiberoptic colonoscopy and prostaglandin F2alpha. Am J Gastroenterol 87:207–210, 1992.
30. Lopez MJ, Memula N, Doss LL, et al: Pseudo-obstruction of the colon during pelvic radiotherapy. Dis Colon Rectum 24:201–204, 1981.
31. Roman RJ, Loeb PM: Massive colonic dilation as initial presentation of mesenteric vein thrombosis. Dig Dis Sci 32:323–326, 1987.
32. Golden GT, Chandler JG: Colonic ileus and cecal perforation in patients requiring mechanical ventilatory support. Chest 68:661–664, 1975.
33. Caccese WJ, Bronzo RL, Wadler G, et al: Ogilvie's syndrome associated with herpes zoster infection. J Clin Gastroenterol 7:309–313, 1985.
34. Shrestha BM, Darby C, Fergusson C, et al: Cytomegalovirus causing acute colonic pseudo-obstruction in a renal transplant recipient. Postgrad Med J 72:429–430, 1996.
35. Nomdedeu JF, Nomdedeu J, Martino R, et al: Ogilvie's syndrome from disseminated varicella-zoster infection and infracted celiac ganglia. J Clin Gastroenterol 20:157–159, 1995.
36. Rex D: Acute colonic pseudo-obstruction (Ogilvie's syndrome). Gastroenterologist 2:233–238, 1994.
37. Fahy BG: Pseudoobstruction of the colon: Early recognition and therapy. J Neurosurg Anesthesiol 8:133–136, 1996.
38. Ohri SK, Patel T, Desa L, et al: Drug-induced colonic pseudo-obstruction. Dis Colon Rectum 34:346–350, 1991.
39. Lee JT, Taylor BM, Singleton BC: Epidural anesthesia for acute pseudo-obstruction of the colon (Ogilvie's syndrome). Dis Colon Rectum 31:686–691, 1988.

40. Hutchinson R, Griffiths C: Acute colonic pseudo-obstruction: A pharmacologic approach. Ann R Coll Surg Engl 74:364–367, 1992.

41. Stephenson BM, Morgan AR, Drake N, et al: Parasympathomimetic decompression of acute colonic pseudo-obstruction. Lancet 342:1181–1182, 1993.

42. Johnson CD, Rice RP, Kelvin FM, et al: The radiologic evaluation of gross cecal distension: Emphasis on cecal ileus. AJR 145:1211–1217, 1985.

43. Schermer CR, Hanosh JJ, Davis M, et al: Ogilvie's syndrome in the surgery patient: A new therapeutic modality. J Gastrointest Surg 3:173–177, 1999.

44. Kyne L, Farrell R, Kelly C: Clostridium difficile. Gastroenterol Clin North Am 30:753–777, 2001.

45. Banerjee S, Peppercorn M: Inflammatory bowel disease: Medical therapy of specific clinical presentations. Gastroenterol Clin North Am 31:185–202, 2002.

46. Eisen GM, Baron TH, Dominitz JA, et al: Acute colonic pseudo-obstruction. Gastrointest Endosc 56:789–792, 2002.

47. Martin FM, Robinson AM, Thompson WR: Therapeutic colonoscopy in the treatment of colonic pseudo-obstruction. Am Surg 54:519–522, 1988.

48. Messmer JM, Wolper JC, Loewe CJ: Endoscopic-assisted tube placement for decompression of acute colonic pseudo-obstruction. Endoscopy 16:135–136, 1984.

49. Burke G, Shellito PC: Treatment of recurrent colonic pseudo-obstruction by placement of a fenestrated overtube. Dis Colon Rectum 30:615–619, 1987.

50. Stephenson KR, Rodriguez-Bigas MA: Decompression of the large intestine in Ogilvie's syndrome by a colonoscopically placed long intestinal tube. Surg Endosc 8:116–117, 1994.

51. Harig JM, Fumo DE, Loo FD, et al: Treatment of acute nontoxic megacolon during colonoscopy: Tube placement versus simple decompression. Gastrointest Endosc 34:23–27, 1988.

52. Vantrappen G: Acute colonic pseudo-obstruction. Lancet 341:152–153, 1993.

53. Rex DK: Colonoscopy and acute colonic pseudo-obstruction. Gastrointest Endosc Clin N Am 7:499–508, 1997.

54. Neely J, Catchpole B: Ileus: The restoration of alimentary-tract motility by pharmacological means. Br J Surgery 58:21–28, 1971.

55. Turegano-Fuentes F, Munoz-Jimenez F, Dell Valle-Hernandez E, et al: Early resolution of Ogilvie's syndrome with intravenous neostigmine: A simple, effective treatment. Dis Colon Rectum 40:1353–1357, 1997.

56. Trevisani GT, Hyman NH, Church JM: Neostigmine: Safe and effective treatment for acute colonic pseudo-obstruction. Dis Colon Rectum 43:599–603, 2000.

57. Law N, Bharucha AE, Undale AS, et al: Cholinergic stimulation enhances colonic motor activity, transit, and sensation in humans. Am J Physiol Gastrointest Liver Physiol 281:G1228–G1237, 2001.

58. Althausen PL, Gupta MC, Benson DR, et al: The use of neostigmine to treat postoperative ileus in orthopedic spinal patients. J Spinal Disord 14:541–545, 2001.

59. Paran H, Silverberg D, Mayo A, et al: Treatment of acute colonic pseudo-obstruction with neostigmine. J Am Coll Surg 190:315–318, 2000.

60. Abeyta BJ, Albrecht RM, Schermer CR: Retrospective study of neostigmine for the treatment of acute colonic pseudo-obstruction. Am Surgeon 67:265–269, 2001.

61. Loftus CG, Harewood MD, Baron TH: Assessment of predictors of response to neostigmine for acute colonic pseudo-obstruction. Am J Gastroenterol 97:3118–3122, 2002.

62. Cronnelly R, Stanski DR, Miller RD, et al: Renal function and the pharmacokinetics of neostigmine in anesthetized man. Anesthesiology 51:222–226, 1979.

63. Laine L: Management of acute colonic pseudo-obstruction. N Engl J Med 341:192–193, 1999.

64. Amaro R: Neostigmine infusion: A new standard of care for acute colonic pseudo-obstruction? Am J Gastroenterol 95:304–305, 2000.

65. Tollesson PO, Cassuto J, Faxen A, et al: Lack of effect of metoclopramide on colonic motility after cholecystectomy. Eur J Surg 157:355–358, 1991.

66. Bonacini M, Smith OJ, Pritchard T: Erythromycin as therapy for acute colonic pseudo-obstruction (Ogilvie's syndrome). J Clin Gastroenterol 13:475–487, 1991.

67. Armstrong DN, Ballantyne GH, Modlin IM: Erythromycin reflex ileus in Ogilvie's syndrome. Lancet 337:378, 1991.

68. MacColl C, MacCannell KL, Baylis B, et al: Treatment of acute colonic pseudo-obstruction (Ogilvie's syndrome) with cisapride. Gastroenterology 98:773–776, 1990.

69. Wegener M, Borsch G: Acute colonic pseudo-obstruction (Ogilvie's syndrome). Surg Endosc 1:169–174, 1987.

70. Fiorito JJ, Schoen RE, Brandt LJ: Pseudo-obstruction associated with colonic ischemia: Successful management with colonoscopic decompression. Am J Gastroenterol 86:1472–1476, 1991.

71. Pham TN, Cosman BC, Chu P, et al: Radiographic changes after colonoscopic decompression for acute pseudo-obstruction. Dis Colon Rectum 42:1586–1591, 1999.

72. Duh Q, Way LW: Diagnostic laparoscopy and laparoscopic cecostomy for colonic pseudo-obstruction. Dis Colon Rectum 36:65–70, 1993.

73. Hutchinson R: Pharmacologic treatment of colonic pseudo-obstruction. Dis Colon Rectum 36:781–782, 1993.

74. Ponsky JL, Aszodi A, Perse D: Percutaneous endoscopic cecostomy: A new approach to nonobstructive colonic dilation. Gastrointest Endosc 32:108–111, 1986.

75. Chevallier P, Marcy P, Francois E, et al: Controlled transperitoneal percutaneous cecostomy as a therapeutic alternative to the endoscopic decompression for Ogilvie's syndrome. Am J Gastroenterol 97:471–474, 2002.

76. VanSonnenberg E, Varney RR, Casola G, et al: Percutaneous cecostomy for Ogilvie's syndrome: Laboratory observations and clinical experience. Radiology 175:679–682, 1990.

77. Child CS: Prevention of neostigmine-induced colonic activity: A comparison of atropine and glycopyrronium. Anesthesia 39:1083–1085, 1984.

78. Nietsch H, Kimmey MB: Acute colonic pseudo-obstruction. In Waye J, Rex DK, Williams CB (eds): Colonoscopy: Principles and Practice. London, Blackwell Science, 2004, pp 596–602.

Diagnosis and Staging of Esophageal Carcinoma

Ian D. Penman and Nicholas I. Church

Introduction

The incidence of esophageal carcinoma is increasing in many countries and the condition remains highly lethal, because most patients present with advanced disease. Squamous cell carcinoma (SCC) and adenocarcinoma (AC) are the most common subtypes, whereas verrucous carcinoma (a variant of SCC) and small cell carcinoma occur rarely. Nonepithelial tumors of the esophagus are discussed in Chapter 31. This chapter discusses the clinical characteristics of esophageal carcinoma and focuses on diagnosis and staging, with an emphasis on endoscopic techniques.

Epidemiology

Carcinoma of the esophagus ranked as the eighth most common carcinoma worldwide in 1990 and accounts for 7% of gastrointestinal malignancies,[1] most patients in the Western world presenting after the age of 65 years. Approximately 13,900 people in the United States are affected annually with an overall age-adjusted incidence of 4.5 per 100,000, ranging from 2.1 per 100,000 in women to 7.7 per 100,000 in men.[2,3] Overall 5-year survival has improved in recent years but, at 14%, remains unacceptably low. There are significant epidemiologic differences between the two main carcinoma subtypes; therefore, these are considered separately.

SQUAMOUS CELL CARCINOMA

Globally, SCC remains more common than AC with an overall incidence between 2.5 and 5.0 per 100,000 for men and 1.5 and 2.5 per 100,000 for women.[4] However, there are striking geographical variations in incidence. High-risk areas include the Transkei region

of South Africa and the so-called Asian esophageal cancer belt comprising eastern Turkey, India, northern Iran, and northern China, where incidence is greater than 100 per 100,000 of the population.[5] The highest incidence is reported in the Linxian province of northern China where the incidence in the 1980s was more than 700 per 100,000 inhabitants compared with a national incidence of 32 per 100,000 (see Chapter 32).[5,6] Within the United States, African-American men have the highest incidence of any ethnic group (16.8 per 100,000); in general, men are affected two to three times more often than women,[7] although in high-risk areas of the world the incidence is similar in the two groups. The disease is most prevalent among lower socioeconomic groups.

Variations in incidence have been attributed to a number of etiologic factors including environmental exposure, dietary habits, infection, radiation exposure, and associated high-risk conditions. Nitrosamines and other carcinogenic N-nitroso compounds are found in high concentrations in food and water supplies in northern China.[8] Low soil levels of molybdenum have also been linked to SCC in high-incidence regions.[9] A diet low in fresh fruit and vegetables and high in starch, cured meat, and salted or smoked fish has been shown to be high risk,[5] and other postulated dietary factors include the chewing of betel nut and drinking of hot tea.[10]

The most important risk factors for SCC (in the Western world) are tobacco and alcohol use[11,12]; the risk is greatest in those who both smoke and drink. Many carcinogens including nitrosamines and polycyclic hydrocarbons exist in both tobacco smoke and alcohol, and in alcohol abusers the risk may be compounded by concomitant nutritional and immunologic deficiencies.[5] Spirits are associated with greater risk than consumption of wine or beer.[13]

Infective agents such as fungal species have been linked with SCC as has human papillomavirus (HPV). In one study of 700 cancer cases from China, HPV particles were found in 17%,[14] but to date a major role in the pathogenesis of SCC has not been confirmed. Radiation exposure may be a rare cause of SCC; cases have been reported following radiotherapy for breast carcinoma,[15] but the long latency period makes causality difficult to prove.

Numerous high-risk conditions have been described. Achalasia may predispose to SCC in association with chronic stasis of food and debris in the dilated esophagus, with an incidence of SCC of up to 9% after 15 to 20 years.[5] Lye strictures of the esophagus are associated with a 1000-fold increased risk of SCC compared with controls; patients often present 40 to 50 years after lye ingestion. Up to 16% of patients with Plummer-Vinson syndrome (iron deficiency anemia, dysphagia, and postcricoid webs in elderly females) may develop pharyngeal or esophageal carcinoma.[16] Long-standing celiac disease is rarely associated with esophageal and pharyngeal SCC, in addition to enteropathy-associated T-cell lymphoma and AC.[17] Tylosis is a rare autosomal dominant disease consisting of palmar and plantar hyperkeratosis and thickening and fissuring of the skin. Up to 95% of patients develop esophageal SCC by the age of 65 years.[18] Patients with SCC of the head and neck have been reported to develop synchronous esophageal carcinoma in up to 8% of cases[19]; tobacco and alcohol are common risk factors for both. Therefore, it has been suggested that patients with upper aerodigestive tumors should have endoscopic evaluation to detect concurrent asymptomatic esophageal carcinoma.

SCC can arise anywhere in the esophagus with an approximately equal distribution throughout the gullet (Fig. 27–1).

ADENOCARCINOMA

Esophageal ACs predominantly arise in the distal esophagus and at the gastroesophageal (GE) junction (Fig. 27–2). Tumors at the GE junction and gastric cardia were previously considered as primary gastric carcinomas invading the distal esophagus. More recently, these tumors have been reclassified (Fig. 27–3) as type 1 when they arise from the distal esophagus, type 2 when the origin is the gastric cardia, and type 3 when they are subcardial.[20] Although this classification should allow more accurate characterization of tumors at the GE junction into primary esophageal or primary gastric types, changes in terminology and classification over time must be borne in mind when interpreting data from relevant studies.

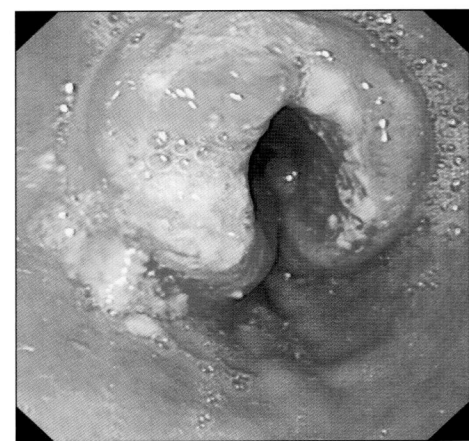

Figure 27–1. Endoscopy in a patient with progressive dysphagia demonstrates a crescentic stenosing squamous cell carcinoma in the midesophagus.

Current evidence suggests that type 1 (and possibly type 2) junctional carcinomas have a similar clinical course to distal esophageal tumors and should be staged as for esophageal carcinoma.[21] Epidemiologic differences between esophageal AC and type 3 junctional AC suggest that these diseases are separate entities,[22] and type 3 tumors are usually staged according to criteria for gastric cancer.

In contrast to SCC, the incidence of esophageal AC has been rising in many parts of the developed world since the 1970s, a consistent finding across the United States, Europe, and Australia.[23–25] The most rapid increases have been reported in the United States at 10% per year,[26] especially in white men, and AC is now more common than SCC.[23] Current incidence in the developed world is approximately 4.0 per 100,000 of the population, varying from less than 1.0 in Eastern Europe to 5.0 to 8.7 cases per 100,000 in Great Britain.[3,4]

The predominant risk factors for AC are GE reflux and Barrett's esophagus (BE). Unlike SCC, lower socioeconomic status and tobacco and alcohol use are not strongly associated with increased incidence.[27] BE is a condition in which the normal squamous epithelium of the distal esophagus is replaced by columnar epithelium with incomplete intestinal metaplasia (see Chapter 28). Chronic gastroesophageal reflux (GERD) predisposes to BE[28] and has also

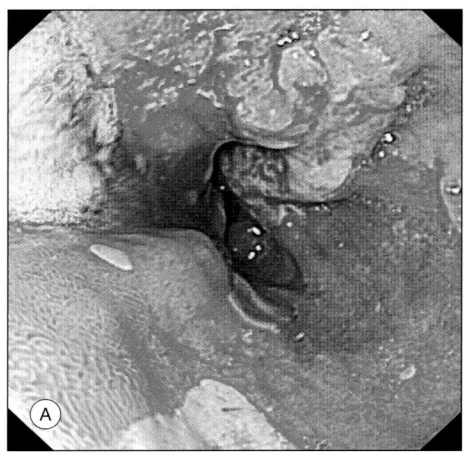

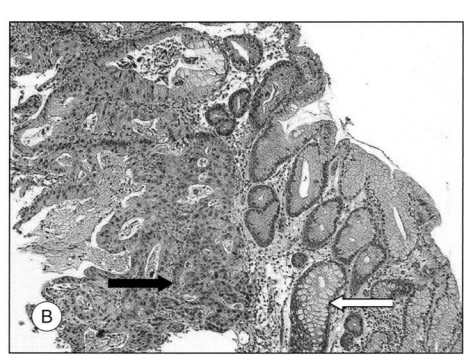

Figure 27–2. *A,* Endoscopy reveals a bulky polypoid distal carcinoma arising on a background of Barrett's esophagus. *B,* Biopsies demonstrate intestinal metaplasia with goblet cells *(open arrow)* and also features of an adenocarcinoma *(closed arrow).*

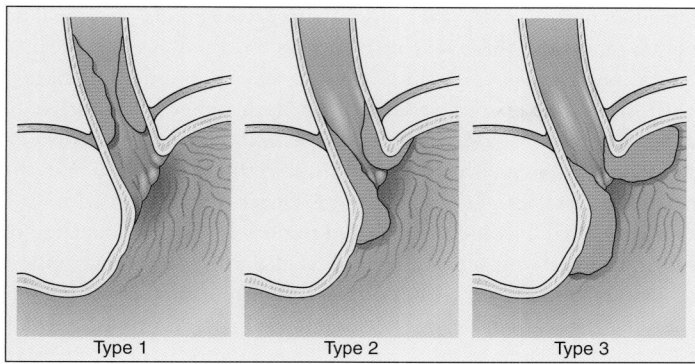

Figure 27–3. Schematic illustration of the proposed classification of carcinomas arising from the esophagogastric junction. Type 1 carcinomas are classified as esophageal in origin, as are type 2 tumors, although this is still debated. Type 3 carcinomas are classified as primary gastric in origin. (From Siewert JR, Stein HJ: Carcinoma of the cardia: Carcinoma of the gastroesophageal junction–classification, pathology and extent of resection. Dis Esoph 9:173–182, 1996).

been associated independently with the development of AC in a large study of Swedish patients.[29] In this population, the development of AC correlated with duration, frequency, and severity of GERD. Obesity has also been implicated in the development of AC, perhaps because of an influence on GERD; one study reported an odds ratio of 7.6 in patients with a high body mass index.[30] There are wide variations in the reported relative risk of cancer development in BE, but it is estimated to be approximately 0.4% to 0.5% per year (i.e., 1 in 200 to 250 patient-years).[28,31] There is a weak correlation between length of the Barrett's segment and malignant potential.[32]

Pathogenesis

SCC usually arises through a sequence of basal cell hyperplasia and increasing degrees of dysplasia. In some cases, this may represent a field change throughout the squamous mucosa of the aerodigestive tract. The molecular genetics are not fully understood, but numerous abnormalities have been demonstrated. These include amplification and overexpression of oncogenes encoding growth factors and/or their receptors (e.g., epidermal growth factor [EGF], epidermal growth factor receptor [EGFR], and transforming growth factor [TGF]-α), tumor suppressor genes (loss of heterozygosity of p53), and cell cycle regulatory genes (e.g., cyclin D1).

Most cases of AC develop within Barrett's epithelium, and evidence supports a metaplasia-dysplasia-carcinoma sequence. BE represents a maladaptive metaplastic response to chronic GE reflux, but, although acid is implicated as the major noxious agent for the epithelium, other components of the refluxate such as pepsin, pancreatic enzymes, and especially bile acids may also play a role. Bile acids induce mucosal injury, stimulate cell proliferation, and are mutagenic in the esophagus, possibly via induction of cyclooxygenase 2 (COX-2) and protein kinase C pathways.[33,34]

BE is characterized histologically by a cellular mosaic consisting of columnar epithelium containing patches of incomplete intestinal metaplasia, the hallmark of which is the presence of goblet cells.

Hyperproliferation of BE is usual, and defects in apoptosis and cell cycle regulation are also commonly reported during progression to malignancy.[35] Many molecular abnormalities have been demonstrated, but the exact relevance of many of these remains to be proven. Up to one third of patients with BE have overexpression of nuclear cyclin D1, a key regulatory step in the transition of cells from the G_1 to S phase of the cell cycle. P53 mutations and/or loss of heterozygosity are common in intestinal metaplasia before dysplasia develops and appears to be an early event. Overexpression of members of the Erb family of receptor tyrosine kinases is frequent (EGF, EGFR, and TGF-α) as are abnormalities in the transforming growth factor-beta (TGF-β)/SMAD signaling pathway. Inactivation of tumor suppressor genes *p16* and *p15* have been reported in Barrett's ACs, as have abnormalities in E-cadherin and β-catenin; nuclear accumulation of β-catenin is a common finding. This may lead to transcription of growth related genes via activation of the T-cell factor (TCF)/LEF-1 family of transcription factors.[34,35] Advances in DNA microarray technology including genomic profiling and cluster analysis have highlighted the potential importance of many novel genes in the development of Barrett's AC recently,[36] and further studies will hopefully unravel the complex sequence of events underlying the pathogenesis of this malignancy.

Clinical Features

SYMPTOMS

The esophagus lacks a serosal covering, and early tumor growth causes asymptomatic dilatation of the smooth muscle. In most patients, dysphagia results only when the lumen has narrowed to 50% to 75% of its normal circumference. By this time, local or nodal spread has often occurred, and the tumor is often incurable. Early cancers can present with dysphagia, but this is uncommon. Dysphagia may be present for several months before medical advice is sought, and subjective localization of the site of obstruction is a poor indicator of the actual site of disease in the esophagus.[37] Symptoms are commonly gradual in onset, with progressive difficulty swallowing solids and then liquids. In rare cases, submucosally infiltrating GE junction tumors affect motility and result in pseudoachalasia with clinical features similar to achalasia and no obvious endoscopic mucosal abnormality.

Anorexia and weight loss, which often precede the onset of dysphagia, are common, and odynophagia may occur with ulcerated tumors. Persistent retrosternal pain, unrelated to swallowing, and back pain are sinister symptoms suggesting mediastinal invasion.[37] Cough worsened by swallowing or recurrent pneumonia suggests esophagobronchial fistulation. This occurs in 5% to 10% of patients and is associated with poor outcomes resulting in a median survival time of 1.5 to 4 months.[38] Hematemesis is uncommon,[39] and exsanguination resulting from aortoesophageal fistula is rare. Tumor involvement of the left recurrent laryngeal nerve results in hoarseness.

SIGNS

Physical examination may reveal evidence of weight loss and dehydration. Examination of the neck may detect cervical or supraclavicular lymphadenopathy. The oral cavity and pharynx should be carefully inspected in patients with SCC for evidence of synchronous head and neck malignancy. Signs of pneumonia may result from aspiration or fistulation into airways, and hepatomegaly or jaundice from liver involvement indicate terminal disease.

PROGRESSION OF DISEASE

Esophageal carcinoma progresses through a combination of direct extension, lymphatic spread, and/or hematogenous metastasis. Lack of a serosal covering facilitates direct extension and invasion of structures in the neck or chest. Early lymphatic spread via rich interconnecting lymphatic networks in the esophageal submucosa is common. Tumors at any site may involve nodes in the neck and mediastinum, although proximal lesions metastasize more commonly to cervical nodes and distal lesions to abdominal nodes.[40] Depth of invasion is a major determinant of lymph node metastasis. Disease confined to the mucosa is associated with nodal involvement in less than 5% of cases,[41] whereas penetration into the submucosa is associated with a 15% to 50% risk of metastases.[42,43] Hematogenous spread occurs to the lungs, liver, adrenals, kidneys, pancreas, peritoneum, bones, and brain. Recent data have suggested that AC may behave as a systemic disease from an early stage, with one study reporting involvement of bone marrow by viable micrometastases in 88% of patients with GE junction carcinoma treated by esophageal resection.[44]

Diagnosis

Flexible videoendoscopy with biopsy and/or brush cytology is the gold standard investigation for the diagnosis of esophageal carcinoma (Figs. 27–1 and 27–2). Endoscopy is more sensitive and specific than double-contrast barium meal for the diagnosis of upper gastrointestinal cancer,[45] and when biopsy and cytology are combined, the accuracy of endoscopy for diagnosis approaches 100%.[46] Rigid esophagoscopy is rarely necessary and is no longer recommended on the grounds of safety and cost effectiveness.[47] In rare patients with pseudoachalasia and repeated negative mucosal biopsy, endoscopic ultrasound with or without fine needle aspiration biopsy may provide supportive evidence for malignancy and a tissue diagnosis.[48]

BARIUM CONTRAST RADIOGRAPHY

Early Carcinoma

Double-contrast barium esophagography is insensitive for the detection of early esophageal tumors that are usually detected at careful endoscopy. Accurate diagnosis can only be made in approximately 73% of barium studies, and specificity is low.[49] Early cancers may appear as centrally ulcerated plaques or polypoid or depressed lesions. Superficial spreading carcinomas may appear as a confluent area of mucosal nodularity or granularity.

Advanced Carcinoma

Double-contrast barium studies may suggest the diagnosis in more than 95% of patients, and tumors may be infiltrative, ulcerating, polypoid, or varicoid. Infiltrating carcinomas generally cause irregular narrowing of the lumen with well-defined margins and nodular mucosa. There may be complete obstruction with proximal dilatation. Occasionally these tumors may mimic benign disease with smooth, tapered strictures or appearances suggestive of achalasia. Pseudoachalasia should be suspected when the history of dysphagia is short, the patient is older than 55 years, and the narrowed distal esophageal segment is longer than 3.5 cm with little or no proximal dilatation.[50] Polypoid tumors are seen as lobulated or fungating intraluminal masses, whereas ulcerating carcinomas appear as well-defined lesions with a rim of radiolucent tumor surrounding the ulcer. In varicoid cancers, submucosal spread produces thick tortuous longitudinal folds, which have an appearance similar to esophageal varices. Mediastinal involvement by tumor may be demonstrated by deformity of the esophageal axis. Angulation or deviation away from the vertical is caused by fixation, tumor retraction, or lymph node metastasis.[51]

Current Role of Barium Studies

Barium esophagography should be performed when esophageal perforation is suspected, either preendoscopy or following esophageal dilatation. It is also useful when there is complete obstruction and when tortuous, complex strictures prevent passage of the endoscope. In these situations, it may be useful to have a radiologic "road map" to facilitate dilatation and subsequent completion of endoscopy or stent insertion. Contrast studies are indicated when esophagobronchial fistulation is suspected, and barium radiology may also be of use in identification and characterization of motility problems such as pseudoachalasia, when endoscopic biopsy is negative but there is a clinical suspicion of malignancy.

ENDOSCOPY

Appearance of Malignant Lesions

Early lesions may appear as minor irregularities of the mucosa; areas of erythema; or depressed, raised, or ulcerated areas (Figs. 27–1, 27–2, 27–4, and 27–5). A high index of suspicion is required, and any such abnormalities should undergo biopsy. Dye staining of the mucosa improves the detection rate and is discussed later. More advanced lesions are usually obvious polypoid or ulcerating masses. The esophageal lumen may be stenosed by tumor bulk or involvement of the muscular layers. A tightly closed distal esophageal sphincter with normal mucosal appearances and resistance to the passage of the endoscope suggests pseudoachalasia.

Diagnostic Technique

Diagnostic endoscopy is performed using topical pharyngeal anesthesia or conscious sedation. Intravenous sedation improves patient tolerance of prolonged procedures and allows esophageal dilatation to be performed if necessary. However, care must be exercised to avoid oversedation and the attendant risks, especially pulmonary aspiration of food and secretions lying above a stenotic tumor. The mouth, pharynx, and larynx should be carefully inspected, particularly in patients with a history of tobacco and alcohol use and those in whom a possible SCC is present. The entire esophagus should be visualized, and the endoscope should be retroflexed in the stomach to examine the GE junction and gastric

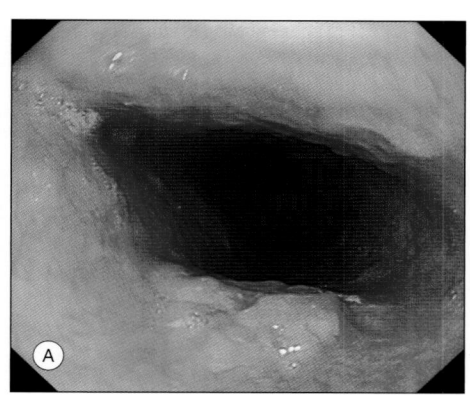 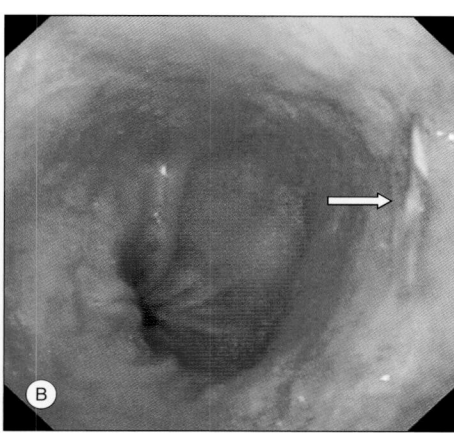

Figure 27-4. Early esophageal cancer. *A,* Early squamous cell carcinoma with an elevated 1-cm lesion in the proximal esophagus. *B,* Surveillance endoscopy in this patient with circumferential long segment Barrett's esophagus demonstrates a 7-mm ulcer *(arrow)*. The lesion was staged T1m,N0 by endoscopic ultrasonography (EUS), and this was confirmed at surgical resection.

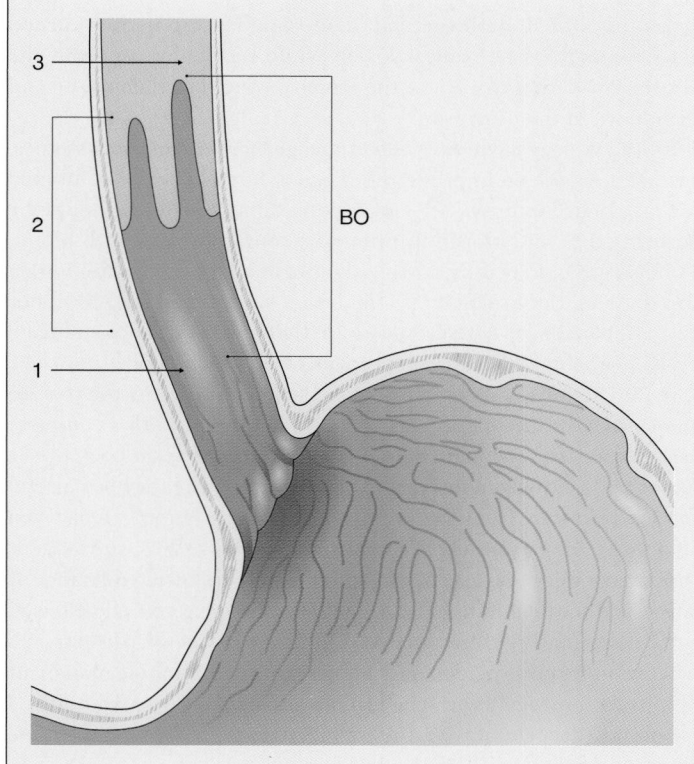

Figure 27-5. Schematic illustration of the relationship of hiatal hernia, gastroesophageal junction, and Barrett's esophagus. The Barrett's segment lies between the top of the gastric folds distally and the most proximal extent of the pink columnar mucosa. These should be carefully documented (in cm from the incisor teeth) at endoscopy along with the location of the diaphragmatic hiatus.

cardia. To complete the procedure, the remainder of the stomach and the duodenum are examined.

When a suspicious lesion is seen, it is important to document the following features, which may provide important information when planning definitive therapy (surgical resection, radiotherapy, or stent insertion):

1. Position relative to the incisor teeth (in cm) with proximal and distal margins
2. Presence and proximal extent of any BE (Fig. 27–5)

3. Presence of a hiatal hernia
4. Involvement of the gastric cardia or extension along lesser curve
5. Presence of metastatic or synchronous lesions elsewhere in the upper gastrointestinal tract
6. Previous gastric or duodenal surgery

Chromoendoscopy

The diagnosis of early carcinoma may be difficult in view of the subtle nature of the lesion. Chromoendoscopy involves the use of agents that enhance the distinction between diseased and normal mucosa, either by filling surface crevices or by differential uptake by diseased epithelium (vital staining). Many chromoendoscopy agents have been studied in the detection of esophageal carcinoma, of which Lugol's iodine and methylene blue have been most widely studied (see Chapter 32).

Lugol's iodine reacts with glycogen in squamous epithelial cells to produce a uniform dark brown coloration. Inflamed, dysplastic, and malignant cells are glycogen depleted and consequently appear minimally stained or unstained.[51,52] One percent to 3% Lugol's iodine is sprayed onto the mucosa using a standard washing catheter inserted through the biopsy channel of the endoscope. Most highly dysplastic or malignant lesions remain unstained (Fig. 27–6), and clinical trials have shown that biopsy of these areas enhances detection of both high grade dysplasia and early carcinoma.[53,54] The sensitivity for high grade dysplasia or carcinoma ranges from 46% to 96% in published series[54,55]; the differences probably reflect differing techniques and populations studied. Despite this, Lugol's staining is straightforward, with unstained areas easy to identify. The technique does not require specialized equipment or additional staff, and there is a case to be made for its routine use in patients with epidemiologic risk factors for SCC.

Particular care must be taken when BE is present. The extent should be documented and biopsies taken to confirm the presence of specialized intestinal metaplasia. Methylene blue is a vital stain taken up by the cytoplasm of absorptive cells. These include goblet cells present in Barrett's epithelium, in addition to normal cells of the colon and small intestine.[56] Methylene blue staining was first shown to selectively stain areas of specialized intestinal metaplasia in BE in 1996,[57] and subsequent studies concluded that dysplasia and cancer were diagnosed in significantly more patients in whom

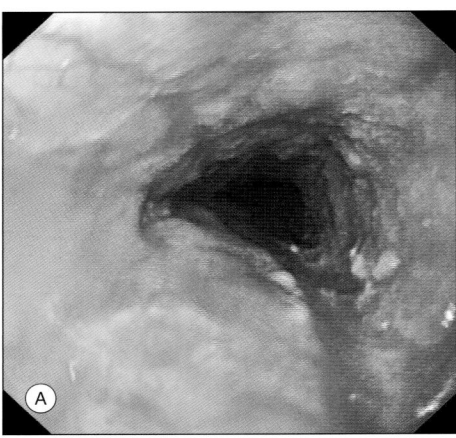 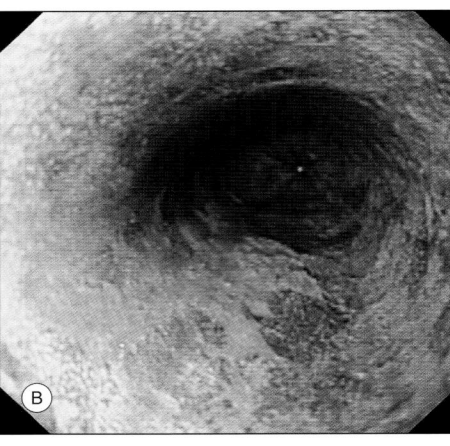

Figure 27–6. Endoscopic view of early superficial squamous cell carcinoma before *(A)* and after *(B)* staining with Lugol's iodine. Before staining, the mucosa appeared rough and irregular, but no focal lesion is evident. After Lugol's iodine, the extent of the lesion is apparent. Histology confirmed intramucosal carcinoma.

staining was used than those in whom only random biopsies were taken.[58] Neoplastic change is associated with a reduction in goblet cell numbers and an increasing nuclear-to-cytoplasm ratio proportional to the degree of dysplasia, and such tissues absorb methylene blue to a lesser extent than surrounding cells. Increasing grades of dysplasia may appear as heterogeneous or unstained areas, allowing targeted rather than random biopsies to be taken.[59]

The technique of methylene blue staining is more complicated than that for Lugol's iodine. Methylene blue uptake is inhibited by surface mucus that must first be removed. To achieve this, a specialized spray catheter is used to spray 10% N-acetylcysteine over the mucosa using a volume of 3 mL per centimeter of Barrett's mucosa. Two minutes are allowed before a 0.5% solution of methylene blue dye is sprayed at a volume of 4 mL per centimeter of Barrett's mucosa. After 2 further minutes, the dye is vigorously washed away using 120 to 300 mL of water. Washing is particularly important because insufficient irrigation results in incorrect staining and reduced sensitivity of targeted biopsy. Staining is deemed to be positive when the noneroded mucosa is stained blue despite vigorous irrigation.[58]

The successful reports of methylene blue staining[57,58] have not always been replicated in other studies,[60] possibly because of different staining techniques. The method is time consuming and requires special equipment and additional staff, and at present, the generalizability of methylene blue staining to standard endoscopic practice remains unclear.

Biopsy and Cytology

Biopsy samples are obtained using forceps inserted via the biopsy channel of the endoscope. The cup volume of standard forceps is 12.4 mm^3, whereas that of the larger "jumbo" forceps is 30.4 mm^3 allowing larger biopsies to be taken; however, an endoscope with a 3.7-mm channel is required. A nonendoscopic balloon device for obtaining esophageal cytology has been developed in China mainly for use in screening high-risk populations.[61]

Jumbo forceps may provide better tissue samples for detection of high grade dysplasia or early carcinoma in BE.[62] Biopsies are taken from the edge of ulcerated lesions to avoid necrotic tissue, and at least six samples are required to confirm the diagnosis in 100% of patients.[63] Larger biopsies can also be obtained by a turn and suction technique, in which the forceps are inserted, opened, and with-

drawn until flush with the endoscope tip. The tip is then turned onto the esophageal wall or lesion while suctioning air from the lumen. This draws tissue into the forceps, which are then closed and withdrawn in the usual way.[64]

Brush cytology alone may detect malignancy and, in some studies, has been shown to improve the diagnostic yield when combined with standard biopsy.[46,65] For best results, brushing should be performed before biopsy to minimize contamination with blood. Samples are obtained by passing the brush catheter into the lumen and drawing the brush across the lesion several times until minor mucosal bleeding is noted. Smears are then made on slides and fixed in alcohol before staining using Papanicolaou's technique.

In 20% to 40% of cases, a malignant stricture prevents the passage of a standard adult endoscope.[66] This may prevent both a complete examination and adequate biopsy from within the main body of the tumor but a cytology brush passed into the stricture may be a useful adjunct to biopsy from the proximal end of the lesion.[67] Dilatation facilitates biopsy, relieves symptoms, and enables subsequent endosonographic staging. Biopsy immediately following dilatation is safe,[68] and for dilatation of malignant strictures the complications of hemorrhage and perforation occur in 2.5% to 10% of patients.[69,70] Dilatation often provides only short-term palliation of malignant dysphagia, however, with the effects lasting days or at the most a couple of weeks. The issue of dilatation before endoscopic ultrasonography (EUS) staging is discussed later.

Future Developments

A number of refinements to standard endoscopic visualization have been reported. These may allow better biopsy targeting and earlier diagnosis of tumors. With the rise in incidence of AC in many parts of the world, most interest has focused on the early detection of dysplasia in BE. The techniques include magnification endoscopy, optical coherence tomography (OCT), and light-induced fluorescence spectroscopy (LIFS).

Magnification Endoscopy

Magnification endoscopes were introduced in 1967, and the latest instruments are able to produce a magnification of 150×. The instruments incorporate a movable lens at the distal tip, which is controlled by an arm on the control unit. Precise tip control is required to avoid blurring of the image, and most endoscopes in clinical applications magnify up to 35 times. Investigators have recently used magnifying endoscopes to assess depth of mucosal invasion of SCC and to detect specialized intestinal metaplasia and high grade dysplasia in BE.[71] Early results are promising, but the use of magnification endoscopes has not yet become standard practice in upper gastrointestinal endoscopy.

Optical Coherence Tomography

OCT is based on the detection of back-reflected infrared light from the mucosal layers of the gut. Catheter probes introduced via the biopsy channel are able to scan end-on or side-on, and considerable mucosal and submucosal detail may be obtained. Initial results of OCT in the esophagus are encouraging,[72] and a recent trial reported a sensitivity of 97% and specificity of 92% for the detection of specialized intestinal metaplasia in BE.[73] The technique has a high resolution, with a limit around 10 μm, but it is currently too early to define what role, if any, OCT will play in the diagnosis or staging of patients with upper gastrointestinal malignancy.

Light-Induced Fluorescence Spectroscopy

LIFS detects emitted photons from molecules in the mucosa, which exhibit fluorescence after excitation by laser light. These "fluorophores" may be endogenous or exogenous. The system uses a catheter probe with a central fiber for delivery of the excitation light surrounded by further fibers to collect the fluorescent light. The received light is amplified and analyzed by spectrophotometry. Normal tissues have characteristic fluorescence spectra, and dysplastic tissue may, therefore, be identified by demonstration of an abnormal spectrum. LIFS has been reported to have a sensitivity of 100% and specificity of 98% in the differentiation of normal from malignant tissue in patients with known esophageal carcinoma.[74] However, subsequent studies investigating the application of LIFS to the detection of dysplasia in BE have been contradictory.[75] Exogenous fluorophores such as topical or oral 5-aminolevulinic acid (5-ALA) preferentially localize in neoplastic tissue, and some initial success has been reported with this agent.[76] The need for specialized equipment and the costs of this time-consuming approach have, to date, limited its uptake and more data are needed.

Staging of Esophageal Carcinoma

IMPORTANCE OF STAGING

Overall, survival in esophageal cancer remains poor. Prospective data from the EUROCARE-2 study in 10 European countries revealed a 1-year survival rate of 33% and an overall 5-year survival of only 10%.[77] Recent registry data from the United Kingdom found that age-standardized relative survival rates at 1 year were 25% and corresponding figures at 5 years were a dismal 4.8% for males and 6.3% for females.[78] Data from the SEER program in the United States estimates a 5-year survival of 14%.[2]

Prognosis is highly dependent on tumor stage at diagnosis. The few fortunate patients with early disease (T1N0M0, stage I) have 5-year survival rates in excess of 90% with surgery alone, but prognosis worsens with advancing stage at diagnosis such that patients with stage IV disease have 5-year survival rates of less than 5%. Five-year survival in patients without nodal involvement at surgery (N0)

is approximately 40% to 60% but only 5% to 17% in those with nodal involvement (N1). Patients undergoing surgery alone for T3N1 disease have 5-year survival of 8% to 10%,[77,78] underlining the harsh reality that although these tumors may be technically resectable they are rarely curable. Thus, accurate staging is essential in determining prognosis and in selecting those for whom surgery alone is likely to be curative and those with advanced disease for whom surgery has little to offer and for whom medical therapy or palliation should be the goal of therapy.

The realization that surgery alone rarely cures patients with locally advanced disease has led to the development of neoadjuvant chemotherapy or chemoradiotherapy protocols for these patients. Although the benefits of neoadjuvant therapy have not yet been conclusively demonstrated,[79-81] it is increasingly used in many countries for patients with locally advanced tumors in an attempt to downstage the disease before surgery and improve long-term survival. The largest prospective randomized trial to date randomized 802 patients to either surgery alone or two cycles of preoperative cisplatin and fluorouracil followed by surgery. The results demonstrated a 9% 2-year survival advantage (43% vs. 34%) for patients undergoing neoadjuvant therapy.[79] A full discussion of the relative benefits of neoadjuvant therapy is beyond the scope of this chapter, but given its increasing use and the considerable morbidity associated with it, it is imperative that patients undergo accurate staging to guide stage-specific therapy with the hope of improving survival. These strategies will vary according to local practice and must be understood by those staging such patients. In addition, to obtain clinically useful and important information from future trials of neoadjuvant therapy, it is essential that study groups are well matched and highly accurate staging is crucial in this regard.

STAGING SYSTEM

Although it is generally true that patients with long malignant strictures and high grade stenosis preventing passage of an endoscope generally have more advanced stage tumors, these clinical features are not an accurate guide to tumor stage and are no longer used in the formal staging process. Tumors are staged using the TNM staging system developed by the International Union against Cancer (UICC) and American Joint Committee on Cancer (AJCC).[82] This system, updated in 2002, describes the anatomic extent of cancer at the time of diagnosis and before therapy and also allows a classification of the stages of cancer for estimation of prognosis and comparison of the results of different treatments. The definition of TNM for all esophageal cancer subtypes and stage groupings are detailed in Table 27–1, based on the depth of invasion of the tumor into the esophageal wall or beyond, the presence or absence of regional lymph node involvement, and identification of distant metastasis. The main regional lymph node stations are shown in Figure 27–7.

For the purposes of staging, the esophagus is arbitrarily divided into four regions because clinical behavior and treatments may vary with the different anatomic segments. These are the *cervical esophagus* (cricoid cartilage to thoracic inlet); the *intrathoracic esophagus* (*upper* portion from the thoracic inlet to the tracheal bifurcation and *midthoracic* portion from the bifurcation to just above the GE junction); and the *lower thoracic and abdominal esophagus*

Table 27–1. TNM Classification and Stage Grouping of Esophageal Carcinoma

TNM Classification of Esophageal Carcinoma

Primary Tumor (T)

TX	Primary tumor cannot be assessed
T0	No evidence of primary tumor
Tis	Carcinoma in situ
T1	Tumor invades lamina propria or submucosa
T2	Tumor invades muscularis propria
T3	Tumor invades adventitia
T4	Tumor invades adjacent structures

Regional Lymph Nodes (N)

NX	Regional lymph nodes cannot be assessed
N0	No regional lymph node metastases
N1	Regional lymph node metastases

Distant Metastases (M)

MX	Distant metastases cannot be assessed
M0	No distant metastases
M1	Distant metastases

Tumors of the lower thoracic esophagus

M1a	Metastases in celiac lymph nodes
M1b	Other distant metastases

Tumors of the midthoracic esophagus

M1a	Not applicable
M1b	Nonregional lymph nodes and/or other distant metastases

Tumors of the upper thoracic esophagus

M1a	Metastases in cervical lymph nodes
M1b	Other distant metastases

Stage Grouping of Esophageal Carcinoma

	T	N	M
Stage 0	Tis	N0	M0
Stage I	T1	N0	M0
Stage IIA	T2	N0	M0
	T3	N0	Mo
Stage IIB	T1	N1	M0
	T2	N1	M0
Stage III	T3	N1	M0
	T4	Any N	M0
Stage IV	Any T	Any N	M1
Stage IVA	Any T	Any N	M1a
Stage IVB	Any T	Any N	M1b

From Greene FL, Page DL, Fleming ID, et al (eds): American Joint Committee on Cancer. Cancer staging manual, 6th ed. New York, Springer, 2002, pp 91–98.

(including the GE junction). The intra-abdominal portion includes type I junctional carcinomas as proposed by Siewert, whereas type III tumors with minimal involvement of the esophagus are considered primary gastric cancers.[82] How best to classify true type 2 junctional tumors remains a subject of debate.

Controversy also exists over how best to classify patients with involvement of distant lymph nodes. Involvement of cervical or celiac axis nodes in patients with intrathoracic tumors signifies a poor prognosis and unresectable disease and is, therefore, classified as M1a or M1b disease depending on exact tumor location. Others have questioned this and suggested that involvement of such nodes is associated with a better prognosis than true visceral metastasis (M1b), but at the present time involvement of celiac axis or cervical lymph nodes in patients with intrathoracic tumors are still classified as stage IV disease.

Pretreatment staging should be performed in conjunction with a detailed assessment of the patient's fitness for major interventions such as surgery or chemoradiotherapy, and full staging is clearly inappropriate in frail patients with significant comorbidity who are only candidates for palliation. Staging should begin with a careful history and examination of the patients to detect cervical lymphadenopathy or hepatomegaly and to assess general fitness and the severity of comorbid disease, particularly cardiorespiratory problems. Detailed cardiac and respiratory investigations are used as appropriate on an individual basis and these investigations can be performed in parallel with staging investigations. Documenting American Society of Anesthesiology (ASA) status and an assessment of performance status (e.g., World Health Organization [WHO] or Karnofsky score) may be clinically useful and are essential for patients entering study protocols.

The principle techniques used for staging esophageal cancer are computed tomography (CT), EUS, and often laparoscopy with or without laparoscopic ultrasonography. Other modalities less frequently used include positron emission tomography (PET), video-assisted thoracoscopy (VATS), and transcutaneous ultrasound scanning of the neck.

In clinical practice, once a diagnosis of esophageal carcinoma is made, staging in patients fit for radical therapy usually begins with noninvasive investigations to detect possible metastases, the finding of which obviates the need for further procedures such as endosonography. Therefore, the assessment of distant metastasis is described before tumor (T) and nodal (N) staging.

ASSESSMENT OF DISTANT METASTASES

Computed Tomography

Distant metastases are present in approximately 20% of patients at diagnosis,[78,83] most commonly involving nonregional abdominal or supraclavicular lymph nodes. CT scanning has been intensively studied over many years, is widely available and noninvasive, and remains the mainstay of initial staging in esophageal cancer. Its role in T and N staging is discussed later, but for distant metastasis CT has overall sensitivity ranging from 41% to 62%, specificity 69% to 83%, and accuracy 63% to 90%.[84,85] Sensitivity for detecting solid organ metastasis over 1 cm in size is approximately 80% but significantly less for smaller lesions (Fig. 27–8). Many of these are benign including simple liver cysts that may be better characterized on ultrasound, but biopsy proof of small metastatic lesions is important because it upstages the patient to stage IV with a major impact on management options.

Diminutive liver lesions are better assessed by laparoscopy, which can also assess peritoneal involvement more accurately than CT (sensitivity 95% vs. 21% for CT).[86,87] However, because of its noninvasive nature, relatively low cost, and availability, CT remains the primary modality for assessment of metastatic disease. The performance of CT is good but not excellent, and, although this may improve with the advent of multidetector CT scanners, little data are currently available.

18F-Fluoro-2-Dexyglucose Positron Emission Tomography

Reported studies of PET in esophageal cancer have demonstrated its superiority over CT for detection of distant metastasis, including those involving nonregional lymph nodes.[83,88–91] In one study of 42

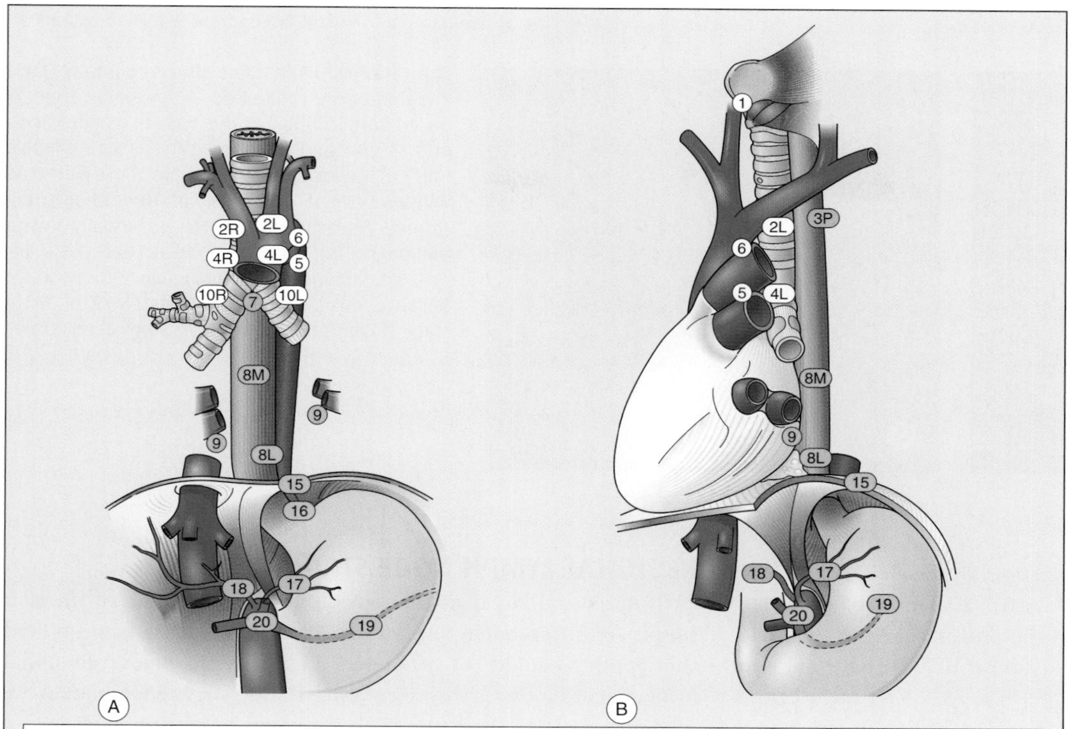

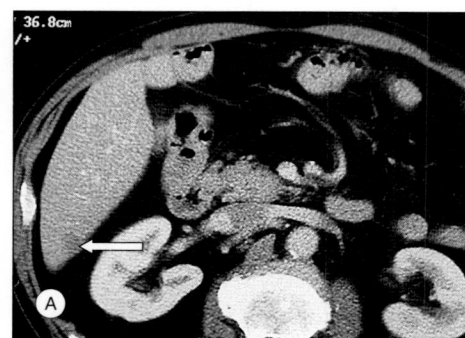

Figure 27-7. Main lymph node drainage stations in the staging of esophageal cancer. (Used with the permission of the American Joint Committee on Cancer (AJCC), Chicago. The original source for this material is the AJCC Cancer Staging Manual, 6th ed. New York, Springer-Verlag, 2002, www.springer-ny.com.)

1	Supraclavicular nodes	Above suprasternal notch and clavicles
2R	Right upper paratracheal nodes	Between intersection of caudal margin of innominate artery with trachea and the apex of the lung
2L	Left upper paratracheal nodes	Between top of arotic arch and apex of the lung
3P	Posterior mediastinal nodes	Upper paraesophageal nodes, above tracheal bifurcation
4R	Right lower paratracheal nodes	Between intersection of caudal margin of innominate artery with trachea and cephalic border of azygous vein
4L	Left lower paratracheal nodes	Between top of aortic arch and carina
5	Aortopulmonary nodes	Subaortic and para-aortic nodes lateral to the ligamentum arteriosum
6	Anterior mediastinal nodes	Anterior to ascending aorta or innominate artery
7	Subcarinal nodes	Caudal to the carina of the trachea
8M	Middle paraesophageal lymph nodes	From the tracheal bifurcation to the caudal margin of the inferior pulmonary vein
8L	Lower paraesophageal lymph nodes	From the caudal margin of the inferior pulmonary vein to the esophagogastric junction
9	Pulmonary ligament nodes	Within the inferior pulmonary ligament
10R	Right tracheobronchial nodes	From cephalic border of azygous vein to origin of RUL bronchus
10L	Left tracheobronchial nodes	Between carina and LUL bronchus
15	Diaphragmatic nodes	Lying on the dome of the diaphragm, and adjacent to or behind its crura
16	Paracardial nodes	Immediately adjacent to the gastroesophageal junction
17	Left gastric nodes	Along the course of the left gastric artery
18	Common hepatic nodes	Along the course of the common hepatic artery
19	Splenic nodes	Along the course of the splenic artery
20	Celiac nodes	At the base of the celiac artery

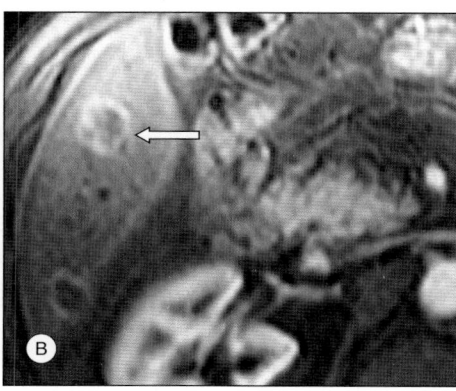

Figure 27-8. A, Contrast-enhanced computed tomography (CT) demonstrates a possible lesion in the right lobe of the liver (arrow). B, The subsequent gadolinium-enhanced magnetic resonance imaging (MRI) scan demonstrates the lesion more clearly and also a separate metastatic lesion (arrow). (Courtesy of Dr. C.L. Kay.)

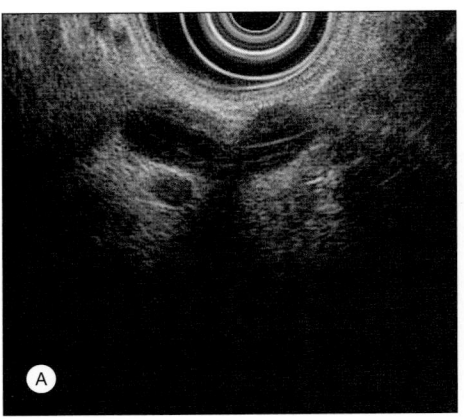
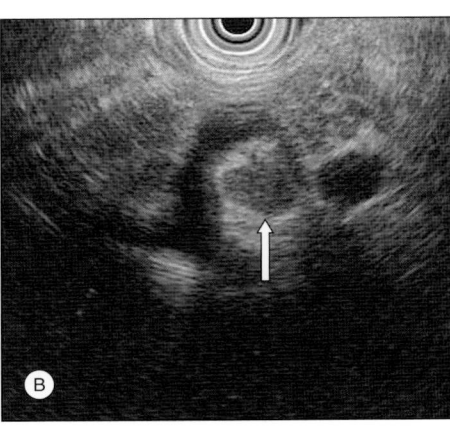

Figure 27–9. Endoscopic ultrasonography (EUS) imaging of the celiac axis. *A,* The celiac trunk is traced from its origin at the aorta to its bifurcation into splenic and hepatic arteries (the "whale's tail"). *B,* Celiac lymph nodes are those detected within 2 cm of the origin of the celiac trunk *(arrow).* Nodes identified here are virtually always malignant, but fine needle aspiration (FNA) for cytologic confirmation of malignancy is important because this upstages patients (M1a or M1b; stage IV) and usually precludes surgical resection.

patients with histopathologic confirmation, the accuracy of PET for distant metastasis (M1a) was 86% with a specificity of 90%.[92] Flamen and coworkers[93] compared the performance of PET with combined helical CT and EUS and found PET to have superior sensitivity, specificity, and accuracy (82% vs. 64%) for stage IV disease. PET led to upstaging to stage IV in 15% of patients with significant impact on management but understaged regional nodal disease in 49% of patients. Other studies have supported these findings, and, although PET appears to be an excellent method for detection of distant metastasis, its costs and lack of availability have so far prevented it becoming an integral part of the staging of patients with esophageal cancer.

Endoscopic Ultrasonography

Because it is only able to visualize the gastrointestinal wall layers and structures immediately adjacent to the gut wall, EUS is not primarily used to perform M staging, but it can provide useful M stage information in some patients without evidence of distant metastasis on CT. Small subcentimeter metastasis in the left lobe of the liver can be detected and are often amenable to EUS-fine needle aspiration (FNA) for tissue confirmation.[94] EUS is also highly sensitive for assessing the celiac axis for nodal involvement (M1a or M1b, Fig. 27–9). The excellent sensitivity and the potential for near 100% specificity through EUS-FNA have been demonstrated in several studies.[85,95–102] In one retrospective study, high-quality thin-slice helical CT only detected 53% of celiac lymph nodes proven to be involved by EUS-FNA.[103] Of the 48 patients, 12 who were felt to be resectable by helical CT had either metastatic lymph node involvement by EUS-FNA or T4 disease. Therefore, EUS can play a complementary role to CT in improving the accuracy of M staging. The impact of the latest multidetector CT scanners on celiac lymph node staging remains to be established, but even with improved sensitivity CT relies solely on size criteria for determining the likelihood for malignant involvement (short axis greater than 10 mm). EUS assesses morphologic features in addition to size and offers the potential for cytologic proof of malignancy through EUS-FNA cytology. Although limited data suggest that PET may be more accurate than combined CT and EUS-FNA,[92,93] further studies are needed and the restricted availability of PET means that CT and EUS-FNA are likely to remain the pivotal imaging techniques for M staging.

REGIONAL LYMPH NODE STAGING

Early spread to locoregional nodes is common because of the rich supply of interconnecting submucosal lymphatic channels and this applies equally to SCC and AC. The prevalence of nodal involvement increases with increasing T stage such that less than 5% of patients with T1m tumors have nodal involvement rising to approximately 25% in T1sm tumors, 60% in T2 tumors, and more than 80% in patients with T3 or T4 disease.[58,59,78] AC micro-metastases, undetectable by routine histologic assessment, may be a common early event, contributing to the poor prognosis in this disease.[44,104,105] Although the presence of peritumoral nodes does not prevent successful tumor resection, it has a major negative impact on prognosis, and cure rates after surgery are only 5% to 10%.[78,106–108] In a study of 94 patients, the prognosis of patients with N1 disease was equally poor regardless of the T stage of the tumor, highlighting the overriding importance of accurate detection of nodal involvement so that such patients can be considered for neoadjuvant therapy.[109] Not only the presence of nodes but the number detected is prognostically important; patients with more than three or four involved regional nodes fare particularly poorly.[34,38,110]

Computed Tomography

CT detection of lymph nodes depends on size criteria alone, and mediastinal nodes are considered likely to be involved if they measure more than 10 mm in short-axis diameter. Accuracy overall for nodal staging is 51% to 70%[85,111] and tends to be better for intra-abdominal lymph nodes compared with those in the mediastinum. Because CT relies on size criteria alone, there are inherent problems with micrometastatic involvement of otherwise normal nodes and also false-positive staging with large but benign reactive lymph nodes, especially in smokers or those with chronic respiratory disease. Although improvements in CT technology might improve this situation, it is likely that inherent limitations in the sensitivity and accuracy of CT for detection of nodes will remain.

¹⁸F-Fluoro-2-Dexyglucose Positron Emission Tomography

¹⁸F-Fluoro-2-Dexyglucose (FDG)-PET depends on glycolytic activity of tissues rather than size criteria. Early data suggest that PET may be superior to CT for detection of distant (e.g., celiac axis)

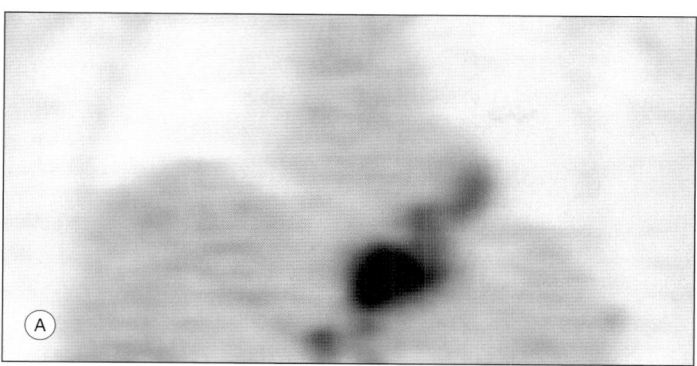
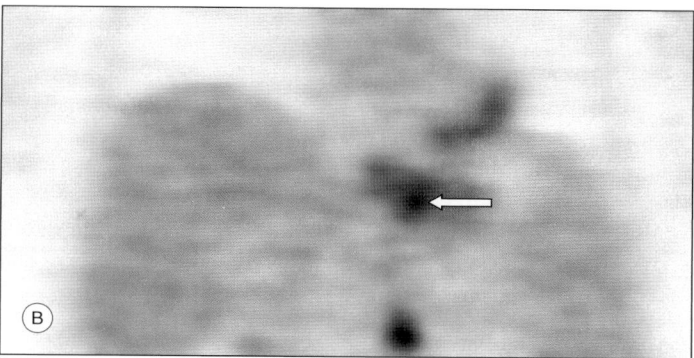

Figure 27–10. Positron emission tomography (PET) scan before *(A)* and after *(B)* neoadjuvant chemoradiotherapy. Before therapy, a bulky but localized tumor is evident. After therapy, there is some PET evidence of tumor response, but now there is evidence of new celiac lymphadenopathy *(arrow)*, confirmed surgically. (Courtesy of Dr. S. Rankin, Clinical PET Centre, Guy's & St. Thomas' NHS Trust, London.)

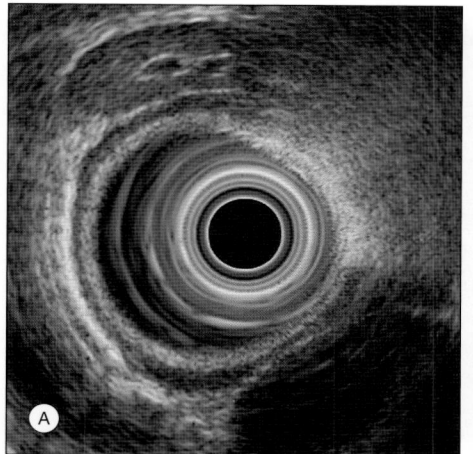
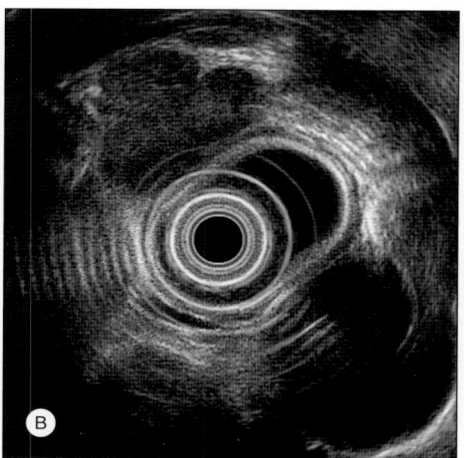
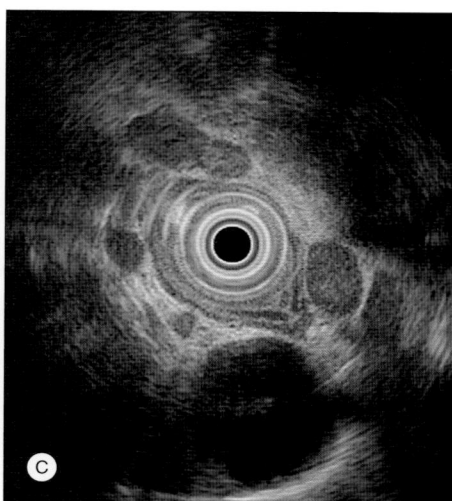
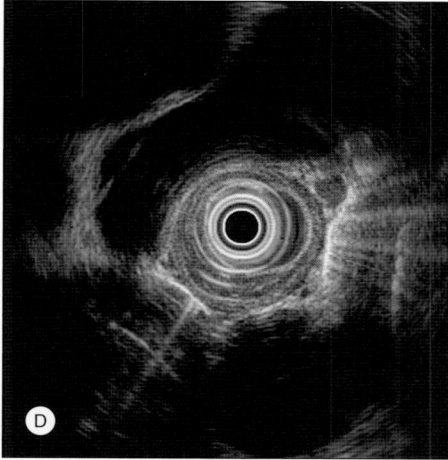

Figure 27–11. Endoscopic ultrasonography (EUS) and lymph nodes in esophageal cancer. *A,* Benign nodes, often in the subcarina, are suggested by a flat or triangular shape, indistinct margin, echo-rich center, and size less than 10 mm. *B,* Malignant nodal involvement is suggested by size over 10 mm, round or oval shape, discrete margins, and hypoechoic sonographic features. *C,* In this case, the nodes are smaller but the number of nodes and their sonographic features suggest malignancy. *D,* Diminutive nodes (in this case 3 mm) are not uncommon, and it is usually impossible to predict whether there is malignant involvement or not at this size.

lymph nodes (Fig. 27–10) but lacks accuracy for staging regional nodal disease. Limited spacial resolution impairs ability to differentiate nodal involvement from the high signal in the adjacent primary tumor, and reactive inflammatory nodes can lead to false-positive results. Flamen and colleagues[93] reported a sensitivity for detection of regional nodes (N1) of only 33% compared with 81% for EUS.

Endoscopic Ultrasonography

EUS not only assesses lymph node size but also assesses morphologic features such as shape, margin, and internal echo features. Normal or reactive nodes in the mediastinum are usually flat or triangular in shape with rather indistinct borders and an echogenic center, whereas malignant involvement is suggested by a size of greater than 10 mm, round shape, distinct outer border, and hypoechoic echo features[112,113] (Fig. 27–11). Although the presence of all of these features is 80% accurate for malignant involvement, this occurs in only 25% to 40% of malignant nodes. Overall, the sensitivity of EUS for detecting nodal involvement ranges from 50% to 75%, and accuracy is approximately 65% to 70%,[85,102] the latter declining with increasing distance from the primary tumor site. The number of nodes detected at EUS correlates well with both the number detected histologically and with prognosis in SCC; thus, it is valuable to document these carefully at EUS.[107] In a multivariate analysis, the detection of malignant-looking nodes by EUS was a statistically significant predictor of poor prognosis with a median survival of 13.5 months compared with more than 25 months in those without nodes.[108]

However, as is the case with CT, size remains a problem despite the ability of the EUS to resolve lymph nodes down to 2 to 3 mm in size. The addition of EUS-FNA can improve the accuracy of lymph node staging, and the overall accuracy of EUS-FNA for detecting malignant involvement in peri-intestinal lymph nodes is high, ranging from 85% to 93%.[114,115] In one retrospective study, the accuracy improved from 70% to 93% with the addition of FNA. This was the result of an improvement in both sensitivity and, to a lesser extent, specificity.[116] Although safe, the addition of FNA prolongs procedure time and may not be possible without traversing the primary tumor, risking contamination of the sample, and obtaining false-positive results. However, it is useful if the information gained will upstage the patient and affect subsequent management. As discussed previously, this is particularly relevant in the assessment of distal nodal involvement especially at the celiac axis where conclusive cytologic proof of involvement usually results in a change in management to a nonsurgical approach in most cases.

TUMOR STAGE

Computed Tomography

The normal esophageal wall is normally less than 3 mm thick, and CT is incapable of demonstrating individual wall layers, invasion of which forms the basis of assessment of T stage. Esophageal carcinomas are usually seen on CT as either areas of focal wall thickening or circumferential irregular thickening of the esophageal wall (Fig. 27–12). The proximal and distal extent of the tumor can also be difficult to measure, and it is often difficult to assess

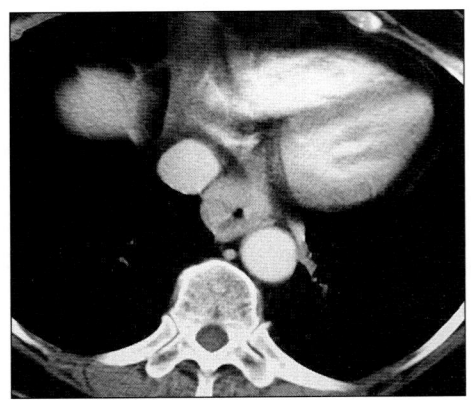

Figure 27–12. A typical helical computed tomography (CT) image in esophageal cancer demonstrating a bulky tumor in close proximity to the descending aorta but detailed T staging is difficult. (Courtesy of Dr. C.L. Kay.)

tumors of the GE junction accurately unless the stomach is adequately distended. The presence of a hiatal hernia can also lead to overstaging. Although invasion of the periesophageal fat may suggest T3 disease and T4 involvement may be suggested by such features as anterior bowing of the posterior wall of the trachea or loss the triangular fat pad between the esophagus, aorta, and spine, these features lack sufficient accuracy to be reliable. Sometimes clear T4 disease can be seen on CT, but its main value lies in assessment of visceral metastatic disease and possibly involvement of nonregional lymph nodes. It is also useful in radiotherapy planning and measurement of initial tumor bulk for subsequent assessment of the response to chemoradiotherapy or chemotherapy protocols.

Endoscopic Ultrasonography

The ability of EUS to image the intestinal wall as a series of concentric layers makes it ideally suited to T staging especially in the esophagus (Figs. 27–13 and 27–14). Multiple studies over the years have repeatedly demonstrated the accuracy of EUS for assessment of T stage in esophageal carcinoma and quoted overall accuracy rates are approximately 80% to 85%.[85,95–102] However, accuracy does vary within each T stage and is generally best for T3

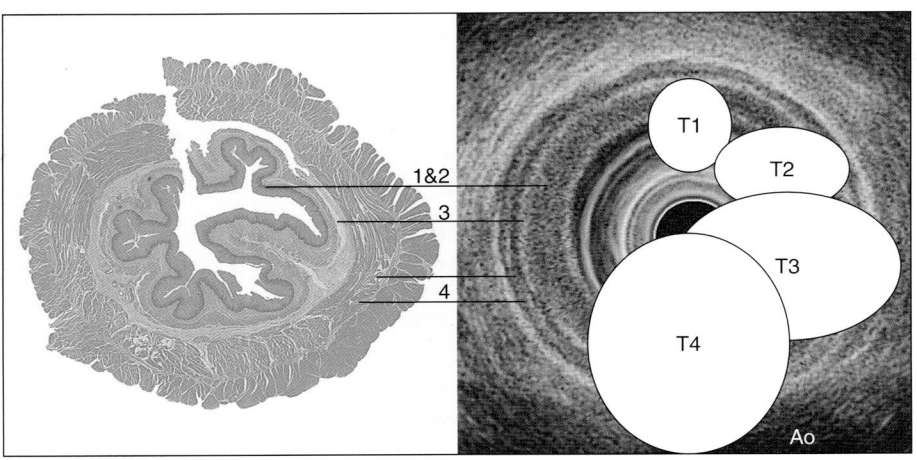

Figure 27–13. Illustration of the esophageal wall layers as seen by endoscopic ultrasonography (EUS) with histologic correlation and the T staging of esophageal cancer: T1 lesions invade but do not penetrate the submucosa, T2 lesions penetrate into but not beyond the muscularis, T3 lesions penetrate through the muscularis (the esophagus lacks a true serosal covering), and T4 lesions invade adjacent structures (e.g., aorta [Ao], trachea, pericardium).

and T4 tumors (Fig. 27–15). Accuracy has generally been reported to be least good for T2 tumors where it ranges from 65% to 73%[85,102] possibly because of difficulty detecting microscopic invasion beyond the muscularis propria.

Nevertheless, to date EUS remains the best available test for assessment of T stage and is significantly superior to CT in this regard, as demonstrated by numerous retrospective and prospective studies.[85,102,103] However, many of these studies compared state-of-the-art EUS with incremental CT; however, recent studies involving high-quality helical CT have confirmed the superiority of EUS.[103] Whether or not new multidetector CT scanning techniques will lead to improved accuracy remains to be seen.

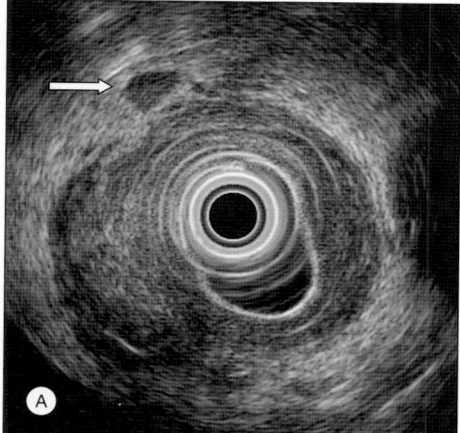
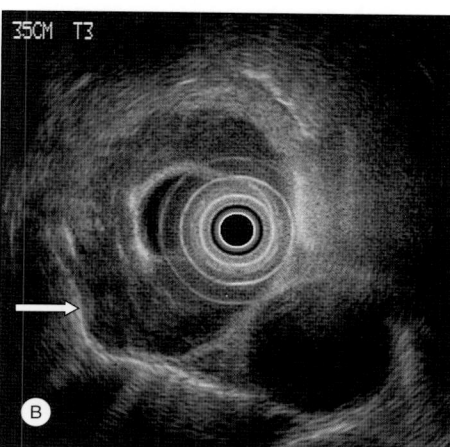

Figure 27–14. Endoscopic ultrasonography (EUS) images of T3 carcinomas. *A,* A bulky tumor extending beyond the muscularis is visible along with a 5mm peri-tumoral lymph node *(arrow). B,* A bulky tumor abuts the pleura *(arrow).*

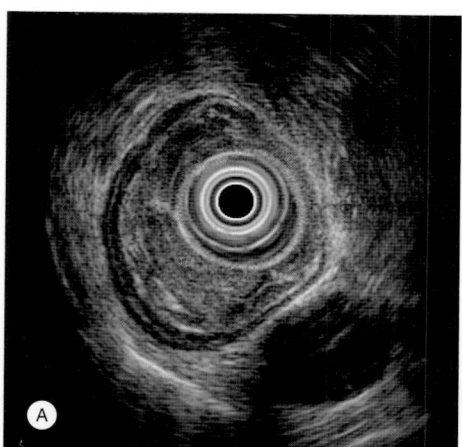
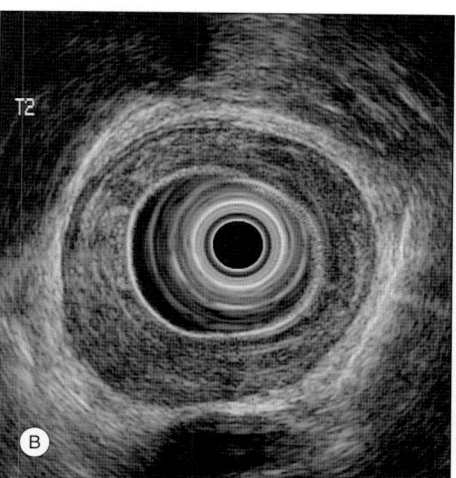
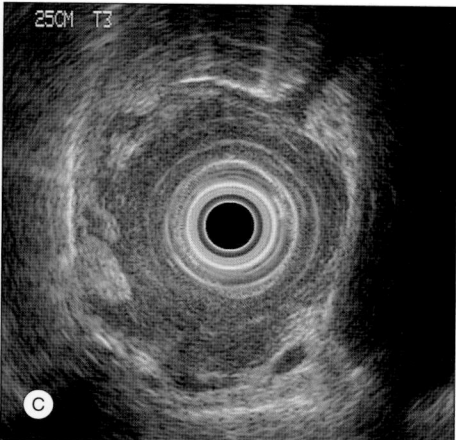
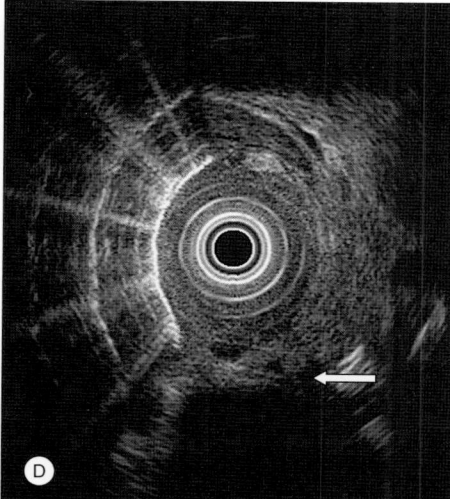

Figure 27–15. Endoscopic ultrasonography (EUS) T staging of esophageal cancer. *A,* T1—the submucosa is infiltrated, but there is no extension into the muscularis. *B,* A circumferential tumor has invaded into but not through the muscularis (T2). *C,* Extensive infiltration beyond the muscularis into the peri-esophageal tissues (T3). *D,* A bulky tumor invades the wall of the aorta with loss of the echo rich plane of separation between the tumor and aorta (T4, *arrow*).

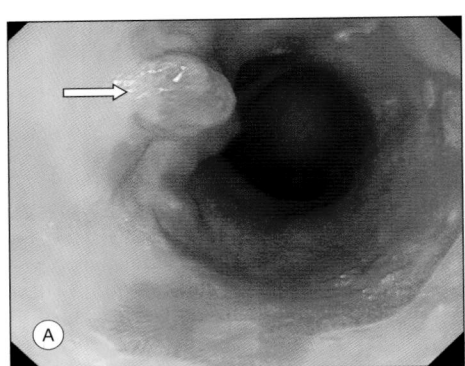
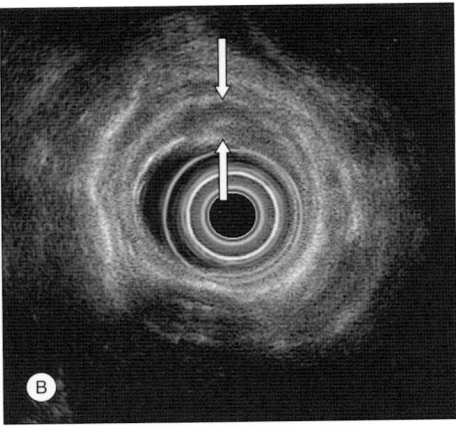

Figure 27–16. *A,* Endoscopically there is extensive Barrett's esophagus with squamous islands but also a superficial polypoid adenocarcinoma *(arrow). B,* Endoscopic ultrasonography (EUS) demonstrates the lesion involving the submucosa *(arrows)* and staged the lesion as T1sm,N0, which was confirmed at surgery.

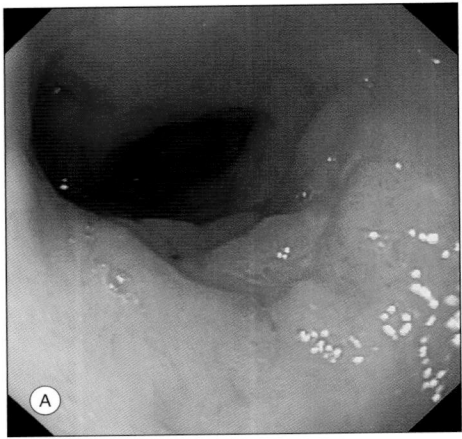
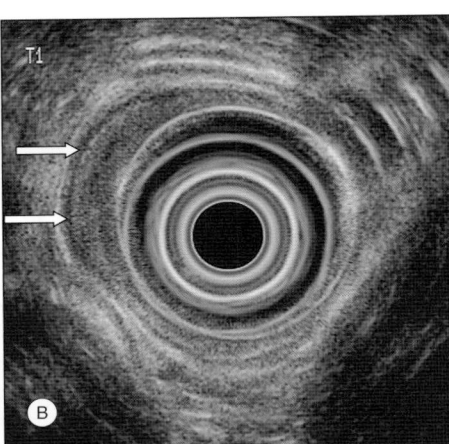

Figure 27–17. *A,* Endoscopic view of an elevated and centrally depressed early adenocarcinoma arising on a background of extensive Barrett's esophagus. *B,* Endoscopic ultrasonography (EUS) demonstrates the lesion involves the submucosa (third layer) but without any involvement of the muscularis propria (fourth layer, *arrows*).

EUS is the only technique currently available for assessing patients with superficial (T1) tumors because these are rarely evident on CT (Figs. 26–16 and 27–17). This is especially important with the increasing use of local endoscopic therapies such as endoscopic mucosal resection and photodynamic therapy as less invasive alternatives to surgical resection. Tumors confined to the mucosa (T1m) are associated with nodal involvement in less than 5% of cases, whereas up to 25% of tumors invading the submucosa (T1sm) may have involved nodes making the latter unsuitable for local endoscopic resection.[116,117] The accuracy of EUS for T1 disease is approximately 85%. Small superficial carcinomas may be subject to compression artefact from the balloon of a dedicated echoendoscope and high-frequency ultrasound catheter probes have proved useful in this setting with greater accuracy reported in some studies.[118,119] Imaging with these miniprobes can be technically challenging, and the optimal method of obtaining satisfactory acoustic coupling between the miniprobe and the esophageal wall must be refined further. Because of the resolution of EUS down to 200 nm, catheter probes are widely used in the assessment of patients with BE and high grade dysplasia, a significant proportion of whom harbor histologically undetected AC. Accurate discrimination of those patients with true high grade dysplasia from those with intramucosal carcinoma or even submucosal invasion is clearly critical. Several small case series have demonstrated the ability of

EUS (with either dedicated echoendoscopes or high-frequency catheter probes) to detect otherwise unsuspected submucosal invasion and/or lymph node involvement.[116,118,120] As such, EUS has become an important part of the assessment of these patients especially if nonoperative therapy is being considered. Data from Japanese groups suggest that ultra high frequency catheter probes (30 MHz) can accurately distinguish superficial submucosal involvement (T1sm-1) from deeper involvement (T1sm-2 or T1sm-3) and that the likelihood of nodal involvement is higher in patients with deeper involvement.[121] This may improve the selection of patients for endoscopic mucosal resection or photodynamic therapy, but experience in Western countries, where such lesions are rare, is limited.

At the opposite extreme, up to 20% to 30% of esophageal cancer patients will have esophageal stenosis of such severity that it is impossible to traverse the stricture with a standard echoendoscope.[66,122–124] Failure to do so and to complete the procedure is associated with significant understaging; however, early studies of EUS reported unacceptably high rates of esophageal perforation, either resulting from the procedure itself or with prior dilatation to 16 to 17 mm.[66] Since these reports, echoendoscope technology has advanced significantly and modern instruments are slimmer, have less bulky ultrasonic transducers at the tip and better video optics, and are rarely associated with esophageal perforation. In a large

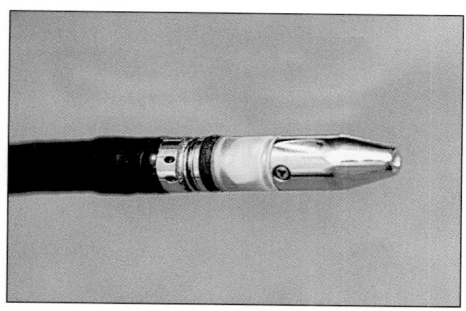

Figure 27–18. Nonoptical 8-mm esophagoprobe (MH-908) for use in patients with tight, stenosing carcinomas.

study of 132 patients, 32% required dilatation up to 14 to 16 mm to complete the procedure in almost all patients and only one perforation occurred.[125] In this study, dilatation allowed detection of advanced disease (either T4 or M1a) in 19% of those undergoing dilatation. If the information gained from completing the EUS procedure is likely to affect patient management, then careful dilatation should be undertaken, in stages if necessary, to allow completion of the procedure. An alternative is the use of the 7.8-mm esophagoprobe (Olympus MH-908, Fig. 27–18). This conical-tipped instrument lacks endoscopic optics and is passed through strictures over a monorail guidewire placed endoscopically. With this instrument, it is possible to pass all but the tightest stenoses with no or minimal dilatation. Several studies have demonstrated the equivalent accuracy of this instrument in comparison with standard echoendoscopes with a reported T staging accuracy of 89%.[122,124] Catheter ultrasound probes have also been used with some success but are not routinely recommended in this situation because of the lack of penetration and suboptimal nodal imaging. If celiac axis nodes are detected by these methods, FNA is usually necessary and this is one argument in favor of the use of dilatation and a standard echoendoscope in preference to other methods.

Endoscopic Ultrasonography Technique

EUS staging of esophageal cancer is usually performed under conscious sedation with the patient in the left lateral position. Careful esophagogastroduodenoscopy is an essential component of the examination and is usually performed immediately before EUS. This allows endoscopic evaluation of the tumor margins and whether or not there is involvement of the GE junction and cardia. The presence of synchronous or satellite lesions can be assessed, the extent of any BE can be measured, and, in SCC, Lugol's iodine staining can be undertaken to look for additional nonstaining areas. Upper endoscopy also allows an assessment of the degree of luminal stenosis and a reasonable idea of the likely ability to traverse the stricture with a standard echoendoscope. Careful dilatation can be performed if necessary or else a guidewire can be placed for subsequent passage of the esophagoprobe.

EUS staging by either radial or linear methods is usually performed in a distal to proximal direction. The echoendoscope is inserted to the duodenal cap and as much of the right lobe of liver

examined as possible before withdrawing to the mid body of the stomach. Air is suctioned out and the balloon inflated to provide adequate acoustic coupling. The splenic artery and vein are identified posterior to the gastric wall, and the splenic artery can be traced back to its origin at the bifurcation of the celiac trunk as it arises from aorta. This bifurcation into the hepatic artery and splenic artery is often visible as a Y-shape, sometimes referred to as the "whale's tail" (Fig. 27–9). This area is examined thoroughly for the presence of lymph nodes at or within 2 cm of the celiac axis. Repeated efforts should be made to visualize this area thoroughly because of the prognostic implications of involved nodes at this site and their impact on patient management. Slow, careful withdrawal of the echoendoscope allows visualization of the left gastric artery territory and the lesser curve for lymph nodes. At this level, the left lobe of the liver is usually seen and should also be examined carefully for small metastases that may not have been apparent on CT. The proximal gastric wall layers should be examined for evidence of tumor involvement, and the endoscope is slowly withdrawn through the GE junction into the distal esophagus and again the wall layers should be carefully examined with care. The presence of a hiatal hernia can cause imaging difficulties because of overlapping gastric folds and the presence of air within the hernia sac. Attempts should be made to distend the layers by inflating the balloon and instilling water through the accessory channel of the instrument to improve image quality. It is often necessary to deflate the balloon slightly when withdrawing through the GE junction into the mediastinum and also if there is any resistance when withdrawing proximally through the tumor itself. The tumor is examined carefully to determine the proximal and distal extent of involvement and to assess the T stage. Care must be taken to avoid overstaging from tangential imaging, and particular attention should be paid to the presence or absence of a hyperechoic plane of separation between the tumor and adjacent structures such as the mediastinal pleura, aorta, pericardium, prevertebral fascia, pulmonary vessels, and main airways. The mediastinum should be carefully assessed from the level of the diaphragm to above the top of the aortic arch, and the number, size, echo characteristics, and location of any lymph nodes should be carefully documented. The location of nodes should be described according to the TNM regional lymph node stations[82] (Fig. 27–7), and consideration should be given to FNA of identified lymph nodes if this will have an impact on management. Nonregional lymph nodes distant from the tumor are more important targets for FNA than those adjacent to the tumor, some of which may be impossible to access for FNA without traversing the primary tumor itself, risking contamination of the sample and a false-positive result. The results of the EUS procedure should be carefully documented both descriptively and according to T, N, and, if applicable, M stage. These results should be discussed in conjunction with the endoscopic findings and results of other staging investigations at a multidisciplinary team meeting where all information can be integrated and inform the discussion about subsequent management.

Some elements of the EUS procedure are undoubtedly subjective and descriptive and where possible standardized terms, definitions, and nomenclature should be used. Minimum standard terminology (MST) definitions for EUS have been developed and should be used where possible.[126]

Other Staging Modalities

Although CT and EUS form the mainstay of esophageal cancer staging, other modalities have an important role to play in selected patients. Patients with distal esophageal or junctional tumors may have significant intra-abdominal disease (tumor extending down the lesser curve, lymphadenopathy, or even peritoneal deposits), and careful laparoscopy with or without laparoscopic ultrasound has been shown to be useful in such cases. Several studies have demonstrated the ability of laparoscopy to upstage a significant percentage of patients and reduce open-close laparotomy rates.[86,87] However, few studies have compared the information provided by a trimodality approach of CT, EUS, and laparoscopy, but this approach may further improve the detection of nonresectable patients.

Although not widely available, VATS is a sensitive and accurate means of detecting mediastinal lymph node involvement and also in assessing T4 involvement, especially of the airways. Few studies have directly compared this form of minimally invasive staging with CT and particularly EUS, but in expert hands it may be superior to EUS in detection of M1 disease.[127] However, it is significantly more invasive than EUS, carries a small but significant complication rate, and requires general anesthesia. Finally, patients with SCC may have clinically undetectable involvement of supraclavicular lymph nodes, and several studies have demonstrated the ability of ultrasound of the neck with FNA biopsy to detect these with high sensitivity and specificity.[128,129] The exact place of cervical ultrasound in the staging algorithm of thoracic esophageal carcinoma remains to be defined, but it is a simple, safe, and relatively inexpensive procedure and one that merits consideration in patients with disease at this location.

Current Issues for EUS in Esophageal Cancer Staging

DO ENDOSCOPIC ULTRASONOGRAPHY FINDINGS CORRELATE WITH PROGNOSIS?

In recent years, a number of studies have assessed the prognostic value of EUS findings in patients with esophageal cancer. The demonstration of celiac axis lymphadenopathy (especially when proven by EUS-FNA) is associated with a poor prognosis irrespective of whether patients undergo surgical resection or not.[130–132] In a multivariate analysis of 203 patients, the presence of malignant looking regional lymph nodes was also a statistically significant predictor of survival.[108] In another study median survival was only 8 months in those with EUS features of malignant lymph node involvement compared with more than 28 months in those with no EUS evidence or nodal involvement.[133] In a large Japanese study of 339 patients, the number of lymph nodes identified by EUS and transcutaneous ultrasound correlated well with prognosis. In this study, 5-year survival rates for patients with 0, 1 to 3, 4 to 7, and 8 or more detected nodes were 53.3%, 33.8%, 17%, and 0%, respectively.[107]

Two retrospective studies also identified T4 stage by endosonography as a marker of poor survival regardless of subsequent

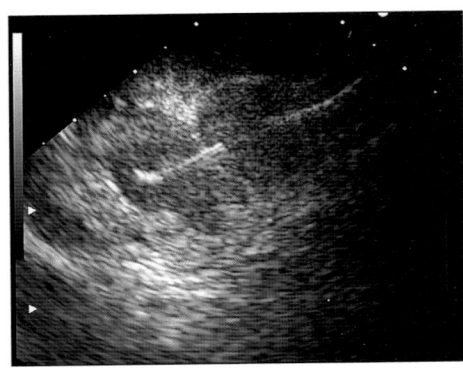

Figure 27–19. The addition of endoscopic ultrasonography fine needle aspiration (EUS-FNA) of lymph nodes increases staging accuracy. In this case, two lymph nodes are seen and FNA confirmed adenocarcinoma (N1).

therapy and demonstrated that survival in these patients was not improved by surgery.[134,135] Thus, the findings of celiac lymph node, regional nodal, or T4 involvement at EUS not only influences management but provides useful prognostic information.

CAN THE ACCURACY OF NODAL STAGING BE IMPROVED?

Given the important prognostic implications of nodal involvement and the potential impact this may have in selecting patients for neoadjuvant therapy, it is essential to improve on the modest accuracy rates of EUS imaging alone. Therefore, EUS-FNA of identified nodes (Fig. 27–19) is logical to improve specificity and accuracy; however, despite numerous reports of its performance, there have been relatively few randomized, prospective studies comparing EUS imaging alone with EUS-FNA of nodes in esophageal cancer.

One retrospective study assessed the impact of EUS-FNA in 64 patients.[116] The addition of FNA increased the accuracy of nodal staging to 93% largely by increasing the sensitivity and, to a lesser degree, specificity. The benefits were not as great for celiac nodes probably because enlarged lymph nodes at this location in esophageal cancer are rarely benign and reactive, a finding confirmed in other studies. The data available from these studies demonstrate that EUS-FNA reduces the rate of both false-positive and false-negative results, and the routine use of FNA sampling of detected nodes in all cases has been advocated by some.

DOES ENDOSCOPIC ULTRASONOGRAPHY HAVE AN IMPACT ON CLINICAL OUTCOME?

Although EUS is the most accurate locoregional staging modality, a major impact of EUS staging on patient management and outcomes remains to be shown, and properly designed outcome studies in this area are relatively few. A prospective UK study examined the effect of EUS on the management of 100 consecutive cases of esophageal and junctional carcinomas.[136] Three specialist surgeons were asked in a blinded fashion to select a management plan after reviewing full staging information before and again after EUS. The additional EUS information led to a significant change in treatment plan in 16%, 18%, and 32% of cases among the three surgeons. Giovannini and coworkers[137] reported that EUS demonstrated distant lymphadenopathy in 40 of 198 patients (20%) with esophageal cancer. FNA was performed with a sensitivity of 97% and a specificity of 100%, and the findings led to a change in treatment in 77.5% of this subgroup of patients (i.e., 16% of all patients). In a prospective study of 108 patients, EUS detected nodal or metastatic involvement in 16.5% of patients, of whom FNA was positive in 86%. When interpreted on an "intention to biopsy" basis, EUS-FNA was relevant to only 8.3% of the entire study population, and the overall impact was 13% in terms of changing the therapeutic strategy.[138] Further large studies of this type are needed as are carefully designed economic studies to bolster the decision modeling analyses that have already suggested the cost effectiveness of an EUS-based strategy for staging esophageal cancer.

IS ENDOSCOPIC ULTRASONOGRAPHY USEFUL FOR RESTAGING AFTER NEOADJUVANT THERAPY?

Initial studies evaluating the accuracy of EUS restaging after neoadjuvant chemoradiotherapy were disappointing and highlighted the inability to differentiate residual tumor from inflammatory or fibrotic changes.[139–141] However, these studies reported T and N stage accuracy rates and were, therefore, not surprisingly disappointing. Alternatively, documenting a reduction in maximal tumor cross-sectional area by EUS may be a promising means of predicting response to therapy. Several small studies have reported that a 50% or greater reduction in cross-sectional area is relatively accurate at predicting response.[142–144] In one study, EUS correctly predicted a tumor response to chemoradiation in 20 of 23 patients (87%) who had pathologic tumor regression, and overall the positive predictive value of EUS for pathologic regression was 80%.[145] Whether or not the use of three-dimensional EUS imaging to estimate tumor volumes will be of value in assessing responses to neoadjuvant therapy is unknown at present. As for nodal involvement, case reports have suggested the potential of EUS-FNA to document nodal downstaging after therapy, but the utility of this approach remains largely unexplored.[146]

Future Trends

Detection of esophageal cancer at an earlier stage is the most likely means by which significant improvements in survival will be achieved, and new imaging techniques in endoscopy are constantly being developed to achieve this. Many of these are still experimental, but the next few years is likely to see important and exciting developments, not only in magnifying endoscopy, high-resolution endoscopy and chromoendoscopy but also in novel means of imaging the gut mucosa. These include fluorescence and light-scattering spectroscopy, OCT, and confocal microscopy.[71,147] Whether or not these will translate into routine practice and help to overcome the inherent limitations of current endoscopy remains to be seen.

EUS technology also continues to evolve with improvements in instrument design, software processing, and better biopsy needles. These will undoubtedly improve even further the ability of EUS to provide accurate and clinically important information in the management of esophageal cancer patients. Other imaging modalities such as multidetector CT and CT-PET are improving rapidly as well, and further carefully designed and adequately powered, prospective studies will be necessary to define the optimal staging strategy for these patients.

REFERENCES

1. Pisani P, Parkin DM, Bray F, Ferlay J: Estimates of the worldwide mortality from 25 cancers in 1990. Int J Cancer 83:18–29, 1999.
2. Ries LAG, Eisner MP, Kosary CL, et al (eds): SEER Cancer Statistics Review, 1975-2000. Bethesda, MD, National Cancer Institute, available at http://seer.cancer.gov/csr/1975_2000, 2003.
3. Bollshweiler E, Wolfgarten E, Gutschow C, Holscher AH: Demographic variations in the rising incidences of esophageal adenocarcinoma in white males. Cancer 92:549–555, 2001.
4. Pisani P, Bray F, Parkin DM: Estimates of the world-wide prevalence of cancer for 25 sites in the adult population. Int J Cancer 97:72–81, 2002.
5. Ribeiro U, Posner MC, Safatle-Ribeiro AV, Reynolds JC: Risk factors for squamous cell carcinoma of the esophagus. Br J Surg 83:1174–1185, 1996.
6. Parkin DM, Laara E, Muir CS: Estimates of the world frequency of 16 major cancers in 1980. Int J Cancer 41:184–197, 1988.
7. Kirkby TJ, Rice TW: The epidemiology of esophageal cancer: The changing face of a disease. Chest Surg Clin North Am 4:217–225, 1994.
8. Yang CS: Research on esophageal cancer in China: A review. Cancer Res 40:2633–2644, 1980.
9. Warwick GP, Harington JS: Some aspects of the epidemiology and etiology of esophageal cancer with particular emphasis on the Transkei, South Africa. Adv Cancer Res 17:81–229, 1973.
10. Khuroo MS, Zargar SA, Mahajan R, Banday MA: High incidence of esophageal and gastric cancer in Kashmir in a population with special dietary and personal habits. Gut 33:11–15, 1992.
11. Wynder L, Mabuchi K: Cancer of the esophagus: Etiological and environmental factors. JAMA 226:1546–1548, 1973.
12. Pottern LM, Morris LE, Blot WJ, et al: Esophageal cancer among black men in Washington, DC: Alcohol, tobacco, and other risk factors. J Natl Cancer Inst 67:777–783, 1981.
13. Tuyns AJ, Pequignot G, Abbatucci JS: Esophageal cancer and alcohol consumption: Importance of type and beverage. Int J Cancer 23:443–447, 1979.
14. Chang F, Syrjanen S, Shen Q, et al: Human papillomavirus involvement in esophageal carcinogenesis in the high-incidence area of China. A study of 700 cases by screening and type-specific in situ hybridisation. Scand J Gastroenterol 35:123–130, 2000.
15. Ahsan H, Neugut AI: Radiation therapy for breast cancer and increased risk of esophageal carcinoma. Ann Intern Med 128:114–117, 1998.
16. Wynder EL, Hultberg S, Jacobsson F, Bross IJ: Environmental factors in cancer of the upper alimentary tract: A Swedish study with special reference to Plummer-Vinson (Paterson-Kelly) syndrome. Cancer 10:470–487, 1957.
17. Ferguson A, Kingstone K: Coeliac disease and malignancies. Acta Paediatr Suppl 412:78–81, 1996.
18. Harper PS, Harper RM, Howel-Evans AW: Carcinoma of the oesophagus with tylosis. Q J Med 39:317–333, 1970.
19. McGuirt WF: Panendoscopy as a screening examination for simultaneous primary tumors in head and neck cancer: A prospective sequential study and review of the literature. Laryngoscope 92:569–576, 1982.
20. Siewert JR, Stein HJ: Carcinoma of the cardia: Carcinoma of the gastroesophageal junction–classification, pathology and extent of resection. Dis Esoph 9:173–182, 1996.

21. van Sandick JW, van Lanschot JJ, Tytgat GN, et al: Barrett oesophagus and adenocarcinoma: An overview of epidemiologic, conceptual and clinical issues. Scand J Gastroenterol 36(Suppl 234):51–60, 2001.

22. El-Serag HB, Mason AC, Petersen N, Key CR: Epidemiological differences between adenocarcinoma of the oesophagus and adeno-carcinoma of the gastric cardia in the USA. Gut 50:368–372, 2002.

23. Devesa SS, Blot WJ, Fraumeni JF Jr: Changing patterns in the incidence of esophageal and gastric carcinoma in the United States. Cancer 83:2049–2053, 1998.

24. Botterweck AA, Schouten LJ, Volovics A, et al: Trends in incidence of adenocarcinoma of the esophagus and gastric cardia in ten European countries. Int J Epidemiol 29:645–654, 2000.

25. Lord RV, Law MG, Ward RL, et al: Rising incidence of oesophageal adenocarcinoma in men in Australia. J Gastroenterol Hepatol 13:356–362, 1998.

26. Blot WJ, Devesa SS, Kneller RW, Fraumeni JF Jr: Rising incidence of adenocarcinoma of the esophagus and gastric cardia. JAMA 265:1287–1289, 1991.

27. Levi F, Ollyo JB, La Vecchia C, et al: The consumption of tobacco, alcohol and the risk of adenocarcinoma in Barrett's oesophagus. Int J Cancer 45:852–854, 1990.

28. Spechler SJ: Esophageal columnar metaplasia (Barrett's esophagus). Gastrointest Endosc Clin N Am 7:1–18, 1997.

29. Lagergren J, Bergstrom R, Lingren A, Nyren O: Symptomatic gastroesophageal reflux as a risk factor for esophageal carcinoma. N Engl J Med 340:825–831, 1999.

30. Lagergren J, Bergstrom R, Nyren O: Association between body mass and adenocarcinoma of the esophagus and gastric cardia. Ann Int Med 130:883–890, 1999.

31. Cameron AJ: Epidemiology of columnar lined esophagus and adenocarcinoma. Gastroenterol Clin North Am 26:487–494, 1997.

32. Rudolph RE, Vaughan TL. Storer BE, et al: Effect of segment length on risk for neoplastic progression in patients with Barrett's esophagus. Ann Intern Med 132:612–620, 2000.

33. Shirbvani VN, Ouata-Lascar R, Kaur BS, et al: Cyclooxygenase 2 expression in Barrett's esophagus and adenocarcinoma: Ex vivo induction by bile salts and acid exposure. Gastroenterology 118:487–496, 2000.

34. Souza, RF, Morales CP, Spechler SJ: Review article: A conceptual approach to understanding the molecular mechanisms of cancer development in Barrett's oesophagus. Aliment Pharmacol Ther 15:1087–1100, 2001.

35. Jankowski JA, Harrison RF, Perry I, et al: Barrett's metaplasia. Lancet 356:2079–2085, 2000.

36. Xu Y, Selaru FM, Yin J, et al: Artificial neural networks and gene filtering distinguish between global gene expression profiles of Barrett's esophagus and esophageal cancer. Cancer Res 62:3493–3497, 2002.

37. Postlethwait RW: Carcinoma of the esophagus. Curr Probl Cancer 2:1–44, 1978.

38. Altorki NK, Migliore M, Skinner DB: Esophageal carcinoma and airway invasion: Evolution and choices of therapy. Chest 104:742–745, 1994.

39. Barrie JR, Goodner JT: Hematemesis from cancer of the esophagus. J Thorac Cardiovasc Surg 56:289–292, 1968.

40. Akiyama H, Masahiko T, Udagawa H, Kihyama Y: Radical lymph node dissection for cancer of the thoracic esophagus. Ann Surg 220:364–373, 1994.

41. Stein HJ, Feith M, Mueller J, et al: Limited resection for early adenocarcinoma in Barrett's esophagus. Ann Surg 232:733–742, 2000.

42. Nigro JJ, Hagen JA, DeMeester TR, et al: Occult esophageal adenocarcinoma: Extent of disease and implications for effective therapy. Ann Surg 230:433–440, 1999.

43. Nigro JJ, Hagen JA, DeMeester TR, et al: Prevalence and location of nodal metastases in distal esophageal adenocarcinoma confined to the wall: Implications for therapy. J Thorac Cardiovasc Surg 117:16–25, 1999.

44. O'Sullivan GC, Sheehan D, Clarke A, et al: Micrometastases in esophagogastric cancer: High detection rate in resected rib segments. Gastroenterology 116:543–548, 1999.

45. Dooley CP, Larson AW, Stace NH, et al: Double contrast barium meal and upper gastrointestinal endoscopy. A comparative study. Ann Intern Med 101:538–545, 1984.

46. O'Donoghue J, Waldron R, Gough D, et al: An analysis of the diag-nostic accuracy of endoscopic biopsy and cytology in the detection of oesophageal malignancy. Eur J Surg Oncol 18:332–334, 1992.

47. Glaws WR, Etzkorn KP, Wenig BL, et al: Comparison of rigid and flexible esophagoscopy in the diagnosis of esophageal disease: Diagnostic accuracy, complications and cost. Ann Otol Rhinol Laryngol 105:262–266, 1996.

48. Faigel DO, Deveney C, Phillips D, Fennerty MB: Biopsy-negative malignant esophageal stricture: Diagnosis by endoscopic ultrasound. Am J Gastroenterol 93:2257–2260, 1998.

49. Moss AA, Koehler RE, Margulis AR: Initial accuracy of esophagograms in detection of small esophageal carcinoma. AJR 127:909–913, 1976.

50. Woodfield CA, Levine MS, Rubesin SE, et al: Diagnosis of primary versus secondary achalasia: Reassessment of clinical and radiographic criteria. AJR 175:727–731, 2000.

51. Schiller W: Early diagnosis of carcinoma of the cervix. Surg Gynecol Obstet 56:210–222, 1933.

52. Sugimachi K, Kitamura K, Baba K, et al: Endoscopic diagnosis of early carcinoma of the esophagus using Lugol's solution. Gastrointest Endosc 38:657–661, 1992.

53. Yokoyama A, Ohmori T, Makuuchi H, et al: Successful screening for early esophageal cancer in alcoholics using endoscopy and mucosa iodine staining. Cancer 76:919–921, 1995.

54. Dawsey SM, Fleischer DE, Wang GQ, et al: Mucosal iodine staining improves endoscopic visualization of squamous dysplasia and squamous cell carcinoma of the esophagus in Linxian, China. Cancer 83:220–231, 1998.

55. Fagundes RB, de Barros SG, Putten AC, et al: Occult dysplasia is disclosed by Lugol chromoendoscopy in alcoholics at high risk for squamous cell carcinoma of the esophagus. Endoscopy 31:281–285, 1999.

56. Carr-Locke DL, Al-Chaws FH, Branch MS, et al: Technology assessment status evaluation: Endoscopic tissue staining and tattooing. Gastrointest Endosc 43:652–656, 1996.

57. Canto MI, Setrakian S, Petras RE, et al: Methylene blue selectively stains intestinal metaplasia in Barrett's esophagus. Gastrointest Endosc 44:1–7, 1996.

58. Canto MI, Setrakian S, Willis J, et al: Methylene blue directed biopsies improve detection of intestinal metaplasia and dysplasia in Barrett's esophagus. Gastrointest Endosc 51:560–568, 2000.

59. Canto MI, Setrakian S, Willis J, et al: Methylene blue staining of dysplastic and non-dysplastic Barrett's esophagus: An in vivo and ex vivo study. Endoscopy 33:391–400, 2001.

60. Wong R, Horwhat J, Maydonovitch C: Sky blue or murky waters: The diagnostic utility of methylene blue. Gastrointest Endosc 54:409–413, 2001.

61. Yang H, Berner A, Mei Q, et al: Cytologic screening for esophageal cancer in a high-risk population in Anyang county, China. Acta Cytol 46:445–452, 2002.

62. Levine DS, Haggitt RC, Blount PL, et al: An endoscopic biopsy protocol can differentiate high-grade dysplasia from early adenocarcinoma in Barrett's esophagus. Gastroenterology 105:40–50, 1993.

63. Lal N, Bhasin DK, Malik AK, et al: Optimal number of biopsy specimens in the diagnosis of carcinoma of the oesophagus. Gut 33:724–726, 1992.

64. Levine DS, Reid BJ: Endoscopic biopsy technique for acquiring larger mucosal samples. Gastrointest Endosc 37:332–337, 1991.

65. Zargar SA, Khuroo MS, Jan GM, et al: Prospective comparison of the value of brushings before and after biopsy in the endoscopic diagnosis of gastroesophageal malignancy. Acta Cytol 35:549–552, 1991.

66. Van Dam J, Rice TW, Catalano MF, et al: High grade malignant stricture is predictive of tumor stage. Risks of endosonographic evaluation. Cancer 71:2910–2917, 1993.

67. Kobayashi S, Kasugai T: Brushing cytology for the diagnosis of gastric cancer involving the cardia or the lower esophagus. Acta Cytol 22:155–157, 1978.

68. Barkin JS, Taub S, Rogers AI: The safety of combined endoscopy, biopsy and dilation in esophageal strictures. Am J Gastroenterol 76:23–26, 1981.

69. Moses FM, Peura DA, Wong RK, Johnson LF: Palliative dilation of esophageal carcinoma. Gastrointest Endosc 31:61–63, 1985.

70. Lundell L, Leth R, Lind T, et al: Palliative endoscopic dilatation in carcinoma of the esophagus and esophagogastric junction. Acta Chir Scand 155:179–184, 1989.

71. Bruno MJ: Magnification endoscopy, high resolution endoscopy and chromoscopy; towards a better optical diagnosis. Gut 52(Suppl IV):7–11, 2003.

72. Jackle S, Gladkova N, Feldchtein F, et al: In vivo endoscopic optical coherence tomography of esophagitis, Barrett's esophagus, and adenocarcinoma of the esophagus. Endoscopy 32:750–755, 2000.

73. Poneros JM, Brand S, Bouma BE, et al: Diagnosis of specialized intestinal metaplasia by optical coherence tomography. Gastroenterology 120:7–12, 2001.

74. Panjehpour M, Overholt BF, Schmidhammer JL, et al: Spectroscopic diagnosis of esophageal cancer: New classification model, improved measurement system. Gastrointest Endosc 41:577–581, 1995.

75. Egger K, Werner M, Meining A, et al: Biopsy surveillance is still necessary in patients with Barrett's esophagus despite new endoscopic imaging techniques. Gut 52:18–23, 2002.

76. Endlicher E, Knuechel R, Hauser T, et al: Endoscopic fluorescence detection of low- and high-grade dysplasia in Barrett's esophagus using systemic or local 5-aminolevulinic acid sensitization. Gut 48:314–319, 2001.

77. Faivre J, Forman D, Esteve J, Gatta G: Survival of patients with oesophageal and gastric cancers in Europe. Eur J Cancer 34:2167–2175, 1998.

78. Newnham A, Quinn MJ, Babb P, et al: Trends in oesophageal and gastric cancer incidence, mortality and survival in England and Wales 1971-1998/1999. Aliment Pharmacol Ther 17:655–664, 2003.

79. Medical Research Council Oesophageal Cancer Working Group: Surgical resection with or without preoperative chemotherapy in oesophageal cancer: A randomised controlled trial. Lancet 359:1727–1733, 2002.

80. Kelsen DP, Ginsberg R, Pajak TF, et al: Chemotherapy followed by surgery compared with surgery alone for localised esophageal cancer. N Engl J Med 339:1979–1984, 1998.

81. Walsh TN, Noonan N, Hollywood D, et al: A comparison of multimodality therapy and surgery for esophageal adenocarcinoma. N Engl J Med 335:462–467, 1996.

82. TNM classification and stage grouping of esophageal carcinoma. In Greene FL, Page DL, Fleming ID, et al (eds): American Joint Committee on Cancer. Cancer Staging Manual, 6th ed. New York, Springer, 2002, pp 91–98.

83. Luketich JD, Friedman DM, Weigel TL, et al: Evaluation of distant metastases in esophageal cancer: 100 consecutive positron emission tomography scans. Ann Thor Surg 68:1133–1136, 1999.

84. Levine MS, Chu P, Furth EE, et al: Carcinoma of the esophagus and esophagogastric junction: Sensitivity of radiographic diagnosis. AJR Am J Roentgenol 168:1423–1426, 1997.

85. Kelly S, Harris KM, Berry E, et al: A systematic review of the staging performance of endoscopic ultrasound in gastro-oesophageal carcinoma. Gut 49:534–539, 2001.

86. Bemelman WA, van Delden OM, van Lanschot JJ, et al: Laparoscopy and laparoscopic ultrasonography in staging of carcinoma of the esophagus and gastric cardia. J Am Coll Surg 181:421–425, 1995.

87. Smith A, Finch MD, John TG, et al: Role of laparoscopic ultra-sonography in the management of patients with oesophagogastric cancer. Br J Surg 86:1083–1087, 1999.

88. Flanagan FL, Dehdashti F, Siegel BA, et al: Staging of esophageal cancer with 18F-fluorodeoxyglucose positron emission tomography. AJR Am J Roentgenol 168:417–424, 1997.

89. Choi JY, Lee KH, Shim YM, et al: Improved detection of individual nodal involvement in squamous cell carcinoma of the esophagus by FDG PET. J Nucl Med 41:808–815, 2000.

90. Meltzer CC, Luketich JD, Friedman D, et al: Whole-body FDG positron emission tomographic imaging for staging esophageal cancer comparison with computed tomography. Clin Nucl Med 25:882–887, 2000.

91. Kato H, Kuwano H, Nakajima M, et al: Comparison between positron emission tomography and computed tomography in the use of the assessment of esophageal carcinoma. Cancer 94:921–28, 2002.

92. Lerut T, Flamen P, Ectors N, et al: Histopathological validation of lymph node staging with FDG-PET in cancer of the esophagus and gastro-esophageal junction. Ann Surg 232:743–752, 2000.

93. Flamen P, Lerut A, Van Cutsem E, et al: Utility of positron emission tomography for the staging of patients with potentially operable esophageal carcinoma. J Clin Oncol 18:3202–3210, 2000.

94. Nguyen P, Feng JC, Chang KJ: Endoscopic ultrasound (EUS) and EUS-guided fine-needle aspiration (FNA) of liver lesions. Gastrointest Endosc 50:357–361, 1999.

95. Tio TL, Cohen P, Coene PP, et al: Endosonography and computed topography of esophageal carcinoma. Gastroenterology 96:1478–1486, 1989.

96. Sugimachi K, Ohno S, Fujishima H, et al: Endoscopic ultrasono-graphic detection of carcinomatous invasion and of lymph nodes in the thoracic esophagus. Surgery 107:366–371, 1990.

97. Vilgrain V, Mompoint D, Palazzo L, et al: Staging of esophageal carcinoma: Comparison of results with endoscopic sonography and CT. AJR Am J Roentgenol 155:277–281, 1990.

98. Ziegler K, Sanft C, Zeitz M, et al: Evaluation of endosonography in TN staging of oesophageal cancer. Gut 32:16–20, 1991.

99. Grimm H, Binmoeller KF, Hamper K, et al: Endosonography for preoperative locoregional staging of esophageal and gastric cancer. Endoscopy 25:224–230, 1993.

100. Grimm H: Endoscopic ultrasonography with the ultrasonic esophagoprobe. Endoscopy 26:818–821, 1994.

101. Souquet JC, Napoleon B, Pujol B, et al: Endoscopic ultrasonography in the preoperative staging of esophageal cancer. Endoscopy 26:764–766, 1994.

102. Rösch T: Endosonographic staging of esophageal cancer: A review of literature results. Gastrointest Endosc Clin N Am 5:537–547, 1995.

103. Romagnuolo J, Scott J, Hawes RH, et al: Helical CT versus EUS with fine needle aspiration for celiac nodal assessment in patients with esophageal cancer. Gastrointest Endosc 55:648–654, 2002.

104. Natsugoe S, Mueller J, Stein HJ, et al: Micrometastases and tumor cell microinvolvement of lymph nodes from squamous cell carcinoma: Frequency, associated tumor characteristics, and impact on prognosis. Cancer 83:858–866, 1998.

105. Hosch SB, Stoecklein NH, Pichlmeier U, et al: Esophageal cancer: The mode of lymphatic tumor cell spread and its prognostic significance. J Clin Oncol 19:1970–1975, 2001.

106. Roder JD, Busch R, Stein HJ, et al: Ratio of invaded to removed lymph nodes as a predictor of survival in squamous cell carcinoma of the esophagus. Br J Surg 81:410–413, 1994.

107. Pfau PR, Ginsberg GG, Lew RJ, et al: EUS predictors of long-term survival in esophageal carcinoma. Gastrointest Endosc 53:463–469, 2001.

108. Natsugoe S, Yoshinaka H, Shimada M, et al: Number of lymph node metastases determined by presurgical ultrasound and endoscopic ultrasound is related to prognosis in patients with esophageal carcinoma. Ann Surg 234:613–618, 2001.

109. Killinger WA, Rice TW, Adelstein DJ, et al: Stage II esophageal carcinoma: The significance of T and N. J Thorac Cardiovasc Surg 111:935–940, 1996.

110. Wang LS, Chow K-C, Chi KH, et al: Prognosis of esophageal squamous cell carcinoma: Analysis of clinicopathological and biological factors. Am J Gastroenterol 94:1933–1940, 1999.

111. Saunders HS, Wolfman NT, Ott DJ: Esophageal cancer. Radiologic staging. Radiol Clin North Am 35:281–294, 1997.

112. Catalano MF, Sivak MV Jr, Rice T, et al: Endosonographic features predictive of lymph node metastases. Gastrointest Endosc 40:442–446, 1994.

113. Bhutani MS, Hawes RH, Hoffman BJ: A comparison of the accuracy of echo features during endoscopic ultrasound (EUS) and EUS-guided fine-needle aspiration for diagnosis of malignant lymph node invasion. Gastrointest Endosc 45:474–479, 1997.

114. Wiersema MJ, Vilmann P, Giovannini M, et al: Endosonography-guided fine-needle aspiration biopsy: Diagnostic accuracy and complication assessment. Gastroenterology 112:1087–1095, 1997.

115. Williams DB, Sahai AV, Aabakken L, et al: Endoscopic ultrasound guided fine needle aspiration biopsy: A large single centre experience. Gut 44:720–726, 1999.

116. Vazquez-Sequeiros E, Norton ID, Clain JE, et al: Impact of EUS-guided fine needle aspiration on lymph node staging in patients with esophageal carcinoma. Gastrointest Endosc 53:751–757, 2001.

117. Holscher AH, Bollschweiler E, Schneider PM, Siewert JR: Early adenocarcinoma in Barrett's oesophagus. Br J Surg 84:1470–1473, 1997.

118. Hasegawa N, Niwa Y, Arisawa T, et al: Preoperative staging of superficial esophageal carcinoma: Comparison of an ultrasound probe and standard endoscopic ultrasonography. Gastrointest Endosc 44:388–393, 1996.

119. Menzel J, Domscke W: Gastrointestinal miniprobe sonography: The current status. Am J Gastroenterol 95:605–616, 2000.

120. Menzel J, Hoepffner N, Nottberg H, et al: Preoperative staging of esophageal carcinoma: Miniprobe sonography versus conventional endoscopic ultrasound in a prospective histopathologically verified study. Endoscopy 31:291–7, 1999.

121. Izumi Y, Inoue H, Kawano T, et al: Endosonography during endoscopic mucosal resection to enhance its safety: A new technique. Surg Endosc 13:358–360, 1999.

122. Mallery S, Van Dam J: Increased rate of complete EUS staging of patients with esophageal cancer using the nonoptical, wire-guided echoendoscope. Gastrointest Endosc 50:53–57, 1999.

123. Pfau PR, Ginsberg GG, Lew RJ, et al: Esophageal dilation for endosonographic evaluation of malignant esophageal strictures is safe and effective. Am J Gastroenterol 95:2813–2815, 2000.

124. Binmoeller KF, Seifert H, Seitz U, et al: Ultrasonic esophagoprobe for TNM staging of highly stenosing esophageal carcinoma. Gastrointest Endosc 41:547–552, 1995.

125. Wallace MB, Hawes RH, Sahai AV, et al: Dilation of malignant esophageal stenosis to allow EUS-guided fine-needle aspiration: Safety and effect on patient management. Gastrointest Endosc 51:309–313, 2000.

126. Aabakken L: Standardized terminology in endoscopic ultrasound. Eur J Ultrasound 10:179–183, 1999.

127. Luketich JD, Schauer P, Landreneau R, et al: Minimally invasive surgical staging is superior to endoscopic ultrasound in detecting lymph node metastases in esophageal cancer. J Thorac Cardiovasc Surg 114:817–821, 1997.

128. van Overhagen H, Lameris JS, Zonderland HM, et al: Ultrasound and ultrasound-guided fine needle aspiration biopsy of supraclavicular lymph nodes in patients with esophageal carcinoma. Cancer 67:585–587, 1991.

129. Doldi SB, Lattuada E, Zappa MA, et al: Ultrasonographic evaluation of the cervical lymph nodes in preoperative staging of esophageal neoplasms. Abdom Imaging 23:275–277, 1998.

130. Catalano MF, Alcocer E, Chak A, et al: Evaluation of metastatic celiac axis lymph nodes in patients with esophageal carcinoma: Accuracy of EUS. Gastrointest Endosc 50:352–356, 1999.

131. Reed CE, Mishra G, Sahai AV, et al: Esophageal cancer staging: Improved accuracy by endoscopic ultrasound of celiac lymph nodes. Ann Thorac Surg 67:319–321, 1999.

132. Eloubeidi MA, Wallace MB, Reed CE, et al: The utility of EUS and EUS-guided fine needle aspiration in detecting celiac lymph node metastasis in patients with esophageal cancer: A single center experience. Gastrointest Endosc 54:714–719, 2001.

133. Hiele M, De Leyn P, Schurmans P, et al: Relation between endoscopic ultrasound findings and outcome of patients with tumors of the esophagus or esophagogastric junction. Gastrointest Endosc 45:381–386, 1997.

134. Chak A, Canto M, Gerdes H, et al: Prognosis of esophageal cancers preoperatively staged to be locally invasive (T4) by endoscopic ultrasound (EUS): A multicenter retrospective cohort study. Gastrointest Endosc 42:501–506, 1995.

135. Fockens P, Kisman K, Merkus MP, et al: The prognosis of esophageal carcinoma staged irresectable (T4) by endosonography. J Am Coll Surg 186:17–23, 1998.

136. Preston SR, Clark GW, Martin IG, et al: Effect of endoscopic ultrasonography on the management of 100 consecutive patients of oesophageal and junctional carcinoma. Br J Surg 90:1220–1224, 2003.

137. Giovannini M, Monges G, Seitz JF, et al: Distant lymph node metastases in esophageal cancer: Impact of endoscopic ultrasound-guided biopsy. Endoscopy 31:536–540, 1999.

138. Mortensen MB, Pless T, Durup J, et al: Clinical impact of endoscopic ultrasound-guided fine needle aspiration biopsy in patients with upper GI tract malignancies. A prospective study. Endoscopy 33:478–483, 2001.

139. Zuccaro G Jr, Rice TW, Goldblum J, et al: Endoscopic ultrasound cannot determine suitability for esophagectomy after aggressive chemoradiotherapy for esophageal cancer. Am J Gastroenterol 94:906–912, 1999.

140. Mallery S, DeCamp M, Bueno R, et al: Pretreatment staging by endoscopic ultrasonography does not predict complete response to neoadjuvant chemoradiation in patients with esophageal carcinoma. Cancer 86:764–769, 1999.

141. Pfau PR, Kochman ML: Pretreatment staging by endoscopic ultrasonography does not predict complete response to neoadjuvant chemoradiation in patients with esophageal carcinoma. Gastrointest Endosc 52:583–586, 2000.

142. Hirata N, Kawamoto K, Ueyama T, et al: Using endosonography to assess the effects of neoadjuvant therapy in patients with advanced esophageal cancer. AJR 169:485–491, 1997.

143. Isenberg G, Chak A, Canto MI, et al: Endoscopic ultrasound in restaging of esophageal cancer after neoadjuvant chemoradiation. Gastrointest Endosc 48:158–163, 1998.

144. Willis J, Cooper GS, Isenberg G, et al: Correlation of EUS measurement with pathologic assessment of neoadjuvant therapy response in esophageal carcinoma. Gastrointest Endosc 55:655–661, 2002.

145. Chak A, Canto MI, Cooper GS, et al: Endosonographic assessment of multimodality therapy predicts survival of esophageal carcinoma patients. Cancer 88:1788–1795, 2000.

146. Penman ID, Williams DB, Sahai AV, et al: Ability of EUS with fine-needle aspiration to document nodal staging and response to neoadjuvant chemoradiotherapy in locally advanced esophageal cancer: A case report. Gastrointest Endosc 49:783–786, 1999.

147. Van Dam J: Novel methods of enhanced endoscopic imaging. Gut 52(Suppl IV):12–16, 2003.

Diagnosis and Surveillance of Barrett's Esophagus

Gary W. Falk

CHAPTER

28

Introduction

Barrett's esophagus is an acquired condition resulting from severe esophageal mucosal injury. It is unclear why some patients with gastroesophageal reflux disease (GERD) develop Barrett's esophagus whereas others do not. The diagnosis of Barrett's esophagus is established if the squamocolumnar junction is displaced proximal to the gastroesophageal junction and intestinal metaplasia is detected by biopsy. However, diagnostic inconsistencies are a problem in Barrett's esophagus, especially in distinguishing short-segment Barrett's esophagus from intestinal metaplasia of the gastric cardia. Barrett's esophagus would be of little importance was it not for its well-recognized association with adenocarcinoma of the esophagus. The incidence of esophageal adenocarcinoma continues to increase, and the 5-year survival rate for this cancer remains dismal. However, the overall disease burden of esophageal cancer remains low and cancer risk for a given patient with Barrett's esophagus is lower than previously estimated. Current strategies for improved survival in patients with esophageal adenocarcinoma focus on cancer detection at an early and potentially curable stage. This can be accomplished either by screening more patients for Barrett's esophagus or with endoscopic surveillance of patients with known Barrett's esophagus. However, current screening and surveillance strategies are inherently expensive and inefficient and of unproved benefit. New techniques to improve the efficiency of cancer surveillance continue to evolve and hold the promise to change clinical practice in the future. Treatment options include aggressive acid suppression, antireflux surgery, chemoprevention, and ablation therapy, but there is still no clear consensus on the optimal treatment for these patients.

Epidemiology

It is estimated that Barrett's esophagus is found in approximately 6% to 12% of patients undergoing endoscopy for symptoms of GERD and in 1% or less of unselected patient populations undergoing endoscopy.[1-5] The prevalence of long-segment Barrett's esophagus, (≥3 cm of intestinal metaplasia) is approximately 5%, whereas that of short-segment Barrett's esophagus (<3 cm of intestinal metaplasia) is approximately 6% to 12% in patients undergoing endoscopy in a variety of settings.[6-8] However, a recent study of Veterans Affairs patients in California found that the prevalence of Barrett's esophagus was 25% in patients without symptoms of GERD.[9] These data, if confirmed at other sites, could dramatically change our understanding of the epidemiology of Barrett's esophagus.

The incidence of Barrett's esophagus has increased markedly since the 1970s, but this increase parallels the increased use of diagnostic upper endoscopy (Fig. 28–1).[10] However, others hypothesize that

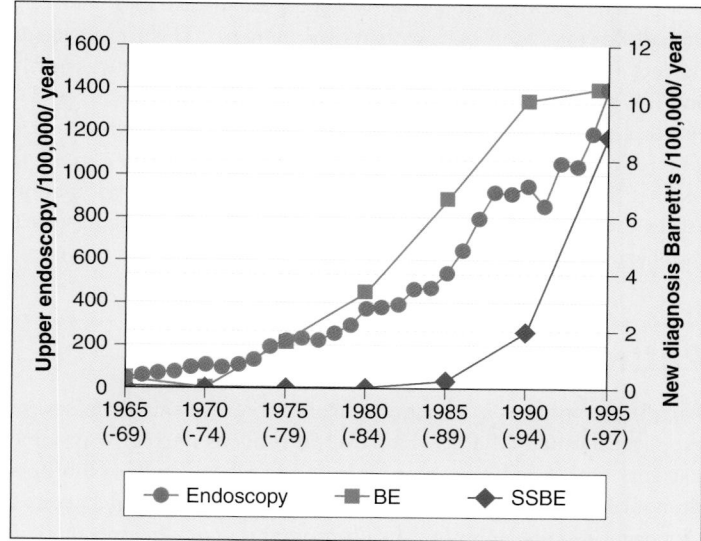

Figure 28–1. Incidence of new diagnosis of Barrett's esophagus (BE) and short-segment Barrett's esophagus (SSBE) in Olmsted County residents between 1965 and 1997 in conjunction with annual utilization rates for upper endoscopy in the same population. (Redrawn from Conio M, Cameron AJ, Romero Y, et al: Secular trends in the epidemiology and outcome of Barrett's oesophagus in Olmsted County, Minnesota. Gut 48:304–309, 2001, with permission of BMJ Publishing Group.)

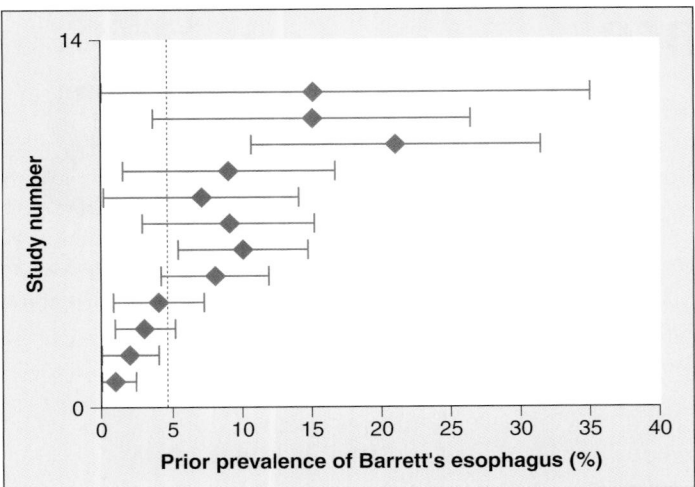

Figure 28–2. Prior prevalence (point estimate with 95% confidence interval) of Barrett's esophagus among patients undergoing resection for incident esophageal adenocarcinoma in 12 studies. The vertical line gives the summary estimate of 4.7%. (Redrawn from Dulai GS, Guha S, Kahn KL, et al: Preoperative prevalence of Barrett's esophagus in esophageal adenocarcinoma: A systematic review. Gastroenterology 122:26–33, 2002, with permission from the American Gastroenterological Association.)

this may be related to the decline in the prevalence of *Helicobacter pylori* infection.[11] Autopsy data from Olmsted County, Minnesota, suggest that most cases of Barrett's esophagus go undetected in the general population, and it is estimated that for every known case of Barrett's esophagus, 20 additional cases go unrecognized.[3] Furthermore, it is estimated that only 5% of patients undergoing resection for esophageal adenocarcinoma have a prior diagnosis of Barrett's esophagus (Fig. 28–2).[12]

Barrett's esophagus is predominantly a disease of middle-aged white men.[4] However, it should be kept in mind that approximately 25% of Barrett's esophagus patients are women.[10] The prevalence of Barrett's esophagus in Hispanics is similar to that in Caucasians,[13] and Barrett's esophagus was diagnosed in 2% of a Taiwanese population undergoing endoscopy for a variety of gastrointestinal symptoms.[14] The prevalence of Barrett's esophagus increases until a plateau is reached between the seventh and ninth decades.[4] One population study estimated that the mean age of development of Barrett's esophagus was 40 years and the mean age at diagnosis was 63 years.[4]

Pathogenesis

Barrett's esophagus is an acquired condition resulting from severe esophageal mucosal injury. However, it remains unclear why some patients with GERD develop Barrett's esophagus whereas others do not. Animal studies suggest that the development of Barrett's esophagus requires injury to the esophageal mucosa accompanied by an abnormal environment of epithelial repair.[15] Epidemiologic data suggest that once injury occurs, Barrett's esophagus develops to its full extent fairly rapidly with little subsequent change in length.[4] The mechanism whereby injury triggers metaplasia, and why this occurs in some but not all individuals is unknown. The cell of origin remains unclear; candidates include esophageal glandular

cells, heterotopic gastric mucosa, or abnormal differentiation of a primordial stem cell in the esophagus.[16] A multilayered epithelium within Barrett's epithelium, with histologic and cytoskeletal features of both squamous and columnar epithelium, provides further support for a multipotential stem cell as the site of origin of Barrett's epithelium.[17]

Barrett's esophagus is clearly associated with severe gastroesophageal reflux. Compared with patients with erosive and nonerosive GERD without Barrett's esophagus, patients with Barrett's esophagus typically have greater esophageal acid exposure based on 24-hour pH monitoring.[18,19] Part of the increase in acid exposure in Barrett's patients may be related to the almost uniform presence of a hiatal hernia, which is typically longer and associated with larger defects in the hiatus than controls or patients with esophagitis alone.[20,21] In addition, patients with Barrett's esophagus have a lower basal lower esophageal sphincter (LES) pressure compared with GERD patients without Barrett's esophagus.[19] Reflux of duodenal contents is also increased in Barrett's esophagus patients compared with GERD patients without Barrett's esophagus.[22] Patients with short-segment Barrett's esophagus tend to have pathophysiologic abnormalities intermediate to those of long-segment Barrett's patients and normal controls.[23,24] Esophageal pH monitoring studies suggest a correlation between the length of Barrett's mucosa and the duration of esophageal acid exposure.[24]

Clinical Features

Patients with Barrett's esophagus are difficult to distinguish clinically from patients with GERD uncomplicated by a columnar lined esophagus.[25] However, some observational studies suggest that features such as the development of reflux symptoms at an earlier age, increased duration of reflux symptoms, increased severity of nocturnal reflux symptoms, and increased complications of GERD such as esophagitis, ulceration, stricture, and bleeding may distinguish Barrett's esophagus patients from GERD patients without Barrett's esophagus.[26,27] Interestingly, similar clinical risk factors have been identified for esophageal adenocarcinoma.[28] Identification of Barrett's esophagus patients may be hampered by the paradox that Barrett's esophagus patients have an impaired sensitivity to esophageal acid perfusion compared with patients with uncomplicated GERD.[29] However, many Barrett's esophagus patients are elderly, and this observation may be related to an age-related decrease in acid sensitivity.[30] A subset of Barrett's esophagus patients may have an inherited predisposition, because several case series have reported on families with multiple affected relatives over successive generations.[31] These reports suggest an autosomal dominant pattern of inheritance in selected individuals with Barrett's esophagus.

Pathology

The columnar lined esophagus is characterized by three different types of columnar epithelium above the LES zone: gastric fundic-type epithelium characterized by parietal and chief cells, cardiac-type mucosa characterized by mucous glands and no parietal cells, and specialized columnar epithelium characterized by a villiform surface and alcian blue staining intestinal-type goblet cells.[32] Currently, the diagnosis of Barrett's esophagus is established if the squamocolumnar junction is displaced proximal to the gastroesophageal junction and intestinal metaplasia (characterized by acid mucin-containing goblet cells using combined hematoxylin and eosin-alcian blue pH 2.5 stain) is detected by biopsy (Fig. 28–3).[33] The emphasis on intestinal metaplasia is based on the observation that cancer risk in Barrett's esophagus appears to be limited to patients with intestinal metaplasia, a finding that may be explained by the increased rate of cellular proliferation encountered in these cells compared with cardiac or fundic type epithelium.[34] In most cases, goblet cells are easily identified on routine hematoxylin and eosin preparations, and special stains such as alcian blue periodic acid–Schiff (PAS) are not necessary. However, in biopsy specimens with few goblet cells, alcian blue PAS stains can help avoid overinterpretation of pseudogoblet cells characterized by distended gastric surface foveolar-type cells that stain for PAS but do not contain alcian blue positive acid mucins and hence are not classified as intestinal metaplasia (Fig. 28–4).[35]

Differential Diagnosis

As stated previously, the diagnosis of Barrett's esophagus is established if the squamocolumnar junction is displaced proximal to the gastroesophageal junction and intestinal metaplasia (characterized by acid mucin-containing goblet cells using combined hematoxylin and eosin-alcian blue pH 2.5 stain) is detected by

biopsy.[33] At the time of endoscopy, landmarks should first be carefully defined. If the squamocolumnar junction is above the level of the esophagogastric junction (as defined by the proximal margin of the gastric folds using partial insufflation), biopsies should be obtained (Fig. 28–5). If intestinal metaplasia is present, the patient is considered to have Barrett's esophagus and should be placed in a surveillance program. Biopsies of the squamocolumnar junction should not be routinely obtained in clinical practice if it is at the level of the gastroesophageal junction.

Despite this relatively simple definition, the diagnosis of Barrett's esophagus is not as straightforward as it might appear. This is because the precise junction of the stomach and the esophagus may be difficult to determine endoscopically, because of the presence of a hiatal hernia, inflammation, and the dynamic nature of the gastroesophageal junction. It is commonly accepted that the proximal margin of the gastric folds is the most useful landmark for the junction of the stomach and the esophagus.[36] Determination of landmarks is facilitated by performing the examination of the esophagus with partial insufflation of air.

Standard endoscopy and biopsy is the current standard for the diagnosis of Barrett's esophagus. However, endoscopy and biopsy have a number of limitations that are not well appreciated. These include endoscopic recognition of the columnar-lined esophagus, adequate targeting of biopsies, and accurate pathologic interpretation. Endoscopists identify landmarks necessary for the diagnosis of Barrett's esophagus inconsistently (Fig. 28–6).[37] Not surprisingly, this leads to inconsistencies in defining the length of the columnar-lined esophagus.[38] One study found that the sensitivity and specificity of endoscopists to correctly identify Barrett's esophagus based on intestinal metaplasia on histology were only 82% and 81%, respectively.[39]

The optimal number of biopsies necessary to find intestinal metaplasia in a columnar-lined esophagus is unknown. However, the yield of intestinal metaplasia in biopsy specimens increases in concert with an increase in the length of the columnar-lined esophagus (Fig. 28–7).[39,40] Furthermore, intestinal metaplasia is more commonly found in biopsies obtained in the proximal portion of the columnar lined segment, where goblet cell density is the greatest.[40] Thus, for a given number of biopsies, the yield of intestinal metaplasia is greatest when biopsies are concentrated in the most proximal part of the columnar-lined segment.[40] The problems involved in the yield of intestinal metaplasia on biopsy have led to further inconsistencies in the diagnosis of Barrett's esophagus. For example, it has been reported that 18% of patients

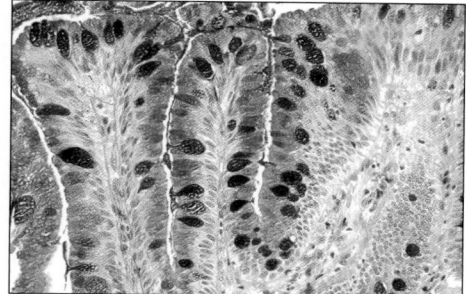

Figure 28–3. Histologic appearance of specialized columnar epithelium, characterized by a villiform appearance, and goblet cells staining positive with periodic acid–Schiff staining. (Courtesy of John Goldblum, MD.)

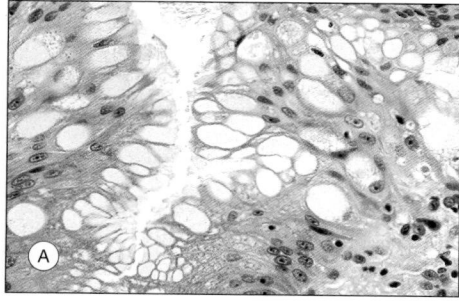
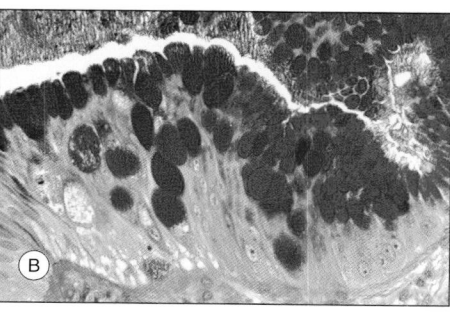

Figure 28–4. Columnar epithelium with pseudogoblet cells characterized by distended gastric surface foveolar-type cells (A) that stain for periodic acid–Schiff (PAS) but do not contain alcian blue positive acid mucins (B). (Courtesy of John Goldblum, MD.)

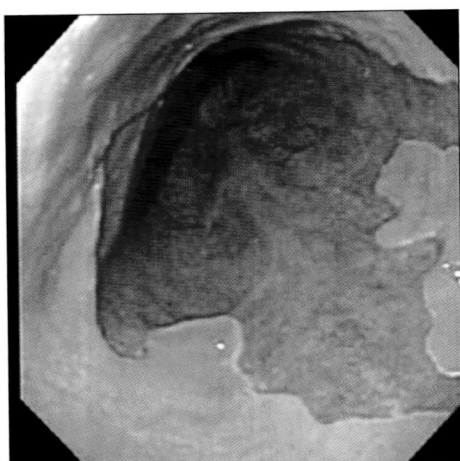

Figure 28–5. Endoscopic appearance of a long segment of Barrett's esophagus.

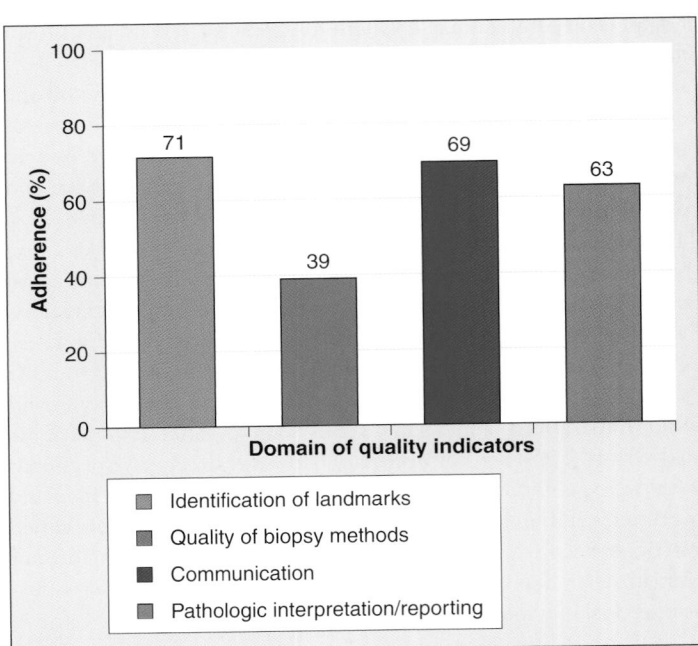

Figure 28–6. Problems in quality of care of Barrett's esophagus: mean proportion of cases adhering to accepted standards in four different domains of care. (Redrawn from Ofman JJ, Shaheen NJ, Desai AA, et al: The quality of care in Barrett's esophagus: Endoscopist and pathologist practices. Am J Gastroenterol 96:876–881, 2001, with permission of Blackwell Publishing Ltd.)

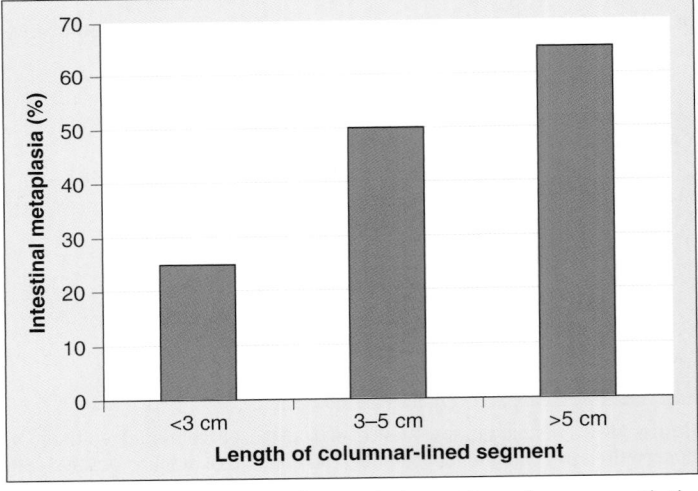

Figure 28–7. Yield of intestinal metaplasia on biopsy increases with the length of the columnar-lined esophagus. (Redrawn from Eloubeidi MA, Provenzale D: Does this patient have Barrett's esophagus? The utility of predicting Barrett's esophagus at the index endoscopy. Am J Gastroenterol 94:937–943, 1999, with permission of Blackwell Publishing Ltd.)

said to have Barrett's esophagus on closely spaced endoscopies had intestinal metaplasia found in only one of the two examinations.[38] Detection of intestinal metaplasia is also a problem in patients with suspected short-segment Barrett's esophagus. In one study, 23% of patients with suspected short-segment Barrett's esophagus, in which the first endoscopy failed to yield intestinal metaplasia, had intestinal metaplasia found at the time of a second endoscopy.[41]

Finally, there is considerable variability in the pathologic diagnosis of intestinal metaplasia without dysplasia. A community-based study of 20 pathologists found that only 35% correctly identified intestinal metaplasia without dysplasia and only 38% could identify gastric metaplasia without intestinal metaplasia![42] Many pathologists continue to classify gastric metaplasia without intestinal metaplasia as Barrett's esophagus, thereby subjecting many individuals to unnecessary surveillance endoscopy.

The evolving concept of short-segment Barrett's esophagus, currently defined as specialized columnar epithelium lining less than 3 cm of the distal esophagus,[43] continues to be a clinical dilemma with respect to where, when, and how to obtain biopsy specimens in patients undergoing upper endoscopy. The prevalence of short-segment Barrett's esophagus has been reported to be 6% to 12% in patients undergoing upper endoscopy in a variety of settings.[6–8] The prevalence of intestinal metaplasia at a normal-appearing gastroesophageal junction varies from 6% to 36%.[6–8,44–46] Routine histopathologic techniques are unable to distinguish among intestinal metaplasia originating in the stomach, a normal gastroesophageal junction, or the cardia.

Patients with short-segment Barrett's esophagus seem to be clinically similar to patients with conventional long-segment Barrett's esophagus. These patients are often white, male, smokers, with longstanding symptoms of GERD.[8] In contrast, there is no clear gender predominance in patients with intestinal metaplasia of the gastroesophageal junction and cardia, because this condition is more common in older patients who are often infected with *H. pylori* and have evidence of gastritis and/or intestinal metaplasia elsewhere in the stomach.[8,44,47] However, a subset of these patients may have

GERD and it is unclear if this condition is a sequela of aging, *H. pylori* infection, GERD, or some combination of these factors. Short-segment Barrett's esophagus is clearly associated with some risk of developing dysplasia and esophageal cancer, which is not substantially lower than that in patients with long-segment Barrett's esophagus.[48] Dysplasia and carcinoma have been reported in patients with intestinal metaplasia of the gastroesophageal junction or cardia, but the magnitude of that risk appears to be less than that of short-segment Barrett's esophagus.[49]

Some studies suggest that methylene blue chromoendoscopy may help direct biopsies in patients with suspected short-segment Barrett's esophagus.[50,51] However, other studies fail to confirm this.[52] These contradictory findings are likely related to methodologic inconsistencies associated with methylene blue chromoendoscopy. A reliable biomarker to distinguish between intestinal metaplasia of the cardia versus intestinal metaplasia of the esophagus would be beneficial. However, techniques advocated such as the Das-1 antibody and cytokeratin immunohistochemical staining patterns do not reliably distinguish between these two entities and are not ready for routine clinical practice.[53]

Barrett's Esophagus and Esophageal Adenocarcinoma

Barrett's esophagus would be of no importance were it not for its well-recognized association with esophageal adenocarcinoma. In the United States, the incidence of adenocarcinoma of the esophagus in white men has increased by 21% per year, a rate greater than that for any other cancer in white men.[54] Similar trends are seen in other Western industrialized countries. However, the overall burden of esophageal adenocarcinoma remains relatively low. It is estimated that there were 13,900 new cases of esophageal cancer (not all of which were adenocarcinoma) in the United States in 2003.[55]

The reason for this increase in the incidence of esophageal adenocarcinoma is unknown. Barrett's esophagus is clearly a risk factor for adenocarcinoma of the esophagus. Epidemiologic studies have identified a variety of other risk factors for the development of esophageal adenocarcinoma. Work from Lagergren and coworkers[28] showed that the more frequent, severe and long-lasting the symptoms of reflux, the greater the risk for esophageal adenocarcinoma. There is increasing evidence of an association between increasing body mass index and esophageal adenocarcinoma.[56,57] Dietary and environmental issues implicated include a diet low in fresh fruit and smoking,[58,59] whereas *H. pylori* infection, especially with *cagA*$^+$ strains, may protect against the development of esophageal adenocarcinoma.[60] There are conflicting data on the role of drugs that relax the LES as a risk factor for esophageal adenocarcinoma.[55]

Despite the alarming increase in the incidence of esophageal adenocarcinoma, the precise incidence of adenocarcinoma in patients with Barrett's esophagus is uncertain, with rates varying from 1 in 52 to 1 in 297 years of follow-up.[61–64] Shaheen and colleagues[64] found a strong inverse relationship between cancer risk and study size, with small studies reporting much higher cancer risks than large studies. This finding suggests that there is a publication bias that has led to an overestimate of cancer risk in Barrett's esophagus: small studies were published or submitted for publication only if they indicated high cancer risk. Most recent studies suggest a much lower risk than what was previously thought, approximately 0.5% or less annually.[63,64] However, there are regional variations of cancer risk in the Western world, and the annual incidence rate in the United Kingdom is approximately twice that found in the United States (1% vs. 0.5%, respectively).[65] The evolving epidemiologic data suggest that despite the alarming increase in the incidence of esophageal adenocarcinoma, most patients with Barrett's esophagus will never develop cancer. Furthermore, the survival of patients with Barrett's esophagus is similar to that of the general population.[66]

Cancer Biology

Cancer risk in Barrett's esophagus appears to be limited to patients with specialized columnar epithelium. Compelling evidence exists for a dysplasia-carcinoma sequence in Barrett's esophagus whereby specialized columnar epithelium progresses to low grade dysplasia, high grade dysplasia, and finally to carcinoma. Foci of carcinoma typically appear adjacent to dysplasia.[67] The time course for this progression is highly variable, and most patients never progress to dysplasia.

It is hypothesized that cancer develops in a subset of patients who have acquired genomic instability in Barrett's epithelium.[68] This predisposes to the development of abnormal clones of cells that then accumulate progressively more genetic errors, which include numerical and structural chromosomal rearrangements, gene mutations, loss of normal cell cycle control, and increased cell proliferation rates.[69–71] However, there is no clearly predictable sequence of genetic abnormalities that leads to the development of cancer. Upregulation of cyclooxygenase-2 (COX-2) expression also occurs in the metaplasia-dysplasia-carcinoma sequence.[72] Increased COX-2 expression is associated with increased cellular proliferation and decreased apoptosis *in vitro*,[73] and administration of selective COX-2 inhibitors can decrease cell growth and increase apoptosis in esophageal adenocarcinoma cell lines.[74] This is a finding that may have implications for chemoprevention.

Screening and Surveillance Strategies for Barrett's Esophagus

Esophageal adenocarcinoma is a lethal disease with a 5-year survival of approximately 14% at present.[55] Survival is stage dependent and early spread before the onset of symptoms is characteristic of this tumor; lymph node metastases may be found in up to 5% of intramucosal carcinoma cases and up to 24% of submucosal carcinoma cases because of the rich lymphatic supply of the esophagus that extends into the lamina propria.[75] There has only been a minor and clinically insignificant improvement in stage of disease at diagnosis and 5-year survival in these patients.[76] Furthermore, approximately 95% of esophageal adenocarcinomas are diagnosed in patients without a prior diagnosis of Barrett's esophagus.[12] Thus, the best hope for improved survival of patients with esophageal adenocarcinoma is detection of cancer at an early and potentially curable stage.

SCREENING

One potential strategy to decrease the mortality rate of esophageal adenocarcinoma further is to identify more patients at risk, namely those with Barrett's esophagus. Current practice guidelines recommend screening all patients with chronic GERD symptoms for Barrett's esophagus.[33] Endoscopy with biopsy is still the only validated technique to diagnose Barrett's esophagus. However, it has clear limitations as a screening tool including cost, risk, and complexity. If applied to the estimated 20% of the population with regular GERD symptoms, the cost implications would be staggering.[77] However, unsedated upper endoscopy using small-caliber instruments may change the economics of endoscopic screening, because this technique may decrease sedation-related complications and costs. Unsedated small-caliber upper endoscopy is feasible, acceptable, and accurate when compared with conventional sedated endoscopy.[78,79] However, only limited information is available on unsedated endoscopy in the evaluation of Barrett's esophagus. Furthermore, it is unclear if endoscopy without sedation will meet with patient acceptance given the cultural preference for sedation in the United States. Otherwise, there are no validated alternative techniques to screen for Barrett's esophagus that overcome the cost and risks associated with endoscopy.

Despite the current practice guidelines, there are no data from randomized controlled trials or observational studies to evaluate the effectiveness or efficacy of screening. A recent decision analysis model by Inadomi and coworkers[80] examined screening of 50-year-old white men with chronic GERD symptoms for Barrett's esophagus and found that one-time screening is probably cost effective if subsequent surveillance is limited to patients with dysplasia on initial examination (Fig. 28–8). This strategy would result in a cost of $10,440 per quality-adjusted life-year saved compared with a strategy of no screening or surveillance. Another modeling study also suggested that screening was a reasonable strategy but only if the following conditions were met: a group of patients at high risk for Barrett's esophagus, high grade dysplasia, or adenocarcinoma; high sensitivity and specificity of endoscopy with biopsy; and little or no reduction in quality of life with esophagectomy.[81] Any variation of these ideal conditions quickly made this strategy cost ineffective. The incremental cost effectiveness of screening deteriorated rapidly once the prevalence of Barrett's esophagus or high grade dysplasia fell to less than 5%.

There is clearly a need to develop either a better profile of patients at high risk for Barrett's esophagus and high grade dysplasia or to develop a far less expensive tool to provide mass population screening. A simple questionnaire and nomogram has been described in an effort to predict Barrett's esophagus in patients with GERD symptoms.[82] However, the sensitivity of this questionnaire for predicting Barrett's esophagus was 77% with a specificity of only 63%. Although clearly cost saving, this model would obviously miss patients with Barrett's esophagus with GERD symptoms and not account for individuals without any symptoms of GERD.

In the future, screening strategies will have to consider the following options: limiting screening to only high-risk patients, offering mass endoscopic screening to all adults older than age 50 as part of a periodic health appraisal preventive strategy, or doing

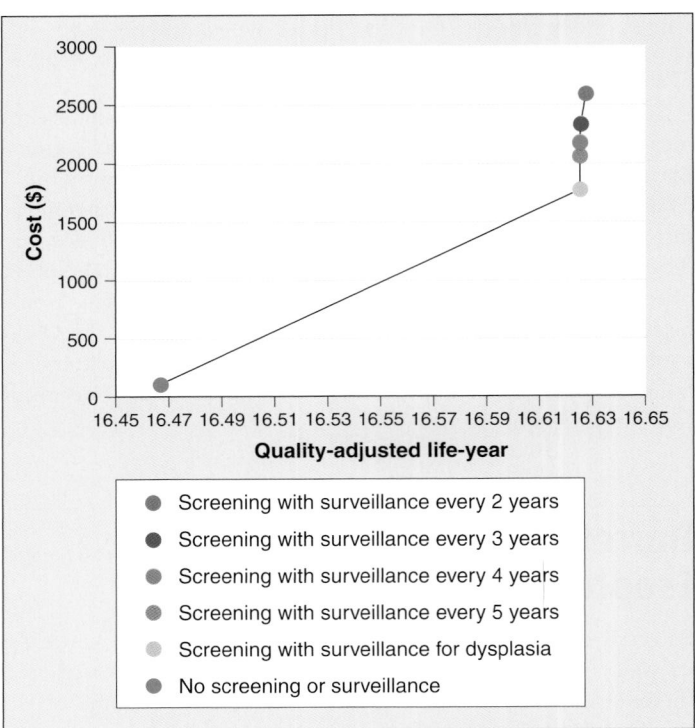

Figure 28–8. Cost and benefit of screening and surveillance for Barrett's esophagus in a hypothetical 50-year-old white man with symptoms of gastroesophageal reflux disease (GERD) compared with no screening or surveillance. (Redrawn with permission from Inadomi JM, Sampliner R, Lagergren J, et al: Screening and surveillance for Barrett esophagus in high risk groups: A cost-utility analysis. Ann Intern Med 138:176–186, 2003.)

nothing until clinical trials provide the evidence to support such a strategy. Problems inherent in demonstrating the utility of a screening program such as healthy volunteer bias, lead time bias, and length time bias will all need to be addressed.

SURVEILLANCE

Current practice guidelines recommend endoscopic surveillance of patients with Barrett's esophagus in an attempt to detect cancer at an early and potentially curable stage.[33] A number of observational studies suggest that patients with Barrett's esophagus in whom adenocarcinoma was detected in a surveillance program have their cancers detected at an earlier stage (Fig. 28–9), with markedly improved 5-year survival compared with similar patients not undergoing routine endoscopic surveillance (Fig. 28–10).[81–88] Furthermore, nodal involvement is far less likely in surveyed patients compared with nonsurveyed patients.[87] Because esophageal cancer survival is stage-dependent, these studies suggest that survival may be enhanced by endoscopic surveillance. Several decision-analysis models support the concept of endoscopic surveillance.[80,89,90] However, the model of Provenzale and coworkers[89] suggests that surveillance every 5 years is the most effective strategy to increase both length and quality of life, whereas the model of Inadomi and colleagues[80] suggests that surveillance should be limited only to individuals with dysplasia at the time of initial endoscopy. Thus, it

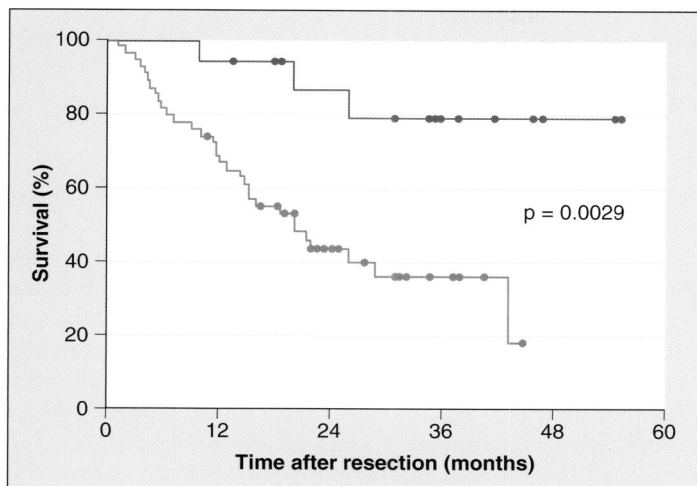

Figure 28–9. Improved postoperative survival in esophageal adenocarcinoma for patients diagnosed during endoscopic surveillance compared with patients diagnosed without prior surveillance. (Redrawn from Van Sandick JW, Lanschot JJ, Kuiken BW, et al: Impact of endoscopic biopsy surveillance of Barrett's esophagus on pathological stage and clinical outcome of Barrett's carcinoma. Gut 43:216–222, 1998, with permission of BMJ Publishing Group.)

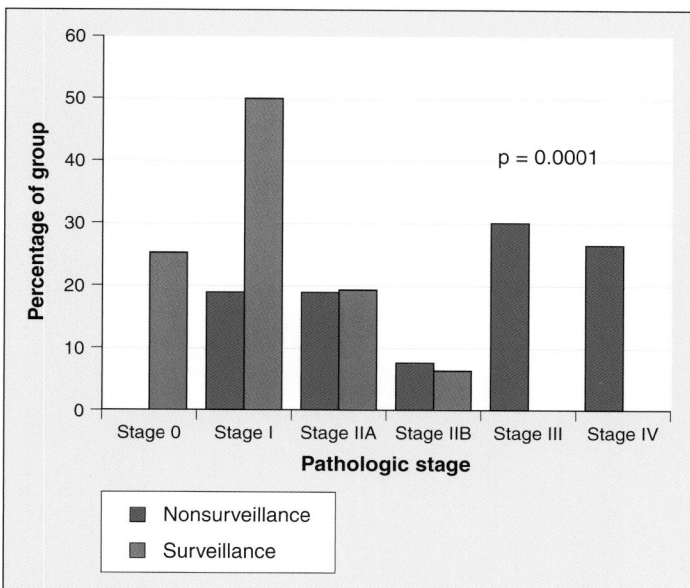

Figure 28–10. Improved pathologic stage at diagnosis of esophageal adenocarcinoma for patients diagnosed during endoscopic surveillance compared with patients diagnosed without prior surveillance. (Redrawn from Van Sandick JW, Lanschot JJ, Kuiken BW, et al: Impact of endoscopic biopsy surveillance of Barrett's esophagus on pathological stage and clinical outcome of Barrett's carcinoma. Gut 43:216–222, 1998, with permission of BMJ Publishing Group.)

appears that current practice guidelines still recommend surveillance too often.

However, others argue that, because most patients with Barrett's esophagus will not die from esophageal cancer, the benefit for surveillance remains uncertain and as such endoscopic surveillance is not warranted until substantiated by prospective studies.[63,91,92] Furthermore, design flaws such as such as selection bias, healthy volunteer bias, lead time bias, and length time bias are inherent in the observational studies that support endoscopic surveillance. The resources encumbered by vigorous endoscopic surveillance are considerable. Despite the concern regarding the esophageal cancer "epidemic," the overall burden of disease is rather limited in the Western world in comparison to other malignancies such as colon cancer. A randomized controlled trial of surveillance versus no surveillance in Barrett's esophagus has not been performed and probably never will be.

Candidates for Endoscopic Surveillance

Only patients at increased risk for the development of carcinoma, that is, those with intestinal metaplasia, should undergo endoscopic surveillance. It is generally agreed that all otherwise healthy patients with Barrett's esophagus should undergo surveillance, with an endpoint of either high grade dysplasia or adenocarcinoma. Elderly patients or patients with comorbid illnesses who are not candidates for esophagectomy generally would not undergo surveillance or would be dropped from surveillance at a certain undetermined age. However, new ablation techniques may make more of these patients eligible for surveillance in the future. This area remains unsettled.

Surveillance Techniques

The aim of surveillance is the detection of dysplasia. The description of dysplasia should use a standard five-tier system: (1) negative for dysplasia, (2) indefinite for dysplasia, (3) low grade dysplasia, (4) high grade dysplasia, and (5) carcinoma.[93] Active inflammation makes it more difficult to distinguish dysplasia from reparative changes. As such, surveillance endoscopy should not be done until any active inflammation related to GERD is controlled with antisecretory therapy.

Current guidelines suggest obtaining systematic four quadrant biopsies at 2-cm intervals along the entire length of the Barrett's segment once inflammation related to GERD is controlled with antisecretory therapy (Fig. 28–11).[33] A systematic biopsy protocol clearly detects more dysplasia and early cancer compared with ad hoc random biopsies.[94] Subtle mucosal abnormalities no matter how trivial, such as ulceration, erosion, plaque, nodule, stricture, or other luminal irregularity in the Barrett's segment, should also be biopsied, because there is an association of such lesions with underlying cancer.[95] The "turn and suction" technique (Fig. 28–12) allows acquisition of biopsies that are significantly larger than those obtained by the traditional techniques of advancing an open biopsy forceps into the lumen and then closing it to obtain the biopsy sample.[96] The safety of systematic endoscopic biopsy protocols has been demonstrated.[97]

The rational for such a comprehensive biopsy program comes from observations that high grade dysplasia and early carcinoma in Barrett's esophagus often occur in the absence of endoscopic abnormalities and from the focal nature of dysplasia. Systematic esophagectomy mapping studies demonstrate just how focal dysplasia and superficial cancer may be.[98] In 30 esophagectomy specimens from patients undergoing surgery for either high grade dysplasia or early invasive adenocarcinoma with no endoscopic evidence of cancer, the median surface area of total Barrett's esophagus was found to be 32 cm^2, low grade dysplasia 13 cm^2, high grade dysplasia 1.3 cm^2, and adenocarcinoma 1.1 cm^2 (Fig. 28–13).[98] The three smallest cancers had surface areas of 0.02, 0.3, and 0.4 cm^2. Because of the focal nature of dysplasia and cancer, some experts recommend that endoscopic surveillance should use a large-particle (jumbo) forceps to obtain biopsies.[99] Studies suggest that a systematic jumbo biopsy protocol at 1-cm intervals plus biopsy of any mucosal abnormalities can reliably distinguish patients with high grade dysplasia alone from those with intramucosal or submucosal adenocarcinoma, thereby avoiding the risk of unnecessary surgery in these patients.[95,99] Reid and coworkers[95] evaluated the utility of this technique in 45 high-grade dysplasia patients who eventually developed cancer. Interestingly, 82% of patients had cancer in only a single 1-cm segment and 69% had cancer in a single biopsy. Furthermore, only 39% of patients with cancer by endoscopic biopsy had cancer found at surgery. Using this "Seattle protocol," 100% of cancers were detected. If biopsies were obtained at 2-cm intervals, only 50% of cancers would have been detected. Others have also found that jumbo biopsies will miss cancer in patients with high grade dysplasia if biopsies are performed at 2-cm intervals.[100] However, this technique requires passage of a therapeutic endoscope, and the generalizability of this technique to clinical practice is problematic. Survey data suggest that only 17% of gastroenterologists in the United States use the jumbo biopsy forceps.[101]

Surveillance Intervals

Surveillance intervals, determined by the presence and grade of dysplasia, are based on our limited understanding of the biology of esophageal adenocarcinoma (Table 28–1). However, these intervals are arbitrary and have never been subject to a clinical trial and likely never will be. Surveillance every 3 years is now recommended as adequate in patients without dysplasia after two negative examinations, whereas annual surveillance is recommended when low grade dysplasia is present.[33] These patients should receive aggressive antisecretory therapy for reflux disease with a proton pump inhibitor to decrease the changes of regeneration that make pathologic interpretation of this category so difficult.

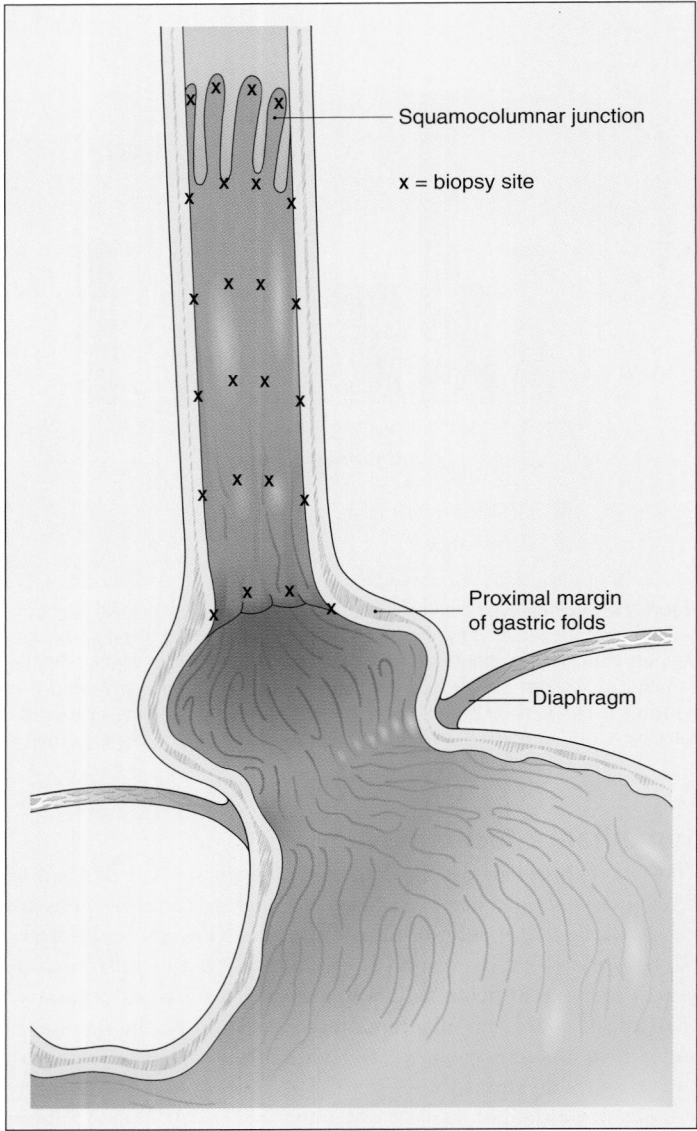

Figure 28–11. Technique of endoscopic surveillance. Landmarks including the diaphragm, proximal margin of gastric folds, and squamocolumnar junction should be identified first. Four-quadrant biopsies should then be obtained every 2 cm in the involved segment. (Redrawn with permission from Falk GW: Endoscopic surveillance of Barrett's esophagus. Tech Gastrointest Endosc 2:186–193, 2000.)

Table 28–1. 2002 American College of Gastroenterology Practice Guidelines for Endoscopic Surveillance of Barrett's Esophagus

Dysplasia Grade	Interval
None	Every 3 years after two are negative
Low grade	Every year until no dysplasia
High grade	Repeat endoscopy Intensive biopsy protocol preferably with therapeutic endoscope and large-capacity biopsy forceps to rule out cancer and document high grade dysplasia. Special attention to mucosal irregularity. Expert pathologist confirmation Focal high-grade dysplasia (<5 crypts): continued surveillance every 3 months Multifocal (>5 crypts): intervention Mucosal irregularity: endoscopic mucosal resection

Adapted from Sampliner RE: Updated guidelines for the diagnosis, surveillance, and therapy of Barrett's esophagus. Am J Gastroenterol 97:1888–1895, 2002, with permission of BMJ Publishing Group.

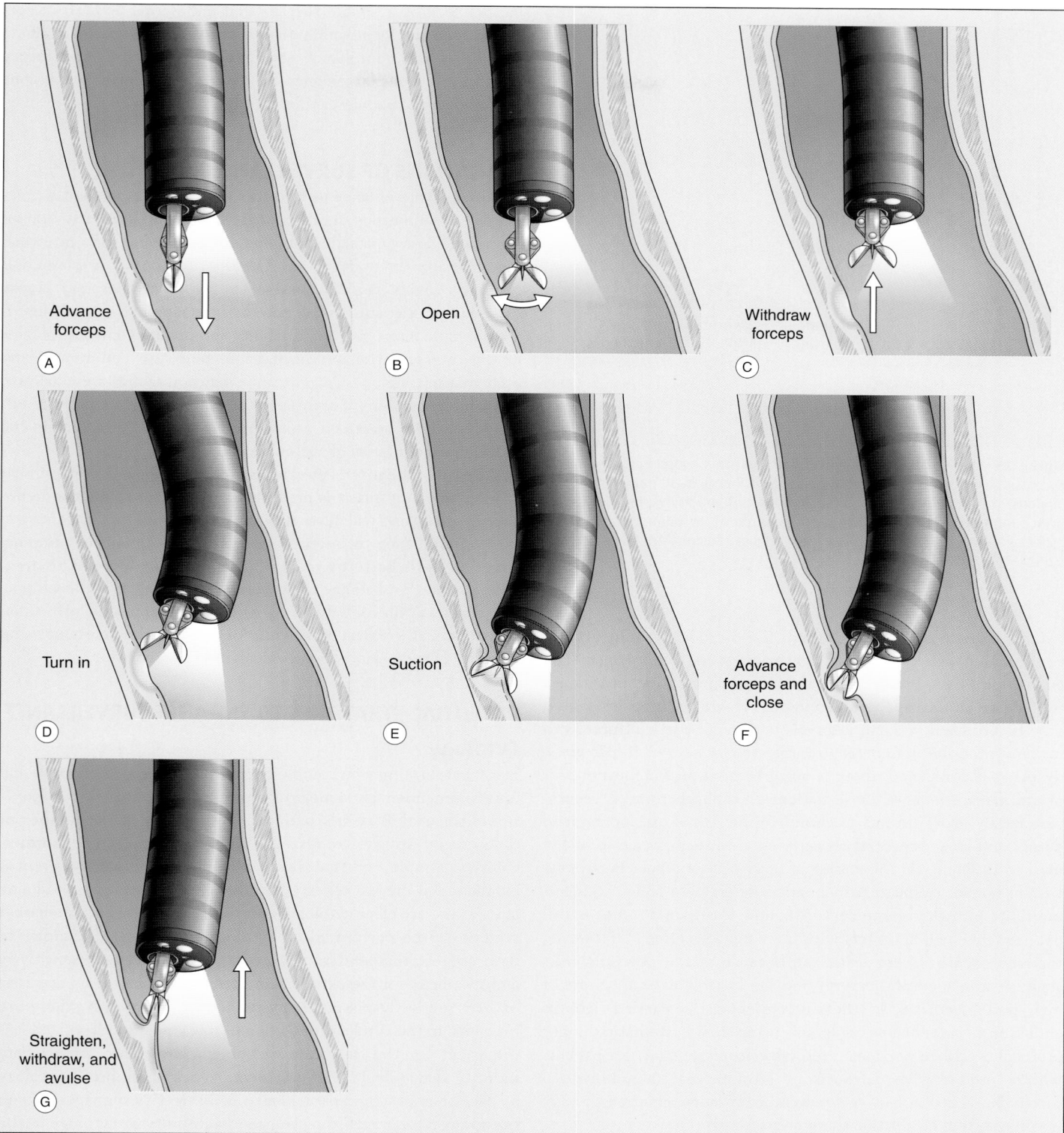

Figure 28–12. Turn and suction technique of obtaining biopsies in Barrett's esophagus. The biopsy forceps are first advanced in the lumen *(A)*, opened *(B)*, and then drawn back into the endoscope until the forceps are flush with the endoscope tip *(C)*. The endoscope is then turned into the esophageal wall *(D)* after which suction is applied *(E)*. The biopsy forceps are advanced slightly and closed *(F)*, after which the endoscope is straightened followed by withdrawal of the forceps to avulse a mucosal sample *(G)*. (Redrawn with permission from Levine DS, Reid BJ: Endoscopic biopsy technique for acquiring larger mucosal samples. Gastrointest Endosc 37:332–337, 1991.)

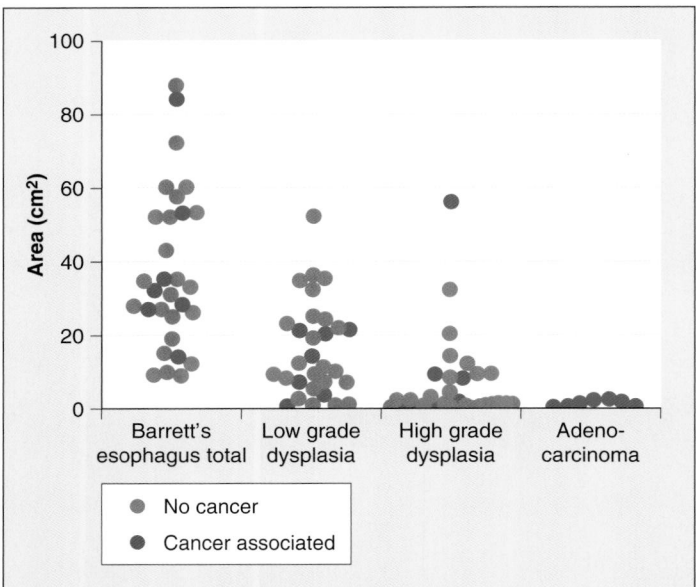

Figure 28–13. Surface area involved with Barrett's esophagus, low grade dysplasia, high grade dysplasia, and adenocarcinoma in 30 patients without obvious carcinoma undergoing resection for high grade dysplasia or superficial adenocarcinoma. (Redrawn from Cameron AJ, Carpenter HA: Barrett's esophagus, high-grade dysplasia and early adenocarcinoma. Am J Gastroenterol 92:586–591, 1997.)

If high grade dysplasia is found, the diagnosis should first be confirmed by an experienced gastrointestinal pathologist. The endoscopic biopsy protocol should then be repeated within 1 month to exclude an unsuspected carcinoma. However, biopsies should now be obtained at 1-cm intervals with large-particle forceps to maximize the ability to detect unsuspected cancer.[95,99] If high grade dysplasia is confirmed, there is no agreement on the most appropriate management of these patients. Esophagectomy is recommended by many authors to eliminate the risk of carcinoma or to detect and treat cancer at an early curable stage, because of the marked variability in the finding of unsuspected cancer in patients with high grade dysplasia, which ranges from 0% to 73%.[102] Surgical mortality in high-volume centers is now less than 5%, but is still unacceptably high in centers with low surgical volume.[100] However, this approach has been criticized because of the potential risks associated with esophagectomy and the variable natural history of high grade dysplasia.[99] Others recommend a continued rigorous endoscopic surveillance program using the systematic biopsy protocol described previously, reserving esophagectomy for patients with a preoperative diagnosis of intramucosal or submucosal carcinoma.[99] Still others recommend endoscopic ablation therapy (see the section on ablation therapy later).

Extent of high grade dysplasia is thought by some to be a risk factor for the subsequent development of adenocarcinoma.[103] However, there are currently no uniform criteria for defining the extent of high grade dysplasia, and there are conflicting data on the clinical significance of extent of high grade dysplasia in biopsy specimens and risk for unsuspected carcinoma.[103,104] The ultimate approach to the patient with high grade dysplasia should consider

factors such as available surgical and endoscopic expertise; age; length of Barrett's epithelium that would require biopsy to eliminate sampling error; compliance with endoscopic surveillance; future need for multiple surveillance endoscopies; and suspicious lesions such as plaques, nodules, and strictures.

LIMITATIONS OF SURVEILLANCE

Endoscopic surveillance of Barrett's esophagus, as currently practiced, has numerous shortcomings. Dysplasia and early adenocarcinoma are endoscopically indistinguishable from intestinal metaplasia without dysplasia. The distribution of dysplasia and cancer is highly variable, and even the most thorough biopsy surveillance program has the potential for sampling error. There is considerable interobserver variability and quality control problems in the interpretation of dysplasia in both the community and academic settings.[42,93] Current surveillance programs are expensive and time consuming. Survey data indicate that, although surveillance is widely practiced, there is considerable variability in the technique and interval of surveillance.[101,105]

Currently, all Barrett's esophagus patients are handled in a similar fashion unless dysplasia is present. However, most patients do not have dysplasia and will never develop cancer. Thus, it is necessary to make surveillance techniques more effective by either sampling larger areas of Barrett's mucosa (targeting our biopsies to areas with a higher probability of harboring dysplasia) or by developing risk stratification tools to allow us to concentrate our efforts on individuals at greatest risk while decreasing the frequency and intensity of surveillance in individuals at lower risk.

POTENTIAL STRATEGIES TO ENHANCE SURVEILLANCE

Cytology

Brush cytology may be complementary to endoscopic biopsies and is recommended by some to be part of the routine endoscopic surveillance of Barrett's patients.[106] Cytology has a number of theoretic advantages compared with routine endoscopic biopsies: ability to sample a greater area of involved epithelium, preferential exfoliation of the less cohesive dysplastic cells, simplicity, and lower cost. There are clear cytologic criteria for dysplasia and biomarker studies can be performed on cytologic specimens.[106] Studies to date suggest that endoscopic cytology has excellent sensitivity and specificity for the extremes of Barrett's esophagus: no dysplasia or high grade dysplasia/adenocarcinoma.[106] However, there are problems in the cytologic detection of low grade dysplasia, and it is imperfect for the detection of goblet cells alone. Survey data indicate that only 17% of gastroenterologists use brush cytology as part of endoscopic surveillance of Barrett's esophagus,[101] and questions remain regarding the generalizability of cytology to the community setting.[107]

Chromoendoscopy

Methylene blue is a vital stain that selectively diffuses into the cytoplasm of absorptive epithelium of the small intestine and colon. The presence of staining in the esophagus indicates the presence of intestinal metaplasia.[50] Some studies suggest that methylene blue chromoendoscopy increases the efficiency of detecting dysplasia: fewer biopsies are required and more patients are identified with dysplasia compared with four-quadrant biopsies obtained at 2-cm intervals.[108] However, others are unable to detect any differences in dysplasia detection between methylene blue directed biopsies compared with a standard biopsy protocol.[109] Chromoendoscopy is appealing because its simple, inexpensive, and safe. However, there is no agreement on application technique in terms of the concentration, volume, and "dwell time" of various reagents, and interpretation of staining is subjective. Methylene blue chromoendoscopy also adds additional procedure time.

Optical Biopsy Techniques

A variety of endoscopic optical techniques including fluorescence spectroscopy, light spectroscopy, optical coherence tomography, light scattering spectroscopy, and light-induced fluorescence endoscopy have the potential to obtain "light" biopsies of Barrett's esophagus. All of these techniques are based on the principle that benign and malignant tissue have different optical qualities. In theory, this would permit optical sampling of larger areas of the columnar-lined esophagus and improve the efficiency of biopsies by targeting areas thought to harbor dysplasia or cancer. However, validation, standardization, and comparison of all of these techniques are still lacking.[110]

Initial work with laser-induced fluorescence spectroscopy in a group of 36 patients had a sensitivity of 100% for high grade dysplasia and a specificity of 70% for no dysplasia, but all six patients with low grade dysplasia were classified as benign by laser-induced fluorescence spectroscopy.[111] A spectroscopic probe that combined the techniques of fluorescence, reflectance, and light scattering spectroscopy in 16 patients with Barrett's esophagus had a sensitivity and specificity of 100% for separating high grade dysplasia from low grade dysplasia and no dysplasia and a sensitivity of 93% with a specificity of 100% for separating any dysplasia from no dysplasia.[112] However, spectroscopic techniques, as currently configured, require a "point and shoot" method of touching the mucosa with the probe followed by biopsy. To be clinically helpful, these techniques will need to image a larger field by "spraying light" followed by targeted biopsies of abnormal optical regions.

Optical coherence tomography uses infrared light to produce high-resolution images of mucosal tissue *in vivo*. Current technology again is limited to a "touch and image" technique and is not yet able to sample large areas rapidly.

Light-induced fluorescence endoscopy is a technique that allows one to "spray" light on the entire esophagus. It is based on the principle that tissue excited by light of a specific wavelength will emit fluorescent light of a longer wavelength and that normal, metaplastic, and dysplastic tissues have different autofluorescence colors visible to the naked eye. This will permit targeting biopsies to areas of abnormal light. In theory, this technique has the potential to rapidly assess large areas of epithelium before targeting biopsies. A preliminary report found that light-induced fluorescence endoscopy identified 14 of 14 early cancers, 7 of 11 severe dysplasias, but only 4 of 22 areas of low grade dysplasia.[113] The system, as currently constituted, is bulky and is configured with fiberoptic endoscopes. Furthermore, once an area is biopsied, the resulting blood can interfere with imaging. Endoscopic fluorescence detection may be enhanced further by using a sensitizer, such as 5-aminolevulinic acid, which accumulates selectively in tumors and dysplasia. Illumination by light of a specific wavelength allows one to see fluorescence from these lesions that is not visible at normal white light endoscopy.

Risk Stratification

A number of clinical and biologic markers may define patients at increased risk for the development of adenocarcinoma. Clinical risk factors for the development of high grade dysplasia or adenocarcinoma include gender, ethnicity, age, dysplasia, hiatal hernia size, length of the Barrett's segment, body mass index, and smoking.[48,114,115] Dysplasia is still the best available marker of cancer risk. Dysplasia is recognized adjacent to and distant from Barrett's esophagus associated adenocarcinoma in resection specimens from patients with Barrett's esophagus.[67,98] Patients progress through a phenotypic sequence of no dysplasia, low grade dysplasia, high grade dysplasia, and adenocarcinoma, although the time course is highly variable.[87]

The natural history of low grade dysplasia is poorly understood. In part, this may be due to the high degree of interobserver variability in establishing this diagnosis and the variable protocols by which these patients are followed.[93] Recent studies suggest that approximately 10% to 28% of low grade dysplasia patients go on to develop high grade dysplasia or adenocarcinoma, whereas regression is seen in approximately 60% to 65%.[116,117] The remainder will have persistent low grade dysplasia.

Unsuspected carcinoma is detected at esophagectomy in approximately 40% of patients with high grade dysplasia, with a range of 0% to 73%.[102] However, although high grade dysplasia remains a worrisome lesion, progression to carcinoma may take many years and is not inevitable. Buttar and coworkers[103] followed 100 patients with high grade dysplasia with continued endoscopic surveillance and found cancer at 1 and 3 years in 38% and 56% of individuals with diffuse high grade dysplasia and in 7% and 14% of individuals with focal high grade dysplasia. Reid and colleagues[118] followed 76 patients for 5 years and encountered cancer in 59%. On the other hand, Schnell and coworkers,[119] in a study of 79 patients, found cancer in 5% during the 1st year of surveillance and in 16% of the remaining patients followed for a mean of 7 years (20% of the total group developed cancer). Others have reported regression of high grade dysplasia over time as well.[119,120]

Unfortunately, dysplasia is not distinguishable endoscopically, and the focal nature of dysplasia makes targeting of biopsies problematic. Furthermore, there is considerable interobserver variability in the grading of dysplasia in both the community and academic settings.[42,93] The ability of pathologists to distinguish between intramucosal carcinoma and high grade dysplasia is problematic even in esophagectomy specimens.[121] Therefore, a less subjective marker for cancer risk that could supplement or replace the current dysplasia grading system is needed.

Biomarkers of Increased Risk

A number of biologic markers may define patients at increased risk for the development of esophageal adenocarcinoma. Among the most often described molecular changes that precede the development of adenocarcinoma in Barrett's esophagus are alterations in p53 (mutation, deletion, or loss of heterozygosity [LOH]), p16 (mutation, deletion, promoter hypermethylation, or LOH), and aneuploidy by flow cytometry. Neoplastic progression in Barrett's esophagus is accompanied by flow cytometric abnormalities such as aneuploidy or increased G_2/tetraploid DNA contents, and these abnormalities may precede the development of high grade dysplasia or adenocarcinoma.[70] The potential importance of flow cytometry as a prognostic biomarker was illustrated in work by Reid and coworkers,[118] who found that, for patients with no flow cytometric abnormalities at baseline and with histology that showed no dysplasia, indefinite, or low grade dysplasia, the 5-year incidence of cancer was 0%.

Mutations of p53 and 17p LOH have been reported in up to 92% and 100%, respectively, of esophageal adencocarcinomas.[122] Furthermore, both abnormalities have been detected in Barrett's epithelium before the development of carcinoma.[122,123] For example, Reid and colleagues[123] found that the prevalence of 17p (p53) LOH at baseline increased from 6% in patients negative for dysplasia to 20% in patients with low grade dysplasia and to 57% in patients with high grade dysplasia. More importantly, the 3-year incidence of cancer was 38% for individuals with 17p (p53) LOH compared with 3.3% for individuals with two 17p alleles. However, techniques to detect p53 mutations and 17p LOH are labor intensive and have not achieved widespread acceptance in clinical practice to date. Immunohistochemistry, a much simpler technique, has been extensively studied in the dysplasia-carcinoma sequence of Barrett's esophagus but is hampered by false-positive and false-negative rates of approximately 25%.[123] Similarly, p16 LOH and inactivation of the p16 gene by promoter region hypermethylation have been reported often in esophageal adenocarcinoma.[69,124] Furthermore, 9p LOH is commonly encountered in premalignant Barrett's epithelium and can be detected over large regions of the Barrett's mucosa.[124] It is hypothesized that clonal expansion occurs in conjunction with p16 abnormalities creating a field in which other genetic lesions leading to esophageal adenocarcinoma can arise.[124]

Unfortunately, none of these biomarkers has been validated in large-scale clinical trials. In the future, it is hoped that risk stratification may be accomplished either by a panel of biomarkers or by genomic or proteomic profiling of Barrett's esophagus patients using rapidly advancing genomic technology. If risk stratification is successful in the future, it is anticipated that endoscopic surveillance intervals will be lengthened for patients at low risk for developing adenocarcinoma and shortened for patients at increased risk of developing adenocarcinoma.

Treatment

MEDICAL THERAPY

Because Barrett's esophagus has the most severe pathophysiologic abnormalities of GERD, it should come as no surprise that proton pump inhibitors are the cornerstone of medical therapy for Barrett's esophagus. Studies show that proton pump inhibitors consistently result in symptom relief, and heal esophagitis in Barrett's esophagus patients.[125,126] However, proton pump inhibitors, even at high doses, result in either no regression of the Barrett's segment or modest

regression that is of uncertain clinical importance.[124–129] Proton pump inhibitors typically increase squamous islands in the Barrett's segment, but biopsies taken from such islands will often show underlying intestinal metaplasia.[130]

Alleviation of reflux symptoms in Barrett's esophagus is not necessarily equivalent to normalization of esophageal acid exposure, despite the use of high-dose proton pump inhibitor therapy. This phenomena is encountered in 15% to 40% on varying doses of proton pump inhibitors.[129,131–133] The importance of complete control of esophageal acid exposure in Barrett's esophagus patients remains unknown. However, some studies provide conceptual support for the concept of aggressive acid suppression in these patients. Normalization of intraesophageal acid exposure in Barrett's patients decreases cellular proliferation rates and increases cellular differentiation rates over 6 months, whereas inability to normalize intraesophageal acid exposure results in no difference in proliferation or differentiation rates.[132] Other studies suggest that complete acid control may result in a decrease in Barrett's esophagus length. Omeprazole, when administered as 40 mg twice daily for 2 years to a group of 26 Barrett's esophagus patients, resulted in normalization of esophageal acid exposure, which was accompanied by a decrease in length by 6.4% and surface area by 7.9%.[127] Both of these changes were greater than that seen in a companion group administered ranitidine 150 mg twice daily for the same time. Another small study of nine patients documented rigorous intraesophageal acid control (with a pH less than 4) of 1.6% over 24 hours on a regimen of twice daily omeprazole 20 mg or lansoprazole 30 mg with or without a nocturnal dose of ranitidine.[134] At a mean follow-up of 54 months, each of the nine patients demonstrated a decrease in length of the Barrett's segment, from a mean of 7.22 cm to 5.22 cm. Thus, preliminary evidence suggests that complete acid suppression may cause regression of the Barrett's segment. However, follow-up of these patients is short and the clinical significance of the modest regression noted to date is uncertain. Any decrease in cancer risk will take years to become evident. Furthermore, medical options for complete acid control in patients failing twice daily doses of proton pump inhibitors are problematic. It remains uncertain if Barrett's esophagus patients should undergo routine 24-hour pH monitoring to assess the response to therapy, although the Bravo probe will make this issue easier for patients to tolerate. However, the costs of such an approach would be substantial and the ability to act on this information in patients already receiving high doses of proton pump inhibitors is uncertain. In summary, it remains unclear how best to administer acid suppression therapy in Barrett's esophagus patients: titration to symptom control or titration to esophageal acid control. It is unknown if either of these strategies affects subsequent cancer risk.

ANTIREFLUX SURGERY

Antireflux surgery effectively alleviates GERD symptoms in Barrett's esophagus patients.[135–138] Studies consistently show the development of squamous islands after antireflux surgery, but complete regression of Barrett's epithelium is uncommon and may well represent "pseudoregression" resulting from surgical repositioning of the esophagus.[137] Some surgical enthusiasts suggest that antireflux surgery decreases the subsequent risk of developing esophageal cancer. However, a large Swedish cohort study found that the risk of developing adenocarcinoma of the esophagus remained elevated after antireflux surgery in GERD patients (Barrett's status unknown) and was no different from GERD patients not undergoing antireflux surgery.[139] In Barrett's esophagus, there are studies both supporting and refuting a protective role for antireflux surgery.[137,140–142] However, the long term durability of antireflux surgery is an ongoing question as demonstrated by the VA cooperative study of patients randomized to medical or open antireflux surgery, in which 62% of the surgical group reported regular use of antireflux medications at a mean follow-up of 10.6 years.[143] Other studies have also found that surgery breaks down over time.[142] Thus, although surgery provides an excellent means of symptom control in Barrett's esophagus patients, it does not appear to influence the natural history of Barrett's esophagus. Furthermore, the overall low incidence of cancer in these patients combined with the problems of surgical breakdown make it difficult to conceive that surgery will influence the natural history of this disease in the future. Finally, the surgical mortality rate of 0.2% associated with antireflux surgery must be balanced against the annual incidence rate of cancer, which is estimated to be 0.05%.[144]

ABLATION THERAPY

Given the limitations of conventional medical and surgical therapy as described previously, a variety of mucosal ablative techniques have been studied including thermal ablation, photodynamic therapy, and endoscopic mucosal resection (Table 28–2). The theory of mucosal ablation therapy is that reinjury of the metaplastic epithelium followed by the regeneration of normal squamous epithelium from a pluripotential stem cell in an environment of decreased acidity may decrease or eliminate the risk of developing esophageal adenocarcinoma. All techniques are able to eliminate much or all of the Barrett's epithelium, but residual intestinal metaplasia underlying the new squamous epithelium is a recurrent theme in most ablation studies to date.[145]

Thermal Ablation

Thermal ablation of Barrett's esophagus can be accomplished by a variety of techniques including laser, multipolar electrocoagulation, heater probe, and argon plasma coagulation. A multicenter study

---

Table 28–2. Ablation Therapy Techniques for Barrett's Esophagus

1. Thermal
   Multipolar electrocoagulation
   Heater probe
   Argon plasma coagulator
   Laser
       Nd:YAG
       Argon
       KTP
2. Photodynamic therapy
   5-aminolevulinic acid
   Porfimer sodium
   Hematoporphyrin derivative
3. Endoscopic mucosal resection
4. Combined endoscopic mucosal resection with photodynamic or thermal therapy

Nd:YAG, neodymium:yttrium-aluminum-garnet; KTP, potassium titanium phosphate.

---

of multipolar electrocoagulation demonstrated complete visual reversal of the Barrett's segment in 85% of patients at 6 months and complete visual and histologic reversal in 78% at the same time point.[146] A subsequent case report demonstrated complete histologic regression of intestinal metaplasia in an esophagectomy specimen from a patient treated with multipolar electrocoagulation, when an esophagectomy was required for complications from antireflux surgery.[147] However, despite the theoretic superficial injury achieved with multipolar electrocoagulation, the esophagus of that patient was fibrotic and friable with adhesions to the pleura. Other studies have reported both complete and incomplete histologic regression with multipolar electrocoagulation.[145] Adverse effects associated with this modality include chest pain and rare strictures. One report of heat probe electrocoagulation reported buried islands of intestinal metaplasia in 23% of patients.[148]

Argon plasma coagulation therapy at a variety of settings has resulted in endoscopic and histologic regression in 61% to 99% of patients.[145,149–152] However, this technique has been associated with significant complications including perforation, chest pain, odynophagia, fever, pleural effusion, strictures, and pneumomediastinum.[150,153] Recent studies have called into question the durability of the neosquamous epithelium that occurs after argon plasma coagulation therapy because both endoscopic and histologic relapse have been described in more than 50% of individuals at both 1 and 2 years after successful treatment.[154,155]

The more interesting role for thermal ablation is for patients with dysplasia or early cancer. Using argon plasma coagulation, Pereira-Lima and coworkers[150] achieved reversal of 14 cases of low grade dysplasia and 1 case of high grade dysplasia with a mean follow-up of 10 months. More recently, Attwood and colleagues[153] administered argon plasma coagulation to 29 patients with high grade dysplasia who either were not surgical candidates or turned down surgery. At a mean follow-up of 37 months, high grade dysplasia resolved in 86%, whereas progression to cancer occurred in 14%.[153] In a case series of six nonoperative candidates with intramucosal carcinoma, Sharma and coworkers[156] achieved a complete response with a combination of neodymium:yttrium-aluminum-garnet (Nd:YAG) laser and multipolar electrocoagulation in five of six patients with a follow-up of 9 to 86 months. Finally, Gossner and colleagues[157] successfully eliminated four cases of low grade dysplasia, four cases of high grade dysplasia, and two superficial cancers using the potassium titanium phosphate (KTP) laser. All ten of these patients had visual reversal of the Barrett's segment, although two patients had underlying intestinal metaplasia.

Photodynamic Therapy

Photodynamic therapy is a process in which a light-sensitive drug concentrates in neoplastic tissue. The drug is activated by laser light of an appropriate wavelength directed at the abnormal tissue producing a cytotoxic substance, singlet oxygen, which then selectively damages neoplastic tissue. Photodynamic therapy has the potential to treat long segments of Barrett's esophagus in which areas of dysplasia are endoscopically indistinguishable from normal epithelium, often multifocal, and unevenly distributed. Furthermore, photodynamic therapy does not require precise aiming of light energy. Photodynamic therapy in Barrett's esophagus has involved a variety of different agents, including porfimer sodium, hematoporphyrin derivative, and 5-aminolevulinic acid (5-ALA). Each of these compounds is characterized by a different depth of tissue destruction and duration of cutaneous photosensitivity. Only sodium porfimer is available in the United States. In a case series of 103 patients treated with sodium porfimer and followed for a mean of 51 months, low grade dysplasia regressed in (93%), high grade dysplasia regressed in 78%, and 44% of early-stage cancers (T1) regressed entirely.[158] Sixty-eight percent of patients had complete regression of Barrett's epithelium.[158] Three cases of adenocarcinoma developed underneath the new squamous epithelium after treatment for high grade dysplasia at 6, 46, and 52 months after treatment. The stricture rate in this study was 30%. Preliminary results of a randomized trial that examined photodynamic therapy with sodium porfimer versus omeprazole in 208 patients with high grade dysplasia demonstrated progression to cancer in 13% of the photodynamic therapy group and 28% of the omeprazole group at a mean follow-up of 24 months.[159] Strictures developed in 37% of these patients.

Oral administration of 5-ALA, a porphyrin precursor, stimulates the endogenous synthesis of protoporphyrin-IX, a potent photosensitizer that accumulates preferentially in the mucosa rather than in the submucosa or the muscularis. There is little photosensitivity because of rapid subsequent metabolism. Encouraging results for photodynamic therapy with 5-ALA have been reported.[160] During a mean follow-up of 9.9 months, all 10 of the patients with high grade dysplasia had complete remission, whereas 17 of 22 patients with early adenocarcinoma (77%) had complete remission.[160] Each of the five failures was characterized by a tumor depth of greater than 5 mm. Partial epithelial reepithelization was accomplished in 21 of 32 patients (68%), and there was no morbidity or mortality. A randomized controlled trial of 5-ALA in 36 patients with low grade dysplasia resulted in regression of dysplasia in 100% of the 5-ALA group compared with 33% in the placebo group.[161] However, this technique resulted in a reduction in surface area of only 30% in the 5-ALA group compared with 10% in the placebo group.

Endoscopic Mucosal Resection

Despite considerable enthusiasm, there is only limited information available on the role of endoscopic mucosal resection in Barrett's esophagus. Nijhawan and Wang[162] performed endoscopic mucosal resection in 25 patients with visible lesions within Barrett's esophagus. Superficial cancer was found in 13, high grade dysplasia in 4, and no dysplasia or carcinoma in 8. Importantly, the technique resulted in reclassification of many patients: eight lesions felt to be benign turned out to have high grade dysplasia or carcinoma, whereas three lesions thought to have cancer or high grade dysplasia had no evidence of dysplasia or carcinoma. Thus, this technique has both therapeutic and diagnostic implications. Ell and coworkers[163] performed endoscopic mucosal resection in 57 Barrett's esophagus patients with either adenocarcinoma (54 patients) or high grade dysplasia (3 patients) that was visible by routine endoscopy, chromoendoscopy, or fluorescence endoscopy. Endoscopic mucosal resection resulted in complete local remission in 34 of 35 (97%) of patients with low risk lesions characterized by the following features: diameter of 20 mm or less, well or moderately differentiated histology, lesion limited to mucosa, or nonulcerated lesion. In contrast, complete local remission was achieved in only 13 of 22

(59%) patients with high-risk lesions characterized by the following features: diameter greater than 20 mm, poorly differentiated histology, lesion extending into the submucosa, or ulcerated lesion. The mean follow-up of the two groups was approximately 12 months. Of importance, subsequent development of metachronous or recurrent high grade dysplasia or cancer was encountered in 17% of the low-risk group and 14% of the high-risk group. Complications, primarily bleeding, occurred in 8 patients (14%). Thus, local curative surgery in these patients is an option. However caveats to keep in mind are the following: (1) follow-up to date is short, (2) lesions must be visible endoscopically or with fluorescence or chromoendoscopy, (3) recurrence in the short term is common, and (4) additional "at risk" mucosa remains behind. The applicability of this technique to invisible lesions or multifocal lesions is still evolving. Circumferential endoscopic mucosal resection of invisible lesions has now been described in a case series of 12 patients during which no recurrent dysplasia, carcinoma, or Barrett's epithelium was encountered.[164] However, larger confirmatory studies are needed.

Combined Endoscopic Mucosal Resection and Photodynamic Therapy

Given the limitations of conventional endoscopic mucosal resection, in which at-risk mucosa remains behind, multimodal therapy in combination of endoscopic mucosal resection with photodynamic therapy has been proposed as a treatment option. Pacifico and coworkers[165] examined such a multimodal approach in patients with intramucosal or submucosal carcinoma judged unfit for surgery or who refused surgery and compared this to standard esophageal resection. At 1-year follow-up, 17% of the combination therapy group still had cancer compared with none of the patients treated surgically. However, surgery was associated with a mortality rate of 2% and a complication rate of 31% compared with 0% and 4% for combination therapy. Furthermore, in patients in whom combination therapy failed, subsequent surgical therapy or chemoradiation therapy was still possible, with good results. Studies such as this are now leading to the concept of tailoring ablation therapy based on length of involved epithelium, presence of nodularity, and the presence of unifocal versus multifocal high grade dysplasia.[166]

Ablation Therapy in Perspective

There is already considerable enthusiasm for ablation therapy for Barrett's esophagus, despite the lack of randomized controlled trials to establish their efficacy. A recent cross-sectional survey of gastroenterologists found that 36% of respondents used ablation therapy despite the fact that only 19% thought its use was supported by the medical literature.[167] Unfortunately, the use of ablation was strongly influenced by the belief that ablation was used by colleagues.[167] Studies to date have significant limitations. They are typically uncontrolled, single-center studies of a relatively small number of patients followed for short periods.[145] Intestinal metaplasia lying beneath the neosquamous epithelium is encountered with all techniques. The concern about cancer developing in these buried islands has now been confirmed by at least three reports.[168–170] Most disturbing is that cancer has developed under the neosquamous epithelium in patients with benign Barrett's epithelium. Potential benefits of ablation therapy must be weighed against risks including strictures, perforation, and incurable cancer developing in otherwise curable patients. The cost effectiveness of ablation therapy also is unknown. Endoscopic surveillance is still warranted in all of these patients, but previous endoscopic landmarks are now obscured making targeting of biopsies problematic. Aggressive antireflux therapy, be it medical or surgical, is suggested to maintain the neosquamous epithelium. However, successful reversal of intestinal metaplasia has been described despite inadequate acid suppression.[171]

Another key remaining question concerns the biologic characteristics of the new squamous lining of patients treated with ablation techniques. Initial biomarker studies suggest that the neosquamous epithelium is similar to normal squamous epithelium after reversal of intestinal metaplasia without dysplasia, but persistent biomarker abnormalities have been described after successful reversal of high grade dysplasia.[172,173]

A recent systematic review of ablation therapy suggests that the only clear indication at present is for nonoperative candidates with high grade dysplasia or superficial adenocarcinoma and that it should be considered as a possible option for patients with high grade dysplasia or superficial adenocarcinoma who refuse surgery.[145] However, given the overall low cancer risk for Barrett's esophagus patients, ablation therapy is not indicated in patients with intestinal metaplasia and no dysplasia.

Chemoprevention

COX-2 expression is increased in intestinal metaplasia, dysplasia, and adenocarcinoma associated with Barrett's esophagus.[72,73] Furthermore, in an *ex vivo* organ culture system, COX-2 expression increased significantly in Barrett's esophagus tissue in response to pulses of acid or bile salts.[72] This effect was attenuated by the use of a COX-2 inhibitor. Administration of a selective COX-2 inhibitor for 10 days to Barrett's esophagus patients reduces COX-2 expression.[174] Furthermore, administration of a selective inhibitor of COX-2 decreases cell growth and increases apoptosis in esophageal adenocarcinoma cell lines.[74] Thus, it is hypothesized that administration of selective or nonselective COX antagonists, with or without aggressive acid suppression, could decrease the risk of esophageal cancer in Barrett's esophagus patients. A systematic review of the literature supports a protective association between the use of aspirin or nonsteroidal anti-inflammatory drugs (NSAIDs) and the risk of developing esophageal adenocarcinoma.[175] Furthermore, greater protection was associated with more frequent use of these compounds. However, a decision analysis model suggested that such a strategy may not be cost effective in the general population of Barrett's esophagus patients but may be worthy of future consideration in high-risk patients (i.e., those with dysplasia be it low grade or high grade).[176] However, given the overall low incidence of esophageal cancer in Barrett's esophagus, it is still premature to administer aspirin or NSAIDs to these patients.

Conclusions and Future Trends

It is clear that Barrett's esophagus is a complication of severe GERD and is associated with an increased risk of esophageal adenocarcinoma. Management of Barrett's esophagus patients should continue to focus on relieving symptoms of GERD and carefully performed endoscopic surveillance at appropriate intervals. However, many questions remain unanswered about Barrett's esophagus. What predisposes only a small subset of patients with GERD to develop Barrett's esophagus and how does it develop? Will there be a simple way to reliably distinguish between short-segment Barrett's esophagus and intestinal metaplasia of the cardia? How can we improve pathologic consistency in interpretation of biopsies from these patients? Will screening GERD patients for Barrett's esophagus prove to be an effective strategy? Will small-caliber endoscopes be accepted and effective? Will we come up with an alternative to endoscopy? Is there an alternative to current time-consuming endoscopic surveillance techniques? In particular, which biomarkers of increased risk will help us stratify patients by individual risk? If biomarkers are validated, can testing be done at an affordable price? Finally, will any treatment be it acid suppression, antireflux surgery, chemoprevention, or ablation have any effect on the natural history of this disease? Answers to these and other questions are eagerly awaited.

REFERENCES

1. Sarr MG, Hamilton SR, Marrone GC, et al: Barrett's esophagus: Its prevalence and association with adenocarcinoma in patients with symptoms of gastroesophageal reflux. Am J Surg 149:187–193, 1985.
2. Winters C, Spurling TJ, Chobanian SJ, et al: Barrett's esophagus: A prevalent occult complication of gastroesophageal reflux disease. Gastroenterology 92:118–124, 1987.
3. Cameron AJ, Zinsmeister AR, Ballard DJ, et al: Prevalence of columnar-lined (Barrett's esophagus). Gastroenterology 99:918–922, 1990.
4. Cameron AJ, Lomboy CT: Barrett's esophagus: Age, prevalence, and extent of columnar epithelium. Gastroenterology 103:1241–1245, 1992.
5. Bonelli L: Barrett's esophagus: Results of a multicenter survey. Endoscopy 25(Suppl):652–654, 1993.
6. Spechler SJ, Zeroogian JM, Antonioli DA, et al: Prevalence of metaplasia at the gastro-oesophageal junction. Lancet 344:1533–1536, 1994.
7. Nandurkar S, Talley NJ: Barrett's esophagus: The long and the short of it. Am J Gastroenterol 94:30–40, 1999.
8. Hirota WK, Loughney TM, Lazas DJ, et al: Specialized intestinal metaplasia, dysplasia, and cancer of the esophagus and esophagogastric junction: Prevalence and clinical data. Gastroenterology 116:277–285, 1999.
9. Gerson LB, Shetler K, Triadafilopoulos G: Prevalence of Barrett's esophagus in asymptomatic individuals. Gastroenterology 123:461–467, 2002.
10. Conio M, Cameron AJ, Romero Y, et al: Secular trends in the epidemiology and outcome of Barrett's oesophagus in Olmsted County, Minnesota. Gut 48:304–309, 2001.
11. El-Serag HB, Sonnenberg A: Opposing time trends of peptic ulcer and reflux disease. Gut 43:327–333, 1999.
12. Dulai GS, Guha S, Kahn KL, et al: Preoperative prevalence of Barrett's esophagus in esophageal adenocarcinoma: A systematic review. Gastroenterology 122:26–33, 2002.
13. Bersentes K, Fass R, Padda S, et al: Prevalence of Barrett's esophagus in Hispanics is similar to Caucasians. Dig Dis Sci 43:1038–1041, 1998.
14. Yeh C, Hsu CT, Ho AS, et al: Erosive esophagitis and Barrett's esophagus in Taiwan. A higher frequency than expected. Dig Dis Sci 42:702–706, 1997.

15. Falk GW: Barrett's esophagus. Gastroenterology 122:1569–1591, 2002.

16. Glickman JN, Chen YY, Wang HH, et al: Phenotypic characteristics of a distinctive multilayered epithelium suggests that it is a precursor in the development of Barrett's esophagus. Am J Surg Pathol 25:569–578, 2001.

17. Boch JA, Shields HM, Antonioli DA, et al: Distribution of cytokeratin markers in Barrett's columnar epithelium. Gastroenterology 112:760–765, 1997.

18. Neumann CS, Cooper BT: 24 hour ambulatory oesophageal pH monitoring in uncomplicated Barrett's oesophagus. Gut 35:1352–1355, 1994.

19. Singh P, Taylor RH, Colin-Jones DG: Esophageal motor dysfunction and acid exposure in reflux esophagitis are more severe if Barrett's metaplasia is present. Am J Gastroenterol 89:349–356, 1994.

20. Cameron AJ: Barrett's esophagus: Prevalence and size of hiatal hernia. Am J Gastroenterol 94:2054–2059, 1999.

21. Wakelin DE, Al-Mutawa T, Wendel C, et al: A predictive model for length of Barrett's esophagus with hiatal hernia length and duration of esophageal acid exposure. Am J Gastroenterol 58:350–355, 2003.

22. Champion G, Richter JE, Vaezi MF, et al: Duodenogastroesophageal reflux: Relationship to pH and importance in Barrett's esophagus. Gastroenterology 107:747–754, 1994.

23. Loughney T, Maydonovitch CL, Wong RK: Esophageal manometry and ambulatory 24-hour pH monitoring in patients with short and long segment Barrett's esophagus. Am J Gastroenterol 93:916–919, 1998.

24. Fass R, Hell RW, Garewal HS, et al: Correlation of oesophageal acid exposure with Barrett's oesophagus length. Gut 48:310–313, 2001.

25. Eloubeidi MA, Provenzale D: Clinical and demographic predictors of Barrett's esophagus among patients with gastroesophageal reflux disease. A multivariable analysis in veterans. J Clin Gastroenterol 33:306–309, 2001.

26. Eisen GM, Sandler RS, Murray S, Gottfried M: The relationship between gastroesophageal reflux disease and its complications with Barrett's esophagus. Am J Gastroenterol 92:27–31, 1997.

27. Lieberman DA, Oehlke M, Helfand M: Risk factors for Barrett's esophagus in community-based practice. Am J Gastroenterol 92:1293–1297, 1997.

28. Lagergren J, Bergstrom R, Lindgren A, et al: Symptomatic gastroesophageal reflux as a risk factor for esophageal adenocarcinoma. N Engl J Med 340:825–831, 1999.

29. Johnson DA, Winters C, Spurling TJ, et al: Esophageal acid sensitivity in Barrett's esophagus. J Clin Gastroenterol 91:23–27, 1987.

30. Grade A, Pulliam G, Johnson C, et al: Reduced chemoreceptor sensitivity in patients with Barrett's esophagus may be related to age and not to the presence of Barrett's epithelium. Am J Gastroenterol 92:2040–2043, 1997.

31. Drovdilic CM, Goddard KA, Chak A, et al: Demographic and phenotypic feature of 65 families segregating Barrett oesophagus and oesophageal adenocarcinoma. J Med Genet 40:651–653, 2003.

32. Paull A, Trier JS, Dalton D, et al: The histologic spectrum of Barrett's esophagus. N Engl J Med 295:476–480, 1976.

33. Sampliner RE: Updated guidelines for the diagnosis, surveillance, and therapy of Barrett's esophagus. Am J Gastroenterol 97:1888–1895, 2002.

34. Reid BJ, Sanchez CA, Blount PL, et al: Barrett's esophagus: Cell cycle abnormalities in advancing stages of neoplastic progression. Gastroenterology 105:119–129, 1993.

35. Weinstein WM, Ippoliti AF: The diagnosis of Barrett's esophagus: Goblets, goblets, goblets. Gastrointest Endosc 44:91–94, 1996.

36. McClave SA, Boyce HW, Gottfied MR: Early diagnosis of the columnar-lined esophagus: A new endoscopic criterion. Gastrointest Endosc 33:413–416, 1987.

37. Ofman JJ, Shaheen NJ, Desai AA, et al: The quality of care in Barrett's esophagus: Endoscopist and pathologist practices. Am J Gastroenterol 96:876–881, 2001.

38. Kim SL, Waring JP, Spechler SJ, et al: Diagnostic inconsistencies in Barrett's esophagus. Gastroenterology 107:945–949, 1994.

39. Eloubeidi MA, Provenzale D: Does this patient have Barrett's esophagus? The utility of predicting Barrett's esophagus at the index endoscopy. Am J Gastroenterol 94:937–943, 1999.

40. Chandrasoma PT, Der R, Dalton P, et al: Distribution and significance of epithelial types in columnar-lined esophagus. Am J Surg Pathol 25:1188–1193, 2001.

41. Jones TF, Sharma P, Daaboul B, et al: Yield of intestinal metaplasia in patients with suspected short-segment Barrett's esophagus on repeat endoscopy. Dig Dis Sci 47:2108–2111, 2002.

42. Alikhan M, Rex D, Khan A, et al: Variable pathologic interpretation of columnar lined esophagus by general pathologists in community practice. Gastrointest Endosc 50:23–26, 1999.

43. Sharma P, Morales TG, Sampliner RE: Short segment Barrett's esophagus-the need for standardization of the definition and of endoscopic criteria. Am J Gastroenterol 93:1033–1066, 1998.

44. Hackelsberger A, Gunther T, Manes G, et al: Intestinal metaplasia at the gastroesophageal junction: *Helicobacter pylori* gastritis or gastro-oesophageal reflux disease? Gut 43:17–21, 1998.

45. Nandurkar S, Talley NJ, Martin CJ, et al: Short segment Barrett's oesophagus: Diagnosis and associations. Gut 40:710–715, 1997.

46. Dias Pereira A, Suspiro A, Chaves P, et al: Short segments of Barrett's epithelium and intestinal metaplasia in normal appearing oesophagogastric junctions: The same or two different entities. Gut 42:659–662, 1998.

47. Goldblum JR, Vicari JJ, Falk GW, et al: Inflammation and intestinal metaplasia of the gastric cardia: The role of gastroesophageal reflux and H. pylori infection. Gastroenterology 114:633–639, 1998.

48. Rudolph RE, Vaughan TL, Storer BE, et al: Effect of segment length on risk for neoplastic progression in patients with Barrett's esophagus. Ann Intern Med 132:612–620, 2000.

49. Sharma P, Weston AP, Morales T, et al: Relative risk of dysplasia for patients with intestinal metaplasia in the distal esophagus and in the gastric cardia. Gut 46:9–13, 2000.

50. Canto MI, Setrakian S, Petras RE, et al: Methylene blue selectively stains intestinal metaplasia in Barrett's esophagus. Gastrointest Endosc 44:1–7, 1996.

51. Sharma P, Topalovski M, Mayo MS, Weston AP: Methylene blue chromoendoscopy for detection of short segment Barrett's esophagus. Gastrointest Endosc 54:289–293, 2001.

52. Wo JM, Ray MB, Mayfield-Stokes S, et al: Comparison of methylene-blue directed biopsies and conventional biopsies in the detection of intestinal metaplasia in Barrett's esophagus: A preliminary study. Gastrointest Endosc 54:294–301, 2001.

53. Morales CP, Spechler SJ: Intestinal metaplasia at the gastroesophageal junction: Barrett's, bacteria, and biomarkers. Am J Gastroenterol 98:759–762, 2003.

54. Bollschweiler E, Wolfgarten E, Gutschow C, et al: Demographic variations in the rising incidence of esophageal adenocarcinoma in white males. Cancer 92:549–555, 2001.

55. Enzinger PC, Mayer RJ: Esophageal cancer. N Engl J Med 349:2241–2252, 2003.

56. Lagergren J, Bergstrom R, Lindgren A, et al: Association between body mass and adenocarcinoma of the esophagus. Ann Intern Med 130:883–890, 1999.

57. Chow WH, Blot WJ, Vaughan TL, et al: Body mass index and risk of adenocarcinoma of the esophagus and gastric cardia. J Natl Cancer Inst 90:150–155, 1998.

58. Brown LM, Swanson CA, Gridley G, et al: Adenocarcinoma of the esophagus: Role of obesity and diet. J Natl Cancer Inst 87:104–109, 1995.

59. Gammon MD, Schoenberg JB, Ahsan H, et al: Tobacco, alcohol, and socioeconomic status and adenocarcinomas of the esophagus and gastric cardia. J Natl Cancer Inst 89:1277–1284, 1997.

60. Chow WH, Blaser MJ, Blot WJ, et al: An inverse relation between *cagA*+ strains of *Helicobacter pylori* infection and risk of esophageal and gastric cardia adenocarcinoma. Cancer Res 58:588–590, 1998.

61. Drewitz DJ, Sampliner RE, Garewal HS: The incidence of adenocarcinoma in Barrett's esophagus: A prospective study of 170 patients followed 4.8 years. Am J Gastroenterol 92:212–215, 1997.

62. O'Connor JB, Falk GW, Richter JE: The incidence of adenocarcinoma and dysplasia in Barrett's esophagus: Report on the Cleveland Clinic Barrett's esophagus registry. Am J Gastroenterol 94:2037–2042, 1999.

63. Conio M, Blanchi S, Lapertosa G, et al: Long-term endoscopic surveillance of patients with Barrett's esophagus: Incidence of dysplasia and adenocarcinoma: A prospective study. Am J Gastroenterol 98:1931–1939, 2003.

64. Shaheen NJ, Crosby MA, Bozymski EM, et al: Is there a publication bias in the reporting of cancer risk in Barrett's esophagus? Gastroenterology 119:333–338, 2000.

65. Jankowski JA, Provenzale D, Moayyedi P: Esophageal adenocarcinoma arising from Barrett's metaplasia has regional variations in the West [letter]. Gastroenterology 122:588–590, 2002.

66. Anderson LA, Murray LJ, Murphy SJ, et al: Mortality in Barrett's oesophagus: Results from a population based study. Gut 52:1081–1084, 2003.

67. McArdle JE, Lewin KJ, Randall G, et al: Distribution of dysplasias and early invasive carcinoma in Barrett's esophagus. Human Pathol 23:479–482, 1992.

68. Reid BJ, Barrett MT, Galipeau PC, et al: Barrett's esophagus: Ordering the events that lead to cancer. Eur J Cancer Prev 5(Suppl 2):57–65, 1996.

69. Klump B, Hsieh CJ, Holzmann K, et al: Hypermethylation of the CDKN2/p16 promoter during neoplastic progression in Barrett's esophagus. Gastroenterology 115:1381–1386, 1998.

70. Reid BJ, Blount PL, Rubin CE, et al: Flow-cytometric and histological progression to malignancy in Barrett's esophagus: Prospective endoscopic surveillance of a cohort. Gastroenterology 102:1212–1219, 1992.

71. Rabinovitch PS, Reid BJ, Haggitt RC, et al: Progression to cancer in Barrett's esophagus is associated with genomic instability. Lab Invest 60:65–71, 1988.

72. Shirivani VN, Ouatu-Lascar R, Kaur BS, et al: Cyclooxygenase 2 expression in Barrett's esophagus and adenocarcinoma: Ex vivo induction by bile salts and acid exposure. Gastroenterology 118:487–496, 2000.

73. Morris CD, Armstrong GR, Bigley G, et al: Cyclooxygenase expression in the Barrett's metaplasia-dysplasia-adenocarcinoma sequence. Am J Gastroenterol 96:990–996, 2001.

74. Souza RF, Shewmake K, Beer DG, et al: Selective inhibition of cyclooxygenase-2 suppresses growth and induces apoptosis in human esophageal adenocarcinoma cells. Cancer Res 60:5767–5772, 2000.

75. Sabik JF, Rice TW, Goldblum JR, et al: Superficial esophageal carcinoma. Ann Thorac Surg 60:896–902, 1995.

76. Farrow DC, Vaughan TL: Determinants of survival following the diagnosis of esophageal adenocarcinoma. Cancer Causes Control 7:322–327, 1996.

77. Shaheen NJ, Provenzale D, Sandler RS: Upper endoscopy as a screening and surveillance tool in esophageal adenocarcinoma: A review of the evidence. Am J Gastroenterol 97:1319–1327, 2002.

78. Sorbi D, Gostout CJ, Henry J, et al: Unsedated small-caliber esophagogastroduodenoscopy (EGD) versus conventional EGD: A comparative study. Gastroenterology 117:1301–1307, 1999.

79. Saeian K, Staff DM, Vasilopoulos S, et al: Unsedated transnasal endoscopy accurately detects Barrett's metaplasia and dysplasia. Gastrointest Endosc 56:472–478, 2002.

80. Inadomi JM, Sampliner R, Lagergren J, et al: Screening and surveillance for Barrett esophagus in high risk groups: A cost-utility analysis. Ann Intern Med 138:176–186, 2003.

81. Soni A, Sampliner RE, Sonnenberg A: Screening for high-grade dysplasia in gastroesophageal reflux disease: Is it cost effective? Am J Gastroenterol 95:2086–2093, 2000.

82. Gerson L, Edson R, Lavori PW, et al: Use of a simple symptom questionnaire to predict Barrett's esophagus in patients with symptoms of gastroesophageal reflux. Am J Gastroenterol 96:2005–2012, 2001.

83. Corley DA, Levin TR, Habel LA, et al: Surveillance and survival in Barrett's adenocarcinomas: A population-based study. Gastroenterology 122:633–640, 2002.

84. Inacarbone R, Bonavina L, Saino G, et al: Outcome of esophageal adenocarcinoma detected during endoscopic biopsy surveillance for Barrett's esophagus. Surg Endosc 16:263–266, 2002.

85. Ferguson MK, Durkin A: Long-term survival after esophagectomy for Barrett's adenocarcinoma in endoscopically surveyed and nonsurveyed patients. J Gastrointest Surg 6:29–36, 2002.

86. Streitz JM, Andrews CW, Ellis FH: Endoscopic surveillance of Barrett's esophagus. Does it help? J Thorac Cardiovasc Surg 105:383–388, 1993.

87. Van Sandick JW, Lanschot JJ, Kuiken BW, et al: Impact of endo-scopic biopsy surveillance of Barrett's esophagus on pathological stage and clinical outcome of Barrett's carcinoma. Gut 43:216–222, 1998.

88. Peters JH, Clark GW, Ireland AP, et al: Outcome of adenocarcinoma arising in Barrett's esophagus in endoscopically surveyed and non-surveyed patients. Thorac Cardiovasc Surg 108:813–822, 1994.

89. Provenzale D, Schmitt C, Wong JB: Barrett's esophagus: A new look at surveillance based on emerging estimates of cancer risk. Am J Gastroenterol 94:2043–2053, 1999.

90. Sonnenberg A, Soni A, Sampliner RE: Medical decision analysis of endoscopic surveillance of Barrett's oesophagus to prevent oesophageal adenocarcinoma. Aliment Pharmacol Ther 16:41–50, 2002.

91. Van der Burgh A, Dees J, Hop WC, et al: Oesophageal cancer is an uncommon cause of death in patients with Barrett's oesophagus. Gut 39:5–8, 1996.

92. MacDonald CE, Wicks AC, Playford RJ: Final results from 10 year cohort of patients undergoing surveillance for Barrett's oesophagus: Observational study. BMJ 321:1252–1255, 2000.

93. Montgomery E, Bronner MP, Goldblum JR, et al: Reproducibility of the diagnosis of dysplasia in Barrett's esophagus: A reaffirmation. Hum Pathol 32:368–378, 2001.

94. Fitzgerald RC, Saeed I, Khoo D, et al: Rigorous surveillance protocol increases detection of curable cancers associated with Barrett's esophagus. Dig Dis Sci 46:1892–1898, 2001.

95. Reid BJ, Blount PL, Feng Z, et al: Optimizing endoscopic biopsy detection of early cancers in Barrett's high-grade dysplasia. Am J Gastroenterol 95:3089–3096, 2000.

96. Levine DS, Reid BJ: Endoscopic biopsy technique for acquiring larger mucosal samples. Gastrointest Endosc 37:332–337, 1991.

97. Levine DS, Blount PL, Rudolph RE, et al: Safety of a systematic endoscopic biopsy protocol in patients with Barrett's esophagus. Am J Gastroenterol 95:1152–1157, 2000.

98. Cameron AJ, Carpenter HA: Barrett's esophagus, high-grade dysplasia and early adenocarcinoma. Am J Gastroenterol 92:586–591, 1997.

99. Levine DS, Haggitt RC, Blount PL, et al: An endoscopic biopsy protocol can differentiate high-grade dysplasia from early adenocarcinoma in Barrett's esophagus. Gastroenterology 105:40–50, 1993.

100. Falk GW, Rice TW, Goldblum JR, et al: Jumbo biopsy forceps pro-tocol still misses unsuspected cancer in Barrett's esophagus with high-grade dysplasia. Gastrointestinal Endosc 49:170–176, 1999.

101. Falk GW, Ours TM, Richter JE: Practice patterns for surveillance of Barrett's esophagus in the United States. Gastrointest Endosc 52:197–203, 2000.

102. Pellegrini CA, Pohl D: High-grade dysplasia in Barrett's esophagus: Surveillance or operation? J Gastrointest Surg 4:131–134, 2000.

103. Buttar NS, Wang KK, Sebo TJ, et al: Extent of high-grade dysplasia in Barrett's esophagus correlates with risk of adenocarcinoma. Gastroenterology 120:1630–1639, 2001.

104. Dar M, Goldblum JR, Rice TW, et al: Can extent of high-grade dysplasia predict the presence of adenocarcinoma at esophagectomy? Gut 52:486–489, 2003.

105. Gross CP, Canto MI, Hixson J, et al: Management of Barrett's esophagus: A national study of practice patterns and their cost implications. Am J Gastroenterol 94:3440–3447, 1999.

106. Falk GW: Cytology in Barrett's esophagus. Gastrointest Endosc Clin N Am 13:335–348, 2003.

107. Alexander JA, Jones SM, Smith CJ, et al: Usefulness of cytopathology and histology in the evaluation of Barrett's esophagus in a community hospital. Gastrointest Endosc 46:318–320, 1997.

108. Canto MI, Setrakian S, Willis J, et al: Methylene-blue directed biopsies improve detection of intestinal metaplasia and dysplasia in Barrett's esophagus. Gastrointest Endosc 51:560–568, 2000.

109. Egger K, Werner M, Meining A, et al: Biopsy surveillance is still necessary in patients with Barrett's oesophagus despite new imaging techniques. Gut 52:18–23, 2003.

110. Wang T, Triadafilopoulos G: S,M, L, XL methods of surveillance for Barrett's oesophagus. Gut 52:5–6, 2003.

111. Panjehpour M, Overholt BF, Vo-Dinh T, et al: Endoscopic fluorescence detection of high-grade dysplasia in Barrett's esophagus. Gastroenterology 111:93–101, 1996.

112. Georgakoudi I, Jacobson BC, Van Dam J, et al: Fluorescence, reflectance, and light-scattering spectroscopy for evaluating dysplasia in patients with Barrett's esophagus. Gastroenterology 120:1620–1629, 2001.

113. Haringsma J, Prawirodirdjo W, Tytgat GN: Accuracy of fluorescence imaging of dysplasia in Barrett's esophagus [abstract]. Gastroenterology 116:A418, 1999.

114. Weston AP, Badr AS, Hassanein RS: Prospective multivariate analysis of clinical, endoscopic, and histological factors predictive of the development of Barrett's multifocal high-grade dysplasia or adenocarcinoma. Am J Gastroenterol 94:3413–3419, 1999.

115. Menke-Pluymers MB, Hop WC, et al: Risk factors for the development of an adenocarcinoma in the columnar-lined esophagus. Cancer 72:1155–1158, 1993.

116. Skacel M, Petras RE, Gramlich TL, et al: The diagnosis of low-grade dysplasia in Barrett's esophagus and its implications for disease progression. Am J Gastroenterol 95:3383–3387, 2000.

117. Weston AP, Banerjee SK, Sharma P, et al: P53 protein overexpression in low grade dysplasia (LGD) in Barrett's esophagus: Immunohistochemical marker predictive of progression. Am J Gastroenterol 96:1355–1362, 2001.

118. Reid BJ, Levine DS, Longton G, et al: Predictors of progression to cancer in Barrett's esophagus: Baseline histology and flow cytometry identify low- and high-risk patient subsets. Am J Gastroenterol 95:1669–1676, 2000.

119. Schnell TG, Sontag SJ, Chejfec G, et al: Long-term nonsurgical management of Barrett's esophagus with high-grade dysplasia. Gastroenterology 120:1607–1619, 2001.

120. Weston AP, Sharma P, Topalovski M, et al: Long-term follow-up of Barrett's high-grade dysplasia. Am J Gastroenterol 95:1888–1893, 2000.

121. Ormsby AH, Petras RE, Hendricks WH, et al: Observer variation in the diagnosis of superficial oesophageal adenocarcinoma. Gut 51:671–676, 2002.

122. Reid BJ: P53 and neoplastic progression in Barrett's esophagus [editorial]. Am J Gastroenterol 96:1321–1323, 2001.

123. Reid BJ, Prevo LJ, Galipeau PC, et al: Predictors of progression in Barrett's esophagus II: Baseline 17p (p53) loss of heterozygosity identifies a patient subset at increased risk for neoplastic progression. Am J Gastroenterol 96:2839–2848, 2001.

124. Wong DJ, Paulson TG, Prevo LJ, et al: p16^{INK4a} lesions are common, early abnormalities that undergo clonal expansion in Barrett's metaplastic epithelium. Cancer Res 61:8284–8289, 2001.

125. Sampliner RE: Effect of up to 3 years of high-dose lansoprazole on Barrett's esophagus. Am J Gastroenterol 89:1844–1848, 1994.

126. Neumann CS, Iqbal TH, Cooper BT: Long term continuous omeprazole treatment of patients with Barrett's oesophagus. Aliment Pharmacol Ther 9:451–454, 1995.

127. Peters FT, Ganesh S, Kuipers EJ, et al: Endoscopic regression of Barrett's esophagus during omeprazole treatment; a randomized double blind study. Gut 45:489–494, 1999.

128. Wilkinson SP, Biddlestone L, Gore S, et al: Regression of columnar-lined (Barrett's) oesophagus with omeprazole 40 mg daily: Results of 5 years of continuous therapy. Aliment Pharmacol Ther 13:1205–1209, 1999.

129. Sharma P, Sampliner RE, Camargo E: Normalization of esophageal pH with high-dose proton pump inhibitor therapy does not result in regression of Barrett's esophagus. Am J Gastroenterol 92:582–585, 1997.

130. Sharma P, Morales TG, Bhattacharyya A, et al: Squamous islands in Barrett's esophagus: What lies underneath? Am J Gastroenterol 93:332–335, 1998.

131. Ortiz A, de Haro LF, Parilla P, et al: 24-h pH monitoring is necessary to assess acid reflux suppression in patients with Barrett's oesophagus undergoing treatment with proton pump inhibitors. Br J Surg 86:1472–1474, 1999.

132. Ouatu-Lascar R, Triadafilopoulos G: Complete elimination of reflux symptoms does not guarantee normalization of intraesophageal acid reflux in patients with Barrett's esophagus. Am J Gastroenterol 93:711–716, 1998.

133. Fass R, Sampliner RE, Malagon IB, et al: Failure of oesophageal acid control in candidates for Barrett's oesophagus reversal on a very high dose of proton pump inhibitor. Aliment Pharmacol Ther 14:597–602, 2000.

134. Srinivasan R, Katz PO, Ramakrishnan A, et al: Maximal acid reflux control for Barrett's oesophagus: Feasible and effective. Aliment Pharmacol Ther 15:519–524, 2001.

135. Ortiz A, Martinez De Haro LF, Parrilla P, et al: Conservative treatment versus antireflux surgery in Barrett's oesophagus: Long-term results of a prospective study. Br J Surg 83:274–278, 1996.

136. Yau P, Watson DI, Devitt PG, et al: Laparoscopic antireflux surgery in the treatment of gastroesophageal reflux in patients with Barrett's esophagus. Arch Surg 135:801–805, 2000.

137. Low DE, Levine DS, Dail DH, et al: Histological and anatomic changes in Barrett's esophagus after antireflux surgery. Am J Gastroenterol 94:80–85, 1999.

138. Farrell TM, Smith CD, Metreveli RE, et al: Fundoplication provides effective and durable symptom relief in patients with Barrett's esophagus. Am J Surg 178:18–21, 1999.

139. Ye W, Chow WH, Lagergren J, et al: Risk of adenocarcinomas of the esophagus and gastric cardia in patients with gastroesophageal reflux diseases and after antireflux surgery. Gastroenterology 121:1286–1293, 2001.

140. Katz D, Rothstein R, Schned A, et al: The development of dysplasia and adenocarcinoma during endoscopic surveillance of Barrett's esophagus. Am J Gastroenterol 93:536–541, 1998.

141. McDonald ML, Trastek VF, Allen MS, et al: Barrett's esophagus: Does an antireflux procedure reduce the need for endoscopic surveillance? J Thorac Cardiovasc Surg 111:1135–1140, 1996.

142. Csendes A, Burdiles P, Braghetto I, et al: Dysplasia and adenocarcinoma after classic antireflux surgery in patients with Barrett's esophagus. Ann Surg 235:178–185, 2002.

143. Spechler SJ, Lee E, Ahnen D, et al: Long-term outcome of medical and surgical therapies for gastroesophageal reflux disease. Follow-up of a randomized controlled trial. JAMA 285:2331–2338, 2001.

144. Richter JE: Antireflux surgery and adenocarcinoma of the esophagus: Let the truth be told. Gastroenterology 121:1506–1508, 2001.

145. Eisen GM: Ablation therapy for Barrett's esophagus. Gastrointest Endosc 58:760–769, 2003.

146. Sampliner RE, Faigel D, Fennerty MB, et al: Effective and safe endoscopic reversal of nondysplastic Barrett's esophagus with thermal electrocoagulation combined with high-dose acid inhibition: A multicenter study. Gastrointest Endosc 53:554–558, 2001.

147. Fennerty MV, Corless CL, Sheppard B, et al: Pathologic documentation of complete elimination of Barrett's metaplasia following endoscopic multipolar electrocoagulation therapy. Gut 49:142–144, 2001.

148. Michopoulos S, Tsibouris P, Bouzakis H, et al: Complete regression of Barrett's esophagus with heat probe thermocoagulation: Mid-term results. Gastrointest Endosc 50:165–172, 1999.

149. Tigges H, Fuchs KH, Maroske J, et al: Combination of endoscopic argon plasma coagulation and antireflux surgery for treatment of Barrett's esophagus. J Gastrointest Surg 5:251–259, 2001.

150. Pereira-Lima JC, Busnello JV, Toneloto EB, et al: High power setting argon plasma coagulation for the eradication of Barrett's esophagus. Am J Gastroenterol 95:1661–1668, 2000.

151. Schulz H, Miehlke S, Antos D, et al: Ablation of Barrett's epithelium by endoscopic argon plasma coagulation in combination with high-dose omeprazole. Gastrointest Endosc 51:659–653, 2000.

152. Van Laethem JL, Cremer M, Peny MO, et al: Eradication of Barrett's mucosa with argon plasma coagulation and acid suppression: Immediate and mid term results. Gut 43:747–751, 1998.

153. Attwood SE, Lewis CJ, Caplin S, et al: Argon beam plasma coagulation as therapy for high-grade dysplasia in Barrett's esophagus. Clin Gastroenterol Hepatol 1:258–263, 2003.

154. Kahaleh M, Van Laethem JL, Nagy N, et al: Long-term follow-up and factors predictive of recurrence in Barrett's esophagus treated by argon plasma coagulation and acid suppression. Endoscopy 34:950–955, 2002.

155. Basu KK, Pick B, Bale B, et al: Efficacy and one year follow up of argon plasma coagulation therapy for ablation of Barrett's oesophagus: Factors determining persistence and recurrence of Barrett's epithelium. Gut 51:776–780, 2002.

156. Sharma P, Jaffe PE, Bhattacharyya A, et al: Laser and multipolar electrocoagulation of early Barrett's adenocarcinoma: Long-term follow-up. Gastrointest Endosc 49:442–446, 1999.

157. Gossner L, May A, Stolte M, et al: KTP laser destruction of dysplasia and early cancer in columnar-line Barrett's esophagus. Gastrointest Endosc 49:8–12, 1999.

158. Overholt BF, Panjehpour M, Halberg DL: Photodynamic therapy for Barrett's esophagus with dysplasia and/or early stage carcinoma: Long-term results. Gastrointest Endosc 58:183–188, 2003.

159. Overholt BF, Lightdale CJ, Wang K, et al: International, multicenter, partially blinded, randomised study of the efficacy of photodynamic therapy using porfimer sodium for the ablation of high-grade dysplasia in Barrett's esophagus: Results of 24-month follow-up [abstract]. Gastroenterology 124:A-20, 2003.

160. Gossner L, Stolte M, Sroka R, et al: Photodynamic ablation of high-grade dysplasia in Barrett's esophagus by means of 5-aminolevulinic acid. Gastroenterology 114:448–455, 1998.

161. Ackroyd R, Brown NJ, Davis MF, et al: Photodynamic therapy for dysplastic Barrett's oesophagus: A prospective, double blind, randomised, placebo controlled trial. Gut 47:612–617, 2000.

162. Nijhawan PK, Wang KK: Endoscopic mucosal resection for lesions with endoscopic features suggestive of malignancy and high-grade dysplasia within Barrett's esophagus. Gastrointest Endosc 52:328–332, 2000.

163. Ell C, May A, Gossner L, Pech O, et al: Endoscopic mucosal resection of early cancer and high-grade dysplasia in Barrett's esophagus. Gastroenterology 118:670–677, 2000.

164. Seewald S, Akaraviputh T, Seitz U, et al: Circumferential EMR and complete removal of Barrett's epithelium: A new approach to management of Barrett's esophagus containing high-grade intraepithelial neoplasia and intramucosal carcinoma. Gastrointest Endosc 57:854–859, 2003.

165. Pacifico RJ, Wang KK, Wongkeesong LM, et al: Combined endoscopic mucosal resection and photodynamic therapy versus esophagectomy for management of early adenocarcinoma in Barrett's esophagus. Clin Gastroenterol Hepatol 1:252–257, 2003.

166. Ginsberg GG: Endoluminal therapy for Barrett's with high-grade dysplasia and early adenocarcinoma. Clin Gastroenterol Hepatol 1:241–245, 2003.

167. Gross CP, Cruz-Correa M, Canto MI, et al: The adoption of ablation for Barrett's esophagus: A cohort study of gastroenterologists. Am J Gastroenterol 97:279–286, 2002.

168. Bonavina L, Ceriani C, Carazzone A, et al: Endoscopic laser ablation of nondysplastic Barrett's epithelium: Is it worthwhile? J Gastrointest Surg 3:194–199, 1999.

169. Van Laetham JL, Peny MO, Salmon I, et al: Intramucosal adenocarcinoma arising under squamous re-epithelialisation of Barrett's oesophagus. Gut 46:574–577, 2000.

170. Shand A, Dallal H, Palmer K, et al: Adenocarcinoma arising in columnar lined oesophagus following treatment with argon plasm coagulation [letter]. Gut 48:580–581, 2001.

171. Kovacs BJ, Chen YK, Lewis TD, et al: Successful reversal of Barrett's esophagus with multipolar electrocoagulation despite inadequate acid suppression. Gastrointest Endosc 49:547–553, 1999.

172. Krishnaduth KK, Wang KK, Taniiguchi K, et al: Persistent genetic abnormalities in Barrett's esophagus after photodynamic therapy. Gastroenterology 119:624–630, 2000.

173. Garewal H, Ramsey L, Sharma P, et al: Biomarker studies in reversed Barrett's esophagus. Am J Gastroenterol 94:2829–2833, 1999.

174. Kaur BS, Khamnehei N, Irvani M, et al: Rofecoxib inhibits cyclooxygenase 2 expression and activity and reduces cell proliferation in Barrett's esophagus. Gastroenterology 123:60–67, 2002.

175. Corley DA, Kerlikowske K, Verma R, Buffler P: Protective association of aspirin/NSAIDs and esophageal cancer: A systematic review and meta-analysis. Gastroenterology 124:47–56, 2003.

176. Sonnenberg A, Fennerty MB: Medical decision analysis of chemoprevention against esophageal adenocarcinoma. Gastroenterology 124:1758–1766, 2003.

Endoscopic Therapy for Superficial Esophageal Carcinoma

Kenneth K. Wang

Summary

Endoscopic therapy of gastrointestinal neoplasms has been a goal of therapeutic endoscopists since the inception of the field. Techniques that initially were used included cautery devices such as argon plasma coagulation (APC) or thermal laser therapy. Technologic improvements in cancer staging have definitely increased the endoscopists ability to determine tumor depth and presence of regional metastasis, which allows endoscopic therapy to become a reality. Endoscopists have been implementing new technologies such as mucosal resection techniques and endoscopic ultrasonography (EUS) to truly stage early cancers with a precision to rival surgical resection. In addition, technologies such as photodynamic therapy (PDT) now allow endoscopists to remove areas of preneoplastic mucosa. These techniques represent the first steps to development of a new field of endoscopic oncologic therapy.

Biology of Early Esophageal Cancer

To treat esophageal cancer, which most often develops in Barrett's esophagus in Western countries, it is important to develop an understanding of the biology of the problem. Barrett's esophagus is a very heterogeneous tissue with metaplastic epithelium overlaying generally altered submucosal components such as increased myocytes in the muscularis mucosa and increased fibroblasts in the lamina propria.

The literature regarding early esophageal carcinoma has primarily concerned the pathogenesis of squamous cell cancer that was the predominant form of cancer in the United States. This is still true in the Far East and has been linked to alcohol and tobacco use. Most of the early esophageal cancers currently found in the United States are adenocarcinoma, associated with Barrett's esophagus. Unlike Asia, where the high incidence of cancer has lead to screening programs, esophageal cancer in the West has primarily been found when patients become symptomatic. With surveillance programs that have been instituted for Barrett's esophagus, early cancers are now being diagnosed with increasing frequency.

Barrett's esophagus related cancers appear to arise from chronically inflamed areas of the mucosa. The mechanism of carcinogenesis appears to be related to inflammation producing increased levels of prostaglandin E2, which is an inflammatory mediator that can cause increased cell proliferation.[1] Cell proliferation has been used as a marker of neoplasia and is an early event in cancer development. Increased cell proliferation drives the cell cycle and progression to cancer in Barrett's esophagus usually involves the loss of cell cycle checkpoint genes such as *p16*. The loss of *p16* function through either promoter inactivation through hypermethylation or loss of heterozygosity occurs early in carcinogenesis and is found almost universally in dysplastic Barrett's mucosa.[2] This loss of cell cycle control leads to further acceleration of the cell cycle that allow further genetic events to occur including loss of *p53*, which is well recognized to be an important tumor suppressor gene that is also involved in promoting apoptosis of cells that have accumulated genetic defects.[3] With the accumulation of these genetic defects, gross chromosomal instability occurs leading to loss of chromosomes and aneuploidy. These are late changes associated with cancer development.

The important aspect of the biology of Barrett's esophagus to the endoscopist is that these genetic changes do not always correlate with histologic changes, especially when ablative therapies have been applied. Ablative therapy has the ability to decrease histologic changes of dysplasia while allowing genetic abnormalities to persist.[4] We have found that these persistent genetic abnormalities lead to recurrence of dysplasia and even cancer over time. This suggests that histologically benign Barrett's esophagus after ablative therapy may be precancerous and that long-term treatment of Barrett's esophagus must involve total elimination of the Barrett's mucosa. These results have been verified by recent data from a randomized prospective study of PDT for Barrett's esophagus with high grade dysplasia. In this study of 208 patients randomized to either PDT in combination with omeprazole or to omeprazole alone, patients who were able to achieve complete elimination of their Barrett's mucosa did not progress to cancer, whereas those with any residual Barrett's mucosa did have a significant chance of developing cancer.

Staging of Early Esophageal Cancer

Endoscopic treatment of early esophageal cancer must involve careful and accurate staging of the malignancy. Previously, early esophageal cancer was primarily defined endoscopically based on size. An example of an early cancer in Barrett's esophagus is shown in Figure 29–1. Cancers that were 2 cm in diameter or less were generally thought to be early cancers.[5] This definition certainly was not very accurate because visualization of local lymph nodes and assessment of the depth of tumor invasion was impossible without surgical resection. In addition, surgical resections have shown physicians that early mucosally based cancers above the muscularis mucosa are rarely associated with metastatic disease. In a survey of European centers that performed a total of 253 esophagectomies for early squamous cell cancers, it was found that those patients with disease confined to the epithelium had a survival rate of 92.8%.[6] With penetration into the mucosa, the 5-year survival rate decreased to 72.8%. Unfortunately, the overall mortality rate for esophagectomy for early cancers in this series was found to be 9.1%. Similar results for squamous cells cancers have also been reported from Japan where, if squamous cell cancer was found to penetrate beyond the muscularis mucosae, there was increased chance of metastasis.[7]

The advent of EUS has certainly affected the need for surgical resection to accurately define the depth of cancer invasion. EUS can be performed with either dedicated echoendoscopes or high-frequency ultrasound probes. The echoendoscopes allow the endoscopist to visualize at 7.5- to 12-MHz frequencies that permit examination of the periesophageal lymph nodes (N1 stage), of celiac lymph nodes (M1A stage), of the nodes of the lesser curve of the stomach (N1 stage), of most of the liver (M1b stage), and for evidence of pleural or vascular involvement (T4 stage) by the tumor. An example of a periesophageal lymph node on ultrasound examination is shown in Figure 29–2. A lymph node is suspicious on EUS examination if it is hypoechoic, rounded, and more than a centimeter in diameter. However, if suspicious lymph nodes are found, they should be sampled by the use of fine needle aspiration performed using a linear array instrument. For mucosally based lesions, the ultrasound probes that can image at 20 to 30 MHz allow the endoscopist to image at the resolution needed to resolve the muscularis mucosa to a greater extent. Unfortunately, the probes cannot image deep into the tissue to visualize lymph nodes so that, to truly stage an early cancer, both probes and echoendoscopes are currently needed. There are some echoendoscopes that image at 7.5 to 20 MHz that are accurate in assessing the mucosa, but further study is needed to see if they can replace the use of probes.

Small case series have been performed of patients with Barrett's esophagus and early cancers staged by EUS before esophagectomy. In one center, the technique was 100% sensitive for detection of submucosal invasion but was only 90% specific for invasion in a group of 22 patients.[8] Inflammatory changes are virtually impossible to differentiate from early cancer invasion by EUS techniques. Overall, it appears that EUS has a tendency to overstage the depth of tumor invasion. A retrospective review of a single center's experience with EUS staging of esophageal cancer from 1991 to 2001 in 222 patients was recently published.[9] It was found that the accuracy of EUS in tumor staging was only 54%, whereas the accuracy of EUS in lymph node staging was 65%. This did not appear to be related to a learning curve in EUS interpretation because the accuracy in the first half of the time period studied was similar to that in the second half of the study period. These results suggest that more accurate staging techniques are needed to allow the implementation of endoscopic therapy.

Fortunately, a new technique termed endoscopic mucosal resection (EMR) has been used to help define the depth of cancer penetration and as a primary treatment for early cancer in Barrett's esophagus. EMR involves the use of a friction fitted cap that attaches to the tip of a standard endoscope. This technique was pioneered in Japan where mucosal resection has become the standard of care for early mucosal esophageal cancers. A survey of over 145 Japanese hospitals found that 76% used EMR for the treatment of early esophageal cancers.[10] The cap technique is the predominant technique used in the United States because of its commercial availability. It currently comes in two styles shown in Figure 29–3; one is completely level, whereas the other has the lip of the cap at an oblique angle.

Regardless of the type of cap selected, the technique of EMR is performed in a similar fashion. For early esophageal cancers, it is critical that the endoscopist is able to obtain adequate lifting of the lesion to be removed using an injection of a saline-epinephrine solution. The area of carcinoma has usually been previously established by biopsy and the area is lifted by positioning an injection

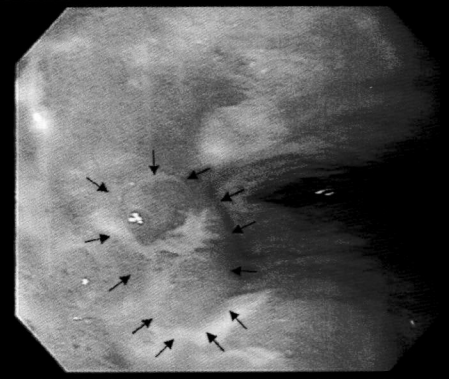

Figure 29–1. An endoscopic view of an early esophageal cancer lesion is outlined by the dark arrows in the setting of chronically inflamed mucosa in Barrett's esophagus.

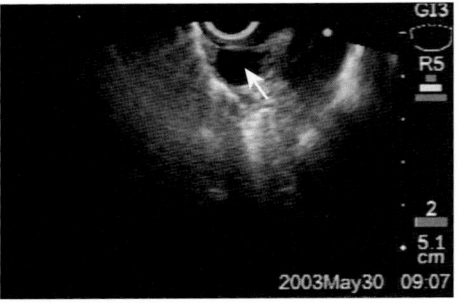

Figure 29–2. Endoscopic ultrasound image demonstrating the presence of a suspicious periesophageal lymph node *(white arrow)* located between the pleural reflection on the left and the aorta on the right. The lymph node is hypoechoic and rounded, which are both features of a malignant node.

needle proximal to the lesion. It is generally not advisable to inject into the lesion because it is theoretically possible to disseminate cancer cells into the submucosa. The sequence of an injection with adequate lifting of the target lesion is shown in Figure 29–4.

Once the target cancer is lifted by the injection, the lesion should be removed with mucosal resection. If this is not accomplished within a few hours, inflammation induced by the injection may cause the cancer to become adherent to the submucosa or muscularis propria, which would make resection difficult if not impossible.

The mucosal resection component of this technique is similar to that of a standard polypectomy except that suction is needed to create the pseudopolyp for mucosal removal. The endoscope with the resection cap attached is advanced into the stomach. It is generally recommended that the snare be positioned in the antrum of the stomach because the mucosa there is smoother and allows easier deflection of the snare around the diameter of the cap. Individuals experienced in this technique can position the snare using mucosa from the esophagus or proximal stomach, although this can be challenging. The sequence of positioning a snare around the lip of a mucosal resection cap is shown in Figure 29–5. This is often the most difficult portion of the mucosal resection because, if the snare is not properly formed, suctioning the tissue into the cap

can result in dislodgment of the snare and improper tissue resection. In addition, the snare is easily deformed and can be twisted during the process of forming the loop around the lip of the resection cap resulting in the need for a new crescent snare.

Once the snare is positioned, it is important that the technician assisting with the snare not move the snare because even slight disruptions in its position can cause the snare to dislodge.

The tissue resection is completed by suctioning the tissue into the cap as shown in Figure 29–6. To accomplish a wider resection, more tissue must be suctioned into the cap similar to what is done in variceal band ligation. The submucosa is often resected with the mucosa during the EMR. Once sufficient tissue is suctioned into the cap, the snare is closed and cautery applied until the tissue is transected. This process does take several more seconds than with the average polypectomy because the amount of tissue to be resected is much greater. The average diameter of resected mucosa is about 1 cm when assessed by the pathologist, and the defect left behind by the resection is often about 2 to 3 cm in diameter. The resection and the residual ulcer are also shown in Figure 29–6. Because tumors are often larger than the size of a single mucosal resection, a second resection can be performed directly adjacent to the first resection so long as care is taken not to suction the muscularis propria exposed at the site of the first resection into the cap. Multiple resections in the same area should only be attempted by endoscopists familiar with the mucosal resection technique.

EMR can be used for diagnosis of unusual-appearing lesions within Barrett's esophagus. In our experience, regions of nodularity or mucosal irregularity have a significantly higher incidence of carcinoma being present. A recent study of agreement among expert pathologists on distinguishing intramucosal carcinoma versus high grade dysplasia found only moderate agreement with a kappa score of less than 0.6 even when the pathologists could agree to standard definitions.[11] It was felt that limited tissue from pinch biopsies often obscured the pathologist's ability to determine invasion. Using EMR, our group has found that the diagnosis of adenocarcinoma increased by 40% in a group of 25 patients with Barrett's esophagus, because it furnishes larger specimens.[12] EMR is also an excellent tool for staging esophageal carcinoma as has been demonstrated in Japan.[13] It has been established that if the tumor can be found to be sm1 or sm2 stage (confined to the lamina propria), the tumor can be safely resected with only rare incidence of metastasis. Metastasis was found in 6% of patients who had cancers that penetrated to the

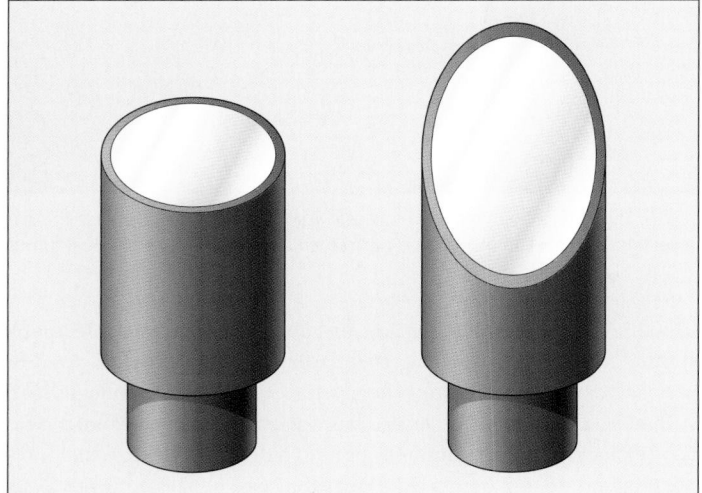

Figure 29–3. The endoscopic mucosal resection cap comes in a straight resection style shown on the left and a angled resection tip as shown on the right.

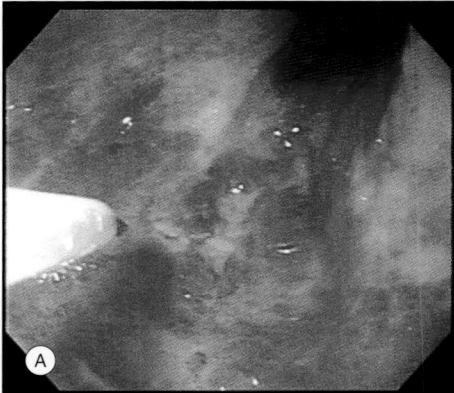
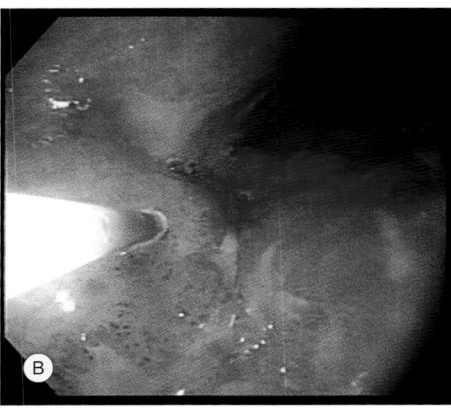

Figure 29–4. *A,* The injection needle poised over the target mucosa. *B,* The injection in process with the lifting of the mucosa with the fluid.

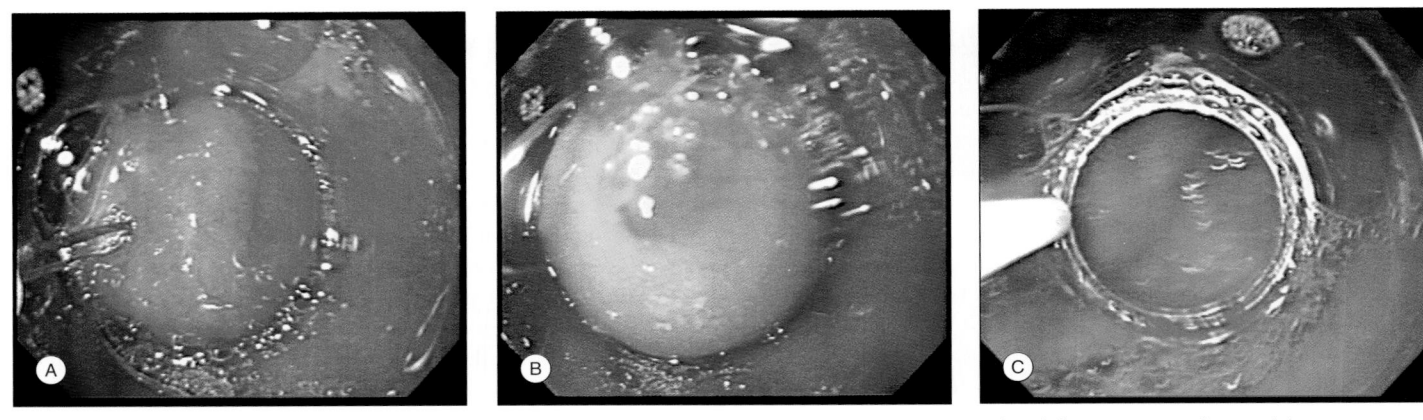

Figure 29–5. *A,* The snare is carefully advanced out while mucosa is suctioned into the cap. The mucosa is used to deflect a point on the tip of the snare toward the lip of the resection cap. *B,* Once the snare is deflected to the side of the cap and the point of the snare safely embedded onto the lip of the cap, the snare can be advanced allowing the loop to be formed around the lip of the cap. *C,* The snare is shown properly positioned around the lip of the mucosal resection cap.

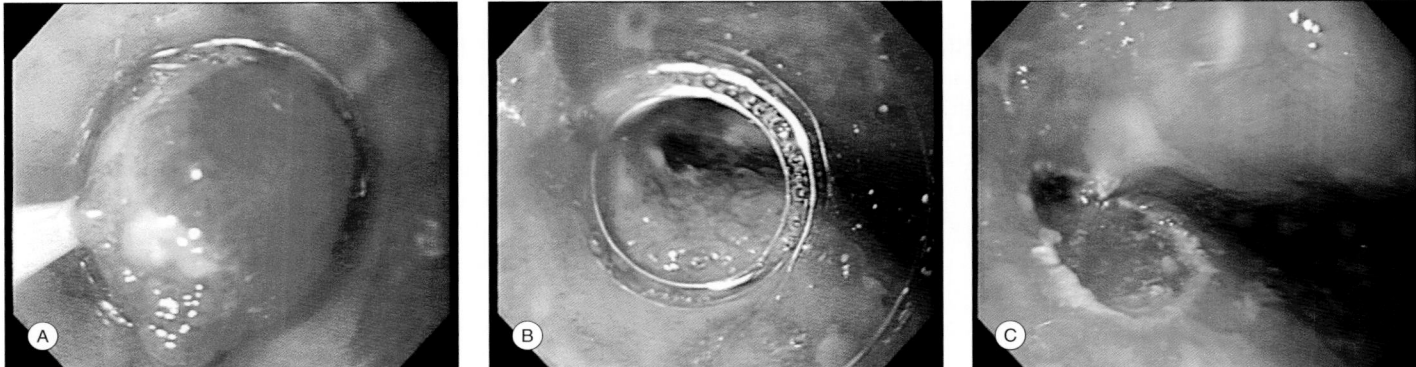

Figure 29–6. *A,* The targeted cancer is suctioned into the cap and the snare is closed. *B,* The defect created by the mucosal resection is shown. Because there is obvious residual cancer, a second resection can be completed adjacent to the first resection. *C,* A second resection is performed and removes the residual tumor.

muscularis mucosa or superficially into the submucosa. The technique of EMR finally gives the endoscopist similar tools to evaluate cancer curability as surgeons have had in the past, the ability to actually obtain a specimen for histology and pathologic depth of staging.

Methods of Endoscopic Treatment of Esophageal Cancer

THERMAL LASERS

One of the early methods of treating esophageal cancer was the application of thermal energy. These techniques originated from therapies developed for palliation of esophageal cancer, which involved the application of laser or intensive thermal energy to create a new lumen through obstructing cancers. Because most (80%–90%) esophageal cancers present as obstructive disease, this was naturally the starting point of most esophageal cancer therapies. Thermal techniques were ideal for this application because they could offer immediate tumor ablation and allowed the endoscopist to fashion a lumen that could pass food easily. However, laser therapies were found to be costly and required several applications

to achieve long-term palliation in contrast to expandable metal stents.[14] It is not surprising that laser therapy was then used as primary treatment of superficial cancers of the esophagus and stomach. The choice of lasers has varied; the initial choice was neodymium:yttrium-aluminum-garnet (Nd:YAG) lasers, which produce infrared laser light (1063 nm) that can penetrate up to 2 cm through tissue. This therapy was used in the 1980s with relative success against predominately superficial squamous cell esophageal cancers. The results of smaller series seemed to suggest that cancers could be eliminated in 73% of 33 patients with superficial cancers of the esophagus and gastric cardia with most patients followed for at least 2 years.[15] The treatment could be repeated up to six times, although the mean number of retreatments was 2.6. The problem with this type of therapy was that the results often depend on endoscopist's skill and experience with the laser. In addition, the determination of the superficial nature of the tumor was solely based on their endoscopic appearance. Unfortunately, during this early time period, the methods of assessing depth of tumor invasion were limited to computed tomography (CT) scans that were of much poorer resolution than what can be obtained today. In addition, assessment of cure was limited to biopsies of the treated sites because assessment of regional lymph nodes and evidence of submucosal disease was impossible without surgical resection. More recent studies using Nd:YAG laser therapy in combination with multipolar coagulation have involved very small numbers of patients. One study enrolled only six patients over a 7-year period and found that the treatment failed in one patient and left residual Barrett's mucosa in three others.[16] An average of three Nd:YAG sessions and three multipolar coagulation treatment sessions were required to treat each patient. Although this form of therapy could be effective, it requires multiple endoscopic treatment sessions and can fail. One case report in the literature suggests that, with Nd:YAG therapy, the failure could occur underneath normal-appearing squamous tissue and may be difficult to detect.[17]

Other laser therapies that have been used to treat superficial cancers include potassium titanyl phosphate:yttrium-aluminum-garnet (KTP:YAG) and argon lasers because they have a more limited depth of penetration than the Nd:YAG lasers. These lasers all operate in the visible green light region (532 nm) spectrum and penetrate tissue to a depth of only about 2 mm. These lasers have been advocated for the treatment of vascular lesions because of their limited depth of penetration and their intense absorption by hemoglobin. Several recent series have reported that these lasers can be used to treat Barrett's esophagus because they offer the safety of superficial therapy. These lasers have been used more for ablation of dysplastic lesions in Barrett's esophagus rather than cancers, but for some very superficial cancers these green lasers may be effective. One case series has found that KTP:YAG laser was able to destroy early cancers in two patients, although this required multiple treatments and also had evidence of intestinal epithelium under squamous mucosa in 2 of 10 patients treated for Barrett's mucosa.[18]

Despite these reports of laser therapy for early esophageal cancer, most endoscopy units no longer operate thermal lasers because they have largely been replaced by newer technologies. The use of thermal lasers for dysphagia has been largely supplanted by the availability of expandable metal stents. The use of thermal lasers for vascular lesions has been replaced by multipolar and APC. It is unlikely that thermal lasers will be used in the future for the treatment of superficial cancers because their availability and expertise level is decreasing in the gastrointestinal endoscopy community.

ARGON PLASMA COAGULATION

APC was originally developed as a hemostatic device that could cauterize bleeding lesions (in a noncontact fashion) that were awkward to reach with traditional probes. It has the ability to treat superficially and has been thought to represent decreased risks of perforation. Mucosal ablative therapy for Barrett's esophagus has been investigated by several investigators who found good to excellent results.[19–27] The technique is shown in Figure 29–7.

The primary goal of APC is to apply a current to the target lesion without producing a perforation. The argon gas is released under pressure, and the endoscopist must be vigilant against allowing the tip of the probe to become embedded into the mucosa during treatment. This could result in submucosa air or, worse, a perforation. For this reason, coagulation performed with the argon plasma coagulator should only be done while the probe is being withdrawn toward the endoscope. This should ensure that the tip of the probe is not embedded in the mucosa. Settings for treating

adenocarcinoma should be in the higher power ranges; 80 to 90 watts has been cited in the literature. Higher output powers seem to be associated with improved outcomes in Barrett's esophagus with high grade dysplasia, although complications such as perforation and strictures are also seen at these doses.[25,28,29]

Treatment of intraepithelial carcinoma in Barrett's esophagus has only been reported in a limited series of patients. In one series of only three intraepithelial cancers, treatment of APC was ineffective and resulted in invasive disease.[29] This cancer also failed treatment with subsequent PDT. Similar results were observed in another small series of three patients with early esophageal cancers who were treated with APC with one recurrence noted that was subsequently treated with PDT.[30] Early squamous cell cancers and high grade dysplasia have been treated with the APC with good results reported in the Asian literature.[31,32] A series of 29 patients with early squamous cancers and 42 cases of high grade dysplasia were first treated with EMR with any residual treated with APC.[32] The early results seem promising with only three of the cancers (10%) found to reoccur after 4 months. Esophageal strictures were found in four of the cases after mucosal resection of the majority of the diameter of the esophagus.

Overall, it appear that, although APC is well tolerated with few described complications, its efficacy in elimination of early esophageal cancer is limited with significant (33%) failure rates in limited numbers of Barrett's esophagus related cancers and lower failure rates (10%) in superficial squamous cell cancers. This is not a surprising finding given the decreased depth of injury associated with this treatment.

ENDOSCOPIC MUCOSAL RESECTION FOR EARLY CANCERS

EMR has been used for the treatment of early esophageal and gastric cancers from its inception in Japan.[33] The technique was performed by Japanese surgeons who had excellent endoscopic skills and the anatomic understanding of cancer surgery. The initial resection were done using an overtube, which was used to anchor tissue. A standard endoscope was then placed within the lumen of the overtube and used to remove the tissue with a snare from the endoscope or one that was preformed around the overtube. The large ulcers that these procedures produced were worrisome, but these ulcers were all

Figure 29–7. Argon plasma coagulation is used to cauterize the mucosa by conduction of the electrical charge alone a stream of ionized argon gas as shown above. The electrical discharge is shown at the *black arrow*. The current can reach areas that are not directly in line with the argon probe.

found to heal within 2 months.[34] The most commonly used of these devices was the Makuuchi tube, which had already been used in 152 cases of superficial esophageal cancer in 1992.[35] These pioneers of mucosal resection established that, when cancers were either intraepithelial or confined to the upper two thirds of the mucosa, vascular invasion or metastasis was extremely rare. Only when cancers penetrated into the bottom one third of the mucosa did vascular invasion or lymph nodes become apparent in 25% of the patients. In their hands, patients with intraepithelial disease had 5-year survivals approaching 100%. However, once the cancers penetrated into the submucosa, the 5-year survival rate dropped to about 55% to 59%. Initially, mucosal resection was only recommended for esophageal cancers that were less than 2 cm and occupied less than one third of the circumference of the esophagus in patients who were not ideal surgical candidates.[36] In one study that correlated the lymph node metastasis to depth of cancer invasion, the presence of lymph node metastasis was found to be 0% if the lesion was confined to the mucosa, 10% if the muscularis mucosae became invaded, and 43% if the submucosa was invaded.[37] Over time, recommendations concerning treatment of early esophageal cancers were altered because about one fourth of all esophageal cancers were classified as early stage because of intensive screening programs.[38] By the late 1990s, a survey of Japanese institutions found that EMR was favored as the treatment of choice for all esophageal cancers confined to the upper two thirds of the mucosa.[39] Interestingly, all patients with mucosally confined disease survived, but disease that penetrated to the submucosa had significantly worse prognosis than disease that remained mucosal.

Mucosal resection techniques in the United States are similar to those described previously. There are other methods of performing EMR such as using a two-channeled therapeutic endoscope. One channel is used to place a snare around the lesion, and then forceps are passed through the other channel to grasp the lesion and tent it toward the endoscope. This positions the tissue within the snare for removal. In addition, another technique that is simple to use is an endoscopic variceal band ligator that can create a pseudopolyp. The lesions is lifted with a saline and epinephrine solution as with the other techniques and followed by banding of the lesion with a variceal band ligation kit. The band ligator creates a pseudopolyp that can then be removed with a small snare. Although this is a simple technique, multiple esophageal intubations are required to accomplish all of the steps, and the cost of the variceal ligation device is typically more than that of the mucosal resection caps discussed earlier. In addition, the variceal band technique requires the snare to be performed as soon as possible after placement of the band because, if there is a large amount of mucosa present, the band will start to slip and fall off of the mucosa. Unlike a varix, there really is no vein for the band to constrict; thus, depending on the density of the tissue, the band may not stay on the lesion at all. All of these techniques are designed to elevate a region of relatively flat mucosa. No specific technique has been established to be better than any other in terms of tissue removal, although the larger sized mucosal resection caps appear to resect larger pieces of tissue.

The results of using EMR for the treatment of adenocarcinoma within Barrett's esophagus have been limited to a few series. At the Mayo Clinic, we have been able to eliminate cancers in a small group of 17 patients treated with a combination of mucosal resection

Table 29–1.	Characteristics of Esophageal Cancers Amenable to Endoscopic Mucosal Resection	
Characteristic	**Favorable Outcome**
Size	Less than 2 cm
Depth of penetration	No penetration of muscularis mucosa
Grade of cancer	Well-differentiated cancer
Appearance	Polypoid, elevated, or flat

followed by PDT.[40] This combination therapy has been undertaken because genetic abnormalities may be found in mucosa that does not appear dysplastic. A total of sixteen (94%) of these patients were cancer free at a median follow-up of 13 months. The complications of this series were primarily due to minor bleeding after EMR in one patient (6%) and stricture formation in five patients (30%). In a larger series from Germany, 64 patients with early cancers and high grade dysplasia were managed with EMR, 97% of those who had lesions favorable for EMR were in remission after a follow-up of about 1 year.[41] However, the endoscopically favorable lesions were those that were polypoid, elevated, or flat, which occurred in only 35 (55%) of the patients. In those that had lesions that were depressed or ulcerated, only 59% were found to be in remission. A serious problem has surfaced during the 3-year follow-up of local therapy from this group. A recent report has indicated that, in the residual Barrett's mucosa that was not originally neoplastic, 30% of patients developed additional neoplastic lesions.[42] The authors now advocate a similar approach to the one used at the Mayo Clinic in treating any residual Barrett's mucosa with additional ablative therapy. The results of these series have led to recommendations about which lesions can be approached with EMR. These are listed in Table 29–1.

PHOTODYNAMIC THERAPY FOR EARLY ESOPHAGEAL CANCER

PDT has been investigated since its origins in 1961 as a treatment for cancers.[43] The therapy has traditional involved the use of a combination of a drug termed a photosensitizer and light of a specific wavelength, which is required to activate the drug. The typical practice is to administer the drug days or hours before light delivery to allow the photosensitizer to concentrate into the neoplastic tissue. Light from a laser is then applied to the mucosa, which causes general tissue destruction and cell death.

Current photosensitizers are derivatives of porphyrin compounds that are generally given intravenously. The normal tissue generally excretes the photosensitizer sooner than the neoplastic tissue. This is the reason that the current commercially available photosensitizer, Photofrin II (sodium porfimer) is given 48 hours before photoradiation. Aminolevulinic acid (ALA) is a prodrug that is often used in Europe. ALA must be converted by the heme synthetic pathway into protoporphyrin IX.[44] Protoporphyrin IX is primarily retained within the mucosal layer, which limits the depth of the photodynamic effect. These photosensitizers can then be activated by red light of 630 nm wavelength or 635 nm (for ALA). Other wavelengths of light can activate these porphyrin compounds, but red light is selected because it can penetrate the tissue significantly better than shorter wavelengths and can avoid absorption by hemoglobin. Generally, lasers deliver the light because it is necessary to channel the light energy through an endoscope. This means the laser light must be "coupled" into a fiber, which requires the coherence and concentration of laser light sources to accomplish. Older laser systems used dye lasers, which basically took light of a short wavelength (e.g., an argon laser 532 nm) and converted into the longer red light. These systems are still available and can produce power of 7 watts. Because the dye lasers required combining two laser systems, there were problems with laser alignment and in the energy requirements of these laser systems. They required special electrical outlets and water cooling systems. Newer solid state diode lasers can be operated on ordinary room current and are air cooled. This has made them much smaller, which allows their transport to be simpler. The current system incorporates a power output meter into the system so that the laser can tune its output to what is needed rather than require the endoscopist to calibrate the system.

The process of photoradiation is usually performed by placing an optical fiber through the biopsy channel of the endoscope. The tip of this has a cylindrical diffusing fiber that can be placed in the lumen of the esophagus. Generally, in the case of an early tumor, the fiber is pressed against the tumor as shown in Figure 29–8.

Treatment parameters for PDT for Barrett's esophagus with a cancer using sodium porfimer involve a drug dosage of 2 mg/kg body weight. This is given 48 hours before PDT. Red light is delivered through a diffusing fiber at a power output of 400 mW/cm fiber for a total energy of around 300 J/cm fiber. If there is no endoscopically apparent disease and mucosal resection has completely removed the lesion, a smaller dose of light such as 200 J/cm fiber can be used to treat the remaining Barrett's mucosa. Patients can experience a number of complications. After injection of the drug, cutaneous photosensitivity can occur and persist for 30 to 90 days. After photoradiation, patients can experience severe chest pain within 24 hours. This pain can require narcotic administration to achieve

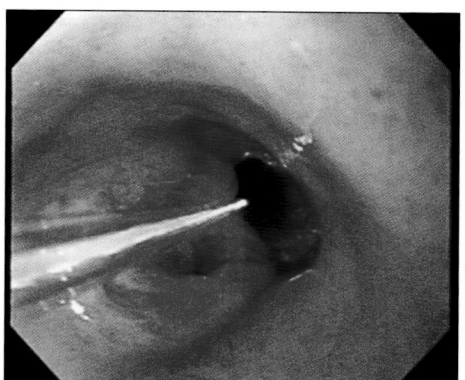

Figure 29–8. Photoradiation of an esophageal cancer.

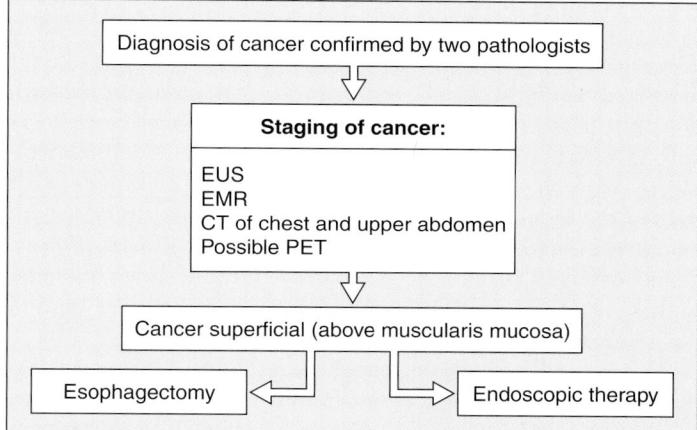

Figure 29–9. Management of early esophageal cancer.

Table 29–2. Results of Photodynamic Therapy for Esophageal Cancer					
Study	Patient Number	Tumor Type	Tumor Stage	Drug	% Success
Jin, et al[47]	207	59% cardia tumors	All advanced	HpD	23% 5-year survival
Sibille, et al.[5]	123	85% squamous 15% adenocarcinoma	"Early"	HpD	74% 5-year disease-free survival
McCaughn, et al.[48]	77	Adenocarcinoma and squamous cancers	Stage I–IV	Photofrin II	Stage I patients 62% 5-year survival
Grosjean, et al.[49]	31	Squamous cancers	87% microscopic cancer	mTHPC	83% microscopic cancers complete response at 15 months
Gossner, et al.[50]	22	Adenocarcinoma	T1 and T2	ALA	77% complete response at 9 months
Tan, et al.[51]	12	Adenocarcinoma	2 T0 10 T1-2	ALA	17%
Panjehpour[52]	13	Adenocarcinoma	12 T1 and 1 T2	Photofrin II	77%
Pacifico[53]	23	Adenocarcinoma	23 T0-T1	HpD and Photofrin II	84%
Wolfsen, et al.[46]	14	Adenocarcinoma	T0-T1	Photofrin II	93%
ALA, aminolevulinic acid; HpD, hematoporphyrin derivative; mTHPC, m-tetrahydroxyphenychlorin.					

pain relief. Usually transdermal administration of narcotics is preferred because patients have odynophagia from the therapy. Dehydration occurs because of the inability to obtain adequate fluid intake and may require intravenous fluids to resolve. Nausea occurs in the first 1 to 3 days after photoradiation and can require administration of antiemetics. Rare side effects include injury to organs that are nearby the esophagus, leading to conditions such as atrial fibrillation and pleural effusions.[45,46] Esophageal strictures have been a major problem because they occur in about a third of patients treated. These strictures are often fibrotic and require multiple dilatations to large diameters to resolve the constriction.

The results of PDT for the treatment of esophageal cancer are shown in Table 29–2. The overall results are quite impressive if only the early cancers are considered. Interestingly, significant (23%) 5-year survival rates were reported in patients who had advanced staged esophageal cancer. Most of the series involved similar photosensitizers such as HpD or Photofrin II although a few involved mTHPC, which is not available in this country and is felt to have a deeper depth of penetration than Photofrin II. Among the series using porphyrin compounds, the survival rates range from 62% to 93% with a median response of about 75%. An important factor illustrated best by the Sibille and coworkers'[5] study is that although disease-free survival was excellent, overall survival over 5 years was only 25%, indicating that these are medically ill patients who have severe comorbidities. These results are very good considering that most of the series contain patients with more invasive disease with penetration of the submucosa and even the muscularis propria. Complications that have been reported in these series is similar to those discussed previously; strictures occur in about one third of the patients.

Our group has recently compared the results of PDT in combination with EMR with surgical resection for early-stage esophageal cancer. This study examined 88 total patients; 64 underwent surgical resection, and 24 were treated endoscopically. Although all patients treated surgically were considered cured of their disease, 88% of those that underwent endoscopic therapy were likewise disease free. However, those that underwent endoscopic therapy had more comorbid medical illnesses that precluded surgical resection. In addition, surgically treated patients had significantly more serious complications including anastomotic strictures and leaks, wound infections, and dumping syndrome. Overall, the study showed that the results of therapy were not statistically significant but that complications were more likely in those treated surgically. These results indicate that endoscopic therapy for early cancers may be a viable alternative to traditional esophagectomy. One possible algorithm for consideration when evaluating patients with esophageal cancer is shown in Figure 29–9. If a patient has early-stage cancer, endoscopic therapy should be considered as a possible option.

The options for endoscopic treatment for early esophageal cancer consists primarily of using EMR alone or in combination with a mucosal ablative therapy such as PDT or a thermal ablative technique such as APC. PDT alone seems to have a reasonable number of reports regarding efficacy, but the use of mucosal resection would decrease the uncertainly about staging this tumor. The decision of whether endoscopic therapy is a viable alternative to surgical treatment depends on further studies in which these modalities are prospectively studied. What will need to be weighed is the benefit of surgical cure versus the risk of surgical complications.

ACKNOWLEDGMENTS

We would like to acknowledge the support of NIH grants CA85992-01 and R01CA097048-01.

REFERENCES

1. Buttar NS, Wang KK, Anderson MA, et al: The effect of selective cyclooxygenase-2 inhibition in Barrett's esophagus epithelium: An in vitro study.[comment]. J Natl Cancer Inst 94:422–429, 2002.
2. Galipeau PC, Prevo LJ, Sanchez CA, et al: Clonal expansion and loss of heterozygosity at chromosomes 9p and 17p in premalignant esophageal (Barrett's) tissue. J Natl Cancer Inst 91:2087–2095, 1999.
3. Prevo LJ, Sanchez CA, Galipeau PC, Reid BJ: p53-mutant clones and field effects in Barrett's esophagus. Cancer Res 59:4784–4787, 1999.
4. Krishnadath K, Wang K, Liu W, et al: Persistent genetic abnormalities in Barrett's esophagus after photodynamic therapy. Gastroenterology 119:624–630, 2000.
5. Sibille A, Lambert R, Souquet JC, et al: Long-term survival after photodynamic therapy for esophageal cancer [see comments]. Gastroenterology 108:337–344, 1995.
6. Bonavina L: Early oesophageal cancer: Results of a European multicentre survey. Group Europeen pour l'Etude des Maladies de l'Oesophage. Br J Surg 82:98–101, 1995.
7. Noguchi H, Naomoto Y, Kondo H, et al: Evaluation of endoscopic mucosal resection for superficial esophageal carcinoma. Surg Laparosc Endosc Percutan Tech 10:343–350, 2000.
8. Scotiniotis IA, Kochman ML, Lewis JD, et al: Accuracy of EUS in the evaluation of Barrett's esophagus and high-grade dysplasia or intramucosal carcinoma. Gastrointest Endosc 54:689–696, 2001.
9. Bosing N, Schumacher B, Frieling T, et al: Endoscopic ultrasound in routine clinical practice for staging adenocarcinomas of the stomach and distal esophagus. [German]. Chirurg 74:214–223, 2003.
10. Kodama M, Kakegawa T: Treatment of superficial cancer of the esophagus: A summary of responses to a questionnaire on superficial cancer of the esophagus in Japan. Surgery 123:432–439, 1998.
11. Ormsby AH, Petras RE, Henricks WH, et al: Observer variation in the diagnosis of superficial oesophageal adenocarcinoma. Gut 51:671–676, 2002.
12. Nijhawan PK, Wang KK: Endoscopic mucosal resection for lesions with endoscopic features suggestive of malignancy and high-grade dysplasia within Barrett's esophagus. Gastrointest Endosc 52:328–332, 2000.
13. Yoshida MMK: [Endoscopic evaluation of the depth of invasion in cases of superficial esophageal cancer in determining indications for endoscopic mucosal resection]. Nippon Geka Gakkai Zasshi 103:337–342, 2002.
14. Dallal HJ, Smith GD, Grieve DC, et al: A randomized trial of thermal ablative therapy versus expandable metal stents in the palliative treatment of patients with esophageal carcinoma. Gastrointest Endosc 54:549–557, 2001.
15. Yang GR, Zhao LQ, Li SS, et al: Endoscopic Nd:YAG laser therapy in patients with early superficial carcinoma of the esophagus and the gastric cardia. Endoscopy 26:681–685, 1994.
16. Sharma P, Jaffe PE, Bhattacharyya A, Sampliner RE: Laser and multipolar electrocoagulation ablation of early Barrett's adenocarcinoma: Long-term follow-up. Gastrointest Endosc 49:442–446, 1999.

17. Fremond L, Bouche O, Diebold MD, et al: [Partial regression of Barrett esophagus with high grade dysplasia and adenocarcinoma after photocoagulation and endocurietherapy under antisecretory treatment]. Gastroenterol Clin Biol 19:112–116, 1995.

18. Gossner L, May A, Stolte M, et al: KTP laser destruction of dysplasia and early cancer in columnar-lined Barrett's esophagus. Gastrointest Endosc 49:8–12, 1999.

19. Dumoulin FL, Terjung B, Neubrand M, et al: Treatment of Barrett's esophagus by endoscopic argon plasma coagulation. Endoscopy 29:751–753, 1997.

20. Maass S, Martin WR, Spiethoff A, Riemann JF: [Barrett esophagus with severe dysplasia in argon beam therapy]. Z Gastroenterol 36:301–306, 1998.

21. Mork H, Barth T, Kreipe HH, et al: Reconstitution of squamous epithelium in Barrett's oesophagus with endoscopic argon plasma coagulation: a prospective study. Scand J Gastroenterol 33:1130–1134, 1998.

22. Van Laethem JL, Cremer M, Peny MO, et al: Eradication of Barrett's mucosa with argon plasma coagulation and acid suppression: Immediate and mid term results [see comments]. Gut 43:747–751, 1998.

23. Byrne JP, Armstrong GR, Attwood SE: Restoration of the normal squamous lining in Barrett's esophagus by argon beam plasma coagulation [see comments]. Am J Gastroenterol 93:1810–1815, 1998.

24. Grade AJ, Shah IA, Medlin SM, Ramirez FC: The efficacy and safety of argon plasma coagulation therapy in Barrett's esophagus. Gastrointest Endosc 50:18–22, 1999.

25. Pereira-Lima JC, Busnello JV, Saul C, et al: High power setting argon plasma coagulation for the eradication of Barrett's esophagus. Am J Gastroenterol 95:1661–1668, 2000.

26. Martin WR, Jakobs R, Spiethoff A, et al: [Treatment of Barrett esophagus with argon plasma coagulation with acid suppression—a prospective study]. [German]. Z Gastroenterol 37:779–784, 1999.

27. Tigges H, Fuchs KH, Maroske J, et al: Combination of endoscopic argon plasma coagulation and antireflux surgery for treatment of Barrett's esophagus. J Gastrointest Surg 5:251–259, 2001.

28. Schulz H, Miehlke S, Antos D, et al: Ablation of Barrett's epithelium by endoscopic argon plasma coagulation in combination with high-dose omeprazole. Gastrointest Endosc 51:659–663, 2000.

29. Van Laethem JL, Jagodzinski R, Peny MO, et al: Argon plasma coagulation in the treatment of Barrett's high-grade dysplasia and in situ adenocarcinoma. Endoscopy 33:257–261, 2001.

30. May A, Gossner L, Gunter E, et al: Local treatment of early cancer in short Barrett's esophagus by means of argon plasma coagulation: initial experience. Endoscopy 31:497–500, 1999.

31. Katsuta M, Tajiri T, Nomura T, et al: Treatment of superficial esophageal cancer by argon plasma coagulation. [Japanese]. Nihon Ika Daigahu Zasshi 69:383–385, 2002.

32. Wang GQ, Wei WQ, Hao CQ, et al: Minimal invasive treatment of early esophageal cancer and its precancerous lesion: endoscopic mucosal resection using transparent cap-fitted endoscope. [Chinese]. Chung-Hua i Hsueh Tsa Chih 83:306–308, 2003.

33. Inoue H, Endo M: Endoscopic esophageal mucosal resection using a transparent tube. Surg Endosc 4:198–201, 1990.

34. Inoue M, Shiozaki H, Tamura S, Monden M: Endoscopic mucosal resection for early esophageal cancer. Review 15 refs. [Japanese]. Nippon Rinsho 54:1286–1291, 1996.

35. Makuuchi H, Machimura T, Mizutani K, et al: Controversy in the treatment of superficial esophageal carcinoma—indications and problems of the procedures. [Japanese]. Nippon Geka Gakkai Zasshi 93:1059–1062, 1992.

36. Endo M, Takeshita K, Inoue H: Endoscopic mucosal resection of esophageal cancer. Review 7 refs. [Japanese]. Gan to Kagaku Ryoho 22:192–195, 1995.

37. Yoshida M, Hanashi T, Momma K, et al: Endoscopic mucosal resection for radical treatment of esophageal cancer. [Japanese]. Gan to Kagaku Ryoho 22:847–854, 1995.

38. Kato H: Diagnosis and treatment of esophageal neoplasms. Jpn J Cancer Res 86:993–1009, 1995.

39. Kodama M, Kakegawa T: Treatment of superficial carcinoma of the esophagus—A review of responses to questionnaire on superficial carcinoma of the esophagus collected at the 49th conference of Japanese Society for Esophageal Diseases. [Japanese]. Nippon Geka Gakkai Zasshi 97:683–690, 1996.

40. Buttar NS, Wang KK, Lutzke LS, et al: Combined endoscopic mucosal resection and photodynamic therapy for esophageal neoplasia within Barrett's esophagus. Gastrointest Endosc 54:682–688, 2001.

41. Ell C, May A, Gossner L, et al: Endoscopic mucosal resection of early cancer and high-grade dysplasia in Barrett's esophagus. Gastroenterology 118:670–677, 2000.

42. May A, Gossner L, Pech O, et al: Local endoscopic therapy for intraepithelial high-grade neoplasia and early adenocarcinoma in Barrett's oesophagus: Acute-phase and intermediate results of a new treatment approach. Eur J Gastroenterol Hepatol 14:1085–1091, 2002.

43. Wang KK: Current status of photodynamic therapy of Barrett's esophagus. Gastrointest Endosc 49:S20–23, 1999.

44. Barr H, Shepherd NA, Dix A, et al: Eradication of high-grade dysplasia in columnar-lined (Barrett's) oesophagus by photodynamic therapy with endogenously generated protoporphyrin IX [see comments]. Lancet 348:584–585, 1996.

45. Overholt BF, Panjehpour M, Ayres M: Photodynamic therapy for Barrett's esophagus: Cardiac effects. Lasers Surg Med 21:317–320, 1997.

46. Wolfsen HC, Woodward TA, Raimondo M: Photodynamic therapy for dysplastic Barrett esophagus and early esophageal adenocarcinoma. Mayo Clin Proc 77:1176–1181, 2002.

47. Jin M, Yang B, Zhang W, Wang Y: Photodynamic therapy for upper gastrointestinal tumours over the past 10 years. Semin Surg Oncol 10:111–113, 1994.

48. McCaughan JS Jr, Ellison EC, Guy JT, et al: Photodynamic therapy for esophageal malignancy: A prospective twelve-year study. Ann Thorac Surg 62:1005–1009; discussion 1009–1010, 1996.

49. Grosjean P, Savary JF, Mizeret J, et al: Photodynamic therapy for cancer of the upper aerodigestive tract using tetra(m-hydroxyphenyl)chlorin. J Clin Laser Med Surg 14:281–287, 1996.

50. Gossner L, Stolte M, Sroka R, et al: Photodynamic ablation of high-grade dysplasia and early cancer in Barrett's esophagus by means of 5-aminolevulinic acid [see comments]. Gastroenterology 114:448–455, 1998.

51. Tan WC, Fulljames C, Stone N, et al: Photodynamic therapy using 5-aminolaevulinic acid for oesophageal adenocarcinoma associated with Barrett's metaplasia. J Photochem Photobiol B 53:81–90, 1999.

52. Panjehpour M, Overholt BF, Haydek JM, Lee SG: Results of photodynamic therapy for ablation of dysplasia and early cancer in Barrett's esophagus and effect of oral steroids on stricture formation. Am J Gastroenterol 95:2177–2184, 2000.

53. Pacifico RJ, Wang KK: Role of mucosal ablative therapy in the treatment of the columnar-lined esophagus. Chest Surg Clin North Am 12:185–203, 2002.

Endoscopic Palliation of Malignant Dysphagia and Esophageal Fistulas

Marjolein Y.V. Homs and Peter D. Siersema

Introduction

Annually, cancer of the esophagus and gastroesophageal junction is diagnosed worldwide in more than 400,000 patients, which makes it the eighth most common malignancy and sixth on the list of cancer mortality causes.[1] It is somewhat difficult to determine its true incidence, because cancer of the gastroesophageal junction is sometimes classified as gastric cancer and sometimes as esophageal cancer. In clinical practice, this distinction is not very important because for both adenocarcinoma of the esophagus or of the gastroesophageal junction, the curative and palliative options for treatment are the same.

Overall, cancer of the esophagus and gastroesophageal junction carries a poor prognosis with a 5-year survival rate of less than 20%.[2] This is at least partly because more than 50% of patients with carcinoma of the esophagus or gastroesophageal junction have already inoperable disease at presentation. Most of these patients require palliative treatment to relieve progressive dysphagia or to treat associated problems such as the presence of a fistula.

This chapter focuses on the epidemiology and pathogenesis of inoperable cancer of the esophagus and gastroesophageal junction. In addition, clinical features and pathologic characteristics of these tumors are reviewed. Then, endoscopic methods for palliation of dysphagia and treatment of esophagorespiratory fistulas are discussed. In the final part of this chapter, we discuss future developments for treatment of malignant dysphagia.

Epidemiology

SQUAMOUS CELL CARCINOMA

The incidence of squamous cell carcinoma varies from country to country; also, within a country it may occur more often in certain regions. About two thirds of new cases of squamous cell carcinoma are detected in China (47%) and Central Asia (19%). This is called the Central Asia Esophageal Cancer Belt. The incidence of squamous cell carcinoma in this area varies from 19 per 100,000 in Azerbaijan to 340 per 100,000 in the northern part of China. The incidence of squamous cell carcinoma in Western Europe and the United States is much lower (i.e., 3 to 6 per 100,000). In Western countries, squamous cell carcinoma of the esophagus is mainly found in the older age group with the highest incidence between 50 and 70 years. The distribution between males and females is 3 to 4:1.[3]

ADENOCARCINOMA

Until about 1970, more than 90% of esophageal cancers were squamous cell carcinomas. However, population based studies have shown a large increase in the incidence of adenocarcinoma of the esophagus and gastroesophageal junction over the last 30 years in North America and Western Europe, especially among white males.[4,5] In males, the incidence of adenocarcinoma of the esophagus and gastroesophageal junction has now surpassed that of squamous cell carcinoma.[6] In the United States, the annual rates per 100,000 population for esophageal adenocarcinoma rose from 0.7 during 1974 to 1976 to 3.2 during 1992 to 1994, an increase of more than 350%.[5] The same trend, although occurring less rapidly, has been reported in other areas, such as Australia, New Zealand, and Western Europe.[7]

Many believe that the increase in esophageal adenocarcinoma is related to an increase in the incidence of Barrett's esophagus. In a report from Scotland, Prach and colleagues[8] found that the incidence of new diagnoses of Barrett's esophagus increased from 1 per 100,000 in 1980 to 48 per 100,000 in 1992. The rate of Barrett's esophagus detection increased over the same years from 1.4 to 42.7 (16.5 if only cases with histologic conformation were included) per 1000 endoscopic procedures.

Multiple reports confirm that adenocarcinoma of the esophagus and gastroesophageal junction occurs more frequently in white males. The distribution between males and females is 4:1. Most patients with esophageal adenocarcinoma are older individuals with a peak incidence around 65 years.[9] The worldwide distribution of esophageal cancer (for males) is shown in Fig. 30–1.

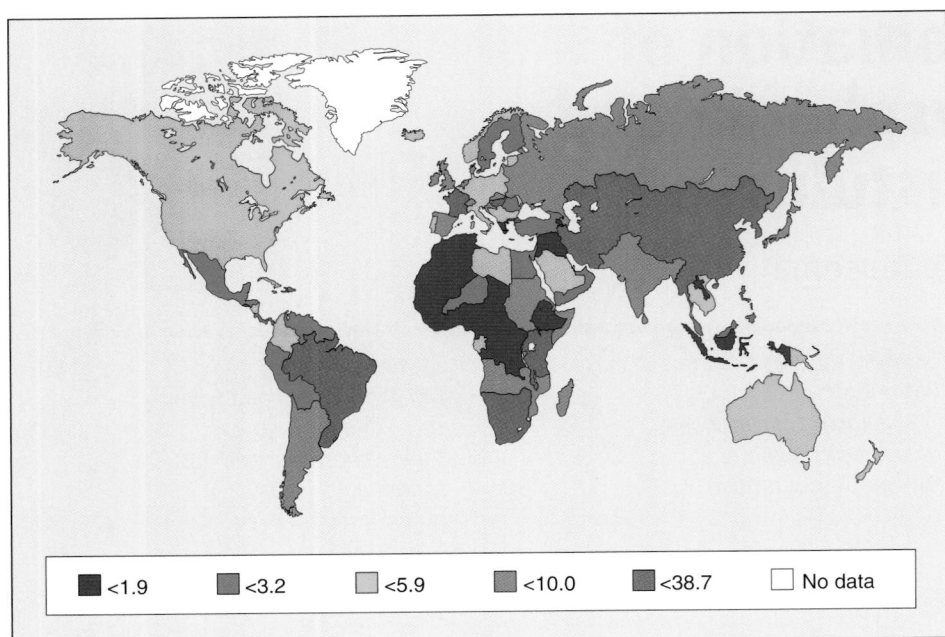

Figure 30-1. Incidence of esophageal cancer: age-standardized rate (world)—male (all ages). (From Parkin DM, Bray FI, Devesa SS: Cancer burden in the year 2000. The global picture. Eur J Cancer 37:4–66, 2001.)

Legend: <1.9   <3.2   <5.9   <10.0   <38.7   No data

Pathogenesis

SQUAMOUS CELL CARCINOMA

Smoking and Alcohol

The most important risk factors for squamous cell carcinoma in Western Europe and the United States are smoking and alcohol intake. The squamous cell carcinoma risk is increased by a factor of 5 for moderate smokers and a factor of 10 for heavy smokers. It has been shown that alcohol intake and smoking are independent risk factors for the development of esophageal squamous cell carcinoma.[10]

Food

In Hong Kong, a correlation has been established between the use of pickled vegetables and the development of squamous cell carcinoma. It was found that this was caused by herbs that were used for these vegetables, which were often contaminated with toxic fungi.[11]

Other Factors

Prior radiation therapy has been associated with an increased squamous cell carcinoma risk. A recent study demonstrated that patients who underwent radiation therapy for breast cancer more than 10 years ago had an increased risk of developing squamous cell carcinoma in the esophagus.[12]

Hot drinks, particularly tea in certain areas in Asia, are associated with an increased risk of developing squamous cell carcinoma. The suggested mechanism is chronic irritation of the esophageal mucosa caused by these hot drinks.[13]

The role played by human papillomavirus (HPV) is unclear. In South Africa, where the incidence of squamous cell carcinoma is high, HPV DNA was detected in more than 50% of cancers.[14] In contrast, in the Netherlands, the presence of HPV in squamous cell carcinoma is rare.[15]

Disorders Associated with an Increased Squamous Cell Carcinoma Risk

Achalasia

In a cohort study from Sweden, in which 1062 patients with achalasia were followed, the risk of squamous cell carcinoma was increased by a factor 16 after a follow-up of 9864 patient-years.[16] Because most tumors were detected at an advanced stage, a curative resection was only possible in a minority of the patients.

Caustic Ingestion

The incidence of esophageal squamous cell carcinoma is increased by a factor 1000 to 3000 in patients with a stricture in the esophagus caused by a caustic ingestion. The risk of developing a malignancy is probably highest after the ingestion of lye.[17] The mean time between ingestion of a corrosive agent and the development of squamous cell carcinoma is 30 to 40 years.

Head and Neck Cancer

Squamous cell carcinoma of the esophagus and the hypopharynx are both associated with smoking and alcohol intake. Therefore, it is not surprising that 1% to 8% of the patients with head and neck cancer also have esophageal cancer or will develop it at a later stage.[18] The risk of esophageal cancer is increased by a factor 3 to 10 in patients with head and neck cancer.

ADENOCARCINOMA

Gastroesophageal Reflux Disease

A direct association between reflux and adenocarcinomas rather than the presumed sequence of reflux disease leading to Barrett's esophagus and this condition leading to adenocarcinoma was found by Lagergren and coworkers.[19] The esophageal adenocarcinoma risk was 7.7 times increased in persons with heartburn and acid reflux occurring at least once per week. For those with severe symptoms for 20 years or longer, the risk was 43.5 times increased for esophageal adenocarcinoma but only 4.4 times increased for adenocarcinoma of the gastric cardia. There was no correlation with squamous cell carcinoma.

Barrett's Esophagus

Barrett's esophagus is a disorder of the distal esophagus in which the squamous epithelium is replaced by metaplastic columnar epithelium. Barrett's esophagus is a complication of long-standing gastroesophageal reflux disease[20] (GERD). A causal relationship between Barrett's esophagus and the development of esophageal adenocarcinoma has been established.

In older reports, the risk of esophageal adenocarcinoma in long segment Barrett's esophagus was 30 to 52 times greater than that of the normal population. Cancer was diagnosed at a median rate of about 1 per 100 patient-years of follow-up. However, these reports were often based on a short period of follow-up with the possibility of including prevalent cancers as incidence cases and, therefore, may have overestimated the cancer risk. More recent reports with longer follow-up found 1 cancer per 180 to 200 patients-years of follow-up.[21] The prevalence of Barrett's esophagus in consecutive patients undergoing endoscopy for any clinical indication varies between 0.3% and 2%.[22] Several studies have shown that Barrett's esophagus is a disorder of whites and is mainly found in Western Europe. The distribution between males and females is 2.5 to 4:1.[9]

Clinical Features

Local effects of esophageal carcinoma include dysphagia, odynophagia, coughing, regurgitation, vomiting, or a vague discomfort in the back of the throat. At the time of diagnosis, tumor length is mostly more than 4 cm and patients often have already 6 weeks to 4 months of dysphagia with accompanying substantial weight loss.[23] Dysphagia is not diagnostic of an esophageal malignancy, because there are also nonmalignant diseases presenting with dysphagia such as achalasia or peptic strictures caused by reflux esophagitis. In case of rapidly progressive dysphagia and weight loss the suspicion of a malignant tumor of the esophagus or gastroesophageal junction is, however, high. Unfortunately, dysphagia is a late symptom of an esophageal malignancy. Only when a mass lesion has come to a critical size will it impair the passage of food. At this time, the tumor has usually invaded the deeper layers of the esophageal wall, making the prognosis poor.

Odynophagia is seen in nearly 50% of esophageal cancer patients. The pain associated with this tumor is usually steady, dull, and substernal and occasionally radiates to the back. Severe or persistent pain is a poor prognostic sign and suggests mediastinal extension of the tumor; pain radiating to the back suggests perineural compression of spinal nerves.

Patients with esophageal cancer may develop iron deficiency anemia. Bleeding from the tumor is usually a slow, occult process. Sometimes patients experience frank hemorrhage. Rarely, when the tumor invades the aorta or another major vessel, the patient may exsanguinate, a not infrequent cause of death.[23]

Physical examination is usually not helpful for a diagnosis at an early stage. When present, weight loss, lymphadenopathy, and hepa-

tomegaly are signs of an advanced stage of disease. Lymphadenopathy can be detected in the cervical, supraclavicular, and axillary node areas, in order of decreasing frequency. Auscultation and percussion may reveal findings of tracheoesophageal fistula, pneumonia, pleural effusions, or a cavitary lung abscess.

There is no evidence that, with the increase in the incidence of adenocarcinoma of the esophagus and gastroesophageal junction in Western countries, the presentation of esophageal cancer has changed; however, more than 50% of patients present with inoperable disease. Reasons for inoperable cancer include the presence of distant metastatic disease in 65%, locally advanced cancer in 20%, or severe comorbidity precluding the possibility of surgery in 15% of patients.

Pathology

SQUAMOUS CELL CARCINOMA

Twenty-four percent of squamous cell carcinomas occur in the upper third, 47% in the middle third, and 29% in the lower third of the esophagus.[24]

It has been demonstrated that squamous cell carcinoma develops from low-grade/high-grade dysplasia to intraepithelial carcinoma and finally invasive esophageal carcinoma. Endoscopic follow-up in 327 Chinese patients with high-grade dysplasia showed that squamous cell carcinoma was diagnosed at a median rate of 4 cases per 100 patient-years of follow-up.[25]

Unfortunately, less than 10% of patients with squamous cell carcinoma in the Western world are diagnosed at an early stage.[24]

ADENOCARCINOMA

Adenocarcinomas of the esophagus and gastroesophageal junction are located in the distal esophagus and proximal stomach.

There is also clear evidence for a dysplasia-carcinoma sequence in Barrett's esophagus, whereby Barrett's esophagus without dysplasia progresses to low-grade dysplasia, high-grade dysplasia, and ultimately carcinoma.[26] Progression from Barrett's esophagus without dysplasia to low-grade dysplasia occurs in 12% to 18% of patients and from low-grade to high-grade dysplasia or adenocarcinoma in 10% to 25% of patients during a mean follow-up of 3.0 to 5.2 years.[27,28] Progression from high-grade dysplasia to carcinoma occurs in 17% to 66% of patients in a time interval ranging from 0.75 to 9 years.[29,30] The distribution of the grade of dysplasia in transversal studies of patients with Barrett's esophagus is 80% no dysplasia, 18% low-grade dysplasia, and 2% high-grade dysplasia/adenocarcinoma.[31,32]

Given the dismal prognosis among patients with symptomatic esophageal cancer, guidelines from the American College of Gastroenterology[33] recommend endoscopic surveillance of patients with Barrett's esophagus in an attempt to prevent death from adenocarcinoma. Retrospective studies have found that patients whose esophageal adenocarcinoma was detected in a surveillance program presented at an earlier stage had better 5-year survival rates than patients who initially presented with cancer.[34] However, a recent study showed that less than 5% of patients who presented with esophageal adenocarcinoma actually underwent endoscopic surveillance.[35]

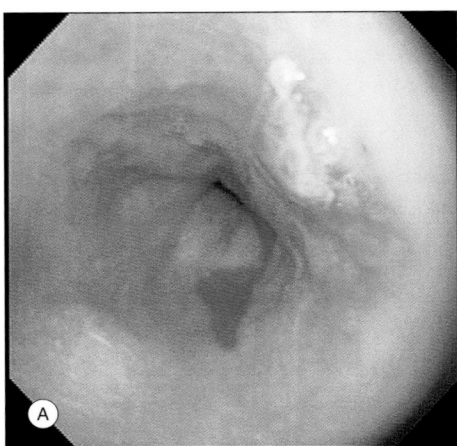 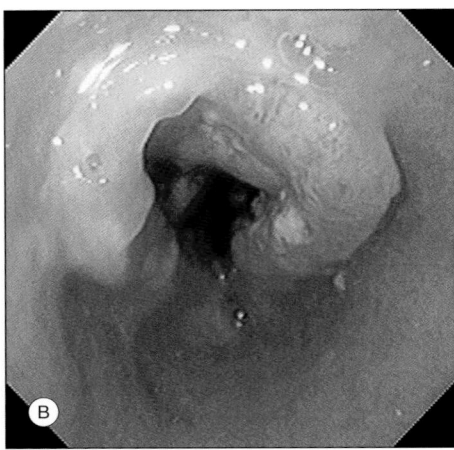

Figure 30–2. Endoscopic view of (A) early and (B) advanced esophageal cancer.

Esophageal cancer grows by intraesophageal spread, direct extension, and lymphatic and hematogenous metastases. The tumor typically invades adjacent structures, and lymph node metastases range from 40% to 70%. Because esophageal lymph node flow is bidirectional, sites of nodal metastases are many. Distant metastases, particularly to liver, lung, and bone, are present in 25% to 30% of patients at diagnosis.[36]

Early esophageal carcinomas are usually slightly elevated, coarse, or polypoid with denuded epithelium at endoscopy (Fig. 30–2A). Gross appearance of squamous cell carcinomas and adenocarcinomas are practically indistinguishable. Adenocarcinoma of the esophagus, especially in its early stage, can be distinguished from squamous cell carcinoma by the presence of Barrett's esophagus. However, if esophageal adenocarcinoma is advanced, it is often impossible to detect Barrett's esophagus because the tumor has presumably overgrown its precursor. The macroscopic features of advanced esophageal cancers can be ulcerative, stenotic, polypoid, or a combination of these (see Fig. 30–2B).

Differential Diagnosis

The differential diagnosis of esophageal carcinoma includes peptic stricture, Schatzki ring, corrosive stricture, and achalasia. Rarely, one should consider bronchogenic carcinoma invading the esophagus.

Patients with a peptic stricture usually have a long history of pyrosis; substantial weight loss, however, is uncommon. Endoscopy reveals a smooth lining of the stricture with inflammation and scar tissue on histologic examination. Peptic strictures are not as common in the Western world as early, probably because of the widespread use of proton pump inhibitors. A Schatzki ring is characterized by the presence of a ringlike stricture at the gastroesophageal junction. If a Schatzki ring is leading to symptoms of odynophagia or dysphagia, it is often associated with GERD and/or a hiatal hernia. The occurrence of symptoms is usually intermittent. A stricture that is the result of a prior corrosive insult is usually short and irregular and sometimes multiple strictures are present in the esophagus. Dysphagia is intermittent and nonprogressive in patients with achalasia. In most patients with achalasia, the esophagus is somewhat elongated and dilated.

Treatment

The preferred treatment for esophageal cancer is a surgical resection. Resection of the esophagus with a gastric pull-up or a colonic interposition is, however, an invasive procedure with significant morbidity and mortality.[36] A discussion on the different surgical techniques, long-term results, and complications following surgery is beyond the scope of this chapter.

In the past decade, endoscopic methods have been developed to remove early cancers in the esophagus via a nonsurgical endoscopic way. Indications and contraindications for endoscopic treatment of early esophageal cancer are discussed in Chapter 29.

In patients with inoperable esophageal cancer resulting from locally advanced or metastatic disease or severe comorbidity, restoration of the ability to eat is the only possible therapy. Because most of these patients live no longer than 6 months, the aim of palliative treatment is to relief dysphagia rapidly with minimal or no hospital stay, to maintain swallowing during life, and to avoid serious complications. It is important to realize that treatment of incurable esophageal cancer should be individualized and based on tumor stage, medical condition and performance status of the patient, and the patient's personal wishes. In addition, both the available expertise and equipment and the results of prospective, randomized studies should be taken into consideration.

There are a variety of palliative techniques currently available (Table 30–1). The main options can be divided into nonendoscopic modalities, of which radiation therapy is most commonly used, and endoscopic procedures, of which the placement of a self-expanding metal stent to relieve obstruction resulting from a malignant stricture in the esophagus is the most frequently used technique. In the following, some of the endoscopic procedures for palliation of malignant dysphagia are discussed.

SELF-EXPANDING METAL STENTS

Placement of a self-expanding metal stent is a frequently used method for palliation of malignant dysphagia. Since 1990, more then 75 studies have been published on the outcome of metal stent placement for palliation of malignant dysphagia and esophageal fistulas (summarized in references 37 to 39).

Table 30-1. Palliative Modalities for Esophageal Carcinoma
Modality
Nonendoscopic Techniques
Surgery
Radiation therapy
External beam radiotherapy
Intraluminal radiotherapy (brachytherapy)
Chemotherapy
Endoscopic Techniques
Stent placement
Self-expanding metal stents
Laser therapy
Thermal (Nd:YAG)
Photodynamic therapy
Dilation
Electrocoagulation (BICAP probe)
Chemical injection therapy
Nutritional support
Nasoenteric feeding tube
Percutaneous endoscopic gastrostomy (PEG)
BICAP, bipolar electrocoagulation probe.

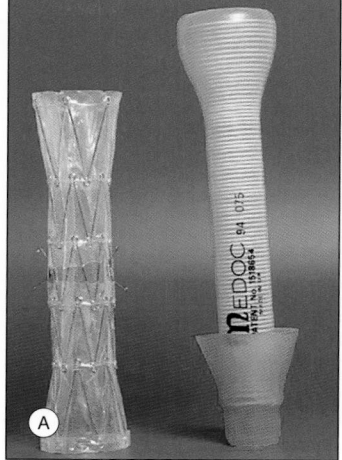

Figure 30-3. *A,* Example of a covered self-expanding metal stent (Z stent) *(left)* and a prosthetic tube (Celestin Pulsion Tube) *(right). B,* Note the difference in internal diameter.

Metal Stents Versus Rigid Plastic Endoprosthetics

Metal stents have several advantages over the previously used prosthetic tubes. They can be inserted with a minimum of dilatation because the diameter of the delivery catheters is only 7 to 11 mm (Fig. 30–3). After placement of a metal stent, the stent expands gradually, which potentially decreases the occurrence of subsequent procedure-related complications. Moreover, the larger lumen achieved from 16 to 24 mm and the flexibility of metal stents should improve the quality of swallowing compared with prosthetic tubes. An advantage of prosthetic tubes is the low cost compared with the rather expensive metal stents.

Several randomized trials have been performed comparing metal stents with prosthetic tubes.[40-45] In summary, these studies have demonstrated that placement of a metal stent is associated with fewer procedure-related complications than placement of a prosthetic tube.[41,42,44,45] In one study, metal stents were also more effective in improving dysphagia.[43] Studies on cost effectiveness have shown that, despite the high initial purchase costs, metal stents were more cost effective than prosthetic tubes because of a shorter hospital stay for procedures for stent-related complications.[40,41,43,46]

Covered Versus Uncovered Metal Stents

A disadvantage of the first-generation metal stents, which were not covered by a membrane, was that tumor ingrowth through the wire mesh of the stent led to recurrent dysphagia in 20% to 30% of patients. Stents were subsequently developed with a membrane to prevent tumor ingrowth. Covered metal stents are now the most commonly used type, to avoid ingrowth of tumor through the metal mesh. It has been suggested that covered metal stents are more likely to migrate than bare metal stents, especially in the region of the distal esophagus and gastric cardia. This increased risk of migration could then be caused by insufficient anchoring of the stent cover to the esophageal wall.

In a prospective randomized trial by Vakil and coworkers,[47] covered and uncovered Ultraflex stents were compared in 62

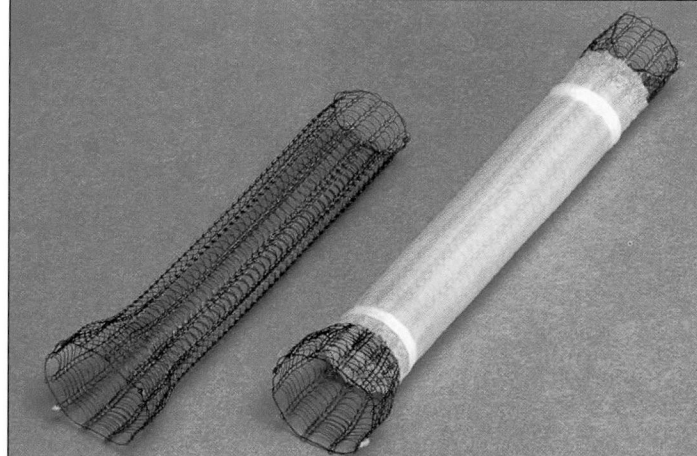

Figure 30-4. An uncovered *(left)* and a covered *(right)* versions of the Ultraflex stent.

patients with obstructing tumors at the gastroesophageal junction (Fig. 30–4). Tumor ingrowth or overgrowth was significantly more common in the uncovered stent group (9/30, 30%) than in the covered stent group (1/32, 3%). Stent migration was, however, not different between the two treatment groups (uncovered stent: 2/30 [7%] vs. covered stent 4/32 [12%]).

It can be concluded that covered stents give better long-term palliation of malignant dysphagia than uncovered stents.

Currently Available Covered Metal Stents

Special stent characteristics are needed for the effective palliation of tumors of the distal esophagus and the gastric cardia. The ideal stent would have the following characteristics:

- It would have a large internal diameter to ensure the passage of a normal diet.

Table 30–2. Characteristics of the Presently Available Types of Metal Stents

Stent Type	Covering	Length (cm)	Diameter (mm)	Release System	Radial Force	Degree of Shortening	Flexibility	Stent Material	Manufacturer
Ultraflex	Partial	10, 12, 15	18, 22	Proximal/distal	Low	30%–40%	High	Nitinol	Boston Scientific, Watertown, MA
Wallstent II	Partial	10, 15	20	Distal	High	20%–30%	Moderate	Cobalt-based alloy	Boston Scientific, Watertown, MA
Flamingo Wallstent	Partial	12 14	prox:24/dist:16 prox:30/dist:20	Distal	High	20%–30%	Moderate	Cobalt-based alloy	Boston Scientific, Watertown, MA
Z-stent	Full	6, 8, 10, 12, 14	18, 22	Distal	Moderate	None	Low	Stainless steel	Wilson Cook, Winston-Salem, NC
Choo-stent	Full	8, 11, 14, 17	18	Distal	Moderate	None	Low	Nitinol	M.I. Tech, Seoul, Korea

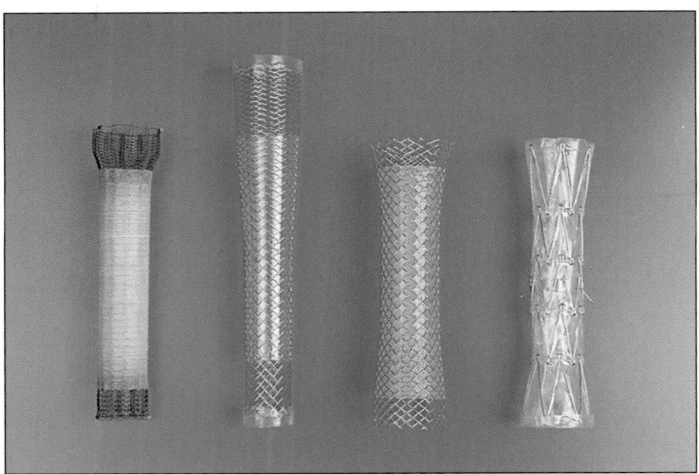

Figure 30–5. Currently available covered metal stents, from left to right: Ultraflex stent, Flamingo Wallstent, Wallstent II, and Z-stent. The Song stent is not shown but has a design that is comparable to the Z-stent.

- It would be flexible and nontraumatic while still achieving full expansion.
- It would not migrate, yet could be repositioned or removed if necessary.

Although this ideal stent does not exist, all available covered metal stents do meet some of these criteria (Table 30–2).

The Ultraflex stent (Boston Scientific, Natick, MA) consists of a knitted nitinol wire tube, and the covered version has a polyurethane layer that covers the midsection of the stent extending to within 1.5 cm of either end of the stent (Fig. 30–5). The stent has a proximal flare with two sizes: 28 mm (distal diameter 23 mm) and 23 mm (distal diameter 18 mm). The stent has an easy-to-use delivery system and can be deployed gradually either from the proximal to the distal end or vice versa. It is important to remember that the degree of shortening after stent placement is 30% to 40%. The radial force of the Ultraflex stent is the lowest amongst the currently available metal stents. Partial obstruction of the stent can occur in stents that are sharply angulated after passing across the gastroesophageal junction.

The Wallstent (Boston Scientific) is made from cobalt-based alloy and is formed into a tubular mesh and is available in two designs: the Wallstent II and the Flamingo Wallstent (available only in Europe) (see Fig. 30–5). Stents of both designs are easy to place. The Wallstent can be repositioned during the procedure because recapture remains possible while less than 50% of the stent is expanded. The degree of shortening after placement is about 20% to 30%. Both designs have a high radial force. The Wallstent II flares to 28 mm at both ends with a diameter of 20 mm at its midsection. It is covered with a silicone polymer layer, with 2 cm left exposed at the proximal and distal ends. The Flamingo Wallstent is designed specifically for use in the distal esophagus and gastric cardia; however, it can be used in the midesophagus as well. This conical shaped stent is designed to apply a variable radial force throughout the length of the stent to address anatomic differences in the distal esophagus and gastric cardia. The stent is covered by a polyurethane layer, which is applied from the inside, extending to within 2 cm of either end of the stent. Both a large-diameter stent (proximal and distal diameters 30 and 20 mm) and a small-diameter stent (proximal and distal diameters 24 and 16 mm) are available. The Wallstent II and the Flamingo Wallstent are both very pliable, with the diameter of the stent being unaffected even when angulated.

The Z-stent (Wilson-Cook Medical, Winston-Salem, NC) with a Korean modification, the Choo stent (M.I. Tech, Seoul, Korea), consists of a wide Z-mesh of stainless steel covered over its entire length by a polyethylene layer (see Fig. 30–5). The Z-stent is available with (Europe) or without (United States) fixing barbs in the central segment. The introduction system is more complex than that of the (Flamingo) Wallstent and the Ultraflex stent. The stent does not shorten on release and is the least flexible of the currently available metal stents. The Z-stent flares to 25 mm at both ends with a diameter at its midsection of either 18 mm or 22 mm.

Comparison of Different Types of Metal Stents

There are two retrospective studies and two prospective randomized trials comparing the outcome of different types of metal stents.

A retrospective study, including 96 patients, compared the uncovered Ultraflex, covered and uncovered versions of the Wallstent, and the covered Z-stent. No differences were found in outcome and complication rate between the different stent types.[48] Covered versions of the Wallstent and the Ultraflex stent were compared in another retrospective study, showing a higher early complication rate with the Wallstent but a higher reintervention rate with the Ultraflex stent.[49]

In a prospective trial, 100 patients were randomized to one of three types of covered metal stents, the Ultraflex stent, the Flamingo Wallstent, and the Z-stent. There were no significant differences in dysphagia improvement and the occurrence of complications or recurrent dysphagia, although there was a trend toward more complication with the Z-stent (Ultraflex stent: 8/34 (24%), Flamingo Wallstent: 6/33 (18%), and Z stent: 12/33 (36%); $p = .23$).[50] In another prospective trial, the Ultraflex stent and the Flamingo Wallstent were compared in patients with distal esophageal cancer. The two stent types were equally effective in the palliation of dysphagia in this patient group, and the complication rate associated with their use was also comparable (Ultraflex stent: 7/31 [23%] and Flamingo Wallstent: 5/22 [23%]).[51]

From these data, it can be concluded that there are only minor differences between the most commonly used stent types. The choice of stent should, therefore, be determined by the location and the anatomy of the malignant stricture on the one hand and the specific characteristics of the stent on the other hand (see Table 30–2).

Metal Stents for Tumors of the Gastroesophageal Junction

Because the incidence of adenocarcinoma of the distal esophagus is rising rapidly,[4,5] it is likely that the deployment of metal stents across the gastroesophageal junction will increase.

However, stent placement for tumors of the distal esophagus and gastroesophageal junction constitutes a particular problem. In comparison with stents placed for more proximally located esophageal tumors, these procedures provide inferior palliation and have higher complication rates.[52]

Migration is more likely with stents placed across the gastroesophageal junction than with stents placed for more proximally located tumors, because the distal part of the stent projects freely into the fundus of the stomach and this part cannot fix itself to the wall. Moreover, an increased incidence of bleeding has been reported for stents placed across the gastroesophageal junction. This could be the result of two factors. First, the lower end of the stent may erode the posterior wall of the stomach, resulting in ulceration and subsequent bleeding. Second, a stent that passes the gastro-

esophageal junction cannot remain straight because of the normal anatomical angle between the esophagus and the gastric cardia. Consequently, the asymmetric lateral force exerted by the proximal part of the stent on the esophagus above the tumor results in an increased rate of pressure-related complications, such as ulceration and subsequent bleeding. This angulation of the stent may also explain the finding that the improvement in quality of swallowing is inferior with stents across the gastroesophageal junction compared with that for more proximally placed stents. Finally, patients with a stent crossing the gastroesophageal junction often experience symptoms of reflux of gastric fluid into the esophagus.

How can migration of metal stents be prevented? The design of the stent may play a role in reducing stent migration. The Flamingo Wallstent has a shift in the braiding angle between the proximal and the distal part of the stent, which allows the distal part of the stent to stretch in response to peristalsis. Both the Ultraflex stent and both versions of the Wallstent are available with proximal and distal uncovered segments that allow the normal mucosa above and below the tumor to project into the stent lumen. The European version of the Z-stent is available with metal barbs on the outside of the stent to anchor it to the tumor. The most significant change in stent design is probably the introduction of stents with a greater proximal flange diameter (30 mm for the Flamingo Wallstent, 28 mm for the Wallstent II, and 28 mm for the Ultraflex stent), and/or an increase in the diameter at the midportion of the stent (22 mm for the Z-stent). A prospective, randomized trial, between covered versions of the Ultraflex stent, the Flamingo Wallstent, and the Z-stent, demonstrated that 12 of 13 migrations occurred with small-diameter stents placed for tumors in the midesophagus. In contrast, only one migration occurred with large-diameter stents placed for tumors of the distal esophagus and gastric cardia (Fig. 30–6).[50] No differences in complications were noted between small-diameter stents in the esophagus and large-diameter stents in the gastric cardia in this trial. On the other hand, in a prospective study comparing 19 large-diameter Flamingo Wallstents with 21 small-diameter Flamingo Wallstents placed for a malignant stricture at various levels in the esophagus, five of the seven complications (mainly perforation and bleeding) occurred with large-diameter stents ($p = .07$).[53] This suggests that the extra pressure exerted by large-diameter stents on the esophageal wall may cause more complications. Therefore, widespread use of the larger diameter stents for tumors above the level of the cardia should wait until

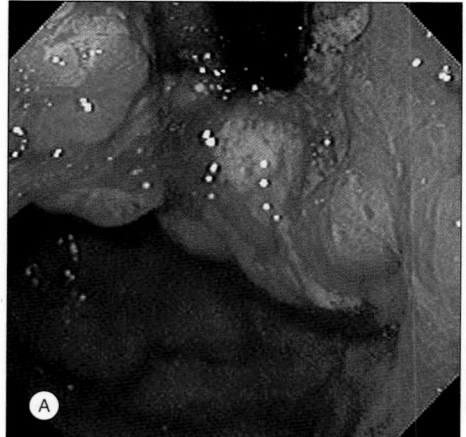
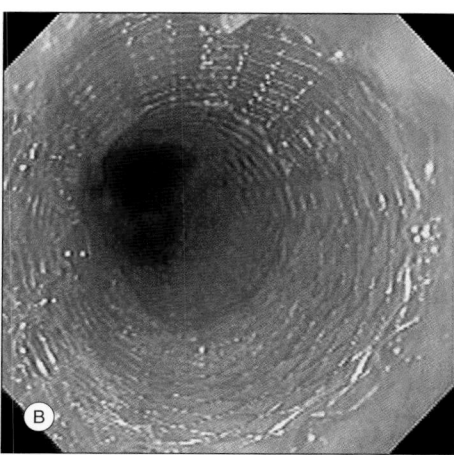

Figure 30–6. Placement of a metal stent to palliate dysphagia caused by carcinoma of the gastric cardia. *A,* Endoscopic view, taken from the stomach, of the tumor. *B,* A large-diameter Flamingo Wallstent was placed. Note that the stent is adjacent to the esophageal wall immediately following placement.

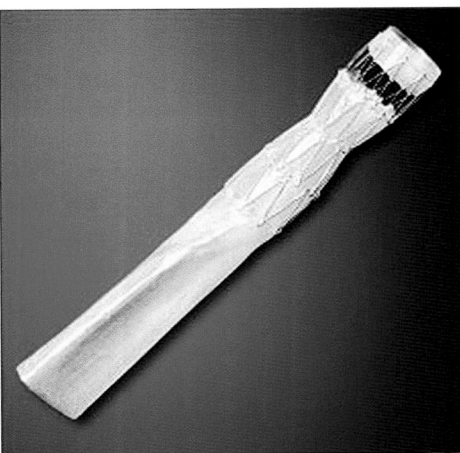

Figure 30–7. The Z-stent with antireflux valve for the prevention of gastro-esophageal reflux.

comparative studies have proven their greater efficacy without compromising safety.

A modification that has recently become available is the Z-stent with a "windsock"-type valve to prevent gastroesophageal reflux, especially when the stent extends below the lower esophageal sphincter[54] (Fig. 30–7). There is as yet only limited experience with this antireflux stent.

To summarize, the currently available evidence suggests that it is probably best to use either the Wallstent (Wallstent II or Flamingo Wallstent) or the Ultraflex stent for tumors at the distal esophagus and cardia. Stent migration, especially if placed across the gastro-esophageal junction, will be reduced, if not eliminated, by using stents of a greater diameter. However, further studies are needed to establish the balance between the advantages of less stent migration and the possible increased risk of complications associated with large-diameter stents. The addition of an antireflux valve may be effective in decreasing gastroesophageal reflux in patients needing stents that extend into the gastric cavity.

Description of the Stent Placement Procedure

Placement of metal stents is usually done with the patient under sedation (Video 30–1). When fluoroscopy is used, the proximal and distal margins of the stricture are demarcated endoscopically by skin markers, tissue clips, or the intramucosal injection of a radiopaque contrast agent. Injection of the lipid-soluble contrast agent lipiodol results in a persistent mark. Accurate placement of the Ultraflex stent is also possible under endoscopic guidance without the aid of fluoroscopy. This can be done by the application of an external marker at the level of the proximal radiopaque marker on the stent, allowing the stent to be placed under direct endoscopic visualization.[55] This technique is at present only feasible with the Ultraflex stent release system. Finally, metal stents can be placed under fluoroscopy alone, without the use of endoscopy.[56]

In most institutions, a stenotic malignant stricture is dilated to a diameter of 9 to 10 mm before stent placement, to measure stricture length and to accurately place a guide wire. Dilation may increase the risk of perforation; however, there is no consensus on whether one or more dilation sessions preceding stent placement will lower this

risk of perforation. The next step is to place a stiff guidewire, for example, a 0.038-inch Savary guidewire, across the stricture into the stomach or, preferably, the duodenum and withdraw the endoscope.

A premounted Ultraflex stent or Wallstent (either a Wallstent II or a Flamingo Wallstent) is then advanced over the wire. The Wallstent is deployed by retracting the constraining outer sheath, whereas the Ultraflex stent is deployed by pulling a ring attached to the suture ring.

As a first step in inserting Z-stents, the Z-stent must be back-loaded into its delivery catheter. Then, the Z-stent is deployed by removing a peel-away sheath and pulling a compression catheter back over a pushing catheter.

Both the Ultraflex stent and the Wallstent shorten during expansion, which must be taken into consideration when positioning the introduction system. To prevent migration of the stent on release from the introduction system, the system should not be advanced too far distally. An advantage of the Wallstent is that it can be recaptured (if not expanded more than 50%) by advancing the constraining sheath and repositioning the entire stent. The stent should be 2 to 4 cm longer than the stricture to allow for a 1 to 2 cm extension above and below the proximal and distal tumor margins. For stents placed across the gastroesophageal junction, stent length is guided by the rule that the proximal covered portion of the stent should lie at least 1 to 2 cm above the tumor margin, whereas the distal covered portion should not overlap the tumor margin by more than 1 cm, to prevent ulceration of the posterior wall of the stomach by the distal end of the stent. There is no objection to confirm endoscopically that the upper end of the stent is in place proximal to the upper tumor margin. However, the endoscope should not be passed through the stent to avoid stent dislodgment from friction with the endoscope.

Thanks to their mechanical properties, both the Ultraflex stent and the Wallstent, whether fully expanded, partially expanded, unexpanded, or migrated after release from the introduction system, are easier to reposition or remove endoscopically than the Z-stent. This is done by pulling at the upper rim of the Wallstent or at the lasso attached inside the proximal flange of the Ultraflex stent, causing the stent's radial diameter to decrease. Stent expansion can best be confirmed by a chest radiograph.

Currently, stent placement may be an outpatient procedure. Placement of a metal stent takes about 15 to 20 minutes in experienced hands.

Variations and Unusual Situations
Fistula Formation

Progressive esophageal carcinoma can infiltrate into surrounding tissue with subsequent development of a fistula, most commonly between the esophagus and the respiratory tract (i.e., the trachea or bronchi) and occasionally between the aorta, the mediastinum, or pleura. In a series of 1943 patients with esophageal cancer, it was found that 5% of patients developed a fistula over time. In the same publication, it was reported that 0.2% of 5714 patients with bronchogenic carcinoma developed an esophagorespiratory fistula.[57] Apart from tumor invasion, fistulas may also develop secondary to radiation and/or laser therapy. Finally, pressure necrosis caused by the proximal edge of a previously placed metal stent sporadically

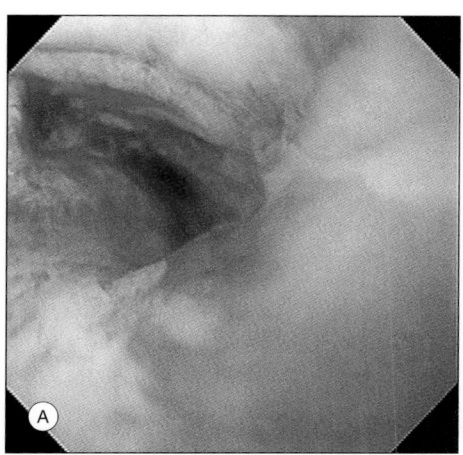
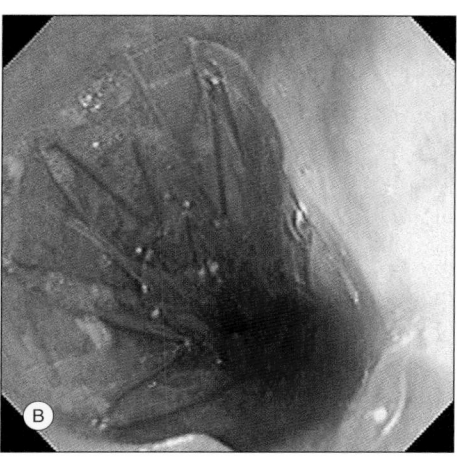

Figure 30–8. Endoscopic view of *(A)* an esophago-respiratory fistula in the midesophagus caused by an infiltrating esophageal carcinoma. *B,* A Z-stent was placed to seal the fistula.

results in the development of a fistula. Treatment of a fistula should be expeditious, as fistula formation is a life-threatening complication, which in case of esophagorespiratory fistulas can result in serious pulmonary infections from aspiration pneumonia.

Esophagorespiratory Fistulas A history of repeated coughing associated with drinking, eating, or both, in combination with worsening dysphagia and dyspnea is highly suggestive of an esophagorespiratory fistula. The fistula can be diagnosed radiographically and/or endoscopically. Curative resection is usually impossible because of the coexistent presence of an advanced tumor stage, whereas palliative surgery (including a combination of cervical esophagostomy and feeding gastrostomy or a bypass operation) is associated with a mortality rate up to 50%.[58]

Until the early 1990s, cuffed prosthetic tubes were used to seal esophagorespiratory fistulas.[59] These devices were effective in 60% to 90% of patients. Cuffed endoprostheses were, however, associated with a complication rate that was comparable to conventional prosthetic tubes. An additional disadvantage of these devices was that the cuff of the tube migrated through the lumen of the fistula into the bronchial lumen in up to 25% of patients, causing acute respiratory distress.[60]

Presently, endoscopic placement of a covered self-expanding metal stent is the treatment of choice for an esophagorespiratory fistula (Fig. 30–8). Several retrospective and prospective series have been published reporting the outcome of endoscopic placement of a covered metal stent for this indication[61–71] (Table 30–3). In most of these publications, complete sealing of the fistula was established in more than 90% of patients with no clear difference between the presently available covered metal stents. Moreover, dysphagia scores improved significantly in most patients. The complication rate (early and late complications) varied between 10% and 30%, whereas recurrent dysphagia was mainly the result of tumor overgrowth or stent migration. The median survival was poor and varied between 35 and 148 days, which undoubtedly reflects the advanced tumor stage in most of these patients.

In conclusion, symptoms from an esophagorespiratory fistula can successfully be treated with one of the presently available covered metal stents. Although studies have not been performed, it can be anticipated that the quality of life in patients with an esophago-respiratory fistula will be improved with this treatment.

Parallel Stent Placement In some patients with esophageal cancers that infiltrate into the trachea, dysphagia and dyspnea may develop simultaneously. Moreover, in some cases, placement of a metal stent in the esophagus to seal a fistula can result in obstruction of the trachea and acute dyspnea. In these circumstances, it is important to consider the placement of a stent in the trachea and/or bronchi in combination with an esophageal stent. Tracheobronchial stents that are placed in the trachea are usually uncovered and embed themselves in the mucosa of the respiratory tract.[72] The reason that these stents are uncovered is that this decreases the risk that the stent will migrate distally leading to acute respiratory distress. Another indication for parallel stent placement is a tracheoesophageal fistula near the upper esophageal sphincter. Esophageal stents alone are not always effective in sealing the fistula at this location. One may then consider placing a covered stent in the proximal part of the trachea in addition to a proximal esophageal stent.[73] Not surprisingly, complications occur more commonly with parallel stent placement. Fatal complications such as perforation and bleeding have been described, which was caused by tissue necrosis resulting from the high radial force exercised by both stents.[74]

Proximal Esophageal Carcinoma

Endoscopic intubation has traditionally been contraindicated for malignancies within a few centimeters below the upper esophageal sphincter because of the risk of foreign body sensation, tracheal compression, and proximal migration of the prosthesis into the hypopharynx. However, positive results have been reported in studies on palliation of proximal lesions with metal stents.[70,75–78] The results are summarized in Table 30–4. Stent characteristics are an important consideration in the treatment of cancers that are located in the cervical esophagus. In our opinion, metal stents should not shorten or minimally shorten to ensure exact placement just below the upper esophageal sphincter. Second, the stent should be covered, to prevent tumor ingrowth and to seal any coexisting fistula. Finally, the stent should have a body diameter of 18 mm or less and be flexible to avoid globus sensation and tracheal compression. Although this stent is not available, the Ultraflex stent and the Wallstent II are probably the stent types that are most preferable in this situation (Fig. 30–9). Other methods for the palliation of malignant strictures near the upper esophageal sphincter include radiation therapy if the patient is fit enough to

Table 30–3. Studies Reporting the Outcome of Placement of a Covered Metal Stent for Esophagorespiratory Fistulas

Author/Year (Ref.)	No. of Patients	Stent Type	Complete Sealing	Dysphagia Improvement	Early Major Complications	Late Major Complications	Recurrent Dysphagia	Median Survival
Do et al., 1993 (61)	8	Z-stent	8/8 100%	? → 1.3	0	1/8 13%	0	Mean: ~10 weeks
Bethge et al., 1995 (62)	6	Wallstent	6/6 100%	4 → 1.2	1/6 17%	1/6 17%	0	64 days
Kozarek et al., 1996* (63)	11	Z-stent	8/11 73%	?	?	?	?	?
Morgan et al., 1997 (64)	39	Wallstent (n = 36) Z-stent (n = 3)	37/39 95% (10 patients 2 stents)	3 → 1	6/39 15%	5/39 13%	4/39 10%	81 days
Nelson et al., 1997 (65)	8	Wall stent	7/8 (88%)	5.0 → 3.2 (1–6 scale)	0	?	5/8 63%	59 days
Low et al., 1998 (66)	13 (plastic)	W. Cook/Atkinson (n = 13)	10/13 77%	3.2 → 0.2	7/13 54%	?	3/13 23%	1.1 months
	12 (metal)	Wallstent/Z-stent (n = 12)	11/12 92%	2.5 → 0.8	2/12 17%		5/12 42%	3.1 months
May et al., 1998 (67)	11	Z-stent	10/11 91%	3 → 0.6	0	1/11 9%	1/11 9%	121 days
Raijman et al., 1998 (68)	13	Wallstent	13/13 100%	?	?	?	?	?
Dumonceau et al., 1999 (69)	17	Wallstent/Z-stent (n = 5)	1/5 20%	2 → 0	2/17 12%	1/17 6%	6/17 35%	98 days
		Ultraflex (n = 12)	12/12 100%	3.1 →0.6				146 days
Siersema, et al., 2001 (70)	16	Z-stent (n = 11) Ultraflex (n = 5)	16/16 100% (2 patients 2 stents)	?	1/16 6%	2/16 13%	6/16 38%	58 days
Abadal et al., 2001 (71)	15	Z-stent (n = 4) Wallstent (n = 9) Ultraflex (n = 2)	14/15 93%	3.4 → ?	0	2/15 13%	3/15 20%	148 days

Publication on metal stent placement for malignant dysphagia and fistulas; outcome data of fistulas not separately presented.

Table 30–4. Placement of a Metal Stent for Proximal Esophageal Carcinoma

Author/Year (Ref.)	No. of Patients	Stent Type	Dysphagia Improvement	Complications (Early and Late) and Recurrent Dysphagia
Bethge et al., 1997 (75)	8	Ultraflex n = 2 Wallstent n = 6	3.5 → 1.6	1/8 distal stent migration 1/8 tumor overgrowth 2/8 fistula formation
Conio et al., 1999 (76)	6	Ultraflex	3.5 → 0.8	3/6 insufficient expansion of stent 1/6 cervical pain 4/6 tumor overgrowth
Macdonald et al., 2000 (77)	22	Metal stent	3 → 2	2/22 technical failure 4/22 foreign body sensation
Siersema et al., 2001 (70)	10	Ultraflex n = 6 Z-stent n = 4	3.6 → 1.9	1/10 insufficient expansion of stent 1/10 perforation 1/10 aspiration pneumonia 2/10 tumor overgrowth
Profili et al., 2002 (78)	10	Ultraflex	3.6 → 1.5	2/10 interference with swallowing 1/10 too distally placed stent 1/10 food impaction 1/10 stent twisting 4/10 tumor ingrowth

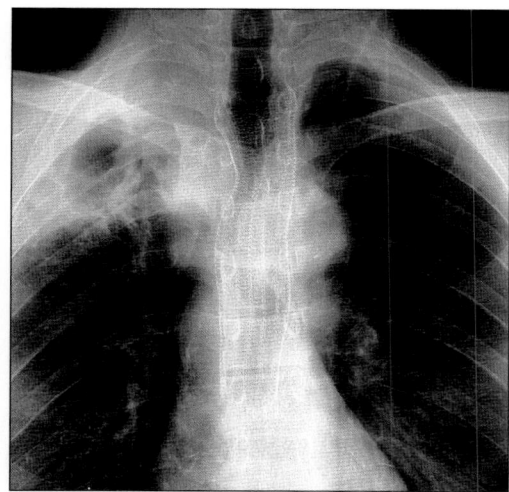

Figure 30–9. Chest radiograph showing an Ultraflex stent, which was placed for inoperable cancer, located 2 cm distal to the upper esophageal sphincter.

undergo a more intensive treatment or laser treatment. In case of failure of these treatments or a poor general condition of the patient, a nasoduodenal feeding tube or placement of a percutaneous endoscopic gastrostomy (PEG) are the safest options.

Extrinsic Compression

A specific problem is dysphagia caused by extraesophageal malignancies that compress the esophagus. The origins of these malignancies are diverse, ranging from bronchogenic carcinoma to metastatic breast cancer, although most are caused by pulmonary malignancies. These patients are mostly not suitable for curative therapy and need

rapid relief of dysphagia to improve the nutritional status. Palliative treatment options include radiation therapy, chemotherapy, and metal stent placement. The effect of radiotherapy and chemotherapy is often too slow in these patients with only a short life expectancy.

The experience with metal stents for palliation of dysphagia resulting from extrinsic compression is limited (Table 30–5).[79–82] In a nonrandomized study, the safety and efficacy of stents for extrinsic compression ($n = 24$) was compared with stents for primary esophageal malignancies ($n = 21$).[81] Dysphagia scores improved significantly in both groups; however, the improvement was greater in patients with primary esophageal tumors ($p = .012$). The frequency of complications was comparable between both groups. Two other studies described the results of metal stent placement for extrinsic compression in 13 and 17 patients, respectively.[79,82] These studies both concluded that dysphagia caused by extraesophageal malignancies can safely and effectively be treated with metal stents. In addition, there is no evidence that uncovered metals stents give better results than covered stents (Fig. 30–10). A characteristic of extrinsic compression is that the lesion is often irregular and noncircumferential. In addition, there is no tumor tissue in the esophageal lumen to fix the stent. Despite these nonfavorable tumor characteristics, stent migration rate in these studies was comparable to that of stents for primary esophageal carcinoma.

Recurrent Dysphagia after Previous Surgery

Surgery is generally considered to offer the best chance for cure in patients with esophageal carcinoma; however, locoregional or systemic tumor recurrence occurs often in these patients.

A few studies have been published in which metal stents were used to improve dysphagia resulting from tumor recurrence after esophagectomy.[70,83–85] In our institution, 21 patients with recurrent

Table 30–5. Metal Stent Placement for Palliation of Dysphagia Caused by Extrinsic Compression of Extraesophageal Malignancies

Author/Year (Ref.)	No. of Patients	Tumor	Stent Type	Mean Dysphagia Improvement	Early Complications	Late Complications	Mean Survival
De Gregorio et al., 1996 (79)	13	Lung $n = 9$ Breast $n = 2$ Laryngeal $n = 1$ Colon $n = 1$	Cov. Z-stent	$3.2 \rightarrow 0.6$	4/13 Chest pain $n = 3$ Migration $n = 1$	2/13 Migration $n = 1$ Benign stricture $n = 1$	2.2 months
Kozarek et al., 1997* (80)	10	Lung $n = 6$ Mesothelioma $n = 1$ Lymphoma $n = 1$ Mediastinal metastases $n = 2$	Cov. Z-stent	?	?	?	?
Bethge et al., 1998 (81)	24	Lung $n = 8$ Recurrent gastric cancer $n = 10$ Breast $n = 3$ Recurrent laryngeal cancer $n = 2$ Thyroid $n = 1$	Uncov. Wallstent $n = 21$ Uncov. Ultraflex $n = 2$ Part. cov. Ultraflex $n = 1$	$3.5 \rightarrow 1.6$	2/24 Migration $n = 1$ Stridor $n = 1$	7/24 Fistula $n = 1$ Tumor ingrowth $n = 3$ Food bolus impaction $n = 3$	3 months
Gupta et al., 1999 (82)	17	Lung $n = 12$ Breast $n = 1$ Larynx $n = 1$ Meloma $n = 1$ Renal cell carcinoma $n = 1$ Unknown $n = 1$	Uncov. $n = 13$ Cov. $n = 6$ (19 in 17 patients placed)	$3.1 \rightarrow 1.3$	7/17 Pneumonia $n = 1$ Migration during placement $n = 1$ Chest pain $n = 5$	4/17 Tumor overgrowth $n = 2$ Food bolus impaction $n = 2$	2.1 months

Part of a larger patient group, no separate data are given.
Cov., covered; Part. cov., partially covered; Uncov., uncovered.

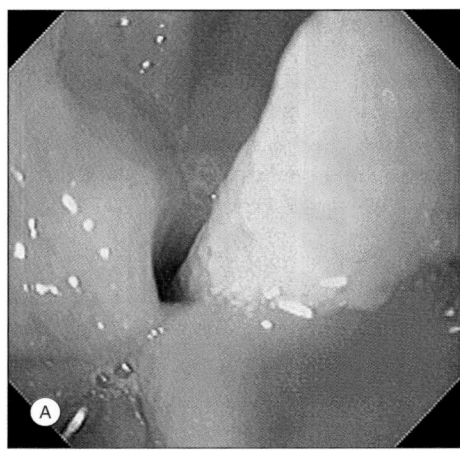
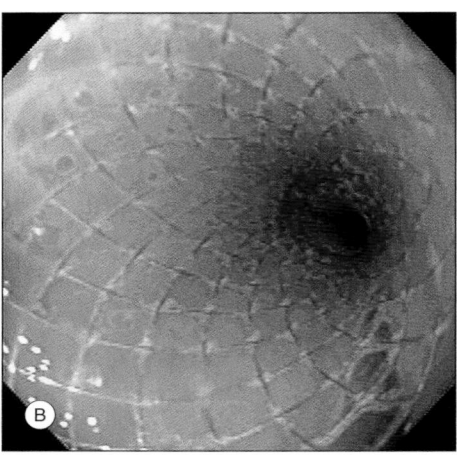

Figure 30–10. Endoscopic view of *(A)* extrinsic compression in the midesophagus resulting from metastatic breast cancer. *B,* A Flamingo Wallstent was placed. Note that the stent has not completely deployed at 1 day after stent placement.

tumor after esophagectomy were treated, of which in 10 patients the tumor was located in the proximal part of the gastric tube interposition (including the anastomosis) and in 11 patients in the mid- or distal portion of the interposition. In most of these patients, a large-diameter metal stent was used to effectively cover the dilated lumen of the neo-esophagus. Dysphagia improved from a mean of 3.2 (only able to drink fluids) to 1.5 (dysphagia for some solids) and median survival was 63 days. Major complications occurred in 4 (19%) patients, consisting of bleeding ($n = 2$), fistula formation ($n = 1$), and severe pain ($n = 1$). Recurrent dysphagia occurred in 8/21 (38%) patients and was due to tumor overgrowth.[70]

Dysphagia caused by recurrent tumor after partial or total gastrectomy presents specific problems because there is often complete luminal obstruction and/or sharp angulation of the luminal axis. We treated 10 patients with recurrent carcinoma after partial ($n = 4$) or total ($n = 6$) gastrectomy with a small diameter Ultraflex stent or Z-stent. Dysphagia improved substantially and median survival was 64 days. Complications occurred in 2/10 patients and consisted of perforation ($n = 1$) and bleeding ($n = 1$).[70]

In summary, although the experience is limited, metal stent placement can be used for the palliation of dysphagia from tumor recurrence after esophagectomy or gastrectomy.

Effect of Prior Radiation and/or Chemotherapy on Outcome of Stent Placement

It has been suggested that prior radiation and/or chemotherapy increases the risk of complications after self-expanding metal stent placement in patients with inoperable cancer of the esophagus and gastroesophageal junction; however, this relationship is controversial. Nine studies addressed this question.[44,83,86–92] Four studies showed an increased risk for the development of complications after prior chemoradiation therapy,[44,83,86,91] whereas five studies did not found such a relationship.[87–90,92] The results of these studies are summarized in Table 30–6. In a study with 200 prospectively followed patients from our institution, it was concluded that the incidence of complications and the outcome after self-expanding metal stent placement for carcinoma of the esophagus and gastroesophageal junction were not affected by prior radiation and/or chemotherapy. Only retrosternal pain occurred more frequently in patients who had undergone prior chemoradiation.[92]

Stent placement in patients with prior radiation and/or chemotherapy is probably as safe as in patients who had not undergone prior treatment; however, patients should be informed that there is an increased risk of chest pain after stent placement.

Limitations and Success Rate

The technical success rate for placement of metal stents is close to 100%. Limitations to successful placement include severe pain during placement; extensive tumor growth in the stomach; failure of the stent to release from the introduction system, as can occur with Ultraflex stents; and immediate stent migration because the stent has been placed too deeply. Almost all patients experience improvement of dysphagia and this is sustained unless and until a specific complication arises. The dysphagia grade usually improves from a mean of 3 (able to eat liquids only) to a mean of 1 (able to eat most solid foods), with no difference in effectiveness between the Ultraflex stent, the Wallstent, and the Z-stent. Some patients with advanced cancer at the distal esophagus or gastric cardia will fail to experience relief of dysphagia following technically successful stent placement because of other (unidentified) sites of intestinal obstruction, often peritoneal carcinomatosis, or gastric paresis resulting from neural involvement by the tumor. These patients usually require feeding through a nasoenteral tube or, preferably, a PEG.

Complications and Recurrent Dysphagia

Procedure-related complications after metal stent placement mainly consist of perforation, aspiration pneumonia, fever, bleeding, and severe pain and occur in 5% to 15% of patients. Delayed complications and recurrent dysphagia following stent placement include hemorrhage, fistula formation, gastroesophageal reflux, stent migration, tumor overgrowth or ingrowth, and food-bolus obstruction and occur in 30% to 45% of patients. Minor complications are mild retrosternal pain and gastroesophageal reflux, which are reported by 10% to 20% of patients.

Perforation

Perforation occasionally occurs after stent placement, sometimes following dilation of an obstructing tumor to facilitate placement of the stent. Perforation is treated with conservative treatment including nasoduodenal tube feeding, nil per mouth, and antibiotics. Placement of a second stent to seal the perforation might be necessary.

Table 30–6. Effect of Prior Radiation and/or Chemotherapy (RTCT) on the Outcome of Stent Placement

Author/Year (Ref.)	No. of Patients with and without Prior RTCT	Type of Study	Type of Stent	Life-Threatening Complications (Prior RTCT vs. No Treatment)
Increased Risk				
Kinsman et al., 1996 (86)	Prior RTCT: n = 22 No treatment: n = 37	Retrospective	Z-stent	8/22 (36%) vs. 1/37 (3%)
Bethge et al., 1996 (83)	Prior RTCT: n = 13 Prior surgery: n = 4 No controls	Prospective	Wallstent	3/17 (18%)
Siersema 1998 (44)	Prior RTCT: n = 28 No treatment: n = 47	Prospective	Prosthetic tubes n = 38 Z-stent n = 37	12/28 (43%) vs. 8/47 (17%)*
Muto et al., 2001 (91)	Prior RTCT: n = 13 No controls	Retrospective	Ultraflex n = 9 Wallstent n = 2 Z-stent n = 2	7/13 (54%)
No Difference				
Kozarek et al., 1996 (87)	Prior RTCT: n = 27 No treatment: n = 11	Retrospective	Z-stent n = 26 Wallstent n = 10 Esophacoil/Ultraflex n = 2	1/27 (4%) vs. 1/11 (9%)
Nelson et al., 1997 (88)	Prior RTCT: n = 6 No/other treatment: n = 15	Retrospective	Wallstent	0/6 (0%)
Raijman et al., 1997 (89)	Prior RTCT: n = 39 No treatment: n = 21	Retrospective	Wallstent	3/39 (8%) vs. 2/21 (10%)
Bartelsman et al., 2000 (90)	Prior RTCT: n = 54 No treatment: n = 99	Retrospective	Song stent	No relation (not further specified)
Homs et al., (92)	Prior RTCT: n = 49 No treatment: n = 151	Prospective	Z-stent n = 70 Wallstent n = 71 Ultraflex stent n = 59	14/49 (29%) vs. 31/151 (21%)†

Device-related complications, most complications from prosthetic tubes (8/12 and 6/8).
†*Stent-related complications.*

Fever

Fever that occurs without evidence of aspiration pneumonia or perforation is most likely to be caused by a mechanical effect of the stent on the tumor, possibly by releasing toxic products from the tumor. Patients usually recover uneventfully after prophylactic treatment with antibiotics.

Hemorrhage

Hemorrhage, including hematemesis and melena, mostly occurs as a late complication of stent placement. It is often unsure whether this is due to the stent placement or progression of the disease. During endoscopy, the precise source of blood loss is often not discovered. Treatment consists of blood transfusions in case of severe hemorrhage, in combination with a short course of external beam radiotherapy (e.g., five sessions of 4 Gy).

Retrosternal Pain

(Transient) retrosternal pain is a frequently reported complication after stent placement, particularly after prior radiation and/or chemotherapy. Golder and coworkers[93] recorded the daily opioid analgesic requirements of 52 patients from 3 days before until 7 days after stent placement. Twenty-six (50%) patients needed opioid analgesia for chest pain within 48 hours of the procedure compared with 11 (21.2%) patients before stent placement ($p < .001$).

In other studies, figures ranging from 5% to 50% for chest pain after stent placement have been reported.[44,81,90,94] In our experience, mild retrosternal pain after stent placement can effectively be treated with acetaminophen or one of the nonsteroidal anti-inflammatory drugs. Only rarely, new opioid analgesics are indicated for a period of a few days to a maximum of 14 days. Severe pain after stent placement occurs in 1% to 2% of patients. In these patients, removal of the stent is sometimes indicated to relieve the pain.

Gastroesophageal Reflux

Gastroesophageal reflux is a common problem among patients with distally located tumors where the distal end of the stent is placed through the lower esophageal sphincter. As a preventive measure, proton pump inhibitors are prescribed to many patients with a stent passing the lower esophageal sphincter. Recently, metal stents with an antireflux mechanism have been developed to prevent gastroesophageal reflux. At the distal end of the stent, the cover of the stent is extended beyond the lower metal cage to form a "wind sock"-type valve (see Fig. 30–7). The first results of this antireflux stent were reported in a study including 11 patients. The authors concluded that the antireflux stent was effective in preventing gastroesophageal reflux.[54] A randomized study comparing antireflux stents (25 patients) with standard open stents (25 patients) showed that 3/25 (12%) versus 24/25 (96%) patients, respectively, reported

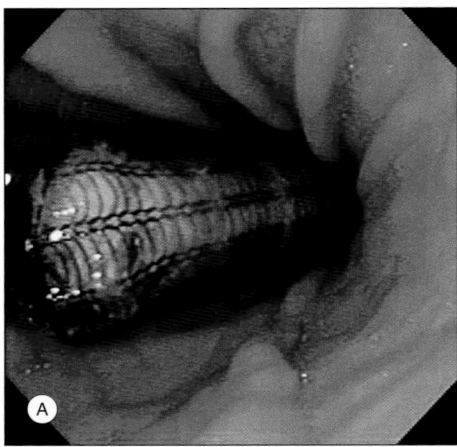
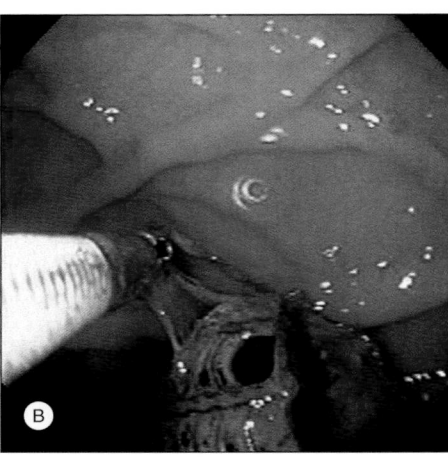

Figure 30–11. Migration of an Ultraflex stent that occurred 2 months after placement. *A,* The migrated Ultraflex stent in the stomach. *B,* The lasso inside the proximal flange of the Ultraflex stent was grasped with a forceps. Subsequently, the stent was repositioned in the distal esophagus.

symptoms of gastroesophageal reflux ($p < .001$), whereas no differences in dysphagia improvement, complications, or reintervention rate were found.[95] These results are promising and will likely reduce the prescription rate of proton pump inhibitors in these patients.

Stent Migration

Stent migration is a common complication with reported incidence rates ranging from 5% to 15%.[50,90,96,97] The most frequently used method for reintervention after stent migration is placement of a second stent. In certain cases, repositioning of a distally migrated stent is possible with the use of a forceps or a snare[98] or by placing the endoscope in a retroflexed position.[99] We do not recommend using the latter technique, because esophageal perforation may occur. In addition, this method may result in damage to the endoscope.[100] If repeated episodes of stent migration occur in the same patient, other palliative treatments such as brachytherapy or laser therapy need to be considered.

From our own experience and from others,[97] it is important to realize that stent retrieval after migration is often not indicated, because perforation or obstruction of the digestive tract is uncommon. If a migrated stent causes obstruction of the pylorus or symptoms of pain, or if successful placement of a second stent is impossible, then stent removal should be performed. Several methods of stent retrieval have been described. In case of an Ultraflex stent, this can be done by collapsing the stent with a grasping forceps using the purse string suture attached to the proximal flange of the stent (Fig. 30–11). The most frequently described method, however, is by decreasing the diameter of the stent with a polypectomy snare at 2 to 5 cm from the proximal end of the stent.[101,102] Others have used a biopsy forceps in combination with a snare, which requires passage of a double-channel therapeutic endoscope.[103] Apart from a snare, one can use Endoloops, which may have a greater constriction force than a polypectomy snare.[104]

Tumor Overgrowth

Tumor overgrowth is the result of progression of the malignancy rather than a failure or a complication of the stent. It affects both ends of the stent at a similar rate and is seen in 10% to 20% of patients after a mean period of 2 to 4 months after stent placement (Fig. 30–12).[48,50,94,96] Tumor overgrowth can be prevented, at least temporarily, by inserting a stent that is, after expansion, approxi-

mately 2 to 4 cm longer than the malignant stricture to allow for a 1 to 2 cm extension above the proximal and below the distal end of the tumor.

The most frequently used method for the treatment of tumor overgrowth is placement of a second stent. In addition, laser therapy or argon plasma coagulation can be used to debulk the tumor. In case of placement of a second stent, the stent is placed proximal or distal to the previously placed stent with a part of the second stent overlapping the primary stent (Fig. 30–13).

In our experience, recurrent dysphagia resulting from non-malignant obstructive tissue, such as granulation tissue, reactive hyperplasia, and fibrosis at the proximal or distal end of the stent is an unlikely event. Mayoral and colleagues[105] have reported this cause of recurrent dysphagia in more than 30% of their patients at a mean interval of 22 weeks after stent placement. We observed the development of this nonmalignant tissue in a number of patients undergoing endoscopy for reasons other than recurrent dysphagia. It was predominantly found at the proximal end of the stent but did not appear to cause dysphagia.

Other Causes of Recurrent Dysphagia

Food bolus obstruction occurs fairly common with reported rates of 5% to 15% (Fig. 30–14).[48,50,94,96] It can successfully be treated by

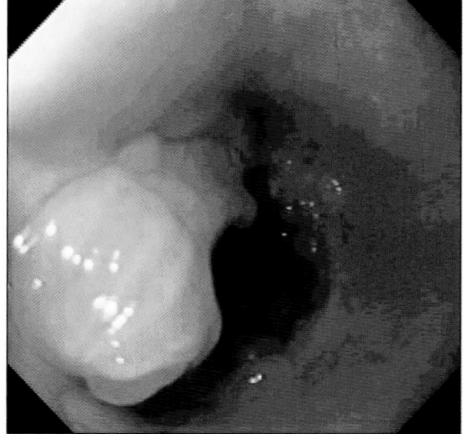

Figure 30–12. Endoscopic view of tumor overgrowth at the proximal end of the stent.

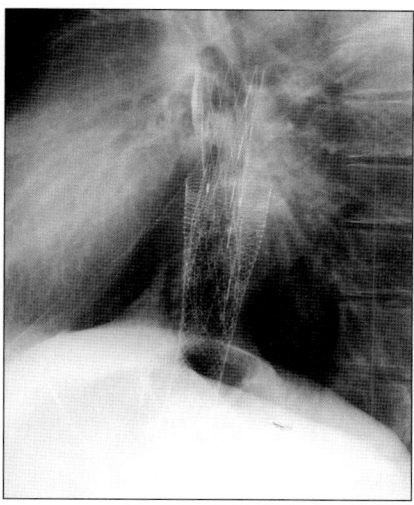

Figure 30–13. A plain radiograph of the abdomen, demonstrating a Flamingo Wallstent in the distal esophagus and proximal stomach placed for inoperable carcinoma of the gastric cardia. After 3 months, a Z-stent was placed for tumor overgrowth at the proximal end of the stent.

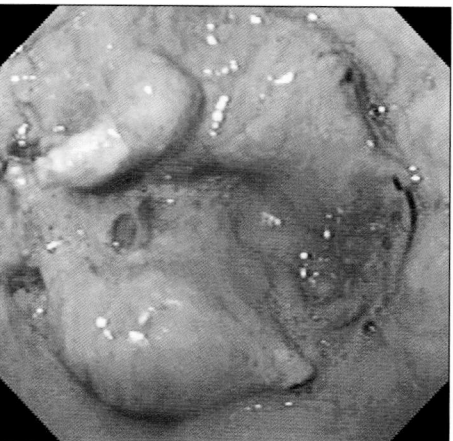

Figure 30–14. Endoscopic view of food bolus obstruction in the lumen of the stent.

endoscopic stent clearance. However, care should be taken to prevent the stent from migrating while doing this. Prevention of food bolus obstruction can be achieved by providing eating instruction, including chewing the food thoroughly and drinking carbonated drinks during and after a meal.

LASER THERAPY
Thermal Therapy

Treatment of obstructing esophageal cancer with the high-power neodymium yttrium-aluminum-garnet (Nd:YAG) laser was first described in 1982.[106] Over the years, the procedure has become an accepted and effective method for palliation of malignant dysphagia. Early investigators used a prograde technique; currently a retrograde approach with initial dilation is preferred.[107] Tumors that are relatively short (<6 cm), nonangulated, exophytic, noncircumferential, and located in the mid- or distal esophagus are most amenable to laser ablation. Laser treatment is unsafe for submucosal tumors, those causing extrinsic compression, and angulated tumors, whereas circumferential tumors are vulnerable to stricture formation. In various studies, technical success was around 90%, whereas functional success was approximately 70%.[108–112] Depending on the length of follow-up, recurrent dysphagia occurs in 40% to 60% of patients between 4 to 10 weeks after initial treatment. Therefore, patients are usually reassessed at 4 to 6 week intervals. Complications include perforation, fistula formation, hemorrhage, and sepsis in 5% to 10% of patients.

Photodynamic Therapy

Photodynamic therapy (PDT) involves the local destruction of tumor tissue by light of a specific wavelength activating a previously administered photosensitizer that is retained in malignant tissue. Porphyrin compounds, such as porfimer sodium (Photofrin), have been the most commonly used photosensitizers for the palliation of malignant dysphagia. As opposed to the thermal destruction induced by the Nd:YAG laser, the damage by PDT is initiated by a photochemical effect. PDT may be useful for long tumors, for tumors that are narrow or angulated, and for flat infiltrating tumors. The costs of PDT are high because of the high costs of a special laser unit and the costs of the photosensitizer Photofrin.[113]

The most frequent complication is prolonged skin photosensitivity. Patients must avoid direct sunlight for at least 6 weeks after treatment. Major complications, including perforation, fistula formation, and strictures have been reported in up to 30% of patients. Other side effects include fever, chest pain, and pleural effusion, probably secondary to a transient, local inflammation, but these side effects are usually mild.[114–118]

Clinical experience with PDT for palliation of malignant dysphagia is limited to a few centers worldwide.[114–116] One or two treatment sessions are usually required for an adequate tumor response. PDT is considered technically easier and less operator dependent than Nd:YAG laser ablation. Two randomized trials have compared PDT with Nd:YAG laser therapy.[117,118] Lightdale and coworkers[117] found equivalent improvements in dysphagia score with a trend toward an improved response with PDT in tumors located in the upper and lower third of the esophagus, in long (>10 cm) tumors, and in patients who had prior chemotherapy and/or radiotherapy. Complications were similar in both treatment groups, but side effects (i.e., skin photosensitivity, nausea, and transient fever) occurred more often after PDT. Heier and colleagues[118] found an improved performance status and a longer duration of response (84 vs. 57 days) after PDT compared with laser therapy, with similar functional results and complications rates.

Because of the high costs of the treatment, the side effects, and the necessity of repeated treatments every 8 weeks, PDT as a sole treatment is not an optimal treatment for palliation of malignant dysphagia.

Laser Therapy in Combination with Brachytherapy

It has been suggested that thermal laser therapy in combination with brachytherapy (intraluminal radiotherapy) should be able to increase the long-term effectiveness of laser therapy. First, laser therapy should be applied to reduce the tumor bulk, followed by a single treatment of brachytherapy with a maximum dose of 10 Gy, leading to a sustained effect of laser therapy with a better improvement of the dysphagia score and a reduction in the need for repeated treatment sessions. In four nonrandomized studies, laser therapy (Nd:YAG) plus brachytherapy was studied prospectively and proved to be both safe and effective.[119–122] Laser therapy plus brachytherapy was compared with laser therapy alone in two prospective, randomized trials in 39 and 22 patients, respectively.[123,124] Both these studies showed a prolonged dysphagia-free interval after the combination of laser and brachytherapy; however, this did not result in a difference in survival between the two treatment groups.

Laser Therapy versus Stent Placement

A few nonrandomized studies[125,126] and two randomized trials compared laser treatment with stent placement.[112,127] Both nonrandomized trials concluded that laser therapy was a safer treatment than stent placement with a similar effectiveness. Dallal and coworkers[112] compared laser treatment (mostly Nd:YAG) with metal stents in 65 patients with esophageal carcinoma in a randomized trial. Median survival was longer for the laser group, but relief of dysphagia was disappointing in both groups with similar complication rates and costs. Adam and colleagues[127] randomized 60 patients to laser therapy, uncovered stent placement, or covered stent placement and concluded that stent placement was more effective for the palliation of malignant dysphagia.

OTHER ENDOSCOPIC METHODS

Dilation

Dilation can relieve dysphagia temporarily, but it provides often palliation for only a few days to 2 weeks. It is frequently used to allow access through the tumor for different forms of palliative treatments such as metal stent placement or laser therapy. Dilation is a simple and cheap method; however, complications, including perforation and hemorrhage, are not uncommon.[128–130]

Some authors advocate gradual dilation of the malignant stricture over several sessions before stent placement to reduce the risk of complications.[42,130] The most commonly used dilators are polyvinyl wire-guided bougies including the tapered dilators (Savary), the rubber dilators (Maloney), and the through-the-scope hydrostatic balloons. There is as yet no study comparing these dilators in patients with malignant strictures.

Because dilation as a sole therapy must be repeated at frequent intervals, it should only be performed in extremely ill patients with a very short lifespan.

Chemical Injection Therapy

Chemical injection therapy for the treatment of malignant dysphagia is an inexpensive alternative requiring no special equipment. Ethanol or polidocanol in aliquots of 0.5 to 1 mL is injected into the tumor, leading to tumor necrosis within several days after therapy. Exophytic tumors are most amenable to injection therapy, whereas firm and fibrotic tumors (after radiotherapy) prove difficult to inject. Studies on injection therapy for malignant dysphagia are limited.[131–134] Dysphagia score improved from 3 (liquids only) to 1 (some difficulties with solid foods). Complications are rare; only

fistula formation ($n = 2$), perforation ($n = 1$), and mediastinitis ($n = 1$) have been reported.[132,133] In general, two sessions were necessary to obtain a maximum effect and retreatment was necessary at 4 to 5 week intervals. A comparative study in 34 patients between injection therapy with polidocanol and Nd:YAG laser therapy concluded that both techniques were safe and equally effectively for the palliation of malignant dysphagia.[132]

NUTRITIONAL SUPPORT

In case of failure of different palliative therapies or if other palliative modalities are technically not possible, nutritional support to maintain an adequate calorie intake should be considered. The overall condition and the prognosis of the patient are important factors to take into consideration before nutritional support is offered to the patient. Placement of a nasoenteral feeding tube is the easiest and least invasive feeding method; however, for patients with a longer life expectancy, placement of a PEG/percutaneous endoscopic jejunostomy (PEJ) is preferred. Rarely, central venous alimentation is indicated for maintaining or restoring an adequate nutritional status.[135]

Placement of a PEG using the classic pull method through a preexisting esophageal stent or in the presence of a malignant tumor can be problematic. In these cases, PEG placement without endoscopy using a nasogastric tube with gastric insufflation, fluoroscopic monitoring, and a direct percutaneous catheter insertion technique (push method) should be considered.[136] Adler and coworkers[137] described the results of nine patients undergoing classic PEG placement after stent placement and reported a good functional result and only one stent migration following PEG placement (11%).

Quality of Life

To evaluate the effectiveness of a palliative treatment modality, it is not only important to assess functional outcome and complications but also to assess the outcome from the perspective of patients, particularly quality of life. The aim of palliative treatment of esophageal cancer is to relieve dysphagia with minimal morbidity and mortality and maximum quality of life.[138] Unfortunately, data on quality of life after palliative treatment for esophageal carcinoma are scarce. Validated measures that can be used to assess quality of life before and after treatment are the oncology-specific European Organization for Research and Treatment of Cancer (EORTC) QLQ-C30 questionnaire[139] and the esophageal carcinoma specific EORTC OES-24 questionnaire.[140]

O'Hanlon and colleagues[141] investigated quality of life at 6 and 16 weeks after treatment in 43 patients undergoing intubation or radiation therapy. Although the dysphagia score improved significantly after treatment, none of the other parameters assessed were significantly improved at 16 weeks after treatment. Barr and coworkers[108] assessed quality of life after palliative Nd:YAG laser treatment for malignant dysphagia in 40 patients at monthly intervals. The linear analogue self-assessment (LASA) questionnaire, assessing 25 items on physical condition, psychological effects, and social interactions and a physician's assessment using a quality of life (QL) index consisting of a structured interview on specific items were performed. The patient swallowing ability, the items on the LASA questionnaire, and the QL-index were all improved at some time after laser therapy. Blazeby and colleagues[142] assessed quality of life among 37 patients after palliative treatment (intubation $n = 30$ or palliative radiation or chemotherapy $n = 7$) and compared these with patients undergoing surgery for esophageal cancer, using the EORTC QLQ C-30 questionnaire at 3-month intervals. Patients with palliative treatment reported worse baseline quality of life scores compared with patients undergoing surgery. However, following palliative treatment, most aspects of quality of life from the EORTC QLQ-C30 were maintained until death.

These studies indicate that more data are necessary on quality of life after palliative treatments and that comparisons between different palliative treatments are needed. The EORTC OES-24 questionnaire addresses issues that are relevant to patients undergoing palliative treatment for esophageal carcinoma and is, therefore, probably a worthwhile tool in combination with the EORTC QLQ-C30 questionnaire and the dysphagia score for assessing quality of life after palliative treatment for malignant dysphagia.

Future Trends

The presently available endoscopic treatments for the palliation of malignant dysphagia are, as yet, not optimal in achieving fast and sustained dysphagia relief with minimal morbidity and mortality. Metal stents are reasonably effective in improving dysphagia; however, the complication rate and number of reinterventions necessary for recurrent dysphagia are still too high. The disadvantage of laser treatment is the need for retreatment every 4 to 6 weeks, and expertise and expensive equipment is needed to perform the procedure. Combination therapies might increase the efficacy of treatments but will likely increase the period of initial hospital stay and/or the frequency of hospital visits. Randomized controlled trials are warranted to compare different treatment modalities or to compare combination modalities with monotherapies, with special reference to dysphagia relief, complications, quality of life after treatment, and costs.

New types of stents are currently being developed and include biodegradable stents, stents with a radioactive coating, and drug-eluting stents. Biodegradable stents have been developed for benign stenoses[143,144]; however, a possible application could be the initial treatment of dysphagia in patients undergoing palliative chemotherapy. Because results of chemotherapy for this indication are improving,[145] stent migration is more likely to occur in patients with a good response to chemotherapy.

The incorporation of beta-emitting agents and cytotoxic agents in esophageal stents may increase the efficacy of stents, particularly in the prevention of (recurrent) tumor overgrowth at both ends of the stent. Clinical experience has been obtained with radioactive stents and drug-eluting stents in coronary arteries of humans. For the esophagus, only experience with animal models is available. In healthy dogs, the radioactive stent caused fibrosis with radiation damage to the normal esophagus, but no serious complications, such as perforation or fistula formation, occurred.[146] The safety and efficacy of radioactive and drug-eluting stents in malignant strictures in the esophagus need to be further evaluated in clinical trials.

REFERENCES

1. Parkin DM, Bray FI, Devesa SS: Cancer burden in the year 2000. The global picture. Eur J Cancer 37:4–66, 2001.
2. Pisani P, Parkin DM, Bray F, Ferlay J: Estimates of the worldwide mortality from 25 cancers in 1990. Int J Cancer 83:18–29, 1999.
3. Polednak AP: Trends in survival for both histologic types of esophageal cancer in US surveillance, epidemiology and end results areas. Int J Cancer 105:98–100, 2003.
4. Pera M, Cameron AJ, Trastek VF, et al: Increasing incidence of adenocarcinoma of the esophagus and esophagogastric junction. Gastroenterology 104:510–513, 1993.
5. Devesa SS, Blot WJ, Fraumeni JF Jr: Changing patterns in the incidence of esophageal and gastric carcinoma in the United States. Cancer 83:2049–2053, 1998.
6. Bollschweiler E, Wolfgarten E, Gutschow C, Holscher AH: Demographic variations in the rising incidence of esophageal adenocarcinoma in white males. Cancer 92:549–555, 2001.
7. Botterweck AA, Schouten LJ, Volovics A, et al: Trends in incidence of adenocarcinoma of the oesophagus and gastric cardia in ten European countries. Int J Epidemiol 29:645–654, 2000.
8. Prach AT, MacDonald TA, Hopwood DA, Johnston DA: Increasing incidence of Barrett's oesophagus: Education, enthusiasm, or epidemiology? Lancet 350:933, 1997.
9. van den Boogert J, van Hillegersberg R, Siersema PD, et al: Barrett's oesophagus: Pathophysiology, diagnosis and management. Scand J Gastroenterol 33:449–453, 1998.
10. Blot WJ: Esophageal cancer trends and risk factors. Semin Oncol 21:403–410, 1994.
11. Cheng KK, Day NE, Duffy SW, et al: Pickled vegetables in the aetiology of oesophageal cancer in Hong Kong Chinese. Lancet 339:1314–1318, 1992.
12. Ahsan H, Neugut AI: Radiation therapy for breast cancer and increased risk for esophageal carcinoma. Ann Intern Med 128:114–117, 1998.
13. Yang CS, Wang ZY: Tea and cancer. J Natl Cancer Inst 85:1038–1049, 1993.
14. Cooper K, Taylor L, Govind S: Human papillomavirus DNA in oesophageal carcinomas in South Africa. J Pathol 175:271–277, 1995.
15. Kok TC, Nooter K, Tjong-A-Hung SP, et al: No evidence of known types of human papillomavirus in squamous cell cancer of the oesophagus in a low-risk area. Rotterdam Oesophageal Tumour Study Group. Eur J Cancer 33:1865–1868, 1997.
16. Sandler RS, Nyren O, Ekbom A, et al: The risk of esophageal cancer in patients with achalasia: A population-based study. JAMA 274:1359–1363, 1995.
17. Appelqvist P, Salmo M: Lye corrosion carcinoma of the esophagus. Cancer 45:2655–2658, 1980.
18. Cooper JS, Pajak TF, Rubin P, et al: Second malignancies in patients who have head and neck cancer: Incidence, effect on survival and implications based on the RTOG experience. Int J Radiat Oncol Biol Phys 449–456, 1989.
19. Lagergren J, Bergstrom R, Lindgren A, Nyren O: Symptomatic gastroesophageal reflux as a risk factor for esophageal adenocarcinoma. N Engl J Med 340:825–831, 1999.
20. Spechler SJ: Barrett's esophagus. N Engl J Med 346:836–842, 2002.
21. van der Burgh A, Dees J, Hop WCJ, van Blankenstein M: Oesophageal cancer is an uncommon cause of death in patients with Barrett's oesophagus. Gut 39:5–8, 1996.
22. Cameron AJ: Epidemiology of Barrett's esophagus and adenocarcinoma. Dis Esophagus 15:106–108, 2002.
23. Moses FM: Squamous cell carcinoma of the esophagus. Natural history, incidence, etiology, and complications. Gastroenterol Clin North Am 20:703–716, 1991.
24. Miller C: Carcinoma of the thoracic oesophagus and cardia: A review of 405 cases. Br J Surg 49:507–522, 1962.

25. Shu YJ: Cytopathology of the esophagus: An overview of esophageal cytopathology in China. Acta Cytol 27:7–16, 1983.

26. Falk GW: Endoscopic surveillance of Barrett's esophagus: Risk stratification and cancer risk. Gastrointest Endosc 49(Part 2):S29–S34, 1999.

27. Hameeteman W, Tytgat GN, Houthoff HJ, van den Tweel JG: Barrett's esophagus: Development of dysplasia and adenocarcinoma. Gastroenterology 96:1249–1256, 1989.

28. Miros M, Kerlin P, Walker N: Only patients with dysplasia progress to adenocarcinoma in Barrett's oesophagus. Gut 32:1441–1446, 1991.

29. Weston AP, Sharma P, Topalovski M, et al: Long-term follow-up of Barrett's high-grade dysplasia. Am J Gastroenterol 95:1888–1893, 2000.

30. Schnell TG, Sontag SJ, Chejfec G, et al: Long-term nonsurgical management of Barrett's esophagus with high-grade dysplasia. Gastroenterology 120:1607–1619, 2001.

31. Katz D, Rothstein R, Schned A, et al: The development of dysplasia and adenocarcinoma during endoscopic surveillance of Barrett's esophagus. Am J Gastroenterol 93:536–541, 1998.

32. O'Connor JB, Falk GW, Richter JE: The incidence of adenocarcinoma and dysplasia in Barrett's esophagus: Report on the Cleveland Clinic Barrett's Esophagus Registry. Am J Gastroenterol 94:2037–2042, 1999.

33. Sampliner RE, and the Practice Parameters Committee of the American College of Gastroenterology: Practice guidelines in the diagnosis, surveillance, and therapy of Barrett's esophagus. Am J Gastroenterol 93:1028–1032, 1998.

34. van Sandick JW, van Lanschot JJ, Kuiken BW, et al: Impact of endoscopic biopsy surveillance of Barrett's oesophagus on pathological stage and clinical outcome of Barrett's carcinoma. Gut 43:216–222, 1998.

35. Corley DA, Levin TR, Habel LA, et al: Surveillance and survival in Barrett's adenocarcinomas: A population-based study. Gastroenterology 122:633–640, 2002.

36. Hulscher JB, van Sandick JW, de Boer AG, et al: Extended transthoracic resection compared with limited transhiatal resection for adenocarcinoma of the esophagus. N Engl J Med 347:1662–1669, 2002.

37. Ell C, May A: Self-expanding metal stents for palliation of stenosing tumors of the esophagus and cardia: A critical review. Endoscopy 29:392–398, 1997.

38. Baron TH: Expandable metal stents for the treatment of cancerous obstruction of the gastrointestinal tract. N Engl J Med 344:1681–1687, 2001.

39. Siersema PD, Marcon N, Vakil N: Metal stents for tumors of the distal esophagus and gastric cardia. Endoscopy 35:79–85, 2003.

40. O'Donnell CA, Fullarton GM, Watt E, et al: Randomized clinical trial comparing self-expanding metallic stents with plastic endoprostheses in the palliation of oesophageal cancer. Br J Surg 89:985–992, 2002.

41. Knyrim K, Wagner HJ, Bethge N, et al: A controlled trial of an expansile metal stent for palliation of esophageal obstruction due to inoperable cancer. N Engl J Med 329:1302–1307, 1993.

42. De Palma GD, di Matteo E, Romano G, et al: Plastic prosthesis versus expandable metal stents for palliation of inoperable esophageal thoracic carcinoma: A controlled prospective study. Gastrointest Endosc 43:478–482, 1996.

43. Roseveare CD, Patel P, Simmonds N, Goggin PM, et al: Metal stents improve dysphagia, nutrition and survival in malignant oesophageal stenosis: A randomized controlled trial comparing modified Gianturco Z-stents with plastic Atkinson tubes. Eur J Gastroenterol Hepatol 10:653–657, 1998.

44. Siersema PD, Hop WC, Dees J, et al: Coated self-expanding metal stents versus latex prostheses for esophagogastric cancer with special reference to prior radiation and chemotherapy: A controlled, prospective study. Gastrointest Endosc 47:113–120, 1998.

45. Sanyika C, Corr P, Haffejee A: Palliative treatment of oesophageal carcinoma: Efficacy of plastic versus self-expandable stents. S Afr Med J 89:640–643, 1999.

46. Nicholson DA, Haycox A, Kay CL, et al: The cost effectiveness of metal oesophageal stenting in malignant disease compared with conventional therapy. Clin Radiol 54:212–215, 1999.

47. Vakil N, Morris AI, Marcon N, et al: A prospective, randomized, controlled trial of covered expandable metal stents in the palliation of malignant esophageal obstruction at the gastroesophageal junction. Am J Gastroenterol 96:1791–1796, 2001.

48. May A, Hahn EG, Ell C: Self-expanding metal stents for palliation of malignant obstruction in the upper gastrointestinal tract. Comparative assessment of three stent types implemented in 96 implantations. J Clin Gastroenterol 22:261–266, 1996.

49. Schmassmann A, Meyenberger C, Knuchel J, et al: Self-expanding metal stents in malignant esophageal obstruction: A comparison between two stent types. Am J Gastroenterol 92:400–406, 1997.

50. Siersema PD, Hop WC, van Blankenstein M, et al: A comparison of 3 types of covered metal stents for the palliation of patients with dysphagia caused by esophagogastric carcinoma: A prospective, randomized study. Gastrointest Endosc 54:145–153, 2001.

51. Sabharwal T, Hamady MS, Chui S, et al: A randomized prospective comparison of the Flamingo Wallstent and Ultraflex stent for palliation of dysphagia associated with lower third oesophageal carcinoma. Gut 52:922–926, 2003.

52. Spinelli P, Cerrai FG, Ciuffi M, et al: Endoscopic stent placement for cancer of the lower esophagus and gastric cardia. Gastrointest Endosc 40:455–457, 1994.

53. Siersema PD, Hop WC, van Blankenstein M, Dees J: A new design metal stent (Flamingo stent) for palliation of malignant dysphagia: A prospective study. Gastrointest Endosc 51:139–145, 2000.

54. Dua KS, Kozarek R, Kim J, et al: Self-expanding metal esophageal stent with anti-reflux mechanism. Gastrointest Endosc 53:603–613, 2001.

55. Austin A, Khan Z, Cole AT, Freeman JG: Placement of self-expanding metallic stents without fluoroscopy. Gastrointest Endosc 54:157–159, 2001.

56. Martin DF: Endoscopy is superfluous during insertion of expandable metal stents in esophageal tumors. Gastrointest Endosc 46:98–99, 1997.

57. Martini N, Goodner JT, D'Angio GJ, Beattie EJ Jr: Tracheoesophageal fistula due to cancer. J Thorac Cardiovasc Surg 59:319–324, 1970.

58. Weigert N, Neuhaus H, Rosch T, et al: Treatment of esophago-respiratory fistulas with silicone-coated self-expanding metal stents. Gastrointest Endosc 41:490–496, 1995.

59. Hordijk ML, Dees J, van Blankenstein M: The management of malignant esophago-respiratory fistulas with a cuffed prosthesis. Endoscopy 22:241–244, 1990.

60. Rosch W, Keller C: The cuffed esophageal prosthesis: A life-threatening instrument. Endoscopy 27:214–215, 1995.

61. Do YS, Song HY, Lee BH, et al: Esophagorespiratory fistula associated with esophageal cancer: Treatment with a Gianturco stent tube. Radiology 187:673–677, 1993.

62. Bethge N, Sommer A, Vakil N: Treatment of esophageal fistulas with a new polyurethane-covered, self-expanding mesh stent: A prospective study. Am J Gastroenterol 90:2143–2146, 1995.

63. Kozarek RA, Raltz S, Brugge WR, et al: Prospective multicenter trial of esophageal Z-stent placement for malignant dysphagia and tracheoesophageal fistula. Gastrointest Endosc 44:562–567, 1996.

64. Morgan RA, Ellul JP, Denton ER, et al: Malignant esophageal fistulas and perforations: Management with plastic-covered metallic endoprostheses. Radiology 204:527–532, 1997.

65. Nelson DB, Axelrad AM, Fleischer DE, et al: Silicone-covered Wallstent prototypes for palliation of malignant esophageal obstruction and digestive-respiratory fistulas. Gastrointest Endosc 45:31–37, 1997.

66. Low DE, Kozarek RA: Comparison of conventional and wire mesh expandable prostheses and surgical bypass in patients with malignant esophagorespiratory fistulas. Ann Thorac Surg 65:919–923, 1998.

67. May A, Ell C: Palliative treatment of malignant esophagorespiratory fistulas with Gianturco-Z stents. A prospective clinical trial and

review of the literature on covered metal stents. Am J Gastroenterol 93:532–535, 1998.

68. Raijman I, Siddique I, Ajani J, Lynch P: Palliation of malignant dysphagia and fistulae with coated expandable metal stents: Experience with 101 patients. Gastrointest Endosc 48:172–179, 1998.

69. Dumonceau JM, Cremer M, Lalmand B, Deviere J: Esophageal fistula sealing: Choice of stent, practical management, and cost. Gastrointest Endosc 49:70–78, 1999.

70. Siersema PD, Schrauwen SL, van Blankenstein M, et al: Self-expanding metal stents for complicated and recurrent esophagogastric cancer. Gastrointest Endosc 54:579–586, 2001.

71. Abadal JM, Echenagusia A, Simo G, Camunez F: Treatment of malignant esophagorespiratory fistulas with covered stents. Abdom Imaging 26:565–569, 2001.

72. van den Bongard HJ, Boot H, Baas P, Taal BG: The role of parallel stent insertion in patients with esophagorespiratory fistulas. Gastrointest Endosc 55:110–115, 2002.

73. Ellul JP, Morgan R, Gold D, Dussek J, et al: Parallel self-expanding covered metal stents in the trachea and oesophagus for the palliation of complex high tracheo-oesophageal fistula. Br J Surg 83:1767–1768, 1996.

74. Binkert CA, Petersen BD: Two fatal complications after parallel tracheal-esophageal stenting. Cardiovasc Intervent Radiol 25:144–147, 2002.

75. Bethge N, Sommer A, Vakil N: A prospective trial of self-expanding metal stents in the palliation of malignant esophageal strictures near the upper esophageal sphincter. Gastrointest Endosc 45:300–303, 1997.

76. Conio M, Caroli-Bosc F, Demarquay JF, et al: Self-expanding metal stents in the palliation of neoplasms of the cervical esophagus. Hepatogastroenterology 46:272–277, 1999.

77. Macdonald S, Edwards RD, Moss JG: Patient tolerance of cervical esophageal metallic stents. J Vasc Interv Radiol 11:891–898, 2000.

78. Profili S, Meloni GB, Feo CF, et al: Self-expandable metal stents in the management of cervical oesophageal and/or hypopharyngeal strictures. Clin Radiol 57:1028–1033, 2002.

79. De Gregorio BT, Kinsman K, Katon RM, et al: Treatment of esophageal obstruction from mediastinal compressive tumor with covered, self-expanding metallic Z-stents. Gastrointest Endosc 43:483–489, 1996.

80. Kozarek RA, Raltz S, Marcon N, et al: Use of the 25 mm flanged esophageal Z stent for malignant dysphagia: A prospective multicenter trial. Gastrointest Endosc 46:156–160, 1997.

81. Bethge N, Sommer A, Vakil N: Palliation of malignant esophageal obstruction due to intrinsic and extrinsic lesions with expandable metal stents. Am J Gastroenterol 93:1829–1832, 1998.

82. Gupta NK, Boylan CE, Razzaq R, et al: Self-expanding oesophageal metal stents for the palliation of dysphagia due to extrinsic compression. Eur Radiol 9:1893–1897, 1999.

83. Bethge N, Sommer A, von Kleist D, Vakil N: A prospective trial of self-expanding metal stents in the palliation of malignant esophageal obstruction after failure of primary curative therapy. Gastrointest Endosc 44:283–286, 1996.

84. Law S, Tung PH, Chu KM, Wong J: Self-expanding metallic stents for palliation of recurrent malignant esophageal obstruction after subtotal esophagectomy for cancer. Gastrointest Endosc 50:427–436, 1999.

85. Lyburn I, Blazeby JM, Barham P, Loveday E: Palliation of malignant gastric outlet obstruction after oesophagectomy by percutaneous transthoracic placement of an expanding metal stent. Clin Radiol 56:82–83, 2001.

86. Kinsman KJ, DeGregorio BT, Katon RM, et al: Prior radiation and chemotherapy increase the risk of life-threatening complications after insertion of metallic stents for esophagogastric malignancy. Gastrointest Endosc 43:196–203, 1996.

87. Kozarek RA, Ball TJ, Brandabur JJ, et al: Expandable versus conventional esophageal prostheses: Easier insertion may not preclude subsequent stent-related problems. Gastrointest Endosc 43:204–208, 1996.

88. Nelson DB, Axelrad AM, Fleischer DE, et al: Silicone-covered Wallstent prototypes for palliation of malignant esophageal obstruction and digestive-respiratory fistulas. Gastrointest Endosc 45:31–37, 1997.

89. Raijman I, Siddique I, Lynch P: Does chemoradiation therapy increase the incidence of complications with self-expanding coated stents in the management of malignant esophageal strictures? Am J Gastroenterol 92:2192–2196, 1997.

90. Bartelsman JF, Bruno MJ, Jensema AJ, et al: Palliation of patients with esophagogastric neoplasms by insertion of a covered expandable modified Gianturco-Z endoprothesis: Experiences in 153 patients. Gastrointest Endosc 51:134–138, 2000.

91. Muto M, Ohtsu A, Miyata Y, et al: Self-expandable metallic stents for patients with recurrent esophageal carcinoma after failure of primary chemoradiotherapy. Jpn J Clin Oncol 31:270–274, 2001.

92. Homs MY, Hansen BE, van Blankenstein M, et al: Prior radiation and/or chemotherapy has no effect on the incidence of life-threatening complications and the long-term outcome of self-expanding metal stent placement for esophagogastric carcinoma. Eur J Gastroenterol Hepatol 16:163–170, 2004.

93. Golder M, Tekkis PP, Kennedy C, et al: Chest pain following oesophageal stenting for malignant dysphagia. Clin Radiol 56:202–205, 2001.

94. Cwikiel W, Tranberg KG, Cwikiel M, Lillo-Gil R: Malignant dysphagia: Palliation with esophageal stents—long-term results in 100 patients. Radiology 207:513–518, 1998.

95. Laasch HU, Marriott A, Wilbraham L, et al: Effectiveness of open versus antireflux stents for palliation of distal esophageal carcinoma and prevention of symptomatic gastroesophageal reflux. Radiology 225:359–365, 2002.

96. Christie NA, Buenaventura PO, Fernando HC, et al: Results of expandable metal stents for malignant esophageal obstruction in 100 patients: Short-term and long-term follow-up. Ann Thorac Surg 71:1797–1801, 2001.

97. De Palma GD, Iovino P, Catanzano C: Distally migrated esophageal self-expanding metal stents: Wait and see or remove? Gastrointest Endosc 53:96–98, 2001.

98. Raijman I, Marcon NE, Kandel G, et al: Repositioning of an esophageal stent after migration using a snare. Gastrointest Endosc 40:652, 1994.

99. Rosen C, Goldberg RI: Repositioning of a migrated esophageal stent using a retroflexed endoscope. Gastrointest Endosc 42:278–279, 1995.

100. Berkelhammer C, Roberts J, Steinecker G: Repositioning a migrated esophageal stent using a retroflexed endoscope: A note of caution. Gastrointest Endosc 44:632–634, 1996.

101. Noyer CM, Forohar F: A simple technique to remove migrated esophageal stents. Am J Gastroenterol 93:1595, 1998.

102. Rollhauser C, Fleischer DE: Late migration of a self-expandable metal stent and successful endoscopic management. Gastrointest Endosc 49:541–544, 1999.

103. Farkas PS, Farkas JD, Koenigs KP: An easier method to remove migrated esophageal Z-stents. Gastrointest Endosc 50:277–279, 1999.

104. Seitz U, Thonke F, Bohnacker S, et al: Endoscopic extraction of a covered esophageal Z-stent with the aid of Endoloops. Endoscopy 30:S91–92, 1998.

105. Mayoral W, Fleischer D, Salcedo J, et al: Nonmalignant obstruction is a common problem with metal stents in the treatment of esophageal cancer. Gastrointest Endosc 51:556–559, 2000.

106. Fleischer D, Kessler F, Haye O: Endoscopic Nd: YAG laser therapy for carcinoma of the esophagus: A new palliative approach. Am J Surg 143:280–283, 1982.

107. Pietrafitta JJ, Bowers GJ, Dwyer RM: Prograde versus retrograde endoscopic laser therapy for the treatment of malignant esophageal obstruction: A comparison of techniques. Lasers Surg Med 8:288–293, 1988.

108. Barr H, Krasner N: Prospective quality-of-life analysis after palliative photoablation for the treatment of malignant dysphagia. Cancer 68:1660–1664, 1991.

109. Mason RC, Bright N, McColl I: Palliation of malignant dysphagia with laser therapy: Predictability of results. Br J Surg 78:1346–1347, 1991.

110. Carter R, Smith JS, Anderson JR: Palliation of malignant dysphagia using the Nd:YAG laser. World J Surg 17:608–613, 1993.

111. Carazzone A, Bonavina L, Segalin A, et al: Endoscopic palliation of oesophageal cancer: Results of a prospective comparison of Nd:YAG laser and ethanol injection. Eur J Surg 165:351–356, 1999.

112. Dallal HJ, Smith GD, Grieve DC, et al: A randomized trial of thermal ablative therapy versus expandable metal stents in the palliative treatment of patients with esophageal carcinoma. Gastrointest Endosc 54:549–557, 2001.

113. Marcon NE: Photodynamic therapy and cancer of the esophagus. Semin Oncol 21:20–23, 1994.

114. Patrice T, Foultier MT, Yactayo S, et al: Endoscopic photodynamic therapy with hematoporphyrin derivative for primary treatment of gastrointestinal neoplasms in inoperable patients. Dig Dis Sci 35:545–552, 1990.

115. Luketich JD, Christie NA, Buenaventura PO, et al: Endoscopic photodynamic therapy for obstructing esophageal cancer: 77 cases over a 2-year period. Surg Endosc 14:653–657, 2000.

116. Moghissi K, Dixon K, Thorpe JA, et al: The role of photodynamic therapy (PDT) in inoperable oesophageal cancer. Eur J Cardiothorac Surg 17:95–100, 2000.

117. Lightdale CJ, Heier SK, Marcon NE, et al: Photodynamic therapy with porfimer sodium versus thermal ablation therapy with Nd:YAG laser for palliation of esophageal cancer: A multicenter randomized trial. Gastrointest Endosc 42:507–12, 1995.

118. Heier SK, Rothman KA, Heier LM, Rosenthal WS: Photodynamic therapy for obstructing esophageal cancer: Light dosimetry and randomized comparison with Nd:YAG laser therapy. Gastroenterology 109:63–72, 1995.

119. Bader M, Dittler HJ, Ultsch B, et al: Palliative treatment of malignant stenoses of the upper gastrointestinal tract using a combination of laser and afterloading therapy. Endoscopy 18:27–31, 1986.

120. Renwick P, Whitton V, Moghissi K: Combined endoscopic laser therapy and brachytherapy for palliation of oesophageal carcinoma: A pilot study. Gut 33:435–438, 1992.

121. Shmueli E, Srivastava E, Dawes PJ, et al: Combination of laser treatment and intraluminal radiotherapy for malignant dysphagia. Gut 38:803–805, 1996.

122. Spencer GM, Thorpe SM, Sargeant IR, et al: Laser and brachytherapy in the palliation of adenocarcinoma of the oesophagus and cardia. Gut 39:726–731, 1996.

123. Sander R, Hagenmueller F, Sander C, et al: Laser versus laser plus afterloading with iridium-192 in the palliative treatment of malignant stenosis of the esophagus: A prospective, randomized, and controlled study. Gastrointest Endosc 37:433–440, 1991.

124. Spencer GM, Thorpe SM, Blackman GM, et al: Laser augmented by brachytherapy versus laser alone in the palliation of adenocarcinoma of the oesophagus and cardia: A randomised study. Gut 50:224–227, 2002.

125. Gevers AM, Macken E, Hiele M, Rutgeerts P: A comparison of laser therapy, plastic stents, and expandable metal stents for palliation of malignant dysphagia in patients without a fistula. Gastrointest Endosc 48:383–388, 1998.

126. Sihvo EI, Pentikainen T, Luostarinen ME, et al: Inoperable adenocarcinoma of the oesophagogastric junction: A comparative clinical study of laser coagulation versus self-expanding metallic stents with special reference to cost analysis. Eur J Surg Oncol 28:711–715, 2002.

127. Adam A, Ellul J, Watkinson AF, et al: Palliation of inoperable esophageal carcinoma: A prospective randomized trial of laser therapy and stent placement. Radiology 202:344–348, 1997.

128. Moses FM, Peura DA, Wong RK, Johnson LF: Palliative dilation of esophageal carcinoma. Gastrointest Endosc 31:61–63, 1985.

129. Lundell L, Leth R, Lind T, et al: Palliative endoscopic dilatation in carcinoma of the esophagus and esophagogastric junction. Acta Chir Scand 155:179–184, 1989.

130. Parker CH, Peura DA: Palliative treatment of esophageal carcinoma using esophageal dilation and prosthesis. Gastroenterol Clin North Am 20:717–729, 1991.

131. Payne-James JJ, Spiller RC, Misiewicz JJ, Silk DB: Use of ethanol-induced tumor necrosis to palliate dysphagia in patients with esophagogastric cancer. Gastrointest Endosc 36:43–46, 1990.

132. Angelini G, Pasini AF, Ederle A, et al: Nd:YAG laser versus polidocanol injection for palliation of esophageal malignancy: A prospective, randomized study. Gastrointest Endosc 37:607–610, 1991.

133. Chung SC, Leong HT, Choi CY, et al: Palliation of malignant oesophageal obstruction by endoscopic alcohol injection. Endoscopy 26:275–277, 1994.

134. Nwokolo CU, Payne-James JJ, Silk DB, et al: Palliation of malignant dysphagia by ethanol induced tumour necrosis. Gut 35:299–303, 1994.

135. Boyce HW Jr: Palliation of dysphagia of esophageal cancer by endoscopic lumen restoration techniques. Cancer Control 6:73–83, 1999.

136. Willis JS, Oglesby JT: Percutaneous gastrostomy: Further experience. Radiology 154:71–75, 1985.

137. Adler DG, Baron TH, Geels W, et al: Placement of PEG tubes through previously placed self-expanding esophageal metal stents. Gastrointest Endosc 54:237–241, 2001.

138. Blazeby JM: Measurement of outcome. Surg Oncol 10:127–133, 2001.

139. Aaronson NK, Ahmedzai S, Bergman B, et al: The European Organization for Research and Treatment of Cancer QLQ-C30: A quality-of-life instrument for use in international clinical trials in oncology. J Natl Cancer Inst 85:365–376, 1993.

140. Blazeby JM, Alderson D, Winstone K, et al: Development of an EORTC questionnaire module to be used in quality of life assessment for patients with oesophageal cancer. The EORTC Quality of Life Study Group. Eur J Cancer 32A:1912–1917, 1996.

141. O'Hanlon DM, Harkin M, Karat D, et al: Quality-of-life assessment in patients undergoing treatment for oesophageal carcinoma. Br J Surg 82:1682–1685, 1995.

142. Blazeby JM, Farndon JR, Donovan J, Alderson D: A prospective longitudinal study examining the quality of life of patients with esophageal carcinoma. Cancer 88:1781–1787, 2000.

143. Fry SW, Fleischer DE: Management of a refractory benign esophageal stricture with a new biodegradable stent. Gastrointest Endosc 45:179–182, 1997.

144. Sandha GS, Marcon NE: Expandable metal stents for benign esophageal obstruction. Gastrointest Endosc Clin N Am 9:437–446, 1999.

145. Polee MB, Verweij J, Siersema PD, et al: Phase I study of a weekly schedule of a fixed dose of cisplatin and escalating doses of paclitaxel in patients with advanced oesophageal cancer. Eur J Cancer 38:1495–1500, 2002.

146. Won JH, Lee JD, Wang HJ, et al: Self-expandable covered metallic esophageal stent impregnated with beta-emitting radionuclide: An experimental study in canine esophagus. Int J Radiat Oncol Biol Phys 53:1005–1013, 2002.

Nonepithelial Tumors of the Esophagus and Stomach

CHAPTER

31

Nicholas Nickl

Introduction

Neoplasms of nonepithelial origin, although uncommon, are not so vanishingly rare that the busy gastrointestinal (GI) endoscopist will not encounter them with troublesome regularity. Although the number of such pathologic entities is manageably small, the spectrum of clinical behavior manifested by these lesions spans from trivial to life threatening. The difficulty in managing patients with such lesions is that the tumor originates from within the GI tract wall and, therefore, often appears as a mass beneath otherwise normal mucosa. Encountering such a seemingly innocent façade behind which lurks a fearsome range of possibilities, the GI endoscopist is challenged to appropriately use new diagnostic tools to direct the patient's care.

have been reported to exhibit a submucosal appearance.[1] Examples of nonepithelial lesions in all four categories are listed in Table 31–1. This discussion centers on neoplasms that primarily originate from nonepithelial GI tract cell lines, but all types of pathology must be taken into account when developing a management plan.

Depending on the clinical circumstances and type of tumor, the lesion may cause symptoms such as bleeding, obstruction, or pain. However, commonly, such lesions are serendipitously found during evaluation for a different, unrelated problem. Because most such lesions are asymptomatic, epidemiologic data are skewed by the nature of their discovery incidental to a different, usually unrelated condition. In one study of 15,104 EGD reports, submucosal tumors were identified in 0.36%.[2] Because most of these were life-threatening tumors, the study database likely under-reported less

Epidemiology

The clinical starting point for patients with such lesions is the discovery of a mass impinging on the GI tract mucosa from beneath, the so-called submucosal tumor (Fig. 31–1). In its classic form, a discrete tumorous appearance is presented with overlying mucosa that, although most commonly bland, may be erythematous, pale, dimpled, or ulcerated. Such lesions are often initially identified at esophagogastroduodenoscopy (EGD), but the patient may also be referred to an endoscopist for evaluation of an abnormal radiograph (e.g., barium-contrast examination).

Applied literally, the term *submucosal* seems to imply the presence of an intramural mass originating in the submucosal layer of the GI wall. However, the term has come to be used for a range of lesions that create a similar appearance, including intramural and extramural structures. Such submucosal tumors may include both neoplastic and non-neoplastic masses, and even mucosal neoplasms

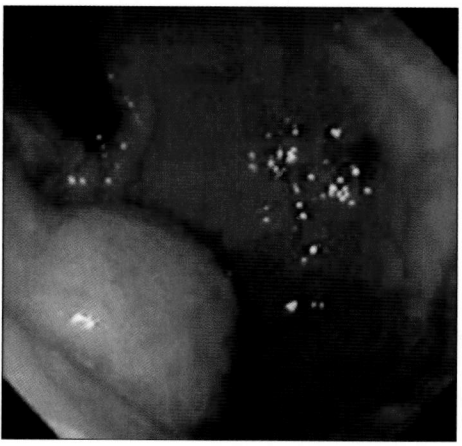

Figure 31–1. Endoscopic view of medium-sized submucosal tumor (retroflexed view).

Table 31–1. Types of Masses Causing Esophageal and Gastric Submucosal Tumors

	Neoplastic Masses	Non-neoplastic Masses
Intramural masses	Stromal cell tumor Lipoma Granular cell tumor Lymphoma Fibrovascular polyp Hemangioma/hemangiosarcoma Lymphangioma/lymphangiosarcoma Metastatic neoplasm	Varices Duplication cyst Inflammatory granuloma Foreign body (e.g., surgical suture or clip) Pancreatic rest
Extramural masses	Primary neoplasm of adjacent organs (benign and malignant) Metastatic lymph node	Benign lymph node Inflammatory mass of adjacent organs (e.g., pancreas, spleen) Organomegaly (e.g., spleen, liver)

serious lesions. In fact, a large number of such lesions turn out to be normal extramural organs. Allgayer[3] found that, among 30 patients referred for submucosal tumors, 14 (47%) were caused by normal extramural structures. Motoo and coworkers[4] also reported normal organs in 16 of 19 submucosal tumors, as did Caletti and colleagues[5] in 10 of 25 tumors; organs identified include the spleen, liver, splenic vessels, and pancreas. Because submucosal tumors are often left *in situ*, the pathologic distribution among tumors is imperfectly known. It is reported that 1% to 3% of resected gastric tumors are stromal cell tumors[6]; it can be inferred that the actual incidence, when including those not resected, is considerably higher. In the American Endosonography Club study,[7] among 45 submucosal tumors, most were found to have a benign appearance that required no follow up. From these available data it may be cautiously concluded that submucosal tumors are found in less than 1% of routine upper endoscopy examinations, as many as half of such lesions are found to be normal extramural structures, most of those remaining are benign, and stromal cell tumors compose most of such neoplasms.

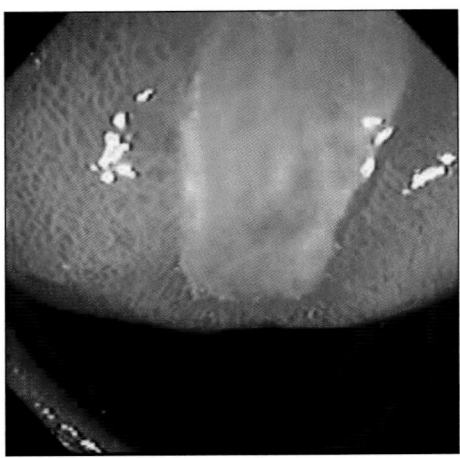

Figure 31–2. Endoscopic view of duodenal lipoma with ulceration at tip.

Clinical Features

Lumps and bumps of all sorts are regularly encountered in endoscopic examinations; the decision regarding which to further evaluate depends on the endoscopic appearance, the clinical circumstances, and the inclination of the endoscopist. Unfortunately, because few standardized guidelines exist to direct such decisions, great variation in practice exists. Symptoms attributed to the mass nearly always drive further investigation, but our own endoscopic ultrasonography (EUS) study of a subset of such lesions found that nearly 90% were asymptomatic.[8] GI bleeding may be seen in many submucosal lesions, most commonly in the form of slow blood loss causing iron deficiency anemia. The surface of the tumor may be ulcerated in such cases (Fig. 31–2). Malignant tumors may be more prone to ulceration and bleeding[9]; indeed, this might be taken as a sign of a potentially malignant form that compels definitive treatment. However, benign lesions may also cause severe bleeding,[10] and occasionally rapid hemorrhage may occur.[11] Less often, GI tract obstruction may be caused by such masses,[12] especially if the lesion is located in a narrow area such as the esophagogastric junction or

pylorus; intussusception caused by such masses has been reported.[13] Pain may be a presenting complaint, especially if the submucosal tumor is neoplastic or malignant.[14]

However, because most lesions are incidentally found during endoscopic examination for another problem, the clinical features of submucosal masses are primarily those that, in the endoscopist's opinion, compel further evaluation. Large size has been proposed as an ominous finding,[15] and lesions with an ulcerated or irregular (lumpy) surface often undergo additional testing or treatment. Patients with submucosal tumors who have a prior history of malignancy should receive further attention to exclude metastatic disease. Finally, patients with submucosal lesions that change appearance on serial examination are usually directed by the alert clinician to further testing.

Pathology

Extramural masses compose up to half of submucosal tumors, and include normal organs, non-neoplastic masses, and extramural neoplasms. Normal liver, spleen, pancreas, gallbladder, colon, and kidney have all been reported to appear as submucosal tumors.[3–5] Vascular structures often produce the appearance of a discrete

Table 31–2. Classification of Gastrointestinal Mesenchymal Tumors[19]

Tumor Type	Examples
Stromal tumors	Smooth muscle tumors (leiomyoma, leiomyosarcoma), glomus tumors, leiomyomatosis, pleomorphic sarcoma
Neural tumors	Neuroma/neurofibroma, paraganglioma, ganglioneuromatosis
Endothelial and vascular tumors	Hemangioma, hemangiosarcoma, Kaposi's sarcoma, lymphangioma
Lipocytic tumors	Lipoma, liposarcoma, lipohyperplasia (ileocecal valve), lipomatosis (colon)
Granular cell tumor	Granular cell tumor
Inflammatory fibroid polyp	Inflammatory fibroid polyp
Fibrohistiocytic tumors	Fibrovascular polyp, fibrous histiocytoma, desmoid tumors (mesentery), fibroepithelial polyp
Striated muscle tumors	Rhabdomyosarcoma

tumor, including normal vessels of the spleen[16] and abnormal vessels such as varices and aneurysms.[17] Neoplasms and non-neoplastic masses involving these same organs can also produce this appearance, as can such masses involving the peritoneum, mediastinum, and the lymph nodes adjacent to the upper GI tract. The various malignancies, cysts, and inflammatory masses of these structures need no further elaboration here, because a large variety of such findings have been noted in the case report literature.

However, masses that arise within the wall of the esophagus and stomach require further discussion, particularly because many are peculiar to the GI tract. Most neoplasms in this category are mesenchymal tumors, meaning that they arise from cells of mesodermal origin. Most of such neoplasms are clinically benign, although, as will be seen, tumor histology may not provide reliable clues to malignant behavior. A dizzying array of such neoplasms have been described (Table 31–2), but, fortunately, most are exceedingly rare. The tumors most likely to be encountered in the esophagus and stomach in a routine clinical setting are discussed here.

GASTROINTESTINAL STROMAL TUMOR

Most mesenchymal GI tumors are pale, firm, spherical, or ovoid structures embedded in the wall of the affected organ. The microscopic appearance of muscle-like eosinophilic, spindle-shaped cells in uniform sheets and the proximity of the tumors to the muscular wall layers led early observers to believe that these tumors were of myogenic origin[18]; hence the name leiomyoma and its variations (leiomyosarcoma, leiomyoblastoma, etc.). However, it soon became clear that these neoplasms are not only not of obvious myogenic origin but also often lack any specific markers of differentiation whatsoever.[19] Immunohistochemical analyses showed variable expression of smooth muscle features such as desmin and actin and neural proteins such as S-100.[20] For clarity's sake, these lesions came to be referred to as gastrointestinal stromal tumors (GISTs), an acknowledgment that they originate in mesenchymal stroma. So matters stood until the discovery that a majority of GI stromal tumors stain positive for a specific membrane protein, designated CD117.[21] This protein has been subsequently identified as KIT, a tyrosine kinase receptor which mediates a variety of growth func-

tions including cell proliferation and apoptotic cell death.[22] Several mutations have been described in the associated proto-oncogene, c-KIT, resulting in gain-of-function changes in the membrane kinase and leading to abnormal cell growth. It has further been observed that the interstitial cells of Cajal (ICC) share some phenotypic and ultrastructural similarities with GIST and, in addition, normally express the KIT receptor; this has led to the current hypothesis that GIST arises from interstitial cells of Cajal[23] or from ICC precursor cells. Finally, it has been noted that this gain-of-function mutation is not found in true leiomyomas.[24] Most pathologists now believe that CD117 positivity is required to confirm a diagnosis of GIST and that stromal tumors negative for this protein should undergo immunohistochemical staining to detect desmin (smooth muscle tumors) or S-100 (neural tumors).[25]

Nearly all upper GI tumors of this type occur in the stomach, but duodenal lesions have been described.[26] Interestingly, most esophageal stromal tumors lack the CD117 protein and are therefore considered true leiomyomata.[25] The endoscopic appearance is of a dome-shaped, firm submucosal mass; central umbilication or frank ulceration are not uncommon, and there may be a lobulated or irregular appearance. They are usually solitary except in the case of specific disease entities such as Carney's triad (GIST, pulmonary chondroma, and extra-adrenal paraganglioma). Giant sizes of greater than 10 cm have been noted, but most are less than 3 cm.

Pathologically the tumor usually consists of uniform pale tissue, although hemorrhagic and necrotic areas may be seen. Microscopically, the cells are spindle shaped with uniform nuclei and general cytologic uniformity. Some cell groups may show epithelioid configurations (closely packed polygonal cells), and there may be nuclear pleomorphism (both noteworthy features discussed later).

Malignant behavior is a definite risk for GIST, but a distinct problem is presented by the relatively bland cytology and slow growth of this neoplasm. Even small benign-appearing stromal tumors have been known to metastasize,[27] making a simple dichotomous classification of biopsies or resection specimens as benign or malignant impossible. Present classification systems categorize GISTs according to their malignant potential as benign, malignant, and indeterminate (or uncertain) with the caveat that tumors meeting criteria for benign may occasionally exhibit malignant potential and vice versa. However, even this classification system is not without controversy, and many of the histologic features used are subject to substantial intraobserver variability. Considerable attention has focused on the number of mitoses observed (mitotic index), at least in part because this is an easily quantifiable finding. In one study of 100 cases, tumors with more than 5 mitoses per 10 high power fields (HPFs) were significantly more likely to metastasize, although 40% of malignant lesions in that study had fewer mitoses.[28] In another study, multivariate analysis of various clinical and pathologic features in 122 specimens showed that more than 10 mitoses/50 HPFs correlated with poor outcome, whereas site, epithelioid histology, and tumor size were not independently predictive.[29] However, the sensitivity and specificity of this cutoff point were not given, marring its practical clinical utility. Attempts to correlate CD117 positivity with malignant behavior have produced generally negative results[30]; some suggested that specific types of KIT mutations (such as at exon 11) correlate with malignant behavior[24] and other investigators have demonstrated poor correlation of these same mutations with prognosis.[31] A consensus conference concluded that intensity of CD117 staining is not a reliable indicator of biologic behavior.[22] However, recent data suggest that the expression of proteins associated with tumor proliferation, including endothelial growth factors and Ki-67 antigen, are strongly associated with malignant behavior[32,33] and may soon emerge as reliable indicators of malignancy. Pending further investigation of biochemical markers, routine histologic and pathologic criteria such as those listed in Table 31–3 represent the current standard for predicting malignant behavior.

The second half of the revolution in GI stromal tumors has been the development of imatinib mesylate, an agent that is effective in reducing the KIT enzyme activity and, therefore, serves as an effective therapeutic drug for tumor treatment. This agent targets the specific abnormal enzyme activity in the neoplasm and does not rely on generalized cytotoxicity for its effect. In an open label study of 147 patients with unresectable malignant GISTs, an overall response rate of 38% was seen.[34] Among responders, results are often dramatic (Fig. 31–3). Thus, the recognition of the malignant potential of GIST, combined with the availability of effective treatment even for unresectable disease, has compelled new thinking in the accurate diagnosis of this neoplasm.

GLOMUS TUMORS

Glomus tumors are paragangliomata that generally occur in the skin; a morphologically similar lesion has long been know in the stomach[35] and is usually classified with the GI stromal tumors. They are typically located in the antrum and are generally small, although they can range up to 5 cm.[36] A recent immunohistochemical study of 32 cases demonstrated that all examined glomus tumors were negative for desmin, S-100, and KIT,[37] suggesting a different histogenesis from leiomyomata, neuromas, and GISTs. In this same study, one patient died of metastatic disease, suggesting a malignancy risk that is low but not zero.

NEURAL TUMORS

Technically, most tumors that appear to be of neural origin continue to be classified as stromal tumors, although the recent revolution in GIST understanding brought about by the discovery of CD117 mutations has left terminology somewhat behind. As previously noted, many experts consider stromal tumors that are positive for S-100 and negative for CD117 to be of neural origin.

Neural tumors may represent glial cell proliferation, sometimes in combination with other neural elements. Neuroma, neurofibroma, and schwannoma are largely interchangable terms, although some pathologists observe differences among these lesions. When ganglion cells are present, the term ganglioneuroma is often applied. They seem to arise from ganglion cells in either the myenteric plexus or submucosal plexus.

Neuroma and Neurofibroma

Neuroma and neurofibroma are well circumscribed, nonencapsulated tumors arising from either the submucosa or the muscularis propria

Table 31–3. System for Malignant Potential of Gastrointestinal Stromal Tumor[19]	
Pathologic Factors	
Unequivocal factors	Metastases Invasion of adjacent organs
High-risk factors	Size: >5.5 cm in stomach, >4 cm elsewhere Mitoses: >5/50 high power fields in stomach, any mitoses elsewhere Tumor necrosis Nuclear pleomorphism Dense cellularity Microscopic invasion (lamina propria, vasculature) Epithelioid pattern
Classification Criteria	
Malignant	1 unequivocal factor or 2 high-risk factors
Indeterminate (uncertain)	1 high-risk factor only
Benign	No high-risk factors

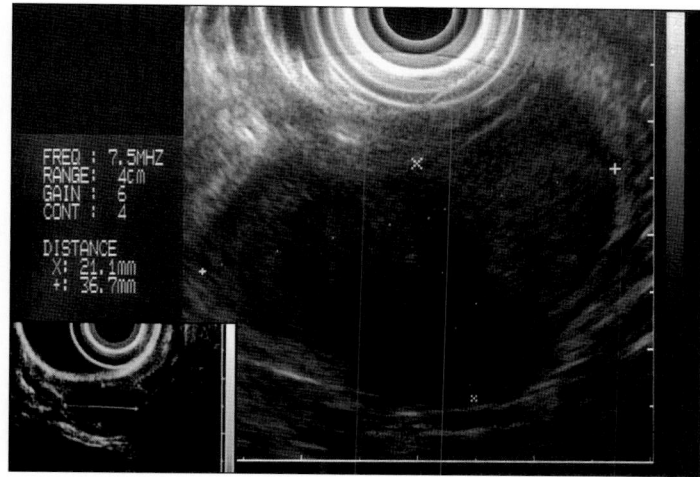

Figure 31-3. Endoscopic ultrasonography (EUS) imaging of a malignant gastrointestinal stromal tumor (GIST) treated with imatinib methylate: large tumor initially measuring 21 by 37 mm *(main image)* that decreased to 7 by 17 mm *(inset)* after 11 months of treatment.

layer. Except in the case of von Recklinghausen's neurofibromatosis, they are usually solitary nodules. They consist of bland spindle-shaped cells and are often currently classified as neuromas (as opposed to GISTs) if neural markers are identified on immuno-histochemical stain.

Gangliocytic Paraganglioma

Gangliocytic paragangliomas are rare tumors that range from 0.5 to 4 cm in size and are found in the periampullary duodenum. They may be present in either the submucosa or muscularis propria layers and consist of a combination of ganglion cells and epithelioid cells; they usually also contain a component resembling carcinoid tumor. Immunocytochemically somatostatin is usually present, and other neuropeptides may also be seen. They are always benign but may be locally infiltrative.

ENDOTHELIAL AND VASCULAR TUMORS

Cavernous hemangiomata are vascular neoplasms that rarely occur in the GI tract and even more rarely in the upper tract. They appear as sessile red or blue nodules and can be difficult to distinguish from vascular ectasias (which are not neoplastic). A malignant counterpart, the hemangiosarcoma, is exceedingly rare but has been described in nearly all parts of the GI tract.[38] Lymphatic tumors are also exceedingly rare in the GI tract, primarily being reported in the duodenum. They are described as having a smooth, sessile, polypoid translucent appearance endoscopically.[39] Histologically, they are mucosal or submucosal and contain hamartomatous rather than true neoplastic elements[38]; therefore, they are always benign.

LIPOCYTIC TUMORS: LIPOMA AND LIPOSARCOMA

Submucosal lipomas are (usually) harmless neoplasms arising from submucosal adipocytes. They are most common in the colon but may appear in any part of the GI tract, particularly the gastric antrum.[40] The typical endoscopic appearance is of a pale yellowish,

soft submucosal tumor; usually a solitary lesion is seen. The overlying mucosa can sometimes be tented up with a biopsy forceps, and the lesion deforms easily when pushed with the forceps. Histologically such tumors are encapsulated and consist of typical benign mature lipocytes. When they contain a large number of blood vessels, they are sometimes called angiolipomas. It is rarely necessary to further evaluate or remove them unless they cause bleeding or obstruction. They are normally small, but giant lipomas have been described[41] that can cause obstruction or intussusception.[42] The malignant form, liposarcoma, is exceedingly rare,[43] which is fortunate because they are clinically aggressive.

GRANULAR CELL TUMOR

The esophagus is the most common site of granular cell tumors, but they may be found throughout the GI tract. They are most often located in the submucosa and often assume a polypoid shape. Multiple tumors are common. They may be of Schwann cell origin and consist of masses of histiocyte-like cells containing periodic acid–Schiff (PAS) positive cytoplasmic granules. A literature review of 117 cases found dysphagia as the most common symptom in roughly half of patients; three fourths were smaller than 2 cm.[44] It is not certain that there is a malignant form of the neoplasm; the same review found that, in four locally invasive cases, distant metastases were not noted. They generally appear as yellowish, plaquelike, round or oval lesions less than 2 cm across.[45] The overlying squamous epithelium of the esophagus may show pseudoepitheliomatous hyperplasia.[46] If this is misinterpreted as metaplastic mucosal transformation, confusion may lead to additional investigations in search of an epithelial neoplasm.

INFLAMMATORY FIBROID POLYP

Inflammatory fibroid polyps are uncommon tumors that can occur anywhere in the GI tract; the stomach is the most common site,[19] but they have been described elsewhere.[47] Pathologically they consist of nonencapsulated myxoid stroma that includes blood vessels, inflammatory cells, and invariably eosinophils. The eosinophilic infiltrate had previously led to the (now discarded) designation of this tumor as localized eosinophilic gastroenteritis. They are often small, but giant tumors have been described that can cause (as usual) bleeding, obstruction, or intussusception.[48] Current theories of their genesis focuses on myofibroblasts or fibroblasts,[49] but the cell of origin is unknown. They tend to originate in the muscle layers of the GI tract wall, beginning as an intramural bulge but later assuming a polypoid shape; there may often be a significant extramural (subserosal) extension. There appears to be no malignant potential.

FIBROUS (FIBROVASCULAR) POLYP

Fibrous polyps are esophageal tumors that can grow to enormous size. They occur predominantly in males, usually originate in the upper esophagus, and often assume a polypoid shape.[50] Tumors in excess of 15 cm have been described[51] and can cause dysphagia, globus, bleeding, and even asphyxiation from laryngeal impaction.

Although they may have ulcerated overlying mucosa, the sheer size of the lesion may make it difficulty to clearly identify endoscopically.[52] Histologically a large variety of cytologic elements are seen, including spindle cells, lipocytes, mononuclear inflammatory cells, and vascular connective tissue. However, because some typical characteristics of inflammatory fibroid polyps are lacking and because of differing epidemiology and location, these lesions are classified separately from inflammatory fibroid polyps and should not be confused with them (despite the similar names). They are of uncertain histogenesis but do not seem to posses malignant potential. Nevertheless, because fatal outcomes have been described arising from the mechanical size of these tumors, removal is considered prudent.

METASTATIC TUMORS

Intramural metastases to the GI tract are distinctly less common than compression or invasion from extramural cancer. In a recent study of gastric mural metastases, the most common primary sites were lung, breast, and esophagus, but malignant melanoma was the most frequent tumor to metastasize to the stomach. Half appeared endoscopically as submucosal tumors, the rest were ulcerated or fungating; one third showed multiple lesions.[53]

CYSTIC TUMORS

A variety of cystic intramural lesions may present as submucosal tumors. In an individual patient, it may not be clear until EUS is performed that these tumors are cystic. However, it is worth collectively listing lesions (some of which have already been discussed) that can assume such an appearance. Small lymphatic ectasias are a common endoscopic finding,[38] particularly in the duodenum, and represent cystic structures less than 5 mm in size; they are, of course, not neoplasms. Duplication cysts are another non-neoplastic intramural cyst that may be seen as a submucosal tumor. These are very rarely encountered lesions in the upper GI tract[54,55] and are due to embryonic epithelial nodules that fail to regress. Brunner's gland hamartomata and heterotopic pancreas have also been described as showing a cystic appearance.[56] Among neoplastic cysts, lymphangiomas[57] and hemangiomas[58] (and hemangiosarcomas) assume a cystic appearance. In addition, any malignant neoplasm with central necrosis may appear as a cystic intramural lesion.

Differential Diagnosis

As has been shown, submucosal tumors may represent the full spectrum of symptomatology and pathology, from innocent to critical. Fortunately, a variety of diagnostic tools are available to sort out the possibilities with substantial confidence.

CONVENTIONAL ENDOSCOPY, COMPUTED TOMOGRAPHY, AND TRANSABDOMINAL ULTRASOUND

Confronted with a submucosal tumor, the alert endoscopist should not permit the presence of mucosa between the endoscopic camera and the mass to preclude preliminary conclusions about the nature of the unseen tumor. Despite the multitude of possibilities already discussed, a short list of half a dozen lesions will cover nearly everything likely to be found in all but the largest referral centers. Moreover, each has distinctive clinical and endoscopic features (Table 31–4) to provide an adequate preliminary assessment, which can be used to direct further management.

Routine endoscopic pinch biopsies are often obtained but rarely yield diagnostic material, even when large size (jumbo) pinch

Table 31–4. Endoscopic Appearance of Typical Upper Gastrointestinal Submucosal Tumors

Clinical Characteristics	Most Likely Tumor
Lower esophagus: <2 cm, plaquelike, firm, yellowish, sometimes multiple	Granular cell tumor
Upper esophagus: firm, large, polypoid	Fibrous (fibrovascular) polyp
Stomach: ovoid, firm, any size, single lesion	Gastrointestinal stromal tumor (GIST)
Stomach: <1 cm, firm, dimpled	Heterotopic pancreas
Any organ: translucent, soft	Lymphangioma
Any organ: soft, yellowish, soft, compressible, any size, single lesion	Lipoma

Table 31–5. Endoscopic Ultrasonography Features of Importance in Intramural Masses

Attribute	Attribute Values
Location	Organ (e.g., stomach) and position (e.g., greater curve)
Size	Measured (in three dimensions if possible)
Background echogenicity	Hypoechoic, hyperechoic, or anechoic
Focal echogenicity	Hypoechoic foci, hyperechoic foci, both, neither
Shape/margin shape	e.g., round, oval, etc; smooth margins, irregular margins
Margin definition	Well-defined margins, poorly defined margins
Position/origin relative to wall layers	e.g., involves mucosa, submucosa, muscularis propria
Tumor extension or invasion	T stage relative to site organ

forceps are used.[59] Other efforts to obtain tissue during routine endoscopy have been described, including standard fine needle aspiration (FNA) needles,[60] a special guillotine aspiration biopsy needle,[61] and mucosal stripping after forceps biopsy[62]; these show variable success but have not yet gained widespread acceptance.

Conventional computed tomography (CT) has traditionally been unhelpful in evaluating intramural tumors because of their small size, but new CT methods show promise. Multidetector high-resolution scanners can identify most tumors larger than 1 cm, although further characterization may be difficult.[63] Three-dimensional computerized reconstruction techniques are also able to reliably detect intramural tumors and may provide useful images.[64] Ongoing improvements in CT resolution may yet result in clinically important images, but current conventional technology is not generally worthwhile.

Conventional transabdominal ultrasonography has likewise been unhelpful in this setting, but like CT useful progress is being reported. High-resolution transabdominal sonography, using transducer frequencies of 5 or 7.5 MHz and a water-filled stomach, provides remarkable imaging of tumors as small as 10 mm and their relationship to the five-layer GI tract wall.[65] Although not suitable for obese patients or many anatomic tumor locations, this technique could potentially replace many endoscopic ultrasound exams of such tumors.

ENDOSCOPIC ULTRASONOGRAPHY

High-resolution scanning from an intraluminal position makes EUS ideally suited for evaluation of submucosal tumors and for the complete characterization of intramural masses that are identified. Extramural impression from normal and abnormal structures can be reliably demonstrated, and intramural masses can be readily characterized. Moreover, the ability to relate intramural tumors to the five-layer wall structure of the GI tract permits conclusions about the origin of the lesion (and hence its probable histology) and, where appropriate, the degree of local invasion (T stage). Table 31–5 lists some important features that can be derived from EUS and that are usually helpful diagnosing the lesion and directing further management.

Several studies have documented the ability of EUS to accurately characterize such lesions. Yasuda and coworkers[66] reported their experience with 308 patients, including 210 submucosal tumors. Characteristic echo features of benign and malignant stromal tumors, varices, cysts, lipomas, lymphoma, and aberrant pancreas were described. Rösch and colleagues[68] described the appearance of 102 submucosal lesions collected in a multicenter German study group. Characterizing the accuracy of EUS for this purpose is difficult and depends on the question being asked. The ability of EUS to accurately measure tumor size has been documented,[69] as has reliability in identifying extramural structures.[67] However, distinguishing among different classes of lesions (cystic, fatty, stromal, etc.) or pathologic entities (stromal tumor, carcinoid, etc.) is hampered by the fact that pathologic confirmation is not uniformly available in these research subject groups. Rösch and coworkers[68] reported sensitivity and specificity figures of 64% to 92% and 80% to 100%, respectively, for various types of pathologic distinctions being examined.

These and other authors have characterized the typical appearance of several intramural lesions. Lipomas (Fig. 31–4) are brightly echogenic structures with uniform echotexture and well demarcated margins, and they are generally associated with the submucosal layer (layer 3). They are easily deformed by compression from the transducer tip. Because they are virtually always benign, identifying continuity of the muscularis propria layer behind the tumor is helpful in confirming the diagnosis. Varices (Fig. 31–5) are also easy to recognize as anechoic vermiform structures. They are nearly always in groups, and extramural varices can usually be seen. When a variceal structure is seen in isolation, a hemangioma or lymphangioma should be considered, because these may have a similar appearance. Cysts such as duplication cysts also have an anechoic internal structure (Fig. 31–6), although debris may be seen as hyperechoic foci within the cyst structure. Aberrant pancreas (Fig. 31–7) is usually suspected by the endoscopic appearance, and the EUS structure of a hypoechoic lesion associated with the submucosal layer is confirmatory. Internal echogenic spots are often observed with this lesion.

The most frequent finding, however, is of a hypoechoic intramural structure (Figs. 31–8 and 31–9). A large variety of tumors, mostly

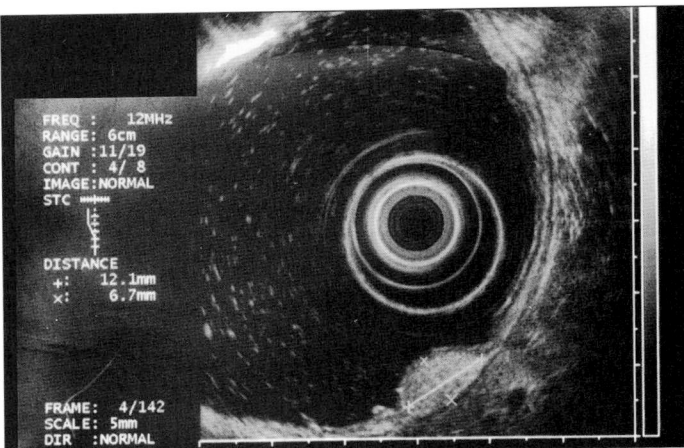

Figure 31–4. Endoscopic ultrasonography (EUS) image of gastric lipoma. Note uniform hyperechoic echogenicity and submucosal position with intact muscularis propria layer.

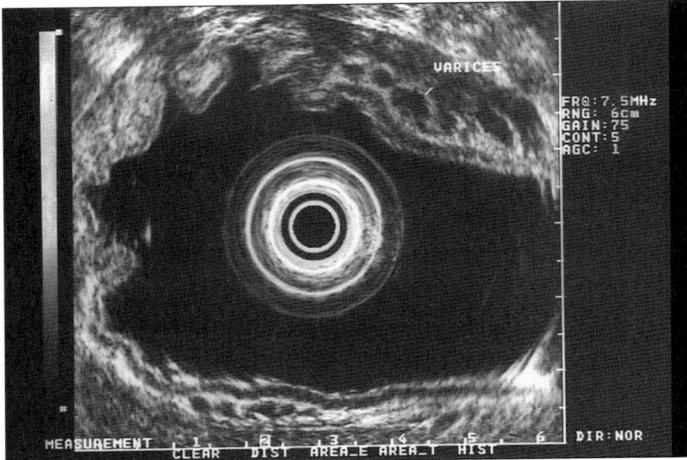

Figure 31–5. Endoscopic ultrasonography (EUS) image of gastric varices. Note multiple anechoic serpiginous structures; on real-time images, the continuous nature of these structures is obvious.

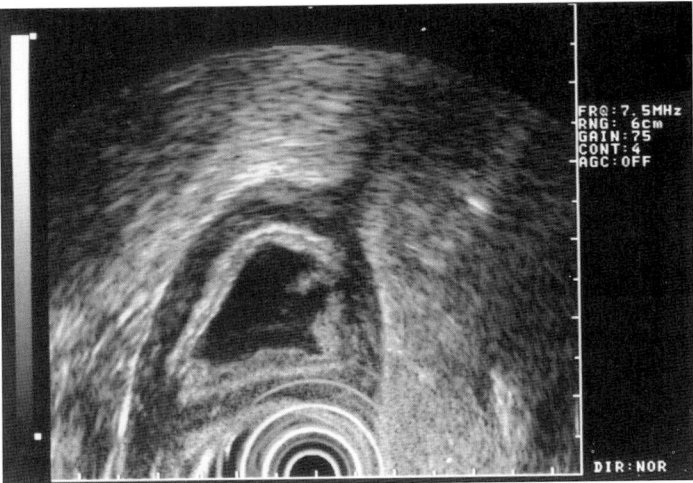

Figure 31–6. Endoscopic ultrasonography (EUS) image of a gastric duplication cyst. Note that the cyst wall contains a multilayer echos similar to the normal wall structure.

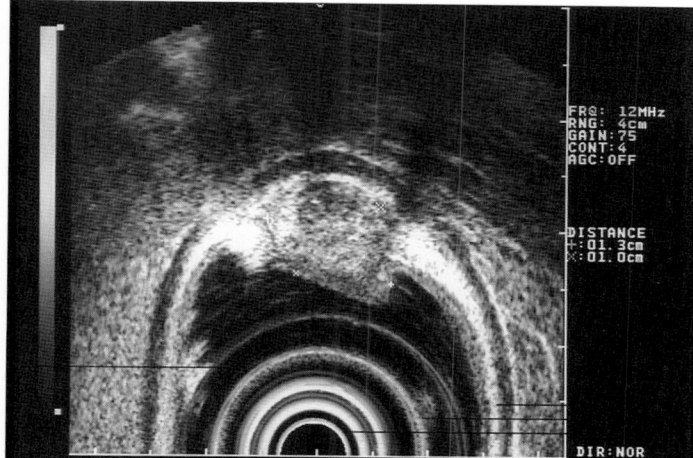

Figure 31–7. Endoscopic ultrasonography (EUS) image of ectopic pancreas. Note heterogeneous structure located in the mucosal layer and submucosal layer.

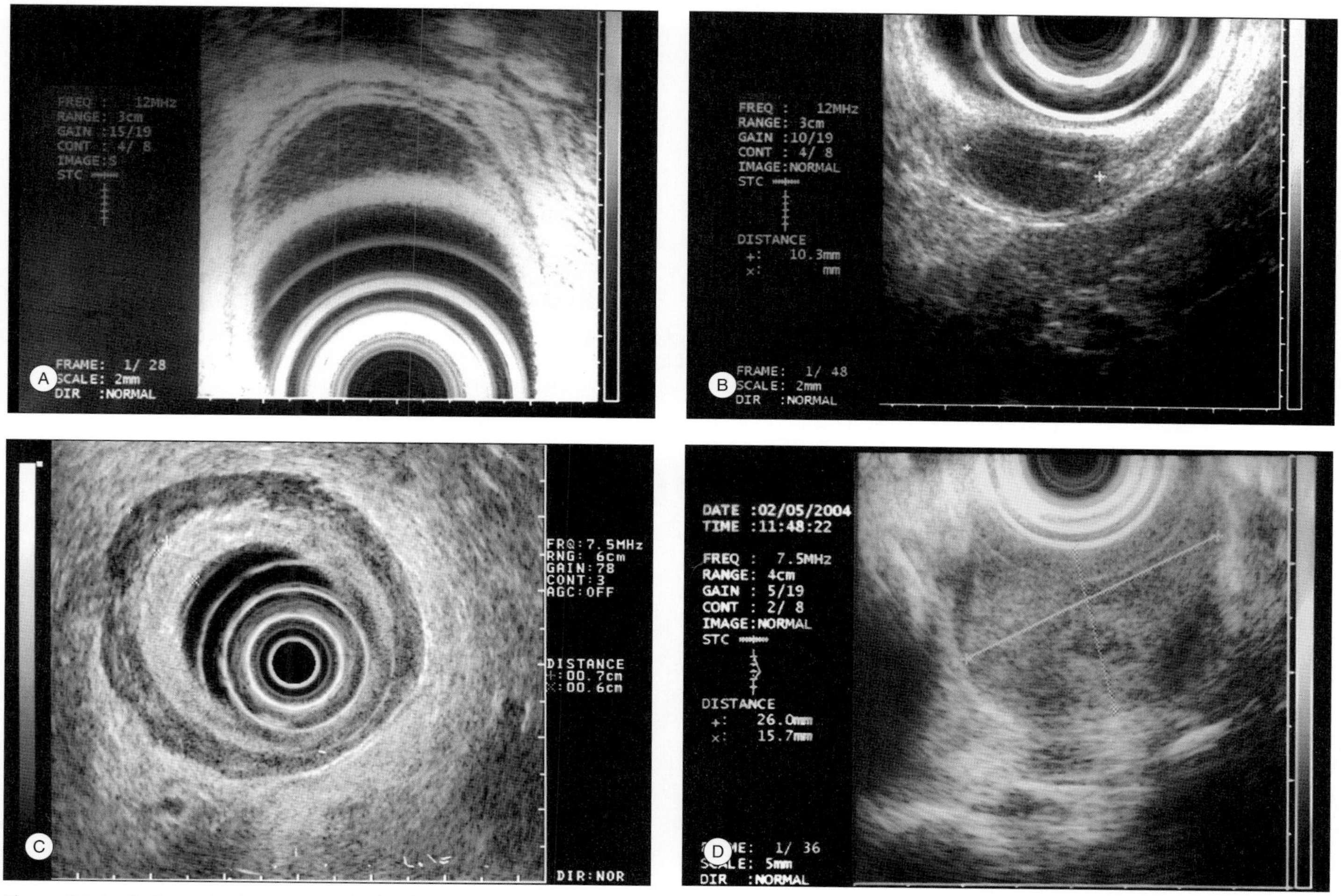

Figure 31–8. Endoscopic ultrasonography (EUS) appearance of intraepithelial neoplasms. *A,* Granular cell tumor of the esophagus, seen as a hypoechoic structure located within the submucosal layer (note intact muscularis propria layer). *B,* Carcinoid tumor of the duodenum, a hypoechoic tumor in the submucosa. *C,* Infiltrating lymphoma causing thickening of both the third and fourth echolayers. *D,* A large metastatic tumor which largely replaces the entire wall locally.

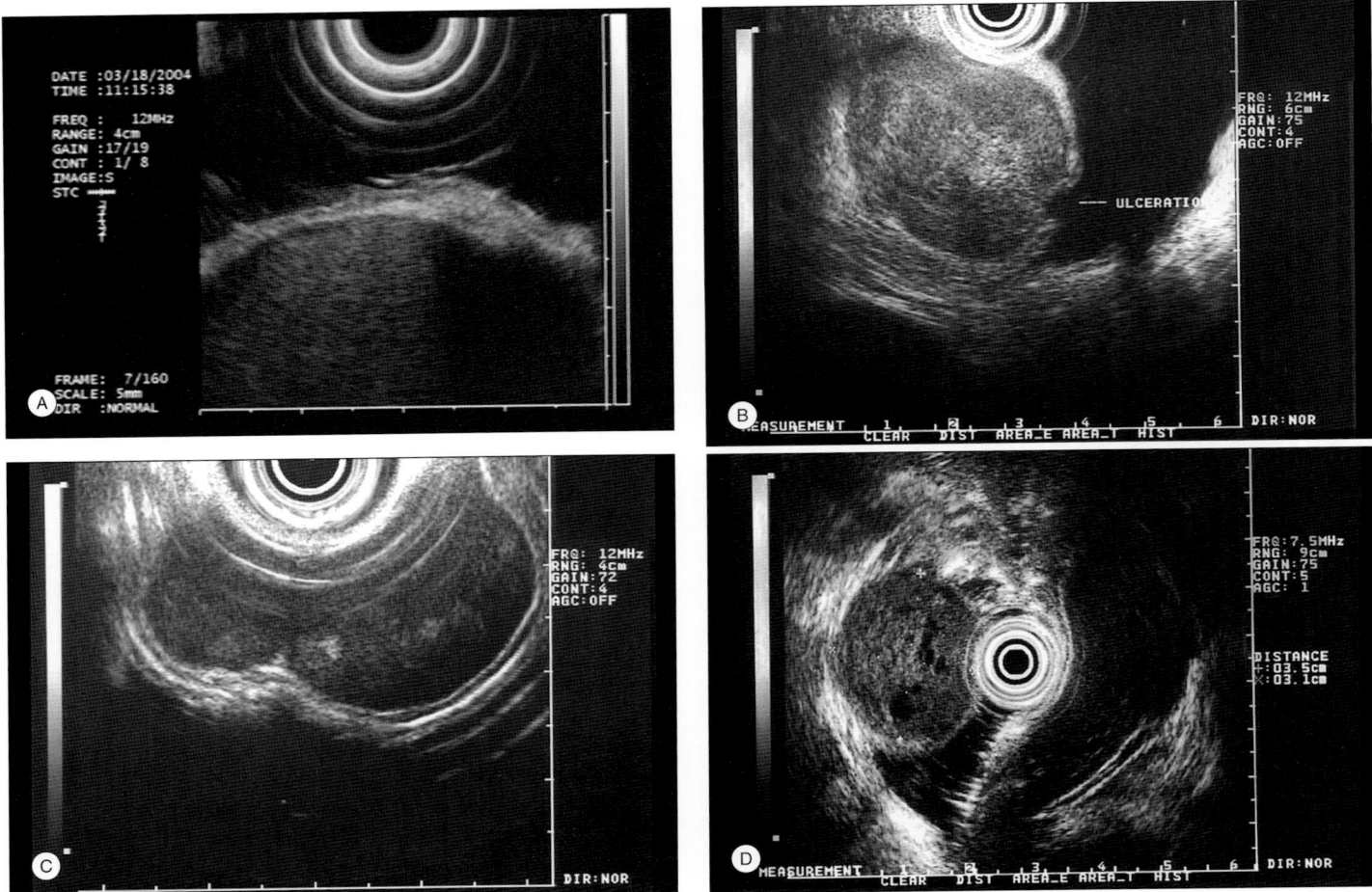

Figure 31–9. Endoscopic ultrasonography (EUS) appearance of gastrointestinal stromal tumors (GISTs). *A,* Benign-appearing GIST. Note small size, layer four (muscularis propria) location, smooth and well-defined margins. *B,* Large gastric GIST greater than 3 cm with surface ulceration and hyperechoic internal foci. *C,* GIST with multilobed irregular margins and hyperechoic foci. *D,* Hypoechoic (anechoic) foci within a large GIST.

neoplasms, can give this appearance, including GISTs, carcinoids, granular cell tumors, lymphomas, and metastatic tumors. These lesions all show generally hypoechoic (ground glass) background echotexture, often containing hyperechoic or hypoechoic/anechoic foci (or both). The tumor margins are typically well defined and smooth, and the overall shape is round or oval. Despite the similarities, some EUS clues may help to distinguish among these. Granular cell tumors, usually located in the esophagus, are typically seen within the third (submucosal) echo layer, and are generally smaller than 2 cm (see Fig. 31–8A). Carcinoid tumors are most common in the mucosal and submucosal layers (see Fig. 31–8B), as are lymphomas (see Fig. 31–8C), whereas metastatic tumors (see Fig. 31–8D) may occupy any layer in any organ.

Stromal tumors (see Fig. 31–9) are typically located in the muscularis propria layer and indistinguishably blend into it. Their most innocent appearance is of rounded, well-circumscribed, smooth tumors of 1 to 2 cm with uniform echogenicity (see Fig. 31–9A). However, other EUS features may be seen, and significant effort has been given to determining whether those features can distinguish benign from malignant behavior. Giant size (see Fig. 31–9B) and

irregular or knobby margins (see Fig. 31–9C) have been imputed to predict malignancy, as have internal foci that are hyperechoic or hypoechoic (see Fig. 31–9D). Early proposals that all these features were ominous[70] have been further investigated with mixed results. Tsai and coworkers[71] recently demonstrated a correlation of each of these features with malignant histology, but no single factor or combination of factors yielded satisfactory diagnostic accuracy. Chak and colleagues[72] demonstrated sensitivity figures of 80% to 100% for malignancy in a retrospective videotape study using these factors, but there were only fair to moderate intraobserver agreement for the factors themselves, especially for hyperechoic and hypoechoic foci; specificity was as low as 80%. A recent multicenter prospective study that attempted to further validate these criteria in what is the largest prospective series to date (198 tumors) found that tumor size, surface ulceration, non-oval shape, and irregular or indistinct margins were associated with malignancy, whereas hyperechoic and hypoechoic internal foci were uncorrelated.[8] The authors also reported that serial surveillance of initially innocent lesions by repeat EUS provided a very low yield of additional malignant neoplasms. Reviewing the literature on the subject collectively, most experts would agree that size greater than 3 cm and irregular or indistinct margins are worrisome features.

FINE NEEDLE ASPIRATION BIOPSY

Given the ambiguous predictive value of EUS morphology in either identifying tissue histology or predicting malignant behavior when considering hypoechoic intramural tumors, efforts to obtain diagnostic tissue assume greater importance. Transcutaneous sampling under CT or ultrasound guidance is possible for some lesions and can yield diagnostic material in up to three fourths.[73] Likewise, endoscopic FNA by direct puncture or under EUS guidance yields adequate diagnostic material in up to 90%[60] and, when combined with immunohistochemical stains, can distinguish GIST from leiomyoma.[74] However, although such specimens are usually adequate to distinguish other neoplasms from GISTs, they are not able to reliably distinguish benign from malignant GISTs. The fact that the cellularity is insufficient to obtain a mitotic index is a major obstacle, but the addition of immunohistochemical stains in biopsy specimens, including c-KIT and Ki-67, improves the diagnostic accuracy of stromal tumors[75] and can strongly suggest malignant risk. A recent modeling study has suggested that biopsy can improve clinical management of hypoechoic tumors,[76] lending support to the routine performance of needle biopsy of hypoechoic tumors, with immunostaining when appropriate.

Treatment

Ultimately, treatment for intramural tumors is reduced to two choices: leave it in place or take it out. Fortunately, new diagnostic and therapeutic options make the decision easier. The use of EUS appearance, combined with FNA biopsies and immunostaining, provide important information to direct the choice. Similarly, new options for removing the tumors have emerged to supplant or replace the traditional choice of open laparotomy or thoracotomy.

INDICATIONS AND CONTRAINDICATIONS

Several clear-cut indications have emerged to direct resection of intramural tumors. Most obvious is the presence of symptoms that are caused by the lesion, such as bleeding, obstruction, or intussusception. Beyond this, lesions that are malignant or pose a significant risk of becoming malignant require resection, whereas clearly benign tumors, such as granular cell tumors and lipomas, pose no meaningful malignant risk and may be safely left *in situ*. Because GISTs compose most intramural tumors, it remains to identify which hypoechoic lesions are GISTs and how high the malignant risk is for a given GIST. For this reason, the aforementioned EUS criteria, combined with FNA biopsy and immunostaining, is emerging as the diagnostic procedure of choice. In a recent study, 71% of resected hypoechoic tumors were GISTs, and of these 12% were malignant GISTs and another 41% were GISTs of indeterminate malignant potential.[8] Given what appears to be a significant malignant risk among such tumors, criteria to direct resection should have high sensitivity, even at the expense of low specificity. It

appears currently reasonable to direct to resection hypoechoic tumors with greater than 3 cm size, irregular or indistinct margins, ulceration, or non-oval shape. Rapid growth on serial examination, although not a validated criterion, is nevertheless a sufficiently alarming finding to also direct removal of the tumor.

PREOPERATIVE HISTORY AND CONSIDERATIONS

In selecting patients with GISTs who should be directed to surgical resection, it is important to maintain perspective on the actual level of malignant risk in comparison to the surgical risk. Despite the suggestion that the proportion of GISTs containing a meaningful malignant risk may approach 50%, the fact is that most GISTs, if left alone, will remain benign and asymptomatic. Among patients with an average surgical risk, it is reasonable to maintain a low threshold for resection of tumors with alarming EUS or histologic features. However, for those with advanced age or significant comorbidities that render surgical resection risky, a higher threshold is warranted. In such patients, a more diligent search for immunohistochemical markers of malignancy, such as MIB-1 or KI-67, would be prudent in directing surgery.

DESCRIPTION OF TECHNIQUES

Some submucosal tumors are appropriate for endoscopic removal. Numerous reports, most from Japan, document success in removal of tumors of the mucosa or submucosa, including lipomas, inflammatory fibroid polyps, carcinoids,[77] and granular cell tumors.[78] Stromal cell tumors that do not involve the muscularis propria can also be successfully removed endoscopically.[79] Generally a snare or inject/snare technique is described. Bleeding is the most common complication and may require transfusion, endoscopic therapy,[77] or surgery.[80] Despite the reported success of this technique, the number of tumors appropriate for endoscopic removal is limited. The most problematic intramural tumors are those that show EUS features of GIST; because most of these involve the muscularis propria, they are not suitable for endoscopic treatment. Endoscopic removal is likely to remain of limited applicability for this condition.

Recent advances in minimally invasive surgery have made laparoscopic removal possible for many such tumors. Several small case series describe successful laparoscopic removal of GISTs various gastric sites,[81,82] including the posterior wall of the stomach.[83] Even large tumors of up to 7 cm can be removed.[84] Surgical techniques described include tumor enucleation, wedge resection, and partial gastrectomy. A combined endoscopic and laparoscopic approach may be required when the tumor cannot be readily identified from the serosal surface.[85] In these small series, few complications are reported,[81] but conversion to open resection may be required.[83] A recent retrospective study comparing open and laparoscopic resection of GISTs found a shorter mean hospital stay for the latter (3.8 vs. 6.2 days) but otherwise comparable technical and safety outcomes,[86] and a smaller prospective study found a similar decrease in hospital stay but also noted hospital costs to be 31% less in the laparoscopy group.[87] It has been emphasized that such resections require a high degree of technical skill in laparoscopic surgery.[86] As experience widens, it is likely that, in the near future, laparoscopic resection will become the procedure of choice for GISTs requiring removal; the convenience and patient acceptance of this method may well come to decrease resistance to resection of GISTs of equivocal malignant potential.

Future Trends

The alert reader, perusing the literature on the subject, must be struck by the extremely variable quality of the data available. It cannot be otherwise, of course; all the lesions discussed here range from "uncommon" to "never in my lifetime," and even the largest of case series rarely contain more than a few dozen subjects. Developing a management algorithm—or even a reasonable plan for a single patient—based on such scant data is a hazardous undertaking.

Despite the dearth of clinical material, however, great strides have been made. The revolution in the understanding of stromal tumors by the discovery of CD117 and its dovetailing with other known oncogene markers has provided great insight into the histogenesis and growth mechanism of these neoplasms and has pioneered a treatment agent, imatinib, of completely novel therapeutic action. Extending this work will provide exciting new insights and

therapies, and the grail of GISTs—a reliable test of benign versus malignant behavior—may be right around the corner. Another revolution has been in the development of laparoscopic surgical approaches to these tumors. The ability to safely and reliably remove intramural masses in what may soon become an outpatient procedure enormously increases the management options. However, this also substantially increases the pressure on GI endoscopists to establish efficacy and cost efficiency in endoscopic management. Multiple endoscopic evaluations and serial surveillance of submucosal lesions, by either EGD or EUS, makes little sense when the tumor can be easily and conveniently dispensed with altogether. A recent modeling suggests that the GI endoscopist who cannot establish definitive patient management in an average of 1.7 EUS examinations is wasting the patient's time and money.[8] This leads to what is, from the GI endoscopist's perspective, a critical need. Clinical studies that reliably define those submucosal tumors that require further investigation and that establish the performance characteristics of EUS and other diagnostic modalities will permit the endoscopist to safely and reliably direct further management of submucosal tumors. A provisional treatment algorithm (fools rush in . . .) is proposed here (Table 31-6), but substantial work remains to be done to validate the steps that will translate this provisional algorithm into a reliable management tool.

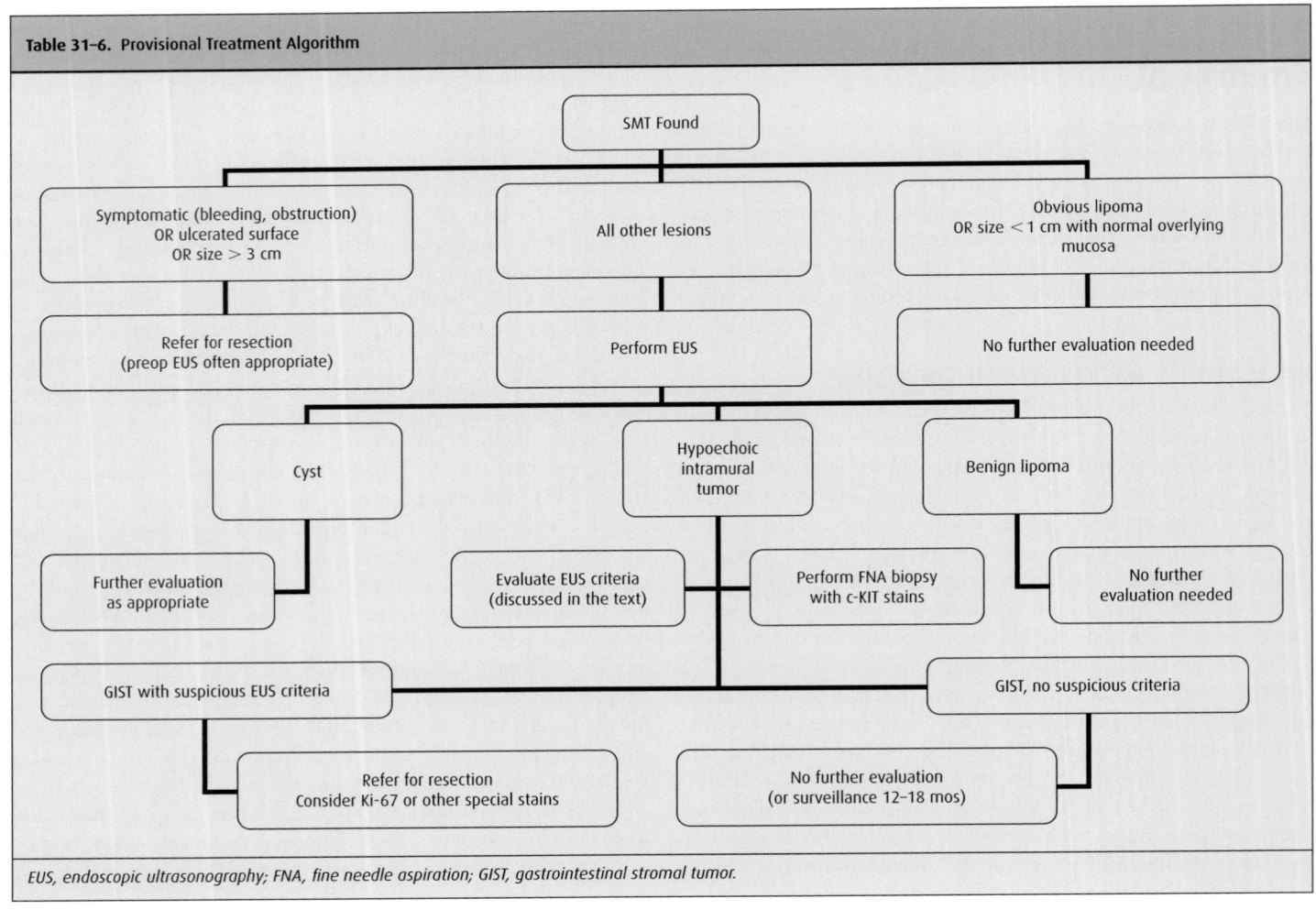

Table 31-6. Provisional Treatment Algorithm

EUS, endoscopic ultrasonography; FNA, fine needle aspiration; GIST, gastrointestinal stromal tumor.

REFERENCES

1. Kume K, Yoshikawa I, Yamazaki M, et al: A case of gastric cancer with features of submucosal tumor. Gastrointest Endosc 53:247–249, 2001.

2. Hedenbro JL, Ekelund M, Wetterberg P: Endoscopic diagnosis of submucosal gastric lesions. The results after routine endoscopy. Surg Endosc 5:20–30, 1991.

3. Allgayer H: Cost-effectiveness of endoscopic ultrasonography in submucosal tumors. Gastrointest Endosc Clin N Am 5:625–629, 1995.

4. Motoo Y, Okai T, Ohta H, et al: Endoscopic ultrasonography in the diagnosis of extraluminal compressions mimicking gastric submucosal tumors. Endoscopy 26:239–242, 1994.

5. Caletti G, Zani L, Bolondi L, et al: Endoscopic ultrasonography in the diagnosis of gastric submucosal tumor. Gastrointest Endosc 35:413–418, 1989.

6. Rohatgi A, Singh KK: Laparoendoscopic management of gastrointestinal stromal tumors. J Laparoendosc Adv Surg Tech 13:37–40, 2003.

7. Nickl N, Bhutani M, Catalano M, et al: Clinical implications of endoscopic ultrasound: The American Endosonography Club Study Gastrointest Endosc 44:371–377, 1996.

8. Nickl N, Gress F, McClave S, et al: Hypoechoic intramural tumor study: Final report. Gastrointest Endosc 55:AB98, 2002.

9. De Waele B, Gillardin J, Creve U, et al: Upper gastrointestinal bleeding due to benign tumours of the stomach. Acta Chir Belg 87:322–325, 1987.

10. Hsu CC, Chen JJ, Changchien CS: Endoscopic features of metastatic tumors in the upper gastrointestinal tract. Endoscopy 28:249–253, 1996.

11. Johnson DC, GeGennaro VA, Pizzi WF, Nealon TF: Gastric lipomas: A rare cause of massive upper gastrointestinal bleeding. Am J Gastroenterol 75:299–301, 1981.

12. Treska V, Pesek M, Kreuzberg B, et al: Gastric lipoma presenting as upper gastrointestinal obstruction. J Gastroenterol 33:716–719, 1998.

13. Moues C, Steenvoorde P, Wiersma J, et al: Jejunal intussusception of a gastric lipoma: A review of the literature. Dig Surg 19:418–420, 2002.

14. Sanders L, Silberman M, Rossi R, et al: Gastric smooth muscle tumors: Diagnostic dilemmas and factors affecting outcome. World J Surg 20:992–995, 1996.

15. Rosch T, Lorenz R, Dancygier H, et al: Endosonographic diagnosis of submucosal upper gastrointestinal tract tumors. Scand J Gastroenterol 27:1–8, 1992.

16. Rosch T, Lorenz R, von Wichert A, Classen M: Gastric fundus impression caused by splenic vessels: Detection by endoscopic ultrasound. Endoscopy 23:85–87, 1991.

17. Sun MS, Wang HP, Lin JT: Gastroduodenal artery aneurysm mimicking a bleeding submucosal tumor. Gastrointest Endosc 54:621, 2001.

18. Golden T, Stout A: Smooth muscle tumors of the gastrointestinal tract and retroperitoneal tissues. Surg Gynecol Obstet 73:784–810, 1941.

19. Lewin K, Riddel RH, Weinstein WM: Mesenchymal tumors. In Gastrointestinal Pathology and Its Clinical Implications. New York, Igaku-Shoin, 1992, pp 284–341.

20. Ma CK, De Peralta MN, Amin MB, et al: Small intestinal stromal tumors: A clinicopathologic study of 20 cases with immunohisto-chemical assessment of cell differentiation and the prognostic role of proliferation antigens. Am J Clin Pathol 108:641–651, 1997.

21. Hirota S, Siozaki K, Moriyama Y: Gain-of-function mutations of c-kit in human gastrointestinal stromal tumors. Science 279:577–580, 1998.

22. Berman JJ, O'Leary TH: Gastrointestinal stromal tumor workshop. Hum Pathol 32:578–582, 2001.

23. Kindblom LG, Remotti HE, Aldenborg F, Meis-Kindblom JM: Gastrointestinal pacemaker cell tumor (GIPACT): Gastrointestinal stromal tumors show phenotypic characteristics of the interstitial cells of Cajal. Am J Pathol 152:2008–2011, 1998.

24. Lasota J, Jasinski M, Sarlomo-Rikala M, Miettinen M: Mutations in exon 11 of c-Kit occur preferentially in malignant versus benign gastrointestinal stromal tumors and do not occur in leiomyomas or leiomyosarcomas. Am J Pathol 154:53–60, 1999.

25. Miettinem M, Sobin LH, Sarlomo-Rikala M: Immunohistochemical spectrum of GISTs at different sites and their differential diagnosis with reference to CD117 (KIT). Mod Pathol 13:1134–1142, 2000.

26. Miettinen M, Kopczynski J, Makhlouf HR, et al: Gastrointestinal stromal tumors, intramural leiomyomas, and leiomyosarcomas in the duodenum: A clinicopathologic, immunohistochemical, and molecular genetic study of 167 cases. Am J Surg Pathol 27:625–641, 2003.

27. Evans HL: Smooth muscle tumors of the gastrointestinal tract: A study of 56 cases followed for a minimum of 10 years. Cancer 56:2242–2250, 1985.

28. Ranchod M, Kempson R: Smooth muscle tumors of the gastrointestinal tract and retroperitoneum: A pathologic analysis of 100 cases. Cancer 34:255–262, 1977.

29. Cunningham RE, Federspiel BH, McCarthy WF, et al: Predicting prognosis of gastrointestinal smooth muscle tumors: Role of clinical and histologic evaluation, flow cytometry, and image cytometry. Am J Surg Path 17:588–594, 1993.

30. Li SQ, O'Leary TJ, Sobin LH, et al: Analysis of KIT mutation and protein expression in fine needle aspirates of gastrointestinal stromal/smooth muscle tumors. Acta Cytol 44:981–986, 2000.

31. Morey AL, Wanigesekera GD, Hawkins NJ, Ward RL: C-kit mutations in gastrointestinal stromal tumors. Pathology 34:315–319, 2002.

32. Takahashi R, Tanaka S, Kitadai Y: Expression of vascular endothelial growth factor and angiogenesis in gastrointestinal stromal tumor of the stomach. Oncology 64:266–274, 2003.

33. Toquet C, Le Neel JC, Guillou L, et al: Elevated (> or = 10%) MIB-1 proliferative index correlates with poor outcome in gastric stromal tumor patients: A study of 35 cases. Dig Dis Sci 47:2247–2253, 2002.

34. Dagher R, Cohen M, Williams G, et al: Approval summary: Imatinib mesylate in the treatment of metastatic and/or unresectable malignant gastrointestinal stromal tumors. Clin Cancer Res 8:3034–3038, 2002.

35. Agawa H, Matsushita M, Nishio A, Takakuwa H: Gastric glomus tumor. Gastrointest Endosc 56:903, 2002.

36. Appleman HD, Helwig EB: Glomus tumors of the stomach. Cancer 23:203–213, 1969.

37. Miettinen M, Paal E, Lasota J, Sobin LH: Gastrointestinal glomus tumors: A clinicopathologic, immunohistochemical, and molecular genetic study of 32 cases. Am J Surg Pathol 26:301–311, 2002.

38. Lewin K, Riddel RH, Weinstein WM: Vascular Disorders. In Gastrointestinal Pathology and Its Clinical Implications. New York, Igaku-Shoin, 1992, pp 33–92.

39. Camilleri M, Satti M, Wood CB: Cystic lymphangioma of the colon. Endoscopic and histologic features. Dis Colon Rectum 25:813–816, 1982.

40. Johnson DC, DeGennaro VA, Pizzi WF, Nealon TF: Gastric lipomas: A rare cause of massive upper gastrointestinal bleeding. Am J Gastroenterol 75:299–301, 1981.

41. Hyun CB, Coyle WJ: Giant gastric lipoma. Gastrointest Endosc 56:905, 2002.

42. Moues CM, Steenvoorde P, Viersma JH, et al: Jejunal intussusception of a gastric lipoma: A review of literature. Dig Surg 19:418–420, 2002.

43. Seki K, Hasegawa T, Konegawa R, et al: Primary liposarcoma of the stomach: A case report and a review of the literature. Jpn J Clin Oncol 28:284–288, 1998.

44. Coutinho DS, Soga J, Yoshikawa T, et al: Granular cell tumors of the esophagus: A report of two cases and review of the literature. Am J Gastroenterol 80:758–762, 1985.

45. Fenoglio-Preiser CM, Lantz PE, Listrom MB, et al: Mesenchymal Tumors. In Gastrointestinal Pathology: An Atlas and Text. New York, Raven Press, 1989, pp 543–585.

46. Morson BC, Dawson IM, Day DW, et al: Polyps and tumors. In Morson & Dawson's Gastrointestinal Pathology, 3rd ed. Oxford, Blackwell Scientific Publications, 1990, pp 53–70.

47. Soon MS, Lin OS: Inflammatory fibroid polyp of the duodenum. Surg Endosc 14:86, 2000.

48. Shimer G., Helwig EB. Inflammatory fibroid polyp of the intestine. Am J Clin Pathol 81:708–714, 1984.

49. Makhlouf HR, Sobin LH: Inflammatory myofibroblastic tumors (inflammatory pseudotumors) of the gastrointestinal tract: How closely are they related to inflammatory fibroid polyps? Hum Pathol 33:307–315, 2002.

50. Lewin K, Riddel RH, Weinstein WM: Polyps and tumors. In Gastrointestinal Pathology and Its Clinical Implications. New York, Igaku-Shoin, 1992, p 482.

51. Patel J, Kieffer RW, Martin M, Avant GR: Giant fibrovascular polyp of the esophagus. Gastroenterology 87:953–956, 1984.

52. Burrell M, Toffler R: Fibrovascular polyp of the esophagus. Am J Dig Dis 18:714–718, 1973.

53. Oda, Kondo H, Yamao T, et al: Metastatic tumors to the stomach: Analysis of 54 patients diagnosed at endoscopy and 347 autopsy cases. Endoscopy 33:507–510, 2001.

54. Woolfolk GM, McClave, Jones WF, et al: Use of endoscopic ultrasound to guide the diagnosis and endoscopic management of a large gastric duplication cyst. Gastrointest Endosc 47:76–79, 1998.

55. Bhutani MS, Hoffman BJ, Reed C: Endosonographic diagnosis of an esophageal duplication cyst. Endoscopy 28:396–397, 1996.

56. Hizawa K, Matsumoto T, Kouzuki T, et al: Cystic submucosal tumors in the gastrointestinal tract: Endosonographic findings and endoscopic removal. Endoscopy 32:712–714, 2000.

57. Kim HS, Lee SY, Lee YD, et al: Gastric lymphangioma. J Korean Med Sci 16:229–232, 2001.

58. Araki K, Ohno S, Egashira A, et al: Esophageal hemangioma: A case report and review of the literature. Hepatogastroenterology 46:3148–3154, 1999.

59. Wegener M, Adamek R: Puncture of submucosal and extrinsic tumors: Is there a clinical need? Puncture techniques and their accuracy. Gastrointest Endosc Clin N Am 5:615–623, 1995.

60. Layfield LJ, Reichman A, Weinstein WM: Endoscopically directed fine needle aspiration biopsy of gastric and esophageal lesions. Acta Cytol 36:69–74, 1992.

61. Spandre M, Cavallero M, Pennazio M: Needle biopsy of submucosal lesions of the gastrointestinal tract. Surg Endosc 4:161–163, 1990.

62. Matsuoka J, Takai K, Kojima K, et al: Endoscopic submucosal tumor biopsy using Stiegmann-Goff endoscopic ligator. Acta Med Okayama 54:233–234, 2000.

63. Nishida T, Kumano S, Sugiura T, et al: Multidetector CT of high-risk patients with occult gastrointestinal stromal tumors. AJR Am J Roentgenol 180:185–189, 2003.

64. Ogata I, Komohara Y, Yamashita Y, et al: CT evaluation of gastric lesions with three-dimensional display and interactive virtual endoscopy: Comparison with conventional barium study and endoscopy. AJR Am J Roentgenol 172:1263–1270, 1999.

65. Tsai TL, Changchien CS, Hu TH, Hsiaw CM: Demonstration of gastric submucosal lesions by high-resolution transabdominal sonography. J Clin Ultras 28:125–132, 2000.

66. Yasuda K, Cho E, Nakamima M, Kawai K: Diagnosis of submucosal lesions of the upper gastrointestinal tract by endoscopic ultrasonography. Gastrointest Endosc 36(2):S17–S20, 1990.

67. Reference deleted in page proofs.

68. Rösch T, Kapfer B, Will U, et al: Accuracy of endoscopic ultrasonography in upper gastrointestinal submucosal lesions: A prospective multicenter study. Scand J Gastroenterol 37:856–862, 2002.

69. Murata Y, Yoshida M, Akimoto S, et al: Evaluation of endoscopic ultrasonography for the diagnosis of submucosal tumors of the esophagus. Surg Endosc 2:51–8, 1988.

70. Rösch T, Lorenz R, Dancygier H, et al: Endosonographic diagnosis of submucosal upper gastrointestinal tract tumors. Scand J Gastroenterol 27:1–8, 1992.

71. Tsai TL, Changchien CS, Hu TH, et al: Differentiation of benign and malignant gastric stromal tumors using endoscopic ultrasonography. Ghang Gung Med J 24:167–173, 2001.

72. Chak A, Canto MI, Rosch T, et al: Endosonographic differentiation of benign and malignant stromal tumors. Gastrointest Endosc 45:468–473, 1997.

73. Ballo MS, Guy CD: Percutaneous fine-needle aspiration of gastrointestinal wall lesions with image guidance. Diagn Cytopathol 24:16–20, 2001.

74. Stelow EB, Stanley MW, Mallery S, et al: Endoscopic ultrasound fine needle aspiration findings of gastrointestinal leiomyomas and gastrointestinal stromal tumors. Am J Clin Pathol 119:703–708, 2003.

75. Ando N, Goto H, Niwa Y, et al: The diagnosis of GI stromal tumors with EUS-guided fine needle aspiration with immunohistochemical analysis. Gastrointest Endosc 55:37–43, 2002.

76. Nickl N, Wackerbarth S, Gress F, et al: Management of hypoechoic intramural tumors: A decision tree analysis of EUS directed vs. surgical management. Gastrointest Endosc 51(4 Pt 2):AB176, 2000.

77. Wei SC, Wong JM, Shieh MJ, et al: Endoscopic resection of gastrointestinal submucosal tumors. Hepatogastroenterology 45(19):114–118, 1998.

78. Fujiwara Y, Watanabe T, Hamasaki N, et al: Endoscopic resection of two granular cell tumors of the oesophagus. Eur J Gastroenterol Hepatol 11:1413–1416, 1999.

79. Hyun JH, Jeen YT, Chun HJ, et al: Endoscopic resection of submucosal tumor of the esophagus: Results in 62 patients. Endoscopy 29:165–170, 1997.

80. Yu JP, Luo HS, Wang XZ: Endoscopic treatment of submucosal lesions of the gastrointestinal tract. Endoscopy 24:229–231, 1992.

81. Ludwig K, Wilhelm L, Scharlau U, et al: Laparoscopic-endoscopic rendezvous resection of gastric tumors. Surg Endosc 16:1561–1565. 2002.

82. Rohatgi A, Singh KK: Laparoendoscopic management of gastrointestinal stromal tumors. J Laparoendosc Adv Surg Tech 13:37–40, 2003.

83. Hepworth CC, Menzies D, Motson RW: Minimally invasive surgery for posterior gastric stromal tumors. Surg Endosc 14:349–353, 2000.

84. Walsh RM, Heniford BT: Laparoendoscopic treatment of gastric stromal tumors. Semin Laparosc Surg 8:189–194, 2001.

85. Agoi K, Hirai T, Mukiada H, et al: Laparoscopic resection of submucosal gastric tumors. Surg Today 29:102–106, 1999.

86. Matthews BD, Walsh RM, Kercher KW, et al: Laparoscopic vs. open resection of gastric stromal tumors. Surg Endosc 16:803–807, 2002.

87. Nickl N, Park A, Chak A, McClave S: A comparison of hospital costs and length of stay between laparoscopic and open resection of GI submucosal tumors. Gastroenterol 166(4 Pt 2):A1336, 1999.

Screening for Esophageal Squamous Cell Carcinoma and its Precursor Lesions

Sanford M. Dawsey and David E. Fleischer

Introduction

Esophageal cancer (EC) is the sixth leading cause of cancer death worldwide.[1] It is estimated that there are about 400,000 new EC cases each year and 338,000 EC deaths, only 35,000 fewer deaths than are caused by breast cancer.[1] About 80% of EC cases occur in developing countries, including almost 50% in China alone.[2] In the United States, EC is the ninth leading cause of cancer death, with about 13,900 new cases and 13,000 deaths resulting from EC in 2003.[3]

One characteristic of EC throughout the world is its prominent geographic variation in incidence, even across small areas: 10-fold differences in incidence have been reported over distances of a few hundred kilometers.[4] Worldwide, the highest risk populations, with age-adjusted incidence rates more than 100 cases per 100,000 inhabitants per year, are found in north central China, northeastern Iran, and the intervening central Asian countries (sometimes called the "Central Asian Esophageal Cancer Belt").[1,5] Intermediate-risk populations, with incidence rates around 20 to 50 per 100,000 per year, are found in eastern and southern Africa, southern Brazil, Uruguay, northern Argentina, and northwestern France.[1,5] Most of the world is considered low risk, with incidence rates less than 10 per 100,000 per year.[5] In the Surveillance, Endoscopy, and End Results (SEER) cancer registries in the United States, the age-adjusted incidence of EC per 100,000 per year in 1996 to 2000 was 7.5 in white males, 2.0 in white females, 11.4 in black males, and 4.2 in black females.[6] In low-risk countries such as the United States, the male-to-female ratio of cases is usually about 3 to 4:1, but in the highest risk populations, this ratio approaches or even falls below 1:1.[1,3–5]

Throughout most of the world, most EC cases are esophageal squamous cell carcinomas (ESCC).[1] In Western countries, however, the incidence of ESCC has been gradually declining and the incidence of esophageal adenocarcinoma (EAC) has been rapidly rising over the last 30 years,[7–9] so that now more than 50% of EC cases in the United States are EAC.[8]

In most low-risk countries, cigarette smoking and alcohol consumption are the dominant risk factors for ESCC.[10,11] In the United States, more than 90% of ESCC cases can be attributed to these two exposures alone.[12] Additional contributing risk factors include a low dietary intake of fruits and vegetables and factors related to low socioeconomic status.[12–15] A few host medical conditions have also been associated with increased risk of ESCC in low-risk populations, including previous or concurrent squamous cell carcinoma of the head and neck region, achalasia, tylosis, caustic esophageal strictures, and the Plummer-Vinson syndrome.[16]

In most high-risk populations, tobacco and alcohol are not major risk factors for ESCC. Tobacco consumption in these groups is typically low, both in terms of the prevalence of smoking and in the amount of tobacco consumed by smokers, and alcohol consumption is even lower.[17,18] In addition, in the highest risk areas, where there are as many ESCC cases in women as in men, virtually none of the women smoke or drink.[17,18] These high-risk groups may, however, be exposed to some of the major tobacco carcinogens, such as polycyclic aromatic hydrocarbons (PAHs) and nitrosamines, in other ways. Recent studies have documented high levels of PAH exposure in Linxian, a county in the center of the high-risk region in north central China[19] and in northeastern Iran.[20] The source of these exposures is not yet known, although in Linxian it may be related to ingestion of ambient soot particles released from heating and cooking with soft coal in unvented stoves.[21] Nitrosamine exposure has also been suggested in Linxian.[22,23] Other risk factors reported in high-risk areas include diets low in fruits and vegetables,[24,25] low levels of certain micronutrients, especially the antioxidants selenium and vitamin E,[26,27] exposure to fungal toxins such as fumonisins,[28] and drinking hot liquids.[24,29]

One of the most consistent risk factors for ESCC in high-risk populations is family history,[30,31] and preliminary molecular studies support a role for genetic susceptibility in the etiology of ESCC in these areas. Recent studies have shown high frequencies of loss of heterozygosity (LOH),[32] characteristic patterns of gene expression,[33] and significant differences in both LOH and gene expression

Table 32–1. Components Needed for a Successful Early Detection and Treatment Program for Esophageal Squamous Cell Carcinoma

Component		Current State of the Art
Identification of precursor lesion		Squamous dysplasia
Primary screen		Cytology? Endoscopy? Molecular?
Endoscopic localization		Iodine staining
Staging		Endoscopic ultrasonography? Optical coherence tomography?
Therapy	High-grade lesions	Endoscopic mucosal resection Focal ablation Esophagectomy
	Low-grade lesions	Chemoprevention?

by family history[33,34] in tumors from north central China, but no major susceptibility gene for ESCC has yet been identified.

Both cell types of EC have a dismal prognosis. In the most recent SEER data, for 1992 to 1999, the overall 5-year relative (disease-specific) survival for EC patients was 14.0%.[6] This has improved from 4.7% in 1975 to 1979,[8] but it is still the third lowest survival rate (after pancreas and liver) among major cancers.

The main reason for poor survival in EC is that most tumors are asymptomatic and go undetected until they have spread beyond the esophageal wall. The esophagus is a distensible organ—it distends to let food pass—so most patients do not complain of dysphagia or other symptoms until the tumor significantly obstructs the lumen, and by that time it has usually invaded through the wall and/or metastasized. Significant reduction in EC mortality, both in low-risk and in high-risk populations, will probably require the development of successful new strategies for screening asymptomatic high-risk individuals that can diagnose and treat more cases at earlier, more curable stages of the disease.

We think that there are five components needed for a successful early detection and treatment program for EC:

1. Identification of the clinically important precursor lesions, which will be the targets for screening and treatment.
2. Accurate, cost-effective, primary screening tests that can detect precursor and early invasive lesions and are acceptable to asymptomatic high-risk individuals.
3. Reliable techniques for endoscopic localization of precursor and early invasive lesions, so we can accurately target diagnostic biopsies and focal therapy.
4. Reliable techniques for accurate staging of early invasive lesions, so we can triage patients to the most appropriate treatment.
5. A spectrum of curative therapies for precursor and early invasive lesions that are acceptable to asymptomatic people.

Table 32–1 summarizes these components for ESCC and our understanding of the current techniques available for each component. Techniques that are possible but are not yet established are followed by a question mark.

Because the subject of this chapter is screening, we cover only the first three of these components. Staging and endoscopic therapy are covered in other chapters of this text.

Precursor Lesions of Esophageal Squamous Cell Carcinoma

In low-risk countries, squamous dysplasia (including carcinoma in situ) is accepted as the histologic precursor of ESCC, because it is the established precursor in other organs lined by squamous epithelium, such as the cervix, and because it is often found adjacent to invasive cancer in esophagectomy specimens.[35] In high-risk populations, squamous dysplasia is also accepted as a precursor of ESCC,[36–40] but other histologic lesions such as chronic esophagitis, atrophy, and basal cell hyperplasia have also been proposed as precursors, based primarily on differences in the prevalence of these lesions in high- and low-risk groups.[37,40,41] These ecologic comparisons, however, have not always been consistent.[42] In the only two prospective studies, in which biopsied patients were followed over time, only squamous dysplasia was significantly associated with the later development of ESCC,[36,38,39] and increasing grades of dysplasia were associated with increasing risk.[36,39] In the larger of these prospective studies, members of our group followed 682 endoscoped Linxian adults without initial evidence of invasive cancer for up to 13.5 years and compared the cumulative incidence and relative risk of developing ESCC among patients with different initial biopsy diagnoses (Fig. 32–1, Table 32–2).

Thus, we believe that squamous dysplasia is the only confirmed, clinically relevant precursor lesion of ESCC in both high- and low-risk populations.

Nonendoscopic Screening Techniques

CYTOLOGIC TECHNIQUES

The most common nonendoscopic screening technique for early detection of EC is cytologic screening in high-risk populations. Two principal types of cytologic samplers have been used in these screenings, an inflatable balloon sampler first developed in China[43–46] and an encapsulated sponge sampler first developed in Japan[47–50] (Fig. 32–2). In the balloon technique, a deflated balloon covered by a cloth net or rubber ribbing is swallowed into the stomach, inflated, and then withdrawn, collecting exfoliated cells and scraping the mucosal surface of the esophagus. At the upper esophageal sphincter, the balloon is deflated and removed. In the sponge technique, a polyurethane mesh is compressed inside a gelatin capsule and attached to a string or a thin plastic stylet. The capsule is swallowed into the stomach, where the gelatin dissolves and the mesh expands. Then the mesh is pulled up the esophagus by the string, collecting exfoliated and scraped mucosal cells. In both methods, the collected cells are processed and stained for cytology

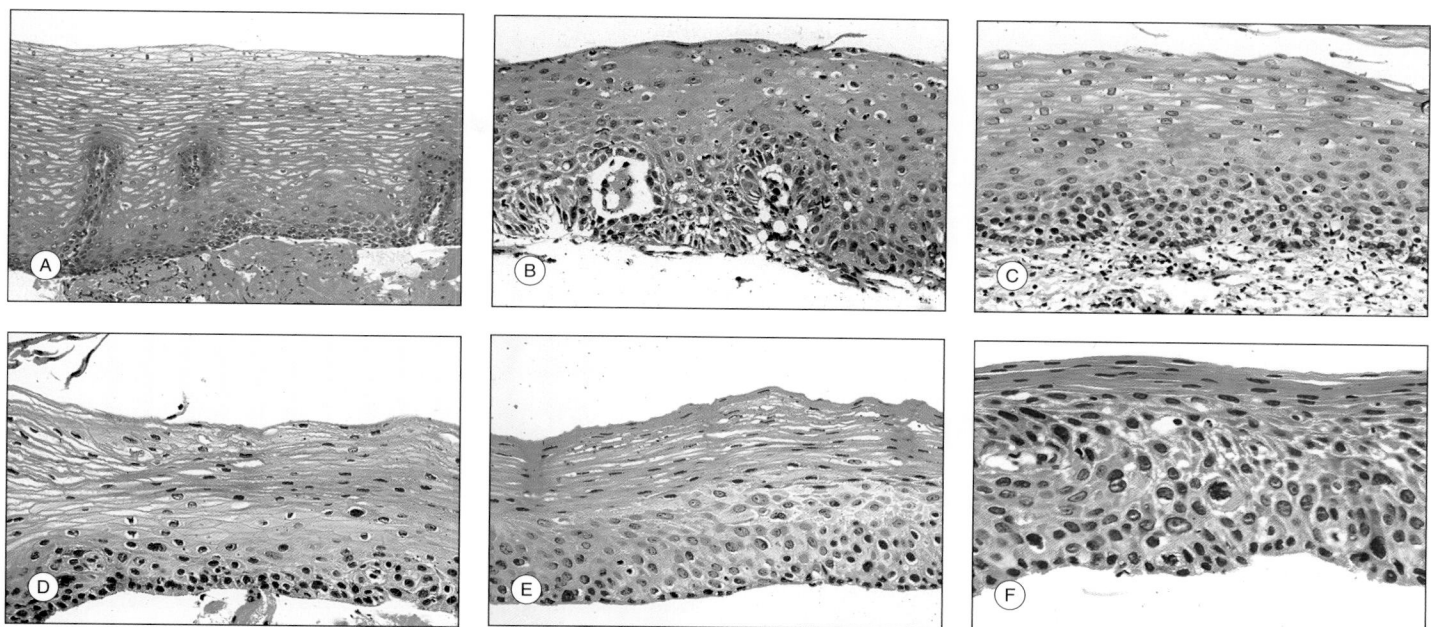

Figure 32–1. Histologic categories used in the endoscopic studies in Linxian, China. *A,* Normal. *B,* Esophagitis: the epithelium is infiltrated by polymorphonuclear leukocytes. *C,* Basal cell hyperplasia: the basal zone is greater than 15% of the epithelial thickness, without cellular atypia. *D,* Mild squamous dysplasia: there is cellular atypia, confined to the lower third of the epithelium. *E,* Moderate squamous dysplasia: there is cellular atypia involving the lower two thirds of the epithelium. *F,* Severe squamous dysplasia: the cellular atypia involves all thirds of the epithelium, without invasion of the lamina propria.

Table 32–2. Incidence and Relative Risk of Esophageal Squamous Cell Carcinoma (ESCC) during 13.5 Years of Follow-Up, by Initial Histology, in an Endoscoped Cohort from Linxian, China

Initial Diagnosis	Number of Patients	Cumulative ESCC Incidence (%)	Relative Risk (95% CI)
Normal	375	8.3	1.0 (ref)
Acanthosis	77	7.8	0.9 (0.4–2.2)
Esophagitis	33	6.1	0.8 (0.2–3.2)
Basal cell hyperplasia	40	15.0	1.9 (0.8–4.5)
Mild dysplasia	76	23.7	2.9 (1.6–5.2)
Moderate dysplasia	30	50.0	9.8 (5.3–18.3)
Severe dysplasia	39	74.4	30.8 (15.3–52.3)
Dysplasia NOS*	12	58.3	12.7 (5.5–29.6)
Total	682	16.7	N/A

Dysplasia not otherwise specified, not graded because of small size or poor orientation of the biopsy.
CI, confidence interval; N/A, not applicable.
Adapted from Wang G, Abnet CC, Liu FS et al: Squamous dysplasia is the histologic precursor of invasive esophageal cell carcinoma. Gastroenterology 124:A297, 2003, with permission from the American Gastroenterological Association.

and read for cellular abnormalities. Several studies of both of these methods have reported high sensitivities for detecting ESCC in symptomatic patients, but there are little data on their accuracy for detecting squamous dysplasia or for detecting ESCC in asymptomatic people, who would be the target group for any population screening effort.

To further investigate the potential of nonendoscopic esophageal cytology for screening asymptomatic high-risk individuals, we performed a study in Linxian to evaluate the screening characteristics of a commonly used Chinese balloon and an American-made encapsulated sponge. In this study, asymptomatic Linxian adults were examined by both samplers, in random order, followed by iodine chromoendoscopy of all participants. The cytology slides were read using the Bethesda System, the standard Western cytologic criteria for diagnosing cervical and vaginal smears, and the cytologic diagnoses were compared with the gold standard biopsy diagnoses. In the 439 patients with complete data, the sensitivities (specificities) of the balloon and sponge for detecting squamous dysplasia or cancer were 47% (81%) and 24% (92%), respectively.[51] These results make us conclude that the cytologic techniques that were used in this study are not accurate enough for a primary screening test in an early detection and treatment program for ESCC.

Figure 32-2. Sponge and balloon cytologic samplers used in Japan and China.

Possible ways to improve these techniques include designing improved cell samplers, developing improved (esophagus-specific) cytologic criteria for dysplasia and early cancer, and using image analysis or molecular tests to assist current methods of morphologic evaluation.

MOLECULAR TECHNIQUES

Molecular markers have several attributes that make them potentially useful for primary screening in an early detection and treatment program for ESCC and its precursor lesions. Molecular changes occur early in the neoplastic process (earlier than morphologic changes); they can sometimes be detected in clinical samples such as blood or stool that can be collected noninvasively. Molecular changes in DNA (e.g., hypermethylation, loss of heterozygosity, and mutations) can be amplified by polymerase chain reaction (PCR), so rare events can be found in complex clinical samples; some molecular changes undergo clonal expansion, so they are present over a much larger field of tissue than the discrete foci of morphologic dysplasia, which should make them easier to detect when mucosal sampling is incomplete. Measurement of molecular changes is more objective and less variable than cytologic or histologic identification of dysplasia.

Blood, or one of its components, would be an ideal clinical sample for primary screening purposes. A few authors have looked for hypermethylated genes in the serum or plasma of ESCC patients and have found them to be present in a minority of cases.[52,53] Hibi and coworkers[52] found hypermethylated p16 in tumor tissue in 31 (82%) of 38 ESCCs and found this same marker in the serum of 7 (23%) of the 31 patients with positive tumors. Kawakami and colleagues[53] found hypermethylated APC in tumor tissue from 16 (50%) of 32 ESCCs and in the corresponding serum from 2 (12%) of the 16 tumor-positive patients. In the latter study, detection of hypermethylated APC in the plasma of esophageal adenocarcinomas was significantly associated with tumor stage: 1/26, (4%) positive in stage I to II tumors and 12/26 (46%) positive in stage III to IV tumors. This should probably also be true of ESCCs. Although the proportion of tumors showing some hypermethylation increases when multiple genes are evaluated,[54,55] it still seems unlikely that

many intraepithelial precursor lesions or stage I ESCCs will shed altered DNA into the serum or plasma that can be detected by such evaluations. Another possible screening technique for identifying the presence of esophageal neoplasia in serum is the analysis of protein patterns.[56] This more complicated analysis has been able to identify ovarian and prostate cancer patients in initial studies,[57,58] but the reproducibility of these methods is uncertain, and their ability to identify precursor lesions has yet to be shown.

Stool is another possible clinical sample that could potentially contain information about the esophagus and could be collected noninvasively. Several authors have shown that neoplasia-specific DNA mutations can be detected in stool from patients with colonic adenomas and patients with both proximal and distal colorectal adenocarcinomas,[59–61] and the sensitivity of these assays can be increased by testing panels of markers.[62–64] There is also one report of detection of other more proximal aerodigestive malignancies, including three esophageal carcinomas, by measuring high molecular weight/"long" DNA (DNA from nonapoptotic cells, which are more commonly sloughed from neoplasms) in stool.[65] Again, detection of esophageal precursor lesions or early invasive ESCCs by these methods may be unlikely, but it should nonetheless be evaluated.

At least for the near future, it appears that nonendoscopic molecular screening for early ESCC and its precursor lesions will probably still need to depend on evaluation of esophageal cell samples. We have shown that current cytologic techniques are not sufficiently sensitive for finding focal squamous dysplasia in these samples, but molecular techniques may be better at finding focal molecular abnormalities, especially DNA changes that can be amplified. The most promising possibility may be the detection of molecular changes that have undergone clonal expansion and affect large areas of the squamous mucosa, similar to the field effects previously documented for p16 and p53 lesions in Barrett's esophagus.[66,67] If such field-wide molecular abnormalities are identified that reliably precede or accompany squamous dysplasia, then a simple, imperfect but patient-acceptable sampler such as an encapsulated sponge may be able to accurately identify or rule out the presence of an abnormal field, which may be sufficient to triage patients appropriately to endoscopy.

Endoscopic Screening Techniques

When endoscopy is used to screen for early ESCC or its precursors, chromoendoscopy may or may not be used as an ancillary technique. A variety of different endoscopes have been used and they differ in size, resolution, and magnification characteristics. The endoscopes may have different diameters. Ultrathin endoscopes (see Chapter 10) of less than 6 mm (with biopsy channels) may be used. A trial with a 3.1-mm stand-alone battery-powered fiberoptic esophagoscope showed that it was feasible and accurate in detecting esophageal pathology.[68] This small endoscope did not have a biopsy channel. Typically, instruments with diameters of 9 mm are used. Standard resolution and magnification instruments suffice, but advantages of higher resolution and magnification have been described.[69] Conventional videoendoscopes are equipped with charge-coupled device (CCD) chips of 100k to 300k pixels, meaning that each image is built up from 100,000 to 300,000 individual pixels. This technical feature, pixel density, determines the resolution. Newer instruments have chips of 400k, and recently 850k chips were introduced. High resolution is distinct from magnification, which can be obtained by moving the lens closer to the mucosa. The degree of magnification may range from 1.5 to 150×. Most of the published literature regarding endoscopic screening describes the use of standard endoscopes.

When screening is performed endoscopically, visual inspection to identify pathology is the first step. If chromoendoscopy is to be used, it generally is delivered before performing biopsies. The accurate use of endoscopy in studying and managing precursor lesions and early ESCC requires a biopsy strategy that will reliably identify the worst mucosal pathology. If dysplasia or cancer is endoscopically visible, these lesions can be targeted directly. If there are no visible lesions, then a larger number of systematic biopsies should be taken.

In the absence of staining, dysplasia may appear as normal mucosa, irregular mucosa, a small white patch, a focal red area, an erosion, or a plaque. Early ESCC is usually seen as an erosion, a plaque, or a nodule[70] (Fig. 32–3). Most of the published literature describes findings using standard endoscopes. It is possible that the higher resolution or higher magnification endoscopes may have higher yields.

When chromoendoscopy is used, Lugol's iodine is the stain that is generally used. The first description of iodine staining was by Schiller in 1933; he used it in the uterine cervix.[71] The first reports using iodine as a supplement to esophagoscopy were by Voegeli, Brodmerkel, and Nothmann.[72-74] Iodine has an affinity for non-keratinized squamous epithelial cells—normal cells which contain glycogen. This cellular affinity causes a brown color change in normal mucosa. Inflamed, dysplastic, or cancerous cells are relatively depleted of glycogen and, therefore, do not take up as much of the dye. Foci of glycogenic acanthosis have more than the usual amount of glycogen and, thus, appear overstained. Therefore, Lugol's iodine can be used to identify abnormal mucosal areas (unstained lesions [USLs]), including esophagitis, dysplasia, and ESCC (Fig. 32–4). In addition, it can be valuable in delineating the margins of these lesions, which is particularly relevant if endoscopic mucosal resection or an ablative treatment is contemplated.

In a typical procedure, the patient is placed in the left lateral decubitus position. Sedation may or may not be used. Often a Cetacaine-type medication is sprayed onto the throat or a Dicaine-type slurry is drunk. If sedation is used, typically a benzodiazepine with or without a narcotic is given. The esophageal mucosa must be assessed in its entirety, so evaluation must begin as soon as the instrument passes the upper esophageal sphincter. The endoscopist searches for mucosal abnormalities as described previously (see Fig. 32–3).

If the initial endoscopy without staining is to be followed by chromoendoscopy, then biopsies are deferred until after the staining. Various concentrations of Lugol's iodine have been used, but in most cases the concentration is between 1% and 2%. The formula of the iodine stain that we use (12 g iodine + 24 g potassium iodide dissolved in 1000 mL of water) was taken from the work of Endo and Ide.[75] This formula is slightly stronger than Lugol's original solution (1 g iodine + 2 g potassium iodide in water to 100 g). The formula we use has been called 1.2% Lugol's by some authors, referring to its elemental iodine content, and 3% Lugol's by other authors, referring to the total (iodine + potassium iodide) iodine content. For this reason, it is important to specify the formula that is used.

Some investigators advocate pretreatment with a water rinse or a mucolytic agent to remove mucus from the esophageal mucosa.[76] It has not been our practice to do so.

The dye is delivered through a spray catheter passed via the biopsy channel of the endoscope. Specifically designed spray catheters can be used (e.g., the Olympus PW-5L spray catheter; Olympus America Inc, Melville, NJ) or endoscopic retrograde cholangiopancreatography (ERCP) catheters. Typically spraying begins distally, at the squamocolumnar junction, and, as the endoscope is withdrawn proximally, it is rotated so that the dye covers the entire mucosal surface. One should be careful not to withdraw proximally all the way to the upper sphincter, to avoid inadvertently spraying proximal to the sphincter. Generally 20 to 25 mL of Lugol's solution is sprayed. If the entire surface is not covered, then further spraying is necessary. The normal mucosa becomes brown in appearance. The dye begins to fade in 5 to 8 minutes, so biopsies should be taken as quickly as possible. If USLs are seen, directed biopsies are taken. If there are no unstained areas, biopsies should be taken in a systematic way. At the end of the examination, the stomach should be carefully suctioned, to remove as much of the iodine solution as possible.

The utility of mucosal iodine staining to improve endoscopic visualization of dysplasia and ESCC was evaluated by us and colleagues in the high-risk population of Linxian, China.[77] For the past 2 decades, Chinese and American researchers have collaborated in conducting prevention, screening, and treatment studies in this area. In our mucosal staining study, 225 patients with evidence of dysplasia or carcinoma found on previous balloon cytology were evaluated with endoscopy before and after staining with 1.2% Lugol's iodine solution. In these patients, 253 USLs, 94 foci of high-grade dysplasia (HGD) (moderate or severe), and 20 invasive ESCCs were found. Before staining, the sensitivity of visible lesions for identifying HGD or ESCC was 62% and the specificity was 79%. After staining, the sensitivity of USLs for identifying HGD or ESCC was 96% and the specificity was 63%. Thus, mucosal iodine staining significantly improved endoscopic detection of HGD and ESCC.

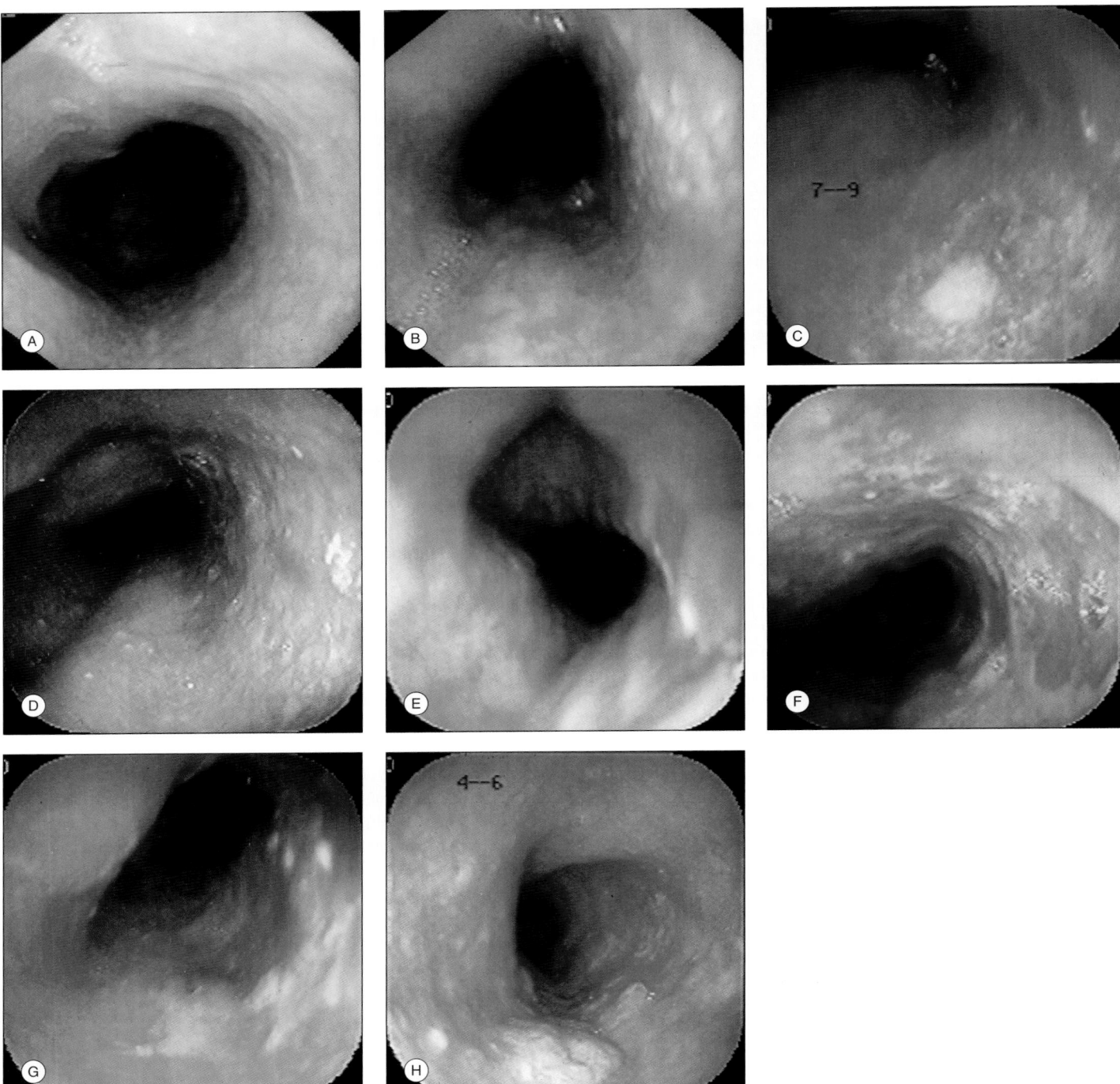

Figure 32–3. Endoscopic categories used in the studies in Linxian, China. *A,* Normal mucosa. *B,* Irregular mucosa, seen focally at the 3:00 position. *C,* Small white patch, at the 6:00 position. *D,* Focal red area, at the 3:00 position. *E,* Small punched-out erosion, at the 3:00 position. *F,* Large broad-based erosion, at the 11:00 to 4:00 position. *G,* Plaque, at the 2:00 to 6:00 position. *H,* Nodules, at the 4:00 and 5:00 to 7:00 positions.

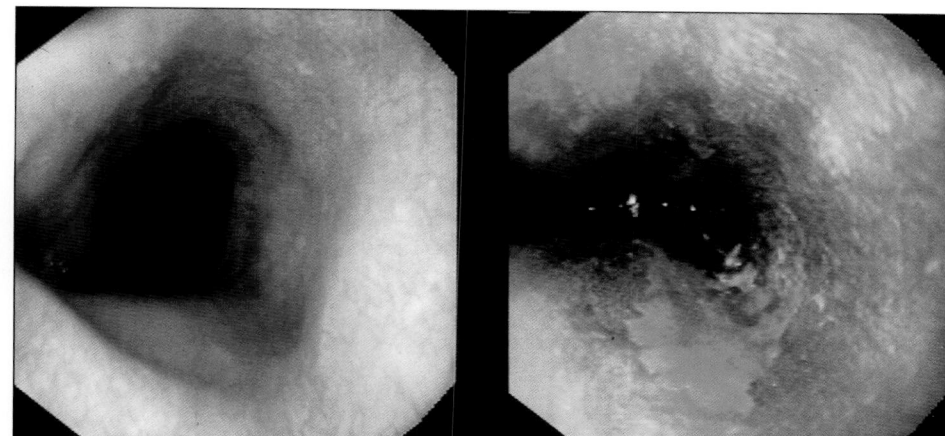

Figure 32-4. Detection of squamous dysplasia by iodine chromoendoscopy. Before staining, all of the mucosa appears normal. After staining, the normal mucosa stains brown, but an abnormal area at the 6:00 position remains unstained. Biopsies of this unstained lesion showed mild dysplasia.

In this study, Lugol's staining also greatly improved delineation of the significant mucosal abnormalities. Examples of dysplastic lesions before and after iodine staining are shown in Fig. 32–5. The outlines of the lesions are much clearer after staining. This is very important when endoscopic treatment is delivered[78] (Fig. 32–6).

Misumi and coworkers[76] evaluated the role of Lugol's dye endoscopy in diagnosing ESCC in 17 lesions in 10 patients. In 14 instances, there was an abnormality before staining, either a color change (redness) or elevation or depression. The lesions ranged in size from 0.7 to 4.0 cm. There was good correlation in all cases between the endoscopic detection of the unstained area and the lesion margins in the final surgical specimen. They concluded that Lugol's staining was useful in diagnosing ESCC because it would find some abnormalities not detected by routine endoscopy and it would also provide more accurate information about the extent of the cancer.

Shiozaki and colleagues[79] used Lugol's iodine to screen asymptomatic patients with head and neck cancer for EC. Nine of the 178 screened patients (5%) had one or more ECs identified. Eight of the nine patients with cancers had early-stage disease, with no lymph node metastases. Only 4 of the 13 cancerous lesions were seen at routine endoscopy. The authors concluded that Lugol's chromoendoscopy should be considered in asymptomatic patients with a history of head and neck cancer and in any other patient populations at high risk for ESCC.

Ina and coworkers[80] also evaluated the utility of Lugol's staining in male patients with oral or oropharyngeal cancer who had no symptoms of esophageal disease. Lugol's dye was used to screen 101 patients with oral cancer and 26 patients with oropharyngeal cancer. Eight of these 127 patients (6%) had EC. In 5 of the 8 cases, no abnormality was seen on routine endoscopy or barium swallow.

Muto and colleagues[81] performed chromoendoscopy with Lugol's solution in 389 patients with head and neck cancer and found 54 (14%) who had a synchronous primary ESCC. They characterized the staining pattern in the 389 patients into four groups. Type I patients had normal brown staining; type II patients had 10 or fewer unstained areas, type III patients had more than 10 unstained areas, and type IV patients had irregularly shaped multiform USLs. In the latter group, 55% of the patients had ESCC. They also followed their patients for more than 1 year, and those who had the type IV pattern were more likely to develop a metachronous lesion during that time. They concluded that the irregularly shaped, multiform lesions likely represented a "field cancerization."

Using iodine staining, Hashimoto found 8 cases of dysplasia (7%) and 10 cases of ESCC (8%) in 118 Brazilian patients with head and neck cancer.[82] Because most reports using Lugol's staining in high-risk patients are from Asia, this Brazilian study lends support to its utility in any patient population at risk throughout the world.

In addition to patients with head and neck cancer, alcoholics are another group at high risk for developing esophageal squamous cancer. Yokoyama and coworkers[83] studied a cohort of 629 male alcoholics by endoscopy with iodine staining. USLs were observed in 162 patients (26%), and 36 USLs in 21 patients (3%) were superficial ESCC. Because these lesions were superficial, endoscopic mucosal resection could be performed in 17 individuals. In a similar group of 255 alcoholic Japanese patients, Ban and colleagues[84] found USLs in 22% and cancer in 4%.

Strader and coworkers[85,86] screened 98 alcoholic American veterans with endoscopy and iodine staining. Twenty-eight (29%) had USLs, but no foci of dysplasia or cancer were found. Screening in this study began at age 40, which may have been too young in this population. Meyer and colleagues[87] prospectively compared the diagnostic accuracy of videoendoscopy with and without Lugol's staining for the detection of EC in 158 alcoholic and smoking patients in France. Before staining, 12 patients had 14 endoscopically identifiable dysplastic or cancerous lesions. After staining, these numbers rose to 13 patients with 17 lesions. The unstained areas were significantly larger than the mucosal abnormalities seen before staining.

In an attempt to better understand staining patterns with Lugol's, Mori and coworkers[88] applied iodine staining to 24 ESCC specimens resected by subtotal esophagectomy. They divided the staining patterns into four groups: type I, hyperstaining; type II, normal brown staining; type III, less intense staining; and type IV, unstained. Most type IV lesions were invasive carcinomas, carcinomas *in situ*, or severe dysplasia. Moderate to mild dysplasia or atrophy appeared as type III staining. They also demonstrated that there was good

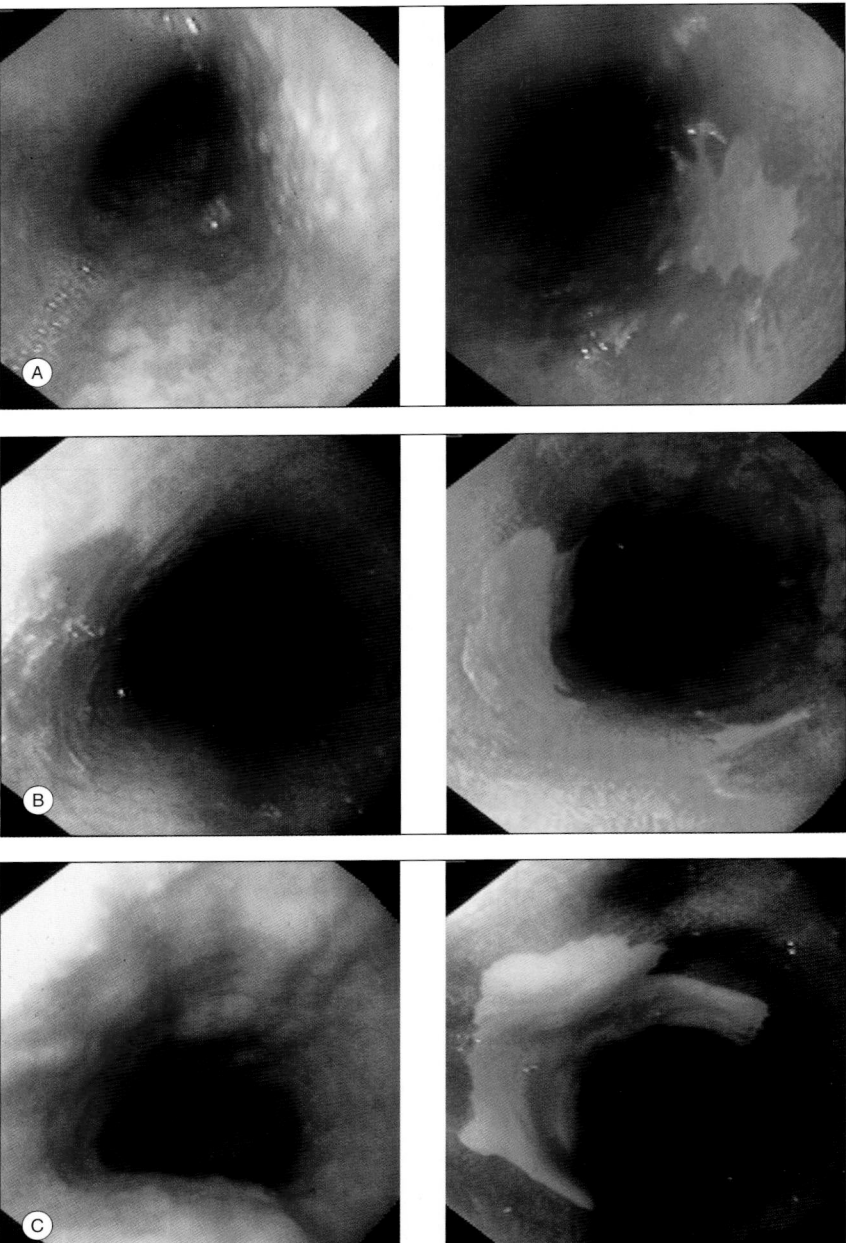

Figure 32–5. Improved delineation of squamous dysplasia by iodine chromoendoscopy. *A,* Before staining, irregular mucosa is seen at the 3:00 position. After staining, the outline of the lesion is much more distinct. Biopsies showed moderate dysplasia. *B,* Before staining, a large broad-based erosion is seen at the 7:00 to 10:00 position. After staining, the borders of this lesion are clearer, and a second lesion is identified at the 5:00 position. Biopsies of both lesions showed severe dysplasia. *C,* Before staining, the mucosa appears normal. After staining, a large unstained lesion with sharp borders is seen. Biopsies showed severe dysplasia.

correlation between the histologic tumor margin and the absence of staining.

Table 32–3 summarizes the detection of significant lesions before and after iodine staining in the studies described previously. In these patients, who had various degrees of risk for developing ESCC, 39% of the lesions were detected only after staining with iodine. This underscores our position that mucosal iodine staining improves endoscopic detection and delineation of high-grade squamous dysplasia and ESCC.

Although the largest experience using dyes to assist with screening for ESCC and its precursor lesions is with Lugol's iodine, there are also some reports using toluidine blue (also called tolonium chloride). Toluidine blue stains cellular nuclei, and it is this property

that makes it useful for identifying malignant tissue, which has an increased DNA content and a higher nuclear-to-cytoplasmic ratio. The mucosa of a normal esophagus does not stain with toluidine blue (Fig. 32–7).

When toluidine blue is used, a proteolytic enzyme (e.g., proteinase) in water is often used.[75] It may be ingested by mouth or sprayed on the mucosal surface. Toluidine blue is delivered as a 2% solution through a spray catheter in a manner identical to Lugol's iodine.

Seitz and coworkers[89] screened 100 patients with a history of alcohol and tobacco abuse using toluidine blue. Two carcinomas and 15 cases of dysplasia were detected. Two studies have looked at the use of toluidine blue dye spraying in patients with head and neck cancers. Hix and Wilson[90] found a 17% prevalence of ESCC in 18

Chapter 32

Screening for Esophageal Squamous Cell Carcinoma and its Precursor Lesions

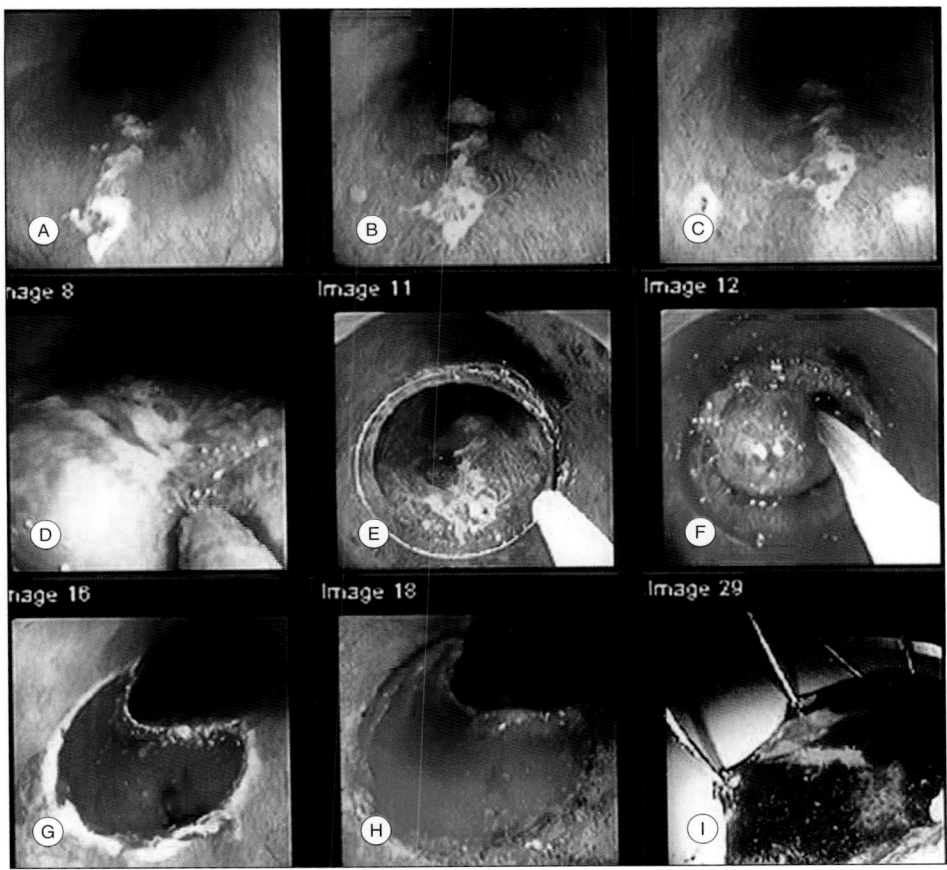

Figure 32–6. Use of chromoendoscopy for endoscopic mucosal resection. *A,* Dysplastic lesion before staining. *B,* Immediately after staining with Lugol's iodine. *C,* Five minutes later; stain is fading; two cautery marks in place. *D,* Injection with saline. *E,* Lesion seen through cap on tip of endoscope for snare technique removal. *F,* Snare now closed around lesion. *G,* Esophageal defect seen after endoscopic mucosal resection (EMR). *H,* Repeat stain with iodine to assess for residual pathology. *I,* Resected specimen.

Table 32–3. Detection of Squamous Dysplasia and Esophageal Squamous Cell Carcinoma (ESCC) in Studies Using Iodine Chromoendoscopy

Study (Ref.)	Population	Number of Lesions	Number Seen Before Stain	Number Seen After Stain	% Seen Only After Stain
Misumi, et al. (76)	Known ESCC	17	14	17	18
Shiozaki, et al. (79)	HN CA	13	4	13	69
Ina, et al. (80)	HN CA	8	3	8	63
Hashimoto, et al. (82)	HN CA	18	8	18	56
Yokoyama, et al. (83)	ETOH	36	12	36	67
Meyer, et al. (87)	ETOH	17	14	17	18
Mori, et al. (88)	Resected ESCC	32	26	32	19
Dawsey, et al. (77)	Asx high risk	114	70	109	34
Total		255	151	250	39

Asx, asymptomatic; ETOH, alcoholics; HN CA, head and neck cancer patients.

asymptomatic patients with a history of ENT malignancy. Contini and colleagues[91] found three esophageal neoplasms, two of which were not seen on routine endoscopy. Additional cases of leukoplakia and esophagitis were also identified.

Complications

Although Lugol's iodine is generally regarded as safe when sprayed onto esophageal mucosa to facilitate early detection of squamous cell carcinoma, some side effects have been reported.[92,93] Mucosal

irritation can be manifested by retrosternal pain, discomfort, or nausea. Free iodine, one of the components of Lugol's, causes these side effects, and the risk of complication is greater with increasing concentrations of iodine.

Sodium thiosulphate (STS), a water-soluble neutral chemical, can be used as an intravenous antidote for cyanide, iodine, arsenic, or heavy metal intoxication. STS spray was first reported as being effective for reducing symptoms caused by staining with iodine solutions in 1993.[93,94] Kondo and coworkers[95] compared the utility of 5% STS to no treatment and to aluminum magnesium hydroxide gel (Maalox) in 120 patients after spraying the esophagus with 3% Lugol's iodine. STS was most effective in reducing adverse

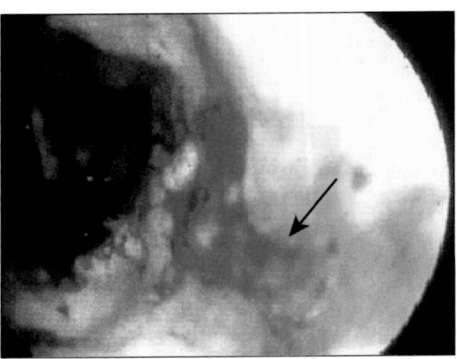

Figure 32-7. Toluidine blue chromoendoscopy.

symptoms, and the authors recommended its routine use after staining with iodine.

To date, no complications have been reported with toluidine blue. Because the dye is absorbed through the gastrointestinal tract and excreted in the urine, caution should be observed in cases with decreased renal function.

Summary

In summary, we think that any serious effort to reduce the mortality of ESCC will probably require the development of practical and accurate screening procedures for high-risk asymptomatic individuals. The feasibility, acceptability, and cost effectiveness of specific screening techniques will vary in different populations; thus, all screening programs will need to be tailored to local conditions. Finding the relatively few affected patients, such as the 6000 people who will develop ESCC in the United States each year, at a T0-T1 stage will be a challenge and will probably require screening large numbers of risk-stratified individuals in primary care settings.

Chromoendoscopy with Lugol's iodine solution is an excellent technique for confirming and localizing squamous dysplasia and early ESCC, and it is probably a practical method for screening very high-risk patients such as those with previous head and neck cancer, but it is impractical for primary screening of most other high-risk groups. The main purpose of nonendoscopic screening is to accurately identify which patients should be triaged to endoscopy. In most settings, current cytologic techniques are not sensitive enough to successfully perform this triage function. New molecular techniques, alone or combined with cytology, may significantly improve the accuracy and practicality of nonendoscopic primary screening, which may then offer hope for early detection and treatment of this disease.

REFERENCES

1. Parkin DM, Bray FI, Devesa SS: Cancer burden in the year 2000. The global picture. Eur J Cancer 37(Suppl 8):S4–66, 2001.
2. Parkin DM, Pisani P, Ferlay J: Estimates of the worldwide incidence of eighteen major cancers in 1985. Int J Cancer 54:594–606, 1993.
3. Jemal A, Murray T, Samuels A, et al: Cancer statistics, 2003. CA Cancer J Clin 53:5–26, 2003.
4. Mahboubi E, Kmet J, Cook PJ, et al: Oesophageal cancer studies in the Caspian Littoral of Iran: The Caspian cancer registry. Br J Cancer 28:197–214, 1973.
5. Munoz N, Day NE: Esophageal cancer. In Schottenfeld D, Fraumeni JF (eds): Cancer Epidemiology and Prevention. New York, Oxford University Press, 1996, pp 681–706.
6. Ries L, Eisner M, Kosary C, et al: SEER Cancer Statistics Review, 1975-2000. http://seer.cancer.gov/csr/1977_2000. 2003. National Cancer Institute, Bethesda, MD.
7. Devesa SS, Blot WJ, Fraumeni JF Jr: Changing patterns in the incidence of esophageal and gastric carcinoma in the United States. Cancer 83:2049–2053, 1998.
8. Polednak AP: Trends in survival for both histologic types of esophageal cancer in US surveillance, epidemiology and end results areas. Int J Cancer 105:98–100, 2003.
9. Powell J, McConkey CC, Gillison EW, Spychal RT: Continuing rising trend in oesophageal adenocarcinoma. Int J Cancer 102:422–427, 2002.
10. Brown LM, Hoover RN, Greenberg RS, et al: Are racial differences in squamous cell esophageal cancer explained by alcohol and tobacco use? J Natl Cancer Inst 86:1340–1345, 1994.
11. Lagergren J, Bergstrom R, Lindgren A, Nyren O: The role of tobacco, snuff and alcohol use in the aetiology of cancer of the oesophagus and gastric cardia. Int J Cancer 85:340–346, 2000.
12. Brown LM, Hoover R, Silverman D, et al: Excess incidence of squamous cell esophageal cancer among US Black men: Role of social class and other risk factors. Am J Epidemiol 153:114–122, 2001.
13. Brown LM, Swanson CA, Gridley G, et al: Dietary factors and the risk of squamous cell esophageal cancer among black and white men in the United States. Cancer Causes Control 9:467–474, 1998.
14. Steinmetz KA, Potter JD: Vegetables, fruit, and cancer. I. Epidemiology. Cancer Causes Control 2:325–357, 1991.
15. Terry P, Lagergren J, Hansen H, et al: Fruit and vegetable consumption in the prevention of oesophageal and cardia cancers. Eur J Cancer Prev 10:365–369, 2001.
16. Enzinger PC, Mayer RJ: Esophageal cancer. N Engl J Med 349:2241–2252, 2003.
17. Joint Iran-International Agency for Research on Cancer Study Group: Esophageal cancer studies in the Caspian littoral of Iran: Results of population studies—a prodrome. J Natl Cancer Inst 59:1127–1138, 1977.
18. Li JY, Ershow AG, Chen ZJ, et al: A case-control study of cancer of the esophagus and gastric cardia in Linxian. Int J Cancer 43:755–761, 1989.
19. Roth MJ, Qiao YL, Rothman N, et al: High urine 1-hydroxypyrene glucuronide concentration in Linxian, China, an area of high risk for squamous oesophageal cancer. Biomarkers 6:381–386, 2001.
20. Kamangar F: Personal communication, November 12, 2003.
21. Roth MJ, Strickland KL, Wang GQ, et al: High levels of carcinogenic polycyclic aromatic hydrocarbons present within food from Linxian, China may contribute to that region's high incidence of oesophageal cancer. Eur J Cancer 34:757–758, 1998.
22. Abnet CC, Qiao YL, Mark SD, et al: Prospective study of tooth loss and incident esophageal and gastric cancers in China. Cancer Causes Control 12:847–854, 2001.
23. Yang CS: Research on esophageal cancer in China: A review. Cancer Res 40(8 Pt 1):2633–2644, 1980.
24. Castellsague X, Munoz N, De Stefani E, et al: Influence of mate drinking, hot beverages and diet on esophageal cancer risk in South America. Int J Cancer 88:658–664, 2000.
25. Cook-Mozaffari PJ, Azordegan F, Day NE, et al: Oesophageal cancer studies in the Caspian Littoral of Iran: Results of a case-control study. Br J Cancer 39:293–309, 1979.
26. Mark SD, Qiao YL, Dawsey SM, et al: Prospective study of serum selenium levels and incident esophageal and gastric cancers. J Natl Cancer Inst 92:1753–1763, 2000.

27. Taylor PR, Qiao YL, Abnet CC, et al: Prospective study of serum vitamin E levels and esophageal and gastric cancers. J Natl Cancer Inst 95:1414–1416, 2003.

28. Turner PC, Nikiema P, Wild CP: Fumonisin contamination of food: Progress in development of biomarkers to better assess human health risks. Mutat Res 443(1–2):81–93, 1999.

29. Ghadirian P: Thermal irritation and esophageal cancer in northern Iran. Cancer 60:1909–1914, 1987.

30. Guo W, Blot WJ, Li JY, et al: A nested case-control study of oesophageal and stomach cancers in the Linxian nutrition intervention trial. Int J Epidemiol 23:444–450, 1994.

31. Hu N, Dawsey SM, Wu M, Taylor PR: Family history of oesophageal cancer in Shanxi Province, China. Eur J Cancer 27:1336, 1991.

32. Hu N, Roth MJ, Polymeropolous M, et al: Identification of novel regions of allelic loss from a genomewide scan of esophageal squamous-cell carcinoma in a high-risk Chinese population. Genes Chromosomes Cancer 27:217–228, 2000.

33. Su H, Hu N, Shih J, et al: Gene expression analysis of esophageal squamous cell carcinoma reveals consistent molecular profiles related to a family history of upper gastrointestinal cancer. Cancer Res 63:3872–3876, 2003.

34. Hu N, Goldstein AM, Albert PS, et al: Evidence for a familial esophageal cancer susceptibility gene on chromosome 13. Cancer Epidemiol Biomarkers Prev 12:1112–1115, 2003.

35. Ohta H, Nakazawa S, Segawa K, Yoshino J: Distribution of epithelial dysplasia in the cancerous esophagus. Scand J Gastroenterol 21:392–398, 1986.

36. Dawsey SM, Lewin KJ, Wang GQ, et al: Squamous esophageal histology and subsequent risk of squamous cell carcinoma of the esophagus. A prospective follow-up study from Linxian, China. Cancer 74:1686–1692, 1994.

37. Munoz N, Crespi M, Grassi A, et al: Precursor lesions of oesophageal cancer in high-risk populations in Iran and China. Lancet 1:876–879, 1982.

38. Qiu SL, Yang GR: Precursor lesions of esophageal cancer in high-risk populations in Henan Province, China. Cancer 62:551–557, 1988.

39. Wang G, Abnet CC, Liu FS, et al: Squamous dysplasia is the histologic precursor of invasive esophageal cell carcinoma. Gastroenterology 124:A297, 2003.

40. Wang LD, Qiu SL, Yang GR, et al: A randomized double-blind intervention study on the effect of calcium supplementation on esophageal precancerous lesions in a high-risk population in China. Cancer Epidemiol Biomarkers Prev 2:71–78, 1993.

41. Crespi M, Munoz N, Grassi A, et al: Precursor lesions of oesophageal cancer in a low-risk population in China: Comparison with high-risk populations. Int J Cancer 34:599–602, 1984.

42. Dawsey SM, Lewin KJ: Histologic precursors of squamous esophageal cancer. Pathol Annu 30(Pt 1):209–226, 1994.

43. Dawsey SM, Shen Q, Nieberg RK, et al: Studies of esophageal balloon cytology in Linxian, China. Cancer Epidemiol Biomarkers Prev 6:121–130, 1997.

44. Shen O, Liu SF, Dawsey SM, et al: Cytologic screening for esophageal cancer: Results from 12,877 subjects from a high-risk population in China. Int J Cancer 54:185–188, 1993.

45. Shu YJ: Cytopathology of the esophagus. An overview of esophageal cytopathology in China. Acta Cytol 27:7–16, 1983.

46. Shu Y: The Cytopathology of Esophageal Carcinoma. New York, Masson, 1985.

47. Jaskiewicz K, Venter FS, Marasas WF: Cytopathology of the esophagus in Transkei. J Natl Cancer Inst 79:961–967, 1987.

48. Leoni-Parvex S, Mihaescu A, Pellanda A, et al: Esophageal cytology in the follow-up of patients with treated upper aerodigestive tract malignancies. Cancer 90:10–16, 2000.

49. Nabeya K, Onozawa K, Ri S: Brushing cytology with capsule for esophageal cancer. Chir Gastroenterol 13:101–107, 1979.

50. Nabeya K: Markers of cancer risk in the esophagus and surveillance of high-risk groups. In Sherlock P, Morson B, Barbara L, Veronesi U (eds): Precancerous Lesions of the Gastrointestinal Tract. New York, Raven Press, 1983, pp 71–86.

51. Roth MJ, Liu SF, Dawsey SM, et al: Cytologic detection of esophageal squamous cell carcinoma and precursor lesions using balloon and sponge samplers in asymptomatic adults in Linxian, China. Cancer 80:2047–2059, 1997.

52. Hibi K, Taguchi M, Nakayama H, et al: Molecular detection of p16 promoter methylation in the serum of patients with esophageal squamous cell carcinoma. Clin Cancer Res 7:3135–3138, 2001.

53. Kawakami K, Brabender J, Lord RV, et al: Hypermethylated APC DNA in plasma and prognosis of patients with esophageal adenocarcinoma. J Natl Cancer Inst 92:1805–1811, 2000.

54. Brock MV, Gou M, Akiyama Y, et al: Prognostic importance of promoter hypermethylation of multiple genes in esophageal adenocarcinoma. Clin Cancer Res 9:2912–2919, 2003.

55. Yamashita K, Upadhyay S, Osada M, et al: Pharmacologic unmasking of epigenetically silenced tumor suppressor genes in esophageal squamous cell carcinoma. Cancer Cell 2:485–495, 2002.

56. Wulfkuhle JD, Liotta LA, Petricoin EF: Proteomic applications for the early detection of cancer. Nat Rev Cancer 3:267–275, 2003.

57. Adam BL, Qu Y, Davis JW, et al: Serum protein fingerprinting coupled with a pattern-matching algorithm distinguishes prostate cancer from benign prostate hyperplasia and healthy men. Cancer Res 62:3609–3614, 2002.

58. Petricoin EF, Ardekani AM, Hitt BA, et al: Use of proteomic patterns in serum to identify ovarian cancer. Lancet 359:572–577, 2002.

59. Sidransky D, Tokino T, Hamilton SR, et al: Identification of ras oncogene mutations in the stool of patients with curable colorectal tumors. Science 256:102–105, 1992.

60. Traverso G, Shuber A, Levin B, et al: Detection of APC mutations in fecal DNA from patients with colorectal tumors. N Engl J Med 346:311–320, 2002.

61. Traverso G, Shuber A, Olsson L, et al: Detection of proximal colorectal cancers through analysis of faecal DNA. Lancet 359:403–404, 2002.

62. Ahlquist DA, Skoletsky JE, Boynton KA, et al: Colorectal cancer screening by detection of altered human DNA in stool: Feasibility of a multitarget assay panel. Gastroenterology 119:1219–1227, 2000.

63. Ahlquist DA, Shuber AP: Stool screening for colorectal cancer: Evolution from occult blood to molecular markers. Clin Chim Acta 315(1–2):157–168, 2002.

64. Dong SM, Traverso G, Johnson C, et al: Detecting colorectal cancer in stool with the use of multiple genetic targets. J Natl Cancer Inst 93:858–865, 2001.

65. Ahlquist D, Cameron A, Jett J, et al: Universal detection of aerodigestive cancers by assays of non-apoptotic human DNA in stool [abstract 4773]. Gastroenterology 118:A855, 2000.

66. Prevo LJ, Sanchez CA, Galipeau PC, Reid BJ: p53-mutant clones and field effects in Barrett's esophagus. Cancer Res 59:4784–4787, 1999.

67. Wong DJ, Paulson TG, Prevo LJ, et al: p16(INK4a) lesions are common, early abnormalities that undergo clonal expansion in Barrett's metaplastic epithelium. Cancer Res 61:8284–8289, 2001.

68. Mokhashi MS, Wildi SM, Glenn TF, et al: A prospective, blinded study of diagnostic esophagoscopy with a superthin, stand-alone, battery-powered esophagoscope. Am J Gastroenterol 98:2383–2389, 2003.

69. Kiesslich R, Jung M, DiSario JA, et al: Perspectives of chromo and magnifying endoscopy: How, how much, when, and whom should we stain? J Clin Gastroenterol 38:7–13, 2004.

70. Dawsey SM, Wang GQ, Weinstein WM, et al: Squamous dysplasia and early esophageal cancer in the Linxian region of China: Distinctive endoscopic lesions. Gastroenterology 105:1333–1340, 1993.

71. Schiller W: Early diagnosis of carcinoma of the cervix. Surg Gynecol Obstet 59:210–222, 1933.

72. Brodmerkel G: Schiller's test: An aid in esophagoscopic diagnosis. Gastroenterology 60:813, 1971.

73. Nothmann BJ, Wright JR, Schuster MM: In vivo vital staining as an aid to identification of esophagogastric mucosal junction in man. Am J Dig Dis 17:919–924, 1972.

74. Voegeli R: Die schillersche jodprobe im rahmen der osophagus-diagnostik. Pract Otorhinolaryngol 28:230–239, 1966.

75. Endo M, Ide H: Endoscopic Staining in Early Diagnosis of Esophageal Cancer. Tokyo, Japan Scientific Societies Press, 1991.

76. Misumi A, Harada K, Murakami A, et al: Role of Lugol dye endoscopy in the diagnosis of early esophageal cancer. Endoscopy 22:12–16, 1990.

77. Dawsey SM, Fleischer DE, Wang GQ, et al: Mucosal iodine staining improves endoscopic visualization of squamous dysplasia and squamous cell carcinoma of the esophagus in Linxian, China. Cancer 83:220–231, 1998.

78. Fleischer DE, Wang GQ, Dawsey SM, et al: Endoscopic therapy for esophageal dysplasia and early esophageal cancer in Linxian, China. Gastrointest Endosc 45:AB68, 1997.

79. Shiozaki H, Tahara H, Kobayashi K, et al: Endoscopic screening of early esophageal cancer with the Lugol dye method in patients with head and neck cancers. Cancer 66:2068–2071, 1990.

80. Ina H, Shibuya H, Ohashi I, Kitagawa M: The frequency of a concomitant early esophageal cancer in male patients with oral and oropharyngeal cancer. Screening results using Lugol dye endoscopy. Cancer 73:2038–2041, 1994.

81. Muto M, Hironaka S, Nakane M, et al: Association of multiple Lugol-voiding lesions with synchronous and metachronous esophageal squamous cell carcinoma in patients with head and neck cancer. Gastrointest Endosc 56:517–521, 2002.

82. Hashimoto C, Moraes-Filho J, Eisig J: High incidence of esophageal cancer in patients of primary head and neck cancer: The role of Lugol's staining method in the establishment of early diagnosis of esophageal cancer [abstract]. Am J Gastroenterol 94:2586, 1999.

83. Yokoyama A, Ohmori T, Makuuchi H, et al: Successful screening for early esophageal cancer in alcoholics using endoscopy and mucosa iodine staining. Cancer 76:928–934, 1995.

84. Ban S, Toyonaga A, Harada H, et al: Iodine staining for early endoscopic detection of esophageal cancer in alcoholics. Endoscopy 30:253–257, 1998.

85. Strader D, Dawsey S, Fleischer DE, et al: Early detection of esophageal cancer/dysplasia in a high-risk population via chromoendoscopy. Gastrointest Endosc 45:AB84, 1997.

86. Strader D: Personal communication, September 9, 2003.

87. Meyer V, Burtin P, Bour B, et al: Endoscopic detection of early esophageal cancer in a high-risk population: Does Lugol staining improve videoendoscopy? Gastrointest Endosc 45:480–484, 1997.

88. Mori M, Adachi Y, Matsushima T, et al: Lugol staining pattern and histology of esophageal lesions. Am J Gastroenterol 88:701–705, 1993.

89. Seitz JF, Monges G, Navarro P, et al: [Endoscopic detection of dysplasia and subclinical cancer of the esophagus. Results of a prospective study using toluidine blue vital staining in 100 patients with alcoholism and smoking]. Gastroenterol Clin Biol 14:15–21, 1990.

90. Hix WR, Wilson WR: Toluidine blue staining of the esophagus. A useful adjunct in the panendoscopic evaluation of patients with squamous cell carcinoma of the head and neck. Arch Otolaryngol Head Neck Surg 113:864–865, 1987.

91. Contini S, Consigli GF, Di Lecce F, et al: Vital staining of oesophagus in patients with head and neck cancer: Still a worthwhile procedure. Ital J Gastroenterol 23:5–8, 1991.

92. Aoyama N, Aruike S, Koizumu H, Aoki M: Investigations of questionnaire about side effects of Lugol's staining. Jpn J Gastroenterol Soc 16:939–940, 1983.

93. Kameyama H, Murakami M, Shimuzu Y, et al: The efficacy and diagnostic significance of sodium thiosulfate spraying after iodine dyeing of the esophagus. Dig Endos 6:181–186, 1994.

94. Yonekawa H, Shima S, Yoshizumi Y: The effect of sodium thiosulfate on endoscopic Lugol staining of the esophagus. Endoscopia Digestiva 5:681–685, 1993.

95. Kondo H, Fukuda H, Ono H, et al: Sodium thiosulfate solution spray for relief of irritation caused by Lugol's stain in chromoendoscopy. Gastrointest Endosc 53:199–202, 2001.

Extraintestinal Endosonography (including celiac block)

Bonnie J. Pollack and Frank G. Gress

Introduction

The use of endoscopic ultrasonography (EUS) has grown over the last 15 years, and it is now a well-established diagnostic modality for the assessment of a range of gastrointestinal (GI) disorders including the evaluation and staging of many types of endoluminal cancers. Several years ago, it would have been unusual to consider the role that EUS currently occupies in detection of disorders outside the limits of the GI tract.

This chapter is devoted to EUS applications relating to extra-intestinal organs and lesions. The objectives of this chapter are to review the utility of EUS for evaluating the mediastinum in both benign and malignant disease processes including the detection of mediastinal lymph node metastases in lung cancer. Mass lesions in the paragastric and retroperitoneal organs (excluding the bile duct, gallbladder, and pancreas) are reviewed, including detection of lesions of the adrenal gland, the liver, and the kidneys. Ascites and pleural fluid are examined along with unusual extraintestinal lesions. In addition, the EUS-guided technique of celiac plexus block (CPB) for chronic pancreatitis and celiac plexus neurolysis (CPN) for managing malignant pain are reviewed.

Lung Cancer

Lung cancer is the leading cause of cancer death in the United States in both men and women and has an overall 5-year survival rate of 15%.[1–2] Treatment decisions are based on the location and extent of the tumor. The presence of extrapulmonary metastasis is crucial, because patients without mediastinal involvement are potential candidates for resection. The distinction between non–small cell lung cancer (NSCLC), which composes 80% of tumors, and small cell lung cancer (SCLC), which composes 20% of tumors,

is important because of the more aggressive nature of SCLC. SCLC is usually classified as limited or extensive disease, although the criteria for these two categories remain controversial.[3–5] The TNM staging system is rarely used for the classification of SCLC, although for tumor registries this system should be used. Metastatic disease is detected in 80% of SCLC cases at the time of diagnosis and tends to spread quickly so that surgery is considered less often in SCLC compared with NSCLC. Although highly responsive to radiotherapy and chemotherapy, SCLC usually recurs within 2 years.

In comparison, half of NSCLC cases are localized or locally advanced and can be treated by surgery, the cornerstone of therapy for NSCLC, or with adjuvant therapy with or without resection.[6–8] NSCLC, which includes adenocarcinoma, squamous cell cancer, and large cell cancer, is staged using the 2002 International Staging System (ISS), which is unchanged from the 1997 revision (Table 33–1).[8–10] This section focuses on EUS applications in the diagnosis and staging of NSCLC, although much of what is covered can be applied to SCLC.

STAGING AND STAGING MODALITIES

Mediastinal lymph node metastases are present in nearly half of all patients with NSCLC. Accurate staging of NSCLC plays a crucial role in determining treatment options because the detection of mediastinal lymph node metastasis preoperatively has therapeutic implications. In the absence of distant metastasis, the documen-tation of mediastinal metastasis is probably the most common deterrent to cure.[11–22] The TNM staging system used for lung cancer (see Table 33–1) designate ipsilateral peribronchial, intrapulmonary, and/or ipsilateral hilar lymph nodes as N1, and ipsilateral medi-astinal and subcarinal lymph node involvement as N2 disease. Although N2 disease is potentially resectable, most patients with N2 disease receive multimodality treatment. Contralateral lymph

Table 33–1. International Staging System for Lung Cancer, 1997 Revision

Primary Tumor (T)
Tx: Primary tumor cannot be assessed
T0: No evidence of primary tumor
Tis: Carcinoma *in situ*
T1: Tumor <3 cm without bronchoscopic evidence of invasion more proximal than the lobar bronchus (not the main bronchus unless superficial tumor of any size with invasion limited to the bronchial wall, which may extend proximal to the main bronchus)
T2: Tumor >3 cm *or* any size with any of the following:
  Involves the main bronchus, (at least 2 cm distal to the carina)
  Invades the visceral pleura
  Associated with atelectasis or obstructive pneumonitis that extends to the hilar region but does not involve the entire lung
T3: Tumor of any size that invades any of the following:
  Chest wall, diaphragm, mediastinal pleura, or parietal pericardium *or* tumor in the main bronchus <2 cm distal to the carina (without involvement of the carina)
  Atelectasis or obstructive pneumonitis of the entire lung
T4: Tumor of any size that invades any of the following:
  Mediastinum, heart, great vessels, trachea, esophagus, vertebral body, or carina
  Separate tumor nodules in the same lobe
  Malignant pleural effusion

Nodal Involvement (N)
Nx: Regional lymph nodes cannot be assessed
N0: No regional lymph nodes metastasis
N1: Metastasis to ipsilateral peribronchial and/or ipsilateral hilar lymph nodes, and intrapulmonary nodes including involvement by direct extension of the primary tumor
N2: Metastasis to ipsilateral mediastinal and/or subcarinal lymph nodes
N3: Metastasis to contralateral mediastinal, contralateral hilar, ipsilateral or contralateral scalene, or supraclavicular lymph node(s)

Metastasis (M)
Mx: Distant metastasis cannot be assessed
M0: No distant metastasis
M1: Distant metastasis present (includes separate tumor nodule(s) in a different lobe)

Stage Grouping
Occult carcinoma: TxN0M0
Stage 0: TisN0M0
Stage IA: T1N0M0
Stage IB: T2N0M0
Stage IIA: T1N1M0
Stage IIB: T2N1M0, T3N0M0
Stage IIIA: T1N2M0, T2N2M0, T3N1M0, T3N2M0
Stage IIIB: Any T N3 M0, T4 Any N M0
Stage IV: Any T any N M1

From references 8 and 9.

node involvement of mediastinal or hilar nodes or either ipsilateral or contralateral scalene or supraclavicular lymph nodes is assigned as N3 disease, which precludes resection (see Tables 33–1 and 33–2; Fig. 33–1).[8–10,22,23]

Various techniques are currently available for the diagnosis and staging of lung cancer. Modalities include plain radiography, computed tomography (CT), magnetic resonance imaging (MRI), positron emission tomography (PET), and EUS. CT of the chest is the current standard by which mediastinal lymphadenopathy is detected. In general, lymph nodes shown on chest CT to be larger than or equal to 1 cm are considered abnormal. A review of previously published studies reveals an accuracy range of CT staging of the mediastinum from 52% to 88%.[24–34] This variation has been attributed to the wide range of correlation of lymph node size to the presence of malignant involvement. Although the general trend is increased risk for metastasis correlating with increasing lymph node size, lymph node size is not an accurate criterion for assessing risk. Problems associated with size as a criterion include the inability to differentiate inflammatory or reactive lymph nodes from malignant involvement. In one study, 37% of mediastinal lymph nodes that ranged in size from 2 to 4 cm were benign,[34] and up to 40% of enlarged nodes in another series were not cancerous.[35] Similarly,

normal-sized lymph nodes can contain foci of cancer. McKenna and colleagues[36] found no correlation between the presence of mediastinal nodal metastases and nodal size. In fact, metastases may be found in 21% of normal-sized nodes.[37]

MRI is perhaps slightly superior to CT in the detection of mediastinal disease,[38] and PET has been shown to be superior to CT for staging for the mediastinum.[39,40] PET does not rely on an arbitrary cutoff of size to diagnose malignant nodes but detects the increased glycolytic rate in metabolically active tumors. In a recent meta-analysis, PET had a sensitivity of 79% and a specificity of 91% compared with CT, which had a sensitivity and specificity of 60% and 77%, respectively, for the detection of mediastinal disease.[39] In another meta-analysis by Toloza and colleagues,[40] the performance characteristics of CT, PET, and EUS for staging the mediastinum in NSCLC were compared. PET scanning was more accurate than CT or EUS for detecting mediastinal metastases with a sensitivity of 84% and a specificity of 89% for PET compared with CT scanning (sensitivity 57% and specificity 82%) and compared with EUS (sensitivity 78% and specificity 71%). However, PET is limited for small lesions (≤1 cm), has false-negative results in tumors with low metabolic activity, and has false-positive results in benign lesions such as granulomatous disease. Although PET has a relatively

Table 33–2. Lymph Node Map Definitions

Nodal Station	Anatomic Landmarks
N2 Nodes: All N2 Nodes Lie Within the Mediastinal Pleural Envelope	
1. Highest mediastinal nodes	Nodes lying above a horizontal line at the upper rim of the brachiocephalic (left innominate) vein where it ascends to the left, crossing in front of the trachea at its midline
2. Upper paratracheal nodes	Nodes lying above a horizontal line drawn tangential to the upper margin of the aortic arch and below the inferior boundary of the No. 1 nodes
3. Prevascular and retrotracheal nodes	Prevascular and retrotracheal nodes may be designated 3A and 3B; midline nodes are considered to be ipsilateral
4. Lower paratracheal nodes	The lower paratracheal nodes on the right lie to the right of the midline of the trachea between a horizontal line drawn tangential to the upper margin of the aortic arch and a line extending across the right main bronchus at the upper margin of the upper lobe bronchus, and contained within the mediastinal pleural envelope; the lower paratracheal nodes on the left lie to the left of the midline of the trachea between a horizontal line drawn tangential to the upper margin of the aortic arch and a line extending across the left main bronchus at the level of the upper margin of the left upper lobe bronchus, medial to the ligamentum arteriosum and contained within the mediastinal pleural envelope. Researchers may wish to designate the lower paratracheal nodes as No. 4s (superior) and No. 4i (inferior) subsets for study purposes; the No. 4s nodes may be defined by a horizontal line extending across the trachea and drawn tangential to the cephalic border of the azygos vein; the No. 4i nodes may be defined by the lower boundary of No. 4s and the lower boundary of No. 4 as described previously
5. Subaortic (aortopulmonary window)	Subaortic nodes are lateral to the ligamentum arteriosum or the aorta or left pulmonary artery and proximal to the first branch of the left pulmonary artery and lie within the mediastinal pleural envelope
6. Para-aortic nodes (ascending aorta or phrenic)	Nodes lying anterior and lateral to the ascending aorta and the aortic arch or the innominate artery, beneath a line tangential to the upper margin of the aortic arch
7. Subcarinal nodes	Nodes lying caudal to the carina of the trachea but not associated with the lower lobe bronchi or arteries within the lung
8. Paraesophageal nodes (below carina)	Nodes lying adjacent to the wall of the esophagus and to the right or left of the midline, excluding subcarinal nodes
9. Pulmonary ligament nodes	Nodes lying within the pulmonary ligament, including those in the posterior wall and lower part of the inferior pulmonary vein
N1 nodes: All N1 Nodes Lie Distal to the Mediastinal Pleural Reflection and Within the Visceral Pleura	
10. Hilar nodes	The proximal lobar nodes, distal to the mediastinal pleural reflection and the nodes adjacent to the bronchus intermedius on the right; radiographically, the hilar shadow may be created by enlargement of both hilar and interlobar nodes
11. Interlobar nodes	Nodes lying between the lobar bronchi
12. Lobar nodes	Nodes adjacent to the distal lobar bronchi
13. Segmental nodes	Nodes adjacent to the segmental bronchi
14. Subsegmental nodes	Nodes around the subsegmental bronchi

From Mountain CF, Dresler CM: Regional lymph node classification for lung cancer staging. Chest 11:1718–1723, 1997.

high sensitivity, because of the importance and implications of staging, specificity is still too low and pathologic staging is still generally sought.[41–43] Fritscher-Ravens and associates[44] performed a prospective comparison of CT, PET, and EUS for the detection of metastatic lymph nodes metastases in patients with lung cancer considered for operative resection. After bronchoscopic evaluation, CT, PET, and EUS were performed to evaluate potential mediastinal involvement with bronchoscopic biopsy/cytology proven (n = 25) or radiologically suspected (n = 8) lung cancer before surgery. Surgical histology was used as "gold standard" and revealed NSCLC in 30 patients, neuroendocrine tumor in 1 patient, and benign disease in 2 patients. With respect to the correct prediction of mediastinal lymph node stage, the sensitivities of CT, PET, and EUS were 57%, 73%, and 94%; specificities were 74%, 83%, and 71%; and accuracies were 67%, 79%, and 82%, respectively. Results of PET could be improved when combined with CT (sensitivity, 81%; specificity, 94%; accuracy, 88%). The specificity of EUS (71%) was improved to 100% by fine needle aspiration (FNA) cytology. The

authors concluded that no single imaging method alone was conclusive in evaluating potential mediastinal involvement. They also suggested that CT may be necessary to evaluate the pretracheal region and the rest of the thorax and that PET may be valuable to detect distant metastases.

Whenever enlarged lymph nodes are seen in the mediastinum on chest CT, standard practice is to perform a lymph node biopsy for more accurate staging. The traditional methods for performing a lymph node biopsy are via CT and/or bronchoscopy. Bronchoscopy with FNA is commonly used to evaluate suspicious paratracheal, hilar, and subcarinal lymph nodes seen on CT.[45–48] Its role in the diagnosis and staging of NSCLC is well established and has a sensitivity of approximately 60%.[49–55] However, bronchoscopy is not able to access the aortopulmonary window or the inferior mediastinal nodes. CT-guided biopsy of the mediastinum is limited by overlying vascular and bony structures. When the lymph node status is not determined with CT and/or bronchoscopy, mediastinoscopy and in some cases limited thoracotomy are performed

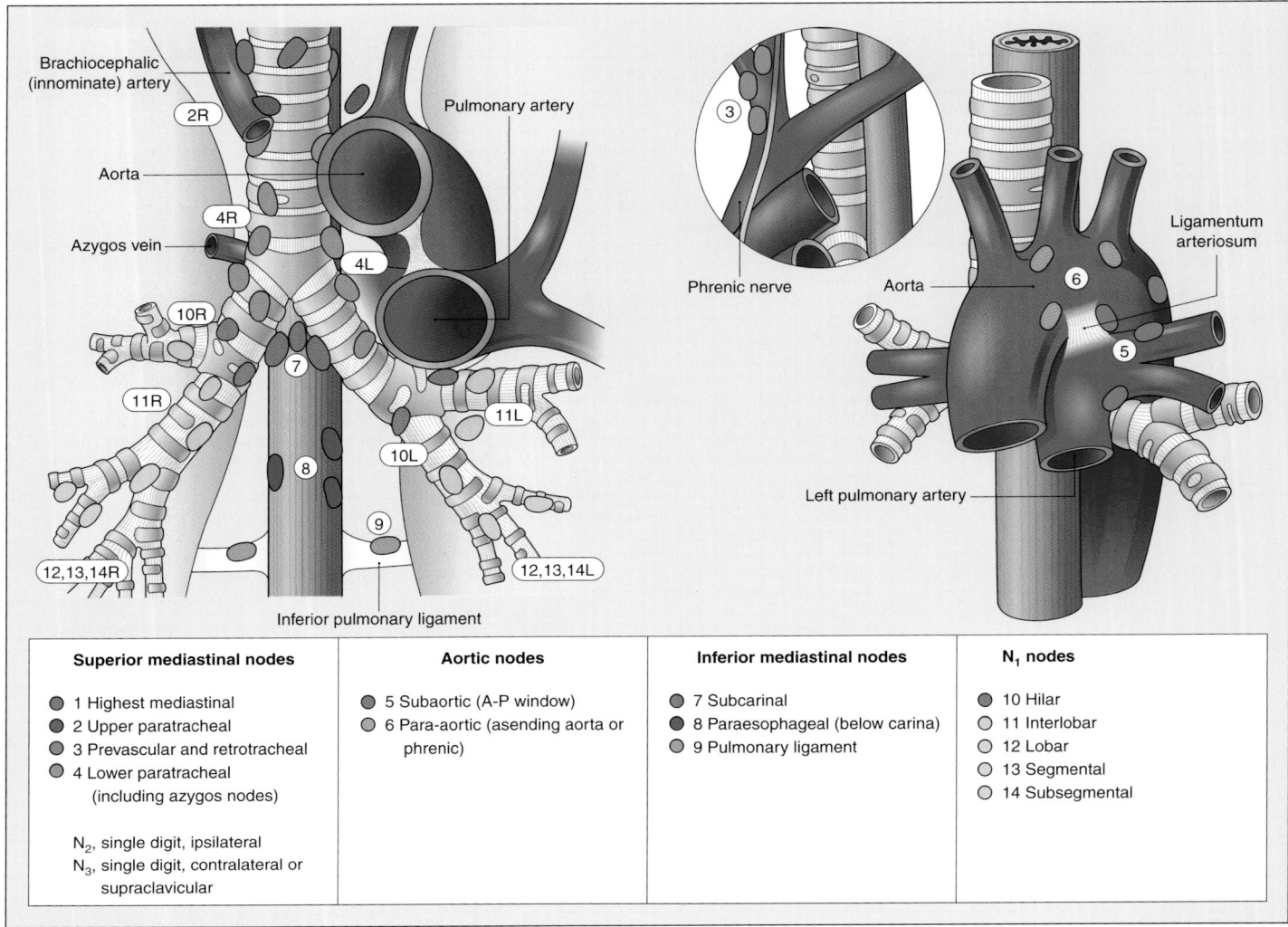

Figure 33–1. Lymph node stations. (From Mountain CF, Dresler CM: Regional lymph node stations for lung cancer staging. Chest 111:1718–1723, 1997.)

Within the figure:

Brachiocephalic (innominate) artery — 2R
Aorta — 4R
Azygos vein — 4L
10R
7
11R
11L
10L
8
9
12,13,14R
12,13,14L
Inferior pulmonary ligament

Pulmonary artery

3
Phrenic nerve — Aorta — 6 — Ligamentum arteriosum
5
Left pulmonary artery

Superior mediastinal nodes	Aortic nodes	Inferior mediastinal nodes	N₁ nodes
1 Highest mediastinal	5 Subaortic (A-P window)	7 Subcarinal	10 Hilar
2 Upper paratracheal	6 Para-aortic (asending aorta or phrenic)	8 Paraesophageal (below carina)	11 Interlobar
3 Prevascular and retrotracheal		9 Pulmonary ligament	12 Lobar
4 Lower paratracheal (including azygos nodes)			13 Segmental
			14 Subsegmental
N_2, single digit, ipsilateral			
N_3, single digit, contralateral or supraclavicular			

to clarify the disease stage.[33,56–58] However, these procedures are more invasive and require general anesthesia and inpatient recovery, thus increasing the time, cost, and risk of the staging process.[59]

ENDOSCOPIC ULTRASONOGRAPHY

The advent of EUS has made it possible to image the GI tract and surrounding extraluminal structures such as the mediastinum with precise resolution. Over the last decade, EUS has played an increasingly important role as an accurate and safe method for staging patients with NSCLC.[60–77] With the advent of transesophageal EUS-guided FNA, suspicious posterior mediastinal lymph nodes, including aortopulmonary window, subcarinal nodes, and inferior (below carina) paraesophageal nodes can be sampled. Tracheal air artifact generally precludes reliable assessment of the anterior mediastinum lesions, pretracheal nodes, and upper paratracheal nodes. The use of EUS technology can enhance the overall accuracy for detecting mediastinal lymph node metastasis.

The results of a pilot study evaluating the role of EUS in 17 patients with lung cancer found EUS to be very accurate at detect-

ing mediastinal lymphadenopathy with an overall accuracy of 71% versus 41% for CT.[75] However, during this initial study the capability of performing EUS-guided FNA was not available. Sampling of suspicious lymph is essential except in N1 nodes. In the mid-to-late 1990s, several prospective studies evaluated the accuracy of EUS, EUS-guided FNA, and chest CT in detecting and staging mediastinal lymph node metastasis in patients with NSCLC based on correlation with surgical staging.[65–67] Gress and colleagues[67] reported a study consisting of patients with NSCLC and enlarged mediastinal lymph nodes (>1 cm) seen on chest CT. EUS-guided FNA was performed for suspicious contralateral posterior mediastinal or subcarinal lymph nodes. EUS criteria used to differentiate benign from malignant lymph nodes resulted in an accuracy of 84% compared with 49% for CT. The sensitivity and specificity of CT was 64% and 35%, respectively, which compared with a sensitivity and specificity of 86% and 83% for EUS. The addition of transesophageal EUS-guided FNA improved the overall accuracy of lymph node staging to 96% with a sensitivity of 93% and a specificity of 100%. The combination of CT and EUS did not improve overall accuracy above that for EUS alone for detecting lymph node involvement. However, the addition of CT did aid in evaluating the extent of the lung cancer, detecting distant metastasis not seen by EUS, and evaluating anterior and pretracheal nodes, which are not imaged by EUS. EUS was best at accurately detecting mediastinal lymph node metastasis in the aortopulmonary window (station 5), subcarinal (station 7), and paraesophageal (station 8) regions (see Fig. 33–1). These findings are similar to the studies reported by Giovannini and colleagues[65] and Silvestri and co-workers[66] who reported sensitivities of 81% and 89%, respectively, and specificities of 100% each. Wallace and colleagues[76] have reported the largest series to date, which included 121 patients with carcinoma of the lung who had EUS staging procedures. The overall sensitivity in this study was 87% for EUS and CT. The specificity of EUS was 100% for the detection of mediastinal lymph nodes, whereas that of CT was 32%. Mediastinal disease was detected in 10 of 24 (42%) patients who did not have enlarged mediastinal lymph nodes on CT. Therefore, the need for more invasive staging procedures was avoided in some patients who had disease detected by EUS-guided FNA; however, up to 30% of patients in this study did have malignant nodes detected at mediastinoscopy after EUS failed to detect lymph nodes. Fritscher-Ravens and colleagues[77] detected lung cancer with a sensitivity of 96% and specificity of 100% for patients undergoing EUS-guided FNA of mediastinal lymph nodes when bronchoscopic methods failed.

ENDOSCOPIC ULTRASONOGRAPHY TECHNIQUE FOR IMAGING THE MEDIASTINUM

After informed consent is obtained, the patient is placed in the left lateral decubitus position. Conscious sedation is administered and the echoendoscope is then passed to the gastroesophageal junction in a manner similar to the passage of a duodenoscope. Many endosonographers first perform staging with a radial scanning echoendoscope, and then switch to a dedicated biopsy echoendoscope or a curved linear array echoendoscope if FNA is to be performed.

When imaging the mediastinum, a thorough understanding of mediastinal anatomy relative to the esophagus is essential to perform a complete examination. Scanning should begin distally below the gastroesophageal (GE) junction while withdrawing the scope proximally as this limits scanning artifacts. It is useful to press the transducer with its balloon partially inflated against the gut wall to minimize air artifacts and help to anchor the transducer. In addition, the suction port is depressed to maintain optimal imaging by minimizing intraluminal air. As the endosonographer withdraws the radial scanning echoendoscope, the aorta should be maintained in the 5- to 6-o'clock position in the ultrasound (US) field, which generally allows proper orientation of the paraesophageal structures. The aorta is easily recognized as the circular anechoic structure, approximately 1.5 to 2 cm in diameter, with a relatively bright border resulting from back wall enhancement (a normal artifact seen in vessels). As the echoendoscope is withdrawn into the distal esophagus, the aorta, spine, left lobe of the liver, inferior vena cava, and heart can be seen. The spine is also easily identified in the 7-o'clock position next to the aorta and has irregular echo features with artifacts produced by poor penetration of echoes through bony structures. The left lobe of the liver appears at the 6- to 12-o'clock

position and often the hepatic veins and inferior vena cava can be seen as they course through the liver. Slightly more proximally, the beating of the heart is appreciated as the left atrium comes into view at the 12-o'clock position. The mitral valve leaflets can be seen as the valve opens from the left atrium into the left ventricle, and the pulmonary veins can be seen entering the left atrium. The left pulmonary artery arches posteriorly to the left of the ascending aorta and tends to be easier to view than the right pulmonary artery, which can be seen just below the carina. The left ventricle, right atrium, and right ventricle lie deep to the left atrium; therefore, it can be more difficult to visualize these structures completely. As the aorta moves toward the left, the spine and azygous vein are seen posteriorly. The aortic outflow tract can be appreciated as the endoscope is withdrawn further. The spine continues to be a useful landmark because it consistently appears as a hyperechoic structure located posteriorly throughout the chest. Careful inspection of this area may reveal the thoracic duct adjacent to the aorta and spine.

The right lung appears as hyperechoic rings emanating from the 9-o'clock position, whereas the left lung appears at the 2-o'clock position. In the midesophagus, the right and left bronchi are easily demarcated by the hyperechoic rings (echogenic air) seen at the 11-and 1-o'clock positions. The two bronchi join together to form the trachea normally at 27 to 28 cm from the incisors. The azygos vein can be seen coming into position to the right of the aorta and moves anterior to the spine and toward the right lung. As the endoscope is withdrawn further, the azygos can be seen to move forward and extend anteriorly into the superior vena cava. The ascending aorta can be difficult to trace because this structure runs deep to the hilar structures (pulmonary vessels) and, because of air within the bronchi and trachea, the ascending aorta is often not fully imaged. In the proximal esophagus, the aortic arch is identified on the left and then moves rightward and anteriorly across the screen. In the cervical esophagus, above the level of the aortic arch, the carotid vessels and, occasionally, the thyroid gland can be seen (Figs. 33–2, 33–3, and 33–4).

Evaluation of the mediastinum using linear EUS requires rotation of the echoendoscope every few centimeters for a thorough evaluation. As in radial endosonography, vascular structures provide the major landmarks for orientation, and the home-base structure is the descending aorta, which is first located approximately 35 cm from the incisors. The echoendoscope is rotated initially clockwise (right) bringing structures anterior to the esophagus into view and then counterclockwise (left) bringing posterior structures into view. The left atrium is found by rotating the shaft of the scope 180 degrees in the distal to midesophagus until a large, echolucent structure is seen within which the mitral valve leaflets are located. By tipping the scope upward and with slight withdrawal, the subcarinal lymph node station is located immediately beneath the endoscope at approximately 27 cm between the left atrium and right pulmonary artery. The aortopulmonary window is located by following the descending aorta cephalad to the arch and then pushing the endoscope in again about 2 cm. The endoscope is then turned 90 degrees clockwise and tipped up slightly until a cross-sectional view of the aortic arch and the more distally located left pulmonary artery are seen. The area between these structures is known as the "AP window." Another potentially important area for FNA of lymph nodes is the celiac axis. This area is located by finding

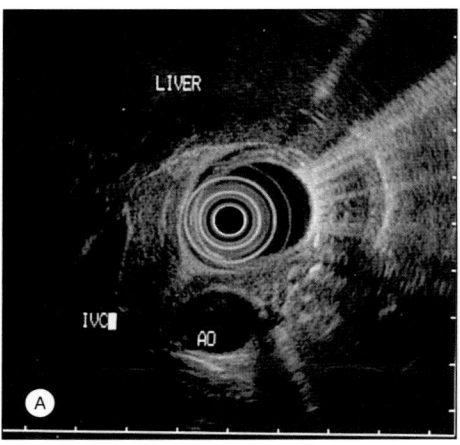
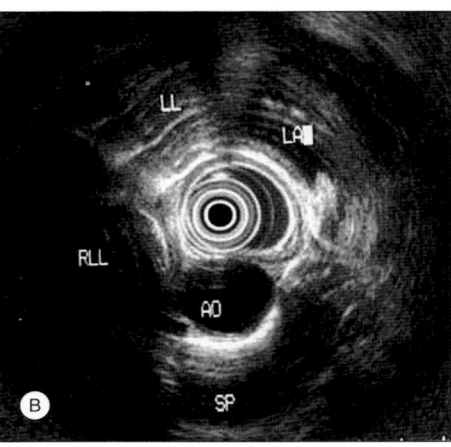

Figure 33-2. *A,* Radial imaging at the distal esophagus showing the liver, inferior vena cava (IVC), and aorta (AO). The spine lies immediately deep to the aorta. *B,* Imaging slightly higher in the distal esophagus, the right lung (RLL), left lung (LL), aorta (AO), spine (SP), and a portion of the left atrium (LA) can be seen.

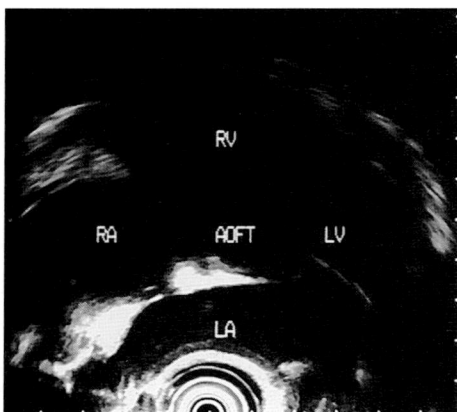

Figure 33-3. Radial endoscopic ultrasonography (EUS) imaging from the distal esophagus. The left atrium (LA), the right atrium (RA), the right ventricle (RV), and the left ventricle (LV) can be seen. The leaflets of the mitral valve and the base of the aortic outflow tract (AOFT) are also visible.

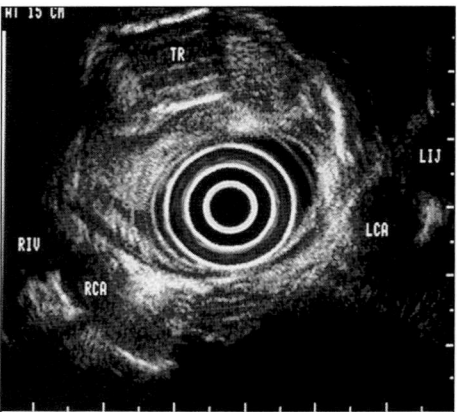

Figure 33-4. Radial endoscopic ultrasonography (EUS) imaging from the most proximal aspect of the esophagus. The left common carotid artery (LCA), the left internal jugular vein (LIJ), the right internal jugular vein (RIV), and right common carotid artery (RCA) are seen. In addition, the thyroid gland is seen on either side of the trachea (TR).

the abdominal aorta at the level of the GE junction and the takeoff of the celiac artery with the superior mesenteric artery just distal to this (Figs. 33–5, 33–6, 33–7, and 33–8).

Techniques for Staging Non–Small Cell Lung Cancer with Endoscopic Ultrasonography

EUS is performed under conscious sedation in an outpatient setting with the radial scanning and/or the linear array scanning echoendoscopes. In experienced hands and with careful planning, EUS of the mediastinum can be quickly accomplished regardless of the type of EUS technology used to perform the examination. When FNA of mediastinal lymph nodes is performed the procedure is slightly prolonged, dependent on the availability of the cyto-pathologist. The preparation of the patient is the same as that used for standard endoscopy. Prophylactic antibiotics are not administered unless recommended by the American Heart Association and/or the American Society of Gastrointestinal Endoscopy because EUS-guided FNA of mediastinal lesions is not associated with significant bacteremia. However, prophylactic quinolone antibiotics are recommended for FNA of cystic mediastinal lesions, which is similar to the recommendations for pancreatic cystic lesions and perirectal lesions.[78–85] After informed consent is obtained and conscious sedation administered (we have found propofol to be effective), the instrument is advanced into the stomach and the celiac axis imaged. The probe is then slowly withdrawn to the GE junction and then cephalad using radially scanning images generally obtained with 7.5-MHz frequencies at each 1-cm interval while keeping the aorta at the 5- or 6-o'clock position. All mediastinal lymph nodes seen are "mapped" by location according to the American Thoracic Society (ATS) classification scheme (see Tables 33–1 and 33–2; Fig. 33–1; Video 33–1).[8–10]

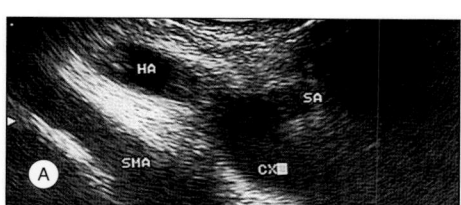
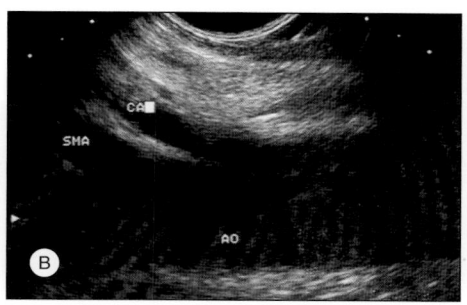
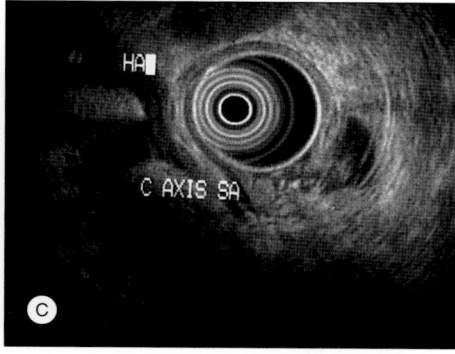

Figure 33–5. *A,* Linear array imaging of the celiac axis is depicted showing the takeoff of the superior mesenteric artery and celiac axis along with the hepatic artery and splenic artery branches. *B,* More typical linear images as seen from the proximal stomach. *C,* Radial imaging showing the celiac axis. CX, celiac axis; HA, hepatic artery; SA, splenic artery; SMA, superior mesenteric artery.

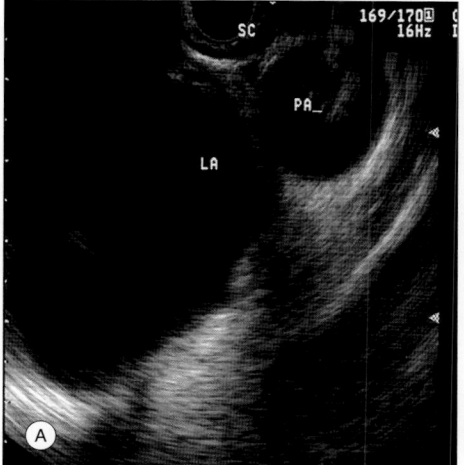
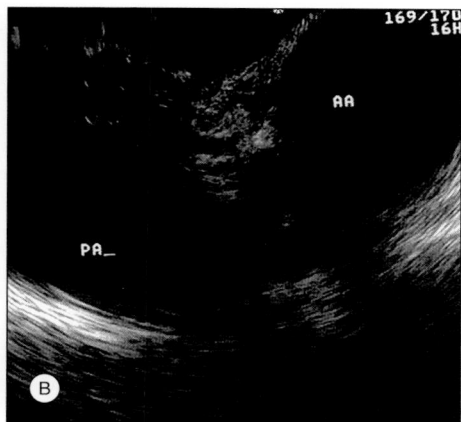
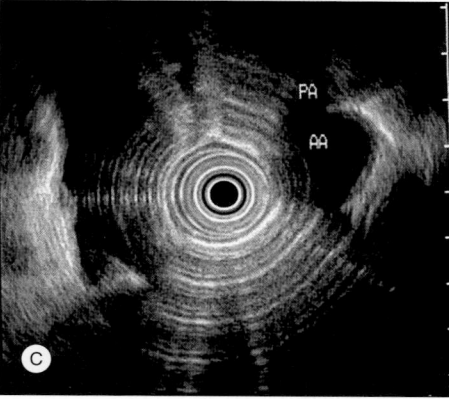

Figure 33–6. *A,* Curved linear array view through the midesophagus of the subcarinal (SC) region. The left atrium (LA) is next to the right pulmonary artery (PA) with the ascending aorta lying deep to these structures. *B,* Linear array view through the midesophagus of the aortic arch (AA) and the pulmonary artery (PA)—the "AP window." *C,* Radial imaging of the area of the AP window. AA, aortic arch; PA, pulmonary artery.

An objective determination is made as to whether the mediastinal lymphadenopathy detected by EUS is consistent with benign or malignant status according to previously reported studies using the same criteria.[74,79,86–92] The EUS criteria used to diagnose malignant lymph nodes are round shape, sharp distinct borders, hypoechoic texture, and a short-axis diameter greater than 5 mm. Each of these parameters should be present for a lymph node to be considered as potentially malignant; however, FNA has significantly improved the sensitivity and specificity of malignant lymph node detection.[65–67,76,77,79,92,93]

Careful inspection is then made of the liver and left adrenal gland and the possible unexpected detection of ascites or pleural fluid. If suspicious lymphadenopathy or other suspicious findings are seen that may represent metastatic disease, the linear echoendoscope is introduced (if not already in use) and EUS-guided FNA is performed. It is noted that many centers have successfully used only linear technology for both diagnostic imaging and for obtaining needle-aspiration cytologic samples.

Technique for Performing Endoscopic Ultrasonography Guided Fine Needle Aspiration

MEDIASTINAL LYMPH NODES

EUS-guided FNA became available after the development of a specially designed needle catheter system consisting of a 4-cm, 23-gauge needle attached to a 180-cm long, 5-French aspiration catheter (Echo Tip, Wilson-Cook Medical, Inc., Winston-Salem, NC) and the 22-gauge, 10-cm needle (GIP, Medi-Globe, Inc., Tempe, AZ). Presently, there are several EUS catheter–FNA needle systems available with various needle lengths (up to 14 cm) and gauges (19 to 25 gauge) available. We routinely perform EUS-guided FNA on all posterior mediastinal lymph nodes that are suspicious for malignant involvement by EUS criteria. Many patients have more than one suspicious lymph node or finding. In our patients, we

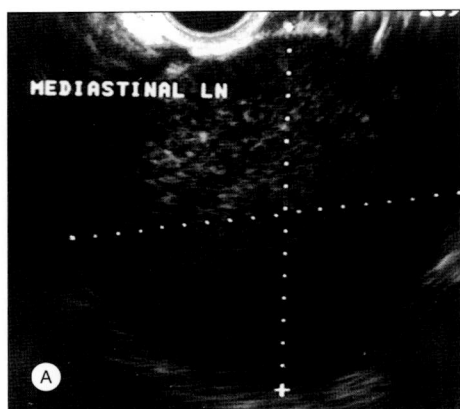

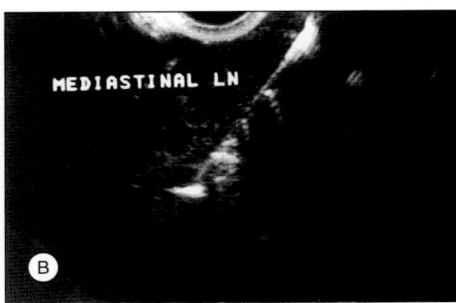

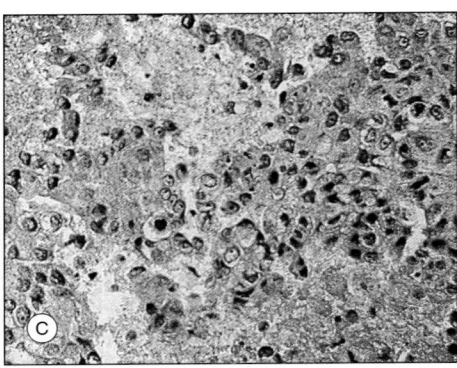

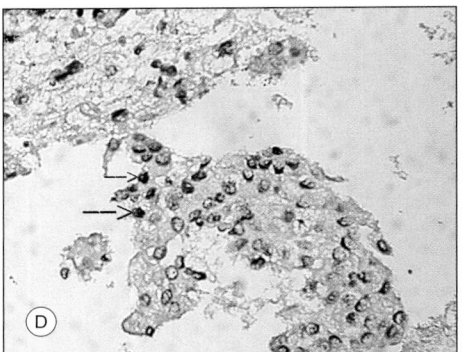

Figure 33-7. *A,* This demonstrates a mediastinal lymph node as imaged with the linear array endoscopic ultrasonography (EUS) system. *B,* This picture shows the fine needle aspiration (FNA) needle exiting the scope and the tip of the needle is seen to be in the center of the lymph node. *C,* High power magnification of hematoxylin and eosin (H&E) stain on cell block revealing metastatic adenocarcinoma. *D,* High power magnification of immunoperoxidase stain on cellblock. Tumor nuclei *(arrows)* are positive for TTF1 antibody consistent with non–small cell lung carcinoma. LN, lymph node.

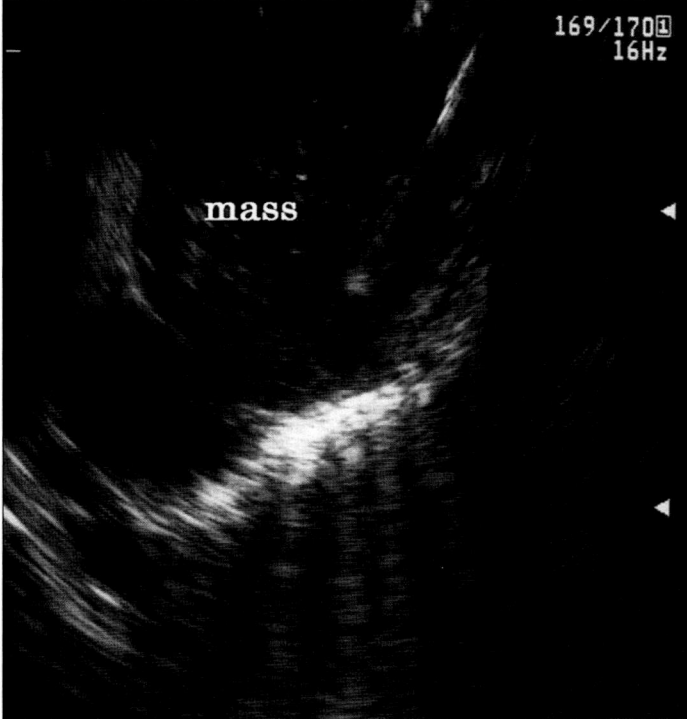

Figure 33-8. Linear endoscopic ultrasonography (EUS) imaging revealing a hypoechoic mass within the mediastinum. EUS-guided fine needle aspiration (FNA) was performed and revealed metastatic non-small cell lung cancer (cytology favored a large cell neuroendocrine type lesion).

sample only the most suspicious lymph node or finding that would have the greatest impact on the clinical staging (i.e., contralateral or subcarinal). The EUS-guided FNA biopsy technique was initially developed for use with the linear array instrument and has been described elsewhere.[87–89,94,95] The unique viewing angle of the linear array transducer allows for observation of the needle as it exits the biopsy channel and enables direction of the needle tip into the target lesion. A similar technique using a radial scanning echoendoscope has been reported; however, serious complications have been described via this technique, and, therefore, it is not recommended.[86,95]

EUS-guided FNA involves the insertion of the FNA catheter device through the accessory channel of the echoendoscope followed by deployment of the needle under EUS guidance into the lymph node to be sampled. The handle mechanism is secured to the accessory port and if the instrument has an elevator, the elevator should be fully released into the down position to allow easy passage of the needle. The elevator can be used during the biopsy to gently direct the needle into the lesion. Doppler is used to identify surrounding vascular structures. The FNA needle is slowly advanced toward the target lesion. The stylet is withdrawn a few millimeters (2 to 3 mm), and the needle and the stylet are then directed into the target. When the needle has entered the lesion, the stylet is advanced (to clear the needle) and then removed. The endosonographer or assistant applies suction to the catheter system using a 5- or 10-mL Luer lock syringe. This is followed by "in and out" movements of the catheter after firmly locking the needle-catheter system to the appropriate depth so that the needle is not advanced beyond a desired depth. Typically, we make 7 to 10 gradual in-and-out movements within the lesion. Before removing the needle, the negative pressure is released slowly and the needle removed from the lesion and subsequently the needle system is unscrewed from the echoendoscope. There has been a suggestion of performing EUS-guided FNA of lymph nodes without the use of suction, because suction may result in a bloody sample that may be more difficult for the cytopathologist to examine.[92]

Preliminary cytology findings are obtained immediately during the FNA procedure by a cytopathologist or cytotechnologist present during the study. We recommend having a cytopathologist or cytotechnologist present during the EUS-guided FNA portion of the procedure because it can improve the efficiency of the technique. If this is not possible, two to three passes should be taken for lymph nodes (or liver metastases) and five to six passes for masses (similar to pancreatic masses) to ensure adequate cellularity in more than 90% of cases.[92,96] However, this approach is associated with a 10% reduction in definitive cytologic diagnoses, increased time and risk, and potentially the need for additional needles.[92] The FNA sample obtained is prepared for reviewing using Diff-Quik stain (Harleco, Gibbstown, NJ) applied to the slide containing the deposited specimen or fixed with ethanol. Additional passes are made until a positive cytology or adequate tissue sample is obtained. When lymphoma is suspected, added material is collected if possible and placed in a preservative solution (RPMI media) for subsequent flow cytometry and immunocytochemistry as indicated.[97,98] If an infection is suspected, a culture media can be used.

OTHER MALIGNANT MEDIASTINAL DISEASE

Arguably, the most important indication for mediastinal imaging is the detection and/or staging of lung cancer. However, there are several reports of EUS-guided FNA in the cytologic diagnosis of mediastinal metastases from various extrathoracic malignancies in which EUS has played a pivotal role in detection or staging. These include metastatic pancreatic, esophageal, gastric, colon, laryngeal, germ cell, renal cell, breast, and ovarian cancers.[68,69,71–73,99–102]

Most of the experience with EUS in patients with lymphoma has been in the setting of gastric lymphoma, although there are reports of mediastinal lymphoma as well.[72,103] In a study by Fritscher-Ravens and colleagues[72] of 153 patients with mediastinal lymphadenopathy undergoing EUS-guided FNA, lymphadenopathy originated from the lung in greater than 80% of patients without a previous cancer diagnosis, whereas in those with a previous malignancy, recurrence of extrathoracic sites was the major cause of mediastinal lymphadenopathy. Benign lesions and treatable second cancers were found in a significant minority of patients. Devereaux and colleagues[102] retrospectively reviewed a large, single-center experience with EUS-guided FNA for the diagnosis of mediastinal mass or lymphadenopathy in the absence of known pulmonary malignancy. In this report, 49 patients were analyzed; in 22/49 (45%) a malignant process was diagnosed, and in 24/49 (49%) a benign process was found. These included four previously undiagnosed lung cancer patients, whereas metastatic breast carcinoma was the most frequent (6/22, 27%) lesion. EUS-guided FNA was diagnostic in 46/49 (94%) patients. Catalano and coworkers[99] reported a multicenter study of 62 patients in which FNA results were classified as benign/infectious, malignant pulmonary, and malignant mediastinal (lymphoma, metastatic malignancy); EUS-guided FNA was diagnostic in 90% of cases. Panelli and associates[104] reported a series of 33 patients with mediastinal masses, which represented 2.3% of the 1447 upper EUS examinations over a 5-year period. EUS-guided FNA was performed in 25/33 (76%), of which 22 (67%) ultimately were determined to be malignant. Wiersema and coworkers[73] reported a series of 82 patients with mediastinal lymphadenopathy and EUS-guided FNA after other nonsurgical techniques failed to provide a diagnosis or could not be used. The sensitivity and specificity of EUS-guided FNA were 96% and 100%, respectively. These studies suggest that in the absence of accessible extrathoracic disease lesions or as an alternative, EUS-guided FNA may be a useful technique for the cytodiagnosis of extrathoracic cancers that are metastatic to the mediastinum. Table 33–3 summarizes the reported studies for EUS-guided FNA of mediastinal lymphadenopathy (Fig. 33–9).

NONMALIGNANT MEDIASTINAL DISEASE

Although commonly present in patients with suspected or known pulmonary malignancy, mediastinal lymph nodes are also present in patients with benign diseases such as histoplasmosis, tuberculosis, and sarcoidosis.[72,102,105–109] In addition, benign cystic structures such as congenital foregut cysts account for approximately 20% of mediastinal masses.[83]

Wiersema and coworkers[105] described three patients with dysphagia from compression of the esophagus by mediastinal masses.

EUS demonstrated that the masses were enlarged lymph nodes with anechoic areas thought to represent caseating necrosis. The EUS-guided FNA finding of reactive lymphocytes along with a positive complement fixation titer was instrumental in making the diagnosis of mediastinal histoplasmosis. Savides and colleagues[107] described 11 patients with dysphagia who had a midesophageal submucosal mass or stricture. EUS findings consisted of large, matted posterior mediastinal lymph nodes in all patients. The diagnosis of histoplasmosis was supported by EUS finding of lymph node calcifications in seven of these patients, symptomatic improvement in response to antifungal medication in all seven who were treated, and a mean follow-up of 20.5 months in which none of the patients developed signs of a malignancy.

EUS has been reported to be an accurate and simple method for the diagnosis of sarcoidosis, a systemic granulomatous disease with a predilection for the lung and mediastinal lymph nodes.[108,109] In most situations, the recommended procedure is a transbronchial biopsy, which has a diagnostic yield of 40% with one biopsy and 90% when four biopsies are obtained.[110] If the transbronchial approach is not successful, more invasive diagnostic procedures such as mediastinoscopy or lung biopsy may be used. Recently, there were several reports describing the utility of EUS-guided FNA in the diagnosis of sarcoidosis presenting with mediastinal lymphadenopathy.[108,109,111] Mishra and coworkers[108] described seven patients with mediastinal lymphadenopathy in which EUS helped confirm the diagnosis of sarcoidosis. Nodes were between 1.8 to 6 cm in the long axis and were elongated and triangular and described as draping around the esophagus. A study reporting the results of EUS-guided FNA evaluation in 19 patients with suspected sarcoidosis revealed enlarged mediastinal lymph nodes (mean size, 2.4 cm) located subcarinally ($n = 15$), in the aortopulmonary window ($n = 12$), and in the lower posterior mediastinum ($n = 5$).[109] The nodes were described as isoechoic or hypoechoic, with "atypical" vessels in five cases. The aspirate obtained using EUS-guided FNA was adequate in all patients and contained blood in excess of normal in some, which was felt to be indicative of a high degree of vascularity. Cytology demonstrated epithelioid cell granuloma formation, and cultures for *Mycobacteria* were negative in all of the patients except

Table 33–3. Diagnostic Characteristics of EUS-FNA for Mediastinal Lymphadenopathy

Author	n	Sensitivity (%)	Specificity (%)	Accuracy (%)
Giovannini, et al. (65)	24	81	100	83
Silvestri, et al. (66)	26	89	100	92
Gress, et al. (67)	24	93	100	96
Hunerbein, et al. (68)	25	89	83	—
Janssen, et al. (69)	35	—	—	91
Serna, et al. (70)	7	86	100	86
Williams, et al. (71)	120	83	100	89
Fritscher-Ravens, et al. (72)	153	92	100	95
Wiersema, et al. (73)	82	96	100	98

EUS, endoscopic ultrasonography; FNA, fine needle aspiration.
Adapted from Norton ID, Wiersema MJ: Endoscopic ultrasound-guided fine needle aspiration biopsy. In Gress F, Bhattacharya I (eds): Endoscopic Ultrasonography. Malden, MA, Blackwell Science, 2001, pp 136–148.

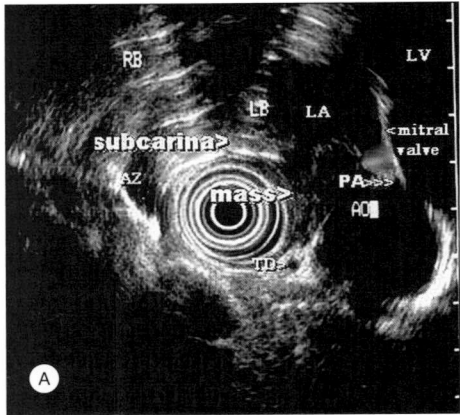
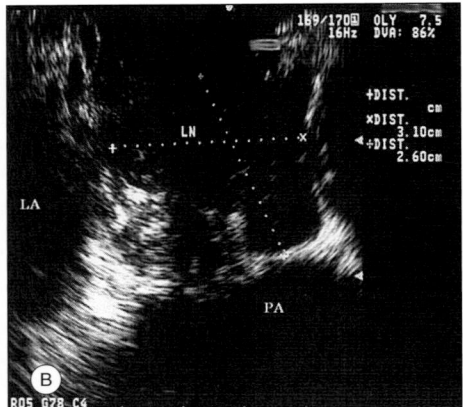
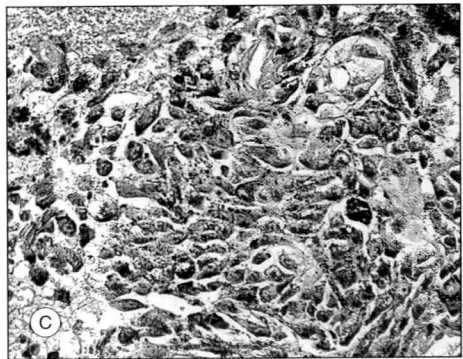

Figure 33–9. A 71-year-old woman with a history of breast cancer and melanoma was found to have mediastinal lymphadenopathy on chest computed tomography (CT). *A,* Radial endoscopic ultrasonography (EUS) revealed a subcarinal 3.1 by 2.6 cm necrotic-appearing lymph node versus mass. *B,* Linear array imaging depicting fine needle aspiration (FNA) of this lesion. *C,* High-power magnification of hematoxylin and eosin (H&E) stain on cell block showing metastatic pigmented melanoma. AO, aorta; AZ, azygous vein; LA, left atrium; LB, left bronchi; LV, left ventricle; PA, pulmonary artery; RB, right bronchi; TD, thoracic duct.

one, in whom the final diagnosis was tuberculosis. The specificity and sensitivity of EUS-guided FNA in the diagnosis of sarcoidosis were 94% and 100%, respectively. Fritscher-Ravens and coworkers[72] found 2 patients with tuberculosis in the 101 patients without a history of cancer who had EUS-guided FNA of mediastinal lymph nodes. This highlights the need for acid-fast staining and culture to exclude tuberculosis in cases of noncaseating granulomas. In addition, there is potential for EUS-guided FNA in the cytologic diagnosis of intra-abdominal and pancreatic sarcoidosis (Figs. 33–10 and 33–11).[112–114]

It is also important to be aware that approximately 4% of regional lymph nodes of carcinomas have noncaseating epithelioid granulomas so that a presumptive diagnosis of sarcoidosis or another granulomatous disease should only be made after careful exclusion of malignancy and close follow-up.[115] Detectable mediastinal lymph nodes may also be present in normal subjects and are often found in patients undergoing EUS examinations for various indications (Fig. 33–12).[74,116] It has been postulated that detectable mediastinal lymph nodes in asymptomatic individuals may be related to prior histoplasmosis or other pulmonary infections.[107] Devereaux and colleagues,[102] in their retrospective study of 49 patients with mediastinal masses in the absence of known pulmonary malignancy, found a benign process in 24/49 (49%) including 8 patients with histoplasmosis, 1 with sarcoid, 2 with leiomyoma, 2 with duplication cyst, 1 teratoma, and 10 with benign lymph node cytology on EUS-guided FNA.

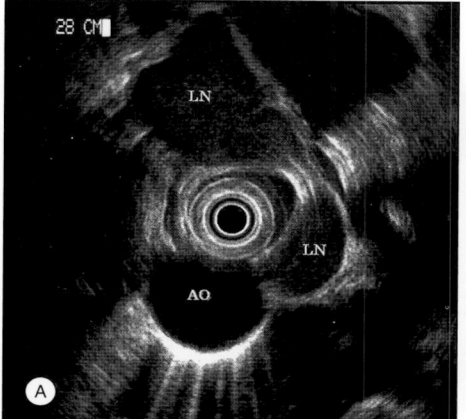
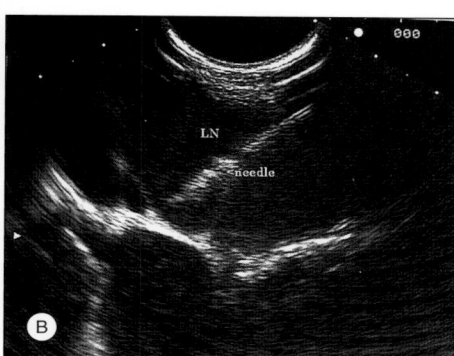
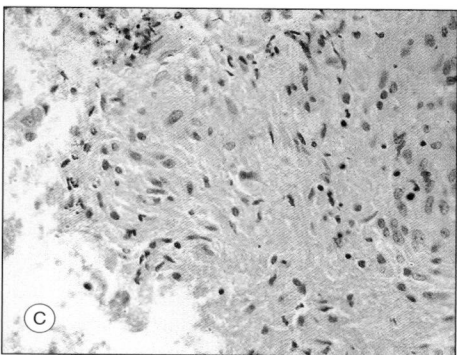

Figure 33–10. *A,* Radial imaging of large hypoechoic, oblong, and tear-drop-shaped mediastinal lymph nodes (measuring up to 3.7 by 3.4 cm) in a patient with fever and elevated angiotensin-converting enzyme (ACE) level. *B,* Fine needle aspiration (FNA) performed with linear array echoendoscope. *C,* High magnification of hematoxylin and eosin (H&E) stain on cell block revealing a noncaseating epithelioid granuloma consistent with sarcoidosis. Special stains (AFB, acid fast bacilli; GMS, Gomori methenamine silver) to rule out tuberculosis and fungal infections were negative. AO, aorta; LN, lymph node.

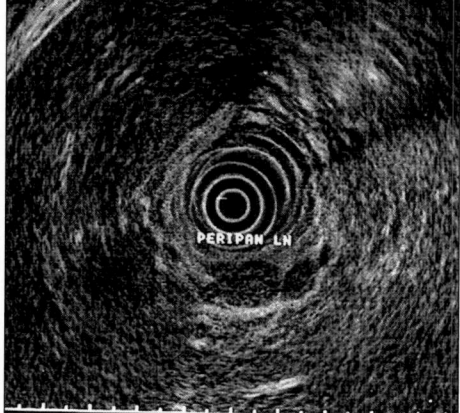
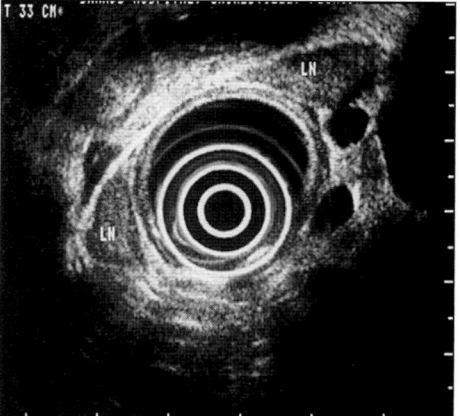

Figure 33–11. Radial endoscopic ultrasonography (EUS) imaging from the body of the stomach in a patient with a history of sarcoidosis with peripancreatic lymphadenopathy that increased in size on serial transabdominal imaging. EUS revealed several hypoechoic lymph nodes. Fine needle aspiration (FNA) yielded tissue with prominent granulomatous inflammation thought to represent abdominal sarcoidosis.

Figure 33–12. Radial imaging of benign-appearing mediastinal lymph nodes.

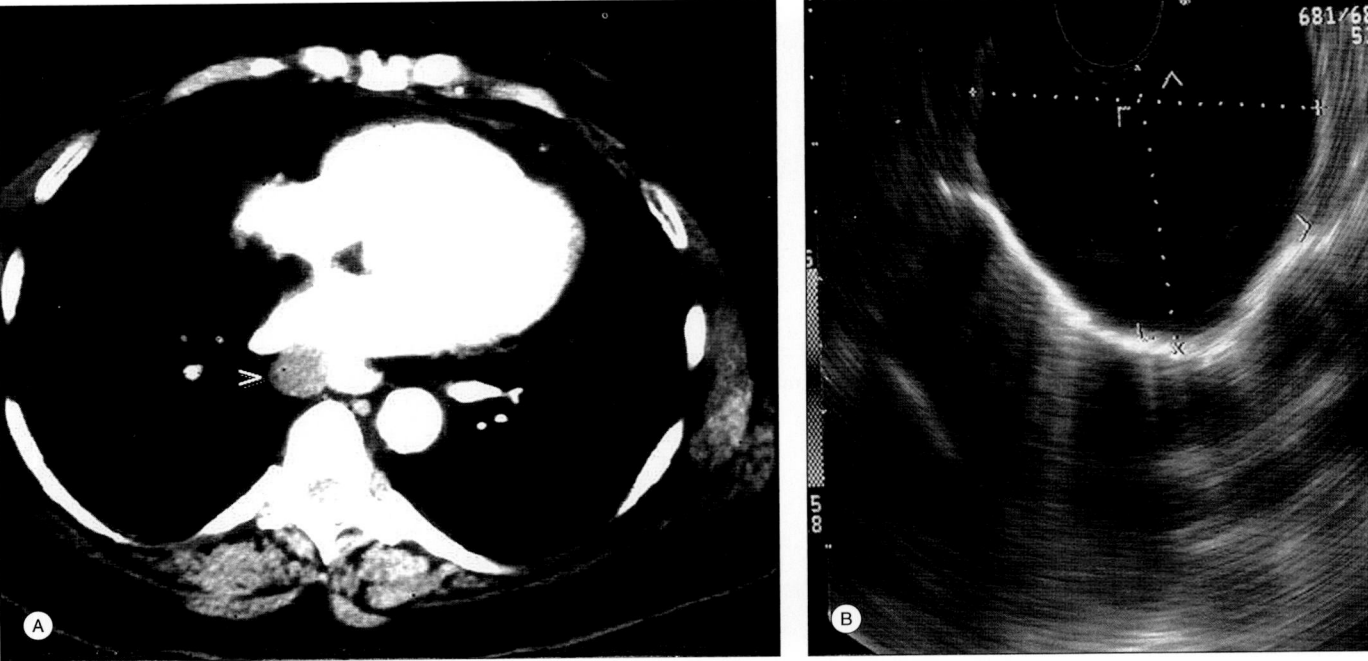

Figure 33–13. *A,* Chest computed tomography (CT) showing an ill-defined soft tissue density adjacent to the midesophagus. *B,* Linear array imaging of this lesion reveals a paraesophageal duplication cyst.

EUS is often useful in distinguishing cystic lesions from solid lesions in the mediastinum, whereas chest CT can have limited utility in providing this distinction.[83,117–122] A recent study by Wildi and coworkers[83] reported on a retrospective review of the results of EUS in 20 patients with suspected mediastinal cysts. The features used to classify cysts were as follows: benign simple cysts appear as anechoic or hypoechoic smooth, spherical structures with well-defined thin walls; esophageal duplications cysts are adherent to the esophagus, whereas cysts originating from the airways are designated as bronchogenic cysts. Cysts that do not fall into either category are termed nonspecific duplication cysts. A layered wall structure supports the diagnosis of duplication cyst but is not mandatory. Simple cysts include mesothelial, lymphogenous cysts, and thoracic duct cysts. Simple cysts do not have a layered wall and do not have a connection to the airways or esophagus and are termed nonspecific simple cysts. When solid tissue is seen within the fluid, the cysts are considered complex (e.g., benign cystic teratoma, thymic cyst) and the diagnosis of a benign simple cyst is excluded. In 19 of 20 patients, definite diagnosis of a mediastinal cyst was established by EUS (12 anechoic, 6 hypoechoic, 1 anechoic with small echoic foci). In only 4 of 18 cases were CT (17 cases) or MRI (1 case) diagnostic of a cyst. In three cases with mixed echo features, EUS-guided FNA was performed with administration of prophylactic antibiotic. In a fourth case, without prior prophylactic administration of an antibiotic, FNA was performed in a solid-appearing duplication cyst misdiagnosed by EUS as extensive lymphadenopathy. Mediastinitis subsequently developed requiring thoracotomy, in which an infected bronchogenic cyst was diagnosed. The authors concluded that aspiration of cysts should be avoided in those lesions with clearly anechoic features because of the risk of infection, whereas for hypoechoic lesions (when a cyst cannot be clearly distinguished from a solid tumor) FNA should be considered, but prophylactic antibiotics should be administered (Fig. 33–13).

ADRENAL AND RENAL LESIONS

EUS can provide early excellent images of the left adrenal gland, but it is more difficult to view the right adrenal gland with EUS; thus, routine evaluation of the right adrenal by EUS is probably not feasible. On the other hand, the left adrenal gland is more difficult to view than the right gland when imaging with transabdominal US.[123–125]

When imaging the left adrenal gland, the echoendoscope is advanced into the proximal stomach and the aorta is identified just below the GE junction. The splenic vein is then imaged by advancing the transducer forward with a clockwise rotation. Following the splenic vein laterally, the splenic hilum is found by further clockwise rotation and slight withdrawal. The left kidney is then imaged by advancing the scope from the splenic hilum with a slight counterclockwise rotation. The left adrenal gland lies just below the splenic vein, between the left kidney (superior and medial to the kidney) and the aorta. In a study by Chang and colleagues,[125] the average long-axis dimension of the adrenal gland was 2.5 cm, and the short-axis dimension was 0.8 cm. The adrenal gland as imaged on EUS is homogeneous and hypoechoic with two basic morphologic types: seagull shape and elliptical shape. Occasionally, in the same patient, the adrenal gland can appear as both shapes with a slight change in the orientation of the EUS probe tip.[125] In some patients, the central region of the gland may appear more echogenic than the peripheral region (Fig. 33–14).

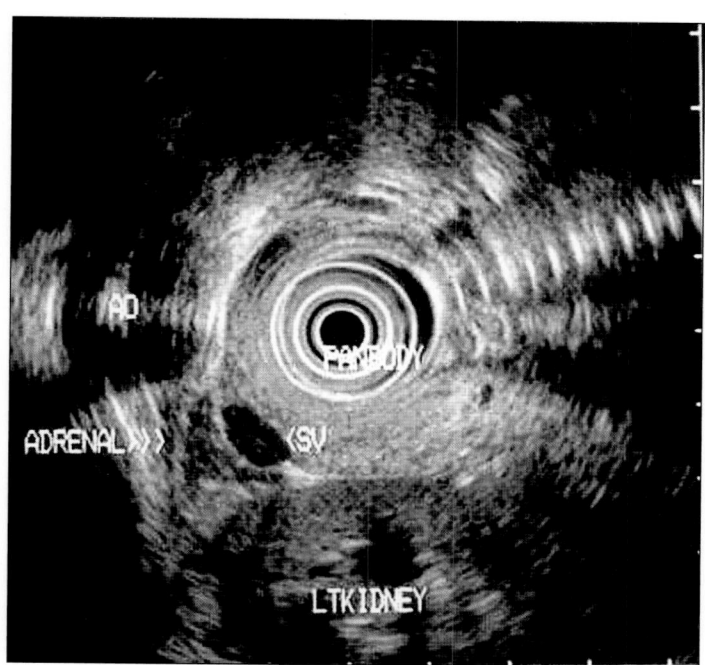

Figure 33–14. Radial imaging from the body of the stomach showing the left adrenal gland, aorta (AO), splenic vein (SV), left (LT) kidney, and body of the pancreas (panbody).

Incidental benign adrenal lesions, the so-called "adrenal incidentalomas," are commonly found on CT scans performed for a variety of indications. Unless unequivocally benign, these lesions should be biopsied in certain scenarios. CT scans performed in the staging workup of lung cancer reveal that more than 16% of patients have adrenal masses on screening examination.[125–129] Metastasis to the adrenal glands as the cause of isolated mass lesions occurs from 32% to 93% in cases of NSCLC as determined by FNA cytology.[127,130] In autopsy series of NSCLC, adrenal metastases are found in up to 59% of cases.[131,132]

EUS-guided FNA may provide an alternative to percutaneous aspiration technology in the evaluation of adrenal lesions. EUS-guided biopsy of an adrenal mass has been reported in a patient in whom CT-guided FNA was unsuccessful.[125] Chang and associates[125] reported the identification of the left adrenal gland in 97% of 31 consecutive patients undergoing EUS for known pulmonary or GI malignancies. In one patient with a history of lobectomy for lung cancer, staged as T1N0, a follow-up CT scan showed interval enlargement of an adrenal mass from 2.5 cm to 4 cm. Previously, a CT-guided FNA was negative for malignancy. An EUS-guided FNA of the left adrenal was performed and revealed metastatic disease. Given the clinical impact of an adrenal metastasis, routine assessment of the left adrenal gland in lung cancer patients is routinely recommended during the EUS evaluation.[125]

EUS imaging of both the right and left kidney is possible because of the immediate approximation between the GI lumen and the kidneys. The right kidney can be imaged by placing the transducer in the second portion of the duodenum and rotating laterally. The left kidney can be imaged from the body of the stomach, posterior to the spleen, as described previously. The left kidney often is easier to demonstrate then right kidney. The kidneys have a hyperechoic central medulla, a hypoechoic outer cortex, and a thin echogenic capsule (Fig. 33–15).

Approximately 85% of renal masses detected on CT are renal cell carcinomas, whereas 15% of CT detected renal masses are benign lesions.[133,134] Malignant-appearing masses that are resectable should not be routinely biopsied. Biopsy of a solitary renal mass is generally accepted in cases with a known primary extrarenal malignancy when the presence of a metastasis would alter management.[133,135] Specimens of renal masses have been obtained traditionally under either transabdominal US or CT guidance with a sensitivity of 62% to 100% and a specificity ranging of 0% to 100% in the diagnosis of renal cell carcinoma.[133,136] No data currently exist as to the frequency with which renal masses are identified during upper EUS examinations. Farrell and Brugge[133] recently reported the first EUS-guided FNA diagnosis of primary renal cell carcinoma in a patient with a large renal mass. The procedure was well tolerated without complications. Further experience is required before the establishment of EUS-guided FNA as modality of performing renal biopsy.

ASCITES AND PLEURAL FLUID

The identification of malignant pleural effusion or malignant ascites is diagnostic of advanced disease in various malignancies. EUS appears to be more sensitive than CT in the detection of small amount of ascitic and pleural fluid. Drainage of pleural or ascitic fluid at the time of EUS is possible and can be helpful if positive for malignancy. The technique of EUS-guided FNA of ascites or pleural fluid is similar to the technique applied to other lesions. Seeding of malignant cells into the fluid through the tract is a concern. The site of the needle penetration in the GI lumen must not be involved with tumor (Fig. 33–16).

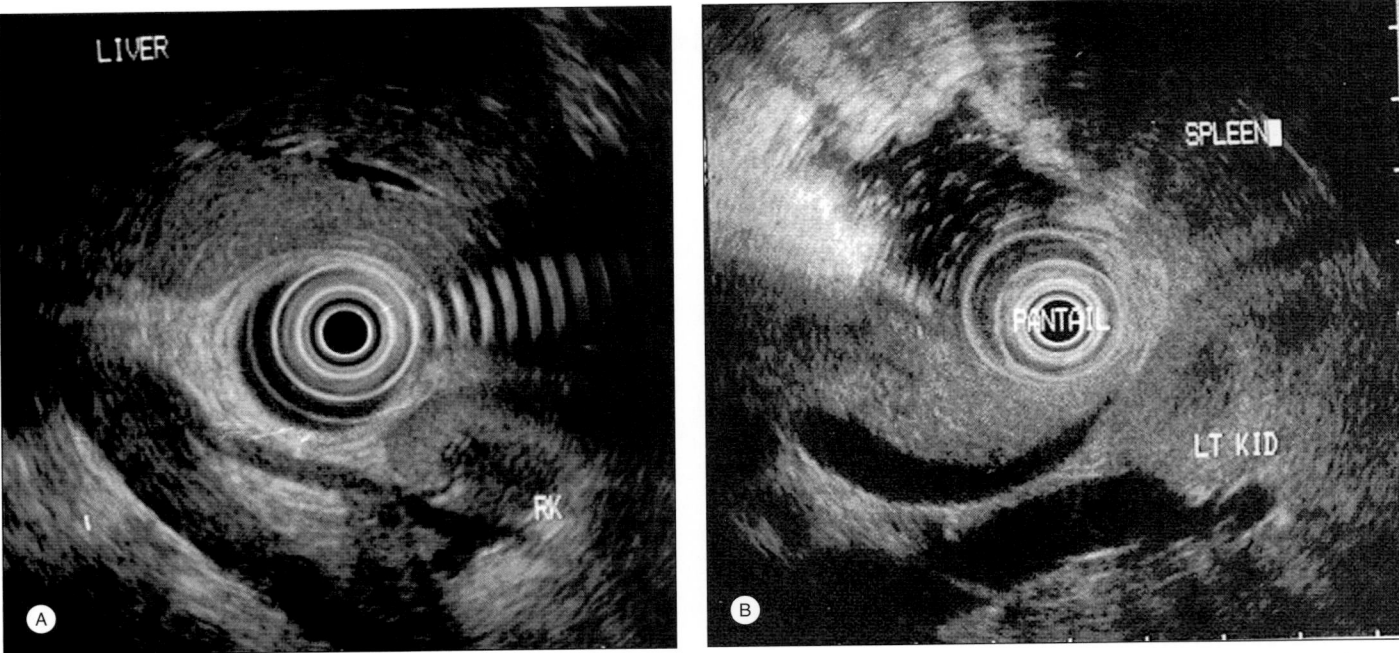

Figure 33–15. *A,* Radial imaging from the duodenum revealing excellent images of the right kidney in this patient with malrotation of the right kidney. The liver is seen in the upper portion of the image. *B,* Radial imaging from the body of the stomach showing the left kidney, spleen, body and tail of the pancreas (closest to the transducer) and above the splenic vein. The left renal vein is seen exiting the kidney.

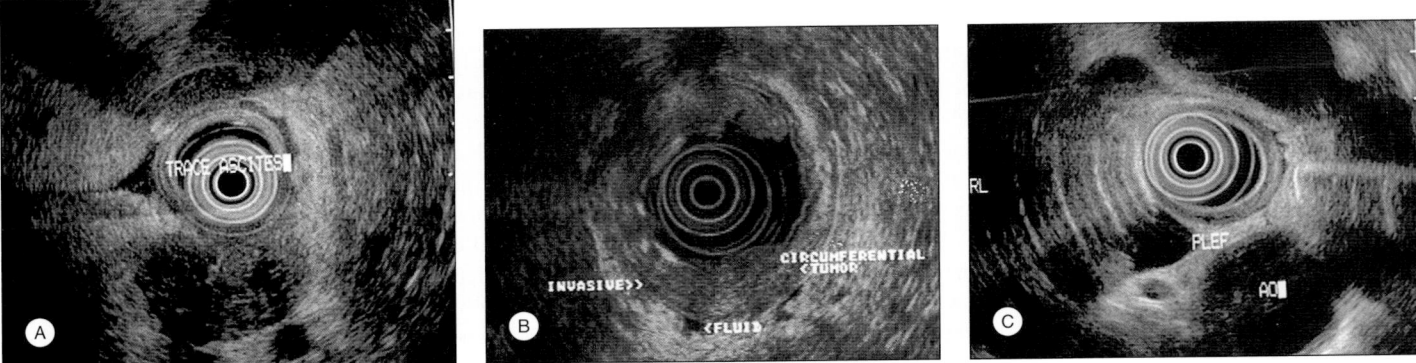

Figure 33–16. Radial imaging of *(A)* trace ascites in a patient with pancreatic cancer. The pancreatic mass is seen below the ascites. *B,* Ascites in a patient with linitis plastica. *C,* Pleural effusion (PLEF) seen adjacent to the right lung (RL). AO, aorta.

Chang and associates[137] first reported the detection of malignant fluid via EUS-guided FNA of pleural effusion and ascitic fluid in patients with gastric cancer. In a larger retrospective study, these same investigators reported the utility of EUS for the detection of ascites and EUS-guided FNA in 571 consecutive patients who underwent upper EUS for various indications.[138] Eighty-five patients (15%) had ascites detected by EUS, whereas CT detected ascites in 14 (18%) of the 79 patients who had pre-EUS CT. Thirty-one of 85 patients underwent EUS-guided FNA paracentesis, and, in 5 of these patients, malignant ascites was diagnosed. These findings have been supported by similar studies, which have described the clinical significance of peritoneal fluid detected by EUS.[139,140]

LIVER LESIONS

EUS provides very good imaging of the left lobe of the liver and a significant portion of the right lobe of the liver. The left lobe and hilum of the liver are examined from the gastric body and fundus. The tip of the echoendoscope is placed in the gastric antrum, then slowly withdrawing the echoendoscope, the tip is deflected up and rightward. When the liver comes into view, the instrument is rotated to evaluate portions of the liver. The right lobe of the liver is best imaged from the duodenum but can also be seen from the antrum. Liver lesions near the second or third portion of the duodenum, peripheral lesions near the dome of the diaphragm, and lesions in the inferior portion of the right lobe of the liver can be difficult to visualize (see Figs 33–2 and 33–15).[141]

CT- and US-guided FNA of liver lesions have been reported to have sensitivities ranging from 83% to 93% for the detection of malignant disease.[141-145] Because EUS has not traditionally been used in evaluation of the liver, little information is available regarding the effectiveness and safety of EUS-guided FNA for the diagnosis of liver lesions. However, several recent reports suggest that EUS-guided FNA of the liver may be effective and safe.[141,146-148] Nguyen and associates[141] conducted a prospective study in which 574 consecutive patients with a history or suspicion of GI or pulmonary tumor undergoing upper EUS examinations underwent EUS evaluation of the liver. They found small focal liver lesions undetected with conventional CT. Fourteen (2.4%) patients were found to have focal liver lesions (five right lobe, nine left lobe) and underwent EUS-guided FNA. The median largest diameter of the liver lesions was 1.1 cm (range 0.8 to 5.2 cm), and the mean number of passes per lesion was 2.0 (range 1 to 5 passes). Fourteen of the 15 liver lesions sampled by means of EUS-guided FNA were malignant and one was benign. Before EUS, CT depicted liver lesions in only 3/14 (21%) patients; in most patients, CT was performed within 2 months of the EUS procedure. In seven patients, the initial diagnosis of cancer was made by means of EUS-guided FNA of the liver. There were no immediate or late complications. Percutaneous FNA of the liver has been associated in rare instances with tumor seeding, intrahepatic hematoma, and hemorrhage.[149-153] As postulated by Nguyen and coworkers,[141] EUS-guided FNA has the possible advantage over the percutaneous route of shorter insertion length of the needle if the liver lesion is deep to the skin surface. With EUS-guided FNA there is continuous visualization of the needle tip, which helps to minimize risk for bleeding when the procedure is performed in conjunction with color flow and Doppler US. tenBerge and colleagues[154] reported a multicenter study of 167 cases of EUS-guided FNA of the liver. Complications were reported in 6 (4%) including death in 1 patient with an occluding biliary stent and biliary sepsis, bleeding (1 case), fever (2 cases), and pain (2 cases). In 23/26 patients, EUS-guided FNA diagnosed malignancy after nondiagnostic FNA with transabdominal US guidance. EUS was able to localize an unrecognized primary tumor in 17/33 (52%) cases after CT demonstrated only liver metastases. Thus, EUS-guided FNA of liver lesions appears to be safe and effective; however, the indications should be limited to cases when other less invasive methods are not feasible, when tumors cannot be accessed by other routes, or when EUS is required to identify the primary tumor site. In addition, in the setting of cholangitis, adequate biliary drainage is recommended before or coincident with the FNA procedure.

Finally, Barclay and colleagues[155] recently reported the first case of EUS-guided ethanol injection of a solid hepatic metastasis, the location of which precluded percutaneous treatment.

MISCELLANEOUS

The close proximity of the intestinal tract to abdominal organs and raises the possibility of EUS-guided FNA of idiopathic abdominal masses. Catalano and coworkers[156] retrospectively evaluated the diagnostic accuracy of EUS-guided FNA of abdominal masses of unknown cause and its impact on subsequent evaluation. Thirty-four patients from five tertiary referral centers with idiopathic abdominal masses underwent EUS-guided FNA after evaluation including CT and/or transabdominal US. CT demonstrated an intra-abdominal mass in all patients. Four patients had a history of intra-abdominal cancer (two cervical, one ovarian, one colon), but these cancers were considered to be in remission. A final diagnosis for the mass lesions was established in all patients by a variety of methods including EUS-guided FNA, surgery, autopsy, or long-term follow-up. Abdominal masses were classified into three categories: infectious, benign/inflammatory, and malignant. EUS-guided FNA established a tissue diagnosis in 29 of 34 patients (85%) (infectious, 80% including abscess and infected pseudocyst; benign/inflammatory, 67% including hematoma/postsurgical inflammatory mass, leiomyoma, and sarcoidosis; malignant, 91% including sarcoma, lymphoma, hepatoma, adenocarcinoma of unknown primary, ovarian cancer, transitional bladder carcinoma, uterine/cervical cancer, recurrent colon cancer, neuroendocrine tumor, paraganglionoma, metastatic lung cancer, and prostate cancer). EUS-guided FNA was instrumental in directing subsequent evaluation in 29 patients (85%) and therapy in 26 (77%). The number of fine needle passes for adequate tissue sampling was lower for nonmalignant (2.2 to 3.2 passes) versus malignant diseases (4.6 passes). A perirectal abscess developed in one patient and was treated successfully with antibiotics. In a study by Erickson and Tretjak[157] of 18 cases of nonpancreaticobiliary and nonadrenal retroperitoneal lesions, EUS-guided FNA was used in 15 cases and in all 15 patients management was significantly altered by the EUS-guided FNA result. In addition, cases of EUS-guided FNA diagnosis of a schwannoma of the mediastinum[158] and a retroperitoneal neurilemoma[159] have been described.

Accessory spleen may be a potential cause of misinterpretation at EUS. Barawi and colleagues[160] described the EUS features of accessory spleen in 10 (8 accessory spleen, 2 lobulated spleen) patients. The mean diameter of these lesions was 2.7 by 3.1 cm. Nine were round and one was oval. All were located inferolateral to the pancreatic tail and medial to the spleen. All of these lesions had a sharp and regular outer margin and homogeneous echo texture; four were hypoechoic and six hyperechoic. CT may be helpful in confirming the presence of lobulated spleen and accessory spleen (Fig. 33–17).

Fritscher-Ravens and associates described EUS-guided FNA of splenic lesions in 12 patients when other modalities were inconclusive (n = 5), not attempted because of small size (0.9 to 1.4 cm) (n = 4), or considered dangerous (adjacent to the splenic hilum or located peripherally) (n = 3).[161] The size of the lesions was 0.8 to 4.2 cm (median 1.4 cm). A positive diagnosis was made in 10/12 patients (83%); cytology was inadequate in one patient. Bacteriology was positive in one patient each for *Staphylococcus aureus* and *Serratia* and for *Mycobacterium tuberculosis* in two patients. Diagnoses included Hodgkin's disease, sarcoidosis, abscesses, tuberculosis, metastatic colon cancer, and infarction in one. One patient experienced pain postprocedure, but no hematoma was demonstrated on subsequent US examination. The authors concluded that EUS-guided FNA cytodiagnosis in patients with unknown splenic lesions appears feasible, when CT- or US-guided biopsy fails.

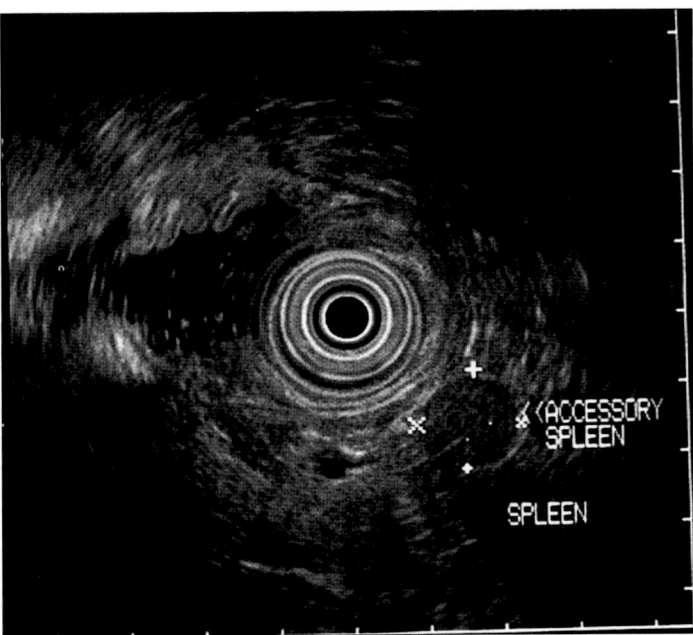

Figure 33–17. Radial imaging from the stomach of an accessory spleen.

COMPLICATIONS

EUS-guided FNA is a relatively safe procedure when compared with CT-guided FNA, bronchoscopy with transbronchial FNA, mediastinoscopy, or open/exploratory procedures. In general, when complications occur, these are usually mild and self-limited. In reports that have addressed complications of EUS-guided FNA, rare complications including endoscope-induced perforations, febrile episodes (after FNA of pancreatic cystic lesions), hemorrhage, pancreatitis, and pneumoperitoneum; false-positive diagnoses have been reported.[71,81,84,85,146,162–164] As alluded to previously, the role of prophylactic antibiotics for EUS-guided FNA remains unclear. The general practice has been to administer antibiotics to any patient undergoing FNA of cystic pancreatic or perirectal lesions. Barawi and colleagues[78] studied 108 consecutive EUS-guided FNA cases and did not demonstrate bacteremia at 30 and 60 minutes postprocedure. However, the study by Van de Mierop and colleagues[85] did reveal a 19% incidence of bacteremia with EUS-guided FNA of solid lesions.

Endosonography-Guided Celiac Plexus Block and Celiac Plexus Neurolysis

Pain resulting from pancreatic cancer and chronic pancreatitis is often difficult to manage. Many approaches have been used to treat these patients including narcotic analgesia, antidepressants, pancreatic enzymes, octreotide, denervation procedures (most commonly CPB), and various palliative or decompression/drainage procedures.[165–178] Not surprisingly, the effectiveness of these therapies is not only highly variable but also often controversial, especially in the treatment of chronic pancreatitis. Opioid analgesics are probably the most often used and can effectively treat pain but

are associated with a number of side effects including constipation, delirium, nausea, and the potential for addiction in patients with chronic pancreatitis.[179,180] Nonpharmacologic methods of pain control may improve quality of life and minimize drug-related side effects.[179]

The celiac plexus lies anterior to the aorta at the level of the celiac artery. Most of the sensory nerves returning from the pancreas and other intra-abdominal viscera pass through the celiac ganglion and splanchnic nerves. Interruption of these fibers may lessen pain in pancreatic malignancies and in chronic pancreatitis.[181] CPB, a temporizing treatment, most commonly refers to a steroid and long-acting local anesthetic injection into the celiac plexus to control pain associated with chronic pancreatitis. In contrast, CPN generally refers to injection of alcohol or phenol, a more permanent agent, into the celiac axis area.[181] This induces a chemical splanchnicectomy that ablates nerve fibers that transmit pain and is used in patients with pancreatic cancer. Neural regrowth may limit the effect.[181] In practice the terms CPB and CPN are often transposable.

The efficacy of CPN for the treatment of cancer pain has been demonstrated in a number of studies. The benefit appears to be similar independent of the method used with pain control in 70% to 90% of patients up to 3 months after the procedure.[182–187] CPB and CPN have traditionally been performed via various percutaneous (most common posterior route) and surgical approaches and most recently under endoscopic guidance.[188] Of the nonsurgical approaches, EUS offers the most direct access to the celiac plexus. Wiersema and coworkers[179,181,189] recognized the anatomic advantage that EUS provides in visualizing the celiac region and were successful in performing transgastric EUS-guided CPN with results similar to more the traditional approaches.

The timing of CPN relative to pain onset appears to be a predictor of response. In one study, CPN was more effective when the block was performed early after pain onset.[183] This was postulated to be related to involvement of visceral and somatic nerves late in the disease and pain appearing to derive mainly from the celiac plexus early on.[181,183]

Studies also suggest that CPB may also have a role in the treatment of pain related to chronic pancreatitis.[190,191] In a study of 18 patients with chronic pancreatitis, reduction in pain was noted in 50% (5/10) of EUS-guided CBP compared with 25% (2/8) of CT-guided blocks.[190] The benefit persisted for up to 24 weeks in 30% of responders. A cost comparison demonstrated a $200 saving for EUS-CPB compared with CT-guided CPB. Another report of 90 patients by the same authors found a significant improvement in overall pain scores in 55% at 4 and 8 weeks of follow-up.[191] A persistent benefit beyond 24 weeks was observed in only 10% of patients. Pain relief was more likely in older patients (>45 years) and those who had not had previous surgery for chronic pancreatitis. Further studies are needed to clarify what role EUS CBP will play in the management of painful chronic pancreatitis.

TECHNIQUE FOR PERFORMING ENDOSONOGRAPHY-GUIDED CELIAC PLEXUS BLOCK AND CELIAC PLEXUS NEUROLYSIS

This section focuses on endoscopic methods of EUS-guided CPB and CPN. Patients with inoperable pancreatic cancer and pain requiring narcotic analgesics are potential candidates for CPN. Selection of patients with pain related to chronic pancreatitis for

CPB is less clear. Patients with pain refractory to high doses of narcotics may be appropriate candidates, although the response may be minimal.

The celiac artery is readily visualized with curvilinear array EUS and provides the important landmark structure when performing EUS-guided CPB and CPN. For practical purposes, the celiac ganglia is located at the origin of the celiac artery, although its exact location has been described any where from 1 cm to 9 mm inferior to the artery takeoff (the right is most commonly 6 mm inferior, and the left ganglion is most commonly 9 mm inferior to the celiac artery origin).[181,183] The celiac axis is not visualized directly but identified by its relative position to the artery. The proximity of the celiac ganglia to the posterior gastric wall ensures an accurate passage of the needle into the ganglia, thereby minimizing the risk of complications and potentially increasing the effectiveness.

After preprocedure hydration with intravenous saline (500 to 1000 mL), the patient is placed in the left lateral decubitus position and sedation is administered. Blood pressure, pulse oximetry, and electrocardiogram are continuously monitored. The linear array echoendoscope is advanced to just below the GE junction. A sagittal view of the aorta is obtained through the posterior gastric wall. The aorta is traced to the celiac trunk, the first large vessel emerging off the aorta, and the second branch is usually easily identified as the superior mesenteric artery. Identifying both the celiac and superior mesenteric artery helps to confirm correct location. Color flow Doppler can be should be used to exclude any intervening vessels.

After the stylet is removed from the 22-gauge FNA needle, the entire system is flushed with normal saline to remove any air because this can interfere with imaging. Using real-time imaging, the sterile FNA needle is inserted immediately lateral and anterior to the aorta at the level of the celiac trunk via a transgastric approach. A small amount (2 mL) of 0.9% saline is injected to clear the needle. An assistant then aspirates a 10-mL syringe filled with 0.9% saline for approximately 10 seconds. This is to confirm that the needle is not within any of the regional blood vessels.

Two techniques are available: one in which injections are performed by rotating to each side of the celiac trunk and the other in which the entire injection is performed just anterior and cranial to the celiac artery takeoff.[179,181] For CPB, 10 mL of preservative-free bupivacaine (0.25%) (Abbott Laboratories, Abbott Park, IL) followed by 1 mL of triamcinolone (40 mg) (Fujisawa USA, Deerfield, IL) are injected on both sides of the celiac trunk. The aspiration test is repeated before each steroid injection. A 3-mL saline flush is performed before needle withdrawal on each side. For CPN, 10 mL of bupivacaine (0.25%) is injected followed by 10 mL of dehydrated 98% absolute alcohol. Before alcohol injection, the 10-second aspiration test is repeated. Again, the needle is flushed with 3 mL of saline before withdrawal of the needle. The procedure is then repeated on the opposite side of the aorta. With alcohol injection, an echo-dense cloud is typically seen, but this is not usually seen with steroid injection.

For the alternative approach, a single site injection at the base of the celiac artery takeoff is performed with the entire amount of the injectant, that is, 20 mL of bupivacaine (0.25%) and 20 mL of dehydrated alcohol in CPN; 20 mL of bupivacaine (0.25%) followed by 80 mg (2 mL) of triamcinolone in CPB. There are no studies comparing the two techniques, but it is believed that they have

similar results. Anatomic variations may decide which technique is used.

The examination, performed on an outpatient basis, is usually completed in 30 minutes. Recovery time is usually 2 hours. Before discharge, orthostatic blood pressure changes should be checked, and patients should be counseled regarding potential complications (Video 33–2).

COMPLICATIONS

CPB and CPN are generally effective, safe, and well-tolerated procedures. The three most common complications are transient hypotension (20% to 40%), transient diarrhea (4% to 38%), and transient increase in pain (9%), which are expected in CPB performed via any route.[181,184,192] Interruption of the plexus can result in a sympathetic blockade.[193] Clinical manifestations of sympathetic blockade can include diarrhea and hypotension resulting from a relative unopposed visceral parasympathetic activity. Mesenteric vasodilation accounts for the hypotension that resolves in approximately 2 days. Diarrhea and increase in baseline pain are also usually limited to 2 days. Less common complications include unilateral paresis or paraplegia, pneumothorax, loss of sphincter function, retroperitoneal bleeding, renal puncture, and prolonged gastroparesis.[179,181,184,185,194] In addition, cephalic spread of the neurolytic agent may result in involvement of the cardiac nerves and plexus.[195] Although not unique to EUS CPN, EUS may decrease the incidence of complications because the needle does not traverse the paraspinal region or somatic nerves or traverse the diaphragm and pleural space.[166,179,181] Another benefit with EUS CPN is the ability to perform the block as part of a single procedure that may include tumor staging and FNA.[192] Infectious complications are uncommon but potentially serious. In a series of 90 patients, only one patient (1/90) developed an infectious complication (a peripancreatic abscess), which resolved with a 2-week course of antibiotics.[191] The authors reasoned that there may have been a predisposition to infection because of gastroduodenal colonization with bacteria because the patient was taking a proton pump inhibitor. They suggested that prophylactic antibiotics should be considered in patients who are receiving acid suppression. The bactericidal nature of ethanol appears to minimize this risk for infection, and some experts do not routinely use antibiotics in this setting, irrespective of concurrent acid suppression.[179]

Conclusion

Over the last decade, EUS has played an increasingly important role as an accurate and safe method for staging patients with NSCLC. EUS is now integrated into the evaluation of non-GI pathology, especially in the assessment of mediastinal pathology. EUS-guided FNA should be considered in those patients in whom a previous attempt at lymph node FNA was unsuccessful using CT or bronchoscopy. Depending on the local expertise, EUS may be considered the primary procedure for biopsying lesions arising from the posterior mediastinum, especially at levels 5 (aortopulmonic), 7 (subcarinal), or 8 (periesophageal) because these are most readily accessed by EUS. This is of particular relevance for staging of

NSCLC in which contralateral mediastinal lymph node metastases preclude curative resection. Identification of ipsilateral mediastinal lymph node involvement may be helpful for identifying patients who could benefit from neoadjuvant therapy. Mediastinoscopy, thoracoscopy, or partial thoracotomy could then be reserved for patients with enlarged anterior lymph nodes or in those patients with suspicious nodes not successfully sampled by CT, bronchoscopy, or EUS. Furthermore, EUS-guided FNA has been shown to be a highly accurate modality for evaluating unknown mediastinal masses and/or lymph nodes including lymphoma, sarcoidosis, and histoplasmosis.

In patients with otherwise operable lung cancer, EUS-guided FNA may be a viable alternative to percutaneous aspiration biopsy of a left adrenal mass. EUS can detect small focal liver lesions and small pockets of ascites or pleural fluid that are not detected at CT. Findings of EUS-guided FNA can confirm a cytologic diagnosis of metastasis and establish a definitive M stage that may change clinical management. EUS-guided FNA of renal masses may be a safe means of confirming the presence or absence of malignancy and may preclude the need for CT-guided studies. EUS-guided FNA provides minimally invasive tissue sampling and may obviate the need for exploratory laparotomy in cases of abdominal masses of undetermined origin. EUS CPN appears to be as safe and effective method for performing CPN. EUS CPN may also allow a diagnostic, staging, and therapeutic procedure all in one setting. Studies also suggest that EUS CPB may also have a role in the treatment of pain related to chronic pancreatitis.

ACKNOWLEDGMENTS

The authors wish to thank Mala Gupta, M.D., Chief of Cytopathology, Winthrop University Hospital for the photomicrographs of the cytologic specimens.

REFERENCES

1. Jemal A, Murray T, Samuels A, et al: Cancer statistics, 2003. Ca Cancer J Clin 53:5–26, 2003.
2. Travis WD, Lubin J, Ries L, Devesa S: Unites States lung carcinoma incidence trends: Declining for most histologic types among males, increasing among females. Cancer 77:2464–2470, 1996.
3. Argiris A, Murren JR: Staging and clinical prognostic factors for small-cell lung cancer. Cancer J 7:437–47, 2001.
4. Simon GR, Wagner H, American College of Chest Physicians: Small cell lung cancer. Chest 123(1 Suppl):259S–271S, 2003.
5. Micke P, Faldum A, Metz T, et al: Staging small cell lung cancer: Veterans Administration Lung Study Group versus International Association for the Study of Lung Cancer—what limits limited disease? Lung Cancer 37:271–276, 2002.
6. Deslauriers J: Current surgical treatment of nonsmall cell lung cancer 2001. Eur Respir J Suppl 35:61s–70s, 2002.
7. Feins RH: Multi-modality treatment of non-small cell lung cancer. Surg Clin North Am 82:611–620, 2002.
8. Greene FL, Page DL, Fleming ID, et al (eds): AJCC (American Joint Committee on Cancer) Cancer Staging Manual, 6th ed. New York, Springer-Verlag, 2002, pp 167–174.
9. Mountain CF: Revisions in the International System for Staging Lung Cancer. Chest 111:1710–1717, 1997.
10. Mountain CF: A new international staging system for lung cancer. Chest 89:225s–233s, 1986.
11. Barker JM, Silvestri GA: Lung cancer staging. Curr Opin Pulm Med 8:287–293, 2002.
12. Jett JR, Scott WJ, Rivera MP, Sause WT: American College of Chest Physicians. Guidelines on treatment of stage IIIB non-small cell lung cancer. Chest 123(1 Suppl):221S–225S, 2003.
13. Robinson LA, Wagner H Jr, Ruckdeschel JC: American College of Chest Physicians. Treatment of stage IIIA non-small cell lung cancer. Chest 123(1 Suppl):202S–220S, 2003.
14. Martini N, Baines MS, McCormick PM, et al: Surgical treatment in non-small cell carcinoma of the lung: The Memorial Sloan-Kettering experience. In Hoogstraten B, Addis BJ, Hansen HH, et al (eds): Treatment of Lung Tumors. Heidelberg, Germany, Springer-Verlag, 1987, pp 111–132.
15. Sandler Ab, Buzaid AC: Lung cancer: A review of current therapeutic modalities. Lung 170:249–265, 1992.
16. Hatter J, Kohman LJ, Mosca RS, et al: Preoperative evaluation of stage I and stage II non-small cell lung cancer. Ann Thorac Surg 58:1738–1741, 1994.
17. Shields TW: Surgical therapy for carcinoma of the lung. Clin Chest Med 14:121–147, 1993.
18. Medina Gallardo JF, Borderas Naranjo F, Torres Cansino M, Rodriquez-Panadero F: Validity of enlarged mediastinal nodes as markers of involvement by non-small cell lung cancer. Am Rev Respir Dis 146:1210–1212, 1992.
19. Van Raemdonck DE, Schneider A, Ginsberg RJ: Surgical treatment for higher staged non-small cell lung cancer. Ann Thorac Surg 54:999–1013, 1993.
20. Naruke T, Goya T, Tsuchiva R, Suemasu K: The importance of surgery to non-small cell carcinoma of lung with mediastinal lymph node metastasis. Ann Thorac Surg 46:603–610, 1988.
21. Martini N, Flehinger BJ: The role of surgery in N2 lung cancer. Surg Clin North Am 67:1037–1049, 1987.
22. Mountain CF: The biological operability of stage III non-small cell lung cancer. Ann Thorac Surg 40:60–64, 1985.
23. Glazer GM, Gross BH, Quint LE, et al: Normal mediastinal lymph nodes: Number and size according to American Thoracic Society mapping. AJR 144:261–265, 1985.
24. Ingram CE, Belli AM, Lewars MD, et al: Normal lymph node size in the mediastinum: A retrospective study in two patient groups. Clin Radiol 40:35–39, 1989.
25. Mann H: CT in the management of lung cancer. Semin Ultrasound CT MR 9:40–52, 1988.
26. Verschakeln JA, Bogaert J, De Wever W: Computed tomography in staging for lung cancer. Eur Respir J Suppl 35:40s–48s, 2002.
27. Patterson GA, Ginsberg RJ, Poon PY, et al: A prospective evaluation of magnetic resonance imaging, computed tomography, and mediastinoscopy in the preoperative assessment of mediastinal node status in bronchogenic carcinoma. J Thorac Cardiovasc Surg 94:679–684, 1987.
28. Aronchick JM: CT of mediastinal lymph nodes in patients with non-small cell lung carcinoma. Radiol Clin North Am 28:573–581, 1990.
29. Glazer GM, Orringer MB, Gross GH, Quint LE: The mediastinum in non-small cell lung cancer: CT-surgical correlation. AJR 142:1101–1105, 1984.
30. Cybulsky IJ, Lanza LA, Ryan MB, et al: Prognostic significance of computed tomography in resected N2 lung cancer. Ann Thorac Surg 54:533–537, 1992.
31. Lewis JW, Pearlberg JL, Beute GH, et al: Can computed tomography of the chest stage lung cancer? Yes and no. Ann Thorac Surg 49:591–596, 1990.
32. Dales RE, Stark RM, Raman S: Computed tomography to stage lung cancer. Approaching a controversy using meta-analysis. Am Rev Respir Dis 141(5 Pt 1):1096–1101, 1990.
33. Staples CA, Muller NL, Miller RR, et al: Mediastinal nodes in bronchogenic carcinoma: Comparison between CT and mediastinoscopy. Radiology 167:367–372, 1988.

34. McLoud TC, Bourgouin PM, Greenberg RW, et al: Bronchogenic carcinoma: Analysis of staging in the mediastinum with CT by correlative lymph node mapping and sampling. Radiology 182:319–323, 1992.

35. Arita T, Matsumoto T, Kuramitsu T, et al: Is it possible to differentiate malignant mediastinal nodes from benign nodes by size? Reevaluation by CT, transesophageal echocardiography, and nodal specimen. Chest 110:1004–1008, 1996.

36. McKenna RJ, Libshitz HI, Mountain CF, McMurtrey MJ: Roentgenographic evaluation of mediastinal nodes for pre-operative assessment in lung cancer. Chest 88:206–210, 1985.

37. Arita T, Kuramitsu T, Kawamura M, et al: Bronchogenic carcinoma: Incidence of metastases to normal sized lymph nodes. Thorax 50:1267–1269, 1995.

38. Miller JD, Gorenstein LA, Patterson GA: Staging: The key to rational management of lung cancer. Ann Thorac Surg 53:170–178, 1992.

39. Dwamena BA, Sonnad SS, Angobaldo JO, Wahl RL: Metastases from non-small cell lung cancer: Mediastinal staging in the 1990s—meta-analytic comparison of PET and CT. Radiology 213:530–536, 1999.

40. Toloza EM, Harpole L, McCrory DC: Noninvasive staging of non-small cell lung cancer: A review of the current evidence. Chest 123(1 Suppl):137S–146S, 2003.

41. Flickling W, Wallace MB: EUS in lung cancer. Gastrointest Endosc 56:S18–S21, 2002.

42. Wallace MB, Silvestri GA, Sahai AV, et al: Endoscopic ultrasound-guided fine needle aspiration for staging patients with carcinoma of the lung. Ann Thorac Surg 72:1861–1867, 2001.

43. Pieterman RM, van Putten JW, Meuzelaar JJ, et al: Preoperative staging of non-small-cell lung cancer with positron-emission tomography N Engl J Med 343:254–261, 2000.

44. Fritscher-Ravens A, Bohuslavizki KH, Brandt L, et al: Mediastinal lymph node involvement in potentially resectable lung cancer: Comparison of CT, positron emission tomography, and endoscopic ultrasonography with and without fine-needle aspiration. Chest 123:442–451, 2003.

45. Schieppati E: Mediastinal lymph node puncture through the tracheal carina. Surg Gynecol Obstet 107:243–246, 1958.

46. Wang KP, Terry P, Marsh B: Bronchoscopic needle aspiration biopsy of paratracheal tumors. Am Rev Respir Dis 118:17–21, 1978.

47. Oho K, Kato H, Ogawa I, et al: A new needle for transfiberoptic bronchoscope use. Chest 76:492, 1979.

48. Wang KP: Flexible transbronchial needle aspiration biopsy for histologic specimens. Chest 88:860–863, 1985.

49. Shure D, Fedullo PF: Transbronchial needle aspiration in the diagnosis of submucosal and peribronchial bronchogenic carcinoma. Chest 88:49–51, 1985.

50. Harrow EM, Oldenburg FA Jr, Lingenfelter MS, Smith AM Jr: Transbronchial needle aspiration in clinical practice: A five-year experience. Chest 96:1268–1272, 1989.

51. Schenk DA, Bower JH, Bryan CL, et al: Transbronchial needle aspiration staging of bronchogenic carcinoma. Am Rev Respir Dis 134:146–147, 1986.

52. Harrow E, Halber M, Hardy S, Halteman W: Bronchogenic and roentgenographic correlates of a positive transbronchial needle aspiration in the staging of lung cancer. Chest 100:1592–1596, 1991.

53. Carlin BW, Harrell JH 2nd, Fedullo PF: False-positive transcarinal needle aspirate in the evaluation of bronchogenic carcinoma. Am Rev Respir Dis 140:1800–1802, 1989.

54. Wang KP, Terry PB: Transbronchial needle aspiration in the diagnosis and staging of bronchogenic carcinoma. Am Rev Respir Dis 127:344–347, 1983.

55. Midthun DE, Cortese DA: Bronchoscopic needle aspiration and biopsy. In Prakash UBX (ed): Bronchoscopy. New York, Raven Press, 1994, pp 147–153.

56. Zwischenberger JB, Savage C, Alpard SK, et al: Mediastinal transthoracic needle and core lymph node biopsy: Should it replace mediastinoscopy?Chest 121:1165–1170, 2002.

57. Jolly PC, Hutchinson CH, Detterbeck F, et al: Routine computed tomographic scans, selective mediastinoscopy, and other factors in evaluation of lung cancer. J Thorac Cardiovasc Surg 102:266–271, 1991.

58. Merav AD: The role of mediastinoscopy and anterior mediastinotomy in determining operability of lung cancer. A review of published questions and answers. Cancer Investig 9:439–442, 1991.

59. Aabakken L, Silvestri GA, Hawes RH, et al: Cost-efficacy of endoscopic ultrasonography with fine-needle aspiration vs. mediastinotomy in patients with lung cancer and suspected mediastinal adenopathy. Endoscopy 31:707–711, 1999.

60. Lee N, Inoue K, Yamamoto R, Kinoshita H: Patterns of internal echoes in lymph nodes in the diagnosis of lung cancer metastasis. World J Surg 16:986–993, 1992.

61. Sugimachi K, Ohno S, Fujishima H, et al: Endoscopic ultrasonographic detection of carcinomatous invasion of lymph nodes in the thoracic esophagus. Surgery 107:366–371, 1990.

62. Schuder G, Isringhaus H, Kubale B, et al: Endoscopic ultrasonography of the mediastinum in the diagnosis of bronchial carcinoma. Thorac Cardiovasc Surg 39:299–303, 1991.

63. Kondo D, Imaizumi M, Abe T, et al: Endoscopic ultrasound examination for mediastinal lymph node metastases of lung cancer. Chest 98:586–593, 1990.

64. Aibe T, Ito T, Yoshida T, et al: Endoscopic ultrasonography of lymph nodes surrounding the upper GI tract. Scand J Gastroenterol 123(Suppl):164–169, 1986.

65. Giovannini M, Seitz JF, Monges G, et al: Fine-needle aspiration cytology guided by endoscopic ultrasonography: Results in 141 patients. Endoscopy 27:171–177, 1995.

66. Silvestri GA, Hoffman BJ, Bhutani MS, et al: Endoscopic ultrasound with fine-needle aspiration in the diagnosis and staging of lung cancer. Ann Thorac Surg 61:1441–1446, 1996.

67. Gress FG, Savides TJ, Sandler A, et al: Endoscopic ultrasonography, fine-needle aspiration biopsy guided by endoscopic ultrasonography, and computed tomography in the preoperative staging of non-small-cell lung cancer: A comparison study. Ann Intern Med 127(8 Pt 1):604–612, 1997.

68. Hunerbein M, Ghadimi BM, Haensch W, Schlag PM: Transesophageal biopsy of mediastinal and pulmonary tumors by means of endoscopic ultrasound guidance. J Thorac Cardiovasc Surg 116:554–559, 1998.

69. Janssen J, Johanns W, Luis W, Greiner L: Clinical value of endoscopic ultrasound-guided transesophageal fine needle puncture of mediastinal lesions. Dtsch Med Wochenschr 123:1402–1409, 1998.

70. Serna DL, Aryan HE, Chang KJ, et al: An early comparison between endoscopic ultrasound-guided fine-needle aspiration and mediastinoscopy for diagnosis of mediastinal malignancy. Am Surg 64:1014–1018, 1998.

71. Williams DB, Sahai AV, Aabakken L, et al: Endoscopic ultrasound guided fine needle aspiration biopsy: A large single center experience. Gut 44:720–726, 1999.

72. Fritscher-Ravens A, Sriram PV, Bobrowski C, et al: Mediastinal lymphadenopathy in patients with or without previous malignancy: EUS-FNA-based differential cytodiagnosis in 153 patients. Am J Gastroenterol 95:2278–2284, 2000.

73. Wiersema MJ, Vazquez-Sequeiros E, Wiersema LM: Evaluation of mediastinal lymphadenopathy with endoscopic US-guided fine-needle aspiration biopsy. Radiology 219:252–257, 2001.

74. Wiersema MJ, Hassig WM, Hawes RH, Wonn MJ: Mediastinal lymph node detection with endosonography. Endoscopy 39:788–793, 1993.

75. Hawes RH, Gress F, Kesler KA, et al: Endoscopic ultrasound versus computed tomography in the evaluation of the mediastinum in patients with non-small cell lung cancer. Endoscopy 26:784–787, 1994.

76. Wallace MB, Silvestri GA, Sahai AV, et al: Endoscopic ultrasound-guided fine needle aspiration for staging patients with carcinoma of the lung. Ann Thorac Surg 72:1861–1867, 2001.

77. Fritscher-Ravens A, Soehendra N, Schirrow L, et al: Role of transesophageal endosonography-guided fine-needle aspiration in the diagnosis of lung cancer. Chest 117:339–345, 2000.

78. Barawi M, Gottlieb K, Cunha B, et al: A prospective evaluation of the incidence of bacteremia associated with EUS-guided fine-needle aspiration. Gastrointest Endosc 53:189–192, 2001.

79. Faigel DO: EUS in patients with benign and malignant lymphadenopathy Gastrointest Endosc 53:593–598, 2001.

80. Wiersema MJ, Vilmann P, Giovannini M, et al: Endosonography-guided fine-needle aspiration: Diagnostic accuracy and complication assessment. Gastroenterology 112:1087–1095, 1997.

81. O'Toole D, Palazzo L, Arotcarena R, et al: Assessment of complications of EUS-guided fine-needle aspiration. Gastrointest Endosc 53:470–474, 2001.

82. Savides TJ, Master SS: EUS in rectal cancer. Gastrointest Endosc 56(Suppl):S12–S18, 2002.

83. Wildi SM, Hoda RS, Fickling W, et al: Diagnosis of benign cysts of the mediastinum: The role and risks of EUS and FNA. Gastrointest Endosc 58:362–368, 2003.

84. Levy MJ, Norton ID, Wiersema MJ, et al: Prospective risk assessment of bacteremia and other infectious complications in patients undergoing EUS-guided FNA. Gastrointest Endosc 57:672–678, 2003.

85. Van de Mierop F, Buorgeois S, Hiel M, et al: Bacteremia after EUS guided puncture: A prospective analysis [abstract]. Gastrointest Endosc 49:A13100, 1999.

86. Ikenberry S, Gress FG, Savides TA, Hawes RH: Fine-needle aspiration of posterior mediastinal lesions guided by radial scanning endosonography. Gastrointest Endosc 43:605–610, 1996.

87. Wiersema M, Hawes R, Tao LC, et al: Endoscopic ultrasonography as an adjunct to fine needle aspiration cytology of the upper and lower gastrointestinal tract. Gastrointest Endosc 38:35–39, 1992.

88. Rex DK, Tarver RD, Wiersema MJ, et al: Endoscopic transesophageal fine needle aspiration of mediastinal masses. Gastrointest Endosc 37:465–468, 1991.

89. Wiersema MJ, Kochman ML, Chak A, et al: Real-time endoscopic ultrasound-guided fine needle aspiration of a mediastinal lymph node. Gastrointest Endos 39:429–431, 1993.

90. Catalano MF, Sivak MV Jr, Rice T, et al: Endosonographic features predictive of lymph node metastases. Gastrointest Endosc 40:442–446, 1994.

91. Bhutani MS, Hawes RH, Hoffman BJ: A comparison of the accuracy of echo features during endoscopic ultrasound (EUS) and EUS-guided fine-needle aspiration of diagnosis of malignant lymph node invasion. Gastrointest Endosc 45:474–479, 1997.

92. Wallace MB, Kennedy T, Durkalski V, et al: Randomized controlled trial of EUS-guided fine needle aspiration techniques for the detection of malignant lymphadenopathy. Gastrointest Endosc 54:441–447, 2001.

93. White P Jr, Ettinger DS: Tissue is the issue: Is endoscopic ultrasonography with or without fine-needle aspiration biopsy in the staging of non-small-cell lung cancer an advance? [comment]. (Comment on Ann Intern Med 127[8 Pt 1]:604–612, 1997). Ann Intern Med 127[8 Pt 1]:643–645, 1997.

94. Villman P, Hancke S, Hendrickson FW, et al: Endosonographic guided fine needle aspiration biopsy of malignant lesions in the upper gastrointestinal tract. Endoscopy 25:523–527, 1993.

95. Gress FG, Hawes RH, Savides TJ, et al: Endoscopic ultrasound guided fine needle aspiration biopsy utilizing linear array and radial scanning endosonography: Results from a large single center experience. Gastrointest Endosc 45:243–250, 1997.

96. Erickson RA, Sayage-Rabie L, Beissner RS: Factors predicting the number of EUS-guided fine-needle passes for diagnosis of pancreatic malignancies. Gastrointest Endosc 51:184–190, 2000.

97. Wiersema MJ, Gatzimos K, Nisi R, Wiersema LM: Staging of non-Hodgkin's gastric lymphoma with endosonography-guided fine-needle aspiration biopsy and flow cytometry. Gastrointest Endosc 44:734–736, 1996.

98. Ribeiro A, Vazquez-Sequeiros E, Wiersema LM, et al: EUS-guided fine-needle aspiration combined with flow cytometry and immunocytochemistry in the diagnosis of lymphoma. Gastrointest Endosc 53:485–491, 2001.

99. Catalano MF, Nayar R, Gress F, et al: EUS-guided fine needle aspiration in mediastinal lymphadenopathy of unknown etiology. Gastrointest Endosc 55:863–869, 2002.

100. Fritscher-Ravens A, Sriram PV, Topalidis T, et al: Endoscopic ultrasonography-guided fine-needle cytodiagnosis of mediastinal metastases from renal cell cancer. Endoscopy 32:531–535, 2000.

101. Hahn M, Faigel DO: Frequency of mediastinal lymph node metastases in patients undergoing EUS evaluation of pancreaticobiliary masses Gastrointest Endosc 54:331–335, 2001.

102. Devereaux BM, Leblanc JK, Yousif E, et al: Clinical utility of EUS-guided fine-needle aspiration of mediastinal masses in the absence of known pulmonary malignancy. Gastrointest Endosc 56:397–401, 2002.

103. Palazzo L, Roseau G, Ruskone-Fourmestraux A, et al: Endoscopic ultrasonography in the local staging of primary gastric lymphoma. Endoscopy 25:502–508, 1993.

104. Panelli F, Erickson RA, Prasad VM: Evaluation of mediastinal masses by endoscopic ultrasound and endoscopic ultrasound-guided fine needle aspiration. Am J Gastroenterol 96:401–408, 2001.

105. Wiersema MJ, Chak A, Wiersema LM: Mediastinal histoplasmosis: Evaluation with endosonography and endoscopic fine-needle aspiration biopsy. Gastrointest Endosc 40:78–81, 1994.

106. Hainaut P, Monthe A, Lesage V, Weynand B: Tuberculous mediastinal lymphadenopathy. Acta Clinica Belgica 53:114–116, 1998.

107. Savides TJ, Gress FG, Wheat LJ, et al: Dysphagia due to mediastinal granulomas: Diagnosis with endoscopic ultrasonography. Gastroenterology 109:366–373, 1995.

108. Mishra G, Sahai AV, Penman ID, et al: Endoscopic ultrasonography with fine-needle aspiration: An accurate and simple diagnostic modality for sarcoidosis. Endoscopy 31:377–82, 1999.

109. Fritscher-Ravens A, Sriram P, Topalidis T: Diagnosing sarcoidosis using endosonography-guided fine-needle aspiration Chest 118:928–935, 2000.

110. Gilman MJ, Wang KP: Transbronchial lung biopsy in sarcoidosis: An approach to determine the optimal number of biopsies. Am Rev Respir Dis 122:721–724, 1980.

111. Larsen SS, Krasnik M, Vilmann P, et al: Endoscopic ultrasound guided biopsy of mediastinal lesions has a major impact on patient management Thorax 57:98–103, 2002.

112. Garcia, C, Kumar V, Sharma OP: Pancreatic sarcoidosis. Sarcoidosis Vasc Diffuse Lung Dis 13:28–32, 1996.

113. Michael H, Ho S, Pollack BJ, et al: Diagnosis of retroperitoneal and mediastinal sarcoidosis using endoscopic ultrasound guided fine-needle aspiration (manuscript in progress).

114. Limaye A, Paauw D, Raghu G, et al: Sarcoidosis associated with recurrent pancreatitis. South Med J 90:431–433, 1997.

115. Brincker H: Sarcoid reactions in malignant tumors. Cancer Treat Rev 13:147–156, 1986.

116. Tio TL, Tytgat GNJ: Endoscopic ultrasonography in analyzing peri-intestinal lymph node abnormality. Scand J Gastroenterol 21(Suppl 123):158–163, 1986.

117. Van Dam J, Rice TW, Sivak MV Jr: Endoscopic ultrasonography and endoscopically guided needle aspiration for the diagnosis of upper gastrointestinal tract foregut cysts. Am J Gastroenterol 87:762–765, 1992.

118. Geller A, Wang KK, DiMagno EP: Diagnosis of foregut duplication cysts by endoscopic ultrasonography. Gastroenterology 109:838–842, 1995.

119. Bhutani MS, Hoffman BJ, Reed C: Endosonographic diagnosis of an esophageal duplication cyst. Endoscopy 28:396–397, 1996.

120. Faigel DO, Burke A, Ginsberg GG, et al: The role of endoscopic ultrasound in the evaluation and management of foregut duplications. Gastrointest Endosc 45:99–103, 1997.

121. Bondestam S, Salo JA, Salonen OL, Lamminen AE: Imaging of congenital esophageal cysts in adults. Gastrointest Radiol 15:279–281, 1990.

122. Mendelson DS, Rose JS, Efremidis SC, et al: Bronchogenic cysts with high CT numbers. Am J Roentgenol 140:463–465, 1983.

123. Marchal G, Gelin J, Verbeken E, et al: High-resolution real-time sonography of the adrenal glands: A routine examination? J Ultrasound Med 5:65–68, 1986.

124. Zappasodi F, Derchi LE, Rizzatto G: Ultrasonography of the normal adrenal glands: A study using linear-array real-time equipment. Br J Radiol 59:759–764, 1986.

125. Chang KJ, Erickson RA, Nguyen P: Endoscopic ultrasound (EUS) and EUS-guided fine-needle aspiration of the left adrenal gland. Gastrointest Endosc 44:568–572, 1996.

126. Harper PG, Houang M, Spiro SG, et al: Computerized axial tomography in the pretreatment assessment of small cell carcinoma of the bronchus. Cancer 47:1775–1780, 1981.

127. Pagani JJ: Non-small cell carcinoma adrenal metastasis: Computed tomography and percutaneous needle biopsy in their diagnosis. Cancer 53:1058–1060, 1984.

128. Sandler MA, Pearlberg JL, Madrazo BL, et al: Computed tomographic evaluation of the adrenal gland in the preoperative assessment of bronchogenic carcinoma. Radiology 145:733–736, 1982.

129. Whittlesey D: Prospective computed tomographic scanning in the staging of bronchogenic cancer. J Thorac Cardiovasc Surg 95:876–882, 1988.

130. Oliver TW, Bernardino ME, Miller JI, et al: Isolated adrenal masses in nonsmall-cell bronchogenic carcinoma. Radiology 153:217–218, 1984.

131. Abrams HL, Spiro R, Goldstein N: Metastasis in carcinoma: Analysis of 1000 autopsied cases. Cancer 3:74–85, 1950.

132. Englemen RM, McNamara WL: Bronchogenic carcinoma: A statistical review of two hundred twenty-four autopsies. J Thorac Surg 27:227–237, 1954.

133. Farrell JL, Brugge WR: EUS-guided fine-needle aspiration of a renal mass: An alternative method for diagnosis of malignancy. Gastrointest Endosc 56:450–452, 2002.

134. Davis CJ: Pathology of renal neoplasms. Semin Roentgenol 22:233–240, 1987.

135. Wood BJ, Khan MA, McGovern F, et al: Imaging guided biopsy of renal masses: Indications, accuracy and impact on clinical management. J Urol 161:1470–1474, 1999.

136. Dechet CB, Sebo T, Farrow G, et al: Prospective analysis of intraoperative frozen needle biopsy of solid renal masses in adults. J Urol 162:1282–1285, 1999.

137. Chang KJ, Albers CG, Nguyen P: Endoscopic ultrasound-guided fine needle aspiration of pleural and ascitic fluid. Am J Gastroenterol 90:148–150, 1995.

138. Nguyen P, Chang K: GE EUS in the detection of ascites and EUS-guided paracentesis. Gastrointest Endosc 54:336–339, 2001.

139. Pollack BJ, Chak A, Canto M, et al: Endoscopic ultrasonography in the detection of malignant ascites: Is it a marker of peritoneal carcinomatosis? [abstract]. Gastrointest Endosc 43:A549, 1996.

140. Canto M, Gislason G: Is extraluminal fluid at endoscopic ultrasonography an accurate marker of peritoneal carcinomatosis? A prospective study [abstract]. Gastrointest Endosc 47:AB142, 1998.

141. Nguyen P, Feng JC, Chang KJ: Endoscopic ultrasound (EUS) and EUS-guided fine-needle aspiration (FNA) of liver lesions. Gastrointestinal Endosc 50:357–361, 1999.

142. Edoute Y, Tibon-Fisher O, Ben Haim S, Malberger E: Ultrasonically guided fine-needle aspiration of liver lesions. Am J Gastroenterol 87:1138–1141, 1992.

143. Samaratunga H, Wright G: Value of fine needle aspiration biopsy cytology in the diagnosis of discrete hepatic lesions suspicious for malignancy. Aust N Z J Surg 62:540–544, 1992.

144. Fornari F, Civardi G, Cavanna L, et al: Ultrasonically guided fine-needle aspiration biopsy: A highly diagnostic procedure for hepatic tumors. Am J Gastroenterol 85:1009–1013, 1990.

145. Sautereau D, Vireo O, Cazes PY, et al: Value of sonographically guided fine needle aspiration biopsy in evaluating the liver with sonographic abnormalities. Gastroenterology 93:715–718, 1987.

146. Wiersema MJ, Vilmann P, Giovannini M, et al: Endosonography-guided fine-needle aspiration: Diagnostic accuracy and complication assessment. Gastroenterology 112:1087–1095, 1997.

147. Bentz JS, Kochman ML, Faigel DO, et al: Endoscopic ultrasound-guided real-time fine-needle aspiration: Clinicopathologic features of 60 patients. Diagn Cytopathol 18:98–109, 1998.

148. Fritscher-Ravens A, Schirrow L, Atay Z, et al: Endosonographically controlled fine needle aspiration cytology-indications and results in routine diagnosis. Gastroenterology 37:343–351, 1999.

149. Livraghi T, Damascelli B, Lombardi C, Spagnoli I: Risk in fine-needle abdominal biopsy. J Clin Ultrasound 11:77–81, 1983.

150. Edoute Y, Ben-Haim S, Brenner B, Malberger E: Fatal hemoperitoneum after fine-needle aspiration of a liver metastasis. Am J Gastroenterol 87:358–359, 1992.

151. Glaser KS, Weger AR, Schmid KW, Bodner E: Is fine-needle aspiration of tumours harmless? Lancet 1:620, 1989.

152. Kowdley KV, Aggarwal A, Sachs PB: Delayed hemorrhage after percutaneous liver biopsy: Role of therapeutic angiography. J Clin Gastroenterol 19:50–53, 1994.

153. Vergara V, Garripoli A, Marucci MM, et al: Colon cancer seeding after percutaneous fine needle aspiration of liver metastasis. J Hepatol 18:276–278, 1993.

154. tenBerge J, Hoffman BJ, Hawes RH, et al: EUS-guided fine needle aspiration of the liver: Indications, yield, and safety based on an international survey of 167 cases. Gastrointest Endosc 55:859–862, 2002.

155. Barclay RL. Perez-Miranda M. Giovannini M: EUS-guided treatment of a solid hepatic metastasis. Gastrointest Endosc 55:266–270, 2002.

156. Catalano MF, Sial S, Chak A, et al: EUS-guided fine needle aspiration of idiopathic abdominal masses Gastrointest Endosc 55:854–858, 2002.

157. Erickson RA, Tretjak Z: Clinical utility of endoscopic ultrasound and endoscopic guided fine needle aspiration in retroperitoneal neoplasms. Am J Gastrointest 95:1188–1194, 2000.

158. McGrath KM, Ballo MS, Jowell PS: Schwannoma of the mediastinum diagnosed by EUS-guided fine needle aspiration Gastrointest Endosc 53:362–365, 2001.

159. Okada N, Hirooka Y, Itoh A, et al: Retroperitoneal neurilemoma diagnosed by EUS-guided FNA Gastrointest Endosc 57:790–792, 2003.

160. Barawi M, Bekal P, Gress F: Accessory spleen: A potential cause of misdiagnosis at EUS. Gastrointest Endosc 52:769–772, 2000.

161. Fritscher-Ravens A, Mylonaki M, Pantes A, et al: Endoscopic ultrasound-guided biopsy for the diagnosis of focal lesions of the spleen. Am J Gastroenterol 98:1022–1027, 2003.

162. Gress F, Michael H, Gelrud D, et al: EUS-guided fine-needle aspiration of the pancreas: Evaluation of pancreatitis as a complication. Gastrointest Endosc 56:864–867, 2002.

163. Wallace MB, Hawes RH, Sahai AV, et al: Dilation of malignant esophageal stenosis to allow EUS guided fine-needle aspiration: Safety and effect on patient management. Gastrointest Endosc 51:309–313, 2000

164. Schwartz DA, Unni KK, Levy MJ, et al: The rate of false-positive results with EUS-guided fine-needle aspiration. Gastrointest Endosc 56:868–872, 2002.

165. Reidenberg MM, Portenoy RK: The need for an open mind about the treatment of chronic nonmalignant pain. Clin Pharmacol Ther 55:367–369, 1994.

166. Fugere F, Lewis G: Coeliac plexus block for chronic pain syndromes. Can J Anaesth 40:954–963, 1993.

167. Hastings RH, McKay WR: Treatment of benign chronic abdominal pain with neurolytic celiac plexus block. Anesthesiology 75:156–158,1991.

168. Leung JW, Bowen-Wright M, Aveling W, et al: Coeliac plexus block for pain in pancreatic cancer and chronic pancreatitis. Br J Surg 70:730–732, 1983.

169. Arner S, Myerson BA: Lack of analgesic effect of opioids on neuropathic and idiopathic forms of pain. Pain 33:11–23, 1988.

170. McQuay HJ, Tramer M, Nye BA, et al: A systematic review of antidepressants in neuropathic pain. Pain 68:217–227, 1996.

171. Malfertheiner P, Mayer D, Buchler M, et al: Treatment of pain in chronic pancreatitis by inhibition of pancreatic secretion with octreotide. Gut 36:450–454, 1995.

172. Halgreen H, Pederson NT, Worning H: Symptomatic effect of pancreatic enzyme therapy in patients with chronic pancreatitis. Scand J Gastroenterol 21:104–108, 1986.

173. Malesci A, Gaia E, Fioretta A, et al: No effect of long-term treatment with pancreatic extract on recurrent abdominal pain in patients with chronic pancreatitis. Scand J Gastroenterol 30:392–398, 1995.

174. Mossner J, Secknus R, Meyer J, et al: Treatment of pain with pancreatic extracts in chronic pancreatitis: Results of a prospective placebo-controlled multicenter trial. Digestion 53:54–66, 1992.

175. Ferrer-Brechner T: Anesthetic management of cancer pain. Semin Oncol 12:431–437, 1985.

176. Stone HH, Chauvin EJ: Pancreatic denervation for pain relief in chronic alcohol associated pancreatitis. Br J Surg 77:303–305, 1990.

177. Bradley EL 3rd: Long-term results of pancreaticojejunostomy in patients with chronic pancreatitis. Am J Surg 153:207–213, 1987.

178. Markowitz JS, Rattner DW, Warshaw AL: Failure of symptomatic relief after pancreatojejunal decompression for chronic pancreatitis. Strategies for salvage. Arch Surg 129:374–379, 1994.

179. Levy MJ, Wiersema MJ: EUS-guided celiac plexus neurolysis and celiac plexus block. Gastrointest Endosc 57:923–930, 2003.

180. Zenz M, Strumpf M, Tryba M: Long-term oral opioid therapy in patients with chronic nonmalignant pain. J Pain Symptom Manage 7:69–77, 1992.

181. Hoffman BJ: EUS-guided celiac plexus block/neurolysis. Gastrointest Endosc 56(4 Suppl):S26–28, 2002.

182. Wong GY, Brown DL: Transient paraplegia following celiac plexus block for cancer pain. Reg Anesth 20:352–355, 1995.

183. Ischia S, Ischia A, Polati E, Finco G: Three posterior percutaneous celiac plexus block techniques. A prospective, randomized study in 61 patients with pancreatic cancer pain. Anesthesiology 76:534–540, 1992.

184. Eisenberg E, Carr DB, Chalmers TC: Neurolytic celiac plexus block for treatment of cancer pain: A meta-analysis. Anesth Analg 80:290–295, 1995.

185. Lillemoe KD, Cameron JL, Kaufman HS, et al: Chemical splanchnicectomy in patients with unresectable pancreatic cancer. A prospective randomized trail. Ann Surg 217:447–455, 1993.

186. Polati E, Finco G, Gottin L, et al: Prospective randomized double-blinded trial of neurolytic coeliac plexus block in patients with pancreatic cancer. Br J Surg 85:199–201, 1998.

187. Kawamata M, Ishitani K, Ishikawa K, et al: Comparison between celiac plexus block and morphine treatment on quality of life in patients with pancreatic cancer. Pain 64:597–602, 1996.

188. Mercadante S, Nicosia F: Celiac plexus block: A reappraisal. Reg Anesth Pain Med 23:37–48i, 1998.

189. Wiersema MJ, Wiersema LM: Endosonography-guided celiac plexus neurolysis. Gastrointest Endosc 44:656–662, 1996.

190. Gress F, Schmitt C, Sherman S, et al: A prospective randomized comparison of endoscopic ultrasound- and computed tomography-guided celiac plexus bloc for managing chronic pancreatitis pain. Am J Gastroenterol 94:900–905, 1999.

191. Gress F, Schmitt C, Sherman S, et al: Endoscopic ultrasound-guided celiac plexus block for managing abdominal pain associated with chronic pancreatitis: A prospective single center experience. Am J Gastroenterol 96:409–416, 2001.

192. Naresh T, Gunaratnam NT, Sarma AV, et al: A prospective study of EUS-guided celiac plexus neurolysis for pancreatic cancer pain Gastrointest Endosc 54:316–324, 2001.

193. Patt RB, Reddy S: Spinal neurolysis for cancer pain. Ann Acad Med 23:216–220, 1994.

194. Davies DD: Incidence of major complications of neurolytic coeliac plexus block. J R Soc Med 86:264–266, 1993.

195. Hardy PA, Wells JC: Coeliac plexus block and cephalic spread of injectate. Ann R Coll Surg Engl 71:48–49, 1989.

Evaluation of Gastric Polyps and Thickened Gastric Folds

Kenneth D. Chi and Irving Waxman

Gastric polyps are detected in up to 3% of upper endoscopic evaluations,[1] but the incidence is higher than in past years because of the introduction of endoscopy for diagnosis and treatment of upper digestive tract diseases.[2] These polyps are usually asymptomatic and are often found incidentally on endoscopic or radiographic examination. They may be sporadic in occurrence or associated with polyposis syndromes. Gastric polyps may be single or multiple in number and pedunculated or sessile in form. Depending on the type of polyp, variable sizes can be encountered ranging from millimeters to several centimeters in diameter. In general, gastric polyps are usually small (diameter <1 cm), well circumscribed, clearly demarcated, and project above the level of surrounding mucosa.

Because of its diagnostic clarity and therapeutic ability, endoscopy is the examination of choice in the diagnosis and treatment of gastric polyps. Gastric polyps can be divided into epithelial and non-epithelial lesions. This chapter reviews the various types of epithelial gastric polyps with a discussion on the endoscopic techniques of gastric polypectomy, surveillance, and management. Nonepithelial gastric tumors including submucosal tumors (SMTs) are discussed in Chapter 31, and the management of upper gastrointestinal (GI) hereditary polyposis syndromes is discussed in Chapter 36. This chapter concludes with a discussion on the evaluation of thickened gastric folds, differential diagnoses, and endoscopic techniques and management.

Epithelial Gastric Polyps

Epithelial gastric polyps are divided into non-neoplastic and neoplastic lesions. In contrast to colonic polyps, most gastric polyps are non-neoplastic. Approximately 80% to 90% of gastric polyps are non-neoplastic and include fundic gland and hyperplastic polyps. Although hyperplastic polyps are not neoplastic, dysplasia and/or gastric adenocarcinoma may rarely develop within the lesion.[3] Neoplastic epithelial gastric polyps include adenomas and polypoid gastric carcinomas.

FUNDIC GLAND POLYPS

Fundic gland polyps (also known as Elster's glandular cysts, cystic hamartomatous epithelial polyps) compose up to 47% of all gastric polyps. They are more common in women and increasingly have been found between 40 and 69 years of age.[4] The pathogenesis is unknown, and usually occurs sporadically but at increased frequency in patients with familial adenomatous polyposis (FAP).[5] Although fundic gland polyps are traditionally considered a condition with little or no malignancy potential, some reports have shown a possible increased association of concomitant colorectal adenomas or carcinomas in patients with fundic gland polyps.[6-8] The development of dysplasia and adenomatous changes in fundic gland polyps have been found in 1% to 1.9% of sporadic cases[5,9] and in 25% to 44% of patients with FAP.[5,7,10] In addition, reports have suggested malignant transformation of fundic gland polyps in patients with FAP, which may occur more often than previously believed.[10,11] Management of FAP syndrome is discussed in Chapter 36. The development of fundic gland polyps have also been associated with long-term proton pump inhibitor use,[12-14] but other studies have shown that a causal pathogenetic relationship is unlikely.[15,16] Histologically, fundic gland polyps are characterized by dilated glands forming microcysts lined with fundic type parietal and chief cells.

Endoscopically, fundic gland polyps are usually found in the fundus or body of the stomach. They may be found as a solitary lesion but are often multiple in closely packed clusters, resembling small round grapes. The size of these lesions are generally 2 to 3 mm in diameter, and, because of their small size, they are sometimes hidden between rugae. The mucosal surface typically resembles the normal surrounding mucosal color but also can be seen pale in coloration; thus, maximal visualization is best when the stomach is fully distended. These polyps may be difficult to distinguish from carcinoid tumors that are similar in shape and location and may be multiple in number. Endoscopically, carcinoid tumors can be distinguished from fundic gland polyps by its commonly yellowish coloration and firmer consistency.

HYPERPLASTIC POLYPS

Hyperplastic polyps are considered the most commonly observed polypoid lesion in the stomach composing 28% to 75% of all gastric polyps.[4,17] The large variability in frequency is likely due to differing definitions of hyperplastic polyps. Men and women are both equally affected, with a predominance in those older than 60 years. These polyps have previously been regarded as having no malignant potential; however, this is no longer true because of the increasing number of dysplastic changes or carcinoma that occur in gastric hyperplastic polyps.[3,18,19] Focal carcinomas have been found to occur in 2.1% of gastric hyperplastic polyps in one large Japanese series.[20] In addition, within the same series, foci of dysplasia were seen in 4.0% of gastric hyperplastic polyps. The prevalence of true dysplasia arising from hyperplastic polyps is debated, with reported rates ranging from 1.9% to 19%.[21] Similarly, other series of adenocarcinoma arising from hyperplastic polyps were variable, ranging from 0% to as high as 13.5%.[21] Unlike gastric fundic gland polyps that tend to arise from otherwise normal gastric mucosa, hyperplastic polyps have been associated with chronic gastritis, particularly with autoimmune gastritis,[21–23] and *Helicobacter pylori* gastritis.[24] It has been recently shown that *H. pylori* eradication may shrink hyperplastic polyps[25,26] and, therefore, may provide an initial medical therapy before endoscopic removal. The histology of gastric hyperplastic polyps is different from that of hyperplastic colorectal polyps in that they have submucosal edema with prominent foveolar hyperplasia and inflammation of the lamina propria.

Endoscopically, hyperplastic polyps can be found throughout the stomach and range in size of small nodules of a few millimeters to a large mass of many centimeters that can be mistaken for carcinoma. They can be solitary or multiple and may be sessile or pedunculated with an associated stalk. If multiple polyps are found, the chance of associated atrophic gastritis may be as high as 20% to 30% and usually are more proximal in location.[21,27] The overlying mucosa may be normal in appearance, but often it has a reddish coloration in larger polyps. Because of local trauma, larger hyperplastic polyps often have a friable ulcerated whitish tip of granulation tissue and may be surrounded by atrophic or inflamed-appearing mucosa. There is no consensus regarding endoscopic removal and surveillance of hyperplastic gastric polyps. Details of management are discussed later.

GASTRIC ADENOMATOUS POLYPS

Adenomatous polyps of the stomach are more uncommon than the non-neoplastic epithelial lesions, representing 7% to 10% of gastric polypoid lesions.[28,29] Gastric adenomas are true neoplasms and are premalignant lesions with increasing risk of developing into adenocarcinoma depending on its size and structure. Up to 40% of gastric adenomas may harbor a focus of adenocarcinoma, especially if greater than 2 cm in diameter.[15] Malignancy, however, can be found in lesions of any size. These lesions often arise in stomachs with a background of mucosal atrophy and are a marker for increased risk of adenocarcinoma elsewhere in the stomach.[29,30] Gastric adenomas have been associated with FAP but not as frequent as fundic gland polyps. Histologically, gastric adenomas are characterized by columnar epithelium that is pseudostratified and shows elongated atypical nuclei and increased mitotic activity and can be divided into tubular, villous, and tubulovillous types. Dysplasia and carcinomatous changes occur most often in villous and tubulovillous adenomas in up to 28.5% to 40%.[31–34]

Endoscopic evaluation of gastric adenomas should consist of a careful complete examination of the surrounding mucosa, with biopsies of any suspicious lesions. These lesions can be found in any location of the stomach but appear to have a predilection for the antrum.[35] Gastric adenomas are found generally larger than hyperplastic polyps, usually around 3 to 4 cm in diameter, but can also range in size from a few millimeters to several centimeters. The mucosal surface is usually smooth with a reddish coloration and often with a cerebriform mucosal pattern. The shape of gastric adenomas can vary, ranging from single round sessile projections to multilobulated lesions. Villous-type lesions are sometimes difficult to detect, because of the flat sessile carpet-like appearance that can blend in with the surrounding rugae. Rarely, flat or even depressed adenomas are encountered.[36] Because of its malignant potential, there is consensus that all gastric adenomatous polyps need to be completely removed, either endoscopically or by laparoscopic wedge resection. In addition, thorough biopsy of the surrounding gastric mucosa should be performed. The recurrence rate of adenomatous polyps may be as high as 16% after polypectomy.[37] Endoscopic techniques and management are further discussed later.

POLYPOID GASTRIC CARCINOMA

Because of similar appearance, endoscopic determination of adenomatous gastric polyps versus genuine malignant lesions is extremely difficult without histologic confirmation. Synchronous or metachronous gastric cancers have been found in 11% of patients with adenomas.[32] Gastric adenocarcinomas may develop as polypoid lesions (Borrmann type A) and are differentiated into type I (protruded, polypoid type) and type IIa (superficial elevated type) (Fig. 34–1).[38]

Subepithelial Gastric Polyps

Subepithelial gastric polyps consist of a heterogenous group of lesions that are usually small and difficult to differentiate between hyperplastic and adenomatous polyps. These non-epithelial lesions are usually covered by normal-appearing mucosa and consist of a variety of causes including carcinoid tumors, lipomas, aberrant pancreas (pancreatic rest, heterotopic pancreas), inflammatory fibroid polyps, and gastrointestinal stromal tumors (GISTs, including leiomyomas, leiomyosarcomas, schwannomas, fibromas, and others). One should refer to Chapter 31 for a complete discussion of non-epithelial tumors of the stomach.

Endoscopic Techniques and Management

Gastric polyps are rarely symptomatic and often incidental on discovery. The first step in the management of a gastric polyp is to identify the tissue histology. Because the endoscopic appearance of a

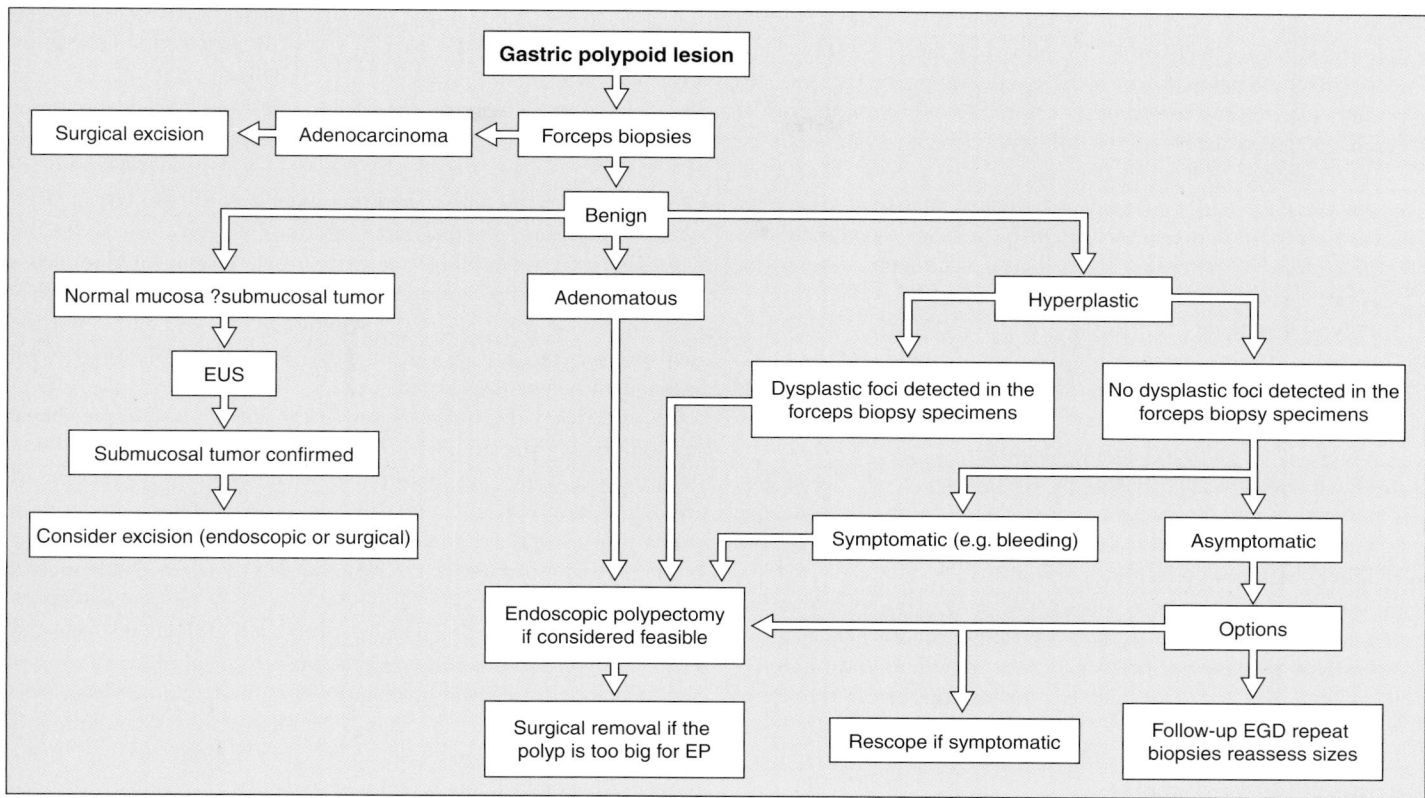

Figure 34–1. Evaluation and management of a gastric polypoid lesion. (Adapted from Lau CF, Hui PK, Mak KL, et al: Gastric polypoid lesions—illustrative cases and literature review. Am J Gastroenterol 93:2559–2564, 1998, with permission from Blackwell Publishing Ltd.)

gastric polyp cannot reliably distinguish histology using a standard endoscope, gastric polypoid lesions found on upper endoscopy should be biopsied or removed. This, however, may change as more studies using magnification or zoom endoscopy are performed to identify mucosal patterns to correlate with histology.[39,40] Although the use of forceps biopsy is a simple method of obtaining polyp tissue, this method may provide inadequate tissue or sampling error. Studies have shown inconsistencies between histologic diagnosis made by forceps biopsy and subsequent snare polypectomy specimen.[41,42] Muehldorfer and coworkers[43] led a prospective multicenter study comparing the diagnostic accuracy of forceps biopsy versus polypectomy of a sample of 222 gastric polyps greater than 5 mm (excluded fundic gland polyps). Relevant differences were found in 2.7% of cases in which there was failure to reveal foci of carcinoma on forceps biopsy in a group of hyperplastic polyps. Therefore, they recommend removal by an experienced endoscopist of all epithelial gastric polyps larger than 5 mm.

If multiple gastric polyps are found, additional risk is presented to the patient if multiple snare excisions are performed. Although complete excision is preferred, this may not be technically feasible or practical; thus, the risks and benefits should be individualized with each patient. In this scenario, resection could be delayed until forceps biopsy results are reviewed, and this delay can also give the endoscopist a chance to bring to attention the additional risks involved to the patient. Although gastric polyps that are found multiple in number are usually of the same histology type,[17] hyperplastic and adenomatous polyps can be found together.[33,37] One strategy to use when dealing with multiple gastric polyps would

be to remove the largest polyps that are feasible and safe by snare excision, combined with multiple forceps biopsies of the smaller polyps. Hopefully, this will give a complete representation of the histologic makeup of the lesions encountered, while minimizing risk of missing a neoplasm.

If one or more foci of dysplasia are detected in a biopsy specimen from a gastric hyperplastic polyp, the polyp should be removed, even if not producing any symptoms. However, controversy exists in the management of incidentally found gastric hyperplastic polyps with no focus of dysplasia on forceps biopsy. Some authors recommend endoscopic removal of all hyperplastic polyps that are encountered because of the small but significant risk of missing an area of dysplasia within the forceps biopsy.[32,42,44] Others propose endoscopically removing small polyps and periodic biopsy of hyperplastic polyps that are too large for polypectomy,[45] depending on the level of endoscopic expertise. Currently, there is no consensus on the most appropriate frequency and duration of endoscopic follow-up of hyperplastic polyps.[46]

Until well-designed long-term prospective studies are available on the management of gastric polyps, the American Society for Gastrointestinal Endoscopy has developed general recommendations[47]:

1. Polypoid defects of any size detected radiographically should be evaluated endoscopically, with biopsy and/or removal of the lesions.
2. Polyps causing symptoms, such as obstruction and bleeding, should be removed, preferably endoscopically.

3. Polyps greater than 2 cm in size should be endoscopically excised wherever feasible. If endoscopic polypectomy is not possible, the polyp should be biopsied. If adenomatous tissue is detected, referral for surgical excision should be considered. If no adenomatous tissue is detected, management must be individualized. If it is felt that there is a reasonable chance that endoscopic biopsy could have overlooked adenomatous change in a mixed polyp (e.g., as might be seen in a pedunculated polyp in which sampling from all areas is difficult), referral for surgical excision is reasonable.

4. Polyps less than 2 cm in size may be initially biopsied or excised. If representative biopsies are obtained and the polyp is nonadenomatous, no further intervention is necessary. If biopsies reveal adenomatous change, endoscopic excision should be considered wherever feasible.

5. When multiple gastric polyps are encountered, the largest polyps should be biopsied or excised, and representative sample biopsies taken from some others. Further management should be based on histologic results.

6. Surveillance endoscopy 1 year after removing adenomatous gastric polyps is reasonable to assess recurrence at prior excision site, new or previously missed polyps, and/or super-vening early carcinoma in gastric mucosa apart from the site of coincident polyps. If this examination is negative, repeat surveillance endoscopy should be repeated no more frequently than 3- to 5-year intervals.

7. No surveillance endoscopy is necessary after removal of nonadenomatous gastric polyps.

Endoscopic Techniques and Considerations

Gastric polypectomy, like all invasive procedures, carries significant potential for injury to the patient. The patient should be aware of the added risks of possible complications before giving informed consent, especially if the diagnosis of gastric polyps is already known. Consideration for antibiotic prophylaxis for the prevention of bacterial endocarditis should be made for high-risk patients. Adequate preparation of available endoscopic devices at the endoscopist's disposal is essential, as well as continuous coordination with the nursing staff to ensure a smooth procedure. Selection of a multichannel gastroscope is helpful, especially if interventional procedures are expected. Pedunculated polyps with thin stalks can be safely removed by snare cautery. For larger polyps on a thick pedicle, the concern of a "feeder vessel" within the stalk can be worrisome. Tio and Tytgat[48] demonstrated a technique of surveying vascular structures within a pedicle of a large pedunculated polyp using endoscopic ultrasonography (EUS) before transaction of the stalk. For pedunculated polyps greater than 1 cm in diameter, endoscopic resection can be assisted by using a grasping forceps through a snare technique, as described by Akahoshi and colleagues.[49] In this technique, utilizing a dual channel endoscope, grasping forceps are inserted in one channel through the detach-able snare loop previously inserted in the second channel. The detachable snare loop is a nylon loop that is deployed to ensnare the target tissue (Endoloop; Olympus America, Melville, NY). The forceps grasp the middle part of the stalk, while the detachable snare is extended and looped over the polyp and tightened around the stalk to provide hemostasis when deployed. When the target tissue displays a cyanotic discoloration after tightening the detach-able loop, it can then be released. Next, an electrosurgical snare loop is extended over the polyp, and the upper part of the stalk is lifted with the grasping forceps while resecting the lesion just above the detached loop. Endoscopic resection using a detachable loop is a useful method of preventing polypectomyrelated bleeding in other parts of the GI tract as well.[50,51] Complications and data reporting inadvertent transaction of the polyp stalk with the snare with subsequent bleeding is limited.[52]

Large gastric polyps that are sessile can be removed in piecemeal fashion, but if a transmural lesion is suspected, EUS can be useful in determining depth of invasion. The Japanese introduction of endoscopic mucosal resection[53] (EMR) is now gaining popularity in the Western world. With the assistance of ultrasonography, EMR is both safe and effective for the management of selected submucosal lesions.[54] EUS is especially helpful in delineating submucosal lesions for assistance in resection and has been used with good success. A more complete discussion on the approach to submucosal tumors and techniques of EMR is in Chapter 31.

The incidence of hemorrhage from endoscopic polypectomy is about 2%.[50,55,56] However, despite careful resection and using preventative endoscopic techniques described previously, compli-cations may arise. Injection of 2 to 4 mL of 1:10,000 epinephrine solution diluted with 3% saline into the stalk before or after resection can be performed for hemostasis. Additional hemostasis can be provided by endoscopically deployed metallic clips (Hemoclip; Olympus America, Melville, NY) to provide mechanical com-pression to the target tissue. Lin and coworkers[57] demonstrates the use of Hemoclips in the excision of a large polyp within a technically difficult angle of the duodenum using a needle knife. Recently, Sobrino-Faya and colleagues[58] published a retrospective study demonstrating that the prophylactic use of hemoclips is associated with a low risk of bleeding (3.3%) after polypectomy of large polyps 15 to 40 mm in diameter. In addition, thermal hemostatic devices such as bipolar electrocautery or heater probe (Olympus America, Melville, NY) can deliver thermal energy to give additional hemostasis.

Resected polyps should be recovered and sent for pathologic examination and is essential when the diagnosis is uncertain. A variety of devices designed for polyp retrieval include grasping forceps, nets, and baskets. The polypectomy snare may be used to lasso the severed polyp,[59] or applying continuous suction while removing the endoscope can be done with smaller polyps that cannot be caught in a specimen trap. A risk during removal of polyps with these methods is the possibility of aspiration or accidental release of the polyp into the airway. Using an overtube be in this situation may be prudent unless more secure polyp retrieval methods are used such as a basket or retrieval net. The Roth retrieval net (United States Endoscopy Group, Inc., Mentor, OH) is a single-use device comprised of a net over a retractable loop that captures the polyp after polypectomy. Finally, polyps that are lost distally by peristalsis, especially when performing a duodenal polypectomy, can possibly be prevented with the use of glucagon.

Table 34–1. Diseases Considered in the Endosonographic Evaluation of Thickened Folds and Layers Principally Involved

Etiology of Thickened Folds	EUS Wall Layer Involved
Gastric varices	2 and 3
Gastritis	2 and 3
Carcinoma and lymphoma	2, 3, 4, and 5
Hypertrophic gastric folds	2 and 3
Zollinger-Ellison syndrome	2 and 3
Ménétrier's disease	2 and 3
Gastritis cystica profunda	3
Hyperrugosity	2 and 3
Rectal ulcer and prolapse syndromes	2, 3, and 4

EUS, endoscopic ultrasonography.

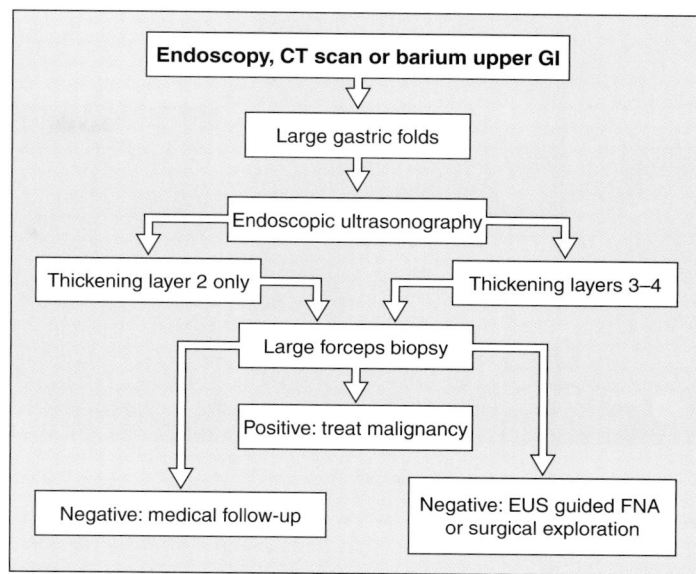

Figure 34–2. Flow chart illustrating the workup of large gastric folds.

Thickened Folds

Thickened folds often present a diagnostic challenge to the endoscopist, particularly in the stomach. Standard endoscopic biopsies are often unrevealing and often only contain superficial mucosa despite repetitive deep biopsies. Although obtaining specimens from deeper layers with a diathermic snare can increase the diagnostic yield, there is increased risk of hemorrhage or perforation.[60,61] In addition, the etiologies of thickened gastric folds are extremely varied and are a common feature in both benign and malignant diseases. The more common and classical etiologies are discussed individually. The diagnosis of thickened gastric folds can be suspected if folds do not flatten during adequate insufflation. What constitutes a thickened fold is debatable as size of folds varies by location, and the precise amount of insufflation varies with each endoscopy. Radiographic criteria for gastric folds have included a width greater than 10 mm.[60] With the introduction of EUS, individual gut wall layers and accurate measurement of wall thickness is possible. Both high-frequency ultrasound probe sonography (HFUPS) and dedicated echoendoscopes are useful for evaluation.[62,63] Normal gastric wall thickness measured by EUS is between 0.8 to 3.6 mm.[64] Therefore, the gastric wall is considered thickened if measured greater than 3.6 mm and is especially true if greater than 4.0 mm.[65,66] In normal gastric folds, there are five wall layers of the GI tract that are roughly proportional in size. The five EUS layers consist of layer 1, the interface between the transducer or the fluid surrounding the transducer and the mucosa; layer 2, the deep mucosa and the mucosa; layer 3, the submucosa; layer 4, the muscularis propria; and layer 5, the serosa adventitia. Different diseases show different levels of infiltration with regional thickening of distinct layers, which can refine potential diagnoses by EUS. Specific causes of thickened folds and their EUS features are listed in Table 34–1. In addition, preservation of layer structures can be determined, and subsequent diagnostic options including needle aspiration, EMR, and surgery with endosonography can be provided.

The initial endosonographic approach to thickened gastric folds should be to evaluate the layer thickness. When EUS abnormalities involve only the mucosal layer or layer 2, endoscopic biopsies are diagnostic.[67] If layers 2 and 3 are involved, deep or large forceps biopsies should be considered. Malignancy should be strongly suspected if layer 4 is involved or the muscularis propria is thickened,

regardless if normal biopsies are returned.[65,67–69] Finally, many experts instill water into the lumen to improve image quality during endosonography, but this may not always be necessary and can lead to aspiration when performed in the upper GI tract. An algorithm for the evaluation of thickened gastric folds is outlined in Fig. 34–2.

GASTRIC VARICES

Gastric varices are seen in the submucosal layer as distinct hypoechoic structures by EUS and are often described as wormlike. The mucosal and submucosal layer may be thickened (layers 2 and 3) in portal hypertension. In addition, engorgement of larger vessels such as the splenic and portal veins, perigastric collateral veins, and gastric perforating veins may also be seen.[70] If gastric varices are identified or suspected, biopsies should not be done, because it could be potentially hazardous.[68] Thickened gastric folds in the cardia or fundus should be evaluated by EUS if indicated. The use of a color Doppler EUS (CD-EUS) can verify blood flow and calculate blood flow volume and velocity, which can be monitored during therapy.[70] In addition, EUS has been used to predict which patients will respond to therapy and which will not, and it can be used to assess the results of therapeutic intervention.[71]

GASTRITIS

Another cause of superficial wall layer thickening is gastritis, which involves the mucosa and submucosal (layers 2 and 3). Infectious etiologies are common, especially *H. pylori*.[65,72] *H. pylori* infection of the gastric mucosa is associated with an active gastritis characterized by infiltration of the mucosa and submucosa with neutrophils, eosinophils, lymphocytes, and macrophages. Avunduk and coworkers[72] demonstrated the endosonographic resolution of *H. pylori* gastritis induced gastric fold thickening after eradication of the organism. Inflammatory conditions have also been implicated, particularly those resulting in granuloma formation such as sarcoidosis[73] and Crohn's disease.[74,75] Hirokawa and colleagues[75] described an endoscopic appearance of a "bamboo joint-like" appearance characterized

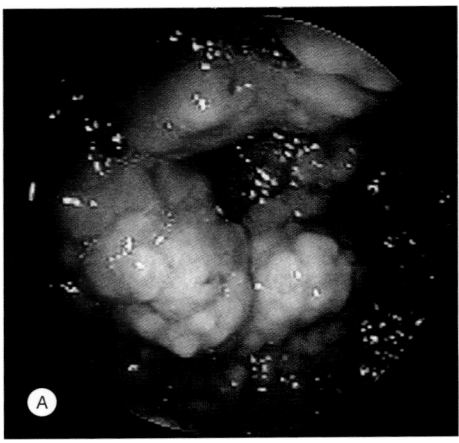 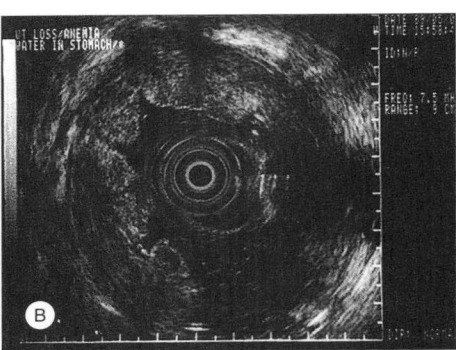

Figure 34–3. *A,* Endoscopic images reveal gastric body thickened folds. Biopsies are nondiagnostic. *B,* EUS reveals marked expansion of acoustic layers one, two, and three, consistent with Ménétrier's disease.

by swollen longitudinal folds traversed by erosive fissures in the stomach of 15 of 23 patients that had Crohn's disease. Mucosal nodularity or cobblestone mucosa with thickening of the antral folds in patients with Crohn's disease has also been described.[74] Endoscopic biopsies are typically positive and thickening may regress with directed therapy and time. When infection or the inflammatory reaction is severe, involvement can sometimes include deeper wall layers as well, raising concern for malignancy.[76]

MÉNÉTRIER'S DISEASE (GIANT HYPERTROPHIC GASTRITIS)

Ménétrier was the first to describe giant gastric folds as a finding in hypertrophic gastritis.[77] Ménétrier's disease is a rare condition whose cause is largely unknown. It involves marked thickening of EUS layers 2 and 3 with histologic features of foveolar hyperplasia and atrophy of glands (Fig. 34–3). Erosions or ulceration may be present on the enlarged folds and may appear convoluted or cerebriform with a reddish coloration. The disease is more common after the age of 50 and more commonly involves men.[65] These patients usually present clinically with weight loss, diarrhea, and edema. Defining Ménétrier's disease has been variable. Criteria that have been used to define authentic cases include (1) giant folds, especially in the fundus and body of the stomach; (2) hypoalbuminemia; and (3) histologic features of foveolar hyperplasia, atrophy of glands, and a marked overall increase in mucosal thickness.[78] Endosonographic differentiation of Ménétrier's disease and lymphoma may be difficult because both display similar echo patterns; therefore, malignancy must be ruled out if Ménétrier's disease is considered. Pinch biopsies are usually insufficient for diagnosis, whereas loop biopsy using a polypectomy snare over a fold yields better results for diagnosis. Submucosal saline injection technique can also be applied to help raise the lesion before removal.

LYMPHOMA AND CARCINOMA

Malignancy should always be considered when evaluating thickened gastric folds. As mentioned previously, involvement of the muscularis propria (EUS layer 4) should prompt concern for malignancy and consideration of surgical biopsy, even if aggressive endoscopic biopsy techniques are performed and return unremarkable. In these situations, the muscularis propria layer can be thickened four- to

six-fold compared with controls.[69,79] Both lymphoma and carcinoma involve the deeper wall layers exclusively, without mucosal disease,[68] so this diagnosis could easily be missed on standard endoscopy. An EUS-guided fine needle aspiration (FNA) or surgical approach should be attempted for obtaining tissue diagnosis.

Diffuse gastric cancers (linitis plastica, scirrhous carcinoma) are seen as diffuse hypoechoic wall thickening covered by normal appearing mucosa, but often with distorted layers and an irregular appearing outer margin on EUS (Fig. 34–4). In contrast, when compared with patients with hypertrophic gastritis, only the mucosal layer is thickened.[79]

Lymphoma more often involves the superficial layers as well, particularly in mucosal-associated lymphoid tissue (MALT) lymphoma. The role of EUS in MALT lymphoma has received considerable attention, primarily because EUS can predict disease, which may respond to *H. pylori* eradication as the sole means of therapy. Complete remission rates of up to 100% have been described for patients with T1 stage low-grade MALT lymphoma (Fig. 34–5).[80] In addition, EUS surveillance helps detect persistent disease, recurrences, and the need for aggressive chemotherapy.[81] Accuracy in staging MALT lymphoma depends on endosonography expertise, with a recommendation of more than 100 procedures to appreciate the subtleties of gastric EUS and to acquire all the technical skills of this procedure.[82] Miniature ultrasound probes have been advocated for initial staging and the follow-up of MALT lymphoma because of increased patient compliance and the advantage of performing the examination in a single session.[63,83] These miniprobes are also considered to be more advantageous than the conventional echoendoscope because of better resolution of superficial lesions.[84,85]

ZOLLINGER-ELLISON SYNDROME

Gastrinoma, or Zollinger-Ellison syndrome (ZES), is a rare condition that can be associated with thick gastric folds. It is estimated to occur in 0.1 to 3 patients per million of the United States' population, with a mean age of diagnosis of 50 years.[86] ZES should be suspected in patients with severe erosive esophagitis, multiple or refractory peptic ulcers, and ulcers in unusual locations and in patients with a family history of multiple endocrine neoplasia type 1 (MEN-1).[87] Most patients with ZES do not present with multiple

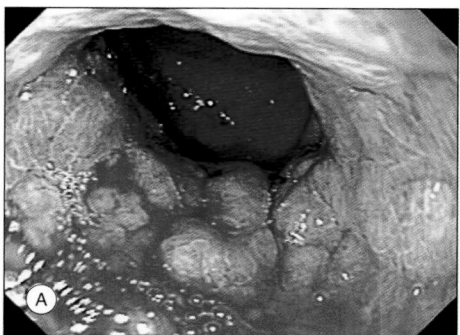
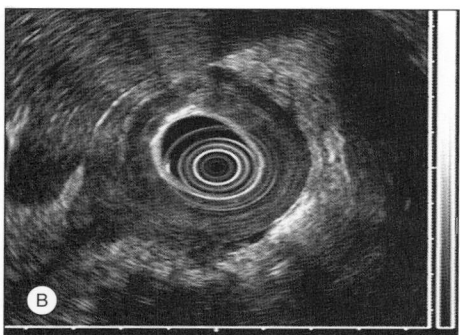
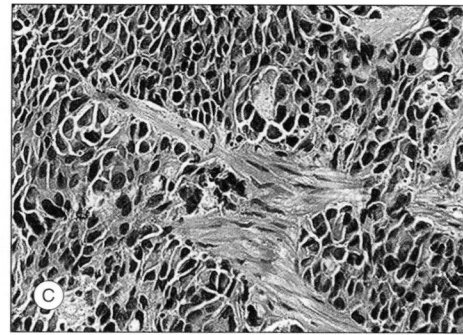

Figure 34-4. *A,* Endoscopic images of thickened folds with negative standard biopsies. *B,* EUS reveals infiltration of layers 3,4 and transmural extension consistent with linitis plastica or lymphoma. *C,* EUS-guided Tru-cut biopsy revealing adenocarcinoma.

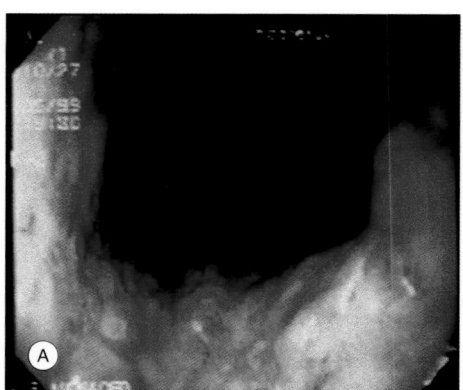
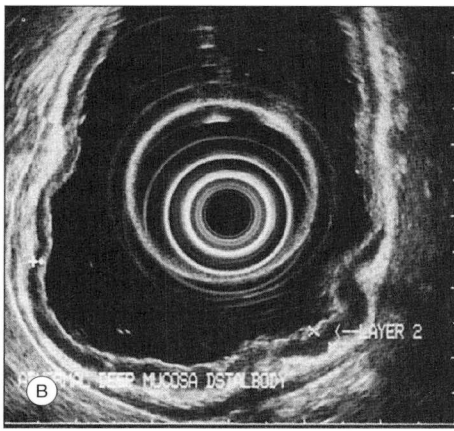

Figure 34-5. *A,* Endoscopic images of severe antral gastritis with biopsies consistent with a MALT lymphoma. *B,* EUS demonstrates the disease limited to layers 1,2 (superficial and deep mucosa) making it amenable to antibiotic therapy.

ulcers as previously described. The ulcers in ZES are usually less than 1 cm in diameter, and approximately 75% of ulcers are located in the first portion of the duodenum but can also be found distally beyond the ligament of Treitz.[27] Histologically, ZES is characterized as hyperproliferation of enterochromaffin-like and parietal cells with glandular hyperplasia resulting from trophic effects of gastrin. In most patients, gastric fold thickening is not excessive. Endosonographic evaluation of thickened folds shows thickening of layers 2 and 3 in the body and fundus. Tumor localization is done by somatostatin receptor scintigraphy, EUS, or both. A combination of scintigraphy and EUS detects greater than 90% of gastrinomas.[87]

MISCELLANEOUS

There are several rare miscellaneous causes of thickened gastric folds. Metastatic disease, particularly from breast cancer, may present as thickening and disruption of the wall layers.[88] Gastritis cystica profunda involves EUS layer 3 and appears as multiple small cysts, which are histologically benign. Of note, malignant infiltration may also result in cystic changes in EUS layers 2 and 3; thus, diagnosis must be based on adequate histologic analysis such as EMR specimens.[89] Hyperrugosity involves EUS layers 2 and 3 and is a term applied to thickening that proves to be idiopathic and benign after biopsies and prolonged clinical observation.[65]

Thickened folds are not unique to the stomach. Large folds in the duodenum, small bowel, and colon are typically related to infectious, infiltrative, neoplastic, or portal hypertensive etiologies.

The causes are often clear based on the clinical scenario. In cases in which there is doubt, EUS probes may be useful to help refine the differential diagnosis, because these areas are often inaccessible to echoendoscopes. In the rectum, EUS and EUS-guided FNA or EMR may be very useful to diagnose thickened folds resulting from genitourinary malignancies. We and others have used FNA to establish a diagnosis of infiltrating prostate carcinoma when endoscopic biopsies have been unrevealing, but EUS demonstrated involvement of the deeper wall layers.[90] Benign conditions such as ulceration and thickened folds felt secondary to rectal prolapse syndromes can be examined thoroughly to rule out concerning features for malignancy such as transmural infiltration and characteristic lymphadenopathy.

Conclusion

The evaluation of gastric polyps and thickened folds present both technical and diagnostic challenges to the endoscopist. Obtaining adequate tissue to secure a diagnosis is crucial in evaluating new lesions. Guidelines for surveillance after polypectomy or monitoring thickened folds are not yet established. With the advancement of technology and the development of new endoscopic techniques, accuracy and ease of diagnosis will only improve when evaluating these lesions, especially in the field of endosonography. Clinical experience and numerous studies have demonstrated EUS as an important tool for diagnosis and characterization of polypoid lesions and large gastric folds. Alone, EUS cannot define histology or determine malignancy in target tissues, nevertheless much information can be obtained by examining individual layers of the gut wall, which can help narrow the differential diagnosis and modify management decisions.

REFERENCES

1. Dekker W: Clinical relevance of gastric and duodenal polyps. Scand J Gastroenterol Suppl 178:7–12, 1990.
2. Sivelli R, Del Rio P, Bonati L, Sianesi M: [Gastric polyps: A clinical contribution]. Chir Ital 54:37–40, 2002.
3. Hattori T: Morphological range of hyperplastic polyps and carcinomas arising in hyperplastic polyps of the stomach. J Clin Pathol 38:622–630, 1985.
4. Stolte M, Sticht T, Eidt S, et al: Frequency, location, and age and sex distribution of various types of gastric polyp. Endoscopy 26:659–665, 1994.
5. Wu TT, Kornacki S, Rashid A, et al: Dysplasia and dysregulation of proliferation in foveolar and surface epithelia of fundic gland polyps from patients with familial adenomatous polyposis. Am J Surg Pathol 22:293–298, 1998.
6. Jung A, Vieth M, Maier O, Stolte M: Fundic gland polyps (Elster's cysts) of the gastric mucosa. A marker for colorectal epithelial neoplasia? Pathol Res Pract 198:731–734, 2002.
7. Eidt S, Stolte M: Gastric glandular cysts—investigations into their genesis and relationship to colorectal epithelial tumors. Z Gastroenterol 27:212–217, 1989.
8. Seifert E, Gross U, Schulte F, Stolte M: [Are stomach polyps an indicator of colonic carcinoma and colonic polyps an indicator of stomach carcinoma?]. Dtsch Med Wochenschr 112:1967–1972, 1987.
9. Kinoshita Y, Tojo M, Yano T, et al: Incidence of fundic gland polyps in patients without familial adenomatous polyposis. Gastrointest Endosc 39:161–163, 1993.
10. Bertoni G, Sassatelli R, Nigrisoli E, et al: Dysplastic changes in gastric fundic gland polyps of patients with familial adenomatous polyposis. Ital J Gastroenterol Hepatol 31:192–197, 1999.
11. Hofgartner WT, Thorp M, Ramus MW, et al: Gastric adenocarcinoma associated with fundic gland polyps in a patient with attenuated familial adenomatous polyposis. Am J Gastroenterol 94:2275–2281, 1999.
12. Stolte M, Bethke B, Seifert E, et al: Observation of gastric glandular cysts in the corpus mucosa of the stomach under omeprazole treatment. Z Gastroenterol 33:146–149, 1995.
13. el-Zimaity HM, Jackson FW, Graham DY: Fundic gland polyps developing during omeprazole therapy. Am J Gastroenterol 92:1858–1860, 1997.
14. Choudhry U, Boyce HW Jr, Coppola D: Proton pump inhibitor-associated gastric polyps: A retrospective analysis of their frequency, and endoscopic, histologic, and ultrastructural characteristics. Am J Clin Pathol 110:615–621, 1998.
15. Oberhuber G, Stolte M: Gastric polyps: An update of their pathology and biological significance. Virchows Arch 437:581–590, 2000.
16. Vieth M, Stolte M: Fundic gland polyps are not induced by proton pump inhibitor therapy. Am J Clin Pathol 116:716–720, 2001.
17. Deppisch LM, Rona VT: Gastric epithelial polyps. A 10-year study. J Clin Gastroenterol 11:110–115, 1989.
18. Rosen S, Hoak D: Intramucosal carcinoma developing in a hyperplastic gastric polyp. Gastrointest Endosc 39:830–833, 1993.
19. Zea-Iriarte WL, Itsuno M, Makiyama K, et al: Signet ring cell carcinoma in hyperplastic polyp. Scand J Gastroenterol 30:604–608, 1995.
20. Daibo M, Itabashi M, Hirota T: Malignant transformation of gastric hyperplastic polyps. Am J Gastroenterol 82:1016–1025, 1987.
21. Abraham SC, Singh VK, Yardley JH, Wu TT: Hyperplastic polyps of the stomach: Associations with histologic patterns of gastritis and gastric atrophy. Am J Surg Pathol 25:500–507, 2001.
22. Krasinskas AM, Abraham SC, Metz DC, Furth EE: Oxyntic mucosa pseudopolyps: A presentation of atrophic autoimmune gastritis. Am J Surg Pathol 27:236–241, 2003.
23. Laxen F: Gastric carcinoma and pernicious anaemia in long-term endoscopic follow-up of subjects with gastric polyps. Scand J Gastroenterol 19:535–540, 1984.
24. Veereman Wauters G, Ferrell L, Ostroff JW, Heyman MB: Hyperplastic gastric polyps associated with persistent Helicobacter pylori infection and active gastritis. Am J Gastroenterol 85:1395–1397, 1990.
25. Ohkusa T, Takashimizu I, Fujiki K, et al: Disappearance of hyperplastic polyps in the stomach after eradication of Helicobacter pylori. A randomized, clinical trial. Ann Intern Med 129:712–715, 1998.
26. Nakajima A, Matsuhashi N, Yazaki Y, et al: Details of hyperplastic polyps of the stomach shrinking after anti-Helicobacter pylori therapy. J Gastroenterol 35:372–375, 2000.
27. Tytgat G: Gastric diseases. In Classen M, Tytgat, GNJ, Lightdale, CJ (eds): Gastroenterological Endoscopy. New York, Thieme, 2002, pp 488–523.
28. Papa A, Cammarota G, Tursi A, et al: Histologic types and surveillance of gastric polyps: A seven year clinico-pathological study. Hepatogastroenterology 45:579–582, 1998.
29. Abraham SC, Montgomery EA, Singh VK, et al: Gastric adenomas: Intestinal-type and gastric-type adenomas differ in the risk of adenocarcinoma and presence of background mucosal pathology. Am J Surg Pathol 26:1276–1285, 2002.
30. Harju E: Gastric polyposis and malignancy. Br J Surg 73:532–533, 1986.
31. Nakamura T, Nakano G: Histopathological classification and malignant change in gastric polyps. J Clin Pathol 38:754–764, 1985.
32. Stolte M: Clinical consequences of the endoscopic diagnosis of gastric polyps. Endoscopy 27:32–37; discussion 59–60, 1995.
33. Tomasulo J: Gastric polyps. Histologic types and their relationship to gastric carcinoma. Cancer 27:1346–1355, 1971.
34. Schmitz JM, Stolte M: Gastric polyps as precancerous lesions. Gastrointest Endosc Clin N Am 7:29–46, 1997.
35. Pisano R, Llorens P, Backhouse C, Palma M: [Anatomopathological study of 86 gastric adenomas. Experience in 14 years]. Rev Med Chil 124:204–208, 1996.
36. Nakamura K, Sakaguchi H, Enjoji M: Depressed adenoma of the stomach. Cancer 62:2197–2202, 1988.
37. Seifert E, Gail K, Weismuller J: Gastric polypectomy. Long-term results (survey of 23 centres in Germany). Endoscopy 15:8–11, 1983.
38. Borrmann R: Geschwulste des magens und duodenums. In Henke F, Lubarsch O (eds): Handbuch der Speziellen Pathologischen Anatomie und Histologie, Vol 4. Berlin, Springer, 1926, p 865.
39. Guelrud M, Herrera I, Essenfeld H, Castro J: Enhanced magnification endoscopy: A new technique to identify specialized intestinal metaplasia in Barrett's esophagus. Gastrointest Endosc 53:559–565, 2001.
40. Yao K, Oishi T, Matsui T, et al: Novel magnified endoscopic findings of microvascular architecture in intramucosal gastric cancer. Gastrointest Endosc 56:279–284, 2002.
41. Seifert E, Elster K: Gastric polypectomy. Am J Gastroenterol 63:451–456, 1975.
42. Ginsberg GG, Al-Kawas FH, Fleischer DE, et al: Gastric polyps: Relationship of size and histology to cancer risk. Am J Gastroenterol 91:714–717, 1996.
43. Muehldorfer SM, Stolte M, Martus P, et al: Diagnostic accuracy of forceps biopsy versus polypectomy for gastric polyps: A prospective multicentre study. Gut 50:465–470, 2002.
44. Batovsky M, Vavrecka A, Pauer M, Valach A: Endoscopic gastroduodenal polypectomy. Czech Med 11:157–167, 1988.
45. De Salvo L, Ansaldo GL, Romairone E, Borgonovo G: [Gastric polyps: Role of endoscopy]. Ann Ital Chir 61:153–156; discussion 157, 1990.

46. Lau CF, Hui PK, Mak KL: Gastric polypoid lesions—illustrative cases and literature review. Am J Gastroenterol 93:2559–2564, 1998.

47. The role of endoscopy in the surveillance of premalignant conditions of the upper gastrointestinal tract. American Society for Gastrointestinal Endoscopy. Gastrointest Endosc 48:663–668, 1998.

48. Tio TL, Tytgat GN: Endoscopic ultrasonography of an arteriovenous malformation in a gastric polyp. Endoscopy 18:156–158, 1986.

49. Akahoshi K, Kojima H, Fujimaru T, et al: Grasping forceps assisted endoscopic resection of large pedunculated GI polypoid lesions. Gastrointest Endosc 50:95–98, 1999.

50. Iishi H, Tatsuta M, Narahara H, et al: Endoscopic resection of large pedunculated colorectal polyps using a detachable snare. Gastrointest Endosc 44:594–597, 1996.

51. Brandimarte G, Tursi A: Endoscopic snare excision of large pedunculated colorectal polyps: A new, safe, and effective technique. Endoscopy 33:854–857, 2001.

52. Matsushita M, Hajiro K, Takakuwa H, et al: Ineffective use of a detachable snare for colonoscopic polypectomy of large polyps. Gastrointest Endosc 47:496–499, 1998.

53. Iishi H, Tatsuta M, Kitamura S, et al: Endoscopic resection of large sessile colorectal polyps using a submucosal saline injection technique. Hepatogastroenterology 44:698–702, 1997.

54. Waxman I, Saitoh Y, Raju GS, et al: High-frequency probe EUS-assisted endoscopic mucosal resection: A therapeutic strategy for submucosal tumors of the GI tract. Gastrointest Endosc 55:44–49, 2002.

55. Rosen L, Bub DS, Reed JF 3rd, Nastasee SA: Hemorrhage following colonoscopic polypectomy. Dis Colon Rectum 36:1126–1131, 1993.

56. Van Gossum A, Cozzoli A, Adler M, et al: Colonoscopic snare polypectomy: Analysis of 1485 resections comparing two types of current. Gastrointest Endosc 38:472–475, 1992.

57. Lin LF, Siauw CP, Ho KS, Tung JC: Hemoclip-assisted endoscopic polypectomy of large superior duodenal angle polyp using a needle knife. Zhonghua Yi Xue Za Zhi (Taipei) 64:731–734, 2001.

58. Sobrino-Faya M, Martinez S, Gomez Balado M, et al: Clips for the prevention and treatment of postpolypectomy bleeding (hemoclips in polypectomy). Rev Esp Enferm Dig 94:457–462, 2002.

59. Waye JD, Lewis BS, Atchison MA, Talbott M: The lost polyp: A guide to retrieval during colonoscopy. Int J Colorectal Dis 3:229–231, 1988.

60. Bjork JT, Geenen JE, Soergel KH, et al: Endoscopic evaluation of large gastric folds: A comparison of biopsy techniques. Gastrointest Endosc 24:22–23, 1977.

61. Komorowski RA, Caya JG, Geenen JE: The morphologic spectrum of large gastric folds: Utility of the snare biopsy. Gastrointest Endosc 32:190–192, 1986.

62. Buscarini E, Stasi MD, Rossi S, et al: Endosonographic diagnosis of submucosal upper gastrointestinal tract lesions and large fold gastropathies by catheter ultrasound probe. Gastrointest Endosc 49:184–191, 1999.

63. Lugering N, Menzel J, Kucharzik T, et al: Impact of miniprobes compared to conventional endosonography in the staging of low-grade gastric malt lymphoma. Endoscopy 33:832–837, 2001.

64. Kimmey MB, Martin RW, Haggitt RC, et al: Histologic correlates of gastrointestinal ultrasound images. Gastroenterology 96:433–441, 1989.

65. Caletti G, Fusaroli P, Bocus P: Endoscopic ultrasonography in large gastric folds. Endoscopy 30(Suppl 1):A72–75, 1998.

66. Botet JF, Lightdale C: Endoscopic sonography of the upper gastrointestinal tract. AJR Am J Roentgenol 156:63–68, 1991.

67. Mendis RE, Gerdes H, Lightdale CJ, Botet JF: Large gastric folds: A diagnostic approach using endoscopic ultrasonography. Gastrointest Endosc 40:437–441, 1994.

68. Chen TK, Wu CH, Lee CL, et al: Endoscopic ultrasonography in the differential diagnosis of giant gastric folds. J Formos Med Assoc 98:261–264, 1999.

69. Songur Y, Okai T, Watanabe H, et al: Endosonographic evaluation of giant gastric folds. Gastrointest Endosc 41:468–474, 1995.

70. Sung JJ, Lee YT, Leong RW: EUS in portal hypertension. Gastrointest Endosc 56:S35–43, 2002.

71. Miller LS: Endoscopic ultrasound in the evaluation of portal hypertension. Gastrointest Endosc Clin N Am 9:271–285, 1999.

72. Avunduk C, Navab F, Hampf F, Coughlin B: Prevalence of Helicobacter pylori infection in patients with large gastric folds: Evaluation and follow-up with endoscopic ultrasound before and after antimicrobial therapy. Am J Gastroenterol 90:1969–1973, 1995.

73. Marcato N, Abergel A, Froment S, et al: [Sarcoidosis gastropathy: Diagnosis and contribution of echo-endoscopy]. Gastroenterol Clin Biol 23:394–397, 1999.

74. Danzi JT, Farmer RG, Sullivan BH Jr, Rankin GB: Endoscopic features of gastroduodenal Crohn's disease. Gastroenterology 70:9–13, 1976.

75. Hirokawa M, Shimizu M, Terayama K, et al: Bamboo-joint-like appearance of the stomach: A histopathological study. Apmis 107:951–956, 1999.

76. Lagasse JP, Causse X, Legoux JL, et al: Cytomegalovirus gastritis simulating cancer of the linitis plastica type on endoscopic ultrasonography. Endoscopy 30:S101–102, 1998.

77. Ménétrier P: Des polyadenomes gastriques et de leurs rapports avec le cancer de l'estomac. Arch Physiol Norm Path 1:236–262, 1888.

78. Appelman H: Localized and extensive expansions of the gastric mucosa: Mucosal polyps and giant folds. In Appelman H (ed): Pathology of the Esophagus, Stomach, and Duodenum. Contemporary Issues in Surgical Pathology, 4th ed. New York, Churchill Livingstone, 1984, p 79.

79. Fujishima H, Misawa T, Chijiwa Y, et al: Scirrhous carcinoma of the stomach versus hypertrophic gastritis: Findings at endoscopic US. Radiology 181:197–200, 1991.

80. Sackmann M, Morgner A, Rudolph B, et al: Regression of gastric MALT lymphoma after eradication of Helicobacter pylori is predicted by endosonographic staging. MALT Lymphoma Study Group. Gastroenterology 113:1087–1090, 1997.

81. Caletti G, Fusaroli P, Togliani T: EUS in MALT lymphoma. Gastrointest Endosc 56:S21–26, 2002.

82. Fusaroli P, Buscarini E, Peyre S, et al: Interobserver agreement in staging gastric malt lymphoma by EUS. Gastrointest Endosc 55:662–668, 2002.

83. Yeh HZ, Chen GH, Chang WD, et al: Long-term follow up of gastric low-grade mucosa-associated lymphoid tissue lymphoma by endosonography emphasizing the application of a miniature ultrasound probe. J Gastroenterol Hepatol 18:162–167, 2003.

84. Waxman I: Clinical impact of high-frequency ultrasound probe sonography during diagnostic endoscopy—a prospective study. Endoscopy 30(Suppl 1):A166–168, 1998.

85. Yanai H, Yoshida T, Harada T, et al: Endoscopic ultrasonography of superficial esophageal cancers using a thin ultrasound probe system equipped with switchable radial and linear scanning modes. Gastrointest Endosc 44:578–582, 1996.

86. Hirschowitz BI: Zollinger-Ellison syndrome: Pathogenesis, diagnosis, and management. Am J Gastroenterol 92:44S–48S; discussion 49S–50S, 1997.

87. Hung PD, Schubert ML, Mihas AA: Zollinger-Ellison syndrome. Curr Treat Options Gastroenterol 6:163–170, 2003.

88. Lorimier G, Binelli C, Burtin P, et al: Metastatic gastric cancer arising from breast carcinoma: Endoscopic ultrasonographic aspects. Endoscopy 30:800–804, 1998.

89. Hizawa K, Suekane H, Kawasaki M, et al: Diffuse cystic malformation and neoplasia-associated cystic formation in the stomach. Endosonographic features and diagnosis of tumor depth. J Clin Gastroenterol 25:634–639, 1997.

90. Bhutani MS: EUS and EUS-guided fine-needle aspiration for the diagnosis of rectal linitis plastica secondary to prostate carcinoma. Gastrointest Endosc 50:117–119, 1999.

Endoscopic Therapy for Gastric Neoplasms

Mainor R. Antillon and Yang Chen

Introduction

Gastrointestinal (GI) endoscopy has continued to evolve at an amazing pace in the past decade. The scope of therapeutic endoscopy has increased dramatically mostly because of advancement in technology. In turn, such technologic breakthroughs have stimulated the proliferation of novel endoscopic techniques for diagnosing and treating GI diseases, including gastric neoplasms.

The development and clinical application of endoscopic ultrasonography (EUS) has enabled the GI specialist to evaluate previously inaccessible intramural gastric lesions and to determine their layer of origin. It is the ability to determine, with almost pinpoint accuracy, the depth of gastric wall layer involvement and to exclude lymph node metastasis that permits the endoscopist to safely proceed to endoscopic removal of a gastric neoplasm.

Introduction of new techniques such as endoscopic mucosal resection (EMR) and thermal ablation techniques such as neodymium:yttrium-aluminum-garnet (Nd:YAG) laser and argon plasma coagulation (APC) have made it possible to safely and completely remove or destroy certain types of gastric neoplasms.[1-5]

Gastric tumor is defined as any mass lesion occurring in the wall of the stomach. Its metastatic potential defines the difference between benign and malignant neoplasms. Epithelial neoplasms include adenomas and carcinomas. Intramural lesions include gastric stromal cell tumors and lymphoma. Table 35–1 shows the classification of gastric neoplasms.

The primary emphasis of this chapter is on endoscopic therapy for early gastric cancer (EGC).

Gastric Cancer

Gastric cancer remains the world's second leading cause of cancer mortality behind lung cancer, despite its worldwide decline in incidence and mortality. It has been estimated that more than 870,000 deaths from the disease occurred in the year 2000, accounting for approximately 12% of all cancer deaths.[6,7] Adenocarcinoma accounts for approximately 90% of gastric cancers; the remainder are due to non-Hodgkin's lymphoma (NHL) and leiomyosarcoma.

EPIDEMIOLOGY

The annual incidence of gastric cancer varies worldwide. It is well known that there is a difference in the prevalence of gastric cancer between the East and the West (Fig. 35–1).

Table 35–1. Gastric Neoplasms

Epithelial neoplasms
• Adenomas
• Carcinomas
  Primary
  Secondary
• Carcinoids

Lymphoma
Stromal tumors

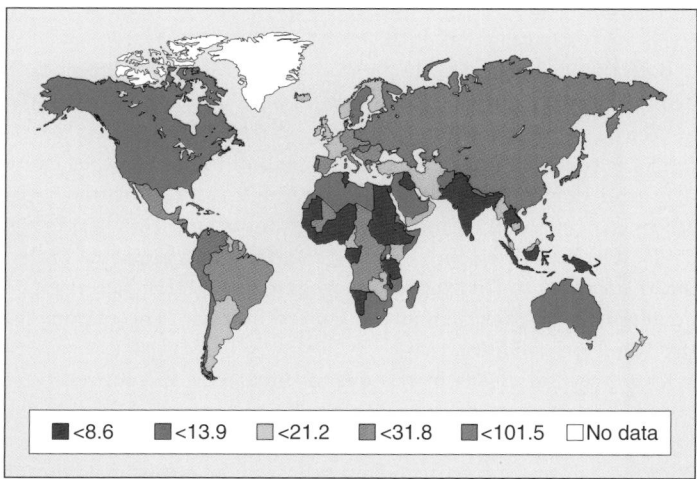

Figure 35–1. Worldwide incidence of gastric cancer.

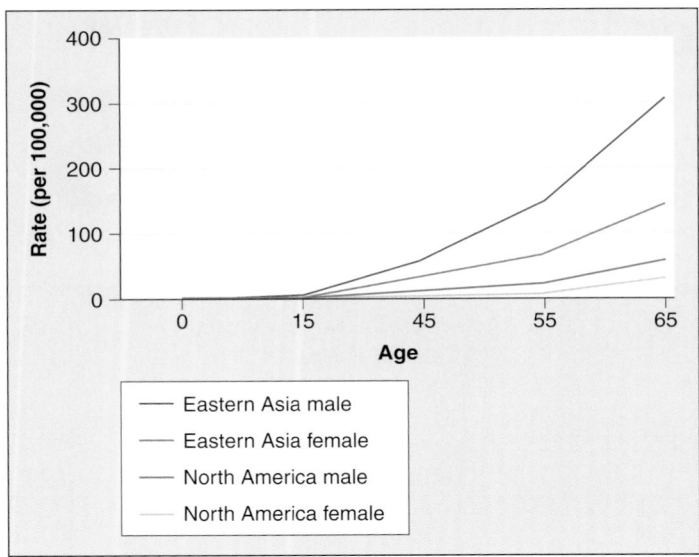

Figure 35-2. Incidence of gastric cancer in East Asia and the United States according to gender and age.

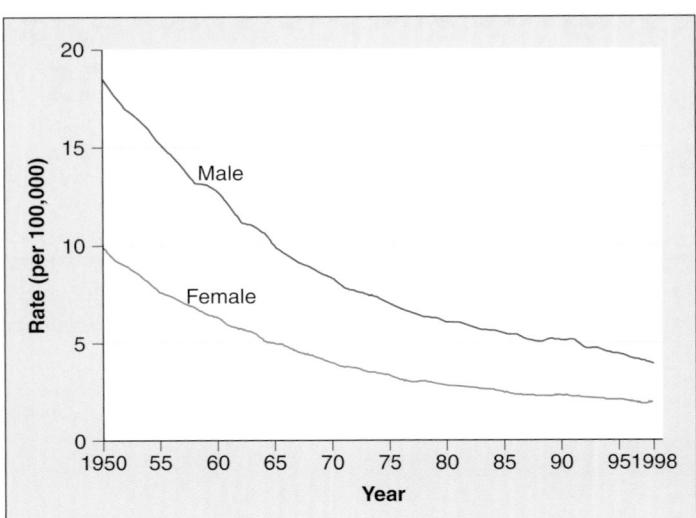

Figure 35-3. Incidence of noncardia gastric cancer in the United States from 1950 to 1990, age-standardized for males and females.

In Eastern Asian countries, such as Japan and China, and in many developing countries, gastric cancer is the most prevalent malignant neoplasm and the leading cause of cancer mortality.[8] The incidence of gastric cancer in Eastern Asia and the United States are shown in Figure 35-2.

There is a high incidence of gastric cancer in the East, the former Soviet Union, some portions of Central and Eastern Europe, and Central America (e.g., Costa Rica) and South America (e.g., Chile). The lowest rates occur in the United States and in some parts of Africa.

The International Agency for Research on Cancer data for 1996 reported an age-standardized incidence rate in males ranging from 95.5/105 in Yamagata, Japan to 7.5/105 in whites in the United States.[8] Most of the geographic variation is due to differences in the incidence of gastric cancer not localized in the cardia, whereas cancer that is localized in the cardia has a more uniform distribution.

Ethnic groups that migrate from a high to a low incidence country have an overall risk intermediate between that of their homeland and that of their new country. First-generation migrants tend to retain their high risk, whereas subsequent generations have risk levels approximating that of their host country.[9]

Both the incidence and the mortality rates for gastric cancer have declined sharply during the last several decades, particularly in the United States and in Western Europe. In the United States, gastric cancer is the 13th most common cancer and the 8th leading cause of cancer death. A steady decline in the incidence of noncardia gastric cancer has occurred since 1930 throughout the world (Fig. 35-3). On the other hand, the incidence of adenocarcinoma involving the cardia and/or the esophagogastric junction has risen in developed countries such as the United States.[10] The reasons for this trend are unknown.

There are variations in the overall incidence and mortality of noncardia gastric cancer between gender and ethnic groups. In the United States, the incidence is higher among Native Americans, Hispanic whites, and African Americans.[11] The ethnic distribution

for cancer of the gastric cardia is also different, with a preponderance in American whites over African Americans.[8] The incidence of gastric cancer increases with age; most patients are between 50 to 70 years of age. The incidence of gastric cancer in patients younger than 36 years has increased, from 1.8% before 1970 to 4.2% after 1970, with the great majority (62.5%) occurring in Hispanics. Noncardia gastric cancer is more common in males than females by a ratio of approximately 2:1. Gastric cancer located in the cardia has an even higher male-to-female ratio of up to 6:1 in U.S. whites.[8] Figures 35-4 and 35-5 summarize the trends in the incidence and mortality of gastric cancer in the United States from approximately 1970 to 2000 according to gender and ethnicity.

PATHOGENESIS

Gastric cancer has a bad prognosis with a 5-year survival of less than 5%. This poor prognosis is mostly because four out of five patients present at an advanced stage.[12] Incidental diagnosis of gastric cancer has been reported to increase patient survival.[13,14]

Japan continues to have the highest incidence of gastric cancer worldwide. However, the establishment of an aggressive mass screening policy has resulted in a remarkably high detection rate of EGC, in the range of 40% to 66.4% of all gastric cancers diagnosed.[15,16] Consequently, the most extensive experience with treatment of EGC has come from Japan.

The Japanese Society of Gastrointestinal Endoscopy defines EGC as cancer confined to the mucosa or submucosa, with or without lymph node metastasis. This designation was based on the observation that this subgroup of patients has an excellent prognosis, with a 5-year survival of greater than 90% after gastrectomy and removal of both the primary and secondary lymph nodes.[1,17] In the West, 10% to 20% of surgical resections for gastric carcinoma are for EGC,[17] whereas in Japan more than 50% of surgical specimens are classified as EGC.[18,19]

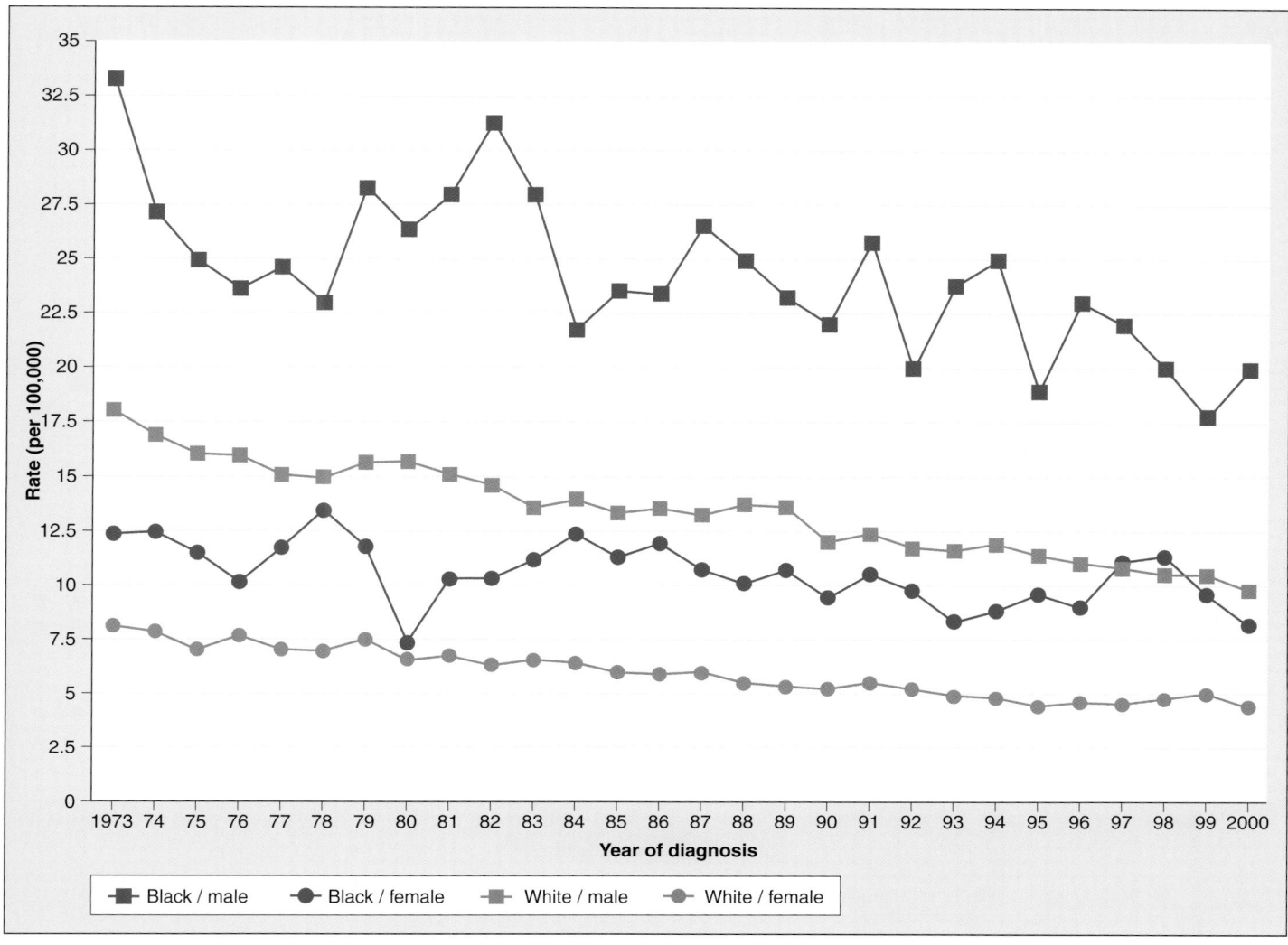

Figure 35–4. Incidence of gastric cancer in the United States from 1973 to 2000 according to gender and race.

Helicobacter pylori

Since *H. pylori* was first reported in 1983, a wealth of evidence has been gathered concerning its role in the etiology of gastric cancer.[20–22] In 1994, the International Agency for Research on Cancer classified *H. pylori* as carcinogenic to humans. Evidence supporting an etiologic association between *H. pylori* and gastric cancer can be found in ecologic studies, case-control studies, and prospective cohort studies.[21,23–25] Meta-analyses of prospective studies suggest that the risk of gastric cancer is increased twofold to threefold in those who are chronically infected with *H. pylori*.[26,27] One prospective, nested case-control study found a significant association between prior *H. pylori* infection and gastric adeno-carcinoma overall, but there was no association with cancer of the cardia.[28] Individuals without *H. pylori* colonization appear to have a minimal risk of gastric carcinoma.[29]

H. pylori contributes to the causation of gastric cancer via mechanisms that involve the development and progression of chronic gastritis.[30] Infection causes chronic gastritis in almost all infected individuals and accounts for almost all cases of chronic gastritis.[31] *H. pylori*-induced gastritis may progress over time from superficial nonatrophic gastritis to more severe forms including severe atrophic gastritis with intestinal metaplasia.

Chronic gastritis is present in most cases of gastric cancer and is associated with an increased cancer risk.[30] The risk of developing gastric cancer increases with the severity of gastritis, with reported risks in excess of 10-fold for severe atrophic antral gastritis.[30,32] Intestinal-type gastric cancer appears to be more strongly associated with severe atrophic gastritis, whereas the diffuse type is more common in nonatrophic gastritis.[30]

There is strong evidence for a role for virulence factors in *H. pylori* carcinogenesis. The Cag A virulence factor is strongly associated with the risk of adenocarcinoma, whereas its absence carries, at most, a low risk of developing diffuse type adenocarcinoma.[33,34]

Peptic Ulcer Disease

H. pylori infection is a common risk factor for gastric ulcer, duo-denal ulcer, and gastric cancer. Thus, an association between peptic ulcer disease and gastric cancer would be expected. However,

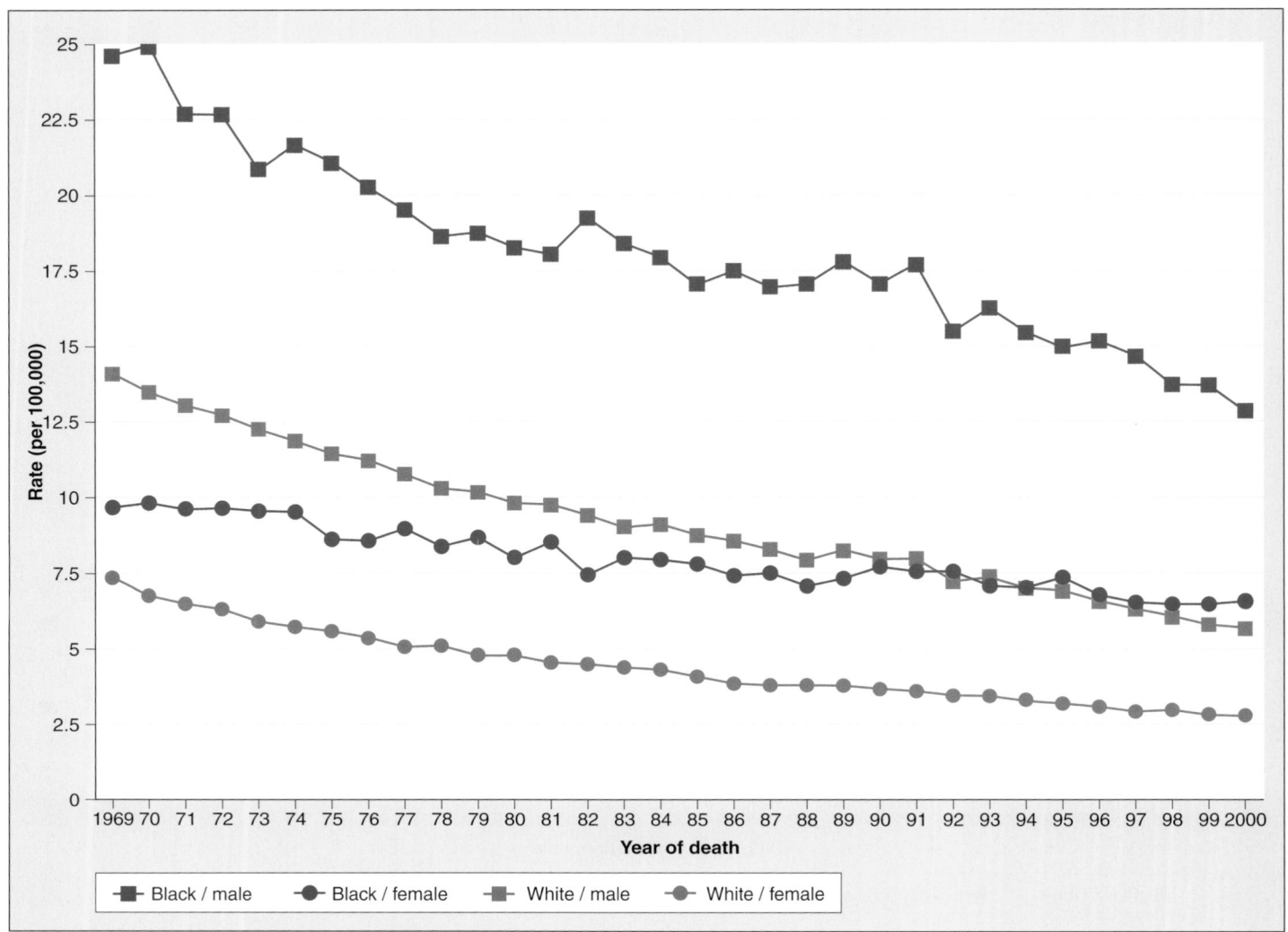

Figure 35–5. Gastric cancer mortality in the United States from 1969 to 2000 according to gender and race.

studies have found duodenal ulceration to be inversely associated with gastric cancer risk.[35]

One possible explanation for this apparent paradox has been suggested by Parsonnet,[34] who has argued that *H. pylori* infection can progress to gastric cancer or duodenal ulcer but seldom to both. Other factors such as the genetic characteristics of the individual and the organism may play a significant role in determining which disease will occur. The age at which infection was acquired may also influence the outcome. It has been suggested that infection early in life predisposes to atrophic gastritis and cancer but reduces duodenal ulcer risk because of decreased acid production associated with the gastritis. If infection is acquired later in life, atrophic gastritis is less likely and the gastric cancer risk is decreased.[34]

Recent evidence supports a moderate association between gastric ulcer and noncardiac gastric cancer.[36,37]

Dietary Factors

Several observational studies have shown a protective association with fresh fruits and vegetables, independent of other dietary factors. The association has been less impressive in limited cohort studies.[38] Possible protective nutrients include vitamin E, carotenoids, selenium, and vitamin C.[38] The evidence is stronger for vitamin C. In a case-control study, a high intake of vitamin C decreased the risk of gastric cancer by half when compared with low vitamin C intake.[39] However, a 5-year intervention trial in China involving a large number of adults did not show any change in the risk of gastric cancer in individuals receiving supplemental vitamin C.[40]

High salt consumption has been fairly consistently associated with an increased risk of gastric cancer in ecologic and case-control studies.[41–43] However, good quantitative data linking salt consumption with gastric cancer are still lacking.

N-nitroso compounds have been shown to be carcinogenic in animal studies.[44] In the human stomach, these compounds may be formed from dietary nitrite or nitrate, leading to the hypothesis that a diet high in nitrite or nitrate predisposes to gastric cancer. Case-control studies examining dietary intake of nitrate and the risk of gastric cancer have consistently found a negative association. Because the major source of nitrate and nitrite are vegetables and preserved meats, nitrate intake was probably an index of vegetable intake and the negative association is therefore not surprising.[38] Case-control studies have reported a weak, statistically insignificant increased risk of gastric cancer (relative risk, 1.12 to 1.28) for high versus low nitrite intake.[45–48] It is thus difficult to isolate the effect of nitrate consumption in gastric cancer because diets high in nitrite may also be high in antioxidants that are frequently found in vegetables and in fruits.[45]

It has been postulated that virulent strains of *H. pylori* release reactive oxygen metabolites that could destroy neighboring glandular cells leading to gastric glandular atrophy, hastened by other factors such as high-salt intake but retarded by antioxidants such as vitamin C.[49]

The invention of refrigeration, the availability of fresh food, and the accompanying decreased consumption of preserved foods may have contributed to a decline in gastric cancer incidence in the second half of the past century.

Socioeconomic Status

Worldwide, a low socioeconomic status has been consistently shown to be associated with an increased risk of gastric cancer.[6] The higher prevalence of gastric cancer among those belonging to a lower socioeconomic status is matched by a similar high prevalence of *H. pylori* infection in these groups.[50,51] Interestingly, an increased incidence of cancer of the cardia has been observed predominantly in higher socioeconomic status populations.[10]

Gastric Surgery

An increased risk of gastric cancer after gastric surgery has been reported, particularly after 15 or more years.[52,53] The association is strongest for gastrectomy performed for gastric ulcer but less persuasive for either vagotomy or gastrectomy performed for duodenal ulcer. This association does not extend to cancer of the gastric cardia.[35]

Gastric Polyps

Single hyperplastic polyps are often found in the background of chronic gastritis, and they are mainly seen in the body of the stomach. At most, 0.3% of hyperplastic gastric polyps may contain a focus of adenocarcinoma. However, approximately 3% of multiple hyperplastic polyps are associated with a synchronous carcinoma elsewhere in the stomach.[54] Thus, the presence of multiple hyperplastic polyps is considered a precancerous condition.

Fundic gland polyps, on the other hand, do not have malignant potential when they occur sporadically or in association with proton pump inhibitor therapy. Hundreds of fundic gland polyps may be present in association with polyposis coli. Dysplasia has been reported in few of these patients.[55] Gastric adenocarcinoma associated with fundic gland polyposis in familial adenomatous polyposis (FAP) has been reported.[56]

Adenomatous polyps occur in the setting of intestinal metaplasia and associated chronic gastritis. Endoscopic features that increase the risk of malignant transformation include large size and a red, erosive surface color. Forty percent of pyloric gland adenomas and in general up to 10% of tubular adenomas may contain a carcinoma.[54,57] Furthermore, approximately 11% of patients with adenomatous polyps have a synchronous or metachronous gastric adenocarcinoma.[54,58]

Genetic Factors

Genetic predisposition may play a role in the development of gastric cancer, with a twofold to fourfold increased risk in first-degree relatives. Similarly, patients who have hereditary lesions such as Lynch syndrome II have an increased risk of gastric cancer.[57,59]

Miscellaneous Factors

A higher risk for gastric cancer has been reported in Menetrier's disease, in ataxia telangiectasia, and in patients with blood type group A.[60–62]

Pernicious anemia and its association with autoimmune chronic gastritis increases the risk of developing gastric cancer by twofold to threefold, according to population-based studies.[63,64] Regular endoscopic surveillance in young patients with pernicious anemia has been advocated.[65]

Smoking may increase the incidence of premalignant gastric lesions and dysplasia; however, a dose-response relation has not been clearly demonstrated.[66–68] No clear relationship between alcohol consumption and gastric cancer has been shown.[25,66,68]

Molecular Abnormalities

Abnormalities at the molecular level have been described in patients who develop gastric cancer. These include allelic deletions of the atrial premature complex (*APC*) gene, the migrating motor complex (*MCC*) gene, and the *p53* tumor-suppressor gene. Allelic deletions of the *p53* tumor-suppressor gene can be found in up to 64% of gastric cancers. These deletions are common late events in gastric cancer.[69] In addition, mutations of the *APC* gene and loss of heterozygosity on chromosomes 1q, 5q, and 17p have been reported in gastric carcinoma.[70]

Loss of E-cadherin-dependent cell-to-cell adhesion resulting from mutation of beta-catenin has been found in gastric cancer.[71] Reduced expression of E-cadherin has been found to be significantly associated with recurrence of cancer and decreased survival.[72] Microsatellite instability has also been found in gastric carcinoma.[73] Higher expression of Sialyl-Tn has been associated with a poor prognosis in patients with gastric cancer.[74] Patients with overexpression of c-erbB protein have been found to have a poorer prognosis than those without c-erbB expression in poorly differentiated gastric adenocarcinoma.[75] Germline truncating mutations in the E-Cadherin gene (*CDH1*) have been found in several families with hereditary diffuse gastric cancer.[76,77]

CLINICAL FEATURES

Early Gastric Cancer

Observational studies have shown that approximately 70% of patients with EGC have symptoms of dyspepsia but no anemia, dysphagia, or weight loss. It is uncommon to find gastric cancer at an early stage (less than 20% of diagnosed cases) in countries with a relatively low risk for the disease. In countries with high risk such as Japan, endoscopic screening has been practiced since the 1960s, and, as a result, the incidence of EGC is 40% to 50%. In the absence of suggestive symptoms, detecting EGC requires a high index of suspicion and a low threshold for endoscopic examination, especially in patients belonging to relatively high-risk groups.

Advanced Gastric Cancer

Most patients with gastric adenocarcinoma present with advanced disease. Accompanying symptoms such as weight loss, vomiting, anorexia, early satiety, abdominal pain, and anemia may mimic peptic ulcer disease and other GI conditions. Typically, patients have been symptomatic for less than 12 months and, in 40%, for less than 3 months. Signs and symptoms are due to cancer invasion beyond the muscularis propria by direct extension or by distant metastasis. Liver and lungs are the most common sites of gastric cancer metastases (40%); bone and peritoneum are less frequent sites (10%). The occasional patient may present with a paraneoplastic syndrome such as Trousseau's syndrome (thrombosis), acanthosis nigricans (pigmented skin lesion, classically of the axilla), or dermatomyositis.[78,79]

PATHOLOGY

Most primary gastric cancers are adenocarcinoma, with an occasional squamous or adenosquamous carcinoma. Other rare gastric cancers include parietal cell carcinoma, choriocarcinoma, and rhabdoid tumor. Cancer metastasizing to the stomach is uncommon, with lung cancer being the most frequent primary tumor. A few cases of gastric carcinosarcoma and spindle cell carcinoma have been reported.[80]

Histologically, gastric adenocarcinoma can be subdivided into two categories[81]:

1. Intestinal type, a well-differentiated neoplastic lesion that forms glandlike structures that ulcerate frequently
2. Diffuse type, characterized by infiltration and thickening of the gastric wall without the formation of a discrete mass

Approximately 16% of gastric cancers cannot be categorized or are of the mixed type.[80]

The decline in incidence of gastric cancer has been predominantly in the distal stomach intestinal type, and a steady rise in the incidence of proximal stomach diffuse type has been observed in the United States and in Europe.[82,83]

There has been inconsistent classification of gastric cardia and distal esophageal cancer in the literature because many or most of these represent distal spread from specialized intestinal metaplasia of the distal esophagus or the esophagogastric junction.

Intestinal Type

Grossly, intestinal adenocarcinoma is a well-demarcated neoplasm that tends to be nodular, polypoid, or ulcerated. Histologically, intestinal adenocarcinoma is characterized by a well-formed glandular pattern, which may contain solid or papillary areas. The malignant cells are columnar or cuboidal, with a basally located nucleus.

Diffuse Type

Grossly, diffuse adenocarcinoma is more likely to have a plaquelike surface and ill-defined infiltrating growth. Histologically, the infiltrating growth is composed of individual cells or cords of cells, and a fibrous or mucoid stroma is present between the cells or cords of cells. Many cells of diffuse carcinoma contain mucin droplets that sometimes produce a signet-ring appearance. Most cases of linitis plastica are classified as diffuse carcinomas. Most diffuse carcinomas are poorly differentiated.

DIFFERENTIAL DIAGNOSIS

Diagnosis of gastric cancer requires histologic confirmation. Gastric carcinoma can mimic peptic ulcer disease, both radiographically and endoscopically. Therefore, it is mandatory to biopsy all gastric ulcers to establish the correct benign or malignant diagnosis. Radiographic or endoscopic detection of EGC can be very difficult, requiring recognition and tissue sampling of very subtle abnormalities such as slight depressions or elevations, minor differences in color or texture, or changes in peristalsis.

Advanced cancer is more commonly encountered at the time of diagnosis. Fifty percent of gastric cancers are located in the antrum, and one out of four are in the body. The remainder involves either the cardia or the entire stomach. Advanced carcinoma may be fungating, polypoid, flat (superficial), ulcerated, or diffusely infiltrating (linitis plastica). Sixty percent to seventy percent of gastric cancers are ulcerating or fungating. Ulcerating types may mimic benign ulcers, but they are usually larger, with more heaped-up edges (rather that appearing "punched out"), and have a more irregular or "shaggy" ulcer base. Linitis plastica or "leather bottle" stomach makes up 10% of cases; there is no luminal mass, but the stomach wall is diffusely infiltrated and usually markedly thickened.

STAGING

Initial staging of gastric cancer should include spiral computed tomography (CT) of the abdomen to determine the presence or absence of metastatic disease. In the absence of metastasis, EUS is helpful for assessing resectability. Determination of surgical resectability for cure using EUS has been found to be 91% accurate.[84]

EGC is defined by the Japanese Society of Gastrointestinal Endoscopy as gastric cancer confined to the mucosa or submucosa, with or without lymph node metastasis. This group of patients has an excellent 5-year survival of more than 90%.[1,85] The risk of lymph node metastasis is 3% for intramucosal lesions (T1m) and 20% if there is submucosal involvement.[86] Other independent risk factors for lymph node metastasis in EGC include lymphovascular invasion on histopathology, histologic ulceration, and tumor diameter more than 3 cm.[87] For T1m tumors less than 3 cm without evidence of lymphovascular invasion or histologic ulceration, the risk of lymph node metastasis is only 0.36%.[87]

TREATMENT

Indications and Contraindications

The main indications for treatment can be divided according to the goal of the therapeutic intervention:

1. Curative—this involves the complete removal or destruction of the lesion.
2. Palliative—this involves the use of endoscopic techniques to improve the life of a patient in whom complete resection is not possible.

Preoperative History and Considerations

Appropriate patient selection and accurate diagnosis and staging are essential to ensure good outcomes from endoscopic therapy. One should avoid unnecessary risks. Is the lesion amenable to surgical or endoscopic removal? Should endoscopic therapy be performed at the same time as the staging procedure or deferred to a subsequent intervention? One should consider referral to a tertiary care center with extensive experience in cancer resection and therapeutic endoscopy. Overnight observation may be appropriate for high-risk endoscopic procedures and for patients who have significant comorbidities.

Gastroscopy

During gastroscopy, the stomach should be well distended to allow full inspection of the entire gastric lining. Intestinal type of gastric cancer is found mostly in the antropyloric region and along the lesser curvature. Areas of discoloration (erythema or pallor), ulceration, nodularity, protrusion, or depression should be biopsied. A high index of suspicion is very important for the diagnosis of EGC.

A morphologic staging classification based on the macroscopic endoscopic appearance of the EGC has been described by Japanese investigators[88]:

Type I—protruding more than 5 mm
Type IIa—slightly raised lesion
Type IIb—irregular but flat
Type IIc—flat but slightly depressed
Type III—excavating ulcerations

Types I, IIa, and IIc are considered to be endoscopically resectable. Certain adjuncts to the morphologic staging also help to predict that a lesion is amenable to minimally invasive (endoscopic) therapy and will likely have the same outcome as surgery: lesions less than 1 cm in size, absence of a scar or ulcer histologically and endoscopically (0.2% lymph metastasis), and a well-differentiated histology (less than 1% lymph metastasis).[1,85]

Endoscopic Ultrasonography and Endoscopic Ultrasonography-Guided Fine Needle Aspiration Cytology

EUS is now established as the best local staging modality for esophageal, gastric, and rectal cancer with a T-stage accuracy of about 90%.[89,90] Kelly and colleagues[84] reported that T-staging by EUS was more accurate for gastric cancer than for esophageal cancer although there was no difference for nodal staging. EUS has been shown to be the most accurate imaging modality for staging EGC,[89,91] with an accuracy of greater than 90% for assessing the depth of tumor invasion.[92,93]

Early-generation conventional echoendoscopes had limited image resolution for the gastric wall because of relatively low transducer frequencies from 7.5 to 12 MHz. Newer echoendoscopes now provide a wider range of frequencies from 5 to 20 MHz. Higher frequencies allow more detailed assessment of superficial lesions.

Long-term disease-free survival in GI malignancies is a function of lymphatic and distant tumor spread. The linear-array echo-endoscope has enabled the endoscopist to precisely place a needle under real-time EUS guidance and obtain tissue samples from both the primary tumor and from transluminal lesions such as lymph nodes and liver metastasis. Other imaging modalities such as CT scan are still necessary to exclude metastases that are more distant. The overall performance of EUS with fine needle aspiration (FNA) cytology for benign versus malignant lymph node involvement has been found to have a sensitivity of 92% (84%–97%), specificity of 93% (75%–100%), and accuracy of 92% (82%–98%).[94]

Disadvantages of dedicated echoendoscopes include inability to traverse critical stenoses and technical difficulty of evaluating superficial lesions in some areas of the stomach such as the cardia.

High-Frequency Ultrasound Probes

High-frequency ultrasound (HFUS) probes provide a higher range of frequencies (12–30 MHz), allowing the gut wall to be visualized in finer detail. These miniature probes can be passed through the operating channel of any standard gastroscope. Acoustic contact is ensured by filling a transparent plastic bag with water around the probe. At high frequencies, a nine-layer wall can be identified, with the muscularis mucosa as the fourth layer. We prefer a double-channel therapeutic gastroscope for catheter probe examination because of its larger working channel; the second channel can be used to immerse the gastric lesion in water for better acoustic contact and for introducing a second device when using the "cut and lift" endoscopic resection technique. It is sometimes technically easier to position a miniature probe at a small target lesion in the gastric fundus that could not be easily accessed with a conventional echoendoscope. However, HFUS probes do not have the depth of penetration to visualize regional lymph nodes or metastases for TNM staging.

The miniature probe can also be used to evaluate a lesion after saline injection, to confirm complete separation of the lesion from the underlying muscularis propria layer of the gastric wall before EMR.[95] Inability to separate the lesion from the muscularis propria after saline injection is a predictor of unresectability and thereby obviates the need for additional imaging to determine endoscopic resectability.

High-Frequency Ultrasound Staging of Early Gastric Cancer

A classification system for EGC has been developed based on depth of tumor penetration into the mucosa (m) and submucosa (sm), as defined by using HFUS probes. The superficial cancers are further divided into upper, middle, and lower third of the layer involvement as m1, m2, m3, sm1, sm2, and sm3.[93]

An overall T-staging accuracy of about 80% has been reported using HFUS in patients with EGC.[93,96,97] T-staging accuracy is higher for Tm1 (92.1%) than for Tsm1 (62.8%) or T2 muscularis propria (42.9%).[98] The curative effect of EMR is excellent for intramucosal cancers (m1, m2, and probably m3) but not for sub-mucosal cancers (sm1 to sm3).[12] Thus, the ability to distinguish between m3 and sm1 lesions is critical. Using a 20-MHz frequency probe, Yanai and coworkers[99] were able to distinguish between EGC involving the mucosa from EGC involving the submucosal with an accuracy of 72.3%.

In 33 patients referred for endoscopic management of superficial or submucosal neoplastic lesions, the usefulness of HFUS was evaluated.[100] The depth of invasion was accurately predicted by HFUS before EMR in 25 out of 26 patients (96%). Of the nine gastric lesions removed, eight had HFUS before EMR. There was 100% agreement between the depth of invasion determined by HFUS and pathologic staging. Almost half of the resected lesions were gastroduodenal including gastric adenocarcinoma, gastric and duodenal adenoma, gastric and duodenal carcinoid, pancreatic rest, fibrovascular submucosal polyp, ampullary adenoma, and duodenal lipoma. The diagnostic accuracy of HFUS probes for small gastric lesions (less than 4 cm) has been found by some researchers to be comparable to dedicated (standard) echoendoscopes.[101]

DESCRIPTION OF TECHNIQUES

Endoscopic Mucosal Resection

EMR involves the lifting of a lesion from the deep muscle layer of the gut wall, either by injection or by suction of the lesion into a cap fitted to the tip of the endoscope, followed by snare removal of the lesion (Fig. 35–6). Complete removal of the lesion "en bloc" during a single therapeutic procedure is ideal, although large lesions may require piecemeal resection. The availability of the resected specimen for pathologic examination is a distinct advantage of EMR over ablation therapies. Because EUS and HFUS cannot reliably distinguish between tumor infiltration and inflammation that may

associated with a malignant lesion, EMR provides both curative benefit and final staging confirmation.

Several EMR techniques have been described[102–104]:

1. Inject and cut technique
2. Inject, lift, and cut technique
3. EMR with ligation (EMRL)
4. Cap-assisted EMR

Inject and Cut Technique

In this technique, the lesion is lifted from the underlying muscularis propria by injecting a solution submucosally to produce a bleb beneath the lesion. The lesion is then captured and resected by using an electrosurgical snare (Fig. 35–7). The required volume of submucosal injection will vary according to the size of the lesion, provided that the bleb is sufficient to ensure a good lift of the entire lesion so that it can be safely captured and resected.

One technical caveat is to perform the initial injection at the periphery and distal margins of the lesion (farthest away from the tip of the endoscope), followed by injection at the lateral margins and at the periphery of the lesion closest to the endoscope. This injection sequence minimizes the problem of obscuring the endoscopic view of the distal margins of the lesion yet to be injected. The submucosal bleb provides a pseudostalk for the snare and a

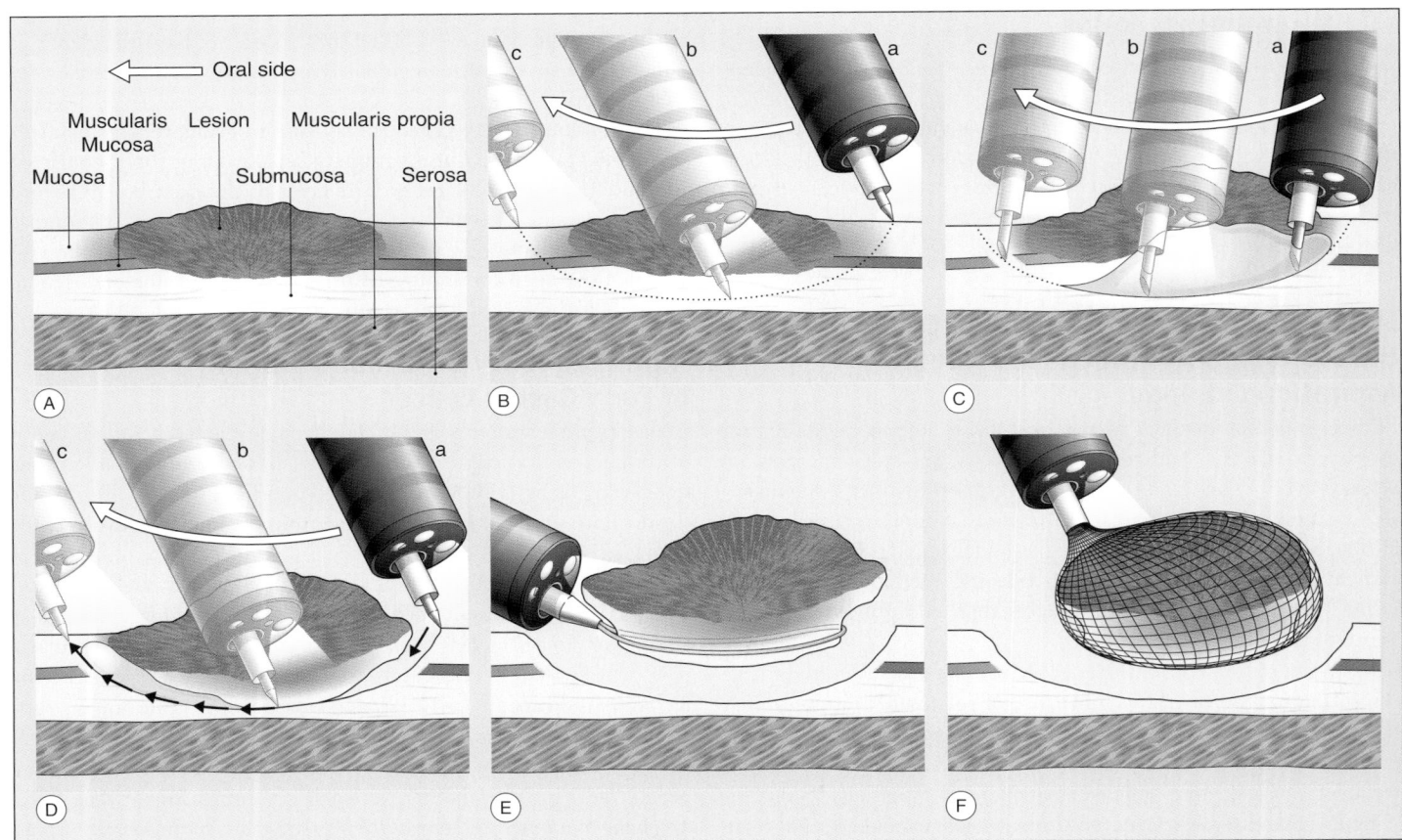

Figure 35–6. En bloc endoscopic mucosal resection (EMR). *A,* Lesion involving the mucosal layer. *B,* Marking of incision around lesion with needle knife from distal to proximal edge. *C,* Submucosal injection of sodium hyaluronate below the lesion and around lesion from distal to proximal edge. *D,* Incision of marked area around lesion with needle knife from distal to proximal edge of lesion. *E,* Snare excision of entire lesion. *F,* Retrieval of lesion with Roth net.

protective cushion beneath the lesion, decreasing tissue resistance and minimizing electrocautery injury to the deeper wall layers. A variety of solutions is available for injection. Hypertonic saline-epinephrine is widely used in the hopes of decreasing the risk of bleeding[105]; other solutions have been used to obtain a more durable lift of the lesion.[106] In addition, a variety of snares and currents (e.g., blended, ERBE) are preferred by different endoscopists. To date, no randomized trials have been conducted to compare the safety and effectiveness of different types of snares and injectants.

The advantage of the inject and cut technique is its simplicity and the fact that it does not require additional equipment. A disadvantage is that most solutions used to lift the lesion dissipate very rapidly thus making it difficult at times to safely capture the lesion with the snare.

Inject, Lift, and Cut Technique (Strip Biopsy)

In this technique the submucosal injection is performed in the standard manner, as already described. A snare and grasping forceps are passed through the operating channels of a dual-channel endoscope. First, the grasping forceps are captured by the open snare and the snare is closed over the forceps. Working as a unit, the forceps are used to grasp the lesion, the snare is opened, and the lesion is pulled through the open snare. The snare is then closed over the lesion and resection of the lesion is performed[107-109] (Fig. 35–8).

This technique is more cumbersome than the inject and cut technique, and requires a dual-channel endoscope and two assistants to perform EMR.

Endoscopic Mucosal Resection with Ligation

In this technique, the lesion is removed with or without previous submucosal injection.[110-112] An endoscopic rubber band variceal ligation device is loaded over the tip of the endoscope. The lesion is ligated, and snare polypectomy is then performed. The standard polypectomy snare is positioned immediately above or below the rubber band[112] (Fig. 35–9).

An advantage of this technique is that only conventional devices and instruments are required. Disadvantages include suboptimal visualization of the margins of the lesion when the variceal ligation device is loaded and the need to reintubate after rubber band ligation.

Cap-Assisted Endoscopic Mucosal Resection

In this technique, a specially designed transparent plastic cap is used.[113,114] The plastic cap is fitted over the tip of the endoscope, and various cap sizes are available. Submucosal injection of the lesion is performed in the standard manner. A crescent-shaped snare is prelooped into the groove of the rim of the specialized cap by gently suctioning normal mucosa into the cap and opening the snare to allow it to rest along the inside groove of the rim of the cap (SD-221L-25 or SD-7P-1, Olympus America, Inc.). After prelooping the snare, the suction is turned off to release the normal mucosa. The cap is now used to suction the lesion while maintaining constant medium to high vacuum. Once the lesion is trapped completely inside the cap, the snare is closed over the lesion. After the lesion is tightly strangulated by the snare, the suction is turned

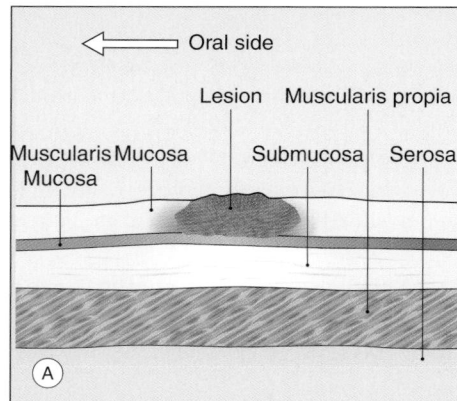

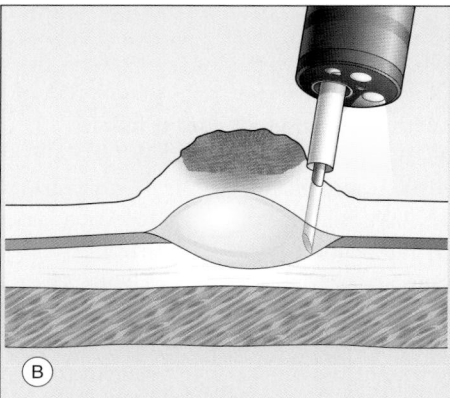

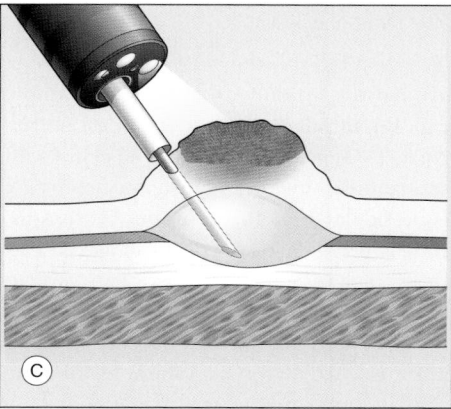

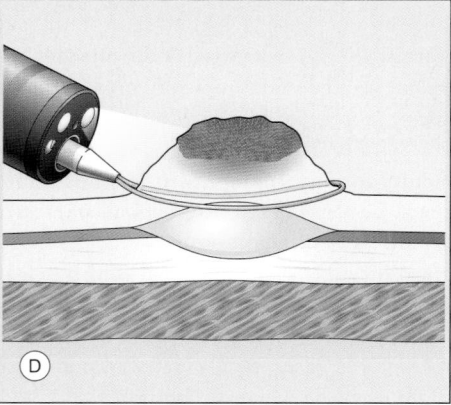

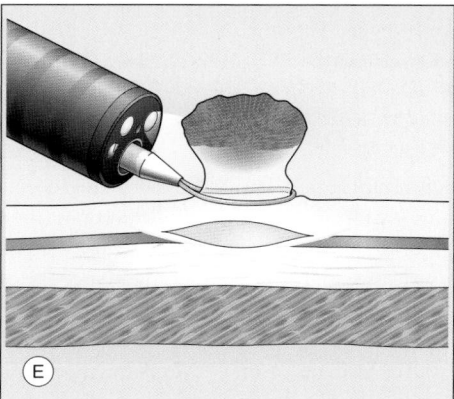

Figure 35–7. Inject and cut. *A,* Lesion involving the mucosal layer. *B,* Submucosal injection at distal edge of lesion. *C,* Submucosal injection at proximal edge of lesion. *D,* Snaring of raised lesion. *E,* Tightening of snare and excision of raised lesion.

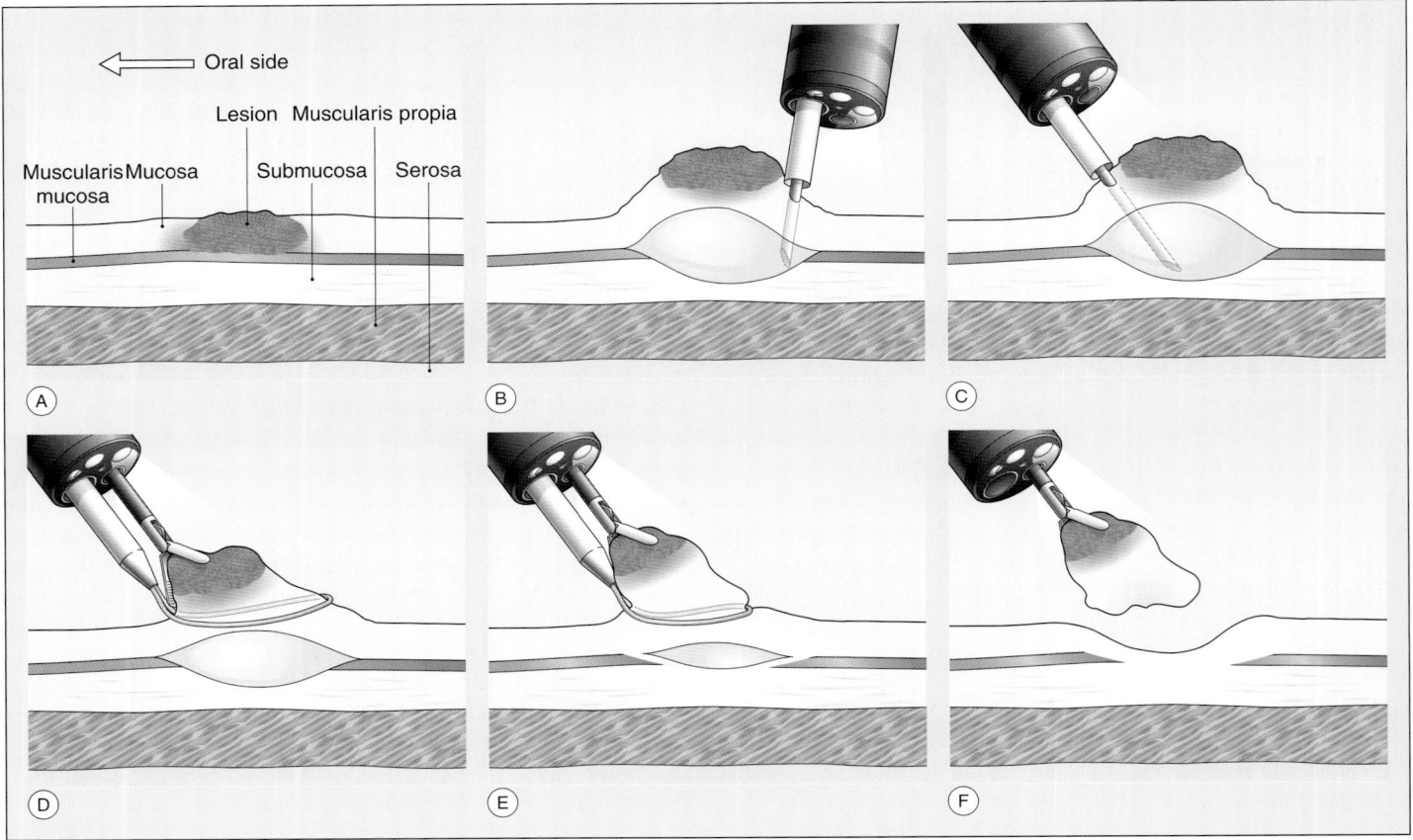

Figure 35–8. Strip biopsy. *A*, Lesion involving the mucosal layer. *B*, Submucosal injection at distal edge of lesion with double-channel endoscope. *C*, Submucosal injection at proximal edge of lesion. *D*, Grasping forceps pulling lesion into open snare. *E*, Tightening of snare and excision of lesion. *F*, Mucosal defect created after removal of lesion.

off and the lesion with the snare around it is allowed to leave the cap. Resection of the lesion is then performed with application of current. Gentle suction of the specimen into the cap will allow safe and complete recovery of the specimen (Fig. 35–10). This technique is particularly useful for upper GI lesions.[113,115,116] Matsuzaki and colleagues[116] have reported the use of a soft, 18-mm diameter cap for en bloc resection of larger gastric lesions (lesions up to 1.4 times the size that can be removed with a standard cap).

For lesions greater than 3 cm, some endoscopists have used a more viscous material, sodium hyaluronate, for submucosal injection. A small-caliber tip transparent hood that accommodates a needle-knife or an insulated thermal knife with a ceramic cap is then used to cut around the lesion on its entire circumference. The final step is the complete removal of the lesion using a large snare.[117,118]

Endoscopic Mucosal Resection for Early Gastric Cancer

EMR is now considered a curative procedure for EGC, and has increasingly replaced surgical resection for this indication in Japan, although the technique is not universally accepted as a first line of treatment in the West. EMR has also been used as a histologic staging technique to assess the depth of penetration in EGC to help determine the best definitive treatment.

Correct diagnosis of the depth of invasion and the absence of lymph node metastasis are crucial for achieving a cure with endoscopic therapy. The important endoscopic points to consider are as follows:

1. The extension of the surface and the morphology. Endoscopic resection is not recommended for lesions greater than 2 cm in size.
2. The depth of invasion should be no deeper than the mucosa. This must be determined by EUS before EMR and should be corroborated by pathologic examination of the resected specimen.
3. High grade dysplasia is the earliest stage of malignancy. A high degree of differentiation favors endoscopic treatment, whereas poorly differentiated lesions have a higher risk of distant spread and should (probably) not be treated endoscopically.
4. Multifocal EGC can be treated endoscopically provided that the entire morphology is compatible with an intramucosal cancer.[119]
5. The degree of difficulty in performing EMR depends on its location in the stomach. Lesions in the posterior wall and lesser curvature technically are more difficult to remove.
6. The success or failure of curative EMR is assessed by clear margins seen on pathology and by endoscopy and biopsy obtained during follow-up.
7. Assessment of the results is based on the rates of complete removal or destruction, rates of recurrence, and survival.

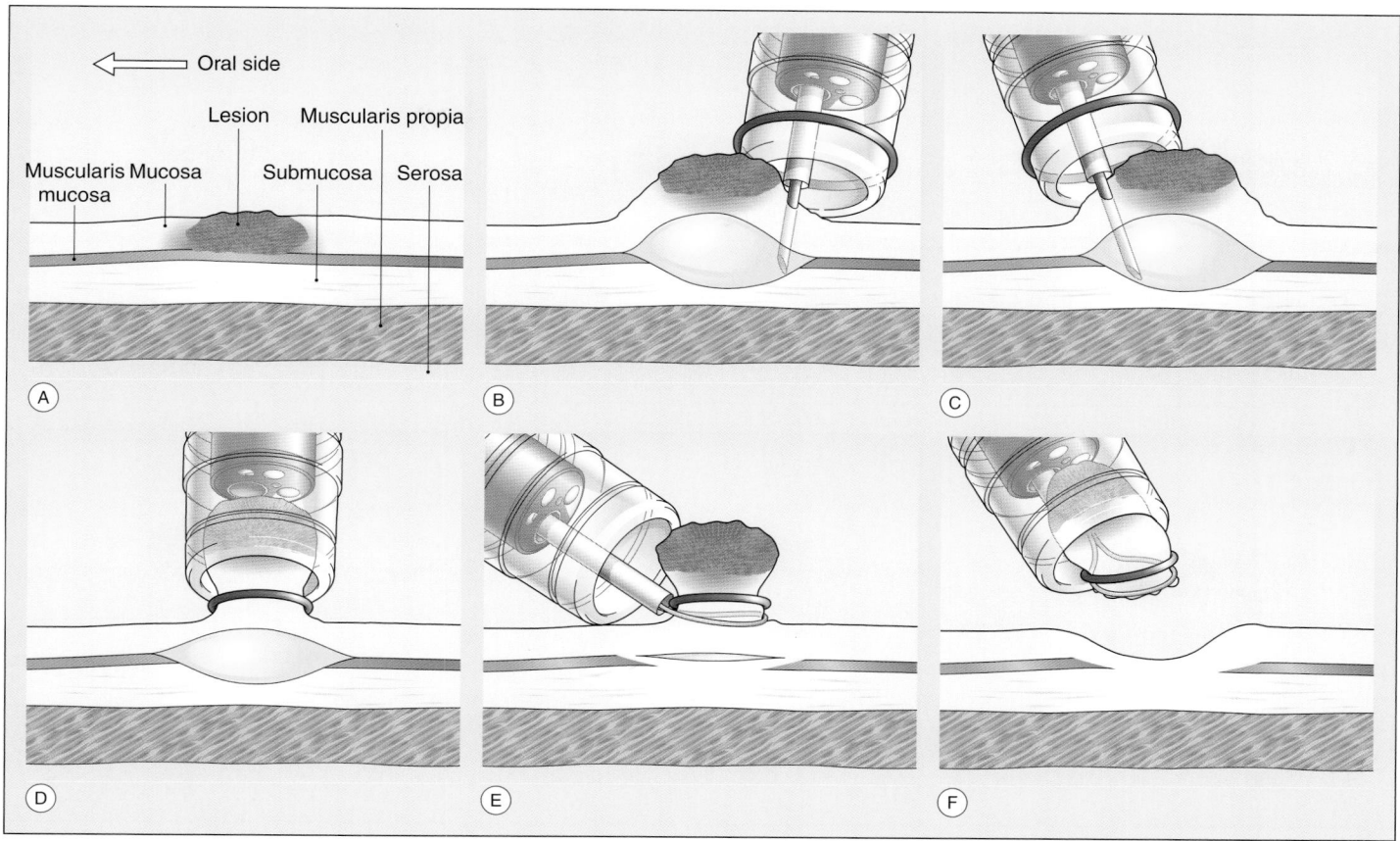

Figure 35–9. Endoscopic mucosal resection with ligation (EMRL). *A,* Lesion involving the mucosal layer. *B,* Submucosal injection at distal edge of lesion. *C,* Submucosal injection at proximal edge of lesion. *D,* Suction of lesion into hood and ligation with rubber band. *E,* Snaring and excision of lesion below the rubber band. *F,* Mucosal defect created after removal of lesion.

The Japanese Research Society for gastric cancer has developed the following criteria for lesions that are suitable for endoscopic resection[88]:

1. Well differentiated, type I or IIa, limited to the mucosa, without histologic ulceration and less than 2 cm
2. Well differentiated, type IIc, limited to mucosa without ulceration and less than 1 cm

When these criteria are followed, the risk of lymph node involvement is only 1.7%. However, the use of morphologic staging is subjective and its generalization has not been evaluated.

A retrospective evaluation of 210 cases of EGC treated with EMR and followed up for 14 years reported a 5-year survival of 86% and a 10-year survival of 56%; there were no cancer-related deaths.[109] EMR as a curative treatment has been evaluated in 102 patients.[103] No distant or local metastases were seen during 9 years of follow-up.

A total of 106 patients with EGC up to 2 cm in diameter were treated with complete resection of the lesion in a single procedure, either by en bloc resection for lesions less than 10 mm (64%) or by piecemeal resection for larger lesions (36%). No recurrence after either technique was found in patients with tumor-negative margins. The overall recurrence rate of cancer in this particular study was 2.8%. Tumors that recurred all were greater than 15 mm initially and were treated with piecemeal resection.[120] Because histologic

reconstruction to confirm complete resection by piecemeal method is often difficult, patients should to be followed very closely after piecemeal resection.

Endoscopic therapy in patients with EGC that do not meet the Japanese Research Society morphologic criteria for lesions suitable for EMR was evaluated by Amano and coworkers[121] in a retrospective study. Endoscopic therapy consisted of EMR, thermal therapy, or both. Poorly and well-differentiated tumors ranging from 1 to 3 cm were included in the study. Some patients with submucosal invasion limited to the most superficial layer (sm1) were included. Curative resection was achieved in 95%. The rate of cure in this group was statistically similar to the cure rate of cases that fulfilled the standard morphologic criteria for EMR resection (98%).[121]

Adequacy of EMR can be assessed by measuring the distance from the edge of the resected specimen to the margin of the cancer. In a prior study, no patient with a distance of more than 2 mm developed recurrence of the cancer, whereas 16% of those patients with a distance of less than 2 mm developed recurrence.[122] Presence of cancer at the edge of the specimen was associated with a recurrence of 45.8%. No recurrence was observed if the distance from the edge of the specimen to the cancer was more than 7 mm, suggesting that adequate distance (preferably at least 2 mm) between the edge of the specimen and the cancer must be achieved to ensure a complete resection.[123] Margin-negative resections are

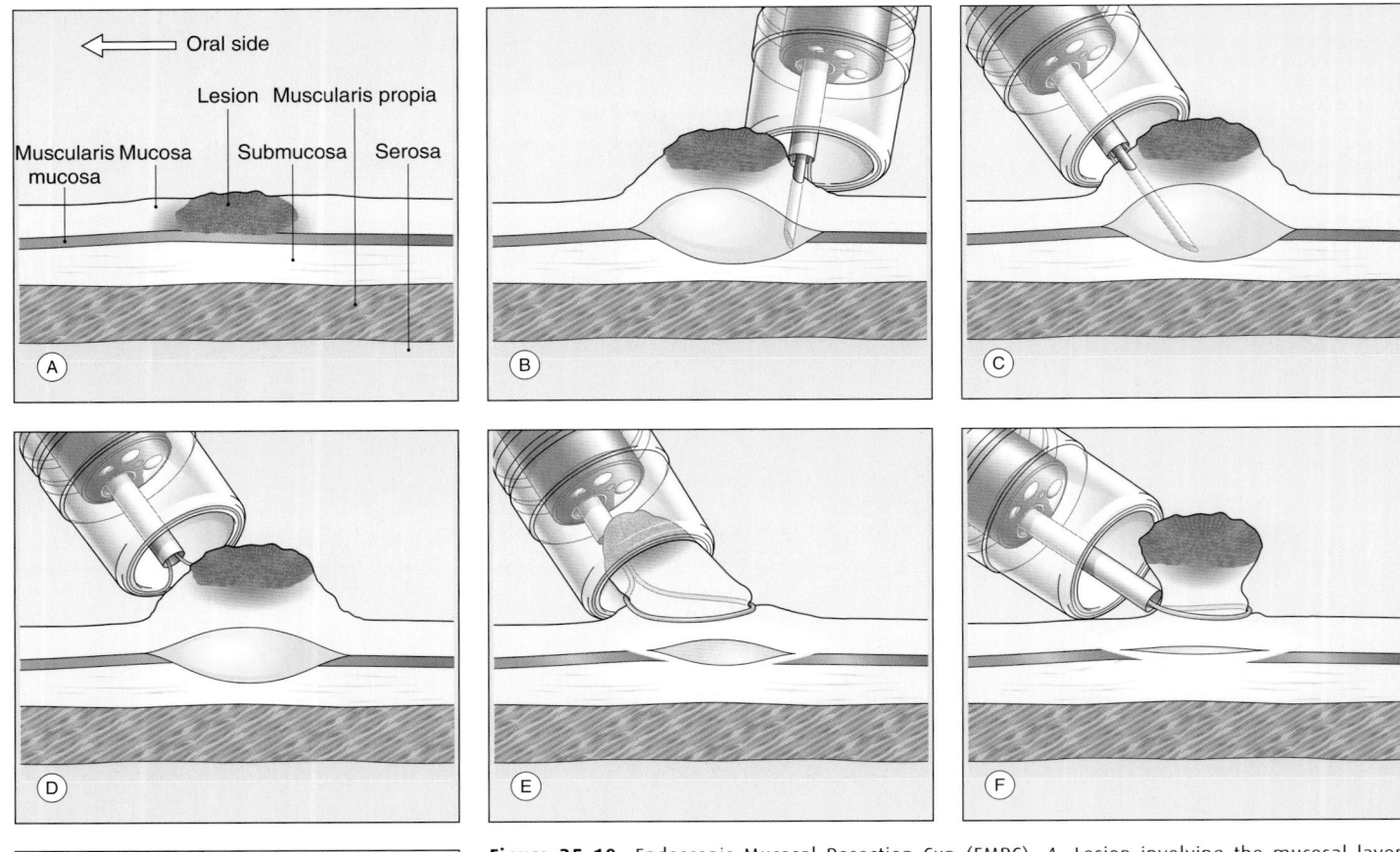

Figure 35-10. Endoscopic Mucosal Resection Cup (EMRC). *A,* Lesion involving the mucosal layer. *B,* Submucosal injection at distal edge of lesion. *C,* Submucosal injection at proximal edge of lesion. *D,* Preloaded snare in groove of endoscopic mucosal resection (EMR) cup. *E,* Suction of ion into EMR cup and capture of pseudostalk by snare. *F,* Release of suction with continuous tight grasp of lesion by snare. *G,* Suction of lesion into EMR cup for retrieval after snare excision.

more likely (81.2%) in cancers that are less than 1 cm in diameter than in cancers that are more than 2 cm in diameter.[123]

In a prospective analysis of 479 EGCs treated with EMR over an 11-year period at Tokyo National Cancer Center, the following selection criteria were used: well or moderately well differentiated gastric cancer; morphologic type I, Iia, and IIc; no histologic evidence of ulceration; diameter of less than 3 cm with histologic confirmation of intramucosal carcinoma; no lymphovascular invasion; and clean margins. A total of 405 patients were treated with EMR, and complete resection was achieved in 69%. The recurrence rate was only 2%, and all were treated successfully with a modified combination therapy of EMR and laser. No subsequent recurrence occurred in any of the 278 patients after a median follow-up period of 38 months (range 3–120 months). No cancer-related deaths were reported. Bleeding and perforation were the two major complications. Bleeding was controlled in all cases with endoscopic treatment. Bowel perforation occurred in 5%; endoscopic clips were effective in 84% (21/25) and surgery was performed in only 16% (4/25) of the patients with perforation.[118]

Postoperative Care

Patients who undergo EMR should be observed in the recovery area during the immediate postoperative period for possible complications. Patients should be placed on a liquid diet during the remainder of the day, especially for patients who had bleeding during the procedure or if there is a concern for other complications. Antisecretory medications, preferably proton pump inhibitors, should be prescribed for 6 to 8 weeks after the procedure.

Complications of Endoscopic Mucosal Resection

Complications of EMR include adverse events secondary to sedation and procedure-related complications that are specific but not exclusive to EMR.

Bleeding. Bleeding is the most common complication of EMR of gastric tumors. The reported incidence of bleeding after EMR has ranged between 0.38% to 16.1%.[123] The discrepancy may be due to differences in definition of bleeding and to study methodology. Most institutions have reported the incidence of bleeding to be between 10% and 16%, although studies based on surveys have reported a much lower incidence. Most bleeding occur during the procedure or within 24 hours after EMR. In the largest retrospective study dealing with predictors of bleeding after EMR of gastric tumors, the overall incidence of bleeding was 17.6%, with delayed bleeding occurring in 5.3%. In this study, the only statistically significant factor for predicting delayed bleeding was the occurrence of immediate bleeding during EMR.[124] Delayed bleeding is probably not due to inadequate initial hemostasis but rather to insufficient coagulation during resection, because in this study the sites of delayed bleeding were not the same as the sites of immediate bleeding.[124] Size greater than 1 to 2 cm has been reported by some authors to be predictive of bleeding[125]; other studies have not found a positive correlation between size of lesion and risk of bleeding.[124,126] No significant association has been found between the risk of bleeding and different techniques used for EMR, morphology of the lesion (flat, raised, or depressed), type of electrocautery current used, amount of saline used, or location of the lesion.

Management of Post-Endoscopic Mucosal Resection Bleeding.

No maneuver has been shown to help prevent post-EMR bleeding. Fortunately, bleeding during EMR usually stops spontaneously. If significant bleeding occurs, the standard methods of endoscopic hemostasis should be attempted. A few caveats are worth remembering when treating this complication endoscopically. Cautery should be applied cautiously, keeping in mind that the site has already received a significant amount of energy. Overvigorous delivery of additional coagulation current may result in a transmural burn or even a perforation. Injection of diluted epinephrine (1 in 10,000 or 1 in 20,000) can also be used to control the bleeding, either as the only measure or to prepare the bleeding site for another maneuver such as cauterization or placement of mucosal hemoclips.[124,125] One potential advantage of the latter is that hemoclips do not cause additional gastric wall injury to the EMR site.

Patients who develop delayed bleeding should be managed as any patient who presents with upper GI hemorrhage. The initial objectives are to establish venous access and achieve hemodynamic stability. Once the situation is under control, urgent endoscopic hemostasis can be attempted.

Perforation. Perforation typically occurs when part of the muscularis proper is inadvertently resected in the specimen. Transmural burns secondary to aggressive cauterization may also result in delayed perforation. The rates of EMR-induced perforation are highest for gastric lesions at 2.5% to 5%, compared with the colon at less than 1%. Reported rates of perforation are higher when performing EMR with an insulation-tipped knife (5.6%) compared with the endoscopic aspiration technique (0.8%).[126]

Some caveats may help to reduce the risk of perforation: (1) one should avoid performing EMR in patients who have had prior attempts at endoscopic resection. This is because scarring secondary to prior cauterization may prevent proper lifting of the lesion from the underlying muscularis propria during submucosal injection; (2) proper technique and an adequate volume of submucosal injection are important to provide a margin of safety; (3) one should avoid resnaring resected tissue; and (4) one should abort the procedure if the patient experiences pain on closure of the snare because this may be an indication of full-thickness capture by the snare.

Management of Perforation.

A surgical consultation should be obtained as soon as perforation is suspected. The earlier that the diagnosis is established (within the first 6 hours), the better is the prognosis. The standard of care for management of a recognized perforation continues to be surgical. However, if the perforation is small and the patient is asymptomatic, hemoclips could be used to close the defect but this should be done early on.[126] Patients should be placed nil per os (NPO) and treated with broad-spectrum antibiotics.

Transmural Burn Syndrome.

Transmural burn syndrome occurs when thermal injury to the muscularis propria and serosa is produced by excessive electrocoagulation during polypectomy or EMR. Transmural burn syndrome has been reported in 0.5% to 1% of colonic polypectomies, but the exact incidence in EMR is still unknown.

Patients often present with symptoms and laboratory abnormalities that are indistinguishable from a perforation. Therefore, it is extremely important to exclude a perforation immediately before resorting to conservative management. A surgical consultation should be obtained. Once a perforation has been excluded, patients should be placed on broad-spectrum antibiotics, intravenous hydration, and bowel rest. Serial abdominal x-ray films should be ordered to monitor for the possibility of a late perforation. Most patients respond very well to conservative management.[127]

Luminal Stenosis.

Luminal stenosis has been described as a delayed complication in patients who have had EMR mainly of an esophageal lesion.[128] This complication tends to occur after extensive resection when the mucosa of more than three fourths of the luminal circumference has been excised. The mechanism of retraction appears to be related to the healing process. Temporary metal stent placement[129] and balloon dilations or a combination of both have been used effectively.[128] Incremental resections in multiple treatment sessions may help to minimize contraction of the lumen.

Ablation Techniques

Lasers (light amplification by stimulated emission of radiation) are devices that produce a light energy that is focused into a unidirectional, single-wavelength beam. The most common medical uses of lasers derive from the conversion of light to heat energy. The laser light beam can be used to cut, coagulate, or vaporize tissue depending on the wavelength of light, power density used to excite the lasing medium, and absorption and scattering. Nd:YAG, CO_2, Nd:holmium, and argon ion laser are the most frequently lasers used in biomedical applications.

When performing laser therapy, safety eyewear is used to avoid ocular damage to endoscopy personnel. Adequate local exhaust ventilation and use of respiratory filter masks have been recommended to avoid respiratory exposure to aerosolized infectious pathogens resulting from the vaporization of tissue.[130] Because of its limited portability, high cost, availability of less costly alternatives, and the need for specific training, laser therapy is not widely used today for endoscopic treatment of gastric neoplasms.

Neodymium:Yttrium-Aluminum-Garnet Laser

Laser energy can be delivered through flexible optic fibers at wavelengths of 1320 and 1064 nm. Because the emission is invisible, a helium-neon aiming beam is used in conjunction with Nd:YAG to visualize the focal target area.[131,132] To obtain photoablation, an optical fiber is passed through the operating channel of the endoscope and the transmitted laser beam can be delivered in a contact or noncontact fashion. Tangential irradiation is not possible with this technique; thus, the location of some lesions may be more difficult to target.[133]

Photodynamic Therapy

Photodynamic therapy (PDT) also delivers energy via flexible optic fibers. The laser light activates a photosensitizing agent, releasing toxic singlet oxygen and causing tissue necrosis. The photosensitizer selectively accumulates in the target tissue. The only commercially available photosensitizer in the United States is porfimer sodium (Photofrin).[134] Other photosensitizers include 5-aminolevulinic acid (5-ALA), zinc II phthalocyanine, aluminum sulfonated phthalocyanine, benzoporphyrin, meta-tetrahydroxyphenylchlorin (mTHPC), N-aspartyl chlorine e6 (NPe6), and motexafin lutetium.

Among these different photosensitizers, mTHPC, porfimer sodium, and ALA have been used extensively in gastroenterology. mTHPC is a potent, highly selective drug that has been used in the treatment of neoplasms, whereas ALA, which induces very superficial necrosis, has been used to treat Barrett's esophagus.[135,136]

Porfimer sodium is administered at a recommended dose of 2 mg/kg intravenously and activated 48 hours later by a tunable dye laser at 630 nm.[134]

ALA is a heme pathway precursor that can be given orally or intravenously. ALA is then converted to the endogenous photosensitized protoporphyrin IX that can be activated by red or green light.

Complications of Laser Therapy

Bleeding is one of the most common complications of Nd:YAG laser therapy. A major bleeding rate of 12.5% after laser treatment of gastric tumors has been reported.[137] Perforations may occur in 1% to 9%, with a procedure-related mortality of up to 1%.[137] Stricture formation as a late complication of laser therapy (Nd:YAG and PDT) has been observed in 5% to 13%.[5] Pulmonary complications have been reported after PDT in up to 15%. Photosensitization lasting up to 3 months and severe sunburn have been reported in 5% to 7% of patients after PDT therapy.[134,138]

Laser Therapy for Early Gastric Cancer

Endoscopic laser therapy has been used to treat inoperable patients with EGC. In 13 patients with EGC, Nd:YAG or PDT achieved a complete response in 85% of the patients.[5] Sibille and coworkers[136] used Nd:YAG laser to treat 18 nonoperative patients with EUS T1 gastric cancer until a complete response (negative endoscopic biopsies) was achieved. The number of sessions varied from 1 to 15 sessions, performed every 2 weeks. Initial complete response was achieved in 16 (89%) of the patients after a mean of 1.7 sessions (range 1–4); two patients (11%) did not respond to therapy.

PDT has been shown to achieve a complete response in eight EGC lesions diagnosed in seven nonoperative patients.[137] In another study, Nakamura and colleagues[138] reported on the use of PDT with an excimer dye laser in 7 patients with 8 EGC. Photodynamic therapy was safely utilized with success in all seven patients.

Nd:YAG laser therapy has also been used to photoablate residual tumor after an incomplete EMR.[3,139]

Laser Therapy for Advanced Gastric Cancer

Laser ablation therapy is more frequently used as a palliative modality in advanced gastric lesions. Successful palliation of bleeding or obstruction resulting from gastric cancer has been reported in 81% to 100%.[5,137,140] Relief of obstructing cancer in the gastric cardia using the Nd:YAG laser has been reported.[141,142] Addition of external beam radiation and brachytherapy was found to increase the interval between laser treatments in advanced esophageal and gastric cardia adenocarcinoma.[143–145]

Argon Plasma Coagulation

APC uses a high-frequency current and an ionized argon gas for coagulating tissue. In the early 1990s, an APC delivery catheter that could be inserted through a flexible endoscope was invented by Farin and Grund.[146] Initially introduced as a hemostatic device, the technology subsequently was used for ablation of superficial neoplastic lesions. A noncontact coagulation device, APC can deliver a tangential current to uniformly coagulate a target lesion.[131]

The standard equipment consists of a high-frequency generator and an automatically regulated argon source. The APC current and argon gas are delivered via a flexible probe introduced through the operating channel of the endoscope. Straight-fire and side-fire probes are available. The recommended settings for ablation of gastric lesions using the APC 300/ICC 200 electrosurgical system (ERBE USA Incorporated Surgical Systems, Marietta, GA) are mode: auto coag; power setting: 60 to 80 watts; coagulation type: forced; and argon plasma flow rate: 1.0 to 2.0 L/minute. The VIO300D-APC2, a new second-generation APC system recently released by the same manufacturer, achieves similar results at power settings approximately half of the APC 300 unit.

Argon Plasma Coagulation for Early Gastric Cancer

Compared with laser therapy, experience with APC for treatment of both early and advanced gastric cancer is limited with a shorter duration of follow-up.[146] APC as a curative treatment for EGC was used by Sagawa and colleagues[4] in 27 patients who were considered poor candidates for either surgical resection (17 patients) or EMR (10 patients) because of comorbidities including severe cardiac failure, marked thrombocytopenia, or anticoagulation therapy. No evidence of recurrence was observed in 26 treated patients (96%) at a median follow-up of 30 months. Only one patient had a tumor recurrence at 6 months and this was successfully retreated with no evidence of recurrence after an additional follow-up of 39 months. Twelve of the 27 patients (44%) had EGCs located in areas more difficult to access endoscopically, such as the posterior wall of the stomach or the cardia.[4]

APC is also commonly used to ablate any residual tumor after EMR.[4,120]

Argon Plasma Coagulation for Advanced Gastric Cancer

APC as part of a multimodality palliative approach for advanced gastric cancer has been reported.[147] Ten patients with gastric carcinoma in whom surgery would not have been curative were treated with APC for debulking of a partially obstructing tumor; a mean of 4.9 treatment sessions were required to achieve effective palliation and symptom relief.[147]

APC has also been used to treat tumor ingrowth within self-expandable metal stents (SEMSs) in patients with obstructing esophagogastric junction tumors.[148]

Complications of Argon Plasma Coagulation

APC therapy in 27 patients with EGC was not associated with any serious complications. Three out of 27 patients (11%) complained of abdominal fullness that was alleviated by intermittent suction or by continuous suction when a dual-channel upper endoscope was used.[4]

Enteral Stents

Enteral stents are indicated for malignant luminal obstruction of the GI tract. Patients who have gastric outlet obstruction secondary to gastric cancer can be treated with surgical palliative bypass (via laparoscopy in some centers).[149] Patients who are not good candidates for surgical palliation may benefit from percutaneous gastrostomy for decompression and enteral feeding.[150] Another alternative is the use of enteral SEMSs. SEMSs have been used as palliative therapy for obstructing gastroesophageal junction tumors.[151] SEMSs are made of a variety of metal alloys in varying sizes and shapes. Covered and uncovered SEMSs are available.[152] Many of the published series on SEMS placement in the upper GI tract have used either modified or standard esophageal stents.[153,154]

There are two basic techniques for inserting a metal stent. A through-the-scope (TTS) technique is used to place an enteral Wallstent (Microvasive Endoscopy, Natick, MA); a non-TTS delivery system is used when deploying esophageal stents. Two important caveats for successful SEMS placement are the ability to pass a guidewire across the stricture and the selection of a stent that is at least 3 to 4 cm longer than the obstruction, to allow an adequate margin at both side of the obstruction.[155]

Other Gastric Neoplasms

GASTRIC POLYPS
See Chapter 34.

GASTRIC LYMPHOMA
Epidemiology

GI lymphoma accounts for 4% to 20% of all NHLs and 30% to 40% of all extranodal cases.[156] The incidence rate for NHL has been rising, with this trend being more prevalent for extranodal disease. Although primary gastric lymphoma accounts for less than 5% of all gastric malignant neoplasms, an increase in incidence of primary gastric lymphoma has been observed in the United States.[157]

Time trend analysis based on a population-based registry has shown increased incidence rates for gastric (6.3%) and small bowel (5.9%) NHL and a concomitant decrease in GI NHL of unknown site, suggesting that at least in part the increased incidence may be a result of more accurate diagnosis. In this particular study, the most common site of GI NHL for all age groups was gastric (43.3%), followed by small bowel (27.4%) and large bowel (11.1%); NHL of unknown site accounted for the remaining 16.1%.[156]

Pathogenesis

An association between *H. pylori* infection and gastric NHL has been shown in several studies.[158,159] Acquired mucosa-associated lymphoid tissue (MALT) in the stomach provides the background for lymphoma to develop. *H. pylori* is the only well-established chronic antigenic stimulus that causes gastric MALT.[160] Parsonnet and coworkers[161] has shown that prior *H. pylori* infection gives a statistically significant sixfold increased risk of developing gastric NHL, with the association being stronger for high-grade lymphoma. Complete regression of MALT following eradication of *H. pylori* infection has been described, with subsequent relapse of the lymphoma following reinfection with the organism.[160,162,163] The link between *H. pylori* gastritis and low-grade gastric lymphoma of the MALT type has also been supported by published data from case control and epidemiologic studies.[163]

Although the rate of *H. pylori* infection in patients with gastric lymphoma has been found to be higher (91%) than in the general population (64%) in some areas throughout the world, the incidence of gastric lymphoma only partially parallels the incidence of *H. pylori* gastritis.[164]

In some areas of Africa, the prevalence of *H. pylori* infection is very high but the incidence of gastric lymphoma is very low. Furthermore, a study using population-based registries demonstrated that the incidence of gastric lymphoma parallels the incidence of all NHL, indicating that *H. pylori* infection is not the only factor in the pathogenesis of MALT lymphoma.[164] A 22% rate of *H. pylori*–negative status based on histologic and serologic tests has been reported in patients with low-grade gastric lymphoma.[165] Rarely, low-grade lymphoma may develop in the background of *Helicobacter heilmanii*–associated gastritis.[166]

In some *H. pylori*–negative gastric MALT lymphomas, association with autoimmune diseases such as Sjögren's syndrome has been described, but no association with viruses known to be present in other types of lymphomas has been detected.[167] Epstein-Barr virus infection, an early pathogen in the development of nodal lymphoma, is only very rarely found in gastric MALT lymphoma.[168]

Occupational exposure to solvents and pesticides has been suggested to play a pathogenic role in some gastric lymphomas in an Italian study.[159] Thus, the development of MALT that gives rise to gastric lymphoma is probably a multifactorial process involving both antigenic and host-related factors, but other mechanisms are not known yet.

Clinical Features

Low-grade gastric lymphoma typically occurs in the fifth decade, whereas high-grade lymphoma occurs in the sixth decade, suggesting that the progression from low-grade to high-grade lymphoma takes about a decade.[169]

Patients with gastric lymphoma generally present with nonspecific dyspepsia or with symptoms suggestive of peptic ulcer disease. Some patients may present with GI bleeding or anemia. The finding of an abdominal mass at presentation is rare.[169]

Endoscopic Diagnosis

Endoscopically, patients with low-grade lymphoma may display normal-appearing gastric mucosa, nonspecific macroscopic gastritis, thickened gastric folds, or ulcerative lesions. Patients with high-grade lymphoma generally display large ulcers on more protruding tumors.[170] The diagnosis is based on gastric biopsies and is enhanced by immunohistochemistry.[171]

Endoscopic Ultrasonography Staging

EUS provides accurate staging of gastric lymphoma. Based on endosonographic criteria, gastric lymphoma can be divided into four types: superficially spreading (with thickening of the second and/or third layers), diffusely infiltrating (diffuse transmural irregular thickening of the gastric wall), mass-forming (localized hypoechoic mass with a clear margin located in the third layer or in the third and fourth layers), and mixed (combination of mass-forming and superficially spreading.[172] Superficially spreading and diffusely infiltrating lymphomas are seen only in patients with low-grade MALT lymphoma. Mass-forming lymphomas are of the same histologic type as intermediate-grade lymphomas, either diffuse large-cell or mixed-cell type.[172]

EUS is considered the most accurate technique for locoregional staging of MALT lymphoma.[172,173] EUS had a T-staging accuracy of 91.5% when resected specimen histology was the gold standard.[173] The accuracy of EUS for detection of lymph node metastasis was reported to be 83% when compared with resected histology in the same study.[173]

A previous study evaluated the accuracy of a 12-MHz miniprobe for the staging of low-grade gastric MALT lymphoma, compared with conventional EUS.[174] A total of 39 patients who had histologically confirmed low-grade MALT lymphoma were reviewed retrospectively before treatment. The accuracy of T and nodal staging using miniprobe and conventional EUS were similar in this study.

The obvious advantage of performing staging with the miniprobe is that this examination can be performed as a single-step procedure during diagnostic gastroscopy. However, we believe that conventional EUS and EUS guided-FNA is the procedure of choice for staging MALT lymphoma because miniprobes cannot detect distant metastatic lymph node involvement (e.g., nodes in the celiac region) or provide a specimen for cytologic evaluation.[174,175]

Pathology

NHLs are malignant neoplasms of the B and T lymphocytes and their precursor cells.[176] In Occidental countries, B-cell lymphoma is more common (>80%). In the Western world, B-cell lymphoma of the MALT type is the most common. Most of these lymphomas arise in the stomach.[163,177-179] In southern Japan on the other hand, T-cell lymphomas predominate, accounting for more than 75% of GI cases.[163,177-179]

In the presence of H. pylori infection, B- and T-lymphoid cells and neutrophils are brought to the gastric mucosa to form acquired MALT. In low-grade lymphoma, the autoreactive B-cell proliferation is secondary to a specific activation of reactive T cells by H. pylori and cytokines rather than to the bacteria per se.[180] The two main groups of gastric lymphomas are extranodal marginal zone B-cell lymphoma (MZBL), MALT type, and diffuse large B-cell lymphoma (DLBCL).[181] MZBL, MALT type is composed of a monotonous, diffuse infiltrate of small lymphoid cells, whereas DLBCL is characterized by a diffuse infiltrate of large malignant lymphoid blasts resembling centroblasts, plasmablasts, and inmunoblasts.[182]

Low-grade MALT lymphoma characteristically displays small cleaved cells or centrocyte-like cells, and it is more frequently found in the stomach. As with nodal NHL, low-grade MALT lymphoma may progress to high-grade lymphoma. In the stomach, low-grade MALT lymphoma may extend over a large area or may be multifocal.[183] A subset of patients with low-grade B-cell MALT lymphoma can have a focal high-grade component histologically. A lower survival rate has been found in this subset of patients.[184] Conventional biopsy specimens do not always yield a histologic diagnosis of low-grade B-cell MALT lymphoma.[171] EUS detection with EMR histologic confirmation has been reported recently in one patient.[185]

Simultaneous coexistence of gastric carcinoma and gastric lymphoma is uncommon but has been reported in the literature.[186–188]

Treatment

The strong association between H. pylori and B-cell lymphoma of MALT dictates that H. pylori eradication should be a routine treatment for superficial gastric lymphoma. A combination of two antibiotics (clarithromycin and metronidazole or amoxicillin) with a proton pump inhibitor results in more than 90% eradication of H. pylori.[189] When H. pylori eradication is achieved, more than 70% of low-grade MALT-type lymphoma regresses at an early stage. Complete histologic remission of lymphoma can be achieved between 2 and 18 months after H. pylori eradication.[162,165,190] In H. pylori–positive patients with localized gastric lymphoma who have no lymph node involvement assessed by EUS, a complete remission can be achieved in 79% of cases. A significant difference in response rate was found between lymphomas restricted to the mucosa and lymphomas involving the deeper layers.[165] Patients who have persistent tumor and are antibiotic failures and those with an H. pylori–negative status could benefit from radiotherapy or radical surgery with curative intent.[191] Patients with advanced age or patients in whom surgery is contraindicated should receive radiotherapy.[169]

Endoscopic Therapy

Present experience using EMR to treat gastric lymphoma is very limited. Toyoda and colleagues[185] reported one patient with low-grade MALT lymphoma diagnosed by EUS and EMR to have a focal high-grade component. The ability of EMR to provide a histologic diagnosis and the confirm the depth of wall layer involvement allowed the appropriate therapy to be instituted (distal subtotal gastrectomy and extended lymph node [D2] dissection with Billroth I anastomosis). In a previous study, low-grade B-cell MALT lymphoma with a focal high-grade component was present in 27 out of 233 (12%) patients. EUS and EMR may prove to be useful for identifying this subset of patients who have a worse postoperative 5-year survival rate than patients who have low-grade MALT lymphoma (80% vs. 96%).[184]

CARCINOID TUMOR

Epidemiology

Epidemiologically, carcinoid tumor is a rare lesion comprising only 0.5% of all malignancies. It is found in fewer than 1% of all cancer autopsy cases, and the approximate incidence is only one to two per 100,000 population.[192,193] The largest epidemiologic series to date indicates that the incidence of gastric carcinoid, as a percentage of the all carcinoid tumors, has increased from 2.25% (1950–1971) to 5.58% (1992–1999).[194] The percentage of gastric carcinoid in relation to all gastric tumors also has increased from 0.4% in the early Surveillance, Epidemiology and End Results (SEER) data (1973–1999) to 1.77% in the late SEER data (1992–1999). However, it is unclear if these findings represent a true increase in the incidence or are a result of increased awareness, more frequent use of endoscopy, or changes in reporting methods.[194]

Pathogenesis

Carcinoid tumors are slow-growing tumors that derive from neuroendocrine cells known as enterochromaffin-like (ECL) cells. The ECL cell is the main endocrine cell type of the corpus-fundus mucosa. ECL cell is known to be highly sensitive to gastrin stimulus and in turn to be able to trigger parietal cell acid secretion by releasing histamine.[195] Gastrin, fibroblast growth factor (FGF), and *H. pylori* all have been shown to have trophic effects on the ECL cell. Potentially, these factors may be relevant in the development of carcinoids.[195,196]

Nearly 67% of carcinoid tumors arise from the GI, with the tracheobronchopulmonary system being the most frequent site for carcinoid formation outside the GI tract.[194] Most carcinoid tumors in the GI tract occur in the small intestines (41.8%), rectum (27.4%), or stomach (8.7%). A slight female predominance for this tumor has been found.[194]

The etiology of carcinoid tumor is unknown. The majority are considered to be due to sporadic somatic mutations, although there have been reports of a familial predisposition to the disease.[197]

Carcinoid tumors have been classified into three types: those associated with chronic atrophic gastritis type A (type 1), those associated with multiple endocrine neoplasia type I (MEN-1) and the Zollinger-Ellison syndrome (type 2), and sporadic gastric carcinoid tumors unaccompanied by hypergastrinemia or any specific gastric pathology (type 3).[198]

Clinical Features

Clinical manifestations of carcinoids tumors are often absent or vague. In approximately 8% to 10% of patients, these tumors present with the carcinoid syndrome (flushing, watery diarrhea, abdominal pain, and wheezing). This syndrome is attributed to secretion of the bioactive mediator serotonin (5-hydroxy-tryptamine) into the systemic circulation from the primary tumor or, more commonly, from metastatic sites.[199]

An association between GI carcinoids and second primary malignancies has been reported with incidence ranging between 12% to 46%.[194,200] In the late SEER subset of data, carcinoid tumors in total were associated with other noncarcinoid tumors in 22.4%. Interestingly, patients with gastric carcinoids had a decrease of 26% in the incidence of additional noncarcinoid neoplasms when the early SEER data (1973–1991) was compared with the late data (1992–1999). This findings prompted the authors to speculate that the decrease might be related to higher identification and removal of these tumors endoscopically.[194] The most common site of second primary malignancy is the GI, which is involved in 32% to 62% of cases, followed by genitourinary (9%–22%) and the lung and bronchial system (9%–13%). Adenocarcinoma of the colon has been reported as the most common second primary malignancy.[201]

It has been speculated that some of the bioactive substances secreted by the carcinoids such as epidermal growth factor, cholecystokinin (CCK), vasoactive intestinal polypeptide (VIP), secretin, bombesin, and gastrin can promote the growth of tumor cells. It is probable that over time, prolonged exposure to such growth factors may promote phenotypic changes in susceptible cells and induce neoplastic transformation.[202]

Metastases from carcinoid tumors have been reported to occur in approximately 29% of patients; the majority (61.2%) originates from the small intestine. After lymph node metastasis (89.9%), the liver is the most frequent site of metastasis (44.1%) followed by lung (13.6%), peritoneum (13.6%), and pancreas (6.8%).[203]

Endoscopic Diagnosis

Endoscopically, gastric carcinoid tumors may be present as polyp-like lesions or more frequently as smooth, rounded, submucosal lesions.[204] The presence of an irregular erythematous depression or ulceration on the lesion has been considered characteristic but not pathognomonic of gastric carcinoids.[205]

Pathology

Type 1 tumors associated with chronic atrophic gastritis type A are the most common type of gastric carcinoids characterized by multiple tumors and hypergastrinemia.[198] The tumors are usually polypoid in appearance, small (<1 cm), and found in the body or fundus of the stomach. Type 1 tumors have a relatively benign course. Nodal involvement is reported in up to 16% of cases and hepatic metastasis is reported in up to 4%.[206,207] Type 2 gastric carcinoids are typically also small lesions, but the adjacent mucosa in nonatrophic. They have a low potential for malignancy. Type 3 carcinoids are usually solitary tumors greater than 2 cm in size. Forty percent are present in the antrum and prepyloric area. There is no hypergastrinemia or chronic gastritis. Type 3 tumors are characterized by deep invasion and high potential for metastasis, even when primary lesions are small.[198,208] Nodal metastasis is present in 55% of patients, and liver metastases are present in 25%. The 5-year survival in only 50%. Histologically, tumors less than 1 cm and/or growth restricted to the mucosa characterize tumors with a benign behavior.[209]

STROMAL CELL TUMOR

Epidemiology

Gastrointestinal stromal tumors (GISTs) are rare; however, they are the most common mesenchymal tumors to arise in the GI tract. According to a population-based sample, the estimated incidence of GISTs is in the vicinity of 10 to 20 per million per year.[210]

The annual incidence in the United States has been estimated to be as high as 5000 to 6000 cases per year.[211] The estimated incidence of malignant GISTs in southern Finland was found to be 4 per million.[212] GISTs rarely occur before age 40 and are slightly more common in men than in women. An association between GISTs and von Recklinghausen's disease has been suggested.[213] GISTs are most commonly located in the stomach (60%), with the remainder being found in the small intestine (20%–25%), colon and rectum (5%), and esophagus (<5%).[211]

Pathogenesis

Morphologically, GISTs are a heterogeneous group of neoplasms that arise anywhere in the GI tract. They represent a family of tumors that probably originates from the intestinal pacemaker cell, also known as the interstitial cell of Cajal (ICC).[214] The ICC serves as a pacemaker system within the muscle layers of the gut and regulates GI motility.[215] In the normal gut, these cells express vimentin, CD34, and CD117. The observation that immunohistochemical staining for several of these markers are identical between ICC and GISTs prompted Kindblom and coworkers[216] to propose that GISTs originate from the ICC or may originate from a pluripotential stem cell. The c-kit protein, or CD117, is now recognized as a very sensitive and specific marker for GI stromal cells.

Clinical Features

Up to one third of patients with GISTs are completely asymptomatic, and tumors are found incidentally during imaging, endoscopic, or surgical procedures being done for unrelated reasons.[210,212] Patients may present with vague symptoms, but the most common manifestations are intestinal bleeding (20%–50%), abdominal pain (40%–50%), or a palpable mass (25%–40%).[212,217] Up to 30% of all GISTs are malignant. The most common site of extraintestinal metastasis is the liver, which is involved in 50% of malignant tumors, followed by lung (10%) and bone (<10%) involvement.[210]

Endoscopic Diagnosis

Most gastric stromal tumors appear as smooth, round, glistening masses covered with normal gastric mucosa. A defect in the overlying mucosa may occur when ulceration and resulting bleeding occur.[217] Endoscopic mucosal biopsies are inadequate to establish the histologic diagnosis in most patients, thus re-emphasizing need for EUS in evaluating suspected GISTs and other subepithelial lesions.

Endoscopic Ultrasonography Diagnosis

Endosonographically, GISTs appear as hypoechoic masses arising from the muscularis propria layer (fourth layer); infrequently, the lesions may originate from the muscularis mucosa layer (second layer).[218] When GISTs are occasionally found in the submucosal (third layer), they are thought to originate from the muscularis propria or the muscularis mucosa with subsequent extension into the submucosa.[219]

EUS features that may help in identifying malignant tumors include size greater than 4 cm, irregular extraluminal borders, and presence of echogenic foci and cystic spaces. If at least two of these three features are present, the sensitivity of EUS for detecting malignancy is 80% to 100%.[220] On the other hand, Palazzo and coworkers[221] found that size less than 3 cm, homogenous echo pattern, and regular margins were 100% specific for benign lesions.

Pathology

The most common histologic variant among gastric GISTs is a cellular, spindle-cell type of tumor consisting of uniform eosinophilic cells. Some of these tumors have a prominent nerve sheath tumor-like nuclear palisading pattern, whereas others show prominent perinuclear vacuolization with moderate to slight interstitial collagen.[211] Malignant GISTs may have a spindled, round cell or epithelioid pattern or a combination of both. Some malignant GISTs histologically resemble leiomyosarcomas, although they usually have a less eosinophilic cytoplasm.[211]

Pathologic features that have been used to predict malignancy include mitotic activity, nuclear pleomorphism, degree of cellularity, nuclear-to-cytoplasmic ratio, tumor size (>5 cm have a high risk), mucosal invasion, ulceration, and tumor necrosis.[222]

Endoscopic Therapy of Submucosal Neoplasms

Submucosal tumors (SMTs) of the stomach are uncommon and are usually found incidentally during endoscopy. These tumors traditionally have been approached in one of two ways:

1. Observation with or without an attempt to make the tissue diagnosis
2. Surgical resection

The advent of EUS has given gastroenterologists the ability to determine the etiology of SMTs noninvasively. Some tumors have EUS characteristics that are so pathognomonic that no additional diagnostic testing is needed. One example is a small lipoma that on EUS demonstrates the classic hyperechoic texture of a lesion arising from the submucosa.[223,224] In other situations, the EUS features alone are not adequate to establish the correct diagnosis. For example, mesenchymal tumors as a group typically arise from the fourth layer of the muscularis propria as a hypoechoic lesion; however, the EUS features alone do not distinguish gastric stromal tumors from other types of mesenchymal tumors. In this situation, cytopathology and immunocytochemistry obtained by EUS-guided FNA are helpful to establish the diagnosis and guide therapy. Of course, patients with symptomatic disease and any SMTs with EUS features suggestive of local invasion will require surgical consideration regardless of FNA results.

A practical problem with EUS-FNA is the fact that small SMTs are often difficult to target. For example, a small leiomyoma with tightly packed spindle cells may not permit adequate sampling using standard techniques. Newly introduced EUS-guided core biopsy needles in theory provide a better tissue sample, but these needles are technically difficult to deploy and often yield suboptimal results and the technique is not feasible for small lesions. In some instances, surgical removal of SMT may be the only practical way to provide a histologic diagnosis and removal may also be curative. On the other hand, small (<1 cm) gastric SMTs rarely involve the lymph nodes, and, in the absence of suspicious EUS characteristics, simple observation and follow-up may be all that is required.

Endoscopic Ultrasonography and High-Frequency Ultrasound Staging

Prior studies have demonstrated the accuracy of EUS for the diagnosis of upper GI tract submucosal lesions.[224] More recently, the efficacy and safety of endoscopic resection of SMTs based on EUS and/or HFUS probe findings also have been reported.[225] Prior reports and unpublished personal experience suggest that 20-MHz HFUS probes are useful for the evaluation of small submucosal lesions before EMR. Lesions larger than 2 cm may require the use of a lower frequency (12 MHz) probe or standard EUS-FNA for cytologic diagnosis and staging.[225]

Endoscopic Mucosal Resection

HFUS probe-assisted EMR has been performed in 26 out of 28 SMTs. A 20-MHz HFUS probe was used to evaluate the lesions and to confirm complete detachment of the lesion from the muscularis propria. All four gastric submucosal lesions (two carcinoids, one heterotopic pancreas, and one fibrovascular polyp) were successfully removed after saline solution injection into the submucosa. Two out of the four (50%) benign gastric lesions involved the lower third of the submucosal (sm3), suggesting that deeply seated submucosal lesions are amenable to EMR therapy. Inability to completely separate the lesion from the muscularis propria by saline solution injection was noted in two rectal submucosal lesions, both of which were incompletely resected. Twenty-one of these lesions were removed by the lift and cut method, and six were removed using the cap technique. No complications occurred. There was no difference in complete resection rate with respect to location of the lesion in the submucosa (sm1, sm2, or sm3).[95] No recurrence was observed during a median follow-up of 21.5 months. These results suggest that even deeply seated benign submucosal lesions (sm3), as delineated by HFUS probe, are equally amenable to complete removal by EMR as mucosal lesions.

More recently, Ichikawa and colleagues[204] have reported on the usefulness of EMR in the management of gastric carcinoid tumors. A total of five patients with type 1 gastric carcinoids underwent successful curative EMR. The depth of invasion was submucosal in three patients and mucosal in two patients by histologic evaluation of the EMR specimens. No evidence of recurrence was found during a mean follow-up of 32.6 months.[204]

Kojima and coworkers[225] also reported on their experience with EMR of SMTs. Twenty-three out of 54 lesions (43%) studied were gastric (10 leiomyomas, 2 lipomas, 6 aberrant pancreas, 1 neurofibroma, 1 neurinoma, 1 leiomyoblastoma, 1 leiomyosarcoma, and 1 granular cell tumor). Eighteen of the 23 (78%) gastric lesions were removed by EMR. The other five patients (22%) had evidence of muscularis propria involvement by EUS and in these patients EMR was used to resect the mucosa and expose the tumor for forceps biopsies. In this series, only one patient had bleeding after gastric EMR; this patient was managed successfully with endoscopic therapy.

Future Trends

In the past decade, we have seen an explosion of technologic advances in the area of therapeutic endoscopy. Our enhanced ability to accurately stage GI neoplasms by using noninvasive or minimally invasive endoscopic techniques has greatly benefited the patient and allowed consideration of nonsurgical options for treating superficial gastric neoplasms. The interventional GI endoscopist is now poised to move beyond the traditional boundaries of endoscopic diagnosis and palliation, to offer curative endoscopic resection for selected patients with gastric neoplasms.

EMR by its very name implies a limitation of the technique to treatment of mucosal disease. More recently, investigators have been pushing the envelope to demonstrate the safety and efficacy of extending endoscopic resection to submucosal lesions, although the cumulative experience to date is still limited.[95,225] Concurrently, preliminary results in animal models indicate that full-thickness endoluminal resection and transluminal endoscopic surgery are technically feasible.[226,227] Successful translation of such innovative techniques into endoscopic practice in the near future will redefine the limits of endoscopic therapy for gastric neoplasms and further blur the boundary between therapeutic endoscopy and surgery.

REFERENCES

1. Okamura T, Tsujitani S, Korenaga D, et al: Lymphadenectomy for cure in patients with early gastric cancer and lymph node metastasis. Am J Surg 155:476–480, 1988.
2. Fujino MA, Morozumi A, Kojima Y, et al: Gastric carcinoma, an endoscopically curable disease. Bildgebung 61(Suppl 1):38–40, 1994.
3. Kojima T, Parra-Blanco A, Takahashi H, Fujita R: Outcome of endoscopic mucosal resection for early gastric cancer: Review of the Japanese literature. Gastrointest Endosc 48:550–554; discussion 554–555, 1998.
4. Sagawa T, Takayama T, Oku T, et al: Argon plasma coagulation for successful treatment of early gastric cancer with intramucosal invasion. Gut 52:334–339, 2003.
5. Spinelli P, Mancini A, Dal Fante M: Endoscopic treatment of gastrointestinal tumors: Indications and results of laser photocoagulation and photodynamic therapy. Semin Surg Oncol 11:307–318, 1995.
6. Howson CP, Hiyama T, Wynder EL: The decline in gastric cancer: Epidemiology of an unplanned triumph. Epidemiol Rev 8:1–27, 1986.
7. Pisani P, Parkin DM, Bray F, Ferlay J: Estimates of the worldwide mortality from 25 cancers in 1990. Int J Cancer 83:18–29, 1999.

8. Parkin DM, Whelan SL, Ferlay J: Cancer Incidence in Five Continents, vol VII. Lyon, International Agency for Research on Cancer, 1997.

9. Haenszel W, Kurihara M: Studies of Japanese migrants. I. Mortality from cancer and other diseases among Japanese in the United States. J Natl Cancer Inst 40:43–68, 1968.

10. Powell J, McConkey CC: The rising trend in oesophageal adenocarcinoma and gastric cardia. Eur J Cancer Prev 1:265–269, 1992.

11. Wiggins CL, Becker TM, Key CR, Samet JM: Stomach cancer among New Mexico's American Indians, Hispanic whites, and non-Hispanic whites. Cancer Res 49:1595–1599, 1989.

12. Allum WH, Powell DJ, McConkey CC, Fielding JW: Gastric cancer: A 25-year review. Br J Surg 76:535–540, 1989.

13. Hundahl SA, Stemmermann GN, Oishi A: Racial factors cannot explain superior Japanese outcomes in stomach cancer. Arch Surg 131:170–175, 1996.

14. Baba H, Maehara Y, Takeuchi H, et al: Effect of lymph node dissection on the prognosis in patients with node-negative early gastric cancer. Surgery 117:165–169, 1995.

15. Hisamichi S: Screening for gastric cancer. World J Surg 13:31–37, 1989.

16. Kampschoer GH, Fujii A, Masuda Y: Gastric cancer detected by mass survey. Comparison between mass survey and outpatient detection. Scand J Gastroenterol 24:813–817, 1989.

17. Jentschura D, Heubner C, Manegold BC, et al: Surgery for early gastric cancer: A European one-center experience. World J Surg 21:845–848; discussion 849, 1997.

18. Hiki Y, Sakakibara Y, Mieno H, et al: Endoscopic treatment of gastric cancer. Surg Endosc 5:11–13, 1991.

19. Roukos DH: Current status and future perspectives in gastric cancer management. Cancer Treat Rev 26:243–255, 2000.

20. Handa Y, Misaka R, Kawaguchi M, Saitoh T: [Clinico-pathological study of Helicobacter pylori in early gastric cancer]. Nippon Rinsho 51:3249–3254, 1993.

21. An international association between Helicobacter pylori infection and gastric cancer. The EUROGAST Study Group. Lancet 341:1359–1362, 1993.

22. Handa Y, Saitoh T, Kawaguchi M, et al: Production of secretory component and pathogenesis of gastric cancer in Helicobacter pylori-infected stomach. J Gastroenterol 34(Suppl 11):37–42, 1999.

23. Nomura A, Stemmermann GN, Chyou PH, et al: Helicobacter pylori infection and gastric carcinoma among Japanese Americans in Hawaii. N Engl J Med 325:1132–1136, 1991.

24. Forman D, Newell DG, Fullerton F, et al: Association between infection with Helicobacter pylori and risk of gastric cancer: Evidence from a prospective investigation. BMJ 302:1302–1305, 1991.

25. Nomura AM, Stemmermann GN, Chyou PH: Gastric cancer among the Japanese in Hawaii. Jpn J Cancer Res 86:916–923, 1995.

26. Danesh J: Helicobacter pylori infection and gastric cancer: Systematic review of the epidemiological studies. Aliment Pharmacol Ther 13:851–856, 1999.

27. Eslick GD, Lim LL, Byles JE, et al: Association of Helicobacter pylori infection with gastric carcinoma: A meta-analysis. Am J Gastroenterol 94:2373–2379, 1999.

28. Siman JH, Forsgren A, Berglund G, Floren CH: Association between Helicobacter pylori and gastric carcinoma in the city of Malmo, Sweden. A prospective study. Scand J Gastroenterol 32:1215–1221, 1997.

29. Uemura N, Okamoto S, Yamamoto S, et al: Helicobacter pylori infection and the development of gastric cancer. N Engl J Med 345:784–789, 2001.

30. Sipponen P, Riihela M, Hyvarinen H, Seppala K: Chronic nonatrophic ('superficial') gastritis increases the risk of gastric carcinoma. A case-control study. Scand J Gastroenterol 29:336–340, 1994.

31. Valle J, Kekki M, Sipponen P, et al: Long-term course and consequences of Helicobacter pylori gastritis. Results of a 32-year follow-up study. Scand J Gastroenterol 31:546–550, 1996.

32. Sipponen P, Kekki M, Haapakoski J, et al: Gastric cancer risk in chronic atrophic gastritis: Statistical calculations of cross-sectional data. Int J Cancer 35:173–177, 1985.

33. Ponzetto A, Soldati T, De Giuli M: Helicobacter pylori screening and gastric cancer. Lancet 348:758, 1996.

34. Parsonnet J: Helicobacter pylori in the stomach—a paradox unmasked. N Engl J Med 335:278–280, 1996.

35. Molloy RM, Sonnenberg A: Relation between gastric cancer and previous peptic ulcer disease. Gut 40:247–252, 1997.

36. Hansson LE, Nyren O, Hsing AW, et al: The risk of stomach cancer in patients with gastric or duodenal ulcer disease. N Engl J Med 335:242–249, 1996.

37. Hole DJ, Quigley EM, Gillis CR, Watkinson G: Peptic ulcer and cancer: An examination of the relationship between chronic peptic ulcer and gastric carcinoma. Scand J Gastroenterol 22:17–23, 1987.

38. Kono S, Hirohata T: [A review of gastric cancer and life style]. Gan No Rinsho Spec No:257–267, 1990.

39. Neugut AI, Hayek M, Howe G: Epidemiology of gastric cancer. Semin Oncol 23:281–291, 1996.

40. Blot WJ, Li JY, Taylor PR, et al: Nutrition intervention trials in Linxian, China: Supplementation with specific vitamin/mineral combinations, cancer incidence, and disease-specific mortality in the general population. J Natl Cancer Inst 85:1483–1492, 1993.

41. Hansson LE, Nyren O, Bergstrom R, et al: Diet and risk of gastric cancer. A population-based case-control study in Sweden. Int J Cancer 55:181–189, 1993.

42. Ramon JM, Serra L, Cerdo C, Oromi J: Dietary factors and gastric cancer risk. A case-control study in Spain. Cancer 71:1731–1735, 1993.

43. Buiatti E, Palli D, Decarli A, et al: A case-control study of gastric cancer and diet in Italy. Int J Cancer 44:611–616, 1989.

44. Hasegawa R, Futakuchi M, Mizoguchi Y, et al: Studies of initiation and promotion of carcinogenesis by N-nitroso compounds. Cancer Lett 123:185–191, 1998.

45. Buiatti E, Palli D, Decarli A, et al: A case-control study of gastric cancer and diet in Italy: II. Association with nutrients. Int J Cancer 45:896–901, 1990.

46. Gonzalez CA, Riboli E, Badosa J, et al: Nutritional factors and gastric cancer in Spain. Am J Epidemiol 139:466–473, 1994.

47. La Vecchia C, Ferraroni M, D'Avanzo B, et al: Selected micronutrient intake and the risk of gastric cancer. Cancer Epidemiol Biomarkers Prev 3:393–398, 1994.

48. Hansson LE, Nyren O, Bergstrom R, et al: Nutrients and gastric cancer risk. A population-based case-control study in Sweden. Int J Cancer 57:638–644, 1994.

49. Dixon MF: Commentary: Role of Helicobacter pylori on gastric mucosal damage, gastric cancer, and gastric MALT lymphoma. Gastroenterology 113(6 Suppl):S65–66, 1997.

50. Banatvala N, Feldman R: The epidemiology of Helicobacter pylori: Missing pieces in a jigsaw. Commun Dis Rep CDR Rev 3:R56–59, 1993.

51. Webb PM, Forman D: Helicobacter pylori as a risk factor for cancer. Baillieres Clin Gastroenterol 9:563–582, 1995.

52. Stalnikowicz R, Benbassat J: Risk of gastric cancer after gastric surgery for benign disorders. Arch Intern Med 150:2022–2026, 1990.

53. Fisher SG, Davis F, Nelson R, et al: A cohort study of stomach cancer risk in men after gastric surgery for benign disease. J Natl Cancer Inst 85:1303–1310, 1993.

54. Stolte M: Clinical consequences of the endoscopic diagnosis of gastric polyps. Endoscopy 27:32–37; discussion 59–60, 1995.

55. Attard TM, Giardiello FM, Argani P, Cuffari C: Fundic gland polyposis with high-grade dysplasia in a child with attenuated familial adenomatous polyposis and familial gastric cancer. J Pediatr Gastroenterol Nutr 32:215–218, 2001.

56. Hofgartner WT, Thorp M, Ramus MW, et al: Gastric adenocarcinoma associated with fundic gland polyps in a patient with attenuated familial adenomatous polyposis. Am J Gastroenterol 94:2275–2281, 1999.

57. Benatti P, Sassatelli R, Roncucci L, et al: Tumour spectrum in hereditary non-polyposis colorectal cancer (HNPCC) and in families with "suspected HNPCC". A population-based study in northern Italy. Colorectal Cancer Study Group. Int J Cancer 54:371–377, 1993.

58. Nakamura T, Nakano G: Histopathological classification and malignant change in gastric polyps. J Clin Pathol 38:754–764, 1985.

59. La Vecchia C, Negri E, Franceschi S, Gentile A: Family history and the risk of stomach and colorectal cancer. Cancer 70:50–55, 1992.

60. Stamatakis JD: Menetrier's disease and carcinoma of stomach. Proc R Soc Med 69:264–265, 1976.

61. Bigalke KH, Dahm HH, Schiemoller M: [Menetrier's disease and carcinoma]. Med Welt 28:1103–1106, 1977.

62. Ho SB: Premalignant lesions of the stomach. Semin Gastrointest Dis 7:61–73, 1996.

63. Brinton LA, Gridley G, Hrubec Z, et al: Cancer risk following pernicious anaemia. Br J Cancer 59:810–813, 1989.

64. Hsing AW, Hansson LE, McLaughlin JK, et al: Pernicious anemia and subsequent cancer. A population-based cohort study. Cancer 71:745–750, 1993.

65. Sjoblom SM, Sipponen P, Jarvinen H: Gastroscopic follow up of pernicious anaemia patients. Gut 34:28–32, 1993.

66. Hansson LE, Baron J, Nyren O, et al: Tobacco, alcohol and the risk of gastric cancer. A population-based case-control study in Sweden. Int J Cancer 57:26–31, 1994.

67. Nomura AM, Hankin JH, Kolonel LN, et al: Case-control study of diet and other risk factors for gastric cancer in Hawaii (United States). Cancer Causes Control 14:547–558, 2003.

68. Stemmermann GN, Nomura AM, Chyou PH, Hankin J: Impact of diet and smoking on risk of developing intestinal metaplasia of the stomach. Dig Dis Sci 35:433–438, 1990.

69. Rhyu MG, Park WS, Jung YJ, et al: Allelic deletions of MCC/APC and p53 are frequent late events in human gastric carcinogenesis. Gastroenterology 106:1584–1588, 1994.

70. Sano T, Tsujino T, Yoshida K, et al: Frequent loss of heterozygosity on chromosomes 1q, 5q, and 17p in human gastric carcinomas. Cancer Res 51:2926–2931, 1991.

71. Kawanishi J, Kato J, Sasaki K, et al: Loss of E-cadherin-dependent cell-cell adhesion due to mutation of the beta-catenin gene in a human cancer cell line, HSC-39. Mol Cell Biol 15:1175–1181, 1995.

72. Mayer B, Johnson JP, Leitl F, et al: E-cadherin expression in primary and metastatic gastric cancer: Down-regulation correlates with cellular dedifferentiation and glandular disintegration. Cancer Res 53:1690–1695, 1993,

73. Rhyu MG, Park WS, Meltzer SJ: Microsatellite instability occurs frequently in human gastric carcinoma. Oncogene 9:29–32, 1994.

74. Werther JL, Rivera-MacMurray S, Bruckner H, et al: Mucin-associated sialosyl-Tn antigen expression in gastric cancer correlates with an adverse outcome. Br J Cancer 69:613–616, 1994.

75. Yonemura Y, Ninomiya I, Tsugawa K, et al: Prognostic significance of c-erbB-2 gene expression in the poorly differentiated type of adenocarcinoma of the stomach. Cancer Detect Prev 22:139–146, 1998.

76. Guilford P, Hopkins J, Harraway J, et al: E-cadherin germline mutations in familial gastric cancer. Nature 392:402–405, 1998.

77. Guilford PJ, Hopkins JB, Grady WM, et al: E-cadherin germline mutations define an inherited cancer syndrome dominated by diffuse gastric cancer. Hum Mutat 14:249–255, 1999.

78. Colombo E, Giorgi S, Sonzini E, et al: Disseminated intravascular coagulation and bone marrow metastases as presenting manifestations of gastric carcinoma. Haematologica 70:187, 1985.

79. Tonouchi H, Miki C, Masato K: [Gastric cancer associated with dermatomyositis accompanied by photoallergy]. Gan To Kagaku Ryoho 28:689–691, 2001.

80. Owens DA: Diagnostic Surgical Pathology. Philadelphia, Lippincott Williams & Wilkins, 1999.

81. Lauren P: The two histological main types of gastric carcinoma: Diffuse and so-called intestinal type. Acta Pathol Microbiol Immunol Scand 64:31–49, 1965.

82. Blot WJ, Devesa SS, Kneller RW, Fraumeni JF Jr: Rising incidence of adenocarcinoma of the esophagus and gastric cardia. JAMA 265:1287–1289, 1991.

83. Fuchs CS, Mayer RJ: Gastric carcinoma. N Engl J Med 333:32–41, 1995.

84. Kelly S, Harris KM, Berry E, et al: A systematic review of the staging performance of endoscopic ultrasound in gastro-oesophageal carcinoma. Gut 49:534–539, 2001.

85. Noguchi Y, Imada T, Matsumoto A, et al: Radical surgery for gastric cancer. A review of the Japanese experience. Cancer 64:2053–2062, 1989.

86. Sano T, Kobori O, Muto T: Lymph node metastasis from early gastric cancer: Endoscopic resection of tumour. Br J Surg 79:241–244, 1992.

87. Yamao T, Shirao K, Ono H, et al: Risk factors for lymph node metastasis from intramucosal gastric carcinoma. Cancer 77:602–606, 1996.

88. Japanese Classification of Gastric Carcinoma. Tokyo, Kanehara and Co., Ltd, 1995.

89. Akahoshi K, Misawa T, Fujishima H, et al: Preoperative evaluation of gastric cancer by endoscopic ultrasound. Gut 32:479–482, 1991.

90. Rice TW, Boyce GA, Sivak MV, et al: Esophageal carcinoma: Esophageal ultrasound assessment of preoperative chemotherapy. Ann Thorac Surg 53:972–977, 1992.

91. Dittler HJ, Siewert JR: Role of endoscopic ultrasonography in gastric carcinoma. Endoscopy 25:162–166, 1993.

92. Ohashi S, Nakazawa S, Yoshino J: Endoscopic ultrasonography in the assessment of invasive gastric cancer. Scand J Gastroenterol 24:1039–1048, 1989.

93. Akahoshi K, Chijiwa Y, Hamada S, et al: Pretreatment staging of endoscopically early gastric cancer with a 15 MHz ultrasound catheter probe. Gastrointest Endosc 48:470–476, 1998.

94. Wiersema MJ, Vilmann P, Giovannini M, et al: Endosonography-guided fine-needle aspiration biopsy: Diagnostic accuracy and complication assessment. Gastroenterology 112:1087–1095, 1997.

95. Waxman I, Saitoh Y, Raju GS, et al: High-frequency probe EUS-assisted endoscopic mucosal resection: A therapeutic strategy for submucosal tumors of the GI tract. Gastrointest Endosc 55:44–49, 2002.

96. Hunerbein M, Ghadimi BM, Haensch W, Schlag PM: Transendoscopic ultrasound of esophageal and gastric cancer using miniaturized ultrasound catheter probes. Gastrointest Endosc 48:371–375, 1998.

97. Maruta S, Tsukamoto Y, Niwa Y, et al: Evaluation of upper gastrointestinal tumors with a new endoscopic ultrasound probe. Gastrointest Endosc 40:603–608, 1994.

98. Kida M, Tanabe S, Watanabe M, et al: Staging of gastric cancer with endoscopic ultrasonography and endoscopic mucosal resection. Endoscopy 30(Suppl 1):A64–68, 1998.

99. Yanai H, Tada M, Karita M, Okita K: Diagnostic utility of 20-megahertz linear endoscopic ultrasonography in early gastric cancer. Gastrointest Endosc 44:29–33, 1996.

100. Waxman I, Saitoh Y: Clinical outcome of endoscopic mucosal resection for superficial GI lesions and the role of high-frequency US probe sonography in an American population. Gastrointest Endosc 52:322–327, 2000.

101. Akahoshi K, Chijiiwa Y, Sasaki I, et al: Pre-operative TN staging of gastric cancer using a 15 MHz ultrasound miniprobe. Br J Radiol 70:703–707, 1997.

102. Rembacken BJ, Gotoda T, Fujii T, Axon AT: Endoscopic mucosal resection. Endoscopy 33:709–718, 2001.

103. Inoue H, Tani M, Nagai K, et al: Treatment of esophageal and gastric tumors. Endoscopy 31:47–55, 1999.

104. Shim CS: Endoscopic mucosal resection. J Korean Med Sci 11:457–466, 1996.

105. Hirao M, Masuda K, Asanuma T, et al: Endoscopic resection of early gastric cancer and other tumors with local injection of hypertonic saline-epinephrine. Gastrointest Endosc 34:264–269, 1988.

106. Yamamoto H, Yube T, Isoda N, et al: A novel method of endoscopic mucosal resection using sodium hyaluronate. Gastrointest Endosc 50:251–256, 1999.

107. Karita M, Tada M, Okita K, Kodama T: Endoscopic therapy for early colon cancer: The strip biopsy resection technique. Gastrointest Endosc 37:128–132, 1991.

108. Tada M, Murakami A, Karita M, et al: Endoscopic resection of early gastric cancer. Endoscopy 25:445–450, 1993.

109. Takekoshi T, Baba Y, Ota H, et al: Endoscopic resection of early gastric carcinoma: Results of a retrospective analysis of 308 cases. Endoscopy 26:352–358, 1994.

110. Suzuki Y, Hiraishi H, Kanke K, et al: Treatment of gastric tumors by endoscopic mucosal resection with a ligating device. Gastrointest Endosc 49:192–199, 1999.

111. Suzuki H: Endoscopic mucosal resection using ligating device for early gastric cancer. Gastrointest Endosc Clin N Am 11:511–518, 2001.

112. Ell C, May A, Gossner L, et al: Endoscopic mucosal resection of early cancer and high-grade dysplasia in Barrett's esophagus. Gastroenterology 118:670–677, 2000.

113. Inoue H, Takeshita K, Hori H, et al: Endoscopic mucosal resection with a cap-fitted panendoscope for esophagus, stomach, and colon mucosal lesions. Gastrointest Endosc 39:58–62, 1993.

114. Tada M, Inoue H, Yabata E, et al: Feasibility of the transparent cap-fitted colonoscope for screening and mucosal resection. Dis Colon Rectum 40:618–621, 1997.

115. Tani M, Sakai P, Kondo H: Endoscopic mucosal resection of superficial cancer in the stomach using the cap technique. Endoscopy 35:348–355, 2003.

116. Matsuzaki K, Nagao S, Kawaguchi A, et al: Newly designed soft prelooped cap for endoscopic mucosal resection of gastric lesions. Gastrointest Endosc 57:242–246, 2003.

117. Yamamoto H, Kawata H, Sunada K, et al: Successful en-bloc resection of large superficial tumors in the stomach and colon using sodium hyaluronate and small-caliber-tip transparent hood. Endoscopy 35:690–694, 2003.

118. Ono H, Kondo H, Gotoda T, et al: Endoscopic mucosal resection for treatment of early gastric cancer. Gut 48:225–229, 2001.

119. Kitamura K, Yamaguchi T, Okamoto K, et al: Clinicopathologic features of synchronous multifocal early gastric cancers. Anticancer Res 17:643–646, 1997.

120. Tanabe S, Koizumi W, Mitomi H, et al: Clinical outcome of endoscopic aspiration mucosectomy for early stage gastric cancer. Gastrointest Endosc 56:708–713, 2002.

121. Amano Y, Ishihara S, Amano K, et al: An assessment of local curability of endoscopic surgery in early gastric cancer without satisfaction of current therapeutic indications. Endoscopy 30:548–552, 1998.

122. Hamada T, Kondo K, Itagaki Y, Nishida J: [Endoscopic mucosal resection for early gastric cancer]. Nippon Rinsho 54:1292–1297, 1996.

123. Mizumoto S, Misumi A, Harada K, et al: [Evaluation of endoscopic mucosal resection (EMR) as a curative therapy against early gastric cancer]. Nippon Geka Gakkai Zasshi 93:1071–1074, 1992.

124. Okano A, Hajiro K, Takakuwa H, et al: Predictors of bleeding after endoscopic mucosal resection of gastric tumors. Gastrointest Endosc 57:687–690, 2003.

125. Ahmad NA, Kochman ML, Long WB, et al: Efficacy, safety, and clinical outcomes of endoscopic mucosal resection: A study of 101 cases. Gastrointest Endosc 55:390–396, 2002.

126. Tsunada S, Ogata S, Ohyama T, et al: Endoscopic closure of perforations caused by EMR in the stomach by application of metallic clips. Gastrointest Endosc 57:948–951, 2003.

127. Waye JD: Management of complications of colonoscopic polypectomy. Gastroenterologist 1:158–164, 1993.

128. Katada C, Muto M, Manabe T, et al: Esophageal stenosis after endoscopic mucosal resection of superficial esophageal lesions. Gastrointest Endosc 57:165–169, 2003.

129. Ohmura K, Nagashima R, Takeda H, Takahashi T: Temporary stenting with metallic endoprosthesis for refractory esophageal stricture secondary to cylindrical resection of carcinoma. Gastrointest Endosc 48:214–217, 1998.

130. Sliney DH: Laser safety. Lasers Surg Med 16:215–225, 1995.

131. Polanyi TG: Physics of surgery with lasers. Clin Chest Med 6:179–202, 1985.

132. Polanyi TG: Laser physics. Otolaryngol Clin North Am 16:753–774, 1983.

133. Hiki Y, Shimao J, Yamao Y, et al: The concepts, procedures, and problems related in endoscopic laser therapy of early gastric cancer. A retrospective study on early gastric cancer. Surg Endosc 3:1–6, 1989.

134. Patrice T, Foultier MT, Yactayo S, et al: Endoscopic photodynamic therapy with hematoporphyrin derivative for primary treatment of gastrointestinal neoplasms in inoperable patients. Dig Dis Sci 35:545–552, 1990.

135. Overholt BF, Panjehpour M, Halberg DL: Photodynamic therapy for Barrett's esophagus with dysplasia and/or early stage carcinoma: Long-term results. Gastrointest Endosc 58:183–188, 2003.

136. Sibille A, Descamps C, Jonard P, et al: Endoscopic Nd:YAG treatment of superficial gastric carcinoma: Experience in 18 Western inoperable patients. Gastrointest Endosc 42:340–345, 1995.

137. Mathus-Vliegen EM, Tytgat GN: Analysis of failures and complications of neodymium: YAG laser photocoagulation in gastrointestinal tract tumors. A retrospective survey of 18 years' experience. Endoscopy 22:17–23, 1990.

138. Nakamura H, Yanai H, Nishikawa J, et al: Experience with photodynamic therapy (endoscopic laser therapy) for the treatment of early gastric cancer. Hepatogastroenterology 48:1599–1603, 2001.

139. Hiki Y, Shimao H, Mieno H, et al: Modified treatment of early gastric cancer: Evaluation of endoscopic treatment of early gastric cancers with respect to treatment indication groups. World J Surg 19:517–522, 1995.

140. Mathus-Vliegen EM, Tytgat GN: Laser photocoagulation in the palliative treatment of upper digestive tract tumors. Cancer 57:396–399, 1986.

141. Fleischer D, Sivak MV Jr: Endoscopic Nd:YAG laser therapy as palliation for esophagogastric cancer. Parameters affecting initial outcome. Gastroenterology 89:827–831, 1985.

142. Fleischer D, Sivak MV: Endoscopic Nd:YAG laser therapy as palliative treatment for advanced adenocarcinoma of the gastric cardia. Gastroenterology 87:815–820, 1984.

143. Sargeant IR, Loizou LA, Tobias JS, et al: Radiation enhancement of laser palliation for malignant dysphagia: A pilot study. Gut 33:1597–1601, 1992.

144. Sargeant IR, Tobias JS, Blackman G, et al: Radiotherapy enhances laser palliation of malignant dysphagia: A randomised study. Gut 40:362–369, 1997.

145. Spencer GM, Thorpe SM, Blackman GM, et al: Laser augmented by brachytherapy versus laser alone in the palliation of adenocarcinoma of the oesophagus and cardia: A randomised study. Gut 50:224–227, 2002.

146. Canard JM, Vedrenne B: Clinical application of argon plasma coagulation in gastrointestinal endoscopy: Has the time come to replace the laser? Endoscopy 33:353–357, 2001.

147. Wahab PJ, Mulder CJ, den Hartog G, Thies JE: Argon plasma coagulation in flexible gastrointestinal endoscopy: Pilot experiences. Endoscopy 29:176–181, 1997.

148. Grund KE, Storek D, Zindel C, Becker HD: [Highly flexible self-expanding metal mesh stents: A new kind of palliative therapy of malignant dysphagia]. Z Gastroenterol 33:392–398, 1995.

149. Choi YB: Laparoscopic gastrojejunostomy for palliation of gastric outlet obstruction in unresectable gastric cancer. Surg Endosc 16:1620–1626, 2002.

150. Khulusi S, Morris T: Endoscopic palliation of gastrointestinal malignancy. Eur J Gastroenterol Hepatol 12:397–402, 2000.

151. Sihvo EI, Pentikainen T, Luostarinen ME, et al: Inoperable adenocarcinoma of the oesophagogastric junction: A comparative clinical study of laser coagulation versus self-expanding metallic stents with special reference to cost analysis. Eur J Surg Oncol 28:711–715, 2002.

152. Chan AC, Shin FG, Lam YH, et al: A comparison study on physical properties of self-expandable esophageal metal stents. Gastrointest Endosc 49:462–465, 1999.

153. Maetani I, Tada T, Shimura J, et al: Technical modifications and strategies for stenting gastric outlet strictures using esophageal endoprostheses. Endoscopy 34:402–406, 2002.

154. Kim JH, Yoo BM, Lee KJ, et al: Self-expanding coil stent with a long delivery system for palliation of unresectable malignant gastric outlet obstruction: A prospective study. Endoscopy 33:838–842, 2001.

155. Baron TH, Harewood GC: Enteral self-expandable stents. Gastrointest Endosc 58:421–433, 2003.

156. Gurney KA, Cartwright RA, Gilman EA: Descriptive epidemiology of gastrointestinal non-Hodgkin's lymphoma in a population-based registry. Br J Cancer 79:1929–1934, 1999.

157. Severson RK, Davis S: Increasing incidence of primary gastric lymphoma. Cancer 66:1283–1287, 1990.

158. Zaki M, Schubert ML: Helicobacter pylori and gastric lymphoma. Gastroenterology 108:610–612, 1995.

159. Fagioli F, Rigolin GM, Cuneo A, et al: Primary gastric lymphoma: Distribution and clinical relevance of different epidemiological factors. Haematologica 79:213–217, 1994.

160. Wotherspoon AC, Doglioni C, Diss TC, et al: Regression of primary low-grade B-cell gastric lymphoma of mucosa-associated lymphoid tissue type after eradication of Helicobacter pylori. Lancet 342:575–577, 1993.

161. Parsonnet J, Hansen S, Rodriguez L, et al: Helicobacter pylori infection and gastric lymphoma. N Engl J Med 330:1267–1271, 1994.

162. Steinbach G, Ford R, Glober G, et al: Antibiotic treatment of gastric lymphoma of mucosa-associated lymphoid tissue. An uncontrolled trial. Ann Intern Med 131:88–95, 1999.

163. Zucca E, Bertoni F, Roggero E, Cavalli F: The gastric marginal zone B-cell lymphoma of MALT type. Blood 96:410–419, 2000.

164. Newton R, Ferlay J, Beral V, Devesa SS: The epidemiology of non-Hodgkin's lymphoma: Comparison of nodal and extra-nodal sites. Int J Cancer 72:923–930, 1997.

165. Ruskone-Fourmestraux A, Lavergne A, Aegerter PH, et al: Predictive factors for regression of gastric MALT lymphoma after anti-Helicobacter pylori treatment. Gut 48:297–303, 2001.

166. Morgner A, Lehn N, Andersen LP, et al: Helicobacter heilmanii-associated primary gastric low-grade MALT lymphoma: Complete remission after curing the infection. Gastroenterology 118:821–828, 2000.

167. Royer B, Cazals-Hatem D, Sibilia J, et al: Lymphomas in patients with Sjögren's syndrome are marginal zone B-cell neoplasms, arise in diverse extranodal and nodal sites, and are not associated with viruses. Blood 90:766–775, 1997.

168. Xu WS, Ho FC, Ho J, et al: Pathogenesis of gastric lymphoma: The enigma in Hong Kong. Ann Oncol 8(Suppl 2):41–44, 1997.

169. Ruskone-Fourmestraux A, Rambaud JC: Gastrointestinal lymphoma: Prevention and treatment of early lesions. Best Pract Res Clin Gastroenterol 15:337–354, 2001.

170. Taal BG, Boot H, van Heerde P, et al: Primary non-Hodgkin lymphoma of the stomach: Endoscopic pattern and prognosis in low versus high grade malignancy in relation to the MALT concept. Gut 39:556–561, 1996.

171. Strecker P, Eck M, Greiner A, et al: [Diagnostic value of stomach biopsy in comparison with surgical specimen in gastric B-cell lymphomas of the MALT type]. Pathologe 19:209–213, 1998.

172. Suekane H, Iida M, Yao T, et al: Endoscopic ultrasonography in primary gastric lymphoma: Correlation with endoscopic and histologic findings. Gastrointest Endosc 39:139–145, 1993.

173. Palazzo L, Roseau G, Ruskone-Fourmestraux A, et al: Endoscopic ultrasonography in the local staging of primary gastric lymphoma. Endoscopy 25:502–508, 1993.

174. Lugering N, Menzel J, Kucharzik T, et al: Impact of miniprobes compared to conventional endosonography in the staging of low-grade gastric malt lymphoma. Endoscopy 33:832–837, 2001.

175. Ribeiro A, Vazquez-Sequeiros E, Wiersema LM, et al: EUS-guided fine-needle aspiration combined with flow cytometry and immunocytochemistry in the diagnosis of lymphoma. Gastrointest Endosc 53:485–491, 2001.

176. Magrath I: Introduction: Concepts and controversies in lymphoid neoplasias. In Magrath I (ed): The Non-Hodgkin's Lymphomas, 2nd ed. London, Arnold, 1997, pp 3–47.

177. Montalban C, Castrillo JM, Abraira V, et al: Gastric B-cell mucosa-associated lymphoid tissue (MALT) lymphoma. Clinicopathological study and evaluation of the prognostic factors in 143 patients. Ann Oncol 6:355–362, 1995.

178. Fischbach W, Kestel W, Kirchner T, et al: Malignant lymphomas of the upper gastrointestinal tract. Results of a prospective study in 103 patients. Cancer 70:1075–1080, 1992.

179. Cogliatti SB, Schmid U, Schumacher U, et al: Primary B-cell gastric lymphoma: A clinicopathological study of 145 patients. Gastroenterology 101:1159–1170, 1991.

180. Hussell T, Isaacson PG, Crabtree JE, Spencer J: Helicobacter pylori-specific tumour-infiltrating T cells provide contact dependent help for the growth of malignant B cells in low-grade gastric lymphoma of mucosa-associated lymphoid tissue. J Pathol 178:122–127, 1996.

181. Jaffe ES, Harris NL, Diebold J, Muller-Hermelink HK: World Health Organization classification of neoplastic diseases of the hematopoietic and lymphoid tissues. A progress report. Am J Clin Pathol 111(1 Suppl 1):S8–12, 1999.

182. de Jong D, Boot H, van Heerde P, et al: Histological grading in gastric lymphoma: Pretreatment criteria and clinical relevance. Gastroenterology 112:1466–1474, 1997.

183. Isaacson PG: Gastrointestinal lymphomas of T- and B-cell types. Mod Pathol 12:151–158, 1999.

184. Nakamura S, Akazawa K, Yao T, Tsuneyoshi M: A clinicopathologic study of 233 cases with special reference to evaluation with the MIB-1 index. Cancer 76:1313–1324, 1995.

185. Toyoda H, Ono T, Kiyose M, et al: Gastric mucosa-associated lymphoid tissue lymphoma with a focal high-grade component diagnosed by EUS and endoscopic mucosal resection for histologic evaluation. Gastrointest Endosc 51:752–755, 2000.

186. Lin JI, Tseng CH, Chow S, et al: Coexisting malignant lymphoma and adenocarcinoma of the stomach. South Med J 72:619–622, 1979.

187. Kelly SM, Geraghty JM, Neale G: H pylori, gastric carcinoma, and MALT lymphoma. Lancet 343:418, 1994.

188. Kanamoto K, Aoyagi K, Nakamura S, et al: Simultaneous coexistence of early adenocarcinoma and low-grade MALT lymphoma of the stomach associated with Helicobacter pylori infection: A case report. Gastrointest Endosc 47:73–75, 1998.

189. Isaacson PG, Diss TC, Wotherspoon AC, et al: Long-term follow-up of gastric MALT lymphoma treated by eradication of H. pylori with antibodies. Gastroenterology 117:750–751, 1999.

190. Neubauer A, Thiede C, Morgner A, et al: Cure of Helicobacter pylori infection and duration of remission of low-grade gastric mucosa-associated lymphoid tissue lymphoma. J Natl Cancer Inst 89:1350–1355, 1997.

191. Radaszkiewicz T, Dragosics B, Bauer P: Gastrointestinal malignant lymphomas of the mucosa-associated lymphoid tissue: Factors relevant to prognosis. Gastroenterology 102:1628–1638, 1992.

192. Richardson CT, Walsh JH: The value of a histamine H2-receptor antagonist in the management of patients with the Zollinger-Ellison syndrome. N Engl J Med 294:133–135, 1976.

193. Oberg K: State of the art and future prospects in the management of neuroendocrine tumors. Q J Nucl Med 44:3–12, 2000.

194. Modlin IM, Lye KD, Kidd M: A 5-decade analysis of 13,715 carcinoid tumors. Cancer 97:934–959, 2003.

195. Hakanson R, Tielemans Y, Chen D, et al: The biology and pathobiology of the ECL cells. Yale J Biol Med 65:761–774; discussion 827–829, 1992.

196. Kidd M, Miu K, Tang LH, et al: Helicobacter pylori lipopolysaccharide stimulates histamine release and DNA synthesis in rat enterochromaffin-like cells. Gastroenterology 113:1110–1117, 1997.

197. Yeatman TJ, Sharp JV, Kimura AK: Can susceptibility to carcinoid tumors be inherited? Cancer 63:390–393, 1989.

198. Rindi G, Bordi C, Rappel S, et al: Gastric carcinoids and neuroendocrine carcinomas: Pathogenesis, pathology, and behavior. World J Surg 20:168–172, 1996.

199. Soga J, Yakuwa Y, Osaka M: Carcinoid syndrome: A statistical evaluation of 748 reported cases. J Exp Clin Cancer Res 18:133–141, 1999.

200. Sandor A, Modlin IM: A retrospective analysis of 1570 appendiceal carcinoids. Am J Gastroenterol 93:422–428, 1998.

201. Godwin JD 2nd: Carcinoid tumors. An analysis of 2,837 cases. Cancer 36:560–569, 1975.

202. Oberg K: Expression of growth factors and their receptors in neuroendocrine gut and pancreatic tumors, and prognostic factors for survival. Ann N Y Acad Sci 733:46–55, 1994.

203. Berge T, Linell F: Carcinoid tumours. Frequency in a defined population during a 12-year period. Acta Pathol Microbiol Scand [A] 84:322–330, 1976.

204. Ichikawa J, Tanabe S, Koizumi W, et al: Endoscopic mucosal resection in the management of gastric carcinoid tumors. Endoscopy 35:203–206, 2003.

205. Nakamura S, Iida M, Yao T, Fujishima M: Endoscopic features of gastric carcinoids. Gastrointest Endosc 37:535–538, 1991.

206. Ahlman H, Kolby L, Lundell L, et al: Clinical management of gastric carcinoid tumors. Digestion 55(Suppl 3):77–85, 1994.

207. Borch K: Atrophic gastritis and gastric carcinoid tumours. Ann Med 21:291–297, 1989.

208. Rindi G, Luinetti O, Cornaggia M, et al: Three subtypes of gastric argyrophil carcinoid and the gastric neuroendocrine carcinoma: A clinicopathologic study. Gastroenterology 104:994–1006, 1993.

209. Rindi G, Azzoni C, La Rosa S, et al: ECL cell tumor and poorly differentiated endocrine carcinoma of the stomach: Prognostic evaluation by pathological analysis. Gastroenterology 116:532–542, 1999.

210. Miettinen M, Sarlomo-Rikala M, Lasota J: Gastrointestinal stromal tumors: Recent advances in understanding of their biology. Hum Pathol 30:1213–1220, 1999.

211. Miettinen M, Lasota J: Gastrointestinal stromal tumors—definition, clinical, histological, immunohistochemical, and molecular genetic features and differential diagnosis. Virchows Arch 438:1–12, 2001.

212. Miettinen M, Sarlomo-Rikala M, Lasota J: Gastrointestinal stromal tumours. Ann Chir Gynaecol 87:278–281, 1998.

213. Schaldenbrand JD, Appelman HD: Solitary solid stromal gastrointestinal tumors in von Recklinghausen's disease with minimal smooth muscle differentiation. Hum Pathol 15:229–232, 1984.

214. Sircar K, Hewlett BR, Huizinga JD, et al: Interstitial cells of Cajal as precursors of gastrointestinal stromal tumors. Am J Surg Pathol 23:377–389, 1999.

215. Sanders KM: A case for interstitial cells of Cajal as pacemakers and mediators of neurotransmission in the gastrointestinal tract. Gastroenterology 111:492–515, 1996.

216. Kindblom LG, Remotti HE, Aldenborg F, Meis-Kindblom JM: Gastrointestinal pacemaker cell tumor (GIPACT): Gastrointestinal stromal tumors show phenotypic characteristics of the interstitial cells of Cajal. Am J Pathol 152:1259–1269, 1998.

217. Davis GB, Blanchard DK, Hatch GF 3rd, et al: Tumors of the stomach. World J Surg 24:412–420, 2000.

218. Tio TL, Tytgat GN, den Hartog Jager FC: Endoscopic ultrasonography for the evaluation of smooth muscle tumors in the upper gastrointestinal tract: An experience with 42 cases. Gastrointest Endosc 36:342–350, 1990.

219. Savides TJ: Gastrointestinal submucosal masses. In Gress F, Bhattacharya I (eds): Endoscopic Ultrasonography. Malden, MA, Blackwell Science, 2001, pp 92–102.

220. Chak A, Canto MI, Reosch T, et al: Endosonographic differentiation of benign and malignant stromal cell tumors. Gastrointest Endosc 45:468–473, 1997.

221. Palazzo L, Landi B, Cellier C, et al: Endosonographic features predictive of benign and malignant gastrointestinal stromal cell tumours. Gut 46:88–92, 2000.

222. Franquemont DW: Differentiation and risk assessment of gastrointestinal stromal tumors. Am J Clin Pathol 103:41–47, 1995.

223. Nakamura S, Iida M, Suekane H, et al: Endoscopic removal of gastric lipoma: Diagnostic value of endoscopic ultrasonography. Am J Gastroenterol 86:619–621, 1991.

224. Boyce GA, Sivak MV Jr, Rosch T, et al: Evaluation of submucosal upper gastrointestinal tract lesions by endoscopic ultrasound. Gastrointest Endosc 37:449–454, 1991.

225. Kojima T, Takahashi H, Parra-Blanco A, et al: Diagnosis of submucosal tumor of the upper GI tract by endoscopic resection. Gastrointest Endosc 50:516–522, 1999.

226. Rajan E, Buess G, Dean R, et al: First endoscopic system for transmural resection of colorectal tissue using a prototype full thickness resection device (FTRD). Gastrointest Endosc 53:AB58, 2001.

227. Kalloo A, Kantsevoy S, Jagannath S, et al: Endoscopic gastrojejunostomy with long-term survival in a porcine model. Gastrointest Endosc 55:AB96, 2002.

Management of Upper Gastrointestinal Familial Adenomatous Polyposis Syndrome and Ampullary Tumors

Ian Norton and David James Koorey

Introduction

Classical familial adenomatous polyposis (FAP) is an autosomal dominant condition resulting in profuse adenomatous polyposis of the gastrointestinal (GI) tract, most marked in the colon. Patients generally undergo prophylactic colectomy during adolescence or early adult life. After colectomy, the proximal duodenum is the commonest site of malignancy in FAP subjects.[1] The periampullary region is especially prone to adenomatous change, presumably related in part to the trophic effects of bile on the mucosa.[2–5] Periampullary adenomas develop in 50% to 100% of FAP patients. Less commonly, periampullary adenomas are sporadic (arising in non-FAP patients). As with adenomatous polyps elsewhere within the GI tract, periampullary adenomas are premalignant. Therefore, surveillance and/or removal of adenomas at this site may be justified. Most upper GI adenomas are within easy reach of endoscopic surveillance and therapy. However, the optimal approach to upper GI surveillance and management of upper GI tumors in patients with FAP and sporadic ampullary neoplasms is yet to be determined.

Multiple reports have documented the outcomes of endoscopic surveillance and endoscopic approaches to treatment of periampullary lesions, including piecemeal resection, snare ampullectomy, and thermal ablation. Surgical options for advanced lesions include local transduodenal resection, pancreaticoduodenectomy, and pancreas-sparing duodenectomy. The appropriate management for each patient depends on many factors including the size and number of lesions, degree of dysplasia, involvement of the pancreaticobiliary system, comorbidity, and local expertise.

FAMILIAL ADENOMATOUS POLYPOSIS SYNDROME

FAP is an autosomal dominant condition with virtually complete penetrance, affecting approximately 1 in 8000 in the United States.[6] Mutation of the *APC* gene on the long arm of chromosome 5 is responsible for most cases of FAP.[7] The condition is classically characterized by the development of hundreds to thousands of adenomatous polyps in the colon with the inevitable progression of one or more of these adenomas to carcinoma. However, it is increasingly apparent that attenuated forms of FAP exist. These generally present with fewer colorectal polyps developing later in life than is typical of classic FAP and often distributed more proximally in the colon. Such patients do develop upper GI disease and in some the upper GI findings may be more marked than those in the colon.[8,9] Mutations in particular regions of the *APC* gene account for the attenuated forms of FAP.[8,10,11]

Extracolonic disease is common in classic FAP but varies in severity from family to family and between individuals within families. At one extreme is Gardner's syndrome characterized by GI adenomatous polyps together with other benign neoplasms such as desmoid tumors, osteomas, and fibromas.[12] Gardner's syndrome also results from germline *APC* mutations and is best regarded as part of the spectrum of FAP. Turcot's syndrome is characterized by central nervous system (CNS) tumors, often glioblastomas or medulloblastomas,[12] together with colonic polyposis. The inheritance of this disorder has been difficult to determine,[12] because the association of CNS tumors and polyposis may arise through germline mutation of more than one gene.[13] Germline *APC* mutations have been identified in some subjects with Turcot's syndrome, particularly those with cerebellar medulloblastomas and profuse

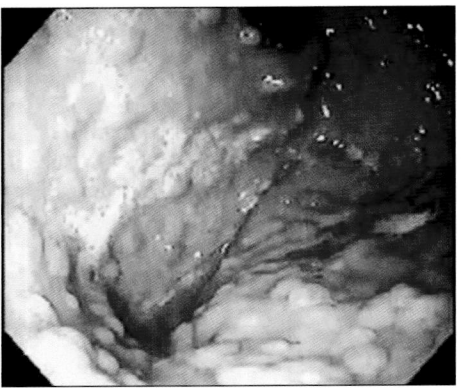

Figure 36–1. Endoscopic view of fundic cystic gland polyps.

colonic polyposis.[13] For the purposes of this chapter, the term FAP incorporates Gardner's syndrome and those cases of Turcot's syndrome attributable to *APC* mutations.

The colonic manifestations of FAP are cured by colectomy (although there remains a risk of rectal cancer after ileorectal anastomosis or in any residual rectal mucosa after restorative proctocolectomy). After colectomy, extracolonic manifestations of FAP therefore assume greater importance. The entire upper GI tract appears to be at risk of malignancy in FAP.[1] In particular, the duodenum is the commonest site of malignancy in postcolectomy patients. Duodenal cancer develops in 4.5% to 8.5% of such patients.[14,15] Adenomas and carcinomas have also been encountered in the distal ileal segment and within ileoanal pouches 5 to 10 years after proctocolectomy.[16]

Gastric polyps are a common finding in FAP. Multiple 3 to 5 mm fundic polypoid lesions are seen in at least 50% of patients (Fig. 36–1).[17] These *fundic gland* or *fundic cystic gland* polyps are hamartomatous lesions and are generally regarded as having very little malignant potential. Histologic examination of fundic gland polyps reveals cystic dilatation of fundic glands with, generally, no epithelial dysplasia.[18] However, a recent case report has described gastric adenocarcinoma and dysplasia arising in the fundic gland polyps of a patient with attenuated adenomatous polyposis suggesting that, rarely, fundic gland polyps might take a more sinister course.[19] Thus, it would seem reasonable to biopsy unusually large fundic gland polyps or those with atypical endoscopic appearances.

Gastric adenomatous polyps (predominantly in the gastric antrum) have been reported in 5% of FAP subjects in a British cohort[1] and 25% in a Japanese series.[20] The risk of gastric malignancy has been estimated at 3.4 times that of controls.[21] However, this report was from Japan where the epidemiology of gastric malignancy differs from that of Western societies. In a British study of 1255 subjects with FAP followed for a mean of 22 years, 7 developed gastric malignancy.[1]

INCIDENCE OF SPORADIC AND FAMILIAL ADENOMATOUS POLYPOSIS RELATED PERIAMPULLARY ADENOMAS

An understanding of the natural history of duodenal neoplasia in FAP patients is essential to the development of surveillance strategies and decisions regarding management in this condition.

Periampullary tumors represent 5% of GI tumors and 36% of resectable pancreaticoduodenal tumors.[22] The periampullary adenoma is an uncommon lesion in clinical practice, although not as rare as previously thought. An early review at the Mayo Clinic by Baggenstoss[23] demonstrated 25 of these lesions in 4000 consecutive autopsies (0.62%), suggesting that the lesion may be subclinical. A review of the case notes in this study suggested that only six of these lesions (24%) might have been symptomatic.

Asymptomatic adenomatous change of the ampulla is extremely common in FAP patients, occurring in up to 100% of subjects.[24] The incidence of FAP-related duodenal and periampullary adenomas depends on the diligence of surveillance (see the section on diagnosis). A review of the Johns Hopkins FAP registry indicated that the relative risk of duodenal adenocarcinoma in FAP compared with the general population was 330 and the relative risk of ampullary cancer was 123.[25] However, the combined absolute risk of duodenal cancer in FAP patients was only 1 per 1698 years. Because follow-up was incomplete and most cancers occur later in life, this risk of malignancy may be an underestimate. A study from the United Kingdom reported development of malignancy in 3 of 70 patients followed over 40 months.[26] Therefore, it is important to remember that although adenomatous change in the duodenum may be almost universal in FAP only a minority of patients appear to develop cancer. Several studies have indicated that the median age at onset of periampullary malignancy complicating FAP is in the 6th decade.[15,25,27] The literature on this subject has often not adequately differentiated sporadic from FAP-related periampullary adenomas.

PATHOGENESIS OF PERIAMPULLARY ADENOMA

As an autosomal dominant condition, all nucleated cells in FAP patients contain one normal and one abnormal *APC* gene (a germline mutation). In the colon, a somatic mutation in the previously normal (wild type) APC allele is generally an early event in carcinogenesis. Accumulation of other somatic mutations (in genes such as *p53* and *K-ras*) drives the progression toward malignancy.[28] The situation with respect to periampullary malignancy appears to be similar except that somatic *APC* mutations may be relatively less frequent and K-*ras* mutations relatively more frequent.[29] Another study has demonstrated *p53* mutations associated with high grade malignant change in periampullary tumors.[22] A recent paper has suggested that other familial factors, possibly unidentified modifier genes, may influence the development of periampullary adenomas in FAP kindreds explaining, at least in part, the familial segregation of periampullary disease observed in their FAP families.[27] This segregation was independent of the kindred's specific *APC* mutation. Spigelman and coworkers[30] have reported a correlation between severity of duodenal polyposis and rectal polyposis after colectomy and ileorectal anastomosis. They have suggested that other factor(s), possibly environmental, may be synergistic in some patients, resulting in more severe polyposis at both sites. However, the authors of this study caution that paucity of rectal polyps does not remove the need for periampullary surveillance.

The periampullary region is the site of most significant small intestinal adenomas in both sporadic and FAP patients. These lesions

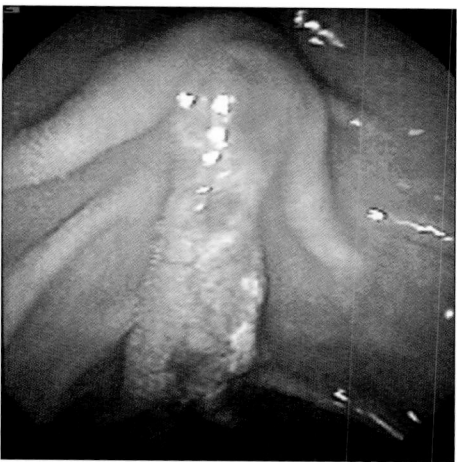

Figure 36–2. Ampullary adenoma with goatee appearance.

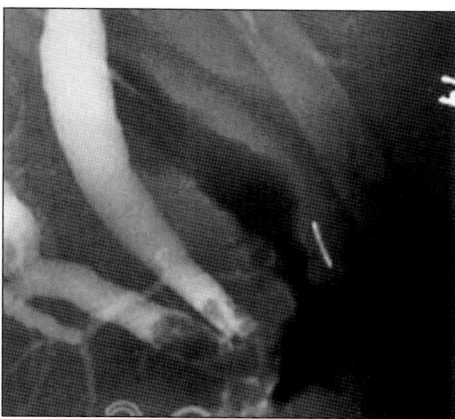

Figure 36–3. Endoscopic retrograde cholangiopancreatography (ERCP) appearance of tumor extending along biliary and pancreatic ducts.

seem to parallel mucosal exposure to bile, particularly with regard to the characteristic inferior extension of early adenomas ("goatee" appearance, Fig. 36–2). Bile has been shown to have proliferative[2-4] and mutagenic[5] effects of gut mucosa. Furthermore, the bile from patients with FAP has been shown to form more DNA adducts both *in vitro* and *in vivo* than bile from controls,[3,31] particularly at low pH (as found in the proximal duodenum).[32] These DNA adducts have the potential to give rise to mutagenesis.[33]

In a situation analogous to that in the colon, these lesions appear to follow the adenoma-carcinoma sequence. In one study, adenomatous tissue was adjacent to or a component of 84% of periampullary cancers studied.[34] A retrospective study by Bleau and Gostout[24] supported the temporal progression of periampullary adenomas to carcinoma, with mean diagnosis of adenoma at age 39, high grade dysplasia at age 47, and malignancy at age 54.

HISTOLOGY

Most periampullary lesions are tubular or tubulovillous adenomas that arise from the intestinal-type epithelium of the ampulla.[35] Foci of severe dysplasia or frank malignancy may be found within a lesion.[36] Other neoplasms of the ampulla are far less common. These include benign lesions (leiomyoma, lipoma, lymphangioma, hemangioma, and carcinoid) and malignancies, both primary and metastatic (lymphoma, melanoma, and metastatic small cell carcinoma).[37]

CLINICAL PRESENTATION

Lesions of the periampullary area may be asymptomatic (discussed earlier) but can also present relatively early with symptoms of pancreaticobiliary origin. Clinical presentation is usually a consequence of obstruction, resulting in abdominal pain, cholangitis or jaundice[37] or, less commonly, recurrent pancreatitis.[38] Courvoisier's sign is occasionally present, suggesting advanced disease.[39] Biochemical evidence of biliary obstruction is common in symptomatic patients.[40] The diagnosis is usually unsuspected before visualization of the ampulla, with most patients thought to have pancreatic malignancy or choledocholithiasis.

Endoscopic Management of Periampullary Adenoma

The endoscopic management of periampullary adenomas can be separated into diagnosis, surveillance, and therapy.

It is important to remember that colonic involvement in FAP can be asymptomatic, that patients with FAP may have no family history (new mutations), and that in attenuated forms of FAP colonic manifestations of the disease may be delayed.[28] For these reasons, all patients with apparently sporadic periampullary adenomas should undergo colonoscopy.

DIAGNOSIS

In patients with FAP, diagnosis of upper GI and particularly periampullary adenomas depends on the vigilance of the endoscopist. Examination with a side-viewing duodenoscope is essential. Two recent studies have demonstrated that duodenoscopy with a forward-viewing endoscopy missed 50% of gross lesions visible with the side-viewer.[24,41] Careful biopsies of the ampulla are also essential to detect early adenomatous change in light of the somewhat frondlike appearance of many normal papillae. In one study, six of eight normal-appearing ampullae demonstrated microscopic adenomatous change at biopsy.[24] Even so, endoscopic biopsies may prove inaccurate. In a recent study, endoscopic biopsy failed to identify infiltrating malignancy in 7 of 23 cases (32%).[42]

Because of the poor sensitivity of endoscopic biopsies with regard to malignant change, endoscopic retrograde cholangiopancreatography (ERCP) is an essential part of the management of a patient with an adenoma involving the ampulla. Sphincterotomy permits sampling of the intra-ampullary mucosa while extension along the pancreaticobiliary system will be revealed by cholangiopancreatography (Fig. 36–3), a situation rendering the patient unsuitable for definitive endoscopic therapy.

The role of endoscopic ultrasonography (EUS) in this condition remains to be determined. There may be difficulty examining this area reliably because of compression of the affected tissues. Despite this, EUS can afford excellent views of the region including the

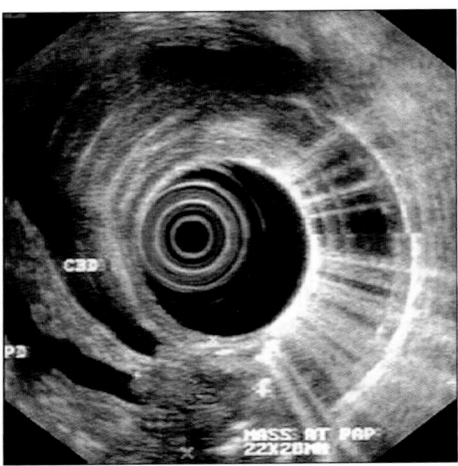

Figure 36–4. Endoscopic ultrasonography (EUS) image of the lesion in Figure 36–3; note extension of the tumor along the common bile and pancreatic ducts.

duct systems (Fig. 36–4). Recent studies have indicated that EUS is useful in the TNM staging of periampullary malignancy, with staging accuracy as high as 84%.[42–46] In another study, however, the diagnostic accuracy of EUS was only 44% in 23 patients with periampullary lesions.[42] Intraductal ultrasound may provide useful information regarding intraductal extension. This approach requires further evaluation.

SURVEILLANCE

As early as 1950, Halsted and coworkers[47] advocated upper GI surveillance of FAP subjects. Given the risk of progression to malignancy, concerns regarding residual adenomatous tissue after ablation or resection, and the ongoing proliferative nature of these lesions, surveillance appears justified, although no studies have demonstrated improved survival as a result. An ideal regimen for surveillance of these lesions is yet to be determined. As discussed earlier, virtually all patients with FAP will eventually have at least microscopic involvement of the ampulla and most will have multiple tiny adenomata spread over the proximal duodenum. It is impossible to remove all adenomatous tissue in FAP patients and the aim of surveillance is to sample tissue to detect advancement to high grade dysplasia. Large lesions are more likely to contain foci of high grade dysplasia or malignancy. Therefore, it is our practice to remove and/or ablate lesions larger than 5 mm and grossly polypoid papillae. Sporadic adenomas, on the other hand, occur as isolated lesions, and the aim of surveillance is to detect recurrence at a previous site of therapy (either endoscopic or surgical).

The optimal time interval for surveillance in FAP patients remains to be determined. Two authors have suggested surveillance every 3 to 5 years.[17,20] Spigelman and coworkers[48] have (retrospectively) developed a scoring system to determine which patients are most likely to progress to malignancy and therefore warrant more intense surveillance (Table 36–1).

It is important to consider that patients with FAP may have adenomas beyond the ampulla that are not seen with standard endoscopy. Therefore, an appropriate surveillance strategy in FAP patients might include extended duodenoscopy with either a colonoscope or push enteroscope.

THERAPY

The ideal endoscopic therapy for periampullary adenomas has not been established. Excision has the advantage of submitting ample tissue for histologic examination. In practice, endoscopic therapy for these lesions usually involves excision of the bulk of the lesion followed by tissue ablation of residual adenoma at the conclusion of the initial endoscopic session and at follow-up examinations. Shemesh and coworkers[49] published their early experience with sphincterotomy and fulguration of adenomatous periampullary tissue in 1989. Four patients with recurrent disease after local surgical resection were treated with fulguration. None had evidence of recurrence with a 12- to 24-month follow-up.

The first step in endoscopic removal of the ampulla is assessment of intraductal extension of the adenoma. Any lesion extending beyond the wall of the duodenum is clearly beyond definitive endoscopic treatment. This is most easily determined by cholangio-pancreatography or possibly EUS.

Endoscopic removal of the ampulla may be performed either in a single piece (snare ampullectomy) or by use of a piecemeal resection technique.

Snare Excision

This technique comprises removal of the tumor using a small snare in one piece (Video 36–1). The procedure may be preceded by submucosal saline injection to increase the distance to the serosal surface and raise the tumor, thus making it more easy to snare. A modification of this technique is to inflate an occlusion balloon in the distal bile duct and retract the tissue toward the snare in an effort to better snare deep tissue.[50] Snare removal of the entire papilla was described in a large cohort by Binmoeller and coworkers in 1993.[51] In a recent report of 28 ampullectomies from the Mayo Clinic immediate complications were minor bleeding ($n = 2$), mild pancreatitis ($n = 4$) and a duodenal perforation ($n = 1$). Papillary stenosis resulting in pancreatitis occurred in two patients (17%) at

Table 36–1. Spigelman Scoring System for Staging of Ampullary Adenoma

Polyp Number	Polyp Size	Histology	Dysplasia	Points
1–4	1–4 mm	Tubular	Mild	1
5–20	5–10 mm	Tubulovillous	Moderate	2
>20	>10 mm	Villous	Severe	3
Stage 0, 0 points; stage 1, 1–4 points; stage 2, 5–6 points; stage 3, 7–8 points; stage 4, 9–12 points.				

4 months and 24 months. Follow-up endoscopy revealed recurrent/residual ampullary adenomatous tissue in two (10%)[52] These recurrence rates after snare ampullectomy compare favorably with transduodenal ampullectomy.[42] Martin and colleagues[53] reported 14 consecutive patients treated with snare ampullectomy. One patient died from necrotizing pancreatitis and another required surgery for hemorrhage. The patient who died did not receive a prophylactic pancreatic stent. Recurrence has occurred in 4 of 10 patients with a mean follow-up of 31 months. Another study of eight patients[54] reported one episode of cholangitis after snare ampullectomy but no other complications. Two patients had invasive malignancy in the snared specimen and went on to have pancreaticoduodenectomy. The remaining six patients remain well with no recurrence at mean follow-up of 12 months.

Clearly, a major concern with snare ampullectomy is the potential for acute pancreatitis. This occurs in about 15% to 20% of cases[51,52] and is potentially fatal.[53] Identification of the pancreatic orifice after snare ampullectomy may not be possible. In the Mayo series, about 50% of patients had a temporary stent placed (at the discretion of the endoscopist), but no difference in pancreatitis rates was reported between those with and without stent insertion. However, it is possible that pancreatic stenting might help modify the severity of subsequent pancreatitis.

Piecemeal Resection

Concerns regarding pancreatitis have led some to adopt a piecemeal technique for adenoma resection performed after the insertion of a pancreatic stent (Video 36–2). The patient initially undergoes a dual biliary and pancreatic sphincterotomy. The pancreatic orifice is then stented. Tissue is then raised on a cushion of submucosal saline and snared piecemeal. A potential concern with this technique is the adequacy of adenoma removal, but small amounts of residual adenoma can usually be adequately removed after piecemeal excision with cautery techniques such as argon plasma coagulation or contact cautery techniques. In a recent report of this approach by Howell and coworkers, 13 patients with ampullary adenomas were treated. Ninety-two percent were disease-free after a mean of 2.7 procedures (mean follow-up 19 months). One patient developed mild pancreatitis.[55]

Laser has been reported to be efficacious in ablation of periampullary adenomas. In a study by Lambert and coworkers,[56] seven of eight lesions treated with neodymium:yttrium-aluminum-garnet (Nd:YAG) laser were completely ablated with follow-up of 14 to 53 months. However, complications such has pancreatitis, transmural burn, and perforation have generally led to the use of less aggressive ablative therapy[24] such as monopolar ablation after sphincterotomy. A fistulatome allows precise targeting of tissue for ablation. Argon plasma coagulation may be an attractive method for destroying residual tissue given its relatively shallow depth of injury.[57]

Surgical Therapy

The long-term results of endoscopic resection and ablative therapy are not known, whereas the limitations of endoscopic biopsy in excluding malignancy are well documented, with false-negative results of up to 56%.[42] The two surgical options for these lesions are pancreaticoduodenectomy (Whipple procedure) and transduodenal excision.

Gray has reported pancreaticoduodenectomy for five patients with benign adenomas and eight with adenomas containing foci of malignancy.[57a] Two of the patients with benign lesions died in the perioperative period, but the three survivors were free of disease at follow-up. Five of eight patients with invasive malignancy were also free of disease at follow-up. The cost of Whipple's procedure is higher potential morbidity and mortality.[42,58] Complications and hospital stay after this surgery are significantly longer than with local resection.[42]

Transduodenal excision is not a new technique, having been reported for ampullary lesions by Halsted in 1899.[47] Transduodenal excision has been used as a less invasive surgical alternative to pancreaticoduodenectomy.[40,42,58–60] Unfortunately, transduodenal resection may be inadequate therapy in many patients. Recurrence of benign adenomas has been reported in 25% to 33%.[40,42,60] In one study, four of four subjects treated had recurrence of adenoma at 24 months' follow-up.[49] In a study of 12 patients, resection margins were inadequate in 50%, leading to conversion to pancreaticoduodenectomy in three patients.[42] FAP patients are a particularly difficult treatment group. Recurrent duodenal adenomas after transduodenal resection (mean recurrence: 13 months) has led one group to conclude that this is inadequate therapy for these patients.[61] Furthermore, the potential for desmoid formation after surgery is another factor favoring the use of nonsurgical (i.e., endoscopic) techniques.

Pharmacologic Treatment

There is randomized controlled data that sulindac (Clinoril) slows the progression of polyps in the colon of patients with FAP syndrome.[62] Similar findings have been reported with the use of the cyclooxygenase-2 (COX-2) specific drug celecoxib (Celebrex).[63] There is less compelling evidence for the use of nonsteroidal anti-inflammatory drugs (NSAIDs) for progression of duodenal disease. The St. Mark's group randomized 24 patients with advanced duodenal disease to 200 mg sulindac twice daily or placebo.[64] After 6 months of treatment, there was a reduction in epithelial proliferation in the sulindac group but no significant regression of large polyps. However, blinded review of videotapes demonstrated significant regression of small polyps (less than 2 mm) compared with the placebo group. This evidence supports the hypothesis that sulindac may also have an effect on polyp proliferation in the duodenum. However, it remains to be seen whether this will translate into a clinically significant benefit.

Summary

It is clear that no optimal approach has yet emerged for the management of sporadic periampullary adenomas and upper GI neoplasia complicating FAP. There are no randomized trials comparing different surgical and/or endoscopic modalities. Such studies may not be feasible given the infrequency of these conditions and the long follow-up period required for such a study. In the meantime, selection of the optimal approach for an individual patient will rely on a careful evaluation of the disease severity and extent in that patient and the use of the best available endoscopic and surgical expertise.

REFERENCES

1. Spigelman AD, Williams CB, Talbot IC, et al: Upper gastrointestinal cancer in patients with familial adenomatous polyposis. Lancet 2:783–785, 1988.
2. Takano S, Matsushima M, Ertuk E, Bryan GT: Early induction of rat colonic orthithinedecarboxylase activity by n-methyl-n-nitro-n-nitrosoguaninidine or bile salts. Cancer Res 41:624–628, 1981.
3. Spigelman AD, Scates DK, Venitt S, Phillips RK: DNA adducts, detected by 32P-postlabelling, in the foregut of patients with familial adenomatous polyposis and in unaffected controls. Carcinogenesis 12:1727–1732, 1991.
4. Deschner EE, Raicht RF: Influence of bile on kinetic behavior of colonic epithelial cells of the rat. Digestion 19:322–327, 1979.
5. Spigelman AD, Crofton-Sleigh C, Venitt S, Phillips RK: Mutagenicity of bile and duodenal adenomas in familial adenomatous polyposis. Br J Surg 77:878–881, 1990.
6. Powell SM, Petersen GM, Krush AJ, et al: Molecular diagnosis of familial adenomatous polyposis. N Engl J Med 328:1982–1987, 1993.
7. Groden J, Thliveris A, Samowitz W, et al: Identification and characterization of the familial adenomatous polyposis gene. Cell 66:589–600, 1991.
8. Lynch HT, Smyrk T, McGinn T, et al: Attenuated familial adenomatous polyposis (AFAP). A phenotypically and genotypically distinctive variant of FAP [see comments]. Cancer 76:2427–2433, 1995.
9. Leggett BA, Young JP, Biden K, et al: Severe upper gastrointestinal polyposis associated with sparse colonic polyposis in a familial adenomatous polyposis family with an APC mutation at codon 1520.Gut 41:518–521, 1997.
10. Soravia C, Bapat B, Cohen Z: Familial adenomatous polyposis (FAP) and hereditary nonpolyposis colorectal cancer (HNPCC): A review of clinical, genetic and therapeutic aspects. Schweiz Med Wochenschr 127:682–690, 1997.
11. Soravia C, Berk T, Madlensky L, et al: Genotype-phenotype correlations in attenuated adenomatous polyposis coli. Am J Hum Genet 62:1290–1301, 1998.
12. Boland CR, Kim YS: Gastrointestinal polyp syndromes. In Sleisenger M, Fordtran J (eds): Gastrointestinal Disease, vol 2. Philadelphia, WB Saunders, 1993, pp 1430–1448.
13. Paraf F, Jothy S, Van Meir EG: Brain tumor-polyposis syndromes: Two genetic diseases? J Clin Oncol 15:2744–2758, 1997.
14. Arvantis ML, Jagelman DG, Fazio VW, et al: Mortality in patients with familial adenomatous polyposis. Dis Colon Rectum 33:639–642, 1990.
15. Jagelman DG, DeCosse JJ, Bussey HJ: Upper gastrointestinal cancer in familial adenomatous polyposis. Lancet 1:1149–1151, 1988.
16. Geller A, Wang KK, Batts KP, Gostout CJ: Ileostomy pouch polyposis in a patient with familial adenomatous polyposis [abstract]. Gastrointest Endosc 41:377, 1995.
17. Sarre RG, Frost AG, Jagelman DG, et al: Gastric and duodenal polyps in familial adenomatous polyposis: A prospective study of the nature and prevalence of upper gastrointestinal polyps. Gut 28:306–314, 1987.
18. Debinski HS, Spigelman AD, Hatfield A, et al: Upper intestinal surveillance in familial adenomatous polyposis. Eur J Cancer 31A:1149–1153, 1995.
19. Zwick A, Munir M, Ryan CK, et al: Gastric adenocarcinoma and dysplasia in fundic gland polyps of a patient with attenuated adenomatous polyposis coli. Gastroenterology 113:659–663, 1997.
20. Sawada T, Muto T: Familial adenomatous polyposis: Should patients undergo surveillance of the upper gastrointestinal tract? Endoscopy 27:6–11, 1995.
21. Iwama T, Mishima Y, Utsonomiya J: The impact of familial adenomatous polyposis on the tumorigenesis and mortality in several organs. Ann Surg 217:100–108, 1993.
22. Scarpa A, Capelli P, Zamboni G, et al: Neoplasia of the ampulla of Vater. Ki-ras and p53 mutations. Am J Pathol 142:1163–1172, 1993.
23. Baggenstoss AH: Major duodenal papilla: Variations of pathologic interest and lesions of the mucosa. Arch Pathol 26:853–868, 1938.
24. Bleau BL, Gostout CJ: Endoscopic treatment of ampullary adenomas in familial adenomatous polyposis. J Clin Gastroenterol 22:237–241, 1996.
25. Offerhaus GJ, Giardiello FM, Krush AJ, et al: The risk of upper gastrointestinal cancer in familial adenomatous polyposis [see comments]. Gastroenterology 102:1980–1982, 1992.
26. Nugent KP, Spigelman AD, Williams CB, et al: Surveillance of duodenal polyps in familial adenomatous polyposis: Progress report. J R Soc Med 87:704–706, 1994.
27. Sanabria JR, Croxford R, Berk TC, et al: Familial segregation in the occurrence and severity of periampullary neoplasms in familial adenomatous polyposis. Am J Surg 171:136–140; discussion 140–141, 1996.
28. Polakis P: The adenomatous polyposis coli (APC) tumor suppressor. Biochim Biophys Acta 1332:F127–F147, 1997.
29. Gallinger S, Vivona AA, Odze RD, et al: Somatic APC and K-ras codon 12 mutations in periampullary adenomas and carcinomas from familial adenomatous polyposis patients. Oncogene 10:1875–1878, 1995.
30. Spigelman AD, Williams CB, Phillips RK: Rectal polyposis as a guide to duodenal polyposis in familial adenomatous polyposis. J R Soc Med 85:77–79, 1992.
31. Scates DK, Spigelman AD, Phillips RK, Venitt S: DNA adducts detected by 32P-postlabelling, in the intestine of rats given bile from patients with familial adenomatous polyposis and from unaffected controls. Carcinogenesis 13:731–735, 1992.
32. Scates DK, Venitt S, Phillips RK, Spigelman AD: High pH reduces DNA damage caused by bile from patients with familial adenomatous polyposis: Antacids may attenuate duodenal polyposis. Gut 36:918–921, 1995.
33. Venitt S. Biological mechanisms. In Raffle PA, Adams PH, Baxter PJ, Lee WR (eds): Hunter's Diseases of Occupations. London, Edward Arnold, 1994, pp 623–654.
34. Spigelman AD, Talbot IC, Penna C, et al: Evidence for adenoma-carcinoma sequence in the duodenum of patients with familial adenomatous polyposis. The Leeds Castle Polyposis Group (Upper Gastrointestinal Committee). J Clin Pathol 47:709–710, 1994.
35. Noda Y, Watanabe H, Iida M, et al: Histologic follow-up of ampullary adenomas in patients with familial adenomatosis coli. Cancer 70:1847–1856, 1992.
36. Yamaguchi K, Enjoji M: Adenoma of the ampulla of Vater: Putative precancerous lesion. Gut 32:1558–1561, 1991.
37. Sobol S, Cooperman AM: Villous adenoma of the ampulla of Vater. An unusual cause of biliary colic and obstructive jaundice. Gastroenterology 75:107–109, 1978.
38. Guzzardo G, Kleinman MS, Krackov JH, Schwartz SI: Recurrent acute pancreatitis caused by ampullary villous adenoma. J Clin Gastroenterol 12:200–202, 1990.
39. Ponchon T, Berger F, Chavaillon A, et al: Contribution of endoscopy to diagnosis and treatment of tumors of the ampulla of Vater. Cancer 64:161–167, 1989.
40. Alstrup N, Burcharth F, Hauge C, Horn T: Transduodenal excision of tumours of the ampulla of Vater. Eur J Surg 162:961–967, 1996.

41. Church JM, McGannon E, Hull-Boiner S, et al: Gastroduodenal polyps in patients with familial adenomatous polyposis. Dis Colon Rectum 35:1170–1173, 1992.

42. Cahen DL, Fockens P, De Wit LT, et al: Local resection or pancreaticoduodenectomy for villous adenoma of the ampulla of Vater diagnosed before operation. Br J Surg 84:948–951, 1997.

43. Tio TL, Tytgat GN, Cikot RJ, et al: Ampullopancreatic carcinoma: Preoperative TNM classification with endosonography. Radiology 175:455–461, 1990.

44. Tio TL, Mulder CJ, Eggink WF: Endosonography in staging early carcinoma of the ampulla of vater. Gastroenterology 102:1392–1395, 1992.

45. Tio TL, Sie LH, Kallimanis G, et al: Staging of ampullary and pancreatic carcinoma: Comparison between endosonography and surgery. Gastrointestinal Endoscopy 44:706–713, 1996.

46. Rosch T, Braig C, Gain T, et al: Staging of pancreatic and ampullary carcinoma by endoscopic ultrasonography. Comparison with conventional sonography, computed tomography, and angiography. Gastroenterology 102:188–199, 1992.

47. Halsted JA, Harris EJ, Bartlett MK: Involvement of the stomach in familial polyposis of the gastrointestinal tract. Gastroenterology 15:763–770, 1950.

48. Spigelman AD, Williams CB, Talbot IC, et al: Upper gastrointestinal cancer in patients with familial adenomatous polyposis. Lancet 2:783–785, 1989.

49. Shemesh E, Nass S, Czerniak A: Endoscopic sphincterotomy and endoscopic fulguration in the management of adenoma of the papilla of Vater. Surg Gynecol Obstet 169:445–448, 1989.

50. Aiura K, Imaeda H, Kitajima M, Kumai K: Balloon-catheter-assisted endoscopic snare papillectomy for benign tumors of the major duodenal papilla. Gastrointest Endosc 57:743–747, 2003.

51. Binmoeller KF, Boaventura S, Ramsperger K, Soehendra N: Endoscopic snare excision of benign adenomas of the papilla of Vater [see comments]. Gastrointest Endosc 39:127–131, 1993.

52. Norton ID, Baron TH, Geller A, et al: Immediate and medium-term outcome of endoscopic snare excision of the ampulla of Vater. Gastrointest Endosc 56:239–243, 2002.

53. Martin JA, Haber GB, Kortan PP, et al: Endoscopic snare ampullectomy for resection for resection of benign ampullary neoplasms. Gastrointest Endosc 45:AB139, 1997.

54. Greenspan AB, Walden DT, Aliperti G: Endoscopic management of ampullary adenomas. Gastrointest Endosc 45:AB133, 1997.

55. Desilets DJ, Dy RM, Ku PM, et al: Endoscopic management of tumors of the major duodenal papilla: Refined techniques to improve outcome and avoid complications. Gastrointest Endosc 54:202–208, 2001.

56. Lambert R, Ponchon T, Chavaillon A, Berger F: Laser treatment of tumors of the papilla of Vater. Endoscopy 20:227–231, 1988.

57. Norton ID, Wang L, Levine SA, et al: In vivo characterization of colonic thermal injury by the argon plasma coagulator. Gastrointest Endosc 55:631–636, 2002.

57a. Gray G, Browder W: Villous tumors of the ampulla of Vater: Local resection versus pancreatoduodenectomy. South Med J 82:917–920, 1989.

58. Knox RA, Kingston RD: Carcinoma of the ampulla of Vater. Br J Surg 73:72–73, 1986.

59. Asbun HJ, Rossi RL, Munson JL: Local resection for ampullary tumors. Is there a place for it? Arch Surg 128:515–520, 1993.

60. Farouk M, Niotis M, Branum GD, et al: Indications for and the technique of local resection of tumors of the papilla of Vater. Arch Surg 126:650–652, 1991.

61. Penna C, Phillips RK, Tiret E, Spigelman AD: Surgical polypectomy of duodenal adenomas in familial adenomatous polyposis: Experience of two European centres. Br J Surg 80:1027–1029, 1993.

62. Giardiello FM, Hamilton SR, Krush AJ, et al: Treatment of colonic and rectal adenomas with sulindac in familial adenomatous polyposis. N Engl J Med 328:1313–1316, 1993.

63. Steinbach G, Lynch PM, Phillips RK, et al: The effect of celecoxib, a cyclooxygenase-2 inhibitor, in familial adenomatous polyposis. N Engl J Med 342:1946–1952, 2000.

64. Debinski HS, Trojan J, Nugent KP, et al: Effect of sulindac on small polyps in familial adenomatous polyposis. Lancet 345:855–856, 1995.

Colorectal Cancer Screening and Surveillance

David Lieberman

Introduction

Colorectal cancer (CRC) is the second leading cause of cancer death in North America and Western Europe. Worldwide, there are more than 875,000 cases per year. In the United States, it is estimated that there will be 147,500 new cases in 2003 and approximately 57,000 deaths, representing about 14% of all cancer deaths.[1]

Survival is directly related to stage at diagnosis. Stage 1 (limited to mucosal and submucosa) has a 5-year survival of nearly 100%. Stage 2 (penetration to muscularis or serosa) has a 5-year survival of 80%. Stage 3 with lymph node involvement has a 5-year survival of 50%, and Stage 4 (distant metastases) has virtually no 5-year survivors. Early discovery improves survival. CRC is usually asymptomatic until late-stage disease. Therefore, the key to early discovery is the identification of high-risk patients before symptoms develop.

Most cancers develop from adenoma precursors. Adenoma prevalence increases steadily with age, ranging from about 25% at age 50 to more than 50% by age 80. There is a 5% to 6% lifetime risk of CRC; thus, it is apparent that most patients with adenomas will not develop clinically apparent cancer during their lifetime. Polyp size and histology are directly associated with malignant risk. The risk of high-grade dysplasia in polyps smaller than 5 mm is 1.1%; for polyps 5 to 9 mm it is 4.6%, and in polyps larger than 9 mm the risk is 20%.[2] The risk of invasive cancer is less than 1% in polyps smaller than 1 cm and more than 10% in larger polyps.[3] These data suggest that the patients most likely to develop cancer are those with advanced adenomas. Recent data from the VA Cooperative Study[4] found that the prevalence of advanced adenomas (defined as adenoma ≥1 cm; adenoma with villous histology or high-grade dysplasia) in asymptomatic men undergoing screening colonoscopy was associated with age. The prevalence was 5.9% at age 50 to 59 years, rising to 12.0% in men age 60 to 69 and to 12.9% in men older than age 69 years. Evidence from the National Polyp Study (NPS)[5] supports the hypothesis that detection and removal of adenomas may prevent cancer incidence. All of these data have important implications for screening. Screening efforts directed at advanced adenomas will target patients with the greatest risk and potentially lead to significant reductions in cancer incidence.

There is now compelling evidence that population-based screening can reduce the mortality from CRC. These data are reviewed in this chapter. Furthermore, there is evidence that screening can lead to incidence reduction, most likely by detection and removal of precursor adenomas.[6]

Screening for diseases in at-risk populations can be costly and ineffective. Ideal screening uses relatively simple, inexpensive tests to risk-stratify patients, and then sensitive tests are directed at individuals with highest risk. The criteria for population-based screening include factors summarized in Table 37–1.

There is considerable variation in screening recommendations in high-risk countries. Some countries (Germany and Australia) have recommended fecal occult blood testing; Canada and the United Kingdom do not yet have national recommendations. The evidence-based United States Preventive Services Task Force[7] has strongly endorsed screening with any of several tests. Other expert panels in the United States, including the American Cancer Society, GI Multi-Society Task Force,[8] American College of Gastroenterology, and the American Society for Gastrointestinal Endoscopy, have strongly endorsed screening.

Despite evidence of effectiveness and consensus among experts in the United States, only 30% to 40% of Americans older than age 50 actually receive any of the recommended screening tests. Issues surrounding poor compliance are of critical importance to program

Table 37–1. The Case for Screening

Criteria	Colorectal Cancer
The disease is common	5%–6% lifetime risk
Early detection can prevent mortality and incidence	Stage I survival: 100%* Stage II survival: 80% Stage III survival: 50% Stage IV survival: nil
Screening methods are shown to be effective	15%–33% reduction in mortality with early cancer detection 18% reduction in CRC incidence
Resources are available to provide screening	Screening can be effectively performed in primary care settings
Resources are available to provide diagnostic tests for patients with positive screening	Colonoscopy resources are limited in United States, Canada, and United Kingdom
Screening is cost effective	Models demonstrate cost effectiveness[47-53]
Screening methods are accepted by patients and providers	30%–40% compliance in United States

*5-year survival by stage.
CRC, colorectal cancer.

Table 37–2. Risk of Incident Invasive Colorectal Cancer and Mortality by Age and Gender

	Male	Female
<40	0.06 (1/1617)	0.06 (1/1630)
40–59	0.88 (1/496)	0.69 (1/687)
60–79	4.00 (1/25)	3.03 (1/33)
Lifetime	5.88 (1/17)	5.56 (1/18)
Risk of death	2.45 (1/41)	2.45 (1/41)

Table 37–3. Incidence and Mortality of Colorectal Cancer by Race and Ethnicity

Race	Incidence*	Mortality*	% Distant Spread	5-Year Survival (%)
White	53.9	21.9	19	63
Black	61.9	29.1	24	53
Asian	47.9	13.7	—	—
Native American	35.2	12.8	—	—
Hispanic	35.7	13.2	—	—

*Per 100,000.

effectiveness. All screening tests share a common final pathway for the evaluation of positive tests: colonoscopy. Therefore, the role of endoscopy in colon cancer detection and prevention is paramount. Effective CRC screening depends on the availability of colonoscopy resources in high-risk countries.

This chapter discusses epidemiology and pathogenesis of CRC and reviews the rationale for screening and surveillance in both high-risk groups and average-risk individuals.

Epidemiology

AGE AND GENDER

CRC represents the third most common form of cancer (excluding skin) among both men and women, and overall, it is the second leading cause of cancer death in the United States. There is a progressive increase in risk associated with age. The age-specific incidence in patients age 40 to 44 is less than 10 per 100,000 in the United States, and this rate rises to 500 per 100,000 by age 80 to 84 years (Table 37–2).

Age-adjusted incidence and mortality of CRC is higher in males. Mortality is 14.6 (men) versus 10.0 (women) per 100,000. Over a lifetime, the risk of developing CRC and risk of death is similar in men and women (see Table 37–2). There is some evidence that women who take hormone replacement therapy (HRT) have a lower risk of death from CRC.[9,10] Risk of incidence and mortality in premenopausal women is very low. These lines of evidence suggest that natural or pharmacologic doses of hormones (estrogen, progestin) may exert some protective effects.

RACE AND ETHNICITY

There is strong evidence that African-American men and women are more likely to die from CRC than whites (Table 37–3). Blacks are more likely to have advanced lesions at the time of diagnosis and more likely to have proximal CRC compared with other races.[11,12]

The reasons for increased black mortality are unknown. Delays in diagnosis could be due to socioeconomic status or access to health care, although there are data to refute this hypothesis.[13] Disparities in survival among blacks and whites have been noted in stage II and III cancers, raising the strong possibility that tumors in blacks are more aggressive.[14] Weber and coworkers[15] studied blacks who met the Amsterdam criteria for hereditary nonpolyposis colorectal cancer syndrome (HNPCC) and black patients with early age onset CRC without a family history. They found novel mismatch repair gene mutations in blacks, raising speculation that these mutations might play some role in the early onset of CRC in blacks.

Theuer and colleagues[11] analyzed Surveillance, Epidemiology and End Results Program (SEER) data and California cancer registry data and found strikingly high rates of CRC in blacks, particularly at a young age. For example, the age-specific CRC risk per 100,000 in California at age 50 years was highest in blacks (56.6) followed by Asians (35.2), whites (33.2), and Latinos (26.6). In contrast, blacks in South Africa[16] have a low age-adjusted rate of CRC (2.2 per 100,000), compared with white South Africans (18.7) and African-Americans (32.8). These data suggest that environmental factors (e.g., diet) may interact with genetic factors to impact risk.

The key point from this discussion is that, for whatever reason, African-Americans represent a high-risk group, tend to develop cancers at a younger age, tend to develop proximal cancers, and are more likely to die when they do have CRC. Future research will likely identify causation. In the meantime, it will be important to develop educational efforts to improve screening rates in this high-risk group.

INCIDENCE AND MORTALITY OVER TIME

There has been a slow but steady decline in incidence and mortality of CRC over the past 15 to 20 years in the United States.[1] The explanation for this decline is not clear. Rates of colon screening remain poor. However, during this period, colonoscopy was more commonly performed for a variety of reasons. Inevitably, colonoscopy will lead to adenoma discovery and removal. The NPS data strongly suggest that polyp detection and removal can reduce CRC incidence.

VARIATION BY COUNTRY

Incidence rates vary around the world. Highest risk is in North America, Western Europe, Australia, New Zealand, Israel, and Japan (mortality 30 to 60 per 100,000). Lowest risk is found in India and most of Africa (mortality <10 per 100,000). Migrant studies have found rapid changes in incidence rates, suggesting that the disease is very sensitive to changes in environment. Incidence rates reach the levels of the host country within one or two generations.

Pathogenesis

GENETICS

In 1990, a stepwise model of CRC tumorigenesis was proposed by Fearon and Vogelstein.[17] This model noted a progression of possible genetic mutations that predispose normal mucosal cells toward a neoplastic phenotype. The observation that not all tumors had each mutation strongly suggested that there were several pathways down the slippery slope to malignant invasion.

Inherited CRC syndromes have taught us about two important genetic pathways to CRC.[18] More than 80% of sporadic CRC is associated with mutation of the adenomatous polyposis coli (APC) gene (chromosome 5). The mutation of this tumor suppressor gene most likely promotes the development of adenomas. In familial adenomatous polyposis (FAP), there is a germline mutation of this gene. Normally, this gene acts to phosphorylate beta-catenin, which

leads to its destruction. Accumulation of beta-catenin leads to unregulated cell proliferation and apoptosis is suppressed.[19] The progression of adenoma to cancer appears to require additional mutations (k-ras, chromosome 18, p53). A second pathway (15% to 20%) of sporadic cancer is due to mutation of mismatch repair genes.[20] These genes normally repair errors in DNA replication. Germline mutations are found in patients with HNPCC. The key feature of this mutation in HNPCC is rapid development of polyps that progress to malignancy. In sporadic cancers, acquired mutation of these genes leads to microsatellite instability and malignant progression.

ENVIRONMENT

A large body of epidemiologic evidence has suggested associations between CRC and a variety of environmental factors. Although evidence for cause and effect are lacking, these factors may enhance risk in genetically predisposed individuals. Factors that have been associated with increased risk include dietary fat, sedentary lifestyle, high body mass index, smoking, alcohol, and prior cholecystectomy. Factors associated with lower risk include dietary calcium, vitamin D, folate, dietary fiber, and use of nonsteroidal anti-inflammatory drugs.

High-Risk Groups

Recognition of inherited syndromes and other high-risk diseases associated with CRC is the key to appropriate screening and management (Table 37–4). It is important for primary care providers to recognize these syndromes and to refer patients for appropriate screening and surveillance.

Perhaps the most important questions in the medical history are (1) do you have a first-degree relative with CRC and, if yes, (2) did any relative have cancer before age 50 years. Patients with an index relative less than 50 years old should be considered at risk for an inherited syndrome and should merit intensive screening at a young age. Recommendations for the specific syndromes are summarized in Table 37–5.

FAMILIAL ADENOMATOUS POLYPOSIS

Patients with FAP have a germline mutation of the APC gene on chromosome 5, predisposing them to adenoma formation. Most affected patients will have more than 100 adenomas. One hundred percent of affected individuals will develop CRC, so that once the phenotype is recognized, colectomy should be considered. The average age of adenoma appearance is 16 years, and the age of CRC is 39 years. In a variant of this syndrome, called attenuated FAP, mutations occur at either the 5′ or 3′ end of the gene. Phenotypically, patients have fewer polyps, with delayed onset of adenoma and cancer formation. Familial colon cancer in Ashkenazi Jews may be the result of a specific germline mutation of the APC gene (I1307K). This mutation appears to predispose to sporadic mutations at distant sites resulting in a high malignant risk.[21]

Table 37–4. Risk Stratification

Risk Level	% of Colorectal Cancer	Recommendations for Screening
High Risk Familial polyposis	1%	Sigmoidoscopy in teenage years Genetic screening can be considered Total colectomy if detected
Hereditary nonpolyposis colorectal cancer	5%	Colonoscopy in 3rd/4th decade at 2-year intervals Genetic screening can be considered
Chronic ulcerative colitis/Crohn's colitis	<1%	Colonoscopy every 2 years beginning at 8–10 years after onset of colitis
Moderate Risk Familial risk First-degree relative	15%–20%	Begin screening at an age 10 years younger than age of index case Consider colonoscopy screening
Personal history of breast, uterine, or ovarian cancer	<1%	No specific recommendation
Average Risk Age >50 years	70%–75%	Begin screening at age 50

Table 37–5. Inherited Forms of Colorectal Cancer

	Genetic Mutation	Lifetime Risk of CRC	Screening Recommendation
FAP	APC	100%	Sigmoidoscopy beginning at age 10–12 Gene testing can be considered Colectomy if phenotype confirmed
HNPCC	MMR	80%	Colonoscopy every 1–2 yr Begin at age 20–25
Peutz Jeghers	STK11	2%–13%	Colonoscopy in teen years
Juvenile polyposis	SMAD4 DPC4	Up to 50%	Colonoscopy in teen years

CRC, colorectal cancer; FAP, familial adenomatous polyposis; HNPCC, hereditary nonpolyposis colorectal cancer.

Screening Recommendation

Family members should be screened with annual sigmoidoscopy beginning at age 10 to 12 years. Genetic counseling and testing should be considered. The current tests detect 80% to 90% of FAP families. These patients are at risk for other malignancies, the most common of which is duodenal or periampullary cancer (5% to 12% lifetime risk). Upper endoscopy with side-viewing instruments to visualize the ampulla is recommended beginning at age 20 to 25 years and should be repeated every 1 to 3 years. There is evidence that colon adenomas regress with cyclo-oxygenase-2 (COX-2) selective inhibition. Many experts recommend that patients use COX-2 inhibitors after colectomy, hoping to reduce the risk of upper gastrointestinal (UGI) malignancy.

HEREDITARY NONPOLYPOSIS COLORECTAL CANCER SYNDROME

The most recent evidence suggests that HNPCC accounts for 1% to 2% of all colon cancers.[22,23] Moreover, there is now evidence that regular screening of kindreds can substantially reduce the risk of CRC.[24] These data reinforce the importance of recognizing affected kindreds and performing surveillance colonoscopy. The clinical

Table 37–6. Criteria for Hereditary Nonpolyposis Colorectal Cancer

Amsterdam Criteria Modified[25]
At least 3 relatives with HNPCC-associated cancer (CRC, endometrium, small bowel, ureter, or renal pelvis) plus
- One affected patient is a 1st-degree relative of the other two
- Two of more successive generations
- One or more received diagnosis of CRC before age 50 years

Bethesda Guidelines[26]
Amsterdam criteria or one of the following:
- Two cases of HNPCC-associated cancer in one patient
- CRC and a 1st-degree relative with HNPCC-associated cancer (before age 45 years) and/or adenoma (before age 40 years)
- Colon or endometrial cancer before age 45 years
- Right-sided colon cancer with undifferentiated or signet-cell features before age 45 years
- Adenomas before age 40 years

CRC, colorectal cancer; HNPCC, hereditary nonpolyposis colorectal cancer.

definitions have been modified over the years from the original Amsterdam criteria[25] to the Bethesda Guidelines[26] that provide a much less rigid clinical definition (Table 37–6).

The findings of the Finnish Cancer Registry[27] reinforce the need to be aware of other cancers that may develop in these kindreds including endometrial (60%); stomach (13%); ovary (12%); bladder, urethra, and ureter (4.0%); brain (3.7%); kidney (3.3%); and biliary tract and gallbladder (2.0%).

The most recent recommendations from the GI Multi-Society Task Force on Colorectal Cancer[8] are to perform colonoscopy every 1 to 2 years beginning at age 20 to 25 years or 10 years earlier than the youngest index case with CRC, whichever comes first. Genetic testing is an option when there is a known inherited mismatch repair gene (approximately 50% to 70% of kindreds). The 2-year interval is recommended because of the rapid development of advanced lesions in this syndrome. In addition, screening for UGI cancers with endoscopy and pelvic examinations with transvaginal ultrasound are recommended every 1 to 2 years.

FAMILIAL RISK

Epidemiologic data[28,29] clearly demonstrate that individuals with a first-degree relative with CRC have an increased risk of CRC. Twin studies estimate that 35% of CRC arose from inherited factors and 65% from environmental factors.[30] A meta-analysis considered risk associated with familial risk.[31] The relative risk of CRC with an affected first-degree relative was 2.4. With more than one relative, the risk was 4.2. If CRC diagnosed before age 45 the risk was 3.8, from 45 to 59 it was 2.2, and older than age 59 it was 1.8.

The odds ratio for CRC risk with one affected relative is 1.7 to 1.8 and with two affected relatives is 2.75 to 5.7. Studies have suggested that, if the index family member was younger than 55 years, risk is higher. The underlying cause of this increased risk is not known. Inherited susceptibility[32] and shared environmental factors could play a role. The risk associated with second-degree relatives is less certain because this is difficult to study. An analysis from the Utah registry found a risk of 1.5 for patients with second-degree relatives with CRC.

There is also evidence that family members of patients discovered to have adenomas before age 60 years may be at increased risk for CRC.[33] The meta-analysis placed the risk at 1.9, similar to the risk in patients with an older first-degree relative with CRC. Recent data from the VA Cooperative Study suggest that this risk may apply only to index family members with advanced adenomas.[34]

In summary, the Multi-Society Task Force[8] has recommended that patients with familial risk be screened with colonoscopy, beginning at an age of at least 10 years younger than the age of diagnosis in the index family member. The panel also recommended that patients with a first-degree relative with adenoma diagnosed before age 60 should be considered high-risk and begin screening at age 40 or 10 years younger than the age of the index family member.

ULCERATIVE COLITIS AND CROHN'S COLITIS

Although patients with inflammatory bowel disease represent less than 1% of all patients who develop CRC, patients with colitis represent a high-risk group. Risk is strongly associated with extent and duration of disease. The risk is very low in the first 8 years of disease. However, in patients with pancolitis, the risk increases by 0.5% to 1% per year, so that after 35 years, the cumulative risk of CRC is 35%.[35]

Cancers that develop in patients with colitis are often flat and infiltrating, making endoscopic detection difficult. Current recommendations are to perform complete colonoscopy, beginning by year 8 of disease, and to obtain four-quadrant biopsies of otherwise flat mucosa at 10 cm intervals throughout the colon to detect dysplasia. Raised lesions should be biopsied more intensively. There are data that patients with low- or high-grade dysplasia in flat mucosa have a high likelihood of having CRC, and colectomy is generally recommended. There is controversy regarding the approach to low-grade dysplasia. As patients age, there are likely to develop sporadic adenomas, which by definition are adenomas with low-grade dysplasia. Distinguishing a sporadic adenoma from a dysplasia-associated lesion or mass (DALM) is often difficult. There is consensus that if a raised lesion is seen, the lesion and surrounding flat mucosa should be biopsied. If the surrounding mucosa is nondysplastic, it is assumed that the raised lesion is most likely a sporadic adenoma.

There are no randomized clinical trials to evaluate surveillance. There is some evidence that survival is better in patients enrolled in surveillance.[36] Recommendations to perform colonoscopy every 1 to 2 years for life are based on the steadily increasing cumulative risk of CRC with time. Patients with colitis limited to the rectum and left colon have a lower risk. Surveillance beginning at 15 years is recommended.

Screening Strategies for Average-Risk Individuals

GOALS OF SCREENING

Cancer screening is traditionally focused on early cancer detection (i.e., breast, prostate). Two important studies provide compelling evidence that detection and removal of premalignant adenomas can prevent cancer. The NPS[5] enrolled 1418 patients with colon adenomas and performed complete colonoscopy with polyp removal. During a 6-year follow-up, only five cancers were detected in this cohort. This represents a 76% to 90% reduction from expected rates when compared with three reference populations. The Minnesota FOBT Study[6] followed their cohort for 18 years and found that, in addition to mortality reduction, there was a 21% reduction in cancer incidence among screened patients compared with controls. The authors believe that this benefit was directly related to polyp discovery and removal.

These studies suggest that there is a unique opportunity to prevent CRC if precursor adenomas can be detected and removed. Patients with advanced adenomas are at greatest risk to develop CRC. In this discussion of screening, each of the potential screening tests is assessed for its ability to reduce mortality from CRC and prevent cancer by detection of advanced neoplasia.

FECAL OCCULT BLOOD TEST

Three randomized-controlled trials[37–39] have demonstrated that, among patients who receive fecal occult blood test (FOBT) compared with controls, cancers are discovered at an earlier stage

Table 37–7. Fecal Occult Blood Test: Randomized Controlled Trials

	Mandel and colleagues[37]	Hardcastle and colleagues[38]	Kronborg and colleagues[39]
Subjects (N)	46,551	152,850	140,000
Frequency of testing	Annual or biennial	Biennial	Biennial
Slide rehydration	Yes	No	No
Duration of follow-up (years)	13	8	10
Rate of positive tests during program (%)	38/28*	4.0	4.3
Reduction of cancer mortality versus control	33%	15%	18%

*Annual/biennial.

and mortality is reduced. Table 37–7 describes the three randomized trials. These studies differ in important ways but reach two similar conclusions. First, cancers discovered in patients who were screened were detected at an earlier stage than cancers in unscreened controls. Second, this early detection resulted in mortality reduction from CRC. Each study operated under the principle that if a test was positive, a structural examination of the colon was warranted.

The European studies using nonrehydrated slides and biennial testing and found lower rates of mortality reduction. The Minnesota study performed annual and biennial tests and rehydrated FOBT slides. Rehydration increases test sensitivity and reduces specificity. Over the 10-year study period, more than 30% of subjects had positive tests. Despite the high rate of positive tests, one half of the discovered cancers were not found as a result of positive tests. These results demonstrate only moderate sensitivity for CRC, even in populations that have regular repeat testing.

Sensitivity issues of FOBT were further addressed in the VA Cooperative Study,[40] which used advanced adenomas as the key endpoint. Nearly 2900 asymptomatic subjects had complete colonoscopy to determine the prevalence of advanced neoplasia (defined as tubular adenoma ≥1 cm, adenoma with villous histology or high-grade dysplasia, and cancer). These patients had FOBT tests (rehydrated, three stool samples) before undergoing colonoscopy. Among patients with advanced neoplasia, only 24% had a positive FOBT. These data suggest that one-time testing is not sensitive for advanced neoplasia and that FOBT programs will need to maintain adherence to repeat testing to be effective.

Fecal Occult Blood Test Recommendations

The Multi-Society Task Force[8] recommends annual testing of three consecutive stools without rehydration and that all positive tests be evaluated with colonoscopy. The VA study[40] confirmed what all other studies have shown: patients with a positive FOBT do have an increased risk of advanced neoplasia—odds ratio (OR) of 3.47 (95% confidence interval [CI] 2.76 to 4.35). One study found that only one in three patients with a positive FOBT had follow-up colonoscopy.[41] Each level of FOBT screening has compliance issues. If testing is not repeated regularly or colonoscopy is not performed when tests are positive, FOBT screening is not likely to be effective.

FLEXIBLE SIGMOIDOSCOPY

Case-control studies[42,43] have found significant reduction in CRC mortality in patients exposed to sigmoidoscopy—a benefit limited to the portion of the colon examined. In these studies, populations exposed to sigmoidoscopy were compared with similar controls (nested cohort). Mortality from CRC was reduced by 60% in the distal portion of the colon. No benefit was seen for patients with proximal colon cancer. These studies used rigid sigmoidoscopy, limited to the distal 25 cm of the colon. Modern flexible sigmoidoscopy permits examination of the distal 55 to 60 cm. If adenomas are found, many experts recommend proceeding to full colonoscopy. Therefore, potential benefit could be extended to the proximal colon, if most patients with cancer and advanced lesions have a distal adenoma that would lead to colonoscopy.

Two recent studies[4,44] used screening colonoscopy to determine prevalence of advanced neoplasia in more than 5000 asymptomatic subjects and to determine whether sigmoidoscopy would have identified the patients. These studies found that patients with either small (<1 cm) or large adenomas in the distal colon have an increased risk of advanced proximal neoplasia. In these studies, the authors assumed that, if an adenoma of any size was found, complete colonoscopy would be performed. With this assumption, sigmoidoscopy would detect 70% to 80% of patients with any advanced neoplasia. However, among patients with advanced proximal neoplasia, 46% to 52% would not be identified.

In a recent study from Norway,[45] 1833 patients with adenomas had flexible sigmoidoscopy followed by colonoscopy. Although the risk of proximal advanced neoplasia was higher in patients with advanced lesions in the distal colon, the authors noted that 38% of patients with proximal advanced neoplasia would not have been detected if colonoscopy was limited to patients with advanced distal lesions.

Based on these studies, a positive sigmoidoscopy is defined as the finding of an adenoma of any size. There is still some debate about the significance of hyperplastic polyps discovered at sigmoidoscopy. The VA study[4] found that that the risk of proximal advanced neoplasia was similar in patients with hyperplastic polyps and patients with no polyps in the distal colon. At this time, the evidence does not support proceeding to colonoscopy if the only finding at sigmoidoscopy is a hyperplastic polyp.

The expert panels recommend that sigmoidoscopy be repeated at 5-year intervals if negative. This recommendation is conservative and based on the results of a case-control study that found that a reduction in cancer deaths was present up to 10 years after the last screening examination.[42]

COMBINED FLEXIBLE SIGMOIDOSCOPY AND FECAL OCCULT BLOOD TEST

The VA Cooperative Study[40] found that the combination of one-time sigmoidoscopy and FOBT would identify 76% of patients with advanced neoplasia (a small incremental improvement over sigmoidoscopy alone). This may represent the most optimistic yield, because this study used rehydrated FOBT and assumed that any distal adenoma would lead to full colonoscopy. As patients age, the tests are less effective, because of the increased prevalence of proximal neoplasia with age.

COLONOSCOPY

Colonoscopy is currently the final step for each of the other screening programs. Some have suggested that is should be the first and only step. Two recent studies performed colonoscopy in more than 5000 asymptomatic individuals.[4,44] The colonoscopy screening studies revealed the high prevalence of advanced neoplasia in asymptomatic subjects. In both studies, 5.6% of patients had either cancer, adenoma with high-grade dysplasia, or adenoma with villous histology, some of whom would not be detected with sigmoidoscopy. In the VA study, an additional 5% had adenomas greater than 9 mm. These studies were not designed to measure mortality reduction or incidence reduction.

There are no clinical trials that have measured incidence or mortality reduction with colonoscopy. However, there are several lines of indirect evidence:

- In the NPS, patients had colonoscopy with removal of all adenomas.[5] During 6 years of follow-up, cancer incidence was reduced by 76% to 90% compared with expected rates in control populations.
- Colonoscopy was used to evaluate positive tests in the FOBT studies. Subsequent mortality reduction was due to colonoscopic discovery of early cancers. Mandel and coworkers[6] found reduced incidence of CRC, which was attributed to colonoscopic detection and removal of premalignant adenomas.
- The sigmoidoscopy case control studies suggest a benefit in that portion of the colon examined. Gondal and colleagues[45] suggest that "going farther" will identify more patients with advanced lesions.

Colonoscopy is the most effective test for detection of adenomas and would be likely to have a greater impact on cancer incidence rates than any other form of screening. Risks and costs of colonoscopy are higher than other forms of screening. Most current data suggest that colonoscopy should only be performed by well-trained experts. Implementation of widespread screening would require careful consideration of resource management.

Colonoscopy is now included among screening options recommended by the American Cancer Society and the Multi-Society Task Force. The United States Preventive Services Task Force (USPSTF) finds the current evidence insufficient to recommend for or against colonoscopy.[7]

IMAGING STUDIES OF THE COLON: BARIUM

Barium enema with air contrast is included in most of the menus of screening recommendations in the United States. There are no direct data evaluating imaging modalities in screening populations. The NPS found that barium studies fail to identify up to 50% of patients with polyps greater than 1 cm.[46] Therefore, if we hold barium enema to the standard of detecting advanced neoplasia, it performs poorly.

Cost and Compliance

Screening is best viewed as program with many components, which include the following:

- Initial screening test
- Evaluation of positive screening test
- Interval rescreening for negative screening test
- Surveillance for patients with neoplasia

Program effectiveness depends on adherence to each component. Program costs should account for each element of the program. During the past few years, there has been considerable discussion about which screening program was most effective. Although this question is far from resolved, we now have several sophisticated cost effectiveness models, all of which show the same thing: screening for CRC with any of the recommended tests is effective (i.e., likely to lead to mortality reduction) and cost effective relative to other medical interventions and treatments[47–53] and perhaps cost-saving.[52,53]

Although more work is needed to clarify the clinical effectiveness of each screening program, it is obvious that no program will be effective if compliance is poor. Rates of adherence to screening in the United States where screening is recommended is dismal—only 30% to 40% of age-eligible patients receive recommended screening. Therefore, more attention should be focused on obstacles to compliance.

Endoscopic Treatment of Cancer and Polyps

When is endoscopic resection of a polyp sufficient during a screening examination? Treatment options for patients with endoscopically removed malignant polyps remain controversial. In general, decisions to perform surgery are driven by several factors. First, is the endoscopist certain of complete removal? If the polyp is pedunculated, complete removal of neoplastic tissue can usually be confirmed with histology. The histologic definition of complete is a margin of normal tissue at the margin that is greater than 1 mm. For patients with large sessile polyps, this determination may not be possible. Second, tumors that are poorly differentiated are much more likely to be more advanced. Third, is there any microscopic evidence of lymphatic or venous invasion in the specimen? If any of the poor prognostics markers are present, surgical resection should be strongly considered. If all of the indicators are favorable, close endoscopic follow-up is sufficient.[54]

Surveillance after Detection of Neoplasia

Recommendations for surveillance have an enormous impact on screening program cost and resource utilization (Table 37–8). After the diagnosis and treatment of cancer, most experts recommend surveillance colonoscopy within 1 to 3 years and if negative every 3 to 5 years thereafter. If a complete examination of the colon was not possible before treatment because of obstruction, a colonoscopy should be completed within 3 to 6 months of surgical treatment to rule out synchronous lesions. Patients with cancer clearly have genetic and/or environmental risk factors that predispose them to malignancy and are the most likely to benefit from surveillance.

The rationale for surveillance after removal of adenomas is based on several lines of evidence, but connecting the dots of evidence is problematic. We know that patients with adenomas have an increased risk of developing CRC. Most (if not all) CRC has an adenoma precursor lesion. Genetic evidence of mutation of the tumor suppressor gene on chromosome 5 (*APC* gene) is found in 80% of CRC and in most adenomas. Therefore, we have a genotype and phenotype that identifies patients who may develop cancer.

The NPS[55] demonstrated that patients with adenomas will commonly be found to have adenomas again within 3 years of a baseline colonoscopy with complete polypectomy. In the NPS, 1418 patients with adenomas had colonoscopy with removal of all visible adenomas. Within 3 years after the "clearing" colonoscopy, 32% to 42% were found to have adenomas (most were small tubular adenomas). Within 3 years, 3.3% had advanced adenomas. We know now that many of these lesions were probably not new but represent missed lesions at the baseline colonoscopy. In a study using back-to-back colonoscopy performed by two endoscopists, Rex and coworkers[56] found that 24% of small adenomas (<1 cm) were not detected on one examination. Nevertheless, it is likely that some of the lesions in the NPS were indeed newly formed adenomas. Therefore, patients with adenomas are likely to form new adenomas within a few years. Because patients with adenomas have an increased risk of CRC, we have a rationale for performing surveillance.

The NPS also found that, after baseline colonoscopy and polyp removal, the subsequent risk of CRC over the next 6 years was reduced by 76% to 90% compared with three reference populations.[5] A recent study from Europe[57] also found a reduced incidence rate of CRC after polypectomy. These data show that the baseline colonoscopy and polypectomy can reduce CRC incidence. Thus, if patients with polyps will grow new polyps, and polyp removal is reduces CRC incidence, surveillance should be beneficial.

However, there are several flaws in this reasoning. Thirty percent to 50% of individuals will develop adenomas in their lifetime, and only 5% to 6% will develop cancer. Therefore, most patients with adenomas will not develop cancer and would be unlikely to benefit from surveillance. How can we identify those patients who are likely to progress to malignancy (and therefore benefit from surveillance)? Risk stratification based on patient characteristics and the index polyp would be ideal. We have some preliminary evidence that patients who have only one to two small tubular adenomas are at low risk for development of new advanced adenomas during 5 to 6 years of follow-up.[55] Indeed, most patients discovered to have adenomas during screening examinations have only small tubular adenomas. The VA cooperative study[4] found that among all patients with neoplasia, 72% had only small tubular adenomas. If surveillance intervals can be extended for this large group, it will reduce the burden of surveillance colonoscopy. Further work is needed to define the appropriate interval for patients with small tubular adenomas. In the future, specific genetic markers or biologic markers within the index polyp may help stratify patients into high- or low-risk groups.

Future Trends
CHEMOPREVENTION

It is beyond the scope of this chapter to review the subject of chemoprevention. However, there has been speculation that chemoprevention, if effective, might preclude the need for colon screening. There are compelling data that aspirin may be an effective chemoprevention agent.[58–67]

Table 37–8. Surveillance Recommendations	
Finding on Baseline Colonoscopy	**Recommended Surveillance Plan**
Advanced adenoma or multiple (≥3) adenomas	F/U at 3 years
1–2 small (<1 cm) tubular adenoma	F/U at 5 years
Invasive cancer	If colon obstructed preoperatively: F/U within 6 months If preoperative colonoscopy complete: F/U within 3 years
F/U, follow-up.	

Recent studies have analyzed the use of aspirin as a chemoprevention agent and asked if aspirin were effective, would screening still be necessary. Two cost effectiveness models concluded that even an effective chemoprevention agent should not replace colon cancer screening.[68,69]

VIRTUAL IMAGING

Computed tomography (CT) colonography has been shown in some studies to be sensitive for detection of lesions greater than 1 cm (>90%). However, there is still considerable variability in polyp detection rates between studies. With technical improvements, sensitivity is likely to improve. However, with improved detection, will come visualization of small polyps, which may or may not be neoplastic. Because 30% to 50% of individuals older than age 50 have adenomas, and another 10% to 15% have hyperplastic polyps, a sensitive CT scan will result in many positive tests, which would require colonoscopy. Currently, CT colonography requires an excellent colon prep. Should the test be positive and colonoscopy recommended, patients would need to undergo two colon preps. Some studies have suggested that one barrier to colonoscopy is the pre-examination cleansing. Sonnenberg and colleagues[70] modeled the cost effectiveness of CT colonography and colonoscopy and found that colonoscopy dominated CT over a broad range of assumptions. Further study is needed before recommending these tests to patients.

GENETIC SCREENING OF STOOL

Cancers and high-risk adenomas harbor genetic mutations. Normal and mutated cells are sloughed into the bowel lumen and excreted with stool. Recent work has found that analyzable DNA can be recovered from stool and can be screened for key mutations associated with colorectal neoplasia.[71-73] Because tumors can have different genetic fingerprints resulting from different pathways toward malignancy, the scientific approach has been to analyze stool for several possible DNA alterations. Preliminary results provide proof-of-principle data. Stool DNA of patients with tumors that have a specific mutation can be detected with high accuracy (91%). Studies are underway to evaluate stool DNA testing to determine the operating characteristics (sensitivity and specificity) in a low-prevalence screening population.

REFERENCES

1. Jemal A, Murray T, Samuels A, et al: Cancer statistics 2003. CA Cancer J Clin 53:5–26, 2003.
2. O'Brien MJ, Winawer SJ, Zauber AG, et al: The National Polyp Study. Patient and polyp characteristics associated with high-grade dysplasia in colorectal adenomas. Gastroenterology 98:371–379, 1990.
3. Muto T, Bussey HJ, Morson BC: The evolution of cancer or the colon and rectum. Cancer 36:2251–2270, 1975.
4. Lieberman DA, Weiss DG, Bond JH, et al and VACSP Group #380: Use of colonoscopy to screen asymptomatic adults for colorectal cancer. N Engl J Med 343:162–168, 2000.
5. Winawer SJ, Zauber AG, Ho MN, et al: Prevention of colorectal cancer by colonoscopic polypectomy. N Engl J Med 329:1977–1981 1993.
6. Mandel JS, Church TR, Bond JH, et al: The effect of screening fecal occult-blood screening on the incidence of colorectal cancer. N Engl J Med 343:1603–1607, 2000.
7. Pignone M, Rich M, Teutsch SM, et al: Screening for colorectal cancer in adults at average risk: A summary of the evidence for the U.S. Preventive Services Task Force. Ann Intern Med 137:132–141, 2002.
8. Winawer S, Fletcher R, Rex D, et al: Colorectal cancer screening and surveillance: Clinical guidelines and rationale—Update based on new evidence. Gastroenterology 124:544–560, 2003.
9. Grodstein F, Martinez E, Platz EA, et al: Postmenopausal hormone use and risk for colorectal cancer. Ann Intern Med 128:705–712, 1998.
10. Rossouw JE, Anderson GL, Prentice RL, et al for the Women's Health Initiative: Risks and benefits of estrogen plus progestin in health postmenopausal women. JAMA 288:321–333, 2002.
11. Theuer CP, Wagner JL, Taylor TH, et al: Racial and ethnic colorectal cancer patterns affect the cost-effectiveness of colorectal cancer screening the United States. Gastroenterology 120:848–856, 2001.
12. Nelson RL, Dollear T, Freels S, et al: The relation of age, race and gender to the subsite location of colorectal carcinoma. Cancer 80:193–197, 1997.
13. Cordice JW, Johnson H: Anatomic distribution of colonic cancers in middle-class black Americans. J Natl Med Assoc 83:730–732, 1991.
14. Chen VW, Fenoglio-Preiser CM, Wu XC, et al: Aggressiveness of colon carcinoma in blacks and whites. Cancer Epidemiol Biomarkers Prev 6:1087–1093, 1997.
15. Weber TK, Chin HM, Rodriquez-Bigas M, et al: Novel hMLH1 and hMSH2 germline mutations in African Americans with colorectal cancer. JAMA 281:2316–2320, 1999.
16. Sitas F, Blaauw D, Terblanche M: Cancer in South Africa, 1992. Johannesburg, National Cancer Registry, South African Institute for Medical Research, 1997.
17. Fearon ER, Vogelstein B: A genetic model for colorectal tumorigenesis. Cell 61:759–767, 1990.
18. Calvert PM, Frucht H: The genetics of colorectal cancer. Ann Intern Med 137:603–612, 2002.
19. Chung DC: The genetic basis of colorectal cancer: Insights into critical pathways of tumorigenesis. Gastroenterology 119:854–865, 2001.
20. Chung DC, Rustgi AK: The hereditary nonpolyposis colorectal cancer syndrome: Genetics and clinical implications. Ann Intern Med 138:560–570, 2003.
21. Laken SJ, Petersen GM, Gruber SB, et al: Familial colorectal cancer in Ashkenazim due to a hypermutable tract in APC. Nat Genet 17:79–83, 1997.
22. Samowitz WS, Curtin K, Lin HH, et al: The colon cancer burden of genetically defined hereditary nonpolyposis colon cancer. Gastroenterology 121:830–838, 2001.
23. Aaltonen LA, Salovaara R, Kristo P, et al: Incidence of hereditary nonpolyposis colorectal cancer and the feasibility of molecular screening for the disease. N Engl J Med 338:1481–1487, 1998.
24. Jarvinen HJ, Aarnio M, Mustonen H, et al: Controlled 15 year trial of screening for colorectal cancer in families with hereditary nonpolyposis colorectal cancer. Gastroenterology 118:829–834, 2000.
25. Vassen HF, Watson P, Mechlin JP, Lynch HT: New clinical criteria for hereditary nonpolyposis colorectal cancer proposed by the international Collaborative group on HNPCC. Gastroenterology 116:1453–1456, 1999.
26. Rodriquez-Bigas MA, Boland CR, Hamilton SR, et al: A National Cancer Institute Workshop on hereditary nonpolyposis colorectal cancer syndrome: Meeting highlights and Bethesda guidelines. J Natl Cancer Inst 89:1758–1762, 1997.

27. Aarnio M, Sankila R, Pukkala E, et al: Cancer risk in mutation carriers of DNA-mismatch repair genes. Int J Cancer 81:214–218, 1999.

28. Fuchs CS, Giovannucci EL, Colditz GA, et al: A prospective study of family history and risk of colorectal cancer. N Engl J Med 331:1669–1674, 1994.

29. St. John JB, McDermott FT, Hopper JL, et al: Cancer risk in relatives of patients with common colorectal cancer. Ann Intern Med 118:785–790, 1993.

30. Lichtenstein P, Holm NV, Verekasalo PK, et al: Environmental and heritable factors in the causation of cancer—analyses of cohorts of twins from Sweden, Denmark and Finland. N Engl J Med 343:78–85, 2000.

31. Johns LE, Houlston RS: A systematic review and meta-analysis of familial colorectal cancer risk. Am J Gastroenterol 96:2992–3003, 2001.

32. Burt RW, Bishop DT, Cannon LA, et al: Dominant inheritance of adenomatous colon polyps and colorectal cancer. N Engl J Med 312:1540–1544, 1985.

33. Winawer SJ, Zauber AG, Gerdes H, et al: Risk of colorectal cancer in families of patients with adenomatous polyps. N Engl J Med 334:82–87, 1996.

34. Lynch KL, Ahnen DJ, Byers T, et al and VA Cooperative Study Group #380: First degree relatives of patients with advanced colorectal adenomas have an increased prevalence of colorectal cancer. Clin Gastroenterol Hepatol 1:96–102, 2003.

35. Ekbom A, Helmick C, Zack M, Adami HO: Ulcerative colitis and colorectal cancer. A population-based study. N Engl J Med 323:1228–1233, 1990.

36. Choi PM, Nugent FW, Schoetz DJ, et al: Colonoscopic surveillance reduces mortality from colorectal cancer in ulcerative colitis. Gastroenterology 105:418–424, 1993.

37. Mandel JS, Bond JH, Church TR, et al: Reducing mortality from colorectal cancer by screening for fecal occult blood. N Engl J Med 328:1365–1371, 1993.

38. Hardcastle JD, Chamberlain J, Robinson MHE, et al: Randomized, controlled trial of fecal occult blood screening for colorectal cancer. Lancet 148:1472–1477, 1996.

39. Kronborg O, Fenger C, Olsen J, et al: Randomized study of screening for colorectal cancer with fecal occult blood test. Lancet 148:1467–1471, 1996.

40. Lieberman DA, Weiss DG and the VACSP #380 Study Group: One-time screening for colorectal cancer with combined fecal occult-blood testing and examination of the distal colon. N Engl J Med 345:555–560, 2001.

41. Lurie JD, Welch HG: Diagnostic testing following fecal occult blood screening in the elderly. J Natl Cancer Inst 91:1641–1646, 1999.

42. Selby JV, Friedman GD, Quesenberry CP Jr, Weiss NS: A case-control study of screening sigmoidoscopy and mortality from colorectal cancer. N Engl J Med 326:653–657, 1992.

43. Newcomb PA, Norfleet RG, Storer BE, et al: Screening sigmoidoscopy and colorectal cancer mortality. J Natl Cancer Inst 84:1572–1575, 1992.

44. Imperiale TF, Wagner DR, Lin CY, et al: Risk of advanced proximal neoplasms in asymptomatic adults according to the distal colorectal findings. N Engl J Med 343:169–174, 2000.

45. Gondal G, Grotmol T, Hofstad B, et al: Grading of distal colorectal adenomas as predictors for proximal colonic neoplasia and choice of endoscope in population screening: Experience from the Norwegian colorectal cancer prevention study. Gut 52:398–403, 2003.

46. Winawer SJ, Stewart ET, Zauber AG, et al: A comparison of colonoscopy and double-contrast barium enema for surveillance after polypectomy. National Polyp Study Work Group. N Engl J Med 342:1766–1772, 2000.

47. Lieberman DA: Cost-effectiveness model for colon cancer screening. Gastroenterology 109:1781–1790, 1995.

48. Wagner, JL, Tunis S, Brown M, et al: Cost effectiveness of colorectal cancer screening in average-risk adults. In Young GP, Rozen P, Levin B (eds): Prevention and Early Detection of Colorectal Cancer. London, Saunders, 1996, pp 321–356.

49. Sonnenberg A, Delco F, Inadomi JM: Cost-effectiveness of colonoscopy in screening for colorectal cancer. Ann Intern Med 133:573–584, 2000.

50. Ness RM, Homes AM, Klein R, Dittus R: Cost-utility of one-time colonoscopic screening for colorectal cancer at various ages. Am J Gastroenterol 95:1800–1811, 2000.

51. Agency for Health Research and Quality: Cost-effectiveness Analysis of Colorectal Cancer Screening and Surveillance Guidelines (AHRQ Publication No. 00-R051). Washington DC, U.S. Government, September, 2000.

52. Loeve F, Brown ML, Boer R, et al: Endoscopic colorectal cancer screening: A cost-saving analysis. J Natl Cancer Inst 92:557–563, 2000.

53. Frazier AL, Colditz GA, Fuchs CS, Kuntz KM: Cost-effectiveness of screening colorectal cancer in the general population. JAMA 284:1954–1961, 2000.

54. Cooper HS, Deppisch LM, Gourley WK, et al: Endoscopically removed malignant colorectal polyps: Clinicopathologic correlations. Gastroenterology 108:1657–1665, 1995.

55. Winawer SJ, Zauber AG, O'Brien MJ, et al: Randomized comparison of surveillance intervals after colonoscopic removal of newly diagnosed adenomatous polyps. N Engl J Med 328:901–906, 1993.

56. Rex DK, Cultler CS, Lemmel GT, et al: Colonoscopic miss rates of adenomas determined by back-to-back colonoscopies. Gastroenterology 112:24–28, 1997.

57. Citarda F, Tomaselli G, Capocaccia R, et al: Efficacy in standard clinical practice of colonoscopic polypectomy in reducing colorectal cancer incidence. Gut 48:812–815, 2001.

58. Thun MJ, Manboodiri MM, Heath CW Jr: Aspirin use and reduced risk of fatal colon cancer N Engl J Med 325:1593–1596, 1991.

59. Rosenberg L, Pamer JR, Zauber AG, et al: A hypothesis: Nonsteroidal anti-inflammatory drugs reduce the incidence of large-bowel cancer. J Natl Cancer Inst 83:355–358, 1991.

60. Giovannucci E, Rimm EB, Stampfer MJ, et al: Aspirin use and the risk for colorectal cancer and adenoma in male health professionals. Ann Intern Med 121:241–246, 1994.

61. Giovannucci E, Egan KM, Hjunter DJ, et al: Aspirin and the risk of colorectal cancer in women. N Engl J Med 333:609–614, 1995.

62. Sandler RS, Galanko JC, Murray SC, et al: Aspirin and nonsteroidal anti-inflammatory agents and risk for colorectal adenomas. Gastroenterology 114:441–447, 1998.

63. Steinbach G, Lynch PM, Phillips RK, et al: The effect of celecoxib, a cyclooxygenase-2 inhibitor in familial adenomatous polyposis. N Engl J Med 342:1946–1952, 2000.

64. Greenberg ER, Baron JA, Freeman DH Jr, et al: Reduced risk of large-bowel adenomas among aspirin users. The Polyp Prevention Study Group. J Natl Cancer Inst 85:912–916, 1993.

65. Sturmer T, Glynn RJ, Lee IM, et al: Aspirin use and colorectal cancer: Post-trial follow-up data from the Physicians' Health Study. Ann Intern Med 128:713–720, 1998.

66. Sandler RS, Halabi S, Baron JA, et al: A randomized trial of aspirin to prevent colorectal adenomas in patients with previous colorectal cancer. N Engl J Med 348:883–890, 2003.

67. Baron JA, Cole BF, Sandler RS, et al: A randomized trial of aspirin to prevent colorectal adenomas. N Engl J Med 348:891–899, 2003.

68. Ladabaum U, Chopra CL, Huang G, et al: Aspirin as an adjunct to screening for prevention of sporadic colorectal cancer: A cost-effectiveness analysis. Ann Intern Med 135:769–781, 2001.

69. Suleiman S, Rex DK, Sonnenberg A: Chemoprevention of colorectal cancer by aspirin: A cost-effectiveness analysis. Gastroenterology 122:78–84, 2002.

70. Sonnenberg A, Delco F, Bauerfeind P: Is virtual colonoscopy a cost-effective option to screen for colorectal cancer? Am J Gastroenterol 94:2268–2274, 1999.

71. Ahlquist DA, Skoletsky JE, Boynton KA, et al: Colorectal cancer screening by detection of altered DNA in stool: Feasibility of a multitarget assay panel. Gastroenterology 119:1219–1227, 2000.

72. Traverso G, Shuber A, Levin B, et al: Detection of APC mutations in fecal DNA from patients with colorectal tumors. N Engl J Med 346:311–320, 2002.

73. Traverso G, Shuber A, Olsson L, et al: Detection of proximal colorectal cancers through analysis of faecal DNA. Lancet 359:403–404, 2002.

Colonoscopic Polypectomy and Endoscopic Mucosal Resection

CHAPTER

38

Roy Soetikno, Shai Friedland, Takahisa Matsuda, and Takuji Gotoda

Introduction

Colorectal cancer is one of the most common causes of cancer death worldwide. In the United States alone in 2002, it accounted for approximately 148,300 new cases and 56,600 deaths. The lifetime risk of developing colorectal cancer in the U.S. population is about 6%, with 90% of cases occurring in people older than 50 years. The incidence of colorectal cancer is slightly higher in men than in women in the United States, but because women live longer than men, the total number of cases is higher in women. In the United States, colorectal cancer incidence and mortality vary by race and ethnicity: the highest rate occurs in African Americans; an intermediate rate in whites and Asian/Pacific Islanders; and the lowest rates in American Indian, Alaska Natives, and Hispanics.[1]

Up to 90% of all colorectal cancer deaths are believed to be preventable with screening colonoscopy and consequent detection and removal of precursor adenomas and early cancers.[2] Most colorectal cancers are thought to arise from polypoid adenomas, through the adenoma to carcinoma sequence.[3] It has been estimated that 25% to 40% of adults older than 50 years in the United States have at least one adenoma. Only a small fraction of these adenomas will progress to cancer. Because it is not possible to predict which adenoma will become malignant, physicians attempt to remove all adenomas during colonoscopy. The National Polyp Study, which showed that removal of adenomas during screening colonoscopy decreases the subsequent development of colorectal cancer by up to 90% in comparison to historical controls, provided partial support to this current standard of practice.[2] An alternative pathway for colorectal cancer development, called the de novo pathway, has also been proposed.[4,5] It is believed that a fraction of cancers develop within nonpolypoid lesions through this pathway.[6] These nonpolypoid lesions can also be detected during colonoscopy, but until recently little attention has been focused on them outside of Japan,[7] where they have been studied for the past 2 decades.[5]

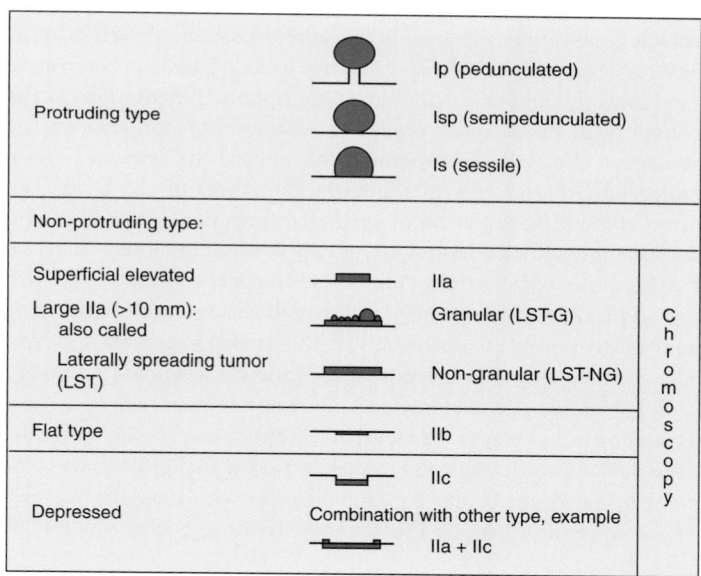

Figure 38–1. Macroscopic classification of early neoplastic lesions of the colon and rectum. This classification provides a more precise schematic description of early neoplastic lesions. In addition to the commonly described pedunculated, semipedunculated, and sessile lesions, the classification provides the appropriate descriptors for flat and depressed lesions, which are increasingly described in the Western countries. The classification is particularly useful for the endoscopist in deciding treatment strategy of early colorectal carcinomas because the risk of submucosal invasion of these lesions corresponds to the endoscopic appearance and size. Chromoscopy is particularly useful to study the surface details and borders of the nonprotruding type.

The focus of therapeutic colonoscopy is the treatment of neoplastic lesions, including adenomas and early cancers. Endoscopically, adenomas and early colorectal cancer can be classified as polypoid (protruded) and nonpolypoid (superficial) types (Fig. 38–1).[8] Colonoscopic polypectomy, a standard procedure throughout the world, is used to remove polypoid lesions. Colonoscopic mucosal resection, a standard procedure in Japan, is increasingly used to remove nonpolypoid lesions in Western countries. Endoscopic mucosal resection (EMR) comprises a variety of techniques intended to remove diseased mucosa by resecting through the middle to deeper layers of the submucosa. It is commonly performed in the treatment of nonpolypoid lesions and is also appropriate for sessile polypoid and submucosal lesions. Recent studies documenting flat and depressed colorectal neoplasms in Western countries highlighted the need for endoscopists to be familiar with these resection techniques.[9–22]

Differential Diagnosis

Colonic lesions are classified as either epithelial or nonepithelial. Epithelial lesions include neoplastic adenomas (tubular, tubulovillous, villous), carcinomas, and non-neoplastic polyps (hyperplastic, juvenile, hamartoma, inflammatory). Occasionally, large numbers of lesions are encountered during colonoscopy of unsuspected patients who have polyposis syndromes, including familial adenomatous polyposis (adenomas), Peutz-Jeghers syndrome (hamartomas), juvenile polyposis (juvenile polyps), or Cowden's syndrome (hamartomas). In addition, patients with hereditary nonpolyposis colorectal cancer may harbor multiple advanced neoplastic lesions. Nonepithelial colonic lesions typically arise in the submucosal, muscularis propria, or serosal layers of the colonic wall. They include lipomas, leiomyomas, carcinoids, lymphomas, and metastatic tumors. Indentations of the colonic wall by adjacent organs or endometrial implants on the serosa can also have the appearance of subepithelial lesions. Careful endoscopic observation of the surface features of the lesion can often allow differentiation of epithelial from nonepithelial origin, because nonepithelial lesions are usually covered by normal mucosa. Furthermore, with current video colonoscopes, and especially with the addition of chromoscopy and magnification endoscopy,[17] it is increasingly possible to distinguish reliably among hyperplastic polyps, adenomatous polyps, and superficial early adenocarcinomas (Fig. 38–2).

Colonoscopic polypectomy and mucosal resection may be viewed as diagnostic procedures. Removal of the entire lesion, when possible, provides the most rigorous evidence that a malignancy was not missed, as it might be due to sampling error with standard biopsies. These procedures provide the definitive treatment when the lesions are removed completely. Subepithelial lesions can at times be removed safely when they are located above the muscularis propria, as evidenced by endoscopic appearance, response to submucosal saline injection, or endoscopic ultrasonography. In general, lesions that are not amenable to endoscopic resection should be biopsied (if possible) to ascertain their histology.

Clinical Features and Pathology

The macroscopic classification of early colorectal neoplasms is critical in the discussion of diagnosis and treatment of early colorectal cancer.[8,23] This classification, which provides a common descriptor of adenomas and early colorectal cancer, should be used by gastroenterologists, radiologists, pathologists, and surgeons worldwide. For endoscopic treatment of early cancer to be successful, endoscopists must recognize the endoscopic features that are associated with superficial malignancies and the characteristics of lesions that are associated with high risk of lymphatic spread and consequent failure of endoscopic treatment.[24]

Based on their endoscopic appearance, we classify adenomas and early colorectal cancers as polypoid, nonpolypoid (superficial), or excavated. The polypoid type consists of pedunculated, semi-pedunculated, and sessile polyps. The nonpolypoid type consists of superficially elevated, flat, and depressed lesions. The excavated type is rarely observed. Superficially elevated nonpolypoid lesions are differentiated from sessile polypoid lesion both endoscopically (the height of the lesion is less than half the diameter) and histologically (the thickness of the lesion is less than twice that of the adjacent normal mucosa).[25] The term *flat* is often used to describe superficially elevated lesions. In the colon, however, flat generally connotes that the surface is flat rather than that the lesion is at the same level as the surrounding mucosa (in the colon and rectum, unlike in the esophagus, early neoplastic lesions are rarely at the same level as the surrounding mucosa). In the Japanese literature, flat lesions (IIa) larger than 10 mm are also called laterally spreading tumors (LSTs), although the term refers more to the growth pattern rather than to the endoscopic appearance. In the United States, these large flat lesions are often called the carpet lesions. LSTs with nodular or coarsely granular surfaces are called

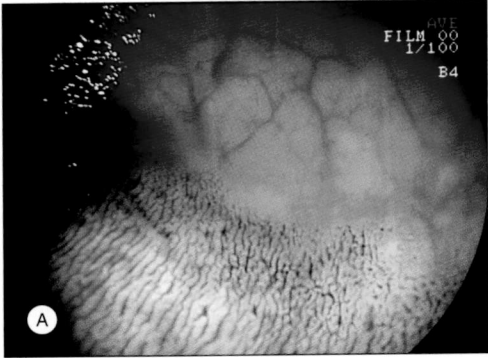
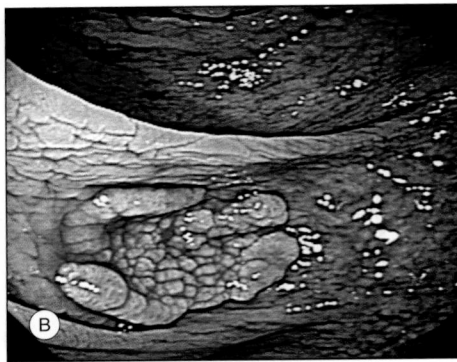
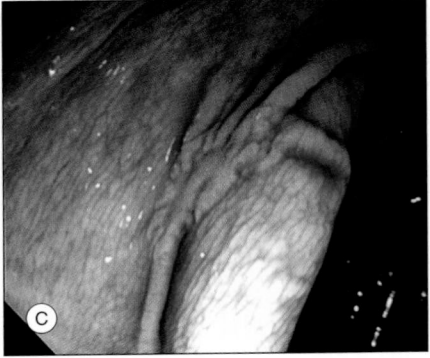

Figure 38–2. Indigo carmine spray can be very useful for detecting and classifying flat and depressed lesions. *A,* Spraying a dilute solution of indigo carmine improves visualization of the grooves on the mucosal surface of the colon (the innominate grooves). *B,* These grooves are also observed in hyperplastic lesions, as in this 15-mm lesion. *C,* Innominate grooves are not observed in neoplastic lesions. Indigo carmine also improves visualization of the border of this 5-mm depressed adenoma. (Figures from Palo Alto.)

LST-granular. Other LSTs are called LST-nongranular. This distinction is important because LST-granular lesions are less likely to contain invasive cancer.[4]

Depressed nonpolypoid lesions, although rare, accounted for almost one third of the invasive cancers that were resected endoscopically by Kudo and colleagues,[4] who observed more than 14,000 colorectal lesions. Confirmatory reports have been published.[26,27] Recent epidemiological studies of flat and depressed lesions in Western countries have also shown that depressed lesions have a high likelihood of containing invasive cancer (Table 38–1).[7,9–20] More than 40% of small (6 to 10 mm) depressed lesions contain submucosal invasive cancer; virtually all large (>2 cm) depressed lesions have submucosal invasion (Table 38–2).[4] In comparison, submucosal invasive cancer is rare in flat lesions smaller than 10 mm. The risk increases to about 30% in LSTs larger than 2 cm.

Protruding (polypoid) lesions have the lowest rate—slightly greater than 2%—of submucosally invasive cancer.[4]

Indications and Contraindications
INDICATIONS
Colonoscopic Polypectomy
Physicians most commonly resect polypoid lesions using either a snare loop or biopsy forceps. Because even small polyps can occasionally harbor high grade dysplasia or cancer and because the malignant potential of an individual polyp is not known, all polyps that are not obviously non-neoplastic are usually removed from otherwise healthy patients. However, the risks of polypectomy must

Table 38–1. Series of Flat and/or Depressed Neoplasms in Patients from Western Countries

Type of Study, Authors (Country)	Number of Patients with F&D Neoplasms/All Patients (%)	Number of F&D Neoplasms/All Neoplasms	Number of F&D Neoplasms with HGD/F&D Neoplasms (%)	Number of F&D Neoplasms with Cancer/F&D Neoplasms (%)	Number of F&D Cancers/All Cancers (%)
Retrospective, Wolber and Owen (Canada)[9]	18/210 (8.6)	29/340 (8.5)	12/29 (41)	2/29 (6.9)	2/2 (100)
Prospective, Lanspa, et al. (U.S.)[10]	18/148 (12.1)	Not stated	0	0	0/1 (0)
Prospective, Jaramillo, et al. (Sweden)[11]	55/232 (23.7)	109/261 (41.7)	12/109 (11)	3/109 (2.7)	3/17 (1.8)
Prospective, Bond (U.K.)[28]	28 F&D lesions/210 patients	28/68 (38.2)	1/28(3.5)	2/28 (7.1)	2/3 (66.7)
Retrospective, Smith, et al. (U.K.)[13*]	9 flat cancers/2198 colonoscopies (0.4)	Not stated	Not stated	Not stated	9/95 (9.4)
Prospective, Rembacken, et al. (U.K.)[14]	123 F&D lesions/1000 patients	123/327 (36.4)	16/123 (13.0)	4/123 (3.2)	4/6 (66.7)
Prospective, Suzuki, et al. (U.K.)[15*]	5 flat cancers/870 colonoscopies (0.6)	Not stated	Not stated	Not stated	5/45 (11.1)
Prospective, Samalin, et al. (France)[16]	74/136 patients with polyps	74/203 (36.4)	0/74	4/74 (5.4)	4/11 (36)
Prospective, Soetikno (U.S.)[29]	48/211 (22.7)	57/139 (41)	Not stated	3/57 (5.2)	3/3 (100)
Prospective, Kiesslich, et al. (Germany)[18]	6/100 (6.0)	6/32 (18.8)	2/6 (33.3)	1/6 (16.7)	1/6 (16.7)
Prospective, Tsuda, et al. (Sweden)[19]	52/866 (6)	66/973 (6.8)	11/66 (16.67)	5/66 (7.5)	5/16 (31.3)

*Study of colorectal cancer only.
F&D, flat and depressed; HGD, high-grade dysplasia; U.K., United Kingdom; U.S., United States.
From Kahng LS, Friedland S, Matsui S, et al: Flat and depressed colorectal neoplasms in the United States of America. Early Colorectal Cancer (Jpn) 8:44–50, 2004.

Table 38–2. The Risk (in %) for Submucosal Invasions Correlated with Endoscopic Appearance and Size of Colorectal Lesions

Appearance	Size				
	Less than 5 mm	6–10 mm	11–15 mm	16–20 mm	>20 mm
Depressed	8.1	40.7	77.8	84.6	90
Flat	0.04	0.2	1.8	10.5	21.4
Protruding	0	1.3	8.5	17.2	31.2

Modified from Kudo S, Kashida H, Tamura T, et al: Colonoscopic diagnosis and management of nonpolypoid early colorectal cancer. World J Surg 24:1081–1090, 2000. Copyright © (2000) Springer-Verlag GmbH & Co. KG.

also be considered: treatment decisions must consider whether substantial risks exist and whether the patient's overall life expectancy is unlikely to be affected by the generally slow progression of colonic adenomas. The natural history of progression through the adenoma to carcinoma sequence is estimated to be approximately 10 years,[28] so patients with advanced comorbid illnesses and limited life expectancy may not benefit from adenoma resection. In general, diminutive polyps measuring up to approximately 6 mm in diameter are easily removed with or without cautery, with use of a biopsy forceps or a snare. Intermediate-sized and larger polyps are most commonly resected via a snare with monopolar cautery. Removal of large sessile polyps may require piecemeal rather than single piece resection. Prophylaxis against postpolypectomy bleeding should be considered with resection of large pedunculated polyps. In addition, when polyps are sessile and particularly when the endoscopic appearance suggests the presence of superficial carcinoma, colonoscopic mucosal resection can be particularly useful to achieve an appropriate submucosal cutting plane and resection margin.

Colonoscopic Mucosal Resection

Colonic mucosal resection is indicated for nonpolypoid and sessile polypoid adenomas. It is also used for the treatment of superficial early cancers, but selection criteria for appropriate tumors are relatively complex and are evolving as more data are collected regarding the risk of lymph node metastasis with submucosal invasive cancers. At present, the indication of mucosal resection for superficial early nonpolypoid or sessile colorectal carcinoma is limited to well or moderately differentiated adenocarcinoma confined to the epithelium without evidence of lymphatic or vascular involvement.[29]

Nonpolypoid lesions can be difficult to capture with standard snare and polypectomy techniques. In addition, it is difficult, if not impossible, to perform en bloc resection of large flat lesions using standard polypectomy techniques; furthermore, application of electrocautery to lesions that can be captured may lead to deep burn into the muscularis propria. Resection of large sessile lesions carries similar risks. Mucosal resection can ameliorate these technical difficulties and risks.

Depressed lesions, including small ones, are most likely to contain submucosally invasive cancer.[4] Thus, complete removal of small, depressed lesions is the only way to accurately determine that no invasive carcinoma is present. Western pathologists rely primarily on evidence of invasion to diagnose invasive carcinoma (as opposed to cellular and glandular morphology, as is common in Japan), which is another strong reason to use mucosal resection as the first-line method to biopsy small, depressed lesions. This is because the superficial submucosa is typically included in these resection specimens, allowing the pathologist to assess for submucosal invasion. Larger truly depressed lesions often are invasive carcinoma. These lesions, after a confirmatory biopsy and tattooing of the site, are usually best managed with operative resection. Mucosal resection is also used increasingly to remove submucosal lesions,[29] especially small (<1 cm) rectal carcinoids in which the risk of metastasis is low.[30,31]

CONTRAINDICATIONS

Colonoscopy is relatively contraindicated in patients who are pregnant or have fulminant colitis, suspected intestinal perforation, fresh intestinal anastomosis, or recent myocardial infarction. Polypectomy and mucosal resection generally should not be performed in patients who have uncorrected bleeding disorders. Good bowel preparation is critical for detection of subtle lesions and for resection of particularly large or difficult lesions when an elevated risk of perforation exists. Thus, poor bowel preparation is also a relative contraindication for performance of complex polypectomy or mucosal resection.

Anticoagulation Therapy

The risks of interrupting anticoagulation for colonoscopic polypectomy or mucosal resection must be balanced against the risks of significant bleeding during and after the procedure.[32,33] The American Society for Gastrointestinal Endoscopy (ASGE) has developed guidelines for management of anticoagulation.[34] In general, patients at relatively low risk of thromboembolic complications can discontinue warfarin 5 days before the procedure and then resume it shortly after standard polypectomy, or 7 to 10 days after complex polypectomy or mucosal resection. The international normalized ratio should be near normal before polypectomy or mucosal resection of a large lesion. High risk patients, such as those with atrial fibrillation and concomitant valvular disease, may receive either standard intravenous heparin until approximately 6 hours before the procedure or other regimens at the cardiologist's discretion. Warfarin generally can be resumed the night after the procedure. Intravenous heparin can be resumed 2 to 6 hours after the procedure. Standard heparin has a short half-life compared with that of low-molecular-weight heparin; thus, it permits swift immediate reversal of anticoagulation should patients develop postpolypectomy bleeding.

Aspirin, Nonsteroidal Anti-inflammatory Drugs, and Antiplatelet Medications

Limited literature suggests that aspirin and other nonsteroidal anti-inflammatory drugs (NSAIDs) in standard doses do not increase the risk of significant bleeding after colonoscopic polypectomy. The ASGE recommends proceeding with standard polypectomy in patients taking these medications.[34] However, we are not aware of any recommendations regarding polypectomy or mucosal resection of large or complex lesions. There also are no guidelines for management of platelet aggregation inhibitors, such as ticlopidine and clopidogrel. The antiplatelet activity of aspirin lasts for 7 to 10 days. Thus, in our practice, when we believe that the risk of bleeding after endoscopic removal of a large or complex lesion is significant, we recommend that most patients refrain from taking aspirin, other NSAIDS, and platelet inhibitors 7 days before the procedure and 7 to 14 days after it.

Antibiotic Prophylaxis for Endocarditis

ASGE and the American Heart Association have published guidelines for antibiotic prophylaxis.[35,36] The risk of bacteremia appears to be low for both diagnostic colonoscopy and colonoscopic polypectomy. The ASGE guidelines note that there are insufficient data to make firm recommendations for antibiotic use even in high-risk patients, such as those with a history of endocarditis or prosthetic valves, and antibiotics should, therefore, be used at the clinician's discretion. For moderate-risk patients, such as those with rheumatic heart disease without a history of endocarditis, the ASGE does not recommend prophylaxis. The risk of bacterial seeding with colonoscopic mucosal resection is not known, but mucosal resection in the upper gastrointestinal tract does not appear to increase the risk of infection.[37]

Instruments

SNARE LOOP

Both the endoscopist and endoscopy assistant must be familiar with the type of snare used. They must understand and have tactile knowledge of the opening and closing of the snare, the closing pressure required to produce optimal coagulation, and the relationship between the size of the tissue being strangulated and the amount of snare being closed. A variety of snares, each with slightly different features, is used for polypectomy and mucosal resection. The choice is made based on personal preference, the size of the lesion, and technique being used. The minisnare is often used for small polyps, and larger snares are used for larger polyps. Stiffer snares are used for colonoscopic mucosal resection so that flat or depressed lesions can be captured in the snare.[29,38]

ELECTROCAUTERY

High-frequency electric current is used to facilitate cutting and to coagulate vessels at the transection margin. Colonoscopic polypectomy or mucosal resection is typically performed with a monopolar snare. The metallic conducting snare serves as the active electrode, and the circuit is completed via a conducting grounding pad that is affixed to the patient's skin. For example, in the case of polypectomy, once the polyp is grasped by the snare, electric current is applied as the snare is closed to transect the stalk. Electric current traveling through tissue heats it. The amount of heat transferred to each point in the tissue (per unit time) is given by the product of the square of the current density and the resistance. The current density is the amount of current passing through a unit area. Therefore, although the same total current passes through the stalk of the polyp and the grounding pad, the current density is much higher at the stalk because the cross-sectional area is smaller. As a result, the stalk is cauterized whereas the bowel wall and the rest of the patient's body generally are left unaffected.[39]

High-frequency electric current greater than 300 kHz (300,000 cycles/second) is used because lower frequencies can stimulate muscles, nerves, and the heart. The effect of the current on the tissue depends on the temperature achieved in the tissue, which in turn depends on the shape of the electrode, the duration and waveform of the current, and the voltage. At temperatures between 50°C and 70°C, irreversible cell damage occurs. Between 70°C and 100°C, the tissue is coagulated: collagen is converted to glucose and the glucose causes the coagulated tissue to become sticky. Above 100°C, the tissue is desiccated: intracellular and extracellular water is vaporized, and the tissue dries out, shrinks, and becomes sticky. During polypectomy, these effects are visualized as a shrinking and whitening of polyp stalks. If low peak voltage (lower than 200 V) is used, the tissue is devitalized, coagulated, and desiccated. As the tissue is dehydrated, the resistance increases until current can no longer flow and no further heat ensues. In this mode, there is little or no cutting; in some clinical situations, the snare can become entrapped in the sticky desiccated tissue.

For efficient electrosurgical cutting, temperatures more than 500°C are required. At these high temperatures, intracellular and extracellular water is vaporized rapidly and the cellular architecture is disrupted by steam pressure. Electrosurgery units generate vaporization by producing electric arcs that jump between the active electrode (snare) and the tissue. The electric arcs focus the current on a small area on the tissue and result in a locally very high current density and temperature. At least 200 V are required to generate these electric arcs; if the tissue is partially desiccated, the voltage required is substantially higher. Electrosurgical cutting is ideally performed without contact between the electrode and the tissue, leaving room for proper arcing to form; cutting then occurs without mechanical pressure as tissue is vaporized. During colonoscopy, however, the snare is typically in contact with the tissue. This contact can lead to lower resistance and high current, in turn causing an inappropriate fall in voltage that prevents electric arcs from forming. The result is an unintended coagulation effect without cutting. Newer cautery units, such as the ERBE (ERBE USA, Marietta, GA), automatically supervise the initial phase of cutting and provide the necessary current and voltage to enhance proper arcing.

During electrosurgical cutting, there is also a coagulation effect, which depends on factors such as the electrode thickness and voltage. Thin electrodes (e.g., a needle knife), low voltages, and rapid cutting result in little coagulation. Thicker electrodes (e.g., a thick snare loop) and higher voltages result in more intense coagulation. Uncontrolled rapid cutting with minimal coagulation can occur if mechanical pressure (e.g., by closing the snare rapidly) is applied; this phenomenon is also familiar to endoscopists with endoscopic retrograde cholangiopancreatography (ERCP) sphincterotomy, where it is called a "zipper" cut. Most electrocautery units allow the endoscopist to choose between various cautery modes that are designed to produce predominantly cutting or predominantly coagulation or a blend of both. However, factors such as the power level, tissue resistance, and speed of snare closure can alter the effect of the cautery. The "cutting" mode delivers a continuous sine-wave voltage pattern. When sufficient voltage is delivered to create electrical arcing, electrosurgical cutting ensues. "Coagulation" and "blended" modes actually deliver a higher voltage, but the delivery is intermittent: short pauses separating brief bursts of delivery. The duty cycle (the total proportion of time that current is delivered) is typically between 5% and 50% in coagulation modes and between 50% and 80% in blended modes. The higher voltages allow deeper coagulation during cutting, particularly in coagulation mode. An additional effect, fulguration (spray coagulation), can occur with very high voltages and low duty cycles when a series of random electrical arcs carbonize the tissue.

The use of submucosal injection during mucosal resection promotes a better distribution of current, because the current can fan out from the resection site to the wide saline cushion. This effect also reduces thermal damage to the part of the colon wall immediately beneath the lesion.[40]

ARGON PLASMA COAGULATION

Argon plasma coagulation (APC) is often used after EMR to cauterize the resection margins. APC generators produce an electrically conducting argon plasma by guiding argon gas through a delivery catheter that also contains an electrode for delivery of high-frequency current. APC generally creates uniformly deep zones of desiccation, coagulation, and devitalization that measure less than 3 mm in total. Because the argon plasma conducts the current, APC can be applied without tissue contact.[41-43]

BIPOLAR INSTRUMENTS

Bipolar instruments, in which current flows between two electrodes in the instrument rather than from one electrode to a grounding pad, have the potential advantage of avoiding damage to deeper structures. Bipolar polypectomy snares are not currently widely used. Bipolar coagulation devices such as the Gold Probe are commonly used to treat bleeding vessels in peptic ulcer disease, and they can be used to treat bleeding areas after polypectomy. Sufficient mechanical pressure should be applied to the vessel to compress it during cauterization to prevent heat dissipation by blood flow.

OTHER INSTRUMENTS

Other instruments that are often used during polypectomy and mucosal resection include the standard sclerotherapy injection needle, Endoclip,[44] Endoloop,[45-47] Roth Net,[48] and Tripod. Detailed examples of use of these instruments are described in the section on techniques.

Techniques

Adequate bowel preparation is important. Techniques to prevent looping of the colonoscope during insertion are essential.[49] Familiarity with the patient, staff, equipment, and accessories are required. A variety of techniques is available to perform sophisticated colonoscopic polypectomy and mucosal resection.[4,29,50,51] These techniques, designed to increase the safety of resection, have allowed resections of lesions that in the past would have necessitated surgery. Pathologic interpretation is vital and is improved by proper orientation of the resected specimen.

ESTIMATION OF MALIGNANT POTENTIAL

Polypectomy and mucosal resection should be performed on appropriate lesions. Assessment to determine the most likely pathologic findings and the depth of invasion is important in planning for polypectomy or mucosal resection. Lesions assessed to be noninvasive are most likely to benefit from endoscopic treatment. Lesions with minimal or moderate risk for submucosal invasion can be treated with endoscopy, provided that the endoscopist believes that the lesion can be safely removed in its entirety and that the potential benefits of endoscopic treatment outweigh the risks. Patients whose lesions have features that are strongly suggestive of invasion should be referred to surgery directly, because endoscopic resection will expose the patients to unnecessary risks. At times, it is appropriate, after assessment of the lesion, to reschedule the patient for a dedicated resection procedure. This allows appropriate discussion of the risks and benefits with the patient and ensures availability of the necessary equipment, endoscopy time, and personnel for the procedure.

Standard endoscopy with and without chromoscopy, endoscopic ultrasonography, and magnification endoscopy can be useful in assessing cancer depth. The assessment is based on several characteristics.

Appearance

The general appearance of the lesion can provide clues as to the likelihood for invasive cancer (Figs. 38–3 and 38–4). As discussed previously, the lesion's size and shape can be predictive of the likelihood for submucosal invasion. Firm consistency, adherence, ulceration, and friability are findings suggestive of invasion. In addition, the appearance of expansion of normal tissue immediately surrounding the lesion may indicate the presence of cancer creeping into the surrounding submucosa. Converging folds (two or more) toward the lesion can also predict submucosal invasion. Saitoh and

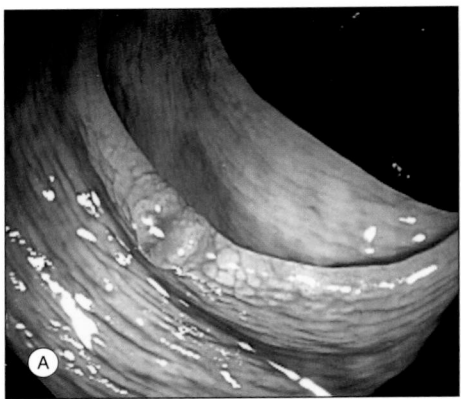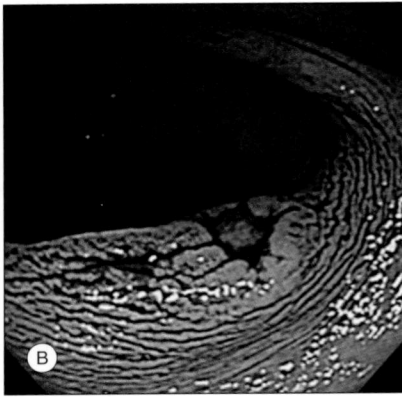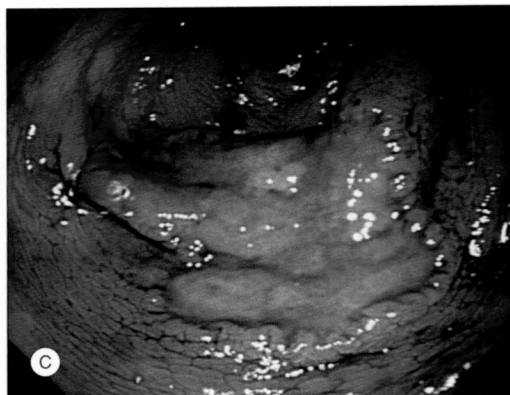

Figure 38–3. Pseudodepression versus true depression. *A,* This adenomatous lesion has small depressions where indigo carmine solution pools. Small depressions without sharp borders, often referred to as pseudodepressions, are typically found in noncancerous adenomas. *B and C,* Extensive depressions with sharp borders are worrisome findings, because they are often observed in cancerous lesions such as these two early adenocarcinomas. (*A and C* from Palo Alto, *B* from Tokyo.)

colleagues[24] have reported the diagnostic operating characteristics of endoscopic findings of depressed colorectal lesions. They observed that patients with one or more findings of expansion appearance, deep depression surface, irregularity of depression surface, or converging folds toward the lesions are more likely to have deep submucosal invasion; the presence of one or more of these findings allowed the endoscopists to determine deep submucosal invasion with a 91% accuracy. These investigators used indigo carmine to improve visualization of lesions, as described later.

Chromoscopy

Chromoscopy is an important technique for visualization and definition of the surface and border of early neoplastic colorectal lesions. In the colon, indigo carmine chromoscopy is widely used in Japan and is increasingly used in Western countries. Indigo carmine chromoscopy is simple to use.[17,52,53] A few milliliters of diluted solution of indigo carmine (0.1 to 0.4%) can be gently sprayed directly from a syringe through the accessory channel onto the tissue surrounding the lesion; direct spraying may cause minor bleeding, which can obscure visualization of the pit pattern. Indigo carmine solution is not absorbed; instead, it pools in mucosal crevices and depressions. The benefits of indigo carmine use are many. For example, innominate grooves, which can be visualized, are present in hyperplastic lesions but are absent in neoplastic lesions. The border of the lesion is delineated by pooling of indigo carmine solution into the crevices at the interface between abnormal and normal tissue. Visualization of surface topography is enhanced. Pooling in depressed areas allows visualization of depressed lesions.

Magnification Endoscopy

The ability to select those lesions that warrant endoscopic removal is important (Fig. 38–5). Diminutive hyperplastic lesions can be left alone, adenomas and superficial early carcinomas are resected endoscopically, and invasive cancers are resected surgically. Closer examination of the surface mucosa, using magnification endoscopy (100×), allows visualization of the pit pattern, which in turn can provide insights as to the pathologic diagnosis of the lesion. Pit patterns, may reflect the tangential structure of the glands within lesion.[54] As the structural organization of the glands becomes disordered or even absent, as it does in invasive carcinoma, the lesion, as seen magnified from its surface, may have a disorderly pattern. Adenomas have their own patterns. Hyperplastic lesions have a specific, orderly, stellar pit pattern.[55,56] Unfortunately, the original classification of the pit pattern may be too complex to apply in

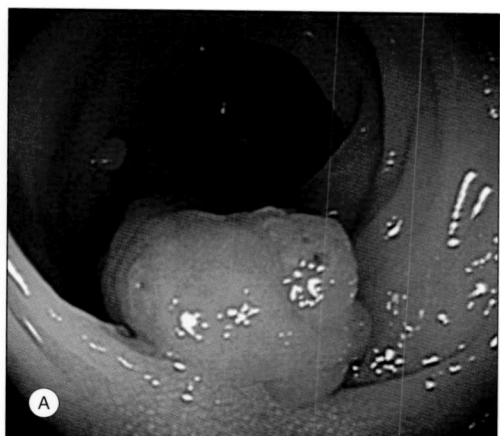
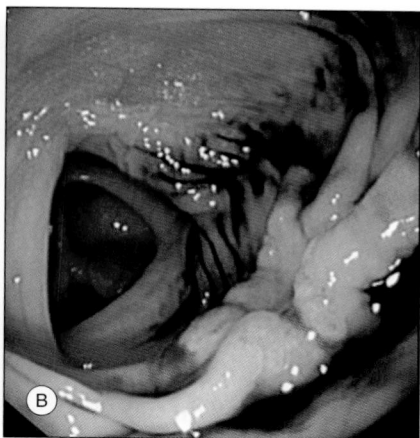

Figure 38–4. Careful observation of the shape of the lesion is crucial to develop an appropriate treatment strategy. A, This sessile lesion has a full or expansive appearance and converging folds, suggesting the presence of invasive carcinoma in the deeper layers of the submucosa. B, Converging folds toward the lesion and central depression are present. The presence of converging folds is specific for invasion deep into the submucosa or beyond. Both of these lesions were treated operatively. (Figures from Tokyo.)

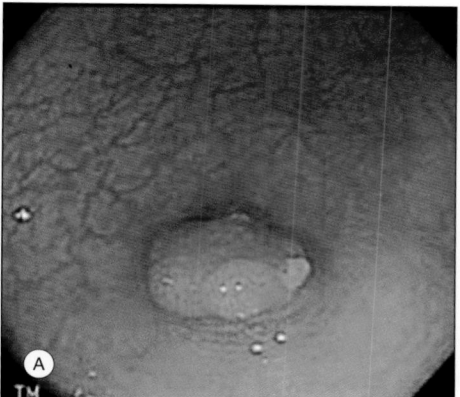
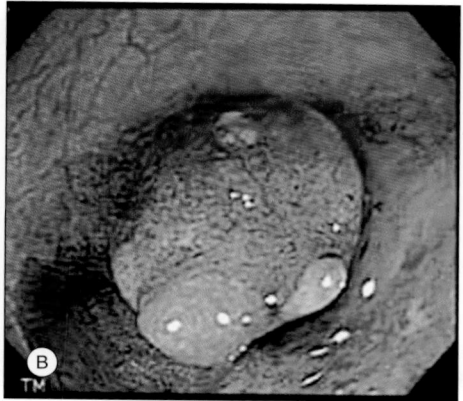
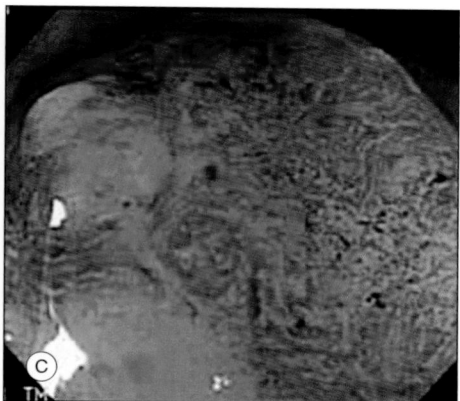

Figure 38–5. Close-up observation of the surface of lesions using magnification endoscopy with crystal violet chromoscopy can improve endoscopic assessment. A, A 7-mm superficial elevated with depression. B, Crystal violet has been applied. C, On close examination using magnification endoscopy (100×), the pit pattern was consistent with deeply submucosal invasive pattern. The patient underwent surgical resection in which a deep, submucosal invasive adenocarcinoma metastatic to local lymph nodes (2/7) was removed. (Figures from Tokyo.)

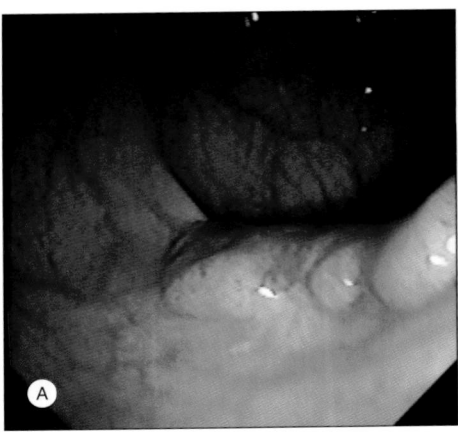
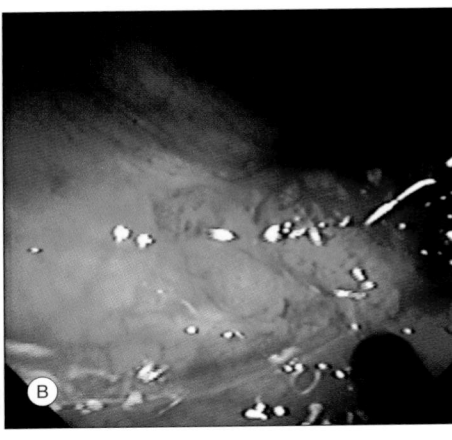

Figure 38-6. *A,* Several previous attempts at endoscopic resection of this sessile rectal lesion were unsuccessful. The lesion has a full appearance that suggests invasive cancer, but prior pathologic examination revealed only villous adenoma. The patient was referred to us. *B,* Nonlifting sign. Injection of saline into the submucosa beneath this lesion does not result in lifting of the lesion; instead, a back flow of injected saline is seen jetting toward the endoscope. Analysis of the operative resection specimen demonstrated adenocarcinoma invading down to the muscularis propria. (Figures from Palo Alto.)

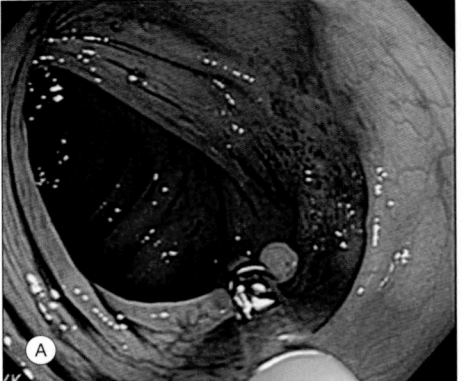
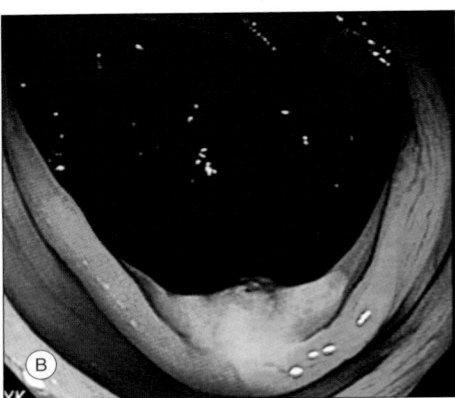

Figure 38-7. Application of hot biopsy forceps to remove and cauterize a 5-mm adenoma. *A,* The lesion was captured using the forceps and coagulation current was applied while the mucosa was tented up to form a pseudopedicle. Tenting causes the cautery effect to be concentrated at the pseudopedicle. *B,* The base of the lesion, which was previously the pseudopedicle, has been coagulated. (Figures from Tokyo.)

routine clinical practice. A simpler classification that groups the patterns as non-neoplastic, noninvasive, and invasive, has been proposed, but is not used widely.

Nonlifting Sign

Observation of the lesion during and after submucosal saline injection is a simple but important method to assess the potential for deeply invasive carcinoma (Fig. 38–6).[57–59] Lesions may not lift because of desmoplastic reaction; invasion from the lesion; or submucosal fibrosis from prior biopsy, cautery, or ulceration. Several studies have reported the diagnostic operating characteristics of the nonlifting sign: the positive predictive value of the nonlifting sign is 83%.

There is a correlate to the nonlifting sign when submucosal injection is not used: it is typically very difficult to capture a deeply invasive lesion in the snare. Difficulties encountered during attempted snare resection should, therefore, alert the endoscopist to the possibility of deep invasion.

Endoscopic Ultrasonography

In general, endoscopic ultrasonography is not used in differentiating nonpolypoid mucosal lesions from submucosally invasive ones.[60–62] The information needed to decide whether or not to perform mucosal resection can usually be collected by observation during conventional colonoscopy, indigo carmine chromoscopy (with standard magnification), and tests for the nonlifting sign. Endoscopic ultrasonography recently was used to locate the blood vessels of large sessile or LST lesions. In that study, the information collected did not significantly change the risk of postpolypectomy bleeding.[63]

TECHNIQUES FOR RESECTION
Polypectomy
Diminutive Polyps

Diminutive polyps can be removed with a variety of techniques: single or repeated use of cold biopsy, hot biopsy, cold snare (snare without cautery),[64] hot snare (snare with cautery; Fig. 38–7), or fulguration. The optimal technique for complete eradication of all polyp tissue is not known and neither is the impact on colon cancer mortality of routine removal during colonoscopy of diminutive (≤ 5 mm) polyps. Documentation of adenoma(s), however, is important for stratification of need for follow-up colonoscopy, which, in turn, is based on assessment of risk of developing colorectal cancer.

Pedunculated, Semipedunculated, and Sessile Lesions

Pedunculated and semipedunculated lesions may be resected by snare loop polypectomy at the middle or upper stalk (Fig. 38–8). Sessile lesions can be resected by a similar technique at the base. Large polyps (>2 cm) or polyps with thick stalk carry a higher risk

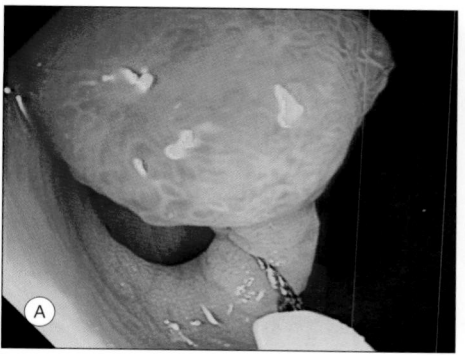
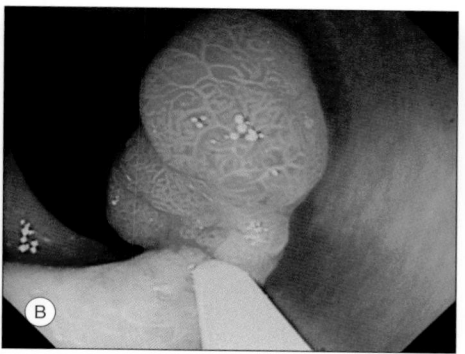
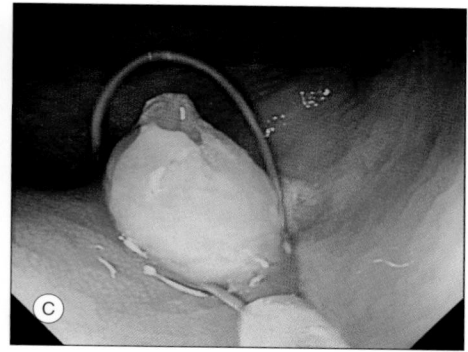

Figure 38–8. Standard polypectomy of a thin-stalked pedunculated polyp. *A,* A snare loop has been position in the middle of the stalk of the polyp. *B,* As electrocautery was applied, the polyp was slightly tented and care was taken to avoid having the head of the polyp touch the opposite wall. Touching the opposite wall could reduce the coagulation at the lower end of the stalk and might cause a contralateral burn. *C,* A stalk remnant with a well-coagulated surface is visible. Leaving some stalk remnant allows application of an endoloop for prevention of bleeding. Alternatively, had bleeding occurred immediately after snaring, the bleeding stalk remnant could have been cauterized further by grasping it with the snare. (Figures from Palo Alto.)

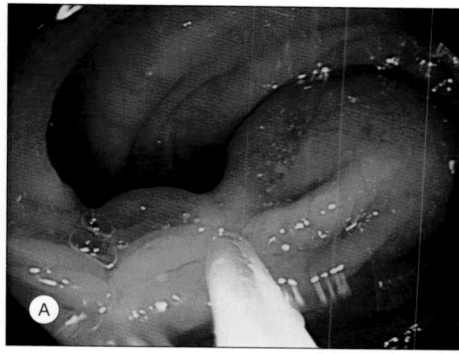
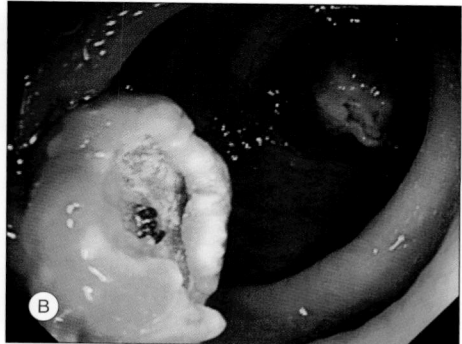

Figure 38–9. Use of the endoloop to prevent postpolypectomy bleeding. The endoloop is used like a snare, except it can be detached after its deployment at the base of the polyp. *A,* The endoloop has been applied at the base of a large pedunculated lesion. The electrocautery snare has been placed above the loop with sufficient room to prevent the endoloop from slipping off after transection. *B,* The resection site immediately after resection. A small blood vessel is visible. There was no bleeding after resection. The diagnosis was lipoma. (Figures from Palo Alto.)

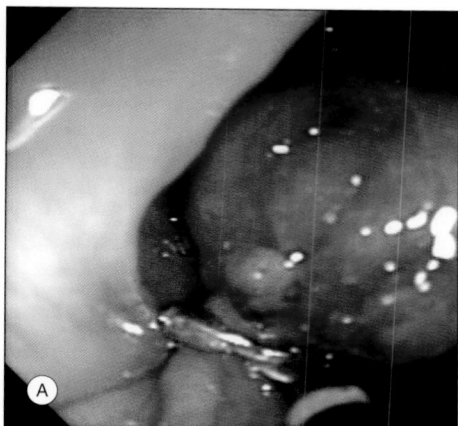
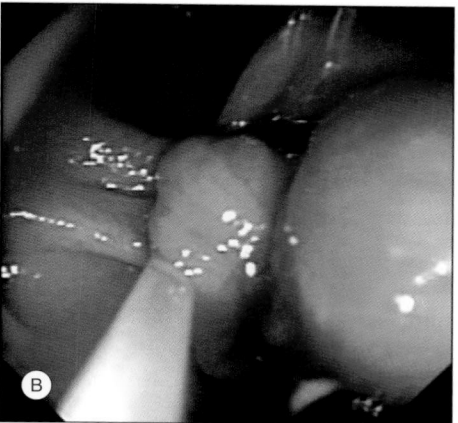

Figure 38–10. Application of the endoloop can be difficult, especially with large pedunculated polyps in a narrow and tortuous sigmoid colon. The double channel technique, also called lift and ligate, can be useful in these cases. *A,* The endoloop has been placed over the large polyp head and a large grasper has been passed through the second accessory channel. *B,* The grasper was used to pull the polyp toward the endoscope and facilitate deployment of the endoloop. The polyp appeared dusky shortly after endoloop application, indicating that there was sufficient tension to cause ischemia of the polyp (not shown). Snare polypectomy was subsequently performed. In addition, the snare was placed well above the endoloop to prevent slippage of the loop. (Figures from Palo Alto.)

of immediate or delayed bleeding. Prophylactic treatment to strangulate the blood vessels before resection prevents immediate or delayed bleeding (Fig. 38–9).[45,46,65–68]

One prophylactic method is application of endoloops, which are detachable loops that are applied to the base of polyp stalk to strangulate the vessels supplying the polyp. Iishi and colleagues[65] reported the use of endoloops in 47 patients and compared the rate of bleeding against 42 patients who did not have endoloop placed before polypectomy of pedunculated polyps with heads larger than 1 cm. No immediate or delayed bleeding was observed among patients who had the endoloop; five patients (12%) in the control group had bleeding (one immediate, four delayed). DiGiorgio and colleagues[66] reported similar results (0% vs. 12% in patients who had and did have the endoloop placed, respectively) in a randomized trial with more patients.

However, placement of the endoloop in pedunculated polyps that have short stalks can be difficult (Fig. 38–10). Massive bleeding can occur if the endoloop slips off immediately after snare polypectomy.[47,69] In addition, the endoloop is made of nylon, which can be too floppy for successful capture of the polyp. Because

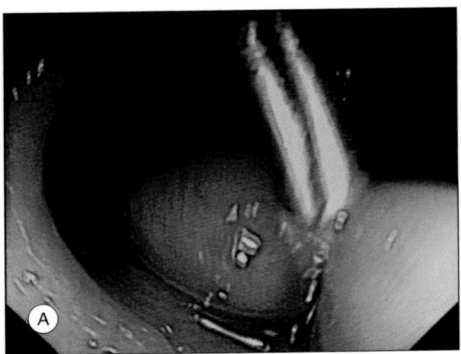
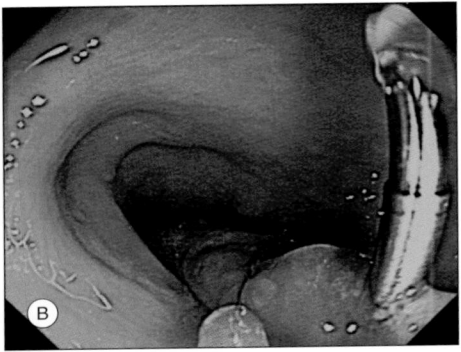

Figure 38–11. An alternative to endoloops for preventing postpolypectomy bleeding is the endoclip. *A,* A single endoclip has been applied at the lower part of a long polyp stalk. *B,* The polyp appeared dusky after the endoclip placement, again effective strangulation of the stalk. The snare was subsequently positioned above the clip and electrocautery was applied. It is important to avoid touching the clip with the snare during electrocautery application. (Figures from Palo Alto.)

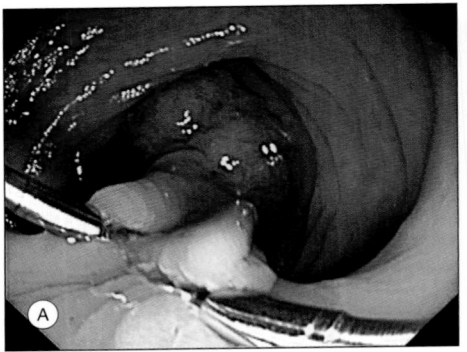
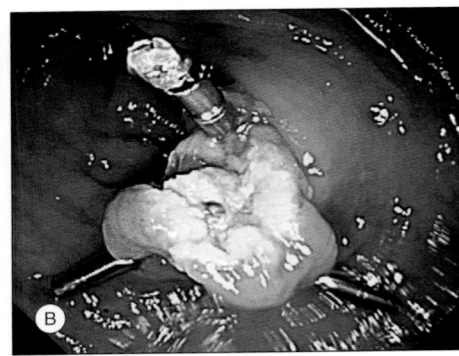

Figure 38–12. Multiple endoclips can be used to prevent postpolypectomy bleeding from a thick stalked polyp. *A,* Two endoclips were placed on opposite sides of the base of the stalk, causing the polyp to become dusky. *B,* A third endoclip was placed on the stalk remnant after transection to prevent bleeding. A sizable blood vessel was visible but was not bleeding. A fourth clip was subsequently placed on the vessel (not shown). (Figures from Palo Alto.)

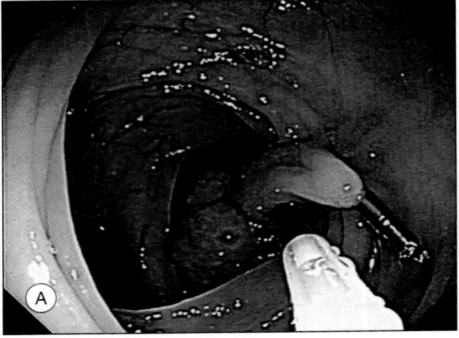
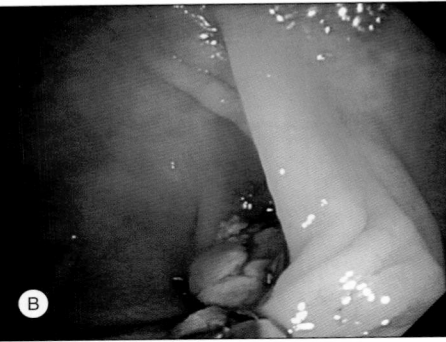

Figure 38–13. The application of endoloops or endoclips may be difficult when the stalk is short. Diluted epinephrine can also be used to prevent immediate bleeding after polypectomy. *A,* A few milliliters of diluted epinephrine (1:10,000) was injected into the base of the stalk before resection. An endoclip had been previously applied to an area believed to contain a blood vessel. *B,* The effect of epinephrine was appreciated with the pale-appearing mucosa seen surrounding the resected site. Multiple endoclips were applied in a zipper-like sequence to clamp any possible large vessels. (Figures from Palo Alto.)

massive colonic bleeding can easily cause immediate loss of visualization, other prophylaxis techniques may be more appropriate (Figs. 38–11 and 38–12).[38,70] Seitz and colleagues[68] used diluted epinephrine to inject to the base of the stalk before polypectomy. Because the effect of epinephrine is transient, the site was then clipped. Others have reported safe use of single or multiple deployment of endoclips before polypectomy (Fig. 38–13).[67,71] The clips did not appear to conduct current, perhaps because care was taken to avoid contact between the snare and the clips.

The use of the endoloop or endoclip to prevent polypectomy bleeding also allows large pedunculated polyps to be resected en bloc rather than piecemeal.[68] In turn, en bloc resection allows a more precise pathologic staging in cases of polyps containing invasive cancer. The endoclip can also function as a marker for the location of polypectomy, because it is radiopaque.

Mucosal Resection

Various resection techniques have been described.[38,51,72–74] The standard inject and cut technique, also called saline-assisted polypectomy, is most common. The inject, lift, and cut technique is also popular in Japan. The simple suction technique has been used in many patients, some of whom had exceptionally large sessile or flat lesions. The mucosal resection technique using a ligation device is particularly useful for resection of submucosal lesions in the rectum.

The inject and cut technique requires submucosal injection to lift the diseased mucosa. The essential aspects of submucosal injection are to inject a sufficient amount and to recognize the presence of the non-lifting sign. The ideal solution, which would form a substantial bulge and would not dissipate quickly, has not been defined. Physicians in the United States routinely use saline (Figs. 38–14, 38–15, and 38–16); those in Japan use Griseol mixed with a small amount of indigo carmine. The use of indigo carmine aids in the

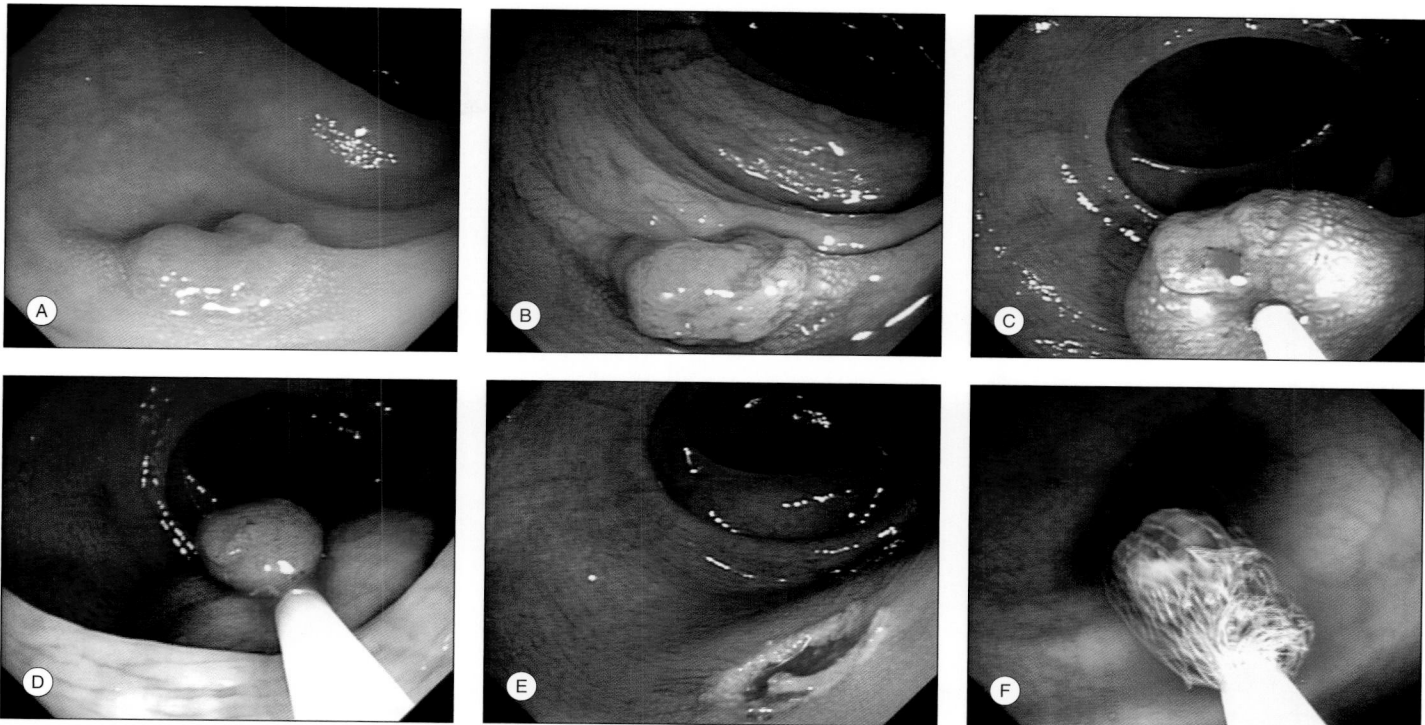

Figure 38–14. The inject and cut endoscopic mucosal resection technique. *A,* The lesion is carefully examined to assess for the potential of malignancy and its depth of invasion. *B,* Indigo carmine was used to define the border of the lesion and to gain insight from the surface appearance. The lesion has a depressed surface, suggesting a high likelihood of malignancy. *C,* Saline solution (approximately 5 mL) was injected into the submucosa, lifting the lesion. *D,* A stiff snare was used to capture the entire lesion with a small rim of surrounding normal mucosa. *E,* The resection site. The site was carefully examined by spraying additional diluted indigo carmine solution to examine for evidence of residual component. *F,* The lesion was carefully removed, without breaking it apart, using a Roth Net. Maintaining the lesion as a single specimen is important to allow the pathologist to determine the resection margin if cancer is found. After the case had been completed, the specimen was pinned at its periphery onto a piece of wood with thin needles (not shown). Endoscopic mucosal resection (EMR) specimens are sectioned at 2-mm intervals to provide accurate staging. (Figures from Palo Alto.)

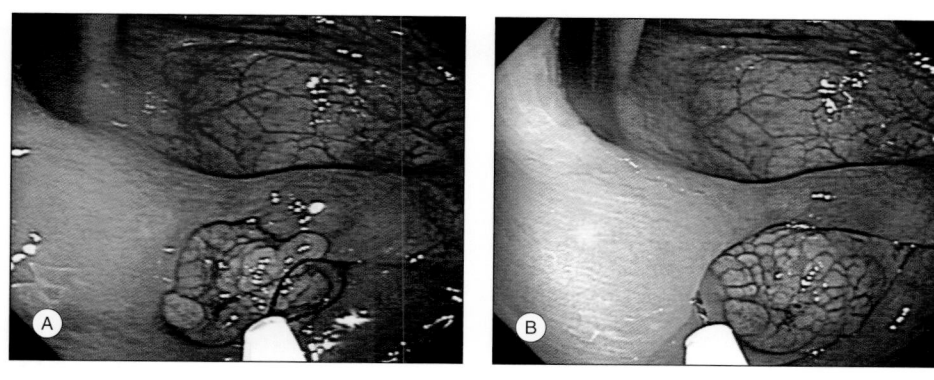

Figure 38–15. The fulcrum technique was used in this case to ensure that the snare was placed in a plane parallel to the fold. Saline had previously been injected to lift the lesion. *A,* The tip of the snare was impacted slightly to the right of the lesion. The snare was then slowly opened as the colonoscope was gently turned to the left. Close coordination between the endoscopist and assistant is required to perform this maneuver. *B,* The snare was pushed toward the lesion and air was suctioned slightly to draw the lesion into the snare. The snare was then slowly closed. Before cautery application, the snare was moved back and forth while examining the effect on the wall to ensure that muscularis propria was not entrapped in the snare. (Figures from Palo Alto.)

assessment of depth during and after resection. The remaining submucosa is a blue-green color, and deeper resections may yield visualization of muscularis propria. Unintentional full-thickness resection may visualize fat or other organs. Standard 25-gauge sclerotherapy needles are used for submucosal injection. Tumor seeding has been reported in only one patient.[75] In our experience, performance of safe and effective mucosal resection demands that all necessary equipment and a trained assistant be present, so that resection can be performed immediately after injection. We use a stiff standard snare. Whenever possible, we complete resections en bloc (Fig. 38–17); if we must remove lesions piecemeal, we

attempt to do so during a single session. Using the inject and cut technique, we are able to resect most colorectal lesions. As mentioned previously, observation during submucosal injection is critical in the performance of the inject and cut technique (Fig. 38–18).

The inject, lift, and cut technique requires a double-channel endoscope and two assistants (Fig. 38–19).[76-78] Submucosal injection is performed as in the inject and cut technique. A grasper is used to pull the lesion gently into the opened snare, and the lesion is resected.

The simple suction technique, developed by Soehendra and colleagues, uses a special, stiff, 0.4-mm monofilament snare.[38,79,80]

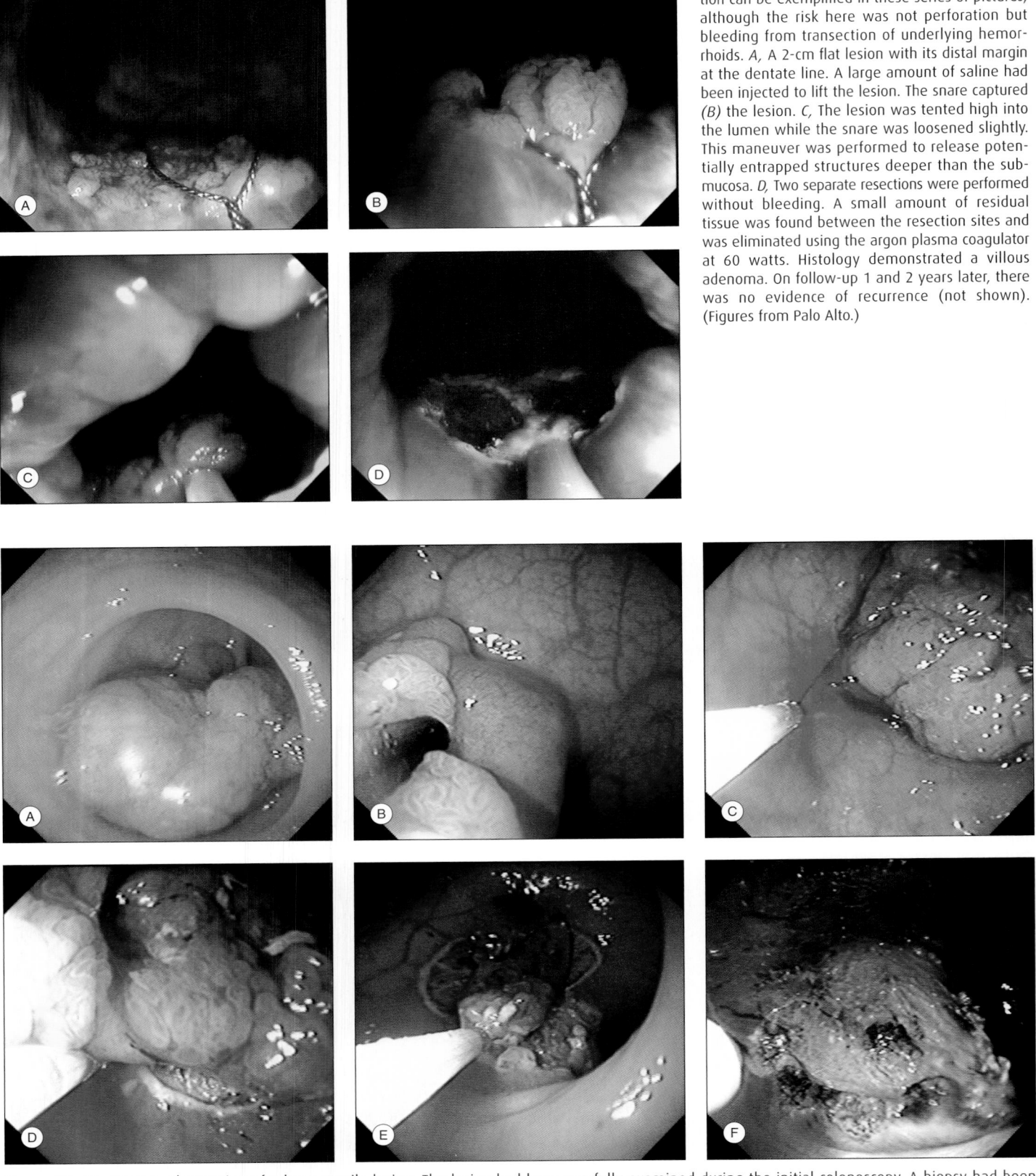

Figure 38-16. The maneuvers to prevent perforation can be exemplified in these series of pictures, although the risk here was not perforation but bleeding from transection of underlying hemorrhoids. *A,* A 2-cm flat lesion with its distal margin at the dentate line. A large amount of saline had been injected to lift the lesion. The snare captured *(B)* the lesion. *C,* The lesion was tented high into the lumen while the snare was loosened slightly. This maneuver was performed to release potentially entrapped structures deeper than the submucosa. *D,* Two separate resections were performed without bleeding. A small amount of residual tissue was found between the resection sites and was eliminated using the argon plasma coagulator at 60 watts. Histology demonstrated a villous adenoma. On follow-up 1 and 2 years later, there was no evidence of recurrence (not shown). (Figures from Palo Alto.)

Figure 38-17. Piecemeal resection of a large sessile lesion. The lesion had been carefully examined during the initial colonoscopy. A biopsy had been performed to document that the lesion was a large villous adenoma, as was suspected from its endoscopic appearance. *A,* The lesion was located at the rectosigmoid junction. *B,* A large amount (40 to 50 mL) of saline was injected to lift the lesion. The initial injections were at the proximal edge of the lesion. *C,* The first piece was resected using a stiff snare at the distal edge of the lesion. The lumen was insufflated with enough air to flatten the wall. By resecting the distal edge (or lateral margins) first, the endoscopist has immediate and easy access to treat any bleeding that might occur. *D,* A small piece of the lesion was resected. It is very important to ascertain the plane of transection in relation to the muscularis propria. In this case, the visible whitish layer is a coagulated deep layer of the submucosa. *E,* Subsequent resections were performed without proceeding deeper than the submucosa. The remaining large piece of the lesion was snared. Note the position of the snare: it is level with the bowel wall. *F,* Appearance after piecemeal resection. Diluted indigo carmine solution has been sprayed to aid visualization of any remnant. Argon plasma was applied to ensure complete eradication of the villous adenoma. (Figures from Stanford.)

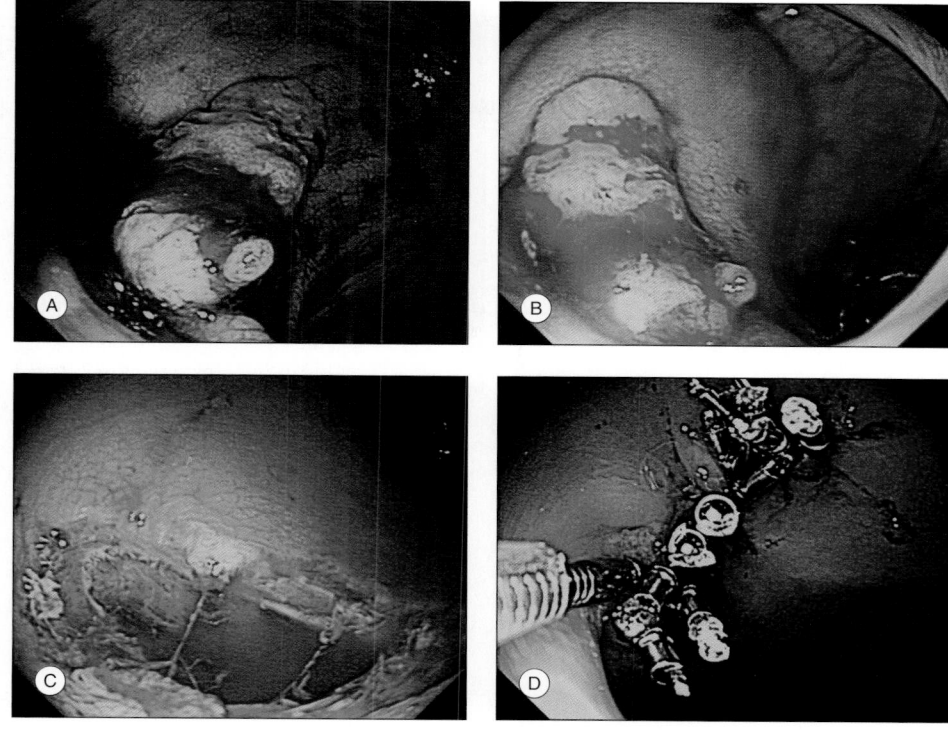

Figure 38–18. Perforation of the bowel wall can occur because of inadvertent entrapment of the muscularis propria. *A,* A 2.5-cm flat lesion on a fold. *B,* After more than 25 mL of saline injection, the lesion appears to have lifted well. *C,* The site after a one-piece resection. Layers of muscularis propria were exposed with minor bleeding occurring concurrently. *D,* The site was carefully closed using serial clipping to approximate the borders of the resected area. The patient did well and had no evidence of perforation. Here a deep resection presumably occurred because it was assumed that there was a thick plane of saline in the submucosa underneath the lesion that the snare would pass through. However, the lesion was a deeply infiltrating adenocarcinoma, and the snare transected the tumor. Subsequent surgery demonstrated a T2N0 tumor, with invasion of the muscularis propria below the endoscopic resection.

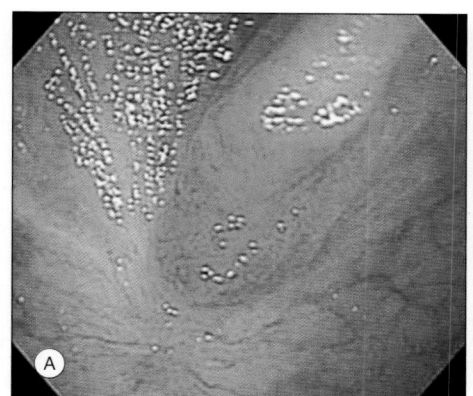
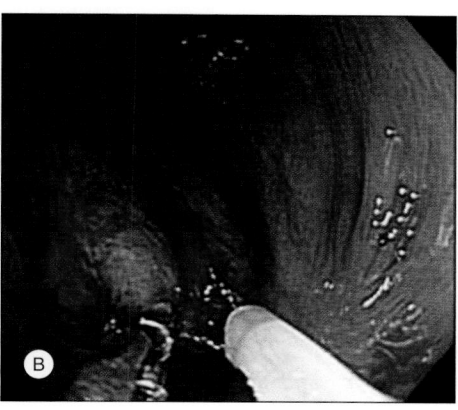

Figure 38–19. Double channel mucosal resection technique. *A,* A small area of residual adenoma was seen next to previous polypectomy scar. *B,* Submucosal injection has been performed. Using a double channel colonoscope, the lesion was lifted further using a grasper while the snare was being closed at the base of the lesion. (Figures from Tokyo.)

The construction of this snare allows consistent placement of the snare parallel to the bowel wall and, with slight pressure, capture of the diseased mucosa. Piecemeal resections are performed without submucosal injections.

Submucosal resection with ligation[81] can be particularly useful for resection of submucosal lesions, such as carcinoid tumors in the rectum (Fig. 38–20).[30,82] After the endoscope is fitted with the ligation device, the target area is ligated, with or without prior deep submucosal injection. Standard polypectomy is then performed below the rubber band. Small submucosal lesions may require prior markings at their periphery, achieved by brief bursts of cautery using the tip of a snare, because such lesions may be difficult to find after the ligation device has been fitted to the endoscope.

Other techniques that have been described but are not widely used include mucosal resection with cap[72,83,84]; inject, precut, and exfoliate using a small-caliber tip cap[85] or insulated-tip needle knife[86]; and use of short endoclips to position the snare.[73] Although popular and efficacious for resection of superficial early cancer in the esophagus and stomach, EMR with cap can be risky to use in the colon.[84] The thin muscularis propria of the colon can easily be suctioned into the cap, potentially leading to perforation.

TECHNIQUES FOR PREVENTION AND TREATMENT OF RESIDUAL LESIONS

Whenever possible, polypectomy and mucosal resection should be completed in a single session. Mucosal resection of lesions that are highly suspicious for carcinoma should be resected en bloc. Such en bloc resection, if possible with surrounding normal mucosa, will provide the ideal specimen for evaluation of involvement of the lateral and vertical margin. APC has been shown to be effective for treating small amounts of residual lesion.[87,88] Large sessile or flat lesions may need more than one session to resect. Small recurrent lesions are often treated with repeat EMR or application of APC.

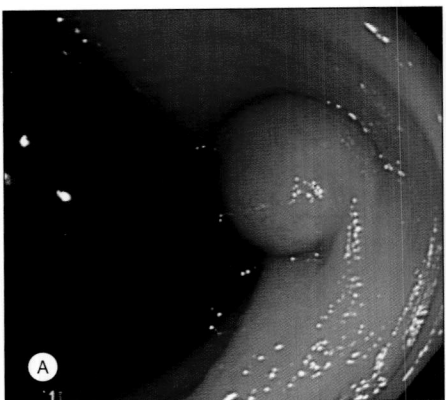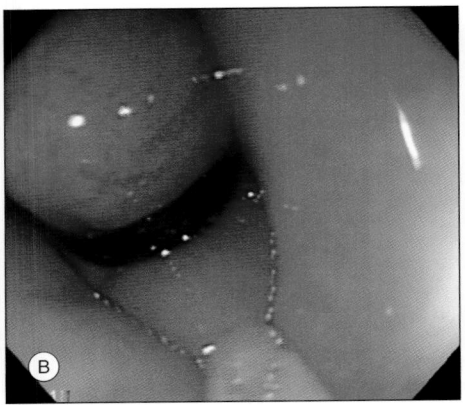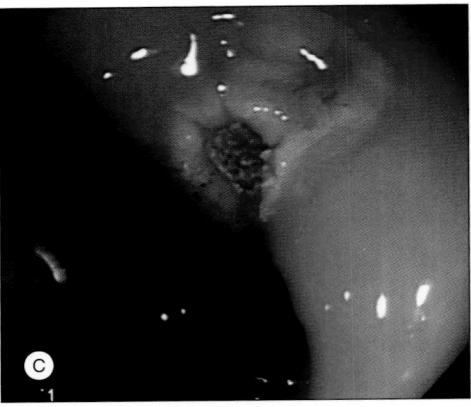

Figure 38–20. Endoscopic submucosal resection of a small carcinoid tumor in the rectum using a band ligation device. *A,* The lesion. *B,* After deep submucosal injection of saline and placement of a band using the ligation device, a snare is seen transecting the lesion as cautery is applied. *C,* After resection. The lesion was contained within the resected specimen with clear margin (not shown). By cutting immediately below the band, a deeper resection can be performed. (Figures from Tokyo.)

TECHNIQUES FOR IDENTIFYING THE SITE OF A LESION OR POLYPECTOMY

The site of a lesion can be marked with a tattooing agent (India ink or carbon black) injected into the submucosa and/or placement of a single endoclip or multiple endoclips (Fig. 38–21).[44,89] Both techniques are safe and relatively simple to perform, although the endoclip may not be palpable and may not stay in place for a prolonged period.

TECHNIQUES FOR RETRIEVING THE SPECIMEN

The benefits of mucosal resection or polypectomy can be assessed only by properly prepared pathologic examination. The Roth Net is useful in recovering specimen[90] from an en bloc resection of a flat or depressed lesion. Recovering such a specimen through the accessory channel may cause the mucosal resection specimen to be torn into smaller pieces. The Roth Net can also aid in efficient recovery of a specimen from piecemeal resection of large sessile or pedunculated lesions. Smaller pieces can be collected through the accessory channel. The net, snare, basket, Tripod, and Pentapod are other accessories that can be useful for removal of large pedunculated polyps.

TECHNIQUES FOR PATHOLOGIC STAGING

The benefits of polypectomy and mucosal resection can be realized only with first-rate pathologic assessment. Orientation of the specimen requires knowledge of the appearance of the lesion before resection. Thus, the orientation of the specimen by the endoscopist, especially in cases of mucosal resections of nonpolypoid lesions, is helpful. To aid orientation, specimens from mucosal resections may be flattened and fixed at their periphery with thin needles inserted into an underlying wood or Styrofoam block before immersion into formalin. Fixed lesions are then sectioned serially at 2-mm intervals. Assessment of a specimen containing carcinoma must include the depth of the lesion, neoplastic involvement of the lateral and vertical margins, histology, and involvement of the lymphatics and/or blood vessels. In the colon, involvement of the vertical margin is particularly important, more so than the involvement of the lateral margin, provided that there is no visible lesion remaining at the conclusion of the resection. The significant cautery effect at

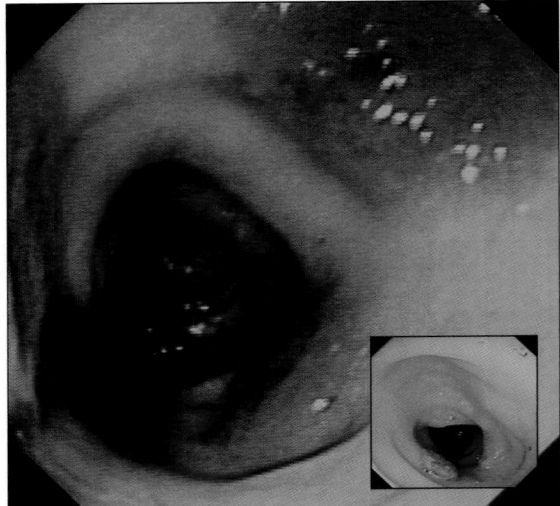

Figure 38–21. India ink injection is used to mark an ulcerated depressed lesion. India ink solution was injected submucosally at three separate points. The depressed lesion was later demonstrated to be an adenocarcinoma invading deep into the submucosa. Locations of the tattoos (distal, proximal, same level of the lesion) must be documented precisely, especially in cases of flat and depressed lesions. These lesions are often not palpable by the surgeon. At times, an endoclip is also used in addition to the use India ink to mark the site on radiographs taken immediately after colonoscopy. This can assist in surgical planning, particularly in cases in which laparoscopic resection is contemplated. (Figures from Palo Alto.)

the lateral margin of the lesion during resection generally ablates any remnant cells. A repeat colonoscopy is needed to rule out evidence of residual or recurrent lesions.

Management and Follow-Up Surveillance after Polypectomy

Reasonable data are available to guide recommendations for post-polypectomy follow-up surveillance after resection of adenomatous polyps. The current guideline published by the U.S. Multisociety Task Force on Colorectal Cancer in 2003 is helpful in directing the

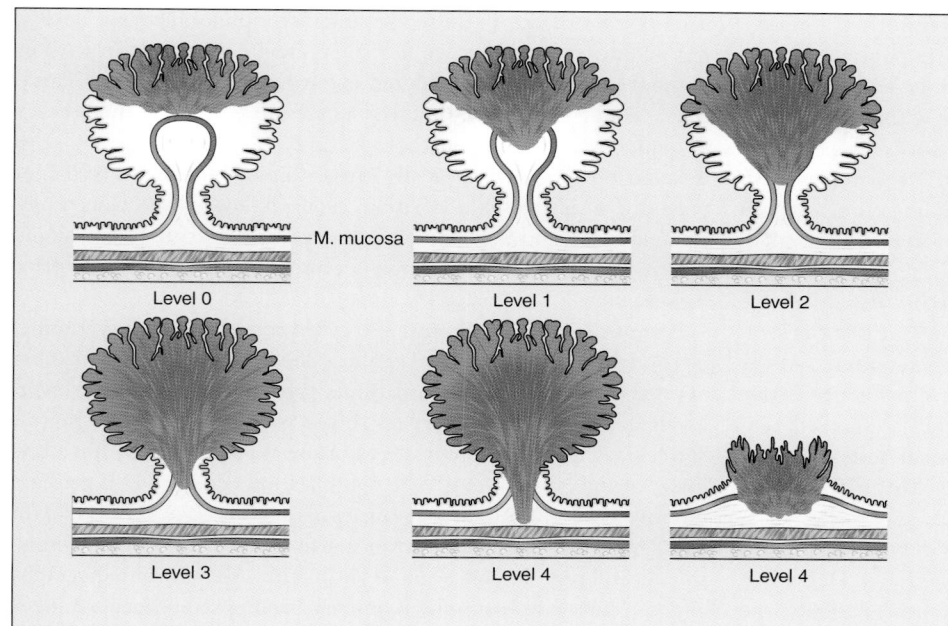

Figure 38-22. Haggitt and colleagues stratified the level of cancer submucosal invasion by the following criteria: level 0, carcinoma in situ (i.e., have not extended below the muscularis mucosa); level 1, carcinoma invading through the muscularis mucosa but limited to the head of the polyp (i.e., above the junction between the adenoma and its stalk); level 2, carcinoma invading the level of the neck (i.e., the junction between adenoma and its stalk); level 3, carcinoma invading any part of the stalk; and level 4 carcinoma invading into the submucosa of the bowel wall below the stalk. In malignant sessile lesions, invasive carcinoma is considered as level 4.

interval for patients who have adenomatous lesions.[91] Patients who have 1 or 2 small (<1 cm) tubular adenomas should have follow-up colonoscopy at 5 years. Patients who have advanced (villous histology or high grade dysplasia) or multiple adenomas (≥ 3) should have follow-up at 3 years. Patients with numerous adenomas, a large sessile adenoma, malignant adenoma, or an incomplete colonoscopy should have a short-interval follow-up examination.

Numerous studies have shown that large sessile, flat, and depressed adenomas can be removed endoscopically with relatively good success.[4,68,80,92-96] However, one should note that these studies were conducted by expert endoscopists in referral centers. Large lesions may require multiple colonoscopy sessions for complete resection.[68,80] After resection, a repeat colonoscopy is typically performed after 8 to 12 weeks to look for recurrence. Recurrent lesions should be examined carefully because they may contain invasive carcinoma, even in cases in which the previously resected specimen was only noted to contain adenoma.[68,97] If there are no residual lesions, another colonoscopy should be performed at 6 to 12 months, and subsequent examinations should be performed every 1 to 2 years to exclude recurrence. The rationale for such an intensive follow-up schedule is the relatively high rate of local recurrence, particularly after piecemeal polypectomy. A recent series of approximately 300 polyps larger than 3 cm that were resected endoscopically demonstrated a recurrence rate of 17%, with most recurrent lesions successfully treated endoscopically.[68]

The management of patients who have polypoid lesions containing invasive carcinoma is not straightforward. The risk of metastases of T1 lesions is approximately 10% to 15%.[98,99] Because most patients will not develop metastases, the decision of whether to perform surgery is complex. Immediate surgery performed shortly after initial local resection of T1 lesions confer a disease-free 5-year survival rate significantly higher than that of patients who had surgery only after local recurrence or lymph node metastasis from rectal cancer.[100] Given the pathologic findings, the endoscopist must assess whether the risk for lymph node metastasis is lower than that

of partial colectomy. A variety of stratification methods have been reported; most distinguish patients at high and low risk to develop recurrence or metastasis. Unfortunately, published data often are collected from small numbers of patients[99]; thus, although they indicate that the absolute fraction of patients who developed metastases was low, great care must be exercised because the upper limit of the confidence interval of this fraction is often higher than the risk of surgery. Furthermore, many studies lumped different types of lesions.

A study by Haggitt and colleagues[101] is often cited. These authors concluded that the level of invasion is the major factor in determining prognosis for the management of a malignant polyp (Fig. 38-22). They found that the risk of metastasis or local recurrence is low when the level is less than 4. This study involved a small number of patients, some of whom had endoscopic treatment and others who had surgery. Thus, the relevance of these data to patients treated with endoscopy can only be inferred. In addition, the Haggitt study lumped into one group (level 4) all patients who had sessile lesions that contained submucosal invasion. Detailed pathologic studies from Japan have found that the absolute depth of invasion within the submucosa should be considered. There appears to be a gradual increase in the risk of lymph node metastasis with the depth of submucosal invasion.[4,102]

Kikuchi and colleagues[102] stratified the risk of metastasis with the depth of carcinoma invasion beyond the muscularis mucosa: sm1 is slight invasion beyond the muscularis mucosa to a depth of 200 to 300 μm, sm2 is intermediate invasion, and sm3 is invasion near the inner surface of the muscularis propria. They found that of 64 patients with sm1 invasion (75% of whom had either subpedunculated or sessile lesions) had no evidence of metastasis during follow-up of at least 5 years.

Other authors have developed stratification systems that combine depth and histology.[99,103] Volk and colleagues[99] stratified patients according to favorable versus unfavorable histology. Favorable histology includes well differentiated and moderately differentiated adenocarcinoma with carcinoma cells at least 2 mm from a clearly visualized margin. Unfavorable histology includes poorly differentiated adenocarcinoma, mucinous adenocarcinoma, and signet-ring cell carcinoma or one with adenocarcinoma cells within 2 mm from a clearly visualized margin. If the margins could not be assessed, the lesion was classified as unfavorable histology. No patients with favorable histology treated with endoscopic polypectomy had an adverse outcome. However, this study also involved only a small number of patients.

Other authors have suggested additional factors that might be important in the stratification of patients who are at risk for local recurrence or metastasis. Tanaka and colleagues[104] reported that the absence of lymphatic or vascular involvement is highly predictive of a successful outcome. Masaki and colleagues[105] showed that unfavorable histology (presence or absence of small nests of cancer cells with poorly differentiated or mucinous histology) at the invasive margin is predictive of adverse outcome.

The management of small, depressed lesions depend on the histology, lymphovascular invasion, and depth of invasion. Depressed lesions larger than 1 cm often contain invasive cancer; patients who have them are often referred directly to surgery.[4]

At present, the stratification of patients with nonpolypoid lesions containing invasive cancer is not resolved. Meticulous specimen examination by an experienced pathologist in close communication with the endoscopist helps optimize the decision whether to recommend surgery. The patient must be well informed of the risks and benefits of endoscopic therapy and surgery, even in cases in which the risk of metastasis is small.

Complications

Complications of polypectomy and mucosal resection include bleeding, transmural burn, and perforation. Familiarity with the endoscopic findings, symptoms and signs of complications, and treatment of complications is a prerequisite for performance of colonoscopic polypectomy and mucosal resection.

Postpolypectomy bleeding can occur during or after the procedure. The reported incidence varies according to the definition of bleeding and the size and type of lesions resected. Significant bleeding was observed in 0.4% of hot biopsies of diminutive polyps in one series. The overall risk is approximately 1% to 2% for snare polypectomy. Rosen and coworkers[106] reported a 0.4% risk of bleeding requiring hospital admission in a retrospective study involving 4721 patients who had polypectomies. Nivatvongs reported 10 episodes of bleeding requiring blood transfusion among 1172 patients.[109] Soehendra reported a 24% risk of bleeding in a series of 176 large (>3 cm) polypectomy. Most of these hemorrhages occurred during the procedure, and all were successfully treated by endoscopic methods.[80]

A variety of techniques are useful for treatment of postpolypectomy bleeding. These include application of the endoclip or endoloop, use of APC, injection of diluted epinephrine, cauterization using monopolar or bipolar instruments, and repeat application of the snare or hot-forceps biopsy to grasp the remnant stalk of pedunculated polyp. In cases in which endoscopic treatment fails, selective angiography with the application of Gelfoam emboli or surgery is used. Our preferred technique for minor bleeding is APC; for significant bleeding, we use the endoclip or endoloop with or without prior injection of diluted epinephrine (Fig. 38–23).[70] Parra-Blanco and colleagues[107] reported a case series showing the efficacy of endoclips to treat postpolypectomy bleeding. In cases with delayed bleeding, we typically purge the bowel using 4 to 6 L of polyethylene glycol solution within 3 hours followed by a colonoscopy, although Rex and colleagues[108] reported successful colonoscopic treatment of delayed postpolypectomy bleeding without prior bowel purge.

Postpolypectomy syndrome, also called transmural burn syndrome, is thought to occur when cautery injury causes full-thickness necrosis of the bowel wall. Patients typically present with fever, localized abdominal tenderness (often with rebound tenderness), and leukocytosis. The onset of symptoms is commonly within a few hours of the polypectomy. The complication occurred in 6 patients out of 1172 (0.5%) in one series[109] and in 9 of 777 (1%) in another.[110] Most patients recover uneventfully after hospital admission, bowel rest, and intravenous antibiotics. Abdominal radiographs and computed tomography scans may demonstrate local changes such as air in the bowel wall but not free air in the abdomen in the amount that would be seen with a perforation.

Perforation can occur when muscularis propria is included in the tissue grasped by a snare; this may happen, for example, when a large sessile polyp that is draped over a fold is grasped in its entirety. Techniques that may decrease the risk of capturing the muscularis propria have been summarized[29] (see also Figs. 38–15 and 38–16). Endoscopic clipping techniques may be useful in cases of fresh small perforation or, prophylactically, in cases in which the resection appears too deep.[70] Delayed perforation can also occur as a result of tissue necrosis from cautery. Most patients with colon perforation are treated surgically, but there are reports of successful nonoperative management.[111,112] Most of the patients who did not require surgery had smaller perforations resulting from polypectomy, rather than the large lacerations that are typically seen with diagnostic colonoscopy perforations. It is possible that endoscopic closure of small perforations seen immediately after snare resection could prevent the need for surgery in some cases, as has been observed in gastric mucosal resections.[113,114]

Future Trends

Advances in the technology and technique of colonoscopy are allowing endoscopists to manage increasingly complex colorectal lesions via endoscopy. Learning and using these new technologies and techniques may be demanding but enables endoscopists to perform endoscopic resection of lesions that previously would have required major abdominal surgery. The more sophisticated approaches can also improve recognition of the nonpolypoid lesions that were previously under-recognized in Western countries and may assist in their treatment. Further developments will increase the potential of colonoscopic polypectomy and mucosal resection. Extensive and long-term databases, using a common terminology for endoscopy and pathology,[115,116] are critically needed. Simplifications in the technology and techniques of the resections will allow them to be used more widely and thus to benefit more patients (Fig. 38–24).

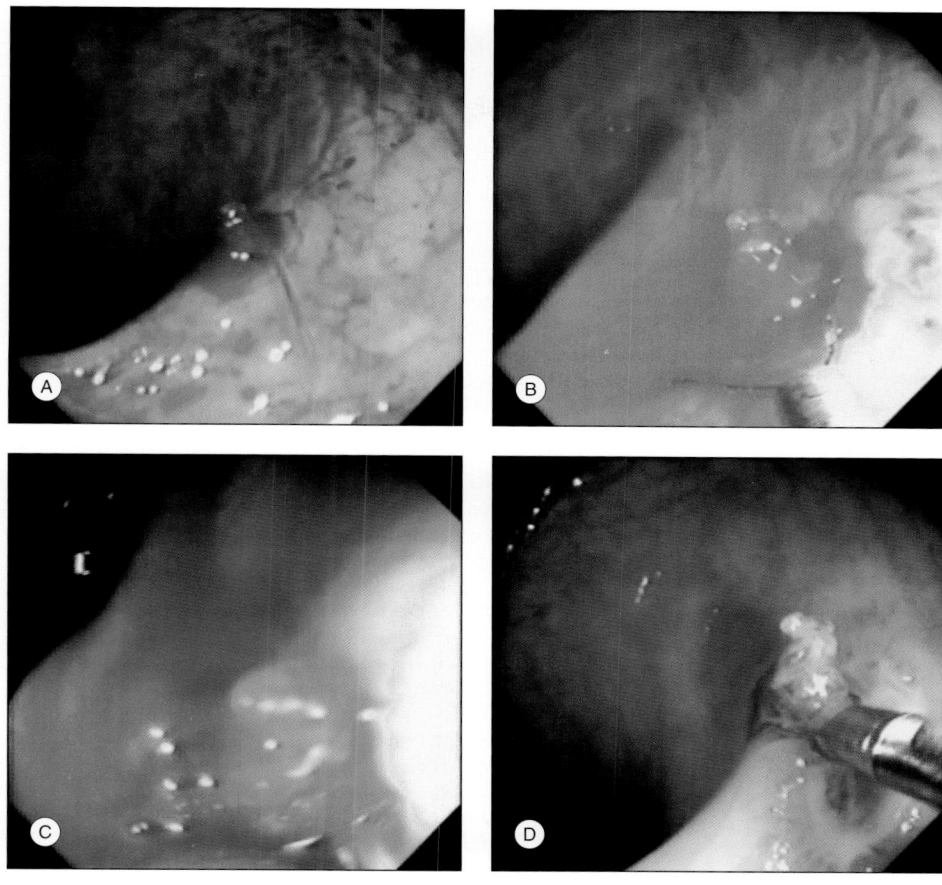

Figure 38–23. The principles of endoscopic clipping in prevention and treatment of postpolypectomy bleeding are shown here. *A,* Spurting arterial bleeding that occurred a few days after snare polypectomy. *B,* The endoclip has been well positioned to capture the bleeding vessel. To obtain the best control and leverage, the tip of the endoclip applicator was positioned very close to the tip of the colonoscope. Application of the endoclip will be more secure when normal underlying tissue is also captured during endoclip deployment. Thus, in this case, the endoclip was positioned slightly distal to the bleeding vessel to allow for capturing tissue underneath the vessel. *C,* To ensure capturing the vessel and its underlying to tissue, the clip was pushed down, the lumen was suctioned, and then the clip was slowly closed. *D,* The endoclip has been placed securely. Sequential application of multiple endoclips may be required in postpolypectomy bleeding from a thick stalk (not shown). (Figures from Palo Alto.)

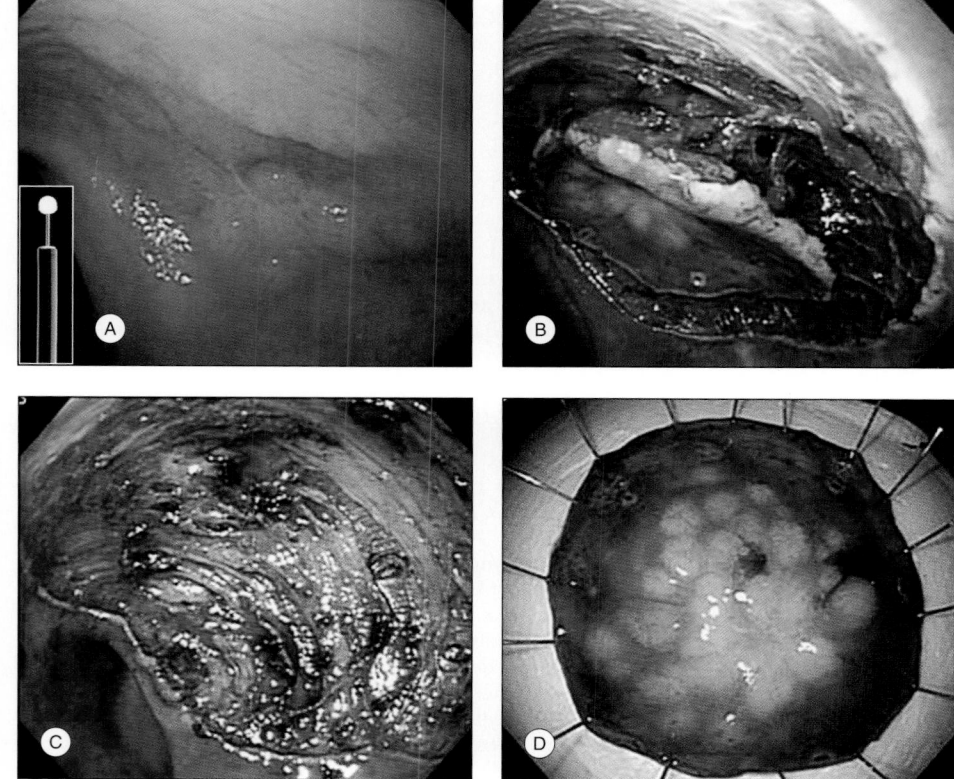

Figure 38–24. En bloc resection of a large rectal localized lymphoma using the IT knife. *A,* The lesion seen after indigo carmine spray. The insulated knife is shown *(inset).* *B,* Submucosal injection with diluted epinephrine and indigo carmine has been performed and a circumferential incision has been made surrounding the lesion. The lesion is shown after further submucosal injection underneath it. *C,* The resection site after the lesion has been removed. *D,* After resection, the lesion is oriented, stretched, and pinned on a piece of Styrofoam by the endoscopist. The lesion was then immersed in formalin. The pathologist sections the specimen at 2-mm intervals and notes their positions relative to each other. Thus, a precise determination of lateral and vertical depth of invasion can be reported. (Figures from Tokyo.)

REFERENCES

1. Cancer Facts and Figures 2002. Atlanta, GA, American Cancer Society, 2001.
2. Winawer SJ, Zauber AG, Ho MN, et al: Prevention of colorectal cancer by colonoscopic polypectomy. The National Polyp Study Workgroup. N Engl J Med 329:1977–1981, 1993.
3. Vogelstein B, Fearon ER, Hamilton SR, et al: Genetic alterations during colorectal-tumor development. N Engl J Med 319:525–532, 1988.
4. Kudo S, Kashida H, Tamura T, et al: Colonoscopic diagnosis and management of nonpolypoid early colorectal cancer. World J Surg 24:1081–1090, 2000.
5. Kudo S: Early Colorectal Cancer. Tokyo, Igaku-Shoin, 1996.
6. Shimoda T, Ikegami M, Fujisaki J, et al: Early colorectal carcinoma with special reference to its development de novo. Cancer 64:1138–1146, 1989.
7. Kahng LS, Friedland S, Matsui S, et al: Flat and depressed colorectal neoplasms in the United States of America. Early Colorectal Cancer (Jpn) 8:44–50, 2004.
8. Japanese Classification of Colorectal Carcinoma. Tokyo, Kanehara & Co, 1997.
9. Wolber RA, Owen DA: Flat adenomas of the colon. Hum Pathol 22:70–74, 1991.
10. Lanspa SJ, Rouse J, Smyrk T, et al: Epidemiologic characteristics of the flat adenoma of Muto. A prospective study. Dis Colon Rectum 35:543–546, 1992.
11. Jaramillo E, Watanabe M, Slezak P, Rubio C: Flat neoplastic lesions of the colon and rectum detected by high-resolution video endoscopy and chromoscopy. Gastrointest Endosc 42:114–122, 1995.
12. Fujii T, Iishi H, Tatsuta M, et al: Effectiveness of premedication with pronase for improving visibility during gastroendoscopy: A randomized controlled trial. Gastrointest Endosc 47:382–387, 1998.
13. Smith GA, Oien KA, O'Dwyer PJ: Frequency of early colorectal cancer in patients undergoing colonoscopy. Br J Surg 86:1328–1331, 1999.
14. Rembacken BJ, Fujii T, Cairns A, et al: Flat and depressed colonic neoplasms: A prospective study of 1000 colonoscopies in the UK. Lancet 355:1211–1214, 2000.
15. Suzuki N, Saunders BP, Talbot IC, et al: Small flat colorectal cancer: Experience in 870 consecutive colonoscopies. Gastrointest Endosc 51:AB149, 2000.
16. Samalin E, Diebold MD, Merle C, et al: Prevalence of colonic flat neoplasia in a French series. Gastroenterology 122(Suppl):W1224, 2002.
17. Fujii T, Hasegawa RT, Saitoh Y, et al: Chromoscopy during colonoscopy. Endoscopy 33:1036–1041, 2001.
18. Kiesslich R, von Bergh M, Hahn M, et al: Chromoendoscopy with indigocarmine improves the detection of adenomatous and nonadenomatous lesions in the colon. Endoscopy 33:1001–1006, 2001.
19. Tsuda S, Veress B, Toth E, Fork FT: Flat and depressed colorectal tumours in a southern Swedish population: A prospective chromoendoscopic and histopathological study. Gut 51:550–555, 2002.
20. Weil R, Ohana G, Halpern M, et al: Small nonpolypoid colorectal carcinoma. World J Surg 26:503–508, 2002.
21. Soetikno RM, Kahng LS, Ono A, Fujii T: Flat and depressed colorectal neoplasms. Curr Opin Gastroenterol 19:69–75, 2003.
22. Hart AR, Kudo S, Mackay EH, et al: Flat adenomas exist in asymptomatic people: Important implications for colorectal cancer screening programmes. Gut 43:229–231, 1998.
23. Schlemper RJ, Hirata I, Dixon MF: The macroscopic classification of early neoplasia of the digestive tract. Endoscopy 34:163–168, 2002.
24. Saitoh Y, Obara T, Watari J, et al: Invasion depth diagnosis of depressed type early colorectal cancers by combined use of videoendoscopy and chromoendoscopy. Gastrointest Endosc 48:362–370, 1998.
25. Sawada T, Hojo K, Moriya Y: Colonoscopic management of focal and early colorectal carcinoma. Baillieres Clin Gastroenterol 3:627–645, 1989.
26. Ajioka Y, Watanabe H, Kazama S, et al: Early colorectal cancer with special reference to the superficial nonpolypoid type from a histopathologic point of view. World J Surg 24:1075–1080, 2000.
27. Togashi K, Konishi F, Koinuma K, et al: Flat and depressed lesions of the colon and rectum: Pathogenesis and clinical management. Ann Acad Med Singapore 32:152–158, 2003.
28. Bond JH: Colon polyps and cancer. Endoscopy 35:27–35, 2003.
29. Soetikno RM, Gotoda T, Nakanishi Y, Soehendra N: Endoscopic mucosal resection. Gastrointest Endosc 57:567–579, 2003.
30. Ono A, Fujii T, Saito Y, et al: Endoscopic submucosal resection of rectal carcinoid tumors with a ligation device. Gastrointest Endosc 57:583–587, 2003.
31. Oshitani N, Hamasaki N, Sawa Y, et al: Endoscopic resection of small rectal carcinoid tumours using an aspiration method with a transparent overcap. J Int Med Res 28:241–246, 2000.
32. Hirsh J, Dalen JE, Anderson DR, et al: Oral anticoagulants: Mechanism of action, clinical effectiveness, and optimal therapeutic range. Chest 114(5 Suppl):445S–469S, 1998.
33. Dunn AS, Turpie AG: Perioperative management of patients receiving oral anticoagulants: A systematic review. Arch Intern Med 163:901–908, 2003.
34. Eisen GM, Baron TH, Dominitz JA, et al: Guideline on the management of anticoagulation and antiplatelet therapy for endoscopic procedures. Gastrointest Endosc 55:775–779, 2002.
35. Infection control during gastrointestinal endoscopy: Guidelines for clinical application. From the ASGE. American Society for Gastrointestinal Endoscopy. Gastrointest Endosc 49:836–841, 1999.
36. Dajani AS, Taubert KA, Wilson W, et al: Prevention of bacterial endocarditis. Recommendations by the American Heart Association. JAMA 277:1794–1801, 1997.
37. Lee TH, Hsueh PR, Yeh WC, et al: Low frequency of bacteremia after endoscopic mucosal resection. Gastrointest Endosc 52:223–225, 2000.
38. Soehendra N, Binmoeller KF, Seifert H, Schreiber HW: Therapeutic Endoscopy. Stuttgart, Thieme, 1998.
39. Farin G, Grund KE: Basic principles of electrosurgery in flexible endoscopy. In Tytgat GNJ, Mulder CJJ (eds): Procedures in Hepatogastroenterology. Great Britain, Kluwer Academic Publishers, 1997:415–436.
40. Norton ID, Wang L, Levine SA, et al: Efficacy of colonic submucosal saline solution injection for the reduction of iatrogenic thermal injury. Gastrointest Endosc 56:95–99, 2002.
41. Farin G, Grund KE: Technology of argon plasma coagulation with particular regard to endoscopic applications. Endosc Surg Allied Technol 2:71–77, 1994.
42. Grund KE, Storek D, Farin G: Endoscopic argon plasma coagulation (APC) first clinical experiences in flexible endoscopy. Endosc Surg Allied Technol 2:42–46, 1994.
43. Grund KE, Straub T, Farin G: New haemostatic techniques: Argon plasma coagulation. Baillieres Best Pract Res Clin Gastroenterol 13:67–84, 1999.
44. Soehendra N, Sriram PV, Ponchon T, Chung SC: Hemostatic clip in gastrointestinal bleeding. Endoscopy 33:172–180, 2001.
45. Hachisu T, Ichinose M, Satoh S, et al: A novel detachable snare for hemostasis after polypectomy. Prog Dig Endosc 36:161–163, 1990.
46. Hachisu T: A new detachable snare for hemostasis in the removal of large polyps or other elevated lesions. Surg Endosc 5:70–74, 1991.
47. Soetikno RM, Friedland S, Lewit V, Woodford S: Lift and ligate: A new technique to treat a bleeding polypectomy stump. Gastrointest Endosc 52:681–683, 2000.

48. Faigel DO, Stotland BR, Kochman ML, et al: Device choice and experience level in endoscopic foreign object retrieval: An in vivo study. Gastrointest Endosc 45:490–492, 1997.

49. Miyaoka M, Sudo I: How to manage difficulties with colonoscope insertion. Dig Endosc 13:111–115, 2001.

50. Kudo S, Tamegai Y, Yamano H, et al: Endoscopic mucosal resection of the colon: The Japanese technique. Gastrointest Endosc Clin N Am 11:519–535, 2001.

51. Rembacken BJ, Gotoda T, Fujii T, Axon AT: Endoscopic mucosal resection. Endoscopy 33:709–718, 2001.

52. Kida M, Kobayashi K, Saigenji K: Routine chromoendoscopy for gastrointestinal diseases: Indications revised. Endoscopy 35:590–596, 2003.

53. Shim CS: Staining in gastrointestinal endoscopy: Clinical applications and limitations. Endoscopy 31:487–496, 1999.

54. Kudo S, Hirota S, Nakajima T, et al: Colorectal tumours and pit pattern. J Clin Pathol 47:880–885, 1994.

55. Kato S, Fujii T, Koba I, et al: Assessment of colorectal lesions using magnifying colonoscopy and mucosal dye spraying: Can significant lesions be distinguished? Endoscopy 33:306–310, 2001.

56. Tanaka S, Haruma K, Ito M, et al: Detailed colonoscopy for detecting early superficial carcinoma: Recent developments. J Gastroenterol 35(Suppl 12):121–125, 2000.

57. Uno Y, Munakata A: The non-lifting sign of invasive colon cancer. Gastrointest Endosc 40:485–489, 1994.

58. Kato H, Haga S, Endo S, et al: Lifting of lesions during endoscopic mucosal resection (EMR) of early colorectal cancer: Implications for the assessment of resectability. Endoscopy 33:568–573, 2001.

59. Ishiguro A, Uno Y, Ishiguro Y, et al: Correlation of lifting versus non-lifting and microscopic depth of invasion in early colorectal cancer. Gastrointest Endosc 50:329–333, 1999.

60. Harada N, Hamada S, Kubo H, et al: Preoperative evaluation of submucosal invasive colorectal cancer using a 15-MHz ultrasound miniprobe. Endoscopy 33:237–240, 2001.

61. Saitoh Y, Obara T, Einami K, et al: Efficacy of high-frequency ultrasound probes for the preoperative staging of invasion depth in flat and depressed colorectal tumors. Gastrointest Endosc 44:34–39, 1996.

62. Friedland S, Soetikno R: Preoperative evaluation of submucosal invasive colorectal cancer using a 15-MHZ ultrasound miniprobe. Gastrointest Endosc 55:959–961; discussion 961, 2002.

63. Polkowski M, Regula J, Wronska E, et al: Endoscopic ultrasonography for prediction of postpolypectomy bleeding in patients with large nonpedunculated rectosigmoid adenomas. Endoscopy 35:343–347, 2003.

64. Tappero G, Gaia E, De Giuli P, et al: Cold snare excision of small colorectal polyps. Gastrointest Endosc 38:310–313, 1992.

65. Iishi H, Tatsuta M, Narahara H, et al: Endoscopic resection of large pedunculated colorectal polyps using a detachable snare. Gastrointest Endosc 44:594–597, 1996.

66. Di Giorgio P, De Luca L, Calcagno G, et al: Detachable snare versus adrenalin stalk injection in the prevention of post-polypectomy bleeding. A controlled randomized study. Gastroenterology A4237, 2001.

67. Iida Y, Miura S, Munemoto Y, et al: Endoscopic resection of large colorectal polyps using a clipping method. Dis Colon Rectum 37:179–180, 1994.

68. Seitz U, Bohnacker S, Seewald S, et al: Long-term results of endoscopic removal of large colorectal adenomas. Endoscopy 35:S41–44, 2003.

69. Matsushita M, Hajiro K, Takakuwa H, et al: Ineffective use of a detachable snare for colonoscopic polypectomy of large polyps. Gastrointest Endosc 47:496–499, 1998.

70. Soetikno R, Gotoda T, Barro J, Soehendra N: Endoscopic Clipping Technique. American Society of Gastrointestinal Endoscopy, 2003.

71. Hachisu T, Yamada H, Satoh S, Kouzu T: Endoscopic clipping with a new rotatable clip-device and a long clip. Dig Endosc 8:127–133, 1996.

72. Inoue H, Endo M, Takeshita K, et al: A new simplified technique of endoscopic esophageal mucosal resection using a cap-fitted panendoscope (EMRC) [letter]. Surg Endosc 6:264–265, 1992.

73. Inatsuchi S: Broadening of the indications for endoscopic surgery: Upper gastrointestinal tract. Dig Endosc 12(Suppl):S2–6, 2000.

74. Shim CS: Endoscopic mucosal resection: An overview of the value of different techniques. Endoscopy 33:271–275, 2001.

75. Zarchy T: Risk of submucosal saline injection for colonic polypectomy. Gastrointest Endosc 46:89–90, 1997.

76. Karita M, Tada M, Okita K, Kodama T: Endoscopic therapy for early colon cancer: The strip biopsy resection technique [see comments]. Gastrointest Endosc 37:128–132, 1991.

77. Karita M, Tada M, Okita K: The successive strip biopsy partial resection technique for large early gastric and colon cancers. Gastrointest Endosc 38:174–178, 1992.

78. Yoshida S: Endoscopic diagnosis and treatment of early cancer in the alimentary tract. Digestion 59:502–508, 1998.

79. Soehendra N, Binmoeller KF, Bohnacker S, et al: Endoscopic snare mucosectomy in the esophagus without any additional equipment: A simple technique for resection of flat early cancer. Endoscopy 29:380–383, 1997.

80. Binmoeller KF, Bohnacker S, Seifert H, et al: Endoscopic snare excision of "giant" colorectal polyp. Gastrointest Endosc 43:183–188, 1996.

81. Suzuki Y, Hiraishi H, Kanke K, et al: Treatment of gastric tumors by endoscopic mucosal resection with a ligating device. Gastrointest Endosc 49:192–199, 1999.

82. Higaki S, Nishiaki M, Mitani N, et al: Effectiveness of local endoscopic resection of rectal carcinoid tumors. Endoscopy 29:171–175, 1997.

83. Inoue H, Takeshita K, Hori H, et al: Endoscopic mucosal resection with a cap-fitted panendoscope for esophagus, stomach, and colon mucosal lesions [see comments]. Gastrointest Endosc 39:58–62, 1993.

84. Inoue H, Kawano T, Tani M, et al: Endoscopic mucosal resection using a cap: Techniques for use and preventing perforation. Can J Gastroenterol 13:477–480, 1999.

85. Yamamoto H, Kawata H, Sunada K, et al: Successful en-bloc resection of large superficial tumors in the stomach and colon using sodium hyaluronate and small-caliber-tip transparent hood. Endoscopy 35:690–694, 2003.

86. Gotoda T, Kondo H, Ono H, et al: A new endoscopic mucosal resection procedure using an insulation-tipped electrosurgical knife for rectal flat lesions: Report of two cases. Gastrointest Endosc 50:560–563, 1999.

87. Brooker JC, Saunders BP, Shah SG, et al: Treatment with argon plasma coagulation reduces recurrence after piecemeal resection of large sessile colonic polyps: A randomized trial and recommendations. Gastrointest Endosc 55:371–375, 2002.

88. Regula J, Wronska E, Polkowski M, et al: Argon plasma coagulation after piecemeal polypectomy of sessile colorectal adenomas: Long-term follow-up study. Endoscopy 35:212–218, 2003.

89. Nizam R, Siddiqi N, Landas SK, et al: Colonic tattooing with India ink: Benefits, risks, and alternatives. Am J Gastroenterol 91:1804–1808, 1996.

90. Miller K, Waye JD: Polyp retrieval after colonoscopic polypectomy: Use of the Roth Retrieval Net. Gastrointest Endosc 54:505–507, 2001.

91. Winawer S, Fletcher R, Rex D, et al: Colorectal cancer screening and surveillance: Clinical guidelines and rationale-Update based on new evidence. Gastroenterology 124:544–560, 2003.

92. Kanamori T, Itoh M, Yokoyama Y, Tsuchida K: Injection-incision-assisted snare resection of large sessile colorectal polyp. Gastrointest Endosc 43:189–195, 1996.

93. Tanaka S, Haruma K, Oka S, et al: Clinicopathologic features and endoscopic treatment of superficially spreading colorectal neoplasms larger than 20 mm. Gastrointest Endosc 54:62–66, 2001.

94. Dell'Abate P, Iosca A, Galimberti A, et al: Endoscopic treatment of colorectal benign-appearing lesions 3 cm or larger: Techniques and outcome. Dis Colon Rectum 44:112–118, 2001.

95. Doniec JM, Lohnert MS, Schniewind B, et al: Endoscopic removal of large colorectal polyps: Prevention of unnecessary surgery? Dis Colon Rectum 46:340–348, 2003.

96. Yokota T, Sugihara K, Yoshida S: Endoscopic mucosal resection for colorectal neoplastic lesions. Dis Colon Rectum 37:1108–1111, 1994.

97. Walsh RM, Ackroyd FW, Shellito PC: Endoscopic resection of large sessile colorectal polyps. Gastrointest Endosc 38:303–309, 1992.

98. Nivatvongs S: Surgical management of early colorectal cancer. World J Surg 24:1052–1055, 2000.

99. Volk EE, Goldblum JR, Petras RE, et al: Management and outcome of patients with invasive carcinoma arising in colorectal polyps. Gastroenterology 109:1801–1807, 1995.

100. Baron PL, Enker WE, Zakowski MF, Urmacher C: Immediate vs. salvage resection after local treatment for early rectal cancer. Dis Colon Rectum 38:177–181, 1995.

101. Haggitt RC, Glotzbach RE, Soffer EE, Wruble LD: Prognostic factors in colorectal carcinomas arising in adenomas: Implications for lesions removed by endoscopic polypectomy. Gastroenterology 89:328–336, 1985.

102. Kikuchi R, Takano M, Takagi K, et al: Management of early invasive colorectal cancer. Risk of recurrence and clinical guidelines. Dis Colon Rectum 38:1286–1295, 1995.

103. Williams CB, Saunders BP, Talbot IC: Endoscopic management of polypoid early colon cancer. World J Surg 24:1047–1051, 2000.

104. Tanaka S, Haruma K, Teixeira CR, et al: Endoscopic treatment of submucosal invasive colorectal carcinoma with special reference to risk factors for lymph node metastasis. J Gastroenterol 30:710–717, 1995.

105. Masaki T, Muto T: Predictive value of histology at the invasive margin in the prognosis of early invasive colorectal carcinoma. J Gastroenterol 35:195–200, 2000.

106. Rosen L, Bub DS, Reed JF 3rd, Nastasee SA: Hemorrhage following colonoscopic polypectomy. Dis Colon Rectum 36:1126–1131, 1993.

107. Parra-Blanco A, Kaminaga N, Kojima T, et al: Hemoclipping for postpolypectomy and postbiopsy colonic bleeding. Gastrointest Endosc 51:37–41, 2000.

108. Rex DK, Lewis BS, Waye JD: Colonoscopy and endoscopic therapy for delayed post-polypectomy hemorrhage. Gastrointest Endosc 38:127–129, 1992.

109. Nivatvongs S: Complications in colonoscopic polypectomy. An experience with 1,555 polypectomies. Dis Colon Rectum 29:825–830, 1986.

110. Waye JD, Lewis BS, Yessayan S: Colonoscopy: A prospective report of complications. J Clin Gastroenterol 15:347–351, 1992.

111. Orsoni P, Berdah S, Verrier C, et al: Colonic perforation due to colonoscopy: A retrospective study of 48 cases. Endoscopy 29:160–164, 1997.

112. Christie JP, Marrazzo J 3rd: "Mini-perforation" of the colon—not all postpolypectomy perforations require laparotomy. Dis Colon Rectum 34:132–135, 1991.

113. Tsunada S, Ogata S, Ohyama T, et al: Endoscopic closure of perforations caused by EMR in the stomach by application of metallic clips. Gastrointest Endosc 57:948–951, 2003.

114. Ono H, Kondo H, Gotoda T, et al: Endoscopic mucosal resection for treatment of early gastric cancer. Gut 48:225–229, 2001.

115. Schlemper RJ, Itabashi M, Kato Y, et al: Differences in diagnostic criteria for gastric carcinoma between Japanese and western pathologists [see comments] [published erratum appears in Lancet 350:524, 1997]. Lancet 349:1725–1729, 1997.

116. Schlemper RJ, Riddell RH, Kato Y, et al: The Vienna classification of gastrointestinal epithelial neoplasia. Gut 47:251–255, 2000.

Endoscopic Palliation of Colorectal Tumors

Charles J. Kahi, Emad Rahmani, and Douglas K. Rex

CHAPTER

39

Introduction

Colorectal cancer (CRC) is the second leading cause of cancer death in the United States.[1] There are an estimated 150,000 new cases and 57,000 deaths in both sexes annually.[1] Many patients are asymptomatic at the time of diagnosis; however, an estimated 7% to 29% present with, or develop, colonic obstruction during their course.[2,3] Malignancy accounts for about 85% of all cases of acute colonic obstruction[3] and usually indicates advanced local and systemic disease.[3,4]

Traditionally, the management of such patients has been surgical, with either resection and primary anastomosis or a two-stage procedure involving initial resection with end colostomy and then colostomy closure later. Both approaches have several limitations: the one-stage procedure is technically demanding,[3] and only 40% of patients with left-sided malignant obstruction are appropriate candidates.[5] The two-stage procedure is usually necessary in left-sided obstruction, and patients in this category tend to be older, debilitated, and with more advanced disease, hence particularly at risk for postoperative morbidity.[3,5,6] This often precludes a second operation for stoma closure, resulting in a permanent colostomy and a negative impact on quality of life.[7]

Regardless of the method used, surgery for malignant colonic obstruction implies a prolonged hospital stay and has a postoperative mortality rate of about 7%.[3] These issues have generated interest in newer, less invasive alternatives and adjuncts to surgery: placement of stents, laser ablation, argon plasma coagulation (APC), photodynamic therapy (PDT), endoscopic dilation, cryotherapy, electrocautery, and endoscopic injection of necrotizing agents.[8] Each of these modalities has been used alone or in combination, either for palliation or in preparation for definitive surgery. None have been evaluated in head-to-head, comparative randomized trials; however, historical data regarding efficacy and complications are substantial and are discussed in detail in the following sections. To compare favorably with emergency surgical intervention, any endoscopic technique should demonstrate at least equivalent efficacy, lower morbidity and mortality rates, availability, and cost effectiveness. Based on these considerations, stenting currently appears to be the leading endoscopic modality for palliation of CRC. This chapter summarizes and discusses the current role of endoscopic techniques in the management of CRC.

Colorectal Stenting

RATIONALE

The use of stents to relieve malignant colorectal obstruction is advantageous in two broad settings. In patients with acute obstruction, emergency surgery carries a high risk of morbidity and mortality because of field contamination with fecal material. Stenting in this situation decompresses the bowel and permits an adequate colonic preparation, thus allowing surgical intervention under better controlled conditions. In patients with unresectable disease, or those who are poor candidates for operative diversion, stents can be inserted for symptomatic relief. The basic idea is to restore luminal patency, either as a bridge to surgery or as a palliative measure. Colorectal stents can be placed by endoscopists, with or without fluoroscopic guidance, or by interventional radiologists using fluoroscopy alone.[9] Certain stents can be passed through the scope (TTS), allowing direct visualization of the procedure. This is a definite advantage for endoscopic stenting, especially when the obstruction is proximal to the sigmoid colon.[9] In general, stents should not be placed within a few centimeters from the anal verge to minimize the risk of chronic tenesmus.[10] The stent anchors should remain proximal to the dentate line to avoid this potential adverse event.

TYPES OF COLORECTAL STENTS

The first description of stenting for malignant colonic obstruction was made by Dohmoto[11] in 1991. Since then, multiple case reports and case series have been published, using a variety of stent types and placement techniques.[12–43] Modern stents are made of metal

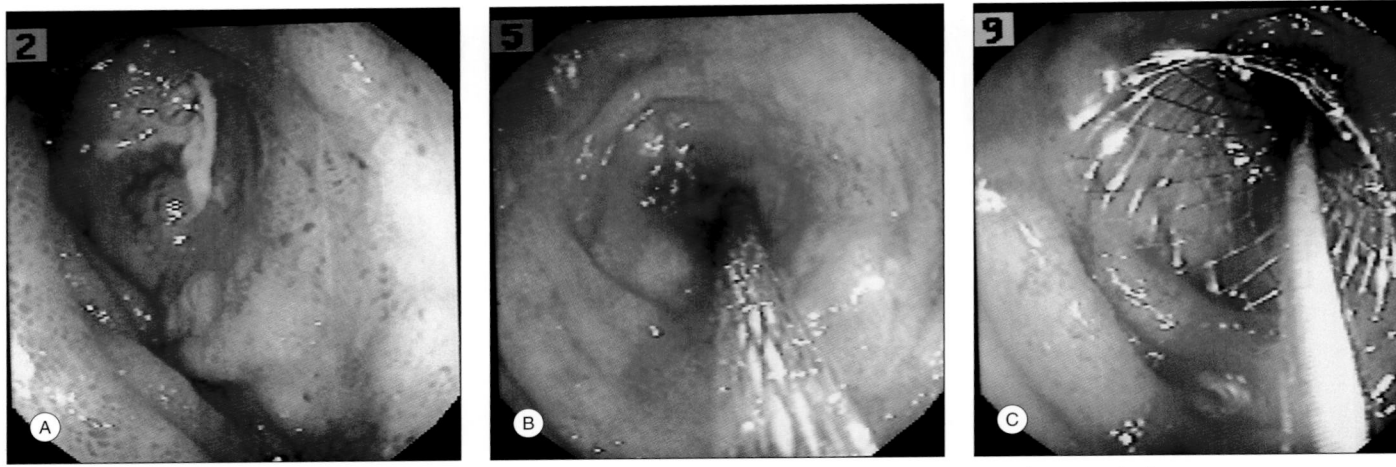

Figure 39–1. *A,* Completely obstructed colon cancer. *B,* Stent placement over radiologically placed guidewire. *C,* After stent deployment.

alloys with different sizes and physical properties, depending on manufacturer specifications and target organ.[9] All trigger pressure necrosis in the tumor and surrounding tissue, ultimately embedding the stent and preventing dislodgement.[9] Most stents used for colonic decompression are uncovered, a property which is thought to facilitate anchoring.[9] Covered stents, such as the esophageal Z-stent (Wilson-Cook Medical, Winston-Salem, NC), and the partially covered esophageal Ultraflex stent (Microvasive Endoscopy, Boston Scientific Corporation, Natick, MA) are better suited to treat malignant colonic fistulas[44–46] and address the problem of tumor ingrowth.[47] Esophageal and biliary stents (e.g., the biliary Wallstent, Microvasive Endoscopy) have been successfully placed in the colon but are not specifically designed for this indication.[8] The choice of stent ultimately depends on local availability, operator experience, and individual patient characteristics. All three colonic stents are sufficiently stiff to withstand the radial pressure exerted by the tumor, yet flexible enough to conform to the curvature of the bowel lumen.[8] The Enteral Wallstent is particularly suitable for use in the proximal colon, given that it can be passed through the endoscope.[9]

TECHNIQUE

Colonic stents can be placed using endoscopic or fluoroscopic techniques or a combination of both. Irrespective of the method chosen, some general principles apply to all patients: First, it is important to exclude perforation with plain abdominal radiographs, because this is an absolute contraindication for colonic stent placement.[9] A retrograde contrast study can also be helpful to assess the extent and degree of the obstruction and to exclude any synchronous lesions that would warrant separate interventions. Bowel preparation with oral solutions should be avoided in the setting of complete obstruction, and tap water enemas given to clean the colon distal to the obstruction. There are no data supporting the routine use of prophylactic antibiotics before stenting[8,48]; however, this seems prudent in case the procedure is complicated by perforation of the bowel. Stent insertion using fluoroscopy alone is described in detail elsewhere[8,49] and is not further discussed. Endoscopic placement begins by inserting a sigmoidoscope or colonoscope, depending on the location of the obstruction. With minimal air insufflation, the instrument is advanced until the site of obstruction is reached. If the endoscope can pass the lesion with minimal or no resistance, a TTS approach is recommended: A stiff guidewire is passed through the accessory channel as far proximal to the lesion as possible. After repositioning the endoscope just distal to the lesion, an enteral endoprosthetic is introduced over the wire and deployed under direct vision (Figs. 39–1 and 39–2). The stent should ideally extend 1 to 2 cm beyond either side of the tumor. If the obstruction is too long to bridge with one stent, a second overlapping stent can be used; again, the proximal end of the tumor should be bridged first. If there is substantial resistance to the passage of the endoscope, the procedure can be completed after exchanging the colonoscope for a thinner upper endoscope. The aim, again, is to pass the tumor and place the guidewire proximal to it. This is also advantageous because the rest of the colon can be examined to exclude any synchronous lesions. If the tumor completely prevents the passage of any type of endoscope, then the procedure can be completed with fluoroscopic guidance. A biliary catheter can be used to gently probe the lesion, attempting to find the lumen.[8] This is recognized fluoroscopically when the wire is visualized in a dilated proximal bowel. After injection of water-soluble contrast to confirm positioning, the wire is replaced with a stiff 0.035-inch guidewire and a stent introduced and deployed under fluoroscopic guidance. Some authors dilate malignant strictures before stent insertion or use the neodymium:yttrium-aluminum-garnet (Nd:YAG) laser to recanalize the tumor, thus avoiding the need for fluoroscopy.[9,50,51] These variations may be effective but may increase the risk of perforation and stent migration, and should only be performed by experts.

POSTPROCEDURAL CARE

Most stenting procedures can be done in the outpatient setting. An abdominal radiograph should be obtained after the procedure to document the position of the stent,[49] and oral intake is usually safe immediately after completion.[9] If surgery is contemplated soon, oral bowel preparation can start within 24 hours.[8] If a waiting period is anticipated, or if no surgery is planned, patients should be advised

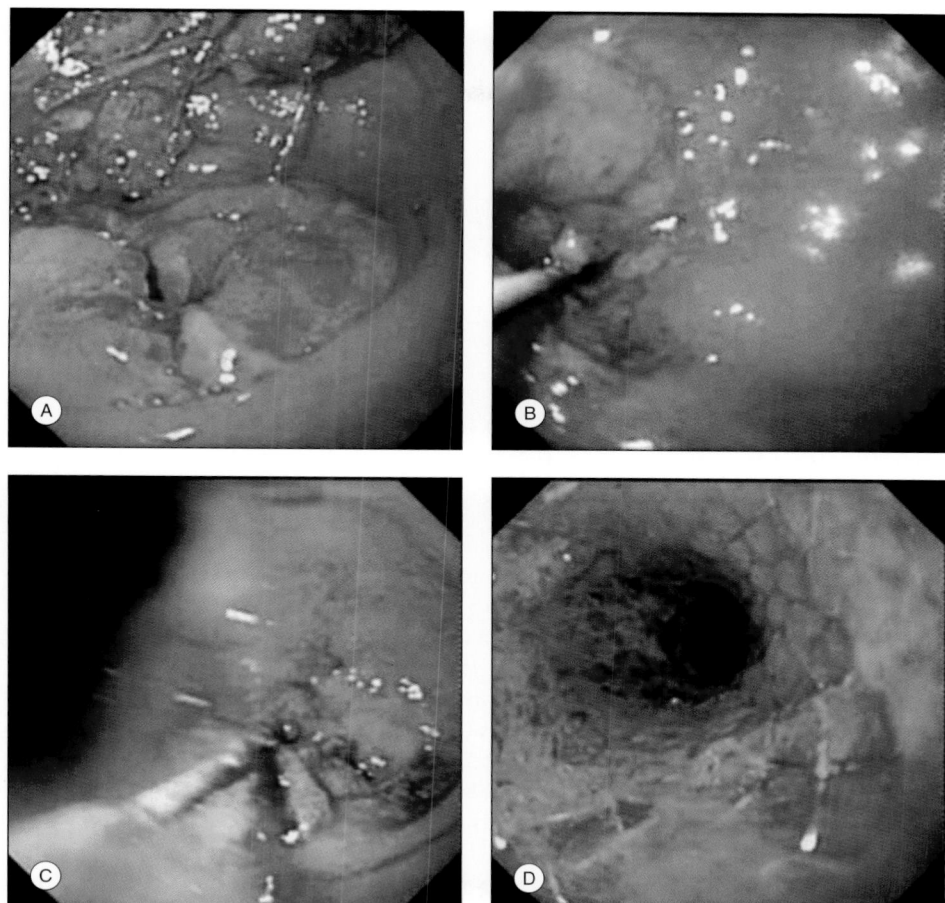

Figure 39–2. *A,* Obstructing sigmoid cancer. *B,* Guidewire through the cancer. *C,* Stent is being advanced over the guidewire. *D,* Stent after deployment with prompt decompression.

to follow a low-residue diet (with or without mild laxatives) to minimize the chance of stool impaction within the stent.[8,9]

OUTCOMES

There is a growing body of literature that shows that colorectal stents are safe and effective, either as a palliative measure or as an adjunct to surgery. Overall, the success rate for stent insertion and decompression ranges from 64% to 100%.[10] In a recent systematic review, Khot and colleagues[52] compiled the data of 29 case series published between 1990 and 2000, representing 598 stent insertions. The procedure was technically successful in 551 (92%) and resulted in appropriate decompression of the bowel in 525 (88%). The indication for stenting (palliation or as a bridge to surgery) did not influence outcome. The mortality rate was 1%, and postprocedural complications included stent migration in 54/551 (10%), pain in 31/598 (5%), bleeding in 27/598 (5%), and perforation in 22/598 (4%). Reobstruction occurred in 52/525 (10%); however, most of these patients had stents placed for palliation, and only 3/223 (1%) patients who had stents placed as a prelude to surgery suffered from this complication. The main factors associated with stent migration were laser pretreatment and chemotherapy, which can shrink the tumor and thus predispose to stent dislodgement. Other studies have confirmed these findings, and listed small stent caliber, covered stents, radiation therapy, benign stric-

tures, and extrinsic lesions as other factors predisposing to stent migration.[8]

Balloon dilation before stenting appears to be the major risk factor for perforation.[52]

Colorectal stenting has not been subjected to the scrutiny of a randomized controlled trial comparing it to surgery, predominantly because of ethical concerns. One study[53] did compare 43 consecutive patients who had stents placed for malignant left-sided obstruction to 29 similar patients who underwent emergency surgery. Morbidity and mortality rates were not significantly different between the two groups; however, the patients who underwent stenting experienced less severe complications and required fewer reinterventions. In addition, the total hospital stay and the number of intensive care unit days were significantly less in the stent group. This is consonant with other analyses,[54] which have found stenting to be more cost effective than surgical decompression regardless of indication.

Argon Plasma Coagulation

APC uses electrical current passed through argon gas to heat and coagulate target tissue. The thermal effect leads to boiling of fluids in the tissue; this creates an insulating layer of steam that decreases electrical conductivity and gradually limits the depth of coagulative

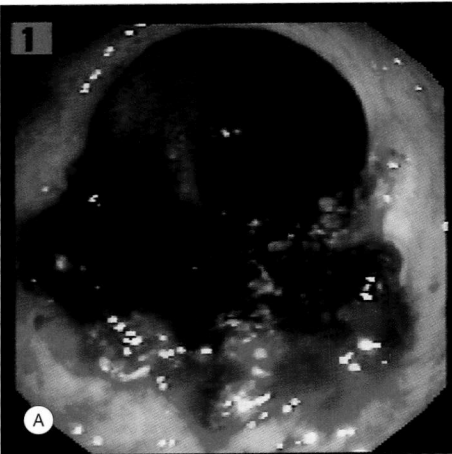
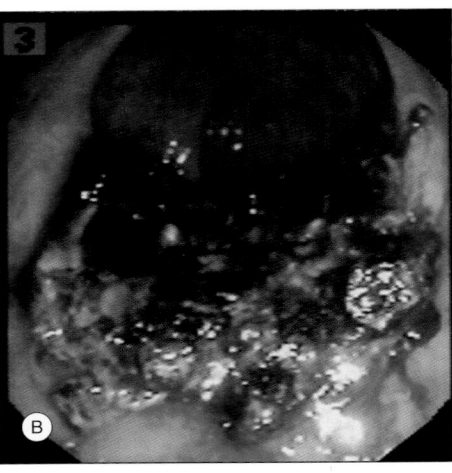

Figure 39-3. *A,* Bleeding rectal cancer. *B,* After argon plasma coagulation (APC).

injury.[55] APC has wide applications in gastroenterology, including the obliteration of angiomata, the treatment of residual or bleeding tissue after snare polypectomy, recanalization of esophageal cancer, and the palliation of radiation proctitis.[56,57] APC is a particularly attractive modality in certain settings for the palliation of CRC: it can be used to destroy remnant neoplastic tissue after tumor excision by other endoscopic means. Given its hemostatic efficacy, it can be used to control bleeding, especially from slowly oozing, friable neoplasms (Fig. 39–3). Finally, it is the procedure of choice to ablate tumor ingrowth and regrowth, particularly after colorectal stent placement. Complications associated with APC are infrequent.[58] However, the depth of tissue injury can be easily underestimated, and there are anecdotal reports of perforation resulting from uncontrolled transmural burns in the colon.

Laser Therapy

RATIONALE

Laser (light amplification by stimulated emission of radiation) has been used as a palliative treatment for esophageal cancer since the early 1980s[59] and has since been used for a variety of other gastrointestinal tumors, including CRC.[59–65] Similar to stenting, the rationale is to recanalize obstructing colorectal tumors, either for palliation or in preparation for surgery. In addition, lasers are useful for the control of tumor bleeding (particularly in nonobstructive tumors)[66] and malignancy-related tenesmus, diarrhea, and fecal incontinence.[67]

However, treatment with lasers is expensive, requires repeated treatment sessions, and is hampered by lack of portability, a significant issue when hemostasis is the goal. This has led to a relative decline of laser therapy in favor of other emerging modalities, such as stenting.

TYPES OF LASERS

Lasers depend on media that release photons when illuminated. These photons are focused by mirrors inside the laser apparatus and released as a monochromatic beam with specific wavelength. The beam is delivered via a probe that can be passed into the accessory channel of most colonoscopes. The media that are most widely used are Nd:YAG, with a wavelength of 1060 nm, and argon gas, with a wavelength of 458 to 514 nm. Both types of lasers exert their effect *in vivo* by heating target tissue, with resultant coagulation or vaporization. Given its higher wavelength, Nd:YAG penetrates deeper than argon and, thus, is preferred for the treatment of colorectal neoplasms. The effect of lasers on tissue also depends on the power setting, distance of the probe from the tumor, and duration of the pulse. Most laser units can deliver up to 120 watts of power, and operators commonly report using 1-second pulses of 50 to 100 watts.[60,67] The optimal distance between the probe and neoplastic tissue is about 1 cm. Contact probes use less power than their noncontact counterparts and thus generate less smoke and can be used to cut through tumor.[68,69] However, noncontact probes are generally preferred because of their higher efficiency.

TECHNIQUE

As with stenting, bowel preparation with oral solutions is not necessary before laser therapy (and contraindicated if complete obstruction is present); an enema is often sufficient to cleanse the distal bowel.[70] Nd:YAG laser therapy for CRC starts at the proximal end of the tumor and proceeds distally. Thus, cancers that have obliterated the lumen need to be dilated before the laser can be used. As noted previously, endoscopists tend to prefer the Nd:YAG laser, delivered via a noncontact probe. The latter is coupled to a red aiming light, which gives the Nd:YAG laser the characteristic red dot when pointed at tissue (argon systems have bluish dots). The high energy of this system tends to produce smoke, hampering vision and slowing the procedure; however, smoke can be suctioned through the endoscope. Therapy proceeds sequentially until blanching of tissue is visualized, indicating coagulation. Laser therapy for tumor hemorrhage proceeds in a similar manner, with particular attention to visualized bleeding sites.

OUTCOMES

Lasers provide effective initial palliation for CRC in 88% to 97% of cases.[60,65,66,71–75] However, the tumor regrows in most instances, mandating repeated sessions at 4- to 8-week intervals. This approach appears to be superior to repeating treatment only when symptoms

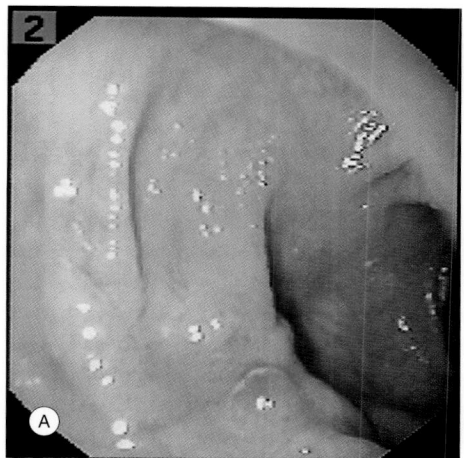 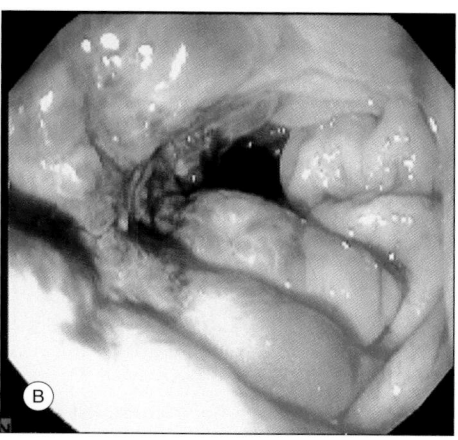

Figure 39–4. *A,* Depressed early colon cancer. *B,* After photodynamic therapy (PDT).

recur.[76] The addition of endocavitary radiation therapy to laser may prolong stenosis-free intervals[77]; however, this is not commonly performed. In a recent large review,[67] 219 patients underwent Nd:YAG therapy for palliation of CRC. Initial success was observed in 92% of cases; however, long-term efficacy depended on the underlying symptom: 83% of the patients with tumor bleeding and 81% of those with other symptoms attributed to CRC (tenesmus, diarrhea, fecal incontinence) were effectively palliated, compared with only 65% of those presenting with obstruction. Another study[78] has confirmed that obstruction was predictive of therapeutic failure and the need for surgical palliation. Mortality directly attributable to Nd:YAG treatment ranges from 2.3% to 8% in most case series.[67,79] Major adverse events include perforation, fistula or abscess formation, and bleeding.[67] Laser therapy has been shown to decrease transfusion requirements in patients with bleeding CRC and to allow elective surgical resection, translating into shorter hospital stays, lower costs, and preserved quality of life.[80–82]

The use of lasers for palliation of CRC has declined in recent years, secondary to the need for repeated treatments, which expose patients to adverse events at every session. In addition, there is increasing operator experience with stenting, which is emerging as the endoscopic modality of choice in CRC therapy. However, lasers are effective and widely available, and they are particularly well suited for certain indications, such as tumor bleeding. Lasers are also used in PDT, which is discussed in the next section. For these reasons, lasers remain an important option in the endoscopic palliation of CRC.

Photodynamic Therapy

RATIONALE

PDT is based on the fact that malignant tissue accumulates photosensitizers selectively. These agents are inert until activated by light of appropriate wavelength, which is applied via an optical fiber. The most widely available photosensitizer in the United States is porfimer sodium (Photofrin, QLT Phototherapeutics Inc, Vancouver, British Columbia), a mixture of hematoporphyrin molecules. This agent is injected intravenously at a dose of 2 mg/kg and cleared by

various tissues; however, skin, organs of the reticuloendothelial system and neoplasms retain it for longer than 72 hours. Subsequent illumination, usually with a 630-nm red light laser, activates the porfimer and leads to oxygen free radical production, with resultant cell death. This modality is attractive given the targeted delivery of therapy and has gained widespread acceptance in the management of patients of esophageal malignancy and Barrett's esophagus with dysplasia.[83,84] There are less data regarding its use specifically for CRC palliation; however, PDT is gaining acceptance in this field as well.

TYPES OF PHOTODYNAMIC THERAPY

As noted previously, porfimer is the main photosensitizer used in the United States. This agent's main drawback is its tendency to accumulate in skin for weeks after administration, resulting in photosensitivity and risk of severe sunburns.[85] A more recently developed photosensitizer is 5-aminolevulinic acid (5-ALA), the natural precursor of protoporphyrin IX. This substance accumulates more selectively and is retained longer in tumor cells. In addition, 5-ALA is administered orally and its brief half-life leads to a much shorter period of photosensitivity for patients.[86,87]

The laser system is essentially the same regardless of the photosensitizer used: it must be approved for stable delivery at a wavelength of 630 nm and deliver sufficient power to the target tissue.[88] This is done via a cylindrical fiberoptic diffuser that can be passed through the endoscope.

TECHNIQUE

As with stenting and laser therapy, PDT can be done after minimal bowel preparation with an enema. Patients receive the photosensitizer (intravenously for porfimer, orally for 5-ALA) and return for their procedure 2 to 3 days later. The colonoscope is guided to the tumor, the diffuser probe inserted into the endoscope until its tip is closely apposed to the lesion (or centered in the lumen in the case of a circumferential tumor), and the light source turned on (Figs. 39–4 and 39–5). A dose of 300 J/cm^2 is recommended for esophageal lesions; however, data are scarce in the case of CRC. Different studies have reported light doses ranging from 50 to 200 J/cm^2.[86,89,90]

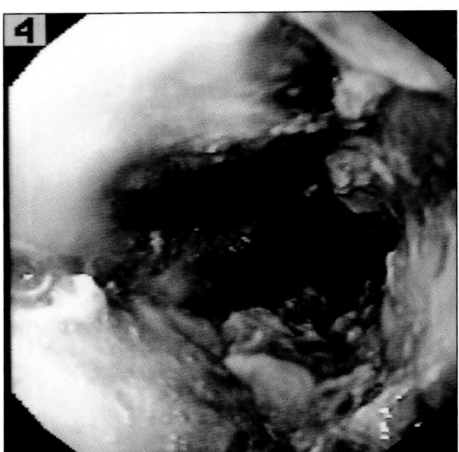

Figure 39–5. After photodynamic therapy (PDT) for obstructive cancer.

OUTCOMES

Most data on the use of PDT for the palliation of CRC come from small case series.[89–91] It is difficult to assess the efficacy of PDT, given the different methodologies used, heterogeneous patient population, and lack of standardized outcome assessment.[90] In one study of 10 patients with inoperable CRC (distances 3 to 70 cm from the anal verge), 6 patients had improvement of symptoms (bleeding, constipation, diarrhea). Another series[91] found a 50% response rate. Overall, a complete response of the local tumor is expected in 35% of patients, with a partial response in 44%.[92] Complications reported with PDT have included perforation, significant hemorrhage, and sunburn related to the photosensitizer.[89–91]

There seems to be an emerging consensus to reserve PDT for small tumors or tumor remnants after treatment with other modalities.[89] This fact, coupled with the high cost of PDT, suggests that this modality will have a very specific niche in the endoscopic palliation of CRC.

Other Modalities

Other modalities in the endoscopic palliation of CRC include bipolar electrocoagulation (BEC), cryotherapy, transanal resection, and injection of chemical agents.

BIPOLAR ELECTROCOAGULATION

BEC involves the application of electric current through a device that contains two electrodes. Current flows from one into the other and leads to tissue desiccation and necrosis. BEC is widely used for hemostasis and is highly effective in that setting. Small rectal carcinomas located below the peritoneal reflection have also been treated with BEC,[93–95] with overall success rates of 77% to 90%. However, BEC probes have otherwise limited usefulness in the palliation of CRC, given the superficiality of tissue injury, requirement for multiple sessions, and tendency of tissue to stick to the probe during therapy. A dedicated Bicap tumor probe has been specifically designed to solve some of these drawbacks; however, perforations were a frequent complication and the device is no longer used in clinical practice. In addition, several major complications resulting from BEC have been reported, including bleeding, rectal stenosis, and perforation. For these reasons, BEC is seldom used for the palliation of CRC.[92]

CRYOTHERAPY

Cryotherapy uses a liquid nitrogen–cooled cryoprobe to freeze neoplastic tissue. After application for 30 to 60 seconds, necrosis occurs to a depth of 4 to 8 mm. Treatment is usually repeated two to three times before a clinical response occurs.[92,96] Effective palliation of obstruction has been reported in 51% to 62% of cases; however, other malignancy-related symptoms are less effectively controlled.[97,98] Cryotherapy is associated with significant risks, including fistula formation, sepsis, and bleeding, in up to 18% of patients.[98] In addition, necrosis and sloughing of tumor tissue leads to rectal discharge that may persist for weeks.[79] Tumors located above the peritoneal reflection are usually not accessible. Thus, cryotherapy has not gained widespread popularity for the palliation of CRC.

TRANSANAL RESECTION

Transanal resection of tumors is usually performed under general or spinal anesthesia by surgeons. The method uses a rigid "resectoscope" with cutting snares (akin to those used for prostate resection), with accessibility limited to lesions within 20 cm from the anal verge. Studies have reported successful palliation in 63% to 76% of cases[99–101]; however, the procedure needed to be repeated at least once in nearly half of the patients. Complications, including bleeding and perforation, occur in about 15% of cases, and the mortality rate is 5%. Gastroenterologists use a less invasive variant, which can be done with standard colonoscopes and under conscious sedation: a diathermy snare is looped around tumor, and current is applied to heat and induce necrosis and sloughing of tissue. The process can be repeated several times until the mass is debulked and luminal patency restored. Arrigoni and colleagues[102] used diathermal snares in conjunction with dilation and laser photoablation to successfully recanalize left-sided tumors in 16/17 (94%) patients. The procedure was best suited for neoplasms with projecting vegetations, which were removed with a blended cutting and coagulating current. Given the need for anesthesia and the relatively high complication rates, the use of transanal resection for CRC palliation is likely to remain restricted to a few specialized centers. However, the endoscopic variant is useful in selected patients with certain tumor types, when used in combination with other modalities.

CHEMICAL INJECTION

Endoscopic injection of agents such as polidocanol, ethanol, and 5-fluorouracil has been reported for the palliation of CRC.[103] These agents can induce tissue necrosis and sloughing and promote hemostasis through vasoconstriction. This method is hampered by poor control of the depth of injury and the lack of immediately visible effects, which mandate repeat procedures to guide therapy. For these reasons, the endoscopic injection of chemicals to palliate CRC has not gained widespread acceptance.

REFERENCES

1. Jemal A, Murray T, Samuels A, et al: Cancer statistics, 2003. CA Cancer J Clin 53:5–26, 2003.
2. Ohman U: Prognosis in patients with obstructing colorectal carcinoma. Am J Surg 143:742–747, 1982.
3. Deans GT, Krukowski ZH, Irwin ST: Malignant obstruction of the left colon. Br J Surg 81:1270–1276, 1994.
4. Gandrup P, Lund L, Balslev I: Surgical treatment of acute malignant large bowel obstruction. Eur J Surg 158:427–430, 1992.
5. Leitman IM, Sullivan JD, Brams D, DeCosse JJ: Multivariate analysis of morbidity and mortality from the initial surgical management of obstructing carcinoma of the colon. Surg Gynecol Obstet 174:513–518, 1992.
6. Deen KI, Madoff RD, Goldberg SM, Rothenberger DA: Surgical management of left colon obstruction: The University of Minnesota experience. J Am Coll Surg 187:573–576, 1998.
7. Nugent KP, Daniels P, Stewart B, et al: Quality of life in stoma patients. Dis Colon Rectum 42:1569–1574, 1999.
8. Lo SK: Metallic stenting for colorectal obstruction. Gastrointest Endosc Clin N Am 9:459–477, 1999.
9. Baron TH, Rey JF, Spinelli P: Expandable metal stent placement for malignant colorectal obstruction. Endoscopy 34:823–830, 2002.
10. Harris GJ, Senagore AJ, Lavery IC, Fazio VW: The management of neoplastic colorectal obstruction with colonic endolumenal stenting devices. Am J Surg 181:499–506, 2001.
11. Dohmoto M: New method-endoscopic implantation of rectal stent in palliative treatment of malignant stenosis. Endosc Dig 3:1507–1512, 1991.
12. Bashir RM, Fleischer DE, Stahl TJ, Benjamin SB: Self-expandable nitinol coil stent for management of colonic obstruction due to a malignant anastomotic stricture. Gastrointest Endosc 44:497–501, 1996.
13. Soonawalla Z, Thakur K, Boorman P, et al: Use of self-expanding metallic stents in the management of obstruction of the sigmoid colon. AJR Am J Roentgenol 171:633–636, 1998.
14. Kozarek RA, Brandabur JJ, Raltz SL: Expandable stents: Unusual locations. Am J Gastroenterol 92:812–815, 1997.
15. Turegano-Fuentes F, Echenagusia-Belda A, Simo-Muerza G, et al: Transanal self-expanding metal stents as an alternative to palliative colostomy in selected patients with malignant obstruction of the left colon. Br J Surg 85:232–235, 1998.
16. Dauphine CE, Tan P, Beart RW Jr, et al: Placement of self-expanding metal stents for acute malignant large-bowel obstruction: A collective review. Ann Surg Oncol 9:574–579, 2002.
17. Vandervoort J, Weiss EJ, Somnay K, et al: Self-expanding metal stent for obstructing adenocarcinoma of the sigmoid. Gastrointest Endosc 44:739–741, 1996.
18. Itabashi M, Hamano K, Kameoka S, Asahina K: Self-expanding stainless steel stent application in rectosigmoid stricture. Dis Colon Rectum 36:508–511, 1993.
19. Feretis C, Benakis P, Dimopoulos C, et al: Palliation of large-bowel obstruction due to recurrent rectosigmoid tumor using self-expandable endoprostheses. Endoscopy 28:319–322, 1996.
20. Keen RR, Orsay CP: Rectosigmoid stent for obstructing colonic neoplasms. Dis Colon Rectum 35:912–913, 1992.
21. Aviv RI, Shyamalan G, Watkinson A, et al: Radiological palliation of malignant colonic obstruction. Clin Radiol 57:347–351, 2002.
22. Aquise M, Tejero E, Mainar A: A new option in the treatment of complete and acute obstruction due to colorectal cancer. Endoscopy 29:229, 1997.
23. Tejero E, Mainar A, Fernandez L, et al: New procedure for the treatment of colorectal neoplastic obstructions. Dis Colon Rectum 37:1158–1159, 1994.
24. Tominaga K, Yoshida M, Maetani I, Sakai Y: Expandable metal stent placement in the treatment of a malignant anastomotic stricture of the transverse colon. Gastrointest Endosc 53:524–527, 2001.
25. Miyayama S, Matsui O, Kifune K, et al: Malignant colonic obstruction due to extrinsic tumor: Palliative treatment with a self-expanding nitinol stent. AJR Am J Roentgenol 175:1631–1637, 2000.
26. Fernandez Lobato R, Pinto I, Paul L, et al: Self-expanding prostheses as a palliative method in treating advanced colorectal cancer. Int Surg 84:159–162, 1999.
27. Liberman H, Adams DR, Blatchford GJ, et al: Clinical use of the self-expanding metallic stent in the management of colorectal cancer. Am J Surg 180:407–411; discussion 412, 2000.
28. Wholey MH, Levine EA, Ferral H, Castaneda-Zuniga W: Initial clinical experience with colonic stent placement. Am J Surg 175:194–197, 1998.
29. Boorman P, Soonawalla Z, Sathananthan N, et al: Endoluminal stenting of obstructed colorectal tumours. Ann R Coll Surg Engl 81:251–254, 1999.
30. de Gregorio MA, Mainar A, Tejero E, et al: Acute colorectal obstruction: Stent placement for palliative treatment—results of a multicenter study. Radiology 209:117–120, 1998.
31. Mainar A, De Gregorio Ariza MA, Tejero E, et al: Acute colorectal obstruction: Treatment with self-expandable metallic stents before scheduled surgery—results of a multicenter study. Radiology 210:65–69, 1999.
32. Mainar A, Tejero E, Maynar M, et al: Colorectal obstruction: Treatment with metallic stents. Radiology 198:761–764, 1996.
33. Choo IW, Do YS, Suh SW, et al: Malignant colorectal obstruction: Treatment with a flexible covered stent. Radiology 206:415–421, 1998.
34. Camunez F, Echenagusia A, Simo G, et al: Malignant colorectal obstruction treated by means of self-expanding metallic stents: Effectiveness before surgery and in palliation. Radiology 216:492–497, 2000.
35. Baron TH, Dean PA, Yates MR 3rd, et al: Expandable metal stents for the treatment of colonic obstruction: Techniques and outcomes. Gastrointest Endosc 47:277–286, 1998.
36. Tejero E, Fernandez-Lobato R, Mainar A, et al: Initial results of a new procedure for treatment of malignant obstruction of the left colon. Dis Colon Rectum 40:432–436, 1997.
37. Saida Y, Sumiyama Y, Nagao J, Takase M: Stent endoprosthesis for obstructing colorectal cancers. Dis Colon Rectum 39:552–555, 1996.
38. Law WL, Chu KW, Ho JW, et al: Self-expanding metallic stent in the treatment of colonic obstruction caused by advanced malignancies. Dis Colon Rectum 43:1522–1527, 2000.
39. Wallis F, Campbell KL, Eremin O, Hussey JK: Self-expanding metal stents in the management of colorectal carcinoma—a preliminary report. Clin Radiol 53:251–254, 1998.
40. Tack J, Gevers AM, Rutgeerts P: Self-expandable metallic stents in the palliation of rectosigmoidal carcinoma: A follow-up study. Gastrointest Endosc 48:267–271, 1998.
41. Canon CL, Baron TH, Morgan DE, et al: Treatment of colonic obstruction with expandable metal stents: Radiologic features. AJR Am J Roentgenol 168:199–205, 1997.
42. Arnell T, Stamos MJ, Takahashi P, et al: Colonic stents in colorectal obstruction. Am Surg 64:986–988, 1998.
43. Campbell KL, Hussey JK, Eremin O: Expandable metal stent application in obstructing carcinoma of the proximal colon: Report of a case. Dis Colon Rectum 40:1391–1393, 1997.
44. Sharma VK, Xie QY, Hassan HA, Howden CW: Placement of a covered metal stent via gastrostomy for management of malignant duodenocolic fistula with duodenal obstruction. Gastrointest Endosc 55:937–940, 2002.
45. Repici A, Reggio D, Saracco G, et al: Self-expanding covered esophageal ultraflex stent for palliation of malignant colorectal anastomotic obstruction complicated by multiple fistulas. Gastrointest Endosc 51:346–348, 2000.
46. Cwikiel W, Andren-Sandberg A: Malignant stricture with colovesical fistula: Stent insertion in the colon. Radiology 186:563–564, 1993.

47. Repici A, Reggio D, De Angelis C, et al: Covered metal stents for management of inoperable malignant colorectal strictures. Gastrointest Endosc 52:735–740, 2000.

48. Saunders BP, Bartram C: Self-expanding, metal stents for malignant colonic obstruction. Clin Radiol 53:237–238, 1998.

49. Lopera JE, Ferral H, Wholey M, et al: Treatment of colonic obstructions with metallic stents: Indications, technique, and complications. AJR Am J Roentgenol 169:1285–1290, 1997.

50. Rey JF, Romanczyk T, Greff M: Metal stents for palliation of rectal carcinoma: A preliminary report on 12 patients. Endoscopy 27:501–504, 1995.

51. Spinelli P, Mancini A: Use of self-expanding metal stents for palliation of rectosigmoid cancer. Gastrointest Endosc 53:203–206, 2001.

52. Khot UP, Lang AW, Murali K, Parker MC: Systematic review of the efficacy and safety of colorectal stents. Br J Surg 89:1096–1102, 2002.

53. Martinez-Santos C, Lobato RF, Fradejas JM, et al: Self-expandable stent before elective surgery vs. emergency surgery for the treatment of malignant colorectal obstructions: Comparison of primary anastomosis and morbidity rates. Dis Colon Rectum 45:401–406, 2002.

54. Binkert CA, Ledermann H, Jost R, et al: Acute colonic obstruction: Clinical aspects and cost-effectiveness of preoperative and palliative treatment with self-expanding metallic stents—a preliminary report. Radiology 206:199–204, 1998.

55. Farin G, Grund KE: Technology of argon plasma coagulation with particular regard to endoscopic applications. Endosc Surg Allied Technol 2:71–77, 1994.

56. Johanns W, Luis W, Janssen J, et al: Argon plasma coagulation (APC) in gastroenterology: Experimental and clinical experiences. Eur J Gastroenterol Hepatol 9:581–587, 1997.

57. Villavicencio RT, Rex DK, Rahmani E: Efficacy and complications of argon plasma coagulation for hematochezia related to radiation proctopathy. Gastrointest Endosc 55:70–74, 2002.

58. Grund KE, Storek D, Farin G: Endoscopic argon plasma coagulation (APC) first clinical experiences in flexible endoscopy. Endosc Surg Allied Technol 2:42–46, 1994.

59. Fleischer D, Kessler F, Haye O: Endoscopic Nd:YAG laser therapy for carcinoma of the esophagus: A new palliative approach. Am J Surg 143:280–283, 1982.

60. Mathus-Vliegen EM, Tytgat GN: Analysis of failures and complications of neodymium: YAG laser photocoagulation in gastrointestinal tract tumors. A retrospective survey of 18 years' experience. Endoscopy 22:17–23, 1990.

61. Nagy AG: Palliative treatment of advanced colorectal carcinoma with the YAG laser. Can J Surg 33:261–264, 1990.

62. Kashtan H, Stern H: The use of lasers in colorectal cancer. Cancer Invest 11:33–35, 1993.

63. Eckhauser ML: The neodymium-YAG laser and gastrointestinal malignancy. Arch Surg 125:1152–1154, 1990.

64. Eckhauser ML: Laser therapy of gastrointestinal tumors. World J Surg 16:1054–1059, 1992.

65. Kiefhaber P, Kiefhaber K, Huber F: Preoperative neodymium-YAG laser treatment of obstructive colon cancer. Endoscopy 18(Suppl 1):44–46, 1986.

66. Mathus-Vliegen EM, Tytgat GN: Laser ablation and palliation in colorectal malignancy. Results of a multicenter inquiry. Gastrointest Endosc 32:393–396, 1986.

67. Gevers AM, Macken E, Hiele M, Rutgeerts P: Endoscopic laser therapy for palliation of patients with distal colorectal carcinoma: Analysis of factors influencing long-term outcome. Gastrointest Endosc 51:580–585, 2000.

68. Radford CM, Ahlquist DA, Gostout CJ, et al: Prospective comparison of contact with noncontact Nd:Yag laser therapy for palliation of esophageal carcinoma. Gastrointest Endosc 35:394–397, 1989.

69. Suzuki S, Aoki J, Shiina Y, et al: New ceramic endoprobes for endoscopic contact irradiation with Nd:YAG laser: Experimental studies and clinical applications. Gastrointest Endosc 32:282–286, 1986.

70. Murray A, Mitchell DC, Wood RF: Lasers in surgery. Br J Surg 79:21–26, 1992.

71. Chia YW, Ngoi SS, Goh PM: Endoscopic Nd:YAG laser in the palliative treatment of advanced low rectal carcinoma in Singapore. Dis Colon Rectum 34:1093–1096, 1991.

72. Brunetaud JM, Maunoury V, Cochelard D: Lasers in rectosigmoid tumors. Semin Surg Oncol 11:319–327, 1995.

73. Brunetaud JM, Maunoury V, Cochelard D, et al: Lasers in rectosigmoid cancers: Factors affecting immediate and long-term results. Baillieres Clin Gastroenterol 3:615–626, 1989.

74. Escourrou J, Delvaux M, Buscail L, et al: Nd:YAG laser in treatment of rectal cancer. Are there features predicting a curative result? Dig Dis Sci 39:464–472, 1994.

75. Loizou LA, Grigg D, Boulos PB, Bown SG: Endoscopic Nd:YAG laser treatment of rectosigmoid cancer. Gut 31:812–816, 1990.

76. Van Cutsem E, Boonen A, Geboes K, et al: Risk factors which determine the long term outcome of Neodymium-YAG laser palliation of colorectal carcinoma. Int J Colorectal Dis 4:9–11, 1989.

77. Mischinger HJ, Hauser H, Cerwenka H, et al: Endocavitary Ir-192 radiation and laser treatment for palliation of obstructive rectal cancer. Eur J Surg Oncol 23:428–431, 1997.

78. Jakobs R, Miola J, Eickhoff A, et al: Endoscopic laser palliation for rectal cancer—therapeutic outcome and complications in eighty-three consecutive patients. Z Gastroenterol 40:551–556, 2002.

79. Tan CC, Iftikhar SY, Allan A, Freeman JG: Local effects of colorectal cancer are well palliated by endoscopic laser therapy. Eur J Surg Oncol 21:648–652, 1995.

80. Unger SW, Stern JD, Arroyo PJ, Russin DJ: Endoscopic Nd-YAG laser treatment of colorectal neoplasms. A four-year longitudinal study. Am Surg 56:153–157, 1990.

81. Farouk R, Ratnaval CD, Monson JR, Lee PW: Staged delivery of Nd:YAG laser therapy for palliation of advanced rectal carcinoma. Dis Colon Rectum 40:156–160, 1997.

82. Eckhauser ML, Imbembo AL, Mansour EG: The role of pre-resectional laser recanalization for obstructing carcinomas of the colon and rectum. Surgery 106:710–716; discussion 716–717, 1989.

83. Overholt BF, Panjehpour M: Photodynamic therapy for Barrett's esophagus. Gastrointest Endosc Clin N Am 7:207–220, 1997.

84. McCaughan JS Jr, Ellison EC, Guy JT, et al: Photodynamic therapy for esophageal malignancy: A prospective twelve-year study. Ann Thorac Surg 62:1005–1009; discussion 1009–1010, 1996.

85. Evrard S, Aprahamian M, Marescaux J: Intra-abdominal photodynamic therapy: From theory to feasibility. Br J Surg 80:298–303, 1993.

86. Fromm D, Kessel D, Webber J: Feasibility of photodynamic therapy using endogenous photosensitization for colon cancer. Arch Surg 131:667–669, 1996.

87. Regula J, MacRobert AJ, Gorchein A, et al: Photosensitisation and photodynamic therapy of oesophageal, duodenal, and colorectal tumours using 5 aminolaevulinic acid induced protoporphyrin IX—a pilot study. Gut 36:67–75, 1995.

88. Kashtan H, Haddad R, Yossiphov Y, et al: Photodynamic therapy of colorectal cancer using a new light source: From in vitro studies to a patient treatment. Dis Colon Rectum 39:379–383, 1996.

89. Barr H, Krasner N, Boulos PB, et al: Photodynamic therapy for colorectal cancer: A quantitative pilot study. Br J Surg 77:93–96, 1990.

90. Kashtan H, Papa MZ, Wilson BC, et al: Use of photodynamic therapy in the palliation of massive advanced rectal cancer. Phase I/II study. Dis Colon Rectum 34:600–604; discussion 604–605, 1991.

91. Patrice T, Foultier MT, Yactayo S, et al: Endoscopic photodynamic therapy with hematoporphyrin derivative for primary treatment of gastrointestinal neoplasms in inoperable patients. Dig Dis Sci 35:545–552, 1990.

92. Dohmoto M, Hunerbein M, Schlag PM: Palliative endoscopic therapy of rectal carcinoma. Eur J Cancer 32A:25–29, 1996.

93. Hoekstra HJ, Verschueren RC, Oldhoff J, van der Ploeg E: Palliative and curative electrocoagulation for rectal cancer. Experience and results. Cancer 55:210–213, 1985.
94. Hughes EP Jr, Veidenheimer MC, Corman ML, Coller JA: Electrocoagulation of rectal cancer. Dis Colon Rectum 25:215–218, 1982.
95. Madden JL, Kandalaft SI: Electrocoagulation as a primary curative method in the treatment of carcinoma of the rectum. Surg Gynecol Obstet 157:164–179, 1983.
96. Meijer S, de Rooij PD, Derksen EJ, et al: Cryosurgery for locally recurrent rectal cancer. Eur J Surg Oncol 18:255–257, 1992.
97. Meijer S, Rahusen FD, van der Plas LG: Palliative cryosurgery for rectal carcinoma. Int J Colorectal Dis 14:177–180, 1999.
98. Geissler N, Mlasowsky B, Jung D, Heymann H: [Results of cryosurgery in the treatment of inoperable tumor stenoses of the anus and rectum]. Zentralbl Chir 116:319–325, 1991.
99. Berry AR, Souter RG, Campbell WB, et al: Endoscopic transanal resection of rectal tumours—a preliminary report of its use. Br J Surg 77:134–137, 1990.
100. Dickinson AJ, Savage AP, Mortensen NJ, Kettlewell MG: Long-term survival after endoscopic transanal resection of rectal tumours. Br J Surg 80:1401–1404, 1993.
101. Sutton CD, Marshall LJ, White SA, et al: Ten-year experience of endoscopic transanal resection. Ann Surg 235:355–362, 2002.
102. Arrigoni A, Pennazio M, Spandre M, Rossini FP: Emergency endoscopy: Recanalization of intestinal obstruction caused by colorectal cancer. Gastrointest Endosc 40:576–580, 1994.
103. Marini E, Frigo F, Cavarzere L, et al: Palliative treatment of carcinoma of the rectum by endoscopic injection of polidocanol. Endoscopy 22:171–173, 1990.

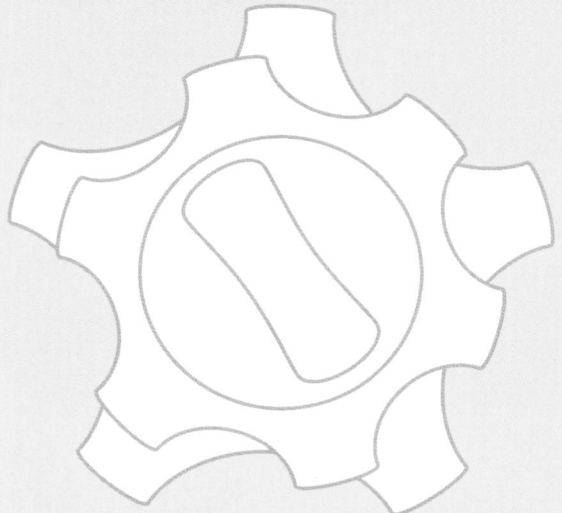

Pancreaticobiliary Disorders

Diagnostic Cholangiography

Evan L. Fogel, Lee McHenry Jr., James L. Watkins,
Stuart Sherman, and Glen A. Lehman

Introduction

Endoscopic cannulation of the major papilla with imaging of the biliary tree and the pancreatic ductal system (endoscopic retrograde cholangiopancreatography [ERCP]) was first successfully accomplished with an end-viewing duodenoscope and reported in 1968.[1] Subsequent development of side-viewing endoscopes with a catheter-deflecting elevator greatly facilitated the technique. Diagnostic studies were supplemented by the first endoscopic sphincterotomies in the early 1970s.[2,3] These developments permitted less invasive diagnostic and therapeutic maneuvers in the bile duct previously limited to open surgical and percutaneous techniques. Although these procedures are more technically demanding than most other gastrointestinal endoscopic techniques, they are now being widely used and are the method of choice for many clinical problems involving the pancreatic ductal and hepatobiliary systems. This chapter focuses on endoscopic retrograde diagnostic cholangiography. Radiographic visualization of the biliary tree is often key to establishing a clinical diagnosis and formulating a therapeutic plan.[4,5] With the aid of noninvasive imaging via transcutaneous ultrasound, computed tomography (CT), and/or magnetic resonance,[6–13] thorough ductal filling at endoscopic retrograde cholangiography (ERC) has become less needed and even contraindicated in select cases. Diagnostic ERC is just one portion of the commonly combined ERCP and associated therapeutic maneuvers.

Endoscopic Retrograde Cholangiopancreatography

INDICATIONS AND CONTRAINDICATIONS

The role for diagnostic ERC alone has nearly disappeared as other less invasive and noninvasive imaging techniques (e.g., CT scans, endoscopic ultrasound, magnetic resonance cholangiopancreatography [MRCP]) have become more widely used. Imaging of the biliary ductal system without anticipated therapy is clinically helpful in only a few clinical settings such as cholestasis without dilated ducts. In select settings, such as inflammatory bowel disease, patients with early sclerosing cholangitis may have ductal changes visible only via invasive cholangiography such as ERC (i.e., missed by noninvasive imaging). ERC is mainly indicated in those clinical settings in which there is significant suspicion of an obstructing, inflammatory, or neoplastic pancreatobiliary lesions that, if detected or ruled out, would alter clinical management. A general classification of indications is listed in Table 40–1.

Most contraindications are relative, and, in such settings, the degree of risk must be balanced against the potential benefit.[14–16] In select settings, even the very ill and unstable patient such as with acute cholangitis with shock or sepsis from bile duct stones or biliary strictures, diagnostic (followed by therapeutic) ERCP may be lifesaving. ERC in patients with necrotizing acute pancreatitis and low clinical suspicion for ductal stones is considered relatively

Table 40–1. Indications for Endoscopic Retrograde Cholangiography

Suspected Biliary Ductal Disorder
Jaundice or cholestasis of suspected obstructive origin
Acute cholangitis
Gallstone pancreatitis
Clarification of biliary lesion seen on other imaging test
Biliary fistula

To Direct Endoscopic Therapy
Sphincterotomy
Biliary drainage

To Direct Endoscopic Tissue and Fluid Sampling
Biopsy, brush, fine-needle aspiration
Bile collection

Preoperative Ductal Mapping
Malignant tumors
Benign strictures
Chronic pancreatitis

To Perform Manometry
Sphincter of Oddi
Ductal

contraindicated because pancreatography may result in bacterial contamination of the pancreatic bed. Other relative contraindications include an unstable cardiopulmonary disease or severe coagulopathy. Patients with comorbid, life-threatening conditions can often have their ERC performed in the intensive care unit (with or without fluoroscopy) if deemed medically necessary. ERC is generally not indicated in type III suspected sphincter of Oddi dysfunction (unless manometry is included).

PREPARATION FOR ENDOSCOPIC RETROGRADE CHOLANGIOGRAPHY

Preparation for ERC involves assembly of a skilled team that includes endoscopists, nursing personnel, and radiology technical and physician support. A quality fluoroscopic unit is needed. A variety of catheters, guidewires, and other therapeutic devices should be available.

Assembling the Team

We recommend that ERCP be done independently only by physicians with prior formal training in ERCP. An adequate number of exams during training will vary greatly with the trainee but should include at least 200 examinations.[17] The latter number includes at least 100 therapeutic examinations. Biliary successful cannulation rates should be at least 85% and preferably 90%. We recommend that nursing personnel have experience with at least 1000 upper gastrointestinal (UGI) and colonoscopy examinations before "graduating up" to the ERCP suite. Nurses should train alongside an experienced ERCP nurse for 100 to 200 examinations before independent guidewire/accessory management is undertaken. Two nursing personnel are needed per examination: one for sedation/analgesia administration and one for accessories management. Radiology technicians working in ERCP should maintain longevity and be team members rather than rotate frequently. Nearly all centers no longer rely on a radiologist to assist in fluoroscopy or image acquisition except in the most difficult cases. Collaborative reading of final images may aid in final interpretation accuracy. Final reading by general radiologists with little pancreatobiliary training, experience, or interest may well be counterproductive.

Patient Preparation

Patient preparation includes an updated medical history and physical examination and recent complete blood cell count, serum liver chemistries, serum amylase, and/or lipase and at least one noninvasive imaging of the upper abdomen, with abdominal ultrasound, CT scan, and/or magnetic resonance cholangiography. Platelet count, prothrombin time, and partial thromboplastin times are usually recommended if therapeutics are anticipated. However, a history of liver disease, renal disease, and bleeding are adequate to detect most patients with increased bleeding risk. Patients with a history of easy bruising, excessive bleeding after dental extraction, other postoperative bleeding, or family history of coagulopathy are best evaluated with the help of hematology consultation. Risk factors such as anticoagulant therapy, prosthetic heart valves, and allergies must be addressed. Iodine allergic patients are probably at very low risk of allergic reaction; nevertheless, they are preferably given prednisone 30 to 40 mg orally 15 and 3 hours before the

examination. Diphenhydramine (Benadryl) 25 mg intravenously may be added if serious past reactions have occurred. Iodine allergy appears to never be a reason to omit a needed examination but limiting volume of contrast media used is logical. Air[18] can be successfully used for cholangiography if needed. If possible, aspirin and nonsteroidal anti-inflammatory drugs should be avoided for 7 days before the procedure. Fasting for 8 hours is generally recommended except for taking oral medications such as for blood pressure medication the morning of the examination. Afternoon examination patients may have a clear liquid breakfast. Patients taking narcotics may need to fast for 12 to 16 hours and/or consume only clear liquids the evening before. Patients with constipation or those who have had recent oral contrast media may benefit from oral laxative purge to clear the transverse colon of material, which may otherwise overlay and obscure viewing of the gallbladder, terminal bile duct, and pancreas. Broad-spectrum antibiotics are recommended (e.g., ciprofloxacin) for patients with obstructive jaundice, cholangitis, pseudocysts, fistulas, or immunosuppressed state. Quinolones are an attractive choice because they can be given orally. Oral simethicone solution is recommended 30 to 60 minutes before examination start time to decrease intraluminal foam, which may obscure visualization.

Informed Consent

Informed consent for ERCP must be obtained. It is both legally and ethically necessary to apprise the patient (and family if applicable) of the risks, benefits, and alternatives of the anticipated procedure. Table 40–2 lists the potential complications of diagnostic and therapeutic ERCP and their relative frequency. While legal standards continue to evolve, we recommend that patients be informed of the potential complications and the relative frequencies of those complications. In addition, we recommend that they be told that a severe complication may possibly result in a prolonged hospital stay, intensive care unit monitoring, or open surgery and may very rarely result in permanent disability or death. Complication rates vary according to patient and procedure risk factors and the disease process being evaluated and treated. Patients with uncomplicated biliary stones, malignancy, or chronic pancreatitis have lower complication rates, whereas patients with acute recurrent pancreatitis and suspected sphincter of Oddi dysfunction have twofold to fourfold higher complication rates. Procedure techniques associated with higher complication rates include repeated cannulation attempts, repeated pancreatic duct injections, pancreatic parenchymal acinarization, and precut sphincterotomy (without associated protective pancreatic stent). Attention to details of the technique and patient selection can minimize but not eliminate complications. Early recognition and treatment of complications helps to limit morbidity.

Endoscopic Equipment

ERC can be performed with fiberoptic or video chip, side-viewing instruments. Endoscopes are 120-cm working length and generally categorized as diagnostic (approximately 10 mm diameter) or therapeutic (12 to 13 mm diameter). Video systems offer the advantage of television monitor viewing by all persons in the endoscopy suite. This offers better teaching capabilities and allows better coordination between the endoscopist and nursing assistants. Some

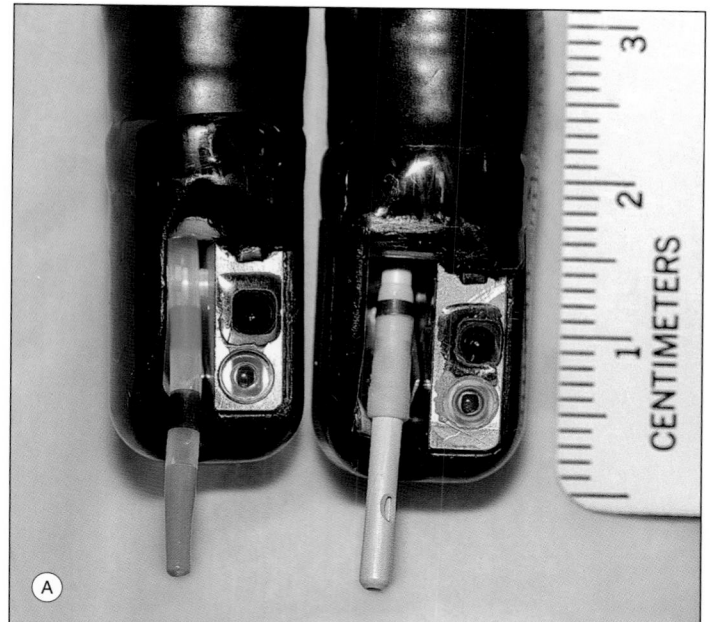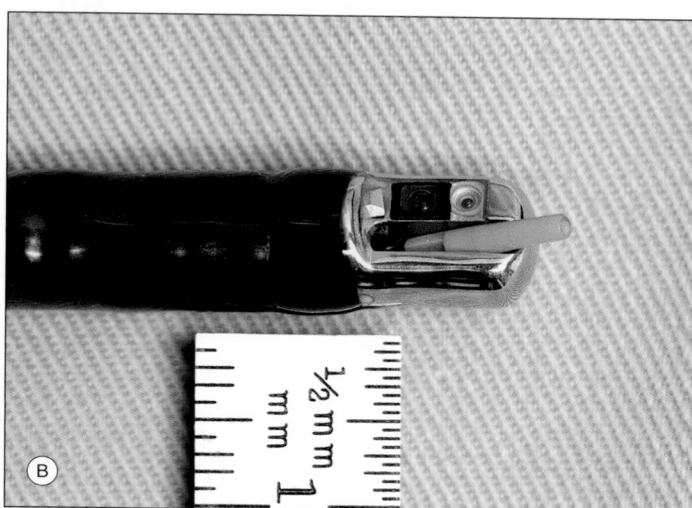

Figure 40–1. *A,* Photograph of two side-viewing endoscopes used for standard endoscopic retrograde cholangiography (ERC). Biopsy channels vary from 3.2 to 4.5 mm to accommodate a wide variety of accessories needed in diagnostic and therapeutic biliary studies. *B,* Newer generation Olympus pediatric video duodenoscope for use in children weighing less than 10 kg.

Table 40–2. Approximate Frequencies of Complications from Endoscopic Retrograde Cholangiography and Sphincterotomy (%)

Complication	Average-Risk Patient		High-Risk Patients*	
	ERCP	Sphincterotomy	ERCP	Sphincterotomy
Pancreatitis	3	5	8	20
Bleeding	0.2	1.5	0.4	3.5
Perforation	0.1	0.8	0.3	1.5
Infection	0.1	0.5	2	2
Sedation reaction or cardiopulmonary	0.5	0.5	2	2
Total %[†]	3.9[‡]	8.3[‡]	12.7[‡]	29[‡]

*Certain patient characteristics and technical aspects of the procedure increase the risk of complications, including suspected sphincter of Oddi dysfunction, recurrent pancreatitis, difficult cannulation, precut sphincterotomy, coagulopathy, renal dialysis, cirrhosis, or advanced cardiopulmonary disease.
[†]Some patients have more than one complication.
[‡]Approximate severity of complications: mild, 70%; moderate, 20%; and severe, 10%.
ERCP, endoscopic retrograde cholangiopancreatography.

newer generation endoscopes combine a large working channel diameter up to 4 mm with a standard 10 to 11 mm outer diameter (Fig. 40–1). A newer generation pediatric videoendoscope with outer diameter less than 7 mm is now available from Olympus America Inc. For Billroth II patients, we generally start with a standard side-viewing duodenoscope, but an end-viewing endoscope is occasionally needed. In patients with a long Roux-en-Y gastro-enterostomy, or choledochojejunostomy, a 160-cm pediatric colono-scope or a 220-cm enteroscope will reach the bile duct in greater than half of patients.[19] The lack of a catheter-deflecting elevator and limited compatibility accessories make end-viewing endoscopy diffi-cult in these settings. Rendezvous with transhepatic wire passage is occasionally helpful (Fig. 40–2).

Current generation endoscopes are capable of undergoing submersion disinfection. Endoscopes should be hung in vertical position to facilitate drying after cleaning. In the past, *Pseudomonas*

infections were directly linked to inadequate ERCP scope dis-infection. Ideally, endoscopes should be cultured periodically. Patients developing post-ERCP infections should be cultured for the presence of *Pseudomonas* species (see Chapter 4).

Radiology Suite

Few endoscopists have a dedicated suite for ERCP. We are aware of no manufacturer who markets a fluoroscopy unit specifically for ERCP. Most endoscopists schedule time in the radiology department and use general purpose or angiographic units. Film documentation will likely disappear in the next decade and digital formats will be viewed only on high-resolution monitors, which are becoming the new standard. Quality digital images now rival film quality. Flat tables with fixed overhead carriage have limited versatility. The preferred x-ray table includes capability to tilt the patient head up and down 30 degrees and has C-arm carriage, which allows axial,

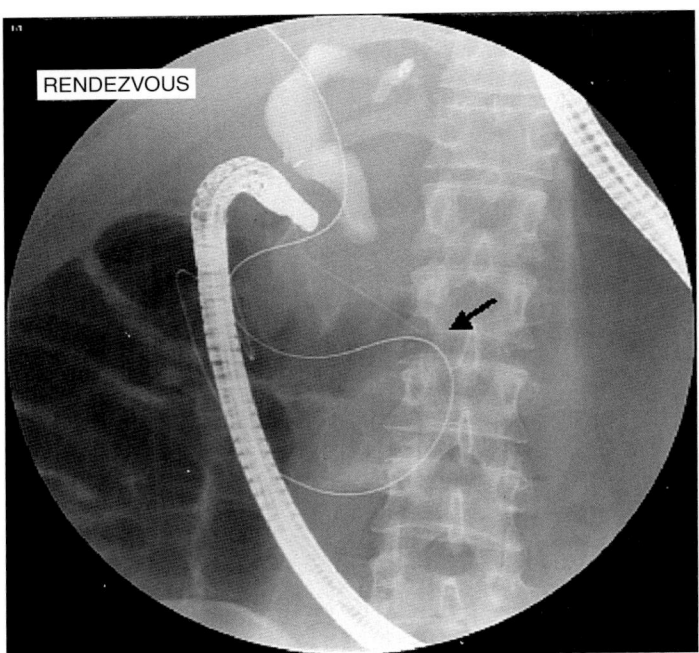

Figure 40-2. A patient underwent gastric bypass surgery for obesity and developed biliary colic and suspected common duct stones. A pediatric colonoscope was passed by mouth but failed to pass retrograde back to the descending duodenum. A guidewire was passed percutaneous transhepatically into the duodenum, beyond the ligament of Treitz *(arrow),* and on down into the jejunum. The wire was then grasped and the endoscope pulled back to the papilla for stone therapy.

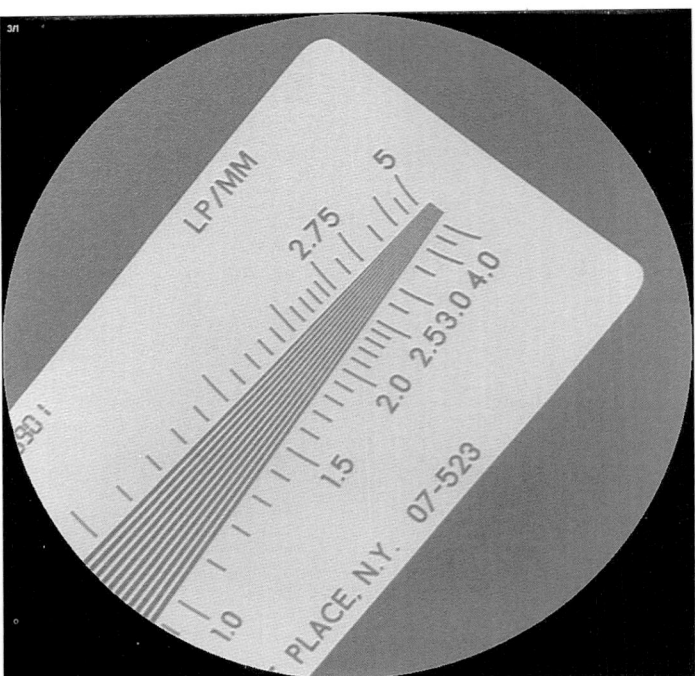

Figure 40-4. Phantom used in determining line pair resolution during fluoroscopy or image acquisition. Greater than 2.5 line pair resolution is recommended for optimal endoscopic retrograde cholangiopancreatography (ERCP) resolution. (Courtesy Joe Edmiston, Indiana University Medical Center.)

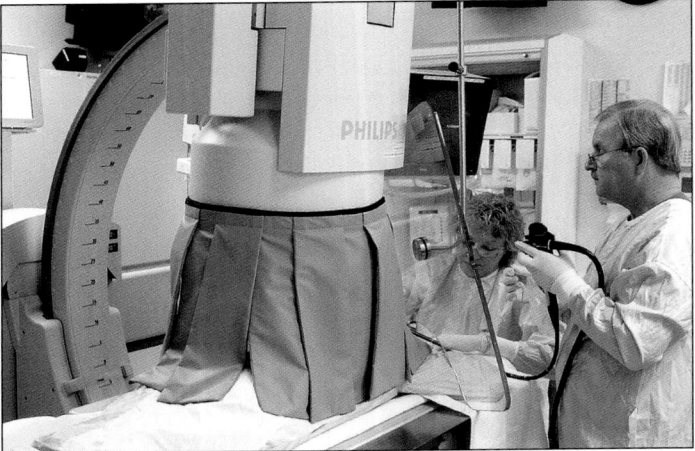

Figure 40-3. Room set-up with C-arm x-ray unit. Table tilt and cradle, C-arm tilt, and rotation offer viewing in multiple angles. Note lead apron drape from image intensifier. Note see-through lead shield near head of patient.

cranial and caudal, vertical and horizontal movements, thereby allowing viewing at multiple angles (Fig. 40–3). Because the patient is usually positioned prone with the head at the "foot" of the table, ability to reverse the viewing image in both the vertical and horizontal axes is helpful.

In the past, endoscopists have accepted use of older generation x-ray units including portable C-arm units with limited image resolution. This is no longer acceptable because fluoroscopy and saved image quality are key to accurate diagnosis and management. High-quality ERCP imaging requires resolution equivalent to that for neuroradiology (brain blood vessels). Resolution of greater than 2.5 line pair per millimeter is strongly recommended for both fluoroscopy and final images (Fig. 40–4). This is best accomplished with smaller diameter image intensifier of 6 to 9 inches. Radiation safety standards should be followed.[20] Monitoring of personal exposure and review of methods to limit exposure are needed. Attention to coning the field of view to the area of interest is good practice. Lead aprons or shields around the patient limit

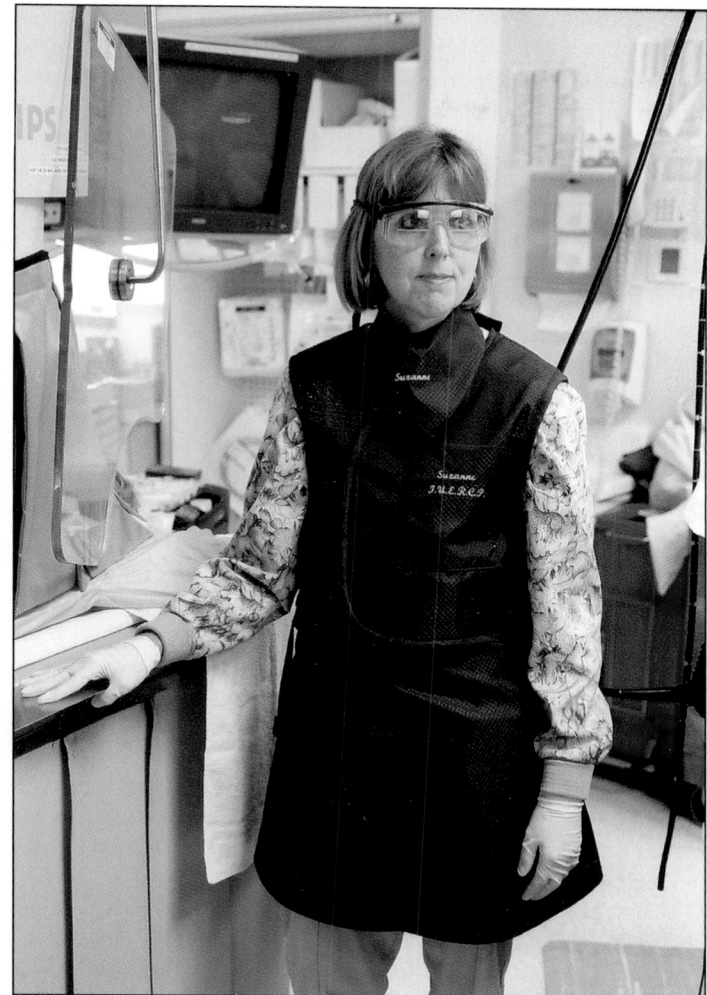

Figure 40–5. Endoscopy assistant with lead apron, thyroid shield, and lead glasses for optimal radiation safety.

x-ray beam scatter. Use of newer generation pulse fluoroscopy gives intermittent viewing, which is slightly jerky, but often adequate with as low as ¹/₁₀ the radiation exposure. Appropriate lead aprons, lead glasses, and thyroid shields are recommended (Fig. 40–5).

TECHNIQUE

Patient Positioning, Preparation, and Sedation

Most centers prefer to have the patient positioned in a prone or slightly left lateral decubitus position on a fluoroscopic table. Less often, the supine position is preferred as in difficult Billroth II patients. Intravenous access and monitoring equipment for blood pressure, pulse, and pulse oximetry are needed. Electrocardiogram (ECG) monitoring is desirable for patients with angina or a history of a cardiac arrhythmia or in other less stable patients. Sedation and analgesia are achieved by *slow* intravenous administration of common agents such as diazepam (10 to 40 mg), midazolam (2 to 10 mg), and meperidine (25 to 150 mg) or fentanyl (50 to 150 mg). The general ranges given here are those given over a 30- to 60-minute

examination. Droperidol (2.5 to 10 mg) is a common supplement or alternative, particularly for alcoholics or persons regularly taking narcotics or benzodiazepines.[21] However, recent concerns about arrhythmias and QT-interval prolongation have limited the use of droperidol for endoscopy. Our policy is to still use droperidol routinely for patients whose baseline ECG has a normal corrected QT interval. More recently propofol has been used for deep sedation and may offer better procedure tolerance and a much shorter recovery time than standard sedation. The complication rate for propofol use, when administered by endoscopists and endoscopy nurses, appears safe for standard UGI endoscopy and colonoscopy but has not been well studied for ERC.[22–24] Visual monitoring in a darkened ERCP room with fluoroscopy equipment draped over the patient gives some safety concerns for ERC use. Topical pharyngeal anesthetic spray probably decreases gagging in suspect patients. An antiperistaltic drug (e.g., glucagon or atropine) to inhibit duodenal motility is commonly needed. Drugs to treat bradycardia (e.g., atropine) and high blood pressure (e.g., labetalol) should be immediately available. Benzodiazepine and narcotic reversal agents should be immediately available in an "easy to administer" format. A fully equipped resuscitation cart must be close by. Pediatric cases can be done with success similar to adults. We prefer to use the pediatric less than 8-mm diameter endoscope for children less than 12 kg, but we use the standard 10-mm diameter endoscope for all larger children.

Upper Gastrointestinal Endoscopy

Initially, a brief endoscopic examination of the esophagus, stomach, duodenum, and major duodenal papilla is done. The finding of a large ulcer or neoplasm may cancel the need for ERCP. One should attempt to exit the stomach with as little residual intragastric air as possible because a deflated stomach permits better en face papilla views. Other findings, such as tumor infiltrating the proximal descending duodenum, varices, a pseudocyst pressing on the gut wall, or edema of the medial wall of the duodenum, help to quantitate or localize disease processes. The major papilla is usually located on the medial aspect of the mid-descending duodenum but may reside anywhere from the duodenal bulb to the transverse duodenum. Care should be taken to observe for major papilla abnormalities (e.g., tumor, edema, enlarged orifice from stone or mucus passage). The location of orifice(s) should be noted. A brief examination of the minor papilla may become helpful later in the examination if initial ERP via the major papilla fails. Before attempts at cannulation, fluoroscopic visualization (or filming) of the field of interest should be performed to look for stents, calcifications, masses, and residual contrast material (Fig. 40–6). Choice of initial cannulation tool is a personal preference (similar to choosing a tennis racket or golf club). One may begin with a simple single-lumen 5-Fr polyethylene catheter, without a guidewire, in many cases. The relative flexibility (not rigid), maneuverability, low cost, and simplicity are attractive features. A manometry catheter is initially used if ERCP findings are likely to be nonspecific or normal and if manometry is likely to be of potential help. If a sphincterotomy is almost certainly needed, a sphincterotome is a good starting tool. If the orifice appears small, a more tapered tip catheter or sphincterotome may be chosen. A few centers prefer various shaped metal tip catheters. Two- or three-lumen catheters or sphincterotomies may be preferred because they have a separate lumen for a guidewire and contrast media. A guidewire may be used at any point to aid cannulation or maintain intraductal stability. For biliary cannulation, .025- or .035-inch diameter wires are preferred. Soft-tipped wires have the advantage of less tissue trauma (e.g., fewer submucosal or other extraductal dissections). The specific device(s) used are much less important than the skill of the endoscopist (Fig. 40–7).

If the major papilla is not initially evident, gentle lifting of folds, greater air distention, and use of glucagon to inhibit peristalsis will likely expose the structure. If duodenal diverticular are present, the major papilla is most commonly on the diverticular rim, but in approximately 5% to 10% of cases the papilla is within the diverticulum per se (Fig. 40–8).

The major papilla is then cannulated. Orientation of the catheter tip toward the 11 to 12 o'clock position (Fig. 40–9) will more likely enter the bile duct; orientation of the catheter toward the 3 to 5 o'clock position will more likely enter the pancreatic duct. Biliary orifice location may vary from 10 o'clock to 2 o'clock. Cannulation may be initially done by gentle impaction of the catheter tip in the papillary orifice. Deep cannulation (greater than 1 cm penetration of the catheter into the duct) more securely establishes an intraductal position, which allows contrast injection, fluid aspiration, patient position changes, and endoscope position changes without loss of access to the duct.

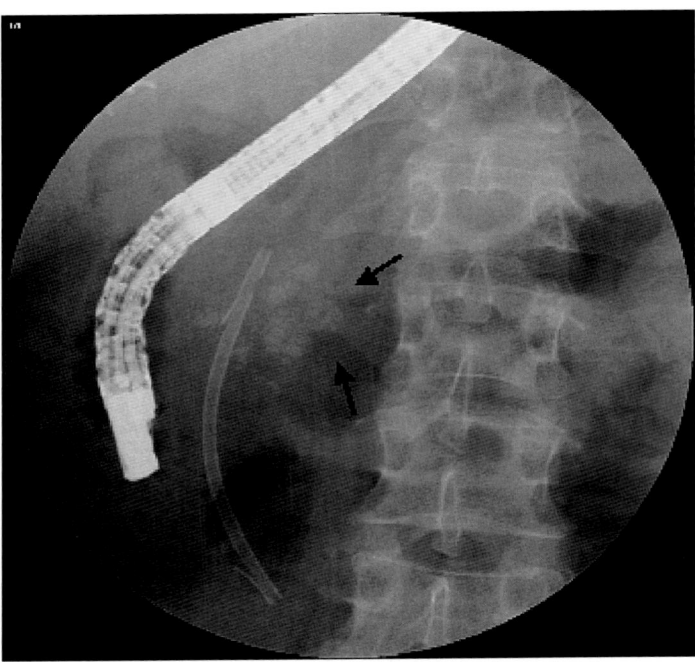

Figure 40–6. Plain x-ray film of right upper quadrant showing post shockwave lithotripsy pancreatic calcifications *(arrows)* and residual biliary stent. This film serves as a background view for all subsequent contrast injections.

Selective Deep Biliary Cannulation

Pancreatic cannulation is easier than biliary. Selective biliary entry is mandatory in most biliary pathology cases. We often start with a standard 5-Fr catheter and next add a guidewire or a sphincterotome for assistance. If the cannulation angle fails to achieve adequate cephalad orientation, a sphincterotome or curved top guidewire will generally help to achieve that angle. In patients with a prominent major papilla (protruding well into the duodenal lumen), the path of the biliary lumen is nearly always somewhat stair stepped. Cannulation is initially cephalad then more perpendicular into the wall and then more cephalad again. This is partially accomplished by pulling the endoscope more cephalad, lowering the elevator, and moving the viewing lens very close to the papilla. Sharp guidewire may puncture the ampullary segment roof at the first cephalad-perpendicular junction. Gentle guidewire manipulations and more perpendicular catheter orientation are required. There are limited data that indicate that cannulation may be facilitated in difficult cases with use of drugs (e.g., nitroglycerin) to relax the sphincter. If biliary entry is mandatory (obstructive jaundice) and initial attempts fail, precut entry is generally required (Chapter 42). In this setting, the endoscopist must balance decisions as to transfer to a more experienced facility,[25,26] consider percutaneous or surgical opinions, or proceed with more aggressive endoscopic techniques.

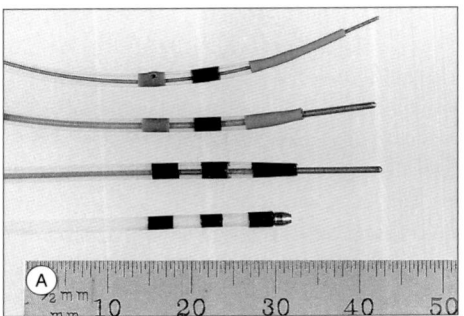
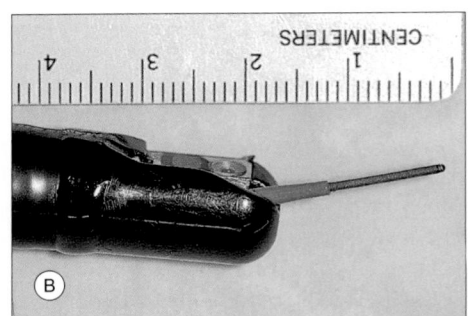
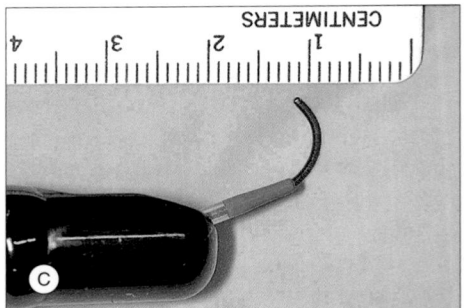

Figure 40–7. *A,* A wide variety of guidewires with varying characteristics, size .018-, .025-, and .035-inch diameter, variable hydrophilic tips and some groomable wires, whose tip shape can be changed are all a part of a well-equipped biliary diagnostic unit. Also shown are 5-Fr catheters with variable tip taper or metal tip (bottom). *B,* Stainless steel wire of .035-inch diameter (with Teflon coating) ungroomed (straight). *C,* Same as *(B)* except tip has been manually groomed to curl cephalad for biliary cannulation assistance.

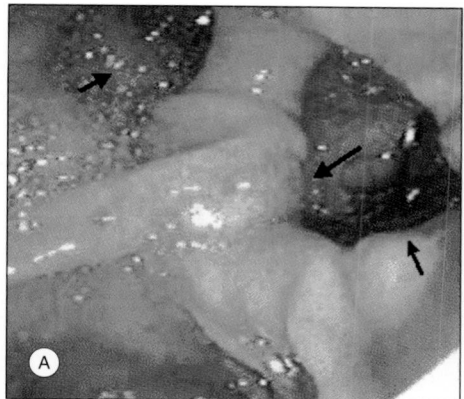 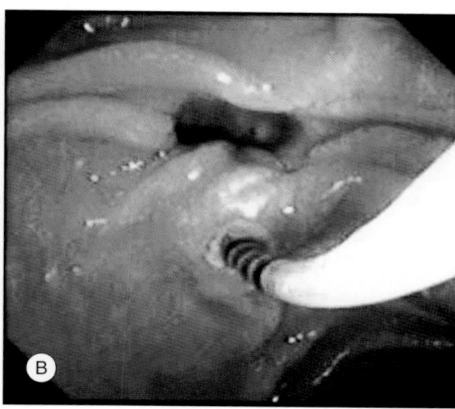

Figure 40–8. *A* and *B,* Difficult biliary cannulation cases. Major papilla associated with duodenal diverticula. The papilla is most commonly on the rim of the diverticulum but may be located fully within the diverticulum and be much more problematic to cannulated. *A,* Bilobed diverticulum *(short arrows).* Major papilla orifice *(long arrow).* *B,* Papilla on 6 o'clock rim of diverticulum.

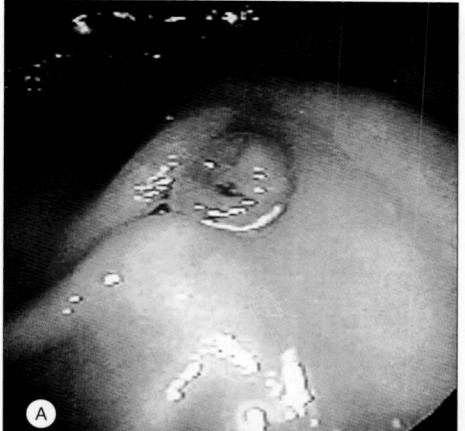 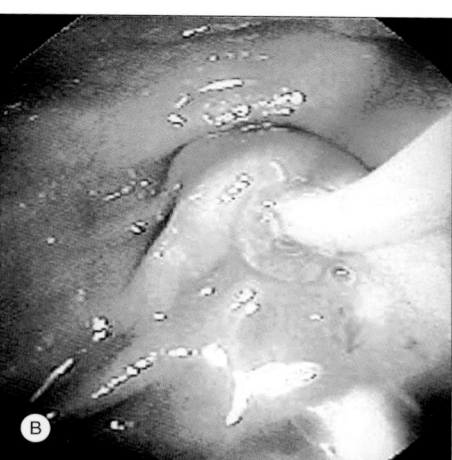 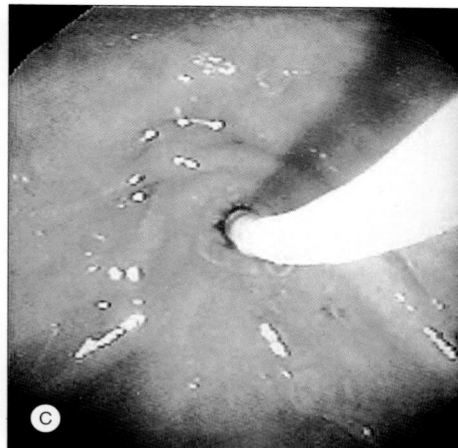

Figure 40–9. *A,* Endoscopic view of 5-Fr catheter oriented toward the 11 o'clock position of the major papilla. *B,* The bile duct has been entered and bile aspiration confirmed by yellow color in catheter lumen. The catheter was oriented more toward the 3 o'clock position to enter the pancreas *(C).*

Precut sphincterotomy[27–31] involves cutting the papilla to gain deep intraductal access to the biliary tree. This technique should be limited to experienced endoscopists and mostly applied in patients when there is a high clinical suspicion of obstructive pathology (e.g., impacted stone (Fig. 40–10*A*) or jaundiced patient with dilated bile duct on noninvasive imaging after standard techniques fail. Precutting can be achieved by impaction of a short-nosed pull-type sphincterotome into the papillary orifice with sequential shallow cephalad cuts until the biliary orifice is identified. Similar sequential shallow cuts can be made with a needle knife. We prefer to place a 3- to 4-Fr, 6-cm long, no intraductal flange polyethylene stent into the pancreatic duct first, if possible, and use the stent to guide needle-knife cutting (see Fig. 40–10*B*).

CONTRAST MEDIA AND IMAGE ACQUISITION

Standard contrast media (e.g., meglumine diatrizoate) at a 25% to 30% concentration is often called half strength and is most commonly used for cholangiography. This permits adequate visualization of small ducts of 2 to 6 mm diameter yet allows filling defects (stones) to be seen in more dilated ducts. However, biliary stricture detail and peripheral intrahepatic ducts are better defined with full-strength contrast (50% to 60% concentration). Nonionic and lower osmolality contrast media, which are more expensive, offer no safety advantage and are not recommended.[32,33] We prefer 20-mL syringes because this avoids need to exchange syringes as often (and potentially introduce air bubbles). With each syringe exchange, one should aspirate back to remove any air bubbles from the Luer connector and flush to be sure that the contrast media extends to the catheter tip. Contrast media injection is done with continuous fluoroscopic monitoring. Contrast media is more dense than bile and will flow along the most dependent route. The left lobe fills more quickly (lowest) with the patient prone (Fig. 40–11*A*), whereas the right anterior segments fill next and right lobe posterior segments fill last (and may remain unfilled unless adequate volume and injection force is applied) (see Fig. 40–11*B*). The extent of ductal filling should be correlated with the clinical history and the need to know the ductal anatomy. High-resolution fluoroscopy is required to see fine detail of small ducts.

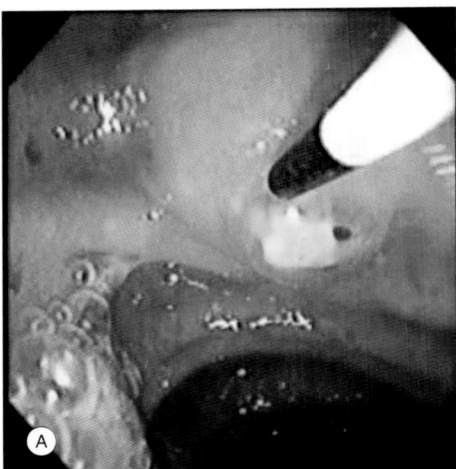

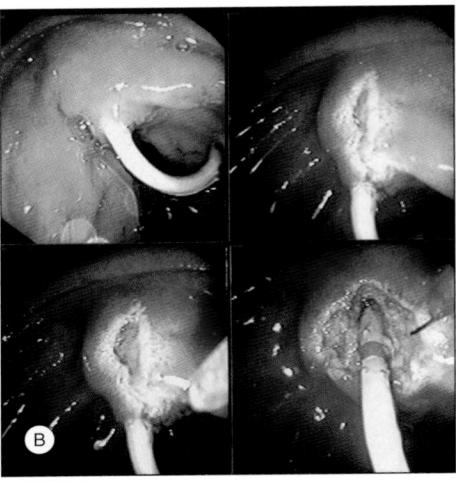

Figure 40–10. *A,* Stone impacted in orifice. Needle-knife cut over stone being initiated. *B,* Endoscopic photos of technique of precut major papilla needle-knife sphincterotomy over indwelling pancreatic stent.

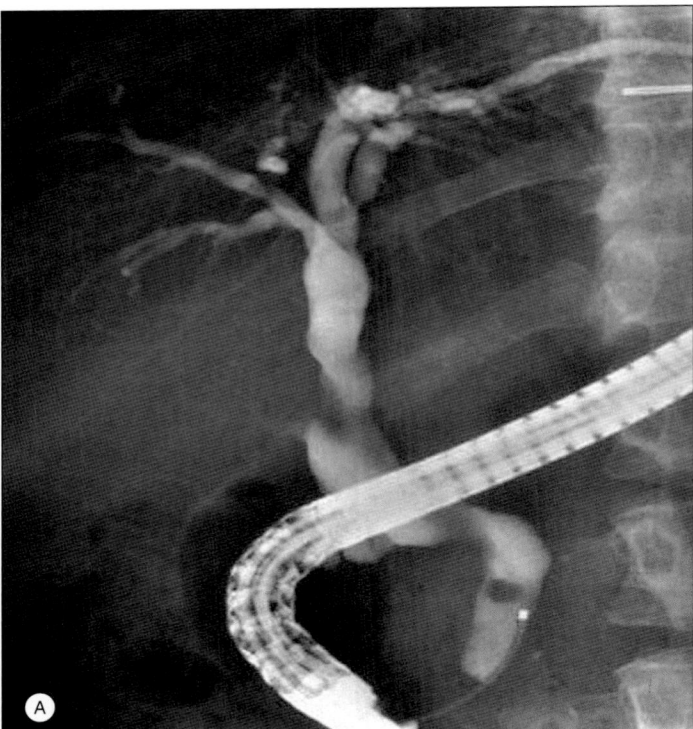

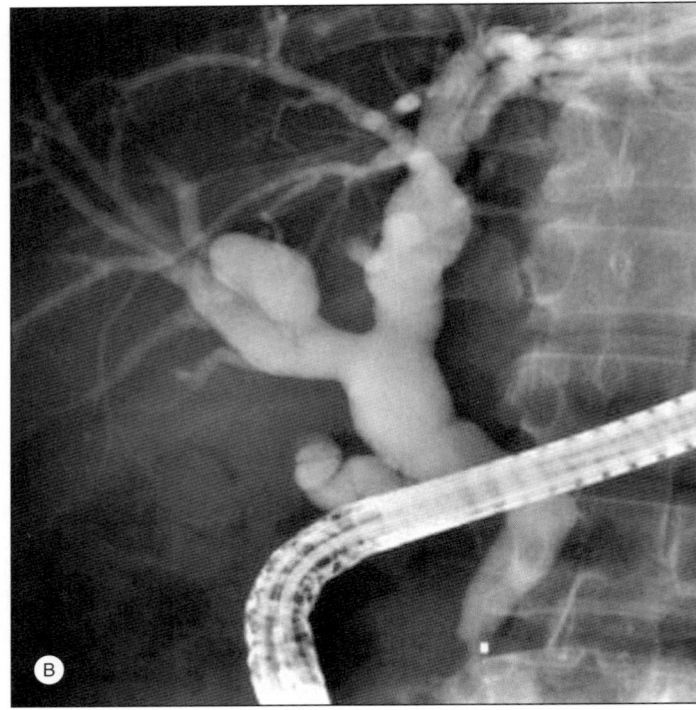

Figure 40–11. *A,* Initial left lobe filling. This fills preferentially as contrast media is heavier than bile and flows down into the dependent left lobe with the patient prone. This could be mistaken for complete biliary filling. *B,* With aid of tilting patient head down 20 degrees and more volume, the right lobe is viewed.

Multiple views of initial distal bile duct filling are recommended to see potential small filling defects (stones) that may be washed upstream (and no longer visible) or masked by more dense contrast concentration in a dilated duct (Fig. 40–12*A* and *B*, Fig. 40–13). Complete cholangiography requires filling of the peripheral intrahepatic radicles. The left lobe is more dependent in the prone position and fills preferentially. Right lobe filling may require tilting the patient's head down 15 to 20 degrees on the fluoroscopy table, more forceful injection (a balloon occlusion catheter is helpful),

selective right lobe cannulation, or turning the patient to the supine position. Contrast media mixes slowly with gallbladder bile. Multiple films during early filling are recommended. Final films may be best taken in the supine position after endoscope withdrawal. Occasionally, delayed gallbladder films taken 4 to 24 hours after completion of the procedure allows for passage of intraluminal gas, giving better diagnostic film quality. In settings of tight biliary strictures, limited contrast filling upstream should be done until catheter access above the stricture is achieved (Fig. 40–14).[34–36]

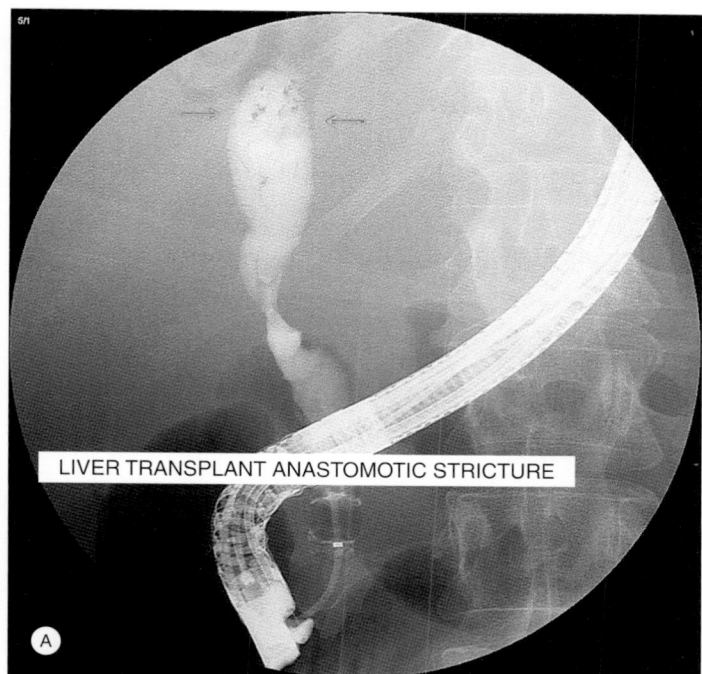

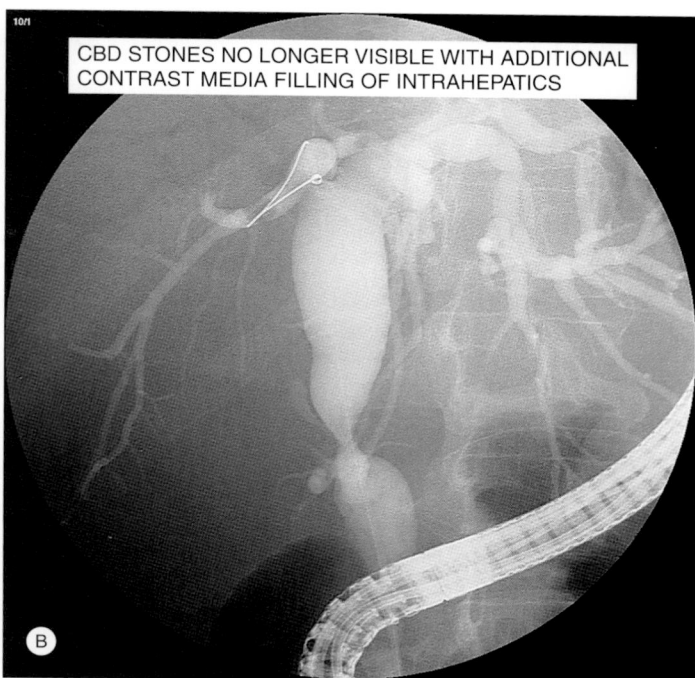

Figure 40–12. Patient with suspected common duct stones (especially those with dilated ducts) should have multiple early filling biliary films taken to observe stones *(A)* before the stones potentially being washed upstream or being masked by dense contrast *(B)*. The patient has had a liver transplant with duct-to-duct anastomosis. There is stricture at the anastomosis.

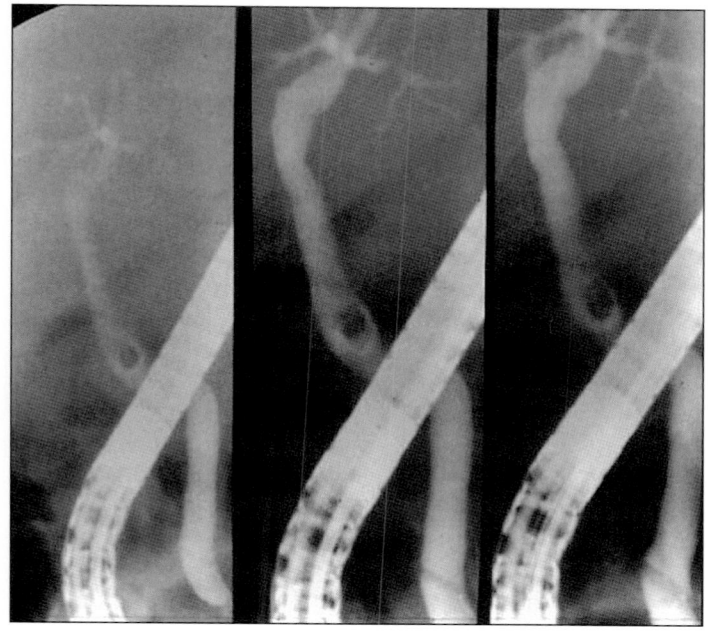

Figure 40–13. Multiple early films with limited contrast injection give best opportunity to see small stones. Filling defect in this patient is "pseudostone" representing the orifice of the cystic duct.

PROBLEM SOLVING

Table 40–3 reviews multiple general problems encountered with ERC and how to potentially solve them.[37–39]

Biliary manometry usually is performed at the time of ERCP. All drugs that relax (e.g., anticholinergics, nitrates, calcium channel blockers, glucagon) or stimulate (e.g., certain narcotics, cholinergic agents) should be avoided for at least 8 to 12 hours before the study and during the manometric session. Manometry is performed using a low-compliance infusion pump system and a 5-Fr catheter (see Chapter 49).

Table 40–3. Common General Problems and Challenges Encountered at Endoscopic Retrograde Cholangiography

Cholangiographic Challenge or Clinical Suspicion	Potential Steps to Solve Problem
Obese patient	Increase kilovoltage (KV). Take extra exposures (a few will probably be adequate). Develop and review still images before deciding on therapy (i.e., do not rely only on fluoroscopy view).
Patient moves frequently	Take multiple exposures (one will likely be clear). Increase KV to shorten exposure time.
Terminal (preampullary) CBD not well seen	If patient has cholangitis with risk of sepsis if greater filling done, pass stone retrieval balloon to mid common bile duct, inflate balloon, and inject contrast downstream to balloon (need appropriate "below the balloon" injection port). Tilt head up 5–20 degrees (Fig. 40–15). If moderate amount of contrast already upstream in intrahepatic ducts, place catheter tip 1 cm above sphincter. Aspirate nonopacified bile until upstream contrast flows back into terminal CBD (Fig. 40–16).
Patient has fairly typical postcholecystectomy pain but ERCP (or MRCP) is normal	Perform manometry.[37–39] Do not initiate ERCP in such patients if ducts are not dilated by noninvasive imaging and liver serum chemistries are normal, unless manometry immediately available.
Cannot find the papilla	Check fluoroscopy to be sure endoscope tip is in descending duodenum. Be sure of surgical anatomy—Roux Y gastrojejunostomy? Bile present—follow trail. Gently lift folds in candidate area. Find minor papilla and search left and inferior. Give cholecystokinin or secretin to stimulate fluid flow.
Left and right hepatic ductal systems overlap at hilum, not well-defined	Fixed fluoroscopy table, roll patient to slight left posterior oblique position. Use C-arm rotation to separate systems.
Bile leak expected	Obtain multiple early images to precisely locate leak site, before leak site contrast obscures view. Limit injection to small amount of spilled contrast (Fig. 40–17A).
Air bubbles introduced	Observe where bubble went and where collected. If distal CBD, tilt head down and aspirate bubbles, bile, and contrast from terminal duct. Consider tilt head up and observe bubble passage into intrahepatic ducts.
Contrast or air in duodenum or stomach detracts from image quality	Aspirate all contrast and air from duodenum before imaging. Do this routinely when injecting contrast (Fig. 40–17B).
Endoscope repeatedly covers area of interest	Use C-arm (or patient positioning to change angles). Move endoscope from short (lesser curve) to long (greater curve) position. Place catheter upstream to hilum, slowly back endoscope into stomach aspirating air and spilled contrast as if nasobiliary tube placement were being done.
Pyloric or duodenal narrowing precludes endoscope passage	Pass a guidewire and 5–7 Fr catheter through the narrowing and ahead into transverse duodenum. An extra-stiff guidewire (Amplatz super stiff guidewire, Boston Scientific, Billerica, MA) is especially helpful. Pass endoscope over wire, paying attention to fluoroscopic alignment more than the endoscopic view.

CBD, common bile duct; ERCP, endoscopic retrograde cholangiopancreatography; MRCP, magnetic resonance cholangiopancreatography.

NORMAL FINDINGS

A normal cholangiogram is shown in Figure 40–18. Although there is controversy, the weight of evidence indicates that the biliary tree does not dilate after cholecystectomy in the absence of obstructing pathology. The common hepatic and common bile duct diameter at ERCP is commonly 2 to 3 mm greater than that seen at CT or ultrasound. This is accounted for by filling (or overfilling) the ductal system with extra fluid (contrast media) under greater pressure than physiologic secretory pressure.[40] Many centers accept the upper limits of normal diameter for the common bile duct as 10 mm in adults. The cystic duct commonly joins the common duct approximately half way from the hilum to the papilla, but this junction may be quite variable. The intrahepatic radicles have a leafless treelike branch pattern with marked variation in distribution. An aberrant, low insertion right hepatic duct, which connects to right posterior hepatic segments, is seen in 5% of patients (Fig. 40–19). These may be transected during laparoscopic cholecystectomy and give rise to problematic bile leaks from the disconnected segmental branch (Fig. 40–20). Because the transected duct does not fill at ERCP, MRCP may be more diagnostic.[41,42] Numerous other anatomic normal variants have been reported[42–44] (Fig. 40–21) and are beyond the realm of this chapter.

BILIARY STONES

In Caucasians and African Americans, most stones are cholesterol or mixed type and occur in the gallbladder. Such patients do not require ERC unless stones also occur or migrate into the bile ducts.[45–50] Figure 40–22A shows a 35-year-old female patient with multiple small stones in the gallbladder (transcutaneous ultrasound). Figure 40–22B shows a single small ductal stone per ERC. Gallstone pancreatitis is one common outcome of small stone (<5 mm diameter) passage. In this latter setting, more than 80% of patients will spontaneously pass their stone(s) from the bile duct and on into the duodenum. Selective use of ERC is recommended for patients who have persistent (≥12 hours) upper abdominal pain, persistent or worsening cholestasis, cholangitis, or dilated extrahepatic bile ducts.[51–59] Meta-analysis of prospective randomized trials shows benefit of therapeutic ERCP in the setting of acute pancreatitis of suspected gallstone origin.[60] Additional noninvasive imaging is

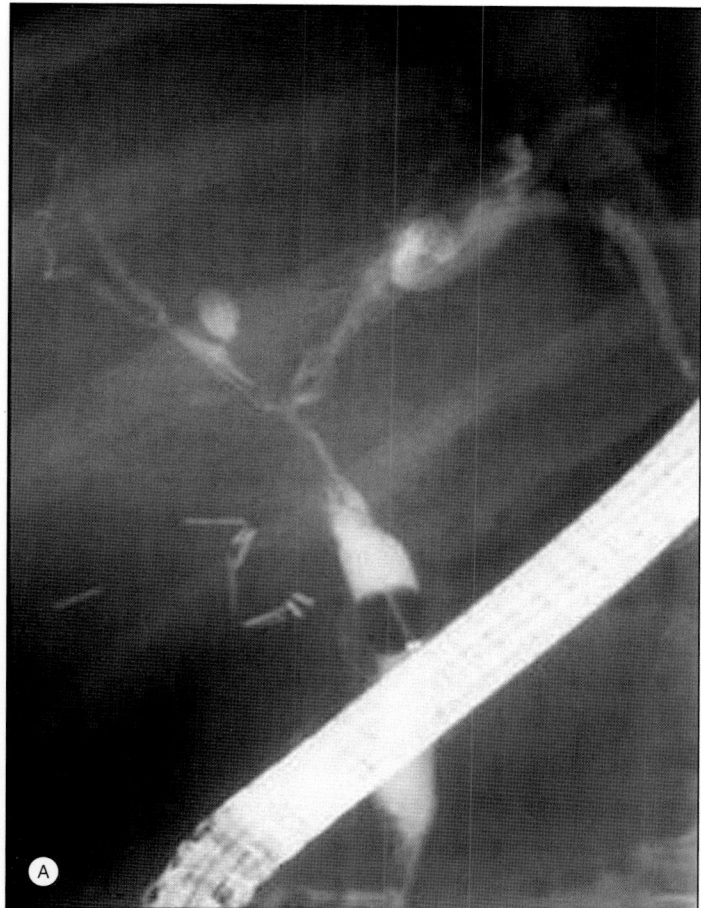

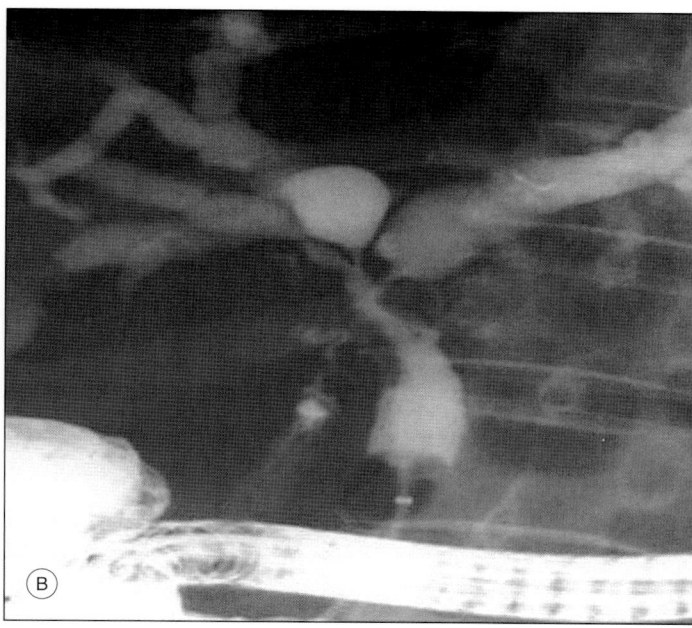

Figure 40–14. *A,* Cholangiocarcinoma involving the hepatic hilum. Only a limited amount of contrast media is injected above the strictures to avoid contamination. Only after the guidewire is advanced above the stricture should more contrast media be injected. If additional upstream information is needed, a magnetic resonance cholangiopancreatography (MRCP) or computed tomography (CT) scan is recommended. *B,* Excessive intrahepatic filling above hilar stricture. Unless bilateral subsequent drainage achieved, the patient is at higher risk of postprocedure cholangitis.

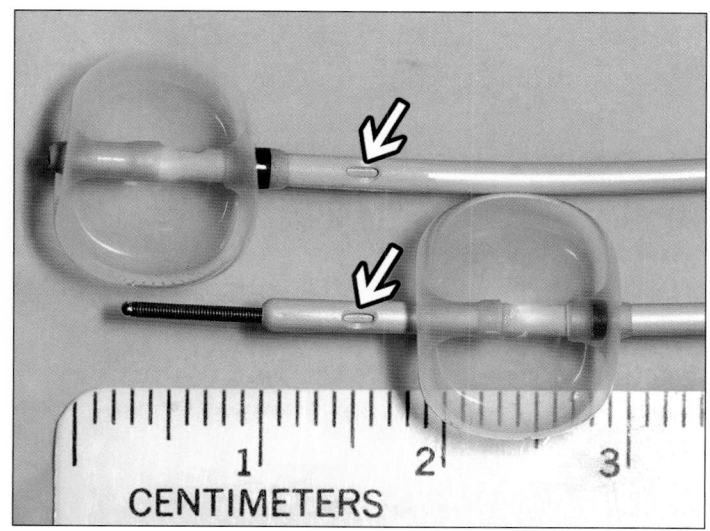

Figure 40–15. Stone retrieval type balloon catheters with injection port *(arrows)* above balloon and below balloon for selective filling of areas of interest above and below balloon.

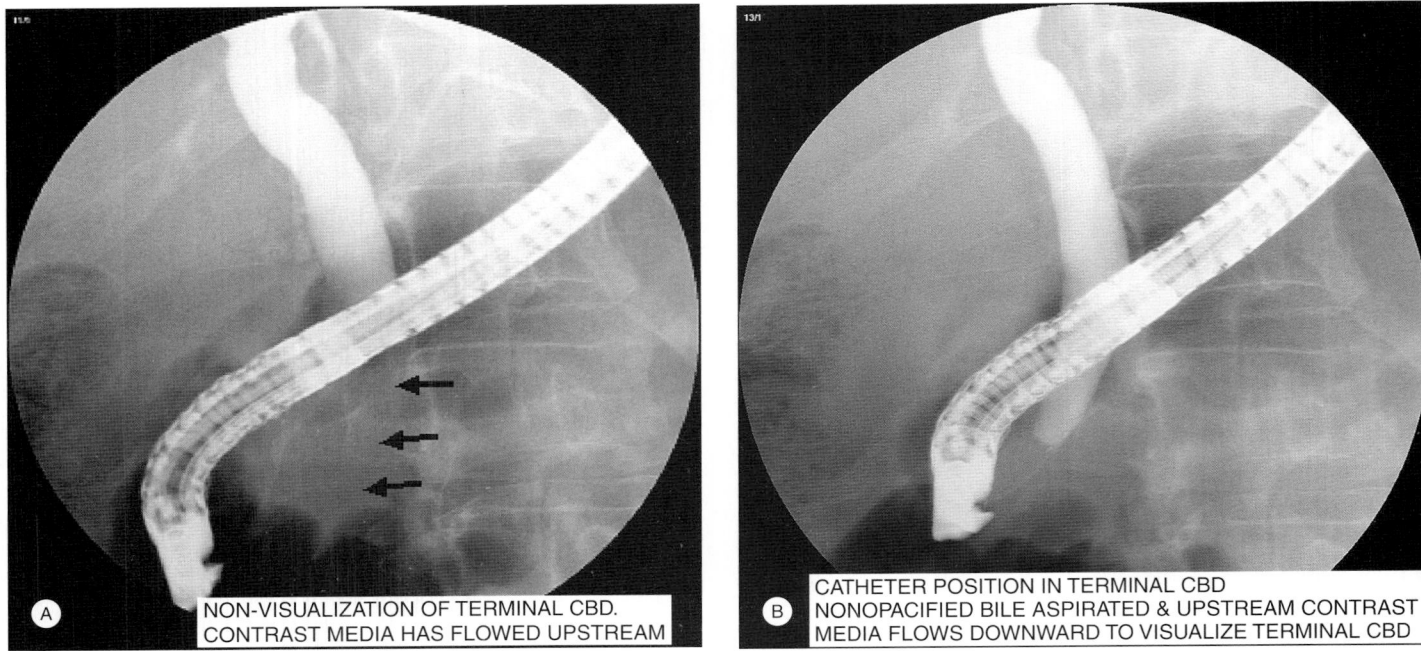

Figure 40-16. *A* and *B,* Terminal bile duct filling using aspiration technique to withdraw nonopacified bile from terminal duct.

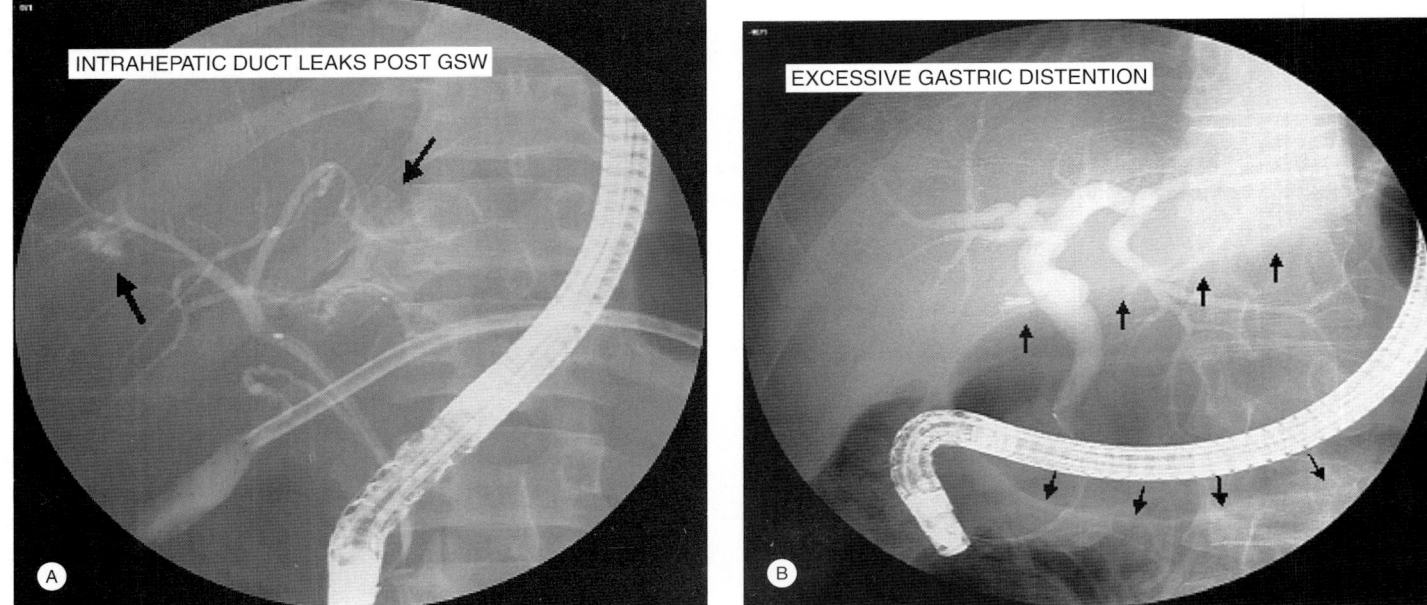

Figure 40-17. *A,* Bile leaks. Patient had gunshot injury to the liver with small leak from right lobe and larger leak from left lobe. *B,* Aspirate duodenal and gastric air to give better ductal imaging. Excessive intragastric air partially obscures the terminal common duct.

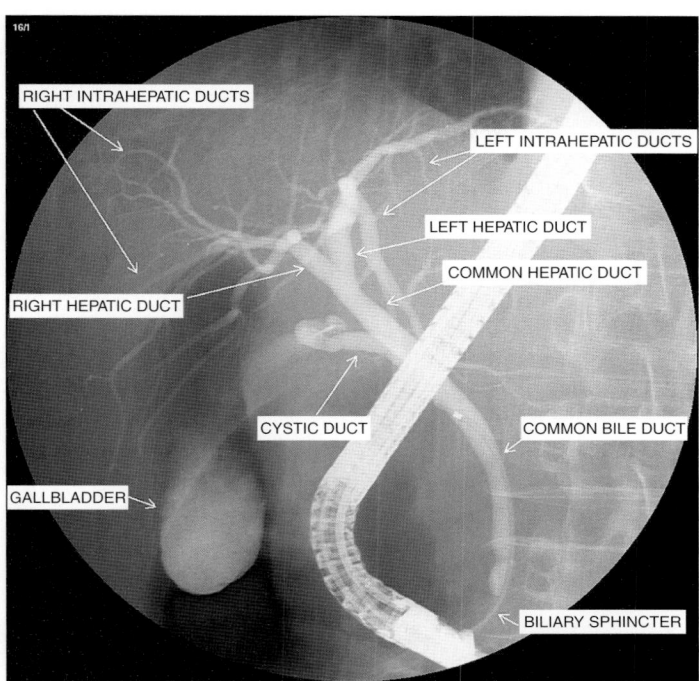

Figure 40-18. Normal cholangiogram with ductal segments labeled. Colon gas overlaps gallbladder making viewing suboptimal.

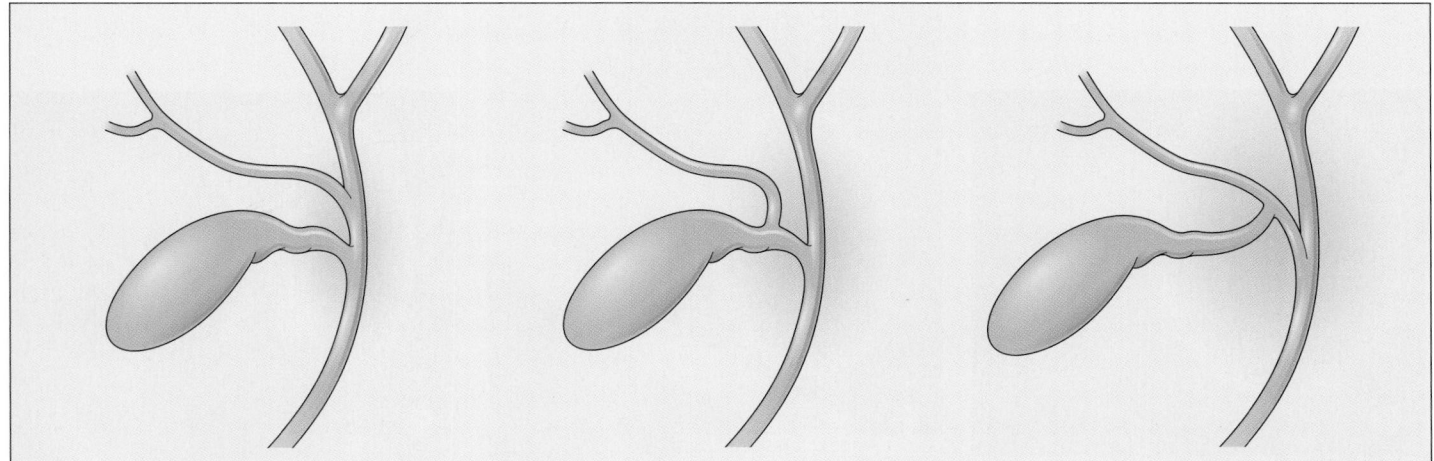

Figure 40-19. Variations of right posterior hepatic segment branch. *Left,* Cystic duct and aberrant right hepatic duct adjacent to each other but both attached to main extrahepatic duct. *Center,* Aberrant right branch arises from cystic duct. *Right,* Cystic duct arises from aberrant right branch.

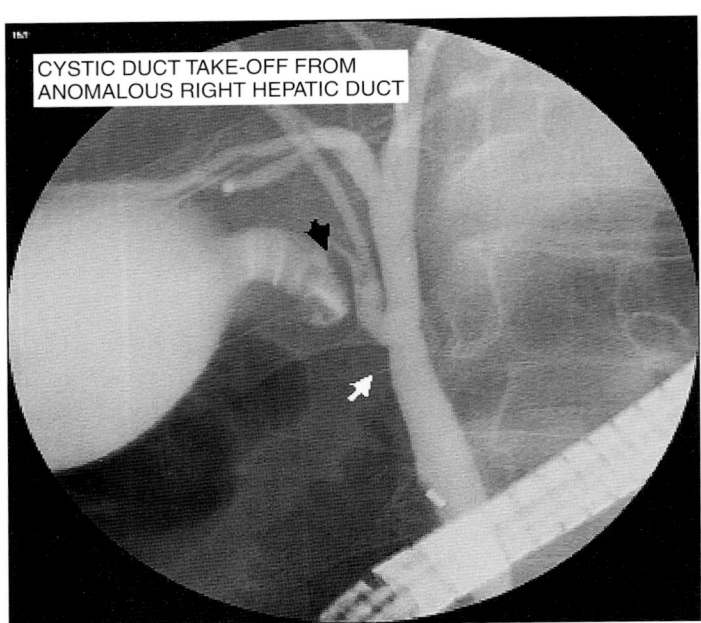

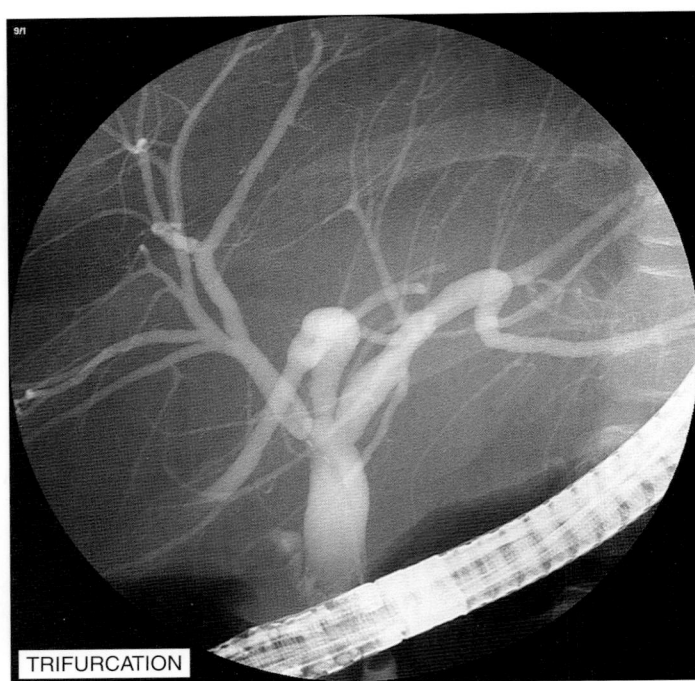

Figure 40–20. Aberrant posterior segmental hepatic branch arising from mid-extrahepatic duct *(white arrow)*. The cystic duct take-off *(black arrow)* is from the aberrant right hepatic duct.

Figure 40–21. Bifurcation of intrahepatic ducts at hilum.

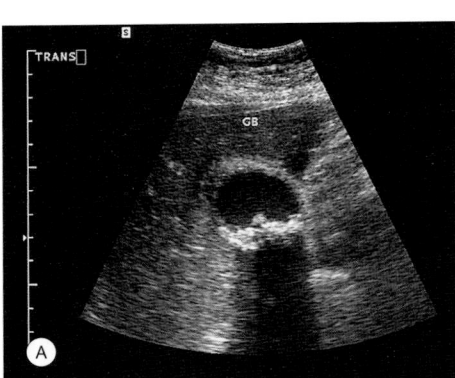

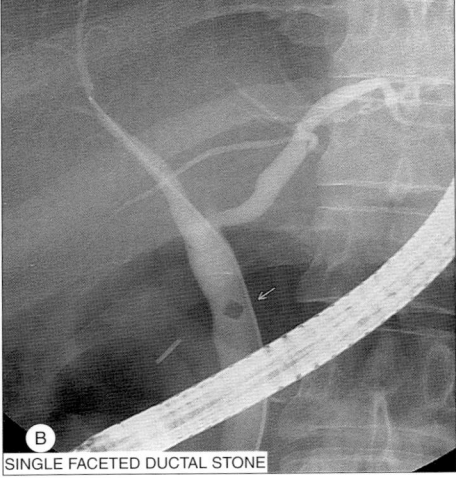

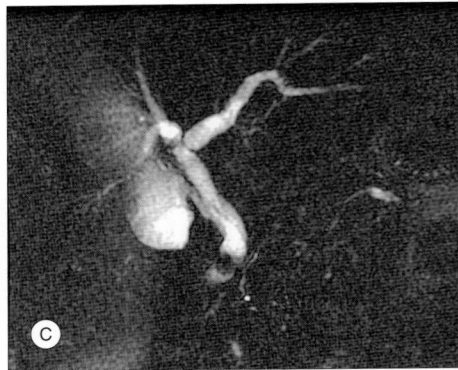

Figure 40–22. *A,* Multiple small shadowing gallbladder stones seen by transcutaneous ultrasound. The gallbladder wall is thickened. *B,* Small common hepatic duct stone in postcholecystectomy patient. *C,* Distal common bile duct stone detected by magnetic resonance cholangiopancreatography (MRCP).

helpful but adds expense and should probably be reserved for higher risk patients (e.g., cardiopulmonary disease) and those with relatively low probability (10% to 25%) of ductal stones. Higher stone probability patients should have ERC without preceding MRCP or endoscopic ultrasonography (EUS) (Fig. 40–23C). A larger ductal stone[61–65] is seen in Figure 40–23 in a postcholecystectomy patient. Intrahepatic stones[66–69] (with or without extrahepatic stones) are common in Asians. Figure 40–24 shows right segmental branches with large fusiform stones. A stone impacted in the cystic duct may compress the common hepatic or common bile duct and cause obstructive jaundice (Mirizzi's syndrome).

Table 40–4 reviews problems encountered in biliary stone cases and how to try to solve them.

BILIARY STRICTURES

Biliary strictures[70–81] are abnormal narrowings of the ductal system from compression (e.g., chronic pancreatitis), scar formation (e.g., postoperative), or neoplasm (e.g., cholangiocarcinoma). These typically clinically present with cholestasis, obstructive jaundice, and/or cholangitis. The etiology of the stricture is usually evident from the history (e.g., recent biliary surgery, ethanol abuse, or

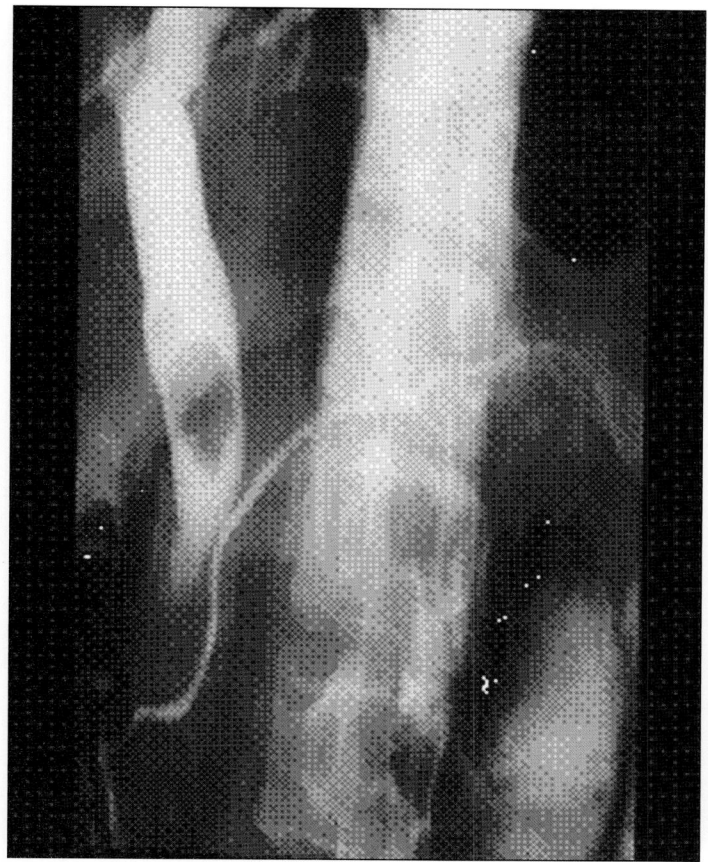

Figure 40–23. Larger common duct stone in an elderly patient with long-standing biliary colic.

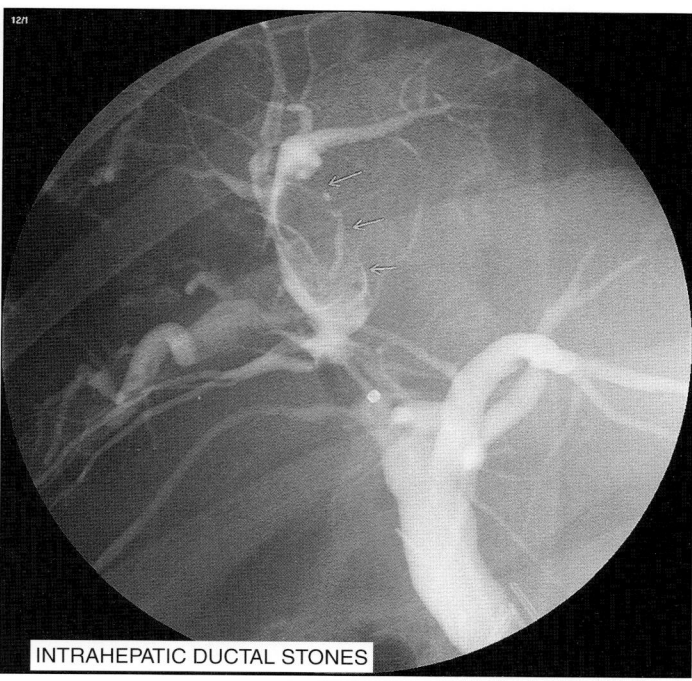

INTRAHEPATIC DUCTAL STONES

Figure 40–24. Large intrahepatic stones in Caucasian patient. Small common bile duct stones were also present. The gallbladder had been removed 5 years previously. These are much more common in Asian population.

Table 40–4. Challenges for Optimal Viewing of Stones

Probable bile duct stones (most are in terminal CBD at beginning of examination)	Inject contrast with catheter tip in sphincter segment (not deeply cannulated). Inject contrast slowly. Take film exposures early after only 1–2 cm of duct filled and again at each 1–2 cm further filling. With patient prone, tilt table head up 5–20 degrees to keep contrast near papilla.
Gallbladder stones?	Take multiple early filling gallbladder films. If overfilled, advance guidewire and catheter into gallbladder and aspirate excess contrast (Fig. 40–25). Take delayed films supine in 4–24 hr.
Probable sludge seen in terminal CBD on early films	Stop contrast injection. Aspirate bile through "see through" (nonopaque) catheter and confirm granular material.
Cholangitis presenting with purulent bile (± sepsis)	Aspirate bile from CBD (send for culture) and replace aspirated bile (e.g., 30 mL with less than ⅓ volume; e.g., 10 mL of contrast media). Limit intrahepatic filling. Do definitive intrahepatic duct and stone evaluation later when cholangitis resolved.
CBD, common bile duct.	

elderly patient with weight loss). Figure 40–26 shows a smooth tapered long narrowing within the head of the pancreas in a patient with calcific chronic pancreatitis. Laparoscopic cholecystectomy[82–84] is associated with thermal or mechanical injury which results in stricture formation in 0.25% to 0.5% of patients. Figure 40–27 shows an example of a typical postlaparoscopy stricture. Injuries at open cholecystectomy occur less frequently. Duct transactions (Fig. 40–28) and duct resections are the most serious injuries. Orthotopic liver transplant with duct-to-duct anastomosis results in pathologic narrowing at the anastomosis in 15% of patients[85,86] (Fig. 40–29). Primary sclerosing cholangitis[87–93] is characterized by multifocal extrahepatic and/or intrahepatic strictures (Fig. 40–30). The gallbladder and cystic duct are spared. The goals of ERC in suspected primary sclerosing cholangitis are (1) establish a diagnosis, (2) identify treatable dominant strictures, and (3) identify (or rule out) concomitant cholangiocarcinoma, which occurs in up to 40% of advanced cases going on to transplantation. Pancreatic ductal cell origin adenocarcinoma is the most common cancer encountered at

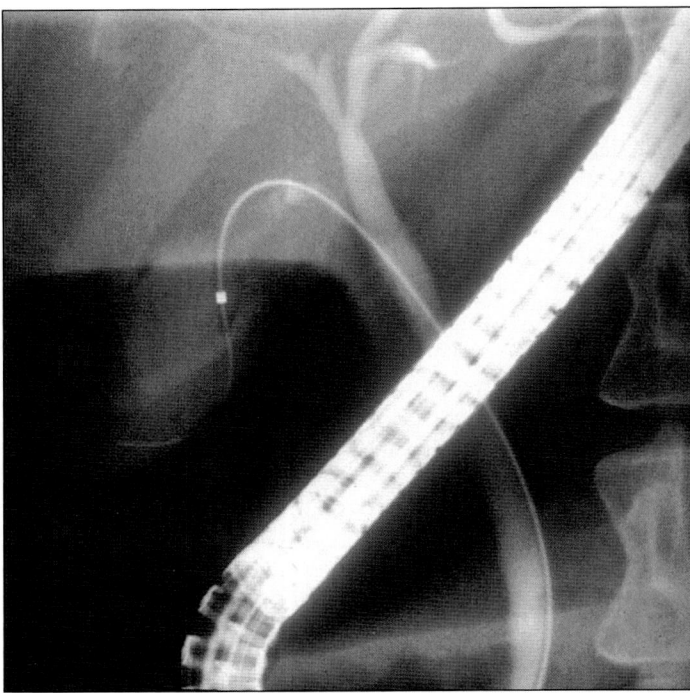

Figure 40–25. Gallbladder aspiration done after passing guidewire into gallbladder. This technique may be used to collect bile for crystals, inject contrast needed, or aspirate excessive bile or contrast media or pus.

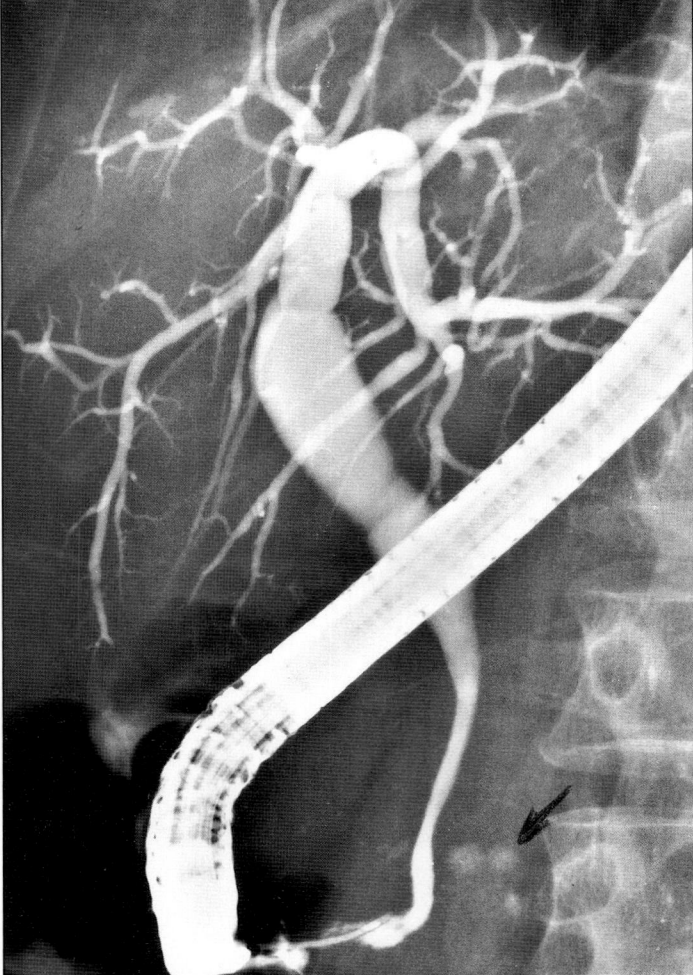

Figure 40–26. Endoscopic retrograde cholangiography (ERC) showing long, smooth, tapered stricture within the pancreas with mild upstream dilatation (the right lobe has not yet filled). Calcified stones (*arrow*) are seen in the head of the pancreas.

ERC. Pancreas cancer[94,95] of the head gives the classic double-duct sign (Fig. 40–31). This sign may also be seen in chronic pancreatitis. Tissue sampling[96–98] should be done on strictures that clinically have any suspicion of neoplasm. Brush cytology is easiest to obtain but will detect cancer when present in only 30% to 50% of cases. Additional sampling with a second brush, forceps, or endoluminal needles each add approximately 10% to the diagnostic sensitivity.

BILIARY LEAKS

Biliary leaks[99–105] occur from surgery complications or trauma (penetrating or nonpenetrating). Laparoscopic cholecystectomy is most commonly associated with leaks from the cystic duct or ducts of Luschka (Fig. 40–32). Bile leaks typically cause right upper quadrant pain, fever, mildly abnormal serum liver chemistries, and leukocytosis. A typical duct of Luschka leak is seen in Figure 40–33 with leak occurring from small intrahepatic duct. A subhepatic

contrast collection is seen in Figure 40–34 from a cystic duct leak occurring after laparoscopic cholecystectomy.

Table 40–5 reviews common problems encountered at ERC when dealing with strictures and leaks.

Gallbladder disease is commonly found at ERC. Figure 40–35 shows stones of less than 2 mm diameter in a partially filled gallbladder. Figure 40–36 shows gallbladder stones and right colon filling via gallbladder fistula to the colon.

ANOMALOUS PANCREATOBILIARY DUCTAL UNION

Anomalous pancreatobiliary ductal union[106,107] occurs in approximately 2% of Asians but only 0.2% of Caucasians. In this condition, the pancreatobiliary junction occurs outside the duodenal wall and simultaneous biductal filling occurs from major papilla injection (Figs. 40–37 and 40–38). Approximately one third of these patients have an associated choledochal cyst (Fig. 40–39). There is also an association with gallbladder cancer.

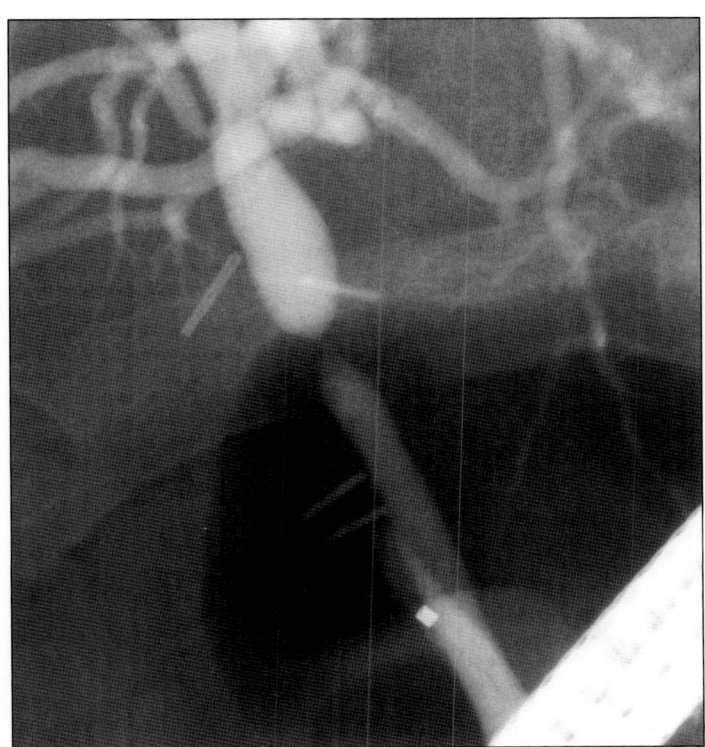

Figure 40–27. Postlaparoscopic cholecystectomy. Short stricture of common hepatic duct seen with upstream dilatation. Stricture occurred near clips and is probably thermal injury in origin.

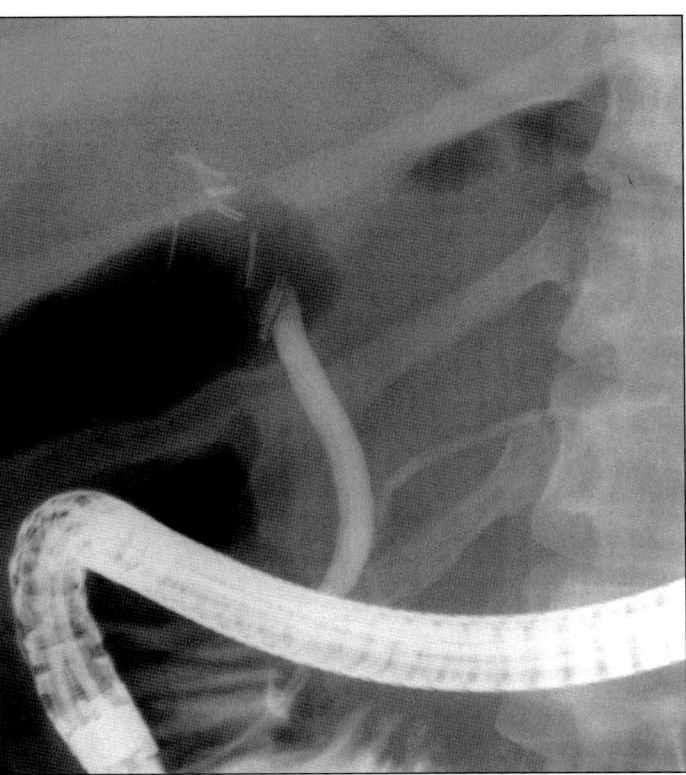

Figure 40–28. Unintentional clip transection of the common bile duct at the cystic duct junction, which occurred at open cholecystectomy in a complicated patient with prior upper abdominal radiation for lymphoma.

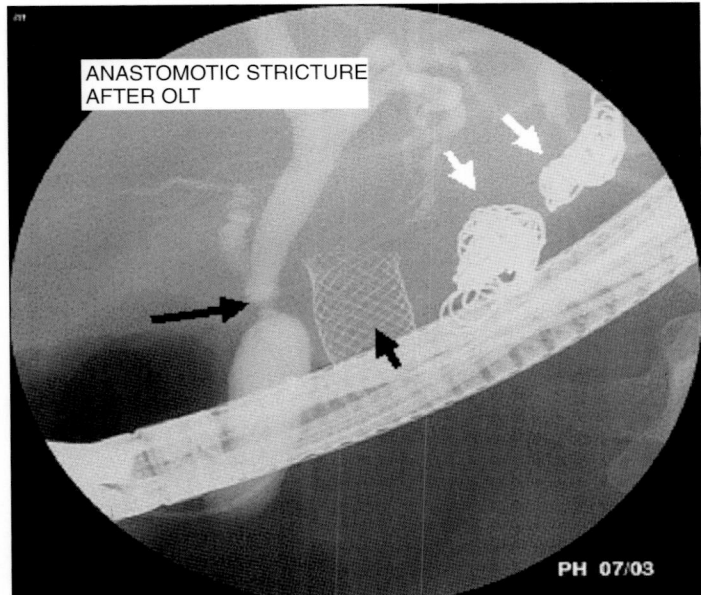

Figure 40–29. Orthotopic liver transplant with duct-to-duct anastomosis. Narrowing of the anastomosis is seen just 10 days postoperatively *(long black arrow)*. Note endovascular metal stent (transjugular intrahepatic porto-systemic shunt [TIPS]) used to treat prior variceal bleeding *(short black arrow)* and endovascular coils in duodenal arcade from bleeding duodenal ulcers *(white arrows)*.

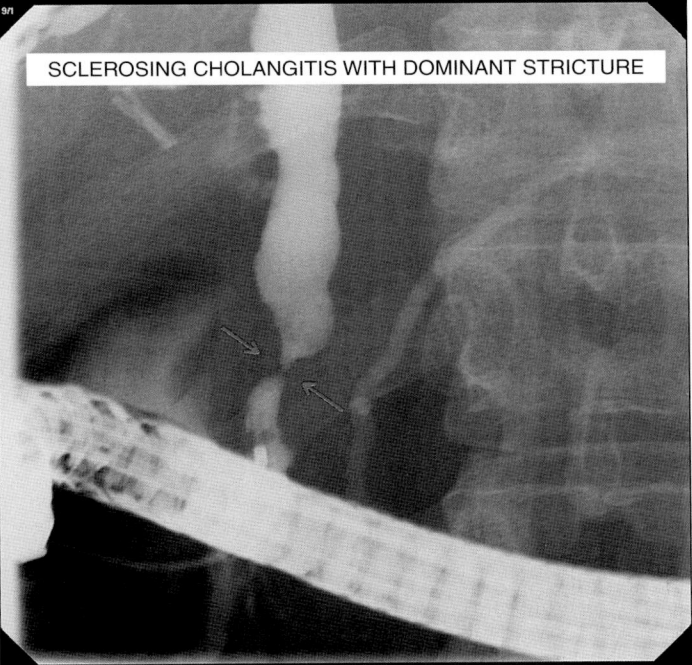

Figure 40–30. Sclerosing cholangitis with dominant stricture. All diagnostic studies were benign.

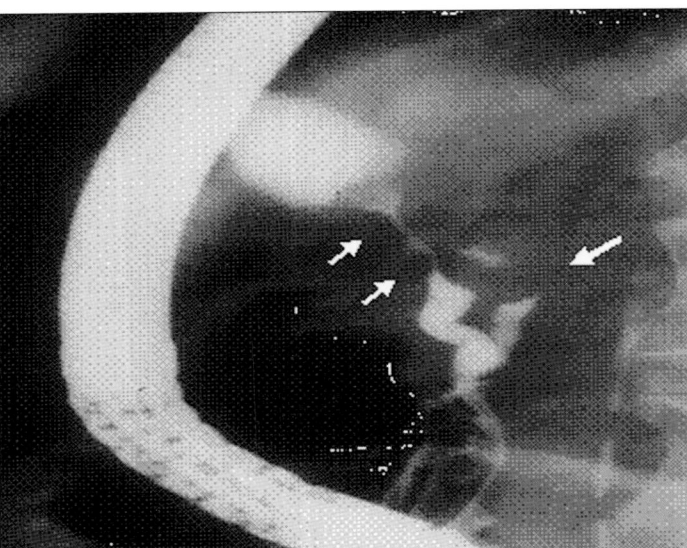

Figure 40–31. Typical double-duct sign of pancreatic cancer. *Double arrows* indicate common bile duct narrowing. *Longer arrow* notes pancreatic duct narrowing. This sign may also be seen in chronic pancreatitis.

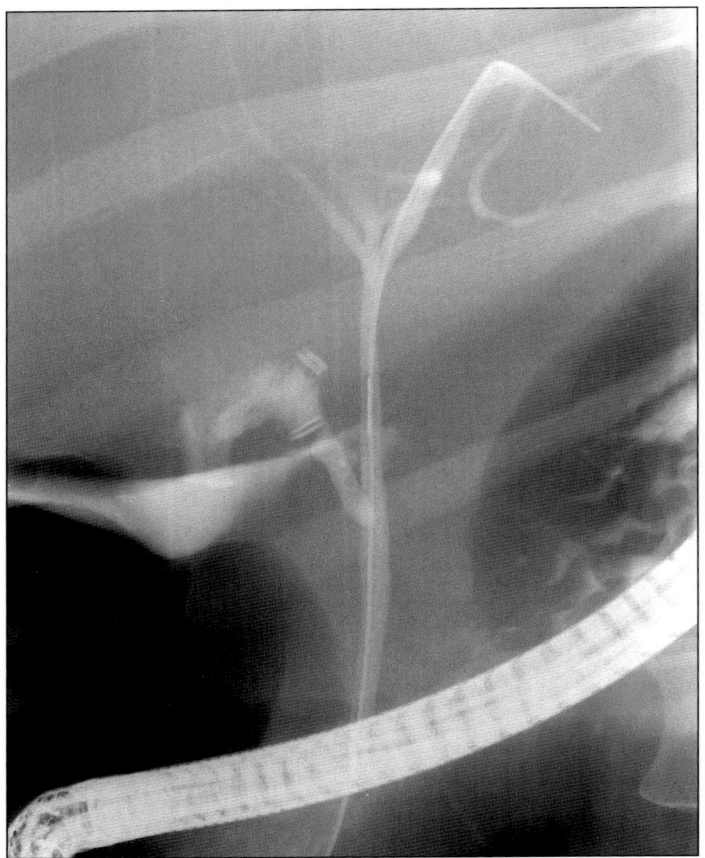

Figure 40–32. Leak from cystic duct seen two days after laparoscopic chole-cystectomy.

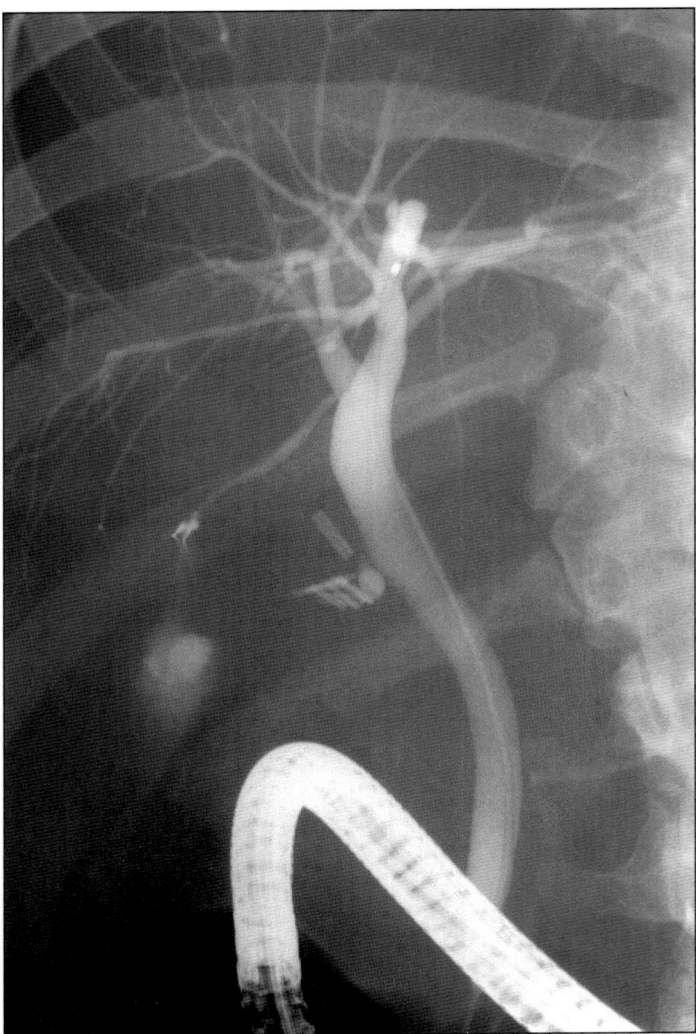

Figure 40–33. Duct of Luschka leak seen 7 days after laparoscopic cholecys-tectomy. These ducts are in close proximity to the gallbladder bed and are exposed with free dissection of the gallbladder.

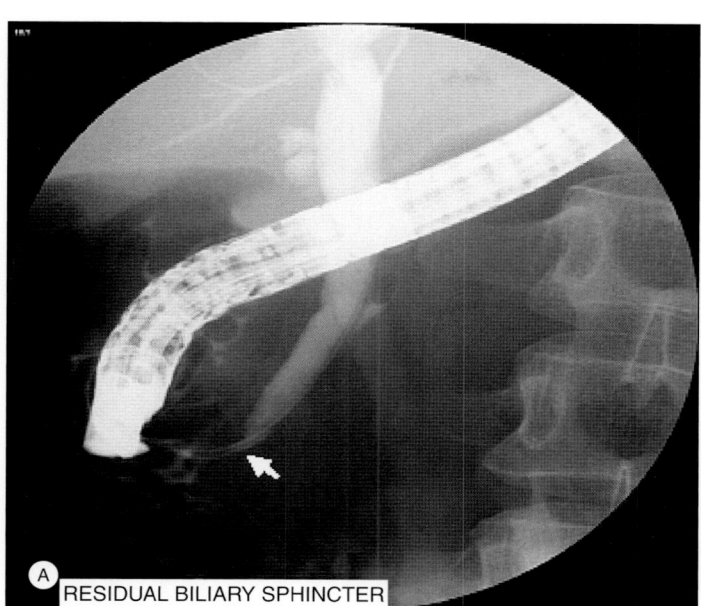

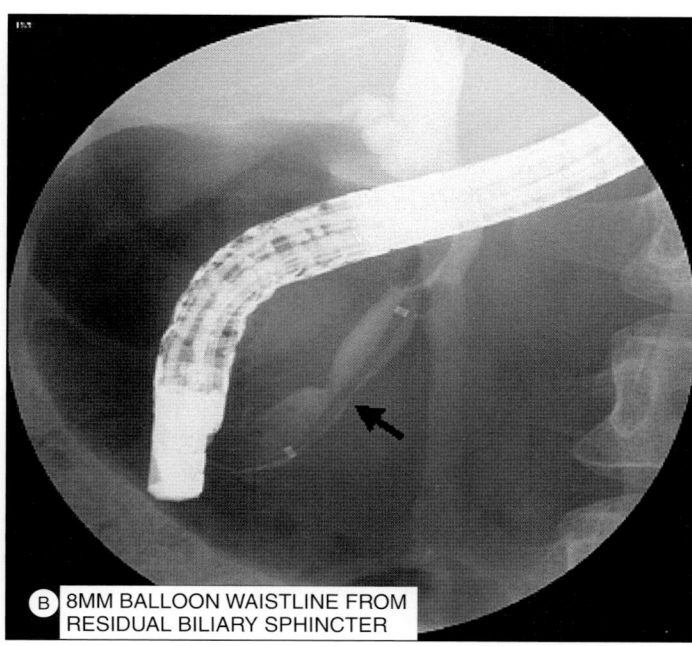

Figure 40-34. *A* and *B,* After biliary sphincterotomy the terminal bile duct may appear somewhat narrowed *(white arrow);* however, true sphincter size is probably best determined by inflation of a hydrostatic balloon within the sphincter segment observing the residual waistline *(black arrow).*

Table 40-5. Challenges in Detection and Optimal Viewing of Strictures

Hilar stricture	Take multiple early filling views with varying degrees of angulation. Especially obtain Y confluens view with left and right main hepatic ducts separated. Fill only a tiny amount of duct upstream, initially; get guidewire upstream before filling more. Avoid thorough upstream filling (rely on MRCP or CT if that information clinically needed) unless guidewire and catheter already passed upstream and full stent drainage is certain.
Common bile or common hepatic duct stricture with obviously dilated upstream ducts (per CT or MRI). Need upper rim of stricture definition	Avoid thorough filling above stricture. Advance large-diameter stone retrieval balloon above stricture, inflate, and fill downstream to balloon to better see upper stricture definition.
Right lobe not filling; is obstruction present?	Inject more contrast with greater force (unless purulent bile). Advance catheter into right duct. Consider aspirating bile from near hilum to "empty" right lobe to make space for contrast. If prior sphincterotomy, use balloon occlusion. Tilt head down 5-20 degrees.
Probable sclerosing cholangitis setting or other intrahepatic stricturing. Contrast preferentially enters gallbladder.	Limit gallbladder filling in primary sclerosing cholangitis because post-ERCP cholecystitis may occur. Inflate balloon catheter above cystic duct takeoff and inject upstream. After more aggressive intrahepatic filling, the patient should remain on broad-spectrum antibiotics for 5-7 days.
The sphincter segment appears narrow.	This is usually a normal finding. A dilated duct upstream or abnormal liver serum chemistries present suggests pathology. Measure length of segment; >12 mm suggests scar or tumor narrowing. Correlate with normal or abnormal appearance of the papilla. Brush cytology, manometry, sphincterotomy with viewing inside ampulla, endoscopic ultrasound may be needed to clarify.
Is postsphincterotomy biliary orifice adequate?	Do manometry, pull through stone retrieval balloon; size with hydrostatic balloon (see Fig. 40-34).

CT, computed tomography; MRCP; magnetic resonance cholangiopancreatography; MRI, magnetic resonance imaging.

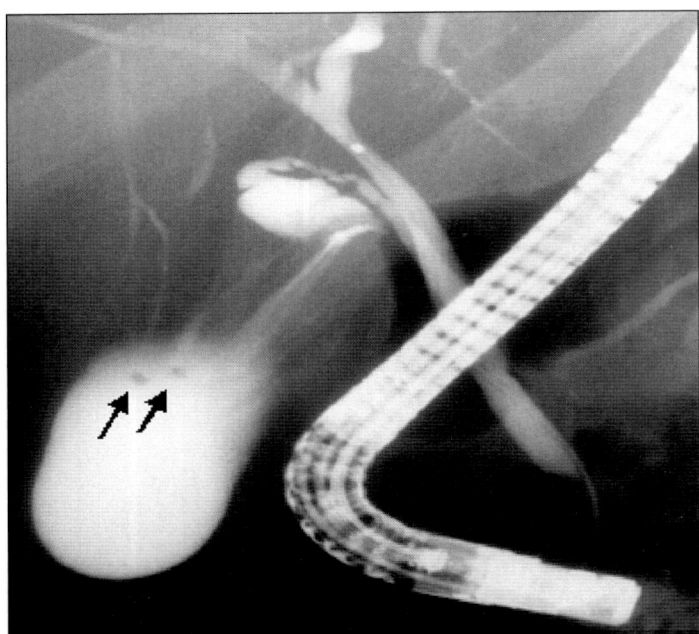

Figure 40–35. Tiny gallbladder stones.

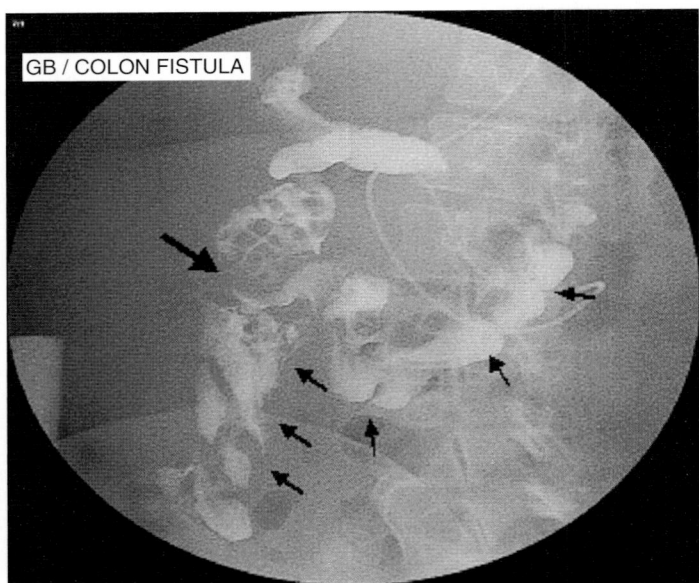

Figure 40–36. Gallbladder colonic fistula *(large arrow)* seen at endoscopic retrograde cholangiography (ERC). Colonic contrast media *(multiple small arrows)*.

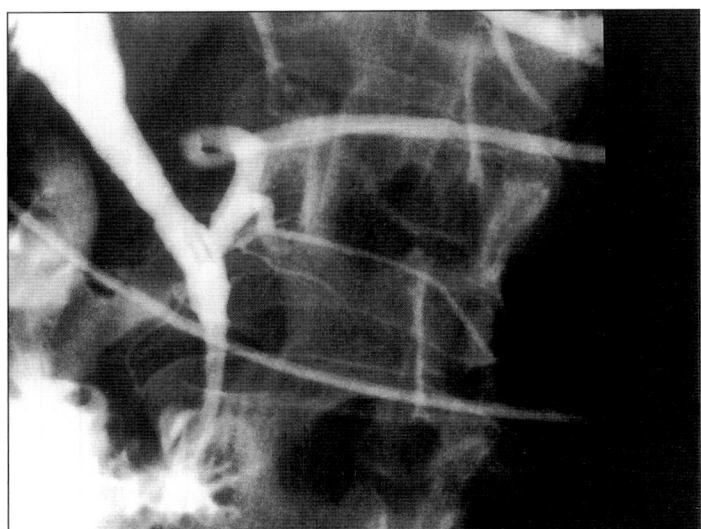

Figure 40–37. Anomalous pancreatobiliary ductal junction with pancreatic duct joining the bile duct well outside the duodenal wall. Note the long common channel of at least 15 mm length.

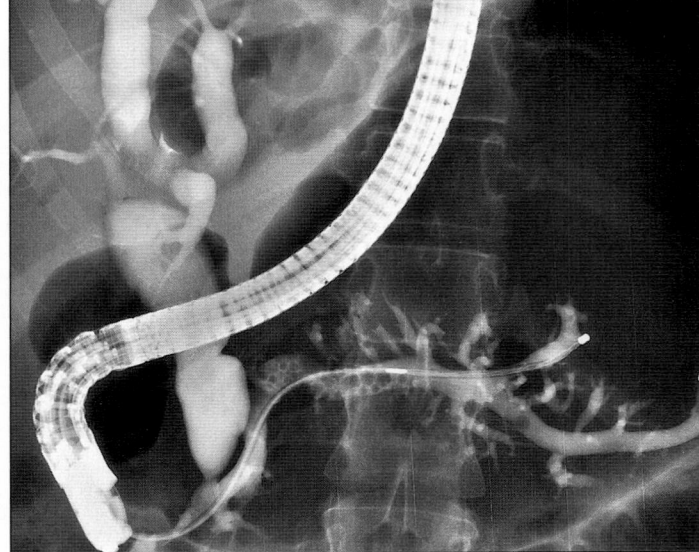

Figure 40–38. Anomalous pancreatobiliary ductal union with (1) long common channel, (2) chronic pancreatitis, (3) bile duct entering apparent pancreatic duct, and (4) stricture at bile duct pancreatic duct junction with dilated bile duct upstream (choledochocyst present at the hilum but not pictured).

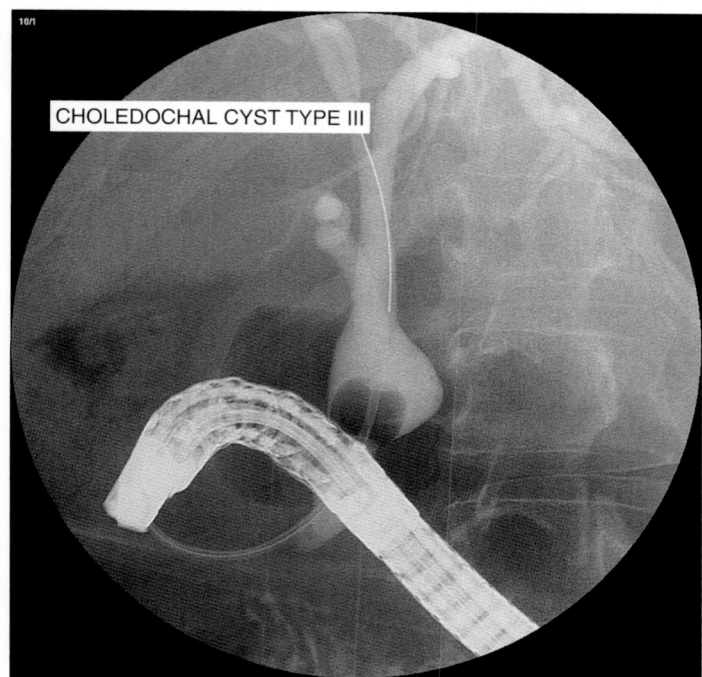

CHOLEDOCHAL CYST TYPE III

Figure 40–39. Small type III choledochal cyst. Eleven millimeter stone retrieval basket is in cyst.

Summary

Obtaining a diagnostic cholangiography at ERC is now less important in view of quality CT, EUS, and MRCP imaging. Nevertheless, the endoscopist should have the skills, knowledge, and associated equipment to obtain excellent quality cholangiogram when clinically relevant. Attention to details, especially during initial ductal filling, and thorough filling will aid in the effort. Appropriate clinical and endoscopic decision making is often possible only after a quality cholangiogram has been obtained.

REFERENCES

1. McCune WS, Shorb PE, Moscovitz H: Endoscopic cannulation of the ampulla of Vater: A preliminary report. Ann Surg 167:752–756, 1968.
2. Classen M, Demling L: [Endoscopic sphincterotomy of the papilla of vater and extraction of stones from the choledochal duct (author's transl)]. Dtsch Med Wochenschr 99:496–497, 1974.
3. Kawai K, Akasaka Y, Murakami K, et al: Endoscopic sphincterotomy of the ampulla of Vater. Gastrointest Endosc 20:148–151, 1974.
4. Arguedas MR, Dupont AW, Wilcox CM: Where do ERCP, endoscopic ultrasound, magnetic resonance cholangiopancreatography, and intraoperative cholangiography fit in the management of acute biliary pancreatitis? A decision analysis model. Am J Gastroenterol 96:2892–2899, 2001.
5. Fayad L, Holland GA, Bergin D, et al: Functional magnetic resonance cholangiography (fMRC) of the gallbladder and biliary tree with contrast-enhanced magnetic resonance cholangiography. J Magn Reson Imaging 18:449–460, 2003.
6. Maniatis P, Triantopoulou C, Sofianou E, et al: Virtual CT cholangiography in patients with choledocholithiasis. Abdom Imaging 28:536–544, 2003.
7. Soto JA, Alvarez O, Munera F, et al: Diagnosing bile duct stones: Comparison of unenhanced helical CT, oral contrast-enhanced CT cholangiography, and MR cholangiography. AJR Am J Roentgenol 175:1127–1134, 2000.
8. Stockberger S, Wass JL, Sherman S, et al: Intravenous cholangiography with helical CT: Comparison with endoscopic retrograde cholangiography. Radiology 192:675–680, 1994.
9. Zidi SH, Prat F, Le Guen O, et al: Performance characteristics of magnetic resonance cholangiography in the staging of malignant hilar strictures. Gut 46:103–106, 2000.
10. Urbach D, Khajanchee YS, Jobe BA, et al: Cost-effective management of common bile duct stones: A decision analysis of the use of endoscopic retrograde cholangiopancreatography (ERCP), intraoperative cholangiography, and laparoscopic bile duct exploration. Surg Endosc 15:4–13, 2001.
11. Textor H, Flacke S, Pauleit D, et al: Three-dimensional magnetic resonance cholangiopancreatography with respiratory triggering in the diagnosis of primary sclerosing cholangitis: Comparison with endoscopic retrograde cholangiography. Endoscopy 34:984–990, 2002.
12. Sackmann M, Beuers U, Helmberger T: Biliary imaging: Magnetic resonance cholangiography versus endoscopic retrograde cholangiography. J Hepatol 30:334–338, 1999.
13. Cabada Giadas T, Sarria Octavio de Toledo L, Martinez-Berganza Asensio MT, et al: Helical CT cholangiography in the evaluation of the biliary tract: Application to the diagnosis of choledocholithiasis. Abdom Imaging 27:61–70, 2002.
14. Freeman ML, Nelson DB, Sherman S, et al: Complications of endoscopic biliary sphincterotomy. N Engl J Med 335:909–918, 1996.
15. Freeman ML, DiSario JA, Nelson DB, et al: Risk factors for post-ERCP pancreatitis: A prospective, multicenter study. Gastrointest Endosc 54:425–434, 2001.
16. Cotton PB, Lehman G, Vennes J, et al: Endoscopic sphincterotomy complications and their management: An attempt at consensus. Gastrointest Endosc 37:383–393, 1991.
17. Jowell PS, Baillie J, Branch MS, et al: Quantitative assessment of procedural competence. A prospective study of training in endoscopic retrograde cholangiopancreatography. Ann Intern Med 125:983–989, 1996.
18. Choudari CP, Fogel E, Kalayci C, et al: Therapeutic biliary endoscopy. Endoscopy 31:80–87, 1999.
19. Wright BE, Cass OW, Freeman ML: ERCP in patients with long-limb Roux-en-Y gastrojejunostomy and intact papilla. Gastrointest Endosc 56:225–232, 2002.
20. Heyd RL, Kopecky KK, Sherman S, et al: Radiation exposure to patients and personnel during interventional ERCP at a teaching institution. Gastrointest Endosc 44:287–292, 1996.
21. Wille RT, Barnett JL, Chey WD, et al: Routine droperidol premedication improves sedation for ERCP. Gastrointest Endosc 52:362–366, 2000.
22. Krugliak P, Ziff B, Rusabrov Y, et al: Propofol versus midazolam for conscious sedation guided by processed EEG during endoscopic retrograde cholangiopancreatography: A prospective, randomized, double-blind study. Endoscopy 32:677–682, 2000.
23. Gillham MJ, Hutchinson RC, Carter R, Kenny GN: Patient-maintained sedation for ERCP with a target-controlled infusion of propofol: A pilot study. Gastrointest Endosc 54:14–17, 2001.
24. Hansen J, Ulmer B, Rex D: Technical performance of colonoscopy in patients sedated with nurse-administered propofol. Am J Gastroenterol 99:52–56, 2004.
25. Kumar S, Sherman S, Hawes RH, Lehman GA: Success and yield of second attempt ERCP. Gastrointest Endosc 41:445–447, 1995.
26. Choudari CP, Sherman S, Fogel EL, et al: Success of ERCP at a referral center after a previously unsuccessful attempt. Gastrointest Endosc 52:478–483, 2000.

27. Heiss FW, Cimis RS Jr, MacMillan FP Jr: Biliary sphincter scissor for pre-cut access: Preliminary experience. Gastrointest Endosc 55:719–722, 2002.

28. Kasmin FE, Cohen D, Batra S, et al: Needle-knife sphincterotomy in a tertiary referral center: Efficacy and complications. Gastrointest Endosc 44:48–53, 1996.

29. Cotton PB: Precut papillotomy—a risky technique for experts only. Gastrointest Endosc 35:578–579, 1989.

30. Binmoeller KF, Seifert H, Gerke H, et al: Papillary roof incision using the Erlangen-type pre-cut papillotome to achieve selective bile duct cannulation. Gastrointest Endosc 44:689–695, 1996.

31. Goff JS: Long-term experience with the transpancreatic sphincter pre-cut approach to biliary sphincterotomy. Gastrointest Endosc 50:642–645, 1999.

32. Sherman S, Hawes RH, Rathgaber SW, et al: Post-ERCP pancreatitis: Randomized, prospective study comparing a low- and high-osmolality contrast agent. Gastrointest Endosc 40:422–427, 1994.

33. Johnson GK, Geenen JE, Bedford RA, et al: A comparison of nonionic versus ionic contrast media: Results of a prospective, multicenter study. Midwest Pancreaticobiliary Study Group. Gastrointest Endosc, 42:312–316, 1995.

34. Hintze RE, Abou-Rebyeh H, Adler A, et al: Magnetic resonance cholangiopancreatography-guided unilateral endoscopic stent placement for Klatskin tumors. Gastrointest Endosc 53:40–46, 2001.

35. De Palma GD, Galloro G, Siciliano S, et al: Unilateral versus bilateral endoscopic hepatic duct drainage in patients with malignant hilar biliary obstruction: Results of a prospective, randomized, and controlled study. Gastrointest Endosc 53:547–553, 2001.

36. Freeman ML, Overby C: Selective MRCP and CT-targeted drainage of malignant hilar biliary obstruction with self-expanding metallic stents. Gastrointest Endosc 58:41–49, 2003.

37. Lehman G, Sherman S: Sphincter of Oddi dysfunction. In Yamada T, Alpers DH, Laine L, et al (eds): Textbook of Gastroenterology. Philadelphia, Lippincott Williams & Wilkins, 1999, pp 2343–2354.

38. Hogan WJ, Sherman S, Pasricha P, Carr-Locke D: Sphincter of Oddi manometry. Gastrointest Endosc 45:342–348, 1997.

39. Sherman S, Gottlieb K, Uzer MF, et al: Effects of meperidine on the pancreatic and biliary sphincter. Gastrointest Endosc 44:239–242, 1996.

40. Blaut U, Sherman S, Fogel E, Lehman GA: Influence of cholangiography on biliary sphincter of Oddi manometric parameters. Gastrointest Endosc 52:624–629, 2000.

41. Kalayci C, Aisen A, Canal D, et al: Magnetic resonance cholangiopancreatography documents bile leak site after cholecystectomy in patients with aberrant right hepatic duct where ERCP fails. Gastrointest Endosc 52:277–281, 2000.

42. Hand B: Anatomy and embryology of the biliary tract and pancreas. In Sivak MV Jr (ed): Gastroenterologic Endoscopy. Philadelphia, WB Saunders, 1987, pp 863–877.

43. Hand B: Anatomy and function of the extrahepatic biliary system. Rev Gastroenterol Mex 2:3–29, 1973.

44. Gazelle GS, Lee MJ, Mueller PR: Cholangiographic segmental anatomy of the liver. Radiographics 14:1005–1013, 1994.

45. Boraschi P, Gigoni R, Braccini G, et al: Detection of common bile duct stones before laparoscopic cholecystectomy. Evaluation with MR cholangiography. Acta Radiol 43:593–598, 2002.

46. Charfare H, Cheslyn-Curtis S: Selective cholangiography in 600 patients undergoing cholecystectomy with 5-year follow-up for residual bile duct stones. Ann R Coll Surg Engl 85:167–173, 2003.

47. Coppola R, Riccioni ME, Ciletti S, et al: Selective use of endoscopic retrograde cholangiopancreatography to facilitate laparoscopic cholecystectomy without cholangiography. A review of 1139 consecutive cases. Surg Endosc 15:1213–1216, 2001.

48. Sherman S, Hawes RH, Lehman GA: Management of bile duct stones. Semin Liver Dis 10:205–221, 1990.

49. Bergman JJ, Rauws EA, Tijssen JG, et al: Biliary endoprostheses in elderly patients with endoscopically irretrievable common bile duct stones: Report on 117 patients. Gastrointest Endosc 42:195–201, 1995.

50. Prat F, Tennenbaum R, Ponsot P, et al: Endoscopic sphincterotomy in patients with liver cirrhosis. Gastrointest Endosc 43(2 Pt 1):127–131, 1996.

51. Folsch UR, Nitsche R, Ludtke R, et al: Early ERCP and papillotomy compared with conservative treatment for acute biliary pancreatitis. The German Study Group on Acute Biliary Pancreatitis. N Engl J Med 336:237–242, 1997.

52. Fan ST, Lai EC, Mok FP, et al: Early treatment of acute biliary pancreatitis by endoscopic papillotomy. N Engl J Med 328:228–232, 1993.

53. Neoptolemos JP, Carr-Locke DL, London NJ, et al: Controlled trial of urgent endoscopic retrograde cholangiopancreatography and endoscopic sphincterotomy versus conservative treatment for acute pancreatitis due to gallstones. Lancet 2:979–983, 1988.

54. Fogel E, Sherman S: Acute biliary pancreatitis: When should the endoscopist intervene? Gastroenterology 125:229–235, 2003.

55. Nowak A, Nowakowska-Dulawa E, Marek TA, et al: Final results of the prospective, randomized, controlled study on endoscopic sphincterotomy versus conventional management in acute biliary pancreatitis. Gastroenterology 108:A380, 1995.

56. Connors P, Carr-Locke D: Endoscopic retrograde cholangiopancreatography findings and endoscopic sphincterotomy for cholangitis and pancreatitis. Gastrointest Endosc Clin N Am 1:27–50, 1991.

57. Kozarek RA: Role of ERCP in acute pancreatitis. Gastrointest Endosc 56:S231–S236, 2002.

58. Uomo G, Manes G, Laccetti M: Endoscopic sphincterotomy and recurrence of acute pancreatitis in gallstone patients considered unfit for surgery. Pancreas 14:28–30, 1997.

59. Boerma D, Rauws EA, Keulemans YC, et al: Wait-and-see policy or laparoscopic cholecystectomy after endoscopic sphincterotomy for bile-duct stones: A randomized trial. Lancet 360:761–765, 2002.

60. Sharma VK, Howden CW: Metaanalysis of randomized controlled trials of endoscopic retrograde cholangiography and endoscopic sphincterotomy for the treatment of acute biliary pancreatitis. Am J Gastroenterol 94:3211–3214, 1999.

61. Adamek HE, Maier M, Jakobs R, et al: Management of retained bile duct stones: A prospective open trial comparing extracorporeal and intracorporeal lithotripsy. Gastrointest Endosc 44:40–47, 1996.

62. Hintze R, Adler A, Velzke W: Outcome of mechanical lithotripsy of bile duct stones in an unselected series of 704 patients. Hepatogastroenterology 43:473–476, 1996.

63. Shaw MJ, Mackie RD, Moore JP, et al: Results of a multicenter trial using a mechanical lithotripter for the treatment of large bile duct stones. Am J Gastroenterol 88:730–733, 1993.

64. Binmoeller KF, Bruckner M, Thonke F, Soehendra N: Treatment of difficult bile duct stones using mechanical, electrohydraulic and extracorporeal shock wave lithotripsy. Endoscopy 25:201–206, 1993.

65. Sackmann M, Holl J, Sauter GH, et al: Extracorporeal shock wave lithotripsy for clearance of bile duct stones resistant to endoscopic extraction. Gastrointest Endosc 53:27–32, 2001.

66. Lee, SK, Seo DW, Myung SJ, et al: Percutaneous transhepatic cholangioscopic treatment for hepatolithiasis: An evaluation of long-term results and risk factors for recurrence. Gastrointest Endosc 53:318–323, 2001.

67. Kim M, Sekijima J, Lee S: Primary intrahepatic stones. Am J Gastroenterol 90:540–548, 1995.

68. Jeng K: Treatment of intrahepatic biliary strictures associated with hepatolithiasis. Hepatogastroenterology 44:342–351, 1997.

69. Kim M, Lim BC, Myung SJ, et al: Epidemiological study on Korean gallstone disease: A nation-wide cooperative study. Dig Dis Sci 44:1674–1683, 1999.

70. Smith MT, Sherman S, Lehman GA: Endoscopic management of benign strictures of the biliary tree. Endoscopy 27:253–266, 1995.

71. Davids PH, Rauws EA, Coene PP, et al: Endoscopic stenting for post-operative biliary strictures. Gastrointest Endosc 38:12–18, 1992.

72. Berkelhammer C, Kortan P, Haber GB: Endoscopic biliary prostheses as treatment for benign postoperative bile duct strictures. Gastrointest Endosc 35:95–101, 1989.

73. Bergman JJ, Burgemeister L, Bruno MJ, et al: Long-term follow-up after biliary stent placement for postoperative bile duct stenosis. Gastrointest Endosc 54:154–161, 2001.

74. Costamagna G, Pandolfi M, Mutignani M, et al: Long-term results of endoscopic management of postoperative bile duct strictures with increasing numbers of stents. Gastrointest Endosc 54:162–168, 2001.

75. Davids PH, Tanka AK, Rauws EA, et al: Benign biliary strictures. Surgery or endoscopy? Ann Surg 217:237–243, 1993.

76. Dumonceau JM, Deviere J, Delhaye M, et al: Plastic and metal stents for postoperative benign bile duct strictures: The best and the worst. Gastrointest Endosc 47:8–17, 1998.

77. Smits ME, Rauws EA, van Gulik TM, et al: Long-term results of endoscopic stenting and surgical drainage for biliary stricture due to chronic pancreatitis. Br J Surg 83:764–768, 1996.

78. Barthet M, Bernard JP, Duval JL, et al: Biliary stenting in benign biliary stenosis complicating chronic calcifying pancreatitis. Endoscopy 26:569–572, 1994.

79. Farnbacher MJ, Rabenstein T, Ell C, et al: Is endoscopic drainage of common bile duct stenoses in chronic pancreatitis up-to-date? Am J Gastroenterol 95:1466–1471, 2000.

80. Ludwig K, Bernhardt J, Steffen H, Lorenz D: Contribution of intraoperative cholangiography to incidence and outcome of common bile duct injuries during laparoscopic cholecystectomy. Surg Endosc 16:1098–1104, 2002.

81. Hirao K, Miyazaki A, Fujimoto T, et al: Evaluation of aberrant bile ducts before laparoscopic cholecystectomy: Helical CT cholangiography versus MR cholangiography. AJR Am J Roentgenol 175:713–720, 2000.

82. A prospective analysis of 1518 laparoscopic cholecystectomies. The Southern Surgeons Club. N Engl J Med 324:1073–1078, 1991.

83. Gouma D, Go P: Bile duct injury during laparoscopic and conventional cholecystectomy. Am Coll Surg 178:229–233, 1994.

84. Bergman JJ, van den Brink GR, Rauws EA, et al: Treatment of bile duct lesions after laparoscopic cholecystectomy. Gut 38:141–147, 1996.

85. Rerknimitr R, Sherman S, Fogel EL, et al: Biliary tract complications after orthotopic liver transplantation with choledochocholedochostomy anastomosis: Endoscopic findings and results of therapy. Gastrointest Endosc 55:224–231, 2002.

86. Morelli J, Mulcahy HE, Willner IR, et al: Long-term outcomes for patients with post-liver transplant anastomotic biliary strictures treated by endoscopic stent placement. Gastrointest Endosc 58:374–379, 2003.

87. Campbell WL, Ferris JV, Holbert BL, et al: Biliary tract carcinoma complicating primary sclerosing cholangitis: Evaluation with CT, cholangiography, US, and MR imaging. Radiology 207:41–50, 1998.

88. Campbell WL, Peterson MS, Federle MP, et al: Using CT and cholangiography to diagnose biliary tract carcinoma complicating primary sclerosing cholangitis. AJR Am J Roentgenol 177:1095–1100, 2001.

89. Ernst O, Asselah T, Sergent G, et al: MR cholangiography in primary sclerosing cholangitis. AJR Am J Roentgenol 171:1027–130l, 1998.

90. Lee S, Kim MH, Lee SK, et al: MR cholangiography versus cholangioscopy for evaluation of longitudinal extension of hilar cholangiocarcinoma. Gastrointest Endosc 56:25–32, 2002.

91. Baluyut AR, Sherman S, Lehman GA, et al: Impact of endoscopic therapy on the survival of patients with primary sclerosing cholangitis. Gastrointest Endosc 53:308–312, 2001.

92. Chalasani N, Baluyut A, Ismail A, et al: Cholangiocarcinoma in patients with primary sclerosing cholangitis: A multicenter case-control study. Hepatology 31:7–11, 2000.

93. Tanaka Y, Koshiyama H, Nakao K, et al: Rapid progress of acute suppurative cholangitis to secondary sclerosing cholangitis sequentially followed-up by endoscopic retrograde cholangiography. Endoscopy 33:633–635, 2001.

94. Costamagna G, Pandolfi M, Mutignani M: Carcinoma of the pancreatic head area. Diagnostic imaging. Direct cholangiography: ERCP. Rays 20:269–279, 1995.

95. Kozarek RA: Endoscopy in the management of malignant obstructive jaundice. Gastrointest Endosc Clin N Am 6:153–176, 1996.

96. De Bellis M, Sherman S, Fogel EL, et al: Tissue sampling at ERCP in suspected malignant biliary strictures (Part 1). Gastrointest Endosc 56:552–561, 2002.

97. de Bellis M, Sherman S, Fogel EL, et al: Tissue sampling at ERCP in suspected malignant biliary strictures (Part 2). Gastrointest Endosc 56:720–730, 2002.

98. Jailwala J, Fogel EL, Sherman S, et al: Triple-tissue sampling at ERCP in malignant biliary obstruction. Gastrointest Endosc 51(4 Pt 1):383–390, 2000.

99. Brooks DC, Becker JM, Connors PJ, Carr-Locke DL: Management of bile leaks following laparoscopic cholecystectomy. Surg Endosc 7:292–295, 1993.

100. Frakes JT, Bradley SJ: Endoscopic stent placement for biliary leak from an accessory duct of Luschka after laparoscopic cholecystectomy. Gastrointest Endosc 39:90–92, 1993.

101. Peters J, Ollila D, Nichols K: Diagnosis and management of bile leaks following laparoscopic cholecystectomy. Surg Endosc 4:163–170, 1994.

102. Barkun A, Rezieg M, Mehta SN, et al: Postcholecystectomy biliary leaks in the laparoscopic era: Risk factors, presentation, and management. McGill Gallstone Treatment Group. Gastrointest Endosc 45:277–282, 1997.

103. Bjorkman DJ, Carr-Locke DL, Lichtenstein DR, et al: Postsurgical bile leaks: Endoscopic obliteration of the transpapillary pressure gradient is enough. Am J Gastroenterol 90:2128–2133, 1995.

104. Barton JR, Russell RC, Hatfield AR: Management of bile leaks after laparoscopic cholecystectomy. Br J Surg 82:980–984, 1995.

105. Raijman I, Catalano MF, Hirsch GS, et al: Endoscopic treatment of biliary leakage after laparoscopic cholecystectomy. Endoscopy 26:741–744, 1994.

106. Samavedy R, Sherman S, Lehman GA: Endoscopic therapy in anomalous pancreatobiliary duct junction. Gastrointest Endosc 50:623–627, 1999.

107. Schmidt HG, Bauer J, Wiessner V, Schonekas H: Endoscopic aspects of choledochoceles. Hepatogastroenterology 43:143–146, 1996.

Diagnostic Pancreatography

Bret T. Petersen

Diagnostic endoscopic retrograde pancreatography (ERP) evolved from a novel and cutting edge procedure in the 1970s to a widely used standard imaging tool in the latter 2 decades of the 20th century. The development of magnetic resonance (MR) imaging and endoscopic ultrasonography (EUS) have contributed to the further evolution of ERP from a stand-alone diagnostic procedure to a highly therapeutic endeavor, the diagnostic uses being largely displaced by these alternative imaging modalities. Nevertheless, familiarity with the applications and findings of pancreatography remain critical to the skillful performance of endoscopic retrograde cholangiopancreatography (ERCP). This chapter reviews the indications for endoscopic pancreatography, techniques involved in its performance, and both normal and pathologic findings.

Indications

Despite the erosion in use of diagnostic pancreatography, legitimate indications remain essentially unchanged over the past decade. As for all endoscopic procedures, ERP is indicated only when the potential findings will alter the management of the patient's condition in a meaningful way.[1,2] Appropriate indications have been published by national societies and interest groups[2] and revised for application in individual practices. Our standard indications for pancreatography are listed in Table 41–1. They include investigation of symptoms strongly suspected as relating to the pancreas on the basis of associated abnormal laboratory or imaging tests, investigation of specific abnormalities on prior imaging or laboratory testing, and investigation of known pancreatic abnormalities for which intervention is needed or anticipated. Diagnostic pancreatography alone is not indicated to confirm findings clearly demonstrated on other testing if therapy will not be changed by its performance. Pancreatography alone also is not indicated for investigation of isolated abdominal pain when other tests are normal. A recent National Institutes of Health (NIH) consensus conference addressing the clinical applications of ERCP emphasized that it is indicated for investigation of isolated abdominal pain only when equipment

and skills are available for concurrent therapy and for manometric investigation for potential sphincter of Oddi dysfunction.[3]

Preparation

Pancreatography may be performed alone or in concert with diagnostic or therapeutic endoscopic cholangiography (ERCP). Patient preparation, sedation, and positioning for pancreatography are all the same as for endoscopic cholangiography. Recommendations for fasting intervals before sedation and intubation are quite variable between centers.[4] Most patients are asked to fast overnight; however, those scheduled for afternoon procedures can generally be allowed a small clear liquid breakfast early in the day. Preprocedure antibiotics are indicated in any patient with known or suspected parenchymal necrosis; duct obstruction; duct leak; or filling of poorly drained fluid collections or spaces, such as peripancreatic fluid collections and pseudocysts.

Sedation for ERCP is usually accomplished by titrated parenteral administration of a narcotic and a benzodiazepine. Fentanyl is the

Table 41–1. Pancreatic Indications for Endoscopic Retrograde Cholangiopancreatography

Abdominal pain and/or laboratory or imaging studies suggesting pancreatic disease
History of acute pancreatitis of uncertain etiology
Current severe acute gallstone pancreatitis
Known pancreatic cancer, for palliation
Known or suspected pancreatic fistula or leak
Pancreatic insufficiency or malabsorption
Chronic pancreatitis, with pain, jaundice, or leak—for therapy or preoperative assessment
Pancreatic pseudocyst—for therapy or preoperative assessment
Recurrent abdominal pain, for manometry for suspected sphincter of Oddi dysfunction

narcotic of choice for most gastrointestinal endoscopy; however, compared with meperidine, it has a shorter half-life and a greater stimulatory effect on the sphincter of Oddi.[5,6] Fentanyl is thus less advantageous for performance of ERCP and meperidine (Demerol) tends to be the narcotic of choice. Midazolam (Versed) is the usual benzodiazepine for all gastrointestinal endoscopy, including performance of ERCP. Midazolam has been shown to reduce sphincter of Oddi pressures,[7,8] and is therefore not recommended during sphincter of Oddi manometry. Diazepam (Valium) does not influence the normotensive sphincter of Oddi, but little is known regarding its effects on the hypertensive sphincter. It is the preferred agent during manometric procedures.[9] Propofol has recently become a popular agent for use during endoscopy by virtue of its extremely rapid induction and reversal and the deep sedation achieved. It is most often used in concert with anesthesia specialists. Propofol does not appear to influence sphincter pressures at commonly used doses and hence can be used for all aspects of ERCP practice.[10]

Optimal positioning for pancreatography is the same as for cholangiography. A fully anterior posterior (AP) view is usually optimal for fluoroscopic and radiographic imaging. When using fixed upright RF (radiography-fluoroscopy) tables, this requires having the patient in a prone or supine position. Either can be used at times; however, endoscopes are adapted for approaching the papilla during prone intubation and the risk for aspiration is least in this position as well. When using radiographic equipment with C-arm capabilities, the patient's position is less critical, because AP views can be obtained from most angles. The lateral decubitus position is better tolerated and potentially safer in many elderly or obese patients and in those with significant respiratory compromise.

Technique

Endoscope positioning within the duodenum is critical for efficient performance of cholangiography or pancreatography. For cholangiography, the optimal lens position is below the papilla looking upward or backward toward the proximal second portion of the duodenum. The cannula then follows an upward and slightly posterior trajectory to access the bile duct located in the 10 to 12 o'clock position relative to the papillary os. In contrast, for pancreatography via the major papilla, the optimal lens position is relatively en face to the papilla with a slightly anterior directed view. The cannula is then directed in a slightly forward and upward trajectory to access the pancreatic duct, which lies roughly between the 1 and 3 o'clock position relative to the papillary os[11] (Fig. 41-1). Cannulation of the major papilla is usually performed with the same equipment as is used in the biliary tree. After apparent cannulation, fluoroscopically guided contrast injection should be more judicious and gradual than in the biliary tree. The normal pancreatic duct has a much smaller volume than the bile duct and overfilling and injury can occur after relatively small volumes of contrast have been injected. Cannulation of normal side branches or of anomalous ductal systems can lead to overfilling of small segments almost immediately after injection is begun. Similarly, wire-guided cannulation must be more circumspect than in the bile duct, because wire-induced perforation of a side branch can occur early, before contrast

injection. Once appropriate position is confirmed within the desired system, more complete filling can commence.

When difficult anatomy, pathology, or pancreas divisum prevent performance of pancreatography from the major papilla, it can be accomplished via the minor papilla approximately 90% of the time.[12] The minor papilla is usually located 2 to 3 cm proximal and slightly anterior to the major papilla. It is usually more subtle than the major papilla and may not have an obvious opening. If identification of either the papilla or the os is difficult, secretin can be administered (0.5 to 1 U/kg intravenous [IV]) to stimulate the flow of pancreatic juice into the duodenum, which occurs within minutes of administration.[13] Methylene blue can be sprayed on the duodenal wall to facilitate visualization of the focal source of drainage of clear pancreatic juice.[14] Once identified, the minor papilla can be approached with a nearly en face view using either a semilong-scope position or an extremely short-scope position with slightly posterior orientation. Cannulation usually follows a slightly posterior and horizontal to mildly cephalad path. Smaller caliber accessories are usually needed to image and access the pancreatic duct via the minor papilla. Accessories working with wires ranging from 0.018- to 0.025-inch caliber are generally used. A catheter with a short blunt needle tip (Cremer Catheter, Wilson Cook Inc., Winston Salem, NC) is often used to obtain a pancreatogram from an impacted position. However, this device does not accept a guidewire. A tapered tip sphincterotome-wire combination may be necessary to allow flexion toward an optimal axis for either impacted contrast injection or wire entry.

Complications of Pancreatography

The complications of diagnostic pancreatography are similar to those seen with therapeutic pancreatography and ERCP in general; the major exception is the rarity of perforation and bleeding. Sedation- and intubation-related complications are undoubtedly similar. Pancreatitis is the dominant concern. The performance of pancreatography during ERCP is one of the most consistently positive risk factors identified in studies of procedural pancreatitis.[15] Some studies note an even higher incidence with overfilling to the point of acinarization. Investigation of patients with past episodes of pancreatitis, particularly if procedure related, and investigation of patients with suspected sphincter of Oddi dysfunction are also both risk factors for post-ERCP pancreatitis. Numerous studies have investigated medications and interventions intended to reduce the incidence of post-ERCP pancreatitis. Their details are beyond the scope of this chapter; however, on rigorous study most interventions have not proven useful.[15] Temporary prophylactic placement of a small-caliber pancreatic stent has been shown to reduce ERCP related pancreatitis or the severity of pancreatitis, in a variety of patient groups including those in whom needle-knife sphincterotomy is used to access the bile duct,[15] sphincterotomy is performed for treatment of sphincter of Oddi dysfunction,[16] sphincter dilation is performed for biliary stone removal,[17] and miscellaneous high-risk indicators including difficult cannulation are present.[18]

Infection is a risk of pancreatography in predictable subgroups of patients, particularly those with necrosis, duct leaks, and communicating

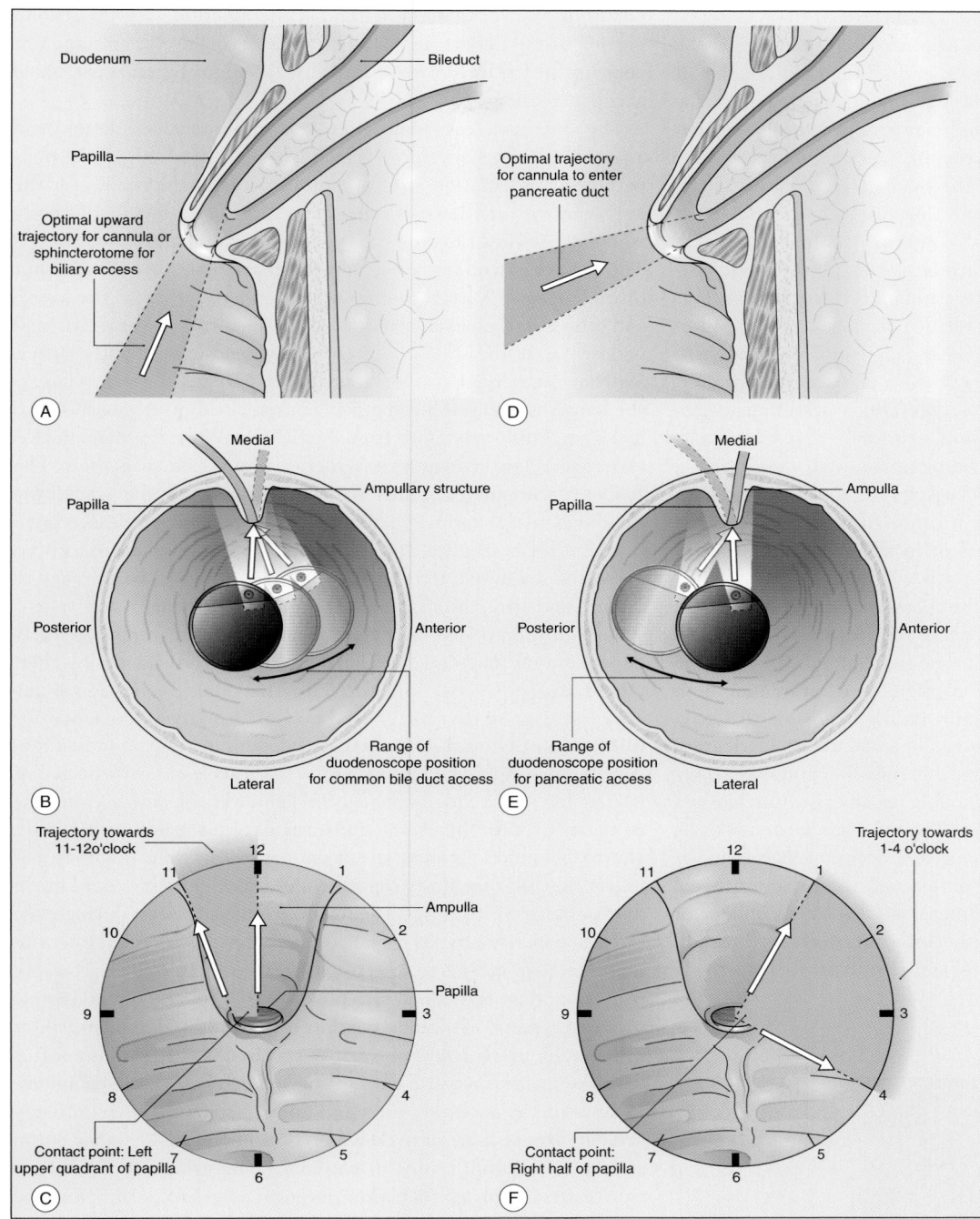

Figure 41–1. Optimal trajectories for cannulation of the bile duct *(A, B, C)* and the pancreatic duct *(D, E, F)* as projected in coronal *(A, D)*, transverse *(B, E)*, and en face *(C, F)* views.

cystic spaces (particularly pseudocysts). Although minimal data exist guiding the use of antibiotics in these settings, risk-to-benefit considerations suggest all of these patients should receive prophylactic antibiotics before and after ERCP. In the past, pancreatic pseudocysts were considered a relative contraindication to ERCP unless surgical drainage was planned within 24 hours. Experience has demonstrated less risk than this approach assumed,[19] but prudent practice uses antibiotic coverage and limits filling of spaces that will not be drained near term.

Normal Pancreatic Ductal Anatomy

Pancreatography provides a contrast enhanced radiographic image of the shape, caliber, and distribution of the pancreatic ducts. It does not image the parenchyma of the gland. Occasionally pancreatography grossly overestimates or underestimates the size of the gland based on the degree of filling accomplished at the time of imaging and the actual length and distribution of the ducts. The ducts of interest usually include: the main pancreatic duct of

Wirsung that drains from the tip of the tail through the pancreatic body and the ventral portion of the head to the major papilla; the accessory duct of Santorini, which extends from a major angle of the main duct, termed the genu, through the dorsal portion of the pancreatic head to the minor papilla; an intermittently present uncinate branch in the ventral portion of the head; and the many small side branches draining into the major and accessory ducts throughout the length of the gland. Terminology for the linear extremes of the pancreatic duct is sometimes confusing, because *proximal* and *distal* sometimes correlate with direction of flow (distal bile ducts are at the major papilla) but in the pancreas *proximal* and *distal* usually refer to relative distance from a point of reference at the duodenal wall (proximal pancreatic duct relative to or near the major papilla). In line with this classical use, surgical terminology uses *distal pancreatectomy* to refer to resections beginning with the tail. To avoid confusion, especially that which may occur among three specialties providing procedural, radiographic, and surgical interpretations, it is clarifying to speak of *upstream* segments or locations as being toward the tail relative to another location, and *downstream* segments or locations as being toward the duodenum.[20]

Globally, in the AP projection, the pancreatogram extends in an oblique fashion from the tail, located left of the spine at the T12 level, to the major papilla located right of the spine at the L2 level (Fig. 41–2). However, there is significant variation in both overall extent and the course of individual portions of the main duct. Within the head, the duct runs cephalad about 15 degrees from parallel to the spine; in the body, it runs horizontally or perpendicular to the spine; and in the tail, it usually rises further at a gentle angle but may even descend.[21] The tail segment tends to be the most variable in course and shape. On occasion, it is bifid, or split, left of the spine. In the AP projection, the retroperitoneal main pancreatic duct appears two-dimensional. However, oblique or lateral views demonstrate that it begins posteriorly in the tail, extends anteriorly around the spine, and then back to a relatively

posterior position at the genu and at the junction with the second portion of the duodenum. This excursion is highly variable and not very useful for interpretation of displacement by adjacent space occupying lesions.[22]

The main pancreatic duct is smooth with minor undulations and a general decline in caliber from the head to the tail. Focal non-pathologic indentations are sometimes noted at the genu, near the approximate junction with the accessory duct, and in the body where it is in close proximity to the superior mesenteric vasculature.[23] The former is well described but uncommon and the latter is not often reported. A large number of studies have reported the length and caliber of the pancreatic duct as obtained from postmortem and endoscopic studies.[24] Postmortem values tend to be slightly higher. With age, the duct caliber appears to increase slightly, whereas the length is stable. The length in normal glands averages about 16 to 17 cm, but it may range from 9 to 24 cm. When the main duct is less than 9 cm in length, obstruction should be suspected. The caliber of the pancreatic duct is most variable within the head of the gland, where the normal diameter is 3 to 4 mm but may range up to 6 mm, after correction for radiographic magnification. Accepted corrected diameters for the body and tail are 2 to 3 mm (range to 5 mm), and 1 to 2 mm (range to 3 mm), respectively.[25]

Visualization of side branches during pancreatography is largely dependent on technique and adequacy of contrast injection. Their visualization may be immaterial to the clinical question being addressed, or it may be critical and of primary importance for resolution of clinical issues. Hence, depending on the indication, lack of side-branch filling may not be indicative of a suboptimal or inadequate study. Side branches are highly variable and asymmetric in the pancreatic head but quite regular and symmetrical, with alternating junctions along the main duct throughout the body and tail. A postmortem study reported a mean of 56 first-order branch ducts (range 52 to 66).[26] Far fewer are usually seen during even forceful pancreatography. A single large inferiorly directed uncinate branch is seen in 55% to 62% of pancreatograms.[23,27] The accessory pancreatic duct is demonstrated in only 14% to 62% of endoscopic pancreatograms, although postmortem studies demonstrate its presence in up to 100% of autopsy specimens.[24] It communicates with the main pancreatic duct in approximately 90% of specimens. Patency of the accessory duct and minor papilla together is highly variable. It is seen in more than 60% of general ERCP studies but in as few as 17% of studies in patients being evaluated for biliary pancreatitis, implying that when patent it serves to decompress the briefly obstructed main pancreatic duct.

Pancreatic Duct Variants

The pancreatic ducts are highly subject to abnormal formation during embryogenesis (Fig. 41–3). Most variants are of no clinical consequence, other than recognition when identified during diagnostic studies. However, several variants are associated with the risk of occurrence of pain or pancreatitis based on partial obstruction to flow of pancreatic juice after major stimulation. The most important and common variants occur as a result of either

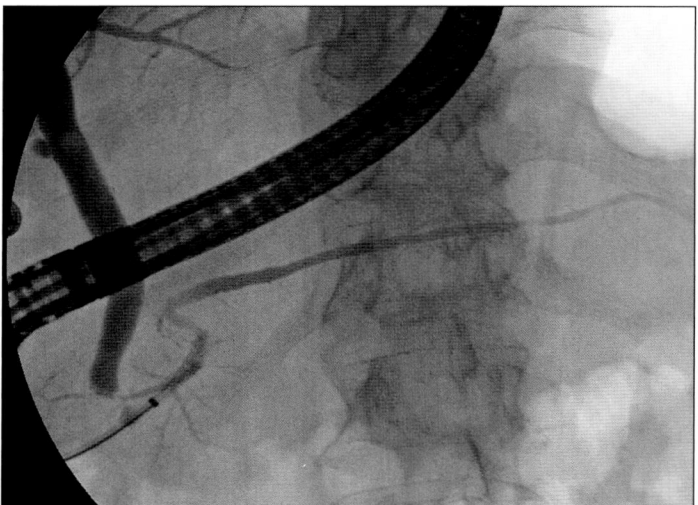

Figure 41–2. Radiograph demonstrating a normal pancreatogram.

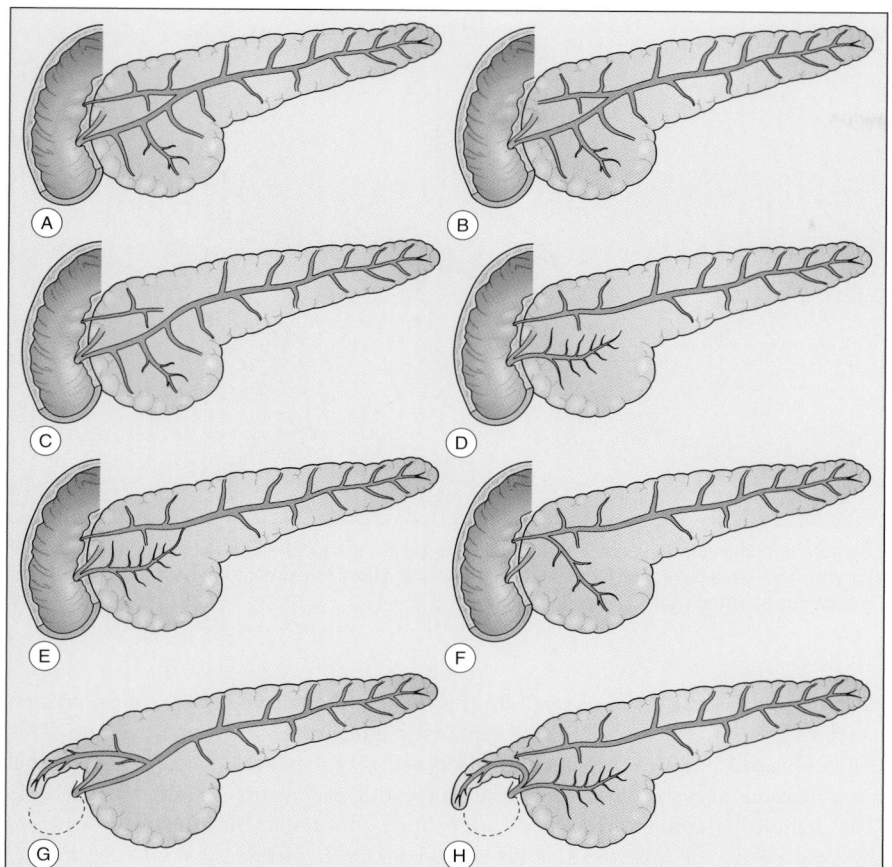

Figure 41-3. Variations in dorsal and ventral duct migration and fusion. *A,* Normal. *B,* Normal with imperforate minor papilla. *C,* Normal with dysjunction of the accessory duct. *D,* Pancreas divisum. *E,* Incomplete pancreas divisum. *F,* Pancreas divisum with no ventral duct. *G,* Annular pancreas with normal fusion. *H,* Annular pancreas with associated pancreas divisum.

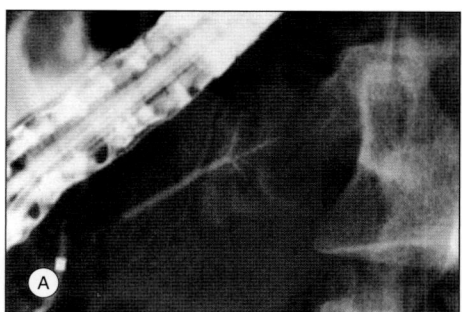

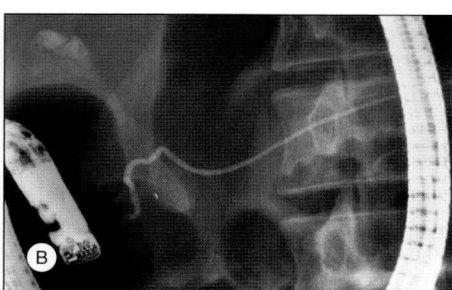

Figure 41-4. Radiograph of a pancreatogram demonstrating pancreas divisum. The ventral duct fills via injection into the duct of Wirsung at the major papilla *(A).* The dorsal duct fills via injection into the duct of Santorini at the minor papilla *(B).*

malrotation or malfusion of the ventral and/or dorsal embryonic pancreatic anlage. Normally, during the 6th to 8th week of embryogenesis, the smaller ventral pancreas rotates posteromedially as the duodenum rotates and migrates laterally. Once in a medial position neighboring the larger dorsal pancreas, the parenchyma and ducts fuse, yielding a main pancreatic duct comprised of both dorsal and ventral segments.

Failure of normal rotation and migration can yield an annular pancreas, in which some portion of the ventral pancreas remains behind in the path of migration. The band of incompletely migrated duct and associated parenchyma typically form a partial to complete

ring around the second portion of the duodenum, just proximal to the major papilla. Many cases remain asymptomatic, but more extreme variants can cause partial duodenal obstruction in infancy, childhood, or even adulthood. The preferred treatment for intestinal obstruction is duodenal bypass, rather than excision of the offending segment. Annular pancreas may also cause episodic pancreatitis, but its association with other abnormalities makes interpretation of the exact etiology uncertain. Approximately one third of cases are associated with pancreas divisum as well.

Pancreas divisum is the most common and important of the congenital variants (Fig. 41–4). It occurs as a result of incomplete

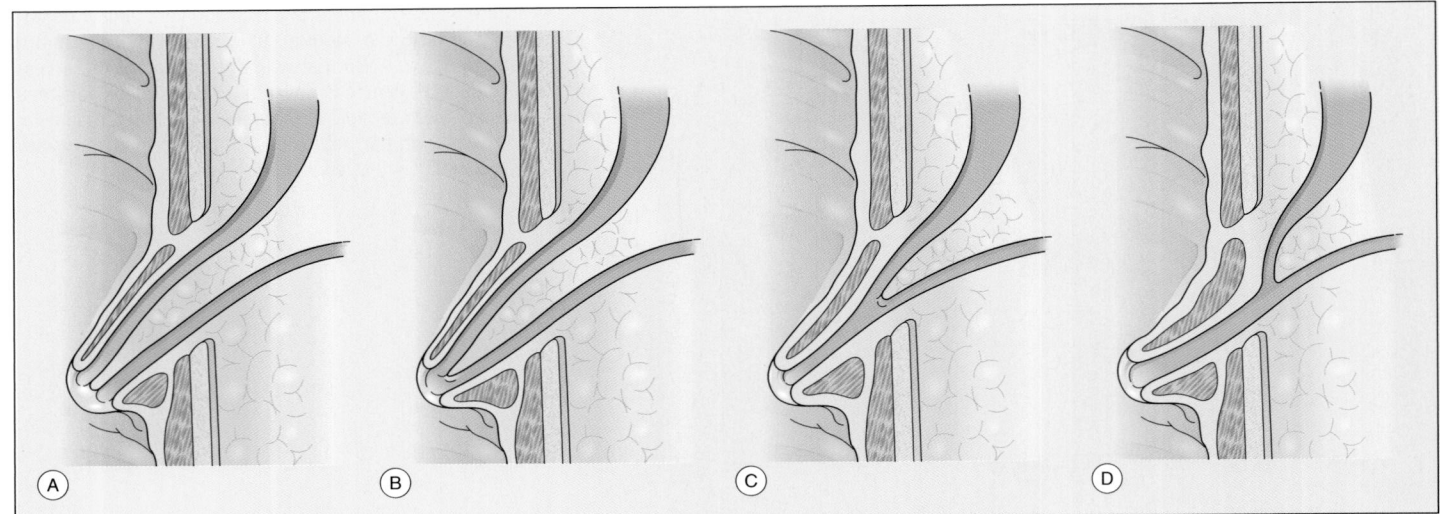

Figure 41–5. Variations in the pancreaticobiliary junction. *A,* Separate openings on one papilla (infrequent). *B,* Fusion immediately at the duodenal surface of the papillary os (common). *C,* Fusion within a combined sphincter with a variable common channel length (usual). *D,* Fusion proximal to the ampullary sphincter yielding a common channel of greater than 15 mm (so-called anomalous pancreaticobiliary junction) (rare).

fusion of the ventral and dorsal ducts after migration of the ventral anlage. Pancreas divisum occurs in approximately 7% (1% to 14%) of autopsy and pancreatography series. Approximately 20% of cases are incompletely divided, with persisting tiny communications via side branches of the dorsal and ventral systems. The technical approach to pancreatography via the minor papillae has been described previously. In pancreas divisum, the ventral duct may be generous, small, or even nonexistent in up to 30% of cases. It should appear finely tapering with gradually smaller side branches, suggesting the appearance of a delicate Christmas tree. Abrupt termination of the main duct should prompt concern about a potential obstructing lesion. Dorsal ductography and EUS usually resolve this question.

The clinical importance of pancreas divisum relates to the fact that it precludes full evaluation of the dorsal ducts during pancreatography via the major papilla, it mimics and must be differentiated from small focal lesions obstructing the ducts near the junction of the ventral and dorsal systems, and, when accompanied by relative stenosis of the minor papillae, it may contribute to partial outflow obstruction resulting in episodes of acute pancreatitis or even solitary pain. Whether pancreas divisum causes important clinical problems is highly controversial. If so, the identification of the subset of patients in whom this relatively frequent anomaly produces clinical symptoms is a persistent challenge, because only a minority have a grossly abnormal dorsal pancreatogram. Delayed drainage during ductography and the use of secretin stimulation to identify prolonged duct dilation attributable to sphincter stenosis have not proven useful.

The junction between the pancreatic duct and the bile duct at the major papilla is also highly variable (Fig. 41–5). Differences in junctional anatomy are primarily important for the challenges they present during selective cannulation of one or the other system during ERCP. A so-called anomalous pancreaticobiliary junction exists when the ducts unite proximal to the pancreatic sphincter and

the duodenal wall. In this setting, there is no barrier for prevention of reflux of bile or pancreatic juice into the alternate system. This abnormality has been associated with the development of choledochal cystic dilation and acute idiopathic pancreatitis. Whether endoscopic sphincterotomy is adequately efficacious remains questionable, because the junction is often above the boundary of safe incision.

Duct duplications, with the resulting appearance of a bifid system, occur most commonly in the body and tail.[28] They may be associated with unusual patterns of glandular parenchyma, but they are generally of no clinical consequence.

Periampullary Pathology Related to Pancreatic Disease

Pathologic appearances of the ampulla, the papilla of Vater, and the medial wall of the duodenum can be due to intrinsic conditions or can reflect underlying pathology within the neighboring pancreas or the pancreatic ducts. The most common extrinsic causes of an abnormal appearance are changes related to underlying malignancy or pancreatitis. Cancer within the head of the pancreas often encroaches on the periampullary region, causing mucosal and ampullary swelling, induration, and inflammation. In the absence of malignant ulceration, the changes are nonspecific and similar to those seen with underlying severe acute or subacute pancreatitis. Severe pancreatitis often produces more prominent and widespread edema of the duodenal mucosa as well.

Changes of the papillary os are relatively uncommon and usually seen after stone passage from the bile duct. Transpapillary passage of white chalky pancreatic stones from the pancreatic duct is rarely seen endoscopically but has been noted during investigation of obstructive cholangitis in patients with chronic calcific pancreatitis and duct stones.[29] Observation of thick plugs of mucus extruding

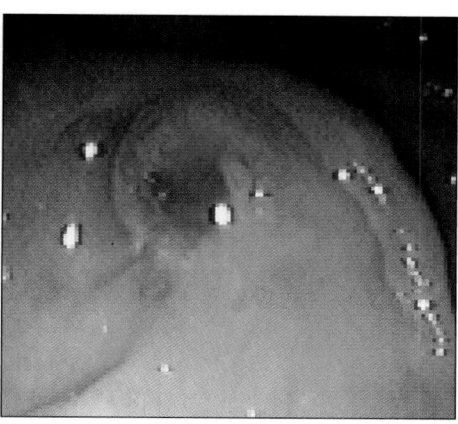

Table 41–2. Pathologic Patterns and Their Common Etiologies Seen During Pancreatography

Filling Defects
Stones (chronic pancreatitis)
Mucus (secreted by intraductal tumors)
Papillary tumors
Parasites

Abnormalities in Duct Caliber or Contour
Obstruction or stricture (tumor, stone, benign inflammatory lesions, extrinsic compression)
Dilation (downstream obstruction, intraductal mucus or stones)
Irregularity (acute or chronic pancreatitis)

Duct Leaks
Free leaks (trauma, surgery, endoscopy, acute or chronic pancreatitis)
Contained leaks (acute or chronic pancreatitis)
Fistulas (surgery, acute or chronic pancreatitis)

Filling into Cystic Spaces
Extrapancreatic spaces (pseudocysts)
Intrapancreatic spaces (pseudocysts, communicating cystic neoplasms, side-branch IPMN)

IPMN, intraductal papillary mucin-producing neoplasm.

Figure 41–6. Endoscopic image of mucus extruding from the major papilla in a patient with intraductal papillary mucin-producing neoplasm (IPMN) of the pancreas.

from a dilated papillary os is pathognomonic of intraductal papillary mucin-producing neoplasm (IPMN) of either the bile duct or the pancreatic duct.[30] The latter is far more common (Fig. 41–6).

Pathologic Patterns Seen During Pancreatography

During pancreatography, recognition of pathologic changes requires familiarity with both normal findings and patterns of abnormalities that might be encountered. The variety of potential findings is relatively limited in spectrum, and includes: (1) filling defects, (2) abnormalities in duct caliber or contour, (3) duct leaks, and (4) filling into cystic spaces. Each abnormality carries a differential of possible causes, many of which overlap or contribute to multiple abnormalities (Table 41–2). Filling defects include stones, parasites, and mucus secreted by IPMNs. Abnormalities in contour include partial or complete obstruction, duct dilation, and focal or diffuse irregularities resulting from malignancy or benign inflammatory processes. Leaks can be free, contained, or communicating with other organs as fistulas and occur as a result of trauma, surgery, endoscopy, and acute or chronic pancreatitis. Filling of cystic spaces can be within or extrinsic to the pancreas and may be associated with pseudocysts, central areas of necrosis within solid lesions, and communicating cystic neoplasms.

Pancreatic Neoplasia

Pancreatography is a key means of identifying neoplastic lesions of the pancreas. Pancreatic carcinoma produces several characteristic duct abnormalities, most of which are nonspecific and must be differentiated from similar changes resulting from chronic pancreatitis. Patterns include complete obstruction, focal stricturing or stenosis, diffuse or lengthy segmental narrowing of moderate degree,

distortion or obliteration of side branches, and stenosis with entry into necrotic cystic spaces.[31] Overt obstruction and focal strictures are the two dominant patterns. Obstruction related to cancer may appear blunt, serrated, or abruptly pointed, whereas that related to chronic pancreatitis may appear more smooth or even rounded, as with a meniscus sign related to intraductal stones. Malignant strictures tend to be more abrupt, with irregular contours, whereas those from chronic pancreatitis are either very short and suggestive of focal weblike scars or lengthy and smoothly tapered.[32] In malignant obstruction or stenosis, the side branches are commonly absent near the lesion, dilated upstream from the obstruction, and normal downstream. In chronic pancreatitis, the side branches are intact but perhaps abnormal near the main duct lesion, and the main duct and side branches exhibit either dilation or chronic distortion upstream and changes of chronic pancreatitis downstream from the obstruction.

The presence of concomitant neighboring abnormalities in both the pancreatic and bile ducts is highly suggestive of malignancy. Findings may include dual obstruction or stenosis (double duct sign), displacement by tethering or compression, and effacement.[33] The double duct sign is highly suggestive and should be considered diagnostic of cancer until proven otherwise (Fig. 41–7). Lesions in the head are often first brought to attention by associated biliary obstruction and jaundice or pruritus. In this setting, ERCP often accesses the biliary obstruction for both tissue sampling and palliative stent placement. If computed tomography (CT) or ultrasonography (US) is diagnostic of cancer, pancreatography is usually not necessary. If no mass has been seen by cross-sectional imaging when ERCP demonstrates a distal biliary stricture, it is very useful to obtain a full pancreatogram at least within the pancreatic head, ideally including both uncinate and accessory branches. Cases of pancreatic carcinoma involving a nonfilling accessory duct, with an otherwise normal pancreatogram, have been reported.[34]

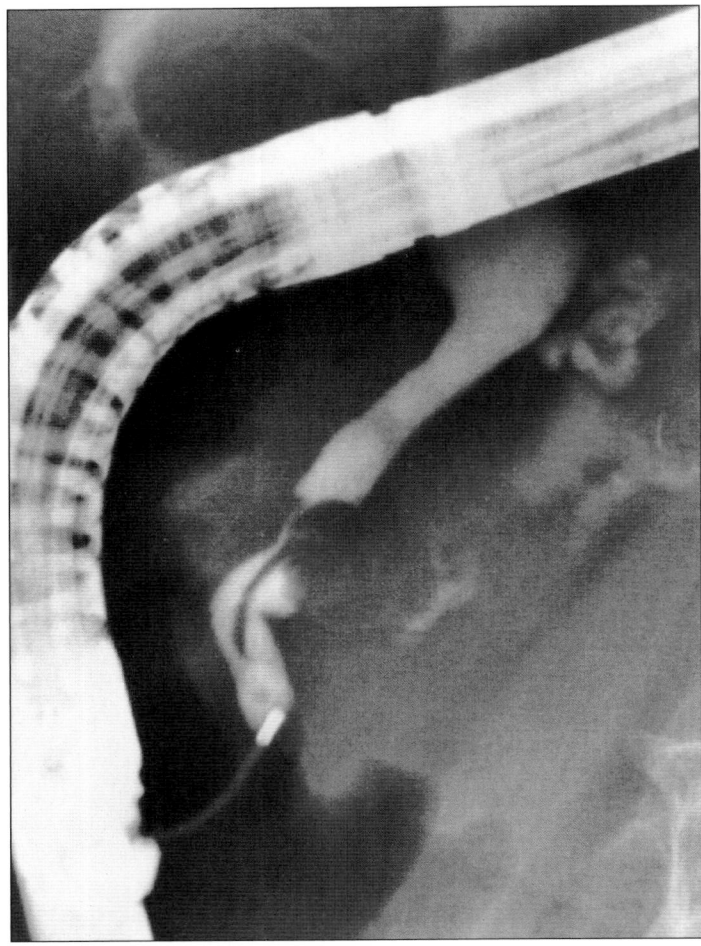

Figure 41-7. Radiograph of the double duct sign showing concurrent biliary and pancreatic duct obstruction, seen here with unusual deviation of both ducts produced by a small tumor of the periampullary region.

Among the pancreatic neoplasms, findings with IPMNs of the pancreatic ducts are among the most specific.[30] The characteristic production of mucus may occur silently, with eventual identification of dilated segments on cross-sectional imaging, or it may present clinically with episodes of pain or pancreatitis related to intermittent obstruction.[35] When IPMN involves the main pancreatic duct, pancreatography typically demonstrates dilation and soft and bulky filling defects that can be stripped from the lumen with an occlusion balloon. When present only in side branches, the diagnosis is commonly suspected after cross-sectional imaging with CT or US. Contrast filling of segments harboring side-branch IPMN may require forceful injection above an occlusion balloon. This maneuver increases the risk of pancreatitis and may not be justified, given the improving identification of this process by EUS. Gross papillary changes of the duct lining mucosa are not often evident radiographically but, when present, can be sampled with transpapillary biopsy and brushing to diagnose IPMN. Transpapillary pancreatoscopy and intraductal ultrasonography (IDUS) during ERCP have both been described as useful in preoperative staging the longitudinal spread of main duct IPMN.[36,37] Mucus markedly distorts the endoscopic view, but wire-guided IDUS identifies both the mucus and papillary changes if they are accessible. None of these endoscopic

tools are highly sensitive for identifying the progression to invasive malignancy.[38]

Pancreatography in Acute Pancreatitis

Relative consensus now exists regarding the use of endoscopic cholangiography for acute pancreatitis. Despite the known risk of pancreatitis as a result of ERCP, performance of cholangiography in the setting of acute pancreatitis has been shown to be generally safe.[39] Cholangiography and sphincterotomy, as indicated by findings, are now accepted in the setting of acute severe pancreatitis with associated biliary obstruction or cholangitis.[40] They may also be beneficial for severe biliary pancreatitis without biliary obstruction; however, data are mixed on this point,[41,42] and one study suggested detrimental effects in this setting.[43]

Subsequent to resolution of one or more episodes of acute pancreatitis, pancreatography is useful for identification of potential etiologies, including biliary stone disease, anomalous anatomy (pancreas divisum, anomalous junction, etc.), occult neoplasia, or chronic pancreatitis among others.[44] Venu reported use of ERCP and sphincter of Oddi manometry in 116 patients with recurrent idiopathic pancreatitis. A treatable cause of pancreatitis was identified in 37%, including a mixture of anatomic abnormalities, stones, and sphincter hypertension. As previously described, evolving guidelines propose that in this elective setting ERCP should only be performed if skills for therapy and performance of sphincter of Oddi manometry are also available.

The use of pancreatography during episodes of severe acute pancreatitis is generally not indicated. However, smoldering pancreatitis that is not resolving and late morbidity related to strictures or leaks after improvement in the most severe inflammatory process are both settings in which pancreatography, and associated therapies, may be of benefit.[45-48] Nonspecific findings that may be seen during acute pancreatitis, for which intervention is not indicated, include increased irregularity in contour of the main duct and side branches; perhaps less prompt filling of side branches; and occasional early parenchymal staining even before side-branch filling, suggestive of local necrosis.

Duct leaks and strictures resulting from acute pancreatitis occur most often near the genu and likely relate to focal necrosis at that site. Leaks identified within the first few weeks appear free within the retroperitoneum, whereas those identified at a later date enter more circumscribed spaces or mature pseudocysts. The timing of onset for duct leaks remains incompletely defined. Data from Neoptolemos and coworkers[49] suggested that most leaks occur after the 4th day. They retrospectively stratified patients to modest versus extensive (>25%) glandular necrosis by CT scan and then determined the incidence and timing of duct leaks, based on pancreatography. No leaks were found among 89 patients with limited necrosis. In contrast, 7 of 16 patients in the extensive necrosis group exhibited leaks, including none of 4 patients studied before day 5 and 7 of 12 studied at day 5 or later. In a prospective study of pancreatic duct integrity during acute pancreatitis, Uomo and colleagues[50] demonstrated a 31% incidence of leaks by pancreatography performed during the 1st week (mean 4.2 days). Leaks did not correlate with need for surgical management. In both acute and chronic pancreatitis, it is useful to clarify whether leaks are being potentiated by downstream obstruction related to strictures or stones, because this has implications for both endoscopic and surgical management. The details of the therapeutic interventions are beyond the scope of this chapter.

There is growing interest in the potential utility of early investigation and prophylactic intervention, or early treatment, for significant duct injury in severe necrotizing pancreatitis.[51] However, there are currently only limited data to support this approach, and the potential for secondary infection of necrosis and peripancreatic tissues mandates that prospective studies be performed before this becomes common practice.

Pancreatography in Chronic Pancreatitis

The indications for pancreatography in chronic pancreatitis have been reviewed. They include: to establish a diagnosis, to characterize the anatomy before surgical management, and as a component of endoscopic therapy. Pancreatography has been the gold standard for diagnosing chronic pancreatitis for several decades. Several classification systems for chronic pancreatitis have been proposed. Although none are perfect or all encompassing, the Cambridge Classification of 1983 proposed a sequential gradation of pancreatograms[20] that remains perhaps the most straightforward and widely used to this day. Pancreatograms are termed normal; equivocal; or indicative of mild, moderate, or marked pancreatitis on the basis of side-branch abnormalities, main duct abnormalities, or additional advanced irregularities including presence of cavities, complete obstruction, filling defects (stones), severe dilation (>1 cm), and segmentation ("chain of lakes") (Figs. 41–8 and 41–9). The severity of pancreatographic findings correlates loosely with progression of disease and decline in pancreatic function. The main challenges in the interpretation of pancreatography for the diagnosis of chronic pancreatitis are the differentiation of normal from early disease with minimal changes and the differentiation of pancreatic carcinoma from chronic disease with focal stricturing. Comments on the latter have been made in prior segments. Mild changes on pancreatography—blunting, dilation, or shortening of the side branches—are the least specific and most subjective as they are highly dependent on technique and adequacy of filling, and potentially a result of age related changes or transient effects of acute injury. Endoscopic pancreatography is more sensitive for early changes of chronic pancreatitis than are CT, transabdominal US, or magnetic resonance cholangiopancreatography (MRCP). Endoscopic ultrasonography (EUS) is both highly sensitive for early chronic pancreatitis and safe.[52] In centers with adequate EUS experience, it is becoming the procedure of choice for making this diagnosis when CT or MRCP are normal.

Pancreatic duct morphology is best characterized by pancreatography; hence, this remains the procedure of choice for anatomic characterization before surgery or in concert with other less invasive therapies for pseudocysts, fistulas, leaks, and pancreatic ascites

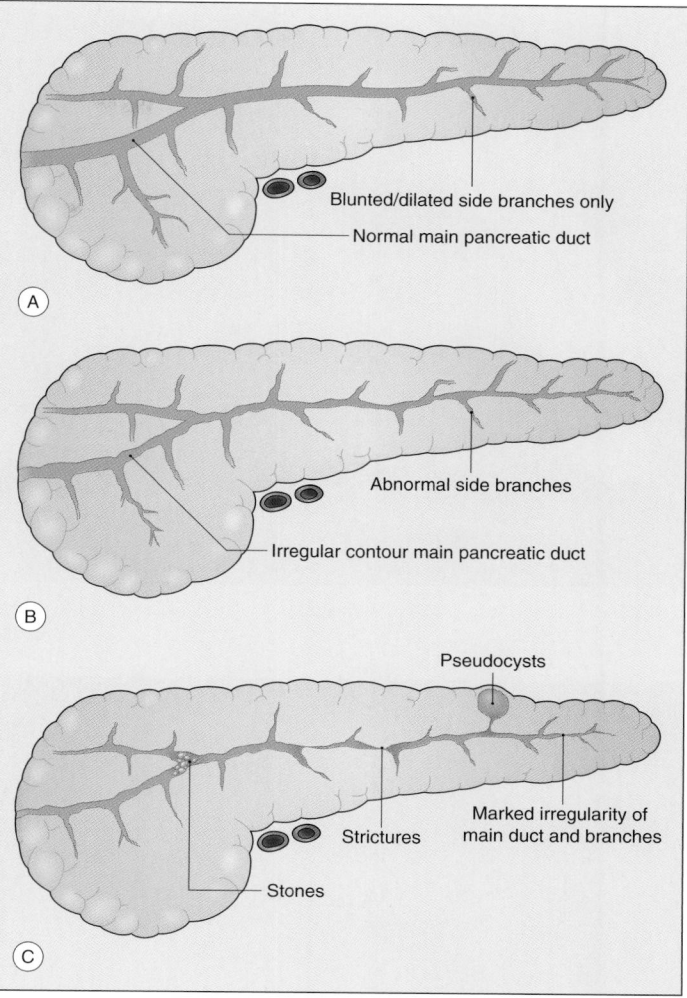

Figure 41–8. Cambridge classification of chronic pancreatitis. *A,* Mild. *B,* Moderate. *C,* Marked.

related to chronic or postnecrotic pancreatitis.[53,54] In a prospectively documented series of 41 patients with pseudocysts associated with chronic or resolving acute pancreatitis, Nealon and coworkers[55] showed that preoperative ERCP led to significant alterations in the surgical management in 24 patients (59%). In particular, ERCP led to pseudocyst drainage combined with concurrent drainage of the pancreatic duct in 19 patients and of the common bile duct in 11 patients with chronic pancreatitis. In the current era of transmural and transpapillary endoscopic drainage of pseudocysts, the role of endoscopic characterization of the pancreatic duct remains incompletely defined. Its utility is likely to be equivalent or greater than when used in concert with surgery.

Miscellaneous Settings

After pancreatic surgery, questions pertaining to anastomotic leaks are often best answered by pancreatography (Fig. 41–10). Duct decompression and drainage are feasible at the same procedure, much like what was described for acute and chronic pancreatitis leaks. Resection procedures generally yield leaks at closure lines of

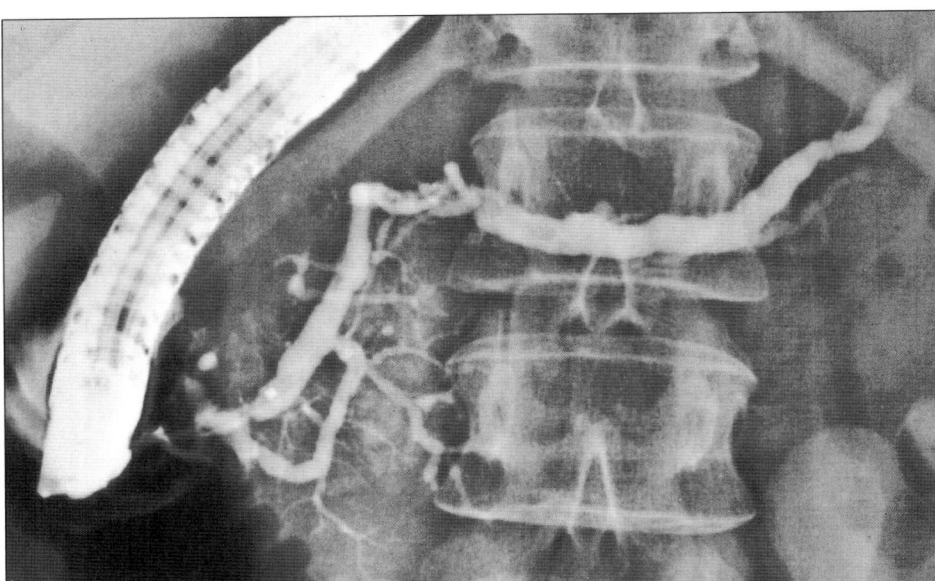

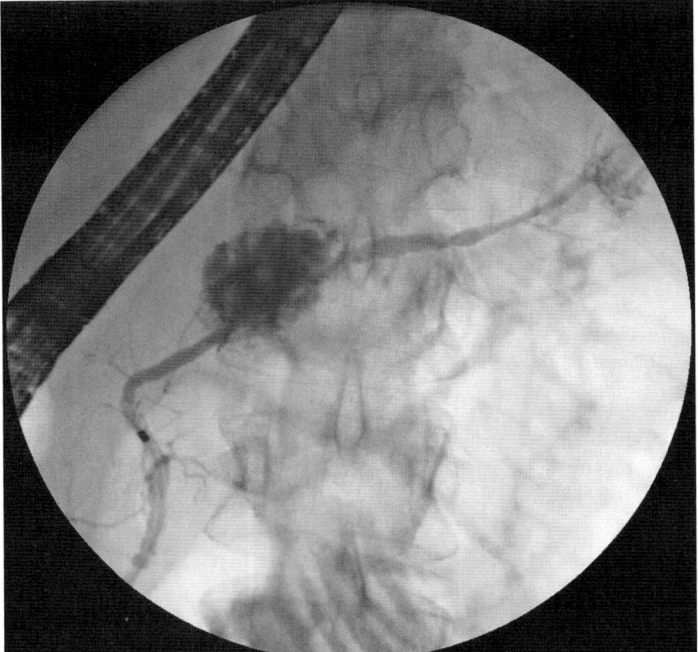

Figure 41-10. Pancreatogram showing a postoperative leak from region of the genu subsequent to enucleation of a neighboring small benign tumor.

main ducts, whereas surgical enucleation or excision procedures are more prone to smaller side branch or lateral main duct leaks. Pancreatography may also be useful for investigation and therapy of late postoperative anastomotic strictures after Whipple resections or lateral pancreatico-jejunostomy drainage. Similarly, pancreatography is very useful during investigation of blunt midabdominal trauma, from which midpancreatic duct leaks can occur because of rupture of the gland over the spine. Identification and localization of traumatic leaks can guide surgical[56,57] or endoscopic management.

Magnetic Resonance Pancreatography

Each of the imaging modalities for the pancreas is imbued with particular benefits and shortcomings. Endoscopic pancreatography is relatively invasive and carries moderate to significant risk, but it also provides the opportunity for efficient therapy of lesions identified during the same study. EUS is relatively invasive but safer than ERCP. EUS offers opportunity for sampling but, to date, negligible therapeutic options other than injection of anesthetics or ablative agents for neurolysis. Both CT and MRCP provide optimal non-invasive imaging of the parenchyma and the neighboring organs. Based on differentiation of fluid density, MRCP more easily provides a diagnostic quality pancreatogram as well. However, neither are therapeutic modalities.

Performance of MRCP is predominantly dependent on the strength of the magnet and the use of sophisticated software algorithms for generating optimal views of the region of interest. Magnetic resonance pancreatography (MRP) has slightly less spatial resolution than does endoscopic pancreatography, but optimal performance approaches that of endoscopic studies and is generally adequate for clinical decision making.[58] MRP is highly accurate for demonstration of pancreas divisum.[59] In chronic pancreatitis, MR can demonstrate glandular and periglandular atrophy and inflammation, in addition to the status of the ducts. The duct distention and higher spatial resolution of ERCP yield more optimal imaging of fine detail and side branches. Secretin stimulation during MRCP can enhance distention and interpretation of both duct detail and assessment of parenchymal function.[60] In a retrospective study of 32 patients who underwent ERCP, CT, and abdominal US for advanced chronic pancreatitis, Varghese and colleagues[61] assessed dual interpretations of MRP. He reported sensitivity, specificity, and diagnostic accuracy for detection of filling defects in the pancreatic duct (56% to 78%, 100%, 87% to 94%), ductal strictures (75% to

88%, 92% to 96%, 88% to 94%), and of pseudocysts (100%, 100%, 100%). MR failed in two patients because of respiratory motion artifacts. Among all others, the duct was completely visualized in 84%, partially in 9%, and not at all in 6%. ERCP failed in two, resulting from Billroth II anatomy in one and a duct stricture and pseudocyst in another. ERCP was inadequate in five (6%) because of poor opacification of the duct, which was insufficient for diagnosis. There was good correlation between MRCP and ERCP with respect to duct size. He concluded that MR is poorly sensitive but specific for duct abnormalities and, when combined with CT or trans-abdominal US, sufficient for planning therapy in most patients with advanced chronic pancreatitis.

Helical CT and optimal MRCP are equivalent techniques for detection of pancreatic neoplasms, vascular invasion, and neighboring lymphadenopathy.[58] Cystic tumors and the contents of tumors and fluid collections are more accurately characterized with MR than with CT. MR to EUS comparisons are not yet available.

Most centers use MRCP (or CT) for diagnosis or characterization of advanced disease and for those patients who are not good candidates for sedation and intubation or in whom the clinical suspicion is quite low. Endoscopic pancreatography is reserved for those patients in whom subtler duct abnormalities are anticipated or endoscopic therapy is planned. Local preferences dictate which study is used for preoperative anatomic characterization.

REFERENCES

1. Lambert R, Rey JF: Appropriateness of diagnostic digestive endoscopy. Dig Dis 20:236–241, 2002.
2. American Society for Gastrointestinal Endoscopy: Appropriate use of gastrointestinal endoscopy. Gastrointest Endosc 52:831–837, 2000.
3. National Institutes of Health State-of-the-Science Conference statement (final statement: June 10, 2002): Endoscopic retrograde cholangiopancreatography (ERCP) for diagnosis and therapy, January 14–16, 2002. Available at: http://consensus.nih.gov/ta/020/020sos_statement.htm.
4. Warner MA, Caplan RA, Epstein BS, et al, for American Society of Anesthesiology: Practice guidelines for preoperative fasting and the use of pharmacologic agents to reduce the risk of pulmonary aspiration: Application to healthy patients undergoing elective procedures. Available at: http://www.asahq.org/publicationsAndServices/NPO.pdf.
5. Radnay PA, Brodman E, Mankikar D, Duncalf D: The effect of equianalgesic doses of fentanyl, morphine, meperidine, and pentazocine on common bile duct pressure. Anaesthetist 29:26–29, 1980.
6. Thune A, Baker RA, Saccone GT: Differing effects of pethidine and morphine on human sphincter of Oddi motility. Br J Surg 77:992–995, 1990.
7. Fazel A, Burton FR: The effect of midazolam on the normal sphincter of Oddi: A controlled study. Endoscopy 34:78–81, 2002.
8. Fazel A, Burton FR: A controlled study of the effect of midazolam on abnormal sphincter of Oddi motility. Gastrointest Endosc 55:637–640, 2002.
9. Ponce Garciia J, Garrigues V, Sala T, et al: Diazepam does not modify the motility of the sphincter of Oddi. Endoscopy 20:87, 1988.
10. Goff JS: Effect of propofol on human sphincter of Oddi. Dig Dis Sci 40:2364–2367, 1995.
11. Petersen BT: Cannulation techniques: Biliary and pancreatic. Tech Gastrointest Endosc 5:17–27, 2003.
12. Benage D, McHenry R, Hawes RH, et al: Minor papilla cannulation and dorsal ductography in pancreas divisum. Gastrointest Endosc 36:553–557, 1990.
13. O'Connor KW, Lehman GA: An improved technique for accessory papilla cannulation in pancreas divisum. Gastrointest Endosc 31:13–17, 1985.
14. Park SH, de Bellis M, McHenry L, et al: Use of methylene blue to identify the minor papilla or its orifice in patients with pancreas divisum. Gastrointest Endosc 57:358–363, 2003.
15. Freeman ML: Prevention of post-ERCP pancreatitis: Pharmacologic solution or patient selection and pancreatic stents? Gastroenterology 124:1977–1980, 2003.
16. Tarnasky P, Palesch YY, Cunningham JT, et al: Pancreatic stenting prevents pancreatitis after biliary sphincterotomy in patients with sphincter of Oddi dysfunction. Gastroenterology 115:1518–1524, 1998.
17. Aizawa T, Ueno N: Stent placement in the pancreatic duct prevents pancreatitis after endoscopic sphincter dilation for removal of bile duct stones. Gastrointest Endosc 54:209–213, 2001.
18. Fazel A, Quadri A, Catalano M, et al: Does a pancreatic duct stent prevent post-ERCP pancreatitis? A prospective randomized study. Gastrointest Endosc 57:291–294, 2003.
19. Kolars JC, O'Connor M, Ansel H, et al: Pancreatic pseudocysts: Clinical and endoscopic experience. Am J Gastroenterol 84:259–264, 1989.
20. Axon AT, Classen M, Cotton PB, et al: Pancreatography in chronic pancreatitis: International definitions. Gut 25:1107–1112, 1984.
21. Classen M, Hellwig H, Rosch W: Anatomy of the pancreatic duct: A duodenoscopic-radiological study. Endoscopy 5:14–17, 1973.
22. Varley PF, Rohrmann CA, Silvis SE, et al: The normal endoscopic pancreatograms. Radiology 118:295–300, 1976.
23. Sivak MV, Sullivan BH: Endoscopic retrograde pancreatography. Analysis of the normal pancreatogram. Dig Dis 21:263–269, 1976.
24. Sivak MV Jr: The normal retrograde pancreatogram and cholangiogram. In Sivak MV Jr (ed): Gastroenterologic Endoscopy, 2nd ed. Philadelphia, WB Saunders, 2000, pp 878–889.
25. Cotton PB: The normal endoscopic pancreatograms. Endoscopy 6:65–70, 1974.
26. Ishibashi T, Matsubara O: Studies on the retrograde pancreatography in autopsy specimens. Bull Tokyo Med Dent Univ 24:43–51, 1997.
27. Rienhoff WF Jr, Pickrell KL: Pancreatitis: An anatomic study of the pancreatic and extrahepatic biliary systems. Arch Surg 51:205–219, 1945.
28. Halpert RH, Shabot JM, Heare BR, Rogers RE: The biphid pancreas: A rare anatomical variation. Gastrointest Endosc 36:60–61, 1990.
29. Little TE. Kozarek RA: Pancreatic stones as a cause of bile duct and ampullary obstruction: Endoscopic treatment approaches.[comment]. Gastrointest Endosc 39:709–712, 1993.
30. Venu RP, Atia G, Brown RD, Rosenthal GM: Intraductal papillary mucinous tumor of the pancreas: ERCP, EUS, and pancreatoscopy findings. Gastrointest Endosc 55:82, 2002.
31. Fukumoto K, Nakajima M, Murakami K, Kawai K: Diagnosis of pancreatic cancer by endoscopic pancreatocholangiography. Am J Gastroenterol 62:210–213, 1974.
32. Rohrmann CA Jr, Silvis SE, Vennes JA: The significance of pancreatic ductal obstruction in differential diagnosis of the abnormal endoscopic retrograde pancreatogram. Radiology 121:311–314, 1976.
33. Freeny PC, Bilbao MK, Katon RM: "Blind" evaluation of endoscopic retrograde cholangiopancreatography (ERCP) in the diagnosis of pancreatic carcinoma: The "double duct" and other signs. Radiology 119:271–274, 1976.
34. Kowdley KV, Variyam EP, Sivak MV Jr: Obstructive jaundice caused by pancreatic carcinoma in the setting of a normal pancreatogram. Gastrointest Endosc 41:158–160, 1995.
35. Loftus EV Jr, Olivares-Pakzad BA, Batts KP, et al: Intraductal papillary-mucinous tumors of the pancreas: Clinicopathologic features, outcome, and nomenclature. Gastroenterology 110:1909–1918, 1996.

36. Hara T, Yamaguchi T, Ishihara T, et al: Diagnosis and patient management of intraductal papillary-mucinous tumor of the pancreas by using peroral pancreatoscopy and intraductal ultrasonography. Gastroenterology 122:34–43, 2002.

37. Yamao K, Ohashi K, Nakamura T, et al: Evaluation of various imaging methods in the differential diagnosis of intraductal papillary mucinous tumor (IPMT) of the pancreas. Hepatic Gastroenterol 48:962–966, 2001.

38. Cellier C, Cuillerier E, Palazzo L, et al: Intraductal papillary and mucinous tumors of the pancreas: Accuracy of preoperative computed tomography, endoscopic retrograde pancreatography and endoscopic ultrasonography, and long-term outcome in a large surgical series. Gastrointest Endosc 47:42–49, 1998.

39. Brambs HJ, Scholmerich J, Gross V, et al: Endoscopic retrograde cholangiopancreatography in acute pancreatitis. Dig Surg 5:156–159, 1988.

40. Fan ST, Lai EC, Mok FP, et al: Early treatment of acute biliary pancreatitis by endoscopic papillotomy. N Engl J Med 328:228–232, 1993.

41. Barkun AN: Early endoscopic management of acute gallstone pancreatitis—an evidence-based review. J Gastrointest Surg 5:243–250, 2001.

42. Neoptolemos JP, Carr-Locke DL, London NJ, et al: Controlled trial of urgent endoscopic retrograde cholangiopancreatography and endoscopic sphincterotomy versus conservative treatment for acute pancreatitis due to gallstones. Lancet 2:979–983, 1988.

43. Foelsch UR, Nitsche R, Luedtke R, et al, and the German Study Group on Acute Biliary Pancreatitis: Early ERCP and papillotomy compared with conservative treatment for acute biliary pancreatitis. N Engl J Med 336:237–242, 1997.

44. Venu RP, Geenen JE, Hogan W, et al: Idiopathic recurrent pancreatitis. An approach to diagnosis and treatment. Dig Dis Sci 34:56–60, 1989.

45. Kozarek RA: Endoscopic therapy of complete and partial pancreatic duct disruptions. Gastrointest Endosc Clin N Am 8:39–53, 1998.

46. Varadarajulu S, Noone T, Hawes R, Cotton PB: Pancreatic duct stent insertion for functional smoldering pancreatitis. Gastrointest Endosc 58:438–441, 2003.

47. Kozarek RA, Ball TJ, Patterson DJ, et al: Endoscopic transpapillary therapy for disrupted pancreatic duct and peripancreatic fluid collections. Gastroenterology 100:1362–1370, 1991.

48. Levy MJ, Geenen JE, Catalano MF, et al: Pancreatic duct stent therapy for "smoldering" pancreatitis. Gastrointest Endosc 51:AB203, 2000.

49. Neoptolemos JP, London NJ, Carr-Locke DL: Assessment of main pancreatic duct integrity by endoscopic retrograde pancreatography in patients with acute pancreatitis. Br J Surg 80:94–99, 1993.

50. Uomo G, Molino D, Visconti M, et al: The incidence of main pancreatic duct disruption in severe biliary pancreatitis. Am J Surg 176:49–52, 1998.

51. Lau ST, Simchuk EJ, Kozarek RA, Traverso LW: A pancreatic ductal leak should be sought to direct treatment in patients with acute pancreatitis. Am J Surg 181:411–415, 2001.

52. Sahai AV: EUS and chronic pancreatitis. Gastrointest Endosc 56:S76–S81, 2002.

53. O'Connor M, Kolars J, Ansel H, et al: Preoperative endoscopic retrograde cholangiopancreatography in the surgical management of pancreatic pseudocysts. Am J Surg 151:18–24, 1986.

54. Kuo Y, Wu C: The role of endoscopic retrograde pancreatography in pancreatic ascites. Dig Dis Sci 39:1143–1146, 1994.

55. Nealon WH, Townsend CM, Thompson JC: Preoperative endoscopic retrograde cholangiopancreatography (ERCP) in patients with pancreatic pseudocyst associated with resolving acute and chronic pancreatitis. Ann Surg 209:532–540, 1989.

56. Sugawa C, Lucas CE: The case for preoperative and intraoperative ERCP in pancreatic trauma. Gastrointest Endosc 34:145–147, 1988.

57. Plancq MC, Villamizar J, Ricard J, Canarelli JP: Management of pancreatic and duodenal injuries in pediatric patients. Pediatr Surg Int 16:35–39, 2000.

58. Reinhold C: Magnetic resonance imaging of the pancreas in 2001. J Gastrointest Surg 6:133–135, 2002.

59. Bret PM, Reinhold C, Taourel P, et al: Pancreas divisum: Evaluation with MR cholangiopancreatography. Radiology 199:99–103, 1996.

60. Manfredi R, Costamagna G, Brizi MG, et al: Severe chronic pancreatitis versus suspected pancreatic disease: Dynamic MR cholangiopancreatography after secretin stimulation. Radiology 214:849–855, 2000.

61. Varghese JC, Masterson A, Lee MJ: Value of MR pancreatography in the evaluation of patients with chronic pancreatitis. Clin Radiol 57:393–401, 2002.

Difficult Cannulation and Sphincterotomy

Juergen Hochberger

Introduction

In the era of magnetic resonance cholangiopancreatography and endosonography, ERCP has become a procedure with primarily therapeutic focus (e.g., access to and over stenoses, removal of stones or drainage of cysts).[1-7] If used as a diagnostic procedure, ERCP is mostly associated with additional sampling of tissue by the introduction of cytology brushes or biopsy forceps. Therefore, major papilla sphincterotomy is mandatory in most cases to achieve an adequate access for the introduction of instruments, drainage catheters, and so forth. General issues on cannulation and sphincterotomy have already been highlighted in Chapter 40. This chapter focuses on variations of the standard technique addressed to the advanced endoscopist. The variations in technique have to be carried out with caution and adapted to the individual case. Important general issues are discussed in the beginning of the chapter.

The Proper Endoscope

The standard endoscope for most indications is a therapeutic side-viewing duodenoscope with an instrumentation channel of 3.7 to 4.2 mm. Among the few situations in which a smaller diagnostic duodenoscope offers certain advantages are duodenal stenoses (e.g., in advanced chronic pancreatitis mostly resulting from scarring plus edema). Furthermore, for the examination of a pediatric patient younger than 2 years and in a case in which the papillary orifice is localized at the inner side of a duodenal diverticulum, a standard 11.5-mm duodenoscope may be advantageous. A disadvantage of the smaller scope is a channel of only 2.8 to 3.2 mm, which makes the implantation of 10- to 12-Fr stents and the use of two guidewires impossible respectively difficult. An argument in former times had always been the better deflection of the elevator (Albarran's lever) using standard 6- to 7-Fr catheters or tiny instruments. Changes in elevator design since the mid-1990s have eliminated this problem with therapeutic duodenoscopes. Thus, grooming of

standard catheters to facilitate cannulation of the common bile duct (CBD) is usually not necessary because the catheter can be deflected sufficiently by the elevator and the catheter automatically bends because of manipulation with the elevator.

Access to and cannulation of the papilla in case of a Billroth II (BII) resection (Figs. 42–1 and 42–2) is generally possible with comparable success rate using a prograde or a side-viewing endoscope and is described later (discussed in the section on the BII situation).[8-10] Although the prograde instrument (standard or therapeutic gastroscope) facilitates an easier intubation of the

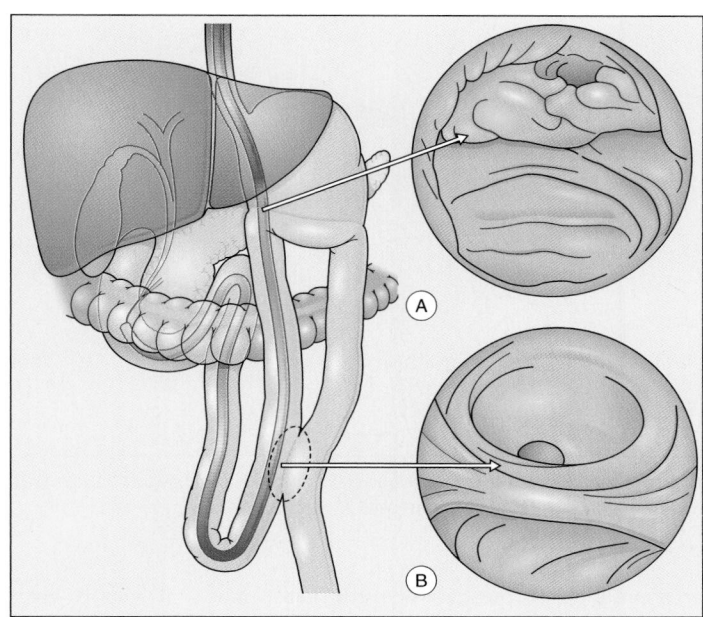

Figure 42–1. Billroth II anatomy: endoscopic access. Endoscopic view at the gastrojejunal *(A)* and enteroenteral (Braun) anastomosis *(B)*. Use afferent loop and stay at the same side of the enteral wall when you pass the enteroenteral anastomosis (oval). (Modified from ref 12, with permission.)

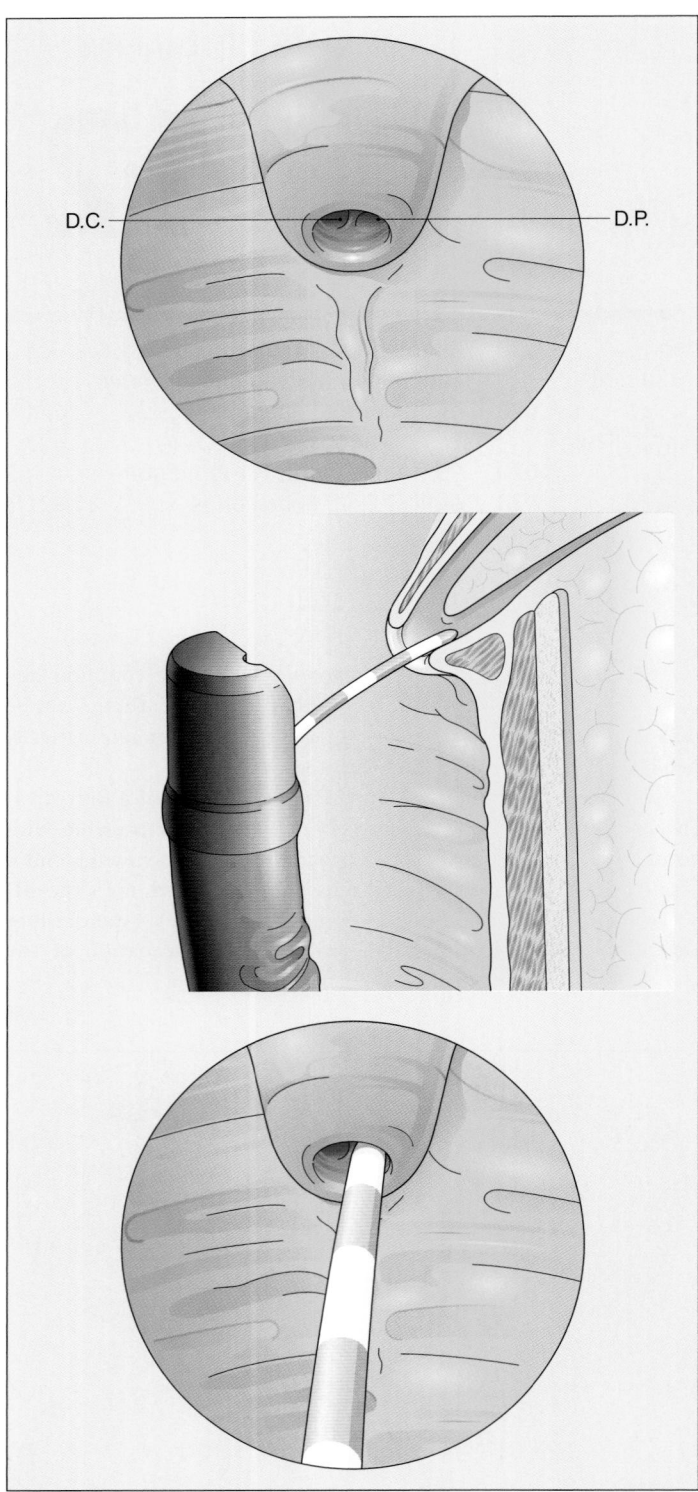

Figure 42-2. Billroth II cannulation. View onto the papilla from below with inverted anatomy. (Modified from ref 12, with permission.)

needle-knife sphincterotome for sphincterotomy. Therefore, the duodenoscope is preferred by many endoscopists if anatomically applicable. In a difficult anatomic situation with a steep angle to the afferent loop, it can be helpful to first place a 0.035-inch 400 to 450 cm Seldinger guidewire (e.g., PNB Medical, Denmark) into the blind proximal end of the duodenal stump with one or two guidewire loops under radiograph control and then to follow the pathfinder with the side-viewing instrument.

In patients with a very long afferent loop and in patients with a post-gastrectomy Roux-en-Y situation, a pediatric colonoscope or an enteroscope longer than 170 cm may be helpful.

Localizing the Papilla

Although the natural position of the papilla is on the inner side of the duodenal C in the middle of the second part of the duodenum, it may be difficult to find. The papilla may be located very caudally toward the lower duodenal knee, which often requires a very long endoscope position. The papilla can be covered by duodenal folds and often only the frenulum, as a caudal longitudinal fold, signals that the papillary orifice may be close. In the search for the papilla, an atraumatic ERCP catheter or sphincterotome can be helpful. Duodenal diverticula have to be inspected carefully, and sometimes the only way to expose the inner side of the diverticulum is to gently push the mucosa from the outer rim of the diverticular opening caudally with an ERCP catheter. Often, the papillary opening is then pulled from the innerside toward the edge of the diverticular opening. Submucosal injection into the bottom of the diverticulum has been described to lift the papillary orifice. However, one should keep in mind the thin wall of the diverticulum with the risk of needle perforation and potential edematous compression of the papillary orifice.[12]

In special cases, it can take 20 minutes or more to find the papilla. Sometimes, the papilla is located very proximally toward the upper duodenal knee. This situation happens after Billroth I resection. Very rarely, the papilla is located in the duodenal bulb. In an edematous duodenum after an acute attack of a chronic pancreatitis or in the case of a cancer of the head of the pancreas with duodenal infiltration, it can be impossible to localize or cannulate the papilla. A temporary radiologic percutaneous-transhepatic access and rendezvous procedure can be necessary in this case.

Parks and coworkers have described an interesting technique using methylene blue to find the papillary orifice of the minor papilla in patients with a complete pancreas divisum.[13,14] After dye spraying onto the papilla, secretion washes away the dye at the papillary orifice.

Cannulation

A well-sedated patient is the prerequisite for a smooth examination. Before cannulation, the papilla should be observed carefully and one should imagine the natural course of the CBD. A long papillary roof pronouncing the distal bile duct above the horizontal fold (plica horizontalis) may be helpful in determining its axis and course. For cannulation of the CBD, the papilla should be viewed from below

afferent loop at the gastroenteric anastomosis, it mostly gives a tangential view onto the papilla.[11] The duodenoscope offers the advantage of more rigidity with a more direct contact to the endoscope tip. Furthermore, the elevator is helpful to keep guidewires in place and better deflect and direct instruments such as a

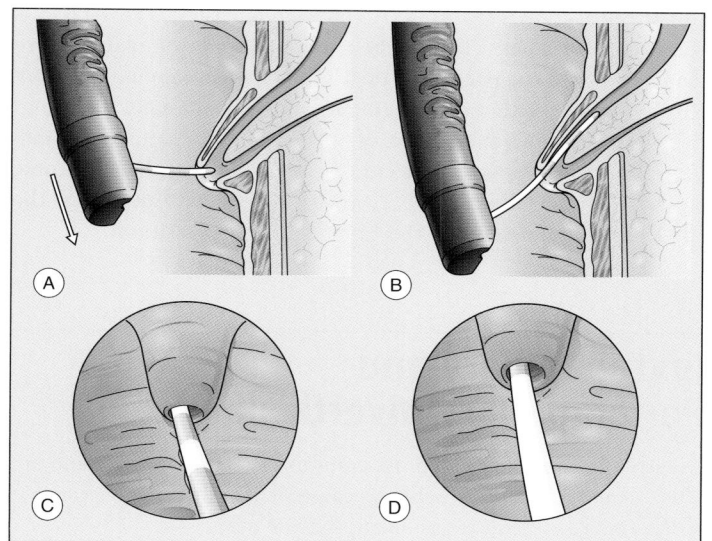

Figure 42–3. For primary cannulation of the common bile duct using a standard catheter and a therapeutic duodenoscope, it often helps to first intubate the papillary orifice with the catheter *(A)* and then to change the angle of the catheter by gently advancing the endoscope *(B)*. Alignment with the axis of the papilla is important in biliary cannulation *(C and D)*. (Modified from ref 12, with permission.)

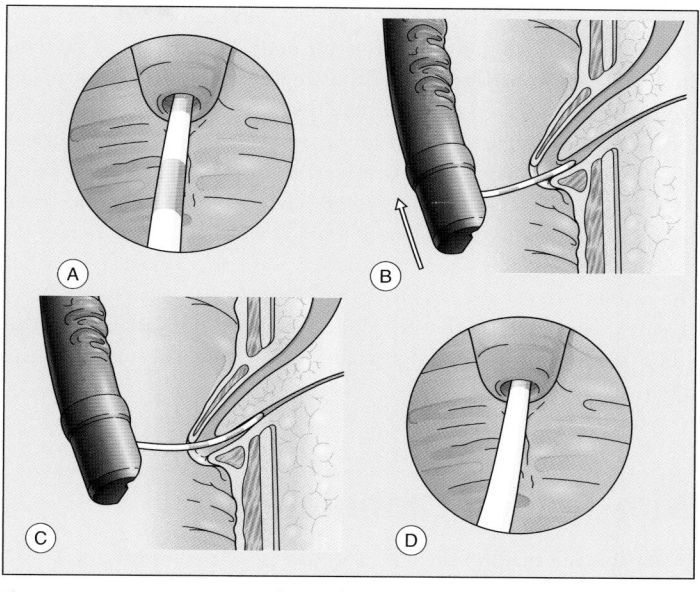

Figure 42–4. Pancreatic cannulation *(A–D)*. Flat position of the catheter facing the papilla at the same level. If common bile duct cannulation was performed first, pulling back the endoscope facilitates cannulation *(B and C)* as well as changing the direction of the catheter within the papilla *(D)*. (Modified from ref 12, with permission.)

and the catheter direction should be steep and within the axis of the papilla. Introducing the catheter tip into the papillary orifice and then gently pushing the catheter forward while opening the elevator will bend the catheter and help achieve a steeper angle for biliary cannulation (Fig. 42–3). Grooming of the catheter often facilitates the achievement of this angle. For primary pancreatic cannulation (Fig. 42–4), the endoscope position remains at the level of the papilla, and the catheter direction is about horizontal. Although the natural course of the pancreatic duct leads toward the 5-o'clock position viewed from directly in front of the papilla, in our experience it is often helpful to turn the small wheel of the endoscope forward and cannulate the papillary orifice from the right to the left for a first, gentle, contrast injection.

Catheter Versus Sphincterotome Cannulation

The primary use of a catheter or a sphincterotome for biliary cannulation is controversial. Traditional first choice is a regular tapered type 6-Fr catheter with a 4-Fr tip accepting a 0.035-inch wire that not only is used for biliary cannulation of the papilla but also may serve directly after for intrahepatic cannulation. The advantage is a high flexibility of the catheter compared with a 6-Fr sphincterotome. Directly after gaining access, it can be used for deep cannulation (e.g., to segment III of the intrahepatic bile ducts) using, for example, a 0.035-inch J-tip stiff hydrophilic guidewire (Terumo type). The same wire can then be left in place during all further interventional procedures such as sphincterotomy, stone extraction, or stent placement.

The use of a regular sphincterotome to initiate cannulation of the bile duct potentially allows variability and therefore improvement of the vertical angle in which the bile duct is cannulated alongside the axial alignment. After correct adjustment is achieved, the catheter or sphincterotome is advanced toward the papilla. It is best to approach the papilla from a distance so that the natural curve of the sphincterotome is obvious on exiting the endoscope. The tip of the sphincterotome is then gently introduced into the common channel. Bowing of the sphincterotome tip usually eases the tip into the mouth of the CBD. When this happens, a characteristic "give" usually occurs. Relaxing the wire to straighten the tip, as well as gently withdrawing the endoscope, results in further anchoring the tip of the sphincterotome within the distal bile duct. Simply advancing the sphincterotome will now invariably lead to deep cannulation.

New devices are constantly being developed to improve the success rate of ERCP.[15] Two studies evaluated the use of a new steerable catheter (SwingTip, Olympus, Tokyo, Japan) to achieve bile duct cannulation. Igarashi and coworkers[16] reported successful cholangiography in 175 of 195 cases (90.5%) with a standard catheter; using the SwingTip catheter in cases in which the standard catheter failed, it was possible to carry out cholangiography in 11 of 17 patients (64.7%), increasing the overall success rate to 95%. Laasch and colleagues[17] carried out a prospective randomized and controlled trial comparing the success rate in achieving cholangiography and bile duct cannulation with three different catheters: a standard ERCP cannula, a short-nosed sphincterotome, and the SwingTip device. At two tertiary referral centers, 312 patients were included in the study. Both steerable catheters were significantly better than the standard catheter for achieving cholangiography ($p = 0.038$), but no differences were found between the SwingTip cannula and the sphincterotome. Steerable catheters were also more effective for deep cannulation of the bile duct, but the improvement did not reach statistical significance. Steerable catheters succeeded in 26% of the cases in which the standard cannula failed. The study also compared differences in the results obtained from an expert and a trainee endoscopist using the three catheters. Trainees experienced greater benefit from using steerable catheters, whereas experts were quicker in achieving cholangiography and deep cannulation with the SwingTip device. The overall success rate was 97%, and pancreatitis occurred in 5.3% of cases. Steerable catheters should be readily available on the ERCP trolley, allowing faster access to the bile duct and success when standard catheters fail.

Wire-Guided Cannulation

When routine maneuvers fail, the next step may be the use of a wire-guided sphincterotome. The endoscopist positions the tip of the sphincterotome at the presumed mouth of the biliary orifice, and the assistant gently turns the wire in a clockwise. The J-tip of a 0.035-inch minimally traumatic Teromo guidewire is usually turned in a clockwise direction. One should note that the tip of even the softest wire becomes stiff if forcefully pushed forward out of a catheter or if the sphincterotome lumen is pressed against tissue. Therefore, one should gently press the sphincterotome or catheter in the suspected CBD direction and leave the tip enough room to slightly flex while the wire is rotated with a cannulation aid (Terumo Corp., Japan). When this fails, the options are to abort the procedure, review the indications and alternatives such as referral to an expert, or proceed to precut sphincterotomy. A good reason to stop at this point is limited experience and a low case volume.

Biliary and Pancreatic Standard Sphincterotomy

Having deeply cannulated the CBD, the exact position of the sphincterotome is confirmed by injection of contrast medium. In case the necessity of a sphincterotomy is confirmed, the instrument is first completely withdrawn from the bile duct leaving a 0.035-inch guidewire in place. The sphincterotome is then gently pushed forward again until about one-fourth of the cutting wire is located inside the papilla. The cut is then performed by smoothly advancing the sphincterotome. The papillary roof is opened always along its axis and its middle. While in former times, exact advices for the direction of the cut have been given orientation along the axis of the papillary roof, and careful cutting just with the tip of the sphincterotome cutting wire seems preferable. Papillary anatomy and axis may vary strongly. It may be necessary to torque the instrument in the opposite direction to maintain the desired cutting direction. There are no precise data on the length of incision, but a depth of 10 mm is usually recommended for insertion of stents; in the case of stone extraction, a larger cut may be required.

In the case of pancreatic duct sphincterotomy, cutting should aim at the 1-o'clock position. An incision length of 5 to 10 mm is considered suitable. The cutting wire should not be placed more than 5 mm into the pancreatic duct. The physician should be aware of the shorter intramural segment of the pancreatic duct and therefore the much higher risk of perforation. To facilitate sphincterotomy, it may be helpful to mold the tip of the sphincterotome on the anatomic situation (e.g., in case of sphincterotomy of the CBD, the tip is curved into the 11- to 12-o'clock position).

Juxtapapillary and Periampullary Diverticula

Diverticula represent the most common type of anomaly and are often found in elderly patients. Because of the distorted anatomy, it is often more difficult to cannulate the bile duct.

Most often, the ampulla is located at the 3-o'clock position within the diverticulum; however, it may be seen anywhere along the inferior rim. Sometimes, aspirating air reveals the site of the papilla. It may also helpful to put the patient in a prone position or to press in the right upper abdominal quadrant. Some authors have good experience with injecting some saline into the contralateral side of the diverticula; this will protrude the papilla and facilitate cannulation.

Precut Sphincterotomy

Although needle-knife sphincterotomy has been considered a risk factor for ERCP-induced complications such as pancreatitis, bleeding, or perforation, series from centers with a high frequency of needle-knife precut sphincterotomies show that in experienced hands the needle-knife procedure does not necessarily have a higher complication rate.[18]

The endoscopist has several choices of the precut technique: three of which involve cutting from the papillary orifice and one involves cutting the roof of the papilla. A standard sphincterotome has been used by inserting the tip into the mouth of the pancreatic duct and using 1 to 2 mm of the wire to cut up into the biliary direction in an incremental fashion. Similarly, if the nose of the papillotome is cut so that only 1 to 2 mm extends beyond the wire, the mouth of the papillary orifice can be entered but the nose of the papillotome does not extend into the pancreatic duct. Short cuts in the biliary direction cut the overlying mucosa and change the angle of the entry into the bile duct. This can be termed an "entry" cut, to distinguish this technique from the following two freehand needle-knife techniques (Fig. 42–5). One is to place the needle tip into the papillary orifice, lift the upper lip of the papilla with slight tension on the needle-knife, and give short bursts of cutting current in the biliary direction. The other approach is careful sequential cutting dissection of the roof of the papilla, starting at the apex of the papillary mound with careful sweeping movements. Subsequent cuts should allow splaying of the cut edges of the mucosa as the

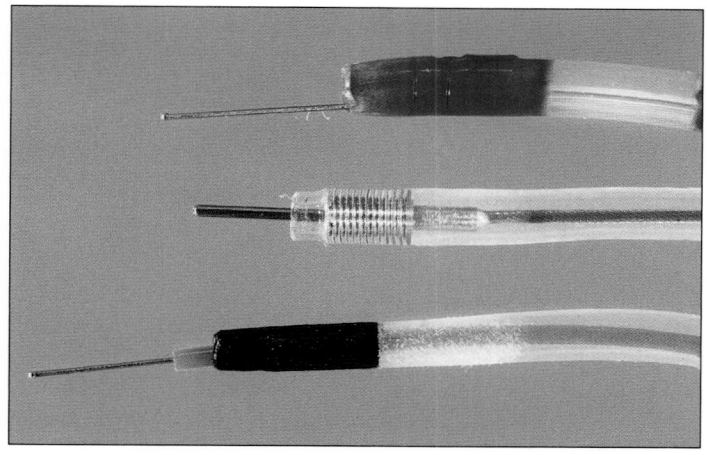

Figure 42–5. Different types of needle knives. Diameter and length of the cutting wire influence cutting properties: the thinner the wire knife, the faster and sharper the cut; the longer the wire, the potentially deeper the cut with relatively high risk of bleeding and perforation.

submucosa is dissected and recognition of the fleshy red appearance as the sphincter muscle is cut; occasionally, the endoscopist may even appreciate a pale white interface between the submucosa and the surface of the muscle. A gush of bile to indicate successful bile duct access should not be expected. Once the initial cut into the muscle is made, it is helpful to switch to a tapered cannula and probe the cut muscle to attempt deeper cannulation. If this is unsuccessful, a further layer should be cut and one can probe again with a cannula until the lumen is reached.

Billroth II Situation

ERCP in a patient with BII resection of the stomach may be very challenging because of the more difficult endoscopic access in a completely altered anatomy. Advantages of the use of a gastroscope and a duodenoscope for cannulation and sphincterotomy are described in the section on the proper endoscope.

The endoscope is introduced alongside the minor curvature of the stomach, which often shows a longitudinal postoperative prominence. Routinely, a short view onto and under the gastrojejunal anastomosis during the ERCP examination can be crucial for the patient even if the problem is jaundice rather than the detection of an early stump cancer in a BII stomach (which is not too rarely found as a side diagnosis in the elderly BII patient). The usual access to the BII papilla is via the afferent loop because of the shorter distance to the papilla and a better direct contact to the tip of the endoscope. The afferent loop, strictly following the minor curvature of the stomach, is the upper "o" of an "8"; unfortunately, the efferent loop, the lower "o" of the "8," is easier to intubate (see Fig. 42–1*A*). One may easily slip back from the afferent loop into the efferent loop without recognizing it because of the steep angle of fixation of the afferent loop to the stomach to prevent gastric and biliary reflux. One should exclude a Whipple resection of the pancreas as the cause of the resection of ⅔ of the stomach; in the Whipple resec-

tion, there is usually a single jejunal loop attached side-to-side to the gastric anastomosis and Roux-en-Y biliary anastomosis.

The afferent loop often must be carefully probed and lifted with the tip of the endoscope. As described previously, the use of a gastroscope is preferable in a case of unclear anatomy because the risk of jejunal perforation in BII anatomy may be increased.[11] Often, the angle of the fixation of the afferent loop to the stomach is very steep and sometimes the opening of the afferent loop is only seen from below looking back in inversion to the stomach.

The access in a BII situation implies that the approach is performed from below instead of from above; thus, there is a reversed anatomy. The bile duct is now located at the 5-o'clock position, and the pancreatic duct is reached via the 11-o'clock position.

Because the afferent loop often enters the stomach at a sharp angle, the use of a side-viewing endoscope is not always possible. However, cannulation may be much more difficult with a forward-viewing endoscope.

It may be difficult to distinguish afferent loop from efferent loop. Usually, the afferent loop is located along the lesser curvature (usually on the right); if three lumens are seen, the middle opening represents the afferent loop.

With regard to the reversed anatomy, the catheter tip should not be curved but should be straight. Often, a tangential approach has to be chosen. As described previously, the use of a guidewire may make it easier to cannulate the papilla in more difficult cases.

Cannulation and Sphincterotomy of the Minor Papilla

The indication for cannulation of the minor papilla is a suspected complete pancreas divisum as a cause for repeated acute episodes or chronic pancreatitis. This fusion anomaly leads to drainage of the major dorsal part of the gland via the small minor papilla, whereas the major papilla drains exclusively the smaller ventral part with pancreatic juice from the head of the organ. Further indications for minor papilla cannulation can be an incomplete pancreas divisum (dominant dorsal duct [DDD]) with just a very fine ductal connection of the ventral and dorsal pancreas or a nonpassable prepapillary obstruction and suspected increased intraductal pressure or infection.

Because of its small size, cannulation of the minor papilla is more challenging. Sometimes, the minor papilla is hard to identify and often is only a 2-mm protrusion with a difficult to identify orifice. The minor papilla is usually located 1.5 to 2 cm above the major papilla, 5 to 10 mm to the right side, often above the first or second horizontal fold on the right. First, the major papilla should be identified, then the endoscope has to be slowly withdrawn; just beyond the superior angle of the duodenum, the minor papilla should appear. It is controversial whether a short or a long endoscope position is preferable. For cannulation, a 3-Fr "Glo tip" or "bottle neck" catheter (e.g., Wilson & Cook, Watertown MN) is helpful. Cannulation and contrast injection should be carried out with caution so that interstitial edema is not created with the fine catheter tip.

Sphincterotomy of the minor papilla is performed preferably over the wire-push sphincterotomy using a mini-sphincterotome (e.g., ¾-Fr Minitome, Wilson & Cook, Watertown, MN). The cut should not exceed 4 mm; some authors even prefer a much shorter cut of 2 to 3 mm. The direction of the cut should aim at the 12-o'clock position (10- to 1-o'clock position). Because the size of the minor papilla is usually very small and the orifice is difficult to cannulate, often a two-step approach is necessary: if primary cannulation fails, a 2-mm precut sphincterotomy is performed toward 12-o'clock with no further attempt to cannulate or opacify the duct. After 2 to 3 days, cannulation is successful in most cases at re-endoscopy.

First, a 5- or 7-Fr stent is inserted. Second, the sphincterotomy is performed by using the stent as a guide rail. Because it is assumed that the stent reduces the risk of pancreatitis, it may be left in place for several days and can be removed in a second session.

Complications

The success rate and complications in ERCP and especially sphincterotomy techniques are volume-dependent, as is seen with many techniques. In sphincterotomy, bleeding, pancreatitis, and perforation are the most feared complications. Reasons for bleeding may be a lateral deviation from the axis of the papilla[19] or an aberrant vessel in the roof of the papilla, which may occur as a variation of the normal anatomy in about 2.5% of cases.

The reported incidence of post-ERCP and sphincterotomy pancreatitis ranges between 1.3% and 24.4% in nonselected series. This varying incidence likely reflects differences in patient populations, indications, and endoscopic expertise and different definitions of pancreatitis and methods of data collection. Among a number of patient-related factors recognized as risks for post-ERCP pancreatitis in recent large prospective studies, including 1966 cases, are the combination of female gender, normal serum bilirubin levels, and recurrent abdominal pain suggesting sphincter of Oddi dysfunction and previous post-ERCP pancreatitis.[20] Combinations of risk factors can substantially increase the odds ratio (e.g., to 16.2 for a difficult cannulation in a female patient with normal bilirubin). Among the technique-related risk factors for post-ERCP pancreatitis, biliary sphincter balloon dilation, difficult cannulation, sphincter of Oddi manometry, and pancreatic sphincterotomy have also been recognized as significant risk factors. However, because the case mix in nonselected series does not significantly differ in the different studies, it is logical to assume that the different criteria adopted for defining the post-ERCP pancreatitis play a key role in the reported wide variation of incidence reported for this complication. The occurrence and duration of pain and the amplitude of serum amylase after ERCP are critical points in the definition of post-ERCP pancreatitis. Although a consensus conference identified 24-hour persisting pain associated with hyperamylasemia greater than three times the upper reference limit as an indicator of pancreatitis, these two parameters are considered in a different manner in the studies available up to now. In a prospective study in which we calculated the incidence of post-ERCP pancreatitis by using the most widely used criteria, for both occurrence and duration of pancreatic pain and serum amylase amplitude, the incidence of postprocedure pancreatitis ranged from 1.9% to 11.7% depending on the criteria adopted.

Pancreatic Stents for Prevention of Post-ERCP Pancreatitis

Acinarization and ductal hypertension caused by injection of contrast medium play an important role and can induce ischemia of the pancreatic tissue.

As a potential prophylaxis, pancreatic drainage with stents or nasopancreatic tubes can reduce the risk of post-ERCP pancreatitis in selected cases. In particular, patients with pancreatic sphincter hypertension benefit from a temporary endoprosthesis.[22,23] As a consequence, the implantation of a protective pancreatic 5- to 7-Fr stent has also been postulated for prevention of pancreatitis after difficult cannulation and/or sphincterotomy.[24,25]

Aizawa and coworkers[26] retrospectively analyzed the efficacy of temporary pancreatic duct stenting for prevention of pancreatitis after endoscopic sphincter dilatation (ESD) for removal of bile duct stones. ESD was performed in 38 patients with a mean number of 2.2 ductal stones and a mean maximum stone size of 12 mm. Bile duct clearance was achieved in 37 patients after 52 sessions, using mechanical lithotripsy in 58% of the cases. Biliary drainage was augmented in 13 cases to prevent cholangitis. The success rate of insertion of pancreatic 5-Fr stents was 95%. Endoscopy was repeated after 3 days for removal of biliary and pancreatic prostheses, with the exception of a few cases in which there was spontaneous passage. Unfortunately, in a historical control group of 92 patients, the success rates for ESD without pancreatic stents were not provided. Medical treatment such as the oral administration of nifedipine 3 hours before treatment or subcutaneous low-molecular-weight heparin showed no benefit compared with placebo in recent studies.[27,28] Awareness of specific patient- and procedure-related risk factors before the procedure, referral of elective high risk cases to an expert center, and, eventually, fine-caliber protective pancreatic stenting are currently the best options for the clinician to reduce the risk of pancreatic post-ERCP complications.

ACKNOWLEDGMENTS

The author thanks his colleagues, Johannes Volk, M.D., Heiko Lorenz, and Ulf Luetkemeier, all from St. Bernward Hospital in Hildesheim, Germany, for their invaluable support in preparing the manuscript and video-sequences.

REFERENCES

1. Adamek HE, Albert J, Weitz M, et al: A prospective evaluation of magnetic resonance cholangiopancreatography in patients with suspected bile duct obstruction. Gut 43:680–683, 1998.

2. Varghese JC, Liddell RP, Farrell MA, et al: The diagnostic accuracy of magnetic resonance cholangiopancreatography and ultrasound compared with direct cholangiography in the detection of choledocholithiasis. Clin Radiol 54:604–614, 1999.

3. Varghese JC, Farrell MA, Courtney G, et al: A prospective comparison of magnetic resonance cholangiopancreatography with endoscopic retrograde cholangiopancreatography in the evaluation of patients with suspected biliary tract disease. Clin Radiol 54:513–520, 1999.

4. Meroni E, Bisagni P, Bona S, et al: Pre-operative endoscopic ultrasonography can optimise the management of patients undergoing laparoscopic cholecystectomy with abnormal liver function tests as the sole risk factor for choledocholithiasis: A prospective study. Dig Liver Dis 36:73–77, 2004.

5. Linghu EQ, Cheng LF, Wang XD, et al: Intraductal ultrasonography and endoscopic retrograde cholangiography in diagnosis of extra-hepatic bile duct stones: A comparative study. Hepatobiliary Pancreat Dis Int 3:129–132, 2004.

6. Wiersema MJ, Wiersema LM: Endosonography of the pancreas: Normal variation versus changes of early chronic pancreatitis. Gastrointest Endosc Clin N Am 5:487–496, 1995.

7. Napoleon B, Dumortier J, Keriven-Souquet O, et al: Do normal findings at biliary endoscopic ultrasonography obviate the need for endoscopic retrograde cholangiography in patients with suspicion of common bile duct stone? A prospective follow-up study of 238 patients. Endoscopy 35:411–415, 2003.

8. Hintze RE, Adler A, Veltzke W, Abou-Rebyeh H: Endoscopic access to the papilla of Vater for endoscopic retrograde cholangiopancreatography in patients with Billroth II or Roux-en-Y gastrojejunostomy. Endoscopy 29:69–73, 1997.

9. Aabakken L, Holthe B, Sandstad O, et al: Endoscopic pancreatico-biliary procedures in patients with a Billroth II resection: A 10-year follow-up study. Ital J Gastroenterol Hepatol 30:301–305, 1998.

10. Costamagna G, Mutignani M, Perri V, et al: Diagnostic and therapeutic ERCP in patients with Billroth II gastrectomy. Acta Gastroenterol Belg 57:155–162, 1994.

11. Kim MH, Lee SK, Lee MH, et al: Endoscopic retrograde cholangiopancreatography and needle-knife sphincterotomy in patients with Billroth II gastrectomy: A comparative study of the forward-viewing endoscope and the side-viewing duodenoscope. Endoscopy 29:82–85, 1997.

12. Soehendra N, Binmoeller KF, Seifert H, Schreiber HW: Therapeutic Endoscopy: Color Atlas of Operative Techniques for the Gastrointestinal Tract. New York, Thieme Medical Publishers, 1997.

13. Park SH, de Bellis M, McHenry L, et al: Use of methylene blue to identify the minor papilla or its orifice in patients with pancreas divisum. Gastrointest Endosc 57:358–363, 2003.

14. Neuhaus H: Therapeutic pancreatic endoscopy. Endoscopy 36:8–16, 2004.

15. Mutignani M, Tringali A, Costamagna G: Therapeutic biliary endoscopy. Endoscopy 36:147–59, 2004.

16. Igarashi Y, Tada T, Shimura J, et al: A new cannula with a flexible tip (Swing Tip) may improve the success rate of endoscopic retrograde cholangiopancreatography. Endoscopy 34:628–631, 2002.

17. Laasch HU, Tringali A, Wilbraham L, et al: Comparison of standard and steerable catheters for bile duct cannulation in ERCP. Endoscopy 35:669–674, 2003.

18. Katsinelos P, Mimidis K, Paroutoglou G, et al: Needle-knife papillotomy: A safe and effective technique in experienced hands. Hepatogastroenterology 51:349–352, 2004.

19. Carr-Locke DL: Biliary access during endoscopic retrograde cholangiopancreatography. Can J Gastroenterol 18:251–254, 2004.

20. Freeman ML, DiSario JA, Nelson DB, et al: Risk factors for post-ERCP pancreatitis: A prospective, multicenter study. Gastrointest Endosc 54:425–434, 2001.

21. Haber GB: Prevention of post-ERCP pancreatitis. Gastrointest Endosc 51:100–103, 2000.

22. Freeman ML: Adverse outcomes of endoscopic retrograde cholangiopancreatography: Avoidance and management. Gastrointest Endosc Clin N Am 13:775–798, xi, 2003.

23. Tarnasky PR, Palesch YY, Cunningham JT, et al: Pancreatic stenting prevents pancreatitis after biliary sphincterotomy in patients with sphincter of Oddi dysfunction. Gastroenterology 115:1518–1524, 1998.

24. Andriulli A, Solmi L, Loperfido S, et al: Prophylaxis of ERCP-related pancreatitis: A randomized, controlled trial of somatostatin and gabexate mesylate. Clin Gastroenterol Hepatol 2:713–718, 2004.

25. Tarnasky PR: Mechanical prevention of post-ERCP pancreatitis by pancreatic stents: Results, techniques, and indications. JOP 4:58–67, 2003.

26. Aizawa T, Ueno T: Stent placement in the pancreatic duct prevents pancreatitis after endoscopic sphincter dilation for removal of bile duct stones. Gastrointest Endosc 54:209–213, 2001.

27. Prat F, Amaris J, Ducot B, et al: Nifedipine for prevention of post-ERCP pancreatitis: A prospective, double-blind randomized study. Gastrointest Endosc 56:202–208, 2002.

28. Rabenstein T, Fischer B, Wiessner V, et al: Low-molecular-weight heparin does not prevent acute post-ERCP pancreatitis. Gastrointest Endosc 59:606–613, 2004.

Endoscopic Retrograde Cholangiopancreatography Tissue Sampling Techniques

CHAPTER

43

Douglas Howell

Introduction

Tissue sampling at endoscopic retrograde cholangiopancreatography (ERCP) has been an area of controversy since the very inception of therapeutic ERCP in 1973. Histologic diagnosis remains the most certain confirmation of the presence of malignancy; however, ERCP has been the only endoscopic procedure in which tissue biopsy and cytology are considered secondary, generally because the main goal of the intervention is to provide drainage for obstructive jaundice.

Nevertheless, ERCP may present a unique opportunity to establish a definite diagnosis of malignancy during a drainage procedure, which may save the patient subsequent unnecessary, painful, and expensive procedures.[1] Despite many years of study, imaging alone cannot make the diagnosis of malignancy.[2]

This chapter covers this controversial topic including a historical background, pathogenesis, techniques in tissue sampling, complications, and finally future trends and potential.

History

ERCP was developed in the late 1960s as a diagnostic technique to provide detailed radiography of the biliary tree and pancreatic ducts. Diagnostic ERCP remained as its principle role until 1973 when endoscopic sphincterotomy was performed in Japan and Germany. One of the first sphincterotomies performed in Germany by Drs. Demling and Classen was to introduce a biopsy forceps to sample a bifurcation stricture (personal communication, Dr. Classen, September 1992).

Because of the technical difficulties of introducing standard front-viewing endoscopic accessories over an elevator for retrograde cannulation, tissue sampling did not develop early in the history of therapeutic ERCP. Initial efforts were limited to simple aspiration of bile and, on occasion, pancreatic juice, when deep cannulation was achieved. After placing a diagnostic catheter just below or into the stricture, aspiration of 10 to 50 mL of bile or 5 to 20 mL of pan-

creatic juice may be collected over 10 to 15 minutes. Shed cells within these biologic fluids occasionally yielded a definite diagnosis. Notably, specificity in early reports was uniformly 100%. Despite early enthusiasm, clinicians noted low yields when the technique was used in a clinical setting. Only, 6% to 32% sensitivity in six published studies[3–8] have caused this technique to fall from practice in favor of the newer, higher yield approaches of brush cytology, fine needle aspiration (FNA) cytology, and endobiliary forceps biopsy.

Pathogenesis

Before discussing the individual and, perhaps most important, the combined techniques of tissue sampling at ERCP, a discussion of pathogenesis is warranted.

Obstruction of the biliary tree by benign or malignant stricturing requiring temporary or palliative bile duct stenting remains a major indication for ERCP, now that diagnostic ERCP has been largely replaced by lower risk imaging techniques of helical computed tomography (CT) and magnetic resonance cholangiopancreatography (MRCP). As discussed elsewhere in this textbook, endoscopic ultrasound has an important role in examining the minority of patients with pancreatic neoplasms whose resectability remains uncertain after radiologic imaging. Many gastroenterologists use endoscopic ultrasonography (EUS) largely to perform tissue sampling in lieu of ERCP, often because of poor yields at their center with ERCP techniques, and to permit an advance tissue diagnosis before metal stent placement. Although this approach to adequate staging of potentially resectable patients is reasonable, most patients will be obviously unresectable because of advanced malignancy, definite metastases, or advanced age and comorbidity. Most general hospitals report that only approximately 15% of patients presenting with malignant obstructive jaundice undergo an attempt at surgical curative resection. The controversy of endoscopic palliative stenting followed by oncologic care versus palliative resection or surgical bypass is beyond the scope of this chapter, but most obstructed patients will need ERCP as part of their treatment strategy.

Malignant biliary obstruction occurs because of three basic disease processes. Most frequent in Western countries, pancreatic cancer obstructs the common duct as it courses through the head of the gland. Body and tail cancers rarely cause obstruction except when metastases involve the lymph nodes in the porta hepatis.

The second major malignancy that causes obstruction is biliary cancer, beginning either in the gallbladder or as a primary tumor of the biliary tree. Worldwide, biliary cancers are the leading cause of malignant obstructive jaundice, probably because of the prevalence of parasitic and environmental carcinogenic factors in less-developed countries.

The final mechanism is obstruction resulting from metastatic disease from a variety of primary tumors including gastrointestinal (GI) (gastric, pancreatic, colon), intra-abdominal (adrenal, renal, bladder, lymphoma), and extra-abdominal (breast, lung) tumors. Central hepatocellular carcinomas represent a particularly challenging problem when central obstruction presents with jaundice, a very common occurrence worldwide where hepatitis B remains pandemic.

These three types of malignant obstruction are pathologically distinct and represent special problems when attempting tissue sampling.

The first major pathologic factor influencing biopsy or cytologic yield is tumor cellularity. Pancreatic carcinoma, in particular, often stimulates an intense desmoplastic fibrotic reaction, making the tumor very dense and of low cellularity. Sampling often produces acellular or false-negative specimens.[9,10] Maximizing yield requires repeated, deep, or large specimen sampling. Occasionally, an immune response or relative ischemia produces ulceration, bleeding, exudate, or debris that can obscure the rare malignant cell recovered in an endoscopic specimen.

Cholangiocarcinoma of the primary type begins in the mucosa of the primary or secondary bile ducts. It is a relatively cellular cancer, and cells are more often shed in bile and can be more readily collected by sampling the superficial epithelium.

Hepatocellular carcinoma often can invade and extend intraductally. Superficial sampling generally obtains diagnostic cells in this setting as well.

As with pancreatic cancer, gallbladder cancer and, especially, metastatic cancer encase or compress the biliary tree, often while preserving intact benign biliary epithelium. Establishing a tissue diagnosis often requires sampling deeper than the surface epithelium.[9,11–13]

Finally, very well differentiated tumors represent a significant minority of malignant pancreaticobiliary tumors and prove very difficult to diagnose by cytologic criteria. Large specimens are often necessary to permit the pathologist to examine and compare these tumors to differentiate them from normal tissue. This fact likely explains why no biopsy technique, even open surgical wedge biopsy, has a 100% yield.

These pathogenetic factors demand refined techniques and devices if adequate specimens are to be obtained to permit a positive cytologic or histologic diagnosis to be made in most cases. These factors explain why no single technique of tissue sampling produces a yield as high as combining superficial and deep sampling in the same patient.

Techniques of Tissue Sampling

Collecting adequate samples for cytologic and histologic review remains a major challenge for the endoscopist during ERCP. It should be remembered that the primary goal of the planned ERCP is to provide endoscopic drainage for a jaundiced obstructed patient. This involves obtaining ductal access, negotiating the obstruction with a guidewire, usually performing sphincterotomy, and, finally, placing a biliary endoprosthesis. Tissue sampling, therefore, has always assumed a secondary position in this sequence, likely explaining the reason for the limited experience generally reported by most endoscopists. Alternatively, an EUS can be scheduled with an FNA as its only or at least a major goal. A cytopathologist can be present at the EUS procedure, and up to 16 needle passes have been used to establish a tissue diagnosis.[14]

Inadequate tissue acquisition at ERCP remains the most common reason for failing to establish an accurate pathologic diagnosis. Technical difficulty, time consideration, patient restlessness, and the need to proceed with the primary goal of biliary drainage, all contribute to limit the time and thoroughness of tissue collection for many endoscopists.

Because of these factors, brush cytology has been the only sampling technique adopted widely into clinical practice. Initially, standard endoscopic brushes were inserted, usually after sphincterotomy, in an attempt to sample from within a malignant-appearing stricture (Fig. 43–1A). These devices can be "groomed" by manually curving their end portions before placement. Most have a blunt smooth metal tip to minimize trauma and the risk of perforation. Nevertheless, negotiation through the stricture was often problematic. This factor and the very superficial nature of this technique of sampling produced disappointing yields, and it never became popular.

Industry responded to these problems by producing a variety of cytology brushes, some of which could be inserted over a guidewire placed through the malignant-appearing stricture before attempted

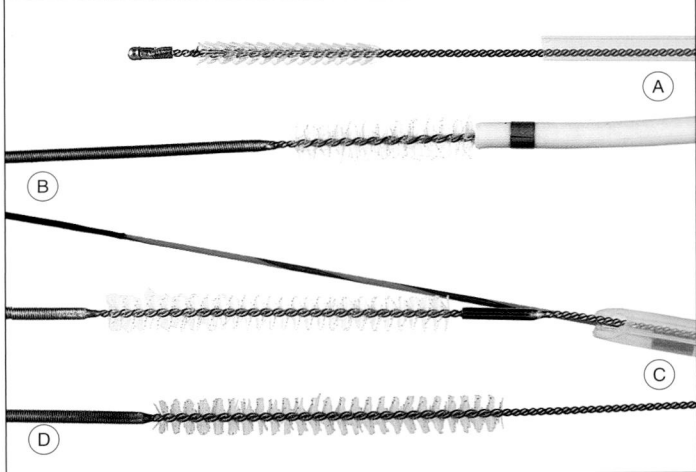

Figure 43–1. Brushes for endoscopic retrograde cholangiopancreatography (ERCP) brush cytology. From top to bottom: *A,* Standard metal tipped brush. *B,* Geenen spring-nosed brush in a diagnostic catheter. *C,* Cytomax 8-Fr brush catheter over a 0.035-inch guidewire. *D,* Large HBIB brush for use in the Howell biliary introducer (HBI).

sampling (see Fig. 43–1). Because most endoscopists concentrate on negotiating a guidewire through the stricture as the first major step in the therapeutic goal of stent placement, tissue sampling may be done at this appropriate time without changing or interrupting this sequence.

Two popular guided brushes are Combo-cath (Microvasive Boston Scientific, Natick, MA) and Cytomax (Wilson-Cook Medical, Winston Salem, NC) (see Fig. 43–1C). These guided devices suffer from their relative large size of 8 Fr and their stiffness. In addition, the length of the bristles must be quite short to fit within the small channel size in these double-lumen devices, a feature that may limit specimen collection. Smaller versions of these two devices have been produced but can only be placed over 0.018-inch guidewires.

An alternative to using these brushes is to insert a catheter over the previously placed guidewire, withdraw the guidewire, and place a brush with a long spring-tip nose (Geenen brush, Wilson-Cook Medical) (see Fig. 43–1B). By slightly withdrawing the catheter while leaving the brush above the stricture, the tissue to be sampled can be accessed. Brushing now would not lose position above the stricture because the long nose maintains position. The principal drawback of the technique is the loss of cells when the brush is withdrawn from the catheter after the catheter is readvanced above the stricture to maintain access.[15] If the entire assembly is withdrawn, reinsertion of the guidewire is required, which is an uncomfortable, and occasionally unsuccessful, challenge.

Another alternative is to create a "monorail" brushing device by piercing a catheter with a sharp 20-gauge needle 1 to 2 cm from its tip and passing the guidewire through its end hole and out this newly produced side hole. The spring-tipped brush is positioned just behind this and the assembled device can be more easily passed into the duct (Fig. 43–2).

Once above the stricture, the catheter is passed beyond the tip of the guidewire. The brush is then free to advance beyond the tip of the catheter, exposing the bristles for specimen collection and leaving the guidewire in place above the stricture. The principal advantage is that the brush can be pulled into the end of the catheter and both components can be withdrawn to minimize cellular loss (Fig. 43–3).[16]

Published yields of ERCP brush cytology devices vary widely for reasons that can only be speculated. In general, series that have a higher proportion of pancreatic adenocarcinomas and, perhaps, earlier smaller tumors have a much lower yield of positive results, compared with those series with more cholangiocarcinomas. Published overall sensitivities using these devices vary from 8% to 57%.[8,17–22] As discussed subsequently, many of these series are also flawed by including patients with "suspicious for malignancy" reports as positive results.

The probable pathologic explanation for these varied yields relates to the observation that the interior of malignant strictures are made of benign epithelium compressed by surrounding neoplastic tissue, with the exception of cholangiocarcinoma of the major bile ducts. This fact explains the low yield of simple bile aspiration for cytology because few, if any, malignant cells are in contact with the bile flow as previously discussed. When the stricture is traumatized by dilation, thereby removing the benign epithelium, the yield of aspirating bile not unexpectedly increases.[23]

The yield of brushing is lower with deeper and more remote encasing tumors. One would predict the lowest yield in metastatic malignancy, followed by pancreatic cancer, with a much higher yield with primary cholangiocarcinoma. In general, this has been confirmed in clinical practice.

The type of brush bristles, the overall brush length, and the amount of time spent brushing all affect yield. Rabinowitz and colleagues[24] emphasized this by using three separate brushes at each ERCP and repeating the procedure with three new brushes when suspicious strictures were initially negative. Positive yield continued to increase until 62% of their patients were eventually diagnosed by brushing alone.

Clearly, additional improvements of techniques and equipment for brush cytology are needed to improve yield. Alternatively, additional techniques and devices can be used, as reviewed in this chapter.

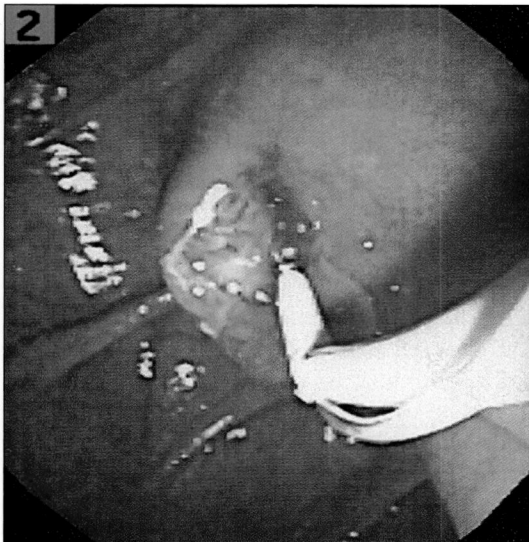

Figure 43–2. The "mono-rail" system being passed into the bile duct. Note the guidewire enters the tip but passes out the newly created side hole at approximately 2 cm behind the tip. The brush is positioned just inside the side hole.

Fine Needle Aspiration Cytology

Chiba needle aspiration cytology was pioneered in Japan in the 1950s using 22-gauge long percutaneous needles. Still the standard for most radiologic guided biopsies, Chiba needle aspiration has proved to be exceedingly safe and widely applied.

However, Warshaw[25] reported a high rate of recovery of intraperitoneal malignant cells in patients undergoing attempted resection for pancreatic cancer who had undergone CT-guided percutaneous transabdominal Chiba needle biopsy 24 to 48 hours preoperatively. This apparent strong potential for intraperitoneal seeding has caused most physicians to seek an alternative to the Chiba technique in patients who might undergo subsequent surgery. In light of these concerns, some centers even advocate proceeding with surgical exploration without any attempts at tissue sampling, if the clinical situation is sufficiently suspicious.[26]

In contradistinction, intraductal FNA cytology during ERCP only traverses tissue that will be resected en bloc. There can be no

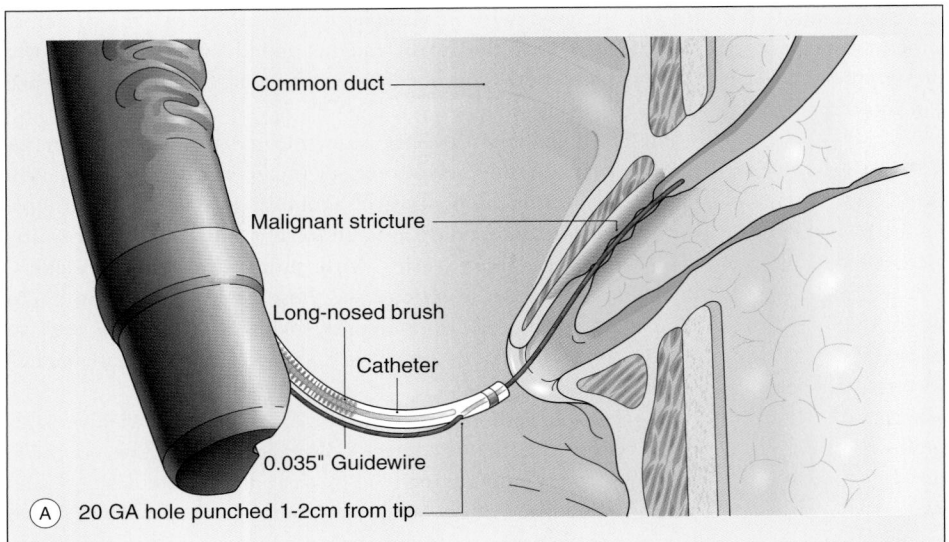

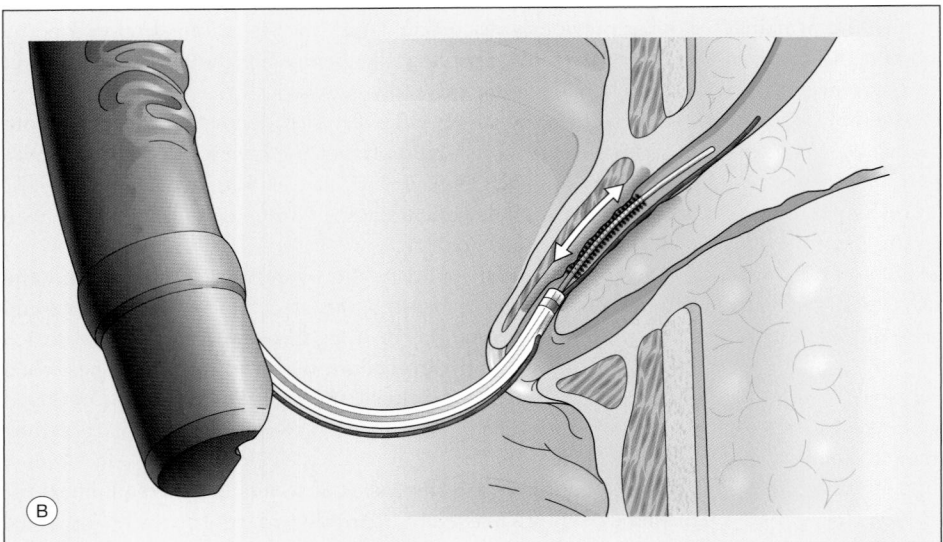

Figure 43-3. *A,* Monorail brush; long-nosed brush is preloaded into a diagnostic catheter and passed with the catheter over a guidewire in a monorail fashion through the stricture. *B,* The monorail catheter has been passed over the end of guidewire well above the stricture. Once off the guidewire the long-nosed brush can be advanced to brush the stricture. The long nose maintains access. The guidewire remains in place.

contamination of the peritoneal cavity including the lesser sac behind the stomach.

Endoscopic needle biopsy of pancreatic head masses was pioneered in 1977 by Tsuchiya and coworkers[27] using straight, 22-gauge needles directed at bulges seen compressing the central duodenal wall. This situation, unfortunately, represents only a small minority of such patients but remains a viable tissue sampling technique throughout the upper GI tract for submucosal tumors.[28]

Intraductal FNA during ERCP required the development of a specifically designed endoscopic accessory device. Howell and colleagues[22] reported on such a device after developing a ball-tipped catheter with a retractable 22-gauge Chiba-type biopsy needle (HBAN-22, Wilson-Cook Medical). The needle extends 7 mm beyond the ball-tip once the catheter is placed within the duct and permits deeper sampling than that afforded by brushing (Fig. 43–4). However, the technique requires sphincterotomy and proves to be technically challenging. The initial high yield of 62% (positives and suspicious) has not been reproduced in more recent series. The true positive sensitivity has been reported to be 27% to 30% of cases in three

series.[20,29,30] Nevertheless, FNA may add to the total yield when added to other techniques, as discussed later in this chapter. To date no complication of this technique has been reported.

Forceps Biopsy

Despite a long history, insertion of forceps to perform endobiliary forceps biopsy has never gained popularity probably because of the technical difficulty of placing the forceps into the bile duct because of their stiffness. Initial efforts used gastroscopic forceps until special flexible-tipped duodenoscopic forceps (Olympus) were developed and proved to work better over the elevator. To pass these forceps retrograde up the duct still required a large sphincterotomy.

The technique of forceps biopsy involves insertion of the device to the lower edge of the stricture. Using fluoroscopy, accurate biopsy can then be obtained from the lower edge of the apparent tumor. Several passes of the forceps are required to produce an

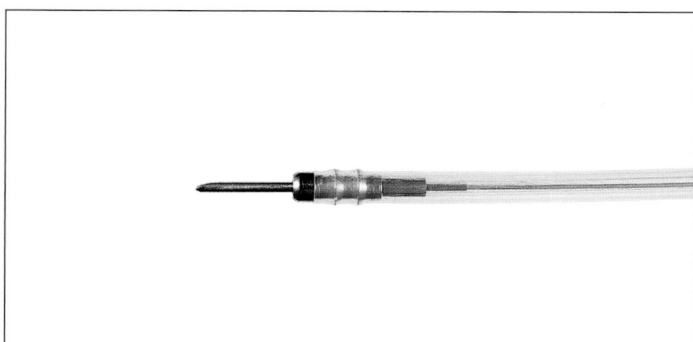

Figure 43-4. Howell biliary aspiration needle (HBAN-22) is a 22-gauge Chiba-type needle mounted in a 7-Fr ball-tipped catheter, precurved for placement into the common bile duct (CBD) after sphincterotomy.

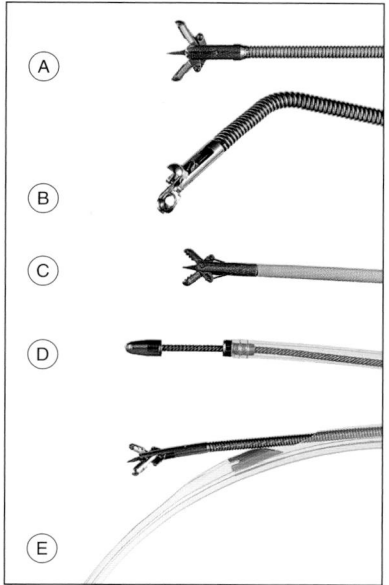

Figure 43-5. Variety of specialized forceps for endoscopic retrograde cholangiopancreatography (ERCP) endobiliary biopsy. Top to bottom: *A,* Standard flexible tip ERCP forceps. *B,* Angled tipped forceps (Maxum Carr-Locke; Wilson-Cook). *C,* 6-Fr pediatric forceps (Microvasive) that can be placed after sphincterotomy. *D,* Mighty-Bite (Wilson-Cook) side-biting specialized ERCP forceps. *E,* 5-Fr reusable HBIN forceps exiting from the Howell biliary introducer (Wilson-Cook).

optimal yield. Reporting on his experience, Ponchon and coworkers[11] suggested a minimum of three forceps bites.

For the technique to be practical, specialized forceps were developed. Several devices have been marketed to permit easier insertion, including two devices that are purported not to need sphincterotomy (Fig. 43-5).

Easier to insert but still unguided, pediatric forceps of 5 to 6 Fr work reasonably well but provide rather small specimens. Disposable 6-Fr pediatric forceps are now available, although they are relatively expensive (see Fig. 43-5C).

Malleable forceps were introduced by Olympus to permit the endoscopist to curve the tip by grooming. In this fashion, cannulation of the duct may be performed without sphincterotomy. Initial experience by Sugiyama and colleagues[7] produced a reported success rate of 87% in establishing a histologic diagnosis in Japanese patients, most of whom had biliary cancers. This experience has not been duplicated, and further safety data, especially the risk of producing post-ERCP pancreatitis, has not been published.

The full-sized angled forceps (Maxum Carr-Locke forceps, Wilson-Cook Medical) designed to permit cannulation without sphincterotomy were also reported to be successful in a small series of patients (see Fig. 43-5B).[31] This larger cup forceps has a pre-made angled tip but is fairly large and, in my experience, is not suitable for cannulation except after sphincterotomy. Again, no data on postprocedural complications have been published.

Two devices have been marketed to enable forceps placement over a guidewire. As previously discussed, the guidewire is generally placed early in therapeutic ERCP to ensure that the major goal of biliary stent placement will be successful. It is then logical to use the in-place guidewire for subsequent tissue sampling.

A side-biting forceps (Mighty-Bite, Wilson-Cook Medical) device has been marketed to go over a small guidewire. The conical-tipped forceps collect tissue at any angle after inserting it through the stricture. Because only a very narrow cup engages tissue during the sampling process, specimens tend to be small. In addition, the guidewire device requires a 0.018-inch guidewire and does not fit over the standard 0.035- or 0.025-inch guidewires generally in use. To use the guidewire function requires beginning with the smaller wire or converting to it—a lengthy and expensive option.

A non-guidewire Mighty-Bite is also available, but it must be inserted freehand into the stricture, making it difficult to place

(see Fig. 43-5D). No comparisons have been made to other forceps. Published experience has been limited to fewer than 10 patients and in abstract form only.[32]

The other guidewire-based device currently in use, developed by the author, is the Howell biliary introducer (HBI, Wilson-Cook Medical) (see Fig. 43-5E).

The 10-Fr device goes over a 0.035-inch or smaller guidewire while permitting the passage of a reusable 5-Fr specially designed long forceps. Multiple passes of the forceps and other sampling devices can be quickly accomplished, once the introducer is in position. At present, I advocate using this forceps as part of a multimodality sampling sequence. Introducing this device, its uses, and results are discussed later in this chapter because it is intended to facilitate the introduction of multiple sampling devices to maximize yield while maintaining guidewire position.

In a recent review published in two consecutive issues of *Gastrointestinal Endoscopy,* the journal of the American Society of Gastrointestinal Endoscopy, deBellis and colleagues[33] tabulated all reports in the literature for the three major techniques including forceps biopsy and ERCP tissue sampling since 1989 (Table 43-1).

Complications of forceps biopsy have been reported but appear to be very uncommon. Among the 502 patients tabulated in Table 43-1, major bleeding requiring transfusion in one cancer patient was reported[34] and a significant perforation of a benign stricture required surgery in one additional patient.[18] The use of a large cup forceps and repeatedly biopsying the same location may have caused the perforation. Pediatric forceps do produce a smaller specimen, but we have experienced no complications in more than 200 cases using them to date. These rare but serious complications have not been noted using endobiliary brushing or ERCP-directed FNA.

Table 43–1. Comparison of Endoscopic Retrograde Cholangiopancreatography Techniques

ERCP Technique	Number of Reports	Number of Patients	Sens	Specificity	PPV	NPV
Brush	8	837	42%	98%	98%	43%
FNA	5	223	34%	100%	100%	22%
Forceps	5	502	56%	97%	97%	57%

ERCP, endoscopic retrograde cholangiopancreatography; FNA, fine needle aspiration; NPV, negative predictive value; PPV, positive predictive value; Sens, sensitivity.

Combining Multiple Sampling Techniques

With the disappointing yields of single technique sampling as presented previously, endoscopists began to report their experience of combining techniques during the same ERCP procedure. This logical approach parallels standard endoscopic practice in which brush cytology and forceps biopsy are usually combined during both upper and lower procedures. Although this approach clearly takes more time than a single technique, improved yields have made the combined approach the preferred sequence in many, particularly academic, centers.

Using standard brushes and non-guidewire forceps, Ponchon and colleagues[11] reported improved combined yields for diagnosing cancer at ERCP. Although brushing had a sensitivity of 43% and forceps biopsy 30%, their combined yield was increased to 63% (a 20% overall gain).

A more comprehensive approach was studied by the Indiana University group. Researchers attempted to perform all three techniques of brush, FNA, and forceps sampling and, in addition, submitted withdrawn indwelling stents for cytology when present. This demanding approach resulted in positive diagnosis in 82% of patients at a single ERCP, the highest success yet reported.[20] Furthermore, when they analyzed their results, each technique contributed to making the diagnosis in at least some patients. In other words, many patients had only one of the techniques positive and the other two or three were negative or equivocal.

Despite this report and the logic of this approach, the technique of triple sampling has not become a standard during ERCP. Several explanations can be advanced.

The first and probably most important reason was previously discussed: triple sampling is technically difficult, time consuming, and ancillary to the main goal of the therapeutic procedure.

The second reason may be a clinical bias that pancreatic cancer and advanced biliary cancers are hopeless diseases and conservative palliation by stenting is all that is required. The case for tissue diagnosis beyond selection for chemotherapy or radiation therapy has been poorly made. A recent proposed algorithm from a major surgical hospital suggests that patients with appropriate images suggestive of resectable pancreatic cancer need only undergo surgical exploration.[26]

Finally, the advent and availability of EUS-guided FNA cytology has caused many authors to advocate a separate EUS procedure before ERCP is done to place a stent. Although this approach may shorten the ERCP, have a higher yield with multiple needle passes, and permit more confident placement of an initial metal stent, an additional invasive procedure is required. In most patients, there remains a role for ERCP tissue sampling.

To enhance the average endoscopist's ability to perform triple sampling with a minimum of time, expense, and risk, we assisted in the development of a multiuse biliary introducer (HBI, Wilson-Cook), mentioned previously. A goal was to permit maximum sampling at various depths to increase the chance of detecting all three types of malignancy and to do so without requiring a sphincterotomy if so desired (Fig. 43–6).

The details of the device and our initial procedural sequence, techniques, and yields were reported in 1996.[35] An overall sensitivity of 69%, despite a large proportion of small early pancreatic cancers, suggested the potential of the device. The HBI introducer is a double-lumen 10-Fr tapered dilator that contains a 0.035-inch channel for a standard ERCP guidewire and a 6-Fr large channel for the introduction of endoscopic accessories. The larger channel exits 3 cm below the tip and is fronted by a metal angled ramp that deflects the advance of devices at a 30-degree angle to assist in device positioning. The purpose of the ramp is to direct sampling away from the axis of the biliary stricture and into the deeper tissues where malignant tissue diagnosis was more likely to lie.

The needle and forceps exits to biopsy at this 30-degree angle into the lower edge of the stricture. With fluoroscopic guidance, repeated biopsy at the same point may also help sample deeply. Care should be taken when using this repeated biopsy technique when a clear mass is not present on pre-ERCP CT scan to minimize the risk of perforation. To date, no perforation has been reported using the 22-gauge needle or the small 5- or 6-Fr biopsy forceps.

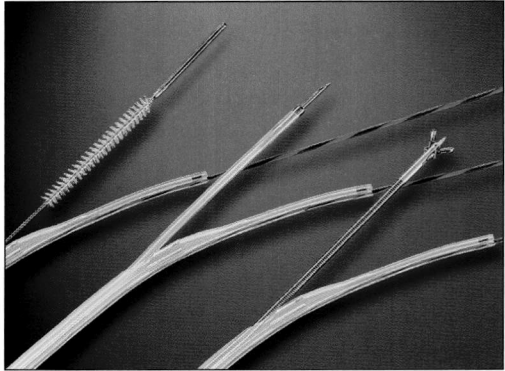

Figure 43–6. Howell biliary introducer (HBI, Wilson-Cook) with three tissue sampling devices advanced to biopsy or cytology position. Each device is placed sequentially to attempt to maximize yield at a single endoscopic retrograde cholangiopancreatography (ERCP). The HBI is placed over a pre-positioned 0.035-inch guidewire.

We advise against ever biopsying the bile duct above a stricture because the bile duct is thinned by obstructive dilation and a bile leak may occur.

Finally, the HBI and the previously mentioned devices serve to remove benign epithelium before introducing the specially designed cytology brush (HBIB, Wilson-Cook Medical). This brush has extra-long, extra-stiff bristles and is mounted on a stiff braided-wire shaft resulting in an aggressive device (see Fig. 43–1D).

We have standardized the technique of triple sampling using the HBI. After placement of a guidewire through the stricture, the preloaded HBI containing the specially designed 22-gauge needle is passed as a unit into the stricture (Fig. 43–7). It is important that the retracted needle within its ball-tipped 5-Fr catheter be kept just

inside the angled port. As this unit is passed over the pre-positioned guidewire (see Fig. 43–7A), the elevator of the duodenoscope is relaxed to prevent damage to the needle. Once positioned under the stricture, the ball tip is advanced, locked, and the needle is then thrust forward into the tumor (see Fig. 43–7B). The stylet is then removed from the needle, 10 mL of syringe vacuum suction is applied, and the needle is thrust in and out using a standard Chiba technique. A second thrust can be made without withdrawing the needle, but we generally perform a single FNA. The specimen is expressed into a cytologic transport medium (Cyto-Rich, Roche, Elon College, NC) that lyses red cells and fixes tissue for cell block. This approach shortens procedure time and avoids improper slide preparation or cellular loss.

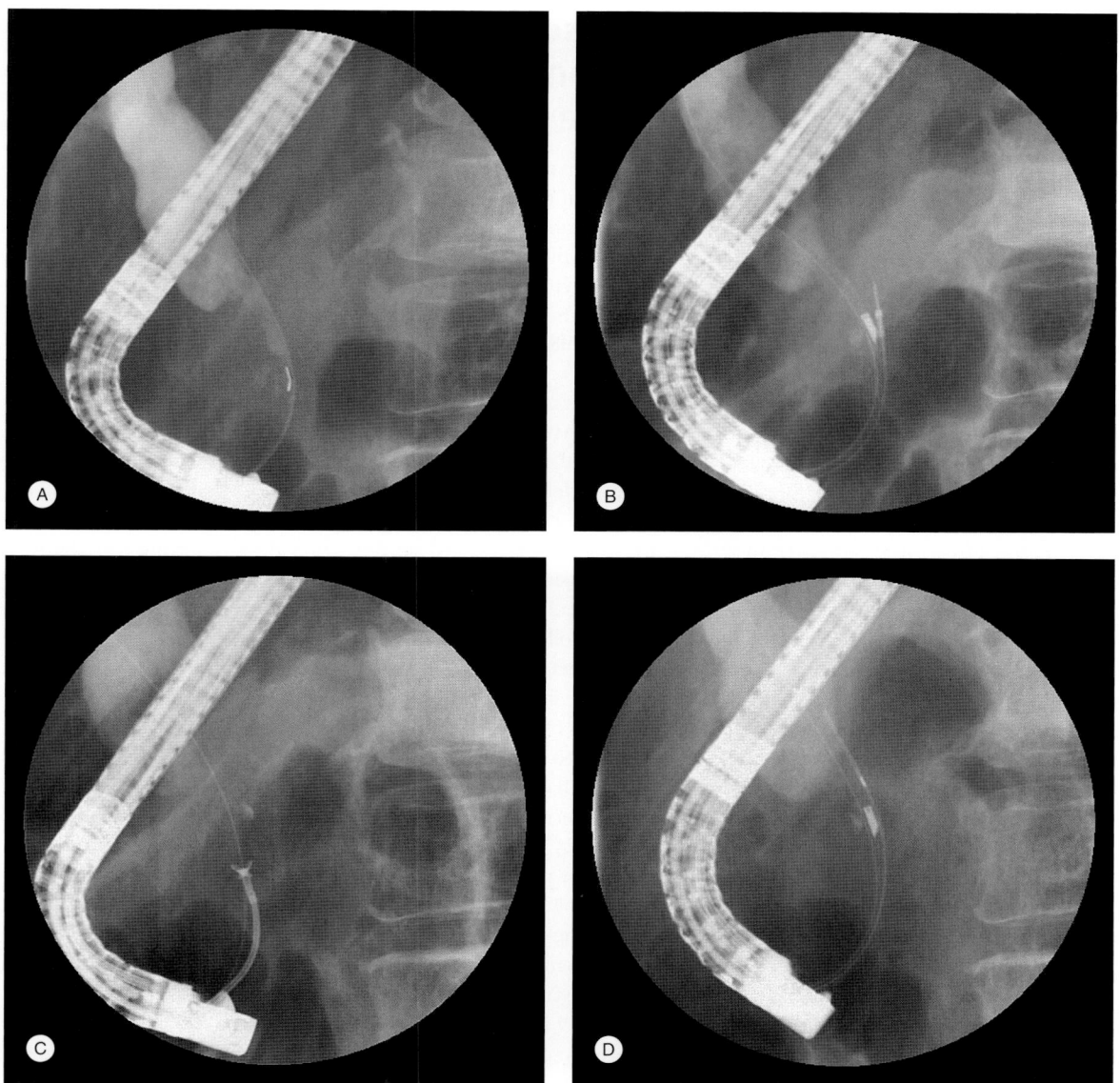

Figure 43–7. Howell biliary introducer (HBI) triple device tissue sampling. *A,* The guidewire is first negotiated through a malignant-appearing stricture. A sphincterotomy is optional. *B,* The HBI preloaded with the 5-Fr 22-gauge needle for fine needle aspiration (FNA) is placed over the guidewire and positioned just beneath the lower edge of the stricture. Here the needle has been thrust into the tumor at 30 degrees from the axis of the guidewire. *C,* The 5-Fr reusable HBIN forceps are then passed for repeat biopsies of the lower edge of the stricture. *D,* To perform brush cytology with the HBI, the introducer is advanced so the metal port lies above the stricture. The special brush (HBIB) is then advanced into the proximal duct. The introducer is then pulled down into the stricture to permit vigorous brushing with adequate side pressure to maximize cellular collection.

The second device is always the 5-Fr HBIN forceps. This can be passed through the HBI and over the elevator, if the angle of entry into the duct is not too sharp (see Fig. 43–7C). If resistance is felt, moving the HBI back into the endoscope permits the forceps to advance to the angled port, and the HBI and forceps can then be advanced again as a unit, to ensure easy forceps placement.

We attempt to open the forceps below the stricture, but often the distal duct is too small to accommodate this action. The HBI containing the forceps can be advanced above the stricture to permit the forceps to be advanced into the dilated proximal duct and opened. The HBI is then pulled down leaving only the narrow tip in the stricture. The open forceps can be pulled through the stricture while open and closed on the appropriate lower stricture edge. Care should be used to never biopsy the duct above the stricture.

On occasion, the hard nature of pancreatic tumors does not permit easy severing of tissue, despite firm biting force. Diagnostic pieces can still be obtained after closing the cups but pushing the HBI forward, which then often shears off the desired sample.

We have generally used three bites as a standard but more biopsies increase yield, as discussed later in the chapter.

Finally, the specially designed brush (HBIB) is introduced while the angled port is advanced above the stricture. Once the brush is advanced into the duct, the HBI is pulled back into the stricture so that the wide 10-Fr portion just in front of the angled port lies inside the stricture. The spring-nosed brush is then vigorously moved to and fro keeping the nose always just above the upper aspect of the stricture (see Fig. 43–7D). The brush will be very tight but will abrade and deeply sample the encasing tumor.

After 60 to 120 seconds of brushing, the brush is pulled back just into the 6-Fr channel and left there while the entire HBI and brush is removed leaving the guidewire in place. Cellular loss is prevented by not withdrawing the brush through the HBI.

The brush is then simply cut off and dropped into the transport medium, again to shorten the procedure time and permit slide preparation in the cytology department.

After some initial experience, this sequence of triple sampling using the HBI takes 12 to 15 minutes and does not interfere with planned stent insertion. The entire sequence is portrayed in the accompanying video clip.

Our initial experience reported a positive yield of 69% using the previously described technique.[35] This sequence demonstrated the value of using all three devices because patients often had only one device sample positive with the others being read as suspicious or falsely negative. For the purposes of the initial report, we considered "suspicious for adenocarcinoma" as positive (45% positive, 24% suspicious, for a total of 69%). In the appropriate study setting of a documented mass, this resulted in maintaining a specificity of 100%.

A comparative trial of the HBI device against standard brushing was recently reported.[36] For the purpose of their study, the authors considered any positive, suspicious, or atypical/suggestive of malignancy to be true positives. The authors used only the HBIN 22-gauge needle and HBI brush and reported an 85% yield compared with a sensitivity of 57% for brushing alone. Presumably, if the HBI forceps had been used in addition, yield would have been greater.

For the diagnosis of malignancy, this method of reporting suspicious, and even atypical/suggestive of malignancy, results has been generally done in reports of ERCP tissue sampling, but a higher standard must be demanded.

We have recently modified our technique of HBI sampling to attempt to increase the true-positive yield. We now take six biopsies and brush for 2 full minutes. This prolongs tissue sampling by about 6 minutes. In our 2003 report, we considered any result but frankly positive to be negative.[37] The true-positive yield increased from 45% to 71.4%. The greatest increase of positives proved to be with the extra forceps biopsies. In this recent series of 35 consecutive patients, 9 cases had only forceps positive, 3 had only FNA positive, and 1 had the brush positive alone. No complications were noted.

Other Methods of Endoscopic Retrograde Cholangiopancreatography Tissue Sampling

A number of less productive or controversial techniques of tissue acquisition have been reported and deserve review.

Leung and coworkers[38] originally reported that examining indwelling plastic biliary stents on their removal may produce a positive cytologic specimen when the diagnosis had not been established at the initial ERCP placement.

Since 1989, only one series has approached Leung and coworkers'[38] initial 70% yield. Most centers report only 11% to 44% positive specimens.[8,14,39]

The most recent report of stent cytology included withdrawn pancreatic stents and those from biliary strictures.[40] The true-positive yield from pancreatic stents was 25% compared with only 11% from biliary stents. In addition, they agreed with other authors that the technique had limited clinical valve because of the long delay in diagnosis when positive results were obtained.

Another approach to tissue acquisition at ERCP has been to attempt collection of specimens from the pancreatic duct. Collection of pancreatic juice has been advocated by a few authors.[41,42] The technique involves deep insertion of a standard ERCP catheter and aspiration of juice below a malignant-appearing stricture. Yields may increase to greater than 50% with the infusion of secretin. This approach has not become popular, perhaps because of its complexity and concern for inducing pancreatitis. Furthermore, Pugliese and coworkers[43] concluded that pancreatic juice collection did not add to positive diagnosis when pancreatic duct strictures were directly sampled by brushing.

Brushing in the pancreatic duct has been reported since 1979.[44] More recent reports emphasize that yields increase very little when a biliary stricture is also present and can be sampled.[45-47] Most concerning has been the report of postprocedural pancreatitis after pancreatic ductal stricture brushing. Vandervoort and colleagues[48] noted a 21.5% pancreatitis rate after such procedures in both benign and malignant cases but noted a marked decrease in risk if pancreatic temporary plastic stents were placed. Others have also advocated postbrushing stent placement, but all studies do not outline the eventual management and outcome of these temporary stents. It seems likely that subsequent procedures for pancreatic

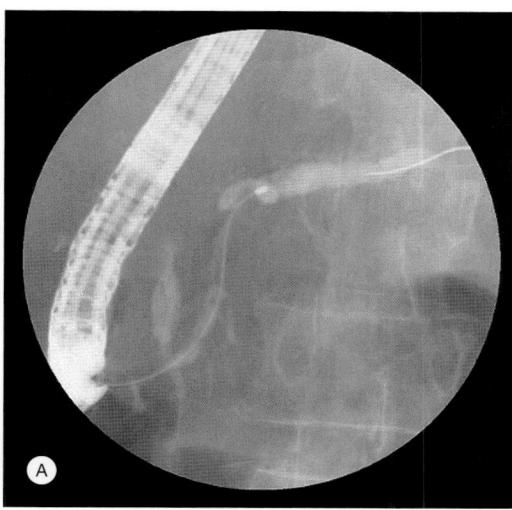

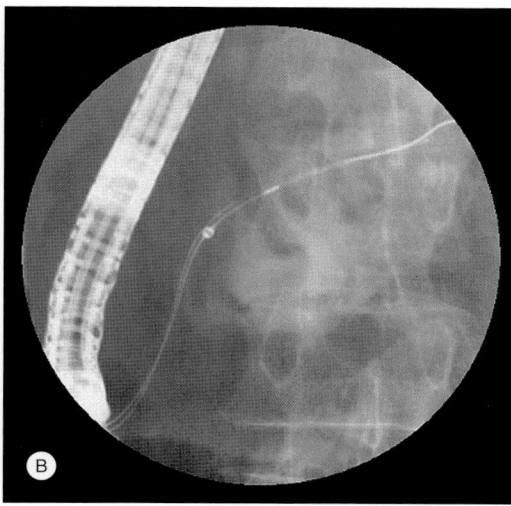

Figure 43–8. *A,* A malignant-appearing midpancreatic duct stricture has produced a pseudocyst from the tail drainage. Here a guidewire has been advanced through the stricture and advanced into the tail, and the stricture is being dilated to 7 Fr. *B,* A monorail-type catheter with a preloaded long-nosed brush has been advanced through the stricture over the upper end of the guidewire. The brush has been advanced and pulled down to brush the stricture. After removal, a decompressing pancreatic stent will be positioned over the guidewire.

stent removal or delayed stent obstruction with resulting pancreatitis or sepsis outweighs their utility and favors other approaches to tissue sampling.

Currently, we only sample from the pancreatic duct when a pancreatic stent is clinically warranted to manage obstructing pancreatitis, fistula, or upstream pseudocyst. We prefer to use the monorail technique for brushing as outlined previously, so that the guidewire, which was placed before tissue sample, can remain in position (Fig. 43–8*A* and *B*).

Specimen Handling and Analysis

Improper handling of collected specimens remains a problem in many endoscopy units. A major cause of uninterpretable smears is air-drying artifact that can occur rapidly after creation of appropriate thin smear.[9] Thick smears and overly bloody specimens are other significant problems.[49] Furthermore, slide preparation requires the time and attention of ERCP team members during a busy and often complex procedure.

As outlined in the section outlining the technique of triple sampling with the HBI device, we prefer to deposit all collected specimens into transport media rather than preparing any smears or slides in the ERCP suite. Available transport media include 95% ethanol or commercially prepared solutions such as CytoLyt (Cytyc Corporation, Boxborough, MA) or CytoRich (UtoCyte, Burlington, NC). Papanicolaou-stained spun smears and, when applicable, hematoxylin and eosin (H&E) stained cell block sections are prepared for cytologic evaluation. In our institution, we prefer CytoLyt solution, which lyses red blood cells and minimizes obscuring debris, with smears prepared via the ThinPrep method (Cytyc Corporation). We have not found it practical to have a cytology technician or a cytopathologist in the room because the precise time during the ERCP procedure when specimens will be collected is highly variable and does not use his or her time efficiently. The exception may be needle biopsying hilar strictures that have been previously negatively sampled and are not amenable to EUS or CT-guided FNA because of their location.

Interpretation of specimens to be clinically useful should follow accepted cytologic criteria. Several such schemes exist with each accepting frankly positive (Fig. 43–9*A*) and negative (see Fig. 43–9*B*) features. Intermediate cytologic abnormalities present on the slides may lead to interpretations such as atypical, in which mild cellular abnormalities are usually associated with inflammation and reparative changes, and suspicious, in which there are rare cells exhibiting cytologic features of malignancy but they are present in insufficient numbers to render a definitive diagnosis of malignancy. As previously stated, suspicious for malignancy should contain adequate features to make the diagnosis highly likely especially when interpreted in the appropriate clinical setting. In our institution, suspicious for adenocarcinoma is equivalent to a true positive when the patient has a malignant-appearing distal biliary stricture at ERCP and a definite mass on CT scan. Suspicious is not adequate in interpreting samples from biliary strictures in patients with primary sclerosing cholangitis (PSC) or postbiliary irradiation resulting in significant false positives. Ponshon and coworkers[11] reported four false-positive ERCP brush cytology specimens among three patients with PSC. A larger series noted only an 80% specificity in this setting.[50]

The findings of "cellular atypia" should include criteria that make the diagnosis of malignancy unlikely and, therefore, demand further attempts at confirmation. We interpret all atypia findings as negative, understanding that many will be falsely negative.

Finally, because of the inherit difficulties in ERCP tissue sampling, negative results can never be accepted as definitive.[10] Sampling problems are often due to the relative hardness of pancreaticobiliary adenocarcinomas that may greatly resist needle puncture and forceps sampling. Furthermore, these desmoplastic tumors can be relatively hypocellular resulting in inadequate numbers of cells for interpretation. A small fraction of adenocarcinomas are so well differentiated they can only be diagnosed histologically in the setting of an excisional biopsy to permit the recognition of invasion. This is also true of lymphoma, which does on occasion produce biliary obstruction. Furthermore, as previously discussed, metastatic lesions obstructing the biliary tree are relatively deep and cannot be readily accessed at ERCP from within the ductal stricture except, on occasion, by intraductal FNA.

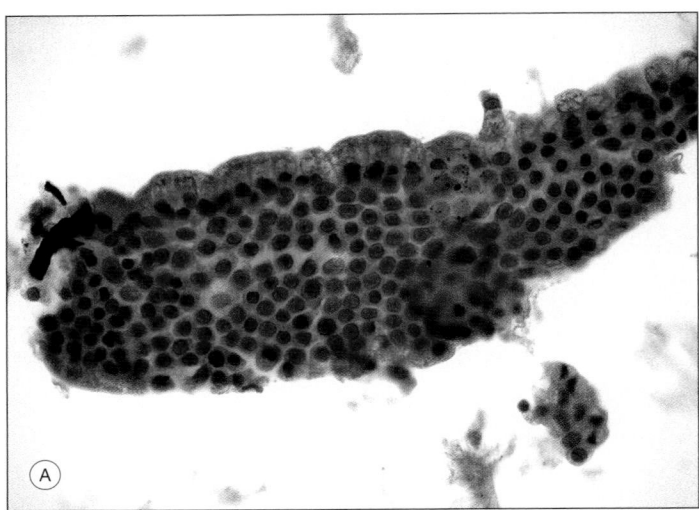 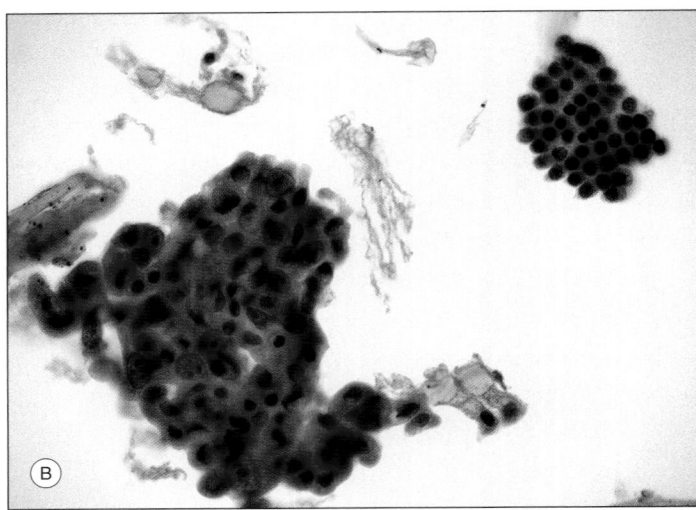

Figure 43-9. *A,* An example of a benign biliary sample collected at endoscopic retrograde cholangiopancreatography (ERCP) by fine needle aspiration (FNA). The specimen demonstrates normal monolayer architecture with cells of high cytoplasm to nuclear ratio. The nuclei are smooth with fine chromation and without obvious nucleoli. *B,* Conversely, this ERCP-collected specimen reveals malignant features diagnostic of adenocarcinomas. Note the clusters of cells with nuclear crowding. The nuclei have irregular membranes, coarse chromatin, and prominent nucleoli. Finally, the nuclei are large, producing high nuclei to cytoplasmic ratio.

All of these factors result in a low negative predictive value in all series reporting techniques of tissue sampling. This should not discourage the endoscopist from developing a preferred sequence of tissue sampling at ERCP because specificity in all reports is generally 100% for true positives. A false-negative result leads to additional invasive tests, procedures, or surgery,[1] the same result as when no effort is made. Using the outlined techniques of endobiliary sampling during ERCP, patients are benefited at a minimum of expense and risk.

Future Trends

Currently, there is a strong trend to apply newer technology to specimen analysis. Once collected, specimens have undergone additional techniques of analysis in an attempt at increasing positive results, but none have been yet established as clinically useful despite considerable attention.

Flow cytometry was one of the first ancillary techniques reported with the hope that cytologically negative specimens might reveal DNA aneuploidy sufficient to advance the diagnosis of cancer. Early reports clearly revealed the problem of poor specificity most likely resulting from the mixed population of inflammatory cells and debris.[51] This problem may be resolved with a technique of digital image analysis, but a large prospective study has yet to be produced.[52]

Techniques of genetic analysis have similarly proved both promising and to date disappointing because of lack of specificity. Researchers have examined the technique of polymerase chain reaction (PCR) to augment and detect genetic mutations that may add to malignant diagnosis.

The K-*ras* mutation has been identified as often present in pancreaticobiliary cancers. Several PCR-based studies to detect K-*ras* mutations in ERCP-collected specimens seemed useful with positive yields increasing by up to 30%.[53] However, as with flow cytometry, specificities proved to be poor when patients with chronic pancreatitis were included. Two studies reported finding K-*ras* mutations in 25% and 36% of chronic pancreatitis patients with subsequently proven benign strictures.[43,54] This potential for false-positive results precludes this technique from use in clinical decision making.

Two other research techniques, namely screening for loss of genetic heterozygosity (LOH) and immunostaining for the *p53* gene have been preliminarily examined but do not have sufficient data to support their use. These techniques are likely to receive further attention, because these techniques are being actively researched for possible use in colon cancer stool specimen screening.[55]

An advance in equipment is another trend that may impact tissue sampling at ERCP. Newer, small endoscopes termed "baby-scopes" of 10 Fr have permitted direct examination of biliary tree and, with the smallest 7-Fr baby-scopes, even pancreatic duct lesions. A 3-Fr biopsy forceps and a long cytology brush can be inserted through the 10-Fr baby-endoscope's 1.0-mm accessory channel to permit directed biopsy, but because of the very small size and their superficial nature this equipment is not likely to increase tissue diagnosis. Nevertheless, efforts are under way to permit accurate visual diagnosis of malignancy using rigid and reproducible criteria.[56]

Intraductal EUS (IDUS) has been used through biliary strictures to this same end. However, specificity is much below that of directed tissue sampling and as such cannot substitute. One report of comparing EUS with tissue sampling and IDUS in 30 patients suggested that IDUS increased accuracy from 68% to 90%.[57] However, the need for accurate tissue determination of the type of malignancy required further efforts at tissue diagnosis. The ERCP tissue diagnosis specificity was 100%.

Optical coherence tomography (OCT) may be adaptable to be used over a guidewire during ERCP and provide a histologic quality image for pathologic interpretation.[58]

A more promising approach to increase the yield and specificity of ERCP tissue sampling will lie in developing better devices to collect larger specimens more successfully. The recent introduction of a cutting needle for EUS-guided biopsy is such an example.[59]

Summary

Tissue sampling at ERCP remains an underused group of techniques that when properly used is safe, rapid, and cost effective. The increasing yield as individual techniques are added, support multimodality sampling or, at minimum, collection of multiple specimens. The consequence of not attempting ERCP sampling commits the patient to other expensive and often uncomfortable biopsy attempts, if a tissue diagnosis is to be established. Based on the literature at present, rapid collection of multiple specimens for cytology and histology is possible during a single therapeutic ERCP and can be recommended.

REFERENCES

1. Howell D, Mazzaglia P, Sheth S, et al: Clinical value of tissue sampling at ERCP [abstract]. Gastrointest Endosc 55:AB196, 2002.
2. Bain VG, Abraham N, Jhangri GS, et al: Prospective study of biliary strictures to determine the predictors of malignancy. Can J Gastroenterol 14:397–402, 2000.
3. Foutch PG, Kerr DM, Harlan JR, et al: A prospective, controlled analysis of endoscopic cytotechniques for diagnosis of malignant biliary strictures. Am J Gastroenterol 86:577–580, 1991.
4. Desa LA, Akosa AB, Lazzara S, et al: Cytodiagnosis in the management of extrahepatic biliary strictures. Gut 32:1188–1191, 1991.
5. Davidson B, Varsamidakis N, Dooley J, et al: Value of exfoliative cytology for investigating bile duct strictures. Gut 33:1408–1411, 1992.
6. Kurzawinski TR, Deery A, Dooley JS, et al: A prospective study of biliary cytology in 100 patients with bile duct strictures. Hepatology 18:1399–1403, 1993.
7. Sugiyama M, Atomi Y, Wada N, et al: Endoscopic transpapillary bile duct biopsy without sphincterotomy for diagnosing biliary strictures: A prospective comparative study with bile and brush cytology. Am J Gastroenterol 91:465–467, 1996.
8. Mansfield JC, Griffin SM, Wadehra V, et al: A prospective evaluation of cytology from biliary strictures. Gut 40:671–677, 1997.
9. Kocjan G, Smith AN: Bile duct brushings cytology: Potential pitfalls in diagnosis. Diagn Cytopathol 16:358–363, 1997.
10. Logrono R, Kurtycz DF, Molina CP, et al: Analysis of false-negative diagnoses on endoscopic brush cytology of biliary and pancreatic duct strictures: The experience at two university hospitals. Arch Pathol Lab Med 124:387–392, 2000.
11. Ponchon T, Gagnon P, Berger F, et al: Value of endobiliary brush cytology and biopsies for the diagnosis of malignant bile duct stenosis: Results of a prospective study. Gastrointest Endosc 42:565–572, 1995.
12. Renshaw AA, Madge R, Jiroutek M, et al: Bile duct brushing cytology: Statistical analysis of proposed diagnostic criteria. Am J Clin Pathol 110:635–640, 1998.
13. Bardales RH, Stanley MW, Simpson DD, et al: Diagnostic value of brush cytology in the diagnosis of duodenal, biliary and ampullary neoplasms. Am J Clin Pathol 109:540–548, 1998.
14. Harewood GC, Wiersema MJ: Endosonography-guided fine needle aspiration biopsy in the evaluation of pancreatic masses. Am J Gastroenterol 97:1386–1391, 2002.
15. Baron TH, Lee JG, Wax TD, et al: An in vitro randomized, prospective study to maximize cellular yield during bile duct cytology. Gastrointest Endosc 40:146–149, 1994.
16. Foutch PG, Harlan JR, Kerr D, Sanowski RA: Wire-guided brush cytology: A new endoscopic method for diagnosis of bile duct cancer. Gastrointest Endosc 35:243–247, 1989.
17. Lee JG, Leung JW, Baillie J, et al: Benign, dysplastic, or malignant-making sense of endoscopic bile duct brush cytology: Results in 149 consecutive patients. Am J Gastroenterol 90:722–726, 1995.
18. Pugliese V, Conio M, Nicolo G, et al: Endoscopic retrograde forceps biopsy and brush cytology of biliary strictures: A prospective study. Gastrointest Endosc 42:520–526, 1995.
19. Glasbrenner B, Ardan M, Boeck W, et al: Prospective evaluation of brush cytology of biliary strictures during endoscopic strictures: A review of 406 cases. J Clin Pathol 54:449–455, 2001.
20. Jailwala J, Fogel EL, Sherman S, et al: Triple tissue sampling at ERCP in malignant biliary obstruction. Gastrointest Endosc 51:383–390, 2000.
21. Macken E, Drijkoningen M, Van Aken E, et al: Brush cytology of ductal strictures during ERCP. Acta Gastroenterol Belg 63:254–259, 2000.
22. Howell DA, Beveridge RP, Bosco J, et al: Endoscopic needle aspiration biopsy at ERCP in the diagnosis of biliary strictures. Gastrointest Endosc 38:531–535, 1992.
23. Glasbrenner B, Ardan M, Boeck W, et al: Prospective evaluation of brush cytology of biliary strictures during endoscopic retrograde cholangiopancreatography. Endoscopy 31:712–717, 1999.
24. Rabinowitz M, Zajko AB, Hassanein T, et al: Diagnostic value of brush cytology in the diagnosis of bile duct carcinoma: A study in 65 patients with bile duct strictures. Hepatology 12:747–752, 1990.
25. Warshaw AL: Implications of peritoneal cytology for staging of early pancreatic cancer. Am J Surg 161:26–29, 1991.
26. Farnell MB, Nagorney DM, et al: The Mayo clinic approach to the surgical treatment of adenocarcinomas of the pancreas. Surg Clin North Am 81:611–623, 2001.
27. Tsuchiya R, Henmi T, Kondo N, et al: Endoscopic aspiration biopsy of the pancreas. Gastroenterology 73:1050–1052, 1977.
28. Kochhar R, Rajwanshi A, Malik AK, et al: Endoscopic fine needle aspiration biopsy of gastroesophageal malignancies. Gastrointest Endosc 34:321–323, 1988.
29. Lo SK, Cox J, Soltani S, et al: A prospective blinded evaluation of all ERCP sampling methods on biliary strictures [abstract]. Gastrointest Endosc 43:386A, 1996.
30. Farrell RJ, Jain AK, Brandwein SL, et al: The combination of stricture dilation, endoscopic needle aspiration, and biliary brushings significantly improves diagnostic yield from malignant bile duct strictures. Gastrointest Endosc 54:587–594, 2001.
31. Vandervoort J, Soetinko RM, Montes H, Carr-Lock DL: Use of a new angled forceps to biopsy pancreatic and biliary strictures [abstract]. Gastrointest Endosc 45:AB41, 1997.
32. Tada M, Isayama H, Sasahira, et al: Definitive diagnosis of malignant biliary tract strictures by introducing Mighty Bite [abstract]. Gastrointest Endosc 55:AB168, 2002.
33. de Bellis M, Sherman S, Fogel EL, et al: Tissue sampling at ERCP in suspected malignant biliary strictures. Gastrointest Endosc 56:552–561 (Part I), 720–730 (Part II), 2002.
34. Schoefl R, Haefner W, Wrba F, et al: Forceps biopsy and brush cytology during endoscopic retrograde cholangiopancreatography for the diagnosis of biliary stenosis. Scand J Gastroenterol 32:363–368, 1997.
35. Howell DA, Parsons WG, Jones MA, et al: Complete tissue sampling of biliary strictures at ERCP using a new device. Gastrointest Endosc 43:498–501, 1996.
36. Farrell RJ, Jain AK, Brandwein SL, et al: The combination of stricture dilation, endoscopic needle aspiration and biliary brushings significantly improves diagnostic yield from malignant bile duct strictures. Gastrointest Endosc 54:587–594, 2001.
37. Howell D, Lukens F, Shah, et al: What is the true yield of tissue sampling at ERCP [abstract]? Gastrointest Endosc 55:AB170, 2002.
38. Leung JW, Sung JY, Chung SC, Chan KM: Endoscopic scraping biopsy of malignant biliary strictures. Gastrointest Endos 35:65–66, 1989.

39. Pescatore P, Heubner C, Heine M, et al: The value of histological analysis of occluded biliary endoprostheses. Endoscopy 27:597–600, 1995.

40. Simsir A, Greenebaum E, Stevens PD, et al: Biliary stent replacement cytology. Diagn Cytopathol 16:233–237, 1997.

41. Devereaux BM, Fogel EL, Bucksot L, et al: Clinical utility of stent cytology for the diagnosis of pancreaticobiliary neoplasms. Am J Gastroenterol 98:1028–1031, 2003.

42. Nakaizumi A, Tatsuta M, Uehara H, et al: Cytologic examination of pure pancreatic juice in the diagnosis of pancreatic carcinoma: The endoscopic retrograde intraductal catheter aspiration cytologic technique. Cancer 70:2610–2614, 1992.

43. Pugliese V, Pujic N, Saccomanno S, et al: Pancreatic intraductal sampling during ERCP in patients with chronic pancreatitis and pancreatic cancer: Cytologic studies and k-ras-2 codon 12 molecular analysis in 47 cases. Gastrointest Endosc 545:595–599, 2001.

44. Osnes M, Serck-Hansenn A, Kristensen O, et al: Endoscopic retrograde brush cytology in patients with primary and secondary malignancies of the pancreas. Gut 20:279–284, 1979.

45. Nakaizumi A, Tatsuta M, Uehara H, et al: Effectiveness of cytologic examination of pure pancreatic juice in the diagnosis of early neoplasia of the pancreas. Cancer 76:750–757, 1995.

46. McGuire DE, Venu RP, Brown R, et al. A brush cytology for pancreatic carcinoma: An analysis of factors influencing results. Gastrointest Endosc 44:300–304, 1996.

47. Ferrari AP Jr, Lichtenstein DR, Slivka A, et al: Brush cytology during ERCP for the diagnosis of biliary and pancreatic malignancies. Gastrointest Endosc 40:140–145, 1994.

48. Vandervoort J, Soetikno RM, Montes H, et al: Accuracy and complication rates of brush cytology from bile duct versus pancreatic duct. Gastrointest Endosc 49:322–327, 1999.

49. Layfield LJ, Wax TD, Lee JC: Accuracy and morphologic aspects of pancreatic and biliary duct brushings. Acta Cytol 39:11–18, 1995.

50. Lindberg B, Arnelo U, Bergquist A, et al: Diagnosis of biliary strictures in conjunction with endoscopic retrograde cholangio-pancreatography, with special reference to patients with primary sclerosing cholangitis. Endoscopy 34:909–909, 2002.

51. Ryan ME, Baldauf MC: Comparison of flow cytometry for DNA content and brush cytology for detection of malignancy in pancreatobiliary strictures. Gastrointest Endosc 40:133–139, 1994.

52. Rumalla A, Baron TH, Leontovich O, et al: Improved diagnostic yield of endoscopic biliary brush cytology by digital image analysis. Mayo Clin Proc 76:29–33, 2001.

53. Sturm PD, Rauws EA, Hruban RH, et al: Clinical value of K-ras codon 12 analysis and endobiliary brush cytology for the diagnosis of malignant extrahepatic bile duct stenosis. Clin Cancer Res 5:629–635, 1999.

54. Iwao T, Hanada K, Tsuchida A, et al: The establishment of a preoperative diagnosis for pancreatic carcinoma using cell specimens from pancreatic duct brushing with special attention to p53 mutations. Cancer 82:1487–1494, 1998.

55. Ahlquisht DA, Skoletsky JE, Boynton KA, et al: Colorectal cancer screening by detection of altered human DNA in stool: Feasibility of a multitarget assay panel. Gastroenterology 119:1219–1227, 2000.

56. Telford JJ, Carr-Locke DL: The role of ECP and pancreatoscopy in cystic and intraductal tumors. Gastrointest Endosc Clin N Am 12:747–757, 2002.

57. Vasquez-Sequeiros E, Baron TH, Clain JE, et al: Evaluation of indeterminate bile duct strictures by intraductal US. Gastrointest Endosc 56:372–379, 2002.

58. Van Dam J: Novel methods of enhanced endoscopic imaging. Gut 52:12–16, 2003.

59. DeWitt J, LeBlan J, McHenry L, et al: Endoscopic ultrasound-guided fine needle aspiration cytology of solid liver lesions: A large single-center experience. Am J Gastroenterol 98:1976–1981, 2003.

Endoscopic Ultrasonography of Pancreatic and Biliary Diseases

Mark D. Topazian

Introduction

Endoscopic ultrasonography (EUS) is a powerful imaging modality that has changed the clinical approach to biliary and pancreatic disease. Because it provides detailed images of the extrahepatic biliary tree and pancreas with very little risk to the patient, EUS can substitute for endoscopic retrograde cholangiopancreatography (ERCP) in the evaluation of obstructive jaundice,[1] biliary dilation,[2] pancreatic masses, and pancreatitis.[3] EUS and ERCP can be performed under the same sedation, with EUS identifying patients likely to benefit from endoscopic therapy. Intraductal ultrasonography (IDUS) performed with a high-frequency probe during ERCP improves diagnostic accuracy for biliary stones and strictures and is useful in some pancreatic diseases, such as intraductal papillary mucinous neoplasm (IPMN). EUS is an increasingly important tool for the biliary and pancreatic endoscopist.

This chapter discusses the use of EUS for diagnosis of common biliary and pancreatic diseases. The technique of EUS-guided fine needle aspiration (FNA) is presented in a subsequent chapter.

Gallbladder Stones, Sludge, and Polyps

EUS is useful for diagnosis of gallbladder sludge or stones missed by transabdominal ultrasound and is more sensitive than bile microscopy in such patients (Fig. 44–1).[4,5] It may be especially useful in obese patients and those with stones in the gallbladder neck, settings in which transabdominal ultrasound is less sensitive for diagnosis. Sludge is visualized as echogenic, nonshadowing, layering material. It should not be confused with gain artifact or

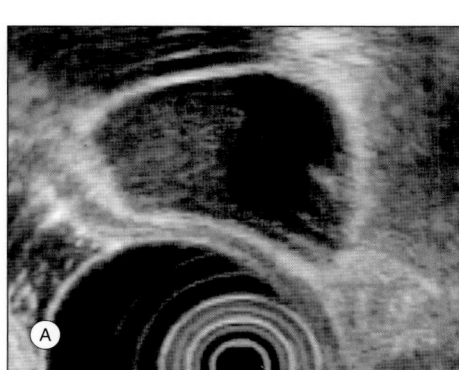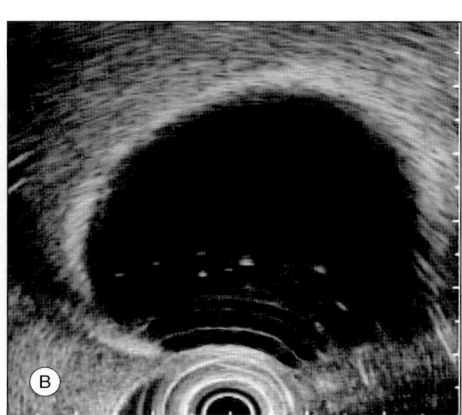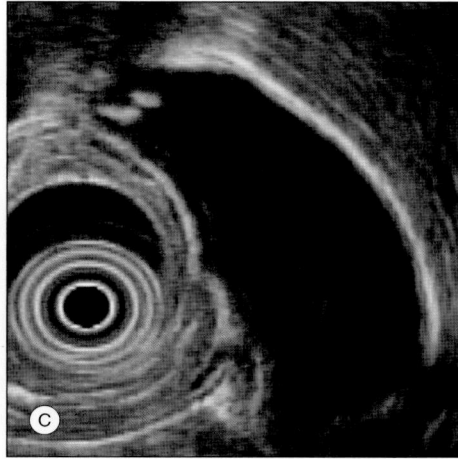

Figure 44–1. Gallbladder findings in patients with recurrent acute pancreatitis and previous normal transabdominal ultrasound. *A,* Layering sludge. *B,* Echogenic cholesterol crystals in gallbladder bile. *C,* Small stones in the gallbladder neck.

Table 44–1. Differential Diagnosis of Gallbladder Polyps

Non-neoplastic	Neoplastic
Cholesterol	Adenoma
Hyperplastic	Adenocarcinoma
Inflammatory	Adenosquamous carcinoma
Fibrous	Neuroendocrine tumor
Adenomyomatosis	

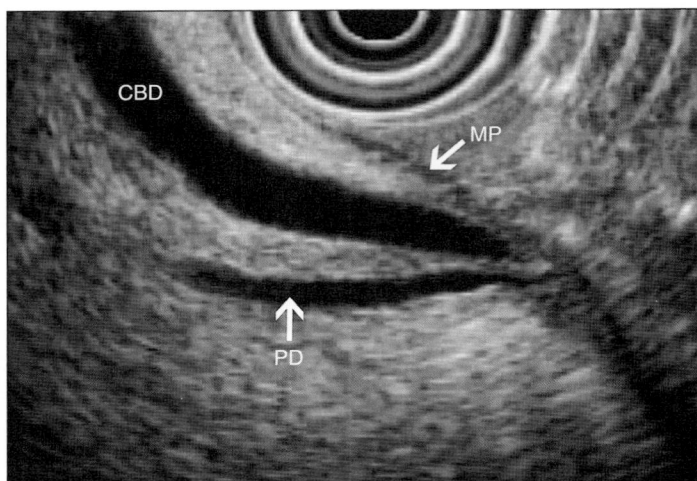

Figure 44–2. Normal bile duct viewed from the duodenal bulb with a radial echoendoscope. CBD, common bile duct; MP, muscularis propria of the duodenal wall; PD, pancreatic duct.

"ring-down artifact," circular bright lines parallel to the transducer seen with mechanical radial scopes. A clear-cut sludge–bile interface is helpful for diagnosis of sludge. Cholesterol crystals have straight edges and are highly echogenic; they appear as bright flecks in bile, sometimes casting "comet's tails." Calcium bilirubinate granules are rounded and much less echogenic and can be missed by EUS unless they are present in sufficient quantity to form layering sludge.

EUS has been used for differential diagnosis of gallbladder polyps. The best clinical studies have been reported from Asia, and their applicability to Western populations has not been well studied. Most gallbladder polyps are readily imaged, although the fundus and cap of the gallbladder may be difficult or impossible to visualize in some patients. Polyps should be distinguished from sludge by turning the patient during EUS to confirm that the lesion is immobile. The differential diagnosis of gallbladder polyps is listed in Table 44–1. The size of gallbladder polyps is the single most important consideration in differential diagnosis. Neoplasm is very unlikely in polyps with a diameter of 5 mm or less but is usually present in polyps greater than 15 mm in diameter.[6–8] Particular echofeatures that predict non-neoplastic polyps have been identified. Cholesterol polyps may contain bright, echogenic spots or demonstrate comet's tail artifacts caused by cholesterol crystals in the lesion. Adenomyomatosis typically contains cystic or anechoic spaces and may also show evidence of cholesterol deposits in the lesion. When these distinctive findings are seen, it appears safe to follow larger gallbladder polyps, at least those less than 20 mm in diameter.[7] Neoplasm should be considered when the characteristic findings of a non-neoplastic lesion are absent and the lesion is greater than 5 mm, even in lesions confined to the mucosa. Loss of gallbladder wall architecture is highly suggestive of an invasive cancer.[9]

Bile Duct Stones

EUS is highly accurate for diagnosis of choledocholithiasis. EUS is useful in patients with an intermediate risk of bile duct stones, refining the use of ERCP and decreasing the overall risks of an endoscopic approach. As EUS equipment and training become more widespread, suspicion of ductal stones will become an increasingly common indication for the procedure.

The accuracy of EUS for diagnosis of biliary stones and sludge relies on both the technical skill of the endoscopist and on patient factors. The common duct is best visualized from the duodenal bulb with either the radial or linear array echoendoscope. The bile duct must be distinguished from adjacent vessels, especially the portal vein, hepatic artery, and gastroduodenal artery. This is accomplished by identifying its convergence with the pancreatic duct as both

ducts taper into the duodenal wall, the so-called stack sign (Fig. 44–2). The cystic duct insertion is another useful landmark. In addition, the bile duct wall has an inner hypoechoic layer that is not present in adjacent vessels. Imaging should also be performed with the endoscope opposite the ampulla in the second part of the duodenum for detection of stones in the ampulla or intramural bile duct.

Stones are identified as echogenic structures casting dark acoustic shadows (Fig. 44–3). Air bubbles in the duct also appear as echogenic, rounded structures but cast hyperechoic acoustic reverberations instead of shadows. Sludge or cholesterol crystals can be visualized in the bile duct much as they are visualized in the gallbladder (see Fig. 44–1).

Diagnosis of ductal stones is easiest when small stones are present in a dilated duct, the very situation in which cholangiography can miss stones. Conversely, sonographic diagnosis may be challenging when a diminutive duct is present or when the common duct is completely filled with stones, obliterating a visible ductal lumen. Care should be taken to visualize the entire bile duct, not skipping over portions. Longitudinal views demonstrating most of the duct in one view are preferable to cross-sectional views, except in the periampullary region. It is important to recognize a technically inadequate or incomplete EUS examination and to consider other imaging tests rather than conclude that no stones are present.

EUS has been compared with ERCP for diagnosis of bile duct stones. Prat and colleagues[10] performed EUS and ERCP in 119 patients with suspected bile duct stones, performing sphincterotomy and balloon sweeps of the bile duct in all subjects to obtain an independent gold standard. The sensitivity and specificity of EUS were 93% and 97%, respectively, compared with 89% and 100% for ERCP. This study suggested that radial EUS was more sensitive than cholangiography for diagnosis of stones. A recent study of similar design using linear array echoendoscopes reported that the sensitivity and specificity of EUS were both 93%.[11]

EUS can be used as the sole imaging study to exclude choledocholithiasis before laparoscopic cholecystectomy. When EUS showed no bile duct stones, recurrent symptoms resulting from

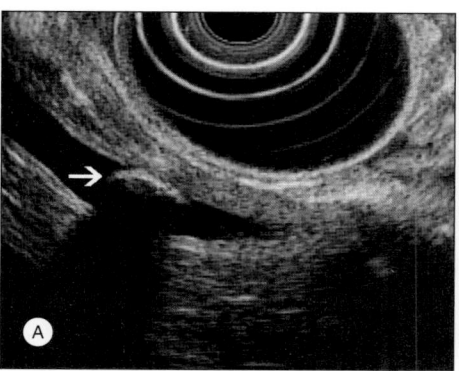 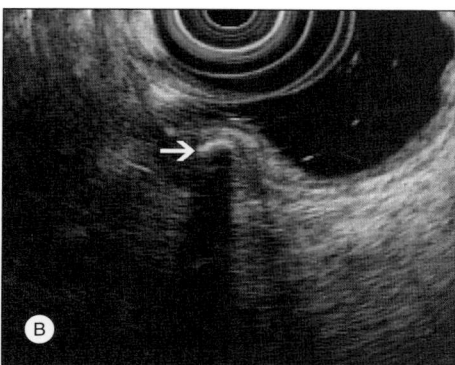 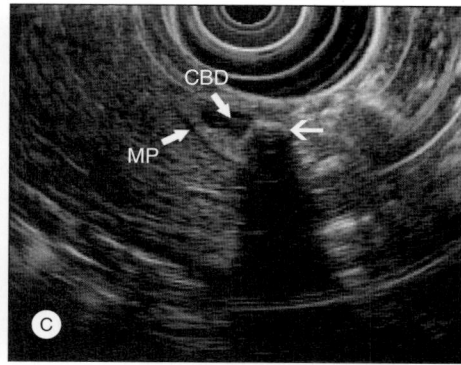

Figure 44-3. Bile duct stones *(arrows)* casting acoustic shadows. *A,* Common bile duct stone. *B,* Ampullary stone. *C,* Ampullary stone with dilation of the obstructed intra-ampullary bile duct. CBD, bile duct; MP, muscularis propria of the duodenal wall.

ductal stones did not occur during almost 3 years of follow-up in a European cohort.[12] Because EUS does not reliably image the intrahepatic ducts, it would not fare as well in a group of patients at risk for intrahepatic stones.

Biliary IDUS is also accurate for diagnosis of bile duct stones and sludge. IDUS requires deep cannulation of the bile duct with the intraductal probe, which can be passed over a guidewire without sphincterotomy. Most investigators have performed IDUS after obtaining a cholangiogram during ERCP. To minimize trauma to the probe and extend its useful life, the operator should use as little elevator as possible and image only during slow probe withdrawal.

Because IDUS uses a high-frequency probe placed directly in the duct, it is probably the best available imaging technique for diagnosis of small stones and ductal sludge. In one direct comparison of cholangiography and IDUS, the sensitivity of IDUS for stones was 97%, compared with 81% for ERCP.[13] Because it is performed during ERCP, IDUS is probably best used to clarify diagnosis in patients with equivocal findings at cholangiography, such as small filling defects, possible air bubbles or polyps in the bile duct, or a dilated bile duct. In such patients, IDUS improves diagnostic accuracy in about a third of patients.[14] However, the need to diagnose and treat small (less than 5 mm) stones detected only with IDUS has been questioned,[15] because such stones often pass spontaneously.[16]

Cost analysis suggests that EUS should be most useful for diagnosis of choledocholithiasis in patients at intermediate risk for ductal stones.[17] Its use is especially appealing as an alternative to ERCP in gallstone pancreatitis. EUS is equivalent to or better than ERCP for diagnosis of ductal stones in acute pancreatitis and allows selective use of ERCP when stones are present.[18,19] ERCP and sphincterotomy can be performed under the same sedation as EUS, when indicated.

Bile Duct Strictures and Cholangiocarcinoma

Biliary strictures may be of indeterminate etiology, especially when cross-sectional imaging is unrevealing and intraductal biopsies and brushings obtained during ERCP are nondiagnostic. The cholangiographic appearance of a stricture and the patient's clinical history

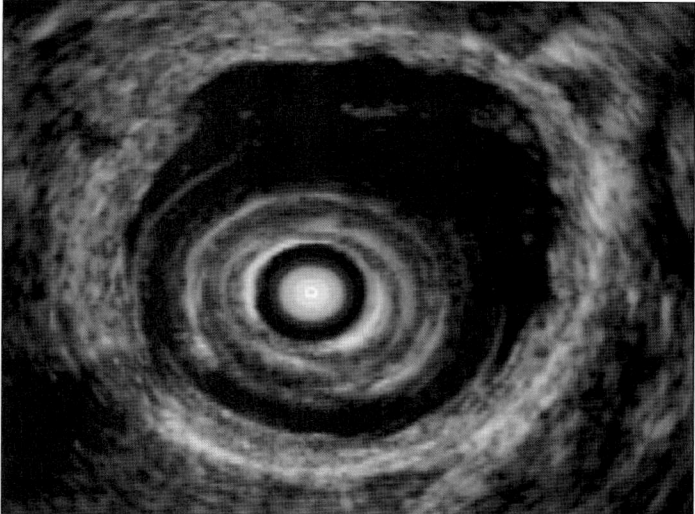

Figure 44-4. Layers of the bile duct wall, demonstrated during intraductal ultrasound in a patient with cholangitis. The inner, hypoechoic layer is markedly thickened because of inflammation. The outer, hyperechoic layer is also visible. Small amounts of nonshadowing sludge are present in the duct lumen.

have traditionally determined whether unexplained bile duct strictures should be resected on suspicion of malignancy. EUS and IDUS may be used to further define biliary strictures and may aid clinical decision making by suggesting a benign or malignant process. Endosonography can also be used for local staging of malignant biliary strictures.

The bile duct wall appears to have two or three layers on EUS and IDUS (Fig. 44-4). An internal, hyperechoic layer is sometimes seen representing an interface echo. Deep to this layer is a hypoechoic layer corresponding to the mucosa, subepithelial connective tissue, muscularis propria, and the fibrous layer of the subserosa. The amount of muscularis varies, with little or no muscularis propria in the proximal bile duct. Deep to this hypoechoic layer is an outer hyperechoic layer formed by the adipose layer of the subserosa, the serosa, and the interface with surrounding tissue.[20] The normal bile duct wall is less than 1 mm thick on EUS,[21] although the presence of a stent or drain in the duct may lead to thickening of the wall up to 2.8 mm.[22]

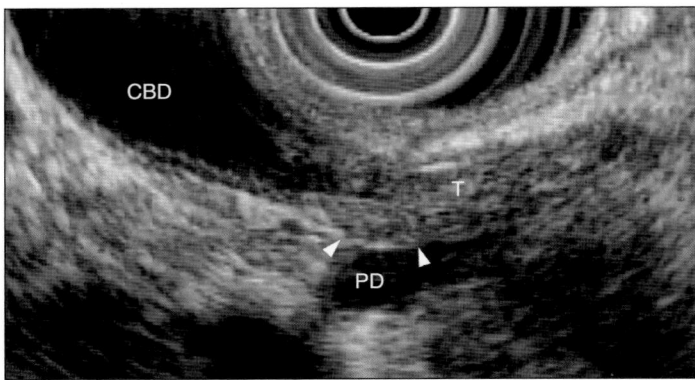

Figure 44–5. T2 distal cholangiocarcinoma (T). The tumor thickens the bile duct wall and focally disrupts the outer, hyperechoic layer of the duct wall *(arrowheads)*. CBD, common bile duct; PD, pancreatic duct.

Box 44–1. Staging of Extrahepatic Cholangiocarcinoma, Including Bifurcation Tumors

TX	Primary tumor cannot be assessed		
T0	No evidence of primary tumor		
Tis	Carcinoma *in situ*		
T1	Tumor confined to the bile duct		
T2	Tumor invades beyond the wall of the bile duct		
T3	Tumor invades the liver, gallbladder, pancreas, and/or unilateral branches of the portal vein (right or left) or hepatic artery (right or left)		
T4	Tumor invades any of the following: main portal vein or its branches bilaterally, common hepatic artery, or other adjacent structures, such as the colon, stomach, duodenum, or abdominal wall		
NX	Regional lymph nodes cannot be assessed		
N0	No regional lymph node metastases		
N1	Regional lymph node metastases		
MX	Distant metastases cannot be assessed		
M0	No distant metastases		
M1	Distant metastases		
Stage 0	Tis	N0	M0
Stage IA	T1	N0	M0
Stage IB	T2	N0	M0
Stage IIA	T3	N0	M0
Stage IIB	T1	N1	M0
	T2	N1	M0
	T3	N1	M0
Stage III	T4	Any N	M0
Stage IV	Any T	Any N	M1

From American Joint Committee on Cancer (AJCC): AJCC Cancer Staging Manual, 6th ed. New York, Springer-Verlag, 2002 (www.springer-ny.com).

The bile duct wall layers can be identified with either EUS or IDUS. Intraductal ultrasound probes can be passed into the central intrahepatic ducts, visualizing portions of the biliary tree not usually accessible to transduodenal EUS, and IDUS also provides high-resolution images of the bile duct wall and adjacent vessels and tissue. EUS with a dedicated echoendoscope can image the extrahepatic biliary tree, including bifurcation tumors,[23] and its deeper depth of penetration permits a thorough assessment of the gallbladder, pancreatic head, and regional lymph nodes. The two techniques are complementary.

Endosonography has been used for differential diagnosis of unexplained bile duct strictures. During IDUS, malignant strictures typically appear hypoechoic with a thickened wall and irregular margins, whereas benign strictures are usually relatively hyperechoic with smooth edges.[24] Two studies have shown IDUS to be more accurate than ERCP and intraductal tissue sampling for diagnosis of malignant bile duct strictures.[25,26] Although one study relied on a single reviewer's retrospective review of both IDUS and ERCP still images, these studies reported IDUS accuracy of 80% to 90%. Another recent study evaluated unexplained distal bile duct strictures with transduodenal EUS and FNA. Malignant strictures were associated with either a pancreatic head mass or an irregular bile duct wall in more than 90% of cases, and a bile duct wall thickness of greater than 3 mm was suggestive of malignant strictures (Fig. 44–5). These imaging criteria were more accurate than EUS-guided FNA cytology for diagnosis.[27] Taken together, these studies suggest that sonographic findings at either EUS or IDUS may help determine whether an unexplained bile duct stricture should be resected.

The current TNM staging system for carcinoma of the extrahepatic bile ducts is shown in Box 44–1. T staging was redefined in 2002 and previously published material used different criteria. Both EUS and IDUS have been used to stage cholangiocarcinoma. The two techniques have similar accuracy of about 80% for T stage, differentiating T1 lesions confined to the bile duct wall (involving the inner hypoechoic layer) from T2 lesions invading beyond the bile duct wall (with disruption of the outer hyperechoic layer) (see Fig. 44–5).[20] IDUS is more useful than EUS for lesions of the proximal biliary tree. IDUS has also been used to estimate the longitudinal extent of cholangiocarcinoma, because cholangiography is well known to underestimate the proximal extent of ductal involvement. Unfortunately, nonspecific thickening of the bile duct wall resulting from the presence of a stent or drain limits the value of IDUS in previously drained patients.[28] Use of intravenous ultrasound contrast may improve the specificity of IDUS for malignancy, demonstrating hyperperfusion of inflammatory lesions and hypoperfusion of tumor,[29] and more studies using contrast agents are needed.

IDUS is probably the most sensitive available imaging test for diagnosis of early cholangiocarcinoma in choledochal cysts. The technique should be considered in adult patients with choledochal cysts, especially if surgical resection of the cyst is not otherwise planned.

Ampulla of Vater

EUS provides detailed images of the papilla of Vater. The papilla is best located during slow withdrawal of the echoendoscope from the third part of the duodenum, using sonographic rather than endoscopic landmarks. The ventral pancreas is visualized, and the bile duct and/or pancreatic duct lumens are identified. The ducts can then be traced to the duodenal wall and papilla. Administration of intravenous glucagon and instillation of water into duodenum may improve visualization once the periampullary region has been located.

The submucosal apparatus of the papilla can be visualized as a round hypoechoic structure in duodenal submucosa, composed of the sphincter of Oddi and the intramural ducts. The normal submucosal mound of the papilla is usually less than 6 mm in transverse cross-sectional diameter. The lumens of the bile duct and pancreatic duct are usually not visible within the papilla; they generally taper and disappear from view as they reach the duodenal wall. The finding of a visible ductal lumen in the papilla suggests obstruction of the papilla by a stone (see Fig. 44–3), stenosis, or tumor but can also be seen in choledochocele and IPMN.

IDUS has been used to study the ampulla and may aid in the local staging of some ampullary tumors. It identifies the sphincter mechanism and permits accurate measurement of its length. However, sonographic features do not distinguish normal from hypertensive sphincters.[30]

AMPULLARY NEOPLASMS

Adenomas of the papilla may occur on the duodenal surface of the papilla, within the papilla in the mucosa of the intra-ampullary ducts, or both. They may spread into or arise from the peri-ampullary bile duct or pancreatic duct. EUS findings can include a mucosal mass on the duodenal surface of the papilla, enlargement of the submucosal ampullary apparatus resulting from intra-ampullary polyp, and thickening of the periampullary duct walls or an intraductal nonshadowing mass. These findings can be seen both in ampullary adenoma and in T1 ampullary cancer, and the two entities are often difficult or impossible to distinguish with EUS.

The TNM staging of ampullary cancers is shown in Box 44–2 and illustrated in Fig. 44–6. T1 carcinoma may be limited to the mucosal surfaces of the ampulla and intra-ampullary ducts but may also involve the sphincter mechanism of the ampulla. The presence of an irregular outer edge of the submucosal ampullary apparatus suggests a T2 lesion invading the duodenal submucosa or muscularis propria. T3 cancers invade the pancreas, extending either through the duodenal wall or directly from the periampullary ducts. A T4 tumor extends into peripancreatic soft tissue or other adjacent structures. Regional lymph nodes include not only those adjacent to pancreatic head but also the porta hepatis and celiac nodes.

In one large series, EUS accuracy for T staging of ampullary malignancies was 78%.[31] Adenomas were considered T1 lesions, highlighting the difficulty in distinguishing adenoma from T1 cancer with EUS. Most errors in staging involved overstaging of T2 lesions or understaging of T3 lesions because of difficulty in assessing the presence of invasion into the pancreas. The presence of peritumoral pancreatitis and edema and shadowing and tissue thickening resulting from an indwelling biliary stent were the major factors limiting the accuracy of EUS. Despite these limitations EUS is considerably more accurate than computed tomography (CT) or magnetic resonance imaging (MRI).[31–33] Because visualization of the ampulla can be technically challenging, EUS accuracy is likely to depend on operator experience.

Box 44–2. Staging of Ampullary Carcinoma

TX	Primary tumor cannot be assessed		
T0	No evidence of primary tumor		
Tis	Carcinoma *in situ*		
T1	Tumor limited to ampulla of Vater or sphincter of Oddi		
T2	Tumor invades duodenal wall		
T3	Tumor invades pancreas		
T4	Tumor invades peripancreatic soft tissues or other adjacent organs or structures		
NX	Regional lymph nodes cannot be assessed		
N0	No regional lymph node metastases		
N1	Regional lymph node metastases		
MX	Distant metastases cannot be assessed		
M0	No distant metastases		
M1	Distant metastases		
Stage 0	Tis	N0	M0
Stage IA	T1	N0	M0
Stage IB	T2	N0	M0
Stage IIA	T3	N0	M0
Stage IIB	T1	N1	M0
	T2	N1	M0
	T3	N1	M0
Stage III	T4	Any N	M0
Stage IV	Any T	Any N	M1

From American Joint Committee on Cancer (AJCC): AJCC Cancer Staging Manual, 6th ed. New York, Springer-Verlag, 2002 (www.springer-ny.com).

IDUS is probably more accurate that transduodenal EUS for T staging of ampullary neoplasms. In one large series, IDUS had an overall accuracy of 89%.[33] It visualized small tumors missed by EUS and was more accurate than endoscopic biopsies for diagnosis of ampullary neoplasm. IDUS was also accurate for differentiation of adenoma from T1 carcinoma. These results were achieved by experienced endosonographers, using IDUS at the patient's initial ERCP and before sphincterotomy, stent placement, or biopsy—an optimal algorithm for tumor imaging but difficult to replicate in most EUS referral centers.

Acute Pancreatitis

EUS has two emerging roles in patients with acute pancreatitis. The first is for timely diagnosis of common bile duct or ampullary stones in patients with acute gallstone pancreatitis, and the second is for differential diagnosis in patients with unexplained bouts of pancreatitis. In both cases, EUS can be used in place of diagnostic ERCP and may identify those patients most likely to benefit from therapeutic ERCP or sphincter of Oddi manometry. A prognostic role for EUS in acute pancreatitis has not been demonstrated, although the use of intravenous sonographic contrast agents may allow EUS diagnosis of pancreatic necrosis.

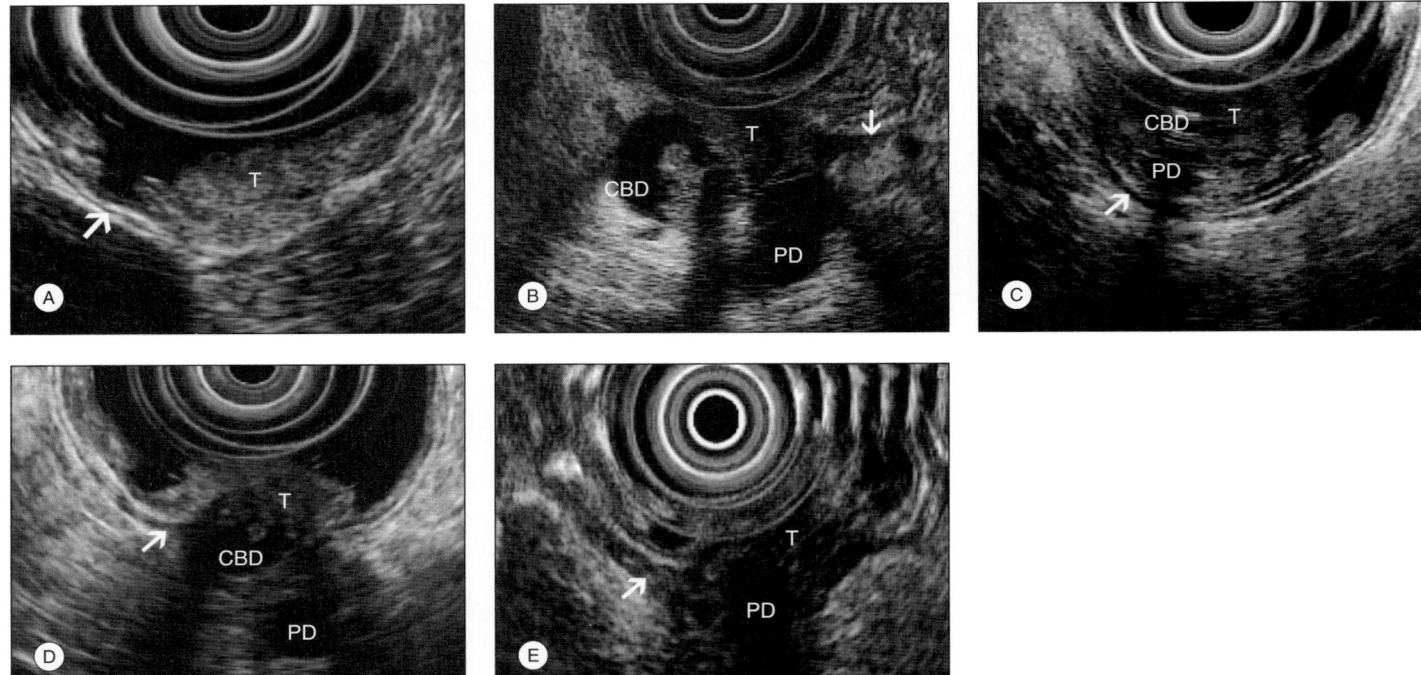

Figure 44-6. Ampullary neoplasms. *Arrows* indicate the duodenal muscularis propria. *A,* Adenoma on the duodenal surface of the ampulla. *B,* Ampullary tumor extending into the distal bile duct. A biliary stent is present. *C,* T1 ampullary carcinoma. This intra-ampullary lesion was mostly adenoma but contained foci of invasive carcinoma. *D,* T2 ampullary carcinoma invading duodenal wall. *E,* T3 ampullary carcinoma invading pancreas, with an irregular outer edge of the muscularis propria. CBD, common bile duct; PD, pancreatic duct; T, tumor.

Table 44-2. Endoscopic Ultrasonography Features of Chronic Pancreatitis

	Parenchymal Features	Ductal Features
	Hyperechoic strands	Stones
	Hyperechoic foci	Main duct irregularity
	Lobularity	Hyperechoic main duct
	Cysts	Visible side branches
		Main duct dilatation

From The International Working Group for Minimal Standard Terminology in Gastrointestinal Endosonography: Minimal standard terminology in gastrointestinal endosonography. Dig Endosc 10:159-184, 1998.

The accuracy of EUS for diagnosis of bile duct stones is discussed earlier in this chapter. When used in acute pancreatitis, the ampulla and the bile duct must be examined for stones. A skilled examiner can perform a focused EUS of the biliary tree in less than 10 minutes, and the patient can undergo therapeutic ERCP under the same sedation if a stone is demonstrated. This strategy allows patients with a suspected ductal stone to avoid the potential complications of ERCP, if they have already passed their stone into the duodenum.

One prospective trial investigating EUS in gallstone pancreatitis reported that it was accurate for diagnosis of gallbladder and ductal stones and predicted longer hospital stay in patients found to have peripancreatic fluid by EUS.[34] In another large series in which ERCP was used selectively, on the basis of EUS findings, patient outcomes were good and recurrent biliary pancreatitis was uncommon.[35] The authors suggested that early EUS in patients with gallstone pancreatitis, followed by selective use of ERCP, might lead to better outcomes than a strategy of no ERCP in mild gallstone pancreatitis and ERCP in all patients with severe gallstone pancreatitis.

EUS is also a useful tool in the evaluation of idiopathic pancreatitis, demonstrating abnormalities in most patients.[3,36,37] Findings include missed biliary stones or sludge (see Fig. 44-1), chronic pancreatitis, pancreas divisum, pancreatic or ampullary malignancy, and pancreatic duct stones. EUS does not diagnose pancreatic sphincter dysfunction but may nevertheless supplant ERCP by diagnosing or excluding previously unsuspected gallbladder pathology, chronic pancreatitis, or pancreatic malignancy.

Chronic Pancreatitis

Endosonographic features of chronic pancreatitis are listed in Table 44-2 and are illustrated in Fig. 44-7. This list of consensus criteria uses minimal standard terminology adopted by an international working group,[38] and good interobserver agreement has been demonstrated for these criteria among experienced American endosonographers.[39] Investigators have also used other terms not

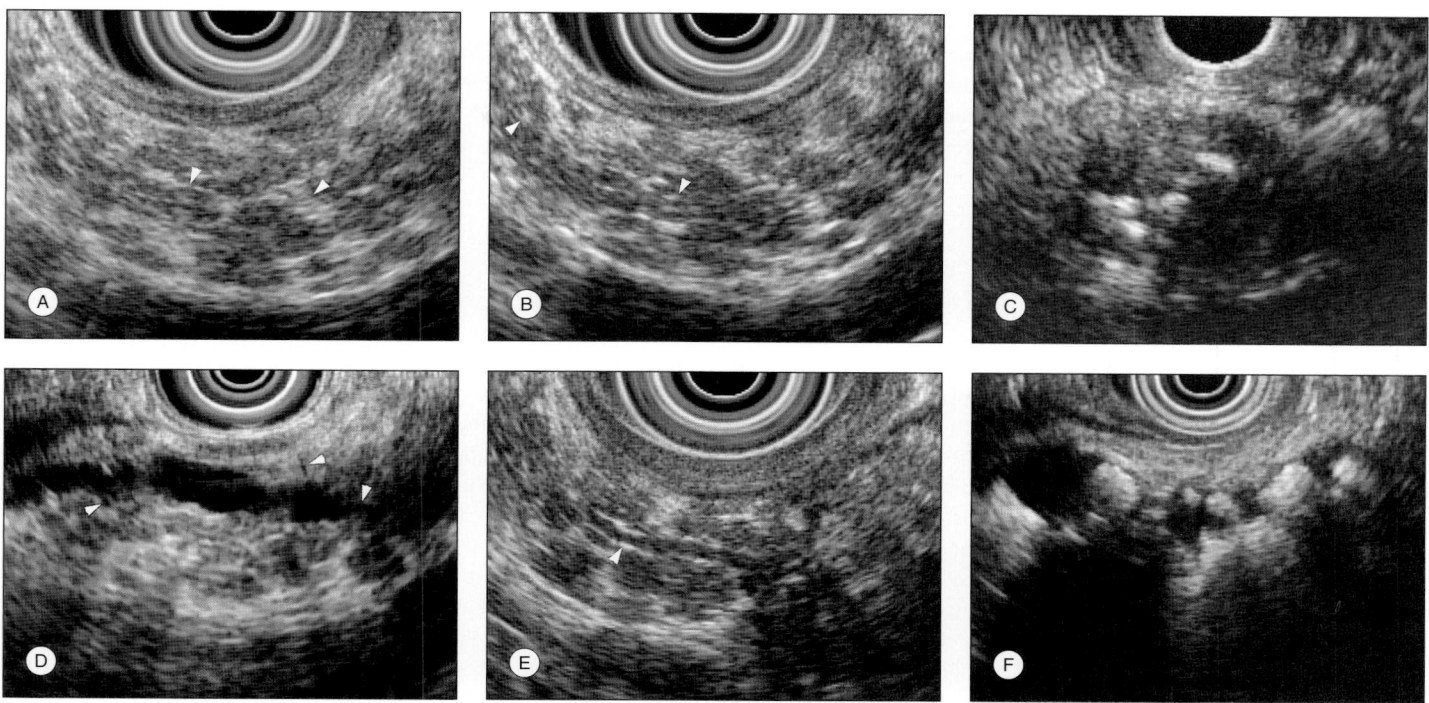

Figure 44–7. Chronic pancreatitis. *A,* Hyperechoic strands *(arrowheads)* and lobularity. *B,* Hyperechoic foci *(arrowheads)* and lobularity. *C,* Large hyperechoic foci in a hypoechoic pancreas. *D,* Dilated, irregular main pancreatic duct with visible side branches *(arrowheads). E,* Hyperechoic, irregular main duct. *F,* Ductal stones.

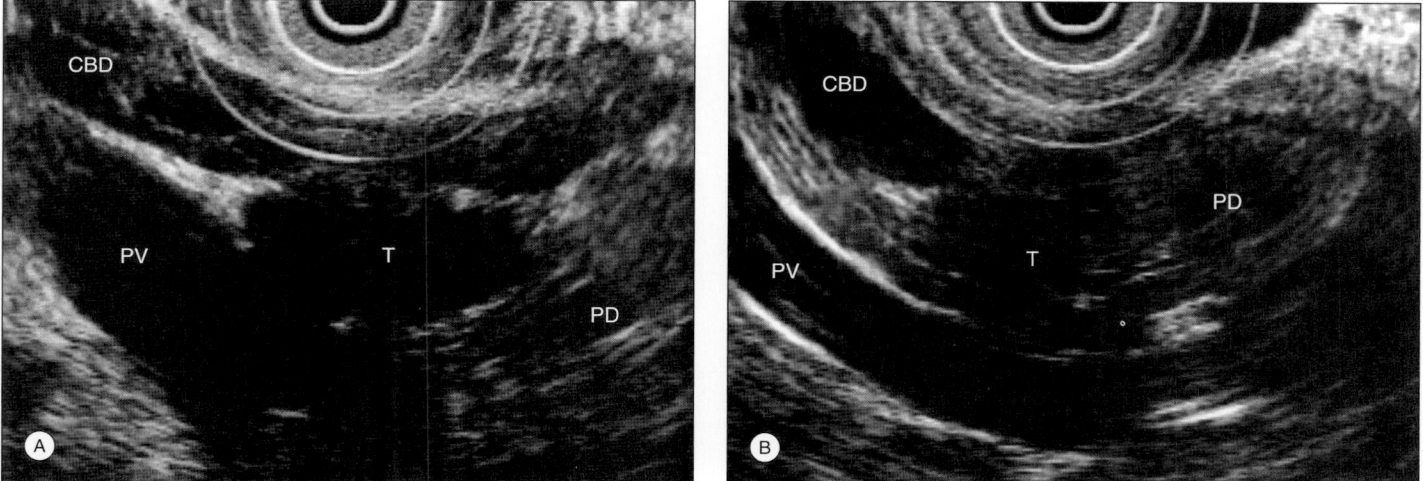

Figure 44–8. Focal pancreatitis versus pancreatic cancer. Both lesions (T) caused biliary obstruction and were resected. *A,* Focal pancreatitis without malignancy. *B,* T1 pancreatic adenocarcinoma. CBD, common bile duct; PD, pancreatic duct; PV, portal vein.

included in this list, including honeycombing (in which multiple parenchymal lobules are encircled by hyperechoic strands), heterogeneous echotexture, focal areas of hypoechogenicity, tortuous pancreatic duct, thickened pancreatic duct wall, and narrowing of the main pancreatic duct. Although usually described in chronic pancreatitis, similar EUS features have been reported in members of a family prone to pancreatic cancer who have widespread dysplasia of pancreatic duct epithelium at resection.[40] Focal areas of pancreatic hypoechogenicity can be due to focal inflammation but may also be due to neoplasm (Fig. 44–8).

Definitions vary for some criteria. Hyperechoic foci have been defined as greater than 3 mm by some investigators[41] but as 1 to 2 mm by most others.[42,43] Main pancreatic duct dilation has been variably defined, although in consensus criteria a diameter of greater than 2 mm in the body or greater than 1 mm in the tail was considered abnormal.[39]

There are caveats regarding use of EUS criteria for diagnosis of chronic pancreatitis. Identified features have been considered abnormal at either 12 or 7.5 MHz by some investigators but at only 7.5 MHz by others. Findings must be interpreted with considerable caution when imaging the pancreatic head, because some features (e.g., hyperechoic strands and visible side branches) are often seen in the normal pancreatic head, whereas others (e.g., cysts and stones) are not. Diagnosis is best made based on features seen in pancreatic body and tail. Visible duct side branches have been seen in the normal pancreatic body by some investigators.[41] Acute pancreatitis may cause decreased parenchymal echogenicity (resulting from edema), accentuating the echogenicity of the pancreatic duct wall and the interlobular septa of the pancreas. When performed for diagnosis of chronic pancreatitis, EUS should therefore be done after an acute episode of pancreatitis has resolved. Finally, ductal dilation and pancreatic fibrosis occur in older persons without clinical pancreatic disease, and age-related endosonographic changes in normal subjects have not been adequately studied.

The accuracy of EUS for diagnosis of chronic pancreatitis has been compared with pancreatography, functional tests, and histology. Histologic comparisons in resection specimens[44] or at autopsy[45] have been reported in abstract form. In one of these studies, individual sonographic criteria had a sensitivity of 67% to 100% for diagnosis of chronic pancreatitis.[44] Comparative studies using pancreatography as a gold standard have shown that EUS is accurate for diagnosis of chronic pancreatitis when more than three sonographic criteria are present,[41–43,46] with a positive predictive value of greater than 85%. The number of sonographic criteria correlates with the severity of disease at ERCP as reflected in the Cambridge criteria,[42,43] and subjects with six or more sonographic criteria are likely to have severe chronic pancreatitis found at ERCP. Secretin testing correlates well with EUS for diagnosis of severe chronic pancreatitis but appeared less sensitive than EUS for diagnosis of milder forms of disease.[42]

The significance of "mild changes" on EUS (only one to three criteria seen) has been debated. In most such cases, endoscopic pancreatography and secretin testing are normal.[42,43] Are mild changes normal, or do they represent an early form of chronic pancreatitis missed by other diagnostic modalities? Several lines of evidence suggest that mild endosonographic changes of chronic pancreatitis are indicative of underlying pathologic changes in the pancreas.

First, EUS may detect pancreatic fibrosis earlier than ERCP because the initial histologic changes of chronic pancreatitis may affect the pancreatic parenchyma rather than the macroscopic ductal system. Intralobular, periacinar fibrosis of the pancreas is an early histologic feature of chronic pancreatitis and is seen at autopsy in most chronic alcohol users with no clinical history of pancreatic disease and in up to a third of nonalcoholic persons older than 65 years.[47–50] EUS in asymptomatic alcoholic patients often demonstrates parenchymal features of chronic pancreatitis.[51] Cytologic findings of chronic pancreatitis on EUS-guided FNA specimens have been shown to correlate with endosonographic findings of chronic pancreatitis,[46] but this technique has not been applied specifically to patients with only one or two EUS features.

Second, studies in normal volunteers have generally demonstrated no parenchymal EUS abnormalities in young, asymptomatic people who do not use alcohol.[41,42,51] Among older patients with no history of pancreatic disease undergoing EUS for other indications, a mean of 1.9 features of chronic pancreatitis were seen.[52] The finding of some features in patients older than 60 years may reflect the occurrence of age-related parenchymal fibrosis and ductal changes. In contrast to these studies, a large study comparing EUS and ERCP found that multiple EUS abnormalities were seen in subjects with chronic abdominal pain and normal pancreatograms. Many of these "normals" were diagnosed with papillary stenosis.[43] It is difficult to conclude that ERCP definitively excluded subtle chronic pancreatitis in such patients. Studies without appropriate controls may underestimate the accuracy of EUS for diagnosis of early chronic pancreatitis.

Third, a longitudinal study suggests that the presence of one or two EUS features of chronic pancreatitis predicts the subsequent development of clear-cut chronic pancreatitis in symptomatic alcoholic patients. Kahl and colleagues[53] studied chronic alcohol users with abdominal pain, a normal pancreatogram, and one or more features of chronic pancreatitis on EUS. Subjects who continued to have pain and/or clinical bouts of pancreatitis underwent follow-up pancreatography a mean of 18 months after their initial, normal ERCP. Follow-up ERCP showed an abnormal pancreatic duct in all subjects. This suggests that EUS was more sensitive than ERCP for early diagnosis of chronic pancreatitis, although repeat EUS was not done at the time of follow-up ERCP to document sonographic progression. A follow-up study of similar design has been reported in patients with alcoholic cirrhosis who (in contrast to the previous study) had no abdominal pain or clinical pancreatitis. The investigators found EUS evidence of chronic pancreatitis in 44%, with abnormal pancreatography in 19%. Imaging studies were repeated after a mean of 22 months and showed no progression on either follow-up EUS or follow-up pancreatography in these asymptomatic subjects.[54] The finding of EUS abnormalities in 44% correlates well with autopsy data showing that 47% to 57% of alcoholic cirrhotics have pancreatic fibrosis.[47,55]

Thus, it seems likely that the presence of one or two parenchymal features of chronic pancreatitis does correlate with histologic pancreatic abnormalities and that the commonest parenchymal endosonographic findings probably reflect underlying perilobular fibrosis. The clinical significance of this finding can be questioned, because these changes may be attributed to age or alcohol use rather than disease. Nevertheless, the finding of two or three features in a young, nonalcoholic patient with unexplained pain does raise the question of an underlying pancreatic process.

Solid Pancreatic Neoplasms

EUS is commonly used for diagnosis of pancreatic neoplasms. It images small tumors missed by other diagnostic modalities, provides local staging information, and permits immediate aspiration or biopsy of pancreatic masses and lymph nodes under real-time ultrasound guidance. This section reviews the role of endosonography in patients with known or suspected pancreatic adenocarcinoma and pancreatic neuroendocrine tumors. Cystic neoplasms are discussed elsewhere in this chapter.

To accurately diagnose and stage pancreatic neoplasms, the endosonographer must have a detailed understanding of sonographic pancreatic anatomy and the ability to reliably identify important adjacent vessels, including the portal vein, portal confluence, hepatic and gastroduodenal arteries, splenic vessels, and superior mesenteric vessels. Educational materials that teach this endosonographic anatomy are available.[56]

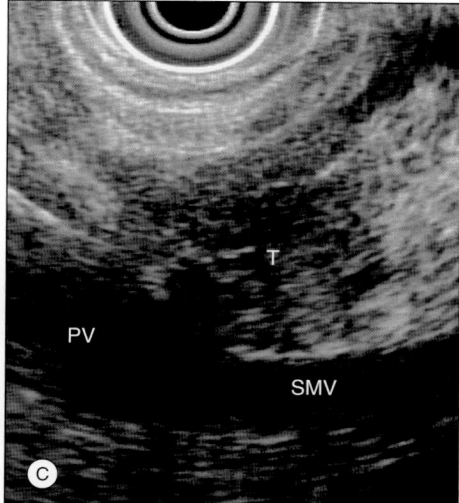

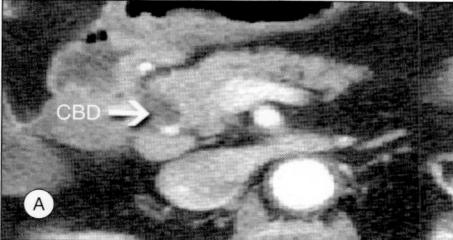 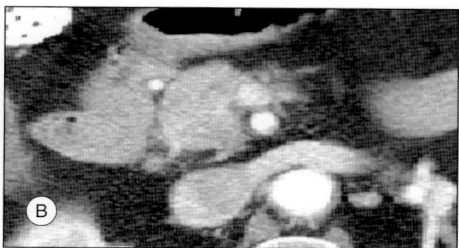

Figure 44–9. Pancreatic adenocarcinoma missed by computed tomography (CT). *A,* Arterial phase contrast-enhanced CT shows a dilated bile duct (CBD) in the pancreatic head. *B,* The next CT slice shows abrupt disappearance of the bile duct, without a focal pancreatic mass. *C,* Endoscopic ultrasonography (EUS) shows a 1.8-cm hypoechoic mass (T) in the pancreatic head with loss of echoplane between the mass and the portal confluence. PV, portal vein; SMV, superior mesenteric vein.

ADENOCARCINOMA

Pancreatic adenocarcinoma typically appears as a hypoechoic mass with poorly defined, somewhat irregular edges. The lesion often appears to obstruct the pancreatic duct. Large tumors may demonstrate poor echopenetration, making assessment for vascular invasion difficult or impossible.[57] Infiltrating adenocarcinomas may present a heterogeneous or hypoechoic parenchymal echotexture without a discrete mass.

The finding of a hypoechoic pancreatic mass is not specific for adenocarcinoma and may also be caused by focal pancreatitis. Acute or chronic pancreatitis can cause this appearance, and a focal mass is often seen in autoimmune pancreatitis. Benign pancreatic masses tend to have better defined edges than malignancies (see Fig. 44–8), and computerized image analysis has been used as an aid in differential diagnosis.[58] Analysis of blood flow in the mass using power Doppler and an echo-enhancing intravenous contrast agent has been reported to accurately distinguish inflammatory masses (which are hyperperfused) from malignant masses (which are hypoperfused).[59] Details of clinical history and EUS-guided aspiration of focal lesions are also useful aids to preoperative differential diagnosis of a hypoechoic pancreatic mass, although a negative cytologic result does not fully exclude malignancy. EUS aspiration cytology has a sensitivity of about 80% for diagnosis of pancreatic cancer.[60,61] K-*ras* analysis of cytologic aspirates may improve the diagnostic yield further.[62]

Early studies comparing CT and EUS showed that EUS was more sensitive for detection of pancreatic adenocarcinoma, particularly lesions less than 2 cm in diameter. Subsequent studies comparing contrast-enhanced helical CT with EUS, taken in aggregate, suggest that EUS remains superior.[63,64] Patients suspected to have pancreatic carcinoma, but with no mass on CT, should undergo EUS (Fig. 44–9).

EUS also permits assessment of the relationship between a pancreatic tumor and adjacent vascular structures. The finding of

normal tissue between a tumor and a vessel, or an intact echo-rich interface (echoplane) between the two, reliably excludes tumor invasion of the visualized vessel. Conversely, other findings suggest possible vascular involvement (Fig. 44–10). These features include loss of the echoplane between tumor and vessel, irregularity of the vessel wall, narrowing of the vessel lumen, echogenic material within the vessel lumen, and the presence of peripancreatic venous collaterals (Fig. 44–11). Although numerous studies have reported EUS accuracy of 75% to 100% for diagnosis of vascular invasion,[63] these studies relied on a reference standard of intraoperative assessment by dissection and palpation. However, the surgeon's intraoperative suspicion of vascular invasion may be incorrect, particularly if a tumor is densely adherent to a vessel without actual invasion.[65] Surgical resection of portal vein or superior mesenteric vein (SMV) at the time of pancreatectomy has become an accepted technique, and patients undergoing venous resection have a survival comparable to those not requiring venous resection.[66] One recent report evaluated preoperative EUS as a predictor of intraoperative vascular resection by pancreatic surgeons experienced with venous resection techniques. Loss of echoplane was a poor predictor of vascular involvement (specificity less than 30%), and only half of resectable tumors with more advanced sonographic features of vascular invasion required vascular resection.[67] A recent blinded review of EUS videotapes suggested that endosonographers were less accurate in their assessment of vascular invasion when they were denied access to other clinical information about the patient, including results of other imaging studies.[68] Taken together these data suggest that EUS features of venous invasion are sensitive but not specific. EUS combined with a cross-sectional imaging study may provide more accurate local staging than either study alone.[69]

The 2002 revision of the TNM staging system for pancreatic carcinoma (Box 44–3) reflects current surgical philosophy and categorizes tumors as unresectable if there is local arterial invasion (stage III) or distant metastases (stage IV).[70] The classification

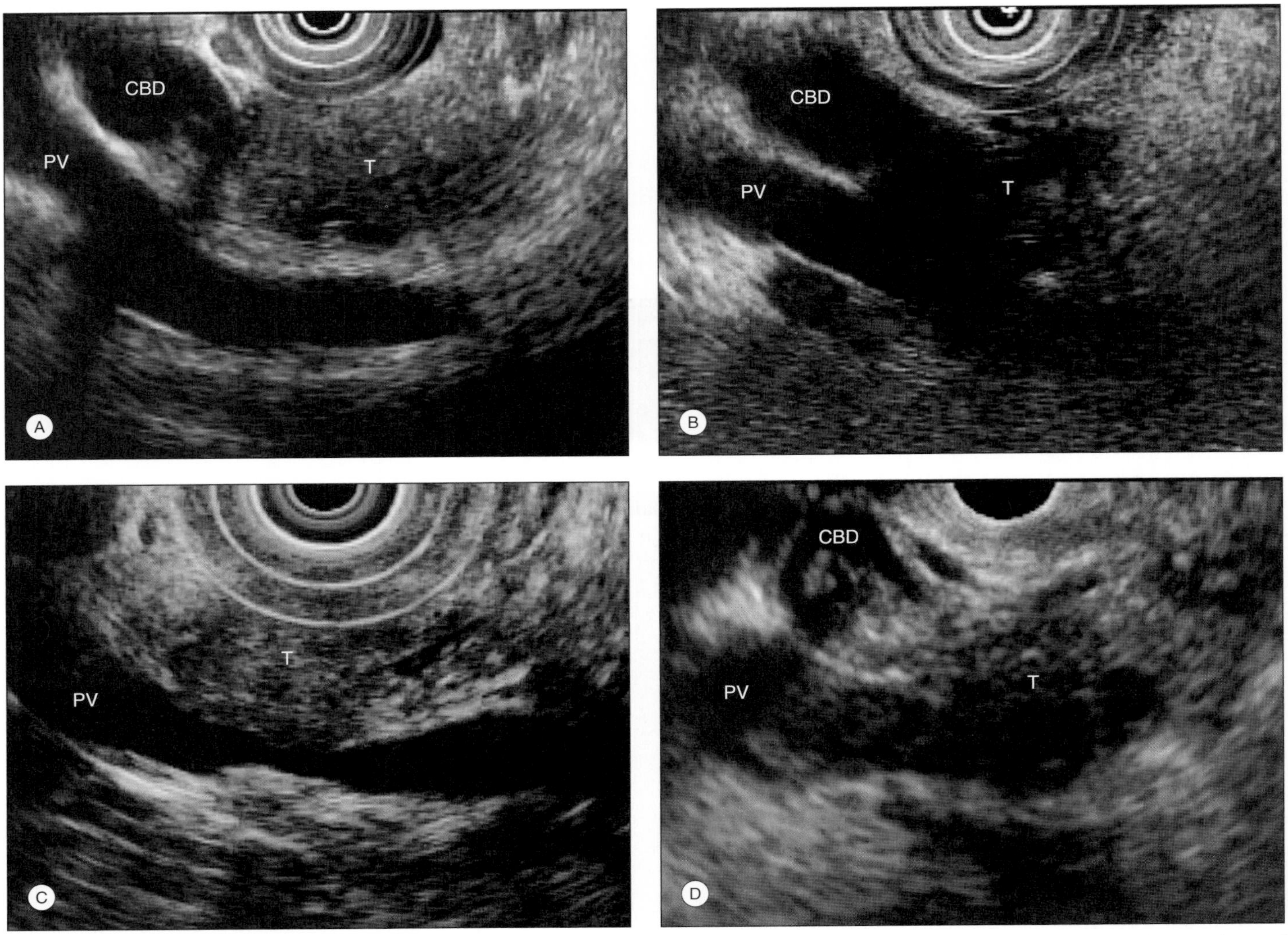

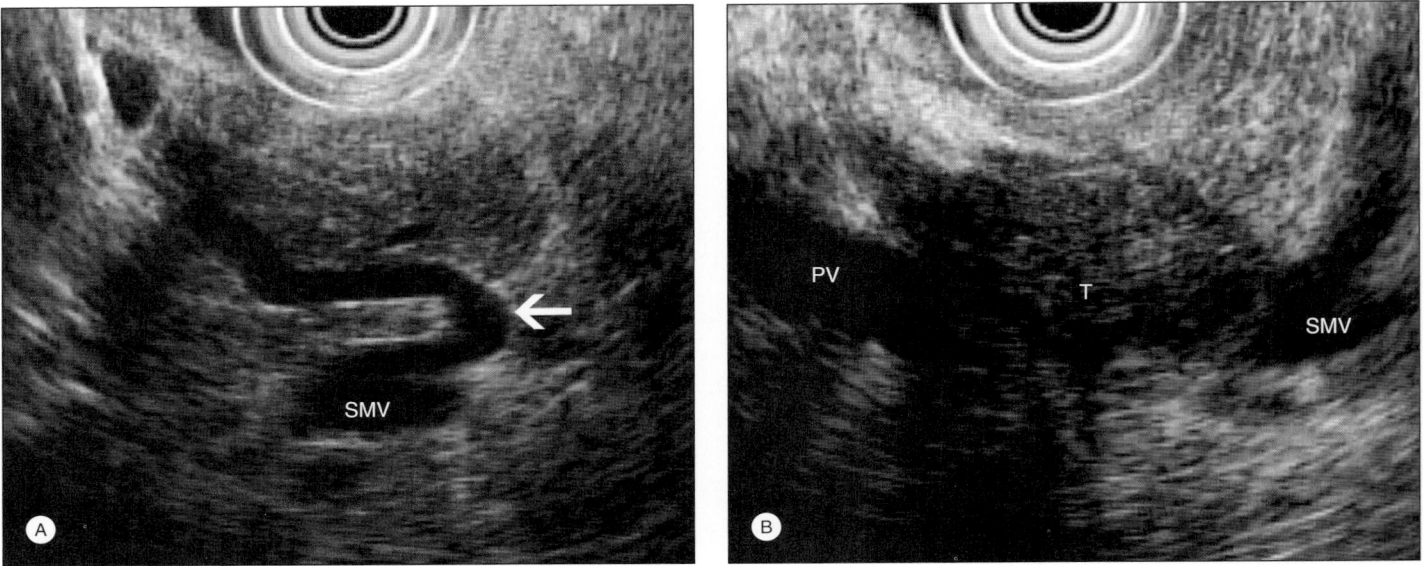

Figure 44–10. Vascular involvement by pancreatic cancer. *A,* Normal tissue between tumor (T) and vessels of the portal confluence, with no evidence of invasion. *B,* Loss of echoplane between tumor and portal vein. *C,* Irregular vein wall and narrowed vein lumen. *D,* Tumor extending directly into vein. PV, portal vein; T, tumor.

Figure 44–11. Venous collaterals in pancreatic cancer. *A,* A large venous collateral *(arrow)* courses through the pancreatic head from superior mesenteric vein (SMV), ultimately joining the proximal portal vein. *B,* In a different image plane, a pancreatic adenocarcinoma (T) is seen obstructing the portal confluence. PV, portal vein.

Box 44–3. Staging of Pancreatic Adenocarcinoma			
TX	Primary tumor cannot be assessed		
T0	No evidence of primary tumor		
Tis	Carcinoma *in situ* (includes PanIN III)		
T1	Tumor limited to the pancreas, 2 cm or less in greatest dimension		
T2	Tumor limited to the pancreas, more than 2 cm in greatest dimension		
T3	Tumor extends beyond the pancreas but without involvement of the celiac axis or the superior mesenteric artery		
T4	Tumor involves the celiac axis or the superior mesenteric artery (unresectable)		
NX	Regional lymph nodes cannot be assessed		
N0	No regional lymph node metastases		
N1	Regional lymph node metastases		
MX	Distant metastases cannot be assessed		
M0	No distant metastases		
M1	Distant metastases		
Stage 0	Tis	N0	M0
Stage IA	T1	N0	M0
Stage IB	T2	N0	M0
Stage IIA	T3	N0	M0
Stage IIB	T1	N1	M0
	T2	N1	M0
	T3	N1	M0
Stage III	T4	Any N	M0
Stage IV	Any T	Any N	M1

From American Joint Committee on Cancer (AJCC): AJCC Cancer Staging Manual, 6th ed. New York, Springer-Verlag, 2002 (www.springer-ny.com).

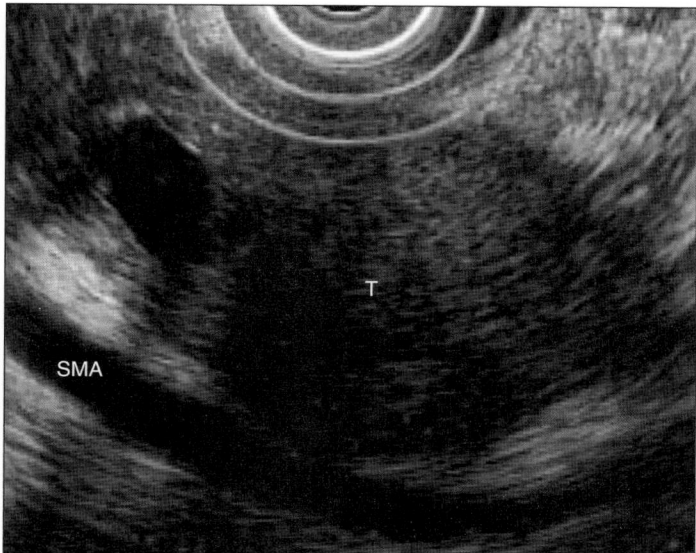

Figure 44–12. Retroperitoneal margin in pancreatic cancer. A large pancreatic head cancer (T) extends close to the superior mesenteric artery (SMA). At surgery, the tumor was not adherent to SMA and was resected, but the retroperitoneal margin was positive for malignancy.

distinguishes between tumors limited to the pancreas (T1 if 2 cm or less, T2 if more than 2 cm) and those that extend beyond the pancreas (T3 if not involving celiac axis or SMA, T4 if involving these arteries). Arterial but not venous invasion is considered when assigning T stage. T3 tumors, which extend beyond the pancreas, are considered resectable.

Extension of tumor beyond the edge of the pancreas has become an important criterion for T staging of pancreatic cancer. Tumor extension is best seen during EUS when the pancreatic parenchyma has a different echotexture than surrounding fat. When the pancreatic parenchyma is isoechoic with surrounding fat, the endosonographer is only able to identify the edge of the pancreas where it abuts major peripancreatic veins or other organs. In such cases, it may be impossible to arrive at an accurate T stage sonographically, and CT or MRI may be more useful. When assessing the edge of the pancreas, particular attention should be given to the "retroperitoneal margin" of the pancreatic head abutting the connective tissue between pancreas and superior mesenteric artery. This is the most likely site for a positive microscopic margin and subsequent local recurrence after resection of pancreatic head cancers (Fig. 44–12).[70] EUS features of arterial invasion may suggest T4 disease, although the true specificity of these features for arterial invasion is not known.

EUS aids in the detection of nodal and liver metastases from pancreatic cancer. Although it is probably less useful than CT or MRI for liver lesions, EUS has equal or greater sensitivity for identification of abnormal lymph nodes and is usually the procedure of choice for sampling abnormal nodes. Regional lymph nodes (considered N1 when malignant) are the peripancreatic nodes, including nodes along the hepatic artery, celiac axis, pyloric, and splenic regions.[70] The presence of N1 disease is not considered a contraindication to resection in many referral centers, because a "complete" resection does appear to lengthen survival in such patients.[66,70] The finding of malignant nodes distant from the primary tumor is considered metastatic disease and generally excludes surgery. In this regard, EUS identifies mediastinal nodal metastases in up to 7% of patients with pancreatic adenocarcinoma.[71]

A standard clinical approach to patients with suspected pancreatic cancer begins with a high-quality, contrast-enhanced CT or MRI. If liver lesions are demonstrated, percutaneous or EUS-guided biopsy is the most direct approach to staging. If a locally unresectable pancreatic mass is demonstrated, EUS can provide confirmation of local staging and permits aspiration for tissue diagnosis. If an apparently resectable mass is demonstrated, the role of EUS is controversial. EUS will detect liver or distant nodal metastases in a minority of such patients, obviating surgery. EUS-guided biopsy of an apparently resectable mass will also show a diagnosis other than adenocarcinoma in up to a fourth of patients, potentially changing management plan.[63,72] If pancreatic cancer is suspected but no mass is demonstrated on CT or MRI, EUS should be strongly considered for diagnosis of a small lesion missed by other modalities. Patients with small masses missed by other imaging techniques are probably those most likely to benefit from surgery.

Despite its overall excellent sensitivity for diagnosis of pancreatic cancer, EUS often misses cancer arising in the setting of underlying chronic pancreatitis[72] or severe acute pancreatitis. Tumor may be difficult to differentiate from areas of inflammation. Use of an intravenous ultrasound contrast agent may improve diagnosis in this setting, and positron emission tomography (PET) has also been advocated. Infiltrating neoplasms can also be missed by EUS, and needle aspiration may be a reasonable diagnostic strategy in the absence of a mass, particularly when performed adjacent to an obstructed bile duct or pancreatic duct.

OTHER SOLID TUMORS

The commonest variant of pancreatic adenocarcinoma is colloid carcinoma, a solid tumor containing pools of mucus. Colloid carcinoma may contain demonstrable cystic spaces on EUS (Fig. 44–13) and has a better prognosis following resection than typical adenocarcinoma. Metastatic cancer may present in the pancreas, including melanoma. Other uncommon solid tumors of the pancreas include lymphoma, acinar cell carcinoma, medullary carcinoma, osteogenic giant cell tumors, and pancreatoblastoma. The EUS features of these rarer tumors are not well described.

In contrast to adenocarcinoma, pancreatic neuroendocrine tumors typically appear as uniform, rounded, homogeneous masses with discrete edges (Fig. 44–14). They may also appear cystic (Fig. 44–15). EUS is the most sensitive preoperative imaging test for diagnosis of pancreatic insulinomas, and is an important modality in multiple endocrine neoplasia type 1 (MEN I) patients who have multiple pancreatic tumors, some of which are visualized only by EUS. EUS features suggestive of a malignant neuroendocrine tumor include an irregular central echogenic area and displacement or obstruction of the main pancreatic duct.[73] EUS-guided needle aspiration is an accurate means of diagnosing functioning neuroendocrine tumors.[74]

Intraductal Papillary Mucinous Neoplasm

IPMN is a papillary growth of neoplastic epithelium in the main pancreatic duct or its side branches. IPMN shares histologic and genetic features with pancreatic intraepithelial neoplasia (PanIN), and both are precursor lesions for pancreatic adenocarcinoma, but IPMN is characterized by ductal dilation, mucin production, and more extensive ductal involvement.[75] IPMN is commonest in the pancreatic head but may be seen anywhere in the pancreas and may be multifocal. Histologically, IPMN varies from a hyperplasia of ductal mucosa (not a true neoplasia) to adenoma, adenoma with borderline features, carcinoma *in situ*, and invasive carcinoma. Carcinoma is seen in more than 50% of resected main duct IPMN but in only about 15% of resected branch duct IPMN,[76–79] and branch duct lesions appear less likely to progress over time.[76,80,81] IPMN has also been termed intraductal papillary mucinous tumor (IPMT), mucinous ductal ectasia, and intraductal cystadenoma.

Diagnosis of IPMN is clear-cut in a symptomatic patient with a markedly dilated main pancreatic duct containing polypoid filling

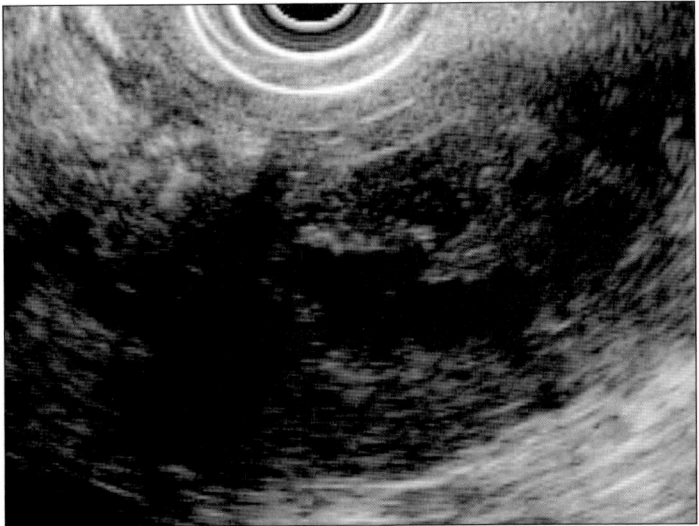

Figure 44–13. Colloid carcinoma of the pancreas. The tumor contains cystic pools of mucus.

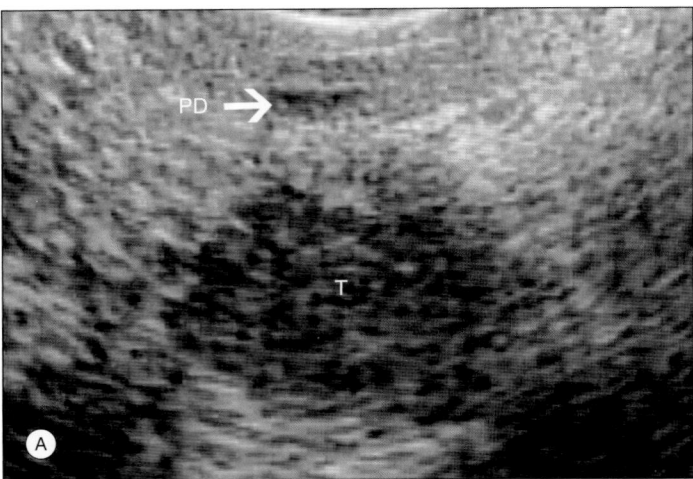

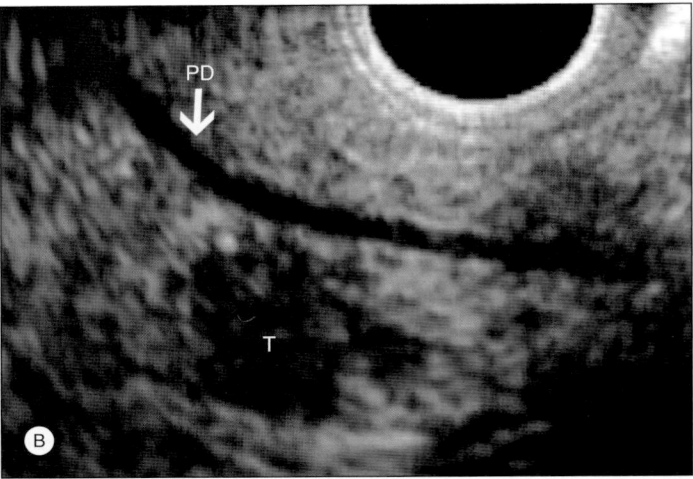

Figure 44–14. Pancreatic neuroendocrine tumors. *A,* Gastrinoma. *B,* Insulinoma. PD, pancreatic duct; T, tumor.

defects, in whom mucus is seen disgorging into the duodenum through a gaping ampullary orifice. Other, less classic presentations of IPMN are increasingly recognized. These include patients with a normal-appearing ampulla who have focal dilation or ectasia of the main pancreatic duct mimicking chronic pancreatitis or isolated branch duct lesions mimicking parenchymal cysts.[82] Branch duct disease may be missed by ERCP because contrast may not enter the mucin-filled side branch, and magnetic resonance cholangio-pancreatography (MRCP) or EUS may be more sensitive for diagnosis.

EUS demonstrates the ductal dilation that is a hallmark of IPMN (Fig. 44–16). In main duct lesions, there is typically marked dilation of the duct without an obstructing mass, stricture, or stone. The main duct wall may be irregular or thickened, with visible side branches that are also involved. Faintly echogenic material may be seen in the duct lumen corresponding to mucin, but this finding is often subtle or absent. The differential diagnosis of main duct dilation includes chronic pancreatitis and downstream ductal obstruction, and the pancreatic duct should be traced during EUS looking for an obstructing lesion or stricture.

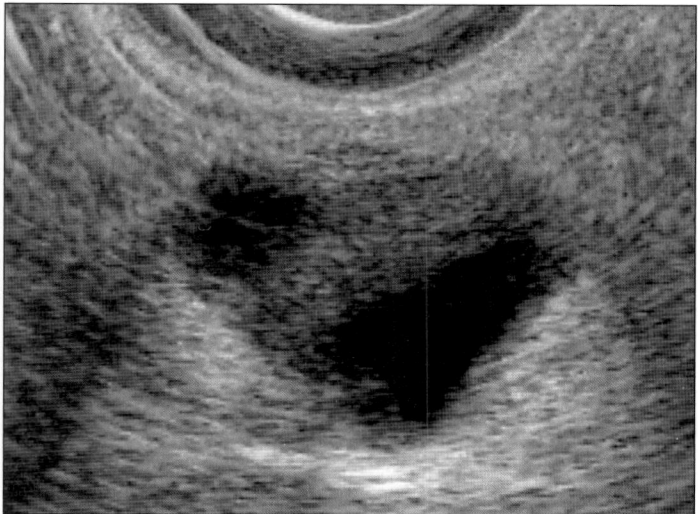

Figure 44–15. Cystic neuroendocrine tumor. There are two locules, a thickened cyst wall, and echogenic material within the cyst.

Some branch duct IPMN lesions have a tubular branching structure that is clearly recognizable as a dilated ductal system, but others appear cystic rather than ductal (Fig. 44–17). Branch duct IPMN can often be distinguished from a cyst by detection of a connecting duct leading to the main pancreatic duct, recognition of pancreatic parenchyma rather than septa between the locules of a lesion, proximity to the pancreatic duct, or the presence of a branching architecture. In some cases, these features are absent and the lesion may be misdiagnosed as a cyst. IPMN should be considered in the differential diagnosis of any mucin-containing pancreatic cyst, particularly in men (in whom mucinous cystic neoplasm [MCN] is rare).

Endosonography may be helpful in distinguishing the presence of invasive malignancy in IPMN. In one multicenter, retrospective study, EUS had poor accuracy for distinguishing between invasive and noninvasive IPMN,[83] but in a larger single center trial useful EUS criteria were identified.[82] These included dilation of the main pancreatic duct to 10 mm or larger, diameter of branch duct lesions greater than 40 mm, irregular thick septa in branch duct lesions, and large (>10 mm) mural nodules in either main duct or branch duct lesions. Malignancy was suspected if any of these four features were seen. Overall, EUS correctly diagnosed the presence or absence of malignancy in 86% of cases. In addition, IDUS appears useful in distinguishing malignant IPMN (see Fig. 44–16). In one large study, intraductal lesions with a maximum tumor height of 4 mm or more were malignant in 88% of cases, and this cutoff had a sensitivity and specificity of 68% and 89%, respectively.[84]

Infiltrating parenchymal malignancy may be present in patients with IPMN and should always be suspected when a patient with IPMN has obstructive jaundice. Hypoechoic pancreatic parenchyma associated with IPMN can be due to inflammation or malignancy, and EUS-guided FNA may clarify diagnosis in such cases.

Pancreatic Cysts and Pseudocysts

EUS is commonly used as an aid in the diagnosis of pancreatic cysts and pseudocysts. The role of EUS in diagnosis and management of these lesions is evolving and has been the subject of recent, comprehensive reviews.[85] Although the differential diagnosis is

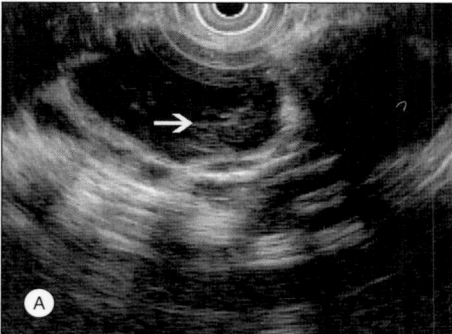
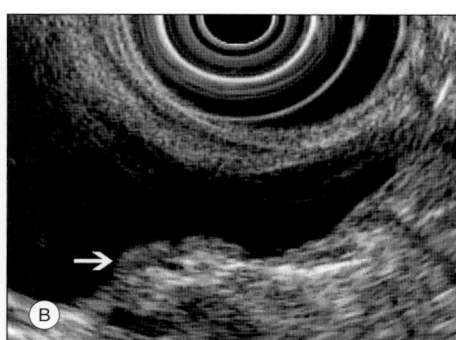
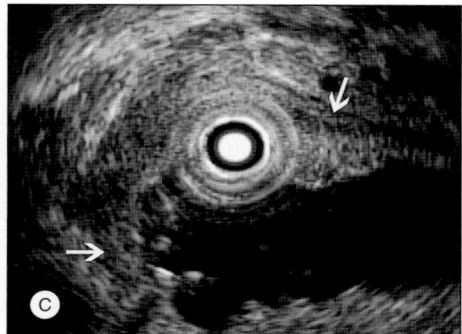

Figure 44–16. Intraductal papillary mucinous neoplasm (IPMN) of the main pancreatic duct. *A,* Dilated pancreatic duct containing mucus *(arrow)*. *B,* Thickened pancreatic duct mucosa *(arrow)*. *C,* Intraductal ultrasonography in IPMN. There is marked thickening of the duct wall *(arrows)*.

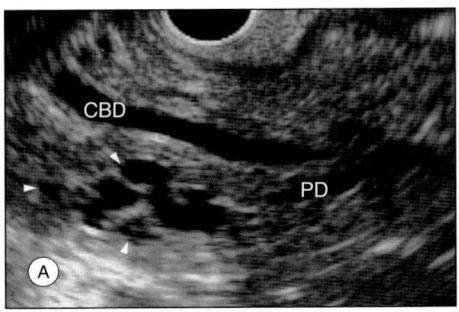
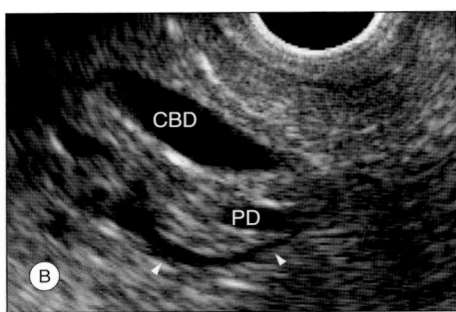
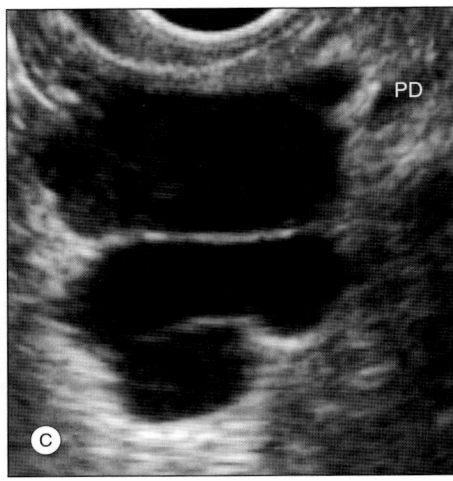

Figure 44–17. Branch duct intraductal papillary mucinous neoplasm (IPMN). *A,* This oligocystic lesion *(arrowheads)* has a branching architecture and pancreatic parenchyma rather than septa between the cystic spaces, suggesting IPMN. In a different image plane *(B),* a connecting duct leading to the main pancreatic duct is seen *(arrowheads)*. *C,* Another branch duct IPMN, this one without distinguishing sonographic features. CBD, common bile duct; PD, pancreatic duct.

Table 44–3. Differential Diagnosis of Pancreatic Cystic Lesions

Inflammatory	Cystic Neoplasms	Non-neoplastic Cysts	Vascular Lesions
Acute fluid collection	Serous cystic neoplasm	Cystic fibrosis	Splenic artery aneurysm
Organized necrosis	Mucinous cystic neoplasm	Polycystic kidney disease	Pseudoaneurysm
Pseudocyst	Intraductal papillary mucinous neoplasm	Lymphoepithelial cyst	
Abscess	Colloid carcinoma	Lymphangioma	
	Ductal adenocarcinoma with cystic degeneration	Epidermoid cyst (intrapancreatic accessory spleen)	
	Cystic neuroendocrine tumor	Endometrioma	
	Acinar cell cystadenocarcinoma	Hemorrhagic cyst	
	Papillary and cystic tumor	Congenital	
	Cystic teratoma	Tuberculosis	
	Leiomyosarcoma	Hydatid cyst	
	Pancreatoblastoma		

Table 44–4. Sonographic Features of Pancreatic Cysts

Architecture	Wall	Lumen
Shape	Presence of a wall	Echogenicity (anechoic/echogenic)
Unilocular/oligocystic/microcystic	Mural thickening (>1 mm)	Heterogeneity
Septa	Mural nodularity/mass	Sludge (layering/mobile)
Branching structure	Mural calcification	Intracystic mass
	Irregularity	Intracystic calcification

extensive (Table 44–3), this discussion focuses on the commonest cystic lesions of the pancreas.

EUS features of pancreatic cystic lesions are listed in Table 44–4. Sonographically, cystic structures are characterized by increased through-transmission, with enhanced echogenicity of the tissue beyond the cyst. The overall cyst architecture, the cyst wall, and the cyst lumen should be assessed during EUS. Unilocular cysts are usually round and have one cyst cavity, with or without incomplete septa. Oligocystic cysts contain more than one cystic space or locule separated by septa, but the individual locules are easily seen during EUS and can be counted. Microcystic cysts contain innumerable cystic spaces, some of which may be too small to be resolved by EUS.

PSEUDOCYST

Pseudocysts lack an epithelial lining and occur as a result of either pancreatitis or pancreatic ductal obstruction or disruption. In contrast to acute fluid collections, pseudocysts have a well-defined fibrous wall. When they occur in a region of recent pancreatic necrosis, they may be considered "organized pancreatic necrosis" and often contain solid necrotic debris.

Pseudocysts have a variable sonographic appearance (Fig. 44–18). They are typically unilocular, although they can appear oligocystic. A wall is invariably present, but its thickness can vary considerably. Mural calcification can be seen in both chronic pseudocysts and cystic neoplasms. The lumen of a pseudocyst may be anechoic or echogenic and can be complex, particularly in cases of organized

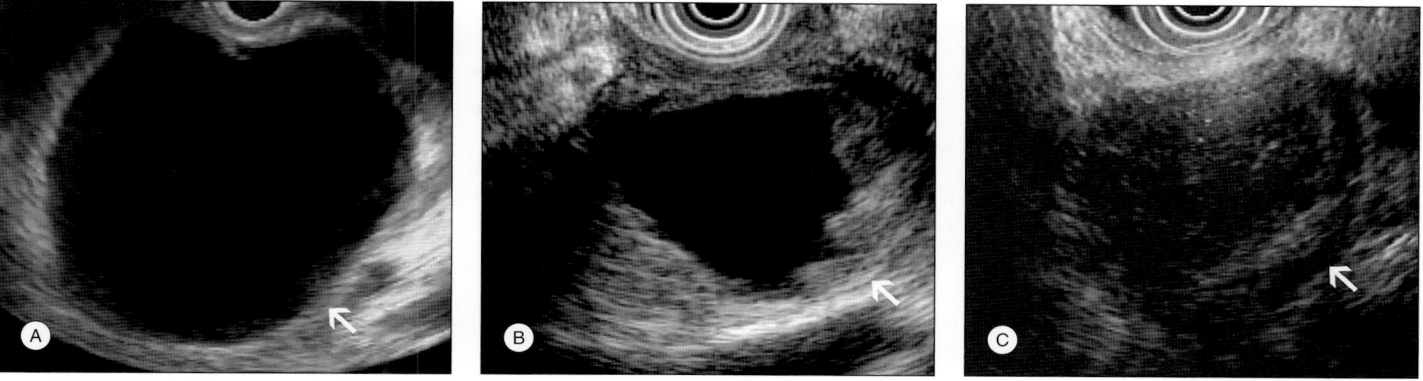

Figure 44–18. Pancreatic pseudocysts. *Arrows* point to the pseudocyst wall. *A,* Large pseudocyst with an anechoic lumen. *B,* Echogenic, partially layering material in a pseudocyst. *C,* Organized pancreatic necrosis with a thick wall and echogenic contents.

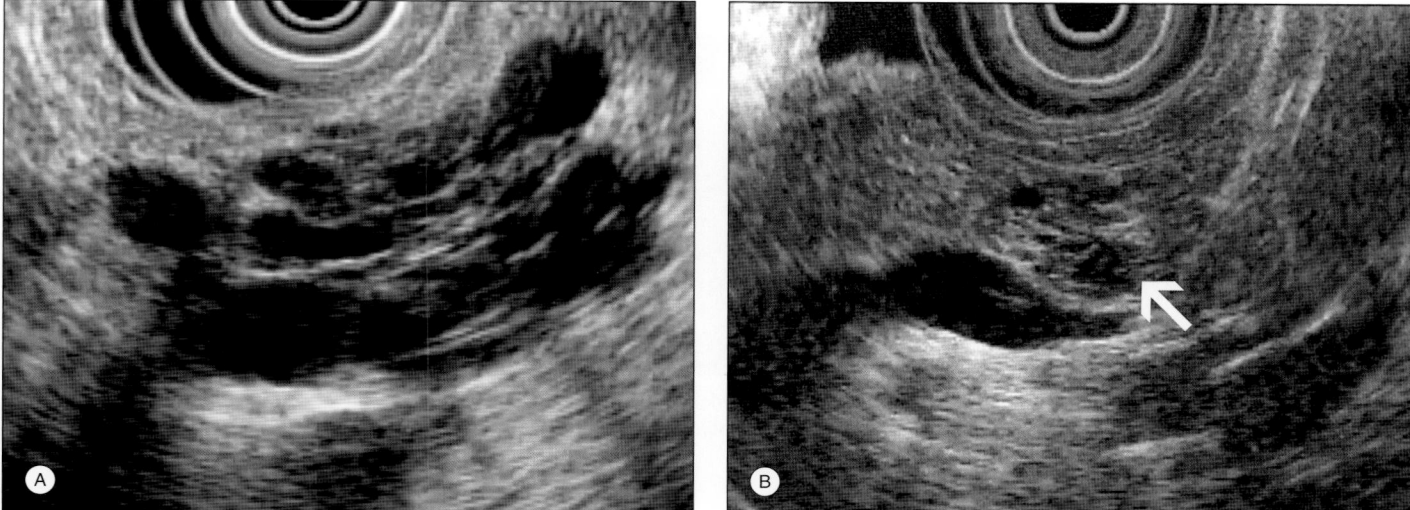

Figure 44–19. Microcystic serous cystadenomas. *A,* Innumerable locules with intervening thin septa. In some areas, septa predominate. There is no well-defined wall. *B,* Some portions of this lesion appear solid because of the microscopic size of individual locules.

pancreatic necrosis (see Fig. 44–18). Echogenic material in the cyst lumen may layer, suggesting sludge, but may also present the appearance of an intracystic mass.

Fluid aspirated from a pseudocyst may be clear or discolored and may contain gritty or particulate matter. A drop placed between two gloved fingers typically does not form a string. Fluid amylase is usually elevated above 5000 U/L. CA 19-9 values vary widely in pseudocyst fluid and are not helpful for diagnosis, but carcino-embryonic antigen (CEA), CA 72-4, and CA 15-3 values are typically low.

SEROUS CYSTIC NEOPLASM

Serous cystic neoplasms are cystic growths that likely arise from centroacinar cells. Most serous cystic neoplasms are serous cystadenomas, although a handful of serous cystadenocarcinomas have been reported in the medical literature. In contrast to mucinous cystic lesions and IPMN, these tumors lack K-*ras* mutations and have very low malignant potential.[75] Mutations of the von Hippel-Lindau (VHL) tumor suppressor gene have been implicated in their pathogenesis.[86] Most serous cystadenomas are microcystic, although they may also be oligocystic, unilocular, or (uncommonly) solid. A fibrous capsule or wall is usually not present.

Sonographically, microcystic serous cystadenoma has a characteristic appearance (Fig. 44–19). The lesion is rounded and contains innumerable small cystic spaces, with the largest individual cyst usually less than 2 cm in diameter. Central calcification may be seen in the lesion with a "sunburst" configuration. There is a discrete edge but typically without an identifiable wall. The absence of a wall is an important feature because mucinous cystic neoplasms typically have a wall. In some portions of the lesion, the individual cysts are too small to resolve with EUS; in these areas, septa predominate, and the tissue has a relatively hypoechoic,

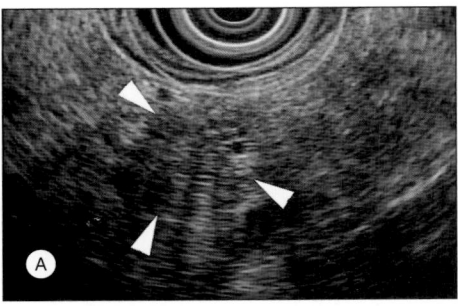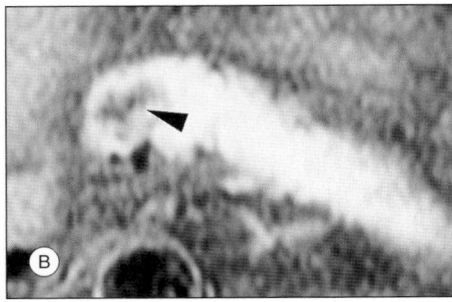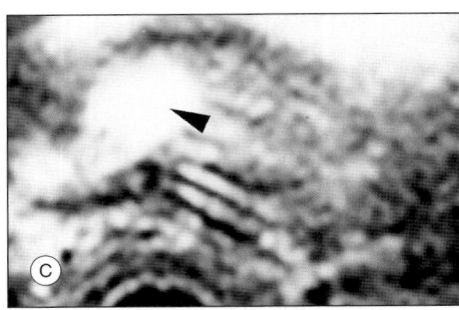

Figure 44–20. Microcystic serous cystadenoma appearing solid on EUS *(A),* but cystic on magnetic resonance imaging (MRI) *(B* and *C). Arrowheads* indicate the lesion.

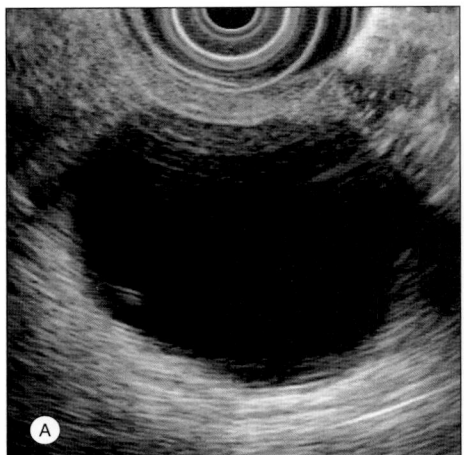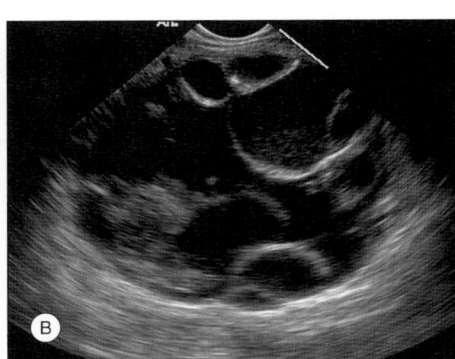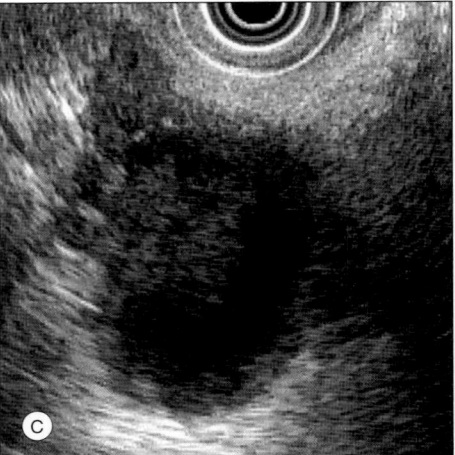

Figure 44–21. Mucinous cystic neoplasms. *A,* Unilocular mucinous cystadenoma. *B,* Oligocystic mucinous cystic neoplasm with borderline features histologically. *C,* Mucinous cystadenocarcinoma, with a thickened wall, an intracystic mass, and extension into adjacent pancreas parenchyma.

solid appearance. Sometimes the majority of the lesion has this appearance, leading to misdiagnosis of a solid mass, but MRI will show the cystic nature of the lesion (Fig. 44–20). Branch duct IPMN may appear similar to oligocystic serous cystadenoma, and the two lesions can be confused with each other, especially when small (see Fig. 44–17). In contrast to the microcystic form, serous cystadenomas that are oligocystic or unilocular do not have sonographic features that distinguish them from mucinous cystadenoma or inflammatory fluid collections.

Fluid aspirated from a serous cystadenoma is typically clear and watery and does not form a string. Little or no fluid may be obtained when the microcystic form is aspirated. Amylase level, CEA, and other tumor marker levels in the fluid are low, even in the macrocystic form.[87,88] CEA is often less than 5 ng/mL. Cytology may show glycogen-containing cells but is often nondiagnostic.[89]

MUCINOUS CYSTIC NEOPLASM

MCNs are cystic growths with well-recognized malignant potential. Ninety percent of MCNs occur in women. They are usually oligocystic, although a single large cyst may dominate. MCNs may

be benign (mucinous cystadenoma), malignant (mucinous cystadenocarcinoma), or have borderline features (MCN with moderate dysplasia).[75] Epidemiologic data suggests that these lesions begin as cystadenomas and grow slowly, because cystadenocarcinoma patients on average are 10 years older than those with cystadenoma.[90] Cystadenocarcinoma is uncommon in MCNs less than 5 cm in size[91] but has been reported.[92]

Sonographically, MCNs may appear oligocystic or unilocular (Fig. 44–21). When oligocystic, some of locules are generally greater than 2 cm in diameter. When the rim and septa of the lesion are thin and smooth, invasive malignancy is unlikely. Thickening, nodularity, or irregularity of these structures suggests the presence of mucinous cystadenocarcinoma, but these findings are not specific and can be present in mucinous cystadenoma as well.

Fluid aspirated from an MCN is often cloudy and tenacious, and a drop placed between two gloved fingers will usually form a string. Amylase level in the cyst fluid is usually low, and tumor marker levels in cyst fluid are elevated. Most (but not all) investigators have found that CEA and CA 72-4 levels are generally elevated in fluid from MCNs.[93,94] Elevated values of CA 15-3 in a mucinous lesion suggest mucinous cystadenocarcinoma.[95]

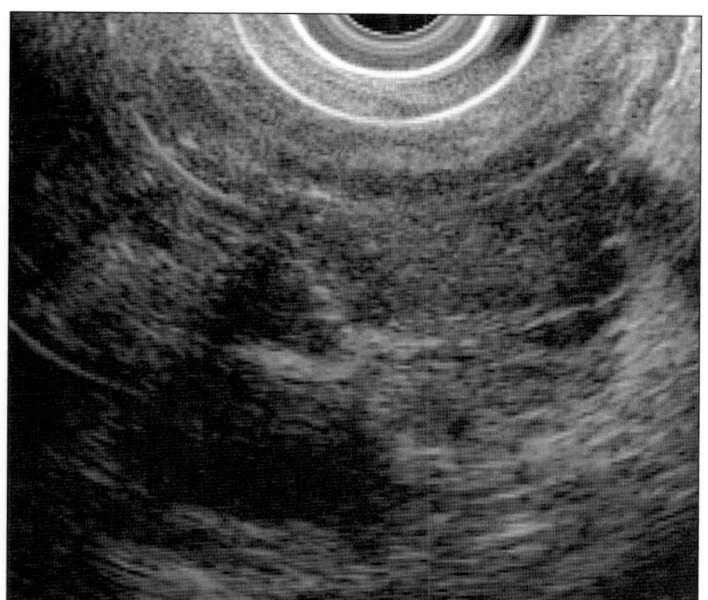

Figure 44–22. Papillary and cystic neoplasm of the pancreatic head.

Occasionally, fluid aspirated from MCNs is not tenacious, perhaps because of digestion of mucins by pancreatic enzymes. A minority of MCNs communicate with the pancreatic duct, and in these cases fluid from the cyst may have high amylase levels without impressive elevations of tumor marker levels. Thus, the absence of typical findings on cyst fluid analysis does not exclude the diagnosis of MCN, particularly in a woman with no antecedent history and imaging findings to suggest a pseudocyst.

INTRADUCTAL PAPILLARY MUCINOUS NEOPLASM

Branch duct IPMN may present the appearance of a cystic lesion on EUS. The lesion typically appears oligocystic and may be rounded. Clues to diagnosis include a branching architecture suggestive of a dilated ductal system and the presence of pancreatic tissue between the locules of the lesion, rather than true septa (see Fig. 44–17). Careful examination may show the connecting duct leading from the lesion to the main pancreatic duct. However, these features are not always present, and IPMN should always be considered in the differential diagnosis of a cystic lesion containing viscous or mucinous fluid, particularly in men (in whom MCN is rare).

Fluid aspirated from an IPMN has variable features. In general, the fluid is either viscous with high tumor marker levels, or thin and watery with low or midrange elevations of tumor marker levels. This variability is probably due to the communication between the lesion and the main pancreatic duct, resulting in a mixture of pancreatic juice and tumor secretions in the lumen of the lesion. Thus, findings may vary from those typically seen in pseudocysts to those associated with MCNs. It seems likely that branch duct lesions more often contain viscous fluid with elevated tumor marker levels, because there is less mixing with normal pancreatic juice in these lesions.

OTHER CYSTIC LESIONS

Solid pancreatic adenocarcinomas may undergo cystic degeneration, perhaps resulting from necrosis and liquefaction of portions of the tumor. About 15% of pancreatic adenocarcinomas are colloid carcinomas containing gelatinous pools of extracellular mucin[96]; these lesions often arise from a MCN or IPMN and may appear heterogeneous or cystic on EUS. Uncommon cystic neoplasms of the pancreas include cystic neuroendocrine tumors (see Fig. 44–14), acinar cell cystadenocarcinomas, and papillary and cystic tumors (Fig. 44–22). These lesions typically have a discrete, thickened wall and a complex internal architecture, raising concern for an invasive neoplasm. The EUS appearance of these lesions is not specific for diagnosis. Acinar cell cystadenocarcinoma may be associated with elevated serum alpha-fetoprotein levels. Little information is available regarding the results of cyst fluid analysis in these less common cystic neoplasms.

Among non-neoplastic cystic lesions, lymphangioma may be distinguished by the finding of milky white lymph fluid when the cyst is aspirated. The finding of squamous cells on cytology may suggest a lymphoepithelial cyst or teratoma.

von HIPPEL-LINDAU SYNDROME

VHL syndrome is characterized by hemangioblastomas of the central nervous system and retina, renal cysts and carcinoma, pheochromocytoma, and multiple pancreatic lesions. The commonest pancreatic findings in VHL are serous cystadenoma and neuroendocrine tumor. The pancreatic lesions may be difficult to diagnose by sonographic features alone, because some microcystic serous neoplasms appear solid with a discrete edge, and conversely some neuroendocrine tumors may be cystic. EUS-guided aspiration and other imaging studies such as MRI and octreotide scanning may be useful.

ACCURACY OF ENDOSCOPIC ULTRASONOGRAPHY FOR DIFFERENTIAL DIAGNOSIS

The sonographic appearance of a pancreatic cystic lesion usually does not provide a specific diagnosis. Characteristic sonographic features do suggest a likely diagnosis when the classic features of microcystic serous cystadenoma or branch duct IPMN are seen. In oligocystic or unilocular lesions, however, sonographic appearance alone is nonspecific for final diagnosis.[97] Within oligocystic or unilocular lesions, the presence of thin walls and septa, an anechoic lumen, and the absence of a mass all suggest that the lesion does not currently contain an invasive malignancy.[92] Unfortunately, these findings do not discriminate cysts of little or no malignant potential (pseudocysts and serous cystadenomas) from those with significant malignant potential over time (mucinous cystadenomas or branch duct IPMNs). Conversely, when the lesion has a thickened wall or septa and a complex luminal echogenicity, the cyst may contain invasive malignancy, but the presence of malignancy cannot be determined from the sonographic appearance alone.[97] In one large surgical series, only 3% of asymptomatic cysts less than 2 cm in size contained malignancy, but half of the lesions were premalignant (MCNs or IPMN).[98] Thus, careful follow-up is warranted in small, benign-appearing cystic lesions that are not resected.

Table 44–5. Cyst Fluid Analysis for Diagnosis of Cystic Lesions*

Diagnostic Test	Pseudocyst	Serous Cystadenoma	Mucinous Cystadenoma	Mucinous Cystadenocarcinoma	IPMN
Amylase	High	Low	Low	Low	Variable
Viscosity	Low	Low	High	High	Variable
String sign	Negative	Negative	Positive	Positive	Variable
CEA	Low	Low	High	High	Variable
CA 72-4	Low	Low	High	High	Variable
CA 15-3	Low	Low	Low	High	—
CA 125	Low	Variable	Variable	High	—
CA 19-9	Variable	—	Variable	Variable	Variable

*Typical findings are shown; results may vary in individual cases, as discussed in the text.
CEA, carcinoembryonic antigen; IPMN, intraductal papillary mucinous neoplasm.
Adapted from references 99–102.

Cyst fluid analysis may aid in the differential diagnosis of cystic lesions. Although EUS-guided aspiration of cystic lesions was reported to result in infection of the cyst in up to 10% of cases, the use of prophylactic antibiotics has markedly decreased this risk. Lesions containing thick mucinous fluid or numerous septa may be difficult to aspirate, with a plug of mucin or tissue filling the needle lumen. When sufficient fluid can be aspirated, multiple diagnostic studies should be obtained, including cytology, amylase, CEA, CA 72-4, CA 15-3, and CA 125. Viscosity should also be assessed, either by measuring fluid viscosity or by placing a drop of fluid between two gloved fingers and determining if the fluid will form a string (the "string sign"). The typical results of fluid analysis for various cystic lesions is shown in Table 44–5.

Unfortunately, cyst fluid analysis alone does not provide a confident diagnosis in many cases. Cytology is specific but insensitive for diagnosis of MCNs and IPMN. The classic MCN has a cyst fluid CEA greater than 400 µg/L and CA 72-4 greater than 40 and a positive string sign or increased fluid viscosity, and a low amylase level.[99] However, lower or normal tumor marker levels may be seen in mucinous lesions, particularly those that communicate with the pancreatic duct, and the cyst fluid amylase may be elevated in such lesions also.[100] Because IPMN lesions always communicate with the pancreatic ductal system, they show variable results of fluid analysis depending in part on the ratio of normal pancreatic juice to mucin in the aspirated specimen. Thus, the absence of typical findings on fluid analysis does not exclude a mucinous lesion.

Despite these shortcomings, EUS helps with clinical decision making in many patients, particularly those with small incidentally detected cysts or multiple cystic lesions and in patients with increased operative risk. The best EUS-guided diagnosis relies on a combination of the clinical history, the sonographic appearance of a cyst, and results of diagnostic studies on cyst fluid. The decision to proceed to cyst resection for definitive diagnosis hinges not only on EUS but also on the clinical presentation, the size of the lesion, and the age, symptoms, general health, and preferences of the patient.

REFERENCES

1. Erickson RA, Garza AA: EUS with EUS-guided fine-needle aspiration as the first endoscopic test for the evaluation of obstructive jaundice. Gastrointest Endosc 53:475–84, 2001.
2. Songür Y, Temuçin G, Sahin B: Endoscopic ultrasonography in the evaluation of dilated common bile duct. J Clin Gastroenterol 33:302–305, 2001.
3. Tandon M, Topazian M: Endoscopic ultrasound in idiopathic acute pancreatitis. Am J Gastroenterol 96:705–709, 2001.
4. Dahan P, Andant C, Levy P, et al: Prospective evaluation of endoscopic ultrasonography and microscopic examination of duodenal bile in the diagnosis of cholecystolithiasis in 45 patients with normal conventional ultrasonography. Gut 38:277–281, 1996.
5. Dill JE, Hill S, Callis J, et al: Combined endoscopic ultrasound and stimulated biliary drainage in cholecystitis and microlithiasis—diagnoses and outcomes. Endoscopy 27:424–427, 1995.
6. Choi WB, Lee SK, Kim MH, et al: A new strategy to predict the neoplastic polyps of the gallbladder based on a scoring system using EUS. Gastrointest Endosc 52:372–379, 2000.
7. Sugiyama M, Atomi Y, Yamato T: Endoscopic ultrasonography for differential diagnosis of polypoid gall bladder lesions: Analysis in surgical and follow up series. Gut 46:250–254, 2000.
8. Azuma T, Yoshikawa T, Araida T, Takasaki K: Differential diagnosis of polypoid lesions of the gallbladder by endoscopic ultrasonography. Am J Surg 181:65–70, 2001.
9. Miziguchi M, Kudo S, Fukahori T, et al: Endoscopic ultrasonography for demonstrating loss of multiple-layer pattern of the thickened gallbladder wall in the preoperative diagnosis of gallbladder cancer. Eur Radiol 7:1323–1327, 1997.
10. Prat F, Amouyal G, Amouyal P, et al: Prospective controlled study of endoscopic ultrasonography and endoscopic retrograde cholangiography in patients with suspected common-bile duct lithiasis. Lancet 347:75–79, 1996.
11. Kohut M, Nowakowska-Dulawa E, Marek T, et al: Accuracy of linear endoscopic ultrasonography in the evaluation of patients with suspected common bile duct stones. Endoscopy 34:299–303, 2002.
12. Berdah SV, Orsoni P, Bege T, et al: Follow-up of selective endoscopic ultrasonography and/or endoscopic retrograde cholangiography prior to laparoscopic cholecystectomy: A prospective study of 300 patients. Endoscopy 33:216–220, 2001.
13. Ueno N, Nishizono T, Tamada K, et al: Diagnosing extrahepatic bile duct stones using intraductal ultrasonography: A case series. Endoscopy 29:356–360, 1997.

14. Catanzaro A, Pfau P, Isenberg GA, et al: Clinical utility of intraductal US for evaluation of choledocholithiasis. Gastrointest Endosc 57:648–652, 2003.

15. Haber GB: Is seeing believing? Gastrointest Endosc 57:712–714, 2003.

16. Frossard JL, Hadengue A, Amouyal G, et al: Choledocholithiasis: A prospective study of spontaneous common bile duct stone migration. Gastrointest Endosc 51:175–179, 2000.

17. Sahai AV, Mauldin PD, Marsi V, et al: Bile duct stones and laparoscopic cholecystectomy: A decision analysis to assess the roles of intraoperative cholangiography, EUS, and ERCP. Gastrointest Endosc 49:334–343, 1999.

18. Prat F, Edery J, Meduri B, et al: Early EUS of the bile duct before endoscopic sphincterotomy for acute biliary pancreatitis. Gastrointest Endosc 54:724–729, 2001.

19. Liu CL, Lo CM, Chan JK, et al: Detection of choledocholithiasis by EUS in acute pancreatitis: A prospective evaluation in 100 consecutive patients. Gastrointest Endosc 54:325–330, 2001.

20. Fujita N, Noda Y, Kobayashi G, et al: Staging of bile duct carcinoma by EUS and IDUS. Endoscopy 30(Suppl 1):A132–A134, 1998.

21. Tamada K, Tomiyama T, Oohashi A, et al: Bile duct wall thickness measured by intraductal US in patients who have not undergone previous biliary drainage. Gastrointest Endosc 48:199–203, 1999.

22. Tamada K, Tomiyama T, Ichiyama M, et al: Influence of biliary drainage catheter on bile duct wall thickness as measured by intraductal ultrasonography. Gastrointest Endosc 47:28–33, 1998.

23. Fritscher-Ravens A, Broering DC, Siriam PV, et al: EUS-guided fine-needle aspiration cytodiagnosis of hilar cholangiocarcinoma: A case series. Endoscopy 52:534–540, 2000.

24. Inui K, Nakazawa S, Yoshino J, et al: Ultrasound probes for biliary lesions. Endoscopy 390(Suppl 1):A120–A123, 1998.

25. Domagk D, Poremba C, Dietl KH, et al: Endoscopic transpapillary biopsies and intraductal ultrasonography in the diagnostics of bile duct strictures: A prospective study. Gut 51:240–244, 2002.

26. Vazquez-Sequeiros E, Baron TH, Clain JE, et al: Evaluation of indeterminate bile duct strictures by intraductal US. Gastrointest Endosc 56:372–379, 2002.

27. Lee J, Salem R, Aslanian H, et al: Endoscopic ultrasound and fine-needle aspiration of unexplained bile duct strictures. Am J Gastroenterol 99:1069–1073, 2004.

28. Tamada K, Kanai N, Wada S, et al: Utility and limitations of intraductal ultrasonography in distinguishing longitudinal cancer extension along the bile duct from inflammatory wall thickening. Abd Imaging 26:623–631, 2001.

29. Hyodo T, Hyodo N, Yamanaka T, et al: Contrast-enhanced intraductal ultrasonography for thickened bile duct wall. J Gastroenterol 36:557–559, 2001.

30. Wehrmann T, Stergiou N, Riphaus A, et al: Correlation between sphincter of Oddi manometry and intraductal ultrasound morphology in patients with suspected sphincter of Oddi dysfunction. Endoscopy 33:773–777, 2001.

31. Cannon ME, Carpenter SL, Elta GH, et al: EUS compared with CT, magnetic resonance imaging, and angiography and the influence of biliary stenting on staging accuracy of ampullary neoplasms. Gastrointest Endosc 50:27–33, 1999.

32. Skordilis P, Mouzas IA, Dimoulios PD, et al: Is endosonography an effective method for detection and local staging of the ampullary carcinoma? A prospective study. BMC Surg 2:1–8, 2002.

33. Menzel J, Hoepffner N, Sulkowski U, et al: Polypoid tumors of the major duodenal papilla: Preoperative staging with intraductal US, EUS, and CT—a prospective, histopathologically controlled study. Gastrointest Endosc 49:349–357, 1999.

34. Chak A, Hawes RH, Cooper GS, et al: Prospective assessment of the utility of EUS in the evaluation of gallstone pancreatitis. Gastrointest Endosc 49:599–604, 1999.

35. Prat F, Edery J, Meduri B, et al: Early EUS of the bile duct before endoscopic sphincterotomy for acute biliary pancreatitis. Gastrointest Endosc 54:724–729, 2001.

36. Norton SA, Alderson D: Endoscopic ultrasonography in the evaluation of idiopathic acute pancreatitis. Br J Surg 87:1650–1655, 2000.

37. Coyle WJ, Pineau BC, Tarnasky PR, et al: Evaluation of unexplained acute and acute recurrent pancreatitis using endoscopic retrograde cholangiopancreatography, sphincter of Oddi manometry and endoscopic ultrasound. Endoscopy 34:617–623, 2002.

38. The International Working Group for Minimal Standard Terminology in Gastrointestinal Endosonography: Minimal standard terminology in gastrointestinal endosonography. Dig Endosc 10:159–84, 1998.

39. Wallace MB, Hawes RH, Durkalski V, et al: The reliability of EUS for the diagnosis of chronic pancreatitis: Interobserver agreement among experienced endosonographers. Gastrointest Endosc 53:294–299, 2001.

40. Kimmey MB, Bronner MP, Byrd DR, et al: Screening and surveillance for hereditary pancreatic cancer. Gastrointest Endosc 56(4 Suppl):S82–86, 2002.

41. Wiersema MJ, Hawes RH, Lehman GA, et al: Prospective evaluation of endoscopic ultrasonography and endoscopic retrograde cholangiopancreatography in patients with chronic abdominal pain of suspected pancreatic origin. Endoscopy 25:555–564, 1993.

42. Catalano MF, Lahoti S, Geenan JE, et al: Prospective evaluation of endoscopic ultrasonography, endoscopic retrograde cholangiopancreatography, and secretin test in the diagnosis of chronic pancreatitis. Gastrointest Endosc 48:11–17, 1998.

43. Sahai AV, Zimmerman M, Aabakken L, et al: Prospective assessment of the ability of endoscopic ultrasound to diagnose, exclude, or establish the severity of chronic pancreatitis found by endoscopic retrograde cholangiopancreatography. Gastrointest Endosc 48:18–25, 1998.

44. Zimerman MJ, Mishra G, Lewin D, et al: Comparison of EUS findings with histopathology in chronic pancreatitis. Gastrointest Endosc 45:AB185, 1997.

45. Bhutani M, Moezzi J, Suryaprasad S, et al: Histopathologic correlation of endoscopic ultrasound findings in chronic pancreatitis. Gastrointest Endosc 45:AB167, 1997.

46. Hollerbach S, Klamann A, Topalidis T, et al: Endoscopic ultrasonography and fine-needle aspiration cytology for diagnosis of chronic pancreatitis. Endoscopy 33:824–831, 2001.

47. Pitchumoni CS, Glasser M, Saran RM, et al: Pancreatic fibrosis in chronic alcoholics and nonalcoholics without clinical pancreatitis. Am J Gastroenterol 79:382–388, 1984.

48. Suda K, Shiotsu H, Nakamura T, et al: Pancreatic fibrosis in patients with chronic alcohol abuse: Correlation with alcoholic pancreatitis. Am J Gastroenterol 89:2060–2062, 1994.

49. Suda K, Takase M, Takei K, et al: Histopathologic study of coexistent pathologic states in pancreatic fibrosis in patients with chronic alcohol abuse: Two distinct pathologic fibrosis entities with different mechanisms. Pancreas 12:369–372, 1996.

50. Kuroda J, Suda K, Hosokawa Y: Periacinar collagenization in patients with chronic alcoholism. Pathol Int 48:857–868, 1998.

51. Bhutani MS: Endoscopic ultrasonography: Changes of chronic pancreatitis in asymptomatic and symptomatic alcoholic patients. J Ultrasound Med 18:455–462, 1999.

52. Sahai AV, Mishra G, Penman ID, et al: EUS to detect evidence of pancreatic disease in patients with persistent or nonspecific dyspepsia. Gastrointest Endosc 52:153–159, 2000.

53. Kahl S, Glasbrenner B, Leodolter A, et al: EUS in the diagnosis of early chronic pancreatitis: A prospective follow-up study. Gastrointest Endosc 55:507–111, 2002.

54. Hastier P, Buckley MJ, Francois E, et al: A prospective study of pancreatic disease in patients with alcoholic cirrhosis: Comparative diagnostic value of ERCP and EUS and long-term significance of isolated parenchymal abnormalities. Gastrointest Endosc 49:705–709, 1999.

55. Martin E, Bedossa P: Diffuse fibrosis of the pancreas: A peculiar pattern of pancreatitis in alcoholic cirrhosis. Gastroenterol Clin Biol 13:579–84, 1989.

56. Topazian M: Endoscopic ultrasound of the pancreas [video]. American Society for Gastrointestinal Endoscopy, Oakbrook, IL, 2001.

57. Yasuda K, Mukai H, Jufimoto S, et al: The diagnosis of pancreatic cancer by endoscopic ultrasonography. Gastrointest Endosc 34:1–8, 1988.

58. Norton ID, Zheng Y, Wiersema MS, et al: Neural network analysis of EUS images to differentiate between pancreatic malignancy and pancreatitis. Gastrointest Endosc 54:625–629, 2001.

59. Becker D, Strobel D, Bernatik T, et al: Echo-enhanced color and power Doppler EUS for the discrimination between focal pancreatitis and pancreatic carcinoma. Gastrointest Endosc 53:784–789, 2001.

60. Williams DB, Sahai AV, Aabakken L, et al: Endoscopic ultrasound guided fine needle aspiration biopsy: A large single centre experience. Gut 44:720–726, 1999.

61. Voss M, Hammel P, Molas G, et al: Value of endoscopic ultrasound guided fine needle aspiration biopsy in the diagnosis of solid pancreatic masses. Gut 46:244–249, 2000.

62. Tada M, Komatsu Y, Kawabe T, et al: Quantitative analysis of K-*ras* gene mutation in pancreatic tissue obtained by endoscopic ultrasonography-guided fine needle aspiration: Clinical utility for diagnosis of pancreatic tumor. Am J Gastroenterol 97:2263–2270, 2002.

63. Hunt GC, Faigel DO: Assessment of EUS for diagnosing, staging, and determining the resectability of pancreatic cancer: A review. Gastrointest Endosc 55:232–237, 2002.

64. Dewitt J, Ciaccia D, Leblanc J, et al: Prospective comparison of EUS and dual-phase helical computed tomography for the preoperative evaluation of known or suspected pancreatic malignancy. Gastrointest Endosc 57:AB 677, 2003.

65. Bold RJ, Charnsangavej C, Cleary KR, et al: Major vascular resection as part of pancreaticoduodenectomy for cancer: Radiologic, intraoperative, and pathologic analysis. J Gastrointest Surg 3:233–243, 1999.

66. Leach SD, Lee JE, Charnsangavej C, et al: Survival following pancreaticoduodenectomy with resection of the superior mesenteric-portal vein confluence for adenocarcinoma of the pancreatic head. Br J Surg 85:611–617, 1998.

67. Aslanian H, Salem R, Lee J, et al: EUS features of vascular invasion in pancreas cancer: Surgical and histologic correlates (in press).

68. Rösch T, Dittler HJ, Strobel K, et al: Endoscopic ultrasound criteria for vascular invasion in the staging of cancer of the head of the pancreas: A blind reevaluation of videotapes. Gastrointest Endosc 52:469–477, 2000.

69. Ahmad NA, Lewis JD, Siegelman ES, et al: Role of endoscopic ultrasound and magnetic resonance imaging in the preoperative staging of pancreatic adenocarcinoma. Am J Gastroenterol 95:1926–1931, 2000.

70. Exocrine pancreas. In Greene FL, Page DL, Fleming ID, et al (eds): AJCC Cancer Staging Manual, 6th ed. Chicago, American Joint Committee on Cancer, 2002, pp 179–187.

71. Hahn M, Faigel DO: Frequency of mediastinal lymph node metastases in patients undergoing EUS evaluation of pancreaticobiliary masses. Gastrointest Endosc 54:331–335, 2001.

72. Fritscher-Ravens A, Brand L, Knöfel T, et al: Comparison of endoscopic ultrasound-guided fine needle aspiration for focal pancreatic lesions in patients with normal parenchyma and chronic pancreatitis. Am J Gastroenterol 97:2768–2775, 2002.

73. Sugiyama M, Abe N, Izumisato Y, et al: Differential diagnosis of benign versus malignant nonfunctioning islet cell tumors of the pancreas: The roles of EUS and ERCP. Gastrointest Endosc 55:115–121, 2002.

74. Ginès A, Vazquez-Sequeiros E, Soria MT, et al: Usefulness of EUS-guided aspiration (EUS-FNA) in the diagnosis of functioning neuroendocrine tumors. Gastrointest Endosc 56:291–296, 2002.

75. Compton CC: Histology of cystic tumors of the pancreas. Gastrointest Endosc Clin N Am 12:673–696, 2002.

76. Matsumoto T, Aramaki M, Yada K, et al: Optimal management of the branch duct type intraductal papillary mucinous neoplasm of the pancreas. J Clin Gastroenterol 36:261–265, 2003.

77. Bernard P, Scoazec JY, Jouber M, et al: Intraductal papillary-mucinous tumors of the pancreas. Arch Surg 137:1274–1278, 2002.

78. Kobari M, Egawa S, Shibuya K, et al: Intraductal papillary mucinous tumors of the pancreas comprise two clinical subtypes. Arch Surg 134:1131–1136, 1999.

79. Terris B, Ponsot P, Paye F, et al: Intraductal papillary mucinous tumors of the pancreas confined to secondary ducts show less aggressive pathologic features as compared with those involving the main pancreatic duct. Am J Surg Pathol 24:1372–1377, 2000.

80. Yamaguchi K, Sugitani A, Chijiiwa K, et al: Intraductal papillary mucinous tumor of the pancreas: Assessing the grade of malignancy from natural history. Am Surg 67:400–406, 2001.

81. Obara T, Maguchi H, Saitoh Y, et al: Mucin-producing tumor of the pancreas: Natural history and serial pancreatogram changes. Am J Gastroenterol 88:564–569, 1993.

82. Kubo H, Chijiiwa Y, Akahoshi K, et al: Intraductal papillary-mucinous tumors of the pancreas: Differential diagnosis between benign and malignant tumors by endoscopic ultrasonography. Am J Gastroenterol 96:1429–1434, 2001.

83. Cellier C, Cuillerier E, Palazzo L, et al: Intraductal papillary and mucinous tumors of the pancreas: Accuracy of preoperative computed tomography, endoscopic retrograde pancreatography and endoscopic ultrasonography, and long-term outcome in a large surgical series. Gastrointest Endosc 47:42–49, 1998.

84. Hara T, Yamaguchi T, Ishihara T, et al: Diagnosis and patient management of intraductal papillary-mucinous tumor of the pancreas by using peroral pancreatoscopy and intraductal ultrasonography. Gastroenterology 122:34–43, 2002.

85. Brugge WR (ed): Cystic disease of the pancreas. Gastrointest Endosc Clin N Am 12:4, 657–812, 2002.

86. Vortmeyer AO, Lubensky IA, Fogt F, et al: Allelic deletion and mutation of the von Hippel-Lindau (VHL) tumor suppressor gene in pancreatic microcystic adenomas. Am J Pathol 151:951–956, 1997.

87. Sperti C, Pasquali C, Perasole A, et al: Macrocystic serous cystadenoma of the pancreas: Clinicopathologic features in seven cases. Int J Pancreatol 28:1–7, 2002.

88. Chatelain D, Hammel P, O'Toole D, et al: Macrocystic form of serous pancreatic cystadenoma. Am J Gastroenterol 97:2566–2571, 2002.

89. Centeno BA: Role of cytology in the diagnosis of cystic and intraductal papillary mucinous neoplasms. Gastrointest Endosc Clin N Am 12:697–708, 2002.

90. Zamboni G, Scarpa A, Bogina G, et al: Mucinous cystic tumors of the pancreas: Clinicopathological features, prognosis, and relationship to other mucinous cystic tumors. Am J Surg Pathol 23:410–422, 1999.

91. Sarr MG, Carpenter HA, Prabhakar LP, et al: Clinical and pathologic correlation of 84 mucinous cystic neoplasms of the pancreas: Can one reliably differentiate benign from malignant (or premalignant) neoplasms? Ann Surg 231:205–212, 2000.

92. Koito K, Namieno T, Nagakawa T, et al: Solitary cystic tumor of the pancreas: EUS-pathologic correlation. Gastrointest Endosc 45:268–276, 1997.

93. Hammel P, Voitot H, Vilgrain V, et al: Diagnostic value of CA 72-4 and carcinoembryonic antigen determination in the fluid of pancreatic cystic lesions. Eur J Gastroenterol Hepatol 10:345–348, 1998.

94. Bassi C, Salvia R, Gumbs AA, et al: The value of standard serum tumor markers in differentiating mucinous from serous cystic tumors of the pancreas: CEA, CA 19-9, CA 125, CA 15-3. Langenbecks Arch Surg 387:281–285, 2002.

95. Rubin D, Warshaw AL, Southern JF, et al: Expression of CA 15-3 protein in the cyst contents distinguishes benign from malignant pancreatic mucinous cystic neoplasms. Surgery 115:52–55, 1994.

96. Adsay NV, Pierson C, Sarkar F, et al: Colloid (mucinous noncystic) carcinoma of the pancreas. Am J Surg Pathol 25:26–42, 2001.

97. Ahmad NA, Kochman ML, Lewis JD, et al: Can EUS alone differentiate between malignant and benign cystic lesions of the pancreas? Am J Gastroenterol 96:3295–300, 2001.

98. Castillo CF, Targarona J, Thayer SP, et al: Incidental pancreatic cysts: Clinicopathologic characteristics and comparison with symptomatic patients. Arch Surg 138:427–434, 2003.

99. Hammel P: Role of tumor markers in the diagnosis of cystic and intraductal neoplasms. Gastrointest Endosc Clin N Am 12:791–801, 2002.

100. Sand JA, Hyoty MK, Mattila J, et al: Clinical assessment compared with cyst fluid analysis in the differential diagnosis of cystic lesions in the pancreas. Surgery 119:275–280, 1996.

101. Van Dam J: EUS in cystic lesions of the pancreas. Gastrointest Endosc 56(Suppl):S91–S93, 2002.

102. Fernandez-del Castillo C, Warshaw AL: Cystic tumors of the pancreas. Surg Clin North Am 75:1001–1016, 1995.

Endoscopic Ultrasonography Guided Fine-Needle Aspiration of Pancreaticobiliary Lesions

Kenneth J. Chang

Introduction

Many of the limitations of endoscopic ultrasonography (EUS) as a pure imaging modality have been overcome by the development of EUS-guided fine-needle aspiration (FNA). This chapter reviews the role of EUS-guided FNA in the diagnosis of pancreaticobiliary lesions such as pancreatic adenocarcinoma and cystic and neuroendocrine tumors of the pancreas and less appreciated applications to biliary and ampullary cancers. We also discuss the specific role of EUS-guided FNA in the staging of various pancreaticobiliary cancers. Finally, we cover some of the exciting emerging applications of EUS-guided therapies, including celiac neurolysis, cyst gastrostomy, and delivery of antitumor agents via EUS-guided fine-needle injection (FNI), including immune, viral, and gene therapies. Technical considerations are also elaborated on.

Endoscopic Ultrasonography-Guided Fine-Needle Aspiration in the Diagnosis of Pancreatic Tumors

PANCREATIC CANCER

Adenocarcinoma is the fifth leading cause for cancer-related death in the United States. Despite improvements in medical and surgical therapy, the overall 5-year survival still remains at 4%. The most favorable outcome is among surgical patients with small tumors without nodal, vascular, or systemic metastasis. These patients have 5-year survivals that range up to 25%. Optimally, earlier detection and precise preoperative staging would best stratify patients who

would most likely benefit from surgery while sparing the remaining patients from exploratory or palliative-only surgery. EUS is considered as one of the most useful diagnostic procedures among the body imaging tools for detecting pancreatic cancer. EUS was shown to be superior (sensitivity 98%) to other imaging modalities, including computed tomography (CT), in 146 patients with pancreatic cancer[1] (Table 45–1). With the more recent introduction of spiral CT with dual-phase contrast, the detection rate for CT is improving. However, recent comparisons between dual-phase spiral CT and EUS still favor EUS. The ability to obtain a cytologic specimen by EUS-guided FNA has overcome the difficulty in differentiating between benign and malignant lesions seen on EUS alone. The application of EUS-guided FNA to the pancreas in particular has great clinical utility. CT or ultrasound (US)-guided percutaneous FNA are the more common methods for diagnosing pancreatic cancer. The sensitivity of percutaneous FNA ranges from 45% to 100%, with a specificity of up to 100%. However, obtaining a tissue diagnosis with CT or US guidance is limited by the ability to visualize the lesion. In our previous multicenter trial, 56% of patients with pancreatic carcinoma had CT scans that did not demonstrate a mass or revealed nonspecific enlargement of the pancreas.[2] ERCP with cytologic brushing also has a relatively low yield, with sensitivities between 30% and 56%. The overall sensitivity, specificity, diagnostic accuracy, negative predictive value (NPV), and positive predictive value (PPV) of EUS-guided FNA for pancreatic cancer was 83%, 90%, 85%, 80%, and 100%, respectively. This was superior to CT alone (without FNA): 56%, 37%, 50%, 28%, and 65%, respectively ($p < .05$). There were four complications in 164 patients (2%), including two major (perforation, bleeding) and two minor (fever). Comparison among the four

Table 45-1. Detection of Pancreatic Carcinoma by Body Imaging Tools

Size	EUS	US	CT	ERCP	AG
Under 20 mm (N = 10)	8/10	3/10	1/10	7/10	3/10
Over 20 mm (N = 136)	135/136	104/132	102/136	121/136	77/80
Total Sensitivity (%)	143/146 (98)	107/142 (75)	103/129 (80)	128/146 (86)	80/90 (89)

AG, angiogram; CT, computed tomography; ERCP, endoscopic retrograde cholangiopancreatography; EUS, endoscopic ultrasonography; US, ultrasound.

centers showed that institutions in which a cytologist was present during the procedure had a significantly higher number of passes, cytologic yield, sensitivity, and diagnostic accuracy. Advantages of EUS-guided FNA include procuring a tissue diagnosis while also obtaining additional tumor and nodal (TN) staging information, avoiding additional diagnostic testing and/or surgery, and obtaining prognostic information relating to accurate TN staging. A another report from a large single-institution study of 144 pancreatic lesions undergoing EUS-guided FNA, showed a sensitivity, specificity, and diagnostic accuracy of 82%, 100%, and 85%, respectively.[3] More recently, helical or spiral CT has improved imaging of the pancreas. However, preliminary studies still show superiority of EUS versus spiral CT. The most difficult diagnosis to make for any imaging test, including EUS-guided FNA, is the differentiation between pancreatic carcinoma and chronic pancreatitis. Although a positive FNA is almost 100% accurate, a negative FNA is about 80% accurate. A clinical outcomes study was performed at a single center comparing the management and survival of 136 patients with pancreatic cancer between the pre and post EUS eras.[4] EUS detected carcinomas that were either not seen or only possibly seen by CT in 34% and there were 75% fewer required operations for diagnosis. The median survival without liver metastases was also longer during the EUS period (102 versus 205 days; *p* < 0.02, log-rank test) probably contributed by secondary to lead-time bias.

We believe that all patients thought to have operable disease based on initial CT imaging should undergo EUS with or without FNA before surgical intervention (see clinical algorithm in Fig. 45–1). At the same time, considering the possibility of a false-negative result (up to 20%, especially in the setting of chronic pancreatitis), we believe that surgical intervention should not be precluded in a patient with a high suspicion of resectable pancreatic carcinoma and a negative FNA cytology.

EUS-guided FNA of pancreatic lesions is also worthwhile in patients with a prior negative tissue diagnosis by endoscopic retrograde cholangiopancreatography (ERCP) or CT of the abdomen. Gress and coworkers[5] reported his experience with EUS-guided FNA of pancreatic mass lesion in 102 patients who had negative cytologic tissue diagnosis by ERCP sampling or CT-guided FNA. Among those patients, 57 of the 61 patients (93.4%) with a final diagnosis of pancreatic cancer had positive cytology results for adenocarcinoma by EUS-guided FNA. The false-positive results were zero.

In an earlier report, we reviewed a series of 44 consecutive patients who underwent EUS with or without FNA as part of their pancreatic cancer evaluation.[6] Surgery and further diagnostic testing were avoided in 41% and 57% of patients, respectively. A substantial cost saving of $3300 per patient was calculated. In a series of 216

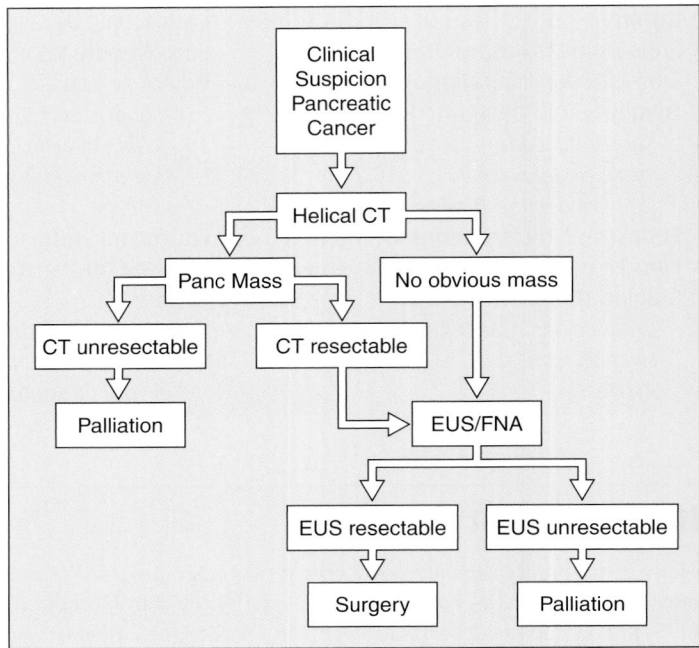

Figure 45-1. Algorithm for diagnosis and staging of pancreatic cancer.

consecutive patients, the use of EUS with EUS-guided FNA as the initial approach to patients with obstructive jaundice was studied by Erickson and coworkers.[7] EUS and FNA proved useful not only as a diagnostic and staging modality but also in directing the need for subsequent therapeutic ERCP, saving approximately $1007 to $1313 per patient. In addition, if EUS and EUS-guided FNA were not used at all, an extra $2200 would be spent per patient. EUS-guided FNA of the pancreas unlike CT-guided FNA can be performed during the initial endosonographic procedure. The overall complication rate of EUS-guided FNA was reported to be 0.5% to 2.9%. It is noteworthy that several case reports have described malignant seeding of the needle tract after transcutaneous FNA. The true incidence has yet to be established. Theoretically, EUS-guided FNA of pancreatic cancers should have a lower chance of malignant seeding because of the short needle tract. In pancreatic head lesions, EUS-guided FNA is usually performed from the second portion of the duodenum, a segment resected surgically along with the tumor during Whipple procedure. This is another theoretical advantage in eliminating the needle tract and decreasing the risk of malignant seeding when compared with the percutaneous approach. However, this may not apply to pancreatic body and tail lesions, where the possibility of malignant seeding of the gastric wall

Table 45–2. Pancreatic Cyst Fluid Analysis

Diagnosis	Cytology	Amylase	CEA
Pseudocyst	Benign	↑↑↑↑	Low
Serous cystadenoma	Benign	Low	Low
Mucinous cystadenoma	Benign	Low	↑↑
Mucinous cystadenocarcinoma	Malignant	Low	↑↑↑↑
CEA, carcinoembryonic antigen.			

Table 45–3. Pancreatic Cyst Cytology (Fluid and Solid) in 12 Patients

Location	Size (cm)	Fluid Cytology	Solid Cytology
Head	3.1 × 2.5	Benign	Benign
Body	5.2 × 6.3	Adenocarcinoma	Adenocarcinoma
Body	1.9 × 2.6	Benign	Benign
Head	2.8 × 2.5	Benign	Benign
Body	3.2 × 1.9	Benign	Benign
Head	1.5 × 1.3	Benign	Adenocarcinoma
Body	5 × 3.5	Benign	Benign
Neck	4 × 4	Benign	Benign
Body	1.1 × 1.7	Benign	Benign
Body	8 × 8	Benign	Adenocarcinoma
Head	2.2 × 1.3	Benign	Benign
Neck	2.7 × 3.7	Benign	Adenocarcinoma

could still exist. The ability to detect vascular structure around the targeted lesion by Doppler flow analysis is another advantage as to minimize the bleeding complication rate. Most of the bleeding is self-limited and resolves spontaneously.

CYSTIC NEOPLASMS

EUS can be helpful in distinguishing cystic neoplasms from pancreatic pseudocyst, although even here, the specificity is not perfect.[8] The more problematic discernment is between serous and mucinous cysts, with the latter considered premalignant. The inter-observer agreement for the interpretation of cystic lesions in the pancreas is quite low. The interobserver agreement on 31 pancreatic cyst cases among eight expert endosonographers was shown to be "fair" between endosonographers for diagnosis of neoplastic versus non-neoplastic lesions (kappa = 0.24).[9] Agreement for individual types of lesions was moderately good for serous cystadenomas (kappa = 0.46) but fair for the remainder. Accuracy rates of EUS for the diagnosis of neoplastic versus non-neoplastic lesions ranged from 40% to 93%. Thus, EUS imaging alone is often inadequate for the clinical management of these patients. EUS-guided FNA of cystic contents can be analyzed for cytology, biochemistry, and tumor markers. Because cytology is a relatively insensitive test, cyst fluid tumor markers such as carcinoembryonic antigen (CEA) have been used to improve the sensitivity for the detection of malignancy. Cyst fluid CEA values are uniformly low in serous cystadenomas, higher in mucinous lesions, and markedly elevated in mucinous cystadenocarcinomas.[10] A recent multicenter European study reported a series of 67 patients who underwent EUS-guided FNA of pancreatic cysts and subsequently went to surgery.[11] EUS alone (no

FNA) correctly identified 49 cases (73%), whereas FNA correctly identified 65 cases (97%). Sensitivity, specificity, positive predictive value, and negative predictive value of EUS and EUS-guided FNA to indicate whether a lesion needed further surgery were 71% and 97%, 30% and 100%, 49% and 100%, and 40% and 95%, respectively. Carbohydrate antigen 19-9 greater than 50,000 U/mL had a 15% sensitivity and a 81% specificity to distinguish mucinous cysts from other cystic lesions, whereas it had a 86% sensitivity and a 85% specificity to distinguish cystadenocarcinoma from other cystic lesions. We routinely send cyst fluid for cytology, amylase, and CEA (Table 45–2). Pseudocysts have very high amylase levels, often greater than 50,000 IU/L, with a normal CEA and benign cytology. Serous cystadenomas usually have benign cytology and normal CEA and amylase. Mucinous cystadenomas usually differ from serous cystadenoma in having a high CEA. Mucinous cystadenocarcinoma classically has malignant cytology, a low amylase, and a very elevated CEA. Although there is still some overlap of the CEA levels in these three entities, we have found a cut-off value of CEA greater than 100 U/mL helpful in stratifying patients to surgical versus conservative management. The cytology from the fluid of malignant cysts may be nondiagnostic. We have found that targeting any solid component, including the cyst wall, may enhance the yield on FNA cytology. We examined 42 pancreatic cystic lesions that underwent EUS-guided FNA.[12] The needle was advanced under EUS guidance into the cyst in the direction of the solid component and aspirated completely. Then without withdrawal, the needle was advanced directly into the solid component. Fluid and solid cytology were analyzed separately. All patients received prophylactic antibiotics. Twelve of the 42 cysts were found to have a solid component (Table 45–3). Nine patients had both fluid and solid cytology showing benign cells. One patient had malignant cells on both fluid and solid cytology. However, three patients had benign fluid cytology but malignant (consistent with cystadenocarcinoma) solid cytology. This suggests a higher yield if the solid component is targeted.

NEUROENDOCRINE TUMORS

EUS is very accurate in the detection of neuroendocrine tumors of the pancreas.

Zimmer and coworkers[13] reported their results in localizing and staging neuroendocrine tumors of the foregut in 40 patients examined by EUS, somatostatin receptor scintigraphy (SRS), CT, magnetic resonance imaging (MRI), and transabdominal US. EUS showed the highest sensitivity in localizing insulinomas compared with SRS, US, CT, and MRI. They suggested that US and EUS should be the first-line diagnostics if insulinoma has been proven by a fasting test. Further diagnostic procedures were unnecessary in most cases. Further diagnostics such as CT or MRI to search for distant metastases are necessary in large tumors or local invasive tumors. EUS shows the highest accuracy to detect or exclude pancreatic gastrinomas but fails to detect extrapancreatic gastrinomas in about 50%. The combination of EUS and SRS may give additional information. They recommended that the first-line diagnostics in gastrinoma patients should be SRS and CT or MRI. If no metastases are detected, EUS should be the next preoperative imaging procedure. In nonfunctional neuroendocrine tumors, EUS provides the best information on local tumor invasion and regional lymph node involvement.

EUS has also been shown to be cost effective in the preoperative localization of pancreatic endocrine tumors. Bansal and colleagues[14] reported a case-control study of 36 patients who underwent preoperative EUS with a matched group of 36 patients who underwent surgical exploration immediately before the introduction of EUS. The EUS group had reduced charges for preoperative localization studies: $2620 versus $4846 per patient ($p < .05$), largely because of reductions in the number of diagnostic angiograms and venous sampling procedures performed. Surgical and total anesthesia times were decreased, as were the number of preoperative admissions for angiographic procedures. The cost-effectiveness ratio for the EUS group was $3144 per tumor localized compared with $5628 per tumor localized for the group treated before EUS became available ($p < .05$). The more specific utility of EUS-guided FNA in these patients was recently reported.[15] Ten patients with clinically suspected functioning neuroendocrine tumors (hormonal disturbances) underwent EUS-guided FNA to determine the location and to confirm the diagnosis cytologically. EUS identified 14 tumors in these 10 patients. In all but one patient, CT did not demonstrate the tumor or missed at least one of multiple lesions. Mean tumor size was 12 mm (range 4 to 25 mm). Tumor locations were pancreas ($n = 13$) and duodenal wall ($n = 1$). Eleven of the 14 detected lesions were aspirated under EUS-guided FNA with accurate diagnosis in all cases. Surgical confirmation of EUS-guided FNA findings was available in seven patients. There were no complications related to EUS-guided FNA. EUS may also be useful in marking these subtle lesions using EUS-guided fine-needle "tattooing" before surgery to assist in intraoperative localization.[16]

Endoscopic Ultrasonography-Guided Fine-Needle Aspiration in the Staging of Pancreatic Cancer

In a prospective analysis, Mortensen and coworkers[17] found 30% overall impact of EUS-guided FNA on clinical management in 99 consecutive patients with pancreatic cancer of whom 20 patients underwent EUS-guided FNA for staging purposes: 5 liver lesions, 1 malignant ascites, 13 lymph nodes, and 1 aspiration from retroperitoneal tumor infiltration. The remaining 25 patients had diagnostic FNA: 22 pancreatic and 3 duodenal. The EUS-guided FNA was only performed if positive results would have a clinical relevant impact on the subsequent management of the patient. The clinical impact of EUS-guided FNA was 12% (12/99) for staging purposes and 86% (18/21) for diagnostic purposes. The economic impact of EUS-guided FNA in the preoperative staging of patients with pancreatic head adenocarcinoma was clearly demonstrated in a decision analysis model.[18] The use of EUS-guided FNA prevented 16 surgeries per 100 patients compared with 8 per 100 patients if CT-guided FNA was performed for non-peritumoral lymph nodes. If the frequency of non-peritumoral lymph nodes was greater than 4%, then EUS-guided FNA is the least costly procedure ($15,938) versus $16,378 for CT-FNA and $18,723 for surgery.

LYMPH NODE ASSESSMENT

According to a multivariate analysis, lymph node metastasis, intrapancreatic perineural invasion, and portal vein invasion are significant prognostic factors in patients with pancreatic cancer after curative resection.[19] A retrospective analysis of 193 patients who underwent curative resection was conducted. Of the 193 patients, 38 (20%) survived for more than 5 years, the 5-year survival rates for stages I, II, III, and IV disease were 41%, 17%, 11%, and 6%, respectively. Subsequently, a subgroup analysis concerning nodal metastasis and intrapancreatic perineural invasion was performed in 126 patients with records of these histologic findings. In the group of patients without nodal metastasis, the 5-year survival rate for those without perineural invasion was 75%, whereas that for those with perineural invasion was 29%, the difference in survival of these subgroups being significant ($p < .02$). In the group of patients with nodal metastasis, the 5-year survival rate for those without perineural invasion was 17%, whereas that for those with perineural invasion was 10%. EUS imaging alone cannot fully distinguish malignant from inflammatory nodes, thus limiting its specificity in lymph node staging. Various EUS criteria have been described to distinguish malignant from benign nodes. However, these parameters including size, shape, borders, and echotexture have lacked specificity. We previously conducted a study correlating EUS features of lymph nodes with the respective EUS-guided FNA diagnosis.[20] Computer analysis of endosonographic images of 48 lymph nodes in 47 patients using both linear array and radial scanning transducers was performed. Parameters included lymph node area, longest diameter, shape factor, and gray scale. There were 22 malignant and 26 benign nodes. When correlated with the FNA cytology results for each node, the only single criterion that was

100% specific for predicting malignancy were a longest diameter greater than 2.5 cm or an area greater than 2.5 cm². However, using this size cut-off, the sensitivity fell to only 18%. Thus, it appears that no single criterion has an acceptable sensitivity and specificity to circumvent the need for a tissue diagnosis by EUS-guided FNA. In a multicenter study 171 patients underwent EUS-guided FNA of 192 lymph nodes (46 benign, 146 malignant).[21] The final diagnosis was ascertained by clinical follow-up (108 lymph nodes) or histopathology correlation (84 lymph nodes). The mean long-axis dimension of benign lymph nodes was less than malignant lymph nodes (18 mm, 5 to 37 mm versus 27 mm, 5 to 80 mm; $p < .001$). On average, two to three needle passes were made for each lymph node. The overall performance of EUS-guided FNA in lymph node assessment was sensitivity 92% (84% to 97% among four centers), specificity 93% (75% to 100%), and accuracy 92% (82% to 98%). If a 15-mm long-axis dimension was used for determining benign (≤15 mm) versus malignant (>15 mm) lymphadenopathy, EUS alone had a sensitivity (67%), specificity (50%), and accuracy (63%) all inferior to EUS-guided FNA ($p < .05$). In 89 patients, 101 lymph nodes underwent EUS-guided FNA for staging of lung cancer (14 patients) or primary gastrointestinal (GI) and pancreatic malignancies (75 patients). When comparing EUS-guided FNA with EUS size criteria (≤10 mm = benign), the sensitivity (90% vs. 91%, p = ns) and accuracy (92% vs. 83%, p = ns) for EUS-guided FNA were similar, whereas the specificity was superior to that of EUS size criteria alone (100% vs. 47%, $p < .001$). EUS-guided FNA not only can improve the specificity of lymph node metastasis with cytologic confirmation but also can detect genetic alterations in cytologic negative nodes. A prospective study was conducted to assess the clinical value of genetic staging of lymph node metastasis in patients with pancreatic adenocarcinoma who underwent curative surgery.[22] K-ras gene mutations were detected in the primary tumors in 18 of 25 patients with pancreatic adenocarcinoma. Among these 18 patients, mutated K-ras gene was also found in at least one lymph node in 13 patients. Of these 13 patients, seven had no evidence of histologic nodal involvement and six had histologic lymph node metastasis. Although there was no significant difference in overall survival rates between the pathologic node-negative and node-positive patients, overall survival of the five patients with nodes negative for the mutated K-ras gene were significantly better than that of the 13 patients with genetically metastasis-positive nodes ($p < .001$). Furthermore, overall survival of the six patients with genetically metastasis-positive nodes limited to peripancreatic area was significantly better than that of seven patients with genetic metastasis in lymph nodes beyond the peripancreatic areas ($p = .018$). These findings suggest that detection of K-ras gene mutations in lymph nodes may be clinically useful to assess the accurate tumor staging and to stratify patients who may be at higher risk for recurrence after curative resection.

LIVER METASTASIS

EUS is not traditionally thought to be clinically applicable in liver imaging. A prospective study was conducted in which 574 consecutive patients with a history or suspicion of GI or pulmonary malignant tumor undergoing upper EUS examinations underwent EUS evaluation of the liver.[23] Fourteen (2.4%) patients were found to have focal liver lesions and underwent EUS-guided FNA. Before EUS, CT depicted liver lesions in only 3 of 14 (21%) patients. Seven of 14 patients had a known cancer diagnosis. For the other seven, the initial diagnosis of cancer was made by means of EUS-guided FNA of the liver. There were no immediate or late complications. This study showed that EUS can detect small focal liver lesions that are not detected at CT. Findings of EUS-guided FNA can confirm a cytologic diagnosis of liver metastasis and establish a definitive M stage that may change clinical management. A retrospective questionnaire study was recently reported, which included 21 EUS/FNA centers around the world regarding indications, complications, and findings of EUS-guided FNA of the liver.[23a] There were 167 cases of EUS-guided FNA of the liver. A complication was reported in 6 (4%) of 167 cases including the following: death in 1 patient with an occluding biliary stent and biliary sepsis, bleeding (1 patient), fever (2 patients), and pain (2 patients). EUS-guided FNA diagnosed malignancy in 23 of 26 (89%) cases after nondiagnostic FNA under transabdominal US guidance. EUS localized an unrecognized primary tumor in 17 of 33 (52%) cases in which CT had demonstrated only liver metastases. EUS image characteristics were not predictive of malignant versus benign lesions. EUS-guided FNA of the liver appears to be a safe procedure with a major complication rate of approximately 1%. EUS-guided FNA should be considered when a liver lesion is poorly accessible to percutaneous FNA or when US or CT-guided FNA fail to make a diagnosis. If EUS detects a liver lesion de novo in the setting of staging pancreatic cancer, EUS-guided FNA should be attempted first, even before taking biopsies of the primary pancreatic tumor. Liver lesions have a much higher cytologic yield (less needle passes requires, less inflammatory and fibrotic reaction) and give the highest staging information (see section on FNA technique).

ASCITES

The utility of EUS and FNA was evaluated for detection and aspiration of scant ascites among patients undergoing EUS for diagnosis and staging of GI malignancies.[24] Eighty-five patients (15% of a series of 571 patients) were found to have ascites by EUS. Pre-EUS CT identified ascites in only 18% of patients with ascites on EUS. Thirty-one of the 85 patients underwent EUS-guided FNA paracentesis, and in 5 patients, malignant ascites was diagnosed by EUS-guided FNA. The clinical impact was high in these patients as surgery was avoided.

Endoscopic Ultrasonography-Guided Fine-Needle Aspiration in Biliary Lesions

DIAGNOSIS AND STAGING OF CHOLANGIOCARCINOMA

Cholangiocarcinoma carries with it a high mortality and it is often difficult to obtain accurate tissue diagnosis; ERCP and brushings of the bile duct is the preferred modality for this purpose. The currently reported diagnostic yield from ERCP varies from 30% to 60%, and the diagnosis of malignant biliary stricture remains a challenge. EUS-guided FNA is now used to diagnose and stage cholangiocarcinoma.[25,26] In one case series, 10 patients with bile duct strictures at the hepatic hilum, diagnosed by CT and/or ERCP, underwent EUS-guided FNA. Adequate material was obtained in nine patients. Cytology revealed cholangiocarcinoma in seven and hepatocellular carcinoma in one. One benign inflammatory lesion identified on cytology proved to be a false-negative finding by frozen section. Metastatic locoregional hilar lymph nodes were detected in two patients, and in one patient the celiac and para-aortic lymph nodes were aspirated to obtain tissue proof of distant metastasis. A recent retrospective series of 238 patients with suspected or known biliary strictures was reported. Thirty-five patients with proximal bile duct strictures were identified, of which 27 were found to be malignant (23 cholangiocarcinoma, 3 gallbladder carcinoma, and 1 metastatic cancer) and 8 were benign. Of the 27 patients with malignancy, 17 had ERCP before EUS and 10 patients had ERCP after. A stricture was considered positive if on EUS a hypoechoic mass was seen around the common bile duct or a positive tissue diagnosis was made by FNA. EUS-guided FNA was not done in one patient because ERCP had established the diagnosis. EUS-guided FNA obtained tissue diagnosis in 12 of 26 (46%) patients, who had negative findings on cytology or had an unsuccessful ERCP. EUS correctly identified the eight benign strictures with clinical follow-up time of at least 8 months. There were no complications associated with EUS-guided FNA. These studies suggest that EUS with FNA is safe and effective in evaluating proximal biliary strictures. When used in combination with ERCP, it helps distinguish benign from malignant strictures and facilitates a definitive diagnosis by increasing tissue yield.

DIAGNOSIS AND STAGING OF AMPULLARY CANCER

Conventional abdominal imaging studies such as CT, MRI, and transabdominal US often fail to detect ampullary lesions. EUS is a sensitive modality for detecting and staging ampullary tumors. Accurate staging may be affected by biliary stenting, which is often performed in these patients with obstructive jaundice. Combined data from two centers reported the accuracy of ampullary tumor staging with multiple imaging modalities in patients with and those without endobiliary stents.[27] Fifty consecutive patients with ampullary neoplasms were preoperatively staged by EUS plus CT (37 patients), MRI (13 patients), or angiography (10 patients) over a 3½-year period. Twenty-five of the 50 patients had a transpapillary endobiliary stent present at the time of endosonographic examination. EUS was shown to be more accurate than CT and MRI in the overall assessment of the T stage of ampullary neoplasms (EUS 78%, CT 24%, MRI 46%). No significant difference in N stage accuracy was noted between the three imaging modalities (EUS 68%, CT 59%, MRI 77%). EUS T stage accuracy was reduced from 84% to 72% in the presence of a transpapillary endobiliary stent. This was most prominent in the understaging of T2 and T3 carcinomas. More recently, a retrospective study was published in which the role of EUS-guided FNA in the diagnosis and staging of ampullary lesions was reported.[28] EUS-guided FNA was performed in 20 of 27 (74%) patients with suspected ampullary

tumors. EUS-guided FNA made the initial ampullary tissue diagnosis in seven patients (adenocarcinoma in five, adenoma in one, neuroendocrine tumor in one). In addition, EUS-guided FNA resulted in a change of the diagnosis from adenoma to adenocarcinoma in one patient. In one patient, EUS-guided FNA diagnosed a liver metastasis not seen on CT. Overall, EUS-guided FNA provided new histologic information in 9 of 27 patients (33%).

Endoscopic Ultrasonography-Guided Therapy for Pancreaticobiliary Lesions

CELIAC NERVE BLOCK

Patients with significant abdominal pain who have unresectable pancreatic cancer may be candidates for EUS-guided celiac plexus neurolysis (CPN). Wiersema and Wiersema[29] described this novel technique and the impact on pancreatic cancer patients' pain management. After visualizing the celiac trunk by the linear array echoendoscope and using a 22-gauge needle, injection of bupivacaine (0.25%) followed ethyl alcohol (98%) can then be performed on either side of the vessel. Up to 88% of patients had persistent improvement in their pain score. Only minor complications were seen and consisted of transient diarrhea in four patients. This anterior transgastric approach for performing CPN is theoretically considered safer when compared with the traditional CT-guided posterior method. This is because of the rare reported cases of paraplegia that occurred with the posterior approach because of its proximity of the spinal column.

Unfortunately, the effect of CPN in controlling abdominal pain from chronic pancreatitis is less evident. Gress and colleagues[30] performed EUS-guided celiac plexus block (CPB) in 80 patients with chronic pancreatitis. A mixture of bupivacaine 0.25% and 80 mg of triamcinolone was injected using the previously described technique. Only 10% had benefit beyond 24 weeks. There were two major complications—peripancreatic abscess and bleeding celiac artery secondary to ethanol-induced arterial pseudoaneurysm.

This technique was less effective in younger patients (<45 years old) and those who had previous surgery for chronic pancreatitis.[30] There was a slight economical advantage of EUS-guided CPB over CT-guided approach ($1200 vs. $1400). Long-term controlled trials in different patient populations need to be performed to better delineate the efficacy and safety of this technique for treatment of patients with pancreatitis.

CYST GASTROSTOMY

Endoscopic technique for pseudocyst drainage is an established alternative for surgical and radiologic approaches. Since the early report of EUS-assisted pseudocyst drainage,[31] the use of EUS as the only tool for draining pseudocysts has been evolving. With the development of larger accessory channels echoendoscopes, this approach became feasible. EUS-guided pseudocyst drainage technique overcame many obstacles faced with the conventional endoscopic approach. In the absence of apparent intraluminal bulge, cyst drainage could still be safely performed after accurate measurement of the distance between the cyst and the GI wall. The EUS/Doppler method can be used to define and avoid any interjecting vessels, thus theoretically reducing the risk of hemorrhage and perforation. In cases in which cystic neoplasms are of concern, cyst fluid aspiration before drainage should be performed. The level of tumor markers in the fluid, mainly CEA, along with the concentration of amylase may assist in differentiating inflammatory from neoplastic cysts.[32,33] Giovannini and coworkers[34] drained 35 pancreatic cysts under EUS-guidance, of which 15 were pseudocysts and 20 were pancreatic abscesses. Of the 33 transgastrically drained cysts, an extrinsic compression was seen in only one patient with the use of a forward-viewing gastroscope. No major complication occurred except a pneumoperitoneum (one case), which was successfully managed medically. No bleeding was encountered. A 7-Fr nasocystic drain was placed in 18 of 20 cases of pancreatic abscess. Surgery was performed in the two other patients. In the pseudocyst group, placement of an 8.5-Fr stent was successful in 10 patients and placement of a nasocystic drain was successful in 5 patients. In one case, only cyst puncture and aspiration was performed. Over a mean follow-up of 27 months (6 to 48 months) one recurrence among the 15 pancreatic pseudocysts and two relapses of the 18 pancreatic abscesses have been observed. The EUS-guided drainage success rate was 88.5% (31/35); only four patients with pancreatic abscesses underwent surgery.

In a related paper, Seifert and coworkers[35] evaluated a new one-step stenting device using a large-channel echoendoscope (3.2 mm) for pseudocyst drainage in six patients. One of them had pancreatic abscess. Transmural drainage was successfully done using modified 7-Fr stents. There were no complications encountered with the endoscopic interventions. One patient with necrotizing pancreatitis, who denied surgery, died secondary to sepsis. At follow-up of 3 to 13 months, the cysts had completely resolved in four patients. This study confirmed the feasibility and effectiveness of EUS-guided one-step technique in draining various cystic lesions; however, larger studies are needed. In a subsequent study using the one-step device through a 3.7-mm channel echoendoscope, the same group was able to place a 10-Fr stent in three patients and 7-Fr in one patient (all patients had peripancreatic cystic lesions). One of the cysts had persisted for more than 3 months and was found to be a ganglioneuroma after surgical enucleation.[36]

DELIVERY OF ANTITUMOR AGENTS

We have examined the feasibility and safety of direct injection of allogenic mixed lymphocyte culture (cytoimplant) in pancreatic adenocarcinoma under EUS guidance.[37] In a phase I clinical trial, eight patients with unresectable pancreatic adenocarcinoma underwent EUS-guided FNI of cytoimplants. Four patients were in stage II, three in stage III, and one in stage IV. The escalating doses of cytoimplants 3, 6, or 9 billion cells were implanted using a novel EUS-guided FNI technique. The median survival was 13.2 months with two partial responders and one minor response. Major complications including bone marrow toxicity and hemorrhagic, infectious, renal, or cardiopulmonary toxicity were absent. Low-grade fever was encountered in seven of the eight patients and was symptomatically treated with acetaminophen. Our study showed

that local immunotherapy is feasible and safe. The technique of EUS-guided FNI was recently applied to deliver antitumor viral therapy.[38] ONYX-015 (dl1520) is an E1B-55kD gene-deleted replication-selective adenovirus that preferentially replicates in and kills malignant cells. Twenty-one patients with locally advanced adenocarcinoma of the pancreas or with metastatic disease, but minimal or absent liver metastases, underwent eight sessions of ONYX-015 delivered by EUS injection into the primary pancreatic tumor over 8 weeks. The final four treatments were given in combination with gemcitabine (intravenous (IV) 1000 mg/m^2). After combination therapy, 2 patients had partial regressions of the injected tumor, 2 had minor responses, 6 had stable disease, and 11 had progressive disease. No clinical pancreatitis occurred despite mild, transient elevations in lipase in a minority of patients. Two patients had sepsis before the institution of prophylactic oral antibiotics. Two patients had duodenal perforations from the rigid endoscope tip. No perforations occurred after the protocol was changed to transgastric injections only. The most recent EUS-guided antitumor therapy involves a novel gene therapy.[39] TNFerade is a replication-deficient adenovector containing human tumor necrosis factor alpha (TNFα) gene, regulated by a radiation-inducible promoter Egr-1. The study design consisted of a 5-week treatment of weekly intratumoral injections of TNFerade ($4 \times 10^{9-11}$ particle units [pu] in 2 mL). EUS-guided FNI was compared with percutaneous approaches (CT or US). TNFerade was combined with continuous intravenous 5-fluorouracil (5-FU) (200 mg/m^2/day × 5 days/week) and radiation (50.4 Gy). TNFerade was delivered with a single needle pass at a single site in the tumor for percutaneous approaches (PTA), and up to four injections were given by EUS. The clinical endpoints included safety and tumor response on spiral CT by a core laboratory. Of 37 patients, 17 had EUS and 20 had PTA (similar TNFerade doses). Baseline tumor stage, nodal staging, tumor size, and CA 19-9 levels were similar in the EUS and PTA groups. One dose-limiting toxicity (grade 3 hypotension) was noted in a PTA patient; all other adverse events potentially related to TNFerade were grade 1 to 2. Procedure related adverse events were all grade 1 to 2 and were similar between the two groups, except for injection site pain: 35% PTA versus 0% EUS ($p = .01$). Tumor responses and disease control were similar (Table 45–4). Four patients underwent resection; one, an EUS patient, had a complete pathologic response. These initial studies have established that EUS-guided FNI is an effective delivery system for antitumor agents.

Technical Considerations

The technique of EUS-guided FNA has been well described in the literature.[21,40–45] Specifically, the area of interest is visualized by EUS and placed within the center (or just slightly left of center on the monitor) of the imaging field. Doppler imaging is used as needed to identify vascularity of the lesion and to assess adjacent vascular structures. The needle is then advanced through the endoscope biopsy channel and advanced into the lesion under direct US visualization. The central stylet is removed and a 10-mL syringe is attached to the hub of the needle and suction applied as the needle is moved back and forth within the lesion. The suction is then slowly

Table 45–4. Results of TNFerade Phase 1/2 Clinical Trial Comparing Endoscopic Ultrasonography and Percutaneous Delivery

	1 month			3 months		
	EUS	PTA	Overall	EUS	PTA	Overall
Tumor stabilization	88%	80%	83%	73%	75%	74%
Objective tumor response						
>25% reduction in tumor area	38%	25%	31%	33%	30%	31%
>50% reduction in tumor area	25%*	0%	11%	13%	10%	11%
Survival without overall progression	56%	68%	63%	53%	42%	47%

*$p = .03$, Fisher's Exact test, for all other comparisons p = NS.
EUS, endoscopic ultrasonography; PTA, percutaneous approach.

Table 45–5. Sequence Priority for Endoscopic Ultrasonography-Guided Fine-Needle Aspiration in Patient with a Pancreatic Tumor

Target Site	Average Number of Passes	Sequence Priority
Ascites or pleural fluid	1	1
Liver	2 (range 1–5)	2
Distant (e.g., celiac) lymph node	2 (range 1–10)	3
Proximal lymph node	2 (range 1–10)	4
Pancreatic tumor	3–5 (range 1–19)	5

released, the needle retracted in the catheter, and the entire assembly removed from the biopsy channel. The aspirated material is then sprayed onto glass slides (using an air-filled syringe); a set of two slides are processed immediately and reviewed by an attendant or nearby cytopathologist if available. If residual material is present within the needle, this is then rinsed into a formalin container that is collected and later processed into a cell block.

In general, placing the FNA needle directly into the center of the targeted lesion is appropriate. However, this may not be the optimal technique for large tumors, especially those arising from the pancreas. The center of large tumors may be necrotic, possibly from decreased oxygenation. Therefore, if initial passes from the center show necrotic cells or acellular material, the endosonographer should realign the needle to target the periphery of the tumor.

PRIORITIZING LESIONS FOR FINE-NEEDLE ASPIRATION

There are situations when more than one lesion in a given patient may be targeted for EUS-guided FNA. For example, the priority and sequence for multiple lesions in a patient with a pancreatic primary is summarized in Table 45–5. The sequence priority is predicated on the principle of confirming the most advanced stage and economizing the number of passes.

Thus, if a patient has a pancreatic mass, a celiac node, and a lesion in the left lobe of the liver (no ascites), the endosonographer should approach the liver lesion first. If this is positive for cancer, this would give the most advanced staging information (an M_1 stage), and the other lesions would not need to be biopsied. However, if this negative, then the celiac node would be biopsied followed by the pancreatic mass. This sequence also happens to be the most efficient from a technical standpoint. The most difficult lesions to obtain adequate cytologic samples are pancreatic tumors and

submucosal tumors. Lymph nodes and liver lesions are relatively easier, in that fewer passes are generally required to obtain an adequate sample.

NUMBER OF PASSES

Pancreatic adenocarcinoma generally requires the most number of FNA passes to obtain an adequate specimen. Approximately three to five passes are required, with a range of 1 to 19.[2] Pancreatic tumors may have extensive fibrosis (desmoplastic reaction) or necrosis that decreases the cellularity of malignant cells. The number of passes required for pancreatic tumors may be related to the differentiation of the tumor. A recent study was designed to prospectively assess whether any patient or endosonographic characteristics could predict the number of EUS-guided FNA passes needed to diagnosis pancreatic malignancy.[46] Among the 95 patients undergoing EUS-guided FNA of a pancreatic mass, the average number of needle passes into the mass (includes head, neck, body, and tail) was 3.44 ± 2.19, with a range of 1 to 10 passes. Tumors that were well-differentiated required an average of 5.5 passes to obtain an adequate specimen. This is significantly different from 2.7 passes for moderately differentiated and 2.3 for poorly differentiated tumors ($p < .001$). Based on this study, it was recommended that without a cytopathologist in attendance, five to six passes should be made for pancreatic masses However, this approach would still be associated with a 10% to 15% reduction in definitive cytologic diagnoses, extra procedure time, increased risk, and additional needles when compared with having "real-time" cytopathology interpretations. Lymph nodes and liver lesions generally require much fewer passes. In an earlier series of 171 patients, the median number of passes for lymph node was 2 (range 1 to 10).[21] Liver lesions in one series showed that the average number of passes was similarly 2 (range 1 to 5).[47] Lymph node and liver metastases in general do not exhibit the desmoplastic or necrotic reaction that is common for primary tumors of the pancreas. Ascites and pleural fluid on average only require a single FNA pass to obtain specimen for cytologic diagnosis.[24] The endosonographer should try to obtain as much fluid as possible (preferably larger than 10 mL). The fluid is spun down to concentrate the cells on a slide. Making the diagnosis of peritoneal metastasis from ascitic fluid has a lower yield than solid lesion (approximately 50% false-negative rate, especially with small amounts of fluid). However, a positive cytology is still very helpful in staging the tumor as unresectable. Ascitic fluid, if present,

Table 45–6. Needle Advancement Technique for Endoscopic Ultrasonography-Guided Fine-Needle Aspiration

Wall Parameter	Lesions Parameter	Vessel Parameter	Needle Advancement Technique	Difficulty Level
Thin wall, taut (e.g., esophagus)	Small (e.g., lymph node)	Vessel immediately behind lesion	Very fine, slow pincer movements	Moderate
Thin wall, taut	Large (e.g., tumor)	No adjacent vessel	Slow, moderate movements	Easy
Thick wall, elastic (e.g., gastric fundus)	Small lesion or scant fluid	Vessel immediately behind lesion	Consider puncturing through stomach first (adjacent to lesion) with a very quick, dart-like motion (or use spring-loaded device), then fine pincer movements to target lesion	Difficult
Thick wall, elastic	Large	No adjacent vessel	Very quick, dart-like motion using wrist action directly into lesion	Moderate
Duodenum	Small	Adjacent vessel	Quick, pincer movement to avoid pushing scope tip away	Difficult
Duodenum	Large, firm tumor	No adjacent vessel	Very quick, hand grasp with elbow and shoulder "ice pick" motion	Difficult

should be aspirated first, especially if there is a possibility of contamination from other lesions undergoing FNA. For example, in the presence of ascites, FNA of the primary pancreas tumor, lymph node, or a liver metastasis has the theoretical potential to contaminate the fluid. In addition, the process of preparing cytology slides from ascitic fluid requires an additional step of concentrating the cells by centrifugation. We often aspirate the fluid first, even before performing our vascular staging, to allow sufficient time for cytologic interpretation before moving on to the second lesion. Thus, both for the reasons of most relevant staging information and efficiency of FNA passes, the priority for FNA is ascites, then liver metastasis, followed by distant and local lymph nodes, and finally, the primary pancreatic tumor.

The importance of dynamic real-time cytologic interpretation has been emphasized in a number of studies.[2,21,41,48] These studies have shown that centers with an attendant cytopathologist had higher cytologic yield and diagnostic accuracy compared with centers that performed passes on an empiric basis. Increasing the number of empiric passes may increase cytologic accuracy but at the expense of performing unnecessary passes with its associated cost, time, and safety issues. A most recent abstract reported the experience of a single endosonographer practicing in two clinical sites, one with an attendant cytopathologist and one without.[49] Seventeen percent of patients in the site without an attendant cytopathologist required repeat procedures compared with 2% where a cytopathologist was present ($p = .015$). This study further confirmed that on-site cytopathologic interpretation during EUS-guided FNA has a significant clinical impact by increasing the diagnostic yield of the FNA and suggests that EUS centers should allocate resources to cover for on-site cytopathologic evaluation.

NEEDLE INSERTION AND SUCTION

The technique of needle advancement can vary considerably from very fine motion of the needle handle, using only the fine motor pincer muscles of the thumb and index finger, to very large motions, using a full hand grasp on the needle handle with gross motor elbow and shoulder movements similar to that of downward thrust with an ice pick. The optimal technique of advancing the needle varies according to three factors: (1) the consistency of the GI wall (wall parameter), (2) the size and consistency of the lesion targeted (lesion parameter), and (3) the proximity of surrounding vessels (vessel parameter). Table 45–6 summarizes the needle advancement technique with respect to these parameters.

The amount of pressure to apply to the suction syringe also needs to be considered. For most lesions, 5 mL of continuous suction applied to a 10-mL syringe is the most optimal. One report assessing various syringe sizes and continuous versus intermittent suction of lymph nodes from an autopsy specimen showed that continuous rather than intermittent suction with smaller syringes (5 to 10 mL) provided optimal cellularity and that use of larger (20 to 30 mL) syringes did not improve the rate of obtaining a diagnostic specimen.[50] If after the first pass, a large amount of blood is present on the smear, one should consider very little (2 to 3 mL) or no suction. At times, too much suction in a vascular lesion may result in an inadequate cytology specimen because of the overwhelming amount of red blood cells.

AVOIDING COMPLICATIONS

An important part of maximizing the yield of EUS-guided FNA is avoiding complications. Three large published series involving a sum of more than 1000 patients have reported on the complication rate of EUS-guided FNA.[3,21,51] One multicenter trial showed that complications associated with the procedure (457 patients) seem to arise predominantly from infectious or hemorrhagic events after puncturing pancreatic cystic lesions.[21] Five nonfatal complications occurred for a rate of 0.5% (95% confidence interval [CI] 0.1% to 0.8%) in solid lesions versus 14% (95% CI 6% to 21%) in cystic lesions ($p < .001$). Another single institution study among 333 patients who underwent EUS-guided FNA experienced only one complication (0.3%): a streptococcal sepsis after puncture of a cystic pancreatic lesion.[3] A small risk (1 in 121 patients) of developing pancreatitis after EUS-guided FNA of the pancreas has been reported.[52] Thus, the risk associated for FNA of solid tumors is extremely low. The general guidelines for the use of antibiotic prophylaxis includes any cystic lesion or lesion adjacent to the rectum or colon. The risk of malignant seeding is felt to be very low. A recent abstract suggests that EUS-guided FNA has a lower potential for peritoneal seeding when compared with CT-guided FNA.[53]

Conclusions

EUS-guided FNA is extremely useful in the diagnosis and staging of pancreaticobiliary lesions such as pancreatic cancers (with associated lymph nodes, liver metastasis, and ascites), cystic tumors, neuroendocrine neoplasms, ampullary carcinomas, and cholangiocarcinomas. In addition, this technique has been extended to therapeutic modalities such as CNB, cyst gastrostomy, and delivery of anti-tumor agents.

REFERENCES

1. Rosch T, Lorenz R, Braig C, et al: Endoscopic ultrasound in pancreatic tumor diagnosis. Gastrointest Endosc 37:347–352, 1991.
2. Chang KJ, Wiersema M, Giovannini M, et al: Multi-center collaborative study on endoscopic ultrasound (EUS) guided fine needle aspiration (FNA) of the pancreas. Gastrointest Endosc 43:A507, 1996.
3. Williams DB, Sahai AV, Aabakken L, et al: Endoscopic ultrasound guided fine needle aspiration biopsy: A large single centre experience. Gut 44:720–726, 1999.
4. Erickson RA, Garza AA: Impact of endoscopic ultrasound on the management and outcome of pancreatic carcinoma. Am J Gastroenterol 95:2248–2254, 2000.
5. Gress F, Gottlieb K, Sherman S, Lehman G: Endoscopic ultrasonography-guided fine-needle aspiration biopsy of suspected pancreatic cancer. Ann Intern Med 134:459–464, 2001.
6. Chang KJ, Nguyen P, Erickson RA, et al: The clinical utility of endoscopic ultrasound-guided fine-needle aspiration in the diagnosis and staging of pancreatic carcinoma. Gastrointest Endosc 45:387–393, 1997.
7. Erickson RA, Garza AA: EUS with EUS-guided fine-needle aspiration as the first endoscopic test for the evaluation of obstructive jaundice. Gastrointest Endosc 53:475–484, 2001.
8. Song MH, Lee SK, Kim MH, et al: EUS in the evaluation of pancreatic cystic lesions. Gastrointest Endosc 57:891–896, 2003.
9. Ahmad NA, Kochman ML, Brensinger C, et al: Interobserver agreement among endosonographers for the diagnosis of neoplastic versus non-neoplastic pancreatic cystic lesions. Gastrointest Endosc 58:59–64, 2003.
10. Brugge WR: Role of endoscopic ultrasound in the diagnosis of cystic lesions of the pancreas. Pancreatology 1:637–640, 2001.
11. Frossard JL, Amouyal P, Amouyal G, et al: Performance of endosonography-guided fine needle aspiration and biopsy in the diagnosis of pancreatic cystic lesions. Am J Gastroenterol 98:1516–1524, 2003.
12. Powis ME, Nguyen PT, Chang KJ: A novel endoscopic ultrasound (EUS) guided fine needle aspiration (FNA) technique for the diagnosis of malignant cystic lesions of the pancreas [abstract]. Gastrointest Endosc 51:164, 2000.
13. Zimmer T, Scherubl H, Faiss S, et al: Endoscopic ultrasonography of neuroendocrine tumours. Digestion 62(Suppl 1):45–50, 2000.
14. Bansal R, Tierney W, Carpenter S, et al: Cost effectiveness of EUS for preoperative localization of pancreatic endocrine tumors. Gastrointest Endosc 49:19–25, 1999.
15. Gines A, Vazquez-Sequeiros E, Soria MT, et al: Usefulness of EUS-guided fine needle aspiration (EUS-FNA) in the diagnosis of functioning neuroendocrine tumors. Gastrointest Endosc 56:291–296, 2002.
16. Gress FG, Barawi M, Kim D, Grendell JH: Preoperative localization of a neuroendocrine tumor of the pancreas with EUS-guided fine needle tattooing. Gastrointest Endosc 55:594–597, 2002.
17. Mortensen MB, Pless T, Durup J, et al: Clinical impact of endoscopic ultrasound-guided fine needle aspiration biopsy in patients with upper gastrointestinal tract malignancies. A prospective study. Endoscopy 33:478–483, 2001.
18. Harewood GC, Wiersema MJ: A cost analysis of endoscopic ultrasound in the evaluation of pancreatic head adenocarcinoma. Am J Gastroenterol 96:2651–2656, 2001.
19. Ozaki H, Hiraoka T, Mizumoto R, et al: The prognostic significance of lymph node metastasis and intrapancreatic perineural invasion in pancreatic cancer after curative resection. Surg Today 29:16–22, 1999.
20. Durbin TE, Chang KJ: Endoscopic ultrasound (EUS) criteria for predicting malignant lymph nodes using linear array and radial scans—correlation with EUS-guided fine needle aspiration (FNA). Gastrointest Endosc 43:418, A510, 1996.
21. Wiersema MJ, Vilmann P, Giovannini M, et al: Endosonography-guided fine-needle aspiration biopsy: Diagnostic accuracy and complication assessment. Gastroenterology 112:1087–1095, 1997.
22. Yamada T, Nakamori S, Ohzato H, et al: Outcome of pancreatic cancer patients based on genetic lymph node staging. Int J Oncol 16:1165–1171, 2000.
23. Nguyen P, Chang K: Endoscopic ultrasound (EUS) and EUS-guided fine needle aspiration (FNA) of liver lesions in patients with gastrointestinal malignancies. Gastrointest Endosc 50:357–361, 1999.
23a. tenBerge J, Hoffman BJ, Hawes RH, et al: EUS-guided fine needle aspiration of the liver: Indications, yield, and safety based on an international survey of 167 cases. Gastrointest Endosc 55:859–862, 2002.
24. Nguyen P, Chang KJ: Endoscopic ultrasound (EUS) in the detection of ascites and EUS-guided paracentesis. Gastrointest Endosc 54:336–339, 2001.
25. Fritscher-Ravens A, Broering DC, Sriram PV, et al: EUS-guided fine-needle aspiration cytodiagnosis of hilar cholangiocarcinoma: A case series. Gastrointest Endosc 52:534–540, 2000.
26. Sharma A, Chang KJ, Nguyen PT: The role of endoscopic ultrasound (EUS) and EUS-guided fine needle aspiration (FNA) in the diagnosis of proximal biliary strictures. Gastrointest Endosc 57:AB681, 2003.
27. Cannon ME, Carpenter SL, Elta GH, et al: EUS compared with CT, magnetic resonance imaging, and angiography and the influence of biliary stenting on staging accuracy of ampullary neoplasms. Gastrointest Endosc 50:27–33, 1999.
28. Muthusamy R, Jafri SF, Jivcu C, et al: Endoscopic ultrasound (EUS) guided fine needle aspiration (FNA) in the diagnosis and staging of ampullary neoplasms [abstract]. Gastrointest Endosc 53:176, 2001.
29. Wiersema M, Wiersema L: Endosonography guided celiac plexus neurolysis (EUS CPN) in patients with pain due to intra-abdominal malignancy (IAM). Gastrointest Endosc 43:A565, 1996.
30. Gress F, Schmitt C, Sherman S, et al: Endoscopic ultrasound-guided celiac plexus block for managing abdominal pain associated with chronic pancreatitis: A prospective single center experience. Am J Gastroenterol 96:409–16, 2001.
31. Grimm H, Binmoeller KF, Soehendra N: Endosonography-guided drainage of a pancreatic pseudocyst. Gastrointest Endosc 38:170–171, 1992.
32. Brugge WR: The role of EUS in the diagnosis of cystic lesions of the pancreas. Gastrointest Endosc 52(6 Suppl):S18–22, 2000.
33. Lewandrowski KB, Southern JF, Pins MR, et al: Cyst fluid analysis in the differential diagnosis of pancreatic cysts. A comparison of pseudocysts, serous cystadenomas, mucinous cystic neoplasms, and mucinous cystadenocarcinoma. Ann Surg 217:41–47, 1993.
34. Giovannini M, Pesenti C, Rolland AL, et al: Endoscopic ultrasound-guided drainage of pancreatic pseudocysts or pancreatic abscesses using a therapeutic echo endoscope. Endoscopy 33:473–477, 2001.

35. Seifert H, Dietrich C, Schmitt T, et al: Endoscopic ultrasound-guided one-step transmural drainage of cystic abdominal lesions with a large-channel echo endoscope. Endoscopy 32:255–259, 2000.

36. Seifert H, Faust D, Schmitt T, et al: Transmural drainage of cystic peripancreatic lesions with a new large-channel echo endoscope. Endoscopy 33:1022–1026, 2001.

37. Chang KJ, Nguyen PT, Thompson JA, et al: Phase I clinical trial of allogeneic mixed lymphocyte culture (cytoimplant) delivered by endoscopic ultrasound-guided fine-needle injection in patients with advanced pancreatic carcinoma. Cancer 88:1325–1335, 2000.

38. Hecht JR, Bedford R, Abbruzzese JL, et al: A phase I/II trial of intratumoral endoscopic ultrasound injection of ONYX-015 with intravenous gemcitabine in unresectable pancreatic carcinoma. Clin Cancer Res 9:555–561, 2003.

39. Chang KC, Senzer N, Chung T, et al: A novel gene transfer therapy against pancreatic cancer (TNFerade) delivered by endoscopic ultrasound(EUS) and percutaneous guided fine needle injection (FNI) [abstract]. Gastrointest Endosc 59, 2004.

40. Vilmann P, Hancke S, Henriksen FW, Jacobsen GK: Endosonographically-guided fine needle aspiration biopsy of malignant lesions in the upper gastrointestinal tract. Endoscopy 25:523–527, 1993.

41. Chang KJ, Katz KD, Durbin TE, et al: Endoscopic ultrasound-guided fine-needle aspiration. Gastrointest Endosc 40:694–699, 1994.

42. Wiersema MJ, Kochman ML, Cramer HM, et al: Endosonography-guided real-time fine-needle aspiration biopsy. Gastrointest Endosc 40:700–707, 1994.

43. Giovannini M, Seitz JF, Monges G, et al: Fine-needle aspiration cytology guided by endoscopic ultrasonography: Results in 141 patients. Endoscopy 27:171–177, 1995.

44. Rosch T: Fine-needle aspiration cytology guided by endoscopic ultrasonography. Results in 141 patients. Gastrointest Endosc 42:380–382, 1995.

45. Erickson RA, Sayage-Rabie L, Avots-Avotins A: Clinical utility of endoscopic ultrasound-guided fine needle aspiration. Acta Cytol 41:1647–1653, 1997.

46. Erickson RA, Sayage-Rabie L, Beissner RS: Factors predicting the number of EUS-guided fine-needle passes for diagnosis of pancreatic malignancies. Gastrointest Endosc 51:184–190, 2000.

47. Nguyen P, Feng JC, Chang KJ: Endoscopic ultrasound (EUS) and EUS-guided fine-needle aspiration (FNA) of liver lesions. Gastrointest Endosc 50:357–361, 1999.

48. Chang KJ: Endoscopic ultrasound-guided fine needle aspiration in the diagnosis and staging of pancreatic tumors. Gastrointest Endosc Clin N Am 5:723–734, 1995.

49. Klapman JB, Logrono R, Dye CE, et al: Clinical impact of on-site cytopathology interpretation on endoscopic ultrasound-guided fine needle aspiration. Am J Gastroenterol 98:1289–1294, 2003.

50. Bhutani MS, Suryaprasad S, Moezzi J, Seabrook D: Improved technique for performing endoscopic ultrasound guided fine needle aspiration of lymph nodes. Endoscopy 31:550–553, 1999.

51. O'Toole D, Palazzo L, Arotcarena R, et al: Assessment of complications of EUS-guided fine-needle aspiration. Gastrointest Endosc 53:470–474, 2001.

52. Gress FG, Hawes RH, Savides TJ, et al: Endoscopic ultrasound-guided fine-needle aspiration biopsy using linear array and radial scanning endosonography. Gastrointest Endosc 45:243–250, 1997.

53. Micames C, Jowell PS, White R, et al: Lower frequency of peritoneal carcinomatosis in patients with pancreatic cancer diagnosed by EUS-guided FNA vs. percutaneous FNA. Gastrointest Endosc 58:690–695, 2003.

Choledocholithiasis

James A. DiSario and Steven R. Granger

Introduction

Gallstone disease affects people from every society, race, gender, and age-group. It is estimated that 15% of Americans have gallstones. Approximately 700,000 cholecystectomies are performed each year in the United States, making it the most common cause for digestive disease admission to Western hospitals. More than 95% of biliary tract disorders are related to gallstones.[1] Most bile duct stones are gallstones that have passed into the bile duct.

Cholelithiasis describes gallbladder stones, and choledocholithiasis means stones in the bile ducts. Stones are noncrumbling concretions larger than 2 mm in diameter and biliary microlithiasis are particles 2 mm or less in diameter, although there is no universally accepted definition. Choledocholithiasis can be classified as primary stones that develop in the bile ducts or secondary stones that pass from the gallbladder. Choledocholithiasis can be further subdivided by the location of the stones, which may be intrahepatic or extrahepatic. Five percent to fifteen percent of patients with symptomatic gallstone disease have bile duct stones. In contrast, more than 90% of patients with choledocholithiasis also have cholelithiasis.[2] Sludge is a suspension of cholesterol monohydrate crystals, calcium bilirubinate granules, and/or other calcium salts with or without microlithiasis in gallbladder mucus. This is a form of gallstone disease and may predispose to macroscopic stones or directly cause pancreatitis and other morbidity.[3]

Epidemiology

CHOLELITHIASIS

Gallstone disease occurs worldwide. It is a major health problem in Westernized countries and the incidence is rising in places where Western diets are becoming more common.

Most gallstones are composed primarily of cholesterol and are nodular and round with a golden color. The minority of gallstones contain mostly calcium bilirubinate are round, hard, and black. However, primary bile duct stones are composed of calcium salts of unconjugated bilirubin with variable amounts of cholesterol, protein, and bacteria. These stones are brown and amorphous, and have an earthy texture. Figure 46–1 shows examples of stones extracted from the bile duct.

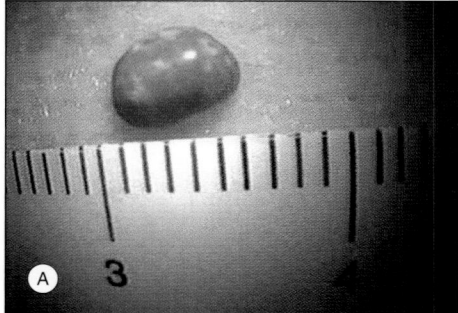
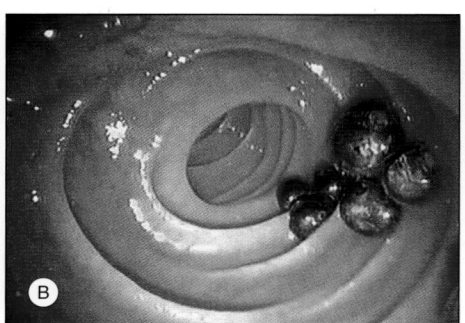
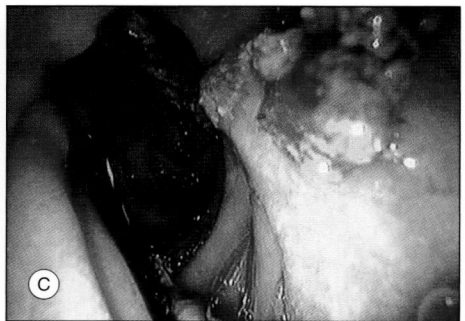

Figure 46–1. *A,* Cholesterol and calcium stone *ex vivo. B,* Calcium bilirubinate stones in the duodenum. *C,* Brown, amorphous, earthy primary bile duct stone material in the duodenum.

The epidemiology of gallstone disease is influenced by biologic and behavioral factors. Biologic factors include race, gender, age, underlying diseases, and serum triglyceride levels. Behavioral factors include physical inactivity, obesity, and rapid weight loss.[1]

Cholesterol Gallstones

The prevalence of cholesterol gallstones varies greatly among ethnic populations. Sub-Saharan Africans, African Americans, and Asians have a lower risk of cholesterol gallstone disease than most Caucasians. In contrast, gallstone disease is more prevalent in Scandinavians, Native Americans, and New World Hispanics particularly all Chileans, and Bolivians of native origin. Although a genetic etiology seems likely, genes linked to gallstone disease have been discovered only in mice.[1]

Women have an incidence of cholesterol gallstones that is twofold to fourfold that of men and the etiology is likely hormonal. Gallstones occur more often in pregnancy. High estrogen levels promote bile secretion with increased saturation of cholesterol, and progesterone promotes gallbladder stasis. Multiparous women develop gallstones twice as often as nulliparous women do. Twenty percent to thirty percent of stones that present during pregnancy are not present postpartum, presumably because they have dissolved.[4]

Older age is associated with an increased risk of gallstone disease, and 30% of Italian women older than age 50 have gallstones.[5] Diet, alcohol, caffeine, and tobacco are not associated with the development of cholesterol stones. Obesity is a risk factor for stones, and physical activity decreases the risk. Weight loss of any etiology is also an independent risk factor for gallstones.

There are several drugs that are associated with gallstone formation including exogenous estrogens, clofibrate, and long-term use of octreotide.[6] Persons on total parenteral nutrition are at increased risk for cholesterol stones because of gallbladder stasis.

There are a number of systemic diseases associated with cholesterol gallstone formation. Hypertriglyceridemia is associated with stones. However, there is no association of gallstones and hypercholesterolemia.[6] Insulin-resistant diabetes appears to be associated with stones.[6] Cholesterol stones may be associated with ileal disease, and a twofold to threefold increase in stones occurs with Crohn's disease.

Pigment Gallstones

Black pigment (bilirubinate) gallstones account for up to 25% of gallstones in the United States but are more prevalent in Asia. They are more common in women, and this increases with age. Pigment stones are associated with hemolytic diseases, hepatic cirrhosis, and ileal disease. Terminal ileal disease may predispose to pigment stones because of the inability reabsorb bile salts that then pass to the colon where they solubilize unconjugated bilirubin and thus promote the absorption of bilirubin and subsequent enterohepatic cycling. Brown pigment stones may occur in the gallbladder or bile duct and are associated with biliary bacterial colonization.[7]

CHOLEDOCHOLITHIASIS

Primary and secondary bile duct stones vary greatly in epidemiology. In parallel with cholelithiasis, the prevalence of secondary duct

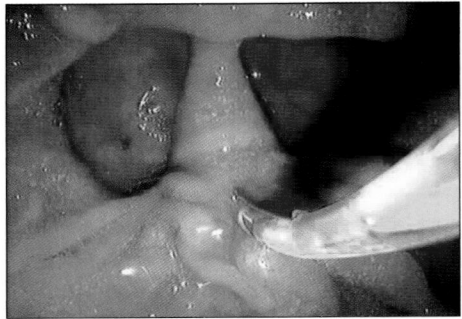

Figure 46–2. A large periampullary diverticulum, which will predispose to choledocholithiasis. The bile duct is cannulated and can be seen traversing the diverticulum.

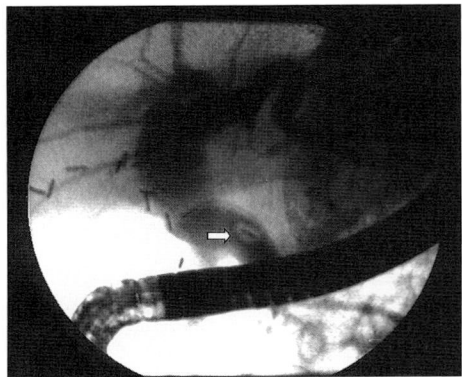

Figure 46–3. Endoscopic cholangiogram with an *arrow* pointing to a radiolucent stone in the common bile duct that has a surgical clip from prior cholecystectomy as the nidus.

stones increases with age. Most bile duct stones are secondary stones in Western societies.

The incidence of primary bile duct stones is generally lower in Western countries than in Asian countries. However, the proportion of brown stones is decreasing as the rates of biliary infection decline. Primary bile duct stones are associated with bacterial contamination of the choledochus by biliary enteric anastomoses, sphincterotomy, stents, instrumentation, or portal bacteremia. Periampullary diverticula provide a site for bacterial proliferation with subsequent reflux into the bile duct (Fig. 46–2).[8] Hemoglobinopathies may induce primary stones by providing a bilirubinate nidus for stone development. Foreign bodies including surgical clips and parasites may also introduce bacteria and be a nidus for stone formation as shown in Figure 46–3.[9]

Pathogenesis
CHOLESTEROL GALLSTONES

A complete discussion of the pathogenesis of gallstone formation is beyond the scope of this chapter. The formation of cholesterol gallstones is multifactor. Bile is composed of water, cholesterol, bile salts, phospholipids (lecithin), calcium, and electrolytes. The principal mechanisms of stone formation are cholesterol supersaturation in the bile, accelerated nucleation, and gallbladder stasis.

PIGMENT STONES

Black stones are mostly comprised of calcium bilirubinate with lesser amounts of calcium carbonate and calcium phosphate. Cholesterol accounts for less than 50% of the makeup of these stones. Bacteria, especially *Escherichia coli* and *Enterococcus*, can be cultured from up to 80% of calcium bilirubinate stones and from the bile in up to 70% of affected patients, but the organisms may be different. Electron microscopy shows bacteria in all layers of a calcium bilirubinate stones but only in the pigment layers of mixed stones. Black stones are associated with hypersecretion of bilirubin conjugates into the bile and acidification defects. There is no associated gallbladder hypomotility.[9]

Brown stones are caused by anaerobic and coliform bacterial contamination of the bile. The bacteria produce beta-glucuronidase, phospholipase A, and conjugated bile acid hydrolase, which produce unconjugated bilirubin, palmitic and stearic acids, and unconjugated bile acids, respectively. These substances bind calcium and form insoluble salts and stones. Many stones from around a nidus including suture material, surgical clips, parasites, and other foreign bodies.[9]

Clinical Features

The clinical presentation of gallstones can be classified into three groups: (1) asymptomatic cholelithiasis and/or choledocholithiasis, (2) symptomatic gallstones (biliary colic), and (3) complications from gallstones (pancreatitis, cholecystitis, obstructive jaundice, cholangitis, gallbladder cancer, gallstone ileus).

Sixty percent to eighty percent of persons with gallstones have no symptoms and the risk of progression to symptoms or complications is small. However, once symptoms occur, persistence and progression to complications is common. About 2% of asymptomatic carriers develop symptoms per year for 5 years. Thereafter, symptoms occur in 15% at 10 years, and 18% at 15 and 20 years, with about 3% developing complications. Somewhat higher rates have also been reported.[1,10,11] Episodes of biliary colic precede complications in 90% of cases. Symptomatic gallstones take a more aggressive course. Thirty-five percent to fifty percent of patients with symptomatic gallstones have recurrence within 1 year and nearly 2% per year have complications.[10]

The natural history of choledocholithiasis is unpredictable and not well described. Many common bile duct (CBD) stones are asymptomatic and pass into the duodenum without incident, whereas others lead to biliary colic, jaundice, cholangitis, and/or pancreatitis.[12–14] Choledocholithiasis associated biliary colic is similar to gallbladder-associated biliary colic. Nausea and vomiting often accompany an episode of severe visceral pain in the epigastrium or right upper quadrant. Jaundice without associated symptoms may also occur with choledocholithiasis. Untreated bile duct stone obstruction can cause secondary biliary cirrhosis, usually after about 5 years.[15] These patients can also present with liver failure and/or portal hypertension.

Biliary pain is often described as steady severe pain with rapid onset. This pain is usually located in the right upper quadrant but may also be referred to the midepigastrium, back, and right subscapular area. Outpatient remedies, flatus, and position or environmental changes do not relieve gallstone pain. It usually is severe enough to interfere with current activities and lasts from 30 minutes to several hours. Food ingestion is commonly associated with the onset of an attack. These attacks can occur at anytime day or night without any associated inciting event. Nausea and vomiting are often associated with the pain.

Differential Diagnosis

Diagnosing biliary tract pathology requires a holistic approach to the patient evaluation. Key clinical features, laboratory findings, and radiographic evaluations are all used. All foregut disorders may have similar symptoms including esophageal, gastric, duodenal, and hepatic and pancreatic lesions. In addition, colonic diseases, diaphragmatic and pleural problems, and musculoskeletal disease may mimic biliary symptoms. It is difficult to accurately assess the segment of the biliary tree affected by stone disease by history and physical examination alone because biliary colic may be present with cholelithiasis or choledocholithiasis. Laboratory evaluation can help with this localization because elevations in serum transaminases, alkaline phosphatase, and total bilirubin suggest bile duct stones as does ductal dilatation on transabdominal ultrasound studies.

Jaundice can occur with choledocholithiasis but cannot clinically be differentiated from jaundice of other etiologies. Cardiac failure can clinically mimic biliary complaints with right upper quadrant tenderness, jaundice, and elevated bilirubin and serum liver tests. Pericarditis can be associated with cardiac congestion and a similar clinical picture. Acute viral hepatitis may also cause acute pain, tenderness, jaundice, and fever.

CBD stones can be present without changes in laboratory values.[16] Total bilirubin levels can range from normal to very high, and time period of obstruction does not correlate with the serum bilirubin. However, complete obstruction may cause a steady increase in serum bilirubin. Alkaline phosphatase is usually elevated by up to fivefold in symptomatic patients. However, acute biliary obstruction usually causes a disproportionate increase in the transaminases.[17]

Imaging studies are the standard for the diagnosis of biliary stone disease. Transcutaneous abdominal ultrasound is the initial imaging study obtained when gallstone disease is suspected with a sensitivity and specificity each above of 95% for cholelithiasis, and about 50% and 98% for CBD stones. Older series have much lower diagnostic rates.[18] Spiral computed tomography (CT) is reported to be up to 82% sensitive and 97% specific for detecting bile duct stones, but many series have lower rates.[19,20] Meta-analysis data show magnetic resonance cholangiopancreatography (MRCP) to be 92% sensitive and 97% specific for stones, but the sensitivity declines for concrements 5 mm or less in diameter (Fig. 46–4).[20,21] Multiple studies demonstrate sensitivities and specificities for endoscopic retrograde cholangiopancreatography (ERCP) of 90% to 100% and 98% to 100%, respectively.[20] Endoscopic ultrasonography (EUS) can be performed with a dedicated echoendoscope with either 360-degree radial imaging, linear imaging or with an intraductal probe. EUS is performed like a standard endoscopy with sonographic imaging of the extrahepatic bile duct done through the duodenal bulb or descending duodenum as shown in Figure 46–5.

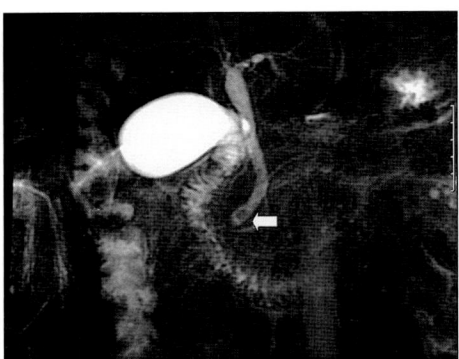

Figure 46–4. Magnetic retrograde cholangiopancreatography (MRCP) with the *arrow* showing a 5-mm distal bile duct stone.

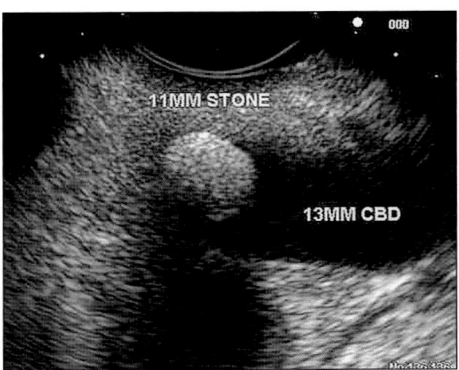

Figure 46–5. Linear endosonographic image of a longitudinal section of the distal bile duct with a round bright echodense structure with shadowing representing a stone. (Courtesy of Iqbal Sandhu, MD.)

Reported sensitivities and specificities are 84% to 100% and 96% to 100%, respectively.[20]

Preoperative diagnosis of CBD stones is not always necessary. Many authors advocate intraoperative cholangiography (IOC) as the diagnostic modality of choice in the setting of cholecystectomy with suspected CBD calculi. Laparoscopic IOC is technically successful in more than 90% of cases, and is about 80% to 90% sensitive and 76% to 97% specific (Fig. 46–6).[22,23] Fluoroscopic IOC has better diagnostic accuracy than static imaging. IOC is also used during cholecystectomy to verify biliary tree anatomy before dividing the cystic duct. IOC generally adds 5 to 25 minutes to the operation, but it is usually less expensive, faster, and better tolerated than other invasive modalities.[23]

Laparoscopic intraoperative ultrasonography (IOUS) is less widely used than IOC. It has no radiation exposure and is touted to be less time consuming than IOC with similar sensitivity and specificity. There appears to be a marginal diagnostic advantage to performing IOUS in addition to IOC.[23,24]

Although 5% to 15% of persons who have cholecystectomy have bile duct stones, it is not cost effective to perform universal ERCP or IOC for detection and treatment. Therefore, clinical, laboratory, and imaging studies are used to stratify for risk of harboring bile duct stones, and numerous studies have identified risk factors and developed scoring formulas for risk. The most commonly detected risk factors are elevations in serum transaminases, alkaline phosphatase, and bilirubin and bile duct dilatation to 8 mm or larger on transabdominal ultrasound. However, only about 50% to 75% of persons predicted to be at high risk have choledocholithiasis.[1,25] EUS or MRCP may be useful to more precisely define the risk; however, these tests add cost and do not allow for therapy. When stones are suspected preoperatively, the options for diagnosis and therapy are preoperative ERCP or IOC with laparoscopic common duct exploration (LCDE). For stones detected at IOC, LCDE, conversion to open common duct exploration (OCDE), or intraoperative or postoperative ERCP can be done. However, OCDE is associated with significant morbidity and prolonged hospital and recovery times and should not be used routinely. Choledocholithiasis may be diagnosed after surgery with transabdominal ultrasound, CT, MRCP, EUS, and/or ERCP depending on the index of suspicion, and treated with ERCP.[23]

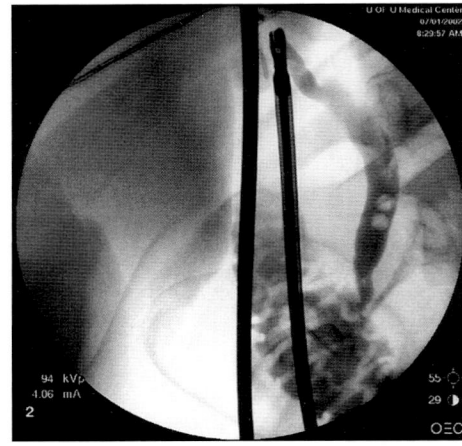

Figure 46–6. Intraoperative cholangiogram with two radiolucent stones seen in the common bile duct. (Courtesy of Robert Glasgow, MD.)

BILIARY SLUDGE, MICROLITHIASIS, AND CRYSTALS

Biliary sludge, microlithiasis, and/or crystals are a form of gallstone disease and appear to have a natural history and clinical associations that are similar to macroscopic stone disease. Over the course of 3 years, 50% of persons with abdominal pain and sludge have spontaneous resolution of the sludge, 20% have asymptomatic persistence, 10% to 15% have symptoms persist or develop, and 5% to 15% acquire stones.[26,27] Sludge, microlithiasis, and crystals account for about 75% cases of acute recurrent pancreatitis in which the etiology is undiagnosed by history, physical examination, blood tests, and noninvasive imaging studies.[27,28] Cholesterol monohydrate crystals and/or calcium bilirubinate granules can be found in gallbladder bile, or bile duct bile after cholecystectomy, in 67% to 89% of these patients.[27–30] These lesions are also associated with cholelithiasis not seen on imaging studies, cholecystitis without macroscopic stones, and cholangitis.

The initial diagnosis of gallbladder sludge is often made by transabdominal ultrasound that has been recently reported to be 86% sensitive at showing a dependent layer of nonshadowing, slowly mobile material.[31] EUS is about 96% sensitive for detecting sludge and finds small gallbladder and bile duct stones missed on other studies.[31,32] MRCP is more sensitive than transabdominal ultrasound for the diagnosis of sludge and microlithiasis.[33] Direct microscopic examination of the bile is considered the diagnostic standard and is more sensitive than transcutaneous ultrasonography or EUS, allows determination of the type of particles in the sludge, and is required to diagnose microlithiasis in the absence of sludge. However, crystals may occur intermittently and false-positive and false-negative results may occur.[3]

Duodenal aspiration after stimulation of gallbladder emptying is cumbersome and yields a contaminated specimen.[34] ERCP with gallbladder cannulation and aspiration provides a relatively pure specimen and has the added advantage of allowing for imaging of the biliary tree and pancreas, and sphincter of Oddi manometry when indicated.[35]

Gallbladder bile (B bile) is opaque dark green or black and is much more informative than the lighter colored hepatic bile (A bile) for diagnosing microlithiasis and crystals (Fig. 46–7). Some authors have collected dark bile with cannulation of only the choledochus, but this may be time consuming and unsuccessful.[36] Radiographic contrast material in the bile may cause false-positive microscopic

examinations. It is our practice to collect a pure bile specimen by gallbladder cannulation under fluoroscopic guidance before contrast injection into the gallbladder.

There is no consensus on the method of preparation, examination, and interpretation of bile specimens for microscopic crystal examination. Some authors have attempted to quantify the findings,[36] but a qualitative examination is appropriate for clinical purposes.[3] One suggested protocol is to centrifuge a 10- to 15-mL specimen at 3000 g for 15 minutes and make a slide from the sediment. The slide is examined by light and polarizing microscopy at 100× (two crystals or granules per field or four per slide is considered a positive test). Cholesterol monohydrate crystals are rhomboid plaques with a notch that are multicolored on polarized examination, and bilirubinate granules are amorphous and red brown colored as shown in Figure 46–8. Leukocytes may be indicative of acute or chronic cholecystitis. It is difficult and unnecessary to strictly maintain the specimen temperature at 37°C. However, the specimen should be centrifuged as quickly as possible. The intact specimen should not be stored because bacterial contamination can occur in room temperature and refrigerated specimens, and cholesterol crystal precipitation develops in frozen bile. However, the sediment may be frozen for later examination if necessary.[3]

GALLSTONE PANCREATITIS

Gallstones cause about 35% cases of acute pancreatitis in the United States, and about 25% of these cases are severe with mortality in up to 10%. Gallstones are recovered from the feces in up to 95% of people with acute pancreatitis; however, only up to 7% of people with gallstones develop pancreatitis.[37] Soon after the onset of pancreatitis, up to 78% of affected persons have bile duct stones found at surgery or ERCP.[38,39] However, delayed operations reveal bile duct and impacted ampullary stones much less frequently.[40]

It is thought that small stones pass more easily through the cystic duct and impact in the sphincter of Oddi; stones less than 5 mm in diameter are the most common.[41] The causal relationship between gallstones and pancreatitis is confirmed by the finding that cholecystectomy or endoscopic sphincterotomy with removal of bile duct stones prevents recurrences.[42] The pathophysiology may be due to obstruction of pancreatic juice outflow and/or reflux of offending substances into the pancreatic duct.

The diagnosis of biliary pancreatitis is usually made by finding gallstones on transabdominal ultrasound in the absence of other

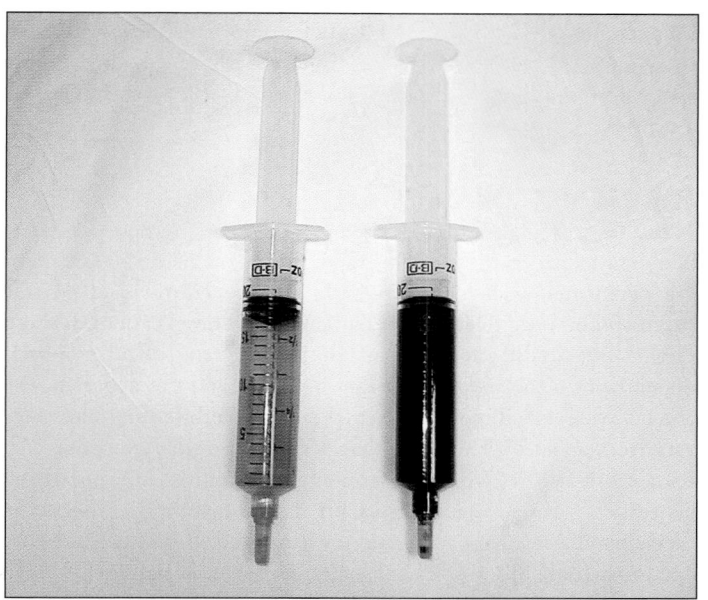

Figure 46–7. Aspiration specimens of yellow hepatic bile (A bile) on the left and black gallbladder bile (B bile) on the right.

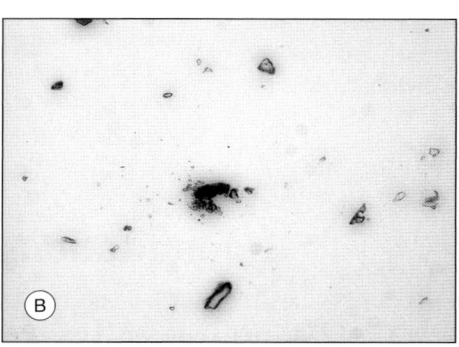

Figure 46–8. *A,* Cholesterol monohydrate crystals seen with polarized microscopy. *B,* Amorphous bilirubinate aggregates seen with light microscopy.

known causes of pancreatitis, although EUS is more sensitive and specific, and provides much better visualization of the bile duct.[38] Abnormal liver enzymes and bilirubin, and bile duct dilatation on transabdominal ultrasound are often found but are nonspecific.[43] It is important to stratify the severity of pancreatitis by various algorithms or failure of one or more organ systems as the prognosis and therapy vary greatly between mild and severe cases.[44] The authors use failure of one or more organ system to categorize severe pancreatitis because the algorithms are cumbersome and difficult to remember, include subjective criteria, and may require 48 hours of observation for a conclusion.[45]

SUPPURATIVE CHOLANGITIS

Acute suppurative cholangitis develops in the setting of bacteria in the biliary system and bile duct obstruction. Bile duct stones are the cause the obstruction in most cases. The bacteria enter the duct from the gut and proliferate resulting in increased intraductal pressure and forced translocation of bacteria and endotoxins into the hepatic sinusoids and bloodstream. In contrast to gallstone disease, women and men are affected equally with a median age of 50 to 60 years. Less frequently, benign and malignant strictures, obstructed stents, and side-to-side surgical anastomoses predispose to cholangitis. Mortality rates approach 100% in persons who fail conservative therapy and do not have an adequate drainage procedure.[46]

The most common organisms are *E. coli, Enterococcus, Klebsiella,* and *Enterobacter*. However, *Pseudomonas*, anaerobes, and skin and oral flora may be found after biliary instrumentation or surgery. Polymicrobial infection is common, and bile cultures are usual.[46] The classical clinical presentation is Charcot's triad including fever, jaundice, and right upper quadrant abdominal pain that occurs in 50% to 100% of patients. Reynold's pentad adds altered mental status and hypotension to Charcot's triad and occurs in less than 14% of patients. Typical laboratory abnormalities include leukocytosis, hyperbilirubinemia, elevated alkaline phosphatase, mildly increased transaminases, and a high amylase on occasion. Imaging findings on transabdominal ultrasound include stones and/or ductal dilatation in 67% of patients. CT scans may show ductal dilatation, the level of obstruction, and occasionally calcified bile duct and/or gallstones. MRCP is reported to show distinctive changes in up to 92% of patients but without therapeutic capabilities; thus, the utility is unclear. EUS has not been studied for this indication and does not appear to impart a potentially significant benefit. Percutaneous transhepatic cholangiography (PTC) is sensitive and specific in 90% or more of affected patients and allows for therapy. However, it should not be considered as a first-line procedure because of high complication rates.[47] ERCP is the procedure of choice because it affords the opportunity to provide the diagnosis and definitive therapy with acceptable morbidity and mortality rates.

Treatment

SURGERY

The management of CBD stones varies widely around the world. Therapeutic determinants include individual patient presentation, operative risk, and available expertise for laparoscopic (LCDE) and open (OCDE) CBD exploration and ERCP.

Laparoscopy cholecystectomy is the preferred initial approach to cholelithiasis with the benefit of decreased pain, shorter length of hospital stay, more rapid return to full activity, and less cost than open surgery. LCDE appears to have similar advantages over OCDE and is cost effective compared with ERCP.[48] A transcystic duct approach is generally preferred to choledochotomy resulting in shorter procedure duration and hospital stays and reduced need for T-tube placement. However, some surgeons use a choledochotomy depending on the stone. Stone extraction is generally achieved under fluoroscopic guidance with medical dilatation of the sphincter of Oddi and flushing of small stones, by retrograde balloon or basket catheter techniques, by pushing stones through the native sphincter of Oddi, or after balloon dilatation or antegrade sphincterotomy. Balloon dilatation should be discouraged because of increased rates of pancreatitis. Choledochoscopic guidance may also be used with or without intracorporeal lithotripsy techniques. LCDE results in stone clearance in 75% to 90% of cases and T-tube placement or antegrade biliary stenting is required for incomplete drainage. LCDE adds about 1 hour to the operation. Transcystic duct LCBE requires hospital stays of about 1.5 days, and transductal procedures generally result in stays of up to 7.5 days. Morbidity and mortality occur in 10% and 1% of cases, respectively.[23] A treatment algorithm for preoperatively suspected bile duct stones managed by standard techniques is shown in Figure 46–9 and those requiring more specialized techniques is shown in Figure 46–10. Stones detected after surgery are best managed by ERCP.

ENDOSCOPIC THERAPY

ERCP with sphincterotomy is the most common method of treating bile duct stones in the United States, and more than 150,000 cases are performed each year. Overall, the procedure is ultimately successful in more than 90% of patients with complications in about 10%.[49] Successful clearance of the biliary tree of all stones is dependent on the size and number of stones and the experience of the endoscopist. Reported rates of successful bile duct clearance vary from about 60% to more than 90% at the initial procedure[50–54] to almost 100% with subsequent procedures at specialized centers.[55–62] Failed cases are usually due to inability to access the major papilla resulting from surgically altered anatomy. Morbidity occurs in only 3% to 5% of patients from initial ERCP with sphincterotomy performed for stones, especially when performed within 30 days of laparoscopic cholecystectomy.[54,63,64] The underlying principle is to open the sphincter choledochus and remove the stones with balloon or basket catheters inserted into the bile duct under fluoroscopic and endoscopic visualization. Difficult and unusual circumstances may require the use of mechanical, intracorporeal electrohydraulic or laser lithotripsy, and/or extracorporeal shockwave lithotripsy (ESWL). Long-term stenting for palliation is appropriate for very high-risk patients.

Indications and Contraindications

ERCP is indicated as the standard of care for patients with known or suspected choledocholithiasis with the exception of those who will have LCDE at the time of laparoscopic cholecystectomy. ERCP

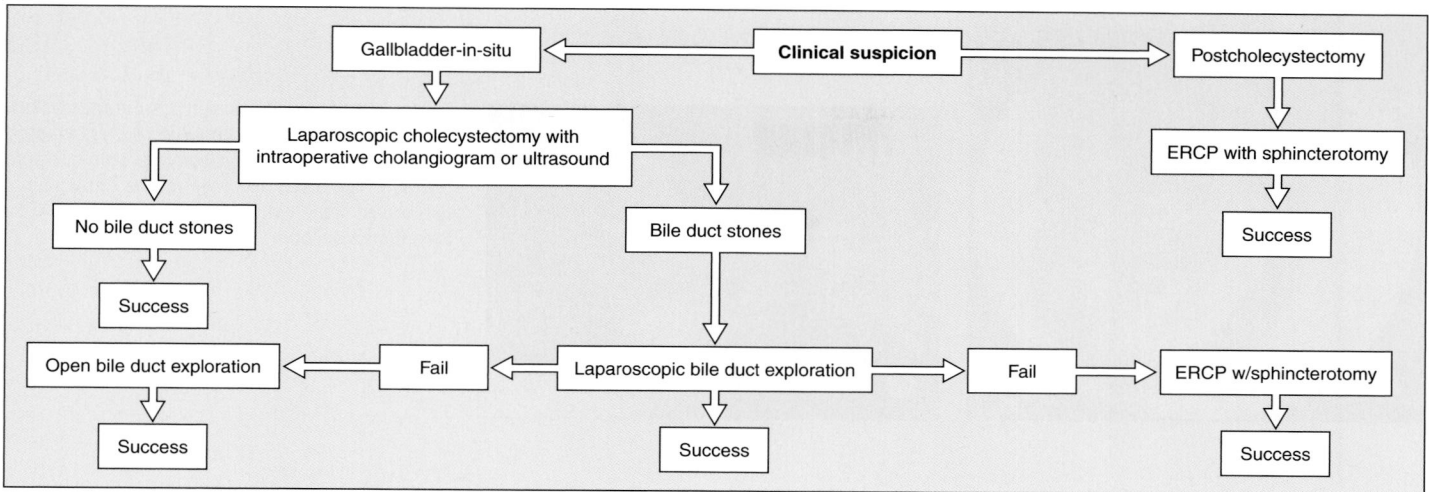

Figure 46–9. Standard treatment for choledocholithiasis.

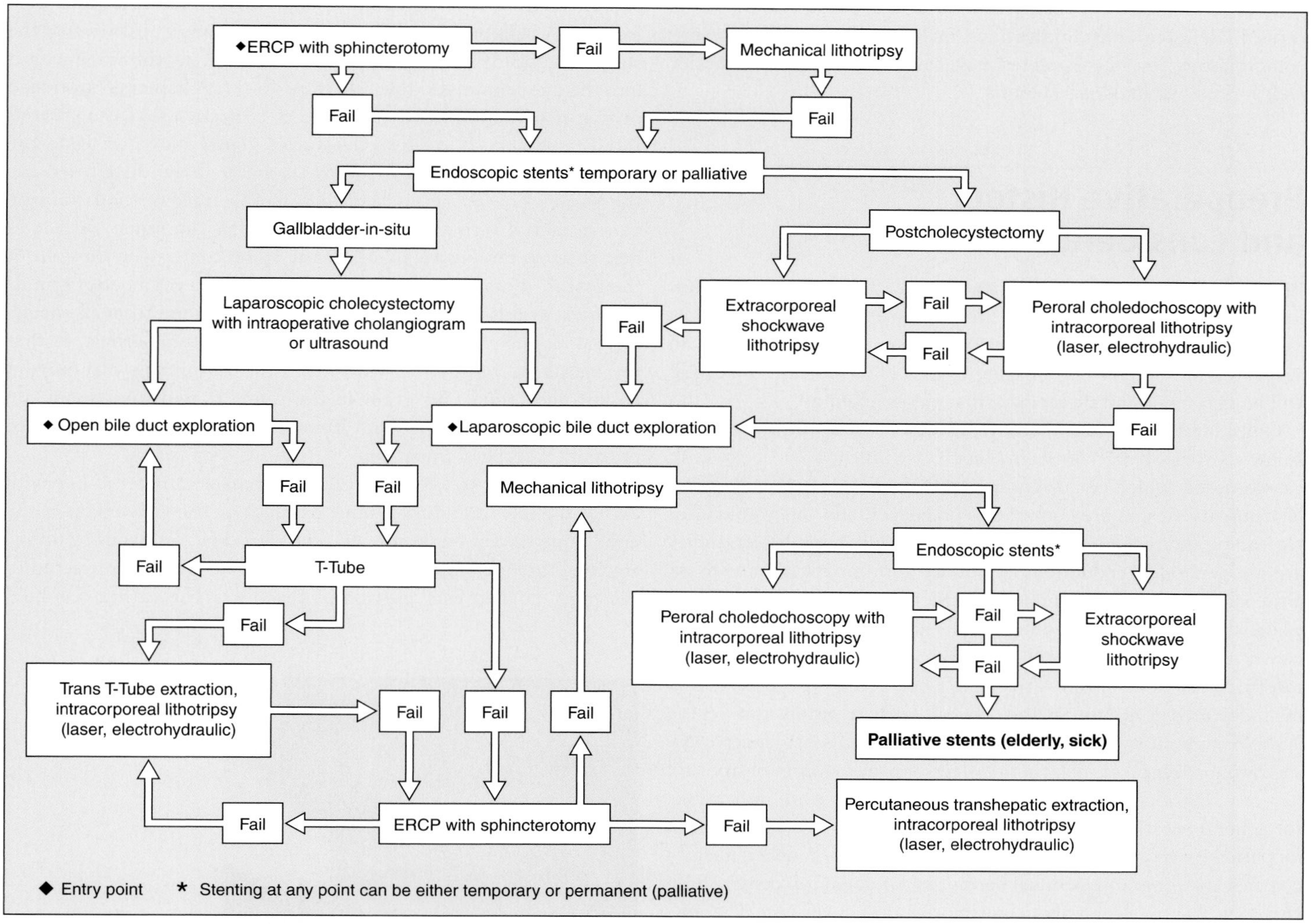

Figure 46–10. Specialized treatment for difficult bile duct stones.

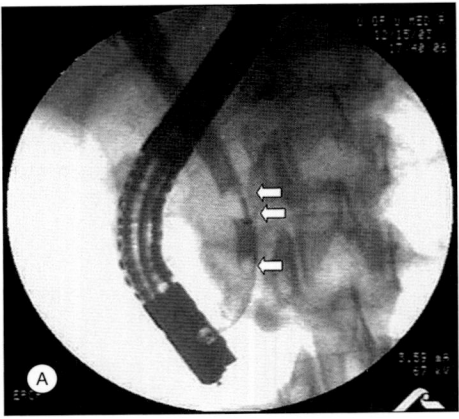
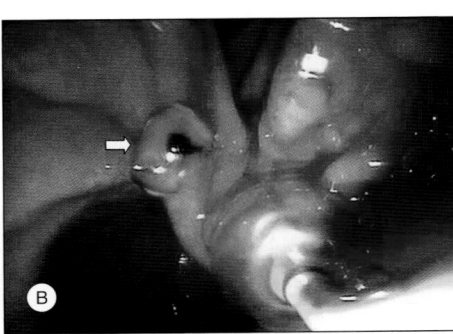

Figure 46-11. *A,* Endoscopic retrograde cholangiogram with a balloon *(double arrows)* inflated in the common bile duct above a stone *(single arrow)* in the distal bile duct. *B,* The *arrow* points to a mixed stone extracted into the duodenum by the inflated balloon.

is also indicated urgently or emergently for persons with severe gallstone pancreatitis and those with acute suppurative cholangitis. Absolute contraindications are those of endoscopy and ERCP in general including bowel obstruction, perforated viscus, and patient refusal. Relative contraindications include coagulopathy, severe comorbidities, recent gastrointestinal anastomosis, and gastric outlet and/or proximal duodenal stenosis.

Preoperative History and Considerations

Bile duct stones are usually diagnosed by clinical history, serum hepatic enzyme levels, and/or imaging studies before ERCP is performed. However, there are circumstances when stones are suspected but not seen on imaging studies in which case the ERCP will be diagnostic and therapeutic if stones are found.

Considerations in the medical history include prior intestinal surgery with altered anatomy such as Billroth or Roux-en-Y anastomoses, which could require a different approach and special instruments. Stones are common in pregnancy, and this would alter the timing and technique of ERCP. Preprocedure coagulation studies are not generally recommended but are appropriate in persons on anticoagulants or with biliary obstruction who may develop a coagulopathy because of vitamin K malabsorption, which is significantly exacerbated in those on warfarin. It is wise to have the international normalized ratio (INR) corrected to 1.2 or less if sphincterotomy is anticipated. Sepsis with hypotension; severe acute pancreatitis; significant cardiopulmonary disease; macroglossia; dysmorphic faces; obstructive sleep apnea; morbid obesity; and narcotic, benzodiazepine, and/or alcohol tolerance are indications for general anesthesia. Other considerations include a bowel purge in patients who have recently had a CT scan or other barium contrast study because residual barium in the colon can compromise cholangiography. Prophylactic antibiotics that cover enteric gram-negative organisms, enterococci, and perhaps *Pseudomonas* are recommended for cases of bile duct obstruction including stone disease.[65]

Therapeutic Techniques

Stones are extracted after cannulation has been achieved, the stone is identified on cholangiography, and the sphincterotomy is performed. A balloon or basket catheter is advanced upstream to the stone. The balloon is inflated and retracted bring the stone with it into the duodenum as shown in Figure 46-11. A basket is positioned so that it will completely open and deploy such that the stone is totally engaged. It is often helpful to gently move or jiggle the basket up and down the affected segment of the duct to entrap the stone. The basket is then left in the fully opened position and retracted into the duodenum bringing the stone with it as demonstrated in Figure 46-12. If the stone continually slips out of the basket, it may be closed around the stone to get a better grip. If this maneuver is done, it is important that the stone be small enough to pass through the distal duct and sphincterotomy orifice, or that the basket be compatible with mechanical lithotripsy, to prevent basket and stone impaction in the duct. If multiple stones are present, the most downstream stone should be removed first also to prevent this type of impaction.

It is important to keep the balloon or basket catheter in line with axis of the bile duct during stone extraction. The viewing tip of the endoscope should be positioned directly below the papillary orifice abutting the opening. The catheter and stone are then retracted to the most downstream portion of the duct. The catheter is held

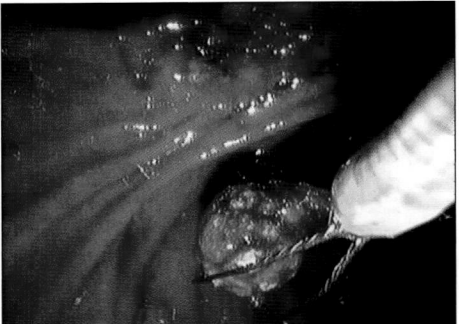

Figure 46-12. A mixed stone is seen extracted within a basket in the duodenum.

tightly against the endoscope with the third through fifth fingers of the left hand and the endoscope is torqued clockwise and pushed inward which directs the catheter and stone straight out of the duct. Alternatively, the endoscope may be pushed in slightly below the sphincterotomy orifice and the tip turned upward against the orifice in a slightly acute angle by turning the large up and down knob counterclockwise. The endoscope is then retracted a little, the catheter is held tightly against the endoscope, and the up and down knob is firmly turned clockwise, which pulls the catheter and stone out along the axis of the duct. If the balloon or basket catheter is simply pulled out with the endoscope in the standard position, the stone is likely to be forced against the superior aspect of the duct deep to the duodenal wall. The catheter will then slip out inferiorly to the stone. The balloon can rupture against the bridge on the endoscope or the basket may slip off the stone and out. Primary bile duct stones have an earthy consistency and crumble with extraction. It is often necessary to repeatedly sweep the duct with a balloon and perhaps irrigate the biliary tree with saline. Brown stone debris extracted into the duodenum is shown in Figure 46–1C.

When a stone is positioned loosely in the hepatic ducts, it may be possible to direct a guide wire upstream, pass a balloon catheter above the stone, and extract it in the usual manner. However, care should be taken to avoid further upstream force on the stone by hydrostatic pressure from contrast injection or from direct pressure from the instruments. If standard extraction is not possible, stones can often be retracted into the extrahepatic bile ducts by positioning a stone extraction balloon just downstream to the stone, inflating it to fit snugly into the duct, and then rapidly retracting it to create downstream suction to dislodge the stone.

Unusual Situations

PREGNANCY

About 8% of pregnant women develop cholelithiasis and often have symptoms. Cholecystectomy can often be postponed until after delivery; however, choledocholithiasis poses significant risks for cholangitis and pancreatitis and generally requires therapy. Potential risks to the fetus are those of the sedatives and analgesics; radiation exposure; and sequela of procedural complications such as hypoxia, pancreatitis, and sepsis. There are at least 76 cases from 36 reports in the literature of ERCP during pregnancy including at least 25 in the first trimester. Biliary sphincterotomy, stone extraction, and stenting were often done. Most patients delivered healthy full-term babies. Therapeutic outcomes were generally successful with minimal morbidity, although there was one death from pulmonary hypertension and sepsis in a neonate whose mother had post-ERCP pancreatitis.[66]

A reasonable approach is to perform a transabdominal ultrasound for pregnant women who develop right upper quadrant and/or epigastric pain, abnormal serum hepatic enzymes, unexplained acute pancreatitis, or biliary sepsis.[67] If gallstones are found and there is no pancreatitis, cholecystectomy may be postponed until after delivery if the symptoms and biochemical tests resolve.[68] ERCP is indicated for choledocholithiasis and/or ductal dilatation seen on ultrasound,

persistent cholestasis, pancreatitis, or cholangitis. The patient should be considered for referral to a high-volume center with experience in these cases. Obstetrical consultation should be obtained and fetal monitoring considered during the procedure. The procedure may need to be performed in the supine or left lateral position. It may be wise to have an anesthesiologist administer the sedation or anesthesia and to consider endotracheal intubation if the patient is to be in the supine position. Fetal radiation exposure should be minimized by lead shielding, using minimal fluoroscopy and avoiding spot films, which have higher exposure. Using these techniques, fetal radiation exposure can be contained to about 310 millirads, which is significantly below the accepted teratogenic dose.[69] Radiation exposure to the fetus may be monitored with a radiation dosimetry badge placed on the mother's abdomen over the uterine fundus.[66] Sphincterotomy and stenting may be safely performed, and transpapillary gallbladder stenting for cholecystitis has been suggested to postpone cholecystectomy until after delivery. Some authorities advocate performing the procedure with no fluoroscopy and perhaps ultrasound guidance, but this may result in a failed procedure or other complications.

BILIARY SLUDGE, MICROLITHIASIS, AND CRYSTALS

Traditional therapy for sludge, microlithiasis and crystals is cholecystectomy, which generally cures relapsing pain and prevents recurrent pancreatitis.[3,27,28] However, ursodeoxycholic acid can dissolve cholesterol microlithiasis and crystals and prevent recurrence of pancreatitis; but the duration of effect remains unknown.[3,27] Endoscopic sphincterotomy prevents or reduces episodes of recurrent pancreatitis resulting from sludge, microlithiasis, and crystals.[28,36]

GALLSTONE PANCREATITIS

The usual therapy for mild to moderate disease is supportive until the pancreatitis resolves and then laparoscopic cholecystectomy with IOC, generally during the same hospital stay. Severe disease is best treated with intensive care monitoring, prophylactic antibiotics, enteral nutritional support, and urgent biliary drainage for jaundice and/or cholangitis. However, early biliary surgery is associated with high rates of morbidity and mortality in severe pancreatitis.[39]

Endoscopic retrograde cholangiography (ERC) with biliary sphincterotomy and stone extraction improves morbidity and mortality rates, and shortens hospital stays in patients with severe pancreatitis and jaundice and/or cholangitis.[44,70] There are four randomized controlled trials of ERC compared with conservative management in patients with acute pancreatitis. These studies have conflicting results[71–74] and are summarized in Tables 46–1 and 46–2.

Neoptolemos and colleagues[71] randomized 121 patients from a single center with suspected biliary pancreatitis to have ERC with sphincterotomy for bile duct stones within 72 hours of admission compared with conservative therapy. Subgroup analysis of patients with severe pancreatitis showed a statistically significant decrease in morbidity and a numerical benefit in mortality. Fan and coworkers[72] randomized 195 patients with pancreatitis of any etiology to receive ERC with sphincterotomy for choledocholithiasis within 24 hours

Table 46–1. Morbidity in Acute Biliary Pancreatitis Treated with Urgent Endoscopic Retrograde Cholangiography with Sphincterotomy Compared with Conservative Therapy

| Reference | Severe* | Stones† | Morbid Events | | RRR | ARR | NNT‡ |
			ERC	Controls			
Neoptolemos, et al.[71] (N = 121)	44%	85%	17%	34%	50%	17%	6
Fan, et al.[72] (N = 195)	42%	66%	18%	29%	39%	11%	9
Nowak, et al.[73] (N = 280)	NR‡	NR‡	17%	36%	53%	16%	6
Fölsch, et al.[74] (N = 238)	14%	46%	46%	51%	20%	5%	20
Pooled data (N = 854)	30%	61%	25%	38%	35%	13%	8

*Severe acute pancreatitis; †bile duct stones; ‡number needed to treat to prevent one morbid event.
ARR, absolute risk reduction; ERC, endoscopic retrograde cholangiography; RRR, relative risk reduction.
Modified from Sharma.[70]

Table 46–2. Mortality in Acute Biliary Pancreatitis Treated with Urgent Endoscopic Retrograde Cholangiography with Sphincterotomy Compared with Conservative Therapy

Reference	Mortality ERC	Mortality Controls	RRR	ARR	NNT
Neoptolemos, et al.[71] (N = 121)	1.7%	8.1%	79%	6.4%	15.6
Fan, et al.[72] (N = 195)	5.2%	9.2%	43.5%	4%	25
Nowak, et al.[73] (N = 280)	2.3%	12.8%	82%	10.5%	9.5
Fölsch, et al.[74] (N = 238)	11.1%	6.3%	−77.4%	−4.8%	−20.8
Pooled data (N = 854)	5.2%	9.1%	42.9%	3.9%	25.6

ARR, absolute risk reduction; ERC, endoscopic retrograde cholangiography; NNT, number needed to treat to prevent 1 death; RRR, relative risk reduction.
Modified from Sharma.[70]

of hospitalization. The overall outcomes were similar for the treatment and control groups, but in those with severe pancreatitis, morbidity was significantly less frequent at 13% versus 54% ($p = .003$), respectively. There was a trend toward improved respective mortality rates in the ERC group at 3% versus 18% ($p = .097$). It is noteworthy that biliary sepsis occurred less commonly in patients with severe disease treated with ERC than conservative management at zero and 29% ($p < .001$), respectively. An issue with this study is the type II error introduced by inclusion of patients with pancreatitis of all causes.

In a multicenter German study, 238 subjects were randomly assigned to ERC with sphincterotomy and stone extraction as needed within 72 hours of symptom onset or conservative management. Patients with cholangitis or a total bilirubin of 5 mg/dL or more were excluded. Twenty of the 112 patients randomized to conservative management went on to ERC and 13 had stones extracted. The overall morbidity rates were similar between the ERC and control groups. However, there were more serious complications, mostly resulting from respiratory failure ($p = .03$), and fewer episodes of cholangitis in the treatment group. Fourteen treatment and seven control patients died, and respiratory failure accounted for the majority of deaths in the treatment group. Pancreatic morbidity rates were similar between the treatment and control groups at 23% and 22%, respectively. The authors concluded that early ERC with sphincterotomy is not beneficial in patients with acute biliary pancreatitis and no obstructive jaundice or cholangitis. Problems with this study are that there are significantly fewer patients with stones and severe disease than in the other studies and that 19 of the 22 centers enrolled less than two subjects per year on average. Respiratory failure was the main problem in the

ERC group, but the rates are much higher than in other studies. Considering the low volume at some of the centers and the undue rates of respiratory failure, questions have been raised about the degree of endoscopic expertise and potential for procedure-related aspiration.[74]

Nowak and colleagues[73] reported in abstract form a single center study of 280 consecutive patients with suspected biliary pancreatitis. Duodenoscopy was performed on all cases within 24 hours of admission, and 75 persons with an impacted stone grossly seen in the papilla had sphincterotomy with extraction. The remaining patients were randomized to have ERC or conservative management. The persons with impacted stones and those that had ERC were combined for the analysis. There were significantly fewer complications and deaths in the treatment group than in the control group for patients with both mild and severe pancreatitis. These authors also found an association between earlier intervention and better outcomes. However, inadequate data are available for rigorous review of this abstract.

From these data, it appears that ERC with sphincterotomy and stone extraction improves outcomes in patients with severe biliary pancreatitis because of avoidance and treatment of cholangitis, without a well-demonstrated effect on pancreatitis.

A rational therapeutic approach is to perform ERC within 24 to 72 hours in patients with severe pancreatitis and concomitant cholangitis and/or other signs of biliary obstruction including jaundice, significant hepatic enzyme elevations, and/or bile duct dilatation. It is also reasonable to consider ERC in patients with mild to moderate biliary pancreatitis that appears to be associated with biliary obstruction as outlined previously and in persons with a persistent or deteriorating course. Sphincterotomy should be performed for stone extraction and in the absence of bile duct stones when cholecystectomy is not anticipated because of comorbidities. This approach also applies during pregnancy to temporize until after delivery when cholecystectomy can be more safely performed. One small study showed that about 90% of gallstone pancreatitis patients do well for about 3 years after sphincterotomy and stone extraction without cholecystectomy.[42] However, close follow-up is prudent in this circumstance. ERCP is not generally indicated for mild to moderate biliary pancreatitis without signs of obstruction. Laparoscopic cholecystectomy with IOC soon after the pancreatitis has resolved is optimal. The role of EUS and MRCP to diagnose stones in a less invasive fashion and then to perform ERC on persons with positive results remains uncertain.[38,44,75]

ACUTE CHOLANGITIS

The initial therapy is medical with supportive care, blood cultures, parenteral vitamin K supplementation, and empiric antibiotics. Up to 90% of patients respond to medical therapy within 12 to 24 hours and may then have semielective biliary drainage by ERC. Those that do not respond require urgent or emergent drainage, preferably by ERC.[46,76] Some appropriate regimens include monotherapy with fluoroquinolones, piperacillin/tazobactam, imipenem/cilastatin, or meropenem, or therapy with extended-spectrum cephalosporins with or without metronidazole or clindamycin for enhanced anaerobic coverage. There are also many other recommended regimens, but aminoglycoside and ampicillin are no longer appropriate because of the increased risk of aminoglycoside nephrotoxicity with obstructive jaundice and bacterial resistance to ampicillin.[46]

PTC is successful in up to 90% of all patients with biliary obstruction, but morbidity including bleeding, pseudoaneurysms, peritonitis, bile fistulas, infections, and strictures occur in 30% to 80%, and mortality occurs in 5% to 17% of those with cholangitis.[9,77] ERC is more effective, has lower morbidity and mortality rates, and is preferred over PTC.[46,63,78–81] However, PTC may be indicated in unusual circumstances such as intrahepatic stones, surgically altered duodenal anatomy, or failed ERC.

The traditional therapy for cholangitis is open surgery, but currently this is rarely performed as first-line therapy because of high rates of morbidity and mortality.[82] Lai and colleagues[79] demonstrated in a randomized controlled trial in cholangitis patients that ERC with sphincterotomy compared with open choledochotomy

was associated with morbidity in 34% and 66% and in-hospital mortality in 10% and 32%, respectively. Operative mortality is associated with the severity of illness at the time of surgery with rates of 40% for emergent, 16% for urgent, and 3% for elective procedures reported.[76] Randomized controlled trials in the setting of laparoscopic cholecystectomy show that laparoscopic bile duct exploration is equivalent to ERC with sphincterotomy for bile duct stone clearance and morbidity and mortality rates but has shorter hospital stays.[82–84] However, the outcomes of laparoscopic bile duct exploration in patients with cholangitis are unknown because only a few patients with mild cholangitis have been studied and none with severe cholangitis.[82] One-stage laparoscopic cholecystectomy with bile duct exploration seems appropriate for cholangitis patients with gallstones who respond to medical therapy, are clinically stable, and are good surgical candidates. Such surgery should not be performed in persons who are unstable or who have had prior cholecystectomy.[82] ERC with sphincterotomy and stone extraction is the preferred procedure for persons with acute cholangitis who are critically ill and/or have had prior cholecystectomy. It is also appropriate for stable persons with cholelithiasis when expertise in laparoscopic bile duct exploration is not available. ERC may be performed in the standard fashion in stable patients with normal coagulation studies. However, persons with cholangitis often have septic shock with associated hypotension, multiorgan failure, disseminated intravascular coagulopathy, and coagulopathy from vitamin K malabsorption because of biliary obstruction. In these circumstances, it is generally best to rapidly provide temporizing biliary drainage with stenting or a nasobiliary drain without sphincterotomy or stone extraction. It is our policy to do these procedures under general anesthesia with endotracheal intubation. It is wise to aspirate and decompress the biliary system before injecting contrast material to avoid further increasing the biliary pressure with potential to exacerbate hematogenous seeding with bacteria and endotoxins. A stent may be placed in the normal fashion by passing a guidewire upstream to the obstructing stone and then inserting the endoprosthesis. Pus under pressure may be seen to emanate around the cannulating catheter and/or through the stent (Fig. 46–13). Nasobiliary drainage entails passing a guidewire above the obstructing stone and then advancing a 7-Fr drainage catheter over the wire and upstream to the stone. Pigtail catheters anchor above the stones and are more stable than straight catheters. The endoscope is then removed over the drainage catheter while

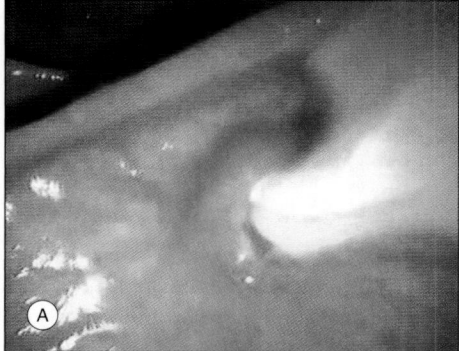
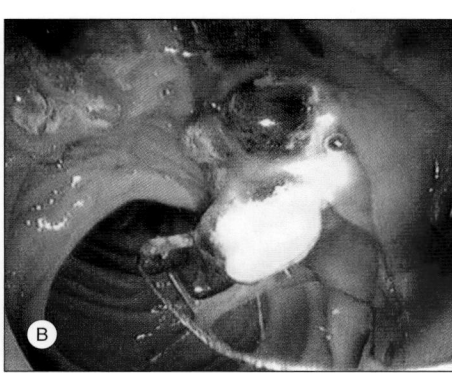

Figure 46–13. *A,* Purulent drainage from the major papilla after cannulation indicative of suppurative cholangitis. *B,* Extracted stone with pus.

Table 46–3. Randomized Controlled Trials of Choledocholithiasis Patients Treated with Endoscopic Sphincterotomy and Stone Extraction Alone Compared with Bile Duct Clearance and Cholecystectomy

	Sphincterotomy			Cholecystectomy	
	N	Symptoms	Surgery	N	Symptoms
Hammarstrom, et al.[91]	39	16 (41%)	14 (36%)	41	2 (5%)
Targarona, et al. [100]	46	10 (22%)	7 (15%)	43	3 (6%)
Boerma, et al.[101]	59	27 (47%)	22 (37%)	49	1 (2%)

Comparisons between the treatment groups for symptoms were each statistically significant with p < .05 or smaller.

advancing the catheter to maintain position, without looping in the stomach, under fluoroscopic guidance. These authors maintain the guidewire in the catheter for additional rigidity to minimize gastric looping. A 14-Fr tube is then passed through a nostril, grasped in the posterior pharynx, and pulled out through the mouth. The drainage catheter is digitally pinioned to the posterior pharynx to prevent dislodgement and the proximal end is inserted into the oral end of the 14-Fr naso-oral catheter. The naso-oral catheter along with the drainage catheter are then pulled outward through the nostril until it is straight in the pharynx while maintaining digital fixation pressure on the drainage catheter in the posterior pharynx. The digital pressure is then released and the drainage catheter is aspirated and irrigated, and a cholangiogram is obtained to verify the position above the stone. The drainage catheter is then fixed to the nose, face, and torso; connected to a bile bag; and set to gravity drainage. The catheter may then be irrigated every 6 to 8 hours to maintain patency. The outcomes of stenting and nasobiliary drainage appear to be similar, and we prefer stenting because in our hands it is quicker and easier and has no external segment of the drain that could lead to accidental displacement.[80] There is often rapid recovery after drainage, and ERCP can be repeated with definitive sphincterotomy and stone extraction once the patient is stable and the coagulopathy has resolved.

ENDOSCOPIC BILE DUCT STONE EXTRACTION AS DEFINITIVE THERAPY WITH THE GALLBLADDER *IN SITU*

Patients with choledocholithiasis who are fit for surgery should have bile duct stone clearance and cholecystectomy. Endoscopic sphincterotomy with bile duct stone extraction will cure the initiating episode related to choledocholithiasis. However, the need for subsequent cholecystectomy in persons with intact gallbladders with or without gallstones has long been debated. After biliary sphincterotomy, there is a marked decrease in lithogenicity of gallbladder and hepatic bile.[85] Results from 14 cohort studies reported over 2 decades involving 1228 patients with choledocholithiasis and *in situ* gallbladders followed for a median of 37 months (range, 2 to 156 months) show that a mean of 14% of patients ultimately went to cholecystectomy.[86–99] Frequent symptoms and complications included biliary colic, jaundice, cholecystitis, cholangitis, choledocholithiasis, pancreatitis, bile leaks, and papillary stenosis. Predisposing factors include gallstones, complete opacification of the gallbladder at ERCP, bile duct dilatation, and periampullary diverticula.[91,95,99]

However, three randomized controlled studies show that rates of symptoms and complications are statistically significantly less for surgery than for sphincterotomy as shown in Table 46–3.[91,100,101]

ENDOSCOPIC BALLOON DILATATION OF THE SPHINCTER OF ODDI FOR EXTRACTION OF BILE DUCT STONES

Endoscopic balloon dilatation of the sphincter of Oddi for stone extraction should be avoided in routine practice. Compared with sphincterotomy, papillary balloon dilatation is associated with increased rates of morbidity and may cause death from pancreatitis.[54] Endoscopic sphincterotomy for removal of bile duct stones is associated with short-term morbidity in about 5% of patients.[63] Medium-term (6 to 15 years) morbidity occurs in 6% to 24% of patients and can usually be managed with endoscopic techniques, but long-term outcomes remain unknown.[97,102,103] Endoscopic balloon dilatation of the sphincter of Oddi has been proposed to prevent late-occurring morbidity from sphincterotomy. Persons who may benefit most from this procedure are the young and healthy laparoscopic cholecystectomy patients who have sphincterotomy for choledocholithiasis.

The technique of endoscopic balloon dilatation involves passing a wire-guided balloon dilatation catheter to the biliary sphincter. The balloon is then inflated with diluted radiographic contrast material to maximum pressure. The technique is not standardized: various authorities inflated the balloon rapidly or slowly, immediately deflated it, or left it inflated for 1 to 2 minutes, and some reinflated the balloon a second time. Fluoroscopy is generally used to document complete inflation with obliteration of the waist in the middle of the balloon. The diameter of the balloon is generally selected to be equal to the diameter of the stone and never larger than the diameter of the bile duct. Stones are then removed with standard balloon and basket techniques, as shown in Figure 46–14. Wire-guided instruments may facilitate the procedure. For large stones, dilatation to a smaller caliber can be performed, and mechanical lithotripsy followed by balloon sweeping is used to crush and extract all of the stone material. Some authorities place a pancreatic duct stent in the standard fashion.

From three uncontrolled series of sphincter of Oddi balloon dilatation involving 435 persons, it appears that initial bile duct clearance was achieved in 68% of patients; the remainder required two or more ERCPs and occasionally sphincterotomy, surgery, or other therapy. Thirty-five percent of these patients required

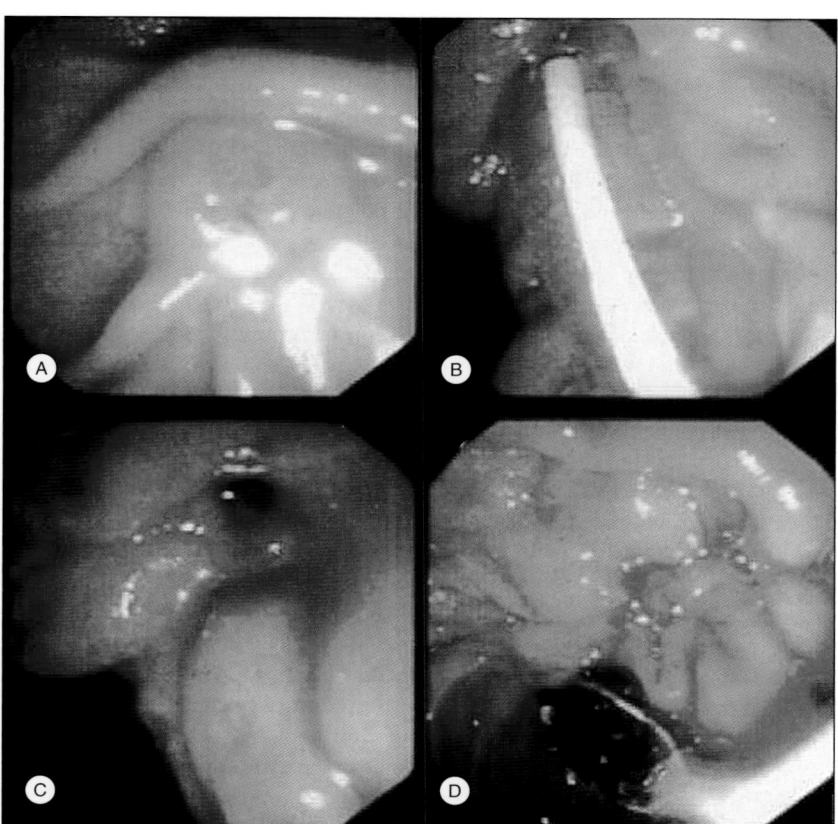

Figure 46–14. *A,* Normal intact papilla. *B,* An inflated dilatation balloon straightens the biliary sphincter. *C,* Opened papilla after dilatation. *D,* Pigment stones are extracted with a basket.

Table 46–4. Randomized Studies with More than 200 Subjects of Balloon Dilation of the Sphincter of Oddi Compared with Sphincterotomy for Stone Removal

	DiSario, et al[54]		Bergman, et al[51]		Fujita, et al[53]		Vlavianos, et al[50]	
	ED	ES	ED	ES	ED	ES	ED	ES
Patients								
Number	117	120	101	101	138	144	103	99
Age, years	47*	54*	72†	71†	67*	68*	61*	62*
Stones								
Size, mm	6*	5*	10†	9†	7*	7.3*	40% ≥ 10 mm	42% ≥ 10 mm
Number	1*	1*	2†	1†	2.5*	2.4*	39% ≥ 3	25% ≥ 3
Procedures								
Success‡	114 (97%)	111 (93%)	90 (89%)	92 (91%)	105 (76%)	113 (78%)	65 (63%)	63(64%)
Cross-over	11 (9%)	0	9 (9%)	0	3 (2%)	0	5 (5%)	1 (1%)
Morbidity								
Total	21 (18%)§	4 (3%)§	17 (17%)§	23 (23%)§	21 (15%)§	17 (12%)§	21 (15%)‖	17 (12%)‖
Severe	8 (7%)§	0§	4 (4%)§	3 (3%)§	¶	¶	≥1 (1%)¶	≥1 (1%)¶
Mortality	2 (1.7%)	0	1 (1%)	0	0	0	0	1 (1%)**

*Mean; †median; ‡removal of all stones at the initial procedure; §consensus criteria[49]; ‖partial consensus criteria[49]; ¶incomplete data reported; **cardiopulmonary arrest.
ED, endoscopic balloon dilatation; ES, endoscopic sphincterotomy.

mechanical lithotripsy. Morbidity occurred in at least 7% to 19% of these patients and was mostly due to pancreatitis.[104–106] Problems with interpreting these studies include the fact that two seem retrospective with potential underestimation of complications.[104,105] All of these reports are from tertiary centers, the patients were relatively old, and standardized morbidity criteria were not consistently used.[49] Another confounding variable was that gabexate

was given to decrease morbidity from pancreatitis in one series[106] and may have been used in another.[104]

There are five randomized controlled clinical trials from tertiary centers comparing balloon dilatation with sphincterotomy; three of these studies with more than 200 subjects are summarized in Table 46–4. The patients were relatively old and sick, harbored large and numerous stones, often had periampullary diverticula, and did not always have cholecystectomy. Multiple procedures were often required, mechanical lithotripsy and precut sphincterotomy were often used, procedures may have been terminated prematurely, and gabexate use was not always specified.[50–53,107] The study methodologies were not always rigorous. They may lack a predefined sample size, not verify sequential enrollment with potential for selection bias, and inconsistently use standardized criteria for overall and severe morbidity.[50,52,53] At least one dilatation patient who suffered morbidity was excluded from analysis.[53] One study found no advantage to balloon dilatation after 24 hours and after 12 months.[50]

DiSario and colleagues[54] performed a randomized, controlled, multicenter, international study involving equal numbers of community-based and academic practices. The patients were representative of those having laparoscopic cholecystectomy in routine clinical practice in that they were younger and healthier, had small stones that were few in number, and did not have complicated anatomy, and most had cholecystectomy before or within 30 days of the ERCP. The procedures were generally straightforward without mechanical lithotripsy or precut sphincterotomy. The study had a predefined primary endpoint and sample size determination and an independent oversight board. The study was stopped at the first interim analysis because a statistically significant difference in the primary endpoint was found with more overall morbidity in the dilatation group. There were also significantly more severe complications, two deaths from pancreatitis, and greater resource utilization and patient days away for normal activities in the dilatation group. Multivariate analysis showed that balloon dilatation was the only factor associated with complications.

The study by DiSario and colleagues[54] and the study by Bergman and coworkers[51] have analogous methodology and the results can be compared. Overall and severe complications after balloon dilatation occurred in 18% and 4% in Bergman and coworkers' series and in 18% and 6.8% in DiSario and colleagues' study, respectively. However, the DiSario and colleagues study had mild to moderate morbidity associated with sphincterotomy in only 3.3% of subjects but Bergman and coworkers detected overall and severe morbidity in 24% and 3%, respectively. These sphincterotomy-related morbidity rates reflect Bergman and coworkers' older, sicker, and more complicated tertiary referral center patients, but these results are very much higher than the rates observed in younger and healthier patients treated in a broad-spectrum of practices. Two large-scale multicenter studies showed less than 5% morbidity after sphincterotomy performed for stones.[49,63] Papillary balloon dilatation was found to the most significant risk factor or pancreatitis found in

another well-designed, multicenter series of 1966 ERCPs with an adjusted odds ratio of 4.5 (95% confidence interval [CI] 1.51 to 113.46, $p = .0027$).[108] A randomized controlled clinical trial by Arnold and colleagues[107] also showed excessive overall and severe complication rates with dilatation compared with sphincterotomy that compelled the authors to terminate the study prematurely.

Balloon dilatation of the sphincter of Oddi may result in edema and/or spasm with obstruction of the pancreatic duct or papillary edema with impaction of stones not extracted. This may cause pancreatitis or cholangitis.[49,107,109,110] However, most retained stones spontaneously pass after sphincterotomy. Some authors have proposed placement of pancreatic duct endoprostheses or medical therapy to minimize balloon dilatation-induced pancreatitis, but these interventions have not been adequately studied.[109,110]

Although papillary balloon dilatation has been proposed to prevent the late-occurring complications of sphincterotomy, there are insufficient data postdilatation to support this concept. There appears to be some incomplete return of function 12 to 15 months after dilatation, but chronic inflammation occurs from 2 to 63 months postdilatation.[52,111–114] Although the clinical outcomes are not known, there may be potential to develop advanced fibrosis and stenosis.

Papillary balloon dilatation may be appropriate for patients with severe coagulopathies and altered surgical anatomy that make standard sphincterotomy more difficult and risky.[115,116] However, this may simply replace bleeding or perforation with pancreatitis, and pancreatic duct stenting seems reasonable if papillary balloon dilatation is used for these conditions.

DIFFICULT STONES

Eighty-five percent to ninety percent of bile duct stones can be removed by standard techniques, and the remainder are considered difficult. What constitutes a difficult stone is subjective, but this may include impacted stones, large stones, intrahepatic stones, recurrent stones, and Mirizzi's syndrome. There are various techniques available for each of these circumstances.

Impacted Stones

Impacted stones at the ampulla should first be approached by attempting to pass a guidewire or catheter upstream into the duct or to slightly dislodge the stone upstream by pushing with a catheter (Fig. 46–15). If a wire or instrument can be passed above the stone, a sphincterotomy can be preformed and the stone extracted in the usual fashion. If the instruments will not pass the impacted stone, an

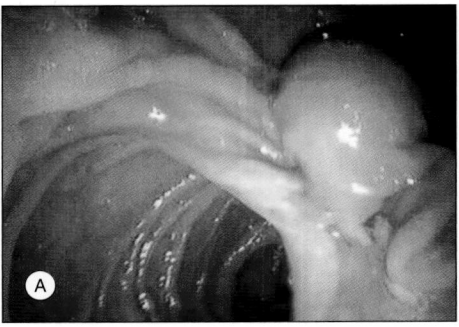
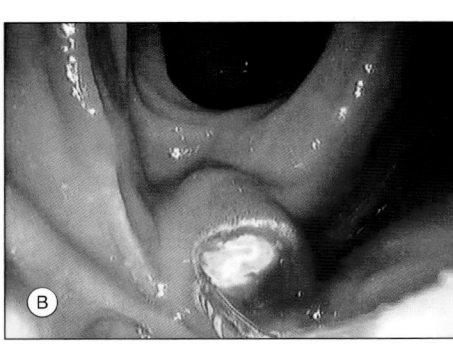

Figure 46–15. *A,* Bulging major papilla resulting from an impacted stone. *B,* An impacted stone is seen at the orifice of the major papilla, and a sphincterotome is inserted below.

access or precut papillotomy may be required. Using a need knife or a sphincterotome with the cutting wire extending over the distal tip, the attenuated papillary tissue encasing the impacted stone is incised in the direction of the bile duct at the 11 o'clock orientation. This requires an experienced endoscopist with excellent control of the instruments. Once the incision alleviates the impaction, the stone usually pops out spontaneously. However, it may be necessary to probe with the precut papillotome or an atraumatic guidewire until an instrument passes above the stone. Extension of the sphincterotomy can then be performed with a standard sphincterotome.

Precut sphincterotomy is associated with increased rates of overall and severe complications compared with standard sphincterotomy. However, precutting is used to gain access to the duct in a complicated situation that requires therapy. The risks for precutting are less with a dilated bile duct and when the incision is made on an attenuated papilla, as is often the case with an impacted stone.[63,117]

Large Stones

Large stones are generally considered to be 10 mm or lager across the greatest span. They are often brown or mixed stones and are often impacted. Endoscopic extraction may be challenging because of the frequent presence of periampullary diverticula, the sheer volume of stone material, and the difficulty in entrapping very large stones in Dormia baskets. One series showed that only 12% of stones larger than 15 mm could be removed with standard sphincterotomy and techniques.[118]

A large sphincterotomy is required to effectively remove large stones. Thus, the first endoscopic maneuver is to create a large sphincterotomy or to extend it if there has been prior failed sphincterotomy. If a guidewire or catheter can be passed upstream to the stone, it can often be removed with standard techniques or mechanical lithotripsy, or a stent can be placed to provide drainage and break the stone over time. Alternatively, transendoscopic electrohydraulic lithotripsy (EHL) or laser lithotripsy, or ESWL may be performed. One series of 108 patients with unsuccessful stone extraction by standard techniques showed success with mechanical lithotripsy in 33, EHL lithotripsy in 65, and ESWL in 7 of 10 with intrahepatic stones.[62]

Intracorporeal Lithotripsy

Mechanical lithotripsy is a technique that is used when the stone is too large to be pulled out of the sphincterotomy and is entrapped in a basket with securely welded wires. The basket is then winched down against a metal sheath until the stone abuts the sheath, and continued pressure from retraction of the basket shatters the stone or breaks the basket (Fig. 46–16). There are devices that pass through the working channel of the duodenoscope. They are manufactured as a single unit or a sheath that can be inserted over the long wire shaft of a basket that has become impacted at the bile duct orifice and then attached to a winch. From a compilation of three series, involving 487 patients, mechanical lithotripsy was successful at clearing the bile duct in 86%, with morbidity in 7%, and eventual biliary drainage surgery in 6%.[59,61,119] Success at lithotripsy is indirectly related to stone size with total clearance in 90% with stones smaller than 10 mm and only 68% with stones larger than 28 mm.[59] Mechanical lithotripsy is a straightforward technology that should be present in all endoscopic units that perform stone extractions.

Intracorporeal lithotripsy can also be performed with EHL or laser probes under direct visualization via a choledochoscope passed through the duodenoscope. The probe can be aimed at stone and correctly positioned to prevent bile duct trauma. These techniques require two endoscopists: one for the mother scope (duodenoscope) and another for the baby scope (4.5- or 3.0-mm miniscope choledochoscope). The baby scopes are very fragile. A light source and processing unit are required for each instrument. There must be an irrigation system to maintain visualization and flush debris out of the bile duct. This can be done with a pneumatic pressure cuff over an intravenous solution bag connected to a nasobiliary drain or the irrigation port of the baby scope. The endoscopist with the mother scope controls most of the motion of the baby scope, mainly with gentle torque on the insertion tube. The baby scope has tip deflection in one axis only allowing minimal capacity for steering. During lithotripsy, stone fragments often obscure visualization in the bile duct and continuous irrigation is required. It is crucial to keep the probe oriented directly at the stone to prevent trauma to the duct.

EHL produces shockwaves by generating high-voltage sparks that vaporize fluid and transmit this energy through a small-caliber (3-Fr/1 mm) probe. The probe is positioned about 1 mm from the stone

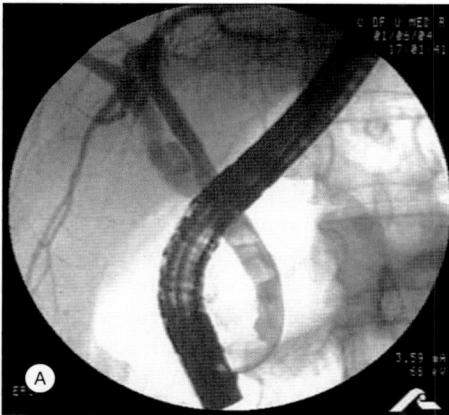
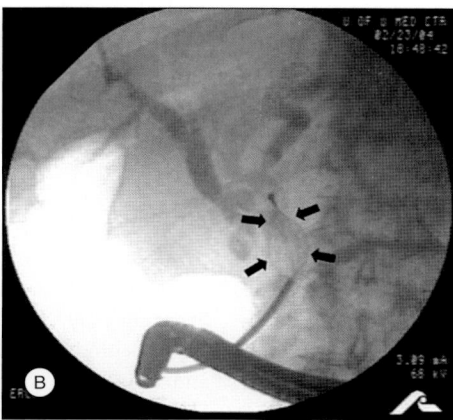

Figure 46–16. *A,* Cholangiogram with medium to large stones. *B,* The *arrows* point to a stone entrapped in a mechanical lithotripsy basket. Note the metal sheath winched against to lower end of the basket.

and aimed directly at it. The shockwave energy is activated by a foot switch and is repeated until the stone is fragmented. Centering balloons and basket catheters are also available to aim the probe under fluoroscopic guidance without choledochoscopy. However, aberrantly aimed shockwaves cause ductal trauma and perforation. Data from five series involving 185 patients with bile duct stones refractory to standard endoscopic therapy exhibit complete ductal clearance in 85% with minimal morbidity. Repeated procedures are sometimes required.[55,62,120–122] Morbidity is reported in about 9% of patients and is usually mild.[121]

There are three endoscopic laser lithotripsy systems for bile duct stones: Q-switched neodymium:yttrium-aluminum-garnet (Nd:YAG), flashlamp pulsed dye, and flashlamp pulsed dye with an automatic stone recognition system. Continuous laser energy generates excessive heat with associated tissue damage and is not appropriate for lithotripsy. Pulsed laser energy shatters stones by a shockwave effect. The Q-switched Nd:YAG laser is more powerful than the others but requires a 600-μm quartz fiber with a coupling device. This fiber is larger and stiffer than those of the flashlamp lasers, and the unit is cumbersome for endoscopic use.[9] The pigment in bile duct stones absorbs laser light of a 504-μm wavelength generated by coumarin dye in the flashlamp pulsed dye laser, and the energy is spread only within the stone. The flashlamp pulsed dye with an automatic stone recognition system uses rhodamine 6-G dye to create a 595-μm wavelength. This laser delivers energy only to the stone that is identified by a spectroscopic analysis of reflected laser light. The flashlamp lasers have a 200 to 320-μm quartz fiber and no coupler making them more suitable to endoscopic use.[9] Both flashlamp lasers have been shown to fragment bile duct stones with equal efficacy and without significant bile duct damage in animals.[121] From a compilation of series involving the 504-μm and the 595-μm flashlamp lasers for refractory bile duct stones, 92% of patients had complete clearance of stones.[58,121,123,124] Higher rates of stone clearance were obtained by performing ESWL on patients with incomplete clearance. One laser procedure was generally sufficient, but a few patients with very large and multiple stones needed two or three sessions. Morbidity is reported in about 7% of patients; is usually mild; and includes transient hemobilia, cholangitis, and pancreatitis.[121] There were no episodes of significant bile duct trauma despite the fact that most cases were only under fluoroscopic guidance. In comparative studies, laser lithotripsy was more effective, required fewer sessions, and had a shorter duration of therapy than did ESWL.[123,124] The holmium:YAG laser is a small, portable unit that requires no special plumbing and is often used for urologic lithotripsy. However, the fibers are somewhat stiff. Although the data are scarce, it appears to also be effective for bile duct stones.[125]

Extracorporeal Shockwave Lithotripsy

ESWL focuses high-pressure shockwave energy at a desired point while minimizing the pressure in the adjacent tissue. The are different methods to generate the shockwaves, but all systems require the shockwaves to travel through water to minimize energy loss. The contact with the patient is with a water-filled compressible bag with a gel. When shockwaves traverse the stone, the surface becomes cavitated, and changes in acoustic impedance release compressive and tensile forces resulting in fragmentation. The properties of the stone that determine fragmentation are the size, microcrystalline structure, and architecture and not the chemical makeup.[126]

The patient is positioned on the lithotripter, and the stone is identified by ultrasonography or fluoroscopy. The shockwaves are usually delivered from the back for the bile duct or over the liver for intrahepatic stones to avoid interposition of gas-filled intestinal loops. This usually requires prior placement of or nasobiliary drain for cholangiography or a biliary stent adjacent to the stone as a target. Prophylactic antibiotics and sedation and analgesia are given. The energy is delivered and cholangiography is performed. If fragmentation has occurred, the debris is usually removed by endoscopic or percutaneous methods. If adequate fragmentation has not occurred, ESWL may be repeated at intervals of about 1 week.

Review of 11 series involving 818 patients with refractory bile duct stones treated with ESWL published over 15 years showed complete stone clearance in 84%.[57,120,123,124,127–132] One to two procedures were generally required (ranging from one to eight procedures). Short-term morbidity occurred in 14% from evaluable studies and included pain, hemobilia, cholangitis, sepsis, hematomas, pancreatitis, hematuria, ileus, and anesthesia problems. Mortality occurred in less than 1% of patients and developed in the setting of advanced age, serious comorbidities, and concomitant cholangitis.[132] It appears that ductal clearance is inversely related to the stone size but not necessarily the number of stones.[130] Stone recurrence documented by symptoms, imaging studies, and/or serum enzyme levels is reported in about 13% of patients at a mean of about 13 months. This may be due to incomplete duct clearance after ESWL.[127,129] Randomized controlled studies show that intracorporeal laser lithotripsy is more effecting at achieving complete ductal clearance than ESWL at about 92% and 66%, respectively.[123,124] However, complete clearance was achieved in similar proportions of patients randomized to ESWL (79%) and EHL (75%).[120] Crossing over to another lithotripsy modality improved the ductal clearance rates to 94% to 100%.[120,123,124]

PTC with antegrade instrumentation, choledochoscopy, and/or the modalities described previously is another option. PTC techniques achieve ductal clearance in 80% to 97% of cases but often require multiple procedures. Percutaneous tubes are usually left in place for several weeks.[133–137] Minor complications are frequent and include pain, fever, and local infections. Serious morbidity from pancreatitis (10%), bleeding (2.5%), sepsis (2.5%), and pneumothoraces (0.5%), and deaths are reported. Other complications include subcapsular hepatic hematomas, hepatic artery aneurysms, cholangitis, peritonitis, bilomas, gallstone ileus, and premature tube displacement and may require surgery or other invasive procedures.[77,133–137] Surgery for bile duct stones is generally reserved as a last resort.

Stents

Biliary drainage with nasobiliary drains or stents is required to prevent cholangitis when large stoned cannot be removed at ERCP as shown in Figure 46–17. However, nasobiliary drains are cumbersome to place, and are uncomfortable and unsightly for the patient. Stenting may be used to temporize until a definitive procedure is performed or as long-term therapy in people with advanced age and/or serious comorbidities and a severely limited life span. However, mid- to long-term morbidity and mortality rates are high,

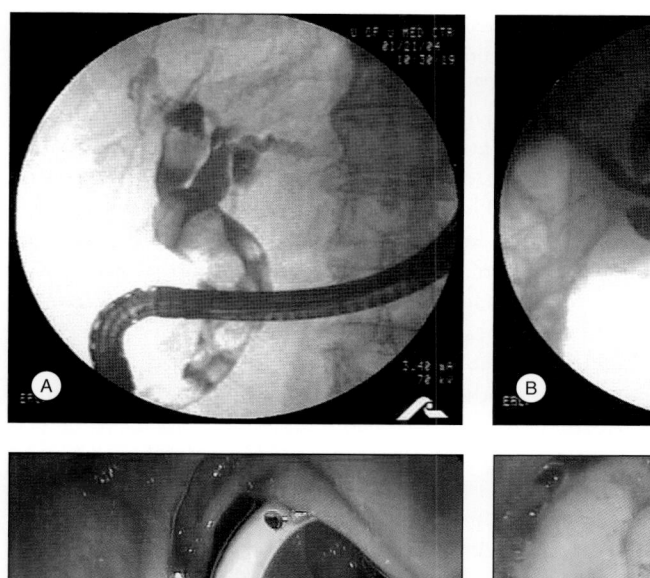

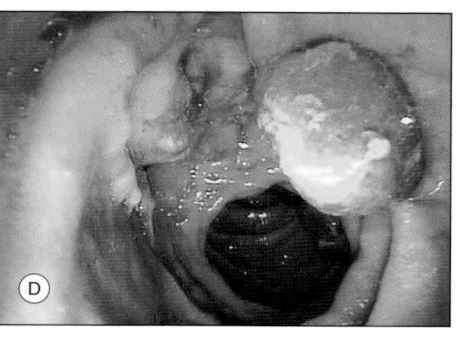

Figure 46–17. *A,* An endoscopic cholangiogram shows several large bile duct stones that could not be extracted with sphincterotomy and mechanical lithotripsy. *B,* A 10-Fr double-pigtailed stent has been placed and is outlined by the *white arrows.* A large stone is demonstrated by the *black arrows. C,* The duodenal end of the pigtailed stent. *D,* A large, mostly cholesterol stone is successfully extracted with a basket 4 weeks later.

and careful patient selection is crucial. The stents may act as a wick allowing bile drainage through or alongside the stent once it becomes obstructed. Friction from the stent may wear down or break stones. Sphincterotomy is performed and one or two straight or pigtailed 7- or 10-Fr stents can be placed in virtually all cases. Stents placed for a mean of 2 to 9 months have been shown to induce stone shrinkage and disappearance and to facilitate removal at a subsequent ERCP.[138] Ursodeoxycholic acid appears to facilitate this process.[139] Recent cohort studies involving 196 elderly and sick patients treated with stenting for refractory stones and followed for means of 2 to 39 months showed serious morbidity in 33%, usually resulting from cholangitis, and related mortality in 6%. Cholangitis developed at means ranging from 2 to 39 months.[138,140–142] In comparative studies, there were significantly higher late morbidity rates with stenting than routine stone extraction (36% vs. 14%), EHL (63% vs. 8%), or surgery (36% vs. 8%) and elevated overall mortality rates with stenting over EHL (74% vs. 41%).[55,140,142]

HEPATOLITHIASIS

Primary intrahepatic stones are associated with ductal strictures and secondary stones are gallstones or bile duct stones that have refluxed into the intrahepatic system. Primary stones occur mainly in eastern Asians who are rural dwellers and of lower socioeconomic status. These stones are associated with parasitic infestations including *Clonorchis sinensis,* biliary infections, congenital factors, ductal abnormalities, and intrahepatic cholangiocarcinoma. In Caucasians, primary intrahepatic stones are associated with prior hepatobiliary surgery, strictures, cystic fibrosis, and Caroli's disease. The intrahepatic ducts are dilated and contain multiple stones, often of

mixed composition. Patients have recurrent bouts of pain, fever, and jaundice that require repeated operations or other invasive therapies.[143] Secondary intrahepatic stones may be treated with ERCP techniques with or without intracorporeal lithotripsy. However, primary stones are difficult to treat from a transpapillary approach because of duct angulation, multiple strictures, and peripheral stone impaction. Sphincterotomy should be avoided unless definitive therapy is assured because of increased risks of recurrent cholangitis. However, clearance of intrahepatic stones was achieved in 64% of 36 patients treated with peroral cholangioscopic lithotripsy with morbidity in 1 (3%) and recurrences in 22% with almost 8 years follow-up.[144]

Recent reports show that PTC with intracorporeal lithotripsy has been reported to result in complete stone clearance in 77% to 85% of patients with morbidity in 1.6% to 22%.[145,146] With 1 to 22 years follow-up, recurrence of stones or cholangitis developed in about 63% and was directly proportional to duration of follow-up at a median of 11 to 18 years. Symptomatic recurrence was more frequent in persons with ductal dilatation and strictures and occurred sooner in those with strictures. Cholangitis and cholangiocarcinoma developed more often in persons with residual stones than those without at 44% and 16% and 6.6% and 0.7%, respectively.[145,146] ESWL has also been used successfully with lesser clearance rates.[56,57,120,124,128,129,131,147] However, in combination with intracorporeal lithotripsy more than 90% of intrahepatic stones can be cleared.[49] Patients with stones associated with strictures do not respond as well.

Hepatic resection or hepaticojejunostomy, usually with intraoperative and/or postoperative choledochoscopy and lithotripsy, may be performed on selected patients with hepatolithiasis.

Resection is generally indicated for segments with parenchymal atrophy, multiple abscesses, and/or intrahepatic cholangiocarcinomas. Patients with resection fare better those with biliary-enteric anastomoses with operative morbidity in 20% and 16%, mortality in 2% and 6%, residual stones in 2% to 60% and 44% to 90%, recurrent stones in 16% and 33%, and cholangitis in 3% and 31%, respectively.[125,148,149]

MIRIZZI'S SYNDROME

The Mirizzi's syndrome is a rare disorder that occurs when a gallstone is entrapped in the gallbladder neck or cystic duct and causes obstruction or fistula of the bile duct. The appearance on direct cholangiography is that of an extrinsic obstruction with smooth tapering of the proximal and distal margins. Making the diagnosis requires an index of suspicion and careful interpretation of direct cholangiography and a high-quality MRCP or intraductal ultrasound scan. Endoscopic therapy is challenging, and standard techniques usually fail. However, bile duct stenting and/or intracorporeal or extracorporeal lithotripsy can be successful.[150] Surgery is often complicated, and open conversion is often required. However, laparoscopic techniques are possible, and it is important to have a preoperative diagnosis to minimize the complications and conversion rates.[151]

SUMP SYNDROME

The sump syndrome is an unusual condition in which there is a choledochoduodenal fistula with downstream impaction of stones and/or food material in the bile duct remnant and sphincter segment. This may cause pain, pancreatitis, and/or cholangitis. Therapy is with endoscopic sphincterotomy with excellent immediate and long-term results.[152]

SMALL STONES

Stones that are 3 mm or less in diameter are generally considered to be small (Fig. 46–18). The clinical significance of these lesions is uncertain and may be negligible. After ESWL, all stone fragments 3 mm or less in diameter, and almost all stones 3.5 mm to 5 mm in

diameter, have been shown to pass into the duodenum with rare symptoms and no complications.[153] In a study of 539 cholecystectomy patients, 12% of those randomized to have IOC had unsuspected bile duct stones detected with equivalent amounts expected in the control group. Similar symptomatic outcomes occurred in the IOC and control groups and none of the control patients had clinically detected retained bile duct stones with 3 years of follow-up.[12] In another study of 163 preoperative gallstone patients with abnormal liver test results and normal ERCs, 49% had sphincterotomy with small bile duct stones found in 26%. With more than 3 years of postoperative follow-up, none of the sphincterotomy or no sphincterotomy patients had biliary complications.[13] In another report, about 5% of 942 laparoscopic cholecystectomy patients who had routine IOCs had filling defects indicative of stones and a biliary catheter was left in place. A normal cholangiogram was seen at 48 hours in 26% and at 6 weeks in another 26%, but 48% had stones detected and then removed by ERCP at 12 weeks.[14] These data seem to indicate that most small bile duct stones, particularly those that are 3 mm or less in diameter, pass spontaneously without adverse sequela. However, if conservative management of these lesions is contemplated, clinical follow-up should be continued because it is the small stones that cause pancreatitis, and secondary biliary cirrhosis may develop in 1 to 3 years with intermittent ductal obstruction.[15,41]

Postoperative Care

Most ERCP patents are observed in a 24-hour holding area or are hospitalized after the procedure. Postoperative management is dependent on the clinical situation and endoscopic maneuvers performed. Most persons who have had an uncomplicated ERCP with sphincterotomy for stones and are not in the perioperative period can be discharged on the same day and advised to avoid anticoagulants, aspirin, and nonsteroidal anti-inflammatory and antiplatelet drugs to prevent hemorrhage. Persons at increased risk for pancreatitis because of younger age, female sex, small-caliber ducts, difficult cannulations, repeated pancreatic injections or instrumentation, and/or precut sphincterotomy should be vigorously

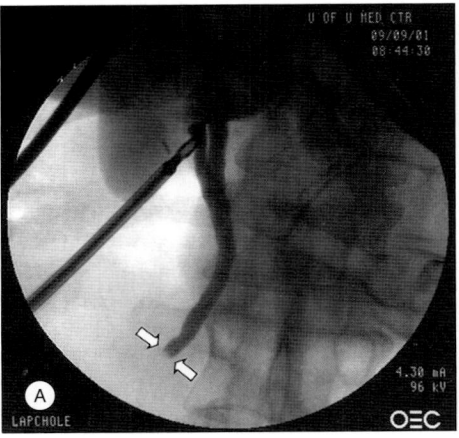
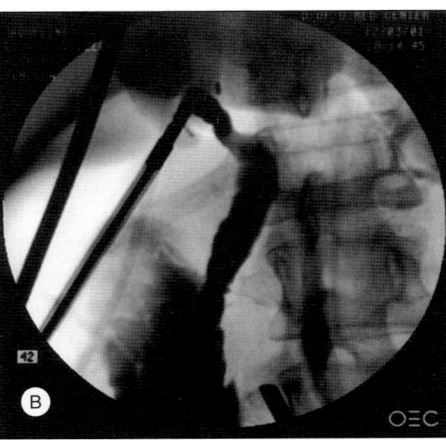

Figure 46–18. *A,* A laparoscopic intraoperative cholangiogram showing a 3-mm stone impacted in the ampullary segment demonstrated by the *arrows. B,* The stone has been flushed through after medical sphincter of Oddi dilatation with glucagon and the contrast material flows freely into the duodenum. (Courtesy of Robert Glasgow, MD.)

hydrated, given only sips of water, and provided with analgesics and antiemetics for 12 to 24 hours after the procedure. Persons with cholangitis who are adequately drained should receive antibiotics for at least 3 days post-ERCP.[154]

OUTPATIENT ENDOSCOPIC RETROGRADE CHOLANGIOPANCREATOGRAPHY

ERCP is increasingly performed on an outpatient basis. Patients considered for same-day discharge must be stratified for risk of complications. Good candidates are patients with few comorbidities and adequate support systems who reside in proximity to the hospital. Additional risk factors include suspected sphincter of Oddi dysfunction, cirrhosis, difficult cannulation, precut sphincterotomy, combined PTC and endoscopic access, and others. About 44% of complications in patients planned for same-day discharge develop within 2 hours and 79% within 6 hours.[155] Recent studies show that up to 19% of planned outpatient procedures resulted in admission with most detected in the endoscopy or recovery units and few returning from home.[156,157]

RECURRENT STONES

Recurrent stones develop in about 10% to 20% of persons who have had sphincterotomy or papillary balloon dilatation for stone extraction.[158–160] Recurrence is usually with brown stones, and the clinical presentation is often cholangitis. The problem may be due to bile stasis and repeated infections. Risk factors for recurrence include older age, periampullary diverticula, a largely dilated bile duct, biliary strictures, mechanical lithotripsy, and a gallbladder *in situ*. Clinical follow-up with serum enzyme levels and trans-abdominal ultrasound with ERCP for abnormal findings may improve stone extraction rates and decrease occurrences of cholangitis.[158,161,162] Surgery may be beneficial to remove stones that cannot be extracted by endoscopic means but has not been shown to decrease recurrence rates.[157,161]

Complications

ERCP with sphincterotomy for stones is successful in more than 90% of patients, with morbidity in about 5% and rare mortality. High-risk patients may safely and successfully undergo ERCP with sedation and analgesia for appropriate indications. Patients with significant comorbidities and morbid obesity who require ERCP benefit from general anesthesia with endotracheal intubation to minimize the risks of cardiopulmonary complications.[163] Patients with severe acute pancreatitis and suppurative cholangitis benefit for urgent ERCP and stone extraction or drainage but often require general anesthesia and maintenance of vital signs. Successful ERCP has been reported in five patients within 15 to 56 days after myocardial infarction for urgent indications without cardiovascular complications.[164] Person with severe coagulopathies and thrombocytopenia with urgent indications for stone extraction should have attempts made to correct the problem with vitamin K, plasma, and/or platelet transfusions. If the deficit cannot be corrected, stent

or nasobiliary drainage may be obtained without sphincterotomy or papillary balloon dilatation may be performed to minimize bleeding risks.

Future Trends

Imaging technology will continue to progress with breakthroughs in tissue harmonic imaging, which improves the signal-to-noise ratio and considerably reduces artifacts seen with conventional transcutaneous ultrasonography.[165] Multidetector CT scanning and new generations of MRI with three-dimensional reconstruction and virtual cholangiography will provide superior resolution and detection of tiny stones.[19] EUS will be more widely used for surveillance of intermediate-risk patients. The technology will improve and ERCP may be performed with side-viewing instruments that allow sonographic imaging and ductal cannulation and instrumentation for stone extraction without fluoroscopy. There will also be improved intraductal ultrasound probes that can be more effectively passed through a duodenoscope to detect stones not seen on cholangiography.

Endoscopic therapy is safe, effective, and well-established for treatment of choledocholithiasis, but technical innovations continue. There will be persistent efforts to minimize short- and long-term complications by devising methods to perform stone extraction without sphincterotomy including medical and mechanical methods to open the sphincter. Intracorporeal lithotripsy technology will progress with more effective lasers that minimize potential tissue damage and do not require direct visualization with choledochoscopes. However, direct intraluminal visualization will become easier and more widely available with steerable small-caliber instruments and optical guidewires that allow simplified instrumentation under direct vision. Surgical therapy will progress with expanded expertise in intraoperative ultrasound and laparoscopic bile duct exploration continuing the transition from ERCP to surgical therapy. In addition, the technical innovations mentioned for ERCP will become available for laparoscopic use as well.

REFERENCES

1. Ko CW, Lee SP: Epidemiology and natural history of common bile duct stones and prediction of disease. Gastrointest Endosc 56(Suppl 6): S165–169, 2002.
2. Soloway RD, Trotman BW, Ostrow JD: Pigment gallstones. Gastroenterology 72:167–182, 1977.
3. Ko CW, Sekijima JH, Lee SP: Biliary sludge. Ann Intern Med 130:301–311, 1999.
4. Gilat T, Konikoff F: Pregnancy and the biliary tract. Can J Gastroenterol 14(Suppl D):55D–59D, 2000.
5. Barbara L, Sama C, Morselli-Labate AM, et al: A population study on the prevalence of gallstone disease: The Sirmione study. Hepatology 7:913–917, 1987.
6. Attili AF, Capocaccia R, Carulli N, et al: Factors associated with gallstone disease in the MICOL experience: Multicenter Italian Study on Epidemiology of Cholelithiasis. Hepatology 26:809–818, 1997.
7. Trotman BW: Pigment gallstone disease. Gastroenterol Clin North Am 20:111–126, 1991.

8. Sandstad O, Osnes T, Skar V, et al: Common bile duct stones are mainly brown and associated with duodenal diverticula. Gut 35:1464–1467, 1994.

9. Lee JG, Leung JW: Choledocholithiasis, bacterial cholangitis, oriental intrahepatic stone disease, and parasitic disorders of the biliary tree. In DiMarino AJ, Benjamin SB (eds): Gastrointestinal Disease. An Endoscopic Approach. Malden, MA, Blackwell Science, 1997, pp 852–870.

10. Gracie WA, Ransohoff DF: The natural history of silent gallstones: The innocent gallstone is not a myth. N Engl J Med 307:798–800, 1982.

11. Attili AF, De Santis A, Capri R, et al: The natural history of gallstones: The GREPCO experience. The GREPCO Group. Hepatology 21:655–660, 1995.

12. Murison MS, Gartell PC, McGinn FP: Does selective preoperative cholangiography result in missed common bile duct stones? J R Coll Surg Edinb 38:220–224, 1993.

13. Siddique I, Mohan K, Khajah A, et al: Sphincterotomy in patients with gallstones, elevated LFTs and a normal CBD on ERCP. Hepatogastroenterology 50:1242–1245, 2003.

14. Collins C, Maguire D, Ireland A, et al: A prospective study of common bile duct calculi in patients undergoing laparoscopic cholecystectomy: Natural history of choledocholithiasis revisited. Ann Surg 239:28–33, 2004.

15. Lakshmi MV, Sridharan GV, Butterworth D: Gallstone cirrhosis: Are we only seeing the tip of the iceberg? Br J Clin Pract 47:164–165, 1993.

16. Goldman DE, Gholson CF: Choledocholithiasis in patients with normal serum liver enzymes. Dig Dis Sci 40:1065–1068, 1995.

17. George GO, Spiegelman GA, Barkin JS: Normal serum alkaline phosphatase: An unusual finding in early suppurative biliary obstruction. Am J Gastroenterol 88:771–778, 1993.

18. Gandolfi L, Torresan F, Solmi L, et al: The role of ultrasound in biliary and pancreatic disease. Eur J Ultrasound 16:141–159, 2003.

19. Mortele KJ, Ji H, Ros PR: CT and magnetic resonance imaging in pancreatic and biliary tract malignancies. Gastrointest Endosc 56:S206–212, 2002.

20. Mark DH, Flamm CR, Aronson N: Evidence-based assessment of diagnostic modalities for common bile duct stones. Gastrointest Endosc 56:S190–194, 2002.

21. Romagnuolo J, Bardou M, Rahme E, et al: Magnetic resonance cholangiopancreatography: A meta-analysis of test performance in suspected biliary disease. Ann Intern Med 139:547–557, 2003.

22. Montariol T, Msika S, Charlier A, et al: Diagnosis of asymptomatic common bile duct stones: Preoperative endoscopic ultrasonography versus intraoperative cholangiography—a multicenter, prospective controlled study. Surgery 124:6–13, 1998.

23. Petelin JB: Surgical management of common bile duct stones. Gastrointest Endosc 56:S183–189, 2002.

24. Catheline JM, Turner R, Paries J: Laparoscopic ultrasonography is a complement to cholangiography for the detection of choledocholithiasis at laparoscopic cholecystectomy. Br J Surg 89:1235–1239, 2002.

25. Sun XD, Cai XY, Li JD, et al: Prospective study of scoring system in selective intraoperative cholangiography during laparoscopic cholecystectomy. World J Gastroenterol 9:865–867, 2003.

26. Lee SP, Maher K, Nicholls JF: Origin and fate of biliary sludge. Gastroenterology 94:170–176, 1988.

27. Ros E, Navarro S, Bru C, et al: Occult microlithiasis in "idiopathic" acute pancreatitis: Prevention of relapses by cholecystectomy or ursodeoxycholic acid therapy. Gastroenterology 101:1701–1709, 1991.

28. Lee SP, Nicholls JF, Park HZ: Biliary sludge as a cause of acute pancreatitis. N Engl J Med 326:589–593, 1992.

29. Perez-Martin G, Gomez-Cerezo, Codoceo, et al: Bilirubinate granules: Main pathologic bile component in patients with idiopathic acute pancreatitis. Am J Gastroenterol 93:360–362, 1998.

30. Gloor B, Stahel PF, Muller CA, et al: Incidence and management of biliary pancreatitis in cholecystectomized patients. J Gastrointest Surg 7:372–377, 2003.

31. Ammori BJ, Boreham B, Lewis P, et al: The biochemical detection of biliary etiology of acute pancreatitis on admission: A revisit in the modern era of biliary imaging. Pancreas 26:e32–35, 2003.

32. Liu CL, Lo CM, Chan JK, et al: EUS for detection of occult cholelithiasis in patients with idiopathic pancreatitis. Gastrointest Endosc 51:28–32, 2000.

33. Calvo MM, Bujanda L, Heras I, et al: Magnetic resonance cholangiography versus ultrasound in the evaluation of the gallbladder. J Clin Gastroenterol 34:233–236, 2002.

34. Choudhuri G, Agarwal DK, Saraswat VA, et al: Is duodenal bile representative of gallbladder bile? A comparative study. Scand J Gastroenterol 28:920–923, 1993.

35. Janowitz P, Swobodnik W, Wechsler JG, et al: Comparison of gallbladder bile and endoscopically obtained duodenal bile. Gut 31:1407–1410, 1990.

36. Kohut M, Nowak J, Nowakowska-Dulawa E, et al: The frequency of bile duct crystals in patients with presumed biliary pancreatitis. Gastrointest Endosc 54:37–41, 2001.

37. Acosta JM, Ledesma CL: Gallstone migration as a cause of acute pancreatitis. N Engl J Med 290:484–487, 1974.

38. Chak A, Hawes RH, Cooper GS, et al: Prospective assessment of the utility of EUS in the evaluation of gallstone pancreatitis. Gastrointest Endosc 49:599–604, 1999.

39. Kelly TR: Gallstone pancreatitis: The timing of surgery. Surgery 88:345–350, 1980.

40. Armstrong CP, Taylor TV, Jeacock J, et al: The biliary tract in patients with acute gallstone pancreatitis. Br J Surg 72:551–555, 1985.

41. Diehl AK, Holleman DR Jr, Chapman JB, et al: Gallstone size and risk of pancreatitis. Arch Intern Med 157:1674–1678, 1997.

42. Kaw M, Al-Antably Y, Kaw P: Management of gallstone pancreatitis: Cholecystectomy or ERCP and endoscopic sphincterotomy. Gastrointest Endosc 56:61–65, 2002.

43. Tenner S, Dubner H, Steinberg W: Predicting gallstone pancreatitis with laboratory parameters: A meta-analysis. Am J Gastroenterol 89:1863–1866, 1994.

44. Fogel EL, Sherman S: Acute biliary pancreatitis: When should the endoscopist intervene? Gastroenterology 125:229–235, 2003.

45. Bradley EL 3rd: A clinically based classification system of acute pancreatitis: Summary of the International Symposium on Acute Pancreatitis, Atlanta, GA, September 11 through 13, 1992. Arch Surg 128:586–590, 1993.

46. Yusoff IF, Barkun JS, Barkun AN: Diagnosis and management of cholecystitis and cholangitis. Gastroenterol Clin North Am 32:1145–1168, 2003.

47. Sirinek KR, Levine BA: Percutaneous transhepatic cholangiography and biliary decompression: Invasive, diagnostic and therapeutic procedures with too high a price? Arch Surg 124:885–888, 1989.

48. Tranter SE, Thompson MH: Comparison of endoscopic sphincterotomy and laparoscopic exploration of the common bile duct. Br J Surg 89:1495–1504, 2002.

49. Cotton PB, Lehman G, Vennes J, et al: Endoscopic sphincterotomy complications and their management: An attempt at consensus. Gastrointest Endosc 37:383–393, 1991.

50. Vlavianos P, Chopra K, Mandalia S, et al: Endoscopic balloon dilatation versus endoscopic sphincterotomy for the removal of bile duct stones: A prospective randomised trial. Gut 52:1165–1169, 2003.

51. Bergman JJ, Rauws EA, Focken P, et al: Randomised trial of endoscopic balloon dilation versus endoscopic sphincterotomy for removal of bile duct stones. Lancet 349:1124–1129, 1997.

52. Ochi Y, Mukawa K, Kiyosawa K, et al: Comparing the treatment outcomes of endoscopic papillary dilation and endoscopic sphincterotomy for removal of bile duct stones. J Gastroenterol Hepatol 14:90–96, 1999.

53. Fujita N, Maguchi H, Komatsu Y, et al: Endoscopic sphincterotomy and endoscopic papillary balloon dilatation for bile duct stones: A prospective randomized controlled multicenter study. Gastrointest Endosc 57:151–155, 2003.

54. DiSario JA, Freeman ML, Bjorkman DJ, et al: Endoscopic balloon dilation compared to spincterotomy for extraction of bile duct stones. Gastroenterology 127:1291–1299, 2004.

55. Hui CK, Lai KC, Ng M, et al: Retained common bile duct stones: A comparison between biliary stenting and complete clearance of stones by electrohydraulic lithotripsy. Aliment Pharmacol Ther 17:289–296, 2003.

56. Sackmann M, Holl J, Sauter GH, et al: Extracorporeal shock wave lithotripsy for clearance of bile duct stones resistant to endoscopic extraction. Gastrointest Endosc 53:27–32, 2001.

57. Ellis RD, Jenkins AP, Thompson RP, et al: Clearance of refractory bile duct stones with extracorporeal shockwave lithotripsy. Gut 47:728–731, 2000.

58. Hochberger J, Bayer J, May A, et al: Laser lithotripsy of difficult bile duct stones: Results in 60 patients using arhodamine 6G dye laser with optical stone tissue detection system. Gut 43:823–829, 1998.

59. Cipolletta L, Costamagna G, Bianco MA, et al: Endoscopic mechanical lithotripsy of difficult common bile duct stones. Br J Surg 84:1407–1409, 1997.

60. Hintze RE, Adler A, Veltzke W: Outcome of mechanical lithotripsy of bile duct stones in an unselected series of 704 patients. Hepatogastroenterology 43:473–476, 1996.

61. Shaw MJ, Mackie RD, Moore JP, et al: Results of a multicenter trial using a mechanical lithotripter for the treatment of large bile duct stones. Am J Gastroenterol 88:730–733, 1993.

62. Binmoeller KF, Bruckner M, Thonke F, et al: Treatment of difficult bile duct stones using mechanical, electrohydraulic and extracorporeal shock wave lithotripsy. Endoscopy 25:201–206, 1993.

63. Freeman ML, Nelson DB, Sherman S, et al: Complications of endoscopic biliary sphincterotomy. N Engl J Med 335:909–918, 1996.

64. Cotton PB, Geenen JE, Sherman S, et al: Endoscopic sphincterotomy for stones by experts is safe, even in younger patients with normal ducts. Ann Surg 227:201–204, 1998.

65. Hirota WK, Petersen K, Baron TH, et al: Standards of Practice Committee of the American Society for Gastrointestinal Endoscopy. Guidelines for antibiotic prophylaxis for GI endoscopy. Gastrointest Endosc 58:475–482, 2003.

66. Cappell MS: The fetal safety and clinical efficacy of gastrointestinal endoscopy during pregnancy. Gastroenterol Clin North Am 32:123–179, 2003.

67. Reece EA, Assimakopoulos E, Zheng XZ, et al: The safety of obstetric ultrasonography: Concern for the fetus. Obstet Gynecol 76:139–146, 1990.

68. Hiatt JR, Hiatt JC, Williams RA, et al: Biliary disease in pregnancy: Strategy for surgical management. Am J Surg 151:263–265, 1986.

69. Tham TC, Vandervoort J, Wong RC, et al: Safety of ERCP during pregnancy. Am J Gastroenterol 98:308–311, 2003.

70. Sharma VK, Howden CW: Metaanalysis of randomized controlled trials of endoscopic retrograde cholangiography and endoscopic sphincterotomy for the treatment of acute biliary pancreatitis. Am J Gastroenterol 94:3211–3214, 1999.

71. Neoptolemos JP, Carr-Locke DL, London NJ, et al: Controlled trial of urgent endoscopic retrograde cholangiopancreatography and endoscopic sphincterotomy versus conservative treatment for acute pancreatitis due to gallstones. Lancet 2:979–983, 1988.

72. Fan ST, Lai EC, Mok FP, et al: Early treatment of acute biliary pancreatitis by endoscopic papillotomy. N Engl J Med 328:228–232, 1993.

73. Nowak A, Nowakowska-Dulawa E, Marek T, et al: Final results of the prospective, randomized, controlled study on endoscopic sphincterotomy versus conventional management in acute biliary pancreatitis. The German Study Group on Acute Biliary Pancreatitis [abstract]. Gastroenterology 108:A380, 1995.

74. Fölsch UR, Nitsche R, Ludtke R, et al: Early ERCP and papillotomy compared with conservative treatment for acute biliary pancreatitis. N Engl J Med 336:237–242, 1997.

75. Fulcher AS: MRCP and ERCP in the diagnosis of common bile duct stones. Gastrointest Endosc 56:S178–182, 2002.

76. Lai EC, Tam PC, Paterson IA, et al: Emergency surgery for severe acute cholangitis: The high-risk patients. Ann Surg 211:55–59, 1990.

77. Winick AB, Waybill PN, Venbrux AC: Complications of transhepatic biliary interventions. Tech Vasc Interv Radiol 4:200–206, 2001.

78. Matzen P, Malchow-Moller A, Lejerstofte J, et al: Endoscopic retrograde cholangiopancreatography and transhepatic cholangiography in patients with suspected obstructive jaundice. A randomized study. Scand J Gastroenterol 17:731–735, 1982.

79. Lai EC, Mok FP, Tan ES, et al: Endoscopic biliary drainage for severe acute cholangitis. N Engl J Med 326:1582–1586, 1992.

80. Lee DW, Chan AC, Lam YH, et al: Biliary decompression by nasobiliary catheter or biliary stent in acute suppurative cholangitis: A prospective randomized trial. Gastrointest Endosc 56:361–365, 2002.

81. Lillemoe KD: Surgical treatment of biliary tract infections. Am Surg 66:138–144, 2000.

82. Suc B, Escat J, Cherqui D, et al: Surgery vs endoscopy as primary treatment in symptomatic patients with suspected common bile duct stones: A multi-center randomized trial. Arch Surg 133:702–708, 1998.

83. Rhodes M, Lussman L, Cohen L, et al: Randomized trial of laparoscopic exploration of common bile duct versus postoperative endoscopic retrograde cholangiography for common bile duct stones. Lancet 351:159–161, 1998.

84. Sgourakis G. Karaliotas K: Laparoscopic common bile duct exploration and cholecystectomy versus endoscopic stone extraction and laparoscopic cholecystectomy for choledocholithiasis. A prospective randomized study. Minerva Chir 57:467–474, 2002.

85. Caroli-Bosch FX, Montet JC, Salmon L, et al: Effect of endoscopic sphincterotomy on bile lithogenicity in patients with gallbladder in situ. Endoscopy 31:437–441, 1999.

86. Jacobsen O, Matzen P: Long-term follow-up study of patients after endoscopic sphincterotomy for choledocholithiasis. Scand J Gastroenterol 22:903–906, 1987.

87. Worthley CS, Toouli J: Gallbladder non-filling: An indication for cholecystectomy after endoscopic sphincterotomy. Br J Surg 75:796–798, 1988.

88. Hansell DT, Millar MA, Murray WR, et al: Endoscopic sphincterotomy for bile duct stones in patients with intact gallbladders. Br J Surg 76:856–858, 1989.

89. Hill J, Martin DF, Tweedle DE: Risks of leaving the gallbladder in situ after endoscopic sphincterotomy for bile duct stones. Br J Surg 78:554–557, 1991.

90. Benattar JM, Caroli-Bosc FX, Harris AG, et al: Endoscopic sphincterotomy for common bile duct calculi in patients without stones in the gallbladder. Dig Dis Sci 38:2225–2227, 1993.

91. Hammarstrom LE, Holmin T, Stridbeck H: Endoscopic treatment of bile duct calculi in patients with gallbladder in situ: Long-term outcome and factors. Scand J Gastroenterol 31:294–301, 1996.

92. Keulemans YC, Rauws EA, Huibregtse K, et al: Current management of the gallbladder after endoscopic sphincterotomy for common bile duct stones. Gastrointest Endosc 46:514–519, 1997.

93. Pedersen FM, Lassen AT, de Muckadell OB: Endoscopic sphincterotomy for common bile duct stones in younger patients. Dan Med Bull 45:533–535, 1998.

94. Lai KH, Lin LF, Lo GH, et al: Does cholecystectomy after endoscopic sphincterotomy prevent the recurrence of biliary complications? Gastrointest Endosc 49:483–487, 1999.

95. Poon RT, Liu CL, Lo CM, et al: Management of gallstone cholangitis in the era of laparoscopic cholecystectomy. Arch Surg 136:11–16, 2001.

96. Adamek HE, Kudis V, Jakobs R, et al: Impact of gallbladder status on the outcome in patients with retained bile duct stones treated with extracorporeal shockwave lithotripsy. Endoscopy 34:624–627, 2002.

97. Sugiyama M, Atomi Y: Risk factors predictive of late complications after endoscopic sphincterotomy for bile duct stones: Long-term (more than 10 years) follow-up study. Am J Gastroenterol 97:2763–2767, 2002.

98. Schreurs WH, Vles WJ, Stuifbergen WH, et al: Endoscopic management of common bile duct stones leaving the gallbladder in situ. A cohort study with long-term follow-up. Dig Surg 21:60–64, 2004.

99. Yi SY: Recurrence of biliary symptoms after endoscopic sphincterotomy for choledocholithiasis in patients with gall bladder stones. J Gastroenterol Hepatol 15:661–664, 2000.

100. Targarona EM, Ayuso RM, Bordas JM, et al: Randomized trial of endoscopic sphincterotomy with gallbladder left in situ versus open surgery for common bile duct calculi in high-risk patients. Lancet 347:926–929, 1996.

101. Boerma D, Rauws EA, Keulemans YC, et al: Wait-and-see policy or laparoscopic cholecystectomy after endoscopic sphincterotomy for bile-duct stones: A randomised trial. Lancet 360:761–765, 2002.

102. Bergman JJ, van der Mey S, Rauws EA, et al: Long-term follow-up after endoscopic sphincterotomy for bile duct stones in patients younger than 60 years of age. Gastrointest Endosc 44:643–649, 1996.

103. Costamagna G, Tringali A, Shah SK, et al: Long-term follow-up of patients after endoscopic sphincterotomy for choledocholithiasis, and risk factors for recurrence. Endoscopy 34:273–279, 2002.

104. Komatsu Y, Kawabe T, Toda N, et al: Endoscopic papillary balloon dilation for the management of common bile duct stones: Experience of 226 cases. Endoscopy 30:12–17, 1998.

105. Mathuna PM, White P, Clarke E, et al: Endoscopic balloon sphincteroplasty (papillary dilation) for bile duct stones: Efficacy, safety, and follow-up in 100 patients. Gastrointest Endosc 42:468–474, 1995.

106. Ueno N, Ozawa Y: Pancreatitis induced by endoscopic balloon sphincter dilation and changes in serum amylase levels after the procedure. Gastrointest Endosc 49:472–476, 1999.

107. Arnold JC, Benz C, Martin WR, et al: Endoscopic papillary balloon dilation vs. sphincterotomy for removal of common bile duct stones: A prospective randomized pilot study. Endoscopy 33:563–567, 2001.

108. Freeman ML, DiSario JA, Nelson DB, et al: Risk factors for post-ERCP pancreatitis: A prospective, multicenter study. Gastrointest Endosc 54:425–434, 2001.

109. Aizawa T, Ueno N: Stent placement in the pancreatic duct prevents pancreatitis after endoscopic sphincter dilation for removal of bile duct stones. Gastrointest Endosc 54:209–213, 2001.

110. Ohashi A, Tamada K, Tomiyama T, et al: Epinephrine irrigation for the prevention of pancreatic damage after endoscopic balloon sphincteroplasty. J Gastroenterol Hepatol 16:568–571, 2001.

111. Yasuda I, Tomita E, Enya M, et al: Can endoscopic papillary balloon dilation really preserve sphincter of Oddi function? Gut 49:686–691, 2001.

112. Mac Mathuna P, Siegenberg D, Gibbons D, et al: The acute and long-term effect of balloon sphincteroplasty on papillary structure in pigs. Gastrointest Endosc 44:650–655, 1996.

113. Sato H, Kodama T, Takaaki J, et al: Endoscopic papillary balloon dilation may preserve sphincter of Oddi function after common bile duct stone management: Evaluation from the viewpoint of endoscopic manometry. Gut 41:541–544, 1997.

114. Kawabe T, Komatsu Y, Isayama H, et al: Histological analysis of the papilla after endoscopic papillary balloon dilation. Hepatogastroenterology 50:919–923, 2003.

115. Kawabe T, Komatsu Y, Tada M, et al: Endoscopic papillary balloon dilation in cirrhotic patients: Removal of common bile duct stones without sphincterotomy. Endoscopy 28:694–698, 1996.

116. Bergman JJ, van Berkel AM, Bruno MJ, et al: A randomized trial of endoscopic balloon dilation and endoscopic sphincterotomy for removal of bile duct stones in patients with a prior Billroth II gastrectomy. Gastrointest Endosc 53:19–26, 2001.

117. Bruins Slot W, Schoeman MN, Disario JA, et al: Needle-knife sphincterotomy as a precut procedure: A retrospective evaluation of efficacy and complications. Endoscopy 28:334–339, 1996.

118. Lauri A, Horton RC, Davidson Br, et al: Endoscopic extraction of bile duct stones: Management related to stone size. Gut 34:1718–1721, 1993.

119. Schneider MU, Matek W, Bauer R, et al: Mechanical lithotripsy of bile duct stones in 209 patients—effect of technical advances. Endoscopy 20:248–253, 1988.

120. Adamek HE, Maier M, Jacobs R, et al: Management of retained bile duct stones: A prospective open trial comparing extracorporeal and intracorporeal lithotripsy. Gastrointest Endosc 44:40–47, 1996.

121. Blind PJ, Lundmark M: Management of bile duct stones: Lithotripsy by laser, electrohydraulic, and ultrasonic techniques. Report of a series and a clinical review. Eur J Surg 164:403–409, 1998.

122. Siegel JH, Ben-Zvi JS, Pullano WE: Endoscopic electrohydraulic lithotripsy. Gastrointest Endosc 36:134–136, 1990.

123. Jakobs R, Adamek HE, Maier M, et al: Fluoroscopically guided laser lithotripsy versus extracorporeal shock wave lithotripsy for retained bile duct stones: A prospective randomized study. Gut 40:678–682, 1997.

124. Neuhaus H, Zillinger C, Born P, et al: Randomized study of intracorporeal laser lithotripsy versus extracorporeal shock-wave lithotripsy for difficult bile duct stones. Gastrointest Endosc 47:327–334, 1998.

125. Uchiyama K, Onishi H, Tani M, et al: Indication and treatment of hepatolithiasis. Arch Surg 137:149–153, 2002.

126. Paumgartner G., Walter B: Cannon lecture. Shock-wave lithotripsy of gallstones. AJR Am J Roentgenol 153:235–242, 1989.

127. Kratzer W, Mason RA, Grammer S, et al: Difficult bile duct stone recurrence after endoscopy and extracorporeal shockwave lithotripsy. Hepatogastroenterology 45:910–916, 1998.

128. Lomanto D, Fiocca M, Nardovino E, et al: ESWL experience in the therapy of difficult bile duct stones. Dig Dis Sci 41:2397–2403, 1996.

129. Testoni PA, Lella F, Masci E, et al: Combined endoscopic and extracorporeal shock-wave treatment in difficult bile duct stones: Early and long-term results. Int J Gastroenterol 26:294–298, 1994.

130. Nicholson DA, Martin DF, Tweedle DE, et al: Management of common bile duct stones using a second-generation extracorporeal shockwave lithotriptor. Br J Surg 79:811–814, 1992.

131. Bland KI, Jones RS, Maher JW, et al: Extracorporeal shock-wave lithotripsy of bile duct calculi. An interim report of the Dornier U.S. Bile Duct Lithotripsy Prospective Study. Ann Surg 209:743–753, 1989.

132. Sauerbruch T, Stern M: Fragmentation of bile duct stones by extracorporeal shock waves. A new approach to biliary calculi after failure of routine endoscopic measures. Gastroenterology 96:146–152, 1989.

133. Yoshimoto H, Ikeda S, Tanaka M, et al: Choledochoscopic electrohydraulic lithotripsy and lithotomy for stones in the common bile duct, intrahepatic ducts and gallbladder. Ann Surg 210:576–582, 1989.

134. Jeng KS, Chiang HS, Shih SC: Limitations of percutaneous transhepatic cholangioscopy in the removal of complicated biliary calculi. World J Surg 13:603–610, 1989.

135. Yamakawa T: Percutaneous cholangioscopy for management of retained biliary tract stones and intrahepatic stones. Endoscopy 21:333–337, 1989.

136. Stokes KR, Falchuk KR, Clouse ME: Biliary duct stones: Update on 54 cases after percutaneous transhepatic removal. Radiology 170:999–1001, 1989.

137. Chen MF, Jan YY, Lee TY: Percutaneous transhepatic cholangioscopy. Br J Surg 74:728–730, 1987.

138. Chan AC, Ng EK, Chung CS, et al: Common bile duct stones become smaller after endoscopic biliary stenting. Endoscopy 30:356–359, 1998.

139. Johnson GK, Geenen JE, Venu RP, et al: Treatment of non-extractable common bile duct stones with combination Ursodeoxycholic acid plus endoprostheses. Gastrointest Endosc 39:528–531, 1993.

140. De Palma GD, Catanzano C: Stenting or surgery for treatment of irretrievable common bile duct calculi in elderly patients? Am J Surg 178:390–393, 1999.

141. Bergman JJ, Rauws EA, Tijssen JG, et al: Biliary endoprostheses in elderly patients with endoscopically irretrievable common bile duct stones: Report on 117 patients. Gastrointest Endosc 42:195–201, 1995.

142. Chopra KB, Peters RA, O'Toole PA, et al: Randomized study of endoscopic biliary endoprosthesis versus duct clearance for bile duct stones in high-risk patients. Lancet 348:791–793, 1996.

143. Kim MH, Sekijima J, Lee SP: Primary intrahepatic stones. Am J Gastroenterol 90:540–548, 1995.

144. Okugawa T, Tsuyuguchi T, K C S, et al: Peroral cholangioscopic treatment of hepatolithiasis: Long-term results. Gastrointest Endosc 56:366–371, 2002.

145. Huang MH, Chen CH, Yang JC, et al: Long-term outcome of percutaneous transhepatic cholangioscopic lithotomy for hepatolithiasis. Am J Gastroenterol 98:2655–2662, 2003.

146. Cheung MT, Wai SH, Kwok PC: Percutaneous transhepatic Choledochoscopic removal of intrahepatic stones. Br J Surg 90:1409–1415, 2003.

147. Adamek HE, Schneider AR, Adamek MU, et al: Treatment of difficult intrahepatic stones by using extracorporeal and intracorporeal lithotripsy techniques: 10 years' experience in 55 patients. Scand J Gastroenterol 34:1157–1161, 1999.

148. Kusano T, Isa TT, Muto Y, et al: Long-term results of hepaticojejunostomy for hepatolithiasis. Am Surg 67:442–446, 2001.

149. Chen MF, Jan YY, Hwang TL, et al: Role of hepatic resection in surgery for bilateral intrahepatic stones. Br J Surg 84:1229–1232. 1997.

150. Tsuyuguchi T, Saisho H, Ishihara T, et al: Long-term follow-up after treatment of Mirizzi syndrome by peroral cholangioscopy. Gastrointest Endosc 52:639–644, 2000.

151. Yeh CN, Jan YY, Chen MF: Laparoscopic treatment for Mirizzi syndrome. Surg Endosc 17:1573–1578, 2003.

152. Caroli-Bosc FX, Demarquay JF, Peten EP, et al: Endoscopic management of sump syndrome after choledochoduodenostomy: Retrospective analysis of 30 cases. Gastrointest Endosc 51:180–183, 2000.

153. Greiner L, Munks C, Heil W, et al: Gallbladder stone fragments in feces after biliary extracorporeal shock-wave lithotripsy. Gastroenterology 98:1620–1624, 1990.

154. van Lent AU, Bartelsman JF, Tytgat GN, et al: Duration of antibiotic therapy for cholangitis after successful endoscopic drainage of the biliary tract. Gastrointest Endosc 55:518–522, 2002.

155. Freeman ML, Nelson DB, Sherman S, et al: Same-day discharge after endoscopic biliary sphincterotomy: Observations from a prospective multicenter complication study. The Multicenter Endoscopic Sphincterotomy (MESH) Study Group. Gastrointest Endosc 49:580–586, 1999.

156. Fox CJ, Harry RA, Cairns SR: A prospective series of out-patient endoscopic retrograde cholangiopancreatography. Eur J Gastroenterol Hepatol 12:523–527, 2000.

157. Tham TC, Vandervoort J, Wong RC, et al: Therapeutic ERCP in outpatients. Gastrointest Endosc 45:225–230, 1997.

158. Lai KH, Lo GH, Lin CK, et al: Do patients with recurrent choledocholithiasis after endoscopic sphincterotomy benefit from regular follow-up? Gastrointest Endosc 55:523–526, 2002.

159. Ueno N, Ozawa Y, Aizawa T: Prognostic factors for recurrence of bile duct stones after endoscopic treatment by sphincter dilation. Gastrointest Endosc 58:336–340, 2003.

160. Ando T, Tsuyuguchi T, Okugawa T, et al: Risk factors for recurrent bile duct stones after endoscopic papillotomy. Gut 52:116–121, 2003.

161. Geenen DJ, Geenen JE, Jafri FM, et al: The role of surveillance endoscopic retrograde cholangiography in preventing episodic cholangitis in patients with recurrent common bile duct stones. Endoscopy 30:18–20, 1988.

162. Cetta F: Do surgical and endoscopic sphincterotomy prevent or facilitate recurrent common duct stone formation? Arch Surg 128:329–336, 1993.

163. Ramirez FC, McIntosh AS, Dennert B, et al: Emergency endoscopic retrograde cholangiopancreatography in critically ill patients. Gastrointest Endosc 47:368–371, 1998.

164. Capell MS: Endoscopic retrograde cholangiopancreatography with endoscopic sphincterotomy for symptomatic choledocholithiasis after recent myocardial infarction. Am J Gastroenterol 91:1827–1831, 1996.

165. Ortega D, Burns PN, Hope Simon D, et al: Tissue harmonic imaging: Is it a benefit for bile duct sonography? AJR Am J Roentgenol 176:653–659, 2001.

Benign Biliary Strictures and Leaks

Guido Costamagna

Introduction

Accidental injuries of the bile ducts leading to biliary leaks and strictures may occur during any surgical procedure involving the biliary tract. Today, however, the main cause of injury of the bile ducts is laparoscopic cholecystectomy (LC). Although LC has proved to be superior to open cholecystectomy in terms of shorter hospitalization, lower overall morbidity, faster recovery, and better cosmetic outcome, the risk of bile duct injury during LC is two to six times higher when compared with open cholecystectomy.[1,2]

Bergman and colleagues[3] described four types of postoperative bile duct injuries:

Type A: cystic duct leaks or leakage from aberrant or peripheral hepatic radicles (minor lesions)
Type B: major bile duct leaks with or without concomitant biliary strictures (major lesions)
Type C: bile duct strictures without bile leakage (major lesions)
Type D: complete transection of the duct with or without excision of some portion of the biliary tree (major lesions)

I refer to this classification in this chapter.

Epidemiology

LC was first performed by Mouret in France in 1987. The technique was then standardized by two other French surgeons, Dubois in Paris and Perissat in Bordeaux.[4,5] This new technique spread very rapidly around the world; in the United States, the percentage of cholecystectomies done laparoscopically grew from 0% in 1987 to almost 80% in 1992.[6] The advent of LC also induced an estimated increase of at least 25% in the overall number of cholecystectomies performed,[7,8] so that today the likely number of cholecystectomies performed in the United States is 800,000 per year.[9] As a result, the number of iatrogenic injuries to the bile duct increased accordingly.[10] Many reasons may explain the increased incidence of biliary complications at the beginning of the laparoscopic era.

Most of them were related to the new technical skills required to perform laparoscopically what had been done by open surgery: bidimensional vision, loss of tactile sensations, different visual approach of the hepatic pedicle, difficult hemostatic maneuvers, abuse of electrocoagulation, lack of confidence with the new instrumentation, and so forth.[11] As a result, the rate of injuries seemed to be related to the surgeon's learning curve and his or her personal experience. Actually, an inversely proportional relationship between the number of cholecystectomies performed and the rate of injuries was suggested by the earlier reported series.[1,12] In a review of 77,604 LCs performed in the United States, the incidence of biliary injuries decreased from 0.6% to 0.4% ($p < .001$) for those surgical teams having an experience of more than 100 LCs.[1] A Belgian survey[11] suggested the number of 50 LCs as the threshold of a completed learning curve; however, the same authors emphasized that one third of the biliary injuries in their country had occurred to surgeons with an experience of more than 100 LCs. When reviewing several multicenter series published before 1995, totaling 198,267 LCs, the incidence of biliary injuries was 0.55% in 13 European series and 0.49% in 17 extra-European series.[13] Therefore, in the mid-1990s the incidence of biliary injury seemed to be three times higher for laparoscopic than for open cholecystectomy. However, these figures most probably underestimated reality because there was a tendency not to declare all the lesions, as revealed by the low rate of reply to most surveys and by the increasing number of reported lesions in direct proportion with the collected replies.[14]

Today, the incidence of biliary injuries has not substantially changed, even if a trend toward reduction has been reported by some authors.[6,15] The estimated overall incidence is between 0.25% and 0.74% for major biliary lesions (Table 47–1) and between 0.1% and 1.7% for minor biliary lesions (Table 47–2). These figures are only partially explained by the still increasing number of LCs performed around the world and by the activity of young surgeons at the beginning of their learning curve. However, as recently shown,[19] at least one third of the biliary injuries may be ascribed to technical mistakes during surgery. Thus, the learning curve is not the only risk factor of LC.

Table 47–1. Incidence of Major Biliary Lesions (Bergman's type B,C, and D) during Laparoscopic Cholecystectomy (Multicenter Surveys)

Author	Country	Year	Number of LC	Major Biliary Lesions (%)
MacFayden et al.[3]	United States	1998	114,005	0.5
Nuzzo[13]	Italy	2002	56,591	0.31
Russell et al.[6]	United States	1996	15,221	0.25
Z'graggen et al.[16]	Switzerland	1998	10,174	0.31
Gigot et al.[11]	Belgium	1997	9959	0.5
Wherry et al[17]	United States	1996	9130	0.41
Adamsen et al.[18]	Denmark	1997	7654	0.74
Richardson et al.[15]	Scotland	1996	5913	0.33

LC, laparoscopic cholecystectomy.

Table 47–2. Incidence of Minor Biliary Lesions (Bergman's type A) during Laparoscopic Cholecystectomy (Multicenter Surveys)

Author	Country	Year	Number of LC	Minor Biliary Lesions (%)
MacFayden et al.[3]	United States	1998	114,005	0.38
Nuzzo[13]	Italy	2002	56,591	0.1
Z'graggen et al.[16]	Switzerland	1998	10,174	0.93
Wherry et al.[17]	United States	1996	9130	0.53
Adamsen et al.[18]	Denmark	1997	7654	1.7
Richardson et al.[15]	Scotland	1996	5913	0.28

LC, laparoscopic cholecystectomy.

Pathogenesis

An unintentional lesion of the bile duct may occur also during an "easy" cholecystectomy performed by an experienced surgeon. Intuitively, the likelihood of injuring the bile duct should increase when the cholecystectomy is difficult and the surgeon is inexpert. Any cholecystectomy may become unexpectedly difficult during surgery; however, there are clinical and morphologic criteria that may be useful in predicting a cholecystectomy at higher risk of bile duct injury. Clinical criteria are obesity; previous abdominal surgery; cirrhosis; portal hypertension; age of the patient; and previous cholecystitis, cholangitis and pancreatitis. Morphologic criteria revealed by preoperative abdominal ultrasonography are related to the gallbladder status (scleroatrophic gallbladder, thickening of the gallbladder wall, gallbladder distension resulting from a stone in the infundibulum) and to the liver (hepatomegaly, atrophy-hypertrophy of the liver lobes). The presence of several criteria raises the chances of being confronted with a difficult cholecystectomy and the risk of concomitant common bile duct (CBD) stones. Unrecognized bile duct stones are one of the major risk factors of cystic duct leakage after LC.

The mechanism and the cause of a biliary injury remain unexplainable in at least one third of the cases.[13] In more than 50% of the cases, the injury occurs during the dissection of the cystic duct or during separation of the gallbladder neck from the CBD. Misinterpretation of the cystic duct and the CBD is the commonest cause of injury.[12] Excessive traction on the gallbladder neck, especially if the tissues are not inflamed, may facilitate the injury of the CBD. Conversely, when the area is acutely or chronically inflamed or when a stone is trapped into the gallbladder infundibulum, the risk of bile duct injury is higher during the dissection of the gallbladder neck from the hepatic pedicle. Other recurrent reasons of bile duct injury are related to incorrect hemostatic maneuvers in case of bleeding from the cystic artery; inappropriate use of electrocautery; and other specific maneuvers such as intraoperative cholangiography, cystic duct dilation, and transcystic CBD instrumental exploration.

The description of anatomic anomalies is often reported by the surgeon as having caused a biliary injury. Actually, variations of the biliary anatomy, especially at the level of the main hepatic confluence, are present in as much as 50% of the subjects (see the section on interpretation of intrahepatic cholangiography). Surgeons must be aware of such variations and must keep in mind the danger of injuring aberrant ducts originating in the right liver during dissection of the gallbladder pedicle. Aberrant ducts must not be interpreted as accessory ducts, because the biliary distribution within the liver parenchyma is of a terminal type. This implies that there are no intrahepatic anastomoses between the ducts and, therefore, that every injury of an aberrant duct will determine functional exclusion of the corresponding liver area. Injury to a small aberrant duct may still be considered a minor lesion; however, it will cause a bile leak into the peritoneal space with all the related consequences.

Another injury modality is clipping or ligation of an aberrant duct. This modality does not imply a bile leak but entails the functional exclusion of the corresponding liver area leading to its progressive atrophy and hypertrophy of the remaining liver parenchyma. This

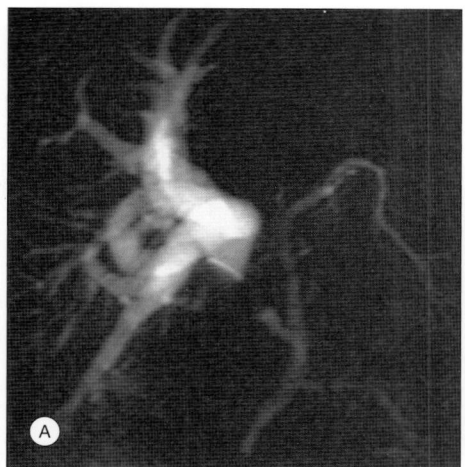

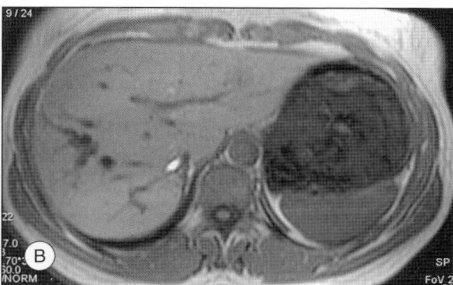

Figure 47-1. Two years after laparoscopic cholecystectomy, this patient presented with only occasional minor right upper quadrant pain with slightly elevated liver function tests. *A,* Magnetic resonance cholangiography showing complete obstruction and dilation of the right biliary ductal system with normal common bile duct and left biliary ductal system. *B,* Abdominal magnetic resonance showing hypotrophy of the right liver and compensatory hypertrophy of the left liver.

possible event may be clinically totally asymptomatic and only witnessed by a raise in biochemical parameters of cholestasis and cytolysis (Fig. 47–1). Although there is no indication of treatment in asymptomatic cases, if the obstructed ducts become infected, recurrent cholangitis is the typical clinical manifestation often requiring operative reestablishment of an adequate bile flow.

Clinical Features

Schematically, three main clinical pictures are characteristic of a bile duct injury: (1) external biliary fistula, (2) choleperitoneum, and (3) obstructive jaundice with or without the features of acute cholangitis. Various combinations of these clinical pictures may also be present. Most importantly, although some of the clinical manifestations, such as uncomplicated jaundice or well-drained external bile leakage, do not require any emergency treatment, the presence of infection must be regarded as an important criterion that requires intensive care and rapid decisions to treat sepsis. Actually, septic complications are the main reason for mortality in these patients in the postoperative period. External biliary fistula and choleperitoneum are both typical features of the immediate postoperative period, whereas obstructive jaundice may occur either immediately after surgery or later, within days to several years. When symptoms arise late after surgery, because of a slow progression from injury to stricture, overt jaundice may be absent and the clinical picture is typically that of anicteric cholestasis, with or without itching, and recurrent bouts of acute cholangitis.

The suspicion of bile duct injury is not always straightforward. When subtle symptoms such as abdominal dull pain, abdominal distension, low-grade fever, and nausea arise in the first days after LC, one should always suspect a possible complication. Intraperitoneal bile collections may initially produce very little or no specific symptoms, but they should be quickly suspected and eventually recognized to identify the cause and to plan the best treatment for the individual patient.

Hemobilia is a rare but alarming clinical presentation of a bile duct injury. The mechanism by which a biliary injury may be associated to hemobilia is often the perforation of a pseudoaneurysm of the right hepatic artery or one of its branches into the bile ducts. These pseudoaneurysms are the result of an inadvertent intraoperative injury of the artery produced by hemostatic maneuvers during a difficult cholecystectomy. In patients with an external biliary drainage or fistula, the bleeding may become suddenly and massively apparent through the drain and may occasionally require emergency treatment.

Differential Diagnosis

Strictures occurring long after surgery may need to be distinguished from malignant strictures and other benign conditions such as primary sclerosing cholangitis. The clinical history may be helpful only in those cases in which the biliary injury had been recognized and eventually treated at the time of surgery. In this setting, the stricture is usually the result of progressive scarring at the site of surgical repair. In all other circumstances, the relationship with cholecystectomy should be questioned. However, clinical presentation may be helpful in discriminating postoperative and malignant stenoses; painless jaundice is in favor of a malignant disease, whereas development of overt jaundice in benign strictures is often heralded by a long period of anicteric cholestasis and relapsing attacks of mild to severe acute cholangitis. Stricture morphology may be very helpful in discriminating scars from neoplastic involvement of the bile duct. Postoperative strictures are usually short, with sharp edges and often asymmetric, and close to the cystic duct stump. Clips may be seen lying over the bile duct or even located medially to it. Biopsy and/or brushing cytology of the stricture may add information but are seldom required because of their low sensitivity.

Treatment

In recent years, endoscopic retrograde cholangiopancreatography (ERCP) has acquired a pivotal role in the management of postsurgical biliary complications. Both of the major typical clinical presentations occurring in this setting may be addressed by ERCP: (1) biliary leak into the peritoneal cavity or external leak and (2) obstructive syndrome with cholestasis, cholangitis, and/or jaundice. ERCP is indicated to confirm the clinical suspicion of biliary injury and to obtain as much morphologic information as possible. ERCP is also increasingly used as a first-line therapeutic tool in those complications that are amenable to endoscopic treatment.

ENDOSCOPIC RETROGRADE CHOLANGIOPANCREATOGRAPHY AND BILIARY LEAK

The presence of a bile leak invariably witnesses a break in the continuity of the biliary system. However, the severity of the injury (ranging from a simple leakage of the cystic stump to a complete transection of the bile duct) and the complexity of its repair are extremely variable. The magnitude of the bile output does not usually help in presuming the origin and the size of the leak. A direct cholangiogram is thus of utmost importance for accurate anatomic depiction and to classify the type of injury to plan therapy. The usefulness of magnetic resonance cholangiopancreatography (MRCP) in the delineation of postoperative biliary leaks has been recently reported.[20] However, MRCP compared with ERCP has no therapeutic potentiality. Therefore, its use may be recommended in those anatomic situations in which the endoscopic approach is presumably difficult or occasionally even impossible, such as in patients with a Billroth II anatomy and with Roux-en-Y hepaticojejunostomy. ERCP has the advantage of providing a detailed morphologic picture of the biliary tree and, when indicated, of offering immediate therapeutic options during the same procedure.

When dealing with biliary leaks, ERCP is usually required in the early postoperative period when the patient has fresh surgical scars (which are potentially painful, especially if surgery has been converted to laparotomy) and carries one or more external abdominal drains placed during surgery or in the postoperative period under ultrasound or computed tomography guidance. This is why the supine position is often preferred to the usual left lateral or prone position in performing ERCP. The supine position, even if a little more demanding for the operator, is also preferable for interpretation purposes, especially in the case of complex hilar lesions. The anteroposterior radiologic projection, with the liver lying on the spine, substantially helps in identifying the anatomy of the main biliary confluence and of the segmental intrahepatic ducts. Doing so also allows changing the patient position obliquely in case of superposition of the biliary branches, which may create difficulties in interpretation.

In case of external biliary fistula through an abdominal drain, it is not advisable to start the procedure by injecting contrast medium through the drain (fistulography). In most instances, especially in minor lesions, the contrast will freely flow into the peritoneal space without depicting the biliary tree. Furthermore, the presence of contrast medium overlapping the area involved by the lesion may hinder the correct interpretation of the following cholangiography and occasionally totally disguise the picture. In contrast, fistulography is indicated whenever the endoscopic cholangiogram shows an incomplete filling of the biliary system resulting from a complete transection of the main bile duct or to lack of visualization of a sectorial or segmental intrahepatic branch. As an alternative to contrast medium, which occasionally might not fill the missing branch, air may be used to obtain a pneumocholangiogram.[21]

The technique of ERCP in the setting of a suspected biliary injury does not substantially differ from the routine examination. However, special attention should be paid to the injection of contrast medium, which should be slow and careful to allow precise delineation of the lesions. Massive injection of the biliary tree should be avoided. Minimal injection and early filling x-ray films are also of importance in detecting small residual CBD stones, which are present in no less than 20% of patients with biliary leakage originating from the cystic duct stump.

If the suspected lesion is located in an intrahepatic biliary branch, it is of paramount importance to obtain a complete intrahepatic cholangiogram; to achieve an adequate pressure of injection, especially if a sphincterotomy has been previously performed, the use of an occlusion balloon catheter is advisable. Intrahepatic biliary anatomy is better demonstrated by multiple x-ray films taken in different projections. Percutaneous transhepatic cholangiography and/or MRCP should be reserved for patients in whom ERCP fails technically or fails to show the intrahepatic biliary anatomy because of proximal ductal disruption.[22]

Interpretation of Intrahepatic Cholangiography

The main biliary confluence is formed by the union of the right and left hepatic ducts that drain the bile originating in the right and the left hemiliver, respectively. The main confluence is often incorrectly called *bifurcation* in the Anglo-Saxon literature; actually, although the portal vein and the hepatic artery, carrying the blood to the liver, have bifurcations, the fusion of ducts collecting the bile from the liver with a flow directed toward the CBD generates a *confluence*. According to the segmental liver anatomy described by Couinaud,[23] the left hepatic duct collects the bile originating from segment II and III (left anatomic liver lobe or left lateral sector) and from segment IV (or quadrate lobe). One or more small ducts originating from segment I (caudate lobe) also join the left hepatic duct close to the main confluence. The anatomic variations occurring in the left hepatic system are very uncommon and, in addition, not relevant in this perspective.

The right hepatic duct is shorter than the left hepatic duct and follows the same axis of the common hepatic duct. The right hepatic duct originates from the confluence of the right anteromedial sectorial duct (segments V and VIII) and of the right posterolateral sectorial duct (segments VI and VII). The right anteromedial duct is recognizable thanks to its orientation, which follows the same axis of the right hepatic duct, whereas the right posterolateral duct joins the right anteromedial duct on its medial aspect with a typical umbrella-handle-like shape. This normal anatomy (called "modal" by Couinaud) is present in approximately 60% of the population (Fig. 47–2).

The main hepatic confluence is usually highly located in the hilar region. A lower position at the level of the hepatic pedicle may also occur, causing a much closer proximity to the insertion of the cystic duct into the hepatic duct (Fig. 47–3).

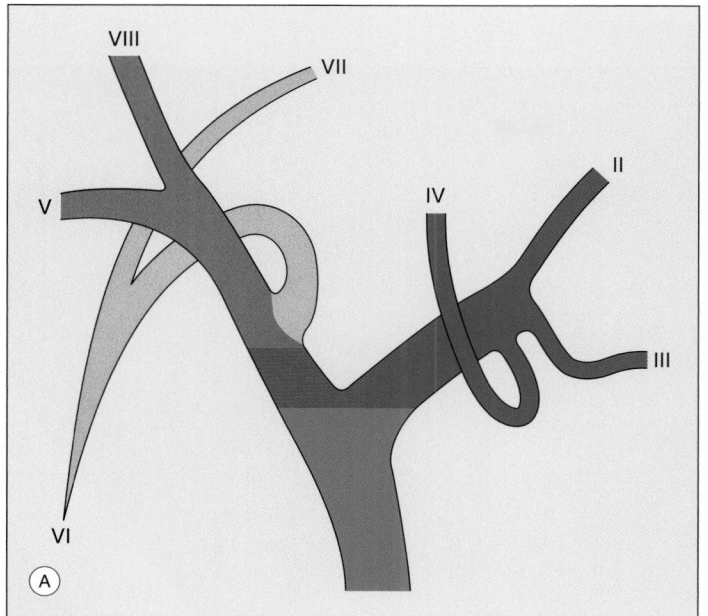

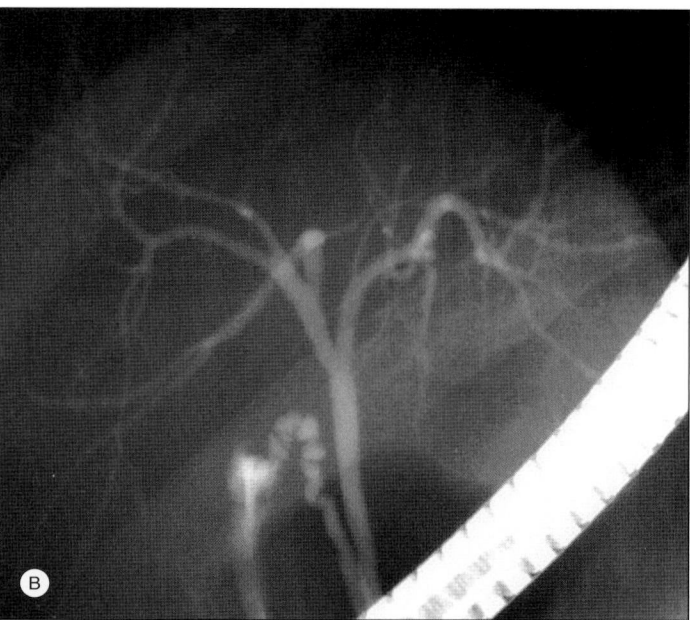

Figure 47–2. *A* and *B,* Normal distribution of intrahepatic bile ducts. Light green, common hepatic duct; blue, left hepatic ducts; dark green, right hepatic duct; red, right anteromedial duct; yellow, right posterolateral duct.

The main variations of the main hepatic confluence are the absence of the right hepatic duct with the anteromedial and posterolateral right ducts joining independently the left duct to form the confluence (Fig. 47–4) or with one of the two right sectorial ducts joining the CBD at a more distal level closer to the insertion of the cystic duct (Fig. 47–5).

More rarely, an isolated segmental or subsegmental duct may join the CBD away from the main confluence, usually on the lateral aspect of the CBD close to the insertion of the cystic duct. Therefore, most aberrant ducts arise from the right liver and drain into the common hepatic duct or cystic duct within 30 mm of the hepatocystic angle.[24] These are the most dangerous anatomic variations for the surgeon during the dissection of the gallbladder pedicle.

Apart from complete transection of the CBD (type D of the Bergman classification) (Fig. 47–6), which is typically an indication for open surgical repair, an attempt at endoscopic treatment may be envisaged in all other circumstances of biliary injury with concomitant bile leak.

The basic principle of endoscopic treatment is abolition of the transpapillary pressure gradient, thus equalizing the bile duct and duodenal pressures and allowing flow of bile into the duodenum.[25]

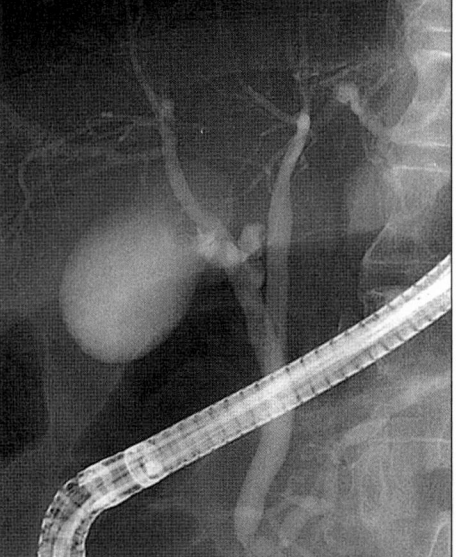

Figure 47–3. Endoscopic retrograde cholangiopancreatography (ERCP) shows low main confluence with the cystic duct joining the right hepatic duct on its medial aspect.

Endoscopic Treatment of Minor Lesions

The largest part of biliary leaks from minor lesions originates from the cystic duct stump (Fig. 47–7).

Bile leakage from the cystic duct stump may be due to different reasons: stump dehiscence resulting from defective technique in clips positioning, inadvertent injury to the cystic wall below the closure, partial disruption of the cystic duct implantation into the bile duct resulting from excessive traction, and so forth. Biliary hypertension resulting from temporary impaction of a residual bile duct stone into the sphincter of Oddi in the early postoperative period is most likely the cause of cystic duct stump dehiscence in almost one fifth of the patients. Similarly, a simple spasm of the sphincter of Oddi may theoretically create enough pressure to induce dislodgement of clips placed on the cystic duct stump. Bile leaks can also originate from severed ducts of Luschka (small

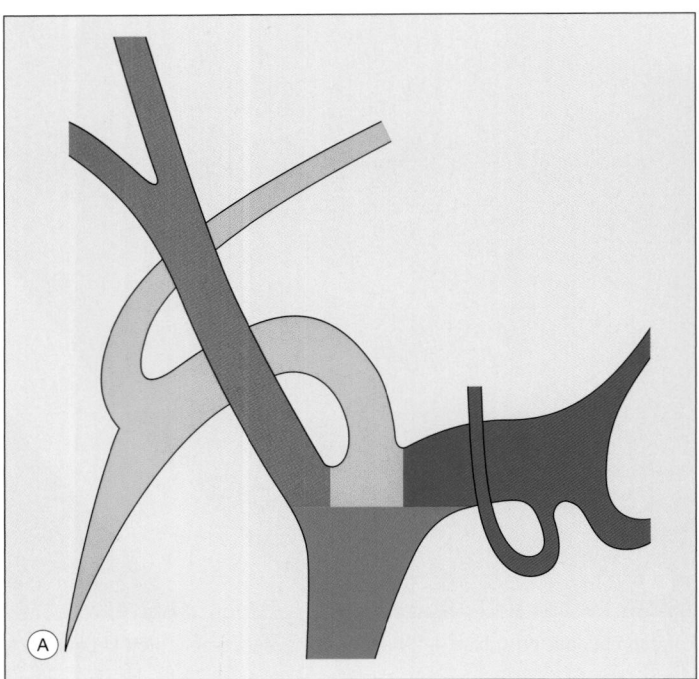
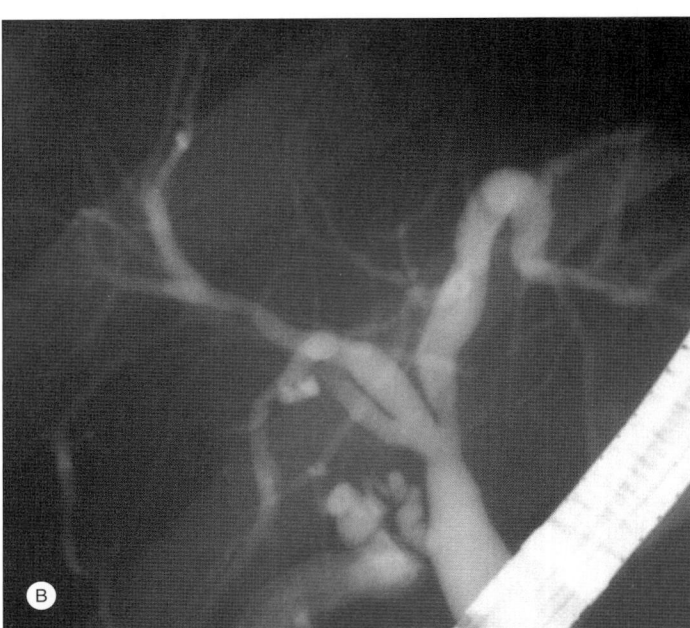

Figure 47–4. *A* and *B,* Absence of the right hepatic duct. Light green, common hepatic duct; blue, left hepatic ducts; red, right anteromedial duct; yellow, right posterolateral duct.

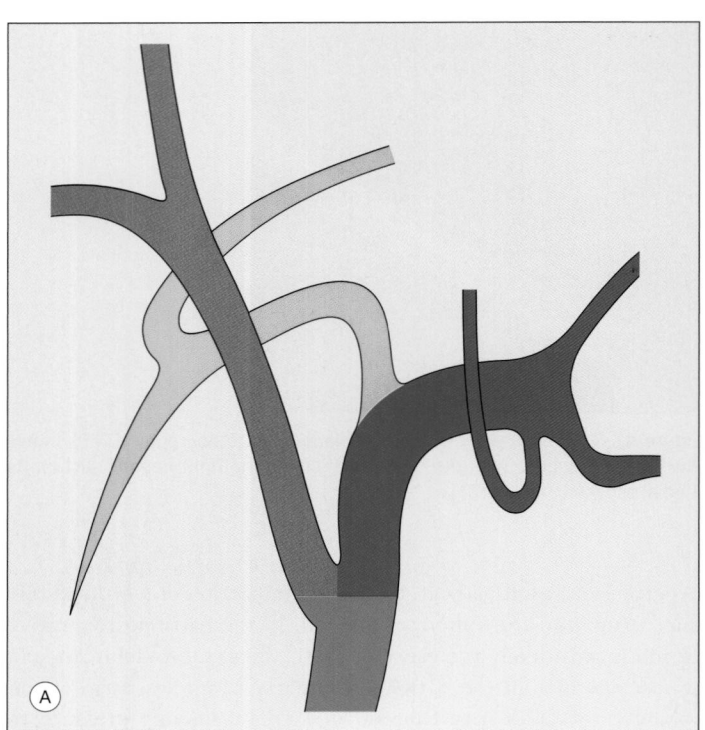
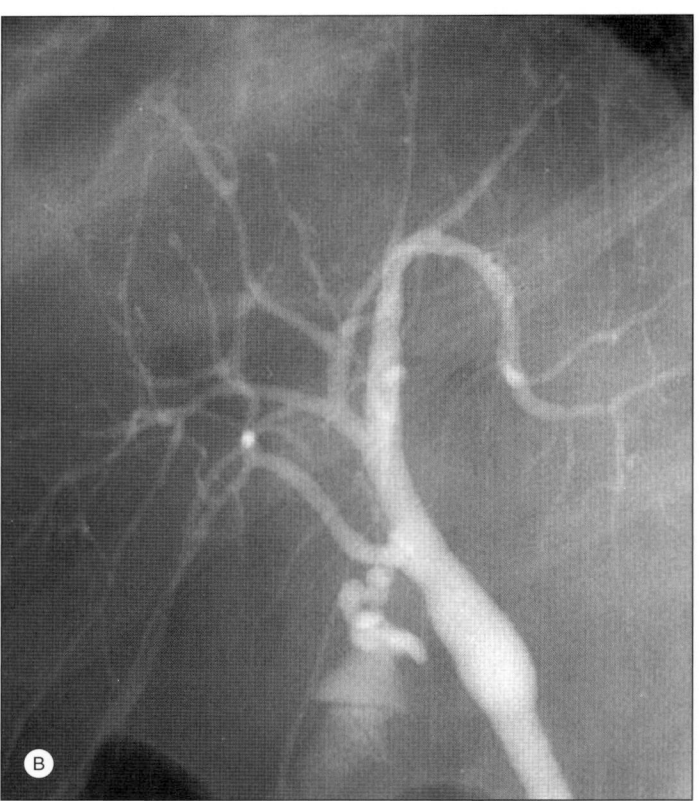

Figure 47–5. *A* and *B,* Absence of the right hepatic duct. Light green, common hepatic duct; blue, left hepatic ducts; red, right anteromedial duct; yellow, right posterolateral duct. On endoscopic retrograde cholangiopancreatography (ERCP), the cystic duct joins the right anteromedial duct on its lateral aspect.

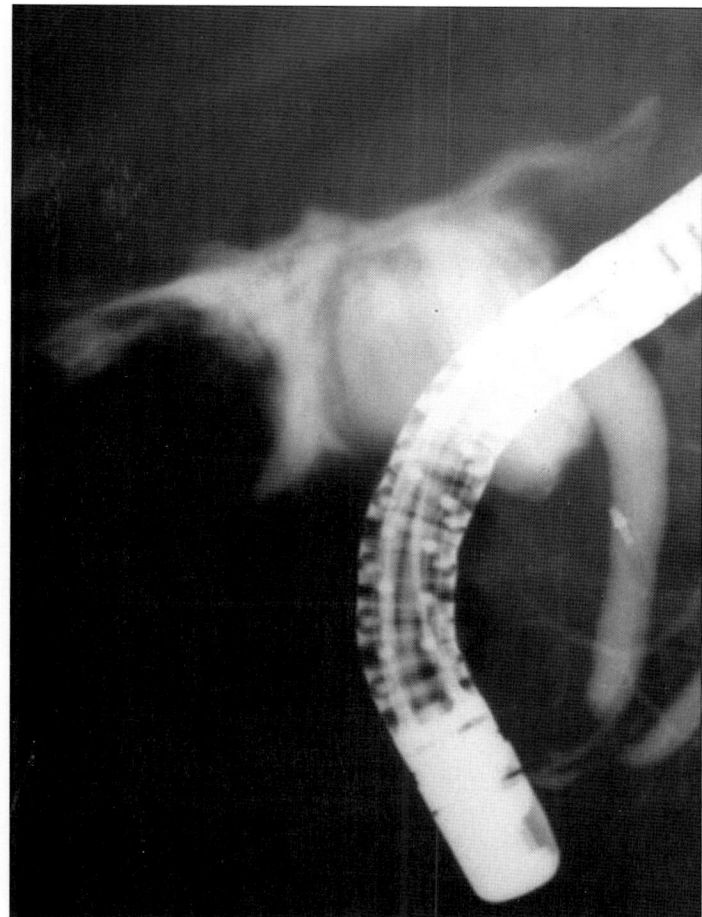

Figure 47–6. Endoscopic retrograde cholangiopancreatography (ERCP) showing complete transection of the common bile duct with contrast medium freely flowing into the subhepatic peritoneal space.

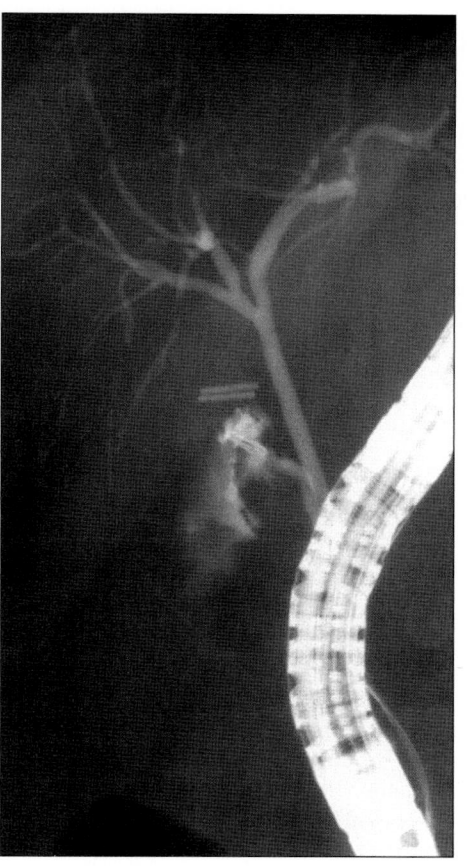

Figure 47–7. Postoperative endoscopic retrograde cholangiopancreatography (ERCP) after laparoscopic cholecystectomy; leakage of contrast medium from the cystic duct stump.

peripheral ducts connecting the intrahepatic system with the gallbladder lumen) (Fig. 47–8), small subsegmental ducts running in the gallbladder bed, and segmental or subsegmental aberrant branches joining the CBD in the proximity of the cystic duct.

As a rule, treatment of these leaks does not differ from that used when the leak arises from the cystic duct stump (Table 47–3).

The transpapillary pressure gradient can be equalized by endoscopic sphincterotomy (ES) alone,[26,27] ES and stent[27] or nasobiliary drain (NBD) placement,[28] and stent[29,30] or NBD alone[31] without preliminary ES (Fig. 47–9).

All methods seem to be equally effective in facilitating the closure of the biliary leak usually within 1 week of treatment.[3,25,29,32] Thus, the endoscopic approach of choice remains controversial. However, if stones are present in the CBD, ES and stone extraction with or without stent or NBD placement seems the most logical attitude. However, each option has its peculiar limitations. ES is associated with inherent immediate and potential long-term complications; stenting requires a second procedure to remove the stent, which can also become clogged or can migrate; and an NBD requires prolonged hospital stay, is uncomfortable for the patient, and may be accidentally

displaced. Advantages and disadvantages of the different options are summarized in Table 47–4.

Endoscopic local injection of botulinum toxin (Botox) to decrease the transpapillary bilioduodenal pressure gradient has also been recently reported.[33] Injection of 100 IU of toxin into the sphincter of Oddi was shown to significantly lower CBD pressure within 24 hours. This effect lasted for 2 weeks on average in the animal model.

In conclusion, postoperative bile leaks from minor lesions (type A) are usually amenable to endoscopic management with a very high success rate. All methods seem to be equally effective in facilitating the closure of the leak within a few days.

Endoscopic Treatment of Major Lesions

In major lesions, the bile leakage originates from a tear on the CBD or on one of the biliary branches that form the main hepatic confluence (type B). In both instances, ES alone may not be adequate to seal the leak. Thus, it is preferable to insert at least one large-bore plastic stent (10 to 11.5 Fr) long enough to bypass the

Table 47–3. Endoscopic Management of Biliary Leaks from Minor Lesions (Type A) after Cholecystectomy

Author	n	LC (%)	Cystic (%)	Luschka (%)	Other (%)	CBDS (%)	ES (%)	ES + EP (%)	EP Only (%)	Success (%)
Bourke 1995	85	62	79	6	15	18	33	67	0	95
Barkun 1997	52	58	77	15	8	22	48	23	15	88
Ryan 1998	50	78	72	8	20	22	12	26	62	100
Hourigan 1999	53	85	68	17	15	11	15	15	70	96

CBDS, common bile duct stones; EP, endoprosthesis or nasobiliary drain; ES, endoscopic sphincterotomy; LC, laparoscopic cholecystectomy.

Table 47–4. Endoscopic Options to Treat Postoperative Bile leaks (Type A according to Bergman)

Procedure	Advantages	Disadvantages
ES	Treatment of associated CBD stones	Complications
Nasobiliary drain (days)	Avoids ES Allows check cholangiography	Uncomfortable Prolongs hospitalization
Stenting (weeks)	Avoids ES	Repeat ERCP required Clogging, dislocation

CBD, common bile duct; ERCP, endoscopic retrograde cholangiopancreatography; ES, endoscopic sphincterotomy.

site of injury. The secondary intent of stent placement is to prevent the development of stricture at the site of the injured bile duct wall.[22,25] For this purpose the stent(s) should be left in place for some months to allow the healing process to stabilize. In case of secondary stricture formation at the site of injury, the presence of a stent already in place will facilitate successive endoscopic maneuvers to dilate the stricture. Therapeutic success may be obtained in 71% to 79% of cases in this setting[3,34,35] (Fig. 47–10).

Biliary stents have also been successfully used to reestablish the continuity of disrupted segmental branches at the level of the main hepatic confluence[21] and for leaks from aberrant bile ducts.[22,36]

In major biliary injury with bile leakage, the primary therapeutic objective is once again to seal the leak to convert an acute problem into a stabilized condition. The high efficacy of the endoscopic approach in this setting justifies its use as a first-line treatment whenever and wherever possible.

Treatment of postoperative bile duct strictures in the pre-laparoscopic era was traditionally surgical. The role of ERCP was limited to the diagnostic phase and particularly to the definition of the level and extent of the lesion.[37] Along with the increasing use of ERCP in the evaluation and treatment of acute complications of LC, therapeutic ERCP has been extensively adopted also to manage postoperative strictures occurring both early and late postoperatively. In fact, the first nonoperative alternative in the management of bile duct strictures has been the percutaneous transhepatic approach. After establishment of a percutaneous access to the intrahepatic bile ducts, the stricture is crossed with a guidewire and a pneumatic balloon dilation is performed. This approach, although instantly very effective, has a very limited value in the long term because of the high rate of stricture recurrence.[38] Approximately one third of the patients undergoing this treatment modality experience complications, and stricture recurrence develops in at least 25% of the cases during follow-up.[39,40] In another series published by the group at The Johns Hopkins University, the

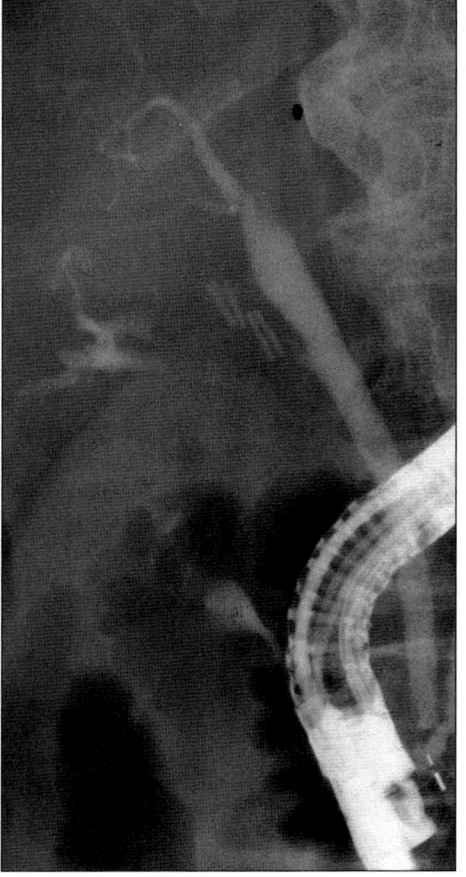

Figure 47–8. Postoperative endoscopic retrograde cholangiopancreatography (ERCP) after laparoscopic cholecystectomy in a case of subhepatic bile collection. The common bile duct is normal. Two clips are visible on the cystic artery and the cystic duct, respectively. A leak of contrast medium into the gallbladder bed originates from a so-called duct of Luschka connecting a subsegmental branch that joins the common bile duct lower than the main confluence.

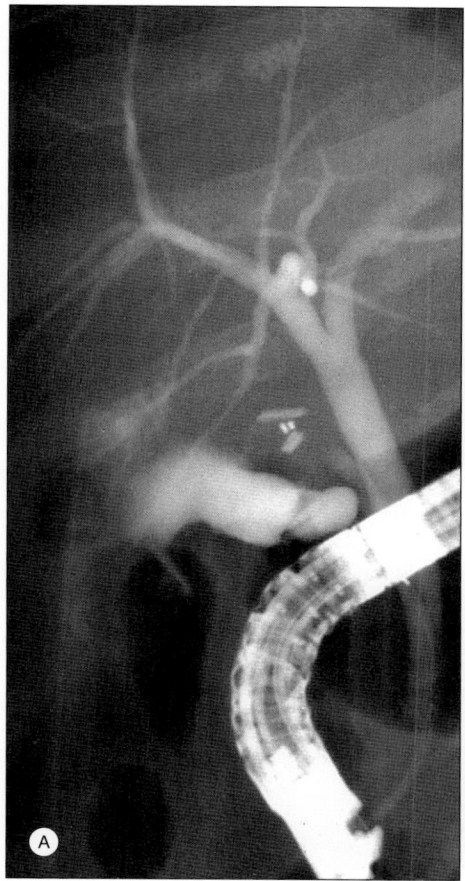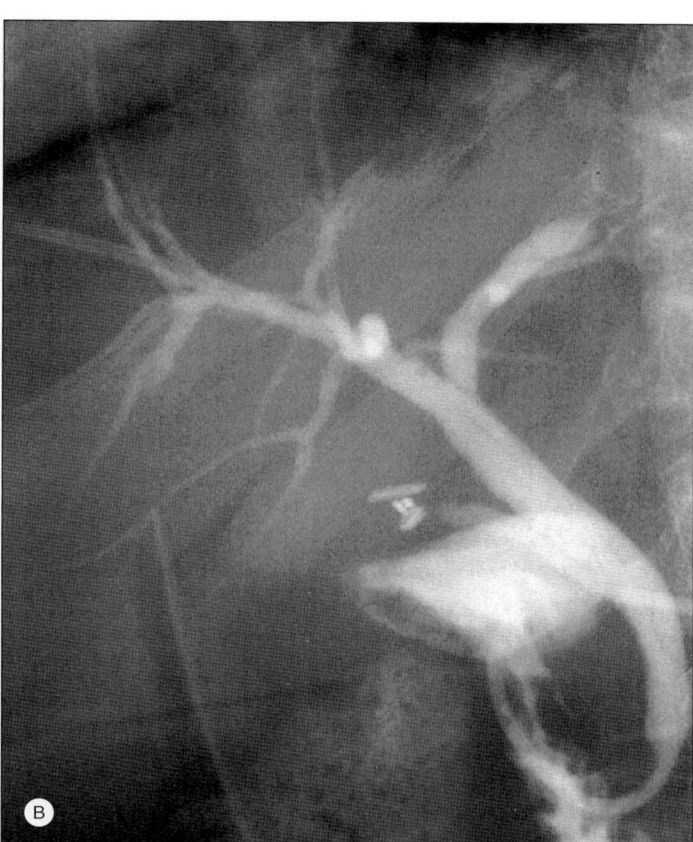

Figure 47–9. Postoperative endoscopic retrograde cholangiopancreatography (ERCP) after laparoscopic cholecystectomy in a case of external biliary fistula through a subhepatic drain. *A,* A leak of contrast medium originating in the gallbladder bed (duct of Luschka) is seen. *B,* Check cholangiography performed 3 days after endoscopic sphincterotomy and nasobiliary drain placement; the leakage is no longer visible.

success rate of these procedure was only 55%, with 20% of the patients having significant hemobilia.[41] The high recurrence rate after percutaneous pneumatic dilation is most probably due to the forceful disruption of the scar, which can add further traumatic damage to the tissue and consequential development of new local fibrogenic reaction.

The percutaneous approach has been progressively replaced by the endoscopic approach. The latter avoids the need for liver puncture, which is the main cause of complications of the percutaneous approach, it is not more difficult when the intrahepatic bile ducts are not dilated or only slightly enlarged, which is often the case in postoperative strictures, and it is also feasible in case of liver cirrhosis, ascites, or coagulopathy. Moreover, the endoscopic approach avoids the need for longstanding percutaneous internal-external catheters, thus improving the patient's comfort and compliance. Therefore, the endoscopic approach is considered today the first-line nonoperative alternative to surgical treatment; in addition, it never hinders the option of a surgical approach as a rescue therapy in case of failure.

Which is the best therapeutic algorithm is still under debate. Both surgery and the endoscopic treatment may obtain good results. However, the two alternatives have never been systematically compared in a prospective randomized trial. It is also very unlikely that

such a study will ever be conducted in the future because of the relatively low incidence of this pathology, its dispersion in several centers, and the heterogeneity of its clinical and morphologic presentation, which would make it very difficult to gather cases in homogeneous groups numerous enough to consent to any comparison.

Description of Technique

Endoscopic treatment of postoperative biliary strictures is based on two technical steps: (1) getting over the stricture, and (2) dilation of the stricture.

GETTING OVER THE STRICTURE

The morphologic requirement that allows getting over the stricture is the continuity of the CBD. In case of complete section or obstruction of the bile duct, the endoscopic option alone is applicable only in a few exceptions. A combined percutaneous and endoscopic approach with an aim at reconstructing the missing segment of the bile duct has been described.[42] Moreover, a similar combined approach has also been described in case of complete obstruction of

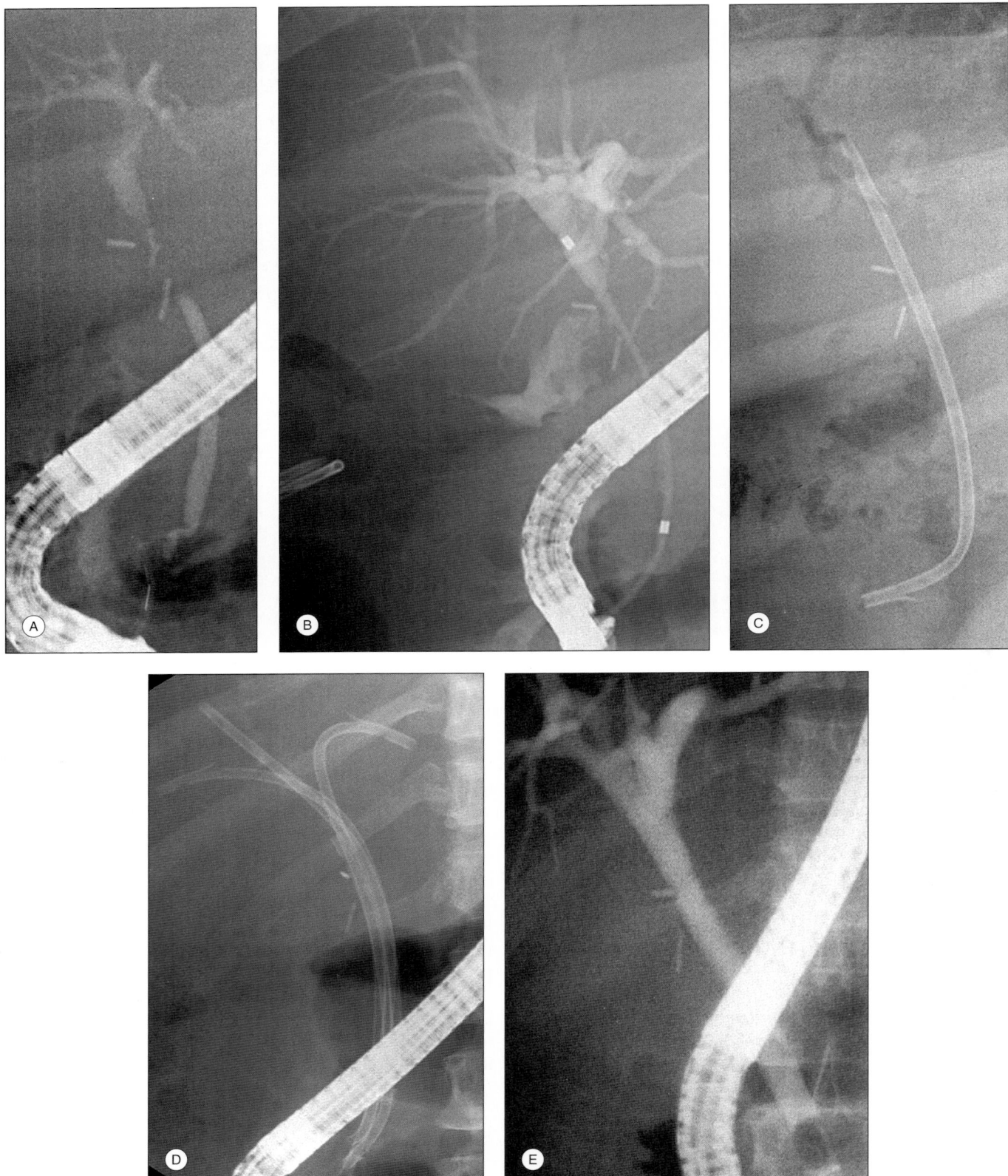

Figure 47-10. Postoperative endoscopic retrograde cholangiopancreatography (ERCP) after laparoscopic cholecystectomy in a case of peritoneal bile collection and cholestasis. *A,* Stricture of the common bile duct with clips overlapping. *B,* A catheter has been passed over the stricture by using a guidewire; injection of contrast medium through the catheter clearly shows the site of biliary injury and the correspondent leak. *C,* A 10-Fr plastic stent has been placed. *D,* During the following months, three 10-Fr stents were inserted to dilate the stricture, one in each main biliary territory (anteromedial right, posterolateral right, and left biliary ducts). *E,* Balloon-occluded check cholangiography after removal of the three stents; the stricture has completely disappeared.

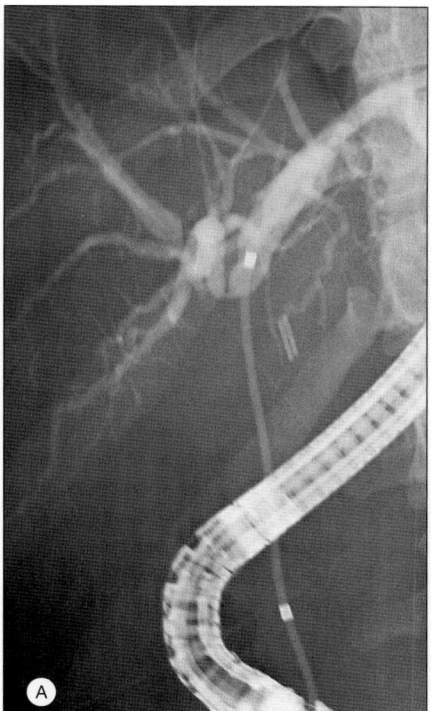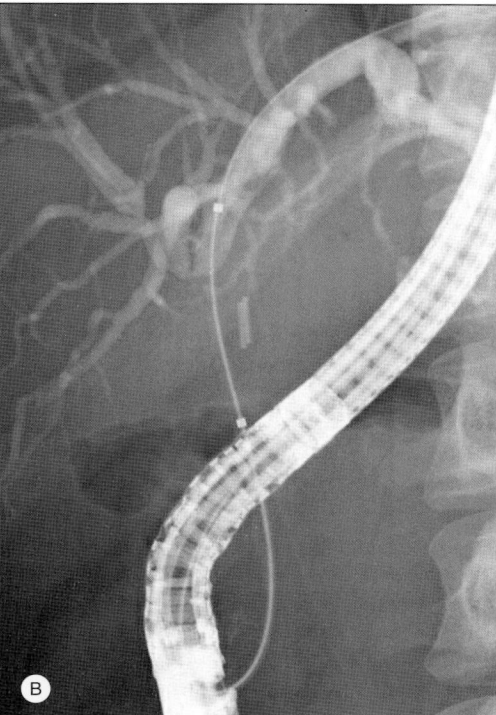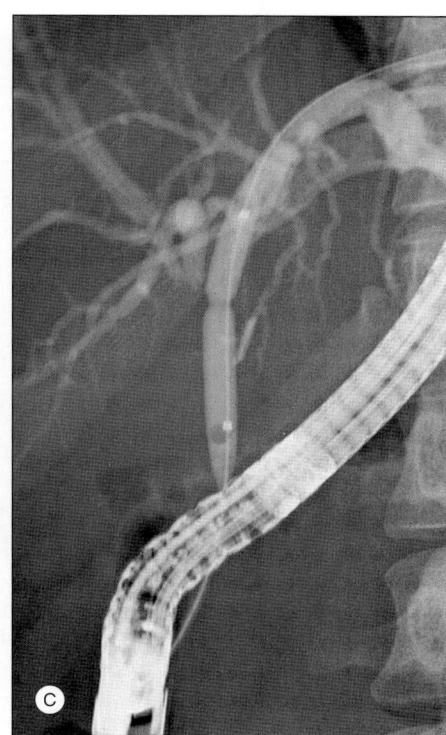

Figure 47–11. Postoperative stricture after laparoscopic cholecystectomy converted to open cholecystectomy. *A,* A very tight stricture located at the level of the main confluence has been overcome by a guidewired catheter. *B,* A balloon dilator has been passed through the stricture over the guidewire. *C,* Balloon dilation is performed; notice the waist on the balloon indicating high stricture firmness.

the distal biliary stump; the percutaneous puncture of the distal stump was performed under radiologic guidance with a device designed for nonbiliary use (a set marketed for placing transjugular intrahepatic portosystemic shunts).[43] However, these approaches, because of the lack of standardization, cannot be recommended on a routine basis.

In most cases, and especially when symptoms develop a long time after surgery, the CBD is accessible by endoscopy, and the stricture is not complete, getting over the stricture is the preliminary step to undertake dilation. This maneuver is often much more difficult in postoperative strictures then in neoplastic strictures because the stenosis, even if commonly very short, may be asymmetric. Furthermore, the fibrosis makes it especially thin and tightened. It is often necessary to use thin hydrophilic guidewires (0.021 or 0.018 inch) with straight or J-type extremity; their manipulation requires patience, skill, and optimal x-ray control. The morphology of the stenosis has to be respected, and forceful maneuvers with stiff guidewires that may create false routes leading to the failure of the procedure should be strictly avoided. Changing the position of the patient may help in identifying radiologically the right pathway to follow with the guidewire. Pulling on a stone retrieval balloon inflated under the stricture may help in stretching the bile duct and thus in modifying the axis of the guidewire. Manipulation of bendable catheters or papillotomes may also be used to change the direction of the guidewire. Once the stricture is passed, the hydrophilic guidewire is exchanged for a stiffer and more stable one to proceed to dilation.

DILATION OF THE STRICTURE

Dilation of the stricture has two objectives: the first one is to reopen the bile duct to achieve a regular bile flow, and the second one is to secure the dilation to avoid restricturing in the long term. In the beginning of endoscopic treatment, only the first objective was pursued; in the percutaneous approach, the mainstay of treatment was pneumatic dilation alone.[44] However, it became very soon clear that even if immediately very effective, pneumatic dilation alone was ineffective in granting good results in a long-term follow-up. Today, pneumatic dilation is mainly used as a preliminary step before placement of one or more plastic stents (Fig. 47–11).

The role of stent placement is to keep the stricture open for a long time (months to years according to different treatment strategies) while allowing scar modeling and its consolidation.[45] Typically, two 10-Fr stents are placed, exchanged every 3 months to avoid cholangitis resulting from stent occlusion, and left in place for 1 year. In a retrospective study from the Amsterdam group reporting on the multidisciplinary experience obtained during a decade (1981 to 1990), the long-term results of endoscopic treatment were compared with the long-term results of surgery.[46] In total, 35 patients had undergone surgery (exclusively represented by Roux-en-Y hepaticojejunostomy), whereas 66 patients had undergone endoscopic treatment. Patients' characteristics, type of initial injury, and level of obstruction were not significantly different in the two groups. At a mean follow-up of 50 and 42 months for the surgical and the endoscopic group of treatment, respectively, 83% of patients in both groups had an excellent (asymptomatic patient with

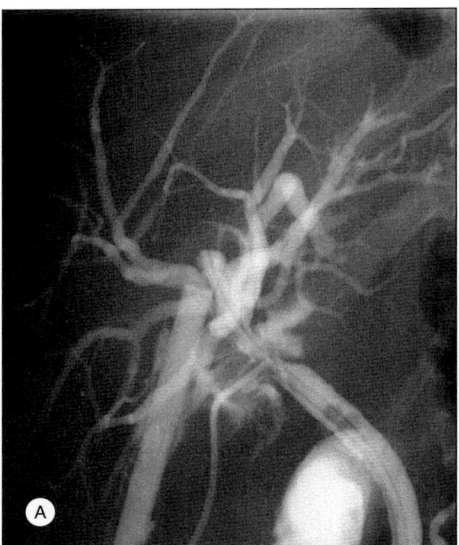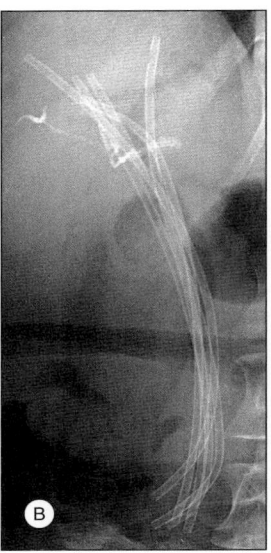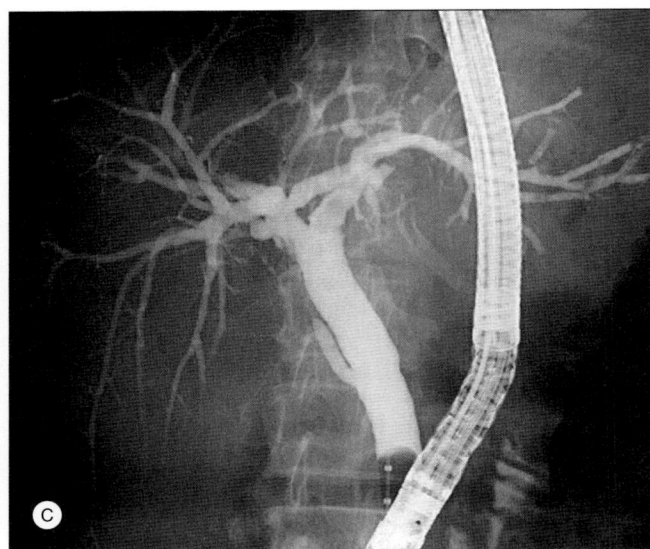

Figure 47–12. Postoperative cholangiography through a T-tube drain placed at cholecystectomy to repair complete transection of the common bile duct at the hilum. *A,* A stricture and a leak of contrast medium around the bile duct are visible. *B,* At the end of treatment 5, 10-Fr stents have been placed. *C,* Balloon-occluded cholangiography after stent removal; complete disappearance of the stricture.

normal or stable laboratory parameters) or good (single episode of cholangitis) result. Immediate complication rate was in favor of the endoscopic treatment (8% vs. 26% for surgical treatment), whereas 21% of the patient had at least one episode of cholangitis resulting from stent malfunction during the stenting period (two 10-Fr stents for 1 year with stent exchange every 3 months). When analyzing the long-term results, it becomes immediately evident how the time interval between the end of treatment and the symptomatic recurrence of the stricture is much shorter in the group with endoscopic treatment when compared with the surgical group (on average 3 ± 11 months vs. 40 ± 11 months), indicating a possible undertreatment in the endoscopy group. However, this important study showed that the endoscopic treatment may be considered at least as effective as the surgical one in terms of long-term results, having the big advantage of not hindering any further surgery if necessary.

Several other experiences of endoscopic treatment with plastic stents of postoperative biliary strictures have been published in the recent years.[3,45–54] However, from the analysis of the available data it appears that this treatment modality is still far from standardized; in fact, the published experiences differ in terms of number of stents placed, their caliber, exchange intervals, and definition of treatment objectives and of outcomes. The following examples, concerning the two largest series published in the literature, exemplify two different methodologic approaches:

- The treatment protocol used by the Amsterdam group in their more recent publication (74 patients) is the classic one, entailing placement of two 10-Fr stents, exchanged every 3 months for 1 year (the period of stenting).[51] Preliminary pneumatic dilation had been performed in approximately one fourth of the patients before stent insertion. A combined percutaneous-endoscopic approach to bypass the stricture with a guidewire was required in only three cases. Stents were removed after 1 year.

- The protocol described by our group (55 patients)[50] involved the placement of the maximum possible number of stents (ideally 10 Fr) in relation to the tightness of the stricture and diameter of the CBD at every treatment session with a trimonthly interval. Treatment was carried on until complete morphologic disappearance of the stricture at cholangiography (Fig. 47–12).

Preliminary balloon dilation was performed in 40% of the patients, almost always at the first treatment session. A combined percutaneous-endoscopic approach was required in three cases. The mean number of stents inserted was 1.7 (range 1 to 4) at the first session, and 3.2 (range 1 to 6) at the end of the treatment. Disappearance of the stricture was checked 24 to 48 hours after removal of the stents by a check cholangiography through an NBD. Early complications developed in four (9%) patients (three cholangitis, one pancreatitis) and stent occlusion that required early stent exchange occurred in eight (18%) patients. Mean duration of treatment was 12.1 ± 5.3 months (range 2 to 24 months). Follow-up included clinical evaluation, laboratory parameters, and liver ultrasonography every 3 months during the 1st year and every 6 months in the following years.

- In the Amsterdam series, the technical success of stenting was 80%; however, only 44 patients (59% of the initial cohort and 75% of patients in whom an initial technical success had been obtained) concluded the 12-month stenting period because of different reasons. At a median follow-up of 9 years, 9 of 44 patients (20%) developed recurrent strictures. In 8 of 9 cases, recurrent strictures developed within the first 6 months of follow-up (median 2.6 months). In conclusion, on an intention-to-treat basis, this protocol was able to definitely solve the bile duct stricture in 47% of the initial cohort. The results of this study suggest that endoscopic stenting is not the best treatment option for patients with low compliance to repeated treatment sessions. Similar results, with 81% of patients free of symptoms at a mean follow-up of 9.5 years, were reported in an abstract form by the Toronto group by using the same treatment protocol.[49]

- In our study, 42 of 55 patients initially considered were evaluable at a mean follow-up of 49 months after the end of treatment. Ten patients were excluded from the protocol because of complete CBD section ($n = 5$) or use of self-expandable metallic stents ($n = 5$). Another three patients were not evaluable because of different reasons. Two patients died of unrelated causes during follow-up. Among the remaining 40 patients, there was no recurrence of symptoms caused by relapsing biliary stricture. One patient sustained two episodes of cholangitis but without stricture recurrence. By an intention-to-treat analysis the success rate was 89% (40/45). Even though the follow-up period in our series is shorter when compared with the Amsterdam series, it is longer then the typical period during which all the recurrences after endoscopic treatment have been described (2 years). In conclusion, this more aggressive approach to endoscopic treatment with stents seems to improve long-term results for patients with postoperative biliary strictures.

According to the published data, endoscopic treatment with stents of major bile duct injuries and strictures is at least as effective as surgical treatment. The advantages of endoscopic treatment are its simplicity, reversibility, and minimal invasiveness. Therefore, endoscopic treatment should always be considered, whenever available, in the therapeutic algorithm of most patients with major bile duct injuries. For most of them, it may be the only treatment required. Endoscopy and surgery should not be considered as alternative but as complementary treatments. This complex and difficult pathology is best managed in centers in which a multidisciplinary approach is available.

Complications

Complications may occur during the first treatment session and are related to the ES (acute pancreatitis, retroperitoneal perforation, and bleeding), which is usually performed to get access to the bile ducts, or during the stenting period. ES-related complications in this setting do not differ in frequency, severity, and management from those encountered in other more common situations, such as treatment of CBD stones. Complications arising during the stenting period are mostly due to stent dysfunction: obstruction, migration, dislocation, and impaction. Acute cholangitis is the typical clinical manifestation of stent dysfunction. Cholangitis is usually mild and often self-limited in this setting but requires prompt endoscopic evaluation and reestablishment of correct bile drainage by stent repositioning. A typical complication of long-lasting stenting is the development of biliary sludge and stones above the stricture. This condition may cause cholangitis, but it may also be totally asymptomatic. In addition, liver function test may also be completely normal. This may lead to unintentional prolongation of the planned stenting period. Removal of all stones and sludge by basket and/or balloon extraction is mandatory before replacement of the new

stent(s) to avoid potential early reocclusion. To avoid stone formation, the trimonthly time schedule of stent replacement should not be prolonged. Therefore, patient compliance is of utmost importance when dealing with postoperative bile duct stricture, and patients should always be fully informed of the inherent risks of not duly following the planned treatment program.

Future Trends

The main limitation of endoscopic treatment of postoperative bile strictures with the current method of multiple plastic stenting is the need for repeat interventions over a long time (1 year on average). The ideal stent would allow progressive dilation of the stricture during weeks or months and would dissolve once the goal had been reached. Self-expanding metal stents (SEMS) have proved to be a bad alternative to plastic stenting for several reasons.[52] First, SEMS invariably induces a hyperplastic response of the inflammatory tissue at the level of the stricture. This hyperplastic reaction ultimately leads to SEMS occlusion, on average less than 1 year after their placement. Second, SEMS are usually not removable; therefore, treatment of secondary stricture resulting from hyperplastic reaction requires repeated balloon dilations and plastic stenting. Third, biliary SEMS have been developed to produce abrupt recanalization of a stricture resulting from neoplastic invasion; thus, the radial force exerted by the stent is much higher than the one desirable to induce progressive dilation of a scar, such as the scar of postoperative bile duct strictures. Self-expandable resorbable plastic stents are under development for esophageal use and may become available in the future for use in the biliary tract. If this technology is able to replace the current method of progressive dilation of postoperative bile duct strictures, it will require appropriate evaluation when these stents become available. Drug-eluting self-expandable stents have been used in the vascular system to inhibit endothelial growth; it is conceivable that this technology might also become available for use in the biliary system. Local release of anti-inflammatory drugs able to control the fibrogenetic process that occurs during healing of a biliary injury may be valuable in this setting.

REFERENCES

1. Deziel DJ, Millikan KW, Economou SG, et al: Complications of laparoscopic cholecystectomy: A national survey of 4292 hospitals and an analysis of 77 604 cases. Am J Surg 165:9–14, 1992.
2. MacFayden BV Jr, Vecchio R, Ricardo AE, et al: Bile duct injury after laparoscopic cholecystectomy. The United States experience. Surg Endosc 12:315–321, 1998.
3. Bergman JJ, van den Brink GR, Rauws E, et al: Treatment of bile duct lesions after laparoscopic cholecystectomy. Gut 38:141–147, 1996.
4. Dubois F, Berthelot G, Levrard H: Cholecystectomy by coelioscopy. La Presse Med 18:980–982, 1989.
5. Perissat J, Collet D, Belliard R, et al: Laparoscopic cholecystectomy: The state of the art. A report on 700 consecutive cases. World J Surg 1074–1082, 1992.
6. Russell JC, Walsh SJ, Mattie AS, et al: Bile duct injuries, 1989-1993. A statewide experience. Arch Surg 131:382–388, 1996.

7. Legorreta AP, Silber JH, Costantino GN, et al: Increased cholecystectomy rate after the introduction of laparoscopic cholecystectomy. JAMA 270:1429–1432, 1993.

8. Shea JA, Healey MJ, Berlin JA, et al: Mortality and complications associated with laparoscopic cholecystectomy. A meta-analysis. Ann Surg 224:609–620, 1996.

9. Moody FG: Bile duct injury during laparoscopic cholecystectomy. Surg Endosc 14:605–607, 2000.

10. Strasberg SM, Hertl M, Soper JN: An Analysis of the problem of biliary injury during laparoscopic cholecystectomy. J Am Coll Surg 180:101–125, 1995.

11. Gigot JF, Etienne J, Aerts R, et al: The dramatic reality of biliary tract injury during laparoscopic cholecystectomy: An anonymous multicenter Belgian survey of 65 patients. Surg Endosc 11:1171–1178, 1997.

12. Davidoff AM, Pappas TN, Murray EA, et al: Mechanisms of major biliary injury during laparoscopic cholecystectomy. Ann Surg 215:196–202, 1992.

13. Nuzzo G: Personal communication, unpublished data, 2002.

14. Fletcher DR: Biliary injury at laparoscopic cholecystectomy: Recognition and prevention. Aust N Z J Surg 63:673–677, 1993.

15. Richardson MC, Bell G, Fullarton GM: Incidence and nature of bile duct injuries following laparoscopic cholecystectomy: An audit of 5913 cases. Br J Surg 83:1356–1360, 1996.

16. Z'graggen K, Wehrli H, Metzger A, et al: Complications of laparoscopic cholecystectomy in Switzerland. A prospective 3-year study of 10 174 patients. Swiss Association of Laparoscopic and Thorachoscopic Surgery. Surg Endosc 12:1303–1310, 1998.

17. Wherry DC, Marohn MR, Malanoski MP, et al: An external audit of laparoscopic cholecystectomy in the steady state performed in medical treatment facilities of the department of defense. Ann Surg 224:145–154, 1996.

18. Adamsen S, Hart Hansen O, Fuch-Jensen P, et al: Bile duct injury during laparoscopic cholecystectomy: A prospective nationwide series. J Am Coll Surg 184:571–578, 1997.

19. Archer SB, Brown DW, Smith D, et al: Bile duct injury during laparoscopic cholecystectomy. Ann Surg 234:549–559, 2001.

20. Vitellas KM, El-Dieb A, Vaswani K, et al: Detection of bile duct leaks using MR cholangiography with mangafodipir trisodium (Teslascan). J Comput Assist Tomogr 25:102–105, 2001.

21. Mutignani M, Shah SK, Tringali A, et al: Endoscopic therapy for biliary leaks from aberrant right hepatic ducts severed during cholecystectomy. Gastrointest Endosc 55:932–936, 2002.

22. Mehta SN, Pavone E, Barkun JS, et al: A review of the management of post-cholecystectomy biliary leaks during the laparoscopic era. Am J Gastroenterol 92:1262–1267, 1997.

23. Couinaud C: Le foie. Etude anatomiques et chirurgicales. Paris, Masson Ed, 1957.

24. Moosman DA, Coller FA: Prevention of traumatic injury to the bile ducts. A study of the structures of the cystohepatic angle encountered in cholecystectomy and supraduodenal choledochostomy. Am J Surg 82:132–143, 1951.

25. Bjorkman DJ, Carr-Locke DL, Lichtenstein DR, et al: Postsurgical bile leaks: Endoscopic obliteration of the transpapillary pressure gradient is enough. Am J Gastroenterol 90:2128–2133, 1995.

26. Liguory C, Vitale GC, Lefevbre JF, et al: Endoscopic treatment of postoperative biliary fistulae. Surgery 100:779–784, 1991.

27. Ponchon T, Gallez JF, Valette PJ, et al: Endoscopic treatment of biliary tract fistulas. Gastrointest Endosc 35:490–498, 1989.

28. Chow S, Bosco JJ, Heiss FW, et al: Successful treatment of post-cholecystectomy bile leaks using nasobiliary tube drainage and sphincterotomy. Am J Gastroenterol 92:1839–1843, 1997.

29. Foutch PG, Harlan JR, Hoefer M: Endoscopic therapy for patients with a postoperative bile leak. Gastrointest Endosc 39:416–421, 1993.

30. Marks JM, Ponsky JL, Shillingstad RB, et al: Biliary stenting is more effective than sphincterotomy in the resolution of biliary leaks. Surg Endosc 12:327–330, 1998.

31. Sugiyama M, Mori T, Atomi Y: Endoscopic nasobiliary drainage for treating bile leaks after laparoscopic cholecystectomy. Hepatogastroenterol 46:762–765, 1999.

32. Binmoeller KF, Katon RM, Schneidman R: Endoscopic management of postoperative biliary leaks. Review of 77 cases and report of two cases with biloma formation. Am J Gastroenterol 86:227–231, 1991.

33. Marks JM, Bower AL, Goormastic M, et al: A comparison of common bile duct pressures after botulinum toxin injection into the sphincter of Oddi versus biliary stenting in acanine model. Am J Surg 181:60–64, 2001.

34. Traverso LW, Kozarek RA, Ball TJ, et al: Endoscopic retrograde cholangiopancreatography after laparoscopic cholecystectomy. Am J Surg 165:581–586, 1993.

35. Woods MS, Traverso LW, Kozarek RA, et al: Characteristics of biliary tract complications during laparoscopic cholecystectomy: A multi-institutional study. Am J Surg 167:27–33, 1994.

36. Mergener K, Strobel JC, Suhocki P, et al: The role of ERCP in diagnosis and management of accessory bile duct leaks after cholecystectomy. Gastrointest Endosc 50:527–531, 1999.

37. Vallon AG, Mason RR, Laurence BH, Cotton PB: Endoscopic retrograde cholangiography in post-operative bile duct strictures. Br J Radiol 55:32–35, 1982.

38. Trambert JJ, Bron KM, Zajko AB, et al: Percutaneous transhepatic balloon dilatation of benign biliary strictures. Am J Radiol 149:945–948, 1987.

39. Mueller PR, van Sonnemberg E, Ferrucci JT Jr, et al: Biliary stricture dilatation. Multicenter review of clinical management in 73 patients. Radiology 160:17–22, 1986.

40. Williams HJ, Bender CE, May GR: Benign postoperative biliary strictures: Dilatation with fluoroscopic guidance. Radiology 163:629–634, 1987.

41. Pitt HA, Kaufman SL, Coleman J, et al: Benign postoperative strictures: Operate or dilate? Ann Surg 210:417–427, 1989.

42. Bezzi M, Silecchia G, Orsi F, et al: Complications after laparoscopic cholecystectomy. Surg Endosc 9:29–36, 1995.

43. Dumonceau JM, Baize M, Devière J: Endoscopic transhepatic repair of the common hepatic duct after excision during cholecystectomy. Gastrointest Endosc 52:540–543, 2000.

44. Geenen DJ, Geenen JE, Hogan WJ, et al: Endoscopic therapy for benign bile duct strictures. Gastrointest Endosc 35:367–371, 1989.

45. Berkelhammer C, Kortan P, Haber GB, et al: Endoscopic biliary prostheses as treatment for benign postoperative bile duct strictures. Gastrointest Endosc 35:95–101, 1989.

46. Davids PH, Tanka AK, Rauws EA, et al: Benign biliary strictures. Surgery or endoscopy? Ann Surg 217:237–243, 1993.

47. Davids PH, Rauws EA, Coene PP, et al: Endoscopic stenting for postoperative biliary strictures. Gastrointest Endosc 38:12–18, 1992.

48. Smith MT, Sherman S, Lehman GA: Endoscopic management of benign strictures of the biliary tree. Endoscopy 27:253–266, 1995.

49. Duvall A, Haber GB, Kortan P, et al: Long term follow up of endoscopic stenting for benign postoperative biliary strictures [abstract]. Gastrointest Endosc 45:AB129, 1997.

50. Costamagna G, Pandolfi M, Mutignani M, et al: Long term results of endoscopic management of postoperative biliary strictures with increasing number of stents. Gastrointest Endosc 54:162–168, 2001.

51. Bergman JJ, Burgmeister L, Bruno MJ, et al: Long term follow up after biliary stent placement for postoperative bile duct stenosis. Gastrointest Endosc 54:154–161, 2001.

52. Dumonceau JM, Devière J, Delhaye M, et al: Plastic and metal stents for postoperative benign bile duct strictures: The best and the worst. Gastrointest Endosc 47:8–17, 1998.

53. Draganov P, Hoffman B, Marsh W, et al: Long term outcome in patients with benign biliary strictures treated endoscopically with multiple stents. Gastrointest Endosc 55:680–686, 2002.

54. Familiari L, Scaffidi M, Familiari P, et al: An endoscopic approach to the management of surgical bile duct injuries: Nine years' experience. Dig Liv Dis 35:493–497, 2003.

Infections of the Biliary Tract

Jennifer J. Telford and David L. Carr-Locke

Introduction

The histologic definition of cholangitis is inflammation of the bile duct. However, when used in practice, cholangitis refers to a characteristic clinical presentation associated with bile duct obstruction and bacterial infection. Other etiologies of bile duct inflammation have a preceding descriptor, for instance, parasitic cholangitis. Furthermore, all types of bile duct inflammation may be complicated by obstruction and secondary bacterial infection. The conditions predisposing to cholangitis are listed in Table 48–1.

Bacterial cholangitis represents most infections of the biliary tract. The underlying cause is usually extrahepatic bile duct obstruction from a stone or stricture and is readily managed by medical and endoscopic therapy. Less common forms of cholangitis include recurrent pyogenic cholangitis, parasitic cholangitis, and acquired immunodeficiency syndrome (AIDS) cholangiopathy. Recurrent pyogenic cholangitis results from obstruction of both the intrahepatic and extrahepatic biliary tract with repetitive episodes of bacterial cholangitis and is almost exclusively observed in eastern Asia. Patients with this condition are seen elsewhere in the world de novo or after emigration. Parasitic cholangitis affects those residing in areas endemic with pathogens that infest the biliary tract. AIDS cholangiopathy is characterized by typical cholangiographic abnormalities together with parasitic or viral infection of the biliary tract. Both parasitic cholangitis and AIDS cholangiopathy may be complicated by secondary bacterial cholangitis.

Cholecystitis usually results from obstruction of bile flow at the level of the cystic duct with subsequent mucosal inflammation of the gallbladder. As with cholangitis, migrated gallstones are the underlying etiology of most cases of cholecystitis. Acalculous cholecystitis is due to cystic duct obstruction from another cause or occurs in the absence of obstruction. Infection of the gallbladder is a common complication of cholecystitis but rarely the underlying cause. Although the treatment of cholecystitis is usually surgical, there is emerging endoscopic experience in patients who are not surgical candidates.

Cholangitis

EPIDEMIOLOGY

The epidemiology of cholangitis depends on the underlying cause of biliary tract obstruction.

PATHOGENESIS

Obstruction of the bile duct leads to bile stasis and increased intraluminal pressure. The normally sterile bile becomes contaminated with bacteria, which either ascend from the duodenum across the papilla or, more likely, cross into the bile duct from the portal venous system (translocation route). With decreased bile flow, Enterobacteriaceae and other colonic bacteria colonize the small intestine and are the primary pathogens in acute obstructive cholangitis by translocation.

CLINICAL FEATURES

Charcot's triad of right upper quadrant pain, fever, and jaundice is present in 70% of patients with acute bacterial cholangitis. The

Table 48–1. Conditions Associated with Cholangitis

Intraluminal Obstruction
Choledocholithiasis and hepatolithiasis
Biliary stent occlusion
Mirizzi syndrome
Biliary parasites
Fungal ball
Hemobilia
Sump syndrome
Choledochal cyst

Non-neoplastic Stricture
Primary sclerosing cholangitis
Chronic pancreatitis
Pancreatic cyst or pseudocyst
Papillary stenosis
Recurrent pyogenic cholangitis
AIDS cholangiopathy
Ischemic stricture
Anastomotic stricture
    Liver transplant
    Bilioenteric anastomosis
Radiation
Postchemoinfusion
Tuberculosis

Neoplastic Stricture
Cholangiocarcinoma
Pancreatic carcinoma
Ampullary adenoma or carcinoma
Duodenal carcinoma
Carcinoid tumor
Small intestinal lymphoma
Kaposi's sarcoma
Metastatic disease

Iatrogenic
Post-ERCP
Postsphincterotomy
Posthepatojejunostomy
Post-transhepatic cholangiography
Post-T-tube cholangiography

AIDS, acquired immunodeficiency syndrome; ERCP, endoscopic retrograde cholangiopancreatography.

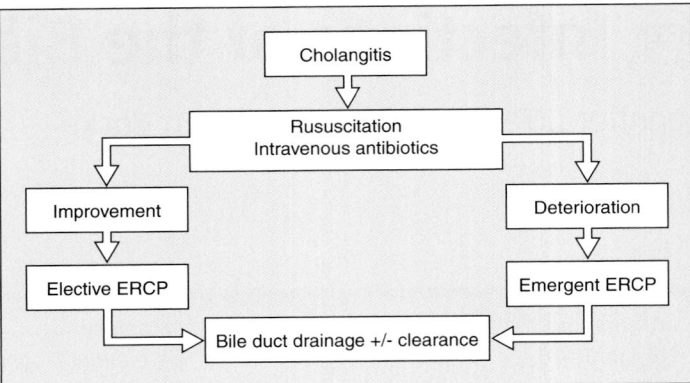

Figure 48–1. Algorithm for management of cholangitis.

addition of hypotension and confusion constitutes Reynold's pentad, which is present in less than 5% of patients with cholangitis but is significantly associated with mortality.[1] Right upper quadrant pain and/or fever may be absent in the elderly, diabetics, or patients treated with systemic corticosteroids. On physical examination, elevated temperature, tachycardia, hypotension, tachypnea, mental status changes, right upper quadrant tenderness, and jaundice may be present.

Laboratory abnormalities include leukocytosis with neutrophilia and elevated liver enzymes with a predominant cholestatic pattern. The pancreatic enzymes are elevated if pancreatitis is also present. Blood cultures are positive in 50% of patients.[2]

The most common organism causing cholangitis is *Escherichia coli*. Other pathogens include *Klebsiella pneumoniae* and the other Enterobacteriaceae, *Pseudomonas aeruginosa*, *Enterococcus* species, and *Streptococcus* species. Anaerobes are rarely isolated, but this may reflect their fastidious culture requirements. Isolation of *Enterococci* or multiple organisms from bile is more common in patients with a biliary endoprosthesis[3] or bilioenteric anastomosis.

Complications of cholangitis include hepatic abscess, distant metastatic abscess, bacteremia, the systemic inflammatory response syndrome, multiple organ dysfunction, and a 10% risk of death. The presence of concomitant medical problems, thrombocytopenia, hypoalbuminemia, and uremia before endoscopic or surgical drainage are prospectively determined independent predictors of mortality in cholangitis resulting from choledocholithiasis, although they have more influence in postsurgical outcome.[4] In cholangitis resulting from any cause, age, female gender, acute renal failure, cirrhosis, hepatic abscess, proximal malignant biliary stricture, and cholangitis after percutaneous cholangiography are independently associated with increased mortality.[1]

DIAGNOSIS

The diagnosis of cholangitis is suspected from the characteristic clinical syndrome described previously. Imaging techniques are used to confirm biliary obstruction, especially in an atypical presentation. Ultrasonography is excellent at detecting cholelithiasis and bile duct dilatation. However, in acute bile duct obstruction, the biliary tract may be of normal caliber and ultrasound is falsely negative. Computed tomography (CT) has limited value in the assessment of a patient with cholangitis.[5] Magnetic resonance (MR) cholangiography has comparable accuracy to endoscopic retrograde cholangiopancreatography (ERCP) in the diagnosis of choledocholithiasis[6] and benign and malignant biliary strictures.[7]

DIFFERENTIAL DIAGNOSIS

The differential diagnosis of cholangitis includes cholecystitis, hepatic abscess, right renal colic, and right lower lobe pneumonia and/or empyema. These entities are usually readily identified by physical examination of the chest for pulmonary processes, urinalysis, and abdominal ultrasound to detect cholecystitis or a liver abscess. In Mirizzi's syndrome, a stone impacted in the gallbladder neck or cystic duct compresses the common hepatic duct and causes both acute cholecystitis and biliary obstruction with or without cholangitis.

TREATMENT OF CALCULOUS CHOLANGITIS

The treatment of acute cholangitis is resuscitation, antimicrobials, and biliary tract drainage (Fig. 48–1). Management of respiratory and circulatory insufficiency in a monitored setting and administration of broad-spectrum antibiotics should precede but not delay definitive biliary tract decompression in the severely ill or deteriorating patient. Initial antibiotic coverage should include gram-negative bacilli and *Enterococci* species. Intravenous ampicillin and gentamicin may be used as initial therapy with addition of metronidazole for critically ill patients or when blood cultures yield multiple organisms or anaerobes. In patients with renal insufficiency, a fluoroquinolone can be used in place of gentamicin to reduce the risk of nephrotoxicity, which may be increased in patients with bile duct obstruction. Once culture and sensitivity results are available, antibiotics specific for the isolated bacteria should be considered depending on the clinical response to that point.

Biliary drainage can be accomplished endoscopically, percutaneously, or surgically. Endoscopic treatment, either sphincterotomy with stone extraction[8,9] or biliary stent or nasobiliary drain insertion, is superior to surgical treatment in severe cholangitis. Endoscopic sphincterotomy with stone extraction resulted in increased survival when compared with surgery in a retrospective cohort of patients with acute calculous cholangitis.[9] This was despite a higher number of concomitant medical problems and increased age in the patients managed endoscopically. Likewise, Lai and colleagues[4] randomized 82 patients with calculous cholangitis requiring emergent therapy to surgery or ERCP with nasobiliary catheter placement. The mortality in the surgical arm was significantly higher than in the endoscopic arm, 32% and 10%, respectively. In addition, there were an increased number of nonfatal complications in the group undergoing surgery.

In current practice, sphincterotomy and stone extraction is usually attempted during the initial ERCP. However, in critically ill patients with acute cholangitis resulting from choledocholithiasis, it may be prudent to achieve biliary drainage endoscopically, by insertion of a stent or nasobiliary catheter, and to defer stone extraction to a later time. Therapeutic response, procedure-related complications, and length of procedure are similar for biliary stents and nasobiliary catheters, but inadvertent catheter removal and patient discomfort are higher in those who receive a nasobiliary catheter.[10]

In a patient with cholangitis and gallstones but no evidence of choledocholithiasis on cholangiography, empiric endoscopic sphincterotomy does not appear to decrease the risk of subsequent episodes of cholangitis and results in a higher ERCP complication rate.[11]

DESCRIPTION OF TECHNIQUES

ERCP is performed in the usual manner. Once biliary cannulation has been accomplished, aspiration of bile and pus should be performed to decompress the biliary tract and lower the risk of bacteremia from the pressure of contrast injection. A specimen of aspirated bile can be placed in a sterile tube and submitted to microbiology for Gram stain and culture.

Cholangiography usually demonstrates the site and cause of biliary obstruction. If choledocholithiasis or another cause of intraluminal obstruction is present, an adequate biliary sphincterotomy is required for removal. Use of a balloon or basket for stone extraction is appropriate. Only the most distal stone is removed on

each sweep to prevent impaction. Approximately 10% of patients have cholangitis resulting from stones that cannot be removed by standard means, including mechanical lithotripsy. These are large stones, stones located proximal to a stricture, or stones greater than the diameter of the distal bile duct. The options are endoscopic electrohydraulic lithotripsy (EHL), extracorporeal shockwave lithotripsy (ESWL), endoscopic laser lithotripsy, and permanent biliary stent placement.[12-14] An occlusion cholangiogram at completion of ERCP may ensure clearance but carries a significant risk of bacteremia in this situation. If all stones or stone fragments cannot be removed during the initial endoscopic session, a stent should be left in place to provide bile drainage and prevent further cholangitis (Fig. 48–2). Long-term stent therapy is no longer advisable because of the high incidence of cholangitis and related deaths.[15,16] Similar techniques can be used in the cystic duct to treat Mirizzi's syndrome.[17-19]

Cholangitis Resulting from a Biliary Stricture

Biliary tract obstruction secondary to a malignant stricture rarely causes cholangitis unless the bile has been contaminated with bacteria during a previous biliary intervention. The incidence of cholangitis in patients with malignant bile duct obstruction is less than 5% and is most common with ampullary tumors.[20]

To treat cholangitis associated with a biliary stricture, a stent is placed across the stricture to relieve obstruction (Fig. 48–3). Although a larger diameter stent is usually preferred, both stent size and type depend on the underlying etiology of the biliary stricture. Balloon or catheter dilatation may be necessary to accommodate stent placement. Patients with strictures involving the biliary hilum should undergo stent placement into both the right and left hepatic ducts when technically possible, because bilateral decompression improves patient survival.[21] This is especially important if the biliary tract proximal to the stricture has filled with contrast.

Before stenting, the stricture should be sampled by brushing and/or biopsy, either fluoroscopically guided or under direct vision during choledochoscopy. Drainage of bile and contrast through the stent should be noted endoscopically and fluoroscopically to ascertain successful decompression.

Cholangitis Resulting from Stent Occlusion

Plastic biliary stents develop a bacterial biofilm on their surface,[22] which leads to stent occlusion and risk of cholangitis. Uncovered self-expandable metal stents, by virtue of their larger diameter and composition, do not develop encrustation at the same rate and have a longer patency.[23,24] If metal stent obstruction does occur, it is usually the result of tumor ingrowth between the metal struts or tumor overgrowth at either end. Metal stents covered with a synthetic coating are a recent development, and their duration of patency has yet to be established (Fig. 48–4).

Postendoscopic Retrograde Cholangiopancreatography Cholangitis

The risk of cholangitis after ERCP is now very low, 0.7% in a large series from a single referral center where drainage of obstructed ducts is practiced aggressively.[25] If diagnostic ERCP is undertaken, without performing biliary drainage when an obstruction is found,

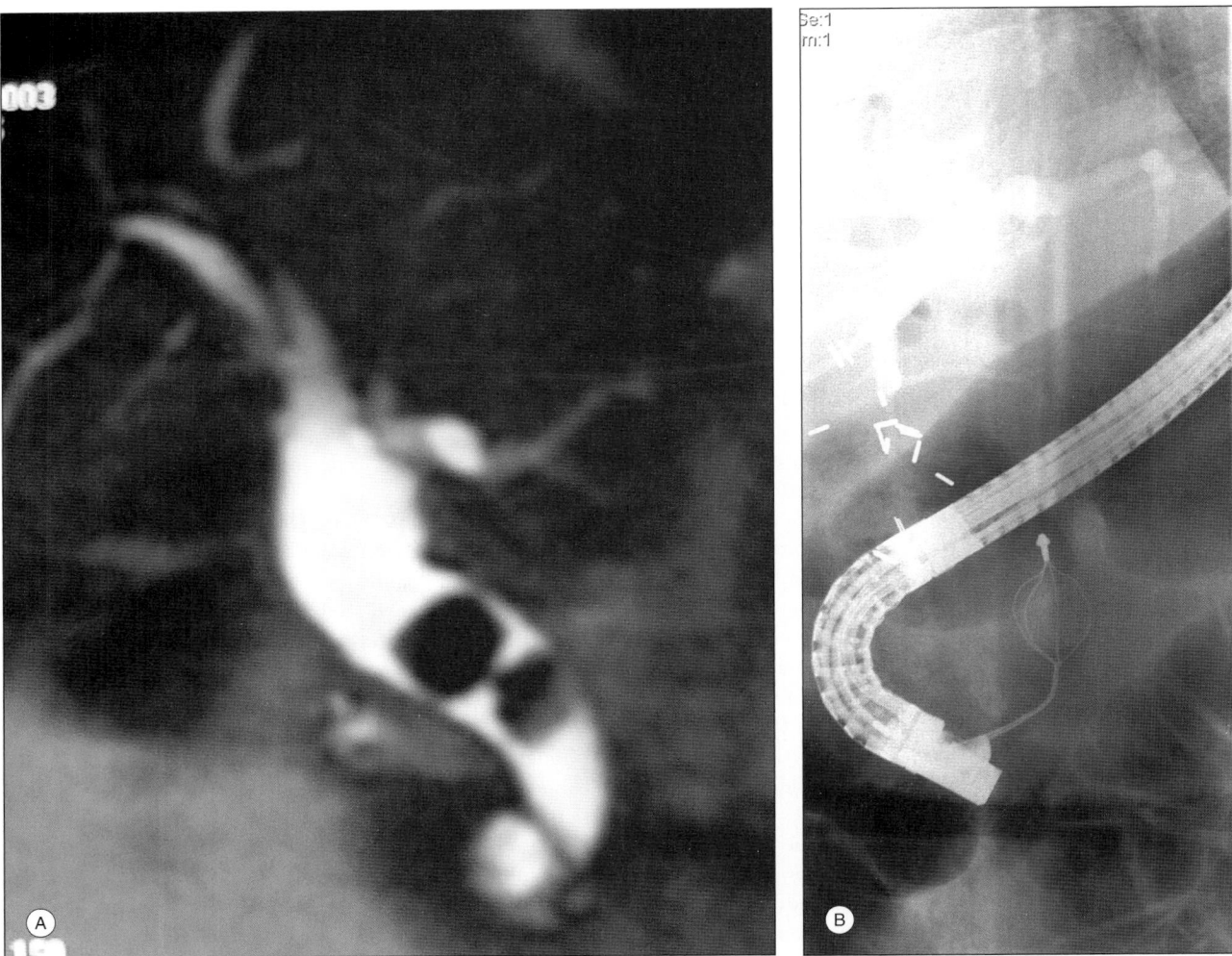

Figure 48–2. Patients with cholangitis showing *(A)* magnetic resonance cholangiopancreatography (MRCP) with two large bile duct stones and *(B)* endoscopic retrograde cholangiopancreatography (ERCP) in the same patient with basket extraction of one of the stones.

Continued

the incidence of cholangitis increases 10-fold.[26] This is due to contaminating sterile bile with enteric bacteria, which in the presence of obstruction will result in cholangitis. Any obstructed segment of the biliary tract opacified during cholangiography should be drained. Biliary obstruction resulting from hilar strictures and intrahepatic duct strictures or calculi may be technically difficult to decompress and care must therefore be taken when performing ERCP in such patients.

A meta-analysis assessing placebo-controlled trials of prophylactic antibiotics in ERCP did not reveal any decrease in bacteremia or cholangitis in the treatment group.[27] Thus, prophylactic antibiotics should not be used routinely in ERCP especially in lieu of establishing bile drainage.

Improper disinfection of duodenoscopes or use of contaminated water also increase the risk of post-ERCP cholangitis and bacteremia, especially with *P. aeruginosa*.[28,29]

Long-Term Postsphincterotomy Cholangitis

Sphincterotomy, either endoscopic or surgical, is a risk factor for bacterial contamination of the biliary tract,[30] likely by facilitating transpapillary migration of enteric bacteria. *E. coli* is the most common organism identified. Furthermore, analysis of postcholecystectomy patients who have undergone sphincterotomy reveals a predisposition for developing brown stones or sludge within the common bile duct in association with bacterobilia.[31]

Post-Transhepatic Cholangiography Cholangitis

Percutaneous transhepatic cholangiography (PTC) is able accurately to diagnose biliary obstruction and provide therapeutic interventions such as stone extraction, stent insertion, and stricture dilatation. PTC is usually used in cases in which ERCP is unsuccessful. Cholangitis is a well-documented complication of PTC, occurring in up to a third of patients.[32–34]

Post-T-Tube Cholangiography Cholangitis

Cholangiography through a surgically placed T-tube after cholecystectomy is performed to assess for retained common bile duct stones. Adverse events, including cholangitis and bacteremia, are documented complications of T-tube cholangiography, occurring in up to 7% of patients.[35] The incidence of adverse events

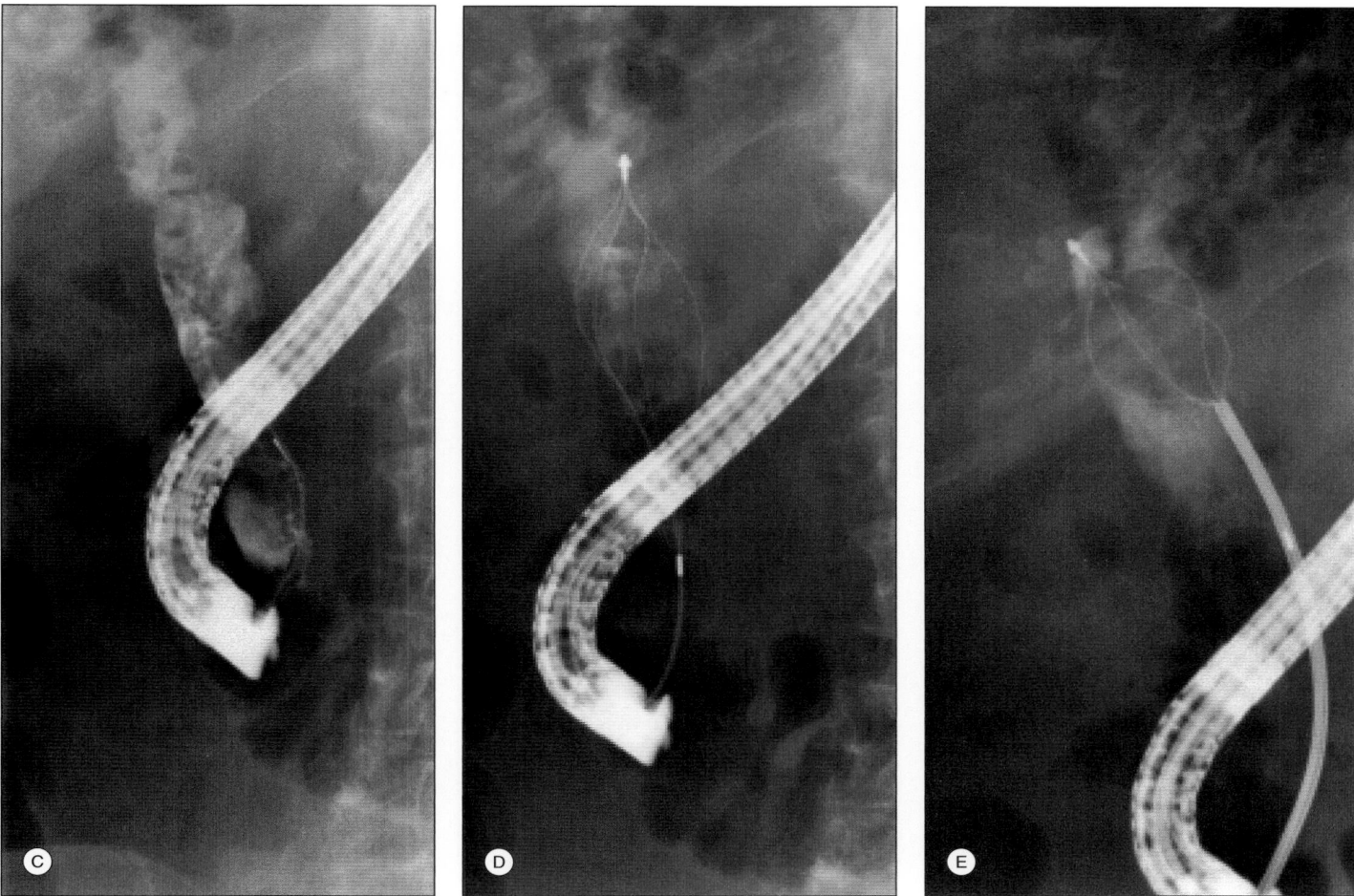

Figure 48–2, cont'd. *C,* ERCP showing dilated bile duct packed with stones. *D,* Basket extraction. *E,* Mechanical lithotripsy.

appears to be reduced by gravity infusion, rather than injection, of contrast to prevent high intraductal pressures and cholangiovenous reflux.[35,36]

Postoperative Cholangitis

Patients who have undergone bile duct reconstruction with creation of a hepatojejunostomy are at risk of postoperative cholangitis. This is especially prevalent in those with biliary atresia.[37] Bacterial colonization of the hepatojejunostomy and stoma obstruction by food debris may be pathogenic factors.

Sump Syndrome

Sump syndrome occurs after creation of a choledochoduodenostomy to manage retained common bile duct stones in a dilated bile duct. The distal bile duct between the papilla and the anastomosis becomes a stagnant reservoir or sump into which sludge, calculi, and/or food collect. The clinical presentation may include recurrent pain, cholangitis, hepatic abscess, or pancreatitis. Endoscopic sphincterotomy with extraction of debris from the bile duct successfully manages most patients.[38] In case series, recurrence of symptoms has been noted in 0% to 19% and results from stenosis of the sphincter of Oddi.[39,40] A repeat sphincterotomy should then be considered.[40]

Cholangitis in Pregnancy

ERCP in pregnancy appears to be safe for both mother and fetus, whereas a delay in definitive treatment of cholangitis may be life threatening. Radiation exposure to the fetus is limited by shielding the uterus with a lead apron, using short periods of fluoroscopy, avoiding magnification, and avoiding hard copy radiographs.[41]

POSTPROCEDURE CARE

If complete endoscopic drainage is not achieved during the initial procedure, then antibiotics should be continued until definitive therapy is performed either by repeat endoscopic, percutaneous, or surgical biliary decompression.

The efficacy of antibiotics after successful endoscopic therapy of cholangitis is unknown. In a retrospective analysis of 80 patients with cholangitis who underwent endoscopic therapy, there was no difference in outcome between the group receiving antibiotics for 3 days or less and the group receiving antibiotics for more than 3 days after ERCP.[42] As yet, there is no placebo-controlled study addressing the use of antibiotics in cholangitis after endoscopic drainage and we generally do not continue antibiotics after successful endoscopic therapy.

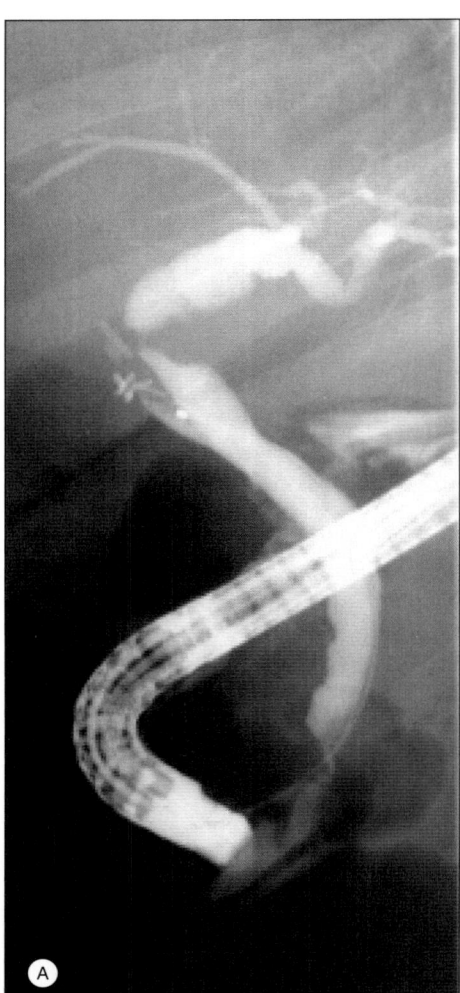 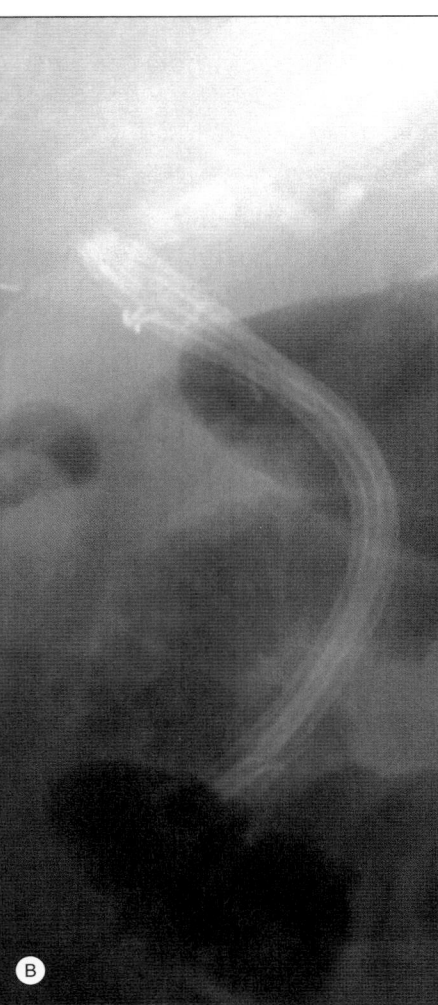

Figure 48–3. Patient with cholangitis resulting from a benign postoperative bile duct stricture shown by endoscopic retrograde cholangiopancreatography (ERCP) *(A)* and *(B)* after placement of three 10-Fr plastic stents.

Recurrent Pyogenic Cholangitis

EPIDEMIOLOGY

Recurrent pyogenic cholangitis, also known as Oriental cholangiohepatitis, is endemic in eastern Asia. In addition to Hong Kong where the disease was first described,[43] recurrent pyogenic cholangitis is commonly seen in individuals of Asian extraction who are living in or have emigrated from southern mainland China, Korea, Taiwan, the Philippines, Malaysia, Singapore, and Japan.[44,45] Amongst the Caucasian population, case reports of recurrent pyogenic cholangitis have been published from Australia, India, Italy, and Central and South America.[45,46] The disease usually presents between ages 20 and 40 years, more commonly in individuals of the lower socioeconomic classes, and both sexes are affected equally.[47,48]

PATHOGENESIS

Recurrent pyogenic cholangitis is a clinical syndrome of repetitive episodes of bacterial cholangitis resulting from intrahepatic biliary obstruction with calcium bilirubinate stones and/or strictures.

Although the etiology and pathogenesis are uncertain, two theories have been proposed. In the first, the initiating event is bacterial contamination from the portal venous system of previously sterile bile. Hematogenous entry is supported by findings on histologic specimens. Portal tract inflammation, in the absence of bile duct abnormalities, and portal pylethrombophlebitis occur with high frequency in early disease.[47] The underlying patient susceptibility factor may be a deficiency of an inhibitor of bacterial beta-glucuronidase, contained in normal bile. This allows deconjugation of bilirubin glucuronide and subsequent precipitation with calcium to create calcium bilirubinate.[47] The resulting biliary obstruction leads to a cycle of cholangitis and further stone formation.

An alternative hypothesis is that recurrent pyogenic cholangitis occurs secondary to biliary parasite infestation. Parasite migration from the duodenum across the papilla allows bacteria to ascend into the biliary system. Parasites may then cause obstruction of the bile duct while their ova and remnants are a nidus for stone formation. Although there are many reports of parasites isolated from the bile ducts of patients with recurrent pyogenic cholangitis, it is unclear whether or not the parasite is an etiologic agent or an incidental finding. In one study, 45% of Chinese patients with recurrent pyogenic cholangitis were infected with *Clonorchis sinensis*, a rate

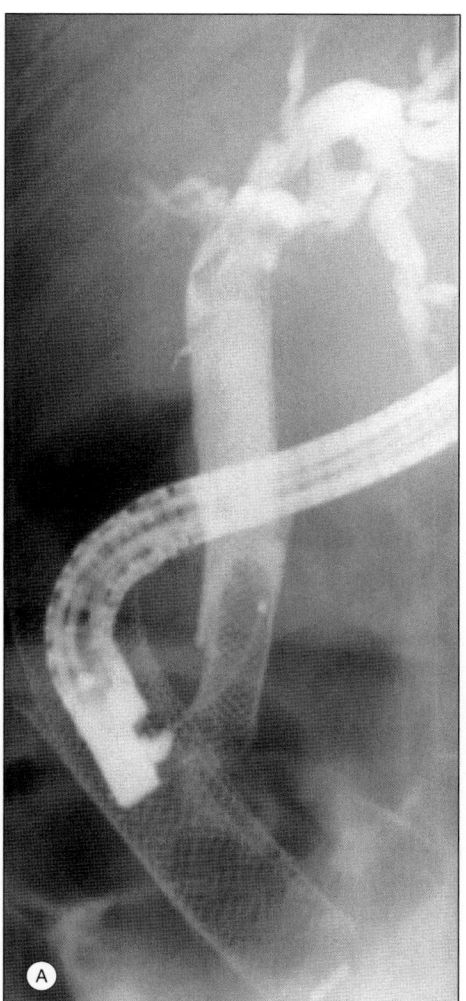
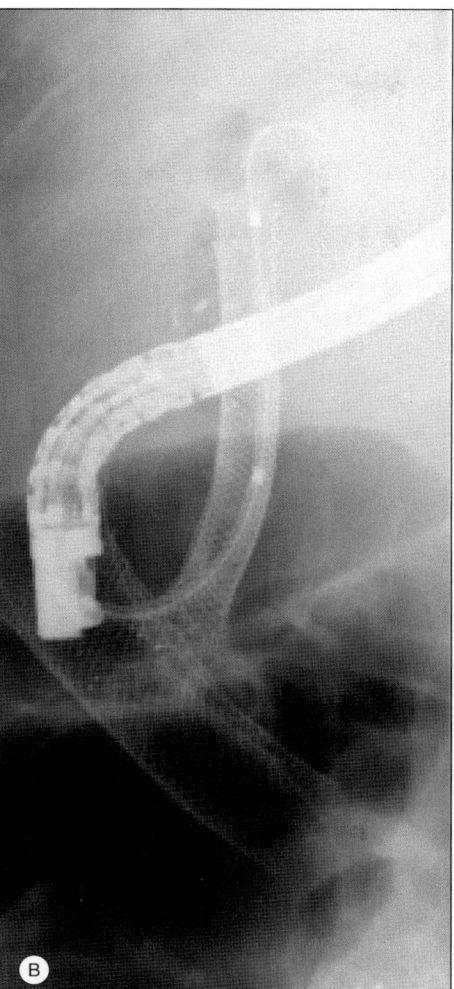
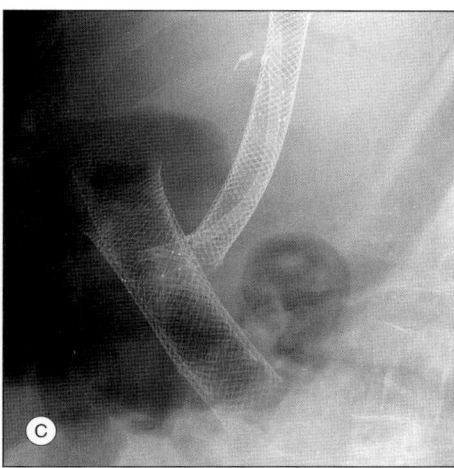

Figure 48–4. Patient with cholangitis secondary to an occluded biliary metal stent (also has three enteral stents in the duodenum) shown at endoscopic retrograde cholangiopancreatography (ERCP) *(A)*, insertion of a 10-Fr plastic stent inside it *(B)*, and the final position *(C)*.

similar to unaffected controls.[47] Other parasites documented in recurrent pyogenic cholangitis patients are *Ascaris*,[47] and *Fasciola* and *Opisthorchis* species.[49]

The cycle of biliary inflammation and healing may lead to secondary stricture formation with exacerbation of bile stasis. The bile ducts in the left lateral segment of the liver are often the only or most severely affected. This segment may be anatomically predisposed to stasis because of duct angulations slowing bile drainage. Chronic obstruction eventually causes permanent dilatation of the proximal biliary tract, often filled with intrahepatic stones. Bile stasis and bacterial contamination may result in the development of multiple hepatic abscesses.

CLINICAL FEATURES

Abdominal pain is the most common symptom, followed by fever and jaundice.[50] Nausea and vomiting, chills, and even rigors may also occur. Acute cholangitis in these patients is indistinguishable from typical obstructive cholangitis. Isolated fever may be present in patients with hepatic abscess, but such individuals invariably give a

history of right upper quadrant abdominal pain and jaundice in the past. Patients may present with acute pancreatitis, presumably resulting from obstruction of the pancreatic duct by a stone or parasite, but this is uncommon. Physical examination findings include an elevated temperature, jaundice, right upper quadrant or epigastric tenderness, hepatomegaly, and a palpable gallbladder.

The clinical course may be complicated by recurrent sepsis, hepatic abscess rupture with peritonitis,[47] portal pylethrombophlebitis, and, rarely, hepatic failure.[44] Longterm, patients are at risk for cirrhosis, atrophy of hepatic segments supplied by thrombosed portal branches, clinical manifestations of portal hypertension, and cholangiocarcinoma.[44,51]

Laboratory studies reveal elevated liver enzymes and white blood cell count.[50] The liver enzymes reflect cholestasis with the most dramatic elevation occurring in the alkaline phosphatase. The aminotransferases are usually less than 1000 U/L with alanine transaminase being greater than aspartate transaminase. The bilirubin level has quite a wide range from normal to more than 50 mg/dL. Between bouts of cholangitis, the liver enzymes are usually normal.

Enterobacteriaceae species are the most frequent bacteria cultured from bile. *P. aeruginosa* may be seen in patients who have previously undergone endoscopic or surgical biliary intervention. Anaerobes are less common. Growth of multiple organisms, although unusual in other causes of cholangitis, often occurs in recurrent pyogenic cholangitis.[46]

DIAGNOSIS

Abdominal ultrasound demonstrates intrahepatic and extrahepatic duct stones in almost all cases of recurrent pyogenic cholangitis. The stones create an echogenic focus sonographically but only rarely cause shadowing.[52] Extrahepatic and intrahepatic duct dilatation is present 96% and 79%, respectively.[52] Intrahepatic duct dilatation involves the primary and secondary branches and may be segmental, and often occurring in left lateral and right posterior segments. Intrahepatic duct dilatation correlates to the location of strictures or impacted stones.[52] Other findings include localized bile duct wall thickening, periportal hyperechoicity, and hepatic abscesses.[48,52] Gallstones may occur in more than half of patients with recurrent pyogenic cholangitis. CT scan is also able to reliably visualize duct dilatation and segmental hepatic atrophy and hepatic abscesses. CT may be less sensitive than ultrasound at detecting stones and, like ultrasound, is unreliable at identifying bile duct strictures. MR cholangiography demonstrates segmental hepatic abnormalities and biliary tract dilatation and strictures. The major advantage of MR cholangiography is complete visualization of the biliary tract including segments obstructed by calculi or strictures[53] that may not be apparent by ERCP.

Cholangiography during ERCP also accurately documents duct dilatation, intraductal stones, and gallstones. The intrahepatic ducts appear straightened and acutely angulated at branches, likely resulting from periductal fibrosis. There is often distinct tapering of the intrahepatic ducts proximally, described as the "arrowhead sign," and decreased duct branching. Complete occlusion of an intrahepatic duct by a stone may be represented by segmental absence of contrast and is better assessed by MR cholangiography. Pancreatic duct abnormalities may also be present.[54]

PATHOLOGY

The hallmark pathologic feature of recurrent pyogenic cholangitis is intrahepatic bile duct calcium bilirubinate stones, casts, sludge, and, in active disease, pus. In one half of patients, the common bile duct and main hepatic ducts contain stones that have migrated distally. Both the intrahepatic and extrahepatic bile ducts are often dilated and have a thickened, fibrotic wall and segmental strictures. Liver abscesses, often multiple, are present in more than 80%.[47]

The predominant histologic finding in recurrent pyogenic cholangitis is a periportal mixed inflammatory infiltrate and thrombophlebitis of the portal vein branches. Pericholangitis follows. Deposition of fibrous tissue within the portal tract and surrounding the bile duct is observed later in the disease course.

DIFFERENTIAL DIAGNOSIS

The differential diagnosis of hepatolithiasis is recurrent pyogenic cholangitis, Caroli's disease, primary sclerosing cholangitis, and post liver transplant. Recurrent pyogenic cholangitis can usually be distinguished from these entities by epidemiologic features and the segmental nature of the disease. Biliary infestation with liver flukes occurs in the same population, causes intrahepatic duct dilatation, and uncommonly precipitates stone formation. However, the extrahepatic ducts are usually of normal caliber. Choledocholithiasis resulting from migration of gallstones into the common bile duct does not follow a chronic relapsing course and is cured by cholecystectomy.

TREATMENT

Treatment of acute cholangitis in recurrent pyogenic cholangitis patients is identical to that of obstructive cholangitis. Patients with recurrent pyogenic cholangitis and risk factors for biliary parasitic infection should have the appropriate diagnostic tests performed and, if positive, undergo antihelminthic therapy.

The management goal in recurrent pyogenic cholangitis is to alleviate biliary stasis, thereby reducing the risk of cholangitis, liver abscess formation, and secondary biliary cirrhosis. This is accomplished by a multidisciplinary approach involving surgery, interventional radiology, and endoscopy. Therapy is customized to the individual patient and to the expertise within an institution. Dilatation of strictures and removal of stones, performed surgically, percutaneously, or endoscopically, is the mainstay of therapy, but segmental hepatic resection may be indicated in localized disease.

For the last 20 years, ERCP has been successfully used in the treatment of recurrent pyogenic cholangitis.[55] ERCP is indicated to provide drainage to obstructed bile ducts when cholangitis is not responding adequately to supportive measures. Otherwise, ERCP in recurrent pyogenic cholangitis should be timed between episodes of acute cholangitis (Fig. 48–5). ERCP was traditionally used to provide a detailed map of the biliary tract, noting the location of stones and strictures, to guide definitive therapy. However, with the development of magnetic resonance imaging (MRI) cholangiography, diagnostic ERCP should be reserved for situations in which MRI expertise is unavailable. Endoscopic sphincterotomy with stricture dilatation and stone extraction is relatively uncomplicated for extrahepatic disease. The soft pigment stones readily deform and fragment, enabling delivery into the duodenum. On the contrary, management of hepatolithiasis is often technically challenging. Accessing intrahepatic branches obstructed by calculi or strictures to perform dilatation or stone removal is often difficult. Furthermore, obstructed intrahepatic ducts requiring treatment may not be apparent to the endoscopist. Intrahepatic ducts that have "vanished" proximal to a high-grade stricture or obstructing calculi are not always appreciated at cholangiography. Duodenoscope-assisted choledochoscopy is very useful in this situation, not only in identifying the presence of the obstructed intrahepatic branch but also in providing further therapy such as EHL. These techniques of endoscopic therapy can also be applied percutaneously or through a surgically created biliary-enteric conduit as described later. In the management of hepatolithiasis, multiple treatment sessions are usually necessary, whether conducted endoscopically or percutaneously, to perform sequential stricture dilatation and to attempt complete stone removal.

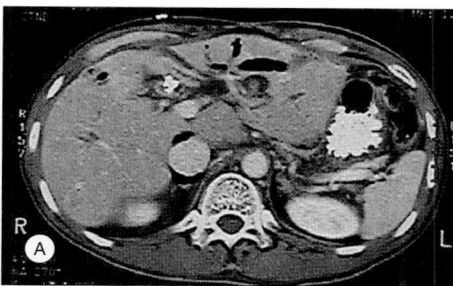

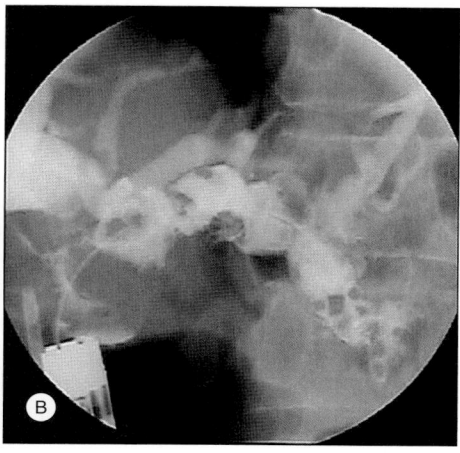

Figure 48-5. Patient with recurrent pyogenic cholangitis demonstrated on computed tomography (CT) scan in *(A)* with dilated air-filled left intrahepatic ductal system with stones and two stents. *B,* endoscopic retrograde cholangiography (ERC) showing multiple lucent stones in the same system.

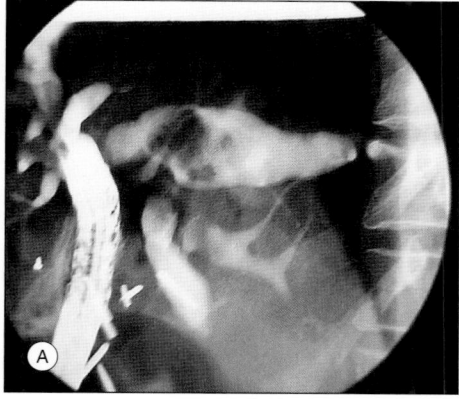

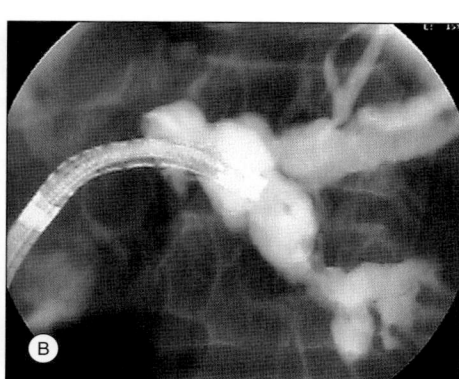

Figure 48-6. Recurrent pyogenic cholangitis, previously treated surgically with the creation of a cutaneous-jejunal-hepatic duct conduit, through which a gastroscope has been passed demonstrating *(A)* a large left intrahepatic duct stone and *(B)* after electrohydraulic lithotripsy and extraction of fragments.

Percutaneous access to the biliary tree can be accomplished by formation of a transhepatic track under ultrasound guidance. As the track matures, biliary dilatation catheters and stone extraction devices are then passed into the biliary tree to provide therapy. Choledochoscopy and EHL are also possible by this route. Complete clearance of hepatolithiasis is attained in 96% of patients after an average of six treatments.[56] However, a third of patients will have recurrent disease by 5 years. Cheung[57] reported 190 patients with residual hepatolithiasis after surgical choledocholithotomy and choledochoscopic lithotripsy who were treated via a T-tube track. Treatment consisted of sequential biliary stricture dilatation with stent placement between dilatation sessions. Once the strictures were adequately treated, choledochoscopy and EHL were performed to fragment intrahepatic calculi with basket retrieval of stone debris. Complete clearance was achieved in 88% of patients. Of these, 15% developed evidence of recurrent disease during a mean follow-up period of 4 years. Complications were mild and included hemobilia and fever.

Biliary enteric bypass procedures for repeated access to the intrahepatic ducts involve creation of a Roux-en-Y hepatojejunostomy or choledochojejunostomy with one jejunal limb brought to the skin as a cutaneous stoma[49,58] or a jejunoduodenostomy.[59] Treatment of strictures and stones is then possible, using a duodenoscope, gastroscope, or choledochoscope (Fig. 48–6). Once treatment is complete, the stoma can be buried subcutaneously but may be reaccessed by a simple surgical procedure in the event of disease recurrence. Avoidance of hepatic resection and resolution of hepatic abscesses can be achieved; however, repeat therapy or hepatic resection will almost certainly be required as stones and strictures recur.[49]

Segmental hepatic resection is often used to treat localized disease, primarily involving the left lateral or right posterior segments. Initial stone clearance is 96% with a disease recurrence of 6% at 5 years.[56] The complication rate is higher than hepatic-preserving procedures and includes hepatic insufficiency, postoperative hemorrhage, and bile leak.

Liver transplantation is rarely performed in recurrent pyogenic cholangitis.[45,60] Appropriate indications are advanced biliary cirrhosis or diffuse hepatic disease unresponsive to the previously mentioned measures. The potential for disease recurrence in the transplanted liver is unknown.

There is no evidence to support the use of long-term antibiotics or ursodeoxycholic acid (UCDA) in the management of recurrent pyogenic cholangitis.

PREPROCEDURE HISTORY AND CONSIDERATIONS

Prophylactic antibiotics have been recommended to decrease the risk of cholangitis during ERCP in patients with recurrent pyogenic cholangitis.[54]

DESCRIPTION OF TECHNIQUES

ERCP is performed in the usual manner. Obtaining a complete cholangiogram may be difficult because of intrahepatic duct obstruction by impacted stones and/or strictures. Occlusion cholangiography using a biliary balloon can be useful in this situation but carries a risk of cholangitis by contaminating obstructed ducts with contrast and of bacteremia by increasing the intraluminal pressure. A complete cholangiogram should not be aggressively pursued if drainage of obstructed ducts is not intended. Noninvasive imaging techniques (ultrasound, CT, and MR cholangiography) will provide similar information without the risk of complications.

An adequate endoscopic sphincterotomy is essential for definitive endoscopic management of recurrent pyogenic cholangitis. After sphincterotomy, standard stone extraction techniques are attempted, but it is often necessary to place a guidewire into the desired hepatic or intrahepatic ducts. Detailed knowledge of intrahepatic segment anatomy is necessary to correlate a CT or MR image to the opacified ducts at ERCP. Careful review of the cholangiogram to note stone position and associated strictures is essential before beginning therapy. Removal of multiple stones is accomplished distal to proximal to reduce the risk of stone impaction. Given the propensity of pigment stones to fragment, extraction balloons or baskets may be used. Balloon catheters have the advantage of wire-guidance, whereas baskets are more flexible and may reach deeply into difficult intrahepatic ducts. When extracting from the smaller caliber intrahepatic ducts, it is necessary to have a variety of balloon diameters available or a multi-step balloon that inflates in a step-wise fashion through a range of sizes. When the size of stone exceeds the caliber of the distal duct, basket lithotripsy can be used to fragment the stone before extraction.

If the previous methods are unsuccessful, choledochoscopy should be considered. The choledochoscope can assist in correct guidewire placement proximal to intrahepatic stones with subsequent exchange of the choledochoscope for an extraction device. Choledochoscopy also provides further therapeutic options for stones resistant to removal by conventional methods such as EHL. The stone debris is removed by balloon or basket extraction.

Strictures occur in the extrahepatic and intrahepatic ducts, often with proximal calculi. At or immediately distal to the hepatic duct confluence is a common site for strictures. It is essential to treat strictures before attempting proximal stone removal to prevent stone impaction at the stricture. Wire-guided balloon or catheter dilatation are both acceptable methods. The ideal post-therapy duct size should be equal to or larger than the proximal stones but is guided by the size of the duct distal to the stricture. If the wire cannot be directed across an intrahepatic duct stricture, aligning the choledochoscope with the duct of interest and passing a guidewire through the accessory channel of the choledochoscope will often provide access. The choledochoscope can then be exchanged for a biliary dilatation balloon or catheter. Multiple endoscopic sessions may be required for adequate stricture dilatation, and a stent should be inserted between procedures.

If a dominant stricture is evident on cholangiogram, then further evaluation to exclude cholangiocarcinoma should be undertaken. This includes biliary cytology brushing and biopsy under fluoroscopy or direct brushing or biopsy through the accessory channel of the choledochoscope. Another endoscopic finding suspicious for cholangiocarcinoma in recurrent pyogenic cholangitis is mucin within the bile duct.[51]

Parasitic biliary infestation may occur concomitant with recurrent pyogenic cholangitis. Endoscopic treatment of parasitic cholangitis is described later.

POSTPROCEDURE CARE

If complete drainage is not achieved, then the patient is at risk of post-ERCP cholangitis and prophylactic broad-spectrum antibiotics should be administered.

Because endoscopic therapy in recurrent pyogenic cholangitis is a temporizing measure and does not cure the underlying disease, repeat interventions will be required as stones and strictures recur.

Parasitic Cholangitis

Ascaris lumbricoides is a nematode or roundworm that matures within the small intestine and causes cholangitis by entering the bile duct across the major papilla. The trematodes *C. sinensis*, *Opisthorchis viverrini* and *Opisthorchis felineus*, and *Fasciola hepatica* mature to adulthood within the human bile duct and are collectively known as liver flukes. Hepatic infection by *Echinococcus* species often involves the biliary tract, by hydatid cyst compression or rupture and direct extension of alveolar echinococcosis.

ASCARIS CHOLANGITIS

Epidemiology

A. lumbricoides exists worldwide but is most prevalent in Asia, Africa, and South America as a result of crowded living conditions and poor sanitation. The highest incidence of *A. lumbricoides* infection occurs in childhood, and both genders are affected equally.[2] There is a higher rate of infection among the lower socioeconomic class.

Pathogenesis

Ova are passed in human feces and are ingested on contaminated fruit or vegetables. The eggs hatch in the small intestine producing larvae, which penetrate the intestinal wall and enter the portal circulation and, subsequently, the pulmonary circulation. Within the alveoli of the lungs, the larvae develop further, proceed through the bronchial tree to the epiglottis, and are swallowed. The worms remain in the small intestine where they fully mature and begin to reproduce. Biliary infection occurs by migration of adult *A. lumbricoides* across the papilla. Previous endoscopic or surgical sphincterotomy and bilioenteric bypass surgery increase the likelihood of biliary involvement.[61] *A. lumbricoides* causes inflammation of the bile duct and secondary bacterial cholangitis by allowing ascending bacterial contamination of bile, obstructing the bile duct and stimulating choledocholithiasis. Migration into the gallbladder appears to be facilitated by a low insertion of the cystic duct at the level of the ampulla and by pregnancy.[62]

Because reproduction is sexual, it is dependent on infection with both male and female worms. If there are no females present, no eggs are produced; if there are no males present, unfertilized eggs are shed. Although *A. lumbricoides* is unable to multiply within an individual host, protective immunity does not develop allowing reinfection to occur and increase the parasite burden.

Clinical Features

Migration of *A. lumbricoides* through the lung may result in transient pulmonary infiltrates and eosinophilia, known as Loffler's syndrome. Patients experience pleuritic substernal chest pain; cough productive of scant, blood-tinged sputum; wheeze; and fever. The sputum may contain immature worms and/or Charcot-Leyden crystals. The pulmonary infiltrates are multiple, bilateral, and migratory. Leukocytosis with eosinophil predominance is most common during this phase of infection.

The clinical manifestations of chronic infection are proportional to the parasite burden. Patients often complain of intermittent, periumbilical abdominal cramps; nausea; and diarrhea. Physical and laboratory examination are usually unremarkable. Less commonly, heavy worm burdens result in malabsorption or mechanical complications such as small bowel obstruction, volvulus, and intussusception. The most common site of obstruction is at the ileocecal valve. Complications include bowel ischemia and perforation.

The most common clinical manifestation of biliary infection is biliary colic. This is generally recurrent and may progress to bacterial cholangitis. The cause of bile duct obstruction is usually one or more worms, but pigment stones and strictures are also often present. Cholecystitis may be acalculous, resulting from worms obstructing the cystic duct, or because of pigment stones, developed around parasite eggs and remnants of deceased worms within the gallbladder. Physical examination findings include elevated temperature, jaundice, right upper quadrant and epigastric abdominal tenderness, and hepatomegaly. *A. lumbricoides* also burrows through the bile duct wall into the liver parenchyma to form hepatic abscesses. Acute pancreatitis has been reported because of worms obstructing the pancreatic duct.

Diagnosis

Diagnosis is suspected by a history of travel to or emigration from endemic countries and typical clinical features. Although serologic tests to detect acute infection with *A. lumbricoides* exist, they are primarily used for research purposes.

Patients occasionally report passing a worm in the stool, sputum, or vomitus or of a worm migrating out the mouth or nose. If the worm is contained, it can be analyzed microscopically. Microscopic examination of concentrated stool specimens for ova and parasites is useful during chronic infection but is negative during acute infection. As previously mentioned, ova are not present if infection consists only of male worms.

Plain abdominal x-ray films or after oral barium may demonstrate adult worms in the intestine and delayed radiographs may show the worm's alimentary canal containing ingested barium. Ultrasound documents dilatation of the biliary tract and possibly the pancreatic duct. The worm may be visible sonographically in the intestine or the biliary tract as a linear or coiled, echogenic tubule that does not produce shadowing and is occasionally mobile. *A. lumbricoides* typically displays an erratic motility pattern best seen within the gallbladder.[62] In a longitudinal view, it may be possible to discriminate an anechoic line within the hyperechoic tube, representing the

digestive tract described as the "four lines sign."[63] CT is useful in demonstrating pneumobilia and hepatic abscesses complicating *A. lumbricoides* cholangitis. Magnetic resonance cholangiopancreatography (MRCP) demonstrates a tubular filling defect within the biliary or pancreatic system, and when the worm is viewed in cross-section, a bull's eye appearance may be observed. The bull's eye describes high signal intensity in the center of the filling defect, which is swallowed bile within the worm.[64]

ERCP is a sensitive and specific test for diagnosing *A. lumbricoides* infection. At duodenoscopy, the adult worm may be observed as a pale white or reddish-yellow tubular structure up to 35 cm in length[2] either within the lumen of the duodenum or crossing the major papilla. On cholangiogram and pancreatogram, *A. lumbricoides* appears as a tubular filling defect with tapered ends. Real-time fluoroscopy may detect movement. Injection of contrast may stimulate the worm to migrate distally into the duodenum. Stones and strictures may also be present in the bile duct, and, if involved, the pancreatic duct is usually dilated.

Treatment

Treatment of secondary bacterial cholangitis is described previously. Parasite eradication should be attempted in all cases of documented infection, regardless of symptoms. Close contacts of infected persons should submit stool specimens for analysis and be treated if positive for parasites. There are a variety of antihelminthic agents effective in treating *A. lumbricoides*. Because larvae are not destroyed, a stool specimen should be analyzed 3 months after therapy to ensure that treatment is complete. Albendazole (400 mg) and mebendazole (500 mg) can both be administered as a single dose with a 100% eradication rate.[65] Higher doses of albendazole (800 mg divided into three doses) have been used to treat biliary *A. lumbricoides* effectively.[66] Albendazole and mebendazole should not be given during pregnancy, because they may be teratogenic. Pyrantel pamoate can be safely used in pregnancy as a single dose of 11 mg/kg body weight (up to a maximum of 1 g). Unlike the benzimidazoles, pyrantel pamoate is only effective against *A. lumbricoides* and does not treat the multiple enteric parasitic infections that commonly occur. Antispasmodics and analgesics may be added to antihelminthic therapy to alleviate symptoms.[66]

Endoscopic removal of worms from the biliary tract may be necessary when antihelminthics are unsuccessful (Fig. 48–7). In addition, the dying worm releases a large number of eggs and these, combined with its own remnants, obstructs the biliary or pancreatic duct and acts as a nidus for stone formation.

Surgical removal of *A. lumbricoides* from the biliary tract was a common practice before the advent of therapeutic endoscopy. Present surgical indications include cholecystitis because of worms or calculi and failure of endoscopic bile duct clearance.

Prevention

A. lumbricoides eggs are destroyed in boiling water and removed by water filtration devices.

Description of Techniques

ERCP is performed in the usual manner. The goal of therapy is complete removal of the parasite and stones and treatment of strictures. If the diagnosis of parasitic cholangitis has not yet been established, aspiration of bile should be performed to evaluate for ova under microscopy.

In most instances, parasite extraction from the biliary tract necessitates an endoscopic sphincterotomy. However, because the enteric reinfection rate for *A. lumbricoides* after eradication is extremely high in endemic areas, sphincterotomy facilitates future biliary tract involvement and is relatively contraindicated. When the major papilla is patulous because of worm migration, access and extraction is uncomplicated. With a papillary orifice of normal or decreased caliber from papillary stenosis, papillary balloon dilatation is a useful compromise.

Worms that appear at the papilla, either spontaneously or in response to contrast injection, can be grasped with a biopsy forceps and pulled into the duodenum, to the opening of the accessory channel on the duodenoscope. Then the endoscope and worm should be withdrawn and the biopsy forceps opened to release the worm into a container for microscopy.

Worms located completely within the biliary tract can be removed with either a biliary extraction balloon or basket. The ideal balloon diameter depends on the size of the bile duct. With either device, the worm should be brought to the papillary orifice and then grasped using the biopsy forceps as described previously. Polypectomy snares are liable to transect the worm and complicate extraction. If a worm is transected during extraction attempt or

debris of deceased worms is present in the bile duct, complete removal of all remnants is vital to prevent further episodes of cholangitis and stone formation.

LIVER FLUKE CHOLANGITIS
Epidemiology
C. sinensis is endemic to eastern Asia, especially Japan, China, Taiwan, Korea, and Vietnam. *O. viverrini* is found in more than 80% of individuals living in Thailand and Laos, and *O. felineus* is present throughout Southeast Asia and Eastern Europe, particularly Siberia. *C. sinensis* and the *Opisthorchis* species reside in fish-eating mammals including humans, cats, and dogs. *F. hepatica* infection occurs worldwide, primarily in sheep and cattle but also in humans. The peak age and gender of infected individuals differs by region, likely related to cultural variation in eating habits. Infection is more prevalent in rural areas, among the lower socioeconomic classes.

Pathogenesis
The eggs of the adult worm pass in the feces of their mammalian host to contaminate fresh water. Miracidia are hatched and consumed by snails. The snail acts as an intermediate host, within which the miracidia develop into mobile cercariae. The cercariae emerge from the snail and either penetrate fish (*Clonorchis* and

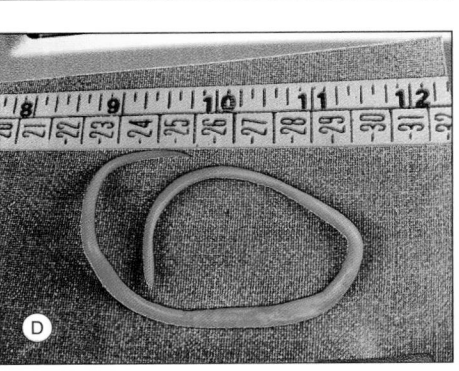

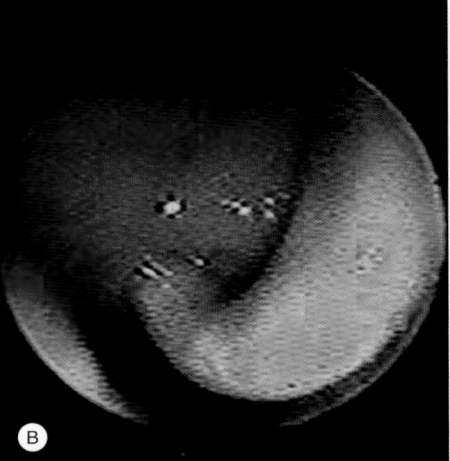

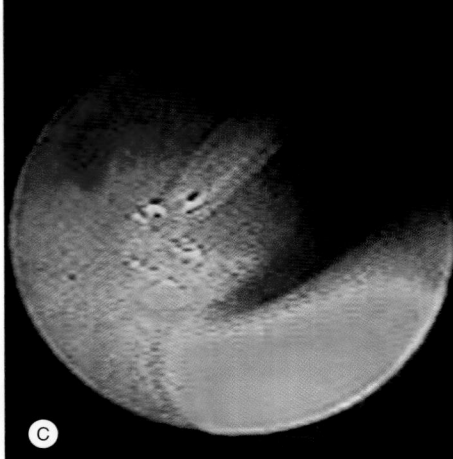

Figure 48–7. *A,* Endoscopic retrograde cholangiopancreatography (ERCP) showing *Ascaris lumbricoides* within the proximal bile duct. *B,* Living *Ascaris* crossing the papilla. *C,* Same as *B* with the motile tip of worm approaching papilla. *D,* Extracted adult *Ascaris.* (*C,* Courtesy of Dr Angelo Ferrari, São Paulo, Brazil; *D,* courtesy of Dr Alok Gupta, Kanpur, India.)

Opisthorchis) or attach to plants (*Fasciola*) where they encyst. Human infection occurs from eating uncooked or undercooked freshwater fish or plants, such as watercress, alfalfa, and parsley. The immature flukes migrate from the small intestine into the bile ducts where they mature and reproduce. *Clonorchis* and *Opisthorchis* enter the biliary tree through the major papilla, whereas *Fasciola* penetrates the intestinal wall into the peritoneal cavity and enters the biliary tree transhepatically. The adult liver flukes most commonly reside in the intrahepatic branches but may be observed in the distal biliary tract. Infection of the gallbladder and pancreatic duct has also been reported.

Immunity does not develop with infection and a single individual may be infected multiple times. Because the adult fluke often lives more than a decade within the bile duct, repeat infection increases the burden of disease and the likelihood of becoming symptomatic.

Parasitic infection causes recurrent inflammation of the bile duct leading to intrahepatic biliary strictures; cholangiocarcinoma can result from *Clonorchis* and *Opisthorchis* infection. The adult parasite may physically obstruct the bile duct, whereas the debris of dead worms and ova act as a nidus for ductal stone formation. In addition to facilitating duct obstruction, passage of the parasite across the papilla allows contamination of the bile with enteric bacteria. Thus, like *A. lumbricoides*, the liver flukes predispose to bacterial cholangitis.

Clinical Features

Initial infection, corresponding to parasite migration from the intestine to the biliary tree, is usually not clinically apparent. The most common fluke to cause symptoms is *F. hepatica*. Those individuals who do have symptoms complain of diarrhea; abdominal pain; urticaria; and flulike symptoms such as fever, lethargy, myalgias, and arthralgias. Physical examination may reveal elevated temperature, dermatographia, lymphadenopathy, and tender hepatomegaly. Eosinophilia is invariably present and often dramatic. Liver enzymes may be mildly elevated.

The presence and severity of chronic symptoms is related to the burden of infection. Chronic or relapsing upper abdominal pain, anorexia with weight loss, and fatigue may be present in between episodes of biliary colic and cholangitis. Right upper quadrant tenderness and hepatomegaly are common findings on physical examination. The gallbladder may be dilated and occasionally palpable. Evidence of chronic liver disease with portal hypertension is a potential complication of longstanding disease. Bouts of cholangitis are similar clinically to typical obstructive cholangitis. Persistent eosinophilia is often present, especially with *F. hepatica*. When bile duct obstruction occurs, liver enzyme levels will reflect cholestasis but are otherwise normal.

Diagnosis

During acute infection, ova are not yet shed in the feces and the diagnosis is made clinically and serologically. Serologic testing for *F. hepatica* with enzyme-linked immunosorbent assay (ELISA) has a sensitivity of 91% to 100% and specificity of 83% to 100%.[67–69] ELISA titers may be used to assess response to therapy because 65% of treated patients had negative serologic testing at 6 months.[70] ELISAs to detect *C. sinensis* and *O. viverrini* are currently under study[71,72] but have not yet been incorporated into clinical practice. In chronic infection, ova and, less commonly, parasites are detected in the feces by microscopic examination. Analyzing concentrated stool specimens may increase the yield.

Imaging is usually not helpful during acute infection. In cases of *F. hepatica* infection, CT scan of the abdomen may show low-density hepatic nodules or tracks corresponding to parasite migration. Ultrasound is excellent at detecting hepatic enlargement, dilatation and wall thickening of the intrahepatic ducts, and gallbladder dilatation present in chronic infection. In addition, ultrasound occasionally demonstrates the worm as a hyperechoic focus that does not shadow and may display subtle movement. This is best seen in the gallbladder.[73] CT scan is more sensitive at detecting abnormalities of the intrahepatic bile ducts including dilatation and wall thickening.

ERCP enables sampling of bile for the presence of ova, which may be more sensitive than stool microscopy,[74] and demonstration of the mature parasite within the biliary system (Fig. 48–8). On cholangiography, there may be saccular dilatation of the intrahepatic ducts, often diffusely with blunted terminal ends.[75] Filling defects may be due to the parasite, secondary stone formation, and mucosal hyperplasia or dysplasia. Filling defects resulting from the worm have a filamentous curvilinear or elliptical shape and may be transient and quickly obscured by the contrast media.[74,75] These are

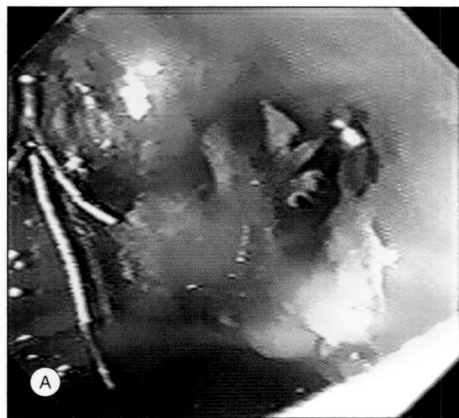

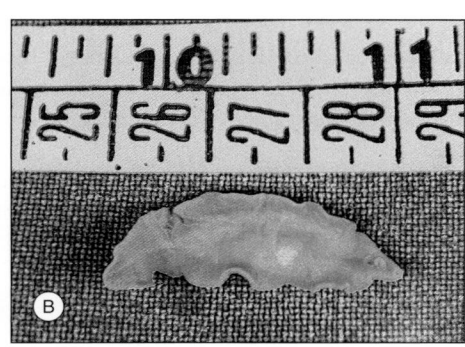

Figure 48–8. *A, Fasciola hepatica* being extracted at endoscopic retrograde cholangiopancreatography (ERCP). *B,* Adult worm after extraction. (*A,* Courtesy of Dr Claudio Navarette, Santiago, Chile; *B,* Courtesy of Dr Alok Gupta, Kanpur, India.)

primarily in the secondary and tertiary branches of the intrahepatic ducts but may appear throughout the biliary tract and in the pancreatic duct. If injection of contrast washes adult flukes distally, they will appear at duodenoscopy as brownish, flat, leaf-shaped, 1 to 2 cm in length and usually less than 1 cm in width.[2] Irregularities in the biliary wall should be sampled to evaluate for cholangiocarcinoma.

Pathology

Inflammation of the bile duct epithelium with eosinophils and lymphocytes extends into the portal tracts and periportal regions.[76] Epithelial ulceration and regenerative hyperplasia are present. With *Clonorchis* and *Opisthorchis*, epithelial adenomatous dysplasia occurs, resulting in an increased risk of cholangiocarcinoma. This risk of malignancy does not appear to be present with *F. hepatica* infection, perhaps because of a shorter duration of habitation within the biliary tree. Recurrent inflammation leads to periductal fibrosis with the formation of multiple intrahepatic biliary strictures. With ongoing disease, hepatic fibrosis develops. Intraductal pigment stones and debris are often present.

Treatment

Superimposed bacterial cholangitis should be treated in the usual manner as described previously. Antihelminthic therapy is indicated in any individual found to be infected. Given the potentially severe complications and ongoing parasite transmission, even asymptomatic individuals should receive eradication treatment. Praziquantel is effective in treating *C. sinensis* and *Opisthorchis* species. The dose is 75 mg/kg body weight divided into three doses over 1 day. The treatment of choice for *F. hepatica* is triclabendazole at a single postprandial dose of 10 mg/kg body weight. In both regimens, a second day of treatment may be required for heavy infestations.

ERCP is indicated to extract obstructing worms, alive or deceased, and stones. Biliary strictures resulting from periductal fibrosis or epithelial hyperplasia or dysplasia may require therapy in their own right.

Surgical intervention is indicated for biliary or pancreatic obstruction after unsuccessful endoscopic therapy and for cholecystitis.

Prevention

Properly cooking or freezing fish before ingestion prevents infection with *C. sinensis* and *Opisthorchis* species. Avoidance of freshwater plants is the most effective way to prevent *F. hepatica* infection.

Description of Techniques

The goals and techniques of endoscopic treatment of liver fluke cholangitis are similar to that of *A. lumbricoides*. Because the liver flukes often inhabit the proximal biliary tree, their clearance can be challenging. Extraction to the papilla may be undertaken with a balloon or basket. The parasite can then be grasped with forceps and removed.[77]

Biliary infusion of povidone iodine, an agent active against *F. hepatica*, through a previously placed nasobiliary tube has been described in the management of *F. hepatica* cholangitis.[78] Nine patients who had failed oral antihelminthic therapy became negative for stool ova after biliary administration of povidone iodine.

ECHINOCOCCAL CHOLANGITIS
Epidemiology

Echinococcus granulosus accounts for up to 95% of all human echinococcal infections and is present throughout the world, particularly in regions where dogs are used to raise livestock. The dog is the definitive host and cattle or sheep the intermediate host. *Echinococcus multilocularis* is found in northern Eurasia, Canada, and Alaska within foxes and wolves with rodents as the intermediate host. Most infected humans participate in farming, hunting, forestry, or gardening.[79] *Echinococcus vogeli* and *Echinococcus oligarthrus* occur in Central and South America and rarely infect humans.

Infection may occur at any age, and the frequency of cyst detection on ultrasound screening increases with age. However, because there is a delay of several years between infection and clinical presentation, the mean age of clinical presentation is usually the 5th or 6th decade.[79] The age of diagnosis is decreasing and will continue to do so with high-risk population screening. Both sexes are affected equally.

Pathogenesis

Ova are passed in the feces of canines (*E. granulosus*, *E. multilocularis*, and *E. vogeli*) or felines (*E. oligarthrus*). Intermediate hosts or humans become infected by inadvertent ingestion. The eggs hatch within the small intestine. The resulting oncospheres penetrate the intestinal mucosa and migrate to distant organ sites via the portal venous and lymphatic systems. The liver, particularly the right lobe, is the most commonly affected organ; the lungs, spleen, kidneys, central nervous system, eyes, and bone can also be affected.

The *E. granulosus* oncosphere forms a unilocular cyst within the infected organ enclosed by three layers. The outermost layer consists of granulation and fibrous tissue produced by the host in reaction to the parasite; this may calcify over time. The middle layer is an acellular laminated membrane, and the innermost layer is the germinal layer of the parasite. This latter layer produces the cystic fluid and brood capsules in which the protoscolices, the head of the adult worm, develop. Daughter cysts form from the germinal layer existing within or separate from the original cyst. Hydatid cysts may remain a constant size or slowly enlarge. Disintegration of the daughter cysts and brood capsules within the original cyst frees the protoscolices. Biliary disease results from compression by the cyst or rupture of the cyst into the biliary tree.

E. multilocularis cysts are not contained by an outer fibrous membrane and budding of daughter cysts occurs exogenous to the original cyst, morphologically resembling the pulmonary alveoli, thus named alveolar echinococcosis. The cystic lesion extends through the liver and into adjacent structures in a malignant fashion. Tissue damage results from pressure necrosis and the host inflammatory response. *E. multilocularis* typically infects the biliary tree by invading into the bifurcation of the right and left hepatic ducts.

E. vogeli and *E. oligarthrus* have a similar life cycle and pathogenesis to *E. granulosus* although they are slightly more aggressive, occasionally invading adjacent organs.

To complete the *Echinococcus* life cycle, the definitive host consumes the protoscolices-containing viscera of the intermediate host. The proctoscolices become mature worms within the small intestine and begin to produce eggs.

Clinical Features

Individuals are asymptomatic during acute *E. granulosus* infection and most remain asymptomatic for several years, if not their entire lives. Most hydatid cysts are diagnosed incidentally by imaging for an unrelated indication. When symptoms occur, they are due to mass effect, secondary bacterial infection with abscess formation, or cyst rupture. Once cysts grow beyond 10 cm, they may produce tender hepatomegaly, nausea, and early satiety. Hepatic cysts may compress the biliary tree (resulting in cholestasis) or adjacent venous structures. Compression of the portal vein causes signs of portal hypertension, whereas compression of the hepatic vein or inferior vena cava may lead to hepatic congestion or, rarely, Budd-Chiari syndrome.

Cyst contents are highly immunogenic and leakage or rupture results in a hypersensitivity reaction, possibly anaphylactic. Intraperitoneal rupture from a subcapsular hepatic cyst carries a very high risk of anaphylaxis and allows dissemination of protoscolices to other organ sites. Contained rupture into adjacent organs, such as the lungs, may result in fistula formation. The most common site of cyst rupture is into the biliary tract leading to echinococcal cholangitis. The daughter cyst membranes and unattached protoscolices obstruct the bile duct lumen causing jaundice, biliary colic, and secondary bacterial cholangitis. Acute pancreatitis after cyst rupture into the biliary tract has also been reported.

Laboratory parameters are normal in asymptomatic disease. Biliary obstruction results in elevated liver enzymes, principally alkaline phosphatase and bilirubin. The eosinophil count and serum globulins are typically normal unless the cyst contents leak in which case eosinophilia and IgE hypergammaglobulinemia are present.

E. multilocularis has a similar spectrum of symptoms to *E. granulosus* including those related to hepatomegaly, bile duct obstruction, and venous obstruction. However, *E. multilocularis* is much more aggressive with an accelerated course and invariable invasion of adjacent structures and distant metastases. The disease is fatal if not treated. Patients often have mild abnormalities in liver enzymes and eosinophilia.

E. vogeli and *E. oligarthrus* produce the clinical features described previously, the severity of which lies between that of *E. granulosus* and *E. multilocularis*.

Unlike the liver flukes and *A. lumbricoides*, protective immunity to *Echinococcus* species does develop in human hosts.

Diagnosis

Diagnosis of echinococcal infection is based on serology and imaging. There is a wide range of serologic tests for *E. granulosus* with sensitivity ranging from 62% to 100% and specificity from 88% to 100%.[80] Serologic testing for *E. multilocularis* using ELISA is reported as 100% sensitive and specific.[81] Titers decrease after surgical resection, eventually becoming undetectable, and rise with disease recurrence.

On ultrasonography, the hydatid cyst must be distinguished from a simple hepatic cyst. It is typically an anechoic round structure contained by a thin wall. There is often hyperechoic "sand" within the cyst cavity, which in many cases is divided by multiple loculations. These findings represent unattached protoscolices and daughter cysts, respectively.[82] More than 80% of hydatid cysts are solitary, and most are located in the right hepatic lobe.[83] Calcifications in the cyst wall produce shadowing on sonography and are also detectable on plain radiographs. Ultrasound is also useful at detecting cyst rupture into the biliary tract. Findings include echogenic material within a dilated biliary tree and loss of cyst wall continuity at the point it approximates the bile duct.[84]

Ultrasound-guided percutaneous cyst puncture and fluid analysis are able to accurately diagnosis hydatid disease. Salama and coworkers[83] examined 54 hepatic cysts in 45 patients and reported that ultrasound characteristics and fluid appearance were correlated to the presence of protoscolices on microscopic examination of the cyst fluid. Round, anechoic cysts with sand yielded clear fluid with chalky sediment, under pressure. Fresh and stained fluid smears demonstrated multiple protoscolices. In contrast, cysts with a calcified lining, elliptical shape indicating collapse or germinal layer detachment ("water-lily sign") contained turbid, yellowish fluid with debris and required negative pressure to aspirate. Protoscolices were not identified on microscopy. In addition to microscopy, detection of hydatid antigen in cyst fluid using latex agglutination has been described with high sensitivity.[85]

CT is comparable to ultrasound in visualizing hepatobiliary hydatid disease[86] and further aids management by mapping the exact location of the cyst and detecting additional cysts not observed by ultrasonography.[82] Alveolar echinococcosis mimics malignancy on CT. The hepatic lesion is usually composed of both cystic and solid components and irregular calcifications and has a poorly defined margin.

MRI does not appear to add information in the characterization of *E. granulosus* disease of the liver but is useful in extrahepatic disease, such as central nervous system involvement.[87] In hepatic *E. multilocularis* infection, MRI is used to determine vascular invasion.[88]

ERCP is indicated to evaluate suspected biliary involvement by *E. granulosus*. Duodenoscopy may demonstrate glistening, white membranes within the duodenum. On cholangiography, three patterns of filling defects have been reported (Fig. 48–9). The membranes appear filiform, the daughter cysts appear round, and hydatid sand appears as debris.[89] In *E. multilocularis* infection, cholangiogram may demonstrate strictures at the bifurcation of the right and left hepatic ducts.[90]

Treatment

Complete surgical excision, by cystectomy, pericystectomy, or partial hepatic resection, is usually curative in *E. granulosus* infection. Albendazole administered before surgery results in a higher number of nonviable cysts[91,92] and may decrease the risk of local recurrence or intraperitoneal seeding should spillage of cyst contents occur. Surgical mortality is 1% to 2%.[93] Complications include infection, bile leak, and leakage of cyst contents with hypersensitivity reaction and dissemination of disease.

Percutaneous evacuation with the ultrasound-guided puncture, aspiration of cyst contents, injection of scolecoidal agent, and

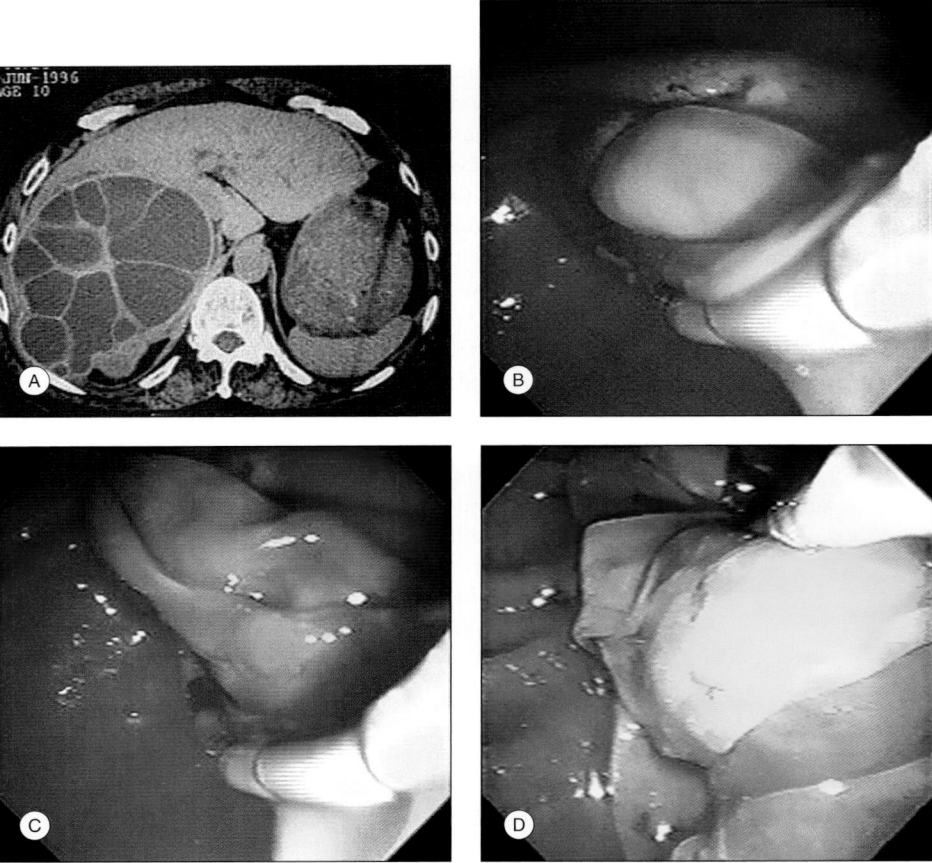

Figure 48-9. Echinococcus (hydatidosis) infection shown *(A)* in right lobe of the liver on computed tomography (CT). *B, C,* and *D,* Sequence of cyst wall extraction at endoscopic retrograde cholangiopancreatography (ERCP) after sphincterotomy. (*A,* Courtesy of Dr Nageshwar Reddy, Hyderabad, India; *B, C,* and *D,* courtesy of Dr Claudio Navarette, Santiago, Chile.)

reaspiration of cyst contents (PAIR) technique is widely used to treat unilocular *E. granulosus* cysts. Scolecoidal agents used for PAIR include 95% ethanol and hypertonic saline.

Khuroo and colleagues[94] randomized 50 patients to undergo cystectomy or PAIR and receive albendazole. At a mean follow-up of 17 months, the cyst diameter was similar in the two groups, but the surgical arm had significantly more complications and a longer length of hospital stay. After PAIR, initial treatment failures occur in less than 1% and probability of relapse ranged from 1% to 4.5%. Complications of PAIR include hypersensitivity reaction, infection, intra-abdominal seeding, and fistula formation to adjacent organs. In a review of 765 abdominal hydatid cysts treated with PAIR, anaphylaxis occurred in four instances with one death and minor complications occurred in 14%.[95] ERCP should be performed before protoscolicide administration to ensure that there is no communication between the cyst and biliary tree because contact with protoscolicidal agents produces sclerosing cholangitis and pancreatitis. Treatment with albendazole at least 4 hours before PAIR and up to 4 weeks following has been recommended.[96]

Oral benzimidazole treatment alone, generally with albendazole (400 mg twice a day), which is better absorbed by the intestine and cyst than mebendazole, is not ideal therapy. Approximately 30% of patients will achieve cure,[97,98] although most will demonstrate degenerative changes in the cyst during therapy and follow-up.[99-101] Successful therapy is more likely with small, simple cysts and treatment duration greater than 3 months.[92,98,100] Albendazole is contraindicated in pregnancy. PAIR has been successfully used during pregnancy to avoid rupture of large cysts during labor.[96] Albendazole should not be used in those with severe underlying liver disease, and liver enzymes should be monitored in all patients.

Radical surgery with complete excision of larvae tissue is the only curative therapy for *E. multilocularis* infection. An additional 2 years of albendazole postoperatively decreases the risk of local recurrence.[97,102] Patients deemed inoperable at diagnosis likely benefit from long-term albendazole therapy[103] and a combination of palliative resection, aimed at lessening the mass of larvae tissue, and benzimidazole therapy is advocated.[104] Liver transplantation is a treatment option for unresectable alveolar echinococcosis. A retrospective study of European transplant centers reported 45 patients who underwent liver transplantation with an overall 5-year survival of 71% and disease-free 5-year survival of 58%.[105] Given the high probability of graft recurrence, long-term benzimidazole therapy should be considered in post-transplant patients.

The indications for ERCP in biliary echinococcosis are listed in Table 48–2. Jaundice, biliary colic, and cholangitis are usually the result of extrinsic compression by a hydatid cyst, cyst contents leaking into the bile duct and causing obstruction, or direct invasion of the biliary tract. Insertion of a biliary endoprosthesis or extraction of the hydatid debris endoscopically will relieve patient symptoms.[106,107]

Prevention

Canines should never be fed livestock offal. Domestic cats and dogs should be routinely dewormed. Proper washing of hands before

Table 48–2. Indications for Endoscopic Retrograde Cholangiopancreatography in Hepatic Echinococcosis

Bile duct obstruction
    Extrinsic compression by hydatid cyst
    Hydatid cyst rupture into the biliary tract
    Biliary tract invasion by alveolar echinococcosis
Before protoscolicide administration
Postprotoscolicide biliary stricture(s)
Postoperative bile leak

eating and washing of vegetables and fruits that are to be eaten uncooked helps reduce infection. One should avoid handling canines in endemic areas.

Description of Techniques

In *E. granulosus* cholangitis, the laminated membranes can be removed with biopsy forceps if protruding from the papilla. Otherwise, the membranes, daughter cysts, and protoscolices should be removed with a biliary extraction balloon or basket, generally after an endoscopic sphincterotomy.[106,107] Saline irrigation facilitates removal of the protoscolices. Biliary strictures resulting from hydatid cyst compression or alveolar echinococcosis invasion can be managed with stent insertion.

Endoscopic therapy may be required after surgical treatment or PAIR to manage bile leaks, communication between the biliary tract and the surgical site with hydatid remnants causing biliary obstruction and/or biliary strictures from scolicidal agents.[106,107]

Acquired Immunodeficiency Syndrome Cholangiopathy

AIDS cholangiopathy is a syndrome of right upper quadrant pain, elevated alkaline phosphatase, and typical cholangiogram findings associated with human immunodeficiency virus (HIV) infection. Opportunistic infection of the biliary tract is likely a causative factor.

EPIDEMIOLOGY

Because those affected may be asymptomatic, the frequency of AIDS cholangiopathy among HIV-infected individuals is not known. AIDS cholangiopathy is most prevalent in homosexual men with a mean age at diagnosis of 37 years.[108,109] Cholangiopathy is the AIDS-defining illness in a few patients, but most have had AIDS for at least a year.[108]

PATHOGENESIS

AIDS cholangiopathy is believed to result from opportunistic infection of the biliary tract. Those affected are immunosuppressed, with a CD4 lymphocyte count of less than 200/mm³. *Cryptosporidium*, most commonly *Cryptosporidium parvum*, is isolated from the bile or stool in up to two thirds of individuals with AIDS cholangiopathy.[110] *Cryptosporidium* is an intracellular parasite that completes a full life cycle within the human host eventually producing oocysts shed in the feces. *Cryptosporidium* oocysts are transmitted orally to humans from other humans, animals, or the environment, for instance, in contaminated water. The organism likely accesses the biliary tract from the duodenum, across the major papilla. The development of cholangiopathy among HIV-infected individuals infected with *Cryptosporidium* is independently associated with a CD4 count of less than 50/mm³.[111] C. *parvum* appears to attach to the apical surface of the biliary epithelial cell, invade, and propagate within the cell while inducing apoptotic cell death of adjacent, uninfected epithelial cells.[112] This results in cholangitis with secondary fibrosis leading to stricture formation and acalculous cholecystitis. Congenital and familial immunodeficiency disorders have been associated with similar biliary abnormalities and infection with *Cryptosporidium*.

Other organisms associated with AIDS cholangiopathy include Cytomegalovirus (CMV), Microsporidia, *Isospora*, *Cyclospora*, and *Mycobacterial avium intracellulare* (MAI).[113,114] Although initially postulated, to date there has been no evidence that direct cholangiocyte infection with HIV is causative in AIDS cholangiopathy.

CLINICAL FEATURES

Patients typically present with right upper quadrant pain. This is the most frequent symptom observed in AIDS cholangiopathy, occurring in more than 90% of patients.[108] Fever and jaundice are less common.[109] Symptoms related to enteritis or colitis may also be present, such as watery diarrhea and weight loss. Acalculous cholecystitis resulting from opportunistic infection of the gallbladder may occur alone or concomitant to cholangiopathy and is associated with similar underlying pathogens. Secondary biliary cirrhosis has not been described as a complication of AIDS cholangiopathy, perhaps because of the shortened life span of this population, but these patients may be at risk of cholangiocarcinoma.[115] Patient survival is dependent on degree of immunosuppression and on the presence of AIDS cholangiopathy.[110]

Marked elevation of the alkaline phosphatase and gamma glutamyltransferase are the most common liver enzyme test abnormalities. There may be a slight increase in bilirubin and aminotransferases as well.

DIAGNOSIS

The differential diagnosis of AIDS cholangiopathy and the management approach are shown in Table 48–3 and Figure 48–10, respectively.

Imaging studies are abnormal in 80% of patients with symptomatic AIDS cholangiopathy.[108] In patients presenting with both abdominal pain and cholestasis, ultrasound had a sensitivity of 96% in identifying biliary abnormalities in ERCP-proven cholangiopathy.[116] Findings include extrahepatic bile duct and gallbladder dilatation and wall thickening and hypoechoic haloing around the intrahepatic bile ducts. The specificity was lower because ultrasound was unable to reliably discriminate AIDS cholangiopathy from other causes of bile duct dilatation.

Cholecystitis, calculous or acalculous, may mimic the clinical presentation of AIDS cholangiopathy, but it is readily distinguished on noninvasive imaging, and appropriate patients may thus be selected for surgical management rather than ERCP. Endoscopic

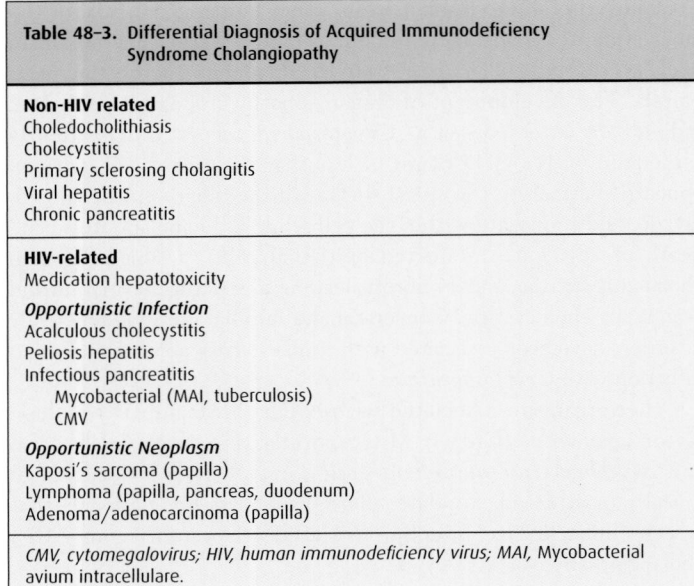

Table 48-3. Differential Diagnosis of Acquired Immunodeficiency Syndrome Cholangiopathy

Non-HIV related
Choledocholithiasis
Cholecystitis
Primary sclerosing cholangitis
Viral hepatitis
Chronic pancreatitis

HIV-related
Medication hepatotoxicity
Opportunistic Infection
Acalculous cholecystitis
Peliosis hepatitis
Infectious pancreatitis
    Mycobacterial (MAI, tuberculosis)
    CMV
Opportunistic Neoplasm
Kaposi's sarcoma (papilla)
Lymphoma (papilla, pancreas, duodenum)
Adenoma/adenocarcinoma (papilla)

CMV, cytomegalovirus; HIV, human immunodeficiency virus; MAI, Mycobacterial avium intracellulare.

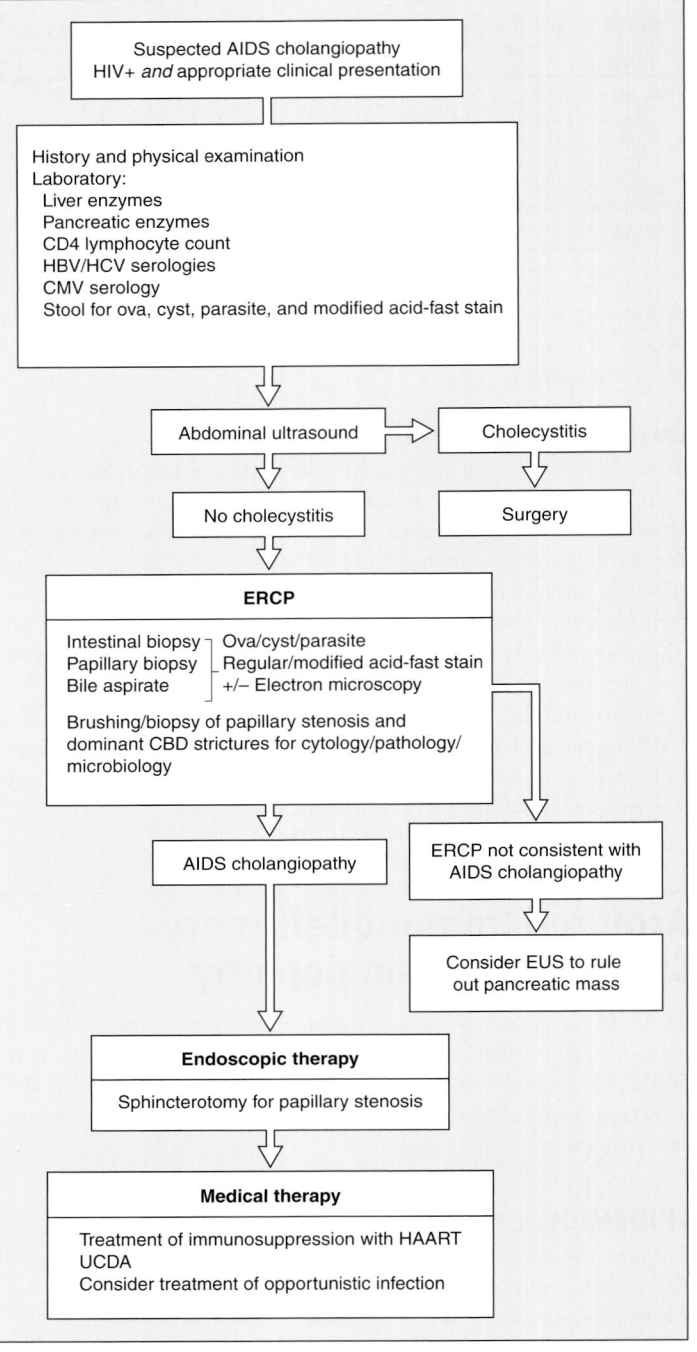

Figure 48-10. Algorithm for management of suspected acquired immunodeficiency syndrome (AIDS) cholangiopathy.

ultrasonography (EUS) may provide additional information in AIDS patients with abdominal pain but without AIDS cholangiopathy by ERCP. Chronic pancreatitis or a pancreatic mass may present in a similar fashion and not be detected by other imaging modalities.[117]

ERCP is the gold standard in diagnosing AIDS cholangiography (Fig. 48-11). Cholangiogram findings have been described as sclerosing cholangitis with segmental stricturing to create a beaded appearance similar to that observed in primary sclerosing cholangitis. The patterns of biliary tract strictures are listed in Table 48-4. Papillary stenosis with intrahepatic strictures is the most common pattern observed.[108,113,116] Other cholangiogram abnormalities reported include adherent polypoid filling defects, biopsies of which demonstrate granulation tissue.[118]

When AIDS cholangiopathy is suspected, attempts should be made to identify an associated infection. Stool specimens, bile specimens, intestinal biopsies, and papillary biopsies should be submitted for examination. In addition to ova, cyst, and parasite examination by microscopy, testing for Microsporidia, C. *parvum*, MAI, and cytomegalovirus (CMV) must be specifically requested. Aspiration of bile for culture and multiple biopsies of the duodenum and papilla reveal an underlying pathogen in up to 92% of cases.[109] One study reported that isolation of *Cryptosporidium* or CMV was more common when intrahepatic duct irregularities were present on cholangiogram.[119]

Pancreatography is abnormal in up to one half of AIDS cholangiopathy patients, revealing pancreatic duct strictures in the head of the pancreas.[109,113] Further imaging is indicated to evaluate for a pancreatic neoplasm or infectious pancreatitis so that appropriate therapy can be initiated.

PATHOLOGY

The pathologic findings in AIDS cholangiopathy are not specific and depend on the associated organism. There is usually a mixed inflammatory infiltrate and fibrosis of the bile ducts. The portal tracts typically have few inflammatory cells.[76] In cryptosporidial infection, there may be an increased number of apoptotic bodies, and the parasite may be seen at the luminal surface of the epithelium. Typical inclusion bodies may not be present in CMV infection of the biliary tract, but immunohistochemical tests make the correct diagnosis.[120] Microsporidia are difficult to detect by light microscopy but may be associated with the presence of foamy macrophages within the lamina propria.[121] Granulomas may be observed with *Cryptosporidia*, Microsporidia, and MAI infection.

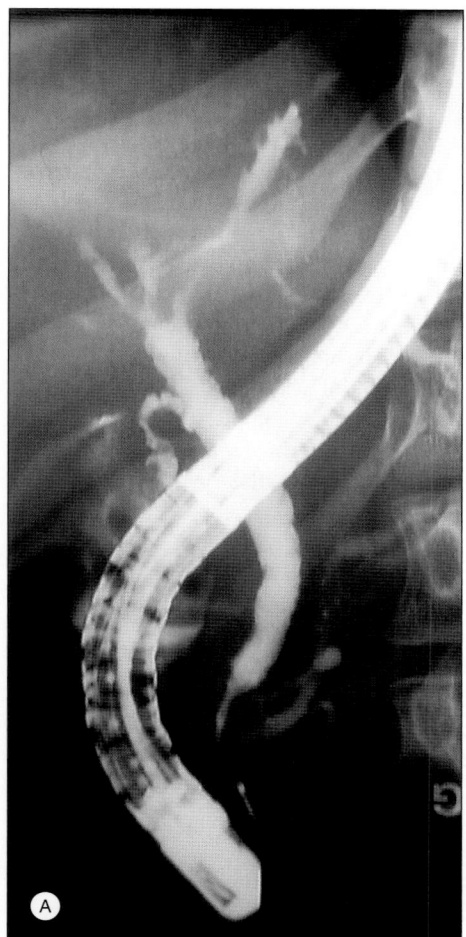
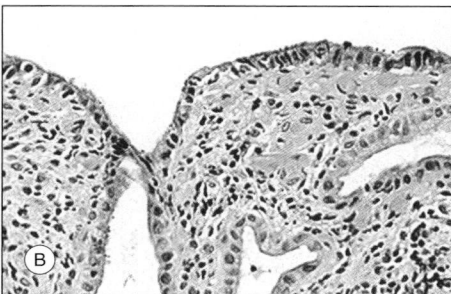
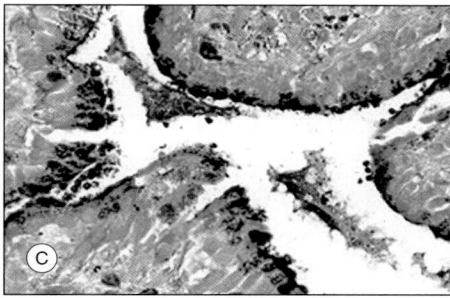

Figure 48–11. Acquired immunodeficiency syndrome (AIDS) cholangiopathy *(A)* shown by endoscopic retrograde cholangiopancreatography (ERCP) with narrowed distal bile duct and irregular bile duct walls with *(B)* a relatively normal bile duct epithelium on biopsy and standard hematoxylin and eosin (H&E) staining but *(C)* Microsporidia demonstrated on the surface as black with silver staining. (Courtesy of Dr. Richard Tilson, Boston, MA.)

Table 48–4. Cholangiogram Findings in Acquired Immunodeficiency Syndrome Cholangiopathy

Finding	Frequency (%)
Papillary stenosis and intrahepatic duct strictures	33
Papillary stenosis alone	21
Papillary stenosis and intrahepatic and extrahepatic duct strictures	20
Intrahepatic duct strictures alone	12
Intrahepatic and extrahepatic duct strictures	8
Extrahepatic duct strictures alone	5
Papillary stenosis and extrahepatic duct strictures	1

From references 108, 109, 113, 119, and 124.

TREATMENT

The medical management of AIDS cholangiopathy is divided into antimicrobial agents directed against the causative organism, highly active antiretroviral therapy directed against the underlying HIV infection, and ursodeoxycholic acid (UDCA). Case series assessing the effect of treatment of CMV, C. *parvum*, and Microsporidia on patient symptoms, liver enzymes, and cholangiogram findings have not been encouraging.[110,111,119] The use of highly active antiretroviral therapy (HAART) to restore the immune system has been effective in suppressing enteritis and, perhaps, cholangiopathy associated with C. *parvum* and Microsporidia, although eradication probably does not occur.[122] Castiella and coworkers[123] treated four AIDS cholangiopathy patients with UDCA (10 mg/kg body weight). At a mean follow-up of 4.5 months, improvement in symptoms and alkaline phosphatase levels was observed in all patients.

Endoscopic therapy has been the most extensively studied treatment in AIDS cholangiography. Endoscopic sphincterotomy in patients with papillary stenosis results in improvement of abdominal pain in 32% to 100% of patients.[109,119,124] Cello and colleagues[125] reported improvement in pain scores at a mean of 9.4 months after sphincterotomy. This did not correspond to an improvement in liver enzymes or cholangiogram abnormalities, both of which appeared to worsen.

Symptomatic extrahepatic bile duct strictures should be sampled to exclude cholangiocarcinoma. Treatment with insertion of plastic stents has been described but, in general, should be avoided to limit migration of enteric pathogens into the biliary tract.

Palliative treatment of abdominal pain associated with AIDS cholangiopathy is generally managed with narcotic analgesics. Other potential therapies include CT-guided celiac plexus block, which was successful in relieving symptoms at 11 months' follow-up in a small case series.[126]

PREPROCEDURE HISTORY AND CONSIDERATIONS

Protease inhibitors and benzodiazepines are both metabolized through the P-450 enzyme complex. The protease inhibitors decrease benzodiazepine metabolism, increasing their serum levels and potentiating their effects including respiratory depression.[127] Because midazolam and diazepam are commonly used for sedation during endoscopic procedures, endoscopists should be cognizant of this drug interaction while administering benzodiazepines in patients receiving protease inhibitors.

DESCRIPTION OF TECHNIQUES

ERCP is performed in the usual manner. The duodenum should be inspected for mucosal abnormalities such as erosions or ulcerations that may indicate enteric infection. Biopsies of lesions or random mucosal biopsies should be performed and sent to microbiology and cytology. Likewise, bile should be sampled after cannulation and submitted for analysis.

Evidence of papillary stenosis should be noted during cannulation and by observing bile drainage after cholangiography. If papillary stenosis is present, an endoscopic sphincterotomy should be performed in a patient with abdominal pain, jaundice, or fever. Sphincterotomy is not beneficial in the absence of papillary stenosis.

Dominant strictures should be sampled for cytology with a cytology brush and/or biopsy forceps to exclude cholangiocarcinoma or another malignant process. In a symptomatic patient, balloon or catheter dilatation of the stricture may be performed, but long-term stenting is not ideal.

Once ERCP is completed, biopsies of the major papilla may be obtained and sent for microbiologic and pathologic analysis.

Cholecystitis

EPIDEMIOLOGY

The epidemiology of cholecystitis depends on the underlying cause. Gallstone disease is more prevalent in premenopausal women and individuals of specific ethnic groups. Other risk factors for cholelithiasis include obesity, rapid weight loss, pregnancy, certain medications, hypertriglyceridemia, chronic hemolysis, and ileal resection. Cholecystitis related to biliary parasitic infections and AIDS cholangiopathy are discussed elsewhere in this chapter.

PATHOGENESIS

The pathogenesis of acute cholecystitis is incompletely understood. Injury to the gallbladder mucosa from bile stasis, ischemia, or infection is thought to stimulate prostaglandin synthesis and an inflammatory response. Bile stasis usually results from cystic duct obstruction by a gallstone or from decreased gallbladder motility. Less common causes of cystic duct obstruction are worms, hemobilia, and tumor. Decreased gallbladder motility and ischemia are implicated in the development of acalculous cholecystitis in the critically ill. Infection of the gallbladder complicates cholecystitis in approximately 50% of cases but is not usually the causative factor, with the exception of parasitic and AIDS cholecystitis.

CLINICAL FEATURES

Patients with acute cholecystitis present with constant right upper quadrant or epigastric abdominal pain that may radiate to the right back and shoulder. There is often associated nausea, vomiting, malaise and fever. There may be a history of biliary colic. Biliary colic is identical in character to the pain of cholecystitis but does not have associated fever, is often less severe, and should resolve within 4 hours.

Acalculous cholecystitis accounts for approximately 10% of acute cholecystitis and is generally seen in the critically ill or those with vascular insufficiency such as atherosclerotic disease, vasculitis, or cholesterol emboli syndrome. Decreased gallbladder motility resulting from fasting, total parenteral nutrition, and medications may also contribute to the development of acalculous cholecystitis.

Complications of cholecystitis usually occur with secondary bacterial infection and include empyema, gallbladder wall necrosis resulting in a gangrenous gallbladder, perforation, and emphysematous cholecystitis. Gallbladder perforation may result in abscess formation, peritonitis, or fistula formation. Migration of a large gallstone through a cholecystoenteric fistula may lead to bowel obstruction, usually at the level of the ileocecal valve, referred to as gallstone ileus. Emphysematous cholecystitis describes gas within the gallbladder wall resulting from infection with gas-producing bacteria.

On physical examination, elevated temperature, tachycardia, and right upper quadrant tenderness to palpation with focal peritoneal signs are frequent findings. Murphy's sign is present if, when the examiner's fingers are hooked under the right rib cage, the patient experiences increased pain in deep inspiration and ceases inspiratory effort. In acalculous cholecystitis, a distended gallbladder may be palpable. Laboratory abnormalities include leukocytosis with a neutrophil predominance and increased proportion of band forms. Liver enzymes and amylase levels are usually normal or mildly elevated.

DIAGNOSIS

Ultrasound is the test of choice to confirm clinical features of acute cholecystitis. Findings include gallbladder wall thickening,

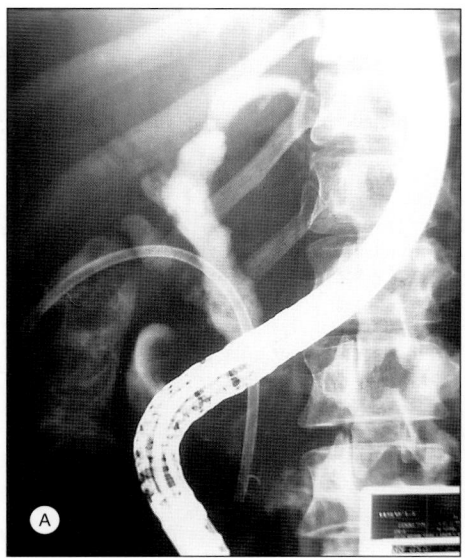 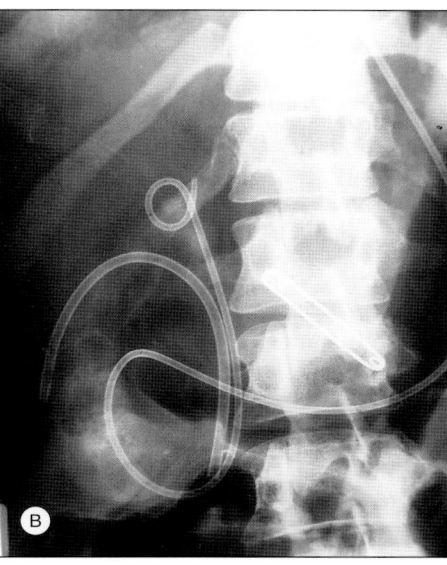

Figure 48-12. Concomitant calculous cholangitis and cholecystitis. *A,* ERCP showing a plastic stent draining the gallbladder. *B,* Radiograph following ERCP showing addition of a nasobiliary tube draining the common bile duct.

pericholecystic fluid, gallbladder sludge, and gallstones. Ultrasound is not able to detect stones reliably in the cystic duct. The sensitivity and specificity of ultrasound in the diagnosis of cholecystitis is 88% and 80%, respectively.[128] A sonographic Murphy sign may also be present.

Cholescintigraphy is a useful adjunct to diagnose cholecystitis in patients without characteristic ultrasound findings because an obstructed cystic duct is then rapidly confirmed or excluded.

PATHOLOGY

The gallbladder is often enlarged and filled with purulent bile, stones, and sludge. The mucosa is edematous with a neutrophil predominant inflammatory infiltrate.[76] There may be necrosis, intramural abscesses, perforation, and fistulas present.

TREATMENT

The initial management of acute cholecystitis is supportive. Fasting, fluid resuscitation, analgesics, and, when secondary bacterial infection is suspected, antibiotics. Antibiotic coverage is directed against Enterobacteriaceae and *Enterococcus* species until directed therapy can be instituted against specific organisms identified in blood or bile cultures. Parenteral administration of prostaglandin inhibitors, such as ketorolac or diclofenac, is often adequate in controlling pain related to acute cholecystitis, but narcotic analgesics may be required.

Cholecystectomy is the definitive therapy. Although patients may recover from an episode of acute cholecystitis, the risk of recurrent symptoms is 70% within the next 2 years.[129] Thus, patients without serious concomitant medical problems should undergo cholecystectomy during the same hospital admission, usually 24 to 48 hours after admission. In particular, diabetics, because of their increased risk of gallbladder necrosis and perforation, should be considered for cholecystectomy after their first attack of cholecystitis.

Patients who are medically unfit for surgery should receive supportive therapy; if they do not improve with conservative management, they should receive gallbladder drainage. This includes critically ill patients who develop acalculous cholecystitis, patients with cholecystitis complicated by sepsis and multiple organ dysfunction, and patients with serious cardiopulmonary conditions precluding general anesthesia. In the nonsurgical patient, gallbladder drainage is generally achieved by percutaneous cholecystostomy tube placement; however, successful endoscopic drainage of the gallbladder has been described.

Placement of a biliary endoprosthesis into the gallbladder during ERCP (Fig. 48–12) can alleviate symptoms resulting from recurrent biliary colic, calculous cholecystitis, acalculous cholecystitis, and gallbladder perforation.[129-131] Endoscopic gallbladder drainage can be performed in the presence of coagulopathy and ascites when percutaneous cholecystostomy tube placement is contraindicated.

DESCRIPTION OF TECHNIQUES

ERCP is performed in the usual manner: cystic duct insertion is identified and entered. A guidewire may facilitate selective cystic duct cannulation. Endoscopic cholecystography identifies calculi within the cystic duct and gallbladder. After careful passage of the guidewire into the gallbladder, wire-guided balloon extraction of stones or placement of a biliary endoprosthesis through the cystic duct and into the gallbladder can then be undertaken. Occasionally, an obstructing stone is dislodged into the gallbladder as instruments are advanced into the cystic duct.[132]

Irrigation of the gallbladder with 1% N-acetylcysteine through a nasobiliary catheter has been described in acalculous cholecystitis.[130] The use of N-acetylcysteine appeared to thin the gallbladder contents and enable gallbladder drainage and collapse around the catheter.

REFERENCES

1. Gigot JF, Leese T, Dereme T, et al: Acute cholangitis. Multivariate analysis of risk factors. Ann Surg 209:435–438, 1989.

2. Mandell G, Bennett J, Dolin R (eds): Mandell, Douglas, and Bennett's Principles and Practice of Infectious Disease, 5th ed. Philadelphia, Churchill Livingstone, 2000.

3. Rerknimitr R, Fogel EL, Kalayci C, et al: Microbiology of bile in patients with cholangitis or cholestasis with and without plastic biliary endoprosthesis. Gastrointest Endosc 56:885–889, 2002.

4. Lai EC, Mok FP, Tan ES, et al: Endoscopic biliary drainage for severe acute cholangitis. N Engl J Med 326:1582–1586, 1992.

5. Balthazar EJ, Birnbaum BA, Naidich M: Acute cholangitis: CT evaluation. J Comput Assist Tomogr 17:283–289, 1993.

6. Chan YL, Chan AC, Lam WW, et al: Choledocholithiasis: Comparison of MR cholangiography and endoscopic retrograde cholangiography. Radiology 200:85–89, 1996.

7. Lee MG, Lee HJ, Kim MH, et al: Extrahepatic biliary diseases: 3D MR cholangiopancreatography compared with endoscopic retrograde cholangiopancreatography. Radiology 202:663–669, 1997.

8. Leung JW, Chung SC, Sung JJ, et al: Urgent endoscopic drainage for acute suppurative cholangitis. Lancet 1:1307–1309, 1989.

9. Leese T, Neoptolemos JP, Baker AR, Carr-Locke DL: Management of acute cholangitis and the impact of endoscopic sphincterotomy. Br J Surg 73:988–992, 1986.

10. Lee DW, Chan AC, Lam YH, et al: Biliary decompression by nasobiliary catheter or biliary stent in acute suppurative cholangitis: A prospective randomized trial. Gastrointest Endosc 56:361–365, 2002.

11. Hui CK, Lai KC, Wong WM, et al: A randomised controlled trial of endoscopic sphincterotomy in acute cholangitis without common bile duct stones. Gut 51:245–247, 2002.

12. Neuhaus H, Zillinger C, Born P, et al: Randomized study of intracorporeal laser lithotripsy versus extracorporeal shock-wave lithotripsy for difficult bile duct stones. Gastrointest Endosc 47:327–334, 1998.

13. Binmoeller KF, Bruckner M, Thonke F, Soehendra N: Treatment of difficult bile duct stones using mechanical, electrohydraulic and extracorporeal shock wave lithotripsy. Endoscopy 25:201–206, 1993.

14. Cotton PB, Kozarek RA, Schapiro RH, et al: Endoscopic laser lithotripsy of large bile duct stones. Gastroenterology 99:1128–1133, 1990.

15. Bergman JJ, Rauws EA, Tijssen JG, et al: Biliary endoprostheses in elderly patients with endoscopically irretrievable common bile duct stones: Report on 117 patients. Gastrointest Endosc 42:195–201, 1995.

16. Chopra KB, Peters RA, O'Toole PA, et al: Randomised study of endoscopic biliary endoprosthesis versus duct clearance for bile duct stones in high-risk patients. Lancet 348:791–793, 1996.

17. Binmoeller KF, Thonke F, Soehendra N: Endoscopic treatment of Mirizzi's syndrome. Gastrointest Endosc 39:532–536, 1993.

18. Baron TH, Schroeder PL, Schwartzberg MS, Carabasi MH: Resolution of Mirizzi's syndrome using endoscopic therapy. Gastrointest Endosc 44:343–345, 1996.

19. Tsuyuguchi T, Saisho H, Ishihara T, et al: Long-term follow-up after treatment of Mirizzi syndrome by peroral cholangioscopy. Gastrointest Endosc 52:639–644, 2000.

20. Nomura T, Shirai Y, Hatakeyama K: Cholangitis in malignant biliary obstruction. Br J Surg 85:407, 1998.

21. Chang WH, Kortan P, Haber GB: Outcome in patients with bifurcation tumors who undergo unilateral versus bilateral hepatic duct drainage. Gastrointest Endosc 47:354–362, 1998.

22. Speer AG, Cotton PB, Rode J, et al: Biliary stent blockage with bacterial biofilm. A light and electron microscopy study. Ann Intern Med 108:546–553, 1988.

23. Davids PH, Groen AK, Rauws EA, et al: Randomised trial of self-expanding metal stents versus polyethylene stents for distal malignant biliary obstruction. Lancet 340:1488–1492, 1992.

24. Carr-Locke DL, Ball TJ, Connors PJ, et al: Multicenter, randomized trial of Wallstent biliary endoprosthesis versus plastic stents [abstract]. Gastrointest Endosc 39:310, 1993.

25. Vandervoort J, Soetikno RM, Tham TC, et al: Risk factors for complications after performance of ERCP. Gastrointest Endosc 56:652–656, 2002.

26. Lai EC, Lo CM, Choi TK, et al: Urgent biliary decompression after endoscopic retrograde cholangiopancreatography. Am J Surg 157:121–125, 1989.

27. Harris A, Chan AC, Torres-Viera C, et al: Meta-analysis of antibiotic prophylaxis in endoscopic retrograde cholangiopancreatography (ERCP). Endoscopy 31:718–724, 1999.

28. Motte S, Deviere J, Dumonceau JM, et al: Risk factors for septicemia following endoscopic biliary stenting. Gastroenterology 101:1374–1381, 1991.

29. Struelens MJ, Rost F, Deplano A, et al: Pseudomonas aeruginosa and Enterobacteriaceae bacteremia after biliary endoscopy: An outbreak investigation using DNA macrorestriction analysis. Am J Med 95:489–498, 1993.

30. Gregg JA, De Girolami P, Carr-Locke DL: Effects of sphincteroplasty and endoscopic sphincterotomy on the bacteriologic characteristics of the common bile duct. Am J Surg 149:668–671, 1985.

31. Cetta F: Do surgical and endoscopic sphincterotomy prevent or facilitate recurrent common duct stone formation? Arch Surg 128:329–336, 1993.

32. Audisio RA, Bozzetti F, Severini A, et al: The occurrence of cholangitis after percutaneous biliary drainage: Evaluation of some risk factors. Surgery 103:507–512, 1988.

33. Sacks-Berg A, Calubiran OV, Epstein HY, Cunha BA: Sepsis associated with transhepatic cholangiography. J Hosp Infect 20:43–50, 1992.

34. Nomura T, Shirai Y, Hatakeyama K: Bacteribilia and cholangitis after percutaneous transhepatic biliary drainage for malignant biliary obstruction. Dig Dis Sci 44:542–546, 1999.

35. Sheen-Chen SM, Cheng YF, Chou FF, Lee TY: Postoperative T-tube cholangiography: Is routine antibiotic prophylaxis necessary? A prospective, controlled study. Arch Surg 130:20–23, 1995.

36. Dellinger EP, Kirshenbaum G, Weinstein M, Steer M: Determinants of adverse reaction following postoperative T-tube cholangiogram. Ann Surg 191:397–403, 1980.

37. Ernest van Heurn LW, Saing H, Tam PK: Cholangitis after hepatic portoenterostomy for biliary atresia: A multivariate analysis of risk factors. J Pediatr 142:566–571, 2003.

38. Baker AR, Neoptolemos JP, Carr-Locke DL, Fossard DP: Sump syndrome following choledochoduodenostomy and its endoscopic treatment. Br J Surg 72:433–435, 1985.

39. Caroli-Bosc FX, Demarquay JF, Peten EP, et al: Endoscopic management of sump syndrome after choledochoduodenostomy: Retrospective analysis of 30 cases. Gastrointest Endosc 51:180–183, 2000.

40. Mavrogiannis C, Liatsos C, Romanos A, et al: Sump syndrome: Endoscopic treatment and late recurrence. Am J Gastroenterol 94:972–975, 1999.

41. Tham TC, Vandervoort J, Wong RC, et al: Safety of ERCP during pregnancy. Am J Gastroenterol 98:308–311, 2003.

42. van Lent AU, Bartelsman JF, Tytgat GN, et al: Duration of antibiotic therapy for cholangitis after successful endoscopic drainage of the biliary tract. Gastrointest Endosc 55:518–522, 2002.

43. Digby K: Common duct stones of liver origin. Br J Surg 17:578–591, 1930.

44. Kusano S, Okada Y, Endo T, et al: Oriental cholangiohepatitis: Correlation between portal vein occlusion and hepatic atrophy. AJR Am J Roentgenol 158:1011–1014, 1992.

45. Sperling RM, Koch J, Sandhu JS, Cello JP: Recurrent pyogenic cholangitis in Asian immigrants to the United States: Natural history and role of therapeutic ERCP. Dig Dis Sci 42:865–871, 1997.

46. Wilson MK, Stephen MS, Mathur M, et al: Recurrent pyogenic cholangitis or "oriental cholangiohepatitis" in occidentals: Case reports of four patients. Aust N Z J Surg 66:649–652, 1996.

47. Chou ST, Chan CW: Recurrent pyogenic cholangitis: A necropsy study. Pathology 12:415–428, 1980.
48. Lim JH: Oriental cholangiohepatitis: Pathologic, clinical, and radiologic features. AJR Am J Roentgenol 157:1–8, 1991.
49. Stain SC, Incarbone R, Guthrie CR, et al: Surgical treatment of recurrent pyogenic cholangitis. Arch Surg 130:527–532; discussion 532–533, 1995.
50. Harris HW, Kumwenda ZL, Sheen-Chen SM, et al: Recurrent pyogenic cholangitis. Am J Surg 176:34–37, 1998.
51. Sheen-Chen SM, Chou FF, Lee CM, et al: The management of complicated hepatolithiasis with intrahepatic biliary stricture by the combination of T-tube tract dilation and endoscopic electro-hydraulic lithotripsy. Gastrointest Endosc 39:168–171, 1993.
52. Lim JH: Radiologic findings of clonorchiasis. AJR Am J Roentgenol 155:1001–1008, 1990.
53. Park MS, Yu JS, Kim KW, et al: Recurrent pyogenic cholangitis: Comparison between MR cholangiography and direct cholangiography. Radiology 220:677–682, 2001.
54. Lam SK, Wong KP, Chan PK, et al: Recurrent pyogenic cholangitis: A study by endoscopic retrograde cholangiography. Gastroenterology 74:1196–1203, 1978.
55. Lam SK: A study of endoscopic sphincterotomy in recurrent pyogenic cholangitis. Br J Surg 71:262–266, 1984.
56. Otani K, Shimizu S, Chijiiwa K, et al: Comparison of treatments for hepatolithiasis: Hepatic resection versus cholangioscopic lithotomy. J Am Coll Surg 189:177–182, 1999.
57. Cheung MT: Postoperative choledochoscopic removal of intrahepatic stones via a T tube tract. Br J Surg 84:1224–1228, 1997.
58. Gott PE, Tieva MH, Barcia PJ, Laberge JM: Biliary access procedure in the management of oriental cholangiohepatitis. Am Surg 62:930–934, 1996.
59. Ramesh H, Prakash K, Kuruvilla K, et al: Biliary access loops for intrahepatic stones: Results of jejunoduodenal anastomosis. Aust N Z J Surg 73:306–312, 2003.
60. Strong RW, Chew SP, Wall DR, et al: Liver transplantation for hepatolithiasis. Asian J Surg 25:180–183, 2002.
61. Gupta R, Agarwal DK, Choudhuri GD, et al: Biliary ascariasis complicating endoscopic sphincterotomy for choledocholithiasis in India. J Gastroenterol Hepatol 13:1072–1073, 1998.
62. Khuroo MS, Zargar SA, Yattoo GN, et al: Sonographic findings in gallbladder ascariasis. J Clin Ultrasound 20:587–591, 1992.
63. Khuroo MS, Zargar SA, Mahajan R, et al: Sonographic appearances in biliary ascariasis. Gastroenterology 93:267–272, 1987.
64. Ng KK, Wong HF, Kong MS, et al: Biliary ascariasis: CT, MR cholangiopancreatography, and navigator endoscopic appearance—report of a case of acute biliary obstruction. Abdom Imaging 24:470–472, 1999.
65. Jongsuksuntigul P, Jeradit C, Pornpattanakul S, Charanasri U: A comparative study on the efficacy of albendazole and mebendazole in the treatment of ascariasis, hookworm infection and trichuriasis. Southeast Asian J Trop Med Public Health 24:724–729, 1993.
66. Gonzalez AH, Regalado VC, Van den Ende J: Non-invasive management of Ascaris lumbricoides biliary tact migration: A prospective study in 69 patients from Ecuador. Trop Med Int Health 6:146–150, 2001.
67. Rokni MB, Massoud J, O'Neill SM, et al: Diagnosis of human fasciolosis in the Gilan province of Northern Iran: Application of cathepsin L-ELISA. Diagn Microbiol Infect Dis 44:175–179, 2002.
68. Cordova M, Herrera P, Nopo L, et al: Fasciola hepatica cysteine proteinases: Immunodominant antigens in human fascioliasis. Am J Trop Med Hyg 57:660–666, 1997.
69. Shaheen HI, Kamal KA, Farid Z, et al: Dot-enzyme-linked immunosorbent assay (dot-ELISA) for the rapid diagnosis of human fascioliasis. J Parasitol 75:549–552, 1989.
70. Shehab AY, Hassan EM, Basha LM, et al: Detection of circulating E/S antigens in the sera of patients with fascioliasis by IELISA: A tool of serodiagnosis and assessment of cure. Trop Med Int Health 4:686–690, 1999.
71. Kim TY, Kang SY, Park SH, et al: Cystatin capture enzyme-linked immunosorbent assay for serodiagnosis of human clonorchiasis and profile of captured antigenic protein of Clonorchis sinensis. Clin Diagn Lab Immunol 8:1076–1080, 2001.
72. Sirisinha S, Chawengkirttikul R, Sermswan R, et al: Detection of Opisthorchis viverrini by monoclonal antibody-based ELISA and DNA hybridization. Am J Trop Med Hyg 44:140–145, 1991.
73. Lim JH, Ko YT, Lee DH, Kim SY: Clonorchiasis: Sonographic findings in 59 proved cases. AJR Am J Roentgenol 152:761–764, 1989.
74. Chan HH, Lai KH, Lo GH, et al: The clinical and cholangiographic picture of hepatic clonorchiasis. J Clin Gastroenterol 34:183–186, 2002.
75. Leung JW, Sung JY, Banez VP, et al: Endoscopic cholangiopancreatography in hepatic clonorchiasis—a follow-up study. Gastrointest Endosc 36:360–363, 1990.
76. Damjanov I, Linder J (eds): Anderson's Pathology, 10th ed. St. Louis, Mosby-Year Book, 1996.
77. Dias LM, Silva R, Viana HL, et al: Biliary fascioliasis: Diagnosis, treatment and follow-up by ERCP. Gastrointest Endosc 43:616–620, 1996.
78. Dowidar N, El Sayad M, Osman M, Salem A: Endoscopic therapy of fascioliasis resistant to oral therapy. Gastrointest Endosc 50:345–351, 1999.
79. Kern P, Bardonnet K, Renner E, et al: European echinococcosis registry: Human alveolar echinococcosis, Europe, 1982-2000. Emerg Infect Dis 9:343–349, 2003.
80. Parija SC: A review of some simple immunoassays in the serodiagnosis of cystic hydatid disease. Acta Trop 70:17–24, 1998.
81. Lanier AP, Trujillo DE, Schantz PM, et al: Comparison of serologic tests for the diagnosis and follow-up of alveolar hydatid disease. Am J Trop Med Hyg 37:609–615, 1987.
82. Suwan Z: Sonographic findings in hydatid disease of the liver: Comparison with other imaging methods. Ann Trop Med Parasitol 89:261–269, 1995.
83. Salama H, Farid Abdel-Wahab M, Strickland GT: Diagnosis and treatment of hepatic hydatid cysts with the aid of echo-guided percutaneous cyst puncture. Clin Infect Dis 21:1372–1376, 1995.
84. Zargar SA, Khuroo MS, Khan BA, et al: Intrabiliary rupture of hepatic hydatid cyst: Sonographic and cholangiographic appearances. Gastrointest Radiol 17:41–45, 1992.
85. Devi Chandrakesan S, Parija SC: Latex agglutination test (LAT) for antigen detection in the cystic fluid for the diagnosis of cystic echinococcosis. Diagn Microbiol Infect Dis 45:123–126, 2003.
86. Pandolfo I, Blandino G, Scribano E, et al: CT findings in hepatic involvement by Echinococcus granulosus. J Comput Assist Tomogr 8:839–845, 1984.
87. Savas R, Calli C, Alper H, et al: Spinal cord compression due to costal Echinococcus multilocularis. Comput Med Imaging Graph 23:85–88, 1999.
88. Fleiner-Hoffmann AF, Pfammatter T, Leu AJ, et al: Alveolar echinococcosis of the liver: Sequelae of chronic inferior vena cava obstructions in the hepatic segment. Arch Intern Med 158:2503–2508, 1998.
89. Doyle TC, Roberts-Thomson IC, Dudley FJ: Demonstration of intrabiliary rupture of hepatic hydatid cysts by retrograde cholangiography. Australas Radiol 32:92–97, 1988.
90. Carpenter HA: Bacterial and parasitic cholangitis. Mayo Clin Proc 73:473–478, 1998.
91. Aktan AO, Yalin R: Preoperative albendazole treatment for liver hydatid disease decreases the viability of the cyst. Eur J Gastroenterol Hepatol 8:877–879, 1996.
92. Gil-Grande LA, Rodriguez-Caabeiro F, Prieto JG, et al: Randomised controlled trial of efficacy of albendazole in intra-abdominal hydatid disease. Lancet 342:1269–1272, 1993.
93. Balik AA, Basoglu M, Celebi F, et al: Surgical treatment of hydatid disease of the liver: Review of 304 cases. Arch Surg 134:166–169, 1999.

94. Khuroo MS, Wani NA, Javid G, et al: Percutaneous drainage compared with surgery for hepatic hydatid cysts. N Engl J Med 337:881–887, 1997.

95. Filice C, Brunetti E, Bruno R, Crippa FG: Percutaneous drainage of echinococcal cysts (PAIR–puncture, aspiration, injection, reaspiration): Results of a worldwide survey for assessment of its safety and efficacy. WHO-Informal Working Group on Echinococcosis-Pair Network. Gut 47:156–157, 2000.

96. Filice C, Brunetti E: Percutaneous drainage of hydatid cysts. N Engl J Med 338:392; author reply 392–393, 1998.

97. Guidelines for treatment of cystic and alveolar echinococcosis in humans. WHO Informal Working Group on Echinococcosis. Bull World Health Organ 74:231–242, 1996.

98. Horton RJ: Albendazole in treatment of human cystic echinococcosis: 12 years of experience. Acta Trop 64:79–93, 1997.

99. Nahmias J, Goldsmith R, Soibelman M, el-On J: Three- to 7-year follow-up after albendazole treatment of 68 patients with cystic echinococcosis (hydatid disease). Ann Trop Med Parasitol 88:295–304, 1994.

100. Liu Y, Wang X, Wu J: Continuous long-term albendazole therapy in intraabdominal cystic echinococcosis. Chin Med J (Engl) 113:827–832, 2000.

101. Franchi C, Di Vico B, Teggi A: Long-term evaluation of patients with hydatidosis treated with benzimidazole carbamates. Clin Infect Dis 29:304–309, 1999.

102. Ammann RW: Improvement of liver resectional therapy by adjuvant chemotherapy in alveolar hydatid disease. Swiss Echinococcosis Study Group (SESG). Parasitol Res 77:290–293, 1991.

103. Ammann RW, Fleiner-Hoffmann A, Grimm F, Eckert J: Long-term mebendazole therapy may be parasitocidal in alveolar echinococcosis. J Hepatol 29:994–998, 1998.

104. Ishizu H, Uchino J, Sato N, et al: Effect of albendazole on recurrent and residual alveolar echinococcosis of the liver after surgery. Hepatology 25:528–531, 1997.

105. Koch S, Bresson-Hadni S, Miguet JP, et al: Experience of liver transplantation for incurable alveolar echinococcosis: A 45-case European collaborative report. Transplantation 75:856–863, 2003.

106. Giouleme O, Nikolaidis N, Zezos P, et al: Treatment of complications of hepatic hydatid disease by ERCP. Gastrointest Endosc 54:508–510, 2001.

107. Bilsel Y, Bulut T, Yamaner S, et al: ERCP in the diagnosis and management of complications after surgery for hepatic echinococcosis. Gastrointest Endosc 57:210–213, 2003.

108. Cello JP: AIDS-Related biliary tract disease. Gastrointest Endosc Clin N Am 8:963, 1998.

109. Bouche H, Housset C, Dumont JL, et al: AIDS-related cholangitis: Diagnostic features and course in 15 patients. J Hepatol 17:34–39, 1993.

110. Forbes A, Blanshard C, Gazzard B: Natural history of AIDS related sclerosing cholangitis: A study of 20 cases. Gut 34:116–121, 1993.

111. Hashmey R, Smith NH, Cron S, et al: Cryptosporidiosis in Houston, Texas. A report of 95 cases. Medicine (Baltimore) 76:118–139, 1997.

112. Chen XM, LaRusso NF: Cryptosporidiosis and the pathogenesis of AIDS-cholangiopathy. Semin Liver Dis 22:277–289, 2002.

113. Farman J, Brunetti J, Baer JW, et al: AIDS-related cholangiopancreatographic changes. Abdom Imaging 19:417–422, 1994.

114. Pol S, Romana CA, Richard S, et al: Microsporidia infection in patients with the human immunodeficiency virus and unexplained cholangitis. N Engl J Med 328:95–99, 1993.

115. Hocqueloux L, Gervais A: Cholangiocarcinoma and AIDS-related sclerosing cholangitis. Ann Intern Med 132:1006–1007, 2000.

116. Daly CA, Padley SP: Sonographic prediction of a normal or abnormal ERCP in suspected AIDS related sclerosing cholangitis. Clin Radiol 51:618–621, 1996.

117. Santo E, Giovannini M: The role of EUS and EUS FNA in evaluating abnormalities of the hepatobiliary tract and pancreas in AIDS patients P286 [abstract]. Gut 41(4S):27E, 1997.

118. Collins CD, Forbes A, Harcourt-Webster JN, et al: Radiological and pathological features of AIDS-related polypoid cholangitis. Clin Radiol 48:307–310, 1993.

119. Benhamou Y, Caumes E, Gerosa Y, et al: AIDS-related cholangiopathy. Critical analysis of a prospective series of 26 patients. Dig Dis Sci 38:1113–1118, 1993.

120. Goldin RD, Hunt J: Biliary tract pathology in patients with AIDS. J Clin Pathol 46:691–693, 1993.

121. Liberman E, Yen TS: Foamy macrophages in acquired immunodeficiency syndrome cholangiopathy with Encephalitozoon intestinalis. Arch Pathol Lab Med 121:985–988, 1997.

122. Carr A, Marriott D, Field A, et al: Treatment of HIV-1-associated microsporidiosis and cryptosporidiosis with combination antiretroviral therapy. Lancet 351:256–261, 1998.

123. Castiella A, Iribarren JA, Lopez P, et al: Ursodeoxycholic acid in the treatment of AIDS-associated cholangiopathy. Am J Med 103:170–171, 1997.

124. Ducreux M, Buffet C, Lamy P, et al: Diagnosis and prognosis of AIDS-related cholangitis. AIDS 9:875–880, 1995.

125. Cello JP, Chan MF: Long-term follow-up of endoscopic retrograde cholangiopancreatography sphincterotomy for patients with acquired immune deficiency syndrome papillary stenosis. Am J Med 99:600–603, 1995.

126. Collazos J, Mayo J, Martinez E, et al: Celiac plexus block as treatment for refractory pain related to sclerosing cholangitis in AIDS patients. J Clin Gastroenterol 23:47–49, 1996.

127. Preston SL, Postelnick M, Purdy BD, et al: Drug interactions in HIV-positive patients initiated on protease inhibitor therapy. AIDS 12:228–229, 1998.

128. Shea JA, Berlin JA, Escarce JJ, et al: Revised estimates of diagnostic test sensitivity and specificity in suspected biliary tract disease. Arch Intern Med 154:2573–2581, 1994.

129. Thistle JL, Cleary PA, Lachin JM, et al: The natural history of cholelithiasis: The National Cooperative Gallstone Study. Ann Intern Med 101:171–175, 1984.

130. Johlin FC Jr, Neil GA: Drainage of the gallbladder in patients with acute acalculous cholecystitis by transpapillary endoscopic cholecystotomy. Gastrointest Endosc 39:645–651, 1993.

131. Baron TH, Farnell MB, Leroy AJ: Endoscopic transpapillary gallbladder drainage for closure of calculous gallbladder perforation and cholecystoduodenal fistula. Gastrointest Endosc 56:753–755, 2002.

132. Feretis C, Apostolidis N, Mallas E, et al: Endoscopic drainage of acute obstructive cholecystitis in patients with increased operative risk. Endoscopy 25:392–395, 1993.

Sphincter of Oddi Dysfunction

Stuart Sherman, Evan L. Fogel, James L. Watkins, Lee McHenry Jr., and Glen A. Lehman

CHAPTER

49

Introduction

Since its original description by Ruggero Oddi in 1887, the sphincter of Oddi (SO) has been the subject of much study and controversy. Its very existence as a distinct anatomic or physiologic entity has been disputed. Hence, it is not surprising that the clinical syndrome of sphincter of Oddi dysfunction (SOD) and its therapy are controversial areas.[1] Nevertheless, SOD is commonly diagnosed and treated by physicians. This chapter reviews the epidemiology and clinical presentation of SOD and currently available diagnostic and therapeutic modalities.

Definitions

Postcholecystectomy pain resembling the patient's preoperative biliary colic occurs in at least 10% to 20% of patients.[2] We assume that these patients will have appropriate noninvasive and invasive (when clinically appropriate) evaluation to rule out common duct stones, tumors, or strictures near the cholecystectomy site. The residual group of patients has a high frequency of SOD. SOD refers to an abnormality of SO contractility. It is a benign, noncalculous obstruction to flow of bile or pancreatic juice through the pancreaticobiliary junction (i.e., the SO). SOD may be manifested clinically by "pancreaticobiliary" pain, pancreatitis, abnormal liver function tests, or abnormal pancreatic enzymes. SO dyskinesia refers to a motor abnormality of the SO, which may result in a hypotonic sphincter but, more commonly, causes a hypertonic sphincter. In contrast, SO stenosis refers to a structural alteration of the sphincter, probably from an inflammatory process, with subsequent fibrosis. Because it is often impossible to distinguish patients with SO dyskinesia from those with SO stenosis, the term SOD has been used to incorporate both groups of patients. In an attempt to deal with this overlap in etiology, and also to determine the appropriate use of sphincter of Oddi manometry (SOM), a biliary clinical classification system has been developed for patients with suspected SOD (Hogan-Geenen SOD classification system; Table 49–1) based

Table 49–1. Hogan-Geenen Biliary Sphincter of Oddi Classification System (Post-Cholecystectomy) Related to the Frequency of Abnormal Sphincter of Oddi Manometry and Pain Relief by Biliary Sphincterotomy

Patient Group Classifications	Approximate Frequency of Abnormal Sphincter Manometry	Probability of Pain Relief by Sphincterotomy If Manometry:		Manometry Before Sphincter Ablation
		Abnormal	Normal	
Biliary Type I Patients with biliary-type pain, abnormal SGOT or alkaline phosphatase greater than two times normal documented on two or more occasions, delayed drainage of ERCP contrast from the biliary tree >45 minutes, and dilated CBD >12 mm diameter	75%–95%	90%–95%	90%–95%	Unnecessary
Biliary Type II Patients with biliary-type pain and only one or two of the previous criteria	55%–65%	85%	35%	Highly recommended
Biliary Type III Patients with only biliary-type pain and none of the three criteria	25%–60%	55%–65%	<10%	Mandatory

CBD, common bile duct; ERCP, endoscopic retrograde cholangiopancreatography; SGOT, serum glutamine-oxaloacetic transaminase.

Table 49–2. Pancreatic Sphincter of Oddi Classification System

Patient Group Classification
Pancreatic Type I Patients with pancreatic-type pain, abnormal amylase or lipase 1.5 times normal on any occasion, delayed drainage of ERCP contrast from the pancreatic duct (PD) >9 minutes, and dilated PD >6 mm diameter in the head or 5 mm in the body
Pancreatic Type II Patients with pancreatic-type pain but only one or two of the previous criteria
Pancreatic Type III Patients with only pancreatic-type pain and no other abnormalities
ERCP, endoscopic retrograde cholangiopancreatography. *Adapted from Sherman S, Troiano FP, Hawes RH, et al: Frequency of abnormal sphincter of Oddi manometry compared with the clinical suspicion of sphincter of Oddi dysfunction. Am J Gastroenterol 86:586–590, 1991.*

on clinical history, laboratory results, and endoscopic retrograde cholangiopancreatography (ERCP) findings.[3] A pancreatic classification has also been developed, but it is less commonly used[4] (Table 49–2). Both the biliary and pancreatic classification systems have been modified,[5] making them more applicable for clinical use, because biliary and pancreatic drainage times have been generally abandoned. A variety of less accurate terms—such as papillary stenosis, ampullary stenosis, biliary dyskinesia, and postcholecystectomy syndrome—are listed in the medical literature to describe this entity. The latter term is somewhat of a misnomer, because SOD may clearly occur with an intact gallbladder.

Anatomy, Physiology, and Pathophysiology

The SO is a small complex of smooth muscles surrounding the terminal common bile duct, main (ventral) pancreatic duct (of Wirsung), and the common channel (ampulla of Vater), when present (Fig. 49–1). It has both circular and figure-8 components. The high-pressure zone generated by the sphincter is variably 4 to 10 mm in length. Its role is to regulate bile and pancreatic exocrine juice flow and to prevent duodenum-to-duct reflux (i.e., maintain sterile intraductal environment). The SO possesses both a variable basal pressure and phasic contractile activity. The former appears to be the predominant mechanism, regulating outflow of pancreaticobiliary secretion into the intestine. Although phasic SO contractions may aid in regulating bile and pancreatic juice flow, their primary role appears to be maintaining a sterile intraductal milieu. Sphincter regulation is under both neural and hormonal control. Phasic wave activity of the sphincter is closely tied to the migrating motor complex (MMC) of the duodenum. Innervation of the bile duct does not appear to be essential because sphincter function has been reported to be preserved after liver transplantation.[6] Although regulatory processes vary among species, cholecystokinin (CCK) and secretin appear to be most important in causing sphincter relaxation, whereas nonadrenergic, noncholinergic neurons, which at least in part transmit vasoactive intestinal peptide (VIP) and nitric oxide, also relax the sphincter.[7] The role of cholecystectomy in altering these neural pathways needs further definition. Luman and colleagues[8] reported that cholecystectomy, at least in the short

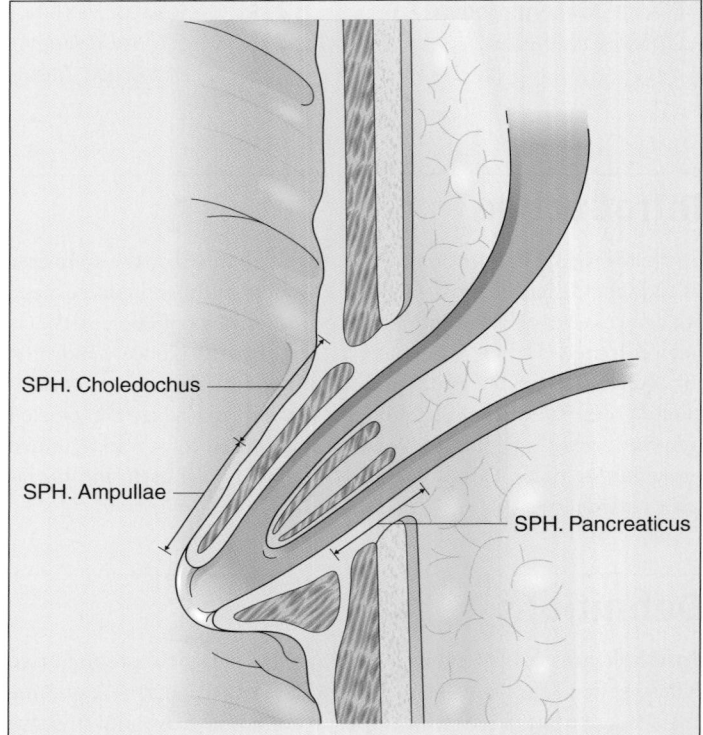

Figure 49–1. Anatomy of sphincter of Oddi.

term, suppresses the normal inhibitory effect of pharmacologic doses of CCK on the SO. However, the mechanism of this effect is unknown.

Wedge specimens of the SO obtained at surgical sphincteroplasty from SOD patients show evidence of inflammation, muscular hypertrophy, fibrosis, or adenomyosis within the papillary zone in approximately 60% of patients.[9] In the remaining 40% with normal histology, a motor disorder is suggested. Less commonly, infections with cytomegalovirus or *Cryptosporidium*, as may occur in acquired immunodeficiency syndrome (AIDS) patients, or *Strongyloides* have caused SOD.

How does SOD cause pain? From a theoretical point of view, abnormalities of SO pressure can give rise to pain by (1) impeding the flow of bile and pancreatic juice resulting in ductal hypertension, (2) inducing ischemia arising from spastic contractions, and (3) resulting in "hypersensitivity" of the papilla. Although unproved, these mechanisms may act alone or in concert to explain the genesis of pain.

Epidemiology

SOD may occur in pediatric or adult patients of any age; however, patients with SOD are typically middle-aged females.[10] Although SOD most commonly occurs after cholecystectomy, it may be present with the gallbladder *in situ*. In a survey on functional gastrointestinal (GI) disorders, SOD appeared to have a significant impact on quality of life, because it was highly associated with work absenteeism, disability, and health care use.[11]

The frequency of manometrically documented SOD in patients before cholecystectomy has received limited study. Guelrud and colleagues[12] evaluated 121 patients with symptomatic gallstones and a normal common bile duct diameter (by transcutaneous ultrasound) by SOM before cholecystectomy. An elevated basal sphincter pressure was found in 14 patients (11.6%). SOD was diagnosed in 4.1% of patients with a normal serum alkaline phosphatase (4 of 96) and in 40% with an elevated serum alkaline phosphatase (10 of 25). Ruffolo and associates[13] evaluated 81 patients with symptoms suggestive of biliary disease but normal ERCP and no gallbladder stones on transcutaneous ultrasound by scintigraphic gallbladder ejection fraction and endoscopic SOM. Fifty-three percent of patients had SOD and 49% had an abnormal gallbladder ejection fraction. SOD occurred with a similar frequency in patients with an abnormal gallbladder ejection fraction (50%) and a normal ejection fraction (57%).

The frequency of diagnosing SOD in reported series varies considerably with the patient selection criteria, the definition of SOD, and the diagnostic tools used. In a British report, SOD was diagnosed in 41 (9%) of 451 consecutive patients being evaluated for postcholecystectomy pain.[14] Roberts-Thomson and Toouli[15] evaluated 431 similar patients and found SOD in 47 (11%). In a subpopulation of such patients with a normal ERCP (except dilated ducts in 28%) and recurrent pain of more than 3 months duration, SOD was diagnosed in 68%. Sherman and colleagues[4] used SOM to evaluate 115 patients with pancreaticobiliary pain with and without liver function test abnormalities. Patients with bile duct stones and tumors were excluded from analysis. Fifty-nine of 115 patients (51%) showed abnormal basal SO pressure greater than 40 mm Hg. These patients were further categorized by the Hogan-Geenen SOD classification system (see Table 49–1). The frequency of abnormal manometry of one or both sphincter segments was 86%, 55%, and 28% for biliary type I, II, and III patients, respectively. These abnormal manometric frequencies were very similar to those reported by others for type I and type II patients.[16,17] In biliary type III patients, the finding of an abnormal basal sphincter pressure has varied from 12% to 59%.[5,18] As noted, patient selection factors may be one explanation for this great variability.

SOD can involve abnormalities in the biliary sphincter, pancreatic sphincter, or both.[5,19] Therefore, the true frequency of SOD depends on whether one or both sphincters are studied. Eversman and colleagues[5] performed manometry of the biliary and pancreatic sphincter segments in 360 patients with pancreatobiliary pain and intact sphincters. In this large series, 19% had abnormal pancreatic sphincter basal sphincter pressure alone, 11% had abnormal biliary basal sphincter pressure alone, and in 31%, the basal sphincter pressure was abnormal in both segments (overall frequency of sphincter dysfunction was 61%). Among the 214 patients labeled type III by a modified Hogan-Geenen SOD classification system, 17%, 11%, and 31% had elevated basal sphincter pressure in the pancreatic sphincter alone, biliary sphincter alone, or both segments, respectively (overall frequency of SOD was 59%). In the 123 type II patients, SOD was diagnosed in 65%: 22%, 11%, and 32% had the elevated basal sphincter pressure in the pancreatic sphincter only, biliary sphincter only or both sphincter segments, respectively. Similar findings were reported by Aymerich and colleagues.[20] In a series of 73 patients with suspected SOD, basal pressures were normal in both segments in 19%, abnormal in both segments in 40%, and abnormal in one segment but normal in the other in 41%. The negative predictive value of normal biliary basal sphincter pressure in excluding SOD was 0.42; when the pancreatic basal sphincter pressure was normal, the negative predictive value was 0.58. These two studies clearly suggest that both the bile duct and pancreatic duct must be evaluated when assessing the sphincter by SOM.

Dysfunction may occur in the pancreatic duct portion of the SO and cause recurrent pancreatitis. As noted earlier, a pancreatic SOD classification system has been developed (see Table 49–2), but it has not been widely used.[5] Manometrically documented SOD has been reported in 15% to 72% of patients with recurrent pancreatitis, previously labeled as idiopathic.[5,18,21] This is discussed later in this chapter.

Clinical Presentation

Abdominal pain is the most common presenting symptom of patients with SOD. The pain is usually epigastric or right upper quadrant, may be disabling, and lasts for 30 minutes to hours. In some patients, the pain is continuous with episodic exacerbations. It may radiate to the back or shoulder and be accompanied by nausea and vomiting. Food or narcotics may precipitate the pain. The pain may begin several years after a cholecystectomy was performed for a gallbladder dysmotility or stone disease and is similar in character to the pain leading to the cholecystectomy. Alternatively, patients may have continued pain that was not relieved by a cholecystectomy. Jaundice, fever, or chills are rarely observed. A symposium on functional disorders of the pancreas and biliary tree established the Rome II diagnostic criteria[10] for SOD. These include episodes of severe abdominal pain located in the epigastrium and/or right upper quadrant, and all of the following: (1) symptom episodes lasting 30 minutes or more with pain-free intervals, (2) symptoms have occurred on one or more occasions in the previous 12 months, (3) the pain is steady and interrupts daily activities or requires consultation with a physician, and (4) there is no evidence of structural abnormalities to explain the symptoms. Physical examination is typically characterized only by mild epigastric or right upper quadrant tenderness. The pain is not relieved by trial medications for acid peptic disease or irritable bowel syndrome. Laboratory abnormalities consisting of transient elevation of liver function tests, typically during episodes of pain, are present in less than 50% of patients. Patients with SOD may present with typical pancreatic pain (epigastric or left upper quadrant radiating to the back) with or without pancreatic enzyme elevation and recurrent pancreatitis.

SOD may exist in the presence of an intact gallbladder.[12,13,22] Because the symptoms of SOD or gallbladder dysfunction cannot be reliably separated, the diagnosis of SOD is commonly made after cholecystectomy or less often after gallbladder abnormalities have been excluded.[10]

Clinical Evaluation

The diagnostic approach to suspected SOD may be influenced by the presence of key clinical features. However, the clinical manifestations of functional abnormalities of the SO may not always be easily distinguishable from those caused by organic ones (e.g., common bile duct stones) or other functional non-pancreaticobiliary disorders (e.g., irritable bowel syndrome).

GENERAL INITIAL EVALUATION

Evaluation of patients with suspected SOD (i.e., patients with upper abdominal pain with characteristics suggestive of a pancreatobiliary origin) should be initiated with standard serum liver chemistries, serum amylase and/or lipase, abdominal ultrasonography or computed tomography (CT) scans. The serum enzyme studies should be drawn during bouts of pain, if possible. Mild elevations (<2 times upper limits of normal) are frequent in SOD, whereas greater abnormalities are more suggestive of stones, tumors, and liver parenchymal disease. Although the diagnostic sensitivity and specificity of abnormal serum liver chemistries are low,[23] recent evidence suggests that the presence of abnormal liver tests in type II biliary SOD patients may predict a favorable response to endoscopic sphincterotomy.[24] CT scans and abdominal ultrasounds are usually normal but occasionally a dilated bile duct or pancreatic duct may be found (particularly in patients with type I SOD). Standard evaluation and treatment of other more common GI conditions, such as peptic ulcer disease, irritable bowel syndrome, and gastroesophageal reflux should be done simultaneously. In the absence of mass lesions, stones, or response to medical therapy trials, the suspicion for sphincter disease is increased.

DIAGNOSTIC METHODS (NONINVASIVE)

Because SOM (considered by most authorities to be the gold standard for diagnosing SOD) is difficult to perform, invasive, not widely available, and associated with a relatively high complication rate, several noninvasive and provocative tests have been designed in an attempt to identify patients with SOD.

Morphine-Prostigmin Provocative Test (Nardi Test)

Morphine has been shown to cause SO contraction, as assessed manometrically. Prostigmin (neostigmine), 1 mg subcutaneously, is added as a vigorous cholinergic secretory stimulant to morphine (10 mg subcutaneously) to make this challenge test. The morphine-

prostigmin test, historically, had been used extensively to diagnose SOD. Reproduction of the patient's typical pain associated with a fourfold increase in aspartate aminotransferase (AST), alanine aminotransferase (ALT), alkaline phosphatase, amylase, or lipase levels constitutes a positive response. The usefulness of this test is limited by its low sensitivity and specificity in predicting the presence of SOD and its poor correlation with outcome after sphincter ablation.[25] This test has largely been replaced by tests thought to be more sensitive.

Radiographic Assessment of Extrahepatic Bile Duct and Main Pancreatic Duct Diameter After Secretory Stimulation

After a lipid-rich meal or CCK administration, the gallbladder contracts, bile flow from the hepatocytes increases, and the SO relaxes, resulting in bile entry into the duodenum. Similarly, after a lipid-rich meal or secretin administration, pancreatic exocrine juice flow is stimulated and the SO relaxes. If the SO is dysfunctional and causes obstruction to flow, the common bile duct or main pancreatic duct may dilate under secretory pressure. This can be monitored by transcutaneous ultrasonography. Sphincter and terminal duct obstruction from other causes (stones, tumors, strictures) may similarly cause ductal dilation and need to be excluded. Pain provocation should also be noted if present. Limited studies comparing these noninvasive tests with SOM or outcome after sphincter ablation[26-31] show only modest correlation. Because of overlying intestinal gas, the pancreatic duct may not be visualized on standard transcutaneous ultrasound. Despite the superiority of endoscopic ultrasonography (EUS) in visualizing the pancreas, Catalano and coworkers[32] reported the sensitivity of secretin-stimulated EUS in detecting SOD to be only 57%. Magnetic resonance cholangiopancreatography (MRCP) can also be performed to noninvasively monitor the pancreatic duct after secretin stimulation. However, preliminary data from Devereaux and colleagues[33] revealed that secretin-stimulated MRCP demonstrated a diminished, rather than exaggerated, ductal dilation response in 28 patients with SOD.

Quantitative Hepatobiliary Scintigraphy

Hepatobiliary scintigraphy (HBS) assesses bile flow through the biliary tract. Impairment to bile flow from sphincter disease, tumors, or stones (as well as parenchymal liver disease) results in impaired radionuclide flow. The precise criteria to define a positive (abnormal) study remain controversial, but a prolonged duodenal arrival time, a prolonged hepatic hilum to duodenal transit time, and a high Johns-Hopkins scintigraphic score are most widely used.[34-36] Four studies[34,37-39] have shown a correlation between HBS and SOM. Taking these four studies as a whole, totaling 105 patients, the overall sensitivity of HBS using SOM as the gold standard was 78% (range 44% to 100%), specificity 90% (range 80% to 100%), positive predictive value 92% (range 82% to 100%), and negative predictive value 81% (range 62% to 100%). However, these promising results have not been reproduced by others. Overall, it appears that patients with dilated bile ducts and high-grade obstruction are likely to have a positive scintigraphic study. Esber and colleagues[40] found that patients with lower-grade obstruction (Hogan-Geenen classification types II and III) generally have normal scintigraphy, even if done after CCK provocation. Pineau and coworkers[41] reported that 8 of 20 asymptomatic control subjects had an abnormal CCK-stimulated study. Using SOM as the gold standard in 29 patients with suspected SOD, two independent reviewers found the Johns Hopkins scintigraphic score to have a sensitivity of 25% to 38%, a specificity of 85% to 90%, a positive predictive value of 40% to 60%, and a negative predictive value of 75% to 79% for diagnosing SOD.[42] The hepatic hilum to duodenal transit time had a sensitivity of 13%, a specificity of 95%, a positive predictive value of 50%, and a negative predictive value of 74%. The duodenal arrival time mirrored the hepatic hilum to duodenal transit time findings.

The value of adding morphine provocation to HBS was recently reported.[39] Thirty-four patients with a clinical diagnosis of type II and type III SOD underwent scintigraphy with and without morphine and subsequent biliary manometry. The standard HBS scan did not distinguish between patients with normal and abnormal SOM. However, after provocation with morphine, there were significant differences in the time to maximal activity and the percentage of excretion at 45 and 60 minutes. Using a cutoff value of 15% excretion at 60 minutes, the use of morphine during HBS increased the sensitivity and specificity for SOD detection to 83% and 81%, respectively.

The Milwaukee group recently reported their retrospective review of fatty-meal sonography (FMS) and HBS as potential predictors of SOD.[43] In this study, 304 postcholecystectomy patients suspected to have SOD were evaluated by SOM, FMS and HBS. A diagnosis of SOD was made in 73 patients (24%) by using SOM as the reference standard. The sensitivity of FMS was 21% and for HBS 49%, whereas specificities were 97% and 78%, respectively. FMS, HBS, or both were abnormal in 90%, 50%, and 44% of patients with Hogan-Geenen SOD types I, II, and III, respectively. Of the 73 patients who underwent biliary sphincterotomy, 40 had a good long-term response. Among these SOD patients, 11/13 patients (85%) with an abnormal HBS and FMS had a good long-term response. This study suggested that while noninvasive tests are not able to predict an abnormal SOM with high sensitivity, they may be of assistance in predicting response to sphincter ablation in SOD patients.

Cicala and colleagues[44] compared the reliability of HBS (hepatic hilum to duodenal transit time was measured) with that of SOM of the biliary sphincter in 30 postcholecystectomy patients (8 type I, 22 type II; 40% were men). The HBS was abnormal in all 15 patients with abnormal maximal basal sphincter pressures and in 7 of 15 with normal maximal basal sphincter pressures. Thirteen of 14 patients with an abnormal HBS who agreed to undergo biliary sphincter-otomy were asymptomatic and had normal liver function tests, amylase levels, and lipase levels at 10 to 13 months' follow-up. All 8 patients with an abnormal HBS who refused to undergo sphinc-terotomy remained symptomatic. A favorable postsphincterotomy outcome was predicted by hepatic hilum to duodenal transit in 93% and by SOM in 57% of patients. Although this study suggested that HBS is a useful and noninvasive test to diagnose SOD and is a reliable predictor of sphincterotomy outcome in postcholecys-tectomy biliary type I and II patients, several concerns exist. Forty percent of enrolled patients were men, which is unusually high in the SOD population, and the frequency of abnormal maximal basal

sphincter pressures in biliary type II patients was exceedingly low (36%). Moreover, if the authors had used the mean basal sphincter pressure, which is the more commonly recommended manometric parameter for diagnosing SOD, the frequency of an abnormal SOM would likely have been even lower. This calls into question the authors' SOM technique and interpretation.

In the absence of more definitive data, we conclude that use of HBS as a screening tool for SOD should not be recommended for general clinical use. As noted, abnormal results may be found in asymptomatic controls.[41] Furthermore, HBS does not address the pancreatic sphincter, which may be dysfunctional and a cause for the patients' symptoms. Use of HBS and other noninvasive methods should be reserved for situations in which more definitive testing (manometry) is unsuccessful or unavailable.

DIAGNOSTIC METHODS (INVASIVE)

Endoscopic Retrograde Cholangiopancreatography

Because of their associated risks, invasive testing with ERCP and manometry should be reserved for patients with clinically significant or disabling symptoms. In general, invasive assessment of patients for SOD is not recommended unless definitive therapy (sphincter ablation) is planned if abnormal sphincter function is found.

Cholangiography is essential to rule out stones, tumors, or other obstructing processes of the biliary tree that may cause symptoms identical to those of SOD. Once such lesions are ruled out by a good quality cholangiographic study, ducts that are dilated or drain slowly suggest obstruction at the level of the sphincter. A variety of methods to obtain a cholangiogram are available. For noninvasive imaging, magnetic resonance cholangiography (MRC) is most promising, but quality varies greatly from center to center. Software development continues and quality of images continues to evolve. Direct cho-langiography can be obtained by percutaneous methods, intra-operative methods, or more conventionally at ERCP. Although some controversy exists, extrahepatic ducts that are greater than 12 mm in diameter (postcholecystectomy) when corrected for magnifica-tion are considered dilated. Drugs that affect the rate of bile flow and relaxation or contraction of the SO influence drainage of contrast. Such drugs must be avoided to obtain accurate drainage times. Because the extrahepatic bile duct angulates from anterior (the hilum) to posterior (the papilla), the patient must be supine to assess gravitational drainage through the sphincter. Although definitive normal supine drainage times have not been well defined,[45] a postcholecystectomy biliary tree that fails to empty all contrast media by 45 minutes is generally considered abnormal.

Endoscopic evaluation of the papilla and peripapillary area can yield important information that can influence the diagnosis and treatment of patients with suspected SOD. Occasionally, ampullary cancer may simulate SOD. The endoscopist should do tissue sampling of the papilla (preferably after sphincterotomy) in suspicious cases.[46]

Radiographic features of the pancreatic duct are also important to assess in the patient with suspected SOD. Dilation of the pancreatic duct (>6 mm in the pancreatic head and >5 mm in the body) and delayed contrast drainage time (9 minutes in the prone position) may give indirect evidence for the presence of SOD.

Intraductal Ultrasonography

Intraductal ultrasonography (IDUS) makes it possible to assess SO morphology during endoscopy. The sphincter appears as a thin hypoechoic circular structure on IDUS.[47] Limited studies thus far reveal no correlation between the basal sphincter pressures (as detected at SOM) and the thickness of the hypoechoic layer.[48] Although IDUS may provide additional information at the level of the sphincter, it cannot be used as a substitute for SOM.

Sphincter of Oddi Manometry

The most definitive development in our understanding of the pressure dynamics of the SO came with the advent of SOM. SOM is the only available method to measure SO motor activity directly. Although SOM can be performed intraoperatively and percutaneously, it is most commonly done in the ERCP setting. SOM is considered by most authorities to be the gold standard for evaluating patients for sphincter dysfunction.[49,50] The use of manometry to detect motility disorders of the SO is similar to its use in other parts of the GI tract. However, performance of SOM is more technically demanding and hazardous, with complication rates (pancreatitis in particular) reported as high as 30%. Questions remain as to whether these short-term observations (2- to 10-minute recordings per pull-through) reflect the 24-hour pathophysiology of the sphincter. Despite some problems, SOM is gaining more widespread clinical application.

Sphincter of Oddi Manometry: Technique and Indications

SOM is usually performed at the time of ERCP. All drugs that relax (anticholinergics, nitrates, calcium channel blockers, glucagon) or stimulate (most narcotics, cholinergic agents) the sphincter should be avoided for at least 8 to 12 hours before manometry and during the manometric session. Current data indicate that benzodiazepines do not affect the sphincter pressure and therefore are acceptable sedatives for SOM. Meperidine, at a dose of 1 mg/kg or less, does not affect the basal sphincter pressure but does alter phasic wave characteristics.[51] Because the basal sphincter pressure is generally the only manometric criterion used to diagnose SOD and determine therapy, it was suggested that meperidine could be used to facilitate conscious sedation for manometry. Droperidol[52] and propofol[53] are increasingly used for SOM, and it appears that these agents also do not affect the basal sphincter pressure. However, further study is required before their routine use in SOM is recommended. If glucagon must be used to achieve cannulation, an 8- to 15-minute waiting period is required to restore the sphincter to its basal condition.

Five-French catheters should be used, because virtually all standards have been established with these catheters. Triple-lumen catheters are state of the art and are available from several manufacturers. A variety of catheter types can be used. Catheters with a long intraductal tip may help secure the catheter within the bile duct, but such a long nose is commonly a hindrance if pancreatic manometry is desired. Over-the-wire (monorail) catheters can be passed after first securing one's position within the duct with a guidewire. Whether this guidewire influences basal sphincter pressure is unknown. Some triple-lumen catheters will accommodate a 0.018-inch diameter guidewire passed through the entire

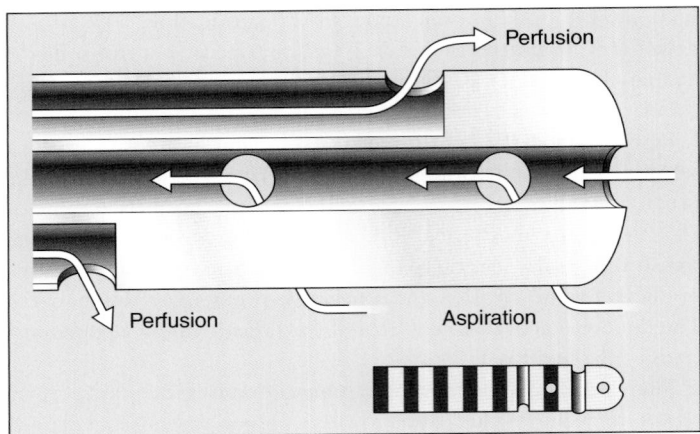

Figure 49–2. A modified triple-lumen aspirating catheter.

length of the catheter and can be used to facilitate cannulation or maintain position in the duct. However, a recent study in our unit found that stiffer shafted nitinol core guidewires used for this purpose commonly increase basal sphincter pressure by 50% to 100%.[54] To avoid such artifacts, such wires need to be avoided or very soft-core guidewires must be used. Guidewire-tipped catheters are being evaluated. Aspiration catheters, in which one recording port is sacrificed to permit both end and side hole aspiration of intraductal juice, are highly recommended for pancreatic manometry (Fig. 49–2). Most centers prefer to perfuse the catheters at 0.25 mL/channel using a low-compliance pump. Lower perfusion rates will give accurate basal sphincter pressures but will not give accurate phasic wave information. A new water perfused sleeve system, similar to that used in the lower esophageal sphincter, awaits further study in the SO.[55] The perfusate is generally distilled water, although physiologic saline needs further evaluation. The latter may crystallize in the capillary tubing of perfusion pumps and must be flushed out often.

SOM requires selective cannulation of the bile duct or pancreatic duct (Fig. 49–3). The duct entered can be identified by gently aspirating on any port. The appearance of yellow-colored fluid in the endoscopic view indicates entry into the bile duct. Clear aspirate indicates that the pancreatic duct was entered. It is preferable to obtain a cholangiogram and/or pancreatogram before performing SOM because certain findings (e.g., common bile duct stone) may obviate the need for SOM. This can be simply done by injecting contrast through one of the perfusion ports. Blaut and colleagues[56] have shown that injection of contrast into the biliary tree before SOM does not significantly alter sphincter pressure characteristics. Similar evaluation of the pancreatic sphincter after contrast injection has not been reported. One must be certain that the catheter is not impacted against the wall of the duct to ensure accurate pressure measurements. Once deep cannulation is achieved and the patient acceptably sedated, the catheter is withdrawn across the sphincter at 1- to 2-mm intervals by standard station pull-through technique. Ideally, both the pancreatic and bile ducts should be studied. The data indicate that an abnormal basal sphincter pressure may be confined to one side of the sphincter in 35% to 65% of patients with abnormal manometry.[5,20,57–60] Thus, one sphincter may be dysfunctional, whereas the other is normal. Raddawi and

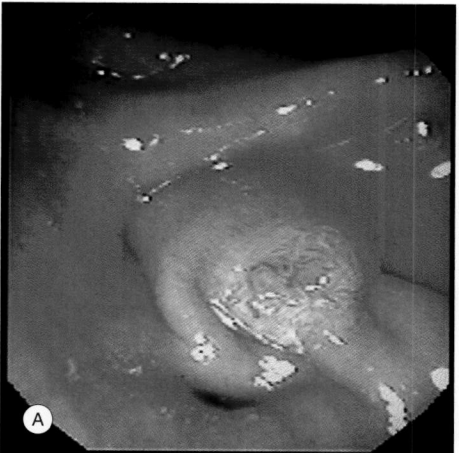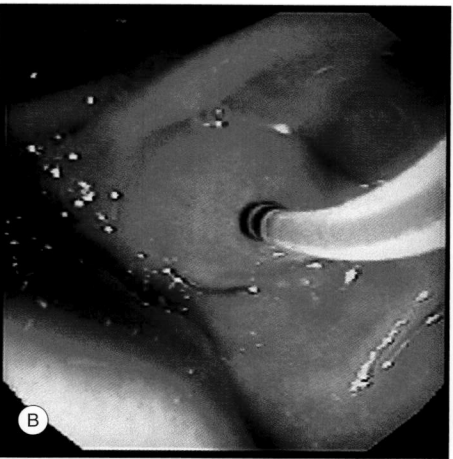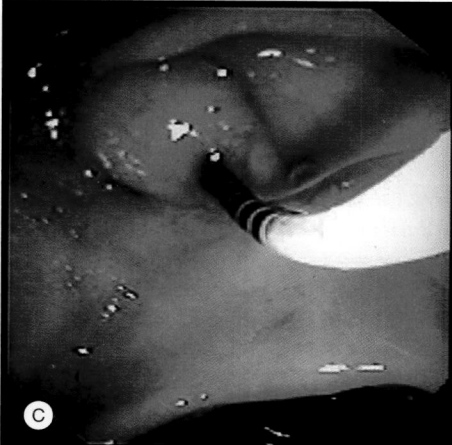

Figure 49–3. Manometry. *A,* Normal major papilla. *B,* Biliary manometry. *C,* Pancreatic manometry.

colleagues[57] reported that an abnormal basal sphincter was more likely to be confined to the pancreatic duct segment in patients with pancreatitis and to the bile duct segment in patients with biliary-type pain and elevated liver function tests.

Abnormalities of the basal sphincter pressure should ideally be observed for at least 30 seconds in each lead and be seen on two or more separate pull-throughs. From a practical clinical standpoint, we settle for one pull-through (from each duct) if the readings are clearly normal or abnormal. During standard station pull-through technique, it is necessary to establish good communication between the endoscopist and the manometrist who is reading the tracing as it rolls off the recorder or appears on the computer screen. This permits optimal positioning of the catheter to achieve interpretable tracings. Alternatively, electronic manometry systems with a television screen can be mounted near the endoscopic image screen to permit the endoscopist to view the manometry tracing during endoscopy. Once the baseline study is done, agents to relax or stimulate the sphincter can be given (e.g., CCK) and manometric or pain response monitored. The value of these provocative maneuvers for everyday use needs further study before widespread application is recommended.

Criteria for interpretation of an SO tracing are relatively standard; however, they may vary somewhat from center to center. Some areas in which there may be disagreement in interpretation include the required duration of basal SO pressure elevation, the number of leads in which basal pressure elevation is required, and the role of averaging pressures from the three (or two in an aspirating catheter) recording ports.[3] Our recommended method for reading the manometry tracings is first to define the zero duodenal baseline before and after the pull-through. Alternatively, intraduodenal pressure can be continuously recorded from a separate intraduodenal catheter attached to the endoscope. The highest basal pressure (defined as the pressure above the zero duodenal baseline; Fig. 49–4) that is sustained for at least 30 seconds is then identified. From the four lowest amplitude points in this zone, the mean of these readings is taken as the basal sphincter pressure for that lead for that pull-through. The basal sphincter pressure for all interpretable observations is then averaged; this is the final basal sphincter pressure. The amplitude of phasic wave contractions is

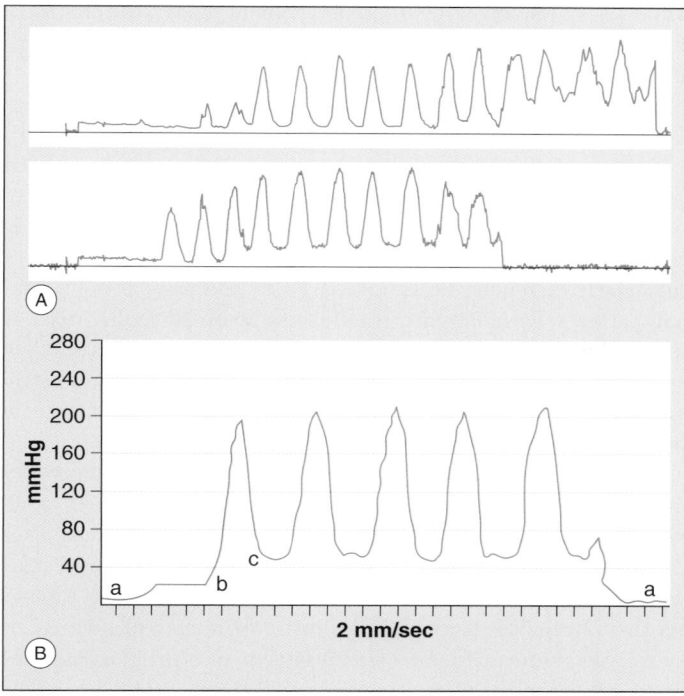

Figure 49–4. *A,* An abnormal station pull-through at sphincter of Oddi manometry. The study has been abbreviated to fit onto one page. *B,* Schematic representation of one lead of the above tracing. (a) Baseline duodenal 0 reference. (b) Intraductal (pancreatic) pressure of 20 mm Hg (abnormal). (c) Basal pancreatic sphincter pressure is 45 mm Hg (abnormal). Phasic waves are 155–175 mm Hg in amplitude and 6 seconds in duration (normal). Redrawn from Fogel EL, Sherman S: Performance of sphincter of Oddi manometry. Clin Perspect Gastroenterol 4:165–173, 2001.

measured from the beginning of the slope of the pressure increase from the basal pressure to the peak of the contraction wave. Four representative waves are taken for each lead and the mean pressure determined. The number of phasic waves per minute and the duration of the phasic waves can also be determined. Most authorities read only the basal sphincter pressure as an indicator of pathology of the SO. However, data from Kalloo and colleagues[61] suggest that intraductal biliary pressure, which is easier to measure than SO pressure, correlates with SO basal pressure. In this study, intrabiliary pressure was significantly higher in patients with SOD than those with normal SO pressure (20 vs. 10 mm Hg; $p < .01$). In a similar study, Fazel and colleagues[62] found that increased pancreatic duct pressure correlated with increased pancreatic sphincter pressure ($p < .001$). Pancreatic duct pressure was significantly higher in patients with SOD as compared with those with normal pressure (18 vs. 11 mm Hg; $p < .0001$). A pancreatic duct pressure greater than 20 mm Hg was 90% specific and 30% sensitive for the diagnoses of SOD. These studies must be confirmed but support the theory that increased intrabiliary and/or intrapancreatic pressure is a cause of pain in SOD.

The best study establishing normal values for SOM was reported by Guelrud and associates.[63] Fifty asymptomatic control patients were evaluated, and the study repeated on two occasions in 10 subjects. This study established normal values for intraductal pressure, basal sphincter pressure, and phasic wave parameters (Table 49–3). Moreover, the reproducibility of SOM was confirmed. Various authorities interchangeably use 35 or 40 mm Hg as the upper limits of normal for mean basal SO pressure.

Several studies have demonstrated that pancreatitis is the most common major complication after SOM.[64-66] Using standard perfused catheters, pancreatitis rates as high as 31% have been reported. Such high complication rates have initially limited more widespread use of SOM. These data also emphasize that manometric evaluation of the pancreatic duct is associated with a particularly high complication rate. Rolny and associates[65] found that patients with chronic pancreatitis were at higher risk of postprocedure pancreatitis after pancreatic duct manometry. They reported an 11% incidence of pancreatitis after manometric evaluation of the pancreatic duct. Twenty-six percent of chronic pancreatitis patients undergoing SOM developed pancreatitis.

A variety of methods to decrease the incidence of postmanometry pancreatitis have been proposed. These include (1) use of an aspiration catheter, (2) gravity drainage of the pancreatic duct after manometry, (3) decrease in the perfusion rate to 0.05 to 0.1 mL/lumen/minute, (4) limitation of pancreatic duct manometry time to less than 2 minutes (or avoid pancreatic manometry), (5) use of the microtransducer (nonperfused) system, and (6) placement of pancreatic stent after manometry and/or sphincterotomy. In a prospective randomized study, Sherman and colleagues[64] found that the aspirating catheter (this catheter allows for aspiration of the perfused fluid from end and side holes while accurately recording pressure from the two remaining side ports) reduced the frequency of pancreatic duct manometry-induced pancreatitis from 31% to 4%. The reduction in pancreatitis rates with the use of this catheter in the pancreatic duct and the very low incidence of pancreatitis after bile duct manometry lend support to the notion that increased pancreatic duct hydrostatic pressure is a major cause of this complication. Thus, when the pancreatic duct sphincter is studied by SOM, aspiration of pancreatic juice and the perfusate is strongly recommended. In a prospective randomized trial, Wehrmann and colleagues[67] found that microtransducer manometry was associated with a significantly lower incidence of postmanometry pancreatitis than standard (nonaspirating) perfusion manometry (13.8% vs. 3.1%; $p = .04$). In another prospective randomized trial, Tarnasky and colleagues[68] showed that stenting the pancreatic duct decreased post-ERCP pancreatitis from 26% to 6% in a group of patients with pancreatic sphincter hypertension undergoing biliary sphincterotomy alone.

SOM is recommended in patients with idiopathic pancreatitis or unexplained disabling pancreaticobiliary pain with or without hepatic enzyme abnormalities. An attempt should be is made to study both sphincters, but clinical decisions can be made when the first sphincter evaluated is abnormal. However, if the other sphincter is dysfunctional and not treated, the outcome of therapy may be suboptimal. Indications for the use of SOM have also been developed according to the Hogan-Geenen SOD classification system (see Table 49–1). In type I patients, there is a general consensus that a structural disorder of the sphincter (i.e., sphincter stenosis) exists. Although SOM may be useful in documenting SOD, it is not an essential diagnostic study before endoscopic or surgical sphincter ablation. Such patients uniformly benefit from sphincter ablation regardless of the SOM results (see the section on endoscopic therapy). Type II patients demonstrate SO motor dysfunction in 55% to 65% of cases. In this group of patients, SOM is highly recommended because the results of the study predict outcome from sphincter ablation. Type III patients have pancreaticobiliary pain without other objective evidence of sphincter outflow obstruction. SOM is mandatory to confirm the presence of SOD. Although not well studied, it appears that the results of SOM may predict outcome from sphincter ablation in these patients.

Table 49–3. Suggested Standard for Abnormal Values for Endoscopic Sphincter of Oddi Manometry Obtained from 50 Volunteers Without Abdominal Symptoms		
Basal sphincter pressure*		>35 mm Hg
Basal ductal pressure		>13 mm Hg
Phasic contractions Amplitude Duration Frequency		>220 mm Hg >8 sec >10/min

Values were obtained by adding three standard deviations to the mean (means were obtained by averaging the results on 2–3 station pull-throughs). Data combine pancreatic and biliary studies.
*Basal pressures determined by (1) reading the peak basal pressure (i.e., the highest single lead as obtained using a three-lumen catheter and (2) obtaining the mean of these peak pressures from multiple station pull-throughs.
Adapted from Guelrud M, Mendoza S, Rossiter G, Villegas MI: Sphincter of Oddi manometry in healthy volunteers. Dig Dis Sci 35:38–46, 1990.

Stent Trial as a Diagnostic Test

Placement of a pancreatic or biliary stent on a trial basis in hope of achieving pain relief and predicting the response to more definitive therapy (i.e., sphincter ablation) has received only limited application. Pancreatic stent trials, especially in patients with normal pancreatic ducts, are strongly discouraged because serious ductal and parenchymal injury may occur if stents are left in place for more than a few days.[69,70] Goff[71] reported a biliary stent trial in 21 type II and III suspected SOD patients with normal biliary manometry. Stents (7-French) were left in place for at least 2 months if symptoms resolved and removed sooner if they were judged ineffective. Relief of pain with the stent was predictive of long-term pain relief after biliary sphincterotomy. Unfortunately, 38% of the patients developed pancreatitis (14% were graded severe) after stent placement. Because of this high complication rate, biliary stent trials are strongly discouraged. Rolny and colleagues[72] also reported a series of bile duct stent placement as a predictor of outcome after biliary sphincterotomy in 23 postcholecystectomy patients (7 type II and 16 type III). Similar to the study by Goff,[71] resolution of pain during at least 12 weeks of stenting predicted a favorable outcome from sphincterotomy irrespective of SO pressure. In this series, there were no complications related to stent placement.

Therapy for Sphincter of Oddi Dysfunction

The therapeutic approach in patients with SOD is aimed at reducing the resistance to the flow of bile and/or pancreatic juice caused by the SO.[10] Historically, emphasis has been placed on definitive intervention (i.e., surgical sphincteroplasty or endoscopic sphincterotomy). This appears appropriate for patients with high-grade obstruction (type I as per Hogan-Geenen criteria). In patients with lesser degrees of obstruction, the clinician must carefully weigh the risks and benefits before recommending invasive therapy. Most reports indicate that SOD patients have a complication rate from endoscopic sphincterotomy of at least twice that of patients with ductal stones.[73,74]

MEDICAL THERAPY

Medical therapy for documented or suspected SOD has received only limited study. Because the SO is a smooth muscle structure, it is reasonable to assume that drugs that relax smooth muscle might be an effective treatment for SOD. Sublingual nifedipine and nitrates have been shown to reduce the basal sphincter pressures in asymptomatic volunteers and symptomatic patients with SOD.[1,75] Khuroo and colleagues[76] evaluated the clinical benefit of nifedipine in a placebo controlled crossover trial. Twenty-one of 28 patients (75%) with manometrically documented SOD had a reduction in pain scores, emergency room visits and use of oral analgesics during short-term follow-up. In a similar study, Sand and associates[77] found that 9 of 12 (75%) type II SOD (suspected; SOM was not done) patients improved with nifedipine. Although medical therapy may be an attractive initial approach in patients with SOD, several drawbacks exist.[1] First, medication side effects may be seen in up to one third of patients. Second, smooth muscle relaxants are unlikely to be of any benefit in patients with the structural form of SOD (i.e., SO stenosis), and the response is incomplete in patients with a primary motor abnormality of the SO (i.e., SO dyskinesia). Finally, long-term outcome from medical therapy has not been reported. Nevertheless, because of the relative safety of medical therapy and the benign (although painful) character of SOD, this approach should be considered in all type III and less severely symptomatic type II SOD patients before considering more aggressive sphincter ablation therapy.

Guelrud and colleagues[78] have demonstrated that transcutaneous electrical nerve stimulation (TENS) lowers the basal sphincter pressure in SOD patients by a mean of 38%, but unfortunately, generally not into the normal range. This stimulation was associated with an increase in serum VIP levels. Electroacupuncture applied at acupoint GB 34 (a specific acupoint that affects the hepatobiliary system) was shown to relax the SO in association with increased plasma CCK levels.[79] Its role in the management of SOD has not been investigated.

SURGICAL THERAPY

Historically, surgery was the traditional therapy of SOD. The surgical approach, most commonly, is a transduodenal biliary sphincteroplasty with a transampullary septoplasty (pancreatic septoplasty). Sixty percent to 70% of patients were reported to have benefited from this therapy during a 1- to 10-year follow-up.[80,81] Patients with an elevated basal sphincter pressure, determined by intraoperative SOM, were more likely to improve from surgical sphincter ablation than those with a normal basal pressure.[81] Some reports have suggested that patients with biliary-type pain have a better outcome than patients with idiopathic pancreatitis whereas others suggested no difference.[80,81] However, most studies found that symptom improvement after surgical sphincter ablation alone was relatively uncommon in patients with established chronic pancreatitis.[81]

The surgical approach for SOD has largely been replaced by endoscopic therapy. Patient tolerance, cost of care, morbidity, mortality, and cosmetic results are some of the factors that favor an initial endoscopic approach. At present, surgical therapy is reserved for patients with restenosis after endoscopic sphincterotomy and when endoscopic evaluation or therapy is not available or technically feasible (e.g., Roux-en-Y gastrojejunostomy). However, in many centers operative therapy continues to be the standard treatment of pancreatic sphincter hypertension.[10,82]

ENDOSCOPIC THERAPY
Endoscopic Sphincterotomy

Endoscopic sphincterotomy is the standard therapy for patients with SOD.[83] Most data on endoscopic sphincterotomy relate to biliary sphincter ablation alone. Clinical improvement after therapy has been reported to occur in 55% to 95% of patients (see Table 49–1). These variable outcomes are reflective of the different criteria used to document SOD, the degree of obstruction (type I biliary patients appear to have a better outcome than type II and III), the methods of data collection (retrospective vs. prospective),

Table 49–4. Biliary Sphincter Ablation in Type I SOD (28-Month Follow-up)*

Basal Sphincter of Oddi Pressure	N	Asymptomatic/Improved after ES/SS
<40 mmHg	6 (35%)	6 (100%)
≥40 mmHg	11 (65%)	11 (100%)

SOD, sphincter of Oddi dysfunction; ES, endoscopic sphincterotomy; SS, surgical sphincterotomy.
*15 ES, 2 SS.
Adapted from Rolny P, Geenen JE, Hogan WJ: Post-cholecystectomy patients with 'objective signs' of partial bile outflow obstruction: Clinical characteristics, sphincter of Oddi manometry findings, and results of therapy. Gastrointest Endosc 39:778–781, 1993.

Table 49–5. Biliary Sphincterotomy for Type II and Type III Sphincter of Oddi Dysfunction Documented by Sphincter of Oddi Manometry: Results of 4 Nonrandomized Controlled Trials

Author (Yr)	Clinical Benefit	
	Type II	Type III
Choudhry et al. (1993)[22]*	10/18 (56%)	9/16 (56%)
Botoman et al. (1994)[17]	13/19 (68%)	9/16 (56%)
Bozkurt et al. (1996)[85]	14/19 (78%)	5/5 (100%)
Wehrmann et al. (1996)[86]	12/20 (60%)	1/13 (8%)

*Six had cholecystectomy.

and the techniques used to determine benefit. Rolny and colleagues[84] studied 17 type I postcholecystectomy biliary patients by SOM (Table 49–4). In this series, 65% had an abnormal SOM (although not specifically stated, it appears that the biliary sphincter was studied alone). Nevertheless, during a mean follow-up interval of 2.3 years, all patients benefited from biliary sphincterotomy. The results of this study suggested that because type I biliary patients invariably benefit from biliary sphincterotomy, SOM in this patient group not only is unnecessary but also may be misleading. However, the results of this study have never been validated at another center. In contrast, results of several nonrandomized controlled trials[17,22,85,86] suggest that performance of SOM is highly recommended in biliary type II and type III patients, because clinical benefit is less certain (Table 49–5).

Although most of the studies reporting efficacy of endoscopic therapy in SOD have been retrospective, three notable randomized trials have been reported. In a landmark study by Geenen and associates,[87] 47 postcholecystectomy type II biliary patients were randomized to biliary sphincterotomy or sham sphincterotomy. SOM was performed in all patients but not used as a criterion for randomization. During a 4-year follow-up, 95% of patients with an elevated basal sphincter benefited from sphincterotomy. In contrast, only 30% to 40% of patients with an elevated sphincter pressure treated by sham sphincterotomy, or with a normal sphincter pressure treated by endoscopic sphincterotomy or sham sphincterotomy, benefited from this therapy. The two important findings of this study were that SOM predicted the outcome from endoscopic sphincterotomy and that endoscopic sphincterotomy offered long-term benefit in type II biliary patients with SOD. Confirming data were seen in a 2-year follow-up study by Toouli and coworkers.[88,89]

In this study, postcholecystectomy patients with biliary-type pain (mostly type II) were prospectively randomized to endoscopic sphincterotomy or sham after stratification according to SOM. Eighty-five percent (11 of 13) of patients with elevated basal pressure improved at 2 years after endoscopic sphincterotomy, whereas 38% (5 of 13) of patients improved after a sham procedure ($p = .041$). Patients with normal SOM were also randomized to sphincterotomy or sham. The outcome was similar for the two groups (8 of 13 improved after sphincterotomy and 8 of 19 improved after sham; $p = .47$).

Sherman and associates[90] reported their preliminary results of a randomized study comparing endoscopic sphincterotomy and surgical biliary sphincteroplasty with pancreatic septoplasty (with or without cholecystectomy) to sham sphincterotomy for type II and III biliary patients with manometrically documented SOD. The results are shown in Tables 49–6A and 49–6B. During a 3-year follow-up period, 69% of patients undergoing endoscopic or surgical sphincter ablation improved compared with 24% in the sham sphincterotomy group ($p = .009$). There was a trend for type II patients to benefit more often from sphincter ablation than type III patients (13/16, 81%, vs. 11/19, 58%; $p = .14$).

Evidence is now accumulating that the addition of a pancreatic sphincterotomy to an endoscopic biliary sphincterotomy in patients with pancreatic sphincter disease may improve the outcome, as preliminarily reported by Guelrud and coworkers.[91] Soffer and Johlin[92] reported that 25 of 26 patients (mostly type II), who failed to respond to biliary sphincterotomy, had elevated pancreatic sphincter pressure. Pancreatic sphincter therapy was performed with overall symptomatic improvement in two thirds of patients. Eversman and colleagues[93] found that 90% of patients with

Table 49–6A. Change in the Mean Pain Score (using a 0 = none to 10 = most severe linear pain scale), Number of Hospital Days per Month Required for Pain and the Percentage Improved in Patients with Manometrically Documented Sphincter of Oddi Dysfunction Randomized to Endoscopic Sphincterotomy, Sham Sphincterotomy, and Surgical Sphincteroplasty with or without Cholecystectomy

Therapy	Follow-up (Yrs)	Mean Pain Score		Hospital Days/Month		% Patients Improved
		Pre-Rx	Post-Rx	Pre-Rx	Post-Rx	
ES (n = 19)	3.3	9.2	3.9*	0.85	0.23†	68%‡
S-ES (n = 17)	2.2	9.4	7.2	0.87	0.89	24%
SSp±CCx (n = 16)	3.4	9.4	3.3*	0.94	0.27†	69%‡

*p < .04; ES and SSp±CCx versus S-ES.
†p = .002; ES and SSp±CCx versus S-ES.
‡p = .009; ES and SSp±CCx versus S-ES.
ES, endoscopic sphincterotomy; Rx, treatment; S-ES, sham sphincterotomy; SSp±CCx, surgical sphincteroplasty with or without cholecystectomy.
Adapted from Sherman S, Lehman GA, Jamidar P, et al: Efficacy of endoscopic sphincterotomy and surgical sphincteroplasty for patients with sphincter of Oddi dysfunction (SOD): Randomized, controlled study. Gastrointest Endosc 40:A125, 1994.

Table 49–6B. Clinical Benefit Correlated with Sphincter of Oddi Dysfunction Type

SOD Type*	Patients Improved/Total Patients		
	ES	S-ES	SSp±CCx
Type II	5/6 (83%)†	1/7 (14%)	8/10 (80%)†
Type III	8/13 (62%)	3/10 (30%)	3/6 (50%)

*SOD type based on Hogan-Geenen SOD classification system.
†p < .02; ES and SSp±CCx versus S-ES.
ES, endoscopic sphincterotomy; S-ES, sham sphincterotomy; SOD, sphincter of Oddi dysfunction; SSp±CCx, surgical sphincteroplasty with or without cholecystectomy.
Adapted from Sherman S, Lehman GA, Jamidar P, et al: Efficacy of endoscopic sphincterotomy and surgical sphincteroplasty for patients with sphincter of Oddi dysfunction (SOD): Randomized, controlled study. Gastrointest Endosc 40:A125, 1994.

Table 49–7. Response to Sphincterotomy in Relation to Sphincter of Oddi Segment Treated (follow-up 17 months)

SO Dysfunction	Biliary Sphincterotomy		Pancreatic Sphincterotomy	
	Total	Response	Total	Response
Biliary	10	8 (80%)	0	0 (0%)
Pancreatic	13	2 (15%)	11	8 (72%)
Combined	10	5 (50%)	5	3 (60%)
Total	33	15 (45%)	16	11 (69%)

Overall benefit 26/33 (79%); patients with pancreatic or combined SO dysfunction who failed to improve after a biliary sphincterotomy underwent pancreatic sphincterotomy.
SO, sphincter of Oddi.
Adapted from Kaw M, Verma R, Brodmerkel GJ: Biliary and/or pancreatic sphincter of Oddi dysfunction (SOD). Response to endoscopic sphincterotomy (ES). Gastrointest Endosc 43:A384, 1996.

persistent pain or pancreatitis after biliary sphincterotomy had residual abnormal pancreatic basal pressure. Five-year follow-up data revealed that patients with untreated pancreatic sphincter hypertension were much less likely to improve after biliary sphincterotomy than patients with isolated biliary sphincter hypertension. Elton and colleagues[94] performed pancreatic sphincterotomy on 43 type I and type II SOD patients who failed to benefit from biliary sphincterotomy alone. During the follow-up period, 72% were symptom-free and 19% were partially or transiently improved. Kaw

and colleagues[95] presented preliminary data demonstrating that response to sphincterotomy also depends on treating the diseased sphincter segment. Patients with pancreatic sphincter hypertension who fail to respond to biliary sphincterotomy can be "rescued" by undergoing pancreatic sphincterotomy (Table 49–7). Recent data from our unit[96] examined the outcome of endoscopic therapy in SOD patients with initial pancreatic sphincter hypertension (with or without biliary sphincter hypertension). Patients were followed for a mean of 43.1 months (range 11-77 months); reintervention was offered for sustained or recurrent symptoms at a median of 8 months after initial therapy. Performance of an initial dual pancreatobiliary sphincterotomy was associated with a lower reintervention rate (70/285, 24.6%) than biliary sphincterotomy alone (31/95, 33%; $p < .05$). Confirmatory outcome studies, preferably in randomized trials, are awaited.

These results clearly indicate that the response rate and enthusiasm for sphincter ablation must be correlated with patient presentation and results of manometry and balanced against the high complication rates reported for endoscopic therapy of SOD. Most studies indicate that patients undergoing endoscopic sphincterotomy for SOD have complication rates two to five times higher than patients undergoing endoscopic sphincterotomy for ductal stones.[73,74] Pancreatitis is the most common complication occurring in up to 30% of patients in some series. A recent prospective, multicenter study examining risk factors for post-ERCP pancreatitis identified suspected SOD as an independent factor by multivariate analysis.[97] A suspicion of SOD tripled the risk of postprocedure pancreatitis to a frequency (23%) that was comparable to that found in other recent prospective studies.[68,74,98–100] Endoscopic techniques are being developed (e.g., pancreatic duct stenting before combined pancreaticobiliary sphincterotomy) to limit such complications.[68,101]

Balloon Dilation and Stenting

Balloon dilation of strictures in the GI tract has become commonplace. In an attempt to be less invasive and possibly preserve sphincter function, adaptation of this technique to treat SOD has been described. Unfortunately, because of the unacceptably high complication rates, primarily pancreatitis, this technology has little role in the management of SOD.[102] Similarly, although biliary stenting might offer short-term symptom benefit in patients with SOD and predict outcome from sphincter ablation, it too has unacceptably high complication rates and cannot be advocated in this setting.[71]

Botulinum Toxin Injection

Botulinum toxin (Botox), a potent inhibitor of acetylcholine release from nerve endings, has been successfully applied to smooth muscle disorders of the GI tract such as achalasia. In a preliminary clinical trial, Botox injection into the SO resulted in a 50% reduction in the basal biliary sphincter pressure and improved bile flow.[103] This reduction in pressure may be accompanied by symptom improvement in some patients. Although further study is warranted, Botox may serve as a therapeutic trial for SOD with responders undergoing permanent sphincter ablation. In a small series,[104] 22 postcholecystectomy type III patients with manometric evidence of SOD underwent Botox injection into the intraduodenal sphincter segment. Eleven of the 12 patients who responded to botulinum toxin injection later benefited from endoscopic sphincterotomy, whereas only 2 of 10 patients who did not benefit from Botox injection later responded to sphincter ablation. However, such an approach does require two endoscopies to achieve symptom relief. Moreover, patients must have relatively frequent episodes of pain to assess the benefit from Botox. Further studies are needed before recommending this technique.

Failure to Achieve Symptomatic Improvement After Biliary Sphincterotomy

There are several potential explanations as to why patients may fail to achieve symptom relief after biliary sphincterotomy is performed for well-documented SOD. First, the biliary sphincterotomy may have been inadequate or restenosis may have occurred. Although the biliary sphincter is commonly not totally ablated,[105] Manoukian and coworkers[106] indicated that clinically significant biliary restenosis occurs relatively infrequently. If no "cutting space" remains in such a patient, balloon dilation to 8 to 10 mm may suffice, but long-term outcome from such therapy is unknown and the risks may be considerable.[102]

Second, the importance of pancreatic sphincter ablation is being increasingly recognized, as noted previously.[91–96]

Third, patients may fail to respond to sphincterotomy because they have chronic pancreatitis. Tarnasky and colleagues[107] reported that SOD patients were four times more likely to have evidence of chronic pancreatitis than those without SOD ($p = .01$). Although SOD appears to be associated with chronic pancreatitis, a causal relationship has not been proven. These patients may or may not have abnormal pancreatograms. Intraductal pancreatic juice aspiration after secretin stimulation may help make this diagnosis.[108,109] EUS may show parenchymal and ductular changes of the pancreas in some of these patients suggesting chronic pancreatitis.[110]

Fourth, some patients may be having pain from altered gut motility of the stomach, small bowel or colon (irritable bowel or pseudo-obstruction variants). There is increasing evidence that upper GI motility disorders may masquerade as pancreatobiliary-type pain (i.e., discrete right upper quadrant pain). Multiple preliminary studies show disordered duodenal motility in such patients.[111–113] This area needs much more study to determine the frequency, significance, and/or coexistence of these motor disorders along with SOD. DeSautels and colleagues[114] suggested that type III patients have duodenal specific visceral hyperalgesia with pain reproduction by duodenal distention. These patients were also shown to have high levels of somatization, depression, obsessive-compulsive behavior, and anxiety compared with control subject.[115]

Sphincter of Oddi Dysfunction in Recurrent Pancreatitis

Disorders of the pancreatic sphincter may give rise to unexplained (idiopathic) pancreatitis or episodic pain suggestive of a pancreatic origin.[82] SOD is a frequent cause of recurrent pancreatitis previously labeled as idiopathic acute recurrent pancreatitis (IARP). It has been manometrically documented in 15% to 72% of such patients (Table 49–8).[5,18,21,116–124] Pancreatic sphincter manometry should be done in patients with IARP, particularly those with normal biliary manometry and in those who have recurrent attacks after a biliary sphincterotomy. It is not surprising that isolated pancreatic sphincter hypertension is common among patients with IARP found to have SOD.[57,125] In addition, pancreatic sphincter hypertension

Table 49–8. Manometrically Documented Sphincter of Oddi Dysfunction Causing Idiopathic Acute Recurrent Pancreatitis

Author (Yr)	Frequency
Toouli et al. (1985)[119]	16/26 (57%)
Guelrud et al. (1986)[120]	17/42 (40%)
Gregg (1989)[121]	38/125 (30%)
Venu et al. (1989)[118]	17/116 (15%)
Sherman et al. (1993)[122]	18/55 (33%)
Choudari et al. (1998)[117]	79/225 (35%)
Kaw et al. (2002)[123]	67/126 (53%)
Coyle et al. (2002)[124]	28/90 (31%)
Total	280/805 (35%)

may explain recurrent pancreatitis despite biliary sphincterotomy or surgical biliary sphincteroplasty.[125] Biliary sphincterotomy alone has been reported to prevent further pancreatitis episodes in more than 50% of patients in some series. From a scientific, but not practical viewpoint, care must be taken to separate out subtle biliary pancreatitis[126] that will similarly respond to biliary sphincterotomy. Moreover, because IARP is an episodic illness, long-term follow-up is necessary to conclude that a patient is "cured."

Sphincter ablation is the recommended therapy for patients with IARP resulting from SOD. Historically, this has been done surgically.[81] However, with increasing experience, endoscopic sphincterotomy has become the treatment of choice. The value of ERCP, SOM, and sphincter ablation therapy was studied in 51 patients with idiopathic pancreatitis.[50] Twenty-four (47.1%) had an elevated basal sphincter pressure. Thirty were treated by biliary sphincterotomy ($n = 20$) or surgical sphincteroplasty with septoplasty ($n = 10$). Fifteen of 18 patients (83%) with an elevated basal sphincter pressure had long-term benefit (mean follow-up, 38 months) from sphincter ablation therapy (including 10 of 11 treated by biliary sphincterotomy) in contrast to only 4 of 12 (33.3%, $p < .05$) with a normal basal sphincter pressure (including 4 of 9 treated by biliary sphincterotomy). However, Guelrud and colleagues[91] found that severance of the pancreatic sphincter was necessary to resolve the pancreatitis (Table 49–9). In this series, 69 patients with idiopathic pancreatitis resulting from SOD underwent treatment by standard biliary sphincterotomy ($n = 18$), biliary sphincterotomy with pancreatic sphincter balloon dilation ($n = 24$), biliary sphincterotomy followed by pancreatic sphincterotomy in separate sessions ($n = 13$), or combined pancreatic and biliary sphincterotomy in the same session ($n = 14$). Eighty-one percent of patients undergoing pancreatic and biliary sphincterotomy had resolution of their pancreatitis compared with 28% of patients undergoing biliary sphincterotomy alone ($p < .005$). Sherman and colleagues[122] reported that only 44% of SOD patients with IARP had no further attacks during a 5-year follow-up interval after biliary sphincterotomy alone. These data are consistent with the theory that many such patients who benefit from biliary sphincterotomy alone have subtle gallstone pancreatitis. The results of Guelrud and colleagues[91] also support the anatomic findings of separate biliary and pancreatic sphincters and the manometry findings of residual pancreatic sphincter hypertension in more than 50% of persistently symptomatic patients who undergo biliary sphincterotomy alone. Kaw and Brodmerkel[123] recently reported that among patients with idiopathic pancreatitis secondary to SOD, 78% had persistent manometric evidence of pancreatic sphincter hypertension despite a biliary sphincterotomy. Toouli and coworkers[127] also demonstrated the importance of pancreatic and biliary sphincter ablation in patients with idiopathic pancreatitis. In this series, 23 of 26 patients (88%) undergoing surgical ablation of both the biliary and pancreatic sphincter were either asymptomatic or had minimal symptoms at a median follow-up of 24 months (range 9 to 105 months). Okolo and colleagues[128] retrospectively evaluated the long-term results of endoscopic pancreatic sphincterotomy in 55 patients with manometrically documented or presumed pancreatic sphincter hypertension (presumption based on recurrent pancreatitis with pancreatic duct dilation and contrast medium drainage time from the pancreatic duct greater than 10 minutes). During a median follow-up of 16 months (range 3 to 52 months), 34 patients (62%) reported significant pain improvement. Patients with normal pancreatograms were more likely to respond to therapy than those with pancreatographic evidence of chronic pancreatitis (73% vs. 58%). Jacob and coworkers[129] postulated that SOD might cause recurrent episodes of pancreatitis, even though SOM was normal, and pancreatic stent placement might prevent further attacks. In a randomized study, 34 patients with unexplained recurrent pancreatitis, normal pancreatic duct SOM, ERCP, secretin testing, and no biliary crystals were treated with pancreatic stents ($n = 19$; 5 to 7 Fr, with stents exchanged three times over a 1-year period) or conservative therapy ($n = 15$). During a 3-year follow-up, pancreatitis recurred in 53% of the patients in the control group and only 11% of the stented patients ($p < .02$). This study suggests that SOM may

Table 49–9. Pancreatic Sphincter Dysfunction and Recurrent Pancreatitis: Response to Sphincter Therapy

Treatment	Patients Improved/Total Patients
Biliary sphincterotomy alone	5/18 (28%)
Biliary sphincterotomy followed by pancreatic sphincter balloon dilation	13/24 (54%)
Biliary sphincterotomy plus pancreatic sphincterotomy at later session	10/13 (77%)*
Biliary sphincterotomy and pancreatic sphincterotomy at same session	12/14 (86%)*

*$p < .005$ versus biliary sphincterotomy alone.
Adapted from Guelrud M, Plaz J, Mendoza S, et al: Endoscopic treatment in Type II pancreatic sphincter dysfunction. Gastrointest Endosc 41:A398, 1995.

be an imperfect test, because patients may have SOD but not be detected at the time of SOM. However, long-term studies are needed to evaluate the outcome after removal of stents and concern remains regarding stent-induced ductal and parenchymal changes.[69,70] Because of the concern of stent-induced injury to the pancreas, trial pancreatic duct stenting to predict outcome from pancreatic sphincterotomy is not recommended.[130] Wehrmann and colleagues[131] recently evaluated the feasibility and effectiveness of botulinum toxin injection in patients with recurrent pancreatitis resulting from pancreatic sphincter hypertension. No side effects of the injection were noted in any of the 15 treated patients. Twelve patients (80%) remained asymptomatic at 3 month follow-up, but 11 developed a relapse at a follow-up period of 6 ± 2 months. These 11 patients underwent pancreatic or combined pancreatobiliary sphincterotomy with subsequent remission after a median follow-up of 15 months. This study showed that injection of botulinum toxin is safe, may be effective short-term, and may predict the outcome from pancreatic sphincter ablation in patients having frequent episodes of pancreatitis, but the need for definitive sphincter ablation in most patients limits its clinical use.

In summary, these data show that SOD is the most common cause of IARP when detailed endoscopic evaluation is performed. SOM should be considered the gold standard for diagnosing SOD. Complete sphincter evaluation requires manometric assessment of both the biliary and pancreatic sphincters. Although the best endoscopic therapy of SOD warrants further investigation, there is mounting evidence that pancreatic sphincter ablation will be necessary in most patients to achieve the best long-term results.

Summary

Our knowledge of SOD, and manometric techniques to assist in this diagnosis, are evolving. Successful endoscopic SOM requires good general ERCP skills and careful attention to the main details listed above. If SOD is suspected in a type III or mild to moderate pain level type II patient, medical therapy should generally be tried. If medical therapy fails or is bypassed, ERCP and manometric evaluation are recommended. The role of less invasive studies remains uncertain owing to undefined sensitivity and specificity. Sphincter ablation is generally warranted in symptomatic type I patients and type II and III patients with abnormal manometry. The symptom relief rate varies from 55% to 95%, depending on the patient presentation and selection. Initial nonresponders require thorough pancreatic sphincter and pancreatic parenchymal evaluation. SOD patients have relatively high complication rates after invasive studies or therapy. Thorough review of the risk-to-benefit ratio with individual patients is mandatory.

REFERENCES

1. Kalloo AN, Pasricha PJ: Therapy of sphincter of Oddi dysfunction. Gastrointest Endosc Clin N Am 6:117–125, 1996.
2. Black NA, Thompson E, Sanderson CF: Symptoms and health status before and six weeks after open cholecystectomy: A European cohort study. ECHSS Group. European Collaborative Health Services Study Group. Gut 35:1301–1305, 1994.
3. Hogan W, Sherman S, Pasricha P, Carr-Locke DL: Position paper on sphincter of Oddi manometry. Gastrointest Endosc 45:342–348, 1997.
4. Sherman S, Troiano FP, Hawes RH, et al: Frequency of abnormal sphincter of Oddi manometry compared with the clinical suspicion of sphincter of Oddi dysfunction. Am J Gastroenterol 86:586–590, 1991.
5. Eversman D, Fogel EL, Rusche M, et al: Frequency of abnormal pancreatic and biliary sphincter manometry compared with clinical suspicion of sphincter of Oddi dysfunction. Gastrointest Endosc 50:637–641, 1999.
6. Richards RD, Yeaton P, Shaffer HA, et al: Human sphincter of Oddi motility and cholecystokinin response following liver transplantation. Dig Dis Sci 38:462–468, 1993.
7. Becker JM, Parodi JM: Basic control mechanisms of sphincter of Oddi motor function. Gastrointest Endosc Clin N Am 3:41–66, 1993.
8. Luman W, Williams AJ, Pryde A, et al: Influence of cholecystectomy on sphincter of Oddi motility. Gut 41:371–374, 1997.
9. Anderson TM, Pitt HA, Longmire WP Jr: Experience with sphincteroplasty and sphincterotomy in pancreatobiliary surgery. Ann Surg 201:399–406, 1985.
10. Corazziari E, Shaffer EA, Hogan W, et al: Functional disorders of the biliary tract and pancreas. Gut 45:48–54, 1999.
11. Drossman DA, Zhiming L, Andruzzi E, et al: US Householder Survey of functional gastrointestinal disorders—prevalence, sociodemography, and health impact. Dig Dis Sci 38:1569–1580, 1993.
12. Guelrud M, Mendoza S, Mujica V, Uzcategui A: Sphincter of Oddi (SO) motor function in patients with symptomatic gallstones. Gastroenterology 104:A361, 1993.
13. Ruffolo TA, Sherman S, Lehman GA, Hawes RH: Gallbladder ejection fraction and its relationship to sphincter of Oddi dysfunction. Dig Dis Sci 39:289–292, 1994.
14. Neoptolemos JP, Bailey IS, Carr-Locke DL: Sphincter of Oddi dysfunction: Results of treatment by endoscopic sphincterotomy. Br J Surg 75:454–459, 1988.
15. Roberts-Thomson IC, Toouli J: Is endoscopic sphincterotomy for disabling biliary-type pain after cholecystectomy effective? Gastrointest Endosc 31:370–373, 1985.
16. Meshkinpoor H, Mollot M: Sphincter of Oddi dysfunction and unexplained abdominal pain: Clinical and manometric study. Dig Dis Sci 37:257–261, 1992.
17. Botoman VA, Kozarek RA, Novell LA, et al: Long term outcome after endoscopic sphincterotomy in patients with biliary colic and suspected sphincter of Oddi dysfunction. Gastrointest Endosc 40:165–170, 1994.
18. Lehman GA, Sherman S: Sphincter of Oddi dysfunction. Int J Pancreatol 20:11–25, 1996.
19. Linder JD, Geels W, Wilcox CM: Prevalence of sphincter of Oddi dysfunction: Can results from specialized centers be generalized? Dig Dis Sci 47:2411–2415, 2002.
20. Aymerich RR, Prakash C, Aliperti G: Sphincter of Oddi manometry: Is it necessary to measure both biliary and pancreatic sphincter pressure? Gastrointest Endosc 52:183–186, 2000.
21. Geenen JE, Nash JA: The role of sphincter of Oddi manometry and biliary microscopy in evaluating idiopathic recurrent pancreatitis. Endoscopy 30:237–241, 1998.
22. Choudhry U, Ruffolo T, Jamidar P, et al: Sphincter of Oddi dysfunction in patients with intact gallbladder: Therapeutic response to endoscopic sphincterotomy. Gastrointest Endosc 39:492–495, 1993.
23. Steinberg WM: Sphincter of Oddi dysfunction: A clinical controversy. Gastroenterology 95:1409–1415, 1988.
24. Lin OS, Soetikno RM, Young HS: The utility of liver function test abnormalities concomitant with biliary symptoms in predicting a favorable response to endoscopic sphincterotomy in patients with presumed sphincter of Oddi dysfunction. Am J Gastroenterol 93:1833–1836, 1998.

25. Steinberg WM, Salvato RF, Toskes PP: The morphine-prostigmin provocative test: Is it useful for making clinical decisions? Gastroenterology 78:728–731, 1980.

26. Darweesh RM, Dodds WJ, Hogan WJ, et al: Efficacy of quantitative hepatobiliary scintigraphy and fatty-meal sonography for evaluating patients with suspected partial common duct obstruction. Gastroenterology 94:779–786, 1988.

27. Simeone JF, Mueller PR, Ferrucci JT Jr, et al: Sonography of the bile ducts after a fatty meal: An aid in detection of obstruction. Radiology 143:211–215, 1982.

28. Troiano F, O'Connor K, Lehman GA, et al: Comparison of secretin-stimulated ultrasound and sphincter of Oddi manometry in evaluating sphincter of Oddi dysfunction. Gastrointest Endosc 35:A166, 1989.

29. Warshaw AL, Simeone J, Schapiro RH, et al: Objective evaluation of ampullary stenosis with ultrasonography and pancreatic stimulation. Am J Surg 149:65–72, 1985.

30. DiFrancesco V, Brunori MR, Rigo L, et al: Comparison of ultrasound-secretin test and sphincter of Oddi manometry in patients with recurrent acute pancreatitis. Dig Dis Sci 44:336–340, 1999.

31. Silverman WB, Johlin FC, Crowe G: Does secretin stimulated ultrasound (SSUS) predict results of sphincter of Oddi manometry (SOM) basal sphincter pressure (BSP) in patients suspected of having sphincter of Oddi dysfunction (SOD)? Gastrointest Endosc 53:A100, 2001.

32. Catalano MF, Lahoti S, Alcocer E, et al: Dynamic imaging of the pancreas using real-time endoscopic ultrasonography with secretin stimulation. Gastrointest Endosc 48:580–587, 1998.

33. Devereaux BM, Fogel EL, Aisen A, et al: Secretin-stimulated functional MRCP: Correlation with sphincter of Oddi manometry. Gastrointest Endosc 51:A197, 2000.

34. Sostre S, Kalloo AN, Spiegler EJ, et al: A noninvasive test of sphincter of Oddi dysfunction in postcholecystectomy patients: The scintigraphic score. J Nucl Med 33:1216–1222, 1992.

35. Kalloo AN, Sostre S, Pasricha PJ: The Hopkins scintigraphic score: A noninvasive, highly accurate screening test for sphincter of Oddi dysfunction. Gastroenterology 106:A342, 994.

36. Cicala M, Scopinaro F, Corazziari E, et al: Quantitative cholescintigraphy in the assessment of choledochoduodenal bile flow. Gastroenterology 100:1106–1113, 1991.

37. Corazziari E, Cicala M, Habib FI, et al: Hepatoduodenal bile transit in cholecystectomized subjects. Relationship with sphincter of Oddi dysfunction and diagnostic value. Dig Dis Sci 39:1985–1993, 1994.

38. Peng NJ, Lai KH, Tsay DG, et al: Efficacy of quantitative cholescintigraphy in the diagnosis of sphincter of Oddi dysfunction. Nuc Med Comm 15:899–904, 1994.

39. Thomas PD, Turner JG, Dobbs BR, et al: Use of 99m Tc-DISIDA biliary scanning with morphine provocation in the detection of elevated sphincter of Oddi basal pressure. Gut 46:838–841, 2000.

40. Esber E, Ruffolo TA, Park H, et al: Prospective assessment of biliary scintigraphy in patients with suspected sphincter of Oddi dysfunction. Gastrointest Endosc 41:A396, 1995.

41. Pineau BC, Knapple WL, Spicer KM, et al: Cholecystokinin-stimulated mebrofenin (99mTc-Choletec) hepatobiliary scintigraphy in asymptomatic postcholecystectomy individuals: Assessment of specificity, interobserver reliability, and reproducibility. Am J Gastroenterol 96:3106–3109, 2001.

42. Craig AG, Peter D, Saccone GT, et al: Scintigraphy versus manometry in patients with suspected biliary sphincter of Oddi dysfunction. Gut 52:352–357, 2003.

43. Rosenblatt ML, Catalano MF, Alcocer E, Geenen JE: Comparison of sphincter of Oddi manometry, fatty meal sonography, and hepatobiliary scintigraphy in the diagnosis of sphincter of Oddi dysfunction. Gastrointest Endosc 54:697–704, 2001.

44. Cicala M, Habib FI, Vavassori P, et al: Outcome of endoscopic sphincterotomy in post cholecystectomy patients with sphincter of Oddi dysfunction as predicted by manometry and quantitative choledochoscintigraphy. Gut 50:665–668, 2002.

45. Elta GH, Barnett JL, Ellis JH, et al: Delayed biliary drainage is common in asymptomatic post-cholecystectomy volunteers. Gastrointest Endosc 38:435–439, 1992.

46. Ponchon T, Aucia N, Mitchell R, et al: Biopsies of the ampullary region in patients suspected to have sphincter of Oddi dysfunction. Gastrointest Endosc 42:296–300, 1995.

47. Itoh A, Tsukamoto Y, Naitoh Y, et al: Intraductal ultrasonography for the examination of duodenal papillary region. J Ultrasound Med 13:679–684, 1994.

48. Wehrmann T, Stergiou N, Riphaus A, Lembcke B: Correlation between sphincter of Oddi manometry and intraductal ultrasound morphology in patients with suspected sphincter of Oddi dysfunction. Endoscopy 33:773–777, 2001.

49. Lehman GA: Endoscopic sphincter of Oddi manometry: A clinical practice and research tool. Gastrointest Endosc 37:490–492, 1991.

50. Lans JL, Parikh NP, Geenen JE: Application of sphincter of Oddi manometry in routine clinical investigations. Endoscopy 23:139–143, 1991.

51. Sherman S, Gottlieb K, Uzer MF, et al: Effects of meperidine on the pancreatic and biliary sphincter. Gastrointest Endosc 44:239–242, 1996.

52. Fogel EL, Sherman S, Bucksot L, et al: Effects of droperidol on the pancreatic and biliary sphincter. Gastrointest Endosc 58:488–492, 2003.

53. Goff JS: Effect of propofol on human sphincter of Oddi. Dig Dis Sci 40:2364–2367, 1995.

54. Blaut U, Sherman S, Fogel EL, et al: The influence of variable stiffness guidewires on basal biliary sphincter of Oddi pressure measured at ERCP. Gastrointest Endosc 55:83A, 2002.

55. Craig AG, Omari T, Lingenfelser T, et al: Development of a sleeve sensor for measurement of sphincter of Oddi motility. Endoscopy 33:651–657, 2001.

56. Blaut U, Sherman S, Fogel E, Lehman GA: Influence of cholangiography on biliary sphincter of Oddi manometric parameters. Gastrointest Endosc 52:624–629, 2000.

57. Raddawi HM, Geenen JE, Hogan WJ, et al: Pressure measurements from biliary and pancreatic segments of sphincter of Oddi. Comparison between patients with functional abdominal pain, biliary, or pancreatic disease. Dig Dis Sci 36:71–74, 1991.

58. Rolny P, Ärlebäck A, Funch-Jensen P, et al: Clinical significance of manometric assessment of both pancreatic duct and bile duct sphincter in the same patient. Scand J Gastroenterol 24:751–754, 1989.

59. Silverman WB, Ruffolo TA, Sherman S, et al: Correlation of basal sphincter pressures measured from both the bile duct and pancreatic duct in patients with suspected sphincter of Oddi dysfunction. Gastrointest Endosc 38:440–443, 1992.

60. Chan YK, Evans PR, Dowsett JF, et al: Discordance of pressure recordings from biliary and pancreatic duct segments in patients with suspected sphincter of Oddi dysfunction. Dig Dis Sci 42:1501–1506, 1997.

61. Kalloo AN, Tietjen TG, Pasricha PJ: Does intrabiliary pressure predict basal sphincter of Oddi pressure? A study in patients with and without gallbladders. Gastrointest Endosc 44:696–699, 1996.

62. Fazel A, Catalano M, Quadri A, Geenen J: Pancreatic ductal pressures: A potential surrogate marker for pancreatic sphincter of Oddi dysfunction. Gastrointest Endosc 55:92A, 2002.

63. Guelrud M, Mendoza S, Rossiter G, Villegas MI: Sphincter of Oddi manometry in healthy volunteers. Dig Dis Sci 35:38–46, 1990.

64. Sherman S, Troiano FP, Hawes RH, Lehman GA: Sphincter of Oddi manometry: Decreased risk of clinical pancreatitis with the use of a modified aspirating catheter. Gastrointest Endosc 36:462–466, 1990.

65. Rolny P, Anderberg B, Ihse I, et al: Pancreatitis after sphincter of Oddi manometry. Gut 31:821–824, 1990.

66. Maldonado ME, Brady PG, Mamel JJ, Robinson B: Incidence of pancreatitis in patients undergoing sphincter of Oddi manometry (SOM). Am J Gastroenterol 94:387–390, 1999.

67. Wehrmann T, Stergiou N, Schmitt T, et al: Reduced risk for pancreatitis after endoscopic microtransducer manometry of the sphincter of Oddi: A randomized comparison with perfusion manometry technique. Endoscopy 35:472–477, 2003.

68. Tarnasky PR, Palesch YY, Cunningham JT, et al: Pancreatic stenting prevents pancreatitis after biliary sphincterotomy in patients with sphincter of Oddi dysfunction. Gastroenterology 115:1518–1524, 1998.

69. Kozarek RA: Pancreatic stents can induce ductal changes consistent with chronic pancreatitis. Gastrointest Endosc 36:93–95, 1990.

70. Smith MT, Sherman S, Ikenberry S, et al: Alterations in pancreatic ductal morphology following polyethylene pancreatic duct stenting. Gastrointest Endosc 44:268–275, 1996.

71. Goff JS: Common bile duct sphincter of Oddi stenting in patients with suspected sphincter of Oddi dysfunction. Am J Gastroenterol 90:586–589, 1995.

72. Rolny P: Endoscopic bile duct stent placement as a predictor of outcome following endoscopic sphincterotomy in patients with suspected sphincter of Oddi dysfunction. Eur J Gastroenterol Hepatol 9:467–4671, 1997.

73. Sherman S, Ruffolo TA, Hawes RH, Lehman GA: Complications of endoscopic sphincterotomy. A prospective series with emphasis on the increased risk associated with sphincter of Oddi dysfunction and nondilated bile ducts. Gastroenterology 101:1068–1075, 1991.

74. Freeman ML, Nelson DB, Sherman S, et al: Complications of endoscopic biliary sphincterotomy: A prospective, multicenter study. N Engl J Med 335:909–918, 1996.

75. Guelrud M, Mendoza S, Rossiter G, et al: Effect of nifedipine on sphincter of Oddi motor activity: Studies in healthy volunteers and patients with biliary dyskinesia. Gastroenterology 95:1050–1055, 1988.

76. Khuroo MS, Zargar SA, Yattoo GN: Efficacy of nifedipine therapy in patients with sphincter of Oddi dysfunction: A prospective, double-blind, randomized, placebo-controlled, cross over trial. Br J Clin Pharmacol 33:477–485, 1992.

77. Sand J, Nordback I, Koskinen M, et al: Nifedipine for suspected Type II sphincter of Oddi dyskinesia. Am J Gastroenterol 88:530–535, 1993.

78. Guelrud M, Rossiter A, Souney P, et al: The effect of transcutaneous nerve stimulation on sphincter of Oddi pressure in patients with biliary dyskinesia. Am J Gastroenterol 86:581–585, 1991.

79. Lee SK, Kim MH, Kim HJ, et al: Electroacupuncture may relax the sphincter of Oddi in humans. Gastrointest Endosc 53:211–216, 2001.

80. Moody FG, Vecchio R, Calabuig R, Runkel N: Transduodenal sphincteroplasty with transampullary septectomy for stenosing papillitis. Am J Surg 161:213–218, 1991.

81. Sherman S, Hawes RH, Madura J, Lehman GA: Comparison of intraoperative and endoscopic manometry of the sphincter of Oddi. Surg Gynecol Obstet 175:410–418, 1992.

82. Chen JW, Saccone GT, Toouli J: Sphincter of Oddi dysfunction and acute pancreatitis. Gut 43:305–308, 1998.

83. Sherman S: What is the role of ERCP in the setting of abdominal pain of pancreatic or biliary origin (suspected sphincter of Oddi dysfunction)? Gastrointest Endosc 56(Suppl):258–266, 2002.

84. Rolny P, Geenen JE, Hogan WJ: Post-cholecystectomy patients with 'objective signs' of partial bile outflow obstruction: Clinical characteristics, sphincter of Oddi manometry findings, and results of therapy. Gastrointest Endosc 39:778–781, 1993.

85. Bozkurt T, Orth KH, Butsch B, Lux G: Long-term clinical outcome of post-cholecystectomy patients with biliary-type pain: Results of manometry, non-invasive techniques and endoscopic sphincterotomy. Eur J Gastroenterol Hepatol 8:245–249, 1996.

86. Wehrmann T, Wiemer K, Lembcke B, et al: Do patients with sphincter of Oddi dysfunction benefit from endoscopic sphincterotomy? A 5-year prospective trial. Eur J Gastroenterol Hepatol 8:251–256, 1996.

87. Geenen JE, Hogan WJ, Dodds WJ, et al: The efficacy of endoscopic sphincterotomy after cholecystectomy in patients with sphincter of Oddi dysfunction. N Engl J Med 320:82–87, 1989.

88. Toouli J, Roberts-Thomson I, Kellow J, et al: Prospective randomized trial of endoscopic sphincterotomy for treatment of sphincter of Oddi dysfunction. J Gastroenterol Hepatol 11:A115, 1996.

89. Toouli J, Roberts-Thomson IC, Kellow J, et al: Manometry based randomized trial of endoscopic sphincterotomy for sphincter of Oddi dysfunction. Gut 46:98–102, 2000.

90. Sherman S, Lehman GA, Jamidar P, et al: Efficacy of endoscopic sphincterotomy and surgical sphincteroplasty for patients with sphincter of Oddi dysfunction (SOD): Randomized, controlled study. Gastrointest Endosc 40:A125, 1994.

91. Guelrud M, Plaz J, Mendoza S, et al: Endoscopic treatment in Type II pancreatic sphincter dysfunction. Gastrointest Endosc 41:A398, 1995.

92. Soffer EE, Johlin FC: Intestinal dysmotility in patients with sphincter of Oddi dysfunction. A reason for failed response to sphincterotomy. Dig Dis Sci 39:1942–1946, 1994.

93. Eversman D, Fogel E, Philips S, et al: Sphincter of Oddi dysfunction (SOD): Long-term outcome of biliary sphincterotomy (BES) correlated with abnormal biliary and pancreatic sphincters. Gastrointest Endosc 49:A78, 1999.

94. Elton E, Howell DA, Parsons WG, et al: Endoscopic pancreatic sphincterotomy: Indications, outcome, and a safe stentless technique. Gastrointest Endosc 47:240–249, 1998.

95. Kaw M, Verma R, Brodmerkel GJ: Biliary and/or pancreatic sphincter of Oddi dysfunction (SOD). Response to endoscopic sphincterotomy (ES). Gastrointest Endosc 43:A384, 1996.

96. Park SH, Watkins JL, Fogel EL, et al: Long-term outcome of endoscopic dual pancreatobiliary sphincterotomy in patients with manometry-documented sphincter of Oddi dysfunction and normal pancreatogram. Gastrointest Endosc 57:483–491, 2003.

97. Freeman ML, DiSario JA, Nelson DB, et al: Risk factors for post-ERCP pancreatitis: A prospective, multicenter study. Gastrointest Endosc 54:425–434, 2001.

98. Gottlieb K, Sherman S: ERCP- and endoscopic sphincterotomy-induced pancreatitis. Gastrointest Endosc Clin N Am 8:87–114, 1998.

99. Tarnasky P, Cunningham T, Cotton P, et al: Pancreatic sphincter hypertension increases the risk of post-ERCP pancreatitis. Endoscopy 29:252–257, 1997.

100. Sherman S, Lehman GA, Freeman ML, et al: Risk factors for post-ERCP pancreatitis: A prospective multicenter study. Am J Gastroenterol 92:A1639, 1997.

101. Fogel EL, Devereaux BM, Rerknimitr R, et al: Does placement of a small diameter, long length, unflanged pancreatic duct stent reduce the incidence of post-ERCP pancreatitis? Gastrointest Endosc 51:A182, 2000.

102. Kozarek RA: Balloon dilation of the sphincter of Oddi. Endoscopy 20:207–210, 1988.

103. Pasricha PJ, Miskovsky EP, Kalloo AN: Intrasphincteric injection of botulinum toxin for suspected sphincter of Oddi dysfunction. Gut 35:1319–1321, 1994.

104. Wehrmann T, Seifert H, Seipp M, et al: Endoscopic injection of botulinum toxin for biliary sphincter of Oddi dysfunction. Endoscopy 30:702–707, 1998.

105. Heinerman PM, Graf AH, Boeckl O: Does endoscopic sphincterotomy destroy the function of Oddi's sphincter? Arch Surg 129:876–880, 1994.

106. Manoukian AV, Schmalz MJ, Geenen JE, et al: The incidence of post-sphincterotomy stenosis in Group II patients with sphincter of Oddi dysfunction. Gastrointest Endosc 39:496–498, 1993.

107. Tarnasky PR, Hoffman B, Aabakken L, et al: Sphincter of Oddi dysfunction is associated with chronic pancreatitis. Am J Gastroenterol 92:1125–1129, 1997.

108. Gregg JA: The intraductal secretin test (IDST)—an adjunct to the diagnosis of pancreatic disease and pancreatic physiology. In Sivak MV (ed): Gastroenterologic Endoscopy. Philadelphia, WB Saunders, 1987, pp 794–807.

109. Sherman S, Hawes RH, Lehman GA: Pure pancreatic juice analysis in patients with pancreatic sphincter stenosis who have undergone sphincter ablation. Am J Gastroenterol 85:A1261, 1990.

110. Wiersema MJ, Hawes RH, Lehman GA, et al: Prospective evaluation of endoscopic ultrasonography and endoscopic retrograde cholangiopancreatography in patients with chronic abdominal pain of suspected pancreatic origin. Endoscopy 25:555–564, 1993.

111. Gottlieb K, Nowak T, Sherman S, et al: Sphincter of Oddi dysfunction (SOD) and abnormal small bowel motility: Analysis of 32 patients. Gastrointest Endosc 40:A109, 1994.

112. Evans PR, Bak YT, Dowsett JF, Kellow JE: Small bowel motor dysfunction occurs in patients with biliary dyskinesia. Gastroenterology 106:A496, 1994.

113. Koussayer T, Ducker TE, Clench MH, Mathias JR: Ampulla of Vater/duodenal wall spasm diagnosed by antroduodenal manometry. Dig Dis Sci 40:1710–1719, 1995.

114. DeSautels SG, Slivka A, Hutson WR, et al: Postcholecystectomy pain syndrome: Pathophysiology of abdominal pain in sphincter of Oddi Type III. Gastroenterology 116:900–905, 1999.

115. Chun A, Desautels S, Slivka A, et al: Visceral algesia in irritable bowel syndrome, fibromyalgia, and sphincter of Oddi dysfunction, Type III. Dig Dis Sci 44:631–636, 1999.

116. Kuo WH, Pasricha PJ, Kalloo AN: The role of sphincter of Oddi manometry in the diagnosis and therapy of pancreatic disease. Gastrointest Endosc Clin N Am 8:79–85, 1998.

117. Choudari CP, Fogel EL, Sherman S, Lehman GA: Idiopathic pancreatitis: Yield of ERCP correlated with patient age. Am J Gastroenterol 93:1654A, 1998.

118. Venu RP, Geenen JE, Hogan W, et al: Idiopathic recurrent pancreatitis: An approach to diagnosis and treatment. Dig Dis Sci 34:56–60, 1989.

119. Toouli J, Roberts-Thomson IC, Dent J, Lee J: Sphincter of Oddi Motility disorders in patients with idiopathic recurrent pancreatitis. Br J Surg 72:859–863, 1985.

120. Guelrud M, Mendoz S, Viera L: Idiopathic recurrent pancreatitis and hypercontractile sphincter of Oddi. Treatment with endoscopic sphincterotomy and pancreatic duct dilation [abstract]. Gastroenterology 90:1443, 1986.

121. Gregg JA: Function and dysfunction of the sphincter of Oddi. In Jacobson IM (ed): ERCP: Diagnostic and Therapeutic Applications. New York, Elsevier, 1989, pp 137–170.

122. Sherman S, Jamidar P, Reber H: Idiopathic acute pancreatitis (IAP): Endoscopic diagnosis and therapy. Am J Gastroenterol 88:1541A, 1993.

123. Kaw M, Brodmerkel GJ: ERCP, biliary crystal analysis, and sphincter of Oddi manometry in idiopathic pancreatitis. Gastrointest Endosc 55:157–162, 2002.

124. Coyle WJ, Pineau BC, Tarnasky PR, et al: Evaluation of unexplained acute and acute recurrent pancreatitis using endoscopic retrograde cholangiopancreatography, sphincter of Oddi manometry, and endoscopic ultrasound. Endoscopy 34:617–623, 2002.

125. Tarnasky PR, Hawes RH: Endoscopic diagnosis and therapy of unexplained (idiopathic) acute pancreatitis. Gastrointest Endosc Clin N Am 8:13–37, 1998.

126. Ros E, Navarro S, Bru C, et al: Occult microlithiasis in "idiopathic" acute pancreatitis: Prevention of relapses by cholecystectomy or ursodeoxycholic acid therapy. Gastroenterology 101:1701–1709, 1991.

127. Toouli J, Di Francesco V, Saccone G, et al: Division of the sphincter of Oddi for treatment of dysfunction associated with recurrent pancreatitis. Br J Surg 83:1205–1210, 1996.

128. Okolo PI 3rd, Pasricha PJ, Kalloo AN: What are the long-term results of endoscopic pancreatic sphincterotomy? Gastrointest Endosc 52:15–19, 2000.

129. Jacob L, Geenen JE, Catalano MF, Geenen DJ: Prevention of pancreatitis in patients with idiopathic recurrent pancreatitis: A prospective nonblinded randomized study using endoscopic stents. Endoscopy 33:559–562, 2001.

130. Testoni PA, Caporuscio S, Bagnolo F, Lella F: Idiopathic recurrent pancreatitis: Long-term results after ERCP, endoscopic sphincterotomy, or ursodeoxycholic acid treatment. Am J Gastroenterol 95:1702–1707, 2000.

131. Wehrmann T, Schmitt TH, Arndt A, et al: Endoscopic injection of botulinum toxin in patients with recurrent acute pancreatitis due to pancreatic sphincter of Oddi dysfunction. Aliment Pharmacol Ther 14:1469–1477, 2000.

Acute Pancreatitis and Peripancreatic Fluid Collections

CHAPTER

50

Todd H. Baron

Introduction

Acute pancreatitis may be clinically mild or severe. Clinically severe acute pancreatitis is usually a result of pancreatic glandular necrosis. The morbidity and mortality of acute pancreatitis are significantly higher when pancreatic necrosis is present, especially when infection of the necrosis occurs.[1] It is important to identify patients with pancreatic necrosis so that appropriate management can be undertaken. The management of patients with necrotizing pancreatitis has shifted from early surgical débridement (necrosectomy) to aggressive intensive medical care. Specific criteria for operative or nonoperative intervention have been developed.[2,3] Advances in radiologic imaging and aggressive medical management with emphasis on prevention of infection have allowed for prompt identification of complications and improvement in outcome for these patients.[4]

Several types of pancreatic and peripancreatic fluid collections may arise because of acute pancreatitis.[5] These include acute fluid collections, acute pancreatic pseudocysts, pancreatic abscesses, and organized pancreatic necrosis.

This chapter reviews the recent advances in the diagnosis and treatment of acute pancreatitis and peripancreatic fluid collections.

Acute Pancreatitis

PRESENTATION AND CLASSIFICATION

Acute pancreatitis usually has a rapid onset manifested by upper abdominal pain, vomiting, fever, tachycardia, leukocytosis, and elevated serum levels of pancreatic enzymes. Gallstone- and alcohol-induced pancreatitis are the most common causes in the United States. Causes of pancreatitis are listed in Box 50–1. Several severity of illness classifications for acute pancreatitis are used to identify patients at risk for developing complications (Box 50–2).[6,7]

Ranson's score consists of 11 clinical signs with prognostic significance: five criteria are measured at the time of admission; six criteria are measured between admission and 48 hours later. There is good correlation between the number of Ranson signs and the incidence of systemic complications and presence of pancreatic necrosis.[6] The Acute Physiology And Chronic Health Evaluation (APACHE) II score is a grading system based on 12 physiologic variables, patient age, and prior history of severe organ system insufficiency or immunocompromised state[6] (see Box 50–2). It allows stratification of illness severity on admission and may be recalculated daily. Severe acute pancreatitis is present if there are three or more Ranson's criteria, if the APACHE II score is 8 or more, or if clinical findings of one or more of shock or renal or pulmonary insufficiency are present.[6] The Glasgow scoring system is yet another classification system[7] (see Box 50–2). Unlike Ranson criteria, the variables apply if they occur at any time within 48 hours.

Box 50–1. Causes of Acute Pancreatitis

Most Common

   Choledocholithiasis
   Ethanol
   Idiopathic

Less Common

   Endoscopic retrograde cholangiopancreatography
   Hyperlipidemia (types I, IV, and V)
   Drugs
   Pancreas divisum
   Abdominal trauma
   Hereditary (familial)
   Sphincter of Oddi dysfunction

Box 50–2. Severity Scores for Acute Pancreatitis

A. Ranson's Criteria of Severity

At admission

Age >55 years

White blood cell count >16,000/mm³

Blood glucose >200 mg/dL

Serum lactate dehydrogenase >350 IU/L

Serum glutamic-oxaloacetic transaminase >250 IU/L

During initial 48 hours

Hematocrit fall >10%

Blood urea nitrogen rise >5 mg/dL

Serum calcium <8 mg/dL

Arterial Pao₂ <60 mmHg

Base deficit >4 mEq/L

Fluid sequestration >6 L

Score ≥3 is considered severe

B. APACHE II Score[5]

= Acute physiology score + Age points + Chronic health points

Score ≥8 is considered severe

C. Glasgow Criteria

Within 48 hours of hospitalization

Age >55 years

White blood cell count >15 000/mm³

Glucose >180 mg/dL

Blood urea nitrogen >45 mg/dL

Lactate dehydrogenase >600 IU/L

Albumin <3.3 g/dL

Calcium <8 mg/dL

Arterial oxygen tension <60 mm Hg

Score ≥3 is considered severe

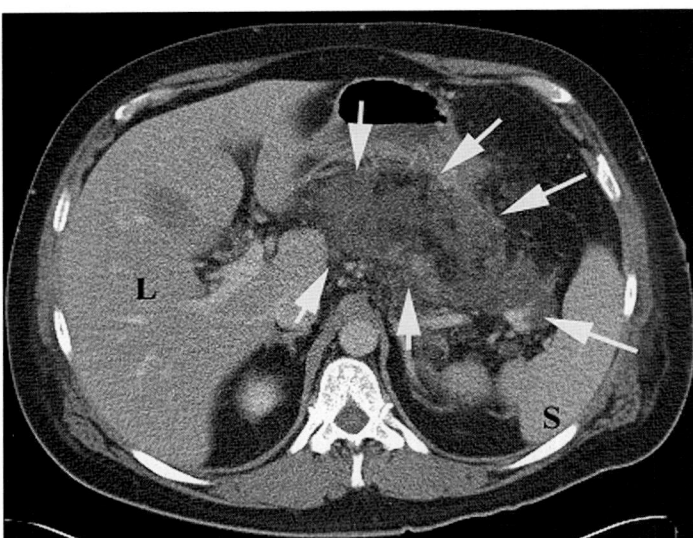

Figure 50–1. Contrast-enhanced abdominal computed tomography (CT) scan of severe necrotizing pancreatitis. Note the contrast enhancement of the liver (L) and spleen (S); the normal enhancing pancreas has a similar density. In this case there is little or no uptake into the pancreas *(arrows).*

Acute pancreatitis may be classified histologically as interstitial-edematous or necrotizing based on the inflammatory changes of the pancreatic parenchyma.[8] According to the International Symposium on Acute Pancreatitis in 1992, pancreatic necrosis is defined as one or more diffuse or focal area(s) of nonviable pancreatic parenchyma (Fig. 50–1).[8] Pancreatic glandular necrosis is usually associated with peripancreatic fat necrosis.[8–10] By definition, the presence of pancreatic necrosis represents a severe form of acute pancreatitis.[8] Approximately 20% to 30% of the 185,000 new cases of acute pancreatitis per year in the United States are necrotizing.[11,12]

MANAGEMENT OF MILD DISEASE

The management of patients with clinically mild or interstitial pancreatitis is almost entirely supportive. This form of pancreatitis generally has a self-limiting course. There is no role for antibiotic therapy or nutritional support. The goal of management is to identify the etiology of the pancreatitis and to treat it appropriately. Identification of gallstones, in the absence of other factors, should be managed with cholecystectomy. Potentially offending drugs should be discontinued and hyperlipidemia should be addressed. If there is alcohol abuse, a rehabilitation program should be offered to the patient.

In some patients, an etiology for acute pancreatitis is not identified and recurrent attacks occur. The management of this patient group is controversial, specifically as it relates to sphincter of Oddi dysfunction and pancreas divisum (Chapters 49 and 51). There are data to support pursuing endoscopic evaluation of these entities,[13] although there are no randomized trials proving effectiveness of endoscopic therapy.[14]

IDENTIFICATION AND CLINICAL IMPORTANCE OF PANCREATIC NECROSIS

Pancreatic necrosis may be pathologically identified at surgery or autopsy. The radiographic diagnosis of pancreatic necrosis is determined by dynamic intravenous contrast-enhanced abdominal computed tomography (CT).[9] Because the normal pancreatic microcirculation is disrupted during acute necrotizing pancreatitis, contrast-enhanced abdominal CT demonstrates a lack of normal contrast enhancement of affected portions of the pancreas (see Fig. 50–1).[15] This may be better detected several days after initial clinical presentation. Contrast-enhanced abdominal CT is the gold standard for noninvasive diagnosis of pancreatic necrosis, with an accuracy of more than 90% when more than 30% glandular necrosis is present.[9] The presence of radiographically detected pancreatic necrosis markedly increases the morbidity and mortality associated with acute pancreatitis.[16] As the percentage of glandular necrosis increases, the morbidity increases. Theoretically, contrast medium may cause significant additional reductions of capillary flow, which has been shown to aggravate acute pancreatitis in experimental studies. However, a recent study in men with severe acute pancreatitis compared a patient group who did not receive contrast medium to those that did. Those who were administered contrast medium did not exhibit a deterioration of acute pancreatitis.[17]

The overall mortality in severe acute pancreatitis is approximately 30%.[12] The mortality occurs in two phases. Early deaths (1 to

2 weeks after onset of pancreatitis) are due to multisystem organ failure from release of inflammatory mediators and cytokines.[1] Late deaths result from local or systemic infections.[18] As long as acute necrotizing pancreatitis remains sterile, the overall mortality is approximately 10%. The mortality rate at least triples if infected necrosis occurs.[11] In addition, patients with sterile necrosis and high severity of illness scores (Ranson's scores, APACHE-II scores) accompanied by multisystem organ failure, shock, or renal insufficiency have a significantly higher mortality.[19]

A myriad of systemic and local complications of acute necrotizing pancreatitis may occur. Systemic complications have been detailed elsewhere[2] but include acute respiratory distress syndrome, acute renal failure, shock, coagulopathy, hyperglycemia, and hypocalcemia. Local complications include gastrointestinal bleeding, infected necrosis, and adjacent bowel necrosis. Late local complications that may require therapy include development of pancreatic abscess or pancreatic pseudocyst. Early therapy of acute necrotizing pancreatitis consists of the combination of aggressive supportive intensive medical care and prevention of infection using prophylactic antibiotics. Late management requires recognition of local infectious complications (pancreatic infection) and the initiation of aggressive débridement strategies. Infected necrosis develops in 30% to 70% of patients with acute necrotizing pancreatitis and accounts for more than 80% of deaths from acute pancreatitis.[1,3] The risk of infected necrosis increases with increasing amounts of pancreatic glandular necrosis and length of time from onset of acute pancreatitis, peaking at 3 weeks.[1,3]

INFECTION IN ACUTE NECROTIZING PANCREATITIS

Because the development of infected necrosis significantly increases the mortality of acute necrotizing pancreatitis, prevention of infection is critical. In experimental acute necrotizing pancreatitis, pancreatic infection occurs primarily as a result of bacterial translocation from the colon.[20] Several animal studies have demonstrated a decrease in pancreatic infection and mortality using orally administered antibiotics to selectively decontaminate the gut or intravenous antibiotics with high pancreatic tissue penetration.[20–22] Similarly, human studies have shown benefits from orally administered antibiotics with or without rectally administered antibiotics to selectively decontaminate the gut.[23,24] Because selective gut decontamination antibiotics must be administered orally and rectally, use of this regimen is problematic from a nursing standpoint and has not gained acceptance. Therefore, the use of systemic antibiotics for the prevention of pancreatic infection has been used almost exclusively.

Schmid and coworkers[25] described efficacy factors for the use of prophylactic antibiotics in the setting of severe pancreatitis. Based on the bacteriology of pathogens found in pancreatic infections, the minimal inhibitory concentrations of the pathogens, and the tissue penetration of the antibiotic, an efficacy factor was assigned to the then available antibiotics (1.0 ideal, 0 no effect). Imipenem was assigned an efficacy factor of 0.98. Indeed, early studies of systemically administered broad-spectrum antibiotics focused on the use of intravenous imipenem-cilastatin (Primaxin).[26,27] Since then, numerous studies have been published in both animals and humans concerning the use of prophylactic antibiotics. A meta-analysis performed using randomized, controlled trials that compared antibiotic prophylaxis with no prophylaxis in patients with acute necrotizing pancreatitis found that antibiotic prophylaxis significantly reduced sepsis by 21.1% and mortality by 12.3% compared with no prophylaxis.[28] There was also a nonsignificant trend toward a decrease in local pancreatic infections.

At present, administration of prophylactic antibiotics using intravenous antibiotics with excellent pancreatic tissue penetration (mezlocillin or imipenem-cilastatin alone or fluoroquinolones with or without clindamycin or metronidazole) is recommended. Antibiotics should begin as soon as the diagnosis of acute necrotizing pancreatitis is made, and there are no data to guide the duration of therapy. It is reasonable to continue antibiotics for at least 2 to 4 weeks. More studies are needed to provide more precise recommendations regarding exact antibiotic regimens and duration of therapy.[29]

Interestingly, since the institution of broad-spectrum antibiotics for prophylaxis of infection, there has been a shift in bacteriology of infected necrosis from gram-negative organisms to gram-positive and fungal organisms.[30] The clinical implications of this finding are unclear at this time but suggest that prophylactic antibiotic therapy for acute pancreatis will continue to evolve.

Sterile and infected acute necrotizing pancreatitis can be difficult to distinguish clinically because both may produce fever, leukocytosis, and severe abdominal pain. The distinction is important, because the mortality in patients with infected acute necrotizing pancreatitis without intervention is nearly 100%.[11] The bacteriologic status of the pancreas may be determined by CT-guided fine needle aspiration of pancreatic and peripancreatic tissue or fluid (Fig. 50–2).[31] This aspiration method is safe and accurate with a sensitivity of 96% and specificity of 99% and is recommended in patients with acute necrotizing pancreatitis who clinically deteriorate or fail to improve clinically despite aggressive supportive care.[2] Ultrasound-guided aspiration may have a lower sensitivity and specificity[32] but can be performed at the bedside. Surveillance aspiration may be repeated on a weekly basis as clinically indicated.

ROLE OF ENDOSCOPIC RETROGRADE CHOLANGIOPANCREATOGRAPHY IN SEVERE ACUTE GALLSTONE PANCREATITIS

Gallstone pancreatitis is caused by impaction of a stone within the common channel of the ampulla of Vater. In most cases the stone passes without therapy. That endoscopic retrograde cholangiopancreatography (ERCP) and biliary sphincterotomy improves the outcome of gallstone pancreatitis is based on the idea that removing an impacted stone will relieve obstruction to the flow of pancreatic secretions. Initial studies using urgent (within 72 hours of admission) ERCP and biliary sphincterotomy (if a stone is identified) in patients with acute gallstone pancreatitis and choledocholithiasis showed an improved outcome in only the group of patients presenting with clinically severe acute pancreatitis.[33] The improvement was attributed to relief of pancreatic ductal obstruction produced by an impacted gallstone in the common biliary–pancreatic channel of the ampulla of Vater.

More recent studies suggest that the improved outcome after ERCP and sphincterotomy in gallstone pancreatitis results from

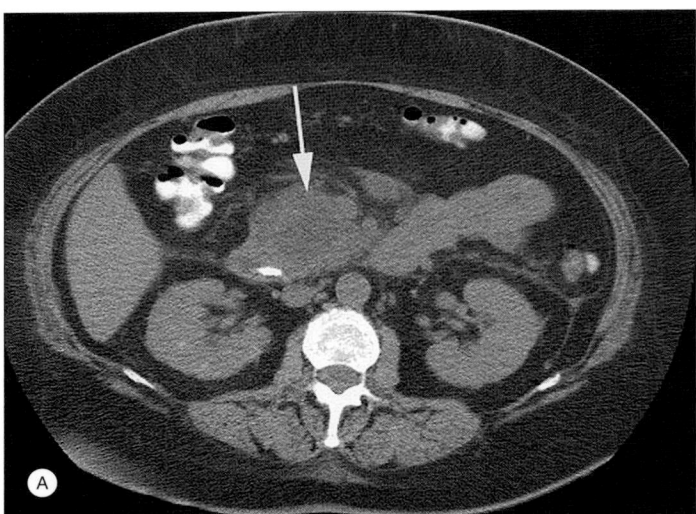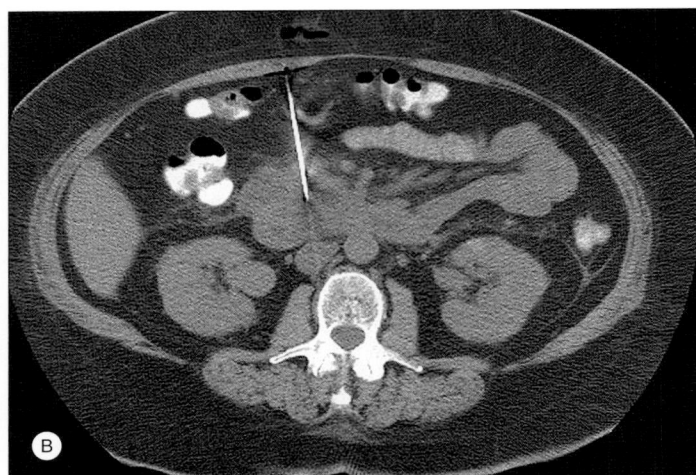

Figure 50–2. Computed tomography (CT)-guided fine-needle aspiration of suspected infected pancreatic necrosis. *A,* CT scan shows necrotic area *(arrow)* within the pancreatic head. *B,* Under CT guidance an 18-gauge needle is passed into the necrotic area.

reduced biliary sepsis rather than from a true improvement in pancreatitis.[34,35] In the presence of pancreatic ductal disruption, a frequent occurrence in acute necrotizing pancreatitis,[36] introduction of infection by incidental pancreatography during ERCP may theoretically occur, transforming acute necrotizing pancreatitis from sterile to infected. Therefore, ERCP must be used judiciously in patients with severe acute gallstone pancreatitis and reserved for patients with suspected biliary obstruction based on hyperbilirubinemia and clinical cholangitis, because it is unlikely that the ampulla is obstructed in the presence of a normal serum bilirubin.[37]

Current evidence supports the use of ERCP for patients with clinically severe gallstone pancreatitis. Further studies are needed to clarify the role of other imaging modalities, such as endoscopic ultrasonography (EUS) and magnetic resonance cholangiopancreatography (MRCP), in patients with severe biliary pancreatitis, with the goal of selectively performing ERCP in patients with documented bile duct stones.[7] An additional question to be answered is whether an empiric biliary sphincterotomy should be performed if no bile duct stones are identified.

NUTRITIONAL SUPPORT FOR ACUTE NECROTIZING PANCREATITIS

To meet increased metabolic demands and to rest the pancreas, total parenteral nutrition (TPN) administered through a central venous catheter is often used for nutritional support in patients with acute necrotizing pancreatitis. TPN does not hasten resolution of acute pancreatitis[38] or preserve gut integrity, an important factor in preventing bacterial translocation. In two randomized prospective studies of patients with severe acute pancreatitis, patients were randomized to either TPN or enteral feeding (through a nasoenteric feeding tube placed radiographically beyond the ligament of Treitz) instituted within 48 hours of illness onset.[39,40] Enteral feeding was well tolerated without adverse clinical effects and resulted in significantly fewer total and infectious complications; the cost of nutritional support was threefold higher in the TPN group.[39] Acute phase

response and disease severity scores were significantly improved after enteral nutrition.[40] It appears that this form of enteral feeding is preferable in patients with acute necrotizing pancreatitis in the absence of a significant ileus.[38,41]

Even more recently, this approach has been extended to nasogastric feeding. In a prospective pilot series, 26 patients with objective evidence of severe acute pancreatitis received nasogastric feeding within 48 hours of hospital admission.[42] It was well tolerated in 22 patients. There was no evidence of clinical or biochemical deterioration with institution of nasogastric feeding. Further study is needed to assess whether this is as safe and efficacious as nasojejunal feeding.

There are a variety of endoscopic techniques for placing nasojejunal feeding tubes in acute pancreatitis.[43] One method avoids the need to transfer the guidewire from the mouth to the nose. An ultrathin endoscope is passed transnasally into the duodenum.[44] A guidewire is then advanced through the endoscope beyond the ligament of Treitz. The endoscope is withdrawn, leaving the guidewire in place. The tube is then passed over the guidewire under fluoroscopic guidance.

INTERVENTIONS FOR NECROSIS

The timing and type of pancreatic intervention for patients with acute necrotizing pancreatitis are controversial. Because the mortality from sterile acute necrotizing pancreatitis is approximately 10% and surgical intervention has not been shown to lower this figure, most investigators recommend supportive medical therapy in this group.[11] Conversely, infected acute necrotizing pancreatitis is traditionally considered uniformly fatal without intervention,[11] although two recent small retrospective studies found that antibiotic therapy alone was effective in a select group of patients.[45,46] Aggressive surgical pancreatic débridement (necrosectomy) remains the standard of care if drainage is undertaken and may require multiple abdominal re-explorations.[41] Necrosectomy should be undertaken soon after confirmation of infected necrosis.

The role of surgery in patients with multisystem organ failure and sterile necrosis remains unproved, although this scenario is often cited as an indication for surgical débridement.[47] In addition, the longer surgical intervention can be delayed from the onset of acute necrotizing pancreatitis, the better the patient survival.[48] This is probably related to improved demarcation between viable and necrotic tissue at the time of operation. The role of delayed necrosectomy (after resolution of multisystem organ failure) in sterile acute necrotizing pancreatitis likewise remains controversial. Some investigators advocate débridement in patients who remain systemically ill 4 to 6 weeks after onset of acute pancreatitis with fever, weight loss, intractable abdominal pain, inability to eat, and failure to thrive.[2,49,50] However, others believe that delayed necrosectomy is unnecessary as long as the process remains sterile.[50]

Surgical Débridement

Surgical methods for treatment of necrosis vary. There are three main types of surgical débridement: conventional drainage, open or semiopen procedures, or closed procedures.[41] Conventional drainage involves necrosectomy with placement of standard surgical drains and reoperation on demand (fever, leukocytosis, lack of improvement by imaging studies). Open or semiopen management uses necrosectomy and either scheduled repeat laparotomies or open packing that leaves the abdominal wound exposed for frequent dressing changes. Closed management involves necrosectomy with extensive intraoperative lavage of the pancreatic bed. The abdomen is closed over large-bore drains for continuous high-volume postoperative lavage of the lesser sac. Most surgeons have abandoned the conventional surgical approach of débridement, because inadequately removed necrotic tissue becomes or remains infected and results in a mortality of approximately 40%.[3]

In all procedures except the closed technique, multiple operations are often required to remove the necrotic pancreatic and peripancreatic material.[3] Leaving the abdomen open avoids the need for formal laparotomies; packing may be changed in the intensive care unit. Repeated débridement and manipulation of the abdominal viscera using the open and semiopen techniques results in a high rate of postoperative local complications such as pancreatic fistulas, small- and large-bowel complications, and bleeding from the pancreatic bed. Pancreatic and/or gastrointestinal tract fistulas occur in up to 41% of patients after surgical necrosectomy and often require additional surgery for closure.[51,52] The mortality using open or closed techniques is approximately 20%.[3]

Alternative Débridement Methods

Alternative methods for débridement of pancreatic necrosis have been very recently described and require considerable technical expertise. As more data become available, the precise role of these techniques in the management of patients with necrotizing pancreatitis will become better defined.

Percutaneous (Interventional Radiology) Therapy

Successful percutaneous therapy for infected acute necrotizing pancreatitis has been described using large-bore percutaneous

catheters up to 28-Fr diameter in conjunction with aggressive irrigation.[53] A total of 34 patients had percutaneous drainage and irrigation catheters inserted into the pancreatic collection at a mean of 9 days after hospital admission for necrotizing pancreatitis with medically uncontrolled sepsis. An average of three separate catheter sites per patient and four catheter exchanges per patient were necessary for removal of necrotic material. Pancreatic surgery was completely avoided in 16 patients (47%). Control of sepsis with delayed elective surgery for repair of external pancreatic fistulas related to catheter placement was achieved in nine patients. Nine patients required immediate surgery for failure of percutaneous therapy. The mortality was 12% in this ill group, many of whom suffered from multisystem organ failure. In a similar fashion, Echenique and colleagues[54] described successful percutaneous drainage of necrosis in 20 patients with documented necrosis. Solid debris was removed percutaneously using basket extraction techniques.

Endoscopic Therapy

Successful endoscopic drainage of symptomatic sterile or infected pancreatic necrosis has been described several weeks after the onset of severe necrotizing pancreatitis.[55] This therapy uses endoscopic placement of internal 10-Fr transmural (transgastric or transduodenal) drainage catheters plus a 7-Fr nasopancreatic irrigation tube into the retroperitoneum. The catheters are placed through a tract dilated up to 20 mm (Fig. 50–3). With this method, solid debris flows around the catheters through the transenteric tract. Complete nonsurgical resolution has been achieved in up to 84% patients with this form of late, or organized pancreatic necrosis.[56]

Complications of endoscopic therapy (described in more detail in the section on peripancreatic fluid collections) include perforation, bleeding, and infection. Adjuvant percutaneous drains are occasionally required to drain peripheral collections away from the body of the pancreas.

Summary

The drainage options for patients with pancreatic necrosis are expanding. The experience using newer, nonsurgical drainage procedures is limited, and no interdisciplinary comparative data exist. When deciding on the timing or treatment modality to be used in these complex patients, the expertise of the local surgeon, interventional endoscopist, and interventional radiologist must be considered. Nonsurgical drainage of pancreatic necrosis, whether performed acutely in the first weeks or subacutely at 1 month or more after the onset of pancreatitis, should be undertaken only by expert interventional endoscopists or interventional radiologists familiar with the potential complications and time required for successful pancreatic drainage. It is important to emphasize that improperly drained sterile necrosis may lead to life-threatening infected necrosis. An upfront team approach in planning pancreatic interventions is useful, because some patients may benefit from multimodality drainage. The decision to intervene should be based on infection of the necrosis or, in the setting of sterile necrosis, severe clinical symptoms such as gastric outlet obstruction, intractable abdominal pain, or failure to thrive.[57]

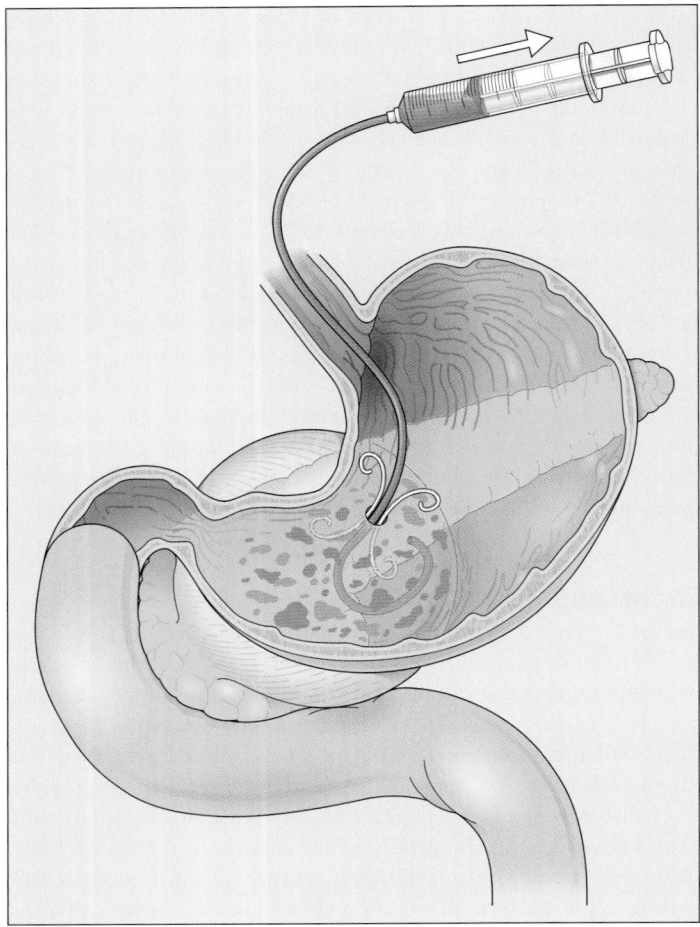

Figure 50–3. Transmural drainage of organized pancreatic necrosis. Two stents are placed transgastrically alongside a nasobiliary irrigation tube. The transgastric tract is dilated to a large caliber (15 to 20 mm) to allow egress of solid material around the stents. (Redrawn with permission from Baron TH, Harewood GC, Morgan DE, Yates MR: Outcome differences after endoscopic drainage of pancreatic necrosis, acute pancreatic pseudocysts, and chronic pancreatic pseudocysts. Gastrointest Endosc 56:7–17, 2002.)

LONG-TERM SEQUELAE OF ACUTE NECROTIZING PANCREATITIS

Despite the enormous cost of caring for patients with acute necrotizing pancreatitis, mean quality of life outcomes up to 2 years after treatment of pancreatic necrosis are similar to those obtained with coronary artery bypass grafting.[58] The long-term clinical endocrine and exocrine consequences of acute necrotizing pancreatitis appear to depend on several factors, including the severity of necrosis, etiology (alcoholic versus nonalcoholic), continued use of alcohol, and the degree of surgical pancreatic débridement.[59,60] Sophisticated exocrine function studies show persistent functional insufficiency in most patients up to 2 years after severe acute pancreatitis.[61] Use of pancreatic enzymes should be restricted to patients with symptoms of steatorrhea and weight loss resulting from fat malabsorption. Although subtle glucose intolerance is frequent, overt diabetes mellitus is uncommon.[62] Follow-up pancreatography often reveals obstructive pancreatic ductal abnormalities that may account for persistent symptoms of abdominal pain or acute recurrent pancreatitis (Fig. 50–4).[63]

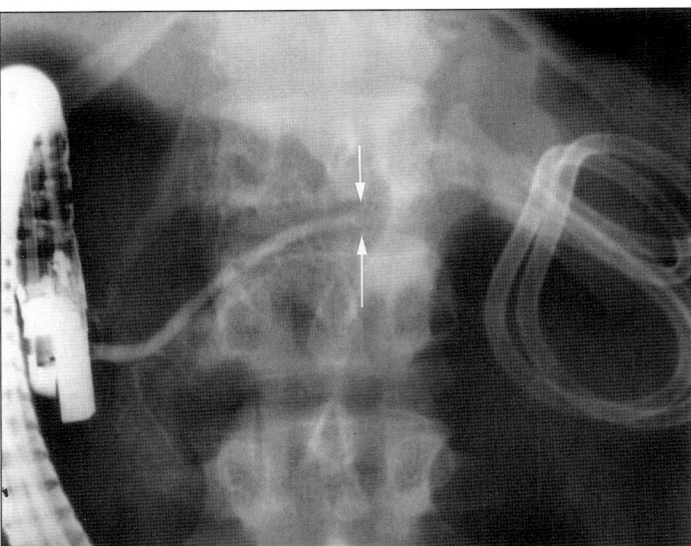

Figure 50–4. Complete cutoff of main pancreatic duct *(arrows)* demonstrated at endoscopic retrograde cholangiopancreatography (ERCP) at the time of removal transgastric double pigtail stents (visible) after successful endoscopic drainage of organized pancreatic necrosis.

OTHER MEDICAL THERAPIES

Platelet-activating factor (PAF), a proinflammatory cytokine, is implicated in the pathophysiology of systemic organ failure in severe acute pancreatitis. PAF antagonists significantly improve both inflammatory changes and survival in animals.[64] An initial randomized trial that compared placebo to a PAF antagonist (lexipafant) showed a significant reduction in the incidence of organ failure at 72 hours.[65] Unfortunately, a subsequent randomized, double-blind, placebo-controlled, multicenter trial of almost 300 patients with severe acute pancreatitis failed to demonstrate any improvement with lexipafant. Lexipafant had no effect on new organ failure, and antagonism of PAF activity on its own does not appear sufficient to ameliorate the severe systemic inflammatory response in severe acute pancreatitis.[66]

SUMMARY OF MANAGEMENT OF SEVERE ACUTE PANCREATITIS

Box 50–3 summarizes the overall approach to the management of acute pancreatitis.

Pancreatic and Peripancreatic Fluid Collections

Pancreatic fluid collections arise as complication of acute and chronic pancreatitis or pancreatic trauma (including postsurgical). Pancreatic fluid collections that occur as a result of acute pancreatitis include acute fluid collections, pancreatic pseudocysts, pancreatic abscesses, and organized pancreatic necrosis (Table 50–1). These collections are amenable to endoscopic drainage. This section outlines the nomenclature, endoscopic drainage methods,

Table 50–1. Types of Pancreatic Fluid Collection Complicating Acute Pancreatitis

Term	Definition
Acute fluid collection	A collection of enzyme-rich pancreatic juice occurring early (within 48 hours) in the course of acute pancreatitis; located in or near the pancreas and always lacks a well-defined wall of granulation tissue or fibrous tissue
Acute pseudocyst	A collection of pancreatic juice enclosed by a wall of nonepithelialized granulation tissue; arises as a consequence of acute pancreatitis, requires at least 4 weeks to form and is devoid of significant solid debris
Pancreatic necrosis (early)	A diffuse or focal area of nonviable pancreatic parenchyma greater than 30% of the gland by contrast-enhanced CT; typically associated with peripancreatic fat necrosis
Organized pancreatic necrosis (late)	Evolution of acute necrosis to a partially encapsulated, well-defined collection of pancreatic juice and necrotic debris
Pancreatic abscess	A circumscribed intra-abdominal collection of pus, usually in proximity to the pancreas, containing little or no pancreatic necrosis; arises as a consequence of acute pancreatitis or pancreatic trauma

Box 50–3. Keys to Successful Management of Acute Necrotizing Pancreatitis

Identify Necrosis

Clinically severe using severity of index scores

Computed tomography (CT) scan demonstrating significant pancreatic necrosis: ≥30% glandular necrosis by contrast-enhanced CT

Intensive Care Unit Management for Clinically Severe Acute Pancreatitis

Supportive care

Antibiotics for radiographically documented pancreatic necrosis

Strongly consider endoscopic retrograde cholangiography for gallstone pancreatitis when jaundice or cholangitis are present

Nutritional support: enteral feeding via nasoenteric tube beyond ligament of Treitz (in the absence of significant ileus)

Identification of Infected Necrosis

CT-guided or sonographically guided fine needle aspiration

Débridement of Infected Necrosis

Operative management

Alternative débridement techniques (percutaneous or endoscopic) in selected centers with expertise

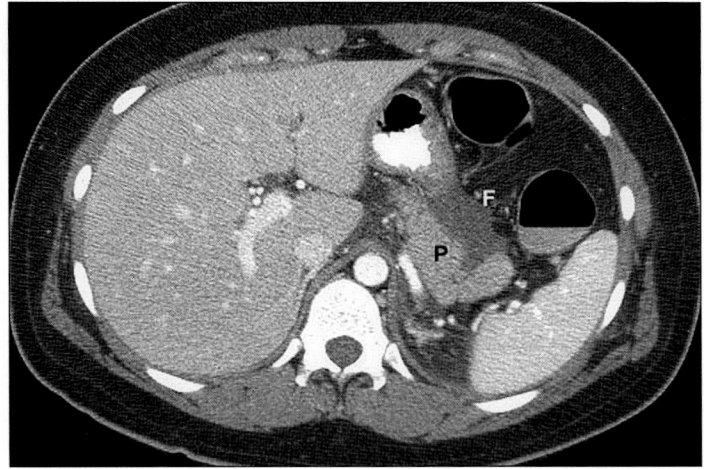

Figure 50–5. Acute fluid collection. Note fluid (F) present adjacent to the pancreas and stomach. Normal enhancement of the pancreas (P) is seen.

and outcomes after endoscopic intervention of pancreatic fluid collections. Although there are other drainage options for these collections (percutaneous and surgical), these are not discussed in detail.

Many gastroenterologists assume that any pancreatic fluid collection arising as a consequence of acute pancreatitis represents a pancreatic pseudocyst. This is incorrect and it is important to recognize that several distinct entities fall under the general terms of peripancreatic and pancreatic fluid collections.

Endoscopic therapy of pancreatic fluid collections is relatively new as compared with percutaneous and surgical therapy. Rogers and coworkers[67] reported the first description of endoscopic intervention of a pancreatic fluid collection in 1973 when simple transgastric aspiration (without successful resolution) of a pancreatic pseudocyst was performed. In 1984, Hershfield[68] described the first successful transpapillary aspiration (via the minor papilla) and resolution of a pancreatic pseudocyst. In 1985, Kozarek and colleagues[69] reported transmural (transgastric and transduodenal) placement of endoprosthesis into pancreatic pseudocysts in four patients. Subsequently, a large body of literature describing endoscopic drainage of pancreatic fluid collections has emerged.

TYPES OF COLLECTION

The types of pancreatic fluid collection occurring as a result of acute pancreatitis are acute fluid collections, pancreatic necrosis, pancreatic abscess, and pancreatic pseudocysts.

Acute Fluid Collections

Acute fluid collections arise early in the course of acute pancreatitis, are usually peripancreatic in location, and usually resolve without sequelae but may evolve into pancreatic pseudocysts (Fig. 50–5). Acute fluid collections rarely require drainage.[5,70]

Acute Pancreatic Pseudocyst

Acute pancreatic pseudocysts arise as a sequela of acute pancreatitis, require at least 4 weeks to form, and are devoid of significant solid debris (Fig. 50–6A). The mechanism of formation of an acute pancreatic pseudocyst is usually a result of limited pancreatic necrosis that produces a pancreatic ductal leak (see Fig. 50–6B and C). Alternatively, areas of pancreatic and peripancreatic fat necrosis may completely liquefy over time and become a pseudocyst.[71] Despite the requirement of at least 4 weeks for a pseudocyst to

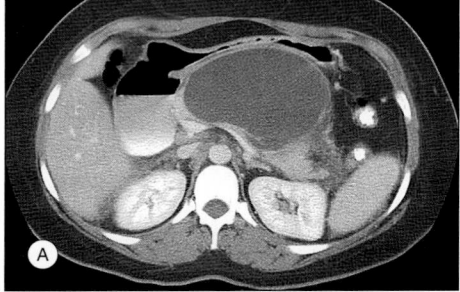

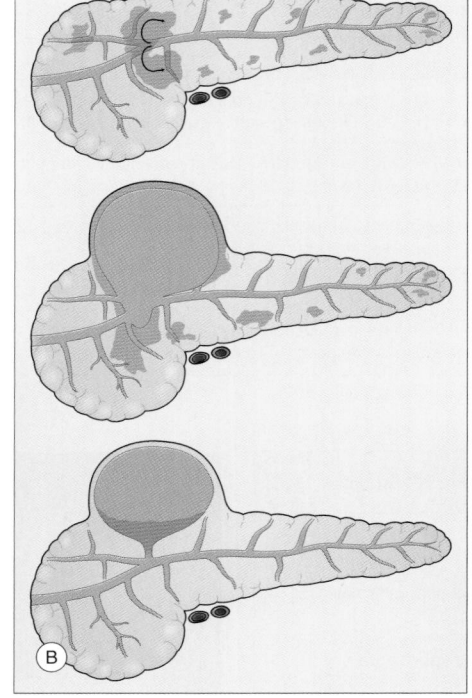

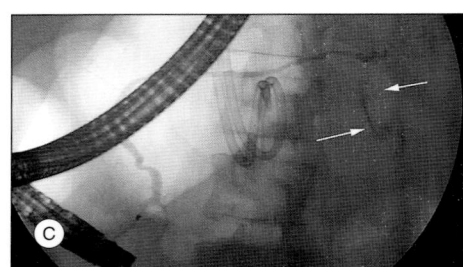

Figure 50–6. Acute pseudocyst. *A,* Computed tomography (CT) demonstrates a homogeneous collection arising 4 weeks after clinically mild acute pancreatitis. *B,* Illustration of the mechanism of formation of an acute pancreatic pseudocyst. Limited necrosis of the main pancreatic duct produces a leak with accumulation of amylase-rich fluid. *C,* Pancreatogram in the same patient as in *A,* showing intact main duct with side-branch leak *(arrows).* (*B* Redrawn with permission from Bradley EL 3rd (ed): Acute Pancreatitis: Diagnosis and Therapy. New York, Raven Press, 1994, p 73.)

form, it is important to note that this time period in and of itself does not define the collection as a pancreatic pseudocyst. Patients with significant pancreatic necrosis (>30%) may evolve the early acute pancreatic necrosis and peripancreatic necrosis into a collection that resembles a pseudocyst radiographically but has been present for 4 or more weeks (see the section on organized pancreatic necrosis). By definition, if these collections contain significant solid debris, they are not pseudocysts and endoscopic treatment of these collections by typical pseudocyst drainage methods may result in infectious complications because of inadequate removal of solid debris.[55,72]

Organized Pancreatic Necrosis

Pancreatic necrosis is defined as nonviable pancreatic parenchyma, usually with associated peripancreatic fat necrosis.[8] In the earliest form, this is detected radiographically on contrast-enhanced CT by the presence of nonenhancing pancreatic parenchyma (see Fig. 50–1). Pancreatic necrosis is often accompanied by the development of major pancreatic ductal disruptions.[73] Over the course of several weeks, the collection may continue to evolve and expand the initial area of necrosis and contain both liquid and solid debris (Fig. 50–7). We have used the term organized pancreatic necrosis to differentiate this process from the early (acute phase) of pancreatic necrosis.[55,56,74] As mentioned in the previous paragraph, the radiographic appearance of organized pancreatic necrosis on CT may be similar to that of an acute pseudocyst. Because the underlying solid debris is often not discernible by CT,[75] its homogeneous appearance may lead one to embark on standard pseudocyst drainage methods,

which do not adequately remove the underlying solid material. This may result in serious infectious complications.[55,72,76]

The distinction between an acute pseudocyst and organized necrosis may be made on clinical, radiologic, or endoscopic findings at the time of drainage. Clinically, if the patient suffered a severe or complicated course of acute pancreatitis, it is likely that pancreatic necrosis occurred and is present within the collection. Radiographically, several features indicate the presence of underlying solid material within the collection. First, if an initial contrast-enhanced CT scan obtained at the time of, or soon after, the initial bout of pancreatitis demonstrated significant glandular necrosis, the collection probably contains solid debris. Second, the evolution of changes on serial CT scans can be traced from the original pancreatic glandular necrosis to the present collection. Third, we have shown that magnetic resonance imaging (MRI) before attempted drainage can delineate the solid debris within the collection (Fig. 50–8).[75] Lastly, a repeat abdominal CT scan after endoscopic drainage will depict solid material once some of the liquid component has been evacuated (Fig. 50–9).[76]

Endoscopic findings at the time of drainage may alert the endoscopist to the presence of necrotic debris within the collection. If the collection is drained transmurally, solid material may be seen to flow from the collection; the presence of chocolate-brown or extremely turbid fluid (in the absence of clinical infection) also suggests the presence of underlying necrosis. During pancreatography, the finding of complete main pancreatic duct disruption suggests that pancreatic necrosis occurred during the initial course of pancreatitis and may be present in the collection. During contrast

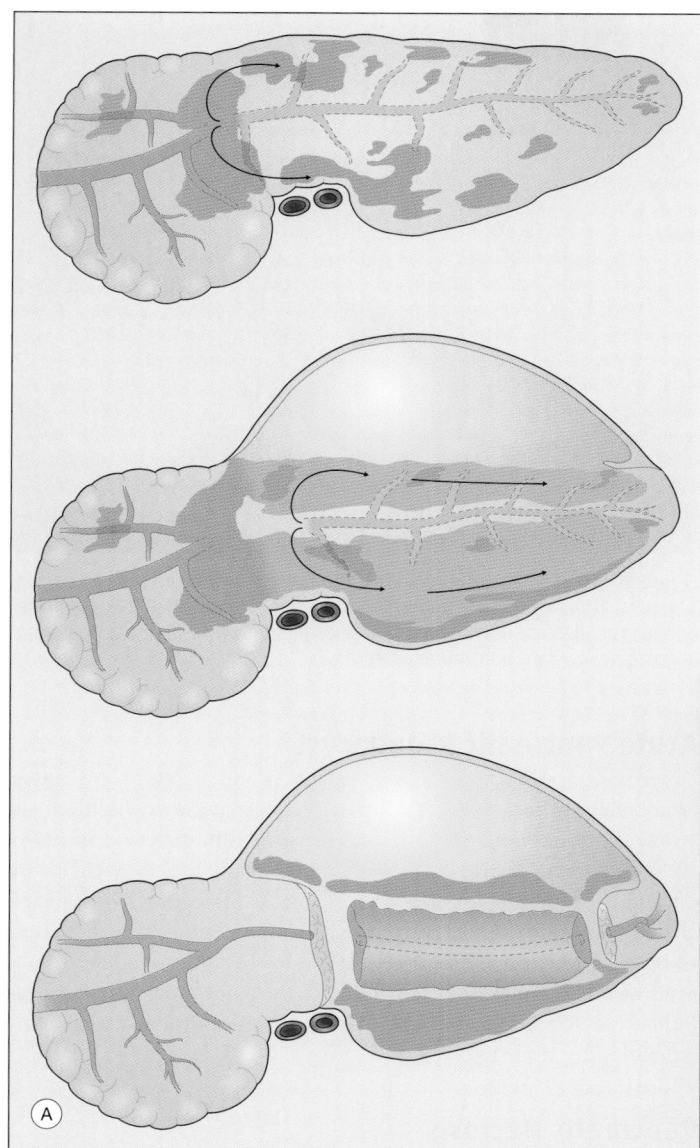

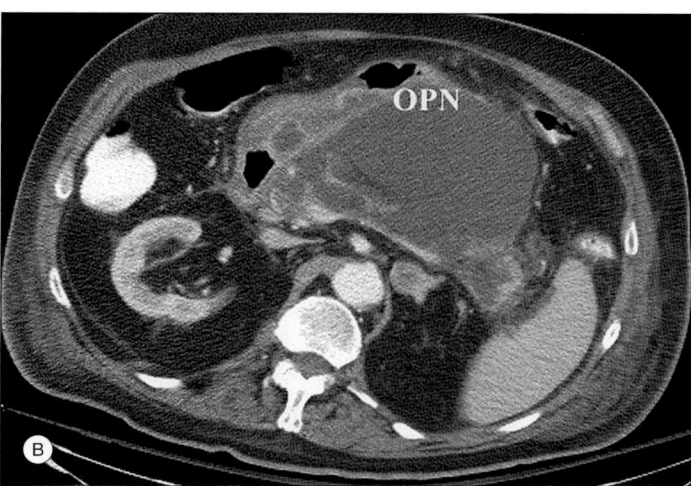

Figure 50–7. Organized pancreatic necrosis. *A,* Formation of organized pancreatic necrosis. Note the mechanism of pancreatic duct disconnection in the lower panel. *B,* Contrast computed tomography (CT) scan demonstrating a large collection that has nearly replaced the pancreatic bed. This collection is consistent with organized pancreatic necrosis. (*A* Redrawn with permission from Bradley EL 3rd (ed): Acute Pancreatitis: Diagnosis and Therapy. New York, Raven Press, 1994, p 73.)

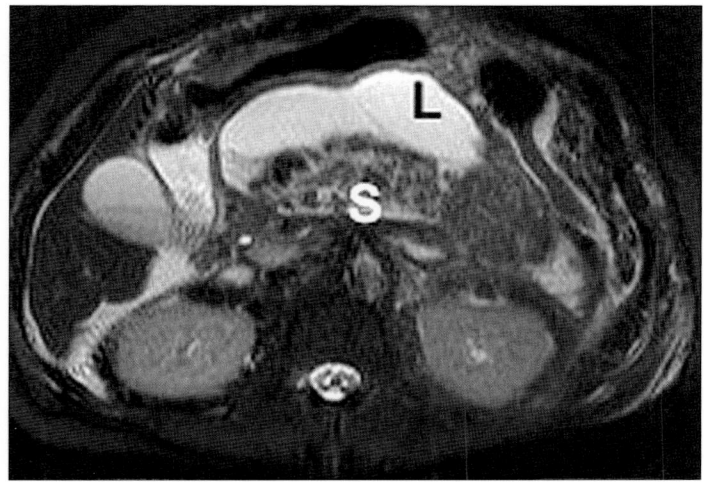

Figure 50–8. Magnetic resonance imaging (MRI) of pancreatic fluid collection that appeared homogenous by computed tomography (CT) scan. The patient had suffered severe necrotizing pancreatitis 6 weeks previously. The liquid component (L) has a whitish appearance, and the solid component (S) appears black.

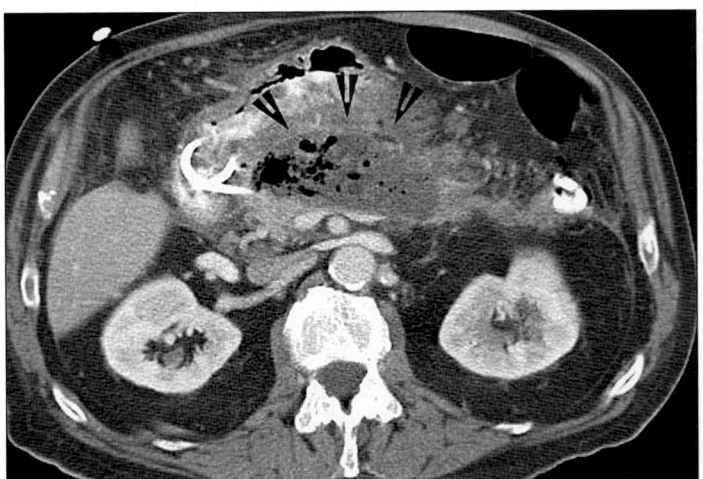

Figure 50–9. Computed tomography (CT) scan obtained several days after endoscopic placement of a transduodenal drainage catheter into a pancreatic fluid collection. *Black arrowheads* denote a collection that contains non-dependent air and debris.

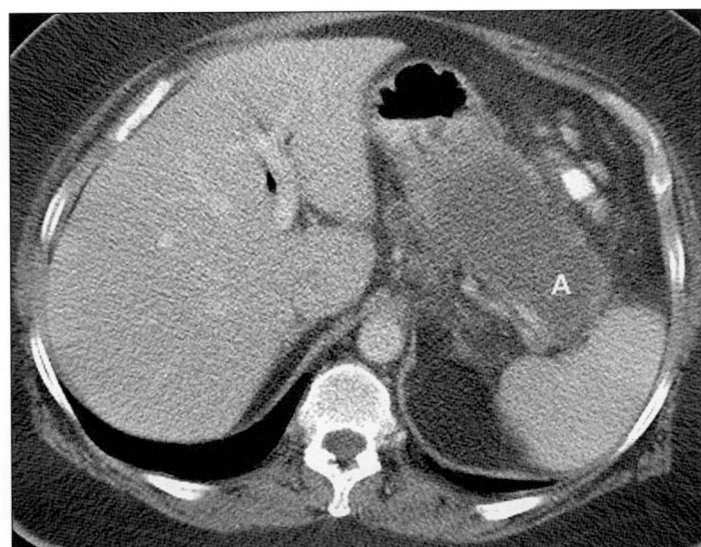

Figure 50–10. Pancreatic abscess (A). This patient developed a septic episode 5 weeks after a bout of moderate acute pancreatitis. Cultures confirmed polymicrobial bacterial infection. The collection was successfully drained endoscopically via a transmural approach.

injection, either through the main pancreatic duct or transmurally, the finding of large filling defects within the collection denotes the presence of solid material. If any or all of the above findings are recognized, then appropriate steps must be taken to evacuate the underlying solid debris to prevent secondary infection (see drainage methods later). Overall, one should consider the evolution of a pancreatic collection from the early phase of acute pancreatic necrosis toward a pseudocyst as a spectrum, with organized pancreatic necrosis as an intermediate stage, but also realize that some collections will never become completely liquefied.

Pancreatic Abscess

A pancreatic abscess is defined as a collection of pus in close proximity to the pancreas (Fig. 50–10). These collections are uncommon and are not synonymous with infected pancreatic pseudocysts or infected pancreatic necrosis. Pancreatic abscesses likely arise from limited pancreatic or peripancreatic fat necrosis, which subsequently liquefies and becomes infected.[5] True pancreatic abscesses are rare.[8]

INDICATIONS FOR DRAINAGE

In general, the indications for drainage of a pancreatic fluid collection are symptom-driven and/or the development of infection. The specific indications for drainage of each collection are discussed separately.

Acute Fluid Collections

Because acute fluid collections usually resolve without sequelae, intervention is not usually indicated unless documented infection occurs and is not responsive to antibiotic therapy. There are no reports in the literature of endoscopic drainage, although it is technically feasible.

Acute Pancreatic Pseudocyst

Pancreatic pseudocysts do not usually produce symptoms unless large enough to compress surrounding structures such as the stomach, duodenum, or bile duct with resultant development of abdominal pain, gastric outlet obstruction, early satiety, weight loss, or jaundice. Pseudocyst size alone is not an indication for drainage, although pseudocysts larger than 6 cm in maximum diameter tend to be symptomatic.[77] Progressive enlargement of a pseudocyst in an asymptomatic patient is considered by some authors to be an indication for drainage.[78] An infected pseudocyst is an absolute indication for drainage.

Pancreatic Necrosis

The indications for, and the timing of, drainage of sterile pancreatic necrosis are controversial. Pancreatic necrosis is not amenable to endoscopic drainage until the process becomes organized, which usually occurs several weeks after the onset of pancreatitis. If the process remains sterile, the general indications for drainage are refractory abdominal pain, gastric outlet obstruction, or failure to thrive (continued systemic illness, anorexia, and weight loss) at 4 or more weeks after the onset of acute pancreatitis.[55] The severity of CT scan findings alone is not an indication for drainage. Because endoscopic drainage of these collections is more technically difficult, carries a higher rate of complications, and tends to involve a more severely ill patient group, the decision to endoscopically intervene in patients with sterile pancreatic necrosis must be carefully considered. Alternative management options to endoscopic drainage include nutritional support with parenteral or enteral jejunal feeding and nonendoscopic drainage methods such as percutaneous or surgical drainage.[57] The final management option is usually based on local expertise and severity of comorbid medical illnesses. Ideally, these patients are best managed by a multidisciplinary approach.[76]

Infected pancreatic necrosis is considered an indication for drainage. Infected necrosis may not be distinguishable clinically from sterile necrosis because of leukocytosis and fever. Percutaneous fine needle aspiration may be required to determine the bacteriologic status of the necrosis.

Pancreatic Abscess

By definition, a pancreatic abscess is infected and is an indication for drainage.

PREDRAINAGE EVALUATION

Before embarking on endoscopic drainage of a pancreatic fluid collection, the endoscopist must always ask the following questions:

- Is the pancreatic collection an inflammatory collection? In other words, did the collection arise as a result of pancreatitis? There are many mimics of pancreatic pseudocysts. These include cystic pancreatic neoplasms, duplication cysts, true pancreatic cysts, pseudoaneurysms, solid necrotic neoplasms (e.g., retroperitoneal sarcoma), and lymphoceles.[70,79,80] If the patient does not have a well-documented history of pancreatitis, the endoscopist should suspect that something other than a pseudocyst is present.[81]
- Could the patient have an underlying pancreatic adenocarcinoma? An elderly patient who either presents with idiopathic pancreatitis complicated by pancreatic pseudocyst formation or develops a documented pancreatic pseudocyst in the absence of clinical pancreatitis should be carefully evaluated to exclude an underlying pancreatic neoplasm causing pancreatic ductal obstruction and upstream ductal leak.[82]

Once the decision has been made to endoscopically intervene on a pancreatic fluid collection, the following imaging and laboratory evaluation should be undertaken:

- Oral and intravenous contrast abdominal CT scan. This allows assessment of the precise location of the collection in relation to the stomach and duodenum in anticipation of possible transmural drainage. In addition, the relationship of the collection to potential intervening vascular structures can be assessed. Surrounding varices from splenic vein or portal vein thrombosis may also be visualized. The finding of inhomogeneity within the collection suggests the presence of underlying solid debris.[75]
- Coagulation parameters.

The following imaging studies should be considered:

- EUS. EUS can be used before considering drainage of a pancreatic fluid collection for two reasons. First, in a patient with a pancreatic collection after a documented episode of pancreatitis, EUS allows assessment of the collection for the presence of significant solid debris that may alter the management strategy. Second, if the endoscopist is uncertain as to whether the collection in question represents a true pseudocyst or other noninflammatory cystic lesion, EUS allows one to obtain a definitive diagnosis by both using the ultrasonographic features and analyzing cyst contents aspirated during EUS.[83] Once the endoscopist is certain that the lesion in question is a

pancreatic fluid collection and the decision has been made to proceed with endoscopic drainage, EUS may be used to guide transmural drainage as discussed in the next section under endoscopic drainage methods.
- MRI to determine the presence of solid debris, to plan for irrigation methods or alternative drainage strategy, depending on local expertise and necrosis drainage preferences.[75]

ENDOSCOPIC DRAINAGE

Methods

The following methods apply to endoscopic drainage of pancreatic fluid collections that do not have significant underlying solid debris (necrosis), such as acute pancreatic pseudocysts. The endoscopic management of organized pancreatic necrosis is addressed separately. The endoscopic approaches to pseudocysts are transpapillary drainage,[84,85] transmural drainage,[86] or combined transpapillary and transmural drainage.[78,87] The decision to proceed with one approach rather than another is based on the anatomic relationship of the collection to the stomach or duodenum, the presence of ductal communication, and the size of the collection. If the stomach or duodenum is not in close apposition to the wall of the collection (within 1 cm by CT), it is not approachable transmurally. If the collection is very large, attempted transpapillary drainage alone in the presence of a ductal communication may result in infection, because the transpapillary drainage process is relatively slow and contrast injection introduces bacteria and/or fungal organisms into the collection. The endoscopic approach to patents with large pseudocysts (>6 cm) using combined transpapillary and transmural drainage is analogous to the treatment of large bilomas complicating laparoscopic cholecystectomy using percutaneous drainage for the biloma and endoscopic therapy to close the biliary ductal leak.

Transpapillary Approach

If the collection communicates with the main pancreatic duct, placement of a pancreatic endoprosthesis with or without pancreatic sphincterotomy is an approach that is useful, especially for collections measuring less than 6 cm that are not otherwise approachable transmurally. The proximal end of the stent (toward the pancreatic tail) may directly enter the collection or bridge the area of leak into the pancreatic duct upstream from the leak (Fig. 50–11). Recent data suggest that complete bridging of the leak is the best approach.[88] The diameter of pancreatic stent used is dependent on the pancreatic ductal diameter but is usually 7 Fr.

The advantage of the transpapillary over the transmural approach is the avoidance of bleeding or perforation that may occur with transmural drainage. The disadvantage of transpapillary drainage is that pancreatic stents may induce scarring of the main pancreatic duct in patients whose pancreatic duct is otherwise normal (i.e., patients with acute pseudocysts and small side-branch disruption).[89,90]

Transmural Approach

Transmural drainage of pancreatic fluid collections is achieved by placing one or more large-bore stents through the gastric or duodenal wall (Fig. 50–12). There is no standardized approach to this method of drainage, and some authorities think that EUS

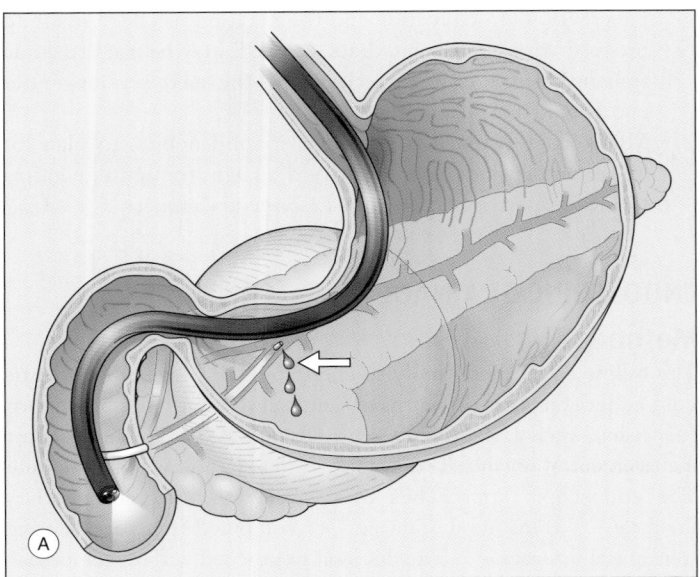
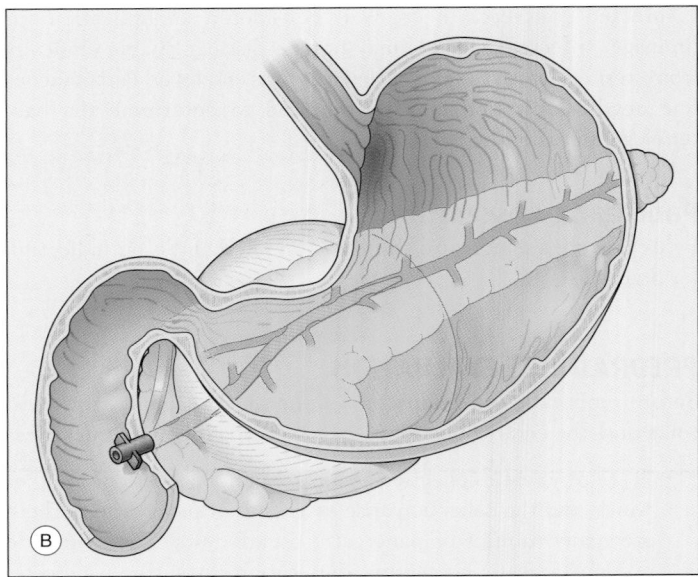

Figure 50–11. Illustration of transpapillary drainage of a pancreatic pseudocyst. *A,* Pancreatogram showing a leak off a side branch of the main pancreatic duct. *B,* A pancreatic duct stent is in place across the leak.

evaluation is mandatory before performing endoscopic transmural drainage of pancreatic fluid collections.[91] EUS-guided and non-EUS-guided drainage are discussed.

Endoscopic Ultrasonography-Guided Transmural Drainage

Although EUS imaging may theoretically reduce complications related to transmural entry of pancreatic fluid collections, this has not been proved in prospective randomized studies. There are two ways EUS can be used for transmural drainage of pancreatic fluid collections.[92] The first is to use an echoendoscope to localize the collection in relationship to surrounding structures and endoscopic landmarks; the echoendoscope is removed and therapeutic endoscope is used to perform transmural drainage by puncturing into the collection as described in the section on non-EUS-guided drainage. The second is to perform the evaluation and entry into the collection using direct EUS guidance.

Early reports of EUS-guided drainage using the first approach to identify intervening vessels did not demonstrate that bleeding complications were avoided.[87,93,94] More recently, Giovannini and coworkers[95] described transmural drainage of pancreatic fluid collections performed entirely under EUS guidance using a Doppler-equipped therapeutic channel echoendoscope. Successful entry was achieved in 35 patients (94%), in 32 of whom there was no endoscopically visible extrinsic compression. No episodes of bleeding occurred, although pneumoperitoneum occurred in one patient. Therefore, if EUS is readily available, it should be used to assist with transmural drainage.

However, unavailability of EUS should not preclude potential transmural drainage except in the following instances:

- Small window of entry based on CT, especially in the absence of an endoscopically defined area of extrinsic compression or unusual location[96] (Fig. 50–13)

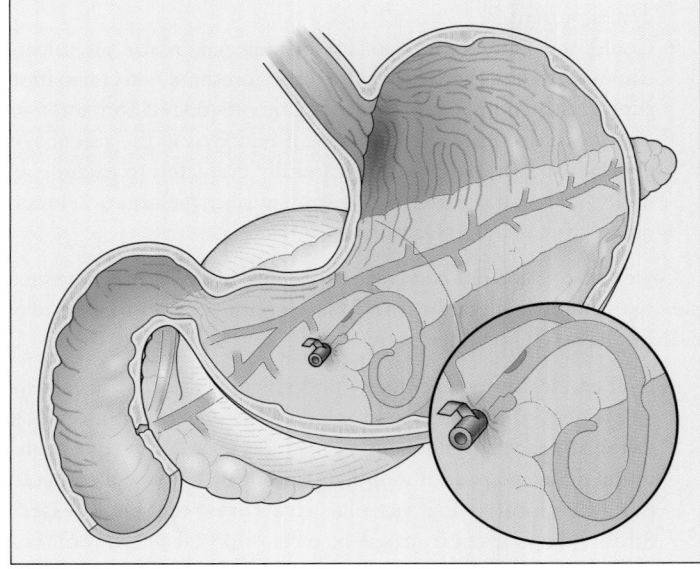

Figure 50–12. Illustration of transmural stent in place through the posterior gastric wall into a pancreatic pseudocyst.

- Marginal, uncorrectable coagulopathy or thrombocytopenia
- Documented intervening varices
- Failed transmural entry using non-EUS-guided techniques

Nonendoscopic Ultrasonography-Guided Transmural Drainage

Many endoscopists enter the collection at the point of maximal endoscopically visible extrinsic compression using needle-knife electrocautery with or without prelocalization using a sclerotherapy needle.[97] Once entry into the collection has been achieved and a

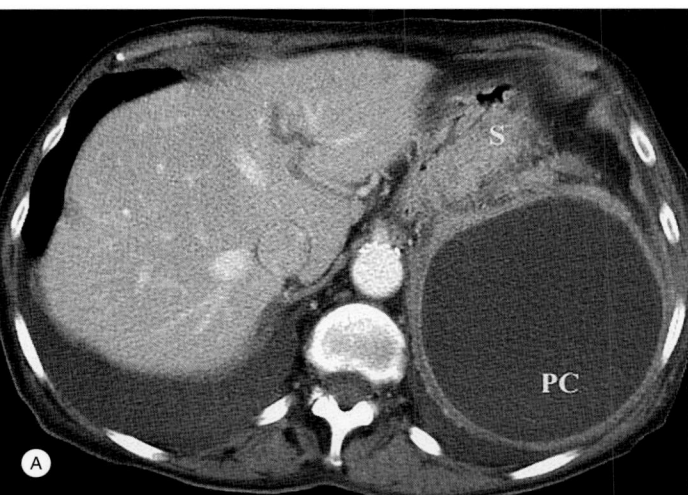
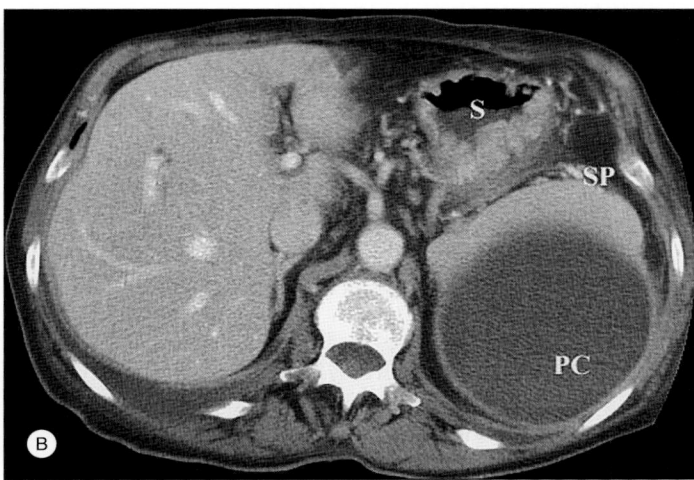

Figure 50–13. Pancreatic pseudocyst best suited for endoscopic ultrasonography (EUS) drainage. *A,* Computed tomography (CT) scan showing a pancreatic pseudocyst (PC) adjacent to the collapsed stomach (S). *B,* CT scan 1 cm below the previous image. Note the spleen (SP). The narrow window would make attempted non-EUS-guided transmural drainage of this pseudocyst dangerous.

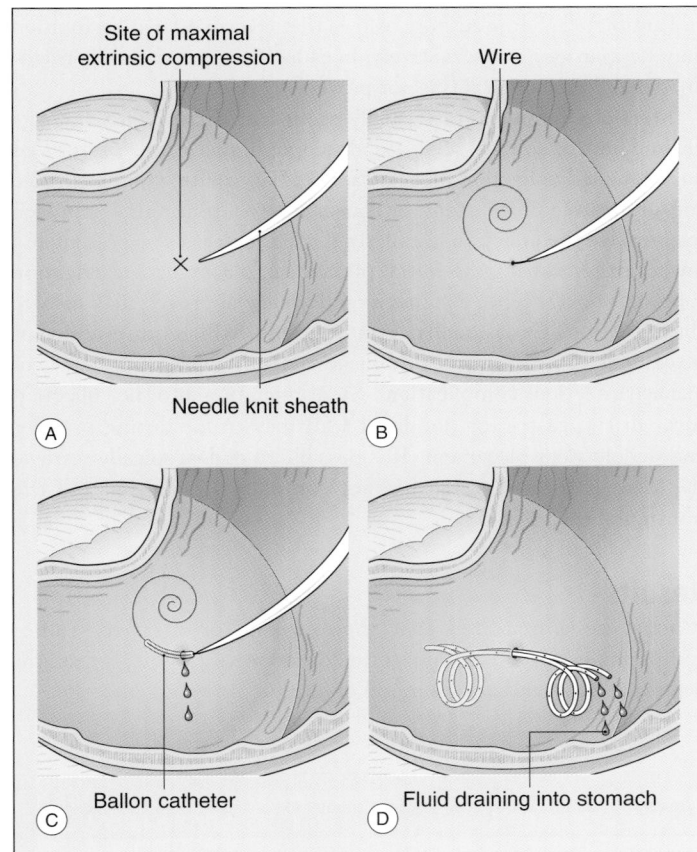

Figure 50–14. Transmural drainage of pancreatic pseudocyst. *A,* A needle is placed through the posterior wall of the stomach or the medial wall of the duodenum at the site of extrinsic compression. *B,* A guidewire is passed through the needle and coiled within the collection. *C,* The transmural tract has been balloon-dilated. *D,* Two double pigtail stents have been placed through the wall into the pancreas. (Redrawn with permission from Baron TH, Morgan DE: Techniques in Gastrointestinal Endoscopy. Philadelphia, WB Saunders, 1999.)

guidewire has been secured, the transmural tract is enlarged with a dilating balloon. Most endoscopists have abandoned the practice of enlarging the transmural tract with a sphincterotome to decrease the risk of bleeding.[98]

Other endoscopists have described both localization and entry into the collection using a large-caliber needle without electrocautery using the Seldinger technique (Video 50–1).[86] This method appears to be safer because, if the collection is not successfully entered with the needle (confirmed by aspiration of fluid and/or injection of radiopaque contrast), the needle is simply withdrawn without adverse sequelae. Similarly, if bleeding occurs on needle entry, if gross blood is aspirated, or if a visible hematoma develops, the needle is withdrawn to allow the vessel to tamponade. Another transmural entry site may be chosen during the same endoscopic session.

Once the collection has been entered as confirmed by aspiration of fluid and/or injection of contrast, a guidewire is passed through the needle-knife or aspiration needle and coiled within the collection (Fig. 50–14). The transmural tract is balloon-dilated to 8 mm using standard biliary dilating balloons to allow placement of one or more double pigtail 10-Fr stents (see Fig. 50–14). One group described using the Seldinger technique for transmural entry reported successful non-EUS-guided transmural entry of pancreatic fluid collections was achieved in 43 patients (95%) in lesions as small as 3 cm and without endoscopically visible extrinsic compression.[86]

Follow-up

After uncomplicated attempted endoscopic drainage of noninfected pancreatic pseudocysts a short-course of oral antibiotics is administered. Most outpatients do not require hospitalization.[99] In the absence of suspected complications or worsening clinical course, a follow-up CT scan is obtained 4 to 6 weeks after the drainage procedure. The internal stents are endoscopically removed after documented radiographic resolution.

Organized Pancreatic Necrosis

Because of the need to evacuate solid material, the endoscopic approach to drainage of organized pancreatic necrosis differs from drainage of other pancreatic fluid collections. In general, the transpapillary approach is not adequate to allow removal of solid debris. Therefore, it is recommended that transmural drainage is the preferred approach for these collections. After transmural entry into the collection, as described previously, the gastric or duodenal wall is dilated to at least 15 mm on the initial endoscopy. This allows egress of solid material around the endoprosthesis. An irrigation system is required to lavage the solid debris. Thus, in addition to two 10-Fr stents, a 7-Fr irrigation tube is placed into the collection (standard nasobiliary tube) for aggressive irrigation (see Fig. 50–3). Up to 200 mL of normal saline is forcefully and rapidly infused via the tube every 2 to 4 hours initially. In patients who are intolerant of nasocystic tubes and/or in whom it is anticipated that irrigation may be required for many weeks, an alternative to nasocystic lavage is the placement of a percutaneous endoscopic gastrostomy tube (PEG) with placement of a jejunal extension tube into the collection (Fig. 50–15).[100] The gastric port may then be used for supplementing nutritional needs.

Patients undergoing attempted endoscopic drainage of organized pancreatic necrosis should receive preprocedural antibiotics. It is recommended that outpatients be admitted to the hospital postprocedurally for observation and irrigation. Patients are discharged home after they are able to tolerate oral intake and care for the

irrigation tube. Oral antibiotics and antifungal agents (e.g., ciprofloxacin and fluconazole) are administered, and irrigation is continued, until the collection has resolved, as documented by follow-up CT. CT scans are obtained weekly or every other week. The internal drains are endoscopically removed several weeks after complete resolution of the collection.

Complications

Life-threatening complications may arise after attempted endoscopic drainage of pancreatic fluid collections and are listed in Box 50–4. Therefore, it is recommended that endoscopic drainage of pancreatic fluid collections should not be performed unless surgical and interventional radiology support is available. The most feared complications of transmural drainage are bleeding and perforation. Bleeding after transmural drainage may be managed supportively, endoscopically, surgically, or with angiographic embolization.[99] If perforation occurs during attempted transgastric drainage and is limited to the gastric wall (does not involve the collection), it may be successfully managed nonsurgically, assuming that a stent has not been placed through the perforation; the gastric wall rapidly closes with conservative treatment consisting of nasogastric suction and antibiotics. Some authors believe that transduodenal perforation may be managed conservatively, because the perforation is retroduodenal,[101] although this is not proven.

Infectious complications usually occur from inadequate drainage of fluid and/or solid debris. If endoscopic drainage was performed on a liquefied collection by the transpapillary route, stent exchange and/or upsizing of the stent, or conversion to a transmural approach may resolve the infection. Similarly, if solid material was present and unrecognized during the initial procedure, placement of irrigation tubes or converting to a transmural drainage approach may resolve the infection. Occasionally, some patients will require adjuvant placement of percutaneous drainage and/or irrigation catheters to manage infectious complications. Stent migration into the collection through the gastric or duodenal wall may occur during or after endoscopic stent placement. It is possible to endoscopically retrieve the stent if the collection has not completely collapsed and the transmural tract is still patent.

Results

It must be emphasized that there are no prospective studies comparing endoscopic drainage to conservative (medical) therapy, percutaneous drainage, or surgical drainage.

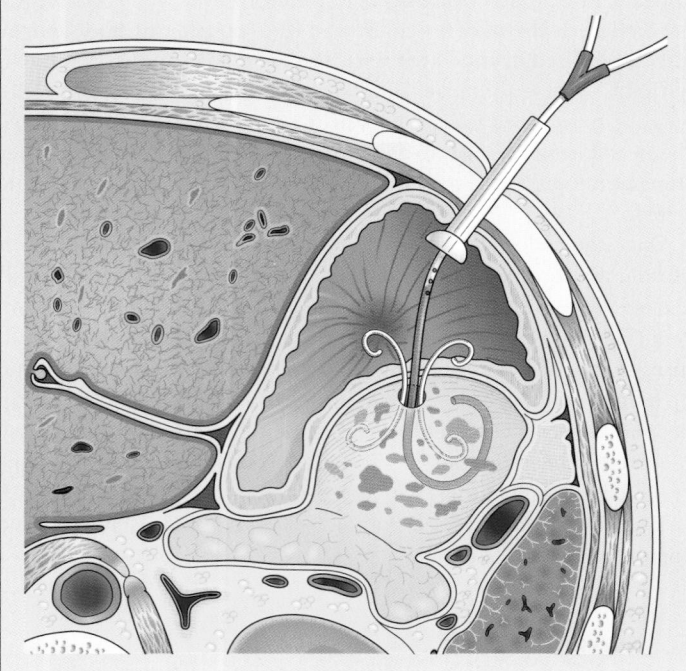

Figure 50–15. Illustration of percutaneous endoscopic gastroscopy tube with jejunal extension tube placed through the posterior gastric wall into a necrotic pancreatic collection to provide irrigation. (Redrawn with permission from Baron TH, Morgan DE: Endoscopic transgastric irrigation tube placement via PEG for débridement of organized pancreatic necrosis. Gastrointest Endosc 50:574–577, 1999.)

Box 50–4. Complications of Endoscopic Therapy of Pancreatic Fluid Collections
Bleeding
Perforation
Infection
Pancreatitis
Sedation complications
Aspiration
Stent migration and occlusion
Pancreatic ductal damage

Pancreatic Pseudocysts

The success rates, recurrence rates, and complication rates after endoscopic drainage of pancreatic pseudocysts are variable. This is probably because most authors have not used standardized criteria for defining pseudocysts, have used variable indications to perform drainage, have tended to lump acute and chronic pseudocysts into a single group, or have combined the results of transpapillary and transmural drainage. Nonetheless, in an excellent review by Beckingham and coworkers[101] in 1997 of the cumulative experience to date of endoscopic drainage of pancreatic pseudocysts, successful drainage was achieved in 82% to 89% of cases with complication rates ranging from 5% to 10% and recurrence rates ranging from 6% to 18%. In addition, from that review there appeared to be slightly lower pseudocyst recurrence rates after transduodenal drainage compared with transgastric drainage. This is probably because of the sustained patency of a transduodenal fistula that allows drainage of the main pancreatic duct. Indeed, we have achieved long-term resolution (>5 years) of a pancreatic pseudocyst using transduodenal drainage after it had rapidly recurred after successful transgastric drainage (unpublished). Therefore, in a patient with severe pancreatic ductal disease we perform transduodenal drainage when possible.

Since the review by Beckingham and coworkers,[101] there have been more recent series of endoscopic drainage of pancreatic pseudocysts with similar results. Libera and colleagues[78] successfully treated 25 patients using transpapillary and transduodenal approaches with a recurrence rate of 4.2% at 42 ± 36 weeks. Complications occurred in 16% and were managed clinically or endoscopically in all cases with no mortality. Sharma and coworkers[102] published long-term follow-up (mean 44 months, range 24 to 80 months) after endoscopic drainage of pancreatic pseudocysts in 38 consecutive patients. Pseudocyst recurrence occurred in six patients (16%); three were symptomatic and were successfully retreated endoscopically. Beckingham and colleagues[103] reported a 7% recurrence rate after successful transmural drainage in 24 patients.

Pancreatic Abscesses

True pancreatic abscesses are rare, although there are many reports of successful endoscopic abscess drainage, that probably represent reports of infected pseudocysts or necrosis. Nonetheless, Park and coworkers[104] described transmural drainage of pancreatic abscesses, which were defined using strict criteria as outlined in the Atlanta Symposium.[8] Successful resolution was achieved in 11 abscess cavities with no mortality. Self-limited bleeding occurred in one patient.

Organized Pancreatic Necrosis

The initial description of successful endoscopic drainage of organized pancreatic necrosis involved 11 patients, of whom 10 were successfully drained using the methods described previously, albeit with dilation of the gastric or duodenal wall to only 8 mm.[55] Subsequent data from the same authors from the same institution have shown successful nonsurgical resolution in 31 of 43 patients (72%).[99] Since that experience, we have changed the drainage strategy to involve dilating the transmural entry tract to more than 15 mm at the initial procedure, which has resulted in nearly uniform nonsurgical resolution in more than 25 patients without complications of bleeding or perforation (unpublished data).

Outcome Differences After Endoscopic Drainage

We recently reviewed the outcome after attempted endoscopic therapy in 138 consecutive patients with symptomatic pancreatic fluid collections.[99] The collections were classified as pancreatic necrosis in 43 patients, acute pseudocyst in 31, and chronic pseudocyst in 64. The median maximal diameter of the collections was 9 cm (range 3 to 27 cm).

A difference in successful endoscopic drainage was noted between the groups. It was achieved overall in 1138 patients (82%), significantly more often in patients with chronic pseudocysts (92%) than acute pseudocysts (74%) or pancreatic necrosis (72%). Complications occurred more commonly in pancreatic necrosis (37%) than with acute pseudocysts (19%) or chronic pseudocysts (17%). Likewise, hospital stay was shorter in patients with chronic pseudocysts, whereas pancreatic necrosis was predictive of a significantly longer stay.

At a median follow-up of 766 days (range 233 to 2122 days) in the 1138 patients whose collections were successfully drained endoscopically, recurrent pancreatic collections occurred in 113 patients (16%). The recurrence rate was significantly higher for patients with pancreatic necrosis (29%) than chronic pseudocyst (12%) or acute pseudocyst (9%).

We believe the differences in success rates, complication rates, recurrences, and hospital stay may be explained by the differences in pathology, pathophysiology, and severity of illness between the groups. Patients with pancreatic necrosis tend to be more seriously ill and endoscopic evacuation of solid debris is less efficient than evacuation of liquid. In terms of recurrence rates, acute pancreatic ductal disruptions occurring in patients with necrosis often lead to a disconnected duct syndrome whereby the head and tail of the pancreas are not in communication.[55,76] This leads to recurrent collections from the undrained viable pancreatic tail. Patients with acute pseudocysts tend to have less severe ductal abnormalities and lower recurrence rates.

In addition to the type of pancreatic collection, the experience of the endoscopist seems to play a role in the success rate of drainage.[105] Future prospective studies assessing skill acquisition are required to define the minimum number of collection drainage procedures at which competence can be achieved.

CONCLUSIONS

Pancreatic necrosis is being increasingly recognized because of physician awareness and improved radiologic imaging. The identification of pancreatic necrosis is important because the morbidity and mortality from acute pancreatitis are markedly increased when necrosis is present. Aggressive medical care with use of antibiotics and limitation of surgery or other types of pancreatic débridement to those patients with infected necrosis are the mainstays of management (see Box 50–2).

Pancreatic fluid collections are heterogeneous, with different underlying pathology and pathophysiology. Each type of pancreatic fluid collection is amenable to drainage, although not in every patient. Collections with only a fluid component that have either apposition to the gastric or duodenal wall by CT or communication with the main pancreatic duct by pancreatography can be drained endoscopically using transmural or transpapillary approaches respectively. Those collections containing significant amounts of solid debris that are treated endoscopically require placement of an irrigation system to evacuate solid debris. Endoscopists considering endoscopic therapy of a pancreatic collection must identify the type of collection being drained and exclude mimics of pancreatic fluid collections such as cystic neoplasms. EUS-guided drainage, if available, may decrease the complications of bleeding and perforation during transmural entry of pancreatic fluid collections. Refinement in endoscopic techniques to improve the safety and efficacy of endoscopic therapy and comparative studies with other drainage methods are needed.

REFERENCES

1. Beger HG, Rau B, Mayer J, Pralle U: Natural course of acute pancreatitis. World J Surg 21:130–135, 1997.
2. Tenner S, Banks PA: Acute pancreatitis: nonsurgical management. World J Surg 21:143–148, 1997.
3. Rau B, Uhl W, Buchler MW, Beger HG: Surgical treatment of infected necrosis. World J Surg 21:155–161, 1997.
4. Foitzik T, Klar E, Buhr HJ, Herfarth C: Improved survival in acute necrotizing pancreatitis despite limiting the indications for surgical débridement. Eur J Surg 161:187–192, 1995.
5. Baron TH, Morgan DE: The diagnosis and management of fluid collections associated with pancreatitis. Am J Med 102:555–563, 1997.
6. Banks PA: Practice guidelines in acute pancreatitis. Am J Gastroenterol 92:377–386, 1997.
7. Fogel EL, Sherman S: Acute biliary pancreatitis: When should the endoscopist intervene? Gastroenterology 125:229–235, 2003.
8. Bradley EL 3rd: A clinically based classification system for acute pancreatitis. Arch Surg 128:586–590, 1993.
9. Balthazar EJ, Freeny PC, vanSonnenberg E: Imaging and intervention in acute pancreatitis. Radiology 193:297–306, 1994.
10. Banks PA: Acute pancreatitis: Medical and surgical management. Am J Gastroenterol 89:S78–S85, 1994.
11. Banks PA: Infected necrosis: Morbidity and therapeutic consequences. Hepatogastroenterology 38:116–119, 1991.
12. Imrie CW: Underdiagnosis of acute pancreatitis. Adv Acute Pancreatitis 1:3–5, 1997.
13. Coyle WJ, Pineau BC, Tarnasky PR, et al: Evaluation of unexplained acute and acute recurrent pancreatitis using endoscopic retrograde cholangiopancreatography, sphincter of Oddi manometry and endoscopic ultrasound. Endoscopy 34:617–623, 2002.
14. Clain JE, Pearson RK: Evidence-based approach to idiopathic pancreatitis. Curr Gastroenterol Rep 4:128–134, 2002.
15. Nuutinen P, Kivisaari L, Schroder T: Contrast-enhanced computed tomography and microangiography of the pancreas in acute human hemorrhagic/necrotizing pancreatitis. Pancreas 3:53–60, 1988.
16. Balthazar EJ, Robinson DL, Megibow AJ, Ranson JH: Acute pancreatitis: Value of CT in establishing prognosis. Radiology 174:331–336, 1990.
17. Uhl W, Roggo A, Kirschstein T, et al: Influence of contrast-enhanced computed tomography on course and outcome in patients with acute pancreatitis. Pancreas 24:191–197, 2002.
18. Gloor B, Muller CA, Worni M, et al: Late mortality in patients with severe acute pancreatitis. Br J Surg 88:975–979, 2001.
19. Karimgani I, Porter KA, Langevin RE, Banks PA: Prognostic factors in sterile pancreatic necrosis. Gastroenterology 103:1636–1640, 1992.
20. Marotta F, Geng TC, Wu CC, Barbi G: Bacterial translocation in the course of acute pancreatitis: Beneficial role of nonabsorbable antibiotics and Lactitol enemas. Digestion 57:446–452, 1996.
21. Foitzik T, Fernandez-del Castillo C, Ferraro MJ, et al: Pathogenesis and prevention of early pancreatic infection in experimental acute necrotizing pancreatitis. Ann Surg 222:179–185, 1995.
22. Mithofer K, Fernandez-del Castillo C, Ferraro MJ, et al: Antibiotic treatment improves survival in experimental acute necrotizing pancreatitis. Gastroenterology 110:232–240, 1996.
23. Luiten EJ, Hop WC, Lange JF, Bruining HA: Controlled clinical trial of selective decontamination for the treatment of severe acute pancreatitis. Ann Surg 222:57–65, 1995.
24. Luiten EJ, Hop WC, Lange JF, Bruining HA: Differential prognosis of Gram negative versus Gram-positive infected and sterile pancreatic necrosis: Results of a randomized trial in patients with severe acute pancreatitis treated with adjuvant selective decontamination. Clin Infect Dis 25:811–816, 1997.
25. Schmid SW, Uhl W, Friess H, et al: The role of infection in acute pancreatitis. Gut 45:311–316, 1999.
26. Pederzoli P, Bassi C, Vesentini S, Campedelli A: A randomized multicenter clinical trial of antibiotic prophylaxis of septic complications in acute necrotizing pancreatitis with imipenem. Surg Gynecol Obstet 176:480–483, 1993.
27. Ho HS, Frey CF: The role of antibiotic prophylaxis in severe acute pancreatitis. Arch Surg 132:487–493, 1997.
28. Sharma VK, Howden CW: Prophylactic antibiotic administration reduces sepsis and mortality in acute necrotizing pancreatitis: A meta-analysis. Pancreas 22:28–31, 2001.
29. Bassi C, Mangiante G, Falconi M, et al: Prophylaxis for septic complications in acute necrotizing pancreatitis. J Hepatobiliary Pancreat Surg 8:211–215, 2001.
30. Gloor B, Muller CA, Worni M, et al: Pancreatic infection in severe pancreatitis: The role of fungus and multiresistant organisms. Arch Surg 136:592–596, 2001.
31. Gerzof SG, Banks PA, Robbins AH, et al: Early diagnosis of pancreatic infection by computed tomography-guided aspiration. Gastroenterology 93:1315–1320, 1987.
32. Rau B, Pralle U, Mayer JM, Beger HG: Role of ultrasonographically guided fine-needle aspiration cytology in diagnosis of infected pancreatic necrosis. Br J Surg 85:179–184, 1998.
33. Neoptolemos JP, Carr-Locke DL, London NJ, et al: Controlled trial of urgent endoscopic retrograde cholangiopancreatography and endoscopic sphincterotomy versus conservative treatment for acute pancreatitis due to gallstones. Lancet 2:979–983, 1988.
34. Fan ST, Lai EC, Mok FP, et al: Early treatment of acute biliary pancreatitis by endoscopic papillotomy. N Engl J Med 328:228–232, 1993.
35. Folsch UR, Nitsche R, Ludtke R, et al: Early ERCP and papillotomy compared with conservative treatment for acute biliary pancreatitis. The German Study Group on Acute Biliary Pancreatitis. N Engl J Med 336:237–242, 1997.
36. Neoptlemos JP, London NJ, Carr-Locke DL: Assessment of main pancreatic duct integrity by endoscopic retrograde pancreatography in patients with acute pancreatitis. Br J Surg 80:94–99, 1993.
37. Baillie J: Treatment of acute biliary pancreatitis. N Engl J Med 336:286–287, 1997.
38. McClave SA, Snider H, Owens N, Sexton LK: Clinical nutrition in pancreatitis. Dig Dis Sci 42:2035–2044, 1997.
39. Kalfarentzos F, Kehagias J, Mead N, et al: Enteral nutrition is superior to parenteral nutrition in severe acute pancreatitis: Results of a randomized prospective trial. Br J Surg 84:1665–1669, 1997.
40. Windsor AC, Kanwar S, Li AG, et al: Compared with parenteral nutrition, enteral nutrition feeding attenuates the acute phase response and improves disease severity in acute pancreatitis. Gut 42:431–435, 1998.
41. Yousaf M, McCallion K, Diamond T: Management of severe acute pancreatitis. Br J Surg 90:407–420, 2003.

42. Eatock FC, Brombacher GD, Steven A, et al: Nasogastric feeding in severe acute pancreatitis may be practical and safe. Int J Pancreatol 8:23–29, 2000.

43. DiSario JA, Baskin WN, Brown RD, et al: Endoscopic approaches to enteral nutritional support. Gastrointest Endosc 55:901–908, 2002.

44. Kulling D, Bauerfeind P, Fried M: Transnasal versus transoral endoscopy for the placement of nasoenteral feeding tubes in critically ill patients. Gastrointest Endosc 52:506–510, 2000.

45. Adler DG, Chari ST, Dahl TJ, et al: Conservative management of infected necrosis complicating severe acute pancreatitis. Am J Gastroenterol 98:98–103, 2003.

46. Ramesh H, Prakash K, Lekha V, et al: Are some cases of infected pancreatic necrosis treatable without intervention? Dig Surg 20:296–300, 2003.

47. Rau B, Pralle U, Uhl W, et al: Management of sterile necrosis in instances of severe acute pancreatitis. J Am Coll Surg 181:279–288, 1995.

48. Mier J, Leon EL, Castillo A, et al: Early versus late necrosectomy in severe necrotizing pancreatitis. Am J Surg 173:71–75, 1997.

49. Rattner DW, Legermate DA, Lee MJ, et al: Early surgical débridement of symptomatic pancreatic necrosis is beneficial irrespective of infection. Am J Surg 163:105–110, 1992.

50. Bradley EL 3rd: Surgical indications and techniques in necrotizing pancreatitis. In Bradley EL 3rd (ed): Acute Pancreatitis: Diagnosis and Therapy. New York, Raven Press, 1994, pp 105–117.

51. Tsiotos GG, Smith CD, Sarr MG: Incidence and management of pancreatic and enteric fistulas after surgical management of severe necrotizing pancreatitis. Arch Surg 130:48–52, 1995.

52. Ho HS, Frey CF: Gastrointestinal and pancreatic complications associated with severe pancreatitis. Arch Surg 130:817–823, 1995.

53. Freeny PC, Hauptmann E, Althaus SJ, et al: Percutaneous CT-guided catheter drainage of infected acute necrotizing pancreatitis: Techniques and results. AJR 170:969–975, 1998.

54. Echenique AM, Sleeman D, Yrizarry J, et al: Percutaneous catheter-directed débridement of infected pancreatic necrosis: results in 20 patients. J Vasc Interv Radiol 9:565–571, 1998.

55. Baron TH, Thaggard WG, Morgan DE, Stanley RJ: Endoscopic therapy for organized pancreatic necrosis. Gastroenterology 111:755–764, 1996.

56. Baron TH, Morgan DE: Organized pancreatic necrosis: Definition, diagnosis, and management. Gastroenterol Int 10:167–178, 1997.

57. Baron TH, Morgan DE: Acute necrotizing pancreatitis. N Engl J Med 340:1412–1417, 1999.

58. Fenton-Lee D, Imrie CW: Pancreatic necrosis: Assessment of outcome related to quality of life and cost of management. Br J Surg 80:1579–1582, 1993.

59. Fernandez-Cruz L, Navarro S, Castells A, Saenz A: Late outcome after acute pancreatitis: Functional impairment and gastrointestinal tract complications. World J Surg 21:169–172, 1997.

60. Nordback IH, Auvinen OA: Long-term results after pancreas resection for acute necrotizing pancreatitis. Br J Surg 72:687–689, 1985.

61. Bozkurt T, Maroske D, Adler G: Exocrine pancreatic function after recovery from necrotizing pancreatitis. Hepatogastroenterology 42:55–58, 1995.

62. Angelini G, Pederzoli P, Caliari S, et al: Long-term outcome of acute necrohemorrhagic pancreatitis. A 4-year follow-up. Digestion 30:131–137, 1984.

63. Angelini G, Cavallini G, Pederzoli P, et al: Long-term outcome of acute pancreatitis: A prospective study with 118 patients. Digestion 54:143–147, 1993.

64. Dabrowski A, Gabryelewicz A, Chyczewski L: The effect of platelet activating factor antagonist (BN 52021) on acute experimental pancreatitis with reference to multiorgan oxidative stress. Int J Pancreatol 17:173–180, 1995.

65. Kingsnorth AN, Galloway SW, Formela LJ: Randomized, double-blind phase II trial of Lexipafant, a platelet-activating factor antagonist, in human acute pancreatitis. Br J Surg 82:1414–1420, 1995.

66. Johnson CD, Kingsnorth AN, Imrie CW, et al: Double blind, randomized, placebo controlled study of a platelet activating factor antagonist, lexipafant, in the treatment and prevention of organ failure in predicted severe acute pancreatitis. Gut 48:62–69, 2001.

67. Rogers BH, Cicurel NJ, Seed RW: Transgastric needle aspiration of pancreatic pseudocyst through an endoscope. Gastrointest Endosc 21:133–134, 1975.

68. Hershfield NB: Drainage of a pancreatic pseudocyst at ERCP. Gastrointest Endosc 30:269–270, 1984.

69. Kozarek RA, Brayko CM, Harlan J, et al: Endoscopic drainage of pancreatic pseudocysts. Gastrointest Endosc 31:322–328, 1985.

70. Adkisson KW, Baron TH, Morgan DE: Pancreatic fluid collections: Diagnosis and endoscopic management. Semin Gastrointest Dis 9:61–72, 1998.

71. Kloppel G: Pathology of severe acute pancreatitis. In Bradley EL 3rd (ed) Acute Pancreatitis: Diagnosis and Therapy. New York, Raven Press, 1994, pp 35–46.

72. Hariri M, Slivka A, Carr-Locke DL, et al: Pseudocyst drainage predisposes to infection when pancreatic necrosis is unrecognized. Am J Gastroenterol 89:1781–1784, 1994.

73. Uomo G, Molino D, Visconti M, et al: The incidence of main pancreatic duct disruption in severe biliary pancreatitis. Am J Surg 176:49–52, 1998.

74. Baron TH, Morgan DE, Vickers SM, et al: Organized pancreatic necrosis: Endoscopic, radiologic, and pathologic features of a distinct clinical entity. Pancreas 19:105–108, 1999.

75. Morgan DE, Baron TH, Smith JK, et al: Pancreatic fluid collections prior to intervention: Evaluation with MR imaging compared with CT and US. Radiology 203:773–778, 1997.

76. Kozarek RA: Endotherapy for organized pancreatic necrosis: Perspectives on skunk-poking. Gastroenterology 111:820–822, 1996.

77. Yeo CJ, Bastidas JA, Lynch-Nyhan A, et al: The natural history of pancreatic pseudocysts documented by computed tomography. Surg Gynecol Obstet 170:411–417, 1990.

78. Libera ED, Siqueira ES, Morais M, et al: Pancreatic pseudocysts: Transpapillary and transmural drainage. HPB Surg 11:333–338, 2000.

79. Boggi U, Candio G, Campatelli A, et al: Nonoperative management of pancreatic pseudocysts. Problems in differential diagnosis. Int J Pancreatol 25:123–133, 1999.

80. Baron TH, Morgan DE, Vickers SM: Endoscopic transgastric drainage of a lymphocele. Gastrointest Endosc 48:309–311, 1998.

81. Beckingham IJ, Krige JE, Bornman PC, et al: Endoscopic management of pancreatic pseudocysts. Br J Surg 84:1638–1645, 1997.

82. Itai Y, Moss AA, Goldberg HI: Pancreatic cysts caused by carcinoma of the pancreas: A pitfall in the diagnosis of pancreatic carcinoma. J Comput Assist Tomogr 6:772–776, 1982.

83. Brugge WR: The role of EUS in the diagnosis of cystic lesions of the pancreas. Gastrointest Endosc 52:S18–S22, 2000.

84. Barthet M, Sahel J, Bodiou-Bertei C, et al: Endoscopic transpapillary drainage of pancreatic pseudocysts. Gastrointest Endosc 42:208–213, 1995.

85. Catalano MF, Geenen JE, Schmalz MJ, et al: Treatment of pancreatic pseudocysts with ductal communication by transpapillary pancreatic duct endoprosthesis. Gastrointest Endosc 42:214–218, 1995.

86. Monkemuller KE, Baron TH, Morgan DE: Transmural drainage of pancreatic fluid collections without electrocautery using the Seldinger technique. Gastrointest Endosc 48:195–200, 1998.

87. Binmoeller KF, Seifert H, Walter A, et al: Transpapillary and transmural drainage of pancreatic pseudocysts. Gastrointest Endosc 42:219–224, 1995.

88. Telford JJ, Farrell JJ, Saltzman JR, et al: Pancreatic stent placement for duct disruption. Gastrointest Endosc 56:18–24, 2002.

89. Kozarek RA: Pancreatic stents can induce ductal changes consistent with chronic pancreatitis. Gastrointest Endosc 36:93–95, 1990.

90. Smith MT, Sherman S, Ikenberry SO, et al: Alterations in pancreatic ductal morphology following polyethylene pancreatic stent therapy. Gastrointest Endosc 44:268–275, 1996.

91. Fockens P, Johnson TG, van Dullemen HM, et al: Endosonographic imaging of pancreatic pseudocysts before endoscopic transmural drainage. Gastrointest Endosc 46:412–416, 1997.

92. Chak A: Endosonographic-guided therapy of pancreatic pseudocysts. Gastrointest Endosc 52:S23–S27, 2000.

93. Smits ME, Rauws EA, Tytgat GN, et al: The efficacy of endoscopic treatment of pancreatic pseudocysts. Gastrointest Endosc 42:202–207, 1995.

94. Norton ID, Clain JE, Wiersema MJ, et al: Utility of endoscopic ultrasonography in endoscopic drainage of pancreatic pseudocysts in selected patients. Mayo Clin Proc 76:794–798, 2001.

95. Giovannini M, Pesenti C, Rolland AL, et al: Endoscopic ultrasound-guided drainage of pancreatic pseudocysts or pancreatic abscesses using a therapeutic echo endoscope. Endoscopy 33:473–477, 2001.

96. Baron TH, Wiersema MJ: EUS-guided transesophageal pancreatic pseudocyst drainage. Gastrointest Endosc 52:545–549, 2000.

97. Howell DA, Holbrook RF, Bosco JJ, et al: Endoscopic needle localization of pancreatic pseudocysts before transmural drainage. Gastrointest Endosc 39:693–698, 1993.

98. Etzkorn KP, DeGuzman LJ, Holderman WH, et al: Endoscopic drainage of pancreatic pseudocysts: Patient selection and evaluation of the outcome by endoscopic ultrasonography. Endoscopy 27:329–333, 1995.

99. Baron TH, Harewood GC, Morgan DE, Yates MR: Outcome differences after endoscopic drainage of pancreatic necrosis, acute pancreatic pseudocysts, and chronic pancreatic pseudocysts. Gastrointest Endosc 56:7–17, 2002.

100. Baron TH, Morgan DE: Endoscopic transgastric irrigation tube placement via PEG for débridement of organized pancreatic necrosis. Gastrointest Endosc 50:574–577, 1999.

101. Beckingham IJ, Krige JE, Bornman PC, et al: Endoscopic management of pancreatic pseudocysts. Br J Surg 84:1638–1645, 1997.

102. Sharma SS, Bhargawa N, Govil A: Endoscopic management of pancreatic pseudocysts: A long-term follow-up. Endoscopy 3:203–207, 2002.

103. Beckingham IJ, Krige JE, Bornman PC, et al: Long term outcome of endoscopic drainage of pancreatic pseudocysts. Am J Gastroenterol 94:71–74, 1999.

104. Park JJ, Kim SS, Koo YS, et al: Definitive treatment of pancreatic abscess by endoscopic transmural drainage. Gastrointest Endosc 55:256–262, 2002.

105. Harewood GC, Wright CA, Baron TH: Impact on patient outcomes of experience in the performance of endoscopic pancreatic fluid collection drainage. Gastrointest Endosc 58:230–235, 2003.

Acute Relapsing Pancreatitis

Adam Slivka

Acute pancreatitis is caused by acute or chronic alcohol intake or cholelithiasis in 80% of cases.[1,2] In the absence of alcohol or gallstones, a number of established and putative etiologies must be considered, any one of which can cause recurrent attacks of acute pancreatitis.[3] In instances in which the underlying etiology eludes detection and leads to a second attack, the term acute relapsing pancreatitis (ARP) is applied. Table 51–1 lists the etiologies of ARP categorized by those typically managed medically versus those that respond to endoscopic therapy to prevent recurrences. This chapter focuses on the etiologies of ARP responding to endoscopic therapy. We also provide a brief update on the newly discovered and expanding body of knowledge of genetic causes of ARP, autoimmune ARP, and celiac-associated ARP. The endoscopic management for the genetic conditions is usually reserved for complications that develop from chronic pancreatitis (CP) and is covered in Chapter 52. For a summary of all etiologies of ARP, the readers are directed to the comprehensive review of Somogyi and coworkers.[4]

The initial workup of a first attack of pancreatitis is a source of some debate and depends on the severity of the attack, special circumstances relating to the presentation, and the demographics of the patient. This workup includes a core, common for all patients, and variations based on the individual case, but the workup must reflect a balance between rigor and reason.

A detailed history is the most important part of the initial evaluation. Clues to alcohol intake, a detailed review of medications, postprandial onset of symptoms suggestive of a biliary source, review of epiphenomenon suggestive of malignancy, a family history, an associated autoimmune or metabolic disorder, and a history of trauma should be sought. Physical examination may detect xanthoma or xanthelasma suggestive of hyperlipidemia, signs of alcohol-related liver disease, or a neck mass of parathyroid origin. Laboratory work and selective imaging should be used to confirm or exclude the differential generated by the history and physical and to direct therapy. An initial complete history and physical examination, routine blood work including liver injury tests, corrected or ionized calcium and triglyceride levels, and transabdominal ultrasound or computed tomography (CT) scan reveals an etiology in 70% to 90% of cases of pancreatitis.[2,5–8] In younger patients (<40 years) a transabdominal ultrasound may suffice, but in older patients, a CT scan of the abdomen is advised because a pancreatic or ampullary neoplasm may present with ARP.[9,10] Without an adequate initial workup and directed therapy, more than half of patients with an initial attack of acute pancreatitis will suffer recurrent attacks or develop CP.[5,11] For example, in patients with gallstone pancreatitis, treatment of the index attack and prevention of further attacks may involve endoscopic sphincterotomy (ES) with bile duct stone extraction and laparoscopic cholecystectomy to remove the stone reservoir.[6,7] Patients who remain untreated have a 33% to 66% chance of a recurrent attack.[8,11–13]

Table 51–1. Putative Etiology of Acute Relapsing Pancreatitis

Medical Management	Endoscopic/Surgical Management
Alcohol	Annular pancreas
Autoimmune	Biliary stones/microlithiasis
Celiac disease	Choledochocyst and choledochocele
Drug induced	Pancreas divisum
Genetic	Pancreatic and ampullary neoplasms
• Hereditary pancreatitis	Periampullary diverticulum
• CFTR mutations	Sphincter of Oddi dysfunction
• SPINK mutations	
• Tropical pancreatitis	
Hypercalcemia	
Hyperlipidemia	
Infectious	
Vascular	

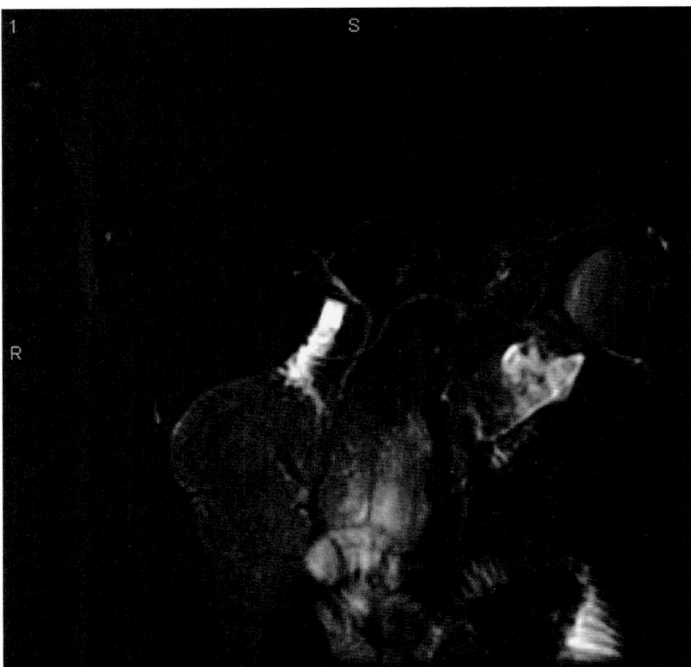

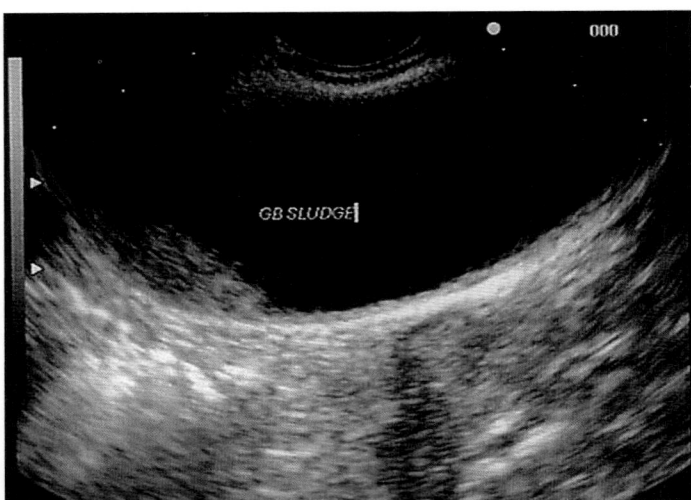

Figure 51–2. Gallbladder sludge was found at endoscopic ultrasound using a convex linear array echoendoscope in a patient with acute recurrent pancreatitis and a normal transabdominal ultrasound. (Photograph courtesy of Dr. Kevin McGrath, University of Pittsburgh Medical Center.)

Figure 51–1. A magnetic resonance cholangiopancreatography (MRCP) in a patient with acute recurrent pancreatitis demonstrating pancreas divisum. The dorsal pancreatic duct is clearly seen crossing over the bile duct and entering the region of the minor papilla. The ventral duct is not seen, and the common bile duct appears normal.

Workup of Acute Relapsing Pancreatitis

If the initial workup after an index attack of pancreatitis is negative and successive attacks occur, a more extensive evaluation reveals a diagnosis in around two thirds of this group of patients. This evaluation may start with a variety of blood tests depending on the individual scenario, followed by magnetic resonance imaging (MRI)/magnetic resonance cholangiopancreatography (MRCP) or endoscopic ultrasonography (EUS), and culminate in endoscopic retrograde cholangiopancreatography (ERCP). At each step of escalating invasiveness, the balance between the yield and the potential complications of the intended investigation should be carefully considered in discussions with the patient.

After an initial unrevealing evaluation for acute pancreatitis, ERCP reveals an etiology in approximately 70% of patients.[5,14] Although some experts advocate performing an ERCP after a single attack of pancreatitis in all patients, most agree that it is warranted only after a severe attack in which the etiology is not obvious or recurrent attacks.[15,16] The utility of this test lies in its unique ability to diagnose and treat biliary microlithiasis, sphincter of Oddi dysfunction (SOD) and pancreas divisum, the most commonly encountered diagnoses in the workup of ARP. Less often, pancreatic and ampullary cancers; duodenal diverticulum; pancreatic duct (PD) strictures or stones; and congenital malformations such as

choledochocele, annular pancreas, and anomalous pancreaticobiliary junction may be encountered.

ERCP is risky because it causes acute pancreatitis in 3% to 20% of patients[17,18] depending on the indication and maneuver performed. Acute pancreatitis is more frequent when ERCP is performed for diagnostic purposes, particularly when coupled with treatment of SOD, compared with other indications, most notably bile duct stones.[19] Other risk factors include multiple or high-pressure injections of contrast into the PD, therapeutic intervention, a past history of pancreatitis, and operator inexperience.[20] In a referral center treating 279 patients with acute pancreatitis over a 5-year period, ERCP was the causal factor in 4% of cases.[21] However, 3 of 11 patients in the subgroup with ERCP-related pancreatitis died.

Because ERCP-related complications, MRCP is replacing diagnostic ERCP in many centers.[22] With heavily T2-weighted images, fluid within the bile and pancreatic ducts produces an image akin to an endoscopically generated cholangiopancreatogram. MRCP is accurate in detecting common bile duct stones,[23,24] and its role in the evaluation of ARP includes the identification of anatomic abnormalities such as pancreas divisum (Fig. 51–1), choledochocysts, annular pancreas, and anomalous pancreaticobiliary junction.[24–27] However, ERCP continues to be used in the diagnostic evaluation of ARP because of the ability to visualize the ampulla, to sample tissue and bile, and to perform sphincter of Oddi manometry (SOM).

EUS uses higher frequencies than conventional abdominal ultrasound, and the image quality is not compromised by intestinal gas providing a higher sensitivity and specificity for detecting cholelithiasis than conventional ultrasonography.[28–30] It has been shown to be as accurate as ERCP in the diagnosis of choledocholithiasis,[31] and the positive predictive value for biliary tract disease including microlithiasis in the gallbladder and biliary sludge[32,33] (Fig. 51–2) is about 98%.[14] It remains the endoscopic procedure of choice for visualizing the pancreas,[34–38] and it is the most accurate technique for the detection and local staging of pancreatic carcinoma.[39,40] EUS is also useful in detecting changes in the pancreatic parenchyma and ducts.[38,39] In patients with ARP, EUS correctly identified a cause of acute pancreatitis in 155 of the 168 patients in whom a cause was found by a multidisciplinary diagnostic approach, involving ERCP, bile crystal analysis, surgery, and medical follow-up. EUS may also be useful in the detection of pancreas divisum,[41] SOD,[42] and anomalous pancreaticobiliary junction,[43] but more data are required before the performance characteristics of EUS for these diagnoses is known. Given the high yield and lower complication rate compared with ERCP, EUS is being used earlier in the workup of ARP. So far, however, a consensus has not been reached as to the exact place for EUS in the diagnostic algorithm for ARP.

Additional laboratory workup after negative routine testing may include genetic testing for hereditary pancreatitis (HP) and cystic fibrosis (CF) and autoimmune markers. The mainstay of management for patients with ARP is to discover the etiology and perform an intervention that prevents recurrence, because there is no specific therapy to treat an acute attack of pancreatitis.

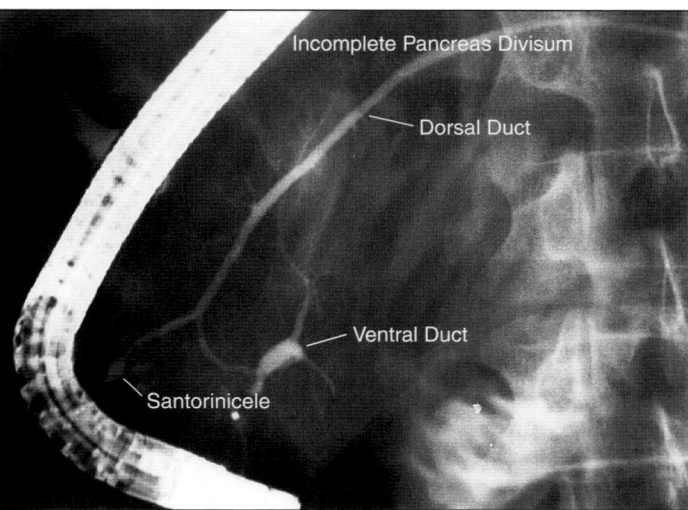

Figure 51-3. An endoscopic retrograde cholangiopancreatography (ERCP) performed on this patient with acute recurrent pancreatitis demonstrates incomplete pancreas divisum. The ventral duct and dorsal duct *(arrows)* are connected by a small branch duct. At the distal most portion of the dorsal duct, a cystic-like outpouching (Santorinicele; *arrow*) is also seen. This patient responded to endoscopic minor papillotomy.

Pancreas Divisum

INTRODUCTION

The term pancreas divisum refers to two pancreatic ductal systems that do not unite during embryologic organogenesis and communicate and separately drain via the two duodenal papillae, the dominant dorsal system through the minor papilla, and the smaller ventral system through the major papilla (see Fig. 51-1). Incomplete pancreas divisum describes a threadlike communication between dorsal and ventral PDs and, when symptomatic, is treated like complete pancreas divisum (Fig. 51-3).

EPIDEMIOLOGY

Pancreas divisum is the most common congenital anomaly of the pancreas and may be found in up to 7% to 14% of autopsy series.[44-46] The frequency of pancreas divisum among ERCP series varies greatly (2.7% to 7.5%) and depends on the population studied and the diligence with which complete pancreatography is pursued. Pancreas divisum is reported to occur less often in Asians (1% to 2%)[47] and blacks (2%).[48] Considerable controversy remains regarding the clinical significance of pancreas divisum. Although estimates reveal that less than 5% of the population with pancreas

divisum ever develops pancreatic symptoms, authorities recognize its association with ARP, CP, and abdominal pain.[49-51] Patients undergoing pancreatography for documented pancreatitis are significantly more likely to have pancreas divisum than those who have incidental pancreatograms during ERCP or for unexplained chronic abdominal pain.[52] Table 51-2 summarizes the larger ERCP series of patients with pancreas divisum and pancreatitis. Caution should be exercised when assigning causation to divisum in patients with ARP given its prevalence in the population, and other known causes of pancreatitis should still be sought for and excluded.

PATHOGENESIS

Because most exocrine flow is routed through the minor papilla in this ductal anomaly, it is hypothesized that in some patients an increased resistance to flow across this small orifice results in dorsal duct hypertension and clinical symptoms.[53-56] The resulting increased dorsal duct pressure may also make the pancreas more prone to injury from alcohol and drugs.[57,58] Thus, procedures aimed at decreasing resistance to flow across the minor papilla, either surgical or endoscopic, have been reported with varying success.

Table 51-2. Reported Incidence of Pancreas Divisum and Associated Acute Relapsing Pancreatitis			
Author	No. of ERCPs	% Incidence of Pancreas Divisum	% Idiopathic Pancreatitis as Indicated for ERCP
Cotton (1980)[48]	810	5.8%	25.6%
Sugawa et al. (1987)[76]	1529	2.7%	2.4%
Delhaye et al. (1985)[207]	5333	5.7%	5.3%
Bernard et al. (1990)[47]	1825	7.5%	50%
Burtin et al. (1991)[208]	1049	5.9%	12%
ERCP, endoscopic retrograde cholangiopancreatography.			

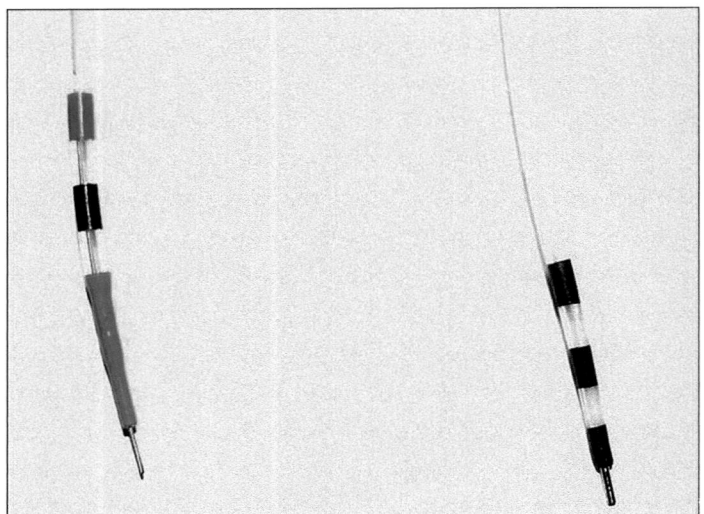

Figure 51–4. A variety of catheters may be used for cannulation of the minor papilla. Two examples are shown above. On the left, the contour endoscopic retrograde cholangiopancreatography (ERCP) cannula (Microvasive/Boston Scientific, Watertown, MA) is a catheter tapered to 3 French at its distal tip. A 0.018-inch guidewire (Roadrunner, Wilson Cook Medical, Winston Salem, NC) is passed through the catheter with its tip protruding several millimeters to facilitate cannulation of the minor papilla. An adapter can be fixed to the proximal end of the catheter that allows simultaneous injection of radiopaque contrast. On the right, a metal tipped catheter (ERCP-LP-23-Lehman, Wilson Cook Medical, Winston Salem, NC) can be used to facilitate minor papilla cannulation and opacification. A guidewire cannot be passed through this catheter.

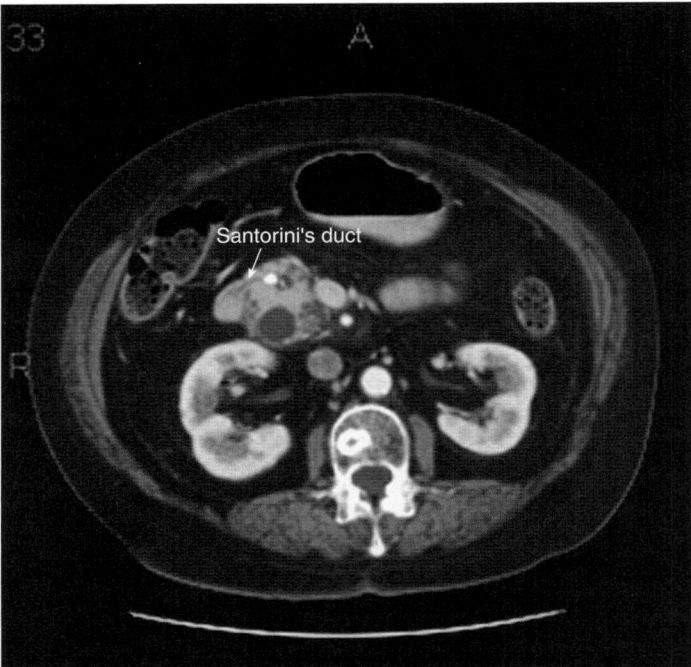

Figure 51–5. A computed tomography (CT) scan obtained in this patient with acute recurrent pancreatitis disclosed chronic pancreatitis and pancreas divisum. Santorini's duct is seen *(arrow)* draining into the area of the minor papilla. A large calcified stone is impacted in Santorini's duct, and the dorsal duct proximal to this is dilated. An intraparenchymal pseudocyst is seen below. This patient was treated with minor papilla sphincterotomy, temporary stenting, hydrostatic balloon dilation, and stone extraction.

DIAGNOSIS

ERCP remain the gold standard for diagnosing pancreas divisum. A characteristic ventral pancreatogram with an attenuated duct that arborizes, strongly suggests pancreas divisum. Caution must be exercised in patients with an obstructed PD that may look like divisum. Confirmation is made by locating the minor papilla and injecting contrast into the dorsal duct (Video 51–1). The minor papilla is usually located 2 cm proximal and 2 cm medial to the major papilla. It is best seen with the duodenoscope passed in a long position, without reducing the loop along the greater curve of the stomach. Occasionally, the minor papilla cannot be identified. The use of intravenous (IV) secretin (0.2 U/kg) during ERCP may stimulate the exocrine pancreas and help identify the minor papilla as a point origin of clear liquid "squirting" into the duodenum.[59] The prior application of methylene blue to the periampullary mucosa before IV secretin has been suggested to assist in the identification of the minor papilla.[60]

Cannulation of the papilla may be difficult, and a variety of tapered or metal-tipped catheters and papillotomes have been developed (Fig. 51–4).

It is my opinion that the success of minor papilla cannulation is optimized when the diagnosis is predetermined. This calls for noninvasive diagnostic modalities to avoid repeat ERCP. MRCP is best suited for this purpose. The use of IV secretin improves PD visualization during MRCP.[61,62] The diagnosis of divisum may be made by CT (Fig. 51–5) or EUS, but the accuracy of diagnosis of these modalities is unknown.

CLINICAL PRESENTATION AND TREATMENT

The earliest attempts of treatment for patients with presumed symptomatic pancreas divisum were surgical. The surgical procedures first performed to reduce resistance to exocrine flow consisted of a transduodenal minor and major sphincteroplasty with cholecystectomy. More recently, a transduodenal minor sphincterotomy or sphincteroplasty alone[63] has evolved as the surgical treatment of choice. The clinical presentation of ARP, the presence of minor papilla stenosis either intraoperatively or by delayed clearance of dye after dorsal ductography during ERCP, and a positive ultrasound (US) secretin test remain the best predictors of outcome after surgical intervention for pancreas divisum.[64]

To avoid laparotomy, a number of endoscopic maneuvers have been applied for the management of symptoms related to pancreas divisum. These have included minor papilla dilation, stenting, and sphincterotomy. The technique of minor papilla stenting involves free selective cannulation of the dorsal duct, placement of a guidewire, and advancement of a stent, specifically designed for use in the pancreas, over the guidewire with a pushing cannula (see Video 51–1). These stents are plastic and vary in diameter from 3 to 10 Fr (Fig. 51–6). Larger stents (7 Fr and 10 Fr) are reserved for patients with dilated PDs and/or CP. Pancreatic stents 5 Fr and larger have multiple side holes to permit drainage from side branches and have external flanges or pigtails to prevent inward migration. Some stents have internal barbs to prevent outward migration. The number and need for multiple stent exchanges has

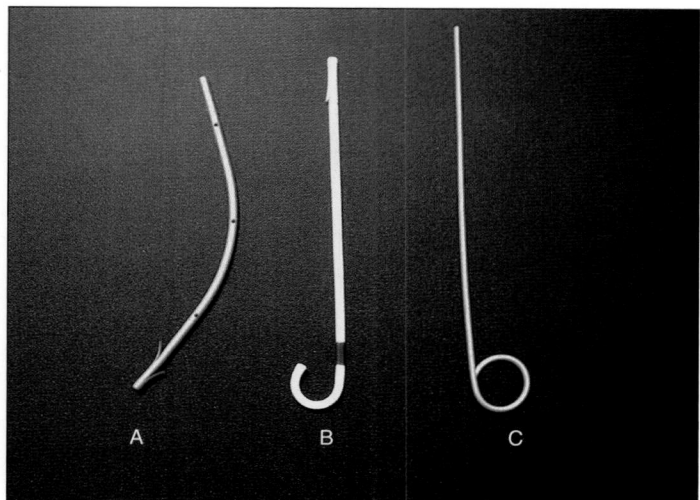

Figure 51–6. A variety of stents can be placed into the pancreatic duct to treat symptomatic pancreas divisum or as prophylaxis against post-endoscopic retrograde cholangiopancreatography (ERCP) pancreatitis. Stent A is the Geenen pancreatic stent (Wilson Cook Medical, Winston Salem, NC). This example is 5 French in diameter and contains a single set of external flaps that allow the stent to migrate out spontaneously over the ensuing days in most patients. A variant of this stent comes with internal flaps, if the stent is intended to stay in the duct for longer periods. Stent B is the Freeman Pancreatic Flexi-Stent (Hobbs Medical, Stafford Springs, CT). This is a soft Silastic stent with an internal flange to prevent outward migration and an external pigtail to prevent inward migration. The example shown is 5 French in diameter. As with the Geenen stent, multiple side holes are present. Stent C is the Zimmon pancreatic stent (Wilson Cook Medical, Winston Salem, NC). This 3-French stent has an external pigtail to prevent inward migration. No side holes are present and this stent will migrate out spontaneously over days in most patients.

not been firmly established nor has the interval necessary for stent exchanges, although most advocate 4 to 8 weeks for stents 5 to 7 Fr in diameter.

Minor papilla dilation may be accomplished with catheter dilators or hydrostatic balloons. The catheter dilators generally vary in diameter from 5 to 10 Fr and are advanced into the dorsal ducts over a preplaced wire. Although balloons vary in diameter, for the sole purpose of dilating the minor papilla, 4 mm over-the-wire hydrostatic balloons are the smallest commercially available devices. Larger balloons should be used with caution, unless concurrent CP exists with need for additional therapy (e.g., stone extraction or stricture dilation; see Chapter 52).

Two techniques have been described for minor papilla sphincterotomy: standard traction papillotomy (see Video 51–1) and needle knife sphincterotomy over a stent. Traction papillotomes with braided or monofilament cutting wires can be used to accomplish traction papillotomy. The papillotome tip in the PD usually directs the wire in a 12 o'clock to 2 o'clock direction, and the length of the cut is dependent on the size of the minor papilla mound, usually about 5 mm. Some advocate the use of pure cutting current to prevent cautery to the pancreatic parenchyma with resulting stenosis of the outflow tract. It is generally advisable to leave a temporary pancreatic stent, which has been shown to decrease the risk of postprocedure pancreatitis for pancreatic sphincterotomy of the major papilla.[65,66] The needle knife technique involves placing a pancreatic stent into the dorsal duct and using it as a guide to create an approximate 5 mm cut over the stent. The stent may be left in place temporarily to reduce the risk of post-ERCP pancreatitis. Minor papilla dilation alone has not been studied in a controlled fashion but has been used in combination with stenting.

Categorizing patients with symptomatic pancreas divisum may help decide management and predict outcome (Table 51–3). There have been two prospective, randomized, controlled trials evaluating endoscopic therapy for patients with pancreas divisum. One looked at the role of minor papilla stenting in patients with pancreas divisum and ARP and reported 90% success over a mean 29-month period.[64] The second trial evaluated the role of minor papillotomy in treating patients with pancreas divisum and chronic abdominal pain and reported symptomatic relief in 44% of the patients.[67] A number of studies looking at dorsal duct stenting and minor papillotomy summarized in Table 51–3[68–71] suggest symptomatic improvement and/or resolution of ARP in 70% to 80% of patients with pancreas divisum; however, these studies suffer from heterogeneous study populations, varied follow-up, and lack of controls. The response in the setting of CP is less satisfactory and, for chronic abdominal pain, suboptimal and, in our opinion, ill advised. Regarding the choice of therapy, most authorities now favor minor papillotomy over dorsal duct stenting.

The overall success rate of endoscopic therapy (stenting, dilation, and/or sphincterotomy) is similar to the results of surgical sphincteroplasty. The restenosis rate in the surgical literature appears less than for endoscopic minor papillotomy, although reports suggesting that patients who have restenosis after ES also restenose after sphincteroplasty.[72] Therefore, endoscopic techniques seem preferable as a first choice, because laparotomy can be avoided. The short-term success rate of minor papilla ES and surgical sphincteroplasty may be similar, but long-term follow-up and comparative trials are needed before firmer recommendations regarding procedure choice and cost effectiveness can be made.

COMPLICATIONS

Complications of stent therapy include acute pancreatitis; the induction of pancreatic ductal changes, many of which may not be reversible[73]; stent occlusion or migration; PD perforation; and the need for repeated procedures. Complications of minor papilla ES including bleeding, perforation, and pancreatitis have been reported and are similar to major papilla ES.[74] Lehman and coworkers[75] reported a 15% procedural complication rate for minor ES, primarily mild pancreatitis. Restenosis is reported to occur with a frequency of 5% to 10%.[76]

Biliary Microlithiasis

INTRODUCTION

A number of terms have been used interchangeably for biliary microlithiasis including biliary sludge and biliary sand. The term biliary microlithiasis typically refers to finding cholesterol monohydrate crystals and calcium bilirubinate granules on light microscopy of an endoscopically acquired centrifuged sample of bile.[77]

Table 51–3. Results of Endoscopic Therapy in Patients with Pancreas Divisum

Author	Study Design	N	Mean F/U Months	Intervention	Symptom Relief				Restenosis	Chronic Duct Changes
					NP	AR	CP	CAP		
Russell et al. (1984)[56]	Retro	5	8	MES	1/5				Not provided	
Soehendra et al. (1986)[209]	Retro	6	3	MES		2/2	4/4		Not provided	
Liquory et al. (1986)[210]	Retro	8	24	MES		5/8			3/8	
McCarthy et al. (1988)[68]	Retro	19	6–36	Stent	17/19					2/19
Prabhu et al. (1989)[69]	Retro	18	12–60	Stent		15/18				NS
Siegel et al. (1990)[70]	Retro	31	24	Stent	26/31					NS
Lans et al. (1992)[211]	RCT	10 (9 controls)	29	Stent		9/10				0/10
Sherman et al. (1994)[67]	RCT	16 (17 controls)	25	MES				7/16	Not provided	
Lehman et al. (1993)[75]	Retro	52	20	MES		13/17	3/11	6/24	10/18	
Coleman 1994[71]	Retro	34	23	Stent		7/9	12/20	2/5	Not provided	NS
Kozarek et al. (1995)[144]	Retro	39	26	MES and/or stent		11/15	6/19	1/5	3/26	10/39
Boerma et al. (2000)[212]	Prosp	16	51	Stent		5/16				NS
Ertan (2000)[213]	Prosp	25	24	Stent		19/25				21/25
Heyries et al. (2002)[214]	Prosp	24	39	MES or stent		22/24	NS			16/16

ARP, acute recurrent pancreatitis; CAP, chronic abdominal pain; CP, chronic pancreatitis; MES, minor papilla endoscopic sphincterotomy; NP, not provided; NS, not significant; Prosp, prospective uncontrolled trial; RCT, randomized controlled trial; Retro, retrospective review.

The criteria for differentiating between biliary microliths and small stones are not entirely clear, but generally a gallstone is defined as a particle with a diameter greater than 2 or 3 mm that cannot be crushed by digital compression.[77] Biliary sludge on the other hand is the ultrasonographic finding of low-level echoes without acoustic shadowing that gravitate toward the dependent portion in the gallbladder[78] and move with positioning. Biliary sludge consists of cholesterol monohydrate crystals and calcium bilirubinate granules suspended in gallbladder mucus. Other calcium salts, proteins, and xenobiotics such as ceftriaxone can also be found.[79]

EPIDEMIOLOGY

Similar to gallstones, the risk of developing biliary microlithiasis is increased in women and in several conditions including pregnancy,[80,81] rapid weight loss,[82] critical illness,[83] prolonged fasting,[84] long-term administration of total parenteral nutrition,[84–87] ceftriaxone[85–90] or octreotide administration,[91–93] and bone marrow or solid organ transplantation.[94–98] It follows that the development of ARP in these clinical situations should prompt an aggressive search for microlithiasis (approximately 31%).

Approximately 31% of patients with nonalcoholic pancreatitis have biliary microlithiasis, and up to 74% of patients with "idiopathic" pancreatitis have been shown to have biliary microlithiasis.[11,99] Two prospective studies of consecutive patients with apparently idiopathic pancreatitis found that two thirds to three fourths had microlithiasis as the presumed cause, as documented by biliary-drainage studies, follow-up sonograms, and ERCP with sphincterotomy or cholecystectomy.[11,99]

PATHOGENESIS

Considerable controversy exists over the clinical significance of biliary microlithiasis. Experts remain divided over whether it is a transient phenomenon or a precursor to gallstones. After chemical dissolution of gallstones, gallbladder sludge is usually seen on ultrasonography before gallstone recurrence,[100] suggesting that the pathogenesis of sludge is similar to that of gallstones.[101–105] On the other hand, sludge resolves spontaneously in most and gallstones form in only a small minority of individuals with sludge. There are few studies of the pathogenesis and natural history of biliary sludge, and most are limited by insufficient follow-up.[100,106,107] Three clinical outcomes were noted in one study, including complete resolution, a waxing and waning course, and gallstone formation.[100] It appears that sludge found in patients with abdominal pain spontaneously disappears in about 50% of cases. Asymptomatic persistence is seen in about 20% of cases over 3 years, and symptoms may develop in 10% to 15% of patients. Gallstones develop in 5% to 15%.[108]

Further support for the role of biliary microlithiasis in producing pancreaticobiliary symptoms comes from the observations that symptomatic patients with gallstones receiving ursodeoxycholic acid had resolution of their symptoms in 3 months, although the number and size of their gallstones remained unchanged.[109] The supposition is that the treatment resolved concurrent biliary microlithiasis, which lead to the symptoms. Asymptomatic patients with gallstones who receive shock-wave lithotripsy have been reported to develop biliary colic, cholecystitis, or acute pancreatitis.[110-114] In this situation, the therapy may have created sludge that in turn produced the symptoms.

Hypothetically, microlithiasis can lead to pancreatitis through a number of mechanisms. Small stones may transiently impact at the papilla leading to PD obstruction and pancreatitis.[115] Recurrent passage of stones may lead to papillary stenosis or SOD, both associated with pancreatitis.[116]

DIAGNOSIS

Biliary sludge remains an ultrasonographic diagnosis. The sensitivity of transabdominal ultrasonography for sludge is approximately 55%, whereas the sensitivity of EUS is approximately 96% (see Fig. 51–2), compared with duodenal bile collection (67%).[117,118] Although clinically less applicable, microscopic examination of gallbladder contents is considered the diagnostic gold standard and also allows the chemical composition of sludge to be defined. The sensitivity is 83% when bile is obtained directly from the common bile duct during ERCP.[119] Bile sampling is indicated only if less invasive studies are negative, the clinical suspicion for microlithiasis is high, and the results will guide management. Techniques vary as to the site of bile collection, cholecystokinin use, sample processing, and criteria for a positive test. The relationship between the quantity of crystals and the clinical outcome remains unproved.

TREATMENT

A number of therapeutic options are available to treat symptomatic biliary microlithiasis including cholecystectomy, ES, and chemical dissolution. The benefit of therapy has been demonstrated by the significant decrease in recurrent episodes of pancreatitis after therapy (<10%) versus a recurrence rate of approximately 66% to 75% in untreated patients.[11,120-125]

Laparoscopic cholecystectomy offers definitive therapy[11,77] and is indicated in good operative candidates of almost any age. Biliary endoscopic sphincterotomy (BES) is an effective alternative in the very elderly or those with significant comorbid illness. The benefits of sphincter ablation[123-129] include enhanced gallbladder motility and reduced stasis, which may persist for years.[130] BES also reduces bile lithogenicity by modifying the bile composition.

Although there is no demonstrable difference in the clinical benefit of cholecystectomy or BES for microlithiasis-induced pancreatitis, the safety profile of laparoscopic cholecystectomy outweighs the immediate and late complications of BES for an indication of ARP in most clinical situations. BES may be used as a temporizing measure in patients who have severe acute pancreatitis secondary to microlithiasis in whom cholecystectomy must be deferred for weeks or months.

Few studies have examined ursodeoxycholic acid for the treatment of biliary sludge. In patients with rapid weight loss, ursodeoxycholic acid has been shown to decrease the incidence of gallstones by 50% to 100%.[131,132] In patients with idiopathic pancreatitis and sludge,[11] maintenance therapy after initial treatment with ursodeoxycholic acid to dissolve cholesterol crystals

successfully prevents the recurrence of sludge and pancreatitis. This form of therapy is a reasonable alternative in poor operative candidates or the elderly.

Sphincter of Oddi Dysfunction

INTRODUCTION

A detailed description of SOD is provided in Chapter 49 and is not stressed in this chapter. Direct evidence of the involvement of the sphincter of Oddi (SO) in the pathogenesis of pancreatitis is lacking. However, experts recognize SOD as a condition that may be associated with ARP. Using probes, surgeons have documented narrowing of the SO in patients undergoing surgery for ARP. Secretin-stimulated ultrasound studies of the PD in patients with SOD have revealed prolonged dilation of the PD compared with controls and are associated with a good outcome after surgical sphincteroplasty.[133] The morphine Prostigmine test has been used to show an association between SOD and abdominal pain associated with pancreatitis. Likewise manometric studies have shown an association between SOD and a proportion of patients with ARP, most commonly an abnormally raised SO basal pressure[134,135]; therefore, intuitively surgeons and endoscopists have devised treatment strategies aimed at relieving obstruction at the SO. The earlier surgical literature suffered from inhomogeneous patient population and mixed results.[136,137] Recent literature using SOM to guide selection of patients with ARP for open sphincteroplasty and septoplasty reveal cessation of attacks in greater than 90% of patients with manometric stenosis; however, in patients with ARP, manometric evidence of SOD varies widely.

SOD can involve either or both the biliary and pancreatic segments. Pancreatic SOD has been implicated in causing recurrent pancreatitis in patients with prior biliary sphincter ablation.[138,139] Recent literature reveals that pancreatic SOD often coexists with biliary SOD; hence, documentation and ablation of both is recommended by a number of centers.[140,141]

Pancreatic sphincterotomy of the major papilla uses the same techniques as described previously for the minor papilla (Video 51–2). Whether concomitant biliary sphincterotomy is required is controversial and currently under investigation. Leaving a temporary pancreatic stent in place after biliary sphincterotomy alone for SOD or after pancreatic sphincterotomy will reduce the incidence and severity of postsphincterotomy pancreatitis.[66,142]

Unfortunately, most data regarding SOD have evolved from studies of the biliary segment and therapy directed at it. Assumptions regarding manipulation of treatment directed at the PD based on such data can be misleading and potentially dangerous. Response to endoscopic stenting of the PD has been used either to treat or to select patients for surgery.[143,144] However, long-term outcome is lacking. In the biliary tree, SO basal pressure has been shown, in a randomized controlled trial, to predict who will respond to biliary sphincterotomy among a group of patients with type II biliary SOD.[145] Corresponding studies for PD manometry have not been performed in ARP; thus, the ability of PD manometry to discriminate between responders and nonresponders to PD sphincterotomy in patients with ARP and PD-SOD has never been demonstrated.

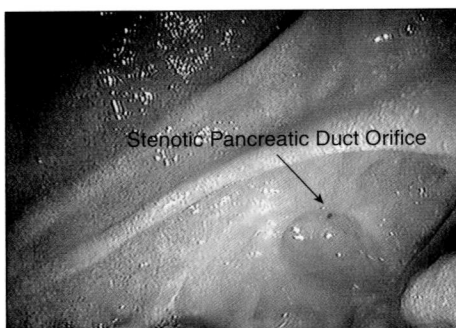

Figure 51-7. This patient presented with acute recurrent pancreatitis 18 months after a biliary and pancreatic surgical sphincteroplasty for sphincter of Oddi dysfunction. At endoscopic retrograde cholangiopancreatography (ERCP), a grossly stenotic pancreatic duct orifice is seen as a pinpoint opening (arrow) within the defect at the site of prior surgery. This was treated successfully with hydrostatic balloon dilation and temporary stenting.

There is circumstantial evidence suggesting a higher incidence of post-ERCP pancreatitis in patients with ARP undergoing ERCP and SOM.[146]

Patients with ARP and a dilated PD in the absence of morphologic criteria for CP (Type 1 SOD) are considered to have stenosis of the pancreatic sphincter[147] (Fig. 51–7), and, akin to the biliary tract, pancreatic sphincterotomy appears reasonable.

Ampullary and Pancreatic Malignancies

In a small subset of patients, malignant or premalignant obstruction of the PD may lead to the development of ARP. This is most commonly due to ductal adenocarcinomas of the pancreas and ampulla but can also be seen with neuroendocrine tumors,[148] metastatic tumors, and ampullary adenomas[149] (Fig. 51–8). Intraductal papillary mucin-secreting tumors (IPMT) of the pancreas are a rarer form of premalignant or malignant tumors that typically present with ARP. Mucin secretion from hyperplastic ductal cells can obstruct the PD and cause ARP. CT scans commonly show a dilated main PD (Fig. 51–9) or isolated side branch dilation (Fig. 51–10). Associated cystic lesions may also be present. At ERCP, a fishmouth papilla held open with mucus is pathognomonic (Fig. 51–11).

Pancreatic stents have been used to palliate obstructive pain and to treat ARP in patients with pancreatic malignancies who are not candidates for surgery.[150] PD ES may allow mucus passage and palliate symptoms in patients with IPMT who are nonoperative candidates. Patients with ARP secondary to ampullary adenomas can be treated with endoscopic or surgical ampullectomy.[151]

Choledochocysts

Choledochocysts are congenital anomalies of the biliary tract that are most often diagnosed in children and often associated with pancreaticobiliary malunion (Fig. 51–12). ARP in children with choledochocysts is usually associated with biliary stones or sludge

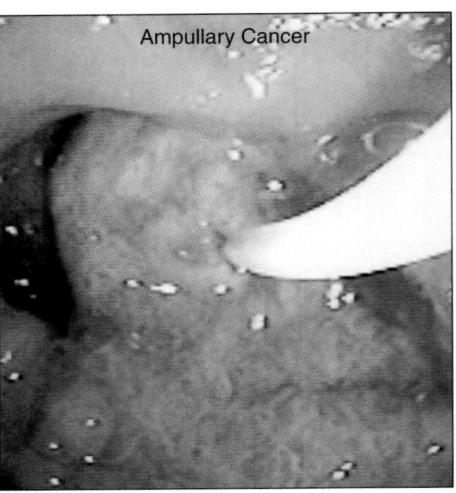

Figure 51-8. This patient with an ampullary cancer presented with cholestatic liver tests and acute recurrent pancreatitis. Fortunately, the lesion was found to be early stage by endoscopic ultrasound and a curative Whipple resection was performed.

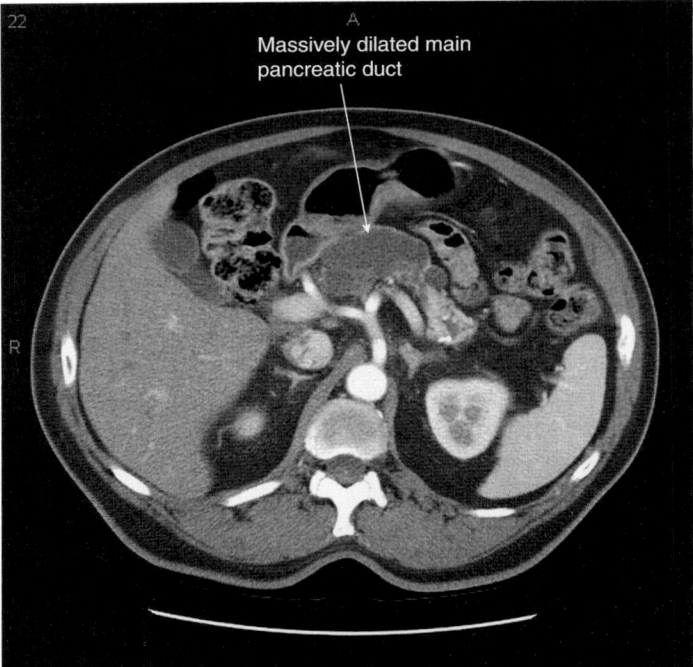

Figure 51-9. Computed tomography (CT) scan obtained in a patient with intraductal papillary mucin-producing tumor. A massively dilated pancreatic duct filled with low-density material is seen (arrow).

that forms in the native or retained cyst.[152] Complete surgical excision is the treatment of choice to prevent pancreaticobiliary symptoms and to prevent the development of biliary cancer, which is increased in the cysts if left in situ. Type 3 choledochocysts (choledochoceles) have been associated with ARP and can be treated with biliary ES through the cyst or via surgical transduodenal marsupialization.[153] They may be recognized at endoscopy as a suprapapillary submucosal bulge and confirmed fluoroscopically at ERCP.

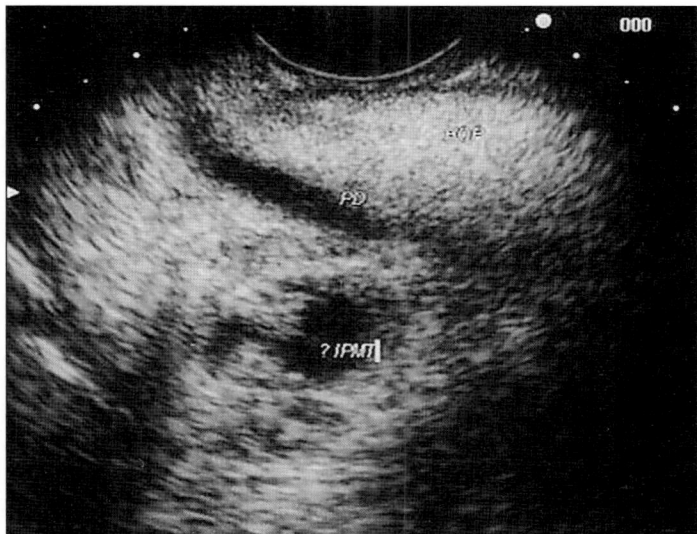

Figure 51–10. An endoscopic ultrasound is performed on a patient with a side-branch variant of intraductal papillary mucin producing tumor. A cystic hypoechoic region (IPMT) is seen immediately caudal to the main pancreatic duct (PD). (Photograph courtesy of Dr. Kevin McGrath, University of Pittsburgh Medical Center.)

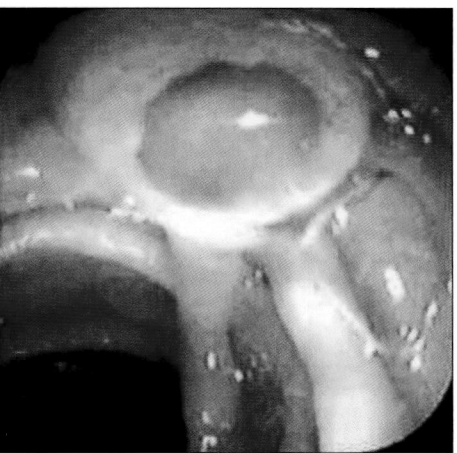

Figure 51–11. This photomicrograph of the endoscopic appearance of the major papilla of a patient with intraductal papillary mucin-producing tumor shows that the pancreatic orifice is held widely patent with intraductal mucus giving the classic fishmouth appearance.

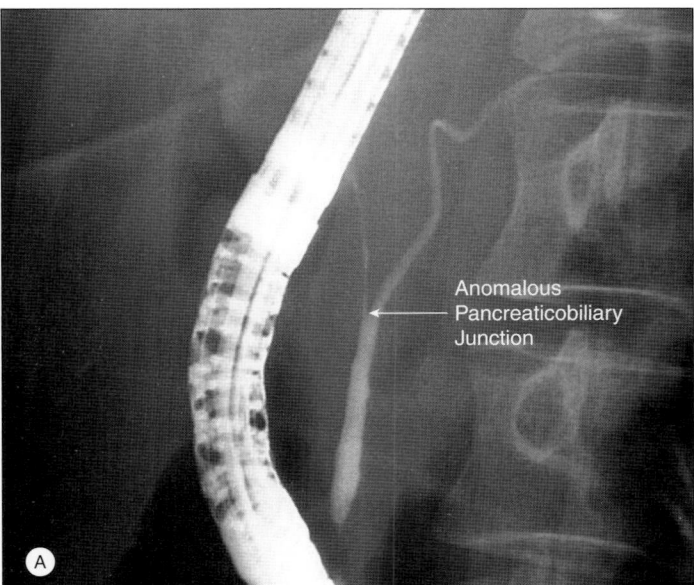

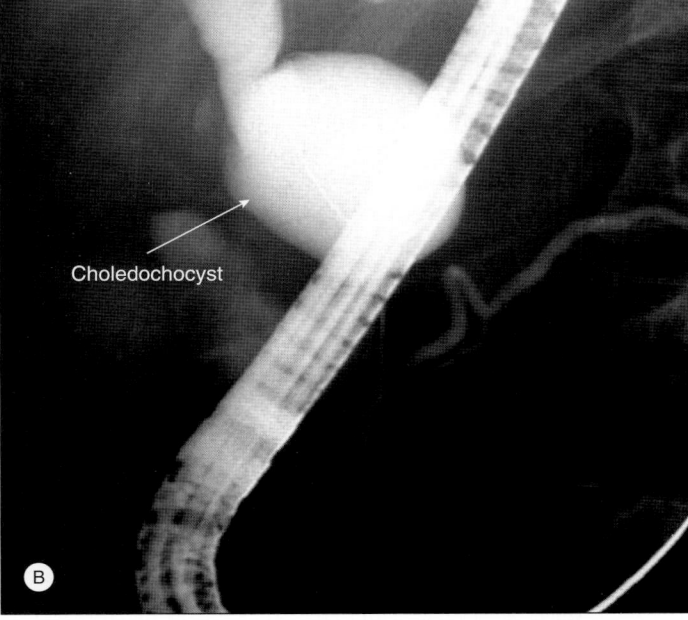

Figure 51–12. This 22-year-old woman presented with acute recurrent biliary pancreatitis. At endoscopic retrograde cholangiopancreatography (ERCP), an anomalous pancreaticobiliary junction *(arrow)* is seen *(A)*. Filling of the distal bile duct is seen via a strictured segment. Further contrast injection into the bile duct fills a classic Type I choledochocyst *(B)*. This patient was taken to surgery and had a complete excision of this cyst with a hepaticojejunostomy and has done well without recurrent symptoms.

Periampullary Duodenal Diverticula

Periampullary diverticula have been indicated in the etiology of ARP. These diverticula are more commonly seen in elderly patients and are more often associated with choledocholithiasis and ARP compared with patients without diverticula.[154] Periampullary diverticula are associated with an incompetent SO with resultant colonization of the bile duct with intestinal bacteria, leading to the generation of mixed pigment bile duct stones.[155] Although direct causative evidence linking periampullary diverticula to ARP are lacking, relative outflow obstruction of bile duct with bacterial colonization and microlith formation or outflow obstruction of exocrine pancreas secretions have been postulated in the pathogenesis of ARP, and a biliary sphincterotomy is generally performed.

Annular Pancreas

Annular pancreas is a rare congenital malformation in which the pancreatic parenchyma encircles the duodenal sweep. It most commonly presents with obstruction of the duodenum and is best treated with a surgical duodenal bypass. Case reports of ARP associated with annular pancreas exist[4,156]; however, causality has not been confirmed.

Genetic Causes

INTRODUCTION

Recent developments in the field of molecular biology have lead to the recognition of a strong genetic predisposition for a significant proportion of patients with idiopathic pancreatitis and evidence for gene-environment interactions for other varieties of pancreatitis including alcohol related. The focus of this section remains on ARP and associated genetic etiologies.

HEREDITARY PANCREATITIS

Epidemiology

Familial pancreatitis refers to pancreatitis of any etiology occurring in a family with an incidence that is greater than expected by chance. HP specifically refers to unexplained pancreatitis in a member of a family in which a pancreatitis-causing gene mutation is expressed in an autosomal dominant pattern. The phenotypic features of HP encompass the spectrum of pancreatic inflammatory diseases. HP typically presents as ARP in childhood and progresses to CP by young adulthood in more than half of cases and is associated with an approximately 40% risk of pancreatic cancer by age 70,[157,158] which is exaggerated by smoking.[159]

Pathogenesis

The gene for HP was mapped to chromosome 7q35[160,161] and was identified as the cationic trypsinogen gene (protease, serine, 1; *PRSS1*; OMIM 276000) by Whitcomb and colleagues in 1996.[162] Two point mutations R122H and N29I[163] occurring in exon3 and exon2 of cationic trypsinogen, respectively, account for most cases. Currently, these are the only mutations for which genetic testing is recommended according to a recent consensus conference.[164,165] The same consensus also provides guidelines for testing.

The R122H mutant cationic trypsin is thought to be resistant to autolysis through elimination of the arginine or lysine residues recognized by trypsin, which is critical in initiating trypsin autolysis.[147] Trypsin is a proteolytic enzyme that activates most pancreatic digestive enzymes within the intestinal lumen and is maintained in the inactive trypsinogen form within the pancreas. Several mechanisms protect the pancreas from the consequences of prematurely activated trypsinogen. When trypsinogen is activated within the pancreas, the first known protective mechanism is inhibition by pancreatic secretory trypsin inhibitor (*PSTI*; unigene symbol *SPINK1*; serine protease inhibitor, Kazal type 1; OMIM 167790), which has the capacity to inhibit approximately 20% of potential trypsin activity.[166] If trypsin activity overwhelms the *SPINK1/PSTI* inhibitory capacity, trypsin inactivation occurs via trypsin autolysis. With mutations that eliminate the autolysis site in HP, the second protective mechanism is lost and pancreatitis occurs.

Studies on families with HP reveal mutations in cationic trypsinogen that enhance autoactivation (N29I), mutations in *SPINK1/PSTI* that likely diminish inhibition of active trypsinogen (e.g., N34S), and mutations in cationic trypsinogen that prevent autolysis (R122H). One third of families with HP have no mutation in either cationic trypsinogen or *SPINK1/PSTI*, suggesting that other genes are also important. For reasons that are unclear, HP disease penetrance is incomplete. A review of large kindred groups worldwide reveals a fairly constant rate of penetrance of 80%.[167–170] A recent study of identical twins with HP[171] suggested that the mechanism of disease penetrance is not one of simple genetics and that the protective element is not a modifier gene or obvious environmental factor.

SPINK1/PSTI mutations are common in the general population and not clearly associated with pancreatitis but may enhance the likelihood of pancreatitis related to other etiologies.[169,170] The most commonly identified mutation in control populations is N34S (1% allele frequency), and the highest frequency is seen in patients with idiopathic CP. Approximately 10% of familial pancreatitis kindreds have identifiable *SPINK1* mutations. The clinical presentations are varied and include ARP or more commonly CP. The age of first presentation is typically before 20 years. Because less than 1% of patients with a heterozygous *SPINK1* mutation alone ever develop pancreatitis, most experts do not recommend genetic testing or screening.[164]

TROPICAL PANCREATITIS

Tropical pancreatitis is a syndrome of ARP progressing to CP, usually developing in children from lower socioeconomic families in tropical regions of Indonesia, Asia, Africa, and South America. There appears to be some variation in presentation; some children suffering from severe calcific CP with late diabetes mellitus, whereas others develop diabetes and pancreatic fibrosis before developing calcification.

The etiology of tropical pancreatitis is uncertain, but some clues are beginning to accumulate. First, diet has been eliminated as a cause of this disease. Second, there appears to be genetic susceptibility because a significant minority of patients have mutations in the pancreatic secretory trypsin inhibitor gene *SPINK1*.[172,173] Third, these children's immune systems and pancreaticobiliary tree are constantly challenged by infectious agents including helminths such as *Ascaris lumbricoides* that are endemic.[174–176] If these infectious agents trigger acute pancreatitis, then an altered immune response may drive pancreatic fibrosis in genetically susceptible individuals.[177] Thus, current evidence suggests that tropical pancreatitis is a complex condition with strong environmental trigger factors and genetic susceptibility and modifier factors that eventually result is irreversible pancreatic damage.

Therapy

Endoscopic therapy for ARP secondary to HP is reserved for complications of CP in general including strictures, stones, fistulas, and pseudocysts and is discussed in detail in Chapter 52.

CYSTIC FIBROSIS

Pathogenesis

Cystic fibrosis (CF, OMIM 219700) is the most common lethal autosomal recessive disorder in Caucasians and is caused by a mutation of the cystic fibrosis transmembrane conductance regulator gene (*CFTR*; OMIM 602421) located on chromosome 7q32.[178] CFTR is a chloride channel located on the luminal surface of the PD cell that is tightly linked to bicarbonate secretion.[179-181] Major mutations in both alleles leads to loss of CFTR function and the ability to hydrate mucus resulting in inspissated glands. Based on their functional impact, *CFTR* gene mutations are classified as either severe (class 1 to 3) or mild (class 4 and 5).[181,182] Severe mutations yield little or no functional protein, whereas mild mutations diminish CFTR function. Pulmonary consequences and abnormal sweat chloride occurs with CFTR function less than 5%; however, pancreatic exocrine function may be maintained down to 1% CFTR function. One or 2 mild CFTR mutations retaining more than 1% CFTR function, therefore, may not lead to pancreatic insufficiency despite the overall disease status.[183,184] Such patients are susceptible to ARP as may be patients with one severe mutation (e.g., delta F508, the most common mutation approximately 70%) and a second milder mutation (e.g., CFTR R117H, R334W, R347W, and so forth) any time the CFTR function falls below 10% of normal.[185,186] It follows that the pancreas behaves differently from the lung and vas deferens, qualitatively depending on the degree of CFTR impairment. Although the spectrum of pancreatic disease ranges from pancreatic insufficiency to ARP and CP, most of the data available pertains to patients with pancreatic insufficiency and idiopathic CP and is based on a select number of the known mutations; therefore, firm recommendations with regards to patients with ARP cannot be made. Patients with ARP resulting from diminished CFTR activity probably reflect an intermediate stage with CP as the result. Studies involving histologic correlation are needed to further elucidate this process. In patients with ARP and suspected CFTR mutations, diminished CFTR function can be confirmed with nasal bioelectric potential difference measurements because many mild CFTR mutations are not included in commercial CFTR tests.

Therapy

As with HP, endoscopic therapy for ARP in CF is reserved for complications of CP and is discussed in Chapter 52.

AUTOIMMUNE PANCREATITIS

Introduction

Pancreatitis associated with hypergammaglobulinemia was first reported in 1965.[187] Since then evidence for an autoimmune basis for recurrent attacks (but more commonly CP) in a subset of patients has been increasing.[188,189]

Epidemiology and Diagnosis

The clinical findings in autoimmune pancreatitis encompass those typical of pancreatitis but often with milder symptoms and usually without acute attacks. Obstructive jaundice appears to be a common feature, and a therapeutic response to steroid therapy has been reported.[190] The sex ratio for autoimmune pancreatitis varies remarkably in literature, probably because of the small study populations.[191,192]

Radiologic findings include diffuse or focal pancreatic parenchymal enlargement, diffuse or focal pancreatic main duct narrowing and beading, and a characteristic absence of pancreatic calcifications or cysts.[193,194]

Laboratory findings in autoimmune pancreatitis may differ between isolated autoimmune pancreatitis and autoimmune pancreatitis associated with an autoimmune disorder. Although both varieties are characterized by elevated serum IgG and the presence of autoantibodies including antinuclear (ANA), anti-lactoferrin (ALF), and anti-carbonic anhydrase II (ACA II), and less commonly anti-smooth muscle (ASMA) and rheumatoid factor.[194] Elevated IgG4 levels, on the other hand, are useful in diagnosing isolated autoimmune pancreatitis.[193,195] IgG4 is the least common of the IgG subclasses and has been considered a noninflammatory protective antibody,[196] and its secretion along with IgE is regulated by T helper-2 cytokines such as interleukin (IL)-4, IL-5, and IL-13.[1] However, the antigens driving the elevated IgG4 antibody titers in isolated autoimmune pancreatitis remain obscure.

Therapy

The finding of elevated IgG4 levels in the appropriate clinical setting may also be useful for deciding on a trial of steroid therapy.[197,198] In addition to the improvement in symptoms and radiographic features, patients with autoimmune pancreatitis and diabetes mellitus display a trend toward normalizing insulin secretion and glycemic control with steroid therapy.[198] Other regimens have been reported including the use of additional immunosuppressive therapy such as azathioprine.

CELIAC DISEASE

A known association between celiac disease and pancreatic insufficiency has been recognized for a number of years,[198-200] and reports exist of improvement in pancreatic function in non-CP cases with gluten-free diet. The postulated mechanisms have included malnutrition[201,202] and reduced gallbladder emptying resulting from impaired cholecystokinin release.[203-205] Recently, an association between ARP and celiac disease has been reported, presumably resulting from duodenal inflammation leading to papillary stenosis.[206] In 169 patients referred for suspected SOD, celiac disease was diagnosed in 12 (3 men, 9 women). Ten had ARP, and two had elevated liver function tests associated with abdominal pain. These patients had manometric evidence of papillary stenosis *and* histologic evidence of periampullary inflammation and celiac disease. Improvement in duodenal inflammation and symptoms was seen on a gluten-free diet; however, all patients had undergone BES and, therefore, the data are somewhat difficult to interpret.

ACKNOWLEDGMENTS

I would like to thank Dr. Asif Khalid for assistance in the preparation of the sections on hereditary and autoimmune pancreatitis.

REFERENCES

1. Steer ML: Classification and pathogenesis of pancreatitis. Surg Clin North Am 69:467–480 1989.
2. Reber HA: Acute pancreatitis: Another piece of the puzzle? N Engl J Med 325:423–424, 1991.
3. Sakorafas GH, Tsiotou AG: Etiology and pathogenesis of acute pancreatitis: Current concepts. J Clin Gastroenterol 30:343–356, 2000.
4. Somogy L, Martin SP, Venkatesan T, et al: Recurrent acute pancreatitis: An algorithmic approach to identification and elimination of inciting factors. Gastroenterology 120:708–717, 2001.
5. Venu RP, Geenen JE, Hogan W, et al: Idiopathic recurrent pancreatitis. An approach to diagnosis and treatment. Dig Dis Sci 34:56–60, 1989.
6. Glazer G, Mann DV on behalf of the working party of the British Society of Gastroenterology: United Kingdom guidelines for the management of acute pancreatitis. Gut 42(Suppl 2):S1–13, 1998.
7. Baillie J: Treatment of acute biliary pancreatitis. N Engl J Med 336:286–287, 1997.
8. Goodman AJ, Neoptolemos JP, Carr-Locke DL, et al: Detection of gall stones after acute pancreatitis. Gut 26:125–132, 1985.
9. Lin A, Feller ER: Pancreatic carcinoma as a cause of unexplained pancreatitis: Report of ten cases. Ann Intern Med 113:166–167, 1990.
10. Gutman M, Inbar M, Klausner JM: Metastases-induced acute pancreatitis: A rare presentation of cancer. Eur J Surg Oncol 19:302–304, 1993.
11. Ros E, Navarro S, Bru C, et al: Occult microlithiasis in 'idiopathic' acute pancreatitis: Prevention of relapses by cholecystectomy or ursodeoxycholic acid therapy. Gastroenterology 101:1701–1709, 1991.
12. Patti MG, Pellegrini CA: Gallstone pancreatitis. Surg Clin North Am 70:1277–1295, 1990.
13. Lo SK, Chen J: The role of ERCP in choledocholithiasis. Abdom Imaging 21:120–132, 1996.
14. Amouyal P, Amouyal G, Levy P: Diagnosis of choledocholithiasis by endoscopic ultrasonography. Gastroenterology 42:225–231, 1994.
15. Bank S, Indaram A: Causes of acute and recurrent pancreatitis. Clinical considerations and clues to diagnosis. Gastroenterol Clin North Am 28:571–589, viii, 1999.
16. Gregor JC, Ponich TP, Detsky AS: Should ERCP be routine after an episode of "idiopathic" pancreatitis? A cost-utility analysis. Gastrointest Endosc 44:118–123, 1996.
17. Thornton J, Axon A: Towards safer endoscopic retrograde cholangiography. Gut 34:721–724, 1993.
18. Sherman S, Hawes RH, Rathgabe SW, et al: Post-ERCP pancreatitis: Randomized, prospective study comparing a low-and High-osmolality contrast agent. Gastrointest Endosc 40:422–427, 1994.
19. Chen YK, Foliente RL, Santoro MJ, et al: Endoscopic sphincterotomy-induced pancreatitis: Increased risk associated with nondilated bile ducts and sphincter of Oddi dysfunction. Am J Gastroenterol 89:327–333, 1994.
20. Roszler MH, Campbell WL: Post-ERCP pancreatitis: Association with urographic visualization during ERCP. J Radiol 157:595–598, 1985.
21. de Beaux AC, Palmer KR, Carter DC: Factors influencing morbidity and mortality in acute pancreatitis; an analysis of 279 cases. Gut 37:121–126, 1995.
22. Baron TH, Fleischer DE: Past, present, and future of endoscopic retrograde cholangiopancreatography: Perspectives on the National Institutes of Health consensus conference. Mayo Clin Proc 77:407–412, 2002.
23. Soto JA, Barish MA, Yucel EK, et al: Magnetic resonance cholangiography: Comparison with endoscopic retrograde cholangiopancreatography. Gastroenterology 110:589–597, 1996.
24. Barish MA, Yucel EK, Gerrucci JT: Magnetic resonance cholangiopancreatography. N Engl J Med 341:258–264, 1999.
25. Taourel P, Bret PM, Reinhold C, et al: Anatomic variants of the biliary tree: Diagnosis with MR cholangiopancreatography. Radiol 199:521–527, 1996.
26. Barish M, Soto J, Ferrucci J: Magnetic resonance pancreatography. Endoscopy 29:487–495, 1997.
27. Bret PM, Reinhold C, Paourel P, et al: Pancreas divisum: Evaluation with MR cholangiopancreatography. Radiology 199:99–103, 1996.
28. Buscail L, Escourrou J, Moreau J, et al: Endoscopic ultrasonography in chronic pancreatitis: A comparative prospective study with conventional ultrasonography, computed tomography and ERCP. Pancreas 10:251–257, 1995.
29. Chak A, Hawes RH, Cooper GS, et al: Prospective assessment of utility of EUS in the evaluation of gallstone pancreatitis. Gastrointest Endosc 49:599–604, 1999.
30. Liu CL, Lo CM, Chan JK, et al: EUS for detection of occult cholelithiasis in patients with idiopathic pancreatitis. Gastrointest Endosc 51:28–32, 2000.
31. Norton SA, Alderson D: Prospective comparison of endoscopic ultrasonography and endoscopic retrograde cholangiopancreatography in the detection of bile duct stones. Br J Surg 84:1366–1369, 1997.
32. Dahan P, Andat C, Levy P, et al: Prospective evaluation of endoscopic ultrasonography and microscopic examination of duodenal bile in the diagnosis of cholecystolithiasis in 45 patients with normal conventional ultrasonography. Gut 38:277–281, 1996.
33. Dille JE: Symptom resolution or relief after cholecystectomy correlates strongly with positive combined endoscopic ultrasound and stimulated biliary drainage. Endoscopy 29:646–648, 1997.
34. Axon AT, Classen M, Cotton PB, et al: Pancreatography in chronic pancreatitis: International definitions. Gut 25:1107–1112, 1984.
35. Prat F, Amouyal G, Amouyal P, et al: Prospective controlled study of endoscopic ultrasonography and endoscopic retrograde cholangiography in patients with suspected common bile duct lithiasis. Lancet 347:75–79, 1996.
36. Frossard JL, Hadengue A, Amouyal G, et al: Choledocholithiasis. A prospective study of spontaneous common bile duct stone migration. Gastrointest Endosc 51:175–179, 2000.
37. Yasuda K, Mukai H, Fujimoto S, et al: The diagnosis of pancreatic cancer by endoscopic ultrasonography. Gastrointest Endosc 34:1–8, 1988.
38. Rosch T, Lorenz R, Braig C, et al: Endoscopic ultrasound in pancreatic tumor diagnosis. Gastrointest Endosc 37:347–352, 1991.
39. Zuccaro G, Sivak MV: Endoscopic ultrasonography in the diagnosis of chronic pancreatitis. Endoscopy 24:347–349, 1992.
40. Nattermann C, Goldschmidt AJ, Dancygier H: Endosonography in chronic pancreatitis—a comparison between endoscopic retrograde pancreatography and endoscopic ultrasonography. Endoscopy 24:565–570, 1993.
41. Bhutani MS, Hoffman BJ, Hawes RH: Diagnosis of pancreas divisum by endoscopic ultrasonography. Endoscopy 31:167–169, 1999.
42. Di Francesco V, Brunori MP, Rigo L, et al: Comparison of ultrasound-secretin test and sphincter of Oddi manometry in patients with recurrent acute pancreatitis. Dig Dis Sci 44:336–340, 1999.
43. Sugiyama M, Atomi Y: Endoscopic ultrasonography for diagnosing anomalous pancreaticobiliary junction. Gastrointest Endosc 45:261–267, 1997.
44. Varshney S, Johnson CD: Pancreas divisum. Int J Pancreatology 24:135–141, 1999.
45. Narisawa R, Asakura H, Niwa M, et al: Morphological study of pancreas divisum using ERCP in Niigata. Digest Endosc 6:158–162, 1994.
46. Smanio T: Proposed nomenclature and classification of the human pancreatic ducts and duodenal papillae: Study based on 200 post mortems. Int Surg 52:125–134, 1969.

47. Bernard JP, Sahel J, Giovanini M, et al: Pancreas divisum is a probable cause of acute pancreatitis: A report of 137 cases. Pancreas 5:248–254, 1990.

48. Cotton PB: Congenital anomaly of pancreas divisum as cause of obstructive pain and pancreatitis. Gut 21:105–114, 1980.

49. Gregg JA: Pancreas divisum: Its association with pancreatitis. Am J Surg 134:539–543, 1997.

50. Krueger KJ, Wootton FT, Cunningham JT, et al: Unexpected anomalies of the common bile and pancreatic ducts. Am J Gastroenterol 87:1492–1495, 1992.

51. Sahel J, Cros RC, Bourry J, et al: Clinico-pathological conditions associated with pancreas divisum. Digestion 23:1–8, 1982.

52. Richter JM, Schapiro RH, Mulley AG, Warshaw AL: Association of the pancreas divisum and pancreatitis and its treatment by sphincteroplasty of the accessory ampulla. Gastroenterology 81:1104–1110, 1981.

53. Cotton PB: Congenital anomaly of pancreas divisum as cause of obstructive pain and pancreatic. Gut 21:104–114, 1980.

54. Bernard JP, Sahel J, Giovannini M, et al: Pancreas divisum is a probable cause of pancreatitis: A report of 137 cases. Pancreas 5:248–254, 1990.

55. Warshaw AL, Richter JM, Schapiro RH: The cause and treatment of pancreatitis associated with pancreas divisum. Ann Surg 198:443–452, 1983.

56. Russell RC, Wong NW, Cotton PB: Accessory sphincterotomy (endoscopic and surgical) in patients with pancreas divisum. Br J Surg 71:954–957, 1984.

57. Lowes JR, Rode J, Lees WR, et al: Obstructive pancreatitis: Unusual causes of chronic pancreatitis. Br J Surg 75:1129–1133, 1988

58. Mairose UB, Wurbs D, Classen M: Santorini's duct an insignificant variant from normal or an important overflow valve? Endoscopy 10:24–29, 1978.

59. Devereaux BM, Lehman GA, Fein S, et al: Facilitation of pancreatic duct cannulation using a new synthetic porcine secretin. Am J Gastroenterol 97:2279–2281, 2002.

60. Park SH, de Bellis M, McHenry L, et al: Use of methylene blue to identify the minor papilla or its orifice in patients with pancreas divisum. Gastointest Endosc 57:358–363, 2003.

61. Khalid A, Peterson M, Slivka A: Secretin-stimulated magnetic resonance pancreaticogram to assess pancreatic duct outflow obstruction in evaluation of idiopathic acute recurrent pancreatitis: A pilot study. Dig Dis Sci 48:1475–1481, 2003.

62. Matos C, Metens T, Deviere J, et al: Pancreatic duct Morphological and functional evaluation with dynamic MR pancreatography after secretin stimulation. Radiology 203:435–441, 1997.

63. Keith RG: Surgery for pancreas divisum. Gastrointest Clin North Am 4:171–180, 1995.

64. Lans JI, Geenen JE, Johanson JF, et al: Endoscopic therapy in patients with pancreas divisum and acute pancreatitis: A prospective, randomized, controlled clinical trial. Gastrointest Endosc 38:430–434, 1992.

65. Tarnasky PR: Mechanical prevention of post-ERCP pancreatitis by pancreatic stents: Results, techniques, and indications. JOP 4:58–67, 2003.

66. Fazel A, Quadri A, Catalano MF, et al: Does a pancreatic duct stent prevent post-ERCP pancreatitis? A prospective randomized study. Gastrointest Endosc 57:291–294, 2003.

67. Sherman S, Hawes R, Nisi R, et al: Randomized controlled trial of minor papilla sphincterotomy (MiES) in pancreas divisum (Pdiv) patients with pain only [abstract]. Gastrointest Endosc 40:A125, 1994.

68. McCarthy J, Geenen JE, Hogan W: Preliminary experience with endoscopic stent placement in benign diseases. Gastrointest Endosc 34:16–18, 1988.

69. Prabhu M, Geenen JE, Hogan WJ, et al: Role of endoscopic stent placement in the treatment of acute recurrent pancreatitis associated with pancreas divisum: A prospective assessment [abstract]. Gastrointest Endosc 34:165, 1989.

70. Siegel JH, Ben-svi JS, Pullano W, et al: Effectiveness of endoscopic drainage for pancreas divisum. Endoscopy 22:129–133, 1990.

71. Coleman SD, Eisen GM, Troughton AB, Cotton PB: Endoscopic treatment in pancreas divisum. Am J Gastroenterol 89:1152–1155, 1994.

72. Kozarek RA: Pancreatic stents can induce ductal changes consistent with chronic pancreatitis. Gastrointest Endosc 36:93–95, 1990.

73. Smith M, Ikenberry S, Uzer M, et al: Alterations in pancreatic duct morphology following pancreatic stent therapy. Gastrointest Endosc 44:268–275, 1996.

74. Lehman GA, Sherman S: Diagnosis and therapy of pancreas divisum. Gastrointest Endosc Clin N Am 8:55–77, 1998.

75. Lehman GA, Sherman S, Nisi R, et al: Pancreas divisum: Results of minor papilla sphincterotomy. Gastrointest Endosc 39:1–8, 1993.

76. Sugawa C, Walt AJ, Nunez DC, et al: Pancreas divisum: Is it a normal anatomic variant? Am J Surg 153:62–67, 1987.

77. Lee SP: Biliary sludge: Curiosity or culprit? [editorial] Hepatology 20:523–525, 1994.

78. Filly RA, Allen B, Minton MJ, et al: In vitro investigation of the origin of echoes with biliary sludge. J Clin Ultrasound 8:193–200, 1980.

79. Allen B, Bernhoft R, Blackaert N, et al: Sludge is calcium bilirubinate associated with bile stasis. Am J Surg 141:51–56, 1981.

80. Maringhini A, Marceno MP, Lanzarone F, et al: Sludge and stones after pregnancy. Prevalence and risk factors. J Hepatol 5:218–223, 1987.

81. Maringhini A, Ciambra M, Baccelliere P, et al: Biliary sludge and gallstones in pregnancy: Incidence, risk factors, and natural history. Ann Intern Med 119:116–120, 1993.

82. Shiffman ML, Sugerman JH, Kellum JM, et al: Gallstone formation after rapid weight loss: A prospective study in patients undergoing gastric bypass surgery for treatment of morbid obesity. Am J Gastroenterol 86:1000–1005, 1991.

83. Murray FE, Stinchcombe SJ, Hawkey CJ: Development of biliary sludge in patients on intensive care unit: Results of a prospective ultrasonographic study. Gut 33:1123–1125, 1992.

84. Bolondi L, Gaiani S, Testa S, et al: Gallbladder sludge formation during prolonged fasting after gastrointestinal tract surgery. Gut 26:734–738, 1985.

85. Messing B, Bories C, Kuntslinger F, et al: Does total parenteral nutrition induce gallbladder sludge formation and lithiasis? Gastroenterology 84:1012–1019, 1983.

86. Gafa M, Sarli L, Miselli A, et al: Sludge and microlithiasis of the biliary tract after total gastrectomy and postoperative total parenteral nutrition. Surg Gynecol Obstet 165:413–418, 1987.

87. Pitt HA, King W 3rd, Mann LL, et al: Increased risk of cholelithiasis with prolonged total parenteral nutrition. Am J Surg 145:106–112, 1983.

88. Schaad UB, Tschappeler H, Lentze MJ: Transient formation of precipitations in the gallbladder associated with ceftriaxone therapy. Pediatr Infect Dis 5:708–710, 1986.

89. Schaad UB, Wedgwood-Krucko J, Tschaeppeler H: Reversible ceftriaxone-associated biliary pseudolithiasis in children. Lancet 2:1411–1413, 1988.

90. Ettestad PJ, Campbell GL, Welbel SF, et al: Biliary complications in the treatment of unsubstantiated Lyme disease. J Infect Dis 171:356–361, 1995.

91. Vance ML, Harris AG: Long-term treatment of 189 acromegalic patients with the somatostatin analog octreotide. Results of the international Multicenter Acromegaly Study Group. Arch Intern Med 151:1573–1578, 1991.

92. Newman CB, Melmed S, Snyder PJ, et al: Safety and efficacy of long-term octreotide therapy of acromegaly: Results of a multicenter trial in 103 patients-a clinical research center study. J Clin Endocrinol Metab 80:2768–2775, 1995.

93. Ezzat S, Snyder PJ, Younge WF, et al: Octreotide treatment of acromegaly. A randomized, multicenter study. Ann Intern Med 117:711–718, 1992.

94. Teefey SA, Hollister MS, Lee SP, et al: Gallbladder sludge formation after bone marrow transplant: Sonographic observations. Abdom Imaging 19:57–60, 1994.

95. Frick MP, Snover DC, Feinberg SB, et al: Sonography of the gallbladder in bone marrow transplant patients. Am J Gastroenterol 79:122–127, 1984.

96. Lorber MI, Van Buren CT, Flechner SM, et al: Hepatobiliary and pancreatic complications of cyclosporine therapy in 466 renal transplant recipients. Transplantation 43:35–40, 1987.

97. Peterseim DS, Pappas TN, Meyers CH, et al: Management of biliary complications after heart transplantation. J Heart Lung Transplant 14:623–631, 1995.

98. Jacobson AF, Teefey SA, Lee SP, et al: Frequent occurrence of new hepatobiliary abnormalities after bone marrow transplantation: Results of a prospective study using scintigraphy and sonography. Am J Gastroenterol 88:1044–1049, 1993.

99. Lee SP, Nicholls JF, Park HZ: Biliary sludge as a cause of acute pancreatitis. N Engl J Med 326:589–593, 1992.

100. Lee SP, Maher K, Nicholls JF: Origin and fate of biliary sludge. Gastroenterology 94:170–179, 1988.

101. Johnston DE, Kaplan MM: Pathogenesis and treatment of gallstones. N Engl J Med 328:412–421, 1993.

102. Paumgartner G, Sauerbruch T: Gallbladder stones: Pathogenesis. Lancet 338:1117–1124, 1991.

103. Carey MC, Cahalane MJ: Whither biliary sludge? Gastroenterology 95:508–523, 1988.

104. Lee SP: Pathogenesis of biliary sludge. Hepatology 12(3 Pt 2):200S–203S, 1990.

105. Cahalane MJ, Neubrand MW, Carey MC: Physical-chemical pathogenesis of pigment gallstones. Semin Liver Dis 8:317–328, 1988.

106. Janowitz, P, Kratzer W, Zemmler T, et al: Gallbladder sludge: Spontaneous course and incidence of complications in patients with stones. Hepatology 20:291–294, 1994.

107. Ohara N, Schaefer J: Clinical significance of biliary sludge. J Clin Gastroenterol 12:291–294, 1990.

108. Ko CW, Sekijima JH, Lee SP: Biliary sludge. Ann Intern Med 130:301–311, 1999.

109. Tint GS, Dyrszka H, Sanghavi B, et al: Lithotripsy plus ursodiol is superior to ursodiol alone for cholesterol gallstones. Gastroenterology 102:2042–2049, 1992.

110. Sauerbruch T, Delius M, Paumgartner G, et al: Fragmentation of gallstones by extracorporeal shock waves. N Engl J Med 314:818–822, 1986.

111. Sackmann M, Weber W, Delius M, et al: Extracorporeal shock-wave lithotripsy of gallstones without general anesthesia: First clinical experience. Ann Intern Med 107:347–348, 1987.

112. Sackmann M, Deluis M, Sauerbruch T, et al: Shock-wave lithotripsy of gallbladder stones. The first 175 patients. N Engl J Med 318:393–397, 1988.

113. Sackmann M, Pauletzki J, Sauerbruch T, et al: The Munich Gallbladder Lithotripsy Study. Results of the first 5 years with 711 patients. Ann Intern Med 114:290–296, 1991.

114. Opie EL: The etiology of acute hemorrhagic pancreatitis. Bull Johns Hopkins Hosp 12:182–188, 1901.

115. Hernandez CA, Lerch MM: Sphincter stenosis and gallstone migration through the biliary tract. Lancet 341:1371–1373, 1993.

116. Chebli JM, Ferrari Junior AP, Silva MR, et al: Biliary microcrystals in idiopathic acute pancreatitis: Clue for occult underlying biliary etiology [In Portugese with English abstract]. Arq Gastroenterol 37:93–101, 2000.

117. Dahan P, Andant C, Levy P, et al: Prospective evaluation of endoscopic ultrasonography and microscopic examination of duodenal bile in the diagnosis of cholecystolithiasis in 45 patients with normal conventional ultrasonography. Gut 38:277–281, 1996.

118. Dill JE, Hill S, Berkhouse L: Combined endoscopic ultrasound and stimulated biliary drainage in cholecystitis and microlithiasis-diagnoses and outcomes. Endoscopy 27:424–427, 1995.

119. Buscail L, Escourrou J, Delvaux M, et al: Microscopic examination of bile directly collected during endoscopic cannulation of the papilla. Utility in patients with suspected microlithiasis. Dig Dis Sci 37:116–120, 1992.

120. Kaufman Z, Shpitz B, Dinbar A: Microlithiasis of the cystic duct. Am J Gastroenterol 81:303–304, 1986.

121. Moreau JA, Zinsmeister AR, Melton LJ 3rd, et al: Gallstone pancreatitis and the effect of cholecystectomy: A population-based cohort study. Mayo Clin Proc 63:466–473, 1988.

122. Tanaka M, Ikeda S, Yoshimoto H, et al: The long-term fate of the gallbladder after endoscopic sphincterotomy. Complete follow-up study of 122 patients. Am J Surg 154:505–509, 1987.

123. Siegel JH, Veerappan A, Cohen SA, et al: Endoscopic sphincterotomy for biliary pancreatitis: An alternative to cholecystectomy in high-risk patients. Gastrointest Endosc 40:573–575, 1994.

124. Welbourn CR, Beckly DE, Eyre-Brook IA: Endoscopic sphincterotomy without cholecystectomy for gall stone pancreatitis. Gut 37:119–120, 1995.

125. Dalian P, Andant C, Levy P, et al: Prospective evaluation of endoscopic ultrasonography and microscopic examination of duodenal bile in the diagnosis of cholecystolithiasis in 45 patients with normal conventional ultrasonography. Gut 38:277–281, 1996.

126. Sharma BC, Agarwal DK, Baijal SS, et al: Effect of endoscopic sphincterotomy on gall bladder bile lithogenicity and motility. Gut 42:288–292, 1998.

127. Rosseland AR, Solhaug JH: Primary endoscopic papillotomy (EPT) is patients with stones in the common bile duct and the gallbladder in situ: A 5-8–year follow-up study. World J Surg 12:111–116, 1988.

128. Agarwal DK, Sharma BC, Dhiman RK, et al: Effect of endoscopic sphincterotomy on gallbladder motility. Dig Dis Sci 42:1495–1500, 1997.

129. Shiffman ML, Kaplan GD, Brinkman-Kaplan V, et al: Prophylaxis against gallstone formation with ursodeoxycholic acid in patients participating in a very-low-calorie diet program. Ann Intern Med 122:899–905, 1995.

130. Sugiyama M, Atomi Y: Longterm effects of endoscopic sphincterotomy on gall bladder motility. Gut 39:856–859, 1996.

131. Broomfield PH, Chopra R, Scheinbaum RC, et al: Effects of ursodeoxycholic acid and aspirin on the formation of lithogenic bile and gallstones during loss of weight. N Engl J Med 319:567–572, 1988.

132. Warshaw AL, Simeone J, Schapiro RH, et al: Objective evaluation of ampullary stenosis with ultrasonography and pancreatic stimulation. Am J Surg 149:65–72, 1985.

133. Toouli J, Roberts-Thomson IC, Dent J, et al: Sphincter of Oddi motility disorders in patients with idiopathic recurrent pancreatitis. Br J Surg 72:859–863, 1985.

134. Hogan WJ, Geenen JE: Biliary dyskinesia. Endoscopy 20:179–188, 1988.

135. Toouli J, Di Francesco V, Saccone G, et al: Division of the sphincter of Oddi for treatment of dysfunction associated with recurrent pancreatitis. Br J Surg 83:1205–1210, 1996.

136. Nardi GL, Michelassi F, Zannini P: Transduodenal sphincteroplasty: 5-25 year follow of 89 patients. Ann Surg 198:453–461, 1983.

137. Stephens RV, Burdick GE: Microscopic transduodenal sphincteroplasty and transampullary septoplasty for papillary stenosis. Am J Surg 142:621–627, 1986.

138. Gregg JA, Carr-Locke DL: Endoscopic pancreatic and biliary manometry in pancreatic, biliary and papillary disease, and after endoscopic sphincterotomy and surgical sphincteroplasty. Gut 25:1247–1254, 1984.

139. Guelrud M, Siegel JH: Hypertensive pancreatic duct sphincter as a cause of pancreatitis: Successful treatment with hydrostatic balloon dilation. Dig Dis Sci 29:225–231, 1984.

140. Eversman D, Fogel EL, Rusche M, et al: Frequency of abnormal pancreatic and biliary sphincter manometry compared with clinical suspicion of sphincter of Oddi dysfunction. Gastrointest Endosc 50:637–641, 1999.

141. Park SH, Watkins JL, Fogel EL, et al: Long-term outcome of endoscopic dual pancreatobiliary sphincterotomy in patients with manometry-documented sphincter of Oddi dysfunction and normal pancreatogram. Gastrointest Endosc 57:483–491, 2003.

142. Freeman ML: Understanding risk factors and avoiding complications with endoscopic retrograde cholangiopancreatography. Curr Gastroenterol Rep 5:145–153, 2003.

143. McCarthy J, Geenen JE, Hogan WJ: Preliminary experience with endoscopic stent placement in benign pancreatic diseases. Gastrointest Endosc 34:16–18, 1988.

144. Kozarek RA, Ball TJ, Patterson DJ, et al: Endoscopic approach to pancreas divisum. Dig Dis Sci 40:1974–1981, 1995.

145. Geenen JE, Hogan WJ, Dodds WJ, et al: The efficacy of endoscopic sphincterotomy after cholecystectomy in patients with sphincter of Oddi dysfunction. N Engl J Med 320:82–87, 1989.

146. Scicchitano J, Saccone GT, Baker RA, et al: How safe is endoscopic sphincter of Oddi manometry? J Gastroenterol Hepatol 10:334–336, 1995.

147. Khandekar S, Disario JA: Endoscopic therapy for stenosis of the biliary and pancreatic duct orifices. Gastrointest Endosc 52:500–505, 2000.

148. Grino P, Martinez J, Grino E, et al: Acute pancreatitis secondary to pancreatic neuroendocrine tumours. JOP 4:104–110, 2003.

149. Heiskanen I, Kellokumpu I, Jarvinen H: Management of duodenal adenomas in 98 patients with familial adenomatous polyposis. Endoscopy 46:1959–1962, 1999.

150. Tham TC, Lichtenstein DR, Vandervoort J, et al: Pancreatic duct stents for "obstructive type" pain in pancreatic malignancy. Am J Gastroenterol 95:956–960, 2000.

151. Martin JA, Haber GB: Ampullary adenoma: Clinical manifestations, diagnosis, and treatment. Gastrointest Endosc Clin N Am 13:649–669, 2003.

152. Komuro H, Makino SI, Yasuda Y, et al: Pancreatic complications in choledochal cyst and their surgical outcomes. World J Surg 25:1519–1523, 2001.

153. Martin RF, Biber BP, Bosco JJ, et al: Symptomatic choledochoceles in adults. Endoscopic retrograde cholangiopancreatography recognition and management. Arch Surg 127:536–538, 1992.

154. Uomo G, Manes G, Ragozzino A, et al: Periampullary extraluminal duodenal diverticula and acute pancreatitis: An underestimated etiological association. Am J Gastroenterol 91:1186–1188, 1996.

155. Lobo DN, Balfour TW, Iftikhar SY, et al: Periampullary diverticula and pancreaticobiliary disease. Br J Surg 86:588–597, 1999.

156. Chevillotte G, Sahel J, Raillat A, et al: Annular pancreas. Report of one case associated with acute pancreatitis and diagnosed by endoscopic retrograde pancreatography. Dig Dis Sci 29:75–77, 1984.

157. Sossenheimer MJ, Aston CE, Preston RA, et al: Clinical characteristics of hereditary pancreatitis in a large family based on high-risk haplotype. The Midwest Multicenter Pancreatic Study Group (MMPSG). Am J Gastroenterol 92:1113–1116, 1997.

158. Lowenfels A, Maisonneuve P, DiMagno E, et al: Hereditary pancreatitis and the risk of pancreatic cancer. J Natl Cancer Inst 89:442–446, 1997.

159. Lowenfels AB, Maisonneuve P, Whitcomb DC, et al: Cigarette smoking as a risk factor for pancreatic cancer in patients with hereditary pancreatitis. JAMA 286:169–170, 2001.

160. LeBodic L, Bignon JD, Raguenes O, et al: The hereditary pancreatitis gene maps to long arm of chromosome 7. Hum Mol Genet 5:549–554, 1996.

161. Whitcomb DC, Preston RA, Aston CE, et al: A gene for hereditary pancreatitis maps to chromosome 7q35. Gastroenterology 110:1975–1980, 1996.

162. Whitcomb DC, Gorry MC, Preston RA, et al: Hereditary pancreatitis is caused by a mutation in the cationic trypsinogen gene. Nat Genet 14:141–145, 1996.

163. Gorry M, Gabbaaizadeh D, Furey W, et al: Multiple mutations in the cationic trypsinogen gene are associated with hereditary pancreatitis. Gastroenterology 113:1063–1068, 1997.

164. Ellis I, Lerch MM, Whitcomb DC: Genetic testing for hereditary pancreatitis: Guidelines for indications, counseling, consent and privacy issues. Pancreatology 1:405–415, 2001.

165. Gates L, Ulrich C, Whitcomb D: Hereditary pancreatitis: Gene defects and their implications. Surg Clin North Am 79:711–722, 1999.

166. Riderknecht H: Activation of pancreatic zymogens: Normal activation, premature intrapancreatic activation, protective mechanisms against inappropriate activation. Dig Dis Sci 31:314–321, 1986.

167. Pfutzer RH, Barmada MM, Brunskill AP: SPINK1/PSTI polymorphisms act as disease modifiers in familial and idiopathic chronic pancreatitis. Gastroenterology 119:615–623, 2000.

168. Witt H, Hennies HC, Becker M: SPINK1 mutations in chronic pancreatitis. Gastroenterology 120:1060–1061, 2001.

169. Witt H, Luck W, Hennies HC, et al: Mutations in the gene encoding the serine protease inhibitor, Kazal type 1 are associated with chronic pancreatitis. Nat Genet 25:213–216, 2000.

170. Chen JM, Mercier B, Audrezet MP, et al: Mutational analysis of the human pancreatic secretary trypsin inhibitor (PSTI) gene in hereditary and sporadic chronic pancreatitis. J Med Genet 37:67–69, 2000.

171. Lebodic L, Bignon JD, Raguenes O, et al: The hereditary pancreatitis gene maps to long arm of chromosome 7. Hum Mol Genet 5:549–554, 1996.

172. Schneider A, Suman A, Rossi L, et al: SPINK1/PSTI mutations are associated with tropical pancreatitis and type II diabetes mellitus in Bangladesh. Gastroenterology 123:1026–1030, 2002.

173. Rossi L, Pfützer RL, Parvin S, et al: SPINK1/PSTI mutations are associated with tropical pancreatitis in Bangladesh: A preliminary report. Pancreatology 1:242–245, 2001.

174. Das S: Pancreatitis in children associated with round worms. Indian Pediatr 14:81–83, 1977.

175. Gilbert MG, Carbonnel ML: Pancreatitis in childhood associated with ascariasis. Pediatrics 33:589–592, 1964.

176. Coelho da Rocha RF, Chapcha P, Aun F: Abdominal complications of ascariasis in children. Prob Gen Surg 18:92–99, 2001.

177. Schneider A, Whitcomb DC: Hereditary pancreatitis: A model for inflammatory diseases of the pancreas. Best Pract Res Clin Gastroenterol 16:347–363, 2002.

178. Riordan JR, Rommens JM, Kerem B, et al: Identification of the cystic fibrosis gene: Cloning and characterization of complementary DNA. Science 245:1066–1073, 1989.

179. Marino CR, Matovcik LM, Gorelick FS, Cohn JA: Localization of the cystic fibrosis transmembrane conductance regulator in pancreas. J Clin Invest 88:712–716, 1991.

180. Shumaker H, Amlal H, Frizzell R, et al: CFTR drives Na+-nHCO-3 cotransport in pancreatic duct cells: A basis for defective HCO-3 secretion in CF. Am J Physiol 276:C16–C25, 1999.

181. Mickle JE, Cutting GR: Genotype-phenotype relationships in cystic fibrosis. Med Clin North Am 84:597–607, 2000.

182. Zielenski J, Tsui LC: Cystic fibrosis: Genotypic and phenotypic variations. Ann Rev Genet 29:777–807, 1995.

183. Cohn JA, Friedman KJ, Noone PG, et al: Relation between mutations of the cystic fibrosis gene and idiopathic pancreatitis. N Engl J Med 339:653–658, 1998.

184. Sheppard DN, Ostedgaard LS, Winter MC, et al: Mechanism of dysfunction of two nucleotide binding domain mutations in cystic fibrosis transmembrane conductance regulator that are associated with pancreatic sufficiency. EMBO J 14:876–883, 1995.

185. Noone PG, Zhou Z, Silverman LM, et al: Cystic fibrosis gene mutations and pancreatitis risk: Relation to epithelial ion transport and trypsin inhibitor gene mutations. Gastroenterology 121:1310–1319, 2001.

186. Gomez Lira M, Patuzzo C, Castellani C, et al: CFTR and cationic trypsinogen mutations in idiopathic pancreatitis and neonatal hypertrypsinemia. Pancreatology 1:538–542, 2001.

187. Yoshida K, Toki F, Takeuchi T, et al: Chronic pancreatitis caused by an autoimmune abnormality. Proposal of the concept of autoimmune pancreatitis. Dig Dis Sci 40:1461–1568, 1995.

188. Khalid A, Whitcomb DC: The importance of autoimmune pancreatitis. Gastroenterology 121:1518–1520, 2001.

189. Ohana M, Okazaki K, Hajiro K, et al: Multiple pancreatic masses associated with autoimmunity. Am J Gastroenterol 93:99–102, 1998.

190. Ito T, Nakano I, Koyanagi S, et al: Autoimmune pancreatitis as a new clinical entity. Three cases of autoimmune pancreatitis with effective steroid therapy. Dig Dis Sci 42:1458–1468, 1997.

191. Hammano H, Kawa S, Horiuchi A, et al: High serum IgG4 concentrations in patients with sclerosing pancreatitis. N Engl J Med 344:732–738, 2001.

192. Okazaki K, Uchida K, Ohana M, et al: Autoimmune-related pancreatitis is associated with autoantibodies and a Th1/Th2-type cellular immune response. Gastroenterology 118:573–581, 2000.

193. Irie H, Honda H, Baba S, et al: Autoimmune pancreatitis: CT and MR characteristics. AJR Am J Roentgenol 170:1321–1327, 1998.

194. Furukawa N, Muranaka T, Yasumori K, et al: Autoimmune pancreatitis: Radiologic findings in three histologically proven cases. J Comput Assist Tomogr 22:880–883, 1998.

195. Chen RY, Adams DB: IgG4 levels in non-Japanese patients with autoimmune sclerosing pancreatitis. N Engl J Med 346:1919, 2002.

196. Erkelens GW, Vleggaar FP, Lesterhuis, W, et al: Sclerosing pancreato-cholangitis responsive to steroid therapy. Lancet 345:43–44, 1999.

197. Tanaka S, Kobayashi T, Nakanishi K, et al: Corticosteroid-responsive diabetes mellitus associated with autoimmune pancreatitis. Lancet 356:910–911, 2000.

198. Pitchumoni CS, Thomas E, Balthazar E, et al: Chronic calcific pancreatitis in association with celiac disease. Am J Gastroenterol 68:358–361, 1977.

199. Regan PT, DiMagno EP: Exocrine pancreatic insufficiency in celiac sprue: A cause of treatment failure. Gastroenterology 78:484–487, 1980.

200. Fernanez LB, DePaula A, Prizont R, et al: Exocrine pancreas insufficiency secondary to gluten enteropathy. Am J Gastroenterol 53:564–569, 1970.

201. Tandon BN, George PK, Sama SK, et al: Exocrine pancreatic function in protein-calorie malnutrition disease of adults. Am J Clin Nutr 22:1476–1482, 1969.

202. Pitchumoni CS: Pancreas in primary malnutrition disorders. Am J Clin Nutr 26:374–379, 1973.

203. Rhodes RA, Tai HH, Chey WY: Impairment of secretin release in celiac sprue. Am J Dig Dis 23:833–839, 1978.

204. Maton PN, Selden AC, Fitzpatrick ML, et al: Defective gallbladder emptying and cholecystokinin release in celiac disease. Reversal by gluten-free diet. Gastroenterology 88:391–396, 1985.

205. Dimagno EP, Go WL, Summerskill WH: Impaired cholecystokinin-pancreozymin secretion, intraluminal dilution, and maldigestion of fat in sprue. Gastroenterology 63:25–32, 1972.

206. Patel RS, Johlin FC Jr, Murray JA: Celiac disease and recurrent pancreatitis. Gastrointest Endosc 50:823–827, 1999.

207. Delhaye M, Engelholm L, Cremer M: Pancreas divisum: Congenital anatomic variant or anomaly? Contribution of endoscopic retrograde dorsal pancreatography. Gastroenterology 89:951–958, 1985.

208. Burtin P, Person B, Charneau J, et al: Pancreas divisum and pancreatitis: A coincidental association? Endoscopy 23:55–58, 1991.

209. Soehendra N, Kempeneers I, Nam VC, et al: Endoscopic dilatation and papillotomy of the accessory papilla and internal drainage in pancreas divisum. Endoscopy 18:129–132, 1986.

210. Liquory C, Lefebvre JF, Canard JM, et al: Le pancreas divisum: Etude clinique et therapeutique chez I'hommeapropos de 87 cas. Gastroenterol Clin Biol 10:820–825, 1986.

211. Lans JI, Geenen JE, Johanson JF, et al: Endoscopic therapy in patients with pancreas divisum and acute pancreatitis: A prospective, randomized, controlled clinical trial. Gastrointest Endosc 38:430–434,1992.

212. Boerma D, Huibregtse K, Gulik TM, et al: Long-term outcome of endoscopic stent placement for chronic pancreatitis associated with pancreas divisum. Endoscopy 32:452–456, 2000.

213. Ertan A: Long-term results after endoscopic pancreatic stent placement without pancreatic papillotomy in acute recurrent pancreatitis due to pancreas divisum. Gastrointest Endosc 52:9–14, 2000.

214. Heyries L, Barthet M, Delvasto C, et al: Long-term results of endoscopic management of pancreas divisum with recurrent acute pancreatitis. Gastrointest Endosc 55:376–381, 2002.

Chronic Pancreatitis, Stones, and Strictures

Shyam Varadarajulu and Robert H. Hawes

Chronic pancreatitis is an inflammatory condition that results in permanent structural changes in the pancreas that can lead to impairment of exocrine and endocrine function.[1] This disorder contrasts with acute pancreatitis in that the latter is nonprogressive and the gland returns to histologic and functional normalcy once the acute event subsides. Most diagnostic and therapeutic efforts in chronic pancreatitis are directed toward evaluation and management of symptoms, primarily abdominal pain and steatorrhea. Although interpretation of data on the role of endoscopic therapy for management of chronic pancreatitis remains difficult, this is an area that is rapidly expanding and one that is of great interest and challenge to the gastrointestinal endoscopist.

Epidemiology

The incidence of chronic pancreatitis appears to be in the range of 3 to 10 per 100,000 population in many parts of the world.[2] The crude incidence rate for chronic pancreatitis per 100,000 population in Germany is 6.4, in Czech Republic is 7.9, and in Japan is 27.9.[3-5] The peak incidence for chronic pancreatitis in Germany is in the age group of 45 to 54 years, 10 years older than the peak age group for acute pancreatitis suggesting that chronic pancreatitis develops during this time frame after first attacks of acute pancreatitis. In a prospective study that evaluated patients with alcoholic chronic pancreatitis, an annual incidence of 8.2 cases per year per 100,000 population and an overall prevalence of 27.4 cases per year per 100,000 population was noted.[6] The incidence rates in retrospective European and North American studies range from 2 to 10 per 100,000 cases per year.[7,8] Chronic pancreatitis is more common in males,[3,5,6] with sex (male-to-female) ratio of 3.5 in Japan.[5] In comparison with whites, blacks are two to three times more likely to be hospitalized for chronic pancreatitis than for alcoholic cirrhosis.[9] The explanation for this observation remains unclear but could be related to racial differences in diet, type or quantity of alcohol consumption, smoking, or ability to detoxify substances harmful to the liver or pancreas. The absence of any screening programs and unresolved debate on the gold standard for diagnosis of chronic pancreatitis makes epidemiologic studies in this area more difficult and explains the wide range of variations noted among studies.

Pathophysiology

The pathogenesis of chronic pancreatitis appears to be multifactorial and is probably initiated by two distinct events (Fig. 52–1). The first is a decrease in bicarbonate secretion resulting from either a mechanical or a functional ductal obstruction. Mechanical causes may include strictures, sphincter of Oddi dysfunction, and tumors. Functional causes may include mutations in the cystic fibrosis transmembrane conductance regulator (CFTR) gene leading to impaired bicarbonate secretion. This has formed the basis for the secretin pancreatic function test. The second involves intraparenchymal activation of digestive enzymes within the pancreatic gland. Ischemia, antioxidant stress, and sphincter of Oddi dysfunction are possible later events involved in perpetuating the disease process. This multifactorial model provides explanation why no single therapy necessarily works in all patients with chronic pancreatitis.

PANCREATIC DUCT OBSTRUCTION

Proteinaceous plugs are one of the earliest findings noted in patients with chronic pancreatitis.[10] It is theorized that increased glandular secretion of pancreatic proteins causes precipitation of proteinaceous plugs within the pancreatic ductal system. These plugs may act as a nidus for calcification that leads to stone formation. As ductal obstruction progresses, inflammatory changes and cell loss is encountered. The importance of these proteinaceous plugs in

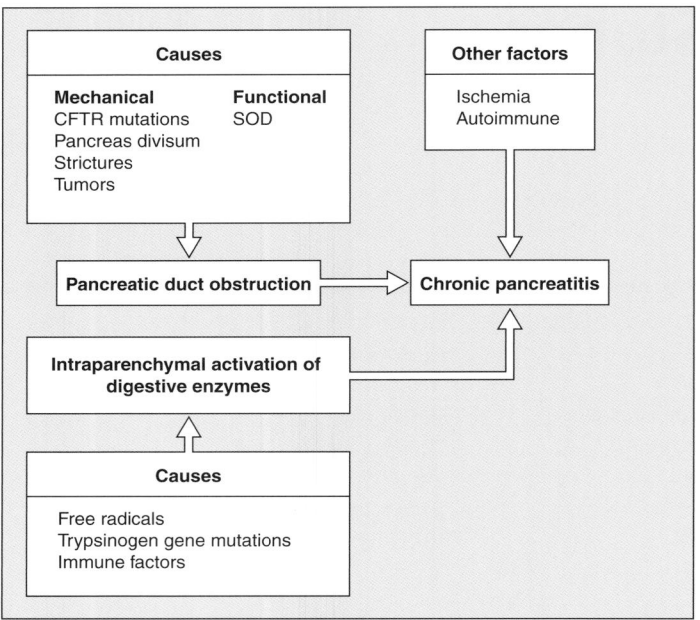

Figure 52–1. Pathophysiology of chronic pancreatitis. The pathogenesis of chronic pancreatitis is initiated by two distinct events. First, a decrease in bicarbonate secretion resulting from either a mechanical or a functional pancreatic duct obstruction. Second, intraparenchymal activation of digestive enzymes occurs within the pancreatic gland. Ischemia and autoimmune factors are postulated to be other important events in this pathway.

perpetuating changes within the pancreas is emphasized by studies that have demonstrated relief of clinical symptoms after endoscopic removal of these plugs in patients with chronic pancreatitis.[11,12] GP2 is a glycosyl phosphatidylinositol anchored protein that is cleaved from the zymogen granules and secreted into the pancreatic juice. This protein has been identified as a major component of intraductal plugs.[13] Pancreatic acinar cells release another protein called lithostatine that prevents calcium carbonate precipitation and therefore stone formation in pancreatic juice.[14] Low levels of these proteins in patients with chronic pancreatitis may be another factor involved in stone formation.

ISCHEMIA

Ischemia may be another important event in the pathogenesis of chronic pancreatitis. Animal models have shown that partial pancreatic duct ligation induces ductal hypertension and increased resistance to blood flow within the pancreas.[15,16] In fact, blood flow was to be found to be 40% of that observed in controls. Secretory stimulus further reduced blood flow as opposed to the normal increase. Moreover, in patients with chronic pancreatitis, pancreatic interstitial pressure rises to a greater degree than in normal individuals because of decreased glandular elasticity. The rapid relief of symptoms achieved by ductal decompression procedures suggests that ischemia plays a central role in the complex mechanisms involved in chronic pancreatitis.

ANTIOXIDANTS

Nutritional depletion is often seen in patients with chronic pancreatis. This is particularly true for antioxidants such as

selenium, vitamin C and E, and methionine.[17,18] An imbalance between a decrease in antioxidants and an increased demand for them in pancreatic cells in chronic pancreatitis may lead to elevation in free radical formation, which in turn is associated with lipid peroxidation and cellular impairment. Increased membrane lipid peroxidation, a marker of oxidative stress and free radical production, can also be seen in alcoholic chronic pancreatitis.[19] It is postulated that alcohol causes disproportionate increase in the secretion of trypsinogen leading to premature activation of digestive enzymes within the acinar or ductal cell systems.[20]

AUTOIMMUNITY

Chronic pancreatitis is also seen in association with autoimmune disorders such as Sjögren's syndrome and primary biliary cirrhosis.[21,22] Autoantibody to pancreatic antigens has been demonstrated in patients with Sjögren's syndrome and idiopathic chronic pancreatitis. Some cases of idiopathic chronic pancreatitis are associated with the expression of novel HLA-DR antigens on duct cells in combination with a localized T-cell inflammatory infiltrate lending further credibility to an autoimmune pathogenesis.[23]

INTERSTITIAL FIBROSIS

It is proposed that repeated episodes of acute pancreatitis initiates a sequence of perilobular fibrosis, duct distortion, and altered secretion and flow of pancreatic juice.[24] Studies on the natural history of pancreatitis have shown that more frequent and more repeated attacks of acute pancreatitis lead to chronic changes as seen in the alcoholic type of chronic pancreatitis.[25]

The exact mechanisms involved in the pathophysiology of chronic pancreatitis still remains elusive and unproved. Multiple exogenous factors may act in a genetically predisposed patient in an appropriate clinical setting, such as alcohol consumption, to trigger a cascade of events culminating in progressive destruction of pancreatic parenchyma and its ensuing sequelae. Although the focus of therapies has been the inhibition of acinar cell secretion, further insights into the role of ductal bicarbonate secretion, ductal obstruction, and the relative contribution of ischemia and oxygen-derived free radicals in this process may provide new therapeutic avenues.

Etiology

ALCOHOL

Alcohol abuse accounts for 70% to 80% of cases of chronic pancreatitis (Table 52–1); the mechanism by which this occurs is unclear. The risk appears to be related to the duration and amount

Table 52–1. Etiology of Chronic Pancreatitis
Alcohol 70%
Idiopathic 10–30%
Other 10–15%
Pancreatic duct obstruction (trauma, divisum, tumor, fibrosis)
Hereditary (*CFTR* gene mutation, trypsinogen gene mutation)
Hyperlipidemia
Tropical

of alcohol consumed rather than to the type of alcohol or the pattern of consumption.[26] Intake of large amounts of alcohol, greater than 50 g/day, has been shown to be associated with a shortened time to pancreatic calcification and survival.[27] There is considerable variation in individual sensitivity to the toxicity of alcohol making it difficult to define a "safe" level of consumption. Only 5% to 10% of alcoholics develop chronic pancreatitis, suggesting that other unidentified factors may be important in the pathogenesis of the disease.[28] Tobacco, although not important in the pathogenesis of alcoholic pancreatitis,[29,30] has been implicated in the development of calcification in those already with chronic pancreatitis.[31]

HEREDITARY PANCREATITIS

Hereditary pancreatitis is characterized by a young age at onset and prominent pancreatic calcifications. It is transmitted as an autosomal dominant trait and nearly 80% of patients with the inherited defect develop chronic pancreatitis.[32] Most affected individuals develop symptoms before the age of 20. In some kindreds, hereditary chronic pancreatitis has been mapped to the long arm of chromosome 7 (7q35), where a cluster of trypsinogen genes is located.[33,34] Several mutations associated with chronic pancreatitis have been identified in this region. Although the exact consequences of these mutations on trypsin activity remain unclear, they are known to interfere with trypsin inactivation or enhance its activation, permitting autodigestion of the pancreas.[35,36] Although mutations in the trypsinogen gene are specific for hereditary pancreatitis, not all affected family members develop chronic pancreatitis. The relationship between mutations of other genes associated with chronic pancreatitis, such as the CFTR and the trypsinogen genes, needs further elucidation.

MUTATIONS OF THE CYSTIC FIBROSIS GENE

Cystic fibrosis is due to mutations in the CFTR gene. Most patients with cystic fibrosis develop progressive pancreatic damage as a result of defective ductular and acinar pancreatic secretion.[37] Mutations in the CFTR gene have been identified, in some series, in 13% to 37% of patients with idiopathic chronic pancreatitis who have no clinical evidence of cystic fibrosis.[38,39] This could be an underestimation because currently available genetic screening tests identify only 18 to 23 of the most severe CFTR mutations that cause classic, childhood cystic fibrosis.

TROPICAL PANCREATITIS

Tropical pancreatitis is a condition of unknown etiology that is seen commonly in younger individuals in south India and other parts of the tropics, where it is the most common cause of chronic pancreatitis. The pathology is characterized by large intraductal calculi, marked dilatation of the pancreatic ducts, atrophy, and fibrosis. Clinically, most patients experience abdominal pain, diabetes mellitus, and fat malabsorption. The etiology of tropical pancreatitis remains unknown. The cassava fruit had been implicated as an etiologic factor in this disorder, although it is no longer thought to be related.[40] Mutations in the serine protease inhibitor SPINK1 have been identified in some patients.[41,42]

DUCTAL OBSTRUCTION

Obstruction of the pancreatic duct from any cause can lead to chronic pancreatitis. The histologic abnormalities that are induced may persist after relief of the obstruction. Sphincter of Oddi dysfunction appears to be associated with chronic pancreatitis. In one study of patients with chronic pancreatitis undergoing sphincter of Oddi manometry, more than 60% had sphincter of Oddi dysfunction.[43]

Pancreas divisum may cause chronic pancreatitis by producing a relative obstruction to flow of pancreatic juice at the minor papilla. It is estimated that less than 5% of patients with pancreas divisum develop pancreatic symptoms. The low frequency of symptoms has created a controversy as to whether pancreas divisum and its associated small minor papilla orifice are ever a cause of obstructive pancreatitis. The arguments against an association are based on two major observations. First, some studies have found that the incidence of pancreas divisum is the same among patients with and without pancreatitis.[44] Second, symptoms occur infrequently in patients with this anomaly. The authors believe that there is a group of patients with pancreas divisum who are subject to recurrent bouts of seemingly idiopathic pancreatitis. In these patients, the minor papilla orifice is so small that excessively high intrapancreatic dorsal ductal pressure occurs during active secretion, which may result in inadequate drainage, ductal distension, pain, and, in some cases, pancreatitis. To support this view, greater than 60% of patients with pancreas divisum and otherwise unexplained abdominal pain had relief of pain after surgical sphincteroplasty suggesting that obstruction to flow of secretion was the proximate cause of symptoms in these patients.[45]

METABOLIC AND ENDOCRINE CAUSES

Elevation of serum triglycerides above 500 mg/dL and hyperparathyroidism are other rare causes of chronic pancreatitis. Recurrent episodes of acute pancreatitis in patients with hypertriglyceridemia lead to chronic glandular damage. The pathophysiology in hyperparathyroidism is thought to be related to increased calcium concentration in pancreatic juice that leads to precipitation of calcium deposits in the pancreatic ducts.

IDIOPATHIC CHRONIC PANCREATITIS

An etiology for pancreatitis cannot be determined in 10% to 30% of patients with chronic pancreatitis despite extensive investigations. Concealed alcohol ingestion, hypersensitivity to small amounts of alcohol, unreported pancreatic trauma, and mutations in the cystic fibrosis and the trypsinogen genes may be contributing factors in at least a small proportion of patients with idiopathic chronic pancreatitis.[46,47] Whereas in the past, patients with idiopathic chronic pancreatitis have been considered as a single group, data from the Mayo Clinic have defined an early and late onset form of idiopathic chronic pancreatitis.[48] Age distribution at onset of symptoms showed a bimodal distribution of patients with early- and late-onset idiopathic chronic pancreatitis with a median age of 19.2 years and 56.2 years, respectively. No gender differences were observed among patients in both groups. Pain was the predominant symptom in 96% of patients with early-onset idiopathic pancreatitis but was only present in 54% of late-onset idiopathic pancreatitis.

Irrespective of whether patients had early- or late-onset idiopathic pancreatitis, pain was the presenting symptom, and endocrine and exocrine insufficiency with pancreatic calcification was seen in both forms of the disease.

Clinical Features

Abdominal pain and pancreatic insufficiency are the two cardinal clinical manifestations of chronic pancreatitis.

ABDOMINAL PAIN

Abdominal pain in chronic pancreatitis is typically centered in the epigastric area and often radiates to the back. The pain is worsened with eating and is sometimes associated with nausea and vomiting. Early in the course of chronic pancreatitis, the pain may occur in discrete attacks; as the condition progresses, pain tends to become more continuous.

The mechanism for this pain is poorly understood. Causes are perhaps multifactorial and include inflammation, duct obstruction, high pancreatic tissue pressure, fibrotic encasement of sensory nerves, and a neuropathy characterized by both increased numbers and sizes of intrapancreatic sensory nerves and by inflammatory injury to the nerve sheaths allowing exposure of the neural elements to toxic substances.[49,50] Pain is not in the spectrum of clinical symptoms in nearly one fourth of patients with chronic pancreatitis.[51]

The view that chronic pain will subside in a substantial number of patients as the disease progresses to the point of organ failure[52] has been widely accepted, but that process may take an unpredictable number of years or may never occur. Some studies suggest that the likelihood of spontaneous pain relief is low.[53] In a study that evaluated the natural history of pain in chronic pancreatitis, pain decreased or disappeared in 67%, 64%, and 77% of early-onset idiopathic, late-onset idiopathic, and alcoholic pancreatitis, over a median time of 25, 13, and 14 years, respectively.[48]

PANCREATIC INSUFFICIENCY

Patients with severe pancreatic exocrine dysfunction cannot properly digest complex foods or absorb digestive breakdown products.

Nevertheless, clinically significant protein and fat deficiencies do not occur until more than 90% of pancreatic function is lost.[54] In a large natural history study, the median time taken for development of pancreatic insufficiency was 13.1 years in patients with alcoholic chronic pancreatitis, 16.1 years in patients with late-onset idiopathic chronic pancreatic, and 26.3 years in those with early-onset idiopathic chronic pancreatitis.[48] Steatorrhea usually occurs before protein deficiencies because lipolytic activity decreases faster than proteolysis.[55,56]

Glucose intolerance occurs with some frequency in chronic pancreatitis, but overt diabetes mellitus usually occurs late in the course of disease. Patients with chronic calcifying disease, particularly those who develop early calcifications, may develop diabetes more often than those with chronic noncalcifying disease.[57,58] Nearly 40% to 70% of patients with chronic pancreatitis develop diabetes on prolonged follow-up. In one study, the median time to develop diabetes was 19.8 years, 11.9 years, and 26.3 years in patients with alcoholic, late-onset idiopathic, and early-onset idiopathic chronic pancreatitis, respectively.[48] In chronic pancreatitis, both insulin-producing beta cells and glucagon-producing alpha cells are destroyed. This is important because when exogenously administered insulin leads to hypoglycemia, the deficiency in glandular glucagon storage fails to correct the serum glucose levels back to normal leading to prolonged and severe hypoglycemia. Hence, the nature of diabetes in this patient population is brittle and its management more complicated than that of patients with type I diabetes.

Pathology

In early stages of chronic pancreatitis, glandular damage is patchy and uneven (Fig. 52–2). Areas of irregularly distributed fibrosis, reduced number and size of acini with relative sparing of the islets of Langerhans, and variable degrees of obstruction of pancreatic ducts of all sizes are seen.[59] A chronic inflammatory infiltrate around lobules and ducts is usually present. The interlobular and intralobular ducts are dilated and contain protein plugs in their lumens. The ductal epithelium may be atrophied or hyperplastic or show squamous metaplasia, and ductal concretions may be evident. Remaining islets become embedded in sclerosed tissue or severely

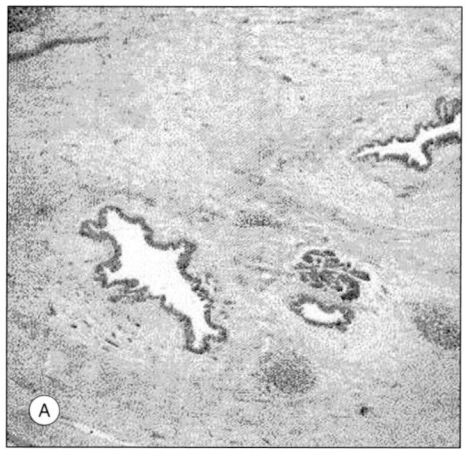
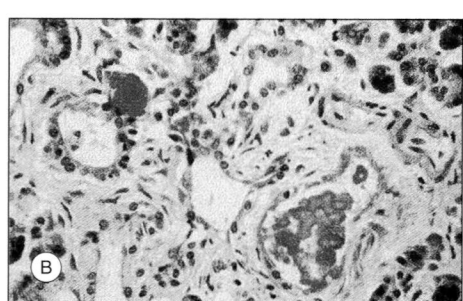

Figure 52–2. Histopathology of chronic pancreatitis. *A,* Extensive fibrosis and atrophy of the pancreatic parenchyma has left only residual islets and ducts, with occasional chronic inflammatory cells and acinar tissue. *B,* A high-power view demonstrating dilated ducts with inspissated eosinophilic ductal concretions.

Table 52–2. Diagnostic Tests for Chronic Pancreatitis

| Structural Tests | Functional Tests | |
	Indirect	Direct
X-Ray Ultrasound CT MRCP ERCP EUS	Serum enzymes (trypsinogen) Fecal tests (fat, elastase, chymotrypsin) Urine tests (Bentiromide, Pancreolauryl)	Secretin stimulation test

CT, computed tomography; ERCP, endoscopic retrograde cholangiopancreatography; EUS, endoscopic ultrasonography; MRCP, magnetic resonance cholangiopancreatography.

damaged lobules, before they too disappear. Grossly, the gland is hard, sometimes with extremely dilated ducts and grossly visible calcified concretions. Pseudocyst formation is common.

Differential Diagnosis

None of the currently available laboratory and radiologic tests is diagnostic of chronic pancreatitis. Thus, a number of disorders such as pancreatic cancer, peptic ulcer disease, irritable bowel syndrome, and symptomatic cholelithiasis must be considered in the differential diagnosis. A careful history and physical examination coupled with judicious use of tests such as gastroscopy and transabdominal ultrasound (US) can establish or exclude the diagnosis in most instances.

Pancreatic cancer is the primary diagnosis that must be strongly considered in patients suspected of having chronic pancreatitis. There are some data to suggest that chronic pancreatitis is associated with an increased risk of developing pancreatic carcinoma. The International Pancreatitis Study Group observed a standardized incidence ratio for pancreatic cancer of 26.3 among patients with chronic pancreatitis compared with an expected ratio of 2.13 that was calculated from country-specific incidence data and adjusted for age and sex.[60]

Similar to chronic pancreatitis, patients with pancreatic cancer can present with abdominal pain, weight loss, and jaundice. Findings suggestive of possible pancreatic cancer in a patient thought or known to have chronic pancreatitis include older age, absence of a history of alcohol use, weight loss, a protracted flare of symptoms, and the onset of significant constitutional symptoms. A high index of suspicion for pancreatic cancer should be entertained particularly in any elderly patient presenting with a new-onset pancreatitis when common causes such as alcohol and gallstones have been excluded. Tumor markers such as CA 19-9 and carcinoembryonic antigen (CEA) are helpful if abnormal, but normal values do not rule out pancreatic cancer. Computed tomography (CT) or endoscopic ultrasonography (EUS)-guided biopsy may be required to establish diagnosis in some patients.

Diagnosis

Tests for chronic pancreatitis can be classified into those that evaluate the structure of the gland (parenchyma, ductal anatomy, or both) or its exocrine function (Table 52–2). The tests most widely used clinically are those that assess structure. The clinical manifestations of pancreatic insufficiency is usually a late event in the course of chronic pancreatitis when more than 90% of the glandular tissue is not functioning because of glandular dysfunction, fibrotic tissue replacement, or proximal pancreatic duct obstruction. The most sensitive and accurate among pancreatic function tests is the secretin stimulation test. However, the test is invasive, its methodology very time consuming and demanding, and its diagnostic accuracy not superior to endoscopic retrograde cholangiopancreatography (ERCP).[61,62] On the other hand, noninvasive pancreatic function tests yield sufficient diagnostic accuracy only in the advanced stages of the disease, and their sensitivity for detection of early or moderate chronic pancreatitis is low.[63] Tests that evaluate pancreatic structure are advantageous in that, although limited by sensitivity, they are more widely available and are better standardized for clinical use.

TESTS OF PANCREATIC FUNCTION

Invasive/Direct Pancreatic Function Tests (Secretin Stimulation Test)

The gold standard for detection of pancreatic functional insufficiency is the secretin stimulation test. The basis for this test is that secretin (with or without cholecystokinin [CCK]) causes the secretion of bicarbonate-rich fluid from the pancreas. The patient swallows a dual-lumen catheter (Dreiling tube) into the duodenum, allowing sampling of the duodenal contents. Intravenous secretin (1 unit/kg) is administered, followed by collection of duodenal juice. A peak bicarbonate concentration less than 80 mEq/L is consistent with pancreatic exocrine insufficiency.

Some studies have shown the secretin stimulation test to be slightly more sensitive than ERCP for the diagnosis of chronic pancreatitis, but the evaluation of all tests in the diagnosis of chronic pancreatitis are suspect because of the lack of a gold standard. The values for sensitivity range from 74% to 97% and specificity from 80% to 90%.[62,64–68] The percentage of patients with an abnormal stimulation test and a normal pancreatogram range from 3% to 20%.[65-68] When such patients were followed, two studies found that 90% of such patients developed chronic pancreatitis.[68,69] Conversely, these studies also identified a small group of patients, averaging less than 10%, with a normal hormonal stimulation test but an abnormal pancreatogram. Long-term follow-up of these patients noted chronic pancreatitis developing in 0% to 26%.[68,69] When the results of pancreatic function tests were compared with pancreatic histology, the overall sensitivity, specificity, and accuracy were 67%, 90%, and 81%, respectively.[70]

Limitations of this test are that it is not well accepted by patients, it is time consuming, it is expensive, and it requires specialized equipment and methodology. The test has not been well standardized, and a consensus on the normal ranges for the test results is yet to be reached. The test is available in very few specialized pancreatic centers around the world.

Noninvasive/Indirect Pancreatic Function Tests

There has been great effort and interest to develop noninvasive tests for evaluating pancreatic function. These tests are designed to measure pancreatic enzymes in blood or stool or the effect of pancreatic enzymes on an orally administered substrate by collection of their metabolites in blood or urine.

Serum Enzymes

Because chronic pancreatitis is a patchy, focal disease with significant parenchymal fibrosis, pancreatic serum enzyme levels (amylase and lipase) are not or only minimally elevated. Very low levels of serum trypsinogen (<20 ng/mL) are reasonably specific for chronic pancreatitis, but levels as low as this are seen only in very advanced stages of the disease in which there is accompanying steatorrhea.[54] In clinical practice, serum enzyme levels are helpful to identify an acute attack of chronic pancreatitis or for monitoring the disease evolution with abnormally low concentration once steatorrhea occurs.

Fecal Tests

Steatorrhea can be diagnosed qualitatively by Sudan staining of feces or quantitatively by determination of fecal fat excretion over 72 hours while the patient is consuming a 100-g/day fat diet for at least 3 days before the test. Excretion of more than 7 g of fat per day is diagnostic of malabsorption, although patients with steatorrhea often have values greater than 20 g/day. On qualitative analysis, more than six globules per high power field is considered positive, but the patient must be ingesting adequate fat to allow measurable steatorrhea. In a landmark study on exocrine insufficiency, steatorrhea did not occur until more than 90% of the pancreas or more than 85% of pancreatic lipase had been destroyed.[54] It is obvious that stool fat analysis has limited sensitivity in chronic pancreatitis, because patients with mild and moderate, and often severe, chronic pancreatitis in the absence of steatorrhea are not detected by this technique.

A novel method, near infrared reflectance analysis (NIRA), may become the procedure of choice for evaluating fat malabsorption.[71-73] NIRA is equally accurate but less time consuming than a 72-hour fecal fat collection and allows for simultaneous measurement of fecal fat, nitrogen, and carbohydrates in a single sample. NIRA is increasingly used in Europe and is also available in some centers in the United States.

The low diagnostic value of fat malabsorption in chronic pancreatitis has lead to the discovery of individual pancreatic enzymes in stool specimen that have increased diagnostic sensitivity. Measurement of fecal chymotrypsin is abnormal in most patients with chronic pancreatitis and steatorrhea.[64] Since inception into clinical use, its utility has been clearly established only in advanced chronic pancreatitis with exocrine insufficiency. This assay is currently not available in the United States.

More recently, an assay to measure human pancreatic elastase in feces has been developed. The assay detects exclusively human elastase; thus, no interference occurs with simultaneous therapeutic pancreatic enzyme supplementation. The diagnostic sensitivity and specificity of the fecal elastase test is superior to the fecal chymotrypsin test, although both are most accurate in advanced chronic pancreatitis.[74] Fecal elastase test may be falsely abnormal in other diseases causing steatorrhea, such as short bowel syndrome or small bowel bacterial overgrowth syndrome. This test is available but not widely used in the United States.

Urine Tests

The principle of these tests is based on the administration of a complex substrate, which is hydrolyzed by a specific pancreatic enzyme with the release of a pancreatic marker substance. This marker is then absorbed from the gut and detected and quantitated either in urine or serum. The bentiromide (N-benzoyl-L-tyrosyl-p-aminobenzoic acid [NBT-PABA]) measures the presence of pancreatic chymotrypsin within the gut lumen and the pancreolauryl test measures the presence of pancreatic arylesterases within the gut lumen. Both tests are accurate in advanced chronic pancreatitis, with sensitivities of 80% to 100%.[64] Limitations of these tests lie in the fact that both tests require anatomic and functional integrity of the digestive systems. Although these tests have reasonable accuracy, neither is currently available for clinical use in the United States.

TESTS OF PANCREATIC STRUCTURE
Plain Abdominal Radiography

Calcifications within the pancreas are present on plain x-ray film in about one third of patients with chronic pancreatitis (Fig. 52–3). Calcifications occur late in the natural history of chronic pancreatitis

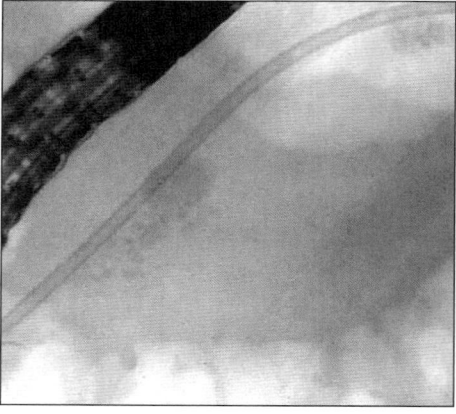

Figure 52–3. Chronic pancreatitis on digital radiography. Anteroposterior digital radiograph obtained as scout image during endoscopic retrograde cholangiopancreatography (ERCP) demonstrates multiple calcifications in the expected location of the pancreas.

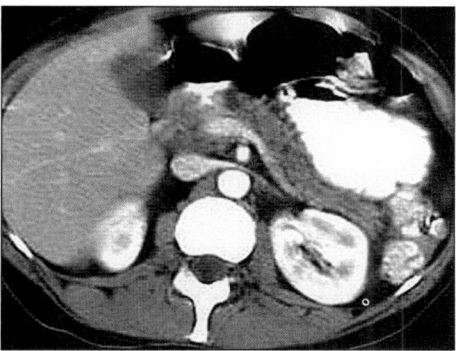

Figure 52-4. Chronic pancreatitis on computed tomography (CT). CT image demonstrates diffusely decreased enhancement relative to the renal cortices.

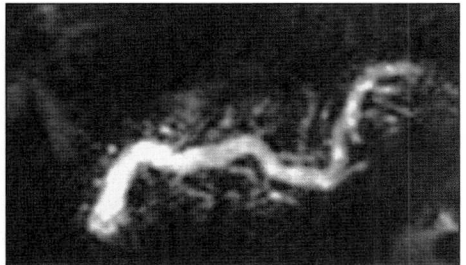

Figure 52-5. Chronic pancreatitis on magnetic resonance cholangiopancreatography (MRCP). Coronal two-dimensional (MRCP) demonstrates diffuse, irregular side-branch dilatation and dilatation of the main pancreatic duct.

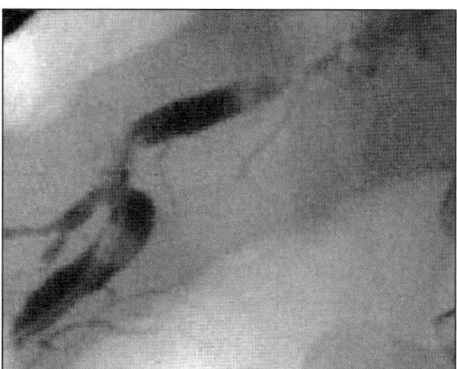

Figure 52-6. Chronic pancreatitis on endoscopic retrograde cholangiopancreatography (ERCP). ERCP image demonstrates irregular narrowing and dilatation of the main pancreatic duct and irregular side-branch dilatation, most prominent in the body and tail.

and may take from 5 to 25 years to develop.[48,52] Both anteroposterior and oblique views should be used because small flecks of calcium can be lost in the spine if oblique views are not obtained. The finding of calcification is pathognomonic of chronic pancreatitis, but the sensitivity of this test is very low.

Abdominal Ultrasound

US was the first technique that allowed complete imaging of the pancreas. There are several morphologic characteristics of chronic pancreatitis detectable by US, which include irregular contours in the margin of the gland, dilatation and irregularity of the main pancreatic duct, heterogeneity of the gland parenchyma, cysts within or adjacent to the pancreas, and the presence of calcifications.[75] The sensitivity and specificity of US for the diagnosis of chronic pancreatitis are 60% to 70% and 80% to 90%, respectively.[76] However, the detail to which the pancreas can be interrogated depends on the body habitus of the patient, presence or absence of overlying bowel gas, and the experience and expertise of the sonographer.

Computed Tomography

The sensitivity and specificity of CT for the diagnosis of chronic pancreatitis are 75% to 90% and 85%, respectively.[64] The main advantage of CT is that it can be standardized and in virtually all cases can visualize the pancreas in its entirety. CT scan is the most

sensitive test for detecting calcification, is accurate in detecting main pancreatic duct dilatation, and can pick up an irregular contour of the gland (Fig. 52–4).[64,77,78] These features are characteristic of advanced chronic pancreatitis, and CT is quite good in detecting these changes. However, it is poor at detecting subtle abnormalities in pancreatic parenchyma or changes in side branches of the pancreatic duct, which is commonly seen in milder forms of the disease. Hence, CT has good specificity but lacks sensitivity for diagnosis of chronic pancreatitis. It is likely that the new spiral CT scanners would produce better sensitivity.

Magnetic Resonance Cholangiopancreatography

Several small studies have reported on the utility of magnetic resonance cholangiopancreatography (MRCP) in assessing pancreatic duct morphology.[79,80] MRCP agrees with ERCP in 70% to 80% of findings, with higher rates of agreement in studies using the most advanced image analysis techniques (Fig. 52–5). In studies that compared MRCP findings with ERCP, MRCP visualized the main pancreatic duct in the head, body, and tail in 79%, 64%, and 53% of cases, respectively.[81] Correlation with ERCP with respect to main pancreatic duct dilatation, narrowing, and filling defects was 83% to 92%, 70% to 92% and 92% to 100%, respectively. The major disadvantage of MRCP compared with conventional cholangiography is a somewhat lower spatial resolution, such that MRCP continues to be partially limited in the assessment in fine detail, such as subtle side branch changes of chronic pancreatitis. Improvements in magnetic resonance (MR) image analysis will continue to improve the image quality of MRCP, and in the future it could approach ERCP in accuracy.

Endoscopic Retrograde Cholangiopancreatography

ERCP is the most widely used structural test for chronic pancreatitis (Fig. 52–6). In 1984, the Pancreatic Society of Great Britain and Ireland reached a consensus on ductographic definitions for chronic pancreatitis termed "the Cambridge criteria," which has become the most widely accepted criteria for interpreting

Table 52–3. Cambridge Grading of Chronic Pancreatitis by Endoscopic Retrograde Pancreatography

Grade	Main Pancreatic Duct	Side Branches
Normal	Normal	Normal
Equivocal	Normal	<3 abnormal
Mild	Normal	<3 abnormal
Moderate	Abnormal	<3 abnormal
Severe	Abnormal, with at least one of the following: Large cavity (>10 mm) Duct obstruction Intraductal filling defects Severe dilation or irregularity	<3 abnormal

Adapted from Axon AT, Classen M, Cotton PB, et al: Pancreatography in chronic pancreatitis. International definitions. Gut 25:1107, 1984.

pancreatography.[82] The criteria are based on abnormalities seen in both the main pancreatic duct and side branches (Table 52–3). In most studies, the sensitivity of ERCP is between 70% and 90%, with a specificity of 80% to 100%.[62,64–68] ERCP is highly sensitive and specific in patients with advanced structural disease; less dramatic pancreatographic changes are less definitive.[83,84]

The ductographic abnormalities of chronic pancreatitis are not absolutely specific: age-related changes, morphologic changes such as in pancreatic cancer or recovery phase of acute pancreatitis, and poststent induced injury can mimic chronic pancreatitis. Furthermore, chronic pancreatitis can involve the pancreatic parenchyma per se and completely spare the radiographically visible portions of the pancreatic ductal system leading to false-negative studies.[85,86] In addition, significant interobserver and intraobserver variability is noted in the interpretation of pancreatography.[87] Much of this is related to interpretation of mild pancreatographic changes rather than to severe abnormalities.

There are several limitations with ERCP as a diagnostic test for chronic pancreatitis. Reliable interpretation of ERCP depends on adequate filling of the pancreatic duct with dye such that the secondary branches are well visualized. However, inadequate opacification of ducts, especially the secondary ducts, occurs in at least 30% of cases.[83] The procedure is invasive and carries a 3% to 7% chance of causing acute pancreatitis.[88] This risk is low in patients with advanced disease and high in those with mild disease, particularly those with underling sphincter of Oddi dysfunction.[89]

Endoscopic Ultrasonography

EUS provides a safe and relatively noninvasive method of obtaining detailed structural information on the pancreatic parenchyma and ducts. There are two main advantages for EUS that make it a very sensitive test for chronic pancreatitis. First, the pancreas lies within a few millimeters of the duodenum and stomach thus obviating the need for deep penetration of the sound waves. Positioning the EUS transducer at this site enables a thorough evaluation of the pancreas in its entirety. Second, positioning of the transducer in the gut lumen eliminates bowel gas as an obstacle for thorough imaging.

A number of EUS criteria for pancreatic disease have been described (Fig. 52–7). Lees and coworkers[90,91] first described endosonographic findings in patients with clinical and radiologic evidence of chronic pancreatitis and characterized endosonographic criteria that distinguish normal from abnormal pancreas. Wiersema and colleagues[92] refined their definitions and found that abnormal endosonographic changes occurred often in patients with abnormal endoscopic pancreatograms and were absent in healthy volunteers.

Criteria for chronic pancreatitis that are specific to EUS can be divided into two groups (Table 52–4): parenchymal and ductal. Parenchymal criteria include inhomogeneity, hyperechoic foci, hyperechoic strands, cysts, and lobularity. Ductal criteria specific to EUS include obvious to more subtle ductal dilatation (≥3 mm in the head, ≥2 mm in the body, ≥1 mm in the tail), hyperechoic main duct margins, irregular main duct margins, and visible side branches. Several studies show that the increasing EUS abnormalities correlate with the severity of pancreatographic changes[93–96] and with

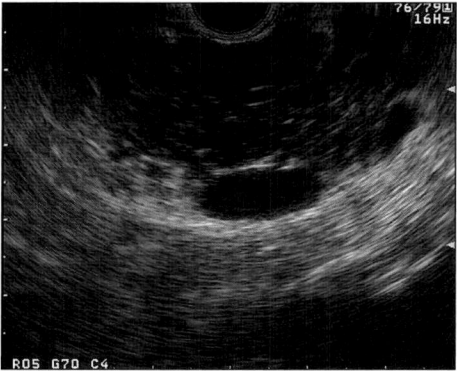

Figure 52–7. Chronic pancreatitis on endoscopic ultrasonography (EUS). EUS demonstrating a pancreatic duct with hyperechoic margins. The pancreatic parenchyma shows stranding, foci, and lobularity.

Table 52–4. Endoscopic Ultrasonography Criteria for Chronic Pancreatitis

Parenchymal Changes	Ductal Changes
Inhomogeneity	Ductal dilation
Hyperechoic foci	Hyperechoic main duct margins
Hyperechoic strands	Irregular main duct margins
Lobularity	Visible side branches
Pseudocysts	

reductions in secretin-stimulated duodenal bicarbonate.[97] A quantitative analysis[93] with nine possible criteria (hyperechoic foci, hyperechoic strands, lobularity, ductal dilatation, ductal irregularity, hyperechoic duct margins, visible side branches, calcifications, and cysts) suggests that, in a population at low to moderate risk of chronic pancreatitis, EUS is most reliable only when it is either clearly normal (≤2 criteria) or clearly abnormal (≥5 criteria). When the threshold for normal is set at two criteria or less and the threshold for abnormal is set at five criteria or more, the predictive values are as high as 85%.[98] Some of the controversy regarding the accuracy of EUS may be due to studies that use three or four criteria (i.e., mild abnormalities) as threshold values to distinguish normal from abnormal EUS. When EUS is only mildly abnormal, endoscopic retrograde pancreatography (ERP) and functional tests are often normal. Whether minimal EUS changes reflect early chronic pancreatic disease is unclear.

Because EUS provides higher resolution imaging than previously used imaging methods and provides information on both the ducts and parenchyma, it is logical to assume that it may detect abnormalities not described previously with tests used traditionally to study pancreatic morphology. Functional testing is said to become abnormal only after greater than 60% to 70% of pancreatic functional reserve is depleted.[99] If this is the case, it may also be reasonable to expect that EUS could detect subtle structural changes that predate functional abnormalities. Finally, it is clear that even severe chronic pancreatitis can be asymptomatic. Therefore, it should not be surprising that EUS may show pancreatic abnormalities in asymptomatic individuals. It has been shown that alcohol consumption is often associated with asymptomatic abnormalities.[100,101]

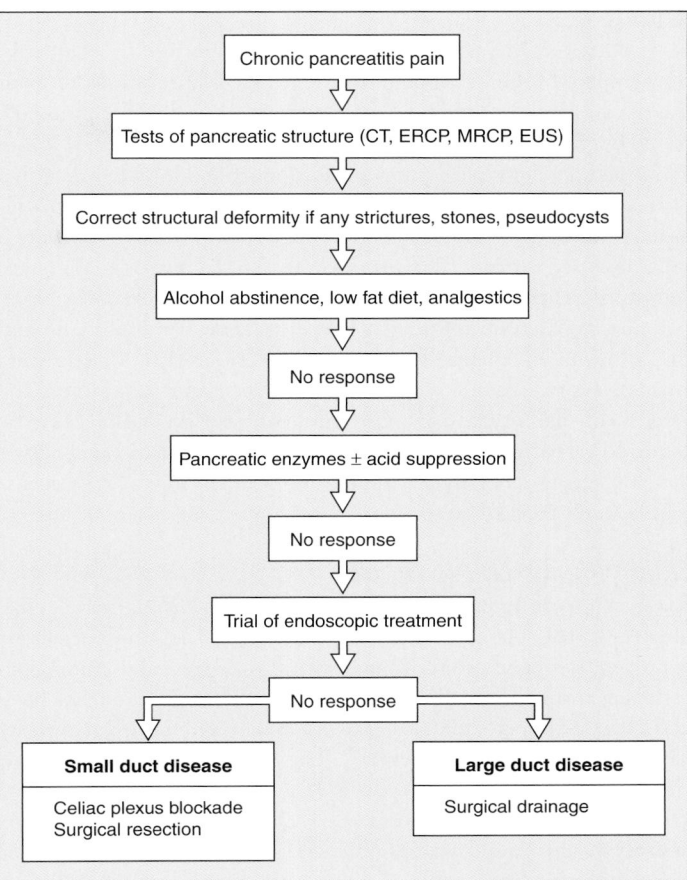

Figure 52–8. Algorithm for the management of pain in chronic pancreatitis.

Treatment

The treatment of chronic pancreatitis may take three approaches. One strategy endeavors to decrease pancreatic exocrine secretion. A second approach aims to decompress the duct. In the third approach, often used after the first two fail, is partial or complete resection of the gland. The goal of all three strategies is to relieve pain, which is the primary symptom of chronic pancreatitis. Pain management is an integral part of the treatment as well and is usually used in parallel with the three approaches listed previously.

MEDICAL MANAGEMENT
Pain Management
Abstinence from Alcohol

Early in the course of chronic pancreatitis, many patients suffer from recurrent acute attacks rather than chronic pain (Fig. 52–8). In these patients with recurrent attacks, a temporal relationship with alcohol binge can be commonly elucidated. In such patients, abstinence from alcohol may be of substantial benefit contrary to those with end-stage disease and chronic pain. Mortality in chronic pancreatitis has been shown to be related to continued alcohol abuse.[102] In a meta-analysis[103] evaluating the effect of abstinence on pain, a substantial reduction in pain was associated with cessation of alcohol (continued pain in 26% of abstinent patients compared with 53% in those who continue to consume alcohol). In addition, in a

large natural history study, continued drinking was associated with a higher risk of painful relapses.[104] It appears that cessation of alcohol has a beneficial effect in preventing alcohol-induced complications and in prolonging life.

Pancreatic Enzyme Supplements

A trial of pancreatic enzyme supplements should be the initial strategy used for patients with pain in chronic pancreatitis. The rationale for this therapy is based on suppression of feedback loops in the duodenum that regulate the release of CCK, the hormone that stimulates digestive enzyme secretion from the exocrine pancreas.[105]

Several randomized control trials have evaluated pancreatic enzymes as a method to provide pain relief. Two of the trials used nonenteric coated enzymes and demonstrated a reduction in pain compared with placebo.[106,107] Four trials used enteric-coated enzymes (which may not be released until they reach the jejunum) and demonstrated no benefit.[108–111] In the two trials that demonstrated pain reduction, female patients, those with idiopathic pancreatitis, and those with less advanced disease seem to benefit most. Despite the lack of proof of clear-cut benefit, a recent consensus review recommended a trial of pancreatic enzymes for pain relief.[112] It should be considered particularly in patients with less advanced disease and in those with idiopathic chronic pancreatitis.

Analgesics

Most patients with painful chronic pancreatitis require analgesics for symptom relief. Although there are no accurate estimates of the risk of narcotic addiction, most experts suggest it occurs in 10% to 20% of patients. This problem is observed to occur more commonly in those with poor social support and in patients with a history of narcotic addiction. A useful strategy is to begin with non-narcotic analgesics such as acetaminophen and nonsteroidal anti-inflammatory agents. If these agents fail to provide adequate symptom relief, narcotic agents may be administered. In many patients, coexistent depression lowers visceral threshold pain and the addition of an antidepressant is often useful. In addition, antidepressants have a direct effect on pain and potentiates the effects of narcotics.[113,114] Chronic narcotic analgesia may be required in patients with persistent significant pain. Long-acting narcotic agents generally are more effective than short-acting agents that last only 3 or 4 hours.

Celiac Plexus Nerve Block

Pancreatic pain is predominantly transmitted through the celiac plexus. Celiac plexus neurolysis, via surgical or transcutaneous approach, has been used for many years to manage abdominal pain resulting from advanced malignancy.[115,116] These approaches have had complications such as paralysis that might be overcome by better visualization of the region. The celiac artery is a landmark structure readily visualized on EUS (Fig. 52–9). Wiersema and Wiersema[117] performed transgastric EUS-guided celiac plexus neurolysis and found that the success was similar to surgical or transcutaneous approaches. An injection of absolute ethanol that permanently destroys the plexus is referred to as a celiac plexus neurolysis, and an injection of corticosteroids that temporarily block the plexus is referred to as celiac plexus block.

EUS-guided celiac plexus block and neurolysis are safe and well-tolerated procedures that can be performed in an outpatient setting with conscious sedation. The procedures can be performed in 10 minutes or less. Mild complications include transient diarrhea (4% to 15%), transient orthostasis (1%), and transient increase in pain (9%). Major complications (2.5%) have included retroperitoneal bleeding and peripancreatic abscess.[118]

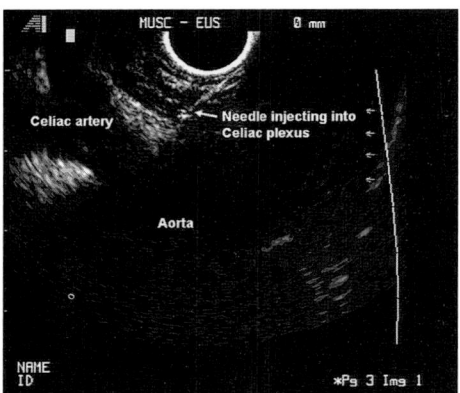

Figure 52–9. Celiac plexus block is being performed with the curvilinear array echoendoscope. The celiac artery is seen emerging from the aorta, and the needle is shown just above this point.

In a prospective study, Wiersema and colleagues[119] evaluated patients with pancreatic malignancy and chronic pancreatitis treated by celiac plexus neurolysis and found that the initial pain scores were similar between the two patient groups. However, after 16 weeks of follow-up, the pain score improvement after celiac plexus neurolysis in patients with chronic pancreatitis was not found to be significant. From these date and because celiac neurolysis may jeopardize future surgery if required (includes significant peri-pancreatic fibrosis), celiac neurolysis is not recommended for chronic pancreatitis. The malignant disease group had a mean pain score of less than baseline. Gress and coworkers[120] used injection of triamcinolone in 90 patients with chronic pancreatitis. At 8 weeks postprocedure, 55% of patients had a decreased score; this dropped off to 10% of patients by 24 weeks. EUS-guided celiac plexus blockade may be somewhat more effective than the transcutaneous approach for treatment of pain in chronic pancreatitis but the effect is short-lived. More study is needed to determine whether EUS-guided celiac plexus blockade may shorten the duration of hospitalization for patients with chronic pancreatitis.

Management of Pancreatic Insufficiency

One approach in patients with steatorrhea is to restrict fat intake to 20 g/day or less. Patients who continue to suffer from steatorrhea after fat restriction require medical therapy.

Lipase Supplementation

Supplemental oral lipase is relatively effective in preventing steatorrhea. Three tablets of nonenteric-coated pills (total of 30,000 units of lipase) with meals is typically sufficient to improve symptoms. The goal of treatment is control of symptoms rather than restoring fat absorption to normal levels.

Enzyme supplements may be inactivated at an acidic pH. Thus, patients who are not responding to the typical dose of medications may benefit from the addition of an histamine-2 (H_2)-antagonist or a proton pump inhibitor. Alternatively, a microencapsulated preparation of pancreatic enzymes with a higher lipase concentration may be effective. There are several explanations for failure of enzyme therapy for steatorrhea. The most common is inadequate dosage, generally resulting from patient noncompliance because of the large number of pills that must be taken. In addition, it is important to ensure that patients taking non–enteric-coated preparations take an acid suppressant to ensure that the enzymes are not denatured by gastric acid or destroyed by proteases. If these measures fail, it is appropriate to search for alternative causes that could cause malabsorption such as celiac sprue or small intestinal bacterial overgrowth.

Medium-Chain Triglycerides

Medium-chain triglycerides may provide extra calories in patients with weight loss and a poor response to diet and pancreatic enzyme therapy. Unlike long-chain triglycerides, which require bile salts and pancreatic lipase, medium-chain triglycerides are readily degraded by gastric and pancreatic lipase and do not require the presence of bile. In addition, medium-chain triglycerides can be directly absorbed by the intestinal mucosa and are less of a stimulant to pancreatic secretion.

In a pilot study of eight patients with chronic pancreatitis and postprandial pain, three to four cans of Peptamen (enriched in medium-chain triglycerides and hydrolyzed peptides) per day for 10 weeks resulted in improvement in pain, which in some patients was sustained after stopping this oral supplement.[121] The mechanism of action may relate to the fact that administration of this enteral formulation resulted in a minimal increase in plasma CCK levels or alternatively may be due to its antioxidant effects.

Management of Complications

Chronic pancreatitis may be associated with a variety of complications. Splenic vein thrombosis, pseudoaneurysm formation, and common bile duct and/or duodenal strictures are occasionally encountered. Other complications such as pseudocyst formation and pancreatic ascites or pleural effusion are discussed in Chapter 50. Intrapancreatic complications such as pancreatic stones and strictures are discussed later.

Splenic Vein Thrombosis

The splenic vein courses along the posterior surface of the pancreas where it can be affected by inflammation and splenic vein thrombosis may result. Affected patients can develop gastric varices as a result of associated portal hypertension. No specific therapy is needed in nonbleeding patients. If bleeding occurs, splenectomy is usually curative.

Pseudoaneurysms

Pseudoaneurysm formation is a rare complication of chronic pancreatitis. Splenic artery is the vessel most commonly involved. Pseudoaneurysms form as a consequence of enzymatic digestion of muscular wall of the artery by a pseudocyst. The presence of unexplained anemia or any degree of gastrointestinal bleeding in a patient with chronic pancreatitis or a known pseudocyst should immediately raise the possibility of a pseudoaneurysm. Once bleeding occurs, the mortality is 40% to 60%.[122] Mesenteric angiography permits confirmation of the diagnosis and also provides a means of therapy by embolization of the pseudoaneurysm. Surgery for bleeding pseudoaneurysms is difficult and associated with a high morbidity and mortality.

Common Bile Duct Strictures

Intrapancreatic common bile duct strictures have been reported in 2.7% to 45.6% of patients with chronic pancreatitis.[123,124] Common bile duct strictures can have serious sequelae of cholangitis, cholelithiasis, choledocholithiasis, intrahepatic stones, and secondary biliary cirrhosis. Deviere and colleagues[124] evaluated the use of biliary stenting in patients with biliary strictures secondary to chronic pancreatitis. They reported that endoscopic biliary drainage is an effective therapy for resolving cholangitis or jaundice in this patient subset. However, the long-term efficacy of this therapy was less than satisfactory as stricture resolution rarely occurred. Preliminary results using metal stents for this indication suggest they could be an effective alternative to surgical biliary diversion. More than 90% of patients had no recurrence of strictures at 3 years, but longer follow-up and controlled trials will be necessary to confirm these findings.[125,126] In a nonrandomized retrospective study that compared surgical drainage procedures with stent insertion, Pitt and coworkers[127] found a significantly higher success rate of 88% in the surgically treated group compared with 55% for patients managed by stent insertion.

Duodenal Obstruction

Duodenal stenosis is seen in around 5% of patients with chronic pancreatitis, particularly those with alcoholic pancreatitis. Coexistent obstruction of the common bile duct may be seen. The diagnosis is made at upper endoscopy or barium swallow. Attempts to dilate the stricture endoscopically are generally futile. The simplest and safest approach is surgical drainage by means of gastrojejunostomy. This may be combined with drainage of the bile duct and/or pancreatic duct.

SURGICAL MANAGEMENT

Surgery for relief of pain in chronic pancreatitis should be considered in patients who fail medical therapy. Other indications for surgical intervention in chronic pancreatitis include pseudocysts, abscess, fistula, ascites, fixed common bile duct obstruction, or variceal hemorrhage secondary to splenic vein thrombosis. Because the manifestations of chronic pancreatitis can mimic that of pancreatic cancer, surgery is required in some instances to exclude malignancy.

The ideal operation for chronic pancreatitis should relieve pain and preserve endocrine and exocrine function. Both pancreatic drainage and resection procedures relieve pain. Pancreatic duct drainage procedures relieve pancreatic hypertension and thereby pain but without sacrificing functioning glandular tissue. However, long-term success requires that the duct be dilated, a dilatation of greater than 8 mm is desirable. Extensive resections should be avoided to prevent endocrine and exocrine insufficiency. There is clearly no one particular procedure that can be applicable to all patients. The approach is tailored to meet the problems posed in each individual patient.

Pancreatic Duct Decompression

In patients with a dilated pancreatic duct, a Roux-en-Y side-to-side pancreaticojejunostomy is performed to drain the entire pancreatic duct from the tail to the duodenum. When necessary, a partial resection of the head of the gland is performed to ensure a complete drainage. Operative mortality for this technique is less than 3%.[128] Substantial improvement in symptoms is seen in 65% to 85% of patients.[128,129] Although some authors report that improvement in symptoms were durable over a follow-up period of 7.9 years,[128] others report recurrence of symptoms in a substantial number of patients within 1 year.[129–132] The explanation for this decline in effectiveness may be that the secondary ducts, which are not amenable to main duct drainage procedures, may subsequently become obstructed. Although improvement in pancreatic endocrine or exocrine function is not expected after pancreaticojejunostomy, steatorrhea and insulin-dependent diabetes arising as a consequence of surgery is not inevitable.[128] Some studies, however, have noted progressive loss of endocrine and exocrine pancreatic function despite a lateral pancreaticojejunostomy.[133–135]

Pancreatic Resection

Pancreatic resection involves resection of a portion of the pancreas, usually the tail or head. This procedure is most appropriate when there is focal disease, particularly in the absence of pancreatic ductal dilatation. In one series of patients who had no benefit from pancreaticojejunostomy, reoperation to resect the head of the pancreas led to a significant improvement in pain in a select group of patients.[136] The reason for the improvement was not clear because there was no evidence of focal pancreatitis. The choice of distal or proximal pancreatectomy and the magnitude of resection are determined by the location and extent of disease. Distal resection is limited to patients with disease involving the tail, which is usually due to trauma. Pancreaticoduodenectomy (Whipple resection) has been advocated because the fibrosis of chronic pancreatitis is often more prominent in the head and uncinate process. This often preserves enough islets in the tail to prevent diabetes. Duodenum-preserving resection of the pancreatic head is another alternative that has alleviated pain with lesser rates of exocrine and endocrine dysfunction.[137] Total pancreatectomy in theory completely removes the source of pain but has severe metabolic consequences. Steatorrhea can develop in 30% to 40% of patients undergoing simple drainage procedures and in 66% of those undergoing extensive pancreatic resections.[138–140] Diabetes mellitus can occur after pancreatic resection either as a consequence of surgery or secondarily from ongoing disease process. Autotransplantation of the tail can be attempted to decrease the risk of diabetes and can be used in association with total pancreatectomy.[141]

ENDOSCOPIC MANAGEMENT

Patients with an established diagnosis of chronic pancreatitis who have failed medical management should undergo ERCP. The goal of ERCP is to evaluate for an obstructive component to the pancreatopathy. Endoscopically treatable causes of obstruction can be at the level of the papilla (papillary stenosis) or along the course of the main pancreatic duct, primarily resulting from stones and/or strictures.

Sphincter of Oddi Dysfunction

The role of sphincter of Oddi dysfunction as a cause of chronic pancreatitis is not completely understood. In a recent study that evaluated 104 patients with unexplained abdominal pain, 29% of patients diagnosed with sphincter of Oddi dysfunction had structural evidence of chronic pancreatitis.[89] Two other studies made similar observations and found that basal sphincter pressures were elevated particularly in the pancreatic segment of the sphincter of Oddi.[142,143] It remains unknown whether the sphincter, at times, becomes dysfunctional as part of the overall general scarring process or has a role in the pathogenesis of chronic pancreatitis. Studies have shown that sphincter ablation therapy benefits 30% to 60% of patients with chronic pancreatitis who have manometrically proven sphincter of Oddi dysfunction.[144,145] Bagley and coworkers[146] reported a series of 67 patients with mild to moderate chronic pancreatitis who underwent empiric sphincterotomy or sphincteroplasty and found that during a 5-year follow-up period 44% of patients had pain relief. The utility of sphincter ablation therapy in patients with chronic pancreatitis awaits further study, probably in randomized controlled trials.

Pancreatic Duct Stones

Approximately one third of patients with chronic pancreatitis have pancreatic stones. There is no close correlation between the presence of pancreatic duct stones and pain; thus, many patients with pancreatic duct stones report no pain. It is unclear if pancreatic calculi aggravate the clinical course of chronic pancreatitis or are the consequence of ongoing glandular destruction from persistent disease processes. It is postulated that pain in chronic pancreatitis is related to increased intrapancreatic pressure arising as a consequence of mechanical duct obstruction by pancreatic stones or strictures.[147,148] This notion is supported by studies that demonstrate improvement in symptoms after ductal clearance of stones.[149–153] Hence, removal of pancreatic duct stones is recommended in patients with symptomatic chronic pancreatitis.

Diagnosis

Most pancreatic duct stones are readily apparent on plain x-ray films of the abdomen because of radio-opacity of the calcium component. However, small stones may not be readily seen. Hence, oblique view on plain x-ray film may uncover stones missed because of the overlying spine on anteroposterior radiograph. Many patients have multiple stones of varying diameters in the main and branch pancreatic ducts in association with strictures. High-resolution CT and MRCP provide the best noninvasive mapping of the duct and may help in selection of patients appropriate for therapy. The main benefit of such imaging is the formulation of an efficient treatment algorithm for these patients. In most patients, however, the suitability for endoscopic therapy is best assessed at ERCP.

Treatment

A small number of mobile stones in the duct without significant strictures are most suitable for endoscopic removal. On the other hand, an impacted stone that impedes injection of contrast into the pancreatic duct usually requires adjunctive therapy using extracorporeal shockwave lithotripsy (ESWL) or intraductal lithotripsy for clearance. Endoscopic management involves sphincterotomy, stricture dilatation, and stone removal by baskets or balloons (Fig. 52–10).

Removal of pancreatic stones requires an adequate opening of the pancreatic orifice. There is often thickening and fibrosis or stenosis of the pancreatic orifice in chronic pancreatitis. A cholangiogram and pancreatogram are obtained initially, and the termination of either duct is correctly assessed. Usually a biliary sphincterotomy is performed first to expose the pancreatic septum and to help assess the necessary extent of the pancreatic cut. Pancreatic sphincterotomy can be done either using a standard pull-type sphincterotome or using a needle-knife to perform sphincterotomy over a previously placed pancreatic stent. In patients with pancreas divisum, a minor papilla sphincterotomy may be required and is usually performed by using a needle-knife over a previously placed dorsal duct pancreatic stent.

The ability to remove a stone by endoscopic methods alone is dependent on stone size and number, duct location, presence of downstream stricture, and the degree of impaction.[151] Downstream strictures may require dilatation either with catheters or hydrostatic balloons. The duct features particular to the pancreas require special consideration. Because of the tortuosity of the main duct and

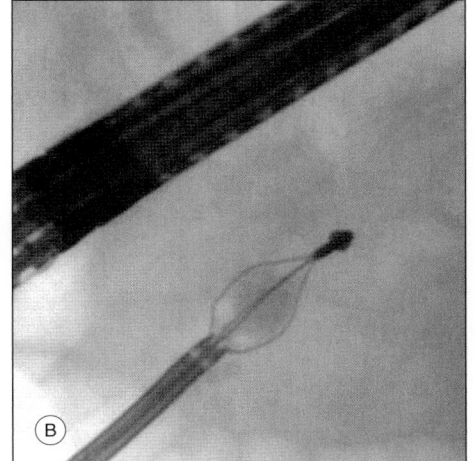
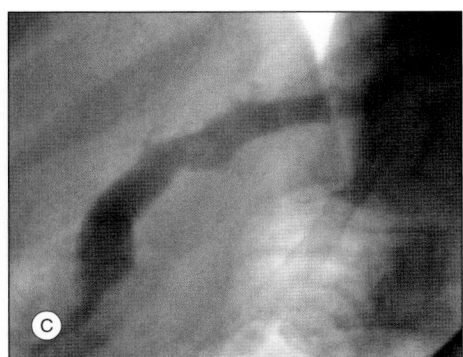

Figure 52–10. Pancreatic stone removal with endoscopic retrograde cholangiopancreatography (ERCP). ERCP images obtained before *(A)*, during *(B)*, and after *(C)* stone removal by lithotripsy. Scout ERCP image *(A)* reveals a large stone within the main pancreatic duct. A second image *(B)* was obtained during basket capture of the stone. A postprocedural ERCP image *(C)* reveals absence of the stone within the duct and no evidence of residual obstruction.

multiple side branches, there is a tendency for the leading tip of a basket to be caught in a side branch. Negotiating around the genu can be particularly difficult because of the sigmoid turn at the junction of the head and body of the pancreas. Soft-wire or wire-guided baskets may be necessary to navigate these tortuous areas of the pancreatic duct. Pancreatic stones are very hard because of their crystalline structure. Care must be taken to assess the adequacy of the ductal system downstream from where the stone is entrapped in the basket to avoid being stuck up the duct with a basket. In a grossly dilated duct, a "through-the-scope" mechanical lithotripsy device can be used, but this is often restricted to stones in the head of the pancreas with a relatively straight line of approach to the stone. Otherwise, the rigidity of this device and its large diameter increase the risk for duct injury. This device can also be used through a very dilated dorsal duct, which permits a straight approach.

Sherman and coworkers[151] reported that endoscopic therapy was effective in 83% of patients presenting with chronic relapsing pancreatitis compared with 46% in those presenting with continuous pain alone. Factors favoring successful endoscopic therapy included those with three or fewer stones, stones confined to head and/or body of pancreas, stone size less than 10 mm, absence of impacted stones, and absence of downstream strictures. After successful stone removal, 25% of patients had regression of ductographic changes of chronic pancreatitis and 42% had a decrease in the main pancreatic duct diameter. The only complication was pancreatitis encountered in 8% of patients. Studies have reported success with endoscopic therapy and improvement in symptoms in the range of 45% to 79% and 60% to 90%, respectively.[151,153,154] One study reported clinical improvement in steatorrhea in 73% of patients after endoscopic management.[153]

Electrohydraulic lithotripsy (EHL) may be an effective adjunct to endoscopic treatment of pancreatic stones. In this technique, shocks are delivered in a fluid medium under direct visualization, because inadvertent firing on tissue can cause perforation or bleeding. This technique requires the use of a "baby" pancreatoscope that is passed up the pancreatic duct to the stone. Although pancreatoscopy can be used to directly visualize probe contact with the stone and

fragmentation, intraductal manipulation remains difficult and very limited.[152,155] These smaller baby scopes have fragile control systems with limited one-way tip deflection. This may hinder accurate placement of the probe. Moreover, the operating channel diameter in these scopes is 0.75 to 1.0 mm and only accepts specialized ultrathin accessories. The EHL probe is 1.9 Fr in diameter and can be used, but channels of 1.0 mm or less do not allow for much coaxial perfusion of saline necessary for lithotripsy. The saline is essential for transmission of the shockwaves (SWs) at the stone surface and for irrigation after the SW. The debris that is created after the SWs obscures visibility and must be flushed away. Thus, placement of a nasopancreatic tube (5 Fr) beyond the stone before pancreatoscopy is helpful for irrigation purposes. Advancing the pancreatoscope requires an ample pancreatic sphincterotomy for insertion and may in addition require a guidewire to advance up a tortuous pancreatic duct. A 450-cm wire is placed into the duct beforehand, and the proximal stiffer end is backloaded into the baby scope. The stiff end of the wire should be slightly bent before backloading to help negotiate the elbow junction of the accessory port and the scope body.

Of late, a new device has been developed, the frequency-doubled yttrium-aluminum-garnet (YAG) laser (FREDDY), which fires with pulses of such short duration that no thermal damage occurs even when the fiber fires directly on the tissue. There is limited clinical experience with this device and more studies are required before its place in the armamentarium against pancreatic stones could be defined.

The main advantage of endoscopic therapy in pancreatic stone management is that recurrence of symptoms resulting from migrated stone can be treated again by endoscopy with or without ESWL. On the other hand, rate of repeat surgery for recurrent pain is high as 20% with a striking increase in morbidity and mortality after repeated surgery.[156] Controlled trials comparing surgical and endoscopic therapies are awaited.

ESWL has become almost indispensable to specialized centers treating many patients with advanced chronic pancreatitis. ESWL should be considered when endoscopic procedures fail to remove

Table 52–5. Technical and clinical results of Extracorporeal Shockwave Lithotripsy for pancreatic stones

Author (Reference)	No. of Patients	Complete or Partial Pain Relief %	Fragmentation %	Complete Clearance %
Dumonceau, et al. (156)	70	68	58	50
Sherman, et al. (151)	32	85	99	58
Delhaye, et al. (157)	123	85	99	59
Sauerbach, et al. (158)	24	83	87.5	42
Farnbacher, et al. (159)	114	93	82	39
Adamek, et al. (160)	80	76	54	ND
Schneider, et al. (161)	50	62	86	60
Ohara, et al. (162)	32	86	100	75
Kozarek, et al. (165)	40	80	100	ND

ND, not determined.

large or impacted stones and for patients with recurrent attacks of pancreatic pain who have moderate to marked changes in the pancreatic ductal system and obstructive ductal stones. Almost all patients are amenable to ESWL because the biochemical composition of stone consists of 95% calcium carbonate on a protein matrix. The procedure is contraindicated only in those who have coagulation disorders or who have bone, calcified aneurysms, or lung tissue in the SW path. Lithotripsy works by concentrating focused SWs on stones, which causes their disruption. Application of several hundred to thousand SWs to the calculi at a focal area permits gradual disintegration of the stone. SWs can be generated by three methods: spark discharge (Dornier system, Germering, Germany), piezoelectric elements (Wolf system, Knittlingen, Germany), and electromagnetic deflection of a metal membrane (Siemens system, Erlangen, Germany). SW generation takes place in degassed water. The SWs are focused by reflection of the primary wave, arraying of the piezoceramic elements on a hemispherical disc or an acoustic lens. SWs are then directed to the body via a water cushion or basin.

In most patients, a radiologic target system is needed, which can be provided by the placement of a stent. Fluoroscopic focusing of densely calcified stones can be achieved without pancreatography. In others, MRCP with secretin or CT can demonstrate pancreatic ductal obstruction related to stones. For very small stones or radiolucent stones, visualization can be improved by instillation of contrast via a naso-pancreatic catheter. Patients require anesthesia, which can be conscious or general. Routine antibiotic prophylaxis is unnecessary. SWs are focused first on the most distal stone and then on other calculi starting from the head to tail, allowing stone fragments to drain downward through the papilla. A total of 3000 to 5000 SWs using the highest possible energy levels are delivered in one treatment session. Pancreatic stones are hard and usually require a higher powered SW (22 to 24 kV). Each session lasts approximately 45 to 60 minutes.

ESWL is an effective adjunct to the nonsurgical endoscopic approach in chronic calcifying pancreatitis with complete or partial relief of symptoms in 80% of patients, which is comparable to the surgical literature.[157,158] In one study, stones were successfully fragmented in 99% of patients resulting in a decrease in duct dilatation in 90%.[157] The main pancreatic duct was cleared of all stones in 59%. However, one of the challenges in pancreatic duct therapy is evaluating treatment efficacy. Disintegration of a stone can be considered successful when a decrease is seen in the radiographic density of the stone and/or the stone surface area. In

addition, the ability to demonstrate relief of ductal obstruction at deep cannulation of the pancreatic duct during ERCP is an indicator of treatment efficacy.[157] Using the previous criteria the success rate of fragmentation has been approximately 76% to 100% in most series regardless of the SW system used.[157–160]

Most patients require endoscopic extraction of stone fragments after ESWL for complete clearance from the ductal system. Some authorities advocate that pancreatic sphincterotomy should be performed before ESWL to facilitate stone passage.[154,161] With the exception of one report[151] in which successful treatment was more frequent in patients with solitary stones (74% vs. 43% for multiple stones), successful fragmentation and stone clearance was not correlated with the initial size or the number of main pancreatic duct stones by others.[159,162,163] Repeat ESWL may be required if stones have incompletely disintegrated, which is often the case in patients with large or multiple stones. The reported mean number of treatment sessions required to complete lithotripsy has ranged from 1.3 to 4.1 per patient in most reports.[154,160,161]

The radiographic success of ESWL has been associated with clinical improvement (Table 52–5). Complete or partial pain relief was observed in 62% to 86% of the patients in the largest series during a mean follow-up ranging from 7 to 44 months.[157,161,164,165] However, complete stone clearance was not required for symptom relief. A considerable number of patients gained weight because of a reduction in postprandial pain attacks, improvement in pancreatic function, or both. The number and location of stones, the presence of a stricture, or continued alcohol use did not appear to be associated with recurrent pain.[157,161] As a result, ESWL does not have to be restricted to patients without these unfavorable clinical characteristics.

One study[156] identified three independent predictors of pain relapse at long-term follow-up after ESWL therapy: a high frequency of pain attacks before treatment (more than or at least two pain attacks during the 2 months before treatment), a long duration of disease before treatment, and the presence of a nonpapillary stenosis of the main pancreatic duct. This suggests that ESWL associated with endoscopic therapy should be performed as early as possible in the course of chronic pancreatitis. Early ductal decompression of the main pancreatic duct may also help prevent further fibrosis, which can lead to pancreatic insufficiency. In addition, it may improve pancreatic function in patients who have already developed pancreatic insufficiency. Three studies investigating this issue found that exocrine pancreatic function improved more often

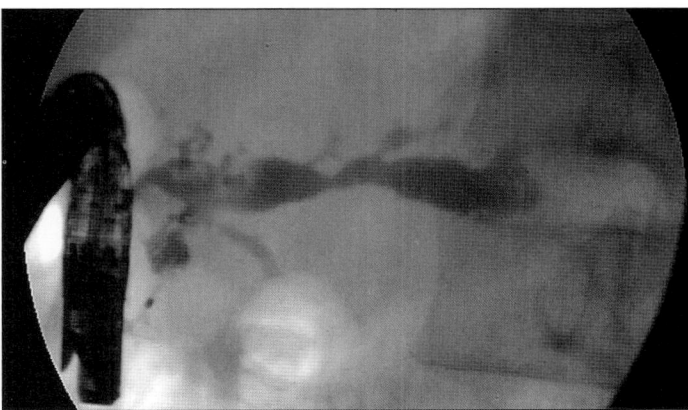

Figure 52–11. Endoscopic retrograde cholangiopancreatography (ERCP) demonstrating changes of chronic pancreatitis with a stricture in the main pancreatic duct.

after treatment compared with endocrine pancreatic function, which remained largely unaffected except for a few patients.[153,157,164] Complications in series using ESWL were primarily related to the endoscopic procedure.

Pancreatic Strictures

Pancreatic duct strictures (Fig. 52–11) may be a complication of previously embedded stone or a consequence of acute inflammatory changes around the pancreatic duct.[166] Pancreatic duct strictures may contribute to pain, recurrent acute pancreatitis, and exocrine insufficiency. Strictures may also be associated with stones, pseudocysts, and pancreatic malignancy.[154,167–169] The mechanism of pain in patients with pancreatic strictures is poorly understood but may, in part, be attributable to pancreatic duct hypertension from obstruction caused by the stricture to the flow of pancreatic juice. Pancreatic duct strictures may be present in association with biliary strictures; thus, liver function test abnormalities, jaundice, and cholangitis may be presenting symptoms.

Diagnosis

The finding of a pancreatic duct stricture often poses a diagnostic dilemma as to the specific cause of the stricture. The cause of a pancreatic duct stricture may be related to acute or chronic pancreatitis, pancreatic neoplasm, pseudocyst, and traumatic injury. Cancer is the most feared cause and should be considered in all patients with pancreatic duct strictures. When evaluating these patients, the background clinical information is paramount. Patients aged older than 50 years presenting with idiopathic or multiple episodes of acute pancreatitis, with pancreatic duct stricture, must have malignancy included in the differential diagnosis, particularly in the absence of alcohol abuse. Thorough evaluation of pancreatic strictures requires multidisciplinary testing.

When evaluating pancreatograms, changes in the ductal anatomy other than strictures should be looked for. This includes irregularity in the contour or dilatation of the pancreatic duct or of the secondary radicles. The presence of a single stricture with proximal dilatation and normal distal ductal anatomy is suggestive of a neoplastic cause. Changes noted throughout the duct, particularly when they occur downstream to the stricture, in addition to the

anticipated upstream changes, are suggestive of chronic pancreatitis. The presence of multiple strictures and dilatations in a "chain-of-lakes appearance" is characteristic of chronic pancreatitis. However, the presence of mucous plugs and a patulous papilla should warn the unwary eye to the possibility of intraductal papillary mucinous tumor of the pancreas. Unfortunately, no pancreatogram findings are absolutely specific for chronic pancreatitis. At ERCP, complete cutoff of the pancreatic duct implies an abrupt stop in the flow of contrast at some point along the length of the pancreatic duct. Incomplete filling of the pancreatic duct can also portray a similar picture. Sufficient contrast must be injected so that the secondary branches of the pancreatic duct can be seen downstream to the blockage. This confirms the presence of a functionally important stricture in the main pancreatic duct because it indicates that the contrast has taken the path of least resistance into the secondary branches. During ERCP, it is vital to attempt to cross the stricture with accessories to allow for improved imaging and tissue sampling by brush cytology, forceps, and needle aspirate. Adjunctive imaging modalities are also important in the differential diagnosis of pancreatic duct strictures. These include conventional studies such as CT and EUS. Both can detect and differentiate chronic pancreatitis and pancreatic neoplasms in their advanced stages and may assist in obtaining tissue diagnosis.

Treatment

Endoscopic therapy for pancreatic duct strictures is primarily indicated for patients presenting with refractory abdominal pain, with or without upstream ductal dilatation. The technique for placing a stent in the pancreatic duct is similar to that used for inserting a biliary stent. A guidewire is first maneuvered beyond the stricture several centimeters. Hydrophilic, flexible-tip wires are generally helpful. Pancreatic stents are similar to biliary stents except for side holes along their length to allow for flow from side branches. Generally, the diameter of the stent should not exceed the size of a normal downstream duct. Therefore, 3-Fr, 4-Fr, 5-Fr stents are used commonly in small ducts, whereas 7-Fr and 10-Fr stents can be used in advanced chronic pancreatitis with dilated pancreatic ducts. Occasionally, in patients with small duct disease who have recurrent strictures, we place multiple 3-Fr stents to dilate the stricture. We believe that stent-induced trauma could be obviated by this method but data on this are still forthcoming. In addition, the severity of the stricture, location, and duct size influence the choice of stent. In general, the best candidates for stenting are those with a distal stricture and upstream dilatation. Other therapy such as pancreatic and/or biliary sphincterotomy, pancreatic duct stone removal, and dilatation of strictures may be required concomitantly at time of stenting. Dilatation to widen single or multiple strictures of the main pancreatic duct in chronic pancreatitis can be performed successfully. Dilating catheters with graded tips are generally used, although dilatation using the torquing motion of the Soehendra stent retriever can be used in tighter strictures. After dilatation, stents of adequate size are left to facilitate drainage and to prevent recurrent stricture formation. If stents larger than 7 Fr are to be used, patients often require biductal sphincterotomy followed by stricture dilatation. For optimal results, therapy must address both the pancreatic duct stricture and duct stones if any are present.

Table 52–6. Stent Therapy for Chronic Pancreatitis with Dominant Strictures

Author (Reference)	No. of Patients	Technical Success	No. of Patients Improved	Mean Follow-up Duration in Months
Cremer, et al. (166)	76	75	41	37
Ponchon, et al. (172)	28	23	12	26
Smits, et al. (173)	51	49	40	34
Binmoeller, et al. (174)	93	84	61	39
TOTAL	248	231 (93%)	154 (62%)	34

The appropriate duration of pancreatic stent placement is currently unknown. Most diagnostic trial or short-term therapy stents are left in place for 2 to 4 weeks. In contrast, long-term therapy stents are left in place for several months. If the patient has improvement in symptoms, then one can remove the stent and follow the patient clinically, continue stenting for a more prolonged period, or perform a surgical drainage procedure. The latter option suggests that the results of endoscopic stenting will predict the surgical outcome. Two preliminary reports support this concept, but more studies are required.[170,171] Quantitating the degree of improvement in pancreatic disorders is often poorly defined. In general, partial or complete symptom improvement indicates that intraductal hypertension was an etiologic factor. Continued improvement in symptoms after stent removal indicates adequate dilatation of the narrowing. The results of stent insertion for dominant pancreatic duct strictures (Table 52–6) has been favorable, with technical success in 72% to 99%, relief of pain in 75% to 94%, and good long-term outcomes in 52% to 81%.[166,172–174] Although long-term symptom resolution has been reported in more than 60% of patients, endoscopic resolution of strictures have been documented in only about one third of patients managed by endoscopic stenting.[172,173] Although these data suggest that stricture resolution is not a prerequisite for symptom improvement, other concomitant therapies at time of pancreatic stenting such as pancreatic sphincterotomy or pancreatic stone removal may account for this successful outcome. It is also likely that pain in chronic pancreatitis tends to decrease over time as glandular destruction of the pancreas progresses in an uninhibited manner.[52]

In a study of 75 patients with pancreatic duct strictures and upstream dilatation managed by placement of 10-Fr stents, Cremer and colleagues[166] reported that over a follow-up of 3 years, 71 patients (94%) were improved, with 40 patients (53%) free of symptoms. Improvement in symptoms was associated with a decrease in the pancreatic duct diameter. In addition, in a prospective study of 23 patients Ponchon and coworkers[172] reported that disappearance of stenosis at stent removal and a reduction in the pancreatic duct diameter by more than 2 mm were predictive of pain relief after pancreatic duct stenting. Binmoeller and colleagues[174] made a similar observation on their study of 93 patients with chronic patients and dominant pancreatic duct strictures managed by pancreatic duct stenting. Although 74% of their patients experienced complete or partial symptom relief, most of them were found to have a regression of ductal dilatation after successful stenting.

Although all the previously mentioned studies used conventional plastic stents, Cremer and coworkers[175] in a pilot study, reported their experience with self-expandable metal stents in patients with chronic pancreatitis. Twenty-two patients with relapsing dominant strictures of the main pancreatic duct underwent stent placement through the major duodenal papilla. A success rate of placement of 100%, associated with an immediate decrease of pancreatic duct diameter and disappearance of pain, was noted. Although no immediate complications were encountered, follow-up of these patients demonstrated a high occlusion rate of these metal stents from mucosal hyperplasia. Hence, use of metal stents in treatment of chronic pancreatitis is not encouraged.

Direct comparative studies evaluating the efficacies of surgery and endoscopic therapy is required to identify subset of patients who would benefit from either treatment modality. Only one prospective, randomized study comparing surgical and endoscopic therapy in chronic pancreatitis has been reported in the literature so far.[176] In this study, 140 patients with obstructive chronic pancreatitis were treated either by endoscopic therapy or by surgical resection and drainage procedures. Although immediate relief of symptoms was identical in both groups (51.6% in the endotherapy group vs. 42.1% in the surgical group), at 5 years' follow-up, complete absence of pain was more frequent after surgery (37% vs. 14%), with partial relief of pain being similar (49% vs. 51%). The increase in body weight was also greater by 20% to 25% in the surgical group, whereas new-onset diabetes mellitus developed with similar frequency in both groups (34% in the surgical group vs. 43% in the endotherapy group). More studies are required to confirm these findings.

Pancreatic stenting is not without consequences. Complications related directly to stent therapy include acute pancreatitis, pancreatic infection, pseudocyst formation, duct injury, stone formation, and migration.[148,177] The rate of pancreatic stent occlusion appears similar to that of biliary stents.[171] However, a majority of these occlusions are without adverse clinical events because pancreatic juice may siphon along the sides of the stent. Morphologic changes of the pancreatic duct directly related to stenting occur in more than 50% of patients.[178–181] It remains uncertain what the long-term consequences of these stent-induced ductal changes are in most patients, although permanent new strictures are seen in a small number. EUS identified parenchymal changes in 68% of patients who underwent short-term pancreatic stenting.[84] Although such changes may have significant long-term consequences in patients with a normal pancreas, the outcomes in patients with advanced chronic pancreatitis appears less certain.

Future Trends

The currently available diagnostic armamentarium for chronic pancreatitis focuses exclusively on pancreatic structure and function with inability to diagnose the disease in its early stages. The association between *CFTR* mutations and idiopathic chronic pancreatitis raises the possibility of genetic testing to evaluate idiopathic chronic pancreatitis. At present, the role of *CFTR* mutation testing is uncertain because no guidelines exist for genetic counseling or altered clinical management of idiopathic chronic pancreatitis based on the results of such testing. As further research clarifies whether idiopathic chronic pancreatitis patients with *CFTR* mutations differ from other idiopathic chronic pancreatitis patients, this information may lead to wider use of genetic testing during the evaluation of patients with idiopathic chronic pancreatitis. Genetic testing may facilitate young patients to seek medical care at an early stage of the disease and also referral to a specialized center for the management of cystic fibrosis.

Although surgery is currently an alternative to endoscopic therapy for management of chronic pancreatitis, randomized studies directly comparing both modalities are required. The often complex morphologic situation in these patients (inflammatory tumor, ductal obstruction resulting from stricture and/or stones) may make an individualized approach necessary. In the future, it may therefore be best to compare directly the two forms of therapy toward more specific conditions. In addition, assessment of costs may yield further data of relevance to clinical decision making.

Clinicians have a keen interest in assessing the effects of medical intervention on outcomes related to morbidity and mortality. Improvements in endoscopic and surgical therapies for chronic pancreatitis have diminished the mortality risk. However, quality of life evaluation remains an area that had long been neglected. Quality of life may be defined as an individual's overall satisfaction with life and one's general sense of well-being.[182] This definition may be further focussed by limiting it to just health-related quality of life. Physicians have always attempted to integrate their patient's well-being into therapeutic plans. However, health care providers have repeatedly been shown to be poor proxies for measuring quality of life.[183] By using instruments that measure quality of life, clinicians can learn if the patient truly benefits from therapeutic interventions, rather than relying solely on clinical indicators. There are currently numerous disease-specific instruments for conditions such as inflammatory bowel disease, arthritis, and cancer but only one for evaluating patients with chronic pancreatitis.[184] Patient-centered outcomes and quality of life assessment are important areas in chronic pancreatitis that must be researched further to evaluate the impact of technical and technologic advances in this area.

REFERENCES

1. Steer ML, Waxman I, Freedman S: Chronic pancreatitis. N Engl J Med 332:1482–1490, 1995.
2. Lankisch PG, Banks PA: Pancreatitis. New York, Springer, 1998.
3. Lankisch PG, Assmus C, Maisonneuve P, et al: Epidemiology of pancreatic diseases in Luneburg County. A study in a defined German population. Pancreatology 2:469–477, 2002.
4. Dite P, Stary K, Novotny I, et al: Incidence of chronic pancreatitis in the Czech Republic. Eur J Gastroenterol Hepatol 13:749–750, 2001.
5. Lin Y, Tamakoshi A, Matsuno S, et al: Nationwide epidemiological screening of chronic pancreatitis in Japan. J Gastroenterol 35(2):136–141, 2000.
6. Copenhagen Pancreatic Study: An interim report from a prospective multicenter study. Scand J Gastroenterol 16:305–312, 1981.
7. Haemmerli UO, Hefti ML, Scmid M: Chronic pancreatitis in Zurich, 1958 through 1962. Bibliotheca Gastroenterologica 7:58–64, 1962.
8. O'Sullivan JN, Noberga FT, Morlock CG, et al: Acute and chronic pancreatitis in Rochester, Minnesota, 1940 to 1969. Gastroenterology 62:373–39, 1972.
9. Lowenfels AB, Maisonneuve P, Grover H, et al: Racial factors and the risk of chronic pancreatitis. Am J Gastroenterol 94:790–794, 1999.
10. Nakamura K, Sarles H, Payan H: Three dimensional reconstruction of the pancreatic ducts in chronic pancreatitis. Gastroenterology 62:942–949, 1972.
11. Harada H, Miyake H, Miki H, et al: Role of endoscopic elimination of protein plugs in the treatment of chronic pancreatitis. Gastroenterol Jpn 17:463–468, 1982.
12. Tsurumi T, Fujii Y, Takeda M, et al: A case of chronic pancreatitis successfully treated by endoscopic removal of protein plugs. Acta Med Okayama 38:169–174, 1984.
13. Freedman SD, Sakamoto K, Venu RP: GP2, the homologue to the renal cast protein uromodulin, is a major component of intraductal plugs in chronic pancreatitis. J Clin Invest 92:83–90, 1993.
14. Guy O, Robles-Diaz G, Adrich Z, et al: Protein content of precipitates present in pancreatic juice of alcoholic subjects and patients with chronic calcifying pancreatitis. Gastroenterology 84:102–107, 1983.
15. Karanjia ND, Widdison AL, Leung FW, et al: Blood flow alterations in chronic pancreatitis: Effects of secretory stimulation [abstract]. Gastroenterology 98:A221, 1990.
16. Karanjia ND, Singh SM, Widdison AL, et al: Pancreatic ductal and interstitial pressures in cats with chronic pancreatitis. Dig Dis Sci 37:268–273, 1992.
17. Rose P, Fraine E, Hunt LP, et al: Dietary antioxidants and chronic pancreatitis. Hum Nutr Clin Nutr 40:151–164, 1986.
18. Uden S, Acheson DW, Reeves J, et al: Antioxidants, enzyme induction, and chronic pancreatitis: A reappraisal following studies in patients on anticonvulsants. Eur J Clin Nutr 42:561–569, 1988.
19. Schoenberg MH, Buchler M, Pietrzyk C, et al: Lipid peroxidation and glutathione metabolism in chronic pancreatitis. Pancreas 10:36–43, 1995.
20. Sahel J, Sarles H: Modifications of pure human pancreatic juice induced by chronic alcohol consumption. Dig Dis Sci 24:897–905, 1979.
21. Epstein O, Chapman RW, Lake-Vakaar G, et al: The pancreas in primary biliary cirrhosis and primary sclerosing cholangitis. Gastroenterology 83:1172–1182, 1982.
22. Nishimori I, Yamamoto Y, Okazaki K, et al: Identification of autoantibodies to a pancreatic antigen in patients with idiopathic chronic pancreatitis and Sjögren's syndrome. Pancreas 9:374–381, 1994.
23. Bovo P, Mirakian R, Merigo F, et al: HLA molecule expression on chronic pancreatitis specimens: Is there a role for autoimmunity? A preliminary study. Pancreas 2:350–356, 1987.
24. Ammann RW, Heitz PU, Kloppel G: Course of alcoholic chronic pancreatitis: A prospective clinicomorphological long-term study. Gastroenterology 111:224–231, 1996.
25. Ammann RW, Muellhaupt B: Progression of alcoholic acute to chronic pancreatitis. Gut 35:552–556, 1994.
26. Gastard J, Jobaud F, Farbos T, et al: Etiology and course of primary chronic pancreatitis in western France. Digestion 9:416–428, 1973.
27. Lankisch MR, Imoto M, Layyer P, et al: The effect of small amounts of alcohol on the clinical course of chronic pancreatitis. Mayo Clin Proc 76:242–251, 2001.
28. Bisceglie AM, Segal I: Cirrhosis and chronic pancreatitis in alcoholics. J Clin Gastroenterol 6:199–200, 1984.
29. Haber PS, Wilson JS, Pirola RC: Smoking and alcoholic pancreatitis. Pancreas 8:568–572, 1993.

30. Levy P, Mathurin P, Roqueplo A, et al: A multidimensional case control study of dietary, alcohol, and tobacco habits in alcoholic men with chronic pancreatitis. Pancreas 10:231–238, 1995.

31. Cavallini G, Talamini G, Vaona B, et al: Effect of alcohol and smoking on pancreatic lithogenesis in the course of chronic pancreatitis. Pancreas 9:42–46, 1994.

32. Sossenheimer MJ, Aston CE, Preston RA, et al: Clinical characteristics of hereditary pancreatitis in a large family, based on high risk haplotype. Am J Gastroenterol 92:1113–1116, 1997.

33. Le Bodic LL, Bignon JD, Raguenes O, et al: The hereditary pancreatitis gene maps to long arm of chromosome 7. Hum Mol Genet 5:549–554, 1996.

34. Whitcomb C, Preston RA, Aston CE, et al: A gene for hereditary pancreatitis maps to chromosome 7q35. Gastroenterology 110:1975–1980, 1996.

35. Whitcomb DC, Gorry MC, Preston RA, et al: Hereditary pancreatitis is caused by a mutation in the cationic trypsinogen gene. Nat Genet 14:141–145, 1996.

36. Teich N, Ockenga J, Hoffmeister A, et al: Chronic pancreatitis associated with an activation peptide mutation that facilitates trypsin activation. Gastroenterology 119:461–465, 2000.

37. Kopelman H, Corey M, Gaskin K, et al: Impaired chloride secretion, as well as bicarbonate secretion, underlies the fluid secretory defect in cystic fibrosis pancreas. Gastroenterology 95:349–355, 1988.

38. Cohn JA, Friedman KJ, Noone PG, et al: Relation between mutations of the cystic fibrosis gene and idiopathic pancreatitis. N Engl J Med 339:653–658, 1998.

39. Sharer N, Schwarz M, Malone G, et al: Mutations of the cystic fibrosis gene in patients with chronic pancreatitis. N Engl J Med 339:645–652, 1998.

40. Sarles H, Augustine P, Laugier R, et al: Pancreatic lesions and modifications of pancreatic juice in tropical chronic pancreatitis. Dig Dis Sci 39:1337–1344, 1994.

41. Bhatia E, Choudhuri G, Sikora SS, et al: Tropical calcific pancreatitis: Strong association with SPINK1 trypsin inhibitor mutations. Gastroenterology 123:1020–1025, 2002.

42. Schneider A, Suman A, Rossi L, et al: SPINK1/PSTI mutations are associated with tropical pancreatitis and type II diabetes mellitus in Bangladesh. Gastroenterology 123:1026–1030, 2002.

43. Vestergaard H, Kruse A, Rokkjaer M, et al: Endoscopic manometry of the sphincter of Oddi and the pancreatic and biliary ducts in patients with chronic pancreatitis. Scand J Gastroenterol 29:188–192, 1994.

44. Delhaye M, Engelholm L, Cremer M: Pancreas divisum: Congenital anatomic variant or anomaly? Contribution of endoscopic retrograde dorsal pancreatography. Gastroenterology 89:951–958, 1985.

45. Lehman GA, Sherman S: Pancreas divisum. Diagnosis, clinical significance, and management alternatives. Gastrointest Endosc Clin N Am 5:145–170, 1995.

46. Witt H, Luck W, Becker M: A signal peptide cleavage site mutation in the cationic trypsinogen gene is strongly associated with chronic pancreatitis. Gastroenterology 117:7–10, 1999.

47. Creighton J, Lyall R, Wilson DI, et al: Mutations in the cationic trypsinogen gene in patients with chronic pancreatitis. Lancet 354:42–43, 1999.

48. Layer P, Yamamoto H, Kalthoff L, et al: The different courses of early- and late-onset idiopathic and alcoholic pancreatitis. Gastroenterology 107:1481–1487, 1994.

49. Bockman DE, Buchler MW, Malfertheiner P, et al: Analysis of nerves in chronic pancreatitis. Gastroenterology 94:1459–1469, 1988.

50. Buchler MW, Weihe E, Friess H, et al: Changes in peptidergic innervation in chronic pancreatitis. Pancreas 7:183–192, 1992.

51. Lankisch PG, Lohr-Happe A, Otto J, et al: Natural course in chronic pancreatitis. Digestion 54:148–155, 1993.

52. Ammann RW, Akovbiantz A, Largiader F, et al: Course and outcome of chronic pancreatitis: Longitudinal study of a mixed medical-surgical series of 245 patients. Gastroenterology 86:820–828, 1984.

53. Lankisch PG, Seidensticker F, Lohr-Happe A, et al: The course of pain is the same in alcohol- and nonalcohol-induced chronic pancreatitis. Pancreas 10:338–341, 1995.

54. DiMagno EP, Go VL, Summerskill WH: Relations between pancreatic enzyme outputs and malabsorption in severe pancreatic insufficiency. N Engl J Med 288:813–815, 1973.

55. Mergener K, Baillie J: Chronic pancreatitis. Lancet 350:1379–1385, 1997.

56. Toskes PP, Hansell J, Cerda J, et al: Vitamin B12 malabsorption in chronic pancreatic insufficiency. N Engl J Med 284:627–632, 1971.

57. Del Prato S, Tiengo A: Pancreatic diabetes. Diabetes Rev 1:260–265, 1993.

58. Malka D, Hammel P, Sauvanet A, et al: Risk factors for diabetes mellitus in chronic pancreatitis. Gastroenterology 119:1324–1332, 2000.

59. Crawford JM, Cotran RS: The pancreas. In Cotran RS (ed): Robbins Pathologic Basis of Disease, 6th ed. Philadelphia, WB Saunders, 1999, pp 902–929.

60. Lowenfels AB, Maisonneuve P, Cavallini G, et al: Pancreatitis and the risk of pancreatic cancer. International Pancreatitis Study Group. N Engl J Med 328:1433–1437, 1993.

61. Malfertheiner P, Buchler M: Correlation of imaging and function in chronic pancreatitis. Radiol Clin North Am 27:51–64, 1989.

62. Bozkurt T, Braun U, Leferink S, et al: Comparison of pancreatic morphology and exocrine functional impairment in patients with chronic pancreatitis. Gut 35:1132–1136, 1994.

63. Lankisch PG: Function tests in the diagnosis of chronic pancreatitis. Int J Pancreatol 14:9–20, 1993.

64. Niederau C, Grendell JH: Diagnosis of chronic pancreatitis. Gastroenterology 88:1973–1995, 1985.

65. Braganza JM, Hunt LP, Warwick F: Relationship between pancreatic exocrine function and ductal morphology in chronic pancreatitis. Gastroenterology 82:1341–1347, 1982.

66. Girdwood AH, Hatfield AR, Bornman PC, et al: Structure and function in noncalcific pancreatitis. Dig Dis Sci 29:721–726, 1984.

67. Malfertheiner P, Buchler M, Stanescu A, et al: Exocrine pancreatic function in correlation to ductal and parenchymal morphology in chronic pancreatitis. Hepatogastroenterology 33:110–114, 1986.

68. Lankisch PG, Seidensticker F, Otto J, et al: Secretin-pancreozymin test (SPT) and endoscopic retrograde cholangiopancreatography (ERCP): Both are necessary for diagnosing or excluding chronic pancreatitis. Pancreas 12:149–152, 1996.

69. Lambiase L, Forsmark CE, Toskes PP: Secretin test diagnoses chronic pancreatitis earlier than ERCP [abstract]. Gastroenterology 104:A315, 1993.

70. Hayakawa T, Kondo T, Shibata T, et al: Relationship between pancreatic exocrine function and histological changes in chronic pancreatitis. Am J Gastroenterol 87:1170–1174, 1992.

71. Stein J: New fecal tests in the diagnosis of exocrine pancreatic insufficiency. In Malfertheiner P, Ditschuneit H (eds): Diagnostic Procedures in Pancreatic Disease. Berlin, Springer Verlag, 1997, pp 277–289.

72. Stein J, Purschian B, Zeuzem S, et al: Quantification of fecal carbohydrates by near-infrared reflectance analysis. Clin Chem 42:309–312, 1996.

73. Bekers O, Postma C, Fischer JC, et al: Fecal nitrogen determination by near-infrared spectroscopy. Eur J Clin Chem Clin Biochem 34:561–563, 1996.

74. Dominguez E, Hieronymus C, Sauerbruch T, et al: Fecal elastase test: Evaluation of a new non invasive pancreatic function test. Am J Gastroenterol 90:1834–1837, 1995.

75. Sarner M, Cotton PB: Classification of pancreatitis. Gut 25:756–759, 1984.

76. Bolondi L, Li Bassi S, Gaiani S, et al: Sonography of chronic pancreatitis. Radiol Clin North Am 27:815–833, 1989.

77. Ferucci JT Jr, Wittenberg J, Black B, et al: Computed body tomography in chronic pancreatitis. Radiology 13:172–182, 1979.

78. Hessel SJ, Siegelman SS, McNeil NJ, et al: A prospective evaluation of computer tomography in ultrasound of the pancreas. Radiology 143:129–133, 1982.

79. Robinson PJ, Sheridan MB: Pancreatitis: Computed tomography and magnetic resonance imaging. Eur Radiol 10:401–408, 2000.

80. Sica JT, Braver J, Cooney MJ, et al: Comparison of endoscopic retrograde cholangiopancreatography with MR cholangiography in patients with pancreatitis. Radiology 210:605–610, 1999.

81. Takehara Y, Ichijo K, Tooyama N, et al: Breath-hold MR cholangiopancreatography with a long-echo-train fast-spin echo sequence in a surface coil in chronic pancreatitis. Radiology 92:73–78, 1994.

82. Axon AT, Classen M, Cotton PB, et al: Pancreatography in chronic pancreatitis: International definitions. Gut 25:1107–1112, 1984.

83. Forsmark CE, Toskes PP: What does an abnormal pancreatogram mean? Gastrointest Endosc Clin N Am 5:105–123, 1995.

84. Sherman S, Hawes RH, Savides TJ, et al: Stent-induced pancreatic ductal and parenchymal changes: Correlation of endoscopic ultrasound with ERCP. Gastrointest Endosc 44:276–282, 1996.

85. Walsh TN, Rode J, Theis BA, et al: Minimal change chronic pancreatitis. Gut 33:1566–1571, 1992.

86. Hayakawa T, Kondo T, Shibata T, et al: Relationship between pancreatic exocrine function and histological changes in chronic pancreatitis. Am J Gastroenterol 87:1170–1174, 1992.

87. Schmitz-Moormann P, Himmelmann GW, Brandes JW, et al: Comparative radiological and morphological study of human pancreas. Pancreatitis-like changes in postmortem ductograms and their morphological pattern. Possible implication for ERCP. Gut 26:406–414, 1985.

88. Sherman S, Lehman GA: Endoscopic therapy of pancreatic disease. Gastroenterologist 1:5–17, 1993.

89. Tarnasky PR, Hoffman BJ, Aabakken L, et al: Sphincter of Oddi dysfunction is associated with chronic pancreatitis. Am J Gastroenterol 92:1125–1129, 1997.

90. Lees WR: Endoscopic ultrasonography of chronic pancreatitis and pancreatic pseudocysts. Scand J Gastroenterol 123:123–129, 1986.

91. Lees WR, Vallon AG, Denyer ME, et al: Prospective study of ultrasonography in chronic pancreatic disease. Br Med J 1:162–164, 1979.

92. Wiersema MJ, Hawes RH, Lehman GA, et al: Prospective evaluation of endoscopic ultrasonography and endoscopic retrograde cholangiopancreatography in patients with chronic abdominal pain of suspected pancreatic origin. Endoscopy 25:555–564, 1993.

93. Sahai AV, Zimmerman M, Aabakken L, et al: Prospective assessment of the ability of endoscopic ultrasound to diagnose, exclude, or establish the severity of chronic pancreatitis found by endoscopic retrograde cholangiopancreatography. Gastrointest Endosc 48:18–25, 1998.

94. Buscail L, Escourrou J, Moreau J, et al: Endoscopic ultrasonography in chronic pancreatitis: A comparative prospective study with conventional ultrasonography, computed tomography, and ERCP. Pancreas 10:251–257, 1995.

95. Dancygier H: Endoscopic ultrasonography in chronic pancreatitis. Gastrointest Endosc Clin N Am 5:795–804, 1995.

96. Natterman C, Goldschmidt AJ, Dancygier H: Endosonography in chronic pancreatitis: A comparison between endoscopic retrograde pancreatography and endoscopic ultrasonography. Endoscopy 25:565–570, 1993.

97. Catalano MF, Lahoti S, Geenen JE, et al: Prospective evaluation of endoscopic ultrasonography, endoscopic retrograde pancreatography, and secretin test in the diagnosis of chronic pancreatitis. Gastrointest Endosc 48:11–17, 1998.

98. Bhutani MS, Hoffman BJ, Hawes RH: Diagnosis of pancreas divisum by endoscopic ultrasonography. Endoscopy 31:167–169, 1999.

99. Toskes PP: Diagnosis of chronic pancreatitis and exocrine insufficiency. Hosp Pract 20:97–100, 1985.

100. Sahai AV, Mishra G, Penman I, et al: EUS to detect evidence of pancreatic disease in patients with persistent or nonspecific dyspepsia. Gastrointest Endosc 52:153–159, 2000.

101. Bhutani MS: Endoscopic ultrasonography: Changes of chronic pancreatitis in asymptomatic and symptomatic alcoholic patients. J Ultrasound Med 18:455–462, 1999.

102. Lowenfels AB, Maisonneuve P, Cavallini G, et al: Prognosis of chronic pancreatitis: An international multicenter study. Am J Gastroenterol 89:1467–1471, 1994.

103. Strum WB: Abstinence in alcoholic chronic pancreatitis: Effect on pain and outcome. J Clin Gastroenterol 20:37–41, 1995.

104. Talamini G, Bassi C, Falconi M, et al: Pain relapses in the first 10 years of chronic pancreatitis. Am J Surg 171:565–569, 1996.

105. Dobrilla G: Management of chronic pancreatitis. Focus on enzyme replacement therapy. Int J Pancreatol 5(Suppl):17–29, 1989.

106. Slaff J, Jacobson D, Tillman CR, et al: Protease-specific suppression of pancreatic exocrine secretion. Gastroenterology 87:44–52, 1984.

107. Isaksson G, Ihse I: Pain reduction by an oral pancreatic enzyme preparation in chronic pancreatitis. Dig Dis Sci 28:97–102, 1993.

108. Halgreen H, Pederson NT, Worning H: Symptomatic effect of pancreatic enzyme therapy in patients with chronic pancreatitis. Scand J Gastroenterol 21:104–108, 1986.

109. Mossner J, Secknus R, Meyer J, et al: Treatment of pain with pancreatic extracts in chronic pancreatitis: Results of a prospective placebo-controlled multicenter trial. Digestion 53:54–66, 1992.

110. Malesci A, Gaia E, Fioretta A, et al: No effect of long-term treatment with pancreatic extract on recurrent abdominal pain in patients with chronic pancreatitis. Scand J Gastroenterol 30:392–398, 1995.

111. Larvin M, McMahon MJ, Thomas WEG, et al: Creon (enteric coated pancreatin microspheres) for the treatment of pain in chronic pancreatitis: A double-blind randomized placebo-controlled crossover trial [abstract]. Gastroenterology 100:A283, 1991.

112. Warshaw AL, Banks PA, Fernandez-Del Castillo C. AGA technical review: Treatment of pain in chronic pancreatitis. Gastroenterology 115:765–776, 1998.

113. Max MB, Schafer SC, Culnane M, et al: Amitryptiline, but not lorazepam, relieves postherpetic neuralgia. Neurology 38:1427–1432, 1988.

114. Ventafridda V, Bianchi M, Ripamonti C, et al: Studies on the effects of antidepressant drugs on the antinociceptive action of morphine and on plasma morphine in rat and man. Pain 43:155–162, 1990.

115. Lillemore KD, Cameron JL, Kaufman HS, et al: Chemical splanchniectomy in patients with unresectable pancreatic cancer. A prospective randomized trial. Ann Surg 217:447–455, 1993.

116. Mercadante S: Celiac plexus block versus analgesics in pancreatic cancer pain. Pain 52:187–192, 1993.

117. Wiersema MJ, Wiersema LM: Endosonography-guided celiac plexus neurolysis. Gastrointest Endosc 44:639–662, 1996.

118. Davies DD: Incidence of major complications of neurolytic celiac plexus block. J R Soc Med 86:224–266, 1993.

119. Wiersema MJ, Harada N, Wiersema LM: Endosonography guided celiac plexus neurolysis efficacy in chronic pancreatitis and malignant disease. Acta Endoscopia 28:67–79, 1998.

120. Gress F, Schmitt C, Sherman S, et al: A prospective randomized comparison of endoscopic ultrasound and computed tomography-guided celiac plexus block for managing chronic pancreatitis pain. Am J Gastroenterol 94:900–905, 1999.

121. Shea J, Bishop M, Parker E, et al: An enteral therapy containing medium chain triglycerides and hydrolyzed peptides reduces postprandial pain associated with chronic pancreatitis. Pancreatology 3:36–40, 2003.

122. Forsmark CE, Wilcox CM, Grendell JH: Endoscopy-negative upper gastrointestinal bleeding in a patient with chronic pancreatitis. Gastroenterology 102:320–329, 1992.

123. Draganov P, Hoffman B, Marsh W, et al: Long-term outcome in patients with benign biliary strictures treated endoscopically with multiple stents. Gastrointest Endosc 55:680–686, 2002.

124. Deviere J, Devaere S, Baize M, et al: Endoscopic biliary drainage in chronic pancreatitis. Gastrointest Endosc 36:96–100, 1990.

125. Deviere J, Cremer M, Love J, et al: Management of common bile duct strictures caused by chronic pancreatitis with metal self-expandable stents. Gut 35:122–126, 1994.

126. Kahl S, Zimmermann S, Glasbrenner B, et al: Treatment of benign biliary strictures in chronic pancreatitis by self-expandable metal stents. Dig Dis Sci 20:199–203, 2002.

127. Pitt HA, Kaufman SL, Coleman J, et al: Benign postoperative biliary strictures. Operate or dilate. Ann Surg 210:417–425, 1989.

128. Prinz RA: Surgical drainage procedures. In Howard J, Idezuki Y, Ihse I, Prinz R (eds): Surgical Diseases of the Pancreas. Baltimore, Williams & Wilkins, 1998, pp 359–366.

129. Frey CF: Why and when to drain the pancreatic ductal system. In Beger HG, Buchler M, Ditschuneit H, et al (eds): Chronic Pancreatitis: Research and Clinical Management. Berlin, Springer-Verlag, 1990, p 415.

130. Prinz RA, Greenlee HB: Pancreatic duct drainage in 100 patients with chronic pancreatitis. Ann Surg 194:313–320, 1981.

131. Adams DB, Ford MC, Anderson MC: Outcomes after lateral pancreaticojejunostomy for chronic pancreatitis. Ann Surg 219:481–487, 1994.

132. Nealon WH, Thompson JC: Progressive loss of pancreatic function in chronic pancreatitis is delayed by main pancreatic duct decompression: A longitudinal prospective analysis of the modified Puestow procedure. Ann Surg 217:458–466, 1991.

133. White TT, Slavotinek AH: Results of surgical treatment of chronic pancreatitis. Ann Surg 189:217–224, 1979.

134. Warshaw AL, Popp JW Jr, Schapiro RH: Long-term patency, pancreatic function, and pain relief after lateral pancreatico-jejunostomy for chronic pancreatitis. Gastroenterology 79:289–293, 1980.

135. Taylor RH, Bagley FH, Braasch JW, et al: Ductal draining or resection for chronic pancreatitis. Am J Surg 141:28–33, 1981.

136. Markowitz JS, Rattner DW, Warshaw AL: Failure of symptomatic relief after pancreaticojejunal decompression for chronic pancreatitis. Strategies for salvage. Arch Surg 129:374–379, 1994.

137. Buchler MW, Freiss H, Muller MW, et al: Randomized trial of duodenum-preserving pancreatic head resection versus pylorus-preserving Whipple in chronic pancreatitis. Am J Surg 169:65–69, 1995.

138. Jimenez RE, Fernandez-del Castillo C, Rattner DW, et al: Outcome of pancreaticoduodenectomy with pylorus preservation or with antrectomy in the treatment of chronic pancreatitis. Ann Surg 231:293–300, 2000.

139. Sakorafas GH, Farnell MB, Farley DR, et al: Long-term results after surgery for chronic pancreatitis. Int J Pancreatol 27:131–142, 2000.

140. Izbicki JR, Bloechle C, Broering DC, et al: Extended drainage versus resection in surgery for chronic pancreatitis. A prospective randomized trial comparing the longitudinal pancreaticojejunostomy combined with local pancreatic head resection with the pylorus-preserving pancreaticoduodenectomy. Ann Surg 228:771–779, 1998.

141. Rossi RL, Soeldner JS, Braasch JW, et al: Long-term results of pancreatic resection and segmental pancreatic autotransplantation for chronic pancreatitis. Am J Surg 159:51–57, 1990.

142. Vestergaard H, Krause A, Rokkjaer M, et al: Endoscopic manometry of the sphincter of Oddi and the pancreatic and biliary ducts in patients with chronic pancreatitis. Scand J Gastroenterol 29:188–192, 1994.

143. Ugljesic M, Bulajic M, Milosavljevic T, et al: Endoscopic manometry of the sphincter of Oddi and pancreatic duct in patients with chronic pancreatitis. Int J Pancreatol 19:191–195, 1996.

144. Sherman S, Hawes RH, Madura JA, et al: Comparison of intraoperative and endoscopic manometry of the sphincter of Oddi. Surg Gyn Obstet 175:410–418, 1992.

145. Williamson RCN: Pancreatic sphincteroplasty: Indications and outcome. Ann R Coll Surg 70:205–211, 1988.

146. Bagley FH, Fraasch JW, Taylor RH, et al: Sphincterotomy or sphincteroplasty in the treatment of pathologically mild chronic pancreatitis. Am J Surg 141:418–422, 1981.

147. Geenen JE, Rolny P: Endoscopic therapy of acute and chronic pancreatitis. Gastrointest Endosc 37:377–382, 1991.

148. Siegel J, Veerappan A: Endoscopic management of pancreatic disorders: Potential risks of pancreatic prosthesis. Endoscopy 23:177–180, 1991.

149. Huibregtse K, Smits ME: Endoscopic management of diseases of the pancreas. Am J Gastroenterol 89:S66–77, 1994.

150. Neuhaus H: Fragmentation of pancreatic stones by ESWL. Endoscopy 23:161–165, 1991.

151. Sherman S, Lehman GA, Hawes RH, et al: Pancreatic ductal stones: Frequency of successful endoscopic removal and improvement in symptoms. Gastrointest Endosc 37:511–517, 1991.

152. Kozarek RA, Ball TJ, Patterson GJ: Endoscopic approach to pancreatic duct calculi and obstructive pancreatitis. Am J Gastroenterol 87:600–603, 1992.

153. Cremer M, Deviere J, Delhaye M, et al: Endoscopic management of chronic pancreatitis. Acta Gastroent Belg 56:192–200, 1993.

154. Smits ME, Rauws EA, Tytgat GNJ, et al: Endoscopic treatment of pancreatic stones in patients with chronic pancreatitis. Gastrointest Endosc 43:556–560, 1996.

155. Neuhaus H, Hoffman W, Classen M: Laser lithotripsy of pancreatic and biliary stones via 3.4mm and 3.7mm miniscopes: First clinical results. Endoscopy 24:208–214, 1992.

156. Dumonceau JM, Deviere J, Le Moine O, et al: Endoscopic pancreatic drainage in chronic pancreatitis associated with ductal stones: Long-term results. Gastrointest Endosc 43:547–555, 1996.

157. Delhaye, M, Vandermeeren, A, Baize, M, et al: Extracorporeal shock wave lithotripsy of pancreatic calculi. Gastroenterology 102:610–620, 1992.

158. Sauerbruch T, Holl J, Sackmann M, et al: Extracorporeal lithotripsy of pancreatic stones in patients with chronic pancreatitis and pain. A prospective follow-up study. Gut 33:969–972, 1992.

159. Farnbacher MJ, Schoen C, Rabenstein T, et al: Pancreatic duct stones in chronic pancreatitis: Criteria for treatment intensity and success. Gastrointest Endosc 56:501–506, 2002.

160. Adamek HE, Jakobs R, Buttmann A, et al: Long term follow up of patients with chronic pancreatitis and pancreatic stones treated with extracorporeal shock wave lithotripsy. Gut 45:402–405, 1999.

161. Schneider HT, May A, Benninger J, et al: Piezoelectric shock wave lithotripsy of pancreatic duct stones. Am J Gastroenterol 89:2042–2048, 1994.

162. Ohara H, Hoshino M, Hayakawa T, et al: Single application extracorporeal shock wave lithotripsy is the first choice for patients with pancreatic duct stones. Am J Gastroenterol 91:1388–1394, 1996.

163. Schreiber F, Gurakuqi GC, Pristautz H, et al: Sonographically-guided extracorporeal shock wave lithotripsy for pancreatic stones in patients with chronic pancreatitis. J Gastroenterol Hepatol 11:247–251, 1996.

164. Brand B, Kahl M, Sidhu S, et al: Prospective evaluation of morphology, function, and quality of life after extracorporeal shockwave lithotripsy and endoscopic treatment of chronic calcific pancreatitis. Am J Gastroenterol 95:3428–3438, 2000.

165. Kozarek RA, Brandabur JJ, Ball TJ, et al: Clinical outcomes in patients who undergo extracorporeal shock wave lithotripsy for chronic calcific pancreatitis. Gastrointest Endosc 56:496–500, 2002.

166. Cremer M, Deviere J, Delhaye M, et al: Stenting in severe chronic pancreatitis: Results of medium-term follow-up in 76 patients. Endoscopy 23:171–176, 1991.

167. Nealon WH, Townsend CJ, Thompson JC: Operative drainage of the pancreatic duct delays functional improvement in patients with chronic pancreatitis. A prospective analysis. Ann Surg 208:321–329, 1988.

168. Barthet M, Sahel J, Bodiou BC, et al: Endoscopic transpapillary drainage of pancreatic pseudocysts. Gastrointest Endosc 42:208–213, 1995.

169. Catalano MF, Geenen GE, Schmalz MJ, et al: Treatment of pancreatic pseudocysts with ductal communication by transpapillary duct endoprosthesis. Gastrointest Endosc 42:214–218, 1995.

170. McHenry L, Gore DC, DeMaria EJ, et al: Endoscopic treatment of dilated-duct chronic pancreatitis with pancreatic stents: Preliminary results of a sham-controlled, blinded crossover trial to predict surgical outcome. Am J Gastroenterol 88:1536A, 1993.

171. DuVall GA, Schneider DM, Kortan P, et al: Is the outcome of endoscopic therapy of chronic pancreatitis predictive of surgical success. Gastrointest Endosc 43:405A, 1996.

172. Ponchon T, Bory RM, Medeluis F, et al: Endoscopic stenting for pain relief in chronic pancreatitis: Results of a standardized protocol. Gastrointest Endosc 42:452–456, 1995.

173. Smits ME, Badiga SM, Rauws AJ, et al: Long-term results of pancreatic stents in chronic pancreatitis. Gastrointest Endosc 42:461–467, 1995.

174. Binmoeller KF, Jue P, Seifert H, et al: Endoscopic pancreatic stent drainage in chronic pancreatitis and a dominant stricture: Long-term results. Endoscopy 27:638–644, 1995.

175. Cremer M, Suge B, Delhoye M, et al: Expandable pancreatic metal stents (Wallstent) for chronic pancreatitis: First world series [abstract]. Gastroenterology 98:215, 1990.

176. Dite P, Ruzicka M, Zboril V, Novotny I: A prospective, randomized trial comparing endoscopic and surgical therapy for chronic pancreatitis. Endoscopy 35:553–558, 2003.

177. Smit MT, Sherman S, Ikenberry SO, et al: Alterations in pancreatic duct morphology following polyethylene pancreatic duct stenting. Gastrointest Endosc 44:268–275, 1996.

178. Kozarek RA: Pancreatic stents can induct ductal changes consistent with chronic pancreatitis. Gastrointest Endosc 36:93–95, 1990.

179. Derfus GA, Geenen JE, Hogan WJ: Effect of endoscopic pancreatic duct stent placement on pancreatic ductal morphology. Gastrointest Endosc 36:206A, 1990.

180. Lehman GA, Sherman S, Nisi R, et al: Pancreas divisum: Results of minor papilla sphincterotomy. Gastrointest Endosc 44:268–275, 1996.

181. Eisen G, Coleman S, Troughton A, et al: Morphological changes in the pancreatic duct after stent placement for benign pancreatic disease. Gastrointest Endosc 40:107A, 1994.

182. Shumaker SA, Anderson RT, Czajkowski SM: Psychological test and scales. In Spilker B (ed): Quality of Life Assessment in Clinical Trials. New York, Raven Press, 1990, pp 95–111.

183. Barofsky I, Sugarbaker PH: Cancer. In Spilker B (ed): Quality of Life Assessment in Clinical Trials. New York, Raven Press, 1990, pp 419–439.

184. Eisen GM, Sandler RS, Coleman SD: Development of a disease specific measure for health related quality of life for individuals with chronic pancreatitis. Gastroenterology 108:A12, 1995.

Pancreatic Duct Leaks and Pseudocysts

Richard Kozarek

Introduction

For the most part, the initial manifestations of acute pancreatitis are caused by local enzyme activation and acute cytokine release. This combination leads to local pain, ileus, peripancreatic burn, and early organ failure including the acute respiratory distress syndrome (ARDS). Perpetuation of the disease process may be a consequence of infection of necrotic tissue or ongoing ductal leak.[1] Chronic pancreatitis may also result in a pancreatic duct leak or fistula as may trauma, surgical or otherwise.[1] In chronic pancreatitis, the consequence of the leak depends on the etiology, size of the ductal disruption, the location of the leak relative to anatomic tissue planes, and the body's success in walling off and containing the disruption. In traumatic pancreatitis, there is usually a smoldering acute inflammatory response and an acute leak. This combination can result in a seriously ill patient after penetrating trauma or in one who remains clinically well after surgical drain placement at time of splenectomy and inadvertent damage to the pancreatic tail.

Pancreatic duct leaks or fistulas have traditionally been defined as internal or external.[2] External leaks (pancreaticocutaneous fistulas) almost always follow percutaneous drainage of internal pancreatic fluid collections or pancreatic surgery. Less commonly, they are the consequence of penetrating abdominal trauma.

Internal pancreatic fistulas include pancreaticoenteric fistulas, pseudocysts, pancreatic ascites, and pancreatic pleural effusions.[3] Pancreatic necrosis, clearly associated with ductal disruption in up to three-fourths of patients, has not traditionally been defined as the cause or consequence of a pancreatic fistula.[4,5] Table 53–1 summarizes the current classification of pancreatic fistulas.

Epidemiology

The incidence of pancreatic duct leaks is uncertain and seems to be independent of the cause of the underlying pancreatitis. Whether caused by alcohol, biliary tract disease, metabolic disorders, or medications, an acute leak seems to be related more to disease severity. As such, multiple reports suggest that 30% to 75% of pancreatic necrosis is associated with ductal disruption, although

Table 53–1. Consequences of Pancreatic Duct Leaks

Acute Disruption
Peripancreatic fluid collection
Pseudocyst
Pancreatic necrosis
? Smoldering pancreatitis

Chronic Disruption
Internal fistula
Pseudocyst
Pancreatic ascites
High amylase pleural effusion
Pancreatic-enteric, biliary, or bronchial fistula

External Fistula
Pancreaticocutaneous fistula

there is considerable debate whether this disruption is a primary or secondary phenomenon.[4-6] It is also known that up to 40% of patients with acute pancreatitis will develop some peripancreatic fluid collection, although less than 5% of the latter will develop a true pseudocyst and a much small percent have decompression of these fluid collections by formation of a pancreaticoenteric fistula.[7] Chronic pancreatitis, in turn, predisposes not only pseudocyst formation but also pancreatic ascites and high amylase pleural effusions. The latter are chronic and have a distinctly different chemical composition and pathophysiology than the ubiquitous acute pleural effusions noted in the setting of severe acute pancreatitis.[2]

Pathogenesis

Pancreatic duct leaks are the consequence of enzyme activation with subsequent necrosis of ductal epithelium, the result of increased intraductal pressure often behind a stricture or stone, or both.[2] Alternatively, leaks may be caused or perpetuated by percutaneous drainage of peripancreatic fluid collections, surgical resection or bypass, tumor disruption of ductal epithelia, or pancreatic trauma particularly penetrating trauma.[8-15] Table 53–2 defines some of the etiologic causes of pancreatic duct leaks.

Table 53–2. Pathogenesis of Pancreatic Fistulas
Internal Fistula
Pseudocyst
• Pancreatic necrosis
• Ductal obstruction
• Stone
• Stricture
• Inflammatory
• Malignant
Pancreatic ascites, high amylase, pleural effusion
• Pancreatic duct stricture, stone, or pseudocyst
Pancreaticoenteric fistula
• Pancreatic necrosis
• Percutaneous tube erosion, contiguous bowel loop
External Fistula
Penetrating trauma
Pancreatic resection or trauma
Percutaneous drainage of pseudocyst or pancreatic fluid collection

Clinical Features

The clinical features of pancreatic duct leaks depend both on the cause of the disruption and its size and site. Pancreatic juice will follow tissue planes and the body will be variably successful in containing this leak contingent on such factors as rate of leak and presence or absence of superinfection. The latter, as well as early cytokine release and extraluminal enzyme activation, will also determine many of the clinical features associated with acute pancreatitis: pain, ileus, nausea and vomiting, tachycardia, oliguria, and hypotension.[16,17]

From an anatomic standpoint, a leak may be low grade and stay within the confines of the parenchyma leading to smoldering pancreatitis or variable degrees of necrosis, the latter often associated with multisystem organ failure and local and systemic infections.[2,18–21] Necrosis may also lead to internal fistulization into contiguous organs including the C-loop, most commonly, but also the bile duct, stomach, transverse colon, or jejunum.[22–24] Depending on the degree of leak and its perpetuation by necrosis or downstream ductal obstruction, as well as ongoing oral feeding and pancreatic stimulation, head leaks will often be associated with right pararenal fluid collections and can track along the psoas musculature to cause pelvic fluid collections that can even track into the scrotum or buttocks.[25] If volumes of juice are sufficient, with resultant pancreatic ascites, I have even seen prolapsed and ulcerated vaginal vaults and uteruses because of increased intra-abdominal pressure. Pancreatic head leak that is successfully walled off by the body, in turn, may cause a pseudocyst localized to the right upper quadrant. Although the latter may be asymptomatic if small, common presentations of larger pseudocysts in this location include postprandial or chronic pain, early satiety or postprandial nausea and vomiting from variable degrees of gastric outlet obstruction, or biliary obstruction. The latter may cause jaundice or occasional cholangitis but is more often associated with liver function abnormalities including variable elevations of transaminases and alkaline phosphatase.

Leaks of the pancreatic duct tail have been associated with left upper quadrant or perisplenic pseudocysts,[26] if contained and walled off. Alternatively, they may track into the retroperitoneum and cause high amylase pleural effusions[27–29] or acute pararenal or pelvic fluid collections. Fistulization into the ligament of Treitz or the transverse colon or splenic flexure are also occasionally seen but almost exclusively in the setting of active necrosis.[9,23] Depending on the rapidity of leak and the presence or absence of concomitant necrosis, clinical signs and symptoms of a tail leak may include shortness of breath, nausea and postprandial pain, or clinical signs of sepsis because of a pancreaticocolonic fistula.

Leaks that occur from the genu to the distal body or proximal tail area of the pancreas occur most commonly in the setting of necrosis and result in lesser sac fluid collections.[8,30–33] Traditionally defined as pseudocysts, these fluid collections are usually more complex, containing considerable saponified fat and tissue debris. Moreover, the consistency and viscosity of lesser sac fluid collections are routinely misinterpreted by abdominal computed tomography (CT) imaging, often leading to therapeutic misadventures with attempts to drain these collections radiographically, endoscopically, or even surgically.[13,34,35] To distinguish these collections from more traditional pseudocysts that can have a similar imaging appearance, Baron and colleagues[36] termed these latter collections "evolving pancreatic necrosis" and suggested that the patient's clinical course may be a better mechanism to define them than traditional abdominal imaging. The lesser sac is often a decompressive site for patients with chronic pancreatitis with downstream duct obstruction from a pancreatic stone or stricture. This can result in a variably sized pseudocyst or even pancreatic pericardial effusion. Additional chest manifestations include pancreatic pleural effusion, as noted previously and pericardiac tamponade or pancreaticobronchial fistulas.[21] Central pancreatic leaks are usually the cause of pancreatic ascites also.[2,28,37] Associated with a concomitant and leaking pseudocyst in 50% of the patients, clinical presentation may include increased pain plus abdominal girth, shortness of breath from diaphragmatic compression or concomitant pleural effusions, and occasional spontaneous bacterial peritonitis from bacterial translocation from the gut.

Pathology

Given the variability of etiology of ductal disruptions, there is no one all-encompassing pathology. Instead, chronic pancreatitis is usually associated with the formation of a leak and its myriad manifestations (pseudocyst, ascites, and pancreatic pleural effusions) by virtue of ductal obstruction by an inflammatory stricture or intraductal calcification.[3] In such settings, acute parenchymal inflammation may be negligible. In contrast, the acute inflammatory response seen in acute pancreatitis, particularly pancreatic necrosis, has been claimed, by some, to be the primary event with subsequent lysis of ductal epithelial cells resulting in a leak.[38] Likely there is a mixture of scenarios in either setting with the resultant pathology depending on the site and size of the disruption, the presence or absence of activated enzymes, and the body's success at walling off the leak, initially with inflammatory cells but later with formation and organization of collagen. The latter is perhaps best represented by a pseudocyst that can further be broken down into acute

Table 53-3. Diagnosis of Pancreatic Leaks
External Fistula
Demonstrable pancreatogram through surgically or percutaneously placed JP drain
Persistent high amylase output through JP drain
Internal Fistula
Pleural effusion: chest x-ray, abdominal and thoracic CT
• High amylase with aspiration
Pancreatic ascites: ground-glass appearance, loss of psoas shadow on flat film. Confirmation via ultrasound, abdominal CT, MRI
• High amylase with aspiration
Pseudocyst ± ductal stone and dilated duct, CT, MRI, EUS, ERCP
Duct disruption ± obstruction, ERCP, S-MRCP
CT, computerized tomography; ERCP, endoscopic retrograde cholangiopancrea-tography; EUS, endoscopic ultrasound; JP, Jackson Pratt; MRI, magnetic resonance imaging; S-MRCP, secretin-magnetic resonance cholangiopancreatography.

Table 53-4. Therapy of Pancreatic Duct Leaks
Minimize pancreatic secretion
• Clear liquids versus NPO and hyperalimentation
• Somatostatin or its analogues
Treat ductal disruption
• Transpapillary stent
• Downsize and reposition external catheter
• Surgery (disconnected gland syndrome)
Treat consequences of ductal disruption
• Ascites and pleural effusion: paracentesis/thoracentesis
• Pseudocyst: endoscopic, radiographic, surgical drainage
NPO, nil per os.

pseudocyst (collection of pancreatic juice enclosed by a wall of nonepithelialized granulation tissue that arises as a consequence of acute pancreatitis, requires at least 4 weeks to form, and is devoid of significant solid debris) and chronic pseudocyst (a collection of pancreatic juice enclosed by a wall of fibrous or granulation tissue that arises as a consequence of chronic pancreatitis).[36]

Differential Diagnosis

The etiology and the benign nature of most pancreatic duct leaks is relatively easy to confirm if one considers the diagnosis in the first place, because of access to excellent abdominal imaging through ultrasound (US), CT scan, magnetic resource imaging (MRI) including secretin-magnetic resonance cholangiopancreatography (S-MRCP), and such endoscopic modalities as endoscopic ultrasonography (EUS) and endoscopic retrograde cholangiopancreatography (ERCP).[7,39–43] As such, routine aspiration of ascites or pleural effusions for amylase and lipase will usually confirm a pancreatic etiology, and a fluid collection in the left upper quadrant after a splenectomy or complicated antireflux procedure can be confirmed as pancreatic in origin if one thinks to check an amylase at time of diagnostic percutaneous aspiration or therapeutic drain placement. In these instances, inadvertent damage to the tail of the pancreas is substantially more common than local perforation of the stomach or splenic flexure of the colon at time of surgery. In addition, the diagnosis of a pancreatic duct leak should not be difficult in patients with a persistent fluid output after a pancreatic resection or percutaneous drainage of an acute, amylase-rich fluid collection in the setting of acute or chronic pancreatitis.

The major differential diagnostic dilemma occurs in patients without a known history of pancreatitis who present with what appears to be a pseudocyst. There have been multiple approaches to distinguish pseudocysts from cystic neoplasms and benign from potentially malignant cystic tumors. Ultrasound and CT characteristics favoring pseudocyst include parenchymal or ductal calcifications, a uniform appearance to the cyst, and lack of calcifications in the lesion itself. Cysts that demonstrate an irregular wall thickness with mass effect, septations, or punctate wall calcification, in turn, are more likely to be neoplastic. Cyst aspirate for amylase, mucus, carcinoembryonic antigen (CEA) level, and cytology can be undertaken under CT, US, or EUS guidance and has been used to distinguish benign and malignant neoplastic cysts from pseudocysts.[44] The latter is covered in detail in other chapters of this text.

As noted previously, S-MRCP has occasionally been used to document a pancreatic duct leak, particularly in the setting of pancreatic necrosis.[40] More commonly, however, ERCP has been the modality used not only to diagnose but also to treat pancreatic duct leaks. Leaks may be demonstrable by abnormal flow of contrast into a pseudocyst, into the peritoneal or thoracic cavity, or into the bile duct or a contiguous loop of bowel in the setting of internal fistulas.[1,2] Alternatively, contrast can often be seen flowing into a surgically or radiologically placed Jackson Pratt (JP) drain in external fistulas.[25,45] In the setting of central pancreatic necrosis or severe chronic pancreatitis, ERCP may simply document a complete obstruction of the main pancreatic duct. In this setting, the leak occurs proximal to the obstruction or from a disconnected portion of the gland.

Table 53–3 summarizes some of the diagnostic tests available for the diagnosis of pancreatic duct leaks.

Treatment

Therapy for pancreatic duct leaks does not occur in an endoscopic vacuum. Strategies include preventing a leak in the first place, using good surgical technique, and using possible intraoperative fibrin glue or stent placement or postoperative octreotide after partial pancreatectomy or decompressive pancreatic surgery.[46–50] The ability to place a transpapillary stent does not mean that this modality is suitable for all patients, and individuals with leaks are best approached by a team consisting of an interventional radiologist, a pancreaticobiliary surgeon, and an endoscopist capable of undertaking both diagnosis and therapy (Table 53–4).[1]

INTERNAL LEAKS

Pseudocysts

Pseudocysts were historically treated surgically, usually by cystenteric or cyst-gastric anastomoses, although pancreatic resection has occasionally been used for pseudocysts in the pancreatic tail.

Likewise, complex cysts with significant internal septations or debris have been treated with external drainage. Morbidity and 30-day mortality rates for open surgery have approximated 25% to 30% and 2% to 5%, respectively, with recurrence rates of 10% to 20%.[43,51,52] These statistics have led some centers to approach surgical decompression laparoscopically and to insist on preoperative MRCP or ERCP to better delineate the ductal anatomy as a guide to type surgery (decompression vs. resection).[42,53,54]

In many centers, percutaneous drainage of pseudocysts with chronic catheter placement has become the standard of care by which other treatment modalities have been judged. Individual series and meta-analyses of the literature suggest 85% successful resolution rates, although catheter occlusions with subsequent bacterial seeding and iatrogenic infection with need for urgent catheter exchange remain problematic.[2,25,55] In addition, in individuals who develop a disconnected gland syndrome from trauma or necrosis, placement of a percutaneous drain may result in a chronic pancreatic external fistula that may necessitate JP drainage for months or even years. Alternatively, attempts at percutaneous injection of glue or fibrin have been used in an attempt to close the fistulous tract, and surgery may be required to resect the distal (tail), disconnected portion of the gland.[56]

Endoscopic pseudocyst drainage was first described by Rogers and coworkers[57] in 1978 using a needle placement through the gut wall to drain a pseudocyst that rapidly recurred. The first successful electrocautery fistulization into a pseudocyst was done more than 2 decades ago and resulted in permanent cure in three of the first four patients in whom it was undertaken.[58] Although the procedure has been refined to take advantage of abdominal CT, EUS, and MRI and MRCP, large pseudocysts still require some form of access, either by needle-knife sphincterotomy or transgastric and transenteric injection followed by placement of one or more guide wires into the cavity proper (Fig. 53–1).[59-64] Historically, the incisions were enlarged using some form of electrocautery (conventional or needle-knife sphincterotomy or an overtube that conducted cautery), but, in most cases currently, 6- to 10-mm hydrostatic balloons are used to enlarge the communication to the stomach or duodenum. Although a variety of stents have been used to maintain the fistulous communication between the gut and pseudocyst, most endoscopists currently use more 7- to 10-Fr double-pigtail stents to minimize migration, leaving them in place for 6 to 8 weeks, or until abdominal imaging has confirmed pseudocyst resolution. Whereas the need for preprocedure antibiotics has not changed, other things have. With the advent of therapeutic EUS scopes, we no longer need to see a "bulge" on the stomach or duodenal wall to ensure that we will enter the fluid collection.[64-69] Therapeutic duodenoscopes are not necessarily required, and concomitant ERCP is usually used to define ductal anatomy including the presence of an ongoing leak or disconnected duct and gland syndrome.[1,2] The former can be treated with transpapillary stents (Fig. 53–2) allowing resolution of small pseudocysts without need for concomitant drainage,[70] and the latter can signal the need for ultimate surgery or long-term indwelling pseudocyst stents in very poor surgical risk patients.[71]

Although there have been many case reports or series describing transpapillary stents or transenteric or transgastric fistulization into pseudocysts with their attendant resolution, one of the better ones has been reported by Baron and colleagues.[36] This group looked at endoscopic drainage techniques and outcomes in acute versus chronic pseudocysts and in pancreatic necrosis. Historically, endoscopic attempts at drainage of necrosis were fraught with bleeding and infectious complications because of increased vascularity at the necrosis–viable tissue interface and because it has proven difficult to drain extremely thick and viscous debris through small-diameter, endoscopically placed stents. These authors instead placed nasocystic tubes and undertook irrigation with large volume saline for prolonged periods (3 to 6 weeks) of irrigation in an attempt to break up the necrotic debris and flush it into the lumen of the gut. Ultimately, they achieved complete resolution of the various pancreatic fluid collections in 113 of 138 (82%) patients, although resolution was more frequent in patients with chronic pseudocyst (59/64, 92%) than those with acute (23/31, 74%, $p = .02$) or necrosis (31/43, 72%, $p = .006$). In addition, complications were more common in necrosis patients who were drained endoscopically (16/43, 37%) than patients with acute pseudocysts (6/31, 19%, $p = $ NS) or chronic pseudocysts (11/64, 17%, $p = .02$). At a median follow-up of 2.1 years, recurrent fluid collections were more common in necrosis patients (9/31, 29%) than for acute pseudocysts (2/23, 9%, $p = .07$) or chronic pseudocysts (7/59, 12%, $p = .047$) (Table 53–5). Whether the recent reports in which necrosis is treated more aggressively by means of retroperitoneal endoscopic debridement after initial fistulization through, and balloon dilation of, the stomach wall,[72] remains to be seen. What is certain, however, is that pseudocyst and necrosis drainage are clearly not risk-free and these therapies must be placed inside the institutional armamentarium of other treatment modalities including surgery and percutaneous drainage. Because it is unlikely that a randomized prospective trial will be done comparing these individual modalities, or that the results can be generalized to institutions with different levels of subspecialty strengths and skills, it is imperative for those who care for such patients to work with a team that includes endoscopy, surgery, and interventional radiology.

For instance, our group has reported 133 patients with severe necrosis (Balthazar score ≥8) treated with multimodality therapy (Fig. 53–3).[4] We demonstrated that 76% of these patients had ductal disruption including side branch or major ductal leak and disconnected gland syndrome. Of the 115 patients to undergo ERCP, 70 (61%) had stent placement, 15 (13%) had cyst-gastrostomy or cyst duodenotomy, 11 (9.6%) had a nasopancreatic drain, and 11 (9.6%) had a nasobiliary drain. In addition, 98/133 (74%) had placement of one or more large JP drains, and 75 patients ultimately required an elective surgery including pancreatic resection in 47 (33%) for glandular disconnection. Mean hospital days approximated a month, and there was a 9% mortality rate in this exceptionally sick group of patients, many with multisystem organ failure. These results equal or exceed previously reported outcomes in surgical series using routine or selective debridement.[73-77]

Pancreatic Ascites and Pleural Effusions

Historically, pancreatic ascites was treated by resting the pancreas to minimize flow and leak. Thus, patients were placed nil per os

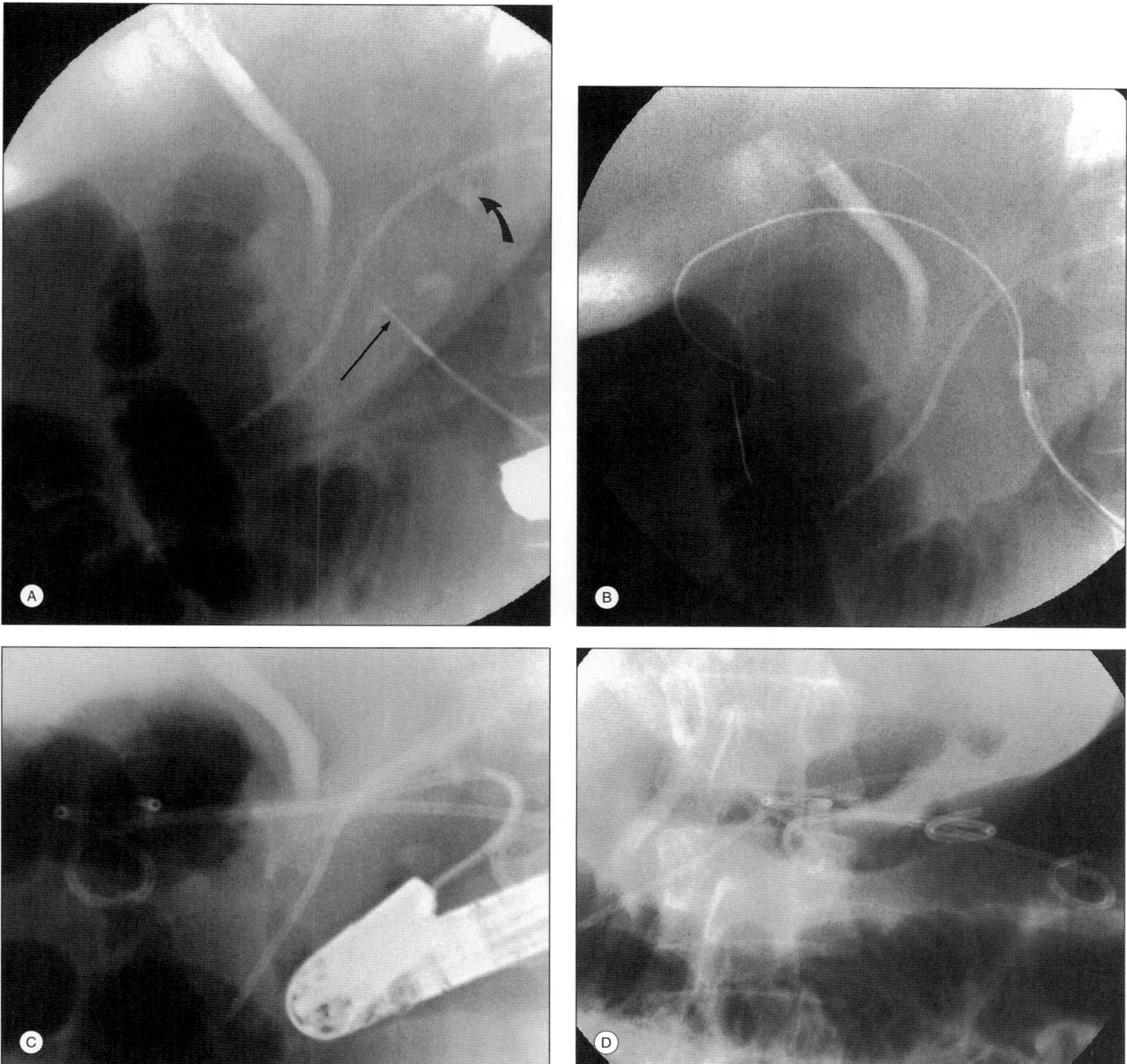

Figure 53–1. Transgastric puncture *(small arrow) (A)* in patient with ductal leak and pseudocyst because of obstructing ductal stone *(large arrow).* Note transpapillary stent. Guidewire placement within pseudocyst *(B)* is followed by placement of two double-pigtail stents *(C, D).*

(NPO), treated with parenteral nutrition, and started on somato-statin analogues.[78–82] Diuretics and large-volume thoracentesis and paracentesis were commonly used before "salvage" operations, usually pancreatic resection or Roux-en-Y cyst-jejunostomy if a concomitant pseudocyst was present. At most, medical therapy was effective in half of the patients, and the subsequent surgical approach, usually predicated on anatomy as defined by preoperative

ERCP, carried an 8% to 15% periprocedural mortality and a 15% recurrence rate.[78–83]

More than a decade ago, we demonstrated that stent placement beyond a ductal disruption, with or without concomitant pseudocyst decompression, was effective therapy in a small group of patients with pancreatic ascites, particularly when combined with large-volume paracentesis (Fig. 53–4).[37,83] Bracker and coworkers[84] have

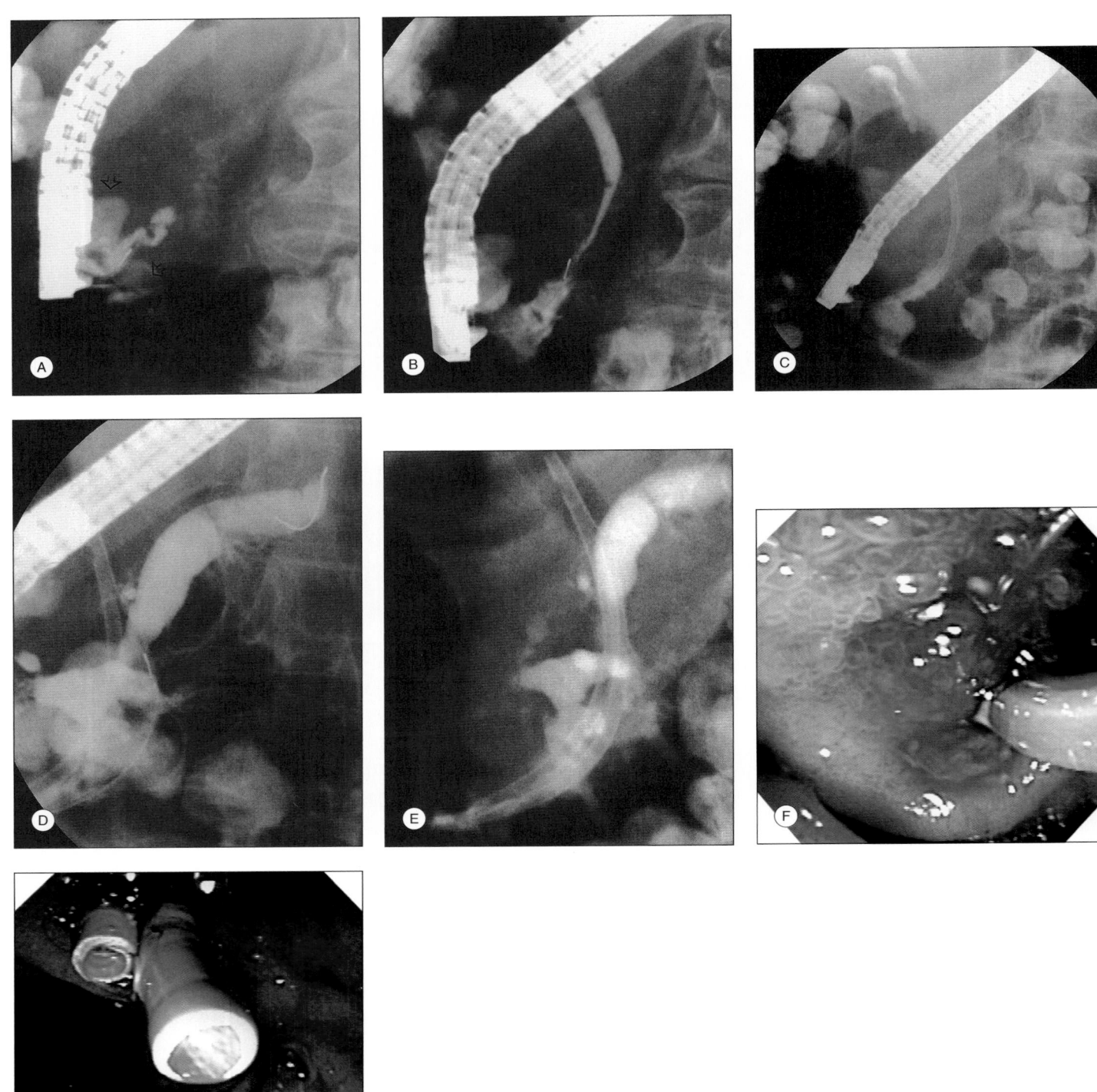

Figure 53–2. Obstructed pancreatic duct *(A)* with intraduodenal pseudocysts *(arrows)* in patient with jaundice, weight loss, and pain. Note biliary stricture *(B)* treated with stent *(C)*. Note guidewire in dilated pancreatic duct *(D)* followed by PD stent insertion *(E, F, G).*

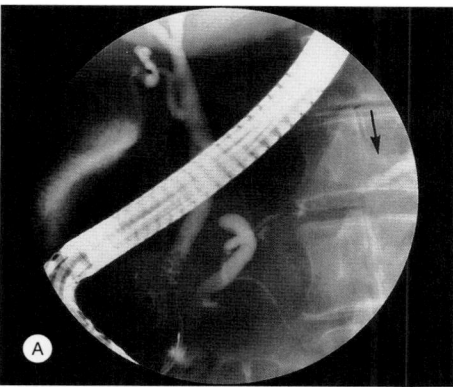 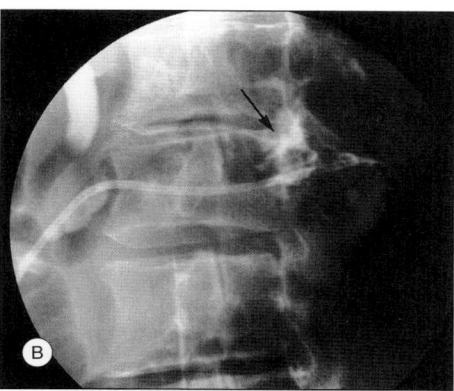 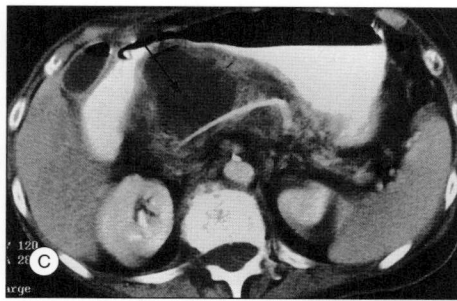

Figure 53–3. Endoscopic retrograde cholangiopancreatography (ERCP) in patient with multisystem failure from pancreatic necrosis demonstrating tight extrinsic stricture of the pancreatic duct *(A)*. Note distal common bile duct stones. Leak at junction of body and tail *(arrow)* was treated with biliary sphincterotomy and transpapillary stent placement *(B)*. Note massive necrosis *(arrow)* (treated percutaneously) and stent in residual pancreatic duct *(C)*. Patient responded to conservative management and required only elective cholecystectomy.

Table 53–5. Outcomes After Attempted Endoscopic Drainage of Patient Fluid Collections*

	Acute Pancreatitis	Chronic Pancreatitis	Pancreatic Necrosis	Necrotic Pancreatitis vs. Acute Pancreatitis	Acute Pancreatitis vs. Pancreatic Necrosis	Chronic Pancreatitis vs. Pancreatic Necrosis
Successful resolution	24/31 (74%)	59/64 (92%)	31/43 (72%)	$p = 0.02$	NS	$p = 0.006$
Complications	6/31 (19%)	11/64 (17%)	16/43 (37%)	NS	NS	$p = 0.02$
Hospital days	9	3	20	$p = 0.0003$	NS	$p = 0.0001$
Recurrence	2/23 (9%)	7/59 (12%)	9/31 (29%)	NS	NS	$p = 0.047$

*Modified from Baron TH, Harewood GC, Morgan DE, et al: Outcome differences after endoscopic drainage of pancreatic necrosis, acute pancreatic pseudocysts, and chronic pancreatic pseudocysts. Gastrointest Endosc 56:7–17, 2002.
NS, not significant.

since confirmed our original findings, and together, 91% of patients resolved their ascites without major complications. Moreover, there were no recurrences in the two series at 60 and 14 months, respectively. This approach appears to work by relieving upstream duct hypertension by bypassing the sphincter or an obstructing stone or inflammatory stenosis. It will not work with a disconnected gland syndrome in which most of the pancreatic juice enters the peritoneal or thoracic cavity from a disconnected tail and the latter is ultimately handled better with surgery.

Pancreaticoenteric Fistula and Acute Pancreatic Trauma

Our group has previously reported successful healing of eight patients with pancreaticoduodenal (five patients) or pancreatico-cutaneous (three patients) fistulas.[45] Three patients healed after downsizing or removal of an external drain, three healed their fistulas with transpapillary stent placement, and two patients ultimately required pancreatic resection. An additional six patients with pancreaticobiliary fistulas have all successfully been treated using a combination of biliary sphincterotomy and pancreaticobiliary stent placement.[4] ERCP has also been used to treat internal fistulas

associated with acute pancreatic trauma. For instance, Kim and colleagues[15] noted injury to the pancreatic duct in 14 of 23 patients, including 8 patients who leaked into the pancreatic parenchyma and resolved spontaneously. An additional 3 patients had a leak from the main pancreatic duct and responded to transpapillary stenting. These authors felt that early ERCP with directed therapy (medical, endoscopic, surgical) was advantageous in the setting of acute pancreatic trauma and potential ductal leak.

EXTERNAL FISTULAS

As previously noted, external pancreatic fistulas are usually iatrogenic. Etiologies include surgical or percutaneous drainage of a pancreatic fluid collection with an ongoing ductal disruption as the consequence of a disconnected gland or downstream obstruction from a stone or stricture. They may also follow partial pancreatic resection or bypass or as a consequence of penetrating abdominal trauma.[1,2,85]

After our initial report using variable length prostheses bridging ductal disruptions for head or body leaks and placing short transpapillary stents alone in postoperative tail disruptions without

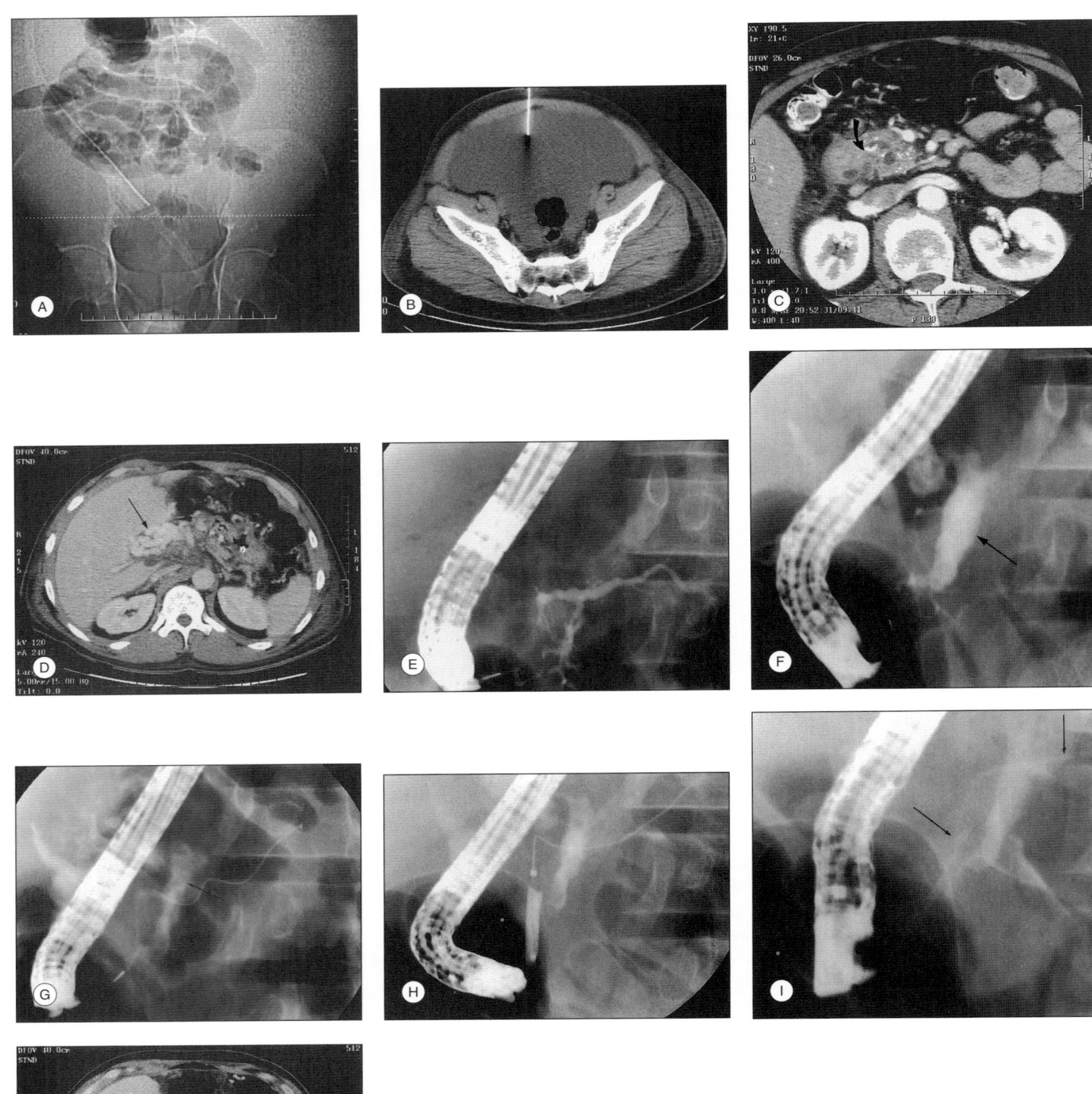

Figure 53–4. Ground-glass appearance in patient with pancreatic ascites *(A)* initially treated with repeated paracentesis *(B)*. Abdominal computed tomography (CT) demonstrates complex cystic inflammatory mass in the head of the pancreas *(C)* with portal vein thrombosis *(D)*. Note porta hepatis varices. Endoscopic retrograde cholangiopancreatography (ERCP) demonstrates stricture and ductal leak *(arrows) (E, F, G)* initially treated with balloon dilation *(H)* and 8-cm, 3-Fr stent placement *(I)*. Note resolution of small pseudocyst on subsequent CT *(J)*.

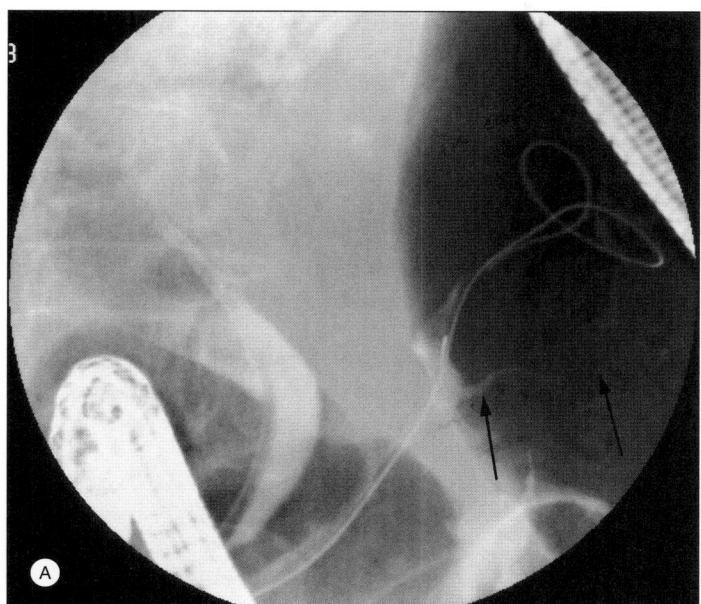 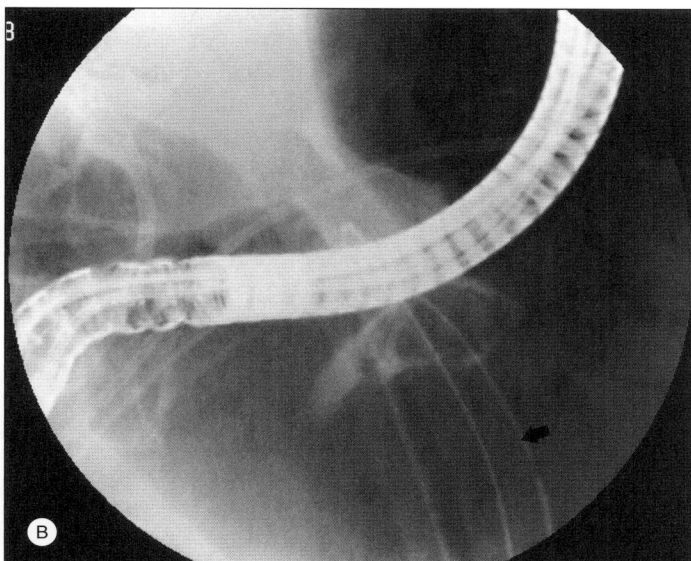

Figure 53–5. Arrows depict actual course of pancreatic duct in patient with acute blowout, pancreaticocutaneous fistula *(A)*. Note guidewire curled in cavity. Leak was treated with transpapillary stent and percutaneous drain *(arrow) (B)*.

downstream obstruction,[86] several additional series have been published in abstract or full manuscript format.[87–89] Taken together, 50/58 patients (86%) with an average fistulous output of 200 mL/day were successfully stented, 46 of whom (92%) had resolution of their fistula within 5 weeks. There were minor flares of pancreatitis in several of the patients and two deaths in one of the series, unrelated to the fistula or endotherapy. Contingent on the series, there were no recurrences in follow-up ranging from 12 to 36 months.

It is currently our practice to treat such patients with enteral nutrition using formula diets or total parenteral nutrition when acutely ill with pancreatic necrosis, usually adding a somatostatin analog if there is persistent high-amylase, high-volume JP output.[90–92] We may also treat postoperative patients with a persistent external fistula this way. However, if there is not dramatic and immediate decrease in fistulous output, our group is now studying these individuals earlier in the course (<1 week) and attempting to place a transpapillary prosthesis if the anatomy is amenable (Fig. 53–5). Alternatively, there are individual reports and case series approaching a subset of such patients, particularly those with disconnected glands, with a variety of interventional radiologic techniques.[85, 93–95]

INDICATIONS AND CONTRAINDICATIONS

The indications for treating a pancreatic duct leak are (1) the persistence of an external fistula, (2) inability to refeed a patient without developing recurrent pain or pancreatitis, (3) an enlarging pancreatic fluid collection (pseudocyst, pancreatic ascites, high amylase, pleural effusion), or (4) a symptomatic fluid collection. Perhaps a fifth indication is uncertainty about diagnosis, which is usually only an issue when attempting to differentiate pseudocyst from cystic neoplasms of the pancreas.[1]

From my perspective, the major contraindication to studying a patient is inability to apply therapy. Thus, it is potentially dangerous to do ERCP in the setting of pancreatic necrosis or pseudocyst because of the potential of iatrogenic infection unless one is prepared to treat this leak. As noted previously, such treatment can be directed either to the leak (transpapillary stent) or to the consequences of the leak (see Table 53–4). Other contraindications are relative and include inability to give informed consent, anaphylaxis with iodinated contrast agents, and a patient so unstable that endoscopic diagnosis or therapy entails prohibitive procedural risk. In this setting, S-MRCP may define anatomy and leak site such that percutaneous drainage may initially be preferable to stabilize the patient.

PREOPERATIVE HISTORY AND CONSIDERATION

The presence of a pancreatic fluid collection or internal or external fistula does not by itself demand therapy. Important considerations include whether duct disruption occurs in the setting of acute or chronic pancreatitis, whether necrosis is present or absent, or whether the patient has a controlled or uncontrolled leak. An example of the former is a low volume fistula through a surgically placed JP drain after distal pancreatectomy. Most of these fistulas resolve within days or weeks. An example of the latter is an individual with rapidly accruing pancreatic ascites or an enlarging pancreatic pseudocyst. What is the etiology of the pancreatic fistula? Is the patient symptomatic? Is there a possibility of infection? Is one sure that the fluid collection in question is not neoplastic? What are the alternatives to diagnosis? EUS? MRI-MRCP? What are the alternatives to treatment and have these been thoroughly discussed with the patient and family? Does the patient and endoscopist have immediate access to a team that includes a pancreaticobiliary surgeon and an interventional radiologist? If not, perhaps the patient would be better served in a setting with these capabilities.

DESCRIPTION OF TECHNIQUE

Placement of a pancreatic duct stent to bridge a ductal disruption is comparable to biliary stent placement for a cystic duct leak but with subtle differences. On the one hand, it should only be undertaken over a hydrophilic wire passed beyond the leak proper.[2] Broad-spectrum antibiotic coverage should be routine, and biliary sphincterotomy will help access by exposing the pancreaticobiliary septum and the pancreatic orifice at the 5 o'clock position at the lower edge of the incision.[3,96] I use pure cutting current if a PD sphincterotomy is needed to improve access to the duct. Stent size is important and one usually chooses 3, 5, 6, or 7 PD stents, depending on the diameter of the duct and lengths that are 1 to 2 cm longer than the leak to be bridged (Video 53–1). Depending on the situation, balloon or catheter dilation of concomitant strictures or stone removal may be necessary. Alternatively, in patients with ductal leaks in the tail, a short transpapillary stent will usually be effective. Stents usually play no, or a limited role, in patients with central pancreatic necrosis and a disconnected gland syndrome. In this latter situation, most of the ongoing leak is from the tail, and small-caliber drains or stents are ineffective in removing large chunks of necrotic debris often present in this situation. When stent placement is done for pancreatic ascites or pleural effusions, a large-volume paracentesis or thoracentesis under ultrasound guidance will speed the healing process considerably.

As previously noted, the endoscopic drainage of pseudocysts can be done in a transpapillary fashion, much like described previously.[2,3] Very large or complex pseudocysts are best drained by fistulizing into the collection using a duodenoscope with therapeutic capabilities.[59–61] Pseudocysts can be localized by defining an extrinsic bulge on the stomach or duodenum or by more precise localization with EUS.[64–69] The latter also has the advantage of Doppler capabilities to define vasculature, particularly in the setting of splenic vein thrombosis and gastric varices. I use a needle-knife sphincterotome with an 0.035-inch wire after initial localization by transgut injection of contrast using a long sclerotherapy needle. Alternatively, localization and access can be done using the Seldinger technique with a needle alone.[36] Once access has been gained into the cavity, I personally add a second guide wire, curling both deep within the pseudocyst proper (Video 53–2). A 6- to 10-mm biliary dilating balloon is used to enlarge the tract followed by placement of at least two 7-to 10-Fr double pigtail stents of variable length. The latter not only prevent migration into or out of the pseudocyst but also allow drainage between the stents if stent occlusion should occur. I routinely aspirate fluid from the cyst for Gram stain, culture and sensitivity, amylase, and cytology at time of drainage, and I routinely do ERCP and place an additional transpapillary stent if an amenable ongoing ductal leak is demonstrated.

VARIATIONS AND UNUSUAL SITUATIONS

The most common scenario that one encounters when draining pseudocysts is the realization that there is considerable necrotic debris interspersed with a liquid interface. This occurs because abdominal CT scan routinely underestimates debris in pancreatic fluid collections.[9] Options once this has occurred are using even larger balloons and retroperitoneal necrosectomy with a therapeutic endoscope,[68] adding multiple large-diameter percutaneous catheters,[25] or leaving one or more nasocystic drains in place and performing large volume and repeated irrigations (Video 53–3).[5] Surgery (debridement) may also be necessary, particularly if one inadvertently infects a necrotic cavity.[4]

Other variations may occur contingent on the location and the consequences of the leak. For instance, ductal disruptions tend to follow anatomic tissue planes, and our institution has had to place concomitant drains in scrotal sacs, buttocks, and inverted vaginal vaults and even to perform pericardial windows for pericardial tamponade as the result of an ongoing leak.

Variations also occur with anatomy, and often one finds that the easiest or only access into the pancreas is the accessory papilla in patients with incomplete or complete pancreas divisum.

POSTOPERATIVE CARE AND COMPLICATIONS

Most common acute complications when using endoscopy to treat pancreatic fistulas are exacerbation of pancreatitis and iatrogenic infection,[2,3] although the full range of potential procedural problems (aspiration, drug reaction, bleeding, perforation, etc.) must be discussed with the patient and family. Postoperative care, therefore, must be anticipatory with routine measurement of pulse, temperature, and constitutional complaints and also blood studies including a complete blood count, amylase, lipase, and a liver profile. Pancreatitis flare is more common with otherwise normal pancreatic ducts and is contingent on the amount of manipulation and the success of the procedure. It approximates 10% in my practice, is close to 0% in patients with extensive chronic pancreatitis, and is usually of the mild variety. Iatrogenic infection often follows placement of small catheters or stents in large, debris-filled cavities, and proactive treatment with larger percutaneous JP drains and a 7- to 10-day course of oral antibiotics is usually indicated. I have also learned to minimize use of antisecretory drugs (proton pump inhibitors, histamine2 [H2] blockers) because the latter are associated with significantly higher intraluminal gastric bacteria counts and seem to increase the risk of bacterial translocation and cavity infection. Finally, the PD stent placement, by itself, is associated with the colonization of bacteria within the duct proper. We have noted that pancreatic sepsis, once thought to be uncommon because of the inhibitory effect of pancreatic enzymes, is noted in a small subset of patients even without a ductal disruption and seems to be more common in patients who occlude their prostheses.[97]

Longer term complications of transpapillary stent placement are iatrogenic ductitis including focal strictures and side branch ectasis.[98] As such, I believe that it is prudent to remove prostheses as soon as feasible after placement. This is relatively easy to define in patients with an external fistula. In this setting, stents can be removed 5 to 7 days after fistula closure, removal of the external JP drain, and abdominal CT scan to ensure that there has been no recurrence of an undrained fluid collection. I usually leave stents in place for internal fistulas for 4 to 6 weeks but can leave 8.5- to 10-Fr stents in place for 3 to 4 months in patients with chronic pancreatic leaks and downstream stones or strictures. Transgastric or transenteric stents are usually left in place for 4 to 6 weeks after ensuring resolution of the pseudocyst at follow-up CT examination. The exception may be the high-risk surgical patient with a disconnected pancreas in whom stent retrieval is usually associated with recurrent pseudocyst.[71] In this setting, and only this setting, a chronic indwelling pancreatic stent is occasionally justified.

Future Trends

Although one can speculate that prostheses will develop that have prolonged patency and cause minimal ductitis thereby obviating the urgency of removal, there are a number of current trends that are likely to be increasingly used in the future. These include the use of S-MRCP to define the presence or absence of a pancreatic fistula and its location. Another trend is likely earlier ERCP in pancreatic necrosis patients with placement of transpapillary prostheses to limit further necrosis and prevent additional local complications. Although our group has currently adopted this practice model, it will require prospective multicenter trials before I recommend widespread acceptance of this approach. Superglue (cyanoacrylate) or fibrin injection to occlude a disconnected duct either percutaneously or by EUS may gain more acceptance in the treatment of disconnected pancreatic duct tail as a means to avoid distal pancreatectomy. In addition, the endoscopic approach to the debridement of pancreatic necrosis may be standardized. This will require new endoscopic accessories, a change in mindset such that multiple endoscopic procedures are the expectation as opposed to the exception, and an even closer working relationship with our surgical colleagues. Finally, one hopes that many of these patients with ductal disruption will be sent to centers with expertise in their treatment. Like all techniques and procedures, data are abundantly clear that endoscopists who have drained more than 20 pseudocysts have significantly better results draining pancreatic fluid collections than those who have drained fewer than 20.[99] In other words, those who dabble in drainage, probably should not.

REFERENCES

1. Lau ST, Simchuk EJ, Kozarek RA, et al: A pancreatic ductal leak should be sought to direct treatment in patients with acute pancreatitis. Am J Surg 181:411–415, 2001.
2. Kozarek RA, Traverso LW: Pancreatic fistulas and ascites. In Brandt JL (ed): Textbook of Clinical Gastroenterology. Philadelphia, Current Medicine 1998, pp 1175–1181.
3. Kozarek RA: Endoscopic therapy of complete and partial pancreatic duct disruptions. Gastrointest Endosc Clin N Am 8:39–53, 1998.
4. Kozarek RA, Attia FM, Traverso LW, et al: Pancreatic duct leak in necrotizing pancreatitis. Role of diagnostic and therapeutic ERCP as part of a multi-disciplinary approach. Gastrointest Endosc 51:AB138, 2000.
5. Baron TH, Morgan DE: Acute necrotizing pancreatitis. N Engl J Med 340:1412–1417, 1999.
6. Uomo G, Molino D, Visconti M, et al: The incidence of main pancreatic duct disruption in severe biliary pancreatitis. Am J Surg 176:49–52, 1998.
7. Balthazar EJ, Robinson DL, Megibow AJ, et al: Acute pancreatitis: Value of CT in establishing prognosis. Radiology 174:331–336, 1990.
8. Sauvanet A, Partensky C, Sastre B, et al: Medial pancreatectomy: A multi-institutional retrospective study of 53 patients by the French Pancreas Club. Surgery 132:836–843, 2002.
9. Memis A, Parildar M: Interventional radiological treatment in complications of pancreatitis. Eur J Radiol 43:219–228, 2002.
10. Halloran CM, Ghaneh P, Bosonnet L, et al: Complications of pancreatic cancer resection. Dig Surg 19:138–146, 2002.
11. Sheehan MK, Beck K, Creech S, et al: Distal pancreatectomy: Does the method of closure influence fistula formation? Am Surg 68:264–268, 2002.
12. Poon RT, Lo SH, Fong D, et al: Prevention of pancreatic anastomotic leakage after pancreaticoduodenectomy. Am J Surg 183:42–52, 2002.
13. Freeny PC, Hauptmann E, Althaus SJ, et al: Percutaneous CT-guided catheter drainage of infected acute necrotizing pancreatitis: Techniques and results. Am J Roentgenol 170:969–975, 1998.
14. Nordback I, Paajanen H, Sand J: Prospective evaluation of a treatment protocol in patients with severe acute necrotizing pancreatitis. Eur J Surg 163:357–364, 1997.
15. Kim HS, Lee DK, Kim IW, et al: The role of endoscopic retrograde pancreatography in the treatment of traumatic pancreatic duct injury. Gastrointest Endosc 54:49–55, 2001.
16. Frakes JT: Biliary pancreatitis: A review. J Clin Gastroenterol 28:97–109, 1999.
17. Enns R, Baillie J: Review article: The treatment of acute biliary pancreatitis. Aliment Pharmacol Ther 13:1379–1389, 1999.
18. Forsmark CE: The clinical problem of biliary acute necrotizing pancreatitis: Epidemiology, pathophysiology, and diagnosis of biliary necrotizing pancreatitis. J Gastrointest Surg 5:235–239, 2001.
19. Ashley SW, Perez A, Pierce EA, et al: Necrotizing pancreatitis: Contemporary analysis of 99 consecutive cases. Ann Surg 234:572–580, 2001.
20. Isenmann R, Rau B, Beger HG: Bacterial infection and extent of necrosis are determinants of organ failure in patients with acute necrotizing pancreatitis. Br J Surg 86:1020–1024, 1999.
21. Büchler MW, Gloor B, Muller CA, et al: Acute necrotizing pancreatitis: Treatment strategy according to the status of infection. Ann Surg 232:619–626, 2000.
22. Oksuz MO, Altehoefer C, Winterer JT, et al: Pancreatico-mediastinal fistula with a mediastinal mass lesion demonstrated by MR imaging. J Magn Reson Imaging 16:746–750, 2002.
23. De Backer AI, Mortele KJ, Vaneerdeweg W, et al: Pancreatocolonic fistula due to severe acute pancreatitis: Imaging findings. JBR-BTR 84:45–47, 2001.
24. Sakorafas GH, Sarr MG, Farnell MB: Pancreaticobiliary fistula: An unusual complication of necrotizing pancreatitis. Eur J Surg 167:151–153, 2001.
25. Szentes MJ, Traverso LW, Kozarek RA: Invasive treatment of pancreatic fluid collections with surgical and nonsurgical methods. Am J Surg 161:600–605, 1991.
26. Heider R, Behrns KE: Pancreatic pseudocysts complicated by splenic parenchymal involvement: Results of operative and percutaneous management. Pancreas 23:20–25, 2001.
27. Salih A: Massive pleural effusion. Postgrad Med J 77:536, 546–547, 2001.
28. Kaman L, Behera A, Singh R, et al: Internal pancreatic fistulas with pancreatic ascites and pancreatic pleural effusions: Recognition and management. ANZ J Surg 71:221–225, 2001.
29. Ito H, Matsubara N, Sakai T, et al: Two cases of thoracopancreatic fistula in alcoholic pancreatitis: Clinical and CT findings. Radiat Med 20:207–211, 2002.
30. Isenmann R, Rau B, Beger HG: Bacterial infection and extent of necrosis are determinants of organ failure in patients with acute necrotizing pancreatitis. Br J Surg 86:1020–1024, 1999.
31. Kozarek RA: Therapeutic pancreatic endoscopy. Endoscopy 33:39–45, 2001.
32. Wyncoll DL: The management of severe acute necrotizing pancreatitis: An evidence-based review of the literature. Intensive Care Med 25:146–156, 1999.
33. Slavin J, Ghaneh P, Sutton R, et al: Management of necrotizing pancreatitis. World J Gastroenterol 7:476–481, 2001.
34. Baron TH, Thaggard WG, Morgan DE, et al: Endoscopic therapy for organized pancreatic necrosis. Gastroenterology 111:755–764, 1996.

35. Roth JS, Park AE: Laparoscopic pancreatic cystgastrostomy: The lesser sac technique. Surg Laparosc Endosc Percutan Tech 11:201–203, 2001.

36. Baron TH, Harewood GC, Morgan DE, et al: Outcome differences after endoscopic drainage of pancreatic necrosis, acute pancreatic pseudocysts, and chronic pancreatic pseudocysts. Gastrointest Endosc 56:7–17, 2002.

37. Kozarek RA, Jiranek GC, Traverso LW: Endoscopic treatment of pancreatic ascites. Am J Surg 168:223–226, 1994.

38. Büchler P, Reber HA: Surgical approach in patients with acute pancreatitis. Is infected or sterile necrosis an indication—in whom should this be done, when, and why? Gastroenterol Clin North Am 28:661–671, 1999.

39. Manfredi R, Costamagna G, Brizi MG, et al: Severe chronic pancreatitis versus suspected pancreatic disease: Dynamic magnetic resonance cholangiopancreatography after secretin stimulation. Radiology 214:849–855, 2000.

40. Urakami A, Tsunoda T, Hayashi J, et al: Spontaneous fistulization of a pancreatic pseudocyst into the colon and duodenum. Gastrointest Endosc 55:949–951, 2002.

41. Carrere C, Heyries L, Barthet M, et al: Biliopancreatic fistulas complicating pancreatic pseudocysts: A report of three cases demonstrated by endoscopic retrograde cholangiopancreatography. Endoscopy 33:91–94, 2001.

42. Nealon WH, Walser E: Main pancreatic ductal anatomy can direct choice of modality for treating pancreatic pseudocysts (surgery versus percutaneous drainage). Ann Surg 235:751–758, 2002.

43. Kozarek RA: Role of ERCP in acute pancreatitis. Gastrointest Endosc 56:S231–S236, 2002.

44. Bounds BC, Brugge WR: EUS diagnosis of cystic lesions of the pancreas. Int J Gastrointest Cancer 50:27-31, 2001.

45. Wolfsen HC, Kozarek RA, Ball TJ, et al: Pancreaticoenteric fistula: No longer a surgical disease? J Clin Gastroenterol 14:117–121, 1992.

46. Sugiyama M, Abe N, Yamaguchi Y, et al: Preoperative endoscopic pancreatic stenting for safe local pancreatic resection. Hepatogastroenterology 48:1625–1627, 2001.

47. Ohwada S, Tanahashi Y, Ogawa T, et al: In situ vs ex situ pancreatic duct stents of duct-to-mucosa pancreaticojejunostomy after pancreaticoduodenectomy with Billroth I-type reconstruction. Arch Surg 137:1289–1293, 2002.

48. Suzuki Y, Fujino Y, Tanioka Y, et al: Selection of pancreaticojejunostomy techniques according to pancreatic texture and duct size. Arch Surg 137:1044–1048, 2002.

49. Li–Ling J, Irving M: Somatostatin and octreotide in the prevention of postoperative pancreatic complications and the treatment of enterocutaneous pancreatic fistulas: A systematic review of randomized controlled trials. Br J Surg 88:190–199, 2001.

50. Suc B, Msika S, Fingerhut A, et al: Temporary fibrin glue occlusion of the main pancreatic duct in the prevention of intra-abdominal complications after pancreatic resection: Prospective randomized trial. Ann Surg 237:57–65, 2003.

51. Vitas GJ, Sarr MG: Selected management of pancreatic pseudocysts: Operative versus expectant management. Surgery 111:123–130, 1992.

52. Yemos K, Laopodis B, Yemos J, et al: Surgical management of pancreatic pseudocysts. Minerva Chir 54:395–402, 1999.

53. Ramachadran CS, Goel D, Arora V, et al: Gastroscopic-assisted laparoscopic cystgastrostomy in the management of pseudocysts of the pancreas. Surg Laparosc Endosc Percutan Technique 12:433–436, 2002.

54. Siperstein A: Laparoendoscopic approach to pancreatic pseudocysts. Semin Laparosc Surg 8:218–222, 2001.

55. Pitchamoni CA, Agarwal N: Pancreatic pseudocysts: When and how should drainage be performed? Gastroenterol Clin 28:615–639, 1999.

56. vanSonnenberg E, Wittich GR, Chen KS, et al: Percutaneous drainage of infected and non-infected pancreatic pseudocysts: Experience in 101 cases. Radiology 170:759–761, 1989.

57. Rogers BH, Cicurel NJ, Seed RW: Transgastric needle aspiration of pancreatic pseudocyst through an endoscope. Gastrointest Endosc 21:133–134, 1975.

58. Kozarek RA, Brayko CM, Harlan J, et al: Endoscopic drainage of pancreatic pseudocyst. Gastrointest Endosc 31:322–327, 1985.

59. Vidyarthi G, Steinberg SE: Endoscopic management of pancreatic pseudocysts. Surg Clin North Am 81:405–410, 2001.

60. Sharma SS, Bhargawa N, Govil A: Endoscopic management of pancreatic pseudocyst: A long-term follow-up. Endoscopy 34:203–207, 2002.

61. DePalma GD, Gallaro G, Puzzielo A, et al: Endoscopic drainage of pancreatic pseudocysts: A long-term follow-up study of 49 patients. Hepatogastroenterology 49:1113–1115, 2002.

62. Mergener K, Kozarek RA: Therapeutic pancreatic endoscopy. Endoscopy 35:48–54, 2003.

63. Howell DA, Elton E, Parsons WG: Endoscopic management of pseudocysts of the pancreas. Gastrointest Endosc Clin N Am 8:143–162, 1998.

64. Fuchs M, Reimann FM, Gaebel C, et al: Treatment of infected pancreatic pseudocysts by endoscopic ultrasonography-guided cystogastrostomy. Endoscopy 32:654–657, 2000.

65. Sanchez Cortes E, Maalak A, Le Moine O, et al: Endoscopic cystenterostomy of nonbulging pancreatic fluid collections. Gastrointest Endosc 56:380–386, 2002.

66. Seifert H, Faust D, Schmitt T, et al: Transmural drainage of cystic peripancreatic lesions with a new large-channel echo endoscope. Endoscopy 33:1022–1026, 2001.

67. Grimm H, Binmoeller KF, Soehendra N: Endosonography-guided pseudocyst drainage. Gastrointest Endosc 38:170–171, 1992.

68. Seifert H, Dietrich C, Schmitt T, et al: Endoscopic ultrasound-guided one-step transmural drainage of cystic abdominal lesions with a large-channel echo-endoscope. Endoscopy 32:255–259, 2000.

69. Giovannini M, Pesenti C, Rolland AL, et al: Endoscopic ultrasound-guided drainage of pancreatic pseudocysts or pancreatic abscesses using a therapeutic echoendoscope. Endoscopy 33:473–477, 2001.

70. Kozarek RA, Ball TJ, Patterson DJ, et al: Endoscopic transpapillary therapy for disrupted pancreatic duct and peripancreatic fluid collections. Gastroenterology 100:1362–1370, 1991.

71. Deviere J, Bueso H, Baize M, et al: Complete disruption of the main pancreatic duct: Endoscopic management. Gastrointest Endosc 42:445–451, 1995.

72. Seifert H, Wehrmann T, Schmitt T, et al: Retroperitoneal endoscopic debridement for infected peripancreatic necrosis. Lancet 356:653–655, 2000.

73. Fernandez-del Castillo C, Rattner DW, Makary MA, et al: Debridement and closed packing for the treatment of necrotizing pancreatitis. Ann Surg 228:676–684, 1998.

74. Takeda K, Matsuno S, Sunamura M, et al: Surgical aspects and management of acute necrotizing pancreatitis: Recent results of a cooperative national survey in Japan. Pancreas 16:316-322, 1998.

75. Schoenberg MH, Rau B, Beger HG: New approaches in surgical management of severe acute pancreatitis. Digestion 60(Suppl S1):22–26, 1999.

76. Kasperk R, Riesener KP, Schumpelick V: Surgical therapy of severe acute pancreatitis: A flexible approach gives excellent results. Hepatogastroenterology 46:467–471, 1999.

77. Rau B, Pralle U, Mayer JM, et al: Role of ultrasonographically guided fine-needle aspiration cytology in diagnosis of infected pancreatic necrosis. Br J Surg 85:179–184, 1998.

78. Torres AJ, Landa JI, Moreno-Azcoita M, et al: Somatostatin in the management of gastrointestinal fistulas. A multicenter trial. Arch Surg 127:97–100, 1992.

79. Parekh D, Segal I: Pancreatic ascites and effusion. Risk factors for failure of conservative therapy and the role of octreotide. Arch Surg 127:707–702, 1992.

80. Uchiyama T, Yamamoto T, Mizuta E: Pancreatic ascites—a collected review of 37 cases in Japan. Hepatogastroenterology 36:244–248, 1989.

81. Pederzoli P, Bassi C, Falconi M, et al: Conservative treatment of external pancreatic fistulas with parenteral nutrition alone or in combination with continuous intravenous infusion of somatostatin, glucagon or calcitonin. Surg Gynecol Obstet 163:428–432, 1986.

82. Martin FM, Rossi RL, Munson JL, et al: Management of pancreatic fistulas. Arch Surg 124:571–573, 1989.

83. Kozarek RA, Patterson DJ, Ball TJ, et al: Endoscopic placement of pancreatic stents and drains in the management of pancreatitis. Ann Surg 209:261–266, 1989.

84. Bracher GA, Manocha AP, DeBanto JR, et al: Endoscopic pancreatic duct stenting to treat pancreatic ascites. Gastrointest Endosc 49:710–715, 1999.

85. Bosscha K, Hulstaert PF, Hennipman A, et al: Fulminant acute pancreatitis and infected necrosis: Results of open management of the abdomen and "planned" reoperation. J Am Coll Surg 187:255–262, 1998.

86. Kozarek RA, Ball TJ, Patterson DJ, et al: Transpapillary stenting for pancreaticocutaneous fistulas. J Gastrointest Surg 1:357–361, 1997.

87. Costamagna G, Mutignani M, Ingrosso M, et al: Endoscopic treatment of postsurgical external pancreatic fistulas. Endoscopy 33:317–322, 2001.

88. Saeed ZA, Ramirez FC, Hepps KS: Endoscopic stent placement for internal and external pancreatic fistulas. Gastroenterology 105:1213–1217, 1993.

89. Ukita T, Moriyama A, Tada A, et al: Successful management of postoperative pancreatic fistula by application of constructed S-type pancreatic stent after operation for abnormal biliary-pancreatic junction. Endoscopy 35:253, 2003.

90. Tulassay Z, Flautner L, Vadasz A, et al: Short report: Octreotide in the treatment of external pancreatic fistulas. Aliment Pharmacol Ther 7:323–325, 1993.

91. Lansden FT, Adams DB, Anderson MC: Treatment of external pancreatic fistulas with somatostatin. Am Surg 55:695–698, 1989.

92. Prinz R, Pickleman J, Hoffman JP: Treatment of pancreatic cutaneous fistulas with a somatostatin analog. Am J Surg 155:36–42, 1988.

93. Cope C, Tuite C, Burke DR, et al: Percutaneous management of chronic pancreatic duct strictures and external fistulas with long-term results. J Vasc Interv Radiol 12:104–110, 2001.

94. Sheiman RG, Chan R, Matthews JB: Percutaneous treatment of a pancreatic fistula after pancreaticoduodenectomy. J Vasc Interv Radiol 12:524–526, 2001.

95. Hirota M, Kamekawa K, Tashima T, et al: Percutaneous embolization of the distal pancreatic duct to treat intractable pancreatic juice fistula. Pancreas 22:214–216, 2001.

96. Kozarek RA, Ball TJ, Patterson DJ, et al: Endoscopic pancreatic duct sphincterotomy: Indications, technique, and analysis of results. Gastrointest Endosc 40:592–598, 1994.

97. Kozarek RA, Hovde O, Attia F, et al: Do pancreatic duct stents cause or prevent pancreatic sepsis? Gastrointest Endosc 58:508–509, 2003.

98. Smith MT, Sherman S, Ikenberry SO, et al: Alterations in pancreatic ductal morphology following polyethylene pancreatic stent therapy. Gastrointest Endosc 44:268–275, 1996.

99. Harewood GC, Wright CA, Baren TH: Impact on patient outcomes of experience in the performance of endoscopic pancreatic fluid collection drainage. Gastrointest Endosc 58:230–235, 2003.

Palliation of Malignant Pancreaticobiliary Obstruction

Anne-Marie van Berkel, Paul Fockens, and M. J. Bruno

Introduction

Pancreaticobiliary malignancies include pancreatic head cancer, gallbladder carcinoma, and proximal cholangiocarcinomas also referred to as Klatskin tumors. Pancreatic head carcinoma comprises tumors that may originate from various tissues and include pancreatic adenocarcinoma, distal cholangiocarcinoma, carcinoma of the ampulla of Vater, and duodenal carcinoma. Although there are marked differences in biologic behavior and clinical outcome between these tumors, the overall prognosis is dismal. At the time of presentation more than 90% of patients have local unresectable disease or distant metastases, which leaves only a minority of patients as suitable candidates for curative resection. Other treatment modalities such as chemotherapy and radiotherapy have little to no effect on survival. Unfortunately, most of these patients can only be offered palliative treatment.

More than 85% of patients with pancreaticobiliary malignancies will develop obstructive jaundice in the course of their disease and often it is a presenting symptom. Relief of jaundice, besides pain management, is the mainstay of palliative therapy. In the past, the gold standard treatment was surgical biliary diversion. Because of associated morbidity and mortality, surgical treatment has been challenged by endoscopic stent placement since the introduction of endoscopic retrograde cholangiopancreatography (ERCP) in 1980. Endoscopic biliary drainage has become the palliative treatment of choice to relieve biliary obstruction in pancreaticobiliary malignancies.

Epidemiology

Of all pancreaticobiliary malignancies, pancreatic adenocarcinoma has the highest incidence, with around 30,000 new cases annually in the United States. It ranks fifth among the leading causes of cancer-related deaths.[1,2] Only 10% of patients are suitable candidates for resection, and the overall 5-year survival rate is less than 4%.[3,4]

The incidence of gallbladder carcinomas is 1 per 100,000 person-years. The survival rate is only slightly higher than that of pancreatic carcinoma.[2] Most probably, the only patients who will survive are those in whom early cancer was detected in a postcholecystectomy specimen.

Klatskin tumors also have a poor prognosis, with less than 10% of patients surviving 5 years after being diagnosed and the vast majority of patients dying in the first year.[5] The number of tumors that are potentially resectable is low, ranging from 5% to 20%.

In ampullary carcinoma, biliary obstruction usually develops relatively early in the course of the disease. Therefore, tumors are usually small and radical resection is possible in most cases, with an overall 5-year survival rate of up to 50%.[6]

Pathogenesis

Although a detailed discussion of the pathogenesis of pancreaticobiliary malignancies is beyond the scope of this chapter, it is interesting to note that several epidemiologic studies have identified risk factors for the development of pancreaticobiliary malignancies.

Tobacco smoking doubles the risk of pancreatic cancer.[7,8] Patients with chronic pancreatitis have an increased risk for developing pancreatic cancer that is estimated at 4% per 20 years.[9] The risk of developing pancreatic cancer in patients with hereditary pancreatitis is as high as 50%, with smoking as an important risk modifier.[10,11] Etiologic factors for cholangiocarcinoma include primary sclerosing cholangitis and hepatolithiasis.[12,13] Gallstone disease is the most important risk factor for gallbladder cancer.[14]

Clinical Features

The most common presenting symptoms of pancreaticobiliary malignancies are painless jaundice with anorexia and weight loss, which are seen in most patients. If pain occurs, it is often located in the epigastric region or right upper quadrant and may radiate to the back. Back pain usually indicates retroperitoneal infiltration with tumor and therefore unresectability. Other symptoms may include dark urine, pale stools, and pruritus. As many as 80% of patients with pancreatic cancer have impaired glucose tolerance or frank diabetes mellitus at the time of presentation. Carcinoma of the body and tail of the pancreas presents with similar features, although jaundice is usually absent or develops very late in the course of the disease.

Pathology

About 90% of pancreaticobiliary malignancies are ductal adenocarcinomas (Fig. 54–1). Most of these tumors arise from the pancreatic head. Other exocrine malignancies are mucinous cyst adenocarcinoma and acinar cell carcinomas. Endocrine tumors include gastrinoma and insulinoma. Metastases of a primary tumor

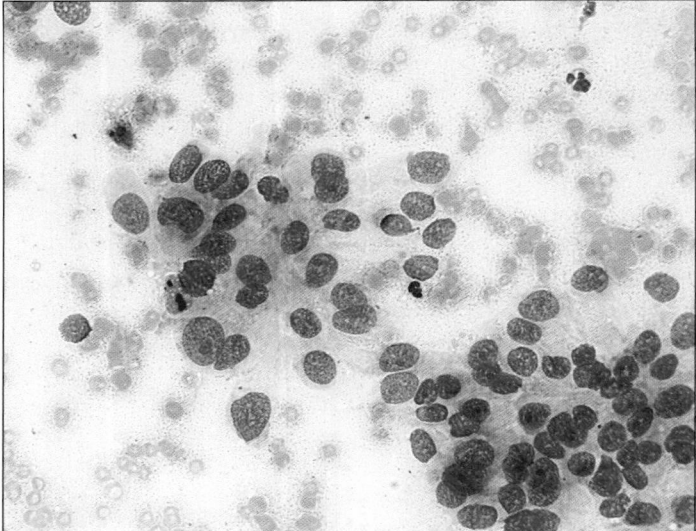

Figure 54–1. Brush cytology of ductal adenocarcinoma of the pancreatic head (Giemsa staining).

(mammary, lung, and melanoma) and lymphoma should be considered because of important treatment implications (e.g., chemotherapy). Mesenchymal tumors are extremely rare.

The definitive diagnosis of malignancy depends on obtaining a tissue diagnosis. Although a number of patients are palliated without definite confirmation of the tumor, in cases of adjuvant therapies such as radiotherapy or chemotherapy a cytologic or histologic biopsy-proven malignancy is a prerequisite. To lower the number of costly and cumbersome ultrasound- or computed tomography (CT)-guided punctures, it is advisable to attempt to obtain a tissue diagnosis during the same ERCP procedure in which a biliary endoprosthesis is inserted for palliation of jaundice. Various techniques can be used to obtain tissue specimens during ERCP including cytologic brushings, forceps biopsy, needle aspiration cytology, and fluid collection from the bile and/or pancreas.

Cytologic brushings are relatively easy to obtain and widely used. Specificity approaches 100% but sensitivity is as low as 30% to 60%.[15,16] The sensitivity in cholangiocarcinoma is higher than in pancreatic carcinoma. Forceps biopsy or needle aspiration cytology requires endoscopic sphincterotomy and therefore carries an increased risk of complications. Ampullary tumors can be directly biopsied. Fine needle aspiration is superior to brush cytology and endobiliary forceps biopsy, with a cancer detection rate of 65%.[17–19] Sampling of ductal fluid is a simple method but its sensitivity is very low; therefore, it is not used very often. Several studies have shown that sensitivity can be increased by combining different techniques of tissue sampling.[16]

Endosonographic fine needle aspiration biopsy results in an excellent sensitivity of 85% to 90% and specificity of virtually 100%.[20] Although these tests may be useful in making the diagnosis of carcinoma, a negative test cannot rule out malignant disease. Percutaneous fine needle aspiration biopsy is another accurate method for confirmation of malignancy, with a sensitivity of 60% to 90%.[21] However, needle-track seeding has been described and this technique should only be used for tissue confirmation in the case of unresectable disease.

Differential Diagnosis

The most important discrimination is the differential diagnosis between benign and malignant lesions. In the case of the former, surgery may not be indicated and may even cause harm to the patient, whereas in the latter case it is the treatment of choice if a lesion is resectable.

An enlarged pancreatic head may be caused either by pancreatitis or by carcinoma. The patient's history and clinical presentation contribute to making a diagnosis. Cystic lesions of the pancreas may be benign (pancreatic pseudocyst or serous cystadenoma), premalignant (mucinous cystadenoma), or malignant (cystadenocarcinoma). Radiologic imaging is used to characterize these lesions. Endoscopic ultrasonography may further increase accuracy of the diagnosis in combination with fine needle aspiration and fluid analysis.

In the case of a suspicious mid or proximal bile duct stricture, a gallbladder carcinoma should be included in the differential diagnosis. It is important to exclude benign causes of strictures such as Mirizzi's syndrome, primary and secondary sclerosing cholangitis,

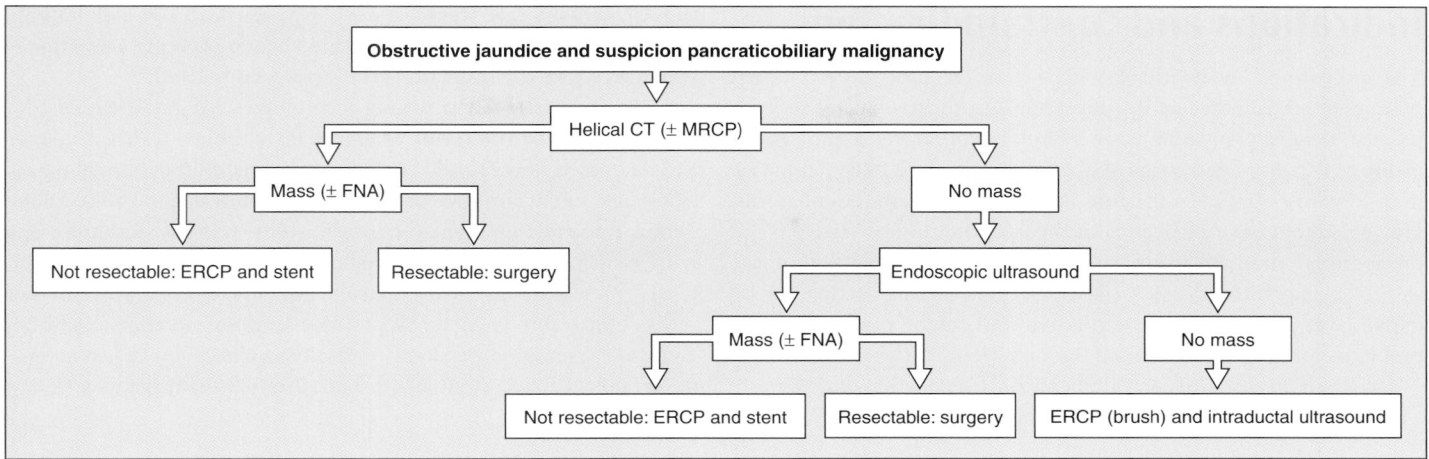

Figure 54-2. Algorithm of diagnosis of pancreaticobiliary cancer.

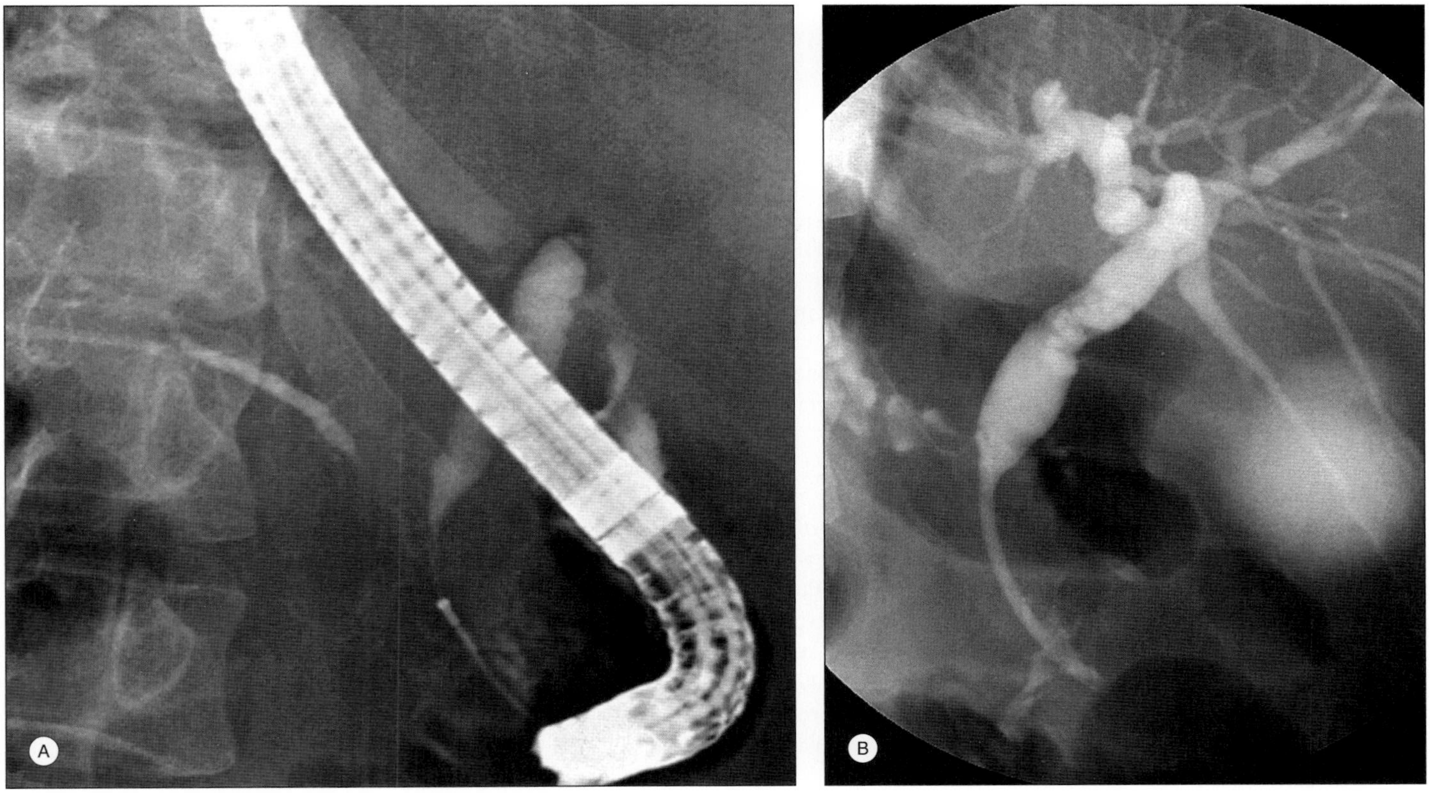

Figure 54-3. *A,* Stenosis of both common bile duct and pancreatic duct, also called a double-duct sign, caused by a pancreatic adenocarcinoma. *B,* A 10-Fr, 9-cm plastic endoprosthesis inserted through a distal bile duct stricture.

and postoperative conditions. An algorithm of the diagnosis of pancreaticobiliary cancer is presented in Fig. 54–2.

Treatment

Since the introduction of endoscopic biliary stenting in 1980, the palliative treatment of pancreaticobiliary malignancies has changed considerably. Currently, endoscopic stenting to relieve jaundice is well established and is considered the preferred treatment (Fig. 54–3). Compared with percutaneous and surgical drainage it is associated with lower morbidity and mortality rates.[22–24] The main problem of endoscopic biliary drainage is late stent occlusion, which necessitates stent exchange. The technical success rate of endoscopic biliary drainage is between 70% to 90% and is higher for distal tumors compared with more proximal malignancies involving the bifurcation. The complication rate of therapeutic ERCP ranges between 5% and 10%.[25,26]

Indications and Contraindications

The indications for an ERCP with a drainage procedure by stent placement are jaundice and/or fever and/or pruritus. Biliary stenting has also been shown to improve symptoms of anorexia and quality of life.[27,28] It has been suggested that preoperative biliary drainage may improve surgical outcome after pancreaticoduodenectomy. However, this has not been substantiated in clinical trials.[29-31] If preoperative drainage is indicated because of cholangitis, drainage should be performed using plastic stents. In this setting, metal expandable stents are too expensive and might cause technical problems for the surgeon during the resection.

There are no absolute contraindications. Coagulation disorders are a relative contraindication and should be corrected before ERCP.

Overview of Stents for Biliary Drainage

PLASTIC STENTS

The median patency of a conventional 10-Fr plastic stent ranges between 3 and 6 months. The incidence of stent occlusion varies between 20% and 50%.[32-34] The initial event in stent blockage is adherence of proteins and bacteria to the inner wall of the stent and subsequent formation of a biofilm. Bacteria are introduced into the biliary system during transpapillary placement of the stent. Sludge then forms from the accumulation of bacteria, which produce β-glucuronidase and form calcium bilirubinate and calcium palmitate.[35-37] Many efforts have been made to prolong stent patency, some of which are discussed in the following paragraphs.

STENT DIAMETER

The first biliary stents which were placed were only 7- or 8-Fr in diameter because of limitations of the diameter of the working channel of the endoscope (2.8 mm). When side-viewing endoscopes with large-diameter working channels (4.2 mm) were introduced in 1980, it became possible to insert large-bore plastic stents.[38] Larger stents (10 Fr) perform better than smaller stents (7 Fr).[39] This appears to be because of the higher flow rate, as predicted by Poiseuille's law, and less stasis with larger-diameter stents. Theoretically, bile flow rate is proportional to the internal diameter raised to the fourth power; thus, even a small increase in diameter results in a substantial increase in flow capacity.[40] Somewhat in contrast to this hypothesis, the use of larger-diameter plastic stents of 11.5 or 12 Fr did not result in further improvements in stent patency.[41-43]

STENT DESIGN

The first biliary stents had a pigtail configuration at the proximal end to provide better anchorage. Straight stents were then developed because of their improved bile flow characteristics compared with pigtail stents[40,44,45] (Fig. 54–4). Huibregtse and Tytgat[46] developed the Amsterdam-type stent—a straight design with two side holes to facilitate biliary drainage and two side flaps to prevent dislocation—which has been the standard type of stent since 1980.

Sludge in plastic stents mainly accumulates around side holes.[35,47] This seems to be the result of higher intraluminal flow turbulence and decreased flow rates.[40] Soehendra postulated that elimination of side holes might improve patency rates and designed the so-called Teflon Tannenbaum stent (a straight stent without side holes and with multiple proximal and distal side flaps to prevent dislocation).[48,49] At first, uncontrolled results were encouraging, with patency rates comparable to metal stents, but randomized trials could not confirm these initial results.[50-52] Omitting side holes in a standard-design polyethylene stent also did not improve stent patency.[53]

STENT MATERIAL

Different materials have been used for stent construction: polyethylene, polyurethane, and Teflon. *In vitro* studies have shown a direct relation between the coefficient of friction and the amount of encrusted material. Teflon has the lowest friction coefficient and therefore the best potential for preventing stent clogging.[35] Initially, Teflon Tannenbaum stents showed a favorable patency rate.[48,49] A randomized study comparing Amsterdam-type stents made from polyethylene and Teflon did not show a difference in stent patency.[54] Other controlled clinical trials could also not confirm the superiority of Teflon material in a Tannenbaum-design stent.[50-52]

Scanning electron microscopy of out-of-package biliary stents has shown that the inner surface smoothness of plastic stents is highly variable. This is possibly a result of the manufacturing process of plastic stents by extrusion. Only the polyurethane stent was found to have an extremely smooth surface.[55]

Two new polymers were introduced with an ultrasmooth surface, Vivathane and Hydromer. Both materials have been shown to reduce bacterial adherence *in vitro*.[56,57] In addition, the Hydromer stent has not only a smooth texture but also a coating that absorbs water and provides a hydrophilic sheath. Because bacteria initially

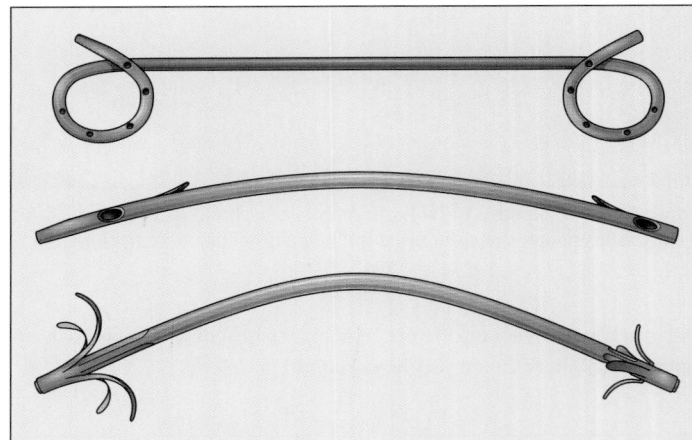

Figure 54–4. Different types of plastic endoprosthesis (from top downward): a double-pigtail stent, an Amsterdam-type stent (one side hole and one side flap at each end), and a Tannenbaum-type stent (without side holes and multiple side flaps at each end).

attach by hydrophobic interactions, this coating could potentially lower bacterial adhesion and therefore increase stent patency. However, the encouraging results of *in vitro* studies could not be confirmed in prospective clinical trials.[58,59]

STENT COATING

Priming the inner surface of a stent with a coating with some form of antiadhesion property may reduce biofilm formation and hence stent clogging. Antibiotics, antithrombotics, silver, and hydrophilic coating were all effective in reducing bacterial colonization *in vitro*.[57,60,61] However, clinical studies using antibiotic-coated or hydrophilic-coated stents did not show any benefit.[59]

STENT POSITION

Placing the stent entirely within the common bile duct has the theoretical advantage of preserving the barrier function of the sphincter of Oddi. This prevents duodenal reflux of food and bacteria into the stent and biliary tree. This so-called inside stent approach can only be performed when a free margin of 1 to 2 cm is maintained between the distal end of the stricture and the papilla. With this in mind, about one third of patients with malignant obstructive jaundice are potential candidates for such treatment.[62] However, in a randomized trial no difference was found in stent performance. In fact, in the inside stent group, stent migration occurred significantly more often.[63]

ANTIBIOTICS

Bacteria can enter the bile duct through the portal circulation but more easily directly from the duodenum. When an endoprosthesis is placed, the barrier function of the sphincter of Oddi is lost and bacteria enter the biliary tract freely. Sludge may then form because these bacteria produce β-glucuronidase and form calcium bilirubinate and calcium palmitate. To prolong stent patency, prophylactic treatment with antibiotics seemed a logical step.

In vitro studies showed that antibiotic treatment reduced bacterial adherence to plastic stents.[64] In a prospective randomized study with ciprofloxacin, no difference in stent patency was found.[65] In another study rotating antibiotics (cycles of two weeks of ampicillin, metronidazole, and ciprofloxacin) were combined with ursodeoxycholic acid, and no difference in stent patency was shown.[66] Only one small pilot study showed a reduced rate of stent blockage with norfloxacin plus ursodeoxycholic acid.[67] Other studies combining antibiotics and bile salts (ofloxacin and ursodeoxycholic, ciprofloxacin, and Rowachol) did not show a longer duration of stent patency.[68,69]

In summary, at this time there is no compelling evidence that stent patency benefits from antibiotic prophylaxis.

ASPIRIN

Animal studies in prairie dogs have shown that aspirin inhibits mucous glycoprotein secretion by blocking prostaglandin synthesis.[70] In a clinical study, the use of aspirin reduced the content of all sludge components, although no effect was shown on stent patency.[71] No further studies using aspirin have been performed.

BILE SALTS

Bile salts have a potent antibacterial effect and may also stimulate bile flow. Because bacteria attach by hydrophobic interactions, hydrophobic bile salts (deoxycholate, taurodeoxycholate) inhibit initial bacterial attachment, as was shown in experimental studies.[72] However, hydrophobic bile salts are not well tolerated. Unfortunately, hydrophilic bile salts such as ursodeoxycholate, which are better tolerated, have a minimal effect on bacterial adhesion. Except for one small pilot study, different prospective clinical studies using ursodeoxycholic acid alone or combining ursodeoxycholic acid with antibiotics could not show a difference in stent patency.[66–69]

STENT EXCHANGE

Some endoscopists prefer to schedule patients for elective stent exchange every 3 to 4 months. The optimal time interval remains an unanswered question.[73,74] Prophylactic stent exchange requires a repeat (clinically not indicated) endoscopy and has to be compared with the risks of watchful waiting and the risk of (severe) cholangitis. Because most patients will not develop stent occlusion before dying of the underlying disease, most endoscopists favor an expectant management strategy.

STENT CLEANING

Some endoscopists have proposed leaving an occluded stent *in situ* and cleaning the obstructed lumen with a cytology brush or flushing with saline instead of performing stent replacement.[75] However, this carries the risk of inducing biliary sepsis by actively introducing the biofilm of the stent and bacteria from the duodenum into the biliary tract. Therefore, stent cleaning is not recommended.

SELF-EXPANDING METAL STENT

The diameter of biliary stents was restricted by the size of the instrumentation channel of the endoscope until the development of self-expanding metal stents. All currently available expandable stents are made of metal. They differ in the way they are braided, the size of the mesh, the metal used, and their rigidity. At present, many different types of self-expanding metal stents are available from different manufacturers (Fig. 54–5). There are two expansion types: self-expanding metal stents with an intrinsic expanding force and balloon-expanding stents deployed by inflation of a balloon.

To date, the most experience has been gained with the self-expanding Wallstent. This stent is delivered in a collapsed configuration on an 8-Fr delivery system. When deployed, it expands to a final diameter of 30 Fr (approximately 10 mm) and shortens about 30% in length. The final diameter is achieved after 1 week, when an equilibrium is achieved between the dilating force of the stent and the resistance of the bile duct wall and tumor.

These large-caliber self-expanding metal stents of 30 Fr remain patent for longer than plastic stents but do not prevent blockage

Table 54–1. Results of Trials Comparing Self-Expandable Stents with Plastic Stents

Author	Number of Patients		Drainage (%)		Occlusion Rate (%)		Median Stent Patency (days)	
	PE	SEMS	PE	SEMS	PE	SEMS	PE	SEMS
Davids et al.[33]	49	56	95	96	54	33	126	273
Carr-Locke et al.[77]	78	86	95	98	13	13	62	111
Knyrim et al.[34]	31	31	100	100	43	22	140*	189*

*Mean.
PE, polyethylene stent; SEMS, self-expanding metal stent.

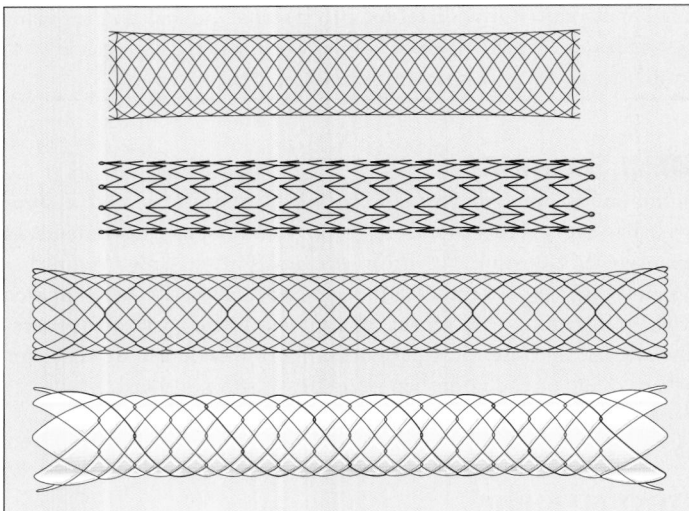

Figure 54–5. Different types of self-expanding metal stents (from top downward): Wallstent (Boston Scientific, Boston, MA), Gianturco Z stent (Wilson Cook, Winston Salem, NC), and Hanaro stent and covered Hanaro stent (MI Tech Corporation, Seoul, South Korea).

indefinitely. Because of their design, self-expanding metal stents have much less surface to which bacteria can adhere. The mechanism of stent blockage differs from that seen in plastic stents and includes tumor ingrowth through the interstices of the stent or overgrowth of the end of the stent and intima hyperplasia. Several studies have shown a median stent patency of about 6 to 9 months[33,34,74,76,77] (Table 54–1).

Self-expanding metal stents are more difficult to insert, they cannot be removed after deployment, and initial costs are high (about $1000). Various types of self-expanding metal stents have been introduced; these are summarized in the following sections. Randomized trials with large groups of patients and long-term follow-up are only available for the Wallstent.

Wallstent

The initial endoscopic placement experience was reported in 1989.[78] The Wallstent (Boston Scientific, Boston, MA) is made from stainless steel alloy filaments braided in a tubular mesh configuration. In the early phase of development, technical problems mainly involved the restraining membrane failing to retract completely, but this is now rarely seen.[79] The first randomized trial comparing plastic stents and the Wallstent was performed by Davids and

coworkers.[33] Wallstent patency was superior to plastic stents, with a median duration of 9 months. These results have been confirmed in several other studies.[34,74,80]

Ultraflex Diamond Stent

Compared with the Wallstent, this stent is more flexible, uses a larger mesh design, has less radial expandable force, and is constructed from nitinol. The name of this stent relates to the appearance of its mesh pattern. Nonrandomized studies comparing the Ultraflex Diamond stent (Boston Scientific, Boston, MA) to the Wallstent suggested an equal or less durable patency.[81,82] One prospective uncontrolled multicenter study showed a stent patency duration of the Ultraflex stent of almost 16 months, a result that has never been documented with any type of biliary stent.[83] This exceptional outcome should be confirmed in a prospective randomized trial, preferably in comparison with the Wallstent.

EndoCoil

This removable self-expanding metal stent is made of a coil spring of nickel-titanium alloy that expands radially (InStent, Eden Prairie, MN). It can only be used for distal stenosis because apposing coils prevent drainage of segmental ducts. Theoretically, the problem of tumor ingrowth should be prevented by the apposing coils. However, stent dysfunction by tumor ingrowth remains a problem and removal of the stent is not without risk.[84,85] No long-term follow-up or comparative data are available.

Gianturco Z-Stent

The Gianturco Z-stent (Wilson Cook, Winston Salem, NC) has wide gaps between the zigzag bands, with greater potential for tumor ingrowth. Advantages of this stent are the fact that it does not shorten on expansion and has no sharp edges at the ends. The Gianturco Z-stent is the second most used expandable stent and it is mostly inserted via the percutaneous route. Patency rates are comparable to the Wallstent.[86–89]

Strecker Stent

This is a balloon-expandable stent, and there are only a few reported studies.[90,91] Technical failures occur in up to 27%. The main disadvantage of this stent is its diameter of only 21 Fr and the absence of an intrinsic radial force.[34,92] These unfavorable features

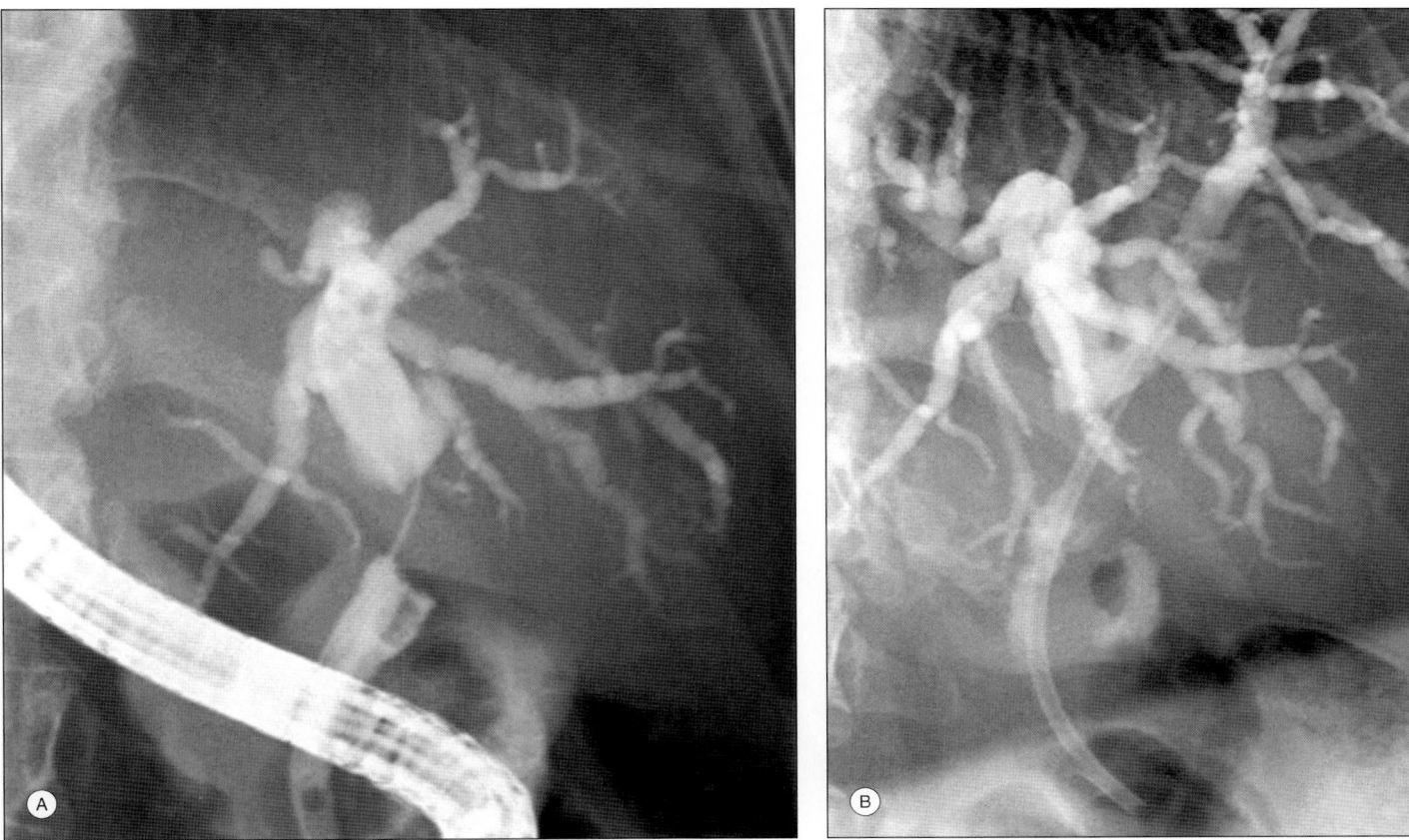

Figure 54–6. *A,* Mid common bile duct stricture caused by gallbladder carcinoma. *B,* With an 11-cm, 10-Fr plastic endoprosthesis inserted.

have prohibited the general use of the Strecker stent (Boston Scientific, Boston, MA), and it is no longer commercially available.

Covered Self-Expanding Metal Stent

Tissue ingrowth through the meshes of the stent is responsible for stent occlusion in about 22% to 33% of patients.[33,34] To overcome this problem, self-expanding metal stents have been covered with a polyurethane or silicone membrane, except for the proximal and distal 5 mm. Results of various stents (MI Tech Corporation, Seoul, South Korea; Wilson Cook, Winston Salem, NC; Boston Scientific, Boston, MA) in various studies are contradictory.[92–94] Major concerns are the risk of stent migration, cholecystitis, and pancreatitis, although these complications have not been reported with any significant frequency. Furthermore, these stents should not be used intrahepatically because of occlusion of hepatic side branches by the covering membrane. The exact role of covered self-expanding metal stents is still under investigation.

PLASTIC OR METAL STENT?

Self-expanding metal stents have a longer duration of patency than plastic stents and ideally should be placed in all patients. The high initial costs have limited their use in different health care settings worldwide.

Therefore, in a cost-effective approach the choice between a plastic or metal stent depends mainly on an estimate of patient survival. Tumor size seems a reliable predictor of survival. Prat and coworkers[95] claim that in the case of a tumor greater than 30 mm, a polyethylene stent should be placed because of shorter expected survival. The presence and number of liver metastases have also been shown to be independently related to prognosis.[96,97] Comparative studies did not show any benefit of self-expanding metal stents compared with polyethylene stents in the first 3 months after insertion.[33,74] Therefore, it seems reasonable to insert a polyethylene stent in patients with a life expectancy of less than 3 months (Fig. 54–6). If expected survival extends to 3 to 6 months, a self-expanding metal stent should be considered (Fig. 54–7). Different authors have shown this strategy to be cost effective.[33,98,99] Patients who present with early clogging of a polyethylene stent (within 1 month) should also receive a self-expanding stent, irrespective of their life expectancy, although this has not been proved in prospective studies.[100]

Procedure of Stent Placement

ANTIBIOTICS

Drainage of the biliary tree is the mainstay of therapy for patients with cholangitis. There is controversy about the routine use of preprocedure antibiotic prophylaxis.[101–103]

Preoperative administration of antibiotics should definitively be started in a patient with fever. Because failure to drain the entire

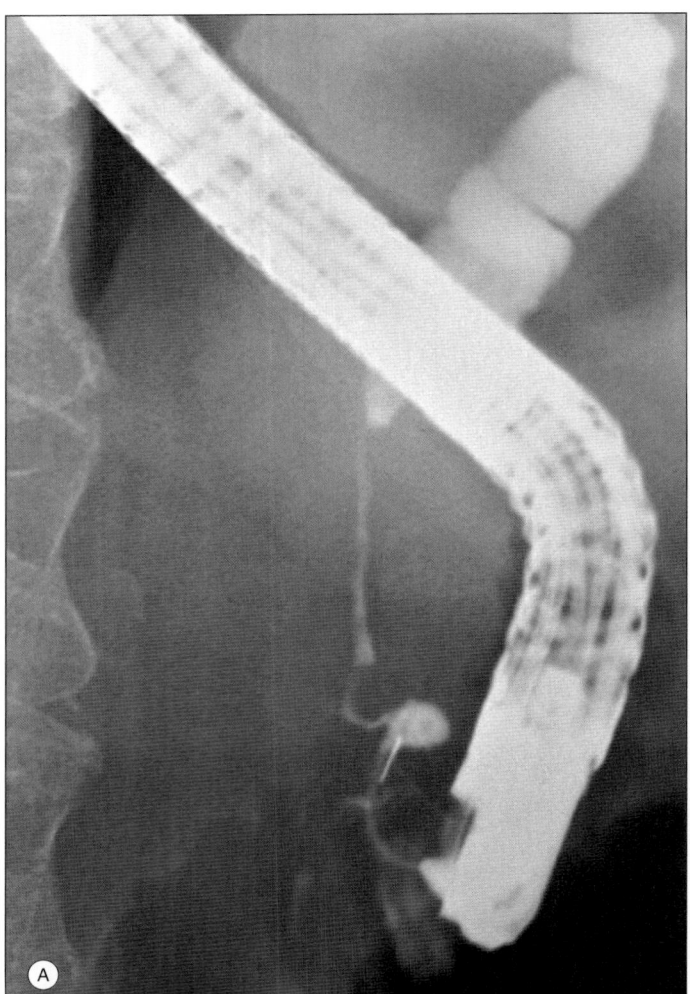
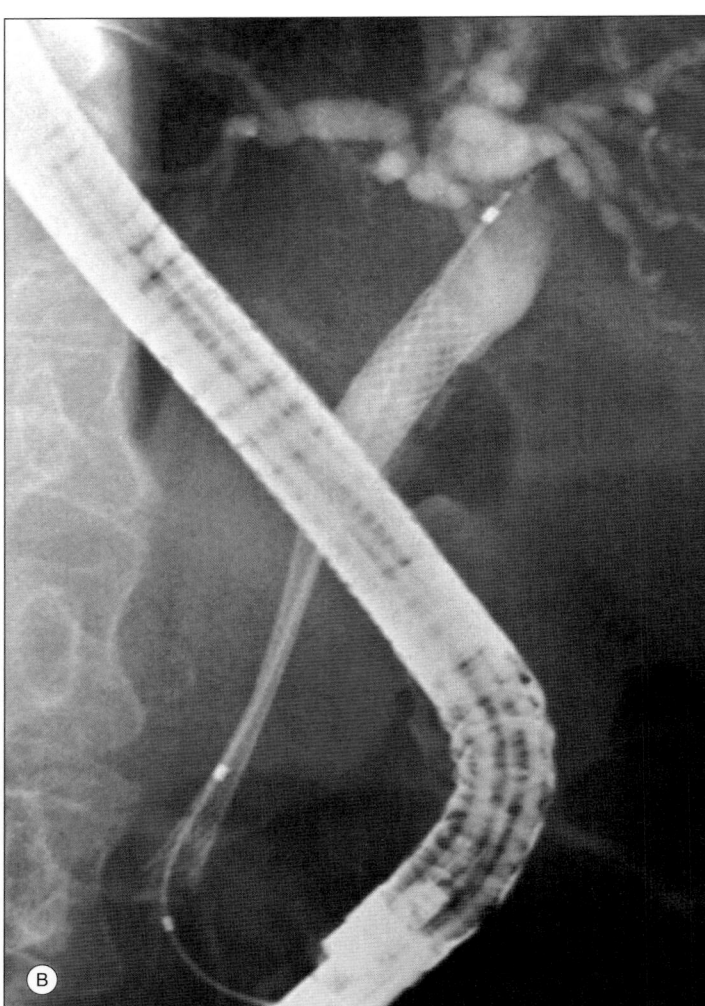

Figure 54–7. *A,* Distal common bile duct stricture caused by a pancreatic adenocarcinoma. *B,* With a self-expanding metal stent inserted.

biliary tree is the most important risk factor associated with cholangitis after ERCP, antibiotic prophylaxis should also be administered in a highly selective group of patients in whom incomplete drainage is anticipated, such as patients with a hilar malignancy or primary sclerosing cholangitis.[104,105] Prophylaxis can be given as a single, adequate dose shortly before the procedure. If contrast is injected in the biliary tract but obstruction cannot be relieved, antibiotic therapy should be continued (or started) until drainage is established.

Gram-negative bacteria are consistently the most common organisms in bile (*Escherichia coli* and to a lesser extent *Klebsiella* spp. and gram-positive *Enterococcus* spp.). Therefore, antibiotics in these cases should be bactericidal and aimed at gram-negative bacteria with good penetration in liver tissue and bile. Ciprofloxacin is currently the first choice of antibiotic in our unit with the caveat that it does not cover enterococci. In case of fever despite ciprofloxacin, the addition of amoxicillin or a switch to piperacillin/tazobactam is advisable.

Technique of Stent Placement

The procedure starts with the introduction of a large-channel (4.2 mm) side-viewing therapeutic endoscope into the second portion of the duodenum. Standard cannulation of the papilla of Vater is performed by a ball-tip or cone-tip catheter; eventually cannulation can be attempted with a guidewire inserted in the ball-tip catheter. If this approach fails, a double-lumen sphincterotome with a guidewire (cannulatome) should be used. Use of this device may aid in achieving an optimal angle for bile duct cannulation. If this is not successful, a precut sphincterotomy is performed to obtain biliary access.[106] With the use of all these different techniques, deep cannulation is achieved in up to 95% of patients.

Once a diagnostic catheter is inserted into the bile duct, contrast is injected. It is essential to define the exact anatomy, location, and nature of the stenosis. To avoid postprocedural cholangitis in patients with complex hilar strictures, contrast filling of segments that will not be drained should be avoided. The next step is to pass a guidewire through the stricture to facilitate introduction of the catheter and enable exchange for other instruments. When passage of a guidewire through the stricture cannot be accomplished, the direction of the guidewire can be changed by manipulating its position with movements of the endoscope similar to those made for standard cannulation. The assistant can help to cross the stricture by moving the guidewire in and out of the catheter. The endoscopist can manipulate the guidewire by moving the guiding catheter.

A variety of guidewires are available with different flexibility, diameter, and tip shape. On the one hand, rigid guidewires facilitate introduction of instruments (e.g., an intraductal ultrasound probe) and small-diameter stents. On the other hand, very slippery guidewires with a hydropolymer coating follow bends easily and are used to pass asymmetric strictures. Once the guidewire is passed through the stricture, a catheter can be advanced and more complete filling can be achieved.

A sphincterotomy is not routinely necessary for introduction of one biliary stent. Previously, it was believed that a sphincterotomy was necessary to facilitate introduction of different devices and also to avoid occlusion of the pancreatic duct by the endoprosthesis. However, in clinical practice this did not prove to be a problem. A sphincterotomy is indicated only in cases in which more than one prosthesis is placed.

PLASTIC STENTS

Once the stricture is passed with a guidewire, a stent can usually be inserted. First, a catheter is introduced over the guidewire through the stricture to ensure a more rigid introductory system to facilitate stent placement. If appropriate, the guidewire can be exchanged for a cytology brush to obtain tissue samples.

The endoprosthesis is positioned over the guiding catheter and inserted into the instrumentation channel. With a pusher tube, the stent is further advanced toward the tip of the endoscope with the elevator bridge closed. When the prosthesis reaches the tip of the instrumentation channel, the elevator bridge is opened and the stent is pushed out of the endoscope by the pusher tube under endoscopic and fluoroscopic control. During further advancement of the stent, it is important to keep the endoscope tip close to the papilla. The stent should be advanced one step at a time by pushing it a little bit further each time into the duodenum. The stent is raised by closing the elevator bridge, and the tip of the endoscope is moved closer to the papilla with the up and down knob, thus introducing the stent. These steps are repeated until the distal side flap has reached the papilla. Finally, the assistant pulls out the catheter and guidewire while the endoscopist keeps the prosthesis in position with the pusher tube.

In most distal and mid common bile duct strictures, it is usually possible to insert a 10-Fr endoprosthesis without prior dilation. However, in proximal strictures, the stricture may have to be dilated to allow stent placement. This can be achieved with the use of progressively dilating catheters, which are introduced over a rigid guidewire. Balloon catheters can be used as well to accomplish this goal. If it is still not possible to insert a 10-Fr stent, a smaller caliber prosthesis (7 Fr) should be inserted, which can be exchanged for a 10-Fr prosthesis a few days later. When both right and left liver lobes have to be drained, it is usually more convenient to place the endoprosthesis draining the left side first, followed by the right side.

The required length of the endoprosthesis can be measured by using the guidewire as a measuring device. First, under fluoroscopic control, the proximal tip of the guidewire is positioned at the level at which the proximal tip of the endoprosthesis is projected. Then, the endoscopy nurse fixes the guidewire between finger and thumb where it exits the catheter. Subsequently, under fluoroscopic control, the guidewire is withdrawn from the catheter until the proximal tip reaches the duodenum. The distance between finger and thumb and the distal margin of the catheter is the required length of the endoprosthesis.

Plastic stents are available in various widths (ranging from 5 to 12 Fr) and lengths (ranging from 5 to 19 cm).

Management of Plastic Stent Occlusion

A clogged plastic stent can be removed by means of a snare or dormia basket. It is important to keep the position of the endscope in line with the common bile duct. When a snare is used, the stent is caught in the snare and removed through the instrumentation channel of the endoscope. When a dormia basket is used, the stent is pulled close to the endoscope and both the endoscope and stent are withdrawn.

When massive tumor invasion is present in the duodenum and difficult stent exchange is anticipated because of a nonoptimal scope position, it can be helpful to leave the occluded stent in place and use it as a guide for common bile duct cannulation and introduction of a second stent.

Soehendra and coworkers[107] described a technique that enables the removal of a clogged stent while maintaining the original pathway to the bile duct. A ball-tip catheter is positioned at the distal end of the stent and the stent is cannulated with the guidewire. A Soehendra retriever is introduced over the guidewire and the tip is screwed into the distal end of the stent. Then, the retriever is pulled out along with the stent, leaving the guidewire in place.

SELF-EXPANDING METAL STENTS

For introduction of a self-expanding metal stent, a stiff guidewire is positioned through the stricture by standard techniques. The insertion device with the constrained stent is then inserted through the instrumentation channel over the guidewire. When the insertion device is in position, with the help of radiopaque markers, the prosthesis can be released by removing the outer catheter while keeping the inner catheter in place. Deployment follows gradually as the outer catheter is withdrawn and can be followed fluoroscopically. If deployment is not proceeding according to plan and repositioning is required, the expanding stent may be constrained again by pushing the outer catheter inward provided the point of no return has not yet been passed. This point may vary with stent type but may extend to 83% of total stent deployment and is indicated by a marker. Deployment reduces the length of the self-expanding metal Wallstent by about 30%. Therefore, it is important to constantly correct the position of the expanding stent under fluoroscopic control, which usually means that one has to pull the insertion device outward while deploying the stent.

When the expanding metal stent bridges the papilla, in the case of a distal stenosis, the endoscopic image is used to keep a fixed distance of about 1 cm between the papillary orifice and the distal margin of the stent.

Stent diameter expands to 8 to 10 mm, and the available deployed lengths are 40, 60, 80, and 100 mm.

In case of a complex hilar stricture in which both liver lobes are drained by two or more self-expanding endoprostheses, the procedure is as follows.[108] The procedure begins with the introduction of two stiff guidewires, one in each liver lobe. If appropriate, dilation of a stricture is performed over one of the guidewires. Then, a expanding metal stent is inserted over the guidewire into the left system and deployed. Finally, an expanding metal stent is inserted into the right system alongside the first stent and deployed under fluoroscopic control (Fig. 54–8).

Although technically difficult, it is also possible to insert a second self-expanding metal stent through the meshes of a former placed self-expanding stent.[109] In that case, a guidewire is introduced and the mesh is dilated using a balloon catheter before passing the second constrained stent and deploying it.

Management of Occlusion of a Self-Expanding Metal Stent

A self-expanding metal stent can be removed within the first 2 to 3 days after deployment by grasping it with a forceps or a snare. After this time the stent becomes embedded in the tumor tissue and cannot be extracted.

Stent obstruction is mainly due to tumor ingrowth through the interstices of the stent or overgrowth of the ends of the stent. Management of stent occlusion consists of placement of a polyethylene stent or a second self-expanding metal stent through the occluded self-expanding metal stent. Another strategy is mechanical cleaning by using a balloon and flushing, but this is only effective in case of sludge formation.

Intrahepatic Biliary Obstruction

Strictures at the level of the hepatic confluence account for about 20% of malignant bile duct obstruction and mainly consist of primary cholangiocarcinoma, gallbladder neoplasms, and metastatic spread to hilar nodes. Cholangiocarcinoma arising at the hilar level is also referred to as a Klatskin tumor and is classified according to the degree of involvement of the intrahepatic bile ducts[110] (Fig. 54–9). Stenting the proximal biliary tree is more challenging and is associated with lower success rates than stenting distal common bile duct stenosis. Drainage can be achieved either endoscopically (retrograde) or percutaneously (antegrade).

Procedure-induced cholangitis caused by contrast injection in undrained biliary branches is the main complication and occurs in up to 30%.[111-113] The current management strategy (depending on local services available) is first to attempt endoscopic drainage; when this strategy is not successful, percutaneous drainage offers additional opportunities.[114,115] When internal drainage fails, an external drain can be left *in situ*, minimizing the risk of cholangitis.

UNILATERAL OR BILATERAL DRAINAGE?

There is controversy whether to drain one or both liver lobes in Bismuth type II, III, and IV strictures. In Bismuth type I, one stent always suffices because the left and right ducts communicate and drainage will be complete. Theoretically, at least 25% of the liver volume must be drained to achieve biochemical improvement and relief of symptoms.[116] Concerns about unilateral drainage include the inability to relieve jaundice and the potential for bacterial contamination in the undrained lobe. Indeed, the worst treatment results seem to be obtained in patients with cholangiographic opacification of both lobes but drainage of only one.[117]

Recently, a prospective randomized trial compared unilateral with bilateral hepatic duct drainage.[118] Unilateral drainage was associated with a significantly higher rate of successful endoscopic stent insertion. Bilateral stent placement was associated with a significantly higher rate of complications because of the higher rate of early cholangitis. In per-protocol analysis the rate of successful drainage, complications, and mortality did not differ between the two groups. Magnetic resonance cholangiopancreatography (MRCP)-guided endoscopic stent placement in Bismuth III and IV malignancies was associated with a low morbidity and mortality in an uncontrolled study.[119] The intention was to place an unilateral stent in one of both lobes, guided by the MRCP picture, and to avoid entry and contrast injection in the contralateral lobe. In those patients in whom, by accident, guidewire entry (50%) or contrast injection (20%) occurred in the contralateral liver lobe, stents were placed bilaterally. This treatment strategy resulted in a very low cholangitis rate of only 6%. A recent study evaluated selective unilateral MRCP- or CT-targeted drainage, and no episodes of cholangitis were observed.[120]

The message seems to emerge that unilateral drainage is appropriate when unilateral cannulation and opacification has been achieved. If the contralateral lobe is (unintentionally) opacified or probed, it should also be drained to avoid cholangitis.

PLASTIC OR SELF-EXPANDING METAL STENT?

By design, expandable stents may be more suitable than plastic stents for draining hilar tumors. The stent lumen is much wider, and, more importantly, intrahepatic side branches can drain through the metal meshes. Indeed, self-expanding metal stents that were inserted via the percutaneous route showed a higher rate of treatment efficacy than plastic stents.[114,121] There are no randomized studies available comparing endoscopic and percutaneous insertion of self-expanding metal stents in hilar strictures.

Additional proof of the superiority of self-expanding metal stents over plastic stents is suggested by a retrospective series of patients with nonresectable hilar cholangiocarcinoma in whom, during stent treatment, plastic stents were replaced by metal expandable stents.[122] Successful palliation without the need for further biliary reintervention was achieved in most patients (69%).

A potential drawback of the placement of a metal stent is that, in the case of treatment failure, introduction of additional stents may become difficult. However, a technique for introducing a second stent through the wire mesh of the first stent has been described.[109]

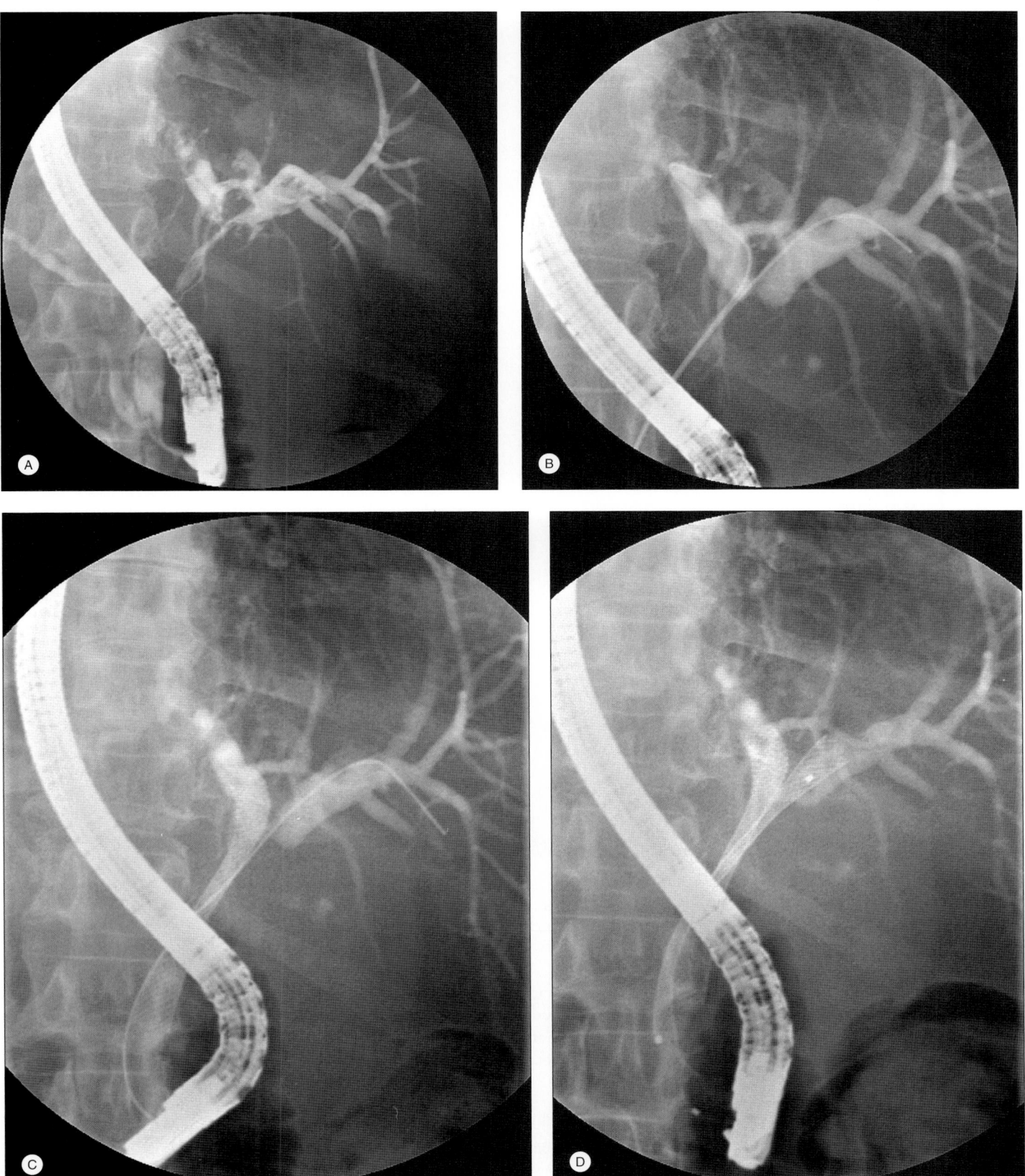

Figure 54–8. *A,* Klatskin type II tumor (unresectable because of vascular involvement). *B,* Guidewires inserted to both the left and right biliary system. *C,* A self-expanding metal stent has been inserted into the left system and deployed. *D,* Bilateral self-expanding metal stent drainage.

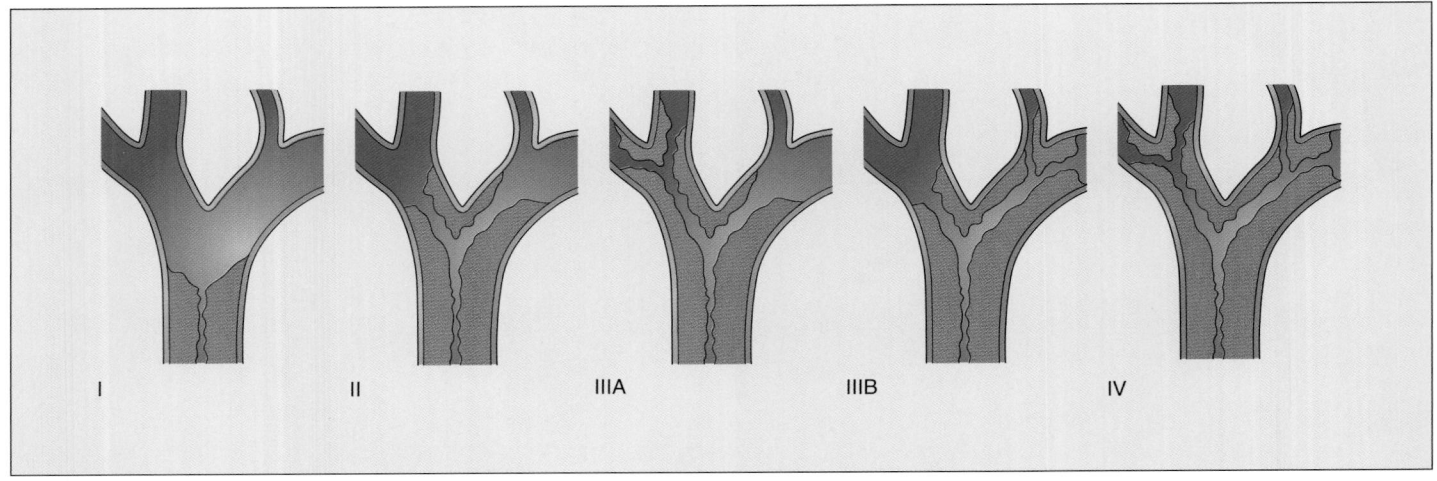

Figure 54–9. Bismuth classification. I: Stricture involving the common hepatic duct. II: Stricture involving both right and left hepatic duct. IIIA: Stricture extending proximally to the right secondary intrahepatic ducts. IIIB: Stricture extending proximally to the left secondary intrahepatic ducts. IV: Stricture involving secondary intrahepatic ducts bilaterally.

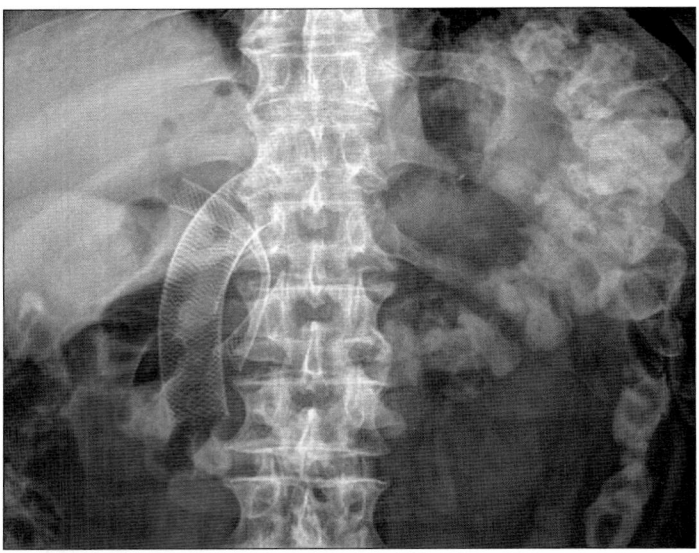

Figure 54–10. Pancreatic adenocarcinoma growing into the duodenum with a self-expanding metal stent (not yet fully deployed) in the biliary tract and a self-expanding metal stent in the duodenum.

Duodenal Stenosis

Duodenal stenosis resulting from pancreaticobiliary malignancies occurs in 10% to 20% of patients.[123] Presenting symptoms include nausea and vomiting resulting from gastric outlet obstruction. Usually, this is a late event and occurs in patients in poor general condition who have already received a biliary endoprosthesis.[124] Surgical bypass has a significant procedure-related mortality of up to 10% and related morbidity and prolonged hospital stay.[24,125,126] Endoscopic stenting for duodenal obstruction together with bile duct stenting may be an effective alternative.

Placement of duodenal stents has a high technical success rate without major procedure-related complications.[127–129] Stenting is carried out under simultaneous endoscopic and fluoroscopic control. Preliminary dilation of the duodenal stenosis can be performed by balloon dilation if necessary. Patients are usually able to tolerate a liquid diet immediately after stent placement. Full stent deployment may take a few days, during which time soft foods are allowed.

One study reported about simultaneous decompression of biliary and duodenal obstruction with similar success rates compared with duodenal stenting alone.[130] Because of the difficulty of accessing the biliary tree endoscopically through the mesh wall of a duodenal stent, an expanding metal biliary stent should preferably be placed before the duodenal stent is introduced (Fig. 54–10). If endoscopic biliary stenting fails, the remaining treatment options are percutaneous stenting, combined percutaneous and endoscopic management, or surgical bypass.

Postprocedural Care

General measures after conscious sedation include observation in a day care unit for several hours with monitoring of blood pressure and oxygen saturation.

When a patient develops fever post-ERCP, efforts should be made to obtain specimens for culture and administration of antibiotics should be started. If fever does not subside, the accuracy of biliary drainage should be reassessed and migration and early stent occlusion should be excluded. In the case of a complex malignant hilar stricture, it is important to check for undrained dilated intrahepatic segments and rule out abscesses by transabdominal ultrasound or CT. Depending on the findings, ERCP should be reattempted or percutaneous drainage achieved.

Complications

EARLY COMPLICATIONS

Early complications are defined as those that occur less than 1 week after the conclusion of the procedure. The rate of complications ranges between 5% and 10% for therapeutic ERCP with a mortality rate of up to 1%.[25,26,131] Cotton and coworkers[25] introduced a complication grading system in which complications are graded as mild, moderate, and severe, and these guidelines are still widely used.

The most frequent early complication is cholangitis, probably resulting from introduction of bacteria into the biliary tract during the procedure. This is reported in approximately 10% to 15% of patients in most series. It occurs more often after endoscopic procedures for complex hilar strictures when incomplete drainage is achieved. The same holds true for patients with primary sclerosing cholangitis. In these high-risk procedures, antibiotics should be administered prophylactically and continued for a few days after the procedure.

Post-ERCP pancreatitis occurs in about 5% to 7% of patients. It is defined as new-onset or increased abdominal pain lasting at least 24 hours after ERCP, with associated elevation in serum amylase or lipase to at least three to five times normal normal.[25,26,132] Most cases are mild, self-limiting, and only require intravenous fluids and gut rest. Serious cases may evolve into (infected) necrotizing pancreatitis with multiorgan failure.

The rate of postsphincterotomy bleeding is about 0.2% to 5% with an associated mortality rate less than 1%.[133] Bleeding is usually obvious immediately after sphincterotomy but can be delayed for hours or even several days. Most episodes of delayed bleeding are managed successfully by conservative measures and blood transfusions if the hemoglobin level drops significantly. Postsphincterotomy bleeding usually occurs at the apex of the sphincterotomy site and can be managed endoscopically with injection of epinephrine (adrenaline).

Retroperitoneal perforation occurs in fewer than 1% in most series. It may be caused by standard sphincterotomy, precut sphincterotomy, or guidewire manipulation. Most cases are diagnosed or suspected during ERCP. These perforations mostly heal with conservative measures and do not usually result in clinical symptoms.[134]

Conservative treatment measures consist of nil by mouth, antibiotic treatment, and nasogastric suction. It is estimated that about 20% to 30% of these patients will require surgery.

In cases of peritoneal perforation caused by the duodenoscope, prompt exploratory laparotomy, with repair or oversewing of the defect in the duodenal wall, is mandatory.[135]

LATE COMPLICATIONS

The primary late complication of stent placement is occlusion of the endoprosthesis, occurring in up to 50% of cases.[33,34] Clinically these patients present with a flulike syndrome with cholestasis, frank cholangitis, or jaundice. Treatment consists of exchange of the occluded stent or, in case of an occluded self-expanding metal stent, insertion of a polyethylene stent or second self-expanding metal stent (see management of plastic stent occlusion and management of self-expanding metal stent occlusion) through the obstructed expanding stent. Plastic stent migration, either proximally or distally, may occur in up to 10% of cases.[136]

Future Trends

PHOTODYNAMIC THERAPY

Photodynamic therapy (PDT) involves the administration of a photosensitizer, which is activated with a laser light and causes necrosis of the exposed tissue. Preliminary results suggest prolonged survival and stent patency for PDT in cholangiocarcinoma at the hilum.[137-139] Controlled trials are in progress. PDT cannot be combined with uncovered expanding stents, because PDT generates necrotic tumor tissue, which sloughs into and occludes the lumen.[140] However, replacement of a plastic stent by a self-expanding metal stent 1 month after PDT could be promising.[137]

DRUG-COATED BILIARY STENTS

Future prospects include development of chemotherapy-impregnated expanding stents. Covering biliary stents with chemotherapeutic agents, delivering chemotherapy directly to the tumor tissue, at least in theory should give protection against tumor ingrowth, overgrowth, or both. For optimal therapeutic effects, these drugs should be released over a longer period of time with good penetration in tissue and without systemic toxicity.

Carboplatin and paclitaxel have shown to inhibit cell proliferation in vitro.[141,142] Carboplatin-coated plastic stents have been used with promising preliminary results in a limited number of patients.[142] Further controlled trials are warranted.

Endoscopic Ultrasonography-Guided Plexus Neurolysis

Celiac plexus neurolysis can improve pain control in patients with pancreatic cancer. The injected agent usually includes a local anesthetic (bupivacaine or lidocaine) and a neurolytic (phenol or alcohol). A meta-analysis showed long-lasting benefit for 70% to 90% of patients; adverse effects were common but generally transient and mild.[143] For best results, it is recommended to perform celiac plexus neurolysis not too late in the course of the disease when pain has become unbearable. This is because the central effects of chronic pain lead to hypersensitization and unresponsiveness to antipain treatments. Endoscopic ultrasonography may reduce neurologic complications (because of the anterior approach) compared with the percutaneous technique, although no comparative studies have been performed.[144] Side effects of celiac plexus neurolysis are usually mild and include postprocedural pain and transient diarrhea.

REFERENCES

1. Ries LA, Wingo PA, Miller DS, et al: The annual report to the nation on the status of cancer, 1973–1997, with a special section on colorectal cancer. Cancer 88:2398–2424, 2000.
2. Michaud DS: The epidemiology of pancreatic, gallbladder, and other biliary tract cancers. Gastrointest Endosc 56(6 Suppl): S195–S200, 2002.
3. Warshaw AL, Fernandez-del Castillo C: Pancreatic carcinoma. N Engl J Med 326:455–465, 1992.
4. Rosewicz S, Wiedenmann B: Pancreatic carcinoma. Lancet 349:485–489, 1997.
5. Bismuth H, Castaing D, Traynor O: Resection or palliation: Priority of surgery in the treatment of hilar cancer. World J Surg 12:39–47, 1988.
6. Monson JR, Donohue JH, McEntee GP, et al: Radical resection for carcinoma of the ampulla of Vater. Arch Surg 126:353–357, 1991.
7. Bueno de Mesquita HB, Maisonneuve P, Moerman CJ, et al: Lifetime history of smoking and exocrine carcinoma of the pancreas: A population-based case-control study in The Netherlands. Int J Cancer 49:816–822, 1991.
8. Gold EB, Goldin SB: Epidemiology of and risk factors for pancreatic cancer. Surg Oncol Clin North Am 7:67–91, 1998.
9. Lowenfels AB, Maisonneuve P, Cavallini G, et al: Pancreatitis and the risk of pancreatic cancer. International Pancreatitis Study Group. N Engl J Med 328:1433–1437, 1993.
10. Lowenfels AB, Maisonneuve P, Whitcomb DC, et al: Cigarette smoking as a risk factor for pancreatic cancer in patients with hereditary pancreatitis. JAMA 286:169–170, 2001.
11. Ghadirian P, Lynch HT, Krewski D: Epidemiology of pancreatic cancer: An overview. Cancer Detect Prev 27:87–93, 2003.
12. Bergquist A, Ekbom A, Olsson R, et al: Hepatic and extrahepatic malignancies in primary sclerosing cholangitis. J Hepatol 36:321–327, 2002.
13. Okuda K, Nakanuma Y, Miyazaki M: Cholangiocarcinoma: Recent progress. Part 1: Epidemiology and etiology. J Gastroenterol Hepatol 17:1049–1055, 2002.
14. Lowenfels AB, Maisonneuve P, Boyle P, Zatonski WA: Epidemiology of gallbladder cancer. Hepatogastroenterology 46:1529–1532, 1999.
15. Mansfield JC, Griffin SM, Wadehra V, Matthewson K: A prospective evaluation of cytology from biliary strictures. Gut 40:671–677, 1997.
16. Jailwala J, Fogel EL, Sherman S, et al: Triple-tissue sampling at ERCP in malignant biliary obstruction. Gastrointest Endosc 51:383–390, 2000.
17. Howell DA, Beveridge RP, Bosco J, Jones M: Endoscopic needle aspiration biopsy at ERCP in the diagnosis of biliary strictures. Gastrointest Endosc 38:531–535, 1992.
18. Pugliese V, Conio M, Nicolo G, et al: Endoscopic retrograde forceps biopsy and brush cytology of biliary strictures: A prospective study. Gastrointest Endosc 42:520–526, 1995.
19. Ponchon T, Gagnon P, Berger F, et al: Value of endobiliary brush cytology and biopsies for the diagnosis of malignant bile duct stenosis: Results of a prospective study. Gastrointest Endosc 42:565–572, 1995.
20. Williams DB, Sahai AV, Aabakken L, et al: Endoscopic ultrasound guided fine needle aspiration biopsy: A large single centre experience. Gut 44:720–726, 1999.
21. Linder S, Blasjo M, Sundelin P, von Rosen A: Aspects of percutaneous fine-needle aspiration biopsy in the diagnosis of pancreatic carcinoma. Am J Surg 174:303–306, 1997.
22. Speer AG, Cotton PB, Russell RC, et al: Randomised trial of endoscopic versus percutaneous stent insertion in malignant obstructive jaundice. Lancet 2:57–62, 1987.
23. Andersen JR, Sorensen SM, Kruse A, et al: Randomised trial of endoscopic endoprosthesis versus operative bypass in malignant obstructive jaundice. Gut 30:1132–1135, 1989.
24. Smith AC, Dowsett JF, Russell RC, et al: Randomised trial of endoscopic stenting versus surgical bypass in malignant low bile duct obstruction. Lancet 344:1655–1660, 1994.
25. Cotton PB, Lehman G, Vennes J, et al: Endoscopic sphincterotomy complications and their management: An attempt at consensus. Gastrointest Endosc 37:383–393, 1991.
26. Freeman ML, Nelson DB, Sherman S, et al: Complications of endoscopic biliary sphincterotomy. N Engl J Med 335:909–918, 1996.
27. Ballinger AB, McHugh M, Catnach SM, et al: Symptom relief and quality of life after stenting for malignant bile duct obstruction. Gut 35:467–470, 1994.
28. Abraham NS, Barkun JS, Barkun AN: Palliation of malignant biliary obstruction: A prospective trial examining impact on quality of life. Gastrointest Endosc 56:835–841, 2002.
29. Lai EC, Mok FP, Fan ST, et al: Preoperative endoscopic drainage for malignant obstructive jaundice. Br J Surg 81:1195–1198, 1994.
30. Sewnath ME, Birjmohun RS, Rauws EA, et al: The effect of preoperative biliary drainage on postoperative complications after pancreaticoduodenectomy. J Am Coll Surg 192:726–734, 2001.
31. Martignoni ME, Wagner M, Krahenbuhl L, et al: Effect of preoperative biliary drainage on surgical outcome after pancreatoduodenectomy. Am J Surg 181:52–59, 2001.
32. Shepherd HA, Royle G, Ross AP, et al: Endoscopic biliary endoprosthesis in the palliation of malignant obstruction of the distal common bile duct: A randomized trial. Br J Surg 75:1166–1168, 1988.
33. Davids PH, Groen AK, Rauws EA, et al: Randomised trial of self-expanding metal stents versus polyethylene stents for distal malignant biliary obstruction. Lancet 340:1488–1492, 1992.
34. Knyrim K, Wagner HJ, Pausch J, Vakil N: A prospective, randomized, controlled trial of metal stents for malignant obstruction of the common bile duct. Endoscopy 25:207–212, 1993.
35. Coene PP, Groen AK, Cheng J, et al: Clogging of biliary endoprostheses: A new perspective. Gut 31:913–917, 1990.
36. Leung JW, Ling TK, Kung JL, Vallance-Owen J: The role of bacteria in the blockage of biliary stents. Gastrointest Endosc 34:19–22, 1988.
37. Speer AG, Cotton PB, Rode J, et al: Biliary stent blockage with bacterial biofilm. A light and electron microscopy study. Ann Intern Med 108:546–553, 1988.
38. Huibregtse K: Endoscopic Biliary and Pancreatic Drainage. Stuttgart, Georg Thieme, 1988.
39. Speer AG, Cotton PB, MacRae KD: Endoscopic management of malignant biliary obstruction: Stents of 10 French gauge are preferable to stents of 8 French gauge. Gastrointest Endosc 34:412–417, 1988.
40. Rey JF, Maupetit P, Greff M: Experimental study of biliary endoprosthesis efficiency. Endoscopy 17:145–148, 1985.
41. Pereira-Lima JC, Jakobs R, Maier M, et al: Endoscopic biliary stenting for the palliation of pancreatic cancer: Results, survival predictive factors, and comparison of 10-French with 11.5-French gauge stents. Am J Gastroenterol 91:2179–2184, 1996.

42. Kadakia SC, Starnes E: Comparison of 10 French gauge stent with 11.5 French gauge stent in patients with biliary tract diseases. Gastrointest Endosc 38:454–459, 1992.

43. Siegel JH, Pullano W, Kodsi B, et al: Optimal palliation of malignant bile duct obstruction: Experience with endoscopic 12 French prostheses. Endoscopy 20:137–141, 1988.

44. Scheeres D, O'Brien W, Ponsky L, Ponsky J: Endoscopic stent configuration and bile flow rates in a variable diameter bile duct model. Surg Endosc 4:91–93, 1990.

45. Leung JW, Del Favero G, Cotton PB: Endoscopic biliary prostheses: A comparison of materials. Gastrointest Endosc 31:93–95, 1985.

46. Huibregtse K, Tytgat GN: Palliative treatment of obstructive jaundice by transpapillary introduction of large bore bile duct endoprosthesis. Gut 23:371–375, 1982.

47. Dowidar N, Kolmos HJ, Matzen P: Experimental clogging of biliary endoprostheses. Role of bacteria, endoprosthesis material, and design. Scand J Gastroenterol 27:77–80, 1992.

48. Seitz U, Vadeyar H, Soehendra N: Prolonged patency with a new-design Teflon biliary prosthesis. Endoscopy 26:478–482, 1994.

49. Binmoeller KF, Seitz U, Seifert H, et al: The Tannenbaum stent: A new plastic biliary stent without side holes. Am J Gastroenterol 90:1764–1768, 1995.

50. Catalano MF, Geenen JE, Lehman GA, et al: 'Tannenbaum' Teflon stents versus traditional polyethylene stents for treatment of malignant biliary stricture. Gastrointest Endosc 55:354–358, 2002.

51. England RE, Martin DF, Morris J, et al: A prospective randomised multicentre trial comparing 10 Fr Teflon Tannenbaum stents with 10 Fr polyethylene Cotton–Leung stents in patients with malignant common duct strictures. Gut 46:395–400, 2000.

52. Terruzzi V, Comin U, De Grazia F, et al: Prospective randomized trial comparing Tannenbaum Teflon and standard polyethylene stents in distal malignant biliary stenosis. Gastrointest Endosc 51:23–27, 2000.

53. Sung JJ, Chung SC, Tsui CP, et al: Omitting side-holes in biliary stents does not improve drainage of the obstructed biliary system: A prospective randomized trial. Gastrointest Endosc 40:321–325, 1994.

54. Van Berkel AM, Boland C, Redekop WK, et al: A prospective randomized trial of Teflon versus polyethylene stents for distal malignant biliary obstruction. Endoscopy 30:681–686, 1998.

55. Van Berkel AM, van Marle J, van Veen H, et al: A scanning electron microscopic study of biliary stent materials. Gastrointest Endosc 51:19–22, 2000.

56. McAllister EW, Carey LC, Brady PG, et al: The role of polymeric surface smoothness of biliary stents in bacterial adherence, biofilm deposition, and stent occlusion. Gastrointest Endosc 39:422–425, 1993.

57. Jansen B, Goodman LP, Ruiten D: Bacterial adherence to hydrophilic polymer-coated polyurethane stents. Gastrointest Endosc 39:670–673, 1993.

58. Costamagna G, Mutignani M, Rotondano G, et al: Hydrophilic hydromer-coated polyurethane stents versus uncoated stents in malignant biliary obstruction: A randomized trial. Gastrointest Endosc 51:8–11, 2000.

59. Van Berkel AM, Bruno MJ, Bergman JJ, et al: A prospective randomized study of hydrophilic polymer-coated polyurethane versus polyethylene stents in distal malignant biliary obstruction. Endoscopy 35:478–482, 2003.

60. Leung JW, Liu Y, Cheung S, et al: Effect of antibiotic-loaded hydrophilic stent in the prevention of bacterial adherence: A study of the charge, discharge, and recharge concept using ciprofloxacin. Gastrointest Endosc 53:431–437, 2001.

61. Leung JW, Lau GT, Sung JJ, Costerton JW: Decreased bacterial adherence to silver-coated stent material: An in vitro study. Gastrointest Endosc 38:338–340, 1992.

62. Liu Q, Khay G, Cotton PB: Feasibility of stent placement above the sphincter of Oddi ('inside-stent') for patients with malignant biliary obstruction. Endoscopy 30:687–690, 1998.

63. Pedersen FM, Lassen AT, Schaffalitzky de Muckadell OB: Randomized trial of stent placed above and across the sphincter of Oddi in malignant bile duct obstruction. Gastrointest Endosc 48:574–579, 1998.

64. Leung JW, Liu YL, Desta TD, et al: In vitro evaluation of antibiotic prophylaxis in the prevention of biliary stent blockage. Gastrointest Endosc 51:296–303, 2000.

65. Sung JJ, Sollano JD, Lai CW, et al: Long-term ciprofloxacin treatment for the prevention of biliary stent blockage: A prospective randomized study. Am J Gastroenterol 94:3197–3201, 1999.

66. Ghosh S, Palmer KR: Prevention of biliary stent occlusion using cyclical antibiotics and ursodeoxycholic acid. Gut 35:1757–1759, 1994.

67. Barrioz T, Ingrand P, Besson I, et al: Randomised trial of prevention of biliary stent occlusion by ursodeoxycholic acid plus norfloxacin. Lancet 344:581–582, 1994.

68. Halm U, Schiefke I, Fleig WE, et al: Ofloxacin and ursodeoxycholic acid versus ursodeoxycholic acid alone to prevent occlusion of biliary stents: A prospective, randomized trial. Endoscopy 33:491–494, 2001.

69. Luman W, Ghosh S, Palmer KR: A combination of ciprofloxacin and Rowachol does not prevent biliary stent occlusion. Gastrointest Endosc 49(3 Pt 1):316–321, 1999.

70. Lee SP, Carey MC, LaMont JT: Aspirin prevention of cholesterol gallstone formation in prairie dogs. Science 211:1429–1431, 1981.

71. Smit JM, Out MM, Groen AK, et al: A placebo-controlled study on the efficacy of aspirin and doxycycline in preventing clogging of biliary endoprostheses. Gastrointest Endosc 35:485–489, 1989.

72. Sung JY, Shaffer EA, Lam K, et al: Hydrophobic bile salt inhibits bacterial adhesion on biliary stent material. Dig Dis Sci 39:999–1006, 1994.

73. Frakes JT, Johanson JF, Stake JJ: Optimal timing for stent replacement in malignant biliary tract obstruction. Gastrointest Endosc 39:164–167, 1993.

74. Prat F, Chapat O, Ducot B, et al: A randomized trial of endoscopic drainage methods for inoperable malignant strictures of the common bile duct. Gastrointest Endosc 47:1–7, 1998.

75. Matsuda Y, Shimakura K, Akamatsu T: Factors affecting the patency of stents in malignant biliary obstructive disease: Univariate and multivariate analysis. Am J Gastroenterol 86:843–849, 1991.

76. Lammer J: Biliary endoprostheses. Plastic versus metal stents. Radiol Clin North Am 28:1211–1222, 1990.

77. Carr-Locke D, Ball TJ, Conners PJ: Multicenter randomized trial of Wallstent biliary prosthesis versus plastic stents. Gastrointest Endosc 39:310–316, 1993.

78. Huibregtse K, Cheng J, Coene PP, et al: Endoscopic placement of expandable metal stents for biliary strictures—a preliminary report on experience with 33 patients. Endoscopy 21:280–282, 1989.

79. Bethge N, Wagner HJ, Knyrim K, et al: Technical failure of biliary metal stent deployment in a series of 116 applications. Endoscopy 24:395–400, 1992.

80. Lammer J, Hausegger KA, Fluckiger F, et al: Common bile duct obstruction due to malignancy: Treatment with plastic versus metal stents. Radiology 201:167–172, 1996.

81. Dumonceau JM, Cremer M, Auroux J, et al: A comparison of Ultraflex Diamond stents and Wallstents for palliation of distal malignant biliary strictures. Am J Gastroenterol 95:670–676, 2000.

82. Ahmad J, Siqueira E, Martin J, Slivka A: Effectiveness of the Ultraflex Diamond stent for the palliation of malignant biliary obstruction. Endoscopy 34:793–796, 2002.

83. Ferlitsch A, Oesterreicher C, Dumonceau JM, et al: Diamond stents for palliation of malignant bile duct obstruction: A prospective multicenter evaluation. Endoscopy 33:645–650, 2001.

84. Goldin E, Beyar M, Safra T, et al: A new self-expandable, nickel–titanium coil stent for esophageal obstruction: Preliminary report. Gastrointest Endosc 40:64–68, 1994.

85. Smits M, Huibregtse K, Tytgat G: Results of the new nitinol self-expandable stents for distal biliary structures. Endoscopy 27:505–508, 1995.

86. Rossi P, Bezzi M, Rossi M, et al: Metallic stents in malignant biliary obstruction: Results of a multicenter European study of 240 patients. J Vasc Interv Radiol 5:279–285, 1994.

87. Coons HG: Self-expanding stainless steel biliary stents. Radiology 170:979–983, 1989.

88. Irving JD, Adam A, Dick R, et al: Gianturco expandable metallic biliary stents: Results of a European clinical trial. Radiology 172:321–326, 1989.

89. Shah RJ, Howell DA, Desilets DJ, et al: Multicenter randomized trial of the spiral Z-stent compared with the Wallstent for malignant biliary obstruction. Gastrointest Endosc 57:830–836, 2003.

90. Bezzi M, Orsi F, Salvatori FM, et al: Self-expandable nitinol stent for the management of biliary obstruction: Long-term clinical results. J Vasc Interv Radiol 5:287–293, 1994.

91. Jaschke W, Klose KJ, Strecker EP: A new balloon-expandable tantalum stent (Strecker-Stent) for the biliary system: Preliminary experience. Cardiovasc Intervent Radiol 15:356–359, 1992.

92. Shim CS, Lee YH, Cho YD, et al: Preliminary results of a new covered biliary metal stent for malignant biliary obstruction. Endoscopy 30:345–350, 1998.

93. Isayama H, Komatsu Y, Tsujino T, et al: Polyurethane-covered metal stent for management of distal malignant biliary obstruction. Gastrointest Endosc 55:366–370, 2002.

94. Smits ME: New Developments in Endoscopic Biliary and Pancreatic Drainage [thesis]. Amsterdam, Thesis Publishers, 1995.

95. Prat F, Chapat O, Ducot B, et al: Predictive factors for survival of patients with inoperable malignant distal biliary strictures: A practical management guideline. Gut 42:76–80, 1998.

96. Kaassis M, Boyer J, Dumas R, et al: Plastic or metal stents for malignant stricture of the common bile duct? Results of a randomized prospective study. Gastrointest Endosc 57:178–182, 2003.

97. Pereira-Lima JC, Jakobs R, Maier M, et al: Endoscopic stenting in obstructive jaundice due to liver metastases: Does it have a benefit for the patient? Hepatogastroenterology 43:944–948, 1996.

98. Yeoh KG, Zimmerman MJ, Cunningham JT, Cotton PB: Comparative costs of metal versus plastic biliary stent strategies for malignant obstructive jaundice by decision analysis. Gastrointest Endosc 49:466–471, 1999.

99. Arguedas MR, Heudebert GH, Stinnett AA, Wilcox CM: Biliary stents in malignant obstructive jaundice due to pancreatic carcinoma: A cost-effectiveness analysis. Am J Gastroenterol 97:898–904, 2002.

100. Van Berkel AM, Bergman JJ, Waxman I, et al: Wallstents for metastatic biliary obstruction. Endoscopy 28:418–421, 1996.

101. Van den Hazel SJ, Speelman P, Dankert J, et al: Piperacillin to prevent cholangitis after endoscopic retrograde cholangiopancreatography. A randomized, controlled trial. Ann Intern Med 125:442–447, 1996.

102. Sauter G, Grabein B, Huber G, et al: Antibiotic prophylaxis of infectious complications with endoscopic retrograde cholangiopancreatography. A randomized controlled study. Endoscopy 22:164–167, 1990.

103. Harris A, Chan AC, Torres-Viera C, et al: Meta-analysis of antibiotic prophylaxis in endoscopic retrograde cholangiopan-creatography (ERCP). Endoscopy 31:718–724, 1999.

104. Motte S, Deviere J, Dumonceau JM, et al: Risk factors for septicemia following endoscopic biliary stenting. Gastroenterology 101:1374–1381, 1991.

105. Deviere J, Motte S, Dumonceau JM, et al: Septicemia after endoscopic retrograde cholangiopancreatography. Endoscopy 22:72–75, 1990.

106. Bruins SW, Schoeman MN, Disario JA, et al: Needle-knife sphincterotomy as a precut procedure: A retrospective evaluation of efficacy and complications. Endoscopy 28:334–339, 1996.

107. Soehendra N, Maydeo A, Eckmann B, et al: A new technique for replacing an obstructed biliary endoprosthesis. Endoscopy 22:271–272, 1990.

108. Dumas R, Demuth N, Buckley M, et al: Endoscopic bilateral metal stent placement for malignant hilar stenoses: Identification of optimal technique. Gastrointest Endosc 51:334–338, 2000.

109. Neuhaus H, Gottlieb K, Classen M: The 'stent through wire mesh technique' for complicated biliary strictures. Gastrointest Endosc 39:553–556, 1993.

110. Bismuth H, Corlette MB: Intrahepatic cholangioenteric anastomosis in carcinoma of the hilus of the liver. Surg Gynecol Obstet 140:170–178, 1975.

111. Deviere J, Baize M, de Toeuf J, Cremer M: Long-term follow-up of patients with hilar malignant stricture treated by endoscopic internal biliary drainage. Gastrointest Endosc 34:95–101, 1988.

112. Ducreux M, Liguory C, Lefebvre JF, et al: Management of malignant hilar biliary obstruction by endoscopy. Results and prognostic factors. Dig Dis Sci 37:778–783, 1992.

113. Polydorou AA, Cairns SR, Dowsett JF, et al: Palliation of proximal malignant biliary obstruction by endoscopic endoprosthesis insertion. Gut 32:685–689, 1991.

114. Stoker J, Lameris JS, van Blankenstein M: Percutaneous metallic self-expandable endoprostheses in malignant hilar biliary obstruction. Gastrointest Endosc 39:43–49, 1993.

115. Gordon RL, Ring EJ, LaBerge JM, Doherty MM: Malignant biliary obstruction: Treatment with expandable metallic stents–follow-up of 50 consecutive patients. Radiology 182:697–701, 1992.

116. Dowsett JF, Vaira D, Hatfield AR, et al: Endoscopic biliary therapy using the combined percutaneous and endoscopic technique. Gastroenterology 96:1180–1186, 1989.

117. Chang WH, Kortan P, Haber GB: Outcome in patients with bifurcation tumors who undergo unilateral versus bilateral hepatic duct drainage. Gastrointest Endosc 47:354–362, 1998.

118. De Palma GD, Galloro G, Siciliano S, et al: Unilateral versus bilateral endoscopic hepatic duct drainage in patients with malignant hilar biliary obstruction: Results of a prospective, randomized, and controlled study. Gastrointest Endosc 53:547–553, 2001.

119. Hintze RE, Abou-Rebyeh H, Adler A, et al: Magnetic resonance cholangiopancreatography-guided unilateral endoscopic stent placement for Klatskin tumors. Gastrointest Endosc 53:40–46, 2001.

120. Freeman ML, Overby C: Selective MRCP and CT-targeted drainage of malignant hilar biliary obstruction with self-expanding metallic stents. Gastrointest Endosc 58:41–49, 2003.

121. Wagner HJ, Knyrim K, Vakil N, Klose KJ: Plastic endoprostheses versus metal stents in the palliative treatment of malignant hilar biliary obstruction. A prospective and randomized trial. Endoscopy 25:213–218, 1993.

122. Cheng JL, Bruno MJ, Bergman JJ, et al: Endoscopic palliation of patients with biliary obstruction caused by nonresectable hilar cholangiocarcinoma: Efficacy of self-expandable metallic Wallstents. Gastrointest Endosc 56:33–39, 2002.

123. Watanapa P, Williamson RC: Surgical palliation for pancreatic cancer: Developments during the past two decades. Br J Surg 79:8–20, 1992.

124. Yates MR 3rd, Morgan DE, Baron TH: Palliation of malignant gastric and small intestinal strictures with self-expandable metal stents. Endoscopy 30:266–272, 1998.

125. Van der Schelling GP, van den Bosch RP, Klinkenbij JH, et al: Is there a place for gastroenterostomy in patients with advanced cancer of the head of the pancreas? World J Surg 17:128–132, 1993.

126. Wong YT, Brams DM, Munson L, et al: Gastric outlet obstruction secondary to pancreatic cancer: Surgical vs endoscopic palliation. Surg Endosc 16:310–312, 2002.

127. Nevitt AW, Vida F, Kozarek RA, et al: Expandable metallic prostheses for malignant obstructions of gastric outlet and proximal small bowel. Gastrointest Endosc 47:271–276, 1998.

128. Soetikno RM, Lichtenstein DR, Vandervoort J, et al: Palliation of malignant gastric outlet obstruction using an endoscopically placed Wallstent. Gastrointest Endosc 47:267–270, 1998.

129. Venu RP, Pastika BJ, Kini M, et al: Self-expandable metal stents for malignant gastric outlet obstruction: A modified technique. Endoscopy 30:553–558, 1998.

130. Kaw M, Singh S, Gagneja H: Clinical outcome of simultaneous self-expandable metal stents for palliation of malignant biliary and duodenal obstruction. Surg Endosc 17:457–461, 2003.

131. Masci E, Toti G, Mariani A, et al: Complications of diagnostic and therapeutic ERCP: A prospective multicenter study. Am J Gastroenterol 96:417–423, 2001.

132. Testoni PA, Bagnolo F: Pain at 24 hours associated with amylase levels greater than 5 times the upper normal limit as the most reliable indicator of post-ERCP pancreatitis. Gastrointest Endosc 53:33–39, 2001.

133. Foutch PG: A prospective assessment of results for needle-knife papillotomy and standard endoscopic sphincterotomy. Gastrointest Endosc 41:25–32, 1995.

134. Enns R, Eloubeidi MA, Mergener K, et al: ERCP-related perforations: Risk factors and management. Endoscopy 34:293–298, 2002.

135. Stapfer M, Selby RR, Stain SC, et al: Management of duodenal perforation after endoscopic retrograde cholangiopancreatography and sphincterotomy. Ann Surg 232:191–198, 2000.

136. Johanson JF, Schmalz MJ, Geenen JE: Incidence and risk factors for biliary and pancreatic stent migration. Gastrointest Endosc 38:341–346, 1992.

137. Dumoulin FL, Gerhardt T, Fuchs S, et al: Phase II study of photodynamic therapy and metal stent as palliative treatment for nonresectable hilar cholangiocarcinoma. Gastrointest Endosc 57:860–867, 2003.

138. Zoepf T, Jakobs R, Arnold JC, et al: Photodynamic therapy for palliation of nonresectable bile duct cancer—preliminary results with a new diode laser system. Am J Gastroenterol 96:2093–2097, 2001.

139. Ortner M: Photodynamic therapy for cholangiocarcinoma. J Hepatobiliary Pancreat Surg 8:137–139, 2001.

140. Shah SK, Mutignani M, Costamagna G: Therapeutic biliary endoscopy. Endoscopy 34:43–53, 2002.

141. Kalinowski M, Alfke H, Kleb B, et al: Paclitaxel inhibits proliferation of cell lines responsible for metal stent obstruction: Possible topical application in malignant bile duct obstructions. Invest Radiol 37:399–404, 2002.

142. Mezawa S, Homma H, Sato T, et al: A study of carboplatin-coated tube for the unresectable cholangiocarcinoma. Hepatology 32:916–923, 2000.

143. Eisenberg E, Carr DB, Chalmers TC: Neurolytic celiac plexus block for treatment of cancer pain: A meta-analysis. Anesth Analg 80:290–295, 1995.

144. Gunaratnam NT, Sarma AV, Norton ID, Wiersema MJ: A prospective study of EUS-guided celiac plexus neurolysis for pancreatic cancer pain. Gastrointest Endosc 54:316–324, 2001.

What's Next in Advanced Therapeutic Endoscopy?

Endoluminal Surgery

Pankaj J. Pasricha

Overview and Introduction

Flexible endoscopy has revolutionized gastroenterology, providing a noninvasive palliative or therapeutic approach to many conditions that had previously necessitated traditional surgery. In the 1st decade or so of its existence, endoscopy made rapid progress as "low-hanging fruit" procedures, such as polypectomy; stenting and simple hemostasis were readily incorporated by the development of relatively crude devices such as snares, plastic tubes, and heaters. At present, however, endoscopy appears to have reached the limits of what current flexible technology can achieve. Despite the introduction of more sophisticated versions of existing devices (e.g., the expandable metal stent), the scope and nature of endoscopic therapy has changed little, if at all, from its inception. Therefore, it is becoming increasingly clear that if luminal approaches are to successfully compete with minimally invasive laparoscopic approaches, fundamental changes in the way one uses current endoscopes will be necessary.

Current Methods of Endoscopic Therapy: A Conceptual Overview

Currently, the endoscope is used in two broad ways for therapeutic purposes: (1) in "ancillary" therapeutic endoscopy, it simply provides access for the accurate placement of a drug (e.g., botulinum toxin) or other device (e.g., a pacing electrode or capsule) and (2) in conventional therapeutic endoscopy, the endoscope plays a more critical role in the therapy itself and its form and function determine how much can be accomplished. Such endoscopic procedures can generally not produce the same anatomic outcome as surgery but rely on clever devices and techniques to *substitute* the surgical technique with an alternative procedure compatible with the endoscope's abilities. Thus, relief of biliary obstruction is provided not by recreating a surgical bypass but by simply placing a stent through the obstructed segment of the bile duct. Unfortunately, many of the more effective surgical techniques have not been easily substituted by conventional endoscopic means and conventional endoscopy.

The Next Frontier in Surgery: "Radical" Endoscopy

A long-held goal of therapeutic endoscopists has been to re-engineer endoscopy so that it can *reproduce* the anatomic outcomes of surgery. This concept justifies the term "radical" to describe this form of therapeutic endoscopy. In limited ways, these techniques are already being practiced for certain specific indications—examples include the near-heroic scale of mucosal resections for superficial gastric carcinomas in Japan. Even bolder and more ambitious procedures are now in various stages of experimentation; as outlined in Table 55–1 these cover a range of techniques and indications including widespread mucosal resection for Barrett's esophagus and gastric restriction (for obesity). Perhaps the most radical concept is that of transluminal endoscopic therapy: accessing the peritoneal cavity via a deliberate incision in the wall of the stomach or other organ and creating organ resections (e.g., appendectomy), anastomoses, or bypasses (e.g., gastrojejunostomy) (Fig. 55–1). Preliminary animal work and anecdotal human experience suggest that this procedure may not be as dangerous as traditional surgical dogma would lead one to believe. Clearly, if validated, this approach has the potential to completely transform abdominal surgery.

Limitations of Current Instruments

Although much excitement has been generated by the previously mentioned concepts, there are many substantial technological challenges that must be addressed before radical endoscopy becomes practical. Over several centuries, three techniques have evolved to become the mainstay of any surgical operation:

1. To precisely and cleanly cut tissue
2. Pari passu, to join cut edges of tissue back together in a manner that approximates the natural condition
3. To control the bleeding that accompanies the previously mentioned procedures

In general, flexible instruments have not yet been able to achieve comparable results with any of these techniques. The current

Table 55-1. Future and Current Endoscopic Procedures

Class of Procedure	Possible Future Procedure			Current Procedure	
	Type of Operation	Therapeutic Target		Conventional Endoscopy	Surgery
"Radical" endoscopy	Bile duct to gut anastomosis	Palliation of obstructive jaundice		Stents	Choledochointestinal anastomoses
	Gastroplasty	Restriction→obesity Cardioplasty→reflux disease		None Bulking, cautery of the LES	Banding Fundoplication
	Vascular suturing	Arterial bleeding		Cautery, injection	Surgical oversew
	Transluminal procedures	Organ resection (appendix, gallbladder, etc.) Gut-to-gut anastomoses Palliation of obstruction Obesity Adhesiolysis		None Endoluminal stents None None	Laparoscopic removal Resection and or bypass Gastrojejunal bypass Laparoscopic or open lysis
"Ancillary" endoscopy	Site-specific delivery of biologicals	Uncomplicated peptic ulcer Inflammatory bowel disease Cancer (adjuvant)		None None Ablation techniques	Not indicated Various Various
	Electrode or other stimulating device	Motility disorders		None	None

LES, lower esophageal sphincter.
From Pasricha PJ: The future of therapeutic endoscopy. Clin Gastroenterol Hepatol 2:286–289, 2004.

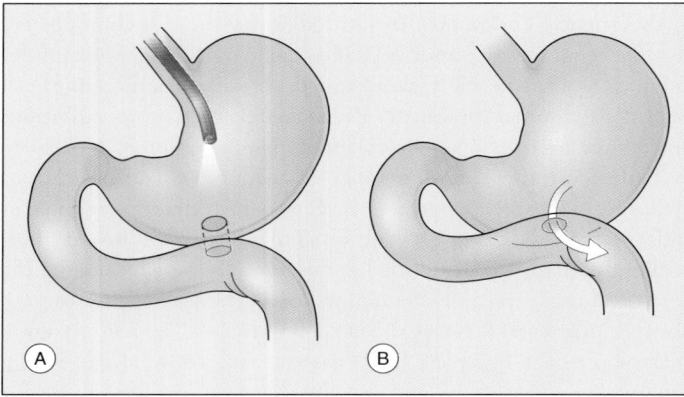

Figure 55-1. Conceptualization of an endoscopically created gastrojejunal anastomosis.

endoscope is constrained by its flexibility and small diameter, which ironically are the two factors most responsible for its success in providing quick and safe access to the gastrointestinal (GI) tract. The net result is that the endoscope itself is incapable of providing an adequate convergence of forces on a given point, a concept called triangulation. Although endoscopic instruments such as the needle knife and the sphincterotome provide good cutting, their use is limited to relatively few applications in which the tissue is relatively fixed and the incision is small (e.g., sphincterotomy). When surgeons cut, the target field is held stationary with various accessories and the scalpel applied with great precision with respect to location and force. During flexible endoscopy, however, the target tissue is constantly moving because of respiration and intrinsic motility.

The biggest unmet challenge to flexible endoscopy is that of tissue anastomosis. The traditional surgical techniques for achieving this require either sewing or stapling or some combination of both. However, these are not simple to transfer to the flexible endoscopy

field in which an inherent limitation is the amount of force that can be exerted through a flexible biopsy channel, usually in the order of a tenth of a kilogram or a few ounces. By contrast, the surgeon's hands exert forces of a magnitude 10 times or more when wielding a suturing needle. Attempts at incorporating both stapling and suturing have been made in the past and are the focus of many research and development efforts; current and planned embodiments, however, go through the biopsy channel and typically require the use of a relatively long rigid piece affixed to the end of the scope, limiting both the visibility and maneuverability.

Finally, hemostasis in endoscopy is usually a simple, relatively blind thermal coaptation method and is not useful for large vessels that are completely severed. This is a major factor limiting the adoption of more aggressive excisional methods in GI endoscopy. Although clips and elastic bands have been developed, they are unreliable for this purpose because of problems such as lack of adequate penetration or strength, imprecision, and ease of slippage.

For radical endoscopy to work, these obstacles have to be overcome by innovations in the fundamental way endoscopes are designed and in a conceptual shift in thinking: one in which the endoscope itself is limited to its primary role of visualization, with the remainder of the apparatus performing complex multidimensional movements, perhaps robotically assisted. Such a conceptual instrument is illustrated in Figure 55–2.

Other Considerations in the Push for Endoscopic Surgery

The reality of today's environment is that most of the costs of research and development for new medical devices are borne by industry. Consequently, market forces play a major role in determining which devices will eventually make it to practice and which

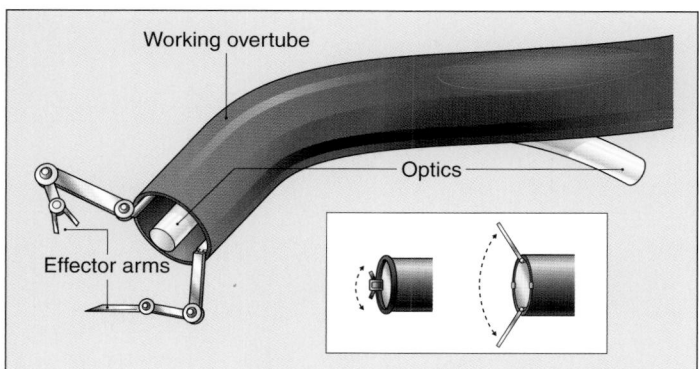

Figure 55-2. A possible configuration for the future "radical" endoscope. Note that the optics occupy a relatively minor portion of the instrument, the bulk of which is devoted to therapeutic tools that can perform traditional surgical tasks such as cutting and suturing. The inset shows how the proposed configuration of this instrument *(bottom)* allows for much more effective triangulation (see text for details) than currently used instruments *(top)*. (From Pasricha PJ: The future of therapeutic endoscopy. Clin Gastroenterol Hepatol 2:286–289, 2004.)

will remain unfulfilled promises despite the best intentions of the inventor. From this perspective, the success of a device or procedure can be seen as being dependent on at least two of three critical components: felt need, simplicity, and efficacy. Procedures that target indications for which highly successful therapies already exist have to score very highly with respect to both simplicity and efficacy. This may be one reason why endoscopic antireflux procedures have not yet met the initial expectations. Conversely, procedures aimed at disorders that are not currently treatable may succeed even with modest efficacy, as long as they are simple and convenient to perform. Examples would include procedures that target functional bowel disease and chronic pain.

Conclusions

Technological developments in endoscopy, particularly in radical procedures, will proceed rapidly in the next few years. These developments will not only introduce exciting new therapies for patients but also have profound implications for our specialty. A proper understanding of these trends in endoscopic technology is necessary for anticipation and preparation of the many challenges that they will bring.

Bioabsorbable Stents

Elizabeth Rajan

Introduction

Gastrointestinal stents have been in use for several decades for the management of gastrointestinal luminal obstruction. Historically, the word *stent* is derived from the name of an English dentist, Dr. Charles T. Stent, who, in 1856, developed a plastic dental compound for obtaining alveolar impressions of edentulous subjects.[1]

Gastrointestinal luminal obstruction and strictures are currently treated using self-expanding metal stents or fixed-diameter plastic stents. Self-expanding metal stents have several well-recognized limitations that include migration and occlusion from tumor ingrowth and epithelial hyperplasia necessitating stent replacement.[2] Nonetheless, these stents provide adequate palliation for patients with a limited life expectancy. Self-expanding metal stents are generally nonremovable, permanent devices and thus are considered unsuitable for benign disease. Fixed-diameter plastic stents are primarily used in benign biliary or pancreatic ductal obstruction. These stents often require frequent exchanges because of bacterial accumulation that forms a biofilm leading to early stent occlusion or cholangitis. The use of plastic stents for benign enteral obstruction is usually not advocated because of awkward delivery systems, associated high complication rate, and tendency to migrate. There is no ideal stent available for the treatment of benign disease.

The advent of bioabsorbable stent technology provides an important alternative for the management of benign luminal obstruction and strictures. The foreseeable advantages of a self-expanding bioabsorbable stent would include nonpermanence, large inner diameter with durable patency, continuous dilatation for 3 to 6 months, and spontaneous bioabsorption over a fixed duration. Furthermore, there is a potential role for impregnation of these self-limited stents with pharmaceuticals such as antineoplastic, anti-inflammatory, and antimicrobials for local drug delivery.

Most research on bioabsorbable stents has been with urologic and cardiovascular applications.

Bioabsorbable Stent Technology

The terms bioabsorbable and biodegradable are used interchangeably. Bioabsorbable defines a material and its end products that are truly absorbed into the body, whereas biodegradable refers to materials and their end products that are merely broken down but not absorbed. However, in practice, stents manufactured from bioabsorbable materials undergo a degree of biodegradation.

The early medical application of bioabsorbable materials was the use of sutures in the early 1970s.[3,4] Since then, bioabsorbable implants have been developed for various applications such as orthopedics, urology, cardiology, and gastrointestinal endoscopy. Polylactide, polyglycolide, and their copolymers have been used in bone fracture treatment for over a decade.[5] Such polymers are used as components of surgical sutures, coronary stents, urethral stents, clips and meshes, and bone prostheses for fracture fixation.[4,6–11]

The two polymers widely used for stent manufacture are polylactide and polyglycolide. Experience with polylactide, polyglycolide, and their copolymers has shown these materials to be biocompatible, toxicologically acceptable, and immunologically inert.[12] These synthetic materials have the added advantages of lot-to-lot uniformity and source of supply. When the stent is deployed, body heat and water degrades the polymer or copolymer into lactic acid and/or glycolic acid, which then enter the Krebs cycle and are broken down to carbon dioxide and water. Other stent materials using natural agents such as cat gut collagen and fibrin were of limited utility because of inadequate radial strength.

The mechanical properties and degradation kinetics of bioabsorbable polymers can be tailored to the specific needs by adjusting characteristics such as chemical composition, structural configuration, molecular weight, and sterilization process. Time of absorption of a stent can be modified by multiple factors such as choice of basic molecule with which the stent is manufactured, selection of mixture of polymers, crystallinity, shape, site of implantation, temperature, and pH.[10,13] Time to anticipated strength loss is different (approximately 3–6 months depending on stent material) than time to anticipated mass loss (i.e., complete absorption); time to anticipated mass loss is generally longer (approximately 18–24 months depending again on stent composition). The degradation products and degradation rates of several polymers have been reported.[14] Rates of degradation vary substantially ranging from 100% in 2 to 3 months for materials such as poly D,L-lactide/glycolide copolymer, which has 85% lactide and 15% glycolide, to 20% or less degradation rate over 6 months for polyhydroxybutyrate/hydroxyvalerate copolymer with 22% valerate.[8,11]

Poly-L-lactide has the longest biodegradation time of the basic molecules[13,15] Lactic acid has an asymmetrically substituted carbon atom and can exist in two enantiomeric forms: L(+) and D(–) lactic acid. The two enantiomers differ from each other significantly in their rate of biodegradation.[7]

Bioabsorbable polymers generally erode by two methods of hydrolysis.[12] One method is homogeneous or bulk degradation in which erosion occurs simultaneously throughout the entire polymer. Hydrophilic and noncrystalline polymers primarily degrade in this way. The other method is heterogeneous or surface degradation in which erosion occurs only on the surface of the polymer. Hydrophobic polymers and highly crystalline polymers primarily undergo surface erosion. Poly-L-lactide is an example of a highly crystalline polymer.

Initial bioabsorbable stent iterations exhibited poor compressibility into a delivery device and the need for balloon expansion following stent deployment were problematic concerns that needed to be addressed before clinical application. Textile manufacturing techniques such as braiding and knitting provided solutions allowing for improved stent flexibility and compressibility.[4,15] Now, with the manufacture of self-expanding bioabsorbable stents, the need for balloon expansion following stent deployment should be minimized or eliminated. Stent expansion rate and speed depend on several factors including stent material, internal arrangement of molecular chains, diameter of stent wire, and processing conditions.[6,16] Stents are stable at room temperature and expansion occurs at body temperature. The level at which expansion will stop also depends on similar factors such as material, crystallinity, and temperature.[17] Expansion rate is generally higher with more crystalline materials such as poly-L-lactide. The challenge lies in designing a stent that is compressible, self-expanding, and yet able to maintain significant radial force over a period of time (6 months or more) and that is eventually absorbed.

To ensure that bioabsorbable stents will not lose their radial strength before healing has occurred, it is important to determine how the bioabsorption process affects the stent mechanical properties *in vitro*. The bioabsorption mechanism for polylactide and polyglycolide polymers is mainly hydrolytic. Authors either have found no differences between *in vitro* and *in vivo* degradation or have reported faster *in vivo* degradation.[5,18,19] These findings have been explained by the cellular and enzymatic activity affecting implanted devices. Although it remains unclear how *in vitro* findings would correlate with *in vivo* results for a given implantation site, *in vitro* testing simulating the clinical environment is essential and should be used as a guideline for planning clinical studies.

Drug impregnation of bioabsorbable stents is a further appeal of these stents. However, drugs in high doses have been reported to reduce the mechanical properties of a stent significantly. This deterioration can be explained by the incompatibility between the drug and polymer phase or the inhibition of polymer crystallization following incorporation of the drug.[20] Studies will be needed to define the relationship between varying drug concentrations and mechanical properties of bioabsorbable stents.

These multiple properties can be used to engineer the ideal stent for specific clinical indications, from fast absorbing self-expanding stents used to keep surgical anastomosis patent for several weeks to longer lasting stents for refractory strictures.

Clinical and Animal Studies

Freeman[21] reported on the preliminary results of a multicenter clinical study using a bioabsorbable biliary stent for the palliation of malignant biliary obstruction. The bioabsorbable stent used was a biliary Wallstent manufactured by Boston Scientific Corporation, Natick, MA. The delivery system was 11-Fr and stent deployment was similar to the wire mesh Wallstent. Biliary sphincterotomy was initially performed and the delivery system passed through the stricture. The outer sheath was withdrawn and the stent deployed (Fig. 56–1A and B). The radial force of these stents was lower than metal stents and thus in this study a poststent deployment balloon dilatation was required, which was reported to result in luminal diameters comparable to metal stents (Fig. 56–1B and C). Incorrectly positioned stents could be easily removed by pulling the stent through the endoscope channel using a snare, a maneuver not possible with metal stents. Preliminary clinical data published on 51 patients showed patency in some stents in excess of 9 months.

Fry and Fleischer[22] described the first placement of a biodegradable esophageal stent in the United States for a refractory benign esophageal stricture. A prototype AB Esophacoil (Fig. 56–2) made of a single wire of poly L-lactide (Instent, Eden Prairie, MN) was studied. The stent was tightly wrapped on an introducer catheter with an external diameter of 9 mm. The stent was 10 cm in length, and no foreshortening was reported following deployment. Full expansion of the coil provided a 16-mm internal diameter. The introducing catheter had radiopaque markers facilitating accurate placement, but the stent was completely radiolucent. At 6 weeks, this patient experienced a sudden return of dysphagia. Endoscopy showed a collapsed proximal stent that would not allow passage of the endoscope. Barium swallow and computed tomography (CT) scan showed that the proximal 25% of the stent had fractured and collapsed under the force of the tightest part of the stricture. The stent was removed endoscopically in a piecemeal fashion using an overtube and rat-tooth grasping forceps. Remodeling of the esophagus had not occurred in the 6 weeks, and dysphagia recurred following stent removal. The authors speculate that it would take 6 months or more to remodel esophageal strictures. The projected stent biologic life was 3 to 6 months, and the projected time to loss of mechanical strength was 4 to 8 weeks.

Goldin and coworkers[23] published an abstract on their experience with a bioabsorbable esophageal stent (InStent Inc). Five self-expanding poly-L-lactide stents were inserted: four for peptic strictures and the other following nasogastric tube trauma. The first three patients had recurrent dysphagia after 2 to 3 weeks. The authors report that the remaining two stents had wires that were stronger; thus, patients were still asymptomatic at 2 months.

A preclinical study conducted by Ginsberg and colleagues[24] looked at a new bioabsorbable biliary stent (Fig. 56–3A) in a porcine model. BioStent (Bionx Implants, Blue Bell, PA) is composed of a polylactide copolymer of 4% D-lactide and 96% L-lactide (96PLA). D-lactide was added to decrease the crystallinity and so accelerate the absorption rate. The polymer filaments were manufactured in a braided configuration and the stent was reinforced with nonbioabsorbable elastomeric axial runners to improve the radial expansion force. To make the stents radiopaque, barium sulfate (~20% weight) was mixed with the 96PLA copolymer.

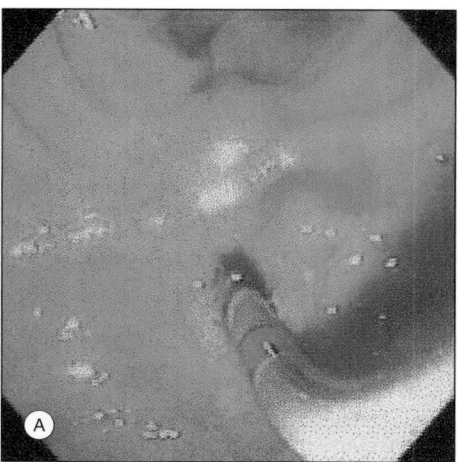
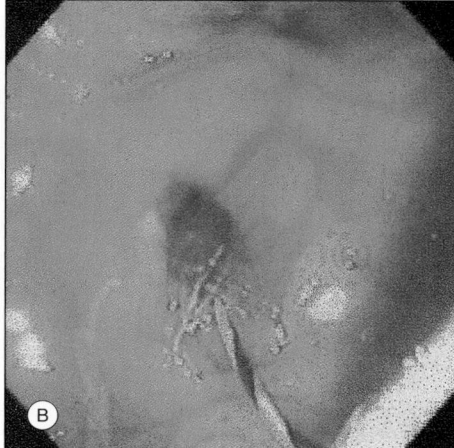
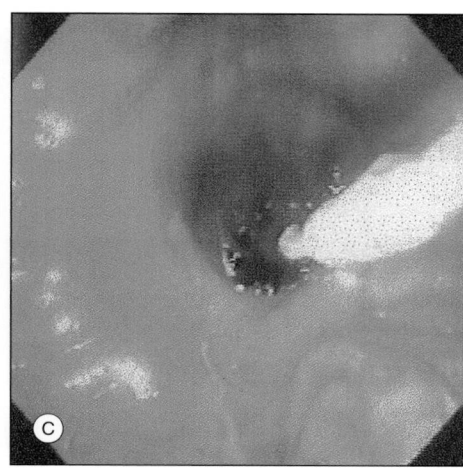
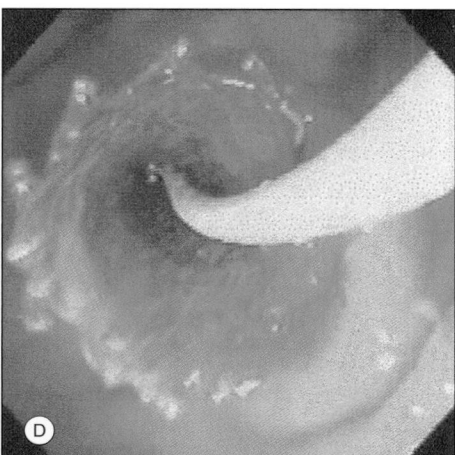

Figure 56–1. *A* and *B*, Initial deployment of bioabsorbable Wallstent. *C* and *D*, Endoscopic view postdilatation of bioabsorbable Wallstent. (From Freeman ML: Bioabsorbable stents for gastrointestinal endoscopy. Tech Gastrointest Endosc 3:120–125, 2001.)

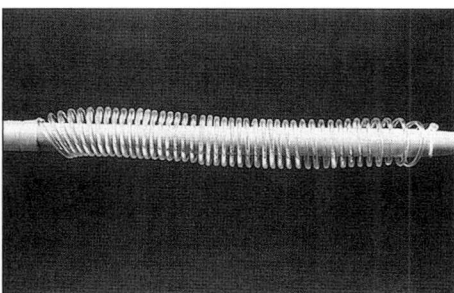

Figure 56–2. AB-Esophacoil on introducer, before winding tightly. (From Fry SW, Fleischer DE: Management of a refractory benign esophageal stricture with a new biodegradable stent. Gastrointest Endosc 45:179–182,1997.)

Stents had a 10-mm diameter and 50-mm length with a 12-Fr delivery device.

The accuracy and ease of stent delivery and deployment, radial expansion, and radiologic visualization were studied in eight animals with healthy bile ducts. Stent function and biotolerance was assessed by cholangiography, serum bilirubin, and histopathology at 2, 4, 6, and 12 months. Results showed that the stents were delivered without need for biliary sphincterotomy and were deployed easily and accurately. Good immediate stent expansion

and radiographic visualization were reported. Stent expansion was rated as 50% to 75% in six animals and greater than 75% in two animals (Fig. 56–3B). At follow-up, stents were functionally patent up to 9 months. Although filling defects were noted to be common at cholangiography, serum bilirubin was normal and animals were clinically asymptomatic. The authors suggest that the observed functional patency may be accounted by bile flow around the exterior of the stent. Histopathologic analysis showed normal bile duct epithelium with no stent impression marks and no stent induced inflammation or epithelial hyperplasia (Fig. 56–3C and D). There was no endothelialization, that is, stent integration into the bile duct lamina propria. The absence of epithelial integration and hyperplasia, a major cause of occlusion for self-expanding metal stents, is promising. These stents were deployed proximal to the ampulla and a concern voiced by the authors is the question of spontaneous migration for stents placed across the ampulla.

Preliminary preclinical studies are also currently under way on the efficacy and feasibility of bioabsorbable esophageal stents. At present, there are no commercially available bioabsorbable stents for use in gastrointestinal endoscopy.

Potential Clinical Applications

Placement of bioabsorbable stents across benign biliary or pancreatic strictures would serve as an important alternative to the current

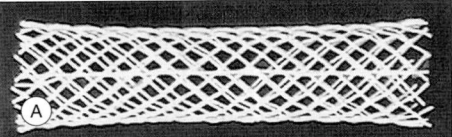
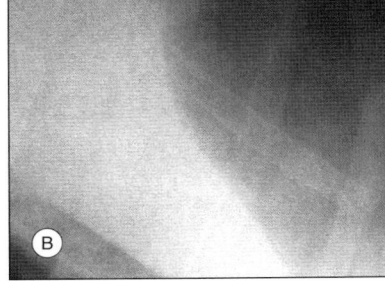
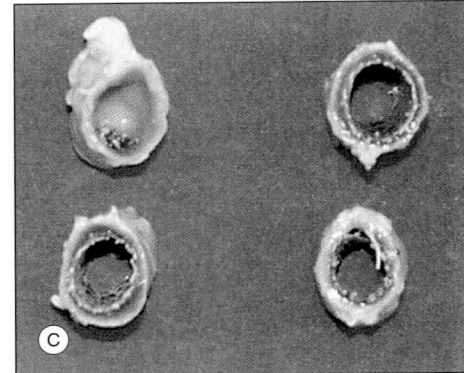
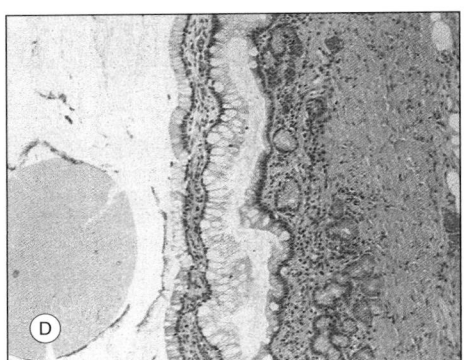

Figure 56–3. *A,* BioStent self-expanding bioabsorbable biliary stent consists of self-reinforced PLA filaments configured in a braided structure with four-quadrant elastomeric axial runners to improve stent diameter recovery and radial force. *B,* Immediate postdeployment stent is readily seen radiographically and is 50% to 75% of fully expanded diameter. *C,* Cross sections of common bile duct with fully expanded and patent stent at 4-month necropsy gross inspection. Note absence of stent integration into the bile duct wall. *D,* 4-month histopathology: normal bile duct epithelium with no stent impression marks, no integration, and no stent-induced inflammation or epithelial hyperplasia; a fragment of stent material is left in the lumen. (From Ginsberg G, Cope C, Shah J, et al: In vivo evaluation of a new bioabsorbable self-expanding biliary stent. Gastrointest Endosc 58:777–784, 2003.)

practice of repeated dilatation, frequent placement of single or multiple plastic stents that commonly occlude, and surgery. Sealing leaks from biliary or pancreatic ducts or sphincters and prevention of restenosis following endoscopic sphincterotomies or surgical sphincteroplasties would be further applications. Retroperitoneal perforation postendoscopic biliary sphincterotomy is traditionally managed conservatively with nasobiliary tubes or surgical drainage. Bioabsorbable stents could close the leak and prevent retroperitoneal contamination. Metal stents are not recommended for benign disease because of permanency, given that long-term safety of such indwelling devices remain unestablished, and potential interference with future surgery.

Bioabsorbable stents would also be the treatment of choice for long-term stenting of benign luminal obstruction or strictures of the esophagus, pylorus, small bowel, and colon. Such strictures would include peptic esophageal strictures, Crohn's strictures, and post-surgical and postradiation strictures. Surgical resection has been the traditional approach to strictures that remain refractory to medication or repeated dilatation. Their use can also be extended to include malignant strictures treated with chemoradiation before surgery and as a temporary bridge in patients in whom resectability is unclear.

Other potential uses include routine prophylactic stenting of surgical anastomoses with a high propensity to stricture such as hepaticojejunostomy, choledochocholedochostomy at orthotopic liver transplantation, and esophagogastrostomy; palliation of strictures suspicious for malignancy without tissue diagnosis; and treatment of persistent fistulas such as tracheoesophageal fistulas.

With the increasing use of endoscopic mucosal resection for removal of premalignant tissue, the prophylactic use of bioabsorb-

able stents in widespread or circumferential endoscopic mucosal resection is particularly significant.[25] The major concern with a circumferential resection is postprocedural stricture formation. Placement of a bioabsorbable stent immediately postprocedure could potentially minimize or eliminate this complication especially in diseases such as Barrett's esophagus with high grade dysplasia for which many patients undergo an esophagectomy.

The potential clinical applications of bioabsorbable stents can be found in Table 56–1.

Potential Benefits and Limitations

The predominant appeal of bioabsorbable stents is the nonpermanence and complete absorption over a predetermined period. This precludes the need for stent removal and eliminates the concern over long-term complications associated with nonremovable devices. The self-expanding component of the stent provides a large internal diameter for prolonged patency. These stents also do not cause imaging artifact.

The use of bioabsorbable stents for palliation of malignant strictures, for which most patients have a limited life expectancy, will likely be determined by cost savings when compared with self-expanding metal stents. Nonetheless, its use would still be preferred over metal stents when there is an indeterminate etiology or when surgery is considered.

The challenges faced by recent iterations of bioabsorbable stents have been suboptimal stent expansion requiring balloon dilatation and insufficient radial force to maintain stent patency. Stent migration is a further problem especially when an adequate tumor

Table 56–1. Potential Clinical Applications of Bioabsorbable Stents

Biliary and Pancreatic Ducts
Benign strictures
Indeterminate strictures
Leaks from biliary and pancreatic ducts or sphincters
Prevention of restenosis of endoscopic sphincterotomies and surgical sphincteroplasties
Retroperitoneal perforation postendoscopic biliary sphincterotomy
Pancreatic cyst-gastrostomies

Esophageal, Pyloric, Small Bowel, and Colon
Benign strictures
Indeterminate strictures
Malignant strictures treated with chemoradiation prior to surgery
Fistulas (e.g., tracheoesophageal fistulas)

Prophylactic Stenting
Surgical anastomoses (e.g., hepaticojejunostomy, choledochocholedochostomy at orthotopic liver transplant, esophagogastrostomy)
Widespread or circumferential endoscopic mucosal resection (e.g., Barrett's esophagus with high grade dysplasia)

shelf does not exist, as in benign strictures. These issues are being addressed with the manufacture of the next generation of stents.

Future of Bioabsorbable Stent Technology

Bioabsorbable polymers are promising new materials. The use of bioabsorbable stents in gastrointestinal endoscopy is an emerging and exciting technology. The ideal stent should provide adequate mechanical support to the wall, maintain luminal patency during healing, and after healing spontaneously bioabsorb into the body. Furthermore, the ideal stent should have a noncumbersome delivery system, be easy to deploy, and preferably be deployed through the working channel of the endoscope. The merits and modifications of such stents are currently being studied to facilitate clinical use.

Interest has accordingly shifted to the local administration of potentially useful drugs at disease sites using bioabsorbable stents. Local delivery poses the theoretical advantage of avoiding adverse systemic effects while maintaining sustained release and high local concentrations of drug. Bioabsorbable stents have the advantage of gradual, sustained, local drug delivery over a finite period. Delivery of potential drugs includes antimicrobials, cytotoxic drugs to tumors, hormones, and more ambitious local delivery of cellular gene therapy. Polymers for drug delivery to targeted organs can degrade by bulk erosion; thus, the potential for dose dumping with large fluctuations in local drug concentrations would be a concern that will need to be studied. The precedent of using bioabsorbable stents for drug delivery has already been established. Wei and colleagues[26] used D,L-lactic acid to evaluate kanamycin release in rabbit femurs; this polymer degraded in 9 weeks with adequate antibiotic concentrations up to 6 weeks after implantation. A more recent study by Rutledge and coworkers[27] showed the effectiveness of antibiotic impregnated bioabsorbable polymers in the treatment of osteomyelitis in rabbits. Yamawaki and colleagues[28] incorporated an antiproliferative agent into a poly-L-lactic acid coronary stent that inhibited the activity of tyrosine kinase. This study showed that neointimal formation was significantly less at the sites where the poly-L-lactic acid stent was loaded with the specific inhibitor. Ye

and coworkers[29] demonstrated the successful transfer and expression of a nuclear-localizing reporter gene in cells within the arterial wall of rabbits after implantation of biodegradable polymer stents impregnated with recombinant adenovirus carrying that gene. The possibility of transferring genes that code for key proteins in the central regulatory pathways of cell proliferation in the gastrointestinal tract using biodegradable stents as vehicles is exciting. The use of bioabsorbable materials undoubtedly represents a new and promising future in the field of therapeutic gastrointestinal endoscopy. Much of current bioabsorbable stent technology is proprietary. Its impact on the future of stent-related therapy remains to be proven through clinical trials.

REFERENCES

1. Sterioff S: Etymology of the world "stent." Mayo Clin Proc 72:377–379, 1997.
2. Baron TH: Expandable metal stents for the treatment of cancerous obstruction of the gastrointestinal tract. N Engl J Med 344:1681–1687, 2001.
3. Tormala P, Pohjonen T, Rokkanen P: Bioabsorbable polymers: Materials technology and surgical applications. Proc Inst Mech Eng 212:101–111, 1998.
4. Nuutinen JP, Valimaa T, Clerc C, et al: Mechanical properties and in vitro degradation of bioresorbable knitted stents. J Biomater Sci Polym Ed 13:1313–1323, 2002.
5. Rokkanen P: Current clinical use of absorbable fracture fixation devices. Ann Chir Gynaecol 80:243–244, 1991.
6. Laaksovirta S, Talja M, Valimaa T, et al: Expansion and bioabsorption of the self-reinforced lactic and glycolic acid copolymer prostatic spiral stent. J Urol 166:919–922, 2001.
7. Isotalo T, Talja M, Hellstrom P, et al: A double-blind, randomized, placebo-controlled pilot study to investigate the effects of finasteride combined with a biodegradable self-reinforced poly L-lactic acid spiral stent in patients with urinary retention caused by bladder outlet obstruction from benign prostatic hyperplasia. BJU Int 88:30–34, 2001.
8. Lincoff AM, Schwartz RS, van der Giessen WJ, et al: Biodegradable polymers can evoke a unique inflammatory response when implanted in the coronary artery [abstract].Circulation 86:I-801, 1992.
9. Gammon RS, Chapman GD, Agrawal GM, et al: Mechanical features of the Duke biodegradable intravascular stent. J Am Coll Cardiol 17:235A, 1991.

10. Lumiaho J, Heino A, Tunninen V, et al: New bioabsorbable polylactide ureteral stent in the treatment of ureteral lesions: An experimental study. J Endourol 13:107–112, 1999.
11. Zidar JP, Lincoff MA, Stack RS: In Topol EJ (ed): Textbook of Interventional Cardiology, 2nd ed. New York, Saunders, 1994, pp 787–802.
12. Tanguay JF, Zidar JP, Phillips HR 3rd, et al: Current status of biodegradable stents. Cardiol Clin 12:699–713, 1994.
13. Korpela A, Aarnio P, Sariola H, et al: Bioabsorbable self-reinforced poly-L-lactide, metallic, and silicone stents in the management of experimental tracheal stenosis. Chest 115:490–495, 1999.
14. Cutright DE, Perez B, Beasley JD 3rd, et al: Degradation rates of polymers and copolymers of polylactic and polyglycolic acids. Oral Surg Oral Med Oral Pathol 37:142–152, 1974.
15. Saito Y, Minami K, Kobayashi M, et al: New tubular bioabsorbable knitted airway stent: Biocompatibility and mechanical strength. J Thorac Cardiovasc Surg 123:161–167, 2002
16. Jedwab MR, Clerc CO: A study of the geometrical and mechanical properties of a self-expanding metallic stent—theory and experiment. J Appl Biomater 4:77–85, 1993.
17. Valimaa T, Laaksovirta S, Tammela TL, et al: Viscoelastic memory and self-expansion of self-reinforced bioabsorbable stents. Biomaterials 23:3575–3582, 2002.
18. Suuronen R, Pohjonen T, Hietanen J, et al: A 5-year in vitro and in vivo study of the biodegradation of polylactide plates. J Oral Maxillofac Surg 56:604–615, 1998.
19. Kangas J, Paasimaa S, Makela P, et al: Comparison of strength properties of poly-L/D-lactide (PLDLA) 96/4 and polyglyconate (Maxon) sutures: In vitro, in the subcutis, and in the Achilles tendon of rabbits. J Biomed Mater Res 58:121–126, 2001.
20. Venkatraman S, Poh TL, Vinalia T, et al: Collapse pressures of biodegradable stents. Biomaterials 24:2105–2111, 2003.
21. Freeman ML: Bioabsorbable stents for gastrointestinal endoscopy. Tech Gastrointest Endosc 3:120–125, 2001.
22. Fry SW, Fleischer DE: Management of a refractory benign esophageal stricture with a new biodegradable stent. Gastrointest Endosc 45:179–182, 1997.
23. Goldin E, Fiorini A, Ratan Y, et al: A new biodegradable and self-expanding stent for benign esophageal strictures [abstract]. Gastrointest Endosc 43:294, 1996.
24. Ginsberg G, Cope C, Shah J, et al: In vivo evaluation of a new bioabsorbable self-expanding biliary stent. Gastrointest Endosc 58:777–784, 2003.
25. Rajan E, Gostout CJ: Widespread endoscopic mucosal resection. Gastrointest Endosc Clin N Am 11:489–97, 2001
26. Wei G, Kotoura Y, Oka M, et al: A bioabsorbable delivery system for antibiotic treatment of osteomyelitis. The use of lactic acid oligomer as a carrier. J Bone Joint Surg Br 73:246–252, 1991.
27. Rutledge B, Huyette D, Day D, Anglen J: Treatment of osteomyelitis with local antibiotics delivered via bioabsorbable polymer. Clin Orthop 1:280–287, 2003.
28. Yamawaki T, Shimokawa H, Kozai T, et al: Intramural delivery of a specific tyrosine kinase inhibitor with biodegradable stent suppresses the restenotic changes of the coronary artery in pigs in vivo. J Am Coll Cardiol 32:780–786, 1998.
29. Ye YW, Landau C, Willard JE, et al: Bioresorbable microporous stents deliver recombinant adenovirus gene transfer vectors to the arterial wall. Ann Biomed Eng 26:398–408, 1998.

New Techniques in Imaging

Shai Friedland and Jacques Van Dam

Development of novel endoscopic imaging techniques including light-scattering spectroscopy, fluorescent spectroscopic imaging, and optical coherence tomography (OCT), has the potential to alter routine clinical practice for the detection of dysplasia, malignancy, and ischemia of the gastrointestinal (GI) tract. Although it is not yet clear which of these optical methods will move from the laboratory to widespread clinical use, each of them has attracted substantial interest in furthering our ability to diagnose disease endoscopically. This chapter reviews the major new optical methods that may have a future role in endoscopic practice. In each instance, the core physical principles are summarized and followed by a discussion of recent results and potential future applications.

Each optical method is similar to conventional endoscopy in that it involves illuminating the mucosa with light and using the light that returns to the endoscope after interacting with the tissue. The differences between the various methods involve the various properties of the light used and the processing of the light signal. For example, in laser-induced fluorescence endoscopy, the light source is relatively short wavelength laser light, and what is measured is the longer wavelength fluorescent light that is emitted by the tissue. Preliminary studies using many of these newer optical techniques were conducted with catheter-based probes capable of insertion via the accessory channel of the endoscope. Such probes typically deliver light to a small spot on the mucosa and analyze the light returning from this small spot; this technique is referred to as point spectroscopy. With further refinement of the devices, it has been possible to build systems that permit independent analysis of a large number of points to create a two-dimensional image much like a conventional endoscopy picture. An example is fluorescence endoscopic imaging in which the physician is able to view the standard endoscopic image with an overlay that indicates areas of relatively high or low fluorescence that may signify dysplasia or other mucosal abnormalities. Other optical methods, such as confocal microscopy and Raman spectroscopy, are not yet at such an advanced stage of development to permit such a seamless integration into routine endoscopic practice.

Reflectance Spectroscopy

Reflectance spectroscopy and light-scattering spectroscopy are conceptually the simplest of the newer optical techniques: both typically rely on illuminating the tissue of interest with light and quantitatively analyzing the light that returns to a detector from the tissue. White light is a mixture of wavelengths between approximately 390 nm and 780 nm. When the mucosa is illuminated by white light, some the light is absorbed by molecules within the tissue, particularly by capillary hemoglobin which is abundant and has high absorbance. To the eye, blood appears red in color because oxygenated hemoglobin preferentially absorbs blue light, allowing a larger proportion of red light to be scattered and reflected back to the observer. Reflectance spectroscopy is typically performed using a catheter-based fiberoptic probe inserted via the accessory channel of an endoscope. White light is used to illuminate the tissue, and the light that is reflected from the tissue is collected by a second optical fiber (or multiple fibers) and transmitted to the detector. Because some wavelengths are preferentially absorbed by molecules such as oxygenated and deoxygenated hemoglobin in the tissue, the spectrum of reflected light can be analyzed for the characteristic absorption signatures of these molecules. Oxygenated and deoxygenated hemoglobin have dramatically different absorption spectra (Fig. 57–1).[1] Using a mathematical algorithm, the ratio of oxygenated to deoxygenated hemoglobin in the superficial tissue can be calculated reliably by analyzing the spectrum of the reflected light.[2] The analysis is typically performed at 500 to 600 nm, where the two forms of hemoglobin differ substantially and where penetration of light into tissue is limited to less than 1 mm (red light penetrates deeper). Because most of the hemoglobin is located in capillary erythrocytes, this analysis yields a reliable estimate of capillary hemoglobin oxygen saturation and thereby allows the endoscopist to evaluate the perfusion status of the GI mucosa.

Reflectance spectrophotometry has been a research tool for the measurement of GI mucosal perfusion for the past 25 years,[3–5] after the pioneering work of Chance and colleagues,[6] who devised a flexible light guide for spectroscopy. In 1979, Sato and coworkers[7] described the first *in vivo* application of reflectance spectroscopy to measure gastric perfusion. In the early 1980s, these investigators used this method to quantify gastric mucosal blood flow in patients in burn and head injury patients, demonstrating that a severe reduction in blood flow preceded the development of gastric ulcers.[8,9] Several groups have investigated the role of perfusion in the healing of gastric and duodenal ulcers. Most gastroduodenal ulcer margins have a higher hemoglobin oxygen saturation than nearby normal mucosa. The fraction of ulcers whose margins have a lower hemoglobin oxygen saturation, 22% in one study of duodenal ulcers, tend to have delayed healing.[10,11]

Reflectance spectrometry has the advantage of permitting very rapid (less than 1 second) measurement and analysis. The ease and rapidity of such systems has lent itself to applications in measuring dynamic changes in perfusion. Temmesfeld-Wollbruck and colleagues[12] demonstrated the ability of reflectance spectroscopy to detect substantial decreases in mucosal hemoglobin oxygen saturation in patients with septic shock. They were then able to demonstrate a partial correction of the oxygen saturation after pharma-

cologic intervention with intravenous dopexamine. Reflectance spectrometry was compared with gastric tonometry, a research technique used to study gastric perfusion by estimating intramucosal pH, and found to be superior in monitoring rapid pharmacologic intervention with dopexamine. In other studies, the response of GI mucosa to epinephrine injection was monitored in real-time. Endoscopic maneuvers such as clipping or looping of polyp stalks before polypectomy have also been monitored by reflectance spectrometry (Fig. 57–2).[2]

Early spectrometric devices were limited by an ability to measure the absorbance at only three wavelengths. With current technology, however, it is possible to simultaneously measure absorption at hundreds of wavelengths and apply more sophisticated analytical software to obtain measurements that are more robust. Reflectance spectrometry has the potential to evolve into a clinical tool for the monitoring of organ perfusion in patients at risk for ischemia. Commercially manufactured catheter-based probes will allow clinicians to measure capillary hemoglobin oxygen saturation in buccal, esophageal, and rectal mucosa. Early experience suggests that major alterations in blood flow, such as during cardiovascular interventions, can be detected. The precise role of this type of monitoring remains to be established by clinical trials.

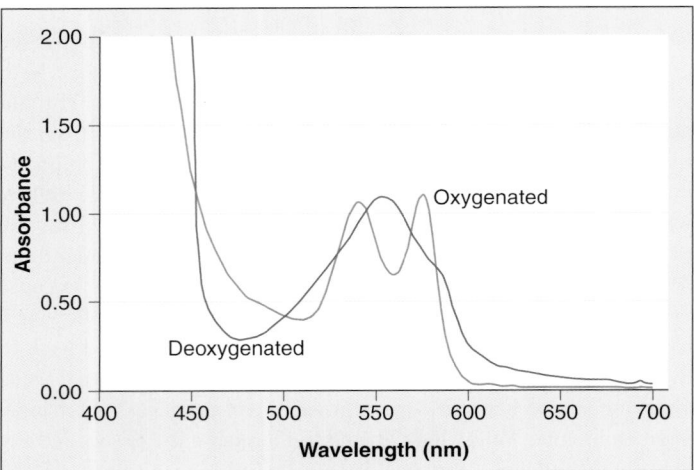

Figure 57–1. Spectra of oxygenated and deoxygenated hemoglobin. (Redrawn from Friedland S, Benaron D, Parachikov I, Soetikno R: Measurement of mucosal capillary hemoglobin oxygen saturation in the colon by reflectance spectrophotometry. Gastrointest Endosc 57:492–497, 2003, with permission from the American Society for Gastrointestinal Endoscopy.)

Light-Scattering Spectroscopy

When light encounters a change in the refractive index, such as at an air-glass interface, a portion of the light is reflected and the remainder enters the second medium at an angle (refraction). When there are multiple interfaces, the reflected and refracted light from multiple scatterers can interfere with one another and yield interference patterns that can be measured. In biologic tissues, there are many structures, such as cell nuclei, that have a higher index of refraction than that of the surrounding cytoplasm.[13,14] The light that is reflected by a nucleus at the mucosal surface can interfere with light that is reflected by a nucleus immediately beneath or adjacent to the first nucleus. The interference is strongest when the path lengths of the two components differ by n + 1/2 wavelengths, where n is an integer; in this case the two light rays are exactly out of phase. By solving Maxwell's equations of electromagnetism, it

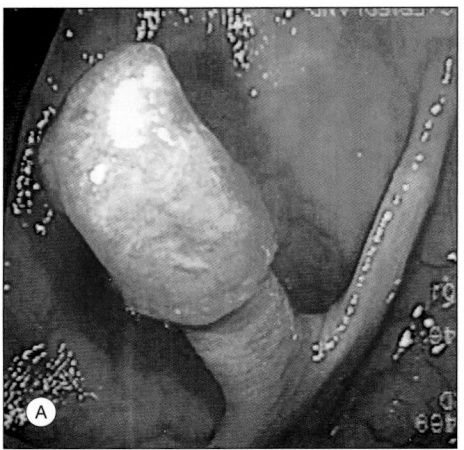

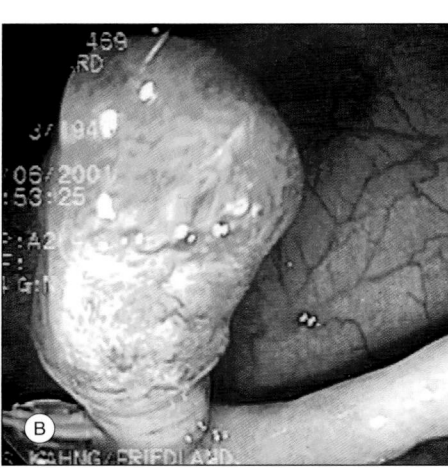

Figure 57–2. Measurement of tissue oxygenation of a pedunculated polyp before *(left)* and after *(right)* placement of a strangulating endoscopic loop around the polyp stalk. The mucosal capillary oxygen saturation decreased from 78% to 36%.

is possible to calculate the scattering behavior of model systems, such as a collection of spherical objects with a particular index of refraction, size, and concentration. These types of calculation were first performed by Gustav Mie in 1908, and the results are known as Mie scattering. For the purposes of gastroenterology, it is sufficient to appreciate that the different size distribution of nuclei in normal and dysplastic epithelium has an appreciable effect on the scattering of light of various wavelengths. Using a model that takes into account exponential attenuation of light in tissue, hemoglobin absorption and scattering, Perelman and coworkers[15] were able to demonstrate that normal and dysplastic Barrett's epithelia had a different periodic fine structure in the reflected light spectra that was attributable to the different size distribution of normal and dysplastic nuclei.

Light-scattering spectroscopy was recently tested in 13 patients undergoing routine surveillance for Barrett's esophagus or evaluation of suspected esophageal adenocarcinoma.[16] In the initial part of the study, eight samples were used to determine the optimal threshold for classifying samples as dysplastic; no distinction was made between low grade and high grade dysplasia. This established the optimal cutoff at a value of 30% of the nuclei greater than 10 μm in diameter. This value was then used prospectively on 68 samples from the same 13 patients. Spectroscopy was found to be 90% sensitive and 90% specific for diagnosing dysplasia in this setting. Further studies are necessary to confirm these results in a more clinically relevant (and challenging) setting such as a cohort with what appears endoscopically to be simple Barrett's without suspicious nodules or masses. The confounding effect of inflammation from gastroesophageal reflux, which may alter the characteristics of cells in the mucosa, also must be investigated. If these initial encouraging results are confirmed and duplicated and if the system can be made readily accessible, it is possible that our ability to detect dysplasia in a variety of clinical settings could be improved substantially. An important further development would be the ability to scan an entire endoscopic visual field for dysplasia, to develop an imaging system for measuring dysplasia using light-scattering spectroscopy. Such a device would enable the endoscopist to scan the entire field at once for abnormalities. Until such a system is developed, light-scattering spectroscopy is likely to remain a research technique.

Fluorescence Spectroscopy

Fluorescence occurs when atoms or molecules absorb relatively short wavelength (high energy) light and subsequently emit relatively long wavelength (lower energy) light. The absorption of a high-energy photon excites the absorbing atom or molecule to a higher energy level. In the process of dissipating the absorbed energy, certain atoms and molecules preferentially emit photons of characteristic wavelengths, typically after a delay of on the order of 10^{-7} seconds. The emitted photons are of lower energy than the original photon that excited the atom or molecule. In biologic tissues, there are numerous endogenous molecules that fluoresce when illuminated by ultraviolet or short wavelength visible light. This is referred to as autofluorescence of tissue, in contrast to fluorescence that occurs when certain fluorescent drugs such as

5-aminolevulinic acid are administered. Both autofluorescence and drug-induced fluorescence have been studied extensively.

Autofluorescence can be elicited from multiple endogenous molecules in biologic tissues, including connective tissue components (collagen, elastin), aromatic amino acids (e.g., tryptophan), porphyrins, coenzymes such as nicotinamide adenine dinucleotide (NADH; only the reduced form is fluorescent), and lipofuscin. Each of these fluorophores has characteristic wavelength regions at which it absorbs light and characteristic wavelength regions at which fluorescent light is emitted. However, because the excitation and fluorescence emission bands are broad and overlap and because there are so many different fluorophores in tissue, it can be difficult to interpret the autofluorescence spectra of tissue. In addition, when fluorescence spectroscopy is performed in vivo, the observed fluorescence is derived from the superficial mucosa and deeper layers. Each layer has a distinct molecular composition, and both the composition and thickness of the layer may be altered in disease. There is also an additional compounding effect of absorption: as the fluorescent emission travels back out of the tissue, some of it is absorbed just as it is in reflectance and light-scattering spectroscopy. Different wavelengths are absorbed at varying rates, and this affects the measured fluorescence spectrum. A particular source of artifact in GI fluorescence studies arises from fluorophores in food residue and in stool.

Because of the difficulty in resolving the fluorescence spectra into their constituent components, most human studies have attempted to characterize typical fluorescence patterns in a variety of disease states, such as in hyperplastic and adenomatous polyps. An observed signal from an unknown polyp is then compared with the hyperplastic and adenomatous patterns, and a mathematical algorithm calculates which type the unknown signal more closely resembles. More advanced systems collect what is termed an excitation-emission matrix, which is a collection of fluorescence spectra that are obtained by exciting the tissue using different excitation wavelengths. For example, one portable device obtains a series of 11 different fluorescence spectra in less than 1 second, each one derived using a different excitation wavelength to illuminate the tissue.

Fluorescence spectroscopy systems consist of an excitation light source, a fiberoptic probe with one or more fibers to carry the excitatory light to the tissue, and one or more fibers that collect the fluorescence signal and transmit it back to a photon detector. The signal is analyzed by computer. The excitation light source is often a short wavelength laser, such as a nitrogen laser, which emits light at a wavelength of 337 nm. Alternatively, a light source that emits a broad range of wavelengths can be used with a filter that only permits transmission of short wavelength light to excite the tissue. The fluorescence signal, which is typically at wavelengths of 350 to 700 nm, is collected and often passed through a filter that eliminates shorter wavelengths to avoid artifacts because of light from the excitation source. In systems in which an excitation-emission matrix is collected, a variety of different excitation sources of different wavelengths are used sequentially. Thus, one can, for example, obtain a fluorescence signal that includes collagen (which is excited at 330 nm) using one excitation source, wait for the signal to taper, and then perform a second excitation at 405 nm, which would elicit a strong signal from porphyrins.

Applications of Fluorescence Point Spectroscopy

Several studies have demonstrated the feasibility of using fluorescence spectroscopy to differentiate between normal colonic mucosa and hyperplastic and adenomatous polyps.[17-21] Kapadia and colleagues[17] used laser-induced fluorescence at 325 nm on recently excised normal colonic tissue, hyperplastic polyps, and adenomatous polyps. After studying 35 normal sites and 35 polyps, they developed a regression model to analyze fluorescence spectra that they then tested on a second collection of specimens. They were able to demonstrate 94% to 100% accuracy in identification of hyperplastic and adenomatous polyps *ex vivo*. *In vivo* laser-induced fluorescence was first demonstrated in the colon by Cothren and coworkers,[18] who used an excitation wavelength of 370 nm and analyzed fluorescence up to 700 nm. They noted that adenomatous tissue tended in general to have a lower fluorescence intensity. By analyzing the fluorescence signal at 460 and 680 nm, adenomatous polyps could be distinguished from normal mucosa with a 100% sensitivity and 97% specificity. In a subsequent blinded endoscopic study by the same group, involving a larger number of polyps, a sensitivity of 90% and a specificity of 95% were observed (Fig. 57–3).[19]

Tissue autofluorescence has also been studied in the esophagus, particularly in the identification of dysplasia in Barrett's esophagus. Panjehpour and colleagues[22,23] demonstrated that high grade dysplasia in Barrett's esophagus can be distinguished from nondysplastic or low grade dysplastic mucosa. They used a nitrogen-pumped dye-laser tuned to generate pulses of light at 410 nm to excite the tissue. The fluorescence spectra were analyzed by a technique based on what the authors term the differential normalized fluorescence index.[24] In this technique, each spectrum is first normalized by dividing by a factor corresponding to the sum of the intensity of fluorescence at all of the wavelengths in the spectrum. A set of normalized spectra from a cohort of normal patients is averaged and used as a reference baseline. Subsequently, in each study patient the reference baseline is subtracted from the normalized measured spectrum. The particular value of this difference at 480 nm was used to classify patients with Barrett's esophagus and various degrees of dysplasia. The authors found that Barrett's adenocarcinoma and Barrett's high grade dysplasia had a lower differential normalized fluorescence at 480 nm than that of Barrett's low grade dysplasia and Barrett's without dysplasia. However, when foci of high grade dysplasia surrounded by low grade dysplasia were analyzed, only 28% were classified as highly dysplastic. In this study, the technique was relatively insensitive in the situation in which it could potentially aid clinicians the most—in detecting worrisome foci of high grade dysplasia that could potentially be missed by standard random biopsy protocols.

Enhanced Fluorescence Using Protoporphyrins

Studies of fluorescence spectroscopy using exogenously administered molecules, such as 5-aminolevlulinic acid (5-ALA), have shown substantial promise in the detection of dysplasia in the GI tract. The basis for these studies is a differential accumulation or bioconversion of prodrugs into photoactive compounds in dysplastic cells compared with adjacent normal cells. Exogenous 5-ALA is taken up by mucosal cells in the GI tract and leads to an accumulation of protoporphyrin IX because of feedback inhibition of the final step of the heme biosynthetic cycle. Protoporphyrin IX is easily detected by fluorescence and has been exploited for therapeutic applications in photodynamic therapy. Depending on factors such as the dose and route of 5-ALA administration, there is an accumulation of protoporphyrin IX in malignant or dysplastic areas of the mucosa compared with normal areas. This difference is the basis for fluorescence spectroscopy and fluorescence imaging using 5-ALA. When tissue exposed to 5-ALA is illuminated with light at 400 nm, which penetrates to a depth of approximately 0.5 mm, distinct peaks of protoporphyrin IX fluorescence are observed at 635 nm and 705 nm. These peaks are easily distinguished from the broad autofluorescence peak at around 480 nm that is due to endogenous fluorescent molecules in the tissue.

Multiple studies have demonstrated the potential application of 5-ALA in the detection of dysplasia in Barrett's esophagus and in the differentiation of adenomatous polyps from normal colon or hyperplastic polyps. Early studies used relatively qualitative assessments of protoporphyrin IX fluorescence, whereas more recently a quantitative measure has been used. In a recent study, using oral administration of 5-ALA 3 hours before endoscopy, high grade dysplasia was detected with 77% sensitivity and 71% specificity in a group of 20 patients (Fig. 57–4).[25] The authors of that study also noted that 5-ALA based fluorescence endoscopy was detected several areas of nonpolypoid high grade dysplasia, which appeared normal by standard endoscopy. These results are encouraging because unlike nodular high grade dysplasia, which is easily found by biopsy of nodular areas in the Barrett's esophagus, foci of high grade dysplasia in nonpolypoid areas of Barrett's esophagus are easily missed even with random biopsy protocols.

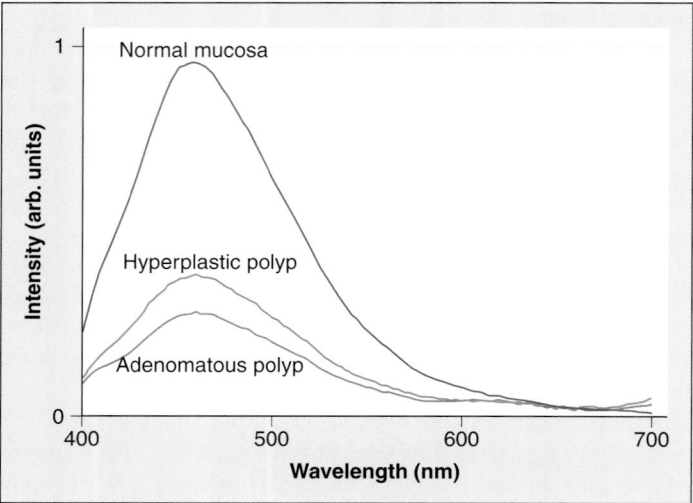

Figure 57–3. Typical point spectroscopy fluorescence spectra of hyperplastic and adenomatous colon polyps. (Redrawn from Cothren RM, Sivak MV Jr, Van Dam J, et al: Detection of dysplasia at colonoscopy using laser-induced fluorescence: A blinded study. Gastrointest Endosc 44:168–176, 1996.)

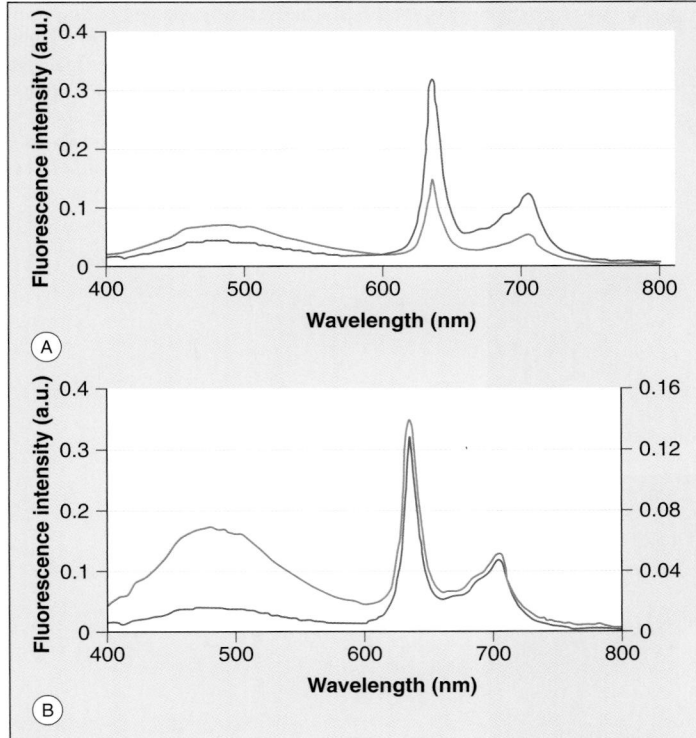

Figure 57–4. Fluorescence spectra of Barrett's esophagus with high grade dysplasia *(blue line)* and Barrett's esophagus without dysplasia *(red line)* after administration of 5-aminolevlulinic acid (5-ALA) are shown in the top graph. The broad peak at 480 nm is due to tissue autofluorescence. The peaks at 635 nm and 705 nm are from protoporphyrin IX fluorescence. In the bottom graph, the spectra have been normalized by the protoporphyrin IX fluorescence to demonstrate a relative decrease in tissue autofluorescence in the Barrett's high grade dysplasia. (Redrawn from Brand S, Wang TD, Schomacker KT, et al: Detection of high-grade dysplasia in Barrett's esophagus by spectroscopy measurement of 5-aminolevulinic acid-induced protoporphyrin IX fluorescence. Gastrointest Endosc 56:479–487, 2002.)

One limitation of early reports that may have led to overly optimistic results was based on tissue morphology and the source of autofluorescence. Specifically, tissue autofluorescence of nodules is lower than that of flat areas because most tissue autofluorescence actually originates in the submucosa; an overlying nodule will decrease the autofluorescence signal by virtue of having a thicker mucosa that overlies and obscures the fluorescent submucosa. Therefore, if one compares a cohort of nodular high grade dysplasia to another cohort of flat nondysplastic Barrett's esophagus, it is relatively easy to differentiate the two. It is much more difficult to obtain a high sensitivity and specificity in a study of patients that all have an endoscopically normal-appearing flat Barrett's in which a proportion have foci of high grade dysplasia. Such limitations were overcome in studies of colonic polypoid dysplasia by using nondysplastic polyps (hyperplastic polyps) as controls.

There are several other factors which can also potentially impact dysplasia screening protocols based on tissue autofluorescence and 5-ALA. These include the effect of blood, food, stool, and other substances in the lumen that can absorb incident or emitted light and, in some cases, fluoresce. In addition, there is increased protoporphyrin IX fluorescence in inflamed tissue, which could lead to difficulty in differentiating inflammation from dysplasia. Although early results are clearly encouraging, large studies involving less highly selected patient populations must be done to evaluate the sensitivity and specificity of these optical methods in a more general gastroenterology setting.

Endoscopic Fluorescence Imaging

Endoscopic fluorescence imaging allows the physician to survey the entire endoscopic field at once, rather than proceeding one spot at a time as in point spectroscopy (Fig. 57–5). To perform fluorescence imaging, it is necessary to use a light source that delivers exclusively short wavelength light. This has typically been achieved with the aid of a filter that blocks nearly all of the light photons that are of a higher than the desired wavelength, typically about 450 nm. In addition, a filter is placed on the receiving end of the endoscope to block all photons except those in the desired fluorescence range, typically about 600 to 700 nm. Because of the relatively weak fluorescence signal when a fiberoptic endoscope is used, the standard videocamera that is typically mounted on the eyepiece is replaced by a more sensitive intensified camera. The overall result is an image that consists entirely of tissue fluorescence, which is usually displayed as a green signal on the video monitor. Prototype systems have been built that alternate rapidly between a white-light endoscopy and fluorescence imaging so that both can be displayed on separate monitors in the endoscopy suite. Recently, a prototype fluorescence endoscopy system that uses the charge-coupled device (CCD) of a modern colonoscope has been demonstrated.[26] Instead of using a separate intensified camera and fiberoptic scope to perform fluorescence imaging, the white light is briefly blocked and the colon is illuminated by an argon laser using a fiberoptic probe in the accessory channel of a standard videocolonoscope. The fluorescence is then imaged with the colonoscope's CCD, exploiting the fact that the CCD is insensitive to the ultraviolet light from the laser and is sensitive enough to detect fluorescence.

The endoscopic fluorescence imaging systems described thus far use steady-state fluorescence, whereby the light source is steadily on while the fluorescence signal is collected. This contrasts with some of the more precise fluorescence point spectroscopy systems that first illuminate the tissue with the excitation wavelength, then turn off the light source and measure the fluorescence signal after a preset delay to ensure that a relatively pure fluorescence signal is collected. In addition, instead of measuring the fluorescence at a large number of individual wavelengths and obtaining a spectrum, imaging systems generally perform only one measurement (or two in some systems) at each spatial point using a detector that is triggered by a wide range of light wavelengths. In addition, fluorescence point spectroscopy systems typically use a pulse of relatively monochromatic laser light and use sophisticated mathematical algorithms to process the measured spectra. However, all of these relative deficiencies of fluorescence imaging systems are offset by the ability to image an entire field at once, allowing instant comparisons of one area of mucosa to another.

Early studies demonstrated that colonic adenomas can be distinguished *in vitro* by virtue of having a lower fluorescence intensity than adjacent normal tissue. Using a threshold of 75% of normal,

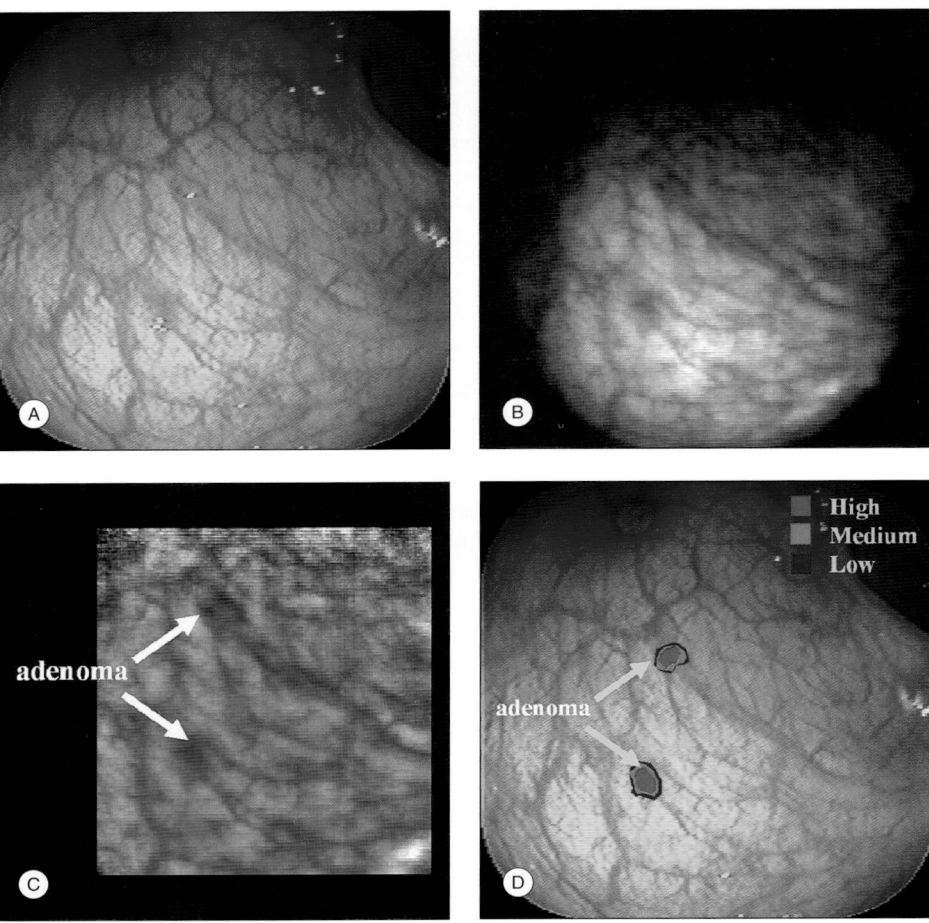

Figure 57-5. Fluorescence imaging during colonoscopy. *A,* Standard endoscopic image of rectum. Two diminutive adenomas are poorly visualized. *B,* Unprocessed fluorescence imaging image. *C,* Processed fluorescence imaging image obtained using a moving average algorithm. The two adenomas are clearly visualized. *D,* Standard endoscopic view with fluorescence overlay demonstrating the two adenomas. (Courtesy of Dr. Thomas Wang, Stanford University, Palo Alto, CA.)

a sensitivity and specificity of approximately 90% was observed during *in vitro* analysis of resected colons of patients with familial adenomatous polyposis.[27] The situation is somewhat more complicated *in vivo,* where for example there is also decreased fluorescence in poorly illuminated areas such as in shadows cast behind mucosal folds and where the orientation of the colonoscope is not as well controlled as it is on the laboratory bench. In a recent study of 30 patients undergoing colonoscopy, a sensitivity of 83% for the detection of adenomatous polyps was achieved using a threshold of 80% of normal fluorescence.[26] The specificity of fluorescence imaging was not assessed in that study, but the authors noted that poor illumination of areas in the shadows of mucosal folds consistently produced a false-positive signal by virtue of their decreased fluorescence. Interestingly, modern endoscopes use two separate illumination bundles located on either side of the CCD detector to reduce this type of artifact in standard white-light endoscopy. Therefore, it may be possible to improve the results by using this type of illumination technique. It should also be noted that unlike dysplastic adenomatous polyps, all six of the hyperplastic polyps in this study were observed to have near-normal fluorescence. This may be partly due to the absorption of the incident ultraviolet light by the higher hemoglobin levels in adenomatous polyps, although other factors could also contribute.[28]

A commercial prototype fluorescence imaging system, LIFE II (Xillix Corporation), has recently been developed for use during endoscopy (Fig. 57–6).[29,30] It uses a fiberoptic endoscope, on which the Xillix camera head is mounted. The system also uses a light source that can be switched between white light for conventional endoscopy and a filtered blue light for fluorescence excitation. Blue light, although somewhat less efficient at inducing fluorescence than ultraviolet light, has the potential advantage of being less mutagenic than ultraviolet light and the practical advantage of being usable with existing lenses and optical elements on available endoscopes. The LIFE II camera is capable of switching between standard white-light imaging and a fluorescence mode within 4 seconds. In the fluorescence imaging mode, blue light (400 to 450 nm) excites the tissue, and the emitted fluorescence in the green wavelength range (490 to 560 nm) is measured by an intensified CCD array while the fluorescence in the red wavelength range (630 to 750 nm) is measured by a second intensified CCD array. The fluorescence image is displayed as a colored image on the video monitor based on the red and green measurements.

Clinical studies of the LIFE II system have been undertaken in several centers, and the results have been published in the form of illustrative cases and photographs.[31] Examples include areas of high grade dysplasia within Barrett's esophagus that appeared as regions of increased red fluorescence surrounded by regions of low fluorescence or green fluorescence. Other examples have included a signet ring gastric carcinoma appearing as an area of faint red fluorescence and a flat colon polyp that also fluoresced red and was surrounded

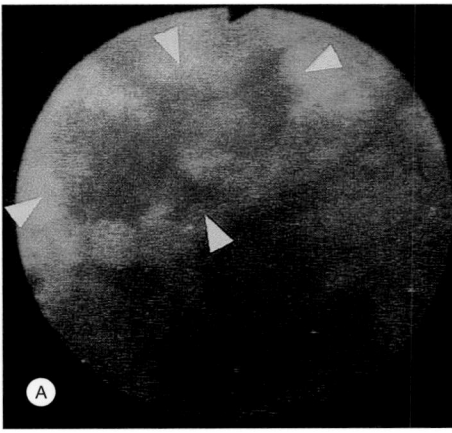
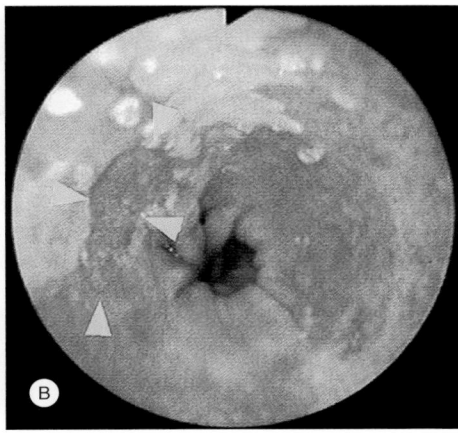

Figure 57-6. Fluorescence images of Barrett's esophagus with high grade dysplasia obtained using the commercial Xillix LIFE II instrument. The dysplastic tissue fluoresces slightly less than normal tissue in the red wavelengths and dramatically less than normal tissue in the green wavelengths. By adjusting the relative gain of the red and green channels on the instrument, the dysplastic area is visible as a faint red color on the viewing screen *(A)*. A standard white-light endoscopic view of the same area is shown in *B*. (Reprinted from Haringsma J, Tytgat GN, Yano H, et al: Autofluorescence endoscopy: feasibility of detection of GI neoplasms unapparent to white light endoscopy with an evolving technology. Gastrointest Endosc 53:642–650, 2001.)

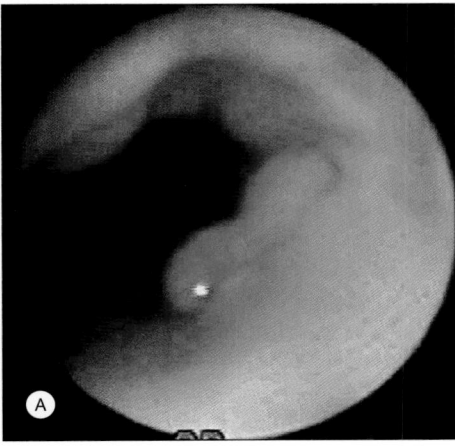
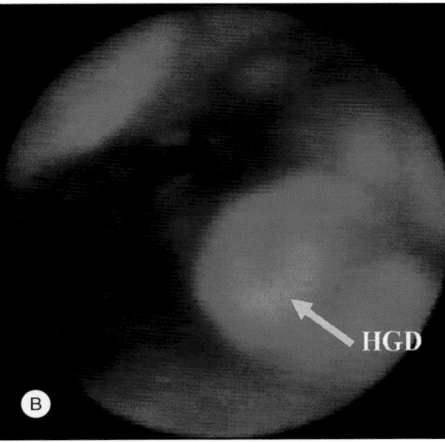

Figure 57-7. Enhanced fluorescence imaging using 5-aminolevlulinic acid (5-ALA). *A,* Standard endoscopic image of the gastroesophageal junction. *B,* Fluorescence image of the same region obtained 3 hours after administration of 5-ALA, demonstrating enhanced fluorescence in an area of high grade dysplasia (HGD). (Courtesy of Dr. Thomas Wang, Stanford University, Palo Alto, CA.)

by normal mucosa that fluoresced in the green wavelengths. Rigorous clinical studies are certainly needed to define the potential role of this system, but it is encouraging that a commercial fluorescence imaging system may become available to clinicians and investigators. In addition, as with fluorescence point spectroscopy, there may be a future role for fluorescence imaging after administration of fluorophores such as 5-ALA. Initial experience with 5-ALA fluorescence imaging has been reported in limited studies of patients with adenomas and carcinomas of the GI tract (Fig. 57–7).[32,33]

Raman Spectroscopy

Raman spectroscopy is a technique based on the inelastic scattering of light. Unlike elastic scattering, in which the incident and scattered light photons are of the same wavelength, in Raman spectroscopy the incident and scattered light are generally of slightly different wavelengths. Because the energy of light photons is proportional to their frequency (inversely proportional to their wavelength), there is either transfer of energy from the incident light to the tissue or vice versa. For most practical endoscopic applications, it is the scattered light that is of slightly lower frequency than the incident light that is analyzed. In the process, a small amount of energy is transferred to the tissue. The molecules in the tissue responsible for the scattering are thereby excited to a higher

vibrational or rotational energy level. Each type of molecule has a specific Raman signature, and the Raman spectrum has a series of sharp peaks corresponding to known molecular transitions.[34] This is in contrast to tissue fluorescence spectra, in which peaks are typically broad and where it is difficult to assign parts of the spectrum to particular chemical species. Thus, using Raman spectroscopy, it is possible, for example, to directly quantify nucleic acids using an ultraviolet laser system. *In vitro* studies of resected colons using Raman have demonstrated that dysplastic areas and areas with invasive cancer typically have a lower adenyl signal and/or a lower amino acid-to-nucleotide ratio compared with normal areas.[35]

Endoscopic applications of Raman spectroscopy use a fiberoptic probe to deliver monochromatic laser light to the tissue. A very small fraction of the laser light undergoes Raman scattering, and the scattered light is collected by optical fibers in the probe. Several factors have combined to make Raman spectroscopy technically challenging. Because only a small percentage of incident light photons undergo Raman scattering, the Raman signal is weak and a relatively strong laser light source must be used. Highly sensitive photon detectors, such as liquid nitrogen cooled charge-coupled devices, are usually needed. In addition, the optical fibers and other optical accessories in the system typically cause some Raman scattering by themselves, producing a signal that competes with the tissue signal. Tissue fluorescence also interferes with the signal, and internal filters and signal processing techniques are used to reduce this effect. For all of these reasons, most studies of Raman spectroscopy have been performed *ex vivo*, where powerful lasers and long collection times (on the order of a minute) can be used. Recently, however, a Raman system has been described that that can be used during endoscopy with reusable optical probes[34] and a 5-second measurement time (Fig. 57–8).

In a pilot study, Raman spectroscopy performed *in vivo* was shown to be useful in differentiating adenomatous from hyperplastic polyps.[34] The study was limited, involving a total of nine polyps in three patients. Nineteen spectra were collected; in some cases, more than one location on the same polyp was measured. A "leave-one-

out" statistical analysis technique was used, whereby all of the other 18 spectra were used to determine whether a given spectrum was dysplastic or hyperplastic. In some cases, this resulted in a situation in which spectra from the same polyp were compared with the "unknown" spectrum. Using this approach, a 95% accuracy in classifying polyps as adenoma or hyperplastic was achieved. Although the small number of patients studied and the inclusion of multiple spectra from the same polyp simultaneously in the algorithm development and analysis are important limitations of this study, the development of an endoscopic Raman system has the potential to permit a rapid diagnosis of tissue abnormalities *in situ*. Studies of Raman spectroscopy in the assessment of dysplasia in Barrett's esophagus and ulcerative colitis are in progress, and the results are eagerly anticipated.

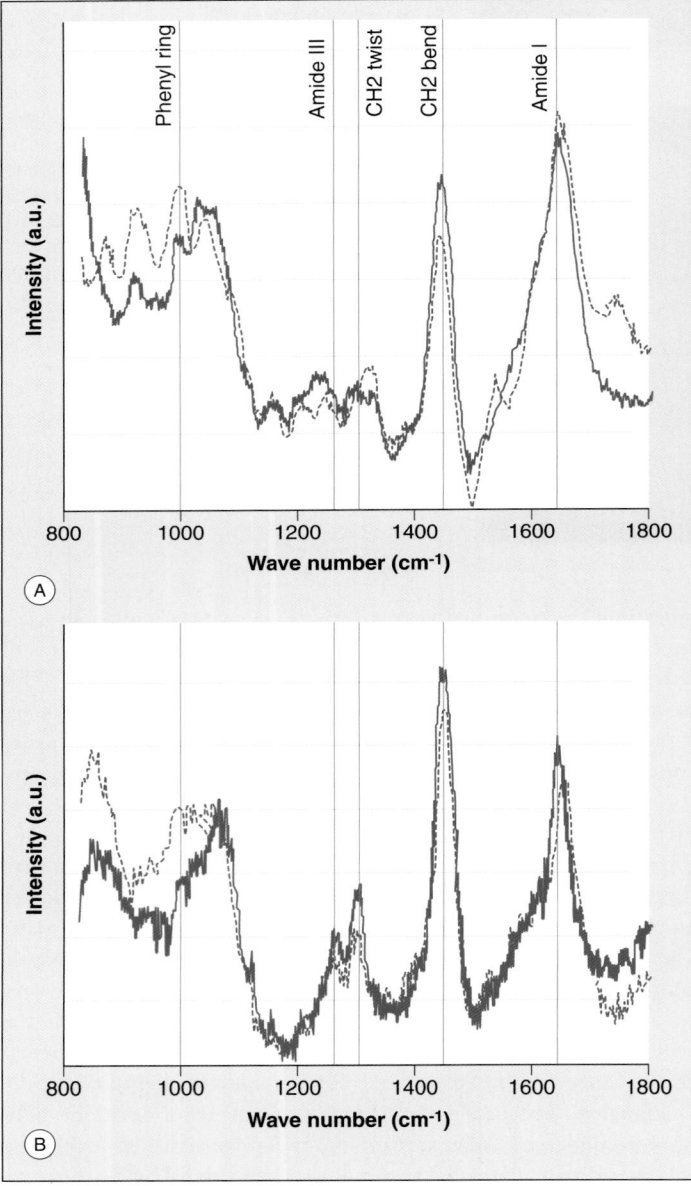

Figure 57–8. Average Raman spectra of hyperplastic *(solid line)* and adenomatous *(broken line)* colon polyps obtained *ex vivo (graph A)* and *in vivo (graph B)*. The spectra have been intensity corrected, wavelength calibrated, and fluorescence background subtracted. (Redrawn from Molckovsky A, Song, LW, Shim MG, et al: Diagnostic potential of near-infrared Raman spectroscopy in the colon: Differentiating adenomatous from hyperplastic polyps. Gastrointest Endosc 57:396–402, 2003.)

Optical Coherence Tomography

OCT is an imaging technique that relies on the backscattering of light to create cross-sectional images of tissue.[36,37] It has many similarities in principle to ultrasonography but uses light waves rather than acoustical waves. As with ultrasound, a quantitative measurement of backscattering is made at each axial depth. The assembly then shifts slightly to a different transverse position, and the measurement process is repeated at the new transverse position. The process is repeated until a two-dimensional map of backscattering strength is acquired. As with endoscopic ultrasound devices, the scanning can be performed in either a linear or a radial configuration.

To measure optical backscattering, a technique called low coherence interferometry is used. The incident light is split in two by a beam splitter. One of the beams is directed to the tissue via an optical fiber, and the other beam is directed to a mirror that is located at a precisely controlled distance. The backscattered light from the tissue is collected by an optical fiber and then combined with the light returning from the mirror. When these two waves interfere, the interference is measured. Significant interference only occurs when both beams have traveled nearly the same distance: the paths of the two beams must differ in length by less than the coherence length of the light source. In this application, a superluminescent diode with a coherence length of approximately 20 μm is typically used. Therefore, by varying the mirror position, it is possible to measure the backscattering from tissue and obtain an axial resolution of approximately 20 μm. A transverse resolution of about 20 μm is achieved by focusing the beam to a small spot and by translating the beam by approximately 20 μm after each axial scan.

OCT is usually performed using near infrared light, which penetrates deeper into tissue than visible light. Light scattering in tissue still limits the scanning depth to 1 to 2 mm in the GI tract, allowing visualization of the mucosa and submucosa. Both linear and radial scanning catheter probes are available for endoscopic use. Unlike ultrasound, a water interface is not required. Tissue contact is also not required.[38] Current devices have a resolution of 7 to 20 μm and provide real-time imaging at approximately four frames per second.

The current resolution of OCT is not sufficient to image individual mammalian cells but is sufficient to visualize mucosal glands, crypts, villi, and various layers of the luminal wall

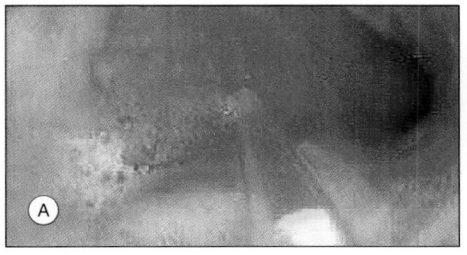
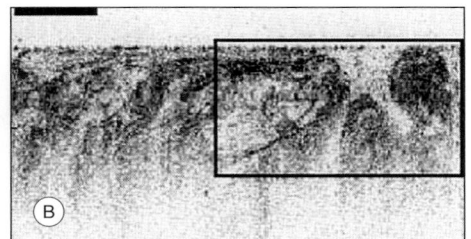
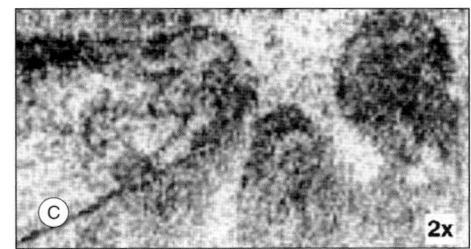
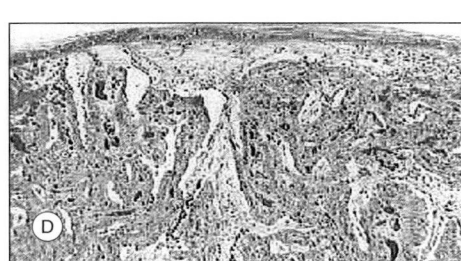

Figure 57–9. Optical coherence tomography image of esophageal adenocarcinoma. *A,* Standard white-light endoscopic view with the optical coherence tomography (OCT) catheter in position. *B,* OCT image demonstrating mucin pockets and an abnormal epithelial morphology. The scale bar corresponds to 500 μm. *C,* Magnified view. *D,* Corresponding histologic section. (Reprinted from Bouma BE, Tearney GJ, Compton CC, Nishioka NS: High-resolution imaging of the human esophagus and stomach in vivo using optical coherence tomography. Gastrointest Endosc 51:467–474, 2000.)

(Fig. 57–9). Much of the early work using OCT has been done in the esophagus, where the wall layers are clearly discernible. In Barrett's esophagus, this layered structure is absent and replaced with areas of inhomogeneous tissue contrast and submucosal gland structures.[39] A prospective OCT study demonstrated 97% sensitivity and 92% specificity for diagnosing Barrett's esophagus.[40] However, in practice the difficulty in diagnosing Barrett's esophagus by visual appearance on endoscopy lies in differentiating it from esophagitis and gastric metaplasia, and several false positives in this study were due to gastric cardia tissue with or without inflammation. Therefore, it is likely that the specificity of OCT would be lower in a more clinically representative setting.

There are as yet no reports to suggest that OCT can detect dysplasia in Barrett's esophagus. Current resolution is not sufficient to image individual dysplastic nuclei; thus, it would be necessary to use multicellular features such as glandular organization to infer dysplasia. This may be possible in esophageal adenocarcinoma, in which there is a generally disorganized appearance to the mucosa and there are large low-scattering pockets corresponding to mucin.[39,41]

There are a few descriptive reports of OCT in the stomach, small bowel, large bowel, and hepatobiliary system.[42–46] In the stomach, there is generally low tissue contrast, making differentiation of mural morphology problematic. Villi are clearly visualized in the small bowel, and crypts are appreciated in the colon. Colonic adenomas have been described as having an uneven surface, mucosal cysts, and expanded glands. Superficial mucosal ulcers have been described in ulcerative colitis. Several tumors have been imaged with OCT, including colonic adenocarcinoma and cholangiocarcinoma. In colon cancer, there appears to be a loss of the normal mucosal architecture. In cholangiocarcinoma, villiform papillary structures were observed.

OCT resolution, although substantially finer than that of ultrasound, is insufficient for assessment of individual human cells and nuclear dysplasia. However, there are recent reports of dramatically higher resolution with systems that use femtosecond laser pulses instead of current light sources.[47] Ultrahigh-resolution OCT has been demonstrated, in a bench-top *ex vivo* system, to achieve an axial resolution of approximately 1 μm.[48] Other ongoing research includes color Doppler OCT, which has been demonstrated in animal models and may permit visualization of bleeding vessels and monitoring of hemostatic interventions.[49] Spectroscopic OCT, in which the frequency content of backscattered light is analyzed in addition to the overall intensity, has also been described recently.[48] As expected, because longer wavelengths penetrate more deeply into tissue, the signal from the superficial mucosa tends to contain more short wavelength light, whereas the signal from the deeper parts of the mucosa contains relatively more longer wavelength light. *Ex vivo*, normal squamous epithelium in the esophagus was shown to have a relatively smooth transition between the superficial and deep mucosa, whereas Barrett's epithelium had more irregularities in spectroscopic content.

Infrared Imaging, Holographic Interferometry, and Confocal Microscopy

Endoscopic imaging using infrared light has the potential to visualize submucosal structures because of the relatively deep penetration of infrared light in tissue. Because the CCDs on electronic endoscopes are sensitive to both red and near-infrared light, it is possible to perform infrared imaging using a near-infrared light source and appropriate filters to allow transmission of infrared light. To increase contrast, which is a major issue with infrared imaging, investigators have used intravenous dyes such as indocyanine green (ICG). After intravenous administration of ICG, which binds to plasma albumin and absorbs near-infrared light, it is possible to observe deep submucosal vessels in detail. A recent study of ICG-enhanced infrared imaging demonstrated that 11 of 11 submucosally invasive gastric cancers had pooling of ICG dye in the tumors that was visible on infrared endoscopy (Fig. 57–10).[50] In addition, poorly differentiated gastric cancers confined to the mucosa also exhibited ICG pooling. The authors noted that these findings could make ICG-enhanced infrared endoscopy useful for determining which

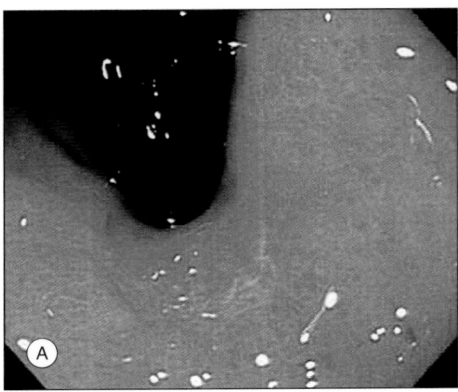

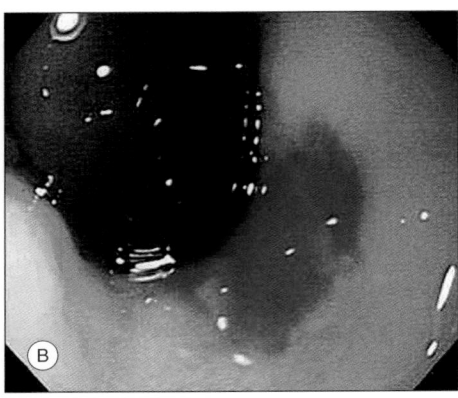

Figure 57–10. Infrared endoscopy images of an early gastric cancer obtained after intravenous administration indocyanine green. *A,* Standard white-light endoscopic image. *B,* Infrared endoscopy image showing pooling of dye in the cancer. (Reprinted from Mataki N, Nagao S, Kawaguchi A, et al: Clinical usefulness of a new infrared video-endoscope system for diagnosis of early stage gastric cancer. Gastrointest Endosc 57:336–342, 2003.)

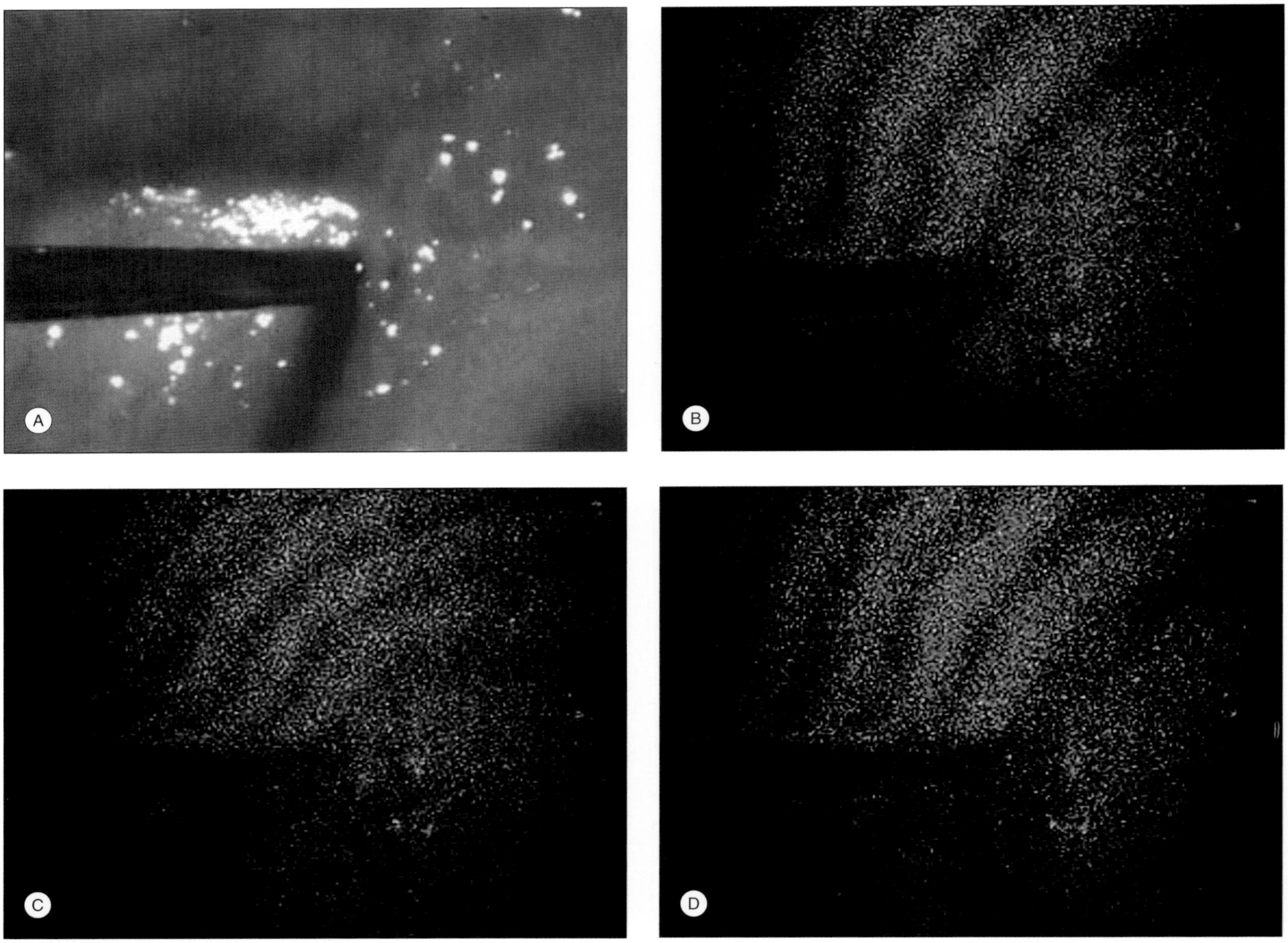

Figure 57–11. Gastric wall elasticity as assessed by holographic interferometry in an excised animal stomach. *A,* Standard white-light laparoscopic view of the stomach being probed and deformed by a wire. *B* to *D,* Corresponding speckle correlation patterns. (Reprinted from Avenhaus W, Kemper B, von Bally G, et al: Gastric wall elasticity assessed by dynamic holographic endoscopy: Ex vivo investigations in the porcine stomach. Gastrointest Endosc 54:496–500, 2001.)

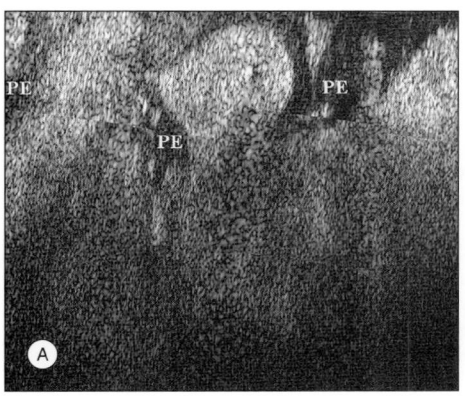 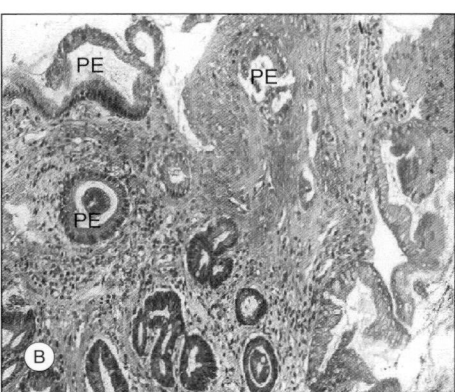

Figure 57–12. *A,* Confocal microscopy image of Barrett's esophagus, performed *ex vivo. B,* Standard hematoxylin and eosin (H&E) histologic section of a nearby area. PE, pit epithelium. (Courtesy of Dr. Thomas Wang, Stanford University, Palo Alto, CA.)

gastric cancers are resectable endoscopically, because two of the major contraindications to endoscopic resection are submucosal invasion and poorly differentiated morphology.

Holographic interferometry is an optical method that has been used widely in industry for nondestructive testing of materials. It relies on interference of holographic images generated during motion of an object and has recently been adapted to study gastric elasticity.[51] By superimposing two images taken a short time apart, an interference pattern is created. The reconstructed image is covered by a series of light and dark lines (fringes) connecting points that are shifted in the same way. In a pilot study, interference images were generated during deformation of an excised porcine stomach while using a probe to push on the wall (Fig. 57–11). The resulting images yielded a different pattern of light and dark lines in normal stomachs compared with stomachs altered by implantation of small metal plates in the muscularis propria. In theory, such a system could develop to the point where an endoscopist could probe the surface of the stomach and obtain a holographic interference image that could provide information about the elasticity of the organ. Patients with tumors infiltrating the gastric wall, such as linitis plastica, would presumably demonstrate a pattern of reduced elasticity.

Confocal microscopy is a technique that is particularly suited to high-resolution tissue imaging. By using a pinhole to block light that is not in the focal plain of the objective lens, an axial resolution of less than 1 μm can be achieved with commonly available desktop confocal microscopes. Recently, advances have been made in the miniaturization of confocal microscopes, and it is likely that an endoscopic confocal microscope will be available in the next few years (Fig. 57–12).[52] In *ex vivo* experiments, it was possible to directly visualize and measure the size of nuclei in esophageal mucosa.[52] It may be feasible in the near future to directly assess GI mucosa for the presence of large dysplastic nuclei using such a system.

Summary

New optical techniques have the potential to significantly expand our ability to diagnose GI disease beyond what is currently possible with conventional endoscopy. Techniques such as confocal microscopy may in the future allow us to examine surface detail at resolution that approaches that of bench-top microscopes, whereas other modalities such as OCT will permit visualization beneath the surface. Spectroscopy and fluorescence techniques offer a glimpse into the molecular contents of tissue, such as hemoglobin oxygenation states and the quantity and types of endogenous fluorophores. Fluorescence using exogenous agents may become a method to assay for specific conditions such as malignancy by highlighting differences in binding, uptake or processing by normal and abnormal tissues. Although none of these modalities have yet achieved prominent clinical acceptance, it seems increasingly likely that future endoscopists will rely on more advanced optical techniques than conventional white-light imaging.

REFERENCES

1. Prahl S: Tabulated molar extinction coefficient for hemoglobin in water. Oregon Medical Laser Center 2001. Available at http://omlc.ogi.edu/spectra/hemoglobin/.
2. Friedland S, Benaron D, Parachikov I, Soetikno R: Measurement of mucosal capillary hemoglobin oxygen saturation in the colon by reflectance spectrophotometry. Gastrointest Endosc 57:492–497, 2003.
3. Leung FW, Slodownik E, Jensen DM, et al: Gastroduodenal mucosal hemodynamics by endoscopic reflectance spectrophotometry. Gastrointest Endosc 33:284–288, 1987.
4. Frank KH, Kessler M, Appelbaum K, Dummler W: The Erlangen micro-lightguide spectrophotometer EMPHO I. Phys Med Biol 34:1883–1900, 1989.
5. Leung FW, Morishita T, Livingston EH, et al: Reflectance spectrometry for the assessment of gastroduodenal mucosal perfusion. Am J Physiol 252:G797–804, 1987.
6. Chance B, Mayevsky A, Goodwin C, Mela L: Factors in oxygen delivery to tissues. Microvasc Res 8:276–282, 1974.
7. Sato N, Kamada T, Shichiri M, et al: Measurement of hemoperfusion and oxygen sufficiency in gastric mucosa in vivo. Gastroenterology 76:814–819, 1979.
8. Kamada T, Sato N, Kawano S, et al: Gastric mucosal hemodynamics after thermal or head injury. A clinical application of reflectance spectrophotometry. Gastroenterology 83:535–540, 1982.
9. Kamada T, Sato N, Kawano S, et al: Studies on the mechanism of acute gastric mucosal lesion. (III). The hemoperfusion and oxygen insufficiency in the gastric mucosa after head-or thermal-injury analyzed by reflectance spectrophotometry. Nippon Shokakibyo Gakkai Zasshi 78:2302–2307, 1981.
10. Kamada T, Kawano S, Sato N, et al: Gastric mucosal blood flow distribution and its changes in the healing process of gastric ulcer. Gastroenterology 84:1541–1546, 1983.
11. Leung FW, Wong DN, Lau J, et al: Endoscopic assessment of blood flow in duodenal ulcers. Gastrointest Endosc 40:334–341, 1994.

12. Temmesfeld-Wollbruck B, Szalay A, Mayer K, et al: Abnormalities of gastric mucosal oxygenation in septic shock: Partial responsiveness to dopexamine. Am J Respir Crit Care Med 157:1586–1592, 1998.

13. Beuthan J, Minet O, Helfmann J, et al: The spatial variation of the refractive index in biological cells. Phys Med Biol 41:369–382, 1996.

14. Sloot PM, Hoekstra AG, Figdor CG: Osmotic response of lymphocytes measured by means of forward light scattering: theoretical considerations. Cytometry 9:636–641, 1988.

15. Perelman LT, Backman V, Wallace MB, et al: Observation of periodic fine structure in reflectance from biological tissue: A new technique for measuring nuclear size distribution. Phys Rev Lett 80:627–630, 1998.

16. Wallace MB, Perelman LT, Backman V, et al: Endoscopic detection of dysplasia in patients with Barrett's esophagus using light-scattering spectroscopy. Gastroenterology 119:677–682, 2000.

17. Kapadia CR, Cutruzzola FW, O'Brien KM, et al: Laser-induced fluorescence spectroscopy of human colonic mucosa. Detection of adenomatous transformation. Gastroenterology 99:150–157, 1990.

18. Cothren RM, Richards-Kortum R, Sivak MV Jr, et al: Gastrointestinal tissue diagnosis by laser-induced fluorescence spectroscopy at endoscopy. Gastrointest Endosc 36:105–111, 1990.

19. Cothren RM, Sivak MV Jr, Van Dam J, et al: Detection of dysplasia at colonoscopy using laser-induced fluorescence: A blinded study. Gastrointest Endosc 44:168–176, 1996.

20. Schomacker KT, Frisoli JK, Compton CC, et al: Ultraviolet laser-induced fluorescence of colonic polyps. Gastroenterology 102:1155–1160, 1992.

21. Schomacker KT, Frisoli JK, Compton CC, et al: Ultraviolet laser-induced fluorescence of colonic tissue: basic biology and diagnostic potential. Lasers Surg Med 12:63–68, 1992.

22. Panjehpour M, Overholt BF, Schmidhammer JL, et al: Spectroscopic diagnosis of esophageal cancer: new classification model, improved measurement system. Gastrointest Endosc 41:577–581, 1995.

23. Panjehpour M, Overholt BF, Vo-Dinh T, et al: Endoscopic fluorescence detection of high-grade dysplasia in Barrett's esophagus. Gastroenterology 111:93–101, 1996.

24. Vo-Dinh T, Panjehpour M, Overholt BF, et al: In vivo cancer diagnosis of the esophagus using differential normalized fluorescence (DNF) indices. Lasers Surg Med 16:41–47, 1995.

25. Brand S, Wang TD, Schomacker KT, et al: Detection of high-grade dysplasia in Barrett's esophagus by spectroscopy measurement of 5-aminolevulinic acid-induced protoporphyrin IX fluorescence. Gastrointest Endosc 56:479–487, 2002.

26. Wang TD, Crawford JM, Feld MS, et al: In vivo identification of colonic dysplasia using fluorescence endoscopic imaging. Gastrointest Endosc 49:447–455, 1999.

27. Wang TD, Van Dam J, Crawford JM, et al: Fluorescence endoscopic imaging of human colonic adenomas. Gastroenterology 111:1182–1191, 1996.

28. Zonios GI, Cothren RM, Arendt JT, et al: Morphological model of human colon tissue fluorescence. IEEE Trans Biomed Eng 43:113–122, 1996.

29. Haringsma J, Tytgat GN, Yano H, et al: Autofluorescence endoscopy: feasibility of detection of GI neoplasms unapparent to white light endoscopy with an evolving technology. Gastrointest Endosc 53:642–650, 2001.

30. Abe S, Izuishi K, Tajiri H, et al: Correlation of in vitro autofluores-cence endoscopy images with histopathologic findings in stomach cancer. Endoscopy 32:281–286, 2000.

31. DaCosta RS, Wilson BC, Marcon NE: Light-induced fluorescence endoscopy of the gastrointestinal tract. Gastrointest Endosc Clin N Am 10:37–69, 2000.

32. Mayinger B, Reh H, Hochberger J, Hahn EG: Endoscopic photodynamic diagnosis: oral aminolevulinic acid is a marker of

33. Messmann H: 5-Aminolevulinic acid-induced protoporphyrin IX for the detection of gastrointestinal dysplasia. Gastrointest Endosc Clin N Am 10:497–512, 2000.

34. Molckovsky A, Song, LW, Shim MG, et al: Diagnostic potential of near-infrared Raman spectroscopy in the colon: Differentiating adenomatous from hyperplastic polyps. Gastrointest Endosc 57:396–402, 2003.

35. Boustany NN, Crawford JM, Manoharan R, et al: Analysis of nucleotides and aromatic amino acids in normal and neoplastic colon mucosa by ultraviolet resonance Raman spectroscopy. Lab Invest 79:1201–1214, 1999.

36. Fujimoto JG, Brezinski ME, Tearney GJ, et al: Optical biopsy and imaging using optical coherence tomography. Nat Med 1:970–972, 1995.

37. Tearney GJ, Brezinski ME, Bouma BE, et al: In vivo endoscopic optical biopsy with optical coherence tomography. Science 276:2037–2039, 1997.

38. Das A, Sivak MV Jr, Chak A, et al: High-resolution endoscopic imaging of the GI tract: A comparative study of optical coherence tomography versus high-frequency catheter probe EUS. Gastrointest Endosc 54:219–224, 2001.

39. Jackle S, Gladkova N, Feldchtein F, et al: In vivo endoscopic optical coherence tomography of esophagitis, Barrett's esophagus, and adenocarcinoma of the esophagus. Endoscopy 32:750–755, 2000.

40. Poneros JM, Brand S, Bouma BE, et al: Diagnosis of specialized intestinal metaplasia by optical coherence tomography. Gastroenterology 120:7–12, 2001.

41. Zuccaro G, Gladkova N, Vargo J, et al: Optical coherence tomography of the esophagus and proximal stomach in health and disease. Am J Gastroenterol 96:2633–2639, 2001.

42. Kobayashi K, Izatt JA, Kulkarni MD, et al: High-resolution cross-sectional imaging of the gastrointestinal tract using optical coherence tomography: preliminary results. Gastrointest Endosc 47: 515–523, 1998.

43. Jackle S, Gladkova N, Feldchtein F, et al: In vivo endoscopic optical coherence tomography of the human gastrointestinal tract—toward optical biopsy. Endoscopy 32:743–749, 2000.

44. Pitris C, Jesser C, Boppart SA, et al: Feasibility of optical coherence tomography for high-resolution imaging of human gastrointestinal tract malignancies. J Gastroenterol 35:87–92, 2000.

45. Seitz U, Freund J, Jaeckle S, et al: First in vivo optical coherence tomography in the human bile duct. Endoscopy 33:1018–1021, 2001.

46. Poneros JM, Tearney GJ, Shiskov M, et al: Optical coherence tomography of the biliary tree during ERCP. Gastrointest Endosc 55:84–88, 2002.

47. Fujimoto JG, Bouma B, Tearney GJ, et al: New technology for high-speed and high-resolution optical coherence tomography. Ann N Y Acad Sci 838:95–107, 1998.

48. Li XD, Boppart SA, Van Dam J, et al: Optical coherence tomography: Advanced technology for the endoscopic imaging of Barrett's esophagus. Endoscopy 32:921–930, 2000.

49. Wong RC, Yazdanfar S, Izatt JA, et al: Visualization of subsurface blood vessels by color Doppler optical coherence tomography in rats: Before and after hemostatic therapy. Gastrointest Endosc 55:88–95, 2002.

50. Mataki N, Nagao S, Kawaguchi A, et al: Clinical usefulness of a new infrared videoendoscope system for diagnosis of early stage gastric cancer. Gastrointest Endosc 57:336–342, 2003.

51. Avenhaus W, Kemper B, von Bally G, et al: Gastric wall elasticity assessed by dynamic holographic endoscopy: Ex vivo investigations in the porcine stomach. Gastrointest Endosc 54:496–500, 2001.

52. Wang TD, Mandella MJ, Contag CH, Kino GS: Dual-axis confocal microscope for high-resolution in vivo imaging. Opt Lett 28:414–416, 2003.

GI cancer and dysplastic lesions. Gastrointest Endosc 50:242–246, 1999.

Index

Page numbers followed by "f" indicate figures; "t," tables; "b," boxes.

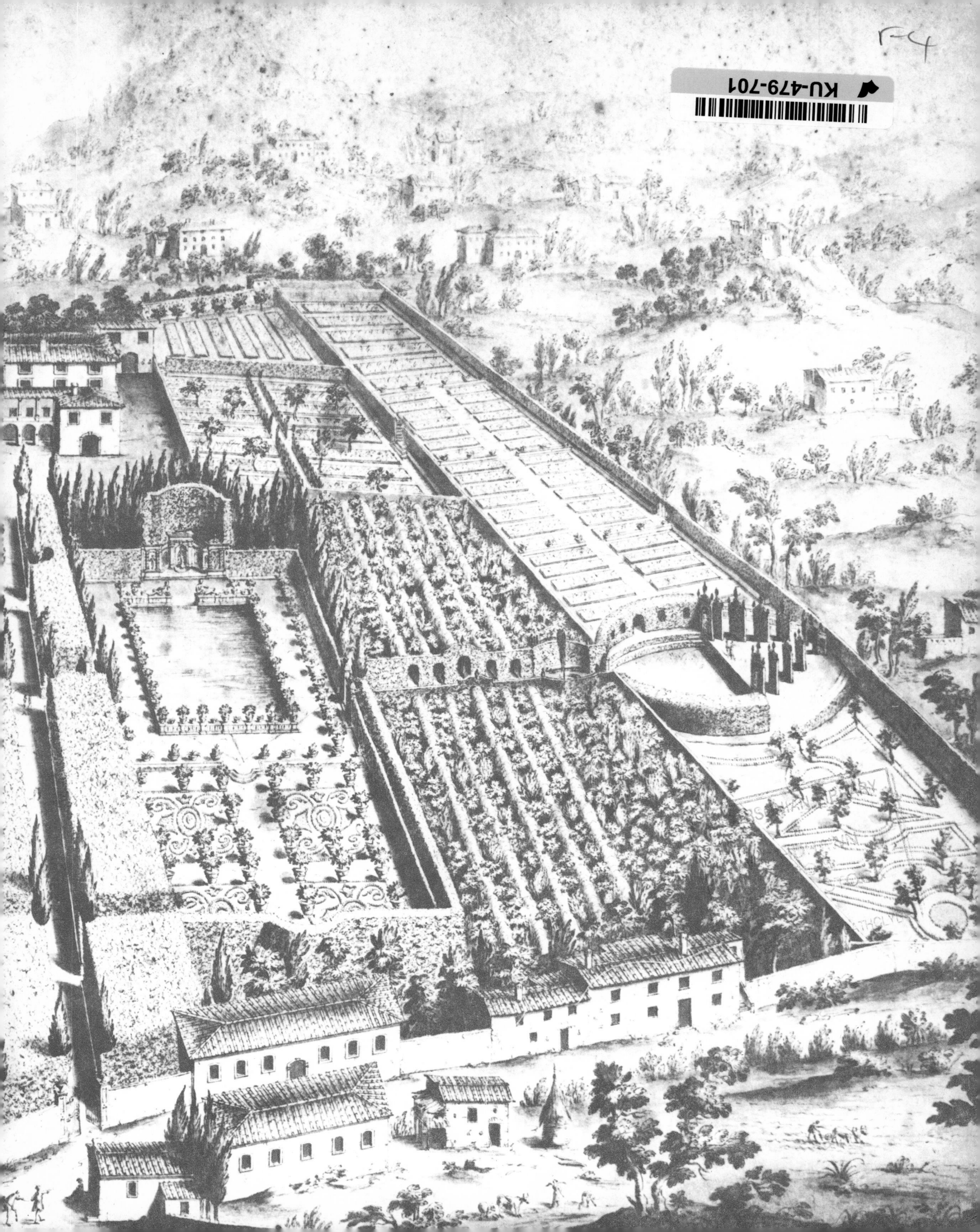

TUSCAN
VILLAS

TUSCAN VILLAS

HAROLD ACTON

with photographs by

Alexander Zielcke

126 plates in photogravure
19 text illustrations
and 34 colour plates

T & H

THAMES AND HUDSON

ISBN 0 500 24085 X

CONTENTS

ACKNOWLEDGMENTS

We wish to acknowledge our gratitude to those who have allowed us to photograph their villas and gardens and who have expressed their interest in many helpful ways. Among these kind friends we are particularly indebted to: the Conti Amati-Cellesi, Professor Ranuccio Bianchi Bandinelli, Mr and Mrs Ernest Boissevain, Marchesa Ginevra Chigi-Bonelli, Mr and Mrs Henry Clifford, Duchessa Simonetta Colonna, Marchese Vieri d'Elci, Contessa Adriana Gardi dell'Ardenghesca, Marchese Giaquili-Ferrini, the Conti Guicciardini Corsi-Salviati, Don Giovanni Guiso, Contessa Laura Mansi-Salom, Ing. Ferruccio and Signora Marchi, Dr Marcello Marchi, Conte Dino Pecci-Blunt and his sisters, Onorevole Comm. Paolo Rossi and Signora Rossi, Signora Marjorie Scaretti, Contessa Sofia Serristori Bossi-Pucci. We hope not to offend protocol by mentioning these friends in alphabetical order.

Our thanks are also due to Dr Riccardo Francovich and Signor Mario Falsini of Scala (Florence) for their invaluable collaboration, and to Mr Ian Greenlees for the loan of a rare book from his private library.

Harold Acton
Alexander Zielcke

To the memory of
ARTHUR M. ACTON

INTRODUCTION

Since more and more of the great country houses are disappearing and doomed to disappear – unless they be preserved by National Trusts in an age of expanding penal taxation – it seemed timely to record those ancient dwellings which survive in Tuscany and which have long been famous for their beauty and historical associations either separate or combined. Those which have had the rare good fortune to remain in private hands are naturally the best cared for. How soon a dwelling loses its warmth, charm, personality, when it is relegated to museum status! How many houses that were designed to be lived in by a particular family or patron of the arts are reduced to pathetic carcases unless their original contents remain *in situ*, and even then the ancestral portraits, tapestries and furniture, intended to serve as a background for their owner's daily life, are roped off like crown jewels.

Certain houses played an important part in the development of humanism and of such dynamic characters as Lorenzo the Magnificent, and it should enhance the visitor's appreciation of a building if he knows enough about its past history to let his imagination wander evocatively beyond its external appearance. The significant form so dear to Roger Fry becomes far more significant when living history is attached to it.

The purpose of this book is to reflect the past life of the most typical Tuscan villas, to treat them as living entities wherever possible, though in many instances they are now void of inhabitants or transformed into quasi-anonymous institutions. Nearly all of them enjoyed periods of high prosperity, of gaiety if not glory, in the social and cultural heyday of bygone Florence. Some of the most celebrated, repeatedly praised in travel books since the sixteenth century, have either vanished utterly, like the central structure and formal garden of Pratolino whose wonders were engraved by Stefano della Bella, or been converted, like Poggio Imperiale, into a genteel school for girls. Others, long left to moulder in a state of desolation, like Castello and Poggio a Caiano, are gradually being restored, the former as a home for the Accademia della Crusca with the apparatus of its vast vocabulary, the latter to serve as a museum of sculpture and paintings of botanical and ornithological subjects which are overlooked among the spectacular masterpieces of the Florentine galleries. Their original residents had a yearning for the countryside and its amenities after toiling at their counters in the city. They were seldom as rigidly urbanized as their descendants but they wanted nature to be tamed into formal gardens and vineyards.

Few modern families can afford to live as they did formerly in manors of such spacious dimensions, hence many old villas are divided into apartments and stables are turned into garages. Even in Italy modern families have a tendency to grow smaller and more nomadic.

Being neither an architect nor a botanist I might be deemed presumptuous. My excuse is that I was born and brought up in a typical Tuscan villa which had always been inhabited since, and perhaps before, the fifteenth century when Francesco Sassetti bought it. Each generation has left a trace but it is essentially Tuscan in its simplicity and adaptability. To have opened one's eyes, physical and mental, in such surroundings, and to have watched the garden grow again as it might have been before the craze for so-called English or landscape gardening overwhelmed it in the nineteenth century, has no doubt influenced my personal vision and attitude.

Italy abounds in imposing mansions, from the Palladian splendours of the Veneto to the spectral palaces of the Sicilian nobility, but few of these are as adaptable to modern conditions as the more modest houses of Tuscany. As in England the grounds are an integral part of the country house, yet what we mean by 'stately homes' does not apply to them in general. The thriving and thrifty Florentine merchants of the early Renaissance revelled in rustic occupations: Cosimo de' Medici the Elder delighted in pruning his vines for hours together; and the oldest villas were castellated farmhouses surrounded by acres of orchards and vineyards. With increasing wealth and security they enlarged their dwellings and paid more attention to garden design. In this as in other artistic developments the Medici were the leaders. The grandest Florentine villas were built by members of this dynasty and are consequently better known than others of equal or greater charm and beauty.

More massive than graceful, these earlier villas were invariably built on healthy sites and had the advantage of harmonizing with the scenery. Hillsides were usually preferred. Ranging from the Mugello to Siena, the landscape has been rendered most exquisitely in the backgrounds of the early Tuscan painters, its craggy hills and fertile valleys where cypress, pine and ilex stand singly or in friendly groups above the silvery olives, neatly cubistic castles trying to look impregnable here and there though they never succeed in frowning under such azure skies. Large areas are still mercifully unspoiled by the rising tide of Philistine speculation. Some of the loveliest villas are hidden behind high walls and are as worthy of attention as the 'showplaces' of the guide-books. The proprietor could say truly that his home was his castle, dependent on its own resources, and in earlier times it had to be a castle for protection against roving bandits and predatory mercenaries.

One is apt to forget how much of the countryside was unsafe for travellers until the nineteenth century. Even in 1817 the road between Rome and Florence was so infested with brigands that travellers from the north chose to return there by the Adriatic route. This did not deter several rich Englishmen from settling in Tuscan villas during the eighteenth century and we hear a lot about them from the gossipy Sir Horace Mann, first Secretary of Legation and then Minister to the Court of Tuscany from 1740 to 1786, described by Lady Holland as 'the most obliging polite man that ever lived, has a charming house, shows away, and lives most elegantly. The mixture of Germans and other strangers' (she added), 'make this place better than Rome or Naples for society.'*

'If I could afford it, I really would take a villa near Florence,' Mann wrote to Horace Walpole in July 1750, 'but I am afraid of its becoming a cheesecake house for all the English, though the King's Arms is vastly frequented by them in town, so that I have not a moment to myself. Sometimes I fancy I should be quieter there, and yet I am afraid to venture, for fear of their friendly visits in the morning, to avoid the heat, and their lasting the whole day.'

The most prominent of eighteenth-century settlers were George Nassau, 3rd Earl Cowper, at the Villa Palmieri, and the equally eccentric Countess of Orford at the Villa Medici of Fiesole. During the nineteenth century the English settlers formed a considerable colony. (Signora Giuliana Artom Treves has described their activities in her fascinating study *Gli Anglo-Fiorentini 1847–1862*, translated by Sylvia Sprigge as *The Golden Ring*, London 1956.) That colony was still flourishing during my childhood and its members were no whit less eccentric than their predecessors, including Mrs Janet Ross of Poggio Gherardo, who wrote one of the most readable, if unwieldy, quartos about Florentine villas (London 1901). Mrs Ross was portrayed as 'Lady Joan' in Ouida's classic *Friendship*, and a rival authoress wrote of her in 1902: 'She no longer traffics in "Murillos" and "Peruginos" with the names of these painters inscribed in large gold letters on their frames – all to be sold for the benefit of distressed Italian families – but has turned her attention to pastoral pursuits, and places her oil and wine on the English market, no doubt as much to the advantage of her customers as to her own, which could hardly be said of the old line of business.' Her fragrant vermouth, concocted according to a 'secret Medicean recipe', used to be on sale at the Army and Navy Stores in London, and the goldfish in my ponds are descended from the long-tailed specimens her husband brought back from China at the time of the Boxer Rebellion – or was it earlier? Alas, they are bastardized and have lost their rococo tails.

Many of these good settlers dabbled in polite literature inspired by their villas, and one villa led to another. In the early 1900s there was an amazing proliferation of books with such titles as *In a Tuscan Garden*, and they contain many a gem of unconscious humour. Nothing could be less Tuscan in tone

* Duchess of Leinster, Correspondence, ed. Fitzgerald, Dublin 1949–57. I, 505.

11

than these naively priggish volumes: their authors did not begin to understand or adapt themselves to their environment. On the contrary. 'Old Italian villas', we read (*In a Tuscan Garden*), 'about which so much has been written, and to the idea of which so much romance clings, are, as a matter of fact, for the most part, gaunt, barren, hideous structures outside, and conspicuous for every kind of inconvenience within. You never see a creeper of any kind planted against their walls to soften their staring outline, and they have a desolate, forlorn look, in strong contrast to our own lovely English houses.'

That benighted craving for creepers . . . Imagine ivy on the superb façade of Artimino or Poggio a Caiano! The same lady confides that after finding a villa to her liking, she 'employed a very good decorator, and the house was stencilled throughout in artistic designs, copied from old Italian brocades.' Very few of the conveniences described by Mr Mark Girouard in *The Victorian Country House* (Oxford 1971), such as bells in each room, luggage lifts, pull-out racks in the airing cupboard, and closets for the ironing of newspapers, were to be found in villas that had scarcely changed since they were built in the fifteenth century, though undoubtedly these expatriates introduced a number of conveniences. When my parents built bathrooms in La Pietra an old Lady Airlie remarked to my mother: 'But isn't it nicer to have a tub brought into the bedroom and let the maid pour warm water over one?' Evidently hip-baths had satisfied the Prussian Minister and his guests when La Pietra served as his legation until Rome became the capital of Italy.

Few have analyzed the emotions of the Anglo-American expatriate with the perspicacity of Henry James. Though he chose to settle in England rather than Italy he understood the lure of the Tuscan villa with a sensibility superior to most of his contemporaries. His article on 'Italy Revisited' published in his *Portraits of Places* (1883) was written, as he confessed, 'with the full consciousness of having no information whatever to offer,' yet his tastes and opinions are reflected on every page, and these are perhaps more precious than the facts of guide-books. After a climb to Bellosguardo in 1877 he noted: 'The villas are innumerable, and if one is a stranger half the talk is about villas. This one has a story; that one has another; they all look as if they had stories. Most of them are offered to rent (many of them for sale) at prices unnaturally low: you may have a tower and a garden, a chapel and an expanse of thirty windows, for five hundred dollars a year. In imagination you hire three or four: you take possession, and settle, and live there. About the finest there is something very grave and stately: about two or three of the best there is something even solemn and tragic. From what does this latter impression come? You gather it as you stand there in the early dusk, looking at the long, pale brown façade, the enormous windows, the iron cages fastened upon the lower ones. Part of the brooding expression of these great houses comes, even when they have not fallen into decay, from their look of having outlived their original use. Their extraordinary largeness and massiveness are a satire upon their present fate. They were not built with such a thickness of wall and depth of embrasure, such a solidity of staircase and superfluity of stone, simply to afford an economical winter residence to English and American families.'

With a few eminent exceptions the latter have departed like the nymphs in T. S. Eliot's *Waste Land*, and no villa can be rented any longer for five hundred dollars a year. As far back as 1902 the authoress of *In a Tuscan Garden* complained that the expenses of living in Italy had increased enormously within the last thirty years, yet an interesting variety of Englishmen of slender means were painting and writing and botanizing in remote country villas. The temptation to dwell on these cultured expatriates must be firmly resisted here though many have played beneficent and recreative roles.

The multitude of villas perched on the verdant hills dominating the valley of the Arno have always been one of the attractions of Florence and we have been confronted by an *embarras de choix*. After mature deliberation we have decided to offer a characteristic selection based on Giuseppe Zocchi's famous book of engraved views, *Vedute delle ville e d'altri luoghi della Toscana*, first published in 1744 and re-issued in 1754, extending these to the neighbourhood of Siena and Lucca and presenting their salient virtues without cramming the reader with indigestible information. While they share a family resemblance that distinguishes them from the country houses of other provinces, they are by no means all of a pattern. The villas near Siena and Lucca are sharply differentiated. Each century has left its seal, but even in the Baroque period, when they grew more ornate, their decoration was more restrained than elsewhere in Italy. Some have no garden to speak of: the many-chimneyed pile of Artimino was surrounded by an extensive hunting park. Others are more garden than house, a series of open-air drawing-rooms. Some with sober exteriors are elaborately decorated within, reflecting the luxury and pomp of their former occupants, who entertained lavishly on special occasions in contrast with the rustic simplicity of the average *villeggiatura*. The essence of their charm is not always amenable to reproduction, especially when the house faced the highway long before the advent of motorized traffic.

All writers about Florence and its vicinity are heavily indebted to Emanuele Repetti's encyclopaedic *Dizionario Geografico Fisico Storico della Toscana* (1833), to D. Moreni's *Notizie istoriche dei contorni di Firenze* (1792), and to Guido Carocci's *I Dintorni di Firenze* (1906), which have been quoted and paraphrased copiously, often without acknowledgment. These are seminal works, profuse in details which are mainly of interest to Florentine readers, recording the builders and purchasers of each house mentioned, including the cost of purchase and subsequent modifications. Students of Florentine topography and history cannot skip them, but they are too particularized for the general reader. Janet Ross, Edward Hutton, H. D. Eberlein, and more recently the two comprehensive volumes of Signor Giulio Cesare Lensi Orlandi Cardini, are as beholden to these valuable sources as we are, since fundamental facts cannot be re-invented. Signora Isa Belli Barsali has dealt exhaustively with the villas near Lucca in her erudite tome *La Villa a Lucca dal XV al XIX Secolo* (Rome 1964), but we have nothing comparable about the great villas of Siena, though Edith Wharton and Miss Georgina Masson have picked the best plums among Sienese country houses in their admirable essays of a more compendious nature. Miss Masson's *Italian Gardens* (1961) is the most important of recent books on the subject but it covers most of the peninsula. We have felt that Tuscany remains worthy of broader treatment, and we trust that Alexander Zielcke's photographs are our justification.

Since the mass migration of land workers to urban factories after the last world war, vast areas of once-flourishing vineyards and olive plantations have been abandoned together with their farmhouses, whose broad arches, turreted dovecotes, roomy interiors and red-tiled roofs are often as handsome as the manor they belonged to. Many of these *case coloniche* have been profitably converted into sophisticated modern dwellings, as their thick walls make them cool in summer and easily heated in winter, and they require little domestic staff – another increasing rarity. Larger and more solid than the average English cottage, they can be made equally cosy with the aid of modern plumbing. The demand for these is rising steadily, especially in the Chianti region renowned for its vintages, and they are coming to cost more than a historic villa in the time of Henry James. Consequently the most recent settlers in Tuscany choose a manageable *casa colonica* in preference to the grander villa, of which many are now for sale, like the fine castle of Montegufoni.

I
MEDICEAN
VILLAS

See notes on pp. 271–275

2

3

4

5

6

7

8    9

10  11

12

POGGIO

13

14

15

16

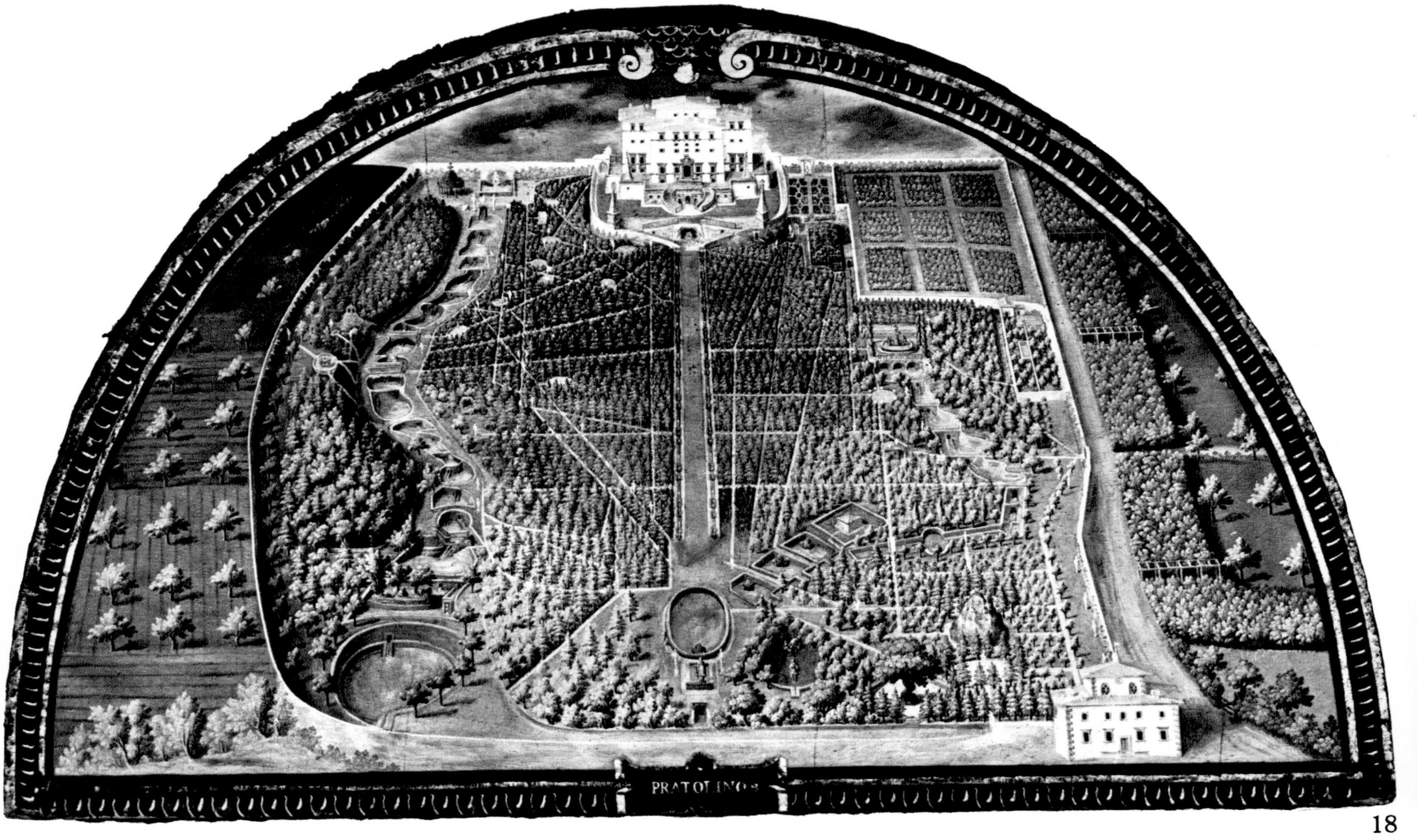

PRATOLINOS

18
19

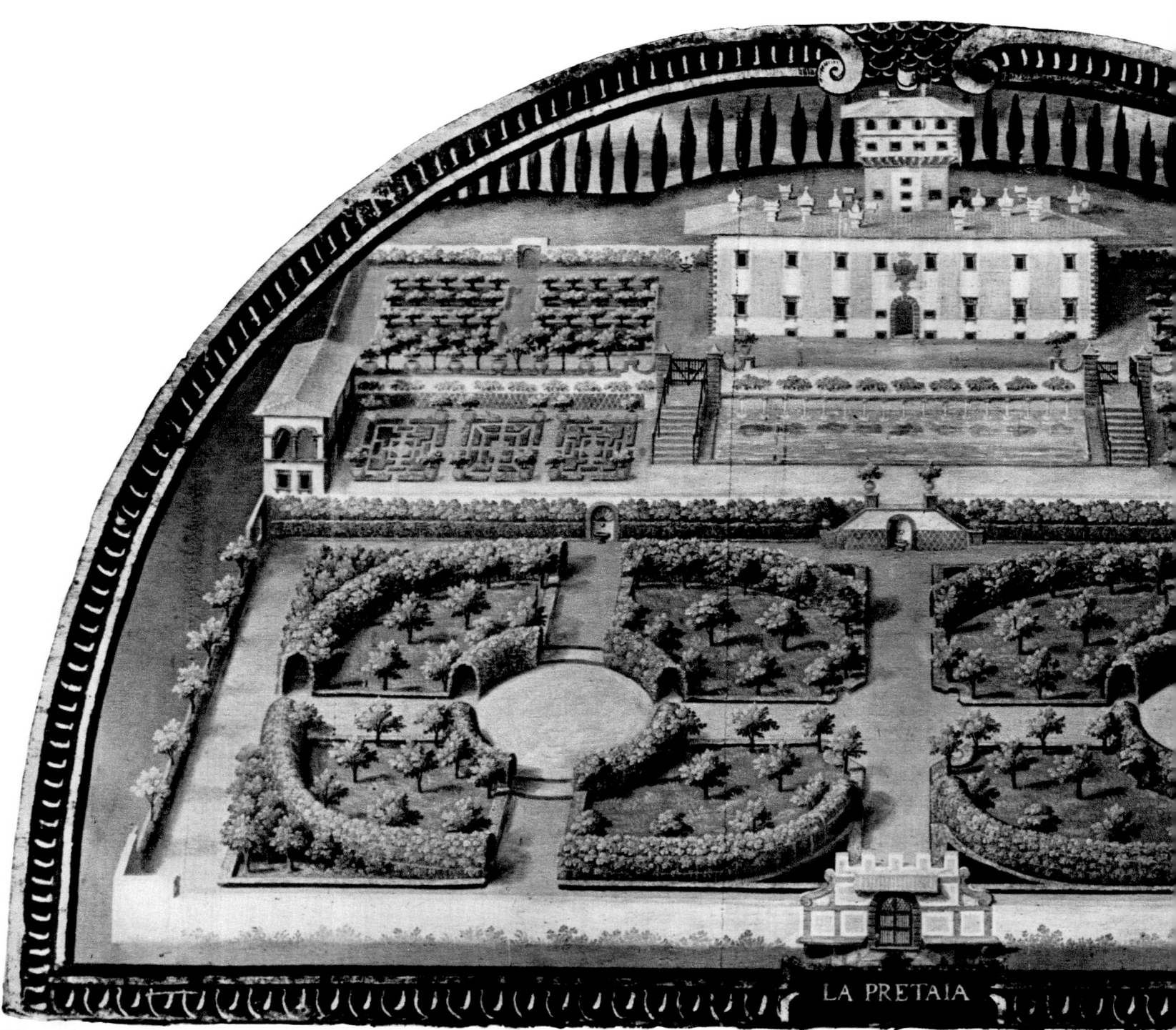

LA PRETAIA

23

24

IMPERIALE VILLA DELL

SERENI · ARCIDVCESSA · DI TOSCANA

Alfonso Parigi. I et f

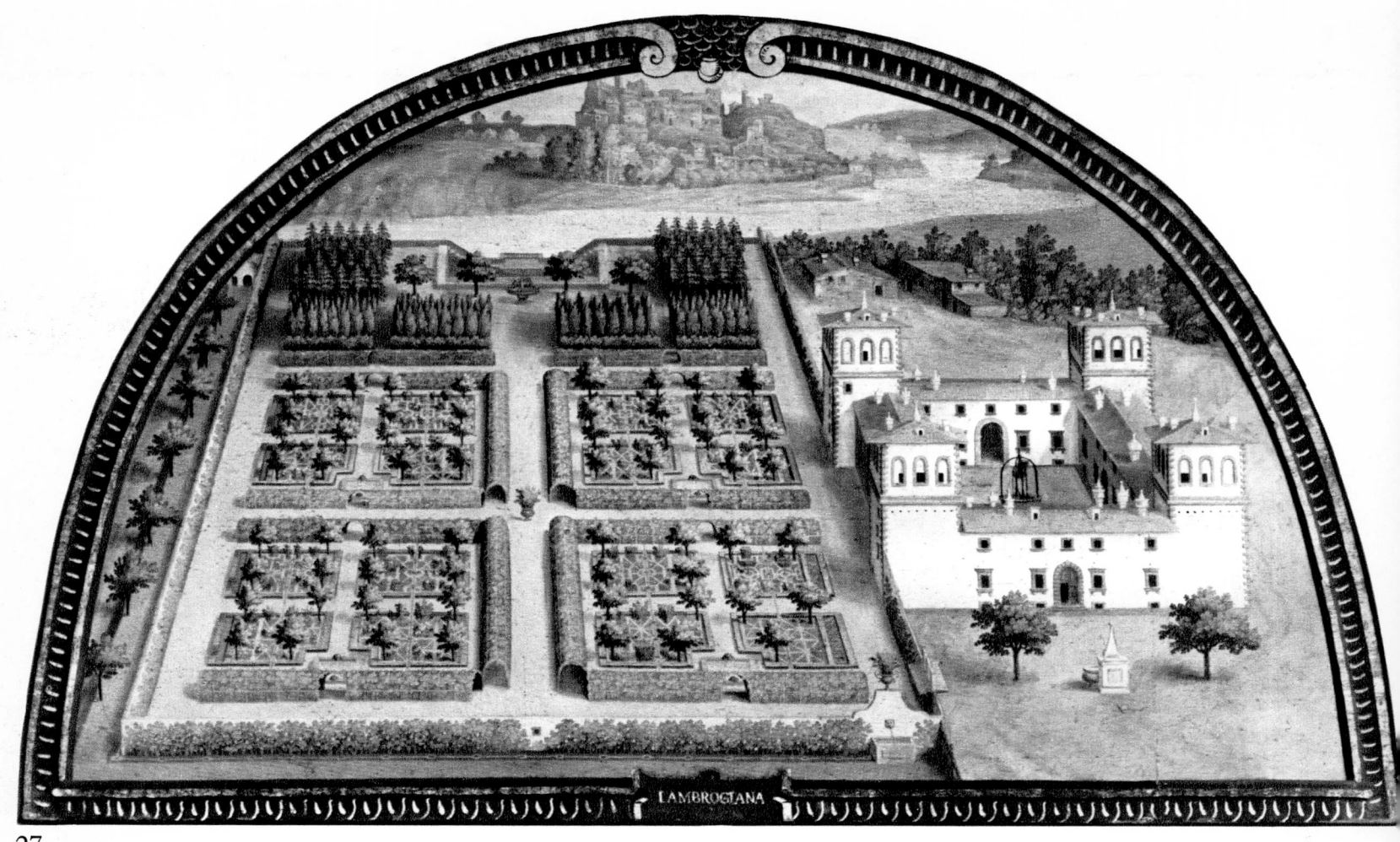

27

LAMBROGIANA

LA PEGGIO

28

MEDICEAN VILLAS

Gaetano Pieraccini's three monumental volumes on the Medici family, unique as a chronology of their physical diseases, are aptly entitled *La stirpe de' Medici di Cafaggiolo* because it was from this part of the mountainous Mugello region north of Florence that the obscure ancestors of this great dynasty migrated to the city to seek and find their fortune during the thirteenth century. Hence both Cafaggiolo and Il Trebbio, castles rather than country houses, are closely connected with the origins of the Medici, who retained an atavistic attachment to them.

To remind his progeny of their distant origin in the Mugello and prolong the image of an ancestral home of his own creation, Cosimo the Elder commissioned his favourite architect Michelozzo Michelozzi to build the castle of Cafaggiolo in the style of a feudal fortress. According to Giorgio Vasari (whose *Lives of the most eminent Painters, Sculptors, and Architects* remains an invaluable work of reference in guiding the scholar to his sources without pedantic dullness', Michelozzo surrounded Cafaggiolo with a moat which has vanished since, together with one of its original towers in the left wing. He also laid out farms, new roads, gardens, fountains with groves around them, thickets for bird-catching, with 'all the requisites of distinguished country houses.' That was in 1451.

We miss the highest tower and the drawbridge before its entrance as portrayed by Zocchi, but it still has a rugged elegance with its battlemented arches under the roof reminding one of the lace cap on an antiquated dame of formidable austerity. It is beautifully framed in the fertile landscape beneath rolling hills so that one regrets the gardens less, which were probably enclosed in medieval style. The interior is disappointing for it has been messed about in the last century. Better gaze at the rectangular masses against the sky and imagine it alive with huntsmen and bright-clad courtiers.

The fortress of Il Trebbio is more spectacular owing to its solitary situation on a wooded hilltop 2 kms above Cafaggiolo. Vasari tells us that Michelozzo executed various improvements but they are not easy to identify. Apparently he respected its initial nucleus in an archaeological spirit, building the courtyard with an outside staircase and loggia, the covered walk round the ramparts and under the roof of the twelfth-century tower. Possibly he added the distinctive crenellations. From its lofty square tower the view over the Mugello in every direction has scarcely changed since Dante took the winding road to exile, and its neat garden still has a medieval accent reminiscent of Pietro Crescenzi's treatise *Opus Ruralium Commodorum*, which had circulated for over a century in manuscript before it was printed in 1471; and of such delicate miniatures as illustrate the 'Romance of the Rose'.

Crescenzi recommended that the garden be square with every species of sweet-scented herb in its borders (sage, basil, marjoram, mint, goat's rue) and paths of grass, pergolas of vine for cool and delectable shade; in the midst of the lawn there should be no trees, but 'the fresh level of the grass left alone

*Cafaggiolo: engraving
after Giuseppe Zocchi*

in a pure and joyful air, and if possible a clear fountain, to add pleasure and gaiety by its beauty.'

Both these fortress-villas were used as summer resorts, especially for the younger generation, by Cosimo the Elder and his descendants. They could serve as strongholds in case of insurrection and as shelters in time of pestilence. Country life is conducive to letter writing, and many letters of the early Medici were written from Il Trebbio and Cafaggiolo. From a selection of these translated by Janet Ross* we gain fugitive impressions of their domestic lives in the Mugello, bucolically placid and even monotonous in contrast with events in the city some eighteen miles distant.

Cosimo the Elder was at Il Trebbio when he was summoned by the hostile Signoria of Florence in September 1433 to attend an urgent meeting in the Palazzo Vecchio. In spite of friendly warnings and private suspicions he risked obeying the summons. As when his grandson Lorenzo risked going into the lion's lair at Naples, he was amply vindicated by the sequel. In the meantime his powerful enemy Rinaldo degli Albizzi was resolved to ruin him. Cosimo's arrest in the course of a quiet conversation; his imprisonment in a tiny cell half-way up the tower of the Palazzo Vecchio; his semi-starvation for fear of poison and effective bribery of the Gonfalonier of Justice; his banishment to Padua for ten years instead of the death sentence his enemies desired: the dramatic details have been related in his diary as well as by the leading historians of Florence. Cosimo's conduct throughout this crisis was supremely self-confident. At the request of the Venetian government he was allowed to move to Venice where, as he wrote, 'I was received like an ambassador, not like an exile . . . It would hardly be believed that, banished from home I should find so much honour, for usually one loses one's friends with one's fortune.'

* *Lives of the Early Medici as told in their Correspondence,* London 1910.

But he had not lost his material fortune for he controlled banking houses in sixteen European cities and lent money to kings and popes. Niccolò d'Este of Ferrara and envoys from Venice pleaded his cause while his party in Florence gathered strength. A year later he was recalled by a majority of the Signoria and, as Machiavelli wrote, 'Seldom has a citizen returning triumphant from a victory been received by such a concourse of people and with such demonstrations of affection as was Cosimo on his return from exile, greeted by all as the benefactor of the people and the father of his country.' *Pater Patriae*: that memorable title was engraved on his simple tomb in San Lorenzo.

He had been followed to Venice by his faithful architect Michelozzo, whom he continued to load with commissions. His handsome town residence, now the Prefecture, the church and convent of San Marco with its noble vaulted library and rows of rhythmical columns, are among Michelozzo's most notable achievements, but we are concerned with the villas he designed and remodelled and these have been much altered since the fifteenth century. Besides Cafaggiolo and Il Trebbio he modernized the villa of Careggi and built the Medici villa of Fiesole for Cosimo's beloved son Giovanni, who predeceased him in 1463.

Careggi, now the mere annexe of a spreading medical centre two miles north-west of Florence, was renowned as the cradle of the Platonic Academy which under Cosimo's patronage was chiefly responsible for the growth of Italian Hellenism. Michelozzo enlarged and restored the building (which Cosimo's brother Lorenzo had acquired in 1417), with a courtyard, loggia, well, dovecote, tower, and walled orchard, preserving its outward character but transforming its interior. However, it conveys the impression of a city mansion transported into the country rather than of a genuine country house. The real Tuscan villa came into being when it was no longer necessary to defend it with castellations, when it had dropped its heavy coat of armour and could appear naked and unashamed.

Vasari describes Careggi as magnificent and tells us that Michelozzo 'conducted the water for the fountains we now see there', but all is changed except for the handsome courtyard. As it was nearer the city Cosimo spent more time at Careggi than in his other villas and it became a centre of cultural and political life, attracting scholars from other parts of Italy as well as from Constantinople. Here he kept his considerable library and filled the rooms with choice examples of the artists he most admired, such as Fra Filippo Lippi and Donatello, and Vasari gives many an amusing anecdote to illustrate his familiarity with these creative contemporaries. Donatello, he tells us, 'was the principal cause of Cosimo's resolve to bring the antiquities now in the Palazzo Medici to Florence, and all of which he restored with his own hand' – a pardonable exaggeration for the sculptor had several pupils working under him. Vespasiano da Bisticci, that earlier chronicler of the lives of eminent Florentines in the fifteenth century, relates that, 'As Donatello did not go dressed in the manner that Cosimo would have liked, the latter caused a mantle and cap to be made for him, with a cape beneath the mantle; and thus providing him with a new suit, he sent it to the master one morning that there was a festival, so that he might wear it on that occasion. Donato wore it once or twice, but after that he sent it back to Cosimo because, as he said, it appeared to him to be too dainty.'

According to Vasari again, Cosimo took care of the master when he became too decrepit to work. 'It is said, that when Cosimo found himself at the point of death, he left Donato in charge to Piero his son, who being a most careful executor of his father's will, bestowed on him a farm at Cafaggiolo, the income from which was of such amount that Donato might have lived on it most commodiously. He made great rejoicings over this gift accordingly, considering himself to be more than secured from the fear of dying of hunger by such a provision; but he had not held the property a year when he returned it to Piero, restoring the farm to him by the proper legal forms, declaring that he would not have his quiet destroyed by thinking of household cares and listening to the troubles and complaints of the farmers, who came pestering him every third day, now because the wind had unroofed the dovecote, then because his cattle had been seized for taxes, and anon because of the storms that had cut up his vines and fruit-trees; with all of which he was so completely worn out and wearied that he would rather die of hunger than be tormented by so many cares. Piero laughed at the simplicity of Donato, and to liberate him from this grievance he resumed possession of the farm (for Donato absolutely insisted upon this), but assigned him an income of equal or larger value, secured on the bank, and to be paid in cash; of this he received the due proportion every week while he lived, an arrangement which rejoiced him greatly. Thus, as the friend and servant of the house of Medici, Donato lived in cheerfulness and free from cares all the rest of his days . . .'

We have quoted this at length because it rings so true. The canny Tuscan farmer is still an inveterate grumbler. But Cosimo, who had a genuine interest in agriculture and understood his peasants, knew how to cope with their complaints and placate them with his dry humour and common sense. 'He could talk to them as if he had never done anything else but farm,' wrote Vespasiano da Bisticci, 'and he enjoyed grafting and pruning with his own hand. Once when an epidemic of plague kept him out of Florence at Careggi, in February when the vines are pruned, as soon as he rose he went to prune the vines, and for two hours he did nothing else. With these exercises of the body he alternated those of the spirit . . . He took no pleasure in any game except chess.'

Ammirato describes him as of medium height, with an olive complexion and of imposing presence. In his personal habits he was frugal, and his wife Contessina de' Bardi, who also belonged to a patrician banking family, was even more so, judging by her letters, which were those of a practical housewife. Thus she wrote to her son Giovanni at Volterra in December 1450: 'Your shoes were ready but they have made them black, so others must be made, and I will send them by the first messenger . . . Although I told you we paid too much for the pigs, I want you to send us a pig or a roe for Christmas, if they are offered to you gratis; if we have to buy them we will not have them. Messer Rosello writes that he is coming to spend Christmas with me, and has sent Cosimo a fine cloak of Polish fashion of marten and sable, a pair of gloves, and the tooth of a fish a foot and a half long. As we have to prepare for the festival of the Three Kings, they will make a little change from my cloth of gold.'

Other letters are concerned with summer and winter clothes, provisions for the family larder, and even stakes for the vineyard. In one she asked Giovanni to search in a cupboard for a pair of scissors belonging to Cosimo, who appreciated her domestic virtues but evidently tired of her chatter. He seldom wasted words and his moods of silent meditation worried her as he grew older. To her anxious questioning he replied: 'When we go to the country you are busy for a fortnight preparing for our departure, but since I am about to leave this life for another, does it not seem to you that I have much to occupy my thoughts?'

Cosimo's library was a great solace to him after the death of his son Giovanni, for whom he built the Medici villa at Fiesole. Giovanni's character resembled that of his nephew Lorenzo the Magnificent: he was an assiduous bibliophile addicted to music and the arts, and successive inhabitants of his villa seem to have shared his inclinations. Vasari described it as 'a splendid and noble palace, the foundations for the lower part of which were sunk at very great expense in the declivity of the hill, but this was not without its equivalent advantage, as there he made various cellars, storerooms, stables, and other handsome and useful accessories to the dwelling of a noble. Above these, and in addition to the usual halls, chambers, and other apartments, Michelozzo arranged special rooms for books and music. In short he gave a clear proof in this palace of his eminent skill as an architect, since it was so well constructed that although much exposed on that hill it has never sunk in the smallest degree.'

Every tourist and most Florentines make a point of climbing to Fiesole for the unparalleled panorama of Florence spread out in the valley below, and the owners of this villa had it all to themselves. Though Giovanni did not live long enough to make the most of it, his nephew Lorenzo spent many a fruitful hour of leisure here with Pico della Mirandola, Marsilio Ficino, Poliziano, and other Platonic friends. According to Poliziano, who often sang its praises, the Pazzi conspiracy to exterminate the Medici was to have started here. The plot had been hatched in Rome by Girolamo Riario, the notorious nephew of Pope Sixtus IV, but he sent his own nephew, the youthful Cardinal Rafaello Riario, to Florence instead of coming in person. The Cardinal went to stay with Jacopo de' Pazzi, head of the clan hostile to the Medici. Jacopo had two brothers and between them they had ten grown sons and many daughters: one of his nephews married Cosimo's grand-daughter Bianca but this did not deter him from his bloody scheme. After attending Mass in the Badia of San Domenico the Pazzi and the young prelate, who seems to have been an innocent pawn, were invited to dine at the villa by Lorenzo, but his brother Giuliano was unable to attend owing to 'an inflammation of the eyes', so the murder was postponed. Neither Lorenzo nor Giuliano, who were immensely popular, harboured any suspicion of their danger. The eventual assassination of Giuliano in the Cathedral has been related by many historians. He was an athletic figure of twenty-five, devoted to Lorenzo whose literary and artistic enthusiasm he shared, and his violent death was deplored by the Florentine majority. Lorenzo, though wounded in the neck, escaped to the sacristy. During the subsequent turmoil he sent his children to Cafaggiolo for safety.

After the extinction of the Medici, the villa at Fiesole was owned by various unusual and gifted personalities. Henry Swinburne wrote in June 1779: 'We dined with Lady Orford at her villa at Fiesole, in a glorious situation for views, and a very convenient, elegant house, perhaps the best furnished in Italy for neatness and propriety, but too high, too much confined, and on a rock which reflects a burning heat in summer.'* This eccentric Lady Orford was a Devonshire heiress whose maiden name was Margaret Rolle. She had married Sir Robert Walpole's eldest son (raised to the peerage in his father's lifetime), and was therefore Horace Walpole's sister-in-law, but she soon left her husband. After a sojourn in Naples she settled in Florence, where the Count de Richecourt, an influential Lorrainer, became one of her lovers. She was a sore trial to Sir Horace Mann, the English Minister, who mentioned her frequently in his letters to Horace Walpole. In October 1741 he wrote: 'The great Maffei (Scipione) writes from Verona (in whose neighbourhood my Lady Walpole is) that many a woman has he known but none so wise and learned as she is. Maffei constantly quarrels with everybody that contradicts him and declares them fools *ipso facto*. My Lady for many reasons will say yes to all the high-flown wisdom he pleases to utter, let him be as unintelligible as he will, and *ipso facto* will be declared wise too.' And in February 1742: 'Lady Walpole was here this morning for the first time she ever set foot in this house. She talks of nothing but Venice; goes about dressed *à la Veneziana*. I am no favourite still.'

In 1773 Sir Horace informed the other Horace that she had bought the villa of Fiesole, while the young Lord Orford, her profligate son, was faced with ruin and insanity in England. 'Cavalier Mozzi, her messenger, told me that she had commissioned him to desire that I would inform you that, if her age and ill health permitted, she would hasten to England, though she does not see in what shape she could be useful to her son . . .' When the news of her son's condition became more alarming, 'She came over to me, and expressed both her concern and her embarrassment, saying she was too old and infirm to take

* Henry Swinburne: *The Courts of Europe at the close of the last century*. London 1895.

46

such a journey, nor could see of what use she could be to him if she was there. . . . She set out yesterday for Naples, I believe, to bring away all her furniture, in order to fix in Tuscany.' Later in the year, being urged to go over to her unhappy son, she again pleaded infirmity, and in June, when her excuses were backed up by the announcement of her resolution not to go to England, desperate as was her son's condition, Mann wrote: 'You know her situation and will easily perceive that stronger motives than those which she alleges, of her age and health, will make her repugnance to return to England insurmountable; therefore, in my opinion, it will be vain to insist upon it.' 'As to Lady Orford's health,' he added, 'she rides for some hours every morning, and is in continual motion the rest of the day, by which she maintains a vivacity not common at her age.'

Lady Orford died in January 1781, leaving the villa and her other possessions to Cavalier Mozzi. 'The whole inheritance will be very considerable, reckoning only what she had here and at Naples,' wrote Mann. 'Neither she nor Mozzi had the least apprehension of the approach of death, till the 10th January, and she died on the 13th. She had indeed been in a declining state for some time, yet she dined and went about as usual, but never complained. . . . Mozzi has often assured me that Lady Orford never confided to him anything relating to her affairs in England; neither do I believe that she knew the detail of them herself; for it was her known custom, never, at least very seldom, to open any letter from her agents there; but threw them into a drawer, where many have been found sealed, as they came; all complaining of her silence and of the prejudice her affairs suffered by it . . . and yet she was very attentive to small expenses . . .

'I never heard of her having had two daughters by Richecourt nor do I believe it. You seem to be mistaken about Mozzi. He is of one of the most ancient families among the *nobiltà* here, and not poor for this country. She, to be sure, chose him for his beauty, which was then great and in its prime, but she wished it to be thought that his learning (for which he was distinguished, and he has published some approved works on the Mathematicks) biased her choice. Richecourt was nothing but what his place here made him, not young and of a very common figure. Mozzi's attention has been greatly rewarded, but his mother and his family, or I should better say his friends, always abused Lady Orford for being the obstacle to his marrying and raising issue to his own family, of which he is the only male.'

Cavalier Mozzi married three years later and sold the Villa Medici to the Buoninsegni family of Siena. In 1780 it had been transformed by the architect Gasparo Paoletti to suit eighteenth-century taste and there is little to remind us of Michelozzo, who would have been astonished by the Chinese wallpaper inside it. In the nineteenth century it was best known as Villa Spence from the name of its versatile and hospitable owner William Blundell Spence, a painter, musician, actor and collector, who entertained all the celebrities who came to

Florence and wrote a guide to the city. His self-portrait used to hang in the Uffizi and he was created a Cavalier like his predecessor Mozzi. During my youth the villa belonged to Lady Sybil Cutting (later Scott and Lubbock), whose richly talented daughter Marchesa Iris Origo, the biographer of Leopardi and Byron's 'Last Attachment', was brought up there. The Marchesa's childhood is vividly evoked in her recent *Images and Shadows*. A determined bluestocking, Lady Sybil was eccentric by modern standards. Like Lady Orford she complained of her health, yet she was remarkably vivacious by fits and starts. Something of the Platonic Academy still lingered in her day at the Villa Medici, with Geoffrey Scott and Percy Lubbock as the pale successors of Ficino and Poliziano.

With his subtle insight, Cosimo the Elder recognized the precocious genius of Marsilio Ficino and took him into his household when Ficino was eighteen. Under the tuition of John Argyropoulos he became an accomplished Greek scholar, especially trained to translate and interpret the works of Plato. Anti-Mediceans detect a serpentine cunning in Cosimo's cult for Platonism, as if he had a sinister intention to pervert the Tuscan character and distract it from political activity. His grandson Lorenzo, according to Signor Eugenio Garin, exploited Ficino 'not only to add brilliance to his house, but also for insidious reasons of political propaganda.' But Cosimo and Lorenzo were sincere humanists and all their efforts as patrons of art and letters prove them so. The rediscovery of Plato and Greek philosophy was as exciting to them as that of classical art to Donatello and Brunelleschi. Cosimo gave Ficino a villa now known as Le Fontanelle near Careggi, where he could pursue his studies in a peaceful atmosphere, and one of his last letters was written to Ficino: 'Yesterday I came to the villa of Careggi, not to cultivate my fields but my soul. Come to us, Marsilio, as soon as possible. Bring with you your Latin translation of our Plato, *De Summo Bono*, for I desire nothing so much as to learn the road to the greatest happiness.'

Cosimo, his son Piero the Gouty, and his grandson Lorenzo the Magnificent, all died at Careggi, which was packed with the works of art they had never ceased collecting. Unfortunately it was looted and partly burned by youthful extremists called the *Arrabbiati* ('the Enraged' – precursors of our 'Angry Brigade') when the Medici were expelled from Florence in 1494. During the reign of the Medici Grand Dukes, who restored it, Careggi was treated as an antiquated suburban dwelling among others far grander and more convenient. The Lorraine dynasty sold it in 1750 to Count Vincenzo Orsi, and Lord Holland rented it when he was Minister to the Tuscan Court in 1845. His guest G. F. Watts frescoed the fine loggia with an apocryphal scene – the murder of Lorenzo's doctor Piero Leoni. In fact the doctor went mad and drowned himself in a well after Lorenzo's death. Hence it was rumoured that he had poisoned Lorenzo and been thrown into a well in revenge, but as a French author pertinently remarked, doctors kill others, not

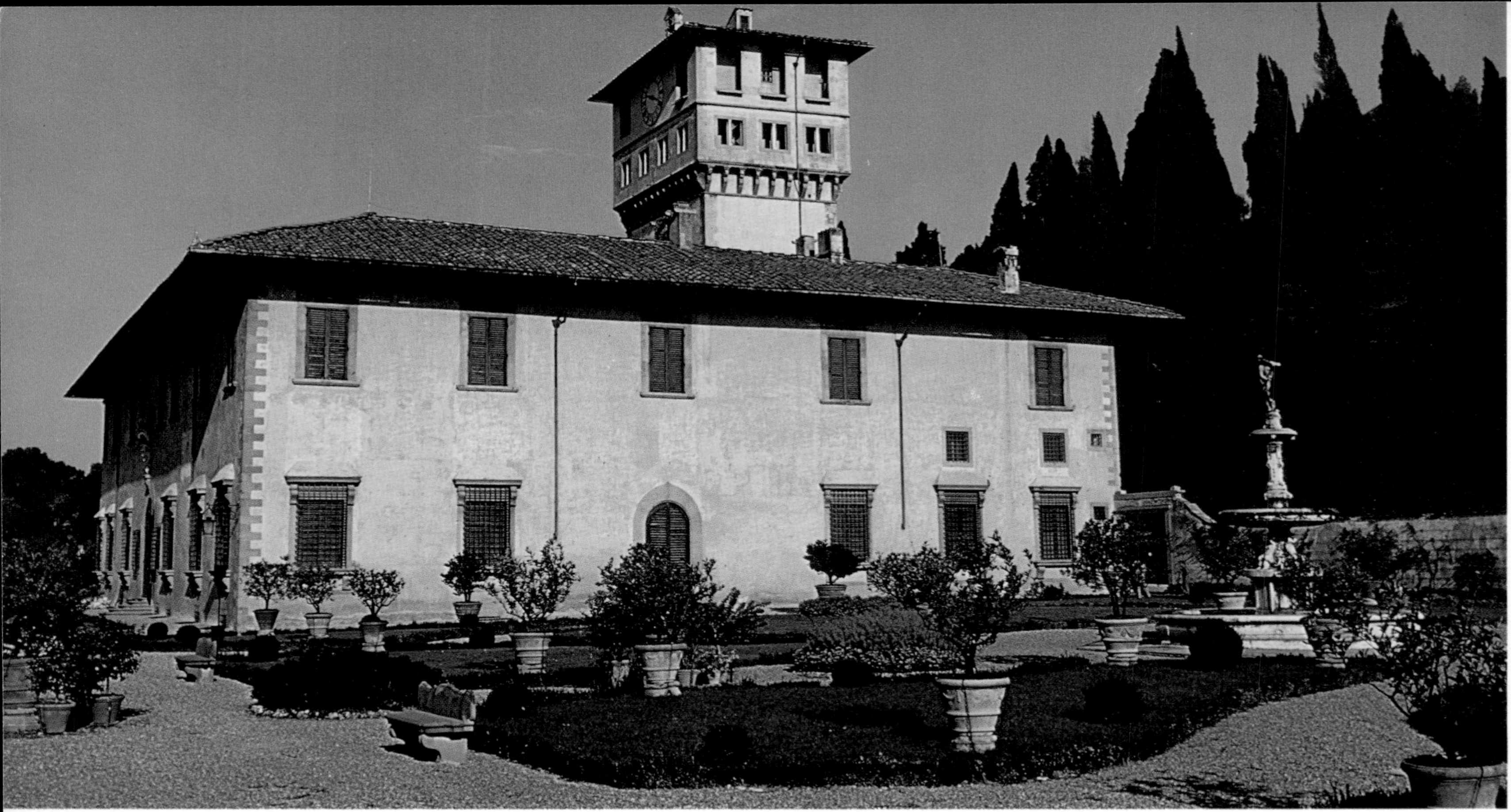

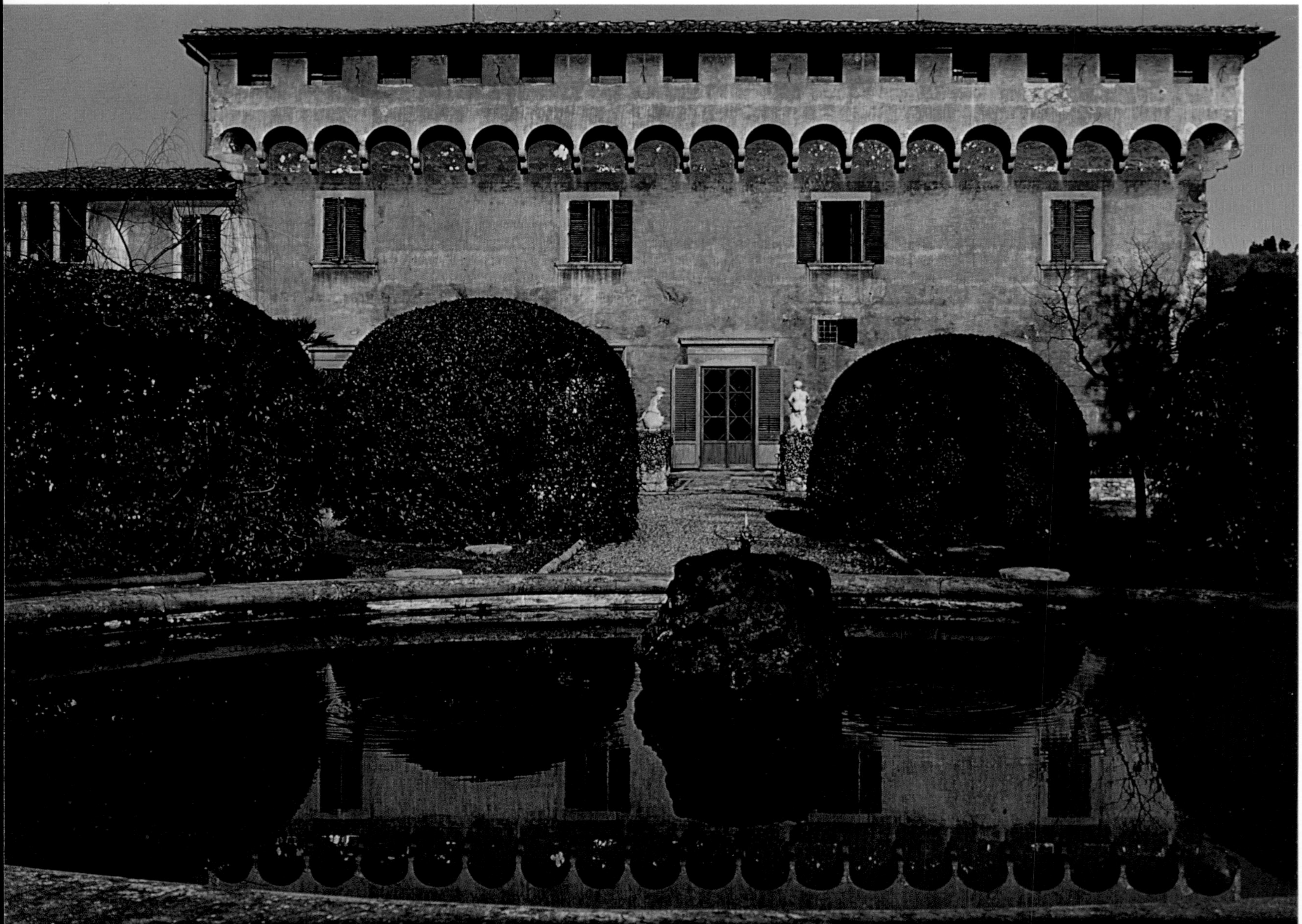

II
II
IV

themselves. On the ground floor of the Pitti Palace in the Museo degli Argenti there is a splendid fresco of Lorenzo and the Platonic Academy at Careggi by Francesco Furini: here the villa can be seen as it was in its halcyon period.

The novelist Elizabeth Sewell, who 'looked down into the well in the courtyard in which the physician who poisoned Lorenzo was thrown,' added (in 1862), 'But, strange to say, the place is not old and dreary, but as gay with paint and marble as English taste of the present day can make it, only there is something ghastly and ghostly in the memories which haunt it; and the long, narrow corridor running along the outside of the house, just under the roof, with the low rooms which open from it, the floors of which are so old as to be unsafe, remind one that the modern dress is only a *dress*, and that Careggi was really the place where the splendour and the guilt of the Medici were concentrated. A broad covered terrace or loggia opens from the rooms which Lorenzo last inhabited. It commands a splendid view over Florence; and there, no doubt, all the great men whom Lorenzo patronized often enjoyed themselves in the summer evenings. . . . People belonging to that period became very real as one stood upon the precise spot where they must have congregated . . .'*

Cafaggiolo and Il Trebbio were favoured as summer resorts for the children, who stayed there with their mother Clarice Orsini at the time of the Pazzi conspiracy. Poliziano was profoundly bored in their company and complained of Clarice's interference with his education of Piero and Giovanni, the later Pope Leo X. We hear less of these castles in the Mugello until Cosimo, the first Grand Duke of the cadet branch, spent part of his boyhood there, and Lorenzino took refuge there after murdering the Duke Alessandro. Later on, in July 1576, Don Pietro, a younger son of the Grand Duke Cosimo, strangled his young wife at Cafaggiolo. Don Pietro had married his maternal cousin Eleonora, or Dionora, a daughter of Don Garzia of Toledo. While her husband neglected her she was said to have consoled herself with several adorers, one of whom entered a monastery; the other, Bernardo Antinori, who had killed his rival Francesco Ginori in a duel, was executed in the Bargello. Pietro's eldest brother, the Grand Duke Francesco, insisted on his avenging the family honour though he – no pattern of propriety – was living openly with his mistress Bianca Cappello. The young wife's corpse was sent to Florence for secret burial with a laconic letter from Pietro to the Grand Duke, informing him that 'this evening at six o'clock my wife died of an accident' (9th July 1576). And the Grand Duke wrote cynically to his brother Cardinal Ferdinando: 'Last night Donna Leonora suffered from so terrible an accident that she choked in bed without Don Pietro or others having any chance to succour her with remedies.' A few days later the Grand Duke's beautiful sister, Isabella Orsini, was also strangled by her husband at Cerreto Guidi for a similar reason. Her alleged lover Troilo Orsini (a cousin of her husband deputed to keep an eye on her) escaped to France where he was killed by hired assassins.

* *Impressions of Rome, Florence and Turin*. By the Author of 'Amy Herbert'. London 1862.

Poggio a Caiano:
engraving after Zocchi

Perhaps on account of the previous murder we hear less of Cafaggiolo as a family residence until it was sold to Prince Borghese in 1864, though it is portrayed in a cheerful hunting scene of the seventeenth century, with the profligate Cardinal Giovan Carlo de' Medici and his courtiers. It is almost better known today for its maiolica. This was perfected in the beginning of the sixteenth century when the Fattorini family from Montelupo were invited by the Medici to settle there. The ceramics of Cafaggiolo continued to flourish till the eighteenth century.

Piero the Gouty, whose abilities have been underestimated on account of his chronic ill-health, stayed longer at Careggi surrounded by his father's coterie of Platonists. Louis XI of France paid him the graceful compliment of letting him add the French Lily to his family coat of arms.

Though Lorenzo the Magnificent and his circle were also closely connected with Careggi, as depicted in Furini's fresco, he seems to have preferred Poggio a Caiano, about ten miles from Florence on the road to Pistoia, for rural relaxation, and it inspired much of his poetry. Considering the multitude of his activities as statesman, banker, diplomatist, head of a great family, fond parent, Platonic lover, patron of the arts and collector of books and antiques, one wonders how or when he found leisure to compose; but his Ovidian allegory *L'Ambra* was even named for an islet formed by the river Ombrone near Poggio a Caiano, which was first known as *Ambra*, according to Michele Verini who described it soon after its foundations were laid. 'The villa', he wrote, 'abounds with quails and other birds, particularly water fowl, so that the diversion of fowling is enjoyed here without fatigue. Lorenzo has also furnished the woods with pheasants and with peacocks, which he procured from Sicily. His orchards and gardens are most luxuriant, extending along the banks of the river. His plantation of mulberry trees is of such extent, that we may hope ere long to have a diminution in the price of silk . . .'

Lorenzo's poem relates that the chaste nymph Ambra, while bathing in the Ombrone, stirs the passion of the river god, son of the Apennines. Fleeing from his embraces, she implores Diana to save her and is changed into a rock. The rock becomes an island in the river. Lorenzo's delight in natural scenery was unusual, if not unique, among his Italian contemporaries. His poems are verbal genre-paintings permeated with this love.

Some critics have denied his authorship of another genial Tuscan pastoral, *La Nencia di Barberino,* but his spirited improvisation on hawking, *La Caccia col Falcone,* evokes the indigenous atmosphere of the Mugello where he had spent his earliest years. From the departure of the company in the morning till their return in the noonday heat, the squabbles of the hawkers and their pungent humour during relaxation, give us not only a striking picture of contemporary manners, as William Roscoe wrote in his classic *Life* of Lorenzo, but also an illustration of the author's *joie de vivre.* He must have composed such poems during the summer *villeggiatura,* with the rustic speech still ringing in his ears, to entertain his friends on wintry evenings.

Whereas Cafaggiolo, Il Trebbio and Careggi were all types of the castellated stronghold, Poggio a Caiano is the first Medicean villa of pure Renaissance design. Thus it stands in relation to earlier villas as the Pazzi Chapel to previous ecclesiastical buildings. Both its exterior and interior are more consciously architectural than the older villas, though like most of them it was built on the site of an ancient house which had belonged to the Cancellieri of Pistoia, then to Palla Strozzi and Giovanni Rucellai, who sold it to Lorenzo in 1479.

Vasari records that Lorenzo commissioned several architects to make models for Poggio a Caiano and that Giuliano da Sangallo's was 'so entirely unlike those of all others and so completely to Lorenzo's taste, that he charged him immediately to put it in execution; and the favour of Giuliano so greatly increased with him in consequence that he ever afterward paid him a yearly stipend.' Sangallo is said to have completed the building in 1485, but the horseshoe stairs leading to the front loggia and the Della Robbia frieze in pseudo-classical style above it were added later.

Instead of the traditional open courtyard Sangallo built a vast hall two storeys high with a gorgeous barrel-vaulted ceiling of gilded stucco. This is the only room in the villa that has not been changed. The allegorical frescoes on the walls were commissioned by Lorenzo's son, Pope Leo X, and Paolo Giovio chose the subjects to correspond with episodes in family history. Thus *Cosimo the Elder's return from exile* is suggested by *Cicero's return to Rome,* begun by Franciabigio in 1521 and finished much later by Allori; while Andrea del Sarto's *Caesar receiving tribute from Egypt,* also completed by Allori, refers to an embassy from the Sultan to Lorenzo in 1487 and includes the popular giraffe led by two Turks, of which a chronicler related that it excited so general a curiosity, even among the nuns, that it was sent round to various convents to be inspected. 'It ate everything, poking its head into every peasant's basket, and would take an apple from a child's hand, so gentle it was. It died on January 2nd 1489, and everybody lamented it, for it was such a beautiful animal.' Artistically these crowded frescoes pale beside Pontormo's idyllic lunette of *Vertumnus and Pomona* (1520). 'As design, as colour, as fancy, the freshest, gayest, most appropriate mural decoration now remaining in Italy,' wrote Berenson in 1896. One regrets that it is so high up above the hall: the whole composition is as lively as Lorenzo's bucolic poems. Among detailed descriptions of it Mary McCarthy's in *The Stones of Florence* is the most accurate.

Most of the rooms in Poggio a Caiano were redecorated and furnished with deplorable taste in the nineteenth century, but Bianca Cappello's bedroom with its Renaissance staircase and fireplace still exist.

Bianca's visits to this villa have given rise to many a lurid legend. The Grand Duke Francesco's passionate devotion to the Venetian adventuress (whose husband was supposed to have been murdered with his complicity) has provided romantic novelists with ample material, culminating with her death soon after the Grand Duke's in 1587. The legendary version was that the Grand Duke and Bianca ate a poisoned tart intended for Cardinal Ferdinando, the Grand Duke's brother and heir, who hated Bianca. Others have accused the Cardinal of this crime. Actually, as Pieraccini has proved, the couple died of malarial fever, then described as double tertian. Bianca, prostrated by the same disease, was unable to nurse Francesco when he was taken ill after hunting, and when he died on 20th October at the age of forty-six she did not long survive him.

Sir John Reresby, who visited Poggio a Caiano in April 1657, was less impressed by it than other travellers. 'The house is nothing so considerable in itself, as in its situation,' he wrote, 'standing betwixt several hills on one side, covered with vines and olive trees, and a valley divided into many walks by rows of trees, leading different ways; one leads to a park where the Great Duke [Ferdinando II] had made a paddock course, by the direction of Signor Bernard Gascoigne, an Italian, who having served our late king in his wars, carried the pattern from England.

'There we found the duke diverting himself in the morning, who, after his return to dinner, according to his usual civility to strangers, sent us two dishes of fish (being Friday) and twelve bottles of excellent wines, to our inn.

'Near to this house is another park, the largest in Italy, or rather a chase, said to be thirty miles in compass.'*

Probably Sir John Reresby did not enter the building, which contained a whole set of tapestries of hunting scenes designed by Stradano and others of wild duck shooting and bullfights designed by Allori. These are now in the Palazzo Vecchio and various museums. It was often used for state receptions and ceremonial entries to Florence, especially for prospective brides such as Eleonora of Toledo, Joan of Austria, Christine of Lorraine, and last, Marguerite-

* Sir John Reresby, Bart: *Memoirs and Travels*. London 1904.

Louise d'Orléans, who fled there from her detested husband Cosimo III before her final return to France. While at Poggio a Caiano, Marguerite-Louise galloped about the country for six or seven hours at a stretch and scandalized the neighbourhood with her loose behaviour, such as tickling her French cook and chasing him round the royal apartments with loud screams.

As if the vast grounds of Poggio a Caiano were not sufficient for his hunting expeditions Francesco I commissioned Buontalenti to enlarge the ancient villa La Magia at Quarrata near Pistoia, which had been built by Vinciguerra Panciatichi in 1318. When this family was defeated by the Cancellieri, who then owned Poggio a Caiano, they fortified their house in self-defence, and in 1536 they entertained the Emperor Charles V and Duke Alessandro de' Medici to a gala hunting party on the estate, as commemorated by an incription on the eastern façade. Niccolò Panciatichi had to sell all his property owing to financial reverses in 1581, and in 1583 the villa was acquired by the Grand Duke Francesco, who had it remodelled in late Renaissance style by Buontalenti.

Fortunately it is in an excellent state of preservation: a massive irregular cubic structure with rudimentary towers at the angles. The discreetly articulated oblong windows framed in stone are characteristic of Buontalenti's work, though his masterpiece at Artimino was built much later in 1594. The graceful courtyard with the central fountain is decorated with diversified geometrical panels in low relief, as fine an example of this sort of wall decoration as that of the Villa Le Maschere in the Mugello and typical of the transition from High Renaissance to Baroque. The double staircase leading to the garden is omitted in Zocchi's engraving.

The villa and grounds were sold by the Grand Duke Ferdinando II to Pandolfo Attavanti in 1645, from whom it passed to the Ricasoli in 1752 and to Giulio Amati of Pistoia in 1766, in whose family it remained, for it is still inhabited by the Counts Amati Cellesi.

Buontalenti also designed the dramatic approach to the severe block of Villa Cerreto Guidi, four staircases on zigzag ramps slotted with mysterious doors and windows like portholes on a ship, much higher and more solid than the two-storeyed building with its few windows and numerous chimneys, on the homonymous hill-town near Empoli, with its breathtaking view of the Val di Nievole. This was the former abode of the Counts Guidi, which came into the possession of the monstrous Duke of Bracciano who murdered his beautiful wife Isabella de' Medici there in 1576.

The Villa Corsini at Mezzomonte – so named because half-way up Monte Oriolo – is an early fifteenth-century structure which belonged to the roystering Cardinal Giovan Carlo de' Medici for fourteen years. He bought it in 1630 and sold it in 1644, before he was elected cardinal at the age of thirty-five, to Marchese Andrea, son of Senator Neri Corsini. Cardinal Giovan Carlo embellished it for the entertainment of his cohort of friends and satellites:

he had the interior frescoed and filled the garden with rare flowers, and it must have been splendid during his occupation. His whole life was a Carnival, but now the imposing villa has a Lenten air.

Bernardo Buontalenti stood in a similar relation to the Grand Duke Francesco I and his brother Ferdinando I as Michelozzo to Cosimo the Elder, and the refined simplicity of his buildings reminds one of Michelozzo rather than of his manneristic forbears and contemporaries. As painter, sculptor, architect civil and military, engineer and theatrical designer and machinist, he was a figure of immense versatility and an epitome of the spirit of the age. He was also a prodigy, for he was only fifteen when he was appointed a sort of tutor-companion to the hereditary Prince Francesco, and it is probable that he encouraged Francesco's naturalistic bent which eventually became an obsession. Francesco as Grand Duke paid more attention to his chemical experiments than to state affairs, and his experiments were mingled with the fantastic pseudo-scientific theories of that period.

Born in Florence in 1531 (though the date is often given as 1536), Buontalenti lost both his parents when his home collapsed during a flood of the Arno. The child was extracted unhurt from a grotto which had formed miraculously under the débris. This episode may have influenced his subsequent designs for grottoes, of which the finest in the Boboli garden is the sole authenticated survivor.* After his rescue Buontalenti was brought up at Cosimo I's expense and he soon showed, as Vasari wrote, 'a very fine genius and extraordinary wealth of felicitous fancies,' which included the construction of machines for lifting weights, a method by which rock crystal could be melted

* See Detlef Heikamp: *La Grotta Grande del Giardino di Boboli* Antichità Viva IV, No. 4, 1965.

Pratolino: etching by Stefano della Bella

58

and purified, ingenious jewellery and automata, many of which were enthusiastically described by Baldinucci.* He was said to have discovered the secrets of Oriental porcelain, and his lapis-lazuli vase in the Museo degli Argenti of the Pitti Palace is a splendid example of his craftsmanship. Happily his copious and elaborate designs for scenery and costumes have been preserved, as well as accounts of the performances for which he designed them. His inexhaustible fantasy found an outlet in these wonderful inventions, but they were ephemeral, unlike his buildings.

It is a tragic irony that Pratolino, the building in which he expressed his versatile talents most successfully, was destroyed in 1822 by the engineer Frichs on the order of the Austrian Grand Duke Ferdinand III, who considered its upkeep too expensive. Instead he wanted a landscape garden and a hunting park. Yet its fame had once been international.**

Francesco I acquired this large property about six miles north of Florence on the old road to Bologna in 1568, at the height of his infatuation for Bianca Cappello. It took fifteen years to complete, though he continued to add fresh wonders to its garden.

'The Grand Duke has used all his five senses to beautify this villa,' wrote Montaigne, who admired it far more than the corpulent Bianca. We must rely on the descriptions of Francesco Vieri, Bernardo Sgrilli and bygone travellers, on the bird's-eye view by Utens in the Museo Topografico and Stefano della Bella's engravings, to visualize it in its prime. The minutest English description is in John Evelyn's *Diary* (1645): 'The house is a square of four pavilions, with a fair platform about it, balustred with stone, situate in

* See F. Baldinucci: *Notizie dei Professori del Disegno,* 1688, ed. Firenze, 1846, II.

** See Luciano Berti's important book *Il Principe dello Studiolo,* Florence 1967, also Detlef Heikamp's excellent article, *Pratolino nei suoi giorni splendidi*, Antichità Viva, Florence, Anno VIII, No. 2, 1969.

Pratolino, the fountain walk: etching by Stefano della Bella

a large meadow, ascending like an amphitheatre, having at the bottom a huge rock, with water running in a small channel, like a cascade; on the other side are the gardens. The whole place seems consecrated to pleasure and summer retirement. The inside of the palace may compare with any in Italy for furniture of tapestry, beds, etc., and the gardens are delicious, and full of fountains. In the grove sits Pan feeding his flock, the water making a melodious sound through his pipe; and a Hercules, whose club yields a shower of water, which, falling into a great shell, has a naked woman riding on the backs of dolphins. In another grotto is Vulcan and his family, the walls richly composed of corals, shells, copper, and marble figures, with the hunting of several beasts, moving by the force of water. Here, having been well washed for our curiosity, we went down a large walk, at the sides whereof several slender streams of water gush out of pipes concealed underneath, that interchangeably fall into each other's channels, making a lofty and perfect arch, so that a man on horseback may ride under it, and not receive one drop of water. This canopy, or arch of water, I thought one of the most surprising magnificences I had ever seen, and very refreshing in the heat of the summer. At the end of this very long walk, stands a woman in white marble, in posture of a laundress wringing water out of a piece of linen, very naturally formed, into a vast laver, the work and invention of M. Angelo Buonarotti [actually by Valerio Cioli]. Hence, we ascended Mount Parnassus, where the Muses played to us on hydraulic organs. Near this is a great aviary. All these waters came from the rock in the garden, on which is the statue of a giant representing the Apennines, at the foot of which stands the villa. Last of all, we came to the labyrinth, in which a huge coloss of Jupiter throws out a stream over the garden. This is fifty feet in height, having in his body a square chamber, his eyes and mouth serving for windows and door.'

In the centre of one octagonal grotto was a fine marble table which often served for the private dinners of the Grand Duke and Bianca Cappello, with six guests. John Keysler FRS, who viewed it in 1760, noted the following inscription on the ceiling of the great hall of the villa: 'This house was adorned with fountains, canals, porticos, and walks by Francesco de' Medici, second Grand Duke of Tuscany, and dedicated to festivity and relaxation of mind, for the use of himself and his friends, in the year 1575.' He also observed that, 'though it is now near 150 years since the Grand Duke Francesco's decease, yet everything is kept up in the same order as he left it, for it is accounted such a complete work that no expense is spared towards keeping it in repair. If the water-works do not equal those of Versailles, they have their beauty, and in summer time are the more agreeable on account of the excessive heat of the climate.'

During the seventeenth century, when it was the frequent residence of Cosimo III's elder son the Grand Prince Ferdinando, an enlightened patron of the arts, Pratolino became a hive of musical activity. In 1697 the architect

Antonio Ferri built him a theatre for which Giovanni Maria Galli, called Bibbiena, provided the scenery. The Prince had a pleasant singing voice, understood counterpoint, and played several musical instruments with distinction. He invited Giacomo Peri, Alessandro and Domenico Scarlatti, Bernardo Pasquini, and even Handel to Pratolino, and his private theatre was considered one of the best in Europe. He invented the libretti for operas, and his correspondence with Alessandro Scarlatti proves that he was far more than an amateur virtuoso.

Despairing of his long-lived father's extravagantly bigoted rule and married to a plain Bavarian Princess whose affection he failed to reciprocate, he took refuge in music and picture collecting. He preferred contemporary Venetian to Florentine painting, which struck him as too timidly conservative, though he did his best to stimulate it with a public exhibition of 250 paintings in the cloister of the SS. Annunziata in 1705, of which the catalogue survives – an innovation in Italy. His private collection of some 300 pictures was distributed among his Pitti Palace apartments, Pratolino, and Poggio a Caiano, where he engaged Sebastiano Ricci to decorate a room for him in 1707, of which nothing remains, as well as a room in the Pitti which survives.

His predilection for Giuseppe Maria Crespi, who spent several months with his family at Pratolino and was appointed his *pittore attuale*, is another proof of his originality, for Crespi's spirited genre scenes, though darker in tone, are more akin to Chardin than to the Italian painters of his age. One of his best works, the *Fair at Poggio a Caiano*, now in the Uffizi, was painted for the Prince, who manifested his friendship by acting as godfather to one of his sons, duly christened Ferdinando. After the Prince's death in 1713 the theatre was closed, though Zocchi's engraving shows that the garden was still kept up. Prince Paul Demidoff bought the estate in 1872 long after the villa and garden had been demolished. Some of the statues were removed to the Boboli gardens, and others were stolen or broken. The present villa has a vague 'period' charm but is un-Italian and unworthy of its ancestor, and Giambologna's colossal *Apennine* is one of the few relics of the original garden. Its most recent owner, Prince Paul of Yugoslavia, would have liked to restore it but the cost was prohibitive.

Both the villas of Castello and Petraia beyond Careggi lost much of their glamour since they were redecorated in the last century under the House of Savoy. Castello had been acquired in 1477 by Cosimo the Elder's great-nephews, Lorenzo and Giovanni di Pierfrancesco de' Medici, the former of whom has been confused by certain art historians with Lorenzo the Magnificent. It was for Lorenzo di Pierfrancesco that Botticelli painted his famous *Spring* and the *Birth of Venus*. These masterpieces adorned the villa of Castello until 1815 when they were removed to the Uffizi (where for a long time they remained unnoticed and forgotten, according to the artist's most scholarly biographer Herbert Horne). Botticelli also produced his wonderful illustrations

Castello: engraving after Zocchi

to Dante's *Divina Commedia* for this Lorenzo, and his *Pallas and the Centaur*, rediscovered by William Spence, has also been traced to the collection formerly at Castello.

When Piero de' Medici fled from Florence in 1494 his possessions were confiscated and sold by order of the Signoria, but his cousins were allowed to keep their property because they had shrewdly joined the popular party. On the death of Lorenzo di Pierfrancesco in 1503, the villa fell to the share of his bellicose nephew Giovanni delle Bande Nere, and after his death, during the siege of Florence, the house was fired and narrowly escaped destruction. Here Cosimo the first Grand Duke of the Medici spent part of his boyhood when he was not hunting at Il Trebbio.

The austere façade with Tuscan windows on consoles and a rusticated doorway separated from the road by a semicircular grass plot, holds little promise of the celebrated garden behind it. The Grand Duke Cosimo I, whose brave mother Maria Salviati died there, ordered Tribolo to design the garden in 1538 and Buontalenti continued the good work when Tribolo expired in 1550; both Giambologna and Ammannati contributed various statues. According to tradition the historian Benedetto Varchi conceived the original plan which was too grandiose to accomplish: an avenue of trees, for instance, was to have led towards the villa from the Arno.

Cosimo was just over seventeen when he dashed to Florence from Il Trebbio to stake his claim to the duchy after the murder of the Duke Alessandro. He stands out as one of the greatest of the Medici for his political flair and energy though his character was far from sympathetic. Victorian historians, mostly of the female sex, loved to portray the Medici as monsters, but the lurid tales about Cosimo had little foundation in fact. As Gaetano Pieraccini has established, he was an excellent ruler by contemporary standards, a conscientious parent and husband who imposed wise laws and restored peace to Tuscany, especially to Florence, after years of chaos and tyranny worse than his. He was prematurely aged when he made young Cammilla Martelli his second wife and appointed his son Francesco regent. His proud sons resented the marriage and treated Cammilla as a low-born concubine. However, she soothed his last years when he retired to Castello and died there in 1574 at the age of fifty-five.

Vasari and Montaigne rhapsodized about the garden, which has suffered from regrettable changes, such as the removal of Giambologna's statue of Venus wringing her hair and the bronzes of animals and birds, some of which are now in the Bargello. But the sloping parterre against the dark ilex wood with which it forms so bright a contrast still contains the superb fountain of Hercules crushing Antaeus, which was begun by Tribolo and finished by Ammannati from Tribolo's model, while the exquisite bronze *putti* round the basin have been attributed to Pierino da Vinci. The pleached alleys with inter-laced branches described by Montaigne have gone, but the retaining wall flanked by lemon-houses and the central surprise grotto, with three marble baths and groups of stone and bronze animals probably by Fancelli, including a unicorn, a camel, a monkey, a stag with real antlers and a wild boar with real tusks, under a ceiling of masks and arabesques in coloured shell-work, remains one of the finest of its kind, and its jets of water under the tessellated pavement are still in working order.

Even in the 1450s Leon Battista Alberti had foreshadowed the future development of Tuscan gardens. 'Before the entrance', he wrote, 'let there be an ample space for carriages and equestrian exercise. . . . In the grottoes of caves the ancients used to make a crust of rough and rocky material, fragments of pumice or sponge and travertine . . . and I have seen some who add green wax to imitate the soft hair of a cavern full of musk. I was delighted by what I observed in a similar cave whence a fountain of water gushed, with an exterior of different shells including those of oysters, arranged according to variety of hue with pleasant artifice. . . . Let there be a most cheerful lawn, and let water flow from divers places where it is least expected. Let the alleys end with fruit trees and evergreens, and enclose that part which is sheltered from the wind with box hedges. . . . Stone vases are excellent ornaments for garden fountains. Trees should be planted in straight lines equidistant and correspon-ding with each other. . . . Gardeners of yore had a charming custom of praising their master by tracing their names on the ground in letters of box and scented herbs. . . . Rose-bushes fastened to pomegranate and dogwood form attractive hedges. . . . I have no objection to statues that make you laugh so long as they contain nothing indecent. . . . I would prefer the houses of nobles not to be situated in the most fertile part of the country but in the most scenic, whence every convenience is available, be they views of the city, land or sea, or an extensive plain, and the familiar hills and mountains.'

Here we have the Tuscan garden in embryo, partly derived from classical imitations. Many such details appeared in the woodcuts illustrating the *Hypnerotomachia Poliphili*, first published by Aldus Manutius in 1499. This strange allegorical romance, attributed to Fra Francesco Colonna of Treviso, was an idealization of antiquity from which Italian sculptors and gardeners, painters and engravers used to borrow freely as from a book of patterns.

Castello was one of the first great formal gardens of Italy which set a fashion for others even in France. Here its main characteristics were summarized, entirely subservient to architecture. Rectangular forms predominate: flower-beds lead by slow degrees to the long screen of the retaining wall with the ilex grove above it. The ground was converted into terraces, stairs, and avenues; plants were trained into arches, columns and labyrinths. Likewise water had to be trained. The joyful fountain as a work of art was polished and perfected in Florence. True, it had flourished in ancient Greece and Rome but it had gone underground, so to speak, during the Middle Ages.

In his introduction to the Third Day of the *Decameron,* Boccaccio describes 'a fountain of white marble, whereon was engraven most admirable workmanship; and within it (I know not whether by a natural vein or artificial) flowing from a figure, standing on a column in the midst of the fountain, such abundance of water, and so mounting up towards the skies, that it was a wonder to behold. For after the high ascent, it fell down again into the womb of the fountain, with such a noise and pleasing murmur, as the stream that glideth from a mill. When the receptacle of the fountain did overflow the bounds, it streamed along the meadow, by secret passages and channels, very fair and artificially made, returning again into every part of the meadow, by the like ways of cunning conveyance, which allowed it full course into the garden.'

No doubt Boccaccio had seen something similar and let his imagination run riot, for the fountains in painted miniatures of the period (1348) are much cruder. Almost a century later Donatello and his disciples developed the fountain in which sculpture played a leading part: a series of circular basins superimposed, the smallest on top surmounted by the figure from which water rose and fell, gushed or trickled. Verrocchio's *putto* with the spouting dolphin, which was brought from the villa of Careggi to the courtyard of the Palazzo Vecchio, is a consummate masterpiece of the kind, dating from 1476. Towards the end of the fifteenth century fountains became more elaborate: transitions between levels of water were emphasized by human bodies, sportive animals, grotesque masks, and the arrangement of jets created a symphonic harmony.

Baroque sculptors were to develop these even further and populate gardens with a hectic mythology of tritons and river gods blowing, splashing and dripping. Bernini was to multiply their histrionic effects but, as usual, the Florentines were the great precursors. When Giambologna's *Oceanus* was

Garden scene from Hypnerotomachia Poliphili, *1499*

erected in the centre of the oval island laid out as a lemon garden, approached by two bridges and surrounded by a balustrade – the magical *Isolotto* of the Boboli garden – Bernini was a child.

The villa of Petraia near Castello was bought by Cardinal Ferdinando in 1575, restored by Buontalenti and frescoed with scenes of Cosimo I's reign by Volterrano and other artists, but the frescoes were damaged and later repaired (none too well) when it was renovated in 1859 by King Victor Emmanuel II, who often stayed there with his morganatic wife, the Countess of Mirafiori. Gaudy timepieces, statuettes, and Japanese vases bear witness to the fatty degeneration of taste. Among the branches of the so-called King's ilex in the garden with a trunk of unusual girth, a corkscrew stair led up to a wooden platform where the Countess used to sit and enjoy the view. But even the view has changed, for Rifredi has become a dull industrial suburb. However, the villa, a simple structure round an inner quadrangle with a graceful tower of an earlier period, and its terrace with large palm trees was much admired by Horace Walpole. Sir Horace Mann mentioned it frequently in his letters to him as 'your favourite Petraia'. The regent under the House of

Lorraine, the Prince de Craon, and his amiable wife, preferred it to the other country houses at their disposal and had to supply all the furniture since it was empty. The Prince was a frequent sufferer from the itch and repaired there to scratch himself, according to Mann. In February 1750 he wrote: 'Except at Poggio Imperiale and Castello there is no furniture worth selling. Most of the other villas are lent out: Count Richecourt [Lady Orford's lover] has two, Careggi and the Imperialino; General Stampa has one, between this and Leghorn [possibly the Ambrogiana]; Prince Craon had two, Artimino and Petraia, to which he was forced to carry chairs, and the Princess her *berceau*.' And many years later, in July 1767: 'You will with difficulty believe that your old friend, the Princess Craon, at the age of eighty-four [actually eighty-one] arrived here lately just to take a peep at the Petraia, and then returned again to Nancy without taking leave of anybody. She . . . expected to find a better reception and more conveniences at the Petraia than she met with, which, I believe, was destitute of common necessaries, and all her own equipage, plate and everything, was at sea towards Leghorn.'

In 1861 Elizabeth Sewell wrote: 'We were at Petraia the other day, – a villa which was the Grand Duke's and is the King's; a dream of beauty it is; – terraces bordered by trellis-work, and orange-trees, with showers of roses, magnolias, and azaleas; a view over Florence, and away to the Carrara mountains; and behind the villa, a hill, planted with trees, commanding another view in a different direction, and having at its base one of those broad, solemn cypress avenues which form the contrast wanting to set off the glory of an Italian sky.'

Now the chief glory of the garden is Giambologna's fountain brought hither from Castello, surmounted by an exquisite figure of Venus wringing out her hair, traditionally based on a design by Tribolo.

Almost every patriarch of the Medici built – in most cases rebuilt – one or more villas which reflected his personal preferences, and there was no dearth of highly skilled architects in Florence. Cosimo the Elder's gravity and reticence seem to have been expressed to perfection by Michelozzo in his buildings; Lorenzo the Magnificent's suave elegance and sense of luxury were equally well expressed by Giuliano da Sangallo. The Grand Dukes of the cadet branch were as fortunate in finding architects who could interpret their progressive grandeur and spaciousness without pompous exaggeration: from Vasari and his pupils to Antonio Maria Ferri (d. 1716) there was a prolific heritage of talent.

During the reign of Ferdinando I, the best of the Grand Dukes, Tuscany enjoyed a period of peace and prosperity fruitful to architecture as well as agriculture. Even the biased Galluzzi had to admit that, 'owing to the improvement of agriculture there was a growing taste for the delight and luxury of gardens, and a desire to attract the rarest plants of Asia and America to Florence. The gardens laid out by Ferdinando served as a model, kindling emulation in private citizens, and the most magnificent and delicious private gardens owed their beginnings to this spirit.' In fact Ferdinando's predecessors, as we have seen, had shown as keen an interest in horticulture and set the earliest examples to their subjects. Ferdinando I's vast villas of Ambrogiana and Artimino were built as hunting-lodges: the former had a garden which has since disappeared, but according to the painted lunette by Utens now in the Museo di 'Firenze com'era' its design was stiffly rectangular, more neat than imaginative, and the cubic structure with its four massive turrets is more imposing than beautiful. Cosimo III filled it with pictures of rare animals and flowers by Andrea Scacciati and Bartolomeo Bimbi of Settignano, but his doctor, the poet Redi, complained that 'the wind blows and will blow for eternity' in that spot, which is now a grim lunatic asylum.

Lack of water was one of the chief drawbacks of Artimino, hence there was no garden. The solemn and majestic villa, so graceful in its simplicity, dominates an extensive hunting preserve, densely wooded and rich in game, which used to include bears, wolves and foxes. Baldinucci relates that Ferdinando I was so fascinated by the site that he ordered Buontalenti to build 'a palace sufficient for me and my whole court without delay', and that this was completed a year later in 1594. For a hunting-lodge it is indeed palatial. It was christened Villa Ferdinanda. One's first impression of the main façade looking eastwards, protected on each side by bastions framed in *pietra serena*, is definitely severe. The sparse windows are elegantly spaced: the three highest with stone jambs surmounted by the Medici arms sculpted in white marble above the central door comprise the sole ornaments of the long white building whose harmonious sobriety grows upon one like a fugue by Bach. There seem to be far more chimneys than windows. The western façade is lighter and gayer in comparison, thanks to the central open loggia of four columns framed by

Ambrogiana: engraving after Zocchi

two pilasters and an architrave, and the balustraded stairs leading up to it (which were added in 1930 from an original sketch by Buontalenti in the Uffizi), though there are solid towers with slightly bent outlines on each side rising as far as the roof. Of the fifty-six rooms this hunting-lodge contains, two high-windowed halls replace the traditional courtyard. Most of these were distinguished by odd names, some of which, like the room of 'the Bodyguard', of 'the Lancers', of 'the Arquebusiers' and 'the Grooms' were explanatory, as also perhaps those of 'the Lion' and 'the Bear', but why were some called of 'the Widows' and the entrance hall of 'the Wars'? Their original furniture has been dispersed since the Medici, and apart from the carved stone-work and the frescoes attributed to Passignano in the loggia there is little interior decoration. The Grand Duke Pietro Leopoldo sold it to Marchese Lorenzo Bartolommei in 1781, since when it has had several occupants, of whom Contessa Maraini was the local Lady Bountiful. The latter restored and improved the property, which her husband had bought in 1911, but now it is empty, an elephantine relic of grander days. Its wine, so highly praised by Francesco Redi in his dithyrambic poem *Bacchus in Tuscany* (ingeniously translated by Leigh Hunt), is still worth more than a sip in the adjacent *trattoria* full of revellers on Sundays.

The villa of Poggio Imperiale, now a fashionable school for girls, must have been truly imperial, judging from Zocchi's engraving. Cosimo I, having confiscated it from the rebellious Salviati, presented it to his beautiful daughter Isabella in 1565 when she married the ruffianly Gian Paolo Orsini, Duke of Bracciano, who strangled her, as we have mentioned, soon after her brother had done the same to his wife at Cafaggiolo. As if he had connived at his sister's murder the Grand Duke Francesco allowed Orsini to keep Poggio Baroncelli (as it was then called after its original owner before the Salviati). In 1619 it was sold to the Grand Duchess Maria Maddalena of Austria, Cosimo II's wife, and renamed Poggio Imperiale in her honour. Giulio Parigi was commissioned to enlarge it as in his son Alfonso's print, and its period of splendour followed. 'The ascent to the house', wrote John Evelyn in 1645, 'is by a stately gallery as it were of tall and overgrown cypress trees for near half a mile. At the entrance of these ranges, are placed statues of the Tiber and Arno, of marble; those also of Virgil, Ovid, Petrarch, and Dante. The building is sumptuous, and curiously furnished within with cabinets of *pietra-commessa* in tables, pavements, etc., which is a magnificence, or work, particularly affected at Florence. The pictures are, Adam and Eve by Albert Dürer, very excellent; as is that piece of carving in wood by the same hand standing in a cupboard. Here is painted the whole Austrian line; the Duke's mother, sister to the Emperor, the foundress of this palace, than which there is none in Italy that I had seen more magnificently adorned, or furnished.'

Court pageantry had become increasingly elaborate since the reign of Cosimo I, and this was the great era of flamboyant theatrical entertainments, ballets, tournaments of stylized combat, multiple masquerades and processions to celebrate weddings and state visits. The Grand Duchesses Christine of Lorraine and Maria Maddalena were joint Regents until the latter's son, Ferdinando II, was considered old enough to govern in 1628. As both Regents were devoutly religious, theatrical shows were intended to be edifying, in the words of the librettist Andrea Salvadori, 'that our souls obtain much more delight and amazement from true and glorious Christian actions than from the empty fables of the pagans.' However, the battle scenes and choreography of ballets were much the same, as when the five intricate acts of the opera *La Regina Sant'Orsola*, recounting the martyrdom of St Ursula and her eleven thousand virgins, was performed for the state visit of Prince Ladislaus Sigismund of Poland in January 1625. The scenery and 'machines' by Giulio Parigi and his son Alfonso were equally fantastic. One operatic ballet with a pagan theme, *La Liberazione di Ruggiero dall'isola d'Alcina*, was given for the Polish Prince on the wide piazza in front of Poggio Imperiale. The two Parigi provided wonderful settings for Neptune's chariot pulled by seahorses in the prologue, wherein the god of the river Vistula also paid homage to the Polish guest; for the witch Alcina's island and castle where Ruggiero had succumbed to her enchantments; and for the final conflagration and transformation of the witch into a winged monster who plunges into the flames. To end on a cheerful note the scene changed into a landscape of rocky peaks whence nymphs emerged from grottoes pursued by liberated knights, dancing for joy at the wicked Alcina's defeat. An equestrian ballet on the piazza before the villa was diversified by the appearance of the good fairy Melissa singing a madrigal on a chariot drawn by centaurs.

Fortunately the engravings of such entertainments remain to help us visualize them, and to inspire such scenic artists as Bakst and Sert in this century. Apart from the cost of production, consummate art was lavished on these shows to dazzle visitors with the opulence of the Medici. Fresh ideas in relation to the scenery were worked out and adopted; stage effects were heightened with such devices as clouds containing goddesses and angels and, as in Ben Jonson's *Masque of Blackness*, inspired by Queen Anne, for which Inigo Jones designed the scenery and costumes in 1605, artificial seas 'raised with waves which seemed to move, and in some places billows to break, as imitating that orderly disorder which is common in nature.' Inigo Jones's designs for masques in the Chatsworth collection bear a close resemblance to those of Buontalenti and his school. In England as in Italy, Court entertainments were more notable as spectacles than as dramatic productions: the art and invention of the architect were of prime importance.

In his villa at Arcetri not far from Poggio Imperiale, Galileo, 'Chief Mathematician to the Grand Duke Cosimo II', spent the last eight years of his life, completed his *Dialoghi delle nuove scienze*, and discovered 'the moon's diurnal and monthly librations' before going blind. Even then he dictated his latest theories to his disciples Viviani and Torricelli and continued his scientific correspondence. Let us not forget that when he discovered Jupiter's satellites with his telescope he named them *Sidera Medicea*, the Medicean stars, in honour of his pupil and patron Cosimo II.

Poggio Imperiale was further enlarged and redecorated by the Grand Duchess Vittoria della Rovere who held court there, but it suffered disastrously from later chops and changes at the hands of mediocre architects whose names are best forgotten. The Austrian Grand Duke Pietro Leopoldo added the vast stables which became military barracks, and it was his second son, the Philistine Ferdinand III, who ruined Giulio Parigi's façade. During Bonaparte's first Italian campaign, King Carlo Emanuele IV of Sardinia and his wife Maria Clotilde, refugees from Turin, were Ferdinando's guests there for a month in 1799, but they soon had to flee to Sardinia while Ferdinando joined his imperial brother in Vienna. Then the widowed Queen of Etruria (that ephemeral kingdom created by Napoleon) was allowed to stay there with her two children till they had to make way for Napoleon's sister, Elisa Baciocchi. Festivities followed in honour of her brother's victories, but in 1814 Ferdinand III came back and Elisa had to slip away by night.

Sir Horace Mann's letters describe the decay of taste and comic opera conditions of Court life after the Medici, when the Prince de Craon acted as regent until the advent of the Empress Maria Theresa's third son, Pietro Leopoldo, as Grand Duke in 1765. 'Sad work in the Pitti Palace and in the garden,' Mann reported in 1764: arrangement of the pictures was to depend upon the freshness of the gilding of the frames. And in May 1765: 'Everything is calculated for the meridian of Germany, nay of Muscovy: stoves and chimneys in every room, in some both. In the furniture the *goût* is not less Gothic. All the freshest gilt frames are to be put together, and in the room where the canopy is, no figure must turn his back to it, and the famous picture of Luther and Calvin by Pordenone [actually Titian's *Concert*] has been discarded from among the Madonnas. The Empress [Maria Theresa] will not permit even a naked leg or arm to defile the walls of any of the apartments she frequents, and for that reason, as Marshal Botta said lately, will never set her foot into a house where the Emperor keeps his virtu, though there is nothing that is indecent.'

The Hapsburg-Lorraine Grand Dukes were conspicuously addicted to domesticity and more frugal than the early Medici without their love and patronage of the fine arts. They sold most of the Medici villas and it was lucky for Florence that the last Medicean Princess, Anna Maria Luisa, bequeathed her family's collection of treasures to Tuscany, on condition that none should ever be removed from Florence, and that it should be 'for the benefit of the people of all nations.' But the Medicean wardrobe was not included in the terms of her bequest and the Grand Duke Pietro Leopoldo sold it. The sale continued monthly for ten years. As Henry Napier related: 'Almost every residence of the Medici throughout Tuscany had its peculiar wardrobe, independent of the great magazine of Medicean splendour in Florence, and all were now exposed to public sale. Velvets, damasks, gold embroideries, chairs and mirror frames of massive silver, gold brocades, rich lace, fringes, and costly silken fabrics, were either sold to the public or condemned to the crucible. Gian Gastone's state bed, embroidered throughout with a profusion of beautiful pearls and other gems, was picked to pieces, and many exquisite works in jewellery and precious metals, the symbols of Medicean taste and magnificence, were all broken up or otherwise disposed of to the amount of half a million of crowns.' Sir Horace Mann wrote more specifically in 1781: 'The sales of late years have consisted of old pictures, tables, chairs, and stools; but there was likewise much blue and white china, no sets, but some pieces, old, and estimable on that account. . . . But what will you say to what the Grand Maitre told me, that with the gold lace and fringe that adorned the hangings, chairs, and stools, he made three sets of plate for the table, of 36 covers each, with three dozen of gold knives, forks, and spoons, for the use of the Princes.'

One of the last eminent guests at Poggio Imperiale, before it was occupied by the Austrian troops who brought the Grand Duke Leopoldo II back to his shaky throne and remained to garrison Florence from 1849 till 1854, was the first King of Italy – as an infant in 1822. Here the baby Victor Emmanuel's cradle caught fire and his nurse died of burns after saving him from the flames. Maddened by the mosquitoes swarming round his net, she had tried to burn them, with this fatal result.

As King in 1860 Victor Emmanuel revisited the apartments he had occupied with his parents, then Princes of Carignano of the cadet line. But in spite of its regal scale it has a woebegone air as a school for tender maidens.

What was once the festive villa of Lappeggi contained the last flickers of gaiety before the Medici vanished in melancholy sterility. Wishing to emulate the fantasies of Pratolino, Cardinal Francesco Maria, the prodigal younger brother of Cosimo III, ordered Antonio Ferri to build it on the site of an old turreted villa that had belonged to the Medici since 1569. Choosing the most ornate of Ferri's plans, he asked what the cost would be. 'Forty thousand crowns, if the building is solid,' the architect replied. 'And if I only wish to spend thirty thousand, yet have my villa built to this design, how long would it last?' When the architect said he would guarantee it for eighteen years the Cardinal told him to proceed.

Work on it started in 1667, and while Zocchi's engraving helps us to visualize its outward grace the poet G. B. Fagiuoli has celebrated its amenities in his *Rime Piacévoli*. To paraphrase some of the latter: 'Where there had not been a drop of water fountains suddenly gushed forth at every corner: pools, reservoirs, fish-tanks, woods, grottoes and greenery were conjured in a twinkling [*Si fanno dal vedere al non vedere*]. Suddenly statues and pictures appeared, galleries, cabinets, and terraces with copious views both far and near.

Gardens were made to sprout like mushrooms; hovels were transformed into noble orangeries, farms into palaces, woods into pleasant highways; in alleys a man could scarcely penetrate singly two teams of horses now may turn together. Everything is accomplished in a trice; there is everything save time, yet this is never lacking, nor is it given for a sample sip. This gentleman, as far I could observe, would adapt himself to the divine, for the words *dixit et facta sunt* do please him well. . . .'

Fagiuoli described with gusto the practical jokes perpetrated by the Cardinal, as when a donkey was served for a banquet in delectable disguise until the bleeding hoofs and hairy head were produced; the noisy games of cards and *pallone* (the ancient ball-game played on a large court near a wall by six players on each side: an inflated leather ball was struck by a wooden armlet shaped like a pineapple and worn over the right arm); the fairs, with country dances on the Cardinal's birthday; the comedies, concerts, marionettes and jugglers, who failed to surprise the poet since 'the talent of changing cards by sleight of hand is by no means uncommon these days.'

A detailed account of King Frederick IV of Denmark's visit to Lappeggi in 1708* affords us a glimpse of Medicean entertainment in the country on gala occasions though the Cardinal, an arrant glutton, was prevented by gout from attending this one. Prince Gian Gastone acted as his deputy, and he drove to Lappeggi with the King and ten ladies in the largest of the Cardinal's coaches, divided into compartments with four windows. Punctually at midday a copious banquet was served in the entrance hall. There were twelve covers at the King's table, including those for the Prince and ten ladies, who were served exclusively by eight pages in Spanish uniforms chosen, we may be sure, by Gian Gastone. Melodious music accompanied the meal without drowning conversation. The table service was of Saxon porcelain and Bohemian glass engraved with the Cardinal's arms. Groups of statuettes in coloured porcelain represented a lover's tryst in a formal garden, and many flasks of generous wine – the flasks swaddled in straw and gold filigree – were placed among them. Prince Gian Gastone made the ladies laugh uproariously with his quips, but their husbands were served at another table in an adjacent hall and perhaps they heard the laughter with some misgiving. A crimson curtain embroidered with the Della Rovere arms divided the two halls. Coffee was served in the garden amid the fragrance of lemon trees in flower and a large coffee-pot shaped like a fountain with four spouts was placed before the King, together with gold dishes containing cups of chocolate and fresh water. After the feast they played games till four o'clock, when they drove about the grounds and visited the greenhouses and farm. Returning to the garden where the Cardinal had raised an Indian pavilion, they found an appetising cold collation, galantine of capon, iced fruit and syrups, sorbets and sweetmeats. The iced fruit, a novelty to the King and his suite, delighted them so much that His Majesty asked leave to present some to his dwarf, who was of noble

* *Visita del Re di Danimarca a Firenze nel 1708*. Firenze, Loescher and Seeber, 1886.

*Lappeggi: engraving
after Zocchi*

birth and a favourite mascot. Another pyramid of flasks in silk napkins with silver foil contained a selection of the most valued Tuscan vintages. Finally Prince Gian Gastone ordered crystal sconces to be hung on the walls to light up the ballroom: musicians were summoned and the dancing began. The *Scarpetta* ('little shoe') and other country jigs enlivened the whole company. His Majesty was in an excellent humour and stayed on till three o'clock after nightfall.

The chronicler fails to mention the pilfering that went on, for the Cardinal was constantly robbed by his retainers and he was aware of it. At Easter he would summon them all to beg his pardon on their knees, after which he would harangue them half in fun: 'Now then, you pack of rascals, run quickly and confess. As for me, I absolve you from your thefts and present you with what you have taken.'

The jollities of Lappeggi ended the same year when the Cardinal was induced to secularize himself for the sake of an heir. A promising bride was found for him, Princess Eleonora of Guastalla, just over twenty. The ex-Cardinal was forty-eight and old for his age, gouty and grossly corpulent, and though he strained himself to please her she could not overcome her disgust. He had sacrificed everything to a sterile marriage which hastened his own dissolution.

Sir Horace Mann, writing to Horace Walpole in September 1742, has related the epilogue: 'the most extraordinary story of an half prince who would have made a very good Grand Duke of Tuscany had he come into the world a little sooner, a young man of twenty years old born of the body of Princess Leonora by one of her footmen (a French running footman) and brought into the world under the nose of the Electress (Anna Maria Luisa, her sister-in-law).

Can you ever forgive her, that all the entreaties, all the handsome young fellows put in her way during the Cardinal's lifetime should not prevail upon her to procure such an advantage to Tuscany, and that after his death she should fu–– with her footman to increase the number of the *innocenti,* for the child was absolutely put into the hospital until he was twelve years old, and then got out with much difficulty by the means of two worthy priests who put him in, and by whom this discovery as well as the forthcoming of the young fellow to dispute his mother's inheritance with the Grand Duke (whom she made her heir) has been made.'*

Lappeggi outlasted the eighteen years guaranteed for it by the architect, and it was an oasis of enjoyment when the Angel of Death was passing over Tuscany. But at the end of the eighteenth century it was let and later sold. The fine elms and cypresses of its avenues within a circumference of four miles were chopped down and the second storey of the house was demolished, as it caused the walls to bulge dangerously. In 1876 it belonged to the Sienese sculptor Giovanni Dupré, whose monument to Cavour in Turin was considered a masterpiece, and his daughter Amalia, also a sculptor, inherited it. But the villa suffered further damage from an earthquake in 1895 and as little of its origins remain as of the Pratolino that inspired it.

All these country houses of the Medici, so modest in comparison with Castle Howard or Blenheim Palace or the châteaux of the Loire, used to form an obligatory part of the curriculum of visiting noblemen on the Grand Tour, and of cultivated Frenchmen who adapted elements of what they had admired in Tuscany to their own buildings, especially in the seventeenth century. From innumerable travellers (some of whom we have quoted) we gather that then as now, when the contents of these villas are dispersed and the buildings have suffered from a century or more of neglect or reconstruction, for those who had eyes to see the thrills of expectancy were seldom disappointed. European taste has been influenced for the better by what they found there: Poggio a Caiano and Pratolino were great precursors in their prime.

Though they were blind to Botticelli and Giotto was deemed barbaric, the Grand Tourists marvelled at the sculptural refinement of Castello and the fantastic grottoes of Pratolino – until the landscape garden was invented and they became blind in turn to the beauty of formal gardens. But the leisure of the Grand Tour is a vanished luxury – how one envies a Beckford in spite of the discomforts of a jolting chaise! – and our contemporaries who are hustled on a little tour of Tuscan villas are often too weary to appreciate what is shown them by the polyglot cicerone. They stumble and sit fanning themselves by the wayside. 'Where were we yesterday, in Venice or Ravenna? And where are we now? In Florence? Already? You don't mean to say!'

More leisure to linger and gaze beside dripping fountains amid fragrant jasmine is essential to the appreciation of villas that were made in order to enjoy it.

* According to Pieraccini, *La stirpe de' Medici di Cafaggiolo,* Florence 1924, II, pp. 705–712, Princess Eleonora was probably the mother of two illegitimate sons.

II
VILLAS IN AND
NEAR FLORENCE

See notes on pp. 275–279

29

33
34

43

48

49

52

53

54 55

61    62

65
66

VILLAS IN AND NEAR FLORENCE

Would the Tuscan villa have developed in a different manner if the Medici had not dominated Florence for three centuries? Until Cosimo the Elder's triumphant return from exile in 1434 the alternative had been the rule of a more rigid oligarchy, that of the Albizzi. Cosimo's ancestors had been associated with the liberties of the Republic and their interests were those of the merchant class concerned with the expansion of Florentine trade. 'They lived as citizens among citizens,' as Armstrong wrote,* 'keeping their private buildings and entertainments, and their personal dress and bearing in republican restraint.' Cosimo's ambitious rival Luca Pitti showed that grandiose building was no monopoly of the Medici when he commissioned the palace that still bears his name; and other great families such as the Acciaiuoli and Salviati built villas as massive and spacious as Careggi. That vanished pleasance known as the *Orti Oricellari* was laid out by Bernardo Rucellai towards the end of the fifteenth century, and the Acciaiuoli had a fine garden in the heart of the city, as well as the castle of Montegufoni and other estates. The rivalry between bankers and merchants could be discerned in their country houses, which were given descriptive names like Belcanto and Schifanoia, equivalent to the French Sans-Souci or the Neapolitan Posillipo ('Banish Care') when they were not named after their owners.

Leon Battista Alberti, whose treatise on architecture, *De Re Aedificatoria*, was composed between 1450 and his death in 1472, recommended that buildings should rely more on beauty of design and convenience of disposition than on size and ornament. He defined beauty as 'the harmony and concord of all the parts achieved in such a manner that nothing could be added or taken away or altered except for the worse.' His *Ten Books on Architecture* (translated into English by James Leoni in 1755) were widely circulated before they were printed in 1485 and their influence was strong in Tuscany while the conditions for building were favourable. Florentine architects continued to act on the principle that beauty was 'innate and diffused throughout the whole, whilst ornament was something added and attached rather than proper and innate.' They were more sparing of ornament than their Venetian and Roman peers. More than elsewhere in Italy their buildings seem to grow out of the landscape, as if in sympathy with the hills and local vegetation. Conditions were less favourable when the Medici were expelled in 1494 and their property was pillaged and confiscated. The next eighteen years of disturbed republican rule ended in a temporary restoration of the Medici under the aegis of Lorenzo the Magnificent's son Cardinal Giovanni, soon to be elected Pope Leo X; their second expulsion in 1527; and their definite reinstatement in 1531.

Cosimo the first Grand Duke was the founder of the Medicean monarchy: he and his descendants cast off republican restraint and ceased to live as plain citizens among citizens. Architecture reflected their desire for glorification, and its leading exponent was Giorgio Vasari, whose fame as an art historian has eclipsed that of his other versatile achievements. He was the father of the

* E. Armstrong: *Lorenzo de' Medici and Florence in the fifteenth century*. London 1900.

Florentine mannerists who prided themselves on their speed and facility of execution. Perhaps the speediest of these was Bernardo Buontalenti, nick-named 'of the Catherine wheels' owing to his precocious skill in pyrotechnics. While there was a growing tendency towards more fanciful design in gardens, country houses were scarcely affected by the mannerists. According to Vasari, 'delicacy, refinement and supreme grace' were 'the qualities produced by the perfection of art'; and refinement was natural to Tuscan architects.

Chronologically it is difficult to date the early villas owing to the habit of remodelling and reconstructing the original. Many have had their faces lifted again and again. A salient example is the castle of Montegufoni, familiar to the readers of Sir Osbert Sitwell's memoirs, since it was his father who bought and restored it after it had been occupied by some three hundred peasants for about fifty years. From a distance it resembles a group of buildings with a tower like that of the Palazzo Vecchio in miniature – almost a village above the old road to Volterra in the hilly country near San Casciano – and one must admire Sir George Sitwell's quixotic enterprise, so vividly and amusingly narrated by his son. In announcing his purchase to the latter Sir George wrote: 'The purchase, apart from the romantic interest, is a good one, as it returns five per cent. The roof is in splendid order, and the drains can't be wrong, as there aren't any.' He also wrote: 'There seem to have been bathrooms and every luxury. We shall be able to grow our own fruit, wine, oil – even cham-pagne.' But even after thirty years or more of cautious restoration, the castle still had 'an air of forlorn grandeur', and this was evidently one of its main attractions for Sir George.

The castle had belonged to the powerful clan of Acciaiuoli since the begin-ning of the thirteenth century. Like the Bardi, Peruzzi, Pitti, and Medici, the Acciaiuoli were the most prominent members of the Guild of Bankers or Moneylenders (*Arte del Cambio*) in the fourteenth century, making large loans to foreign princes and occupying a similar position to that of the Rothschilds in modern history. Philippe de Commines alleged that Edward IV of England owed his crown to Florentine bankers. Matteo Palmieri's biography of Niccolò Acciaiuoli, the most famous member of his family, noted that his father enjoyed 'the supreme honour of the Priorate many times' and that the family 'were great and much honoured not only in Florence, but in Sicily as well.' Niccolò, having gone to Naples on business, soon endeared himself to Catherine, titular Empress of Constantinople and widow of Philip, Prince of Taranto, and he also won the confidence of King Robert, her brother-in-law, who entrusted his nephews, the Princes of Taranto and heirs to the crown of Naples, to his care. For over twenty years he governed the kingdom of Naples with the title of Grand Seneschal, and in 1345, when the King of Hungary, to avenge the violent death of his brother Andrew, the first husband of Queen Giovanna, waged war against the kingdom, Niccolò brought his royal charge Lodovico of Taranto, Queen Giovanna's second husband, to the safety of Montegufoni. There he stayed until Niccolò defeated the Hungarian invaders in 1348, with the help of Pope Clement VI. Created Count of Melfi and other castles in the south, as well as Count of Campagna and Senator of Rome by the Pope, he was further enriched by the duchy of Corinth before he died in Naples in 1366, much regretted by the Angevin dynasty he had served so faithfully.

The Grand Seneschal had been born at Montegufoni, and his nephew Donato erected the tower dominating the castle in 1386. Donato's brother Neri inherited the duchy of Corinth from his uncle Niccolò, and in 1392 he obtained the fief of the duchy of Athens from King Ladislaus of Naples. His descendants remained in Greece until 1463 when Francesco di Antonio, sixth duke of this line, was killed by the Turks. They possessed one castle on the Acropolis of Athens and another on the Acropolis of Corinth, but only that of Montegufoni has survived. It did not acquire its actual shape until the middle of the seventeenth century. Originally it had consisted of seven separate houses surrounded by a fortified wall. Senator Marchese Donato Acciaiuoli, son of Senator Ottaviano and brother of the notorious Cardinal Niccolò, whose cruel persecution of his nephew Roberto and his wife Elisabetta Mormorai was generally execrated, joined the seven houses together and gave them a conglomerate appearance. Cardinal Niccolò added the northern façade and various embellishments, and other members of the family continued to improve the garden, but nobody can improve on Sir Osbert Sitwell's prismatic and humorous descriptions of the place in his autobiography. Its main features of picturesque interest, apart from the tower and the Baroque eastern façade, are the pretty pebbled grotto with the balustraded outside staircase, and many of the rooms contain pleasing eighteenth-century frescoes, as in the former bedroom shaped like a cave, divided in two sections, the outer one painted with fanciful landscapes, while the sky of the ceiling swarmed with volatile cupids, some pink and some dusky with bats'-wings, chasing each other through the fluffy clouds. To these, Sir Osbert and Sacheverell Sitwell added a parlour of their own, delightfully frescoed with figures from the *Commedia dell'Arte* by Gino Severini – very much to their father's distaste. Thanks to the Sitwells the castle recovered a poetical atmosphere entirely *sui generis*.

Here many of the finest pictures from the Florentine galleries and churches were stored during the last world war and Professor Frederick Hartt has described movingly how he found them there when the villa was occupied by the First Battalion, Mahratta Light Infantry, Eighth Indian Division, while the hillside shook with the thunder of British guns and German shells screamed overhead to explode among the neighbouring vineyards and cypresses.* Since Sir Osbert's death and the removal of most of the furniture, Montegufoni has the same air of forlorn grandeur which appealed so strongly to Sir George.

Nearer Florence the Villa Salviati is another impressive pile of venerable age, rising like a rampart on the hill opposite the Badia of San Domenico di

* Frederick Hartt: *Florentine Art under Fire*. Princeton 1949.

Fiesole from which it is clearly visible: a large rectangle crowned with a projecting open gallery on brackets and small arches reminiscent of Careggi, but the later addition of a turret and haphazard windows did not improve it. Evidently it was a thirteenth-century fortress when Alamanno Salviati bought it from the Montegonzi family in 1469. The Salviati were a long-established clan of merchants from the Santa Croce quarter, very wealthy and prominent in the chief magistracies: they appeared constantly in the Signoria and various embassies. Though connected with the Medici by marriage, many of them were anti-Medicean, for they were also intermarried with the Pazzi. Francesco Salviati, who had been appointed Archbishop of Pisa by Sixtus IV, joined the Pazzi conspiracy from spite because he was prevented from occupying his see. This is hardly surprising if Poliziano's account of him was reliable: 'an ignoramus, a contemner of all law human and divine, a man steeped in crime and disgrace of every sort.' After the murder of Giuliano de' Medici in the Cathedral, Francesco was hung in his ecclesiastical robes from a window of the Palazzo Vecchio.

Lorenzo the Magnificent's sister Lucrezia was married to Jacopo Salviati, and their daughter Maria married the brave condottiere Giovanni de' Medici, surnamed Delle Bande Nere, whose son became Grand Duke Cosimo I. Three of Maria's brothers joined the anti-Medicean faction while Alamanno, the youngest, was a trusted counsellor of both Dukes Alessandro and Cosimo and left a considerable fortune.

In 1527 the Salviati were declared rebels because they were suspected of attachment to the Medici. Hence their villa was set on fire and sacked by republican vandals. Vasari tells us that Giovan-Francesco Rustici had executed a large medallion in marble for the chapel of the villa, besides 'numerous medallions filled with figures of terracotta in full relief, to say nothing of many other beautiful decorations which were, for the most part, nay rather, almost all, destroyed by the soldiery in the year of the siege, when the villa was set on fire by those who were adverse to the party of the Medici.' Vasari adds that Rustici had a great love for the Villa Salviati and would sometimes stroll up there in his *lucco*, or long gown. 'Having cleared the city, he would throw the gown over his shoulder, and thus accoutred would march slowly forward lost in thought, until he reached his favourite resort. One day he was going along that road when, feeling too hot, he concealed that long robe of his in a sloe-bush, and never thought of it again until he had been at the villa two days. He then sent one of his servants to look for the gown, and seeing the man return after finding it he exclaimed: "Ah, the world is getting too good. It must be coming to its end, and cannot last much longer!" '

Clement VIII created Alamanno's grandson a marquis, and Urban VIII created his great-great-grandson Jacopo Duke of Giuliano. This Jacopo restored the villa lavishly in honour of his bride Veronica, a daughter of the Prince of Massa. The wedding was celebrated on a regal scale, but the bride

Salviati: engraving
after Zocchi

was plain as well as haughty and, as a chronicler wrote, the Duke Salviati had little pleasure with her. After eight years or more of unhappy marriage, the gallant and handsome Duke sought consolation in the arms of Caterina Canacci, the youthful wife of a repulsive old man with several grown sons. Having got wind of this affair from Bartolomeo Canacci (who was said to have courted his stepmother in vain), the jealous Duchess promised him a good pension and protection if he avenged his family's dishonour. She then hired four assassins from her native Massa and gave them secret instructions. On the night of 31st December 1638 Bartolomeo and the assassins stabbed Caterina to death in her husband's house. Her maid was also murdered to prevent her from giving evidence – a crime witnessed by two terrified neighbours. Parts of their bodies were thrown into a well; others into the Arno where they were discovered. But Caterina's head had been sawn off and consigned to the Duchess by the assassins. On the first of January the Duchess sent her husband this grisly relic in a silver basin of fresh linen. His shock may be imagined. What was left of the murdered woman had been identified in the meantime. Caterina's husband and stepsons were arrested and imprisoned. After torture Bartolomeo was executed in the Bargello, his accomplices having escaped. As the daughter of a reigning prince the Duchess felt sure of her immunity: she was merely exiled. Her husband refused to see her again. A legend persists that when the basin containing the head of his beloved was presented to him he dropped it in horror, and the head rolled slowly down the staircase where the thumping of its descent may still be heard. This may help to account for the present owner's reluctance to show the villa.

When the Salviati died out with Cardinal Gregorio in 1794 the villa was left to his niece, Princess Borghese. Her sons inherited it, and their descendants sold it in 1844 to an Englishman, Arthur Vansittart. It was subsequently sold to

Mario, Count of Candia, the most famous tenor of the nineteenth century, who retained the grace and charm of youth long after his mellifluous voice showed signs of decay. He married the equally famous soprano Giulia Grisi, by whom he had three daughters, and retired from the stage in 1871 after Grisi's death. In 1867 Charles Richard Weld wrote: 'The Villa Salviati, abounding in works of art and curiosities, which literally crowd the vast and numerous apartments – gifts, for the most part, to Mario and Grisi, to whom this villa belongs – is remembered by me more for its setting in terraced gardens, and for the views from these, than for its art treasures; with, however, let me add, one exception. This is a portrait of Grisi, representing her in the fulness of her beauty, pronounced to be the best likeness of that long regnant queen of song. It hangs, as is fitting, in Mario's study.'* Weld omits to mention that Garibaldi paid a visit to Mario and Grisi at the villa, where an absurdly bad painting commemorated the scene. The property was later sold to a Swedish Mr Hagermann, who sold it to the Swiss Mr Turri. It remains a tantalizing vision to expectant sightseers, especially as glimpsed from San Domenico. But the frustrated sightseer may be compensated with better specimens of this type of architecture at Careggi and Cafaggiolo, which still bear traces of the great Michelozzo. Otherwise Zocchi's engraving will have to suffice.

Opposite this haunted fastness stands the extensive Villa Palmieri, as celebrated for its sylvan situation on the hill slope below San Domenico as for its bygone occupants. Boccaccio's description of a garden in his introduction to the Third Day of the *Decameron* has often been identified with that of Villa Palmieri, and it is amusing to imagine Boccaccio spinning his frisky stories in a spot twice hallowed by the presence of our solemn Queen Victoria. But Boccaccio's description seems an idealized picture of fourteenth-century gardens, which were simpler, to judge from paintings before the Renaissance.

The house had belonged to several Florentine families when Marco Palmieri bought it in 1454. His descendant Palmiero Palmieri transformed it in 1697, creating the oval lemon garden. Always a 'showplace', its subsequent owners have trimmed it to the prevailing wind of fashion, and what we now see is a fifteenth-century villa with a superficially Baroque superstructure, a broad southern terrace overlooking the garden and family chapel. The Renaissance style prevails, for it was built on three sides of a courtyard, while the enclosure of the fourth side was completed by the loggia added by Matteo di Marco Palmieri in 1469. The latter is separated from the terrace by a curtain wall. The interior is also of Renaissance origin with typical vaulted ceilings, carved fireplaces and doorways, and one doorway in the courtyard is even earlier. The balustraded terrace with a double ramp sweeping down to the elaborate parterre of cut box patterns is the most prominent feature of the garden, which was grandly laid out in both Italian and English styles by the Earl of Crawford and Balcarres in the 1870s. Only the lemon garden is unchanged.

* Charles Richard Weld: *Florence the New Capital of Italy*. London 1867.

Of the Palmieri family, Matteo (1406–1474) was one of the leading Platonists of Cosimo the Elder's circle, an eloquent orator and prolific writer in Latin and Italian. The grandson of a rich apothecary who invested his profits in real estate like most of the merchant class, he held various important posts in the government. Having no children of his own, he adopted his brother Bartolomeo's two orphan sons, who managed his family business when he was sent abroad on special missions. The bookseller-biographer Vespasiano da Bisticci wrote that he 'ennobled his family by his singular virtues' and that he was honoured for his learning wherever he went. Antonio Rossellino's bust of him in the Bargello portrays an open and generous countenance: Vespasiano adds that he was tall, his hair had turned prematurely white and he had an imposing presence. Among his writings was a history of Pisa, a biography of the Grand Seneschal Acciaiuoli in florid Latin, a funeral oration on his master Carlo Marsuppini, Chancellor of the Florentine Republic, which drew tears from the congregation, a dialogue on government, and a Dantesque poem entitled *Città di Vita*, highly praised by his friends but never published, as the theologians who examined it after his death decided that it was heretical – on the grounds that it renewed Origen's error concerning the pre-existence of souls. The Inquisition even wanted to destroy it with Palmieri's remains but the manuscript was kept by the Pro-Consul of Notaries and consequently preserved in the Laurentian Library. An *Assumption of the Virgin* by Botticini, now in the National Gallery at London, was originally painted for the Palmieri chapel. According to Vasari, who attributed it erroneously to Botticelli, Matteo Palmieri suggested its design, with himself and his wife in the foreground, but he was accused of heresy by 'malicious and evil speaking persons', so that the picture was removed to the villa and walled up. Finally it was taken out and sold. After passing into the Duke of Hamilton's collection, it was bought for the National Gallery in 1882. Matteo's heirs continued to prosper and embellish their villa near San Domenico.

Florence was already a cultural goal of the English when the third Earl Cowper bought the villa in the 1760s. Having fallen in love with a Florentine married lady, not even the entreaties of his dying father could induce him to return to England. Eventually he married Miss Hannah Gore, an attractive young Englishwoman visiting Florence with her father, and he is frequently mentioned in Sir Horace Mann's correspondence with Horace Walpole. Referring to Zoffany's crowded picture of the Tribuna in the Uffizi, Horace Walpole wrote in 1779: 'I do allow Earl Cowper a place in the Tribune; an Englishman who has never seen his earldom, who takes root and bears fruit in Florence, and is proud of a pinchbeck principality in a third country, is as great a curiosity as any in the Tuscan collection.' Though Earl Cowper had become an MP for Hertford in 1759 when he went to Italy, he lost his seat through failing to return. He became a friend of the Grand Duke Pietro Leopoldo (later Emperor Leopold of Austria), who was fascinated by his wife, and he played an active role in Florentine society. He organized concerts, collected paintings ancient and modern, exerting his influence with the Grand Duke in favour of English artists who wished to copy in the gallery, cultivated scientists and kept a laboratory and physics cabinet. He also contributed towards Galileo's monument in Santa Croce, corresponded with Alessandro Volta, and was a member of various learned academies. But he was ridiculed for attaching an exaggerated importance to titles.

As his mother was the youngest daughter and co-heiress of Henry de Nassau d'Overquerque, Earl of Grantham and a descendant of Maurice de Nassau, his heart was set on acquiring the title of Prince of Nassau. There were many hitches, however. As Sir Horace Mann wrote in March 1778, 'The great Nassaus objected to his bearing their name with the title of Prince. The Emperor therefore thought he had found a medium, by substituting Overquerque, but his cousins of that family have likewise put their negative to that; so that it is now to be reduced to plain Prince Cowper; for which he must pay ten thousand zecchins (about 500 l.). The Heralds of the Empire have, like King William, in the cases of Lords Rochford and Grantham, objected to his bearing the arms of Nassau. They don't allow such a right from females; and more particularly when there is any male branch of the family. Neither the Emperor nor my Lord seems to know what they were about, when it was asked and granted, and I believe that both now repent of it.' At length he received the Imperial Diploma, hence Walpole's reference to a pinchbeck principality. His portrait by Mengs's pupil Giuseppe Antonio Fabrini (known as official painter to H. H. George Cowper) represents a robust figure in an ermine cloak with the Bavarian Order of St Hubert round his neck – a great contrast with Rossellino's bust of Matteo Palmieri.

The Earl of Crawford and Balcarres bought Villa Palmieri in 1874 and restored the place so that, as the Misses Horner wrote,* it 'combined the beauty of an Italian garden with the care and order of an English home.' Queen Victoria stayed there twice, in 1888 and 1893, and the cypress she planted in 1888 is flourishing, though in many parts of Tuscany a disease has recently attacked cypresses and made them wither. We have had much ado to protect those at La Pietra, most of which were planted by my father in the early years of this century.

A clear plan of La Pietra as it was in the fifteenth century may be found in the Uffizi Gallery's department of drawings and has been reproduced recently in Giorgio Vasari Junior's *Plans for Churches, Palaces and Vills of Tuscany*.** The central courtyard with a well was covered over when the house was remodelled in the seventeenth century, probably by Fontana and Ruggeri who built the Capponi Palace in the city, and a handsome staircase of elliptical shape was introduced. Where the well had stood my father placed a marble fountain which has been attributed to Benedetto da Maiano. Of the two gardens mentioned in Vasari Junior's notes (*giardino grande, giardino segreto*),

* Susan and Joanna Horner: *Walks in Florence and its Environs*. London 1884.

** Giorgio Vasari il Giovane. *La Città Ideale. Piante di Chiese (Palazzi e Ville) di Toscana e Italia a cura di Virginia Stefanelli*. Officina Edizioni. Rome 1970.

*Palmieri: engraving
after Zocchi*

the one facing south was demolished in the nineteenth century and restored by my father as he imagined it might have been; whereas that facing north was surrounded by a wall and is now a lemon garden ending in a spacious *limonaia*, or orangerie, decorated with rocaille work in the seventeenth century and surmounted like the walls by busts and a central balustrade.

The name La Pietra is derived from a stone pillar which indicated the distance of one mile from the old city gate of San Gallo, and the villa is much older than its Tuscan Baroque exterior suggests. Many of the rooms are pure Quattrocento, and even in the drawing-room the plaster relief decorations were applied without changing the original lunette vaulting.

In the fourteenth century the estate belonged to the Macinghi family, eight of whom were Priors of the Republic, and their descendants sold it to the Sassetti family in 1460. The Sassetti boasted of their descent from Saxon kings and belonged to the Ghibelline party. Francesco di Tommaso, who remodelled the villa in Renaissance style, married twice into the Strozzi and Pazzi families, and by his second wife he became the father of Francesco, the financial genius of the family.

Born in 1420, this Francesco won such a reputation for business acumen that he was sent to Avignon in 1440 as Cosimo de' Medici's banking partner. Later Lorenzo the Magnificent entrusted him with all his affairs in France, where he had an establishment at Lyons. After his return to Florence in 1468 he married Nera dei Corsi and had ten children. He entertained lavishly, amassed a large library of manuscripts, and cultivated the friendship of Marsilio Ficino and other famous scholars. In 1481 he commissioned Domenico Ghirlandaio to paint the frescoes in the family chapel in Santa Trinità where he was buried. These represent episodes in the life of St Francis and contain portraits of Lorenzo the Magnificent and his sons accompanied by their tutors, Luigi Pulci and Agnolo Poliziano, with views of the Piazza della Signoria and Piazza Santa Trinità. Francesco Sassetti and his wife are also portrayed kneeling on each side of the altar. They are among the finest of Ghirlandaio's works: a realistic evocation of prosperous Florence in the age of Lorenzo the Magnificent. As Berenson wrote, his talent in portraiture almost rises to genius in the Sassetti chapel. There is also a brilliant bust of Francesco by Antonio Rossellino in the Bargello Museum.

Francesco died in 1491, and his heirs sold the villa to Giuliano di Piero di Gino Capponi in 1546, to whose family it belonged for the next three centuries. Giuliano was the son of the famous Piero who in 1494 resisted Charles VIII of France's threat to 'sound his trumpets' with: 'If you sound your trumpets we shall ring our bells.' The villa owes its restrained Baroque exterior to Luigi Capponi who, born in 1583, became a cardinal in 1608. After serving as Papal Legate in the Romagna, he lived in retirement at La Pietra until his death in 1659. During this period the villa was rebuilt and redecorated, and the cardinal's hat surmounts the Capponi coat of arms behind the house. In spite of his alterations much of the fifteenth-century building was left intact. The Sassetti arms remain on many corbels of the vaulted ceilings and the narrow windows with bars, as in the ground-floor libraries, evoke the original aspect of these lofty rooms, which belong to the early Renaissance in form and spirit. As well as the Baroque exterior the Cardinal built handsome lodges at the outer gate, whence a long avenue of cypresses leads to the north-west façade of the villa, the central portion of which was raised to accommodate a spacious ballroom. That the Cardinal's architects merely overlaid the original structure and adapted their designs to it is apparent on several doorways, where Baroque pediments have been imposed on fifteenth-century lintels. The stuccoed walls of the exterior are of a mottled amber tint, the shutters green, and the windows of cool grey *pietra serena*, the local sandstone.

The process of 'tuscanizing' the so-called English garden began in 1904. The main plan consists of a series of broad terraces, levelled from the slope descending behind the house. The first is a long platform with a stone balustrade for statues at regular intervals, flanked by stairs on each side, which run down to the central terrace, enclosed by low walls and clipped hedges with niches for other statues. In the centre of this and the lowest terrace are fishpond fountains with circular basins, surrounded by stone benches and geometrical plots of grass contained by clipped hedges of box. A mossy staircase paved with coloured pebbles leads to the long grass alley between, with a colonnade roofed in by banksia roses above it on the right. Both terraces are planted mainly with evergreens. A peristyle of Corinthian columns separates the lowest terrace from the adjacent vineyard and a statue of Hercules stands vigorously in the centre with a couple of ancient cypresses behind him. Many paths running parallel with the hillside lead to stone arches and circular plots enclosed by hedges and statues. On June nights these are illuminated by myriads of fireflies.

The whole garden is essentially green; other colours are episodic and incidental. Sunlight and shade are as carefully distributed as the fountains, terraces
and statues, and in no other private Florentine garden have I seen statues of
such individual strength and grace, from the lone colossus by Orazio Marinali
to the Venetian figures by Francesco Bonazza which have stepped on to the
open-air theatre as for one of Goldoni's comedies. The wings of this little
theatre are of clipped yew, the globed footlights of box. The statues, collected
by my father for decades, deserve a separate monograph. It is a garden for all
seasons, independent of flowers. Most visitors are unaware that my father
recreated it during this century. Its central axis faces the hills towards Vallom-
brosa; Fiesole and San Domenico loom northward on the left, and southward,
below, the domes and belltowers of Florence in the echoing valley.

The approach to many Florentine villas of the fifteenth century seldom
suggests the spaciousness and tranquillity behind their solid entrance, which
seems to immunize them from the outside world. Villa Capponi at Arcetri,
for instance, is approached by a narrow road winding uphill between crumbling
walls from Poggio Imperiale. The façade is reticent and unpretentious, yet
behind it a lofty passage leads to one of the best kept lawns in Florence, a true
tapis vert, while the other leads to the vast saloon which opens on to a broad
terrace with a stupendous view of the city. This dazzles and dominates the
garden, which consists of three small parterres at different levels with geometrical box hedges and trim topiary work, laid out between undulating pink walls
of climbing jasmine, surmounted by vases and urns. Circular shapes prevail:
globes of box spring like green bubbles from the gravel, and the flowers bloom
in pots to save precious water. On the lowest level is a swimming pool concealed by cypresses. Beyond are sloping olive groves where iris and anemone
luxuriate in spring.

The place was acquired by Gino di Ludovico Capponi in 1572 and subsequent owners have respected the simplicity of the building with its modest
tower. The two loggias, one on the southern terrace, another on the northern
side, were added in 1882 by Lady Scott, a daughter of the Duke of Portland,
and are most convenient in summer when dinner may be served in one and
tea in the other. Their *pietra serena* columns were salvaged from the old market
place, demolished to make way for the present Piazza della Repubblica. No
doubt it was Lady Scott who planted the smooth lawn running behind the
house like the bowling alley at Villa Gamberaia. A hedge and gate surmounted
by griffins separate it from the lemon garden with conventional pots of lemon
trees and clipped box, the walls festooned with wistaria and roses. The villa
has been kept in excellent repair by Mr and Mrs Henry Clifford.

Another charming villa of about the same period owes its revival and
restoration to the imaginative enthusiasm of Mr and Mrs Ernest Boissevain.
Like many an old house outside the city – and this stands above a sloping avenue
of cypresses beyond the Certosa on the way to Impruneta – it was probably a

fortified farm when Niccolò degli Antinori acquired it for a country residence in 1487. Still called Villa Antinori delle Rose, it remained in the family until 1937. Badly scarred by military occupation during the last world war, it was the ghost of its former self when Mr and Mrs Boissevain were captivated by its eroded charm and rustic situation among fields of vine and olive – apart from its piazza-like courtyard and the adaptability of its interior. Undeterred by its rickety condition, they bought it in 1958 and restored it in meticulous detail with the assistance of Count Niccolò Rucellai: even windows that had been enlarged in the last century were replaced as they had been during the sixteenth. The large courtyard between the main villa and the more ancient structure with the square tower was entirely repaved; the lawns and parterres that had run to seed were replanted; and a round swimming pool was built on the plot of ground below the tower.

The two-storeyed main building is distinguished by its graceful open loggia with slim grey columns brightened by masses of azalea and gardenia in season. The whole place has a festive atmosphere, emphasized by the seventeenth-century ballroom with *trompe l'œil* painted doors evoking rococo follies: the real doors framed in stucco might be confused with the false ones at a casual glance. The glazed door leading into it is repeated in *trompe l'œil* and there is a raised balcony under the vaulted ceiling for the violinists of a bygone era: beside this is a music room frescoed with landscapes and architecture *à la* Bibbiena. On the other side is a dining room frescoed with Apollo and his chariot on the ceiling, Diana and her hunting party on the walls, in frivolous eighteenth-century fashion; a smaller dining room is adorned with traditional grotesques, winged animals, griffins and medallions. Birds, insects and butterflies are a-flutter on the cream and ochre walls of the card room in Pompeian style. This is one of the most cheerful of Florentine villas, and its hospitable owners are generous in sharing its delights.

Were I asked which garden near Florence is the most poetical, I would answer without hesitation that of the Villa Gamberaia. And were I asked which villa is superlative as pure Tuscan-blooded architecture, I would answer the Collazzi. These have been so deservedly praised by discriminating experts that one can only add wholehearted assent. Both have been copiously described and reproduced, and both possess that quality of inevitability reserved for those triumphs where the gardener and the architect have so felicitously solved the problem they have set themselves that the critic can conceive of no happier solution.

In its homely simplicity the Villa Gamberaia is a perfect foil, as it were, to the elaborate embroidery of its garden. From a distance, as in Zocchi's engraving, the latter is invisible, approached by a narrow lane from Settignano, the birthplace of so many great fifteenth-century sculptors. With its projecting eaves and coigned angles in *pietra serena*, the two-storeyed structure differs from others of the species by the addition of flying arcades to north and south.

Though it has the characteristics of a sixteenth-century building it dates from the beginning of the seventeenth. One would never guess that it has arisen like the phoenix from its ashes (since it was wholly gutted during the last world war) because its present owner has restored it with such scrupulous integrity that it is, if anything, finer than it was before – a miracle of aesthetic reconstruction.

All its previous owners must have loved the place, for its supreme quality is a serene harmony of liquid mirrors and rhythmical plants. Its name is reputedly derived from a pool of crayfish (*gamberi*), if not from the Gambarelli family which produced the fine sculptor-architects Bernardo and Antonio Rossellino, both born near by; but an inscription dated 1610 records that it belonged to Zanobi Lapi, described as its founder. Contracts for the purchase of springs and the right to convey water through neighbouring properties suggest that the Lapi family spared no expense to provide their garden with abundant water, enabling their successors, Antonio and Piero Capponi, to lay out the garden in sophisticated eighteenth-century style. Owing to this wise forethought, it has an air of perennial freshness. No bowling green could be greener, and it runs the whole length of the grounds like a corridor between the back façade of the house and a sloping wall crowned with statues and vases – a wall which would stimulate a Leonardo da Vinci to make marvellous discoveries. The silhouettes of plants against it remind one of Chinese paintings. Among gnarled old cypresses at one end of this verdant alley there is an arched fountain of rusticated stonework encrusted with stalactites and overhung by an ilex grove as at Castello, but on a more intimate scale: nymphs and fauns undoubtedly frequent it. At the far opposite end is a balustrade with a statue between stone obelisks commanding a vast prospect of the Arno valley and distant hills. A wrought-iron gate with an intricate design of Florentine lilies in the retaining wall opens on to a ravishing secret garden: a grotto fountain, rococo statues, obelisks, and balustraded steps, which lead up to a lemon orchard and sheltering *stanzone*. This grotto garden is one of the prettiest open-air boudoirs imaginable. But the main saloon of the garden is spectacular: an oblong parterre of geometrical pools framed in box of varied design round a circular central fountain, divided by paths with terracotta jars of lemons and stone vases of geraniums. The pools reflect such a feast of shimmering colour that the eye is dazzled before it can absorb so many precious details: the star in mosaic on the pavement, the carved stone and immaculate topiary work. It is a hall of horizontal mirrors terminating in a theatrical arcade of clipped cypresses, with stone benches for contemplation above a semicircular pond of water-lilies.

Though all the flowers have been judiciously selected they are not indispensable, for the arrangement of symmetrical pools protected by a screen of clipped yew and the terminal arcade overlooking the blue valley and the pale-blue distant hills fuse nature with art to a supreme degree. Nowhere else in my recollection have the liquid and solid been blended with such refinement on a scale that is human yet grand without pomposity. The length of the bowling alley contrasts with the breadth of the water garden, and both move towards a panoramic climax. It leaves an enduring impression of serenity, dignity, and blithe repose. All garden lovers are indebted to its present owner for healing its war wounds with such consummate art.

The villa of I Collazzi has had the same good fortune as the Gamberaia. Here is a complete example of High Renaissance architecture as applied to a country house – of petrified rather than frozen music. One is instantly reminded of Sir Henry Wotton's maxim: 'Well-building hath three conditions: Commodity, Firmness, and Delight.' Above all the Tuscan villas I know, not excluding those of the Medici, I Collazzi is a focus where these separate purposes have converged in a unique result. It does not bear the architect's name, but it is written throughout in the hand of a great master.

Situated superbly on the pine- and oak-clad hills on the old road winding to Montegufoni and Volterra, it is the inevitable cynosure of all who pass it. A stately home if ever there was one, the tradition ascribing its design to Michelangelo might well be correct, since he was a familiar of Agostino Dini who built it. If he was not on the spot he was there in spirit. Its design is the only evidence we possess, but this will not satisfy those critics who attribute it to Santi di Tito (1526–1603), a pupil of Bronzino and Baccio Bandinelli. From our acquaintance with Santi di Tito's achievement, an interesting example of which stands in the chapel of I Collazzi, it is hard to believe that he was wholly responsible for this masterpiece of 'well-building', though it is quite possible that he worked under Michelangelo's inspiration and also, one might add, Brunelleschi's, for it stems from the same pure spring. The lines of the building give an exhilarating sense of nobility and elevation. A low parapet over high bastioned walls encloses the terrace from which it rises: on the north a double row of loggias surround three sides of an open *cortile* or stone-flagged terrace with two well-heads, a majestic balustrade, and a double stairway guarded by two stone lions bearing shields. One door in this court leads into the Dini family chapel with Santi di Tito's altarpiece depicting *The Marriage of Cana*, dated 1593 and evidently painted on the spot, for the artist introduced the long arcade in the courtyard which he could see from the chapel window. The walls and ceiling of the chapel are frescoed by Vincenzo Meucci and Rinaldo Botti in the style of Sebastiano Ricci. The southern façade contains a memorably handsome open loggia of triple arches divided by slender coupled shafts. The rusticated entrance and its escutcheon are equally worthy of note. A building of such monumental quality needs no elaborate garden and the ridge on which it stands is comparatively narrow: a spacious lawn with a pool reflect it, and a grove of cypress separates it from the neighbouring vineyards.

A stronghold of the Buondelmonti (notorious for their medieval feuds) had stood here till Baccio and Agostino Dini bought it from their descendants

I Collazzi: engraving after Zocchi

in the sixteenth century. The Dini family had the privilege of adding *della Libertà* to their coat of arms since 1375 when Messer Giovanni Dini was a member of the Board of Eight (*Gli Otto della Guerra*), also nicknamed 'the Eight Saints' owing to their firmness and ability in the war against Pope Gregory XI – a war leading to the transfer of the papal court from Avignon. Like the Medici, the Dini had moved to Florence from the Mugello in the early 1300s and prospered as bankers. Though they held important posts at home and abroad they remained steadfast republicans, contemptuous of titles. Their intentions were practical as well as artistic when they acquired this estate surrounded by fertile olive trees and vineyards: their country house was to be combined with a productive farm. Hence the ample cellars, the store-rooms for grain, the oil-press still intact with its massive millstones to crush the olives and the wheels set in motion by a donkey at the helm. All the rain-water was collected in a cistern under the open courtyard. All the stone used was quarried from caves in the neighbourhood. Every detail from the foundations to the roof was carefully calculated, yet the total effect is a triumph of aesthetic logic, without any hint of revision or experiment. The Dini continued to strengthen it for over half a century but possibly their funds ran short, for the left wing was unfinished until the present owners, who acquired it in 1933, completed the façade. Both wings are now symmetrical, and so cleverly have the windows with *pietra serena* cornices been introduced that one would never guess they were such recent additions. In Zocchi's engraving the unfinished wing adjoins rustic buildings which belonged to the old farm.

The interior of the villa is worthy of its exterior: the lofty vaulted rooms retain their original walnut doors with brass mountings and monumental fireplaces of *pietra serena*, and they lead to each other in telescopic vistas splendidly proportioned. Practically nothing was changed till the eighteenth century when Medea Castelli married a Dini. It was she who added the double

147

stairway leading up from the outer terrace to the courtyard, and who commissioned Meucci to fresco the chapel with an 'Assumption of St Augustine', the patron saint of the Dini family, and furnished it in contemporary style. Moreover she had a penchant for commemorative inscriptions. Near the well in the courtyard we read in Latin: 'This ancient atrium was restored by Maria Medea Castelli Dini at her own expense [*proprio aere*] A D 1754'. Other inscriptions are suitably edifying, as in the main entrance, 'God has granted us this leisure', and to the right of the main hall, 'Now go ye to bed and sleep soundly.' Above another door we read: 'Soon a joyful feast in the old tradition, and diversions after dinner.' Whereas on a door to the left of the hall we are adjured: 'Go, for the solemn rite of religion is prepared. Hasten, ye ministers!'

The Dini family occupied the villa till the first half of the nineteenth century. As a rule trees were seldom planted close to Tuscan villas because they were considered unhealthy, but the last of the Dini to own I Collazzi in the early 1800s was born Countess Boutourline of Russian origin (there was a large Russian colony in Florence until the First World War) – and she yearned nostalgically for more trees near the house. The trees she planted grew to a great height, but many were shattered by shell fire during the last war.

After the Dini, the Counts Bombicci owned I Collazzi for nearly a century, and when the Marchi brothers bought it from their successors in 1933 most of the original furniture made for the Dini family, including gargantuan beds, remained inside the house – to the great advantage of its authentic 'period' atmosphere. Though placed out of bounds and respected by the military during the last war, the villa suffered from incessant shell fire in August 1944. Not irreparably, for the Marchi family restored it meticulously and planted other trees to replace casualties. All honour to those who have done so much for Florence!

Both Gamberaia and I Collazzi are fairly remote from the city and in the days before motor cars their distance would have seemed much greater.

Santi di Tito, admirable for his contribution to I Collazzi, has also left his imprint on a villa nearer Florence whose tunnel-like loggia may be seen for many a mile. On a rocky ledge against the wooded hillside of Fiesole, in a situation as romantic as that of the neighbouring Villa Medici and commanding as magnificent a view, the Villa San Michele alla Doccia had a long history before it became an ideal resort for honeymoon couples.

In 1411 Niccolò Davanzati bought the property for some monks of the Third Order of St Francis. It consisted of 'a farm with house, courtyard, oven, fountain and grounds, with vineyards, trees and woods in the place called *alla Doccia*' (at the douche) because a stream flowed beneath it from a conduit descending from Fiesole. The conditions stated in the deed of sale specified that Brother Francesco and Brother Ventura should build an oratory and a dormitory for at least six friars within thirty months and 'as an acknowledgement of the patronage of the Davanzati, the friars are expected to dedicate the

VII
VIII
IX

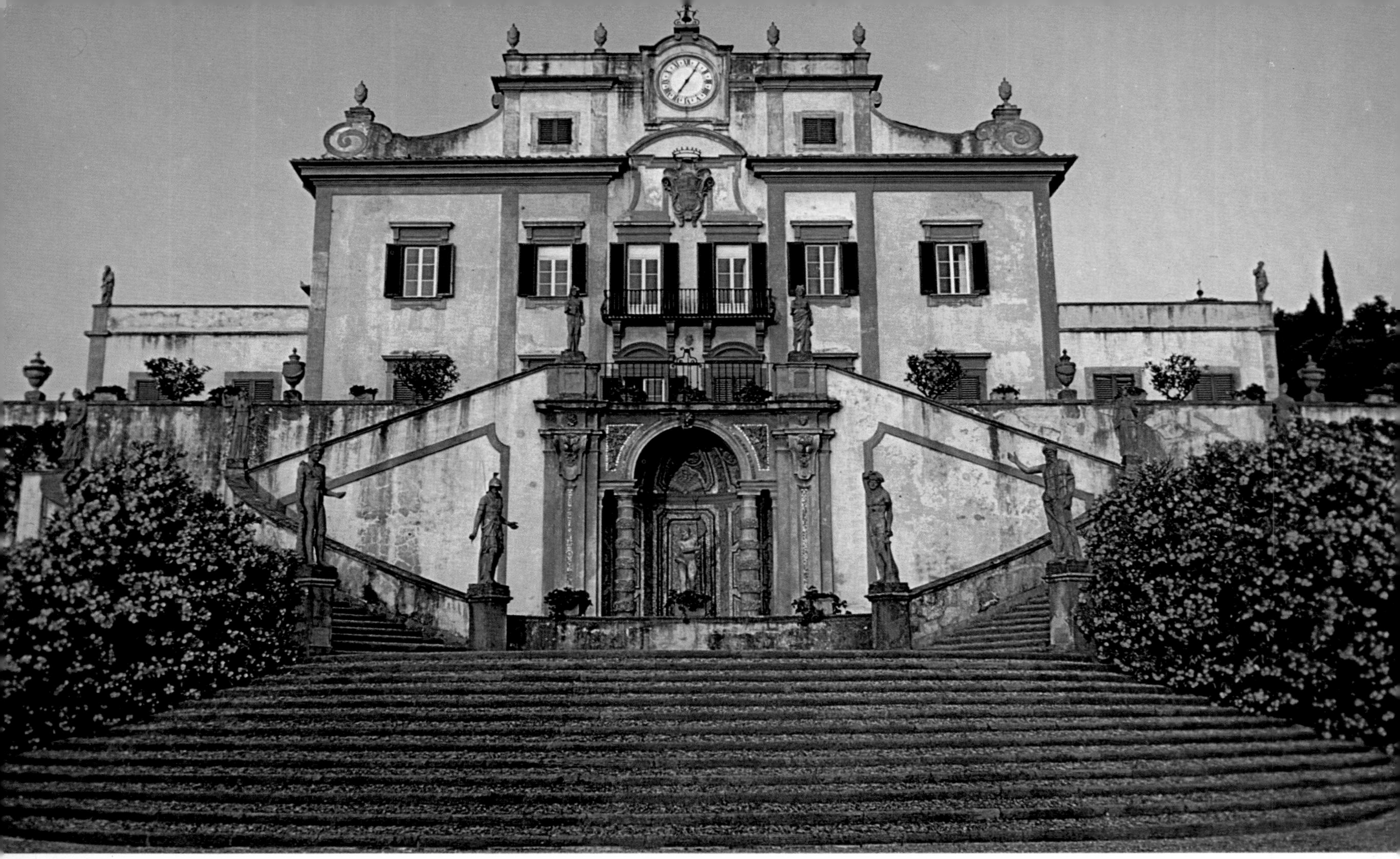

XVII XVIII

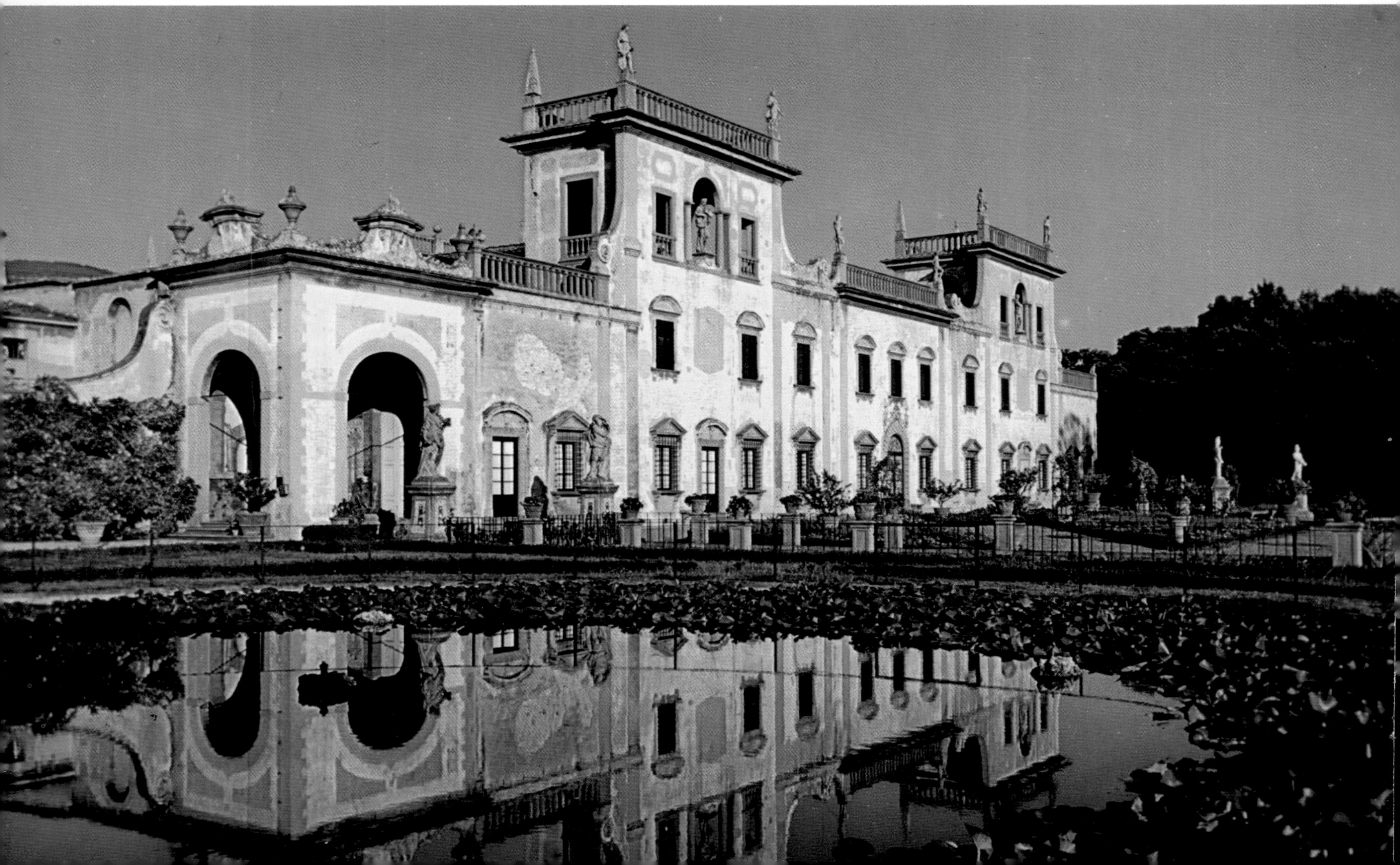

oratory to St Michael the Archangel and also to give their patrons every year, on the day of St Michael, a pound of wax.' A curious detail of the deed of purchase was: 'In order to give the buyer possession of his new property, the notary opens and closes the door of the house, places the cross-bar of the door in the hand of the buyer, takes some earth and some grass and a small branch picked on the same property, and places them on the lap of the buyer; then the buyer, entering the house and the grounds, declares, as a sign of his true possession, that he will keep these goods, not only with his soul but also with his body.'

According to an ancient chronicle* the place was deserted for a while after a monk was murdered by one of his brethren, and in 1483 it was bestowed on the Minori Osservanti (strict followers of the Franciscan Rule), in whose charge it remained until their suppression in 1808.

Giovanni Davanzati restored and enlarged the monastery in 1596, and according to a contract found among his papers all the work on it was entrusted to Michele del Barba, stonecutter in Fiesole, for a settled price, from designs by Santi di Tito. Various artists were employed on the Davanzati coat of arms and other details.**

When Napoleon's troops occupied Florence in 1808 their General Dauchy ordered the suppression of religious communities and the French prefect of the department of the Arno used it as a *maison de plaisance*. On his return from exile, the Grand Duke Ferdinand III allowed some nuns of the Benedictine Order to settle there until 1817, when he ordered it to be sold to the highest bidder. It was bought by Dr Frosini-Martinucci who divided it into apartments which he let furnished. Though most of its contents had been removed, the church was preserved, and a formal parterre with solid retaining walls replaced the monks' kitchen garden.

A steep path winds up to the mellow monastic façade, on the right of which a loggia of eleven arches runs the whole length of the building towards the garden and ilex grove looking south. This unusually long arcade is the glory of San Michele. In 1901 it was acquired by Mr Henry White Cannon of New York who introduced modern comforts with more enthusiasm than discretion, covering the pretty cloister with a glass roof. Owing to its strategic position it was occupied by troops during the last war with inevitable damage, since when it has been tastefully restored by M. and Mme Lucien Teissier, who have adapted it for travellers of discrimination.

The city has advanced inexorably towards other villas which were situated in the open country when they were built. Sesto Fiorentino, as its name implies, was the sixth milestone on the old Roman road to Prato, beyond industrialized Rifredi and the Medici villas above it, now more than ever a busy thoroughfare with modern constructions monopolizing the vineyards and olive groves – a place famed for the porcelain first manufactured at Doccia in 1735 owing to the enterprise of Count Carlo Ginori who brought artisans

* *A History of the Suppressed Convent of San Michele alla Doccia,* compiled and arranged by Eugenia Levi, Florence 1909–1911, page 48.

** *Op. cit.,* pp. 70–75. Apart from which, Doctors Frey, Steinmann and Thode unanimously attributed the design to Santi di Tito.

*Corso–Salviati: engraving
after Zocchi*

from Vienna as well as local sculptors and painters to decorate the productions of his factory. Here one would hardly expect to find a garden of exquisite sophistication hidden behind a rather dull grey stucco façade. Yet we should grow used to such surprises in Tuscany, where we have many examples of concealment behind impersonal exteriors.

The Villa Corsi-Salviati at Sesto was purchased by Simone di Jacopo Corsi from the Carnesecchi family in 1502, and from a fresco by Bernardino Poccetti inside the house we may visualize it as it was then: an irregular fifteenth-century structure surmounted by a spacious loggia with dovecote tower behind it. A red doorway with a rusticated stone border stood in the middle of the façade with niches on each side containing stone watch-dogs; four symmetrical windows with kneeling consoles opened on the ground floor and two smaller ones at the side. A square plot of grass, criss-crossed by paths ending in a basin with a triton, constituted the original garden. There is also a fresco of the original courtyard flanked on three sides by an arcade supporting an open terrace, but this, and the fountain of Fame springing from a triangular base, might have been imagined by the painter though it roughly corresponds with the actual *cortile*. The heirs of the Corsi continued to enlarge and embellish it until both house and garden were completely transformed in the seventeenth century.

All the grace of the building is concentrated in the south front facing the garden: here we see Tuscan Baroque at its apogee, two symmetrical belvederes with niched statues rising above the two-storeyed central block, the lines of the roof surmounted by balustrades punctuated by statues. The elaboration of its parterres on a long tract of level ground, instead of the more usual hillside, compensates for the lack of any ulterior view. Gravelled walks and box-edged beds of flowers, fountains and statues, lemons in terracotta pots, a canal-like pool from the loggia west of the parterres and beyond it more flowers and a park. Zocchi's engraving – one of his most successful – records its appearance in about 1740 not long after it had been remodelled in Baroque style. There is a felicitous fusion of earlier with later elements, and the past bestows its blessing on the present.

The names of the architects and sculptors are unknown but it is likely that the architect-sculptor Gherardo Silvani (1579–1675) had a hand in it. Unfortunately the interior decorations by Baccio del Bianco have vanished. Both house and garden succumbed to nineteenth-century fashion: the large hall on the ground floor was plastered with academic frescoes of the four elements in 1865, while the statues, box hedges and topiary work outside were removed as insufficiently romantic, in favour of palm trees and other exotic plants. Camellia, gardenia, carnation, double jasmine from Goa, the Arabian jasmine (known as *mugherino del Granduca* as it was introduced by Cosimo III) and the ranunculus called *rosellino di Firenze*, became the specialities of this new landscape garden. Their blend of perfume and colour was delightful, but from an aesthetic point of view they were out of place. Marchese Giulio Guicciardini Corsi-Salviati, who inherited the villa in 1907, had the wisdom to restore its eighteenth-century character as much as feasible, reinstating the central fountain, box hedges and lemon trees in pots, and removing the hot-houses and botanical accessories. Horticulturalists may sigh but the beauty of design has been enhanced, while a fragmentary sample of the 'English' section survives between dense ilexes and a miniature lake.

Gherardo Silvani undoubtedly designed the impressive villa known as L'Ugolino on the road towards Chianti. Its façade is strikingly different from that of other seventeenth-century country houses; in fact its triple arched central portico was added in the eighteenth century. Though the latter may suggest the entrance to a chapel it relieves the austerity of the older building without introducing a discordant note, and all who pass it are tempted to peer inside. A tablet over the door records that this was built in 1714 and restored by Giorgio Ugolini in 1744. In other respects it belongs to the Buontalenti tradition, very sober and dignified. All his fantasy was reserved for gardens, theatricals and fireworks: his buildings were remarkably staid, like the south façade of L'Ugolino overlooking the walled garden. The main hall within is frescoed with allegories framed in stucco, painted and signed by Attanasio Bimbacci in 1691, a prolific decorator and stage designer who was patronized by the merry Cardinal Francesco Maria de' Medici. The long avenue of cypress east of the villa enhances its dignity.

In these later villas one cannot fail to notice the great changes that had occurred since the castellated farmhouses of the early fifteenth century – changes due not only to growing prosperity but also to the increase of security since the reign of Grand Duke Cosimo I. More peaceful conditions are apparent in the free approach to these houses surrounded by olives and vineyards.

The buildings seem to expand in space, and to acquire more polished manners. Instead of local masons the best architects were employed, whose plans were designed in sympathy with the background. The proprietor spent more of his time in the country, enjoying nature for its own sake – apart from its products whose sale augmented his income. And the architect had grown in importance and prestige. The Grand Duke Francesco stood in the presence of a seated Michelangelo, and he treated Buontalenti as a boon companion.

Gradually the traditional projecting eaves and central courtyard disappeared, the latter to be replaced by barrel-vaulted halls with fireplaces and doorways of more vigorous design. While the walls were usually of stone coated with stucco, many were decorated with geometrical panels in *sgraffito* (drawn on plaster with a pointed tool) indicated by varied bands of deeper grey or brown. The stuccoed projections of doors and window-mouldings became more pronounced, with brackets, scrolls, cartouches, balconies, balustrades, parapets with statuary (as at Villa Corsi-Salviati) and operatic external staircases (as at La Tana). The *stuccatore* or plasterer gave rein to his fertile ingenuity in a riot of flowers and foliage, cupids, vases, emblems, urns, armorial bearings among looped draperies. The narrow staircase of the fifteenth century was enlarged, broadened and emphasized, and became a commanding feature.

Within the same area as the Villa Corsi-Salviati, in the plain below Petraia, stands another fine example of Tuscan Baroque, the Villa Corsini. It is a two-storeyed building with an elegant central gable, clock and balcony over the front door, flanked by balustrades with four vases. The symmetrical windows of varied design are divided by rudimentary stucco pilasters. Unfortunately it has long been uninhabited, which gives it a somewhat derelict air. Since the Strozzi sold it to the Rinieri in 1460 it was owned by several noble families including the Medici and Lanfredini, until the Corsini acquired it in 1687. Probably the Corsini commissioned Antonio Ferri, who built the grand staircase and state saloon of their regal palace on the Lungarno, to enlarge and modernize it.

The princely house of Corsini has been inseparably associated with Florentine history since the twelfth century. The Emperor Charles IV created the head of the house a count palatine in 1371; Andrea, the holy bishop of Fiesole, was canonized in 1629; in 1730 Cardinal Lorenzo Corsini was elected pope as Clement XII and conferred the rank of Roman princes on his family; in 1732 they were created grandees of Spain. The Villa Rinieri was only one of their minor acquisitions, but it is of interest to Englishmen because Sir Robert Dudley (1574–1649) lived and died there – one of the most adventurous of our expatriates. A son of Queen Elizabeth's Earl of Leicester who repudiated his secret marriage to Dudley's mother, Lady Douglas Sheffield, his character and career were influenced by this repudiation which cast a slur on his legitimacy. Eager to compete with the great navigators, he distinguished himself in an expedition to the Orinoco and won his spurs in the storming of Cadiz,

Rinieri (Corsini):
engraving after Zocchi

but he fell from Court favour owing to his association with the Earl of Essex. His lingering hopes of advancement were blighted when his father died. Leicester recognized him as his heir and left him his property, but after the failure of a suit to prove his legitimacy, he obtained licence to travel abroad and left England in 1605.

It was more of a flight than a departure, for he was accompanied by one of the Queen's maids of honour, his nineteen-year-old half-cousin Elizabeth Southwell, disguised as a page. Since he already had a wife and five daughters this elopement created a scandal, which was increased when he became a Roman Catholic and married the fair page, presumably by papal dispensation. Assuming the titles of Earl of Warwick and Leicester, he appealed to the Grand Duke Ferdinando I de' Medici for protection and permission to settle in Florence. His conversion proved a practical as well as a spiritual advantage, for the Grand Duke as a former cardinal retained much influence in Rome. Dudley's experience of naval matters and his knowledge of shipbuilding were a further recommendation to Ferdinando, who was determined to crush the Barbary pirates infesting the Mediterranean. Dudley stated his qualifications without false modesty in a punctilious letter promising to make Tuscany mistress of the Levant.

Having investigated his pretensions, the Grand Duke decided to employ him. In 1607 he reached Leghorn, which Ferdinando had developed into a free port and refuge for all who were persecuted for their creed. At their first meeting in Florence the Grand Duke was so impressed by Dudley's personality that he put him in charge of the shipyards and arsenal of Pisa as well as Leghorn.

After a period in Pisa, Dudley took a house in Florence, where he and his wife were graciously received by the Grand Duchess Christine, a daughter of Duke Charles of Lorraine. When reports of Dudley's activities reached home he was sent a Royal Warrant of Privy Seal recalling him to England. Dudley rejected it with scorn because it was not addressed to him as Earl of Warwick, thus derogating, as he explained, 'from my due pretenses and right which I claim, being lawful son and heir to my father'. King James retaliated by confiscating his estates.

In the meantime Dudley was building a galleon of sixty-four guns, recruiting English shipwrights and crews, and collecting armament. The Tuscan fleet was largely manned with English sailors, who preferred foreign service to the risks of being press-ganged at home. Bona in Algeria, the strategic base of the pirates, was stormed in the year of Dudley's appointment, and in 1608 Dudley's new galleon, the *San Giovanni Battista*, helped to defeat a Turkish armada, when nine vessels, seven hundred prisoners, and treasure valued at two million ducats were captured.

Dudley was also employed in draining the marshes near Leghorn and improving the harbour. His brain teemed with practical projects: in 1610 he was granted a patent for an invention to improve the manufacture of silk. He even invented a curative powder called *Pulvis Comitis Varvincensis*, of which the Pisan professor of medicine Cornacchini wrote, 'clearing the Italian seas of barbarous and evil pirates was not a greater benefit to mankind than his fighting and exterminating the evil humours which molest humanity and cause disease.'

Dudley's position at the Tuscan Court was strengthened by the affection of the Grand Duchess Christine and her Austrian daughter-in-law, the Archduchess Maria Maddalena, for his wife and children, so that when Ferdinando died in 1609 his influence increased, free from the usual jealousies and intrigues. The young Grand Duke Cosimo II regarded him as invaluable and kept him fully occupied. In his spare time he composed treatises on naval architecture and the fortification of ports. He was appointed Grand Chamberlain to both the Grand Duchesses, and he was given the life-long tenancy of the stately Villa Rinieri. To please his Tuscan sister, the Emperor Ferdinand II conferred on him the title of Duke of Northumberland, thereby recognizing him as the legitimate heir of his grandfather. Pope Urban VIII created him a Roman patrician. Such honours helped to console him for the loss of Kenilworth and his English estates, but his emoluments barely covered his expenses.

When Cosimo II died in 1621 the Grand Duchesses became joint Regents and Dudley remained their trusted counsellor during the Grand Duke Ferdinando II's minority. Ten years later plague broke out. His eighteen-year-old daughter died of it and her death was followed by that of his eldest son Cosimo, a promising captain of the Grand Duke's bodyguard, in his twentieth year. These were fatal blows to Elizabeth Southwell, who had recently given birth to her thirteenth child. The loss of his devoted companion in exile was the hardest to bear. Dudley retired to his country villa to rewrite his treatises on navigation and shipbuilding in Italian: he beguiled his sorrow by drawing hundreds of maps, charts, diagrams and designs for nautical instruments. This monumental production, entitled *Dell'Arcano del mare*, was printed in 1646–47; though its technical information has been superseded it is valued by bibliophiles for its excellent engravings. Dudley was justly proud of his *magnum opus*: after the title page he printed the Emperor's patent confirming his right to be Duke of Northumberland. He died at the Villa Rinieri in 1649, a typical Elizabethan who had outlived that heroic age.

Of the same period as this now deserted villa is the admirably preserved La Tana ('The Den') whose suave eighteenth-century façade of golden brown and rosy stucco soars above Candeli beside the Arno south of the city. It is known to have replaced a fifteenth-century house with four towers at each corner of which one survives, but it has changed very little since Zocchi engraved it, though he took liberties with the foreground in his design. The Bucelli of Montepulciano and the Landi of Castellina in Chianti had been its owners until it was bought by Pietro di Ser Zenobi Buonaventuri and his wife Bianca Cappello in 1570 when Bianca, aged twenty-seven, was already the mistress of Grand Duke Francesco I, who evidently helped them to buy it. Two years after her dissolute husband was killed in a brawl – some said with Francesco's connivance in 1574 – Bianca sold it to the hospital of Santa Maria Nuova. It was then a conventional two-storeyed structure with a central hall, surrounded by fortress-like walls. In 1631 it was leased by the hospital to Baron Ricasoli of ancient Lombard stock, whose successors modified its sixteenth-century austerity, but the most thorough alterations were made in the first half of the eighteenth century by the architect Filippo Billi (1700–81). The main façade was decorated with statues and vases in terracotta surmounted by a clock, and the central hall was heightened by demolishing the ground floor and two open arcades with wrought-iron balconies were built to lead up to the first floor. Curved double stairways to the entrance were added as at Poggio a Caiano, and a columned portico with symmetrical doors on each side led to the vaulted cellars. Breezy frescoes of harbours with sailing vessels, inspired by the old Leghorn, adorn the central salon, stuccoed in pastel shades. The frescoes are signed by Antonio Cioci, 1770. Further changes, including a chapel on the right of the façade, were made by Marchese Fossi in the nineteenth century. The present owner has restored and beautified it, devoting especial care to the garden behind the house, which has become famous for its opulent variety of iris and azalea. A row of slim cypresses leads towards a dense wood on the summit of the hill. The villa now contains a collection of early Chinese ceramics unique in Italy.

Among the villas with late seventeenth-century features but in fact a good century older, that with the curious name of Selva e Guasto, is one of the most alluring. Situated below the Villa Capponi of Arcetri in the vicinity of Viale Michelangelo, its name was probably derived from one or more farms that were built where a wood had been cut down. A solid screen of cypress gives it an air of isolation which is soon dispelled upon entering the formal garden, illuminated by glowing lemons symmetrically disposed in pots among semicircles of topiary work and beds planted with box hedges in decorative patterns. The long low many-windowed façade, crowned by a curvilinear gable with vases approached by a double staircase, is graceful, gay and welcoming. A seventeenth-century private chapel festooned with wistaria stands beside it on the right.

Originally it belonged to the Galilei family, but its present owners inherited it from Princess Dolgoroukoff in 1919, and the spacious drawing-room overlooking the garden contains romantic nineteenth-century portraits of her parents as well as of the Venezuelan heroes, Simon Bolivar 'The Liberator' and General Francisco Miranda, from whom the present owners are descended on the distaff side. Thus imperial Russia and revolutionary South America meet in a Florentine villa – to the amazement of the last King of Spain when he visited the place.

Delectable villas of this type began to proliferate in the eighteenth and nineteenth centuries. Obviously we could not include them all as we have had to deal with our subject by representative selection. Tuscany had become placidly provincial since the extinction of the Medici and even some time before that sad event. It was ever so faintly touched by that unifying wand (where the fine arts were concerned) which we associate with the *douceur de vivre* before the French Revolution. The wand waved over Europe from Rome with varying vibrations, crescendo here and diminuendo there. While the Grand Style survived in parts of Italy, it had been chiselled and filed and manicured in the France of Gabriel's Petit Trianon, which has come to typify eighteenth-century good taste in architecture. Compared with the France of Madame de Pompadour, the Tuscany of Empress Maria Theresa's progeny was dull and prosaic. Only in melody was Italy still supreme, though Germany was soon to overtake her.

During the half-century Sir Horace Mann remained in Florence as British Minister, he wrote hundreds of letters to his friend Horace Walpole which, in spite of their 'damnable iteration' and slipshod style, provide us with detailed vignettes of Florentine life at that period. It was not till the Florentines saw Mann's family tree suspended in the hall of his house, we are told, that they were fully satisfied of his gentility. Yet Florentine society was no more genteel than the French as described in Diderot's letters to Sophie Volland, and far less amusing.

The Princess de Craon, wife of the absent Grand Duke's vice-regent, had been a peasant lass driving turkeys in a field before Duke Leopold of Lorraine took her as a mistress, and she had married his son's tutor M. de Beauvau, raised to the dignity of Prince of the Holy Roman Empire by his former pupil. With such a leading lady the tone of society was no more refined than under the crapulent Gian Gastone de' Medici, and Mann's letters report such petty scandals as the following. In August 1748 he wrote: 'An accident has happened that has soured my temper extremely and almost made me determine to give over my *conversations*. . . . It is time to tell you that a certain Countess Ubaldini who for her pranks has been banished the Pope's state, imagined she saw the Bocchineri do something upon a bench in a side walk [of Mann's garden] with Count Acciaiuoli the canary bird [because he came from Madeira] that would have offended any other's modesty, but that vile woman not only feasted her eyes and her imagination, but carried several people into the same walk to observe what only she herself could see. The affair made no noise that evening, nor did I hear anything of it, but that wretch soon made it public, and engaged a vile poet, a *garde noble* (in the service of the Emperor as Grand Duke) to make a *sonetto* in which everything was represented in the strongest light, and which was soon handed about. One was brought to me which I suppressed, but being at Prince Craon's at Petraia, where the calumny and the *sonetto* were mentioned, it was that very evening represented in town that I had mentioned it and publicly read the sonnet. The vile reporters of this were two people to whom I have had opportunities to do many civilities. I was, however, the last to know how angry the *dame* were with me, or that their husbands had forbid them to come to my garden for fear of being exposed to the same calumny, etc., etc. To conclude, the Regency did find out the author of the *sonetto* as well as the disperser, both of the *garde noble*, and have banished them for six months, and it is believed they will be turned out of the corps.'

A century later, oh the respectable difference! On the one hand Florence is described (by William Wetmore Story) as 'nothing but a Continental Boston in its spirit.' On the other, Hawthorne was writing: 'I hardly think there can be a place in the world where life is more delicious for its own simple sake than here.' The Brownings were in residence but Walter Savage Landor had preceded them, for he had bought the fifteenth-century Villa Gherardesca at San Domenico, a rectangular building surmounted by a 'central turret, round which the kite perpetually circles in search of pigeons or smaller prey, borne onward, like the Flemish skater, by effortless will in motionless progression.' Now called La Torraccia, the house must have had charm when Landor lived there, collecting those Primitives with gold backgrounds at which his friends scoffed but which have been more valued since, planting trees and filling his garden with flowers he would not allow to be picked. The story of his anguished concern for the violets when he had thrown the cook out of the window – 'I forgot the violets!' – is well known. As cantankerous in his conduct as he was classical in his *Imaginary Conversations*, he was undoubtedly sincere when he wrote of Florence: 'He who hath lived in this country can enjoy no distant one. He breathes here another air; he lives more life; a brighter sun invigorates his studies, and serener stars influence his repose.'

The sprawling pseudo-medieval castle of Vincigliata above Settignano is the most solid relic of the golden age of the foreign colony, predominantly

English. This was a heap of ruins when John Temple Leader bought it and had it totally rebuilt in 1855 by a young architect he had helped through the university. Previously he had acquired the ancient Villa Pazzi and several farms and houses at Maiano, but the rebuilding of Vincigliata was his life's vocation. The young architect Giuseppe Fancelli was the son of his bailiff. According to Carocci* he was 'the faithful interpreter of the cultured and studious gentleman's wishes', but he died prematurely in 1867 before his arduous labour was completed. The reconstruction was continued by others, perhaps with different criteria. Now that it is over a century old it has the picturesque quality of a stage setting for a romantic opera.

Before emigrating to Florence, Temple Leader had been a Radical Member of Parliament and it is ironical that he should have devoted so much time and money to recreating a feudal atmosphere: he even coined medals to celebrate his seigniory of Vincigliata and the names of his numerous royal visitors – including that of Queen Victoria who painted with watercolours in the park – were engraved in stone upon his castle walls. We are indebted to him for replanting the hills with trees and protecting the landscape, which seems identical with the background of Benozzo Gozzoli's frescoes of the procession of the Magi. Unfortunately he set a fashion for building villas in pseudo-medieval style, but these are less offensive than the prefabricated cottages of today.

Lord Westbury inherited Vincigliata together with its adjoining farms and villas, most important of which, thanks to its recent owner, was I Tatti. This was a modest dwelling with a few old cypresses and lemon trees on a straggling hill slope above San Martino a Mensola when Bernard Berenson acquired it in 1905. Berenson transformed it. He engaged the English architect Cecil Pinsent to rebuild the house and design the garden between 1908 and 1915, using the lemon house as a connecting link between the enclosed garden and the new formal one descending in terraces to an ilex grove. It is almost contemporary with the garden of La Pietra, but like the equally delightful gardens of Papiniano and Villa Sparta, it has the Pinsent touch. In other words it is Anglo-Florentine; its Tuscan elements have been cleverly adapted rather than absorbed. The scale as well as the dainty precision of the details is more English than Florentine.

Berenson spoke of his house as a library with rooms attached, and everything gravitates about the Quattrocento-style library leading to more and more book-lined rooms and corridors as the accumulation of international art publications continues to grow. Otherwise the interior is quietly and comfortably furnished with little to distract the eye from the magnificent collection of fourteenth- and fifteenth-century Italian paintings, except the view. Here for over half a century Berenson worked and meditated and entertained his many friends of all nationalities, and for those who knew him the place is still vibrant with his personality. Indeed that was its principal attraction.

* Guido Carocci, *I Dintorni di Firenze*. Florence 1908.

Le Falle: engraving after Zocchi

Long before he died Berenson had become, as he laughingly but truthfully said, 'an instootion – one of the sights which the traveller to Florence has to see.' By bequeathing the property to Harvard University he has benefited hundreds of art students and created a living shrine.

The most successful of the other villas remodelled and improved by Cecil Pinsent is the handsome Villa Sparta belonging to HM Queen Helen of Roumania, whose talent and enthusiasm for gardening are truly royal. Originally a fifteenth-century house, it had been tastelessly restored at the beginning of this century. Thanks to Queen Helen it has recovered its former beauty, suddenly disclosed at the end of a winding avenue, surrounded by immaculate parterres of box and cypress hedges. The whole district of San Domenico below Fiesole, above and beyond it, is dotted with civilized buildings – civilized in that they blend harmoniously with the landscape.

Farther east of Florence near Compiobbi are two memorable villas off the beaten track. Since Zocchi engraved the Villa Le Falle the cypresses climbing towards it in long avenues from both left and right have grown to their fullest height but the railway to Pontassieve has spoiled their approach to the house. This is yet another example of a turreted castle totally rebuilt and improved by its transformation. It had belonged to the wealthy Pazzi family till the failure of their conspiracy against the Medici in 1478, when all their property was confiscated. And when it was acquired by the Guadagni family in 1599 it was in a dilapidated condition. The Guadagni engaged Gherardo Silvani, one of the last great architects in the Buontalenti tradition, to reconstruct it as it stands today. While preserving the old square tower, he introduced two symmetrical loggias superimposed on opposite façades and rounded it with a terrace reminiscent of I Collazzi, set high above its park on a broad stone pedestal. The interior courtyard was replaced by a grand

171

saloon. But it was gothickally bedevilled in the nineteenth century when the Guadagni sold it to a Cavalier Danti who had a mania for medievalizing the local farmhouses with turrets and crenellations. Its present owner has wisely restored its seventeenth-century character.

Not far from Le Falle on the southern slope of Monte Loro stands another fine villa called Gricigliano which was acquired in 1478 by the Martelli family who proceeded to rebuild it. Surrounded by a moat of clear water, it is entered across a bridge by a loggia of singular grace, with three arches and two internal columns corresponding with the external ones to support the vault. This arcade between two barred windows opens on the left of the façade: on the right there is an expanse of wall beneath a row of small square windows near the roof – a lack of symmetry which is almost a relief. It contains a seventeenth-century grotto and an eighteenth-century chapel, and for five centuries the same family has continued to own it. This is an Arcadian setting for a *villeggiatura*, deliciously cool in the summer heat, the murmur of flowing water in one's ears.

'The Commodity, Firmness, and Delight' of such villas is never ostentatious: compared with French *châteaux* they are in a minor key. *Grandiosa*, *stupenda*, *signorile*, are adjectives so often applied to them by Carocci and his heirs that one is stunned for lack of more precise definitions. *Signorile* in the sense of noble and refined they certainly are, but they have not the stateliness of Palladio's buildings. Speaking for myself, I can only say that their simple proportions and quiet harmony heighten my enjoyment of both architecture and landscape. The size and calculated distance of doors and windows, the expanse of weathered wall, the faintness of shadows, the importance of the terrace as a pedestal, the balance and grace of the whole structure: one might compare them with the rules of proportion governing Greek sculpture as expounded by Winckelmann. They satisfy a desire for blitheness and repose without pandering to hollow rhetoric.

Still farther from Florence at Figline, a little walled town in the upper valley of the Arno seldom visited by tourists, is a fascinating mansion, half palace, half villa, which has belonged to the Serristori family since the fourteenth century. Known locally as the *Casa Grande*, or Big House, its modest exterior is deceptive. Enter the cloistral courtyard and you are amazed to find an exquisite formal garden, like a Persian carpet delicately woven with geometrical patterns. A hedge of slim cypress surrounds it on the south-west under the castle walls and Guelf battlements, while an arcade forms a suitable boundary on the south-east. The crossed arches of the loggia rest on firm yet elegant columns with sober capitals. A fine staircase with broad circular steps ascends to an upper loggia where the rhythm of the columns in the portico is repeated in lighter manner to support the wooden beams of the ceiling. Old inscriptions and ancestral arms are scattered between the pendentives of the arcade. A slender pillar with a cross in the middle of the garden enhances the monastic

Rospigliosi: engraving after Zocchi

impression and a growing sense of spiritual peace. Upon entering the house one is transported more completely into the distant past, for the rooms are furnished in pure fifteenth-century style, wedding chests, credence and refectory tables, Savonarola chairs and heavy carved cupboards, with terracotta Madonnas, a bas-relief by Rossellino, and other treasures arranged with impeccable taste.

It is almost certain that this *Casa Grande* was built by the Ser Ristoro who went to Florence in 1384 and became notary to the Signoria. His descendants provided the Republic with ten Gonfaloniers and twenty-seven Priors. They were adherents of the Medici until the reign of the dissolute Duke Alessandro when they were exiled as rebels. Under the later Grand Dukes they returned to favour and filled responsible positions in the government.

During the eighteenth century the noble house at Figline was used as a depository for oil and wine and as a factory for wine flasks and glasses. Count Umberto Serristori restored its pristine beauty – no pun intended – in 1904. Hence Edward Hutton was mistaken when he wrote in 1927: 'There is little to be seen in Figline today.' If he admired the piazza named after the great Platonist Marsilio Ficino who was born there in 1433, he would have been enchanted by this villa.

Last but not least of the villas engraved by Zocchi which are still worthy of a visit is the Villa Rospigliosi at Lamporecchio near Pistoia, famed for its biscuits flavoured with aniseed, called *brigidini* because they were invented by the nuns of St Bridget, as well as for its puff pastry. The actual desolation of this majestic building has a poignancy worthy of Claude Lorrain, a close friend of Pope Clement IX who caused it to be built. There is a tradition that it was designed by Gian Lorenzo Bernini: possibly his assistant Mattia de' Rossi designed it after one of his sketches. Unfortunately Clement IX died in

1669, the same year he commissioned the villa near the home of his ancestors. While a cardinal at the court of Urban VIII he had distinguished himself as a poet and patron of the arts who, to quote Professor Haskell's scholarly *Patrons and Painters*,* 'was almost alone among Roman patrons in showing as great an appreciation for the wistful poetry of Claude as for the grand austerities of Poussin.' In 1667 he commissioned Bernini's figures of angels carrying symbols of the Passion for the Ponte S. Angelo which must have monopolized his efforts at this period, though he was as prodigious an artist as he was versatile.

Perhaps because it was never completed according to the original plan the villa used to be known as Il Spicchio – a segment, as of an orange – but others maintain that Spicchio was an old name for the district dating from 1200. Be that as it may, the building consists of a solid square central block, the three storeys of which contain circular saloons, and two rectangular side wings. The latter project beyond the two main façades like truncated towers, framing the central body and limiting the top storey, which was crowned by a balustrade supporting statues, visible in Zocchi's engraving but vanished since. Triangles of steps lead to both balustraded entrances, surmounted by the papal arms in marble. The outer walls, doors and windows are demarcated by bands of *pietra serena* which relieve the surface from monotony. But neglect has played havoc with the front lawn; the fountain is dry and the handsome chapel is overgrown with weeds. Poetical and pathetic in its abandonment, it lies like a sleeping beauty, and one wonders who will ever come to waken and restore the roses to her pallid cheeks.

* Francis Haskell: *Patrons and Painters, A study in the relations between Italian Art and Society in the Age of the Baroque.* London 1963.

III
VILLAS
NEAR LUCCA

See notes on pp. 279–282

81

87

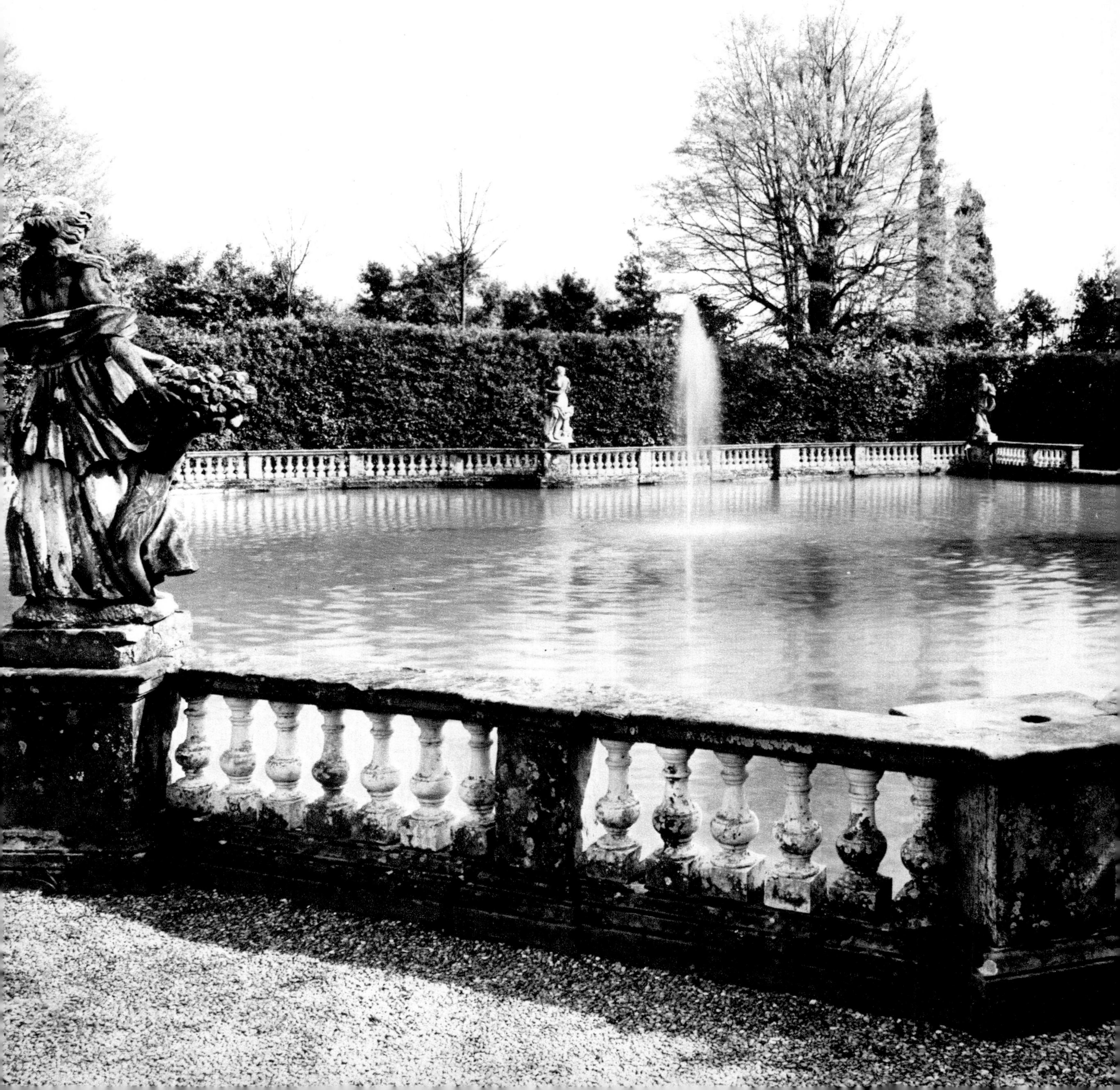

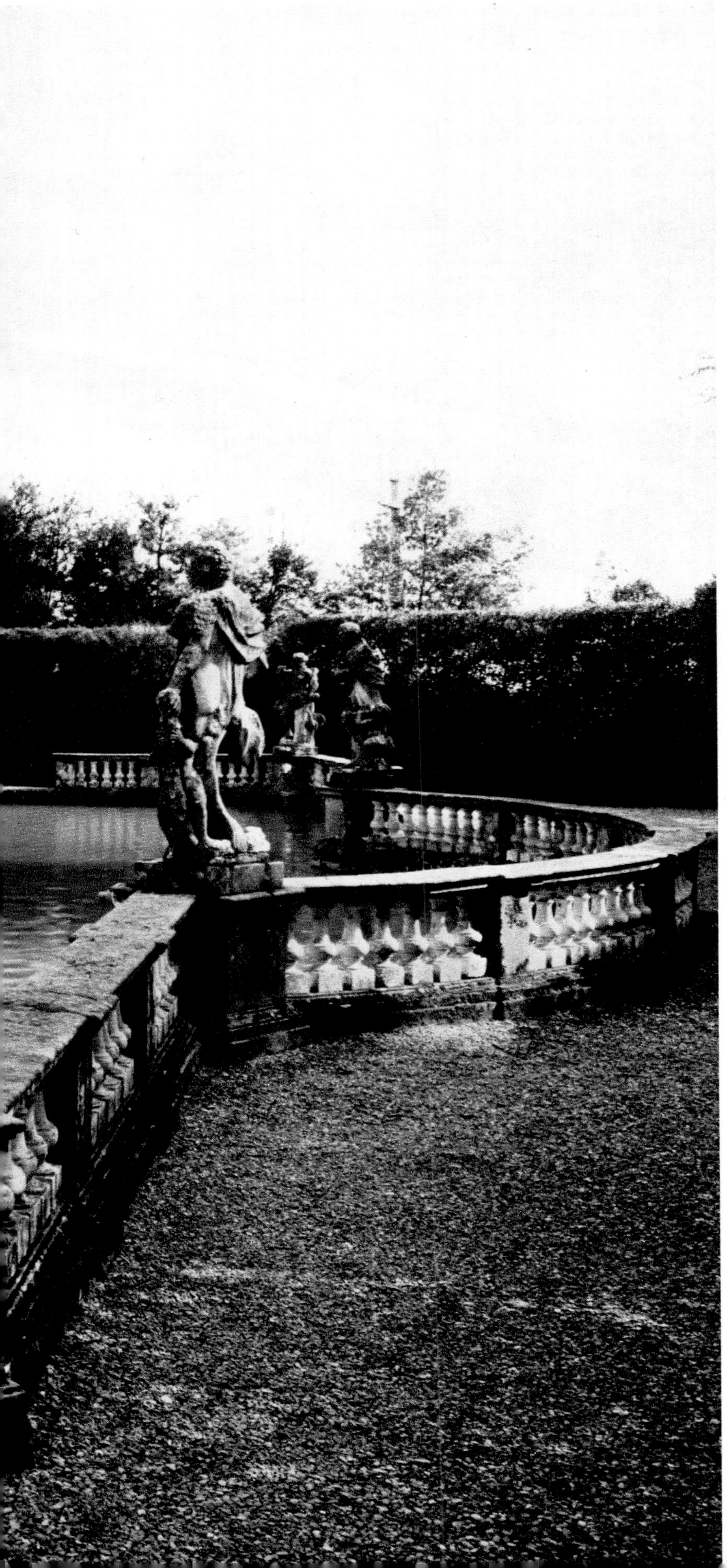

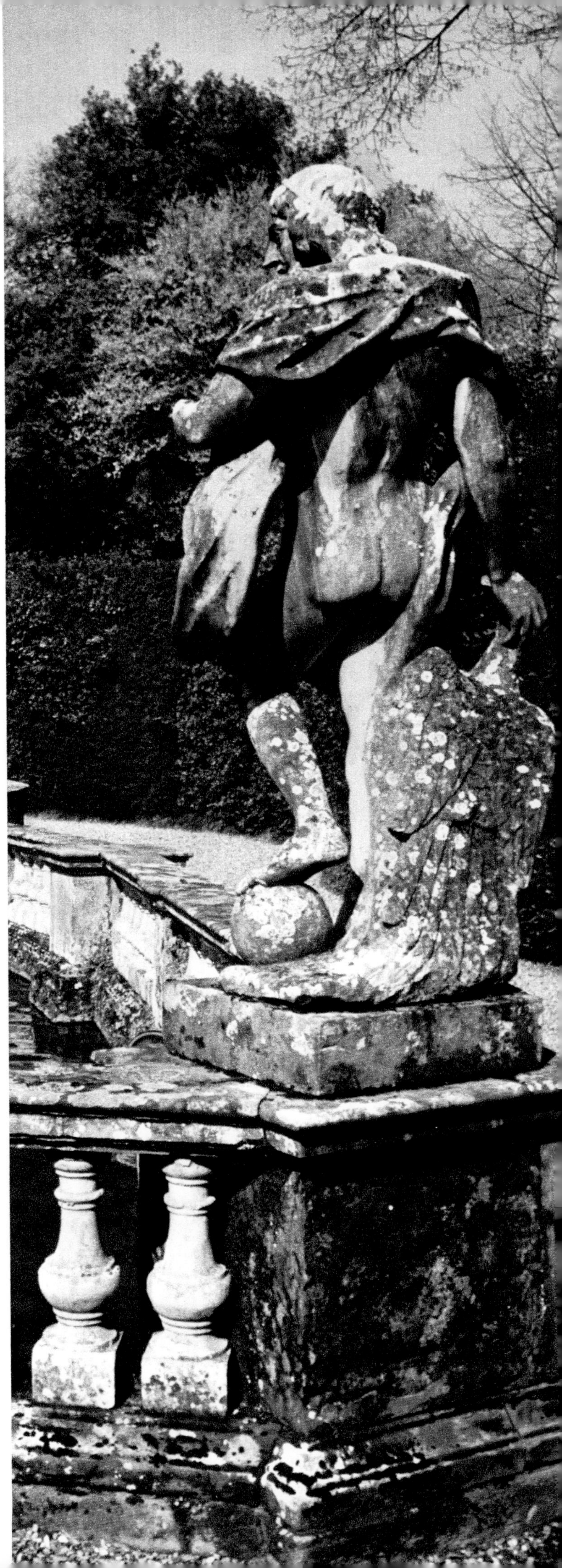

Villa Torrigiani a Camigliano

90   91

93

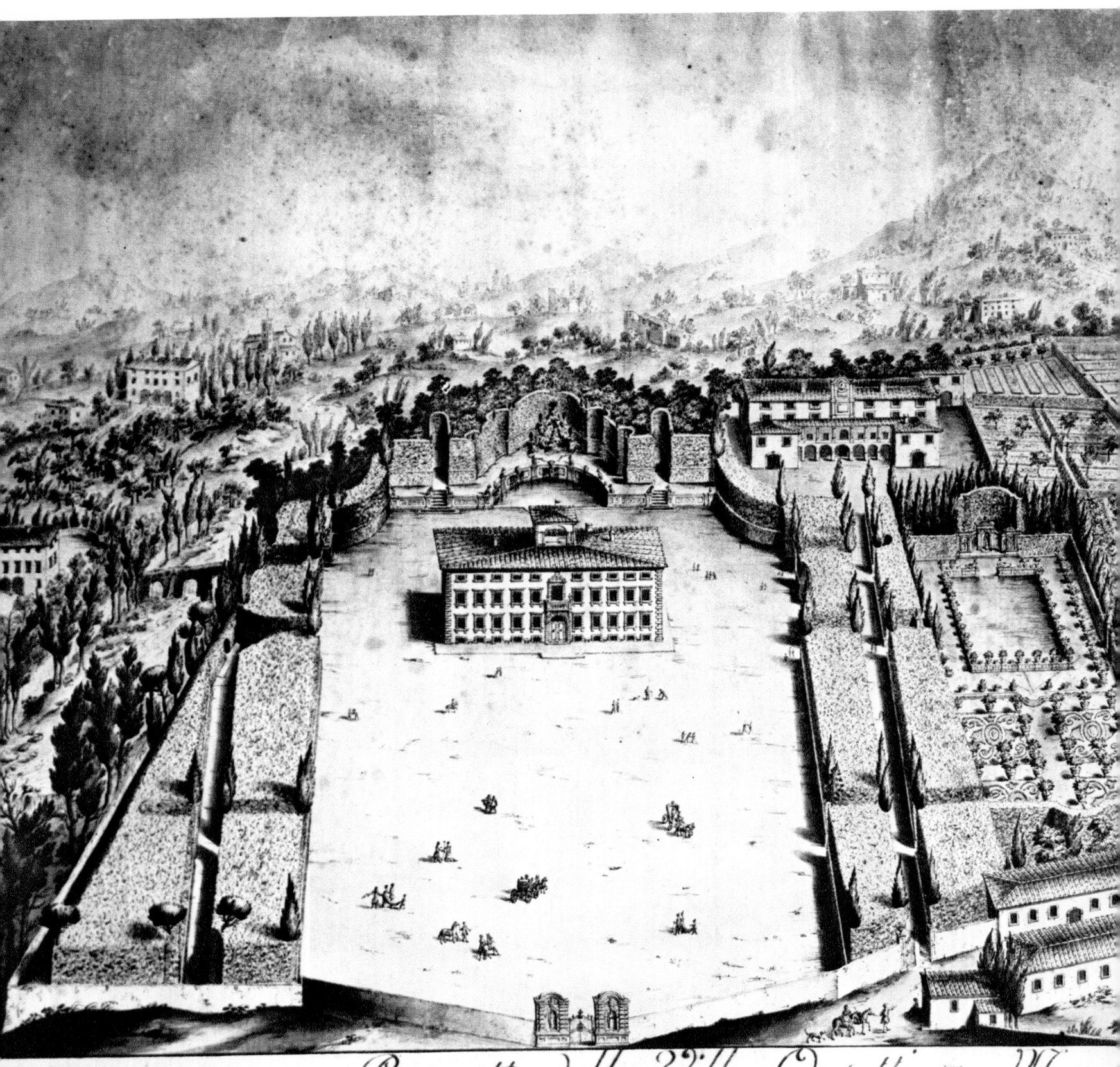

Prospetto della Villa Orsetti a Mar...

97

98

99

VILLAS
NEAR LUCCA

The prolonged prosperity of Lucca is indicated by the great variety of patrician villas in the hills and dales surrounding that walled but welcoming city. Though only some fifty miles from Florence, the luxuriance of its scenery, so different from the rocky heart of Tuscany, reminds one of Northern Italy, even of Austria, yet its architecture remains essentially Tuscan with idiosyncratic local additions.

John Evelyn described Lucca in 1645 as 'a small but pretty territory and state of itself. The city is neat and well fortified, with noble and pleasant walks of trees on the works, where the gentry and ladies used to take the air. It is situate on an ample plain by the river Serchio, yet the country about it is hilly. . . . The inhabitants are exceedingly civil to strangers, above all places in Italy, and they speak the purest Italian. It is also cheap living, which causes travellers to set up their rest here more than in Florence, though a more celebrated city; besides, the ladies here are very conversable, and the religious women not at all reserved. . . . The circuit of this state is but two easy days' journey, and lies mixed with the Duke of Tuscany's, but having Spain for a protector (though the least bigoted of all Roman Catholics), and being one of the fortified cities in Italy, it remains in peace. The whole country abounds in excellent olives, etc.'

Evelyn might have added, like Montaigne, who rode into the country with some gentlemen of Lucca in 1581: 'All round about I saw quantities of delightful villas for the distance of three or four miles with porticoes and loggias, which add greatly to their beauty.' These villas are more self-consciously stylish than those near Florence but even the most flamboyant, such as the Villa Mansi at Segromigno and the Villa Torrigiani at Camigliano, have a firm sixteenth-century bone-structure under a Baroque veneer. Towards the nineteenth century the Neo-classical style predominated, and this is peculiarly suited to the lushness of the landscape, just as the Palladian buildings are suited to the Venetian mainland.

Most of the fine formal gardens, of which a few tantalizing plans survive, were swallowed up by the growing preference for landscape gardens in the so-called English style, but the general landscape is so carefully terraced and cultivated, the vegetation so exuberantly fertile, that one scarcely misses the vanished parterres and fountains, though where they have weathered the storm of fashion the contrast with the background is all the more enjoyable. For the truth is that these villas owe a great deal of their charm to their romantic situation rather than to their architectural features, albeit these may have much to recommend them. In many cases the names of their architects have been forgotten: several were imported from other cities. Often the owner himself designed the building and supervised the stages of its construction. The influence of Ammannati was widely diffused after 1550: the earliest villas had Gothic details, notably in mullioned windows, but even these were affected by the Florentine Renaissance. The geometrical severity, balance, and simple surface, the treatment of stone window frames and columns, the colour schemes of mural decorations and arrangement of sculpture, were characteristically Tuscan. Walls were plastered or whitewashed, and a grey local stone, usually from Gonfolina, replaced the Florentine *pietra serena* for cornices and columns and the corners of façades. A few retain traces of frescoes, as at Forci. But only the Bishop's villa in the grounds of Marlia retains an inside courtyard.

The most imposing of the sixteenth-century country seats, the Villa Rossi at Gattaiola, is a solid square three-storeyed structure in a richly wooded park which had been a formal garden before the vogue for English gardens engulfed it. The building dates from about 1540 and has been attributed to the Lucchese architect Nicolao Civitali (1480– *d.* after 1560), son of the more famous Matteo, and it is known to have belonged to Francesco Burlamacchi, the republican Gonfalonier of Justice who was beheaded in the Sforza castle of Milan in 1548 after the failure of his conspiracy against the Medici. It was presented to Ferrante Gonzaga, Duke of Amalfi, who put it up for auction in 1556, whereupon it was bought by the thriving Santini family. During the next century the Santini continued to embellish it. They commissioned the Lucchese Bartolomeo de Santi to fresco two splendid halls on the first floor: the ballroom, containing their coat of arms, is very sumptuous with painted statues of divinities on the pilastered walls, above which a *trompe l'œil* portico opens to a sky where the Hours dance merrily round the Sun's chariot, and personifications of Dawn, Spring Showers, and Time float suavely beneath them. The second hall was frescoed with luminous perspectives by a different painter: Juno and Iris are depicted on the ceiling among the fluffy clouds, ubiquitous in this type of decoration.

The spacious portico with six Tuscan columns on the back façade is the most striking feature of the exterior, but this was frescoed later, in 1719, when a double outside staircase was added to it as in other Lucchese villas of the period, and the statuesque figures in monochrome by the Lucchese painter Francesco Antonio Cecchi represent Agriculture and Astronomy in much the same posture. The frescoes in other rooms on the first floor above depict four episodes from Tasso's *Gerusalemme Liberata*, five pastoral scenes (the best of a sturdy young shepherd gazing tenderly towards a peasant lass with a pitcher, lambs nestling below by a stream, the Lucchese hills in the background), suggestive of Gobelin tapestry, and views of classical ruins à la Hubert Robert. These also belong to the eighteenth century when the Montecatini owned it. Altogether these are some of the grandest frescoes to be seen in the area.

The formal garden was destroyed in the nineteenth century when it became the property of Alfred-Émilien, Comte de Niewerkerke, who should be elected patron saint of gigolos. Known as '*le beau Batave*' on account of his Dutch ancestry and his handsome physique – he was over six feet tall with a full fair beard and a lofty brow – he owned his successful career as Director General of Museums and Fine Arts in France, as Senator and Member of the Institute in Paris, more to his twenty-three years' liaison with Napoleon III's

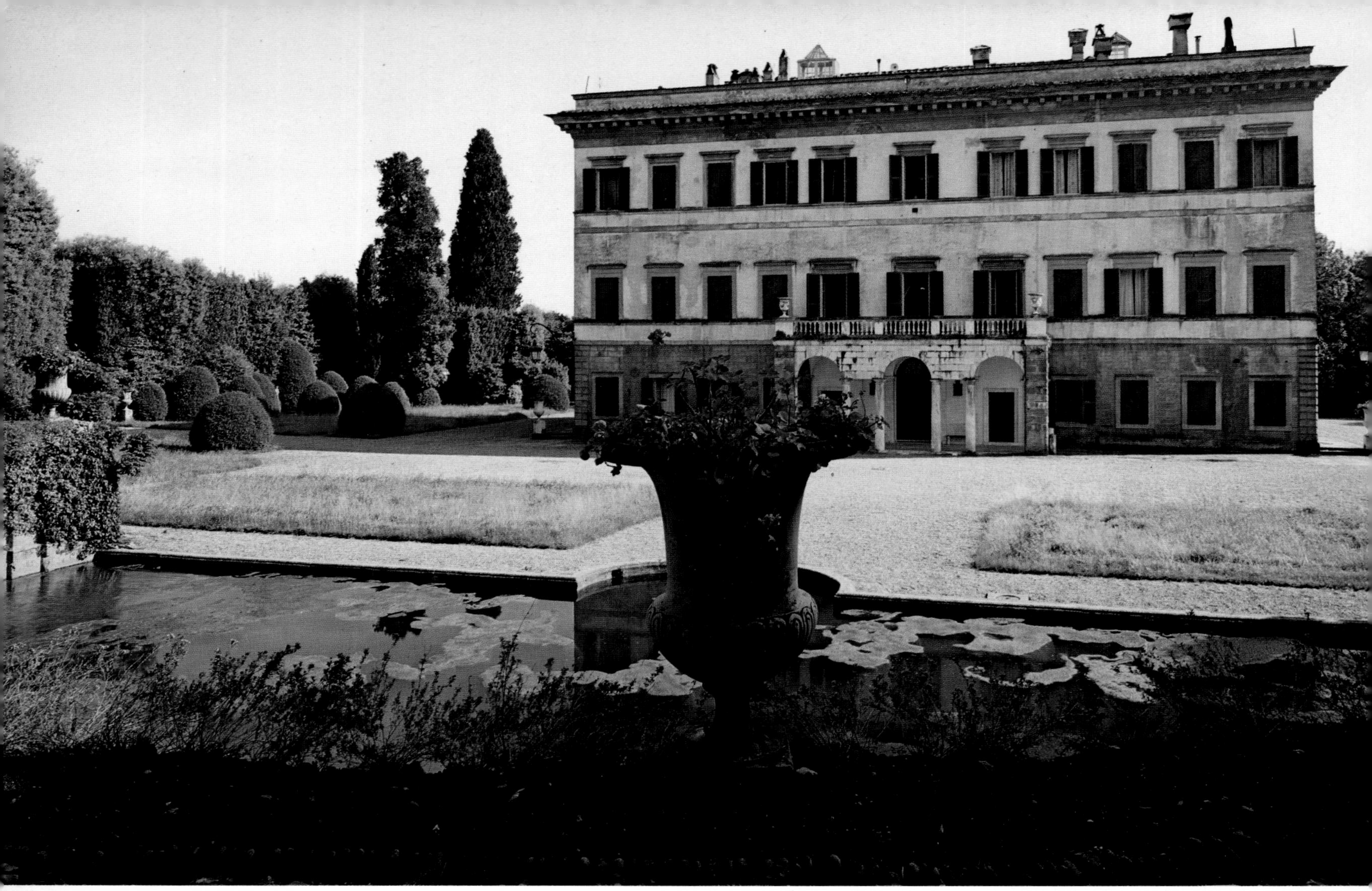

XXIX XXX

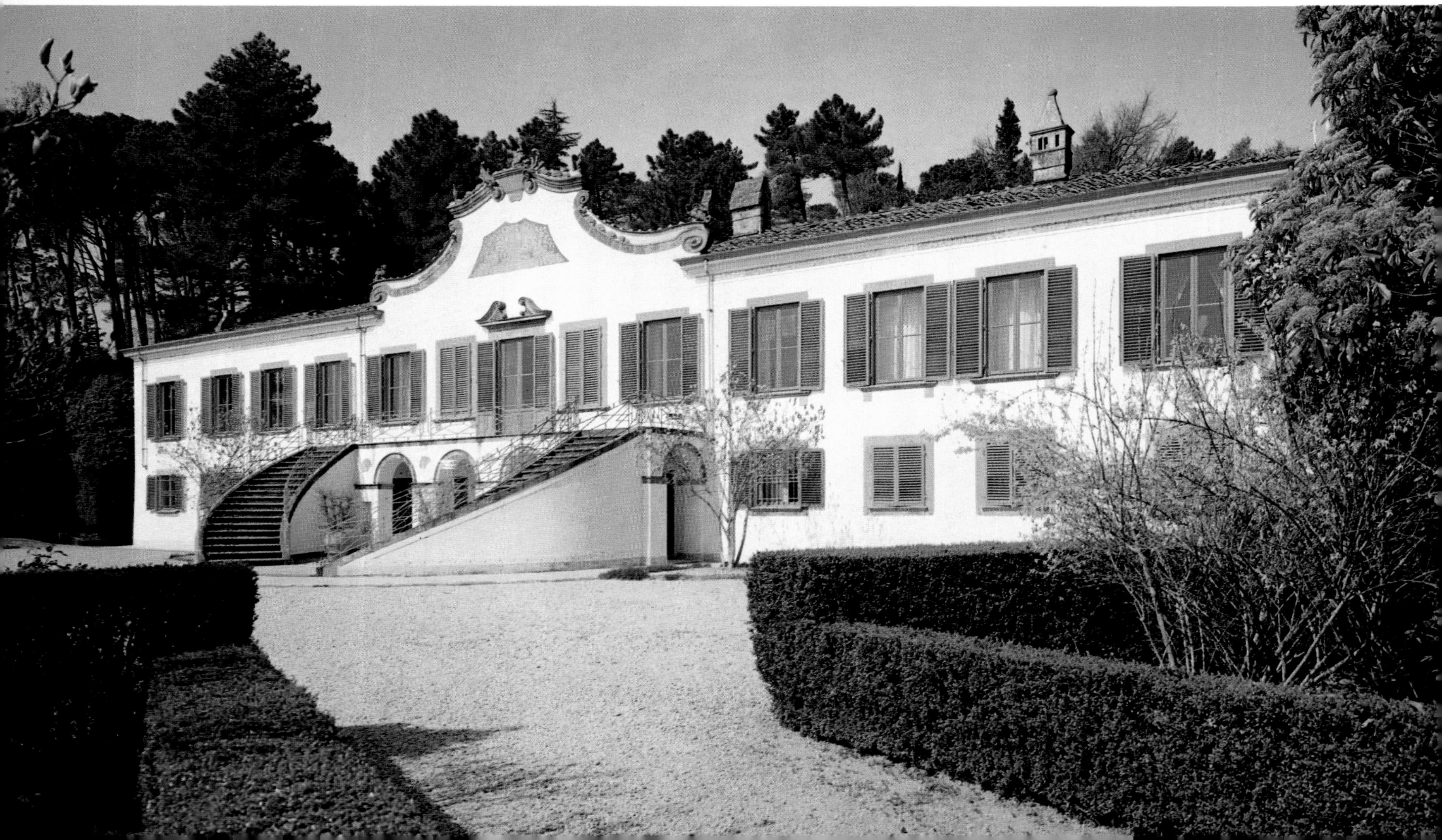

cousin Princess Mathilde than to his artistic or intellectual talents, though he was an amateur sculptor. Horace de Viel-Castel, that sour memorialist of the Second Empire, described him as 'a careerist rather than an artist. Art has only been a means to him. . . . Niewerkerke likes brilliance, show, appearance, in short he has too many little vanities ever to be a serious man.' He was only serious about his amorous conquests. Installed as Princess Mathilde's *amant en titre*, he was seldom faithful to that generous lady, whom he had seduced when she was twenty-five, unhappily married to Prince Anatole Demidoff.

After the fall of the Second Empire, Niewerkerke was dismissed from his various posts. He sold his Parisian house and his valuable collection of armour and weapons, which now form part of the Wallace Collection in London, and retired to the Villa Gattaiola. Lady Paget, wife of the British Ambassador to Rome, happened to stay in the neighbourhood in 1874, and she relates in her memoirs* that he was living with two ladies who were regarded with suspicion by the Lucchese nobility. 'The ladies were an old, very bourgeoise Princess Cantacuzène and her very sympathetic adopted daughter Olga, authoress of many charming novels. . . . She painted and played exquisitely, in fact there was nothing she could not do. She might then have been twenty-five. Niewerkerke, an old man, called her *ma chère enfant*. She married a year later Don Lorenzo Altieri, a clever and cultivated Roman . . .' Lady Paget concluded that Olga Cantacuzène was the daughter of Niewerkerke and Mathilde: they had 'found this good dull little Princess Cantacuzène and induced her to adopt the child.' But as Miss Joanna Richardson pointed out in her biography of Princess Mathilde** this is hardly credible at the height of the Second Empire when Mathilde had been Niewerkerke's mistress for thirteen years. She suggests that Olga was Niewerkerke's daughter by some other woman, possibly Princess Cantacuzène, and that she might even have been his mistress. He was still gallant in old age and Lady Paget considered him 'very agreeable'. According to her he had made Gattaiola 'perfect'. The house still contains interesting relics of his occupation, life-size portraits of Napoleon III and the Empress Eugénie, the latter by Winterhalter, a bust of the Prince Imperial by Carpeaux, and various portraits of Princess Mathilde. The old dandy died there in January 1892, at the age of eighty-two.

Several other sixteenth-century villas near Lucca are associated architecturally with the elegant Villa Rossi but none can evoke the existence of its past residents so convincingly. Industrial and mercantile activity were flourishing in the first half of the sixteenth century; banking chiefly during the second; and agriculture at all times, for this is the land of the olive, the vine, and the mulberry. Though Lucca was nominally a republic with the word Libertas on its coat of arms, political control soon became a patrician monopoly as in the republics of Genoa and Venice, and the ruling class invested in landed property on a large scale. Lucca minted its own money, and its silken products were in demand all over Europe. Woollen stuffs were manufactured there as

* Walburga, Lady Paget:
The Linings of Life. London
1928.

** Joanna Richardson:
Princess Mathilde. London
1969.

215

early as 846. During the sixteenth century the Buonvisi bank had agents in Nüremberg, Lisbon and Constantinople, as well as in many French cities, and it was in their mansion at Lyons that Maria de' Medici awaited her husband Henri IV.

Of the many villas once belonging to the Buonvisi, their hunting lodge at Forci, now called Villa Giustiniani, seems *primus inter pares*, if not unique for its grace and panoramic splendour. Its supreme effectiveness is mainly due to the simplicity of its design and the subtle use of stone for its mullioned windows, so elegantly spaced in rectangles beside the arched front door. Frescoed figures peer from two imitation windows in the wall of the north façade. The rusticated corners harmonize with the smooth texture of the plastered surface worthy of Buontalenti. But the long portico with double staircase overlooking the plain of Lucca excels the north façade in beauty of design, the columns entwined with delicate creepers, heightened by dadoes over the capitals. A dense wood of ilex and pine creeps close to the building, and the steepness of the hill it stands on, besides the scarcity of water and waning wealth of the Buonvisi, saved it from being transformed by later fashion.

The original building was entirely restored in the sixteenth century, possibly by Vincenzo Civitali (1523–97). It was recorded in 1532, when the Buonvisi left it for Lucca to quell a popular rebellion known as that of the *Straccioni*, or Ragamuffins. A little later the learned Ortensio Lando was a guest of the Buonvisi and celebrated his visit, especially the witty conversations and succulent banquets held there, in *Forcinianae quaestiones*, a Latin composition printed in Naples in 1536. 'It has never occurred to me', he wrote, 'to find so delightful a place, or one better adapted to studious concentration. Should anyone be vexed with care, he will immediately be rid of it and all his worries will vanish.'

The superstructure over the north façade, together with the decorative bell above the roof and a clock supported on tiles that raise the Baroque moulding, were added in the eighteenth century, likewise the frescoes by Francesco Antonio Cecchi in the saloon which represent the Vintage and the Gathering of Olives, emphasizing the chief activities of Forci.

Another Villa Buonvisi, now Oliva, at S. Pancrazio dates from the end of the sixteenth century: here the high portico was raised by another storey with square windows above each arch, and the total effect is Florentine. We are told that the property was much enlarged and improved in 1770 by Francesco Buonvisi, who introduced exotic plants into the garden while respecting the formality of its design, but it was 'anglicized' when his family died out in 1800 and it passed into other hands, including those of Prince Charles Poniatowski. During the last world war it was seriously damaged. Its present owners have restored it with taste, and we may still enjoy such fragments of the original garden as the walled Fountain of the Siren, a romantic grotto, and pillared gates with masks.

The neighbouring Villa Cittadella belongs to the same period: it is a simple square building with a triple arched portico and two upper storeys crowned with terracotta sculpture. Here again the garden was transformed in nineteenth-century fashion, but the remaining fragments of its predecessor are fascinating, especially the long lemon-house with arched rusticated doors and round windows like portholes above them; the two fine gates and straight avenue of cypresses; the oval enclosed by wavy hedges with a fountain in a terminal niche; and two other fountains with bronze masks of Midas with magnificent ass's ears. One fountain representing a monstrous half-human bat on the back of a tortoise recalls the grotesque fantasies of Bomarzo.

The stately Villa Marchi, formerly Arnolfini, at Gragnano, is a seventeenth-century structure with sixteenth-century features, such as the turreted corners and double staircase of one façade reminiscent of Artimino, and an open loggia on the other. The last survivor of the Arnolfini family (an ancestor of which was perpetuated by Jan van Eyck in one of the loveliest gems of London's National Gallery) remodelled the house in 1803, raising the top storey with windows somewhat large in proportion to those beneath them. Towards the end of the seventeenth century the main hall was decorated by the prolific Bolognese, Angelo Michele Colonna (1600–87), with *trompe l'œil* porticoes in meticulous perspective and allegorical statues in the ceremonial tradition of Baroque scenography.

The foremost examples of seventeenth- and eighteenth-century domestic architecture near Lucca are the Villa Mansi at Segromigno, Villa Torrigiani at Camigliano, and Villa Garzoni at Collodi. While the first two are very similar in design, the latter is exceptional as the most spectacular Baroque creation in Tuscany.

The Villa Mansi was built by Muzio Oddi in about 1634, and though it is usually labelled Baroque it is more properly a High Renaissance structure with Mannerist additions. The double staircase ascending to the triple portico between projecting side-wings surmounted by a balustrade with statues; the central superstructure repeating the same theme; every feature underlined, as it were, with stone mouldings, has the air of a sumptuous wedding cake dumped in a public park. The lawn before the arcaded façade slopes down to a curvilinear balustraded pool with graceful statues at intervals protected by high green hedges. The dense trees around it produce the effect of a forest glade, half hiding a rustic pond where a marble Diana and her nymphs enliven the dank water. But of the magnificent formal garden in the tradition of Versailles designed by Filippo Juvara in 1732 only an engraving survives. House and garden are open to the public for whose benefit a restaurant-cum-bar with a juke box (or am I dreaming?) has been installed on the ground floor. Recently a boutique has been added and dress shows have been advertised.

The entrance gates of Villa Torrigiani at Camigliano, about two miles distant, are even more monumental than those of Villa Mansi, between two ornate piers with square and oval gratings crowned with stone vases and obelisks at each rusticated end. A long straight avenue of cypresses leads up to them. The house rises in front with steps leading to the central arched portico flanked by statues, a theme repeated in the lofty alcove above, the first and second storeys rimmed with balustrades of statues, to which a small upper storey was added with another balustrade and more statues ending in a delicate peaked cupola. This has so many features in common with Villa Mansi that Muzio Oddi might well have been its architect. It was designed over an earlier building of the same period, as if an intricate mask had been clapped on to a simpler frame – a mask of varied materials and tints. Lions on the steps, niches containing busts over the flanking statues, carved plaques, sculptured coats of arms, and squadrons of statues: the effect of one square superimposed on another is still more Mannerist than Baroque.

The formal garden beside the villa was 'anglicized' in the nineteenth century. However, the sunken Garden of Flora, protected by four high walls with a fanciful grotto at one end and a retaining wall on the other, resembling a pavilion adorned with three arches and copious double stairs with balustrades and statues, leading to the higher lemon garden graced with an oblong pool reflecting a group of cypresses, is a ravishing *coup d'œil*. This shows what many villas of Lucca have lost by nineteenth-century transformations, for such elaborate architecture looks incongruous in a so-called English setting. A subterranean passage leads from the retaining wall to the house. Everywhere hidden springs are ready to spout water, from the open dome of the grotto, from the steps and the pebbled mosaics of the paths, and even from the statue of Flora, as in the grotto of Castello and those described by John Evelyn at Pratolino. Miss Georgina Masson concludes that this cleverly conceived but otherwise crude practical joke 'probably saved this little garden from destruction, for *giochi d'acqua* have held an irresistible appeal to Italian humour from Roman times until today.'*

Albeit nearer Pescia than Lucca, the far-famed Villa Garzoni belonged formerly to the republic of Lucca, when the fortified castle that stood there was often besieged by the Florentines. The Garzoni had been Ghibellines throughout the fourteenth century and had emigrated to Lucca after losing their property at Pescia, of which they had long been overlords. As citizens of Lucca they were able to keep their estates in the Valdinievole, including Collodi, which had not been seized by the Florentines. Though loaded with honours by Lucca, they preferred to settle near their native Pescia from which they were banned. Their stronghold at Collodi was an overt act of defiance. The present villa, commissioned by Romano Garzoni early in the seventeenth century, was built over the foundations of the medieval castle. Formerly the village of Collodi could be reached only by passing through its gates. It is a vast four-storeyed rectangular building with a graceful belvedere crowning the roof. The arched doorway surmounted with the Garzoni arms and classical

* Georgina Masson: *Italian Gardens*. London 1961.

Collodi.
Villa Garzoni, sulla pescia di Collodi, veduta dal Cancello.

Garzoni: drawing by Ettore Romagnoli

trophies relieve its austere monotony. An ample portico at the back stands level with the first floor and from this two broad staircases climb to the *piano nobile* between frescoed columns and balconies in clever perspective. The gallery over the portico is adorned with trophies, bucolic scenes, allegories, and foreshortened architecture by Angelo Michele Colonna, who also frescoed the central saloon in conventional Baroque style with gilded and stuccoed mouldings.

Behind the main building stands a coral-tinted rococo summer house with a convex centre and concave wings, which looks as if it had been imported from eighteenth-century Sicily. The gorgeous garden, built in terraces against a steep hillside, stands quite apart from the house, with which it is connected only by a rustic bridge. Its general design can be taken in at a glance. A succession of balustraded steps and terraces lead up to the central cascade which replaces the usual dwelling. Above the cascade is a flamboyant statue of Fame blowing into a shell, from which water gushes into a pool before her pedestal, and thence over more steps and more pools. Massive figures of Florence and Lucca recline at Fame's feet, and in a lower pool figures of quaint birds pour water from their bills. Water plays a prominent role on this elaborately chiselled hillside, so that hidden showers are abundant for those that seek them.

In a cypress grove behind the figure of Fame is an eighteenth-century bathhouse with separate compartments for dames and cavaliers as well as rooms, gaily frescoed and upholstered in faded silks, where the bathers could enjoy refreshments and conversation, while in a minstrels' gallery discreetly placed above musicians played for the bathers they could not see – no doubt arias by Boccherini who came from Lucca – a sophisticated derivation from the old Roman *thermae*.

There is also an open-air theatre with wings of clipped box and a niched fountain in the background bordered with statues, but the stage is too small for practical use, though an Italian enthusiast wrote that it 'permitted cunning disguises' – *maliziosi travestimenti*. A labyrinth of hedges leading to a grotto with more liquid surprises was added for the entertainment of guests, and the ladies who pretended to get lost could not escape without a cool aspersion. The numerous statues in stucco and terracotta are naively rustic in style: they have the air of stage properties, but as the whole garden is eminently theatrical they are not meant for too critical a scrutiny. All the same one could wish for more eloquent products of the sculptor's art.

A poetical ode to 'The Splendours of Collodi' by the Lucchese, Francesco Sbarra, enables us to date the garden from the first half of the seventeenth century, but the statues and waterworks were added during the eighteenth century when an engraving of it was made especially for King Stanislas Poniatowski of Poland. The Lucchese patrician Ottaviano Diodati, who collaborated in the local edition of the French Encyclopaedia, was the inventor of the waterworks whose wonders had spread to Warsaw. Since then it has only suffered from becoming a tourist resort. One cannot but deplore the discordant sign-posts and lamp-posts, the kiosks for Coca Cola and picture postcards, and the municipal park arrangement of the parterre at the entrance.

The more recent popularity of Collodi is due to the author who chose it as a pseudonym because his mother was born there. Carlo Lorenzini (1826–90) wrote many books for children, the most famous of which is *Pinocchio*. And it is rather for the sake of this long-nosed wooden puppet than for the Villa Garzoni that juvenile excursions are made to his reputed birthplace. His statue dominates a children's playground, and of course he has been televised, arousing passionate polemics worthy of *Alice* or *Peter Pan*.

The royal villa of Marlia, nearer Lucca, had belonged to the Orsetti family for centuries until it was acquired by Napoleon's sister, Elisa Baciocchi, in 1806. All the beauties of the original Baroque garden which have survived Elisa's drastic transformations date from the seventeenth century, and these are particularly fine. The open-air theatre is the prettiest of its kind, with its deep green close-clipped wings, the terracotta figures of Columbine, Harlequin and Pulcinella at the back of the stage, its stand in topiary work for the conductor of the orchestra, its rows of grass-covered seats, and the fountain playing outside the little entrance gate precisely on a line with the stage. And the water garden is dazzling, with its long balustraded fishpool guarded by statues of the Arno and Serchio rivers and ending in a triumphant *nymphaeum*

Màrlia

villa cosi ridotta dalla G. D. Elisa Baciocchi circa il 1809.

Marlia: drawing by Romagnoli, c. 1809

of majestic proportions. Great pots of lemons glow on the balustrade, and the whole design is reflected in the water.

Furious at having to sell his ancestral property to the upstart princess, Count Lelio Orsetti was said to have changed the money received for its purchase (more than 700,000 francs of the period) into silver-plate which was paraded on an ox-cart before Elisa's palace, with a message that she might watch the villa of Marlia passing under her windows.

A Russian friend reminds me that Tolstoy's *War and Peace* begins with the sentence: 'Well, prince, Genoa and Lucca are now no more than private estates of the Bonaparte family.' Napoleon had turned the republic of Lucca into a principality for his ambitious sister Elisa and her submissive husband, Count Felice Baciocchi, in 1805, since she had considered the crown of Piombino 'too small for her head'. She was free to administer it as a sort of sub-prefecture of which she was absolute sovereign. Talleyrand ironically dubbed her the 'Semiramis of Lucca'. She modelled her court on that of Saint-Cloud with ladies-in-waiting, chamberlains, equerries, pages, chaplains, and almoners with resounding titles, ruling public and private receptions with the solemn frivolity of a Ruritanian musical comedy. It was almost a parody of Napoleon's court. She preferred the illusion of power to the reality of her fleshly lovers. Though she had appointed her husband Minister of War and General-in-Command of the small army, she reviewed the troops on horseback with martial gestures to emulate her brother. Her husband obeyed her orders and winked at her infidelities. Elisa wore the trousers. According to the guide-books she transformed the villa of Marlia into a 'little Versailles', but this is an exaggeration. Nor was its name derived from the Château de Marly, but from Marilla, an ancient name of the district.

The new duchess enlarged the Orsetti residence, adding an upper storey with a new cornice, a projecting portico and terrace against the façade in stiff Neo-classical style. The whole interior was redecorated and remodelled in the same fashion under the supervision of Théodore Bienaimé, and while most of the furniture was imported from Paris, local talent was patronized in the brothers Agostino and Stefano Tofanelli who frescoed several rooms. The latter, senator of Lucca and 'first painter to Her Imperial Highness', frescoed the ballroom ceiling with a Ballet of the Hours. (Other paintings of his adorn the Villa Mansi but they require a special 'period' taste for their appreciation: to my eye they seem tritely academic.)

Elisa's transformation of the grounds began in 1811 after Napoleon had promoted her to the Grand Duchy of Tuscany, but she had not time to carry out all the naturalistic 'improvements' suggested by the French architect Morel, who had designed the park of Malmaison. An imposing entrance to the domain was built with two Palladian guard-houses in a semicircular court-yard surrounded by Neo-classical vases of flowers on pedestals. The neighbour-ing 'Bishop's villa' – a pleasing sixteenth-century house with an inside court-yard, an outside staircase, and a *nymphaeum* called Pan's Grotto, exquisitely decorated with arabesques and pebble mosaics in the style of Buontalenti – was incorporated in the grounds as well as more land to widen the space in front of the villa, but further enlargements were nipped in the bud by Napoleon's downfall. The hydraulic works involved considerable expense: 438,583 francs were spent on the estate between 1811 and 1814. The stables were filled with thoroughbred horses and the meadows with merino sheep. Racine's *Phèdre* was performed in the open-air theatre, and while Elisa reclined on a chaise-longue in the park Paganini played for her behind a screen of yew. She ap-pointed him her musical director and we can well believe that, as he wrote, she fainted away when he played his thrilling cadenzas. But her seductive Grand Equerry, Bartolomeo Cenami (nicknamed her '*cher ami*'), was usually in attendance to revive her. Often they went riding together and rested to bill and coo on a mossy bank, unconscious of indiscreet eyes behind the bushes. The impression she made on Marlia remains, but her ambitions were curtailed by the approach of an English force under Lord William Bentinck in 1814. Bentinck told her bluntly that he did not recognize her authority and that he was in command until the future of Tuscany was decided by the Allies. Her negotiations with Murat, then King of Naples, whose fortune seemed more secure than that of her brother, had failed as Murat's were to fail upon his desertion to the Allies, who could not trust him. Nine months pregnant, she had to flee but could only travel by short stages. She gave birth to a son in a squalid inn, 'just when she ceased to require an heir to her crown.' Arrested by Austrian troops in Bologna, she was taken to Brünn as a prisoner of war. After dismal wanderings under the title of Countess of Campignano, she died near Trieste in 1820 at the age of forty-two.

When the Congress of Vienna allotted the duchy of Lucca to Maria Luisa, the Bourbon Duchess of Parma, in compensation for Parma which was awarded to Napoleon's Empress of the same name, Marlia became one of her favourite residences during the last eight years of her short and harassed life. A daughter of Goya's good-natured model Charles IV of Spain, she had married Duke Lodovico of Parma in 1795 when she was thirteen years old. Her only son, Carlo Lodovico, was born in 1799. Though singularly lacking in personal charm she had endeared herself to her cultured husband, who died soon after his father in 1803.

For a few years Tuscany had been converted into the kingdom of Etruria for the Duke Lodovico, but his widow was soon ousted from this ephemeral realm by Elisa Baciocchi when she became the Grand Duchess. Maria Luisa returned to Madrid and then joined her parents in captivity at Compiègne. After futile attempts to return to Parma and to join her sister in Sicily, she was transferred to Rome, where she lingered until she was given the duchy of Lucca during the ex-Empress's lifetime. She was plainer and less intelligent than her predecessor but her solid virtues were appreciated and her statue by Lorenzo Bartolini still stands outside her former palace. She built new roads, a three-mile aqueduct with 459 arches to bring pure drinking-water from the hills, an observatory, a dockyard at Viareggio, and she tried seriously to develop her little duchy.

Maria Luisa died in 1824, and was succeeded by her son, who ceded Lucca to the Grand Duke of Tuscany in 1847, two months before inheriting Parma. Owing to his chequered childhood and education, Carlo Lodovico was restless and neurotic but he was an excellent linguist with many hobbies, chief of which was theology. His penchant for Protestantism and interest in biblical studies led Metternich to doubt his sanity. He was even rumoured to be a Carbonaro since he tolerated Liberal refugees from other parts of Italy. Thanks to him Lucca, and the neighbouring resort of Bagni di Lucca, became centres of attraction for foreigners, since he was the most cosmopolitan and broad-minded of contemporary princes. In 1820 he married Maria Teresa of Savoy, a daughter of Victor Emmanuel I of Sardinia, dignified, melancholy, and deeply religious. Their only son, Carlo Ferdinando, was born in 1823. While Maria Teresa preferred to live in pious seclusion with her son, Carlo Lodovico was fond of travel. During his absence he left the government in the hands of Marchese Ascanio Mansi, a capable and sensible moderate. Lucca was an oasis of peace and prosperity, unaffected by the revolutionary movements outside it.

Though extravagant by fits and starts, the Duke had simple tastes: he abhorred formality. Consequently he preferred his hunting-lodge at Pieve S. Stefano to the grandeur of Marlia. Viewing it merely as a building in a superb situation, we are inclined to sympathize with this preference. Designed by the Neo-classical architect Lorenzo Nottolini on a steep hill in the midst of a pine forest, it is the least Neo-classical of his constructions: a long two-storeyed façade with two graceful curved staircases on each side of a pilastered portico sweeping up to the first-floor balcony. The curves of the double stairs are repeated and completed by a scroll-work pediment which gives it an eighteenth-century twist, though the long row of windows is strictly symmetrical without decorations. The panorama of the plain is comparable to that of Forci, and the present owners of this refined *casino di caccia* have kept it in good repair. This is a villa with a stronger personal flavour than others of the same period near Lucca and one feels certain that the restless Duke enjoyed some relaxation there. His Duchess Maria Teresa preferred her modest residence at S. Martino in Vignale, where she vegetated with her confessor and homeopathic physicians. This also had a splendid view to compensate for its lack of grandeur.

After the death of Marchese Ascanio Mansi in 1841 the Duke's valet, Thomas Ward, became his *fidus Achates*. This shrewd and honest Yorkshire-man, who had been employed in Vienna as a jockey and a head groom, accompanied the Duke to London for Queen Victoria's coronation and was entrusted with many political and private missions. Evidently Ward was a refreshing contrast with the obsequious courtiers who bored the Duke with their intrigues. In 1845 he was appointed Controller of the ducal household, and he was so successful in curbing expenses and increasing efficiency that he was appointed temporary Director of Finance the following year. As Ward's humble origin was notorious, he and his master were ridiculed by the clan-destine press. But the Duke's odd choice was justified, for the erstwhile jockey restored a semblance of order to his muddled finances. The Grand Duke Leopoldo of Tuscany was so impressed by his ability that he bestowed on him the Order of St Joseph and tried to secure his services for Florence. Carlo Lodovico proved his satisfaction by conferring on him the hereditary title of Baron and designing his coat of arms.

The Duke opened his heart in his letters to Ward, which provide us with an insight into his curious character. 'The stormy nature of my life,' he wrote, 'my inexperience, my good faith – the first tossing me hither and thither, the second causing me to fall into the errors common to youth, the third united with too noble a manner of feeling and acting, fatal to my interests – have unfortunately resulted, to my own detriment, in a complete lack of faith in myself, and a diffidence, often involuntary but none the less inevitable, towards others.' And of his marriage he wrote: 'It is a cross to be borne with love, and we must be grateful even for this.'* He hated to leave Lucca for Parma and complained of the change as if it were a cruel sacrifice. Pride in his Bourbon ancestry was his greatest consolation. 'What a family of gentlemen ours has always been!' he exclaimed. Founding a Greek Chapel at the Villa Marlia and a gambling casino at Bagni di Lucca, translating biblical texts and studying Arabic, he had indulged a medley of hobbies in spite of his moods of depression and self-abasement. Moreover, he had enjoyed his popularity.

After the unification of Italy, King Victor Emmanuel II granted the royal villa of Marlia to Penelope Smyth, the Irish widow of the Prince of Capua whose marriage had never been recognized by his brother, King Ferdinando II of the Two Sicilies. Unfortunately their son became insane and remained so for thirty years until his death in 1919. In 1923 the whole estate was bought by Count and Countess Pecci-Blunt and restored most lavishly.

The beautiful remains of formal gardens near Lucca make one deplore that so many were submerged by the 'back to nature' movement which gathered impetus in the nineteenth century. All over Europe it became the fashion to rave about nature, and to condemn the work of formal architects as sacrilege, so that even Catherine the Great remarked to Voltaire: '*à présent l'anglomanie domine dans ma plantomanie*.' But as Sir Reginald Blomfield wrote, lamenting the mass destruction of formal gardens: 'It is not an exhilarating thought that in the one instance in which English taste in a matter of design has taken hold on the Continent, it has done so with such disastrous results.' For the word 'garden', as he pointed out, means an enclosed space, as opposed to unenclosed fields and woods. 'The lone majesty of untamed nature' had nothing to do with it. Even that great arbiter of landscape gardening, Humphry Repton, had to confess that 'a garden is a work of art, using the materials of nature.' The aim of formal gardening was to make the house grow out of its surroundings and to modify the grounds so as to bring nature into harmony with the house. This aim was often realized in Tuscany until the nineteenth century when '*le faux naturel*' was mistaken for the natural.

The obliteration of Juvara's noble design for Villa Mansi is particularly regrettable, and one must be grateful for the luxuriance and variety of Villa Marlia where both styles are happily combined. The grounds of Marlia are so extensive that their appeal is obvious and universal. Prince Metternich, who visited the place in 1817, wrote that it was 'truly divine. The house recalls the most comfortable châteaux in France. The garden is planted *à l'anglaise* to perfection; it is large and offers an appearance that is perhaps unique in its kind, for I know of no other English garden on this side of the Alps with such luxuriant trees and exotic flowers; there are, for instance, groves full of magnolias.' Like Montaigne and John Evelyn before him and dozens of foreigners since, Metternich was captivated by Lucca and he was inclined to envy the life of its Prince: there was everything – town, country

* Jesse Myers: *Baron Ward and the Dukes of Parma*. London 1938.

villa, curative baths, the sea – and nothing to excess. 'As you can see,' he continued, '*l'embarras de richesses* is not excessive, and the question of choice does not present itself . . . ambition and pleasure being concentrated on a single object, the one remains always limited, and the other unceasing.'

In this age *l'embarras de richesses* seems greater, as many a cultured Englishman has discovered. Duke Carlo Lodovico's hunting lodge at Pieve S. Stefano is now in the possession of Mr and Mrs Roworth, and other attractive villas off the beaten track are being occupied by foreign residents who delight in cultivating their gardens. Several of these deserve honourable mention but here we are limited to the most representative, if not the most celebrated. The Villa Garzoni at Collodi has the only Baroque garden near Lucca that remains intact in most of its details – at the risk of becoming a sort of Luna Park. One should overlook its recent excrescences. Those who are repelled by its theatrical flamboyance and by what Vernon Lee called its 'imperishable blossoms of variegated pebbles and chalk', will turn to the more numerous landscape gardens elsewhere. Lovers of the picturesque will discover their Promised Land among the green wooded hills and secluded valleys near Lucca even if Heinrich Heine's eulogy may seem somewhat exaggerated today. *Nirgends Philistergesichter*, he wrote of this territory in his *Reisebilder*: nowhere may you see the face of a Philistine!

IV
SIENESE VILLAS

See notes on pp. 282–285

106

107

118

119

122

123

124

125

SIENESE
VILLAS

The historians of Siena are wont to dwell nostalgically on its feudal age and the emergence of its free Commune; on its civic spirit and victory over Florence in the battle of Montaperti (1260); but most of them are reticent about its more placid period under the Medici when the villas we are concerned with were built or rebuilt on the foundations of ancient castles. The central Campo with its rosy semicircle of palaces facing the Gothic Palazzo Pubblico (1288–1308) and its 'flower-stalk' Torre del Mangia 101 metres high, is the most eloquent monument to its medieval pride. And the annual horse races known as the Palio are medievalism made visible and audible – to the delight of most spectators and the disapproval of a minority. The popular associations called *contrade* into which Siena is still divided evoke medieval factions and their animosities.

During the thirteenth and fourteenth centuries Siena had rivalled Florence in banking and the wool trade, and its Monte dei Paschi is one of the oldest banks in Italy. The countryside bristled with castles like that depicted by Simone Martini in his portrait of the warrior Guidoriccio dei Fogliani in the Palace of the Commune. Such castles were purely functional, with small gardens more for utility than pleasure. 'The plot of ground between the inner and outer rows of walls, where corn and hay might be grown for the horses,' as Vernon Lee divined, 'is not likely to be given up exclusively to her ladyship's lilies and gillyflowers; salads and roots must grow there, and onions and leeks, for it is not always convenient to get vegetables from the villages below, particularly when there are enemies or disbanded pillaging mercenaries about; hence, also, there will be fewer roses than vines, pears, or apples, spaliered against the castle wall.'

The Tuscan villa, as we have seen, was evolved during the Renaissance, which came late to ultra-medieval Siena. The Chigi and Piccolomini families had obtained great wealth through trade in other cities but this naturally benefited their own. The banker Agostino Chigi, who had gone to Rome in 1485, amassed a vast fortune there as a moneylender in the Contrada dei Banchi and later as treasurer, equivalent to finance minister, under Pope Julius II. In his private business he competed with the Medici, for he had ramifications throughout Italy and warehouses all over Europe. He owned a fleet of 100 ships and had 20,000 employees, besides controlling the papal mint, supplying grain to the Papal States – his exclusive privilege – and managing the monopoly of alum at the Tolfa mines. The munificence of this merchant prince was legendary and his Roman villa, now known as the Farnesina, remains a glorious relic of his patronage of the arts. His compatriot Baldassare Peruzzi (1481–1536) was commissioned to design it at the age of twenty-five and Raphael's mistress, La Fornarina, was installed to keep him company while he frescoed its walls with the loves of Cupid and Psyche. It was so crammed with treasures that the Spanish ambassador was reputed to have spat at his majordomo since 'he could find no other empty space'. No doubt this was as apocryphal as the story of the gold dishes he had flung into the Tiber during a banquet he offered the Pope, who happened to see them fished up in a net the next morning. Small wonder that his family flourished. Fabio Chigi, one of his descendants, became Pope Alexander VII.

Agostino Chigi died in 1520, before Siena was subjugated by Florence. Duke Cosimo I de' Medici (he became Grand Duke in 1570) made his triumph-ant entry into the city in 1561 after a prolonged siege whose atrocities have been chronicled with masochistic relish. Though many regretted their lost republic, the Sienese enjoyed the blessings of comparative security, which are reflected in the villas that blossomed in the fertile countryside.

The finest of these had been designed by their great architect Peruzzi, whom Sigismondo and Agostino Chigi had launched on his career. None of his buildings in Siena are as beautiful as the Farnesina or his later Roman masterpiece, the curved Palazzo Massimo alle Colonne. But what William J. Anderson wrote of the latter applies to the bulk of his achievement: 'it seems as if Peruzzi were attempting to infuse into the Roman methods some of the Grecian refinement which was his partly by instinct.' The antithesis of seven-teenth-century architects, his refinement was almost unobtrusive. Perhaps he is best described as an architect's architect, too subtle for the layman's apprecia-tion. We know from Vasari that his personal modesty was such that he never reaped the rewards he deserved, whether in designing palaces or stage settings for Cardinal Bibbiena's comedy *Calandra*, performed before Pope Leo X, when he was supposed to have invented movable scenery, first used on this occasion. Vasari praised his paintings but few have survived in their pristine state. Old critics like Lanzi agree that he was unsurpassed in perspective and that he excelled in the grotesque: in the Farnesina he was a pioneer of *trompe l'œil* decoration.

After being imprisoned and tortured by the Spaniards during the terrible sack of Rome in May 1527, he escaped by the skin of his teeth and returned to Siena. Vasari tells us that on his way home he was so plundered and completely stripped that he entered Siena deprived of all but his shirt. 'He was nevertheless honourably received and clothed anew by his friends; nor did any long time elapse before he entered the service of the Republic, and was appointed superintendent of all works connected with the fortifications of the city.' At this period he 'made numerous designs for the houses of his fellow citizens'. Though Vasari fails to specify these they may be identified as his work by internal evidence. Even when they were reconstructions or modifications like the fortress-villa of Belcaro they bear the peculiar stamp of his personality.

The history of Belcaro is so ancient that the names of its earliest owners mean little today: Marescotti in the thirteenth century, Salimbeni and Savini in the fourteenth when Nanni Savini gave it to St Catherine to be converted into a convent. It was frequently demolished and rebuilt until it was acquired in 1525 by the rich banker Crescenzio Turamini who commissioned Peruzzi

254

to design the present villa, loggia and chapel on one side of the fortress. Unfortunately Peruzzi's frescoes of amorous mythological scenes and arabesques in the loggia and entrance hall were spoiled by clumsy restoration, yet one may easily imagine what they must have been, similar to those in the Farnesina.

Superbly situated on a high hill-top a few miles west of Siena above a dense grove of ilexes, 'in a region of deep lanes and golden green oak-woods, with cypresses and stone-pines, and little streams in all directions flowing over the brown sandstone,' as J. A. Symonds aptly described it, Belcaro is visible from afar, and the view from its battlements is unforgettable. A stroll along these battlements, surrounded by the flickering foliage of ilexes, may be a Hamletish experience. The restricted space at Peruzzi's disposal somewhat cramped his style, which is most evident in the elongated quadrangle of the brick-paved inner court. The south front of the villa, opposite the long lower building for its dependents, is enclosed by elegant arched screens of tawny brick and marble at the east and west ends. Beyond the eastern screen (containing two handsome pilastered gates and an arched well-head in the centre) lies a typical walled garden with an arcaded loggia and family chapel behind it.

A trophy of cannon balls with an inscription on the battlements records the great siege of Siena when Belcaro was held by the forces of the Republic. On 4th April 1554, it was attacked by 2000 Spanish infantry and 50 horsemen. A group of French soldiers defended it till noon, when their officer was killed; the rest surrendered, and the castle was sacked. During the last days of the siege Marchese di Marignano, Duke Cosimo's general who was blockading the city, had his headquarters here and received the Sienese ambassadors who came to arrange the surrender in April 1555. Though Belcaro had been badly battered it was restored by the Turamini; and when they died out in 1721 it was acquired by the Camaiori, who restored it again during the nineteenth century.

Traditionally Peruzzi had a hand in the design of seven or eight country seats near Siena, such as Vicobello, Celsa, Saracini, Le Volte Alte, Santa Regina, Santa Colomba, Anqua, and the elegant farmhouse called L'Apparita. In spite of his versatility he could not have designed all the houses attributed to him, which were probably built under his influence. His creations are characterized by purity of proportion and perspective, by compressed delicacy and vital compactness. There is beauty of surface, of tone, of detail, yet all is as austere as Swinburne's line: 'Siena the bride of Solitude'. Here and there bits of medievalism linger, as in the battlements and fortified gateways of Belcaro, but equilibrium triumphs, as in its quadrangular courtyard. The weather-stained stucco and local limestone like Roman travertine and faded brickwork have a relaxed charm after the zebra-striped Cathedral and Gothic crenellations of the city. But extreme purity of composition may pass unnoticed since it is seldom striking and never theatrical. Peruzzi's fantasy was reserved for his painting but even in his grotesques, as Lanzi wrote, he bridled his caprice by his judgment: 'he distorts and connects those images with a surprising symmetry, and adapts them as devices emblematic of the stories which they surround.' In his architecture he was usually restrained, foreshadowing the Neo-classical.

Like an oasis on its raised ridge of land north of the city, Vicobello is the next most famous villa attributed to him. So modern does it appear that some have questioned this attribution, but its stylistic unity is typical of his work and it has scarcely been altered since the eighteenth century. Apart from which, the Chigi family were among the first to employ him in Siena and in Rome.

The house is a rectangle coated with creamy stucco and, as at Belcaro, a courtyard connects it with the former stables, storage-rooms and servants' quarters, but it is on a bigger scale. A fine gateway with statues in a semicircular wall faces the arched entrance, and the walled gardens lie west of the villa, bounded by a vast lemon-house which prolongs the line of outbuildings on the courtyard. Another gateway leads from the upper to the lower terrace garden, with pools and conventional box borders. The garden is scrupulously kept and even today Edith Wharton's description of it in 1904 cannot be bettered.* 'The descending walled gardens with their different levels', she wrote, 'give opportunity for many charming architectural effects – busts in niches, curving steps, and well-placed vases and statues; and the whole treatment of Vicobello is remarkable for the discretion and sureness of taste with which these ornamental touches are added. There is no excess of decoration, no crowding of effects, and the garden-plan is in perfect keeping with the simple stateliness of the house.' Most memorable are the monumental wellhead between columns in the courtyard wall and the arched gateway leading into the upper parterre, with its terminal niche or tribune crowned with the Chigi arms against a background of venerable cypresses. The enormous terracotta pots of lemon and orange trees and the spreading cedars are equally monumental.

Among the attractive rooms in the interior, guarded by a garrulous whistling parrot, is a spacious salon with *trompe l'œil* curtains in fresco by a certain Spampani, of whom we should like to know more. A fluently painted boudoir contains figures of Dresden porcelain poised on wall brackets. The chatelaine, Marchesa Ginevra Chigi-Bonelli, keeps these rooms alive and warm with her gracious hospitality. A pretty table containing the 36 curious counters of the old game of *biribissi*, so popular in the eighteenth century, is a relic of Casanova's visit to Vicobello.

In his formidable *Memoirs*, Giacomo Casanova has described a delicious dinner at Vicobello (which he mistakenly attributed to Palladio) in May 1770. His hostess, Marchesa Violante Chigi, was a cheerful widow of forty-seven with literary inclinations. Some of her *vers de société* were found among Casa-

* Edith Wharton: *Italian Villas and their Gardens.* New York 1904.

nova's papers at Dux. She had married Marchese Flavio Chigi Zondadori in early youth and presented him with ten children. Since his death in 1769 her motto had become *Carpe diem*, and one of her cronies, the witty Dominican Father Stratico of Pisa, had given Casanova a letter of introduction to her. He had also given him a letter to the librarian of Siena university, Abbé Ciaccheri, 'a philosopher without affectation, and a member of our flock,' who escorted him to her villa. Casanova wrote that this lady took him by storm: 'The Marchesa was still handsome, though her beauty had begun to wane; but her sweetness, grace, and ease of manner supplied the lack of youth. She knew how to make a compliment of the slightest expression, and was totally devoid of any pose of superiority.' And Casanova added that the older he grew the more he became attached to the intellectual charms of women – one suspects with his tongue in his cheek.

In a few pages he affords us a clear glimpse of literary life in Siena with the Abbé Ciaccheri as his mentor. He was taken to the house of two sisters, Maria and Teresina Fortuna, the elder very ugly and the younger very pretty, but the ugly one had acquired ephemeral fame as the 'shepherdess' Isidea Egirena of the Arcadian Academy. They all exchanged verses to set rhymes, and Casanova was dazzled by her skill. Upon discovering her identity he remembered having read 'the beautiful stanzas she had written in praise of Metastasio. I told her so, and she brought me the poet's reply in manuscript. Full of admiration I addressed myself to her alone, and all her plainness vanished.'

This meeting led Casanova into one of his interesting digressions about improvisation and the virtues of Italian, though his autobiography was written in French 'because the French language is more widely known than mine.' He concluded that the Sienese dialett was sweeter and more energetic than the Florentine; though the latter could claim classical purity, an advantage which it owed to its academy. This was the heyday of literary academies and poetical improvisers, who corresponded to the champions of modern quiz programmes on television. Speaking of the renowned Corilla Olimpica, who improvised verses to the accompaniment of her own violin held on her knees and was crowned poetess-laureate in the Roman Capitol, Casanova opined that 'though her merit was considerable it was more tinsel than gold, and not such as to place her on a par with Petrarch or Tasso. . . . Henceforth no man of genuine merit will accept the honour which was once so carefully guarded by the giants of the human intellect.'

We have many accounts of her amazing performances, as well as of her even more famous predecessor, the Sienese Cavalier Bernardino Perfetti, a knight of the Order of St Stephen and professor of jurisprudence in his native city, which certainly regarded him worthy of the crown worn by Petrarch. The Président de Brosses wrote of him in 1739: 'You have heard of the class of poets who think nothing of composing an extempory poem on any subject one may propose to them. The subject we gave to Perfetti was the

Aurora Borealis. He meditated, looking downwards, for at least half a quarter of an hour, to the sound of a harpsichord preluding *sotto voce*. Then he rose, and began to declaim in rhymed octaves, softly, and stanza by stanza, the harpsichord continuing to play chords while he was declaiming, and preluding during the intervals between the stanzas. At first they succeeded each other slowly enough, but little by little the poet became more animated, and in proportion to his doing so the harpsichord also played louder and louder, till at length this extraordinary man declaimed like a poet full of enthusiasm. The accompanist on the harpsichord and himself went on together with surprising rapidity. When it was over Perfetti seemed fatigued; he told us that he does not care to improvise often, as it exhausts his mind and body. His poem pleased me very much; in his rapid declamation it seemed to me sonorous, full of ideas and imagery. . . . You may be sure, however, that it consisted in reality of much more sound than sense: it is impossible that the general construction should not be most often maimed and tortured, and that the filling up be not mere grandiloquent rubbish.'

One digression begets another, and it is tempting to quote Casanova's because he excels in conjuring the social climate of eighteenth-century Siena.* But his visit to Vicobello has led us astray from the other Sienese villas in this chapter.

The scholarly Joseph Forsyth, who ventured into Italy during the Napoleonic occupation to study antiquities and suffered a long captivity in France for his temerity, visited the Chigi villas of Cetinale and Celsa in 1802. He formed a poor opinion of Sienese landholders, however. 'Born and bred in the city,' he wrote, 'they seldom visit their estates but for the *villeggiatura* in autumn; and then, not to inspect or improve their possessions; not even to enjoy the charms of nature or the sports of the field; but to loiter round the villa just as they loiter round the town. . . . Those villas are necessarily large to accommodate the swarm of bachelors, which must result from the system established among this nobility. In general, the uncles and brothers of the heir inherit, as their patrimony, a right to board and lodging in every house belonging to the family.

'None of these possess so many villas as the Chigi. Cetinale, which lies in a wide scraggy oak-wood about ten miles from Siena, owes its rise and celebrity to the remorse of an amorous cardinal who, to appease the ghost of a murdered rival, transformed a gloomy plantation of cypress into a penitential Thebais, and acted there all the austerities of an Egyptian hermit. Another cardinal of the Chigi family, afterwards Alexander VII, made this his favourite retreat, and has left marble tiaras at every corner. . . .

'From Cetinale we rode to Celsa, another large and still more neglected villa, where mouldy pictures and disjointed furniture were thinly scattered to make up a show. We passed through the richest vineyards, over hills clad with olive-trees, and on roads lined with wild myrtle; but we looked in vain for

* *Mémoires de J. Casanova de Seingalt*, Tome XI, Ch. VII, Paris 1932.

258

that thick-matted herbage, and those umbrageous masses of wood which distinguish an English landscape from all others.'

Cetinale, south-west of Siena, still belongs to the Chigi family but it is in a sad state of disrepair and seems to be going the way of the romantic Désert de Retz. It was designed for Cardinal Flavio Chigi, a nephew of Pope Alexander VII, by Bernini's famous pupil Carlo Fontana who, as we learn from a contemporary engraving of the plan, had 'the good fortune to execute the ideas of His Eminence for the embellishment of Villa Cetinale' in 1637.

The distinguished mathematician Professor G. H. Hardy once told me that he considered there was nothing more beautiful than a straight line. He would have been delighted by the plan of Cetinale, which extends in a long straight line from a colossus of Hercules facing the villa at one end of an avenue hemmed in by vegetation so dense you can hardly discern it, widening towards a crossroad with statues and a bas-relief of Cardinal Chigi receiving the Grand Duke Cosimo III, who stayed there in 1691. The line continues to the south front of the villa through the garden flanked by a lemon-house. The second part of the main axis runs from the north façade of the villa along a double row of cypresses, opening through gateways towards a steep flight of stone steps cut vertically through the ilex wood, right up to a square Baroque hermitage-chapel, the focal point of this domain. The ilex wood, with scattered chapels and statues, is the Thebaid referred to by James Forsyth.

The south façade of the villa, a square with projecting wings and a triple-arched loggia on the ground floor, reminds one of the villas near Lucca. Apparently the loggia above this was walled in later with florid escutcheons over each arched window. The north façade, with its double flight of steps ascending to the massive doorway of the first floor, is more Baroque in style and store-rooms. A few pots of lemons and bedraggled flower-beds are the sole remnants of the original parterre, but two concave, ivy-clad stone piers with busts and obelisks facing the north front suggest what it might have been when the Grand Duke Cosimo III stayed there. That morbidly pious prince must have enjoyed the hill-top hermitage.

Joseph Forsyth noted a curious Latin inscription on the porch of Cetinale, of which this is a literal translation:

> *Whoever you are who approach,*
> *That which may seem horrible to you*
> *Is pleasing to myself.*
> *If it appeals to you, remain.*
> *If it bores you, go away!*
> *Each is equally agreeable to me.*

This was probably composed by Cardinal Chigi, and it reminded Forsyth of another inscription he had picked up at the gate of a villa near Maddaloni which, as he remarked, has more salt in it:

> *Open to my friends*
> *And lest these be few,*
> *Even to false friends.*

Vernon Lee suspected it was a hunting-box or place of gallant rendezvous which Cardinal Chigi turned into a spiritual retreat, and she pictured him toiling thither in his litter when 'His Eminence was waxed too old and gouty, or even prone to fits, to lust any more after the World and the Flesh. . . . And, lest the memories of its former mundane pleasures should perhaps awaken sinful regrets as he watched it from the palace window below, he took the strange precaution of covering its façade with a colossal cross, niches and busts of saints, dominating the neighbourhood and reminding himself that he had installed a holy hermit in the commodious rooms and kitchen where, a sprightly prince of the Church, he had been wont to play at pastoral simplicity, dressing and cooking the game he had shot, with stomachered nymphs and high-booted gentlemen building up the fire and larding the roast meat.'*

Cetinale in its decay evokes the legend of the Sleeping Beauty. Even the charcoal-burners have left its ilex woods. A mile beyond Cetinale the castel-lated pile of Celsa soars above the wooded valley of Rosia. It has been considerably restored since Forsyth saw it, a happy merger of medieval with Baroque. Originally a fortress belonging to the now extinct Celsi family, its foundations were laid in the thirteenth or fourteenth century. In the first decades of the sixteenth century it was reconstructed by Mino Celsi, an advo-cate of Luther, but it was devastated by the Austro-Spanish troops on 18th May 1554, sharing the fate of Belcaro. Repetti has attributed its design to Peruzzi, but this is improbable. Only the isolated chapel bears the master's authentic signature. The rugged fortress was converted into a civilized villa with a formal garden during the Baroque period, but the crenellations and mullioned windows were added much later under the influence of the Gothic Revival without spoiling the older structure. A view of the castle was sketched by the Sienese historian Ettore Romagnoli, who was also a meticulous draughtsman, about the same time it was visited by Forsyth; and a comparison with its actual appearance shows that the Neo-Gothic additions (though the Bargello-like eastern tower is open to criticism) are an improvement on the cubic masonry in Romagnoli's sketch.**

The turreted medieval buildings extend on three sides of an irregular open courtyard, which is separated from the road and gardens by a lower screen with three pilastered bays surmounted by a rippling balustrade. Strangely enough, this harmonizes with the older structure. Though some consider it Baroque, on account of the balustrade, it has an affinity with Peruzzi's

* Vernon Lee: *The Golden Keys and other essays on the Genius Loci*. London 1925.

** Two volumes of drawings entitled *Varie bozze di vedute fatte da Ettore Romagnoli* are preserved in Siena's communal library. Some are reproduced in *Casabella* 330, November 1968.

other screens and might be earlier. A walled terrace runs outside it with an entrance gate on the road. Another balustraded wall opposite protects the sloping formal garden on each side of a broad path with steps at intervals ending in a semicircular pool, untouched by the winds of fashion, lightening the effect of the rough stone castle above. From here the view – in a landscape of singular serenity – is certainly one of the finest.

The circular chapel with its superimposed roofs and elegant lantern, standing apart near the south-east angle of the castle, is Peruzzi's most probable contribution to this ensemble. The arrangement of niches and square grilled windows between the slim pilasters, the round window over the door, and the plain but graceful mouldings and panels, are definitely in his style. The charm of this eclectic conglomeration is romantically compelling though it might not appeal to the purist.

Of the other villas attributed to Peruzzi that of remoter Anqua on a hill to the left of the river Cecina is the most arresting in its antique grandeur, like a Roman palace transported to a humble hamlet. It still belongs to the descendants of its original owners, the Pannochieschi d'Elci, who take good care of it. The squared, U-shaped Villa Chigi-Mieli at Le Volte Alte, which dates from 1505, was evidently a forerunner of the supreme Farnesina, and all its details, cornices and jambs of windows and doorways, are redolent of the master.

The daring spiral staircase inside the Villa at Santa Colomba is also ascribed to Peruzzi's design. A fortress of the Petrucci in the fourteenth century, it was remodelled in the beginning of the seventeenth century by Archbishop Petrucci, who adorned it with statues in niches, variegated pediments, and rusticated columns. Cosimo III presented it to the 'Noble Tolomei Boarding School', which owned it until the nineteenth century, when it became a national institute for the deaf and dumb. The interior was ruined by military occupation during the last world war and the whole building has suffered from ages of neglect, but it is now under timely restoration. The formal garden had disappeared even in Romagnoli's day.

Thanks to its present owner, who has converted it into a sophisticated private dwelling, the very superior farmhouse called L'Apparita fully deserves Romagnoli's praise of its beautiful proportions. The graceful rhythm of its double row of arches and pilasters in mellow brick, the upper row taller than the lower, forms an open loggia of rare distinction and an ideal *maison de plaisance* with a belvedere facing Siena. This is a gem of sixteenth-century architecture without additions or detractions or superfluous ornament – a pavilion of 'frozen music'.

Like most castles in the neighbourhood of Siena, that of Sovicille was often sacked and burned by invading Florentines since the thirteenth century. It has undergone many transformations but still preserves fragments of its ancient walls, notably round the tower of its main entrance. Rising above the clustered

L'Apparita: drawing by Romagnoli

village and dominating the hilly landscape with its lofty convex façade, whose salient feature is the elaborately winding late Baroque stairway, with arch over arch and an open gate connecting the castle with the garden and outer landscape, Villa Palmieri-Nuti, now Lechner, contains an inviting restaurant called *Vecchio Maniero*, where restaurants are few and far between. It shares with the Villa Garzoni at Collodi the picturesque distinction of serving as a screen or shield to protect the village behind it. The entrance stands on a lower level than the cliff-like garden front with its panoply of theatrical staircases. Peruzzi was born near Sovicille in 1481.

Practically none of these villas preserves its original décor and furniture intact. The Villa Bianchi-Bandinelli at Geggiano is a remarkable exception, for it has scarcely been altered since the 1790s. A few miles north-east of Siena on a hill-top, the house is a three-storeyed structure with an attic of simple dignity in a formal garden of lemon trees and box hedges. When the Bandinelli acquired it through marriage in about 1530 it was a rustic residence with a medieval tower and the usual cellars for vats and olive press, but it was reconstructed as it stands between 1780 and 1790, incorporating parts of the older building. The square garden and open-air theatre belong to the same period. The twin arches of the proscenium, bearing the arms of the Bianchi-Bandinelli and Chigi-Zondadori to commemorate a marriage between the two families, contain statues of Tragedy and Comedy by the Maltese sculptor Bosio on each side of the stage, with a huge cypress in the background and olive-clad hills beyond.

Here Alfieri's tragedies were performed when their first edition was printed in Siena in 1783 and it is said that the poet chose to act the tyrant's role. The corner room where he slept when visiting his friend Mario Bianchi-Bandinelli contains an elaborately carved and painted bed made in Siena, with silk hangings and embroidered bedspread of the same period, and it is strange to visualize the red-haired firebrand in such surroundings. But although he was a precursor of Cavour and Victor Emmanuel II in reviving the national spirit of Italy, he was a product of the eighteenth century. Richard Garnett has justly observed that he belonged 'to a type more common in England than elsewhere, the patrician republican . . . animated by an unaffected passion for liberty, and yet arrogant, exacting, domineering; fired by a disinterested love of man, and always quarrelling with men.' Inevitably he reminds one of Savage Landor, who introduced him in two of his *Imaginary Conversations*. He was widely read in England and his influence on Byron is well known: their characters were strikingly similar. The last two acts of Alfieri's *Mirra* threw Byron into convulsions: 'I do not mean by that word a lady's hysterics,' he wrote, 'but the agony of reluctant tears and the choking shudder which I do not often undergo for fiction.' Even in style he tried to be 'as simple and severe as Alfieri'. One would like to know which of his tragedies was performed in the open-air theatre of Geggiano, no doubt by amateurs. Most of them contain only four or five protagonists in dramatic situations, with political undercurrents which thrilled the younger generation. They would thrill nobody now, but in the eighteenth-century Italy of academies, *cicisbei* and Arcadian conceits they seemed revolutionary. Besides, Alfieri's long liaison with the Countess of Albany, as wife and then widow of Prince Charles Edward Stuart the Young Pretender, enhanced his personal glamour.

The lighter side of eighteenth-century life is reflected in the interior of Geggiano from the moment we enter the long vaulted hall. This is entirely frescoed with bucolic scenes of the seasons interspersed with portraits of the Bianchi-Bandinelli family, Alessandra Mari of Arezzo who led an anti-French expedition called 'Viva Maria' at the end of the century, and Perellino, a popular singer who belonged to Alfieri's circle of Sienese friends. Painted doors continue the composition on the walls and leafy branches bend over the curved ceiling. Apart from the individual portraits, the Tyrolese painter Ignazio Moder based his designs on Bartolozzi prints after Giuseppe Zocchi. It seems odd that a Maltese sculptor and a Tyrolese painter should contribute to the adornment of a Sienese country house, and that a poet from Piedmont should enliven its open-air theatre, but Mario Bianchi-Bandinelli was evidently cosmopolitan.

A corridor-like reception room runs out of the vaulted hall with an unusually long sofa monopolizing the whole of one side. But for the Louis XVI style arabesques, one might be in a luxurious railway carriage reserved for royalty many a mile from Siena. The brackets holding japanned trays and the painted cupboards would make any interior decorator's mouth water, but indeed the whole place is an interior decorator's dream come true.

Next to the flowery chamber where the tragic poet slept is a light blue room with furniture painted to match: its rare wallpaper, patterned with white Corinthian columns and arches against a pale turquoise ground, was bought in Paris in 1790 from a shop called *Au Grand Balcon*. A contiguous drawing-room contains painted panels which imitate Flemish tapestry and graceful green furniture depicted with bright blossoms. Another bedroom is entirely upholstered with chinoiserie-patterned linen, russet on creamy white, derived from a design by Pillement, and its cupboards and chairs repeat the fabric's design, all of which appears to be in mint condition despite its age. Walls, doors, ceilings and furniture have been practically untouched since the eighteenth century. In addition to these the present owner has brought in some original Empire-style pieces from another Bianchi-Bandinelli villa near Siena: they were designed by Agostino Fantastici (*circa* 1820), an album of whose drawings is preserved in Siena's communal library. The library of Geggiano contains an interesting portrait of Mario Bianchi-Bandinelli (1799–1854) with his step-brothers crowning a bust of his father, in the same style as Giuseppe Cammarano's portrait of Francesco I of Naples and his family with his father Ferdinando's bust. This Mario was a nephew of Alfieri's friend; he was also acquainted with Stendhal. Hence the library of Geggiano is full of intimate associations, both literary and historical. Those connected with the republican Alfieri make one forget that Tuscany was one of the best-governed states of Europe under the Hapsburg Grand Duke Pietro Leopoldo, a conscientious reformer who realized many advanced philanthropic ideas.

Would that other country seats near Siena were as scrupulously preserved as Geggiano! Compared with other provinces, however, the rural landscape of Siena has been spared hitherto by the octopus tentacles of land-development companies and speculators. The nightingales are still vociferous in the ilex woods at sunset.

Indeed, the city of Siena, that 'outpost of medieval civilization', became a model for urban planning when it banned motor traffic from its historic centre. It is a profound satisfaction, even when one is far away, to know that the unique shell-shaped Campo is not used as a parking lot. But the Spanish *parador* system might yet save some of its crumbling country houses.

POSTSCRIPT

Of course there are more, many more, Tuscan villas and gardens that might have been included in this book. Already we anticipate the disappointed murmurs of those who had visited a nice villa (where was it exactly?) belonging to an Uncle Alfred or Aunt Jemima donkey's years ago . . .

Why not L'Ombrellino, for instance, the house at Bellosguardo inhabited by Galileo between 1617 and 1631; by Marcellin Desboutin in the 1860s, better known for his raffish appearance in Degas's *L'Absinthe* than for his drypoint etchings or for his play *Maurice de Saxe*, performed at the Comédie Française in 1870; and, in this century, by the witty and hospitable Mrs George Keppel? However interesting and agreeable its associations, L'Ombrellino suffered from drastic transformation in the nineteenth century, presumably when it belonged to the Russian Zoubows. Mrs Keppel removed the excrescences from its front terrace and replaced the tawdry Victorian palms with Venetian statues. Even so, the house is a pretentious pastiche. Its interior was only enlivened by the hostess and her stream of guests. When her daughter, Violet Trefusis, inherited the place she tried to infuse into it some of that Parisian atmosphere she hankered after, with the aid of exotic *papiers peints*, chinoiseries, a Houdonesque bust, a silver sturgeon, and minor fallals about which she delighted to weave fantasies in the manner of her friend Louise de Vilmorin. Mrs Keppel was wont to practise her Italian on the gardener with the repeated injunction: '*Bisogna begonia!*' The garden, however, is hardly more than a parterre-pedestal for an overwhelming view of Florence. Perhaps it is too all-embracing. Personally we prefer the view of the city from Villa Capponi.

Architecturally the neighbouring Villa Mercedes on the piazza of Bellosguardo is more distinguished, owing to its handsome courtyard by Baccio d'Agnolo, but we have included other courtyards of similar type, and its sprawling asymmetrical façade is rather dull.

Others may ask, what about Villa Stibbert? It has a quaint 'period' flavour of a histrionic-historical kind, with its windows of stained glass and its umbrageous park *all'inglese*, where HBM Consul entertains the diminished English colony annually on the Queen's birthday. Bequeathed to Florence by

Frederick Stibbert who fought for Garibaldi, it contains an intriguing assortment of paintings, tapestry, maiolica, European and Japanese armour, and such relics as Napoleon's robes when he was crowned King of Italy – great fun for growing children. But it is Tuscan only by adoption.

Among rustic sixteenth-century villas, that of Bagazzano with its graceful loggia was worthy of inclusion for it remains unspoiled. Its remoteness on a wooded hill of ilex and cypress has saved it from later bedevilment, but its austere fascination is scarcely photogenic. It would require another Corot to convey its particular aura.

By way of contrast, one garden entirely dedicated to flowers grouped in exquisite colour-schemes was tempting to include – that of the Casa San Martino at Arcetri. The prospect of olive plantations and vineyards rolling beyond it is impeccably Tuscan, but the garden itself is evocative of Sussex.

The whole of the Chianti region and the vicinity of Siena and Lucca offer a tantalizing variety of country-houses large and small in poetical situations, in secluded corners far from any main road or on solitary hill-tops. Many are forsaken, their closed shutters wrapped in cobwebs, the plaster peeling in patches from their mottled walls, their gardens running wild, their fountains dry, their armorial gateways rusty; and these are not the least interesting, haunted by owls and bats and nightingales. Like the recently restored L'Apparita near Siena, some forgotten house designed by a Peruzzi may still be waiting for an adventurous occupant. Alas, the flimsy bungalow and prefabricated cottage are becoming more popular than the fine old Tuscan farmhouse with its solid walls and noble proportions, though some good examples of the latter have been cleverly adapted to modern requirements. And ancient castles that might still be made habitable are slowly collapsing.

The villas we have selected are, in our opinion, the most representative for one reason or another – the most typically Tuscan. We have had no intention to compete with Signor Lensi Orlandi's compendious volumes or with Signora Belli Barsali's *Le Ville Lucchesi*, invaluable as works of reference. There is nothing of comparable utility about the villas of Siena. Ours has been simply a labour of love.

As elsewhere in Italy, too many villas have suffered from the depopulation of the countryside and are decaying through sheer neglect. We earnestly hope that these may be rescued from total ruin, while they could still be used for residential purposes, for schools or cultural centres as in England *faute de mieux*. May this book serve as a stimulus to state-sponsored organizations as well as to aesthetic humanitarians with money to invest. It would indeed be sad if it were merely a memento of vanished monuments of the versatile Tuscan genius.

NOTES
ON THE PLATES

Arabic numbers after the names of villas refer to the black-and-white photographs, Roman numerals to the colour plates, and page numbers to the text illustrations.

MEDICEAN VILLAS

Il Trebbio (1)

Cosimo de' Medici the Elder engaged Michelozzo to convert this square fourteenth-century castle with an inner courtyard and watchtower into a habitable villa, and the wise architect achieved it with respect for its medieval origins. For a while it was the residence of the famous *condottiere* Giovanni delle Bande Nere and his wife Maria Salviati. Their son Cosimo was staying at Il Trebbio when he heard of the Duke Alessandro's assassination, whereupon he promptly left it to assume power in Florence in 1537. In 1644 it was sold to Giuliano Serragli who bequeathed it to the Philippine Fathers. In 1864 it was bought from the state by Prince Marcantonio Borghese and in 1936 it was religiously restored by its late owner, Dott. Enrico Scaretti. The fifteenth-century garden is practically unchanged. A romantic cypress grove was planted here in the nineteenth century.

Cafaggiolo (2, 3, and p. 42)

Cosimo de' Medici the Elder commissioned Michelozzo to build this villa like a fortified castle in 1451, design the garden, and neighbouring farms and roads; he also had it surrounded with walls and a moat, which have disappeared together with one of the towers during the nineteenth century. The original design was a simple square with three internal courtyards and two towers.

For many years it remained a summer resort of the Medici who entertained distinguished guests there, including Pope Eugenius IV in 1436 and Pius II in 1459; Lorenzo and Giuliano de' Medici spent much of their early youth there, and later Pico della Mirandola, Marsilio Ficino and Poliziano were frequent guests – the latter acting as tutor to Lorenzo the Magnificent's children. The Grand Duke Cosimo I kept his menagerie of rare animals in the park. In 1576 it was the scene of a family tragedy, for his dissolute son Pietro murdered his young wife Eleonora of Toledo in her bedroom 'to avenge his honour'. The Grand Duke Francesco and his mistress Bianca Cappello used it occasionally as a hunting lodge. The Hapsburg-Lorraine successors of the Medici continued the tradition, and King Francis I of the Two Sicilies was entertained there as a guest. In 1864 it was acquired by Prince Borghese along with the villa of Il Trebbio on the hill behind it. His architect was responsible for the destruction of walls and the central tower and for filling in the moat – to the detriment of Michelozzo's design. The park and the fountains surrounding it no longer exist. A good idea of its original situation can be gained from the seventeenth-century lunette by Justus Utens in the Museo di 'Firenze com'era'.

271

The ancient square fortress which stood here originally was converted into a solid stately villa by Michelozzo for his patron Cosimo the Elder. It is crowned with an open battlemented gallery under the roof which gives it a medieval style. Lorenzo di Giovanni di Bicci de' Medici acquired it from Tommaso Lippi in 1417 and bequeathed it to his son Pier Francesco. During a division of the family property it was allotted to Cosimo the Elder who spent the last years of his life there, and it became the most famous of Florentine villas as a meeting place of the scholars and artists attracted by Medicean liberality, and as a centre of the Platonic Academy founded by Marsilio Ficino. After the expulsion of the Medici in 1494 the villa was set on fire by their extremist opponents. The Grand Duke Cosimo I of the cadet branch had it restored and redecorated with frescoes by Pontormo and Bronzino, but it was neglected by his successors. The Hapsburg-Lorrainers sold it in 1799, since when it has had many proprietors. At present it is an annexe of the vast Careggi hospital.

Careggi (4–7, III)

Cosimo the Elder bought this spectacular property from the Baldi family in 1458 and engaged Michelozzo to rebuild it, but its fifteenth-century character has been greatly altered by subsequent owners. Yet it retains its pristine charm, owing to its hanging garden with a magnificent view. During the reign of Lorenzo the Magnificent it shared with Careggi the reputation of being a centre of Florentine humanists, where the most famous artists, philosophers and men of letters used to congregate. Poliziano composed his *Rusticus* there, and the Pazzi conspiracy to murder Lorenzo and his brother Giuliano at a banquet was postponed because Giuliano was indisposed. It passed through various hands after Cosimo III sold it in 1671, until the Countess of Orford bought it in 1772. In the nineteenth century it belonged to the versatile English painter William Spence, Colonel Harry Macalmont, and eventually to Lady Sybil Cutting and her daughter Marchesa Iris Origo.

Villa Medici (Fiesole) (8, 9, IV)

This austere square villa stands on the summit of a hill, approached by double ramps designed by Bernardo Buontalenti for the Grand Duke Cosimo I in 1565–67. A corridor passes from the front of the house to the adjacent church and farm. Originally it belonged to the Counts Guidi. It became notorious on account of the murder of the beautiful Isabella de' Medici, Cosimo I's daughter, who was strangled here by her husband Giordano Orsini, Duke of Bracciano, because of her liaison with his cousin Troilo Orsini.

Cerreto Guidi (10, 11)

This grandiose and elegant villa was designed in 1480 by Giuliano da Sangallo in an H-shaped plan with a façade containing an open loggia. The curved double staircase leading up to it was added by Stefano di Ugolino of Siena somewhat later. The central loggia with its Della Robbia frieze and the Medici coat of arms was added by Lorenzo the Magnificent's son Giovanni, who became Pope Leo X. It had belonged to the Cancellieri of Pistoia who sold it to Palla Strozzi in 1420. Lorenzo the Magnificent acquired it from the Rucellai and called it *Ambra* (from a stream that formed a small island with the Ombrone River) and celebrated its charm in verse, as did Poliziano, who was tutor to his children. The Medici family continued to embellish it and Pope Leo X commissioned the frescoes in the great hall. Montaigne visited and described it in 1581. The Grand Duke Francesco I and his second wife Bianca Cappello both died there in 1587, in circumstances that seemed suspicious to their contem-

Poggio a Caiano (12–14, I, and p. 54)

poraries. When Florence became capital of Italy the villa and garden were considerably transformed by King Victor Emmanuell II who used to stay there with his morganatic wife, the Countess of Mirafiori. The villa now belongs to the state and is undergoing timely restoration.

La Magia (15–17)

The villa was originally built in 1318 by Vinciguerra Panciatichi as a stronghold near Quarrata west of Florence. Early in the sixteenth century his descendants fortified themselves there after being defeated by the Cancellieri of Pistoia. The castle had been converted into a country residence when the Duke Alessandro de' Medici entertained the Emperor Charles V there in 1536, as is recorded by a tablet near the entrance. It was acquired by the Grand Duke Francesco I in 1583 who engaged Buontalenti to modernize it: an irregular square structure with a handsome interior courtyard and an angular tower. The park adjoined the estate of Poggio a Caiano where the Medici often hunted. The villa was sold to Pandolfo Attavanti in 1645 and later to the Ricasoli until it was acquired by the Amati of Pistoia whose descendants have kept it in a good state of preservation.

Pratolino (18–20, and pp. 58, 59)

This must have been one of the finest villas belonging to the later Medici, about six miles from Florence on the old road to Bologna over the Futa Pass. The Grand Duke Francesco de' Medici commissioned Buontalenti to design it, but his building was destroyed and only sparse remnants of the original garden exist. The engravings of Stefano della Bella and Giuseppe Zocchi, and Justus Utens's painted lunette provide records of its original appearance, as well as detailed descriptions by Montaigne (1580 before it was finished), John Evelyn (1645) and other travellers. The garden with its fountains, statues, grottoes, lakes, avenues, groves and cascades, was one of the wonders of Florence. Giambologna's colossal statue of the Apennine has been massive enough to survive the holocaust. Cosimo III's eldest son Prince Ferdinando commissioned Antonio Ferri to built a theatre in the villa where operas by Scarlatti and other great composers were performed to perfection, but after his death in 1713 the property was sadly neglected. It was in a deplorable condition when the Austrian Grand Duke Ferdinand III decided in 1814 to demolish it and convert the fantastic garden with its many 'beautiful and stupendous inventions ... set in motion by diverse hidden machines driven by water' into a huge hunting park. Prince Paul Demidoff bought the estate in 1872 and restored the old *paggeria* or 'villa of the pages' for his own residence. Recently it has been improved by his descendant Prince Paul of Yugoslavia.

Castello (21, 22, V, and p. 62)

This austere and solid villa with a slightly curved façade stands at the foot of Monte Morello and the magnificent garden rises behind it. Though it had belonged to the Medici since Cosimo the Elder's great-nephews had acquired it and filled it with works of art the garden was beautified by the Grand Duke Cosimo I, who commissioned Tribolo to improve it on a larger scale with fountains and waterworks, statues in marble and bronze (some by Giambologna and Ammannati), grottoes, orchards and labyrinths described enthusiastically by Vasari and Montaigne (*Journal de Voyage en Italie, 1580*) who observed there, *inter alia*, the chimera of Arezzo before it was restored, unaware of its great antiquity. Buontalenti continued Tribolo's work. Cosimo I lived here after his retirement with his second wife Cammilla Martelli and died there in 1574, at the age of fifty-five, after a reign of thirty-seven years. It is now under restoration as the seat of the Accademia della Crusca.

Originally this was a castle with towers belonging to the Brunelleschi, who defended it gallantly against the attacks of the Pisans and their Anglo-German mercenaries under Sir John Hawkwood in 1364. Cardinal Ferdinando de' Medici acquired it from Lisabetta Tornabuoni, Filippo Salutati's widow, in 1575 and commissioned Buontalenti to convert it into an elegant villa surrounded by a spacious garden. It is a solid square structure with a projecting roof and a medieval watchtower. The interior was frescoed by Volterrano with scenes from Cosimo I's career which were restored by Victor Emmanuel II after they had been whitewashed by his predecessors. Victor Emmanuel lived here with his morganatic wife, the Countess of Mirafiori. Giambologna's famous fountain of Venus wringing out her hair, which is the chief glory of the garden, was moved here from the neighbouring villa of Castello in the eighteenth century. The villa has belonged to the state since 1919.

La Petraia (23, 24, II)

This majestic rectangular building with buttresses at each corner and innumerable chimneys was built as a hunting lodge by Buontalenti for the Grand Duke Ferdinand I in 1594, and it challenges comparison with his other masterpiece in Florence, the Fortezza di S. Giorgio (or di Belvedere) built 1590–95. A graceful loggia relieves the heaviness of the white façade. The staircase approaching it was added during this century from a sketch by Buontalenti in the Uffizi. Originally it was called Villa Ferdinanda, from the Grand Duke who commissioned it and who preferred this region for his hunting expeditions. The interesting series of lunettes representing Medicean villas by Justus Utens in the Museo di 'Firenze com'era' used to adorn the central hall of Artimino.

Artimino (25)

A fine avenue from the Porta Romana leads up to the large semicircular piazza in front of this imposing villa, whose exterior has been completely transformed by Neo-classical architects of mediocre talent in the nineteenth century. It has been a fashionable school for girls since 1864. Originally it was a castle belonging to the Baroncelli but it had belonged to the rebellious Salviati when Cosimo I confiscated it in 1565 and gave it to his daughter Isabella Orsini, Duchess of Bracciano. The Orsini inherited it after her tragic death. Cosimo II's wife, the Grand Duchess Maria Maddalena of Austria, acquired it in 1619, hence its 'imperial' name. Giulio Parigi was commissioned to enlarge it in the style of Buontalenti, as can be seen from Zocchi's engraving. Being so near the city it was a favourite residence of the Medici and their successors.

Poggio Imperiale (26)

This majestic villa was rebuilt upon the foundations of an older mansion belonging to the Ardinghelli when the Grand Duke Ferdinando I bought it in 1587. Buontalenti or one of his pupils must have been responsible for its design: a square plan with four imposing towers at each of the four angles and four entrances with avenues of plane trees above the junction of the Arno and Pesa rivers at Montelupo, west of Florence. The Grand Duke Cosimo III filled the rooms with paintings of rare animals and flowers which have since been dispersed. Occasionally it served as a hunting-lodge and Medicean hostel for distinguished visitors but it was less popular than their other country villas owing to its windy situation, as Francesco Redi the poet and court physician complained in a letter from there in 1683. It is now a criminal lunatic asylum in a wretched state of preservation.

Ambrogiana (27, and p. 67)

Very little survives of the attractive villa and elaborate garden recorded in Zocchi's engraving. Justus Utens's lunette in the aforesaid series depicts it as it was when

Lappeggi (28, and p. 73)

Cosimo III's brother Cardinal Francesco Maria engaged Antonio Ferri to transform it. The happy-go-lucky Cardinal wanted to emulate the wonders of Pratolino but apparently he also wanted to build it in a hurry. During his lifetime – until his death in 1711 – it was entirely dedicated to festivity, as recorded by the poet Fagiuoli and by Francesco Redi. Princess Violante of Bavaria, Cosimo III's daughter-in-law, lived there after 1714. In 1816 it was sold at auction but it has deteriorated rapidly since then.

VILLAS IN AND NEAR FLORENCE

Montegufoni (29–31, VI)

In the thirteenth century this dramatic fortress-villa already belonged to the Acciaiuoli family whose most celebrated member became Grand Seneschal of Naples, having won the favour of King Robert and Queen Giovanna. When the King of Hungary invaded Naples, Niccolò Acciaiuoli brought his ward Lodovico of Taranto, Queen Giovanna's second husband, to Montegufoni for safety while Queen Giovanna fled to Avignon. The castle underwent many transformations through the centuries: the seven houses of which it consisted were combined in a single structure. The central tower, reminiscent of the Palazzo Vecchio, was built in 1386 and restored at various periods, and the Baroque façade was added in the seventeenth century with a formal garden, fountains and a handsome grotto. The private chapel on the eastern side was built in 1680. Its recent owner Sir Osbert Sitwell has described it most eloquently in his autobiography, and it now belongs to his heirs.

Palmieri (32, and p. 141)

Traditionally this handsome villa in a splendid position just below San Domenico di Fiesole was the refuge of Giovanni Boccaccio and his group of young friends who escaped from the plague in 1348, as related in the *Decameron*. But Boccaccio's description of the garden was probably imaginary, an idealization of the gardens he had seen. It is known to have belonged to Nuccio Solosmei in 1350, and in 1454 it was sold to the rich apothecary Marco Palmieri, father of the distinguished statesman and man of letters, Matteo Palmieri, who wrote the *Città di Vita*. In 1697 his descendant Palmerio Palmieri enlarged the villa and garden, adding the spacious loggia and the curved double staircase from the terrace to the garden. In 1766 the eccentric Earl Cowper lived there, and in 1824 Miss Mary Farhill acquired it, bequeathing it to the Grand Duchess Maria Antonia of Tuscany who sold it to the charitable and scholarly Earl of Crawford. The latter built a new road to San Domenico instead of the old one which divided the estate and planted the hillside behind the villa with magnificent trees. Queen Victoria stayed here twice when she visited Florence.

La Pietra (33–42, VII–XI)

A stately avenue of cypresses leads up to the house from a massive gate with the Capponi arms. The lofty façade was rebuilt in sober Tuscan Baroque style during the seventeenth century, but the formal garden surrounding it was laid out during the present century by Arthur Acton, who collected the seventeenth- and eighteenth-century statues and stonework for the terraces on the hillslope and planted the varied cypresses, stone-pines, hedges of cut yew and box. The *pomario*, or walled orchard north of the house, ends with an ornate lemon-house, which formed the original *giardino segreto*. An original plan of the villa by Giorgio Vasari Junior (1598) is preserved in the Drawing and Print Department of the Uffizi and was published in 1970 by Officina Edizioni, Rome (Giorgio Vasari il Giovane, *La Città Ideale, a cura di Virginia Stefanelli. Introduzione di Franco Borsi.*) This represents its fifteenth-century aspect with a characteristic open courtyard and well in the centre. The villa had belonged to the prosperous Sassetti family who sold it to the Capponi in the sixteenth century. A cardinal of the family enlarged and modernized it in the seventeenth century retaining most of the interior on the ground floor, and the modifications were probably entrusted to Fontana and Ruggeri who built the Capponi palace in the city. The Marchesi Incontri inherited it from the historian Marchese Gino Capponi, and the villa was acquired by Arthur and Hortense Acton in the beginning of this century.

The plain exterior of this turreted sixteenth-century villa, which follows the curve of the road, conceals a delightful interior with one corridor leading to a long green lawn and lemon garden and another towards the vast terrace from which you descend to a walled garden and others beneath it, ending in a swimming pool hedged in by cypresses. It had several owners since the early fifteenth century until it was bought in 1572 by Gino di Lodovico Capponi, whose heirs continued to enlarge and embellish it. The villa was acquired by Lady Scott, a daughter of the Duke of Portland, in 1882, and she added the two loggias which were built with columns from the ancient market (demolished with the former ghetto to make way for the present Piazza della Repubblica). The private chapel contains an altarpiece by Tommaso di Stefano. Mr and Mrs Henry Clifford acquired this attractive property in 1928.

Capponi (Arcetri) (43, XII)

In the fifteenth century this characteristically Tuscan square villa, with a classical open loggia on a spacious open courtyard like a piazza, belonged to the Rossi, who sold it to Niccolò di Tommaso Antinori in 1487. For the next four centuries it remained in the possession of his family. The large central hall with the minstrels' gallery was frescoed in 1629 and other rooms were frescoed with *trompe l'œil* architecture and arabesques in the eighteenth and nineteenth centuries. The views of the Tuscan countryside from each room are particularly attractive. The whole place had been seriously damaged during the last world war, since when Mr and Mrs Ernest Boissevain fell in love with the place and decided to restore it. This has been done with consummate taste and sensitive feeling for its original charm, thanks to the co-operation of the talented architect Count Niccolò Rucellai.

Antinori delle Rose (44–47, XIII–XV)

This classical villa in sixteenth-century style has been totally rebuilt by its present owner as it was before its destruction in the last world war, but it has always been more famous for its enchanting garden than for its architecture. Traditionally the property once belonged to the stone-mason Matteo Gamberaia, the father of the famous sculptor-architects Antonio and Bernardo Rossellino. However, an inscription dated 1610 attributes its creation to Zanobi Lapi, at whose death nine years later it was claimed by his creditors. In 1717 it was acquired by the Capponi who enlarged the house, beautified the garden with fountains and statues, and laid out the long bowling alley and grotto-garden leading up to the orchard. Probably it assumed its actual form at this period, but after a long interval of neglect it was recreated with a splendid water parterre by Princess Giovanna Ghyka, who acquired it at the end of the nineteenth century. It is generally considered the most perfect small garden in Tuscany.

Gamberaia (50–53)

I Collazzi
(54–58, and p. 147)

Attributed to Michelangelo and altogether in the master's spirit, architecturally this is one of the finest Tuscan villas, a few miles south of Florence on the old road to Volterra. Owing to a statement by Baldinucci it has also been attributed to Santi di Tito, who painted the altarpiece in the private chapel in 1593. But the villa was built in about 1560 for Agostino Dini who was a personal friend of Michelangelo. The design of the villa, with its two rows of loggias above a large courtyard enclosed on three sides and open on a fourth, approached by an imposing flight of steps, is magnificent in scale; the opposite façade looking south has a front door in rusticated *pietra serena* surmounted by the Dini arms, and its upper storey is adorned with two graceful triple-arched loggias. Giovanni Dini's wife, *née* Boutourline, planted the trees in the garden which had been bare till then. The left wing was unfinished, as in Zocchi's engraving, when the Messrs Marchi acquired it in 1933. Thanks to them it has been completed in accordance with the original plan.

San Michele alla Doccia
(59, 60)

Niccolò Davanzati, who belonged to the prosperous old family of bankers and money-lenders, bought this property on the slopes of Fiesole in 1411 and presented it to some Franciscan monks. The original farmhouse and grounds were transformed into a monastery, together with an oratory dedicated to St Michael the Archangel. After one of the monks was murdered, the Davanzati family handed it over to Franciscans of a stricter Order who settled there until they were suppressed in 1808. It was enlarged and beautified in 1596 according to the designs of Santi di Tito, who had been influenced by Michelangelo. The Grand Duke Ferdinand III ordered it to be sold at auction in 1817, when it was purchased by Dr Frosini-Martinucci, who divided it into apartments and laid out the garden with solid retaining walls and a winding private road. His heirs owned it until it was acquired by Mr Henry White Cannon of New York in 1901. After the last world war, when it suffered from military occupation, it was bought by M. and Mme Lucien Teissier who eventually transformed it into a luxurious hotel. In spite of all these changes it still preserves the fine elements of its original character. The view of Florence from its extensive loggia is breathtaking.

L'Ugolino (61, 62)

The Ugolini family who acquired this villa on the Via Chiantigiana in 1444 engaged Gherardo Silvani to transform it in High Renaissance style during the seventeenth century. The portico in the façade on the highway was added in the eighteenth century yet it harmonizes with the earlier structure. The formal garden is notable for its fine avenue of cypresses. In 1691 Attanasio Bimbacci frescoed the large salon, and in 1744 the house was further restored and embellished by Giorgio Ugolini.

Rinieri (Corsini)
(63, and p. 165)

This is a rare example of Florentine Baroque but both the villa and garden have suffered from neglect since the last world war. The ornate façade was designed by Antonio Ferri, and Tribolo is reputed to have designed the garden, but a dusty road runs through the former esplanade in front of the house, dividing it from the old entrance gate and crumbling walls. In the fifteenth century it belonged to the Strozzi until Palla Strozzi's daughter-in-law Alessandra sold it to the Rinieri in 1460, hence its name, for it remained in their possession till 1571. After passing through several hands it was acquired by

277

Cosimo II de' Medici in 1618, who lent it to Sir Robert Dudley, son of the Earl of Leicester by his second wife Douglas Howard, widow of Lord Sheffield. Sir Robert was a versatile sailor, designer of ships and engineer. After being created Duke of Northumberland by the Emperor Ferdinand II to please his sister the Grand Duchess Maria Maddalena, he died at the villa in 1649. Eventually the Corsini family acquired it in 1687 and it remained in their possession until this century.

From a painting ascribed to Poccetti inside this supremely decorative eighteenth-century villa, it would appear to have been a modest country house of irregular design when Simone di Jacopo Corsi acquired it from Luca di Andrea Carnesecchi in 1502. Even then it had a pretty formal garden. It was frequently modified and restored by members of the Corsi family, above all by Antonio di Giovanni Corsi, who contributed the Baroque façade and arranged the garden with pools and fountains as engraved by Zocchi. The garden was 'anglicized' in the fashionable romantic style during the first half of the nineteenth century and partly converted into a botanical garden with hothouses and exotic plants. Marchese Giulio Corsi-Salviati (author of the monograph *La Villa Corsi a Sesto*, Florence 1937) has most admirably restored its eighteenth-century design. It is unusually situated in the midst of a plain but its rich variety compensates for its lack of panorama.

Corsi-Salviati (64, XVIII, and p. 162)

This striking sixteenth-century villa with a seventeenth-century façade and a handsome double staircase, on a height south of Florence commanding a superb view, was a temporary abode of the beautiful Bianca Cappello before she married the Grand Duke Francesco I. In 1576 she sold it to the hospital of Santa Maria Nuova, which leased it to Baron Giulio Ricasoli in 1631. His heirs enlarged the villa in sumptuous eighteenth-century style and redecorated the interior. The central hall was frescoed by Antonio Cioci. During the last century it belonged to the Marchese Fossi, but it owes its actual state of perfection to its present owner Marchese Giaquili Ferrini.

La Tana (65–72, XVI, XVII)

Originally, as its name suggests, this charming villa must have been in a wild woody situation. The late seventeenth-century façade extending horizontally is flanked by two gardens on different levels with carefully trimmed box hedges, clipped yew and pots of lemons. It has had many respectable owners since it belonged to the Galilei in the early fifteenth century, including the Rucellai. Early in this century it belonged to Princess Dolgoroukoff who bequeathed it in 1919 to the Costa de Suarez, descendants of General Francisco Miranda, the great leader of South American independence.

Selva e Guasto (73)

This handsome villa was rebuilt in the sixteenth century with elegant loggias over a moat of running water. Originally it had been a glorified farmhouse belonging to the Guadagni, who left it to the Captains of Or San Michele in the fifteenth century. In 1478 Niccolò d'Ugolino of the noble Martelli family leased it in perpetuity, paying 100 florins down and pledging himself to pay 18 lbs of wax annually. Since then it has always belonged to the same family, who have restored and enlarged it at intervals. Its charm has been celebrated in a Latin poem entitled *Gricilianum Martelli*.

Gricigliano (74, 75)

Le Falle (76, and p. 171)

Le Falle, whose name is derived from a neighbouring stream, was confiscated from the opulent Pazzi family after the failure of their conspiracy against the Medici in 1478, but in 1539 Giovan Battista Nasi succeeded in claiming it as the dowry of his wife Camilla de' Pazzi. Next year she sold it to Simone del Nero who left it to his daughter Maria, wife of Alessandro Guadagni, in 1599. The Guadagni commissioned Gherardo Silvani to transform it. He designed the symmetrical loggias on opposite façades and the terrace around the building, and he incorporated the early tower in the new structure. He was also responsible for the large interior hall. During the nineteenth century it suffered from the varying caprices of different owners who added fake ruins and other absurdities, but its present owner has restored it as it appears in Zocchi's engraving.

Rospigliosi (Il Spicchio) (77, and p. 173)

Traditionally this stately villa was designed by the great Gian Lorenzo Bernini; possibly it was executed by his assistant Mattia de' Rossi under his influence. It consists of a square central block flanked by two rectangular wings. The outer walls are subdivided into bands of *pietra serena*, and the original structure (as portrayed by Zocchi) was crowned with a balustrade and statues, now replaced by an ordinary roof. The Rospigliosi family had owned property at Lamporecchio, not far from Pistoia, since the fifteenth century, and the cultured Pope Clement IX, a friend and patron of Bernini, commissioned this villa in 1669 and died in the same year. Of the former park only a fine avenue of ilexes survives, and the whole place is in a melancholy state of abandonment.

Serristori ('Casa Grande') (78–80)

The modest approach to this surprising mansion from the town is in striking contrast with its noble interior, which opens on a lovely fifteenth-century courtyard with a view of a neat formal garden bounded by cypresses, the town wall and a watchtower. An early Renaissance staircase ascends to the upper loggia of the same period, and a suite of rooms in the same style contains many works of art, also of the same period. Ancient inscriptions and coats of arms in the loggia record episodes in the history of the Serristori under the Florentine republic, and they include the arms of Niccolò Machiavelli, who was a family connection. The villa, which already existed in 1427, is known locally as the *Casa Grande*, or the Big House. Pope Leo X and his court stopped there on his way to Florence. During the eighteenth century it was used as a silk factory and general depository. Count Umberto Serristori restored its former dignity and furnished it in period style.

VILLAS NEAR LUCCA

Cittadella (81, XXII)

This square three-storeyed villa, with a triple-arched portico (now closed) on the ground floor, was built on the site of a medieval stronghold in the second half of the sixteenth century. Most of the garden and part of the house were transformed during the last century. The original roof had projecting eaves and the portico was open: now the roof is balustraded with statues. The garden was transformed into a so-called English park but part of the old formal garden has survived, such as the decorative long arched lemon-house with round windows, the theatre, fine gates, transversal avenue, and Baroque fountains with masks of satyrs.

According to G. C. Martini who described it in the eighteenth century, the villa was built by a French architect, but it bears a suggestive resemblance to the Villa Bellavista near Pescia which was designed by Antonio Ferri in 1672. The two towers were added to corners of the façade near the end of the seventeenth century; the top storey of the north façade is decorated with a loggia with architraves. The main salon inside is frescoed with fascinating perspectives and allegorical figures by the Bolognese painter A. M. Colonna. A fine double staircase leads to the front door of the south façade and an inscription records that Silvestro Arnolfini enlarged the house by adding a third storey in 1803.

Marchi (Arnolfini) (83)

This solid square structure of classical design has preserved its original grandeur. A superb columned portico at the back with a fine staircase opens towards the lush Lucchese valley, and the interior is full of delightful frescoes – those in the central salon on the ground floor by Bartolomeo de Santi are especially fine. The villa once belonged to Francesco Burlamacchi, who was beheaded in 1548 for conspiring against the Medici. It was then ceded to Don Ferrante Gonzaga, Duke of Amalfi, who put it up for auction in 1556. In the seventeenth century it belonged to the opulent Santini who commissioned Bartolomeo de Santi to redecorate the interior. In the eighteenth century it belonged to the Montecatini, who added the outside staircase in 1719 and had the portico frescoed with allegorical figures of Agriculture and Astronomy by Francesco Antonio Cecchi. A fine circular labyrinth was removed in the early nineteenth century to make way for a romantic landscape garden, possibly by Alfred Niewerkerke, who retired here after the fall of Napoleon III.

Rossi (Gattaiola) (84, XX, XXI)

Built as a hunting lodge in a splendid position on a hilltop with a glorious view of the Lucchese plain, this singularly attractive villa with a long sixteenth-century portico approached by a double staircase was first recorded in 1532 when the Buonvisi went to Lucca to quell the revolt of the *Straccioni* or 'Ragamuffins'. The fine portico was probably built in the second half of the sixteenth century and must have been there when Montaigne visited it in 1580. It was also recorded by Ortensio Lando in 1536. Early in the eighteenth century Alessandro Buonvisi invited Domenico Martinelli to Forci, and he probably designed the chapel which was built much later in 1775 by Francesco Buonvisi. The interior salon contains frescoes of topical rustic scenes by Francesco Antonio Cecchi.

Giustiniani (Buonvisi) (85, XIX)

A lofty five-arched portico is the most prominent feature of this late sixteenth-century villa which is somewhat reminiscent of Gricigliano near Florence. The projecting eaves are typically Florentine. Though its interior was considerably modified in the eighteenth century when Francesco Buonvisi laid out the garden, its exterior remains much as it was originally. The garden is crossed by a central road on an axis with the house, and was embellished by fountains, a fishpond with statues, rococo bas-reliefs and grottoes. The monumental gates, stables, a church and various dependencies were completed in 1770. When the Buonvisi became extinct in 1800 it became the property of Prince Charles Poniatowski and later of the Rossellini, who presented it to Giuseppe Cottolengo's charitable 'House of Divine Providence'. The house and particularly the garden were badly damaged during the last world war.

Oliva (Buonvisi) (86, 87)

This elaborate villa has a quadrangular plan with projecting wings on each side of the façade, adorned with a handsome portico and statues between coupled columns.

Mansi (88, 89, XXIII, XXIV)

The upper storey is likewise adorned with coupled columns repeating the design of the portico. The raised central attic is surmounted by a pediment with more statues. Formerly a sixteenth-century residence of the Benedetti, it was acquired by the Cenami in the seventeenth century. Countess Felice Cenami engaged the Urbino architect Muzio Oddi, who had been employed by the republic of Lucca to strengthen the city walls since 1625, to remodel the entire villa in 1634. He contributed the Mannerist façade, but the top pediment was added in the eighteenth century when the villa belonged to the Mansi who set up their coat of arms in 1742. Ottavio Guido Mansi engaged Filippo Juvara to design the garden with greater splendour between 1725 and 1732. Flower beds, box hedges, fountains, a fishpond adorned with statues, a so-called 'Bath of Diana' formed part of this ambitious design. He also built a small 'clock palace'. But in the nineteenth century the garden was converted into a romantic English park. The formal fishpond and the Bath of Diana are the sole relics of Juvara's plan. Between 1784 and 1792 the highly esteemed Neo-classical painter Stefano Tofanelli painted the mythological panels for the main salon.

Torrigiani (90–92, XXV, XXVI)

As ornate as the Villa Mansi, this magnificent square structure of High Renaissance design is encrusted with graceful statues in arched alcoves, the last word in seventeenth-century sophistication. A fan-shaped staircase leads to the monumental entrance. The attic is surmounted by a pediment with a small cupola. Yet the architect is unknown, though his style had much in common with that of Muzio Oddi. The interior is in perfect harmony with the exterior. Like so many other fine Lucchese villas this belonged to the Buonvisi in the sixteenth century; in the seventeenth century it was acquired by the Santini who redecorated the façade. The interior is fully worthy of the exterior, with a spiral staircase, *trompe l'œil* perspectives and ingenious stuccoes. The beds have sumptuous baldaquins, the dining room exquisite porcelain from Saxony and Capodimonte. The garden was laid out in French style at the same period. Though part of it in front of the house was transformed *all'inglese*, a ravishing sunken garden with lemon trees, flower beds and paths of pebble mosaics concealing jets of water remains intact. Since 1816 when Vittoria Santini married Marchese Torrigiani, it has belonged to the latter family.

Garzoni (93–96, XXVII, XXVIII, and p. 219)

The massive Baroque villa, as impressive as the Villa d'Este at Tivoli, is equally famous for its spectacular garden which extends on the steep slope to the right of it in a dazzling succession of balustraded steps and terraces leading to the cascade framed by dense groves of trimmed ilex, with a row of cypresses above. The cascade is further enlivened by figures of birds. A huge statue of Fame stands higher up with personifications of Florence and Lucca at her feet, but so many details cannot be summarized briefly. A fortified castle had stood here originally. The builder of the present villa, Romano Garzoni, had a plan of it made in 1633, proving that its actual proportions existed then but that the garden was much smaller. In 1652 the garden was already terraced and planted, as described in a florid ode by Francesco Sbarra. Ten years later it was visited by the Emperor Ferdinand of Austria and Anna de' Medici, but the garden was not completed till 1692. The distinguished Lucchese architect and man of letters, Ottaviano Diodati, was responsible for hydraulic innovations in 1786, and at this time the rococo summer pavilion behind the villa was also added. After the death of the second Romano Garzoni in 1756 his estate was inherited by the collateral Garzoni Venturi, since when it has had half a dozen owners. Though in private hands it is open to the public.

Originally this famous property belonged to the Buonvisi, from whom it was acquired by the Orsetti in 1651. The latter remodelled it and created a Baroque garden with an open-air theatre, fishpond, lemon garden, *nymphaeum*, statues and parterres of box on a lavish scale. When Napoleon's sister Elisa Baciocchi became Duchess of Lucca she forced Count Lelio Orsetti to sell it to her and in 1811 she began to modernize it in the fashionable style of the day, adding a stiff portico to the north façade and raising the top storey with a perfect regard for symmetry. The interior was redecorated under the supervision of Théodore Bienaimé, and in 1812 Elisa's official painter Stefano Tofanelli started frescoing the ballroom with a 'Ballet of the Hours'. The French architect Morel was commissioned to modernize the garden which was enlarged with additional land including the old 'Bishop's villa', and vast sums were spent on the waterworks. The villa became Elisa's favourite residence until her brother's downfall and she held receptions on a grand scale, with theatricals and Paganini playing in the park. Both Lamartine and Metternich praised its manifold delights. Under the Restoration Marlia was inherited by the Bourbons of Parma and eventually belonged to the House of Savoy. During this century it was purchased by Count and Countess Pecci-Blunt, who revived its former splendour.

Marlia (97–102, XXIX, and p. 221)

This surprisingly elegant hunting-lodge on a hilltop in the midst of a pine forest has an extremely long façade of two storeys, with a pilastered portico in the lower centre between two sweeping flights of stairs. The central row of windows is surmounted by a curling scrolled pediment which is almost rococo, completing, as it were, the grand curves of the stairs. It was built for the genial Prince Carlo Lodovico of Bourbon-Parma (1824–47) while Duke of Lucca, by the Neo-classical architect Lorenzo Nottolini – one of the few Lucchese examples of a fine building *ex novo* during this period. Since the last world war it has belonged to Colonel and Mrs Roworth.

Pieve S. Stefano (XXX)

SIENESE VILLAS

This is generally considered the most attractive of the rectangular Renaissance villas designed by Baldassare Peruzzi on a hill-top near Siena and its plan has a certain similarity to that of Belcaro (see below), the courtyard being treated as a connecting space between the main residence and its group of dependencies. To the north the courtyard is open towards a park of ilexes; to the south it is separated from the parterre by a wall with a handsome gateway. The well-head in the courtyard beside the arched entrance is also very fine. The gardens descend from the parterre at different levels with ancient trees, shadowy walks, but far too much ivy on the walls. Viewed from the city on an axis with the villa, the general design was intended to compose the Chigi coat of arms. During the last century Marchese Chigi was responsible for various modifications, as can be seen by comparison with ancient designs of the villa, but not so extreme as to alter its classical character. The garden contains many rare plants of botanical interest.

Vicobello (103, 104, XXXI, XXXIV)

The Renaissance villa still retains the appearance of the fortress it was originally, in a position of strategic importance overlooking an ilex grove, some three miles south-west of Siena. Its records go back to 1199 and it has passed through many vicissitudes,

Belcaro (105–107)

alternately dismantled and rebuilt, until it was acquired by the Sienese banker, Crescenzio Turamini, in 1525. Turamini commissioned Baldassare Peruzzi to convert it into a country house in 1535 and he adapted his design to the space at his disposal within the ancient walls. The solid and sober villa stands on the north side of a long brick-paved courtyard facing its dependencies, while the east and west are closed by stone screens containing gateways and a well – a design that differs totally from Tuscan tradition. Beyond the eastern screen is the modest orchard, with a chapel on one side in an angle of the outer walls. The chapel and the villa were frescoed by Peruzzi, but the frescoes have been badly restored and, except for their subject-matter, look mid-Victorian. Owing to the circuit of walls and battlements Belcaro never lost its military character. It was fortified again by the Sienese in 1554 when it was captured by the Grand Duke Cosimo I de' Medici and the Imperial forces. After the extinction of the Turamini family in 1721 it was acquired by the Camaiori, who restored it during the first half of the nineteenth century, and it has not changed since then. The last Grand Dukes of Tuscany Ferdinando III and Leopoldo II often stayed there.

Cetinale (108–110)　The Baroque plan of this extensive garden and villa was designed by the famous Carlo Fontana for Cardinal Flavio Chigi, Pope Alexander VII's nephew, some time before 1680 when it was built. The house is a compact rectangle except for the two projecting wings of the south façade with a triple-arched loggia between them. The north façade is adorned with a superb double staircase ascending from the garden parterre, which is crossed by a very long avenue on an axis with the house, flanked by the dense wood of the so-called 'Thebaid', sown with chapels and statues by Bartolomeo Mazzuoli which are now in a lamentable state of decay. This leads to a steep flight of stone steps and the hermitage or chapel on the crest of the hill. Edith Wharton has aptly noted that Fontana 'was wise enough to profit by the natural advantage of the great forest of oak and ilex which clothes this part of the country, and to realize that only the broadest and simplest lines would be in harmony with so noble a background.' A bas-relief in the garden represents Cardinal Flavio Chigi welcoming the Grand Duke Cosimo III to the villa in 1691. The interior contains several antique statues, frescoes by Zondadari, and portraits of the Chigi family.

Celsa (111, 112)　A frowning fortress stood here in the fourteenth century. Eventually this was converted into a country house by Mino Celsi, an early champion of Protestantism. The Renaissance additions and improvements were probably due to Baldassare Peruzzi, to whom the elegant round chapel near the villa is attributed with greater certainty. The main buildings extend on three sides of the wedge-shaped courtyard, separated from the road and the garden by a stone screen with a wrought-iron gate and two flanking arches with grilles which lighten the austerity of the older structure. In 1554 the castle-villa was devastated by Imperial troops but has often been restored, in Gothic Revival style during the nineteenth century and recently, since the last war, by its present owner Prince Aldobrandini. Its isolated position in the magnificent Sienese landscape adds to its enchantment. The formal garden was laid out in the seventeenth century and its present owner has restored a semicircular pool of the same period in front of a wood at some distance from the castle-villa – since bandits used to lurk behind trees.

Anqua (113, 114)　This spacious country house has the noble air of a city mansion transported to the summit of a hill overlooking a vast landscape. It appears to date from the sixteenth century when it was evidently designed by Baldassare Peruzzi, for it has all his characteristics; but it was restored during the seventeenth century by the Counts Pannochieschi d'Elci whose descendants still own it and keep it in an excellent state of preservation. The villa is entered from a small courtyard flanked by two walls with gates, one of which leads to the orchard. The courtyard is embellished by a beautiful sixteenth-century well.

An imposing quadrangular structure with buttresses at the angles of the façade, its stateliness enhanced by porticoes and statues, panels and columns, situated on a height with a fine view of Siena. The handsome spiral staircase inside it is generally attributed to Peruzzi, but no trace of the garden has survived. Originally this had been a castle belonging to the powerful Petrucci who engaged Peruzzi to convert it into a worthy country house in 1516. (Many of his Sienese buildings were designed while he was in Rome and they were executed from models. It was hardly necessary or possible for him to inspect every site before construction.) The Archbishop Petrucci, however, is known to have remodelled the façade in the beginning of the seventeenth century. The villa was inherited by the Medici and the Grand Duke Cosimo III presented it to the 'Noble Tolomei Boarding School' which owned it till the nineteenth century. Later it belonged to the national institute for the deaf and dumb, and suffered seriously from neglect and war damage. At present it is being restored. During the last century a church and several houses stood near the villa; a chapel containing paintings by Francesco Vanni still remains.

Santa Colomba (115–117)

This dignified yet cheerful villa of typical sixteenth-century design was enlarged towards the end of the eighteenth century when even the façade was transformed, but it has preserved its classical restraint. Since 1560 it has belonged to the Bianchi-Bandinelli family who redecorated the interior in exquisite eighteenth-century taste, and the furnishings are still blessedly intact. The poet Alfieri was an honoured guest, and his tragedies were performed in its open-air theatre. The latter consists of a proscenium with two Baroque arches surmounted by statues by the Maltese sculptor Bosio; the wings and stage are formed by cypress and laurel, harmonizing with the rest of the formal eighteenth-century garden. The lively frescoes of rustic scenes with portraits in the long arched hall by the Tyrolese painter Ignazio Moder are especially worthy of note. The villa now belongs to the eminent archaeologist and art historian Professor Ranuccio Bianchi-Bandinelli.

Bianchi-Bandinelli (Geggiano) (118, 119, XXXII, XXXIII)

Architecturally this is an unusual structure, towering above the walls of Sovicille village, formerly in the diocese of Volterra but in the state of Siena and about seven miles distant from that city. Peruzzi was born near by in Ancaiano. The façade of the castle is curved, following the line of the ancient walled enclosure, and the original towers were incorporated in the massive pile. A florid Baroque staircase leads from the castle to the garden below. Throughout the Middle Ages the castle belonged to Siena but it was often captured by Pisan and Florentine troops. Only two truncated towers of that period have survived. It belonged to the Nuti and Palmieri families before it was acquired by Signor Lechner.

Sovicille (120, 121)

This picturesque villa on the outskirts of Siena was remodelled in romantic Neo-Gothic style after it had been damaged by the earthquake of 26th May 1798. Pope Pius VI

Torre Fiorentina (122, 123)

took refuge here for several days following the Constitution of the Roman Republic as a result of French military intervention under General Berthier. The villa is the property of the Sergardi family.

Chigi–Mieli (Le Volte Alte) (124, 125)

This handsome Renaissance villa on a hilltop was commissioned by Mariano Chigi in 1492 but a tablet records that it was built in 1505. It was probably one of Baldassare Peruzzi's first important buildings, on the basis of which he designed the Farnesina in Rome. A double square with two projecting wings on each side of the porticoed façade, its classical refinement is emphasized by terracotta cornices. Pope Julius II stayed there in 1510 and Pope Paul III in 1541. Inside the villa a bas-relief by Paolo Olivieri portrayed the death of Caesar.

L'Apparita (126, and p. 266)

This was formerly part of a farmhouse built in red brick whose beautiful design has been generally attributed to Peruzzi, and it is probably one of his early works. It consists of two simple storeys with porticoes which form a double loggia of rare refinement open to the lovely Sienese countryside. W. W. Kent mentioned it in his *Life and Works of Baldassare Peruzzi of Siena* (New York 1925) as 'worthy of preservation'. After centuries of neglect it has recently been restored by its present owner, Signor Guiso, who has scrupulously respected its classical design while adapting its interior to modern standards of comfort with discrimination.

INDEX

Figures in italic refer to text illustrations; Arabic numbers in bold type refer to black-and-white photographs, Roman numerals to the colour plates.

286